FLORA OF THE NORTHEAST

A Manual of the Vascular Flora
of New England and
Adjacent New York

FLORA OF THE NORTHEAST

A Manual of the Vascular Flora of New England and Adjacent New York

Dennis W. Magee

AND

Harry E. Ahles

Drawings by Abigail Rorer

University of Massachusetts Press

AMHERST

Copyright © 1999 by
The University of Massachusetts Press
All rights reserved
Printed in the United States of America
ISBN 1–55849–189–9
LC 98–49300

Designed by Jack Harrison
Set in Adobe Minion
Printed and bound by R. R. Donnelley & Sons Company

Library of Congress Cataloging-in-Publication Data

Magee, Dennis W., 1942–
Flora of the Northeast : a manual of the vascular flora of New
England and adjacent New York / Dennis W. Magee and Harry E. Ahles ;
illustrated by Abigail Rorer.
p. cm.
Includes bibliographical references and index.
ISBN 1–55849–189–9 (cloth : alk. paper)
1. Botany—New England. 2. Botany—New York (State) 3. Plants—
Identification. I. Ahles, Harry E. II. Title.
QK121.M34 1999
581.974—dc21   98–49300
                                                       CIP

Dedicated to my wife, Helen, and sons, Tim and Brian,
and to family members of the late Harry Ahles,
his sister, the late Marge Armstrong,
and his niece, Patricia Matera

CONTENTS

PREFACE

Background and Scope of the Manual

The work on this manual was begun by Harry Ahles in the mid-1970s. As an instructor of courses in field identification of vascular plants at the University of Massachusetts he prepared keys to various plant groups as a teaching aid. Renowned for his abilities in field taxonomy, Mr. Ahles emphasized identification of plants in sterile as well as reproductive condition in his teaching. Accordingly, his approach in designing his keys was to construct them using vegetative as well as flowering and fruiting characters whenever possible, and to make them as simple as possible. Prior to joining the University of Massachusetts' botany department he had co-authored the "Vascular Flora of the Carolinas" and had also authored or co-authored other botanical books and journal articles. His goal was to produce a manual similar to the Carolinas' "Flora" for New England, using a similar format and design. However, Mr. Ahles felt that the scope of the work should be based more on natural physiogeographic boundaries and plant distribution limits than on cultural or political boundaries. The area of treatment of this manual, therefore, extends slightly beyond New England, from Canada, to and including Long Island, west to the Hudson River.

At the time of Mr. Ahles' untimely death in early 1981, he had prepared a preliminary draft of keys for many of the taxa. A copy of his preliminary draft of keys has been placed in the University of Massachusetts main library archives in the faculty manuscripts section. He had also completed an herbarium search to gather distribution information, visiting all of the major herbaria throughout New England and New York. This distribution information resides in 12 ring-binder notebooks at the University of Massachusetts herbarium. In 1983 I was approved by the head of the University of Massachusetts' botany department and Mr. Ahles' family to complete the work.

Preparation of a finished flora from the preliminary draft of keys and distribution information left by Mr. Ahles required completing the keys, updating the plant names, updating the distributions and preparing distribution maps, coordinating preparation of the illustrations, and writing all other sections that are necessary parts of a finished flora.

Although Mr. Ahles had intended to publish a book containing only keys and distribution information, I have also prepared descriptions of the families and genera in the interest of producing a more complete work that will fulfill a wider range of needs. The descriptions pertain only to those taxa represented in the greater New England area, and do not include information for taxa occurring beyond the range limits of this manual.

Diagnostic Keys

Preparation of the keys involved testing keys written by Mr. Ahles, making changes wherever review of plant material revealed inaccuracies or identified a clearer approach, completing keys that were only partly finished, and writing keys that were missing. Throughout this process I have, to the extent possible, attempted to preserve Mr. Ahles' understanding of the various plant groups as represented in his approach to design and construction of the keys, but I have exercised license wherever necessary, in the interest of a better treatment. In brief, I have attempted to glean all information of

ix

value from the preliminary keys and notes left by Mr. Ahles in preparing this manual.

Consistent with Mr. Ahles' goal for this flora, I have attempted to make the work a four-season manual, with keys designed to be as simple and "user friendly" as possible. To this end, the general keys to the manual include separate keys for plant groups such as aquatics, vines, woody plants that flower prior to leaf-out, and woody plants in winter condition. There are also keys for woody and herbaceous plants in flower or in fruit. Certain taxa are repeated in various keys as often as necessary where an observer's judgment or the condition of the plant could lead in more than one direction.

This book has been prepared to serve as a field manual as well as a reference work, therefore all keys have been written using characters observable with a ten-power hand lens (except for Isoetes where a compound microscope is necessary to observe megaspore characteristics). In writing the keys virtually all observations were made on herbarium material, using fresh material only when its availability coincided with the season in which particular keys were being written, and depending on the relative ease or difficulty in obtaining material. Out of necessity I have, throughout most of the keys, used characters that do not change after a specimen has been dried, however in some cases use of characters such as color or latex was unavoidable. All measurements made on herbarium specimens and used in keys were checked against published descriptions to account for any shrinkage or shriveling. Where a given taxon occurs only occasionally in greater New England, herbarium material from regions where the taxon is more abundant was used in the interest of observing as many sheets as possible. These keys have been field tested by professional botanists in the environmental consulting field as well as by students and faculty at several universities.

The herbaria as well as the recent literature contain records of various "fugitive taxa" such as waifs from other regions of our country and from other countries, escapes from vegetable and flower gardens, and so on. Many of these records are old and the plants have not been observed for years. To account for such taxa without cluttering the keys with plants that are not really part of our flora, and that the vast majority of users will not encounter, I have, in each case, placed the plant near a similar taxon in the manual to which it will key, and included a brief discussion on how it differs from the similar taxon.

Plant Names

The sequence of the families follows the Englerian arrangement. Although a more modern arrangement could have been used, such as the one presented in Gleason and Cronquist's "Manual of Vascular Plants of Northeastern United States and Adjacent Canada" (1991) it seemed more practical to use the familiar system that is most generally used by taxonomists and field botanists.

Recent years have seen numerous changes in plant nomenclature and systematics, as well as major revisions within certain groups, the ferns and Liliaceae in particular. The taxonomy of many of the ferns is in a constant state of revision, and the treatments presented in this manual reflect the views held at the time that it went to press. The current thinking with regard to the concept of the Liliaceae in the old broad sense, in familiar usage, is that it is a large, unnatural assemblage of genera, and should be replaced by smaller, more uniform family units. Such smaller family units were described as long ago as the last century, and a preponderance of new information supports this earlier view. Subsequently, I have adopted this line of thinking in this flora and split the old Liliaceae into the smaller family units (for a fuller explanation see "Rearrangement of Petaloid Monocot Families at Kew" by Brian Mathew in "Lilies and Related Plants" of the Royal Horticultural Society Lily Group, 1988-89 [David Reed ed.]).

As most botanists are aware, the taxonomy of Crataegus and Rubus is very complex and not well understood. Other floras covering the greater New England region have described several hundred species. The treatments of these genera presented in this manual are based largely on Mr. Ahles' work; these treatments are highly condensed and are subject to substantial modification as future studies shed light on these difficult groups. All species recognized for our range have been provided for in this work as synonyms or hybrids.

As this work was in progress the plant names were reviewed by Dr. John Kartesz.[1] As part of his ongoing work to maintain an updated data base of plant names for North America, Dr. Kartesz collaborates extensively with specialists working on various plant groups and stays abreast of the current literature in the United States and abroad. Accordingly, I have accepted the vast majority of his recommendations and incorporated them into this work because I feel that they reflect the nomenclatural and systematic views of the taxa occurring in our range currently held by most plant taxonomists. Synonyms are provided for all changes, particularly with respect to the names used in the 8th edition of "Grays Manual" and the two editions of Gleason and Cronquist. Consistent with current convention, all specific epithets in this manual are lower case.

As this manual was going to press portions of the "Flora of North America" were being completed. Unfortunately availability of the completed sections of the flora did not coincide with the timing for final production of this manual. If the completed "Flora of North America" reveals major differences in the treatment of a significant number of taxa, this manual will be revised as appropriate to take them into account.

Plant Distributions

Most of the information on plant distributions for this manual was obtained by Mr. Ahles from herbaria at the University of Massachusetts, the New England Botanical Club, the University of Connecticut, the University of Rhode Island, the University of Vermont, the University of Maine, the University of New Hampshire, Smith College, New York State Museum, and Mr. Ahles' personal collection of over 10,000 sheets for New York State.

The distribution information has been presented in the form of county range maps for a majority of the species. In the interest of space, the location information for species with but one or two county records throughout the range treated in this manual is provided in the accounts for most of these species. Similarly, location information for species additions to our range that has been identified from the literature subsequent to Mr. Ahles' work is provided in the accounts for such species. Mr. Ahles' distribution data were updated from a variety of literature sources such as "Rhodora" (1980-1991); "Atlas of New York State Flora" (1991) by the New York Flora Association; "Catalog of Vascular Plants of Berkshire County" Massachusetts (1991) by Pamela Weatherbee; "Atlas of Vermont Pteridophytes" (1988) by David Barrington; and county lists of rare plant species of Massachusetts (1991) by Bruce Sorrie; as well as verified personal accounts of field botanists working throughout greater New England. In addition, current distribution data for the New England states was supplied by Dr. John Kartesz (October 1992) and was used as a final check to ensure that the scope of the manual is as complete as possible relative to taxa verified for our area. Distribution information is in a constant state of change; however, I feel that the information presented in this manual represents a fair accounting of the taxa of New England and the adjacent New York counties.

For species with known occurrences in other parts of the world, such occurrence is indicated in the species account along with status of origin in the United States, as to whether introduced, adventive, or naturalized. Introduced species are those intentionally brought into the United States, adventive species are those that have come into our region from other countries or other parts of the United States but not by human intent, and naturalized species are those that have become firmly established. All other species are indigenous in our area.

---

[1] The Biota of North America Program, The North Carolina Botanical Garden, CB #3280, Coker Hall, University of North Carolina, Chapel Hill, N.C. 27599-3280.

Illustrations

All illustrations used in this manual were prepared by Abigail Rorer. The illustrations (995) are diagnostic in nature and mostly accompany the keys. My intention was that illustrations, presented near the keys, would assist the user in understanding certain important distinctions and concepts, to facilitate working through the keys. For this reason the proportions of various parts depicted in some drawings may not always be true to nature. Some illustrations do not accompany the keys and are provided as general reference figures for given taxa.

Species Accounts

Each species account includes synonyms, habitat information, and federal and state endangered status where applicable. Dates of the various state rare plant lists used in preparing this flora are as follows: Maine—Jan. 1992; New Hampshire—1987; Vermont—Jan. 1992; Massachusetts—Jan. 1992, Connecticut—1980; Rhode Island—Feb. 1992; New York—April 1992.

Consistent with Mr. Ahles' and my own views on the content of a field oriented botanical manual, and in the interest of appealing to a wider readership, other notes of interest have also been added to the species accounts. These include:

Wetland Site Index: Given increased public awareness of the unique values of wetlands, and given the wetland indicator value of many plant species, the modifiers in the U.S. Fish and Wildlife Service list of plant species that occur in wetlands[2] have been added at the end of the species accounts wherever applicable. These modifiers are —OBL (obligate, the plant virtually always occurring under saturated conditions); —FACW (facultative, the plant occurring half the time under saturated soil conditions and half the time in uplands); —FACU (facultative upland, the plant occurring approximately three-quarters of the time in uplands); UPL (the plant virtually never occurring under saturated soil conditions). Intermediate categories are indicated by a - or + added to the modifier.

Wildlife Food Value: The potential food value of a plant genus or species for wildlife is indicated by the code Wildl. 1, 2, 3, or 4, with 1 representing the lowest and 4 the highest value. These codes were derived from the values cited in Martin, Zim, and Nelson[3] for the Northeast. A fuller understanding of the basis for these values should be sought in this work.

Poisonous Properties: Information on the known poisonous properties of plants and plant parts has been included.

Food Value for Humans: Information on known food values has been included. Some plants are poisonous in various growth stages, or some parts may be poisonous and other parts edible. In some cases cooking is required to eliminate the poisonous property. Prior to experimenting with plants that are cited in this book as edible, more informative works on this subject should be sought.

Medicinal Value: Information on plants with known medicinal value has also been added, including aboriginal and early colonial usage. In many cases plants having medicinal value are poisonous if improperly prepared or if used at the wrong time of year. In other cases recent research has demonstrated that plants formerly thought to provide cures for various ailments are ineffective or harmful. As was stated for the plants having food value, more informative works should be sought before experimenting with plants reported as having medicinal uses.

---

[2] U.S. Fish and Wildlife Service, Department of the Interior. 1988. National List of Plant Species that Occur in Wetlands: Northeast (Region I). Biological Report 88(26.1).

[3] Martin, A.C., H.S. Zim, and A.L. Nelson. 1951. American Wildlife and Plants: A Guide to Wildlife Food Habits. New York: McGraw-Hill.

Other Information

Near the beginning or end of the book other information of potential value to the user has been included.

Bibliography for Useful Plants: A partial bibliography for plants reported to have poisonous properties or to be of food or medicinal value has been added.

Excluded Taxa: Taxa attributed to the geographic area treated in this manual but for which occurrences have not been verified are listed.

Matrix of Diagnostic Characteristics for Dicots: During the process of preparing the keys for the dicot families and genera a matrix of diagnostic characters was constructed for use as a tool. This matrix could be used to group taxa by any of the 40 odd characters listed down the left margin as in identifying a plant on which only certain structures are present, or in seeking examples for teaching. For example, the list of possibilities might be greatly shortened in attempting to identify a plant by referring to the column under leaf type, ovary characteristics, or fruit type. Using computer technology this manner of plant identification may eventually come to replace traditional methods of keying.

Matrix of Diagnostic Characteristics for Woody Plants in Winter Condition: Similarly, preparation of the key to woody plants in winter condition involved construction of a matrix of characteristics of diagnostic value. The user may find this of value in identifying a plant using a limited number of characteristics visible in winter condition or as a teaching tool.

Future Editions

It is anticipated that with usage, this manual will establish its place in the botanical reference literature for the greater New England region. It is hoped that the format developed for the manual will provide a basis for periodic revisions of the text as well as the distribution information over the long term by future authors as new information helps refine our understanding of the flora of our region.

Dennis Magee
Normandeau Associates, Inc.
Bedford, New Hampshire

ACKNOWLEDGMENTS

I owe special gratitude to my family, Helen, Tim, and Brian for their patience and support over the many years that this manuscript was in preparation. Special thanks to Bruce Wilcox, Jack Harrison, and other staff at University of Massachusetts Press for their labors to produce this book. I am especially indebted to Abigail Rorer for her patience and dedication in preparing the illustrations for this book from herbarium material.

I gratefully acknowledge the financial support provided by Dr. George Hatsopoulos, chairman of the board and chief financial officer at Thermo Electron Corporation, Dr. John Appleton, president and chief executive officer at Thermo Terrotech Inc., Ms. Pamela Hall, president of Normandeau Associates, Patricia Matera, Margaret E. Barr Bigelow, and the National Wildlife Federation. I wish to thank Pam Hall and Peter Kinner, my supervisors at Normandeau Associates, for their support and encouragement. Thanks also to Joe Larson for valuable suggestions and ideas on fund raising. I owe a special debt of gratitude to several current and former Normandeau Associates staff, including Ethel Hartman for her patience and dedication in assuming overall responsibility for producing the electronic manuscript, which involved numerous revisions and additions as the work evolved, the late Becky Grass for her assistance on one of the drafts of the work, Susan Byrd for typing the first handwritten draft, Lena Morgan for preparing the matrices of diagnostic characteristics, and Jane Bouchard for her role in completing the electronic manuscript.

I owe a special debt of gratitude to John Kartesz for time generously spent in providing much valuable assistance with the nomenclature for this book, and for providing an update on plant distributions for all New England. Special thanks to William Countryman for reviewing an early version of the entire manuscript and providing many valuable suggestions. Thanks to George Wilder for critically reviewing the Pteridophyte, Gymnosperm, and Monocot portions of the work, for offering many important suggestions and comments, and for field testing certain keys. Thanks to Ray Angelo for reviewing portions of the manuscript and offering valuable advice and suggestions, and to Dave Boufford for advice during the start-up years of this project. Thanks to Bruce Sorrie for supplying supplemental distribution information for Massachusetts and Dave Barrington for providing the same for Vermont. Thanks also to Pam Weatherbee for sharing her distribution data for Berkshire County, Massachusetts, and to Rick Van de Poll for providing location records for portions of New Hampshire and for field testing certain keys. Thanks to George Newman for the use of his personal library of floras and periodicals.

I wish to thank Ed Davis for his assistance in getting me nominated to undertake this work. Thanks to Jim Walker for affording me unlimited access to the University of Massachusetts Herbarium and to Karen Searcy and Roberta Lombardi for assisting me in accessing and replacing herbarium material. Thanks to the technical staff of the Terrestrial/Wetlands Group at Normandeau Associates, who field tested various keys throughout the preparation of the manuscript.

Finally, thanks to the many friends who have provided encouragement and moral support to sustain me throughout the 15 years this work was in progress, particularly George and Rebecca Wilder, George and Sally Newman, Patricia and Matt Matera, Joyce and Pete Willette, Norm and

Joy Komich, Garry and Brenda Hollands, Gerry and Liz Scanlon, Jon and Chitra Staley, Pat and Monica Fairbairn, Martin Michener, Pat and Tom Nadherney, Mike and Bev Kalagher, Weldon Bosworth, Bill and Carlha Vickers, Bruce and Anna Aune, Don and Valerie Bartron, Bob and Hilary Keating, Dave and Martha Williams, Ray Rogers, the Piekarski Family, the Yokubaitis Family, the LaValley Family, and the McKenzie Family.

COUNTIES OF NEW ENGLAND AND ADJACENT NEW YORK

MAINE
1. Aroostook
2. Penobscot
3. Piscataquis
4. Somerset
5. Franklin
6. Oxford
7. Washington
8. Hancock
9. Waldo
10. Knox
11. Lincoln
12. Kennebec
13. Androscoggin
14. Sagadahoc
15. Cumberland
16. York

NEW HAMPSHIRE
17. Coos
18. Carroll
19. Grafton
20. Strafford
21. Sullivan
22. Belknap
23. Merrimack
24. Rockingham
25. Hillsboro
26. Cheshire

VERMONT
27. Essex
28. Orleans
29. Franklin
30. Grand Isle
31. Caledonia
32. Lamoille
33. Chittenden
34. Orange
35. Washington
36. Addison
37. Windsor
38. Rutland
39. Windham
40. Bennington

MASSACHUSETTS
41. Essex
42. Middlesex
43. Suffolk
44. Norfolk
45. Bristol
46. Plymouth
47. Barnstable
48. Dukes
49. Nantucket
50. Worcester
51. Franklin
52. Hampshire
53. Hampden
54. Berkshire

RHODE ISLAND
55. Providence
56. Bristol
57. Kent
58. Newport
59. Washington

CONNECTICUT
60. Windham
61. Tolland
62. New London
63. Hartford
64. Middlesex
65. New Haven
66. Litchfield
67. Fairfield

NEW YORK
68. Suffolk
69. Nassau
70. Queens
71. Kings
72. Bronx
73. Westchester
74. Putnam
75. Dutchess
76. Columbia
77. Rensselaer
78. Washington

SUMMARY OF THE TAXA OF NEW ENGLAND AND ADJACENT NEW YORK

Families and Higher Levels	Genera	Species	Subspecies and Varieties	Named Hybrids
DIVISION I PTERIDOPHYTA				
Fam. 1. Equisetaceae	1	9		
2. Lycopodiaceae	3	17	4	3
3. Selaginellaceae	1	3		
4. Isoetaceae	1	7	1	3
5. Ophioglossaceae	2	12	3	
6. Osmundaceae	1	3	1	1
7. Schizaeaceae	2	2		
8. Dennstaedtiaceae	2	2	2	
9. Adiantaceae	5	8		
10. Polypodiaceae	1	2		
11. Blechnaceae	1	2		
12. Aspleniaceae	1	8	1	2
13. Thelypteridaceae	2	5		
14. Dryopteridaceae	11	27	2	2
15. Marsiliaceae	1	1		
16. Salviniaceae	1	1		
17. Azollaceae	1	2		
DIVISION II SPERMATOPHYTA				
Class I. Gymnospermae				
Fam. 18. Taxaceae	1	3		
19. Pinaceae	5	20		
20. Taxodiaceae	1	1		
21. Cupressaceae	3	6	2	
Class II. Angiospermae				
Subclass I. Monocotyledoneae				
Fam. 22. Typhaceae	1	2		1
23. Sparganeaceae	1	8		
24. Zosteraceae	1	1		
25. Potamogetonaceae	1	31	2	2
26. Ruppiaceae	1	1		
27. Najadaceae	1	5	1	
28. Zannichelliaceae	1	1		
29. Juncaginaceae	1	2		
30. Scheuchzeriaceae	1	1		
31. Alismataceae	3	13		
32. Butomaceae	1	1		
33. Hydrocharitaceae	3	4		
34. Poaceae	100	344	52	1
35. Cyperaceae	14	321	24	9
36. Araceae	6	7	2	
37. Acoraceae	1	2		
38. Lemnaceae	4	10		
39. Eriocaulaceae	1	2		
40. Xyridaceae	1	4		
41. Commmelinaceae	2	7	1	

Families and Higher Levels	Genera	Species	Subspecies and Varieties	Named Hybrids
42. Pontederiaceae	2	3		
43. Juncaceae	2	44	12	2
44. Liliaceae	7	15		
45. Colchicaceae	1	1		
46. Hemerocallidaceae	1	2		
47. Convallariaceae	7	16	1	1
48. Alliaceae	1	11	2	
49. Melanthiaceae	7	8		
50. Funkiaceae	1	3		
51. Hyacinthaceae	3	5		
52. Trilliaceae	1	4		
53. Asparagaceae	1	1		
54. Agavaceae	1	1		
55. Smilacaceae	1	6	1	
56. Haemodoraceae	1	1		
57. Dioscoreaceae	1	3		
58. Iridaceae	4	25		
59. Orchidaceae	21	59	2	4

Subclass II Dicotyledoneae

Families and Higher Levels	Genera	Species	Subspecies and Varieties	Named Hybrids
Fam. 60. Saururaceae	1	1		
61. Salicaceae	2	43	5	16
62. Myricaceae	2	3	1	
63. Juglandaceae	2	9	1	1
64. Betulaceae	5	21	4	2
65. Fagaceae	3	21	2	31
66. Ulmaceae	2	8	2	
67. Moraceae	4	5		
68. Cannabaceae	2	3	1	
69. Urticaceae	5	10	1	
70. Santalaceae	3	3		
71. Viscaceae	1	1		
72. Aristolochiaceae	2	5		
73. Polygonaceae	8	62	12	
74. Chenopodiaceae	14	60	3	
75. Amaranthaceae	4	21		
76. Nyctaginaceae	1	5		
77. Phytolaccaceae	1	1		
78. Aizoaceae	2	2		
79. Molluginaceae	1	1		
80. Portulacaceae	5	10		
81. Caryophyllaceae	24	92	4	
82. Ceratophyllaceae	1	2		
83. Cabombaceae	2	2		
84. Nelumbonaceae	1	1		
85. Nymphaeaceae	2	4	3	
86. Cercidiphyllaceae	1	1		
87. Ranunculaceae	17	74	11	
88. Berberidaceae	3	5		1
89. Lardizabalaceae	1	1		
90. Menispermaceae	1	1		
91. Magnoliaceae	2	4		

Summary of the Taxa of New England and Adjacent New York *(Continued)*

Families and Higher Levels	Genera	Species	Subspecies and Varieties	Named Hybrids
Fam. 92. Calycanthaceae	1	1	1	
93. Lauraceae	2	2		
94. Papaveraceae	7	11	2	
95. Fumariaceae	4	11		
96. Brassicaceae	45	115	4	4
97. Capparaceae	2	3	1	
98. Resedaceae	1	4		
99. Sarraceniaceae	1	1		
100. Droseraceae	1	5	2	
101. Podostemaceae	1	1		
102. Crassulaceae	4	21		
103. Hydraneaceae	4	10		
104. Grossulariaceae	1	13		
105. Saxifragaceae	7	16		
106. Hamamelidaceae	2	2		
107. Platanaceae	1	2		
108. Rosaceae	35	166	22	26
109. Fabaceae	55	151	9	4
110. Linaceae	2	10		
111. Oxalidaceae	1	5	1	
112. Geraniaceae	2	23	2	
113. Zygophyllaceae	1	1		
114. Rutaceae	5	6		
115. Simaroubaceae	1	1		
116. Polygalaceae	1	10	2	
117. Euphorbiaceae	7	31	1	
118. Callitrichaceae	1	5		
119. Buxaceae	2	2		
120. Empetraceae	2	3	1	
121. Limnanthaceae	1	1		
122. Anacardiaceae	3	9	1	1
123. Aquifoliaceae	2	6		
124. Celastraceae	2	8	1	
125. Staphyleaceae	1	1		
126. Aceraceae	1	11	2	1
127. Hippocastinaceae	1	2		
128. Sapindaceae	2	2		
129. Balsaminaceae	1	4		
130. Rhamnaceae	3	6		
131. Vitaceae	3	11	1	1
132. Tiliaceae	1	5	1	1
133. Malvaceae	15	26		
134. Actinidiaceae	1	1		
135. Clusiaceae	2	18		
136. Elatinaceae	1	3		
137. Tamaricaceae	1	2		
138. Cistaceae	3	14	1	
139. Violaceae	2	32	6	7
140. Loasaceae	1	1		
141. Cactaceae	1	1		

Families and Higher Levels	Genera	Species	Subspecies and Varieties	Named Hybrids
Fam. 142. Thymelaeaceae	2	2		
143. Elaeagnaceae	2	7		
144. Lythraceae	4	9		
145. Melastomataceae	1	2		
146. Onagraceae	8	38	2	2
147. Trapaceae	1	1		
148. Haloragaceae	2	13	1	
149. Hippuridaceae	1	1		
150. Araliaceae	4	10		
151. Apiaceae	39	61	2	
152. Cornaceae	1	8	1	2
153. Nyssaceae	1	1		
154. Clethraceae	1	1		
155. Monotropaceae	2	3		
156. Pyrolaceae	4	9		
157. Ericaceae	18	52	3	
158. Diapensiaceae	3	3		
159. Primulaceae	8	23	1	2
160. Plumbaginaceae	1	1		
161. Ebanaceae	1	1		
162. Styracaceae	1	1		
163. Oleaceae	5	17	1	1
164. Buddlejaceae		2	2	
165. Menyanthaceae	2	4		
166. Gentianaceae	8	20	1	
167. Apocynaceae	3	7		1
168. Asclepiadaceae	3	13	1	
169. Cuscutaceae	1	9		
170. Convolvulaceae	3	15	1	
171. Polemoniaceae	6	17		
172. Hydrophyllaceae	3	13		
173. Boraginaceae	18	47	1	
174. Verbenaceae	3	11	1	2
175. Lamiaceae	40	104	18	6
176. Solanaceae	16	42	1	
177. Scrophulariaceae	32	92	14	
178. Bignoniaceae	2	4		
179. Pedaliaceae	2	2		
180. Orobanchaceae	3	3		
181. Lentibulariaceae	2	14		
182. Acanthaceae	1	1		
183. Plantaginaceae	2	13	2	
184. Rubiaceae	10	35	4	1
185. Caprifoliaceae	10	38	12	1
186. Valerianaceae	2	5		
187. Dipsacaceae	5	8		
188. Cucurbitaceae	8	12		
189. Campanulaceae	16	25	2	
190. Asteraceae	118	359	105	14
Totals:	1048	3573	401	159

EXCLUDED TAXA

The following taxa have been attributed to New England but their occurrences have not been substantiated, therefore they have been excluded from this treatment. The italicized portions of plant names indicate that only the subtaxon is excluded from treatment, not the typical phase. The abbreviations in parenthesis refer to the state(s) to which the taxon has been attributed.

Lycopodium x issleri (ME)
Pteridium aquilinum *var. pubescens* (VT)
Asplenium trichomanes-dentatum (VT)
Athyrium filix-femina *subsp. cyclosorum* (All New England States)
Gymnocarpium disjunctum (RI)
Woodsia oregana (VT)
Salvinia auriculata (MA)
Potamogeton filiformis *var. occidentalis* (ME)
Sagittaria australis (ME)
S. latifolia *var. pubescens* (VT)
S. montevidensis (CT)
Agropyron desertorum (MA)
Leymus mollis *subsp. villosissimus* (MA, ME, NH)
Bromus inermis *subsp. pumpellianus var. arcticus* (ME)
Festuca vivipara (CT)
Arrhenatherum elatus *var. biaristatum* (RI)
Sphenopholis x pallens (ME, NH, VT, MA, CT)
Andropogon glomeratus *var. hirsutior* (RI)
Andropogon g. *var. pumilis* (MA, RI)
Schizachyrium scoparium *subsp. neomexicana* (ME)
Panicum sonorum (ME, RI, VT)
Dichanthelium aciculare (MA)
Aristida longispica *var. longispica*
Calamagrostis perplexa (MA)
Cenchrus carolinianus (CT, MA, ME, RI)
Carex muhlenbergii *var. australis* (CT)
C. salina (MA, ME, NH)
C. heteroneura (VT)
C. striata var. striata (MA, RI)
C. viridula *subsp. brachyrrhyncha* (RI)

C. emoryi (CT)
C. maritima (MA, ME, NH)
Cyperus entrerianus (MA, VT)
C. polystachyos *var. macrostachyus* (All New England States)
Eleocharis flavescens var. flavescens (VT)
Kobresia sibirica (VT)
Lemna minuta (RI)
Murdannia nudiflora (MA, VT) (Commelinaceae)
Juncus brachyphyllus (CT)
J. effusus *var. effusus* (ME)
J. interior (All New England States)
J. nodosus *var. meridianus* (All New England States)
Melanthium virginicum (RI)
Platanthera flava *var. flava* (RI)
P. hyperborea *var. hyperborea* (All New England States)
Spiranthes brevilabris (RI)
Salix caroliniana (ME, NH, MA, RI, CT)
S. commutata (ME)
S. reticulata subsp. nivalis (NH)
S. x solheimii (ME)
Quercus margarettiae (MA)
Q. falcata (RI)
Urtica dioica *subsp. holosericea* (VT)
Oxytheca dendroidea (ME) (Polygonaceae)
Corispermum orientale (RI)
Chenopodium botryodes (ME)
C. dessicatum (All New England States)
C. vulvaria (ME)
Celosia argentea (CT, VT)
Amaranthus polygonoides (ME)

Silene acaulis *var. acaulis* (ME)
Cerastium brachypetalum (ME)
Ceratophyllum muricatum (All New England States)
Arabis schistacea (VT)
Philadelphus caucasicus (MA)
Saxifraga cespitosa *subsp. cespitosa* (VT)
Heuchera americana *var. hirsuticaulis* (CT)
Rosa acicularus *subsp. acicularis* (CT, ME, NH, VT)
R. carolina *var. sabulosa* (ME)
R. nutkana (ME)
Rubus jugosus (ME)
R. macvaughii (ME)
R. mundus (ME)
R. pubifolius (ME)
R. scambens (MA)
Crataegus calpodendron (RI)
Argentina egedii *subsp. egedii* (ME, MA, RI)
Invesia petallifera (ME) (Rosaceae)
Robinia x margarettiae (All New England States)
Lathyrus japonicus *var. japonicus* (MA, NH)
Vicia ervilia (CT, MA, ME, VT)
Trifolium reflexum (RI)
T. stoloniferum (VT)
Oxalis latifolia (MA)
Ptelea trifoliata *subsp. pallida* (RI)
Polygala brevifolia (RI)
P. polgama *var. polygama* (RI)
Crotonopsis linearis (CT)
Acalypha virginica *var. deamii* (RI)
Toxicodendron pubescens (RI)
Ilex ambigua (CT, MA)
Acer saccharum *var. schneckii* (ME)
Impatiens noli-tangere (RI)
Rhamnus davurica *subsp. davurica* (MA)
Melia azedarach (ME)
Cnidium monnieri (RI)
Osmorhiza purpurea (RI)
Harrimanella stelleriana (RI)
Phyllodoce aleutica (VT)
Lyonia ligustrina *var. foliosiflora* (ME)
Gentiana prostrata (VT)
G. saponaria (RI)
Cuscuta cuspidata (CT)
C. obtusiflora (CT)
Myosotis canescens (RI)
Ballota nigra *var. alba* (CT)
Limosella aquatica (All except VT)

Agalinis obtusifolia (RI)
Ruellia carolinensis subsp. ciliosa var. cinerascens (MA)
Diodia teres *var. hystricina* (ME)
Houstonia canadensis (ME)
Viburnum dentatum *var. scabrellum* (ME)
V. molle (RI)
Lonicera caerulea (All New England States)
L. korolkowii (MA)
Ambrosia psilostachya (ME, NH, VT, MA, CT)
Flaveria bidentis (MA)
Helianthus debilis *subsp. debilis* (CT, MA, ME, VT)
Hieracium gracile (RI)
Artemisia cana subsp. cana (ME, VT)
Cotula australis (ME)
Achillea ligustica (VT)
A. millefolium *var. alpicola* (ME)
A. millefolium *var. litoralis* (ME, NH)
Pluchea odorata *var. odorata* (CT, MA, RI)
Gnaphalium obtusifolium *var. praecox* (RI)
Trimorpha acris *var. asteroides* (ME)
T. acris *var. debilis* (ME)
Aster drummondii *var. texanus* (RI, VT)
A. lanceolatus subsp. lanceolatus *var. interior* (ME, RI)
Lactuca floridana (MA)
L. hirsuta *var. hirsuta* (ME)
Solidago arguta *var. boottii* (RI)
S. simplex subsp. simplex *var. chlorolepis* (RI)
S. spathulata (ME, NH, RI, VT)
S. speciosa *var. rigidiuscula* (RI)
S. stricta (RI)
S. tortifolia (RI)
Helenium autumnale *var. montanum* (CT)
Brickellia oblongifolia (VT)

ABBREVIATIONS OF THE MORE FREQUENTLY CITED BOTANICAL AUTHORS

Adans.   Adanson, Michel
Ait.   Aiton, William
Ait. f.   Alton, William Townsend
Al   Al-Shehbaz & Bates
Alef.   Alefeld, Friedrich
All.   Allioni, Carlo
Anderss.   Andersson, Nils Johan
Andr.   Andrews, Henry C.
Andrz.   Andrzejowski, Anton Lukianowicz
Angstr.   Angstrom, Johan
Applegate   Elmer Ivan
Arcang.   Arcangeli, Giovanni
Arn.   Arnott, George Arnold Walker
Arnold   Johann Franz Xaver
Arthur   Joseph Charles
Aschers.   Ascherson, Paul
Aschers. & Graebn.   Ascherson, Paul A. and
   Graebner, Paul
Ashe   William Willard
Aubl.   Aublet, Jean Baptiste Christophe
   Fusee
Aust.   Austin, Coe Finch
B.S.P.   Britton, Nathaniel Lord, Sterns,
   Emerson Ellick, and Poggenberg, Justus
   Ferdinand
Bab.   Babington, Charles Cardale
Bailey   Liberty Hyde
Baker   John Gilbert
Balbis   Giovanni Battista
Baldw.   Baldwin, William
Banks   Sir Joseph
Barneby   Rupert Charles
Barnh.   Barnhart, John Hendley
Bart.   Barton, Benjamin Smith
Bartr.   Bartram, William
Batsch   August Johann Georg Karl
Baumg.   Baumgarten, Johann Christian
   Gottlob

Bayer   Johann Nepomuk
Beal   William James
Beauv.   Beauvois, Ambroise Marie Francois
   Joseph Palisot de
Beck, G.   Beck Von Mannagetta, Gunther
Bellardi   Carlo Antonio Ludovico
Benn. Ar.   Bennett, Arthur
Benson   Lyman
Benth.   Bentham, George
Benth. & Hook.   Bentham, George, and
   Hooker, Joseph Dalton
Berg   Otto Karl
Bernh.   Bernhardi, Johann Jacob
Berth.   Berthelot, Sabin
Bess.   Besser, Wilibald Swibert Josef Gottlieb
Besser   Wilibald Swibert Josef Gottlieb
Betcke   Ernst Friedrich
Bickn.   Bicknell, Eugene Pintard
Bieb.   Bieberstein, Friedrich August,
   Marschall von
Bigel.   Bigelow, Jacob
Bigelow   Jacob
Bisch.   Bischoff, Gottlieb Wilhelm
Blake or Blake, S. F.   Blake, Sidney Fay
Blanch.   Blanchard, William Henry
Blume   Karl Ludwig
Boeckl.   Boeckeler, Otto
Boenn.   Boenninghausen, Clemens Maria
   Friedrich von
Boiss.   Boissier, Edmond
Boiv., B.   Boivin, Joseph Robert Bernard
Bong.   Bongard, Heinrich Gustav
Boott   Francis
Boott   William
Boreau   Alexandre
Borkh.   Borkhausen, Moritz Balthasar
Br., A.   Braun, Alexander
Br., P.   Browne, Patrick

Br., R.   Brown, Robert
Brack.   Brackenridge, William D.
Brainerd   Ezra
Braun   Alexander
Briot   Charles
Briq.   Briquet, John
Britt.   Britton, Nathanial Lord
Britton   Nathanial Lord
Brot.   Brotero, Felix de Avellar
Buch. & Fern.   Buchenau, Franz, and
Fernald, Merritt Lyndon
Buchenau   Franz
Buckl.   Buckley, Samuel Botsford
Bunge   Alexander von
Burm. f.   Burmann, Nikolaus Laurens
Buse   L. H.
Butters   Frederic King
Campd.   Campdera, Francois
Carr.   Carriere, Elie Abel
Cass.   Cassini, Henri
Cav.   Cavanilles, Antonio Jose
Celak.   Celakovsky, Ladislav
Chaix   Dominique
Cham.   Chamisso, Ludolf Adalbert von
Chapm.   Chapman, Alvan Wentworth
Chapman   Alvan Wentworth
Chase   Agnes
Chatclaim
Chev.   Chevallier, Auguste
Choisy   Jacques Denis
Clairv.   Clairville, Joseph Phillippe de
Clarke   Charles Baron
Clausen   Robert Theodore
Clayton   John
Cockerell   Theodore Dru Alison
Coult.   Coulter, John Merle
Crantz   Heinrich Johann Nepomuk von
Crepin   Francois
Cronq.   Cronquist, Arthur
Curt.   Curtiss, William
DC   DeCandolle, Augustin Pyramus
DC, A.   DeCandolle, Alphonse Louis Pierre
Pyramus
Darl.   Darlington, William
Davenp.   Davenport, George Edward
Dcne.   Decaisne, Joseph
Desf.   Desfontaines, Rene Louiche
Desr.   Desrousseaux, Louis Auguste Joseph
Desv.   Desvaux, Augustin Nicaise

Dewey   Chester
Dickson   Edward Dalzell
Dieck   George
Dietr. or Dietr., A.   Dietrich, Albert
Dill.   Dillenius, Johann Jacob
Don, D.   Don, David
Don, G.   Don, George
Donn   James
Drej.   Drejer, Salomon Thomas Nicolai
Druce   George Claridge
Drude   Carl George Oscar
Du Roi   Johann Philipp
Duchesne   Antoine Nicolas
Dufr.   Dufresne, Pierre
Dum. -Cours.   Dumont de Courset, Georges
Louis Marie
Dum. or Dumort.   Dumortier, Bathelemy
Charles
Dunal   Michel Felix
Dur.   Durieu De Maisonneuve, M.C.
Durand   Elias Magloire
Eames   Edward Ashley
Eat.   Eaton, Amos
Eat., D. C.   Eaton, Daniel Cady
Eat., H. H.   Eaton, Hezekiah Hulbert
Egglest. & Sheld.   E. and Sheldon, Edmund
Perry
Ehrh.   Ehrhart, Friedrich
Ell.   Elliott, Stephen
Ellis   John
Engelm.   Engelmann, George
Engelm. & Gray   E. and Gray, Asa
Engl.   Engler, Heinrich Gustav Adolph
Epl.   Epling, Carl Clawson
Epling   Carl Clawson
Fabr.   Fabricius, Philipp Konrad
Farw.   Farwell, Oliver Atkins
Fassett   Norman Carter
Fenzl   Eduard
Fern.   Fernald, Merritt Lyndon
Fern. & Brack.   F. and Brackett, Amelia Ellen
Fern. & Gale.   F. and Gale (Cross), Shirley
Fern. & Grisc.   F. and Griscom, Ludlow
Fern. & Schub.   F. and Schubert, Bernice
Giduz
Fern. & Wieg.   F. and Wiegand, Karl McKay
Fisch.   Fischer, Friedrich Ernst Ludwig von
Fisch. & Ave-Lall   F. and Ave-Lallemant,
Julius Edward Leopold

Fisch & Mey. or C. A. Mey   F. and Meyer, Karl Anton

Flugge or Fluegge   Johann

Focke   Wilhelm Olbers

Forsk.   Forskal, Pehr

Forst.   Forster, Thomas Furly

Foster, M.   Foster, Sir Michael

Foug.   Fougeroux, Auguste Denis

Franch.   Franchet, Adrien

Fries   Elias Magnus

Fritsch   Karl

Froel.   Froelich, Joseph Aloys

Gaertn.   Gaertner, Joseph

Gattinger   August

Gaud.   Gaudichaud-Beaupre, Charles

Gay, J.   Gay, Jacques

Gill.   Gillies, John

Gl.   Gleason, Henry Allan

Gleason   Henry Allan

Gmel., J. F.   Gmelin, Johann Friedrich

Gmel.   Gmelin, Samuel Gottlieb

Gmel., K. C.   Gmelin, Karl Christian

Godr.   Godron, Dominique Alexandre

Goodenough   Samuel

Gouan   Antoine

Gray   Asa

Gray, S. F.   Gray, Samuel Frederick

Greene   B.D.

Greene   Edward Lee

Grev. & Hook.   Greville, Robert K., and Hooker, William Jackson

Gronov.   Gronovius, Jan Fredrik

Guss.   Gussoni, Giovanni

HBK.   Humboldt, Friedrich Wilhelm Heinrich Alexander von, Bonpland, Aime, and Kunth, Carl Sigismund

Hack.   Hackel, Eduard

Haller   Albrecht von

Hand.-Maz.   Handell-Mazzetti, Heinrich

Hara   Hiroshi

Hartm.   Hartman, Carl Johan

Hartman   Carl Johan

Harv.   Harvey, William Henry

Hassk.   Hasskarl, Justus Carl

Haw.   Haworth, Adrian Hardy

Hayek   August

Hayne   Friedrich Gottlob

Hegelm.   Hegelmaier, Friedrich Joseph

Heist.   Heister, Lorenz

Heller   Amos Arthur

Herrm.   Herrmann, W.

Heynh.   Heynhold, Gustav

Hiern   William Philip

Hill   John

Hill, J.   Hill, John

Hitchc. or Hitch., A. S.   Hitchcock, Albert Spear

Hitchc., A. S. & Chase   H. and Chase, Agnes

Hitchc., E.   Hitchcock, Edward

Hochst.   Hochstetter, Christian Friedrich

Hoffm.   Hoffmann, Georg Franz

Holmb.   Holmberg, Otto Rudolph

Holz.   Holzinger, John M.

Honckeny   Gerhard August

Hook.   Hooker, William Jackson

Hook., J. D.   Hooker, Joseph Dalton

Hoppe   D. H.

Hornem.   Hornemann, Jens Wilken

Hort.   Hortorum. Designatum for names current among horticulturists

Host   Nicolaus Thomas

House   Homer Doliver

Houtt.   Houttuyn, Martin

Hubbard, F. T.   Hubbard, Frederic Tracy

Huds.   Hudson, William

Hull   John H.

Jackson   B. D.

Jacq.   Jacquin, Nicolaus Joseph

Jacques   Henri Antoine

James   Edwin

Johnst.   Johnston, Ivan Murray

Jones   Marcus Eugene

Juss.   Jussieu, Antoine Laurent de

Juss., B.   Jussieu, Bernard de

Karst.   Karsten, Hermann

Kartesz & Gandhi   Kartesz, John T., and Gandhi

Keck & J. Clausen

Ker or Ker - Gawl   Ker, John Bellenden (first known as John Gawler)

Klotzsch   Johann Friedrich

Knight   Joseph

Koch   Karl Heinrich Emil

Koch, K.   Koch, Karl

Koch, W .D. J. or Koch, W.   Koch, Wilhelm Daniel Joseph

Koehne   Emil

Koel.   Koeler, George Ludwig

Krecz. Kreczetowicz, V.

Kuhn Maximilian Friedrich Adalbert

Kukenth. Kukenthal, Georg

Kunth Carl Sigesmund

Kuntze Otto

L'Her. L'Heritier De Brutelle, Charles Louis

L. Linnaeus, Carolus, or Linne, Carl von

L. f. Linne, Carl von (the son)

Lag. Lagasca, Mariano

Lag. & Rodr. L. and Rodriquez, Jose Demetrio

Lam. Lamarck, Jean Baptiste Pierre Antoine de Monet de

Lamb. Lambert, Alymer Bourke

Lange Johan Martin Christian

Lat. Latourette, Marc Antoine Louis Claret de

Laxm. Laxmann, Eric

Ledeb. Ledebour, Carl Friedrich von

Lehm. Lehmann, Johann Georg Christian

Lej. Lejeune, Louis Simon

Lepechin Ivan

Lesp. & Thev. Lespinasse, Gustave, and Theveneau

Less. Lessing, Christian Friedrich

Leyss. Leysser, Friedrich Wilhelm von

Lightf. Lightfoot, John

Lindl. Lindley, John

Lindm. Lindman, Carl Axel Magnus

Link Johann Heinrich Friedrich

Llave & Lex. Llave, Pablo de la, and Lexarza, Juan

Lodd. Loddiges, Conrad

Loefl. Loefling, Pehr

Loes. Loesener, Ludwig Eduard Theodore

Loisel. Loiseleur-Deslongchamps, Jean Louis Auguste

Loud. Loudon, John Claudius

Lour. Loureiro, Juan

Macbr., J. F. Macbride, James Francis

Mackenz. Mackenzie, Kenneth Kent

Mackenz. & Bush M. and Bush, Benjamin Franklin

Mackenzie Kenneth Kent

MacM. MacMillan, Conway

Makino Tomitaro

Marsh. Marshall, Humphrey

Mart. Martius, Karl Friedrich Philipp von

Martens Martin

Mattf. Mattfield, Johannes

Maxim. Maximowicz, Carl Johann

Medic. Medicus, Friedrich Casimir

Meerb. Meerburgh, Nicolaas

Meisn. Meisner, Carl Friedrich

Merr. Merrill, Elmer Drew

Mert. & Koch. Mertens, Franz Carl, and Koch, Wilhelm Daniel Joseph

Mett. Mettenius, Georg Heinrich

Mey. Meyer, Ernst Heinrich Friedrich

Mey., C. A. Meyer, Carl Anton

Mey., G. F. Meyer, George Friedrich

Meyer, E. Meyer, Ernst Heinrich Friedrich

Michx. Michaux, Andre

Michx. f. Michaux, Francois Andre

Mill. or Mill. P. Miller, Philip

Miq. Miquel, Friedrich Anton Wilhelm

Mitchell John

Moench Conrad

Moldenke Harold N.

Molina Juan Ignacio

Moore Thomas

Moq. Moquin-Tandon, Alfred

Moquin -Tandon, Alfred

Morren & Decne. Morren, Charles Jacques Edouard, and Decaisne, Joseph

Muell. Arg Mueller, Jean (of Aargau)

Muenchh. Muenchhausen, Otto Freiherr von

Muhl. Muhlenberg, Gotthilf Henry Ernest

Munro William

Murr. Murray, Johann Andreas

Nakai Takenoshi

Nash George Valentine

Nees Nees von Esenbeck, Christian Gottfried

Nees & Eberm. N. and Ebermaier, Karl Heinrich

Nels. Nelson, Aven

Neum. Neuman, Leopold Martin

Nieuwl. Nieuwland, Julius Arthur

Nutt. Nuttall, Thomas

Nyman Carl Frederik

Oakes William

Ohwi Jisaburo

Olney Stephen Thayer

Opiz Philipp Maximilian

Ostenf. Ostenfeld, Carl Emil Hansen

Paine John Alsop

Pall. Pallas, Peter Simon
Pallas Peter Simon
Palmer Ernest Jesse
Palmer & Steyermark P. and Steyermark, Julian Alfred
Paris Cathy A.
Parl. Parlatore, Filippo
Peck Morton Eaton
Pennell Francis Whittier
Perry & Fern. Perry, Lily May, and Fernald, Merritt Lyndon
Pers. Persoon, Christian Hendrik
Phil. Philippi, Rudolf Amandus
Pilger Robert Knud Friedrich
Piper Charles Vancouver
Planch. Planchon, Jules Emile
Poir. Poiret, Jean Louis Marie
Poll. Pollich, Johann Adam
Pollard Charles Louis
Porter Thomas Conrad
Pourret Pierre Andre
Prantl K. A. E.
Presl, C. Presl, Carel Borowag
Presl, K. Presl, Karel Borowog
Pursh Frederick T.
R. & S. Roemer, Johann Jakob, and Schultes, Joseph August
R. & P. Ruiz Lopez, Hipolito, and Pavon, Joseph
Roemer & J. A. Schultes Roemer, Johann Jacob, and Schultes, Josef August
Raeusch Raeuschel, Ernest Adolph
Raf. or Rafn. Rafinesque-Schmaltz, Constantine Samuel
Regel Edward von
Rehd. Rehder, Alfred
Rehder Alfred
Reichard Johann Jacob
Reichenb. Reichenbach, Heinrich Gottlieb Ludwig
Retz. Retzius, Anders Johan
Rich., A. Richard, Achille
Rich., L. C. Richard, Louis Claude Marie
Richards. Richardson, John
Riddell John Leonard
Robins. or Robins., B. L. Robinson, Benjamin Lincoln
Robins., B. L. & Fern. R. and Fernald,

Merritt Lyndon
Roem & Schult or Roemer & J.A.
  Schultes Roemer, Max J., and Schultes, Joseph August
Roemer Max J.
Rostk. Rostkovius, Friedrich Wilhelm Gottlieb
Rostk. & Schmidt. R. and Schmidt, Wilhelm Ludwig Ewald
Roth Albrecht Wilhelm
Rottb. Rottboell, Christen Fries
Rowlee Willard Winfield
Royle John Forbes
Rudge Edward
Ruiz & Pavon Ruiz Lopez, Hipolito, and Pavon, Joseph
Rupr. Ruprecht, Franz Joseph
Ruprecht Franz Joseph
Rusby Henry Hurd
Ryd. or Rydb. Rydberg, Per Axel
Salis. or Salisb. Salisbury, Richard Anthony
Sarg. Sargent, Charles Sprague
Savi Gaetano
Schaffn. Schaffner, John Henry
Scheele George Heinrich Adolph
Schinz Hans
Schinz & Thellung S. and Thellung, Albert
Schk. Schkuhr, Christian
Schleich. Schleicher, Johann Christoph
Schleid. Schleiden, Matthias Jacob
Schmidt, F. Schmidt, Franz
Schneid. or Schneid, C. K. Schneider, Camillo Karl
Schott Heinrich Wilhelm
Schrad. Schrader, Heinrich Adolph
Schrank Franz von Paula von
Schreb. Schreber, Johann Daniel Christian von
Schub. Schubert, Bernice Giduz.
Schult. Schultes, Joseph August
Schultes, J. A. Schultes, Joseph August
Schultz Bip. Schultz, Carl Heinrich of Zweibrucken (Bipontinus)
Schum. Schumann, Karl
Schur Philipp Johann Ferdinand
Schwarz Otto
Schweigg. & Koerte Schweigger, August Friedrich, and Koerte, Franz
Schwein. Schweinitz, Lewis David de

Schwein. & Torr.   S. and Torrey, John
Scop.   Scopoli, Johann Anton
Scribn.   Lamson-Scribner, Frank
Scribn. & Ball or C. R. Ball.   L.-S. and Ball, Carleton Roy
Seem.   Seemann, Berthold Carl
Sellow   Friedrich
Sendt.   Sendtner, Otto
Ser.   Seringe, Nicolas Charles
Seringe   Nicolas Charles
Sheldon   Edmund Perry
Sibth.   Sibthorp, John
Sibth. & Smith   S. and Smith, James Edward
Sieb.   Siebold, Phillipp Franz von
Sieb. & Zucc.   S. and Zuccarini, Joseph Gerhard
Siebold   Philipp Franz von
Sims   John
Sm.   Smith, James Edward
Sm., J. G.   Smith, Jared Gage
Small   John Kunkel
Smith or Smith, J. E.   Smith, James Edward
Sobol.   Sobolewski, Gregor
Soland.   Solander, Daniel
Solander   Daniel
Sommier & Levier   Sommier, Stefano, and Levier, Emile
Spach   Edouard
Spenner   Fridolin Karl Leopold
Spreng.   Sprengel, Kurt
St. Hil.   Saint Hilaire, August de
St. John   Harold
Standl.   Standley, Paul Carpenter
Stearn   Stearn, W. T.
Sternb. & Hoppe   Sternberg, Caspar M. von, and Hoppe, David Heinrich
Steud.   Steudel, Ernst Gottlieb
Steyerm.   Steyermark, Julian Alfred
Stokes   Jonathan
Sudw.   Sudworth, George Bishop
Sulliv.   Sullivant, William Starling
Sullivant   William Starling
Sur.   Suringar, Jan Valckenier
Sw.   Swartz, Olof
Swartz   Olof
Sweet   Robert
Syme   Boswell-Syme, J. T. I.
T. & G.   Torrey, John, and Gray, Asa
Tausch   Ignaz Friedrich

Ten.   Tenore, Michele
Tenore   Michele
Thell.   Thellung, Albert
Thellung   Albert
Thuill   Thuillier, Jean Louis
Thunb.   Thunberg, Carl Pehr
Todaro   Agostino
Torr.   Torrey, John
Torr. & Gray   Torrey, John, and Gray, Asa
Torr. & Hook.   T. and Hooker, William Jackson
Torr., G. S.   Torrey, George Safford
Torrey & Gray   Torrey, John, and Gray, Asa
Tratt.   Trattinick, Leopold
Trautv.   Trautvetter, Ernst Rudolf von
Trel.   Trelease, William
Trev.   Treviranus, Christian Ludolf
Trevisan   Conte Victore
Trin.   Trinius, Karl Bernhard von
Tuckerm.   Tuckerman, Edward
Tuckerman   Edward
Turcz.   Turczaninow, Nicolaus
Turra   Antonio
Turrill   W. B.
Urban   Ignatius
Vahl   Martin
Vasey   George R.
Vell.   Vellozo de Conceicao, Jose Marianno
Vent.   Ventenat, Etienne Pierre
Vest.   Vest, L. Chr. von
Vill.   Villars, Dominique
Villars   Dominique
Vilm.   Vilmorin (several generations of botanical authors)
Vitm.   Vitman, Fulgenzio
Vitman   Fulgenzio
Voss   Andreas
Wahl   Herbert Alexander
Wahl. or Wahlenb.   Wahlenberg, Georg (Goran)
Waldst. & Kit.   Waldstein, Franz de Paul Adam Graf von, and Kitaibel, Paul
Wall.   Wallich, Nathanial
Wallr.   Wallroth, Carl Friedrich Wilhelm
Walp.   Walpers, Wilhelm Gerhard
Walt.   Walter, Thomas
Wang. or Wangenh.   Wangenheim, Friedrich Adam Julius von
Wats.   Watson, Sereno

Wats. & Coult.   W. and Coulter, John Merle
Wats., S.   Watson, Sereno
Weath.   Weatherby, Charles Alfred
Weatherby   Charles Alfred
Webb & Berth.   Webb, Philip Barker, and Berthelot, Sabin
Weber, G. H.   Weber, Georg Heinrich
Wedd.   Weddell, Hugh Algernon
Weddell   Hugh Algernon
Weston   Richard
Wettst.   Wettstein, Richard von
Wherry   Edgar Theodore

Wieg.   Wiegand, Karl McKay
Willd.   Willdenow, Karl Ludwig
Wimm. & Grab.   Wimmer, Friedrich, and Grabowski, Heinrich
With.   Withering, William
Wood   Alphonzo
Woot. & Standl.   Wooton, Elmer Otis, and Standley, Paul Carpenter
Wormsk.   Wormskjold, Morten
Wulfen   Franz Xaver von
Zabel   Hermann

FLORA OF THE NORTHEAST

A Manual of the Vascular Flora
of New England and
Adjacent New York

General Keys

KEY TO GROUPS

A. Plants with branched stems composed of flattened, suborbicular to ovoid
    segments separated by constrictions, usually also with spines and glochids
    (smaller barbed bristles) (*Opuntia humifusa*) .... *Cactaceae*
A. Plant not as above.
  B. Plant early in the growing season exhibiting only a spathe (pouch-like leaf
      open on 1 side) and spadix, nearly sessile and barely rising out of the
      ground, maroon and greenish spotted and striped, with a strong,
      skunk-like odor (*Symplocarpus foetidus*) .... *Araceae*
  B. Plant not as above.
    C. Insectivorous plants with rosulate, hollow, pitcher-shaped leaves, usually partly
        filled with water and decayed insects (*Sarracenia purpurea*). .... *Sarraceniaceae*
    C. Plant without this combination of characters.
      D. Plants aquatic; free-floating, submerged, or with floating or emersed leaves .. Group 1, p. 2
      D. Plants emergent, growing at least partly out of water, or entirely out
          of water.
        E. Plants parasitic or saprophytic on stems or roots of other plants,
            often without green color .... Group 2, p. 6
        E. Plants not parasitic or saprophytic on other plants, with stems, leaves
            or other parts usually green.
          F. Plant a vine climbing by twining or by tendrils (or by tendril-like
              compound leaves) or adhesive roots, or plant trailing on the
              ground for 3 or more feet without rooting. .... Group 3, p. 6
          F. Plant erect or leaning but not a climbing vine, or if trailing, stems less
              than 3 feet long or rooting at intervals shorter than 3 feet.
            G. Plants not producing flowers or seeds, entirely free-sporing.
                Pteridophytes (Ferns and Fern Allies) .... Group 4, p. 9
            G. Plants producing flowers and/or seeds in season, or flowers
                replaced by vegetative buds, bulblets or leafy tufts.
                Spermatophytes (Seed Plants).
              H. Plant herbaceous.
                I. Plants producing sterile inflorescences only, i.e. the flowers
                    replaced by vegetative buds, bulblets or leafy tufts. .... Group 5, p. 11
                I. Plants producing flowers and seeds.
                  J. Leaves usually parallel-veined; parts of the flowers usually
                      in 3s, 6s, 9s or many, rarely in 2s or 4s, never in 5s:
                      certain Monocotyledons (few Dicotyledons) .... Group 6, p. 11
                  J. Leaves usually net-veined; parts of the flowers usually in 4s,
                      5s, multiples thereof, or many: certain herbaceous
                      Dicotyledons (few Monocotyledons).
                    Plants scapose, the scape naked or with one to few bracts. .. Group 7, p. 14
                    Plants with leafy stems.
                      Plants with leaves opposite or whorled .... Group 8, p. 19
                      Plants with leaves alternate .... Group 9, p. 29

1

H. Plant woody (trees or shrubs).

GROUP 1

Herbaceous Aquatic Plants;
Free-Floating, Submerged or With Floating or Emersed Leaves

A. Plant free-floating on or near the surface, not attached to the bottom.
  B. Plant moss-like, with 2-ranked leaves.
    Stems simple; leaves 2-ranked, mostly 1 cm or more long (*Salvinia minima*). .... *Salviniaceae*
    Stems dichotomously branched; leaves imbricated, minute, mostly 1 mm or
      less long .... *Azollaceae*
  B. Plant an ovoid, ellipsoid or linear body resembling a leaf, or plant with cordate
      leaves, or with leaves in rosettes, not moss-like.
    Plant an ovoid, ellipsoid or linear body up to 1 cm long resembling a tiny leaf,
      several plants often attached together. .... *Lemnaceae*
    Plant with cordate leaves more than 1 cm long, not attached together nor in
      rosettes or radiating (*Nymphoides*) .... *Menyanthaceae*
    Plant with leaves in rosettes or radiating, not cordate.
      Leaf petioles spongy-inflated at base; blades orbicular to reniform;
        flowers not in spadices (*Eichornia crassipes*). .... *Pontederiaceae*
      Leaf petioles not spongy-inflated; blades oblong; flowers in spadices in the
        leaf axils (*Pistia stratiotes*) .... *Araceae*
A. Plant attached to the bottom or free-floating beneath the surface.
  C. Petioles or leaf rachis inflated, or stems spongy-thickened.
    Petioles or leaf rachis inflated; stems not spongy-thickened.
      Leaf rachis inflated, blade with ultimate segments finely divided; flowers
        irregular; fruit lacking spines (*Utricularia*). .... *Lentibulariaceae*
      Leaf petioles inflated, blade not divided, entire or merely toothed.
        Leaves toothed; flowers regular; fruit with 2-4 stout spines (*Trapa natans*) . *Trapaceae*
        Leaves entire; flowers irregular; fruit capsular, not as above
          (*Eichornia crassipes*) .... *Pontederiaceae*
    Petioles or leaf rachis not inflated; stems spongy-thickened. (*Hottonia inflata*) .. *Primulaceae*
  C. Petioles or leaf rachis not inflated; stems not spongy-thickened.
    D. Plant attached to stones in current by fleshy discs (*Podostemum ceratophyllum*) *Podostemaceae*
    D. Plant rooted or free-floating, not attached by fleshy discs.
      E. Stems leafless, or with minute entire leaves or bracts, not growing in
          grass-like patches.
        Flowers regular; ovary inferior (*Myriophyllum*). .... *Haloragaceae*
        Flowers irregular; ovary superior. (*Utricularia*). .... *Lentibulariaceae*
      E. Stems leafy, with divided, toothed or entire leaves, or plants acaulescent,
          or if stems present and leafless then growing in grass-like patches.
        F. Plant lacking submerged leaves, with floating or emersed leaves only.
          G. Leaves with 4 leaflets, resembling a 4-leaved clover
              (*Marsilea quadrifolia*) .... *Marsileaceae*
          G. Leaves simple.
            H. Leaves equitant and ensiform or linear (Iris). .... *Iridaceae*
            H. Leaves not as above.

I. Blades peltate.
    Blades oval, 1 dm or less wide, floating (*Brasenia schreberi*). .... *Cabombaceae*
    Blades orbicular, 3 dm or more wide, raised above the water
        (*Nelumbo lutea*) .... *Nelumbonaceae*
I. Blades not peltate.
  J. Blades cordate, sagittate or hastate at base.
    K. Blades sagittate or hastate.
      Blades parallel-veined (*Sagittaria*) .... *Alismataceae*
      Blades pinnately-veined (*Peltandra virginica*) .. . . *Araceae*
    K. Blades cordate.
      Flowers umbellate below the blade, often accompanied by
        a cluster of tubers; corolla 5-parted (*Nymphoides*) ... *Menyanthaceae*
      Flowers solitary, not accompanied by a cluster of tubers;
        corolla of numerous petals.
        Blades more than twice as long as wide
          (*Pontederia cordata*). .... *Pontederiaceae*
        Blades less than twice as long as wide.
          Leaves acute at tip; flowers on a spadix subtended by
            a flat, white spathe (*Calla palustris*) .... *Araceae*
          Leaves rounded at tip; flowers solitary, not on a
            spadix nor subtended by a spathe.
            Flowers yellow to red or purple; leaves pinnately-
              veined (*Nuphar*). .... *Nymphaeaceae*
            Flowers white or pink; leaves with veins mostly
              radiating from base of sinus (*Nymphaea*) ..... *Nymphaeaceae*
  J. Blades truncate to obtuse or acute at base.
    Plant with leaves sessile in rosettes (*Pistia statiotes*). .... *Araceae*
    Plant not as above.
      Blades truncate at base; flowers purple (*Pontederia*
        cordata). .... *Pontederiaceae*
      Blades obtuse to acute at base; flowers yellow
        (*Orontium aquaticum*) .... *Araceae*
F. Plant with submerged leaves only, or with both submerged and floating
  or emersed leaves, or plant with leafless stems growing in grass-like
  patches.
  L. Submerged leaves divided, deeply dissected or lobed.
    M. Submerged leaves divided into narrow, much longer than wide
      segments.
    N. Leaves opposite or whorled.
      O. Leaves whorled.
        P. Submerged leaves divided into finely forked segments.
          Leaves bearing bladders; flowers with conspicuous
            irregular corolla (*Utricularia*) .... *Lentibulariaceae*
          Leaves lacking bladders; flowers lacking a corolla
            (*Ceratophyllum*). .... *Ceratophyllaceae*
        P. Submerged leaves once pinnately divided (*Myriophyllum*) ...... *Haloragaceae*
      O. Leaves opposite.
        Submerged leaves petioled, fan-shaped, with flattened
          divisions; floating leaves peltate, entire
            (*Cabomba caroliniana*) .... *Cabombaceae*
        Submerged leaves sessile, with numerous thread-like
          divisions; floating or emersed leaves not peltate,
            toothed (*Megalodonta*). .... *Asteraceae*
    N. Leaves alternate, scattered, subopposite or basal.
      Q. Leaves principally alternate, scattered or subopposite, basal
        leaves sometimes also present.
        R. Submerged leaves pinnately divided.
          S. Submerged leaves repeatedly pinnately divided
            (*Armoracia lacustris*). .... *Brassicaceae*
          S. Submerged leaves once pinnately divided.

Flowers and fruits corymbose-paniculate; ovary
superior (*Rorippa*). .... *Brassicaceae*
Flowers and fruits solitary or in small clusters in the
upper leaf axils; ovary inferior. .... *Haloragaceae*
R. Submerged leaves divided into finely forked segments.
Leaves branching from the base into 2 main divisions;
bladders frequently present; flowers irregular
(*Utricularia*). .... *Lentibulariaceae*
Leaves not branching from the base into 2 main divisions;
bladders absent; flowers regular (*Ranunculus*) .... *Ranunculaceae*
Q. Leaves principally basal, in a rosette (*Sium suave*) . ... *Apiaceae*
M. Submerged leaves divided into elliptic or round segments, nearly
as wide as to wider than long.
Stems rooting at the lower nodes; basal rosettes absent, leaves
principally alternate (*Rorippa*) .... *Brassicaceae*
Stems, when present, not rooting at the lower nodes; basal
rosettes present at the base of or separate from the stem,
stem leaves alternate (*Cardamine*). .... *Brassicaceae*
L. Submerged leaves undivided.
T. Leaves coming up from the bottom, or at the base of a stem or
scape, or leaves absent and stems growing in grass-like patches.
U. Leaves limp and filiform or ribbon-like, up to a meter long, not
in a rosette.
V. Leaves with a fine-veined, lightly-colored center stripe
(*Vallisneria americana*) .... *Hydrocharitaceae*
V. Leaves lacking a center stripe.
W. Leaves with cross veins present between the parallel veins.
Leaves with numerous, crowded parallel veins and cross
veins forming minute, squarish cells .... *Sparganiaceae*
Leaves with scattered cross veins between the parallel
veins, not forming distinct squarish cells
(*Sagittaria*). .... *Alismataceae*
W. Leaves lacking cross veins between the parallel veins.
X. Leaves arising in a flat, fan-line plane along a stout
rhizome (*Butomus umbellatus*) .... *Butomaceae*
X. Leaves not arising in a flat, fan-like plane from a rhizome.
Y. Leaves filiform, bases not sheathing.
Leaves with swollen, bulb-like bases containing
sporangia (*Isoetes*). .... *Isoetaceae*
Leaves without swollen, bulb-like bases, not
containing sporangia (*Scirpus*). .... *Cyperaceae*
Y. Leaves broader, ribbon-like, frequently with sheathing
bases (*Alisma*) *Alismataceae*; (*Glyceria, Zizania*)
Poaceae; (*Pontederia cordata*) .... *Pontederiaceae*
U. Leaves short and stiff in a distinct rosette or directly from an
underground rhizome, or absent and the plant composed
of numerous fine stems occurring in grass-like patches.
Z. Leaves present, short and stiff.
a. Roots with conspicuous cross markings; flowers in small,
dense, terminal heads (*Eriocaulon*) .... *Eriocaulaceae*
a. Roots lacking cross markings; flowers not in heads.
b. Leaves (actually phyllodes) transversely septate; flowers in
umbels (*Lilaeopsis chinensis*) .... *Apiaceae*
b. Leaves not transversely septate; flowers not in umbels.
c. Leaves with swollen, bulb-like bases containing
sporangia (*Isoetes*). .... *Isoetaceae*
c. Leaves without swollen, bulb-like bases, not
containing sporangia.
Leaves fleshy, hollow; stems mostly more than
1 dm long; sepals 5; flower 1 cm or more long
(*Lobelia*) .... *Campanulaceae*

Leaves linear or subulate, not fleshy or hollow;
  stems 1 dm or less long; sepals 4 or fewer;
  flower less than 1 cm long.
  Plant monoecious; scapes usually much
      overtopped by the leaves; fruit an achene
      (*Littorella americana*) .... Plantaginaceae
  Plant hermaphrodite; scapes usually over-topping
      the leaves; fruit a silicle (*Subularia
      aquatica*) .... Brassicaceae
Z. Leaves absent, stems thin, soft; growing in grass-like patches.
  d. Ovary many-seeded; fruit a capsule (*Juncus*). .... Juncaceae
  d. Ovary one-seeded; fruit an achene.
    Achene crowned by a tubercle or swollen style base
        (*Eleocharis*). .... Cyperaceae
    Achene not crowned by a tubercle or swollen style base
        (*Scirpus*.). .... Cyperaceae
T. Leaves occurring along an elongate stem.
  e. Leaves opposite or whorled.
    f. Leaves whorled.
      g. Leaves minutely serrulate, mostly in whorles of 3-4 or if
          more numerous, more than 5 mm wide (*Elodea*) .... Hydrocharitaceae
      g. Leaves entire, mostly in whorles of 4-6 or more, 3 mm or
          less wide.
        Leaves in whorles of 6 or more, the lowest scale-like;
            flowers solitary in the upper leaf axils
            (*Hippuris vulgaris*). .... Hippuridaceae
        Leaves in whorles of 6 or fewer, the lowest not scale-like;
            flowers in a usually solitary, terminal head
            (*Sclerolepis uniflora*). .... Asteraceae
    f. Leaves opposite.
      h. Stems long and slender, floating, creeping or decumbent.
        i. Leaves linear.
          j. Leaves widened below into a sheathing base (*Najas*). ..... Najadaceae
          j. Leaves tapered to rounded or truncate at base, not
              sheathing.
            Leaves 2.5 cm or more long, with sheathing
                stipules; stigma broad and flat; achenes
                flattened, falcate, often toothed on back
                (*Zannichellia palustris*). .... Zannichelliaceae
            Leaves less than 2.5 cm long, without sheathing
                stipules; stigma not broad and flat; fruit of
                mericarps, not as above (*Callitriche*) .... Callitrichaceae
        i. Leaves lanceolate to ovate.
          Lower leaves opposite, upper alternate; capsule
              2-lobed (*Chrysosplenium americanum*) .... Saxifragaceae
          Leaves all opposite; capsule globose or 4-sided.
            Flowers regular; capsule 4-sided (*Ludwigia*). .... Onagraceae
            Flowers irregular; capsule globose (*Hemianthus
                micranthemoides*). .... Scrophulariaceae
      h. Stems short and erect or ascending.
        k. Leaves petioled, petioles dilated and clasping at the
            base; sepals 2, petals 3 (*Montia fontana*) .... Portulacaceae
        k. Leaves sessile; sepals and petals of the same number.
          l. Leaves mostly 1 cm or more long; flowers on pedicels
              5 mm or more long; sepals 5 (or leaves often less
              than 1 cm long, sharply acuminate, linear-
              lanceolate in the submersed, dwarf, sterile form).
              (*Gratiola*). .... Scrophulariaceae
          l. Leaves less than 1 cm long, mostly 5 mm or less long;
              flowers sessile or on shorter pedicels; sepals
              fewer than 5.

Leaves linear, connate-based; ovary of 3-4 distinct
carpels; usually tidal waters (*Crassula
aquatica*) .... *Crassulaceae*
Leaves obovate or oblong to linear-lanceolate, not
connate-based; ovary of a single,
2-3-locular carpel; fresh water (*Elatine*) .... *Elatinaceae*
  e. Leaves alternate.
    m. Leaves, at least some of them, lanceolate or broader.
      n. Leaves reniform to suborbicular, wider than long
(*Heteranthera reniformis*). .... *Pontederiaceae*
      n. Leaves not as above, longer than wide.
        Stems with swollen joints and sheathing stipules
(ocreae); leaves net-veined (*Polygonum*) .... *Polygonaceae*
        Stems without swollen joints or ocreae; leaves parallel-
veined or net-veined.
          Leaves net-veined, at least some spatulate (*Drosera*) .... *Droseraceae*
          Leaves parallel-veined, none spatulate *(Potamogeton)* . *Potamogetonaceae*
    m. Leaves all linear or filiform.
      o. Flowers with perianth present (*Heteranthera dubia*). .... *Ponterderiaceae*
      o. Flowers with perianth lacking.
        Fruits in spadices enclosed in the sheath-like leaf bases
(*Zostera marina*). .... *Zosteraceae*
        Fruits in peduncled spikes or heads, or each on an
elongate pedicel.
          Fruits sessile, in peduncled spikes or heads. .... *Potamogetonaceae*
          Fruits pedicelled, in umbels or cymes (*Ruppia
maritima*). .... *Ruppiaceae*

GROUP 2
Herbaceous Plants Parasitic on Stems or Roots of Other Plants,
Often Without Green Color

A. Plant a twining vine with filiform stems, white, yellow or orange (*Cuscuta*). .... *Cuscutaceae*
A. Plant not a twining vine.
  B. Leaves well developed; plants with green color .... *Santalaceae*
  B. Leaves reduced to scales.
    C. Plants 2 cm or less long, parasitic on the branches of coniferous trees
(mostly *Picea mariana*) with green color (*Arceuthobium pusillum*) .... *Viscaceae*
    C. Plants longer than 2 cm, terrestrial root parasites or saprophytes, without
green color, often blackened on drying.
      D. Corolla regular; stamens 8-10; capsule 5-valved; plants usually arising from
a dense ball of mycorhizae .... *Monotropaceae*
      D. Corolla bilabiate or irregular; stamens 4 or fewer; capsule 2 or 3-valved;
plants not arising from a dense ball of mycorhizae.
        Corolla bilabiate, 4-5-lobed; stamens 4; capsule 2-valved. .... *Orobanchaceae*
        Corolla irregular, with 3 petals, 1 dissimilar; stamen 1; capsule 3-valved
(*Corallorhiza*) .... *Orchidaceae*

GROUP 3
Woody or Herbaceous Vines Climbing by Twining or by Tendrils or Adhesive Roots,
or Plant Trailing on the Ground for 3 or More Feet Without Rooting

A. Climbing by tendrils or adhesive roots.
  B. Leaves simple.
    Plant climbing by adhesive roots.
      Leaves opposite.
        Evergreen; stems 4-lined; flowers 4-merous in axillary cymes (*Euonymus*) . *Celastraceae*
        Deciduous; stems not 4-lined; flowers 7-10-merous, in terminal clusters
(*Decumaria barbata*) .... *Hydraneaceae*
      Leaves alternate.

Evergreen; flowers and fruits in umbels (*Hedera helix*). .... *Araliaceae*
Deciduous; flowers and fruits in compound cymes or panicles of cymes
    (*Parthenocissus*) .... *Vitaceae*
Plant climbing by tendrils.
    Tendrils modified stipules (*Smilax*) .... *Smilacaceae*
    Tendrils modified branches.
        Plants herbaceous .... *Cucurbitaceae*
        Plants woody .... *Vitaceae*
B. Leaves compound, with 2 or more leaflets.
    Climbing by tendrils that are usually apical extensions of the leaf rachises.
        Leaves opposite (*Clematis*) .... *Ranunculaceae*
        Leaves alternate.
            Leaves once pinnately compound .... *Fabaceae*
            Leaves ternately-pinnately decompound.
                Polygamodioecious; flowers and fruits in small clusters; sepals 4; fruit
                    bladdery-inflated (*Cardiospermum halicacabum*). .... *Sapindaceae*
                Hermaphrodite; flowers and fruits in panicles; sepals 2 or absent; fruit
                    not bladdery-inflated (*Adlumia fungosa*). .... *Fumariaceae*
    Climbing by adhesive roots or branches.
        Leaves pinnately compound, with 5 or more leaflets (*Campsis radicans*). .... *Bignoniaceae*
        Leaves ternately or palmately compound, usually with 5 or fewer leaflets.
            Adhesive roots with discs; fruit blue to purple. .... *Vitaceae*
            Adhesive roots without discs; fruit white to yellowish (*Toxicodendron*
                radicans) .... *Anacardiaceae*
A. Climbing by twining, or leaf rachis twisting or plant trailing.
  C. Leaves simple.
    D. Leaves opposite or whorled.
      E. Leaves whorled.
        Leaves ovate; petioles 1 cm or more long (*Dioscorea villosa*). .... *Dioscoreaceae*
        Leaves elliptic, linear or lanceolate; leaves sessile or petioles 7 mm or less
            long.
            Leaves fleshy, in whorles of 3 (*Sedum*). .... *Crassulaceae*
            Leaves not fleshy, in whorles of 4 or more (*Galium*). .... *Rubiaceae*
      E. Leaves opposite.
        F. Pistils and styles 4 or more (*Sedum*). .... *Crassulaceae*
        F. Pistils and/or styles fewer than 4.
          G. Leaves distinctly toothed, lobed or cordate.
            Stems retrosely prickly (*Humulus*) .... *Cannabaceae*
            Stems not retrorsely prickly.
               Stems climbing, herbaceous; flowers and fruit in involucrate
                heads (*Mikania scandens*) .... *Asteraceae*
              Stems trailing, or if climbing then woody; flowers not in
                involucrate heads.
                Flowers irregular; fruit a schizocarp of 4 mericarps; plant with
                  a strong odor when crushed .... *Lamiaceae*
                Flowers regular; fruit a capsule; plant lacking strong odor when
                  crushed (*Chrysosplenium americanum*) .... *Saxifragaceae*
          G. Leaves entire or remotely toothed.
            H. Flowers and fruit in pairs, the ovaries often united, or uppermost
              pair of leaves connate.
              Leaves orbicular, mostly 2 cm or less long (*Mitchella repens*). .... *Rubiaceae*
              Leaves elliptic, ovate or oblong, mostly more than 2 cm long
                 (*Lonicera*). .... *Caprifoliaceae*
            H. Flowers and fruit separate, not paired; leaves not connate.
              Plant twining or climbing .... *Asclepiadaceae*
              Plant trailing.
                Calyx 2-4 parted.
                  Petals united, white; fruit a schizocarp (*Diodia*) .... *Rubiaceae*
                  Petals absent or separate and yellow, fruit a capsule.
                    Style 1; disc lacking (*Ludwigia*) .... *Onagraceae*

Styles 2; conspicuous 8-lobed disc present
 (*Chrysosplenium americanum*). .... *Saxifragaceae*
Calyx 5-parted.
 Corolla bilabiate; fruit a schizocarp of 4 mericarps; plant
  with a strong odor when crushed (*Thymus praecox*) .... *Lamiaceae*
 Corolla symmetrical; fruit a capsule or follicle.
  Corolla lobes truncate to oblique at apex; ovaries 2; fruit
   a pair of follicles (*Vinca*) .... *Apocynaceae*
  Corolla lobes rounded or notched at apex; ovary 1; fruit a
   capsule.
   Leaves subulate; corolla pink, white, lavender or blue
    (*Phlox subulata*). .... *Polemoniaceae*
   Leaves orbicular; corolla yellow (*Lysimachia*
    nummularia). .... *Primulaceae*
D. Leaves alternate.
 I. Leaves scale-like, less than 5 mm long (*Bartonia paniculata*). .... *Gentianaceae*
 I. Leaves not scale-like, more than 5 mm long.
  J. Leaves with sheathing stipules (ocreae) at petiole bases (*Polygonum*). .... *Polygonaceae*
  J. Leaves lacking ocreae.
   K. Leaves cordate, sagittate, hastate or lobed at base, or peltate.
    L. Inflorescence internodal or opposite a leaf; flowers violet; fruit a red
     berry (*Solanum dulcamara*) .... *Solanaceae*
    L. Inflorescence axillary or terminal; flowers not violet; fruit not a
     berry or not red.
    M. Leaves peltate near the margin; fruit a bluish-black drupe
     (*Menispermum canadense*) .... *Menispermaceae*
    M. Leaves not peltate; fruit a berry, drupe, capsule or achene.
     Sepals 3; flowers perfect; fruit 3 cm or more long (*Aristolochia*). . *Aristolochiaceae*
     Sepals more than 3 or flowers imperfect; fruit less than 3 cm
      long.
      Flowers imperfect; fruit a drupe or a capsule 1.5 cm or
       more long.
      Sepals and petals each 5; fruit a bluish-black drupe
       (*Menispermum canadense*). .... *Menispermaceae*
      Sepals and petals each 3; fruit a capsule (*Dioscorea villosa*). . *Dioscoreaceae*
      Flowers perfect; fruit an achene or berry or a capsule less
       than 1.5 cm long.
      Corolla rotate or petals separate or absent; fruit a berry or
       achene.
      Petals separate or absent; fruit an achene (*Dalibarda*
       repens). .... *Rosaceae*
      Petals united; fruit a berry (*Epigaea repens*) .... *Ericaceae*
      Corolla bilabiate or united and funnelform; fruit a capsule.
       Corolla bilabiate, spurred; fruit longer than broad,
        ellipsoid or oblong. .... *Scrophulariaceae*
       Corolla funnelform, not spurred; fruit as long as broad
        or broader, ovoid or oblate .... *Convolvulaceae*
   K. Leaves rounded or cuneate at base, not peltate.
    N. Leaves deciduous, or if evergreen an upright climbing shrub.
     Mat-forming; styles and/or pistils 2 or more.
     Leaves fleshy; pistils and styles 4 or more (*Sedum*). .... *Crassulaceae*
     Leaves not fleshy; pistil 1, styles 2 (*Chrysosplenium americanum*). *Saxifragaceae*
     Not mat-forming; stems long and shrubby; style and pistil 1,
      rarely several (*Actinidiaceae*).
     Plant dioecious; stamens numerous; styles several-many
      (*Actinidia arguta*). .... *Actinidiaceae*
     Plant hermaphrodite, or if dioecious stamens 5 and style 1.
     Corolla lavender to violet or yellowish; fruit a berry. .... *Solanaceae*
     Corolla greenish or absent; fruit a capsule (*Celastrus*). .... *Celastraceae*
    N. Leaves evergreen; low growing ground covers.

Flowers paired; fruit 1-seeded (*Linnaea borealis*) .... *Caprifoliaceae*
Flowers not paired; fruit 2 or more-seeded. .... *Ericaceae*
C. Leaves compound, with 2 or more leaflets.
  O. Plant climbing by twining or by twisting of a part of the leaf (e.g. petiole).
    P. Leaves opposite (*Clematis*) .... *Ranunculaceae*
    P. Leaves alternate.
      Plant woody.
        Leaves ternate or palmate.
          Climbing by twining (*Akebia quinata*). .... *Lardizabalaceae*
          Climbing by adhesive roots.
            Inflorescence axillary (*Toxicodendron radicans*). .... *Anacardiaceae*
            Inflorescence terminal or opposite a leaf (*Parthenocissus*). .... *Vitaceae*
        Leaves pinnate, with 5 or more leaflets.
          Stems spiny or thorny (*Rosa*) .... *Rosaceae*
          Stems without spines or thorns (*Wisteria*). .... *Fabaceae*
      Plant herbaceous
        Leaflets 2, palmately lobed; plants free-sporing, not producing seeds
          (*Lygodium palmatum*) .... *Schizaeaceae*
        Leaflets 3 or more; not palmately lobed; plants producing seeds.
          Leaves biternate or bipinnate (*Adlumia fungosa*). .... *Fumariaceae*
          Leaves once-ternate or once-pinnate.
            Flowers irregular, corolla of mostly separate petals; fruit a legume. *Fabaceae*
            Flowers regular, corolla sympetalous, shallowly lobed; fruit a
              capsule (*Ipomoea*) .... *Convolvulaceae*
  O. Plant trailing.
    Leaves pinnate, leaflets 4 or more.
      Leaflets serrate; stems spiny (*Rosa*). .... *Rosaceae*
      Leaflets entire; stems not spiny.
        Leaves opposite, one of each pair larger than the other
          (*Tribulus terrestris*). .... *Zygophyllaceae*
        Leaves alternate (*Coronilla varia*) .... *Fabaceae*
    Leaves ternate, leaflets 3 or leaves palmate.
      Leaflets entire or serrulate; corolla yellow; fruit not in aggregates. .... *Fabaceae*
      Leaflets serrate; corolla not yellow; fruit in aggregates .... *Rosaceae*

GROUP 4

Herbaceous Plants Not Producing Flowers or Seeds, Entirely Free-Sporing: Pteridophytes (Ferns and Fern Allies)

A. Plants free floating; foliage leaves 2-ranked; sporangia borne in sporocarps (fruit
    cases) on submerged, dissected leaves or on the lower leaf lobes.
  Stems simple; leaves 2-ranked; mostly 1 cm or more long (*Salvinia minima*). .... *Salviniaceae*
  Stems dichotomously branched; leaves imbricated, minute, mostly 1 mm or less
    long (*Azolla*) .... *Azollaceae*
A. Plants rooting, on land or underwater; foliage leaves not 2-ranked; sporangia not
    borne as above.
  B. Stems jointed, the joints covered by toothed sheaths (*Equisetum*). .... *Equisetaceae*
  B. Stems neither jointed nor covered by toothed sheaths.
    C. Leaves divided into 4 leaflets (*Marsilea quadrifolia*) .... *Marsileaceae*
    C. Leaves not divided into 4 leaflets.
      D. Leaves scale-like or subulate, very numerous, overlapping in 4 or more
        ranks on an elongate simple or branched stem.
        Plants moss-like, heterosporous, the smaller sporangia containing
          numerous reddish or orange microspores, the larger containing
          usually 4 yellowish megaspores (*Selaginella*) .... *Selaginellaceae*
        Plants not moss-like, homosporous .... *Lycopodiaceae*
      D. Leaves not as above.
        E. Foliage leaves linear and grass-like.
          Sporangia contained in the swollen leaf bases (*Isoetes*) .... *Isoetaceae*

Sporangia borne on reduced pinnae terminating a slender petiole (*Schizaea pusilla*) .... *Schizaeaceae*
E. Foliage leaves (fronds) with dilated blades.
  F. Fronds twining, pinnae palmate (ours), alternating in pairs (*Lygodium palmatum*) .... *Schizaeaceae*
  F. Fronds not twining, pinnae neither palmate nor alternating in pairs.
    G. Fertile fronds or portions of fronds highly modified, unlike the sterile.
      H. Sterile portion of frond simple (*Ophioglossum vulgatum*). .... *Ophioglossaceae*
      H. Sterile portion of frond divided.
        I. Fertile fronds with margins inrolled and concealing the sporangia, the modified pinnae cylindric or with berry-like divisions. .... *Dryopteridaceae*
        I. Fertile frond not as above, the sporangia naked.
          Rhizome well developed, with the fronds clustered at the summit; sporangia not 2-ranked (*Osmunda*) .... *Osmundaceae*
          Rhizome not well developed, fronds not clustered; sporangia 2-ranked (*Botrychium*) .... *Ophioglossaceae*
    G. Fertile fronds or portions of fronds not highly modified, the sterile, differing sometimes only in size.
      J. Fronds filmy and delicate in texture, translucent. .... *Hymenophyllaceae*
      J. Fronds not filmy, delicate or translucent.
        K. Sori borne at or just inside the margin, with indusia formed entirely or in part by the revolute margin of the frond, not (except sometimes in Dennstaedtiaceae) individually indusiate.
          Rhizomes and fronds lacking scales, with hairs only; rhizomes elongate; fronds large, usually 4 dm or more tall. .... *Dennstaedtiaceae*
          Rhizomes and often also the blades scaly, sometimes also pubescent; rhizomes often short; fronds (except sometimes in one genus) mostly shorter than 4 dm. .... *Adiantaceae*
        K. Sori borne on the interior part of the pinnule, with or without an indusium, or individually indusiate, indusia not formed by the revolute margin of the frond.
          L. Indusia wanting; fronds simply pinnatifid, the segments entire or merely denticulate (*Polypodium virginianum*). .. *Polypodiaceae*
          L. Indusia present, or if absent then the fronds pinnate-pinnatifid or tripinnate.
            M. Sori elongate, crescent-shaped or straight.
              Sori paralleling midrib (*Woodwardia*). .... *Blechnaceae*
              Sori divergent from midrib.
                Fronds less than 2 dm long or less than 5 cm wide (*Asplenium*). .... *Aspleniaceae*
                Fronds more than 3 dm long, more than 5 cm wide. ... *Dryopteridaceae*
            M. Sori circular, reniform or cup-like.
              N. Indusium superior, over center of sporangium.
                O. Pinnae or pinnules truncate or rectangular at base, auricled on upper edge near base, entire, serrulate or with bristle-tipped teeth. .... *Dryopteridaceae*
                O. Pinnules not truncate or rectangular at base, not auricled, or if lower pinnules slightly auricled, teeth not bristle-tipped.
                  Rhizomes short and stout, with all the fronds in a cluster at the apex; stipes more than 2 mm broad or stipe very chaffy (*Dryopteris*). .... *Dryopteridaceae*
                  Rhizomes long and slender, with fronds spaced apart or few in groups; stipes less than 2 mm broad, without chaff or remotely chaffy (*Thelypteris*). .... *Thelypteridaceae*

N. Indusium inferior, marginal or absent.
 Frond about as long as wide or bases of the lower
  pinnae adnate to the rachis; indusium lacking.
 Frond ternate with 3 principal rachi
  (*Gymnocarpium dryopteris*). .... *Dryopteridaceae*
 Frond pinnate to bipinnatifid with 1 central rachis. *Thelypteridaceae*
 Frond longer than wide, the bases of the lower pinnae
  not adnate to the rachis; indusium present ...... *Dryopteridaceae*

GROUP 5

Herbaceous Plants Producing Inflorescences Only, The Flowers Replaced By Vegetative Buds, Bulblets or Leafy Tufts

A. Leaves terete, linear, linear-lanceolate, or grass-like, or if broader then parallel-
 veined; Monocotyledons.
 B. Plant with distinct odor of onion (*Allium*). .... *Alliaceae*
 B. Plant without onion-like odor.
  C. Leaves septate-nodulose at intervals; inflorescence a diffuse panicle (*Juncus*) ..... *Juncaceae*
  C. Leaves not septate-nodulose; inflorescence compact.
   D. Inflorescence a compact head with imbricated bracts terminating a naked
    scape (*Xyris*) .... *Xyridaceae*
   D. Inflorescence a panicle or umbel.
    Inflorescence a panicle; leaf sheaths split .... *Poaceae*
    Inflorescence an umbel; leaf sheaths closed (*Cyperus*). .... *Cyperaceae*
A. Leaves lanceolate or broader, net-veined; Dicotyledons.
 E. Reproductive buds moniliform, borne in the axils of opposite, punctate-dotted
  leaves (*Lysimachia terrestris*). .... *Primulaceae*
 E. Reproductive buds or bulblets not moniliform, in terminal clusters; leaves basal
  or alternate, not punctate-dotted.
  F. Rosette leaves covered with stalked glands (*Drosera*). .... *Droseraceae*
  F. Rosette leaves, if present, not covered with stalked glands.
   Leaves lobed or toothed, at least at apex; stems lacking sheathing stipules
    (*Saxifraga*) .... *Saxifragaceae*
   Leaves entire; stems with sheathing stipules (ocreae) (*Polygonum*). .... *Polygonaceae*

GROUP 6

Herbaceous Plants With Leaves Usually Parallel-Veined; Parts of the Flowers Usually in 3s, 6s, 9s or Many, Rarely in 2s or 4s, Never in 5s: Certain Monocotyledons. (Few Dicotyledons)

A. Perianth absent, or inconspicuous, i.e. chaffy, scale-like or bristle-like.
 B. Flowers in spadices (fleshy spikes), which are each subtended by a large white or
  colored spathe (bract) (*Orontium* has a yellow spike, the spathe
  inconspicuous); leaves compound or simple with a dilated blade, never
  linear or grass-like. .... *Araceae* (in part)
 B. Flower clusters, if spicate, not subtended by a spathe, or if so, this appearing as
  a continuation of the stem with the spike appearing lateral and divergent;
  leaves linear or grass-like.
  C. Flowers each in the axil of 1 or more scales, usually concealed by them or
   stamens and style exserted.
   D. Plants either with cauline leaves or sheathing scales, or if scapose with
    more than 1 spike, spikelet or head of flowers on each scape.
    Each flower usually subtended by 2 or more distichous scales; perianth
     none or of 2 or 3 minute scales (lodicules); leaf sheaths usually
     open; culms (aerial stems) round or flat, usually hollow; fruit a
     grain or utricle. .... *Poaceae*
    Each flower subtended by a single scale (in *Carex* each pistillate flower
     also in a perigynium [tiny sac]); perianth none or of bristles or
     scales; leaf sheaths usually closed; culms often triangular, usually
     solid; fruit an achene .... *Cyperaceae*

    D. Plants with linear basal leaves only, scapose, each naked scape terminated
        by a small, button-like head (*Eriocaulon*). .... *Eriocaulaceae*
   C. Flowers not concealed by scales.
      E. Inflorescence a dense, elongate spike.
         F. Spike divergent at junction of scape and spathe (*Acorus calamus*). .... *Acoraceae*
         F. Spike erect.
            Spike 1, of perfect flowers; leaves terete to half-rounded, basal;
               perianth scale-like (*Triglochin*) .... *Juncaginaceae*
            Spikes more than 1 and superposed, the lowermost spike pistillate,
               the upper ones staminate; leaves flat, linear, basal and
               cauline; perianth of bristles (*Typha*) .... *Typhaceae*
      E. Inflorescence of globose heads, racemes, cymes or loose open clusters
        (a spiciform panicle in *Luzula spicata*, but not a dense, elongate
        spike).
         G. Flowers unisexual, the lower heads pistillate, the upper smaller heads
            staminate; fruit an achene (*Sparganium*). .... *Sparganiaceae*
         G. Flowers perfect, heads, if present, uniform; fruit a capsule or follicle.
            Ovary 1; fruit a dehiscent capsule .... *Juncaceae*
            Ovaries 3, connivent but separating at maturity and becoming follicles
               (*Scheuchzeria palustris*) .... *Scheuchzeriaceae*
A. Perianth present, at least the inner segments (and usually all of the segments)
    conspicuous and petal-like.
   H. Flowers in 1 or more globose or subglobose heads; flowers sessile or nearly so.
      Head solitary; leaves mostly near the base; sepals and petals each 3 (*Xyris*). .... *Xyridaceae*
      Heads several; leaves cauline as well as basal; sepals and/or petals each 5.
        Leaves coriaceous, bristly-margined; flowers uniform, white to greenish.
          (*Eryngium*) .... *Apiaceae*
        Leaves not coriaceous or bristly-margined; flowers of 2 kinds, 1 tubular,
          5-lobed and perfect, the other strap-shaped, pistillate, both kinds
          yellow (*Pityopsis falcata*) .... *Asteraceae*
    H. Flowers not in globose or subglobose heads, often pedicellate.
      I. Stamens and style united with the prolonged central axis to form a column,
        anthers 1 or 2, sessile; one petal different from the other 2 in size, shape
        or color, sometimes spurred or pouch-like. .... *Orchidaceae*
      I. Stamens and style not united with a prolonged central axis into a column;
        anthers 3 or more, on filaments (sessile in *Juncaginaceae*); petals all alike
        (one smaller than the other two in one genus of *Commelinaceae*).
        J. Ovaries 3 or more in each flower.
          K. Ovaries 3, or 6 and flowers spicate.
            Stem leaves present with a terminal pore; inflorescence a loose,
               bracted raceme (*Scheuchzeria palustris*) .... *Scheuchzeriaceae*
            Stem leaves absent, the leaves all basal, lacking a terminal pore;
               inflorescence a spiciform, bractless raceme (*Triglochin*). .... *Juncaginaceae*
          K. Ovaries 6 or more; flowers in panicles, racemes or umbels.
            Flowers in panicles or racemes; sepals green, petals white or pink. .... *Alismataceae*
            Flowers in umbels; sepals and petals all pink (*Butomus umbellatus*). .... *Butomaceae*
        J. Ovary one in each flower.
          L. Ovary inferior or partly inferior.
            Perianth densely woolly outside; plant with red juice (*Lachnanthes*
               caroliniana) .... *Haemodoraceae*
            Perianth not woolly outside; juice of plant not red.
               Stamens 3; leaves equitant (*Iris*) .... *Iridaceae*
               Stamens 6; leaves not equitant.
                 Flowers in a spike-like raceme; perianth with a mealy surface
                   (*Aletris farinosa*) .... *Melanthiaceae*
                Flowers solitary or umbelled; perianth without a mealy surface. . *Liliaceae*
         L. Ovary superior.
           M. Calyx lobes and petals each 4.
             Leaves opposite; inflorescences cymose; petals showy, pink or
               purple (*Rhexia*). .... *Melastomataceae*

Leaves basal (opposite in 1 species of *Plantago*); inflorescences
spicate; petals not showy, membranous .... *Plantaginaceae*
M. Calyx lobes and petals each 3 (perianth of 4 tepals in 1 genus of
Convallariaceae with leaves alternate; leaves opposite or basal
in the above 2 taxa).
N. Sepals and petals differentiated, the former green, the petals
colored and of a different texture.
Leaves in a single whorl of usually 3 below the flower.
(*Trillium*). .... *Trilliaceae*
Leaves alternate .... *Commelinaceae*
N. Sepals and petals undifferentiated, essentially alike in color and
texture.
O. Flower irregular, bilabiate (*Pontederia cordata*). .... *Pontederiaceae*
O. Flower regular
P. Inflorescence subtended by a spathe-like leaf; perianth
united below into a slender tube; stamens 3 .... *Pontederiaceae*
P. Inflorescence not subtended by a spathe-like leaf, or if so,
perianth not united into a slender tube; stamens 4-6.
Q. Stem woody; leaves evergreen, thick and leathery,
sword-like; inflorescence a large terminal panicle of
showy flowers. (*Yucca filamentosa*). .... *Agavaceae*
Q. Plant without the above combination of characters (the
families in the remainder of the key to Group 6
comprise the Liliaceae in the old, broad sense,
presented to reflect the current view of this
assemblage of genera). [go to R]
R. Leaves principally basal or near the base, the stems scapose, or bracteate, or with
leaves gradually or abruptly reduced upward (absent at anthesis in *Alliaceae*).
S. Leaves large and lanceolate; flowers with a long narrow tube, the base arising
from below ground. (*Colchicum autumnale*). .... *Colchicaceae*
S. Leaves various; flowers not arising from below ground.
T. Flower solitary on a scapose stem. (*Erythronium americanum*). .... *Liliaceae*
T. Flowers 2 or more, or if solitary, stem bracteate or leafy.
U. Inflorescence of 2 or 3 helicoid cymes or an umbel.
Inflorescence of 2 or 3 helicoid cymes; perianth segments more than
5 cm long, orange or yellow. (*Hemerocallis*) .... *Hemerocallidaceae*
Inflorescence an umbel; perianth segments less than 4 cm long, white or
greenish yellow. (Fig. 299).
Leaves elliptic, without an odor like onion or garlic, 2 cm wide or
wider, present at anthesis; fruit a berry. (*Clintonia borealis*) .... *Convallariaceae*
Leaves terete or linear, with an odor like onion or garlic, less than
2 cm wide or absent at anthesis if leaf elliptic and wider;
fruit a capsule. (*Allium*). .... *Alliaceae*
U. Inflorescence racemose, spicate, or paniculate.
V. Inflorescence paniculate, or racemose and leaves equitant, distichous,
the bases overlapping as in *Iris* .... *Melanthiaceae*
V. Inflorescence a spike or raceme; leaves not equitant or distichous.
W. Perianth segments united for half or more their length.
Perianth well over 1 cm long .... *Funkiaceae*
Perianth 1 cm or less long.
Scape arising from a sheath at the base of 2 leaves. (*Convallaria
majalis*). .... *Convallariaceae*
Scape arising from center of rosette or cluster of leaves.
Scape bractless; perianth blue or purple. (*Muscari*). .... *Hyacinthaceae*
Scape bracted; perianth white. (*Aletris farinosa*). .... *Melanthiaceae*
W. Perianth segments free to base or nearly so.
Scape bractless.
Leaves elliptic-lanceolate to oblong. (*Clintonia borealis*). .... *Convallariaceae*
Leaves narrowly linear. (*Ornithogalum*). .... *Hyacinthaceae*
Scape bracted. .... *Melanthiaceae*

R. Leaves principally cauline, alternate or whorled, basal leaves absent.
  X. Leaves whorled.
    Leaves in a single whorl. (*Trillium*) .... *Trilliaceae*
    Leaves in 2 or more whorls.
      Perianth segments less than 1 cm long, greenish; fruit a berry.
        (*Medeola virginiana*) .... *Convallariaceae*
      Perianth segments more than 1 cm long, yellow, red or orange; fruit a
        capsule. (*Lilium*) .... *Liliaceae*
  X. Leaves alternate.
    Y. Flowers or inflorescence terminating the stem or branches.
      Z. Perianth white or bluish; fruit a berry. (*Maianthemum*). .... *Convallariaceae*
      Z. Perianth green, yellow, orange or red; fruit a capsule.
        Flowers numerous in a terminal panicle; leaves strongly plaited.
          (*Veratrum viride*) .... *Melanthiaceae*
        Flowers solitary or few, not in panicles; leaves not strongly plaited.
          Perianth yellow, unspotted; stem usually forking; capsule 3 cm or less
            long. (*Uvularia*) .... *Convallariaceae*
          Perianth red or orange, or if yellow, heavily spotted; stem simple;
            capsule usually more than 3 cm long. (*Lilium*). .... *Liliaceae*
    Y. Flowers or inflorescence in the axils of stem leaves.
      Leaves reduced to inconspicuous scales; ultimate branchlets filiform.
        (*Asparagus officinalis*) .... *Asparagaceae*
      Leaves normal, dilated; filiform branchlets lacking. .... *Convallariaceae*

GROUP 7
Scapose Herbaceous Plants, the Scape Naked or With One to Few Bracts

A. Flowers or fruit in globose or hemispherical heads, not surrounded by a solitary
    spathe; leaves not orbicular.
  Leaves trifoliate (*Trifolium repens*) .... *Fabaceae*
  Leaves not trifoliate.
    Heads in whorles of 3 in a raceme; sepals 3 (*Sagittaria*). .... *Alismataceae*
    Heads not in whorles in a raceme; sepals 5 or perianth of bristles or scales
      (3 in *Xyridaceae*).
      Leaves linear with entire margins.
        Heads white, 7 mm or less wide; leaves in a rosette around the base of the
          scape (*Eriocaulon*) .... *Eriocaulaceae*
        Heads brown or wider than 7 mm.
          Perianth present, yellow; leaves ensiform (*Xyris*). .... *Xyridaceae*
          Perianth absent or of bristles or scales; leaves grass-like. .... *Cyperaceae*
      Leaves not linear, or linear and with toothed, lobed or dissected margins.
        Petals separate; fruit a schizocarp; leaves spiny-serrate (*Eryngium*). .... *Apiaceae*
        Petals united; fruit an achene; leaves not spiny-serrate. .... *Asteraceae*
A. Flowers or fruit not in globose or hemispherical heads (although sometimes in
    heads that are not globose or hemispherical) or if so, surrounded by a solitary
    spathe or leaves oval to orbicular.
  B. Flowers or fruiting structures solitary.
    C. Leaves oval to orbicular; plant aquatic, rooting under water. .... *Nymphaeaceae*
    C. Leaves not oval to orbicular, or if so, plant not aquatic.
      D. Leaves rosulate, hollow, pitcher-shaped, usually partly filled with water
        and decayed insects (*Sarracenia purpurea*). .... *Sarraceniaceae*
      D. Leaves not as above.
        E. Plant in flower.
          F. Corolla irregular.
            Corolla united, spurred; ovary superior. .... *Lentibulariaceae*
            Corolla of separate petals, or united in part and ovary inferior.
              Sepals petaloid, usually colored; ovary inferior. .... *Orchidaceae*
              Sepals green, not petaloid; ovary superior (*Viola*). .... *Violaceae*
          F. Corolla regular or absent.
            G. Pistils separate, usually 3 or more.

Leaves with stipules, these free at least at apex. .... *Rosaceae*
Leaves lacking stipules or if present, completely adnate to petiole. ... *Ranunculaceae*
G. Pistil 1, often compound, with the carpels united at least half their
    length.
    Sepals 3; petals or corolla lobes 3 or absent; stamens 3 or 6.
      Sepals brownish or maroon; petals absent (*Asarum canadense*). ... *Aristolochiaceae*
      Sepals not brownish or maroon; petals present, resembling
        the sepals.
        Ovary inferior .... *Liliaceae*
        Ovary superior.
          Leaves elliptic, their petioles sheathing base of the scape
            (*Erythronium americanum*) .... *Liliaceae*
          Leaves linear, their bases or petioles not sheathing
            (*Heteranthera dubia*). .... *Pontederiaceae*
    Sepals more or less than 3; petals or corolla lobes 4 or more;
      stamens not 3 or 6.
      Stamens 2 or 4.
        Corolla 5-lobed, white (*Limosella australis*). .... *Scrophulariaceae*
        Corolla 4-lobed, greenish or brownish (*Littorella americana*). *Plantaginaceae*
      Stamens 5 or more.
        Scape usually with 1 ovate bract; stamens 5; stigmas 4
          (*Parnassia glauca*). .... *Saxifragaceae*
        Scape bractless; stamens 10 or more; stigmas 2 or 5.
          Petals 8 or more; stamens more than 10
            (*Sanguinaria canadensis*). .... *Papaveraceae*
          Petals 5; stamens 10.
            Leaves trifoliate (*Oxalis*) .... *Oxalidaceae*
            Leaves simple (*Moneses uniflora*) .... *Pyrolaceae*
E. Plant in fruit.
  H. Fruits indehiscent, 1-seeded, in aggregates (except *Littorella*).
    Plant monoecious; fruits not in aggregates, sessile at base of leaves;
      sepals 4 (*Littorella americana*) .... *Plantaginaceae*
    Plant hermaphrodite; fruits in aggregates, not sessile at base of leaves;
      sepals 5 or more.
      Leaves stipulate, stipules free, at least at apex. .... *Rosaceae*
      Leaves exstipulate, or stipules united to petioles for their entire
        length. .... *Ranunculaceae*
  H. Fruits dehiscent, or if indehiscent (*Heteranthera*) more than 1-seeded,
    not in aggregates.
    I. Leaves or leaf segments 6 mm or less wide.
      Fruits sessile in the leaf axils (*Heteranthera dubia*). .... *Pontederiaceae*
      Fruits pedicelled.
        Ovary inferior.
          Fruit 1-celled .... *Orchidaceae*
          Fruit 3-celled .... *Liliaceae*
        Ovary superior.
          Scape more than 2 cm tall (*Utricularia*). .... *Lentibulariaceae*
          Scape 2 cm or less tall (*Limosella australis*). .... *Scrophulariaceae*
    I. Leaves or leaf segments more than 6 mm wide.
      Fruit 1 or 2 carpellate.
        Leaves parallel veined; ovary inferior. .... *Orchidaceae*
        Leaves net-veined; ovary superior.
          Scape usually with a solitary ovate bract; stigmas 4
            (*Parnassia glauca*). .... *Saxifragaceae*
          Scape without a bract; stigmas 1 or 2.
            Leaves entire, sessile in rosettes (*Pinguicula vulgaris*). .... *Lentibulariaceae*
            Leaves lobed, petioled, 1 or 2 on the side of the scape
              (*Sanguinaria canadensis*) .... *Papaveraceae*
      Fruit 3 to 5 or 6-carpellate.
        Fruit 3 or 6-carpellate.

Sepals absent in fruit; fruit 3-celled. .... *Liliaceae*
Sepals present in fruit; fruit 1 or 6-celled.
    Ovary inferior; sepals 2 or 3 (*Asarum canadense*). .... *Aristolochiaceae*
    Ovary superior; sepals 5 (*Viola*) .... *Violaceae*
Fruit 5-carpellate.
    Leaves trifoliate (*Oxalis*) .... *Oxalidaceae*
    Leaves simple (*Moneses uniflora*) .... *Pyrolaceae*
B. Flowers or fruiting structures 2 or more in an inflorescence.
  J. Flowers and fruit in umbels.
    K. Leaves compound.
      Leaves pinnately dissected or compound (*Erodium*). .... *Geraniaceae*
      Leaves ternate.
        Leaves twice-divided, each division 3-5-foliate; fruit a berry (*Aralia*). ..... *Araliaceae*
        Leaves once-divided, 3 foliate; fruit a legume or capsule.
          Corolla irregular; fruit a 1-carpellate legume (*Trifolium repens*). .... *Fabaceae*
          Corolla regular; fruit a 5-carpellate capsule (*Oxalis*). .... *Oxalidaceae*
    K. Leaves simple.
      Leaves orbicular to reniform, oblanceolate or elliptic.
        Leaves orbicular to reniform (*Hydrocotyle*). .... *Apiaceae*
        Leaves oblanceolate to elliptic.
          Calyx 5-parted, present in fruit; fruit a capsule (*Primula*). .... *Primulaceae*
          Calyx 3-parted, absent in fruit; fruit a berry (*Clintonia borealis*). .... *Convallariaceae*
      Leaves linear, terete or angled (or absent at anthesis in some *Allium*).
        Ovary inferior .... *Liliaceae*
        Ovary superior.
          Sepals and petals differentiated; plant lacking onion-like odor
            (*Butomus umbellatus*) .... *Butomaceae*
          Sepals and petals similar; plant with onion-like odor (*Allium*). .... *Alliaceae*
  J. Flowers and fruit not in umbels.
    L. Leaves compound or dissected to midrib or nearly so, present at anthesis.
      Leaves 2 or more times dissected, or with more than 3 leaflets or
        segments.
      Leaves once pinnately compound.
        Flowers in dense spikes; fruit a legume or circumscissile capsule.
          Flowers irregular; fruit a legume (*Oxytropis campestris*). .... *Fabaceae*
          Flowers regular; fruit a circumscissile capsule (*Plantago*). .... *Plantaginaceae*
        Flowers in racemes; fruit a capsule, not circumscissile. .... *Brassicaceae*
      Leaves pedately compound or decompound, not once-pinnate.
        Leaves pedately compound; flowers enclosed in a spathe; fruit
          a fleshy drupe. (*Arisaema*) .... *Araceae*
        Leaves decompound; flowers not enclosed in a spathe; fruit a capsule.
          Corolla 2-spurred; fruit ellipsoid (*Dicentra*). .... *Fumariaceae*
          Corolla 1-spurred; fruit ovoid or globose (*Utricularia*). .... *Lentibulariaceae*
      Leaves with 3 leaflets or segments.
        Leaves narrowly sagittate; petals 3, white (*Sagittaria*). .... *Alismataceae*
        Leaves not sagittate; petals more than 3 or absent.
          Flowers in a head enclosed in a spathe; fruit red, fleshy drupes
            (*Arisaema triphyllum*) .... *Araceae*
          Flowers not in a head enclosed by a spathe; fruit not red, fleshy drupes.
            Corolla irregular, persistent in fruit (*Trifolium repens*). .... *Fabaceae*
            Corolla regular, absent in fruit.
              Flowers in racemes (*Menyanthes trifoliata*). .... *Menyanthaceae*
              Flowers in cymes .... *Rosaceae*
    L. Leaves simple, not deeply dissected, absent or present at anthesis.
      M. Leaves linear to narrowly lanceolate, more than 5 times as long as wide.
        N. Inflorescence with 2 main branches (*Hemerocallis*). .... *Hemerocallidaceae*
        N. Inflorescence a spike, raceme, panicle or spadix, consisting of
          only 1 rachis.
          O. Plant in flower.
            P. Corolla irregular.

Corolla lobed, the petals all united.

 Corolla long-spurred (*Utricularia*) .... *Lentibulariaceae*

 Corolla not spurred (*Lobelia*) .... *Campanulaceae*

Corolla not or only partly lobed, the petals at least some of

  them, separate. .... *Orchidaceae*

P. Corolla regular or absent.

 Perianth united for half or more its length.

  Perianth white, mealy or pebbly (*Aletris farinosa*). .... *Melanthiaceae*

  Perianth blue, rarely white, not mealy or pebbly (*Muscari*). .... *Hyacinthaceae*

 Perianth not united or united less than half its length.

  Corolla white, pink or blue.

   Sepals 2; petals 5 (*Talinum teretifolium*). .... *Portulacaceae*

   Sepals and petals of the same number.

    Sepals and petals each 4 or 5.

     Sepals, petals and stamens 4 or 5; styles 3, deeply

      divided; leaves covered with stalked glands

      (*Drosera*) .... *Droseraceae*

     Sepals and petals 4; stamens 6; style 1, not deeply

      divided; leaves not covered with stalked glands *Brassicaceae*

    Sepals and petals each 3.

     Sepals white or blue, at least in part, similar to the

      petals.

      Inflorescemce a raceme; leaves not equitant or

       distichous, scape bractless; style 1

       (*Ornithogalum*) .... *Hyacinthaceae*

      Inflorescence paniculate, or if racemose leaves

       equitant and distichous or scape bracted;

       styles 3 .... *Melanthiaceae*

     Sepals green, smaller than the petals. .... *Alismataceae*

  Corolla green or brown or absent.

   Petals and sepals each 4 (*Plantago*) .... *Plantaginaceae*

   Petals 3 or absent; sepals 3.

    Leaves 4 mm or less wide, plant not aromatic

     (*Triglochin*). .... *Juncaginaceae*

    Leaves 6 mm or more wide, plant aromatic (*Acorus*

     calamus*). .... *Acoraceae*

O. Plant in fruit.

 Q. Fruit a dehiscent capsule, more than 1-seeded.

  Sepals 2, 4 or 5.

   Leaves covered with stalked glands (*Drosera*). .... *Droseraceae*

   Leaves not covered with stalked glands.

    Capsule circumscissile (*Plantago*) .... *Plantaginaceae*

    Capsule opening by pores or longitudinal slits.

     Capsule opening by pores (*Lobelia*) .... *Campanulaceae*

     Capsule opening by slits.

      Fruit solitary or racemose.

       Leaves flat; capsule 1-locular (*Utricularia*). .... *Lentibulariaceae*

       Leaves terete; capsule 2-locular .... *Brassicaceae*

      Fruits cymose (*Talinum teretifolium*). .... *Portulacaceae*

  Sepals 3 or absent at fruiting time.

   Ovary inferior .... *Orchidaceae*

   Ovary superior or partly inferior.

    Style 1, ovary superior; capsule not enclosed by persistent

     withered perianth. .... *Hyacinthaceae*

    Styles 3, or if 1 ovary partly inferior and capsule enclosed

     by the persistent withered perianth .... *Melanthiaceae*

 Q. Fruit indehiscent, 1-seeded, or a schizocarp splitting into 3 or 6

  mericarps.

  Fruit a schizocarp, not in aggregates or multiples, in racemes

   or spikes (*Triglochin*) .... *Juncaginaceae*

Fruit not a schizocarp, in aggregates or multiples.
  Fruits borne in a whorl on a receptacle or in heads; ovaries
      superior; plant not aromatic .... *Alismataceae*
  Fruits borne on an elongate, linear spadix; ovaries inferior;
      plant aromatic (*Acorus calamus*) .... *Acoraceae*
M. Leaves not linear or lanceolate or if so, less than 5 times as long as wide
    or absent at anthesis.
  R. Inflorescence branched, a panicle or cyme.
    Petals 3; pistils several; fruit achenes in a whorl on a receptacle
        (*Alisma*). .... *Alismataceae*
    Petals more or less than 3 or pistil 1; fruit an achene, capsule, follicle
        or utricle, not in a whorl on a receptacle.
      Sepals distinct, 2 or 5; fruit several-seeded.
        Sepals 2; leaves terete (*Talinum teretifolium*). .... *Portulacaceae*
        Sepals 5; leaves flat .... *Saxifragaceae*
      Sepals 5 and united or 4 and distinct; fruit 1-seeded.
        Calyx of 5 sepals united to near apex (*Limonium carolinianum*). *Plumbaginaceae*
        Calyx of 4 sepals separate to near base (*Oxyria digyna*). .... *Polygonaceae*
  R. Inflorescence not branched, a spike or raceme.
    S. Leaves covered with stalked glands (*Drosera*). .... *Droseraceae*
    S. Leaves not covered with stalked glands.
      T. Flowers in dense spikes or heads (spadix) surrounded by a spathe,
          or spathe absent and scape white just below the spadix; fruit
          fleshy in multiples or closely crowded on the spadix .... *Araceae*
      T. Flowers not in dense spikes or heads or if so, spathe lacking and
          scape not white just below; fruit not fleshy or not closely
          crowded on a spadix.
        U. Flowers and fruit sessile in a spike or axillary.
          Perianth of 3 petals and 3 sepals; fruit a longitudinally
              dehiscent capsule.
            Corolla irregular; fruit completely 3-celled. .... *Orchidaceae*
            Corolla regular; fruit incompletely 3-celled (*Heteranthera
                reniformis*). .... *Pontederiaceae*
          Perianth of 4 sepals and 4 petals; fruit circumscissile
              (*Plantago*). .... *Plantaginaceae*
        U. Flowers and fruit pedicellate in racemes.
          Ovary inferior; leaves parallel-veined; sepals 3; fruit a capsule. *Orchidaceae*
          Ovary superior or if inferior, leaves net-veined.
            Sepals and petals each 4 or 5; fruit a capsule.
              Sepals and petals 4; fruit with a membranous partition
                  in the center (a silicle or silique) .... *Brassicaceae*
              Sepals and petals 5; fruit without a membranous
                  partition in the center.
                Ovary and fruit 3-celled. (*Galax urceolata*). .... *Diapensiaceae*
                Ovary and fruit not 3-celled.
                  Leaves distinctly pubescent; fruit less than 5-celled. *Saxifragaceae*
                  Leaves glabrous; fruit 5-celled (*Pyrola*). .... *Pyrolaceae*
            Sepals and petals each 3, sometimes all united; fruit a
                berry, capsule or an aggregate of achenes.
              Sepals colored, similar to petals; fruit a capsule or berry.
                Perianth segments united for half or more their length.
                  Perianth 2 cm or more long; fruit a capsule (*Hosta*). *Funkiaceae*
                  Perianth 1 cm or less long; fruit a berry
                      (*Convallaria majalis*). .... *Convallariaceae*
                Perianth segments free to base or nearly so.
                  Scape bractless; fruit a berry (*Clintonia borealis*). ..... *Convallariaceae*
                  Scape bracted; fruit a capsule (*Chamaelirium
                      luteum*). .... *Melanthiaceae*
              Sepals green; petals white and larger than the sepals;
                  fruit an aggregate of achenes (*Sagittaria*) .... *Araceae*

GROUP 8
Herbaceous Plants With Leaves Opposite or Whorled

A. Flowers or fruit in involucrate heads.
    Stems spiny; leaves, at least the median ones, connate (*Dipsacus*). .... *Dipsacaceae*
    Stems not spiny or leaves not connate.
        Stamens united by their anthers or absent. .... *Asteraceae*
        Stamens separate, present.
            Leaves whorled.
                Flower clusters subtended by 4, usually white petaloid bracts; fruit a
                    dense cluster of red drupes (*Cornus*) .... *Cornaceae*
                Flower cluster not subtended by petaloid bracts; fruit a capsule or
                    indehiscent.
                Flowers perfect; plant without latex; flowers not in cyathia. .... *Rubiaceae*
                Flowers imperfect; plant with latex; flowers in cyathia (*Euphorbia*). .... *Euphorbiaceae*
            Leaves opposite.
                Plant with latex; flowers in cyathia (*Euphorbia*). .... *Euphorbiaceae*
                Plant without latex; flowers not in cyathia.
                      Corolla absent; calyx corolloid (*Mirabilis*). .... *Nyctaginaceae*
                    Corolla present; calyx green.
                            Flowers or fruits enveloped by an epicalyx of bracteoles; ovary not
                            4-lobed .... *Dipsacaceae*
                        Flowers or fruits not enveloped by an epicalyx; ovary 4-lobed. .... *Lamiaceae*
A. Flowers or fruit not in involucrate heads.
  B. Leaves whorled or subwhorled.
    C. Stem with only 1 whorl of leaves.
        Leaves dissected or compound.
            Flowers in racemes (*Cardamine*) .... *Brassicaceae*
            Flowers in umbels or solitary.
                Flowers in umbels; ovaries inferior; fruit a berry (*Panax*). .... *Araliaceae*
                Flowers solitary; ovaries superior; fruit an aggregate of achenes. .... *Ranunculaceae*
         Leaves simple, not dissected, at most lobed.
            Flowers or fruit solitary; leaves 3, rarely 4 (*Trillium*). .... *Trilliaceae*
            Flowers or fruit 2 or more or leaves more than 4.
                Flowers and fruit in a terminal, head-like cluster; flowers 4-merous;
                    fruit a red drupe (*Cornus*) .... *Cornaceae*
                Flowers and fruit solitary or in umbels; flowers 5 or more-merous;
                    fruit a capsule or follicle.
                    Stamens easily visible; fruit a capsule less than 1 cm long
                      (*Trientalis borealis*) .... *Primulaceae*
                    Stamens not easily visible; fruit a follicle more than 1 cm long
                      (*Asclepias*). .... *Asclepiadaceae*
    C. Stem with 2 or more whorles of leaves.
      D. Plant in flower.
        E. Perianth none; flowers solitary in the upper axils; hypanthium completely
          enclosing ovary (*Hippuris vulgaris*). .... *Hippuridaceae*
        E. Perianth present; flowers lacking the above combination of characters.
          F. Flower irregular.
             Corolla or calyx spurred (*Impatiens*). .... *Balsaminaceae*
             Corolla or calyx spurless.
                Corolla united; stamens 2, distinct (*Veronica*). .... *Scrophulariaceae*
                Corolla, at least in part, of separate petals; stamens 6-8, united by
                  their filaments (*Polygala*) .... *Polygalaceae*
          F. Flower regular.
            G. Corolla 3 or 4-parted, united.
               Corolla rotate or funnelform; flowers not in racemes or spikes. ...... *Rubiaceae*
               Corolla tubular; flowers in racemes or spikes (*Veronicastrum*
                  virginicum). .... *Scrophulariaceae*
           G. Corolla 5 or more-parted, or 3-4-parted and of separate petals, or
              absent and sepals 5.

Corolla of united petals.
  Stamens visible; plant lacking latex.
    Flowers solitary in the leaf axils, yellow, style 1 (*Lysimachia*)... *Primulaceae*
    Flowers cymose, white to pink, styles 2 (*Rubia tinctoria*). .... *Rubiaceae*
  Stamens hidden; plant with latex (*Asclepias*). .... *Asclepiadaceae*
Corolla of separate petals, or absent and perianth comprised of
    calyx only.
  Corolla absent, perianth consisting of 5 sepals (*Mollugo*
    verticillata). .... *Molluginaceae*
  Corolla and calyx both present.
    Sepals and petals each 3 or sepals 5.
      Sepals and petals each 3; leaves parallel-veined.
        Perianth segments less than 1 cm long, greenish; fruit a
          berry. .... *Convallariaceae*
        Perianth segments more than 1 cm long, yellow, red or
          orange; fruit a capsule. .... *Liliaceae*
      Sepals 5, petals 3; leaves net-veined (*Lechea*). .... *Cistaceae*
    Sepals and petals each 4-6.
      Sepals and petals attached to rim of hypanthium or
        perianth tube. .... *Lythraceae*
      Sepals and petals not attached to a hypanthium or
        perianth tube.
        Carpels separate, at least above; leaves mostly 3 in each
          whorl (*Sedum*). .... *Crassulaceae*
        Carpels united to apex; leaves 4 or more in each
          whorl. .... *Caryophyllaceae*
D. Plant in fruit.
  H. Fruit indehiscent, a berry or schizocarp or nut-like.
    Leaves in only 2 whorles; fruit a berry (*Medeola virginiana*). .... *Convallariaceae*
    Leaves in 3 or more whorles; fruit a schizocarp or nut-like.
      Fruit a schizocarp of 2 mericarps, these not beaked. .... *Rubiaceae*
      Fruit nut-like, beaked by the persistent style (*Hippuris vulgaris*). .... *Hippuridaceae*
  H. Fruit dehiscent.
    I. Fruit a follicle; plant with latex (*Asclepias*). .... *Asclepiadaceae*
    I. Fruit not a follicle or if so, plant without latex.
      J. Calyx absent at fruiting.
        Leaves serrate (*Impatiens*) .... *Balsaminaceae*
        Leaves entire or merely scabrous on the margins.
          Fruit 3-carpellate, more than 1 cm long (*Lilium*). .... *Liliaceae*
          Fruit 2-carpellate, less than 1 cm long (*Polygala*). .... *Polygalaceae*
      J. Calyx present at fruiting.
        Calyx 4-parted; fruit a 2-locular capsule.
          Leaves in whorles of 3 (*Veronica*) .... *Scrophulariaceae*
          Leaves in whorles of 4 or more (*Veronicastrum virginicum*). .... *Scrophulariaceae*
        Calyx 5 or more-parted, or if 4-parted (some *Sedum*) fruit of 4-5
          follicles.
        Carpels or valves of fruit separate for half their length.
          Fruit of 4-5 distinct follicles; leaves fleshy (*Sedum*). .... *Crassulaceae*
          Fruit a 3-valved capsule; leaves not fleshy (*Lechea*). .... *Cistaceae*
        Carpels or valves of fruit united to apex.
          Calyx, at least in part, colored other than green (*Polygala*). ...... *Polygalaceae*
          Calyx green.
            Fruits axillary.
              Fruit surrounded by a hypanthium or perianth tube. ...... *Lythraceae*
              Fruit not surrounded by a hypanthium or perianth tube,
                the calyx evident at the base.
                Plant prostrate, mat-forming; leaves 3 cm or less long
                  (*Mollugo verticillata*). .... *Molluginaceae*
                Plant erect, not mat-forming; leaves longer than 3 cm
                  (*Lysimachia*). .... *Primulaceae*
           Fruits terminal.

Fruits in a panicle or cyme .... *Caryophyllaceae*
Fruits in spikes (*Veronicastrum virginicum*). .... *Scrophulariaceae*
B. Leaves opposite or subopposite.
    K. Leaves dissected or compound.
        L. Leaves compound, the leaflets with petiolules.
            Sepals and petals both 5; fruit a capsule or schizocarp of 5 mericarps.
                Flowers solitary in the axils; ovary not prolonged into a long beak;
                    mericarps bearing sharp spines (*Tribulus terrestris*). .... *Zygophyllaceae*
                Flowers paired or umbellate in the axils; ovary prolonged into a long
                    beak; mericarps not spiny .... *Geraniaceae*
            Sepals and petals not both 5; fruit a silique or an achene.
                Sepals and petals 4, petals rarely lacking; fruit a silique (*Cardamine*). ..... *Brassicaceae*
                Sepals 4-many, petals none; fruit an achene. .... *Ranunculaceae*
        L. Leaves simple or if compound, the leaflets sessile.
            M. Flowers solitary or clustered in the leaf axils, or solitary and terminal.
                N. Leaves palmately dissected into more than 3 lobes; fruit a berry, achene,
                    or a cluster of carpels prolonged into beaks (schizocarp of
                    mericarps in *Molluginaceae*).
                    Plant prostrate, mat-forming, stems forked; leaves palmately dissected
                        so as to appear whorled (*Mollugo verticillata*). .... *Molluginaceae*
                    Plant erect, not mat-forming, leaves distinctly opposite.
                        Pistils numerous in a subglobose to cylindric head (*Anemone*). ...... *Ranunculaceae*
                        Pistils 5 or fewer, not in a head.
                            Flowers or fruits solitary; stems glabrous; fruit a berry
                                (*Podophyllum peltatum*) .... *Berberidaceae*
                            Flowers or fruits 2 or more or the stem pubescent; fruit an
                                achene or a cluster of carpels.
                                Flowers perfect, paired on axillary peduncles; fruit a cluster
                                    of carpels prolonged into beaks. (*Geranium*) .... *Geraniaceae*
                                Flowers imperfect, in axillary clusters; fruit an achene
                                    enclosed within a glandular bract (*Cannabis sativa*) .... *Cannabaceae*
                N. Leaves ternately or pinnately dissected; fruit a capsule or schizocarp of
                    mericarps not prolonged into beaks (a cluster of beaked capsules
                    in *Erodium*).
                    O. Plant in flower.
                        Flowers in umbels (*Erodium*) .... *Geraniaceae*
                        Flowers solitary or not in umbels.
                            Corolla very irregular (*Teucrium botrys*) .... *Lamiaceae*
                            Corolla regular or nearly so.
                                Corolla of separate petals, yellow (*Tribulus terrestris*). .... *Zygophyllaceae*
                                Corolla of united petals, white to pinkish.
                                    Stamens 2 or 4.
                                        Stamens 2; flowers in dense axillary clusters
                                            (*Lycopus americanus*). .... *Lamiaceae*
                                        Stamens 4; flowers solitary in the leaf axils or
                                            inflorescence terminal.
                                            Flowers solitary in the leaf axils (*Aureolaria*). .... *Scrophulariaceae*
                                            Flowers in terminal spikes .... *Verbenaceae*
                                    Stamens 5 (*Ellisia nyctelea*) .... *Hydrophyllaceae*
                    O. Plant in fruit.
                        Fruit a cluster of carpels prolonged into beaks (*Erodium*). .... *Geraniaceae*
                        Fruit a capsule or schizocarp of mericarps not prolonged into beaks.
                            Fruit a capsule.
                                Calyx cleft to near base; capsule 1-locular (*Ellisia nyctelea*). .... *Hydrophyllaceae*
                                Calyx campanulate-tubular; not cleft to near base; capsule
                                    2-locular (*Aureolaria*) .... *Scrophulariaceae*
                            Fruit a schizocarp of 4 or more mericarps.
                                Mericarps 4 mm or more long, bearing sharp spines
                                    (*Tribulus terrestris*). .... *Zygophyllaceae*
                                Mericarps less than 4 mm long, lacking spines. .... *Lamiaceae*
            M. Flowers in terminal inflorescences.

Inflorescence a spike or a raceme.
Stems prickly (*Dipsacus*) .... *Dipsacaceae*
Stems not prickly.
Corolla very irregular, or if only slightly irregular ovary not
4-lobed and fruit a capsule; flowers in leafy-bracteate
spikes or racemes.
Ovary not 4-lobed; fruit a capsule .... *Scrophulariaceae*
Ovary 4-lobed; fruit a schizocarp of 4 mericarps. .... *Lamiaceae*
Corolla regular or nearly so; ovary 4-lobed; fruit a schizocarp of 4
mericarps; flowers in scaly-bracteate spikes. .... *Verbenaceae*
Inflorescence an umbel or panicle of cymes.
Corolla bilabiate; fruit 2-carpellate, 2-locular. (*Scrophularia*). .... *Scrophulariaceae*
Corolla regular or slightly irregular but not bilabiate; fruit 1, 3 or
5-carpellate, 1 or 5-locular.
Corolla of separate petals; fruit 5-carpellate (*Erodium*). .... *Geraniaceae*
Corolla of united petals; fruit 1-3 carpellate, 1-locular (*Valeriana*). *Valerianaceae*
K. Leaves simple, not dissected.
P. Leaves toothed or lobed.
Q. Plant in flower.
R. Corolla present.
S. Corolla or calyx spurred.
Sepals 3, the same color as the petals, one of them prolonged into
a spur (*Impatiens*) .... *Balsaminaceae*
Sepals 5, a different color than the petals, none spurred. .... *Scrophulariaceae*
S. Corolla or calyx spurless.
T. Petals united.
Stems prickly (*Dipsacus*) .... *Dipsacaceae*
Stems not prickly.
Ovary inferior .... *Valerianaceae*
Ovary superior.
Ovary 4-lobed or 4-parted; stems usually square.
Inflorescence a spike or raceme; pedicels less than 1 mm
long; calyx less than 5 mm long (*Verbena*) .... *Verbenaceae*
Inflorescence not a spike or raceme or if so, pedicels
more than 1 mm long or calyx more than 5 mm
long .... *Lamiaceae*
Ovary not parted or lobed or at most, 2 parted.
Ovary 4-locular (*Sesamum orientale*) .... *Pedaliaceae*
Ovary 1 or 2-locular.
Ovary 2-locular. .... *Scrophulariaceae*
Ovary 1-locular.
Corolla subequally 5-lobed; ovary with 1 ovule
(*Phryma leptostachya*) .... *Verbenaceae*
Corolla bilabiate; ovary with few to many ovules
(*Proboscidea louisianica*). .... *Pedaliaceae*
T. Petals separate.
Ovary inferior or enclosed in a hypanthium; petals 2 or 4.
Anthers opening by terminal pores (*Rhexia*). .... *Melastomataceae*
Anthers not opening by terminal pores. .... *Onagraceae*
Ovary superior or nearly so, not enclosed in a hypanthium;
petals 5(4) or more.
Leaves less than 1 cm long, coarsely ciliate (*Saxifraga
oppositifolia*). .... *Saxifragaceae*
Leaves more than 1 cm long, or not coarsely ciliate.
Carpels 2; petals laciniate (*Mitella diphylla*). .... *Saxifragaceae*
Carpels 1, 3 or more; petals not laciniate.
Stamens 10 or more; leaves lobed.
Flower solitary; leaves 2 (*Podophyllum peltatum*). .... *Berberidaceae*
Flowers 2 or more; leaves more than 2 (*Geranium*). *Geraniaceae*
Stamens mostly fewer than 10; leaves not lobed
(*Sedum*). .... *Crassulaceae*

R. Corolla absent.
    Styles 3 or sepals more than 1 cm long and white.
        Plant with latex; sepals less than 1 cm long; flowers in cyathia
            (*Euphorbia*). .... *Euphorbiaceae*
        Plant lacking latex; sepals 1 cm or more long; flowers not in
            cyathia (*Podophyllum peltatum*) .... *Berberidaceae*
    Styles 1 or 2, or 2-parted; sepals less than 1 cm long or green.
        Ovary inferior; style 1 .... *Onagraceae*
        Ovary superior or styles 2 or 2-parted.
            Flowers in terminal racemes or solitary or in cymes, sometimes
                appearing axillary (*Chrysosplenium*) by proliferation of
                the stem.
                Flowers in spike-like racemes (*Salvia lyrata*). .... *Lamiaceae*
                Flowers solitary or in cymes (*Chrysosplenium americanum*). ... *Saxifragaceae*
            Flowers in axillary inflorescences, or terminal and not solitary
                or in cymes or racemes.
                Flowers imperfect, the pistillate enclosed by valvate bracts
                    (*Atriplex*). .... *Chenopodiaceae*
                Flowers perfect, or imperfect and the pistillate not enclosed
                  by valvate bracts.
                  Style 1; stamens 5 or fewer .... *Urticaceae*
                  Styles 2; stamens 8 or more (*Mercurialis annua*). .... *Euphorbiaceae*
Q. Plant in fruit.
    U. Stems prickly (*Dipsacus*) .... *Dipsacaceae*
    U. Stems not prickly (although with stinging hairs in some Urticaceae).
        V. Fruit 1-seeded, indehiscent, not in a schizocarp.
            Fruit with uncinnate hairs (*Circaea*). .... *Onagraceae*
            Fruit lacking uncinnate hairs.
                Fruit enclosed by valvate bracts (*Atriplex*). .... *Chenopodiaceae*
                Fruit not enclosed by valvate bracts.
                  Ovary superior; sepals not plumose.
                    Calyx 2-lipped, 5-lobed (*Phryma leptostachya*). .... *Verbenaceae*
                    Calyx not 2-lipped, 2-4-lobed .... *Urticaceae*
                  Ovary inferior; sepals sometimes plumose with cilia
                    (*Valeriana*). .... *Valerianaceae*
        V. Fruit 2 or more-seeded, or 1-seeded and in a schizocarp.
            W. Fruit a berry or schizocarp.
                Fruit a berry (*Podophyllum peltatum*). .... *Berberidaceae*
                Fruit a schizocarp.
                  Mericarps fused more than half their length; plants not
                    aromatic (*Verbena*). ,... *Verbenaceae*
                Mericarps fused only at base or less than half their length;
                    plants usually aromatic .... *Lamiaceae*
            W. Fruit a capsule or follicle.
             X. Seed with a coma (*Epilobium*) .... *Onagraceae*
            X. Seed without a coma.
                Y. Plant with latex; fruit 3-carpellate (*Euphorbia*). .... *Euphorbiaceae*
                Y. Plant without latex; or fruit 2, 4 or more-carpellate.
                  Z. Leaves coarsely bristly-ciliate (*Saxifraga oppositifolia*). .... *Saxifragaceae*
                Z. Leaves not coarsely bristly-ciliate.
                    a. Inflorescence terminal, or sometimes appearing axillary
                      (*Chrysosplenium*) by proliferation of the stem.
                    Inflorescence a panicle or spike, or a raceme and stem
                      leaves in more than 1 pair .... *Scrophulariaceae*
                  Inflorescence a solitary flower, a cyme, or a raceme
                    and stem with 1 pair of leaves.
                    Inflorescence an elongate raceme; stem with 1 pair
                      of leaves (*Mitella diphylla*) .... *Saxifragaceae*
                    Inflorescence a solitary flower or a cyme; stem with
                    more than 1 pair of leaves.

Fruit enclosed in a hypanthium (*Rhexia*). .... *Melastomataceae*
Fruit not enclosed in a hypanthium.
     Carpels 2 (*Chrysosplenium americanum*). .... *Saxifragaceae*
     Carpels 4-5 (*Sedum*) .... *Crassulaceae*
a. Inflorescence axillary.
    Capsule 4-celled, sometimes 4-sided, velvety
       (*Sesamum orientale*). .... *Pedaliaceae*
    Capsule not 4-celled, 4-sided or velvety.
      Fruit a dry, 2-carpellate capsule.
        Capsule more than 2-seeded; style 1 .... *Scrophulariaceae*
        Capsule 2-seeded; styles 2 (*Mercurialis annua*). ... *Euphorbiaceae*
      Fruit a fleshy capsule or dry and more than
        2-carpellate.
        Sepals present in fruit; fruit dry, 5-carpellate
          (*Geranium*). .... *Geraniaceae*
        Sepals absent in fruit; fruit a fleshy capsule
          (*Impatiens*). .... *Balsaminaceae*
P. Leaves entire or at most undulate.
  b. Plant in flower.
    c. Petals present, united.
      d. Corolla strongly irregular.
        Ovary 4-lobed or parted ....*Lamiaceae*
        Ovary not 4-lobed or parted.
          Ovary inferior (*Triosteum*) .... *Caprifoliaceae*
          Ovary superior.
            Leaves ovate to orbicular, cordate, the larger ones 10 cm or
              more long; ovary 1-locular; flowers racemose
              (*Proboscidea louisianica*). .... *Pedaliaceae*
            Leaves not ovate to orbicular or cordate, or if so less than
               10 cm long; ovary 2-locular.
            Calyx 5-lobed, regular, the lobes longer than the tube;
              flowers in axillary spikes (*Justicia americana*) .... *Acanthaceae*
            Calyx 4-lobed or 5-lobed and irregular, or the lobes
              shorter than the tube, or flowers not in axillary
              spikes .... *Scrophulariaceae*
      d. Corolla regular or nearly so.
        e. Plant with latex.
          Flowers in umbels (*Asclepias*) .... *Asclepiadaceae*
          Flowers in cymes or solitary .... *Apocynaceae*
        e. Plant lacking latex.
          f. Corolla 4-lobed.
            Ovary inferior .... *Rubiaceae*
            Ovary superior.
              Stamens 2 (*Veronica*) .... *Scrophulariaceae*
             Stamens 4 or more.
                Leaves linear, 1 cm or more long and 3 mm or less wide.
                 Flowers in heads; plant pubescent (*Plantago psyllium*). *Plantaginaceae*
                 Flowers in dichotomous cymes; plant glabrous
                    (*Polypremum procumbens*). .... *Buddlejaceae*
                Leaves not linear, or less than 1 cm long or more than 3
                 mm wide. .... *Gentianaceae*
          f. Corolla 5-lobed.
            Ovary inferior.
            Stems upright; plant deciduous; flowers cymose,
              corymbose or paniculate. .... *Valerianaceae*
            Stems trailing; plants evergreen; flowers in pairs (*Linnaea*
              borealis). .... *Caprifoliaceae*
           Ovary superior.
            Stamens 2 or 4.
             Ovary 4-lobed or 4-parted .... *Lamiaceae*
             Ovary not lobed .... *Scrophulariaceae*

Stamens 5.
    Ovaries 2, with a common style (*Vinca*). .... *Apocynaceae*
    Ovary 1 (or appearing like 4 in *Asperugo*).
        Stigmas 3; corolla pink or white, salverform. .... *Polemoniaceae*
        Stigmas 2, or 1 and capitate; flowers not pink or
            white, or if so, campanulate or rotate.
            Ovary 4-lobed (*Asperugo procumbens*) .... *Boraginaceae*
            Ovary not lobed.
                Ovary 1-celled; corolla campanulate or rotate. ...... *Primulaceae*
                Ovary completely or partly 2-celled; corolla
                    usually not rotate. .... *Gentianaceae*
c. Petals separate, or united only at the base or absent.
  g. Petals present.
    h. Petals 4 or fewer.
      Sepals 2 (*Montia fontana*) .... *Portulacaceae*
      Sepals 3 or more.
        Ovary superior, not enclosed in a hypanthium.
          Flowers solitary, lateral or axillary; petals green
            or white.
            Flowers pedicelled; pistil 1 (*Sagina*). .... *Caryophyllaceae*
          Flowers sessile or subsessile; pistils 3 or 4 (*Crassula*
            aquatica). .... *Crassulaceae*
          Flowers in cymes or panicles, axillary or terminal; petals
            yellow, white or red.
            Sepals 5, petals 3, red (*Lechea*) .... *Cistaceae*
            Sepals and petals both 4; petals yellow or white.
                Petals yellow; sepals dimorphic; stamens numerous. ... *Clusiaceae*
                Petals white; sepals undifferentiated; stamens 4
                    (*Radiola linoides*). .... *Linaceae*
        Ovary inferior or enclosed in a hypanthium.
          Stamens 8; anthers opening by terminal pores (*Rhexia*). ...... *Melastomataceae*
          Stamens 4 or if 8, anthers not opening by terminal pores.
            Flowers axillary; petals white or pink
               (*Rotala ramosior*). .... *Lythraceae*
            Flowers terminal or axillary and petals yellow. .... *Onagraceae*
    h. Petals 5(4) or more.
      Petals and sepals arising from a hypanthium much above the
        ovary. .... *Lythraceae*
      Petals and sepals not on a hypanthium, attached near base of
        ovary.
        Sepals 2. .... *Portulacaceae*
        Sepals 4-5.
          Leaves fleshy; carpels separate for at least half their length
            (*Sedum*). .... *Crassulaceae*
          Leaves not fleshy; carpels united to apex.
            Leaves coarsely ciliate; petals purple (*Saxifraga*
              oppositifolia). .... *Saxifragaceae*
            Leaves not coarsely ciliate or petals not purple.
              Petals yellow.
                Stamens 10 or more, or stigmas 3 or fewer. .... *Clusiaceae*
                Stamens 5; stigmas 5 (*Linum*) .... *Linaceae*
             Petals white, pink, lavender, blue or green.
                Ovary 1-locular .... *Caryophyllaceae*
                Ovary 4 or more-locular (*Linum*) .... *Linaceae*
  g. Petals absent.
    i. Plant with latex (*Euphorbia*) .... *Euphorbiaceae*
    i. Plant lacking latex.
      j. Calyx of 3 sepals; leaves 2, reniform (*Asarum canadense*). .... *Aristolochiaceae*
      j. Calyx of 4 to 6 sepals, or lacking; leaves more than 2 or not
        reniform.
        k. Calyx brightly colored and corrolloid.

Calyx not tubular at base, campanulate, without an
   involucre, the lobes unappendaged (*Glaux*
   maritima) .... *Primulaceae*
Calyx tubular at base, subtended by an involucre, or each
   lobe bearing a short horn near the apex.
   Calyx united more than half its length; ovary inferior
      (*Mirabilis*). .... *Nyctaginaceae*
   Calyx not united or united less than half its length;
      ovary superior (*Sesuvium maritimum*) .... *Aizoaceae*
k. Calyx green, or at least not corolloid.
   Calyx lobes spine-tipped; rosette leaves numerous; upper
      leaves spine-tipped; flowers in compact axillary
      clusters (*Chorizanthe pungens*). .... *Polygonaceae*
   Plant lacking the above combination of characters.
      Flowers solitary or mostly so, axillary (appearing
         axillary but actually terminal in *Chrysosplenium*).
         Sepals 5 or leaves spine-tipped.
            Leaves spine-tipped (*Salsola australis*). .... *Chenopodiaceae*
            Leaves not spine-tipped.
               Leaves linear, less than 3 mm wide (*Sagina*). .... *Caryophyllaceae*
               Leaves wider, more than 3 mm wide (*Sesuvium*
                  maritimum). .... *Aizoaceae*
         Sepals 4 or absent; leaves not spine-tipped.
            Sepals absent (*Callitriche*) .... *Callitrichaceae*
            Sepals present.
               Leaves linear, less than 3 mm wide (*Sagina*). .... *Caryophyllaceae*
               Leaves lanceolate to ovate, 3 mm or more wide.
                  Hypanthium present, roundly 4-sided, disc
                     lacking, ovary 4-locular (*Ludwigia*) ...... *Onagraceae*
                  Hypanthium absent, conspicuous 8-lobed
                     disc present, ovary 2-locular
                     (*Chrysosplenium americanum*) .... *Saxifragaceae*
      Flowers several in terminal inflorescences.
         Flowers in spikes or compact panicles, or the flowers
            unisexual.
            Entire plant silky-pubescent (*Froelichia gracilis*). ..... *Amaranthaceae*
            Entire plant glabrous or remotely pubescent. .... *Chenopodiaceae*
         Flowers in cymes or racemes; flowers perfect. .... *Caryophyllaceae*
b. Plant in fruit.
   l. Fruit 1-seeded or a schizocarp of 2 or more mericarps, indehiscent.
      m. Fruit a schizocarp of 2 or more mericarps.
         Mericarps 2; stipules forming a ring around the stem with
            marginal bristles (*Diodia*) .... *Rubiaceae*
         Mericarps 4 or more; stipules, if present, not forming a ring,
            around the stem with marginal bristles.
            Mericarps 5 or more, or mericarps and sepals 4. .... *Linaceae*
            Mericarps 4; sepals 2 or 5 or absent.
               Sepals absent; stems flattened or round, unarmed
                  (*Callitriche*). .... *Callitrichaceae*
               Sepals present; stems square or prickly-hispid.
                  Plant with mint-like or spicy odor; stems square, unarmed. *Lamiaceae*
                  Plant without mint-like or spicy odor; stems round,
                     prickly-hispid (*Asperugo procumbens*) .... *Boraginaceae*
      m. Fruit not a schizocarp, 1-seeded.
         Caylx lobes spine-tipped; rosette leaves numerous; upper leaves
            spine-tipped; fruiting calyces in compact axillary-clusters
            (*Chorizanthe pungens*). .... *Polygonaceae*
         Plant lacking the above combination of characters.
            Fruits in spikes or rarely in subglobose heads.
               Plant densely silky-pubescent (*Froelichia gracilis*). .... *Amaranthaceae*
               Plant not silky-pubescent or remotely so. .... *Chenopodiaceae*

Fruits axillary, or in cymes or loosely arranged, not in spikes or
    subglobose heads.
    Calyx present, the ovary inferior or apparently so.
        Leaves less than 2 mm wide .... *Caryophyllaceae*
        Leaves 3 mm or more wide.
            Stems upright; plants deciduous; fruits cymose,
                corymbose or paniculate. .... *Valerianaceae*
            Stems trailing; plants evergreen; fruits in pairs (*Linnaea*
                borealis). .... *Caprifoliaceae*
    Calyx absent, or where present, the ovary obviously superior.
        Leaves spine-tipped or fruit enclosed by a pair of valvate
            bracts. .... *Chenopodiaceae*
        Leaves not spine-tipped; fruit not enclosed by a pair of
            bracts.
            Leaves more than 2 cm long or more than 1 cm wide
                (*Mirabilis*). .... *Nyctaginaceae*
            Leaves less than 2 cm long and less than 1 cm wide. .... *Caryophyllaceae*
l. Fruit a capsule, follicle or berry, 2 or more-seeded, or if 1-seeded,
    circumscissile.
    n. Fruit a fleshy berry, indehiscent, ovary inferior.
        Berry with 2 calyces (or remmants) on top, the product of 2
            united ovaries (*Mitchella repens*) .... *Rubiaceae*
        Berry with 1 calyx on top, the product of a single ovary.
            Sepals 5; stems erect (*Triosteum*) .... *Caprifoliaceae*
            Sepals 3; stems trailing (*Asarum canadense*) .... *Aristolochiaceae*
    n. Fruit not as above.
      o. Fruit with a hooked beak more than 2 cm long (*Proboscidia*
          louisianica). .... *Pedaliaceae*
      o. Fruit without a long hooked beak.
        p. Fruit a follicle, or a capsule opening on 1 side, or with valves
            separate for half or more their length.
            Fruit solitary; plant less than 1 dm tall.
                Fruit terminal; sepals 5; leaves obovate (*Saxifraga*
                    oppositifolia). .... *Saxifragaceae*
                Fruit axillary; sepals 3 or 4, leaves linear (*Crassula*
                    aquatica). .... *Crassulaceae*
            Fruits several or if solitary, plant more than 1 dm tall.
                Inflorescence terminal or if axillary, calyx 6-toothed;
                    plant lacking latex.
                  Fruit 2-locular; calyx 6-toothed (*Cuphea viscosissima*). ..... *Lythraceae*
                  Fruit more than 2 locular; calyx of 4-5 sepals.
                    Fruit of 4-5 distinct follicles; leaves fleshy (*Sedum*). ...... *Crassulaceae*
                    Fruit a 3-valved capsule; leaves not fleshy (*Lechea*). ...... *Cistaceae*
                  Inflorescence axillary, calyx 5-lobed, or if terminal, plant
                    with latex.
                  Follicle less than 5 mm in diameter; leaves more than
                    1 cm wide. .... *Apocynaceae*
                  Follicle more than 5 mm in diameter, or less and leaves
                    less than 1 cm wide. .... *Asclepiadaceae*
        p. Fruit a capsule, the carpels or valves united to apex.
          q. Capsule circumscissile; calyx 5-lobed; fruits not in heads or
             spikes.
             Capsule 3-locular (*Sesuvium maritimum*). .... *Aizoaceae*
             Capsule 1-locular (*Anagallis*) .... *Primulaceae*
          q. Capsule not circumscissile, or calyx 4-lobed, or fruits in
             heads or spikes.
            r. Ovary inferior, or enclosed in a hypanthium, and/or calyx
               sometimes absent.
               Plant with latex (*Euphorbia*) .... *Euphorbiaceae*
               Plant lacking latex.

Calyx present, 3-lobed (*Asarum canadense*). .... *Aristolochiaceae*
Calyx absent, or present and 4 or more lobed.
   Fruit with a slender neck; seed not comose
     (*Rhexia*). .... *Melastomataceae*
   Fruit without a slender neck or seed comose.
     Stipules present .... *Rubiaceae*
     Stipules absent.
       Capsule bilobed or obcordate .... *Saxifragaceae*
       Capsule not bilobed or obcordate.
         Calyx teeth lacking appendages; capsule
           opening by a terminal pore, or seed
           comose .... *Onagraceae*
         Calyx teeth alternating with as many
           appendages in the sinuses; capsule
           not opening by a terminal pore;
           seed not comose. .... *Lythraceae*
    r. Ovary superior, not enclosed in a hypanthium, or enclosed
       only at the base, calyx evident. [go to s]
s. Calyx 2 or 4-lobed.
  t. Stems winged or 2-edged. .... *Clusiaceae*
  t. Stems not winged or 2-edged.
    Calyx 2-lobed. .... *Portulacaceae*
    Calyx 4-lobed.
      Sepals separate to base; calyx regular.
        Fruit notched at apex (*Veronica*) .... *Scrophulariaceae*
        Fruit not notched at apex.
          Fruit in a head or spike (*Plantago psyllium*). .... *Plantaginaceae*
          Fruit not in a head or spike.
            Fruits solitary or few, axillary (*Sagina*). .... *Caryophyllaceae*
            Fruits in terminal cymes or slender panicles.
              Leaves less than 5 mm long and 2 mm wide; fruits in a slender
                panicle (*Bartonia*) .... *Gentianaceae*
              Leaves more than 10 mm long and more than 2 mm wide; fruits
                in cymes (*Polypremum procumbens*) .... *Buddlejaceae*
      Sepals united well above the base or calyx irregular.
        Fruit enclosed in a remnant of corolla. .... *Gentianaceae*
        Fruit not enclosed by corolla, corolla absent. .... *Scrophulariaceae*
s. Calyx 5 or more-lobed.
  u. Fruit obviously 2-carpellate and completely or partly 2-locular.
    Leaves less than 1 cm long, coarsely ciliate (*Saxifraga oppositifolia*). .... *Saxifragaceae*
    Leaves more than 1 cm long or not coarsely ciliate.
      Calyx teeth alternating with as many appendages in the sinuses. .... *Lythraceae*
      Calyx teeth lacking appendages.
        Inflorescence of pedunculate, axillary spikes (*Justicia americana*). .... *Acanthaceae*
        Inflorescence terminal or axillary and not of pedunculate spikes.
          Inflorescence terminal, cymose or compact and head-like; withered
            corolla present. .... *Gentianaceae*
          Inflorescence of axillary or terminal racemes, spikes or panicles, or if
            cymose, corolla not persistent .... *Scrophulariaceae*
  u. Fruit not 2-carpellate; 1 or 3 or more-locular.
    Fruit opening by 5 or 10 terminal teeth, the lower 3/4 of the capsule not
      splitting. .... *Caryophyllaceae*
    Fruit not as above.
      Calyx or hypanthium united more than half its length, may split on 1 side
        when capsule dehisces. .... *Lythraceae*
      Calyx of 5, distinct sepals or sepals separate at least half their length.
        Fruit 1-locular, equally as long as broad or broader. .... *Primulaceae*
        Fruits 3 to 5-locular, or 1-locular and longer than broad.
          Calyx with tubular base. .... *Polemoniaceae*
          Calyx lobes free to base. .... *Clusiaceae*

GROUP 9
Herbaceous Plants With Leaves Alternate

A. Leaves compound or deeply dissected and appearing compound.
  B. Flowers or fruit in heads or umbels (including fruiting specimens with aggregate
    fruits with a head-like appearance).
    C. Flowers or fruit in umbels.
      Ovary inferior; sepals persistent in fruit but small; fruit a berry or schizocarp
        of 2 mericarps.
        Stigmas 2; fruit a schizocarp of 2 mericarps. .... *Apiaceae*
        Stigmas 3 or more; fruit a berry (*Aralia*). .... *Araliaceae*
      Ovary superior; sepals often absent; fruit a legume or capsule.
        Leaves ternately compound with 3 leaflets.
          Leaflets not obcordate; flowers irregular; fruit a legume. .... *Fabaceae*
          Leaflets obcordate; flowers regular; fruit a capsule (*Oxalis*). .... *Oxalidaceae*
        Leaves compound with 5 or more leaflets, or palmately or pinnately
          dissected.
          Corolla regular, with 4 petals; sepals absent in fruit (*Chelidonium*
            majus). .... *Papaveraceae*
          Corolla irregular, or regular and with 5 petals; sepals present in fruit.
            Corolla irregular; fruit 1-carpellate and locular. .... *Fabaceae*
            Corolla regular or nearly so; fruit 5-carpellate and locular. .... *Geraniaceae*
    C. Flowers or fruit in heads.
      Stipules present.
        Stigma 1; fruit not in aggregates .... *Fabaceae*
        Stigmas 2 or more; fruit in aggregates. .... *Rosaceae*
      Stipules absent.
        Leaf segments or leaflets ternate or palmate, entire (*Arisaema*). .... *Araceae*
        Leaf segments or leaflets not ternate or palmate, or if so, toothed.
          Plant in flower.
            Ovary inferior.
              Ovaries hidden by involucral bracts .... *Asteraceae*
              Ovaries not hidden by bracts .... *Apiaceae*
            Ovary superior.
              Stamens 10 or more .... *Ranunculaceae*
             Stamens 5 or fewer.
              Calyx lobes not spinulose-tipped; corolla none. .... *Chenopodiaceae*
              Calyx lobes spinulose-tipped; corolla present, colored.
                (*Navarretia leucocephala*) .... *Polemoniaceae*
          Plant in fruit.
            Fruit in aggregates; heads not surrounded by bracts; ovary superior. .. *Ranunculaceae*
            Fruit not in aggregates, or if so, heads surrounded by bracts and
              ovary inferior.
            Heads surrounded by bracts and the fruit hidden. .... *Asteraceae*
            Heads not surrounded by bracts or the fruit not hidden.
              Ovary inferior; fruit a schizocarp .... *Apiaceae*
             Ovary superior; fruit an achene .... *Chenopodiaceae*
  B. Flowers or fruit not in heads or umbels.
    D. Leaves ternately or palmately dissected or compound.
      E. Leaves palmately divided into more than 3 segments or leaflets.
        F. Flowers and fruit in racemes.
          Petals 4, uniform in shape and size; fruit with stipe more than 5 mm
            long (*Cleome spinosa*) .... *Capparidaceae*
          Petals not 4, or if so, of various sizes and shapes; fruit not long-stipitate.
            Leaf compound, leaflets entire (*Lupinus*). .... *Fabaceae*
            Leaf simple, segments toothed or divided. .... *Ranunculaceae*
        F. Flowers and fruit not in racemes.
          G. Plant in flower.
            Flowers on a spadix surrounded by a spathe (*Arisaema*). .... *Araceae*
            Flowers not on a spadix nor surrounded by a spathe.

Ovary inferior or absent, or corolla absent.
  Flowers in involucrate heads .... *Asteraceae*
  Flowers not in involucrate heads.
    Flowers unisexual (*Cannabis sativa*) .... *Cannabaceae*
    Flowers bisexual (*Alchemilla*) .... *Rosaceae*
Ovary superior; corolla present.
  Stamens united in a column (*Sida hermaphrodita*). .... *Malvaceae*
  Stamens not united.
    Corolla united (*Hydrophyllum*) .... *Hydrophyllaceae*
    Corolla of separate petals.
      Pistil 1; stigmas 5 (*Geranium*) .... *Geraniaceae*
      Pistils several to many, each with a single stigma.
        Stipules present .... *Rosaceae*
        Stipules absent .... *Ranunculaceae*
G. Plant in fruit.
  Fruit fleshy, red to blackish.
    Stipules prominent (*Rubus*) .... *Rosaceae*
    Stipules absent (*Arisaema*) .... *Araceae*
  Fruit dry, not red.
    Fruit in aggregates or heads.
      Stipules present .... *Rosaceae*
      Stipules absent.
        Fruit in a ring consisting of usually 10 carpels (*Sida*
            hermaphrodita). .... *Malvaceae*
        Fruit not in a ring.
          Fruit plainly visible, not surrounded by bracts. .... *Ranunculaceae*
          Fruit not visible, surrounded by bracts. .... *Asteraceae*
    Fruit not in aggregates or heads.
      Fruit 5-seeded, 1 seed per carpel (*Geranium*). .... *Geraniaceae*
      Fruit 1-4 seeded, 1 or more carpellate.
        Stipules present .... *Rosaceae*
        Stipules absent.
          Leaves compound, with distinct leaflets (*Cannabis sativa*). . *Cannabaceae*
          Leaves not compound, merely palmately lobed
            (*Hydrophyllum*). .... *Hydrophyllaceae*
E. Leaves ternately divided into 3 segments or leaflets.
  H. Plant in flower.
    Flowers in involucrate heads, with inferior ovaries, or on a spadix
      surrounded by a spathe.
      Inflorescence surrounded by a spathe (*Arisaema triphyllum*). .... *Araceae*
      Inflorescence surrounded by an involucre of bracts. .... *Asteraceae*
    Flowers not in involucrate heads, or the ovary superior; inflorescence
      not surrounded by a spathe.
      Corolla and/or calyx irregular.
        Petals uniform in size and shape (*Polanisia dodecandra*). .... *Capparidaceae*
        Petals of different sizes and shapes. .... *Fabaceae*
      Corolla and calyx regular.
        Flowers in racemes.
          Corolla of 5 separate petals .... *Rosaceae*
          Corolla of 4 separate or 5 united petals.
            Corolla of 4 separate petals.
              Leaflets toothed or dissected; stamens 6; stems glabrous
                to short-pubescent (*Cardamine*) .... *Brassicaceae*
              Leaflets entire; stamens 8 or more; stems glandular-
                pubescent (*Polanisia dodecandra*) .... *Capparidaceae*
            Corolla united, 5-lobed (*Menyanthes trifoliata*). .... *Menyanthaceae*
        Flowers not in racemes.
          Pistils united, 5 or fewer.
            Leaflets obcordate; ovary 5-locular (*Oxalis*). .... *Oxalidaceae*
            Leaflets linear; ovary 2-locular (*Eschscholtzia californica*). .... *Papavaraceae*
          Pistils separate, more than 5 .... *Rosaceae*

H. Plant in fruit.
    Fruit in heads, short spikes or aggregates.
        Fruit a legume .... *Fabaceae*
        Fruit an achene, follicle or fleshy, not a legume.
            Fruit fleshy, red (*Arisaema triphyllum*) .... *Araceae*
            Fruit dry, not red.
                Stipules present .... *Rosaceae*
                Stipules absent .... *Asteraceae*
    Fruit not in heads, short spikes or aggregates.
        Rachis of inflorescence viscid (*Polanisia dodecandra*). .... *Capparidaceae*
        Rachis of inflorescence not viscid.
            Leaflets obcordate; stipules less than 1 mm long or obsolete
                (*Oxalis*). .... *Oxalidaceae*
            Leaflets not obcordate, or stipules present and more than 2 mm
                long.
                Fruit 1-carpellate; stipules free from petiole for more than half
                    their length .... *Fabaceae*
                Fruit 2-carpellate; stipules adnate to petiole for more than half
                    their length or absent.
                    Leaflets entire.
                        Fruit ovoid (*Menyanthes trifoliata*) .... *Menyanthaceae*
                        Fruit long and slender (*Eschscholtzia californica*). .... *Papaveraceae*
                    Leaflets or primary divisions crenate-toothed; (*Cardamine*). .. *Brassicaceae*
D. Leaves pinnately, bipinnately, or bi or tri-ternately dissected or compound.
  I. Plant in flower.
    J. Flowers in involucrate heads .... *Asteraceae*
    J. Flowers not in involucrate heads.
      K. Flowers irregular.
        Stamens 4 or 6.
            Stamens 4 (*Pedicularis*) .... *Scrophulariaceae*
            Stamens 6 .... *Fumariaceae*
        Stamens 5 or more but not 6.
            Style and stigma 1; stamens not borne on a disc above the petals. ... *Fabaceae*
            Style and stigmas 3 or more; stamens borne on a 1-sided disc
               above the petals (*Reseda*) .... *Resedaceae*
      K. Flowers regular.
        L. Leaves bi or tri-ternately or pinnately compound or dissected.
            Petals yellow, denticulate (*Ruta graveolens*). .... *Rutaceae*
            Petals not yellow, or yellow and not denticulate, or rarely absent.
                Stamens 6; flowers perfect (*Caulophyllum thalictroides*). .... *Berberidaceae*
                 Stamens more than 6 or flowers imperfect.
                    Hypanthium present, saucer-shaped, appearing like a calyx
                      tube.
                      Stamens 10, carpels 2; stem glandular-pubescent above
                        (*Astilbe japonica*). .... *Saxifragaceae*
                      Stamens 15 or more; carpels 3 or more; stem not
                        glandular-pubescent (*Aruncus dioicus*) .... *Rosaceae*
                  Hypanthium none, sepals distinct. .... *Ranunculaceae*
        L. Leaves once-pinnately dissected or compound.
            Corolla united.
                Styles or stigmas 3 .... *Polemoniaceae*
                Styles or stigmas 2 .... *Hydrophyllaceae*
                Style 1, stigma shallowly 2-lobed .... *Solanaceae*
            Corolla of separate petals or absent.
                Sepals 2 or 3, or if falling early (*Papaveraceae*) plant with
                  colored juice.
                  Sepals 3; petals none, styles 3-4 (*Proserpinaca*). .... *Haloragaceae*
                  Sepals 2 or 3; petals present; style 1.
                    Sepals and petals both 3; plant lacking colored juice
                      (*Floerkea proserpinacoides*) .... *Limnanthaceae*
                    Sepals 2; petals 4; plant with colored juice. .... *Papaveraceae*

Sepals 4 or more; plant lacking colored juice.
    Petals unequal; stamens borne on a 1-sided disc above the
        petals (*Reseda*). .... *Resedaceae*
    Petals equal; stamens not borne on a disc above the petals.
        Petals 4; style 1; ovary 2-locular; stamens 6 or fewer. .... *Brassicaceae*
        Petals 5 or none, or if 4, styles 4 and ovary 4-locular;
            stamens mostly more than 6.
            Leaves with conspicuous stipules .... *Rosaceae*
            Leaves without stipules.
                Leaves divided into capillary segments
                    (*Myriophyllum*). .... *Haloragaceae*
                Leaves with ovate leaflets (*Dictamnus albus*). .... *Rutaceae*

I. Plant in fruit.
  M. Fruit 1-seeded.
    Fruit in involucrate heads .... *Asteraceae*
    Fruit not in involucrate heads.
      Leaves once-pinnate.
        Sepals 3 (*Floerkea proserpinacoides*). .... *Limnanthaceae*
        Sepals 4 or more .... *Rosaceae*
      Leaves bi or tri-ternate or pinnate.
        Inflorescence axillary, and often also terminal (*Fumaria*
          officinalis). .... *Fumariaceae*
        Inflorescence only terminal.
          Fruit (seed) blue and globose (*Caulophyllum thalictroides*). .... *Berberidaceae*
          Fruit brown, green or blackish, elongate (*Thalictrum*). .... *Ranunculaceae*
  M. Fruit 2 or more-seeded.
    N. Leaves once-pinnately dissected or compound.
      Fruit a capsule, 3-6 lobed and with 3-6 horns, opening at the top
        (*Reseda*). .... *Resedaceae*
      Fruit sometimes lobed and/or opening at the top but without horns.
        Leaves with stipules; leaflets or segments serrate (*Filipendula*). .... *Rosaceae*
        Leaves without stipules, or if stipules present, leaflets or segments
          entire.
        Fruit quadrangular, eventually splitting into 4 mericarps
          (*Myriophyllum*). .... *Haloragaceae*
        Fruit not quadrangular, indehiscent, or not splitting into
          mericarps.
          Fruit 3-carpellate and 3-locular.
             Fruit dehiscent, not triangular .... *Polemoniaceae*
             Fruit indehiscent, triangular (*Proserpinaca*). .... *Haloragaceae*
          Fruit 1 or more-carpellate and 1 or more locular.
             Fruit a capsule topped by a sessile crown, opening by pores
                under the crown. .... *Papaveraceae*
             Fruit a capsule opening by valves, or indehiscent, or a
                legume.
                Fruit less than twice as long as broad.
                    Leaves lacking translucent dots; ovary unlobed. .... *Hydrophyllaceae*
                    Leaves with translucent dots; ovary 5-lobed
                      (*Dictamnus albus*). .... *Rutaceae*
                Fruit 2 or more times as long as broad.
                    Calyx completely absent in fruit .... *Brassicaceae*
                  Calyx, or a remnant of it, present in fruit.
                    Inflorescence axillary, or stipules present. .... *Fabaceae*
                    Inflorescence terminal; stipules absent
                      (*Pedicularis*). .... *Scrophulariaceae*
    N. Leaves bi or tri-ternately or pinnately dissected or compound.
      Sepals present in fruit.
        Stipules absent; leaf segments entire (*Ruta graveolens*). .... *Rutaceae*
        Stipules present; leaf segments or leaflets serrate (*Astilbe*
          japonica). .... *Saxifragaceae*
      Sepals absent in fruit.

Flowers not 2-4-merous; fruit a berry, achene or follicle. .... *Ranunculaceae*
Flowers 2-4-merous; fruit a capsule.
  Inflorescence umbellate or cymose, or fruits solitary;
        plants with colored juice .... *Papaveraceae*
  Inflorescence racemose; plants with watery juice. .... *Fumariaceae*
A. Leaves simple, obviously not compound, although sometimes lobed or dissected.
  O. Plant in flower.
    P. Corolla united but separate from the calyx.
      Q. Corolla irregular, or in a head with some of the flowers irregular.
        Flowers in involucrate heads ....*Asteraceae*
        Flowers not in involucrate heads.
          Stem leaves scale-like, 2 mm or less long (*Utricularia*). .... *Lentibulariaceae*
          Stem leaves not scale-like, or more than 2 mm long.
            Stems with sharp, stiff, pustulate hairs (*Echium vulgare*). .... *Boraginaceae*
            Stems without sharp, stiff, pustulate hairs.
              Calyx of 3 small and 2 larger sepals colored like the petals;
                stamens united by their filaments forming a split sheath,
                this united with the corolla (*Polygala*) .... *Polygalaceae*
              Calyx not as above; stamens separate or united by their anthers.
                Stamens 5, united by their anthers (*Lobelia*). .... *Campanulaceae*
                Stamens 4 or fewer, or 5 and separate.
                  Ovary 4-locular (*Sesamum orientale*)... *Pedaliaceae*
                  Ovary 1 or 2-locular.
                    Leaves not ovate to orbicular or cordate, or if so less than
                      1 dm long; ovary 2-locular.. *Scrophulariaceae*
                    Leaves ovate to orbicular, cordate, the larger ones 1 dm or
                      more long; ovary 1-locular; flowers racemose
                      (*Proboscidea louisianica*). .... *Pedaliaceae*
      Q. Corolla regular or nearly so; if in a head none of the flowers irregular.
        R. Anther-bearing stamens more numerous than the corolla lobes.
          Leaves deciduous; stamens united in a tube; corolla lobes united only
            at base. .... *Malvaceae*
          Leaves evergreen; stamens separate; corolla united for a quarter or
            more its length .... *Pyrolaceae*
        R. Anther-bearing stamens the same as or fewer in number than the
          corolla lobes.
          S. Stamens united by their anthers.
            Plant with latex; ovary inferior, 2 or more-locular; flowers not in
              involucrate heads .... *Campanulaceae*
           Plant without latex; ovary superior, or if inferior 1-locular; flowers
              in involucrate heads .... *Asteraceae*
          S. Stamens separate (hidden in horn-like structures in *Asclepias*).
           T. Stamens hidden in horn-like structures (*Asclepias*). .... *Asclepiadaceae*
           T. Stamens visible or in the tube of the corolla.
             U. Ovary deeply 4-lobed or parted, and/or 4-locular. .... *Boraginaceae*
             U. Ovary at most 2-lobed, not 4-locular.
               V. Ovary 3 to 5-locular.
                 Ovary inferior ....*Campanulaceae*
                 Ovary superior.
                   Stamens epipetalous, as many as the corolla lobes; ovary
                     3-5 locular.
                     Leaves entire, stigmas 3 (*Collomia linearis*). .... *Polemoniaceae*
                     Leaves coarsely toothed; stigma 1 .... *Solanaceae*
                   Stamens free, twice as many as the corolla lobes; ovary
                     5-locular. .... *Ericaceae*
             V. Ovary 1 or 2-locular.
               Leaves minute and scale-like, 5 mm or less long; stems wiry,
                often spiral or twining (*Bartonia*) .... *Gentianaceae*
               Leaves foliaceous, larger; stems not as above.
                Corolla lobes interspersed with staminodes. .... *Primulaceae*
                Corolla lobes not interspersed with staminodes.

Plant with latex; ovaries 2 (*Amsonia tabernaemontana*). .. *Apocynaceae*
Plant lacking latex; ovary 1.
    Style forked; stigmas 2; stamens 5 .... *Hydrophyllaceae*
    Style capitate; stigma(s) 1 or 2; stamens 2, 4 or 5.
        Ovary 1-locular .... *Primulaceae*
        Ovary 2-locular.
            Flowers not in spike-like racemes, or if so
                corolla funnelform; stamens 4-5 .... *Solanaceae*
            Flowers in spike-like racemes, corolla rotate, or
                stamens 2. .... *Scrophulariaceae*
P. Corolla of separate petals, corolla and calyx adnate or corolla absent.
  W. Corolla irregular.
    Ovary inferior or leaves parallel-veined.
      Inflorescence enclosed in a spathe (*Commelina*). .... *Commelinaceae*
      Inflorescence not in a spathe.
        Stamens 6, with distinct filaments (*Pontederia cordata*) .... *Pontederiaceae*
        Stamens 3 or fewer; filaments absent. .... *Orchidaceae*
    Ovary superior; leaves net-veined.
      Flowers or inflorescences axillary.
        Sepals and petals similarly colored; calyx not green; stipules absent
          (*Impatiens*) .... *Balsaminaceae*
        Sepals and petals dissimilarly colored, or the calyx green; stipules
          present .... *Violaceae*
      Flowers or inflorescences terminal.
        Stamens borne on a 1-sided disc above the petals (*Reseda*). .... *Resedaceae*
        Stamens not borne on a disc above the petals.
          Stamens 5 or 10.
            Stamens, at least in part, fused; petals yellow. .... *Fabaceae*
            Stamens not fused; petals white to pinkish (*Saxifraga*). .... *Saxifragaceae*
          Stamens 6 or 8 (*Polygala*) .... *Polygalaceae*
  W. Corolla regular or absent.
    X. Corolla and calyx adnate.
      Anther-bearing stamens 2 or 3.
        Perianth woolly (*Lachnanthes caroliniana*). .... *Haemodoraceae*
        Perianth not woolly.
          Inflorescence axillary or leaf blades ovate to elliptic. .... *Pontederiaceae*
          Inflorescence terminal; leaf blades linear. .... *Iridaceae*
      Anther-bearing stamens 4 or more.
        Perianth united half or more its length, or ovary 2 or more-ovulate.
          Calyx lobes 4 .... *Onagraceae*
          Calyx lobes 3 (*Polygonatum*) .... *Convallariaceae*
        Perianth united only at base; ovary 1-ovulate. .... *Polygonaceae*
    X. Corolla and calyx separate, or corolla absent.
      U. Sepals and petals borne on the rim of a hypanthium; calyx
        4-6-toothed, alternating with as many appendages in the sinuses
        (*Lythrum*). .... *Lythraceae*
      U. Sepals and petals not borne on the rim of a hypanthium, or if so,
        calyx lacking appendages in the sinuses.
      Z. Corolla of 4 petals.
        Ovary inferior.
          Flowers in a terminal head-like cluster subtended by 4, usually
            white petaloid bracts (*Cornus*) .... *Cornaceae*
          Flowers not in a head-like cluster subtended by petaloid
            bracts.
            Style 1; leaves with expanded blades. .... *Onagraceae*
            Styles 4; leaves reduced to scales (*Myriophyllum*). .... *Haloragaceae*
        Ovary superior.
          Leaves minute and scale-like, 5 mm or less long; stems wiry,
            often spiral or twining (*Bartonia*) .... *Gentianaceae*
          Leaves foliaceous, larger; stems not as above.

Sepals 4; plants without colored juice; stamens 6 or fewer. ...... *Brassicaceae*
Sepals 2 or absent and plants with colored juice, and/or
    stamens 8 or more.
Sepals 2 or absent at flowering; plants with colored juice. .... *Papaveraceae*
Sepals 4, present at flowering; plants without colored juice.
    Pistils 4, separate (*Sedum*) .... *Crassulaceae*
    Pistil 1 (*Radiola linoides*) .... *Linaceae*
   Z. Corolla of more or less than 4 petals, or petals absent. [go to a]
a. Sepals and petals each 5.
  b. Plants monoecious, only the staminate flowers with 5 sepals and 5 petals; plants
     densely stellate-pubescent and scaly (*Crotonopsis elliptica*). .... *Euphorbiaceae*
  b. Plants hermaphrodite; plants not stellate-pubescent and scaly.
    c. Leaves densely covered with stalked, reddish glands (*Drosera*). .... *Droseraceae*
    c. Leaves not covered with stalked reddish glands.
      d. Stigmas 2 or 3.
        Stigmas 3.
          Corolla white.
          Leaves petioled, glandular-serrate; ovary 3-locular; lowers umbellate
            (*Ceanothus*) .... *Rhamnaceae*
          Leaves sessile, entire; ovary 1-locular; flowers cymose
            (*Corrigiola littoralis*) .... *Caryophyllaceae*
          Corolla yellow or red.
          Leaves entire; flowers small; ovary superior. .... *Cistaceae*
          Leaves coarsely toothed; flowers large and showy; ovary inferior
            (*Mentzelia oligosperma*) .... *Loasaceae*
        Stigmas 2.
          Flowers in heads or umbels. .... *Apiaceae*
          Flowers in racemes, panicles or solitary. .... *Saxifragaceae*
      d. Stigmas 1, 4 or more.
        Stamens hidden in horn-like structures (*Asclepias tuberosa*). .... *Asclepiadaceae*
        Stamens not hidden in horn-like structures.
          Flowers in umbels .... *Araliaceae*
          Flowers not in umbels.
            Stamens united into a tube around the styles. .... *Malvaceae*
            Stamens not united into a tube.
              Pistils or stigmas more than twice as many as the sepals.
                Sepals 5, the 2 outer smaller than the 3 inner. .... *Cistaceae*
                Sepals more or less than 5, or 5 and uniform.
                  Leaves not stipulate; hypanthium none. .... *Ranunculaceae*
                  Leaves stipulate; hypanthium present (*Rubus*). .... *Rosaceae*
              Pistils or stigmas twice as many as the sepals or fewer.
                Stem bearing only 1 leaf (*Parnassia glauca*). .... *Saxifragaceae*
                Stem bearing more than 1 leaf.
                  Leaves thick and fleshy (*Sedum*) .... *Crassulaceae*
                  Leaves thin, not fleshy.
                    Ovary 1-locular; stigma 1 (*Lysimachia*). .... *Primulaceae*
                    Ovary 5 or more locular or carpellate; stigmas 5 or more.
                      Stipules present.
                        Flowers more than 1; hypanthium none. .... *Geraniaceae*
                        Flowers solitary; hypanthium present (*Rubus*). .... *Rosaceae*
                    Stipules obsolete.
                        Stigmas sessile (*Penthorum sedoides*). .... *Crassulaceae*
                        Stigmas terminating styles, the latter distinct or
                          united (*Linum*). .... *Linaceae*
a. Sepals and petals more or fewer than 5, or petals absent.
  e. Sepals and petals each 3.
    Leaves pinnately lobed or dissected (*Floerkea proserpinacoides*). .... *Limnanthaceae*
    Leaves entire or merely toothed.
      Petals delicate, purple, pink or white. .... *Commelinaceae*
      Petals hard, or green or brown and papery. .... *Juncaceae*
  e. Sepals and petals not both in 3s.

f. Sepals and petals present, the sepals different in color than the petals.
　Sepals and petals 3-6 or more.
　　Petals unequal; carpels 3; stamens borne on a 1-sided disc above the petals
　　　　(*Reseda*) .... *Resedaceae*
　　Petals equal; carpels 6 or more; stamens not borne on a disc.
　　　Sepals 3-5; carpels numerous in a head; basal leaves, if present, not
　　　　　forming a rosette (*Ranunculus*) .... *Ranunculaceae*
　　　Sepals 6 or more; carpels the same number as the sepals, in a circle; basal
　　　　　leaves present, forming a dense rosette (*Sempervivum tectorum*). .... *Crassulaceae*
　Sepals 2, or absent at anthesis; petals 2 or more.
　　Petals 3 or 5 .... *Portulacaceae*
　　Petals 4 or 6 or more .... *Papaveraceae*
f. Sepals and/or petals absent, or both present and alike in appearance.
　g. Leaves parallel-veined.
　　Sepals and petals each 2; stamens 4 (*Maianthemum canadense*). .... *Convallariaceae*
　　Sepals, petals and stamens not all as above.
　　　Flowers perfect, in racemes (*Scheuchzeria palustris*). .... *Scheuchzeriaceae*
　　　Flowers imperfect, or not in racemes.
　　　　Flowers in spherical heads or elongate dense spikes, the staminate above
　　　　　　the pistillate.
　　　　　Flowers in elongate, dense spikes.
　　　　　　Flowers each in the axil of a scale; ovary surrounded by a sac; stigmas
　　　　　　　　2 or 3 (*Carex*) .... *Cyperaceae*
　　　　　　Flowers not each in the axil of a scale; ovary not surrounded by a
　　　　　　　　sac; stigma 1 (*Typha*) .... *Typhaceae*
　　　　　Flowers in spherical heads (*Sparganium*). .... *Sparganiaceae*
　　　　Flowers in an open inflorescence, or the staminate not above
　　　　　　the pistillate.
　　　　　Anthers versatile; each flower usually subtended by 2 or more
　　　　　　　bract-like structures. .... *Poaceae*
　　　　　Anthers basifixed; each flower subtended by a single scale. .... *Cyperaceae*
　g. Leaves net-veined.
　　h. Ovary inferior.
　　　Flowers in umbels. .... *Apiaceae*
　　　Flowers not in umbels.
　　　　Leaves 1.5 cm or less long, ovate to rotund (*Chrysosplenium*
　　　　　americanum). .... *Saxifragaceae*
　　　　Leaves 2 cm or more long.
　　　　　Leaves ovate, cordate, entire (*Aristolochia*). .... *Aristolochiaceae*
　　　　　Leaves serrate (*Proserpinaca*). .... *Haloragaceae*
　　h. Ovary superior.
　　　i. Stamens 10 or more; flowers perfect.
　　　　Plant with yellow or orange juice. .... *Papaveraceae*
　　　　Plant without colored juice.
　　　　　Leaves fleshy, terete (*Talinum teretifolium*). .... *Portulacaceae*
　　　　　Leaves flat, not fleshy.
　　　　　　Pistils several to many in each flower, not in a ring.
　　　　　　　Pistils separate to the base. .... *Ranunculaceae*
　　　　　　　Pistils united nearly to the middle (*Penthorum sedoides*). .... *Crassulaceae*
　　　　　　Pistil 1 in each flower, or if more numerous (*Phytolacca*) in a ring.
　　　　　　　Calyx rotate; flowers in elongate, leafless racemes (*Phytolacca*
　　　　　　　　americana). .... *Phytolaccaceae*
　　　　　　　Calyx campanulate or urceolate; flowers not in elongate,
　　　　　　　　leafless racemes. .... *Cistaceae*
　　　i. Stamens fewer than 10, or if 10 or more, flowers imperfect.
　　　　j. Perianth absent.
　　　　　Flowers perfect (*Saururus cernuus*) .... *Saururaceae*
　　　　　Flowers imperfect.
　　　　　　Flowers in catkins; plant alpine (*Salix*). .... *Salicaceae*
　　　　　　Flowers not in catkins, inflorescence various; plant not alpine.

Sepals not scarious; flowers not each subtended by 3 scarious
bracts. .... *Euphorbiaceae*
Sepals scarious; flowers each subtended by 3 scarious bracts
(*Amaranthus*). .... *Amaranthaceae*
j. Perianth present.
  k. Perianth not 5-parted, of if so, flowers all unisexual.
    l. Flowers unisexual.
Leaves evergreen, crowded toward the summit of the stem;
plant suffrutescent. (*Pachysandra terminalis*) .... *Buxaceae*
Leaves deciduous, not crowded toward the summit of the stem;
plants herbaceous.
Stigmas 3-parted; stamens more than 5. .... *Euphorbiaceae*
Stigmas simple or 2-parted (3-parted in Amaranthaceae and
some Chenopodiaceae); stamens 5 or fewer.
Plant with stinging hairs (*Laportea canadensis*). .... *Urticaceae*
Plant lacking stinging hairs.
Stipules in the form of a sheath around stem. .... *Polygonaceae*
Stipules absent or not in a sheath around the stem.
Plant with stellate hairs (*Crotonopsis elliptica*). .... *Euphorbiaceae*
Plant with simple hairs.
Sepals and bracts scarious .... *Amaranthaceae*
Sepals and bracts herbaceous.
Stigmas 2 or 3 .... *Chenopodiaceae*
Stigma 1, unbranched (*Parietaria pensylvanica*). .. *Urticaceae*
    l. Flowers perfect.
Stipules large and foliaceous, toothed or lobed; leaves reniform to
orbicular, palmately lobed (*Alchemilla*) .... *Rosaceae*
Stipules and leaves not as above.
Stipules in the form of a sheath around stem and/or basal
rosettes present. .... *Polygonaceae*
Stipules absent, or not in a sheath around the stem; basal
rosettes lacking.
Flowers axillary or in spikes; stamens fewer than 6.
Ovary 2 or more-locular; stamens in small groups
(*Tetragonia tetragonioides*). .... *Aizoaceae*
Ovary 1-locular; stamens not in groups.
Stigmas 2 or 3 .... *Chenopodiaceae*
Stigma 1, unbranched (*Parietaria pensylvanica*). .... *Urticaceae*
Flowers in terminal racemes; stamens usually 6. .... *Brassicaceae*
  k. Perianth of 5 sepals; flowers (or at least 1 in the flower cluster) perfect.
Stipules in the form of a sheath around stem and/or basal rosettes
present. .... *Polygonaceae*
Stipules absent, or not in a sheath around the stem; basal rosettes
lacking.
Flowers in loose racemes, panicles, cymes, umbels or solitary
and terminal.
Calyx white, the lobes spreading; ovary inferior. .... *Santalaceae*
Calyx green, the lobes erect; ovary superior. .... *Cistaceae*
Flowers in compact spikes, fascicles or glomerules.
Sepals of 2 sizes; ovary 3-locular (often incompletely). .... *Cistaceae*
Sepals uniform or ovary 1-locular.
Each flower subtended by 3 bracts; sepals scarious. .... *Amaranthaceae*
Each flower not subtended by bracts, or if so, bracts fewer
than 3; sepals usually not scarious .... *Chenopodiaceae*
O. Plant in fruit.
  m. Fruit 1-seeded; not in schizocarps or aggregates, or if in aggregates, sepals
present and surrounding each fruit.
    n. Fruit fleshy.
Leaves once pinnately dissected (*Floerkea proserpinacoides*). .... *Limnanthaceae*
Leaves not pinnately dissected.

Leaves parallel-veined (*Maianthemum*) .... *Convallariaceae*
Leaves net-veined.
    Fruit red, in aggregates (*Hydrastis canadensis*). ....,............... *Ranunculaceae*
    Fruit not red, not in aggregates.
        Stems with stinging hairs (*Laportea canadensis*). .... *Urticaceae*
        Stems glabrous .... *Santalaceae*
n. Fruit not fleshy.
  o. Leaves linear or lanceolate, parallel-veined.
    Calyx present, 5-parted .... *Chenopodiaceae*
    Calyx absent, or not 5-parted.
        Terminus of inflorescence naked (where staminate portion of
            inflorescence has been present).
        Fruit in globose heads (*Sparganium*) .... *Sparganiaceae*
        Fruit in loose, elongate to short, compact spikes.
            Each fruit subtended by a bract as long or longer than the fruit
                (*Carex*). .... *Cyperaceae*
            Each fruit not subtended by a bract, but surrounded at base
                with fine bristles (*Typha*) .... *Typhaceae*
        Terminus of inflorescence not naked.
        Fruit with vertical, dentate ribs (*Pontederia cordata*). .... *Pontederiaceae*
        Fruit not ribbed or ribs not dentate.
            Seed not fused to fruit wall .... *Cyperaceae*
            Seed fused completely to fruit wall .... *Poaceae*
  o. Leaves not linear or lanceolate, or if so, net-veined.
    p. Fruit in involucrate heads .... *Asteraceae*
    p. Fruit not in involucrate heads.
      q. Plant stellate-pubescent and scaly (*Crotonopsis elliptica*). .... *Euphorbiaceae*
      q. Plant not stellate-pubescent and scaly.
        Each fruit surrounded by 5 sepals; ovary superior.
            Stipules present or fruit trigonous.
                Fruit a utricle, ovoid or globose (*Corrigiola littoralis*). .... *Caryophyllaceae*
                Fruit an achene, lenticular or trigonous. .... *Polygonaceae*
            Stipules absent; fruit not trigonous.
                 Calyx subtended by 3 bracts (*Amaranthus*). .... *Amaranthaceae*
                Calyx not subtended by 3 bracts.
                      Fruit in compact heads (*Ranunculus*) .... *Ranunculaceae*
                    Fruit not in compact heads .... *Chenopodiaceae*
        Each fruit not surrounded by 5 sepals, or if so, the ovary
            obviously inferior.
            Leaves palmately, ternately or pinnately lobed or dissected.
                Leaves pinnately dissected (*Floerkea proserpinacoides*). .... *Limnanthaceae*
                Leaves ternately or palmately lobed or dissected.
                    Stipules present (*Alchemilla*) .... *Rosaceae*
                    Stipules absent (*Ranunculus*) .... *Ranunculaceae*
            Leaves not lobed or dissected.
                Fruit in compact heads (*Ranunculus*) .... *Ranunculaceae*
                Fruit not in compact heads.
                  Fruit trigonous or very lustrous .... *Polygonaceae*
                  Fruit not trigonous, dull.
                    Ovary superior.
                      Fruit in axillary clusters; stem sometimes with
                        stinging hairs (*Laportea*) stigma 1,
                        unbranched .... *Urticaceae*
                      Fruit in spikes or panicles, mostly terminal, or
                        occasionally in axillary clusters; stem with
                        out stinging hairs; stigmas 2 or 3.
                        Calyx subtended by 3 bracts (*Amaranthus*) .... *Amaranthaceae*
                        Calyx not subtended by 3 bracts .... *Chenopodiaceae*
                    Ovary inferior.

Fruits spherical, not in elongate racemes. .... *Santalaceae*
Fruits prismatic or angular, in elongate racemes
    or spikes (*Gaura*). .... *Onagraceae*
m. Fruit 2 or more-seeded, or fruit in schizocarps or aggregates.
  r. Fruit a berry or berry-like.
    Leaves parallel-veined, entire or at most minutely toothed.
      Leaves reduced to inconspicuous scales; ultimate branchlets filiform. .... *Asparagaceae*
      Leaves normal, dilated; filiform branchlets lacking. .... *Convallariaceae*
    Leaves obviously net-veined or pinnately dissected.
      Fruits in a terminal, single aggregate.
        Fruit a head of berries or drupes not on a receptacle.
          Leaves 5-lobed, the lobes incised or serrate (*Hydrastis canadensis*).. *Ranunculaceae*
          Leaves not lobed, entire (*Cornus*) .... *Cornaceae*
        Fruit a cluster of drupelets on a receptacle resembling a berry
          (*Rubus*). .... *Rosaceae*
      Fruit in axillary inflorescences, or terminal and not in aggregates.
        Fruit in umbels.
          Leaves palmately lobed ....*Araliaceae*
          Leaves not palmately lobed.
            Umbels in leaf axils (*Smilax*) .... *Smilacaceae*
            Umbels opposite a leaf or internodal (*Solanum*). .... *Solanaceae*
        Fruit not in umbels.
          Calyx 3-lobed or parted (*Floerkea proserpinacoides*). .... *Limnanthaceae*
          Calyx 5 or more lobed or parted.
            Parts of fruit in 1 plane in a ring, lustrous dark purple or black;
              leaves entire (*Phytolacca americana*) .... *Phytolaccaceae*
            Parts of fruit or fruits on more than 1 plane, not in a ring, not
              lustrous dark purple or black; leaves usually toothed or
              lobed. .... *Solanaceae*
  r. Fruit not a berry or berry-like.
    s. Leaves densely covered with stalked, reddish glands (*Drosera*). .... *Droseraceae*
    s. Leaves not covered with stalked, reddish glands.
      t. Fruit a 3-carpellate capsule or 3 follicles in an aggregate.
        u. Fruit indehiscent, triangular; leaves, at least the lower ones,
          pinnately dissected (*Proserpinaca*) .... *Haloragaceae*
        u. Fruit dehiscent, not triangular; leaves toothed or entire but not
          pinnately dissected.
          v. Fruit of 3 follicles or mericarps, separate to base.
            Leaves entire; fruit of 3 follicles (*Scheuchzeria palustris*). .... *Scheuchzeriaceae*
            Leaves pinnately divided; fruit of 3 mericarps (*Floerkea*
              proserpinacoides). .... *Limnanthaceae*
          v. Fruit a capsule, the 3 carpels united more than half their length.
            w. Each carpel 1-seeded, the seed filling more than half of the
              locule.
              Leaves parallel-veined; sepals and petals each 3, chaffy or
                scale-like, similar (*Luzula*) .... *Juncaceae*
              Leaves net-veined; sepals and petals not each 3, not chaffy
                or scale-like, dissimilar, or perianth entirely lacking.
                Fruit in peduncled, axillary corymbs or racemes
                  (*Ceanothus*). .... *Rhamnaceae*
                Fruit sessile, or not in corymbs or racemes. .... *Euphorbiaceae*
             w. Each carpel with 2 or more seeds, or the seed filling much less
              than half of the locule.
             x. Leaves evergreen, crowded toward the summit of the stem;
              plants suffrutescent (*Pachysandra terminalis*). .... *Buxaceae*
             x. Leaves deciduous, not crowded toward the summit of the
               stem; plants herbaceous.
              y. Sepals evident, 5.
               Ovary inferior.

Fruit opening by pores .... *Campanulaceae*
Fruit opening at the summit by valves
    (*Mentzelia oligosperma*). .... *Loasaceae*
Ovary superior.
    Leaves stipulate, distinctly petioled. .... *Violaceae*
    Leaves not stipulate, sessile or subsessile.
        Outer 2 sepals smaller than the inner 3. .... *Cistaceae*
        Outer and inner sepals the same size. .... *Polemoniaceae*
y. Sepals not evident, or more or less than 5.
    Fruit borne at the base of a leafy stem near the ground
        (*Aristolochia*). .... *Aristolochiaceae*
    Fruit terminal or in the axils of leaves.
        Sepals 4 or more, evident in fruit.
            Fruit in terminal racemes (*Reseda*) .... *Resedaceae*
            Fruits 1-3, axillary .... *Violaceae*
        Sepals 2 or 3, or not evident in fruit.
            Fruit densely pubescent (*Lachnanthes tinctoria*). . *Haemodoraceae*
            Fruit glabrous or essentially so.
                Seeds minute, dust-like .... *Orchidaceae*
              Seeds not minute and dust-like.
                  Fruit 5 mm or less long; perianth parts
                      separate to base. .... *Juncaceae*
                  Fruit more than 5 mm long, or perianth
                      parts united or absent.
                      Leaves equitant .... *Iridaceae*
                      Leaves not equitant.
                        Styles 3, distinct; leaves strongly
                          plaited, inflorescence paniculate
                          (*Veratrum viride*) .... *Melanthiaceae*
                      Style 1, deeply 3 cleft or uncleft; leaves
                        not strongly plaited;
                        inflorescence not paniculate.
                      Capsule 3 cm or less long; style
                        deeply 3-cleft (*Uvularia*). ...... *Convallariaceae*
                      Capsule usually more than 3 cm
                        long; style uncleft (*Lilium*). .. *Liliaceae*
t. Fruit not a 3-carpellate capsule or 3 follicles in an aggregate.
  z. Fruit a schizocarp.
    Leaves pinnately dissected (*Floerkea proserpinacoides*). .... *Limnanthaceae*
    Leaves entire, or toothed, or palmately lobed or dissected.
      Ovary inferior or calyx absent.
        Leaves reduced to scales; fruit quadrangular (*Myriophyllum*). . *Haloragaceae*
        Leaves with expanded blades; fruit not quadrangular.
           Leaves petioled; fruit in spikes (*Saururus cernuus*). .... *Saururaceae*
           Leaves sessile; fruit in umbels .... *Apiaceae*
      Ovary superior; calyx evident.
        Mericarps 4 or fewer .... *Boraginaceae*
        Mericarps 5 or more.
           Leaves entire, linear, sessile .... *Linaceae*
           Leaves usually toothed, lobed, or cordate, not linear,
             petioled.
             Carpels united in a ring around the base of the style. .... *Malvaceae*
             Carpels coiling outwardly or spiralling from the base,
                 remaining attached to the style toward the tip ..... *Geraniaceae*
  z. Fruit a capsule, legume, follicle, or indehiscent.
    aa. Leaves parallel-veined, not fleshy.
      Fruit pedicellate or enclosed in a pedunculate bract. .... *Commelinaceae*
      Fruit sessile or if enclosed in a bract the bract sessile. .... *Pontederiaceae*
    aa. Leaves pinnately or net-veined or fleshy.
      bb. Plant with latex.

Ovary inferior; sepals present .... *Campanulaceae*
Ovary superior; sepals sometimes absent.
  Seed with long, silky hairs much longer than the seed body
    (*Asclepias*). .... *Asclepiadaceae*
  Seed without long hairs.
    Leaves lobed .... *Papaveraceae*
    Leaves toothed or entire (*Amsonia tabernaemontana*). .... *Apocynaceae*
bb. Plant lacking latex.
  cc. Fruit several-many in aggregates.
    Leaves as long as or shorter than wide; sepals deciduous. *Ranunculaceae*
    Leaves longer than wide; sepals present. .... *Crassulaceae*
  cc. Fruit not in aggregates.
    dd. Fruit opening by pores.
      Ovary inferior; sepals sometimes absent.
        Sepals absent or 4 (*Ludwigia*) .... *Onagraceae*
        Sepals present, 5 .... *Campanulaceae*
      Ovary superior; sepals present .... *Scrophulariaceae*
    dd. Fruit opening by sutures, or carpels separating, or
      fruit indehiscent. [go to ee.]
ee. Fruit 4 or more locular, or if 2-locular, indehiscent and tubercled.
ff. Leaves evergreen; plants suffrutescent. .... *Pyrolaceae*
ff. Leaves deciduous; plants herbaceous.
gg. Stem with only 1 leaf, the others basal (*Parnassia glauca*). .... *Saxifragaceae*
gg. Stem with 2 or more leaves, basal leaves present or absent.
hh. Fruit with united styles longer than the body. .... *Geraniaceae*
hh. Fruit with short styles, or styles absent in fruit.
ii. Longest leaves 5 mm or less long, not fleshy (*Harrimanella hypnoides*). ...... *Ericaceae*
ii. Longest leaves more than 1 cm long, or shorter and fleshy.
jj. Fruit indehiscent, tubercled (*Tetragonea tetragonioides*). .... *Aizoaceae*
jj. Fruit dehiscent, or if indehiscent, not tubercled.
kk. Fruit 6-locular; stigma 6-lobed (*Aristolochia*). .... *Aristolochiaceae*
kk. Fruit more or less than 6-locular; stigma not 6-lobed.
ll. Fruit in racemes or spikes or solitary.
Sepals absent in fruit or represented by a flaring collar;
  fruit 4-locular.
  Capsule prickly, subtended by a flaring collar (*Datura*). .... *Solanaceae*
  Capsule not prickly, not subtended by a flaring collar. .... *Onagraceae*
Sepals present in fruit; fruit 5 or more-locular.
  Calyx subtended by an involucre of bracts. .... *Malvaceae*
  Calyx not subtended by bracts (*Reseda*). .... *Resedaceae*
ll. Fruit not in racemes or spikes, not solitary.
Inflorescence axillary; sepals 3; fruit dehiscing elastically
  (*Impatiens*). .... *Balsaminaceae*
Inflorescence axillary or terminal; sepals 4 or more; fruit not
  dehiscing elastically.
Fruit in terminal cymes or corymbs.
  Leaves thick and fleshy (*Sedum*). .... *Crassulaceae*
  Leaves thin, not fleshy.
    Leaves lanceolate, obovate or oblong; capsule 5-locular or
      fruit follicular. .... *Crassulaceae*
    Leaves linear; capsule 10-locular (*Linum*). .... *Linaceae*
Fruit axillary or terminal but not in cymes or corymbs.
  Capsule 5 or more-locular, not 4-sided or velvety; calyx
    subtended by an involucre of bracts. .... *Malvaceae*
  Capsule 4-locular, 4-sided and velvety; calyx not subtended
    by an involucre (*Sesamum orientale*) .... *Pedaliaceae*
ee. Fruit 1 or 2-locular, dehiscent, or if indehiscent, not tubercled.
m.m. Fruit 1-locular.
n.n. Fruit circumscissile.
Leaves thick and fleshy; fruit solitary or in small glomerules terminating
  the stem and branches; ovary half-inferior (*Portulaca*). .... *Portulacaceae*

Leaves thin, not fleshy; fruit solitary in the leaf axils or in spikes;
ovary superior.
Fruit in spikes; leaves 2 cm or more long (*Celosia*). .... *Amaranthaceae*
Fruit solitary in the leaf axils; leaves less than 1.5 cm long (*Anagallis*). .... *Primulaceae*
nn. Fruit not circumscissile.
oo. Fruit in axillary inflorescences, dehiscing elastically; leaves serrate
(*Impatiens*) .... *Balsaminaceae*
oo. Fruit terminal or in terminal inflorescences, or if axillary or lateral, leaves
not serrate; fruit not dehiscing elastically.
pp. Fruit bilobed or of 2 unequal valves and/or ovary inferior, or stigmas 4 ... *Saxifragaceae*
pp. Fruit not as above, ovary superior or stigmas 1 or 2.
qq. Leaves distinctly toothed or lobed, or auriculate or sagittate at base;
fruit lacking a hooked beak.
Fruit indehiscent, or 2 or more times as long as broad. .... *Brassicaceae*
Fruit dehiscent, less than 2 times as long as broad. .... *Hydrophyllaceae*
qq. Leaves entire, undulate or obscurely denticulate, or if with a basal
sinus (*Proboscidea*), fruit with a hooked beak.
Fruit with a hooked beak more than 2 cm long
(*Proboscidea louisianica*). .... *Pedaliaceae*
Fruit without a long hooked beak.
Leaves terete, succulent (*Talinum teretifolium*). .... *Portulacaceae*
Leaves flat, not succulent.
Fruit 1 cm or less long.
Leaves minute and scale-like, 5 mm or less long.
Stems wiry, often spiral or twining; sepals 4 (*Bartonia*). ...... *Gentianaceae*
Stems not wiry, spiral or twining; sepals 2 (*Utricularia*). ..... *Lentibulariaceae*
Leaves foliaceous, larger.
Fruit dehiscent .... *Primulaceae*
Fruit indehiscent (*Gaura*) .... *Onagraceae*
Fruit 1.5 cm or more long .... *Fabaceae*
mm. Fruit 2-locular.
rr. Locules separated by a thin septum, this persistent on the pedicel after the
2 valves fall away .... *Brassicaceae*
rr. Locules not separated by a septum.
ss. Corolla remaining until maturity of fruit; seed with bract-like arils
(*Polygala*) .... *Polygalaceae*
ss. Corolla absent at maturity of fruit; seed lacking bract-like arils.
tt. Fruit surrounded by a hypanthium or perianth tube (*Lythrum*). .... *Lythraceae*
tt. Fruit not surrounded by a hypanthium or perianth tube.
uu. Stem leaves 1 or 2; basal leaves palmately (often shallowly) lobed. .... *Saxifragaceae*
uu. Stem leaves more than 2, or basal leaves absent or not
palmately lobed.
vv. Stem leaves scale-like or basal leaves present (*Utricularia*). .... *Lentibulariaceae*
vv. Stem leaves not scale-like or basal leaves absent.
ww. Calyx absent in fruit (*Salix*) .... *Salicaceae*
ww. Calyx, or its remnants, present in fruit.
xx. Carpels free at apex, the lobes erect or divergent. .... *Saxifragaceae*
x.x. Carpels united to apex.
Fruit solitary, terminal, usually prickly or inflorescence
opposite a leaf. .... *Solanaceae*
Fruit in terminal racemes or panicles, or solitary in the
leaf axils.
Calyx not 5-lobed, or if so, irregular. .... *Scrophulariaceae*
Calyx 5-lobed, regular.
Leaves lobed.
Calyx tube equalling or longer than capsule. .... *Solanaceae*
Calyx tube shorter than capsule .... *Scrophulariaceae*
Leaves unlobed.
Capsule ovoid, leaves entire .... *Solanaceae*
Capsule globose, or ovoid and leaves toothed. .... *Scrophulariaceae*

GROUP 10

Woody Plants Not Producing Flowers, the Seeds Naked (Not Enclosed in an Ovary); Leaves Linear, Needle or Scale-Like, Mostly Evergreen: Gymnosperms

A. Evergreen shrub, 2 m or less tall (rarely a tree); leaves spirally arranged and spreading in 2 ranks; seed surrounded by an orange-red, fleshy covering (aril) (*Taxus*) .... *Taxaceae*
A. Evergreen or deciduous trees or shrubs; if shrubs leaves scale-like and opposite or in whorles of 3; seeds in cones with few to many scales, the cone sometimes berry-like and bluish.
    B. Leaves opposite and scale-like or in whorles of 3 and needle-like. .... *Cupressaceae*
    B. Leaves 2-ranked, spirally arranged, in fascicles of 2-5, or numerous and clustered on short spurs.
        Leaves 2-ranked on slender deciduous branchlets, pointed, uniformly colored; male cones numerous in drooping terminal panicles; 2-ranked female cones globose (*Taxodium distichum*) .... *Taxodiaceae*
        Leaves clustered or if appearing 2-ranked, rounded or notched at the tip, and with 2 white lines beneath; male cones not in panicles; female cones ellipsoidal or cylindric .... *Pinaceae*

GROUP 11

Woody Plants in Flower, Leaves Not Yet or Not Fully Developed

A. Leaves whorled, opposite or subopposite.
    B. Flowers in elongate catkins or heads, the heads not surrounded by petaliferous bracts.
        Plants monoecious (*Betula*) .... *Betulaceae*
        Plants dioecious.
            Calyx present; plant with milky latex; bud scales several (*Broussonetia papyrifera*) .... *Moraceae*
            Calyx absent; plant without milky latex; bud scale single (*Salix*). .... *Salicaceae*
    B. Flowers not in catkins or heads, or if in heads, the heads surrounded by white petaliferous bracts.
        Flowers in heads surrounded by 4 petaliferous bracts (*Cornus florida*). .... *Cornaceae*
        Flowers not in heads.
            Corolla united.
                Flowers in panicles; trees (*Paulownia tomentosa*). .... *Scrophulariaceae*
                Flowers axillary or in whorles, not paniculate; shrubs (*Lonicera*). .... *Caprifoliaceae*
            Corolla of separate petals or petals absent.
                Plant a shrub, covered with reddish scales; hypanthium present, saucer-shaped to tubular (*Shepherdia canadensis*) .... *Elaeagnaceae*
                Plant a tree, not covered with reddish scales; hypanthium lacking.
                    Stamens 2, 3 or 4, or only a pistil present; calyx minute; petals absent (*Fraxinus*) .... *Oleaceae*
                    Stamens 5 or more, rarely only a pistil present; calyx 1.5 mm or more long; petals often present (*Acer*) .... *Aceraceae*
A. Leaves alternate.
    C. Corolla irregular.
        Petals all united (*Rhododendron*) .... *Ericaceae*
        Petals, at least in part, separate.
            Petals of essentially 3 different shapes. .... *Fabaceae*
            Petals essentially the same shape (*Rhododendron canadense*). .... *Ericaceae*
    C. Corolla regular or absent.
        D. Corolla united .... *Ericaceae*
        D. Corolla of separate petals or absent.
            E. Petals 4; plants flowering in the autumn or winter (*Hamamelis virginiana*). ... *Hamamelidaceae*
           E. Petals 5 or absent (if sometimes 4 in *Rutaceae* twigs with stipular spines, these lacking in *Hamamelis*); plants flowering in spring.
                F. Petals white or pink .... *Rosaceae*
                F. Petals yellow or absent.

    G. Flowers in heads (more than 5-flowered) spikes or catkins, at least the
        staminate if monoecious or dioecious plants.
      H. Flowers in spherical heads.
          Twigs very pubescent (*Broussonetia papyrifera*). .... *Moraceae*
          Twigs glabrous or essentially so.
             Leaf scars completely encircling the buds (*Platanus*). .... *Platanaceae*
             Leaf scars not encircling the buds (*Liquidambar styraciflua*). .... *Hamamelidaceae*
      H. Flowers in spikes or catkins.
        I. Flowers mostly perfect; perianth of sepals and petals (*Rhus*
          aromatica). .... *Anacardiaceae*
        I. Flowers imperfect; perianth of sepals only or obsolete.
          J. Plants monoecious.
            Pistillate flowers in clusters.
              Twigs with a spicy odor when crushed. .... *Myricaceae*
              Twigs without a spicy odor when crushed.
                Pistillate flowers in the axils of scales in terminal buds
                  (*Corylus*). .... *Betulaceae*
                Pistillate flowers solitary or in small clusters, not
                  arranged as above.
                  Pith of twig star-shaped; buds clustered at the tips of
                    the twigs (*Quercus*). .... *Fagaceae*
                  Pith of twig round, buds solitary at the tips of the
                    twigs. .... *Juglandaceae*
             Pistillate flowers in elongate spikes or catkins. .... *Betulaceae*
          J. Plants dioecious or flowers perfect.
            Sepals present, 4 .... *Moraceae*
            Sepals obsolete.
              Twigs with a spicy odor when crushed and with resinous
                yellow dots. .... *Myricaceae*
             Twigs without a spicy odor or resinous yellow dots. .... *Salicaceae*
    G. Flowers not in heads, spikes or catkins, or in heads fewer than
        5-flowered.
      Twigs with stipular spines (*Zanthoxylum americanum*). .... *Rutaceae*
      Twigs without spines.
        Flowers in racemes, the pedicels less than 2 mm long. .... *Salicaceae*
        Flowers not in racemes, or the pedicels longer.
          Anthers red to brown; flowers perfect (*Ulmus*) .... *Ulmaceae*
          Anthers yellow; flowers perfect or plants dioecious.
            Calyx 5-6-parted; twigs with a spicy odor when crushed. .... *Lauraceae*
            Calyx 4 or fewer-parted; twigs without a spicy odor.
              Calyx tube cylindric, longer than or equaling the lobes. .. *Thymeliaceae*
              Calyx tube saucer-shaped, shorter than or equaling the
                lobes (*Hamamelis virginiana*) .... *Hamamelidaceae*

GROUP 12

Woody Plants With Whorled, Opposite or Subopposite Leaves

A. Leaves evergreen, awl-shaped or scale-like, less than 3 mm wide.
    Corolla urceolate, persistent in fruit. .... *Ericaceae*
    Corolla salverform, absent in fruit (*Phlox subulata*). .... *Polemoniaceae*
A. Leaves deciduous or evergreen and of a broader shape, or more than 3 mm wide.
    B. Mat-forming shrubs, mostly less than 1 dm tall.
      C. Flowers in pairs, the ovary inferior.
        Ovaries fused; fruit a berry (*Mitchella repens*). .... *Rubiaceae*
        Ovaries separate; fruit a capsule (*Linnaea borealis*). .... *Caprifoliaceae*
      C. Flowers not in pairs, the ovary superior.
        Corolla and calyx bilabiate; fruit a schizocarp of 4 mericarps; plants aromatic
          (*Thymus praecox*) .... *Lamiaceae*
        Corolla and calyx not bilabiate; fruit a berry, follicle or capsule.

Corolla white to pinkish; fruit a berry; leaves very pubescent
    (*Epigaea repens*) .... *Ericaceae*
Corolla blue to purple; fruit a capsule or follicle; leaves glabrous or
    essentially so.
    Petals separate, purple; fruit a bilobed capsule 10 mm or less long
        (*Saxifraga oppositifolia*) .... *Saxifragaceae*
    Petals united, blue or white; fruit a pair of follicles more than 10 mm
        long or a subglobose, unlobed capsule.
        Petals blue; fruit a pair of slender follicles, each 1-locular; other
            habitats (*Vinca*) .... *Apocynaceae*
        Petals white; fruit a 3-locular, subglobose capsule; alpine (*Diapensia*
            lapponica) .... *Diapensiaceae*
B. Upright or ascending shrubs or trees more than 2 dm tall.
  D. Leaves compound.
    E. Leaves palmately compound with 5 or more leaflets (*Aesculus*). .... *Hippocastanaceae*
    E. Leaves pinnately compound.
      F. Plant in flower.
        Flowers with 4 sepals and 2 stamens or only a pistil present. .... *Oleaceae*
        Flowers with 4 or 5 sepals and more than 2 stamens; if only a pistil
           present sepals 5 or more.
          Petals white to pinkish or absent.
            Corolla united (*Sambucus*) .... *Caprifoliaceae*
            Corolla of separate petals or absent.
              Leaves trifoliolate (*Staphylea trifolia*). .... *Staphyleaceae*
              Leaves with more than 3 leaflets (*Acer negundo*). .... *Aceraceae*
          Petals green to yellow.
            Flowers in panicles; ovary 5-locular (*Phellodendron*). .... *Rutaceae*
            Flowers in drooping racemes or umbel-like fascicles; ovary
              2-locular (*Acer negundo*) .... *Aceraceae*
      F. Plant in fruit.
        Fruit winged.
          Fruit a samara (1 wing; *Fraxinus*) .... *Oleaceae*
          Fruit a schizocarp of 2 mericarps (2 wings; *Acer negundo*). .... *Aceraceae*
        Fruit not winged.
           Fruit a berry or drupe.
             Buds glabrous; leaflets serrate; plant a shrub (*Sambucus*). .... *Caprifoliaceae*
             Buds pubescent; leaflets crenate to entire; plant a tree
               (*Phellodendron*) .... *Rutaceae*
          Fruit a capsule.
            Capsule inflated and bladdery, 3-locular (*Staphylea trifolia*). .... *Staphyleaceae*
            Capsule not inflated or bladdery, 2-locular (*Forsythia*). .... *Oleaceae*
  D. Leaves simple.
    G. Flowers in elongate catkins or in heads.
      Heads subtended by an involucre; staminate and pistillate flowers in
        same head (*Iva*) .... *Asteraceae*
      Heads not subtended by an involucre; flowers perfect or staminate and
        pistillate flowers in separate heads.
        Plants hermaphrodite; flowers and fruit in globose heads; heads
          eventually separating into indehiscent nutlets; sap not milky
          (*Cephalanthus occidentalis*) .... *Rubiaceae*
        Plants monoecious or dioecious; flowers and fruit not in globose
          heads, or if so, heads not separating and sap milky.
          Plants monoecious (*Betula*) .... *Betulaceae*
          Plants dioecious.
            Calyx present; plant with milky latex; bud scales several
              (*Broussonetia papyrifera*) .... *Moraceae*
            Calyx absent; plant without milky latex; bud scale single (*Salix*). .... *Salicaceae*
    G. Flowers not in catkins or heads.
      H. Leaves entire.

I. Leaves mostly whorled.
　　Leaves cordate at base; plant a tree (*Catalpa*). .... *Bignoniaceae*
　　Leaves cuneate or rounded at base; plant a shrub.
　　　　Corolla united; capsule 4 mm or less broad (*Kalmia angustifolia*). .. *Ericaceae*
　　　　Corolla of separate petals; capsule more than 4 mm broad
　　　　　　(*Decodon verticillatus*) .... *Lythraceae*
I. Leaves opposite.
　　J. Leaves cordate at base; stamens 2 or 4; fruit a capsule.
　　　　Trees; flowers irregular.
　　　　　　Stamens 4; flowers white or bluish; capsule less than 1 dm long
　　　　　　　　(*Paulownia tomentosa*) .... *Scrophulaciaceae*
　　　　　　Stamens 2; flowers white or yellow mottled with purple or
　　　　　　　　yellow; capsule more than 1 dm long (*Catalpa*) .... *Bignoniaceae*
　　　　Shrubs; flowers regular (*Syringa vulgaris*). .... *Oleaceae*
　　J. Leaves cuneate or rounded at base, or if subcordate (some
　　　　　Caprifoliaceae and *Elaeagnaceae*) stamens 5 or more and fruit a
　　　　　berry or drupe.
　　　　K. Plant in flower.
　　　　　　L. Perianth of numerous segments, undifferentiated into sepals
　　　　　　　　and petals (*Calycanthus floridus*) .... *Calycanthaceae*
　　　　　　L. Perianth differentiated into sepals and petals, or petals absent
　　　　　　　　and sepals 5 or fewer.
　　　　　　　　M. Corolla and/or calyx regular, the lobes, petals or sepals
　　　　　　　　　　usually 4.
　　　　　　　　　　Petals present, separate.
　　　　　　　　　　　　Ovary 4-locular; styles 4 (*Philadelphus*). .... *Hydraneaceae*
　　　　　　　　　　　　Ovary 1-2-locular; styles 1-4.
　　　　　　　　　　　　　　Style 1; ovary inferior (*Cornus*) .... *Cornaceae*
　　　　　　　　　　　　　　Styles 2 or more; ovary superior (*Hypericum*). .... *Clusiaceae*
　　　　　　　　　　Petals united (sometimes only at the base) or absent.
　　　　　　　　　　　　Stamens 8; plants covered with reddish scales
　　　　　　　　　　　　　　(*Shepherdia canadensis*). .... *Elaeagnaceae*
　　　　　　　　　　　　Stamens 2 or 4; plants not covered with reddish scales.
　　　　　　　　　　　　　　Stamens 2. .... *Oleaceae*
　　　　　　　　　　　　　　Stamens 4-5
　　　　　　　　　　　　　　　　Ovary inferior. .... *Caprifoliaceae*
　　　　　　　　　　　　　　　　Ovary superior (*Buxus sempervirens*) .... *Buxaceae*
　　　　　　　　M. Corolla and/or calyx irregular or the lobes 5.
　　　　　　　　　　Corolla irregular .... *Caprifoliaceae*
　　　　　　　　　　Corolla regular.
　　　　　　　　　　　　Petals yellow, separate (*Hypericum*) .... *Clusiaceae*
　　　　　　　　　　　　Petals white, pink or purple, united.
　　　　　　　　　　　　　　Corolla urceolate, bell-shaped or funnelform, about
　　　　　　　　　　　　　　　　as long as broad or longer; leaves deciduous,
　　　　　　　　　　　　　　　　not revolute-margined. .... *Caprifoliaceae*
　　　　　　　　　　　　　　Corolla rotate or saucer-shaped, broader than long;
　　　　　　　　　　　　　　　　leaves evergreen, revolute-margined .... *Ericaceae*
　　　　K. Plant in fruit.
　　　　　　N. Fruit dry.
　　　　　　　　Leaves evergreen.
　　　　　　　　　　Leaves revolute-margined .... *Ericaceae*
　　　　　　　　　　Leaves not revolute-margined (*Buxus sempervirens*). .... ˙*Buxaceae*
　　　　　　　　Leaves deciduous.
　　　　　　　　　　Leaves punctate beneath with translucent dots. .... *Clusiaceae*
　　　　　　　　　　Leaves not punctate beneath.
　　　　　　　　　　　　Ovary inferior, 4-locular (*Philadelphus*). .... *Hydraneaceae*
　　　　　　　　　　　　Ovary superior, 2-locular .... *Oleaceae*
　　　　　　N. Fruit fleshy.
　　　　　　　　Inflorescence axillary; fruit 1-seeded; plants covered with
　　　　　　　　　　reddish scales (*Shepherdia canadensis*) .... *Elaeagnaceae*

Inflorescence terminal or axillary; fruit 2 or more-seeded, or
    if 1-seeded, plants not covered with reddish scales.
    Ovary superior.
        Fruits in small panicles (*Ligustrum*). .... *Oleaceae*
        Fruits solitary (*Calycanthus floridus*). .... *Calycanthaceae*
    Ovary inferior.
        Fruit a drupe (1 large seed); sepals 4 (*Cornus*). .... *Cornaceae*
        Fruit a berry (2 or more-seeded) or if a 1-seeded drupe,
            sepals 5. .... *Caprifoliaceae*
H. Leaves lobed, crenate or toothed.
    O. Flowers and fruit in flat-topped, terminal cymes (*Viburnum*). .... *Caprifoliaceae*
    O. Flowers and fruit not in flat-topped terminal cymes.
        P. Plant with short shoots; leaves subcordate; perianth lacking; fruit a
            follicle (*Cercidiphyllum japonicum*) .... *Cercidiphyllaceae*
        P. Plant without the above combination of characters.
            Q. Corolla united two-thirds its length; fruit a red or white berry, a
                capsule or an achene.
                Flowers and fruit in axillary and terminal clusters or (rarely)
                    heads. .... *Caprifoliaceae*
                Flowers and fruit in slender panicles (*Buddleia davidi*). .... *Buddlejaceae*
            Q. Corolla of separate petals or united at base only; fruit a
                schizocarp, aggregate of achenes, a black drupe or a capsule.
                Leaves palmately lobed (*Acer*) .... *Aceraceae*
                Leaves unlobed (sometimes slightly pinnately lobed in some
                    Hydraneaceae).
                    Twigs 4-lined or winged; inflorescence axillary only
                        (*Euonymus*). .... *Celastraceae*
                    Twigs not lined or winged; inflorescence terminal and/or
                      axillary.
                    Flowers unisexual, greenish or yellowish; fruit a black
                        drupe; leaves distinctly pinnate-veined (*Rhamnus*) . *Rhamnaceae*
                    Flowers perfect, white (yellow in *Forsythia*); fruit a
                        schizocarp or capsule; leaves not distinctly pinnate-
                        veined.
                      Stipules present; fruit a schizocarp of 4 mericarps or
                        achenes (*Rhodotypos scandens*) .... *Rosaceae*
                      Stipules absent; fruit a capsule.
                        Sepals 4 or 5; stamens 8 or more; styles 2 or
                          more; flowers white. .... *Hydraneaceae*
                      Sepals 4; stamens 2; style 1; flowers yellow
                        (*Forsythia*). .... *Oleaceae*

GROUP 13

Woody Plants With Alternate Leaves

A. Leaves compound or deeply dissected to midrib.
    B. Flowers in small, dense heads subtended by an involucre (*Artemisia*). .... *Asteraceae*
    B. Flowers not in small, dense heads subtended by an involucre.
        C. Leaves ternate, bi or tri-ternate, or palmate.
            D. Leaves bi or tri-ternate.
                Stems spiny or prickly, at least below; ovary inferior; fruit a berry
                    (*Aralia*) .... *Araliaceae*
                Stems not spiny or prickly; ovary superior; fruit a capsule (*Ruta
                    graveolens*). .... *Rutaceae*
            D. Leaves once-ternate or palmate.
                Twigs sharply angled, green (*Cytisus scoparius*). .... *Fabaceae*
                Twigs terete, or angled and not green.
                    Leaves stipulate; stems usually bristly or prickly (*Rubus*). .... *Rosaceae*
                    Leaves not stipulate; stems not bristly or prickly.

Terminal leaflet sessile.

    Flowers on leafy branches; fruit a samara (*Ptelea trifoliata*). .... *Rutaceae*

    Flowers axillary, or terminal on leafless branches; fruit a drupe
        (*Rhus aromatica*) .... *Anacardiaceae*

Terminal leaflet with a petiolule (*Toxicodendron radicans*). .... *Anacardiaceae*

C. Leaves one or more times pinnate.

  E. Inflorescence axillary, or if axillary and terminal, of 2 types.

    Stems with spines or thorns.

      Stamens 10; corolla regular or irregular; fruit more than 1-seeded. .... *Fabaceae*

      Stamens fewer than 10; corolla regular; fruit 1-seeded (*Zanthoxylum
        americanum*) .... *Rutaceae*

    Stems without spines or thorns.

      Inflorescence an open panicle; flowers perfect; fruit less than 1 cm long
        (*Toxicodendron vernix*) .... *Anacardiaceae*

      Inflorescence of staminate flowers catkins, of pistillate flowers solitary
        or in spikes; fruit more than 1 cm long. .... *Juglandaceae*

  E. Inflorescence terminal, or if axillary and terminal, of 1 type.

    F. Stems spiny, bristly or prickly.

      Leaves once compound; flowers solitary or cymose; ovary superior. .... *Rosaceae*

      Leaves 2-3 times compound; flowers umbellate, in a compound
        panicle; ovary inferior (*Aralia*) .... *Araliaceae*

    F. Stems not spiny, bristly or prickly.

      G. Flowers or fruit in or subtended by an involucre (*Artemisia*). .... *Asteraceae*

      G. Flowers or fruit not in or subtended by an involucre.

        H. Plant in flower.

          Corolla irregular .... *Fabaceae*

          Corolla regular or absent.

            Petals white, pink or yellow; stamens more than 10 (rarely 10);
              flowers perfect.

              Leaves stipulate .... *Rosaceae*

              Leaves estipulate (*Dictamnus albus*) .... *Rutaceae*

            Petals yellow to greenish or absent; stamens 10 or fewer (or
              none in female trees of *Ailanthus*).

            Leaflets with 1-3 basal teeth on each margin, each tooth with
              a bright green gland on the underside (*Ailanthus
              altissima*). .... *Simaroubaceae*

            Leaflets more uniformly toothed, or teeth absent or few but
              lacking glands.

              Ovary 3-locular (*Koelreuteria paniculata*). .... *Sapindaceae*

              Ovary 1 or 4-5 locular, or pistils separate.

                 Principal leaves 2-3 times pinnatifid; petals present;
                  wood not yellow.

                 Plant not dioecious, flowers perfect (*Ruta graveolens*). *Rutaceae*

                 Plant dioecious or polygamo-dioecious, flowers
                   (or some of them) imperfect (*Gymnocladus
                   dioicus*). .... *Fabaceae*

               Principal leaves once pinnatifid or (sometimes in
                Ranunculaceae) bipinnate with petals absent
                and wood yellow.

               Flowers with 5 or more pistils; wood yellow; plants
                 lacking latex (*Xanthorhiza simplicissima*) .... *Ranunculaceae*

               Flowers with 1 pistil; wood not yellow; plants with
                 latex (*Rhus*). .... *Anacardiaceae*

        H. Plant in fruit.

          Fruit winged, samaroid (*Ailanthus altissima*). .... *Simaroubaceae*

          Fruit wingless, not samaroid.

            Fruit an inflated, papery, 3-locular capsule containing 3 seeds
              (*Koelreuteria paniculata*) .... *Sapindaceae*

           Fruit not as above, or if capsular, 4-5 locular and many-seeded.
            Principal leaves 2-3 times pinnatifid.

Fruit a capsule (*Ruta graveolens*) .... *Rutaceae*
Fruit a legume (*Gymnocladus dioicus*). .... *Fabaceae*
Principal leaves once pinnatifid.
    Twigs with latex; fruit a dry, 1-seeded drupe (*Rhus*). .... *Anacardiaceae*
    Twigs lacking latex; fruit not a dry, 1-seeded drupe.
        Fruit of fleshy drupelets, a pome, or a head of achenes. ... *Rosaceae*
        Fruit a follicle, legume (sometimes indehiscent) or
          capsule.
        Leaflets with translucent dots; fruit a 5-lobed
          capsule (*Dictamnus albus*). .... *Rutaceae*
        Leaflets lacking translucent dots; fruit a follicle or
          legume.
        Leaflets regularly serrate or lobed; fruit a follicle.
          Principal leaflets 10 or more; stipules present;
            follicles more than 1-seeded (*Sorbaria
            sorbifolia*) .... *Rosaceae*
          Principal leaflets mostly 5; stipules lacking;
            follicles 1-seeded (*Xanthorhiza
            simplicissima*) .... *Ranunculaceae*
        Leaflets entire or remotely toothed, or minutely
          serrulate; fruit a legume. .... *Fabaceae*
A. Leaves simple.
  I. Leaves evergreen.
    J. Leaves without blades, consisting only of spiny petioles, these numerous and
      crowded (*Ulex europaeus*) .... *Fabaceae*
    J. Leaves scale-like or with blades.
      K. Leaves scale-like, less than 3 mm wide.
        Corolla yellow, of separate petals; fruit 2 or 3-carpellate (*Hudsonia*). .... *Cistaceae*
        Corolla white or pink, of united petals; fruit 5-carpellate (*Harrimanella
          hypnoides*) .... *Ericaceae*
      K. Leaves not scale-like.
        Plant forming a compact cushion, the branches mostly hidden (*Diapensia
          lapponica*) .... *Diapensiaceae*
        Plant not forming a compact cushion, the branches mostly visible.
          Flowers 3-merous, or 4 or more-merous and petals lacking; fruit a
            drupe or 3-beaked capsule.
          Leaves revolute-margined; flowers not in spikes; fruit a drupe. .... *Empetraceae*
          Leaves toothed; flowers in terminal spikes; fruit a 3-beaked capsule
            (*Pachysandra terminalis*) .... *Buxaceae*
          Flowers 4 or more-merous, petals present; fruit a berry or a capsule
            and not 3-beaked.
          Corolla rotate; berry black and leaves serrate or red and leaves spiny-
            margined (*Ilex*) .... *Aquifoliaceae*
          Corolla campanulate or urceolate; berry red, or if black leaves
            entire, or fruit a capsule; leaves not spiny-margined.
          Plants woody; leaves not subverticillate. .... *Ericaceae*
          Plants suffrutescent; leaves subverticillate (*Chimaphila*). .... *Monotropaceae*
  I. Leaves deciduous.
    L. Leaves scale-like (*Tamarix*) .... *Tamaricaceae*
    L. Leaves not scale-like.
      M. Leaves lobed.
        N. Plant in flower.
          O. Flowers in heads, spikes or catkins; petals absent.
            P. Flowers (at least the pistillate) in heads.
              Heads subtended by an involucre, this not bur-like (*Artemisia*). ..... *Asteraceae*
              Heads not subtended by an involucre, or if so (*Myrica*) involucre
                bur-like.
              Twigs with a spicy odor when crushed and with yellow resin
                dots; colonial shrub less than 5 feet tall (*Comptonia
                peregrina*). .... *Myricaceae*

Twigs without a spicy odor or yellow resin dots; trees or shrubs
usually more than 5 feet tall.
　　Twigs very pubescent (*Broussonetia papyrifera*). .... *Moraceae*
　　Twigs glabrous or essentially so.
　　　　Leaf scars completely encircling buds (*Platanus*). .... *Platanaceae*
　　　　Leaf scars not encircling buds (*Liquidambar styraciflua*). ...... *Hamamelidaceae*
P. Flowers in elongate spikes or catkins.
　　Buds clustered at the tips of the twigs; plants monoecious;
　　　　staminate flowers in catkins; pistillate flowers solitary or
　　　　2 to 3 in a cluster (*Quercus*). .... *Fagaceae*
　　Buds not clustered at the tips of the twigs; plants monoecious or
　　　　dioecious; staminate and pistillate flowers (when present)
　　　　both in catkins or spikes. .... *Moraceae*
O. Flowers not in heads, spikes or catkins; petals usually present.
　　Margin of lobes entire.
　　　　Stamens 5; corolla violet, rarely white (*Solanum dulcamara*). .... *Solanaceae*
　　　　Stamens 9 or more or absent; corolla yellow or yellowish or absent.
　　　　　　Stamens 9 or absent; petals less than 2 cm long (*Sassafras*
　　　　　　　　albidum). .... *Lauraceae*
　　　　　　Stamens 10 or more; petals more than 2 cm long (*Liriodendron*
　　　　　　　　tulipifera). .... *Magnoliaceae*
　　Margin of lobes toothed.
　　　　Sepals 4 (*Hamamelis virginiana*) .... *Hamamelidaceae*
　　　　Sepals 5.
　　　　　　Stamens united into a tube around the styles (*Hibiscus syriacus*). *Malvaceae*
　　　　　　Stamens separate.
　　　　　　　　Inflorescence terminal .... *Rosaceae*
　　　　　　　　Inflorescence axillary (*Ribes*) .... *Grossulariaceae*
N. Plant in fruit.
　　Q. Fruit fleshy or in multiples and the sepals often fleshy.
　　　　Fruit in multiples; sepals often fleshy (*Morus*). .... *Moraceae*
　　　　Fruit not in multiples, or if in aggregates (some *Rosaceae*) sepals
　　　　　　not fleshy.
　　　　Ovaries superior.
　　　　　　Fruit in aggregates, drupelets (*Rubus odoratus*). .... *Rosaceae*
　　　　　　Fruit not in aggregates, drupes or berries.
　　　　　　　　Fruit a red berry (*Solanum dulcamara*). .... *Solanaceae*
　　　　　　　　Fruit a blue-black drupe (*Sassafras albidum*). .... *Lauraceae*
　　　　Ovaries inferior.
　　　　　　Inflorescence terminal (*Crataegus*) .... *Rosaceae*
　　　　　　Inflorescence axillary (*Ribes*) .... *Saxifragaceae*
　　Q. Fruit not fleshy; if in multiples the sepals not fleshy.
　　　　R. Fruit dehiscent, more than 1-seeded.
　　　　　　Fruit 2-carpellate, sometimes in multiples. .... *Hamamelidaceae*
　　　　　　Fruit 3 or more-carpellate, not in multiples.
　　　　　　　　Inflorescence terminal; seed smooth (*Physocarpus opulifolius*). ... *Rosaceae*
　　　　　　　　Inflorescence axillary; seed long-ciliate (*Hibiscus syriacus*) .... *Malvaceae*
　　　　R. Fruit indehiscent, 1-seeded.
　　　　　　Fruit in heads subtended by an involucre (*Artemisia*). .... *Asteraceae*
　　　　　　Fruit not in heads, or if so, not subtended by an involucre.
　　　　　　　　Fruit winged, or with a tuft of hairs or bristles at base.
　　　　　　　　　　Fruit, including wing, more than 2 cm long (*Liriodendron*
　　　　　　　　　　　　tulipifera). .... *Magnoliaceae*
　　　　　　　　　　Fruit less than 2 cm long, not winged, with a tuft of hairs or
　　　　　　　　　　　　bristles at base (*Platanus*) .... *Platanaceae*
　　　　　　　　Fruit not winged and without a tuft of hairs or bristles at base.
　　　　　　　　　　Fruit with a cup-like involucre around its base; twigs without
　　　　　　　　　　　　a spicy odor, not resinous dotted (*Quercus*) .... *Fagaceae*
　　　　　　　　　　Fruit completely enclosed by a bur-like involucre; twigs with
　　　　　　　　　　　　a spicy odor when crushed and with yellow resin dots
　　　　　　　　　　　　(*Comptonia peregrina*). .... *Myricaceae*

M. Leaves unlobed.
  S. Plant in flower.
    T. Plant with spines at the nodes (*Berberis*). .... *Berberidaceae*
    T. Plant not spiny at the nodes, although sometimes with scattered thorns
        or with twigs ending in a sharp tip.
      U. Flowers (at least the staminate) in catkins or spikes.
        Plants dioecious.
          Twigs with latex .... *Moraceae*
          Twigs without latex.
            Twigs with a spicy odor when crushed and with yellow
              resinous dots. .... *Myricaceae*
            Twigs without a spicy odor or yellow resinous dots. .... *Salicaceae*
        Plants monoecious.
          Staminate catkins moniliform; pith usually 5-angled in
            cross-section. .... *Fagaceae*
          Staminate catkins contiguous; pith round or triangular in
            cross-section. .... *Betulaceae*
      U. Flowers not in catkins or spikes.
        V. Inflorescence attached to a long, narrow bract; leaves widely
          ovate, cordate to truncate at base (*Tilia*) .... *Tiliaceae*
        V. Inflorescence not attached to a long, narrow bract; leaves not
          shaped as above.
        W. Leaves inequilateral at base .... *Ulmaceae*
        W. Leaves not inequilateral at base.
          X. Flowers in large, terminal panicles that appear plumose due
            to the plumose pedicels of numerous aborted flowers
            (*Cotinus coggyria*). .... *Anacardiaceae*
          X. Flowers solitary, or in axillary, lateral or terminal
            inflorescences not appearing plumose.
            Y. Flowers in heads subtended by an involucre; twigs lacking
              latex (*Baccharis halimifolia*) .... *Asteraceae*
            Y. Flowers not in heads or if so, not subtended by an
              involucre and twigs with latex.
              Z. Petals of essentially 3 different shapes. .... *Fabaceae*
              Z. Petals the same, or not of 3 different shapes, or lacking.
                a. Flowers in racemes.
                  Flowers with a hypanthium, stamens more or less
                    than 10.
                  Stamens more than 10; plants not polygamous;
                    not parasitic. .... *Rosaceae*
                  Stamens 4 or 5; plants polygamous; root
                    parasites (*Pyrularia pubera*). .... *Santalaceae*
                  Flowers lacking a hypanthium; stamens 10.
                  Petals separate; style 3-cleft (*Clethra alnifolia*). .... *Clethraceae*
                  Petals united; style simple .... *Ericaceae*
                a. Flowers not in racemes.
                  b. Flowers solitary, terminal, 3 cm or more broad, of
                    numerous undifferentiated segments; pistils
                    numerous, separate, on an elongated
                    receptacle (*Magnolia*). .... *Magnoliaceae*
                  b. Flowers without the above combination of
                    characters.
                    c. Calyx (or hypanthium) campanulate or tubular,
                      shallowly lobed.
                      Twigs and leaves silvery-scaly; stamens 4
                        (*Elaeagnus*). .... *Elaeagnaceae*
                      Twigs and leaves not silvery-scaly; stamens 5
                      or more.
                      Branches arched or climbing, sparsely
                        thorny (*Lycium*). .... *Solanaceae*
                      Branches not arched or climbing, unarmed.

Leaves entire; petals lacking; ovary
　　　superior, 1-locular. .... *Thymelaeaceae*
Leaves serrulate; petals present; ovary
　　　inferior, 4-locular (*Halesia
　　　carolina*) .... *Styracaceae*
c. Calyx absent, or not tubular (sometimes
　　campanulate), deeply lobed.
　　Flowers in heads; twigs with latex .... *Moraceae*
　　Flowers not in heads; twigs without latex.
　　　Stamens opening by pores.
　　　　Twigs with a spicy odor when crushed. .... *Lauraceae*
　　　　Twigs without a spicy odor when
　　　　　crushed. .... *Ericaceae*
　　　Stamens opening by lines or slits.
　　　　Petals united (*Diospyros virginiana*). .... *Ebenaceae*
　　　　Petals distinct or absent.
　　　　　Stamens more than 10.
　　　　　　Dioecious or polygamous; leaves
　　　　　　　broadly ovate, abruptly
　　　　　　　acuminate; flowers in
　　　　　　　axillary cymes or solitary
　　　　　　　(*Actinidia arguta*). .... *Actinidiaceae*
　　　　　　Plant without the above
　　　　　　　combination of characters. ... *Rosaceae*
　　　　　Stamens 10 or fewer.
　　　　　　Stamens opposite the petals; style
　　　　　　　divided above the middle. ...... *Rhamnaceae*
　　　　　　Stamens alternate with the petals;
　　　　　　　stigma nearly sessile or
　　　　　　　style not divided above the
　　　　　　　middle.
　　　　　　　Flowers cymose, terminal,
　　　　　　　　sometimes also axillary
　　　　　　　　(*Cornus*). .... *Cornaceae*
　　　　　　　Flowers not cymose, axillary.
　　　　　　　　Stigma terminating a coiled
　　　　　　　　　or curved style; stamens
　　　　　　　　　more numerous than
　　　　　　　　　the calyx lobes (*Nyssa
　　　　　　　　　sylvatica*) .... *Nyssaceae*
　　　　　　　　Stigma nearly sessile; stamens
　　　　　　　　　as many as the calyx
　　　　　　　　　lobes. .... *Aquifoliaceae*
S. Plant in fruit.
　d. Fruit fleshy or covered with a heavy layer of white or grayish wax, or in
　　　multiples with the sepals fleshy.
　　e. Fruit in multiples, the sepals forming the fleshy portion; twigs with
　　　　latex. .... *Moraceae*
　　e. Fruit not in multiples; sepals not fleshy; twigs without latex.
　　　f. Fruit more than 1-seeded.
　　　　g. Plant with spines at the nodes (*Berberis*). .... *Berberidaceae*
　　　　g. Plant not spiny at the nodes, although twigs sometimes sparsely
　　　　　thorny or ending in a sharp tip.
　　　　　h. Ovary inferior.
　　　　　　Seeds less than 1 mm long, or leaves yellow resinous-dotted
　　　　　　　beneath. .... *Ericaceae*
　　　　　　Seeds more than 1 mm long; leaves not yellow resinous-
　　　　　　　dotted beneath. .... *Rosaceae*
　　　　　h. Ovary superior.
　　　　　　Fruit ellipsoid; seeds more than 10; branches sometimes
　　　　　　　sparsely thorny (*Lycium*) .... *Solanaceae*

Fruit globose or oblate; seeds mostly fewer than 10;
 branches not thorny, although sometimes ending
 in a sharp tip.
 Fruit more than 1 cm broad; seed more than 1 cm long
  (*Diospyros virginiana*). .... *Ebenaceae*
 Fruit less than 1 cm broad, or seed less than 1 cm long.
  Plants 2 dm or less tall with leaves crowded toward
   the tip, or stem prostrate; fruit red or white
   (*Gaultheria*). .... *Ericaceae*
  Plants taller than 2 dm; leaves not crowded toward
   the tip; stem not prostrate.
   Leaves with minute, persistent stipules or fruiting
    pedicels 2 cm or more long; fruit red or
    orange; twigs not ending in a sharp tip. .... *Aquifoliaceae*
   Leaves lacking minute stipules; fruiting pedicels
    1.5 cm or less long; fruit usually black;
    twigs sometimes ending in a sharp tip
    (*Rhamnus*). .... *Rhamnaceae*
f. Fruit 1-seeded.
 i. Fruit covered with white or grayish wax (*Myrica pensylvanica*). ... *Myricaceae*
 i. Fruit not covered by wax.
  Leaves uniformly toothed.
   Leaf bases oblique; pulp of fruit dry (*Celtis occidentalis*). ..... *Ulmaceae*
   Leaf bases cuneate to rounded; pulp of fruit juicy (*Prunus*) *Rosaceae*
  Leaves entire or remotely toothed.
   Leaves with spicy fragrance when crushed. .... *Lauraceae*
   Leaves without spicy fragrance when crushed.
    Twigs and leaves silvery-scaly (*Elaeagnus*). .... *Elaeagnaceae*
    Twigs and leaves not silvery-scaly.
     Fruit in terminal racemes (*Pyrularia pubera*). .... *Santalaceae*
     Fruit not in terminal racemes.
      Fruit sessile or pedicels less than 1 mm long. .... *Thymelaeaceae*
      Fruit pedicellate or pedunculate, the pedicels or
       peduncles more than 1 mm long.
       Fruit in cymes (*Cornus*) .... *Cornaceae*
       Fruit sessile on the ends of long peduncles
        (*Nyssa sylvatica*). .... *Nyssaceae*
d. Fruit dry, hard, not covered with a wax.
 j. Fruit spirally arranged on a receptacle, follicles (*Magnolia*). .... *Magnoliaceae*
 j. Fruit not spirally arranged on a receptacle, not follicles (except in
  some *Rosaceae*).
 k. Fruit more than 1-seeded, often dehiscent.
  Fruit 1-carpellate .... *Fabaceae*
  Fruit 2 or more carpellate.
   Fruit a 4-winged drupe (*Halesia carolina*). .... *Styracaceae*
   Fruit not a drupe or if so not 4-winged.
    Fruit 4 to 5-carpellate.
     Carpels separate toward apex.
      Fruit an aggregate of follicles (*Spiraea*). .... *Rosaceae*
      Fruit a 5-winged capsule (*Exochorda racemosa*). .... *Rosaceae*
     Carpels united to apex .... *Ericaceae*
    Fruit 2 to 3 carpellate.
     Fruit 3-carpellate.
      Inflorescence a panicle of umbellate cymes
       (*Ceanothus*). .... *Rhamnaceae*
      Inflorescence racemose (*Clethra alnifolia*). .... *Clethraceae*
     Fruit 2-carpellate.
      Seed densely long-pubescent; capsule in racemes or
       spikes. .... *Salicaceae*
      Seed glabrous; capsules solitary or in clusters of 2 or 3
       (*Hamamelis virginiana*) .... *Hamamelidaceae*

k. Fruit 1-seeded, indehiscent.
  l. Fruit in catkins, racemes or spikes.
      Fruit winged, each on a pedicel (*Ulmus*). .... *Ulmaceae*
      Fruit not winged, or not on pedicels.
         Leaves with a spicy odor when crushed and with yellow,
            resinous dots beneath, less than 2 cm wide, cuneate
            (*Myrica gale*). .... *Myricaceae*
         Leaves without a spicy odor or yellow, resinous dots
            beneath, or wider, or not cuneate .... *Betulaceae*
  l. Fruit not in catkins, racemes or spikes.
    m. Fruit winged, a samara (*Ulmus*) .... *Ulmaceae*
    m. Fruit wingless, a nut or dry drupe.
      n. Fruit enclosed by a spiny involucre or surrounded at base
         by a scaly cup. .... *Fagaceae*
      n. Fruit not enclosed by a spiny involucre nor surrounded at
         base by a scaly cup.
        o. Fruit in or subtended by an involucre.
           Leaves cuneate at base; fruit an achene with a tuft of
              long hairs at the apex (*Baccharis halimifolia*) ... *Asteraceae*
           Leaves rounded to cordate at base; fruit a nut without
              a tuft of long hairs at the apex (*Corylus*) .... *Betulaceae*
        o. Fruit not in or subtended by an involucre.
           Inflorescence attached to a long, narrow bract (*Tilia*).   *Tiliaceae*
           Inflorescence not attached to a bract.
              Fruits solitary or paired in the leaf axils (*Celtis*
                occidentalis). .... *Ulmaceae*
             Fruits in plumose, terminal panicles (*Cotinus*
                coggyria). .... *Anacardiaceae*

GROUP 14

Woody Plants in Winter Condition, Lacking Leaves and Flowers, Fruits Present or Absent

A. Leaf scars opposite, subopposite or whorled.
  B. Twigs and buds densely covered with reddish-brown scales (*Shepherdia*
    canadensis) .... *Elaeagnaceae*
  B. Twigs and buds not covered with reddish-brown scales.
    C. Twigs, at least some of them, ending in spines (*Rhamnus*). .... *Rhamnaceae*
    C. Twigs not ending in spines.
      D. Bundle trace 1, round, crescent-shaped or transverse, sometimes indistinct.
        Leaf scars nearly round, prevalently whorled; buds in depressions above
           the leaf scars; globose heads of nutlets often present (*Cephalanthus*
           occidentalis) .... *Rubiaceae*
        Leaf scars half round, shield-shaped, crescent-shaped or triangular,
           prevalently opposite; buds not in depressions; fruits, if present,
           not globose heads of nutlets.
        Buds cylindric, collateral at many of the nodes; pith hollow or
           chambered; twigs 4-sided or lined, with conspicuous lenticels
           (*Forsythia*). .... *Oleaceae*
        Plants without the above combination of characters.
          Bark, even on twigs, exfoliating; twigs slender and very numerous;
            plants low, bushy; pith minute; leaf scars triangular or
            flattened-triangular. .... *Clusiaceae*
          Bark not exfoliating or if so, only on older growth; twig and plant
            characteristics not as above; pith moderate; leaf scars half
            round, shield or crescent-shaped.
           Leaf scars connected by stipular lines, usually torn, indistinctly
             outlined (*Symphoricarpos*) .... *Caprifoliaceae*
           Leaf scars not connected by stipular lines, not torn, distinctly
            outlined.
             Twigs usually green, 4-lined or winged; pith spongy (*Euonymus*). *Celastraceae*
             Twigs brownish or grayish; pith continuous.

Fruit a berry; leaf scars 2 mm or less wide at the top
    (*Ligustrum*). .... Oleaceae
Fruit a capsule; leaf scars more than 2 mm wide at the top
    (*Syringa vulgaris*). .... Oleaceae
D. Bundle traces several, or in several compound groups, or numerous and
  forming a U-shaped line, circle or ellipse.
  E. Bundle traces numerous, forming a U-shaped line, circle or ellipse.
    Stipule scars present; terminal bud absent; fruit an inflated, bladdery
      capsule (*Staphylea trifolia*) .... Staphyleaceae
    Stipule scars lacking; fruit a samara or a capsule that is not inflated or
      bladdery.
      Terminal bud present (*Fraxinus*) .... Oleaceae
      Terminal bud lacking.
        Pith chambered or hollow; buds usually superposed; fruit an
          ovoid capsule (*Paulownia tomentosa*) .... Scrophulariaceae
        Pith continuous; buds solitary; fruit a long, linear capsule
          (*Catalpa*). .... Bignoniaceae
  E. Bundle traces several, or in several compound groups.
    F. Buds apparently lacking, partly or entirely covered by the leaf scars
      (*Philadelphus*) .... Saxifragaceae
    F. Buds exposed.
      G. Leaf scars horseshoe-shaped, nearly surrounding bud.
        Twigs spicy-aromatic when broken; buds closely superposed;
          inner bark not yellow (*Calycanthus floridus*) .... Calycanthaceae
        Twigs not aromatic; buds solitary; inner bark yellow
          (*Phellodendron amurense*). .... Rutaceae
      G. Leaf scars not horseshoe-shaped nor nearly surrounding bud.
        H. Buds lacking scales, densely pubescent.
          Twigs spicy-aromatic when broken; buds sessile, closely
            superposed (*Calycanthus floridus*) .... Calycanthaceae
          Twigs not aromatic; buds stalked, not superposed (*Viburnum*
            lantanoides). .... Caprifoliaceae
        H. Buds with 1, 2 or more scales, glabrous or pubescent.
          I. Bud scale 1.
            Buds oblong, flattened toward the tip (*Salix purpurea*). .... Salicaceae
            Buds ovoid, not flattened (*Viburnum*). .... Caprifoliaceae
          I. Bud scales 2 or more.
            J. Stipule scars prominent; fruit an inflated, bladdery capsule
              (*Staphylea trifolia*) .... Staphyleaceae
            J. Stipule scars absent or if present, leaf scars ciliate at top
              (*Rosaceae: Rhodotypos*) or twigs stout with warty
              lenticels and leaf scars large (*Caprifoliaceae: Sambucus*)
              (*Staphylea* lacks these features); fruit not an inflated,
              bladdery capsule.
              K. Bud scales 2, valvate.
                Terminal pair of leaf scars raised on persistent petiole
                  bases, connected on each side by a V or deeply
                  U-shaped line (*Cornus*). .... Cornaceae
                Terminal pair of leaf scars not raised on persistent
                  petiole bases.
                Buds ovoid, sessile; terminal bud lacking
                  (*Philadelphus*). .... Saxifragaceae
                Buds oblong to linear, stalked, terminal bud present.
                  First year's twigs reddish or greenish, puberulent
                    or older bark white-striped; fruit a samaroid
                    schizocarp of 2 mericarps simulating a pair
                    of samaras (*Acer*). .... Aceraceae
                  First year's twigs grayish or brownish, glabrous,
                    older bark not striped; fruit a drupe
                    (*Viburnum*) .... Caprifoliaceae
              K. Bud scales 3 or more, imbricated.[go to L.]

L. Leaf scars broad and conspicuous; twigs stout; bundle traces usually 5 or more
    (usually 3 in *Saxifragaceae: Hydrangea*).
    Terminal bud lacking; twigs with prominent, warty lenticels; bundle traces
        usually 5 or more (*Sambucus*) .... *Caprifoliaceae*
    Terminal bud usually present, or if lacking bundle traces usually 3; twigs
        lacking conspicuous lenticels.
        Bundle traces usually 3; terminal bud moderate (*Hydrangea*). .... *Saxifragaceae*
        Bundle traces usually in 3 compound groups or 5 or more in a single series;
            terminal bud enlarged (*Aesculus*) .... *Hippocastanaceae*
L. Leaf scars small or moderate, V, U, crescent shaped or triangular; twigs slender
    to moderate; bundle traces 3 (occasionally more in *Aceraceae*).
    Pith excavated; twigs covered with stellate hairs (*Deutzia scabra*). .... *Saxifragaceae*
    Pith continuous or if excavated (some *Lonicera*) twigs not covered with
        stellate hairs.
        Twigs with 2 or 4 ridges decurrent from the leaf scars; buds with 4 or more
            pairs of scales; leaf scars low (*Diervilla lonicera*). .... *Caprifoliaceae*
        Twigs lacking ridges or if ridges present, buds with3 or fewer pairs of scales
            (*Caprifoliaceae: Viburnum*) or leaf scars conspicuously raised
            (*Caprifoliaceae: Lonicera*).
            Leaf scars and the line connecting them ciliate; terminal bud absent; fruit
                a cluster of black drupes (*Rhodotypos scandens*). .... *Rosaceae*
            Leaf scars and connecting line not ciliate, or if so, terminal bud present;
                fruit not a cluster of drupes (except in *Viburnum*).
                Leaf scars conspicuously raised on persistent leaf bases; buds often
                    superposed (*Lonicera*) .... *Caprifoliaceae*
                Leaf scars not conspicuously raised; buds not superposed.
                    Pith large; buds globose to oblong; inflorescence of sterile flowers
                        often persistent; fruit a capsule (*Hydrangea*). .... *Saxifragaceae*
                    Pith moderate; buds not globose or if so, bud scales and twigs red
                        (these are brown to gray in *Hydrangea*); inflorescence of
                        sterile flowers lacking; fruit a samaroid schizocarp of
                        2 mericarps simulating a pair of samaras, or a drupe.
                        Leaf scars meeting or buds globose and sometimes collaterally
                            multiple; fruit a samaroid schizocarp of 2 mericarps
                            simulating a pair of samaras (*Acer*) .... *Aceraceae*
                        Leaf scars usually not meeting; buds neither globose nor multiple;
                            fruit a drupe (*Viburnum*) .... *Caprifoliaceae*
A. Leaf scars and/or buds alternate (when leaf scars are absent or indistinct leaves are
    represented by spines (*Fabaceae: Ulex*) or scales (*Tamaricaceae*) or leaf scars
    are conspicuously raised (*Rosaceae: Rubus, Potentilla*).
    M. Stems armed with thorns or prickles.
        N. Twigs and buds covered with silvery and sometimes brown scales (*Elaeagnus*). *Elaeagnaceae*
        N. Twigs and buds not covered with silvery or brown scales.
            O. Thorns present, representing modified leaves as indicated by their position
                (i.e. subtending buds or spur shoots).
                Twigs as well as leaves modified as thorns, the stems densely thorny
                    (*Ulex europaeus*) .... *Fabaceae*
                Only the leaves modified as thorns, occurring only at the nodes (*Berberis*). *Berberidaceae*
            O. Thorns, when present, not representing modified leaves (not subtending
                buds or spur shoots), or prickles or bristles instead of thorns present
                (prickles are superficial and easily detached whereas thorns are not;
                bristles are very slender and often flexible whereas thorns are rigid).
                P. Thorns present, representing modified stipules or branches as indicated
                    by definite position (i.e. occurring at the sides of the leaf scars or in
                    their axils).
                    Thorns representing modified stipules (occurring in pairs, one thorn
                        on each side of the leaf scar).
                        Buds concealed beneath the leaf scar, this often splitting (*Robinia*). .... *Fabaceae*
                        Buds not concealed, red-woolly (*Zanthoxylum americanum*). .... *Rutaceae*
                    Thorns representing modified branches (occurring in axils of leaf scars
                        or terminating twigs).

Thorns, or some of them, branched or with 1 or more prongs; buds
  sunken and partly concealed by the leaf scar and sunken in
  the bark above it when in a superposed pair (*Gleditsia
  triacanthos*). .... Fabaceae
Thorns simple, not branched or pronged; buds clearly visible.
  Pith spongy; branches long and spreading (*Lycium*). .... Solanaceae
  Pith continuous; branches not particularly long and spreading.
    Thorns merely short, sharp branches or spinescent twigs (as
      indicated by presence of leaf scars and sometimes buds),
      not highly modified.
      Leaf scars linear; buds and often twigs woolly (*Malus; Pyrus
        communis*). .... Rosaceae
      Leaf scars half-elliptic; buds and twigs not woolly (*Prunus*). ..... Rosaceae
    Thorns highly modified, branch or twig origins not evident.
      Leaf scars narrowly crescent-shaped; bundle traces 3; bud
        scales fleshy; sap not milky (*Crataegus*) .... Rosaceae
      Leaf scars half round or triangular; bundle traces more than
        3 or fused into 1; sap milky (*Maclura pomifera*) .... Moraceae
P. Thorns absent, prickles or bristles present instead as indicated by
  random, scattered occurrence instead of at sides or in axils of leaf
  scars, and by other distinctions noted above.
  Leaf scars conspicuously raised on persistent petiole bases (*Rubus*). .... Rosaceae
  Leaf scars not or only slightly raised.
    Twigs very stout; leaf scars nearly encircling twig; bundle traces
      numerous (*Aralia spinosa*) .... Araliaceae
    Twigs slender to moderate; leaf scars not nearly encircling twig;
      bundle traces 3.
      Buds globose, red-woolly; leaf scars broad (*Zanthoxylum
        americanum*). .... Rutaceae
      Buds ovoid to fusiform, not red-woolly; leaf scars linear to U or
        cresent-shaped.
        Twigs decurrently ridged from the nodes; bark often exfoliating
          (*Ribes*). .... Saxifragaceae
        Twigs not ridged; bark not exfoliating (*Rosa*). .... Rosaceae
M. Stems unarmed.
  Q. Leaf scars absent, or inconspicuous and conspicuously raised on persistent
    petiole bases.
    Leaf scars absent; buds subtended by persistent leaf base (*Tamarix*). .... Tamaricaceae
    Leaf scars inconspicuous, conspicuously raised on persistent
      petiole bases.
      Bark exfoliating; bundle trace 1 (*Pentaphylloides floribunda*). .... Rosaceae
      Bark not exfoliating; bundle traces 3 (evident when petiole base is cut)
        (*Rubus*) .... Rosaceae
  Q. Leaf scars present, conspicuous.
    R. Bundle trace 1.
      S. Twigs and buds covered with silvery and sometimes brown scales
        (*Elaeagnus*). .... Elaeagnaceae
      S. Twigs and buds not covered with silvery or brown scales.
        T. Pith chambered or spongy (at least at the nodes).
          Stipules persistent (*Pentaphylloides floribunda*). .... Rosaceae
          Stipules lacking or not persistent.
            Stipule scars present; buds closely appressed (*Celtis occidentalis*). ... Ulmaceae
            Stipule scars lacking; buds not closely appressed.
              Branches long and spreading, 5-ridged; buds small, indistinctly
                scaly; bundle trace not C-shaped (*Lycium*) .... Solanaceae
              Branches not particularly long and spreading, not ridged; buds
                moderate, with 2 scales; bundle trace C-shaped
                (*Diospyros virginiana*). .... Ebenaceae
        T. Pith continuous.
          U. Stipules or stipule scars present.
            Twigs green and ribbed or grooved (*Cytisus, Genista*). .... Fabaceae

Twigs brownish or grayish, round or angled, not green and
 ribbed or grooved.
 Freshly cut twigs with milky sap; terminal bud lacking; buds
  depressed-globose (*Maclura pomifera*) .... *Moraceae*
 Without the above combination of characters.
  Leaf scars much raised on persistent petiole bases.
   Bark exfoliating; stipules sheathing stem; buds moderate
    solitary (*Pentaphylloides floribunda*) .... *Rosaceae*
   Bark not exfoliating; stipules not sheathing stem; buds
    small, usually superposed (*Colutea arborescens*) .... *Fabaceae*
  Leaf scars, at most, moderately raised.
   Stipules persistent as minute pointed spines; buds usually
    superposed (*Ilex*). .... *Aquifoliaceae*
   Stipules lacking or not as above; buds solitary.
    Low, weak shrubs; fruit a capsule, the disc-like bases
     persistent in clusters (*Ceanothus*) .... *Rhamnaceae*
    Moderate or tall, robust shrubs; fruit a drupe, usually
     persistent in clusters (*Rhamnus*) .... *Rhamnaceae*
U. Stipules or stipule scars lacking.
 V. Terminal bud present.
  Twigs green, spicy-aromatic when broken (*Sassafras albidum*). .. *Lauraceae*
  Twigs brown or gray, not spicy-aromatic.
   Buds clustered toward the tips of the twigs; twigs of the past
    1-several season's growth usually clustered so as to
    appear nearly whorled (*Rhododendron*) .... *Ericaceae*
   Bugs and twigs not clustered.
    Terminal bud much larger than laterals; bundle trace large
     and protruding (*Clethra alnifolia*) .... *Clethraceae*
    Terminal bud not or only slightly larger than laterals;
     bundle trace not protruding.
     Twigs purplish, glaucous, round; bud scales 2, ciliate
      (*Nemopanthus mucronatus*) .... *Aquifoliaceae*
     Twigs brownish or grayish, not glaucous, somewhat
      angled; bud scales 3 or more, not ciliate (*Daphne*
      mezereum) .... *Thymelaeaceae*
 V. Terminal bud absent.
  W. Flower buds distinct from foliar buds on the basis of size,
   shape or position.
   Flower buds in dense, bracteate racemes (*Leucothoe*
    racemosa). .... *Ericaceae*
   Flower buds not in racemes, distinguishable from foliar buds
    primarily on the basis of size and/or shape.
    Twigs greenish, reddish or warty; bud scales usually
     distinctly mucronate (*Vaccinium*) .... *Ericaceae*
    Twigs brown or grayish, not warty; bud scales acute but
     not mucronate (*Gaylussacia*) .... *Ericaceae*
  W. Flower buds not distinct from foliar buds.
   Bud scales more than 3; leaf scars often conspicuously raised;
    fruiting inflorescences usually persistent; fruit a
    follicle (*Spiraea*). .... *Rosaceae*
   Bud scales 2 (or if more leaf scars not raised and fruit a
    capsule).
    Bundle trace not C-shaped; bud scales 3 or more or if 2,
     not overlapping; fruit a capsule, usually persistent
     (*Lyonia*). .... *Ericaceae*
    Bundle trace C-shaped; bud scales 2, overlapping; fruit a
     berry, not persistent (*Diospyros virginiana*) .... *Ebenaceae*
R. Bundle traces 3 or more.
 X. Bundle traces scattered, clustered in small groups, forming a circle or
 ellipse, or nearly confluent in a line.

Y. Stipule scars or stipules present.
    Z. Stipule scars completely or nearly encircling twig.
        Mature buds long and narrowly cylindric; bud scales numerous
            (*Fagus*). .... *Fagaceae*
        Mature buds not long and narrowly cylindric; bud scales 1 or 2.
            Terminal bud compressed and 2-edged, with 2 valvate scales
                (*Liriodendron tulipifera*) .... *Magnoliaceae*
            Terminal bud not compressed or 2-edged, with a single keeled
                scale (*Magnolia*). .... *Magnoliaceae*
    Z. Stipule scars extending less than half way around twig.
        Buds indistinct, barely or not evident; fruit a capsule (*Hibiscus*
            syriacus). .... *Malvaceae*
        Buds distinct, well developed (at least the terminal ones); fruit a
            nut or fleshy and multiple.
            Buds clustered toward the tips of the twigs (*Quercus*). .... *Fagaceae*
            Buds not clustered toward the tips of the twigs.
                Buds conical, with 1-3 striate scales; pith with diaphrams at
                    the nodes; sap milky (*Broussonetia papyrifera*) .... *Moraceae*
                Buds ovoid or depressed-globose, scales not striate; pith
                    lacking diaphrams.
                    Buds depressed-globose; sap milky (*Maclura pomifera*). ...... *Moraceae*
                    Buds ovoid.
                        Buds with 3 or fewer scales.
                          Pith star-shaped in cross-section (*Castanea*). .... *Fagaceae*
                          Pith terete in cross-section (*Tilia*). .... *Tiliaceae*
                      Buds mostly with 4 or more scales.
                          Sap milky; catkins lacking; fruit multiple, berry-like
                            (*Morus*). .... *Moraceae*
                        Sap not milky; catkins often present; fruit a nut
                          subtended by an involucre (*Corylus*) .... *Betulaceae*
Y. Stipule scars and stipules absent.
    Leaf scars round, much elevated, concealing the buds; twigs
        aromatic when broken; sap milky (*Rhus aromatica*) .... *Anacardiaceae*
    Twigs without the above combination of characters although sap
        sometimes milky.
        Leaf scars C or U-shaped and surrounding the bud on at least 3
            sides; buds indistinctly scaly due to dense pubescence;
            dense, terminal clusters of red fruits usually present; sap
            milky (*Rhus*). .... *Anacardiaceae*
        Without the above combination of characters.
            Pith chambered (*Juglans*) .... *Juglandaceae*
            Pith not chambered.
                Twigs and branches covered with dark dots, lustreless,
                  appearing dead; loose, terminal clusters of whitish
                  fruits usually present; poisonous to touch
                  (*Toxicodendron vernix*) .... *Anacardiaceae*
                Twigs and fruits not as above; not poisonous to touch.
                  Terminal bud absent; lateral buds solitary, sessile
                    (*Koelreuteria paniculata*). .... *Sapindaceae*
                Terminal bud present; lateral buds often stalked or
                  superposed (*Carya*). .... *Juglandaceae*
X. Bundle traces 3 or more, separate, in a single open line.
    a. Pith chambered or diaphragmed.
        Stipule scars encircling twig; bud scale single (*Magnolia*). .... *Magnoliaceae*
        Stipule scars absent or not encircling twig; bud scales 2 or more.
            Terminal bud absent; stipule scars present (*Celtis occidentalis*). .... *Ulmaceae*
            Terminal bud present; stipule scars absent.
                Pith chambered, brown (*Juglans*) .... *Juglandaceae*
                Pith continuous, diaphragmed, white (*Nyssa sylvatica*). .... *Nyssaceae*
    a. Pith not chambered or diaphragmed.

b. Buds apparently lacking, partly or entirely covered by the
    leaf scars (bud characteristics visible by removing leaf scar layer).
    Buds with yellow pubescence; fruit a dense cluster of red,
        pubescent drupes; fresh twigs aromatic when broken,
        with latex (*Rhus aromatica*). .... *Anacardiaceae*
    Buds glabrous or pubescence not yellow; fruit a samara or
        legume; twigs lacking latex, not aromatic (except
        Rutaceae: Ptelea).
        Buds with silvery pubescence; fruit a samara (*Ptelea trifoliata*). ... *Rutaceae*
        Buds glabrous or pubescence not silvery; fruit a legume.
            Buds glabrous, partly hidden beneath leaf scars, evident
                (*Gleditsia triacanthos*) .... *Fabaceae*
            Buds pubescent, completely hidden beneath leaf scars, not
                evident (*Robinia*). .... *Fabaceae*
b. Buds clearly present.
    c. Leaf scars horseshoe or C-shaped, completely surrounding bud
        or mostly surrounding it (on at least 3-sides).
        Stipule scars encircling twig (*Platanus*). .... *Platanaceae*
        Stipule scars not encircling twig.
            Twigs jointed and swollen at the nodes, each node having a
                short, upward-pointing spur (*Dirca palustris*) .... *Thymelaeaceae*
            Twigs not as above.
                Buds glabrous, evidently scaly (*Gleditsia triacanthos*). .... *Fabaceae*
                Buds naked or indistinctly scaly due to pubescence.
                    Bundle traces 5 or more.
                        Buds superposed; sap not milky; fruit a legume
                            (*Cladrastis kentukea*). .... *Fabaceae*
                        Buds not superposed; sap milky; fruit a red,
                            pubescent drupe in dense clusters (*Rhus*) .... *Anacardiaceae*
                    Bundle traces 3.
                        Buds silvery-pubescent; fruit a samara (*Ptelea*
                            trifoliata). .... *Rutaceae*
                      Buds pubescent but not silvery; fruit a legume
                            (*Robinia*). .... *Fabaceae*
    c. Leaf scars not horseshoe or C-shaped, not completely or mostly
        surrounding the bud.
        d. Buds naked or indistinctly scaly due to pubescence.
            Buds stalked; fruit a persistent, woody capsule (*Hamamelis*
                virginiana). .... *Hamamelidaceae*
            Buds sessile; fruit a drupe or pome, often not persistent.
                Stipules or small stipule scars present; fruit a 2-3 seeded
                    drupe (*Frangula alnus*) .... *Rhamnaceae*
                Stipules and stipule scars lacking; fruit a 1-seeded drupe
                  or a pome.
                  Terminal bud absent; sap milky; fruit a red, pubescent
                    drupe in dense clusters (*Rhus*) .... *Anacardiaceae*
                  Terminal bud present; sap not milky; fruit a pome, not
                    in dense clusters (*Pyrus, Malus*) .... *Rosaceae*
        d. Buds evidently scaly, with 1 or more scales.
            e. Bud scale single.
                 Stipule scars encircling twig (*Magnolia*). .... *Magnoliaceae*
                 Stipule scars absent or not encircling twig (*Salix*). .... *Salicaceae*
            e. Bud scales 2 or more.
                f. First (lowermost) bud scale centered over leaf scar
                    (*Populus*). .... *Salicaceae*
                f. First bud scale not centered over leaf scar.
                    g. Bundle traces 5 or more.
                      Twigs very stout; leaf scars large and shield-shaped;
                        terminal bud lacking (*Ailanthus altissima*) .... *Simarubaceae*
                      Twigs slender to moderate; leaf scars not as above;
                      terminal bud present.

Bundle traces 8 or more; leaf scars encircling more
than half the twig; wood yellow
(*Zanthorhiza simplicissima*) .... Ranunculaceae
Bundle traces 5; leaf scars encircling half or less of
the twig; wood not yellow.
Twigs ridged from the leaf scars; stipule scars
present (*Physocarpus opulifolius*) .... Rosaceae
Twigs not ridged from the leaf scars; stipule
scars absent (*Sorbus*). .... Rosaceae
g. Bundle traces 3.[go to h.]
h. Terminal bud present.
i. Stipule scars or stipules present.
Mature buds long and narrowly cylindric; stipule scars nearly or completely
encircling twigs (*Fagus*) .... Fagaceae
Mature buds and stipules not as above.
Pith star-shaped in cross-section (*Castanea*). .... Fagaceae
Pith rounded or angled but not star-shaped.
Pith occupying approximately half the twig diameter; fruit a capsule, the
disc-like bases persistent; plant 1m or less tall (*Ceanothus*). .... Rhamnaceae
Pith occupying less than half the twig diameter; fruit not as above; plant
more than 1m tall (except some Betulaceae [*Betula*] and
Rosaceae [*Prunus*]).
Buds with 4 or more scales and/or twigs with decurrent lines or ridges
from the leaf scars.
Buds usually superposed, the upper often soon developed as twigs;
stipules persistent; fruit an inflated, bladder-like legume;
twigs not malodorous (*Colutea arborescens*) .... Fabaceae
Buds solitary or collateral, usually not superposed; stipules
deciduous; fruit a fleshy drupe; twigs, when broken,
sometimes malodorous (*Prunus*). .... Rosaceae
Buds with 2 or 3 scales; twigs mostly lacking distinct lines or ridges
from the leaf scars.
Buds stalked (except in *A. crispa*); pith triangular; scales of pistillate
catkins woody, persistent, unlobed or erose; twigs not
developed as short shoots, lacking wintergreen
odor (*Alnus*). .... Betulaceae
Buds sessile; pith flat or angled but not triangular; scales of
pistillate catkins not woody, deciduous, 3-lobed; twigs
often developed as short shoots, sometimes with a
wintergreen odor when broken (*Betula*). .... Betulaceae
i. Stipule scars or stipules absent.
j. Leaf scars linear or narrowly U or crescent-shaped.
Pith spongy.
Buds red, flattened against the twig; twigs not ridged or lined from the
nodes, not malodorous (*Aronia*) .... Rosaceae
Buds brown or grayish, not flattened against the twig; twigs ridged or
lined from the nodes, often malodorous when broken
(*Ribes*). .... Grossulariaceae
Pith not spongy.
Buds lanceolate or elongate-oblong, the terminal (and often the lateral
buds) 4 or more times as long as broad or if shorter, then lateral
buds flattened against the twig.
Buds lanceolate, the lateral ones not flattened against the twig, scales
sometimes twisted (*Amelanchier*) .... Rosaceae
Buds elongate-oblong, the lateral ones flattened against the twig, scales
not twisted (*Aronia*) .... Rosaceae
Buds ovoid, less than 3 times as long as broad, the lateral ones not
flattened against the twig.
Leaf scar a narrow, nearly straight line extending about half way
around the stem (*Rosa*) .... Rosaceae
Leaf scar not as above.

Buds round-ovoid to globose, with fleshy scales; twigs
    glossy (*Crataegus*). .... *Rosaceae*
Buds ovoid-oblong, scales not fleshy; twigs not glossy.
    Bark exfoliating; twigs slender; bud scales 8 or more
        (*Exochorda racemosa*). .... *Rosaceae*
    Bark not exfoliating; twigs moderately stout; bud scales
        5 or fewer (*Pyrus, Malus*) .... *Rosaceae*
j. Leaf scars crescent-shaped, half round or elliptic, or triangular.
    Pith star-shaped in cross-section; bundle traces circled with white rings;
        twigs often with corky wings (*Liquidambar styraciflua*). .... *Hamamelidaceae*
    Pith round or angled but not star-shaped; bundle traces not as above; twigs
        lacking corky wings.
        Leaf scars half round or broadly crescent-shaped; twigs and buds lacking
            resin drops.
            Twigs green with a spicy odor when broken, without resinous sap;
                pith white (*Sassafras albidum*) .... *Lauraceae*
            Twigs brown, lacking a spicy odor, with resinous sap; pith brown
                (*Cotinus coggria*) .... *Anacardiaceae*
        Leaf scars narrowly crescent-shaped, or if somewhat broader (some
            Myricaceae: *Myrica*) twigs and buds with resin drops.
            Leaf scars on persistent petiole bases, those toward the twig tip
                forming a half V when viewed from the side; bud scales 2,
                valvate; twigs arranged in a flat plane; twigs and buds lacking
                resin drops (*Cornus alternifolia*). .... *Cornaceae*
            Leaf scars not as above, bud scales more numerous or if 2, not valvate;
                 twigs not in a flat plane; twigs and buds with minute resin
                 drops (*Myrica*). .... *Myricaceae*
h. Terminal bud absent (except on short shoots i.e. *Betula*).
  k. Stipule scars or stipules present.
    Pith star-shaped in cross-section (*Castanea*). .... *Fagaceae*
    Pith rounded or angled but not star-shaped.
        Twigs and buds with minute resin drops; twigs pubescent, with a spicy odor
            when broken; buds globose (*Comptonia peregrina*). .... *Myricaceae*
        Twigs and buds without the above combination of characters.
        Buds with 3 or fewer scales.
            Twigs angled or ridged; buds superposed; fruit a legume
                (*Amorpha fruticosa*). .... *Fabaceae*
            Twigs not angled or ridged; buds not superposed; fruit not a legume.
                Buds ovoid, oblique over leaf scar; twigs not developed as
                    short shoots, lacking a wintergreen odor; fruit on a
                    peduncle arising from the middle of a narrow foliaceous
                    bract (*Tilia*) .... *Tiliaceae*
                Buds ovoid-fusiform, centered over leaf scar; twigs often developed
                    as short shoots, sometimes with a wintergreen odor when
                    broken; fruit in catkins or spikes (*Betula*) .... *Betulaceae*
        Buds with 4 or more scales.
            Twigs with milky sap when freshly cut (*Morus*). .... *Moraceae*
            Twigs lacking milky sap.
                Twigs often developed as short shoots, sometimes with a
                  wintergreen odor when broken; bark with horizontally
                  elongate lenticels; fruit in catkins or spikes (*Betula*) .... *Betulaceae*
                Without the above combination of characters.
                  Leaf scars and buds in 2 ranks.
                    Buds closely appressed; pith chambered, at least at some of the
                      nodes (*Celtis occidentalis*) .... *Ulmaceae*
                  Without the above combination of characters.
                    Bud scales 2-ranked; bundle traces sunken in a corky-layered
                      leaf scar; fruit a samara (*Ulmus*) .... *Ulmaceae*
                  Bud scales not 2-ranked; bundle traces not sunken; fruit in
                    catkins or spikes, not samaroid.

Bud scales longitudinally striate; bark scaly
(*Ostrya virginiana*). .... *Betulaceae*
Bud scales not striate; bark not scaly.
Bud scales 9 or more, 4-ranked; scales of terminal buds
not subtending pitillate flowers; trunk fluted
(*Carpinus caroliniana*). .... *Betulaceae*
Bud scales 6 or fewer, not 4-ranked; scales of terminal
buds each subtending a pistillate flower with
red, exserted stigmas; trunk not fluted (*Corylus*). *Betulaceae*
Leaf scars and buds in more than 2 ranks.
Bud scales uniformly dark brown to black; fruit a 2-3 seeded
drupe; bark not malodorous (*Rhamnus*) .... *Rhamnaceae*
Bud scales greenish or light brown, or buds with bicolored
scales; fruit a 1-seeded drupe; twigs sometimes
malodorous when broken (*Prunus*). .... *Rosaceae*
k. Stipule scars or stipules absent.
Twigs with decurrent ridges from the leaf scars; buds encased in hardened
resin; inflorescence remnants or involucres usually present
(*Baccharis halimifolia*) .... *Asteraceae*
Without the above combination of characters.
Buds mostly superposed and/or leaf scars minutely fringed along upper margin.
Twigs green to olive, spicy-aromatic when broken; globose, collateral flower
buds usually present; leaf scars not fringed (*Lindera benzoin*). .... *Lauraceae*
Twigs brownish, not spicy-aromatic; collateral flower buds lacking; leaf
scars minutely fringed along upper margin (*Cercis canadensis*). .... *Fabaceae*
Buds not superposed; leaf scars not fringed.
Twigs and buds with minute resin drops; twigs with a spicy odor when
broken; leaf scars half-elliptic (*Myrica*) .... *Myricaceae*
Without the above combination of characters.
Leaf scars half round to round; fruit a cluster of follicles
(*Sorbaria sorbifolia*) .... *Rosaceae*
Leaf scars linear to narrowly crescent-shaped; fruit a pome.
Twigs glossy; buds round-ovoid to globose, with fleshy scales
(*Crataegus*). .... *Rosaceae*
Twigs not glossy; buds ovoid to conical or oblong, scales not fleshy
(*Pyrus, Malus*) .... *Rosaceae*

Descriptive Flora

Division I. PTERIDÓPHYTA
(Ferns and Fern Allies)
Plants not producing flowers or seeds, entirely free-sporing.

Family 1. Equisetáceae (Horsetail Family)

Perennial, rhizomes subterranean, branched, jointed, bearing roots at the joints, long and creeping. Stems ridged, simple or with branches in whorles, jointed at the solid nodes, internodes hollow, usually having a large central cavity (centrum) surrounded by an outer whorl of smaller cavities (vallecular cavities); joints covered by toothed sheaths which are modified scale-like leaves united at the base. Sporangia clustered on the inner surfaces of the scales of terminal spike-like cones.

1. *Equisétum* L. (horse bristle) Horsetail.

Same characters as the family. Stems contain silica and can be used for scouring. —Wildl. 1

a. Stems evergreen, unbranched or with a few short apical branches.
   b. Teeth of sheaths promptly deciduous, stems more than 3 mm in diameter. .... 1. *E. hyemale*
   b. Teeth of sheaths persistent; stems less than 3 mm in diameter.
      Teeth of sheaths 3; stems usually contorted .... 2. *E. scirpoides*
      Teeth of sheaths 5 or more; stems usually straight. (Fig. 1). .... 3. *E. variegatum*
a. Stems deciduous, often branched.
   c. Teeth of sheaths on main stem cohering, at least in part, and fused into 3 or 4
      lobes; lateral branches branched. (Fig. 2). .... 4. *E. sylvaticum*
   c. Teeth of sheaths on main stem all separate; lateral branches usually simple.
      d. Plant in reproductive condition.
         e. Cone-bearing stems lacking green color, unbranched. .... 5. *E. arvense*
         e. Cone-bearing stems green, branched or unbranched.
            f. Hollow center (centrum) four-fifths diameter of main stem. .... 6. *E. fluviatile*
            f. Centrum approximately one-sixth diameter of stem.
               Cones occurring in spring; cavities surrounding centrum nearly as
                  large as centrum. .... 7. *E. palustre*
               Cones occurring in summer; cavities surrounding centrum much
                  smaller than centrum. .... 8. *E. pratense*
      d. Plant in vegetative condition.
         g. Teeth of sheaths on central stem below the lowest branches mostly white-
            hyaline. (Fig. 3) .... 8. *E. pratense*
         g. Teeth of sheaths on central stem below the lowest branches mostly black or
            dark brown.
            h. Teeth of sheaths on central stem white-margined. .... 7. *E. palustre*

h. Teeth of sheaths on central stem black or dark brown.
Stems up to 4 mm in diameter; central cavity up to two-thirds diameter
of stem, branches solid .... 5. *E. arvense*
Stems more robust, generally 5 mm or more in diameter; central cavity
four-fifths diameter of stem, branches hollow. .... 6. *E. fluviatile*

1. *E. hyemále* L. (of winter; because evergreen). Scouring-Rush. In wet areas, sandy embankments and roadsides. May-June. Map 1. Our plants are var. *affine* (Engelm.) A.A. Eat. [*E. affine; E. hyemale* var. *pseudohyemale; E. prealtum; E. robustum*]. Poisonous. —FACW

E. laevigátum A. Br. Resembling *E. hyemale* but with sheaths distinctly longer than broad and with only an apical dark band (sheaths barely longer than broad and with both basal and apical dark bands in *E. hyemale*). Reported for CT. [*E. hyemale* var. *intermedium; E. kansanum*]. Poisonous. —FACW

E. x ferríssii Clute. A hybrid between *E. laevigatum* and *E. hyemale.*

2. *E. scirpoídes* Michx. (like Scirpus). Dwarf Scouring-rush. Moist, often swampy woodlands, wet hillsides. May-June. Map 2. (N. Europe). —FAC

3. *E. variegátum* Schleich. (variegated). Variegated Horsetail. Wet, often calcareous sandy areas, riverbanks, wet depressions, bogs and shores. May-June. Fig. 1, Map 3. (Eurasia). Our plants are var. *variegatum.* —FACW

E. x nélsonii (A.A. Eat.) Schaffn. A hybrid between *E. variegatum* and *E. laevigatum.* [*E. variegatum* var. *nelsonii*].

E. x máckaii (Newm.) Brichan. A hybrid between *E. hyemale* and *E. variegatum* (*E. variegatum* var. *jesupi*).

4. *E. sylváticum* L. (of woodland). Wood-Horsetail. Woodlands, wooded swamps, open meadows and moist grassy areas. May. Fig. 2., Map 4. (Eurasia). Poisonous. —FACW

5. *E. arvénse.* L. (typical). Common-Horsetail. Roadsides, sandy embankments, dry to moist meadows, damp woodlands. April-June. Map 5. (Eurasia). Poisonous. —FAC

6. *E. fluviátile* L. (of a river). Water-Horsetail. Shallow-water, lake shores, riverbanks, moist woods, bogs and swamps. May-July. Map 6. (Eurasia). —OBL

E. x litorále. Kuhlewein ex Rupr. A hybrid between *E. fluviatile* and *E. arvense.*

7. *E. palústre* L. (of marshes). Marsh-Horsetail. Shallow water, marshes, meadows, moist woodlands, streambanks and shores. July-August. Map 7. (Eurasia). Poisonous. —FACW

8. *E. praténse* Ehrh. (of the meadows). Meadow-Horsetail. Moist streambanks, riverbanks, meadows and abandoned fields, moist woods. May-June. Fig. 3, Map 8. (Eurasia). —FACW

Family 2. Lycopodiáceae (Club-Moss Family)

Low, coarsely moss-like perennial plants, erect, trailing, or creeping. Stems subterranean or on the surface, branched, with numerous scale-like or subulate imbricated or crowded evergreen leaves in 4 or more ranks. Sporangia and spores of uniform size, solitary in the axils of the foliage leaves or in axils of the upper, modified leaves (sporophylls, or bracts) which are imbricated in sessile or stalked strobili (cones).

a. Sporangia borne in the leaf axils, not in cones (Fig. 4). .... 1. *Huperzia*
a. Sporangia borne in terminal cones (Figs. 5,7).
  b. Plants creeping; cones terminating peduncles arising directly from the creeping
    stem, with green, leaf-like bracts similar to the foliage leaves (bracts yellowish
    and scale-like in *Pseudolycopodiella*).
    Leaves of the creeping stem monomorphic; peduncles with crowded leaves,
      similar to those of the creeping stem; bracts of the cone green and
      resembling the foliage leaves .... 2. *Lycopodiella*
    Leaves of the creeping stem dimorphic, the lateral larger than the median;
      peduncles with scattered, scale-like leaves; bracts of the cone yellowish
      and scale-like .... 3. *Pseudolycopodiella caroliniana*

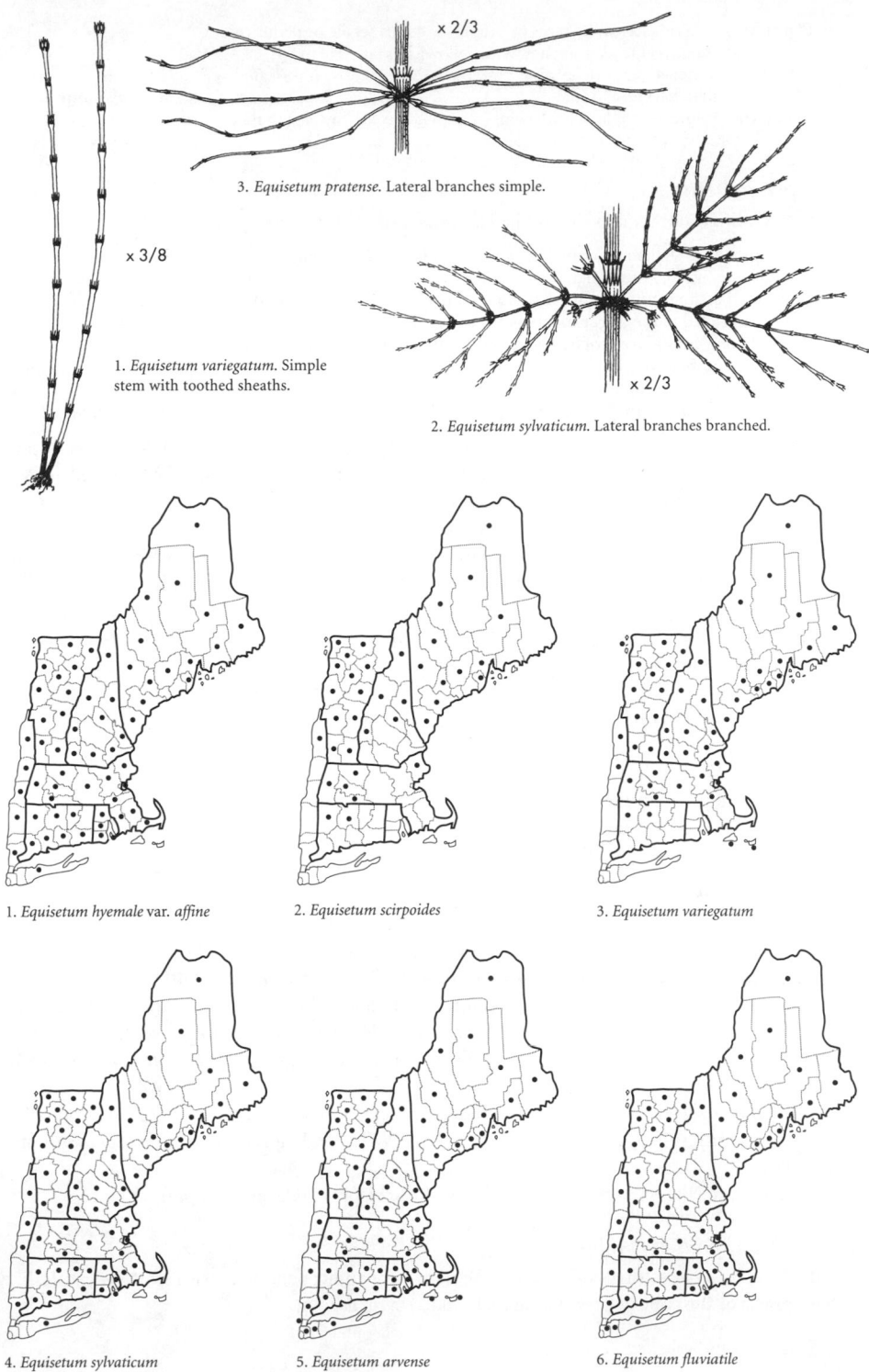

x 2/3

3. *Equisetum pratense.* Lateral branches simple.

x 3/8

1. *Equisetum variegatum.* Simple stem with toothed sheaths.

x 2/3

2. *Equisetum sylvaticum.* Lateral branches branched.

1. *Equisetum hyemale* var. *affine*

2. *Equisetum scirpoides*

3. *Equisetum variegatum*

4. *Equisetum sylvaticum*

5. *Equisetum arvense*

6. *Equisetum fluviatile*

b. Plants with erect or ascending stems or branches; cones sessile or peduncled,
   terminating erect leafy branches, with yellowish, scale-like bracts.
   Branches flattened, appearing wing-margined; leaves mostly imbricated,
      scale-like (Fig. 6) .... 4. *Diphasiastrum*
   Branches rounded, not appearing wing-margined; leaves linear-subulate,
      bristly, not imbricated or scale-like .... 5. *Lycopodium*

1. *Hupérzia* Bernh.

Stems ascending; sporangia borne in the leaf axils, not in cones [*Lycopodium*].

a. Plants with a short, slender, rooting base mostly to about 1.5 cm long; leaves
      lanceolate, up to 8 mm long.
   Plants with distinct annual constrictions; gemmae (small vegetative buds)
      restricted to the upper parts of the stem and branches. .... 1. *H. selago*
   Plants lacking annual constrictions; gemmae scattered throughout the stem
      and branches .... 2. *H. appalachiana*
a. Plants with a prostrate, rooting, marcescent, leafy base mostly 1.5 dm or longer;
      larger leaves oblanceolate, mostly 8-12 mm. long. .... 3. *H. lucidula*

1. *H. selágo* (L.) Bernh. ex Mart. & Schrank (old generic name). Mountain Club-moss. Alpine tundra and barrens. July-September. Map 9. (Eurasia, Mexico, S. Amer.). Endangered in Ma. [*Lycopodium s.*] Our plants are var. s*elago.* —FAC

var. *dénsa* has also been attributed to our range.

H. porophíla (Lloyd & Underwood) Holub. Resembling *H. selago* but with leaves slightly unequal, broadest near the middle and obscurely toothed above (leaves equal, broadest at or near base and entire in *L. selago*).

From farther south. Reported for VT. [*Lycopodium porophyllum; L. selago var. patens*]. —FACU-

2. *H. appalachiána* Beitel & Mickel. Reported for ME, NH, VT, MA.

3. *H. lucídula* (Michx.) Trevisan (somewhat shining). Shining Club-moss. Rich, moist woodlands and wooded swamps. July-October. Fig. 4, Map 10. (Asia). [*Lycopodium lucidulum*].

2. *Lycopodiélla* Holub.

Plants creeping; leaves monomorphic; erect fertile shoots (peduncles) unbranched, with crowded leaves similar to those of the creeping stem, each with a solitary terminal, sporangia-bearing cone, bracts of the cone green and resembling the foliage leaves [*Lycopodium*].

Leaves entire to sparingly ciliate-denticulate; cone slender, 0.5-1.2 cm thick .... 1. *L. inundata*
Leaves strongly ciliate-denticulate; cone stout, 0.8-2.2 cm thick. .... 2. *L. alopecuroides*

1. *L. inundáta* (L.) Holub (inundated). Bog Club-moss. Wet sandy open soil, sandy shores and bogs. July-October. Fig. 5, Map 11 (Eurasia). [*Lycopodium inundatum*]. —OBL

L. appréssa (Chapman) Cranfill. Resembling *L. inundata* but erect fertile branches (peduncles) taller than 1 dm and leaves 1 mm or more wide (peduncles up to 1 dm tall and leaves less than 1 mm wide in *L. inundata*). Scattered locations mostly in MA and CT. [*Lycopodium inundatum* var. *bigelovii; L. appressum*]. —FACW+

2. *L. alopecuroídes* (L.) Cranfill. (resembling *Alopecurus*). Foxtail Club-moss. Coastal, on sandy shores, wet sandy soil. August-October. Map 12. (W.I.) Endangered in Ma. [*Lycopodium a.*]. —FACW+

L. x copelándii (Eig.) Cranfill. A hybrid between *L. alopecuroides* and *L. appressa*.

3. *Pséudolycopodiella* Holub.

Similar to *Lycopodiella*; leaves of the creeping stem dimorphic; peduncles with scattered, scale-like leaves; bracts of the cone yellowish and scale-like. [*Lycopodium*].

1. *P. caroliniána* (L.) Holub (of Carolina). Carolina Club-moss. Wet sandy open soil, pastures and moist sandy pine barrens. August-October. Map 13. (Tropical Amer., Australia). Endangered in NY. [*Lycopodium carolinianum*]. Our plants are var. *caroliniana.* —FACW+

4. *Diphasiástrum* Holub.

Plants with erect or ascending stems or branches; branches flattened and appearing wing-margined (round in *D. sitchense*); leaves mostly imbricated, scale-like (linear-subulate and bristly in *D. sitchense*); cones sessile or peduncled, terminating erect leafy branches, with yellowish, scale-like bracts. [*Lycopodium*].

Horizontal stem deep in ground; leaves of lower surfaces of branches about equalling
 lateral ones; plants bluish-green. .... 1. *D. tristachyum*
Horizontal stem at or near surface; leaves of lower surfaces of branches smaller than
 lateral ones; plants green or yellow-green. .... 2. *D. complanatum*

1. *D. tristáchyum* (Pursh) Holub (three spiked). Ground Pine. Dry fields and woodlands, pine woods. August-September. Map 14 (Europe). [*Lycopodium t.*].

D. x zeílleri (Rouy) Holub. A hybrid between *L. tristachyum* and *L. complanatum*. [*Lycopodium x z.*].

2. *D. complanátum* (L.) Holub (flattened). Ground-cedar. Dry woodlands and fields. July-September. Fig. 6, Map 15. (Eurasia). [*Lycopodium c.*]. —FACU-

D. digitátum (Dill. ex A. Braun) Holub. Resembling *L. complanatum* but horizontal stems superficial, branches without annual constrictions, cones usually with sterile tips (horizontal stems mostly subterranean, branches with annual constrictions and appearing irregular, cones bearing sporangia to tip in *L. complanatum*). [*Lycopodium complanatum* var. *flabelliforme; L. c.* var. *digitatum; L. dillenianum; L. flabelliforme*].

D. x habéreri (House) Holub. A hybrid between *D. digitatum* and *D. tristachyum*. [*Lycopodium x h.*].

3. *D. sitchénse* (Rupr.) Holub (of Sitka). Sitkan Club-moss. Mountain slopes and northern spruce woodlands. July-September. Map 16. Endangered in NY and Me. [*Lycopodium s.; L. sabinaefolium* var. *sitchense*]. This species keys most readily under *Lycopodium* and so for convenience has been placed in that key.

D. x sabinifólium (Willdenow) Holub. A widespread hydrid between *D. sitchense* and *D. tristachyum*. Map 17. [*Lycopodium sabinaefolium; L.s.* var *sitchense*].

5. *Lycopódium* L. (resembling a wolf's foot).

Similar to *Diphasiastrum*; branches rounded, not appearing wing-margined; leaves linear-subulate, bristly, not imbricated or scale-like.

a. Leaves terminated with a soft hair-like bristle; cones stalked. .... 1. *L. clavatum*
a. Leaves not terminated with a bristle, or if so a hard sharp one; cones sessile.
 b. Horizontal stem deep in ground; upright stem with horizontal to ascending,
  bushy branches. (Fig. 7).
  c. Leaves in the rank along the underside of the branch much smaller than those
   in the other 5 ranks .... 2. *L. obscurum*
  c. Leaves all uniform
   Leaves in 2 ranks on the upper and lower sides of the branch and in 1 rank
    on each lateral side; leaves on the main stem below the branches
    spreading, stiff and bristly .... 3. *L. dendroideum*
   Leaves in 1 rank on the upper and lower sides of the branch and in 2 ranks
    on each lateral side; leaves on the main stem below the branches
    appressed, soft to touch .... 4. *L. hickeyi*

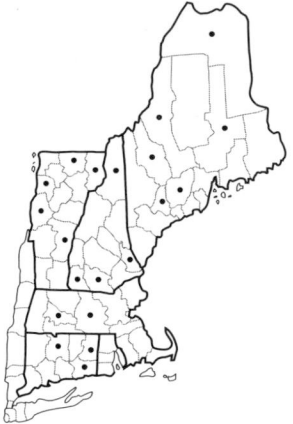

7. *Equisetum palustre*

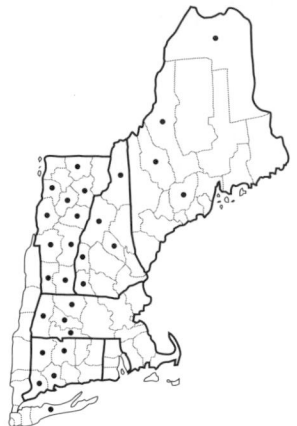

8. *Equisetum pratense*

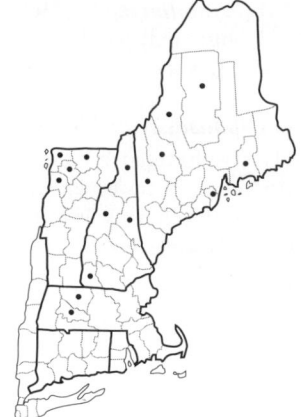

9. *Huperzia selago*

10. *Huperzia lucidula*

11. *Lycopodiella inundata*

12. *Lycopodiella alopecuroides*

13. *Pseudolycopodiella caroliniana*

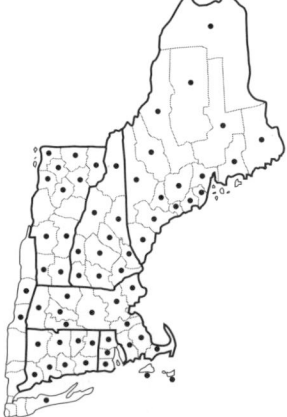

14. *Diphasiastrum tristachyum*

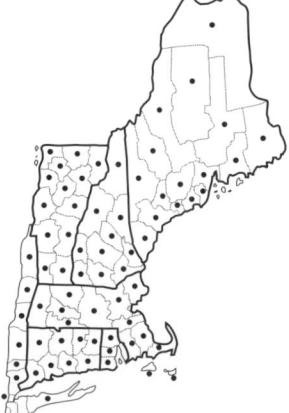

15. *Diphasiastrum complanatum*
and *D. digitatum*

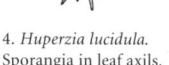

× 3/8

4. *Huperzia lucidula.*
Sporangia in leaf axils.

× 1/2

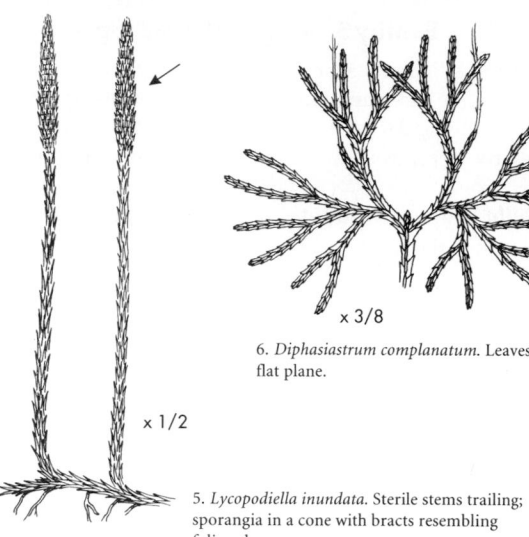

× 3/8

6. *Diphasiastrum complanatum.* Leaves arranged in a flat plane.

5. *Lycopodiella inundata.* Sterile stems trailing; sporangia in a cone with bracts resembling foliage leaves.

b. Horizontal stem at the surface; upright stem simple or sparsely branched,
    branches erect to ascending and dichotomous (Fig. 8).
    Leaves 6 or more-ranked, 3-10 mm long. .... 5. *L. annotinum*
    Leaves 4-5-ranked, 3 mm or less long. .... *Diphasiastrum*
                                  sitchense
                                  (see 3. *D. sitchense*
                                  under
                                  Diphasiastrum).

    1. *L. clavátum* L. (club shaped). Running Club-moss. Dry woods, thickets, abandoned fields and clearings. July-October. Map 18 (Eurasia). Our plants are var *clavatum.* Spores are used as a dusting powder to prevent chafing, for skin diseases and as a base for face powder; spores of this and other species are highly flammable. —FAC
    L. lagópus (Laestadius ex. C. Hartman) G. Zinserling ex Kuzeneva-Prochorova. Resembling *L. clavatum* but leaves ascending to appressed, cone 1 per peduncle (leaves spreading and cones 2 or more per peduncle in *L. clavatum*). [*L.c.* var *monostachyon*].
    2. *L. obscúrum* L. (obscure). Tree Club-moss. Dry or moist woodlands and clearings. July-October. Fig. 7, Map 19 (Asia). —FACU
    3. *L. dendroídeum* Michx. Habitats and distribution similar to *L. obscurum.* [*L. obscurum* var. *d.*]. —FACU
    4. *L. híckeyi* W.H. Wagner, Beitel & R.C. Moran. Habitats and distribution similar to *L. obscurum* [*L. obscurum* var. *isophyllum*].
    5. *L. annótinum* L. (a year old). Bristly Club-moss. Northern hardwood woodlands and clearings. August-September. Fig. 8, Map 20. (Eurasia).
    Our plants include var. *annotinum* and the following 3 vars.:
    var. *acrifólium* Fern. Leaves entire to obscurely serrate (distinctly serrate in var. *annotinum*).
    var. *púngens* (La pylaie) Desv. Leaves strongly ascending to appressed, 6 mm or
    less long (spreading to reflexed and 6 mm or longer in the above vars.).
    var. *alpéstre* Hartm. Resembling var. *pungens* but leaves linear to lance-attenuate, dorsally convex, entire (leaves lanceolate to lance-oblong, flat, obscurely serrate in var. *pungens*). —FAC

Family 3. Selaginelláceae (Spikemoss Family)

Small (ours), moss-like annual or perennial plants, prostrate or erect, with branching stems having numerous scale-like 4 to many-ranked, evergreen leaves. Sporangia of two sizes in the leaf axils of cylindric or quadrangular cones, the smaller containing numerous reddish or orange powdery microspores, the larger usually containing 4 yellowish megaspores.

1. *Selaginélla* Beauv. (Diminutive of *Selago*). Spikemoss.
Same characters as the family.

a. Stem leaves alternately large and small. (Fig. 9). .... 1. *S. apoda*
a. Stem leaves uniform in size.
    Cones quadrangular; leaves with hair-like apices... . ... 2. *S. rupestris*
    Cones cylindric; leaves merely acute. .... 3. *S. selaginoides*

1. *S. ápoda* (L.) Spring. (footless, from the sessile spikes). Creeping Spikemoss. Dry or moist meadows and low woodlands. July-September. Fig. 9, Map 21. (S. America). Endangered in MA. [*S. eclipes*]. —FACW

16. *Diphasiastrum sitchense*

17. *Diphasiastrum x sabinifolium*

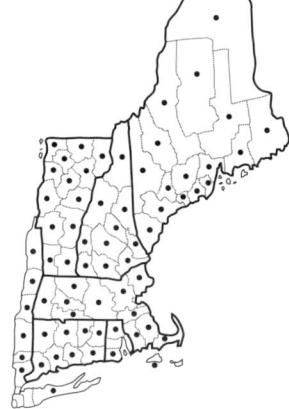

18. *Lycopodium clavatum*

19. *Lycopodium obscurum*

20. *Lycopodium annotinum*

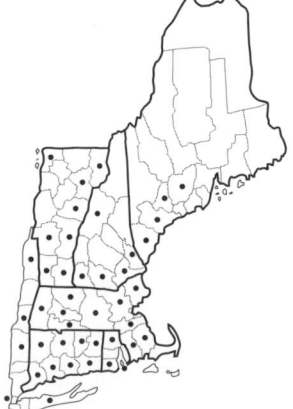

21. *Selaginella apoda*

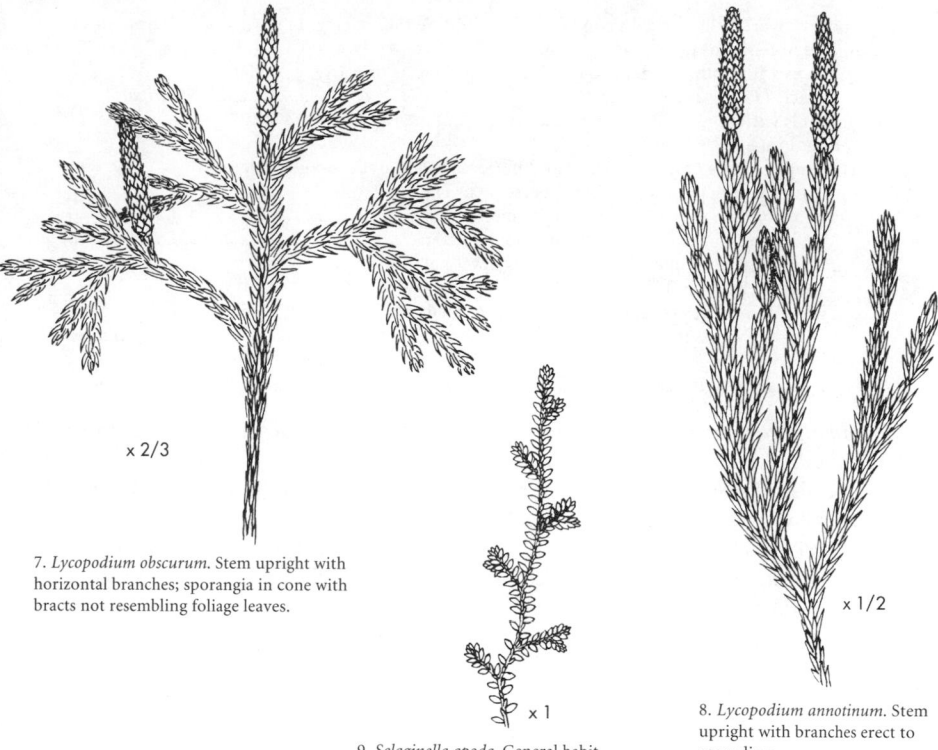

× 2/3

7. *Lycopodium obscurum.* Stem upright with horizontal branches; sporangia in cone with bracts not resembling foliage leaves.

× 1

9. *Selaginella apoda.* General habit.

× 1/2

8. *Lycopodium annotinum.* Stem upright with branches erect to ascending.

2. S. rupéstris (L.) Spring (of rocks). Rock Spikemoss. Rock outcrops, ledges, open or sparsely wooded gravelly soil. July-October. Map 22. (Eurasia).

3. S. selaginoídes (L.) Link (resembling *Selago*). Low Spikemoss. Shores, gravelly or rocky beaches and open, mossy northern woodlands. July-August. Map 23. (Eurasia). Endangered in MA. —FACW

Family 4. Isoetáceae (Quillwort Family)

Perennial, mostly aquatic or amphibious plants with a short, thick corm bearing roots from the underside, and a cluster of linear, grass-like, awl-shaped leaves from the flattened top. Sporangia occurring in the swollen leaf bases, partly or entirely covered by the velum (a fold of leaf tissue), some sporangia containing the minute powdery microspores, others containing the much larger megaspores. Megaspores divided into upper and lower halves by a median ridge, the upper half further divided by 3 equally spaced ridges. Both halves are variously sculptured, the sculpturing diagnostic for the species, which can be distinguished only in reproductive condition using a compound microscope.

1. Isòetes L. Quillwort (Ancient name originally used for a species of *Sedum*).
Same characters as the family.

In addition to the following species *I. x brittonii* is another hybrid that has been distinguished.

a. Megaspores spinulose. (Fig. 10) .... 1. *I. echinospora*
a. Megaspores not spinulose.

b. Megaspores covered all over with convolute, labyrinthine ridges. (Fig. 11). .... 2. *I. x eatoni*
b. Megaspores not as above.
  c. Megaspores with both distinct and confluent jagged crests or warty, granular
      surface. (Figs. 12 & 13) .... 3. *I. riparia*
  c. Megaspores with regular or nearly regular ridges and pits; surface not warty
     or granular.
    d. Three upper faces of megaspore with thin, somewhat parallel-walled ridges,
       lower half honeycombed with coarse pits. (Fig. 14)
      Megaspores mostly 0.6-0.8 mm in diameter. .... 4. *I. lacustris*
      Megaspores mostly less than 0.6 mm in diameter. .... 5. *I. tuckermanii*
    d. Three upper faces of megaspore as well as lower half honeycombed with
      coarse pits. (Fig. 15).
      Three main ridges separating upper faces of megaspore distinctly raised,
        high, pits in lower half shallow; sporangia unspotted .. .. 6. *I. engelmannii*
      Three main ridges barely raised, low and rounded, pits in lower half deep;
        sporangia heavily spotted .... 7. *I. x foveolata*

1. *I. echinóspora* Durieu (with short hard points). Shallow water or wet shores. June-October. Fig. 10, Map 24. [*I. braunii; I. muricata; I. setacea*]. —OBL

2. *I. x eátonii* Dodge. (for its discoverer). Fresh ponds, wet shores or tidal flats. June-October. Fig. 11, Map 25. A hybrid between *I. echinospora* and *I. engelmannii*. [*I. eatonii; I. gravesii*]. —OBL

3. *I. ripária* Engelm. ex A. Braun (occurring on banks of rivers). Shallow water and fresh or tidal shores. June-October. Figs. 12 & 13, Map 26. [*I. canadensis; I. saccharata*]. Our plants include var. *riparia* and the following hybrid and var.:

I. x dòdgei A. A. Eat. A hybrid between *I. riparia* and *I. echinospora*. Distinguishable from *I. riparia* var. *riparia* in having surface of megaspores with remote crests, the smooth spore surface visible between (surface of megaspores with crests crowded and mostly confluent in *I. riparia* var. *r.*) [*I. riparia* var. *robbinsii; I. r.* var. *canadensis*].

var. *ámesii* (A.A. Eat.) Proctor. Surface of megaspores finely granular (surface of megaspores with jagged, irregular crests in var. *riparia* and *I. x dodgei*). [*I. saccharata* var. *a.*]. —OBL

4. *I. lacústris* L. (large-spored). Shallow water or wet shores. June-October. Fig. 14, Map 27. Endangered in MA. [*I. hieroglýphica; I. macrospora*]. —OBL

5. *I. tuckermánii* A. Braun ex Engelmann (for its discoverer). Shallow water or wet shores, frequently tidal. June-October. Map 28. —OBL

I. acadiénsis Kott. Similar to *I. tuckermanii* but with lower side of median ridge smooth (in *I. tuckermanii* the lower side of the median ridge is ornamented with papillae). Canadian. Recently reported from scattered locations in Maine, Vermont and Massachusetts. Endangered in MA.

6. *I. engelmánnii* A. Braun (for its discoverer). Shallow water or wet shores. June-October. Fig. 15, Map 29. Our plants are var. *engelmannii*. —OBL

7. *I. x foveoláta* A.A. Eat. ex Dodge (with small pits). Shallow water or wet shores. June-October. A hybrid between *I. lacustrus* and *I. tuckermanii*. Map 30. [*I. foveolata*]. —OBL

x 25

10. *Isoetes echinospora.* Megaspore with spinulose surface.

x 25

11. *Isoetes x eatonii.* Meagaspore with convolute, labyrinthine ridges.

x 25

12. *Isoetes riparia.* Megaspore with distinct and confluent jagged crests.

x 25

13. *Isoetes riparia.* Megaspore with warty, granular surface.

x 20

14. *Isoetes lacustris.* Three upper faces of megaspore with parallel walled ridges.

x 25

15. *Isoetes engelmannii.* Entire megaspore honeycombed with coarse pits.

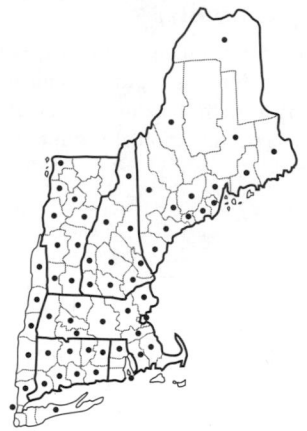

22. *Selaginella rupestris*

23. *Selaginella selaginoides*

24. *Isoetes echinospora*

25. *Isoetes x eatonii*

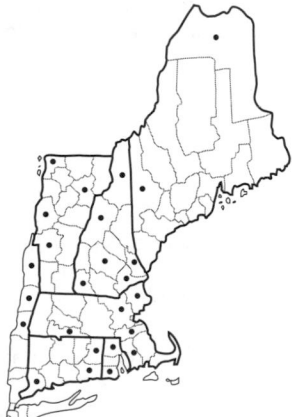

26. *Isoetes riparia*

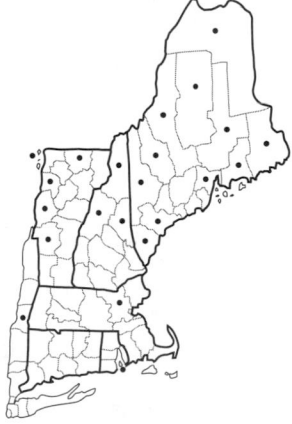

27. *Isoetes lacustris*

28. *Isoetes tuckermanii*

29. *Isoetes engelmannii*

30. *Isoetes x foveolata*

Family 5. Ophioglossáceae (Adder's-Tongue Family)

Perennial, with a short, erect, simple rhizome bearing numerous thick roots and one or two leaves. Sterile leaf consisting of a simple to variously dissected blade; fertile leaf exhibiting a spike or panicle having naked 2-ranked sporangia. Stipe of the spike or panicle arising from the base of the stipe of the sterile blade, or positioned above the sterile blade and appearing as a continuation of a common stipe, with the sterile blade sessile or stalked below the spike or panicle.

Sterile leaf blade compound or dissected, lobed or toothed; sporangia distinct in
  spikes or panicles .... 1. *Botrychium*
Sterile leaf blade simple and entire; sporangia cohering in a simple spike. (Fig. 20) .... 2. *Ophioglossum*
  pusillum

1. *Botrýchium* Sw. Grape-Fern. (Diminutive of "cluster grapes").

Sterile blade mostly compound, or variously dissected or lobed, seldom entire; fertile portion a pinnate spike or a panicle, the sporangia 2-ranked and distinct.

a. Leaves ternately dissected, triangular in outline.
  b. Sterile blade free from fertile below or just above ground level.
    Pinnules mostly acute, 2-4 times as long as wide, serrulate to laciniate. (Fig. 16) 1. *B. dissectum*
    Pinnules mostly obtuse, less than twice as long as wide, entire to crenate or
      dentate (Fig. 17) .... 2. *B. multifidum*
  b. Sterile blade free from fertile 1/3 the distance up the stem or higher.
    Sterile blade 2-3 times pinnately compound, 4 or more times as large as the
      fertile portion; spring.. 3. *B. virginianum*
    Sterile blade once compound with pinnatafid divisions, 3 or less times as large
      as the fertile portion; summer or fall .... 4. *B. lanceolatum*
a. Leaves simple or pinnately dissected.
  c. Pinnae seldom lobed or pinnatifid, fan shaped to obovate, rounded at apex.
    Sterile blade with 3-7 pairs of similar, fan-shaped pinnae. (Fig. 18). .... 5. *B. lunaria*
    Sterile blade simple or with 1-6 pairs of dissimilar, mostly obovate pinnae. .... 6. *B. simplex*
  c. Pinnae usually lobed to pinnatifid, oblong or ovate to lanceolate, acute at
    apex. (Fig. 19).
    Sterile blade usually sessile; pinnae lanceolate. .... 4. *B. lanceolatum*
    Sterile blade usually stalked; pinnae oblong or ovate ... . 7. *B. matricariifolium*

  1. *B. disséctum* Spreng. (dissected). Cut-leaved Grape-Fern. Woodlands, abandoned fields, and meadows. August-September. Fig. 16, Map 31. —FAC.
  B. biternàtum (Savigny) Underw. Similar to *B. dissectum* but with blade less dissected, mostly bipinnate, the ultimate segments cuneate at the base (blade mostly tri or quadripinnate, ultimate segments rounded to truncate at base in *B. dissectum*). From farther south and west. Reported for CT. —FAC.
  2. *B. multifidum* (Gmel.) Rupr. (much divided). Leathery Grape-Fern. Meadows, abandoned fields and woodlands. August-September. Fig. 17, Map 32. (Eurasia). [*B. matricariae; B. silaifolium*]. —FACU
  B. oneidénse (Gilbert) House. Resembling *B. multifidum* with pinnules obtuse and entire to crenate or dentate but differing in being 2-3 times as long as wide (pinnules less than twice as long as wide in *B. multifidum*). Similar distribution.
  B. rugulósum W.H. Wagner. Pinnules less than twice as long as wide as in *B. multifidum* but with ultimate segments acute and coarsely toothed (ultimate segments entire to crenate or dentate in *B. multifidum*). Reported for NH, CT.
  3. *B. virginiánum* (L.) Sw. (Virginian). Rattlesnake-Fern. Rich woodlands. June-July. Map 33. (E. Asia). —FACU
  4. *B. lanceolátum* (Gmel.) Angstr. (lanceolate). Lance-leaved Grape-Fern. Meadows, rich, moist, woodlands and wooded swamps. July-August. Map 34. (Eurasia). Our plants include var. *lanceolatum* [*B. hesperium*] and the following var.:

var. *angustisegméntum* Pease & Moore. Lobes of the pinnae narrow at the base, acute at the apex (lobes broad at the base and round at the apex in var. *lanceolatum*). —FACW

5. B. lunária (L.) Sw. (old generic name). Moonwort. Open meadows, slopes and shores. June-August. Fig. 18, Map 35. (Eurasia, Australia, New Zealand). Endangered in ME, NY and VT. [*B. minganense; B. onondagense*]. —FACW

B. minganénse Victorin. Resembling *B. lunaria* but with longer blade, more cleft, with less distinctly flabellate segments, and often attached below the middle of the axis. Reported for VT. [*B. lunaria* var. *m.*].

6. B. símplex E. Hitchc. (simple). Little Grape-Fern. Open meadows, shores and woodlands. May-June, Map 36. (Eurasia). Our plants include var. *simplex* and the following vars.:

var. *laxifólium* Clausen. Pinnae with 3-6 pairs of lateral lobes, these remote, at least the lower ones narrow at the base (pinnae with 3 or fewer pairs of lateral lobes, these approximate, broad at the base in var. *simplex*).

var. *tenebrósum* (A.A. Eat.) Clausen. Blade borne above the middle of the axis, the stipe 5 cm or more long (blade borne at or below the middle, the stipe less than 5 cm long in the above vars.). [*B. tenebrosum*]. —FACU

7. B. matricariifólium (Döll) A. Braun ex Koch (with leaves of Matricaria). Grape-Fern. Rich or moist woodlands. June-August. Fig. 19, Map 37. (Eurasia). [*B. neglectum; B. oblanceum; B. pseudopinnatum; B. ramosum*].—FACU

2. Ophioglóssum L. (Serpent tongue). Adder's Tongue.

Sterile blade simple and entire, mostly elliptical; fertile portion spicate, the sporangia 2-ranked and coherent.

1. O. pusillum Raf. Moist meadows and woodlands. April-August. Fig. 20, Map 38. Eurasia. [*O. arenarium; O. vulgatum* var. *pseudopodum*] —FACW

Family 6. Osmundáceae (Flowering Fern Family)

Tall swamp or lowland ferns with stout, creeping rhizomes covered with clumps of persistent leaf bases and fibrous roots and bearing leaves in clusters. Stipe naked, winged at the base, blade scaleless, hairy; sterile and fertile fronds separate, or sterile and fertile portions occurring on the same frond; sterile frond once or twice pinnate. Sporangia numerous, naked, and borne on modified, contracted pinnae.

1. Osmúnda L. Flowering Fern (For the Saxon equivalent of the god Thor).

Same characters as the family.

a. Fronds bipinnate, the pinnules serrulate; fertile frond with reproductive portion
  terminal .... 1. *O. regalis*
                                                                                                     var. *spectabilis*
a. Fronds once pinnate, the pinnae pinnatifid; fertile frond separate or reproductive
  portion not terminal.
    Fertile fronds separate from the sterile; mature sterile pinnae with a tuft of
      brownish tomentum at base .... 2. *O. cinnamomea*
    Fertile pinnae in the middle of the frond, the sterile pinnae above and below;
      mature pinnae not tomentose at base. (Fig. 21). .... 3. *O. claytoniana*

1. O. regális L. (royal). Royal Fern. Bogs, swamps, wet thickets and low moist woods. May-July. Map 39. (Eurasia). Represented with us as var. *spectabilis* (Willd.) Gray. Reportedly used to make compresses for external application to areas of the body affected by rheumatism; fiddleheads edible when cooked. —OBL

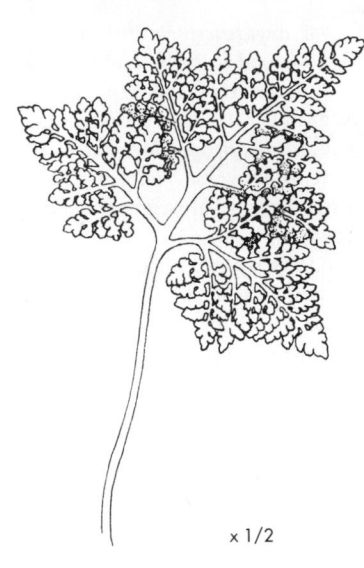

x 1/2

x 1/2

16. *Botrychium dissectum.* Sterile blade with acute pinnules; fertile portion paniculate.

17. *Botrychium multifidum.* Sterile blade with obtuse pinnules.

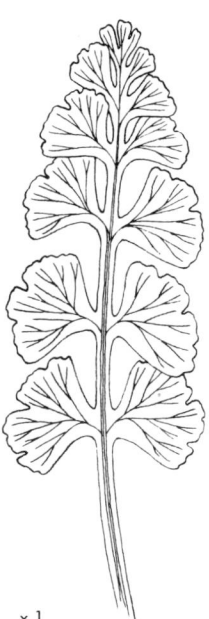

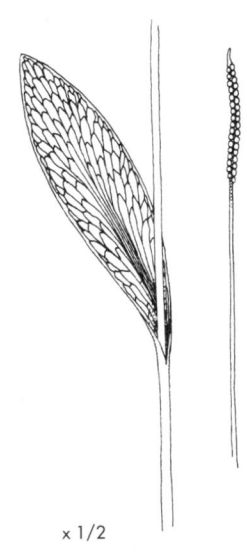

x 1

x 1

x 1/2

18. *Botrychium lunaria.* Sterile blade with unlobed fan-shaped pinnae.

19. *Botrychium matricariifolium.* Sterile blade with lobed pinnae.

20. *Ophioglossum pusillum.* General habit; sporangia 2-ranked in spike.

31. *Botrychium dissectum*

32. *Botrychium multifidum*

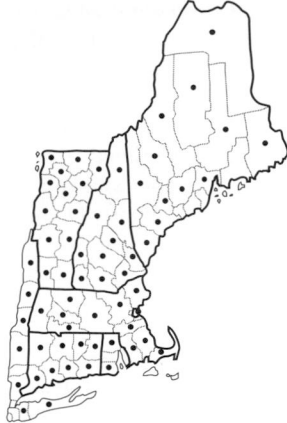

33. *Botrychium virginianum*

34. *Botrychium lanceolatum*

35. *Botrychium lunaria*

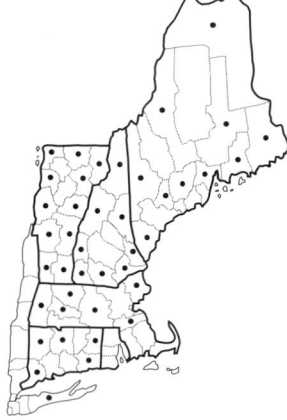

36. *Botrychium simplex*

37. *Botrychium matricariifolium*

38. *Ophioglossum pusillum*

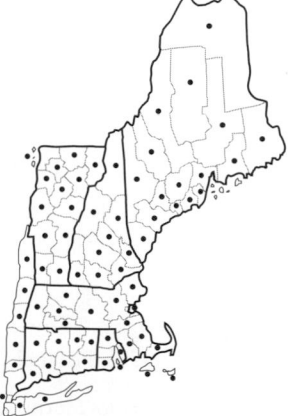

39. *Osmunda regalis* var. *spectabilis*

2. O. cinnamómea L. (cinnamon-colored). Cinnamon-Fern. Swamps, stream-banks and low moist woods. May-June. Map 40. (Tropical and Subtropical America, E. Asia). Our plants include var. *cinnamomea* and the following var.:

var. *glandulósa* Waters. Pinnules and upper part of rachis glandular (eglandular in var. *cinnamomea*). —FACW

3. O. claytoniána L. (for its discoverer). Interrupted Fern. Low moist woods, margins of swamps, thickets, meadows and open roadside areas. May-July. Fig. 21, Map 41. (Asia). Our plants are var. *claytoniana*. Reported to be poisonous. —FACU

O. x rúggii Tryon. A hybrid between *O. regalis* and *O. claytoniana*.

Family 7. Schizaeáceae (Curly-grass Family)

Perennial, unfernlike in appearance, rhizomes short. Sterile fronds tufted and grass-like, the fertile fronds or parts unlike the sterile, having a separate one-sided terminal spike. Sporangia 2-ranked on the narrow, modified divisions, covered by the recurved pinnule margin.

1. Schizáea Sm. Curly-grass (to split).

Rhizome short and erect; sterile fronds densely tufted, linear and grass-like, curling; fertile frond consisting of a very slender stipe terminated by a one-sided spike of about 5-6 pairs of narrow pinnae, the sporangia 2-ranked, partly covered by the recurved pinnule margin.

1. S. pusílla Pursh (very small). Moist open soil, bogs and mossy open woodlands. July-September. Suffolk County NY. Fig. 22, Map 42. Endangered in NY. —OBL

Family 8. Lygodiáceae (Climbing Fern Family)

Perennial, unfernlike in appearance, rhizomes long and creeping. Sterile fronds vine-like and climbing, with alternate, stalked, paired, palmately-lobed pinnae; the fertile fronds or parts unlike the sterile, having a panicle of contracted, forked pinnules toward the apex of the frond. Sporangia 2-ranked, covered by the indusia.

1. Lygódium Sw. Climbing Fern (Flexible).

Rhizome long and creeping, branched; sterile frond vine like, twining and climbing, with alternate stalked, paired, palmately-lobed pinnae; fertile pinnae toward the apex of the frond, contracted, several times forked, forming a panicle, the sporangia 2-ranked on the narrow divisions, each covered by a scale like indusium.

1. L. palmátum (Bernh.) Sw. (palmate or hand-like). Moist woodlands, thickets and pastures. August-September. Fig. 23, Map 43. Endangered in VT and NY. —FACW

Hymenophylláceae (Filmy Fern Family)

Fronds scattered along a creeping rhizome. Petiole and rachis winged, blades bipinnatifid. Sori marginal, sunken, with a tubular indusium, sporangia on a bristle-like receptacle within the indusium.

1. Trichómanes L. Filmy Fern.

Same characters as the family.

1. T. boschiánum Sturm. Gametophytes only have been reported from several locations in the northeast. Rare, southern.

Family 9. Dennstaedtiáceae

Perennial. Rhizomes elongate, lacking scales, with hairs only. Fronds large, lacking scales, with hairs only. Sori borne at the leaf margin or appearing submarginal, indusium formed both by the revolute margin of the leaf and by a scale-like membranous structure on the ventral leaf surface just inside the margin, or true indusium somtimes hidden by the revolute leaf margin. [*Polypodiaceae*].

Sori linear, confluent, covered by the reflexed leaf margin; blade broadly triangular,
with 3 main branches .... 1. *Pteridium aquilinum*

Sori round, borne within a cup formed by fusion of the true indusium and a modified
tooth of the leaf margin; blade lanceolate, with 1 main rachis. .... 2. *Dennstaedtia punctilobula*

1. *Pteridium* Gleditsch ex Scopoli. Bracken (Diminutive of Pteris, a wing).

Rhizome long and creeping; stipe glabrous, brownish, to 1 m long, blade to 1.2 m long and 1 m wide, broadly triangular with 3 main branches, the lower segments twice pinnate, the upper twice pinnate to simple; sori linear, confluent in a continuous line beneath the reflexed leaf margin.

    1. *P. aquilínum* (L.) Kuhn (of an eagle; from the wing-shaped fronds). Bracken Fern. Dry to moist woods, thickets and clearings. July-September. Fig. 24, Map 44. (Europe and Africa). Represented with us by the following vars.:

    var. *latiúsculum* (Desv.) Underw. ex Heller. Longest entire leaf segment or part of a segment about 4 times as long as broad, the terminal segments mostly 5-8 mm wide; margins of ultimate segments moderately pubescent. [*Pteridium l.*].

    var. *pseudocaudátum* (Clute) Heller. Longest entire leaf segment or part of a segment 8 or more times as long as broad, the terminal segments mostly less than 5 mm wide; margins of ultimate segments glabrous or nearly so. Fiddleheads edible when cooked; fronds poisonous when mature; rhizome edible when cooked. —FACU

2. *Dennstáedtia* Bernh. (for A. Dennstedt).

Rhizome long and slender, creeping; stipe to 3 dm, dark brown at base, yellowish above, pilose, blade lanceolate to lance-ovate, acuminate, to 1 m, bipinnate, pilose; sori marginal, small, roundish, borne within a cup formed by a fusion of the true indusium and a modified tooth of the leaf margin.

    1. *D. punctilóbula* (Michx.) Moore (with dotted lobules). Hay-scented Fern. Mixed woods, damp woods, rocky slopes, clearings, woodland borders, meadows, etc. July-October. Map 45. [*Dicksonia p.*].

Family 10. Pteridáceae (Maidenhair Fern Family)

Perennial. Rhizomes often short, scaly, sometimes also pubescent. Blade often scaly and/or pubescent. Sori borne at or just inside the margin, with indusia formed entirely or in part by the revolute margin of the frond. [*Adiantaceae; Polypodiaceae*].

    In addition to those species treated under the genera below *Vittaria lineata* (*Vittariaceae*) has been reported for CT.

a. Fronds palmately divided, the pinnules lobed on only the upper side. (Fig. 25) .... 1. *Adiantum*
a. Fronds pinnately or ternately divided, the pinnules entire or evenly lobed or toothed
      on both sides.
    b. Blade densely hirsute, especially beneath. .... 2. *Cheilanthes lanosa*
    b. Blade glabrous or essentially so.
        Median and upper portion of rachis green. .... 3. *Cryptogramma stelleri*
        Median and upper portion of rachis black or purplish. .... 4. *Pellaea*

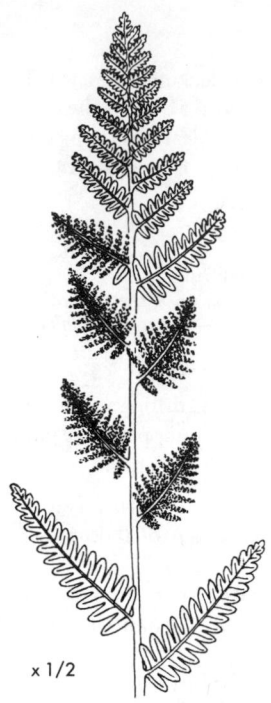

× 1/2

21. *Osmunda claytoniana.* Section of
frond with fertile pinnae.

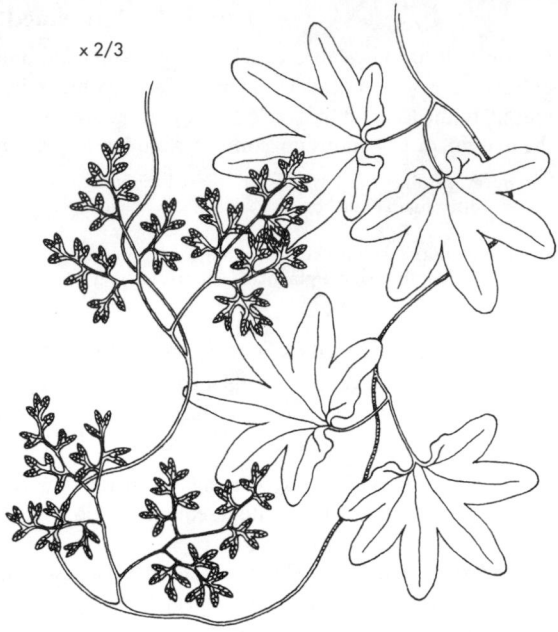

× 2/3

23. *Lygodium palmatum.* General habit.

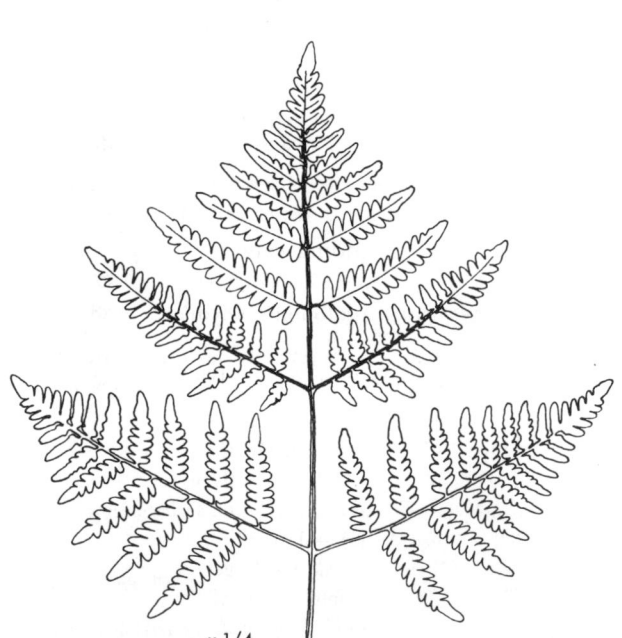

× 1/4

24. *Pteridium aquilinum.* Blade with three main divisions.

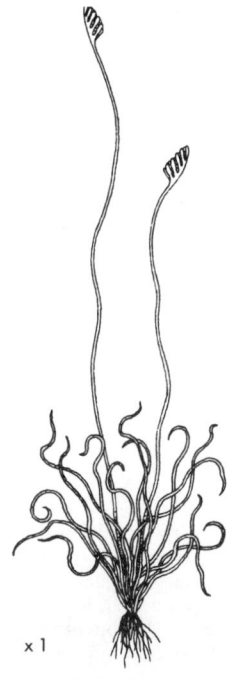

× 1

22. *Schizaea pusilla.* General habitat.

40. *Osmunda cinnamomea*

41. *Osmunda claytoniana*

42. *Schizaea pusilla*

43. *Lygodium palmatum*

44. *Pteridium aquilinum*

45. *Dennstaedtia punctilobula*

1. Adiántum L. Maidenhair. (Unwetted, the foliage shedding water).

Rhizome short and creeping; frond to 0.8 m tall, stipe equalling to longer than the blade, glabrous, lustrous, dark brown, blade (in ours) reniform-suborbicular in outline, 4.5 dm wide, the rachis divided into 2 main branches, the pinnae palmately arranged on the upper sides of each branch, and the pinnules lobed on only the upper side; sori linear, concealed beneath the reflexed margin of the pinnule which forms a false indusium.

1. *A. pedátum* L. (palmately forking). Maidenhair-Fern. Moist, rich hardwood forests and along streams. July-September. Fig. 25, Map 46. Said to be poisonous. (It has recently been concluded that *A. pedatum* in eastern North America is a complex composed of *A. pedatum* and the following 2 species [Cathy A. Paris, Rhodora Vol. 93, No. 874, April 1991]). —FAC

A. aleúticum (Ruprecht) Paris. Distinguishable from *A. pedatum* largely in having medial ultimate segments of the frond long-triangular (medial ultimate segments are ± oblong in *A. pedatum*). On serpentine soils. (Ne. Asia). Reported for ME and VT. [*A. pedatum* var. *aleuticum*].

A. viridimontánum Paris. Similar to *A. aleuticum* but distinguishable largely in having medial ultimate segments of the frond borne on stalks generally longer than 0.9 mm. (medial ultimate segments borne on stalks shorter than 0.9 mm in *A. aleuticum*). Serpentine soils. Reported for Lamoille County, VT.

2. Cheilánthes Sw. Lip Fern (Marginal flower; from the marginal sori).

Rhizome short, creeping; small evergreen ferns, fronds tufted, stipe dark and shining, pubescent, blade lanceolate, 2-3 times pinnate, in ours densely hirsute, especially beneath, with jointed, rusty hairs; sori roundish, marginal, covered by the reflexed margins of the leaf segments.

   1. *C. lanósa* (Michx.) D. C. Eat. (clothed). Hairy Lip-Fern. Rocks, cliffs and outcroppings. July-September. Map 47. Endangered in CT.

3. Cryptogŕamma R. Br. Rock-brake (Hidden line; from the lines of sporangia concealed by the reflexed leaf margins).

Rhizome (in ours) slender and creeping; small, glabrous, evergreen ferns, stipe greenish or straw colored, rachis green except at base, blade ovate, twice pinnate; fertile fronds taller than the sterile, with narrow, entire segments, sori marginal, in a confluent line, covered by the reflexed margins of the leaf segments.

   1. *C. stélleri* (Gmel.) Prantl (for its discoverer). Slender Cliff-Brake. Moist, calcareous cliffs, rocks and ledges. June-September. Fig. 26, Map 48. (Asia). Endangered in CT. —FACU-

4. Pellaéa Link Cliff-Brake (from the Greek meaning dusky).

Rhizome short; small to medium-size evergreen ferns, fronds tufted, stipe and rachis glabrous or hirsute, or purplish, shining, blade once-3 times pinnate; fertile frond taller than the sterile, with narrower divisions, sori marginal, in a confluent line, covered by the reflexed margins of the leaf segments.

Rachis strongly pubescent, at least on the upper side. .... 1. *P. atropurpurea*
Rachis glabrous, or only slightly pubescent. .... 2. *P. glabella*

   1. *P. atropurpúrea* (L.) Link (blackish-purple). Purple Cliff-Brake. Exposed to shaded calcareous rocks, cliffs and ledges. June-September. Fig. 27, Map 49. Endangered in RI.
   2. *P. glabélla* Mett. ex Kuhn (smoothish). Smooth Cliff-Brake. Damp, shaded calcareous rocks, cliffs and ledges. June-September. Map 50. Endangered in CT. [*P. atropurpurea* var. *bushii*]. Our plants are subsp. *glabella*.

Family 11. Polypodiáceae (Polypody Family)

Perennial. Rhizome creeping and branching. Stipe glabrous (in ours), blade evergreen, deltoid to oblong-lanceolate, pinnatifid. Sori large and round, without an indusium.

1. Polypódium L. (early Greek name) Polypody.
Same characters as the family.

   1. *P. virginiánum* L. (virginian). Rock-Polypody. Rocks, rocky woods and slopes. July-September. Map 51. (E. Asia). [*P. vulgare* var. *virginianum*].
   Rhizome is apparently used as a sweetener and in relief of respiratory problems; also used as a purgative for children.
   P. appalachiánum Haufler & Windham. Recently recognized as distinct from *P. virginianum*, this species has also been attributed to our range. It may be distinguished from the latter species in having blades widest near the base and pinnules acute to narrowly rounded (blades widest near middle and pinnules obtuse to rounded in *P. virginianum*).

Family 12. Blechnáceae (Chain-Fern Family)

Perennial. Rhizome long, creeping, branched. Stipe as long or longer than blade, glabrous and shiny, straw colored to purplish, blade oblong-lanceolate. Sterile and fertile frond similar or dimorphic, 1-2 times pinnatifid or pinnate-pinnatifid. Sori elongate, in chain-like rows along the midrib of pinnae and segments, each covered by an indusium. [*Polypodiaceae*].

1. Woodwárdia Smith (for T. Woodward) Chain-Fern.
Same characters as the family.

Sterile and fertile fronds dissimilar; sterile frond deeply pinnatifid, the pinnae merely
          crenate or serrulate .... 1. *W. areolata*
Sterile and fertile fronds similar; sterile frond pinnate, the pinnae pinnatifid. (Fig. 28) .. 2. *W. virginica*

    1. W. areoláta (L.) Moore (with areoles). Netted Chain-Fern. Acid swamps and moist to wet woods. July-October. Map 52. Endangered in NH. [*Lorinseria a.*]. —FACW+
    2. W. virgínica (L.) Smith (Virginian). Virginia Chain-Fern. Bogs, deciduous or coniferous swamps, often in shallow water, and damp woods. June-August. Fig. 28. Map 53. [*Anchistea v.*]. —OBL

Family 13. Aspléniaceae (Spleenwort Family)

Perennial. Rhizome short-creeping to erect. Small, mostly evergreen ferns, fronds clustered, stipe wiry, glabrous, green to black, blade pinnatifid to bipinnate, or (in *A. rhizophyllum*) fronds simple and entire, rooting at tip. Sori inside the leaf margin, elongate, straight or slightly curved, separate, but becoming confluent with age, indusia superior. [*Polypodiaceae*].

1. Asplénium L. Spleenwort (early Greek name for a fern supposed to cure diseases of the spleen).
Same characters as the family

a. Fronds simple and entire, rooting at tip. (Fig. 29) .... 1. *A. rhizophyllum*
a. Fronds pinnate or pinnatifid, not rooting at tip.
  b. Rachis black to mahogany colored, at least below the middle.
    c. Pinnae less than 2 times as long as wide. .... 2. *A. trichomanes*
    c. Pinnae 2 times or more as long as wide.
      Fertile and sterile fronds not differentiated; at least the lowest
        pinnae pinnatifid .... 3. *A. bradleyi*
      Fertile frond stiffly erect, sterile frond arched or recurved; pinnae usually
        not pinnatifid, merely with 1 basal lobe and crenate or serrate. .... 4. *A. platyneuron*
  b. Rachis green throughout.
    d. Fronds once pinnate, the pinnae merely crenate. .... 5. *A. trichomanes-*
                                                                  ramosum
    d. Fronds bipinnate or pinnate-pinnatifid.
      Pinnules rhombic to deltoid; stipe green throughout. .... 6. *A. ruta-muraria*
                                                                          var. *cryptolepis*
      Pinnules ovate to elliptic; stipe brown at base.
        Fronds lanceolate to ovate, not caudate, pinnae cleft or compound. .... 7. *A. montanum*
        Fronds lance-linear, long-attenuate to a caudate tip, pinnae
          merely toothed. .... 8. *A. pinnatifidum*

    1. A. rhizophýllum L. (rooting leaf). Walking Fern. Shaded, mostly calcareous rock and ledges. June-October. Fig. 29, Map 54. Endangered in RI. [*Camptosorus rhizophyllus*].
    2. A. trichómanes L. (placed in the genus *Trichomanes* by pre-Linnaean botanists). Maidenhair-Spleenwort. Rock crevices, mostly calcareous, in rich, shaded woods. June-September. Map 55. (Eurasia).

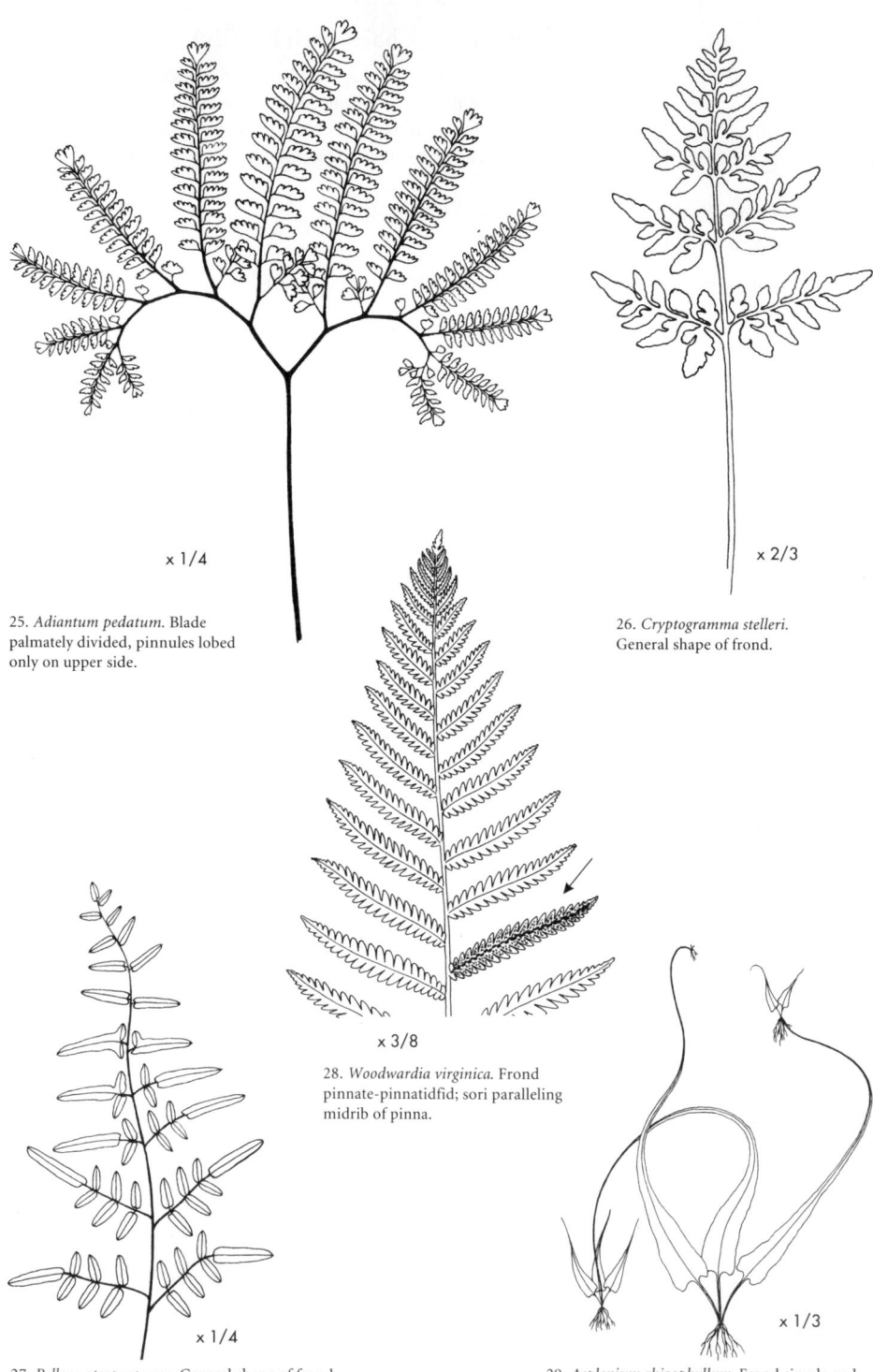

x 1/4

25. *Adiantum pedatum*. Blade palmately divided, pinnules lobed only on upper side.

x 2/3

26. *Cryptogramma stelleri*. General shape of frond.

x 3/8

28. *Woodwardia virginica*. Frond pinnate-pinnatidfid; sori paralleling midrib of pinna.

x 1/4

27. *Pellaea atropurpurea*. General shape of frond.

x 1/3

29. *Asplenium rhizophyllum*. Frond simple and entire, rooting at tip.

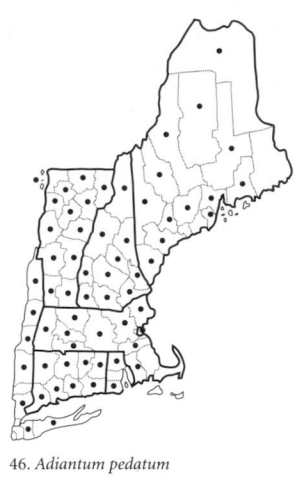

46. *Adiantum pedatum*

47. *Cheilanthes lanosa*

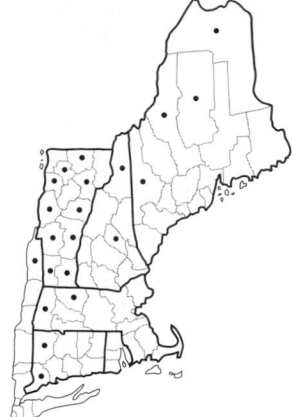

48. *Cryptogramma stelleri*

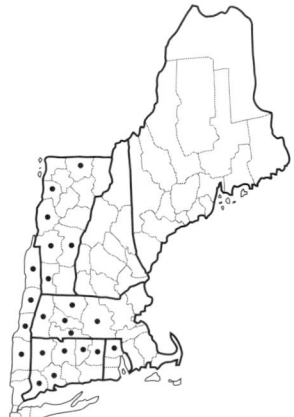

49. *Pellaea atropurpurea*

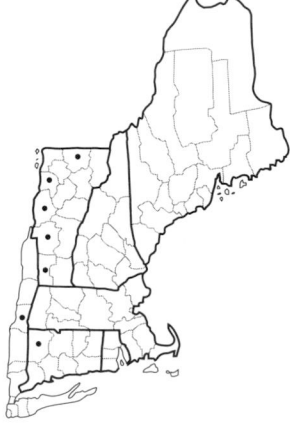

50. *Pellaea glabella*

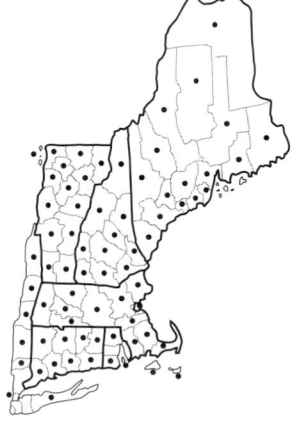

51. *Polypodium virginianum*

52. *Woodwardia areolata*

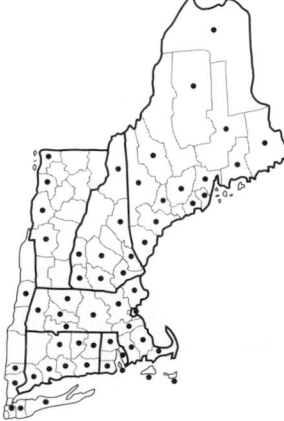

53. *Woodwardia virginica*

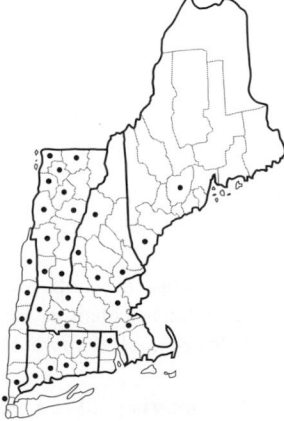

54. *Asplenium rhizophyllum*

3. *A. brádleyi* D. C. Eat. (for its discoverer). Bradley's Spleenwort. Crevices in acidic rocks and cliffs. June-September.

4. *A. platyneúron* (L.) B.S.P. (broad-nerved). Ebony-Spleenwort. Rich or rocky woods, rocky banks, wooded slopes, rocks and crevices in ledges. July-September. Map 56. Our plants include var. *platyneuron* and the following var.:

var. *incísum* (Howe) Robins. Pinnae linear to linear-lanceolate, tapering to acute tips (pinnae narrowly ovate to oblong or oblong-lanceolate in the typical var.). —FACU

A. x ebenoídes R. R. Scott ex Berkeley is a hybrid between *A. platyneuron* and *A. rhizophyllum*.

5. *A. trichómanes-ramósum* L. Green Spleenwort. Crevices and talus of calcareous rocks and ledges. June-September. Map 57. (Eurasia, Greenland). Endangered in ME and NY. [*A. viride*].

6. *A. rúta-murária* L. Wall-Rue Spleenwort. Calcareous rock crevices, cliffs and ledges. June-September. Map 58. Represented with us as var. *cryptólepis* (Fern.) Wherry. [*A. cryptolepis*]. A lotion made with the fronds can be used in treating eye discomfort; also reported as useful in stopping bleeding of small wounds.

A. x clermòntiae Syme. A hybrid between *A. ruta-muraria* and *A. trichomanes*.

7. *A. montánum* Willd. (montane). Mountain Spleenwort. Shaded or sheltered crevices of non-calcareous rocks and cliffs. June-September. Map 59. Endangered in MA and RI.

8. *A. pinnatífidum* Nutt. (*pinnatifid*). Rock crevices and acid soil. June-September. Reported for CT.

Family 14. Thelypteridáceae (Marsh Fern Family)

Perennial. Rhizomes long and slender, scaly and sometimes pubescent. Stipe scaly and hairy to glabrous, sterile and fertile fronds similar or nearly so, bipinnatifid or pinnate-pinnatifid. Sori round, indusium present or absent. [*Polypodiaceae*].

Indusium superior, in center of sporangium. .... 1. *Thelypteris*
Indusium lacking .... 2. *Phegopteris*

1. Thelýpteris Schmidel.

Same characters as the family; indusium present. [*Dryopteris*].

Lowest pinnae rudimentary, less than 2 cm long. .... 1. *T. noveboracensis*
Lowest pinnae well developed, more than 2 cm long.
    Veins all simple; indusia glandular-margined; lowest pinnae usually pointing
        downward .... 2. *T. simulata*
    Veins, or many of them, forked; indusia ciliate, rarely glabrous; lowest pinnae
        horizontally spreading. .... 3. *T. palustris* var.
                                                  pubescens

1. *T. noveboracénsis* (L.) Nieuwl. (of New York). New York Fern. Rich, moist deciduous woods, mixed woods, streambanks, wooded slopes and thickets. Map 60. July-September. [*Dryopteris n.; Aspidium n.; T. thelypteroides*]. —FAC

2. *T. simuláta* (Davenp.) Nieuwl. (imitating). Massachusetts Fern. Deciduous and coniferous swamps, swamp borders and mixed woods. July-September. Map 61. [*Aspidium s.; Dryopteris s.*]. —FACW

3. *T. palústris* Schott. Marsh Fern. Wooded swamps, wet woods and thickets, marshes, bog margins. June-September. Represented throughout our range. [*Dryopteris thelypteris; Aspidium t.; T. thelypteroides*]. Represented with us as var. *pubescens* (Lawson) Fern. —FACW+

2. Phegópteris (C. Presl) Fee.

Similar to *Thelypteris*; indusium lacking. [*Dryopteris; Thelypteris*].

Lowest pair of pinnae spreading horizontally or slightly upward, usually confluent
   with the pair immediately above by their bases; fronds about as wide
   as long. (Fig. 30) .... 1. *P. hexagonoptera*
Lowest pair of pinnae usually pointing downward, separated from the pair
   immediately above; fronds usually longer than wide. .... 2. *P. connectilis*

1. *P. hexagonóptera* (Michx.) Fee. (six-cornered fern). Broad Beech-Fern.
Rich, often moist woods and wooded slopes. July-September. Fig. 30, Map 62. [*Dryopteris h.; Thelypteris h.*]. —FAC

2. *P. connectilis* (Michx.) Watt. Long Beech-Fern. Rich, moist woods and moist cliffs. July-August. Map 63. (Eurasia). [*Dryopteris phegopteris; Phegopteris polypodioides; Thelypteris phegopteris*].

Family 15. Dryopteridáceae (Wood Fern Family)

Perennials with creeping or erect rhizomes. Fronds hairy or scaly, blades simple to variously divided. Sporangia mostly borne in dot-like to elongate clusters (sori) on the undersides of the blades, inside from the margin, often with a membrane (indusium), this either covering, beneath or at one side of the sorus and mostly entire (cleft into segments in *Woodsia*). Sterile and fertile fronds mostly alike in appearance, differing sometimes only in size except in *Onoclea* and *Pteretis* in which the fertile fronds are modified, the margins inrolled and concealing the sporangia, forming berry-like or cylindric divisions which are brown at maturity. [*Polypodiaceae*].

a. Fertile fronds modified, the margins inrolled and concealing the sporangia, brown
     at maturity, the modified pinnae with berry-like divisions or cylindric.
   Fertile pinnae with distinct berry-like divisions; sterile frond with lowest pinnae
      longer than the median. (Fig. 24). .... 1. *Onoclea sensibilis*
   Fertile pinnae cylindric; the divisions cohering, not berry-like; sterile frond with
      lowest pinnae shorter than the median .... 2. *Matteuccia*
                                                         struthiopteris
a. Fertile fronds only slightly or not at all modified, green at maturity, the sporangia
     not enclosed in pinnae with berry-like divisions or cylindric pinnae.
  b. Sori elongate, cresent-shaped or straight.
    c. Fronds bipinnate or pinnate-pinnatifid.
      Fronds bi to tripinnate; sori curved to horseshoe-shaped. .... 3. *Athyrium*
                                                filix-femina
      Fronds pinnate-pinnatifid; sori straight or nearly so. .... 4. *Deparia*
                                                acrostichoides
    c. Fronds simply pinnate, the pinnae at most denticulate or serrulate. .... 5. *Diplazium*
                                                pycnocarpon
  b. Sori circular, reniform or cup-like.
    d. Indusium superior, in center of sporangium.
      e. Pinnae or pinnules truncate or rectangular at base, auricled on upper edge
         near base, entire, serrulate or with bristle-tipped teeth (Fig. 31).
        Fronds bipinnately dissected or once pinnate and dimorphic, the fertile
          frond narrowed at the apex and bearing sori. .... 6. *Polystichum*
        Fronds once pinnate and monomorphic, the fertile frond not narrowed
          at the apex, usually all of the pinnae bearing sori. .... 7. *Cyrtomium*
                                                falcatum
      e. Pinnules not truncate or rectangular at base, not auricled, or if lower
         pinnules slightly auricled, teeth not bristle tipped. .... 8. *Dryopteris*
    d. Indusium inferior, marginal, or absent.
      f. Frond about as long as wide, ternate with 3 principal rachi; indusium lacking. 9. *Gymnocarpium*
      f. Frond longer than wide, pinnate or pinnatifid, with 1 principal rachis;
         indusium present. (Fig. 33).
        Stipe jointed near base, the old stipes remaining as a tuft, or stipe not
          jointed and rachis stipitate-glandular; indusium inferior,
          split into segments .... 10. *Woodsia*
        Stipe not jointed; rachis without scales; indusium hood-shaped, attached
         by its base at one side of sorus .... 11. *Cystopteris*

1. *Onocléa* L. Sensitive Fern.

Rhizome stout, long and creeping, branched; fronds dimorphic, with naked stipes as long or longer than the blades, the sterile to 1 m tall, with deeply pinnatifid, broadly triangular blades, the fertile to 0.6 m tall, bipinnate, with pinnules rolled into distinct, berry-like divisions enclosing the sporangia.

    1. *O. sensíbilis* L. (sensitive; to early frost). Wet open soil, shrub swamps, wooded swamps. June-October. Fig. 31., Map 64. (E. Asia). Poisonous. —FACW

2. *Matteúccia* Todaro Ostrich-Fern.

Rhizome coarse, erect, with underground stolons; fronds dimorphic, the sterile to 2 m tall, forming a circle, stipe scaly, blade pinnate-pinnatifid, oblong-lanceolate, gradually reduced toward the base, abruptly reduced at the tip; fertile fronds to 0.6 m tall, borne in the center of the sterile fronds, stipe sparsely scaly or naked, blade once-pinnate, the pinnae cylindric, crowded and twisted, with cohering divisions enclosing the sporangia. [*Pteretis*].

    1. *M. struthiópteris* (L.) Todaro. Bottomlands and wooded swamps. July-October. Map 65. (Europe, Africa). [*M. pensylvanica; Onoclea s.; Pteretis nodulosa; P. pensylvanica*]. Edible in fiddle-head stage; rhizome edible when cooked. —FACW

3. *Athýrium* Roth (early Greek name).

Rhizome thick, short and creeping; stipe and rachis greenish to straw-colored, sparsely scaly, glabrous or silvery pubescent, blade lanceolate to ovate, pinnatifid or 1-3 times pinnate; sori inside the leaf margin, curved to horseshoe-shaped, indusia superior, shaped like the sori.

x 1/4

30. *Phegopteris hexagonoptera.*
Lowest pair of pinnae confluent with
next pair by their basis.

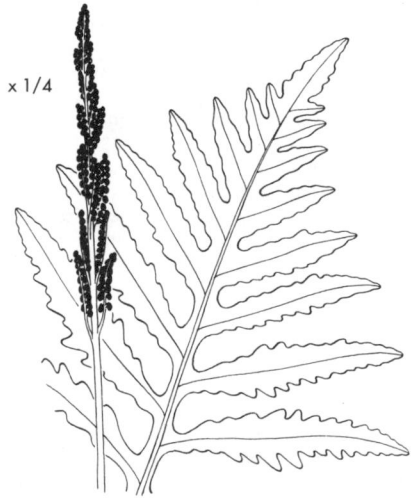

x 1/4

31. *Onoclea sensibilis.*
Sterile and fertile fronds.

55. *Asplenium trichomanes*

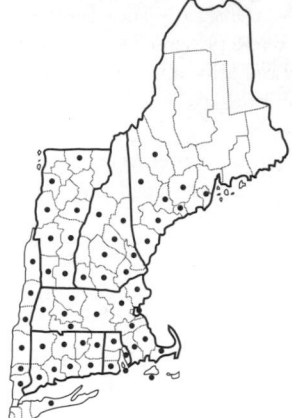

56. *Asplenium platyneuron*

57. *Asplenium trichomanes-ramosum*

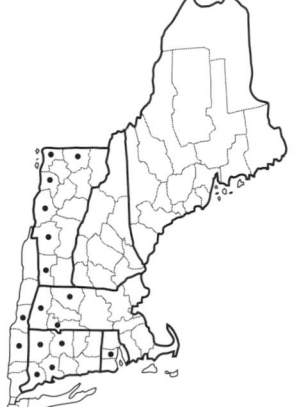

58. *Asplenium ruta-muraria* var. *cryptolepis*

59. *Asplenium montanum*

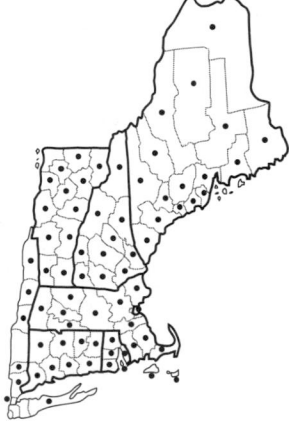

60. *Thelypteris noveboracensis*

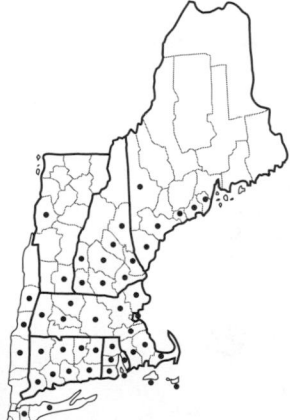

61. *Thelypteris simulata*

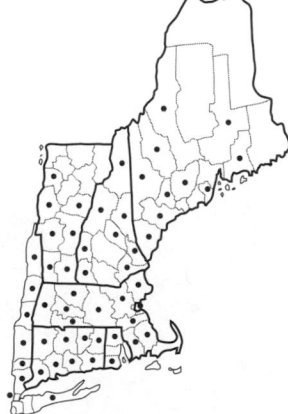

62. *Phegopteris hexagonoptera*

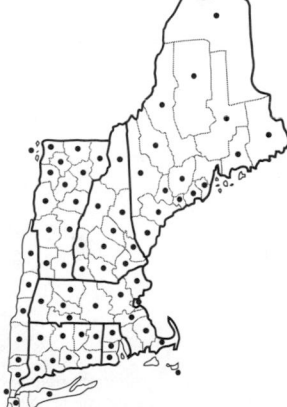

63. *Phegopteris connectilis*

1. *A. filix-fémina* (L.) Roth ex Mertens. Lady-Fern. Moist woodlands, streambanks, swamps and meadows. June-September. Map 66. Represented with us by the following 2 vars.:

var. *angústum* (Willd.) G. Lawson. Stipe about half as long as the blade; basal scales brown to blackish; blade widest near middle; indusia toothed or ciliate, cilia not gland-tipped. [*A. filix-femina var. michauxii; A. angustum*].

var. *asplenioídes* (Michx.) Farwell. Stipe often as long as the beak; basal scales pale to brownish; blade widest near base; indusia with gland-tipped cilia. [*A. filix-femina* var. *a.; A. asplenioides*]. —FAC

4. *Depária* Hook & Grev.

Similar to *Athyrium*; differs primarily in the sori being straight or nearly so. [*Athyrium*].

1. *D. acrostichoídes* (SW.) M. Kato. Silvery Spleenwort. Rich, moist woods and shaded slopes. July-September. Map 67. [*Asplenium a.; Athyrium thelypteroides; Diplazium t.*]. —FAC

5. *Diplázium* Sw.

Similar to *Athyrium* and *Deparia*; differs in the fronds being simply pinnate instead of bipinnate or pinnate-pinnatifid as in the latter 2 genera. [*Athyrium*].

1. *D. pycnocárpon* (Spreng.) M.Brown (with crowded fruits). Glade-Fern. Rich wooded slopes, ravines and rocky woods. July-September. Map 68. Endangered in NH and CT. [*Asplenium p.; Athyrium p.; Homalosorus p.*]. —FAC

6. *Polýstichum* Roth Shield-Fern (early Greek name).

Rhizome stout, erect or short and creeping; stipe densely scaly, blade linear to oblong-lanceolate, once pinnate and dimorphic with fertile frond narrowed at the apex and bearing sori, or bipinnate; rachis and veins scaly, pinnae or pinnules truncate or rectangular at base and auricled on upper edge near base, teeth sometimes bristle-tipped; sori round, indusium superior, in center of sporangium.

a. Fronds bipinnately dissected .... 1. *P. braunii*
a. Fronds once pinnate .... 2. *P. acrostichoides*

1. *P. bráunii* (Spenner) Fee (for its discoverer). Braun's Holly-Fern. Rich woods, wooded slopes and shaded rock slides. June-September. Fig. 32, Map 69. Endangered in MA.

P. x pòtteri Barrington. A hybrid between *P. braunii* and *P. acrostichoides*.

2. *P. acrostichoídes* (Michx.) Schott (resembling *Acrostichum*). Christmas Fern. Woods and rocky slopes. June-September. Map 70. Our plants are var. *acrostichoides.* —FACU

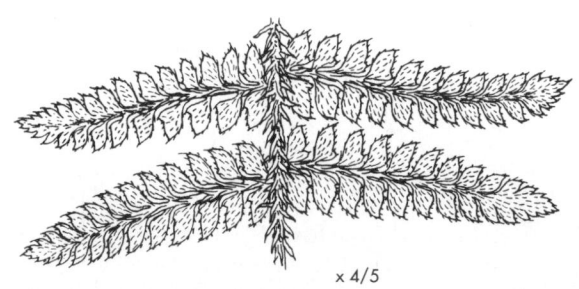

x 4/5

32. *Polystichum braunii.* Frond bipinnate; pinnules rectangular at base.

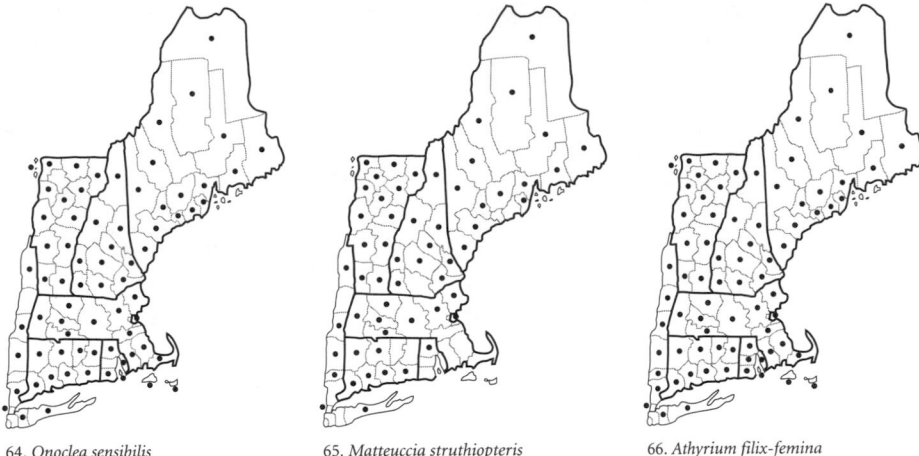

64. *Onoclea sensibilis*   65. *Matteuccia struthiopteris*   66. *Athyrium filix-femina*

7. *Cyrtómium* C. Presl.

Similar to *Polystichum*; fronds are once pinnate and monomorphic, the fertile frond not narrowed at the apex, usually all of the pinnae bearing sori. [*Polystichum*].

   1. *C. falcátum* (L.f.) C. Presl (sickle-shaped). Spreading to walls and urban roadsides. June–September. (Introduced from E. Asia). Reported for CT. [*Polystichum f.*].

8. *Dryópteris* Adans. Shield-Fern (early Greek name).

Rhizome stout, short and erect to slender, long and creeping; frond lanceolate to elliptic, stipe stout to slender, glabrous to scaly, blade ternately compound, pinnatifid or 1-3 times pinnate; sori round, usually set in from margin (infrequently marginal), indusium superior, in center of sporangium. Hybrids abound.

a. Pinnae less than 3 cm long .... 1. *D. fragrans*
a. Pinnae more than 3 cm long.
   b. Sori marginal .... 2. *D. marginalis*
   b. Sori set in from margin.
      c. Frond bipinnate-pinnatifid to tripinnate, the teeth spine- or bristle-tipped.
         d. Basal upper and lower pinnules of lowest pinnae remote, 4 mm or more
            apart; first lower pinnule usually exceeding the one next to it. .... 3. *D. campyloptera*
         d. Basal upper and lower pinnules of lowest pinnae subopposite, rarely more
            than 4 mm apart.
            Blade eglandular; first lower pinnule of lowest pinnae longer than the
               one next to it .... 4. *D. carthusiana*
            Blade glandular; first lower pinnule of lowest pinnae as long or shorter
               than the next one .... 5. *D. intermedia*
      c. Frond pinnate-pinnatifid, the teeth scarcely or not at all bristle-tipped.
         e. Rachis densely chaffy .... 6. *D. filix-mas*
         e. Rachis not or only remotely chaffy.
            Most fronds at least 2 dm wide at widest point. .... 7. *D. goldiana*
            Most fronds less than 2 dm wide at widest point.
               Pinnae more than 8 cm long .... 8. *D. clintoniana*
               Pinnae 8 cm or less long .... 9. *D. cristata*

   1. *D. frágrans* (L.) Schott (fragrant). Fragrant Cliff-Fern. Cliffs and ledges, often calcareous. June–September. Map 71. (Europe). Our plants are var. *remotiúscula* Komarov

   2. *D. marginális* (L.) Gray (marginal). Marginal Shield-Fern. Woods and rocky slopes. June–September. Map 72. [*Aspidium m.*]. —FACU-

67. *Deparia acrostichoides*   68. *Diplazium pycnocarpon*   69. *Polystichum braunii*

70. *Polystichum acrostichoides*   71. *Dryopteris fragrans* var. *remotiuscula*   72. *Dryopteris marginalis*

3. *D. campylóptera* (Kunze) Clarkson. Woods and thickets. June-August. Represented through-out our range. [*D. austriaca; D. spinulosa* var. *americana*]. —FAC+

4. *D. carthusiána* (Vill.) H. P. Fuchs (with minute spines). Spinulose Wood-Fern. Moist woods, thickets and swamp borders. June-August. Map 73.

(Eurasia). Endangered in CT. [*D. spinulosa; D. austriaca* var. *s.*]. —FAC+

5. *D. intermédia* (Muhl. ex Willd.) Gray (intermediate). Woods and thickets. June-August. Represented throughout our range. [*D. austriaca* var. *i.; D. spinulosa* var. *i.*]. —FACU

6. *D. fílix-más* (L.) Schott (old generic name, Male Fern). Male Fern. Rich woods and rocky hillsides, often calcareous. July-September. Map 74. (Greenland; Eurasia; N. Africa). Endangered in ME. [*Aspidium f.*].

Highly effective in treating tapeworm infestations, but also poisonous; works on medicinal plants should be consulted before using.

7. *D. goldiána* (Hook. ex Goldie) Gray. (for its discoverer). Goldie's Fern. Rich, often calcareous woods and rocky hillsides. June-September. Map 75. —FAC+

8. D. clintoniána (D. C. Eat.) Dowell. Rich moist woods. June-August. Map 76. [*D. cristata* var. *clintoniana*]. —FACW+

9. D. cristàta (L.) Gray (crested). Crested Wood-Fern. Rich moist woods, swamps and marshes. June-August. Map 77. (Europe). [*Aspidium c.*]. —FACW+

9. *Gymnocárpium* Newm.

Similar to *Dryoperis*; differs primarily in having no indusium. [*Dryopteris*].

1. G. dryópteris (L.) Newm. Oak-Fern. Rich, deciduous woods, rocky woods and wooded slopes. July-September. Map 78. [*Dryopteris disjuncta; Phegopteris d.*].

G. robertiánum (Hoffm.) Newm. Similar to *G. dryopteris* but with rachis and blades moderately to densely glandular-puberulent on one or both sides (glabrous or sparsely glandular on both sides in *G. dryopteris*). Reported for Vermont. [*Dryopteris r; Phegopteris r.*].

G. jessoénse (Koidzumi) Koidzumi. Similar to *G. robertianum* but with blades glabrous on one surface and basal pinnae and their basal pinnules curving toward apex of leaf and pinna respectively (blades moderately glandular on both sides and basal pinnae and their pinnules straight in *G. robertianum*). Reported for VT, ME and CT. Represented with us as subsp. *párvulum* Sarvela.

10. *Woódsia* R. Br. Woodsia (for J. Woods).

Rhizomes densely tufted; small to medium-size ferns with densely-clustered fronds, stipe often jointed above the base, glabrous or scaly, blade linear-lanceolate to lanceolate, pinnatifid to once or twice pinnate, scaly or scaleless, often hairy or glandular; sori round, indusium inferior, divided into few broad to many filiform lobes.

a. Stipe jointed near base, the old stipes remaining as a tuft; rachis not glandular.
  b. Blade permanently covered with rusty chaff. (Fig. 33). .... 1. *W. ilvensis*
  b. Blade glabrous or nearly so.
    Stipe and rachis glabrous, green or stramineous. .... 2. *W. glabella*
    Stipe and rachis somewhat chaffy, brown to blackish. .... 3. *W. alpina*
a. Stipe not jointed; rachis stipitate-glandular. .... 4. *W. obtusa*

1. W. ilvénsis (L.) R. Br. (of the Island of Elba). Rusty woodsia. Dry exposed rocks, cliffs and ledges. June-September. Fig. 33, Map 79. (Eurasia).

2. W. glabélla R. Br. ex Richards. (smooth). Smooth Woodsia. Moist, mossy calcarious rocks. June-August. Map 80. Endangered in MA and NH.

3. W. alpína (Bolton) S. F. Gray (alpine). Northern Woodsia. Shaded or exposed, damp to dry rocks, cliffs and ledges. June-August. Map 81. (Eurasia). Endangered in VT.

W. x grácilis (Lawson) Butters. A hybrid between *W. alpina* and *W. ilvensis*. (Apparent hybrids between *W. alpina and W. glabella* are also known to occur).

4. W. obtúsa (Spreng.) Torr. (obtuse). Blunt-lobed Woodsia. Cliffs, ledges and rocky woods. May-September. Map 82. Represented with us as subsp. *obtusa*.

11. *Cystópteris* Bernh. Bladder-fern (from the Greek).

Rhizome short and stout to long and creeping; delicate ferns, stipe slender, scaly only toward base, blade lance-linear to lance-ovate or oblong, acute, acuminate or long-attenuate, 2-3 times pinnatifid or pinnate, sparsely hairy on the veins, otherwise glabrous; sori round, indusium hood-shaped, attached by its base at one side of sorus.

Bulbils present on the underside of the frond; blades usually more than 2.5 dm
    long (Fig. 34) .... 1. *C. bulbifera*
Bulbils absent on the underside of the frond; blades usually shorter than 2.5 dm .... 2. *C. fragilis*

1. *C. bulbífera* (L.) Bernh. (bearing bulbs). Bulblet-Fern. Shaded ravines, calcareous rocky slopes, cliffs and rich woods. June-August. Fig. 34, Map 83. [*Filix bulbifera*]. —FAC

2. *C. frágilis* (L.) Bernh. (fragile). Fragile Fern. Rocks and ledges, wooded slopes and moist open woods. June-August. Map 84. (Eurasia). [*C. dickieana*]. Poisonous. —FACU

C. ténuis (Michx.) Desv. Very similar to *C. fragilis* but distinguishable in having pinnae at an angle to the rachis, usually curving toward the blade apex and basal pinnules cuneate at the base (pinnae usually not angled to rachis nor curving toward the blade apex, horizontal and basal pinnules rounded at the base in *C. fragilis*). Throughout our range. [*C. fragilis* var. *mackayi*].

C. protrúsa (Weatherby) R. F. Blasdell. Resembling *C. fragilis* and *C. tenuis* but distinguishable in having an elongate rhizome, sparsely scaly but densely villous with yellow hairs, the growing tip produced several cm beyond the fronds of the season (rhizome short, densely scaly but glabrous, the growing tip not produced beyond the fronds of the season in *C. fragilis* and *C. tenuis*). Reported for CT and MA. [*C. fragilis* var. *p.*].

Family 16. Marsileáceae (Water-Clover Family)

Perennial aquatic or marsh plants, rooting in the mud, having creeping, superficial rhizomes and filiform or (in ours) long petioled, commonly floating leaves which are divided into 4 leaflets. Sporangia enclosed in sporocarps (fruit cases) these borne singly or in small clusters on a peduncle much shorter than the leaf petiole, arising from the rhizome near or at the base of the petiole, or borne laterally on the petiole.

1. *Marsílea* L. (for L. Marsigli).
Same characters as the family.

1. *M. quadrifólia* L. Shallow water of lakes and quiet streams. June-December. Fig. 35, Map 85. (Introduced from Europe). —OBL

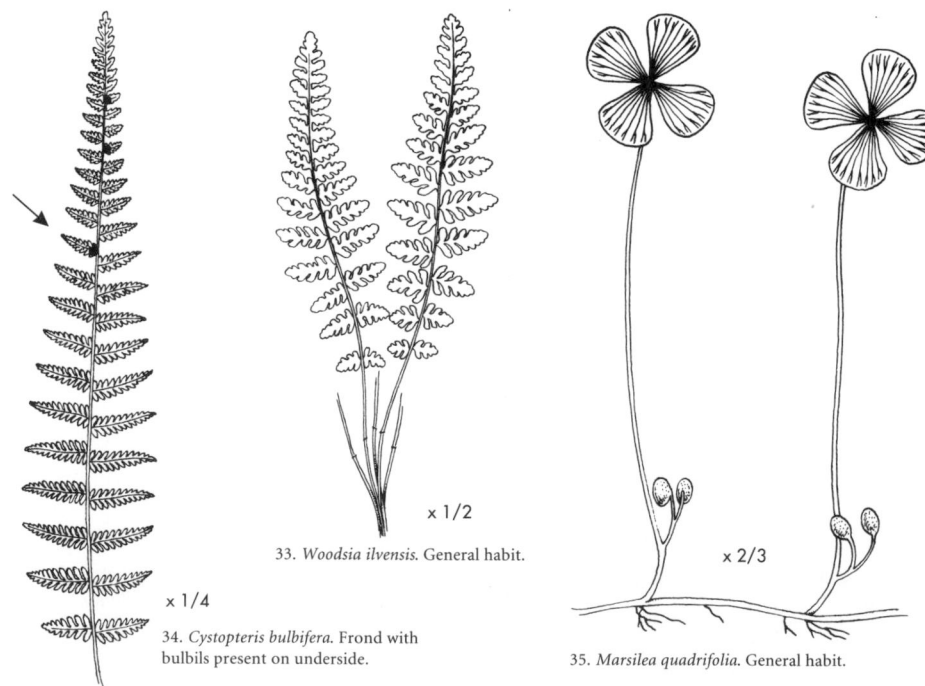

x 1/4

33. *Woodsia ilvensis.* General habit.

x 1/2

34. *Cystopteris bulbifera.* Frond with bulbils present on underside.

x 2/3

35. *Marsilea quadrifolia.* General habit.

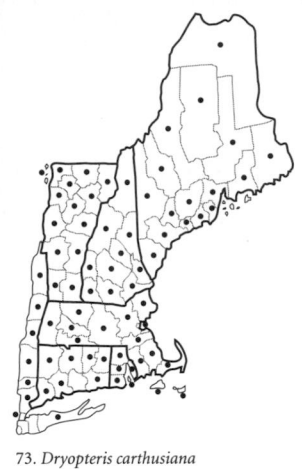

73. *Dryopteris carthusiana*

74. *Dryopteris filix-mas*

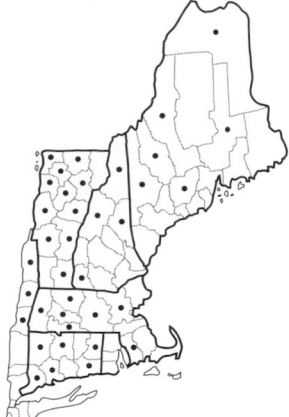

75. *Dryopteris goldiana*

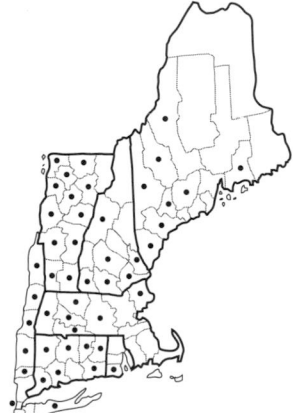

76. *Dryopteris clintoniana*

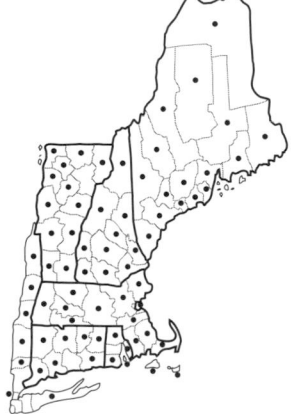

77. *Dryopteris cristata*

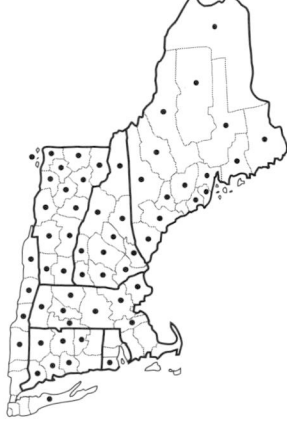

78. *Gymnocarpium dryopteris*

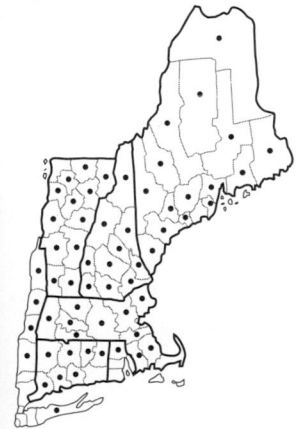

79. *Woodsia ilvensis*

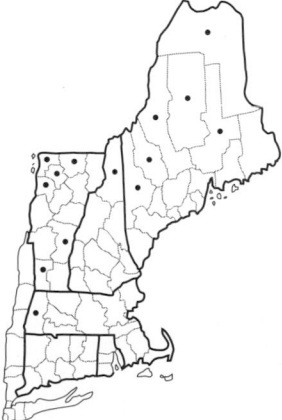

80. *Woodsia glabella*

81. *Woodsia alpina*

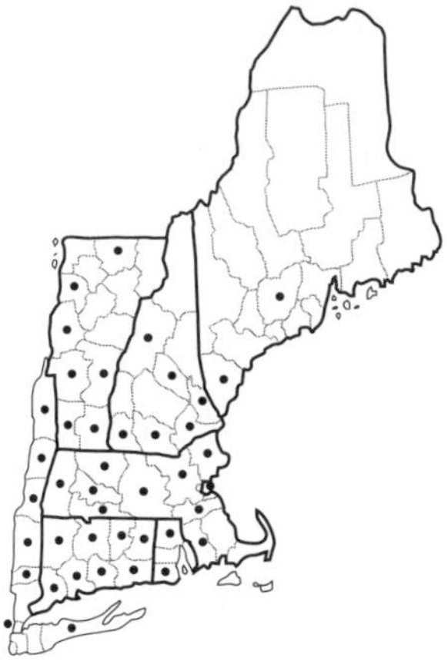

82. *Woodsia obtusa*

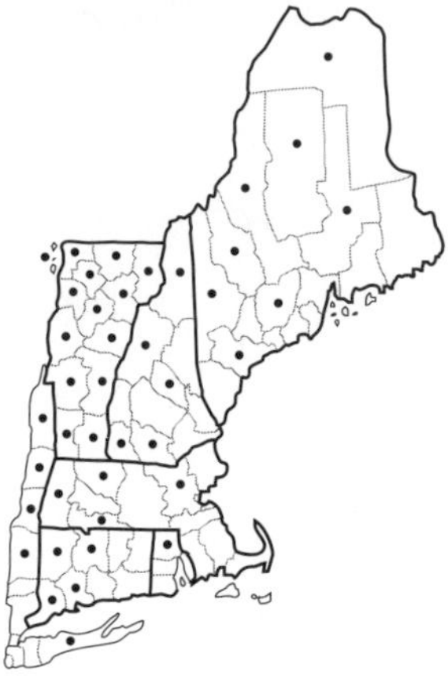

83. *Cystopteris bulbifera*

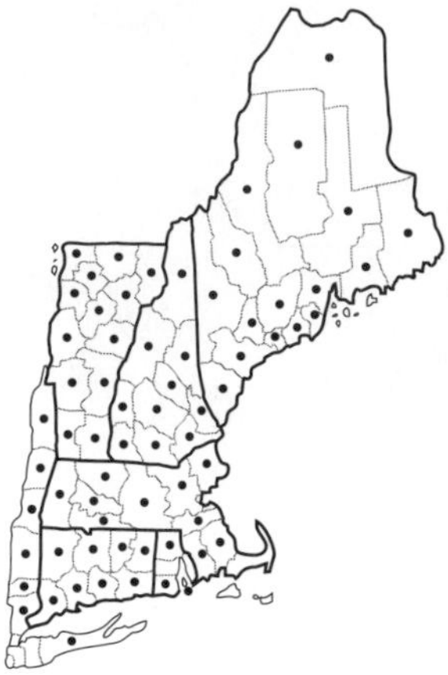

84. *Cystopteris fragilis* and *C. tenuis*

85. *Marsilea quadrifolia*

86. *Salvinia minima*

87. *Azolla caroliniana*

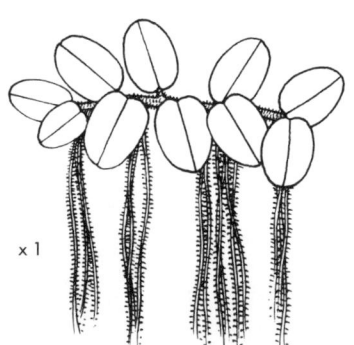

36. *Salvinia minima.* General habit.

37. *Azolla caroliniana.* General habit.

Family 17. Salviniáceae (Floating Fern Family)

Small, annual, floating plants having slender, simple stems bearing clusters of root-like structures beneath. Leaves 2-ranked. Sporangia enclosed in sporocarps (reproductive cases) borne on submerged, dissected leaves.

1. *Salvínia* Seguier Salvinia (For A. Salvini).
Same characters as the family.

    1. *S. mínima* Baker. Ponds, pools and marshes. Fig. 36, Map 86. (Introduced from Mexico). [*S. auriculata; S. natans; S. rotundifolia*].

Family 18. Azolláceae (Water Fern Family)

Small, annual, floating, moss-like plants, often in dense mats, having slender dichotomously branched stems bearing clusters of rootlets beneath. Leaves minute, 2-ranked, imbricated, 2-lobed. Sporangia enclosed in sporocarps borne on the lower leaf lobes.

1. *Azólla* Lam. Water-fern.
Same characters as the family.

Leaves nearly orbicular; 0.5 mm or less long. (Fig. 37). .... 1. *A. caroliniana*
Leaves oblong to ovate; more than 0.5 mm long. .... 2. *A. filiculoides*

    1. *A. caroliniána* Willd. (Carolinian). Lakes and quiet streams. Fig. 37, Map 87. (W.I.). —OBL
    2. *A filiculoídes* Lam. (resembling Filicula). Lakes and quiet streams; escaped from cultivation. Suffolk County NY. (Introduced from farther west or from S. Amer.). —OBL

Division II.
SPERMATÓPHYTA
(Seed-Bearing Plants and Flowering Plants)

Plants producing flowers and/or seeds in season, or flowers replaced by vegetative buds, bulblets or leafy tufts.

Class I. GYMNOSPÉRMAE (Gymnosperms)

Flowers not produced, the seeds naked (not enclosed in an ovary); leaves linear, needle-like or scale-like, mostly evergreen.

Family 19. Taxáceae (Yew Family)

Evergreen trees, or shrubs up to 6 feet tall. Leaves flat, linear, short-petioled, mucronate, spirally arranged, twisted at the petiole so as to form a flat spray with leaves appearing 2-ranked. Plants dioecious, the male cones globose, small, solitary and axillary, consisting of a few scaly, peltate microsporophylles; the ovuliferous short shoot bearing a usually solitary, erect ovule which becomes a bony seed at maturity, the seed surrounded by an aril (globose, fleshy, berry-like orange-red covering open at the end).

1. *Táxus* L. Yew (from the Greek, meaning Yew-tree).
Same characters as the family.

    1. *T. canadénsis* Marsh. (of Canada). American Yew. Deciduous or mixed woodlands. April-May. Fig. 38, Map 88. —FAC

    T. baccàta L. English Yew. Distinguishable from American Yew in being a small
tree with leaves gradually acuminate (*T. canadensis* is a low shrub with leaves abruptly acuminate). Rarely escaped from cultivation. Reported for MA, Nassau and Suffolk counties NY. Foliage and seeds poisonous; pulp of fruit edible.

    T. cuspidáta Sieb. & Zucc. Japanese Yew. A small tree resembling *T. baccata* but with leaves abruptly acuminate. Rarely escaped from cultivation in our range. Reported for MA.

Family 20. Pináceae (Pine Family)

Resinous, mostly evergreen trees. Foliage leaves flat and linear or needle-like, in fascicles, spirally arranged (sometimes appearing 2-ranked) or clustered on short spurs. Plants monoecious, the male cone consisting of an axis bearing spirally arranged microsporophylls, each microsporophyll with 2 microsporangia on its lower surface, the female cone consisting of an axis bearing spirally arranged bracts, each bract subtending a free ovuliferous scale, the scales spirally arranged to form a dry, often woody cone that opens and releases winged seeds.

    Entire family produces edible products; inner bark, young shoots, young cones are all edible. Tea can be made from the needles, which are high in vitamin C. The gums of many of the species, particularly spruce, can be used for chewing.

a. Leaves numerous and clustered on short spurs, or in fascicles of 2-5.
    Leaves numerous, clustered on short spurs, deciduous. (Fig. 39). .... 1. *Larix*
    Leaves in fascicles of 2-5 evergreen. (Fig. 40). .... 2. *Pinus*
a. Leaves neither on spurs nor in fascicles, borne singly.

Leaves flat, attached directly to the twig, leaving a smooth surface on
   falling. (Fig. 41) .... 3. *Abies*
Leaves flat or angular, attached to small, persistent stubs.
   Leaves flat in cross section, with 2 whitish lines beneath. .... 4. *Tsuga canadensis*
   Leaves angular in cross section, uniformly colored. .... 5. *Picea*

1. *Lárix* P. Mill. (Latin name for an old world species). Larch.

Trees with horizontal or ascending branches; leaves deciduous, narrowly linear and needle-like, numerous in circular clusters on short, lateral spurs or scattered along the long shoots of the current year; cones lateral, on short spurs of a previous years growth, globose or subglobose, the male from leafless buds, the female mostly leafy at the base. —Wildl. 1

Mature seed cones more than 1.75 cm long. .... 1. *L. decidua*
Mature seed cones less than 1.75 cm long. .... 2. *L. laricina*

   1. *L. decidua* P. Mill. (deciduous). European Larch. Occasionally spread from cultivation. Map 89. Introduced from Europe. Reported for Putnam, CT. Leaves contain vitamin C.
   2. *L. laricina* (Du Roi) K. Koch (larch-like). American Larch. Swampy woods, damp hillsides and bogs. March-April. Fig. 39, Map 90. —FACW

2. *Pínus* L. Pine (the classical name).

Evergreen trees; primary leaves scale-like, subtending minute branchlets, each bearing a fascicle of 2-5 needle-shaped foliage leaves, the base of the fascicle surrounded by a sheath of 1 or more membranous scale leaves, the fascicle eventually deciduous after 2 or more years; male cones borne in clusters at the base of the current years growth, mature female cones woody, solitary or clustered,

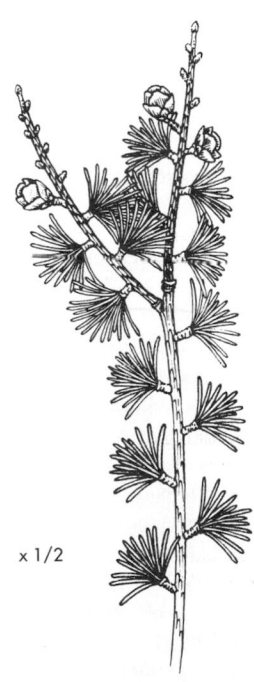

x 2/3

x 1/2

38. *Taxus canadensis.* Branch with male cones and arils.

39. *Larix laricina.* Branch with leaves clustered on short spurs; cones.

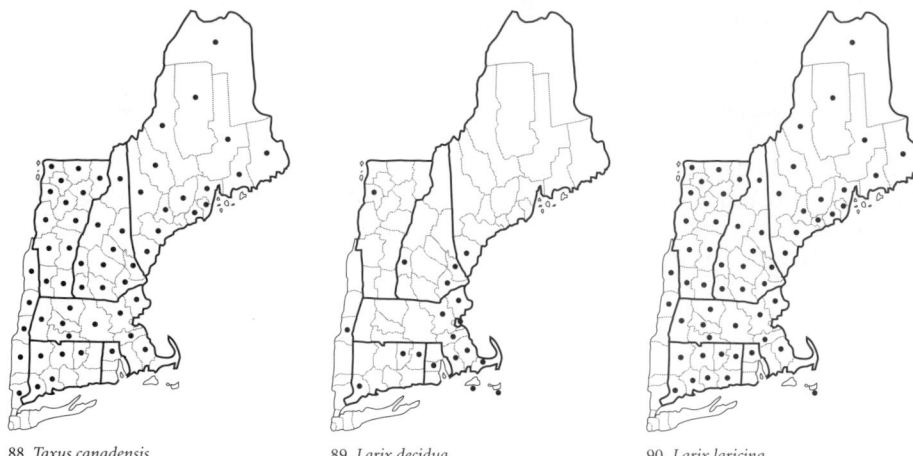

88. *Taxus canadensis*   89. *Larix decidua*   90. *Larix laricina*

borne on the twigs of the preceding years growth, often long persisting, the upper portion of each ovuliferous scale thickened and with a ridge (umbo) which is sometimes spine-bearing. —Wildl. 3

a. Needles in fascicles of 5 .... 1. *P. strobus*
a. Needles in fascicles of 2 or 3.
  b. Needles in fascicles of 3 .... 2. *P. rigida*
  b. Needles in fascicles of 2. (fascicles occasionally with 3 needles in *P. echinata* but most fascicles bearing 2 needles).
    c. Longest needles 7 cm or less in length.
      Mature, unopened seed cones curved, erect; needles 2-3.5 cm long. .... 3. *P. banksiana*
      Mature, unopened seed cones symmetrical, reflexed; needles 3-7 cm long. .... 4. *P. sylvestris*
    c. Longest needles more than 8 cm in length.
      Umbo of ovuliferous scales with a prickle. .... 5. *P. nigra*
      Umbo of ovuliferous scales unarmed .... 6. *P. resinosa*

1. *P. stróbus* L. (ancient name for an incense-bearing tree). White Pine. Woodlands, especially in fertile or well-drained sandy soil but also found in a variety of soil moisture and fertility conditions. May-June. Fig. 40, Map 91. Inner bark can be used to make cough syrup. —FACU

2. *P. rígida* P. Mill. (stiff). Pitch-Pine. Dry sandy or rocky soil. April-May. Map 92. —FACU

3. *P. banksiána* Lamb. (for Sir Joseph Banks). Jack-Pine. Dry sandy or rocky, barren soil. May-June. Map 93. —FACU

4. *P. sylvéstris* L. (of woodland). Scotch Pine. Much cultivated and occasionally escaped. Map 94.

P. múgo Turra. Swiss Mountain Pine. Closely resembling *P. sylvestris* but differing in having nearly sessile cones (cones short-stalked in *P. sylvestris*). Rarely spread from cultivation. Reported for MA, ME and Cheshire, Coos and Merrimack Counties, NH.

P. virginiána P. Mill. Jersey Pine. Resembling *P. sylvestris* and *P. mugo* but distinguishable in having umbo of ovuliferous scales with a prickle (umbo unarmed in the latter 2 species). Southern. Endangered in NY; reported for Nassau and Westchester counties.

5. *P. nígra* Arnott (black). Austrian Pine. Occasionally escaped from cultivation. Map 95. (Introduced from Europe).

P. echináta P. Mill. Yellow Pine. Resembling *P. nigra* but distinguishable in having glaucous twigs, flexible leaves and dull brown cones (twigs not glaucous, leaves stiff and cones yellowish and glossy in *P. nigra*). Southern. Reported for Suffolk County NY.

P. thunbérgiana Franco. Distinguishable from *P. nigra* and *P. echinata* in having sheath at base of fascicle terminating in 2 long filaments (sheath not ending in long filaments in the latter 2 species).

Rarely spread from cultivation. Reported for Hampshire and Nantucket Counties MA, Nassau and Suffolk Counties, NY. [*P. thunbergii*]

6. *P. resinósa* Ait. (resinous). Red Pine. Dry woodlands. May-June. Map 96. Endangered in CT. —FACU

3. *Ábies* P. Mill. Fir (Latin name for an old world species).

Evergreen trees; leaves flat, linear, sessile and leaving a smooth round scar on falling, spirally arranged but twisted at the base and forming a flat spray with the leaves appearing 2-ranked; male cones pendulous on short stalks from the axils of the previous year's leaves, female cones erect on the upper sides of the branches, the ovuliferous scales individually deciduous from the persistent axis at maturity. —Wildl. 2

In addition to the species below *A. x phanerolepis* has been reported for our range.

1. *A. balsàmea* (L.) P. Mill. (balsamic). Balsam-Fir. Moist woodlands and swamps. May-June. Fig. 41, Map 97. Endangered in CT. —FAC

A. cóncolor (Gordon & Glendinn.) Hildebr. White Fir. Distinguishable from *A. balsamea* in having curved, light blue-green leaves 3.5 cm or more long (leaves straight, dark green above and less than 3.5 cm long in *A. balsamea*). Western; rarely escaped from cultivation in our range. Reported for ME, MA.

4. *Tsúga* (Endlicher) Carr. Hemlock (the Japanese name for one of the species).

Evergreen trees with slender horizontal or drooping branches; leaves flat, linear, with 2 white lines beneath, attached to small, persistent stubs, spirally arranged but twisted at the base and forming a flat spray with the leaves appearing 2-ranked; male cones globose or subglobose, on short stalks from the axils of the previous year's leaves, female cones pendulous, terminal on the previous year's lateral branches. —Wildl. 2

1. *T. canadénsis* (L.) Carr. (of Canada). Moist, often rocky woodlands and hillsides, wooded swamps. April-May. Map 98. —FACU

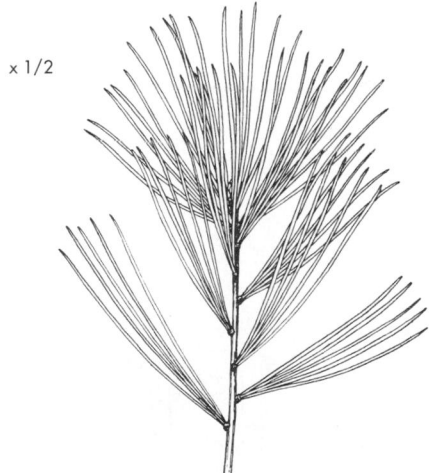

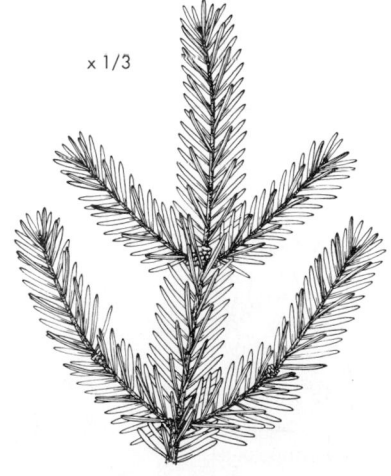

x 1/2

x 1/3

40. *Pinus stobus.* Branch with leaves in fascicles.

41. *Abies balsamea.* Branch showing flat leaves.

5. *Pícea* A. Dietr. Spruce (Latin name for one of the pines).

Evergreen, conical trees; leaves linear, needle-shaped, 4-sided, attached to small, persistent stubs, spreading in all directions; male and female cones borne at the ends of the previous year's branchlets, the female becoming pendulous. Wildl. 2

a. Young twigs pubescent.
  Leaves glaucous; ovuliferous scales with jagged margins. .... 1. *P. mariana*
  Leaves green; ovuliferous scales with entire or barely denticulate margins. .... 2. *P. rubens*
a. Young twigs glabrous.
  Mature seed cones less than 7 cm long; branches erect to spreading. .... 3. *P. glauca*
  Mature seed cones more than 8 cm long; branches pendulous. .... 4. *P. abies*

 1. *P. mariána* (P. Mill.) B.S.P. (of Maryland). Black Spruce. Typical form largely in sphagnum bogs, prostrate form alpine, near timberline. Map 99. Our plants are var. *mariana.* —FACW-

 2. *P. rúbens* Sarg. (reddish). Red Spruce. Coniferous and mixed woodlands and hillsides. May-June. Map 100. [*P. australis; P. rubra*]. —FACU

 3. *P. glaúca* (Moench) Voss (blue-green). White, or Cat Spruce. Typical form in rich, moist soil, depressed form alpine. April-May. Map 101. [*P. canadensis*]. —FACU

 P. púngens Engelm. Colorado Blue Spruce. Distinguishable from *P. glauca* in having blue leaves, not glaucous, lacking strong odor, and mature cones 5.5 cm or more long, (leaves blue-green and glaucous, with strong, disagreeable odor when crushed, mature cones mostly 5 cm or less long in *P. glauca*). Western; rarely escaped from cultivation in our range. Reported for MA, ME.

 4. *P. ábies* (L.) Karst. Norway Spruce. Cultivated as a shade or ornamental tree, occasionally escaped. Map 102. (Introduced from Europe).

Family 21. Cupressáceae (Cypress Family)

Evergreen trees or shrubs. Leaves persistent (some branchlets deciduous in *Taxodium*), opposite or whorled (spirally arranged but appearing 2-ranked in *Taxodium*), mostly small and scale-like or needle-like. Plants monoecious or dioecious, the male cones small, terminal or axillary with few scales (in *Taxodium* male cones clustered in terminal panicles, with spirally arranged scales), the female cones small, terminal or lateral, with few opposite, whorled, or spirally arranged ovuliferous scales closely fused to their subtending bracts, woody, leathery, or fleshy and berry-like (ovuliferous scales then fused together).

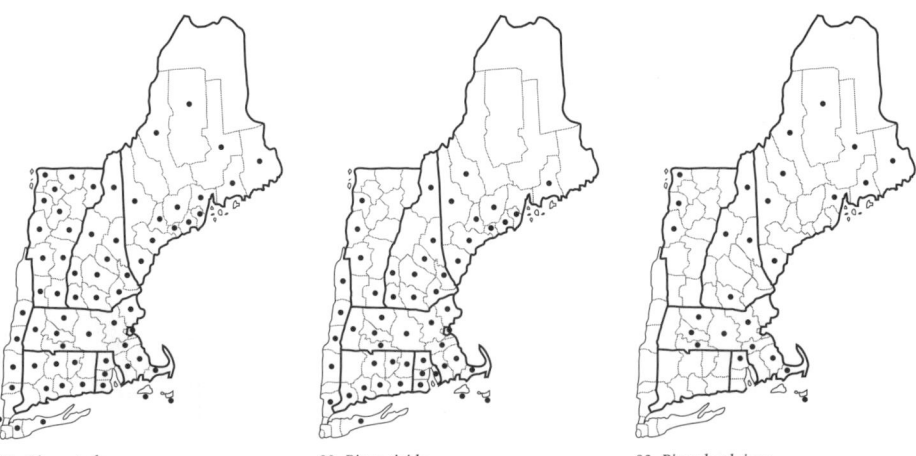

91. *Pinus strobus*   42. *Pinus rigida*   93. *Pinus banksiana*

94. *Pinus sylvestris*

95. *Pinus nigra*

96. *Pinus resinosa*

97. *Abies balsamea*

98. *Tsuga canadensis*

99. *Picea mariana*

100. *Picea rubens*

101. *Picea glauca*

102. *Picea abies*

Leaves needle-like, spirally arranged but appearing 2-ranked; male cones numerous in
    terminal panicles .... 1. *Taxodium*
    distichum
Leaves opposite and scale-like, or needle-like and in whorles of 3; male cones not in
    terminal panicles.
    Female cones elongate, 1 1/2 or more times as long as broad. .... 2. *Thuja occidentalis*
    Female cones globose or subglobose.
        Female cones leathery or woody, of separate ovuliferous scales. .... 3. *Chamaecyparis*
        Female cones berry-like, of fused ovuliferous scales. .... 3. *Juniperus*

1. *Taxódium* Richard Bald Cypress (from the Greek, meaning resembling yew).

Deciduous trees, with a long, bare trunk and horizontal or drooping branches, the trunk base swollen with columnar "knees" in regularly flooded soils; branchlets dimorphic, some persistent, others deciduous in autumn with the leaves; leaves sessile, twisted at the base and forming a flat spray with the leaves appearing 2-ranked; male cones small, globose, numerous in long drooping terminal panicles, female cones with thick, angular ovuliferous scales, in small clusters on the previous year's branches, seeds angled or winged. —Wildl. 1

   1. *T. dístichum* (L.) Richard (two-ranked). Swamps and along rivers and streams. March-April. Fig. 42. Our plants are var. *distichum.* —OBL

2. *Thúja* L. Arbor Vitae (ancient name for a resin-bearing evergreen).

Trees with flat, 2-ranked sprays and small, scale-like imbricated, descussately opposite leaves, the upper and lower flat with a prominent resin gland, the branchlets aromatic when crushed; trees monoecious, the male and female cones on different branches, cones terminal on the branchlets, the male globose, the female ovoid or oblong, with opposite, overlapping scales, seeds winged. —Wildl. 1

   1. *T. occidentális* L. (western). Northern White Cedar. Moist or wet soil, especially in mixed or coniferous swamps. May-June. Fig. 43, Map 103. Endangered in MA. Tea made from the foliage is said to be beneficial in treating rheumatism and as a diuretic. Overdoses (more than several cups at a time) may be toxic. —FACW

3. *Chamaecýparis* Spach White Cedar (from the Greek meaning ground cypress).

Trees with numerous branchlets forming flattened sprays and small, scale-like, imbricated, decussately opposite leaves, the upper and lower flat to rounded, often with a prominent resin gland on the back; trees monoecious, the male and female cones on different branches, cones terminal, the male similar to *Thuja*, the female globose, with opposite scales, seeds narrowly winged. —Wildl. 1

   1. *C. thyoídes* (L.) B.S.P. (like *Thuja*). Atlantic White Cedar. Conifer swamps and bogs, mostly near the coast. April-May. Map 104. —OBL
   C. pisifera (Sieb. & Zucc) Endl. Sawara Cypress. Resembling *C. thyoides* but leaves whitened beneath and cones brown (leaves not whitened beneath and cones bluish in *C. thyoides*). Rarely escaped from cultivation. Reported for MA.

4. *Juníperus* L. Juniper (the classical name).

Shrubs or small trees; leaves scale-like, imbricated, decussately opposite, or linear-subulate and in whorles of 3, both kinds commonly found on the same plant, the scale-like leaves often with a dorsal gland; plants dioecious or occasionally monoecious, cones terminal or axillary, the male oblong or ovoid, with numerous microsporophylls, the female ovoid or globose, the ovuliferous scales coalescent and somewhat fleshy, bluish with a white bloom, the cone resembling a berry, seeds

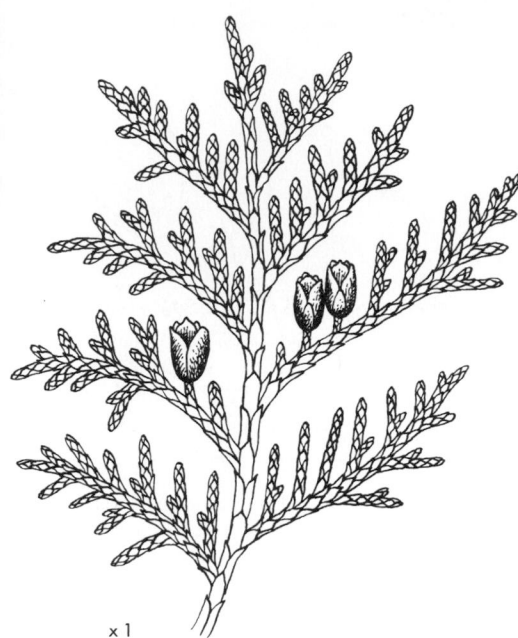

x 1

43. *Thuja occidentalis*. Branch showing
flattened aspect; female cones.

x 1/2

42. *Taxodium distichum*. Branch showing
general arrangement of leaves.

103. *Thuja occidentalis*

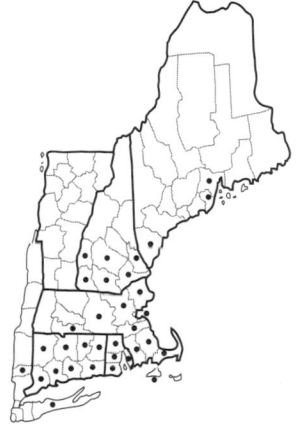

104. *Chamaecyparis thyoides*

wingless, bony, 1-12 per cone. Ripe fruits edible, but should be eaten in small quantities; in large quantities is a kidney irritant; used in flavoring gin and when dried as a coffee substitute. Tea rich in vitamin C can be made from the leaves. —Wildl. 1

Leaves white on upper surface, green below. .... 1. *J. communis*
Leaves green or whitish, but the same on both surfaces.
   Erect tree, more than 1 m tall .... 2. *J. virginiana*
   Prostrate or trailing shrub, usually less than 1 m tall. .... 3. *J. horizontalis*

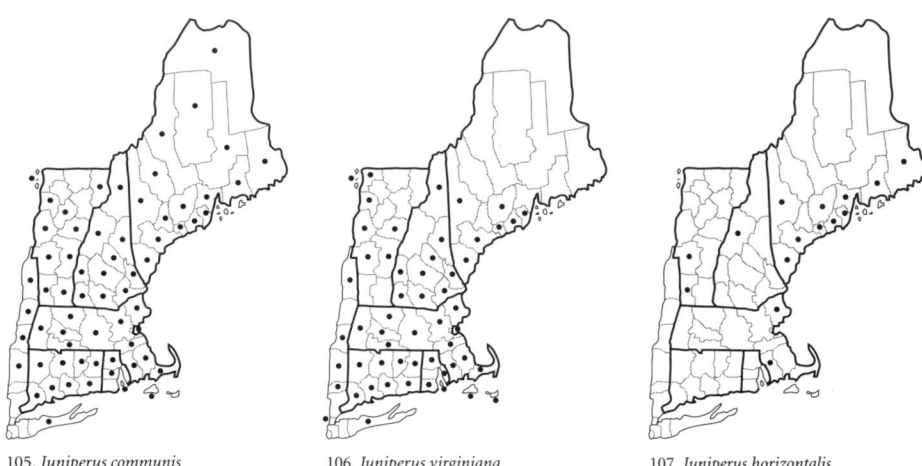

105. *Juniperus communis*   106. *Juniperus virginiana*   107. *Juniperus horizontalis*

1. *J. commúnis* L. (in clumps). Common Juniper. Pastures, dry open woodlands and hillsides. April-May. Map 105. (Europe). Represented with us by the following vars.:

var. depréssa Pursh. Plant decumbent, forming circular patches up to several m wide and 2 m high; leaves straight or nearly so, 1 cm or more long.

var. montána Ait. Plant prostrate and trailing; leaves curved, up to 1 cm long. [*J. communis* var. *alpina*; *J.c.* var. *saxatilis*; *J. nana*; *J. sibirica*].

2. *J. viginiána* L. (Virginian). Red Cedar. Pastures, dry open woodlands and hillsides, barrens. April-May. Map 106. —FACU. Represented with us as var. *virginiana*.

3. *J. horizontális* Moench (lying flat). Creeping Cedar. Rocky or sandy soils, especially along the coast. April-May. Reported for Manchester VT and scattered locations in NH and ME. Map 107. Endangered in NY and NH. —FACU. Represented with us as var. *virginiana*.

Class II. ANGIOSPÉRMAE (Angiosperms)

Flowers produced, the seeds borne within a closed ovary which becomes a fruit or part of a fruit at maturity; leaves mostly deciduous.

Subclass 1.
MONOCOTYLEDÓNEAE (Monocotyledons)

Leaves usually parallel-veined; parts of the flowers usually in 3s, 6s, 9s or many, rarely in 2s or 4s, never in 5s.

Family 22. Typháceae (Cat-tail Family)

Monoecious, perennial marsh or aquatic herbs with creeping rhizomes and fibrous roots. Stems erect, to 2.5 m. Leaves long and linear, erect, those at the base sheathing, appearing before the stems, the stem leaves sessile, alternate, 2-ranked. Flowers imperfect, densely crowded in a long, cylindric, terminal spike, the staminate portion uppermost; perianth represented by bristles, the staminate flowers of 2-7 stamens borne directly on the axis and subtended by long, silky hairs, the pistillate of a single, stipitate, 1-locular, superior ovary containing one ovule, the stipe bearing numerous silky hairs, sterile flowers intermixed with the fertile ones. Fruit a minute, long-stipitate nutlet containing a single seed.

1. Týpha L. Cat-tail (ancient Greek name).
Same characters as the family. Roots, young shoots and young spikes edible; pollen can be used as a flour substitute. —OBL; Wildl. 1

Leaves 7 mm or more wide; pistillate spike 1.5 cm or more in diameter.
   Staminate and pistillate portions usually contiguous; leaves green. (Fig. 44). .... 1. *T. latifolia*
   Staminate and pistillate portions usually separated; leaves glaucous. .... 2. *T. x glauca*
Leaves less than 7 mm wide; pistillate spike less than 1.5 cm in diameter. .... 3. *T. angustifolia*

   1. T. latifólia L. (broad-leaved), Common Cat-tail. Marshes. May-July. Figure 44, Map 108. (Eurasia, N. Africa).
   2. T. x glaúca Godr. A vigorous hybrid between *T. latifolia.* and *T. angustifolia*, often in large sterile stands. Map 109. (Europe, Guatemala). [*T. glauca*].
   3. T. angustifólia L. (narrow-leaved). Narrow-leaved Cat-tail. Marshes, mostly along the coast. June-July. Map 110. (Eurasia).

Family 23. Sparganiáceae (Bur-reed Family)

Monoecious, perennial marsh or aquatic herbs with creeping rhizomes and fibrous roots. Stem erect or floating, simple or branched. Leaves linear, occurring at the base of the stem or before the stems develop, the stem leaves alternate, 2-ranked, sessile and sheathing at the base, submerged forms with narrow, ribbon-like leaves, emergent and submerged leaves with numerous cross veins between the parallel veins, forming squarish cells. Flowers imperfect, densely crowded in globose sessile or peduncled heads in or above the axils of bracteal leaves, forming a spicate or branched inflorescence with the staminate heads uppermost; perianth represented by 3-6 membranous, sepal-like scales, the staminate flowers of usually 5 stamens, the pistillate of a single, superior 1 or 2 locular ovary containing one ovule, with a single style and 1 or 2 stigmas. Fruit an achene with a hard, bony covering containing 1 seed per locule.

1. Spargánium L. Bur-reed (ancient Greek name).
Same characters as the family. —OBL; Wildl. 2

a. Stigmas 2; achenes broadly obpyramidal. .... 1. *S. eurycarpum*
a. Stigma 1; achenes fusiform or elliptic.
   b. Beak of fruit 1.5 mm or less long; fruiting head up to 1.2 cm wide. .... 2. *S. minimum*
   b. Beak of fruit 2 mm or more long; fruiting head more than 1.2 cm wide.
      c. Lowest pistillate head supra axillary. (Fig. 45).
         d. Plant usually erect, emergent; beak of achene about as long as the body. .... 3. *S. erectum*
         d. Plant with weak, floating stems and leaves, aquatic; beak of achene shorter
           than body (except sometimes in no. 4).
           Sepals attached near the base of the stipe; achenes not reddish at base. .... 4. *S. fluctuans*
           Sepals attached at the summit of the stipe; achenes often reddish at base. .. 5. *S. angustifolium*
      c. Lowest pistillate head axillary. (Fig. 46).
         Bracts ascending; body of achene lustrous, more than 5 mm long, beak
           mostly more than 4.5 mm long .... 6. *S. androcladum*
         Bracts spreading; body of achene dull, less than 5 mm long, beak mostly
           less than 4.5 mm long .... 7. *S. americanum*

   1. S. eurycárpum Engelm. ex Gray (broad-fruited). Broad-fruited Bur-reed. Marshes, mud and shallow water. May-August. Map 111.

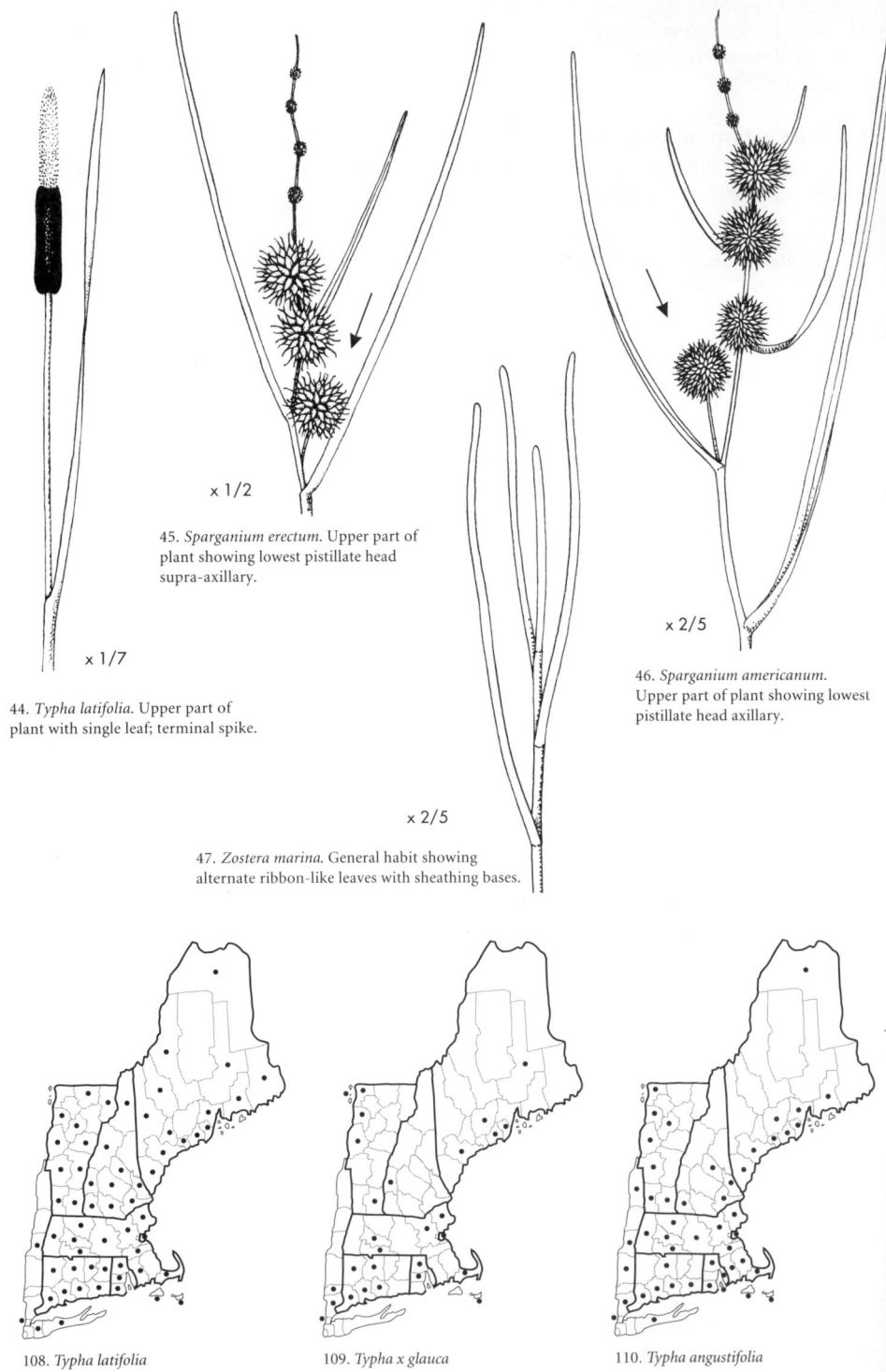

× 1/2

45. *Sparganium erectum.* Upper part of plant showing lowest pistillate head supra-axillary.

× 1/7

44. *Typha latifolia.* Upper part of plant with single leaf; terminal spike.

× 2/5

46. *Sparganium americanum.* Upper part of plant showing lowest pistillate head axillary.

× 2/5

47. *Zostera marina.* General habit showing alternate ribbon-like leaves with sheathing bases.

108. *Typha latifolia*

109. *Typha x glauca*

110. *Typha angustifolia*

2. *S. mínimum* (Hartm.) Wallr. (smallest). Small Bur-reed. Shallow water, in ponds and along streams. June-August. Map 112. (Eurasia). Endangered in MA.

3. *S. eréctum* L. (green-fruited). Green-fruited Bur-reed. Marshes, mud and shallow water. July-September. Fig. 45, Map 113. [*S. chlorocarpum*].

4. *S. flúctuans* (Morong) Robins (fluctuating). Floating Bur-reed. Lakes and ponds. July-September. Map 114.

5. *S. angustifólium* Michx. (narrow-leaved). Narrow-leaved Bur-reed. Deep or shallow water. July-September. Map 115. (Eurasia).

S. emérsum Rehmann. Similar to *S. angustifolium* but with leaves 6 mm or more wide, flat or keeled toward the base (leaves up to 6 mm wide, rounded on the back in *S. angustifolium*). Similar habitats. Northern New England. Represented with us as var. *multipedunculatum* (Morong) Reveal. [*S. multipedunculatum*].

6. *S. andrócladum* (Engelm.) Morong (with staminate branches). Branching Bur-reed. Marshes, mud and shallow water. June-August. Map 116. [*S. lucidum*].

7. *S. americánum* Nutt. (American). Marshes, mud and shallow water. June-August. Fig. 46, Map 117.

Family 24. Zosteráceae (Eelgrass Family)

Submersed, monoecious, grass-like, marine perennial with creeping rhizomes. Stems jointed, flattened, simple or branched. Leaves alternate, 2-ranked, long and linear, ribbon-like, entire and obtuse, sheathing the joints of the stem. Flowers imperfect, naked, the staminate and pistillate flowers alternating in 2 rows on one side of a short, flat spadix enclosed within the sheathing base of a leaf; staminate flowers consisting of a single sessile, 1-celled anther, pistillate flowers a single one-locular, superior, 1-ovulate ovary with a short style and 2 slender stigmas; fruit an oblong-ovoid, beaked achene. [*Najadaceae*].

1. *Zostéra* L. Eelgrass (from the Greek, meaning belt, referring to the sheathing bases of the leaves at the joints of the stem).
Same characters as the family. —Wildl. 2

1. *Z. marína* L. (of the sea). Shallow water in sheltered bays and in seaside ditches and streams. Summer. Fig. 47, Map 118. Represented with us as var. *stenophýlla* Aschers. & Graebn. [*Z. stenophylla*]. —OBL

Family 25. Potamogetonáceae (Pondweed Family)

Monoecious perennials of fresh (rarely brackish or saline) ponds and streams with slender rhizomes, these sometimes producing tubers at the apex. Stems jointed, simple or branched. Leaves alternate (or the uppermost opposite), 2-ranked, petiolate or sessile, stipulate, the stipules free or connate with the base of the leaf or petiole, the floating leaves, if present, lanceolate or ovoid, the submerged linear to lanceolate. Flowers perfect, in heads or cylindric spikes with 1-several whorles of separate or approximate flowers, the spikes peduncled, axillary, usually above water at flowering; stamens 4, the anthers sessile, ovaries 4, one-locular, superior, 1-ovulate, separate, styles short or absent, the stigmas sessile. Fruit of 4 ovoid or subglobose, usually beaked achenes. [*Najadaceae*].

In addition to the taxa treated below *Cymodocea filiformis* (*Cymodoceaceae*) has been reported for NH.

111. *Sparganium eurycarpum*

112. *Sparganium minimum*

113. *Sparganium erectum*

114. *Sparganium fluctuans*

115. *Sparganium angustifolium*

116. *Sparganium androcladum*

117. *Sparganium americanum*

118. *Zostera marina*

1. *Potamogéton* L. Pondweed (ancient Greek name).

Same characters as the family. —OBL; Wildl. 4

a. Submerged leaves filiform, ribbon-like or linear, less than 5 mm wide.
  b. Leaves auricled at base, stiffly 2-ranked, serrulate toward tip. (Fig. 48). .... 1. *P. robbinsii*
  b. Leaves not as above.
    c. Stipules adnate to the leaf base, forming a sheath.
      d. Stipules adnate for a distance of 10 mm or more; peduncles 2 cm or longer,
        flowers in separated whorles; achenes plump.
        e. Stem dichotomously branched from most joints; leaves sharp
          pointed. (Fig. 49). .... 2. *P. pectinatus*
        e. Stem not dichotomously branched; leaves blunt or short apiculate.
          Sheaths loose and inflated, much thicker than the stem. .... 3. *P. vaginatus*
          Sheaths tightly clasping, only slightly thicker than the stem. .... 4. *P. filiformis*
                                          var. *alpinus*
      d. Stipules adnate for less than 10 mm; peduncles mostly less than 2 cm,
        flowers in continuous spikes; achenes strongly flattened.
        f. Leaves linear, 0.5-2 mm wide, obtuse or acute.
          Leaves rounded at tip, adnate part of stipule at least as long
             as the free tip .... 5. *P. spirillus*
          Leaves pointed, adnate part of stipule shorter than the free tip. .... 6. *P. diversifolius*
        f. Leaves setaceous, up to 0.6 mm wide, tapered to a long point. .... 7. *P. bicupulatus*
    c. Stipules free from the base.
      g. Stems strongly flattened, two-thirds to three-fourths as wide as the leaves. ...... 8. *P. zosteriformis*
      g. Stems terete, or if somewhat flattened less than half as wide as the leaves.
        h. Submerged leaves with a conspicuous reticulate band along the midrib,
          readily seen by holding leaf to the light. (Fig. 50). .... 9. *P. epihydrus*
        h. Submerged leaves lacking a conspicuous median band.
          i. Floating leaves usually present. (Fig. 51).
            j. Floating leaves not more than 8 mm wide.
              Floating leaves 2-4 mm wide, submerged leaves tapering to a bristle
                tip; fruit not keeled .... 10. *P. lateralis*
              Floating leaves 4-8 mm wide, submerged leaves merely acute;
                fruit with a low, rounded keel .... 11. *P. vaseyi*
            j. Floating leaves 1 cm or more wide.
              Floating leaves cordate at the base. (Fig. 51). .... 12. *P. natans*
               Floating leaves tapered or rounded at the base.
                 Submerged leaves 1 mm or less wide .... 13. *P. oakesianus*
                 Submerged leaves 3 mm or more wide .... 14. *P. gramineus*
          i. Floating leaves none.
            k. Many or all of the leaves with a pair of small glands at the base.
               (Fig. 52).
             l. Stipules strongly fibrous, becoming whitish.
               Leaves thin, rounded at tip .... 15. *P. friesii*
               Leaves firm, acute at tip .... 16. *P. strictifolius*
             l. Stipules delicate, green or brownish.
               Many of the leaves with bristle tips; peduncles recurved. .... 17. *P. hillii*
               Leaves rounded, obtuse, acute or apiculate but not bristle-tipped;
                peduncles straight.
                 Leaves 2-4 mm wide, rounded at tip .... 18. *P. obtusifolius*
                 Leaves rarely over 2 mm wide, acute to obtuse at tip. .... 19. *P. pusillus*
            k. Leaves glandless.
             m. Leaves less than 0.5 mm wide .... 20. *P. confervoides*
             m. Leaves more than 0.5 mm wide.
              n. Stipules strongly fibrous, becoming whitish. .... 16. *P. strictifolius*
              n. Stipules not strongly fibrous.
                 Leaves less than 3 mm wide.
                 Many of the leaves with bristle tips .... 17. *P. hillii*
                 Leaves acute but not bristle tipped .... 21. *P. foliosus*
                 Leaves 3 mm wide or wider .... 14. *P. gramineus*

a. Submerged leaves ribbon like to lanceolate or ovate, 5 mm wide or wider.
  o. Stems strongly flattened, two-thirds to three-fourths as wide as the leaves. .... 8. *P. zosteriformis*
  o. Stems terete, or if somewhat flattened less than half as wide as the leaves.
    p. Submerged leaves with a conspicuous reticulate band along the midrib, readily
      seen by holding leaf to the light. (Fig. 50). .... 9. *P. epihydrus*
    p. Submerged leaves lacking a conspicuous median band.
      q. Leaves ribbon like, stiffly 2-ranked; stipules adnate to the leaf base. (Fig. 49) . 1. *P. robbinsii*
      q. Leaves lanceolate to ovate, not stiffly 2-ranked; stipules free.
        r. Leaf margins undulate-crisped and serrate. .... 22. *P. crispus*
        r. Leaves entire or merely undulate.
          s. Submerged leaves cordate or rounded at the base, clasping; without
            floating leaves. (Fig. 53).
            t. Stems zigzag, white, stipules firm and persistent. .... 23. *P. praelongus*
            t. Stems not zigzag or white, stipules delicate and disappearing with age
              or disintegrating into persistent fibers.
              Leaves ovate-lanceolate to suborbicular; stipules delicate and
                disappearing with age .... 24. *P. perfoliatus*
              Leaves lanceolate; stipules disintegrating into persistent fibers. .... 25. *P. richardsonii*
          s. Submerged leaves petioled or sessile and tapered at the base, not
            clasping; floating leaves present or absent.
            u. Stem and leaf petioles conspicuously black spotted. .... 26. *P. pulcher*
            u. Stem and petioles not black spotted.
              v. Submerged leaves petioled.
                w. Submerged leaves folded and curved. (Fig. 54). .... 27. *P. amplifolius*
                w. Submerged leaves not folded or curved.
                  Submerged leaves on petioles less than 2 mm long. .... 28. *P. illinoensis*
                  Submerged leaves on petioles 2 mm long or longer. .... 29. *P. nodosus*
              v. Submerged leaves sessile.
                x. Plant reddish tinged; submerged leaves obtuse; floating leaves
                  delicate, blade tapering without sharp distinction to the
                  petiole .... 30. *P. alpinus*
                x. Plant not reddish tinged; submerged leaves acute and sharp
                  pointed or mucronate; floating leaves coriaceous, blade
                  distinct from petiole.
                  Submerged leaves less than 1.5 cm wide. .... 14. *P. gramineus*
                  Submerged leaves 1.5 cm wide or wider. .... 28. *P. illinoensis*

    1. *P. robbínsii* Oakes (for James Watson Robbins). Robbins' Pondweed. Lakes, ponds and quiet rivers. July-September. Fig. 48, Map 119.
    2. *P. pectinátus* L. (comb-like). Sago Pondweed. Fresh, calcarious, brackish or salt water, shallow lakes, ponds and quiet rivers. June-September. Fig. 49, Map 120. (Africa, Eurasia, S. Amer.).
    3. *P. vaginátus* Turcz. (sheathed). Deep fresh or brackish quiet waters. August-October. Reported for Aroostook County ME. (Eurasia).
    4. *P. filifórmis* Pers. (thread-like). Filiform Pondweed. Calcareous or brackish water, shallow ponds, lakes and quiet rivers. July-September. Map 121. (Eurasia, Greenland). Represented with us as var. *alpínus* (M.N. Blytt) Aschers. & Graebn. [*P. filiformis* var. *borealis*; *P. interior*].
    5. *P. spiríllus* Tuckerman (coiled). Shallow, quiet lakes, ponds and rivers. July-November. Map 122. [*P. dimorphus*].
    6. *P. diversifólius* Raf. (diverse-leaved). Rafinesque's Pondweed. Shallow, quiet water. June-September. Reported for Berkshire County MA. Map 123. [*P. bicupulatus*; *P. capillaceus*; *P. hybridus*].
    7. *P. bicupulátus* Fern. (having two cups). Quiet water. July-September. Map 124.
    8. *P. zosterifórmis* Fern. (similar to *Zostera*). Flat-stem Pondweed. Ponds and sluggish streams. July-September. Map 125. [*P. compressus*; *P. zosterifolius*].
    9. *P. epihýdrus* Raf. (upon the water). Nuttall's Pondweed. Ponds, lakes and slow streams and rivers. June-September. Fig. 50, Map 126.

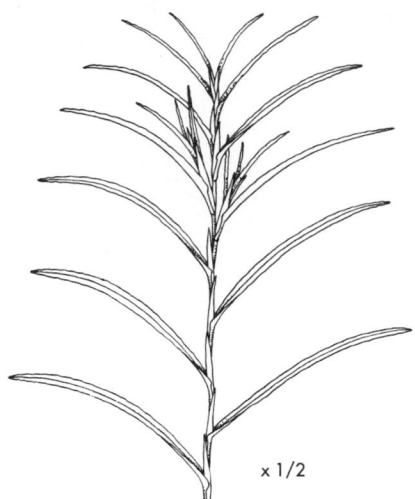

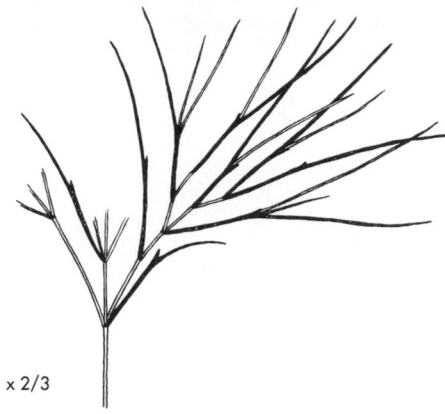

x 2/3

49. *Potamogeton pectinatus.* General habit.

x 1/2

48. *Potamogeton robbinsii.* General
habit showing leaves stiffly 2-ranked.

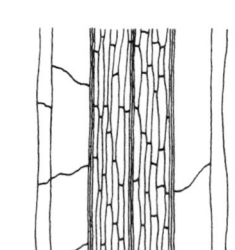

x 5

50. *Potamogeton epihydrus.* Section of submerged
leaf showing reticulate band.

119. *Potamogeton robbinsii*

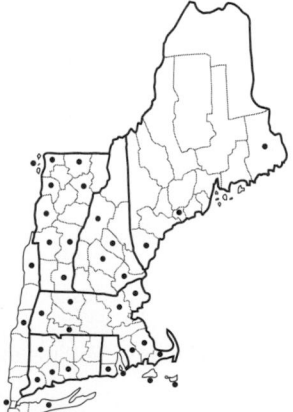

120. *Potamogeton pectinatus*

121. *Potamogeton filiformis* var. *alpinus*

122. *Potamogeton spirillus*

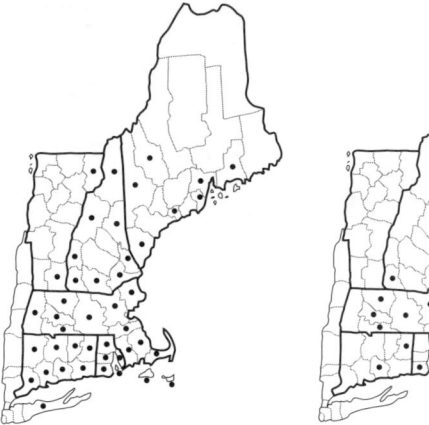

123. *Potamogeton diversifolius*

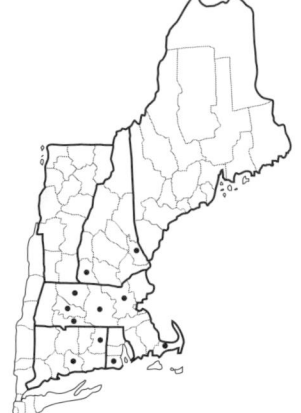

124. *Potamogeton bicupulatus*

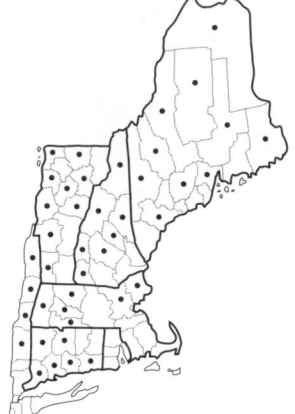

125. *Potamogeton zosteriformis*

126. *Potamogeton epihydrus*

127. *Potamogeton lateralis*

128. *Potamogeton vaseyi*

10. *P. laterális* Morong (one-sided). Opposite-leaved Pondweed. Lakes and slow streams. July-August. Map 127. [*P. pusillus* var. *pusillus*].

11. *P. váseyi* J. W. Robbins (for its discoverer). Vasey's Pondweed. Quiet water. July-September. Map 128. Endangered in ME. [*P. lateralis*].

12. *P. nátans* L. (swimming). Common Floating Pondweed. Ponds, lakes and slow streams. July-September. Fig. 51, Map 129. (Eurasia).

13. *P. oakesiánus* J. W. Robbins (for its discoverer). Oakes' Pondweed. Quiet acid water. July-September. Map 130.

14. *P. gramíneus* L. (grass-like). Various-leaved Pondweed. Lakes, ponds, rivers and streams. July-September. Map 131. (Eurasia, Greenland). [*P. heterophyllus*].

15. *P. friésii* Rupr. (for Elias Magnus Fries). Fries' Pondweed. Calcareous or brackish quiet water. July-September. Fig. 52, Map 132. (Europe). Endangered in ME.

16. *P. strictifólius* Benn (straight-leaved). Slender Pondweed. Calcareous ponds and quiet streams. July-September. Map 133. Endangered in CT. [*P. longiligulatus*; *P. rutilus*].

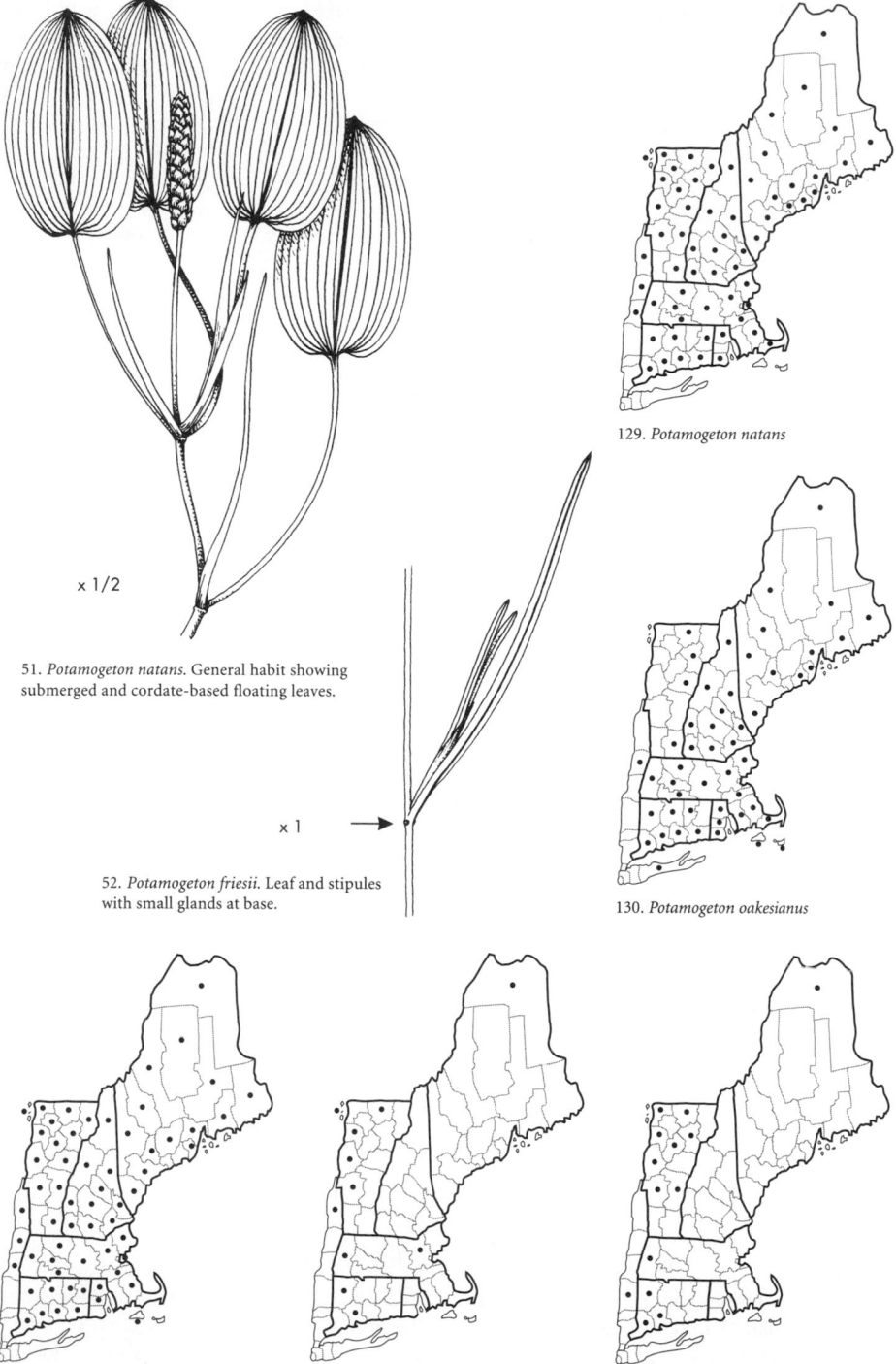

× 1/2

51. *Potamogeton natans*. General habit showing submerged and cordate-based floating leaves.

× 1

52. *Potamogeton friesii*. Leaf and stipules with small glands at base.

129. *Potamogeton natans*

130. *Potamogeton oakesianus*

131. *Potamogeton gramineus*

132. *Potamogeton friesii*

133. *Potamogeton strictifolius*

P. ógdenii Hellquist & Hilton. Ogden's Pondweed. Resembling *P. strictifolius* but with leaves usually 5 or more-veined, stipules wrapped around the stem and split, and fruit 2.5 mm or more long (leaves usually 5 or fewer-veined, stipules connate and sheathing the stem, and fruit less than 2.5 mm long in *P. strictifolius*). Reported for MA, VT.

P. x háynesii Hellquist & Crow. A hybrid between *P. strictifolius* and *P. zosteriformis*. [*P. longiligulatus*].

17. P. híllii Morong (for its discoverer). Hill's Pondweed. Shallow, calcareous ponds and lakes. July-September. Map 134. Endangered in CT. [*P. porteri*].

18. P. obtusifólius Mert & Koch (blunt-leaved). Blunt-leaved Pondweed. Ponds, springs and streams. July-September. Map 135. (Eurasia).

19. P. pusíllus L. (very small). Small Pondweed. Ponds, lakes and sluggish streams and rivers. July-September. Map 136. (Azores, Eurasia, W.I.). Our plants include var. *pusillus* [*P. berchtoldii; P. panormitanus*] and the following vars.:

var. *tenuíssimus* Mert. & Koch. Stipules wrapped around the stem and split, peduncles more than 3 per plant, inflorescence crowded (stipules connate and sheathing the stem, peduncles 3 or fewer per plant and inflorescence of distinct, interrupted, whorles, in var. *pusillus*). [*P. tenuissimus*].

var. *gemmíparis* J. W. Robbins. Leaves bristle-tipped, 1-veined (not bristle-tipped and 3 or more-veined in the above vars.). [*P. gemmiparus*].

20. P. confervoides Reichenb. (like *Conferva*). Alga-like Pondweed. Shallow, acid waters often in bogs; alpine ponds and pools. July-September. Map 137.

21. P. foliósus Raf. (leafy). Leafy Pondweed. Fresh, often calcareous or brackish ponds and streams. July-September. Map 138. (Mexico, W.I.). Endangered in NH. Our plants are var. *foliosus*.

22. P. críspus L. (crimped). Curly Muck-weed. Fresh calcareous, brackish salt and polluted lakes and rivers. June-September. Map 139. (Naturalized from Europe).

23. P. praelóngus Wulfen (greatly prolonged). White-stem Pondweed. Lakes and streams in deep water. June and July. Fig. 53, Map 140. (Eurasia).

24. P. perfoliátus L. (with leaf clasping stem). Clasping-leaved Pondweed. Fresh, (often calcareous) to brackish ponds and sluggish streams. July-September. Map 141. (Australia, Eurasia, N. Africa).

P. x mýsticus Morong. A hybrid between *P. perfoliatus* and *P. pusillus*.

25. P. richardsónii (Benn) Rydb. (for its discoverer). Red-head Pondweed. Calcareous to brackish ponds, lakes, streams and rivers. July-September. Map 142.

26. P. púlcher Tuckerman (handsome). Spotted Pondweed. Shallow, acid ponds and pools and muddy shores. July-September. Map 143.

27. P. amplifólius Tuckerman (large-leaved). Large-leaved Pondweed. Ponds, lakes and streams, usually in deep water. July-September. Fig. 54, Map 144.

28. P. illinoénsis Morong (of Illinois). Illinois Pondweed. Calcareous ponds, lakes and streams. July-September. Map 145. [*P. angustifolius; P. lucens*].

29. P. nodósus Poir. (knotty). Long-leaved Pondweed. Shallow or deep ponds and streams. July-September. Map 146. (Africa, Eurasia, S. Amer., W.I.). [*P. americanus; P. fluitans*].

30. P. alpínus Balbis (alpine). Northern Pondweed. Calcareous ponds and slow streams. July-September. Map 147. (Europe; W. Asia).

Family 26. Ruppiáceae (Ditch-grass Family)

Submersed, monoecious rhizomatous, marine perennial with jointed, filiform, forking stems. Leaves alternate, 2-ranked, capillary, sheathing at the base. Flowers perfect, 2 together on a short stalk enclosed in the leaf sheath, consisting of 2 sessile stamens, each with 2 separate anther locules, and 4 sessile, one-locular, superior, 1-ovulate ovaries with sessile stigmas, the stalk elongating and

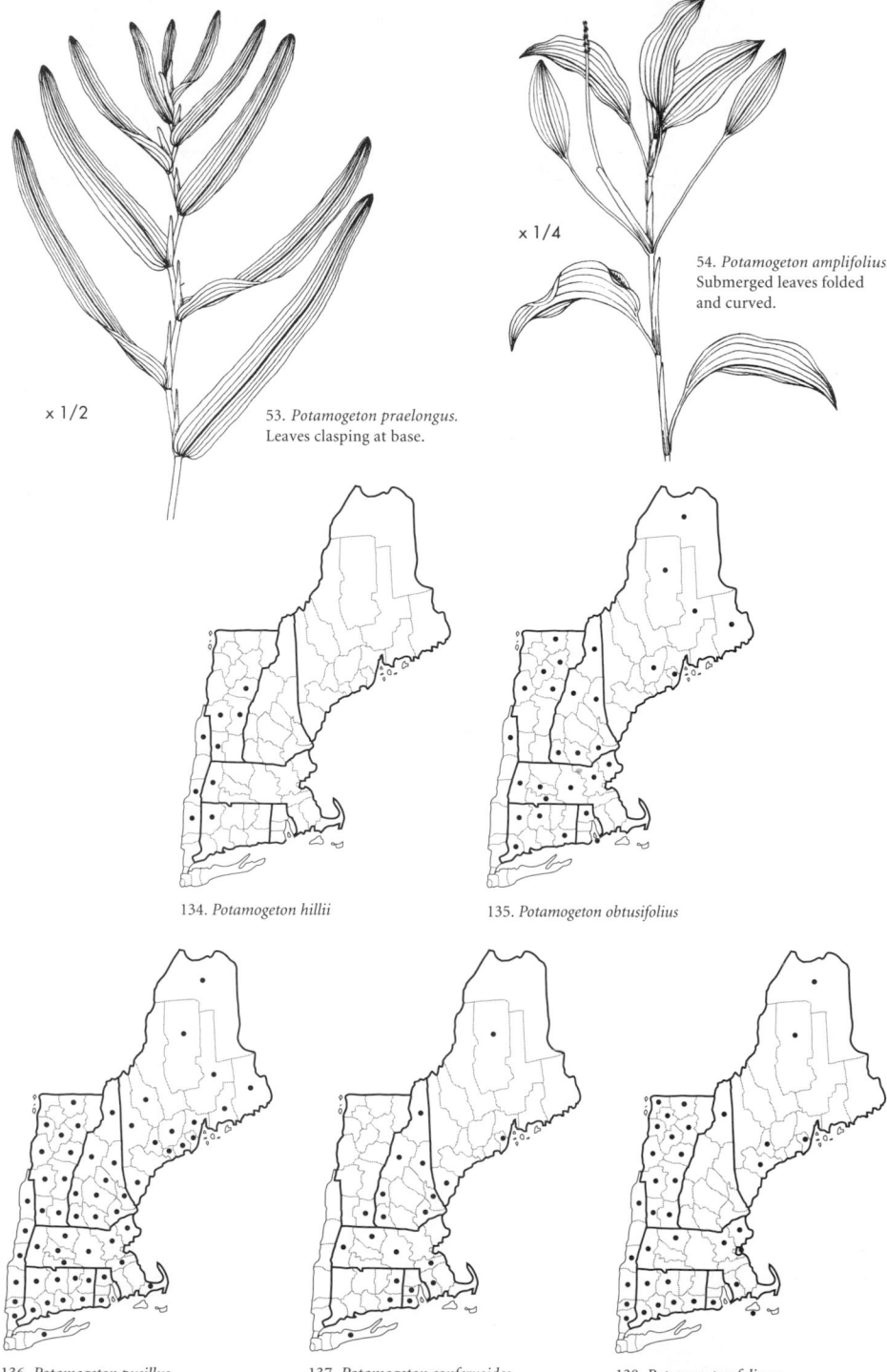

x 1/2

53. *Potamogeton praelongus.*
Leaves clasping at base.

x 1/4

54. *Potamogeton amplifolius.*
Submerged leaves folded
and curved.

134. *Potamogeton hillii*

135. *Potamogeton obtusifolius*

136. *Potamogeton pusillus*

137. *Potamogeton confervoides*

138. *Potamogeton foliosus*

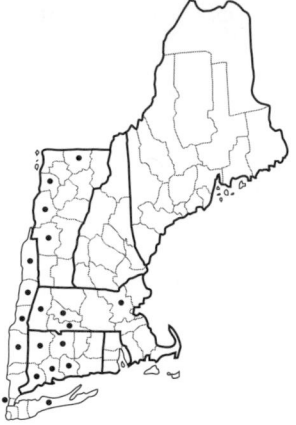

139. *Potamogeton crispus*

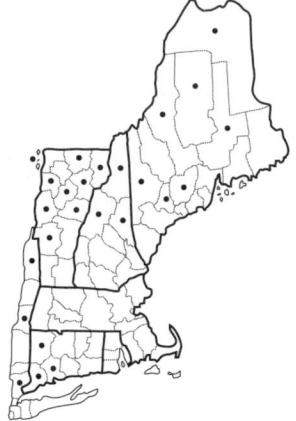

140. *Potamogeton praelongus*

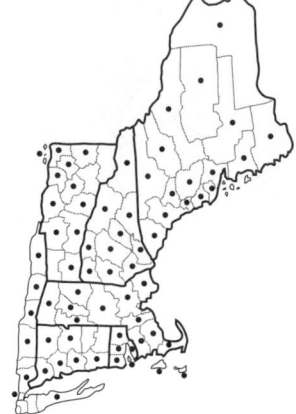

141. *Potamogeton perfoliatus*

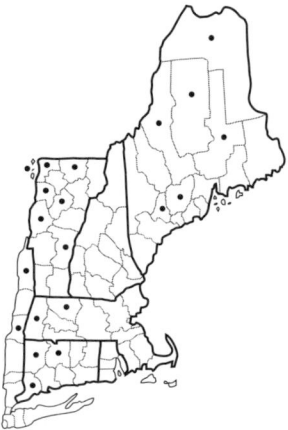

142. *Potamogeton richardsonii*

143. *Potamogeton pulcher*

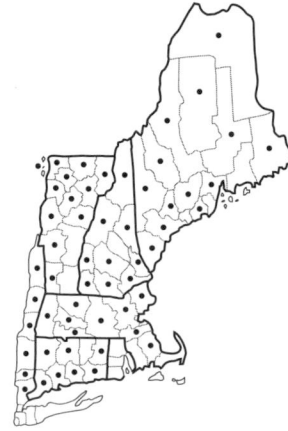

144. *Potamogeton amplifolius*

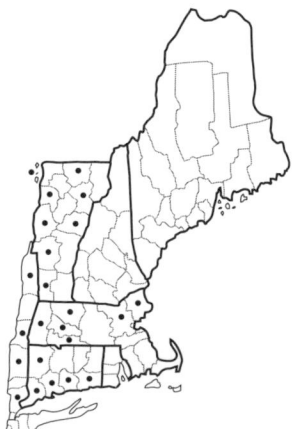

145. *Potamogeton illinoensis*

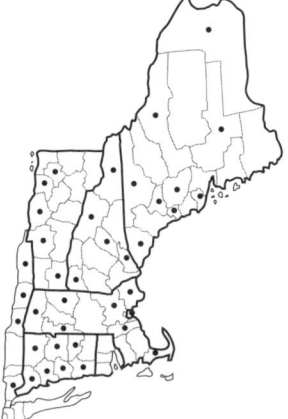

146. *Potamogeton nodosus*

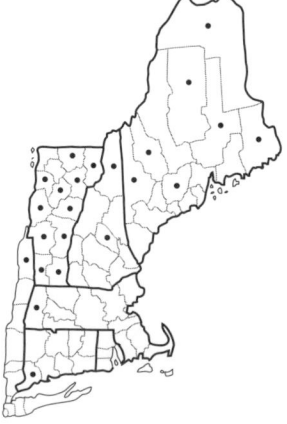

147. *Potamogeton alpinus*

each ovary becoming elevated on a capillary pedicel after flowering. Fruits ovoid, slender-stalked drupes in umbels or cymes. [*Najadaceae*].

1. *Ruppia* L. Ditch-grass (for H. Ruppius).
Same characters as the family. —Wildl. 1

    1. *R. marítima* L. (of the sea). Tidal pools and ditches. July-August. Fig. 55, Map 148. (Europe). —OBL

Family 27. Najádaceae (Naiad Family)

Submersed, monoecious or dioecious (*N. marina*), fresh to brackish water annuals with fibrous roots and jointed, slender, branching stems. Leaves opposite, 2-ranked, narrow and linear, widened below into a sheathing base. Flowers imperfect, solitary in the axils of the branches and leaves, the staminate consisting of a single stamen enclosed in an involucre-like membrane, the pistillate of a single, naked, one-locular, superior, 1-ovulate ovary terminated by 2 or 3 stigmas. Fruit a sessile, fusiform achene.

1.*Najas* L. Naiad. (from the Greek, meaning water nymph).
Same characters as the family. —OBL; Wildl. 2

a. Leaf margins visibly toothed. (Fig. 56).
    Leaf teeth coarse, triangular, projecting 0.5-1 mm. .... 1. *N. marina*
    Leaf teeth barely visible without magnification, projecting 0.1-0.4 mm. .... 2. *N. minor*
a. Leaf margins apparently entire but minutely spinulose, the spinules projecting less
    than 0.1 mm, and usually barely visible at 10 x magnification.
    b. Sheathing leaf base with a truncate, coarsely jagged lobe on each side at the
        summit. (Fig. 57) .... 3. *N. gracillima*
    b. Sheathing leaf base with gradually sloping, spinulose-margined lobes.
        Leaves gradually tapered to tip; seed lustrous. (Fig. 58). .... 4. *N. flexilis*
        Leaves obtuse or acute but not gradually tapered; seed dull. .... 5. *N. guadalupensis*

    1. *N. marína* L. (of the sea). Large Najas. Deep or shallow alkaline lakes and streams. August-October. Fig. 56. (Eurasia, Tropics).

    2. *N. minor* All. (smaller). Locally established in rivers (i.e., the Hudson) and lakes. August-October. Map 149. (Naturalized from the old world).

    3. *N. gracíllima* (A. Br.) Magnus (very slender). Thread-like Najas. Pools and ponds. July-October. Fig. 57, Map 150.

    4. *N. fléxilis* (Willd.) Rostk. & Schmidt (flexible). Slender Najas. Shallow fresh to brackish ponds and streams. July-October. Fig. 58, Map 151. (N.W. U.S., Europe).

    5. *N. guadalupénsis* (Spreng.) Magnus (of the island of Guadalupe). Guadalupe Najas. Ponds, lakes and rivers. August-October. Map 152. (Tropical Amer.). Our plants include var. *guadalupensis* and the following var.:

    var. *muénscheri* (Clausen) Hayes. Seed with more than 50 rows of areolae barely visible at 10 x magnification (seed with up to 20 rows of clearly visible areolae in var. *guadalupensis*). [*N. muenscheri*].

Family 28. Zannichelliáceae (Horned Pondweed Family)

Submersed, monoecious, perennial aquatic with slender rhizomes and jointed, branched, filiform stems. Leaves opposite, 2-ranked, long and very narrow, with sheathing stipules. Flowers imperfect, axillary, the staminate and pistillate adjacent in the same axil, the staminate of a single stamen, the pistillate of up to usually 4 separate, one-locular, superior, 1-ovulate ovaries, each with a short style

x 1/2

55. *Ruppia maritima*. General habit.

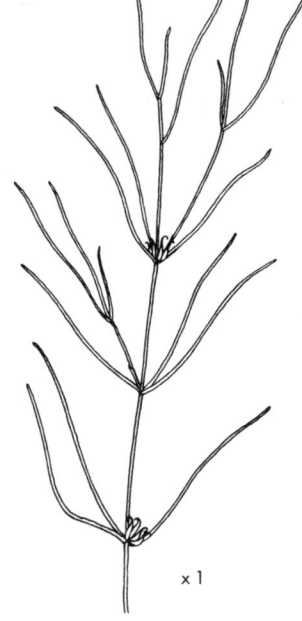

x 1

59. *Zannichellia palustris*. General habit.

x 1

56. *Najas marina*. Toothed leaf margins.

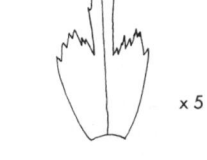

x 5

57. *Najas gracillima*. Leaf showing base with
truncate, coarsely jagged lobes.

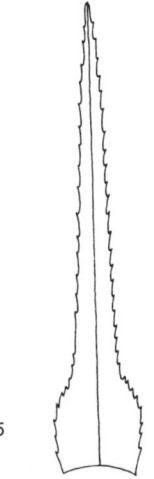

x 5

58. *Najas flexilis*. Leaf showing base with
sloping, spinulose-margined lobes.

148. *Ruppia maritima*

149. *Najas minor*

150. *Najas gracillima*

151. *Najas flexilis*

152. *Najas guadalupensis*

153. *Zannichellia palustris*

tipped by a broad, flat stigma. Fruit a sessile or short-stipitate, flattened, falcate achene which is often toothed or ribbed on the back, and tipped by the persistent, beak-like style, the cluster of fruits sessile or sometimes stalked. [*Najadaceae*].

1. *Zannichéllia* L. Horned Pondweed (for G. Zannichelli).

Same characters as the family. —Wildl. 1

1. *Z. palústris* L. (of marshes). Fresh, brackish, salt or alkaline rivers, lakes and bays. July-October. Fig. 59, Map 153. (Europe). —OBL

Family 29. Juncagináceae (Arrow-grass Family)

Monoecious, perennial marsh herbs with rhizomes producing fibrous roots or stolons, which are sometimes bulb-bearing. Leaves basal, rush-like, linear and bladeless, half-rounded to flat, sheathing and ligulate at the base. Flowers perfect, in terminal bractless spikes or racemes, perianth regular, of 3 sepals and 3 similar petals, stamens 3-6, ovaries 3 or 6, weakly united until maturity, one-locular, superior, containing 1-several ovules, stigma sessile or on a very short style, plumose. Fruit of 3 or 6 follicles.

1. Triglóchin L. Arrow-grass (Greek name based on fruit characteristics of *T. palustre*). Marsh herbs, the rhizomes with or without bulb-bearing stolons; leaves half rounded, sheathing the base of the naked scape; flowers in a long, bractless spiciform raceme terminating the long, naked scape, perianth of 3 or 6 similar segments, stamens 3-6, with sessile anthers, ovaries 3-6, closely approximate, attached to an elongate axis, style absent or very short, stigma plumose; follicles separating from the base upward, from each other and the persistent axis when ripe. Poisonous. —OBL

Ovaries 3; follicles linear, 6-9 mm long. .... 1. *T. palustre*
Ovaries 6; follicles ovoid, not over 5 mm long. .... 2. *T. maritima*

1. T. palústre L. (of marshes). Marsh Arrow-grass. Bogs and brackish or fresh, sometimes calcareous marshes. July-September. Figure 60, Map 154. (Eurasia; S. Amer.). [*T. palustris*].

2. T. marítima L. (of the sea). Seaside Arrow-grass. Bogs and salt, brackish or fresh marshes. July-September. Map 155. (Eurasia, N. Africa, Patagonia). *T. gaspense* has been reported as occurring in the intertidal zone along the coast of Maine.

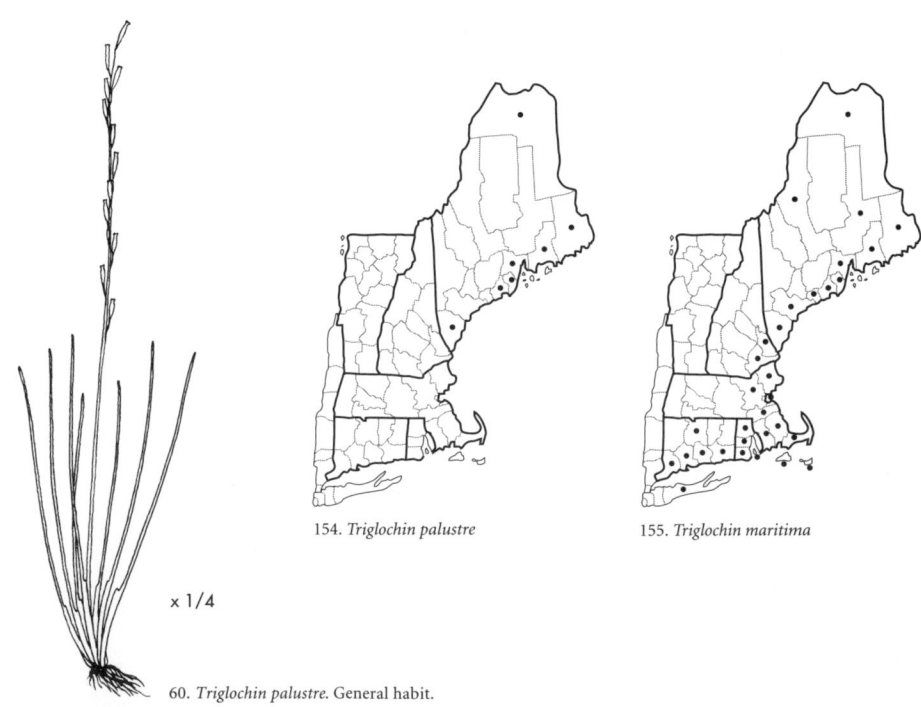

154. *Triglochin palustre*

155. *Triglochin maritima*

x 1/4

60. *Triglochin palustre.* General habit.

Family 30. Scheuchzeriáceae

Monoecious perennial, low, rush-like bog herbs with creeping rhizomes and unbranched, leafy, somewhat zigzag stems. Leaves alternate, rush-like, linear and bladeless, distichous, with inflated basal sheaths, half-rounded below and flat above, with a terminal pore. Flowers perfect, in a short, terminal, few-flowered raceme, the lower subtended by foliaceous bracts, perianth of 6 similar segments, stamens 6, with short filaments, ovaries 3, one-locular, superior, containing 1-several ovules, distinct or slightly united at the base, divergent, stigma sessile, papillose. Fruit of 3 follicles, these divergent, inflated. [*Juncaginaceae*].

1. *Scheuchzéria* L. (for J. Scheuchzer).
Same characters as the family.

    1. *S. palústris* L. (of marshes). Bogs. May-June. Fig. 61, Map 156. Endangered in RI and CT. Represented with us as subsp. americána (Fern) Hulten. —OBL

Family 31. Alismatáceae (Water-plantain Family)

Monoecious or dioecious, annual or perennial, aquatic or marsh herbs with fibrous roots, often rhizomatous. Stems scape-like, leaves basal, long petioled, sheathing at the base, erect or floating, bladeless or with blade varying from linear to ovate or with sagittate bases. Flowers perfect or imperfect (in *Sagittaria*), pedicelled, the pedicels subtended by bracts, usually in whorles, regular, the perianth of 3 greenish, persistent sepals and 3 larger, white or pinkish deciduous petals; stamens 6-many, ovaries 6-many, free, in heads or in a single, flattened whorl (*Alisma*), superior, one-locular, containing one ovule. Fruit an achene.

Flowers in panicles; ovaries in a single, strongly flattened ring. (Fig. 62). .... 1. *Alisma*
Flowers in racemes, the lowest whorls sometimes branched; ovaries in globose heads.
    Upper flowers mostly staminate, only the lower whorles bearing fruiting heads;
        achenes flattened, winged .... 2. *Sagittaria*
    Flowers all perfect and bearing fruiting heads; achenes plump, ribbed but not
        winged. (Fig. 66) .... 3. *Echinodorus*
                                                                parvulus

1. *Alisma* L. Water-or Mud-plantain (from the Greek).
Perennial aquatic or marsh herbs, erect or lax in deep water forms; leaves erect, long petioled, the blade lanceolate, elliptic or ovate, with attenuate, rounded or subcordate base, the deep water forms with lax, narrow, ribbon-like leaves; flowers perfect, in panicles of whorled branches, small and numerous on unequal, bracteolate pedicels, ovaries in a single, strongly flattened ring; achenes flattened, ribbed. —OBL

Plants submerged with leaves long and ribbon-like, or emergent with leaves lanceolate
    and attenuate at base; stamens up to as long as the ovaries. .... 1. *A. gramineum*
Plants emergent; leaves typically rounded to subcordate at base; stamens longer than
    the ovaries.
    Sepals 3-4 mm, petals 3-6 mm long .... 2. *A. triviale*
    Sepals 1.5-2.5 mm, petals 1-2.5 mm long. .... 3. *A. subcordatum*

    1. *A. gramíneum* Lej. (grass-like). Deep water, muddy shores. August-September. (Eurasia, N. Africa). Reported for Addison, Chittenden and Grand Isle Counties VT. [*A. geyeri*].
    2. *A. triviále* Pursh (ordinary). Ponds and streams in shallow water, muddy shores, ditches, and marshes. June-September. Fig. 62, Map 157. [*A. brevipes; A. plantago-aquatica* var. *americana*].
    3. *A. subcordátum* Raf. (somewhat heart-shaped). Shallow water, muddy shores, ditches and marshes. June-September. Map 158. [*A. plantago-aquatica* var. *parviflorum*]. Said to be poisonous; however has been used as a diuretic and by Indians for application to skin wounds.

2. Sagittária L. Arrowhead (name based on shape of the leaves).

Monoecious, dioecious or hermaphrodite, perennial aquatic or marsh herbs with rhizomes bearing apical tubers; leaves erect, long petioled, the blade varying from linear to ovate, sometimes sagittate at the base, lobed and unlobed leaves often occurring on the same plant, submerged forms with narrow, ribbon-like leaves (bladeless phyllodia) having scattered cross veins between the parallel veins; flowers perfect or imperfect, racemose, in whorls of 3s, the staminate uppermost, or the lower part of the raceme sometimes bearing branches, ovaries in globose or subglobose heads; achenes flattened and winged. Tubers are edible when cooked. —OBL; Wildl. 2.

a. Fruiting pedicels strongly thickened; sepals closely appressed to the fruiting heads;
    lower heads perfect .... 1. *S. calycina*
                                                             var. *spongiosa*
a. Fruiting pedicels not strongly thickened; sepals not closely appressed to the fruiting
    heads; lower heads imperfect.
    b. Pistillate heads sessile or subsessile, the pedicels shorter than the sepals. (Fig. 63) .. 2. *S. rigida*
    b. Pistillate heads on pedicels longer than the sepals. (Fig. 64).
        c. Leaves sagittate or hastate. (Fig. 64).
            d. Bracts subtending pedicels ovate, obtuse; sepals obtuse; beak of
                achene horizontal .... 3. *S. latifolia*
            d. Bracts subtending pedicels lanceolate, acute to acuminate; sepals acute to
                acuminate; beak of achene erect to arching.
                Lamina of leaf less than 3 cm wide; beak of achene 0.5 mm or
                    more in length. .... 4. *S. engelmanniana*
                Lamina of leaf more than 3 cm wide; beak of achene less than
                    0.5 mm in length. .... 5. *S. cuneata*
        c. Leaves unlobed. (Fig. 65).
            e. Leaves terete and quill-like .... 6. *S. teres*
            e. Leaves flat.
                 f. Bracts subtending pedicels separate, acute to acuminate. .... 4. *S. engelmanniana*
                 f. Bracts subtending pedicels united or only partly separated, obtuse to acute.
                    Pedicels of fruiting heads reflexed, stouter than staminate
                    pedicels. (Fig. 65) ....7. *S. subulata*
                  Pedicels of fruiting heads ascending or spreading but not reflexed,
                    no stouter than the staminate pedicels .... 8. *S. graminea*

1. *S. calycina* Engelm. In mud on margins of brackish ponds, estuaries and tidewater marshes and streams. July-September. Map 159. Endangered in MA. [*S. montevidensis* subsp. *c.; S.m.* var. *spongiosa; S. spathulata; S. spatulata; Lophotocarpus c.; L. depauperatus; L. spongiosus; L. spatulatus*]. Represented with us as var. *spongiósa* Engelm.

2. *S. rigida* Pursh (stiff). Sessile-fruited Arrow-head. Swamps and fresh or brackish mud or shallow to deep water. July-September. Fig. 63, Map 160. Reported for Hampshire County MA, Washington County NY. [*S. heterophylla*].

3. *S. latifólia* Willd. (broad-leaved). Broad-leaved Arrow-head. Marshes and shallow to deep water. July-September. Fig. 64, Map 161. Our plants are var. *latifolia*.

4. *S. engelmanniána* J. G. Sm. (for G. Engelmann). Engelmann's Arrow-head. Pond margins and shallow water. July-September. Map 162.

5. *S. cuneáta* Sheldon (wedge-shaped). Arum-leaved Arrow-head. In mud on pond and river margins and in shallow water. July-September. Map 163. Endangered in MA. [*S. arifolia*].

6. *S. téres* S. Wats. (quill-like). Slender Sagittaria. Pond margins and shallow water. July-September. Map 164. Endangered in RI and NY.

7. *S. subuláta* (L.) Buchenau (awl-shaped). Subulate Sagittaria. In mud of fresh to brackish tidal rivers, pond margins and shallow water. July-September. Fig. 65, Map 165. Endangered in MA.

S. stagnórum Small. Similar to *S. subulata* but with leaves more than 3 dm long, flexuous, plant non-tidal (leaves 3 dm or less long, firm and curved, mostly tidal in *S. subulata*). Reported for CT, MA, ME, RI. [*S. subulata* var. *gracillima; S. lorata*].

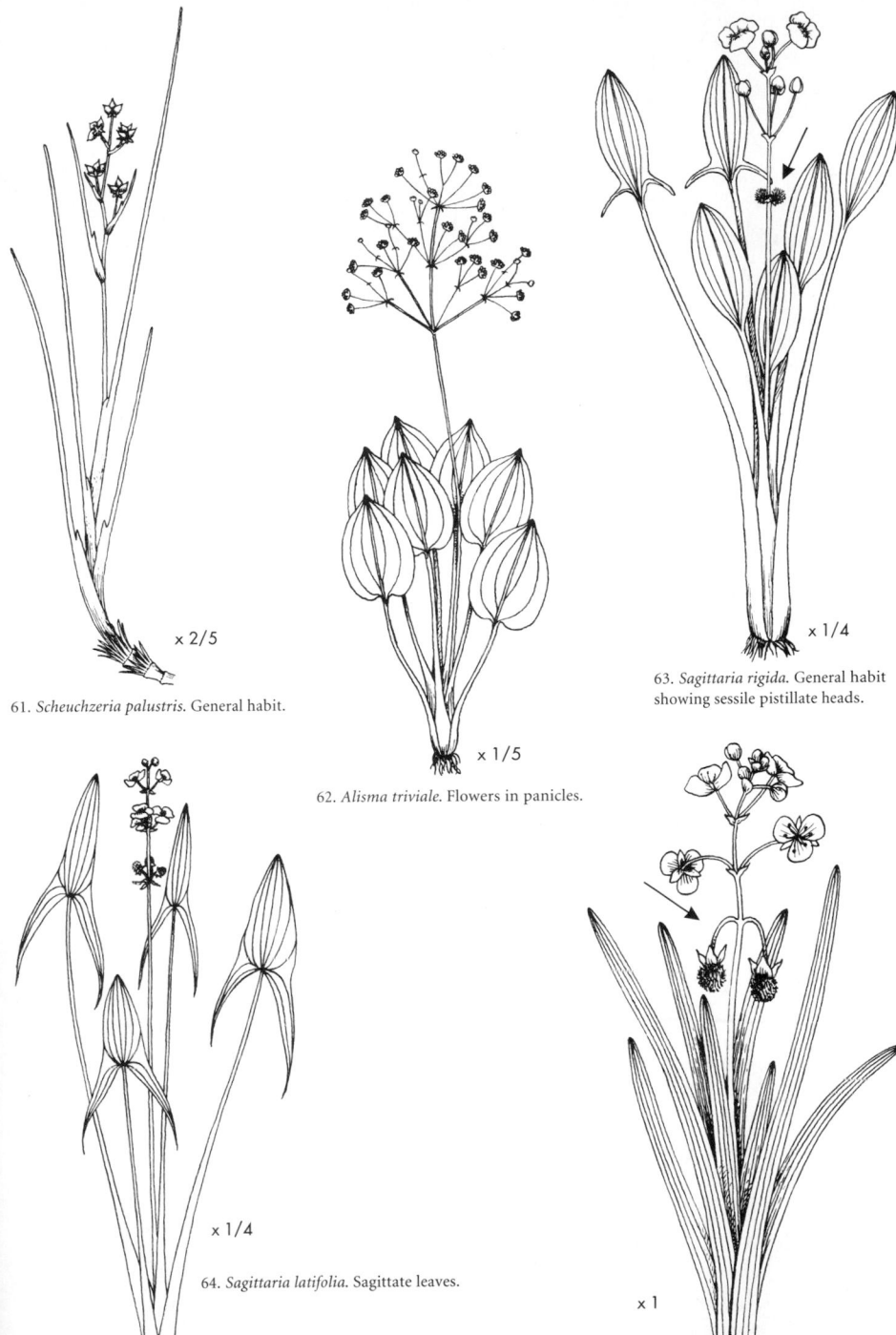

61. *Scheuchzeria palustris*. General habit.
× 2/5

62. *Alisma triviale*. Flowers in panicles.
× 1/5

63. *Sagittaria rigida*. General habit showing sessile pistillate heads.
× 1/4

64. *Sagittaria latifolia*. Sagittate leaves.
× 1/4

65. *Sagittaria subulata*. Leaves unlobed; pedicels of fruiting heads reflexed.
× 1

156. *Scheuchzeria palustris* subsp. *americana*

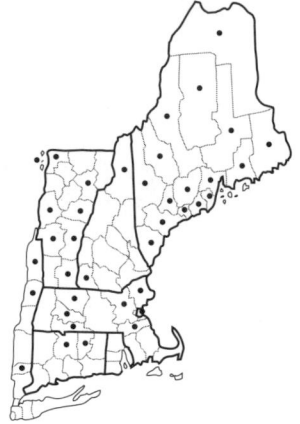

157. *Alisma triviale*

158. *Alisma subcordatum*

159. *Sagittaria calycina* var. *spongiosa*

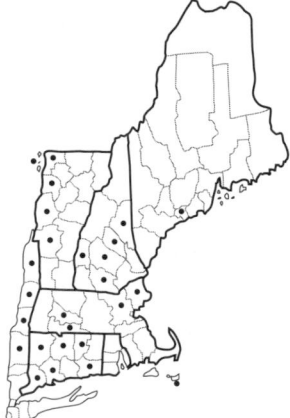

160. *Sagittaria rigida*

161. *Sagittaria latifolia*

162. *Sagittaria engelmanniana*

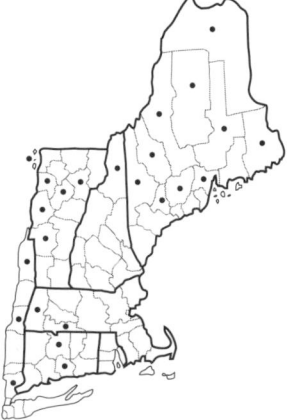

163. *Sagittaria cuneata*

164. *Sagittaria teres*

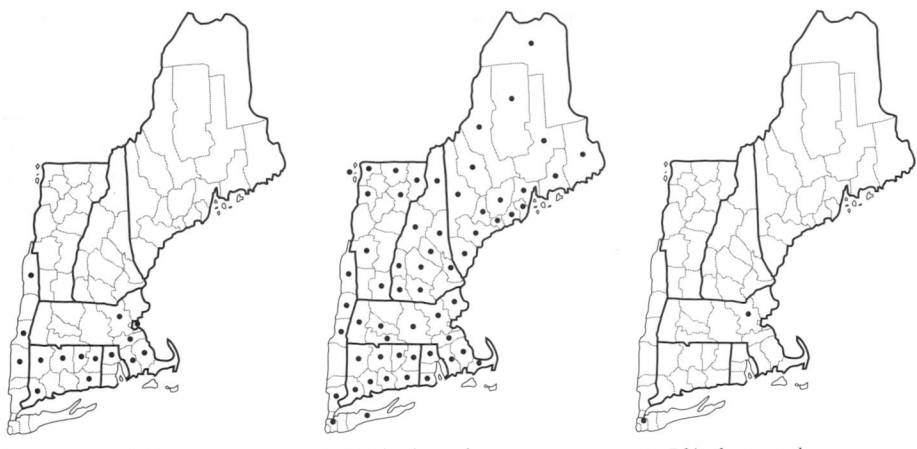

165. *Sagittaria subulata*   166. *Sagittaria graminea*   167. *Echinodorus parvulus*

8. S. gramínea Michx. (grass-like). Grass-leaved Sagittaria. In mud of pond margins and shallow water. July-September. Reported for Columbia County NY. Map 166. [*S. eatoni*]. Our plants are var. *graminea*.

3. Echinodórus L. C. Rich. ex Engelm. Burhead (from the Greek based on condition of the fruit).

Annual or short-lived perennial marsh or aquatic herbs with creeping or erect scapes; submerged leaves, when present, linear to narrowly lanceolate, emergent leaves petioled and (in ours) with a lanceolate, acute blade; flowers perfect, in 1-many verticels of 3 or more, the fruiting pedicels sometimes recurved, ovaries in globose heads; achenes plump, ribbed, beaked or beakless.

1. E. párvulus Engelm. Dwarf Water-plantain. In mud and shallow water. July-September. Fig. 66, Map 167. (Mexico, W.I., S. Amer.). Endangered in CT. [*E. tenéllus* var. *p.*; *Helianthium parvulum*]. —OBL

Family 32. Butomáceae (Flowering Rush Family)

Monoecious, perennial, aquatic or marsh herbs with fibrous roots from a stout rhizome. Leaves basal, erect and sword like (in ours), flat, or petioled and with dilated blades or in the sterile, deep water form long, limp and ribbon-like. Flowers perfect, solitary or in umbels subtended by large bracts terminating long scapes, regular, the perianth of 3 green or colored, persistent sepals and 3 colored, deciduous petals, stamens 6 or more, ovaries 6 or more, free or only coherent at the base, whorled, superior, 1-locular, containing numerous ovules. Fruit a whorl of follicles.

1. Bútomus L. Flowering Rush (from the Greek based on the sword-like leaves).

Flowers in umbels, subtended by 3 large purple-tinged bracts, long pedicelled, the sepals nearly as large as the petals, both sepals and petals persistent, rose colored, the sepals tinged with green; follicles inflated, long-beaked.

1. B. umbellátus L. (with an umbel). Mud and shallow to deep water of rivers and lakes. June-September. Fig. 67, Map 168. (Naturalized from Europe). —OBL

Family 33. Hydrocharitáceae (Frog's-bit Family)

Monoecious, dioecious or polygamous, perennial, submerged or occasionally free-floating aquatic or marsh herbs, often stoloniferous. Leaves basal and (in ours) long and ribbon like, or whorled or opposite, sessile, and crowded on a simple or branched stem. Flowers perfect or imperfect, solitary (pistillate) or numerous (staminate), arising from a spathe of 1-2 bracts or leaves, the spathe sessile or long pedunculate, the peduncles often spirally coiled; flowers regular, sepals 3, petals 3, the perianth forming a tube in the pistillate flowers, staminate flowers with 3-many stamens, pistillate flowers with one, inferior, one-locular ovary (appearing to be 3 or more celled due to the intrusion of placentae into the locule), containing numerous ovules. Fruit indehiscent, berry-like, ripening under water.

a. Leaves cauline, opposite or whorled, less than 4 cm long. (Fig. 68).
    Leaves in whorles of 3, less than 2 cm long. .... 1. *Elodea*
    Leaves in whorles of 5 or more, longer than 2 cm. .... 2. *Egeria densa*
a. Leaves basal, long and ribbon-like, more than 4 cm long. (Fig. 69). .... 3. *Vallisneria americana*

1. *Elodèa* Michx. Waterweed (from the Greek, meaning marshy).

Dioecious or polygamous submerged aquatic herbs with elongate simple or branched stems arising from stolons, the stems brittle, sometimes breaking off and floating; leaves opposite or whorled, elliptic, linear or oblong, serrulate, sessile, and crowded on the stems, becoming imbricated toward the apex; flowers (seldom found) perfect or imperfect, small and white, solitary, arising from a sessile or subsessile, axillary ovoid or tubular, 2-cleft spathe, the pistillate or perfect flowers raised to the surface of the water during flowering by elongation of the slender perianth tube, which resembles a pedicel. —OBL; Wildl. 1

Leaves oblong or ovate, obtuse, the larger 5 times or less as long as wide. .... 1. *E. canadensis*
Leaves narrowly lanceolate, acute, the larger 6 times or more as long as wide. .... 2. *E. nuttallii*

1. *E. canadénsis* Michx. (Canadian). Ponds and quiet streams. July-September. Fig. 68, Map 169. [*Anacharis c.; A. planchonii; Philotria c.*].

2. *E. nuttállii* (Planch.) St. John (for T. Nuttall). Nuttall's Waterweed. Shallow water of ponds and slow rivers, often in brackish, tidal estuaries. July-September. Map 170. [*Anacharis n.; A. occidentalis; Philotria angustifolia; P. minor*].

2. *Egéria* Planch.

Similar to *Elodea*; distinguished in having leaves longer than 2 cm in whorles of 5 or more. [*Elodea*]. —OBL; Wildl 1

1. *E. dénsa* Planch. (dense). Spread from cultivation to ponds, lakes, and quiet streams and rivers. July-September. Map 171. (Naturalized from S. Amer.). [*Elodea d.; Anacharis d.*].

3. *Vallisnéria* L. Tapegrass.

Dioecious, submerged, stoloniferous aquatic herbs; leaves basal, in small clusters along the stolon, long and ribbon-like, with light colored center stripes paralleling the midvein, entirely submerged or the upper portions floating; flowers imperfect, the staminate minute, of usually 2 stamens, numerous in a head enclosed in an ovoid, short peduncled spathe arising among the leaf bases, breaking free and floating to the surface during flowering, the pistillate solitary and sessile in a tubular spathe which is raised to the water surface by elongation of the peduncle; fruit elongate, cylindric, retracted under water to ripen by spiral coiling of the peduncle. —Wildl. 2

1. *V. americána* Michx. (American). Water-celery. Lakes and quiet streams and rivers. July-September. Fig. 69, Map 172. Our plants are var. *americana*. —OBL

66. *Echinodorus parvulus.* General habit.

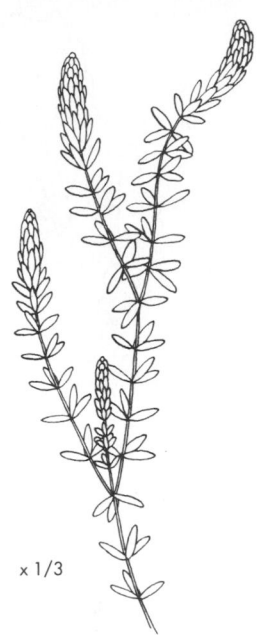

68. *Elodea canadensis.* Leaves whorled, imbricated toward tip of stem.

67. *Butomus umbellatus.* General habit.

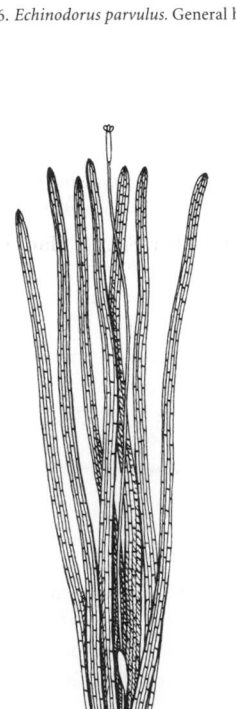

69. *Vallisneria americana.* Leaves basal, long and ribbon-like.

168. *Butomus umbellatus*

169. *Elodea canadensis*

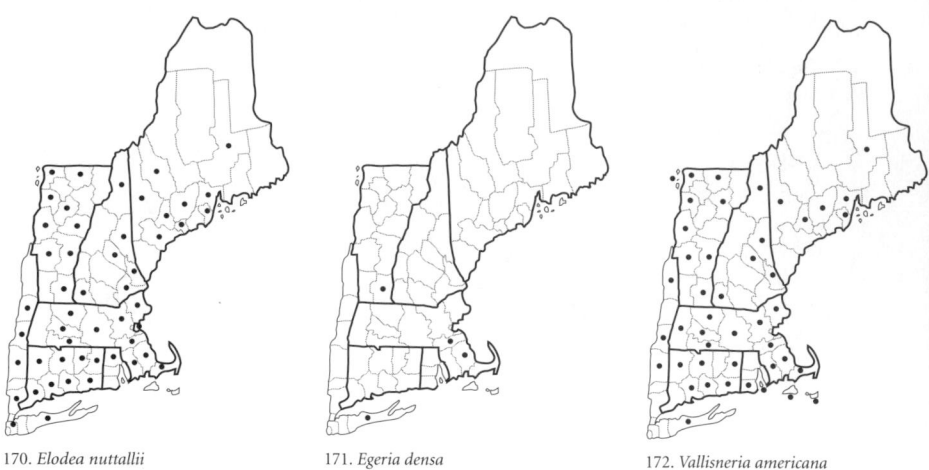

170. *Elodea nuttallii*   171. *Egeria densa*   172. *Vallisneria americana*

Family 34. Poáceae (Grass Family)

Monoecious, dioecious, polygamous, or with flowers all perfect (sometimes accompanied by 1 or more reduced flowers without stamens or pistils). Annual or perennial herbs (ours) with fibrous roots, with or without rhizomes. Stems erect, prostrate or creeping, with solid, often swollen nodes and usually hollow internodes. Leaves solitary at the nodes, 2-ranked, composed of a sheath which is usually split to the base, and a linear to lanceolate blade with parallel veins; at the inner margin of the junction of sheath and blade on the side opposite the split in the leaf sheath an appendage, the ligule, is usually present, which is membranous or cartilaginous, prolonged or truncate, or represented by a row of bristles. The basic unit of the inflorescence is a spikelet, the structure of which is the basis for the identification of the grasses; spikelets sessile or on a stalk termed the pedicel, few to many, aggregated into spikes, racemes or panicles, the axis of the inflorescence or its branches termed the rachis; spikelet typically composed of 2-many bracts alternating in 2 distichous rows along an axis (the rachilla); at the base of the spikelet are 2 empty bracts, the lower (1st glume) often smaller than the upper (2nd glume), one or (rarely) both glumes reduced or obsolete in some genera; articulation of the spikelets is either above the glumes, leaving them as persistent husks or below, leaving a naked pedicel when the spikelet drops; the glumes are followed by the succeeding bracts (lemmas) which are often keeled, rounded, nerved, awned or awnless, and are opposite to, subtend and enclose a second bract (the palea), which is generally 2 nerved, and encloses the flower, the palea obsolete in some genera, the lemma, palea and flower collectively termed the floret; sterile lemmas may be present above or below the fertile, and may be smaller or larger than the fertile; at the base of the flower between the lemma and palea are usually 2 (rarely 3) scales, (lodicules) which are remnants of the perianth, and distend during flowering, opening the floret; at the base of the floret there is often a swollen callousity (the callus) which may be glabrous or pubescent. Flowers perfect, pistillate or staminate, stamens 1-6, usually 3, ovary superior, one-locular, containing one ovule, with usually 2 lateral styles or stigmas, the stigmas usually plumose. Fruit a seed-like grain (caryopsis) or rarely a utricle.

Pseudosása Makino ex Nakai *japónica* (Sieb. & Zucc. ex Steud.) Makino ex Nakai. Culms woody at least at the base and leaf blades petioled. Rarely escaped from cultivation. Reported for Fairfield County CT. [*Arundinaria japonica*].

Pappóphorum Schreb. *vaginátum* Buckl. Pappusgrass. Lemmas divided at the summit into numerous bristle-like awns; spikelets with 1 or 2 fertile and 2 or 3 sterile florets. Southwestern. Wool waste. Reported for York County Maine. [*P. mucronulatum*].

KEY TO THE GROUPS

a. Spikelets enclosed in a prickly bur, the burs falling from plant intact. (Fig. 183) .... 80. *Cenchrus*
a. Spikelets not enclosed in a prickly bur.
  b. Spikelets all unisexual, the staminate and pistillate on the same plant in
      separate inflorescences or in different parts of the same inflorescence.
    c. Staminate spikelets below, pistillate above, the latter linear, pedicelled,
      in a contracted panicle. (Fig. 184). .... 81. *Zizania*
    c. Staminate spikelets above, pistillate below, the latter ovoid or oblong, sessile,
      in hollows in the rachis or in rows on a thickened axis.
      Staminate spikelets in a terminal panicle, pistillate in 1-several axillary
        spikes. (Fig. 185) .... 82. *Zea mays*
      Staminate and pistillate spikelets in one spike. (Fig. 186). .... 83. *Tripsacum*
                                                                  dactyloides
  b. Spikelets perfect, or staminate mixed with perfect in the same part of the
      inflorescence, or staminate and pistillate spikelets on separate plants.
    d. Spikelets or groups of spikelets irregularly clustered or in 2 or more rows
      concentrated along one side of the rachis, forming 1-sided spikes or
      spike-like racemes .... Group 1
    d. Spikelets not irregularly clustered or in rows concentrated along one side
      of the rachis.
      e. Spikelets or groups of spikelets in 2 rows on opposite sides of the rachis
        forming a bilateral spike .... Group 2
      e. Spikelets in panicles or racemes, or if in spikes then not in 2 rows on
        opposite sides of the rachis.
        f. Spikelets with 2 or more functional florets (including staminate florets
          if present).
          g. Glumes shorter than the lowest lemma; awn of lemma, when present,
            terminal or from a bifid apex .... Group 3
          g. Glumes as long or longer than the lowest lemma, often as long as the
            spikelet; awn of lemma, when present, dorsal.
            Central floret perfect, the lower 2 staminate .... 50. *Hierochloe*
            All florets perfect or the uppermost staminate. .... Group 4
        f. Spikelets with one functional floret, this either perfect, pistillate
          or staminate.
          h. Glumes absent; spikelets very strongly flattened. (Fig. 187). .... 84. *Leersia*
          h. Glumes present, or rarely with 1 absent; spikelets sometimes
            compressed but not strongly flattened.
            i. Fertile floret with 2 sterile ones below, these sometimes minute. .... Group 5
            i. Fertile floret without associated sterile florets.
              j. Spikelets in 2s or 3s at each joint of the rachis of the raceme,
                one usually sessile and perfect, the other(s) pedicelled and
                staminate or neutral and represented by empty glumes or a
                pedicel, or both spikelets perfect and pedicelled .... Group 6
             j. Spikelets not arranged as above, solitary.
                Spikelets round in cross section or dorsiventrally compressed,
                  with a sterile lemma resembling the second glume present
                  below the fertile. (1st glume sometimes absent so that the
                  second glume and sterile lemma appear as 2 glumes of
                  nearly equal length); disarticulation below the glumes;
                  glumes membranous .... Group 7
                Spikelets laterally compressed in cross section, without a sterile
                  lemma below the fertile one; disarticulation above or below
                  the glumes; (if dorsiventrally compressed disarticulation
                  above the glumes; if round and disarticulation below
                  glumes then glumes indurated) .... Group 8

GROUP 1

a. Spikelets dorsiventrally compressed; sterile lemma resembling second glume present
    below fertile.
  b. Second glume or sterile lemma awned or cuspidate; spikelets usually beset with
       coarse hairs; spikelets in irregular clusters, not in rows. (Fig. 70). .... 1. *Echinochloa*
  b. Second glume or sterile lemma not awned or cuspidate; spikelets not beset with
       coarse hairs; spikelets in rows.
      Spikelets elliptic, pointed, margins of fertile lemma not inrolled, fertile lemma
          usually dark colored .... 2. *Digitaria*
      Spikelets ovoid or orbicular, blunt, margins of fertile lemma inrolled, fertile
          lemma usually light colored .... 3. *Paspalum*
a. Spikelets laterally compressed; sterile lemma, if present, of a different form than
    2nd glume and positioned above fertile lemma.
  b. Spike 1, terminal. (Fig. 73) .... 4. *Nardus stricta*
  b. Spikes 2 or more.
    c. Spikes digitate or closely approximate at the tip of the stem. (Figs. 74, 75).
      d. Spikelets each with one perfect floret.
        Sterile lemmas none .... 5. *Cynodon dactylon*
        Sterile lemma(s) present, different from the fertile .... 6. *Chloris*
      d. Spikelets each with 2 or more perfect florets.
        Rachis of spike extending beyond the terminal spikelet .... 7. *Dactyloctenium*
                                                    aegyptium
        Rachis of spike not extending beyond the terminal spikelet. .... 8. *Elusine indica*
    c. Spikes racemose or paniculate. (Fig. 77).
    e. Spikelets each with one fertile floret (perfect or staminate).
      Fertile lemma awnless, sterile lemmas none. .... 9. *Spartina*
      Fertile lemma with 3 short awns or points, sterile lemma(s) present. .... 10. *Bouteloua*
    e. Spikelets each with 2 or more fertile florets. .... 11. *Leptochloa*

GROUP 2

a. Spikelets solitary at each joint of the rachis.
  b. Spikelets positioned edgewise to the rachis. (Fig. 80). .... 12. *Lolium*
  b. Spikelets positioned flatwise to the rachis. (Fig. 83).
    c. Lemmas excentrically keeled, the keel much nearer one margin than the other;
      annuals.
      Glumes ovate, 3-nerved; lemmas not ciliate. .... 13. *Triticum*
      Glumes linear-subulate, 1-nerved; lemmas ciliate on the keel and margins. ... 14. *Secale cereale*
    c. Lemmas with keel or midnerve in the center; perennials.
      Rhizomes absent or not more than 1 cm long. .... 15. *Agropyron*
      Rhizomes elongate and extensively creeping. .... 16. *Elytrigia*
a. Spikelets 2 or 3 at each joint of the rachis. (Fig. 84).
    Spikelets in 3s, 1-flowered, the lateral pair (except in cultivated barley) pedicelled
       and sterile, usually reduced to awns, the central spikelet sessile & perfect ... 17. *Hordeum*
    Spikelets 2 or more at each joint, each with 2 or more perfect flowers, all alike
      and sessile.
    Lemmas awned, or if awnless or with an awn up to a third as long as the body,
       rhizomes absent and glumes (excluding awns) less than 2 cm long. .... 18. *Elymus*
    Lemmas awnless; rhizomes present, extensively creeping; glumes (excluding awns)
      2 cm or more long .... 19. *Leymus*

GROUP 3

a. Tall, stout reeds with large, plumose panicles; rachilla with long, brownish hairs
    overtopping the lemmas. (Fig. 88). .... 20. *Phragmites*
                                                     australis
a. Low to tall grasses, the panicle, if present, not plumose; rachilla or lemma hairs
    shorter than the lemmas or absent.
  b. Spikelets of 2 kinds, sterile and fertile paired on a common stalk in a spiciform
      panicle, the sterile fan-shaped, nearly concealing the terete
      fertile one. (Fig. 89). .... 21. *Cynosurus*
  b. Spikelets all alike.

c. Spikelets in dense, 1-sided clusters at the ends of 2 or 3 stiff, naked panicle
    branches. (Fig. 90) .... 22. *Dactylus*
                        glomerata
c. Spikelets not in dense, 1-sided clusters.
    d. Spikelets as broad as long; lemma cordate, as wide as long. (Fig. 91). .... 23. *Briza*
    d. Spikelets longer than broad; lemma not cordate, longer than wide.
        e. Spikelets with 1-4 sterile lemmas below the fertile. .... 24. *Chasmanthium*
                                            laxum
        e. Spikelets with no sterile lemmas below fertile.
            f. Callus, or nerves, or base of lemma densely bearded. (Fig. 94).
                g. Lemmas with 3 distinct nerves. (Fig. 98).
                    h. Lemmas with a cottony web at the base, the nerves glabrous. .... 25. *Poa*
                    h. Lemmas without a cottony web at the base, the nerves densely
                      pubescent.
                    Keels of palea densely bearded on the upper half. .... 26. *Triplasis*
                                          purpurea
                    Keels of palea glabrous on upper half. .... 27. *Tridens flavus*
              g. Lemmas with 5 or more distinct nerves. (Fig. 96).
                  Callus densely short-bearded; lemma awned from the notch of the
                    bifid summit. .... 28. *Schizachne*
                                          purpurascens
              Callus not bearded but lemmas cobwebby at base; lemma awnless . 25. *Poa*
            f. Callus, or nerves or base of lemma glabrous, ciliate or minutely
              pubescent, not densely bearded.
              i. Plant dioecious; spikelets unisexual. (Fig. 101). .... 29. *Distichlis spicata*
              i. Plant not dioecious; spikelets with at least one perfect flower.
                j. Lemmas 2-toothed at the tip, often awned from the notch.
                    Lemmas 5 or more nerved .... 30. *Bromus*
                    Lemmas 3 nerved .... 11. *Leptochloa*
                j. Lemmas not 2-toothed, the awn, when present, terminal.
                k. Lemmas 1-3 nerved.
                    l. Ligules membranous; alpine plants .... 25. *Poa*
                    l. Ligules ciliate; habitats various.
                      Spikelets strongly flattened; glumes keeled .... 31. *Eragrostis*
                      Spikelets subterete; glumes keel-less. .... 32. *Molinia caerulea*
                k. Lemmas 5 or more nerved, the lateral nerves sometimes faint.
                  m. Lemmas keeled or with midrib prominent. .... 25. *Poa*
                  m. Lemmas keel-less, midrib no more prominent than
                    lateral nerves.
                    n. Lateral nerves of lemma converging at the summit.
                      Perennial; stems densely cespitose with crowded
                      basal leaves. .... 33. *Festuca*
                      Annual; stems solitary or loosely cespitose. .... 34. *Vulpia*
                    n. Lateral nerves of lemma parallel, not converging at
                    the summit.
                    Lemmas strongly nerved; second glume 1-nerved
                    (except in *T. pallida*).
                    Second glume 1-nerved; lemmas 7-9 nerved. .... 35. *Glyceria*
                    Second glume 3-nerved; lemmas 5-nerved. .... 36. *Torreyochloa*
                                            pallida
                    Lemmas faintly nerved; second glume 3-nerved. .... 37. *Puccinellia*

GROUP 4

a. One or more lemmas with an awn arising at or below the middle.
    b. Lower floret staminate .... 38. *Arrhenatherum*
                      elatius
    b. Lower floret perfect.
        c. Awn clavate, with a short-hairy joint near the middle. (Fig. 118). .... 39. *Corynephorus*
                      canescens
         c. Awn not clavate, lacking a short-hairy joint near the middle.

d. Glumes longer than 1 cm .... 40. *Avena*
d. Glumes shorter than 1 cm.
    Lemma tapering into 2 slender teeth .... 41. *Aira*
    Lemma obtuse or truncate with 2-4 short teeth.
        Glumes shorter to barely longer than the lemmas. .... 42. *Deschampsia*
        Glumes much longer than the lemmas .... 43. *Vahlodea*
                                                                                     atropurpurea
a. Awn absent or terminal, or arising between the lemma teeth, or from the back of
    the lemma above the middle.
  e. Lemmas densely pubescent on the mid and lateral nerves; spikelets purplish. .... 27. *Tridens flavus*
  e. Lemmas glabrous or if pubescent, pubescence not confined to nerves; spikelets
      not purplish.
    f. Lemmas bidentate.
      g. Lemmas awned from between the teeth. .... 44. *Danthonia*
      g. Lemmas awned on the back below the teeth.
          Glumes longer than 1 cm .... 40. *Avena*
          Glumes shorter than 1 cm .... 45. *Trisetum*
    f. Lemmas not bidentate.
      h. Spikelets with 2 florets, the lower perfect, the upper staminate; glumes
          about equal, greatly exceeding lemmas; plant velvety all over. .... 46. *Holcus*
      h. Spikelets with 2 or more perfect florets; glumes subequal, the same length
          as or shorter than lemmas; plant not velvety all over.
        i. Glumes dissimilar, the second obovate. (Fig. 127). .... 47. *Sphenopholis*
        i. Glumes similar, the second not obovate.
          Panicle loose and open; callus and rachilla bearded. (Fig. 125) .... 45. *Trisetum*
          Panicle spike-like; callus and rachilla glabrous. (Fig. 128). .... 48. *Koeleria*
                                                                macrantha

GROUP 5

Glumes very unequal, the second about twice the length of the first. .... 49. *Anthozanthum*
Glumes nearly equal.
    Sterile florets exceeding the fertile, about as long as the glumes. .... 50. *Hierochloe*
    Sterile florets scale-like, much shorter than the fertile floret. .... 51. *Phalaris*

GROUP 6

a. Leaf blade ovate-lanceolate with a cordate base; creeping annual. (Fig. 133) .... 52. *Arthraxon*
                                                                    hispidus
a. Leaf blade linear-lanceolate, without a cordate base; upright perennial.
  b. Spikelets alike, perfect, in pairs along the rachis. .... 53. *Miscanthus*
  b. Spikelets not alike, the sessile one perfect, the pedicelled one staminate or neutral.
    c. Inflorescence of 1-several solitary, digitate, or aggregated, spike-like racemes
        of several to many joints. (Figs. 135, 136).
      Racemes 2 or more on each peduncle .... 54. *Andropogon*
      Raceme solitary at the summit of each peduncle. .... 55. *Schizachyrium*
                                                               scoparium
    c. Inflorescence an open panicle of abbreviated racemes having 1-few joints.
      Pedicelled spikelet well developed, usually staminate. (Fig. 137). .... 56. *Sorghum*
      Pedicelled spikelet represented only by the pedicel. (Fig. 138). .... 57. *Sorghastrum*
                                                                 nutans

GROUP 7

a. Spikelets subtended by an involucre of persistent bristles.
    Spikelets articulated above the bristles, these remaining on the inflorescence;
        bristles fewer than 5, or if 5 or more plant perennial and first glume a
        third as long as spikelet. .... 58. *Setaria*
    Spikelets articulated below the bristles, these falling with the spikelets or
        articulated above the bristles and bristles below each spikelet 5 or more,
        plant annual and first glume half or more as long as spikelet .... 59. *Pennisetum*

a. Spikelets not subtended by an involucre.
  b. Second glume or sterile lemma awned or cuspidate; spikelets usually beset with
    coarse hairs .... 1. *Echinochloa*
  b. Second glume or sterile lemma not awned or cuspidate; spikelets not beset with
    coarse hairs.
    c. Spikelets nearly sessile in slender, spiciform racemes. (Figs. 71, 72).
      d. Spikelets plano-convex .... 3. *Paspalum*
      d. Spikelets not plano-convex.
        e. Margins of fertile lemma involute.
          Blades of the basal and stem leaves similar and elongate, not crowded
            andforming a rosette or cushion; annual or perennial, bearing
            a terminal primary panicle and sometimes also axillary
            secondary panicles, the primary and secondary panicles
            uniform or nearly so. .... 60. *Panicum*
          Blades of the basal and stem leaves usually different in shape, the
            former crowded and forming a rosette or cushion; perennial,
            early in the season with simple stems and a terminal primary
            panicle, later in the season usually branching and bearing
            axillary leafy fascicles or smaller secondary panicles (often
            hidden by the leaves), of mostly cleistogamous, fertile flowers. ... 61. *Dichanthelium*
        e. Margins of fertile lemma flat, not involute .... 2. *Digitaria*
    c. Spikelets in panicles.
      f. Margins of fertile lemma flat, not involute; spikelets on pedicels mostly
        longer than 2 cm; first glume absent or very tiny. (Fig. 152). .... 62. *Leptoloma*
                                                                cognatum
      f. Margins of fertile lemma involute; spikelets on pedicels mostly shorter than
        2 cm; first glume at least 1/4 length of spikelet.
        Blades of the basal and stem leaves similar and elongate, not crowded and
          forming a rosette or cushion; annual or perennial, bearing a
          terminal primary panicle and sometimes also axillary secondary
          panicles, the primary and secondary panicles uniform or nearly so. 60. *Panicum*
        Blades of the basal and stem leaves usually different in shape, the former
          crowded and forming a rosette or cushion; perennial, early in the
          season with simple stems and a terminal primary panicle, later in
          the season usually branching and bearing axillary leafy fascicles or
          smaller secondary panicles (often hidden by the leaves), of mostly
          cleistogamous, fertile flowers. .... 61. *Dichanthelium*

GROUP 8

a. Leaf blade ovate-lanceolate with a cordate base. .... 52. *Arthraxon*
                                                             hispidus
a. Leaf blade not ovate-lanceolate, without a cordate base.
  b. Inflorescence a dense, symmetrical, cylindric to ovoid, spike-like panicle.
    (Figs. 153-156).
    c. Lemma surrounded at the base by a tuft of callus hairs. .... 63. *Ammophila*
    c. Lemma glabrous or pubescent but without basal callus hairs.
      d. Glumes awned or awn-tipped.
        Glumes prominently folded and keeled, their awns less than 2 mm;
          panicle not appearing silky; lemmas awnless .... 64. *Phleum*
        Glumes not prominently folded and keeled, their awns 3 mm or longer
          causing panicle to appear silky; lemmas awned. .... 65. *Polypogon*
      d. Glumes rounded at the tip or acute to acuminate but not awned or
        awn-tipped.
        e. Glumes longer than and enclosing the lemma.
          Lemma membranous, with dense, woolly pubescence .... 66. *Mibora minima*
          Lemma indurated, appressed-pilose to sericeous but not woolly-
            pubescent. .... 51. *Phalaris*
        e. Glumes shorter than or equalling lemma.
          Spike-like panicle partly included in inflated leaf sheaths; lemmas
            awnless; ligule a ring of hairs. (Fig. 157) .... 67. *Crypsis*
                                      schoenoides

Spike-like panicle exserted; lemmas awned on the back below middle;
ligule membranous. (Fig. 158) .... 68. *Alopecurus*
b. Inflorescence a branched panicle, either loose and open or contracted, spike-like,
and lobed or asymmetrical in outline.
f. Lemma indurated, unlike the glumes in texture, conspicuously harder.
g. Lemma awnless.
h. Spikelets dorsiventrally compressed. .... 69. *Milium effusum*
h. Spikelets laterally compressed.
Glumes longer than and enclosing lemma. .... 51. *Phalaris*
Glumes about as long as the lemma .... 70. *Oryzopsis*
g. Lemma awned (awn sometimes weak or deciduous).
i. Awn 3-forked (lateral branches sometimes short). (Fig. 161). .... 71. *Aristida*
i. Awn simple.
Awn less than 3.5 times as long as the lemma; callus short, obtuse. .... 70. *Oryzopsis*
Awn 4 or more times as long as the lemma; callus long and acuminate. . 72. *Piptochaetium*
avenaceum
f. Lemma membranous, like the glumes in texture, not conspicuously harder.
j. Floret raised above glumes on a short slender stipe; spikelet disarticulating
below the glumes, falling intact. .... 73. *Cinna*
j. Floret not stipitate; spikelet disarticulating above the glumes leaving them
as empty husks.
k. Lemma awned from the tip or mucronate.
Rachilla prolonged behind palea; glumes minute. .... 74. *Brachyelytrum*
Rachilla not prolonged; at least 1 glume well developed. .... 75. *Muhlenbergia*
k. Lemma awnless or awned from the back or just below the tip.
l. Lemma surrounded at the base by a tuft of callus hairs. (Fig. 172).
m. Lemma with a short, sometimes delicate dorsal awn. .... 76. *Calamagrostis*
m. Lemma awnless.
Spikelets longer than 8 mm .... 63. *Ammophila*
Spikelets (excluding awns on glumes) shorter than 8 mm. .... 75. *Muhlenbergia*
l. Lemma glabrous or pubescent but without a tuft of callus hairs.
n. Lemma 1-nerved; seed loose within the pericarp. .... 77. *Sporobolus*
n. Lemma 3-nerved; seed adnate to the pericarp.
o. First glume (excluding awn) shorter than to equalling lemma;
glumes and lemma usually acuminate to a sharp tip;
lemma awnless. .... 75. *Muhlenbergia*
o. First glume exceeding lemma; glumes and lemma not acuminate
to a sharp tip; lemma awned from the back or below tip,
or awnless.
Lemmas awnless or with awns exserted less than 2 times the
length of the spikelets and inserted at or near middle or
base of lemma (Fig. 178), or if inserted near tip palea
minute or wanting; rachilla not prolonged behind palea
as a slender bristle .... 78. *Agrostis*
Lemmas awned, the awns exserted 2 or more times the length
of the spikelets and inserted near tip of lemma (Fig. 182);
palea nearly as long as lemma; rachilla prolonged behind
palea as a slender bristle. .... 79. *Apera*

1. *Echinochloa* Beauv. (from the Greek based on the bristly appearance of the panicle).
Tall, coarse annuals (ours); leaves with compressed sheaths and long, flat blades, ligules obsolete;
inflorescence a terminal, rather compact panicle of short, stout, densely flowered, one-sided
racemes along a central axis; spikelets with one perfect and one sterile flower, disarticulating below
the glumes, ovoid to lanceolate, dorsally flattened, plano-convex, solitary or in irregular clusters in
the racemes, subsessile, usually hispid; first glume up to half as long as the spikelet, acute, second
glume and sterile lemma equal, as long as the spikelet, mucronate or awned, the sterile lemma
enclosing a palea and sometimes a staminate flower; fertile lemma indurated, shining, acute to
cuspidate, the margins inrolled below; palea nearly as long as the lemma; stamens 3. —Wildl. 2

a. Sheaths, at least the lower, pubescent; grain 2.5 or more times as long as broad .... 1. *E. walteri*
a. Sheaths glabrous; grain 2 or less times as long as wide.
  b. Hairs of second glume and sterile lemma, particularly those on the margins,
    with thick, swollen bases .... 2. *E. muricata*
  b. Hairs of second glume and sterile lemma not decidedly swollen at the base.
    Second glume and sterile lemma strigose, most of the hairs about 1 mm long. .... 3. *E. crus-galli*
    Second glume and sterile lemma pilose or short-pubescent, none of the
    hairs over 0.5 mm .... 4. *E. colonum*

1. *E. wálteri* (Pursh) Heller (for T. Walter). Ditches, marshes, wet soil and shallow fresh to brackish marshes, particularly along the coast. August–October. Map 173. (W.I.). —FACW+

2. *E. muricáta* (Beauv.) Fern. (spiny). Barnyard Grass. Wet open ground and waste areas. August-September. Map 174. Our plants include var. *muricata* and the following vars.:

var. *wiegándii* Fassett. Panicle contracted, with ascending to appressed branches, glumes and sterile lemma puberulent (panicle open, with lower branches spreading, glumes and sterile lemma with pustular based hairs in var. *muricata*). [*E. pungens* var. *ludoviciana*].

var. *microstáchya* Wieg. grain 3.5 mm or shorter, awns 3 mm or shorter (in the above vars. grain longer than 3.5 mm and awns longer than 3 mm). (W.I.). [*E. microstachya; E. pungens* var. *m.*]. —FACW+

3. *E. crus-gálli* (L.) Beauv. Barnyard Grass. Cultivated ground, roadsides, waste areas and damp soil. July-October. Fig. 70, Map 175. (Introduced from E. Asia). Our plants are var. *crus-galli*. —FACU

4. *E. colóna* (L.) Link. Jungle Rice. Fields, roadsides, waste places and moist soil. July-October. Map 176. (Naturalized from the old world). [*E. colonum*]. —FACW

2. *Digitària* Haller Crabgrass (finger).

Annual or perennial, erect or prostrate, often branched from the base; leaves with flat blades and membranous ligules; inflorescence a terminal, digitate or subdigitate cluster of few-several, spike-like, one-sided racemes having a winged or 3-angled and wingless rachis; spikelets one-flowered, disarticulating below the glumes, lanceolate or elliptic, dorsally flattened, plano-convex, sessile or short-pedicelled, in twos or threes, alternate in 2 rows on one side of the rachis; first glume minute or wanting, second glume acute, equalling or shorter than the acute, sterile lemma; fertile lemma cartilaginous, often shining, acute, about as long as the sterile lemma; palea of similar texture as the fertile lemma, about as long; flower perfect, stamens 3. —Wildl. 2

a. Sheaths and nodes glabrous .... 1. *D. ischaemum*
a. Sheaths (at least the lower) and/or nodes pubescent.
  b. Rachis of raceme flat, broadly winged; spikelets 2.5 mm or longer. .... 2. *D. sanguinalis*
  b. Rachis of raceme triangular, wingless or slender margined; spikelets less
    than 2.5 mm.
    Stem very slender, less than 1 mm thick. .... 3. *D. filiformis*
    Stem stout, more than 1 mm thick .... 4. *D. texana*

1. *D. ischaémum* (Schreb.) Muhl. Small Crabgrass. Cultivated ground, roadsides and waste places. July-September. Fig. 71, Map 177. (Naturalized from Europe). [*D. humifusa*]. Our plants are var. *ischaemum*.

D. violáscens Link. Resembling *D. ischaemum*; distinguishable in having spikelets shorter than 1.7 mm, the hairs not capitellate (spikelet 1.7 mm or longer with capitellate hairs in *D. ischaemum*). Reported for MA.

2. *D. sanguinális* (L.) Scop. Large Crabgrass. Cultivated ground, roadsides and waste places. July-September. Map 178. (Naturalized from old world). [*D. adscendens*]. Seeds can be eaten or ground into flour. —FACU-

D. ciliáris (Retz.) Koel. Resembling *D. sanguinalis* but distinguishable in having spikelets 3-3.5 mm long with longer cilia (1 mm or more long); (spikelets 2.5-3 mm long with cilia less than 1 mm long in *D. sanguinalis*). Reported for CT, MA. [*D. sanguinalis* var. *c.; D. adscendens*].

4. D. filifórmis (L.) Koel. (thread-like). Slender Crabgrass. Fields, roadsides and waste places in sandy soil. July-September. Map 179. [*D. laeviglumis*]. Our plants are var. *filiformis*.
   4. D. texána A. S. Hitchc. Deciduous woods and open ground in sandy soil.

3. Páspalum L. (from the Greek, meaning meal).

Perennials (ours) usually tufted or branched from the base; leaves with flat blades and membranous ligules; inflorescence of one to many spike-like racemes, digitate or racemose along a common axis at the summit of the stem, secondary racemes often occurring on axillary peduncles from the upper sheaths; spikelets 1-flowered, disarticulating below the glumes, ovate, elliptic or obovate, dorsiventrally flattened or plano-convex, subsessile, solitary or in pairs in 2 or 4 rows on one side of a flattened or 3 angled rachis, placed with the convex side toward the rachis; first glume usually absent, second glume and sterile lemma of about equal length, the former rarely absent or suppressed, acute to rounded, membranous; fertile lemma usually obtuse, indurated and lustrous, its margins inrolled over the indurated palea, subtending a perfect flower with 3 stamens. —Wildl. 2

   Eremóchloa Buse *ophiuroídes* (Munro) Hack. Similar to *Paspalum* but distinguishable in having stems creeping and rooting at the nodes, inflorescence a spikelike terminal raceme, rachis flat, spikelets solitary, sessile, first glume winged at apex. Cultivated in the south, rarely occurring in our range. Reported for Franklin County MA.

Spikelets 2.5 mm or longer; glume and sterile lemma 5-nerved. .... 1. *P. laeve*
Spikelets less than 2.5 mm; glume and sterile lemma 2-3 nerved. .... 2. *P. setaceum*

   1. P. laéve Michx. (smooth). Old fields, thickets, lake shores, pine or mixed woodlands and woods openings, and roadsides. July-October. Fig. 72, Map 180. Endangered in CT. [*P. angustifolium; P. longipilum; P. plenipilum*]. Our plants include var. *laeve* and the following var.:
      var. *circuláre* (Nash) Fern. Spikelets about as long as broad, more than 2.5 mm broad (spikelets longer than broad, 2.5 mm or less broad in var. *laeve*). [*P. circulare*]. —FAC+
   2. P. setáceum Michx. (bristle-like). Dry or sandy fields, pastures, open pine or mixed woodlands and woods openings, waste places and roadsides, mostly on the coastal plain. June-October. Map 181. (Mexico). [*P. debile; P. muhlenbergii; P. pubescens; P. psammophilum*]. —FACU+

4. Nárdus L. Matgrass (Greek name for Spikenard).

Low, densely matted, rhizomatous, wiry perennial; leaves mostly crowded toward base of stem, fewer on the upper part of stem, lower sheaths bladeless or with reduced blades, the upper with slender, involute, somewhat stiff blades, ligule membranous; inflorescence a slender one-sided, terminal spike; spikelets 1-flowered, subulate, solitary, sessile, disarticulating above the glumes, alternating in notches on two sides of a 3 sided rachis; first (inner) glume lacking, second (outer) glume minute, adnate to the rachis; lemma lance-subulate, acuminate or short-awned, margins tightly inrolled; palea about the same length as the lemma (excluding awns); flowers perfect, stamens 3.

   1. N. strícta L. (straight). Dry, open sandy soil. June-September. Fig. 73, Map 182. (Eurasia; Greenland).

5. Cýnodon L. C. Rich. Bermuda Grass (from the Greek meaning dog tooth, from the appearance of the spikelets).

Low, diffusely branched perennial, widely spreading by stolons and rhizomes, bladeless sheaths of the rootstalk in pairs resembling dogs teeth; stems arising along the rootstalk, upright from a geniculate base, flattened, wiry; leaves with short, flat blades, the ligule a conspicuous ring of white hairs; inflorescence a terminal, digitate cluster of several slender spikes; spikelets disarticulating above the glumes, 1-flowered, laterally compressed, sessile in 2 rows along one side of a slender

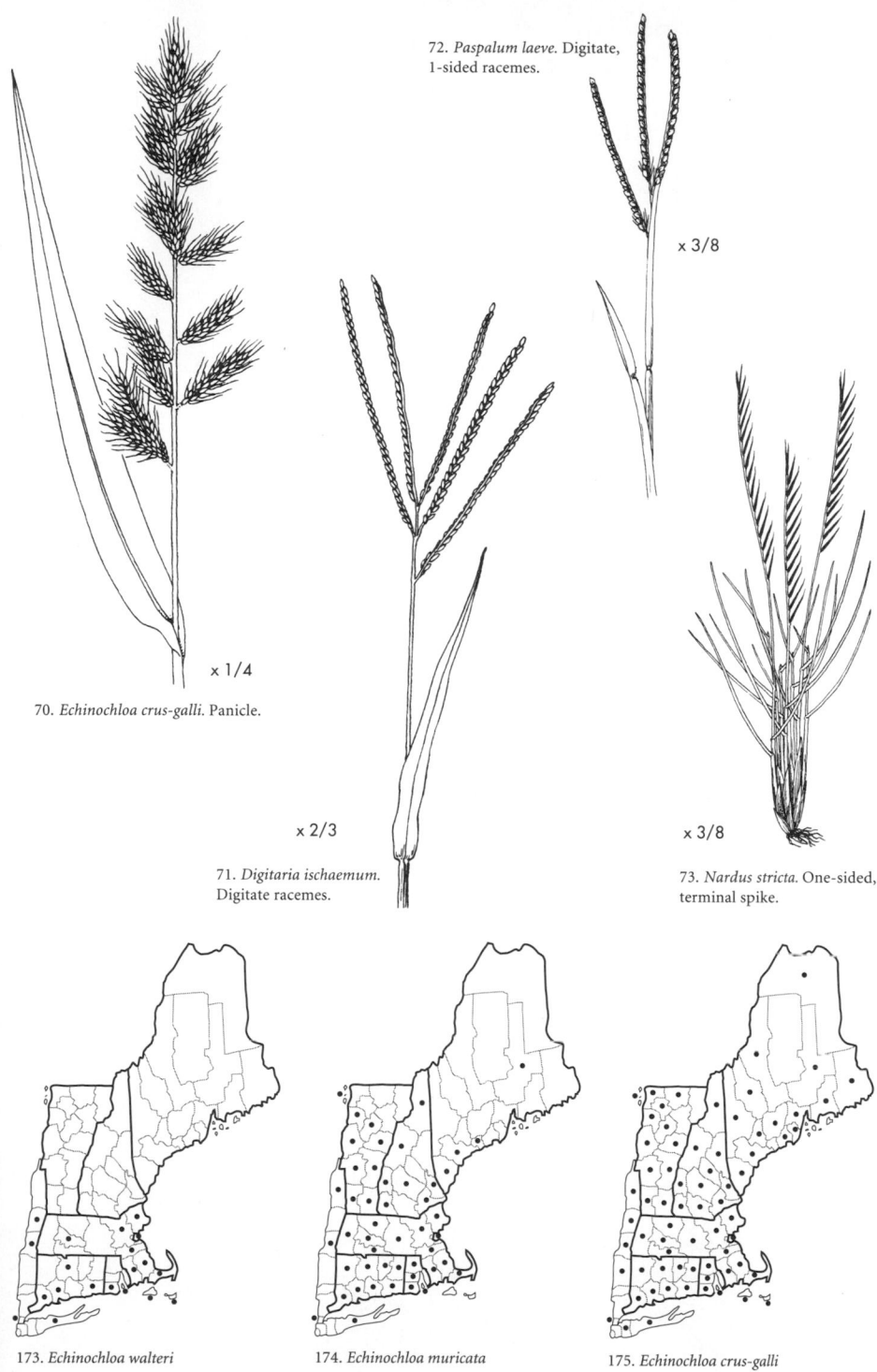

72. *Paspalum laeve*. Digitate,
1-sided racemes.

x 3/8

x 1/4

70. *Echinochloa crus-galli*. Panicle.

x 2/3

71. *Digitaria ischaemum*.
Digitate racemes.

x 3/8

73. *Nardus stricta*. One-sided,
terminal spike.

173. *Echinochloa walteri*

174. *Echinochloa muricata*

175. *Echinochloa crus-galli*

176. *Echinochloa colona*

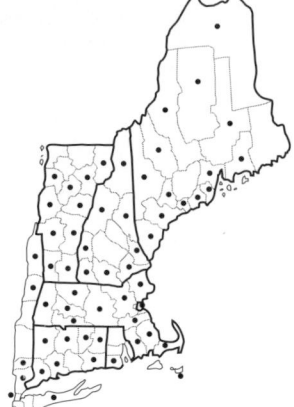

177. *Digitaria ischaemum*

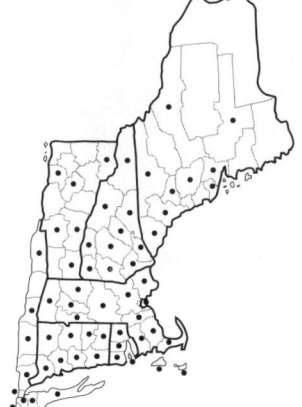

178. *Digitaria sanguinalis*

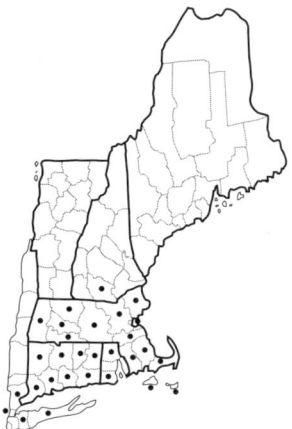

179. *Digitaria filiformis*

180. *Paspalum laeve*

181. *Paspalum setaceum*

182. *Nardus stricta*

183. *Cynodon dactylon*

flattened rachis and appressed to it; glumes narrow, acute or acuminate, subequal, shorter than the lemma; lemma broader than the glumes, acute, ciliate on the keel, awnless; palea nearly as long as the lemma; flowers perfect, stamens 3.—Wildl. 1

1. *C. dáctylon* (L.) Pers. (with fingers). Fields, pastures and waste places. July-September. Fig. 74, Map 183. (Naturalized from Europe). [*Capriola d.*]. —FACU

6. *Chlóris* Sw. Finger Grass (named for a Greek goddess).

Annual or perennial, tufted, stems erect or decumbent and rooting at the nodes; leaves with flat or folded blades, mostly crowded at the base, stem leaves few; inflorescence a terminal, digitate cluster of elongate sometimes feathery and showy spikes; spikelets sessile, in two rows on two sides of a slender, triangular rachis, disarticulating above the glumes, 2-several flowered, the lowest fertile, the second smaller, sterile, often truncate, other sterile lemmas, if present, progressively smaller and enclosed in the first sterile lemma; glumes unequal, narrow, acute, acuminate or short-awned; fertile lemma keeled, usually awned just below the tip, often ciliate on the callus and on the back or margins, sterile lemmas awned or awnless; palea about as long as the lemma; stamens 3.

a. Awns shorter than the spikelets .... 1. *C. cucullata*
a. Awns longer than the spikelets.
  b. Lemma with a tuft of long silky hairs at the tip, the spikes appearing feathery .... 2. *C. virgata*
  b. Lemma without long silky hairs.
    Lemmas at least a third longer than the glumes. .... 3. *C. gayana*
    Lemmas shorter than the glumes or only slightly longer. .... 4. *C. verticillata*

1. *C. cucullàta* Bisch. Dry, sandy waste areas. Fig. 75. Reported for York County ME.

2. *C. virgáta* Sw. (wand-like). Old fields and waste areas. Reported for York County ME, Suffolk County MA. (Adventive from the southwest and the Tropics).

3. *C. gayána* Kunth (for J. Gay). Rhodes Grass. Spread from cultivation. (Introduced from Africa).

4. *C. verticilláta* Nutt. (whorled). Windmill Grass. Plains and prairies. Reported for New London County CT.

7. *Dactylocténium* Willd. Crowfoot Grass (from the Greek meaning finger comb, based on the appearance of the spikes).

Cespitose annual, stems flattened, geniculate, decumbent at the base, creeping and rooting at the nodes, the tips ascending, branching and forming mats; leaves with flat blades and short, membranous, usually ciliate ligules; inflorescence of 2-several short, thick, sessile, terminal spikes, digitate and widely spreading; spikelets laterally compressed, disarticulating above the glumes and between the lemmas, several flowered, sessile and closely imbricated in 2 rows on one side of the rachis, the tip extended beyond spikelets as a point; glumes unequal, shorter than the spikelet, broad, compressed and keeled, the first acute, the second mucronate or short-awned below the tip; lemmas broadly ovate, compressed and keeled, abruptly acuminate or short-awned; palea equalling the lemma; flowers perfect, stamens 3.

1. *D. aegýptium* (L.) Willd. (Egyptian). Fields, roadsides and waste places. August-October. Fig. 76. (Naturalized from the Old World). Reported for Middlesex County MA.

8. *Eleusíne* Gaertn. Goose Grass (from the Greek, referring to the town, Eleusis, where a goddess was worshipped).

Coarse, cespitose annual with compressed stems; leaves with flat, keeled sheaths, flat blades, and membranous ligules; inflorescence a cluster of 2-several stout digitate or approximate spikes, sometimes consisting of a single spike; spikelets several flowered, the flowers all perfect or the upper

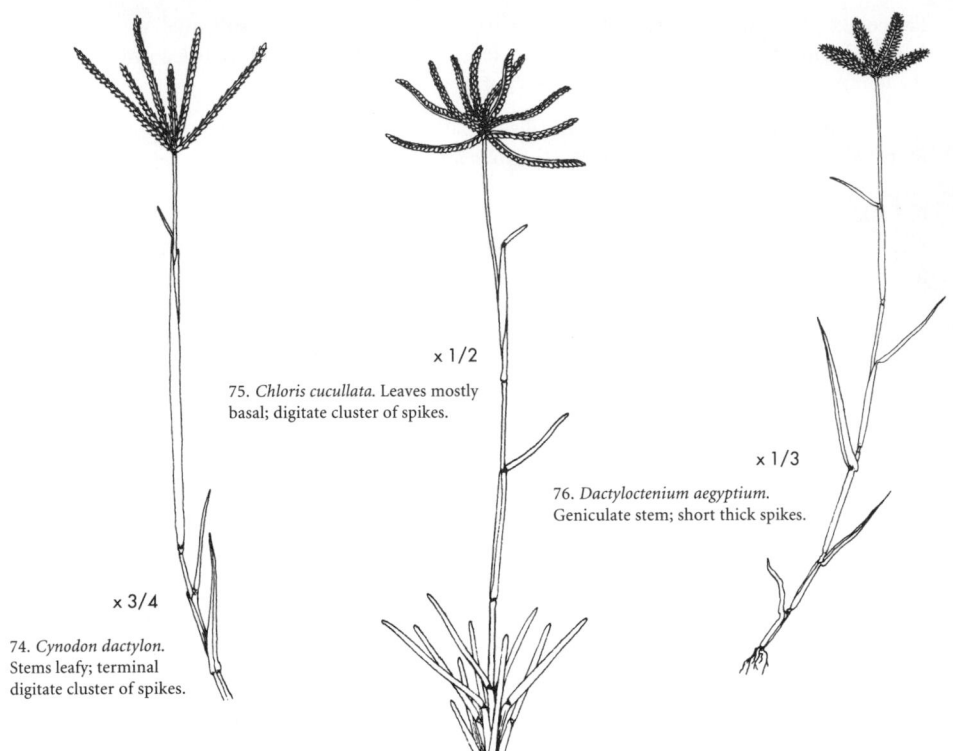

x 1/2

75. *Chloris cucullata.* Leaves mostly basal; digitate cluster of spikes.

x 1/3

76. *Dactyloctenium aegyptium.* Geniculate stem; short thick spikes.

x 3/4

74. *Cynodon dactylon.* Stems leafy; terminal digitate cluster of spikes.

staminate, disarticulating above the glumes and between the lemmas, laterally compressed, sessile and crowded in 2 rows along one side of the rachis; glumes unequal, shorter than the spikelet, keeled, acute to cuspidate; lemmas keeled, acute to acuminate; palea shorter than lemma; stamens 3.

1. *E. índica* (L.) Gaertn. (of India). Fields, yards, cultivated ground and waste places. July-October. Map 184. (Naturalized from the Old World). Seeds can be dried and eaten. —FACU-

9. *Spartína* Schreb. Cord Grass (from the Greek, meaning cord).

Perennials, often stout and tall, from stout, creeping rhizomes; leaves with long, flat or involute blades and very short, ciliate ligule; inflorescence of few to many dense, one-sided spikes, appressed or spreading, racemose along a common axis, the tips of the rachises naked; spikelets 1-flowered, strongly flattened laterally, disarticulating below the glumes, sessile and loosely to closely imbricated in 2 rows on 2 sides of a continuous, triangular rachis; glumes indurated, unequal, keeled, acute, acuminate or awned, the second usually exceeding the lemma; lemma keeled, obtuse, thinner than the glumes; palea equalling or exceeding lemma; flowers perfect, stamens 3. —Wildl. 2

Beckmánnia Host. Differing from *Spartina* in having very broad glumes and suborbicular spikelets. Represented by *B. syzigachne* (Steud.) Fern. From farther west. Wet Soil. Reported for Cumberland County ME. —OBL

a. Spikes mostly 5 or fewer; fresh leaves involute, 3 mm or less wide. .... 1. *S. patens*
a. Spikes mostly more numerous; fresh leaves flat, wider than 3 mm
    (sometimes involute when dry).
   b. Spikes appressed to axis of panicle, smooth when rubbed backward; spikelets
      in the same row on the rachis 4 mm or more apart. (Fig. 77). .... 2. *S. alterniflora*

b. Spikes ascending to divergent, usually not appressed; harsh when rubbed
   backward; spikelets in the same row on the rachis less than 4 mm apart.
   Second glume awned; most spikes separated from each other along the rachis
   by 1 cm or more .... 3. *S. pectinata*
   Second glume acute or acuminate but not awned; most spikes separated from
   each other along the rachis by less than 1 cm. .... 4. *S. cynosuroides*

1. S. pátens (Ait.) Muhl. (spreading). Salt-meadow Cord Grass. Salt marshes inundated during high tide and sea beaches. July-October. Map 185. [*S. juncea*]. —FACW+

S. x caespitósum A. A. Eat. (pro. sp.). A hybrid between *S. patens* and *S. pectinata*, differing from both in having poorly developed rhizomes. [*S. caespitosa; S. patens* var. *caespitosa*]. —OBL

2. S. alterniflóra Loisel (alternate-flowered). Salt-water Cord Grass. Salt marshes, usually growing in the water. July-September. Fig. 77, Map 186. —OBL

3. S. pectináta Link. (comb-like). Fresh-water Cord Grass. Fresh water or brackish marshes and shores. July-September. Map 187. (Europe). [*S. michauxiana*]. —OBL

4. S. cynosuroídes (L.) Roth (spikes like those of *Cynosurus*). Salt Reed-Grass. Salt and brackish marshes. August-October. Map 188. —OBL

10. *Bouteloúa* Lag. Grama-Grass (for C. Boutelou).

Low to tall, cespitose, annual or (ours) perennial, sometimes rhizomatous; leaves with narrow, flat or convolute blades and membranous ligules; inflorescence of few to many short spikes which are nearly sessile, loosely racemose along a common axis; spike with few to many spikelets, these loosely arranged or crowded and overlapping, sessile in 2 rows along one side of a flattened rachis which usually projects beyond the spikelets; spikelets disarticulating above the glumes, with 1 perfect flower and 1 or more sterile rudiments; glumes unequal, narrow, acuminate to awn-pointed, keeled; fertile flower with lemma as long or longer than the glumes, 3 of the nerves extended into short awns, the palea about as long as the lemma, sometimes 2-awned; sterile rudiment on a short extension of the rachilla at the base of the fertile lemma, reduced to an empty, 1-3 awned lemma, a second or third rudiment often present; stamens 3. —Wildl. 1

1. B. curtipéndula (Michx.) Torr. (short-hanging). Tall Grama-Grass. Dry hills, plains and woodlands. July-September. Fig. 78. Map 189. Endangered in NY and CT. [*Atheropogon c.*]. Our plants are var. *curtipendula*.

Six other species, rarely adventive in our range from the west and southwest differ from B. curtipendula in having 12 or fewer spikes in the inflorescence; *B. curtipendula* typically has 15 or more spikes. *B. grácilis* (Willd. ex Kunth) Lag. ex Griffiths. Reported for CT, MA, York County ME, Essex County MA; *B. hirsúta* Lag. Reported for York County Me; *B. radicósa* (Fourn.) Griffiths. Reported for York County ME, Suffolk County MA; *B. répens* (H.B.K.) Scribn. & Merrill. Reported for MA; *B. rigidiséta* (Steud.) A. S. Hitch. Reported for Suffolk County MA; *B. símplex* Lag. Reported for ME.

11. *Leptóchloa* Beauv. Feathergrass (from the Greek, meaning slender grass, from the long, slender racemes).

Tall or moderately tall, often branched, annual or perennial; leaves with flat blades and membranous ligules; inflorescence a long, simple, terminal panicle composed of numerous long, slender, spike-like racemes disposed along the central axis; spikelets 2-several flowered, the flowers all perfect or the upper staminate or rudimentary, disarticulating above the glumes, sessile or short-pedicelled, in 2 rows along one side of the slender rachis or scattered, approximate or distant; glumes membranous, acute or mucronate, unequal, usually shorter than the lemmas; lemmas 3 nerved, obtuse, acute, or bifid and mucronate or short-awned from between the teeth, or the lateral nerves sometimes excurrent into minute points; palea broad, nearly as long as the lemma; stamens 3.

x 1/4

77. *Spartina alterniflora.* Spikes
appressed to axis of panicle.

x 2/3

79. *Leptochloa fascicularis.* Panicle of
numerous, long, spike-like racemes.

x 1/3

78. *Bouteloua curtipendula.* Raceme of 1-sided spikes.

184. *Eleusine indica*

185. *Spartina patens*

186. *Spartina alterniflora*

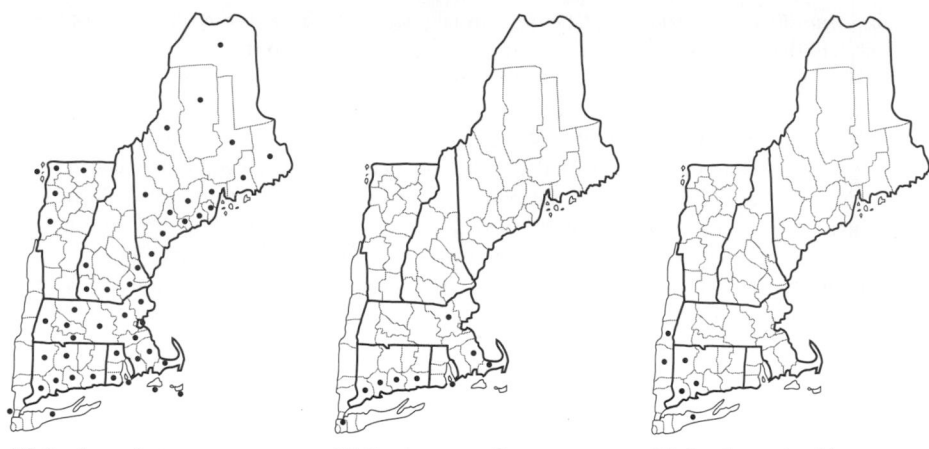

187. *Spartina pectinata*   188. *Spartina cynosuroides*   189. *Bouteloua curtipendula*

Sheaths papillose-pilose; lemmas 1.7 mm or less long. .... 1. *L. filiformis*
Sheaths smooth or scabrous; lemmas 1.8 mm or more long.
   Lemmas 3 mm or more long, short awned. .... 2. *L. fascicularis*
   Lemmas less than 3 mm long, mucronate but not awned. .... 3. *L. uninervia*

1. *L. filifórmis* (Lam.) Beauv. (Thread-like). Cultivated fields, in moist, sandy soil. July-October. (Mexico; S. Amer.; W.I.). From farther south. Reported for Middlesex County MA. [*L. attenuata*]. —FACW

2. *L. fasciculáris* (Lam.) Gray. Clustered Salt-grass. Brackish marshes along the coast and occasionally in waste areas. August-September. Fig. 79. Map 190. (S. Amer.; W.I.). [*Diplachne f.*]. Our plants include var. *fascicularis* and the following var.:

   var. *marítima* (Bickn.) Gl. Plant 5 dm or more tall; awns on lemmas usually not over 1 mm long (plant usually not over 5 dm tall and awns on lemmas 1 mm or more long in var. *fascicularis*). [*L. maritima; D. maritima*]. —FACW

3. *L. uninérvia* (J. Presl.) A. S. Hitchc. & Chase. Ditches and moist soil. From south and west. Reported for Middlesex County MA. —FACW-

12. *Lólium* L. Darnel (ancient name).

Annuals or perennials; leaves with narrow, flat blades, usually auricled at the base, and membranous ligules; inflorescence a slender, terminal, elongate, usually flat spike; spikelets laterally flattened, several-flowered, disarticulating above the glumes and between the lemmas, sessile and alternate on opposite sides of the rachis, placed edgewise, one edge fitting in a groove in the rachis; first glume none on the side resting in the groove, second glume equalling or exceeding second floret, narrowly lance-oblong, terminal spikelet with both glumes; lemmas rounded on the back, obtuse or acute, awned or awnless; palea as long as the lemma; flowers perfect, stamens 3. —Wildl. 1

Glumes (excluding awns) as long or longer than spikelets; annual. .... 1. *L. temulentum*
Glumes (excluding awns) distinctly shorter than spikelets; perennial. .... 2. *L. perenne*

1. *L. temuléntum* L. (drunken; from narcotic grains). Poison Darnel. Grainfields and waste places. June-August. Map 191. (Adventive from Europe). Poisonous.

2. *L. perénne* L. (perennial). Ryegrass. Fields, roadsides and waste places. June-August. Fig. 80, Map 192. (Naturalized from Europe). Our plants include subsp. *perenne* and the following subsp.:

subsp. *multiflórum* (Lam.) Husnot. Lemmas usually awned, rachis scabrous on the side opposite the spikelets (lemmas awnless and rachis smooth on the side opposite the spikelets in subsp. *perenne*). Map 192a [*L. multiflorum; L. perenne* var. *aristatum; L.p.* var. *italicum*]. —FACU-

13. *Tríticum* L. Wheat (classical name).

Low to tall, cespitose annual; leaves with flat blades and membranous ligules; inflorescence a thick, dense terminal spike; spikelets 2-5 flowered, plump, sessile and solitary, alternating on opposite sides at each joint of the rachis with wide side appressed to the rachis, disarticulating above the glumes; glumes ovate, excentrically keeled, pointed at the tip or awned, the broader side truncate or notched at the summit; lemmas broad, excentrically keeled, rounded at the tip, abruptly pointed or awned; palea acute, the same length as the lemma body; flowers perfect, stamens 3. —Wildl. 3

1. *T. aestívum* L. (of summer). Cultivated fields, roadsides and waste places.Fig. 81, Map 193. (Introduced from Eurasia).

T. spélta L. Rachis disarticulating, each joint bearing a spikelet in which the scales permanently enclose the grain (in *T. aestivum* the rachis remains continuous and the spikelet scales open, exposing the grain). Reported for VT.

14. *Secále* L. Rye (ancient name).

Tall, erect, cespitose annual, branched from the base; leaves with flat blades and membranous, erose to ciliate ligule; inflorescence a thick, dense terminal spike; spikelets usually 2-flowered, disarticulating above the glumes, sessile and solitary, flattened, alternate on opposite sides of the rachis with the flat side appressed to the rachis; glumes rigid, narrow, acuminate or subulate, subequal, shorter than the lemmas; lemmas broader than glumes, excentrically keeled, ciliate on keel and margins, 5-nerved, tapering to a long awn; palea about as long as lemma. —Wildl. 1

1. *S. cereále* L. (cereal). Cultivated; often escaped in fields, roadsides and waste places. Fig. 82, Map 194. (Introduced from Eurasia).

15. *Agropýron* Gaertn. Wheatgrass (the Greek name for wild wheat).

Perennials (ours without creeping rhizomes); stems cespitose, simple and usually erect; leaf blades flat or involute, ligule minute or absent; inflorescence a terminal, solitary spike; spikelets 3-several flowered, flattened, sessile, solitary, in alternate notches of the rachis, the flat side appressed to the rachis, disarticulating above the glumes and between the lemmas; glumes equal or nearly so, opposite or edge to edge on the outer side of the spikelet, several nerved, usually shorter than the lemmas, acute or awned; lemmas rounded on the back, 5-7 nerved, acute or awned from the tip; palea nearly as long as the lemma, 2-keeled, the keels minutely ciliate; flowers perfect, stamens 3. —Wildl. 1

Eremóchloa Buse *ophiuroídes* (Munroe) Hack. Similar to *Agropyron*. Spikelets solitary, sessile, 1-flowered, dorsiventrally flattened (see description under *Paspalum, Genus 3*).

Aégilops L. Goat grass. Similar to *Agropyron* and *Eremochloa* but distinguishable in having cylindric spikes with spikelets fitting closely into the concavities of the rachis (in *Agropyron* the spikes are slender and spikelets are broader than the rachis, not fitting into the concavities; in *Eremochloa* spikelets are 1-flowered and first glume is winged at the apex). Western; 2 species rarely occuring in our range: *A. cylíndrica* Host. having 1-awned glumes is reported for Westchester and Kings Counties NY, and *A. trunciális* L. with 3-awned glumes is reported for Westchester County NY.

Most spikes less than 6 cm long; 1 cm or more broad (including awns). .... 1. *A. cristatum*
Most spikes more than 6.5 cm long; if shorter, less than 1 cm broad. .... 2. *A. trachycaulum*

×1

80. *Lolium perenne*. Spike with spikelets placed edgewise.

×1/3

×1/2

82. *Secale cereale*. Spike of awned spikelets.

81. *Triticum aestivum*. Spike of awned spikelets.

190. *Leptochloa fascicularis*

191. *Lolium temulentum*

192. *Lolium perenne* subsp. *perenne*

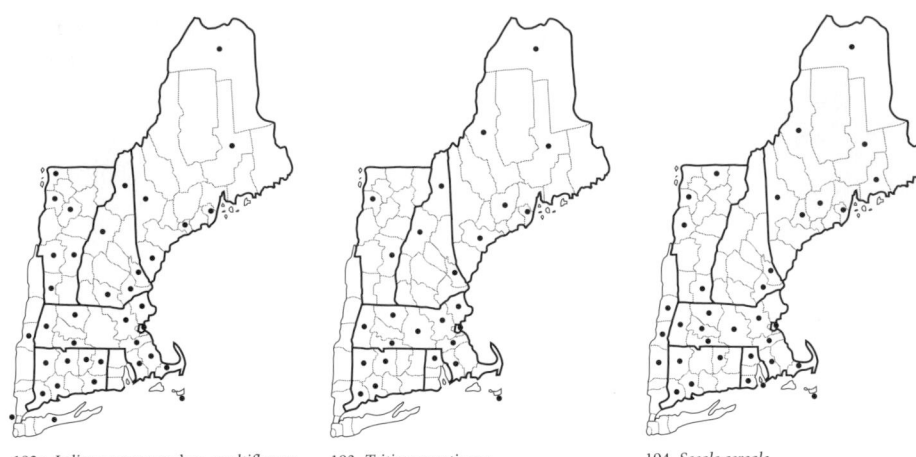

192a. *Lolium perenne* subsp. *multiflorum*   193. *Triticum aestivum*   194. *Secale cereale*

1. A. cristátum (L.) Gaertn. (crested). Roadsides, waste areas. July-August. (Adventive from Eurasia). Reported for Carroll County NH, Suffolk County NY.

2. A. trachycaúlum (Link) Malte (rough-stemmed). Slender Wheatgrass. Dry, gravelly and rocky soil, waste areas. July-August. Fig. 83, Map 195. [*Elymus trachycaulus*]. Our plants include the following vars.:

var. *trachycaulum*. Distinguishable from the other vars. by the following combination of characters: Lemmas awnless or with an awn up to half as long as the lemma, spikelets barely imbricated, internodes of rachis often 4-sided (spikelets closely imbricated and internodes of rachis 2-sided in vars. *majus* and *novae angliae*; lemmas with an awn as long or longer than the body in vars. *glaucum* and *unilaterale*). [*Elymus trachycaulus* subsp. *subsecundus*].

var. *màjus* (Vasey) Fern. Spikes dense, stout, averaging 7 mm thick; lemmas awnless or short awned; glumes (excluding awns) 10-16 mm. [*Elymus trachycaulus* subsp. *trachycaulus*].

var. *novae ángliae* (Scribn.) Fern. Spikes slender, 3-6 mm thick; lemmas awnless or short-awned; glumes (excluding awns) 7-10 mm. [*Elymus trachycaulus* subsp. *trachycaulus*].

var. *glaúcum* (Pease & Moore) Malte. Plant green or glaucous; spikes slender, averaging 5 mm thick; lemmas with awns as long or longer than the body; body of glume averaging 9 mm. [*Elymus trachycaulus* subsp. *subsecundus*].

var. *unilaterále* (Cassidy) Malte. Spikes stout, averaging 9 mm thick; lemmas with awns as long or longer than the body; body of glume averaging 13.5 mm. [*Elymus trachycaulus* subsp. *subsecundus*]. —FACU

16. *Elytrígia* Desv.

Similar to *Agropyron* but with elongate, extensively creeping rhizomes. [*Agropyron*]. —Wildl. 1

In addition to the species treated below *E. pycnanthes* has been reported for MA.

Spikes square; internodes of rachis thick, 4 angled. .... 1. *E. pungens*
Spikes not square, flattened; internodes of rachis thin, rounded on the back. .... 2. *E. repens*

1. E. púngens (Pers.) Tutin (pungent). Coast Wheatgrass. Sandy beaches, borders of salt marshes. July-August. Map 196. (Europe). [*Agropyron p.*].—FACW

2. E. répens (L.) Desv. ex B. D. Jackson (creeping). Quack grass. Fields, roadsides, waste areas. July-September. Map 197. (Europe). [*Agropyron r.*]. Our plants include var. *repens* and the following var.:

var. *vailantiána* Wulfen & Schreb. Glumes lanceolate, gradually tapering from near the middle (glumes oblong, rounded at the apex or abruptly narrowed in var. *repens*). [*Agropyron r.* forma *v.*]. Young shoots edible; rhizome starchy, used to make flour when dried and also to make home-brewed beer. —FACU-

E. intermédia Nevski. Similar to the other 3 species of *Elytrigia* but distinguishable in having obtuse, awnless glumes and lemmas (glumes and lemmas acute to acuminate or awned in the 3 other species of *Elytrigia*). European; a waif in our range. Reported for Westchester County NY.

E. smithii (Rydb.) A. Löve. Similar to the above species of *Elytrigia* but differs in having glumes attenuate to the tip from below the middle (rounded at tip or narrowed from near middle in the above species). Reported for Hampshire County MA, Coos County NH. [*Agropyron s.; Pascopyrum s.*].

17. *Hórdeum* L. Barley (ancient name).

Low to relatively tall annuals or perennials; leaves with flat blades and membranous ligules; inflorescence a dense, bristly, cylindric, terminal spike which disarticulates at each joint (except in cultivated species), the rachis segments falling with the spikelets attached; spikelets 1 (rarely 2) flowered, usually in 3s at each node, alternating on opposite sides of the rachis, the lateral spikelets stalked or sessile, imperfect, (perfect in cultivated species) often reduced to awns, the middle spikelet sessile and perfect; glumes elongate, narrow, awned or awn-like, positioned side by side in front of the lemma, the 6 glumes of the 3 spikelets (where the lateral spikelets are sessile), or the 2 glumes of the fertile spikelet and the 2 stalks of the sterile spikelets (where the lateral spikelets are stalked) simulating a bristly involucre at each joint of the rachis; lemma of the lateral spikelets reduced or absent, that of the central spikelet indurated, its back facing opposite the rachis, usually long-awned; palea slightly shorter than lemma; rachilla prolonged behind the palea as a bristle and sometimes bearing a rudimentary floret; stamens 3. —Wildl. 2

a. Glumes (or most of them) flattened and widened above the base.
    Awns of most of the fertile lemmas 1-5 cm long. .... 1. *H. pusillum*
    Awns of most of the fertile lemmas longer than 5 cm or lemmas awnless. .... 2. *H. vulgare*
a. Glumes all setaceous throughout .... 3. *H. jubatum*

1. H. pusíllum Nutt. (very small). Little Barley. Waste places, roadsides, ballast, often in alkaline soil. June-July. Reported for Tolland County CT, York County ME. Our plants are subsp. *pusillum*. Grazing causes mechanical injury to livestock. —FAC

H. murínum L. Similar to *H. pusillum* but differs in having auriculate leaf blades and lemmas of the lateral spikelets longer than the glumes (leaf blades exauriculate and lemmas of the lateral spikelets shorter than the glumes in *H. pusillum*). Western. Reported for New Haven County CT, York County ME, Middlesex and Suffolk Counties MA. Bronx County NY. Our plants include subsp. *murinum* and the following subsp.:

subsp. *leporínum* (Link.) Arcang. Floret of central spikelet raised on a rachilla joint, equal or nearly so to the pedicels of the lateral spikelets (floret of central spikelet sessile or subsessile, much shorter than pedicels of the lateral spikelets in subsp. *murinum*). [*H. leporinum*].

2. H. vulgáre L. (common). Barley. Occasionally found in fields, roadsides and waste areas. Map 198. (Introduced from Eurasia). Cultivated for the grain which is used in making beer and whiskey; also can be used as a coffee substitute.

3. H. jubátum L. (with a mane). Foxtail Barley. Cultivated ground, fields, roadsides, waste places, upper borders of salt marshes, usually in dry soil. July-August. Fig. 84, Map 199. (Europe; S. Amer.; Siberia). Our plants are subsp. *jubatum*. Grazing causes mechanical injury to livestock. —FAC

H. brachyántherum Nevski. Similar to *H. jubatum* but distinguishable in having spikelets 2 cm or less long including awn (spikelets longer than 3 cm in *H. jubatum* including awns). (Ne. Asia). Southwestern. Reported for ME, NH, Westchester County NY. [*H. boreale; H. nodosum*]. —FAC+

H. márinum Huds. Resembling *H. brachyantherum* but annual, with the rachis of the spike continuous, not readily disarticulating (*H. brachyantherum* is a cespitose perennial with the rachis not continuous, readily disarticulating). [*H. hystrix*]. Our plants are subsp. *gussonianum* (Parl.) Thellung. European. Reported for MA.

18. Élymus L. Wild Rye (Greek name for a type of grain).

Tufted, usually tall, mostly cespitose perennial, ours lacking rhizomes; leaves with flat blades and membranous ligules; inflorescence a dense, terminal spike; spikelets usually 2-6 flowered, disarticulating above the glumes and between the lemmas, in pairs (sometimes solitary below, occasionally 3 or 4), alternate on opposite sides of the rachis, overlapping (except in *E. hystrix*), the uppermost flowers imperfect; glumes equal, usually rigid, narrow, acute to awn-tipped, placed side by side and forming a false involucre to the lemmas, which are more or less dorsiventral to the rachis of the spike (glumes reduced to awns, the first usually obsolete in *E. hystrix*); lemmas indurated, rounded on the back, acute or awned; palea nearly as long as lemma; stamens 3.—Wildl. 1

Taeniátherum Nevskii *capút-medúsae* (L.) Nevskii. Similar to *Elymus* but distinguishable in being annual, with spikes nearly as broad as long (plants perennial, with spikes much longer than broad in *Elymus*). From the west coast. Reported for CT. [*Elymus c.m.*].

a. Spike loose, the rachis visible between the divergent spikelets; glumes absent or
  reduced to 2 short bristles. (Fig. 85). .... 1. *E. hystrix*
a. Spike dense, the rachis concealed by the ascending spikelets; glumes well developed.
  b. Lemmas awnless, or with an awn up to a third as long as the body. .... 2. *E. virginicus*
  b. Lemmas conspicuously awned, the awn as long as the body or longer.
    c. Glumes strongly indurated, bowed out at the base. (Fig. 86). .... 2. *E. virginicus*
    c. Glumes, not strongly indurated or if so, only toward the base, the latter not
      bowed out.
      d. Awns curved outward at maturity; palea more than 8 mm long. (Fig. 87). ..... 3. *E. canadensis*
      d. Awns straight at maturity; palea 8 mm or less long.
        Spikelets hirsute, the hairs longer than 0.5 mm; leaf blades pilose above. ..... 4. *E. villosus*
        Spikelets scabrous, the hairs less than 0.5 mm; leaf blades glabrous. .... 5. *E. riparius*

1. E. hýstrix L. Rich, damp, dry or rocky deciduous woods, thickets and riverbanks. June-August. Fig. 85, Map 200. [*Hystrix patula*]. Our plants include var. *hystrix* and the following var.:

var. *bigeloviána* (Bern.) Bowden. Lemmas pubescent (glabrous in var. *hystrix*). [*Hystrix patula* var. *b.*]

2. E. virginicus L. (Virginian). Moist, rich soil, particularly along streams. July-August. Fig. 86, Map 201. Our plants include var. *virginicus* and the following 2 vars.:

var. *halóphilus* (Bickn.) Wieg. Spikelets whitish-green; blades sometimes involute (spikelets green and leaves flat in var. virginicus).

var. *submúticus* Hook. Glumes and lemmas awnless or nearly so (awned in var. *virginicus*). —FACW-

3. E. canadénsis L. (of Canada). Sandy, gravelly or moist soil, often along riverbanks. July-September. Fig. 87. Our plants include var. *canadensis* (Map 202) and the following 2 vars.: —FACU+

var. *brachystáchys* (Scribn. & Ball) Farwell. Lemmas glabrous or nearly so (*hirsute* in var. *canadensis*). [*E. canadensis* forma *glaucifolius*].

var. *wiegándii* (Fern.) Bowden. Leaves thin, pilose above (thick and firm, glabrous or merely scabrous above in the latter 2 vars.). Map 202a. [*E. wiegandii*]. —FAC

4. E. villósus Muhl. ex Willd. (softly hairy). Woodlands, riverbanks and waste areas. July-August. Map 203. —FACU-

5. E. ripárius Wieg. (of river banks). Riverbanks, moist woodlands, meadows and waste areas. July-September. Map 204. —FACW

19. *Léymus* Hochst.

Similar to *Elymus*; distinguishable in having extensively creeping rhizomes and awnless lemmas. [*Elymus*].

1. *L. móllis* (Trin.) Hara (soft to touch). American Dunegrass. Sand dunes along the coast and shores of the Great Lakes. June-July. Map 204a. (E. Asia). Endangered in MA. [*Elymus m; E. arenarius* var. *villosus*]. Our plants are subsp. *mollis.*

L. arenárius (L.) Hochst. (of sand). Resembling *L. mollis* but with summit of culm and glumes glabrous (summit of culm pubescent and glumes scabrous or pubescent in *E. mollis*). Eurasian. Reported for CT, MA, NH. [*Elymus a.*]

20. *Phragmites* Adans. Reed (Greek name, meaning growing in hedges).

Tall, coarse, perennial reeds from stout rhizomes forming extensive colonies; leaves with long, broad, flat blades and short, truncate, ciliate ligules; inflorescence a large, dense terminal panicle; spikelets several-flowered, disarticulating above the glumes and at the base of the rachilla segments between the lemmas, the lowest floret staminate or sterile, the others perfect, becoming successively smaller upward, the rachilla with long, silky hairs; glumes unequal, lanceolate, acute, shorter than the spikelet; lemmas narrow, long-acuminate; palea much shorter than lemma; stamens 3.

1. *P. austràlis* (Cav.) Trin. ex Steud. Common Reed. Fresh marshes, upper borders of salt marshes, bogs, roadside ditches, waste places. August-September. Fig. 88, Map 205. Formerly thought to be introduced but stems have been found in peat deposits dating several thousand years. [*P. communis*]. Rhizome edible. Stems yield sugar which was extracted by Indians as a gum or dried, ground and sifted. —FACW

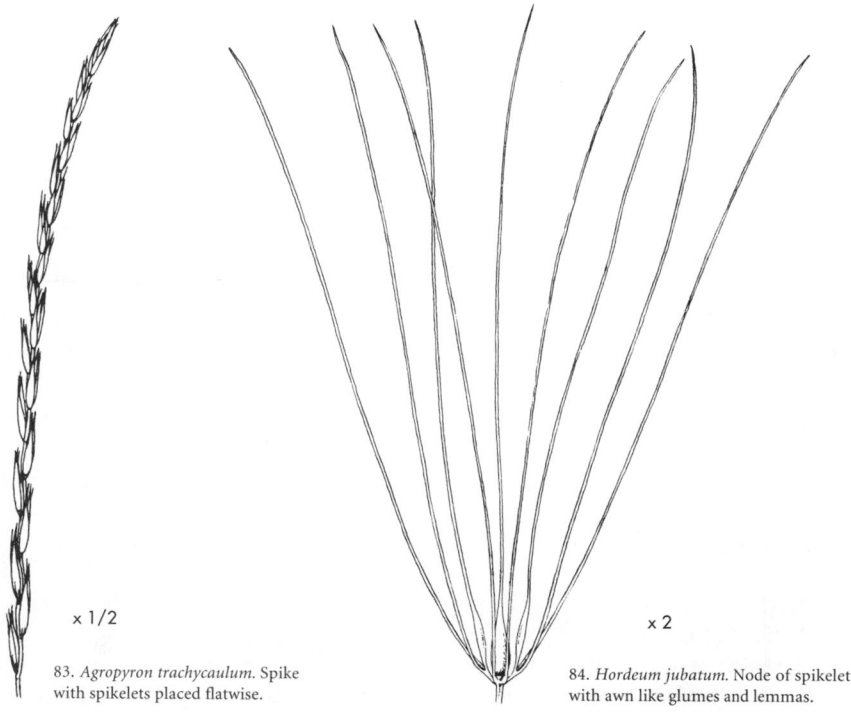

× 1/2

× 2

83. *Agropyron trachycaulum.* Spike with spikelets placed flatwise.

84. *Hordeum jubatum.* Node of spikelet with awn like glumes and lemmas.

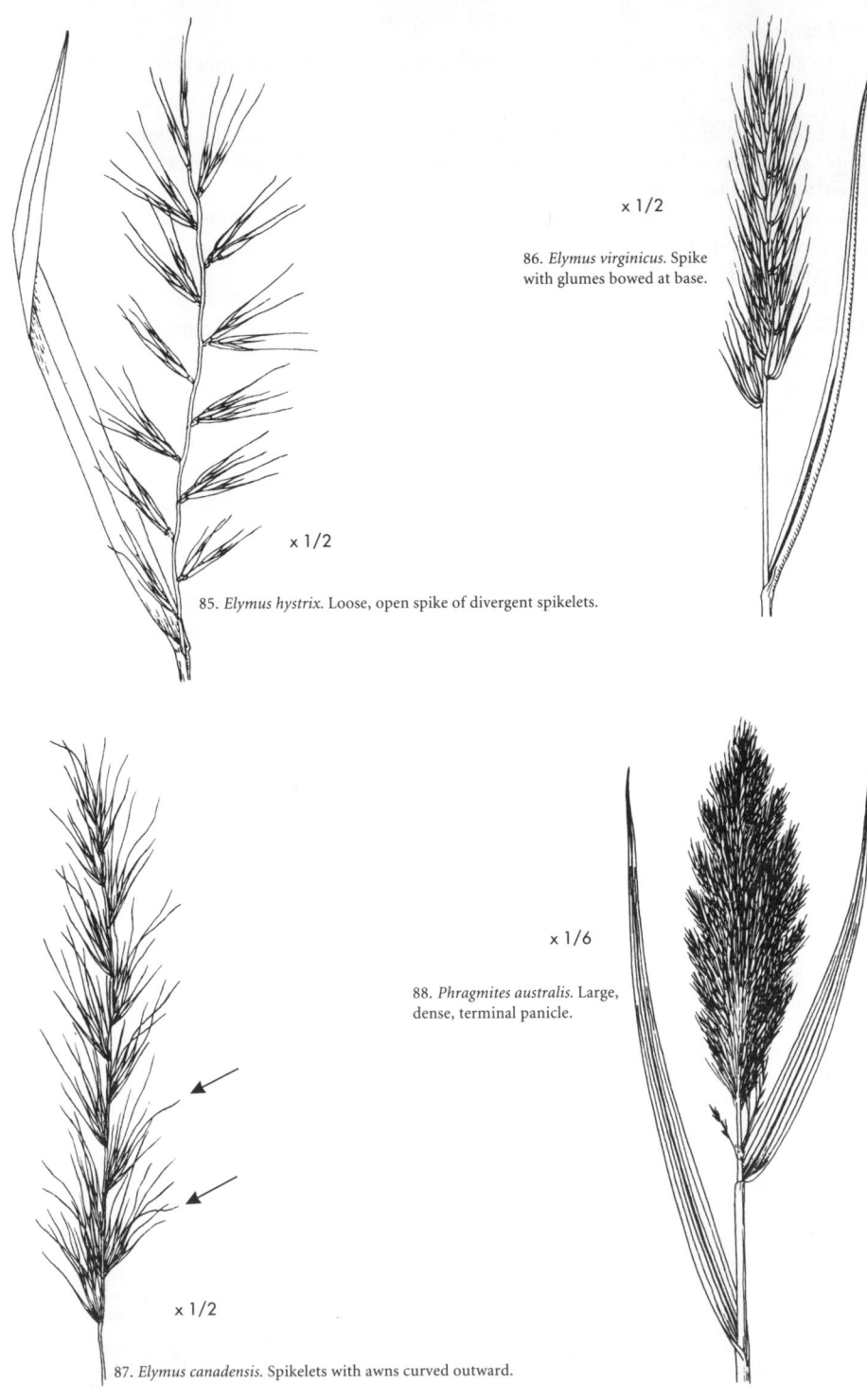

× 1/2

86. *Elymus virginicus*. Spike with glumes bowed at base.

× 1/2

85. *Elymus hystrix*. Loose, open spike of divergent spikelets.

× 1/6

88. *Phragmites australis*. Large, dense, terminal panicle.

× 1/2

87. *Elymus canadensis*. Spikelets with awns curved outward.

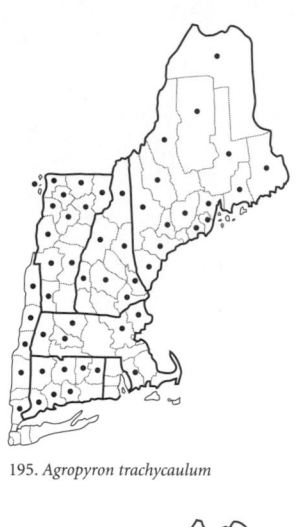

195. *Agropyron trachycaulum*

196. *Elytrigia pungens*

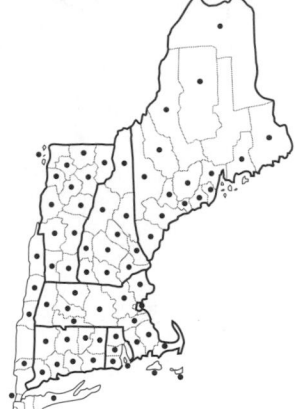

197. *Elytrigia repens*

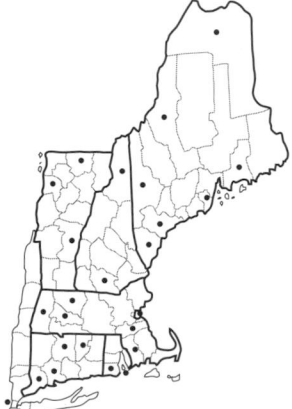

198. *Hordeum vulgare*

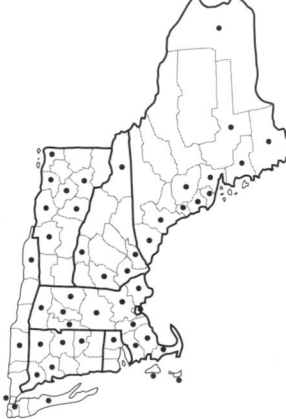

199. *Hordeum jubatum*

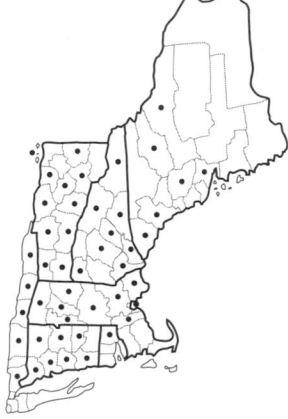

200. *Elymus hystrix*

201. *Elymus virginicus*

202. *Elymus* var. *canadensis*

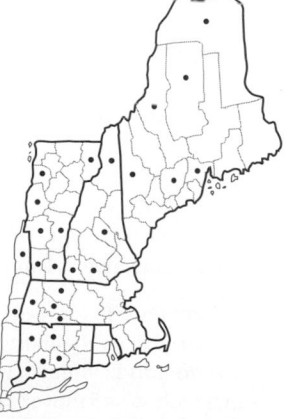

202a. *Elymus canadensis* var. *wiegandii*

203. *Elymus villosus*   204. *Elymus riparius*   204a. *Leymus mollis*

205. *Phragmites australis*   206. *Cynosurus cristatus*   207. *Dactylus glomerata*

21. *Cynosúrus* L. Dog's-tail (from the Greek).

Annual or rhizomatous perennial, cespitose, with simple stems; leaves with flat, narrow blades, primarily basal, with only a few reduced blades on the stem or primarily cauline; inflorescence a terminal, slender, dense, 1-sided, spike-like or subcapitate panicle; spikelets of 2 kinds, sterile and fertile, paired on a common stalk in the same cluster, the sterile spikelet rigid and fan-shaped, consisting of 2 glumes and several narrow, acuminate or awned lemmas, borne in front of and nearly concealing the fertile spikelet, this disarticulating above the glumes, several flowered, the fan-like clusters of paired sterile and fertile spikelets imbricated in the panicle; glumes of fertile spikelet acute to short-awned, subequal, shorter than the lemmas, lemmas broader than glumes, mucronate or awned, palea as long as lemma, stamens 3.

   1. *C. cristátus* L. (crested). Crested Dog's tail. Fields, roadsides and waste places. June-August. Fig. 89, Map 206. (Naturalized from Europe).

   C. echinátus L. Annual, with a subcapitate panicle up to 4 cm long and 2 cm or more thick, lemmas with awns 5 mm or more long (panicle 3-10 cm long and 1 cm thick, lemmas with awns less than 5 mm long in *C. cristatus*). Adventive from Europe. Reported for CT.

22. Dáctylis L. Orchard Grass (Greek name for a grass with digitate spikes).

Tall, cespitose perennial with simple stems; leaves with compressed sheaths, long, membranous ligules, and long, flat blades; inflorescence an open panicle consisting of a main axis and 2-3 erect or divergent branches, the main axis and branches naked at the base and bearing dense, one-sided clusters of spikelets towards the ends; spikelets nearly sessile and strongly overlapping in the clusters, flat, disarticulating above the glumes and between the lemmas, 2-5 flowered, the flowers all perfect or the upper staminate; glumes unequal, shorter than the lemmas, keeled, ciliate on the keel, acute or mucronate; lemmas keeled, ciliate on the keel, acute or mucronate; palea slightly shorter than the lemma; stamens 3.—Wildl. 1

1. **D. glomeráta** L. (gathered in bunches). Meadows, fields, roadsides and waste places. Fig. 90, Map 207. (Naturalized from Europe). Our plants are subsp. *glomerata.* —FACU

23. Bríza L. Quaking Grass (Greek name for a type of grain).

Low annuals or perennials with erect stems; leaves with flat blades and membranous ligules; inflorescence an open, terminal panicle with very slender branches and pedicels bearing nodding or pendulous spikelets; spikelets disarticulating above the glumes and between the lemmas, several flowered, round or triangular, flattened, the florets crowded and spreading horizontally, purplish or brownish; glumes about equal, broad, firm-membranous, scarious margined, shorter than the series of lemmas; lemmas resembling the glumes but broader than long and cordate at the base, imbricated, the uppermost reduced and often empty; palea membranous, shorter than the lemma; stamens 3, fruit dorsally compressed.

Ligule 2 mm or less long, truncate; spikelets 4-5 mm long. .... 1. *B. media*
Ligule 5 mm or more long, acute; spikelets less than 4 mm long. .... 2. *B. minor*

1. **B. média** L. (intermediate). Fields, roadsides and waste places. June-August. Fig. 91, Map 208. (Introduced from Europe). —FAC
2. **B. mínor** L. (smaller). Waste places. From Europe, mostly occurring farther south. (Introduced from Europe). Reported for Greenwich, CT. —FACW
B. máxima L. Spikelets more than 1 cm long (less than 1 cm long in the latter 2 species). Mediterranean; a waif in our range. Reported for MA and VT; also for Suffolk and Queens Counties, NY.

24. Chasmánthium Link. Spikegrass.

Tall perennials from short or long rhizomes; leaves with flat or convolute blades and membranous, often ciliate ligules; inflorescence a narrow or open terminal panicle; spikelets laterally flattened, disarticulating above the glumes and between the lemmas, 3-many flowered, the lower 1-5 florets and the uppermost sterile; glumes subequal, shorter than to nearly equalling spikelet, compressed and keeled, usually narrow, acute or acuminate; lemmas compressed and keeled, acute or acuminate, the lower sterile ones resembling the glumes but usually longer, fertile lemmas lanceolate to ovate; palea shorter than the lemma; stamens 1-3. [*Uniola*].

1. **C. láxum** (L.) Yates (loose). Wooded swamps, moist woods and meadows, mostly near the coast. July-September. Fig. 92. [*Uniola laxa*]. —FAC

25. Póa L. Bluegrass (Greek name for grass).

Annuals or perennials; leaves with flat, folded, or involute blades ending in a boat-shaped tip, and membranous ligules; inflorescence an open or contracted terminal panicle; spikelets 2-several flowered, laterally flattened, disarticulating above the glumes and between the lemmas, the uppermost floret imperfect or rudimentary, the others perfect; glumes acute, keeled, unequal, shorter than the spikelet; lemmas keeled, awnless, 3 or 5 nerved, usually scarious on the margins and tip, usually with a tuft of long, cobwebby hairs at the base; palea slightly shorter than the lemma; stamens 3. —Wildl. 2

a. Stems strongly flattened, 2-edged, especially above, solitary or few together .... 1. *P. compressa*
a. Stems terete or slightly flattened, not 2-edged, generally cespitose.
  b. Spikelets modified into bulblets with elongate tips; stems and leaf tufts with
    bulbous-thickened bases. (Fig. 93). .... 2. *P. bulbosa*
  b. Spikelets not modified into bulblets; stems and leaf tufts not bulbous at base.
    c. Lemmas cobwebby at base. (Fig. 94).
      d. Lower panicle branches in fascicles of 2-3 or solitary.
        e. Lemmas glabrous on the keel and marginal nerves. .... 3. *P. saltuensis*
        e. Lemmas pubescent on the keel and marginal nerves. (Fig. 95).
          Annual; lower panicle branches flowered to or below the middle; fields
          and open ground of lower altitudes .... 4. *P. chapmaniana*
          Perennial; lower panicle branches flowered only at the tip; alpine. .... 5. *P. fernaldiana*
      d. Lower panicle branches mostly in fascicles of 4 or more.
        f. Lemmas glabrous on the marginal nerves.
          Most panicle branches densely flowered to below the middle; lemmas
          with 5 distinct nerves; sheaths scabrous. (Fig. 96). .... 6. *P. trivialis*
          Most panicle branches loosely flowered at the tip; lemmas with
          3 distinct nerves; sheaths glabrous. (Fig. 97) .... 7. *P. alsodes*
        f. Lemmas pubescent on the marginal nerves.
          g. Lemmas with 5 distinct nerves .... 8. *P. pratensis*
          g. Lemmas with 3 distinct nerves.
            Ligule of stem leaves truncate, less than 1 mm long .... 9. *P. nemoralis*
            Ligule of stem leaves elongate, longer than 1 mm................................ 10. *P. palustris*
    c. Lemmas not cobwebby at base.
      h. Lemmas with 5 distinct nerves; plant annual. .... 11. *P. annua*
      h. Lemmas with 3 distinct nerves; plant perennial.
        i. Panicle pyramidal, about as broad as long; glumes ovate, more than half
          as wide as long .... 12. *P. alpina*
        i. Panicle ellipsoid or ovoid, longer than broad; glumes lanceolate, less than
        half as wide as long.
          Ligule 2.5 mm long or longer; plant green. .... 5. *P. fernaldiana*
          Ligule less than 2.5 mm long; plant glaucous. .... 13. *P. glauca*

1. P. compréssa L. (flattened). Canada Bluegrass. Waste places, roadsides, meadows and open woodlands, in dry sandy or gravelly soil. June-August. Map 209. (Naturalized from Eurasia). —FACU

2. P. bulbósa L. (bulbous). Bulbous Bluegrass. Lawns and dry fields. April-June. Fig. 93. (Adventive from Eurasia). Reported for Hampshire County MA.

3. P. saltuénsis Fern. & Wieg. (of bushy pastures). Dry open woods, thickets, clearings and roadsides. June-August. Fig. 94, Map 210. Endangered in MA. [*P. languida*].

4. P. chapmaniána Scribn. (for A. Chapman). Waste places, cultivated ground and fields. April-July. Fig. 95, Map 211.

5. P. fernaldiána (Steud.) Vasey (for M. L. Fernald). Alpine summits. July-August. Map 212. Endangered in ME and NH. [*P. laxa*].

P. paludigéna Fern. & Wieg. Similar to *P. fernaldiana* but distinguishable in being a tall plant of bogs and wet woods, the stem leafy above the middle (*P. fernaldiana* is a low, cespitose plant of alpine summits, the stem leafy only below the middle). From farther west. Endangered in NY. Reported for Bronx County, NY. —FACW+

6. P. triviális L. (ordinary), Rough Bluegrass. Meadows, roadsides and waste places. June-August. Fig. 96, Map 213. —FACW

7. P. alsódes Gray (of woods). Rich or moist woods or thickets. May-June. Fig. 97, Map 214. —FACW-

89. *Cynosurus cristatus.* Fan-like cluster of sterile and fertile spikelets.

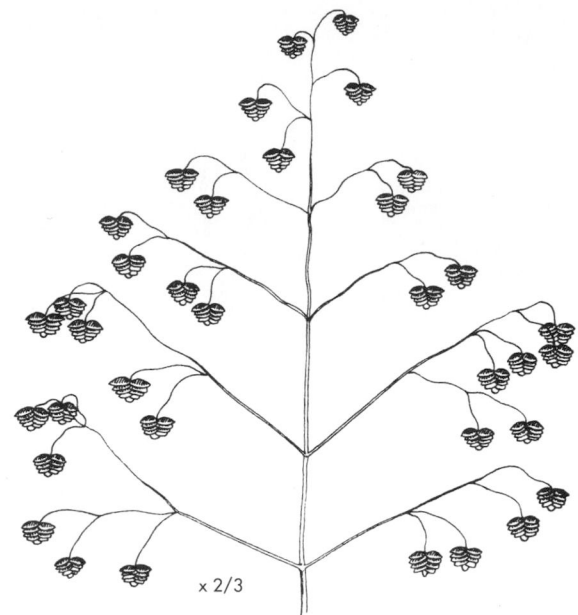

× 2/3

91. *Briza media.* Panicle of rounded, pendulous spikelets.

× 1/2

90. *Dactylis glomerata.*
Open, paniculate inflorescence.

× 1/3

92. *Chasmanthium laxum.* Narrow panicle.

× 1

93. *Poa bulbosa.* Panicle of spikelets modified into bulblets.

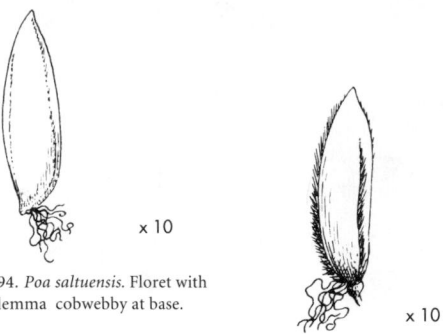

94. *Poa saltuensis.* Floret with lemma cobwebby at base.

95. *Poa chapmaniana.* Floret with lemma pubescent on keel and marginal nerves.

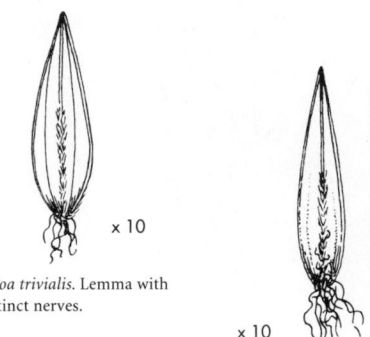

96. *Poa trivialis.* Lemma with 5 distinct nerves.

97. *Poa alsodes.* Lemma 3 distinct nerves.

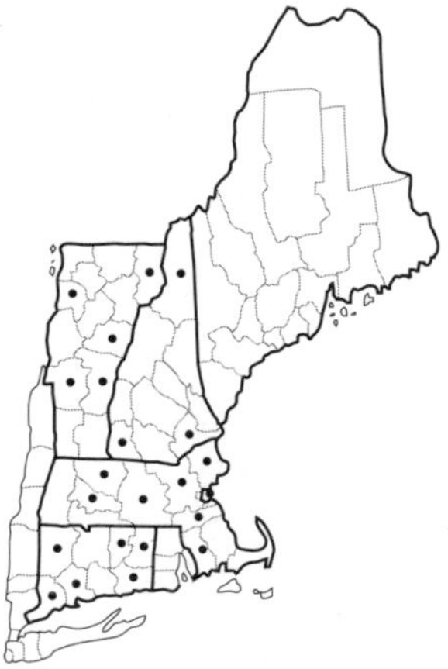

208. *Briza media*

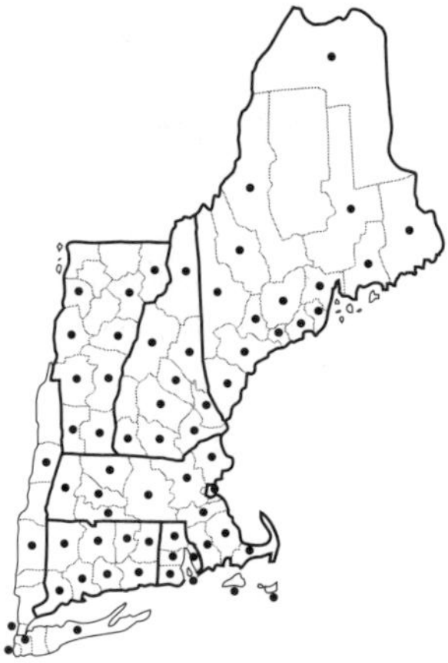

209. *Poa compressa*

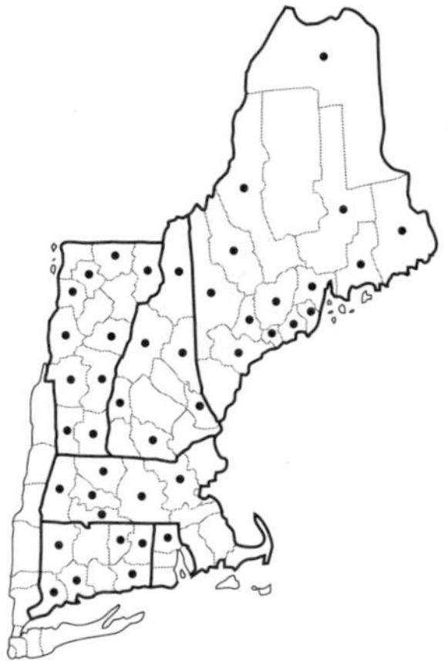

210. *Poa saltuensis*

211. *Poa chapmaniana*

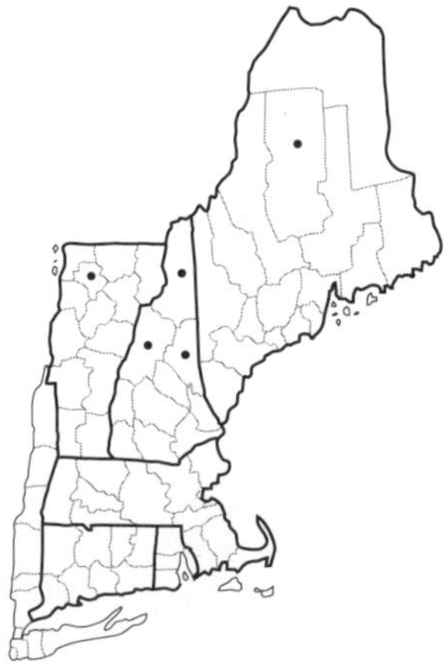

212. *Poa fernaldiana*

213. *Poa trivialis*

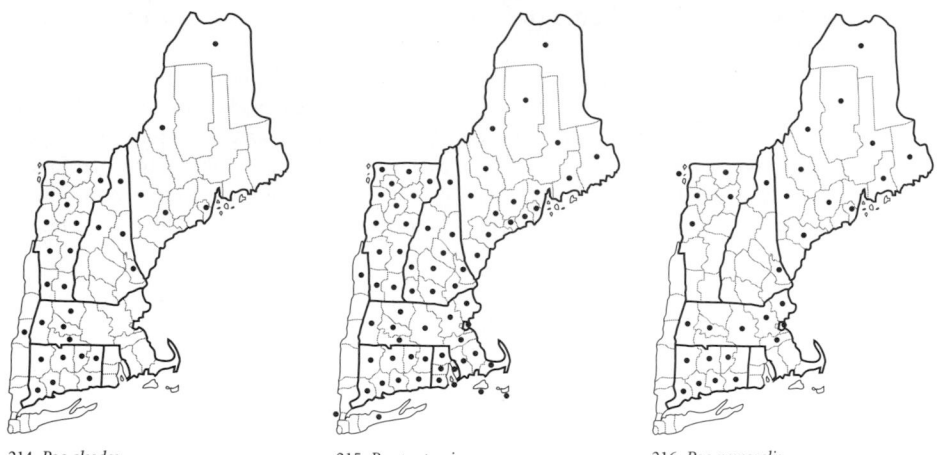

214. *Poa alsodes* 215. *Poa pratensis* 216. *Poa nemoralis*

8. P. praténsis L. (of meadows). Kentucky Bluegrass. Fields, lawns, open deciduous or pine woodlands, roadsides and waste places. June-August. Map 215. (Eurasia). [*P. angustifolia; P. alpigena; P. arctica; P. subcaerulea*].—FACU to FACW-

9. P. nemorális L. (of woodland). Wood Bluegrass. Meadows and roadsides. June-September. Map 216. (Eurasia). —FAC

P. intérior Rydb. Resembling *P. nemoralis* but distinguishable in having the first glume about as wide as the first lemma (much narrower than first lemma in *P. nemoralis*). From farther north and west. Reported for VT.

10. P. palústris L. (of marshes). Fowl meadow-grass. Wet meadows and marshes. June-August. Map 217. (Eurasia, N. Africa). —FACW

11. P. ánnua L. (annual). Annual Bluegrass. Roadsides, waste places, lawns, meadows and cultivated ground, often in moist soil. April-November. Map 218. (Naturalized from Eurasia). —FACU

12. P. alpína L. (alpine). Alpine Bluegrass. Alpine summits. June-August. (Eurasia). [*P. gaspensis*]. —FACU

15. P. glaúca Vahl (blue-green). Alpine summits. June-August. Map 219. (Eurasia). [*P. glaucantha; P. scopulorum*]. Our plants are subsp. *glauca*.

26. Tríplasis Beauv. Sand Grass (Greek name, based on the lemma).

Slender, cespitose annuals or perennials with numerous short internodes, the stems disarticulating at the nodes; leaves with inflated sheaths, narrow, flat or involute, short blades and a ligule of short hairs; inflorescence a short, terminal, few-flowered, purple panicle at first included in the upper sheath, eventually exserted, open, with spreading branches, and small, cleistogamous panicles or spikelets within the inflated sheaths, the mature cleistogenes remaining within the sheaths when the stems disarticulate; spikelets somewhat wedge-shaped, 2-6 flowered, the florets becoming remote, the lowest pedicelled, perfect, the uppermost sometimes only staminate, disarticulating above the glumes and between the lemmas; glumes subequal, keeled, acute, shorter than the spikelet; lemmas 2-lobed, the midnerve excurrent as a short awn, the midnerve and lateral nerves long-ciliate; palea shorter than and soon diverging from the lemma, the 2 keels densely long-ciliate on the upper half; stamens 3.

1. T. purpúrea (Walt.) Chapm. (purple). Dry sand on or near the coast, sea beaches, waste places. August-October. Fig. 98, Map 220.

27. *Trídens* Roemer & J. A. Schultes (from the Greek meaning 3-toothed, based on the tip of the lemma).

Perennial, often tufted; leaves with long somewhat narrow, usually flat blades and ligule of short hairs; inflorescence a large, open (ours) to contracted or spike-like panicle; spikelets purplish, 3-many flowered, disarticulating below the glumes and between the lemmas; glumes subequal, keeled, shorter than the spikelet, oblong or ovate, obtuse or frequently mucronate; lemmas broad, rounded on the back, obtuse or 2-lobed, the nerves often excurrent as short points, the midnerve and lateral nerves densely hairy, at least in the lower half; palea nearly as long as the lemma; flowers perfect or the upper staminate, stamens 3. [*Triodia*].

    1. *T. flávus* (L.) A. S. Hitchc. (yellow). Tall Red Top. Old fields, open woods and roadsides. July-September. Fig. 99, Map 221. [*Triodia flava*]. Our plants are var. *flavus.* —FACU+

28. *Schizáchne* Hack. (from the Greek meaning to split).

Rather tall, slender perennial; leaves with flat blades and membranous ligule; inflorescence a terminal, open, rather few-flowered panicle of large spikelets; spikelets several flowered, disarticulating above the glumes and between the lemmas; glumes unequal, shorter than the lemmas; lemmas lanceolate, strongly 7-nerved, bifid at the tip with an awn just below the teeth, densely short-bearded on the callus, the uppermost lemma reduced and sterile; palea much shorter than lemma, with pubescent, submarginal keels; flowers (except the terminal) perfect, stamens 3.

    1. *S. purpuráscens* (Torr.) Swallen (purplish). False Melic. Dry, rocky or sandy thickets and woodlands. June-August. Fig. 100, Map 222. —FACU-

29. *Distíchlis* Raf. Saltgrass (from the Greek meaning 2-ranked).

Dioecious, low perennial from extensively creeping rhizomes, with stiff, erect stems, forming dense mats; leaves distichous, with overlapping sheaths, membranous ligules, and usually involute blades; inflorescence a rather short, dense, spike-like panicle of large spikelets; spikelets flattened, few to many-flowered, the pistillate disarticulating above the glumes and between the lemmas, the staminate with rachis continuous; glumes shorter than the lemmas, unequal, acute, keeled; lemmas closely imbricated, acute, the pistillate coriaceous; palea as long or nearly as long as lemma; stamens 3. —Wildl. 1

    1. *D. spicáta* (L.) Greene (spiked). Salt marshes, generally in the portion exposed during low tide. July-September. Fig. 101, Map 223. (S. Amer.). Our plants are var. *spicata.* —FACW+

30. *Brómus* L. Brome-Grass (Greek name meaning food).

Low to tall, annual or perennial; leaves with closed sheaths, flat blades and membranous ligules, erose or lacerate at the summit; inflorescence a terminal, usually lax, open panicle of large, drooping spikelets; spikelets disarticulating above the glumes and between the lemmas, few to many flowered, oval to narrowly oblong, round or laterally flattened; glumes unequal, acute, the first 1-3 nerved, the second usually 3-7 nerved, shorter than the spikelet; lemmas rounded on the back or keeled, 5-9 nerved, usually 2-toothed (sometimes minutely) at the tip, awned from the notch or just below, or awnless; palea usually shorter than the lemma, 2-keeled, ciliate on the keels; flowers perfect, stamens 3. —Wildl. 1

    Brachypódium Beauv. *pinnátum* (L.) Beauv. Similar to *Bromus* but with subsessile spikelets in a strict raceme. Rare; adventive from Europe. Reported for Hampshire County MA.

a. Awns as long or longer than the body of the lemma.
    b. Longest awns 3.5 cm or more long, twice as long as body of lemma. .... 1. *B. diandrus*
    b. Longest awns less than 3.5 cm long, equalling to slightly exceeding lemma.

Second glume usually longer than 1 cm; awns 2 cm or longer; lemmas
    scabrous to hispidulous ....2. *B. sterilis*
Second glume usually less than 1 cm; awns less than 2 cm; lemmas strigose
    or hispid .... 3. *B. tectorum*
a. Awns shorter than the body of the lemma or absent.
  c. First glume 1-nerved, or with 2 short lateral nerves sometimes present;
    second glume 3-nerved.
    d. Lemmas awnless or with awns less than 3 mm; long creeping rhizomes present. 4. *B. inermis*
    d. Lemmas with awns mostly 3 mm or longer; long, creeping rhizomes none.
      e. Panicle contracted, with short, erect branches. (Fig. 102). ....5. *B. erectus*
      e. Panicle open, with branches spreading or drooping.
        f. Lemmas pubescent.
          g. Lemmas pubescent only on the margins. ....6. *B. ciliatus*
          g. Lemmas pubescent over the entire surface.
            Leaf sheaths overlapping, most of them covering the nodes. ....7. *B. latiglumis*
            Leaf sheaths not overlapping, most of the nodes exserted from
              the sheaths. ....8. *B. pubescens*
        f. Lemmas glabrous or minutely scabrous.
          Palea minutely pubescent throughout ....8. *B. pubescens*
          Palea ciliate on the 2 marginal ribs. ....6. *B. ciliatus*
  c. First glume 3-nerved, second glume 5 or more nerved.
    h. Lemmas compressed and keeled. ....9. *B. marginatus*
    h. Lemmas rounded on the back.
      i. Pedicels mostly shorter than the spikelets. (Fig. 103). ....10. *B. hordeaceus*
      i. Pedicels mostly as long or longer than the spikelets. (Fig. 104).
        j. Lemmas densely pubescent, with long, silky hairs. ....11. *B. kalmii*
        j. Lemmas glabrous or scabrous.
          k. Leaf sheaths glabrous (the lower sometimes puberulent); lemma
            margins inrolled at maturity ....12. *B. secalinus*
          k. Leaf sheaths pubescent; lemma margins not inrolled (somewhat
           inrolled in *B. japonicus*).
           l. Lemmas awnless or with awns less than 2 mm long, nearly as
            broad as long. ....13. *B. briziformis*
           l. Lemmas with awns longer than 2 mm, much longer than broad.
            m. Awns mostly horizontally divergent, strongly flattened. (Fig. 105). 14. *B. squarrosus*
            m. Awns erect or spreading, not strongly flattened.
              n. Branches of panicle straight, stiffly ascending or spreading,
                not flexuous. (Fig. 106)
                Lowest lemma 7 mm or less long ....15. *B. racemosus*
                Lowest lemma 8 mm or more long...16. *B. commutatus*
              n. Branches of panicle flexuous, widely spreading. (Fig. 107).
                Palea distinctly shorter than lemma; margins of lemma
                  somewhat inrolled at maturity ....17. *B. japonicus*
                Palea nearly as long as lemma; margins of lemma not
                  inrolled at maturity. ....18. *B. arvensis*

1. *B. diándrus* Roth. Ripgut Grass. Waste places. May-June. Map 224. (Adventive from Europe).
[*B. rigidus*].

2. *B. stérilis* L. (sterile). Waste places, roadsides, fields and ballast. June-August. Map 225.
(Naturalized from Europe).

3. *B. tectórum* L. (of roofs). Downy Brome-Grass. Roadsides, waste places, and fields. May-June.
Map 226. (Naturalized from Europe). Reported as causing injury to livestock when grazed.

B. rúbens L. Similar to the later 3 species but distinguishable in having a dense panicle with
branches 1 cm or less long (panicle is open with longer branches in the latter 3 species). From Europe.
Reported for MA.

4. *B. inérmis* Leyss. (unarmed, without awns). Smooth Brome. Roadsides, fields and waste places.
June-July. Map 227. (Naturalized from Europe). Our plants include subsp. *inermis* var. *inermis* and
the following infrataxa:

× 3

98. *Triplasis purpurea.* Spikelet.

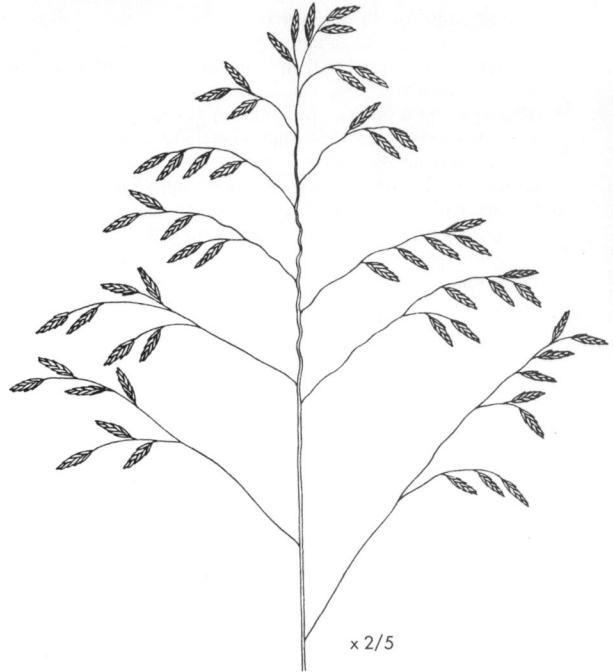

× 2/5

99. *Tridens flavus.* Large open panicle.

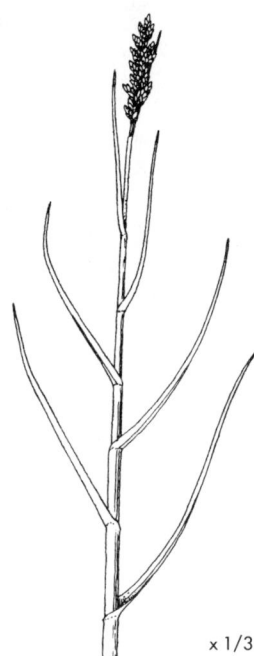

× 1/3

101. *Distichlis spicata.* Distichous leaves and short, spike-like panicle.

× 2/3

100. *Schizachne purpurascens.* Open panicle with awned spikelets.

217. *Poa palustris*

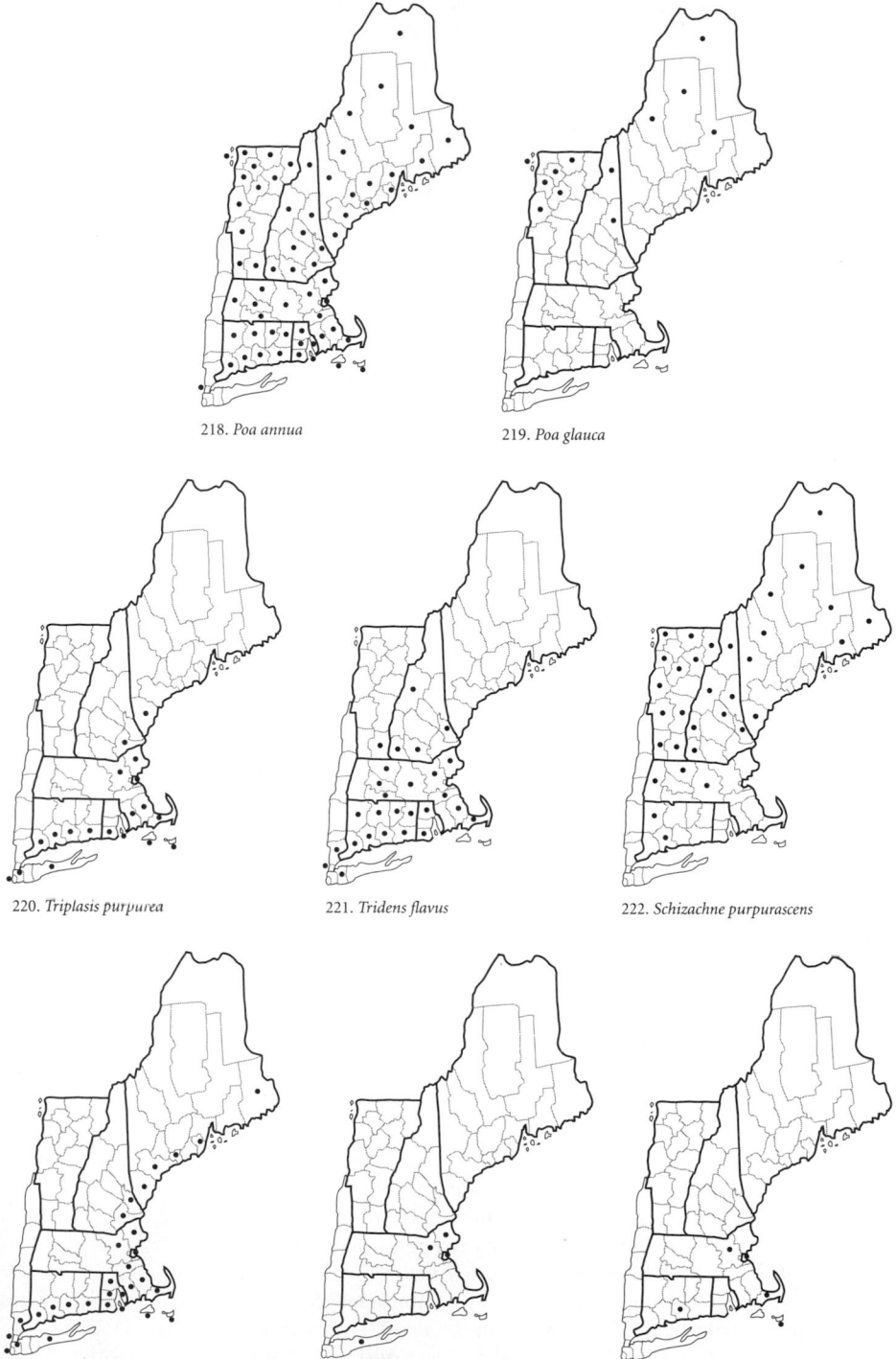

218. *Poa annua*

219. *Poa glauca*

220. *Triplasis purpurea*

221. *Tridens flavus*

222. *Schizachne purpurascens*

223. *Distichlis spicata*

224. *Bromus diandrus*

225. *Bromus sterilis*

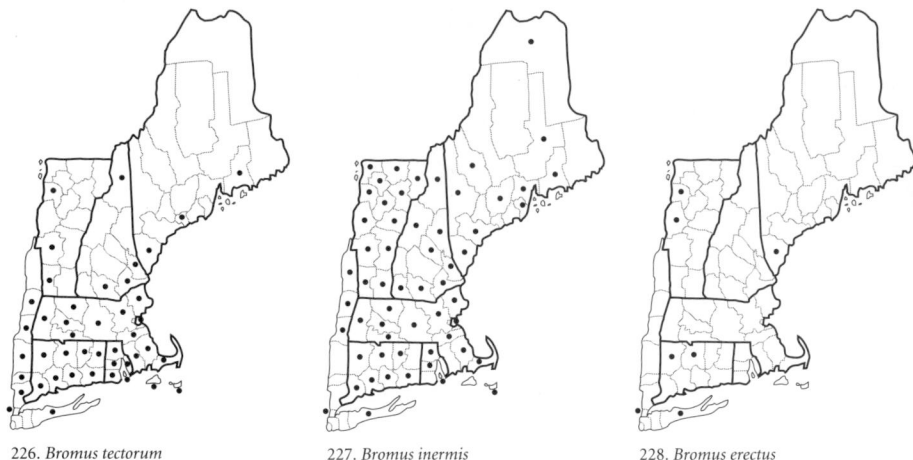

226. *Bromus tectorum*   227. *Bromus inermis*   228. *Bromus erectus*

subsp. *inermis* var. *divaricátus* Rohlena. Panicle loose and open, its branches elongate, widely spreading to reflexed (panicle contracted, with branches ascending to suberect in var. *inermis*).

subsp. *pumpelliánus* (Scribn.) Wagnon. Lemmas pubescent, at least on the margins; nodes and upper leaf surfaces pubescent (lemmas glabrous to scabrous; nodes and leaf blades glabrous in subsp. *inermis*). [*B. pumpellianus*].

5. B. eréctus Huds (erect). Upright Brome-Grass. Fields, roadsides and waste places. June-August. Fig. 102, Map 228. (Adventive from Europe).

6. B. ciliátus L. (ciliate). Fringed Brome. Moist woods, thickets, rocky slopes and roadsides. Map 229. [*B. dudleyi*]. —FAC+ to FACW

B. canadénsis Michx. Similar to *B. ciliatus* and often confused with it; leaf sheaths not overlapping, not auricled at the summit (leaf sheaths overlapping, auricled at the summit in *B. ciliatus*).

7. B. latiglúmis (Shear) A. S. Hitchc. (broad-glumed). Rich or alluvial thickets and woodlands. August-September. Map 230. ([*B. altissimus*].

8. B. pubéscens Muhl. ex Willd. Hairy Brome. Rich, moist woods and thickets, rocky wooded slopes and banks, occasionally waste areas. June-August. Map 231. Endangered in ME. [*B. purgans*]. —FACU

B. ramósus Huds. Keying to *B. pubescens* but distinguishable in having lemmas 12 mm or more long (lemmas up to 12 mm long in *B. pubescens*) From Europe. Reported for CT, MA, VT.

9. B. marginátus Nees (margined). Open ground, waste places. From farther west. Reported for MA, New Haven County, CT, York County ME, Strafford County NH. [*B. carinatus*]. Our plants are var. *marginatus*.

10. B. hordeáceus L. (soft to touch). Soft Chess. Roadsides, abandoned fields and waste places, frequently in sandy soil. July-August. Fig. 103. Map 232. (Naturalized from Europe). [*B. mollis*]. Our plants are subsp. *hordeaceus*.

B. lépidus Holmberg (elegant). Keying to *B. hordeaceus* but distinguishable in having lemmas less than 7 mm long (7 mm or longer in *B. hordeaceus*). From Europe. Reported for CT, MA.

11. B. kálmii Gray (for its discoverer). Kalm's Chess. Sandy or gravelly open soil, open woodlands and thickets. July-August. Map 233. (Endangered in ME and NH). —FAC-

B. grándis (Shear) Hitchc. Keying to *B. kalmii* but distinguishable in having a panicle 12 cm or more long, lemmas longer than 1 cm, with an awn 5 mm or longer (panicle up to 10 cm long, lemmas 1 cm or shorter, with an awn 2-3 mm long in *B. kalmii*). From California. Reported for NH.

12. B. secalínus L. (rye-like). Chess. Grainfields, roadsides and waste places. June-August. Fig. 104, Map 234. (Naturalized from Europe).

13. B. brizifórmis Fisch. & C. A. Mey. (resembling *Briza*). Quake-Grass. Sandy fields, roadsides and waste places. June-August. Map 235. (Introduced from Europe).

14. B. squarrósus L. (with spreading tips), Corn Brome. Waste places. July-August. Fig. 105. (Adventive from Europe). Reported for New Haven County, CT, Chittenden County VT.

15. B. racemósus L. (racemose). Upright Chess. Roadsides, fields and waste places. June-August. Fig. 106. Map 236. (Adventive from Europe).

16. B. commutátus Schrad. (variable). Hairy Chess. Roadsides, fields and waste places, occasionally open woodlands. June-August. Map 237. (Naturalized from Europe).

17. B. japónicus Thunb. ex Murr. (Japanese). Japanese Chess. Roadsides and waste places. June-August. Map 238. (Naturalized from Eurasia). —FACU-

18. B. arvénsis L. (of cultivated land). Field Chess. Fields, cultivated ground, roadsides, waste places. June-July. Fig. 107, Map 239. (Adventive from Europe).

31. *Eragróstis* Von Wolf. Love Grass (Greek name for love grass).

Flowers perfect (ours), annual or perennial, low to tall, from short rhizomes or hardened bases; leaves with flat blades, sheaths which are usually pilose or pubescent at the summit and a ligule consisting of a ring of short hairs; inflorescence an open, diffusely branched, or dense, contracted panicle; spikelets strongly flattened laterally, 2-many flowered, the florets closely imbricated, disarticulating above the glumes and between the lemmas, the lemmas deciduous, paleas persistent, flowers perfect, except uppermost floret sterile; glumes unequal, shorter than the spikelet, acute to acuminate, keeled; lemmas acute to acuminate, awnless, keeled or rounded on the back; palea about as long as or shorter than lemma; stamens 2-3.

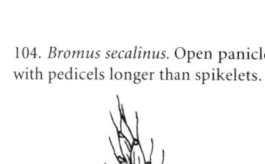

104. *Bromus secalinus.* Open panicle with pedicels longer than spikelets.

x 1

103. *Bromus hordeaceus.* Contracted panicle with pedicels shorter than spikelets.

x 2/3

102. *Bromus erectus.* Contracted panicle with short erect branches.

x 1

106. *Bromus racemosus.* Panicle with straight, stiffly ascending branches.

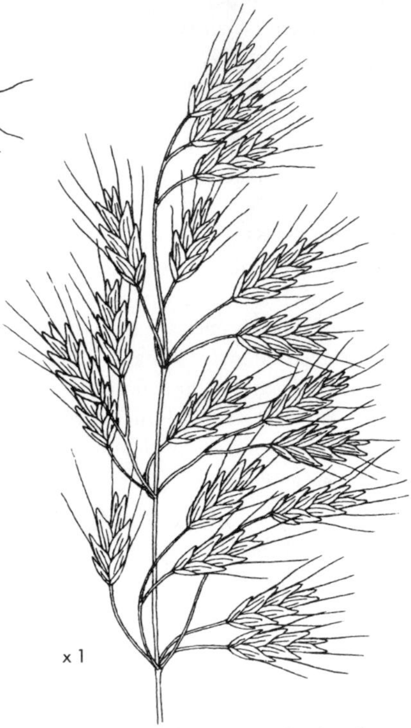

x 3/4

x 1

105. *Bromus squarrosus.* Spikelets with horizontally divergent awns.

x 1

107. *Bromus arvensis.* Panicle with flexuous, spreading branches.

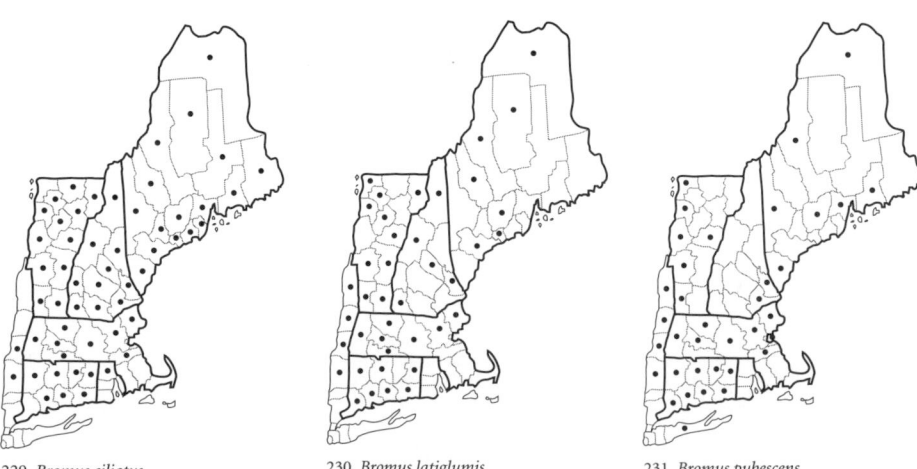

229. *Bromus ciliatus*

230. *Bromus latiglumis*

231. *Bromus pubescens*

232. *Bromus hordeaceus*

233. *Bromus kalmii*

234. *Bromus secalinus*

235. *Bromus briziformis*

236. *Bromus racemosus*

237. *Bromus commutatus*

238. *Bromus japonicus*

239. *Bromus arvensis*

a. Plant trailing, rooting at the nodes, forming mats. (Fig. 108). .... 1. *E. hypnoides*
a. Plant upright, not rooting at the nodes and forming mats.
    b. Perennial with tough, rather stout roots; stem unbranched (sometimes branched
        at the lower nodes in *E. curvula*).
        Lemmas with prominent lateral ribs.
            Spikelets purple; in an open panicle. .... 2. *E. spectabilis*
            Spikelets gray, greenish or drab, approximate in a condensed panicle. .... 3. *E. curvula*
        Lemmas with obscure lateral ribs .... 4. *E. hirsuta*
    b. Annual with delicate roots; stem often branched.
        c. Plant glandular or warty along the leaf margins and on the ultimate branches
            of the panicle.
            Lemma more than 2 mm long, keel glandular; sheath glabrous. .... 5. *E. cilianensis*
            Lemma less than 2 mm long, keel not or sparsely glandular; sheath sparsely
               long-pilose .... 6. *E. minor*
        c. Plant not glandular or warty on the leaf margins or panicle branches.
            d. Panicle two-thirds or more the height of the plant; sheaths long-pilose. .... 7. *E. capillaris*
            d. Panicle less than two-thirds height of the plant; sheaths glabrous or pilose
               only at the top.
               e. Most spikelets 4 or fewer flowered. .... 8. *E. frankii*
               e. Most spikelets 5 or more flowered.
                   Most panicle branches spikelet-bearing from near the base. (Fig. 109). .. 9. *E. pectinacea*
                   Most panicle branches naked at the base for a third to half their length.
                   (Fig. 110) .... 10. *E. pilosa*

1. *E. hypnoídes* (Lam.) B.S.P. (like Hypnum; moss-like). Creeping Love Grass. Sandy riverbanks and shores, mud flats, wet soil. August-October. Fig. 108, Map 240. —OBL

2. *E. spectábilis* (Pursh) Steud. (showy). Purple Love Grass. Dry, sandy soil of open woodlands, fields, roadsides and waste places. July-October. Map 241. [*E. pectinacea*].

3. *E. cúrvula* (Schrad.) Nees. Weeping Love Grass. Escaped from cultivation, mostly in the south. Reported for Barnstable County MA, Suffolk County NY.

4. *E. hirsúta* (Michx.) Nees (hairy). Dry sandy soil of open woodlands, fields, roadsides and waste places. August-October. Reported for Suffolk County MA, ME.

E. intermédia Hitchc. Resembling *E. hirsuta* but distinguishable in having leaf sheaths glabrous (except for the pilose throat) and leaf blades less than 4 mm wide (sheaths hirsute on the surface and/or margins and leaf blades 4 mm or wider in *E. hirsuta*). Southwestern. Reported for MA.

5. *E. cilianénsis* (All.) Lut. ex Janchen. Stinkgrass. Fields, cultivated ground, roadsides and waste areas. July-September. Map 242. (Naturalized from Europe). [*E. major; E. megastachya*]. Reported as poisonous. —FACU

6. *E. minor* Host Beauv. Waste ground, roadsides. July-September. Map 243. (Naturalized from Europe). [*E. poaeoides*].

7. *E. capilláris* (L.) Nees (hair-like). Lace Grass. Dry soil of open woods, fields and waste areas. August-September. Map 244. Endangered in ME.

8. *E. fránkii* C. A. Mey. ex Steud. (for its discoverer). Sand bars, riverbanks, moist open soil and waste areas. August-September. Map 245. —FACW

9. *E. pectinácea* (Michx.) Nees ex Steud. (comb-like). Fields, cultivated ground, sandy or muddy shores, roadsides and waste areas. August-September. Fig. 109, Map 246. Our plants are var. *pectinacea*. —FAC

10. *E. pilósa* (L.) Beauv. (hairy). India Love Grass. Fields, cultivated ground, river shores, roadsides and waste places. August-September. Fig. 110, Map 247. (Naturalized from Europe and E. Asia). [*E. multicaulis; E. peregrina*]. Our plants are var. *pilosa*. —FACU

E. mexicána (Hornem.) Link. Keying to either of the latter 2 species but with spikelets ovate to oblong, 2 mm or more wide (spikelets linear to lanceolate, less than 2 mm wide in the latter 2 species). Southwestern. Reported for ME. Our plants are subsp. *mexicana*.

32. *Molínia* Schrank. Moor Grass (for J. Molina).

Hard-based, cespitose perennial with simple stems; leaves with long, flat blades and a ligule consisting of a ring of short hairs; inflorescence a narrow, elongate, contracted or spreading terminal panicle with lower and middle branches often spaced; spikelets 2-5 flowered, disarticulating above the glumes and between the lemmas, the florets somewhat distant, the uppermost reduced or rudimentary, the others perfect; glumes unequal, much shorter than the spikelet, acute; lemmas coriaceous, rounded on the back, obtuse; palea about equalling the lemma; stamens 3.

   1. *M. caerúlea* (L.) Moench (sky-blue). Fields and roadsides. August-September. Map 248. (Adventive from Europe).

33. *Festúca* L Fescue (ancient name).

Low to tall, perennial; leaves with flat or involute blades and membranous ligules; inflorescence a narrow, contracted or open terminal panicle; spikelets few-several flowered, disarticulating above the glumes and between the lemmas, the uppermost floret reduced; glumes narrow, acute to cuspidate, keeled, unequal, shorter than the lemmas; lemmas membranous or somewhat indurated, rounded on the back, obtuse, acute, awnless or awned from the tip; palea about equalling the lemma; stamens 3. —Wildl. 1

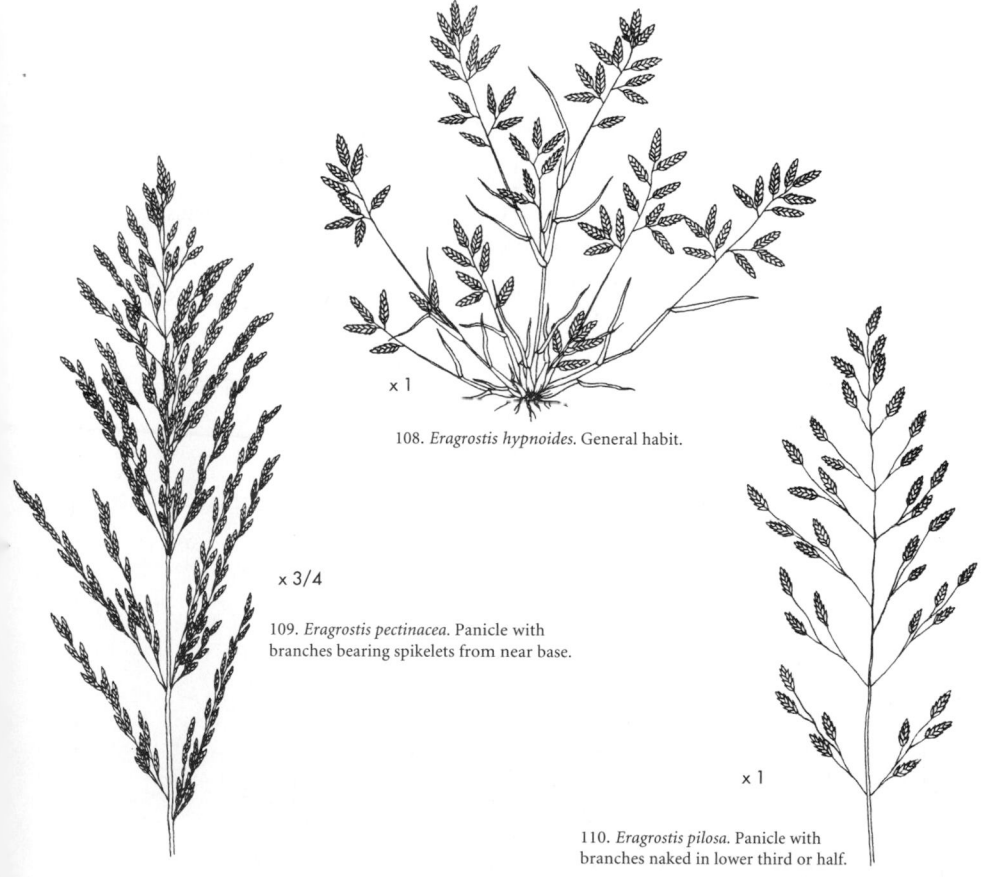

x 1

108. *Eragrostis hypnoides.* General habit.

x 3/4

109. *Eragrostis pectinacea.* Panicle with branches bearing spikelets from near base.

x 1

110. *Eragrostis pilosa.* Panicle with branches naked in lower third or half.

240. *Eragrostis hypnoides*

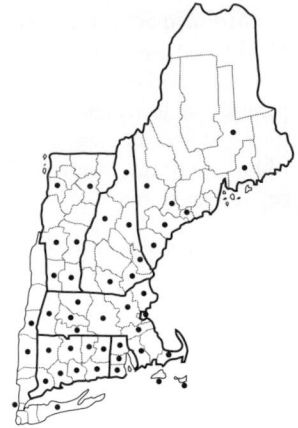

241. *Eragrostis spectabilis*

242. *Eragrostis cilianensis*

243. *Eragrostis minor*

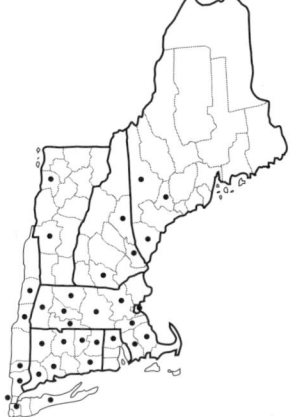

244. *Eragrostis capillaris*

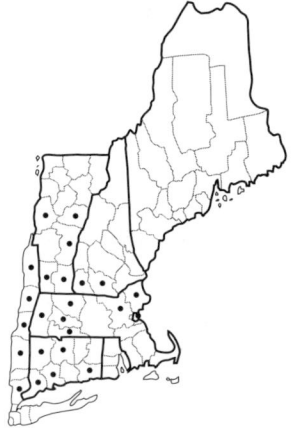

245. *Eragrostis frankii*

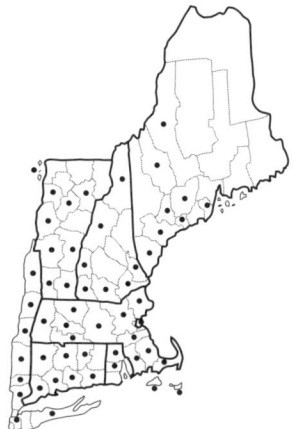

246. *Eragrostis pectinacea*

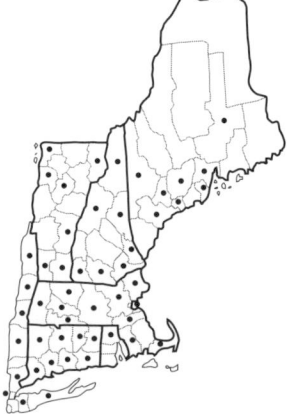

247. *Eragrostis pilosa*

248. *Molinia caerulea*

Desmazéria Dumort. *rígida* (L.) Tutin. Resembling *Festuca*; inflorescence branches spikelet-bearing to the base, spikelets up to 8 mm. long, lemmas awned. Adventive from Europe. Reported for Suffolk County MA, Washington County RI. [*Catapodium rigidum; Scleropoa rigida*].

a. Leaf blades flat, mostly more than 3 mm wide.
  b. Spikelets 8 mm or less long; lemmas less than 5 mm long. .... 1. *F. subverticillata*
  b. Spikelets longer than 8 mm; lemmas 5 mm or more long.
    c. Lemmas short-awned (awns 2 mm or less long) or awnless.
      Spikelets 5 or fewer-flowered and lemmas 7-10 mm long. .... 2. *F. arundinacea*
      Spikelets 6 or more flowered and lemmas 5-7 mm long. .... 3. *F. pratensis*
    c. Lemmas long-awned, the awns as long or longer than the lemmas. .... 4. *F. gigantea*
a. Leaf blades involute, or if flat less than 3 mm wide.
  d. Veins of lower leaf sheaths prominent, persisting as fibers when sheaths
    disintegrate .... 5. *F. rubra*
  d. Veins of lower sheaths neither prominent nor persisting as fibers.
    e. Lemmas awnless or merely mucronate. .... 6. *F. filiformis*
    e. Lemmas distinctly awned.
      f. Panicle loosely open, its branches divergent at anthesis.
        Spikelets 5-7 mm long .... 7. *F. ovina*
        Spikelets 7-10 mm long .... 8. *F. trachyphylla*
      f. Panicle contracted spiciform, linear-cylindric to lanceolate.
        Plants dwarf, 2 dm or less tall; panicle dense, 1-4 cm long; lemmas
          purplish to bronze .... 9. *F. brachyphylla*
        Plants larger, taller than 2 dm; panicle interrupted, 2-10 cm long;
          lemmas greenish .... 10. *F. saximontana*

1. *F. subverticilláta* (Pers.) Alexeev. Nodding Fescue. Moist, often rocky woods, thickets and river floodplains. June-July. Map 249. [*F. nutans; F. obtusa*]. —FACU

2. *F. arundinácea* L. Schreb. Meadow Fescue. Fields, roadsides and waste places. July-August. Fig. 111. Map 250. (Naturalized from Europe). [*F. elatior* var. *arundinacea*]. —FACU

3. *F. praténsis* Huds. Fields, roadsides, waste places. July-August. From Eurasia. [*F. elatior*]. —FACU-

4. *F. gigantéa* (L.) Vill. From Europe. Reported for Hartford County, CT, Bronx and Westchester Counties NY.

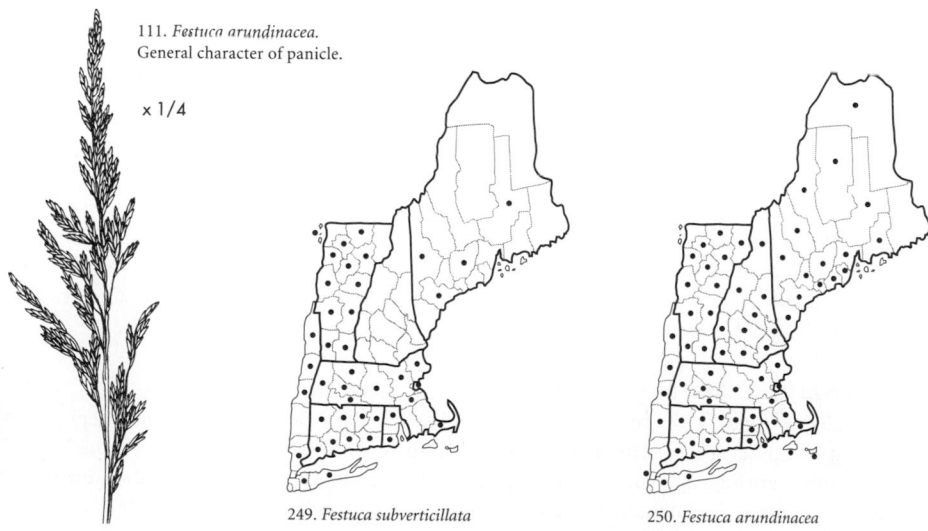

111. *Festuca arundinacea*.
General character of panicle.

x 1/4

249. *Festuca subverticillata*

250. *Festuca arundinacea*

5. *F. rúbra* L. (red). Red Fescue. Fields, thickets, roadsides, and waste places in sandy soil, and in fresh or brackish marshes, coniferous swamps and bogs. June-July. Map 251. Our plants include subsp. *rubra* and the following subsp:

subsp. *árctica* (Hack.) Govor. Florets mostly replaced by leafy tufts; rare, white mountains of New Hampshire. (Scotland). Endangered in NH. [*F. prolifera; F. rubra* var. *prolifera*].

subsp. *fállax*. Thuill. Basal offshoots all erect (all or mostly spreading or decumbent, forming loose mats in subsp. *rubra*) [*F. rubra* var. *commutata*].

subsp. *arenária* (Osbeck) Syme. Lemmas pubescent with long soft hairs (lemmas glabrous or with pubescence of coarse stiff hairs in subsp. *rubra*).

Another subsp. that has been distinguished is subsp. *pruinosa*. —FACU

F. heterophýlla Lam. Similar to *F. rubra* but with involute basal leaves and flat stem leaves (leaves all folded or involute or all flat in *F. rubra*). [*F. rubra* var. *h.*]. Reported for CT.

F. diffúsa Dumort has been attributed to our range. It has a higher ploidy level than *F. rubra* and is not easily distinguished morphologically.

6. *F. filifórmis* Pourret. Dry open soil. June-July. (Naturalized from Europe). [*F. ovina* var. *capillata; F. capillata; F. tenuifolia*].

7. *F. ovína* L. Sheep Fescue. Fields, roadsides, waste places in dry sandy soil. June-July. Map 252. (Naturalized from Eurasia).

8. *F. trachyphýlla* (Hack.) Krajina. Fields, roadsides, waste places. (Naturalized from Europe). [*F. brevipila; F. longifolia; F. ovina* var. *duriuscula; F. duriuscula*].

9. *F. brachyphýlla* J.A. Schultes ex J.A. & J.H. Schultes. Alpine. July. (Arct. Eurasia). [*F. ovina* var. *b.; F. brachyphylla*]. Reported for VT. Our plants are subsp. *brachyphylla*.

10. *F. saximontána* Rydb. Dry slopes, open areas. June-July. Reported for VT. [*F. brachyphylla* var. *rydbergii; F. ovina* var. *s.*].

34. *Vúlpia* K.C. Gmel. (name for fox, from the appearance of the panicle).

Similar to *Festuca* but annual, the stems solitary or loosely cespitose. [*Festuca*].

a. First glume up to half length of second; awns 1 1/2 or more times as long as the
      lemmas .... 1. *V. myuros*
a. First glume more than half length of second.
      Awns not longer, or shorter than the lemmas .... 2. *V. octoflora*
      Awns longer than the lemmas .... 3. *V. bromoides*

1. *V. myúros* (L.) K. C. Gmel. (mouse-tail). Rats-tail Fescue. Fields, roadsides and waste places, usually dry or sandy soil. June-July. Map 253. (Naturalized from Europe). [*Festuca m.*].

2. *V. octoflóra* (Walt.) Rydb. (eight-flowered). Slender Fescue. Roadsides and waste places, in dry, sandy soil. June-July. Map 254. Endangered in VT. [*Festuca o.*]. Our plants include var. *octoflora* and the following var.:

var. *glaúca* (Nutt.) Fern. Panicle dense with crowded, strongly overlapping spikelets, spikelets up to 5.5 mm long (panicle open, spikelets not crowded and strongly overlapping, spikelets 5.5 mm or longer in var. *octoflora*). [*Festuca o.* var. *glauca*].

3. *V. bromoídes* (L.) S. F. Gray. Introduced from Europe. Reported for Worcester County MA; Nassau and Suffolk Counties NY. [*Festuca b.; F. dertonensis; Vulpia d.*]. —FACW

35. *Glycéria* R. Br. Manna Grass (from the Greek meaning sweet).

Usually tall, perennial, with creeping rhizomes and simple stems which are erect or creeping and rooting at the base; leaves with usually closed sheaths, flat blades and membranous ligules; inflorescence a terminal open or contracted panicle; spikelets disarticulating above the glumes and between the lemmas, few to many flowered, ovoid to linear, laterally flattened or subterete; glumes unequal, shorter than the lemmas, obtuse or acute; lemmas broad, convex on the back, awnless, usually obtuse, with 5-9 parallel, usually prominent veins; palea equalling the lemma; flowers perfect, stamens 2 or 3.

Seeds reported as edible when boiled or can be dried and ground into flour. —OBL; Wildl. 1

a. Spikelets linear, mostly 1 cm or more long. (Fig. 112).
  b. Lemma long-acuminate; palea extended 1.5 mm or more beyond lemma. .... 1. *G. acutiflora*
  b. Lemma obtuse; palea as long as lemma or extended much less than 1.5 mm.
    c. Lemmas mostly longer than 5 mm .... 2. *G. fluitans*
    c. Lemmas 5 mm or shorter.
      Lemmas mostly glabrous between the minutely scaberulous nerves. .... 3. *G. borealis*
      Lemmas puberulent between distinctly scabrous nerves. .... 4. *G. septentrionalis*
a. Spikelets ovate or oblong, less than 1 cm long.
  d. Panicle contracted, narrow, with strict, ascending branches.
    Panicle thick-cylindric to oblong; spikelets 4.5 mm long or longer; lemmas
      3-4 mm long. (Fig. 113) .... 5. *G. obtusa*
    Panicle linear-cylindric; spikelets less than 4.5 mm long; lemmas less than
      3 mm long .... 6. *G. melicaria*
  d. Panicle open, lax, with spreading to loosely ascending branches. (Fig. 114).
    e. Most spikelets 3 mm or more wide.
      Palea broadly elliptic, its sides not covered by the lemma; hyaline tip of
        lemma projecting 0.5-1 mm beyond palea. .... 7. *G. canadensis*
      Palea narrowly elliptic, completely covered by the lemma, or if slightly longer,
        projecting less than 0.5 mm beyond palea .... 8. *G. laxa*
    e. Most spikelets less than 3 mm wide.
      f. Nerves of lemma evident but not prominent, palea less than twice as long
        as wide .... 8. *G. laxa*
      f. Nerves of lemma raised and prominent; palea 3-5 times as long as wide.
        First glume 1 mm or less long; lower part of stem (including sheaths) 4 mm
          or less wide .... 9. *G. striata*
        First glume more than 1 mm long; lower part of stem (including sheaths)
          wider than 4 mm .... 10. *G. grandis*

1. G. acutiflóra Torr. (acute-flowered). Sharp-scaled Manna Grass. Shallow water of ponds and streams or wet soil. June-July. Map 255. (Ne. Asia). Endangered in VT and NH.

2. G. flúitans (L.) R. Br. (floating). Floating Manna Grass. Shallow water and wet soil. July-August. Map 256. (Eurasia).

3. G. boreális (Nash) Batchelder (northern). Northern Manna Grass. Shallow water and wet soil. June-August. Fig. 112, Map 257.

4. G. septentrionális A. S. Hitchc. (northern). Eastern Manna Grass. Shallow water, wet soil of meadows and wooded swamps. June-August. Map 258.

G. declináta Brebiss. Similar to *G. septentrionalis* but distinguished in having leaves with open sheaths and blades less than 6 mm wide (sheaths closed and blades mostly 6 mm or more wide in *G. septentrionalis*). Western. Reported for Queens County NY.

5. G. obtúsa (Muhl.) Trin. (obtuse). Blunt Manna Grass. Shallow water, coniferous and deciduous wooded swamps, and bogs. August-September. Fig. 113, Map 259.

6. G. melicária (Michx.) F. T. Hubbard (similar to *Melica*). Long Manna Grass. Deciduous wooded swamps and wet woods. July-August. Map 260. [*G. torreyana*].

7. G. canadénsis (Michx.) Trin. (of Canada). Rattlesnake Grass. Wet meadows, shallow marshes, shores, bogs and deciduous wooded swamps. June-August. Figure 114, Map 261.

8. G. láxa (Scribn.) Scribn. (loose). Wet meadows, shallow marshes, bogs and deciduous wooded swamps. July-August. Map 262. [*G. canadensis* var. *laxa*].

9. G. striáta (Lam.) A. S. Hitchc. (with longitudinal lines). Fowl-meadow Grass. Wet meadows, shallow marshes, deciduous wooded swamps and wet woods. June-September. Map 263. Our plants include var. *striata* and the following var.:

var. *strícta* (Scribn.) Fern. Generally lower than var. *striata* with ascending panicle branches; spikelets purple (green or purple in var. *striata*).

10. G. grándis S. Wats. (large). Reed Manna Grass. Wet meadows, shallow marshes, ditches, wooded swamps, pond margins and shallow-water. June-August. Map 264. [*G. maxima* subsp. *grandis*]. Our plants are var. *grandis.*

36. *Torreyochlóa* Church.

Similar to *Glyceria* and *Puccinellia* but with second glume 3-nerved, lemmas strongly 5-nerved. [*Glyceria*].

1. T. pállida (Torr.) Church (pale). Pale Manna Grass. Marshes, bogs, pond margins and shallow water. June-August. Map 265. (E. Asia). [*Glyceria p.; Puccinellia p.*]. Our plants include var. *pallida* and the following var.:

var. *fernáldii* (A. S. Hitchc.) Dorc ex Koyama & Kawano. Larger leaves up to 3.5 mm wide; ligules up to 4 mm long; spikelets 3-5 mm long (larger leaves 4 mm or more wide; ligules 5 mm or more long; spikelets 5-7 mm long in var. *pallida*). [*Glyceria pallida* var. *fernaldii; G. fernaldii*].

37. *Puccinéllia* Parl. Alkali-Grass (for B. Puccinelli).

Tufted annuals or perennials; leaves with narrow flat or involute blades and membranous ligule; inflorescence a narrow, contracted to open panicle; spikelets several flowered, terete or subterete, disarticulating above the glumes and between the lemmas; glumes unequal, shorter than the lemmas, acute or obtuse; lemmas rounded on the back, acute or obtuse, usually hyaline toward the tip, with 5 parallel, obscure nerves; palea about as long as or somewhat shorter than lemma; flowers perfect, stamens 3. [*Torreyochloa*].

In addition to the species treated below *P. kurilensis* has been reported for CT and MA.

a. Lowest branches of panicle bearing spikelets nearly from the base. (Fig. 115).
    Spikelets up to 4 mm long; lemmas up to 2.5 mm long. .... 1. *P. fasciculata*
    Spikelets 5 mm or more long; lemmas 3 mm or more long. .... 2. *P. rupestris*
a. Lowest branches of panicle naked below the middle. (Fig. 116).
  b. Lemmas 2.8 mm or longer.
    Anthers linear, 1.5 mm long or longer. .... 3. *P. maritima*
    Anthers oblong, shorter than 1.5 mm .... 4. *P. tenella*
  b. Lemmas shorter than 2.8 mm.
    c. Lemmas truncate or broadly rounded. .... 5. *P. distans*
    c. Lemmas acute or obtuse but not truncate or broadly rounded.
      Lemmas 2.4 mm long or longer; grain longer than 1.5 mm. .... 4. *P. tenella*
      Lemmas 2.3 mm long or shorter; grain shorter than 1.5. mm. .... 6. *P. nuttalliana*

1. P. fasciculáta (Torr.) Bickn. (with clusters). Salt marshes and sandy shores. May-July. Fig. 115, Map 266. (Europe). [*P. borreri*]. —OBL

2. P. rupéstris (With.) Fern. & Weatherby. Ballast; from Europe. Reported for Bronx County NY.

3. P. marítima (Huds.) Parl. (of the sea). Salt marshes, sea beaches and dunes. June-August. Fig. 116, Map 267. (Europe). —OBL

4. P. tenélla (Lange) Holmb. Tidal flats and shores inundated at high tide. June-September. Map 268. Endangered in NH.[*P. langeana; P. paupercula; P. pumila*]. Our plants include subsp. *tenella* and the following subsp:

subsp. *alascána* (Scribn. & Merr.) Tzvelev. Ligule more than 1 mm long; first glume 1.5-2 mm long; lemma 2.5-4 mm long (ligule less than 1 mm long; first glume 1-1.5 mm long; lemma 2-2.5 mm long in subsp. *tenella*). [*P. paupercula* var. *a.*].

Another subsp. that has been distinguished is subsp. *langeana*. —FACW+

5. P. dístans (Jacq.) Parl. (remote). Salt marshes, sea beaches and saline or alkaline waste places and roadsides. June-October. Map 269. (Naturalized from Europe). Our plants include subsp. *distans* and the following subsp.:

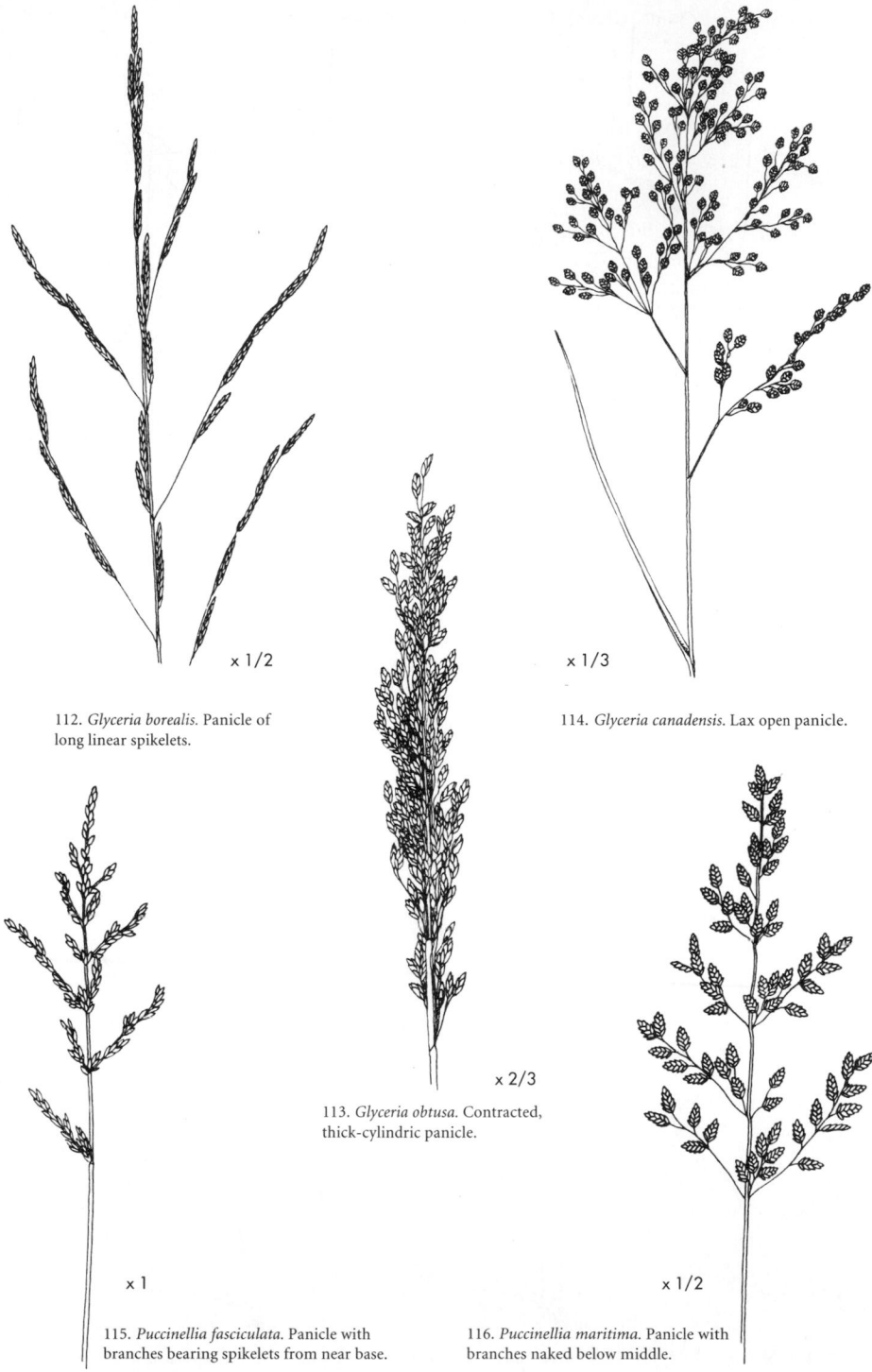

x 1/2

112. *Glyceria borealis.* Panicle of
long linear spikelets.

x 1/3

114. *Glyceria canadensis.* Lax open panicle.

x 2/3

113. *Glyceria obtusa.* Contracted,
thick-cylindric panicle.

x 1

115. *Puccinellia fasciculata.* Panicle with
branches bearing spikelets from near base.

x 1/2

116. *Puccinellia maritima.* Panicle with
branches naked below middle.

251. *Festuca rubra*

252. *Festuca ovina*

253. *Vulpia myuros*

254. *Vulpia octoflora*

255. *Glyceria acutiflora*

256. *Glyceria fluitans*

257. *Glyceria borealis*

258. *Glyceria septentrionalis*

259. *Glyceria obtusa*

260. *Glyceria melicaria*

261. *Glyceria canadensis*

262. *Glyceria laxa*

263. *Glyceria striata*

264. *Glyceria grandis*

265. *Torreyochloa pallida*

266. *Puccinellia fasciculata*

267. *Puccinellia maritima*

268. *Puccinellia tenella*

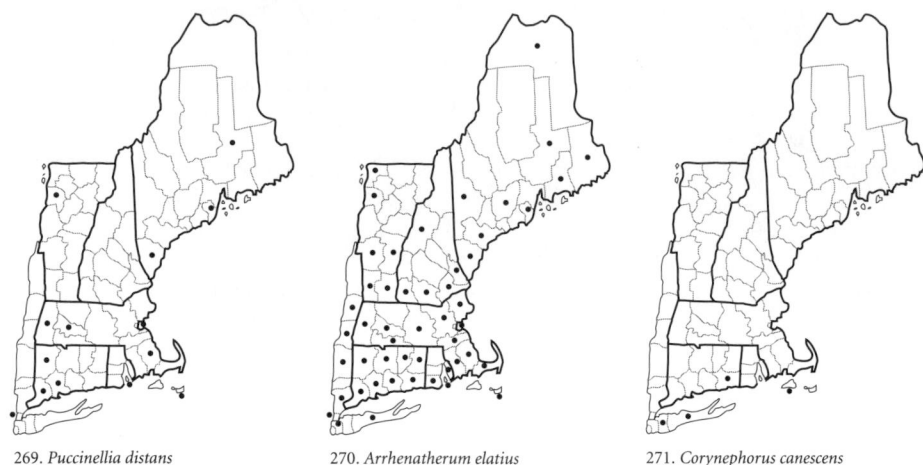

269. *Puccinellia distans*   270. *Arrhenatherum elatius*   271. *Corynephorus canescens*

subsp. *boreális* (Holmb.) W. E. Hughes. Stem leaves 2 mm or less wide, becoming involute (2 mm or wider and flat in subsp. *distans*). [*P. distans* var. *angustifolia*]. —OBL

6. *P. nuttalliána* (J. A. Schultes) A. S. Hitchc. (for T. Nuttall). Nuttall Alkali-grass. Reported for Hancock and York Counties ME, Orleans County VT. [*P. airoides; P. laurentiana; P. lucida*]. —FAC

38. *Arrhenathérum* Beauv. Oat-Grass (from the Greek, referring to the awned staminate floret).

Tall, tufted perennials; leaves with long, flat blades and membranous ligules; inflorescence a long, narrow, open panicle; spikelets disarticulating above the glumes, 2-flowered, the lower staminate, its lemma bearing on the back near the base a twisted, geniculate, exserted awn, the upper perfect, bearing a short straight slender awn near the tip; glumes acute, membranous, the second longer than the first and about equalling the spikelet; lemmas of firmer texture than the glumes, 5-7 nerved, pubescent on the callus; palea membranous, nearly as long as the lemma; stamens 3.

1. *A. elátius* (L.) J. & K. Presl. (rather tall). Tall Oat-Grass. Fields, roadsides and waste places, often in moist soil. June-July. Fig. 117, Map 270. (Naturalized from Europe). Our plants include var. *elatius* and the following var.:

var. *bulbósum* (Willd.) Spenner. Stems with lower internodes short, thickened into subglobose corms. —FACU

39. *Corynéphorus* Beauv. (from the Greek, referring to the club-shaped awns).

Rather short, slender perennial, densely cespitose, branching at the base, stems sometimes geniculate; leaves mostly crowded near the base, with erect, involute-filiform blades, the sheaths often purplish; inflorescence a dense, narrow, terminal silvery panicle; spikelets disarticulating above the glumes and between the lemmas, with 2 perfect flowers; glumes subequal, membranous, acute or acuminate, longer than the lemmas; lemmas membranous, acute, pubescent at the base, awned from near the base, the awn jointed about the middle, with a ring of hairs at the joint, the lower half stout, straight, brown, the upper half slender, pale, gradually thickened toward the tip and club shaped; palea as long or nearly as long as the lemma; stamens 3.

1. *C. canéscens* (L.) Beauv. (grayish). Dry, sandy fields, roadsides and waste places along the coast. June-July. Fig. 118, Map 271. (Naturalized from Europe).

40. Avéna L. Oat (the classical name).

Mostly annuals, low to moderately tall; leaves with broad, flat blades and membranous ligules; inflorescence a narrow or (ours) loose, open, terminal panicle of large spikelets; spikelets disarticulating above the glumes and between the lemmas, 2-3 flowered (ours); glumes about equal, membranous, many nerved, acuminate, exceeding the florets; lemmas indurated except toward the tip, obscurely nerved to prominently nerved distally, acute and 2-toothed at the tip, glabrous or hirsute, bearing a basally twisted straight or geniculate awn from the back near the middle, or awnless, palea membranous, nearly as long as the lemma, nerves ciliate; lower flowers perfect, the upper sometimes staminate, stamens 3; grain hirsute. —Wildl. 1

Helictotríchon Besser. Similar to *Avena* but differing in that the spikelets are erect instead of pendulous as in *Avena* and glumes are 5 or fewer nerved (6 or more nerved in *Avena*). Two species rarely found in our range: *H. pubéscens* (Huds.) Pilger, introduced from Europe, lower sheaths and the blades pubescent, reported for CT, VT, [*Avena pubescens*] and *H. hookeri* (Scribn.) Henr. Spike Oat, from the west, lower sheaths and blades glabrous, reported for Chittenden County VT. [*Avena pratensis*].

Most spikelets with 3 florets, at least 2 awns exceeding 5 mm, the awns geniculate; lemmas pubescent with long, brownish hairs .... 1. *A. fatua*
Most spikelets with 2 florets, only 1 or none of the awns exceeding 5 mm, the awns straight; lemmas glabrous or scabridulous. .... 2. *A. sativa*

1. A. fátua L. (foolish, useless). Wild Oat. Fields, roadsides, railroad tracks, and waste areas. July-September. Fig. 119, Map 272. (Naturalized from Europe).

A. stérilis L. Animated Oats. Resembling *A. fatua*; distinguishable in having glumes 3.5-4 cm long, awns 4.5 or more cm, rachilla not readily disarticulating between the lemmas (glumes 3 cm or less long, awns 4 cm or less, rachilla readily disarticulating in *A. fatua*). Reported for VT.

2. A. sativa L. (cultivated). Oat. Cultivated fields, roadsides, railroad tracks, and waste areas. Map 273. (Introduced from Eurasia). Commercially grown as a cereal grain.

A. strigósa Schreb. Similar to *A. sativa* but with panicle 1-sided and lemmas scabrous toward the apex (panicle symmetrical or nearly so and lemmas glabrous in *A. sativa*). Reported for MA.

41. Áira L. Hairgrass (Greek name for some type of grass).

Small, delicate, tufted annuals; stems slender, upright or frequently geniculate; leaves with short, very narrow blades, ligule membranous, lacerate; inflorescence a diffuse or spike-like panicle; spikelets small, 2-flowered, disarticulating above the glumes and between the lemmas; glumes about equal, obscurely 1-3 nerved, acute to acuminate, thin and membranous, boat-shaped, exceeding the florets; lemmas firm, rounded on the back, tapering into 2 teeth, obscurely nerved, one or both lemmas bearing a delicate awn on the back below the middle, the awn twisted at the base, bent, the straight lower part about equalling the body of the lemma; palea nearly as long as the lemma; callus pubescent; flowers both perfect, stamens 3.

Panicle contracted, narrow and spike-like. .... 1. *A. praecox*
Panicle open and diffusely branched .... 2. *A. caryophyllea*

1. A. praécox L. (precocious). Early Hairgrass. Dry, sandy soil near the coast. May-June. Map 274. (Naturalized from Europe).

2. A. caryophylléa L. (like *Caryophyllus* or *Dianthus*; from the tufts of slender leaves). Silvery Hairgrass. Fields and waste places in sandy soil, mostly near the coast. Fig. 120, Map 275. (Naturalized from Europe).

A. elegantíssima Schur. Similar to the latter species but distinguishable in having pedicels mostly 2 or more times as long as the spikelets (pedicels mostly up to twice as long as the spikelets in *A. caryophyllea*). (Introduced from Europe). Reported for MA. [*A. capillaris; A. elegans*].

x 12

118 *Corynephorus canescens*. Spikelet with 2
florets having awns thickened toward the tip.

x 1

117. *Arrhenatherum elatius*. Panicle of
spikelets with one awn exserted,
geniculate.

x 1

120. *Aira caryophyllea*. Open,
diffusely branched panicle.

x 2/3

119. *Avena fatua*. Panicle of large, several-flowered spikelets.

272. *Avena fatua*

273. *Avena sativa*

274. *Aira praecox*

275. *Aira caryophyllea*

276. *Deschampsia caespitosa*

42. *Deschámpsia* Beauv. Hairgrass (for J. Deslongchamps).

Low or moderately tall, cespitose, annual or perennial; leaves with flat narrow, or involute blades; inflorescence a narrow or open panicle; spikelets disarticulating above the glumes and between the lemmas, 2-flowered, both flowers perfect; glumes membranous, acute, shining, about equal, equaling or slightly longer than the lemmas; lemmas membranous, obtuse or truncate and 2-4 toothed at summit, bearing a slender awn at or below the middle, the awn straight, bent or twisted; palea narrow; callus bearded; stamens 3.

a. Panicle narrow, with appressed branches. .... 1. *D. elongata*
a. Panicle loose and open. (Fig. 121).
    Leaf blades flat or folded; awns included or slightly exserted, straight. .... 2. *D. cespitosa*
    Leaf blades filiform, involute; awns well exserted, geniculate, twisted below the
        middle .... 3. *D. flexuosa*

1. *D. elongáta* (Hook.) Munro. Slender Hairgrass. Western; Recorded for York County ME.

2. *D. cespitósa* (L.) Beauv. (bunched). Tufted Hairgrass. Wet soil, riverbanks and shores. July-August. Map 276. (Europe). Our plants include subsp. *cespitosa* and the following subsp.:

subsp. *parviflóra* (Thuil.) Jarmolenko & Soo. Leaves persistently flat, spikelets less than 3.5 mm long (leaves sometimes folded and spikelets longer than 3.5 mm in subsp. *cespitosa*).

subsp. *glaúca* (Hartman) Hartman. Leaves very narrow, less than 2 mm wide (2-5 mm wide in subsp. *cespitosa*). Endangered in MA. —FACW

3. *D. flexuósa* (L.) Trin. (zigzag). Common Hairgrass. Dry woods, fields, waste areas and in the mountains. July-August. Map 277. (Eurasia). Our plants are var. *flexuosa*.

43. Vahlódea Fries

Similar to *Deschampsia* but with glumes much longer than the lemmas. [*Deschampsia*].

1. *V. atropurpúrea* (Wahlenb.) Fries ex Hartman (dark purple). Mountain Hairgrass. Alpine meadows and wet rocks. July-August. Fig. 121, Map 278. (Eurasia). [*Deschampsia a.*]. —FACW

44. Danthónia DC. Wild Oat Grass (for E. Danthoine).

Low to moderately tall, erect, densely cespitose perennial; leaves with narrow, flat blades, those at the base frequently curled and involute and occasionally twisted, ligule a tuft of hairs; inflorescence a terminal, few-flowered open or contracted panicle of large spikelets; spikelets disarticulating above the glumes and between the lemmas, several flowered, the florets densely crowded, all perfect or the uppermost staminate; glumes longer than the lemmas, subequal, acute; lemmas glabrous to sparsely or densely pubescent, bifid, with a geniculate awn arising between the acute or awned teeth, the awn straw colored to brownish and twisted basally, the upper part straight, usually divergent from the spikelet; palea as long as lemma excluding the awn; stamens 3.

Teeth of lemmas less than 2 mm; awn at spirally twisted base purplish to dark brown;
    lowest branch of panicle erect. (Fig. 122). .... 1. *D. spicata*
Teeth of lemmas longer than 2 mm; awn at spirally twisted base yellowish to pale
    brown; lowest branch of panicle spreading to divergent. (Fig. 123). .... 2. *D. compressa*

1. *D. spicáta* (L.) Beauv. ex Roemer & J. A. Schultes. (spiked). Fields, roadsides and waste places. July-September. Fig. 122, Map 279.

2. *D. compréssa* Aust. ex Peck. (compressed). Woodlands, meadows, roadsides and waste places. July-September. Fig. 123, Map 280. [*D. alleni*]. —FACU

D. serícea Nutt. Will key to *D. compressa* but is distinguishable in having an awn 1 cm or more long (awn less than 1 cm long in *D. compressa*). From farther south. Reported for MA, NH. —FACU

D. califórnica Boland. California Oatgrass. Differing from the latter 3 species in having lemmas glabrous except for pilosity on the lower part of the margin and on the callus (lemmas pilose over the back, sometimes sparsely so in the latter 3 species). Western. Reported for MA.

45. Trisétum Pers. (from the Greek meaning 3 bristles, from the bifid, awned lemma).

Tufted perennials (ours); leaves with flat blades and membranous ligules; inflorescence a contracted, spike-like or open shining, terminal panicle; spikelets 2 or 3 flowered, the terminal floret, when present, rudimentary, rachilla prolonged behind the upper floret, disarticulating above or below the glumes; glumes unequal, equalling or longer than the lowest lemma, acute to aristate; lemmas 2-toothed, the teeth often setaceous, dorsally awned below the teeth with a bent or straight awn or entire and awnless, densely short-bearded at the base; palea shorter than lemma, 2-toothed; flowers perfect or the uppermost staminate; stamens 3.

a. Lemmas awnless, or rarely with a minute awn just below the tip. .... 1. *T. melicoides*
a. Lemmas (at least the upper) with a bent awn often twisted at the base.
    Panicle dense and spike-like, sometimes interrupted near the base. (Fig. 124). .... 2. *T. spicatum*
    Panicle somewhat loose and open with elongate branches, not
        spike-like. (Fig. 125) .... 3. *T. flavescens*

1. *T. melicoídes* (Michx.) Vasey ex Scribn. (resembling *Melica*). Rocky or gravelly lake shores and river banks. July-August. Map 281. Endangered in NE and NY. —FAC

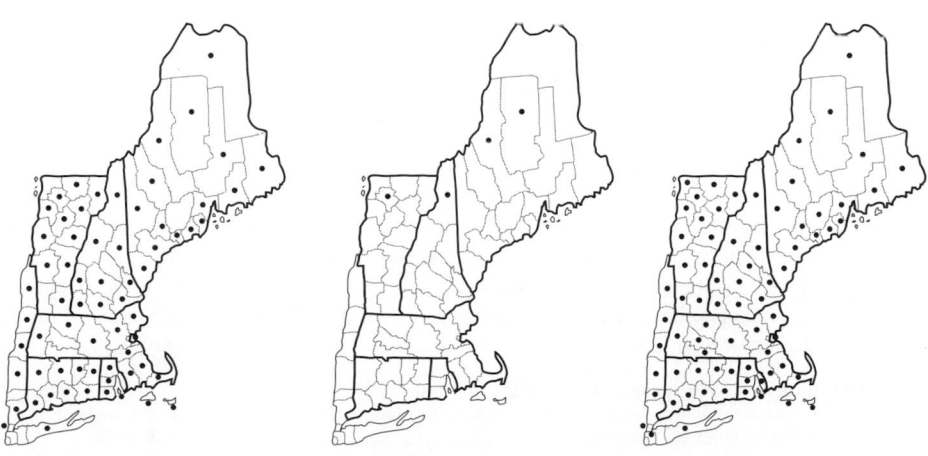

x 2/3

121. *Vahlodea atropurpurea.* Loose, open panicle.

x 1-1/2

122. *Danthonia spicata.* Panicle with lowest branch erect.

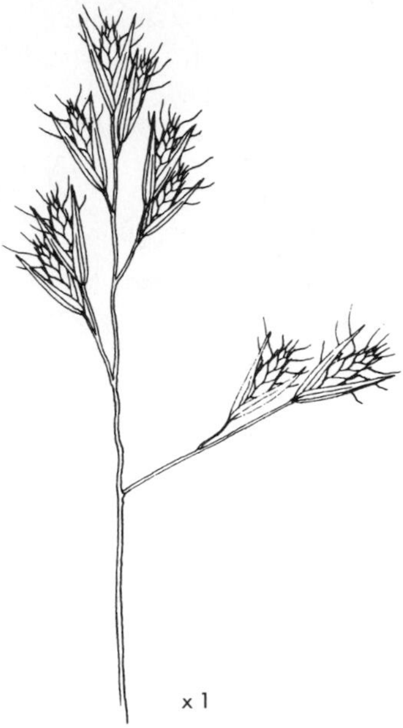

x 1

123. *Danthonia compressa.* Panicle with lowest branch divergent.

277. *Deschampsia flexuosa*

278. *Vahlodea atropurpurea*

279. *Danthonia spicata*

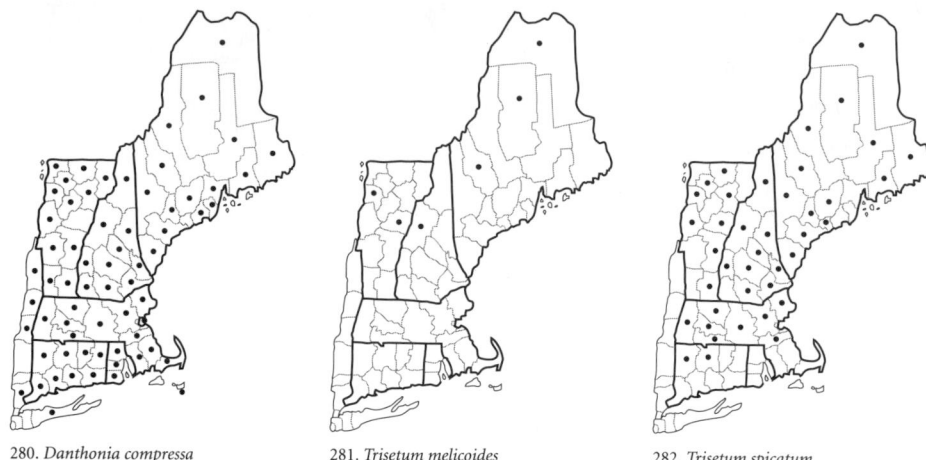

280. *Danthonia compressa*   281. *Trisetum melicoides*   282. *Trisetum spicatum*

2. T. spicátum (L.) Richter (spiked). Spike Trisetum. Lake shores, river banks and alpine meadows. June-August. Fig. 124, Map 282. Endangered in MA and ME. [*T. triflorum*]. —FACU

3. T. flavéscens (L.) Beauv. (Yellowish). Yellow Oats. Fields, roadsides and waste places. June-July. Fig. 125, Map 283. (Naturalized from Europe).

46. Hólcus L. (Greek name for a type of grass). Velvet Grass.

Erect perennials, with or without rhizomes; leaves with relatively wide blades and membranous ligules; inflorescence a dense, contracted, ovoid or subcylindric, terminal panicle; spikelets disarticulating below the glumes, 2-flowered, the lower perfect, awnless, the upper staminate, awned from below the tip; glumes nearly equal, longer than and enclosing the lemmas, acute, keeled; lemmas lustrous; paleas nearly as long as the lemmas; stamens 3. Poisonous.

Awn of staminate floret hooked, less than 2 mm long; glumes villous; rhizomes none ... 1. *H. lanatus*
Awn of staminate floret bent, 3-4 mm long; glumes glabrous except on keel;
    rhizomes present .... 2. *H. mollis*

1. H. lanátus L. (woolly). Meadows, roadsides and waste places. June-July. Fig. 126, Map 284. (Naturalized from Europe). —FACU

2. H. móllis L. (soft). Waste places. Reported for Essex County MA. (Adventive from Europe).

47. Sphenópholis Scribn. Wedgegrass (from the Greek, referring to the obovate second glume).

Slender, tufted perennials; leaves with rather short, usually flat blades and membranous ligule; inflorescence a dense, narrow, shining terminal panicle; spikelets mostly 2 (rarely 3) flowered, disarticulating below the glumes and between the lemmas; glumes subequal, equalling or longer than the lowest lemma, the first narrow, acute, the second much broader, obovate, obtuse or rounded at the tip, or sometimes acute, both somewhat coriaceous, the margins hyaline; lemmas narrow, firm, acute, papillose, usually awnless (except in *S. pensylvanica*); palea hyaline, about as long as lemma; flowers perfect, stamens 3.

a. Second lemma scabrous-papillose, at least on the upper half.
    Upper and sometimes also the lower lemma bearing an awn just below the tip. ..... 1. *S. pensylvanica*
    Upper and lower lemmas awnless ....2. *S. nitida*
a. Second lemma papillose but not scabrous.

Second glume broadly obovate, rounded to truncate, more than half as wide
    as long. (Fig. 127) .... 3. *S. obtusata*
Second glume narrowly obovate to oblanceolate, acute, half or less than half as
    wide as long .... 4. *S. intermedia*

   1. *S. pensylvánica* (L.) A. S. Hitchc. (of Pennsylvania). Swamp Oats. Wooded swamps, wet woods and wet meadows. May-July. Map 285. [*S. palustris; Trisetum pensylvanicum*]. —OBL
   2. *S. nítida* (Biehler) Scribn. (shining). Dry or mesic deciduous woods. April-June. Map 286. Endangered in VT.
   3. *S. obtusáta* (Michx.) Scribn. (blunt). Prairie Wedgegrass. Dry or moist old fields, open woods, borders of brackish marshes, roadsides and waste places. June-August. Fig. 127, Map 287. (Bermuda). Endangered in VT. —FAC-
   4. *S. intermédia* (Rydb.) Rydb. (intermediate). Slender Wedgegrass. Dry or moist woodlands, borders of brackish or salt marshes and waste places. June-August. Map 288. [*S. pallens*]. —FAC

48. *Koeléria* Pers. (for G. Koeler).

Tufted perennial (ours); leaves with narrow, flat or involute blades and membranous ligules; inflorescence a contracted, densely flowered, terminal, spike-like, silvery-pale green panicle; spikelets 2-4 flowered, flattened laterally, disarticulating above the glumes and between the lemmas; glumes subequal, slightly shorter than the lemmas, acute, the first narrow, the second wider than the first, broadest above the middle; lemmas acute to short awned, rounded on the back; palea nearly as long as lemma; callus and rachilla bearded, the rachilla prolonged behind the upper palea as a bristle, or occasionally bearing a reduced floret at the tip; stamens 3.

   1. *K. macrántha* (Ledeb.) J. A. Schultes. Junegrass. Dry sandy soil, open woods. July-September. Fig. 128, Map 289. (Eurasia). [*K. cristata; K. gracilis; K. nitida; K. pyramidata*].

49. *Anthoxánthum* L. Sweet Vernal Grass (from the Greek meaning yellow-flower).

Fragrant, tufted, annual or perennial with slender, erect or decumbent, simple or branched stems; leaves with flat blades and membranous, erose-truncate ligules; inflorescence a short, dense, spike-like panicle; spikelets laterally compressed, with 1 perfect, central floret and 2 sterile lemmas, disarticulating above the glumes, the sterile lemmas falling attached to the fertile; glumes acute or mucronate, very unequal, much exceeding the lemmas; sterile lemmas subequal, brownish pubescent, the first awned on the back near the tip, the second near the base, its awn twisted below, geniculate near the tip of the lemma; fertile floret shorter than and enclosed within the sterile, its lemma broadly rounded, at first membranous, becoming brownish and shining, awnless; palea resembling lemma, smaller and enclosed within it; stigmas elongated, plumose, stamens 2.

Plant perennial; awn of lower sterile lemma straight. .... 1. *A. odoratum*
Plant annual; awns of both sterile lemmas geniculate. .... 2. *A. aristatum*

   1. *A. odorátum* L. (fragrant). Sweet Vernal Grass. Abandoned fields, pastures, meadows, roadsides and waste places. May-July. Fig. 129, Map 290. (Naturalized from Europe). Our plants are subsp. *odoratum.* —FACU
   2. *A. aristátum* Boiss. Long-awned Vernal Grass. Abandoned fields and waste places. June-August. Map 291. [*A. puelii*].

50. *Hieróchloe* R. Br. Holy Grass (from the Greek meaning sacred grass).

Fragrant, slender, erect, rhizomatous perennial; sterile shoots with elongate, basal leaves, fertile shoots with long basal leaves and rather short, flat blades, ligules membranous; inflorescence a terminal panicle of broad spikelets; spikelets disarticulating above the glumes, with 2 staminate

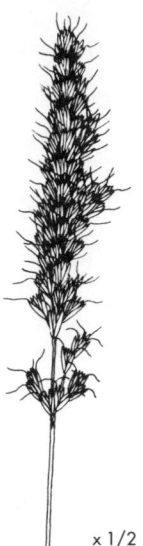

× 1/2

124. *Trisetum spicatum*. Dense, spike-like
panicle interrupted at base.

× 2/3

125. *Trisetum flavescens*. Somewhat open
panicle with elongate branches.

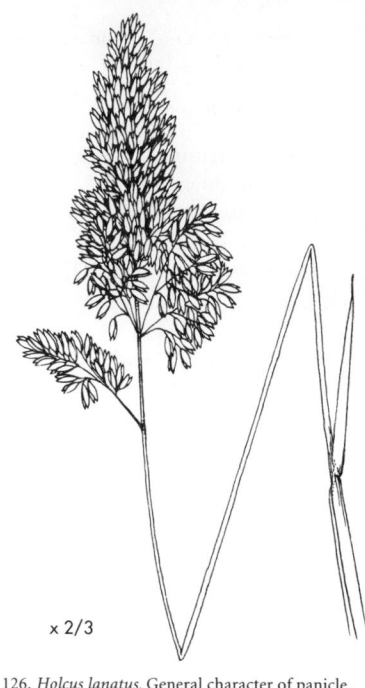

× 2/3

126. *Holcus lanatus*. General character of panicle.

128. *Koeleria macrantha*.
General character of panicle.

× 3/4

× 6

Single spikelet showing glumes

× 1/2

127. *Sphenopholis obtusata*. General character of panicle.

× 3/4

129. *Anthoxanthum odoratum*.
General character of panicle.

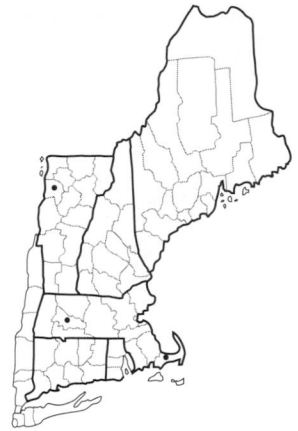

283. *Trisetum flavescens*

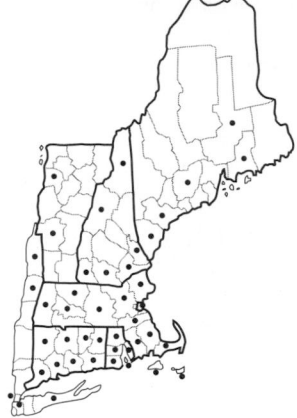

284. *Holcus lanatus*

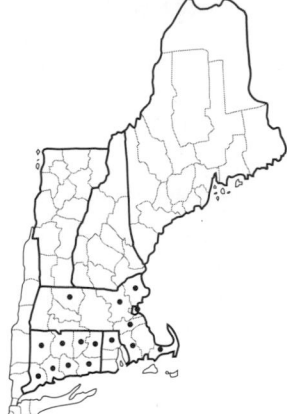

285. *Sphenopholis pensylvanica*

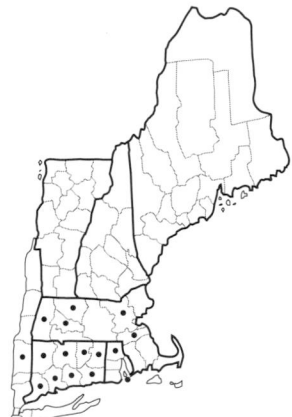

286. *Sphenopholis nitida*

287. *Sphenopholis obtusata*

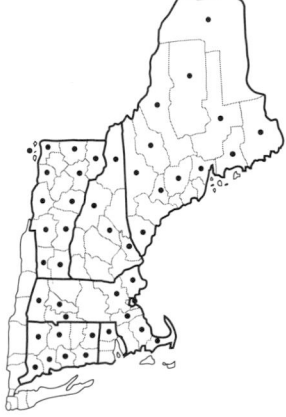

288. *Sphenopholis intermedia*

289. *Koeleria macrantha*

290. *Anthoxanthum odoratum*

291. *Anthoxanthum aristatum*

flowers and 1 terminal, perfect flower; glumes subequal, about as long as the lemmas, membranous, shining, acute; staminate lemmas boat shaped, brown, hairy, awned below the tip or awnless, enclosing a palea and 3 stamens, fertile lemma smaller, somewhat indurated, pubescent toward the tip, glabrous below, enclosing a palea of nearly equal length, and a perfect flower with 2 stamens. Sweet scented.

Staminate lemmas bearing exserted awns; rhizomes absent or very short. .... 1. *H. alpina*
Staminate lemmas awnless, merely sharply acute; rhizomes long and creeping. .... 2. *H. odorata*

    1. *H. alpína* (Sw.) ex Willd. Roemer & J. A. Schultes (alpine). Alpine Holy Grass. Alpine meadows. July-August. Fig. 130. Map 292. (Eurasia). [*Savastana a*]. Our plants are subsp. *alpina.*
    2. *H. odoráta* (L.) Beauv. (fragrant). Sweet Grass. Fresh marshes, borders of salt marshes, open wooded swamps and swamp borders, bog margins, lowland and alpine meadows, shrubby clearings and fresh or brackish shores. June-August. Map 293. (Eurasia). [*H. nashii*]. Our plants are subsp. *odorata.* —FACW

51. *Phaláris* L. Canary Grass (ancient name).

Tufted annuals or perennials; leaves numerous, with flat blades and large, membranous ligules; inflorescence a dense narrow or spike-like panicle of crowded spikelets; spikelets disarticulating above the glumes, laterally flattened, with 1 perfect flower and 2 (rarely 1) small, sterile lemmas attached at its base; glumes subequal, compressed and keeled, acute, exceeding the florets; fertile lemma awnless, indurated and often shining, appressed pilose to sericeous, sterile lemmas reduced to minute entire or plumose scales at the base of the fertile lemma; palea similar to the lemma and the same length; stamens 3. —Wildl. 1

Perennial; panicle lobed or branched, 5 cm long or longer; keel of glume wingless.
    (Fig. 131) .... 1. *P. arundinacea*
Annual; panicle not lobed or branched, less than 5 cm long; keel of glume winged.
    (Fig. 132) .... 2. *P. canariensis*

    1. *P. arundinácea* L. (reed-like). Reed Canary Grass. Wet meadows, marshes, stream and pond margins. June-August. Fig. 131, Map 294. (Eurasia). —FACW+
    2. *P. canariénsis* L. (of the Canary Islands). Canary Grass. Waste places and roadsides. June-October. Fig. 132, Map 295. (Adventive from Europe). —FACU
    P. mínor Retz. Glumes about 5 mm long, fertile lemma 3 mm and sterile lemma 1 (glumes 7 mm, fertile lemma 5 mm and sterile lemmas 2 in *P. canariensis*).

52. *Arthráxon* Beauv. (from the Greek, referring to the disarticulating racemes).

Low, slender, decumbent or creeping annual, branching and rooting at the lower nodes; leaves with hispid sheaths (ours) broad, lance-ovate, cordate-clasping acuminate blades, and membranous, ciliate ligules; spikelets in spike-like racemes, digitate and terminating the branches of a dichotomously forking, somewhat fan-shaped panicle, the axillary panicles often reduced; spikelets disarticulating below the glumes, 1 flowered, the perfect spikelet sessile, with or without an accompanying pedicel of a rudimentary sterile spikelet (the spikelet itself rare); perfect spikelets with glumes equal or subequal, acute to aristate, cartilaginous-indurated, distinctly nerved, hispidulous; lemma shorter than the glumes, membranous or firm, bearing a slender geniculate awn from the back near the base or (ours) awn minute, slightly exserted, or absent; palea absent.

    1. *A. híspidus* (Thunb.) Makino. Damp soil in pastures, ditches, alluvial woods, roadsides and waste places. September-October. Fig. 133. Reported for Franklin County MA, Bronx County, NY. (Adventive from E. Asia).

53. Miscánthus Anderss. (from the Greek, referring to the pedicelled flowers).

Tall, robust perennial; leaves with long, flat blades and membranous, long-ciliate ligules; inflorescence a terminal, fan-shaped panicle of numerous spreading long, slender, spiciform racemes; spikelets in pairs along the rachis, both perfect, one of each pair short-pedicelled, the other long-pedicelled, disarticulating below the glumes, callus bearded, the hairs equalling or exceeding spikelet; glumes about equal, somewhat coriaceous, narrow, acuminate, sparsely long-hairy, exceeding the floret; sterile and fertile lemmas membranous, the fertile shorter than the sterile, bidentate, awnless, or bearing a bent and twisted awn from between the teeth; palea membranous, slightly shorter than lemma; stamens 3.

Eulália Kunth. *vimínea* (Trin.) Kunth. Similar to *Miscanthus* but distinguishable in being a weak annual with leaf blades less than 10 cm long and spikelets subtended by hairs less than 1 mm long (*Miscanthus* is a tall perennial with leaf blades longer than 10 cm and spikelets subtended by a ring of hairs longer than 1 mm.) Asian. Reported for CT and Dutchess County NY. [*Microstegium viminium*]. —FAC

Eriánthus Michx. *gigantéus* (Walt.) Muhl. Similar to *Miscanthus* but differing from it and *Eulalia* in having the racemes occuring along an elongate panicle axis (panicle axis shorter than the racemes in the latter 2 genera). From farther south. Reported for Suffolk County NY. [*E. compactus; E. saccharoides*]. —FACW+

Fertile lemma with a bent and twisted awn; callus hairs not over 1.5 times
      spikelet length .... 1. *M. sinensis*
Fertile lemma awnless; callus hairs 2 or more times length of spikelet. .... 2. *M. sacchariflorus*

1. M. sinénsis Anderss. (Chinese). Eulalia. Cultivated and escaped to fields, roadsides and waste places. September-November. Fig. 134, Map 296. (Naturalized from E. Asia). —FACU

2. M. sacchariflórus (Maxim.) Franch. Cultivated and escaped to roadsides and waste places. August-November. Map 297. (Naturalized from E. Asia).

54. Andropógon L. Beardgrass (from the Greek, referring to the bearded rachis and pedicels).

Coarse, tufted perennials from hardened bases or short rhizomes with solid stems; leaves with long, narrow blades and membranous ligules which are ciliate or erose; spikelets disarticulating below the glumes, in racemes, these paired, digitate or in panicles, lateral and terminal on peduncles which are exserted from or enclosed within spathe-like leaves, the rachis and usually the pedicels villous with long, silky hairs; spikelets in pairs at each joint of the articulate rachis, one sessile and perfect, the other (sometimes 2) pedicelled and staminate, neuter or sometimes simply reduced to the pedicel; glumes of the fertile spikelet subequal, coriaceous, acute, narrow; lemmas shorter than the glumes, hyaline, narrow, 1 lemma in the fertile spikelet empty, sterile, the other lemma fertile, bearing a bent and twisted awn from the apex; palea hyaline, minute or absent; callus bearded; stamens 3. —Wildl. 1

Lycúrus Kunth *phleoídes* Kunth. Similar to *Andropogon*. Lower spikelet sterile, the upper fertile, first glume 2-3 awned, second glume 1-awned. (see also *Polypogon*, Genus 65). Western. Reported for York County ME.

a. Trichomes of rachis and pedicel longer than body of spikelet; pedicelled spikelet
      similar to fertile (dissimilar or abortive in *A. glomeratus*); lower leaf sheaths
      keeled.
    Inflorescence long and slender, simple or slightly branched. .... 1. *A. virginicus*
    Inflorescence strongly compact, corymbiform, densely much-branched. .... 2. *A. glomeratus*
a. Trichomes of rachis and pedicel shorter than body of spikelet; pedicelled spikelet
      abortive, unlike fertile; lower leaf sheaths rounded. .... 3. *A. gerardi*

130. *Hierochloe alpina*. Panicle of spikelets with exserted awns.

× 2/3

131. *Phalaris arundinacea*. Lobed panicle.

× 1/4

× 1/3

134. *Miscanthus sinensis*. General character of panicle.

× 2/5

132. *Phalaris canariensis*. Unlobed panicle.

× 1/2

133. *Arthraxon hispidus*. General habit showing leaves, forked panicle.

292. *Hierochloe alpina*   293. *Hierochloe odorata*   294. *Phalaris arundinacea*

295. *Phalaris canariensis*   296. *Miscanthus sinensis*   297. *Miscanthus sacchariflorus*

1. A. vírginicus L. Broom Sedge. Abandoned fields, waste places, open sandy soil, dry open woods. September-October. Fig. 135, Map 298. Our plants are var. *virginicus.* —FACU

2. A. glomerátus (Walt.) B.S.P. Low, damp soils, often on the margins of bogs. September-October. Reported for MA, RI. [*A. virginicus* var. *abbreviatus*]. Our plants are var. *glomeratus.* —FACW+

3. A. gerárdi Vitman (for L. Gerard). Big Bluestem. Dry open soil, abandoned fields, low moist, meadows and open woodlands. August-September. Map 299. [*A. furcatus; A. provincialis*]. —FAC

55. *Schizáchyrium* Nees.

Similar to *Andropogon* but with raceme solitary at the summit of each peduncle. [*Andropogon*].

1. S. scopárium (Michx.) Nash. Little Bluestem. Abandoned fields, dry sandy soil, waste areas, roadsides and open woodlands. September-October. Fig. 136, Map 300. [*Andropogon scoparius*]. Our plants include subsp. *scoparium* and the following subsp.

subsp. *littorále* (Nash) Gandhi & Smeins. Leaf sheaths prominently keeled; hairs on rachis 4-5 mm long (leaf sheaths not prominently keeled, hairs on rachis 4 mm or less long in subsp. *scoparium*). [*S. littoralis; Andropogon littoralis; A. scoparius* var. *littoralis*]. —FACU

56. Sórghum Moench (old oriental name).

Tall, coarse annuals or perennials; leaves with long, broad flat blades and membranous, usually ciliate ligule; inflorescence a large, terminal, branched panicle of short, 1-several jointed, peduncled racemes, each containing 1-several spikelets; spikelets similar to *Sorghastrum*, in pairs, one sessile and fertile, ovoid, the other pedicillate, well developed, usually staminate, the terminal sessile spikelet with 2 pedicillate spikelets; glumes of the sessile spikelet indurated, those of the narrower pedicillate spikelet membranous; fertile and sterile lemmas thin and membranous, shorter than the glumes, the fertile usually awned; palea absent; stamens 3. Cultivated for the grain; roots and stems also made into mash for poultry; grown also for use in making brooms; fresh foliage may cause poisoning in livestock.

Plant perennial, with rhizomes; grain ellipsoid. .... 1. *S. halepense*
Plant annual, without rhizomes; grain nearly globose. .... 2. *S. bicolor*

1. S. halepénse (L.) Pers. (of Aleppo). Johnson Grass. Fields and waste places. July-September. Fig. 137, Map 301. (Naturalized from Eurasia). [*Holcus h.; S. miliaceum*]. —FACU

2. S. bicolor (L.) Moench (common) Sorghum. Casual weed of waste places. Map 302. (Introduced from Eurasia). [*S. vulgare*]. Our plants include subsp. *bicolor* and the following subsp:

subsp. *drúmmondii* (Nees ex Steud.) deWet & Harlan. Leaf blades up to 5 cm wide; panicle elongate and narrow (blades 2 cm or less wide, panicle long and open in subsp. *bicolor*). [*S. vulgare* var. *d.*].

57. Sorghástrum Nash Indian Grass (named for its similarity in appearance to *Sorghum*).

Tall, coarse, erect perennials from rhizomes or hardened bases; leaves with long, narrow, flat blades tapered to the base, auricled sheaths, and membranous ligule; inflorescence a narrow, terminal panicle of short peduncled racemes, each 1 to several-jointed and containing 1 to 6 spikelets; spikelets in pairs at each joint of the raceme, one sessile, perfect, subterete, long and somewhat fusiform, disarticulating below the glumes, the other sterile, represented only by a hairy pedicel; glumes about equal, indurated and shining, brown or yellowish, the first hirsute, the second glabrous; fertile and sterile lemmas thin and membranous, shorter than the glumes, the fertile terminating in a well developed, bent and twisted awn; palea absent; stamens 3.

1. S. nútans (L.) Nash (nodding). Moist or dry mixed or deciduous open woods, fields, roadsides and waste places. August-September. Fig. 138, Map 303. [*S. avenaceum*]. —Wildl. 1

58. Setária Beauv. Foxtail Grass (Name based on the bristles subtending the spikelets).

Annual or perennial; leaves with flat, linear or lanceolate blades and membranous, ciliate ligule; inflorescence a narrow, cylindric, dense, spike-like (ours) terminal panicle; spikelets with 1 perfect flower, dorsiventrally compressed, subtended by an involucre of 1-many slender bristles, disarticulating above the bristles; glumes unequal, the first usually less than half as long as the spikelet, second glume as long or nearly as long as the spikelet, equal or subequal to the sterile lemma, which often encloses a membranous palea, and rarely a staminate flower; fertile lemma indurated, smooth or transversely rugose, the margins inrolled; palea indurated, as long as the lemma; stamens 3. Seeds are edible. —Wildl. 4

a. Bristles subtending spikelets retrorsely barbed, causing panicles to cling together ...... 1. *S. verticillata*
a. Bristles subtending spikelets antrorsely barbed, the panicles not clinging together.
    b. Upper leaf surfaces strigose or pubescent; panicle conspicuously nodding. .... 2. *S. faberi*
    b. Upper leaf surfaces glabrous or sparsely long-pilose; panicle erect or
        slightly nodding.
        c. Fertile lemma coarsely transversely rugose; bristles below each spikelet 5 or
            more; spike usually erect. (Fig. 139). .... 3. *S. parviflora*

x 1/3

136. *Schizachyrium scoparium*. Single raceme on axillary and terminal peduncles.

x 1/2

135. *Andropogon virginicus*. Two or more digitate racemes on axillary and terminal peduncles.

x 1/3

137. *Sorghum halepense*.
General character of panicle.

x 1/3   x 3

138. *Sorghastrum nutans*. Panicle; pair of spikelets, 1 fertile, 1 sterile.

298. *Andropogen virginicus*

299. *Andropogon gerardi*

300. *Schizachyrium scoparium*

301. *Sorghum halepense*

302. *Sorghum bicolor*

303. *Sorghastrum nutans*

    c. Fertile lemma papillose, finely cross-lined, or nearly smooth; bristles fewer
        than 5; spike often nodding. (Fig. 140).
        Panicle lobulate, rounded at tip; grain readily detached from glumes. .... 4. *S. italica*
        Panicle not lobulate, tapered to tip; grain not readily detached from glumes. . 5. *S. viridis*

    1. S. verticilláta (L.) Beauv. (whorled). Bur Bristlegrass. Waste places and roadsides. July-September. Map 304. (Naturalized from Eurasia). Our plants are var. *verticillata.* —FAC

    2. S. fabéri Herrm. (for its discoverer). Fields, roadsides and waste places. August-October. Map 305. (Naturalized from E. Asia).

    3. S. parviflóra (Poir.) Kerguelen. Bristlegrass. Fields and cultivated areas, open deciduous woods and thickets, upper borders of salt marshes, in moist or dry soil, roadsides and waste places. July-October. Fig. 139, Map 306. (Tropical Amer.; temperate S. Amer.). [*S. geniculata*]. —FAC

    4. S. itálica (L.) Beauv. (Italian). Foxtail Millet. Cultivated soil, fields, roadsides and waste places. July-September. Map 307. (Introduced from Eurasia). Our plants include var. *italica* and the following var:

    var. *stramineofrúcta* Bailey. German Millet. Grains yellow (variously colored in var. *italica*). Another var. that has been distinguished is var. *metzeri.*

    5. S. víridis (L.) Beauv. (green). Green Foxtail. Cultivated soil, roadsides and waste places. July-September. Fig. 140, Map 308. (Naturalized from Eurasia). Our plants are var. *viridis.*

59. *Pennisètum* L.C. Rich. ex Pers.

Similar to *Setaria* but with spikelets articulated below the bristles and falling with the spikelets or (in *P. glaucum*) articulated above the bristles; bristles below each spikelet 5 or more, plant annual, and first glume half or more as long as the spikelet. [*Setaria*].

Spikelets articulated below the bristles, these falling with the spikelets. .... 1. *P. alopecuroides.*
Spikelets articulated above the bristles, these remaining on the inflorescence .... 2. *P. glaucum*

    1. *P. alopecuroídes* (L.) Spreng. Rarely escaped from cultivation in our range. Reported for Nassau County NY. [*Setaria a.*].
    2. *P. glaúcum* (L.) R. Br. Yellow Bristlegrass. Fields, cultivated soil, waste places and roadsides. June-September. Map 309. (Naturalized from Eurasia). [*Setaria glauca; S. lutescens; S. pumila*]. —FAC

60. *Pánicum* L. Panic Grass (from the Latin meaning an ear of millet).

Annuals or perennials with simple or branched stems; inflorescence usually an open or contracted panicle, terminal and sometimes also axillary, essentially uniform; spikelets with 1 perfect and 1 sterile flower, lanceolate to ovate, obovate or globose, usually somewhat dorsiventrally compressed; glumes herbaceous, usually very unequal, the first very short (but sometimes nearly as long as the second), the second about equalling the spikelet; sterile lemma similar to and the same length as the second glume and simulating a third glume, enclosing a palea and sometimes a staminate flower; fertile lemma indurated, light colored, shining, usually obtuse, the margins thick and inrolled; palea of the same texture as the lemma; stamens 3. —Wildl. 3

    Amphicárpum Kunth. *púrshii* Kunth. Similar to *Panicum* but distinguishable in having dimorphic spikelets, those of the terminal panicle perfect but not fertile, the fertile spikelets subterranean. From farther south in the pine barrens. Reported for Nantucket County MA. —FACW
    Brachiária (Trin.) Griseb. *texána* (Buckl.) S. T. Blake. Will key to *Panicum* but is distinguishable in having spikelets with the first glume turned toward the rachis of the raceme, the back of the fertile lemma away from the rachis (first glume turned away from the rachis, back of the fertile lemma toward the rachis in *Panicum*). Southwestern. Reported for MA.

a. Spikelets warty .... 1. *P. verrucosum*
a. Spikelets glabrous to scabrous but not warty.
  b. Plant annual, from a cluster of fibrous roots; stems often branched from
    near the base. (Fig. 141).
    c. Leaf sheaths glabrous .... 2. *P. dichotomiflorum*
    c. Leaf sheaths pubescent.
      d. Spikelets more than 4 mm long .... 3. *P. miliaceum*
      d. Spikelets less than 4 mm long.
        e. Terminal panicle half as broad as long or narrower. (Fig. 142). .... 4. *P. flexile*
        e. Terminal panicle more than half as broad as long. (Fig. 143).
          f. Terminal panicle more than half height of plant . ... 5. *P. capillare*
          f. Terminal panicle less than half height of plant.
            Axillary pulvini in panicle pilose .... 6. *P. philadelphicum*
            Axillary pulvini in panicle glabrous.
              Leaf blades wider than 6 mm; spikelets up to 0.7 mm wide. .... 5. *P. gattingeri*
              Leaf blades 6 mm or narrower; spikelets 0.8-1.1 mm wide. .... 6. *P. philadelphicum*
  b. Plant perennial, from a rhizome or knotty crown; stems simple.
    g. Stems strongly compressed, leaf sheaths keeled. .... 7. *P. rigidulum*
    g. Stems rounded or only slightly compressed, leaf sheaths not keeled.
      Spikelets subsecund along the branchlets. .... 8. *P. anceps*
      Spikelets not at all secund.
        Panicle open, diffuse and spreading. (Fig. 144). .... 9. *P. virgatum*
        Panicle contracted, with appressed branches. (Fig. 145). .... 10. *P. amarum*

1. *P. verrucósum* Muhl. (warty). Warty Panic Grass. Wet sandy and peaty soil, pond margins, mostly along the coast. August-September. Map 310. —FACW

2. *P. dichotomiflórum* Michx. (with forking inflorescence). Spreading Witch Grass. Waste places, moist soil of pond margins. July-September. Fig. 141, Map 311. Our plants include var. *dichotomiflorum* and the following var.:

var. *puritanórum* Sven. Stems slender and weak; spikelets 2.2 mm or less long, obtuse (stems firm and rather stout; spikelets longer than 2.2 mm and tapered at the tip in var. *dichotomiflorum*). [*P. dichotomiflorum* var. *geniculatum*]. —FACW-

3. *P. miliáceum* L. (millet). Broomcorn Millet. Roadsides and waste places. July-September. Map 312.

4. *P. fléxile* (Gattinger) Scribn. (pliant). Wiry Witch Grass. Moist or dry, often calcareous soils of meadows and open woods, often associated with cedar, and along sandy pond margins. August-October. Fig. 142. Reported for Suffolk County MA, Grand Isle County VT. Endangered in VT. —FACU

5. *P. capilláre* L. (hair-like). Old Witch Grass. Waste places, roadsides, cultivated ground and occasionally along pond margins. July-September. Map 313. (Bermuda). [*P. barbipulvinatum*]. —FAC-

P. gattíngeri Nash. Resembling *P. capillare* with terminal panicle less than half the height of the plant (terminal panicle more than half the height of the plant in *P. capillare*). [*P. capillare* var. *campestre*]. —FAC

6. *P. philadélphicum* Bernh. ex Trin. (of Philadelphia). Wood Witch Grass. Roadsides, woodland borders and open woodlands, usually in dry soil. August-September. Fig. 143, Map 314. Endangered in NH. [*P. tuckermani*]. —FAC-

7. *P. rigídulum* Bosc. ex Nees. Long-leaved Panic Grass. Moist peaty or sandy open soil, pond margins. August-September. Map 315. —FACW+ to OBL. We have the following vars.:

Ligule erose or lacerate.
  Spikelets 1.7-2.4 mm; grain subsessile.
    Lower and middle panicle branches divergent [*P. agrostoides* var. *agrostoides*]. .... var. *rigidulum*
    Panicle branches all ascending to appressed [*P. agrostoides* var. *condensum*;
      P. condensum]. .... var. *condensum*
          (Nash) Molenbrock
  Spikelets 2.4 mm or longer; grain distinctly stipitate [*P. agrostoides* var. *elongatum*;
    P. stipitatum] .... var. *elongatum*
          (Pursh) Lelong
Ligule long-ciliate.
  Leaf sheaths usually densely villous, blades villous to the tip [*P. longifolium*
    var. *pubescens*]. .... var. *pubescens*
          (Vasey) Lelong
  Leaf sheaths glabrous or nearly so, blades glabrous or villous only near the base
    P. longifolium var. *combsii*; *P. combsii*]. .... var. *combsii* (Scribn.
          & Ball) Lelong

8. *P. ánceps* Michx. (two-edged). From farther south and west. Reported for Suffolk County NY. [*P. rhizomatum*]. —FAC

9. *P. virgátum* L. (wand-like). Switchgrass. Edges of salt marshes, beaches, river shores, meadows, open woods, and waste places in moist or dry soil. August-September. Fig. 144, Map 316. (Bermuda; S. Amer.). Our plants include var. *virgatum* and the following var.:

var. *spíssum* Linder. Stems cespitose from short, stout knotty rhizomes (stems solitary or in loose tussocks, from long, creeping rhizomes in var. *virgatum*). —FAC

10. *P. amárum* Ell. (bitter). Smaller Sea-beach Grass. Sandy beaches and dunes along the coast. August-October. Fig. 145, Map 317. [*P. amaroides; P. amarulum*]. —FACU-

61. *Dichanthélium* (A.S. Hitchc. & Chase) Gould.

Similar to *Panicum* but blades of the basal and stem leaves usually different in shape, the former crowded and forming a rosette or cushion; stems simple early in the season, bearing a terminal primary panicle, later in the season usually branching and bearing axillary fascicles of smaller leaves or smaller secondary panicles of fertile cleistogamous flowers. [*Panicum*]. —Wildl. 2

a. Leaf blades elongate, 20 times as long as wide, 5 mm or less wide. (Fig. 146).
    Spikelets 2.7 mm or less long, obtuse or rounded at tip. .... 1. *D.linearifolium*
    Spikelets longer than 2.7 mm, acute to beaked .... 2. *D. depauperatum*
a. Leaf blades not elongate, or if so, more than 5 mm wide.
  b. Ligule a conspicuous brush of hairs 2 mm long or longer.
    c. Spikelets 1 mm or less long .... 3. *D. wrightianum*
    c. Spikelets longer than 1 mm.
      d. Stem and sheaths (at least the upper) glabrous or sparsely pilose.
        Panicle not more than half as broad as long; most of the lateral spikelets
          of the panicle branches equalling or exceeding their pedicels. .... 4. *D. spretum*
        Panicle two-thirds to fully as broad as long; most of the lateral spikelets
          of the panicle branches shorter than their pedicels.
          Spikelets 1.4 mm or more long .... 5. *D. acuminatum*
                         var. *lindheimeri*
          Spikelets 1.3 mm or less long .... 6. *D. longiligulatum*
      d. Stem and sheaths strongly pubescent.
        e. Stems and sheaths pubescent but not papillose. (Fig. 147).
          Axis of panicle glabrous to minutely puberulent .... 7. *D. meridionale*
          Axis of panicle pilose
            First glume one third to half as long as the spikelet. .... 5. *D. acuminatum*
                         var. *acuminatum*
            First glume one third or less as long as the spikelet. .... 8. *D. scabriusculum*
        e. Stems and sheaths papillose-pubescent, or at least partly so.
          First glume truncate to obtuse or rounded, or if acute spikelets less than
             2 mm long.
            Axis of panicle pilose .... 5. *D. acuminatum*
                         var. *fasciculatum*
            Axis of panicle glabrate or sparsely pilose in the axils. .... 8. *D. scabriusculum*
            First glume acute, spikelets 2 mm or more long. .... 9. *D. villosissimum*
  b. Ligule absent, inconspicuous, or a brush of hairs less than 2 mm long.
    f. Stems leaves cordate-auriculate and clasping at base. (Fig. 149).
      g. Spikelets globose or subglobose, up to 1.8 mm long. .... 10. *D. sphaerocarpon*
      g. Spikelets ellipsoid, ovoid or obovoid, longer than 2 mm.
        h. Nodes distinctly retrorse-bearded; spikelets 3.8 mm or longer. .... 11. *D. boscii*
        h. Nodes not distinctly bearded; spikelets 3.7 mm or less long.
          i. Leaf sheaths papillose-pubescent .... 12. *D. clandestinum*
          i. Leaf sheaths not papillose-pubescent.
            Primary veins of the leaf blades raised and clearly differentiated
               from the secondary ones; spikelets 3 mm or longer. .... 13. *D. latifolium*
            Primary veins of leaf blades (excluding midvein) not clearly
               differentiated from the secondary ones; spikelets less
               than 3 mm long. .... 14. *D. commutatum*
    f. Stem leaves narrowed, rounded or subcordate at base.
      j. Upper leaf surface pubescent.
        Stem with a viscid ring below the nodes; leaf sheaths glabrous and viscid
          along middle toward summit; spikelets abruptly
          pointed. (Fig. 150). .... 15. *D. scoparium*
        Stem and sheaths not as above; spikelets rounded or obtuse.
          Leaf blades up to 6 mm wide .... 7. *D. meridionale*
          Leaf blades 7 mm wide or wider .... 16. *D. dichotomum*
      j. Upper leaf surface glabrous or with scattered hairs.
        k. Spikelets 2.8 mm long or longer.

l. Spikelets less than 1.4 mm broad.
  Stem glabrous to puberulent; ligule none. .... 17. *D. boreale*
  Stem pubescent; ligule a brush of hairs 1 mm long. .... 18. *D. ovale*
                                                                                                       var. *addisonii*

l. Spikelets 1.4 mm broad or broader.
  Spikelets elliptic, half as broad as long, pointed . ... 8. *D. scabriusculum*
  Spikelets obovoid, more than half as broad as long, blunt.
    Panicle ovoid, with spreading-ascending branches .... 19. *D. oligosanthes*
    Panicle narrow, with strict-erect branches .... 20. *D. xanthophysum*
k. Spikelets less than 2.8 mm long.
  m. Leaf blades typically 15 times as long as wide. .... 17. *D. boreale*
  m. Leaf blades typically 10 or 12 times as long as wide.
    n. Stems mostly densely pubescent, the hairs of 2 lengths.
      Stems short-pubescent, most of the hairs (except toward the
        summit of the lower internodes) less than 1 mm .... 21. *D. sabulorum*
      Stems long-pilose, most of the hairs 1 mm or longer. .... 18. *D. ovale*
                                                                                                       var. *addisonii*

    n. Stems glabrous or with scattered hairs (except sometimes at the
        nodes), the hairs of uniform length.
      Sheaths long-pilose, with spreading to retrorse hairs. .... 22. *D. laxiflorum*
      Sheaths glabrous to minutely or sparsely pilose.
        Leaf blades of stem mostly erect or ascending (Fig. 151). .... 17. *D. boreale*
        Leaf blades of stem mostly spreading. .... 16. *D. dichotomum*

1. *D. linearifolium* (Schrib. ex Nash) Gould (linear-leaved). Dry fields, river shores and open woodlands. May-October. Figure 146, Map 318. [*Panicum werneri*].

2. *D. depauperátum* (Muhl.) Gould (impoverished). Dry, sandy soil in open woods, roadsides, waste areas and occasionally sand dunes. May-October. Map 319. [*Panicum d.*].

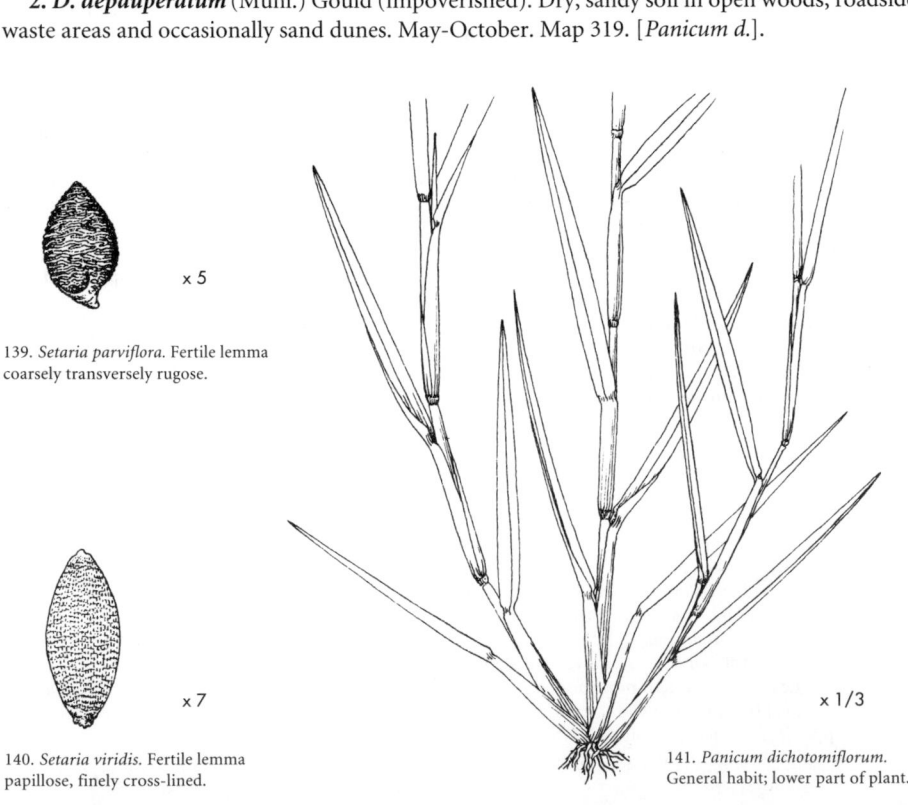

x 5

139. *Setaria parviflora*. Fertile lemma coarsely transversely rugose.

x 7

140. *Setaria viridis*. Fertile lemma papillose, finely cross-lined.

x 1/3

141. *Panicum dichotomiflorum*. General habit; lower part of plant.

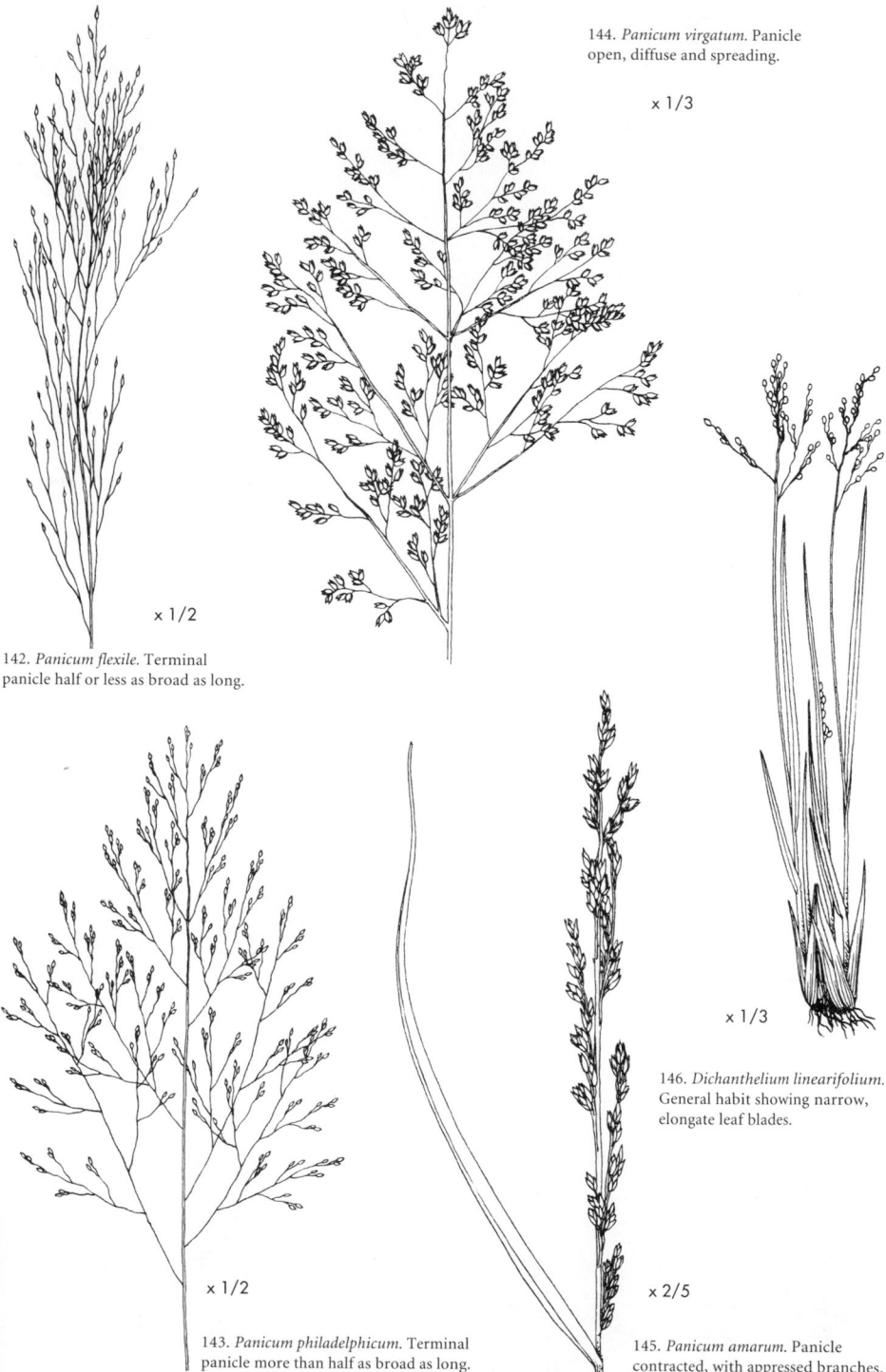

144. *Panicum virgatum.* Panicle open, diffuse and spreading.

x 1/3

x 1/2

142. *Panicum flexile.* Terminal panicle half or less as broad as long.

x 1/3

146. *Dichanthelium linearifolium.* General habit showing narrow, elongate leaf blades.

x 1/2

143. *Panicum philadelphicum.* Terminal panicle more than half as broad as long.

x 2/5

145. *Panicum amarum.* Panicle contracted, with appressed branches.

304. *Setaria verticillata*

305. *Setaria faberi*

306. *Setaria parviflora*

307. *Setaria italica*

308. *Setaria viridis*

309. *Pennisetum glaucum*

310. *Panicum verrucosum*

311. *Panicum dichotomiflorum*

312. *Panicum miliaceum*

313. *Panicum capillare*   314. *Panicum philadelphicum*   315. *Panicum rigidulum*

316. *Panicum virgatum*   317. *Panicum amarum*   318. *Dichanthelium linearifolium*

3. D. wrightiánum (Scribn.) Freckmann (for its discoverer). Sandy or peaty pond and stream margins along the coastal plain. June-October. Reported for Barnstable and Plymouth Counties MA. (W.I.). [*D. acuminatum* var. *w.*].

4. D. sprétum (J. A. Schultes) Freckmann (spurned; originally described without a name). Sandy and peaty soils of pond and river margins. June-October. Map 320. [*Panicum eatonii; D. acuminatum* var. *densiflorum*].

5. D. acuminátum (Sw.) Gould & C. A. Clark. Dry to moist fields, open woods. Map 321. Our plants include var. *acuminatum* [*D. lanuginosum; Panicum auburne; P. lanuginosum* var. *l.; P. chrysopsidifolium*] and the following vars.:

var. *lindheimeri* (Nash) Gould & C. A. Clark. Stems and sheaths glabrous or sparsely pilose (strongly pubescent in vars. *acuminatum* and *fasciculatum*). [*Panicum lanuginosum* var. *lindheimeri; P. lindheimeri; P. longiligulatum*].

var. *fasciculátum* (Torr) Freckmann. Sheaths and stems papillose-pubescent or at least partly so (sheaths and stems pubescent but not papillose in var. *acuminatum*). [*D. acuminatum* var.

implicatum; Panicum lanuginosum var. f.; P.l. var. implicatum; P. implicatum; P.l. var. tennesseense; P. tennesseense; P. glutinoscabrum; P. huachucae; P. languidum]. —FAC

6. D. longiligulátum (Nash) Freckmann. Dry to moist fields and open woods. Reported for CT, MA.

7. D. meridionále (Ashe) Freckmann (southern). Dry, especially sandy soil of open deciduous woods and fields; waste places. June-October. Fig. 147, Map 322. [Panicum albemarlense; P. columbianum var. oricola and var. thinium; P. leucothrix; P. oricola].

8. D. scabríusculum (Ell.) Gould & C. A. Clark. Woolly Panic Grass. Roadsides, waste places, river and pond margins, old fields and open woodlands in moist or dry soil. July-October. Fig. 148, Map 323. [Panicum aculeatum; P. cryptanthum; P. lanuginosum var. septentrionale]. —OBL

9. D. villosíssimum (Nash) Freckmann (very long-hairy). Dry open mixed woodlands, thickets and sandy openings. June-October. Map 324. (Centr. Amer.). [D. acuminatum var. villosum; Panicum benneri; P. ovale; P. praecocius; P. pseudopubescens; P. scoparioides; P. subvillosum]. Our plants are var. villosissimum. —FACU

10. D. sphaerocárpon (Ell.) Gould (spherical-fruited). Dry, sandy soil of waste areas, roadsides, pastures and fields, open deciduous woods and openings, thickets. May-October. Fig. 149, Map 325. Endangered in NH. Our plants include var. sphaerocarpon and the following var.:

var. isóphyllum (Schrib.) Gould & C. A. Clark. Nodes glabrous or puberulent; panicle two or more times as long as wide (nodes pubescent, panicle nearly as wide as long in var. sphaerocarpon). [P. microcarpon var. isophyllum; P. polyanthes; P. sphaerocarpon var. isophyllum]. —FACU

11. D. bóscii (Poir.) Gould & C. A. Clark (for its discoverer). Woodlands, woodland edges, and occasionally roadsides. May-October. Map 326.

12. D. clandestínum (L.) Gould (hidden). Deer Tongue Grass. Moist, mostly sandy thickets, open woods and woodland borders, and waste places. May-October. Map 327. —FAC+

13. D. latifólium L. (broad-leaved). Dry, rich, often rocky woods, woodland borders, openings and thickets. May-October. Map 328. —FACU-

14. D. commutátum Shultes (changeable). Dry, deciduous or mixed woods, thickets, and openings; sandy or rocky open areas. May-October. Map 329 (Mexico; W.I.). [Panicum ashei; P. joorii; P. mutabile; P. recognitum]. —FACU+

15. D. scopárium Lam. (broom-like). Meadows, thickets and ditches in moist soil and sometimes in open sandy areas. June-October. Fig. 150, Map 330. (W.I.). —FACW

16. D. dichòtomum (L.) Gould. Dry, sandy or rocky open deciduous woods and borders of thickets on the coastal plain. June-October. Reported for Barnstable County MA, Queens County NY. Map 331. [Panicum annulum; P. barbulatum; P. clutei; P. lucidum; P. mattamuskeetense; P. microcarpon; P. nitidum; P. roanokense]. —FAC

17. D. boreále (Nash) Freckmann. Dry deciduous woodlands, thickets and openings; roadsides and waste places. May-September. Fig. 151, Map 332. [Panicum bicknellii; P. boreale; P. bushii; P. calliphyllum]. —FACU

18. D. ovále (Ell.) Gould & C. A. Clark. Dry, sandy soil on the coastal plain, often in pine woods. May-October. Map 333. [Panicum addisonii; P. commonsianum; P. mundum]. Represented with us as var. addisónii (Nash) Gould & C. A. Clark. [Panicum commonsianum var. a.]. —FACU

19. D. oligosánthes (J. A. Schultes) Gould (few-flowered). Dry, often sandy soil of deciduous woods, fields, dunes, waste areas and roadsides. May-October. Map 334. [Panicum helleri; P. macrocarpon]. Our plants include var. oligosanthes and the following var.:

var. scribneriánum (Nash) Gould. Culms glabrous to obscurely puberulent; leaves glabrous (culms distinctly puberulent and leaves pubescent beneath in var. oligosanthes). [Panicum scribnerianum]. —FACU

20. D. xanthophýsum (Gray) Freckmann (with yellow bladders, referring to the plump fruits). Sandy roadsides, disturbed soil. June-September. Map 335.

147. *Dichanthelium meridionale.* Section of stem showing pubescent stem and sheath.

x 1

x 1/3

148. *Dichanthelium scabriusculum.* General habit showing basal leaves different from stem leaves.

x 1/3

x 1/3

151. *Dichanthelium boreale.* Leaf blades erect or ascending.

x 3/8

149. *Dichanthelium sphaerocarpon.* Stem leaves cordate-auriculate.

x 3/8

150. *Dichanthelium scoparium.* Stem leaves rounded to subcordate, stem with ring below nodes.

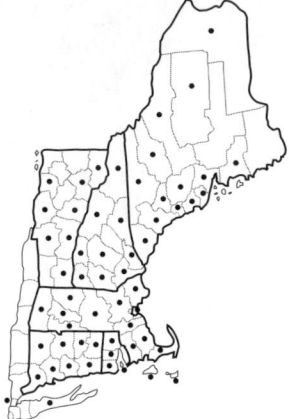

319. *Dichanthelium depauperatum*

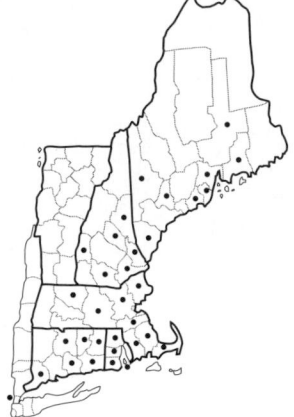

320. *Dichanthelium spretum*

321. *Dichanthelium acuminatum*

322. *Dichanthelium meridionale*

323. *Dichanthelium scabriusculum*

324. *Dichanthelium villosissimum*

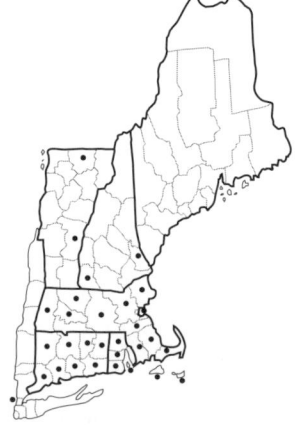

325. *Dichanthelium sphaerocarpon*

326. *Dichanthelium boscii*

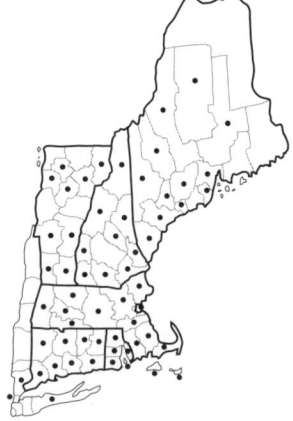

327. *Dichanthelium clandestinum*

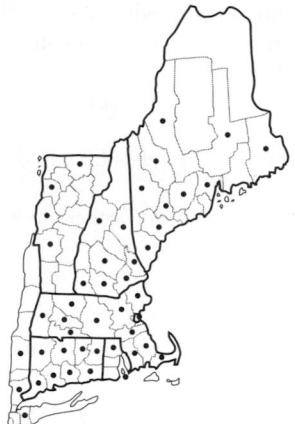

328. *Dichanthelium latifolium*

329. *Dichanthelium commutatum*

330. *Dichanthelium scoparium*

331. *Dichanthelium dichotomum*

332. *Dichanthelium boreale*

333. *Dichanthelium ovale* var. *addisonii*

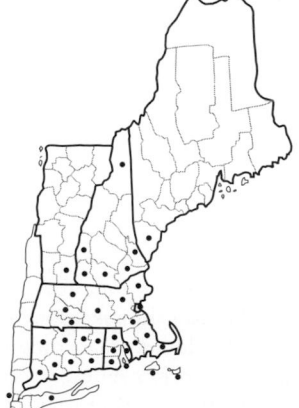

334. *Dichanthelium oligosanthes*

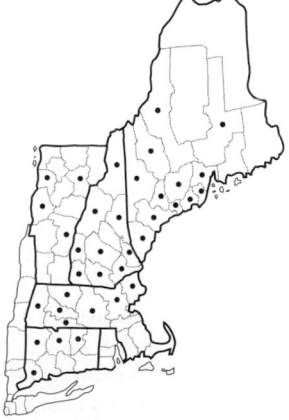

335. *Dichanthelium xanthophysum*

21. *D. sabulórum* (Lam.) Gould & C. A. Clark. Dry, sandy fields, open deciduous woods, woodland borders and roadsides. May-October. Map 336. [*P. tsugetorum; P. oricola*]. Represented with us by the following vars.:

var. *pátulum* (Scribn. & Merrill) Gould & C. A. Clark. Leaf blades ciliate, at least at the base, spikelets mostly longer than 1.9 mm. [*Panicum lancearium*].

var. *thínum* (A. Hitchc. & Chase) Gould & C. A. Clark. Leaf blades eciliate, spikelets 1.9 mm or less long. [*Panicum columbianum*]. —FACU

22. *D. laxiflórum* (L.) Gould. Open woods, clearings. July-September. (W.I.). From farther south and west. Reported for R.I. [*Panicum xalapense*]. —FACU

62. *Leptolóma* Chase (from the Greek referring to the hyaline margins of the lemma).

Perennial, often forming large bunches; stems branched and decumbent at base; leaves with lower sheaths densely pubescent, flat blades and membranous ligules; inflorescence a diffuse, open, purplish panicle with elongate branches, the panicle breaking away when mature and becoming a tumble-weed; spikelets dorsiventrally flattened, 1-flowered, disarticulating below the glumes, solitary on long, slender pedicels; first glume minute or obsolete, second glume nearly as long and of the same texture as the sterile lemma, fertile lemma indurated-cartilaginous, brownish, the margins not inrolled; palea as long as and the same color as the lemma. [*Digitaria*].

1. *L. cognátum* (Schult.) Chase (related). Fall Witchgrass. Sandy fields, roadsides and waste places. July-September. Fig. 152, Map 337. [*Digitaria c.*].

63. *Ammóphila* Host. Beachgrass (from the Greek meaning sand-loving).

Coarse, erect perennials from long, creeping rhizomes; leaves with long, involute blades and cartilaginous or chartaceous ligules; inflorescence a long, dense, cylindric, yellowish, spike-like panicle; spikelets 1-flowered, strongly flattened, disarticulating above the glumes; glumes chartaceous, subequal, lance-linear, acute, keeled, the first 1-nerved, the second 3-nerved; lemmas similar, shorter, with a ring of short callus hairs at the base, obscurely 3-5 nerved; palea nearly as long as the lemma; flowers perfect, stamens 3. —FACU-; Wildl. 1

Ligule firm and cartilaginous, rounded, 3 mm or less long.
   Panicle 19 cm or more long, gradually tapering at both ends; glumes attenuate,
      the lower 11 mm or more long, the upper 12 mm or more long. .... 1. *A. breviligulata*
   Panicle 16 cm or less long, abrupt at both ends; glumes merely acute, the lower
      less than 11 mm long, the upper less than 12 mm long. .... 2. *A. champlainensis*
Ligule thin and chartaceous, tapering, 1 cm or more long. .... 3. *A. arenaria*

1. *A. breviguláta* Fern. (with short ligule). American Beachgrass. Dunes and dry sandy areas along the coast and on the shores of the Great Lakes. July-September. Fig. 153, Map 338.

2. *A. champlainénsis* F.C. Seymour. Sandy shore, Lake Champlain VT. Endangered in VT.

3. *A. arenária* (L.) Link (of sand). European Beachgrass. Sand dunes along the coast. (Introducted from Europe).

64. *Phléum* L. Timothy (Greek name for a kind of reed).

Cespitose, erect annuals or perennials; leaves with flat blades and elongate membranous ligules; inflorescence a dense, terminal, ovoid to cylindric, spike-like panicle; spikelets disarticulating above the glumes, with 1 perfect flower, strongly flattened laterally; glumes equal, compressed and keeled, rounded to truncate and short-awned, ciliate on the keels, membranous, exceeding the lemma; lemma broad and truncate, membranous, awnless; palea membranous, nearly as long as the lemma; stamens 3. —Wildl. 1

Upper leaf sheath inflated at the middle; panicle usually less than 5 cm long; awns
    1.6 mm or longer .... 1. *P. alpínum*
Upper leaf sheath not inflated; panicle usually longer than 5 cm; awns less than
    1.6 mm long .... 2. *P. pratense*

1. P. alpínum L. (alpine). Mountain Timothy. Mountain meadows. July-August. Map 339. (Eurasia). —FACW

2. P. praténse L. (of meadows). Timothy. Fields, roadsides and waste places, commonly cultivated for hay and pasturage. July-August. Fig. 154, Map 340. (Naturalized from Europe). Our plants include subsp. *pratense* and the following subsp.:

    subsp. *nodósum* Areang. Leaves up to 5 mm wide; panicle up to 6 mm thick (leaves wider than 5 mm and panicle thicker than 6 mm in var. pratense). —FACU

    Two other species, both European, rarely occur on ballast. *P. arenárium* L. is similar to *P. alpinum*. Reported for Essex County MA, Manhattan NY; *P. subulátum* (Savi) Aschers. & Graebn. Resembling *P. pratense* but differing in having glumes less than 2.5 mm long (glumes longer than 2.5 mm in *P. pratense*). Reported for Essex County MA.

65. Polypógon Desf. Beardgrass (from the Greek referring to the bristly panicle).

Cespitose decumbent annuals or perennials; leaves with flat blades and elongate, membranous ligule; inflorescence a dense, cylindric to ovoid, bristly, spike-like, terminal panicle of small spikelets; spikelets 1-flowered, disarticulating below the glumes; glumes equal, entire or 2-lobed, bearing a slender awn from the tip or between the lobes; lemma much shorter than the glumes, hyaline, broad, usually bearing a short, slender awn from below the tip; palea shorter than or nearly as long as the lemma; flowers perfect, stamens 1-3.

    Lycúrus Kunth. *phleóides* Kunth. Similar to *Polypogon*. Spikelets in pairs, the lower sterile, the upper fertile, first glume 2-3-awned. Western. Reported for York County ME. (See also *Andropogon*, Genus 54).

    1. P. monspeliénsis (L.) Desf. (of Montpellier). Annual Beardgrass. Roadsides, waste places and moist soil of marsh edges and creekbeds, mostly near the coast. June-September. Fig. 155, Map 341. (Naturalized from Europe). —FACW+

    P. interrúptus H.B.K. Perennial with awns 3-5 mm long (*P. monspeliensis* is an annual with awns 6-8 mm long). Western. Reported for Westchester County NY.

66. Míbora Adans. (unexplained).

Tiny, delicate, tufted vernal annual with simple filiform stems; leaves basal and on the lower parts of the stems, with short flat blades, membranous ligule, and inflated, somewhat membranous sheaths; inflorescence a short, slender, terminal spiciform raceme of 6-8 appressed, purple spikelets; spikelets 1-flowered, disarticulating above the glumes; glumes about equal, overtopping the floret, oblong-ovate, rounded at the tip; lemma membranous, awnless, with dense, woolly pubescence; palea similar to lemma, slightly shorter; rachilla prolonged behind palea as a long hairy bristle; flowers imperfect, containing 2-3 stamens and an aborted pistil or a pistil and aborted stamens in separate spikelets in the same raceme.

    1. M. mínima (L.) Desv. (tiny). Nurseries in Massachusetts and New York, occasionally escaping. Fig. 156. (Adventive from Europe).

67. Crýpsis Ait.

Low, cespitose annuals with decumbent or erect, branching stems; leaves with inflated sheaths, rather short, flat blades and a ligule consisting of a ring of hairs; inflorescence a short, dense, spike-like panicle, these numerous and partly included in the leaf sheaths; spikelets small, 1-flowered,

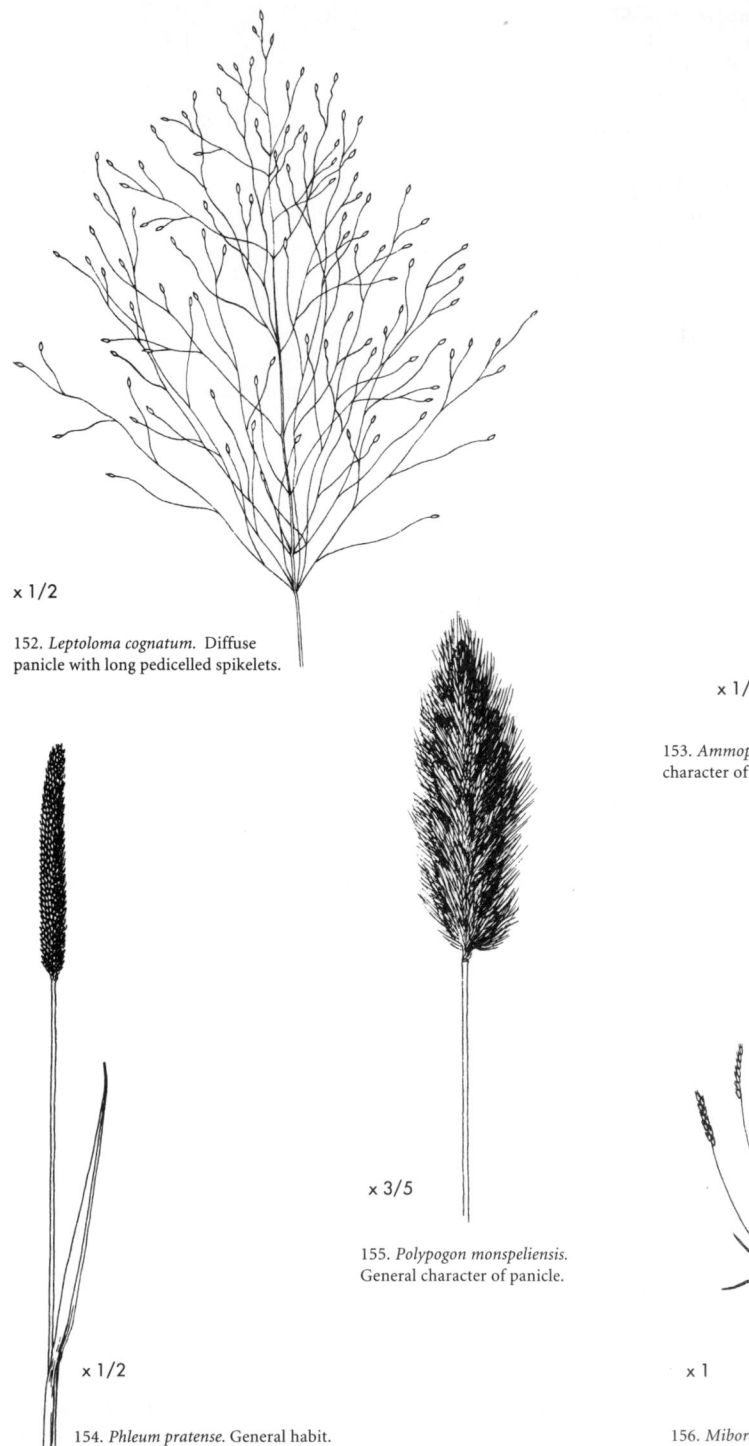

x 1/2

152. *Leptoloma cognatum*. Diffuse
panicle with long pedicelled spikelets.

x 1/4

153. *Ammophila breviligulata*. General
character of panicle.

x 3/5

155. *Polypogon monspeliensis*.
General character of panicle.

x 1/2

154. *Phleum pratense*. General habit.

x 1

156. *Mibora minima*. General habit.

336. *Dichanthelium sabulorum*

337. *Leptoloma cognatum*

338. *Ammophila breviligulata*

339. *Phleum alpinum*

340. *Phleum pratense*

341. *Polypogon monspeliensis*

flattened, disarticulating above the glumes; glumes subequal, shorter than the lemma, narrow, acute, compressed and keeled; lemma broader than glumes, acute, keeled, awnless; palea about as long as the lemma; flowers perfect, stamens 3. [*Heleochloa*].

1. *C. schoenoídes* (L.) Lam. (resembling *Schoenus*). Rush-like Timothy. Waste places. July-August. Fig. 157. Reported for Suffolk County MA, Oak Point NY, Woodbury, VT. (Naturalized from Europe). [*Heleochloa s.*].

68. *Alopecúrus* L. Foxtail (from the Greek meaning fox tail).

Annuals or perennials with erect or decumbent stems; leaves with flat blades, ligule membranous; inflorescence a dense, narrow, cylindric, spike-like panicle; spikelets 1-flowered, strongly flattened, disarticulating below the glumes; glumes equal, acute, 3-nerved, keeled, ciliate on the keel; lemma about as long as the glumes, obtuse, 5-nerved, the margins united at the base, bearing a slender awn on the back below the middle, the awn included or conspicuously exserted; palea (in ours) absent; flowers perfect, stamens 3.

a. Awns of lemmas inconspicuous, included or exserted less than 0.5 mm. .... 1. *A. aequalis*
a. Awns of lemmas conspicuous, exserted from the spikelets 1.5 mm or more. (Fig. 158).
  b. Spikelets, excluding awns, 4.5 mm or more long.
    Panicle 6 mm or less wide, tapered at both ends; glumes merely scabrous on
      the keel above the middle .... 2. *A. myosuroides*
    Panicle 7 mm or more wide, rounded at both ends; glumes long-ciliate on the
      keel above the middle, with hairs 1 mm or more long. .... 3. *A. pratensis*
  b. Spikelets, excluding awns, 3.5 mm or less long.
    Perennial, stems decumbent, sometimes rooting at the lower nodes;
      stem leaves 4 or more .... 4. *A. geniculatus*
    Annual, stems erect or ascending, not rooting; stem leaves 3 or fewer. .... 5. *A. carolinianus*

    1. A. aequális Sobol. (equal, referring to glumes and lemma). Short-awned Foxtail. Shallow water, mud and wet soil, shores, wet meadows. June-August. Map 342. (Eurasia). Our plants are var. *aequalis.* —OBL

    2. A. myosuroídes Huds. (resembling *Myosurus,* Mouse-tail). Slender Foxtail. Fields, waste places, ballast. June-August. Fig. 158, Map 343. (Adventive from Europe). —FACW

    3. A. praténsis L. (of meadows). Meadow Foxtail. Moist meadows, fields and waste places. June-July. Map 344. (Naturalized from Europe). —FACW

    4. A. geniculátus L. (bent like the knee-joint). Marsh Foxtail. Shallow water, mud and wet soil. June-August. Map 345. (Naturalized from Europe). Our plants are var. *geniculatus.* —OBL

    5. A. carolinánus Walt. (of Carolina). Abandoned fields, moist meadows, wet soil, waste places. May-July. Map 346. —FACW

69. Mílium L. Millet Grass. (ancient name for Millet, from resemblence of the grain of *Milium* to that of *Panicum miliaceum*).

Moderately tall, erect perennial (ours), with simple stems; leaves with broad, flat blades and membranous ligule; inflorescence a lax, open, terminal panicle with spreading branches; spikelets 1-flowered, disarticulating above the glumes, dorsiventrally compressed; glumes about equal, slightly longer than the floret, obtuse or acute; lemma indurated, shining, obtuse, awnless, margins inrolled; palea of similar texture, slightly shorter; flowers perfect, stamens 3.

    1. M. effúsum L. (spread out). Rich, moist or dry deciduous woods and openings. June-August. Fig. 159, Map 347. (Eurasia).

70. Oryzópsis Michx. Mountain Rice (from the Greek, referring to resemblence of the grains to those of rice).

Cespitose perennials; leaves with flat or involute blade, and membranous ligules or ligules absent; inflorescence a terminal narrow or open panicle; spikelets 1-flowered, disarticulating above the glumes; glumes about equal, broad, obtuse to acuminate, herbaceous, about equaling the lemma; lemma indurated, its margins involute, oval or oblong, nearly terete, usually pubescent, bearing a straight or twisted, long or short, deciduous awn; palea of the same texture as the lemma and about as long; flowers perfect, stamens 3.

a. Leaves flat, 3 mm or more wide; glumes longer than 5 mm.
    Blades of basal leaves reduced, blade of uppermost stem leaf 10 cm or longer. .... 1. *O. racemosa*
    Blades of basal leaves elongate, blade of uppermost stem leaf not more than
      2 cm long .... 2. *O. asperifolia*
a. Leaves involute and/or 2 mm or less wide; glumes 5 mm or less long.
    Lemmas awnless or awns 2 mm or less long, straight . ... 3. *O. pungens*
    Lemmas with awns longer than 5 mm, twisted and bent. .... 4. *O. canadensis*

    1. O. racemósa (Sm.) Ricker ex A. S. Hitchc. (racemose). Black-fruited Mountain Rice. Dry, rocky or rich deciduous woodlands. July-August. Fig. 160, Map 348.

2. O. asperifólia Michx. (harsh-leaved), White-fruited Mountain Rice. Rich, deciduous woodlands. May-June. Map 349. —Wildl. 1

3. O. púngens (Torr. ex Spreng.) A. S. Hitchc. (sharp-pointed). Slender Mountain Rice. Dry, sandy or rocky soil of mixed woodlands, open areas, and shores. May-June. Map 350.

4. O. canadénsis (Poir.) Torr. (of Canada). Dry, rocky or sandy deciduous woodlands, slopes, open areas and shores. June-July. Map 351. Endangered in NY and NH. [*Stipa c.*].

71. *Arístida* L. Three-awned Grass, Needlegrass (name referring to the awns of the lemmas).

Annual or perennial, mostly slender and tufted; stems frequently geniculate, branching from some or all of the nodes; leaves with narrow, often involute blades, and minute ligule; inflorescence a narrow, dense, spike-like or lax, open raceme or panicle, lateral and/or terminal; spikelets narrow, 1-flowered, disarticulating above the glumes; glumes equal or unequal, narrow, acute, acuminate or short-awned, the first sometimes deciduous; lemmas shorter than at least 1 of the glumes, narrow, indurated, terete, convolute, terminating in 3 similar or dissimilar awns; palea absent or minute; callus pointed, bearded; flowers perfect, stamens 3. Several species cause injury to livestock from grazing.

a. Awns united into a twisted column more than 6 mm long. (Fig. 161). .... 1. *A. tuberculosa*
a. Awns separate or united for less than 5 mm; column, if present, not twisted.
  b. Glumes (including awns) 2 cm or more long; awns 3.5 cm or more long. .... 2. *A. oligantha*
  b. Glumes less than 2 cm long; awns less than 3.5 cm long.
    c. Plant perennial; stems strict .... 3. *A. purpurascens*
    c. Plant annual; stems branched, at least at base.
      d. Central awn (and sometimes also the lateral) spirally twisted at base. (Fig. 162).
        Central awn 7 mm or less long; lateral awns less than half as long
          as the central .... 4. *A. dichotoma*
        Central awn longer than 7 mm; lateral awns half or more as long as
          the central. .... 5. *A. basiramea*
      d. Central awn not spirally twisted at base, merely bent or curved
        outward. (Fig. 163).
        Terminal panicle less than 10 cm long. .... 5. *A. basiramea*
        Terminal panicle 10 cm or longer. .... 6. *A. longespica*

1. A. tuberculósa Nutt. (bearing tubercles, from the enlarged bases of the branches). Sea-beach Needlegrass. Dry sandy soil, especially beaches and dunes. August-September. Fig. 161, Map 352. (Mexico). Endangered in NH.

2. A. oligántha Michx. (few-flowered). Few-flowered Aristida. Dry, sterile, open soil. August-September. Map 353.

3. A. purpuráscens Poir. (purplish). Arrow-grass. Dry, sandy or gravelly soil. September-October. Map 354. (W.I.). Represented with us as var. *purpurascens*.

4. A. dichótoma Michx. (forked). Poverty-grass. Dry, sterile, sandy soil. August-September. Fig. 162, Map 355. Our plants are var. *dichotoma*.

5. A. basirámea Engelm. ex Vasey (branching from base). Forked Needlegrass. Dry, sandy soil. August-September. Map 356.

6. A. longespíca Poir. (with long spike), Slender Needlegrass. Dry sterile, sandy soil. August-September. Fig. 163, Map 357. Represented with us as var. *geniculáta* (Raf.) Fern. Endangered in NH. [*A. gracilis; A. intermedia; A. neocopina*].

A. adscensiónis L. Similar to *A. longespica* but distinguishable in having awns flattened at the base (awns terete throughout in *A. longespica*). Tropical. Rarely found in our range. Reported for Westchester County NY.

157. *Crypsis schoenoides.* General habit.

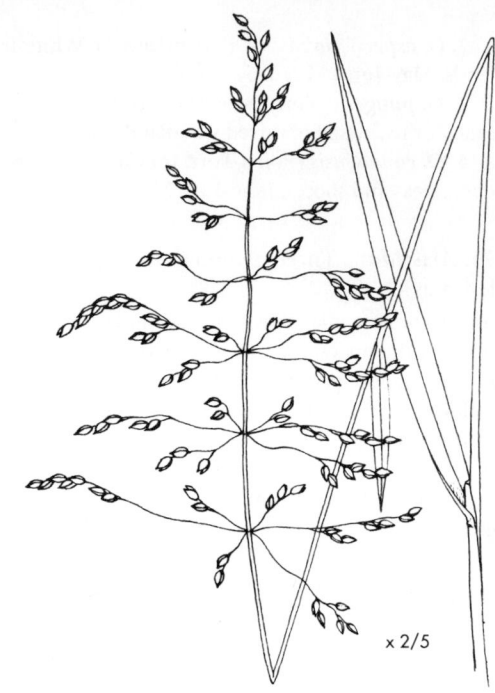

159. *Milium effusum.* Upper part of plant
showing wide leaves, open panicle.

158. *Alopecurus myosuroides.*
Panicle showing spikelets with
exserted, conspicuous awns.

160. *Oryzopsis racemosa.* General character
of upper part of plant, inflorescence.

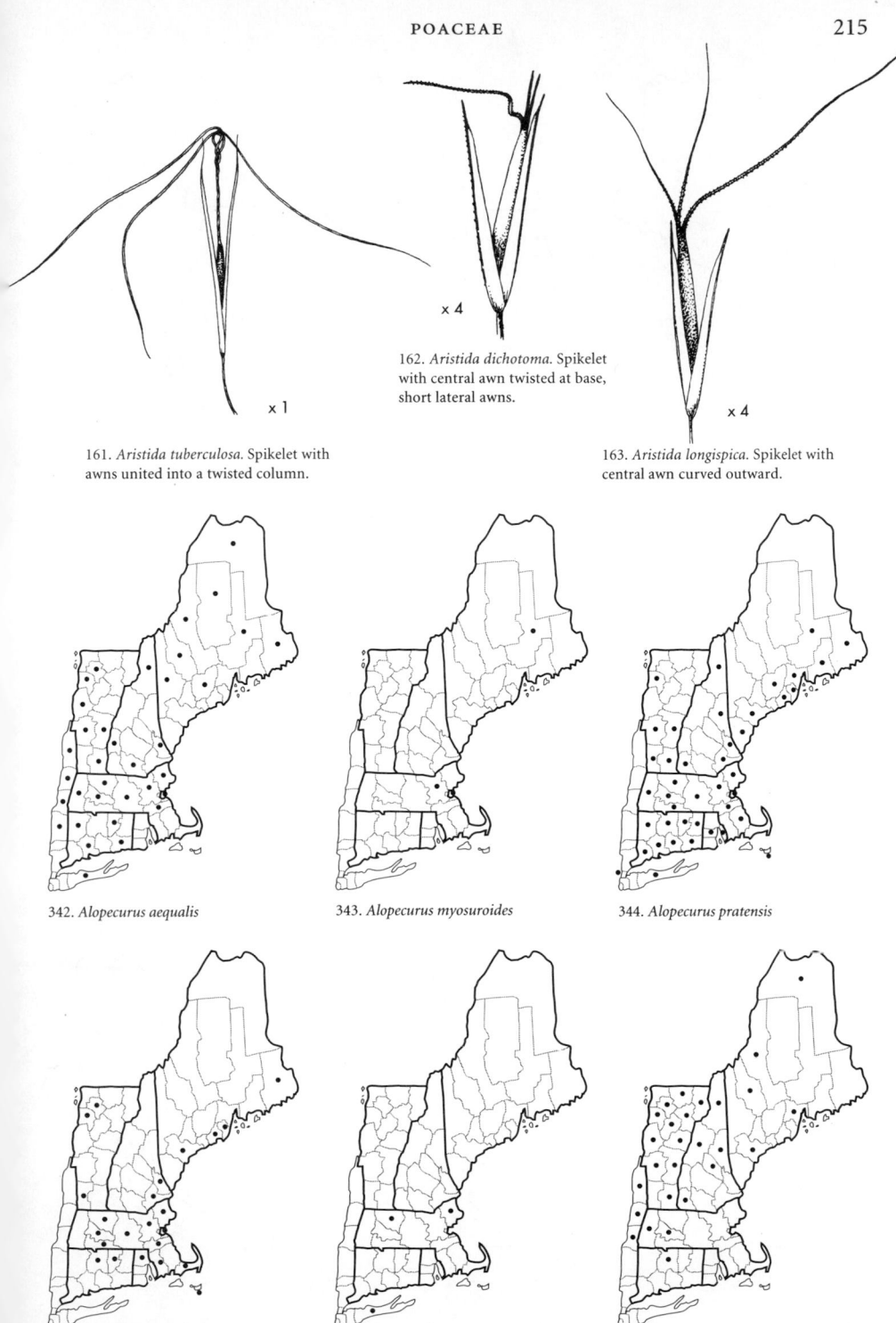

162. *Aristida dichotoma.* Spikelet with central awn twisted at base, short lateral awns.

161. *Aristida tuberculosa.* Spikelet with awns united into a twisted column.

163. *Aristida longispica.* Spikelet with central awn curved outward.

342. *Alopecurus aequalis*

343. *Alopecurus myosuroides*

344. *Alopecurus pratensis*

345. *Alopecurus geniculatus*

346. *Alopecurus carolinianus*

347. *Milium effusum*

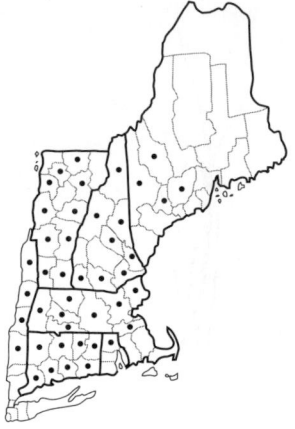

348. *Oryzopsis racemosa*

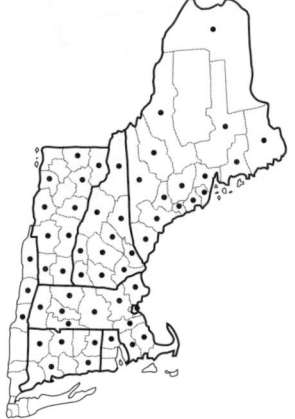

349. *Oryzopsis asperifolia*

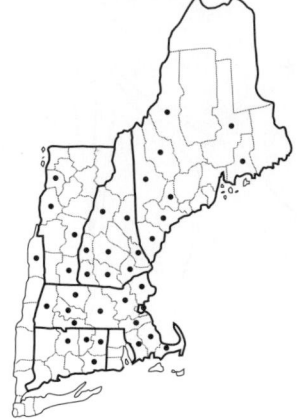

350. *Oryzopsis pungens*

351. *Oryzopsis canadensis*

352. *Aristida turberculosa*

353. *Aristida oligantha*

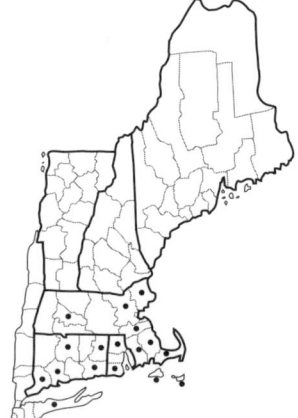

354. *Aristida purpurascens*

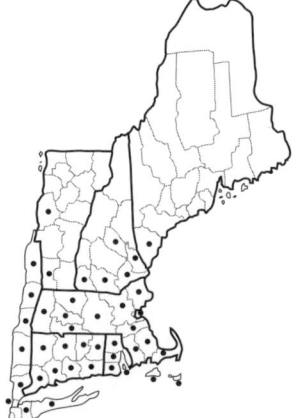

355. *Aristida dichotoma*

356. *Aristida basiramea*

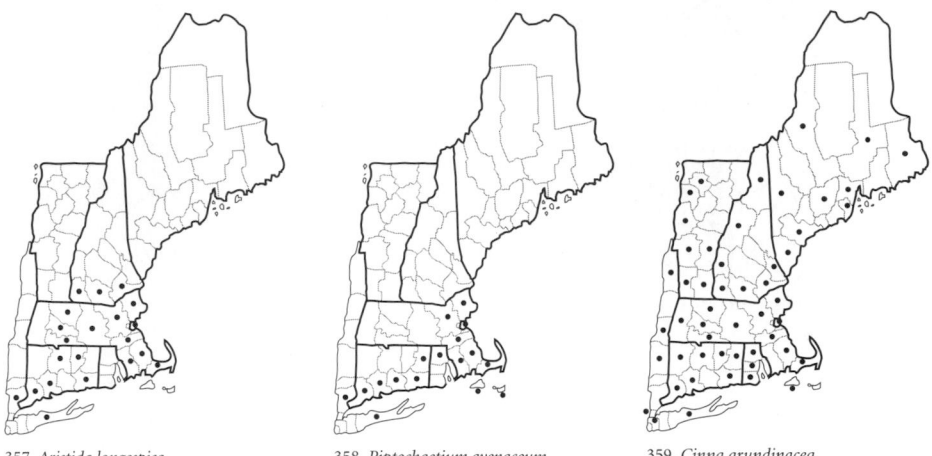

357. *Aristida longespica*   358. *Piptochaetium avenaceum*   359. *Cinna arundinacea*

72. *Piptochaètium* J. Presl. Needlegrass.

Generally tall, tufted perennial; leaves with long, narrow, usually convolute blades and membranous ligules; inflorescence an open or contracted, usually narrow, terminal panicle of rather large spikelets; spikelets narrow, 1-flowered, disarticulating above the glumes; glumes membranous, long and narrow, about equal, acute, acuminate or bristle-tipped; lemma indurated, narrowly fusiform, terete, strongly convolute, brownish, appressed-pubescent, the callus long-bearded, the summit (in ours) bearing a ring of short hairs, terminating in a long, usually twice-geniculate persistent awn which is spiralled at the base; palea about the same length as the lemma and enclosed within it; flowers perfect, stamens 3. [*Stipa*].

Stipa L. *comáta* Trin. & Rupr. Resembling *Piptochaetium* but distinguishable in having glumes 1.5 cm or more long (glumes shorter in *Piptochaetium*). From farther west. Reported for RI. Represented with us as var. *comata*. Reported to cause injury in livestock from grazing.

1. P. avenáceum (L.) Parodi (oat-like). Black Oat Grass. Dry, open deciduous, coniferous or mixed woodlands. May-June. Fig. 164, Map 358. [*Stipa avenacea*].

73. *Cínna* L. Wood Reedgrass (Greek name for a type of grass).

Tall, rhizomatous perennial with simple stems; leaves with wide, flat blades and long, membranous, usually lacerate ligules; inflorescence a terminal, nodding, contracted or open panicle of numerous, small spikelets; spikelets disarticulating below the glumes, 1-flowered; glumes equal or subequal, narrow, keeled, acute or acuminate; lemma similar to the glumes, nearly as long, stipitate above the glumes, bearing a short, straight awn just below the tip; palea slightly shorter than the lemma, keeled; flower perfect, stalked, stamens 3. —Wildl. 1

Panicle densely flowered, with crowded branches; spikelets 4.5 mm or longer;
    second glume 3-nerved. (Fig. 165) .... 1. *C. arundinacea*
Panicle loosely flowered, branches not crowded; spikelets shorter than 4.5 mm;
    second glume 1-nerved (Fig. 166) .... 2. *C. latifolia*

1. C. arundinácea L. (reed-like). Swamps and moist deciduous woods. August-September. Fig. 165, Map 359. Our plants are var. *arundinacea*. —FACW+

2. C. latifolia (Trev. ex Goepp.) Griseb. (broad-leaved). Swamps, moist deciduous woods and meadows. July-September. Fig. 166, Map 360. (Eurasia). —FACW

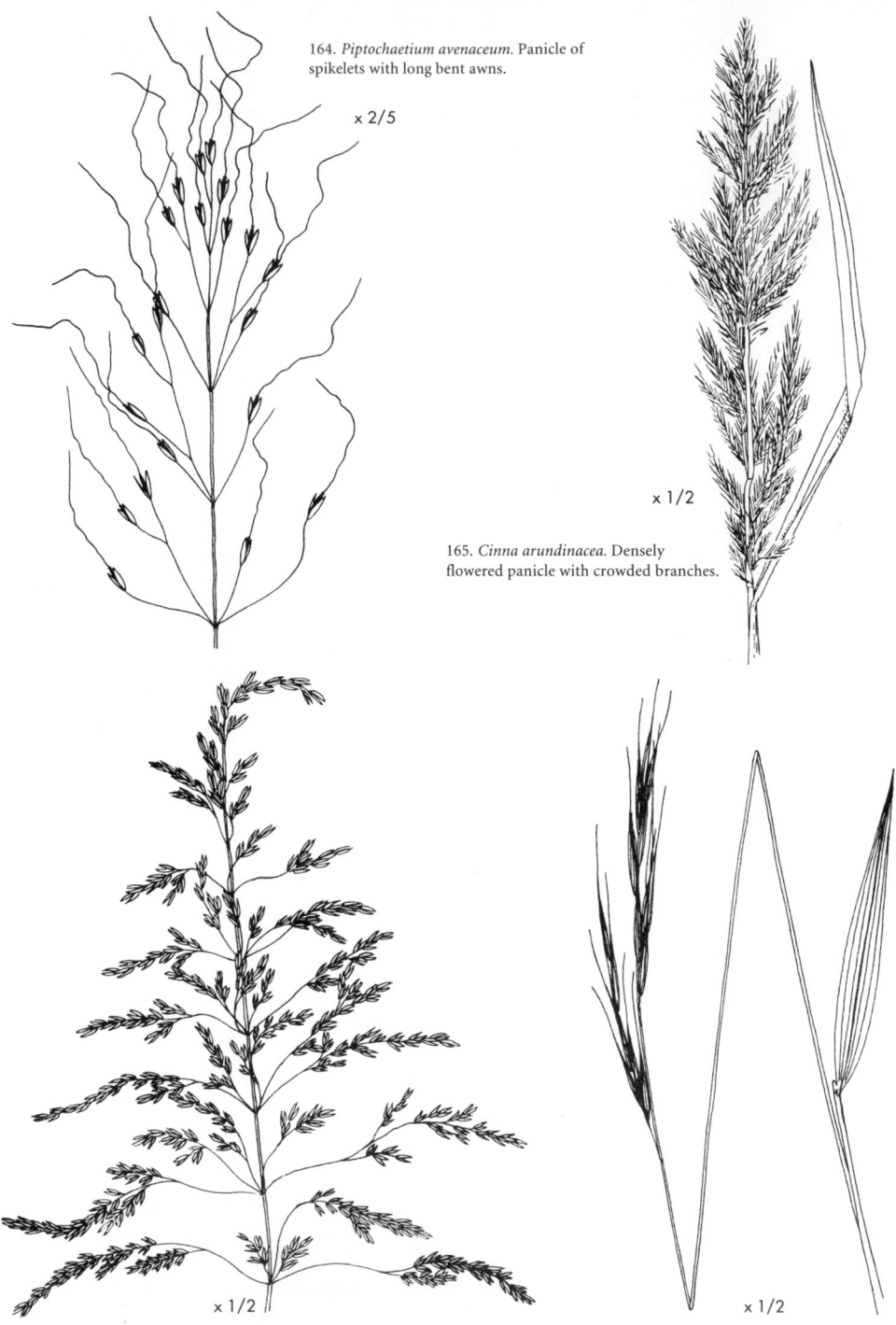

164. *Piptochaetium avenaceum*. Panicle of
spikelets with long bent awns.

x 2/5

x 1/2

165. *Cinna arundinacea*. Densely
flowered panicle with crowded branches.

x 1/2

166. *Cinna latifolia*. Loosely flowered
panicle with branches not crowded.

x 1/2

167. *Brachyelytrum erectum*. General
character of panicle.

360. *Cinna latifolia*

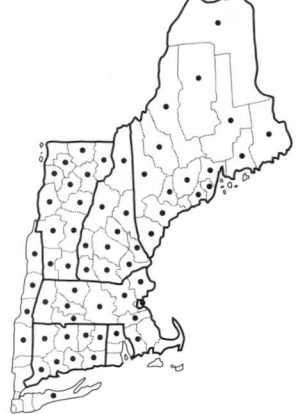

361. *Brachyelytrum erectum*

74. *Brachyélytrum* Beauv. (from the Greek, referring to the minute glumes).

Tall, erect, slender perennial from short, knotty rhizomes with simple stems; leaves with broad flat scabrous blades and a short, membranous ligule; inflorescence a narrow, open, few-flowered panicle; spikelets disarticulating above the glumes, 1-flowered; glumes minute, unequal, acute, the second sometimes aristate, the first sometimes wanting; lemma firm, narrow, 5-nerved, acuminate into a long awn; palea firm, nearly as long as the lemma; floret with a pronounced, short-bearded callus, rachilla prolonged into a long, slender bristle appressed to the palea; flowers perfect, stamens 2.

Lemmas hispid, with hairs 0.2-0.6 mm long. .... 1. *B. erectum*
Lemmas glabrous, or puberulent with hairs less than 0.2 mm long. .... 2. *B. septentrionale*

    1. *B. eréctum* (Schreb.) Beauv. Moist mesic woods. July-August. Fig. 167, Map 361.
    2. *B. septentrionále*(Babel) G. Tucker. Woodlands, often in moist soil. July-August. [*B. erectum* var. *septentrionale; B.e.* var. *glabratum*].

75. *Muhlenbérgia* Schreb. Muhly Grass (for G. Muhlenberg).

Perennial (ours), mostly rhizomatous, low to moderately tall; stems erect or decumbent at base, simple or branched; leaves with flat or involute leaves and membranous, sometimes ciliate ligules; inflorescence a narrow, contracted or open panicle of small spikelets; spikelets 1-flowered, rarely 2-flowered, disarticulating above the glumes; glumes equal or unequal, longer or shorter than lemma, obtuse to acuminate or awned, the first glume sometimes short or rarely absent; lemma membranous, narrow, acute, mucronate or awned, usually pilose at the base; palea slightly shorter than the lemma; flower perfect, stamens 2-3.

    Gastrídium Beauv. Annual with dense, spike-like inflorescence; similar to *Muhlenbergia* but differing in that the glumes are much longer than the lemmas. One species introduced from Europe is rarely found in our range: *G. ventricósum* (Gouan) Schinz & Thell. Reported for ME, Middlesex and Suffolk Counties MA. [*G. australe*]. —FACU

    Lagúrus L. Panicle nearly as broad as long, plumose, spikelets woolly; glumes much exceeding lemmas. Represented by *L. ovátus* L. Occasionally escaped from cultivation. Reported for Fairfield County CT.

a. Panicle loose and open, its branches spreading; pedicles mostly 2 or more times
    length of spikelets. (Fig. 168).
    Lemmas awned .... 1. *M. capillaris*
    Lemmas awnless .... 2. *M. uniflora*
a. Panicle narrow and contracted, with appressed or ascending branches;
    spikelets sessile or subsessile. (Fig. 169).
    b. Leaf blades involute, mostly 1.5 mm or less wide; lemmas glabrous at base. .... 3. *M. richardsonis*
    b. Leaf blades flat, mostly wider than 1.5 mm; lemmas pilose at base.
        c. Glumes a third or less the length of the body of the lemma. .... 4. *M. schreberi*
        c. Glumes half or more the length of the body of the lemma.
            d. Glumes, including their awns, much longer than lemma.
                Stems glabrous below the nodes; leaf sheaths keeled. .... 5. *M. racemosa*
                Stems puberulent below nodes; leaf sheaths not keeled. .... 6. *M. glomerata*
            d. Glumes shorter than to barely exceeding lemma.
                e. Glumes ovate, abruptly narrowed to a short tip.
                    Stems glabrous below the nodes; lemma awnless or awn-tipped.
                        (Fig. 170). .... 7. *M. sobolifera*
                    Stems puberulent below nodes; lemma with an awn 2-5 times
                        length of body. .... 8. *M. tenuiflora*
                e. Glumes linear-lanceolate, gradually tapering from base to tip. (Fig. 171).
                    f. Stems glabrous below the nodes .... 9. *M. frondosa*
                    f. Stems puberulent below the nodes.
                        Spikelets closely imbricated on panicle branches, sessile or subsessile;
                            glumes and lemmas firm, green or purple. .... 10. *M. mexicana*
                        Spikelets loosely imbricated, at least some with pedicels as long as
                            the spikelet; glumes and lemmas membranous, whitish. .... 11. *M. sylvatica*

1. *M. capilláris* (Lam.) Trin. (hair-like). Hairgrass. Sandy or rocky woods, clearings and borders. September-October. Fig. 168, Map 362. Endangered in CT. Our plants are var. *capillaris*. —FACU-

2. *M. uniflóra* (Muhl.) Fern. (one-flowered). Bogs, wet meadows, sandy or peaty pond and river shores, damp fields, occasionally damp, open deciduous woodlands. August-October. Map 363. [*Sporobolus u.*]. —OBL

M. torreyána (Schult.) A. S. Hitchc. Similar to *M. uniflora* but differing in having the second glume two thirds to nearly or fully as long as the lemma (second glume about half as long as the lemma in *M. uniflora*). From farther south along the coastal plain. Reported for Suffolk County NY. [*Sporobolus t.; S. compressus*]. —FACW+

3. *M. richardsónis* (Trin.) Rydb. (for its discoverer). Mat Muhly. Wet, gravelly, often calcareous soil, often along pond and river shores. July-September. Reported for Aroostook and Kennebec Counties ME. —FAC

4. *M. schréberi* J. F. Gmel. (for von Schreber). Nimble Will. Moist, often shady places, waste areas, roadsides, lawns and gardens. August-October. Fig. 169, Map 364. [*M. palustris*]. —FAC

5. *M. racemósa* (Michx.) B.S.P. (racemed). Satin Grass. Meadows, rocky slopes, waste places, river shores, occasionally wet meadows. August-September. Map 365. —FAC

6. *M. glomeráta* (Willd.) Trin. (in clustered heads). Roadsides, waste places, rocky slopes, river and lake shores, wet meadows, bogs and wet deciduous woods. August-October. Map 366. —FACW

7. *M. sobolífera* (Muhl. ex Willd.) Trin. (bearing sprouts). Rock Dropseed. Dry, rocky or gravelly woodlands, rich deciduous woods. August-October. Fig. 170, Map 367. Endangered in ME.

8. *M. tenuiflóra* (Willd.) B.S.P. (slender-flowered). Slender Satin Grass. Rocky or gravelly woodlands and slopes. August-September. Map 368. Our plants are var. *tenuiflora*.

9. *M. frondósa* (Poir). Fern. (leafy). Wirestem Muhly. Roadsides, waste places, damp woodlands, thickets, river and lake shores. August-October. Fig. 171. Map 369. [*M. commutata*]. —FAC

10. *M. mexicána* (L.) Trin. (Mexican). Roadsides and waste places, damp woodlands and clearings, pond and stream margins. August-October. Map 370. [*M. ambigua; M. foliosa*]. Our plants are var. *mexicana*. —FACW

11. *M. sylvática* Torr. ex Gray (of woodland). Moist thickets, woodlands and streambanks. July-October. Map 371. [*M. umbrosa*]. Our plants include var. *sylvatica* and the following var.:

var. *robústa* Fern. Stem stiff, panicle branches densely flowered, glumes broadly lanceolate and shorter than blade of lemma (stem weak and loosely ascending, panicle loosely flowered, glumes narrowly lanceolate and equalling or exceeding blade of lemma in var. *sylvatica*). —FAC+

76. *Calamagróstis* Adans. Reed-Bentgrass (from the Greek meaning reed grass).

Moderately tall, perennial, ours mostly with creeping rhizomes; leaves with long, narrow, usually flat blades; inflorescence a loose, open or contracted, spike-like terminal panicle; spikelets disarticulating above the glumes, 1-flowered, the rachilla prolonged behind the palea as a slender, usually pubescent bristle; glumes subequal, acute or acuminate; lemma shorter than the glumes and usually more delicate, with a slender awn from the back usually at or below the middle, surrounded at the base by white hairs arising from the callus, these often copious and as long or longer than lemma; palea shorter than the lemma, membranous; flowers perfect, stamens 3.

a. Callus-hairs much exceeding the lemma. .... 1. *C. epigeios*
a. Callus-hairs shorter than to barely exceeding lemma.
  b. Awn inserted well above the middle of the lemma; prolongation of rachilla
    with a tuft of long hairs only at the tip. (Fig. 172). .... 2. *C. cinnoides*
  b. Awn inserted at or below middle of the lemma; prolongation of rachilla hairy
    its whole length. (Fig. 173).
    c. Awn conspicuous, bent near middle, the tip frequently protruding
      sidewise from spikelet.
      d. Callus-hairs one-fourth or less the length of the lemma. .... 3. *C. pickeringii*
      d. Callus-hairs half the length of the lemma or longer.
        Callus-hairs in 2 lateral tufts at sides of lemma. .... 4. *C. stricta*
                                                          subsp. *inexpansa*
        Callus-hairs evenly surrounding base of the lemma. .... 5. *C. canadensis*
    c. Awn inconspicuous, thin and resembling the callus hairs, straight or slightly
      arched, included in spikelet.
      e. Panicle open, its branches spreading or ascending; callus hairs mostly as
        long as lemma. (Fig. 175) .... 5. *C. canadensis*
      e. Panicle contracted and spike-like, its branches ascending to appressed;
        callus hairs mostly shorter than lemma. (Fig. 174).
        Leaf blades scabrous; ligule 3.5 mm or longer. .... 4. *C. stricta*
                                                           subsp. *inexpansa*
        Leaf blades smooth; ligule less than 3.5 mm long. .... 4. *C. stricta*
                                                           subsp. *stricta*

1. *C. epigeíos* (L.) Roth. (upon the ground; from its rhizomatous habit.). Feathertop. Sandy soil near the coast in woodlands, fields, upper edges of salt marshes, roadsides and waste places. August-September. Map 372. (Adventive from Eurasia or N. Africa). —FAC

2. *C. cinnoídes* W. Bart. (like *Cinna*). Nuttal's Reed-grass. Wet meadows, open wet woods, bogs, and damp roadsides. July-September. Fig. 172, Map 373. —OBL

3. *C. pickeríngii* Gray (for its discoverer). Pickering's Reed-grass. Wet meadows, bogs, wet shores, mainly alpine. July-September. Fig. 173, Map 374. Endangered in ME. —FACW

4. *C. stricta* (Timm.) Koel. Marshes, sandy shores, alpine areas. Fig. 174. (Eurasia). Endangered in ME. [*C. neglecta*]. Our plants include *C. stricta* subsp. *stricta* var. *stricta* (Map 375) and the following subsp:

subsp. *inexpánsa* (Gray). C. W. Greene. Ligule 3 mm or more long; leaf blades usually scabrous beneath (ligule less than 3 mm long and blades smooth or nearly so in subsp. *stricta* var. *stricta*). Sandy shores, wet meadows, marshes, bogs, alpine areas. Map 376. Endangered in VT and NH. [*C. fernaldii; C. inexpansa; C. lacustrus; C. porteri*]. —FACW to OBL

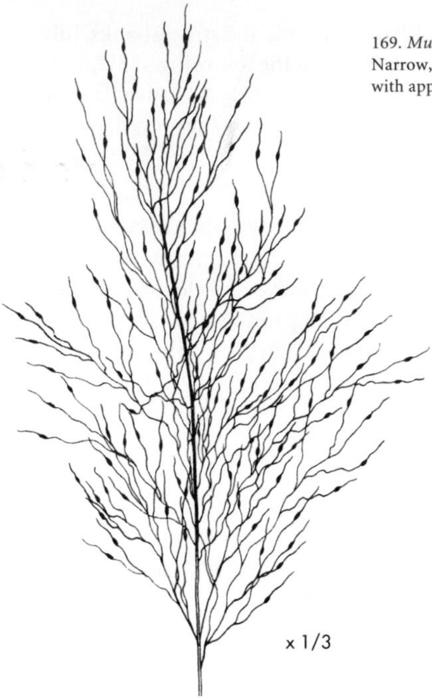

169. *Muhlenbergia schreberi.*
Narrow, contracted panicle
with appressed branches.

x 2/3

x 12

170. *Muhlenbergia sobolifera.*
Spikelet with glumes ovate,
abruptly pointed.

x 10

171. *Muhlenbergia frondosa.*
Spikelet with glumes linear-
lanceolate, gradually tapering.

x 1/3

168. *Muhlenbergia capillaris.* Loose, open
panicle with spreading branches.

174. *Calamagrostis stricta* subsp.
inexpansa. Panicle contracted,
with appressed branches.

x 2/3

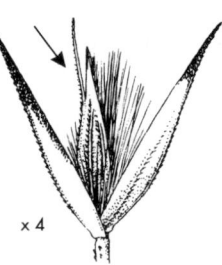

x 4

172. *Calamagrostis cinnoides.*
Spikelet with awn inserted
on lemma above middle,
long callus hairs.

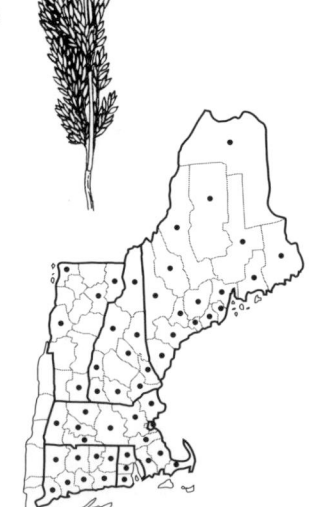

x 10

173. *Calamagrostis pickeringii.*
Spikelet with awn inserted on
lemma below middle, short
callus nairs.

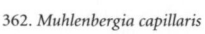

362. *Muhlenbergia capillaris*

363. *Muhlenbergia uniflora*

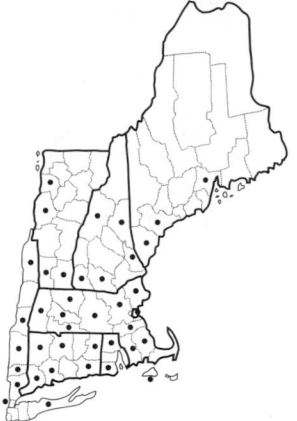

364. *Muhlenbergia schreberi*

365. *Muhlenbergia racemosa*

366. *Muhlenbergia glomerata*

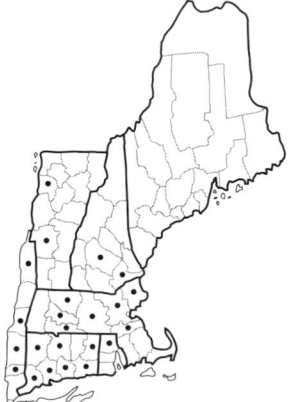

367. *Muhlenbergia sobolifera*

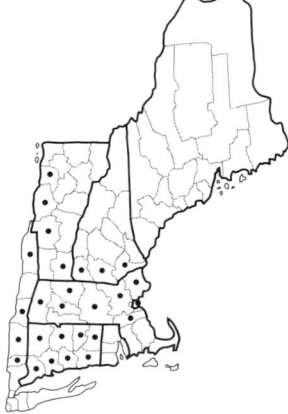

368. *Muhlenbergia tenuiflora*

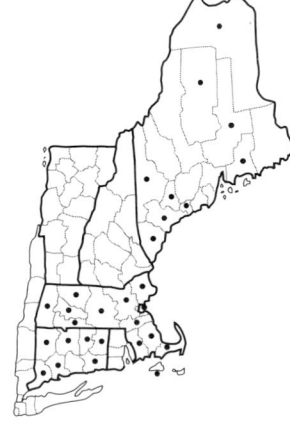

369. *Muhlenbergia frondosa*

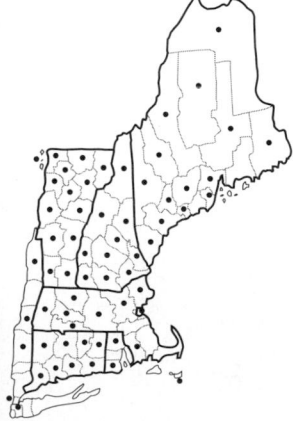

370. *Muhlenbergia mexicana*

371. *Muhlenbergia sylvatica*

372. *Calamagrostis epigeios*

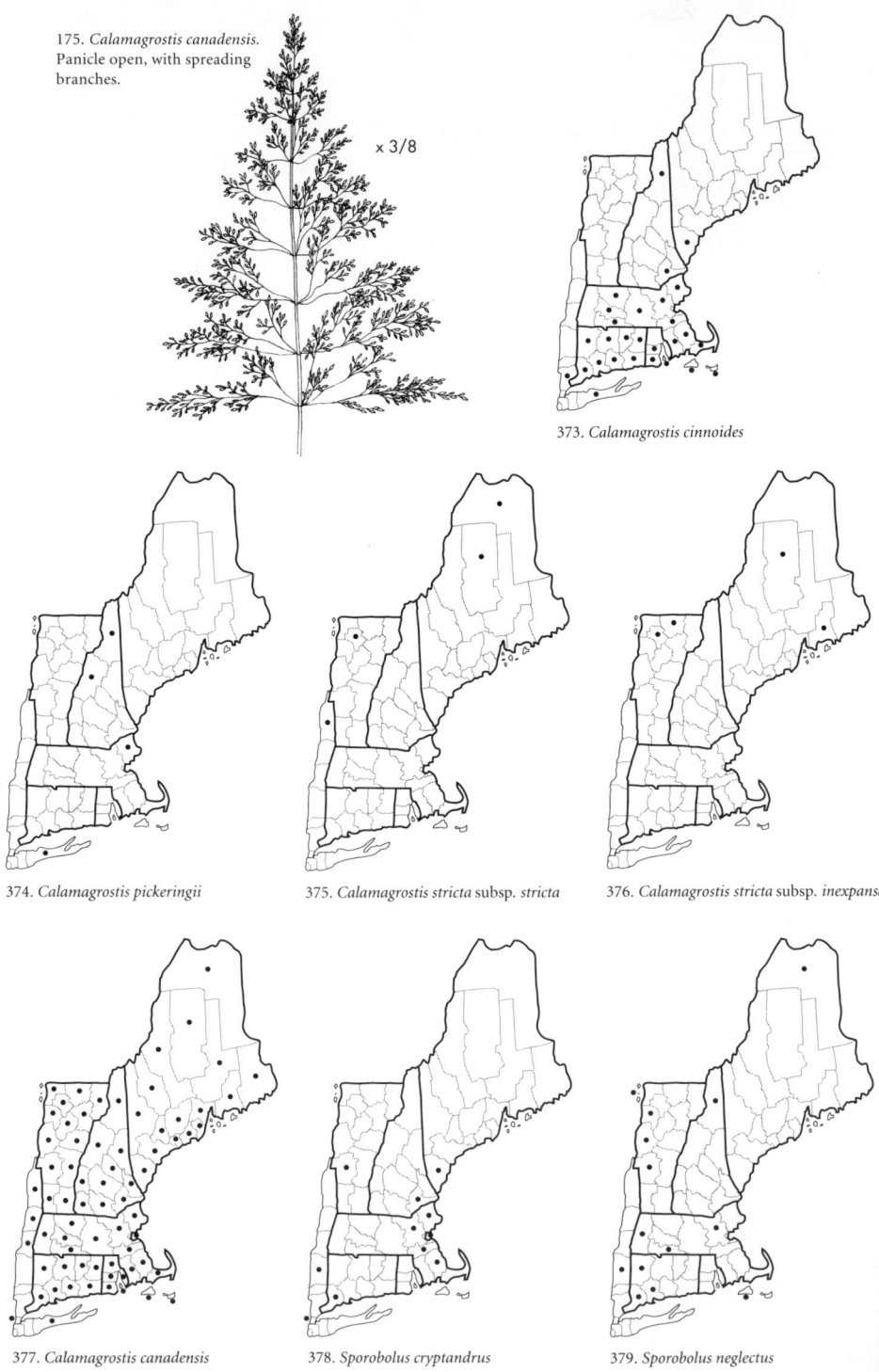

175. *Calamagrostis canadensis.*
Panicle open, with spreading branches.

x 3/8

373. *Calamagrostis cinnoides*

374. *Calamagrostis pickeringii*

375. *Calamagrostis stricta* subsp. *stricta*

376. *Calamagrostis stricta* subsp. *inexpansa*

377. *Calamagrostis canadensis*

378. *Sporobolus cryptandrus*

379. *Sporobolus neglectus*

5. C. canadénsis (Michx.) Beauv. (Canadian). Blue-joint. Wet meadows, marshes, open wet woods, and wet soil in alpine areas. June-August. Fig. 175, Map 377. Our plants include var. *canadensis* and the following 2 vars.:

var. *langsdórfii* (Link) Inman. Awn conspicuous, bent near middle, or inconspicuous and inserted on lower third of lemma and spikelets 4.5 mm or more long (awn inconspicuous and inserted near middle of lemma and spikelets less than 3.8 mm long. in var. canadense). [*C. canadense* var. *scabra; C. nubila; C. langsdorfii*].

var. *macouniána* (Vasey) Stebbins. Panicle more densely flowered than in var. *canadensis*; spikelets mostly less than 2.8 mm long (longer than 2.8 mm in var. *canadensis*). [*C. macouniana*]. —FACW+

77. *Sporobólus* R. Br. Dropseed (from the Greek, referring to the seed).

Annuals or perennials; leaves with flat, narrow or involute blades and minute, ciliate ligule or ligule absent; inflorescence an open or contracted panicle of small spikelets, often enclosed in the leaf sheaths; spikelets 1-flowered, disarticulating above the glumes; glumes usually unequal, lanceolate to ovate, from shorter to longer than the lemma; lemma membranous, awnless, obtuse to acuminate; palea as long or longer than lemma and sometimes wider, often splitting between the nerves at maturity; fruit a utricle, the pericarp free from the seed and easily removed when moist; flowers perfect, stamens 2-3. —Wildl. 2

a. Panicle open, with spreading to ascending branches, not spike-like. (Fig. 176).
    Spikelets mostly shorter than 3 mm .... 1. *S. cryptandrus*
    Spikelets mostly longer than 3 mm .... 2. *S. heterolepis*
a. Panicle contracted and spike-like with erect or appressed branches. (Fig. 177).
  b. Glumes about equal; plant annual.
      Lemmas glabrous; spikelets mostly 3 mm or less long. .... 3. *S. neglectus*
      Lemmas pubescent; spikelets mostly longer than 3 mm. .... 4. *S. vaginiflorus*
  b. Glumes very unequal; plant perennial.
    c. Spikelets mostly shorter than 3 mm. .... 1. *S. cryptandrus*
    c. Spikelets 3.5 mm long or longer.
      Palea about as long as lemma; lemmas glabrous. .... 5. *S. asper*
      Palea much longer than lemma; lemmas pubescent. .... 6. *S. clandestinus*

1. S. cryptándrus (Torr.) Gray (with flowers hidden). Sand Dropseed. Dry, sandy fields, shores and waste places. July-October. Fig. 176, Map 378. Endangered in CT.

S. néalleyi Vasey. Resembling *S. cryptandrus* but distinguishable in having the base a loose cluster of knotty rhizomes (base of plant a small, close tuft in *S. cryptandrus*). Southwestern. Reported for ME.

S. airoídes Torr. Similar to *S. cryptandrus* and *S. nealleyi* but distinguishable in having the sheaths naked or merely pilose at the summit (densely bearded at the summit in the above 2 species). Western. Reported for Westchester County NY. Our plants are var. *airoides*.

S. contráctus Hitchc. Panicle contracted and spike-like (open or somewhat so in the above 3 species). Western. Reported for CT and ME. [*S. cryptandrus* var. *strictus*].

S. pyramidátus (Lam.) A. S. Hitchc. Differing from the above 4 species in having the lower panicle branches in distinct whorles. Southwestern. Reported for Westchester County NY. [*S. argutus*].

2. S. heterólepis (Gray) Gray (with unequal glumes). Northern Dropseed. Dry, open soil. August-October. Reported for New Haven County CT, Worcester County MA. Endangered in CT.

3. S. negléctus Nash (neglected or overlooked). Dry, sandy fields, roadsides and waste places. August-October. Fig. 177, Map 379. Endangered in MA and NH. [*S. ozarkensis*]. —FACU-

4. S. vaginiflórus (Torr. ex Gray) Wood (with flowers in the sheaths). Poverty Grass. Dry, sandy fields, roadsides and waste places. August-October. Map 380.

5. S. ásper (Michx.) Kunth (rough). Dry, sandy fields, open woods, roadsides and waste places. August-October. Map 381. Endangered in ME and VT. Our plants are var. *asper*.

6. S. clandestínus (Biehler) A. S. Hitchc. (concealed). Dry, sandy or rocky fields and open woods, roadsides and waste places. August-October. Reported for Fairfield and New Haven Counties CT. [*S. asper* var. *c.*; *S. canovirens*].

78. Agróstis L. Bentgrass (old Greek name for grass).

Annual or perennial, with or without rhizomes, usually cespitose; leaves with scabrous blades and membranous ligules; inflorescence an open or contracted panicle of small spikelets; spikelets 1-flowered, disarticulating above the glumes, the glumes equal or nearly so, acute, keeled, usually scabrous on the keel or occasionally over the entire surface, longer than the lemma; lemma acute to obtuse, awnless or awned from near the base, middle or just below the tip; palea as long as or shorter than the lemma or wanting, rachilla not prolonged behind the palea as a slender bristle (in ours), flowers perfect, stamens 3.

a. Spikelet bearing well exserted awns, at least as long as the spikelet. (Fig. 178).
  b. Palea present, half to fully as long as the lemma. .... 1. *A. capillaris*
  b. Palea wanting or minute.
    c. Annual; lemma minutely 2-toothed at apex, awned just below the tip,
      the awn 6 mm or more long, flexuous but not bent. .... 2. *A. elliotiana*
    c. Perennial; lemma not toothed at apex, awned near the middle, the awn 6mm
      or less long, bent.
      d. Panicle branches forked at or below the middle.
        Branches of the panicle smooth; alpine species .... 3. *A. mertensii*
        Branches of the panicle scabrous; species not alpine. .... 4. *A. canina*
      d. Panicle branches forked above the middle. .... 5. *A. geminata*
a. Spikelet awnless, or awns not as long as the spikelet.
  e. Panicle branches forked well above the middle. (Fig. 179).
    f. Spikelets less than 2 mm long, subsessile in small clusters terminating
      the branchlets; lemma less than 1.3 mm long. .... 6. *A. hyemalis*
    f. Spikelets 2 mm or more long, distinctly pedicelled and more loosely arranged;
      lemma 1.3 mm or more long.
      Mature panicle diffuse, one third or more the height of the plant. .... 7. *A. scabra*
      Mature panicle scarcely diffuse, rarely up to one third the
        height of the plant .... 5. *A. geminata*
  e. Panicle branches forked at or below the middle. (Fig. 181).
    g. Palea wanting or minute .... 8. *A. perennans*
    g. Palea present, half to fully as long as the lemma.
      h. Ligule truncate, wider than long, less than 2 mm long. .... 1. *A. capillaris*
      h. Ligule ovate to lanceolate, longer than wide, more than 2 mm long.
        i. Glumes scabrous over their entire surface; panicle lobulate, with
          spike-like branches. (Fig. 180) .... 9. *A. semiverticillata*
        i. Glumes smooth or scabrous only on midrib; panicle not
          lobulate. (Fig. 181).
          Panicle cylindric, with closely appressed branches. .... 10. *A. stolonifera*
          Panicle open, the branches ascending or spreading. .... 11. *A. gigantea*

1. A. capilláris L. (slender). Rhode Island Bent. Roadsides, pastures and abandoned fields. July-September. Map 382. (Naturalized from Europe). [*A. tenuis*].

2. A. elliotiána Schult. Open woods, fields, roadsides April-May. From farther south and west. Reported for MA, ME.

3. A. merténsii Trin. Red Bentgrass. Mountain summits, in rocky or gravelly soil. July-August. Fig. 178, Map 383. (Eurasia). [*A. borealis*]. —FACU

4. A. canína L. (of a dog). Brown Bentgrass. Meadows and abandoned fields. July-September. Map 384. (Europe). —FACU

x 1

177. *Sporobolus neglectus.* Panicle
contracted, with erect branches.

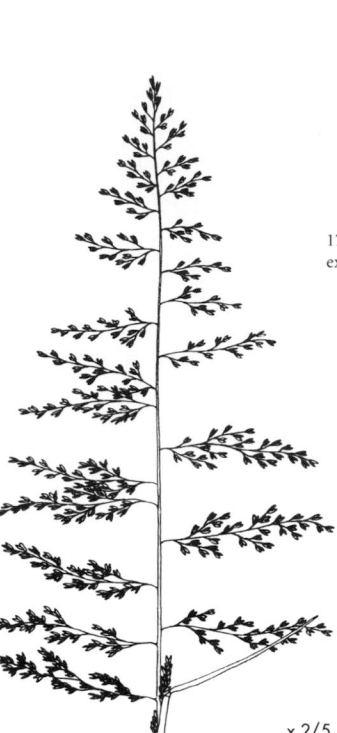

x 2/5

176. *Sporobolus cryptandrus.* Panicle open, with spreading branches.

x 8

178. *Agrostis mertensii.* Spikelet with awn
exserted from middle of lemma.

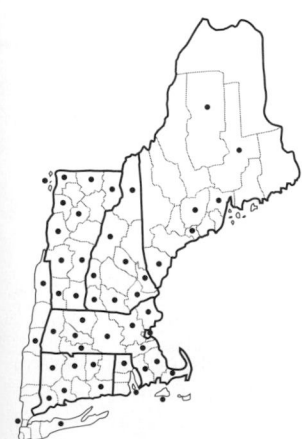

380. *Sporobolus vaginiflorus*

381. *Sporobolus asper*

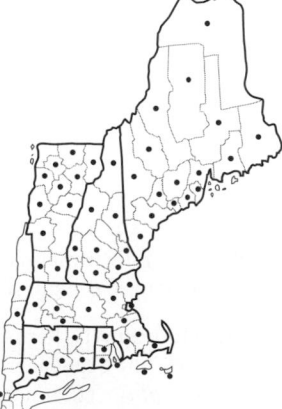

382. *Agrostis capillaris*

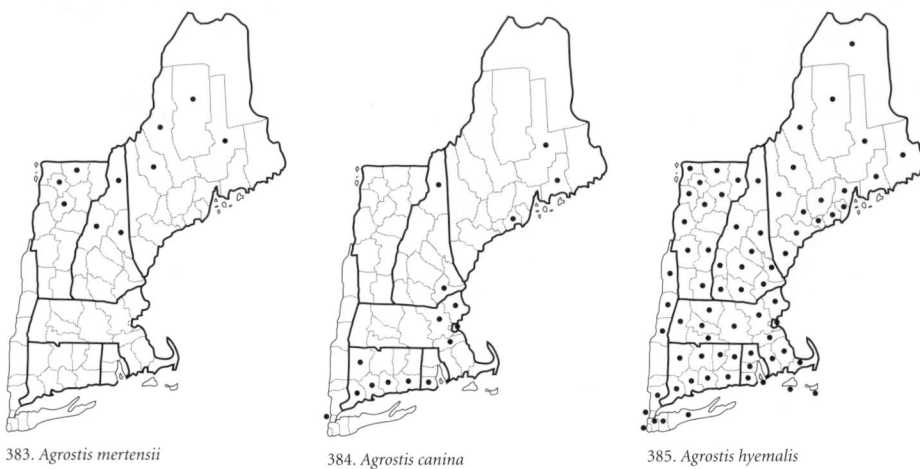

383. *Agrostis mertensii*

384. *Agrostis canina*

385. *Agrostis hyemalis*

A. exárata Trin. Similar to *A. canina* but distinguishable in having glumes 2.5 mm or more long and appressed-ascending panicle branches (glumes are up to 2 mm long and panicle branches are loose and spreading in *A. canina*). Western. Reported for Wallingford, VT. Represented with us as var. *monólepis* (Torr.) A. S. Hitchc.

5. A. gemináta Trin. (twin). Shores, barrens, rocky areas, frequently at high altitudes. July-August. From farther west. Reported for ME, NH. Hybridizes with *A. scabra* and *A. mertensii*.

6. A. hyemális (Walt.) B.S.P. (of winter). Dry to moist fields, roadsides. March-June. Fig. 179, Map 385. —FAC

7. A. scábra Willd. Ticklegrass. Dry to moist soil, roadsides, waste areas. June-November. [*A. hyemalis* var. *scabra; A.h.* var. *tenuis*]. —FAC

8. A. perénnans (Walt.) Tuckerman (perennating). Upland Bentgrass. Dry to moist open woodlands, roadsides, abandoned fields, waste areas. August-October. Map 386. [*A. oreophila; A. schweinitzii*]. —FACU

A. pállens Trin. Dune Bent. Will key to *A. perennans* but is distinguishable in being rhizomatous, with panicle contracted and somewhat spikelike (*A. perennans* is not rhizomatous and has an open panicle). From the west coast. Reported for MA.

9. A. semiverticilláta (Forsk.) C. Chr. Waste areas, roadsides. June-July. Fig. 180. (Adventive from Europe). Reported for New London County CT. [*A. verticillata; Polypogon viridis*]. —FACW

10. A. stolonífera L. Damp swales, roadsides and meadows. June-September. Map 387. (Europe). [*A. stolonifera* var. *compacta; A. palustris*]. —FACW

11. A. gigántea Roth. Redtop. Culms erect, rhizomes present. Fig. 181, Map 388. (Eurasia). [*A. alba; A. stolonifera* var. major).

79. Ápera Adans.
Similar to *Agrostis*; lemmas with long awns inserted near the tip, palea nearly as long as the lemma, rachilla prolonged behind palea as a slender bristle. [*Agrostis*].

1. A. spíca-vénti (L.) Beauv. (wind-spike; the panicle teetering in the wind). Ballast, roadsides and waste places. July-September. Fig. 182, Map 389. (Adventive from Europe). [*Agrostis s.*].

A. interrúpta (L.) Beauv. Resembling the latter species but distinguishable in having a contracted inflorescence with short branches (inflorescence open with long spreading branches in *A. spica-venti*). European. Reported for Amherst, MA. [*Agrostis i.*].

80. *Cénchrus* L. Sandbur (based on the early Greek name for *Setaria*).
Annual or perennial, often decumbent at base or low and branching; leaves with flat blades, loose, frequently overlapping sheaths, and ciliate ligules; inflorescence of simple, spike-like racemes of spiny burs terminating the stem and branches; spikelets ovoid, sessile, 2-flowered, the lower sterile, often containing a staminate flower, the upper perfect, the spikelets solitary or several together, permanently surrounded and enclosed by a spiny bur composed of numerous spines which are flattened and fused in the lower half tapering to a sharp point and retrosely barbed apically, deeply cleft on one side, the bur short peduncled, subglobose, deciduous and falling with the spikelets inside; glumes membranous, shorter than the lemmas; sterile lemma and palea membranous, fertile lemma and palea firmer, somewhat indurated; stamens 3. Spines can cause inflamation and infection.

Trágus Haller. Low annuals with terminal, slender, spiciform racemes of bur-like, 1-flowered spikelets covered with rows of stout, hooked prickles. Differing from *Cenchrus* in that the bur is composed of the enlarged, spiny, second glumes, the spines hooked at the tip. In *Cenchrus* the bur is composed of numerous concrescent bristles, these not hooked at the tip. Two species, adventive from Europe, rarely occur in our range on wool waste, ballast and refuse piles: *T. berteroniánus* J.A. Schultes. Spikelets nearly sessile, 3 mm or less long. Reported for MA, York County ME, Suffolk County MA, and Westchester County NY, and *T. racemósus* (L) All. Spikelets distinctly pedicelled, 4 mm or more long. Reported for MA, York County ME, Bronx and Westchester Counties NY.

1. *C. longispínus* (Hack.) Fern. (long-spined). Field Sandbur. Dry, sandy soil of fields, roadsides, waste areas, beaches and river flats. July-September. Fig. 183, Map 390. Endangered in ME. [*C. pauciflorus*].

C. tribuloídes L. Similar to *C. longispinus* but distinguishable in having burs with spikelets included, scarcely exposed through a narrow-cleft on one side (burs widely cleft on one side exposing the spikelets in *C. longispinus*). From farther south on the coastal plain. Reported for MA and Bronx, Kings, Nassau, Queens and Suffolk Counties NY. (Tropical America).

81. *Zizánia* L. Wild Rice (Greek name for a weed occurring in wheat fields).
Tall, robust, monoecious annual (ours); stem leaves with long, broad flat blades and membranous ligules, underwater leaves of immature plants with ribbon-like blades up to 4 feet long with floating tips; inflorescence a large, terminal panicle, the lower branches spreading and bearing the pendulous staminate spikelets, the upper branches ascending to erect and bearing the appressed pistillate spikelets; spikelets 1-flowered, disarticulating from the pedicel, glumes absent; staminate spikelet early deciduous, the lemma narrowly lanceolate, acuminate or awn pointed, membranous, palea about as long as the lemma; pistillate spikelets tardily deciduous from a cup-shaped depression at the summit of clavate pedicels, linear, terete but becoming angular at maturity, lemma membranous, hispid, short to long-awned, palea as long as lemma, grain long-cylindric, blackish; staminate flowers with 6 stamens. Grain edible. —OBL; Wildl. 4

Pistillate lemmas subcoriaceous, coarsely corrugated, strigose only in the furrows
        between the broad ridges .... 1. *Z. palustris*
Pistillate lemmas thin, delicate, finely ribbed, glabrous or strigose over the surface .... 2. *Z. aquatica*

1. *Z. palústris* L. Shallow borders of lakes, streams and rivers (fresh to brackish), and fresh to brackish marshes. June-September. Fig. 184, Map 391. [*Z. aquatica* var. *angustifolia*]. Our plants are var. *palústris*.

2. *Z. aquática* L. (aquatic). Habitats similar to *Z. palustris.* June-September. Our plants include var. *aquatica* and the following var.:

var. *brévis* Fassett. Ligules less than 5 mm long; mature pistillate lemma 1 cm or less long, with an awn less than 1 cm long (ligules 5 mm or longer, mature pistillate lemma 1 cm or more long, with an awn 1 cm or more long in var. *aquatica*).

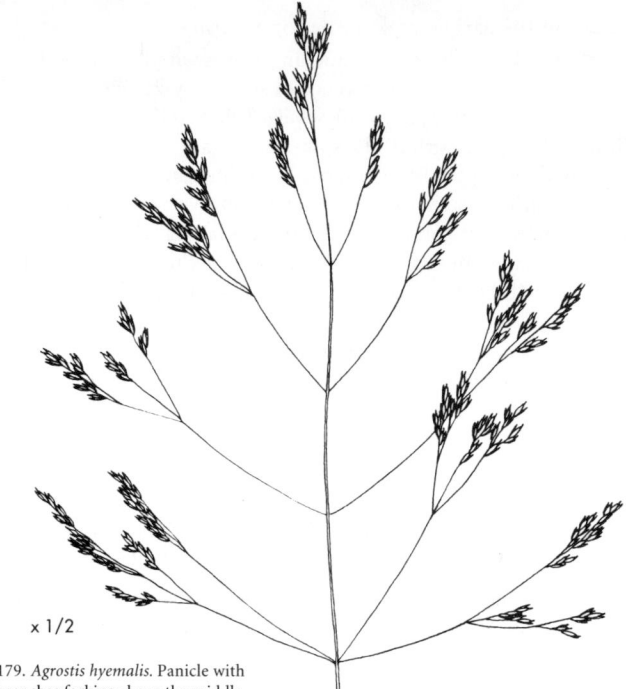

x 1/2

179. *Agrostis hyemalis*. Panicle with branches forking above the middle.

x 1/2

180. *Agrostis semiverticillata*. Panicle lobulate with spike-like branches.

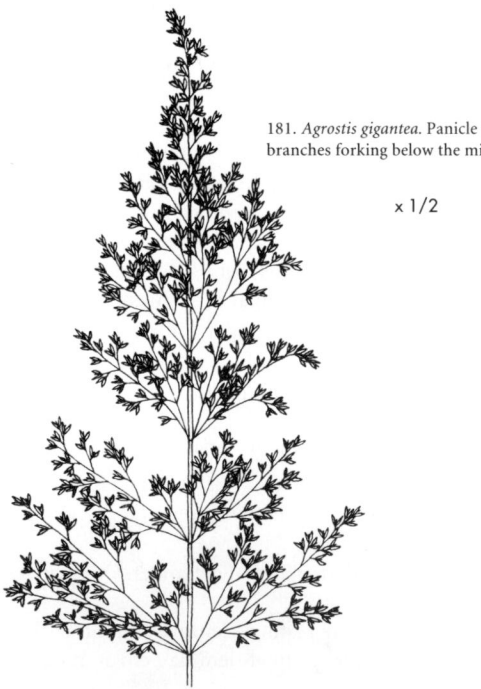

181. *Agrostis gigantea*. Panicle with branches forking below the middle.

x 1/2

x 8

182. *Apera spica-venti*. Spikelet with awn exserted from tip of lemma.

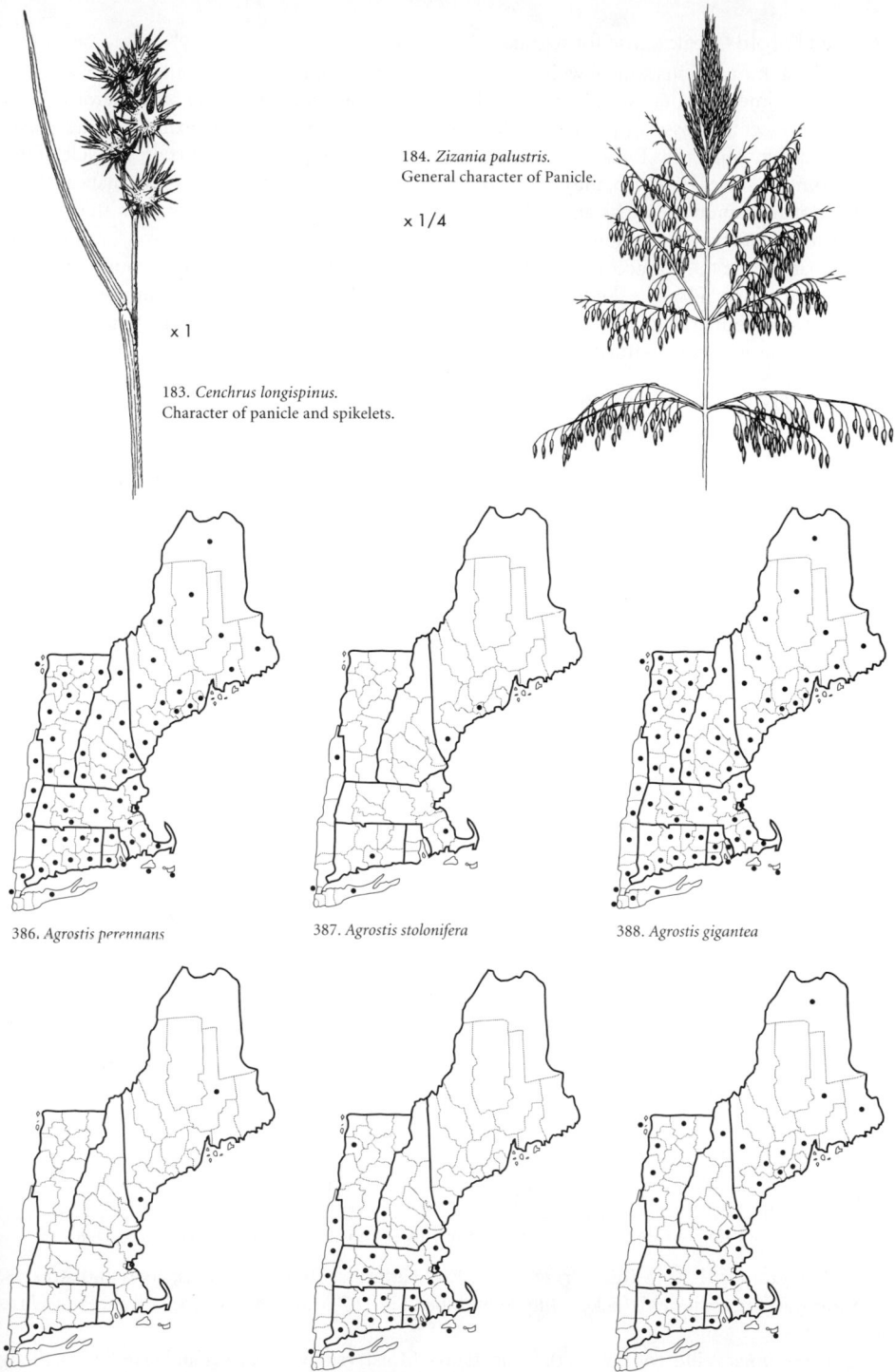

183. *Cenchrus longispinus.*
Character of panicle and spikelets.

x 1

184. *Zizania palustris.*
General character of Panicle.

x 1/4

386. *Agrostis perennans*

387. *Agrostis stolonifera*

388. *Agrostis gigantea*

389. *Apera spica-venti*

390. *Cenchrus longispinus*

391. *Zizania palustris*

82. Zéa L. (old Greek name for a grass).

Tall, robust, monoecious annual with long, broad, flat distichous blades and membranous ligules which are sometimes pubescent; staminate inflorescence a terminal panicle of numerous, long, spike-like racemes (tassels), pistillate inflorescence of 1 to several dense, axillary spikes (ears) surrounded by numerous foliaceous bracts (husks); staminate spikelets in pairs on one side of the rachis, one sessile or nearly so, the other pedicellate, each 2-flowered; glumes somewhat cartilaginous to membranous, lemmas and paleas membranous, nearly equal, shorter than the glumes; pistillate spikelets sessile, in numerous rows on a thickened axis (cob); glumes broad, rounded or emarginate at the tip, coriaceous, about equal; florets 2, the lower usually sterile, but sometimes developed as a second fertile floret, the upper pistillate, the lemmas and paleas membranous; styles very long, protruding from the summit of the spike as a mass of silky threads (silk), the grains greatly exceeding the glumes at maturity; staminate flowers with 3 stamens. —Wildl. 3

1. Z. máys L. (aboriginal name). Maize. Waste places, roadsides, dumps. Fig. 185, Map 392. Cultivated for the grain; young stems can also be boiled and eaten. —Wildl. 3

83. Trípsacum L. Gama Grass (from the Greek, referring to the polished appearance of the spike).

Tall, stout, monoecious perennial, in clumps, from thick, creeping rhizomes; leaves with long, broad flat blades and short, ciliate ligules; inflorescence a spike, these 2-4 together at the summit of the stem or solitary in the leaf axils, separating into joints at maturity, the lower portion pistillate, the upper staminate; staminate spikelets in pairs at each joint of the rachis, each 2-flowered or the first lemma often empty; glumes about equal, the first dorsally flattened, coriaceous, the second cartilaginous, boat-shaped; lemmas and paleas membranous, subequal, shorter than the glumes; pistillate spikelets solitary, embedded in hollows in each segment of the rachis; first glume ovate, coriaceous, fitting into and closing the hollow in the rachis, second glume similar, smaller, boat-shaped; florets 2, the lower sterile, the upper pistillate, sterile lemma, fertile lemma and palea boat-shaped, membranous, each scale slightly smaller than the one preceding, shorter than the glumes; staminate flowers with 3 stamens.

1. T. dactyloídes (L.) L. (with fingers, like Dactylon, an ancient name for a grass). Dry to wet meadows and woodland borders, ditches, roadsides and waste places. June-September. Fig. 186, Map 393. Endangered in MA. —FACW

84. Leérsia Sw. Cutgrass (for J. Leers).

Weak perennials from creeping rhizomes; leaves with flat blades, scabrous on both surfaces and on the margins, and membranous ligules; inflorescence an open panicle of short racemes with overlapping spikelets on short pedicels; spikelets 1-flowered, laterally compressed, disarticulating at the base of the spikelet; glumes none; lemmas oblong to oval, boat-shaped, keeled, cuspidate, the keel and marginal nerves usually hispid-ciliate; palea as long as the lemma, much narrower; flowers perfect, stamens 1-6. —Wildl. 2

Spikelets mostly longer than 4 mm, wider than 1.3 mm; lower panicle
    branches fascicled .... 1. *L. oryzoides*
Spikelets mostly 4 mm or shorter, 1.3 mm or narrower; lower panicle branches solitary 2. *L. virginica*

1. L. oryzoídes (L.) Sw. (like *Oryza*, Rice). Rice Cutgrass. Shores of ponds, lakes and streams, shallow water, marshes and thickets. July-September. Fig. 187, Map 394. (Europe). [*Homalocenchrus o.*]. —OBL

2. L. virginica Willd. (of Virginia). White Grass. Moist, rich woods, river and lake shores, shady roadsides and marshes. August-September. Map 395. [*Homalocenchrus v.*]. —FACW

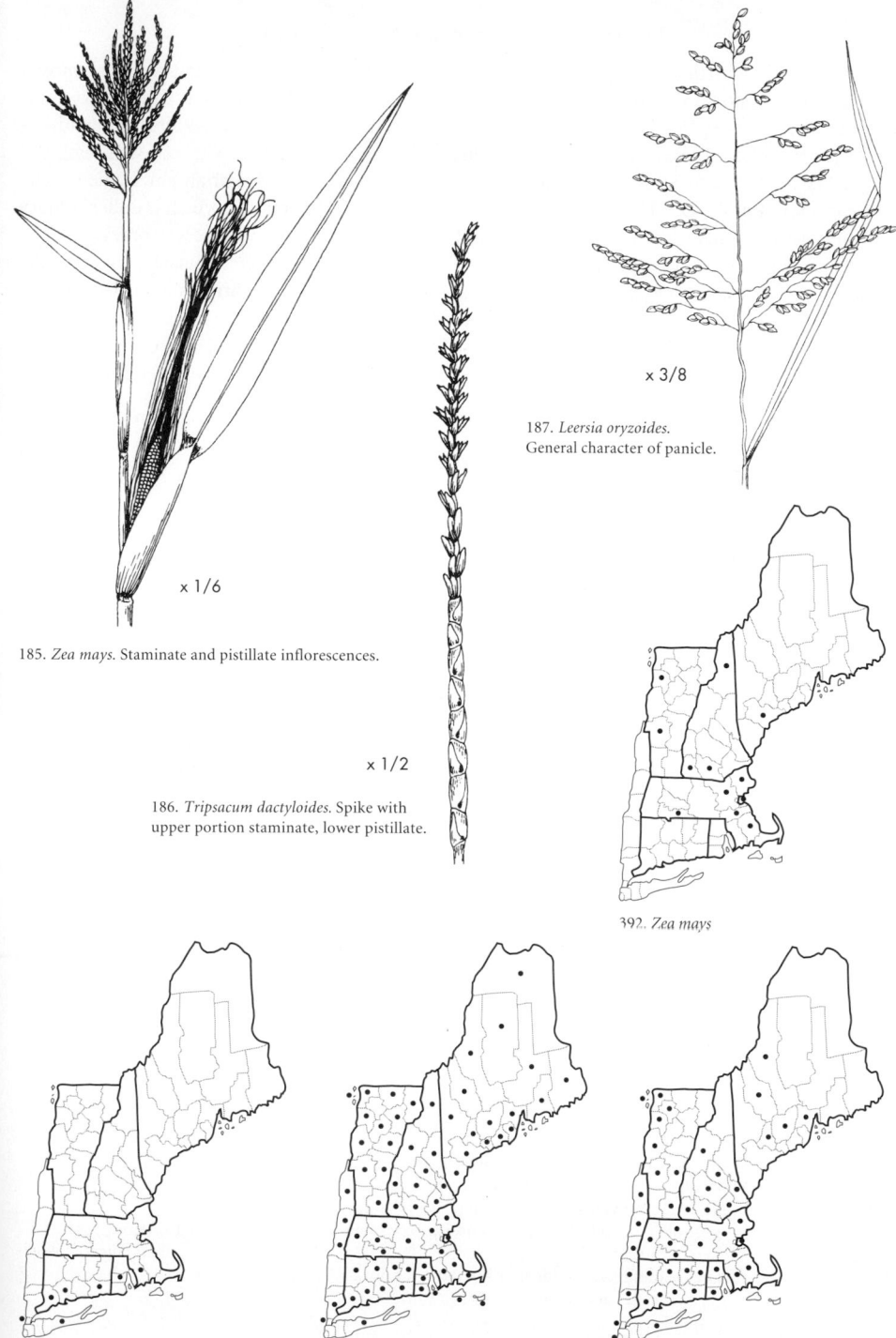

x 1/6

185. *Zea mays*. Staminate and pistillate inflorescences.

x 1/2

186. *Tripsacum dactyloides*. Spike with upper portion staminate, lower pistillate.

x 3/8

187. *Leersia oryzoides*. General character of panicle.

392. *Zea mays*

393. *Tripsacum dactyloides*

394. *Leersia oryzoides*

395. *Leersia virginica*

Family 35. Cyperáceae (Sedge Family)

Monoecious or with flowers all perfect (sometimes accompanied by 1 or more empty scales), mostly perennial (occasionally annual), grass-like or rush-like herbs with fibrous roots from a very short or long and creeping rhizome. Stems usually solid, often triangular, sometimes terete or quadrangular, often leafless. Leaves in basal tufts, or when cauline, usually 3-ranked, with a closed sheath and grass-like blade (sometimes channeled) or the blade sometimes reduced or absent, ligule usually absent (except in *Carex*). The basic unit of the inflorescence is the spikelet, which is either solitary or variously arranged in racemes, panicles or umbels, often subtended by foliaceous bracts; spikelet composed of one to many spirally imbricated or 2-ranked scales. Flowers reduced, solitary in the axils of the scales, the perianth lacking or represented by hypogynous bristles or scales; flowers perfect or imperfect, stamens 1-3, ovary superior (in *Carex* enveloped by a sac-like pouch, the perigynium), 1-locular, containing one ovule, style 2-cleft and the fruit flattened or lenticular, or style 3-cleft and fruit 3-angled. Fruit an achene, sometimes beaked when style is persistent.

a. Achene enclosed in a perigynium (sac-like covering). .... 1. *Carex*
a. Achene not enclosed in a perigynium.
  b. Stamens and pistils (or achenes) in separate flowers; achene bony,
    with a basal disk .... 2. *Scleria*
  b. Stamens and pistils (or achenes) in the same flowers; achene not bony,
    without a basal disk.
    c. Spikelet scales 2-ranked; spikelets clustered into heads or spikes.
      Inflorescence axillary; achene subtended by bristles, beaked. .... 3. *Dulichium*
                                                         arundinaceum

      Inflorescence terminal; achene without bristles, beakless.
        Spikelets with 2 or more fertile florets. .... 4. *Cyperus*
        Spikelets with only 1 fertile floret. .... 5. *Kyllingia*
    c. Spikelet scales spirally imbricated or spikelets not clustered into heads or spikes.
      d. Fertile flowers or achenes 1 or 2 per spikelet, terminal.
        Achene with a tubercle; perianth bristles usually present. .... 6. *Rhynchospora*
        Achene lacking a tubercle; perianth bristles absent. .... 7. *Cladium*
                                                          mariscoides

      d. Fertile flowers or achenes few to many per spikelet, not restricted to
        terminal part.
        e. Achene subtended by a perianth of scales, or bristles or both.
          f. Achene subtended by bristles only.
            g. Achene crowned by a tubercle.
              Spikelet solitary .... 8. *Eleocharis*
              Spikelets in cymose clusters .... 6. *Rhynchospora*
           g. Achene not crowned by a tubercle.
              Bristles shorter than 1 cm, scarcely evident in most species
                without dissecting spikelet .... 9. *Scirpus*
              Bristles longer than 1 cm .... 10. *Eriophorum*
          f. Achene subtended by bristles, or scales, or both.
           Achene subtended by 3 broad, stipitate scales alternating with 3 bristles. 11. *Fuirena pumila*
           Achene subtended by a minute, transluscent scale. .... 12. *Lipocarpha*
                                                             micrantha
        e. Achene not subtended by a perianth of scales or bristles.
          h. Achene crowned by a tubercle or swollen style base.
            i. Spikelet solitary, terminal; involucre wanting. .... 8. *Eleocharis*
           i. Spikelets 2-many, if solitary then appearing lateral; involucre present.
             Leaf blades capillary; scales obtuse; achenes trigonous. .... 13. *Bulbostylis*
                                                           capillaris

            Leaf blades linear, folded, or involute but not capillary;
              scales acuminate or achenes lenticular .... 14. *Fimbristylis*
                                                           autumnalis
        h. Achene not crowned by a tubercle or swollen style base.
          j. Longest bract looking like a continuation of the stem, the
           inflorescence appearing lateral.

Achenes well over 1 mm long .... 9. *Scirpus*
Achenes well under 1 mm long .... 12. *Lipocarpha*
                                                                                               micrantha
j. Bracts 2-several, foliaceous or setaceous, the inflorescence terminal.
  k. Principal leaf blades wider than 3 mm. .... 9. *Scirpus*
  k. Principal leaf blades 3 mm wide or narrower.
    Leaf blades capillary; scales obtuse; achenes trigonous. .... 13. *Bulbostylis*
                                                                                               capillaris
    Leaf blades linear, folded, or involute but not capillary; scales
      acuminate or achenes lenticular .... 14. *Fimbristylis*
                                                                                               autumnalis

1. *Cárex* L. Sedge (the classical Latin name).

Monoecious (rarely dioecious) perennials, mostly with triangular stems; leaves with long, usually narrow blades and a sheath and ligule, the upper foliaceous or reduced and scale-like, usually subtending the inflorescence as a single bract, or the bract sometimes wanting; inflorescence a capitate to elongate spike of few to many unisexual flowers, the staminate and pistillate in separate spikes, in different parts of the same spike, or scattered within the same spike; flowers without a perianth, each in the axil of a scale, the staminate consisting of 3 stamens, the pistillate consisting of a solitary pistil enclosed in a sac (the perigynium) with a 2 or 3-cleft style protruding from the tip; fruit an achene, trigonous with a 3-cleft style, or lenticular with a 2-cleft style.

In addition to the species treated below another hybrid that has been distinguished is *C. x grahamii.* —Wildl. 3

KEY TO THE GROUPS

a. Spike 1 on a stem, terminal, rarely with 1 or 2 smaller lateral ones at its base .... Group 1
a. Spikes 2 or more on a stem.
  b. Achenes lenticular or plano-convex; stigmas 2.
    c. Spikes all essentially uniform, mostly short, the lateral ones sessile.
      d. Plant with long, creeping rhizomes, the stems arising singly or few
        together. .... Group 2
      d. Plant lacking rhizomes or these short, the stems cespitose.
        e. Some or all of the spikes androgenous (staminate flowers terminal),
          often represented by filaments or empty scales), not tapered
          to the base. .... Group 3
        e. Some (especially the terminal) or all of the spikes gynaecandrous
          (staminate flowers basal or scattered but not terminal), at least the
          terminal spike tapered to the base (plants with some terminal spikes
          pistillate, staminate or gynaecandrous in the same colony are
          included here). (Fig. 197).
          Perigynia with rounded or thin, sharp margins but not winged;
            if apparently winged perigynia widely spreading or reflexed. .... Group 4
          Perigynia with winged margins at least above the middle, not widely
            spreading or reflexed .... Group 5
    c. Spikes differentiated, the lower and uppermost unlike, the lateral ones
      peduncled, or if sessile, then elongate. .... Group 6
  b. Achenes trigonous to nearly round; stigmas 3.
    f. Perigynia pubescent or scabrous-puberulent. .... Group 7
    f. Perigynia glabrous.
      g. Leaf sheaths and/or blades pubescent. .... Group 8
      g. Leaf sheaths and blades glabrous.
        Beak of perigynium prominently toothed, the teeth mostly 0.4 mm
          long or longer. (Fig. 223) .... Group 9
        Beak of perigynium toothless or teeth not prominent, less than 0.4 mm long.
          Bract of the lowest pistillate spike with a well developed sheath. (Fig. 211). Group 10
          Bract of the lowest pistillate spike sheathless or nearly so.
            (Fig. 212). .... Group 11

GROUP 1

a. Spike subtended by a leafy bract, commonly as long or longer than the spike; staminate flowers terminal, pistillate basal.

  b. Pistillate scales all foliaceous, green throughout, at least the lowest 3 mm or more wide .... 1. *C. backii*

  b. Pistillate scales with scarious margins, all less than 3 mm wide. (Fig. 188) .... 2. *C. willdenowii*

a. Spike not subtended by a leafy bract, or if so, the staminate flowers basal, pistillate terminal.

  c. Staminate flowers basal, pistillate terminal, or spike wholly staminate or pistillate.

    d. Spike wholly staminate or pistillate.

      e. Achene lenticular or plano-convex; style 2-cleft.

        Perigynium plano-convex, with sharp edges; plants cespitose; rhizomes, if present, very short .... 3. *C. exilis*

        Perigynium biconvex, with rounded edges; plants solitary or few from creeping rhizomes .... 4. *C. gynocrates*

      e. Achene trigonous; style 3-cleft.

        Spikes mostly longer than 12 mm; pistillate scales purplish; beak of perigynium less than 0.5 mm long .... 5. *C. scirpoidea*

        Spikes mostly shorter than 12 mm; pistillate scales greenish or brownish; beak of perigynium 0.5 mm long or longer .... 6. *C. umbellata*

    d. Spike bearing staminate flowers at the base, the pistillate flowers terminal. (Fig. 189).

      f. Pistillate portion of spike 1 cm wide or wider; leaves flat, 2 mm wide or wider; achene trigonous.

        Spikes oval to subglobose; pistillate scales acuminate or awned. .... 7. *C. squarrosa*

        Spikes oblong-cylindric; pistillate scales obtuse to acute. .... 8. *C. typhina*

      f. Pistillate portion of spike much narrower than 1 cm; leaves involute, 1 mm or less wide; achene lenticular .... 3. *C. exilis*

  c. Staminate flowers terminal, the pistillate basal. (Figs. 191, 192).

    g. Perigynia strongly reflexed at maturity, more than 5 mm long. (Fig. 191). .... 9. *C. pauciflora*

    g. Perigynia ascending or spreading to slightly reflexed, 5 mm or less long. (Fig. 192).

      h. Perigynia beakless; achene trigonous; style 3-cleft. .... 11. *C. leptalea*

      h. Perigynia short-beaked; achene lenticular; style 2-cleft.

        Plants cespitose; perigynia faintly nerved; alpine plants. .... 12. *C. capitata*

        Plants scattered along creeping rhizomes; perigynia strongly nerved; plant of sphagnum bogs .... 4. *C. gynocrates*

1. *C. báckii* Boott (for G. Back). Dry rocky or sandy soil in open woods. May-July. Map 396. [*C. durifolia; C. saximontana*].

2. *C. willdenówii* Schkuhr ex Willd. (for K. L. Willdenow). Rich hardwood forests. May-July. Fig. 188, Map 397.

3. *C. exílis* Dewey (meagre). Mostly sphagnum bogs and wet meadows. May-July. Fig. 189, Map 398. —OBL

4. *C. gynócrates* Wormsk. ex Drej (dominantly female; from the stout pistillate spike). Sphagnum bogs, white cedar swamps, larch swamps. June-August. Reported for Aroostook and Piscataquis Counties ME. (N. Eurasia). [*C. dioica* var. *g.*]. —OBL

5. *C. scirpoídea* Michx. (like *Scirpus*). Turf, cliffs, ledges, talus, gravel and dry, especially calcareous soil in alpine areas. June-August. Map 399. (Eurasia). Our plants are var. *scirpoidea*. —FACU

6. *C. umbelláta* Schkuhr ex Willd. (bearing umbels). Deciduous woodlands, river and pond margins, waste places and roadsides in dry, sandy or gravelly soil. May-July. Fig. 190, Map 400. Endangered in NH. [*C. abdita; C. rugosperma; C. tonsa*].

    C. rugospérma Mackenzie. Similar to *C. umbellata* but with pistillate scales lance-ovate, tapering into acuminate tips, perigynia ellipsoid, with beak about three quarters as long as the body (pistillate scales broadly ovate, with short, acute tips, perigynia subglobose, with beak about half as long as the body in *C. umbellata*). Reported for MA. [*C. umbellata*].

C. tónsa (Fern.) Bickn. (shaved). Similar to *C. umbellata* and *C. rugosperma* but distinguishable in having leaves 3-5 mm wide and perigynia glabrous to slightly pubescent (broadest leaves to 3 mm wide and perigynia usually distinctly puberulent in latter 2 species). [*C. umbellata* var. *tonsa*].

7. **C. squarrósa** L. (wide-spreading). Wet meadows, wet, deciduous woods, bottomlands and stream-banks. June-September. Map 401. —FACW

8. **C. typhína** Michx. (resembling *Typha*, Cat-tail). Wet meadows, wet, deciduous woods, and bottomlands. June-September. Map 402. FACW+

9. **C. pauciflóra** Lightf. (few-flowered). Sphagnum bogs. June-August. Fig. 191, Map 403. (Eurasia). Endangered in MA. —OBL

10. **C. microglóchin** Wahlenb. (with minute bristle). Similar to *C. pauciflora* but lowest sheaths are blade-bearing and perigynia are less than 6 mm long (lowest sheaths bladeless and perigynia 6 mm or longer in *C. pauciflora*). (Canada; Eurasia; S. Amer.). Reported from Penobscot County ME.

11. **C. leptálea** Wahlenb. (delicate). Bogs, deciduous and coniferous wooded swamps, wet woods and wet meadows. June-August. Fig. 192, Map 404. [*C. harperi*]. —OBL

12. **C. capitáta** L. (head-like). High alpine areas. July-August. (Eurasia; S. Amer.). Reported for Coos and Grafton Counties NH. Represented with us as subsp. *arctógena* (H. Smith) Boecker ex M. F. Colson Ined. [*C. arctogena*]. —FAC

GROUP 2

Perigynia distinctly wing-margined, the beak half or more as long as the body. .... 13. *C. foenea*
Perigynia not wing-margined, the beak a third or less as long as the body
    (half as long in *C. praegracilis*).
    Spikes aggregated in a head .... 14. *C. chordorrhiza*
    Spikes remote (at least the lower) or the uppermost approximate. .... 15. *C. disperma*

13. **C. foénea** Willd. Var. foénea. Fields and open coniferous or deciduous woods in dry, sandy soil. May-July. Endangered in VT. [*C. aenea; C. argyrantha; C. siccata*]. Our plants are var. *foena*.

14. **C. chordorrhíza** Ehrh. ex L. f. (with cord-like roots). Sphagnum bogs. May-August. Map 405. (Eurasia). Endangered in MA; VT. —OBL

C. praegrácilis W. Boott (very slender). Similar to *C. chordorrhiza* but distinguishable in having a long black rhizome and perigynia with a beak half as long as the body (stems arising from prostrate culms covered with remnants of old leaves and perigynia with beak a third or less as long as the body in *C. chordorrhiza*). (S. Amer.). Western. Reported as spreading eastward along highways and now occurring in NY.

15. **C. dispérma** Dewey (2 seeded). Moist or rich woods, wet woods and bogs. June-August. Map 406. (Eurasia). [*C. tenella*]. —FACW+

GROUP 3

a. Inflorescence unbranched, bearing a single spike at each node. (Fig. 194).
  b. Perigynia nearly terete in cross-section. .... 15. *C. disperma*
  b. Perigynia flattened, biconvex or plano-convex.
    c. Stem wing-angled, soft and easily flattened. .... 16. *C. alopecoidea*
    c. Stem not wing-angled, firm.
      d. Leaf sheaths loose, usually mottled green and white and/or septate-nodulose
        on the back. (Fig. 193) .... 17. *C. cephaloidea*
      d. Leaf sheaths tight, not conspicuously mottled or septate-nodulose.
        e. Inflorescence densely capitate, the individual spikes scarcely
          distinguishable .... 18. *C. cephalophora*
        e. Inflorescence spicate, the spikes clearly distinguishable.
          f. Ligule much longer than broad .... 19. *C. contigua*
          f. Ligule not or only slightly longer than broad.
            g. Perigynia spongy-thickened at the base.
              Margins of perigynia smooth .... 20. *C. retroflexa*
              Margins of perigynia serrulate .... 21. *C. rosea*

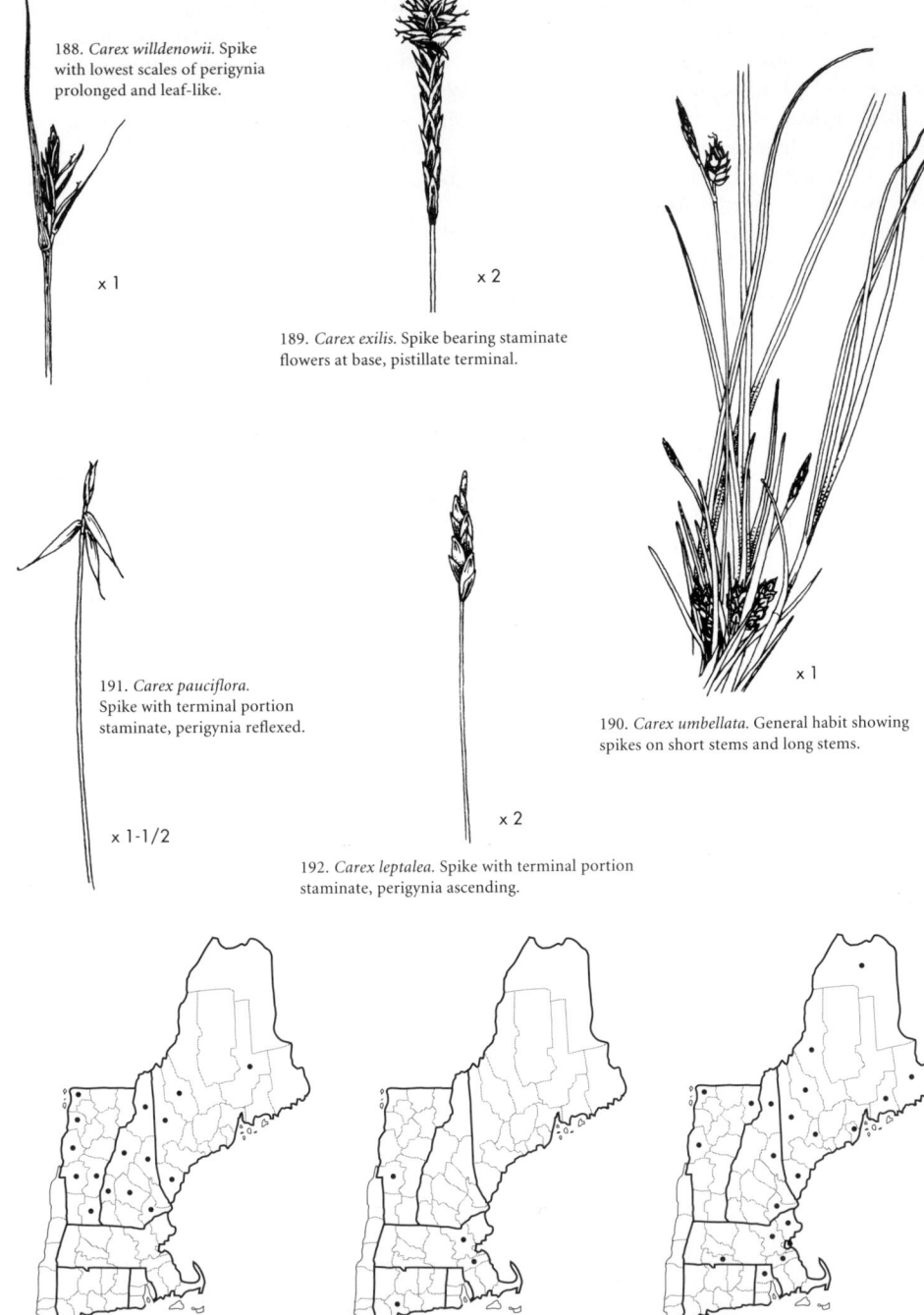

188. *Carex willdenowii.* Spike with lowest scales of perigynia prolonged and leaf-like.

x 1

x 2

189. *Carex exilis.* Spike bearing staminate flowers at base, pistillate terminal.

191. *Carex pauciflora.* Spike with terminal portion staminate, perigynia reflexed.

x 1-1/2

190. *Carex umbellata.* General habit showing spikes on short stems and long stems.

x 1

x 2

192. *Carex leptalea.* Spike with terminal portion staminate, perigynia ascending.

396. *Carex backii*

397. *Carex willdenowii*

398. *Carex exilis*

399. *Carex scirpoidea*

400. *Carex umbellata*

401. *Carex squarrosa*

402. *Carex typhina*

403. *Carex pauciflora*

404. *Carex leptalea*

405. *Carex chordorrhiza*

406. *Carex disperma*

g. Perigynia not spongy-thickened at the base.
  h. Spikes usually contiguous, the tip of each surpassing the base
    of the next above; pistillate scales not conspicuously bicolor,
    at least some long-awned. .... 22. *C. muehlenbergii*
  h. Spikes usually remote, at least at the base; pistillate scales tinged
    with green and brown, acuminate or merely mucronate,
    not long-awned.
    Perigynia less than 3.5 mm long, more than half as wide,
      widely spreading. .... 23. *C. muricata*
    Perigynia 3.5 mm long or longer, less than half as wide,
      appressed-ascending. .... 24. *C. divulsa*
a. Inflorescence branched, at least at the lowest node, bearing 2 or
  more spikes. (Fig. 196).
  i. Perigynia lanceolate, broadest and truncate at the base, spongy-thickened.
    Inner band of leaf sheath usually cross-puckered, the summit
      prolonged. (Fig. 195) .... 25. *C. stipata*
    Inner band of leaf sheath rarely cross-puckered, the summit concave. .... 26. *C. laevivaginata*
  i. Perigynia ovate, rounded at the base, or if lanceolate and broadest at base not
    spongy-thickened.
    j. Pistillate scales awned, the awn as long or longer than body of scale; inner
      band of leaf sheath cross-puckered.
      Leaves mostly equalling or longer than stems; beak of perigynium half
        or more as long as the body .... 27. *C. vulpinoidea*
      Leaves mostly shorter than stems; beak of perigynium less than half as
        long as the body .... 28. *C. annectens*
    j. Pistillate scales acute, acuminate, or with a cusp usually less than half as long
      as body of scale; inner band of leaf sheath not cross-puckered
      (except in *C. conjuncta*).
      k. Stem wing-angled, soft and easily flattened, perigynia corky at base. .... 16. *C. alopecoidea*
      k. Stem not wing-angled, firm; perigynia not corky at base.
        l. Leaves 4 mm wide or wider; perigynia with winged margins. .... 17. *C. cephaloidea*
        l. Leaves narrower than 4 mm; perigynia with rounded margins.
          Leaf sheath strongly brownish-tinged at the summit; perigynia
            brown, flat on the inner face, convex on the outer .... 29. *C. prairea*
          Leaf sheath pale at the summit, often brownish dotted; perigynia
            nearly black, convex on both faces .... 30. *C. diandra*

16. *C. alopecoidea* Tuckerman (like a fox). Wet meadows. June-July. Map 407. Endangered in ME. —FACW

C. conjúncta W. Boott. Similar to *C. alopecoidea* but differing in having sheaths cross-puckered on the ventral band. From farther south and west. Reported for Rensselaer County NY. —FACW

17. *C. cephaloídea* (Dewey) Dewey. Rich, often damp deciduous woods. May-July. Fig. 193, Map 408. Endangered in ME, NH. [*C. sparganioides* var. *cephaloidea*]. —FAC+

C. sparganioídes Muhl. (like *Sparganium*). Similar to *C. cephaloidea* but distinguishable in having a moniliform inflorescence 4 cm or more long, the lower spikes well separated (inflorescence a compact head 4 cm or less long in *C. cephaloidea*, the spikes not separated). Our plants are var. *sparganioides*. —FACU.

18. *C. cephalóphora* Muhl. Rich or moist deciduous woods, dry woods, occasionally in meadows. May-July. Map 409. —FACU

C. mesochórea Mackenzie. Resembling *C. cephalophora* but with perigynia 3 mm or more long, 2 mm or more broad (perigynia are up to 3 mm long and less than 2 mm broad in *C. cephalophora*). [*C. cephalophora* var. *mesochorea*].

19. *C. contígua* Hoppe. Waste places, roadsides and lake margins, in the open. May-August. Map 410. (Naturalized from Eurasia). [*C. muricata; C. spicata; C. sterilis*].

20. *C. retrofléxa* Muhl. ex Willd. (bent backward). Rich deciduous woods, dry, sandy or rocky woods, alluvial woods. May-July. Fig. 194, Map 411. Our plants are var. *retroflexa*.

21. C. rósea Schkuhr ex Willd. (rose-like; from rosettes of perigynia). Rich, often low, damp deciduous woods. June-July. Map 412. [*C. convoluta*].

C. appaláchica J. M. Webber & P. Ball. Very similar to *C. rosea* but with broadest leaves up to 1.5 mm wide (broadest leaves wider than 1.5 mm in *C. rosea*). Reported for MA. [*C. radiata*].

C. radiáta (Wahlenb.) Dew. Closely resembling *C. rosea* and *C. appalachica* but distinguishable in having the achene occupying only the upper half of the perigynium, stigmas straight or merely twisted, not coiled (achene also extending into the lower half of the perigynium, stigmas evidently 1-several times coiled in the latter 2 species. Throughout our range. [*C. rosea* var. *radiata*].

22. C. muhlenbérgii Schkuhr ex Willd. (for G.H.E. Muhlenberg). Fields, waste places and open deciduous woods in dry, sandy or sterile soil. June-July. Map 413. Our plants include var. *muhlenbergii* and the following var.:

var. *enérvis* Boott. Perigynia nerveless on the upper face (nerved on both faces in var. muhlenbergii [*C. m.* var. *muhlenbergii; C. plana*].

23. C. muricáta L. Fields and roadsides. June-July. Map 414. (Eurasia). [*C. angustior; C. cephalantha; C. echinata; C. josselynii; C. pairaei; C. stellulata*]. —OBL

24. C. divúlsa Stokes. Dry fields. June. (adventive from Eurasia). [*C. virens*].

25. C. stipáta Muhl. ex. Willd. (crowded). Wet meadows, deciduous wooded swamps and wet woods. June-August. Fig. 195, Map 415. (E. Asia). Our plants are var. *stipata*. —OBL

26. C. laevivagináta (Kukenth.) Mackenzie. Deciduous wooded swamps and wet woods. June-July. Map 416. —OBL

27. C. vulpinoídea Michx. (resembling *C. vulpina*). Wet meadows and ditches. June-August. Fig. 196, Map 417. [*C. setacea*]. Our plants are var. *vulpinoidea*. —OBL

28. C. annéctens (Bickn.) Bickn. (connecting). Dry to moist fields. June-August. Map 418. [*C. brachyglossa; C. vulpinoidea* var. *ambigua*]. —FACW

29. C. praírea Dewey ex Wood (of prairie). Wet meadows, wooded swamps, shrub swamps and bogs, often calcareous. June-July. Map 419. [*C. diandra* var. *ramosa*]. —FACW

30. C. diándra Schrank (with 2 stamens). Wet meadows, wooded swamps, bogs and pond or lake margins, often calcareous. Map 420. (Eurasia). Endangered in NH. June-August. —OBL

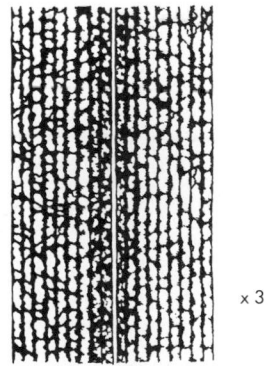

x 3

193. *Carex cephaloidea*. Section of leaf sheath showing septate-nodulose pattern.

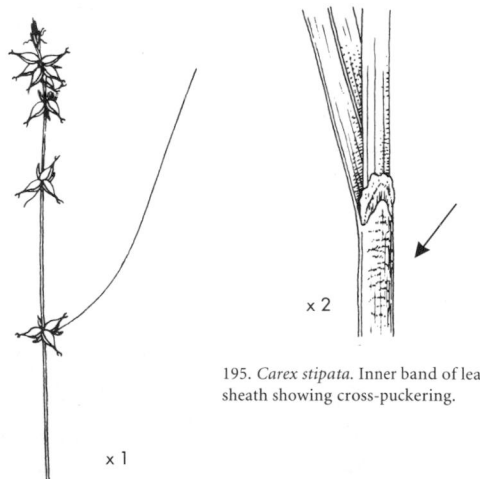

x 2

195. *Carex stipata*. Inner band of leaf sheath showing cross-puckering.

x 1

194. *Carex retroflexa*. Inflorescence unbranched, bearing a single spike at each node.

407. *Carex alopecoidea*

408. *Carex cephaloidea*

409. *Carex cephalophora*

410. *Carex contigua*

411. *Carex retroflexa*

412. *Carex rosea*

413. *Carex muhlenbergii*

414. *Carex muricata*

415. *Carex stipata*

GROUP 4

a. Perigynia with rounded margins, each margin often with a low ridge but not thin-margined, usually appressed or ascending, not spongy at the base.
  b. Perigynia mostly longer than 4 mm, up to a third as wide, with a beak a third or more as long as the body.
    Perigynia strongly nerved on the upper face; leaves mostly 2 mm or less wide. .... 31. *C. bromoides*
    Perigynia nerveless or weakly nerved on upper face; leaves mostly wider than 2 mm .... 32. *C. deweyana*
  b. Perigynia mostly shorter than 4 mm, about half as wide, with a beak less than a third as long as the body.
    c. Spikes closely approximate in an ovoid or subglobose head. .... 33. *C. tenuiflora*
    c. Spikes, at least the lower, separated or if somewhat approximate, head oblong or elongate.
      d. Perigynia ovate, broadest near base; spikes closely aggregated in an oblong head .... 34. *C. arcta*
      d. Perigynia broadest near middle; spikes, at least the lower, separated. (Fig. 198).
        e. Terminal spike with prolonged staminate base; stem smooth; perigynia stipitate; plant of salt or brackish marshes. .... 35. *C. mackenziei*
        e. Terminal spike not greatly prolonged at base; stem scabrous above, or if smooth, spikes with 5 or fewer perigynia; plants of freshwater wetlands.
          f. Perigynia 10 or more per spike; plants gray-green and glaucous. .... 36. *C. canescens*
          f. Perigynia 10 or fewer per spike; plants green.
            Spikes 2 or 3; perigynia 5 or fewer per spike, 2.5 mm or less long. .... 37. *C. trisperma*
            Spikes 3 or more; perigynia 5 or more per spike, longer than 2.5 mm. .... 38. *C. brunnescens*
a. Perigynia with thin margins, usually horizontally spreading or reflexed at maturity (appressed in *C. sterilis*), spongy at the base. (Fig. 200).
  g. Perigynia appressed or strongly ascending, less than 1 mm wide. .... 39. *C. sterilis*
  g. Perigynia divergent or reflexed, 1 mm wide or wider.
    h. Perigynia broadest near the middle. .... 40. *C. seorsa*
    h. Perigynia broadest near the base. (Fig. 199).
      i. Beaks of most perigynia with very short teeth, less than 0.3 mm long.
        Leaves up to 1 mm wide, equalling or exceeding stems; perigynia strongly nerved on outer face .... 41. *C. atlantica* subsp. *capillacea*
        Leaves 1-2 mm wide, shorter than stems; perigynia weakly nerved on outer face. .... 42. *C. interior*
      i. Beaks of most perigynia strongly bidentate, the teeth 0.3-0.7 mm long.
        j. Perigynia broadly ovate, more than half as wide as long. .... 41 *C. atlantica* subsp. *atlantica*
        j. Perigynia ovate or narrowly ovate, less than half as wide as long.
          Scales half to two-thirds as long as perigynium body. .... 43. *C. wiegandii*
          Scales equalling or exceeding perigynium body. .... 44. *C. echinata*

31. *C. bromoídes* Schkuhr ex Willd. (like Bromus). Wooded swamps, wet woods, floodplain forests, bogs and wet meadows. May-July. Map 421. (Mexico). Our plants are var. *bromoides*. —FACW

32. *C. deweyána* Schwein. (for C. Dewey). Dry, moist or rich woods. May-August. Map 422. Our plants are var. *deweyana*. —FACU

33. *C. tenuiflóra* Wahl. (thin-flowered). Bogs and wet coniferous or deciduous woods. June-July. Map 423. (Eurasia). —OBL

34. *C. árcta* Boott (contracted). River and lake margins, alluvial woods, wet woods. June-September. Map 424. Endangered in VT. —OBL

35. *C. mackénziei* Krecz. (for K. K. Mackenzie). Salt and brackish marshes. June-August. Map 425. (Eurasia). [*C. norvegica*].

C. x pseudohélvola Kihlm. A hybrid between *C. mackenziei* and *C. canescens.*

36. C. canéscens L. Swamps, bogs, marshes, wet meadows and wet woods. June-August. Fig. 197, Map 426. (Eurasia). Our plants include subsp. *canescens* and the following subsp.

subsp. *disjúncta* (Fern.) Toivonen. Spikes, except for the uppermost, all distant. (all but the lowest spikes approximate or only slightly distant in subsp. *canéscens*). —OBL

C. lappónica O. F. Lang. Resembling *C. canescens* but with spikes short-ovoid to subglobose and perigynia 2 mm or less long (spikes oblong to cylindric and perigynia longer than 2 mm in *C. canescens*). [*C. canescens* var. *subloliacea*].

37. C. trispérma Dewey (three-seeded). Bogs, deciduous or coniferous swamps and wet deciduous or mixed woods. June-August. Fig. 198, Map 427. Our plants include var. *trisperma* and the following var.:

var. *billíngsii* Knight. Leaves 0.5 mm or less wide; spikes 1 or 2; perigynia 1 or 2, 3.3 mm or less long (leaves wider than 0.5 mm, spikes 2-3, perigynia more than 2 and longer than 3.3 mm in var. *trisperma*). —OBL

C. x trichína Fern. A hybrid between *C. trisperma* and *C. tenuiflora.*

38. C. brunnéscens (Pers.) Poir. (brownish). Wooded swamps, wet woods and alpine areas. June-August. Map 428. (Eurasia). Our plants include subsp. *brunnescens* and the following subsp.:

subsp. *sphaerostáchya* (Tuckerman) Kalela. Leaves and stems lax and arching; spikes distant, the lowest 1 cm or more apart (leaves and stems stiff and erect; spikes approximate, the lowest up to 1 cm apart in subsp. *brunnescens*). —FACW

39. C. stérilis Willd. River shores. June-July. Reported for CT, MA, ME and VT. [*C. elachycarpa; C. muricata* var. *sterilis*]. —OBL

40. C. seórsa Howe (separated). Wet woods and deciduous swamps. May-July. Map 429. Endangered in NH. —FACW

41. C. atlántica Bailey (Atlantic). Swamps and bogs along the coast. May-July. Fig. 199, Map 430. Our plants include subsp. *atlantica* [*C. incomperta*] and the following subsp.:

subsp. *capillácea* (Bailey) Reznicek. Bogs, deciduous or coniferous swamps and wet woods. [*C. howei*]. —FACW+

42. C. intérior Bailey (inland). Wet meadows, bogs, swamps and wet woods. May-July. Fig. 200, Map 431. —OBL

43. C. wiegándii Mackenz. (for K. M. Wiegand). Wet coniferous woods and bogs. June-August. Map 432. Endangered in MA, NY. —OBL

44. C. echináta Murr. Wet meadows, bogs, deciduous swamps and wet woods. June-August. Map 433. (Eurasia). [*C. angustior; C. cephalantha; C. josselynii; C. laricina; C. muricata* var. *angustata; C. muricata* var. *cephalantha; C. stellulata*]. Our plants are subsp. *echináta.* —OBL

GROUP 5

a. Perigynia up to a third as wide as long.
  b. Pistillate scales as long and as wide as the perigynia, covering them.
      Perigynia up to 4.5 mm long, the wing almost obsolete near base. .... 45. *C. oronensis*
      Perigynia longer than 4.5 mm, the wing distinct near base. .... 46. *C. praticola*
  b. Pistillate scales shorter and narrower than the perigynia, exposing the tips
        and margins.
    c. Scales dark brown .... 45. *C. oronensis*
    c. Scales greenish or straw-colored, tan, or green and tan.
      d. Leaves 3 mm wide or wider.
          Tips of perigynia appressed or strongly ascending; spikes usually
              crowded in a continuous head. (Fig. 201) .... 47. *C. tribuloides*
          Tips of perigynia spreading or weakly ascending; spikes usually
              separate, the head moniliform, at least below. (Fig. 202). .... 48. *C. projecta*
      d. Leaves up to 3 mm wide.

Perigynia 4-5 mm long, wider than 1 mm. .... 49. *C. scoparia*
Perigynia up to 4 mm long and 1 mm wide. .... 50. *C. crawfordii*
a. Perigynia more than a third as wide as long.
  e. Pistillate scales as long as the perigynia or only very slightly shorter.
    f. Pistillate scales about as wide as the perigynia.
      Achene about 1 mm wide .... 51. *C. leporina*
      Achene 1.5 mm wide or wider... 52. *C. adusta*
    f. Pistillate scales conspicuously narrower than the perigynia.
      g. Body of perigynium obovate, broadest at or beyond tip of the achene.
        (Fig. 203) .... 53. *C. albolutescens*
      g. Body of perigynium elliptic or ovate, broadest below tip of the achene.
        (Fig. 204).
        h. Perigynia appressed; plants of coastal sands. .... 54. *C. silicea*
        h. Perigynia spreading-ascending; plants of other habitats.
          i. Perigynia abruptly narrowed to short beak; 2.5 mm wide or wider. .... 55. *C. brevior*
          i. Perigynia gradually narrowed to longer beak; less than 2.5 mm wide.
            Perigynia nerveless, faintly-nerved or short-nerved on inner face;
              perigynia hard and thick; spikes greenish or brownish
              but not silvery. .... 56. *C. aenea*
            Perigynia strongly nerved on inner face; perigynia thin; spikes
              silvery green or greenish brown .... 57. *C. argyrantha*
  e. Pistillate scales distinctly shorter than the perigynia.
    j. Perigynia less than 2 mm wide.
      k. Tips of mature perigynia rosulate-spreading, concealing the scales. .... 58. *C. cristatella*
      k. Tips of mature perigynia ascending to spreading but not concealing
        the scales.
        l. Pistillate scales tipped by awn-like points. .... 59. *C. straminea*
        l. Pistillate scales acute to subacuminate but not tipped by awn-like points.
          m. Perigynia widest at or beyond the middle of the body, half or more
            as wide as long.
            Perigynia spreading to ascending; pistillate scales shorter than
              perigynia. .... 60. *C. festucacea*
            Perigynia usually appressed; pistillate scales as long or nearly as
              long as perigynia .... 53. *C. albolutescens*
          m. Perigynia widest below the middle of the body, half or less as
            wide as long.
            n. Beak of perigynium abruptly tapered. .... 60. *C. festucacea*
            n. Beak of perigynium gradually tapered.
              o. Perigynia 4 mm long or longer, ascending to erect............................ 49. *C. scoparia*
              o. Perigynia shorter than 4 mm, or if 4 mm or longer, then spreading.
                p. Spikes closely aggregated into a compact head.
                  Perigynia distinctly nerved on inner face; spikes, at least
                    the terminal, usually clavate at base .... 61. *C. normalis*
                  Perigynia nerveless or faintly nerved on inner face; spikes
                    rounded at base, not distinctly clavate .... 62. *C. bebbii*
                p. Spikes separated, at least at the base, the head moniliform.
                  Leaves less than 3 mm wide.. 63. *C. tenera*
                  Leaves 3 mm wide or wider .... 61. *C. normalis*
    j. Perigynia 2 mm wide or wider.
      q. Pistillate scales tipped by awn-like points.
        Lateral spikes obtuse at base, usually approximate. (Fig. 206). .... 64. *C. alata*
        Lateral spikes tapering to base, usually separated, at least at the base
          of the head. (Fig. 205) .... 59. *C. straminea*
      q. Pistillate scales acute to acuminate but not awn-tipped.
        r. Perigynia and subtending scales spreading-ascending.
          s. Perigynia nerved only on the outer face, nerveless or obscurely
            nerved on inner face .... 55. *C. brevior*
          s. Perigynia usually distinctly nerved on both faces.
            t. Pistillate scales as long or nearly as long as perigynia. .... 53. *C. albolutescens*
            t. Pistillate scales much shorter than perigynia.

Perigynia up to 4 mm long and 2.1 mm wide. .... 60. *C. festucacea*
Perigynia longer than 4 mm, 2.3 mm wide or wider. .... 65. *C. bicknellii*
r. Perigynia and subtending scales appressed.
  u. Perigynia usually less than half as wide as long, widest below
    the middle. .... 49. *C. scoparia*
  u. Perigynia usually half or more as wide as long, widest at or above
    the middle.
    v. Lateral spikes long-clavate; perigynia widest at about the middle
      of the body; head usually moniliform; plant of coastal sands. ...... 54. *C. silicea*
    v. Lateral spikes rounded at base or little clavate; perigynia widest
      above the middle of the body; head usually compact; plants
      of various habitats.
    Pistillate scales as long or nearly as long as perigynia;
      perigynia nerved on both faces .... 53. *C. albolutescens*
    Pistillate scales much shorter than perigynia; perigynia
      nerveless on the inner face .... 66. *C. cumulata*

45. *C. oronénsis* Fern. (of Orono, ME). Fields and clearings. June-July. Map 434. Penobscot River Valley and Moosehead Lake area, ME. Endangered in ME.

46. *C. praticola* Rydb. (prairie-dweller). Meadows, open woods and clearings. June-August. Reported for Aroostook County ME. [*C. pratensis*]. —FAC

47. *C. tribuloídes* Wahlenb. (like Tribulus, the Caltrop). Wet woods, meadows and waste places. July-September. Fig. 201. Map 435. —FACW+

48. *C. projécta* Mackenzie (projected). Deciduous swamps, wet woods, bottomlands, pond and river margins. June-August. Fig. 202, Map 436. [*C. tribuloides* var. *reducta*]. —FACW

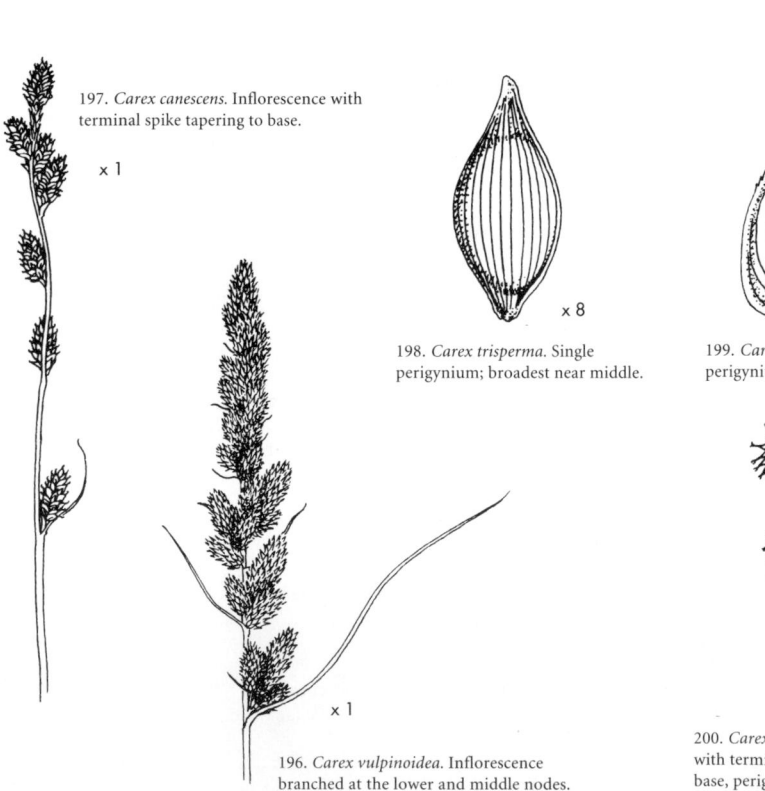

197. *Carex canescens.* Inflorescence with terminal spike tapering to base.

x 1

198. *Carex trisperma.* Single perigynium; broadest near middle.

x 8

199. *Carex atlantica.* Single perigynium; broadest near base.

x 10

196. *Carex vulpinoidea.* Inflorescence branched at the lower and middle nodes.

x 1

200. *Carex interior.* Inflorescence with terminal spike tapering to base, perigynia spreading.

x 1

416. *Carex laevivaginata*

417. *Carex vulpinoidea*

418. *Carex annectens*

419. *Carex prairea*

420. *Carex diandra*

421. *Carex bromoides*

422. *Carex deweyana*

423. *Carex tenuiflora*

424. *Carex arcta*

425. *Carex mackenziei*

426. *Carex canescens*

427. *Carex trisperma*

428. *Carex brunnescens*

429. *Carex seorsa*

430. *Carex atlantica*

431. *Carex interior*

432. *Carex wiegandii*

433. *Carex echinata*

49. C. scopária Schkuhr ex Willd. (broom-like). Wet meadows, open deciduous swamps, dry fields, roadsides and waste places. June-August. Map 437. Our plants are var. *scoparia.* —FACW

50. C. crawfórdii Fern. (for E. A. Crawford). Fields, roadsides and waste places in moist to dry soil. June-September. Map 438. —FAC

51. C. leporína L. (of a hare). Wet meadows, dry fields and roadsides. June-August. Map 439. (Naturalized from Europe). [*C. ovalis*]. —FAC

52. C. adústa Boott (swarthy). Dry open woods and clearings, dry riverbanks. June-August. Map 440. Endangered in ME.

53. C. albolutéscens Schwein. (whitish-yellow). Wooded swamps, bogs and wet woods, mostly along the coast, and in dry soil of roadsides and waste places inland. June-September. Fig. 203, Map 441. [*C. straminea*]. —FACW

C. lóngii Mackenz. Will key to *C. albolutescens* but is distinguishable in having spikes crowded to subapproximate, scales obtuse to acute and perigynium subelliptical (spikes separated in head, scales acuminate and perigynium obovate in *C. albolutescens*). [*C. albolutescens*]. —OBL

54. C. silícea Olney (of sand). Sands along the coast, particularly sea beaches and dunes. June-August. Fig. 204, Map 442.

55. C. brévior (Dewey) Mackenzie ex Lunell (shorter). Dry open soil such as fields and roadsides. June-August. Map 443. [*C. festucacea; C. merritt-fernaldii; C. molesta*]. The following 2 species resemble *C. brevior*, the latter species distinguished by having spikes narrowed at the base and pistillate scales nearly as long as the perigynia (spikes are rounded at the base and pistillate scales distinctly shorter than perigynia in the following 2 species).

C. molésta Mackenz. Spikes approximate, inflorescence up to 3 cm long.

C. mérritt-fernáldii Mackenz. Spikes, at least the lower ones, spaced, inflorescences mostly 3-8 cm long.

56. C. aénea Fern. (bronzy). Open woods and slopes in dry sandy or gravelly soil. June-August. Map 444. Endangered in VT.

57. C. argyrántha Tuckerman (silvery-flowered). Open woods and clearings in dry sandy or rocky soil. June-August. Map 445. [*C. foena*].

58. C. cristatélla Britt. (with small crests). Meadows, rich deciduous or mixed woods, and pond margins in dryish to wet soils. July-August. Map 446. [*C. cristata*]. —FACW

59. C. straminea Willd. ex Schkuhr. (straw-colored). Dry to wet meadows, roadsides and waste places. May-July. Fig. 205, Map 447. [*C. richii*]. Our plants are var. *straminea.* —OBL

C. hormathódes Fern. Resembling *C. straminea* but distinguishable in having perigynium body suborbicular to obovate, gradually tapering to the beak; plant of brackish and salt marshes (perigynium body ovate to orbicular, abruptly tapering to the beak; plant of dry to fresh water habitats in *C. straminea*). [*C. straminea* var. *invisa.*]. —OBL

60. C. festucácea Schkuhr ex Willd. (like fesque). Wet to dry meadows, wooded swamps, wet woods. June-July. [*C. straminea*]. —FAC

61. C. normális Mackenzie (at right angles). Rich dry to wet woods, swamps, thickets and meadows. June-August. Map 448. [*C. mirabilis; C. tincta*]. —FACU

C. tíncta Fern. (tinged). Closely resembling *C. normalis;* distinguishable in having leaf sheaths closely fitting stem and scales exceeding body of perigynium (leaf sheaths loose and scales shorter than body of perigynium in *C. normalis*). —FACU

62. C. bébbii Olney ex Fern. (for M. S. Bebb). Wet meadows and wet woods, especially in calcareous soil. June-August. Map 449. —OBL

63. C. ténera Dewey (slender). Wet to dry meadows, woodlands and clearings. June-August. Map 450. [*C. straminea; C. tincta*]. —FAC

64. C. aláta Torr. (winged). Wooded swamps and wet woods. June-August. Fig. 206, Map 451. Endangered in CT.

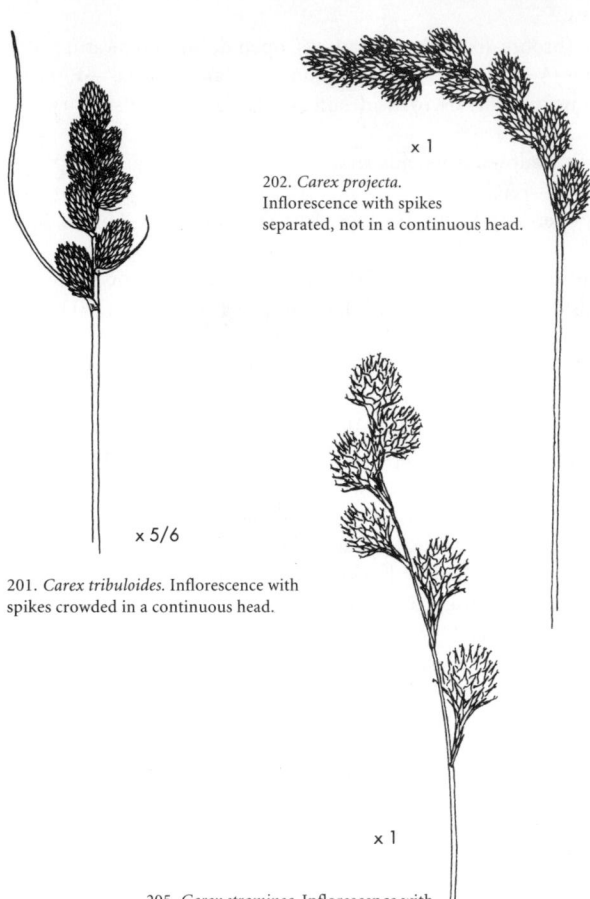

x 1

202. *Carex projecta.*
Inflorescence with spikes
separated, not in a continuous head.

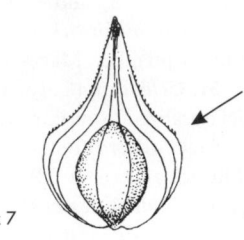

x 7

203. *Carex albolutescens.*
Single perigynium; broadest beyond
tip of achene.

x 5/6

201. *Carex tribuloides.* Inflorescence with
spikes crowded in a continuous head.

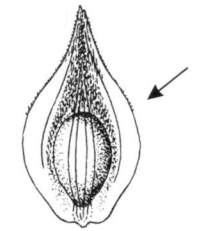

x 7

204. *Carex silicea.* Single perigynium;
broadest below tip of achene.

x 1

205. *Carex straminea.* Inflorescence with
lateral spikes tapering to base.

434. *Carex oronensis*

435. *Carex tribuloides*

436. *Carex projecta*

437. *Carex scoparia*

438. *Carex crawfordii*

439. *Carex leporina*

440. *Carex adjusta*

441. *Carex albolutescens*

442. *Carex silicea*

443. *Carex brevior*

444. *Carex aenea*

445. *Carex argyrantha*

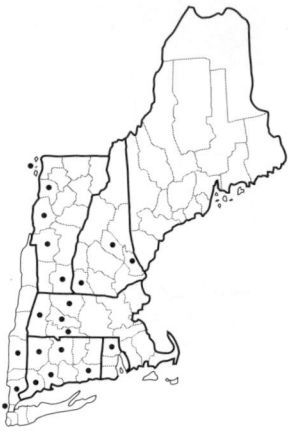

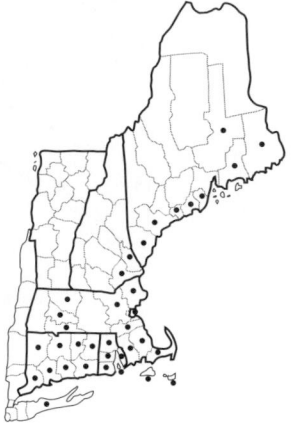

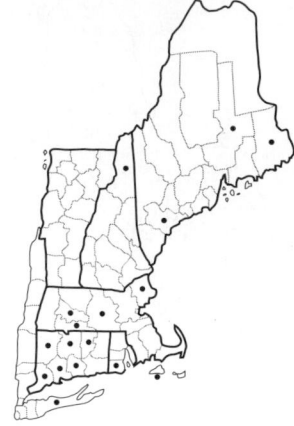

446. *Carex cristatella*   447. *Carex straminea*   448. *Carex normalis*

65. *C. bicknéllii* Britt. (for E. P. Bicknell). Woodlands, thickets and fields, in moist to dry soil. June-August. Map 452. Our plants are var. *bicknellii.* —FACU

66. *C. cumuláta* (Bailey) Fern. (piled up). Moist to dry sandy or rocky soil, mostly in the open. July-September. Map 453. —FACU

GROUP 6

a. Bracts, at least the lowest, sheathing; perigynia in fresh specimens orange
    or white; beakless. (Fig. 207).
   Mature perigynia whitish; pistillate scales obtuse. .... 67. *C. garberi*
   Mature perigynia orange; pistillate scales abruptly acute to cuspidate. .... 68. *C. aurea*
a. Bracts sheathless, or essentially so (lowest bract somewhat sheathing in
   C. lenticularis); perigynia brownish or greenish, usually
   short-beaked. (Fig. 208).
  b. Pistillate scales, at least the lower and middle, distinctly awned. (Fig. 209).
     Pistillate spikes pendulous (if occasionally erect in *C. paleacea*, scales
       with awns longer than the blades).
       Plant stoloniferous, the stems 1 to few from each crown; halophytic. .... 69. *C. paleacea*
       Plant cespitose, the stems few to many; fresh water habitats. .... 70. *C. crinita*
     Pistillate spikes erect; scales with awns shorter than the blades. .... 71. *C. recta*
  b. Pistillate scales obtuse, acute or acuminate, but not awned.
    c. Achene strongly constricted on one side. .... 71. *C. recta*
    c. Achene not constricted.
     d. Beak of perigynium twisted; lower pistillate spikes drooping or spreading. ...... 72. *C. torta*
     d. Beak of perigynium straight; lower pistillate spikes erect (sometimes
       drooping in *C. saxatilis* var. *miliaris*).
      e. Stems numerous in dense tussocks and stolons short or none
        (except sometimes in *C. stricta*); pistillate scales with a broad,
        green or light colored center; sheaths not nodulose.
       f. Perigynia obovate, broadly rounded above; pistillate scales
         acuminate. (Fig. 210) .... 73. *C. haydenii*
       f. Perigynia ovate, tapered to tip; pistillate scales obtuse to acute.
        Inner band of leaf sheaths fibrillose; pistillate spikes often
         staminate at tip; perigynia faintly nerved or nerveless. .... 74. *C. stricta*
        Inner band of leaf sheaths not fibrillose; pistillate spikes usually
         not staminate at tip; perigynia distinctly nerved. .... 75. *C. lenticularis*
      e. Stems solitary or few from small crowns and stolons elongate;
       pistillate scales dark purple throughout or with a very narrow
       green center (if stems sometimes numerous and/or scales

with broad centers in *C. aquatilis*, sheaths nodulose).
g. Style continuous with the achene, strongly contorted at base. .... 76. *C. saxatilis*
g. Style jointed with the achene and readily disarticulating, the achene
    then beakless or with a short straight point.
    h. Perigynia with several nerves on each face. .... 77. *C. nigra*
    h. Perigynia nerveless or obscurely nerved on one or both faces.
        Bracts equalling or overtopping inflorescence. .... 78. *C. aquatilis*
        Bracts rarely equalling inflorescence. .... 79. *C. bigelowii*

67. *C. gárberi* Fern. (for its discoverer) River shores and banks, frequently calcareous. June-August. Map 454. Endangered in NH. [*C. bicolor*]. —FACW

C. hássei Bailey. Similar to *C. garberi* but with spikes mostly separated, the terminal one staminate throughout, pistillate scales equalling to slightly surpassing the perigynia (spikes, at least the upper ones, crowded, the terminal one staminate only at the base, pistillate scales shorter than perigynia in *C. garberi*). Reported for ME, NH. —FACW

68. *C. aúrea* Nutt. (golden). Wet meadows, lake and river margins and wet, usually calcareous soil and rocks. June-July. Fig. 207, Map 455. [*C. garberi; C. hassei*]. —FACW

69. *C. paleácea* Schreb. ex Wahlenb. (chaffy). Salt marshes, meadows and coastlines. June-August. Map 456. (Europe). —OBL

70. *C. criníta* Lam. (long haired). Wet meadows, marshes, wooded swamps and low wet woods. June-August. Figs. 208 and 209, Map 457. [*C. crinita* var. *gynandra*].

Our plants include var. *crinita* and the following vars.:

var. *brevicrínis* Fern. Lower scales, including awns, up to twice as long as the perigynia; pistillate spikes often staminate at tip (lower scales, including awns, 2 or more times as long as the perigynia; pistillate spikes rarely staminate at tip in var. *crinita*).

var. *pórteri* (Olney) Fern. Resembling the last var. but with perigynia not inflated, scarcely longer than the achene (perigynia inflated, distinctly longer than the achene in var. *brevicrinis*). —OBL

C. gynándra Schwein. Similar to *C. crinita* but leaf sheaths are rough-hispidulous (leaf sheaths smooth and glabrous in *C. crinita*). [*C. crinita* var. *gynandra*]. —OBL

C. mitchelliána M. A. Curtis. Resembling *C. gynandra* but perigynia minutely granular and achene not constricted (perigynia smooth or nearly so and achene constricted on one side in *C. gynandra*). [*C. crinita* var. *mitchelliana*]. —OBL

71. *C. récta* Boott. Salt or brackish coastal marshes. July-August. Map 458. (Europe). [*C. salina; C. subspathacea*]. —OBL

72. *C. tórta* Boott ex Tuckerman (twisted). Rocky or sandy streambeds and streambanks, pond margins. June-July. Map 459. —FACW

73. *C. haydénii* Dewey (for its discoverer). Wet meadows, marshes, bogs, open wet woods and along rivers. June-August. Fig. 210, Map 460. —OBL

74. *C. strícta* Lam. (erect). Wet meadows, marshes, wooded swamps, wet woods, river and pond margins, bogs. June-August. Map 461. [*C. strictior*]. —OBL

75. *C. lenticuláris* Michx. (lens-shaped). Lake shores and wet meadows. June-August. Map 462. Our plants are var. *lenticularis*. —OBL

76. *C. saxátilis* L. Lake or river margins in sandy or gravelly soil. July-August. Reported for ME. Represented with us by the following vars.:

var. *miliáris* (Michx.) Bailey. Leaves 2.5 mm wide; perigynia to 3.5 mm long; staminate spike 1, rarely 2. [*C. miliaris*].

var. *rhomálea* Fern. Leaves to 4 mm wide; perigynia to 5 mm long; staminate spikes 2 or 3, rarely 1. —FACW+

77. *C. nígra* (L.) Reichard (black). Wet meadows, turf and gravel near the coast. June-August. Map 463. (Eurasia). [*C. acuta*]. —FACW+

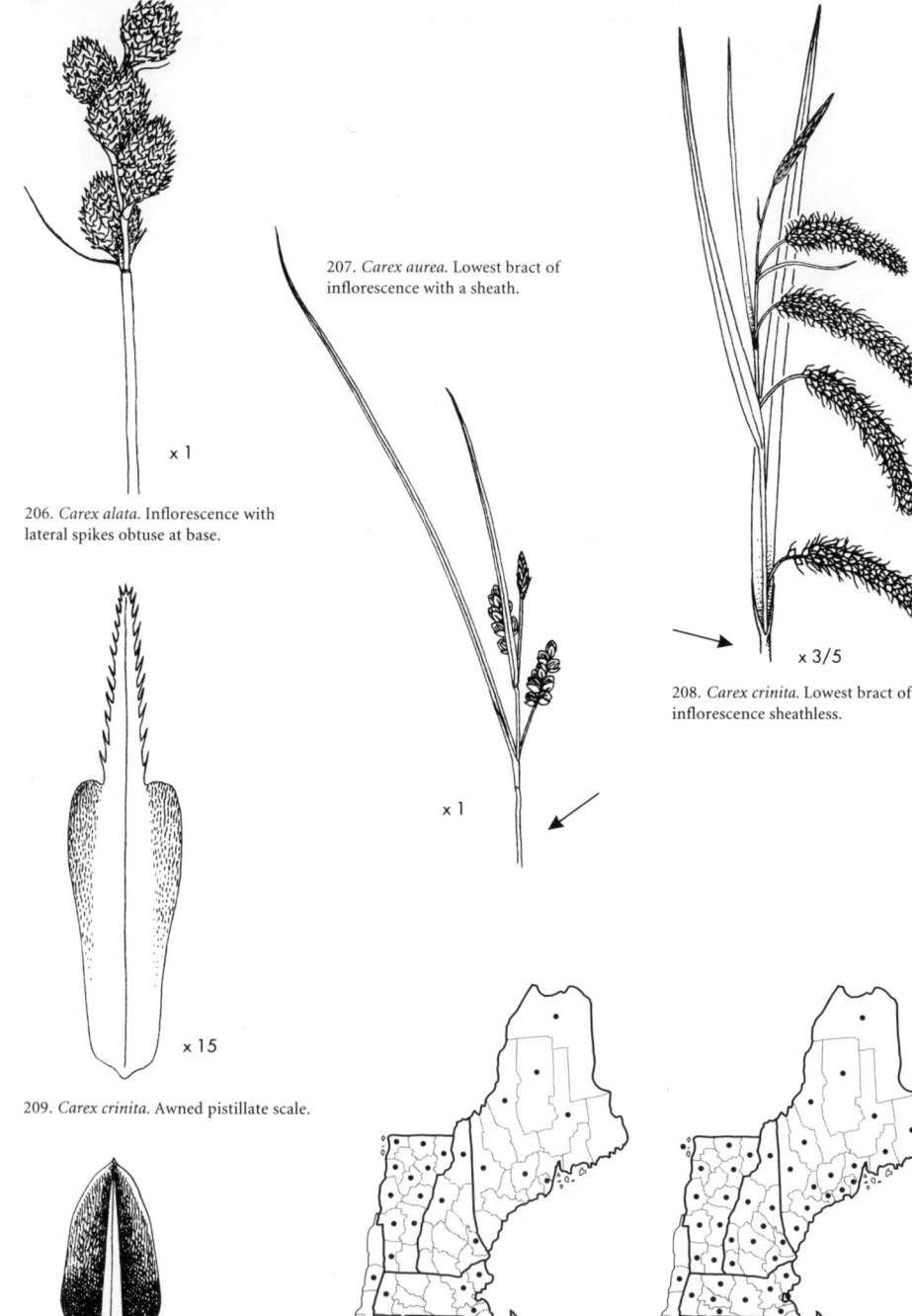

× 1

206. *Carex alata*. Inflorescence with
lateral spikes obtuse at base.

207. *Carex aurea*. Lowest bract of
inflorescence with a sheath.

× 1

× 3/5

208. *Carex crinita*. Lowest bract of
inflorescence sheathless.

× 15

209. *Carex crinita*. Awned pistillate scale.

× 8

210. *Carex haydenii*. Single perigynium
subtended by acuminate scale.

449. *Carex bebbii*

450. *Carex tenera*

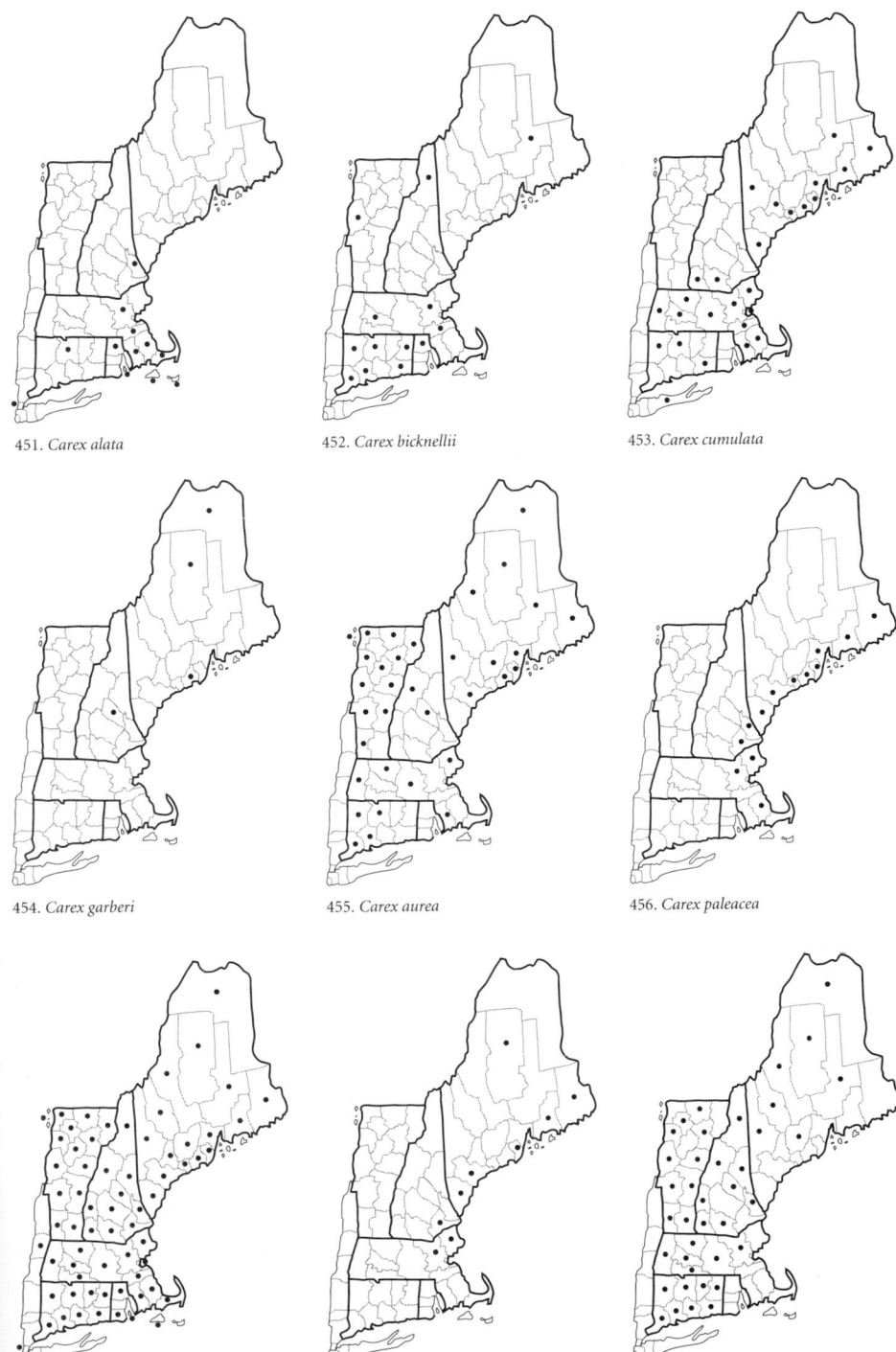

451. *Carex alata*

452. *Carex bicknellii*

453. *Carex cumulata*

454. *Carex garberi*

455. *Carex aurea*

456. *Carex paleacea*

457. *Carex crinita*

458. *Carex recta*

459. *Carex torta*

460. *Carex haydenii*   461. *Carex stricta*   462. *Carex lenticularis*

463. *Carex nigra*   464. *Carex aquatilis*   465. *Carex bigelowii*

78. C. aquátilis Wahlenb. (aquatic). Pond and river margins, wet meadows, marshes, often alpine. June-August. Map 464. (Arctic). [*C. substricta*]. Our plants are var. *aquatilis.* —OBL

79. C. bigelówii Torr. ex Schwein (for its discoverer). Alpine meadows and barrens. July-September. Map 465. (Europe). [*C. concolor*]. —FACW-

GROUP 7

a. Terminal spike gynaecandrous (pistillate flowers terminal, staminate basal).
 Pistillate spikes up to 1.5 cm long, closely flowered at the base. .... 80. *C. swanii*
 Pistillate spikes mostly longer than 1.5 cm, loosely flowered at the base. .... 81. *C. virescens*
a. Terminal spike androgenous (staminate flowers terminal, pistillate basal).
 b. Leaf sheaths and/or blades pubescent.
  Perigynia less than 5 mm long; sheath of bract subtending lowest spike
   absent or less than 5 mm long, the blade usually less than 3 times
   as long as the spike .... 82. *C. hirtifolia*
  Perigynia usually longer than 5 mm; sheath of lowest bract longer than
   5 mm, the blade usually more than 3 times as long as the spike. .... 83. *C. hirta*
 b. Leaf sheaths and blades glabrous.

c. Pistillate spikes globose or nearly so, more than 2 cm thick. .... 84. *C. grayi*
c. Pistillate spikes cylindric, less than 2 cm thick.
  d. Beak of perigynium firm, with well developed teeth, these mostly 0.5 mm
     long or longer. (Fig. 213).
    e. Bract at base of lowest spike with a sheath longer than 5 mm; style
      continuous with the achene, not jointed. (Fig. 211). .... 85. *C. trichocarpa*
    e. Bract at base of lowest spike sheathless or sheath shorter than 5 mm;
      style not continuous with achene, jointed at base. (Fig. 212).
      Perigynia up to 4.5 mm long, the nerves obscured by dense
        pubescence. .... 86. *C. lasiocarpa*
                                           var. *americana*
      Perigynia longer than 4.5 mm, the nerves plainly visible .... 87. *C. houghtoniana*
  d. Beak of perigynium entire or minutely toothed, the teeth inconspicuous,
     less than 0.5 mm long (beak splitting in some species in which case
     it is hyaline tipped). (Fig. 214).
    f. Bract subtending the lowest non-basal pistillate spike with a well
      developed, tubular sheath, this bladeless or with small, scale-like
      blade; staminate spike stalked .... 88. *C. richardsonii*
    f. Bract subtending lowest non-basal pistillate spike with sheath scarcely
      developed (except sometimes in *C. caryophyllea*), with distinct
      blades, or if bladeless staminate spike sessile or nearly so.
      g. Perigynia conspicuously and strongly several-many nerved.
        Pistillate spikes sessile or nearly so, ellipsoidal or short-cylindric,
          often staminate at tip; perigynia densely pubescent. .... 89. *C. vestita*
        Pistillate spikes, at least the lower, long-stalked, long-cylindric,
          not staminate at tip; perigynia scabrous-puberulent. .... 90. *C. scabrata*
      g. Perigynia nerveless, inconspicuously nerved, or 2-ribbed, but not
        strongly several-many nerved.
        h. Beak of perigynium shorter than 0.5 mm; lowest pistillate scales
          rough-awned; summit of achene with a distinct ring. .... 91. *C. caryophyllea*
        h. Beak of perigynium 0.5 mm long or longer; pistillate scales smooth;
          summit of achene lacking a ring.
          i. Some of the spikes terminating very short stems, crowded among
            the basal leaf sheaths and nearly obscured, others on
            elongate stems.
            j. Staminate spikes mostly 5 mm or less long; plant barely or
              not fibrillose at base; pistillate scales shorter than body
              of perigynium. .... 92. *C. deflexa*
            j. Staminate spikes mostly longer than 5 mm; plant strongly
              fibrillose at base, the fibers often in stiff tufts; pistillate
              scales longer than body of perigynium.
              Each stem producing a single peduncle bearing 2 or more
                spikes near the top. .... 93. *C. albicans*
              Each stem producing 2 or more peduncles, each bearing
                1 or 2 spikes. .... 6. *C. umbellata*
         i. Stems all elongate, none crowded among the basal leaf sheaths.
          k. Perigynium body subglobose, about as long as thick.
            Plant with long rhizomes; old leaf bases fibrillose; pistillate
              scales usually purplish .... 94. *C. pensylvanica*
            Plant without rhizomes or these very short; leaf bases not
              fibrillose; pistillate scales usually greenish .... 95. *C. communis*
          k. Perigynium body ellipsoid to obovoid, longer than thick.
           l. Pistillate scales shorter than body of perigynium.
             Pistillate scales with purple margins. .... 92. *C. deflexa*
             Pistillate scales with whitish margins. .... 93. *C. albicans*
           l. Pistillate scales at least as long as body of perigynium.
            Lowest pistillate spike sessile; lower pistillate spikes
             often overlapping; plant short-rhizomatous .... 95. *C. communis*
            Lowest pistillate spike short-peduncled; lower pistillate
             spikes remote; plant with long rhizomes .... 96. *C. novae-angliae*

80. *C. swánii* (Fern.) Mackenz. (for C. W. Swan). Dry deciduous woods, fields and pastures. June-July. Map 466. [*C. virescens* var. *minima*]. —FACU

81. *C. viréscens* Muhl. ex Willd. (greenish). Dry, rich deciduous woods and openings. June-August. Map 467.

82. *C. hirtifólia* Mackenzie (hairy leaved). Mixed mesic woods, thickets and meadows. May-July. Map 468.

C. x sullivántii Boott. A hybrid between *C. hirtifolia* and *C. gracillima.*

83. *C. hírta* L. (rough). Waste places, roadsides and dry fields. June-September. Map 469. (Naturalized from Europe).

84. *C. gráyi* Carey (for A. Gray). Wet meadows, wooded swamps, moist deciduous woods, alluvial woods. June-September. Map 470. —FACW+

85. *C. trichocárpa* Muhl. ex Willd. (hairy fruited). Wet meadows and marshes. June-August. Fig. 211, Map 471. —OBL

86. *C. lasiocárpa* Ehrh. Wet meadows, marshes, wooded swamps, bogs, wet woods, lake and river margins. June-August. Fig. 212, Map 472. [*C. lanuginosa*]. Represented with us as var. *americána* Fern. —OBL

C. lanuginósa Michx. Similar to *C. lasiocarpa* but with leaves flat, 2 mm or more wide (leaves involute-filiform, up to 2 mm wide in *C. lasiocarpa*). [*C. lasiocarpa* var. *latifolia*]. —OBL

87. *C. houghtoniána* Torr. ex Dewey (for its discoverer). Roadsides, waste areas, beaches and dunes in dry sandy or gravelly soil. June-August. Fig. 213, Map 473. [*C. houghtonii*].

88. *C. richardsónii* R. Br. (for its discoverer). Dry sandy or rocky deciduous or pine woods. May-June. Endangered in VT; reported for Bennington County.

C. brúnnea Thunb. (brown). Keying to *C. richardsonii* but distinguishable in having spikes all pistillate, usually with staminate tips and strongly ribbed perigynia (*C. richardsonii* has 2 or 3 pistillate spikes and a terminal staminate spike, perigynia not strongly ribbed). (Adventive from Asia, Malasia or Australia.) Reported for MA.

89. *C. vestíta* Willd. (clothed). Dry sandy deciduous woods and clearings, roadsides and waste areas. May-August. Map 474.

90. *C. scabráta* Schwein (rough). Moist deciduous woods, particularly along streams, wooded swamps and low, wet woods. June-August. Fig. 214, Map 475. —OBL

91. *C. caryophylléa* Lat. (leaf tufts resembling *Caryophyllus* or *Dianthus*). Dry meadows and roadsides. May-June. Map 476. (Naturalized from Europe).

C. flácca Schreb. Resembling *C. caryophyllea* but with perigynia minutely apiculate and achenes distinctly angled (perigynia beaked and achenes obscurely angled in *C. caryophyllea*). (Naturalized from Europe). Reported for Dutchess County NY. [*C. glauca*].

92. *C. defléxa* Hornem. (bent down). Moist deciduous woods and clearings. May-August. Map 477. (Greenland). (*C. peckii* and *C. nigromarginata* may sometimes key to *C. deflexa*; see descriptions under *C. albicans*).

93. *C. álbicans* Willd. ex Spreng. Dry, mixed deciduous woods and clearings. April-July. Map 478. [*C. artitecta; C. nigromarginata* var. *muhlenbergii; C. pensylvanica* var. *m.; C. varia*]. Our plants are var. *albicans.*

C. péckii Howe. Similar to *C. albicans* but with pistillate scales shorter than body of perigynium, or culms up to 2 dm tall, typically much shorter than the blades (pistillate scales about as long as body of perigynium and culms 2 dm or more tall, conspicuously longer than the blades in *C. albicans.*) [*C. albicans* var. *emmonsii; C. emmonsii; C. nigromarginata* vars. *elliptica* and *minor*].

C. nigromargináta Schw. Similar to *C. peckii* but pistillate scales usually dark purple except for narrow midnerve (pistillate scales green or with a purple band on either side of midnerve in *C. peckii*). Reported for CT.

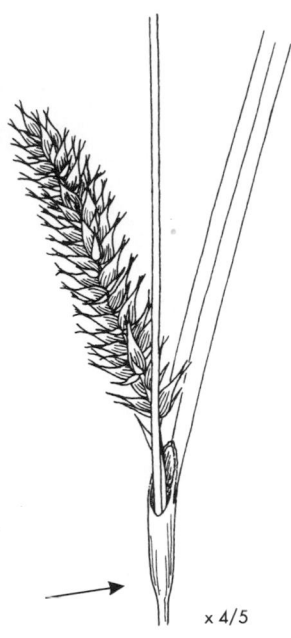

x 5

213. *Carex houghtoniana*. Single peryginium
showing beak with well developed teeth.

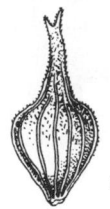

x 4-1/2

214. *Carex scabrata*. Single peryginium
showing beak with minute teeth.

x 4/5

211. *Carex trichocarpa*. Bract at base
of lowest spike with a sheath.

x 3/4

212. *Carex lasiocarpa* var. *americana*.
Bract at base of lowest spike sheathless.

466. *Carex swanii*

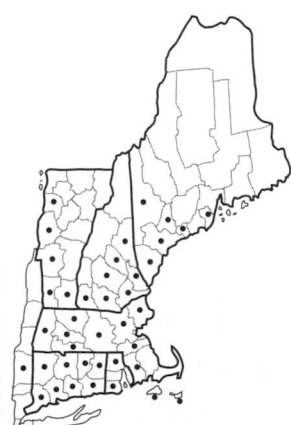

467. *Carex virescens*

468. *Carex hirtifolia*

469. *Carex hirta*

470. *Carex grayi*

471. *Carex trichocarpa*

472. *Carex lasiocarpa* var. *americana*

473. *Carex houghtoniana*

474. *Carex vestita*

475. *Carex scabrata*

476. *Carex caryophyllea*

477. *Carex deflexa*

478. *Carex albicans*

94. *C. pensylvánica* Lam. Dry to rich open deciduous or pine woods, open dry soil. April-June. Map 479. Our plants are var. *pensylvanica*.

C. lucórum Willd ex Link. Similar to *C. pensylvanica* but with perigynia 3-4 mm long, the beak two-fifths to two-thirds as long as the body (perigynia up to 3 mm long, beak up to two-fifths as long as the body in *C. pensylvanica*). [*C. pensylvanica* var. *distans*]. Our plants are var. *lucorum*.

C. ínops Bailey. Similar to the latter 2 species but with perigynia 1.5-2 mm in diameter, suborbicular (perigynia 1-1.5 mm in diameter, obtusely triangular in *C. pensylvanica* and *C. lucorum*). From farther west. Reported for MA, ME, NH. Represented with us as subsp. *heliophila* (Mackenzie) Crins [*C. heliophila; C. pensylvanica* var. *digyna*].

95. *C. commúnis* Bailey (growing in colonies). Dry to moist open deciduous woods and clearings. May-July. Map 480.

96. *C. nóvae-ángliae* Schwein (of New England). Moist deciduous woods. June-August. Map 481. —FACU

GROUP 8

a. Terminal spike gynaecandrous (pistillate flowers terminal, staminate basal or scattered). (Fig. 215).
  b. Bract subtending the lowest pistillate spike with a sheath more than 3 mm long.
    c. Perigynium up to 3.5 mm long.
      Perigynium beakless; spikes densely flowered. .... 97. *C. aestivalis*
      Perigynium short-beaked; at least the lower spikes loosely flowered. .... 98. *C. x aestivaliformis*
    c. Perigynium longer than 3.5 mm.
      Pistillate scales prominently awned .... 99. *C. davisii*
      Pistillate scales obtuse, acute, or short-cuspidate, but not awned. .... 100. *C. formosa*
  b. Bract subtending lowest pistillate spike sheathless, or sheath less than 3 mm long.
    Perigynium flattened, much wider than thick. .... 101. *C. hirsutella*
    Perigynium turgid, nearly or quite as thick as wide, nearly round in cross section .... 102. *C. bushii*
a. Terminal spike androgenous (staminate flowers terminal, pistillate basal) or staminate. (Fig. 216).
  d. Perigynia conspicuously 2-toothed, the teeth 1 mm long or longer. .... 103. *C. atherodes*
  d. Perigynia not 2-toothed, or if so, the teeth inconspicuous, less than 0.5 mm long.
    e. Pistillate spikes drooping on thread-like peduncles; perigynium with a beak at least half as long as the body, the beak with 2 minute teeth. .... 104. *C. castanea*
    e. Pistillate spikes erect; perigynium with a beak less than half as long as the body, the beak entire.
      Bract subtending lowest pistillate spike sheathless, or sheath less than 3 mm long .... 105. *C. pallescens*
      Bract subtending lowest pistillate spike with a sheath longer than 3 mm. .... 106. *C. hitchcockiana*

97. *C. aestivális* M. A. Curtis ex Gray (of summer). Deciduous mountain woods and rocky wooded slopes. June-August. Map 482.

98. *C. x aestivalifórmis* Mackenzie (resembling *C. aestivalis*). Alpine meadows. June-July. A hybrid between *C. aestivalis* and *C. gracillima*. [*C. aestivaliformis*].

99. *C. davísii* Schwein & Torr. (for E. Davis). Rich, often calcareous deciduous woods, meadows and river shores. May-July. Map 483. Endangered in MA, CT. —FAC-

100. *C. formósa* Dewey (handsome). Rich, moist, often calcareous deciduous woods and meadows. May-July. Map 484. —FAC

101. *C. hirsutélla* Mackenzie. Dry to moist, sandy alluvial woods, upland deciduous woods, wooded swamps and fields. May-July. Fig. 215, Map 485. Endangered in NH. [*C. complanata* var. *hirsuta*]. —FACU

102. *C. búshii* Mackenzie. Moist, open deciduous woods and fields. May-July. Map 486. Endangered in MA. —FACW

103. *C. atheródes* Spreng. (resembling an ear of wheat). Marshes, wet meadows, bogs and river and lake shores, often in shallow water. June-August. (Eurasia). Reported for Knox County ME. —OBL

104. *C. castánea* Wahlenb. (chestnut colored). Margins of streams and ponds, bogs, wet meadows and wet woods. June-July. Map 487. Endangered in MA, NH. —OBL

105. *C. palléscens* L. (rather pale). Dry to moist meadows and fields. May-August. Fig. 216, Map 488.

106. *C. hitchcockiána* Dewey (for E. Hitchcock). Rich, moist deciduous woods. May-July. Map 489.

GROUP 9

a. Body of perigynium globose, abruptly contracted to a beak as long as the body.
      (Fig. 217) .... 107. *C. sprengellii*
a. Body of perigynium ovoid to lanceolate or obovoid, gradually tapering to the beak.
   b. Perigynia subulate to slenderly lanceolate, very gradually tapered to beak. (Fig. 218).
      c. Perigynia horizontal to reflexed, teeth of beak reflexed. .... 108. *C. collinsii*
      c. Perigynia spreading to ascending, teeth of beak erect or ascending. (Fig. 219).
         Leaf blades wider than 4 mm; summits of bract sheaths prolonged;
            pistillate scales awned .... 109. *C. folliculata*
         Leaf blades up to 4 mm wide; summits of bract sheaths concave;
            pistillate scales acute to acuminate but not awned. .... 110. *C. michauxiana*
   b. Perigynia broadly lanceolate to broadly ovoid, more abruptly contracted to
      beak (if doubtful perigynia less than 8 mm long or inflated; perigynia are
      8 mm or longer and scarcely inflated in the above 3 species). (Fig. 220).
   d. Perigynia with fewer than 12 conspicuous nerves.
      e. Pistillate scales with scabrous awns longer than the body. (Fig. 221).
         Staminate scales with long, rough awns. .... 111. *C. lurida*
         Staminate scales acuminate, smooth .... 112. *C. schweinitzii*
      e. Pistillate scales acute or acuminate to cuspidate, the awn, if present
         shorter than body and smooth.
         f. Achene deeply indented in the middle of one angle. .... 113. *C. tuckermanii*
         f. Achene not deeply indented on any of the angles, symmetrical.
            g. Beak of perigynium scabrous on the edges. .... 114. *C. bullata*
            g. Beak of perigynium smooth.
               h. Perigynia ascending at maturity; stems slender. .... 115. *C. vesicaria*
               h. Perigynia horizontally spreading to reflexed at maturity; stems
                  stout, especially at base.
                  Bract of lowest pistillate spike less than twice as long as
                     inflorescence; leaves septate-nodulose; perigynia
                     horizontally spreading to ascending. .... 116. *C. rostrata*
                  Bract of lowest pistillate spike more than twice as long as
                     inflorescence; leaves not septate-nodulose; perigynia
                     horizontally spreading to reflexed. .... 117. *C. retrorsa*
   d. Perigynia with 12 or more conspicuous nerves.
      i. Perigynia with lacerate, winged margins. .... 118. *C. kobomugi*
      i. Perigynia not wing margined.
         j. Pistillate spikes up to 1 cm thick; teeth of perigynium blunt; style
            jointed at the base, not persistent. (Fig. 222). .... 119. *C. striata*
                                                                                                              var. *brevis*
         j. Pistillate spikes 1 cm or more thick (if narrower, perigynia reflexed;
            ascending in *C. striata* var. *brevis*); teeth of perigynium sharp;
            style not jointed at base, persistent. (Fig. 223).
            k. Staminate spikes 2 or more to a stem; leaf sheaths conspicuously
               fibrillose on the inner side .... 120. *C. lacustris*
            k. Staminate spike 1 to a stem; leaf sheaths not fibrillose.
               l. Perigynia less than 1 cm long, less than 3 mm wide, scarcely inflated.
                  m. Mature perigynia spreading to ascending. .... 121. *C. hystericina*
                  m. Mature perigynia reflexed.

Teeth of perigynium beak 1.2 mm or more long,
  arched-divergent. .... 122. *C. comosa*
Teeth of perigynium beak 1 mm or less long, straight, erect. .... 123. *C. pseudocyperus*
l. Perigynia 1 cm long or longer, 3 mm wide or wider, much inflated.
  n. Pistillate spikes globose or subglobose, the perigynia on a
    shortened axis; style straight or slightly curved.
    Perigynia narrowed at the base, dull, radiating in all
      directions. .... 84.*C. grayi*
    Perigynia rounded at the base, lustrous, spreading to
      ascending .... 124. *C. intumescens*
  n. Pistillate spikes thick-cylindric, the perigynia along an elongate
    axis; style contorted near base.
    Achene as wide as long or wider, each angle with a prominent
      tubercle. .... 125. *C. lupuliformis*
    Achene longer than wide, the angles not prominently
      tubercled. .... 126. *C. lupulina*

107. *C. sprengéllii* Dewey ex Spreng. (for K. Sprengel). River thickets, woods and banks, meadows, and rocky open deciduous woods. May-July. Fig. 217, Map 490. Endangered in ME. [*C. longirostris*]. —FACU

108. *C. collínsii* Nutt. (for Z. Collins). Bogs and wooded swamps, particularly *Chamaecyparis* swamps, mostly near the coast. June-September. Fig. 218. Endangered in R.I. Reported for Middlesex County CT, Washington County RI. —OBL

109. *C. folliculáta* L. (bearing follicles). Deciduous and coniferous wooded swamps, wet woods, streamsides and bogs. June-August. Fig. 219, Map 491. Our plants are var. *folliculata*. —OBL

110. *C. michauxiána* Boeckl. (for A. Michaux). Bogs, pond margins and wet meadows, often in alpine areas. June-August. Map 492. (E. Asia). Endangered in MA. —OBL

111. *C. lúrida* Wahlenb. (sallow). Wet meadows, wooded swamps and wet woods. June-October. Figs. 220 and 221, Map 493. —OBL

112. *C. schweinítzii* Dewey ex Schwein. (for L. D. de Schweinitz). Deciduous and coniferous calcareous swamps, wet woods and wet meadows. June-August. Map 494. Endangered in MA. —OBL

113. *C. tuckermánii* Dewey (for E. Tuckerman). Deciduous swamps and wet meadows. June-August. Map 495. Endangered in MA. —OBL

114. *C. bulláta* Schkuhr. ex Willd. (inflated). Wooded swamps, bogs and wet meadows, mostly near the coast. June-September. Map 496. —OBL

C. x ólneyi Boott. A hybrid between *C. bullata* and *C. rostrata*.

115. *C. vesicária* L. (bladdery). Wet meadows, marshes, bogs, pond margins and wooded swamps. June-August. Map 497. (Eurasia). Our plants include var. *vesicaria* and the following vars., the first 3 distinguishable in having perigynia with subglobose to ovoid bodies, abruptly beaked (perigynia ovoid-conical, gradually tapered to beak in var. *vesicaria*).

var. *moníle* (Tuckerm.) Fern. Pistillate spikes 2 or 3, to 7.5 cm long.

var. *disténta* Fries. Pistillate spikes 1 or 2, to 2.5 cm long.

var. *jejúna* Fern. Pistillate spikes less than 1 cm thick, perigynia to 5 mm long (pistillate spikes 1 cm or more thick and perigynia 5 mm or longer in the latter 2 vars.).

var. *raeána* (Boott) Fern. Perigynia not or only slightly inflated, lanceolate, 2 mm or less thick (perigynia strongly inflated, ovoid to globose, 2 mm or more thick in the above vars.). —OBL

116. *C. rostráta* Stokes (beaked). Wet meadows, marshes, bogs and wooded swamps. July-September. Map 498. (Eurasia). [*C. utriculata*]. —OBL

C. utriculáta Boott. Similar to *C. rostrata* but with pistillate scales tapering to an acuminate tip (pistillate scales obtuse to acute, not prolonged at tip in *C. rostrata*). [*C. rostrata* var. *utriculata*]. —OBL

215. *Carex hirsutella.*
Terminal spike showing
gynaecandrous condition.

x 1

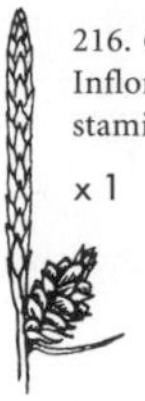

216. *Carex pallescens.*
Inflorescence with
staminate terminal spike.

x 1

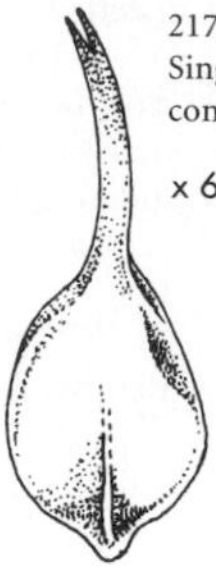

217. *Carex sprengellii.*
Single perigynium abruptly
contracted to beak.

x 6

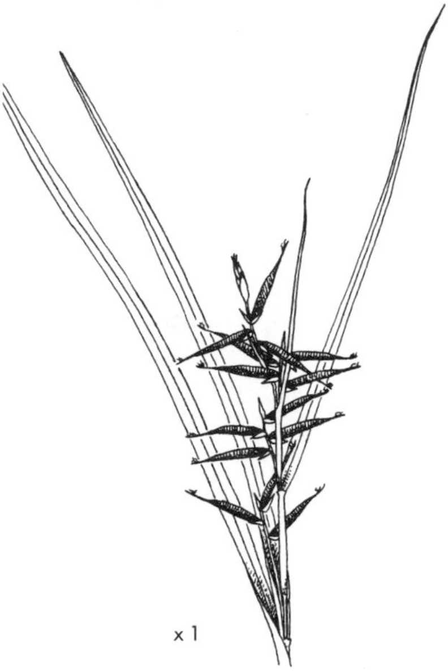

x 1

218. *Carex collinsii.*Perigynia
horizontal, gradually tapered.

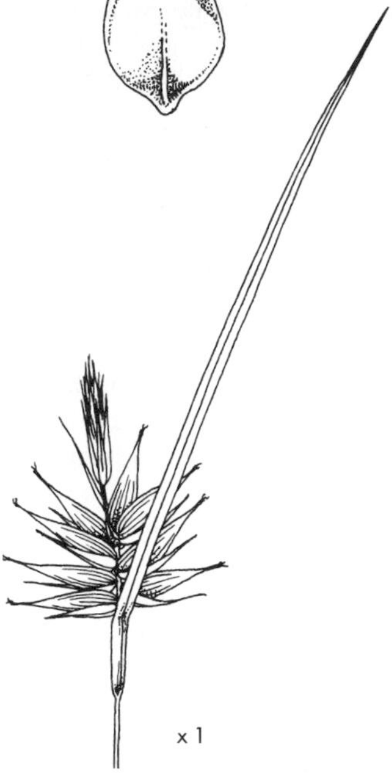

x 1

219 *Carex folliculata.*
Perigynia ascending.

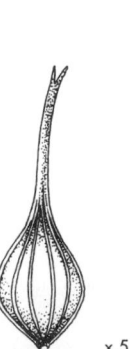

x 5

220. *Carex lurida.*Single perigynium
abruptly contracted to beak.

x 9

221. *Carex lurida.* Single pistillate scale
with scabrous awn longer than the body.

479. *Carex pensylvanica*

480. *Carex communis*

481. *Carex novae-angliae*

482. *Carex aestivalis*

483. *Carex davisii*

484. *Carex formosa*

485. *Carex hirsutella*

486. *Carex bushii*

487. *Carex castanea*

488. *Carex pallescens*

489. *Carex hitchcockiana*

490. *Carex sprengellii*

491. *Carex folliculata*

492. *Carex michauxiana*

493. *Carex lurida*

494. *Carex schweinitzii*

495. *Carex tuckermanii*

496. *Carex bullata*

497. *Carex vesicaria*

117. *C. retrórsa* Schwein (turned backward). Wet meadows, wooded swamps and wet woods. July-September. Map 499. —FACW+

C. x hártii Dew. A hybrid between *C. retrorsa* and *C. lurida.*

118. *C. kobomúgi* Ohwi (Japanese). Coastal sands. May-July. (Naturalized from Asia).

119. *C. striáta* Bailey. Pond margins. May-August. Fig. 222. Endangered in RI, MA; reported for Nantucket and Plymouth Counties MA. [*C. walteriana* var. *brevis*]. Represented with us as var. *brévis* Bailey. —OBL

120. *C. lacústris* Willd. (of lake margins). Deciduous and cedar swamps, bogs. May-August. Fig. 223, Map 500. —OBL

121. *C. hystericína* Muhl. ex Willd. (porcupine-like). Wet meadows, marshes, deciduous swamps, wet woods, and river margins. June-August. Map 501. [*C. hystricina*]. —OBL

122. *C. comósa* Boott (bearded). Pond margins, wet meadows and deciduous or cedar swamps. June-September. Map 502. —OBL

123. *C. pseudocyperus* L. (false Cyperus). Wooded swamps and bogs. June-August. Map 503. (Eurasia and N. Africa). Endangered in CT. —OBL

124. *C. intuméscens* Rudge (swollen). Wet meadows, wet deciduous woods and pond margins. May-September. Map 504. —FACW+

125. *C. lupulifórmis* Sartwell ex Dewey (with form of *C. lupulina*). Wooded swamps and wet woods (often calcareous). July-September. Map 505. —FACW+

126. *C. lupulína* Muhl. ex Willd. (hop like). Wet meadows, marshes, pond margins, wooded swamps and wet woods. June-September. Map 506. —OBL

GROUP 10

a. Sheaths subtending the non-basal pistillate spikes bladeless, or with a scale-like
    blade shorter than the sheath or not over 1.5 cm long. (Fig. 224).
    Leaf blades 1 cm or more wide .... 127. *C. plantaginea*
    Leaf blades not over .5 cm wide.
        Leaf blades mostly involute, less than 1 mm wide; perigynia less than
            2.5 mm long .... 128. *C. eburnea*
        Leaf blades flat, 2 mm or more wide; perigynia more than 2.5 mm long. .... 129. *C. pedunculata*
a. Sheaths subtending non-basal pistillate spikes bearing well developed blades longer
    than the sheath or longer than 1.5 cm.
  b. Pistillate spikes spreading or drooping on long, capillary peduncles. (Fig. 225).
    c. Perigynia beakless, obtuse or rounded at tip. (Fig. 226). .... 130. *C. gracillima*
    c. Perigynia gradually or abruptly narrowed to a beak. (Fig. 227).
      d. Pistillate spikes usually not over 1.5 cm long; stems drab or brown at base. .... 131. *C. capillaris*
      d. Pistillate spikes longer than 1.5 cm; stems reddish-tinged at base.
        e. Beak of perigynium about as long as the body. .... 132. *C. sylvatica*
        e. Beak of perigynium much shorter than the body.
          f. Achene sessile .... 133. *C. arctata*
          f. Achene stipitate.
            Perigynia with numerous strong nerves from base to tip; pistillate
              spike densely flowered .... 134. *C. venusta*
            Perigynia with 2 or 3 strong nerves from base to tip and several
              faint nerves at the base; pistillate spike loosely flowered. .... 135. *C. debilis*
  b. Pistillate spikes erect or ascending (if drooping on capillary peduncles stems not
    reddish tinged at base and perigynia distinctly many nerved; stems reddish
    tinged at base or perigynia with only 2 or 3 distinct nerves in the above
    6 species).
    g. Perigynia strongly divergent to reflexed. (Fig. 229).
      h. Leaves involute; sheaths red-dotted on ventral side; perigynia divergent to
        ascending, not yellowish .... 136. *C. extensa*
      h. Leaves flat; ventral side of sheaths not red-dotted; perigynia divergent to
        reflexed, yellowish.

    Perigynia longer than 3 mm; achene occupying only the lower half of the
      perigynium .... 137. *C. flava*
    Perigynia 3 mm long or shorter (rarely longer); achene filling the
      perigynium nearly to the tip .... 138. *C. viridula*
g. Perigynia ascending or not strongly divergent. (Fig. 230).
  i. Plant arising from elongate rhizomes; perigynia with a few strong nerves,
    otherwise faintly or obscurely nerved (often conspicuously nerved in
    C. crawii and *C. tetanica*).
    j. Perigynia with a distinct beak 1/4 or more the length of the body.
      Basal leaves with well developed blades; pistillate spikes loosely
        flowered, the perigynia mostly in 2 rows; pistillate scales
        mostly acute. .... 19. *C. vaginata*
      Basal leaves bladeless or with rudimentary blades; pistillate spikes
        densely flowered, the perigynia in 3 or more rows; pistillate
        scales mostly obtuse. .... 140. *C. polymorpha*
    j. Perigynia beakless, or beak very short, less than 1/4 the length of the body.
      k. Perigynia oblong-ovoid, rounded at the base.
        Perigynia usually covered with reddish resinous dots. .... 141. *C. crawii*
        Perigynia without resinous dots .... 142. *C. panicea*
      k. Perigynia fusiform, narrowed at the base.
        Leaves whitish-glaucous, involute or folded; perigynia with a few
          strong nerves, otherwise faintly nerved .... 143. *C. livida*
                                        var. *radicaulis*

        Leaves green, flat or becoming revolute; perigynia with many
          strong nerves. .... 144. *C. tetanica*
  i. Plant cespitose; perigynia with numerous conspicuous nerves
    (few in *C. leptonervia*).
    l. Perigynia rounded at the base, not tightly filled to the tip by the achene,
      the upper 1/4 to 1/3 empty. (Fig. 231).
      m. Peduncles of pistillate spikes scabrous. .... 145. *C. conoidea*
      m. Peduncles of pistillate spikes smooth.
        n. Perigynium with a short but distinct beak, strongly nerved. .... 146. *C. granularis*
        n. Perigynium beakless, at most acute or pointed, finely many striate.
          o. Lowest pistillate scales much shorter than the perigynia, acute to
            cuspidate or very short awned .... 147. *C. flaccosperma*
          o. Lowest pistillate scales usually exceeding perigynia, with awns as
            long or longer than the body .... 148. *C. amphibola*
    l. Perigynia tapered to the base, tightly filled nearly to the tip by the achene
      (except in *C. extensa* in which perigynium beak is .5 mm long or
      longer; perigynium beakless or beak less than .5 mm in the above
      4 species). (Fig. 228).
      p. Pistillate spikes subglobose to thick- cylindric, densely flowered,
        the upper approximate, sessile, sheathless; leaves involute. .... 136. *C. extensa*
      p. Pistillate spikes linear-cylindric to oblong, mostly loosely flowered,
        all spikes usually separated, stalked, sheathing (if 1 or more of
        these distinctions doubtful, plant lacking the above combination
        of characters); leaves flat.
        q. Awns of the pistillate scales rough; nerves of perigynia impressed,
          the surface appearing longitudinally wrinkled. .... 149. *C. oligocarpa*
        q. Awns of the pistillate scales smooth or absent (often rough in
          C. laxiflora with most of the pistillate scales obtuse or truncate;
          pistillate scales mostly tapered to the awn in *C. oligocarpa*):
          nerves of perigynia elevated.
          r. Perigynia obtusely triangular (with rounded angles); most of the
            pistillate scales obtuse or truncate, usually awned or
            cuspidate. (Fig. 232).
            Perigynia with 2 or 3 distinct nerves, otherwise nerveless
              or obscurely nerved .... 150. *C. leptonervia*
            Perigynia with numerous distinct nerves. .... 151. *C. laxiflora*

r. Perigynia acutely triangular (with sharp angles); most of the
    pistillate scales acute or acuminate, awned or awnless.
    (Fig. 233).
s. Leaves of the sterile and fertile stems distinctly unlike in
    size, the sterile 1 cm or more wide, the fertile less than
    5 mm wide; blade of lowest bract up to 4 times the
    length of its sheath. .... 152. *C. platyphylla*
s. Leaves of the sterile and fertile stems similar in width, or the
    latter only moderately narrower; lowest bract many times
    the length of its sheath.
    t. Perigynia elliptic-fusiform, tapering to both ends, with a
        beak 1 mm or more long, broadest at the middle .... 153. *C. styloflexa*
    t. Perigynia obovoid, beakless or beak shorter than 1 mm,
        broadest above the middle.
        u. At least the lower peduncles long and drooping, longer
            than their sheaths; staminate spike usually peduncled.
            Leaves up to 5 mm wide; pistillate spikes without
            staminate flowers at the base .... 154. *C. digitalis*
            Leaves wider than 6 mm; pistillate spikes with 2 or 3
            staminate flowers at the base .... 155. *C. laxiculmis*
        u. Peduncles not long and drooping, mostly shorter than
            their sheaths; staminate spike sessile or nearly so. .... 156. *C. abscondita*

127. *C. plantagínea* Lam. (plantain-like). Rich, moist deciduous woods. April-June. Fig. 224, Map 507.

128. *C. ebúrnea* Boott ex Hook (like ivory). Dry sandy or gravelly calcareous soil and cliffs, in the open or in thin, deciduous woods. May-August. Map 508. —FACU

129. *C. pedunculáta* Muhl. ex Willd. (peduncled). Rich damp or dry, often calcareous deciduous woods. April-May. Map 509.

130. *C. gracíllima* Schwein (very slender). Moist deciduous woods and meadows, occasionally wooded swamps, roadsides. May-July. Figs. 225 and 226, Map 510. —FACU

131. *C. capilláris* L. (hair-like). Alpine regions. July-August. Map 511. (Eurasia). —FACW

132. *C. sylvática* Huds. (of woods). Deciduous woods. (Naturalized from Europe).

133. *C. arctáta* Boott ex Hook. (contracted). Moist rich deciduous or mixed woods. June-August. Fig. 227, Map 512.

C. x knieskérnii Dew. A hybrid between *C. arctata* and *C. castanea*.

134. *C. venústa* Dewey (pleasing, graceful). Bogs, wooded swamps and wet woods. May-July. [*C. oblita*]. Represented with us as var. *mínor* Boeckl. —OBL

135. *C. débilis* Michx. (weak). Wooded swamps, moist to wet deciduous woods, occasionally in bogs. May-August. Map 513. Our plants include var. *debilis* and the following vars.:

var. *rúdgei* Bailey. Perigynia averaging 6 mm in length, broadest at or near the middle (perigynia averaging 7 mm in length, broadest below the middle in var. *debilis*). [*C. flexuosa*].

var. *stríctior* Bailey. Similar to the last var. but with basal leaves 4 mm or more broad; perigynia about a third longer than the scales (basal leaves 4 mm or less broad; perigynia about twice as long as the scales in var. *rudgei*). —FAC

136. *C. exténsa* Goodenough (stretched out). Coastal sands and borders of salt marshes. June-August. Fig. 228. (Naturalized from Europe). —OBL

137. *C. fláva* L. (yellowish). Wet meadows, bogs and pond margins. June-September. Fig. 229, Map 514. (Europe). [*C. laxior*]. —OBL

138. *C. virídula* Michx. (greenish). Boggy, gravelly or muddy, often calcareous pond margins and springy areas. June-September. Map 515. Endangered in CT. [*C. chlorophila; C. demissa; C. oederi; C. serotina*]. Represented with us as subsp. *viridula*.

subsp. *oedocarpa* has also been attributed to our range. —OBL

222. *Carex striata* var. *brevis.*
Single perigynium; teeth blunt.

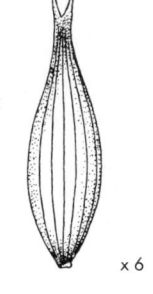

223. *Carex lacustris.* Single
perigynium; teeth sharp.

226. *Carex gracillima.* Single
perigynium; beakless.

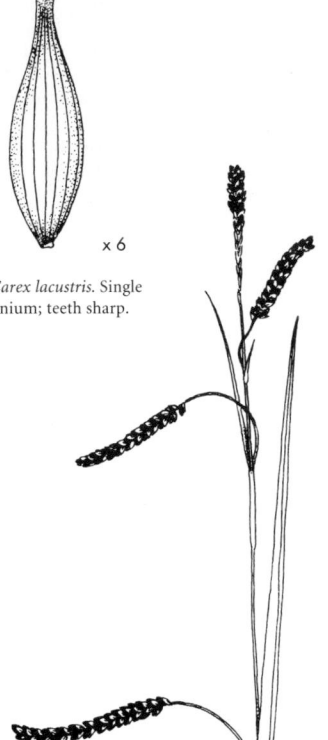

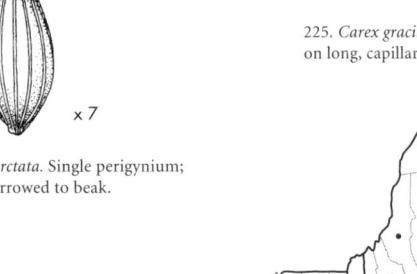

224. *Carex plantaginea.* Sheaths subtending
pistillate spikes with short scale-like blades.

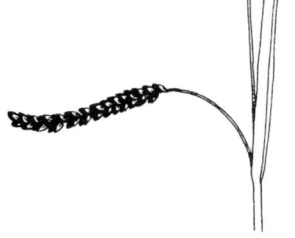

225. *Carex gracillima.* Pistillate spikes drooping
on long, capillary peduncles.

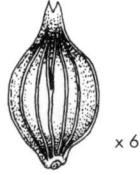

227. *Carex arctata.* Single perigynium;
gradually narrowed to beak.

228. *Carex extensa.* Single
perigynium; tapered to base.

498. *Carex rostrata*

499. *Carex retrorsa*

500. *Carex lacustris*

501. *Carex hystericina*

502. *Carex comosa*

503. *Carex pseudocyperus*

504. *Carex intumescens*

505. *Carex lupuliformis*

506. *Carex lupulina*

507. *Carex plantaginea*

508. *Carex eburnea*

509. *Carex pedunculata*

510. *Carex gracillima*

511. *Carex capillaris*

512. *Carex arctata*

513. *Carex debilis*

514. *Carex flava*

515. *Carex viridula*

516. *Carex vaginata*

517. *Carex polymorpha*

C. hostiána DC. Similar to *C. flava* and *C. viridula* but with all bracts long-sheathed; achenes about 2 mm long and 1.4 mm or more broad (only the lowest bract sheathed, the others sheathless or nearly so; achenes up to 1.8 mm long and 1.4 mm broad in the latter 2 species). Reported for MA. —OBL

139. *C. vagináta* Tausch (sheathed). Bogs, *Thuja* swamps, wet woods, usually calcareous. June-August. Fig. 230, Map 516. (Eurasia). Endangered in VT. [*C. saltuensis*]. —OBL

140. *C. polymórpha* Muhl. (of many forms). Dry open woods. June-August. Map 517. Endangered in MA, RI, CT. —FACU

141. *C. cráwei* Dewey (for its discoverer). Lake shores, wet meadows and ledges, in calcareous soil. May-July. Endangered in CT. Reported for Litchfield County CT, Aroostook County ME. —FACW

142. *C. panícea* L. (like Millet). Fields, meadows and lawns. May-July. Map 518. (Naturalized from Europe).

143. *C. lívida* (Wahlenb.) Willd. (pale lead colored). Bogs and wet meadows, usually calcareous. May-July. Map 519. (N. Europe). Represented with us as var. *radicaúlis* Paine [*C. livida* var. *grayána*]. —OBL

C. flácca Schreb. Similar to *C. livida* and *C. panicea* but distinguishable in having peduncled pistillate spikes, at least the lower somewhat drooping (spikes sessile to short peduncled and erect in the latter two species). (Naturalized from Europe). Reported for Dutchess County NY. [*C. glauca*].

144. *C. tetánica* Schk. (rigid). Meadows, moist to wet woods and bogs, usually calcareous. May-July. Map 520. —FACW

C. woódii Dewey. Lower sheaths purple, bladeless, pistillate spikes loosely flowered, at least at the base (lower sheaths green, blade-bearing; pistillate spikes densely flowered in *C. tetanica*). [*C. colorata; C. tetanica* var. *woodii*]. —FACW

C. meádii Dewey. Resembling *C. tetanica* but distinguishable from it and *C. woodii* in having pistillate spikes 5 mm or more thick with 5 or 6 rows of perigynia (spikes 5 mm or less thick and perigynia in 3 or 4 rows in the latter 2 species). Reported for RI. [*C. tetanica* var. *meadii*]. —FAC

145. *C. conoídea* Schkuhr ex Willd. (cone shaped). Wet or dry meadows, pond margins, pastures and abandoned fields. May-July. Fig. 231, Map 521. [*C. katahdinensis*]. —FACU

146. *C. granuláris* Muhl. ex Willd. (granular). Damp or rich deciduous woods, meadows and pastures, often calcareous. May-July. Map 522. [*C. rectior; C. shriveri*]. Our plants include var. *granularis* and the following var.:

var. *haleána* (Olney) Porter. Perigynia up to 1.5 mm thick (1.5 mm or more thick in var. *granularis*). [*C. haleana*]. —FACW+

147. *C. flaccospérma* Dewey. Rich deciduous woods and meadows. May-July. Map 523. Endangered in MA, NH. [*C. glaucodea*]. Represented with us as var. *glaucòidea* (Tuckerman ex Olney) Kukenth. —FAC

148. *C. amphíbola* Steud. (ambiguous). Alluvial woods, mixed woods, fields, wooded swamps. May-June. Map 524. Represented with us by the following vars.:

var. *túrgida* Fern. Perigynia inflated when mature, obscurely angled, rounded at base and tip. [*C. bulbostylis; C. corrugata; C. grisea*].

var. *rígida* (Bailey) Fern. Perigynia scarcely inflated, obtusely angled, slightly tapering to base and tip. —FAC

149. *C. oligocárpa* Schkuhr ex Willd. (few fruited). Rich deciduous woods. May-July. Map 525, Endangered in VT, CT.

150. *C. leptonérvia* (Fern.) Fern. (finely nerved). Damp woods, rich deciduous woods, pond margins, dry open ground. May-July. Map 526. —FACW

151. *C. laxiflóra* Lam. (loosely flowered). Rich deciduous woods. April-June. Fig. 232, Map 527. Our plants include var. *laxiflora* and the following var.:

var. *serruláta* F. J. Herm. Sheaths of bracts with serrulate angles (sheaths smooth or with irregularly cut or toothed angles in var. *laxiflora*). —FACU

The following complex of species resemble *C. laxiflora* and are distinguishable on minor differences.

C. albursína Sheldon. Pistillate scales obtuse, awnless (most of the pistillate scales awned or cuspidate in *C. laxiflora*). [*C. laxiflora* var. *latifolia*].

C. ormostáchya Wieg. Perigynium abruptly contracted to a short beak (gradually tapered to a longer beak in *C. laxiflora*). [*C. laxiflora* var. *ormostachya*].

C. blánda Dewey. Resembling *C. ormostachya* and distinguished from it by having densely flowered pistillate spikes. [*C. laxiflora* var. *blanda*]. —FAC

C. graciléscens Steud. Staminate spike long peduncled (short peduncled or sessile in the above 4 species). Endangered in MA. [*C. laxiflora* var. *gracillima*].

C. striátula Michx. Resembling *C. gracilescens* and distinguished from it by sterile shoots forming only tufts of leaves and fertile stems being greenish or brownish at base (sterile shoots forming stems and fertile stems purplish at base in *C. gracilescens*). Reported for CT. [*C. laxiflora* var. *angustifolia*].

152. *C. platyphýlla* Carey (broad leaved). Rich deciduous woods. May-June. Fig. 233, Map 528.

153. *C. stylofléxa* Buckl. (with curved style). Wet woods and bogs. May-June. Map 529. —FACW-

154. *C. digitális* Willd. (of a finger). Dry deciduous or mixed woods. May-July. Map 530.

155. *C. laxicúlmis* Schwein. (loose stemmed). Rich, deciduous, usually calcareous woods. May-June. Map 531. Endangered in ME. Our plants include var. *laxiculmis* and the following var.:

var. *copuláta* (Bailey) Fern. An apparent hybrid between *C. laxiculmis* and *C. digitalis*. [*C. copulata*].

156. *C. abscondíta* Mackenzie (concealed). Damp to dry rich, deciduous woods, alluvial woods. June-July. Map 532. [*C. ptychocarpa*]. —FAC

GROUP 11

a. Bracts of the non-basal pistillate spikes bladeless, consisting of the sheath only,
    or with a much reduced, scale-like blade. .... 129. *C. pedunculata*
a. Bracts of the pistillate spikes bearing well developed blades.
  b. Perigynia strongly flattened-trigonous, beakless or very short beaked. (Fig. 234).
    c. Terminal spike staminate; roots covered with a dense, felt-like pubescence
      (except in *C. acutiformis*).
      d. Lowest spikes longer than 2.5 cm; perigynia short beaked. .... 157. *C. acutiformis*
      d. Lowest spikes 2.5 cm or shorter; perigynia beakless or merely apiculate.
        e. Pistillate scales long acuminate, much longer and narrower than
          perigynia. .... 158. *C. magellanica*
        e. Pistillate scales elliptic, about as wide and long as perigynia.
          Pistillate scales enfolding the bases of the perigynia, usually dark
            purple to black; stems smooth .... 159. *C. rariflora*
          Pistillate scales not enfolding the bases of the perigynia, usually
            straw colored or tan; stems rough above .... 160. *C. limosa*
    c. Terminal spike gynaecandrous; roots not covered with dense, felt-like
      pubescence.
      f. Spikes drooping on slender peduncles; scales conspicuously longer and
        narrower than the perigynia .... 158. *C. magellanica*
      f. Spikes erect, or if drooping scales equalling or barely longer than the
        perigynia and about as wide.
        Pistillate spikes sessile or nearly so; scales awned or acuminate. .... 161. *C. buxbaumii*
        Pistillate spikes peduncled, often drooping; scales obtuse or acute. .... 162. *C. atratiformis*
  b. Perigynia not strongly flattened, obscurely to sharply trigonous or nearly round
    in cross section, short or long beaked.
    g. Scales of at least the lower perigynia of most of the spikes prolonged and
      leaf-like, much exceeding the perigynium and sometimes the entire
      spike (Fig. 188); staminate scales clasping the rachis, their margins
      united at the base.

h. Pistillate scales green throughout, without conspicuous hyaline margins, enveloping and mostly hiding the perigynia. .... 1. *C. backii*

h. Pistillate scales with conspicuous hyaline margins, scarcely enveloping perigynia .... 2. *C. willdenowii*

g. Scales not leaf-like (although longer than the perigynia in some species); staminate scales not clasping the rachis, their margins free.

  i. Terminal spike gynaecandrous.

    j. Perigynium distinctly beaked; pistillate spikes erect.

      k. Spikes 1 cm wide or wider, on short peduncles.

        Perigynia widely divergent to reflexed; pistillate scales acuminate or awned. .... 8. *C. squarrosa*

        Perigynia ascending or the lower reflexed; pistillate scales obtuse to acute. .... 9. *C. typhina*

      k. Spikes less than 1 cm wide, all but sometimes the lowest sessile or nearly so.

        Perigynia mostly 3.5 mm or less long, divergent to ascending, not reflexed, the beak up to half the length of the body. .... 138. *C. viridula*

        Perigynia mostly 3.5 mm long or longer, reflexed, the beak more than half the length of the body .... 137. *C. flava*

    j. Perigynium beakless or beak poorly differentiated; if distinctly beaked pistillate spikes drooping.

      Pistillate spikes linear cylindric, spreading or drooping, at least the lower on long peduncles (Fig. 235) .... 163. *C. prasina*

      Pistillate spikes oblong or thick cylindric, erect, sessile or short peduncled .... 143. *C. livida* var. *radicaulis*

  i. Terminal spike staminate.

    l. Perigynia widely divergent to reflexed.

      m. Leaves involute; sheaths red-dotted on ventral side; perigynia divergent. .... 136. *C. extensa*

      m. Leaves flat; sheaths not red-dotted on ventral side; perigynia divergent to reflexed.

        n. Perigynia mostly 3.5 mm or less long, divergent, the beak up to half the length of the body .... 138. *C. viridula*

        n. Perigynia mostly 3.5 mm long or longer, reflexed, the beak more than half the length of the body.

          Pistillate scales light or dark brown, conspicuous; beak of perigynium rough or serrulate on the margins .... 137. *C. flava*

          Pistillate scales pale, relatively inconspicuous; perigynium beak smooth. .... 164. *C. cryptolepis*

    l. Perigynia ascending or not strongly divergent.

      o. Some of the spikes terminating very short stems, crowded among the basal leaf sheaths and nearly obscured, others on elongate stems. (Fig. 190). .... 6. *C. umbellata*

      o. Stems all elongate, none crowded among the basal leaf sheaths.

        p. Body of perigynium subglobose, abruptly narrowed to a beak as long or longer than the body.

          Perigynia 2-ribbed, otherwise nerveless; stems strongly fibrillose at the base .... 109. *C. folliculata*

          Perigynia with 8 or more conspicuous nerves; stems not fibrillose at the base. .... 165. *C. baileyi*

        p. Body of perigynium ovoid or lanceolate, gradually tapered to a beak up to half as long as the body.

          q. Pistillate spikes spreading or drooping, at least the lower on long peduncles.

            Pistillate scales hyaline or greenish .... 163. *C. prasina*

            Pistillate scales purple or dark brown. .... 166. *C. barrattii*

          q. Pistillate spikes erect.

            r. Perigynia beakless or beak poorly differentiated. .... 143. *C. livida* var. *radicaulis*

r. Perigynia with a short or long but clearly differentiated beak.
   s. Staminate spike sessile or nearly so; plant cespitose. .... 136. *C. extensa*
   s. Staminate spike usually long peduncled; plant rhizomatous.
      t. Style jointed at or near base; leaves wider than 3 mm, flat
         or becoming revolute .... 140. *C. polymorpha*
      t. Style continuous; leaves up to 3 mm wide, involute.
         Perygynium beak conspicuously toothed .... 167. *C. x mainensis*
         Perygynium beak merely emarginate .... 168. *C. oligosperma*

157. *C. acutifórmis* Ehrh. (like *C. acuta*). Wet meadows. June-August. (Naturalized from Europe). Reported for New London County CT, Suffolk County MA. —OBL

158. *C. magellánica* Lam. Bogs and *Thuja* swamps, June-August. Fig. 234, Map 533. [*C. paupercula*]. Our plants include subsp. *magellanica* and the following subsp.:

subsp. *irrígua* (Wahlenb.) Hulten. Pistillate spikes 1 cm or more long (less than 1 cm long in subsp. *magellanica*). [*C. paupercula* var. *i.*]. —OBL

159. *C. rariflóra* (Wahlenb.) Sm. July-August. (scantily flowered). (Eurasia). Reported for Mt. Katahdin, and Piscataquis and Washington Counties ME. Our plants are var. *rariflóra.* —OBL

160. *C. limósa* L. (growing in mud). Bogs. June-August. Map 534. (Eurasia). Endangered in CT. —OBL

161. *C. buxbaúmii* Wahlenb. (for J. C. Buxbaum). Wet meadows, wooded swamps, pond and river shores. June-July. Map 535. (Eurasia). Endangered in VT, NH, CT. —OBL

C. norvégica Retz. Will key to *C. buxbaumii* but is distinguishable in having a compact inflorescence up to 3 cm long and obtuse to acute pistillate scales (inflorescence more open, longer than 3 cm, and pistillate scales acute to acuminate and often awned in *C. buxbaumii*). (Eurasia). From farther north and west. Reported for ME. [*C. halleri; C. media; C. vahlii*]. Represented with us as subsp. *inferalpína* (Wahlenb.) Hulten.

162. *C. atratifórmis* Britt. (having the form of *C. atrata*, blackish). Wet meadows and wet ledges. June-August. Map 536. Endangered in NY.

163. *C. prásina* Wahlenb. (leek green). Moist to wet woods and streamsides. May-July. Fig. 235, Map 537. —FACW

164. *C. cryptolépis* Mackenzie. Wet meadows and lake margins, calcareous. Summer. Map 538. [*C. flava* var. *fertilis*]. —OBL

165. *C. baíleyi* Britt. (for L. H. Bailey). Wet meadows, ditches and wet swampy woods. June-August. Map 539. Endangered in MA. —OBL

166. *C. barráttii* Schwein & Torr. (for J. Barratt). Wet woods and pine barren swamps, mostly near the coast. May-June. Endangered in NY. Reported for Fairfield and Hartford Counties, CT. —OBL

167. *C. x mainénsis* Porter ex Britt (pro sp.). (of Maine). Lake and river shores. Summer. Reported for Piscataquis County ME. A hybrid between *C. saxatilis* and *C. vesicaria.*

168. *C. oligospérma* Michx. (few seeded). Bogs and wet meadows. June-August. Map 540. Our plants are var. *obigosperma.* —OBL

2. *Scléria* Berg. Nut Rush (from the Greek based on the bony or enameled achene).

Monoecious, annual, or perennial from creeping rhizomes, with leafy, triangular stems, one or more of the upper leaves forming an involucre to the inflorescence; inflorescence of small, compact, terminal, or terminal and axillary cymes, the axillary clusters often peduncled, or interruptedly spicate; spikelets small, with spirally imbricated scales, the staminate and pistillate usually borne in the same cluster, the pistillate 1-flowered, with lower scales empty, the staminate few-flowered; perianth none, stamens 1-3, style 3-cleft; fruit a globose to ovoid achene, usually white, bony or enameled, subtended (in our species) by a hypogynium (disc).

230. *Carex vaginata.* Pistillate spike with perigynia ascending.

x 1

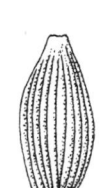

x 6

x 1

229. *Carex flava.* Pistillate spikes with perigynia divergent to reflexed.

231. *Carex conoidea.* Single perigynium; rounded at base.

x 7

232. *Carex laxiflora.* Single perigynium; obtusely triangular.

x 5

233. *Carex platyphylla.* Single perigynium; acutely triangular.

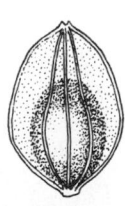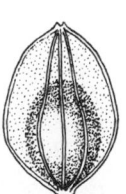

x 7

234. *Carex magellanica.* Single perigynium; strongly flattened-trigonous.

x 3/4

235. *Carex prasina.* Pistillate spikes linear, drooping, the lower long-peduncled.

518. *Carex panicea*

519. *Carex livida* var. *radicaulis*

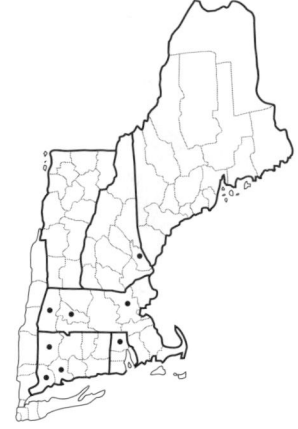

520. *Carex tetanica*

521. *Carex conoidea*

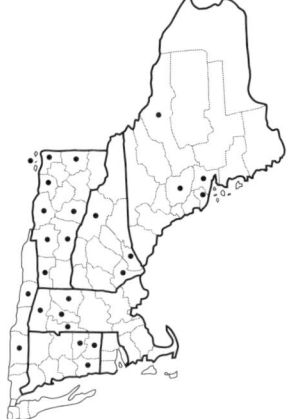

522. *Carex granularis*

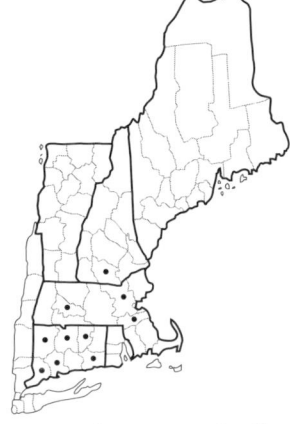

523. *Carex flaccosperma* var. *glaucoidea*

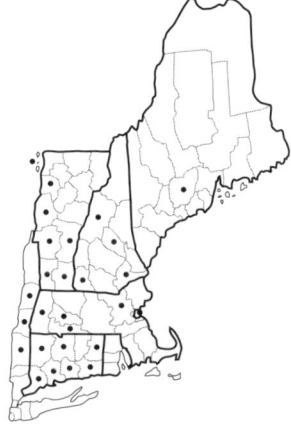

524. *Carex amphibola*

525. *Carex oligocarpa*

526. *Carex leptonervia*

527. *Carex laxiflora*

528. *Carex platyphylla*

529. *Carex styloflexa*

530. *Carex digitalis*

531. *Carex laxiculmis*

532. *Carex abscondita*

533. *Carex magellanica*

534. *Carex limosa*

535. *Carex buxbaumii*

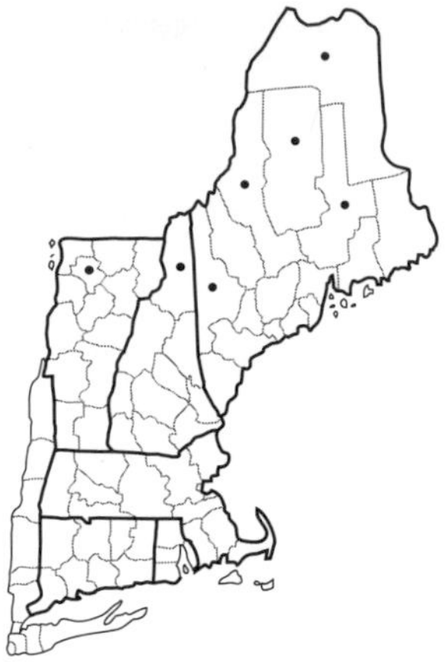

CYPERACEAE

536. *Carex atratiformis*

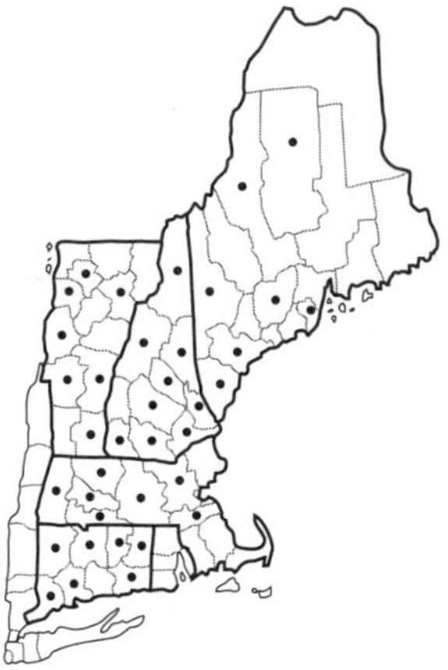

537. *Carex prasina*

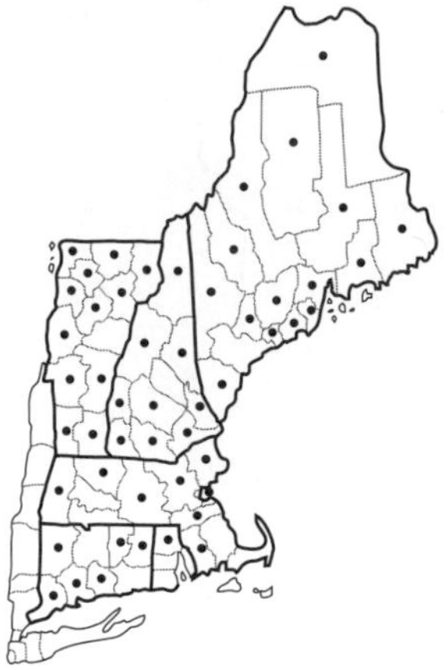

538. *Carex cryptolepis*

539. *Carex baileyi*

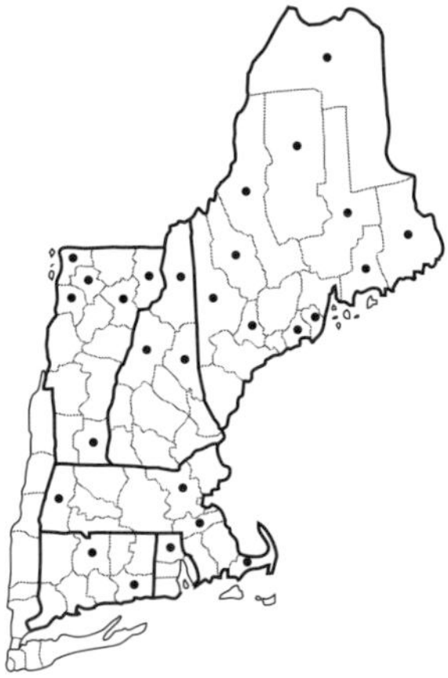

540. *Carex oligosperma*

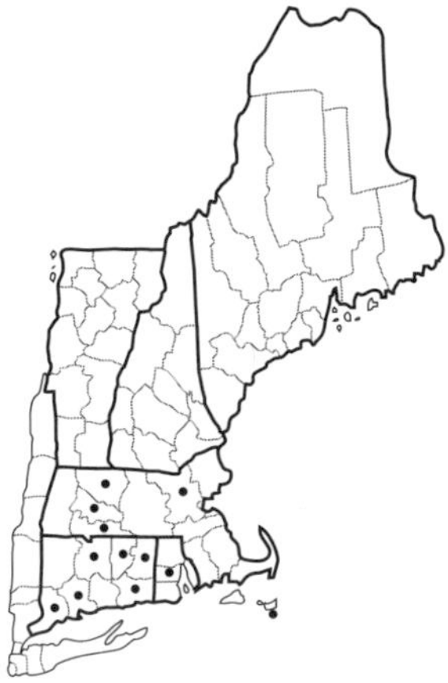

541. *Scleria triglomerata*

542. *Scleria reticularis*

543. *Scleria pauciflora*

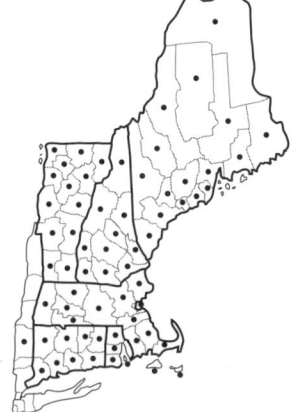

544. *Dulichium arundinaceum*

a. Body of achene smooth .... 1. *S. triglomerata*
a. Body of achene pitted, papillose or ridged.
   b. Achene minutely hairy .... 2. *S. reticularis*
   b. Achene glabrous.
      c. Hypogynium with 6 rounded tubercles; achene body warty or papillose.
         (Fig. 237) .... 3. *S. pauciflora*
      c. Hypogynium without rounded tubercles; achene body pitted in rows or
         transversely ridged. (Fig. 236).
         Achene body pitted in rows; hypogynium with 3 elongate lobes
            appressed to the base of the achene .... 2. *S. reticularis*
         Achene body transversely ridged; hypogynium narrow and flattened. .... 4. *S. verticillata*

1. *S. triglomeráta* Michx. (with three clusters). Moist to dry meadows, thin woods and openings. June-September. Map 541. Endangered in MA, RI, CT. [*S. flaccida; S. nitida*]. —FAC

S. mínor (Britt.) Stone. Similar to *S. triglomerata* but distinguishable in having leaves 3 mm or less wide and achenes up to 2 mm long (leaves 4 mm or more wide and achenes longer than 2 mm in *S. triglomerata*). From farther south on the coastal plain. Endangered in NY; reported for Nassau and Suffolk Counties. [*S. triglomerata* var. *gracilis*]. —FACW

2. *S. reticuláris* Michx. (reticulate). Moist meadows and pond margins in sandy soil, and wet pine barrens. July-September. Fig. 236, Map 542. (Mexico). Endangered in CT. [*S.r.* var. *pubescens; S. muhlenbergii; S. setacea*]. —OBL

3. *S. pauciflóra* Muhl. ex Willd. (few-flowered). Moist to dry open pine or deciduous woods, openings and waste places. June-September. Fig. 237, Map 543. (W.I.). Endangered in MA, RI. Our plants include var. *pauciflora* and the following var.:

    var. *caroliniána* (Willd.) Wood. Culms and leaves densely pilose (glabrous to sparsely pubescent in var. *pauciflora*). —FACU+

4. *S. verticilláta* Muhl. ex Willd. (in whorles). Wet, sandy pond margins and pine barrens. July-September. Endangered in NY; also reported for Litchfield County CT. —OBL

3. *Dulíchium* Pers.

Tall perennial, from a horizontal rhizome, with a terete, simple, hollow, jointed stem; leaves numerous, to the summit of the plant, with conspicuous sheaths, short, flat, conspicuously 3-ranked blades, and a short, membranous ligule, the lower leaves reduced to sheaths only; inflorescence of numerous peduncled spikes, solitary in the upper leaf axils; spikelets linear, flattened to subterete, pinnate in 2 ranks, scales 3-10, 2-ranked, with hyaline margins decurrent on the rachilla as wings below the base; flowers perfect, perianth of 6-9 retrorsely barbed bristles, stamens 3, style 2-cleft above the base; fruit a flattened, linear-oblong achene with the style base persistent as a long, linear beak.

1. *D. arundináceum* (L.) Britt. (reed-like), Three-way Sedge. Freshwater marshes, bogs, wooded swamps, and shallow-water of pond margins. July-October. Fig. 238, Map 544. —OBL

4. *Cypérus* L. Umbrella Sedge (ancient Greek name).

Annual, or perennial from rhizomes or swollen bases, sometimes with stolons, often robust, with stems mostly triangular, simple; leaves basal or low on the stem, shorter to longer than the stem, and 1 or more leaves at the summit, unequal in length, forming an involucre to the inflorescence, shorter than or exceeding the inflorescence; inflorescence a terminal head or an umbel of loose or dense spikes or heads composed of few to many spikelets, the spikelets digitate or pinnate in the spikes, the umbel simple with the central spike sessile or subsessile and the lateral spikes on simple rays of unequal lengths, or compound, with the rays branched, each ray of the umbel enclosed at the base by a tubular sheath; spikelets flattened, subtended by 2 small bracts, composed of few to many scales, the scales concave or conduplicate, 2-ranked, distichous, rachilla often with thin wings running to the scale above it, each scale subtending a flower; flowers perfect, perianth none, stamens 1-3, style 2-3 cleft; fruit a lenticular or triangular, beakless achene.

a. Spikelets closely imbricated in dense globose or subglobose heads.
    Spikelets with 1-3 florets.
        Longest spikelet scale 3 mm or longer; heads mostly more than 1 cm in diameter .... 1. *C. echinatus*
        Longest spikelet scale 2.5 mm or less long; heads mostly less than 1 cm in diameter .... 2. *C. retrorsus*
    Spikelets with more than 3 florets .... 3. *C. filiculmis*
a. Spikelets somewhat loosely arranged, or not in globose or subglobose heads.
  b. Spikelets radiating from a short axis forming a subglobose or digitate spike, or if radiating from an elongate axis then not pinnately arranged. (Fig. 239).
    c. Scales with 7 or more strong nerves more or less evenly distributed from the midrib to or nearly to the margins. (Fig. 240).
      d. Tips of scales acuminate and distinctly recurved; plant fragrant on drying. .... 4. *C. squarrosus*
      d. Tips of scales not distinctly recurved; plant not fragrant.
        e. Scales suborbicular, half as wide as long, or wider; spikelets ascending.
          Scales prominently mucronate, 2.8 mm long or longer; stems rough. .... 5. *C. schweinitzii*
          Scales obtuse or barely mucronate, less than 2.8 mm long; stems smooth. .... 6. *C. houghtonii*
        e. Scales ovate to elliptic, less than half as wide as long; spikelets, at least in part, divergent or horizontal.
          f. Scales closely overlapping, with appressed tips; spikelets in dense, cylindric heads mostly less than 1 cm in diameter. (Fig. 239). .... 2. *C. retrorsus*
          f. Scales with free tips, the spikelet appearing serrated; spikelets somewhat loosely arranged in subglobose spikes mostly more than 1 cm in diameter. (Fig. 241).
            Scales sharply acute; leaves flat; rachilla joints winged. .... 1. *C. echinatus*
            Scales obtuse or sometimes also mucronulate.
              Leaves folded, those of the involucre smooth; rachilla broadly winged; scales narrowly margined .... 7. *C. grayii*
              Leaves flat, those of the involucre rough-margined; rachilla wingless; scales with broad, hyaline margins .... 3. *C. filiculmis*
    c. Scales with 3-5 nerves close to the midrib or to a point half way between the midrib and margins, the lower half to three quarters of each side nerveless. (Fig. 242).
      g. Achenes trigonous; style 3-cleft.
        Scales light green to brown, 2 mm long or longer; perennial. .... 8. *C. dentatus*
        Scales dark brown to black, not over 1.5 mm long; annual. .... 9. *C. fuscus*
      g. Achenes lenticular; style 2-cleft.
        h. Achenes black, transversely wrinkled; scales broadly ovate, slightly more than twice as long as wide .... 10. *C. flavescens*
        h. Achenes not transversely wrinkled; scales narrower, substantially more than twice as long as wide.
          i. Scales yellow or pale brown, mucronate, their tips free, giving the spikelet a serrated appearance. .... 11. *C. polystachyos*
          i. Scales tinged with purple or dark brown, blunt, their tips appressed.
            Style united only at the base, its 2 branches extending beyond the scales, persistent; scales with widest area of dark coloration toward tip. .... 12. *C. diandrus*
            Style united to about the middle, barely extending beyond the scales, deciduous; scales with widest area of dark coloration toward base. .... 13. *C. bipartitus*
  b. Spikelets more or less pinnately arranged on an elongate axis. (Fig. 243).
    j. Scales 2 mm long or longer, with 7 or more strong nerves more or less evenly distributed from the midrib to or nearly to the margins.
      Scales mostly longer than 3 mm; base with knotty swellings. .... 14. *C. strigosus*
      Scales 3 mm long or shorter; base of fibrous roots or with rhizomes ending in tubers.

Annual with tufted, fibrous roots .... 15. *C. odoratus*
Perennial with slender rhizomes ending in small tubers. .... 16. *C. esculentus*
j. Scales less than 2 mm long, with 3-5 nerves close to the midrib or to a point
half way between the midrib and margins.
k. Scales broadly obovate, truncate .... 17. *C. amuricus*
k. Scales lanceolate to ovate.
Scales with broad, hyaline margins; achenes black, lenticular; styles
2-cleft; roots not red .... 18. *C. flavicomus*
Scales with narrow, light brown margins; achenes grayish, trigonous;
styles 3-cleft; roots red .... 19. *C. erythrorhizos*

1. *C. echinátus* (L.) Wood. Dry, often sandy woodlands and cleared woodlands, fields, roadsides and barrens; low, swampy woods, marshy ditches and lake margins. July-September. Endangered in NY. Reported for CT, RI, Suffolk County MA, also Bronx, Queens, Westchester Counties NY. [*C. globulosus; C. ovularis*]. —FACU

2. *C. retrórsus* Chapm. (turned backward). Dry sandy barrens, dry river and seashores, cutover woods and woodland openings, fields and roadsides. August-October. Fig. 239. [*C. torreyi; C. cylindricus; C. ovularis* var. *c.*]. —FAC-

3. *C. filicúlmis* Vahl (with thread-like stems). Dry sandy or gravelly soil. August-October. Fig. 240, Map 545. [*C. bushii; C. martindalei*].

C. lupulínus (Spreng.) Marcks. Similar to *C. filiculmis* but with scales up to 2.8 mm long and achenes up to 1.8 mm long (scales 2.8 mm or more long and achenes 1.8 mm or more long in *C. filiculmis*). Throughout our range. Represented with us as subsp. *maciléntus* (Fern.) Marcks [*C. filiculmis* var. *m.*].

C. pseudovégetus Steud. Similar to the latter 2 species but annual or perennial with soft bases and filbrous roots or short rhizomes (*C. filiculmis* and *C. lupulinus* are perennial with tuberous-thickened rhizomes). Wet soil; from farther south. Reported for Norfolk County MA. (Tropical Amer.). [*C. virens*]. —FACW

C. acuminátus Torr. & Hook. Similar to *C. pseudovegetus* but with oblong to ellipsoid achenes (achenes linear in *C. pseudovegetus*). Western. Reported for Westchester County NY. —OBL

4. *C. squarrósus* L. Damp sandy soil of river and lake shores, sand bars. July-September. Map 546. [*C. aristatus; C. inflexus*]. —FACW+

5. *C. schweinítzii* Torr. (for L.D. deSchweinitz). Dry or wet sandy soil, especially bordering lakes and streams, and on beaches, dunes, roadsides and barrens. July-September. Reported for Franklin County MA. —FACU

6. *C. houghtónii* Torr. (for D. Houghton). Sandy soil of barrens, fields, lake shores and waste places. July-September. Map 547. Endangered in MA. [*C. bushii; C. lupulinus; C. macilentus; C. filiculmis* var. *m.*].

7. *C. gráyii* Torr. (for A. Gray). Dry sandy soil along the coast, particularly beaches and dunes. July-October. Fig. 241, Map 548. Endangered in NH.

8. *C. dentátus* Torr. (toothed). Sandy or gravelly lake shores, river borders and sand dunes. July-October. Fig. 242, Map 549. —FACW+

9. *C. fúscus* L. (dusky). Damp sandy soil, waste places. July-September. Reported for CT and Suffolk County MA. —FAC

10. *C. flavéscens* L. (yellowish). Wet, particularly sandy soil of stream borders, pond margins, sand bars and marshes, and in fields and along roadsides. July-October. Reported for MA and Bronx County NY. —OBL

11. *C polystáchyos* Rottb. (many-spiked). Salt and brackish marshes, beaches, pond margins. August-October. (Tropical Amer.; Philippines). Map 550. [*C. gatesii; C. microdontus; C. paniculatus*]. Represented with us as var. *filicínus* (Vahl) C. B. Clarke [*C. filicinus; C. gatesii; C. microdontus; C. nuttallii; C. polystachyos* var. *texensis; C. paniculatus*]. —FACW to OBL

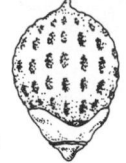

x 12

236. *Scleria reticularis*. Surface of achene pitted in rows.

x 10

237. *Scleria pauciflora.* Surface of achene warty-papillose.

x 1/2

238. *Dulichium arundinaceum.* Peduncled spikes solitary in the upper leaf axils.

x 1

239. *Cyperus retrorsus*. Spikelets radiating in dense, cylindric heads.

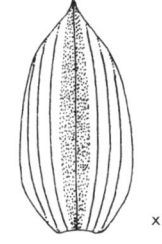

x 12

240. *Cyperus filiculmis.* Single spikelet scale with 7 strong evenly distributed nerves.

x 1

243. *Cyperus strigosus.* Spikelets pinnately arranged on an elongate axis.

x 1 1/2

241. *Cyperus grayii.* Spikelets loosely arranged in subglobose spikes on a short axis.

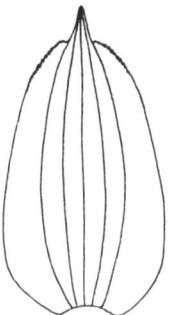

x 20

242. *Cyperus dentatus.* Single spikelet scale with 2 nerves bilaterally, half way between midrib and margins.

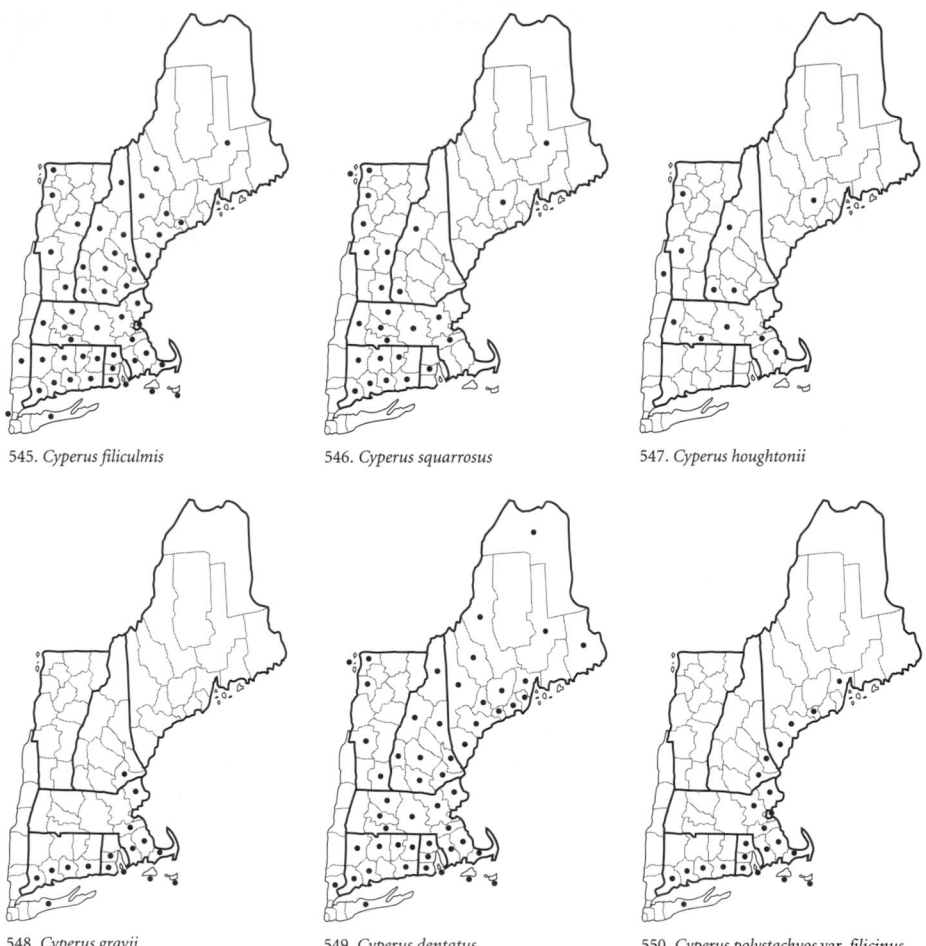

545. *Cyperus filiculmis*   546. *Cyperus squarrosus*   547. *Cyperus houghtonii*

548. *Cyperus grayii*   549. *Cyperus dentatus*   550. *Cyperus polystachyos* var. *filicinus*

12. *C. diándrus* Torr. (with two stamens). Wet soil, especially of pond and stream margins. July-October. Map 551. Endangered in VT. —FACW

13. *C. bipártitus* Torr. Wet soil, particularly along streams and pond margins. July-October. Map 552. [*C. niger* var. *castaneus*; *C. rivularis*]. —FACW+

14. *C. strigósus* L. (lean). Pond and stream margins, moist fields, roadsides and waste places. August-October. Fig. 243, Map 553. —FACW

15. *C. odorátus* L. (fragrant). Moist or wet open or woodland soil, especially along pond margins. August-October. Map 554. (Tropical Amer.). [*C. engelmannii*; *C. ferax*; *C. ferruginescens*; *C. speciosus*]. —FACW

16. *C. esculéntus* L. (edible). Yellow Nut Grass. Damp, often sandy soil of lake and river shores, fields, roadsides, waste places and frequently as a weed in cultivated ground. August-October. Map 555. (Tropical Amer.; Old world). Our plants are var. *esculentus*. Tubers at the ends of the rhizomes are edible; sometimes also roasted and used as a coffee substitute. —FACW

17. *C. amurícus* Maxim. Abandoned fields, cultivated fields and waste places. August-October. Reported for Middlesex County MA.

C. íria L. Similar to *C. amuricus* but rachilla is wingless (narrowly winged in *C. amuricus*). (Naturalized from the Old World). Southern. Reported for Nassau and Queens Counties NY. [*C. microiria*]. —FACW

18. *C. flavicómus* Michx. Damp soil of fields and roadsides. July-October. (Africa; Australia; Tropical Amer.). Reported for Suffolk County NY. [*C. albomarginatus; C. sabulosus*]. —FAC

19. *C. erythrorhízos* Muhl. (red-rooted). Damp or wet soil, particularly along pond and river margins. August-October. Map 556. Endangered in ME. —FACW+

5. *Kyllíngia* Rottb.

Similar to *Cyperus* but spikelets have only 1 fertile floret. [*Cyperus*].

In addition to the species treated below *K. squamulata* has been reported for ME.

Tufted annual from fibrous roots; spikelets to 2 mm long. .... 1. *K. pumila*
Perennial from elongate rhizomes; spikelets 3 mm or more long. .... 2. *K. brevifolia*

1. *K. púmila* Michx. Moist sandy or muddy soil of creek margins and beds, and lake shores. August-October. Fig. 244. [*Cyperus tenuifolius; C. densicaespitosus*]. —FACW

2. *K. brevifólia* Rottb. Pond and stream margins, fresh marshes and springy places, fields and roadsides. August-October. From farther south; reported for CT. [*Cyperus brevifolius*]. —FACW

K. *brevifolioídes* (Thieret & Delahoussaye) Tucker. Similar to *K. brevifolia* but with spikelets longer than 3.5 mm (spikelets 3.5 mm or less long in *K. brevifolia*). [*Cyperus b.; C. brevifolius*]. From farther south; reported for CT.

6. *Rhynchóspora* Vahl Beak-rush (from the Greek based on the beaked achene).

Annual or perennial, with triangular or terete leafy stems; leaves with flat or involute, narrowly linear to filiform blades; inflorescence of terminal and axillary cymose spikelets; spikelets ovoid, fusiform or subglobose, solitary or in glomerules, 1-several flowered, with spirally imbricated scales, the lower scales empty, the upper longer and each subtending a flower, or sometimes all scales subtending a flower; lower (sometimes all) flowers perfect, the uppermost often staminate, perianth of mostly 6 bristles (0-20), stamens commonly 3 (1 or 2), style 2-cleft; fruit a lenticular, flat or swollen achene capped by a tubercle or beak.

a. Perianth lacking.
    Tubercle of achene higher than broad, nearly or quite as long as the body. .... 1. *R. scirpoides*
    Tubercle of achene broader than high, much shorter than the body. .... 2. *R. nitens*
a. Perianth of bristles present.
  b. Spikelets longer than 1 cm; leaves mostly wider than 3 mm.
    c. Bristles shorter than the achene ....3. *R. corniculata*
    c. Bristles longer than the achene.
      Plant stoloniferous; body of achene shorter than 5 mm. .... 4. *R. inundata*
      Plant non-stoloniferous; body of achene 5 mm long or longer. .... 5. *R. macrostachya*
  b. Spikelets shorter than 1 cm; leaves mostly narrower than 3 mm.
    d. Bristles inconspicuous or caducous or much shorter than body of achene.
      (Fig. 246).
      Body of achene transversely rugose .... 6. *R. torreyana*
      Body of achene smooth .... 7. *R. pallida*
    d. Bristles conspicuous, longer than body of achene. (Fig. 247).
      e. Spikelets whitish to very pale brown. .... 8. *R. alba*
      e. Spikelets dark brown.
        f. Longest spikelets not over 5 mm long. .... 9. *R. capitellata*
        f. Longest spikelets longer than 5 mm.
          Body of achene 2 or more times as long as broad. .... 10. *C. capillacea*
          Body of achene less than twice as long as broad. .... 11. *R. fusca*

1. R. scirpoídes (Torr.) Gray (like Scirpus). Sandy and peaty pond margins. July-October. Fig. 245, Map 557. Endangered in RI, CT. [*Psilocarya s.*]. —OBL

2. R. nítens (Vahl) Gray (shining). Wet sandy soil and bogs. July-October. Reported for Plymouth County MA, Suffolk County NY. [*Psilocarya n.*]. —OBL

3. R. corniculáta (Lam.) Gray (horned). Wooded swamps, marshes and ditches. July-September. (W.I.). —OBL

4. R. inundáta (Oakes) Fern. (inundated). Horned Rush. Wooded swamps and pond margins. July-September. Map 558. Endangered in RI, NY. —OBL

5. R. macrostáchya Torr. ex Gray (large-spiked). Horned Rush. Pond margins and wet sand and peat. July-October. Map 559. Endangered in CT. Our plants are var. *macrostachya*. —OBL

6. R. torreyána Gray (for its discoverer). Damp to dryish sand and peat in pine woods near the coast. July-September. Fig. 246, Map 560. Endangered in MA, RI. —FACW+

R. globuláris (Chapm.) Small. Similar to *R. torreyana* but with achene thickened distally and tubercle deltoid-conical (achene and tubercle flattened in *R. torreyana*). From farther south on the coastal plain. Reported for Suffolk County NY. Represented with us as var. *recognita* Gale [*R. cymosa*]. —FACW

7. R. pállida M. A. Curtis (pale). Wet pine barrens and bogs near the coast. July-September. From farther south; reported for Suffolk County NY. —OBL

8. R. álba (L.) Vahl (white). Bogs, and wet sand and peat. July-September. Map 561. (Eurasia; W.I.). —OBL

9. R. capitelláta (Michx.) Vahl (with small heads). Wet sand, muddy and sandy pond and stream margins, bogs, ditches. July-October. Fig. 247, Map 562. —OBL

R. chalarocéphala Fern. & Gale. Similar to *R. capitellata* but differing in having spikelets 1-flowered and fruited (*R. capitellata* has 2 fertile flowers per spikelet). From farther south on the coastal plain. Reported for Suffolk County NY. —OBL

10. R. capilácea Torr. (hair-like). Damp calcareous ledges, lake margins and bogs. July-September. Map 563. Endangered in ME, MA, NH, CT. —OBL

11. R. fúsca (L.) Ait. f. (sooty). Pond margins, bogs, wet meadows, and wet sand and peat. July-October. Map 564. (Europe). —OBL

7. Cládium P. Br. Twig Rush (from the Greek, based on the branched cyme).

Perennial, from stout rhizomes, with leafy stems; leaves with narrow, involute blades, the uppermost reduced and forming an involucre of 2 or more bracts to the terminal inflorescence; inflorescence of 2-4 compound cymes, the 1-3 axillary cymes remote, on long, slender peduncles, the spikelets borne in capitate clusters of 2-10 at the ends of the raylets; spikelets ovoid to lanceolate, 1-several flowered, with loosely imbricated scales, the lower scales empty, the middle bearing staminate or abortive flowers, the uppermost subtending a perfect flower; perianth none, stamens 2, style 2-3 cleft; fruit a brown achene, ovoid or globose, contracted or truncate at the base, pointed distally but lacking a tubercle.

1. C. mariscoídes (Muhl.) Torr. (like Mariscus). Pond margins (fresh or brackish), coniferous or deciduous wooded swamps, marshes and bogs. July-October. Fig. 248, Map 565. [*Mariscus m.*]. —OBL

8. Eleócharis R. Br. Spike Rush (from the Greek, based on the marsh habitat of many of the species).

Annual or perennial from rhizomes, with tufted, simple stems; leaves reduced to bladeless basal sheaths, inflorescence a single, elliptic to linear, terminal, few to many flowered spikelet, not subtended by an involucre; scales usually spirally imbricated, often deciduous at maturity, the lower

1 or 2 sterile, the others fertile; flowers perfect, perianth mostly of 6 (occasionally fewer, more, or obsolete), usually retrorsely barbed bristles, stamens 2-3, style 2 or 3 cleft; fruit a lenticular or triangular achene, with the style base expanded and persistent as a tubercle. Mature achenes are necessary for identification of most of the species. —FACW+ to OBL; Wildl. 2
In addition to the following species *E. decumbens* has been reported for VT.

a. Spikelet barely or not at all thicker than the stem.
  b. Stems triangular or quadrangular.
    Stems triangular .... 1. *E. robbinsii*
    Stems quadrangular .... 2. *E. quadrangulata*
  b. Stems terete.
    Stems septate by cross partitions 1-5 cm apart, warty between the septa. .... 3. *E. equisetoides*
    Stem neither septate at regular intervals nor warty. .... 4. *E. palustris*
a. Spikelet distinctly thicker than the stem.
  c. Achene lenticular or biconvex; style 2-cleft. (Fig. 250).
    d. Upper leaf sheaths at base of stem loose, with prolonged white scarious
      tips .... 5. *E. olivacea*
    d. Upper sheaths close, oblique, truncate, or toothed, not scarious.
      e. Tubercle closely fitting summit of achene, flat-deltoid; annual. (Fig. 250).
        Base of tubercle about 2/3 as wide as summit of achene. .... 6. *E. ovata*
        Base of tubercle nearly or quite as wide as summit of achene.
          Bristles none or much shorter than summit of achene, rarely
            reaching the tubercle .... 7. *E. engelmanni*
          Bristles usually present and much surpassing the tubercle. .... 8. *E. obtusa*
      e. Tubercle constricted at base above summit, not flat, conic; perennial,
        often rhizomatous.
        f. Sterile basal scales of spikelet 2 or 3, not completely encircling base
          of spikelet. (Fig. 249).
          Tubercle much longer than broad .... 4. *E. palustris*
          Tubercle as broad or broader than long. .... 9. *E. smallii*
        f. Sterile basal scale 1, encircling base of spikelet.
          g. Tubercle wider than high; achenes prominently reticulate. (Fig. 251). .... 10. *E. fallax*
          g. Tubercle as high or higher than wide; achenes smooth or obscurely
            reticulate.
            Scales longer than 3 mm, acute; spikelet less than 30 flowered.
              Achenes broadly obovoid; tubercle often higher than broad,
                the base rarely half as wide as summit of achene .... 11. *E. halophila*
              Achenes elliptical to narrowly obovoid; tubercle about as high
                as broad, half to 2/3 as wide as summit of achene .... 12. *E. uniglumis*
            Scales 3 mm or shorter, obtuse; spikelet 30 or more flowered. .... 13. *E. erythropoda*
  c. Achene trigonous, plano-convex or nearly terete; style 3-cleft. (Fig. 252).
    h. Tubercle confluent with summit of the achene, but often of a different
      texture, not forming a cap or separated by a constriction. (Fig. 252).
      i. Spikelets plump, more than 8 flowered. .... 14. *E. rostellata*
      i. Spikelets flattened, 8 or fewer flowered.
        Achene 1.5 mm long or shorter; longest scale not longer than 2.5 mm. ...... 15. *E. parvula*
        Achene longer than 1.5 mm; longest scale longer than 2.5 mm. .... 16. *E. quinqueflora*
    h. Tubercle distinct from summit of the achene and forming a cap, often
      separated by a constriction. (Fig. 253).
      j. Achene truncate at the summit, black; tubercle low and flat, covering the
        entire top of the achene, not separated from it by a constriction.
        (Fig. 253). .... 17. *E. melanocarpa*
      j. Achene not truncate at the summit; tubercle not covering entire top of the
        achene or if so, then separated from it by a constriction.
        k. Surface of achene reticulated, roughened, or pitted. (Fig. 254).
          l. Plant with elongate rhizomes; sheaths usually reddish.
            Achene 1.2 mm long or longer .... 10. *E. fallax*
            Achene less than 1.2 mm long .... 18. *E. tenuis*
        i. Plant without elongate rhizomes; sheaths drab.
          Tubercle as long and broad as achene or nearly so. .... 19. *E. tuberculosa*

Tubercle much shorter and narrower than achene. .... 20. *E. tortilis*
k. Surface of achene not reticulated, roughened or pitted.
   m. Achene nearly terete, with straight, longitudinal lines. (Fig. 255). .... 21. *E. acicularis*
   m. Achene trigonous, without longitudinal lines.
      n. Achene pale greenish-gray to whitish. .... 22. *E. microcarpa*
      n. Achene yellowish or brown.
         Tubercle depressed-pyramidal; bristles none; achene shorter
            than 1 mm. ....23. *E. tricostata*
         Tubercle conic-subulate, a third to half as long as the achene;
            bristles present; achene longer than 1 mm .... 24. *E. intermedia*

1. *E. robbínsii* Oakes (for J. Robbins). Mud or shallow water of ponds, along the coast. August-October. Map 566.

2. *E. quadranguláta* (Michx.) R. & S. (four-angled). Shallow water of ponds and creeks, sometimes tidal. June-October. Map 567.

3. *E. equisetoídes* (Ell.) Torr. (like *Equisetum*). Shallow water, near the coast. July-October. Map 568. Endangered in CT. [*E. interstincta*].

4. *E. palústris* (L.) R. & S. (of marshes). Muddy and sandy pond, lake and river margins, ditches, shallow water. July-September. Fig. 249, Map 569. (Eurasia). [*E. macrostachya; E. smallii; E. uniglumis*].

5. *E. olivácea* Torr. Muddy, sandy and peaty pond margins and shallow water, near the coast. June-October. Map 570. (Mexico, S. Amer. W.I.). [*E. flavescens* var. *olivacea*]. Our plants are var. *olivacea.*

6. *E. ováta* (Roth) R. & S. (ovate or egg-shaped). Muddy and sandy lake and river margins, wet meadows, wet woods, ditches. July-October. Fig. 250, Map 571. (Eurasia; Hawaii). [*E. diandra; E. engelmanni; E. obtusa*].

7. *E. engelmánni* Steud. (for G. Engelmann). Pond margins. May-October.

8. *E. obtúsa* (Willd.) Schultes (blunt). Wet, muddy open areas. May-October. (Hawaii).

9. *E. smállii* Britt. (for J. Small). Shallow river and pond margins. July-September.

10. *E. fállax* Weath. (deceitful). Pond margins and marshes, near the coast. June-July. Fig. 251, Map 572. [*E. ambigens*].

11. *E. halóphila* (Fern. & Brack.) Fern. & Brack. (lover of salt). Upper borders of salt marshes, shores. July-September. Map 573.

12. *E. uniglúmis* (Link) Schultes (with one glume). Wet shores, wet meadows, marshes. June-September. (Eurasia).

13. *E. erythropóda* Steud. Lake and river shores. June-September. Map 574. (E. Asia; Hawaii). [*E. calva*].

14. *E. rostelláta* (Torr.) Torr. (with small beak). Saline, brackish and calcareous marshes and wooded swamps near the coast. July-October. Fig. 252, Map 575. (W.I.). Endangered in ME.

15. *E. párvula* (R. & S.) Link ex Bluff, Nees & Schauer (very small). Wet saline or brackish soil along the coast. July-October. Map 576. (Europe; N. Africa; S. Amer.; W.I.). Our plants are var. *parvula.*

16. *E. quinqueflóra* (F. Hartman) Schwarz. River and lake margins, often calcareous. July-September. Map 577. Endangered in MA; ME; NH. [*E. pauciflora*].

17. *E. melanocárpa* Torr. (black-fruited). Sandy or peaty pond margins and wet sand near the coast. July-October. Fig. 253, Map 578. Endangered in RI.

18. *E. ténuis* (Willd.) Schult. (slender). Wet meadows, bog margins, wet or damp sand and gravel. May-September. Fig. 254, Map 579. Our plants are var. *tenuis.*

E. ellíptica Kunth. Similar to the latter species but with achenes yellow to orange (olivaceous in *E. tenuis*). [*E. tenuis* var. *borealis*].

E. nítida Fern. Similar to the latter species but with 4 angled stems (*E. elliptica* has 6-8 angled stems).

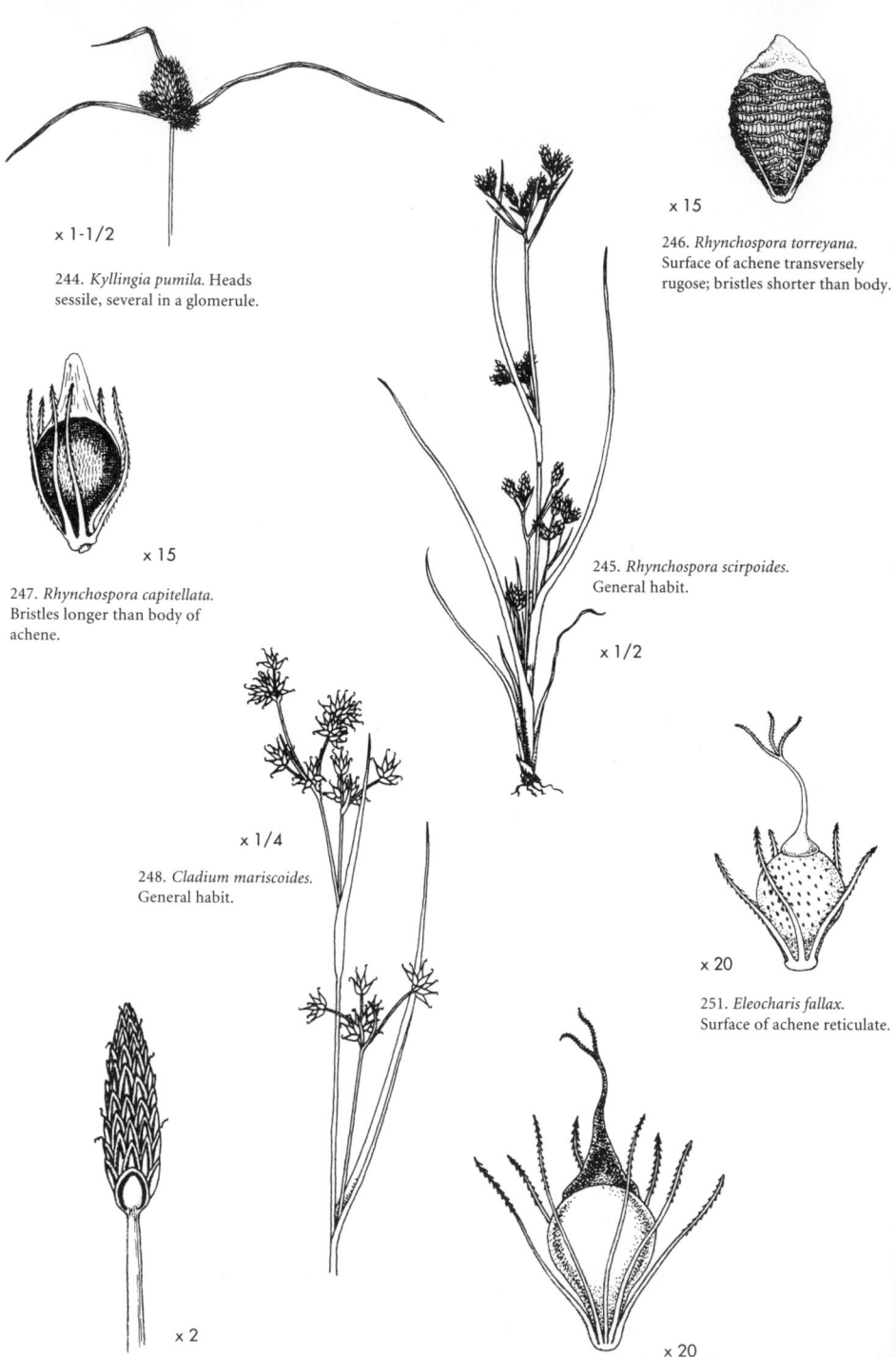

× 1-1/2

244. *Kyllingia pumila.* Heads
sessile, several in a glomerule.

× 15

246. *Rhynchospora torreyana.*
Surface of achene transversely
rugose; bristles shorter than body.

× 15

247. *Rhynchospora capitellata.*
Bristles longer than body of
achene.

245. *Rhynchospora scirpoides.*
General habit.

× 1/2

× 1/4

248. *Cladium mariscoides.*
General habit.

× 20

251. *Eleocharis fallax.*
Surface of achene reticulate.

× 2

249. *Eleocharis palustris.* Spikelet with 2 scales
not completely encircling base.

× 20

250. *Eleocharis ovata.* Achene with
tubercle closely fitting the summit.

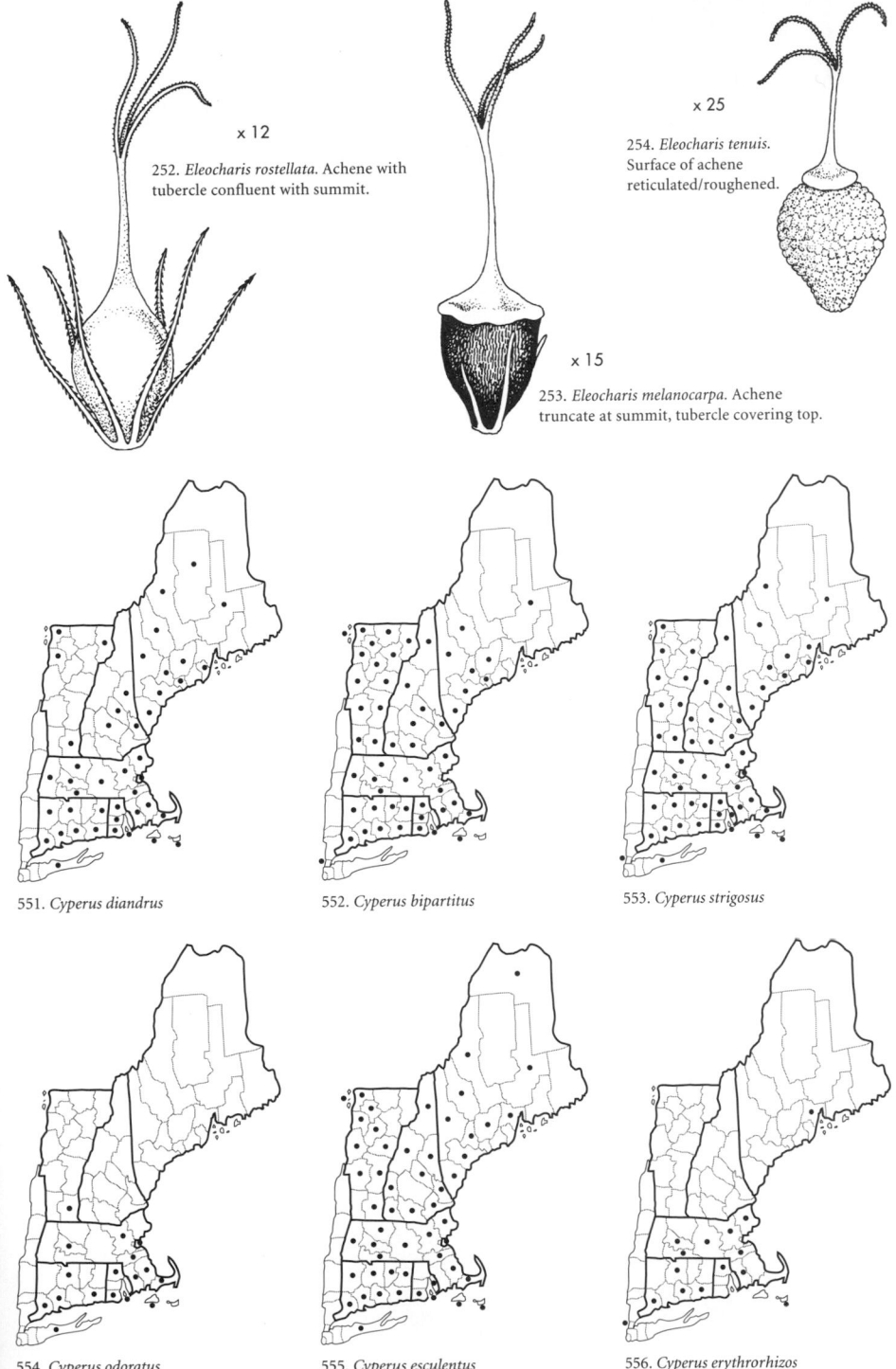

x 12

252. *Eleocharis rostellata.* Achene with tubercle confluent with summit.

x 25

254. *Eleocharis tenuis.* Surface of achene reticulated/roughened.

x 15

253. *Eleocharis melanocarpa.* Achene truncate at summit, tubercle covering top.

551. *Cyperus diandrus*

552. *Cyperus bipartitus*

553. *Cyperus strigosus*

554. *Cyperus odoratus*

555. *Cyperus esculentus*

556. *Cyperus erythrorhizos*

CYPERACEAE

557. *Rhynchospora scirpoides*

558. *Rhynchospora inundata*

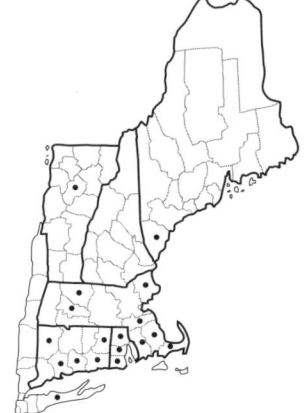

559. *Rhynchospora macrostachya*

560. *Rhynchospora torreyana*

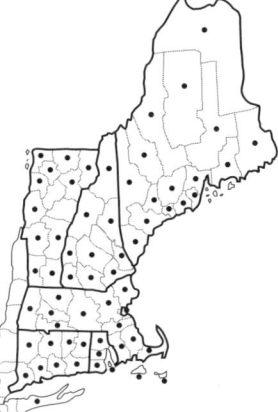

561. *Rhynchospora alba*

562. *Rhynchospora capitellata*

563. *Rhynchospora capillacea*

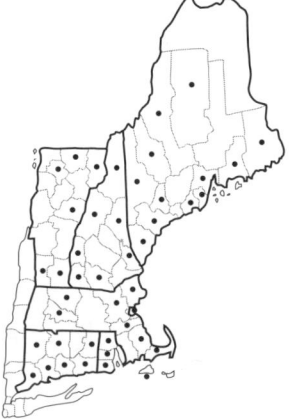

564. *Rhynchospora fusca*

565. *Cladium mariscoides*

566. *Eleocharis robbinsii*

567. *Eleocharis quadrangulata*

568. *Eleocharis equisetoides*

569. *Eleocharis palustris*

570. *Eleocharis olivacea*

571. *Eleocharis ovata*

572. *Eleocharis fallax*

573. *Eleocharis halophila*

574. *Eleocharis erythropoda*   575. *Eleocharis rostellata*   576. *Eleocharis parvula*

577. *Eleocharis quinqueflora*   578. *Eleocharis melanocarpa*   579. *Eleocharis tenuis*

19. E. tuberculósa (Michx.) R. & S. (with a tubercle). Wet sandy and peaty shores, pond margins, ditches, and wet, sandy soil near the coast. June-September. Map 580. Endangered in NH.

20. E. tórtilis (Link.) Schult. (twisted). Wet woods and wooded swamps near the coast. June-September. Reported for Plymouth County MA. [*E. simplex*].

21. E. aciculáris (L.) R. & S. (needle-shaped). Sandy and muddy pond and lake margins, shallow water. July-October. Fig. 255, Map 581. (Eurasia). Our plants include var. *acicularis* and the following var.:

var. *submérsa* (Hj. Nilss.) Svenson. Stems without angles or furrows (stems usually angular and with longitudinal furrows in var. *acicularis*).

22. E. microcárpa Torr. (tiny-fruited). Damp sandy soil, wet meadows and wooded swamps near the coast. June-September. (W.I.). Reported for MA, New London County CT, Nassau County NY. Endangered in MA. [*E. brittonii; E. torreyana*].

23. E. tricostáta Torr. (three-ribbed). Wet sandy or peaty soil and shallow water along the coast. August-October. Map 582. Endangered in MA, ME, RI.

24. E. intermédia Schult. (intermediate). Wet meadows, sandy or muddy pond and stream margins. August-October. Map 583. [*E. macounii*].

9. *Scírpus* L. Bulrush (Latin name for bulrush).

Annual or perennial, stems leafy or leaves reduced to basal sheaths, 1 or more leaves forming an involucre to the inflorescence (when single often appearing like a continuation of the stem) or the involucre lacking in some species; inflorescence terminal, consisting of a solitary spikelet, or spikelets few to many and variously arranged; spikelets few to many flowered, the scales spirally imbricated, usually all subtending a flower, or the 1 or 2 lowest scales sometimes empty; flowers perfect, perianth mostly of 1-6 bristles or sometimes absent, stamens 2-3, style 2-3 cleft, completely deciduous or its base persistent as a slender tip on the fruit; fruit a lenticular or triangular achene. In a number of rhizomatous species, particularly *S. acutus, S. tabernaemontani, S. robustus, S. maritimus*, the rhizomes have been dried and ground into flour by the Indians. —Wildl. 4

a. Bract subtending inflorescence 1, erect or nearly so, or absent; if 2 or more the secondary bracts much smaller.
  b. Longest or only bract less than 1 cm long.
    c. Stem terete, smooth.
      Involucral bract consisting merely of the slightly larger, awn-tipped lowest scale of the spikelet; erect, terrestrial plant. .... 1. *S. cespitosus*
      Involucral bract foliaceous, not a modified spikelet scale; lax, floating aquatic plant (rarely emergent) .... 2. *S. subterminalis*
    c. Stem triangular, scabrous on the angles.
      All of the scales awn-tipped; leaves about as long as the stems. .... 3. *S. verecundus*
      Only the lowest scale awn-tipped; leaves shorter than the stems. .... 4. *S. clintonii*
  b. Longest or only bract 1 cm long or longer, looking like a continuation of the stem.
    d. Spikelets 1-12, sessile or subsessile and appearing lateral at one point on the stem. (Fig. 256).
      e. Stem sharply 3-angled, at least toward the tip just below the inflorescence.
        Achene trigonous; upper leaf sheath membranous on the inner side and ruptured before maturity .... 5. *S. torreyi*
        Achene plano-convex; upper leaf sheath firm on the inner side, straight or concave at the oriface .... 6. *S. americanus*
      e. Stem terete or obscurely 3-angled.
        f. Spikelet solitary; achene trigonous; flaccid aquatic (rarely emergent) perennial .... 2. *S. subterminalis*
        f. Spikelets usually several; achene plano-convex; erect terrestrial annual.
          Achene strongly corrugated transversely. .... 7. *S. hallii*
          Achene smooth or only slightly corrugated. .... 8. *S. smithii*
    d. Spikelets in a branched cluster. (Fig. 257).
      g. Achene trigonous, style 3-cleft; scales pale brown to whitish. .... 9. *S. heterochaetus*
      g. Achene lenticular or plano-convex; style 2-cleft; scales reddish brown.
        Culm firm, not easily compressed; scales with reddish atoms along the midrib .... 10. *S. acutus*
        Culm soft, easily compressed; scales lacking reddish atoms. .... 11. *S. tabernaemontani*
a. Bracts subtending inflorescence 2 or more, spreading, foliaceous, the blades flat. (Fig. 258).
  h. Spikelets mostly longer than 1 cm and 5 mm or more broad.
    i. Bristles equalling or exceeding achene, persistent; achene acutely 3-angled; plant of freshwater habitats .... 12. *S. fluviatilis*
    i. Bristles shorter than achene or early deciduous (persistent in *S. cylindricus*); achene lenticular, plano-convex, or obscurely 3-angled; plant of brackish habitats.
      Bristles usually persistent; achene gradually tapered to beak. .... 13. *S. cylindricus*
      Bristles usually deciduous; achene abruptly differentiated from beak.
        Lower leaf sheaths convex to trucate or slightly concave at the oriface, strongly nerved just below .... 14. *S. robustus*
        Lower leaf sheaths concave to v-shaped at oriface, delicately nerved. .... 15. *S. maritimus*
  h. Spikelets mostly shorter than 1 cm and less than 5 mm broad.

j. Bristles at maturity greatly exceeding and often hiding the scales, the spikelet
    appearing woolly.
    Base of involucre glabrous; achene whitish, gray or drab.
        Involucels and scales blackish .... 16. *S. atrocinctus*
        Involucels brown or reddish-brown.
            Spikelets in glomerules, sessile or subsessile. .... 17. *S. cyperinus*
            Spikelets, at least the lateral ones, distinctly pedicelled. .... 18. *S. pedicellatus*
    Base of involucre viscid or glutinous; achene reddish-brown. .... 19. *S. longii*
j. Bristles at maturity included behind scales, spikelet not appearing woolly.
    k. Bristles strongly curled or contorted. (Fig. 259).
        l. Spikelets not over 4 mm long; scales about equalling achenes. .... 20. *S. polyphyllus*
        l. Spikelets longer than 4 mm; scales much longer than achenes.
            Spikelets reddish-brown; achene brownish; scales conspicuously
                mucronate.
                Bristles less than 5 mm long; inflorescence rays often with
                    axillary bulblets. .... 21. *S. lineatus*
                Bristles 5 mm or more long; rays lacking axillary bulblets. .... 22. *S. pendulus*
                Spikelets purplish-brown; achenes tan or cream colored; scales
                inconspicuously mucronulate .... 23. *S. x peckii*
    k. Bristles straight or nearly so or absent. (Fig. 260).
        m. Lower leaf sheaths (at least) red, summit of sheath lacking a v-shaped
            oriface.
            Most leaf sheaths red at the base; achenes lenticular; stigmas 2; scales
                obtuse or acute .... 24. *S. microcarpus*
            Only the lower leaf sheaths red at the base; achenes trigonous;
                stigmas 3; scales acuminate .... 25. *S. expansus*
        m. Lower leaf sheaths green; summit of sheath with a v-shaped orifice.
            Bristles 3 or fewer or absent .... 26. *S. georgianus*
            Bristles 5 or 6.
                Lower leaves and sheaths usually strongly nodulose-septate;
                bristles often exceeding achene .... 27. *S. atrovirens*
                Lower leaves and sheaths smooth, not nodulose-septate; bristles
                usually shorter than achene .... 28. *S. hattorianus*

1. S. cespitósus L. (in tussocks). Alpine tundra and bogs. June-August. Map 584. (Eurasia). —OBL

2. S. subterminális Torr. (nearly terminal). Ponds and streams in shallow water. August-October. Map 585. —OBL

3. S. verecúndus Fern. (bashful). Dry to mesic deciduous woods and clearings. May-June. Map 586. Endangered in VT. [*S. planifolius*].

4. S. clintónii Gray (for G. Clinton). Dry fields and open woods. June-July. Map 587. Endangered in NY. —FACU

5. S. tórreyi Olney (for J. Torrey). Muddy pond and river shores. July-September. Map 588. — OBL

6. S. americánus Pers. (American). Chair-maker's Rush. Pond and river shores and fresh, brackish or saline marshes. June-September. Fig. 256, Map 589. (Eurasia). [*S. olneyi*]. —OBL

S. púngens Vahl. Similar to *S. americanus* but distinguishable in having an involucral bract 4 cm or more long (bract is less than 4 cm long in *S. americanus*). [*S. americanus*]. Our plants are var. *pungens*. —FACW+

7. S. hállii Gray (for E. Hall). Muddy or sandy pond and river shores. August-September. Reported for Essex and Middlesex Counties MA. [*S. supinus* var. *hallii*]. —OBL

8. S. smíthii Gray (for C. Smith). Muddy and sandy pond and river shores, bogs. August-October. Map 590. —OBL

S. purshiánus Fern. Bristles persistent, surpassing achene; achene unequally biconvex; involucral bract often divergent at maturity (bristles reduced or absent; achene flat on one surface; bract erect in *S. smithii*). [*S. smithii* var. *williamsii*; *S. debilis*]. —OBL

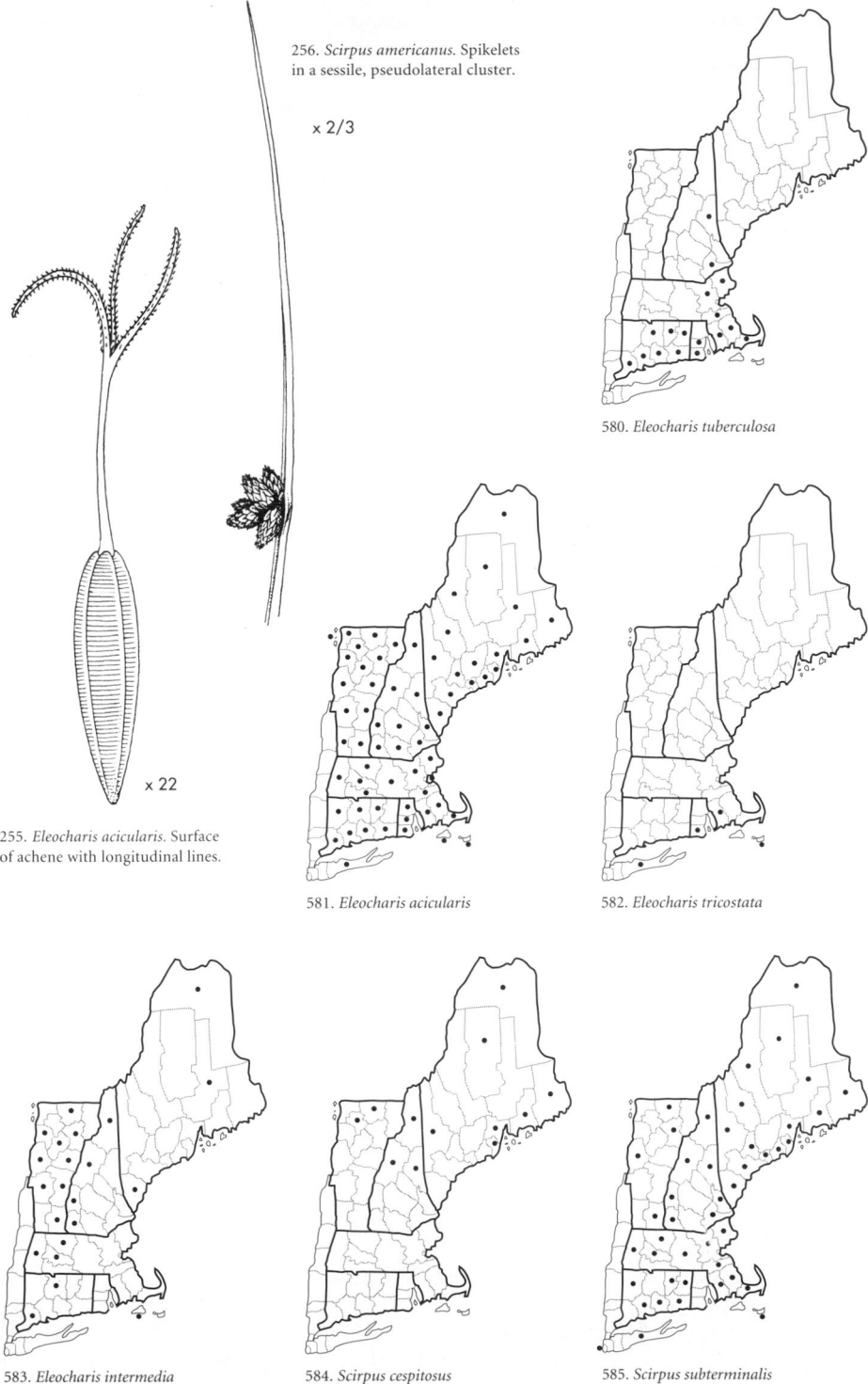

256. *Scirpus americanus.* Spikelets in a sessile, pseudolateral cluster.

× 2/3

× 22

255. *Eleocharis acicularis.* Surface of achene with longitudinal lines.

580. *Eleocharis tuberculosa*

581. *Eleocharis acicularis*

582. *Eleocharis tricostata*

583. *Eleocharis intermedia*

584. *Scirpus cespitosus*

585. *Scirpus subterminalis*

586. *Scirpus verecundus*   587. *Scirpus clintonii*   588. *Scirpus torreyi*

589. *Scirpus americanus*   590. *Scirpus smithii*   591. *Scirpus heterochaetus*

9. S. heterochaétus Chase (with diverse bristles). Great Bulrush. Pond shores, shallow water and marshes. July-September. Map 591. —OBL

S. etuberculàtus (Steud.) Kuntze. Similar to *S. heterochaetus* but distinguishable by the sharply triangular stems (stems terete in *S. heterochaetus*). From farther south on the coastal plain. Endangered in RI. —OBL

10. S. acútus Muhl. ex Bigelow (acute). Hard-stem Bulrush. Pond margins, shallow water and marshes. August-September. Map 592. [*S. occidentalis*]. —OBL

11. S. tabernaemontáni K. C. Gmel. Soft-stem Bulrush. Muddy pond and stream margins, shallow water and marshes. June-September. Fig. 257, Map 593. [*S. steinmetzii; S. validus*]. —OBL

12. S. fluviátilis (Torr.) Gray (of rivers). River Bulrush. River and lake margins, shallow water and marshes. July-September. Fig. 258, Map 594. —OBL

13. S. cylíndricus (Torr.) Britt. Brackish river shores. July-October. [*S. novae-angliae; S. robustus* var. *n.*]. —OBL

14. S. robústus Pursh (stout). Coastal river shores and brackish to saline marshes. July-October. Map 595. (e. S. Amer.; W.I.). Endangered in NY. [*S. cylindricus; S. novae-angliae*]. —OBL

15. S. maritímus L. (of the sea). Fresh, brackish and saline marshes and shores of tidal rivers. July-October. Map 596. (Adventive from Europe). [*S. fernaldii; S. paludosus* var. *atlanticus*]. Our plants are var. *maritimus.* —OBL

16. S. atrocínctus Fern. (black-girdled). Wet meadows, marshes, wooded swamps. June-September. [*S. cyperinus* var. *brachypodus*]. —FACW+

17. S. cyperínus (L.) Kunth (like Cyperus). Wool Grass. Marshes, wet meadows, bogs, wooded swamps, pond and stream borders. July-October. Map 597. [*S. atrocinctus; S, eriophorum; S. pedicellatus; S. rubricosus*]. —FACW+

18. S. pedicellátus Fern. (borne on pedicels). Marshes, river and stream borders, wooded swamps. July-September. [*S. cyperinus* var. *p.; S. eriophorum; S. rubricosus*]. —OBL

19. S. lóngii Fern. (for B. Long). Wet meadows and marshes. June-July. Map 598. Endangered in ME, MA, RI. —OBL

20. S. polyphýllus Vahl (many-leaved). Pond margins, marshes, wooded swamps, and rich, moist, deciduous woods. July-September. Fig. 259, Map 599. Endangered in VT, NH. —OBL

21. S. lineátus Michx. (marked with lines, referring to the keels on the scales). Wet meadows, marshes, and stream margins. June-September. Map 600. Endangered in ME. [*S. fontinalis*]. —OBL

22. S. péndulus Muhl. Wet meadows, marshes, stream borders. July-September. [*S. lineatus*]. —OBL

23. S. x péckii Britt. (for its discoverer). Wet meadows and bogs. July-September. Map 601. Perhaps a hybrid between *S. cyperinus* and *S. atrovirens.*

24. S. microcárpus J. & K. Presl. Wet meadows, marshes, ditches and pond margins. August-September. Fig. 260, Map 602. [*S. rubrotinctus*]. —OBL

25. S. expánsus Fern. (spread-out). Pond and brook margins, wet meadows and marshes. August-September. Map 603. [*S. sylvaticus* var. *bissellii*]. —OBL

26. S. georgiánus Harper. Wet meadows and marshes. July-September. [*S. atrovirens* var. *g.*]. —OBL

27. S. atrovírens Willd. Wooded swamps, stream borders and wet meadows. June-August. Map 604. [*S. georgianus; S. hattorianus*]. —OBL

S. ancistrochaétis Schuyler. Similar to *S. atrovirens* but with narrower leaves; bristles less rigid, often delicate and wrinkled with round-tipped barbs; achenes approximately 1 mm long (leaves 12-20 mm wide, bristles straight or nearly so, sharply barbed, achenes 1 mm or more long in *S. atrovirens*). Reported for Windham County VT and Franklin County MA. Endangered in MA, VT. —OBL

28. S. hattoriánus Makino. Wet meadows and marshes. July-September. [*S. atrovirens* var. *georgianus*]. —OBL

10. **Eriophórum** L. Cotton Grass (from the Greek meaning wool-bearing).

Perennial, with narrow leaves, or with leaves reduced to bladeless sheaths, 1 or more leaves forming an involucre to the inflorescence, or the involucre absent in species having only 1 spikelet; inflorescence terminal, consisting of a solitary spikelet or with spikelets few to many in a capitate cluster or an umbelliform cyme; spikelets many flowered, the scales spirally imbricated, all subtending a flower, or a few of the lower scales often empty; flowers perfect, subtended by 6-many, silky, elongate bristles, stamens 1-3, style 3-cleft, completely deciduous; fruit a triangular achene. OBL; Wildl. 1

a. Perianth of 6 crinkled bristles. (Fig. 261). .... 1. *E. alpinum*
a. Perianth of numerous straight bristles.
   b. Spikelet solitary; leafy involucre none. (Fig. 262). .... 2. *E. vaginatum*
                                                 var. *spissum*
   b. Spikelets 2 or more, in a capitate cluster or umbelliform cyme; involucre of
      1 or more leafy bracts. (Fig. 263).

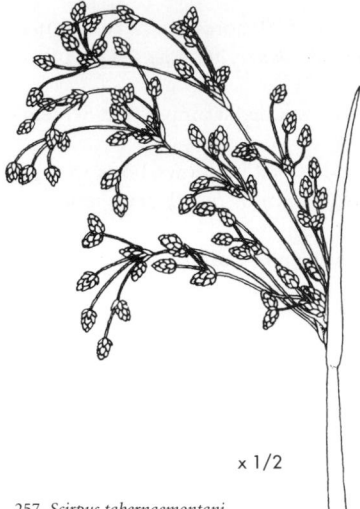

x 1/2

257. *Scirpus tabernaemontani.*
Spikelets in a branched cluster
subtended by a long bract.

x 1/2

258. *Scirpus fluviatilis.* Inflorescence
subtended by several foliaceous bracts.

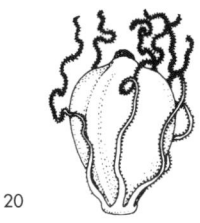

x 20

259. *Scirpus polyphyllus.* Achene with
bristles curled and contorted.

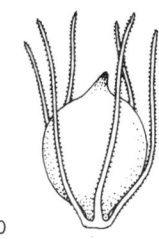

x 20

260. *Scirpus microcarpus.* Achene
with bristles straight or nearly so.

592. *Scirpus acutus*

593. *Scirpus tabernaemontani*

594. *Scirpus fluviatilis*

595. *Scirpus robustus*

596. *Scirpus maritimus*

597. *Scirpus cyperinus*

598. *Scirpus longii*

599. *Scirpus polyphyllus*

600. *Scirpus lineatus*

601. *Scirpus x peckii*

602. *Scirpus microcarpus*

603. *Scirpus expansus*

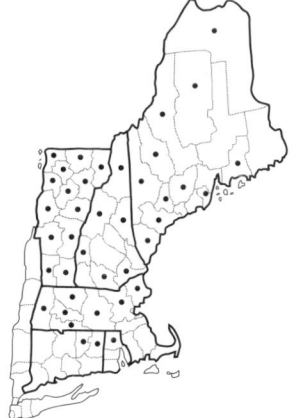
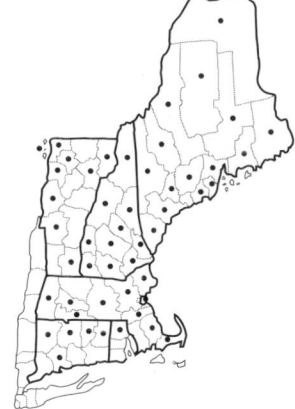

604. *Scirpus atrovirens*   605. *Eriophorum alpinum*   606. *Eriophorum vaginatum* var. *spissum*

    c. Leaves channeled throughout; involucre usually of 1 leafy bract.
        Blade of uppermost stem leaf as long or longer than its sheath. .... 3. *E. tenellum*
        Blade of uppermost stem leaf shorter than its sheath. .... 4. *E. gracile*
    c. Leaves flat, at least below the middle, involucre usually of 2 or more
        leafy bracts.
        d. Spikelet scales brown to whitish, usually with several strong nerves. .... 5. *E. virginicum*
        d. Spikelet scales blackish, drab, or olive green, usually with only the midvein
            prominent.
            Midrib of scale extending to or beyond apex, usually widening distally. ..... 6. *E. viridicarinatum*
            Midrib of scale ending before the apex, narrow, not widening distally. .... 7. *E. angustifolium*

    1. E. alpínum L. Bogs, wet meadows, cedar swamps and deciduous wooded swamps. June-July. Fig. 261, Map 605. (N. Eurasia). [*Scirpus hudsonianus*].
    2. E. vaginátum L. Hare's Tail. Bogs and peat. May-July. Fig. 262. Map 606. [*E. callithrix*]. Represented with us as var *spíssum* (Fern.) Boivin. [*E. spissum*].
    3. E. tenéllum Nutt. (delicate). Bogs, wet meadows, borders of pools and rivers and open wooded swamps. June-September. Fig. 263, Map 607.
    4. E. grácile W. Koch (slender). Bogs, wet meadows and peat. May-July. Map 608. Our plants are var. *gracile.*
    5. E. virginicum L. (Virginian). Tawny Cotton Grass. Bogs, wet meadows and pond margins. July-October. Map 609. (Eurasia).
    6. E. víridicarinátum (Engelm.) Fern. (green-keeled). Wet meadows, bogs and wooded swamps. June-August. Map 610.
    7. E. angustifólium Honckeny (narrow-leaved). Bogs and wet meadows. June-August. Map 611. (Eurasia). [*E. polystachion*].

11. *Fuiréna* Rottb. Umbrella Grass (for G. Fuiren).

Tufted annual (ours) with obtusely triangular, leafy stems; leaves with relatively wide blades and sparsely pubescent sheaths, 1-several leaves forming an involucre to the inflorescence; inflorescence a terminal, sessile, solitary spikelet or head-like cluster of few spikelets, often accompanied by 1 or more peduncled axillary clusters; spikelets ovoid, many-flowered, with spirally imbricated scales, the scales usually setose, and/or puberulent, rounded to truncate distally, conspicuously awned, each subtending a perfect flower; perianth of 3 bristles alternating with 3 ovate, awned scales, these on short stalks, stamens 3, style 3-cleft; fruit a trigonous, stalked, and apiculate achene.

1. **F. púmila** (Torr.) Spreng. (dwarf). Pond margins, wet meadows and marshes, in wet sandy or peaty soil. July-October. Fig. 264, Map 612. Endangered in RI. [*F. squarrosa*]. —OBL

F. squarrósa Michx. Resembling *F. pumila* but distinguishable in being perennial with deltoid, short-awned perianth scales, the awns straight or slightly curving (plant annual and perianth scales ovate, with a strongly curving awn as long as the body in *F. pumila*). From farther south. Reported for Suffolk County NY. (W.I.). [*F. hispida*]. —OBL

12. Lípocarpha Nees (from the Greek, based on the thickness of the perianth scales of some species).

Dwarf, cespitose annual with erect or spreading filiform stems; leaves filiform, basal, and 1 or more foliaceous bracts of unequal length forming an involucre to the inflorescence, the lowest appearing like a continuation of the stem; inflorescence of 1 to several small, sessile spikelets, terminal, but appearing lateral; spikelets many flowered, the scales spirally imbricated, all subtending a perfect flower; bristles none, the perianth consisting of a minute, translucent scale (easily overlooked) between the flower and axis of the spikelet, stamen 1, style 2-cleft; fruit a cylindric, brownish, minutely papillose achene. [*Hemicarpha*].

1. **L. micrántha** (Vahl) G. Tucker (tiny-flowered). Sandy or gravelly lake and river shores and sand bars. August-October. Fig. 265, Map 613. (Tropical Amer.). Endangered in CT. [*Hemicarpha m.*]. —FACW+

13. Bulbostýlis Kunth (name based on the bulbous base of the style).

Small, cespitose annual with slender stems; leaves basal or sub-basal, with filiform blades, 1-several leaves also forming an involucre to the inflorescence; inflorescence a capitate cluster of spikelets, or a simple or compound cyme; spikelets ovoid, few to many flowered, with spirally imbricated scales, each subtending a perfect flower; perianth none, stamens 2-3, style 3-cleft, its base swollen and persisting as a minute (ours) tubercle; fruit a trigonous achene with a colored tubercle.

1. **B. capilláris** (L.) Kunth ex C.B. Clarke (hair-like). Waste places and roadsides, usually in sandy soil. August-October. Fig. 266, Map 614. [*Stenophyllus c.*]. Our plants are subsp. *capillaris.* —FACU

14. Fimbristýlis Vahl (name based on the fringed style of some species).

Cespitose annuals or perennials with narrow flat, involute or folded leaves, these few, toward the base of the stem, 1-several leaves also forming an involucre to the inflorescence; inflorescence a terminal simple or compound cyme with spikelets sessile and on peduncles or pedicels of different lengths; spikelets ovoid to cylindric, many-flowered, with spirally imbricated scales, each subtending a perfect flower; perianth none, stamens 1-3, style 2-3 cleft, usually with a swollen base, completely deciduous; fruit a lenticular or trigonous achene lacking a tubercle.

Achene trigonous; style 3-cleft; plant annual. .... 1. *F. autumnalis*
Achene lenticular; style 2-cleft; plant perennial.
   Spikelet scales glabrous .... 2. *F. castanea*
   Spikelet scales puberulent .... 3. *F. caroliniana*

1. **F. autumnális** (L.) R. & S. (autumnal). Roadsides, pond margins and waste areas in moist, usually sandy soil. July-October. Fig. 267, Map 615. Endangered in VT. [*F. frankii; F. geminata*]. —FACW+

2. **F. castánea** (Michx.) Vahl (chestnut-colored). Shores and salt marshes along the coast. July-October. (W.I.). Reported for Suffolk County NY. [*F. puberula*]. —OBL

3. **F. caroliniána** (Lam.) Fern. (of Carolina). Marshes, sand dune hollows, flats and wet or dry soil along the coast. July-October. [*F. drummondii; F. interior*]. —FACW+

x 1-1/2

261. *Eriophorum alpinum.*
Spikelet subtended by short
bract, bristles crinkled.

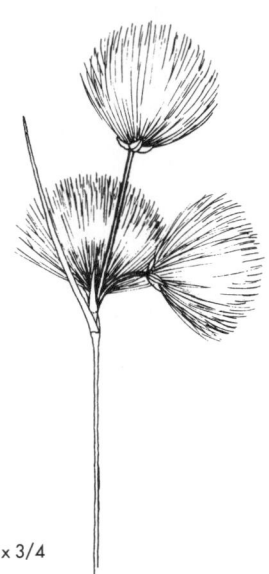

x 1

262. *Eriophorum vaginatum* var. *spissum.*
Solitary spikelet with no leafy involucre.

x 3/4

263. *Eriophorum tenellum.* Cluster of several
spikelets, involucre of 1 leafy bract.

x 1/2

264. *Fuirena pumila.* General habit.

x 3/4

265. *Lipocarpha micrantha.*
General habit.

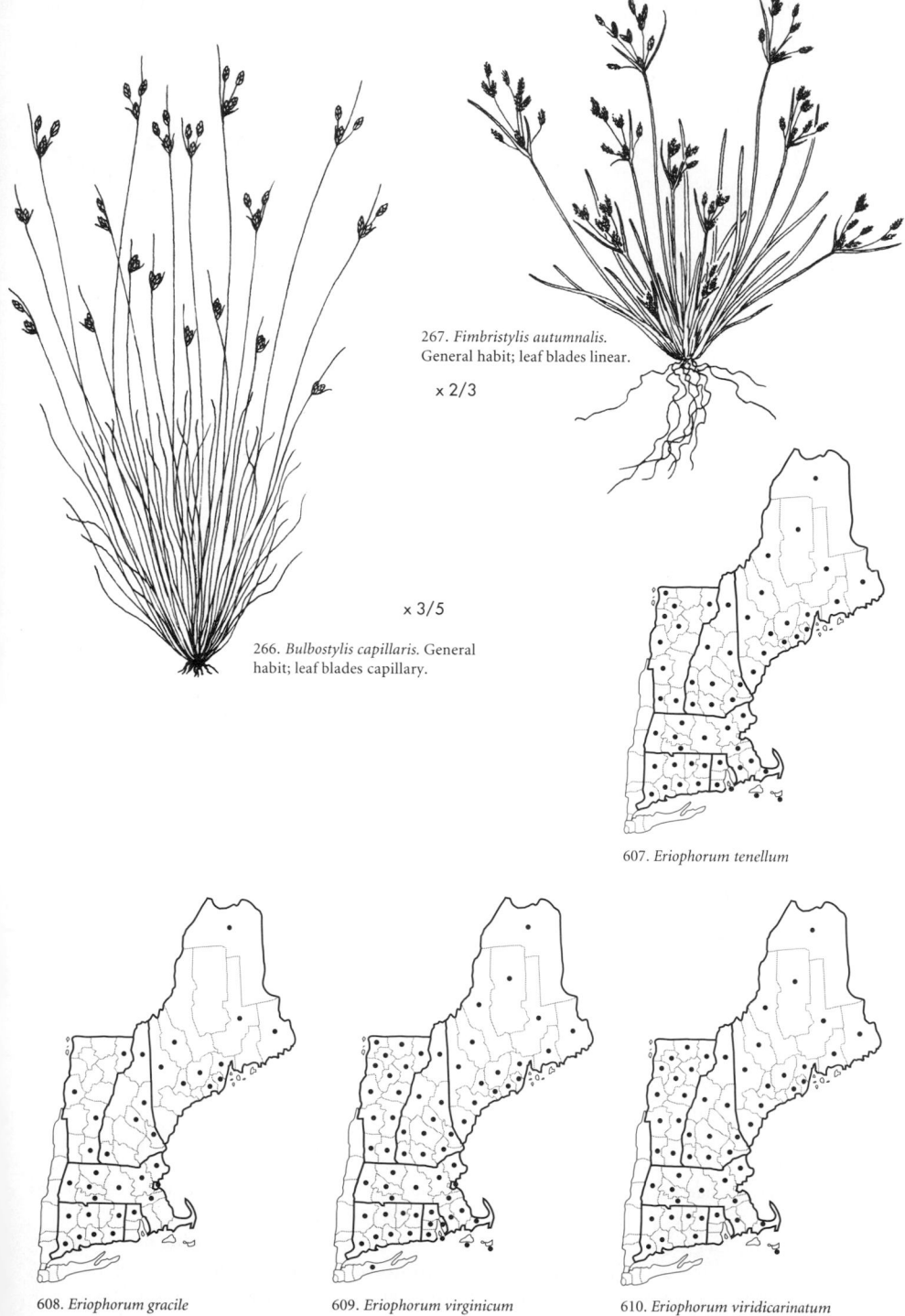

267. *Fimbristylis autumnalis.*
General habit; leaf blades linear.

x 2/3

x 3/5

266. *Bulbostylis capillaris.* General
habit; leaf blades capillary.

607. *Eriophorum tenellum*

608. *Eriophorum gracile*

609. *Eriophorum virginicum*

610. *Eriophorum viridicarinatum*

611. *Eriophorum angustifolium*   612. *Fuirena pumila*   613. *Lipocarpha micrantha*

614. *Bulbostylis capillaris*   615. *Fimbristylis autumnalis*

Family 36. Aráceae (Arum Family)

Monoecious, (rarely dioecious) or hermaphrodite perennial herbs of wetlands or damp habitats, mostly from rhizomes or corms. Stem lacking (in ours), the leaves and scape arising from the rootstalk. Tissues of plant generally containing calcium oxalate crystals. Leaves basal, with basal sheaths, long petioled, simple or compound. Flowers small, imperfect or rarely perfect, crowded on a fleshy spadix and forming a dense spike or head, the staminate flowers above, the pistillate below, the spadix usually subtended by a foliaceous or colored spathe; perianth lacking, or of 4-6 short, free or connate segments, stamens usually 4-6 (up to 10 in *Peltandra*), the filaments very short, staminodes sometimes present, pistil 1, the ovary superior or somewhat embedded in the spadix, 1-4 celled, with 1-several ovules per cell, style short or absent, stigma minute and often sessile. Fruit usually a berry or berry-like. The members of this family that occur in our range are considered poisonous if eaten fresh; poisonous properties are removed by drying.

Pístia L. *stratiótes* L. Water Lettuce. Differing from all other Araceae in being a free-floating aquatic (or sometimes rooting in mud) with simple, entire leaves in rosettes and long, hanging roots, the spathes small, white, sessile in the leaf axils. Rarely escaped from cultivation. Reported for Suffolk County NY. —OBL

a. Leaves compound, ternately or pedately divided. .... 1. *Arisaema*
a. Leaves simple, not divided.
   b. Leaves sagittate or hastate .... 2. *Peltandra virginica*
   b. Leaves cordate, ovate or elliptic.
      c. Leaves elliptic; spadix lacking a spathe. .... 3. *Orontium*
         aquaticum
      c. Leaves cordate or ovate; spadix subtended by a well developed spathe.
         Spathe white, flat, not enclosing spadix; leaves not having a skunk-like
            odor; fruit red .... 4. *Calla palustris*
         Spathe green or brown, enclosing spadix; leaves having a skunk-like odor
            when crushed; fruit blackish green .... 5. *Symplocarpus*
         foetidus

1. *Arisaéma* Mart. Indian Turnip (Greek name for an arum with spotted leaves).

Monoecious or dioecious (by abortion of the staminate flowers) herbs of damp or wet habitats, from a corm, the corm acrid; leaves long petioled, ternately or pedately compound; scape elongate, spathe enclosing the spadix, tubular and convolute below, with an arched limb above, purplish or green, the spadix included or exserted, cylindric, the flowers covering the basal part of the spadix, the terminal part sterile; perianth lacking, the staminate flowers each consisting of a cluster of 2-5 subsessile anthers, the pistillate composed of a 1-locular ovary with 1-several ovules and a broad stigma; fruit a subglobose cluster of red berries, each containing 1-3 seeds. Corms edible but must first be roasted or cut in thin slices and dried for 6 months; fresh corms very acrid due to oxalate crystals. Has also been used to treat pulmonary congestion. —Wildl. 1

Pinèllia Tenore *ternáta* (Thunb.) Breit. Similar to *Arisaema* but distinguishable in having the spadix adnate to the spathe on one side at the base and leaves often bearing bulblets at the base of the leaflets. Adventive from Japan. Reported for Kings County NY.

Leaves ternately 3-parted; spathe arched over the spadix, the latter blunt,
    included .... 1. *A. triphyllum*
Leaves pedately 5 or more parted; spadix tapering into a long slender appendage
    exserted beyond the spathe .... 2. *A. dracontium*

1. *A. triphýllum* (L.) Schott (three leaved). Jack-in-the-pulpit. Wooded swamps, rich or wet woods and thickets. May-July. Map 616. Our plants include subsp. *triphyllum* [*A. atrorubens*] and the following subsp.:

subsp. *stewardsónii* (Britt.) Huttlest. Leaflets green beneath; tubular part of spathe sharply and deeply corrugated, the ridges white (leaflets glaucous beneath; tubular part of spathe obscurely or shallowly corrugated in var. *triphyllum*). [*A. stewardsonii*].

subsp. *pusíllum* (Peck) Huttlest. Leaflets green beneath; tubular part of spathe obscurely or shallowly corrugated, the expanded part of the spathe less than twice as wide as tubular part (expanded part of spathe more than twice as wide as the tube in the above vars.). —FACW-

2. *A. dracóntium* (L.) Schott (a kind of Arum). Green dragon. Rich wet or mesic upland and alluvial woods. Uncommon. May-June. Map 617. [*Muricanda d.*].—FACW

2. *Peltándra* Raf. Arrow Arum (from the Greek, based on the shape of the stamen).

Monoecious, from thick, fibrous roots; leaves long petioled, usually with sagittate or hastate blades having 3 main veins with parallel lateral veins; scape elongate, spathe elongate, convolute below and enclosing the pistillate portion of the spadix, open above and exposing the staminate part, the flowers covering the entire spadix, or only the tip naked; perianth absent, the staminate flowers each consisting of 6-10 stamens beneath a sterile ovary, the pistillate composed of a 1-locular ovary with 1-several ovules, the ovary surrounded by 4-5 white, scale-like staminodia; fruit a 1-3 seeded green or amber berry, the seeds surrounded by gelatinous material, the berries aggregated in a globose head enveloped by the leathery spathe, the head terminating a recurved scape. —Wildl. 1

1. *P. virgínica* (L.) Schott (Virginian). Tuckahoe. Shallow water, mud of ponds or sluggish streams, and deciduous swamps. May-July. Fig. 268, Map 618. [*P. luteospadix*]. Roots edible but first must be roasted or cut into slices and dried for several months. Can then be ground into meal. Spadix was reportedly eaten by Indians after boiling. —OBL

3. *Oróntium* L. Golden Club.

Hermaphrodite, from a deep, thick rhizome; leaves long petioled, erect or floating, in a basal cluster, with an oblong-elliptic blade; scape elongate, terminated by a cylindric spadix, spathe consisting of a tubular sheath at the base of the scape bearing a short, scale-like blade, the flowers covering the entire spadix; flowers perfect, bright yellow, the lower flowers with 6 scale-like sepals, the upper with 4, stamens as many as the sepals, ovary partly embedded in the spadix, 1-locular, with 1 ovule; fruit a green or brown utricle containing a single seed, the fruits aggregated in a conic structure at the end of the scape.

1. *O. aquáticum* L. (aquatic). Pond and river margins, shallow water. May-June. Map 619. Endangered in MA and RI. Rhizome edible after roasting or cutting into slices and drying for several months. Seeds were eaten by Indians after several boilings and then drying. —OBL

4. *Cálla* L. Water Arum (ancient Greek name).

Monoecious, from an elongate rhizome; leaves long petioled, with ovate to suborbicular blades which are cordate at the base and short acuminate; scape elongate, spathe flat, white, not enclosing the spadix, ovate, abruptly contracted to a long narrow tip, spadix cylindric, much shorter than the spathe, the flowers covering the entire spadix; perianth absent, flowers perfect or the uppermost staminate, stamens 6, ovary 1-locular, with several ovules; fruit a red, few seeded berry, the seeds surrounded by gelatinous material, the berries aggregated in a large ovoid head.

1. *C. palústris* L. (of marshes). Wild Calla. Pond margins, deciduous swamps and bogs. June-August. Map 620. (Eurasia). Rhizome edible after roasting or being cut into slices and drying for several months. —OBL

5. *Symplocárpus* Salisb. ex Nutt. Skunk Cabbage (from the Greek, based on the aggregated nature of the fruiting structure).

Hermaphrodite, from a thick erect rhizome, having a strong, skunk-like odor; leaves short to long petioled, in a basal cluster, the blades very large and broad, ovate, cordate; scape short, partly underground, the spathes appearing before the leaves in springtime, nearly sessile and barely rising out of the ground, (the scape later elongating) fleshy, ovate, pointed, with inrolled margins, maroon and greenish spotted and striped, completely enclosing the spadix, spadix subglobose, completely covered by the flowers; perianth present, of 4 fleshy segments, flowers perfect, stamens 4, opposite the perianth segments, ovary embedded in the spadix, 1-locular, 1-ovuled, style thick and elongate, 4-sided; fruiting structure a subglobose mass roughened with the persistent perianth segments and styles, composed of a fleshy spadix with seeds embedded just beneath the surface, the structure persisting on the curved scape after the leaves have disappeared in fall. —Wildl. 1

1. *S. foétidus* (L.) Salisb. ex Nutt. Wooded swamps, wet woods and streamsides. February-May. Map 621. (E. Asia). [*Spathyema f.*]. Rhizome edible after peeling, cutting into thin slices, and drying for 6 months; young tightly-rolled leaves also edible after cutting into thin slices and drying for 6 months. A tea made from the dried rhizome has been used as cough syrup. Powder made from the dried rhizome was used by Indians to dress wounds. Plant often confused with *Veratrum viride*, which is poisonous. —OBL

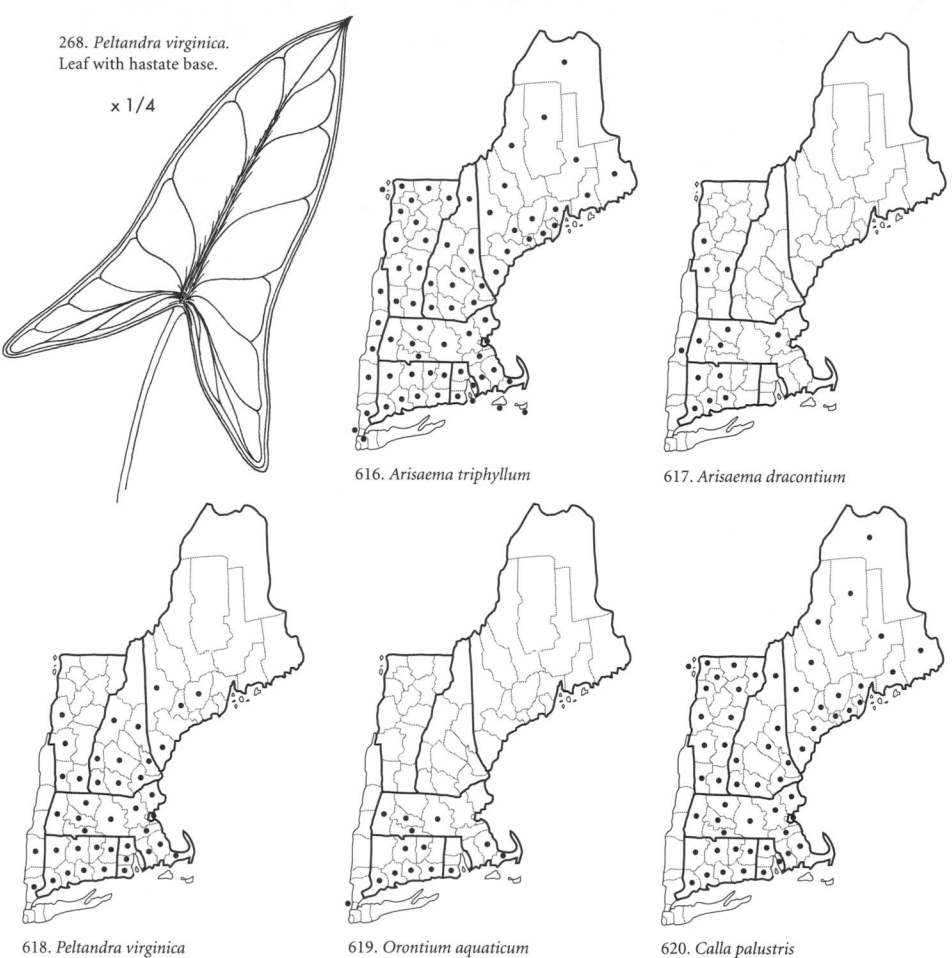

268. *Peltandra virginica.*
Leaf with hastate base.

× 1/4

616. *Arisaema triphyllum*

617. *Arisaema dracontium*

618. *Peltandra virginica*

619. *Orontium aquaticum*

620. *Calla palustris*

Family 37. Acoráceae (Sweetflag Family)

Hermaphrodite, aromatic, from long, thick, creeping rhizomes. Leaves erect, long and linear, sword-shaped, the midvein usually off center. Scape elongate, 3-angled, the spathe prolonged above spadix and appearing as an extension of the scape, the spadix laterally divergent, cylindric, the flowers covering the entire spadix; perianth present, consisting of 6 short concave segments, flowers perfect, stamens 6 with linear filaments, ovary 2-3 locular, with several ovules per locule. Fruit a hard, dry, obpyramidal berry, gelatinous inside and containing 1-3 seeds. [*Araceae*].

1. Ácorus L. Sweetflag (Latin name for an aromatic plant).
Same characters as the family.

1. A. americánus (Raf.) Raf. Deciduous swamps, marshes and shallow water. May-July. Fig. 269, Map 622. (Europe). Bases of the plants edible after cutting in thin slices and boiling; can also be candied. Young shoots edible raw. Rhizome edible after drying; was also eaten raw by Indians in small amounts for indigestion; in large quantities it is said to be hallucinogenic. —OBL

A. cálamus is European and usually sterile; *A. americanus* is North American. Reported for ME.

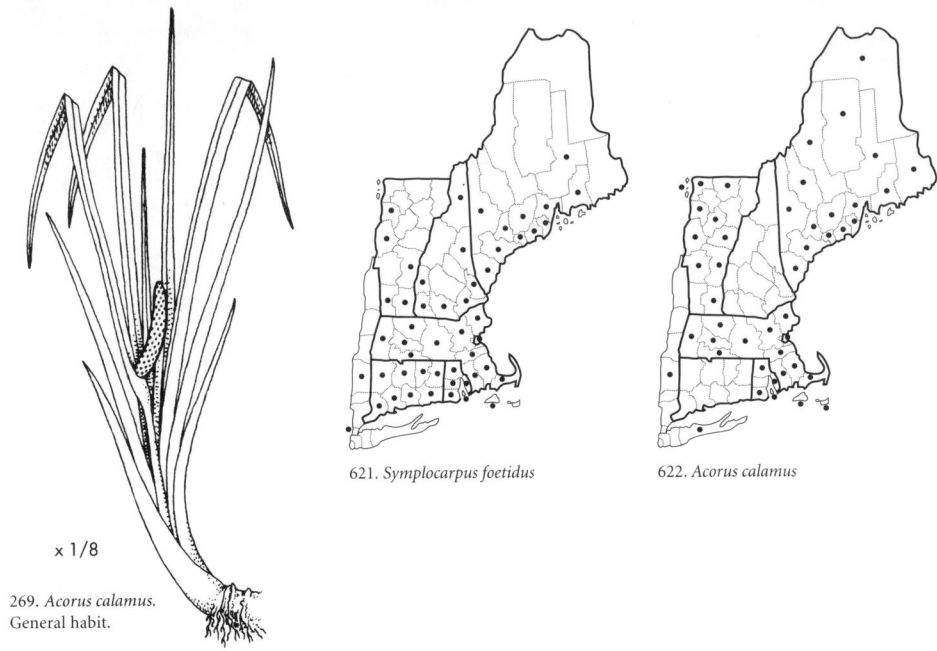

621. *Symplocarpus foetidus*

622. *Acorus calamus*

× 1/8

269. *Acorus calamus*.
General habit.

Family 38. Lemnáceae (Duckweed Family)

Monoecious, perennial, usually free floating on the water surface. Plants minute, the body consisting of 1 or more flattened, leaf-like thalli (fronds), often bearing 1 or more simple, unbranched roots from the under surface, usually multiplying vegetatively by laterally branching from buds, the branches soon separating. Flowers imperfect, borne at the edge or upper surface of the plant, seldom seen; perianth lacking, flowers minute, enclosed in a pouch or spathe, consisting of a single stamen or pistil. Fruit a 1-several seeded utricle.

a. Thalli with roots present, borne on the underside.
    Each thallus with 3 or more roots, usually purple beneath. (Fig. 270). .... 1. *Spirodela polyrhiza*
    Each thallus with 1 root, usually green beneath. (Fig. 271). .... 2. *Lemna*
a. Thalli lacking roots.
    Thallus oval, oblong or ellipsoid, 1.5 mm or less long or wide. (Fig. 272). .... 3. *Wolffia*
    Thallus narrowly linear, much longer than 1.5 mm. (Fig. 273). .... 4. *Wolffiella gladiata*

1. Spirodéla Schleid. Duckweed (from the Greek, based on the thallus roots).
Thallus oval to narrowly obovate, dark green above, 5 or more nerved, purple beneath, with 2 or more roots; young plants remaining attached and forming small colonies. —OBL; Wildl. 2

    1. S. polyrhíza (L.) Schleid. (many-rooted). Ponds, lakes, pools and quiet rivers. Fig. 270, Map 623. (Tropics).
    S. punctáta (Mey.) C. H. Thompson. Similar to *S. polyrhiza* but with 4 or fewer roots and thallus narrowly obovate to oblong (roots 5 or more and thallus broadly obovate to ovate in *S. polyrhiza*). From farther west. Reported for MA. [*S. oligorrhiza*].

2. Lémna L. Ducks Meat (Greek name for a water plant).
Thallus oval, obovate or elliptical, green above and below, 1 to several nerved, with 1 root; young plants often remaining attached and forming small colonies. —OBL; Wildl. 2

a. Thallus tapering at the base to a long stalk, 5 mm or more long
(including stalk) .... 1. *L. trisulca*
a. Thallus sessile or nearly so, less than 5 mm long.
  b. Thalli 2 or more times as long as wide, nerveless or 1 nerved. .... 2. *L. valdiviana*
  b. Thalli less than twice as long as wide, 3 nerved.
    Thallus symmetrical or nearly so .... 3. *L. minor*
    Thallus asymmetrical .... 4. *L. perpusilla*

1. *L. trisúlca* L. (three furrowed). Ponds and ditches. Fig. 271, Map 624. (Old World).

2. *L. valdiviána* Phil. (of Valdivia). Ponds and rivers. Map 625. (Tropical Amer.). [*L. cyclostasa*].

3. *L. mínor* L. (smaller). Ponds and streams. Map 626. (Old World).

L. turionífera Landolt. Similar to *L. minor* but distinguishable by the presence of several papillae on the thallus (thallus with 1 papule in *L. minor*).

4. *L. perpusílla* Torr. (very tiny). Ponds and rivers. Map 627. [*L. trinervis*].

3. **Wólffia** Horkel. ex Schleid. Water Meal (for J. Wolff).

Thallus thick, globose or subglobose to ellipsoid, thick, lacking nerves and roots. —OBL; Wildl. 2

Thalli not punctate .... 1. *W. columbiana*
Thalli brown punctate over both surfaces. .... 2. *W. brasiliensis*

1. *W. columbiána* Karst. (of Colombia). Stagnant pools and ponds, quite water. Fig. 272, Map 628. (Tropical Amer.).

2. *W. brasiliénsis* Weddell. Quiet water. Map 629. (Mexico; W.I.). [*W. borealis; W. papulifera; W. punctata*].

4. **Wolffiélla** Hegelm.

Thallus thin, linear, falcate, much longer than wide, lacking nerves and roots; young plants remaining attached and forming small, radiating colonies. —OBL; Wildl. 2

1. *W. gladiáta* (Hagelm.) Hagelm. Quiet water. Fig. 273. Reported for Middlesex and Plymouth Counties MA. [*W. floridana*].

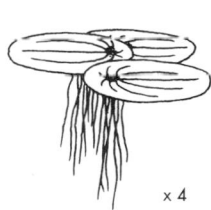

270. *Spirodella polyrhiza*. Several thalli, each with several roots from the underside.

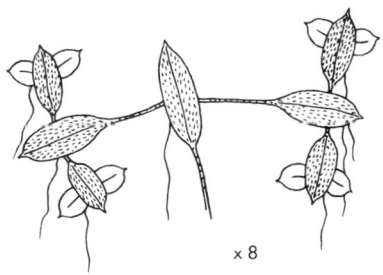

271. *Lemna trisulca*. Cluster of attached thalli, each with 1 root from the underside.

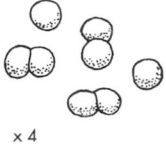

272. *Wolffia columbiana*. Several oval thalli.

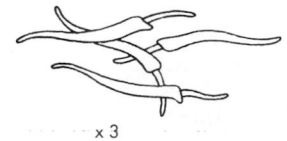

273. *Wolfiella gladiata*. Several linear thalli.

623. *Spirodela polyhiza*

624. *Lemna trisulca*

625. *Lemna valdiviana*

626. *Lemna minor*

627. *Lemna perpusilla*

628. *Wolffia columbiana*

629. *Wolffia brasiliensis*

630. *Eriocaulon aquaticum*

Family 39. Eriocauláceae (Pipewort Family)

Monoecious (ours) perennial herbs of aquatic or marsh habitats, from fibrous roots, these white with conspicuous cross markings. Stem lacking or very short, the leaves basal. Leaves linear, grass-like, tufted, sheathing the base of the naked scape. Flowers small, imperfect, crowded in a dense, terminal, solitary head on a long, slender scape, the head subtended by an involucre of bracts, each flower in the axil of a scarious bract; perianth chaffy or membranous, in 2 series but not differentiated into a calyx and corolla, the outer segments 2 or 3, distinct or sometimes connate, the inner segments 2 or 3, often united below into a tube (rarely absent), staminate flowers with 4-6 stamens inserted on the inner segments, often with a vestigial ovary present, pistillate flowers of 1 pistil, ovary 2-3-loculed, superior, each locule with 1 ovule, style 1, stigmas 2 or 3. Fruit a membranous, 2-3 celled, 2-3 seeded, loculicidal capsule.

1. Eriocaúlon L. Pipewort (from the Greek, based on wool at the base of the scape of another species).

Head flattened or subglobose, the bracts and perianth segments usually white bearded, inner perianth segments of the staminate flowers united below into a tube; those of the pistillate flowers separate. —OBL

Outer flowers of head spreading to reflexed; bracts and perianth densely
  white-pubescent .... 1. *E. aquaticum*
Outer flowers of head ascending to erect; bracts and perianth glabrous or
  sparsely pubescent .... 2. *E. parkeri*

1. E. aquáticum (Hill) Druce. White Buttons. Shallow water of fresh ponds and lakes. July-September. Fig. 274, Map 630. (Ireland and Scotland). [*E. articulatum; E. pellucidum; E. septangulare*].

2. E. párkeri Robins (for its discoverer). Tidal flats and shallow water. July-September. Map 631. Endangered in MA, CT.

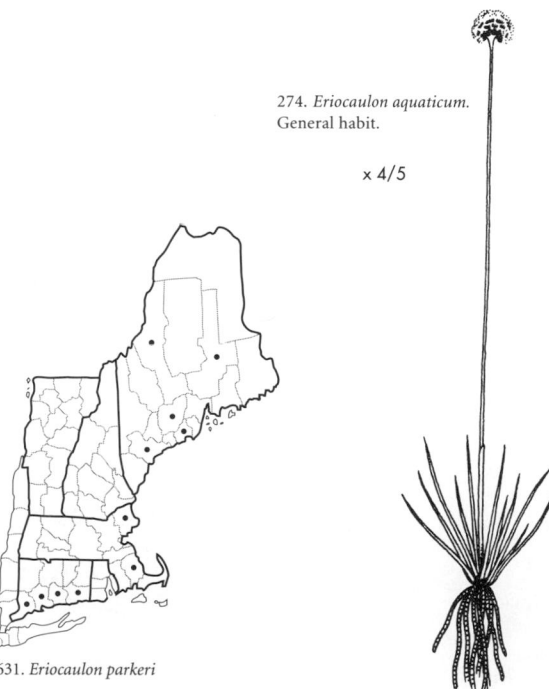

274. *Eriocaulon aquaticum.*
General habit.

x 4/5

631. *Eriocaulon parkeri*

Family 40. Xyridáceae (Yellow-eyed Grass Family)

Monoecious, perennial or annual herbs from a short rhizome, this sometimes bulbous, or from a tuft of fibrous roots. Stem lacking, the leaves basal. Leaves narrow, tufted, sheathing the base of the naked scape. Flowers perfect, in a terminal, solitary, ovoid, globose or cylindric head on a long scape, the head with few to many spirally imbricated, coriaceous bracts, the lower empty, the upper each subtending a flower; calyx irregular, the 2 lateral sepals small, persistent, boat shaped and keeled, the third one larger, deciduous, corolla regular, clawed, persistent, with 3 lobes, usually yellow, stamens 3, inserted on the petals, usually alternating with 3 bifid, plumose or bearded staminodes, ovary superior, 1 celled or imperfectly 3 celled at the base, with numerous ovules, style 3 branched above. Fruit an oblong, 3 valved, loculicidal capsule with many seeds.

1. Xyris L. Yellow-eyed Grass (Greek name for a plant with 2-edged leaves).
Same characters as the family. —OBL

a. Leaves and scapes spirally twisted; base of plant bulbous-thickened. .... 1. *X. torta*
a. Leaves and scapes not conspicuously spirally twisted; base of plant not
    bulbous-thickened.
    b. Tips of the lateral sepals covered by the subtending bracts, included. .... 2. *X. difformis*
    b. Tips of the lateral sepals usually exserted from the subtending bracts
        (if sometimes included in *X. montana*, keel of sepals entire or minutely
        dentate at tip; keel lacerate beyond middle in *X. difformis*). (Fig. 275).
        Head less than 1 cm long; leaves less than 3 mm wide; keel of lateral sepals
        entire or minutely dentate at the tip .... 3. *X. montana*
        Head 1 cm long or longer; leaves 3 mm wide or wider; keel of lateral sepals
        lacerate or fimbriate. (Fig. 275) .... 4. *X. smalliana*

    1. *X. tórta* Sm. (twisted). Bogs, and wet sandy soil, especially pond margins. July-September. Map 632. [*X. flexuosa*].
    2. *X. difförmis* Chapm. (of two forms). Sandy pond margins and bogs, wet sandy soil. July-September. Map 633. [*X. elata*]. Our plants are var. *difformis*.
    3. *X. montána* Ries (of mountains). Bogs, wet sandy soil, pond margins. June-September. Map 634. Endangered in CT. [*X. papillosa*].
    4. *X. smalliána* Nash (for its discoverer) Bogs, pond margins, wet sandy soil and pond margins. July-October. Fig. 275, Map 635. Endangered in ME, CT. [*X. congdoni*].

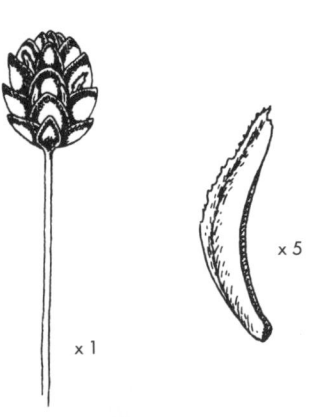

275. *Xyris smalliana.* Solitary head; single sepal with keel minutely dentate.

632. *Xyris torta*

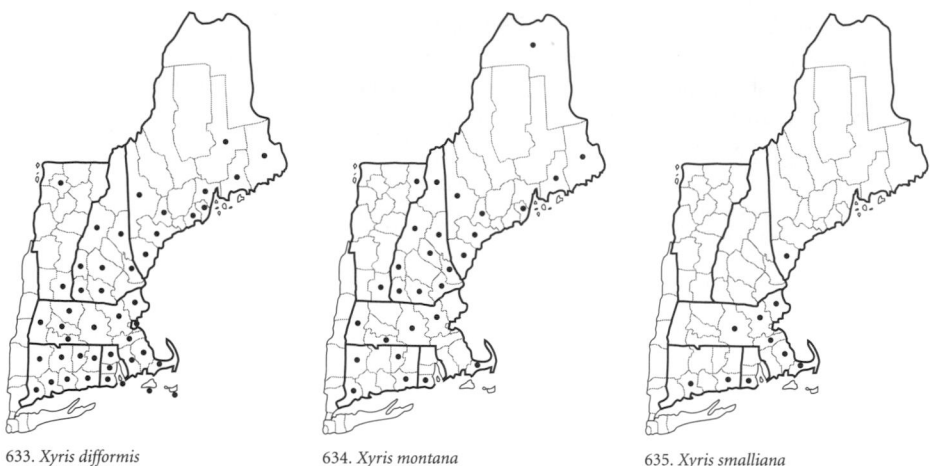

633. *Xyris difformis*   634. *Xyris montana*   635. *Xyris smalliana*

Family 41. Commelináceae (Spiderwort Family)

Monoecious, annual or perennial, often succulent herbs from fibrous or thickened roots. Stems jointed, often branching, leafy. Leaves alternate, parallel veined, dilated at the base into a tubular sheath. Flowers perfect, in cymes or rarely solitary, subtended by foliaceous bracts or spathes; flower regular or irregular, with a green, herbaceous calyx of 3 persistent, separate sepals, and a corolla of 3 membranous, white or colored, equal or unequal petals which are free or united into a tube, deciduous, stamens 6, all fertile or several reduced to staminodes, ovary superior, 2-3 loculed, ovules 1-few per locule, style 1, stigma 1. Fruit a 2-3 valved loculicidal capsule with 3-several seeds.

Inflorescence enclosed in a folded spathiform bract less than 3.5 cm long;
    leaves ovate. (Fig. 276) .... 1. *Commelina*
Inflorescence (terminal) not enclosed in a folded spathiform bract, subtended
    by usually 2 bracts longer than 3.5 cm; leaves linear lanceolate. (Fig. 277). .... 2. *Tradescantia*

1. Commelína L. Dayflower (based on a dedication to early Dutch botanists).

Annual or perennial, erect or procumbent and rooting at the nodes; leaves with dilated, lance-ovate blades distinct from the sheaths; inflorescence enclosed in a folded, clasping, cordate spathe; flowers irregular, sepals unequal, the 2 lateral partly united, petals unequal, the 2 upper ones blue, on long claws, the lower one smaller and often white or absent, fertile stamens 3, larger than the 3 sterile ones, their filaments glabrous, ovary sessile, 2-3-locular, one locule often abortive or empty; flowers ephemeral.

Margins of spathe united at the base .... 1. *C. erecta*
Margins of spathe free to the base.
    Corolla with all three petals blue, shorter than 8 mm. .... 2. *C. diffusa*
    Corolla with 2 large blue petals 8 mm or more long and 1 small white petal. .... 3. *C. communis*

    1. C. erécta L. (erect). Loamy or sandy soil in fields or deciduous or pine woods. June-October. Reported for R.I. [*C. elegans; C. virginica*]. Our plants are var. *erecta.* —FACW
    2. C. diffúsa Burm. f. (spreading). Bottomlands and wet woods. July-October. (Pan Tropical and warm Temperate). Reported for VT. [*C. nudiflora*]. —FACW
    3. C. commúnis L. (growing in colonies). Waste places, roadsides, gardens. June-October. Fig. 276, Map 636. (Naturalized from Asia). Reportedly used as a potherb in other countries. Our plants include var. *communis* and the following var.:
    var. *lúdens* (Miq.) Clarke. Lateral petals 1 cm or less long, deep blue-violet (lateral petals 1 cm or longer and pale violet blue in var. *communis*). —FAC-

2. *Tradescántia* L. Spiderwort (for J. Tradescant).

Perennial, leaves linear lanceolate, not distinctly dilated above the sheaths; involucral bracts resembling the foliage leaves; flowers regular, sepals herbaceous, petals all alike, blue to pink, stamens all fertile, the filaments usually bearded.

a. Upper leaf blades wider than the opened, flattened sheath, usually less than
    10 times as long as wide .... 1. *T. subaspera*
a. Upper leaf blades as wide as or narrower than the opened, flattened sheath,
    usually more than 10 times as long as wide.
    Sepals pilose over the entire surface .... 2. *T. virginiana*
    Sepals glabrous or pilose only at the base and tip. .... 3. *T. ohiensis*

    1. *T. subáspera* Ker (somewhat harsh). Deciduous woods and thickets. June-July. Reported for VT. [*T. pilosa*]. Our plants are var. *subaspera*.

    2. *T. virginiána* L. (of Virginia). Deciduous woods and thickets in rich soil, roadsides and waste places. May-July. Fig. 277, Map 637. —FACU

    3. *T. ohiénsis* Raf. (of Ohio). Deciduous woods, roadsides and waste places. May-July. Map 638. [*T. barbata; T. canaliculata; T. reflexa*]. —FAC

    T. bracteáta Small ex Britt. (bracted). Similar to the latter 2 species but sepals pubescent with glandular hairs (sepals glabrous in latter 2 species, or if pubescent, hairs not glandular). From farther west. Reported for Franklin County MA.

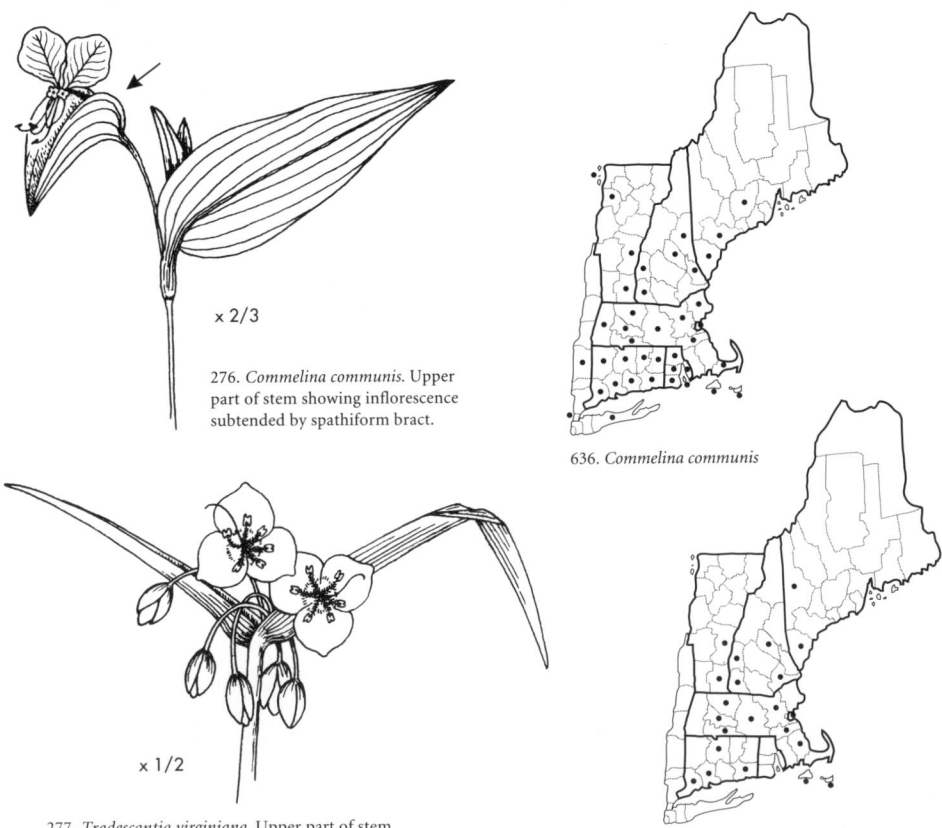

x 2/3

276. *Commelina communis*. Upper part of stem showing inflorescence subtended by spathiform bract.

636. *Commelina communis*

x 1/2

277. *Tradescantia virginiana*. Upper part of stem showing inflorescence subtended by 2 foliaceous bracts.

637. *Tradescantia virginiana*

Family 42. Pontederiáceae (Pickerelweed Family)

Monoecious, perennial herbs of aquatic or marsh habitats, floating or rooting in the substrate, from short or long, creeping rhizomes. Stems branched or unbranched, with sheathing leaves. Leaves narrow and grass like or broad, petioled or sessile, sheathing the base of the stem and/or cauline and alternate. Flowers perfect, solitary, spicate or paniculate, the inflorescence (or flower) subtended by a leaf-like spathe; flowers regular or irregular, perianth of 6 petaloid segments, united below into a tube, stamens 3 or 6, inserted on the tube, unequal or dissimilar, ovary superior, 1 or 3 locular, ovules 1-many, style 1, stigma 3-6 lobed. Fruit a 3-locular, many seeded capsule or a tooth-ridged utricle containing 1 seed.

Eichórnia Kunth. crássipes (Mart.) Solms. Water-hyacinth. Aquatic usually floating, with pendent roots and a cluster of radiating leaves, the bases of the petioles spongy-inflated, the blades orbicular to reniform, flowers bilabiate, bluish or purple. Southern. Adventive in NY. (Introduced from S. Amer.). Reported for Bronx and Suffolk Counties. Young foliage and buds reported as edible after cooking.

Leaves reniform to suborbicular, wider than long, or linear, and not over
5 mm wide. (Figs. 278, 279) .... 1. Heteranthera
Leaves deltoid to lanceolate, longer than wide, 1 cm or more wide. (Fig. 280). .... 2. Pontederia cordata

1. Heteránthera R.&P. Mud Plantain (from the Greek, based on the dissimilar anthers of another species).

Plants creeping in the mud, submersed or floating in shallow water, with long, branched stems, often rooting at the nodes; leaves cauline, sessile or with long petioles sheathing at the base, the blades reniform or suborbicular, wider than long, or elongate and linear; spathe sheathing, bladeless, caudate-acuminate, 1-several flowered, exserted from the base or side of the leaf petiole, flower regular, perianth tube long and slender, the lobes linear to lanceolate, yellow or blue, stamens 3, 1 larger than the other 2 or all alike, ovary 1-locular or incompletely 3-locular by intrusion of 3 parietal placentae, with several to many ovules; capsule ovoid.

Leaves linear, not over 5 mm wide; flowers yellow. (Fig. 278). .... 1. H. dubia
Leaves reniform, suborbicular, 1 cm or more wide; flowers blue. (Fig. 279). .... 2. H. reniformis

1. H. dúbia (Jacq.) MacM. Quiet waters. July-September. Fig. 278, Map 639. (Tropical Amer.). Endangered in ME, NH. [Zosterella d.]. —OBL

2. H. renifórmis R. & P. (kidney shaped). Creeping in mud or floating in shallow water. August-October. Fig. 279. (Tropical Amer.). Endangered in CT. Reported for Fairfield County CT, Dutchess County NY. —OBL

2. Pontedéria L. Pickerelweed (for G. Pontedera).

Marsh or shallow water plants, from a thick, creeping rhizome; leaves long petioled, thick, several sheathing the base of the stem, 1 leaf on the stem, deltoid or cordate/ovate, varying to linear lanceolate or ribbon like (submersed leaves); inflorescence a spike of blue (rarely white) flowers, the spike peduncled and subtended by a bladeless spathe, flower irregular, bilabiate, the 3 lower lobes spreading, their claws free to the base such that the tube is not fused, the 3 upper lobes united for part of their length, the middle lobe larger than the lateral and marked with yellow, stamens 6, inserted on the perianth tube, 3 long and exserted, 3 short and included and sometimes sterile, ovary 3-locular, 2 empty, the other with 1 ovule; fruit a tooth-ridged utricle containing 1 seed. —Wildl. 1

1. P. cordáta L. (heart shaped). Marshes, pond margins in mud or shallow water. June-October. Fig. 280, Map 640. [P. lanceolata]. Seeds edible; vegetative parts of plant also reported as edible after cooking. —OBL

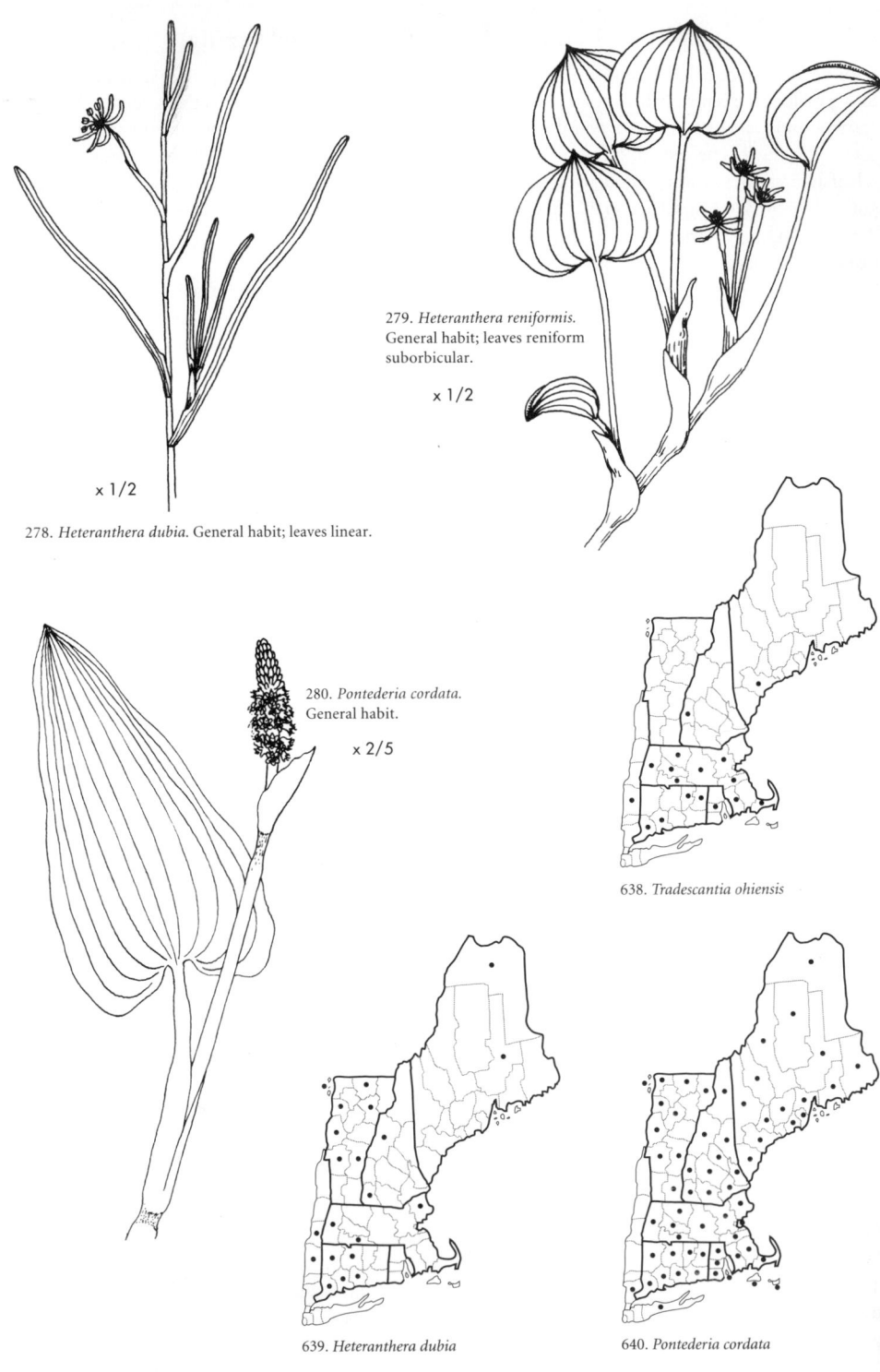

279. *Heteranthera reniformis.*
General habit; leaves reniform
suborbicular.

x 1/2

x 1/2

278. *Heteranthera dubia.* General habit; leaves linear.

280. *Pontederia cordata.*
General habit.

x 2/5

638. *Tradescantia ohiensis*

639. *Heteranthera dubia*

640. *Pontederia cordata*

Family 43. Juncáceae (Rush Family)

Monoecious (ours), usually perennial, sometimes annual, grass-like, usually tufted herbs, often from a short or long rhizome. Stems usually simple, with basal or cauline, alternate leaves. Leaves flat, narrow and grass-like or terete, sometimes with cross partitions at intervals, or reduced to bladeless sheaths. Flowers perfect (ours), in a terminal, branched, compact or open cyme or umbel, or spicate, the flowers solitary on the branches or glomerulate; flowers regular, small, green or brown, with or without a subtending pair of bracteoles, with 6 similar perianth parts (tepals) stamens 3 or 6, ovary superior, 1 or 3-locular, with 3-many ovules, style 1, stigmas 3. Fruit a 1-3 celled loculicidal capsule of 3-many seeds.

Ovary or capsule containing many ovules or seeds; plant glabrous. .... 1. *Juncus*
Ovary or capsule containing 3 ovules or seeds; plant frequently pubescent. .... 2. *Luzula*

1. *Júncus* L. Rush.

Glabrous herbs with stems bearing flat or terete leaves, or with bladeless sheaths or leaves basal; inflorescence an open or compact cyme, terminal but sometimes appearing lateral by continuation of the involucral bract, the flowers solitary or in glomerules, each pedicel or peduncle with a bractlet at the base, stamens 3 or 6, ovary 1 or 3-locular, containing many ovules or seeds, the seeds often 1 or 2 tailed.

a. Inflorescence appearing lateral, the main involucral bract erect, terete, not
    channeled, appearing like a continuation of the stem. (Fig. 281).
  b. Flowers in subglobose heads, without subtending bracteoles, each with a single
    bracteole only at the base of the pedicel. .... 1. *J. subnodolosus*
  b. Flowers solitary or not in subglobose heads (although entire inflorescence may
    be subglobose in vars. of *J. effusus*), each subtended by a pair of bracteoles
    at the base of the perianth in addition to one at the base of the pedicel.
    c. Tepals with a conspicuous dark stripe on either side of the pale midrib. .... 2. *J. balticus*
                                var. *littoralis*
    c. Tepals lacking sharply contrasting stripes.
      Stems mostly scattered or slightly tufted along long, creeping rhizomes;
        involucral bract more than half as long as the stem. .... 3. *J. filiformis*
      Stems densely cespitose, not from long creeping rhizomes; involucral
        bract less than half as long as the stem .... 4. *J. effusus*
a. Inflorescence appearing terminal, the main involucral bract not erect or if so
    then conspicuously channeled and not appearing like a continuation
    of the stem. (Figs. 282, 290).
  d. Plant creeping or floating .... 5. *J. subtilis*
  d. Plant erect.
    e. Leaves septate/nodulose at regular intervals; flowers without subtending
      bracteoles, in glomerules (solitary or 2-3 and appearing to have
      subtending bracteoles in *J. pelocarpus*). (Figs. 283, 284).
      f. Seeds with a distinct tail on each end. (Fig. 285).
        g. Petals obtuse to acute .... 6. *J. brachycephalus*
        g. Petals and sepals lance-subulate.
          h. Seeds 1.3 mm long or longer, the tails more than half the length
            of the body .... 7. *J. canadensis*
          h. Seeds 1.2 mm long or shorter, the tails less than half the length of
          the body.
          Inflorescence narrow, with erect branches, 3-6 times as long as
            broad. .... 8. *J. brevicaudatus*
          Inflorescence open, the branches spreading, less than 3 times as
            long as broad .... 9. *J. subcaudatus*
      f. Seeds lacking tails, blunt or merely pointed.
        i. Fully developed stem leaf 1, conspicuously overtopping inflorescence. .... 10. *J. militaris*
        i. Fully developed stem leaves more than 1, not conspicuously overtopping
          inflorescence.

j. Capsule 1/2-2/3 as long as the perianth. .... 11. *J. brachycarpus*
j. Capsule about equalling or longer than the perianth.
   k. Capsule subulate, long beaked; flowers in spherical heads. (Fig. 286).
      Petals conspicuously shorter than the sepals; auricles of the
         leaf sheaths 2.5 mm long or longer .... 12. *J. torreyi*
      Petals and sepals equal or nearly so; auricles of the leaf sheaths
         less than 2.5 mm long .... 13. *J. nodosus*
   k. Capsule not subulate, oblong, acute to short beaked; flowers usually
      in hemispherical heads. (Fig. 288).
      l. Flowers single or in pairs (3). (Fig. 287). .... 14. *J. pelocarpus*
      l. Flowers in heads of 3 or more.
         m. Sepals obtuse .... 15. *J. alpinoarticulatus*
         m. Sepals and petals acuminate.
            n. Perianth equalling or barely shorter than capsule. .... 16. *J. acuminatus*
            n. Perianth distinctly shorter than capsule, the capsule exserted.
               Capsule chestnut brown or purple brown; tepals subequal.   17. *J. articulatus*
               Capsule straw colored to tan; tepals equal. .... 18. *J. debilis*
e. Leaves not septate/nodulose; flowers often with subtending bracteoles,
   solitary or 2-3 (glomerulate and lacking subtending bracteoles in
   J. marginatus and *J. biflorus*). (Fig. 289).
  o. Seeds with a well developed, distinct tail on each end.
     Seeds 2 mm or longer, the tails thick; flowers lacking subtending
        bracteoles. .... 19. *J. stygius* subsp.
                                                                    americanus
     Seeds shorter than 2 mm, the tails slender; flowers with subtending
        bracteoles .... 20. *J. vaseyi*
  o. Seeds lacking tails, merely pointed or apiculate.
    p. Leaves terete, not channeled.
      Flowers single or in pairs (3), often replaced by bulblets. .... 14. *J. pelocarpus*
      Flowers in heads of 3 or more .... 15.*J. alpinoarticulatus*
    p. Leaves flat, involute, or terete and channeled.
      q. Flowers lacking subtending bracteoles, glomerulate.
         Widest leaves 1-3 mm wide; heads less than 30 per stem. .... 21. *J. marginatus*
         Widest leaves wider than 3 mm; heads usually more than 30 per stem.   22. *J. biflorus*
      q. Flowers with subtending bracteoles, solitary or 2-3 (4). (Fig. 289).
        r. Stem leaves present, occupying the upper two thirds of the stem.
            Inflorescence simple, 1-4 flowered; auricles of leaf sheaths
               deeply fringed; arctic-alpine .... 23. *J. trifidus*
            Inflorescence branched, many flowered; auricles of leaf sheaths
               entire; coastal or occasionally on railroad tracks. .... 24. *J. gerardi*
        r. Stem leaves absent (except involucral bracts), the leaves basal or
            extending less than 1/3 of the way up the stem.
           s. Inflorescence at least 1/3 the height of the plant; annual. .... 25. *J. bufonius*
           s. Inflorescence less than 1/3 the height of the plant; perennial.
              t. Leaves terete or channeled.
                 Capsule twice as long as broad, conspicuously longer
                    than the perianth. ....26. *J. greenei*
                 Capsule less than twice as long as broad, as long or shorter
                    than the perianth ....27. *J. dichotomous*
             t. Leaves flat, but sometimes involute in drying.
               u. Auricles of leaf sheaths prolonged or tongue-like.
                 Auricles scarious, pale, 2 or more times as long as
                    broad. ....28. *J. tenuis*
                 Auricles firm, dark, about as long as broad. ....27. *J. dichotomous*
               u. Auricles of leaf sheaths gradually rounded, not prolonged
                 or tongue-like.
                 Inflorescence not or barely exceeded by the involucre;
                    flowers secund; auricles membranous ....29. *J. secundus*
                 Inflorescence conspicuously exceeded by the involucre;
                    flowers not secund; auricles cartilaginous .... 30. *J. dudleyi*

1. J. subnodolósus Schrank. Brackish marshes. September-October. Reported for Barnstable County MA. [*J. pervetus*]. —OBL

2. J. bálticus Willd. (of the Baltic) Engelm. Sandy, fresh to brackish shores, beaches and marshes, and also on roadsides and railroad tracks. June-September. Map 641. [*J. arcticus* subsp. *littoralis*]. Represented with us as var. *littorális*. Engelm. —FACW+

3. J. filifórmis L. (thread like). Pond and river shores, marshes, bogs and alpine meadows. June-September. Map 642. (Eurasia). —FACW

4. J. effúsus L. (loosely spreading). Fresh marshes, wet meadows, pond margins, ditches. July-September. Fig. 281, Map 643. (Eurasia). Represented with us by the following vars.:

var. *conglomerátus* (L.) Engelm. Inflorescence compact; culms distinctly grooved near summit; perianth spreading from base. [*J. conglomeratus*].

var. *pyláei* (Laharpe) Fern. & Wieg. Inflorescence open and freely branched to slightly compact; culms distinctly furrowed or grooved, perianth ascending [*J.e.* var. *costulatus; J. pylaei*].

var. *decípiens* Buchenau. Inflorescence open and freely branched to slightly compact, culms not grooved near summit, although sometimes finely striate; perianth spreading from base. [*J.e.* var. *compactus*].

var. *solútus* Fern. & Wieg. Inflorescence open and freely branched; culms finely striate; perianth ascending to appressed. —FACW+

J. infléxus L. Similar to *J. effusus* but distinguishable in having 6 stamens and a capsule tapering to a beak (stamens 3 and capsule rounded and beakless in *J. effusus*). (Naturalized from Europe). Reported for Berkshire County MA. —FACW

5. J. subtílis E. Mey. (slender). Muddy shores of ponds and streams. August-September. (Greenland). Reported for Aroostook and Somerset Counties ME. —OBL

J. bulbósus L. Resembling *J. subtilis* but distinguishable in having flowers in glomerules of 3 or more (flowers solitary or in pairs in *J. subtilis*). Reported for MA. [*J. supinus*].

6. J. brachycéphalus (Engelm.) Buch. (short-headed). Shores of ponds, and rivers, wet meadows, marshes and deciduous swamps. August-September. Fig. 282, Map 644. —OBL

7. J. canadénsis J. Gay ex Laharpe (Canadian). Shores of ponds and rivers, wet meadows and marshes. July-October. Figs. 283 and 284, Map 645. —OBL

8. J. brevicaudátus (Engelm.) Fern. (short-tailed). River and pond margins, wet meadows and marshes. July-September. Fig. 285, Map 646. —OBL

9. J. subcaudátus (Engelm.) Coville & Blake (somewhat tailed). Wooded swamps and wet woods near the coast. August-October. Map 647. Our plants are var. *subcaudatus.* —OBL

10. J. militáris Bigelow (soldierly). Pond and river margins in shallow water; occasionally in bogs. July-September. Map 648. Endangered in VT.

In deep water rhizome often producing numerous long capillary leaves. —OBL

11. J. brachycárpus Engelm. (short-fruited). Sea beaches and salt marshes. July-September. Map 649. —FACW

12. J. tórreyi Coville (for J. Torrey). River margins, ditches, wet roadsides and railroad tracks. July-September. Fig. 286, Map 650. —FACW

13. J. nodósus L. (knotty). Pond and river margins, wet meadows. July-September. Map 651. Our plants are var. *nodosus.* —OBL

J. scirpoídes Lam. (resembling Scirpus). Very similar to J. nodosus, but auricles are longer than 1 mm and stamens 3 (auricles 1 mm or less long and stamens 6 in J. nodosus). Reported for RI; also Bronx, Nassau and Suffolk Counties NY. —FACW

14. J. pelocárpus E. Mey. (fruit of mud). Pond and lake margins. August-September. Fig. 287, Map 652. Our plants are var. *pelocarpus.* —OBL

15. J. alpinoarticulátus Chaix. Sandy or gravelly lake shores. July-September. Map 653. (Eurasia). [*J. alpinus*]. Represented with us by the following subsp.:

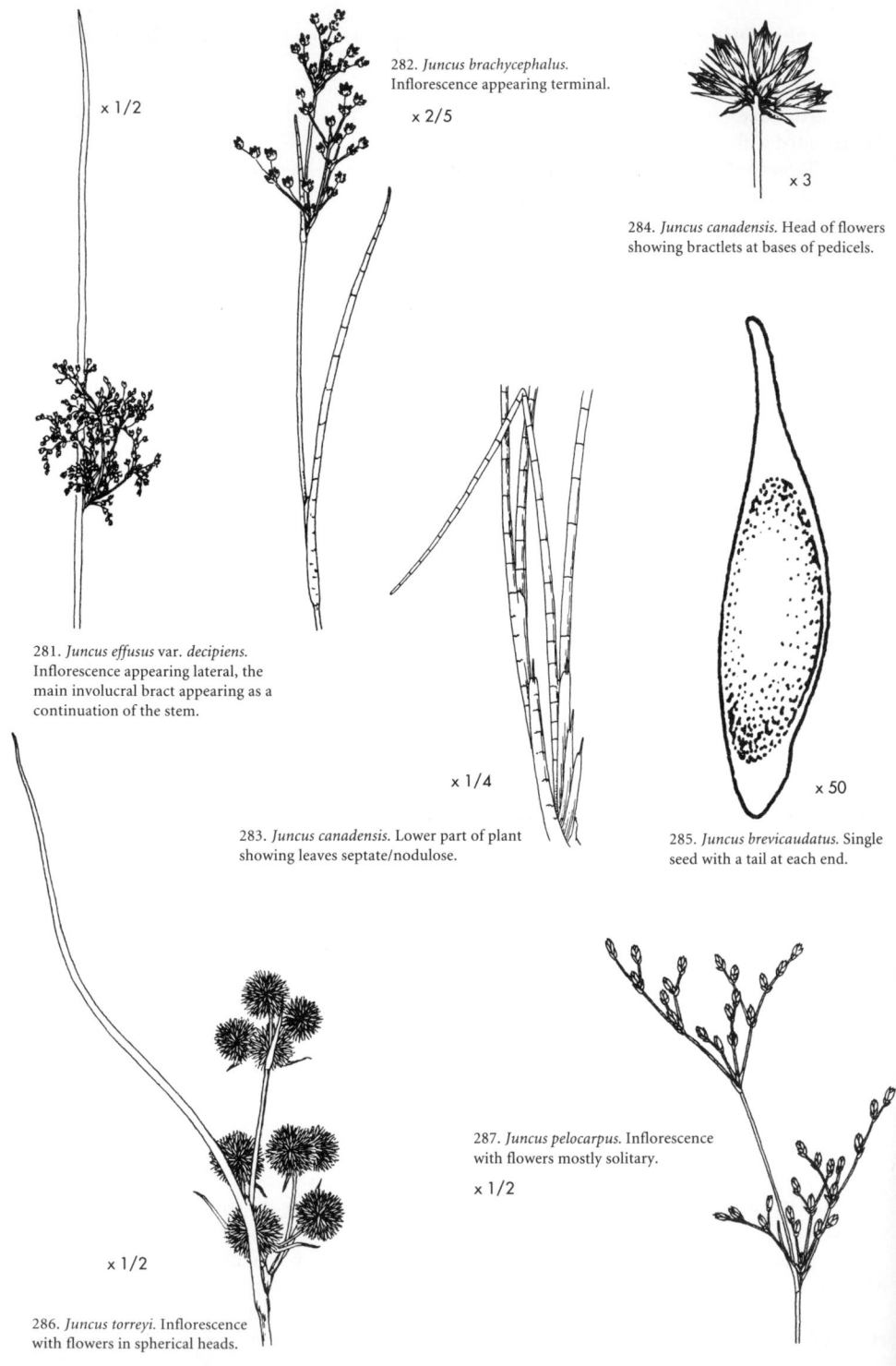

× 1/2

282. *Juncus brachycephalus.*
Inflorescence appearing terminal.

× 2/5

284. *Juncus canadensis.* Head of flowers
showing bractlets at bases of pedicels.

× 3

281. *Juncus effusus* var. *decipiens.*
Inflorescence appearing lateral, the
main involucral bract appearing as a
continuation of the stem.

× 1/4

283. *Juncus canadensis.* Lower part of plant
showing leaves septate/nodulose.

× 50

285. *Juncus brevicaudatus.* Single
seed with a tail at each end.

287. *Juncus pelocarpus.* Inflorescence
with flowers mostly solitary.

× 1/2

× 1/2

286. *Juncus torreyi.* Inflorescence
with flowers in spherical heads.

641. *Juncus balticus* var. *littoralis*

642. *Juncus filiformis*

643. *Juncus effusus*

644. *Juncus brachycephalus*

645. *Juncus canadensis*

646. *Juncus brevicaudatus*

647. *Juncus subcaudatus*

648. *Juncus militaris*

649. *Juncus brachycarpus*

JUNCACEAE

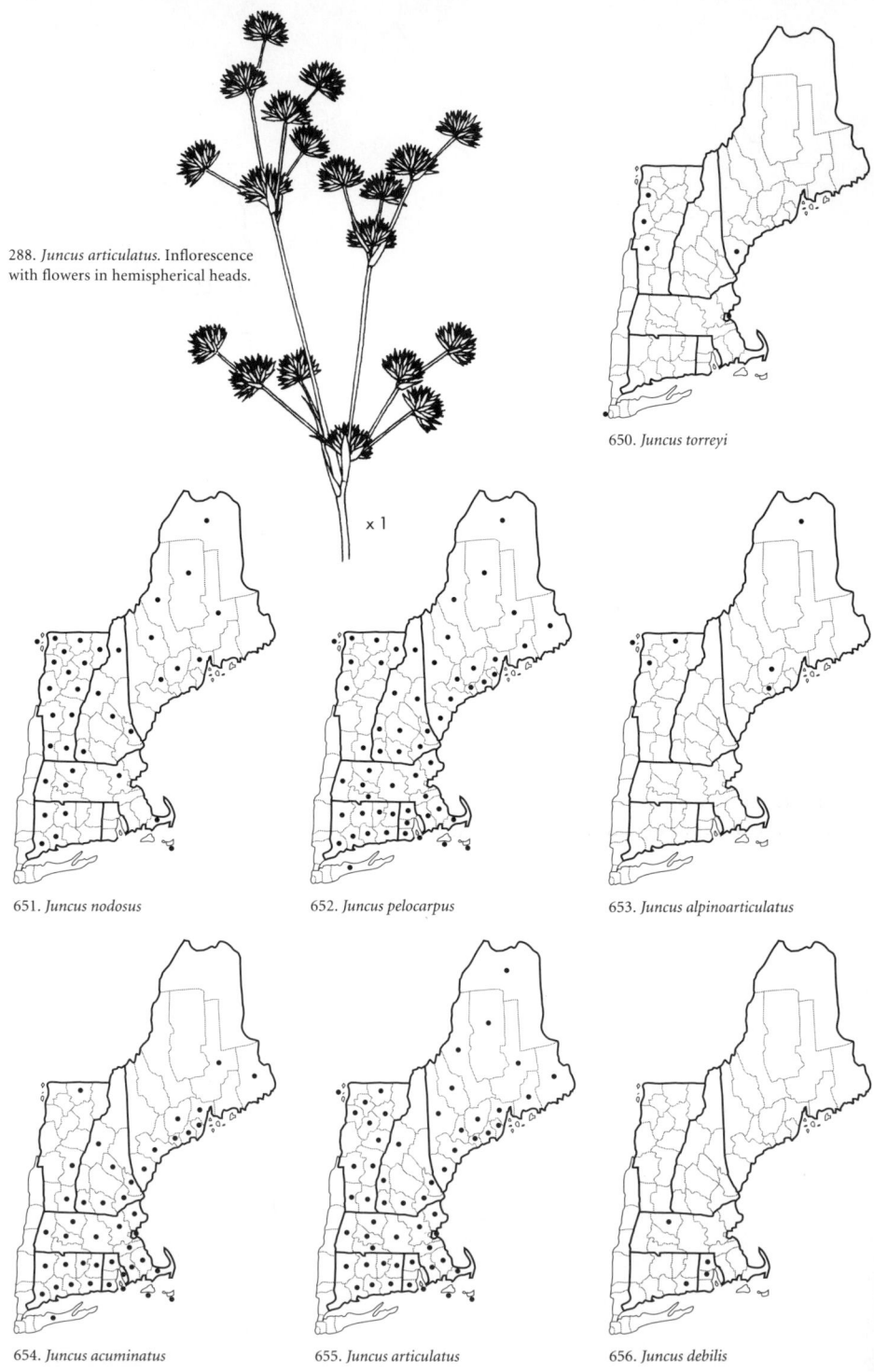

288. *Juncus articulatus*. Inflorescence with flowers in hemispherical heads.

× 1

650. *Juncus torreyi*

651. *Juncus nodosus*

652. *Juncus pelocarpus*

653. *Juncus alpinoarticulatus*

654. *Juncus acuminatus*

655. *Juncus articulatus*

656. *Juncus debilis*

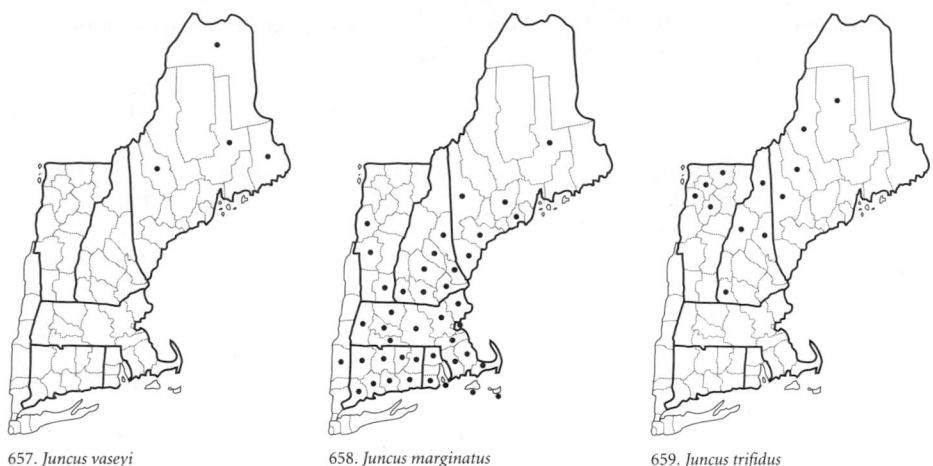

657. *Juncus vaseyi*   658. *Juncus marginatus*   659. *Juncus trifidus*

subsp. *fuscéscens* (Fern.) Hamet-Ahti. Heads hemispherical. [*J. alpinus* var. *fuscescens*].

subsp. *americánus* Farw. Hamet-Ahti. Heads ellipsoid or ellipsoid-hemispherical; some of the flowers often elevated on long pedicels above the others in the head. [*J. alpinus* var. *rariflorus*]. —OBL

16. *J. acuminátus* Michx. (tapering to tip). Pond and river margins, ditches, wet meadows, wooded swamps. July-September. Map 654. —OBL

17. *J. articulátus* L. (jointed). Pond and river margins, beaches, wet meadows, bogs and wet depressions along roadsides and railroads. July-September. Fig. 288, Map 655. (Eurasia). —OBL

J. x fulvéscens Fern. A hybrid between *J. articulatus* and *J. brevicaudatus.*

18. *J. débilis* Gray (weak). Pond margins, ditches, moist sandy soil. June-September. Map 656. Endangered in MA; RI. —OBL

19. *J. stýgius* L. (of the Styx, from its boggy habitat). Bogs and marshes, shallow pools. July-August. (Europe). Reported for Aroostook County ME. Represented with us as subsp. *americánus* Buch.—OBL

20. *J. váseyi* Engelm. (for its discoverer). River margins, wet thickets. July-August. Map 657. —FACW

J. x oronénsis Fern. Petals attenuate; capsule overtopped by perianth (petals obtuse to acute and capsule exserted in *J. vaseyi*). A hybrid between *J. vaseyi* and *J. tenuis.* Reported for ME.

21. *J. marginátus* Rostk (margined). River and pond margins, wet meadows and disturbed wet soil. July-September. Map 658. Our plants are var. *marginatus.* —FACW

22. *J. biflórus* Ell. (two flowered). Pond margins, wet meadows, wet sandy soil. June-September. Endangered in MA; reported for Barnstable and Nantucket Counties. [*J. aristulatus*]. —FACW

23. *J. trífidus* L. (three forked). Alpine meadows and barrens. June-August. Map 659. (Eurasia).

24. *J. gerárdi* Loisel. (for L. Gerard). Black Grass. Salt marshes, and occasionally along railroads. June-September. Map 660. (Eurasia, N. Africa). Our plants include var. *gerardi* and the following var.:

var. *pedicellátus* Fern. Flowers on pedicels 3 mm or more long (flowers sessile or subsessile in var. *gerardi*). —FACW+

J. compréssus Jacq. (compressed). Differing from *J. gerardi* in having a distinctly exserted capsule (capsule equalling or but slightly exceeding perianth in *J. gerardi*). (Canada, Eurasia). Reported for Chittenden County VT.

25. *J. bufónius* L. (of toads). Toad Rush. Pond and river shores, wet meadows, moist roadsides, waste places and disturbed areas. July-September. Map 661.

Our plants include var. *bufonius* and the following vars.:

var. *congéstus* Wahlenb. Similar to var. *bufonius* but with flowers in clusters of 2-4 (scattered in var. *bufonius*).

var. *halóphilus* Buch. & Fern. Petals obtuse (acute in the above vars.). Salt marshes. —FACW

26. *J. greénei* Oakes & Tuckerman (for its discoverer). Dry open soil, sand dunes, mostly near the coast. July-September. Map 662. Endangered in VT. —FAC

27. *J. dichotómous* Ell. (2 parted). Pond margins, ditches, open sandy soil, mostly near the coast. July-September. Map 663. (Tropical Amer.). [*J. tenuis* var. *d.*; *J. platyphyllus*]. —FACW

28. *J. ténuis* Willd. (slender). Path Rush. Damp to dry woodland paths and roadsides. July-September. Figs. 289 and 290, Map 664. (Europe, N. Africa). Our plants are var. *tenuis*. —FAC-

29. *J. secúndus* Beauv. ex Poir. (one-sided). Dry open soil and rocky places. June-September. Map 665. Endangered in VT, NH. —FACU

30. *J. dúdleyi* Wieg. (for W. R. Dudley). Damp to dry meadows and pastures, river shores, roadsides and waste areas. July-September. Map 666. [*J. tenuis* var. *d.*].

2. *Lúzula* DC Woodrush.

Low often pubescent herbs with stems bearing flat, usually hairy, grass-like leaves; inflorescence umbellate or spiciform, terminal, the flowers solitary or in spikes or glomerules, subtended by 1 or 2 bracteoles, these usually lacerate; stamens 6, ovary and capsule 1-locular, the capsule loculicidal, 3-seeded, the seeds usually appendaged.

a. Flowers solitary (rarely paired) at the tips of the branches of the inflorescence.
    Inflorescence a simple, unbranched umbel; plant pubescent. .... 1. *L. acuminata*
    Inflorescence branched; plant glabrous or nearly so. .... 2. *L. parviflora*
a. Flowers in glomerules.
  b. Glomerules in diffuse, open panicles; flowers mostly 6 or fewer in each
     glomerule. (Fig. 291) .... 3. *L. luzuloides*
  b. Glomerules in spikes or close panicles; flowers mostly more than 6 in each
     glomerule.
    c. Glomerules in a nodding, spike-like, often interrupted panicle; bracts
      subtending glomerules conspicuously longer than the glomerules.
      (Fig. 292). .... 4. *L. spicata*
    c. Glomerules in an erect, subcapitate cluster, or some peduncled; bracts
      subtending glomerules scarcely longer than the glomerules. (Fig. 293).
      d. Bracts subtending flowers ciliate; seeds scarcely appendaged. .... 5. *L. confusa*
      d. Bracts subtending flowers entire or lacerate; seeds conspicuously
        appendaged.
        e. Flowering stems solitary from crowns connected by short stolons. .... 6. *L. campestris*
        e. Flowering stems cespitose, not stolonferous, 2-many.
          f. Base of plant producing bulb-like tubers. .... 7. *L. bulbosa*
          f. Base of plant not producing tubers.
            g. Rays of inflorescence horizontally divergent. .... 8. *L. echinata*
            g. Rays of inflorescence ascending to erect.
              h. Mature spikes up to 5 mm thick; seeds up to 1.5 mm long. .... 6. *L. campestris*
                                          var. *pallescens*
             h. Mature spikes 6 mm or more thick; seeds 1.5 mm or more long.
               Umbels somewhat open, some of the spikes on rays. .... 9. *L. multiflora*
               Umbels compact, the spikes mostly sessile or subsessile,
                 rarely with a few rays .... 10. *L. congesta*

1. *L. acumináta* Raf. (tapering to a point). Open deciduous woods and thickets. May-July. Map 667. [*L. saltuensis*]. Our plants are var. *acuminata*. —FAC

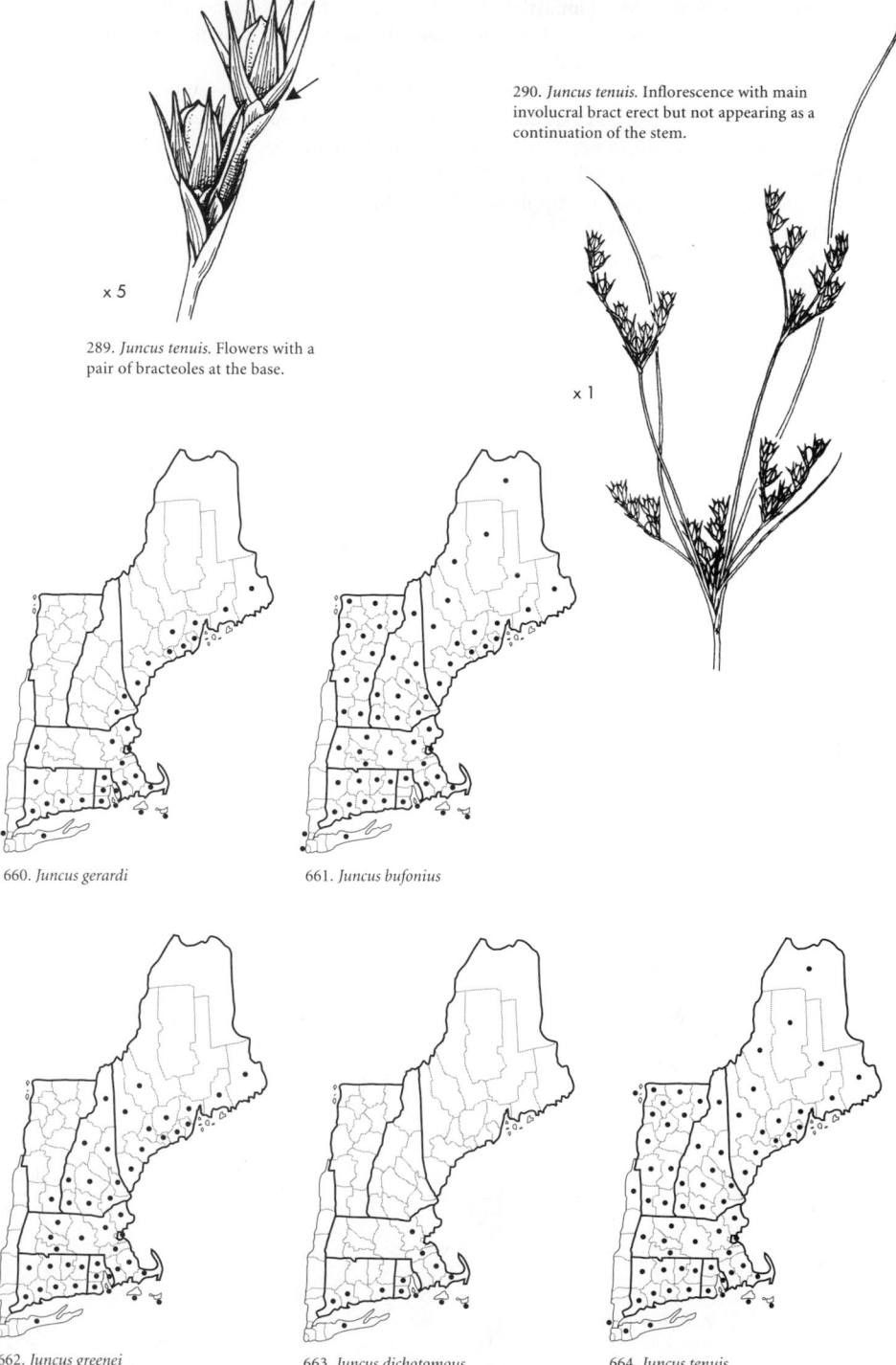

289. *Juncus tenuis.* Flowers with a pair of bracteoles at the base.

x 5

290. *Juncus tenuis.* Inflorescence with main involucral bract erect but not appearing as a continuation of the stem.

x 1

660. *Juncus gerardi*

661. *Juncus bufonius*

662. *Juncus greenei*

663. *Juncus dichotomous*

664. *Juncus tenuis*

2. *L. parviflóra* (Ehrh.) Desv. (small flowered). Mountains, in thickets and in the open. June-July. Map 668. (Eurasia). Endangered in MA. Our plants include subsp. *parviflora* and the following subsp.:

subsp. *melanocárpa* (Michx.) Hamet-Ahti. Perianth brownish to straw-colored; capsule brown to black (perianth brownish and capsule chestnut-colored in subsp. *parviflora*). —FACU

3. *L. luzuloídes* (Lam.) Dandy & Wilmott (resembling *Luzula*). Open woods and roadsides. June-July. Fig. 291, Map 669. (Naturalized from Europe). [*L. nemorosa*].

4. *L. spicáta* (L.) DC. (spiked). Alpine meadows, talus and tundra. June-August. Fig. 292, Map 670. (Eurasia). Endangered in ME.

5. *L. confúsa* Lindeberg (confused). Alpine meadows. July-August. Fig. 293. (Eurasia). Reported for ME, NH, VT. Endangered in ME, NH.

6. *L. campéstris* (L.) DC. (of low fields). Open woods, fields and roadsides. May-June. (Eurasia). Reported for ME, MA, NH, VT. Represented with us by the following var.:

var. *pallescens* Wahlenb. Flowering stems cespitose, 2-many; rays ascending (flowering stems solitary from crowns connected by short stolons and rays divergent in the typical phase). [*L. palléscens; L. pallidula*].

7. *L. bulbósa* (Wood) Rydb. (bulb-bearing). Open woods and fields. April-June. Reported for CT, MA [*L. campestris* var. *b.*]. —FACU

8. *L. echináta* (Small) F. J. Herm. (resembling a hedgehog). Woods and clearings. April-June. Reported for CT, MA. [*L. campestris* var. *e.*]. Our plants are var. *echinata*. —FACU

9. *L. multiflóra* (Retz.) Lejeune (many flowered). Fields, open woods. April-June. Reported throughout our range. [*L. campestris* var. *m.*]. Our plants include subsp. *multiflora* var. *m.* and the following subsp.

subsp. *frígida* (Buch.) Krecz. Sepals deep brown to grayish; capsules deep brown to blackish (sepals pale brown in center and capsules medium brown to tawny in subsp. multiflora [*L. multiflora* var. *fusconigra*]. —FACU

10. *L. congésta* (Thuill.) Lej. Damp thickets, shores. July-August. (Eurasia). From farther north. Reported for MA, ME, VT. [*L. multiflora* var. *c.*].

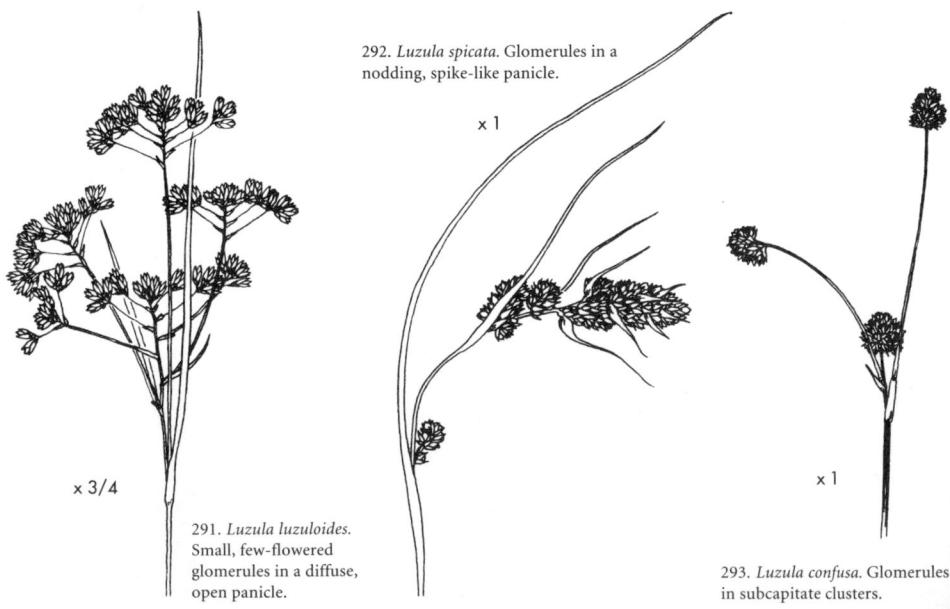

292. *Luzula spicata*. Glomerules in a nodding, spike-like panicle.

x 1

x 3/4

291. *Luzula luzuloides*. Small, few-flowered glomerules in a diffuse, open panicle.

x 1

293. *Luzula confusa*. Glomerules in subcapitate clusters.

665. *Juncus secundus*

666. *Juncus dudleyi*

667. *Luzula acuminata*

668. *Luzula parviflora*

669. *Luzula luzuloides*

670. *Luzula spicata*

Family 44. Liliáceae (Lily Family)

Hermaphrodite, perennial herbs from a rhizome, corm or bulb. Stems erect or absent. Leaves basal or cauline, alternate or whorled, usually narrow but occasionally broad. Flowers perfect solitary or in various kinds of inflorescences; flowers regular, the perianth generally of 6 segments in 2 series of 3, the series undifferentiated, separate or united, stamens as many as the perianth segments, hypogynous or borne on the perianth, ovary inferior or superior, 3-locular, with few to many ovules, style usually 1, stigmas 3 or 1 with 3 lobes. Fruit a capsule or indehiscent.

a. Ovary inferior.
    Flower with a saucer shaped crown (corona) at the summit of a long tube at
        the junction with the tepals. (Fig. 294) .... 1. *Narcissus*
    Flower without a corona.
        Perianth segments glabrous, white with green tips; leaves glabrous. .... 2. *Leucojum aestivum*
        Perianth segments pubescent, yellow; leaves pubescent. .... 3. *Hypoxis hirsuta*
a. Ovary superior.
    Leaves principally basal or near the base; flower solitary on a scapose stem. .... 4. *Erythronium*
                                                       americanum
    Leaves principally cauline, alternate or whorled, basal leaves absent. .... 5. *Lilium*

1. *Narcíssus* L. Narcissus (from Greek mythology).

Leaves and scapes arising from a tunicated bulb; flowers 1-few, conspicuous, terminating long scapes, white or yellow, the flower or umbel subtended by a membranous sheath, perianth with a long, slender tube at the base, with a saucer-shaped crown (corona) at the junction of tube and perianth segments, this of the same or a different color than the perianth, stamens included or barely exserted. [*Amaryllidaceae*]. Poisonous, particularly the bulbs.

Flower white, corona much shorter than perianth segments. .... 1. *N. poeticus*
Flower yellow, corona about as long or longer than perianth segments. .... 2. *N. pseudo-narcissus*

    1. *N. poéticus* L. (of the poets). Poets' Narcissus. Occasionally escaped from cultivation into fields and meadows. April-June. Fig. 294, Map 671. (Introduced from Europe).

    2. *N. pseúdonarcissus* L. (false Narcissus). Daffodil. Occasionally escaped from cultivation into fields and meadows. April-May. (Introduced from Europe). Reported for Strafford County NH.

    N. incomparábilis Mill. Corona half as long as tepals (corona as long as tepals in the latter species) infrequently escapes.

    N. jonquílla L. Corona less than a quarter as long as the tepals, flowers usually 2 or more, leaves cylindrical (corona as long as tepals, flower solitary, leaves flat in *N. pseudonarcissus*).

2. *Leucójum* L. Snowflake (from the Greek meaning white violet).

Leaves and scapes arising from a tunicated bulb; flowers solitary or umbeled, terminating long scapes, subtended by a membranous sheath, nodding, exserted from the sheath on long pedicels, perianth campanulate, its segments distinct nearly to the base, white with green tips, stamens included. [*Amaryllidaceae*].

    Galánthus L. *nivális* L. (snowy). Snowdrop. Differing from *Leucojum* in that the inner perianth-segments are much shorter than the outer. Rarely escaped from cultivation. Reported for Hampshire County MA and RI.

    1. *L. aestívum* L. (of summer). Summer Snowflake. Escaped from cultivation to fields and meadows. April-May. Fig. 295, Map 672. (Naturalized from Europe). Our plants are subsp. *aestivum*.

3. *Hypóxis* L. Yellow Star-grass (slightly acid).

Low plants, the slender scapes and hairy, grass-like leaves arising from a short corm-like rhizome; flowers solitary-few, terminal on short or long scapes, the scapes usually exceeded by the leaves, subtended by 2-several inconspicuous, setaceous bracts, long pedicelled, perianth rotate, separate down to the summit of the ovary, spreading, yellow, greenish on the back, pubescent on the outside, withering-persistent, stamens included. [*Amaryllidaceae*].

    1. *H. hirsúta* (L.) Cov. (stiffly hairy). Fields and open woods. May-July. Fig. 296, Map 673. [*H. leptocarpa*]. Preparation made from the rhizome reported to be of value in treatment of ulcers. —FAC

4. *Erythrónium* L. Trout Lily (Greek name for a purple flowered European species).

Low herbs from a deep, scaly corm, colonial, often propagating by offshoots, producing sterile and fertile plants; stem simple, about half underground, in sterile plants bearing 1 leaf, in fertile plants 2 leaves, leaves elliptic to lanceolate or oblong, shining, mottled with brown, tapering into petioles, sheathing the stem below the middle and thus appearing basal; flower solitary, terminal, nodding, yellow, suffused with purple below, perianth segments separate, lanceolate-elliptic, spreading to recurved, deciduous, stamens hypogynous, shorter than the perianth, style clavate, with 3 short stigmas; capsule ellipsoid to obovoid, loculicidal.

    1. *E. americánum* Ker.-Gawl. (American). Rich, moist deciduous woods and thickets. April-May. Fig. 297, Map 674.

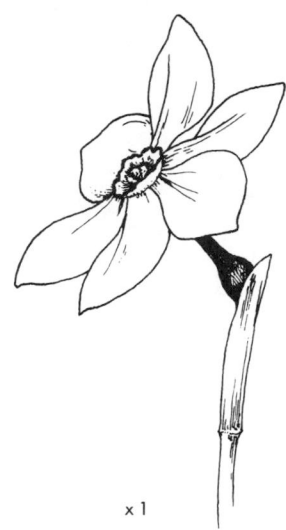

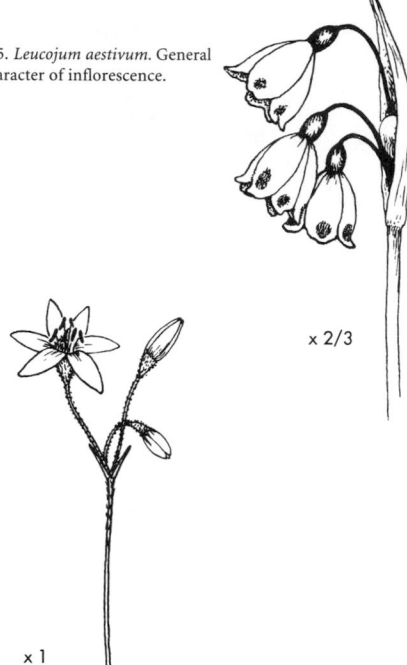

295. *Leucojum aestivum.* General character of inflorescence.

x 2/3

x 1

294. *Narcissus poeticus.* Flower with corona at junction with tepals.

x 1

296. *Hypoxis hirsuta.* General character of inflorescence.

x 1/2

297. *Erythronium americanum.* General habit.

671. *Narcissus poeticus*

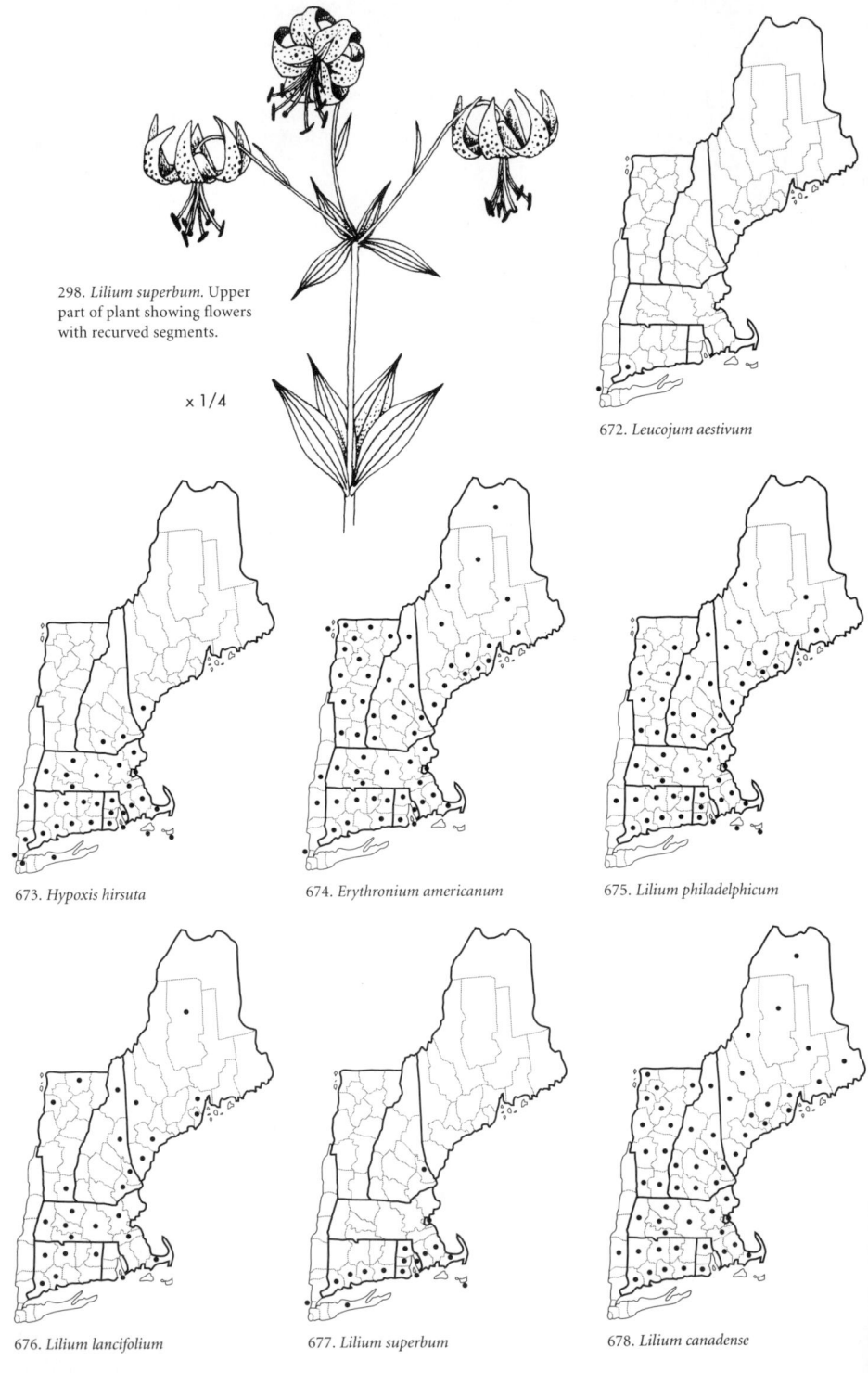

298. *Lilium superbum*. Upper part of plant showing flowers with recurved segments.

x 1/4

672. *Leucojum aestivum*

673. *Hypoxis hirsuta*

674. *Erythronium americanum*

675. *Lilium philadelphicum*

676. *Lilium lancifolium*

677. *Lilium superbum*

678. *Lilium canadense*

5. Lílium L. Lily (classical Latin name).

Tall herbs with erect, unbranched, leafy stems from a scaly bulb; leaves numerous, alternate or whorled, sessile, narrow; flowers 1-few, showy, terminal, erect or nodding, yellow to red, perianth campanulate, tubular at the base, its 6 segments spreading or recurved, clawed or sessile, deciduous, stamens hypogynous, style elongate, stigma 3-lobed; capsule oblong to obovoid, loculicidal with numerous flat seeds. Bulbs reported as having been used by Indians for food.

Túlipa L. Distinguishable from *Lilium* in having only 2 or 3 leaves on each stem (leaves more numerous in *Lilium*). Two species adventive from Europe are reported for MA: *T. sylvéstris L.*, with buds usually nodding, stamens hairy at the base and *T. gesneriána L.*, with buds erect and stamens glabrous.

a. Flowers erect.
    Leaves, at least the middle or upper, in whorles. .... 1. *L. philadelphicum*
    Leaves all alternate .... 2. *L. bulbiferum*
a. Flowers nodding.
    b. Leaves all alternate, the upper with bulblets in the axils. .... 3. *L. lancifolium*
    b. Leaves, at least some of them, in whorles, none with bulblets in the axils.
        Perianth segments strongly recurved, the stamens and style long-exserted;
            leaf margins entire, smooth. (Fig. 298) .... 4. *L. superbum*
        Perianth segments ascending to slightly spreading but not strongly recurved,
            the stamens and style included or slightly exserted; leaf margins
            glandular-serrate or scabrous .... 5. *L. canadense*

1. L. philadélphicum L. (of Philadelphia). Wood Lily. Dry open woods and clearings, meadows and pastures. June-August. Map 675. Our plants are var. *philadelphicum*. —FACU+

2. L. bulbíferum L. (bearing bulbs). Orange Lily. Occasionally escaped to roadsides and fields. June-July. (Introduced from Europe).

3. L. lancifólium Thunb. (spotted, like a tiger). Tiger Lily. Escaped to roadsides and waste places. July-August. Map 676. (Naturalized from E. Asia). [*L. tigrinum*].

4. L. supérbum L. (superb). Turk's-cap Lily. Moist woods and thickets, wet meadows. July-August. Fig. 298, Map 677. Endangered in NH. —FACW+

5. L. canadénse L. (Canadian). Wild Yellow-Lily. Moist to wet meadows. July. Map 678. Our plants are subsp. *canadense*. —FAC+

Family 45. Colchicáceae (Autumn Crocus Family)

Similar to *Liliaceae*. Represented with us by the following species. [*Liliaceae*].

Colchicum L. *autumnale* L. Autumn Croccus. Leaves large and lanceolate, appearing in spring; flowers purple, funnelform, with a long narrow tube, the base arising from below ground. Escaped from cultivation to fields. Reported for Middlesex County MA, Cheshire County NH. Poisonous.

Family 46. Hemerocallidáceae (Day Lily Family)

Similar to Liliaceae. Represented with us by the following genus [*Liliaceae*].

1. Hemerocállis L. Day Lily (from the Greek meaning day beauty).

Tall, glabrous, showy herbs from fleshy-fibrous roots or tubers; stem lacking; leaves basal, numerous, long and linear, keeled; inflorescence of 2-3 helicoid cymes, each with several bracted, large, orange or yellow flowers, each lasting for only 1 day, perianth broadly campanulate with a

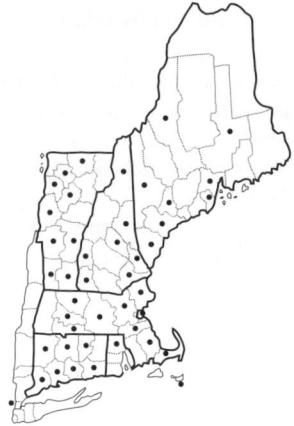

679. *Hemerocallis fulva*

680. *Hemerocallis lilioasphodelus*

x 1/3   x 1/2

299. *Hemerocallis fulva*. Basal leaf; inflorescence.

short cylindrical tube and 6 spreading or recurved, oblong to spatulate lobes, style 1, with a capitate stigma, stamens inserted at the summit of the perianth tube; capsule oblong to ovoid, 3-angled, loculicidal.

Flowers tawny orange .... 1. *H. fulva*
Flowers yellow .... 2. *H. lilioasphodelus*

1. H. fúlva (L.) L. (reddish-yellow). Orange Day Lily. Spread from cultivation to roadsides and waste places. June-July. Fig. 299, Map 679. (Naturalized from Eurasia). Our plants are var. *fulva*. Tubers, young shoots, unopened flower buds edible; buds and withered flowers can also be dried and eaten.

2. H. lilioasphodélus L. (yellow). Yellow Day Lily. Spread from cultivation to roadsides and waste places. May-June. Map 680. (Introduced from Asia). [*H. flava*].

Family 47. Convallariáceae (Lily of the Valley Family)

Rhizomatous, scapose or simple-stemmed. Leaves basal or cauline, alternate or whorled. Flowers solitary or in an umbel, raceme or panicle, ovary superior, flowers otherwise as in *Liliaceae*. Fruit a berry or capsule. [*Liliaceae*].

a. Leaves principally basal or near the base, the stems scapose or bracteate.
    Perianth segments free to base or nearly so. .... 1. *Clintonia borealis*
    Perianth segments united for half or more their length. .... 2. *Convallaria majalis*
a. Leaves principally cauline, alternate or whorled, basal leaves absent.
    b. Leaves whorled. (Fig. 302) .... 3. *Mediola virginiana*
    b. Leaves alternate.
        c. Flowers or inflorescence terminating the stem or branches. (Fig. 303).
            Perianth white or bluish; fruit a berry .... 4. *Maianthemum*
            Perianth yellow; fruit a capsule .... 5. *Uvularia*
        c. Flowers or inflorescence in the axils of stem leaves.
            d. Flowers solitary, or more and separated by one or more intervening leaves
                without axillary flowers; fruit a capsule. .... 5. *Uvularia*
            d. Flowers in 2 or more successive leaf axils; fruit a berry (capsule in *Tricyrtis*)
                Peduncle arising from center of leaf axil, mostly 2 or more-flowered;
                    berry black or blue. (Fig. 306) .... 6. *Polygonatum*
                Peduncle arising from side of leaf axil, mostly 1-flowered; berry red.
                  (Fig. 307) .... 7. *Streptopus*

1. *Clintónia* Raf. (for D. Clinton).

Scapose herbs from a slender, creeping rhizome; leaves 2-4, elliptic, short-acuminate, attenuate to bases which sheath the leafless scape; inflorescence a terminal, few flowered umbel, (a lateral flower or cluster also sometimes present), flowers yellowish-white, campanulate, the 6 perianth segments distinct, elliptic-lanceolate to oblong, stamens inserted at the bases of the perianth segments, as long as the perianth, style equalling or longer than stamens, stigma obscurely 3-lobed; fruit a blue or black, few-seeded berry.

    1. *C. boreális* (Ait.) Raf. (northern). Bluebead-lily. Rich, moist woods and conifer bogs. May-June. Fig. 300, Map 681. —FAC

2. *Convallária* L. Lily of the Valley (a valley).

Rhizomatous, short-stemmed herb; stem bearing several bladeless sheaths near the base and 2 or 3 widely elliptic leaves above, these acute to slightly acuminate, cuneate to attenuate at the base; inflorescence a bracteate raceme terminating a scape arising from one of the middle or upper bladeless sheaths, flowers white, fragrant, nodding on recurved pedicels, perianth globose-campanulate, deciduous, the segments united nearly to the apex, its 6 short lobes reflexed, stamens included, inserted on the perianth near the base, style short, included, stigma capitate; fruit an orange, few-seeded berry.

    1. *C. majális* L. (blooming in May). Escaped from cultivation to deciduous or coniferous woods, thickets, roadsides and waste places. May-June. Fig. 301, Map 682. (Naturalized from Europe). Poisonous.

3. *Medéola* L. Indian Cucumber-root (for the sorceress Medea for its supposed medicinal value).

Herb from a white, tapering, horizontal, tuber-like rhizome; stem slender, unbranched, deciduous-floccose, particularly near the base; leaves in 2 whorles, the lower of 5-10 elliptic or oblanceolate leaves, the upper of 3-5 smaller, ovate leaves, red at the base when plant in fruit, subtending the sessile umbel (young or weakened plants have only 1 whorl and usually do not flower that season); inflorescence a terminal, sessile umbel of small, greenish-yellow flowers, the pedicels declined or recurved in flower, erect in fruit, perianth of 6 separate, elliptic, spreading to reflexed, deciduous segments, stamens hypogynous, styles 3, spreading; fruit a few-seeded, dark purple berry.

1. *M. virginiána* L. (Virginian). Rich woods. May-July. Fig. 302, Map 683. Rhizome edible; crisp, with taste of cucumber.

4. *Maiánthemum* G. H. Weber ex Wiggers (composed from Latin and Greek meaning May flower).

Simple-stemmed herbs from a long, creeping rhizome; leaves alternate, sessile or short-petioled, ovate to elliptic or lanceolate; inflorescence a terminal raceme or panicle of small white flowers, perianth of 4-6 spreading, separate segments, these narrowly lanceolate to elliptic or oblong, often persistent, withering, stamens 4-6, hypogynous, shorter or longer than perianth, ovary 2-3 locular, style short, stigma obscurely 2-3 lobed; fruit a 1 or 2 seeded berry, this at first greenish or yellowish, often speckled, eventually turning red. Berries edible, although somewhat bitter. —Wildl. 1

a. Perianth 4-parted; berry 2-carpellate. .... 1. *M. canadense*
a. Perianth 6-parted; berry 3-carpellate.
  b. Inflorescence a panicle of racemes .... 2. *M. racemosum*
  b. Inflorescence a simple raceme.
    Leaves 6 or more; raceme nearly sessile .... 3. *M. stellatum*
    Leaves 4 or fewer; raceme long-peduncled. .... 4. *M. trifolium*

1. *M. canadénse* Desf. (Canadian). False Lily of the Valley. Moist deciduous or coniferous woods and clearings. May-June. Fig. 303, Map 684. Our plants are var. *canadense.* —FAC-

2. *M. racemósum* (L.) Link (racemed). Rich deciduous woods. May-July. Fig. 304, Map 685. [*Smilacina racemosa; Vagnera racemosa*]. Our plants are subsp. *racemosum.* —FACU-

3. *M. stellátum* (L.) Link (starry). Sandy, alluvial woods, thickets and meadows. May-July. Map 686. [*Smilacina stellata; Vagnera stellata*]. —FACW

4. *M. trifólium* (L.) Sloboda (three-leaved). Bogs, wet coniferous or mixed woods. May-July. Map 687. (Siberia). [*Smilacina trifolia; Vagnera trifolia*]. —OBL

5. *Uvulária* L. Bellwort (name based on the flowers hanging like a palate).

Herbs, from a slender short or elongate rhizome; stem simple, or usually forking above, the lower part bearing several bladeless sheaths, the upper bearing leaves with blades; leaves alternate, sessile or perfoliate, elliptic or ovate; flowers 1-few, solitary at the ends of the branches, appearing axillary due to elongation of the branches, peduncled, nodding, yellow or greenish, perianth narrowly bell-shaped, the 6 segments separate, narrowly elliptic, deciduous, stamens hypogynous or attached to the bases of the perianth segments, much shorter than the segments, ovary 3-lobed, style trifid above the base; capsule 3-angled, ovoid or obovoid, loculicidal.

Leaves perfoliate. (Fig. 305).
  Perianth segments glandular-papillose on inner surface; leaves glabrous
    beneath .... 1. *U. perfoliata*
  Perianth segments smooth on inner surface; leaves pubescent beneath. .... 2. *U. grandiflora*
Leaves sessile, not perfoliate .... 3. *U. sessilifolia*

1. *U. perfoliáta* L. (base of leaf surrounding stem). Dry to moist, typically acid woodlands. May-June. Fig. 305, Map 688. Endangered in NH. Young shoots reportedly can be cooked and used as a substitute for asparagus; rhizome edible when cooked. —FACU

2. *U. grandiflóra* Sm. (large-flowered). Rich, typically calcareous, often rocky woodlands. April-May. Map 689. Endangered in CT, NH.

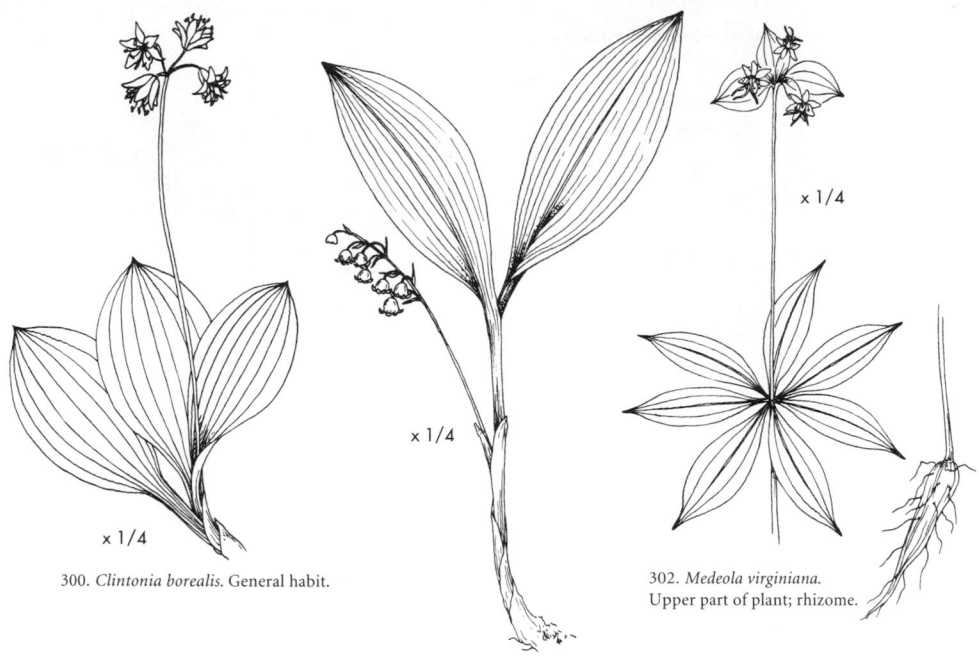

x 1/4

x 1/4

x 1/4

300. *Clintonia borealis*. General habit.

302. *Medeola virginiana*.
Upper part of plant; rhizome.

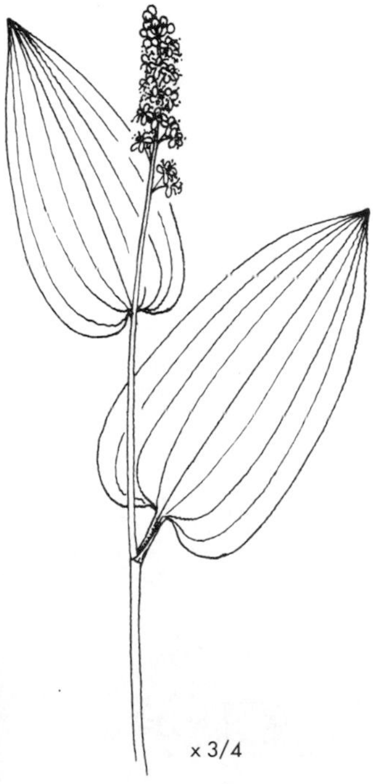

301.*Convallaria majalis*.
General habit.

x 3/4

x 2/5

303. *Maianthemum canadense*.
Alternate leaves; terminal raceme.

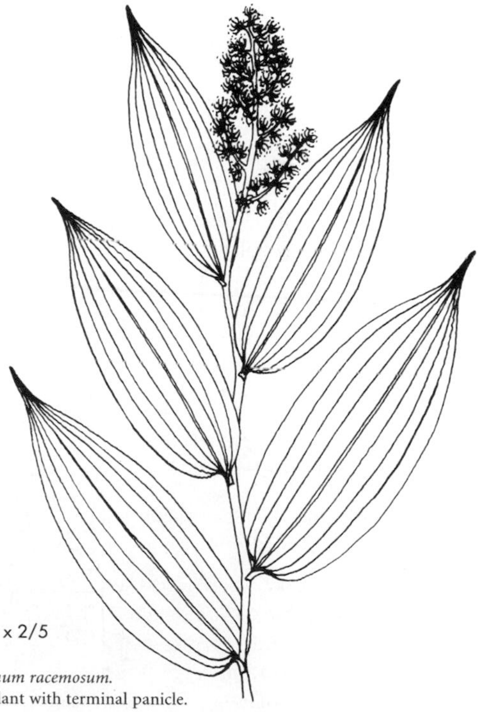

304. *Maianthemum racemosum*.
Upper part of plant with terminal panicle.

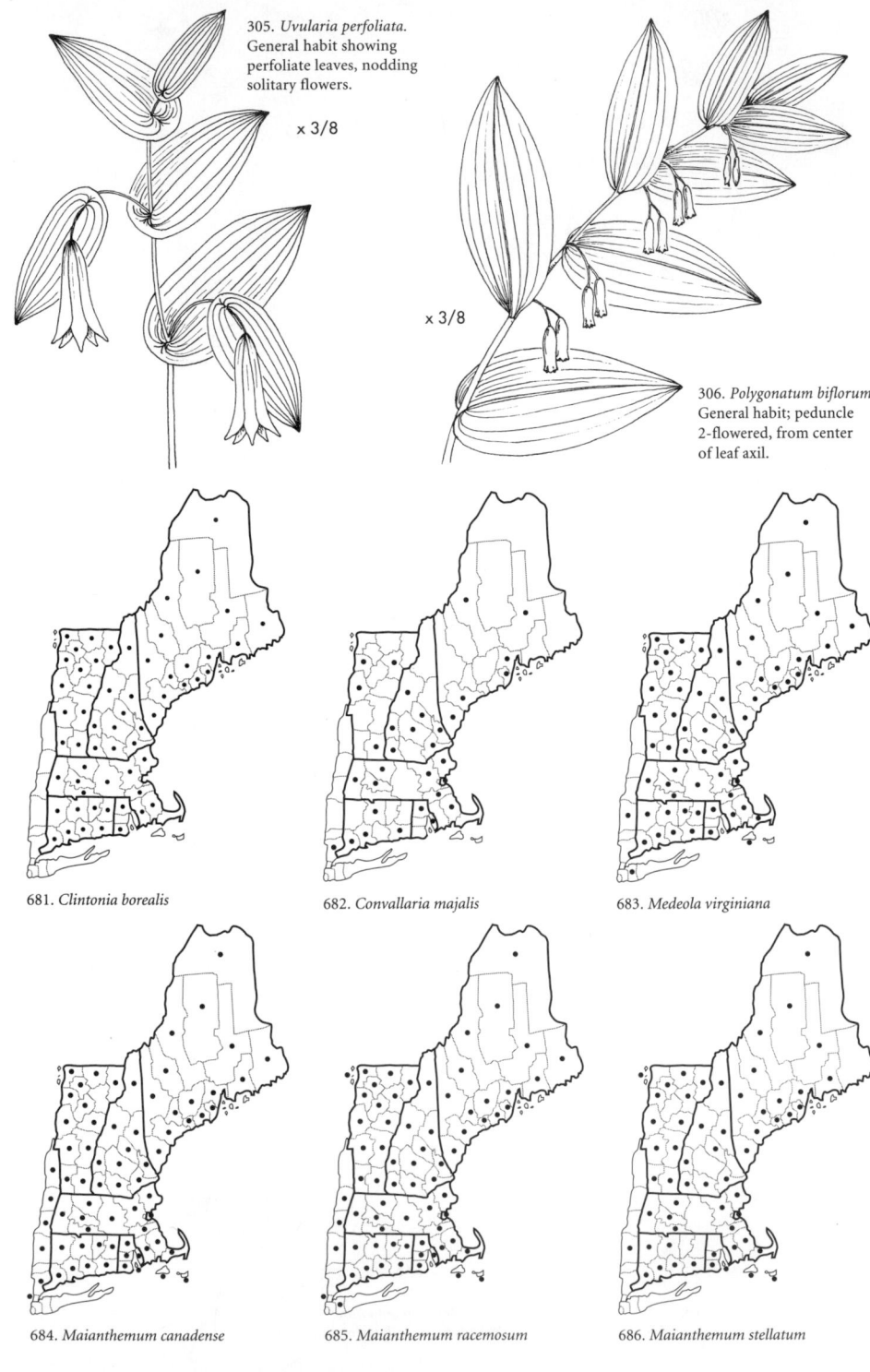

305. *Uvularia perfoliata.*
General habit showing
perfoliate leaves, nodding
solitary flowers.

x 3/8

x 3/8

306. *Polygonatum biflorum.*
General habit; peduncle
2-flowered, from center
of leaf axil.

681. *Clintonia borealis*

682. *Convallaria majalis*

683. *Medeola virginiana*

684. *Maianthemum canadense*

685. *Maianthemum racemosum*

686. *Maianthemum stellatum*

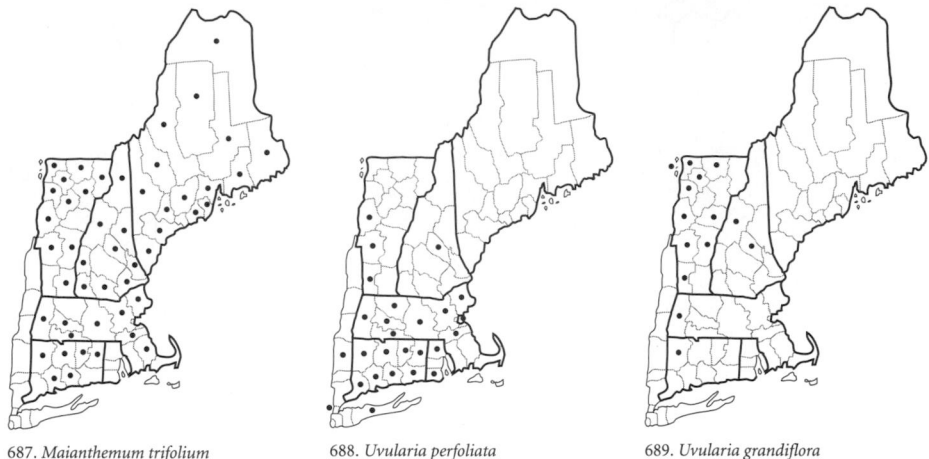

687. *Maianthemum trifolium*   688. *Uvularia perfoliata*   689. *Uvularia grandiflora*

3. U. sessilifólia L. (sessile-leaved). Dry to moist woods and thickets. May-June. Map 690. [*Oakesia s.; Oakesiella s.*]. —FACU-

U. pudíca (Walt.) Fern. Similar to *U. sessilifolia* but with leaves green beneath, styles separate to below the middle and fruit sessile (leaves glaucous beneath, styles separate above the middle and fruit stipitate in *U. sessilifolia*). On the coastal plain. Endangered in NY; reported for Suffolk County. [*Oakesia puberula; Oakesiella puberula; U. puberula*].

6. *Polygonátum* P. Mill. Solomon's Seal (from the Greek, referring to the knotty rhizome).

Herbs, from a stout, elongate, knotty rhizome; stem erect or arching, usually simple, bracteate or naked below, leafy above; leaves alternate, ovate to lanceolate, acute or obtuse, cuneate or rounded to clasping at the base, strongly nerved; inflorescence an axillary, pedunculate umbel, often reduced to 1 or 2 flowers, flowers whitish-green or yellowish, nodding, perianth oblong-cylindric, its segments united nearly to the apex, its 6 short lobes directed forward or slightly spreading, stamens attached to the perianth tube above the middle, included, style slender, stigma capitate, included; fruit a blue or black berry.

Tricýrtis Wall. *hírta* Hooker. Toad-Lily. Will key to *Polygonatum* but differs in having erect flowers and a capsular fruit. Reported for MA.

Leaves pubescent along the veins beneath.
Stem, peduncles and pedicels glabrous .... 1. *P. pubescens*
Stem, peduncles and pedicels pubescent .... 2. *P. latifolium*
Leaves glabrous on both surfaces .... 3. *P. biflorum*

1. P. pubéscens (Willd.) Pursh (hairy). Moist woods and thickets. May-July. Map 691. [*P. biflorum; P. boreale*].

2. P. latifólium (Jacq.) Desf. (broad-leaved). Roadsides. (Introduced from Europe). Reported for Middlesex County MA, Strafford County NH, Suffolk County NY.

3. P. biflórum (Walt.) Ell. (two-flowered). Rich moist woods, thickets, alluvial woods, roadsides. May-July. Fig. 306, Map 692. Our plants include var. *biflorum* and the following var.:

var. *commutátum* (J. A. & J. H. Schultes) Morong. Plants mostly 1-2 m tall, with flowers more than 15 on each peduncle (plants mostly up to 1 m tall, peduncles with up to 15 flowers in var. *biflorum*. [*P. canaliculatum; P. commutatum*]. Young plants and rhizomes reported as edible when cooked. Berries poisonous. —FACU

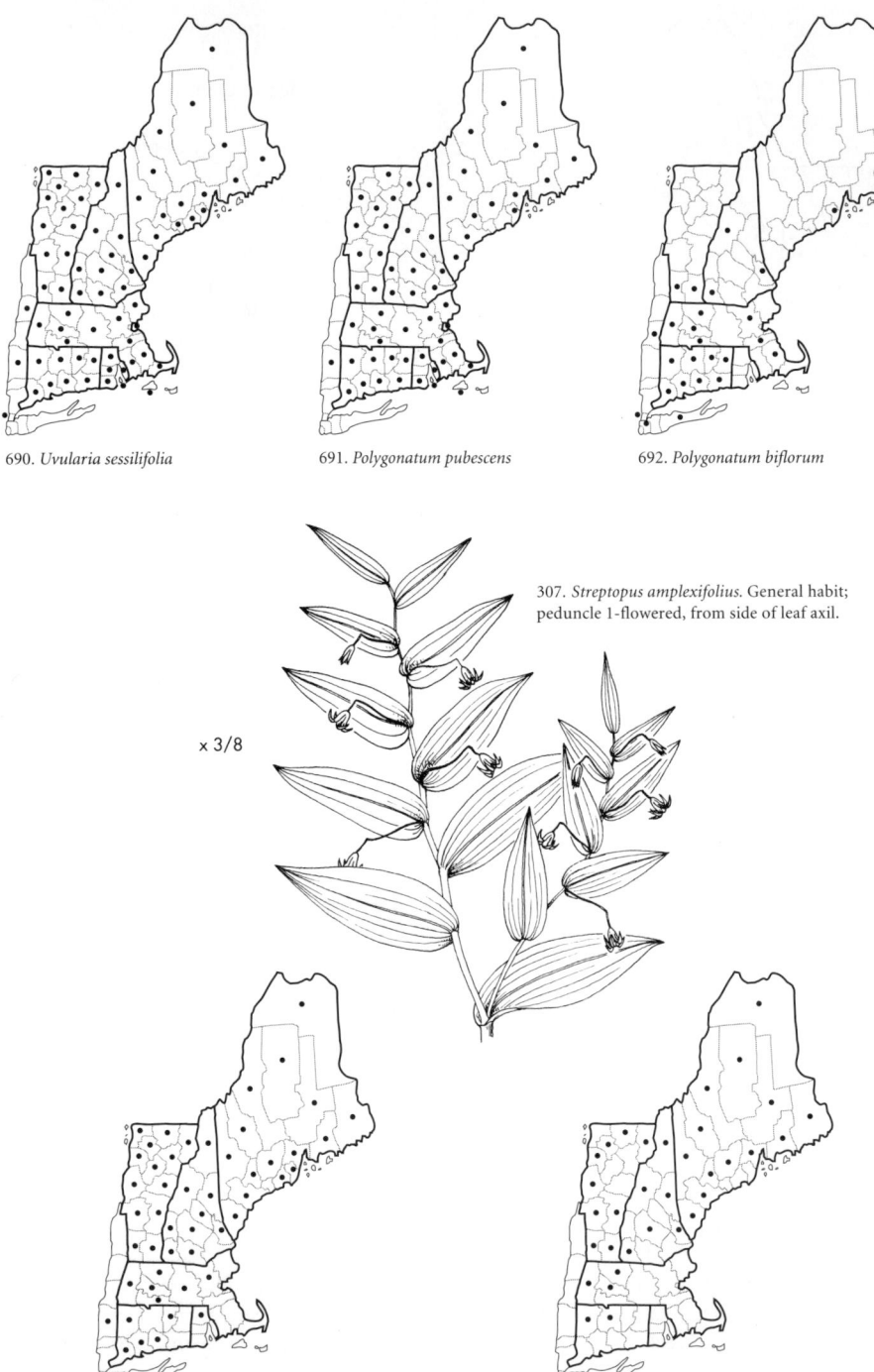

690. *Uvularia sessilifolia*

691. *Polygonatum pubescens*

692. *Polygonatum biflorum*

307. *Streptopus amplexifolius.* General habit; peduncle 1-flowered, from side of leaf axil.

× 3/8

693. *Streptopus roseus* var. *perspectus*

694. *Streptopus amplexifolius*

7. *Stréptopus* Michx. Twisted-stalk (from the Greek, referring to the bent or twisted peduncle).

Rhizomatous herbs with a somewhat stout, often branched stem; leaves alternate, ovate or lance-ovate, acuminate, sessile or clasping, strongly nerved; flowers small, greenish white to purple, extra-axillary, nodding, solitary or peduncle bearing 2 flowers, the peduncle bent or twisted at about the middle, perianth campanulate, the 6 segments separate, lanceolate, acuminate, spreading or recurved toward the apex, deciduous, stamens attached to the bases of the perianth segments, shorter than the perianth, style slender, 3-cleft or entire; fruit a red, many-seeded berry. Young shoots and leaves reportedly useable as salad vegetable; berries have cathartic qualities.

Leaves coarsely ciliate, green on both sides or slightly paler beneath but not glaucous ... 1. *S. roseus*
var. *perspectus*
Leaves not ciliate, glaucous beneath .... 2. *S. amplexifolius*
var. *americanus*

    1. *S. róseus* Michx. (rose-colored). Rich, moist woods. May-June. Map 693. Represented us as var. *perspéctus* Fassett. —FAC-
    2. *S. amplexifólius* (L.) DC. (clasping-leaved). Rich, moist woods. May-July. Fig. 307, Map 694. [*Tortipes a.*]. Represented with us as var. *americanus* J. A. Schultes. —FAC+
    S. x oreópolus Fern. A hybrid between *S. amplexifolius* and *S. roseus*. [*P. amplexifolius* var. *o.*].

Family 48. Alliáceae (Onion Family)

Similar to Liliaceae. Represented with us by the following genus. [*Liliaceae*].

1. *Állium* L. Onion (the ancient Latin name for garlic).

Glabrous scapose-stemmed herbs with strong odor of onion or garlic, from a coated bulb; leaves fleshy, terete or flat, linear to lanceolate, sheathing, basal or on the lower part of the stem, sometimes absent at anthesis; inflorescence a terminal, simple umbel subtended by 1-3 spathiform bracts, flowers green, white, pink or purple, sometimes replaced by bulblets, perianth segments distinct or united at the base, persistent, withering, stamens attached to the perianth segments at the base, style 1, stigma capitate; capsule ovoid or obovoid to globose, 3-lobed, loculidical. Bulbs edible raw or cooked; various medicinal uses are also cited, particularly for garlic, which eaten raw reduces blood cholesterol and blood pressure.

a. Leaves terete or subterete although easily flattened, hollow at least toward the
    base, present at anthesis.
  b. Stem with a distinct inflated segment about a third of the distance above the
      base .... 1. *A. cepa*
  b. Stem lacking a distinct inflated segment.
      Pedicels longer than the perianth; umbel bearing or completely of bulblets. ... 2. *A. vineale*
      Pedicels shorter than the perianth; umbel with flowers only .... 3. *A. schoenoprasum*
a. Leaves flat, not hollow, present or absent at anthesis.
  c. Leaves elliptic-lanceolate, 2-6 cm wide, absent at anthesis; bulblets absent .... 4. *A. tricoccum*
  c. Leaves narrowly linear, mostly 2 cm or less wide, present at anthesis; bulblets
      usually present (except in similar species *A, porrum* and *A. ampeloprasum*
      which occur as waifs in our range). (Fig. 308).
      Outer bulb coat fibrous; stem leafy in the lower third. .... 5. *A. canadense*
      Outer bulb coat membranous; stem leafy from a third to the middle. .... 6. *A. oleraceum*

    1. *A. cépa* L. (onion). Domestic Onion. Cultivated; occasionally escaped to waste places. Map 695. [*A. cepa* var. *bulbifera*].
    Our plants include var. *cepa* and the following var.:

var. *vivíparum* M.C. Mentz. Underground bulb small and undeveloped, bulblets borne in the flower cluster (bulb-large and flower cluster not bearing bulblets in var. *cepa*).

2. *A. vineále* L. (of vineyards). Field Garlic. Fields, pastures and waste places. June-July. Map 696. (Naturalized from Europe). Our plants are subsp. *vineale.* —FACU-

3. *A. schoenóprasum* L. (rush-leak). Domestic Chives. Cultivated, occasionally escaped to waste places. Map 697. (Introduced from Eurasia). Our plants include var. *schoenoprasum* and the following var.:

var. *sibíricum* (L.) Hartm. Leaves rarely reaching umbel (equalling or surpassing umbel in var. *schoenoprasum*). Our native plants of gravelly river shores and fields. June-August. —FACU

4. *A. tricóccum* Ait. (3-locular). Wild Leek. Rich moist woods. June-July. Map 698. Our plants are var. *tricoccum.* —FACU+

A. burdíckii (Hanes) A. G. Jones. Similar to *A. tricoccum* but with scape less than 2 dm tall, leaves less than 5 cm wide, bracts subtending the inflorescence up to 2 cm long (scape mostly more than 2 dm tall, leaves mostly 5 cm or more wide, bracts 2-3 cm long in *A. tricoccum*). From farther west. Reported for ME, NH, VT. [*A. tricoccum* var. *b.*]. —FACU+

5. *A. canadénse* L. (Canadian). Wild Garlic. Low wet woods and thickets, rich woods. May-June. Fig. 308, Map 699. Endangered in NH. [*A. mutabile*]. Our plants are var. *canadense.*

***A. pórrum* L.** Leek. Will key to *A. canadense* but is distinguishable in having unbels without bulblets (umbels produce bulblets in *A. canadense*).

***A. fistulósum* L.** Welsh Onion. Bulbs fascicled; leaves and stem inflated (bulb solitary; leaves and stem not inflated in *A. porrum*).

6. *A. oleráceum* L. (like a vegetable). Wild Garlic. Woodland borders and roadsides. July-August. (Naturalized from Europe). Reported for Suffolk County MA.

***A. satívum* L.** Garlic. Differing from *A. oleraceum* in having leaves 5 mm or more wide and compound bulbs (leaves less than 5 mm wide and bulbs simple in *A. oleraceum*). (Introduced from the Old World). Rarely escaped from cultivation. Reported for Chilmark MA.

***A. ampeloprásum* L.** Wild Leek. Differing from the latter two species in having umbels without bulblets (umbels produce bulblets in *A. sativum* and *A. oleraceum*). Adventive in the south from Europe. Reported for Suffolk County NY.

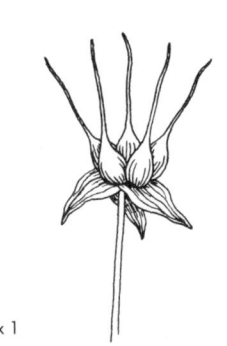

× 1

308. *Allium canadense.* Umbel with bulblets instead of flowers.

695. *Allium cepa*

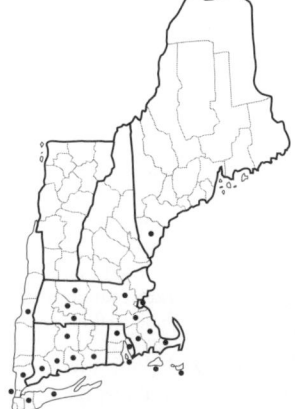

696. *Allium vineale*

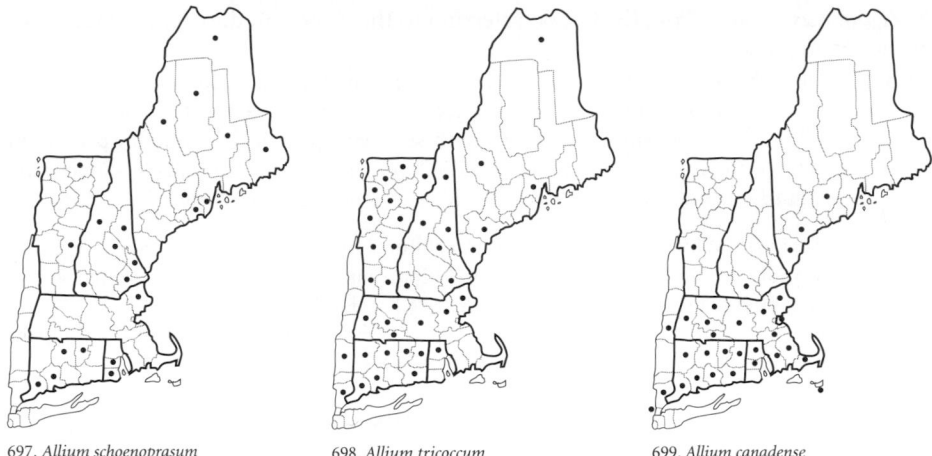

697. *Allium schoenoprasum*   698. *Allium tricoccum*   699. *Allium canadense*

Family 49. Melanthiáceae (Bunch-flower Family)

Similar to *Liliaceae*. Scapose or simple-stemmed. Leaves basal or cauline and alternate. Flowers perfect or rarely dioecious, inflorescence a spike, raceme or panicle, perianth segments separate or united, ovary superior, rarely partly inferior, styles 3, distinct. [*Liliaceae*].

a. Leaves principally basal or near the base, the stem scapose or bracteate, or with
  leaves gradually or abruptly reduced upward.
  b. Leaves equitant, distichous, the bases overlapping as in Iris (Fig. 309). .... 1. *Tofieldia glutinosa*
  b. Leaves not equitant or distichous.
    c. Inflorescence paniculate. (Fig. 311).
      Rachis of inflorescence glabrous; perianth segments not clawed. .... 2. *Zigadenus*
      Rachis of inflorescence pubescent; perianth segments abruptly narrowed
        to basal claws .... 3. *Melanthium latifolium*
    c. Inflorescence a spike or raceme.
      d. Perianth segments united for half or more their length; ovary partly
        inferior .... 4. *Aletris farinosa*
      d. Perianth segments free to base or nearly so; ovary superior.
        Leaves long and linear; pedicels bracted. .... 5. *Amianthium muscitoxicum*
        Leaves elliptic to oblanceolate; pedicels not bracted. .... 6. *Chamaelirium luteum*
a. Leaves cauline, alternate, basal leaves absent. (Fig. 315). .... 7. *Veratrum viride*

1. Tofiéldia Huds. False Asphodel (for T. Tofield).

Slender herb with an unbranched stem from a short or creeping rhizome; leaves linear, 2-ranked, several clustered at or near the base of the stem, the stem sometimes bearing a bract-like leaf near the middle; inflorescence a dense, terminal raceme, each flower subtended by an involucre of 3 small connate bracts, perianth segments separate, spreading, persistent in fruit, styles 3, each terminated by a stigma, stamens free from the perianth segments; capsule septicidal, subtended by the persistent perianth and tipped by the persistent, beak-like styles.

  1. *T. glutinósa* (Michx.) Pers. (sticky). Damp ledges, river and lake shores, bogs and other wet places. June-July. Fig. 309, Map 700. Our plants are subsp. *glutinosa*. —OBL

2. Zigádenus Michx. (from the Greek, referring to the glands on the ovary sometimes occurring in pairs).

Glabrous herb with unbranched stem from a thick rhizome or bulb; leaves long and linear, grass-like, mostly basal or sub-basal, the stem leaves reduced upward; inflorescence a terminal, bracteate, panicle (ours) of white or greenish flowers, perianth segments spreading, fused to the base of the ovary, persistent, withering, each usually bearing 1 or 2 small glands below the middle, stamens free from the perianth segments; capsule 3-lobed, ovoid, each lobe with a persistent style. Poisonous.

   1. Z. élegans Pursh. White Camass. Calcareous lake shores and swamps. July-September. Fig. 310. Reported for Addison County VT. (not seen since 1912; presumed extirpated). Represented with us as subsp. *glaúcus* (Nutt.) Hulten [*Z. glaucus; Anticlea g.*]. —FAC

   Z. leimanthoídes Gray. Tepals less than 6 mm long (7 mm or more long in *Z. elegans*). Along the coastal plain. Reported for Nassau and Suffolk Counties NY. [*Oceanoros l.*]. —OBL

3. Melánthium L. Bunch-flower (from the Greek referring to the darker color of the perianth after expanding).

Tall, polygamous herbs with leafy stems, pubescent above, glabrous below, from a thick rhizome; leaves elongate, linear to narrowly oblanceolate, gradually reduced upward, sheathing or the upper sheathless; inflorescence a large, terminal, bracteate panicle of racemes of greenish flowers, perianth segments spreading, ovate, contracted at the base into claws, bearing 2 glands at the base of the blade, the stamens adnate to the claws, perianth persistent, withering; capsule ovoid, septicidal.

   1. M. latifólium Desr. Open deciduous woodlands. June-July. Fig. 311. Reported for Fairfield County CT. [*M. hybridum*]. —FACU

4. Áletris L. Colic-root (from the mealy appearance of the perianth).

Glabrous, bitter herbs with unbranched stems from fibrous roots; leaves in a basal rosette, lanceolate to narrowly elliptic, those of the stem greatly reduced and bract-like; inflorescence a terminal, spike-like, bracteate raceme of small white (ours) flowers, perianth cylindric to campanulate, the segments united, adnate to the lower part of the ovary, free only at the apex, 6 lobed, roughened with numerous scale-like points giving it a mealy appearance, persistent, withering, stamens attached to the perianth just below the lobes, included, ovary partly inferior, style minutely 3 lobed, stigmas capitate; capsule ovoid, tapered to a long beak, enclosed by the persistent, withered perianth, loculicidal.

   1. A. farinósa L. (mealy, from its granular perianth). Sandy, moist to dry open woods, fields, pond margins and waste places. June-July. Fig. 312, Map 701. Preparation made from the dried ground roots is reported to be useful in treating rheumatism. —FAC

5. Amiánthium Gray Fly poison (from the Greek, referring to the lack of glands on the perianth).

Glabrous herb with unbranched stem from a thick bulb; leaves mostly basal, numerous, long and linear, blunt, the stem leaves greatly reduced upward; inflorescence a dense, terminal raceme of white, bracteate flowers, perianth segments ovate or obovate, spreading, persistent in fruit, stamens attached to the base of the perianth segments; capsule deeply 3-lobed, each tipped with a persistent style, septicidal.

   Scilla sibirica in the *Hyacinthaceae* may also key to *Amianthium;* (see description under Hyacinthaceae).

   1. A. muscitóxicum (Walt.) Gray. Dry, sandy, open woods. June-July. Fig. 313. Reported for Suffolk County NY. [*Chrosperma m.*]. Poisonous. —FAC

311. *Melanthium latifolium.*
Oblanceolate leaves;
terminal panicle.

× 1/5

× 1/4

× 1/5

310. *Zigadenus elegans.* General habit.

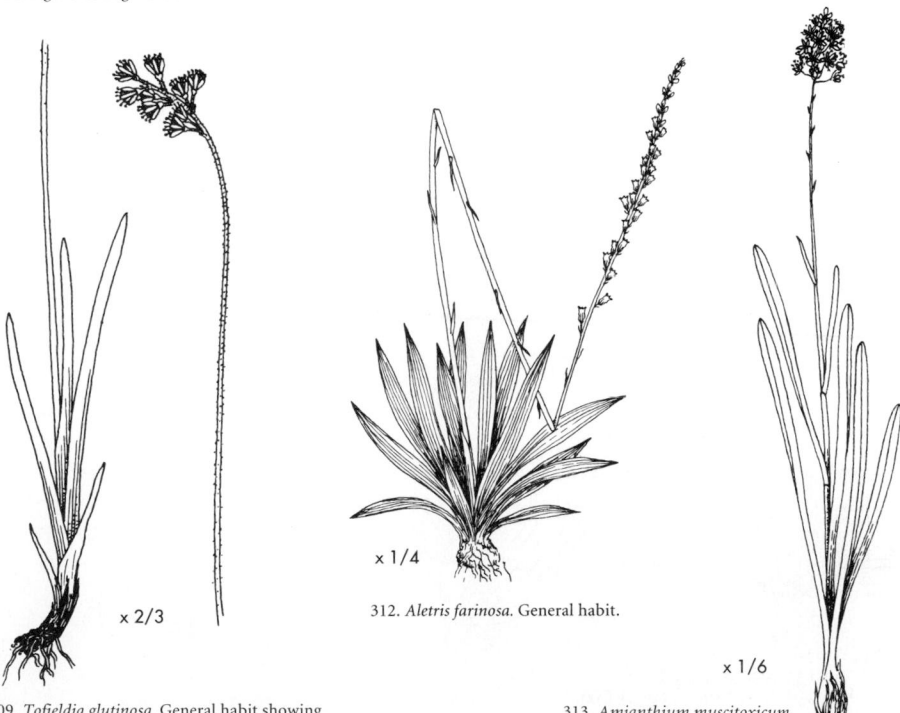

× 1/4

312. *Aletris farinosa.* General habit.

× 2/3

309. *Tofieldia glutinosa.* General habit showing
distichous basal leaves, terminal raceme.

× 1/6

313. *Amianthium muscitoxicum.*
General habit.

6. Chamaelírium Willd. Blazing Star (from the Greek, based on a dwarf specimen).

Dioecious herb with an unbranched stem from a bitter, tuberous rhizome; basal leaves numerous, spatulate, stem leaves alternate, lanceolate; inflorescence a long, narrow, terminal, dense raceme of small, white, bractless flowers, perianth segments linear-spatulate, spreading, persistent, withering, staminate and pistillate flowers on separate plants, the pistillate with 3 sessile stigmas, staminodes present, the staminate with stamens free from the perianth segments; capsule ellipsoid, loculicidal.

    1. **C. lúteum** (L.) Gray (Yellow). Moist or dry mesic woods. May-July. Fig. 314, Map 702. Endangered in MA, CT. [*C. obovale.*]. —FAC

7. Verátrum L. False Hellebore (Latin name for Hellebore).

Tall, coarse, polygamous herbs with unbranched, pubescent stems from a short, stout rhizome; leaves broad, elliptic, clasping at the base, strongly veined and plaited, 3-ranked; inflorescence a large, terminal, bracteate panicle of racemes of green or purple flowers, perianth segments spreading, elliptic to oblong, persistent, withering, stamens free from the perianth segments; capsule 3-lobed, each lobe with a persistent style, septicidal. All parts poisonous.

    1. **V. víride** Ait. (green). Deciduous swamps and wet woods. May-July. Fig. 315, Map 703. Poisonous. —FACW+

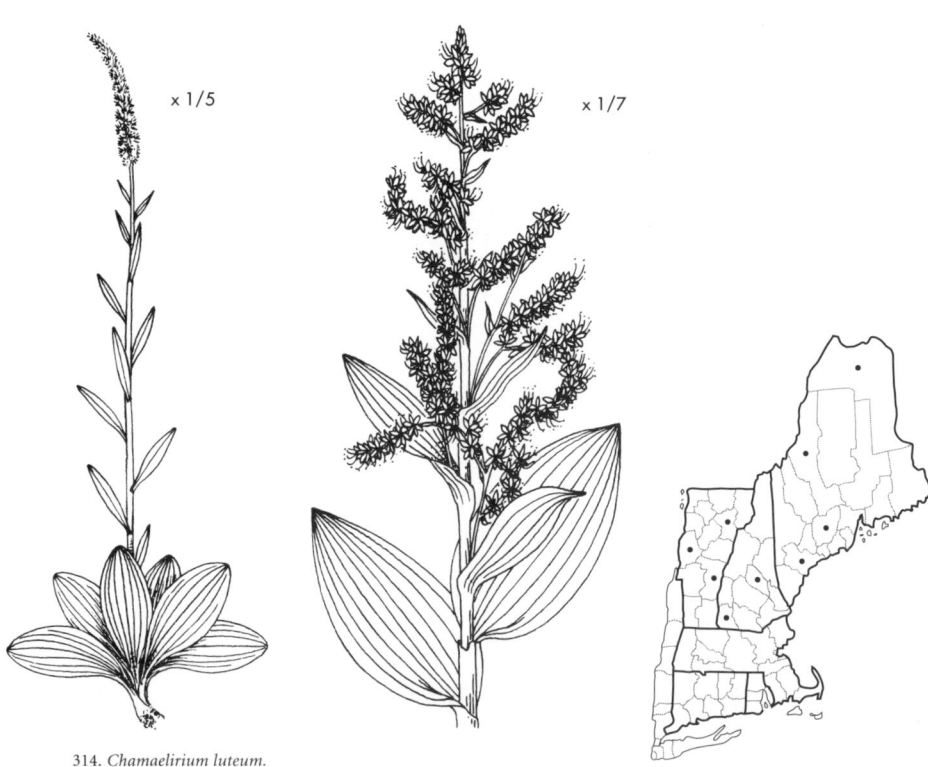

x 1/5

x 1/7

314. *Chamaelirium luteum.*
General habit.

315. *Veratrum viride.* General habit.

700. *Tofieldia glutinosa*

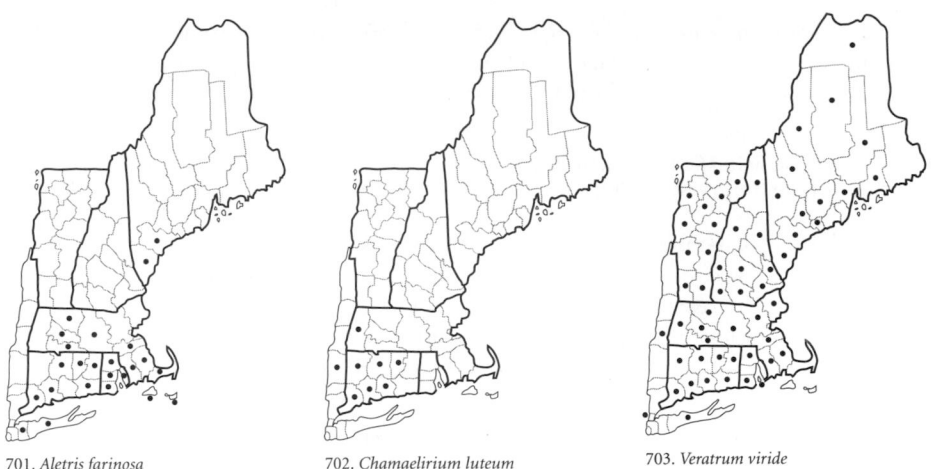

701. *Aletris farinosa*   702. *Chamaelirium luteum*   703. *Veratrum viride*

Family 50. Funkiáceae (Plantain Lily Family)

Similar to *Liliaceae*; represented with us by the following genera. [*Liliaceae*].

1. *Hósta* Tratt. Plantain Lily (for N. Host).

Glabrous, scapose herbs from a cluster of thick roots; leaves basal, broad petioled, ovate or cordate, strongly ribbed; inflorescence a raceme of bracted white to purple flowers, perianth broadly campanulate, with a long tube and 6 erect or spreading oblong lobes, style 1, with a capitate stigma, stamens hypogynous or borne on the perianth tube; capsule elongate, cylindric, septicidal.

Chionodóxa Boiss. *lúciliae* Boiss. Will key to *Hosta* but is distinguishable in arising from a bulb, leaves linear and grass-like to oblanceolate, flowers in a short raceme, blue with white center, perianth with a short tube, capsule 3-angled, loculicidal. Rarely escaped from cultivation in our range. Reported for MA.

Flower 5 cm long or longer, its tube abruptly expanded into the throat; leaves
    cordate or ovate, 6 cm wide or wider. (Fig. 316.).
    Flowers white, very fragrant, 10 or more cm long. .... 1. *H. plantaginea*
    Flowers blue or purple, not fragrant, about 5-6 cm long. .... 2. *H. ventricosa*
Flower about 4 cm long, its tube gradually expanded into the throat; leaves
    lanceolate, usually not over 5 cm wide .... 3. *H. lancifolia*

    1. *H. plantagínea* (Lam.) Aschers. (Plantain-leaved). Spread from cultivation to roadsides and waste places. August-October. (Introduced from E. Asia).

    2. *H. ventricósa* (Salisb.) Stearn (bellied out). Spread from cultivation to roadsides and waste places. July-September. Fig. 316, Map 704. (Naturalized from E. Asia).

    3. *H. lancifólia* Engl. (with lanceolate leaves). Spread from cultivation to roadsides and waste places. July-September. Reported for Fairfield County CT. (Introduced from E. Asia).[*H. japonica*].

Family 51. Hyacintháceae

Similar to *Liliaceae*. Scapose herbs from a scaly bulb. Leaves basal, linear to oblanceolate. Inflorescence a bracteate raceme of blue or white flowers, the segments separate or united nearly to the apex, stigma 1 or 3-lobed. Represented with us by the following genera. [*Liliaceae*].

Scílla L. *sibírica* Haw. ex Andr. (Siberian). Inflorescence a short raceme of several (about 3) deep blue flowers with a rotate perianth; leaves oblanceolate. Occasionally escaped from cultivation to fields and roadsides. (Introduced from Eurasia). Reported for Essex, Hampshire and Middlesex Counties MA.

Perianth segments united for half or more their length. .... 1. *Muscari*
Perianth segments free to base or nearly so. .... 2. *Ornithogalum*

1. *Muscári* P. Mill. Grape Hyacinth (from the flowers sometimes musk-scented).

Slender, glabrous, scapose herbs from a scaly bulb; leaves basal, linear; inflorescence a dense, terminal, bracteate raceme of small, blue, nodding flowers, perianth globose or urceolate, the segments united nearly to the apex, the 6 lobes short, resembling teeth, stamens inserted on the perianth, included, style 1, short, stigma 1; capsule 3-angled, loculicidal.

Leaves 3-8 mm wide, erect; perianth globose to subglobose or ellipsoid. .... 1. *M. botryoides*
Leaves up to 3 mm wide, recurved at the tip; perianth oblong or cylindric. .... 2. *M. neglectum*

1. *M. botryoídes* (L.) P. Mill. (like a cluster of grapes). Escaped from cultivation to fields, roadsides and waste places. April-May. Map 705. (Naturalized from Europe).

2. *M. negléctum* Guss. ex Ten. (of the Atlantic Ocean). Escaped from cultivation to fields, roadsides and waste places. April-May. Fig. 317, Map 706. (Naturalized from Europe). [*M. atlanticum; M. racemosum*].

2. *Ornithógalum* L. Star of Bethlehem (from the Greek, meaning bird milk).

Slender, glabrous, scapose herbs from a scaly bulb; leaves basal, linear; inflorescence a few flowered, terminal, bracteate raceme of white flowers, perianth segments separate, spreading, elliptic-lanceolate, persistent, stamens hypogenous, shorter than the perianth, style short, stigma 3-lobed; capsule subglobose, 3-angled, loculicidal. Poisonous.

Perianth segments up to 2 cm long .... 1. *O. umbellatum*
Perianth segments longer than 2 cm .... 2. *O. nutans*

1. *O. umbellátum* L. (umbelled). Meadows, roadsides and waste places. May-June. Fig. 318, Map 707. (Naturalized from Europe). —FACU

2. *O. nútans* L. (nodding). Reported for Groton and E. Haddam CT. (Introduced from Europe).

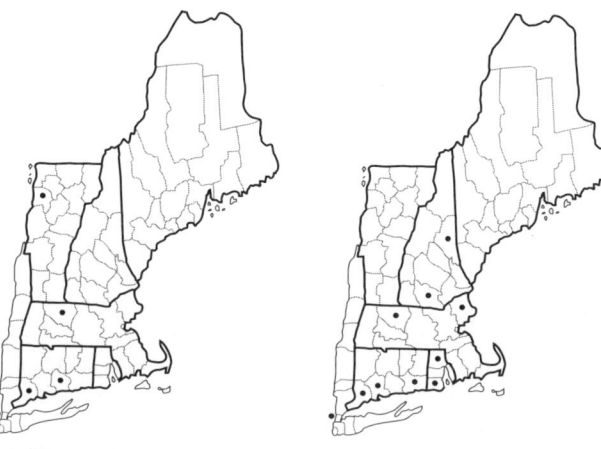

704. *Hosta ventricosa*   705. *Muscari botryoides*

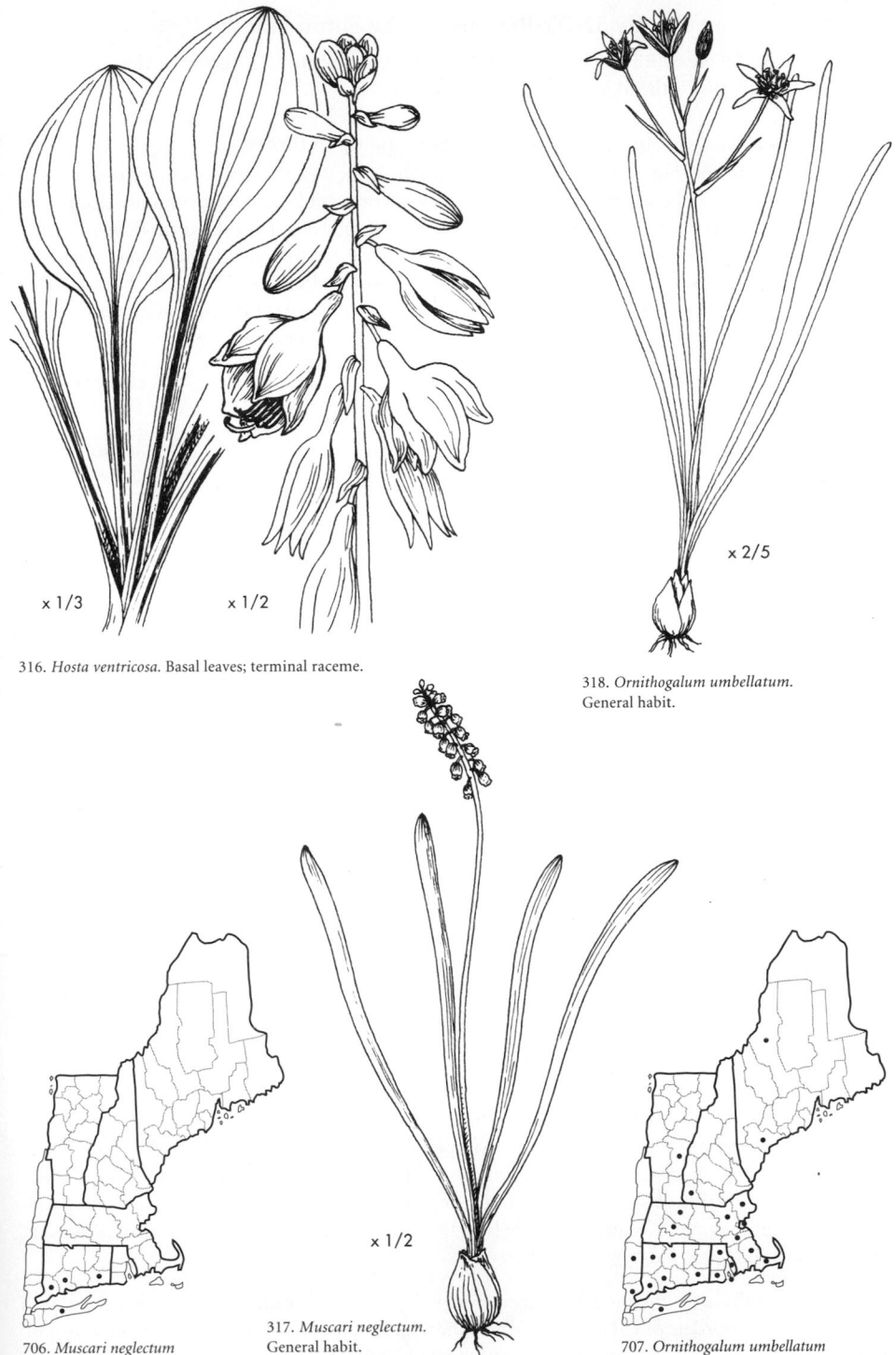

316. *Hosta ventricosa*. Basal leaves; terminal raceme.

× 1/3   × 1/2

318. *Ornithogalum umbellatum*.
General habit.

× 2/5

317. *Muscari neglectum*.
General habit.

× 1/2

706. *Muscari neglectum*

707. *Ornithogalum umbellatum*

Family 52. Trilliáceae (Wake-robin Family)

Similar to the *Liliaceae*. Rhizomatous. Leaves whorled. Perianth of 2 distinct series; stigmas 3. Represented with us by the following genus. [*Liliaceae*].

1. *Tríllium* L. Wake-robin (name based on parts being in threes).

Herbs, from a short, stout rhizome with a short, simple stem; leaves usually 3 (exceptionally fewer or more) in a whorl at the summit of the stem, sessile or short petiolate, ovate, acuminate, immature plants with a solitary, long petioled leaf sometimes arising directly from the rhizome; flower solitary, terminal, sessile or peduncled, perianth of 2 distinct series, the sepals 3, green, spreading or reflexed, persistent, petals 3, white, purple or pink, withering, (sepals and/or petals reduced or increased in number, or leaf-like in aberrant forms), stamens hypogynous, shorter than the perianth segments, ovary usually angulate, stigmas 3, sessile or subsessile; fruit a many seeded berry.

a. Peduncle recurved, hiding flower beneath the leaves. (Fig. 319). .... 1. *T. cernuum*
a. Peduncle straight, erect or divergent, not hiding flower beneath the leaves.
  b. Petioles more than 4 mm long.
    Petals white with red or purple streaks at the base, 2-4 cm long. .... 2. *T. undulatum*
    Petals uniformly white or pink, 4-8 cm long. .... 3. *T. grandiflorum*
  b. Petioles less than 4 mm long or absent.
    Stigmas straight or merely arched; petals imbricate at the base, forming a
      short tube, normally white or pink .... 3. *T. grandiflorum*
    Stigmas strongly recurved; petals not imbricate or overlapping and not
      forming a tube, normally purple .... 4. *T. erectum*

1. *T. cérnuum* L. (nodding). Nodding Trillium. Rich, damp woods and thickets. May-June. Fig. 319, Map 708. Reported to be of medicinal value, including use by Indians to aid childbirth. —FACW

2. *T. undulátum* Willd. (wavy). Painted Trillium. Moist, rich deciduous or mixed woodlands. May-June. Map 709. Also producing forms with dimerous flowers, or sepals enlarged and resembling foliage leaves, or sepals white-striped. —FACU

3. *T. grandiflórum* (Michx.) Salisb. (large-flowered). Rich, moist, usually calcareous woods. May-June. Map 710. A variable species producing forms with dimerous leaves and flowers, or parts of flower in 4s or 5s, or leaves petioled or wanting, or petals green or green and white-striped, or stamens and carpels changed to white petals.

4. *T. eréctum* L. (erect). Stinking Benjamin. Rich, moist, deciduous or mixed woods. April-June. Map 711. A variable species producing forms with parts of flower in 4s, or petals purple at the base and white above, or petals green, yellow, pink or white. —FACU-

Family 53. Asparagáceae (Asparagus Family)

Similar to the *Liliaceae*. Represented with us by the following genus. [*Liliaceae*].

1. *Aspáragus* L. Asparagus (ancient Greek name).

Dioecious herbs from a thick rhizome; stems simple and fleshy at first, becoming bushy-branched; leaves inconspicuous, scale-like, subtending clusters of filiform branchlets resembling leaves; flowers small, greenish-yellow, axillary, solitary or paired, pendant on jointed pedicels, campanulate, of separate segments, stamens inserted on the base of the perianth, included, style slender, stigmas 3; fruit a large, red, few-seeded berry.

1. *A. officinális* L. (of the shops). Escaped from cultivation to dry sandy soil of fields, roadsides, waste places and borders of salt marshes. May-June. Fig. 320, Map 712. (Introduced from Europe). Eating raw shoots can cause dermatitis; berries toxic. —FACU

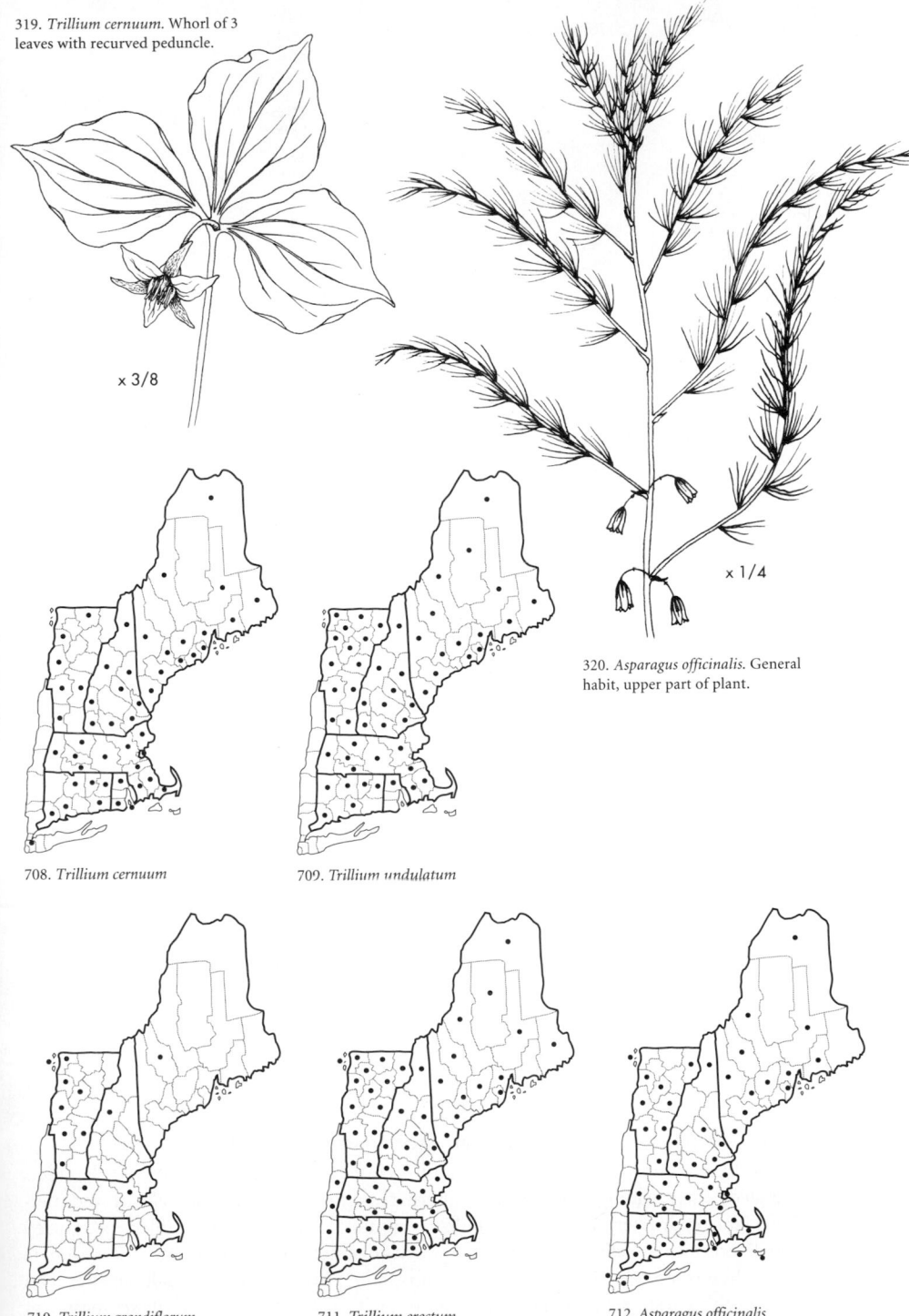

319. *Trillium cernuum*. Whorl of 3 leaves with recurved peduncle.

x 3/8

x 1/4

320. *Asparagus officinalis*. General habit, upper part of plant.

708. *Trillium cernuum*

709. *Trillium undulatum*

710. *Trillium grandiflorum*

711. *Trillium erectum*

712. *Asparagus officinalis*

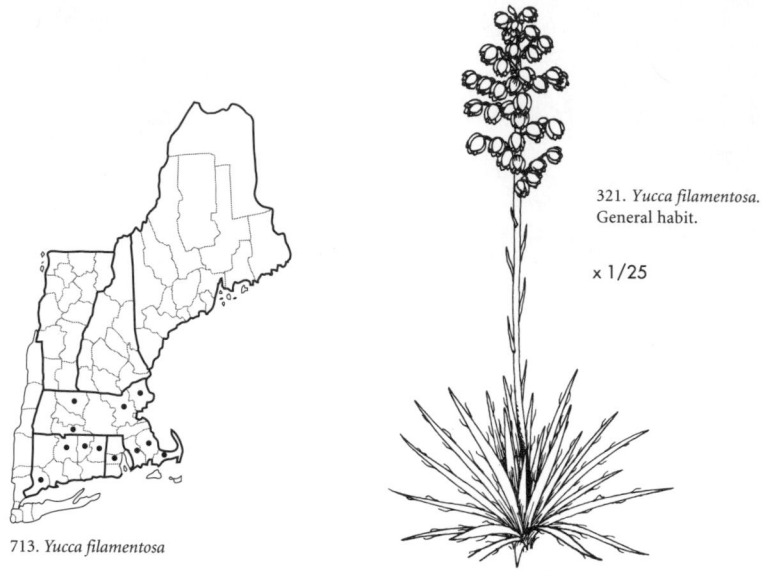

321. *Yucca filamentosa.*
General habit.

x 1/25

713. *Yucca filamentosa*

Family 54. Agaváceae (Beargrass Family)

Similar to the *Liliaceae.* Represented with us by the following genus. [*Liliaceae*].

1. Yúcca L. Beargrass (native Haitian name).
Woody plants with a short, stout, stem unbranched below the inflorescence; leaves linear or lance-linear, tapered to sharp points and clasping bases, evergreen, thick and leathery, numerous and crowded at the summit of the stem; inflorescence a large, terminal panicle borne on a long, bracteate peduncle (ours), flowers large, whitish, broadly companulate, pendulous, the lobes lanceolate or elliptic, persistent, withering, ovary superior, stamens hypogenous, shorter than the perianth, style shorter than the stamens, stigmas 3; fruit a capsule (ours), this oblong, 3-locular or imperfectly 6-locular, loculicidal.
    1. Y. filamentósa L. (bearing threads). Escaped from cultivation to dry sandy soil of roadsides, waste places, and disturbed areas. June-September. Fig. 321, Map 713. [*Y. concava; Y. smalliana*]. Flower stalks edible before buds expand; fruits also edible; roots produce a lather when cut and mashed.

Family 55. Smilacáceae L. (Greenbriar Family)

Similar to the *Liliaceae.* Represented with us by the following genus. [*Liliaceae*].

1. Smilax L. Greenbriar (ancient Greek name for an evergreen oak).
Dioecious, herbaceous or woody vines from a stout rhizome, climbing by stipular tendrils; stems terete or angled, often twining, prickly; leaves alternate, with broad, longitudinally nerved, net-veined blades, and tendrils terminating the stipules, deciduous (ours); flowers in axillary, peduncled umbels, small, greenish or yellowish, perianth segments distinct, spreading, deciduous, staminate flowers with 6 hypogenous, included stamens and no ovary, pistillate flowers usually smaller than the staminate, with 1-6 staminodes, the ovary superior, with 1-3 sessile or subsessile stigmas; fruit

a few-seeded black or blue-black (ours) berry. Young shoots edible raw or cooked. Rhizomes of species 2, 4 and 5 yield a starchy substance when pounded, washed and strained that was used as food by Indians. —Wildl. 2

a. Stems herbaceous, unarmed; peduncles usually more than 4 cm long.
 Leaves ovate, side margins convex; anthers shorter than filaments; longest
  fruiting pedicels nearly 2 or more times as long as fruit. .... 1. *S. herbacea*
 Leaves deltoid-ovate to subhastate, side margins straight or concave; anthers
  as long or longer than filaments; longest fruiting pedicels shorter
  to slightly longer than fruit .... 2. *S. pseudochina*
a. Stems woody, often prickly; peduncles usually less than 4 cm long.
 b. Leaves glaucous beneath .... 3. *S. glauca*
                           var. *leurophylla*
 b. Leaves green beneath.
  c. Peduncles more than 1.5 times as long as the petioles of subtending leaves,
   usually more than 1.5 cm long.
   Leaves thin, the margins lacking a wire-like thickening, finely serrulate
    or ciliate .... 4. *S. tamnoides*
   Leaves thick, subcoriaceous, the margins with a finely raised wire-like
    edge, entire or prickly but not serrulate or ciliate. (Fig. 322). .... 5. *S. bona-nox*
  c. Peduncles 1.5 or less times as long as the petioles of subtending leaves,
   usually less than 1.5 cm long.
   Leaf margins lacking a thickened, wire-like edge, entire. .... 6. *S. rotundifolia*
   Leaf margins with a finely raised, wire-like edge, entire or prickly. .... 5. *S. bona-nox*

1. *S. herbácea* L. (herbaceous). Moist, open, deciduous or mixed woods, thickets, roadsides and waste places. May-June. Map 714. Our plants include var. *herbacea* and the following var.:
 var. *pulverulénta* (Michx.) Gray. Leaves short-acuminate, often puberulent beneath (leaves obtuse or acute, glabrous beneath in var. *herbacea*). —FAC
2. *S. pseudochína* L. Moist woods, woodland borders and thickets along the coast. May-June. Endangered in NY. [*S. tamnifolia*]. —FAC+
3. *S. gláuca* Walt. (whitened). Open woodlands, woodland borders, thickets, roadsides and waste places. May-July. Map 715. Represented with us as var. *leurophýlla* Blake. —FACU
4. *S. tamnoídes* L. Deciduous woods, bottomlands, thickets. May-July. Reported for Fairfield County CT, Strafford County NH and Eastern NY. [*S. hispida; S. pseudochina*]. —FAC
5. *S. bóna-nóx* L. (good night). Damp woods, thickets, old fields, roadsides and waste places. May-June. Fig. 322. Reported for Nantucket County MA. —FACU
6. *S. rotundifólia* L. (round-leaved). Open woods, thickets, roadsides and waste places. May-June. Map 716. —FAC

Family 56. Haemodoráceae (Bloodwort Family)

Monoecious, perennial herbs, often with red sap, from a rhizome, with an erect stem. Leaves linear, alternate, equitant. Flowers perfect, ours in dense, terminal, cymose panicles, small, regular, woolly, yellowish, the perianth of 6 segments, united at the base into a tube, fused to the ovary, persistent, stamens 3, inserted on the base of the perianth, ovary inferior (ours), 3-locular, few to many seeded, style 1, stigma small. Fruit a loculicidal, 3-valved capsule, enclosed by the persistent perianth.

1. *Lachnánthes* Ell. Redroot (from the Greek, based on the woolly flowers).
Rhizome short, roots fibrous, red; upper part of stem pubescent; leaves clustered at the base longer than those on the stem; flowers numerous, perianth segments free down to the top of the ovary, sepals smaller than the petals, stamens and style exserted; capsule subglobose.

 1. *L. caroliniána* (Lam.) Dandy. Sandy, gravelly or peaty pond margins. July-August. Fig. 323, Map 717. (W.I.). Endangered in CT. [*L. tinctoria; Gyrotheca t.*]. Poisonous.—OBL

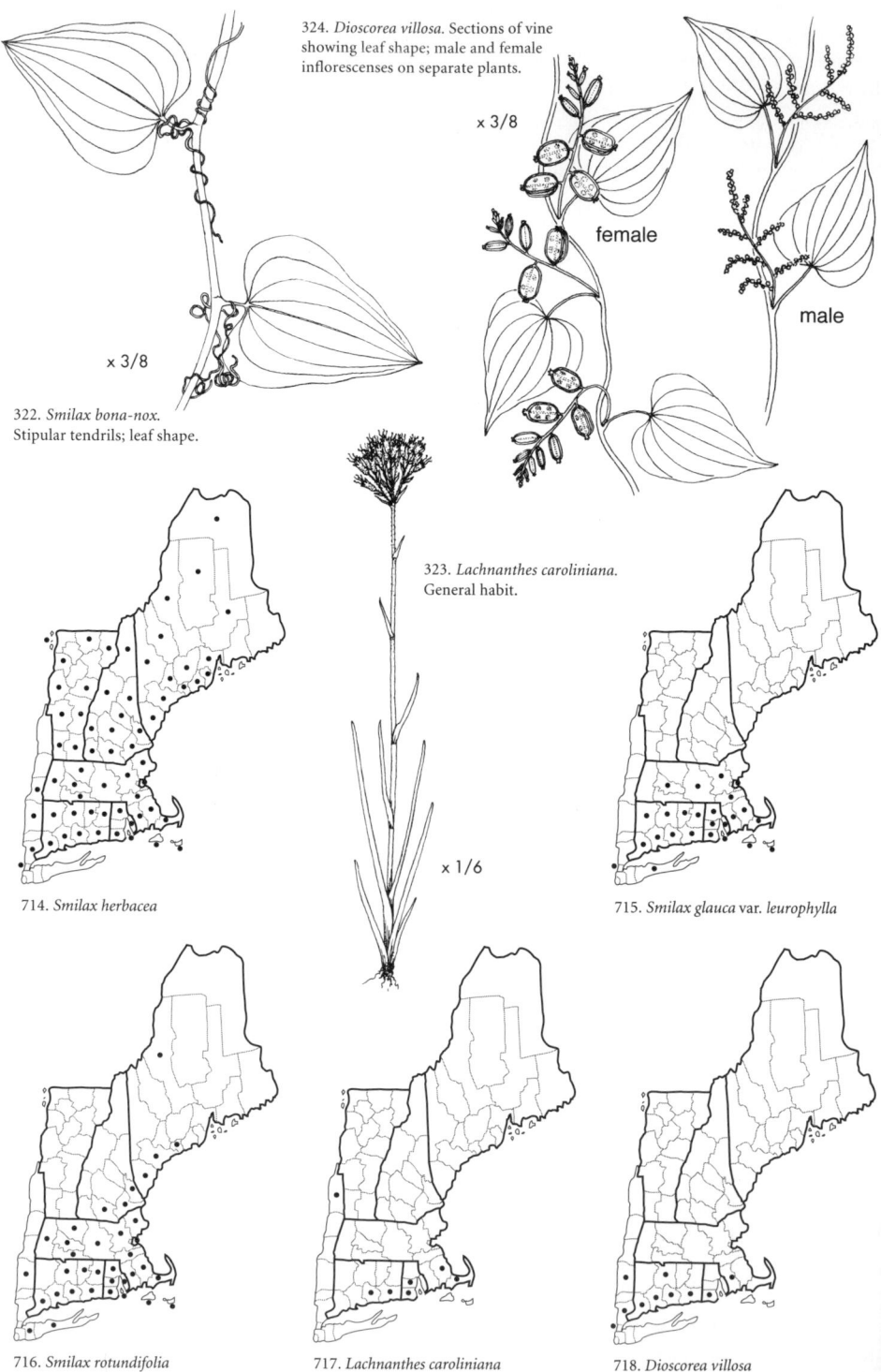

324. *Dioscorea villosa*. Sections of vine showing leaf shape; male and female inflorescenses on separate plants.

× 3/8

female

male

× 3/8

322. *Smilax bona-nox*.
Stipular tendrils; leaf shape.

323. *Lachnanthes caroliniana*.
General habit.

× 1/6

714. *Smilax herbacea*

715. *Smilax glauca* var. *leurophylla*

716. *Smilax rotundifolia*

717. *Lachnanthes caroliniana*

718. *Dioscorea villosa*

Family 57. Dioscoreáceae (Yam Family)

Dioecious, perennial herbs (ours) from thick rhizomes or tuberous roots. Stems slender, twining. Leaves alternate or the lower opposite or whorled, petioled, usually cordate, ribbed and netted-veined. Flowers imperfect, the staminate and pistillate in separate plants, inflorescence an axillary panicle, raceme or spike of small, white flowers; flowers regular, of 6 similar segments, which are adherent to the ovary in pistillate flowers, staminate flowers with 6 stamens, 3 often reduced to staminodia, pistillate flowers with a single, inferior, 3-loculed ovary, styles 3, simple or branched, sometimes also with staminodia. Fruit a 3-valved, 3-angled capsule.

1. Dioscórea L. Yam (for Dioscorides, an early Greek naturalist).

Leaves ovate, cordate based, acute to acuminate; flowers white to greenish, the staminate solitary or in small glomerules in the panicle, the pistillate solitary in a short raceme; capsule loculicidal.

Leaves cordate-ovate, with convex sides.
    Leaves all alternate or only the lowest approximate. .... 1. *D. villosa*
    Leaves all or at least the lower in 1 or more whorles of 4-7. .... 2. *D. quaternata*
Leaves halberd-shaped, with concave sides. .... 3. *D. oppositifolia*

    1. D. villósa L. (soft-hairy). Wild Yam. Moist open woods, thickets, roadsides and waste places. June-August. Fig. 324, Map 718. The root, dried and ground, reportedly useful in treating nausea in pregnant women and for various intestinal disorders.—FAC+

    2. D. quaternáta (Walt.) Gmel. Wild Yam. Rich woods. From farther south. Reported for RI. —FACU

    3. D. oppositifólia L. Chinese Yam. Escaped from cultivation to thickets and waste places. (Naturalized from Asia). Reported for New Haven County CT, Windham County VT. [*D. batatus*].

Family 58. Iridáceae (Iris Family)

Monoecious, perennial herbs, from fibrous roots, rhizomes, bulbs, or corms. Stems solitary, several, or absent. Leaves mostly basal, equitant, linear to ensiform, stem leaves, if present, smaller. Flowers perfect, usually showy, solitary or in racemose, paniculate, cymose or umbellate inflorescences, subtended by 1 or 2 or more spathe-like bracts, regular or irregular, perianth of 6 petaloid segments, the 3 inner tepals sometimes distinguished from the 3 outer by size or color, united, at least basally, withering-persistent, stamens 3, inserted on the perianth, ovary inferior, 3-locular, many seeded, style 1, usually 3 cleft, its branches sometimes also divided. Fruit a 3-locular, loculicidal capsule.

a. Flowers borne from the ground without an evident stem; fruit at or below the
    ground surface .... 1. *Crocus vernus*
a. Flowers and fruit borne on an upright stem.
    b. Stems flattened and winged .... 2. *Sisyrinchium*
    b. Stems neither flattened nor winged.
        Sepals recurved or spreading, usually larger than the spreading to erect
            petals; style branches broad and petal-like. .... 3. *Iris*
        Sepals and petals similar, the perianth rotate; style branches neither broad
            nor petal-like .... 4. *Belamcanda chinensis*

    1. Crócus L. **vérnus** (L.) Hill (of spring). Rarely escaped from cultivation to fields. Reported for Hartford County CT, Barnstable County MA.

2. Sisyrínchium L. Blue-eyed Grass (Greek name).

Low, slender, cespitose, grass-like perennials from fibrous roots; stems flattened, 2-edged or winged; simple or branched; leaves linear and grass-like or narrowly lanceolate; flowers rather small, blue or

white with a yellowish center, terminal, in an umbellate cluster from a 2-bracted spathe, the outer usually the longer, delicate and fugacious, sepals and petals equal and similar, separate to the base, spreading, often mucronate or notched, stamens united to the summit.
In addition to the following species *S. acre* has been reported for ME.

a. Spathes sessile or subsessile, solitary or paired at the summit of the scape.
    (Fig. 325).
  b. Outer bract with margins free to base. .... 1. *S. albidum*
  b. Outer bract with margins united above base.
    c. Scapes less than 3 mm wide; plant usually staying green on drying. .... 2. *S. mucronatum*
    c. Scapes usually 3 mm wide or wider; plant usually darkened on drying.
      Widest leaves more than 3 mm wide .... 3. *S. angustifolium*
      Widest leaves 3 mm or less wide .... 4. *S. montanum*
a. Spathes peduncled from the axils of leaf-like bracts. (Fig. 326).
  d. Old leaf bases persisting as tufts of erect, bristle-like fibers. .... 5. *S. fuscatum*
  d. Old leaf bases not persisting or sparsely persisting as loose irregular shreds.
    Scapes 3 mm wide or wider; widest leaves more than 3 mm wide; plant
      usually darkened on drying .... 3. *S. angustifolium*
    Scapes less than 3 mm wide; widest leaves 3 mm or less wide; plant usually
      staying green on drying .... 6. *S. atlanticum*

    1. S. álbidum Raf. (whitish). Dry open woods and fields. From south and west. Reported for CT and York County ME.
    2. S. mucronátum Michx. (with a short straight point). Fields, roadsides, waste places. May-June. Fig. 325, Map 719.—FACU
    3. S. angustifólium P. Mill. Fields and open woods. May-July. Map 720. [*S. bermudiana; S. graminoides; S. gramineum*].—FACW-
    4. S. montánum Greene (of mountains). Fields, roadsides and waste places. May-July. Map 721. [*S. strictum*]. Our plants are var. *crébrum* Fern. [*S. angustifolium*].—FAC
    5. S. fuscátum Bickn. Fields and open pine or mixed woods in sandy soil, mostly near the coast. May-July. Map 722. [*S. arenicola; S. farwellii*].—FACU
    6. S. atlánticum Bickn. (atlantic). Dry to wet meadows. May-July. Fig. 326, Map 723. [*S. apiculatum; S. strictum*].—FACW

3. Íris L. Iris (rainbow).

Erect, perennial herbs from short or long horizontal rhizomes, with linear or ensiform leaves; flowers large and showy, terminal, solitary or several, subtended by spathaceous, usually foliaceous bracts, perianth united below into a tube, the segments clawed at the base, sepals larger than the petals, lanceolate to oblanceolate, spreading to recurved, petals spatulate to oblanceolate, erect or arching, style branches broad and petal-like, arched over the stamens, each style branch 2 lobed at the apex, stigma a short band at the base of the 2 lobes on the under side, lower part of the style adnate to the perianth tube; capsule 3-6 angled, ellipsoid to oblong. Poisonous, especially the rhizomes, if eaten in large quantities.

a. Plant in flower.
  b. Sepals bearded.
    Stems less than 2 dm tall .... 1. *I. pumila*
    Stems more than 2 dm tall.
      Rhizome stout; flowers usually fewer than 5; beard yellow. .... 2. *I. germanica*
      Rhizome slender; flowers numerous in a long raceme, beard whitish. .... 3. *I. tectorum*
  b. Sepals beardless.
    c. Perianth yellow .... 4. *I. pseudacorus*
    c. Perianth blue, violet, or rarely white.
      d. Leaves less than 1 cm wide.

e. Petals bristle tipped, much reduced and involute, less than 2 cm
long. (Fig. 328) .... 5. *I. setosa*
var. *canadensis*
e. Petals not bristle tipped, not reduced or involute, more than 2 cm long.
Leaves less than 6 mm wide; stem near base less than 3 mm thick. .... 6. *I. prismatica*
Leaves more than 6 mm wide; stem near base more than 3 mm
thick. .... 7. *I. sibirica*
d. Leaves more than 1 cm wide.
f. Petals bristle tipped, much reduced and involute, less than 2 cm
long. (Fig. 328) .... 5. *I. setosa*
var. *canadensis*
f. Petals not bristle tipped nor reduced or involute, more than 2 cm long.
Spathe solitary, terminal .... 3. *I. tectorum*
Spathes usually lateral as well as terminal. (Fig. 329). .... 8. *I. versicolor*
a. Plant in fruit.
g. Capsules, at least some, arching or pendulous. (Fig. 327). .... 4. *I. pseudacorus*
g. Capsules erect.
h. Capsule sharply 3-angled.
Stem near base less than 3 mm thick; plants loosely rhizomatous. .... 6. *I. prismatica*
Stem near base more than 3 mm thick; plants cespitose. .... 7. *I. sibirica*
h. Capsule rounded on the angles.
i. Stem usually less than 3 dm tall.
Leaves less than 1 cm wide .... 5. *I. setosa*
var. *canadensis*
Leaves more than 1 cm wide .... 1. *I. pumila*
i. Stem more than 3 dm tall.
j. Spathe solitary, terminal .... 3. *I. tectorum*
j. Spathes usually lateral as well as terminal.
Capsule (seldom produced) sessile or on a stipe less than 1 cm
long. .... 2. *I. germanica*
Capsule on a stipe more than 1 cm long .... 8. *I. versicolor*

1. *I. púmila* Wild. (dwarf). Commonly cultivated and infrequently escaped to roadsides and waste places. Reported for York County ME.

2. *I. germánica* L. (of Germany). Commonly cultivated and occasionally persistent on roadsides or waste places. Probably represents a series of hybrids of several European species. Map 724.

I. variegáta L. Similar to the latter species but with stems about as long as the leaves (stems exceeding the leaves in *I. germanica*). Infrequently escaped from cultivation. Reported for MA.

3. *I. tectórum* Maxim. (of roofs). Commonly cultivated and infrequently escaped to roadsides and waste places. Map 725.

I. cristáta Ait. Will key to *I. tectorum* in flower but is distinguishable in having only 1-2 flowers and strongly crested sepals (flowers more numerous and sepals not crested in *I. tectorum*). From farther south. Reported for MA.

4. *I. pseudácorus* L. (false Acorus). Yellow Iris. Pond and stream borders, marshes. May-June. Fig. 327, Map 726. (Introduced from Europe).—OBL

5. *I. setósa* Pallas ex Link. Rocky shores, ledges and beaches along the coast. June-July. Fig. 328. Map 727. Our plants are var. *canadénsis* (M. Foster ex B. L. Robins & Fern.) Hulten. [*I. hookeri*].

6. *I. prismática* Pursh ex Ker-Gawl. (like a prism, from the sharply angled ovary and capsule). Brackish to fresh wet meadows, bogs, pond margins and wooded swamps along the coast. June-July. Map 728.—OBL

I. cristáta Ait. Will key to *I. prismatica* in fruit but is distinguishable in having leaves 1 cm or more wide (leaves less than 6 mm wide in *I. prismatica*). See note under *I. tectorum*.

7. *I. sibírica* L. (of Siberia). Commonly cultivated and escaped to roadsides and waste places. June-July. Map 729.

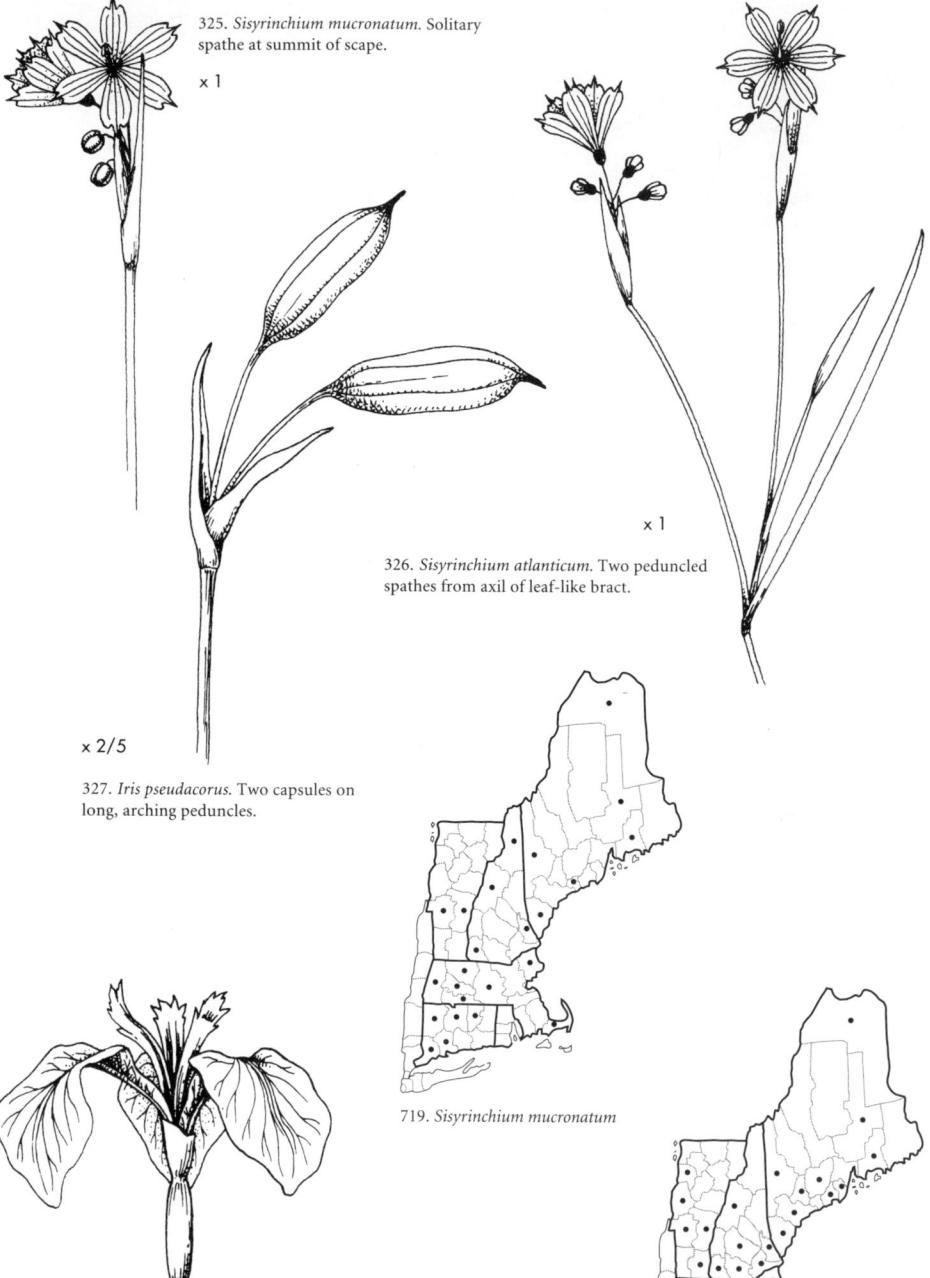

325. *Sisyrinchium mucronatum.* Solitary
spathe at summit of scape.

× 1

× 1

326. *Sisyrinchium atlanticum.* Two peduncled
spathes from axil of leaf-like bract.

× 2/5

327. *Iris pseudacorus.* Two capsules on
long, arching peduncles.

719. *Sisyrinchium mucronatum*

× 1/2

328. *Iris setosa* var. *canadensis.* Single flower
with reduced, involute, bristle-tipped petals.

720. *Sisyrinchium angustifolium*

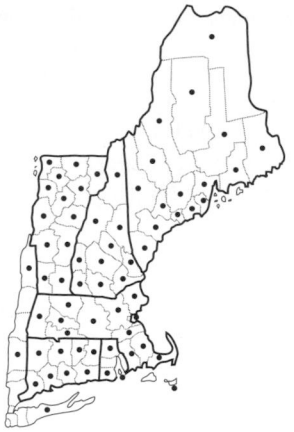

721. *Sisyrinchium montanum* var. *crebrum*

722. *Sisyrinchium fuscatum*

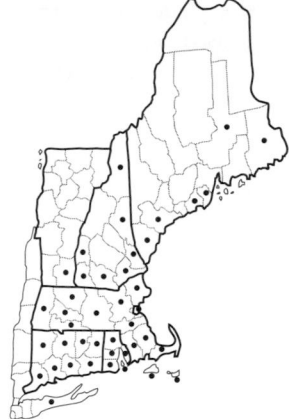

723. *Sisyrinchium atlanticum*

724. *Iris germanica*

725. *Iris tectorum*

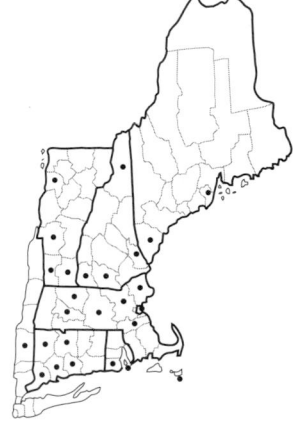

726. *Iris pseudacorus*

727. *Iris setosa* var. *canadensis*

728. *Iris prismatica*

729. *Iris sibirica*

8. *I. versícolor* L. (variously colored) Blue Flag. Wet meadows, marshes, pond and stream margins, deciduous swamps. May-July. Fig. 329, Map 730. Our plants are var. *versícolor*. Preparations made from the rhizomes were used by Indians to soothe burns and skin irritations, and for coughs and colds. Also reported as an irritant of the digestive tract if eaten.—OBL

I. virgínica L. Southern Blue Flag. Resembling *I. versicolor* but with sepal blades oblong with a bright yellow spot at the base (sepal blades ovate to reniform with a greenish-yellow spot at the base in *I. versicolor*). On the coastal plain. Reported for Kings and Suffolk Counties NY. [*I. caroliniana; I. georgiana*].—OBL

Several cultivated species, rarely escaped in our range are similar to the latter two species but differ in having 1 or 2 much reduced cauline leaves (in *I. versicolor* and *I. virginica* cauline leaves are several and elongate); *I. énsata* Thunb. Sepals longer than petals, leaf with prominent midrib. Reported for CT and Windham County VT. [*I. kaempferi*]. *I. laevigáta* Fisch. Sepals and petals the same length, leaf without prominent midrib. Reported for Hartford County CT. *I. spúria* L. Differing from *I. ensata* and *I. laevigata* in having ovary with 2 ridges extending down each of the 3 angles (ovary 3-angled but lacking the ridges in the latter 2 species). Reported for CT. Represented with us as subsp. *ochroleuca* Dykes. *I. orientális* Mill. Similar to *I. spuria* but with white flowers (bluish-purple in *I. spuria*). Reported for CT.

4. *Belamacánda* Adans. Blackberry Lily (East Indian name).

Perennial herb from a thickened horizontal rhizome with a leafy stem; leaves ensiform, as in Iris, rapidly reduced upward; inflorescence a bracteate, loosely many flowered, often widely branched panicle of cymes, perianth of 6 nearly equal, elliptic, widely spreading segments, distinct nearly to the base, orange spotted with red, withering-persistent, stamens about half as long as the perianth, style 3 cleft for nearly half the length; capsule pyriform, its 3 valves recurving when ripe and eventually deciduous, exposing the mass of shiny, black, fleshy seeds on an erect central axis, the whole resembling a blackberry.

1. *B. chinénsis* (L.) D.C. (of China). Roadsides, fields, thickets and open woods. June-July. Fig. 330, Map 731. (Naturalized from Asia). [*Gemmingia c.*].

Family 59. Orchidáceae (Orchid Family)

Hermaphrodite, perennial, terrestrial or semi-aquatic (ours) autotrophic or saprophytic herbs, from rhizomes, corms, bulbs or tuberous roots. Stems naked, bracteate or leafy. Leaves sheathing at the base, basal or cauline or both, sometimes lacking or reduced to scales, alternate or apparently opposite or whorled, simple, the blade linear to orbicular, membranous to coriaceous, sometimes plaited. Flowers perfect, small and inconspicuous to large and showy, solitary or in a spike, raceme, or panicle, sessile or pedicelled, bracteate, irregular, perianth adnate to the ovary, of 6 segments, sepals 3 or 2 by fusion, green, or colored and resembling the 2 lateral petals, petals 3, usually white or colored, the 2 lateral ones similar, the third (lip) dissimilar, differing only slightly to greatly in size, form or coloration from the laterals, often spurred, sometimes inferior or directed downward (resupinate) by a twist of the ovary or pedicel, stamens and style united with the prolongation of the central axis to form a column bearing 1 or 2 sessile anthers at or near the summit or laterally, a small, beak-like structure (the rostellum, a sterile, modified stigma) at the base of the terminal anther and 2 confluent stigmas on the anterior surface near the base, ovary inferior, usually long and twisted, 1-locular, with numerous seeds. Fruit a 3-valved capsule or fleshy pod.

a. Flowers or fruits in spikes or racemes.
   b. Perianth with a distinct, elongate spur (short and sac-like in *Coeloglossum* with leafy stems). (Fig. 331).
      c. Leaf usually absent at anthesis, purple beneath; raceme bractless. .... 1. *Tipularia discolor*
      c. Leaf (ves) present at anthesis, green beneath; raceme bracteate.

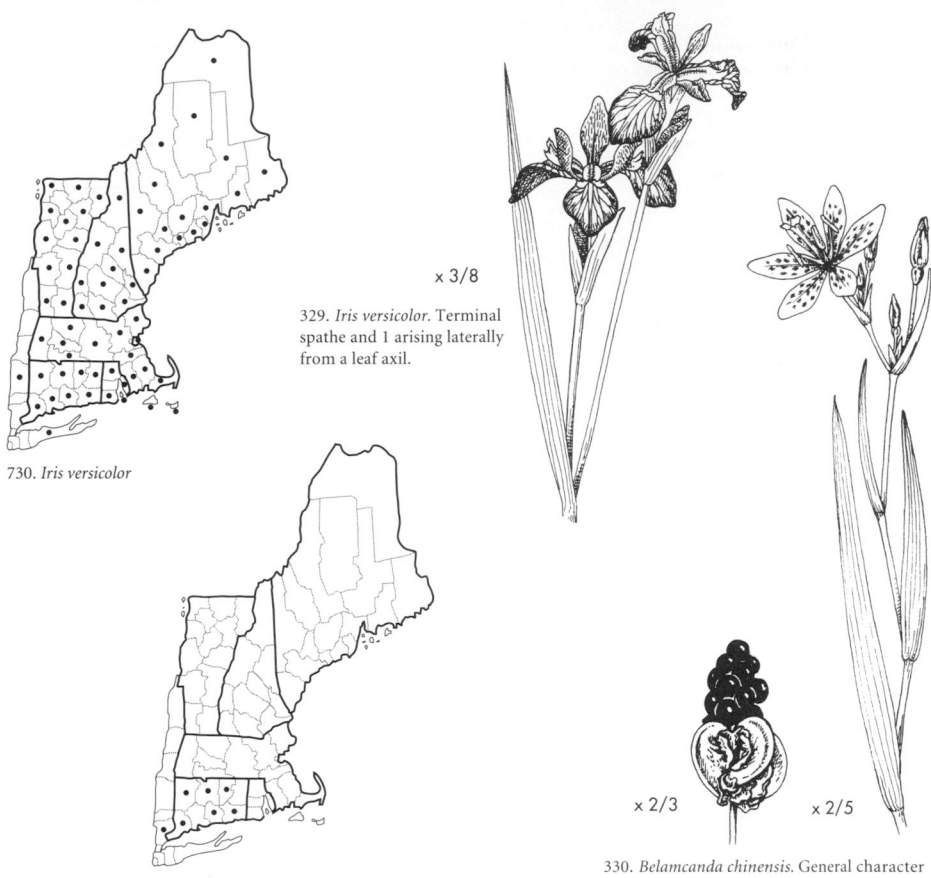

x 3/8

329. *Iris versicolor*. Terminal
spathe and 1 arising laterally
from a leaf axil.

730. *Iris versicolor*

731. *Belamcanda chinensis*

x 2/3   x 2/5

330. *Belamcanda chinensis*. General character
of plant; detail of a ripe capsule.

d. Perianth bicolored, the lip white or white spotted with purple, the
  remainder purple.
  Leaf 1; lateral sepals spreading; lip 3-lobed. (Fig. 332). 2.*Amerorchis
                                                                                  rotundifolia*
  Leaves 2; all sepals and petals connivent; lip not lobed. .... 3. *Galearis spectabilis*
d. Perianth uniformly colored.
  Spur long and slender. (Fig. 336) .... 4. *Platanthera*
  Spur short and sac-like .... 5. *Coeloglossum
                                                                                    viride*
b. Perianth spurless or merely with a small, basal swelling (prominent and
    spur-like in *Corallorhiza maculata*, with leaves reduced to sheathing
    scales).
  e. Leaf solitary or undeveloped at anthesis (rarely 2 leaves in *Calopogon*, with
      lip uppermost part of flower; lip always lowermost in plants under
      second part of couplet).
    f. Leaf usually undeveloped or absent at anthesis, if present basal.
      g. Stem arising from a tuberous root or cluster of roots, not from a
          corm or coral-like rhizome; lip without ridges or keels;
          flower white, or lip with a green center .... 6. *Spiranthes*
      g. Stem arising from a corm or coral-like rhizome; lip with 1-3 basal keels;
          flower variously colored green, yellow and/or purple.

Stem arising from a corm; leaf, if present, elliptic. .... 7. *Aplectrum hyemale*
Stem arising from a coral-like rhizome; leaves reduced to sheathing
    scales. (Fig. 343) .... 8. *Corallorhiza*
  f. Leaf well developed at anthesis, cauline.
    Leaf blade oval or elliptic; lip lowermost part of flower. .... 9. *Malaxis*
    Leaf blade linear; lip uppermost part of flower. (Fig. 345). .... 10. *Calopogon*
                     tuberosus
  e. Leaves 2 or more.
    h. Leaves 2, opposite.
      Leaves basal or sub-basal; lip unlobed. .... 11. *Liparis*
      Leaves near the middle of the stem; lip lobed. (Fig. 347). .... 12. *Listera*
    h. Leaves more than 2.
      i. Lip saccate or concave at the base.
        Leaves basal or sub-basal. (Fig. 348) .... 13. *Goodyera*
        Leaves alternate along the stem. (Fig. 349). .... 14. *Epipactus*
                      helleborine
      i. Lip not saccate.
        Flowers few, from the axils of reduced leaves; leaves cauline. .... 15. *Triphora*
                      trianthophora
        Flowers numerous in a bracted spike; leaves basal or sub-basal.
          (Fig. 339). .... 6. *Spiranthes*
a. Flowers or fruits solitary or infrequently 2 or 3, not in spikes or racemes.
  j. Leaves whorled at the summit of the stem. (Fig. 351). .... 16. *Isotria*
  j. Leaves not as above, basal, or cauline and solitary or alternate, or undeveloped.
    k. Lip inflated and pouch-like or scoop-shaped. (Fig. 352).
      Plant with a solitary basal leaf; margins of lip folded outward and
        forming a white apron .... 17. *Calypso bulbosa*
      Plant with 2 or more basal or cauline leaves; margins of lip inrolled. .... 18. *Cypripedium*
    k. Lip not inflated or pouch-like or scoop-shaped.
      l. Stem leaf solitary, elliptic, borne about halfway up the stem, (flower
        subtended by a foliaceous bract not counted as a stem leaf). .... 19. *Pogonia*
                      ophioglossoides
      l. Stem leaves several, alternate, small and ovate, or undeveloped, or if
        solitary, then linear and borne below the middle.
        m. Stem leaves several, alternate, small and ovate. .... 15. *Triphora*
                      trianthophora
        m. Stem leaf solitary (rarely 2), linear, or undeveloped at anthesis.
          Stem leaf usually developed at anthesis; lip uppermost part of
            flower. .... 10. *Calopogon*
                      tuberosus
          Stem leaf usually undeveloped at anthesis; lip lowermost part of
            flower. (Fig. 356) .... 20. *Arethusa bulbosa*

1. *Tipulária* Nutt. (name based on resemblence of flowers to insects of the genus *Tipula*).

Slender, scapose herbs from a corm, these connected by short rhizomes; leaf solitary, basal, slender petioled, ovate, acute to acuminate, purplish beneath, produced in autumn after the scape has withered, withering in summer as the inflorescence develops, scape naked except for one-several sheathing scales toward the base; inflorescence a long, loose, bractless, many-flowered raceme of slender-pedicelled, nodding, greenish-purple flowers, perianth parts spreading, separate, the sepals and lateral petals oblong-oval, lip 3-lobed, the lateral lobes basal, the middle lobe linear-oblong, lip prolonged into a long, slender, basal spur, column erect, wingless; capsule ovoid, reflexed.

    1. *T. discolor* (Pursh) Nutt. (2-colored, from the differently colored upper and lower leaf surfaces). Cranefly Orchis. Rich, moist deciduous woods. July-August. Fig. 331, Map 732. Endangered in MA. [*T. unifolia*].—FACU

2. Amerórchis Hulten.

Scapose herbs from short rhizomes and thickened roots; leaf solitary, basal, elliptic to ovate, 1 or 2 sheathing scales below; inflorescence a loose, few flowered, bracteate raceme, bracts lance-linear, sepals and lateral petals ovate or oblong, pink or purplish, the petals slightly narrower, the upper sepal and 2 lateral petals connivant, the 2 lateral sepals spreading, lip white spotted with purple, 3-lobed, the 2 lateral lobes short, the middle lobe larger, 2-lobed at the apex, lip produced below into a slender spur shorter than itself, column short; capsule oblong. [*Orchis*].

    1. A. rotundifólia (Banks ex Pursh) Hulten (round-leaved). Small Round-leaved Orchis. Thuja swamps, bogs. June-July. Fig. 332, Map 733. (Greenland). Very rare in our range. [*Orchis r.*].—OBL

3. Galeáris Raf.

Scapose herbs from short rhizomes and thickened roots; scape 4-5 angled, with 2 large, basal, subopposite, suborbicular-obovate leaves, and 1 or 2 sheathing scales below; inflorescence a loose, few-flowered, bracteate raceme, bracts foliaceous, elliptic to lanceolate, longer than the flowers, sepals and lateral petals elliptic to lanceolate, pink to purple, connivent and forming a hood over the column, lip white, ovate to ligulate, with an undulating margin, produced below into a stout spur about as long as itself, column short; capsule ellipsoid. [*Orchis*].

    1. G. spectábilis (L.) Raf. (showy). Showy Orchis. Rich, deciduous woods. May-June. Map 734. Endangered in RI. [*Galeorchis s; Orchis s.*].

4. Platánthera Rich.

Terrestrial or semi-aquatic, glabrous, simple-stemmed herbs from tubers, rhizomes or a cluster of thickened roots; leaves 1 or more, basal or cauline, sessile, sheathing at the base; inflorescence a terminal, bracteate, loose or dense spike or raceme of green or colored small, inconspicuous or showy flowers, the 2 lateral sepals spreading, similar, the upper sepal and 2 lateral petals erect, usually connivent, the lip simple, entire, toothed, fringed or trilobed (the divisions entire or variously toothed or fringed), extended at the base into a spur, this longer or shorter than the lip, column short; capsule ellipsoid. [*Habenaria*].

a. Leaves 2, basal, orbicular or nearly so. (Fig. 333).
    Stem bractless or with 1 bract; lip curved upward; spur tapered to tip. .... 1. *P. hookeri*
    Stem with several bracts; lip curved downward; spur thickened distally.
        (Fig. 333) .... 2. *P. orbiculata*
a. Leaves not paired at base of stem and not orbicular.
  b. Lip divided into 3 segments, each segment fringed. (Fig. 334).
    c. Perianth pink or lavender, or if white, lateral divisions of lip fringed at most
        half way to the base and spur usually less than 2.5 cm long.
        Central segment of lip less than 1 cm wide; raceme up to 4.5 cm thick. .... 3. *P. psycodes*
        Central segment of lip more than 1 cm wide; raceme 5 cm or more
            thick. .... 4. *P. grandiflora*
    c. Perianth white, greenish-white or greenish-yellow; lateral divisions of lip
        fringed 2/3 or more the way to the base.
        Perianth greenish-white or greenish-yellow; lateral petals linear-spatulate,
            entire; spur less than 2.5 cm long .... 5. *P. lacera*
        Perianth white; lateral petals broadly obovate, toothed; spur usually
            more than 2.5 cm long .... 6. *P. leucophaea*
  b. Lip not divided into 3 segments, fringed, or merely short-lobed, toothed,
    or entire.
    d. Lip fringed; flowers yellow, orange or white. (Fig. 335).
      e. Flowers white .... 7. *P. blephariglottis*
      e. Flowers yellow or orange.

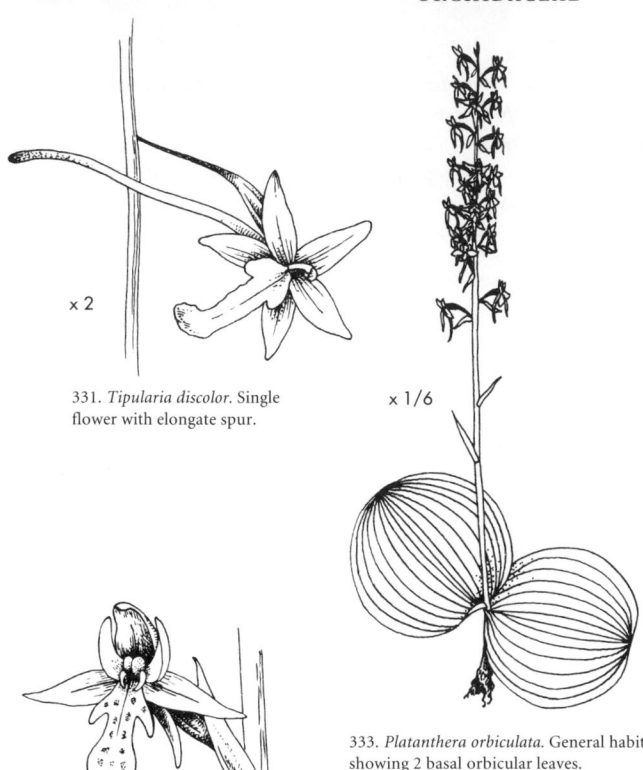

× 2

331. *Tipularia discolor.* Single
flower with elongate spur.

× 1/6

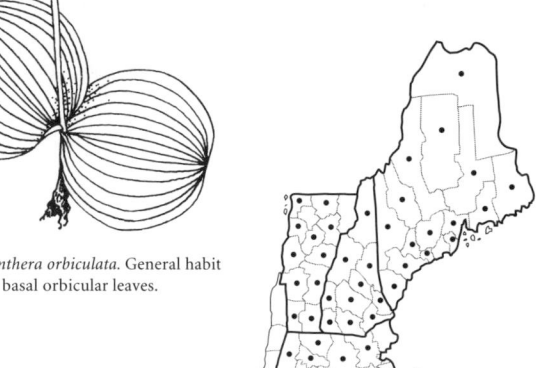

× 2

334. *Platanthera grandiflora.* Single flower
with lip 3-segmented and fringed.

333. *Platanthera orbiculata.* General habit
showing 2 basal orbicular leaves.

× 2

332. *Amerorchis rotundifolia.* Single
flower with lateral sepals spreading,
lip 3-lobed.

735. *Platanthera hookeri*

732. *Tipularia discolor*

733. *Amerorchis rotundifolia*

734. *Galearis spectabilis*

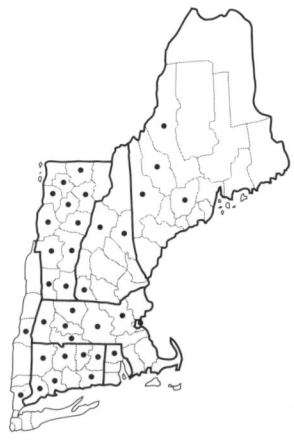

Spur less than 1 cm long .... 8. *P. cristata*
Spur more than 1 cm long .... 9. *P. ciliaris*
d. Lip not fringed, merely short-lobed, toothed or entire; flowers green or white.
  f. Lip truncate, 2 or 3 lobed or toothed at the apex; spur clavate. (Fig. 336). .... 10. *P. clavellata*
  f. Lip rounded or tapered, entire or merely crenulate; spur not clavate.
    g. Leaf solitary, basal, sometimes with a bracteal leaf on the stem. .... 11. *P. obtusata*
    g. Leaves 2 or more, cauline, gradually reduced upward.
      h. Lip with a prominent tubercle on the upper surface below the
        middle and usually with a pair of basal lobes. (Fig. 337). .... 12. *P. flava*
                                                                                                           var. *herbiola*
      h. Lip lacking a tubercle or basal lobes.
        Lip abruptly dilated at base; flowers white. .... 13. *P. dilatata*
        Lip gradually widened at base; flowers green. .... 14. *P. hyperborea*
                                                                                                           var. *huronensis*

1. P. hoókeri (Torr. ex Gray) Lindl. (for W. J. Hooker). Hooker's Orchid. Rich, moist or dry deciduous woods. May-July. Map 735. Endangered in RI. [*Habenaria h.; Lysias h.*].—FAC

2. P. orbiculáta (Pursh) Lindl. (rounded). Large Round-leaved Orchid. Rich deciduous, mixed or coniferous woods. June-August. Fig. 333, Map 736. [*Habenaria o.; Lysias o.*]. Our plants include var. *orbiculata* and the following var.:
  var. *macrophýlla* (Goldie) Luer. Spur 3 cm or more long (less than 3 cm long in var. *orbiculata*). [*Habenaria m.*].—FAC

3. P. psycódes (L.) Lindl. (like a butterfly). Small Purple Fringed Orchid. Wet meadows, wet open deciduous, mixed or coniferous woods, pond and stream borders, bogs. July-August. Map 737. [*Habenaria p.; Blephariglottis p.*].—FACW
  P. x andréwsii M. White. A hybrid between *P. psycodes* and *P. lacera.*

4. P. grandiflóra (Bigelow) Lindl. (large-flowered). Large Purple Fringed Orchid. Same habitats as *P. psycodes*, and also wet, unmowed roadsides. June-August. Fig. 334, Map 738. [*Habenaria psycodes* var. *grandiflora; H. fimbriata; Blephariglottis g.*].—FACW

5. P. lácera (Michx.) G. Don (torn or lacerated). Ragged Fringed Orchid. Dry to wet meadows and moist to wet deciduous woods. June-August. Map 739. [*Habenaria l.; Blephariglottis l.*]. Our plants are var. *lacera.*—FACW

6. P. leucophaéa (Nutt.) Lindl. (ashy). Prairie Fringed Orchid. Bogs and conifer swamps. June-August. Endangered in ME; reported for Aroostook County. [*Habenaria l.; Blephariglottis l.*]. Our plants are var. *leucophaea.*—FACW+

7. P. blephariglóttis (Willd.) Lindl. (eyelid-tongued, from the fringed lip). White Fringed Orchid. Bogs and conifer swamps. July-August. Fig. 335. Map 740. Endangered in CT. [*Habenaria b.; Blephariglottis b.; B. albiflora*]. Our plants are var. *blephariglottis.*—OBL

8. P. cristáta (Michx.) Lindl. (crested). Crested Yellow Orchid. Wet meadows, bogs and deciduous or coniferous woods. July-August. Endangered in MA; also reported for Bristol County NH. [*Habenaria c.; Blephariglottis c.*].—FACW+

9. P. ciliáris (L.) Lindl. (fringed). Yellow Fringed Orchid. Bogs, wet to dry meadows and deciduous or coniferous woods. July-August. Map 741. Endangered in RI. [*Habenaria c.; Blephariglottis c.*].—FACW

10. P. clavelláta (Michx.) Luer. (like a little club, from the clavate spur). Small Green Wood Orchid. Bogs, wet meadows, wet deciduous woods, roadside seeps and pond margins. July-August. Fig. 336, Map 742. [*Habenaria c.; Gymnadeniopsis c.; Denslovia c.*].—FACW+
  Gymnadénia R. Br. *conópsea* R. Br. Will key to *P. clavellata* but is distinguished in having several stem leaves, pink-purplish flowers and long slender spur (*P. clavellata* has 1 stem leaf, white or greenish-yellow flowers and clavate spur). From Europe. Reported for CT.

11. P. obtusáta (Banks ex Pursh) Lindl. (blunt). Blunt-leaf Orchid. Bogs and damp northern coniferous or deciduous woods. July-August. Map 743. [*Habenaria o.; Lysiella o.*].—FACW

x 2

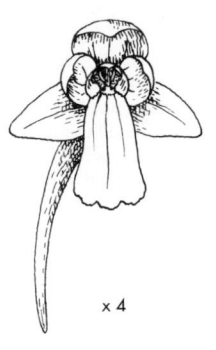

x 4

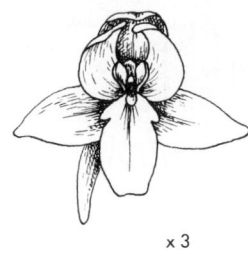

x 3

335. *Platanthera blephariglottis.*
Single flower with lip not
3-segmented, fringed.

336. *Platanthera clavellata.*
Single flower with truncate,
3-toothed lip.

337. *Platanthera flava var herbiola.* Single
flower with lip 2-lobed at base.

736. *Platanthera orbiculata*

737. *Platanthera psycodes*

738. *Platanthera grandiflora*

739. *Platanthera lacera*

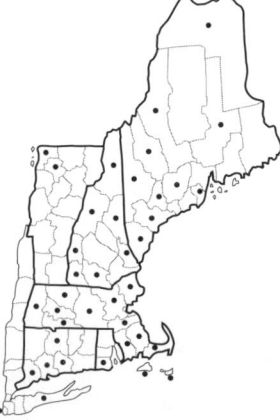

740. *Platanthera blephariglottis*

741. *Platanthera ciliaris*

742. *Platanthera clavellata*

743. *Platanthera obtusata*

744. *Platanthera flava* var. *herbiola*

745. *Platanthera dilatata*

746. *Platanthera hyperborea* var. *huronensis*

12. P. fláva (L.) Lindl. (yellow). Tubercled Orchid. Wet meadows, wet deciduous woods, and floodplains. June-August. Fig. 337, Map 744. Endangered in RI. [*Habenaria f.; Perularia f.; P. scutellata*]. Our plants are var. *herbíola* (Lindl.) Correll.—FACW

13. P. dilatáta (Pursh) Lindl. ex Beck (dilated). Tall Leafy White Orchid. Bogs, wet meadows, wet deciduous or coniferous woods and pond margins. June-August. Map 745. (Iceland). [*Habenaria d.; Limnorchis d.; L. media; L. borealis*]. Our plants are var. *dilatata*.—FACW

P. x média (Rydb.) Niles. A hybrid between *P. dilatata* and *P. hyperborea* var. *huronensis*.

14. P. hyperbórea (L.) Lindl. (far-northern). Bogs, wet deciduous woods and wet meadows. June-August. Map 746. (Iceland, N.e. Asia). [*Habenaria h.; Limnorchis h.; L.huronensis*]. Our plants are var. *huronénsis* (Nutt.) Farw.—FACW

5. Coeloglóssum Hartman.

Terrestrial herbs with fleshy roots from a thick rhizome; leaves several, cauline, clasping, the lowest 1 or 2 reduced to bladeless sheaths, the median obovate to oblanceolate, the upper oblong to lanceolate, progressively reduced and passing into the bracts; inflorescence a terminal spike of inconspicuous green flowers subtended by linear lanceolate, acuminate bracts much exceeding the length of the flowers, lateral sepals oblong, the terminal ovate, the 3 forming a hood, lateral petals lanceolate, nearly concealed by the sepals, lip narrowly oblong-spatulate, 2-3 toothed apically, (the middle tooth short and often obscure), with a thickened keel, spur abbreviated, sac-like, column short; capsule ellipsoid. [*Habenaria*].

1. C. víride (L.) Hartman (green) Long-bracted Orchid. Rich, moist, deciduous or sometimes coniferous woods. May-August. Fig. 338, Map 747. (N.e. Asia). (*C. viride* subsp. *bracteatum; Habenaria viridis* var. *bracteata; H. bracteata; Coeloglossum b.*]. Our plants are var. *viréscens* (Muhl. ex Willd.) Luer.—FACU

6. Spiránthes L. C. Rich. Ladies' tresses (from the Greek based on the spirally twisted spike).

Slender or coarse terrestrial herbs from a fleshy solitary root or cluster of roots; leaves basal or sub-basal, oval or elliptic to linear, reduced above to sheathing bracts; inflorescence a terminal, bracted, more or less spirally twisted spike of small white flowers tinged with green or yellow, in 1-3 rows, sepals free, similar to the lateral petals, these connivent with the upper sepal and forming a hood over the lip, the lip sessile or with a short claw, concave below the middle and embracing the column, spreading or recurved at the apex and crisped, sinuate, or rarely toothed or lobed, with a small callosity on each side at the base, the middle often a different color than the rest of the lip, column short; capsule ellipsoid to ovoid, erect.

In addition to the following species *S. x intermedia* has been attributed to our range.

a. Basal leaves absent during anthesis or ovate.
    Roots solitary, unbranched (rarely 2); lip completely white. .... 1. *S. tuberosa*
    Roots 3 or more; lip white with a green center. .... 2. *S. lacera*
a. Basal leaves present during anthesis, elliptic to linear.
    b. Leaves narrowly elliptic, 12 times or less as long as wide; lip white with a broad
        yellow center. (Fig. 339) .... 3. *S. lucida*
    b. Leaves linear, usually more than 12 times as long as wide; lip white, cream
        colored, or yellowish.
        c. Rachis of inflorescence conspicuously twisted, the flowers appearing
            secund. (Fig. 340).
            d. Lip granular-pubescent outside; ovary densely pubescent, the trichomes
                pointed.
                Rachis of inflorescence with light-colored, non-glandular pubescence;
                    lip white or yellowish .... 4. *S. vernalis*
                Rachis of inflorescence with reddish, glandular pubescence; lip cream
                    colored. .... 5. *S. casei*
            d. Lip glabrous outside; ovary glabrous or sparsely pubescent, the trichomes
                capitate .... 6. *S. praecox*
        c. Rachis of inflorescence not conspicuously twisted, the flowers completely
            around the axis. (Fig. 341).
            Lip distinctly constricted near the middle; sepals and lateral petals
                united below and forming an upward-arching hood .... 7. *S. romanzoffiana*
            Lip not or but slightly constricted near the middle; lateral sepals free,
                the upper sepal and lateral petals adherent .... 8. *S. cernua*

1. S. tuberósa Raf. (tuberous). Little Ladies' tresses. Dry, sandy fields and open woods. August-September. Map 748. Endangered in RI. [*S. beckii; S. grayi*].—FACU-

2. S. lácera (Raf.) Raf. (irregularly cleft). Slender Ladies' tresses. Dry fields, barrens and open woods. July-September. Map 749. Our plants include var. *lacera* and the following var.:

var. *grácilis*. (Bigelow) Luer. Plant glabrous, leaves rarely present during anthesis, flowers closely spaced (plant pubescent, leaves present during anthesis and flowers distantly spaced in var. *lacera*). [*S. gracilis*].—FACU-

3. S. lúcida (H. H. Eat.) Ames (shining). Shining Ladies' tresses. Riverbanks and wet meadows. May-July. Fig. 339, Map 750. Endangered in NH. [*S. plantaginea*].—FACW

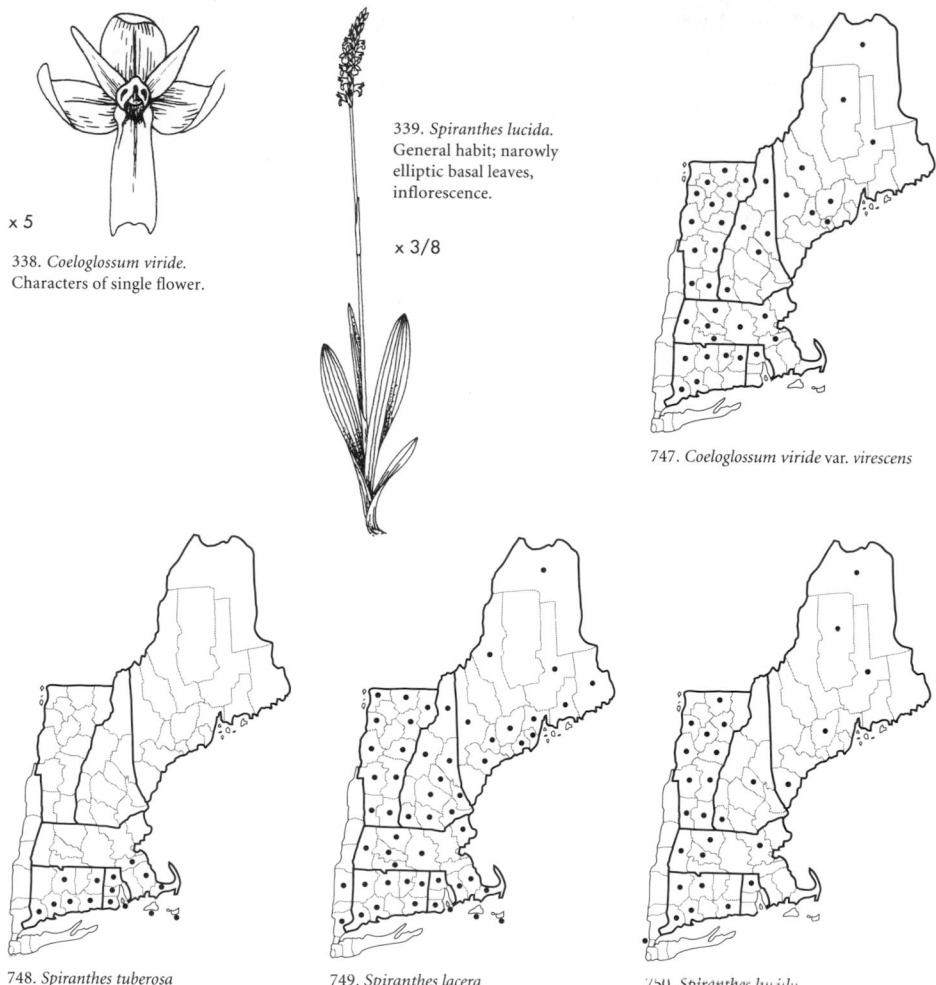

× 5

338. *Coeloglossum viride.*
Characters of single flower.

339. *Spiranthes lucida.*
General habit; narowly
elliptic basal leaves,
inflorescence.

× 3/8

747. *Coeloglossum viride* var. *virescens*

748. *Spiranthes tuberosa*

749. *Spiranthes lacera*

750. *Spiranthes lucida*

4. S. vernális Engelm. & Gray (of spring, the description based on southern specimens which bloom in spring). Early Ladies' tresses. Dry to moist meadows. August-September. Fig. 340, Map 751. [*S. neglecta*].—FAC

5. S. cásei Catling & Cruise (for F. Case). Case's Orchid. Dry fields and open areas. August-September. Map 752. Our plants are var. *casei.*

6. S. praécox (Walt.) S. Wats. (precocious). Grass-leaved Ladies' tresses. Dry to wet meadows. August-September. Reported for CT.—OBL

7. S. romanzoffiána Cham. (for Count Romanzoff). Hooded Ladies' tresses. Bogs, pond and stream margins, wet meadows. July-September. Map 753. (Scotland and Ireland). Endangered in MA. [*S. stricta*].—OBL

8. S. cérnua (L.) Richard (nodding, from the declined flowers). Nodding Ladies' tresses. Roadsides, waste places, dry to wet meadows, pond margins and bogs. August-September. Fig. 341, Map 754. [*S. ochroleuca*].—FACW

S. odoráta (Nutt.) Lindl. Similar to *S. cernua* but distinguishable in being more robust, with a stem 3 mm or more thick at base, leaves gradually reduced up the stem, and lip marked with a broad area of yellow (stem up to 3 mm thick at base, leaves rapidly reduced, and lip white in *S. cernua*). [*S. cernua* var.*o.*]. From farther south. Reported for RI.—OBL

7. *Apléctrum* Torr. (without a spur).

Scapose herbs from a horizontal rootstalk consisting of several subglobose, glutinous corms connected by slender stolons, a new corm produced each year, which gives rise to a flowering scape in late spring and a solitary leaf in autumn; scape stout, naked except for several remote, linear-oblong, sheathing bracts; leaf basal, petioled, elliptic, plaited, bluish-green, often shrivelled in early spring before the scape appears; inflorescence a terminal, bracteate raceme of pedicelled greenish, yellowish or whitish flowers marked with purple, perianth parts separate, spreading, the sepals and lateral petals similar, narrowly oblong-spatulate to oblong-elliptic, lip broadly obovate, 3-lobed, undulate-margined, narrowed to a claw, white marked with purple, with 3 ridges in the lower half, column compressed, undulate at the apex; capsule ellipsoid, pendant.

1. *A. hyemále* (Muhl.ex Willd.) Torr. (of winter, from the overwintering leaf). Putty-root. Rich, deciduous woods. May-June. Fig. 342, Map 755. Endangered in MA.—FAC

8. *Corallorhíza* Gagnebin Coral-root (Greek derivation).

Yellowish, brownish or purplish saprophytes from short or long, branched and toothed, coral-like rhizomes; stem simple, with leaves reduced to sheathing scales; inflorescence a terminal raceme of small, colored flowers, lateral sepals united with the base of the column, forming a short spur or gibbous protuberance at the summit of the ovary, the third sepal free, lip simple or with 2 lateral lobes below the middle, the face bearing 1 or 2 short longitudinal ridges near or below the middle, column shorter than the perianth, bearing a single, terminal anther; capsules pendant.

a. Plant in flower.
    b. Lip oblong or oval, with a lobe or tooth on each side at or below the middle.
        Lateral lobes of lip very small, spur-like swelling lacking, lip unspotted,
            perianth 5 mm or less long; flowering in June or earlier. .... 1. *C. trifida*
        Lateral lobes of lip and spur-like swelling prominent, lip usually
            purple-spotted, perianth longer than 5 mm; flowering in July
            or later. .... 2. *C. maculata*
    b. Lip widely oval or suborbicular, merely undulate-margined, not lobed or
        toothed .... 3. *C. odontorhiza*
a. Plant in fruit.
    c. Longest capsules less than 8 mm long .... 3. *C. odontorhiza*
    c. Longest capsules 8 mm or more long.
        Uppermost leaf sheath with free portion 1 cm or less long. .... 1. *C. trifida*
        Uppermost leaf sheath with free portion more than 1 cm long. .... 2. *C. maculata*

1. *C. trifida* Chatclain (3-parted). Early Coral-root. Wet coniferous or mixed woods, swamps and thickets. May-June. Map 756. (Eurasia). [*C. corallorhiza*].-FACW

2. *C. maculáta* (Raf.) Raf. (spotted). Spotted Coral-root. Upland coniferous or mixed woods. July-September. Fig. 343, Map 757.—FACU

3. *C. odontorhíza* (Willd.) Nutt. (tooth-rooted). Late Coral-root. Rich mixed upland woods. August-October. Map 758. Endangered in ME.

C. wisteriana Conrad. Wister's Coral-root. Similar to *C. odontorhiza* but distinguishable in having a perianth 6 mm or more long, notched lip, and flowering in April-May (perianth up to 5 mm long, lip not notched, flowering in August-October in *C. odontorhiza*). Reported for MA.—FAC

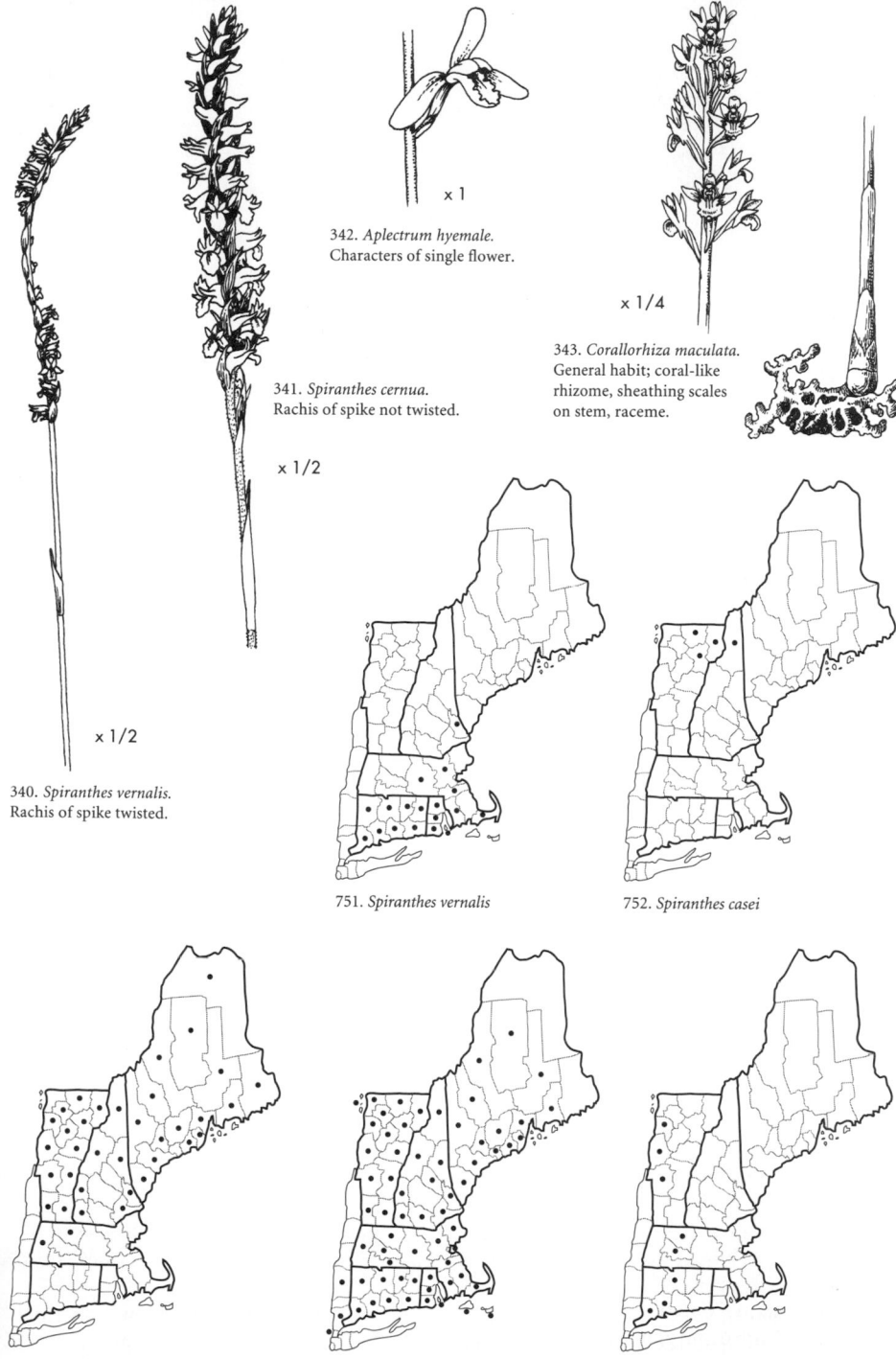

342. *Aplectrum hyemale.*
Characters of single flower.

× 1

× 1/4

343. *Corallorhiza maculata.*
General habit; coral-like
rhizome, sheathing scales
on stem, raceme.

341. *Spiranthes cernua.*
Rachis of spike not twisted.

× 1/2

× 1/2

340. *Spiranthes vernalis.*
Rachis of spike twisted.

751. *Spiranthes vernalis*

752. *Spiranthes casei*

753. *Spiranthes romanzoffiana*

754. *Spiranthes cernua*

755. *Aplectrum hyemale*

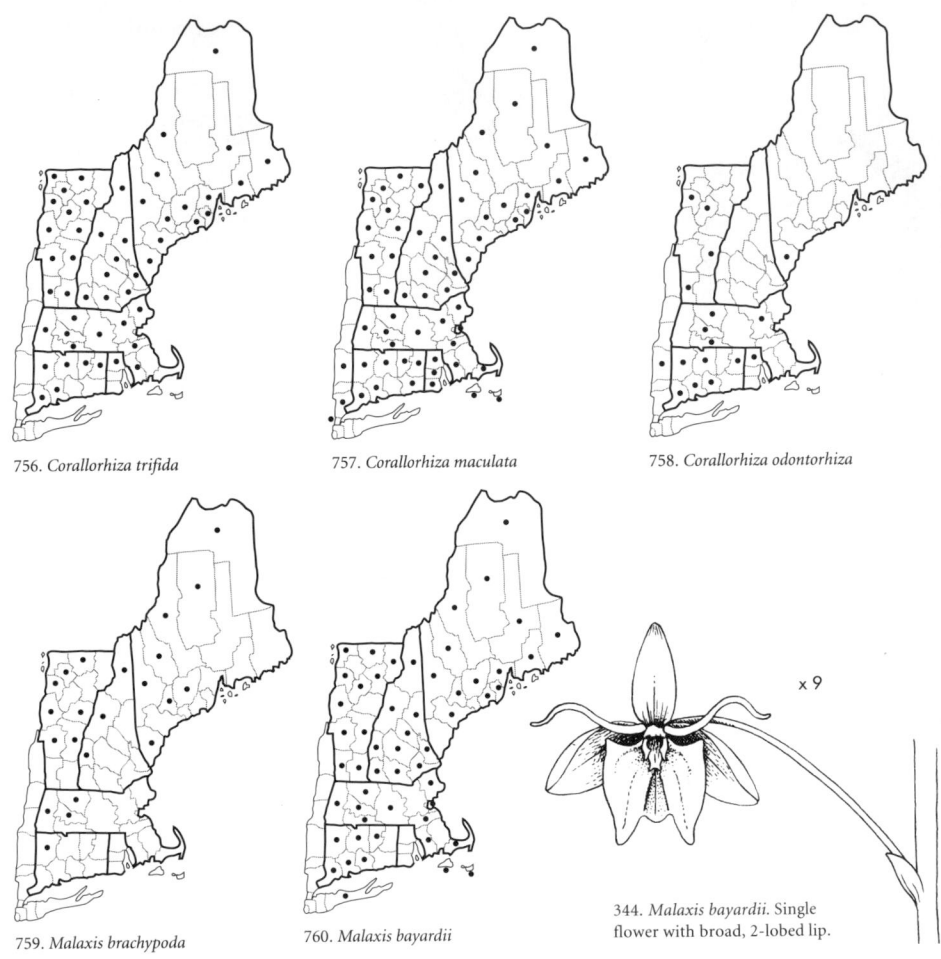

756. *Corallorhiza trifida*   757. *Corallorhiza maculata*   758. *Corallorhiza odontorhiza*

759. *Malaxis brachypoda*   760. *Malaxis bayardii*

×9

344. *Malaxis bayardii.* Single
flower with broad, 2-lobed lip.

9. Maláxis Solander ex Sw. Adder's Mouth (delicate).

Small, terrestrial or wetland herbs from a solid bulb; stem bearing a single oval to elliptic leaf
sheathing at the base or near the middle and 1 or 2 sheathing scales at the base; inflorescence a
terminal, bracteate raceme of small greenish or yellowish flowers, perianth parts spreading, sepals
ovate to elliptic or lanceolate, lateral petals lanceolate to linear, lip oblong, auricled at the base, lobed
or erose at the apex, column very small; capsule ellipsoid.

Pedicels 3 mm or less long; lip narrowly pointed, not lobed; leaf sheathing stem
    below the middle .... 1. *M. brachypoda*
Pedicels longer than 3 mm; lip broad and 2-lobed at the apex; leaf sheathing
    stem at about the middle (Fig. 344) .... 2. *M. bayardii*

    1. *M. brachypóda* (Gray) Fern. (short-pedicelled). White Adder's-mouth. Wet mixed or Thuja
woods and bogs. June-July. Map 759. Endangered in CT, NH. [*M. monophyllos* var. *b.; Microstylis
monophyllos*].—FACW
    2. *M. bayárdii* Fern. Green Adder's-mouth. Rich deciduous woods, meadows, deciduous
swamps, wet coniferous woods, bogs. July-August. Fig. 344, Map 760. Endangered in RI, CT. [*M.
unifolia; Microstylis u.*].—FAC

10. Calopógon R. Br. ex Ait. f. Grass-pink (from the Greek meaning beautiful beard).
Slender herbs from a small, bulbous corm; scape with 1-3 sheathing bracts near the base and 1 (rarely 2) long, linear, sheathing, grass-like leaf just above; inflorescence a short, loosely flowered, bracteate raceme of 2-several, rose-purple (rarely white) flowers, sepals and petals separate and spreading, nearly alike, ovate or oblong to lanceolate, the lateral petals short-clawed and narrower than the sepals, narrowly fiddle-shaped, lip forming the uppermost segment of the perianth, linear-oblong at the base with 2 minute lateral lobes, strongly dilated at the apex, bearded on the upper side with long, clavate hairs with yellow tips, column slender, elongated and somewhat incurved, 2-winged at the summit; capsule ellipsoid, ridged.

1. *C. tuberósus* (L.) B.S.P. (tuberous). Bogs, and wet, peaty meadows. June-July. Fig. 345, Map 761. [*C. pulchellus; Limodorum tuberosum*]. Our plants are var. *tuberosus.*—FACW+

11. Líparis L. C. Rich. Twayblade (from the Greek shining, based on the lustrous leaves).
Low, succulent, scapose herbs arising from a bulbous corm; base of the stem bearing several sheathing scales and a pair of broad, sheathing leaves just above; inflorescence a laxly few to many flowered bracteate raceme of yellowish, greenish or yellowish and purple flowers on filiform pedicels, perianth parts of nearly equal length, spreading, sepals oblong-lanceolate, lateral petals narrowly linear to filiform, lip narrowly cuneate to oblong or suborbicular, arcuate-recurved, entire to erose or apiculate, column curved, narrowly winged above; capsule ellipsoid or obovoid.

Perianth parts 7 mm or more long; lip 7 mm or more wide, purple; capsule on
    a stipe as long or longer than the body .... 1. *L. liliifolia*
Perianth parts less than 7 mm long; lip less than 7 mm wide, yellowish-green;
    capsule on a stipe half or less the length of the body. .... 2. *L. loeselii*

1. *L. liliifólia* (L.) L. C. Rich. ex Ker-Gawl. (with leaves of Lilia). Lilia-leaved Twayblade. Rich, mostly deciduous woods. June-July. Fig. 346, Map 762. Endangered in CT.—FACU
2. *L. loesélii* (L.) L. C. Rich. (for J. Loesel). Loesel's Orchid. Wet to dry meadows, thickets, and woods. June-July. Map 763. (Europe).—FACW

12. Lístera R. Br. Twayblade (for M. Lister).
Small, delicate herbs from fibrous roots; stem slender, glabrous below the leaves, more or less pubescent above; leaves 2, opposite or subopposite, sessile at or somewhat above or below the middle, elliptic, ovate or ovate-cordate, base of stem bearing 1 or 2 sheathing scales; inflorescence a terminal, bracted raceme of small, greenish or purplish flowers, sepals and lateral petals nearly alike, lance-ovate to oblong, or petals linear in *L. convallarioides*, separate, spreading or reflexed, lip longer than the other perianth parts, declined, linear, toothed or auricled on each side near the base, 2-lobed or 2-cleft at the apex, column shorter than petals or very minute; capsule ovate to ellipsoid.

a. Lip divided to or below the middle into 2 linear-setaceous prongs (sometimes
        not cleft to the middle in *L. australis*). (Fig. 347).
    Lip 5 mm or less long; pedicels and axis of raceme glabrous. .... 1. *L. cordata*
    Lip longer than 5 mm; pedicels and axis of raceme glandular. .... 2. *L. australis*
a. Lip not divided to the middle, the lobes broad and round-tipped.
    Lip oblong, broad at the base, with auricles clasping the column. .... 3. *L. auriculata*
    Lip obovate, narrowed at the base to a slender claw, not auricled. .... 4. *L. convallarioides*

1. *L. cordáta* (L.) R. Br. ex Ait. f. (heart-shaped). Heart-leaved Twayblade. Mossy, spruce-fir forests, Thuja swamps and bogs. June-July. Fig. 347, Map 764. (Eurasia). Endangered in MA. [*Ophrys c.*].—FACW+

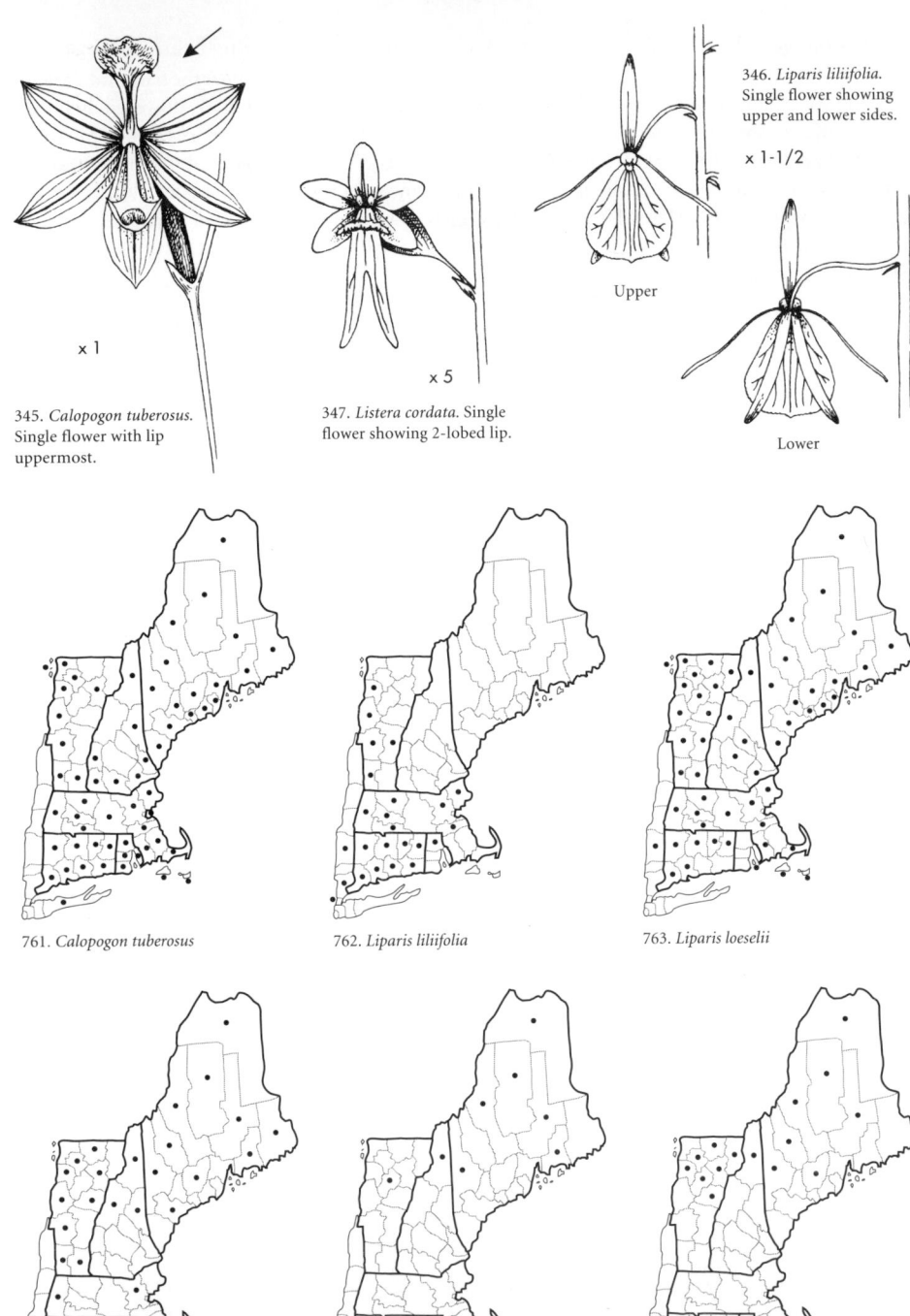

× 1

345. *Calopogon tuberosus.*
Single flower with lip
uppermost.

× 5

347. *Listera cordata.* Single
flower showing 2-lobed lip.

346. *Liparis liliifolia.*
Single flower showing
upper and lower sides.

× 1-1/2

Upper

Lower

761. *Calopogon tuberosus*

762. *Liparis liliifolia*

763. *Liparis loeselii*

764. *Listera cordara*

765. *Listera auriculata*

766. *Listera convallarioides*

2. L. austrális Lindl. (southern). Southern Twayblade. Shaded bogs. June-July. Endangered in VT; reported for Lamoille County. [*Ophrys a.*].—FACW

3. L. auriculáta Wieg. (eared). Auricled Twayblade. Alluvial thickets, associated with alder, and Thuja swamps. June-July. Map 765. Endangered in VT, NY, NH. [*Ophrys a.*].—FACW

4. L. convallarioídes (Sw.) Nutt. ex Ell. (resembling *Convallaria*). Broad-lipped Twayblade. Damp, mossy or wet woods, and Thuja swamps. July-August. Map 766. [*Ophrys c.*].

L. x *vellmánii* Case. A hybrid between *L. convallarioides* and *L. auriculata.*-FACW

13. Goodyéra R. Br. ex Ait. f. Rattlesnake plantain (for J. Goodyer).

Terrestrial herbs from creeping rhizomes bearing thick, fibrous roots; stem scapose, glandular-pubescent; leaves in a basal rosette or alternate and clustered toward the lower part of the stem, ovate to lanceolate, narrowed to a broadly petiolar, sheathing base, evergreen, often reticulated with white, abruptly reduced above to sheathing, scale-like bracts; inflorescence a glandular-pubescent, lax or dense, terminal, spiciform, cylindrical or secund, bracteate raceme of small white or greenish flowers, lateral sepals free, the upper one united with the lateral petals and forming a column (galea) over the hood and lip, the lip saccate or concave, prolonged into a straight or recurved beak, anther 1, borne on the back of the short column; capsule erect, ovoid to ellipsoid.

a. Beak of the lip less than half as long as the body; raceme densely cylindric .... 1. *G. pubescens*
a. Beak of the lip more than half as long as the body; raceme secund or loosely
   spiralling.
   b. Galea 7 mm or more long .... 2. *G. oblongifolia*
   b. Galea less than 6 mm long.
      Raceme secund; lip strongly saccate, the pouch about as deep as long;
         column with beak shorter than body of stigma; leaves usually
         shorter than 3 cm .... 3. *G. repens*
      Raceme loosely spiralling; lip shallowly saccate, the pouch about half as
         deep as long; column with beak as long or longer than body of
         stigma; leaves usually longer than 3 cm .... 4. *G. tesselata*

1. G. pubéscens (Willd.) R. Br. ex Ait. f. (pubescent). Downy Rattlesnake plantain. Dry deciduous or mixed woods. July-August. Map 767. [*Epipactis p.; Peramium p.*].—FACU-

2. G. oblongifólia Raf. (oblong-leaved). Giant Rattlesnake plantain. Dry coniferous or mixed woods. July-August. Map 768. Endangered in ME. [*G. decipiens; Epipactis d.; Peramium d.*]. —FACU-

3. G. répens (L.) R. Br. ex Ait. f. (creeping). Dwarf Rattlesnake plantain. coniferous woods and Thuja swamps. July-August. Map 769. Endangered in MA. [*Epipactis r.*].—FACU+

4. G. tesseláta Lodd. (like a mosaic). Tesselated Rattlesnake plantain. Coniferous or mixed woods. July-September. Fig. 348, Map 770. [*Epipactis t.; Peramium t.*].—FACU-

14. Epipáctis Zinn Helleborine (ancient name for Hellebore).

Tall herbs from fibrous roots with simple, leafy stems; leaves numerous, spirally arranged, clasping, ovate or elliptic-lanceolate, progressively reduced above and grading into the floral bracts; inflorescence a few to many-flowered, terminal raceme of small flowers, sepals strongly keeled, these and the lateral petals similar, ovate-lanceolate, separate, greenish with purple veins, lip purple and pink, 2-parted by a constriction near the middle, the basal half saccate, the upper half broadly ovate and petal-like, column short and thick, stamen 1; capsule obovoid-ellipsoid, pendant.

1. E. helleboríne (L.) Crantz (Greek name for Hellebore). Rich deciduous or coniferous woods and thickets, roadsides. July-August. Fig. 349, Map 771. (Naturalized from Europe). [*E. latifolia; Serapias h.*].

15. Tríphora Nutt. (from the Greek, based on the inflorescence frequently bearing 3 flowers).

Small, delicate herbs from ovoid tubers, these produced at the ends of short stolons; stem succulent, fragile, slender or stout; leaves alternate, small and ovate, clasping; inflorescence of 1-several pedicellate, nodding, pink to white, ephemeral flowers, perianth parts separate, ascending, the sepals and lateral petals elliptic to oblong-spatulate, similar, lip obovate, narrowed to a slender claw, 3 lobed, the middle lobe the largest and sinuate-margined, lip with 3 prominent green ridges broken into teeth or tubercles, column subterete at base, laterally dilated near the middle; capsule ellipsoid, pendent.

    1. T. trianthóphora (Sw.) Rydb. (bearing 3 flowers). Three-birds orchid. Rich, moist, deciduous woods, often in pure beech stands. August-September. Fig. 350, Map 772. Endangered in MA. [*Pogonia t.*].

16. Isótria Raf. (from the Greek based on the 3 equal sepals).

Terrestrial herbs from a cluster of fibrous roots; leaves 5 or 6 in a whorl near the top of the slender stem; flower solitary (rarely 2) just above the leaves, yellow-green, or yellow-green and purple, perianth parts distinct, ascending, sepals linear, elongate, the lateral petals usually shorter and broader, lip erect, 3 lobed, bearing a prominent, crested, median ridge, column with a denticulate summit; capsule ellipsoid.—FACU

Sepals purplish, more than 3 cm long; peduncle as long or longer than ovary. .... 1. *I. verticillata*
Sepals greenish, less than 3 cm long; peduncle shorter than ovary. .... 2. *I. medeoloides*

    1. I. verticilláta Raf. (whorled). Large Whorled Pogonia. Acidic deciduous or mixed woods. May-June. Fig. 351, Map 773. [*Pogonia v.*].
    2. I. medeoloídes (Pursh) Raf. (resembling Medeola). Small Whorled Pogonia. Acidic deciduous woods. May-June. Map 774. Federally Endangered.

17. Calýpso Salis. (named for the goddess Calypso).

Low, delicate herb from a bulbose corm, this sometimes bearing coralloid roots, producing a single basal leaf in autumn, which persists through the next anthesis, and the following spring giving rise to a leafless scape; scape enveloped to about half-way by 2 or 3 membranous sheaths; basal leaf petioled, round-ovate, with numerous veins, shrivelling soon after anthesis; flower showy, terminal, solitary on a slender pedicel subtended by a linear bract, sepals and lateral petals lance-linear, similar, ascending and spreading over the lip, pinkish-purple, lip saccate, scoop-shaped, pendant, narrowed to a bifid summit, streaked with purple, the margins of the sac folded outward and forming a delicate, whitish apron which is spotted with purple and crested with 3 rows of yellow bristles, column petaloid, ovate, overhanging the lip; capsule ellipsoid, erect, tipped by the withered perianth.

    1. C. bulbósa (L.) Oakes (with a bulb). Calypso. Deep, moist, mossy coniferous woods, most often associated with Thuja. May-June. Fig. 352, Map 775. (Eurasia). [*Cytherea b.*]. Represented with us as var. *americána* (R. Br.) Luer—FACW

18. Cypripédium L. Lady's Slipper (derived from the Latin).

Glandular-pubescent, terrestrial herbs from tufted, coarsely fibrous roots; leaves large and broad, plaited, sheathing at the base, 2 or more, basal or cauline; flowers solitary or several, mostly large and showy, sepals spreading, 2 of them usually fused, the other free, petals free and spreading, 2 usually narrow, the lip a large, inflated pouch, column bearing a pair of lateral fertile stamens and a dilated, petaloid, sterile stamen above, stigma terminal, somewhat 3 lobed; capsule obovoid to ellipsoid. Handling stems of certain species, particularly *C. reginae*, is reported to cause skin irritation.

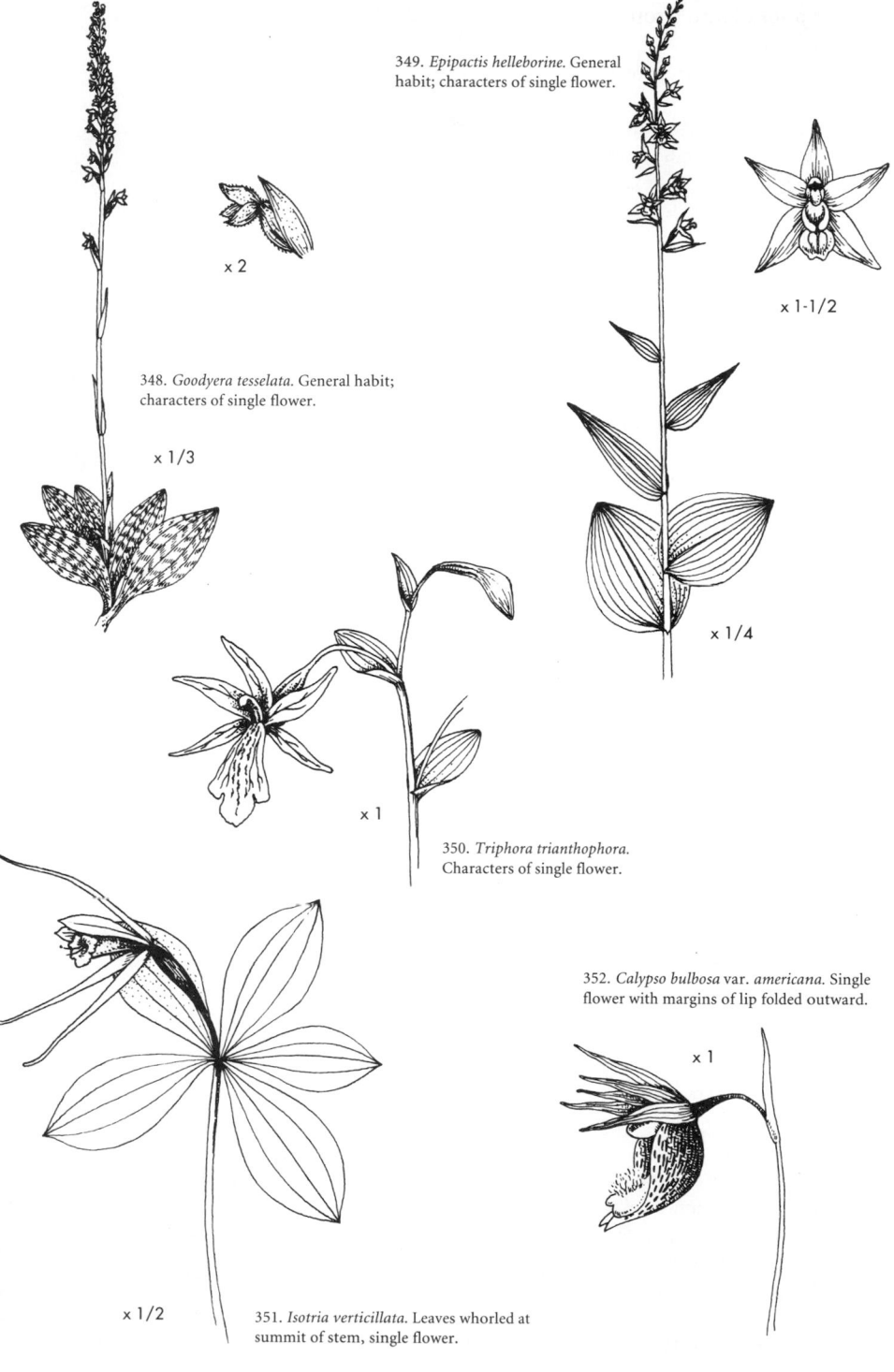

349. *Epipactis helleborine.* General habit; characters of single flower.

x 2

348. *Goodyera tesselata.* General habit; characters of single flower.

x 1/3

x 1-1/2

x 1/4

x 1

350. *Triphora trianthophora.* Characters of single flower.

352. *Calypso bulbosa* var. *americana.* Single flower with margins of lip folded outward.

x 1

x 1/2

351. *Isotria verticillata.* Leaves whorled at summit of stem, single flower.

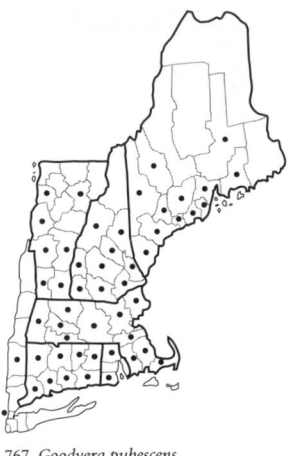

767. *Goodyera pubescens*

768. *Goodyera oblongifolia*

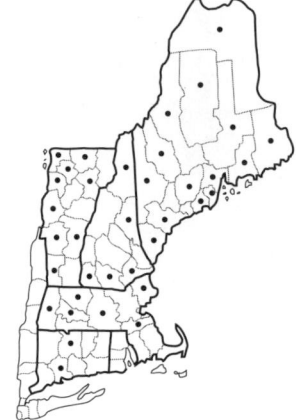

769. *Goodyera repens*

770. *Goodyera tesselata*

771. *Epipactis helleborine*

772. *Triphora trianthophora*

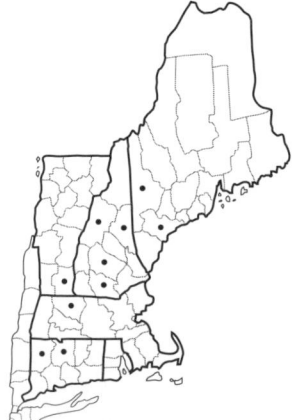

773. *Isotria verticillata*

774. *Isotria medeoloides*

775. *Calypso bulbosa* var. *americana*

a. Leaves basal, 2 (rarely 3), the flowering stem a naked scape. .... 1. *C. acaule*
a. Leaves cauline.
  b. Lateral sepals free almost to the base; leaves glabrous except for ciliate margin;
    lip irregularly cone-shaped. (Fig. 353). .... 2. *C. arietinum*
  b. Lateral sepals fused for their entire length or nearly so; leaves pubescent, at
    least above; lip slipper-shaped. (Fig. 354).
    c. Lip pink or pink and white, rarely pure white; lateral petals white, straight,
      oblong, shorter than the lip. .... 3. *C. reginae*
    c. Lip yellow or white; lateral petals greenish-yellow or purplish-brown,
      twisted, lance-linear, longer than the lip.
      Lip yellow.
        Sepals and lateral petals greenish-yellow, often streaked with
          purple lines; lip 3 cm long or longer .... 4. *C. pubescens*
        Sepals and lateral petals purplish-brown; lip shorter than 3 cm. .... 5. *C. parviflorum*
      Lip white, purple-striped inside .... 6. *C. candidum*

1. *C. acaúle* Ait. f. (stemless). Pink Lady's Slipper. Dry pine or mixed woods, bogs and wet, mossy woods. May-June. Map 776. [*Fissipes a.*].
  forma *albiflórum* Rand and Redfield. Lip white (pink in the typical phase). -FACU

2. *C. arietínum* Ait. f. (like a ram's head). Ram's-head Lady's Slipper. Wet Thuja woods, wooded swamps, moist deciduous woods. May-June. Fig. 353, Map 777. (e. Asia). Endangered in MA. —FACW+

3. *C. regínae* Walt. (of the queen). Showy Lady's Slipper. Deciduous swamps, Thuja swamps, calcareous bogs and wet slopes. June-July. Map 778. Endangered in CT. [*C. hirsutum*].—FACW

4. *C. pubéscens* Willd. (pubescent). Large Yellow Lady's Slipper. Moist, rich to dry deciduous woods. May-June. Fig. 354, Map 779. Endangered in NH. [*C. calceolus* var. *pubescens*].—FAC+

5. *C. parviflórum* Salisb. (small-flowered). Small Yellow Lady's Slipper. Wet Thuja woods, calcarious deciduous swamps and moist, deciduous woods. May-June. Endangered in MA. [*C. calceolus* var. *parviflorum*; *C. flavescens*; *C. parviflorum*].—FAC+

6. *C. cándidum* Muhl. (white). Small White Lady's Slipper. Calcareous wet meadows and bogs. May-June. From farther west. Reported for CT.—OBL

19. *Pogónia* Juss. (from the Greek meaning bearded).

Low, slender herbs from a cluster of thickened roots, often reproducing by root shoots which give rise to new basal leaves and upright, flowering stems; leaf solitary, about half way up the stem, ovate-lanceolate, 1 or 2 long-petioled, lanceolate or obovate basal leaves, sometimes also present, floral

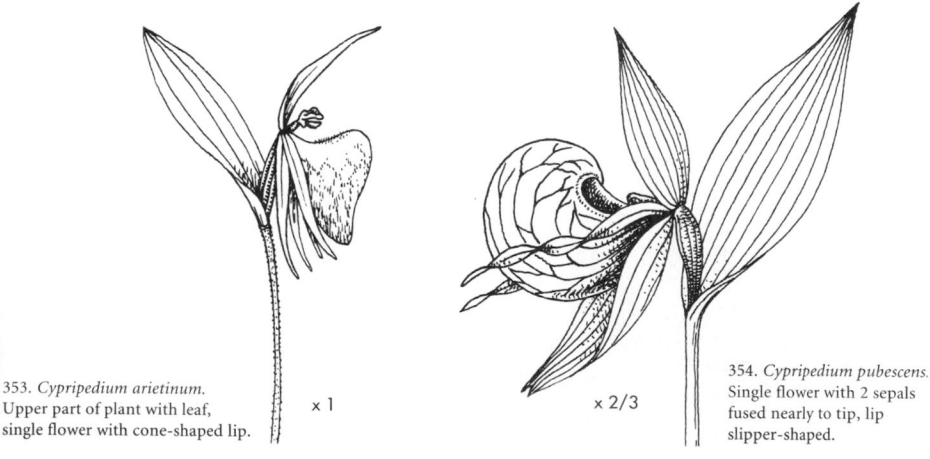

353. *Cypripedium arietinum.*
Upper part of plant with leaf,
single flower with cone-shaped lip.

× 1

× 2/3

354. *Cypripedium pubescens.*
Single flower with 2 sepals
fused nearly to tip, lip
slipper-shaped.

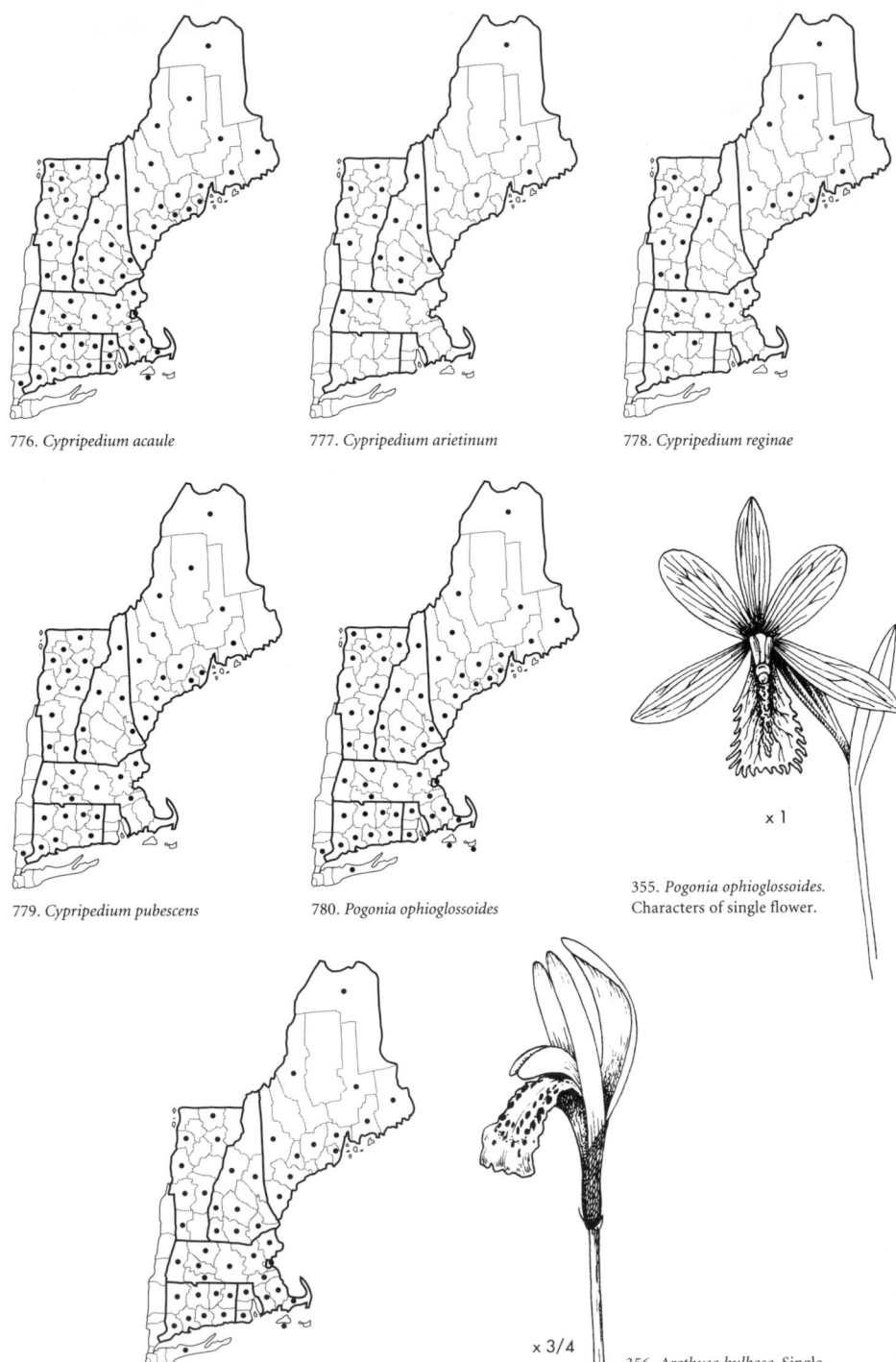

776. *Cypripedium acaule*

777. *Cypripedium arietinum*

778. *Cypripedium reginae*

779. *Cypripedium pubescens*

780. *Pogonia ophioglossoides*

× 1

355. *Pogonia ophioglossoides.*
Characters of single flower.

781. *Arethusa bulbosa*

× 3/4

356. *Arethusa bulbosa.* Single
flower with lip lowermost.

bract foliaceous, oblong lanceolate; flower 1, occasionally 2, somewhat nodding, rose colored or white, perianth parts separate, spreading, sepals linear-oblong to elliptic, lateral petals shorter and wider, oblong-elliptic, lip declined, spatulate and narrowed to the base, lacerate-toothed along the apical margin, prominently bearded in 3 rows with fleshy, yellow bristles, column pink, clavate, curved, apically toothed; capsule ellipsoid.

1. *P. ophioglossoídes* (L.) Ker-Gawl. (like *Ophioglossum*). Rose Pogonia. Bogs, wet meadows and cedar swamps. June-July. Fig. 355, Map 780.—OBL

20. Arethúsa L. Arethusa (named for the nymph Arethusa).
Slender herbs from a small, bulbous corm; scape with 1-3 loose, sheathing bracts, leaf solitary, grass-like, enclosed in the upper bract and arising after flowering; flower terminal, solitary (rarely 2), subtended by a pair of minute bracts, rose pink, (rarely white or lavender) sepals and lateral petals oblong to lanceolate, united at the base, connivent above and arched over the column, lip often spotted or streaked with purple, with a short claw, oblong, arcuate-recurved, often somewhat 3-lobed at the apex, margins crenulate-undulate or erose, crested on the face with 3 fleshy-fringed, yellow ridges, column compressed, narrowly linear-spatulate, petaloid, erose apically; capsule ellipsoid, strongly ridged.

1. *A. bulbósa* L. (bulbous). Dragon's mouth. Bogs and wet, peaty meadows. May-June. Fig. 356, Map 781. Endangered in CT.—OBL

Subclass II Dicotyledoneae (Dicotyledons)

Leaves usually net-veined; parts of the flowers usually in 4s, 5s, multiples thereof, or many.

Family 60. Saururáceae (Lizard's-tail Family)

Monoecious, perennial herbs from a creeping, fleshy rhizome, with jointed stems. Leaves alternate, with sheathing petiole, broad, entire, ovate-cordate, acute to acuminate. Flowers perfect, bracteate, small and white, in one or more dense, slender, elongate, peduncled spikes which are opposite the leaves; perianth lacking, stamens 2-8, hypogynous; ovary superior to half-inferior, of 3-4 carpels which are distinct or united at the base, each with a short, recurved style and 1-4 ovules. Fruit globose, rugose, separating into 3-4 indehiscent carpels.

1. Saurúrus L. Lizard's-tail (from the Greek meaning lizard tail).
Same characters as the family.

1. *S. cérnuus* L. (nodding). Marshes, swamps and shallow water. June-August. Fig. 357, Map 782. Endangered in Ct, RI.—OBL

Family 61. Salicáceae (Willow Family)

Dioecious trees or shrubs with soft, brittle wood. Leaves deciduous, alternate, or rarely subopposite, simple, toothed or entire, petiolate, stipulate, the stipules minute and falling early or leaf-like and persistent. Flowers imperfect, the pistillate and staminate in separate erect to pendulous catkins, perianth lacking, each flower subtended by a small, scale-like bract; staminate flowers of 1-many stamens; pistillate flowers consisting of a single, 1-locular, superior ovary containing many ovules, style short, elongate or absent, stigmas 2-4. Fruit an ovoid to oblong, 2-4 valved capsule; seeds numerous, each bearing a tuft of cottony hairs. The inner bark of both willow and poplar may be eaten raw, boiled in strips, or dried and made into flour. The outer bark, although bitter (contains salicin, the active ingredient in aspirin), can be chewed or a tea made to produce the same effect as aspirin, relief of pain and fever. The young trailing stems of the first 3 species of willow can also be peeled and eaten. The roots of willow and poplar seek water and should not be planted near the home as they may clog drainpipes.

Bud scale single; leaf blades mostly linear, elliptic or narrowly ovate, on petioles
    less than 1/4 the length of the blade; catkins erect, or if pendulous
    (rarely) sessile or on bracted peduncles; each flower with 1-4 glands
    at base. .... 1. *Salix*
Bud scales several; leaf blades deltoid to widely ovate, on petioles 1/3 to as
    long as the blade; catkins pendulous, on naked peduncles; each flower
    with a cup-like disk at base .... 2. *Populus*

1. *Sálix* L. Willow (classical Latin name).

Erect or ascending trees or shrubs (shrubs rarely prostrate); buds covered by a single scale, usually appressed, flat on the side facing the twig, leaf scars u-shaped, bundle traces 3, stipule scars short or absent, pith white, end bud lacking (pseudo-terminal); leaves narrow to broad, short petioled; catkins mostly ascending to spreading (rarely drooping), sessile or on bracted peduncles, their scales entire to shallowly toothed or erose, usually pubescent, staminate flowers with 2-8 stamens, subtended by 1-2 glands, pistillate flowers each subtended by 1-4 glands; capsule 2-valved, glabrous or pubescent.—WILDl. 2

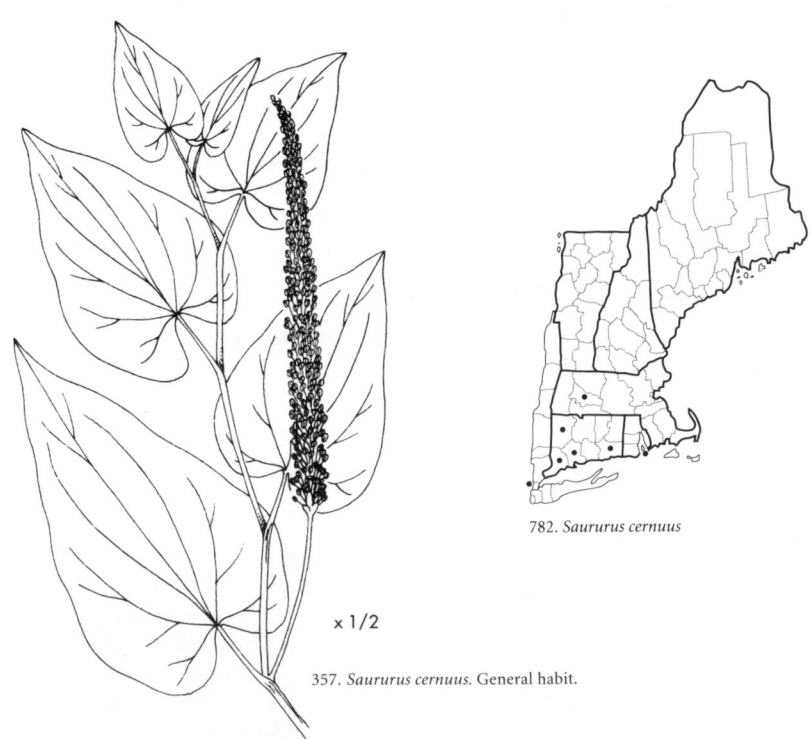

782. *Saururus cernuus*

x 1/2

357. *Saururus cernuus*. General habit.

A. Mature leaves present; catkins present or absent.
  B. Prostrate, creeping or trailing shrubs or near herbs of alpine areas.
    C. Rooting at the nodes; subherbaceous; leaves orbicular or oval, green
      beneath .... 1. *S. herbacea*
    C. Not rooting at the nodes; woody; leaves elliptic or obovate, glaucous
      beneath.
      Leaves finely glandular-crenate; fruit up to 4 mm long, glabrous;
        stamen 1 by cohesion (rarely 2) .... 2. *S. uva-ursi*
      Leaves entire or nearly so, not glandular-crenate; fruit 5 mm or more
        long, usually pubescent (glabrous in 1 form); stamens 2, free. .... 3. *S. arctophylla*
  B. Ascending or erect shrubs or trees; habitats various.
    D. Leaves opposite or subopposite (at least some pairs); catkins subopposite;
      stamens united into 1 .... 4. *S. purpurea*
    D. Leaves and catkins alternate (or if sometimes subopposite in *S. viminalis*,
      then at least 10 times as long as wide; leaves not more than 6 times as
      long as wide in the above species); stamens free, 2 or more.
      E. Leaves entire to undulate-crenate, often revolute-margined, not serrate,
        serrulate, dentate or denticulate; ovary pubescent
        (except in *S. pedicellaris*).
        F. Blades covered beneath with dense, usually tomentose pubescence.
          G. Branchlets usually whitish-pruinose; fruit 4-6 mm long. .... 5. *S. pellita*
          G. Branchlets not whitish-pruinose; fruit 6-9 mm long.
            Blades strongly reticulate veined and grayish-pubescent
              beneath, usually not more than 5 times as long as wide;
              pedicels 1-2 mm long. .... 6. *S. humilis*
            Blades not strongly reticulate veined beneath, white-tomentose,
              usually 5 or more times as long as wide; pedicels less than
              1 mm long. .... 7. *S. candida*
        F. Blades glabrous beneath or covered with silvery or fuscous pubescence,
        not tomentose (sometimes tomentose in *S. viminalis* but leaves
        generally 8 or more times as long as wide; leaves are less than 8
        times as long as wide in the above species).
        H. Branchlets usually whitish-pruinose.
          Blades 4 or more times as long as wide; non-alpine. .... 5. *S. pellita*
          Blades less than 4 times as long as wide; alpine. .... 8. *S. planifolia*
        H. Branchlets not whitish-pruinose (or if sometimes so in *S. petiolaris*
        blades not revolute margined and more than 4 times as long as
        wide; blades revolute margined and/or less than 4 times as long
        as wide in the above 2 species).
        I. Blades more than 4 times as long as wide.
          J. Blades not whitened beneath, green or merely paler, glabrous. .... 7. *S. candida*
               var. *denudata*
          J. Blades distinctly whitened and/or pubescent beneath.
            K. Blades revolute margined; pedicels 2 mm or less long.
              Blades lance-linear, 8 or more times as long as wide;
                fruit subsessile, 4-6 mm long (Fig. 358) .... 9. *S. viminalis*
              Blades elliptic to oblanceolate, 4-5 times as long as wide;
                fruit pedicelled, 7-9 mm long .... 6. *S. humilis*
            K. Blades not revolute margined; pedicels longer than 2 mm. .... 10. *S. petiolaris*
        I. Blades up to 4 times as long as wide.
          L. Blades strongly reticulate veined beneath (sometimes
            questionable in *S. humilis*, in which blades are revolute
            margined and usually gray-pubescent beneath; species
            13-15 lack this combination; *S. argyrocarpa* is silvery
            pubescent beneath). (Fig. 359).
            Blades revolute margined; pedicels 1-2 mm long; scales
              black. .... 6. *S. humilis*
            Blades not revolute margined; pedicels 3 mm or longer;
              scales greenish-yellow or tan .... 11. *S. bebbiana*
          L. Blades not strongly reticulate veined beneath.

M. Blades usually silvery-silky beneath; fruit 2-4 mm long;
    alpine shrub. .... 12. *S. argyrocarpa*
M. Blades glabrous beneath or with rusty or gray pubescence,
    not silvery-silky; fruit 6 mm or longer; non-alpine tree
    or shrub.
    N. Blades distinctly revolute margined, entire to undulate;
        ovary glabrous; peduncle 2-4 cm long; bogs .... 13. *S. pedicellaris*
    N. Blades not or only slightly revolute margined, mostly
        crenate; various habitats.
        O. Blades up to 2 times as long as wide, gray-tomentose
            beneath. .... 14. *S. caprea*
        O. Blades 2-4 times as long as wide, glabrous or loosely
            rusty-pubescent beneath.
            Ovary glabrous; catkins peduncled; pedicels 1-1.5
                mm long. .... 15. *S. myricoides*
            Ovary pubescent; catkins sessile; pedicels 1.5-3 mm
                long. .... 16. *S. discolor*
E. Leaves serrate, serrulate, dentate or denticulate, not revolute margined
    (except *S. humilis*); ovary glabrous or pubescent (all counts of teeth
    per cm of leaf margin are taken at the middle).
  P. Petioles bearing glands at the junction with the blade. (Fig. 362).
    Q. Branchlets pendulous, or blades with 6 or fewer teeth per cm of
        margin, or mature blades sericeous or glaucous beneath with
        7-10 teeth per cm of margin; plant a large tree when mature.
        R. Branchlets pendulous; stamens 3 or more; fruit up to 2.5 mm
            long. .... 17. *S. babylonica*
        R. Branchlets spreading but not pendulous; stamens 2; fruit 3 mm
            or longer.
            Mature blades glabrous with 3-6 teeth per cm of margin;
                pedicels .5-1 mm long .... .18. *S. fragilis*
            Mature blades usually sericeous beneath with 7 or more teeth
                per cm of margin; pedicels less than .5 mm long .... 19. *S. alba*
    Q. Branchlets often spreading but not pendulous; blades with more
        than 6 teeth per cm of margin; mature blades glabrous and
        green beneath (if sometimes glaucous in *S. serissima* teeth more
        than 10 per cm of margin); plant a shrub or small tree when
        mature.
        S. Blades long-acuminate into caudate tips. (Fig. 362). .... 20. *S. lucida*
        S. Blades acute or short-acuminate.
            Blades with 10 or fewer teeth per cm of margin, green beneath;
                fruit 5-6 mm long .... 21. *S. pentandra*
            Blades with more than 10 teeth per cm of margin, subglaucous
                beneath; fruit 7-10 mm long .... 22. *S. serissima*
  P. Petioles lacking glands.
    T. Blades green or merely paler beneath, not distinctly whitened;
        glabrous.
      U. Blades remotely spinulose-denticulate, the teeth usually fewer
        than 4 per cm of margin; petioles usually less than 4 mm long.
        (Fig. 363). .... 23. *S. interior*
      U. Blades more densely serrulate or serrate, the teeth coarser and 4
        or more per cm of margin; petioles 4 mm or longer.
        V. Tree when mature; blades lance-linear to lanceolate, 6 or more
            times as long as wide, tapering to wedge-shaped base,
            long-acuminate, stipules present or absent; scales yellow.
            (Fig. 364) .... 24. *S. nigra*
        V. Shrubs (sometimes tall) when mature; blades lance-ovate to
            lanceolate, usually less than 6 times as long as wide,
            broadly rounded to subcordate at base, short-acuminate;
            stipules usually present; scales brown.
            (Fig. 365).

Blades lance-ovate to ovate, 3 or less times as long as wide;
        catkins 5-8 cm long; peduncles 1-2.5 cm long .... 25. *S. cordata*
Blades lanceolate, more than 3 times as long as wide;
        catkins 2-5 cm long; peduncles 1 cm or less long .... 26. *S. rigida*
T. Blades distinctly whitened and/or pubescent beneath.
  W. Blades coarsely or remotely few-toothed, with 4 or fewer teeth
     per cm of margin, and/or irregularly toothed, the teeth
     differing in size and/or spacing.
    X. Blades spinulose-denticulate, 6 or more times as long as wide.
      (Fig. 363). .... 23. *S. interior*
    X. Blades coarsely toothed, usually not over 5 times as long as
      wide. (Fig. 361).
      Y. Blades up to 2 times as long as wide. .... 14. *S. caprea*
      Y. Blades 2-5 times as long as wide.
        Z. Blades up to 3 times as long as wide, gray-pubescent on
          both faces, not revolute-margined; twigs permanently
          tomentose; fruit to 7 mm long. .... 27. *S. cinerea*
        Z. Blades 2.8-5 times as long as wide, glabrous above,
          pubescent or glabrous beneath; twigs glabrous, or if
          pubescent, blades revolute margined or
          rusty-pubescent beneath; fruit 7-10 mm long.
          Blades revolute margined, usually densely
            gray-pubescent (rarely glabrous) and strongly
            reticulate veined beneath .... 6. *S. humilis*
          Blades not or barely revolute margined, glabrous or
            loosely rusty-pubescent and not strongly
            reticulate veined beneath. .... 16. *S. discolor*
  W. Blades with numerous teeth, generally more than 4 per cm of
     margin, evenly toothed, the teeth uniform in size and spacing.
    a. Blades rounded or subcordate at base. (Fig. 360).
      b. Stipules usually present.
        Blades lanceolate, more than 3 times as long as wide,
          usually glabrous beneath; catkins 2-5 cm long;
          peduncles 1 cm or less long. .... 26. *S. rigida*
        Blades lance-ovate to ovate, 3 or less times as long as
          wide, usually pubescent beneath; catkins 5-8 cm
          long; peduncles 1-2.5 cm long. .... 25. *S. cordata*
      b. Stipules absent (sometimes present in *S. glaucophylloides* with
        leaves glabrous and strongly whitened beneath; leaves
        not strongly whitened in *S. rigida*, usually pubescent
        beneath in *S. cordata*).
        Blades strongly reticulate veined beneath, with fragrance
          of balsam; peduncles 1-3 cm long; pedicels
          2.5-3.5 mm long. .... 28. *S. pyrifolia*
        Blades not strongly reticulate veined beneath, without
          fragrance of balsam; peduncles 1 cm or less long;
          pedicels 1-1.5 mm long. .... 15. *S. myricoides*
    a. Blades tapering to a wedge-shaped base. (Fig. 366).
      c. Blades pubescent, at least beneath.
        Blades up to 6 times as long as wide, with dense, minute,
          silvery pubescence beneath; fruit 3-5 mm long;
          pedicels .5-2 mm long. .... 29. *S. sericea*
        Blades 6 or more times as long as wide, loosely white
          or rusty-pubescent beneath; fruit 5-8 mm long;
          pedicels 2-5 mm long. .... 10. *S. petiolaris*
      c. Blades glabrous.
        d. Blades tapering to a caudate-acuminate tip; fruit up to
          5 mm long; stamens 3 or more. (Fig. 366) .... 30. *S. amygdaloides*
        d. Blades acute to acuminate but not caudate-tipped; fruit
          5-9 mm long; stamens 2.

Blades narrowly lanceolate, 5 or more times as long
as wide.
Stipules usually absent or if present, minute. .... 10. *S. petiolaris*
Stipules usually present, large .... 26. *S. rigida*
Blades lanceolate or lance-ovate, less than 5 times
as long as wide. .... 15. *S. myricoides*
A. Leaves absent; catkins present.
  e. Buds and catkins opposite or subopposite; stamens united into 1. .... 4. *S. purpurea*
  e. Buds and catkins alternate; stamens 2.
    f. Branchlets, buds and capsules covered with a dense, white flocculent
      tomentum .... 7. *S. candida*
    f. Branchlets, buds and capsules glabrous or pubescent but not densely white
      flocculent-tomentose.
      g. Branchlets usually whitish-pruinose; capsules sessile or pedicel not
        over .5 mm long.
        Capsules 5-7 mm long; alpine .... 8. *S. planifolia*
        Capsules mostly not over 5 mm long; non-alpine. .... 5. *S. pellita*
      g. Branchlets not whitish-pruinose; pedicels mostly longer than .5
        (except in *S. viminalis*).
        h. Capsules sessile or subsessile; styles .7-1.2 mm long. .... 9. *S. viminalis*
        h. Capsules distinctly pedicelled; styles up to .7 mm long.
          i. Mature capsules 7-12 mm long.
            j. Scales of catkins greenish-yellow or tan, often with a red tip;
              pedicels 3-5 mm long .... 11. *S. bebbiana*
            j. Scales of catkins dark brown or black, without a red tip; pedicels .
              1-3 mm long.
              Branchlets usually cinereous-pubescent or if glabrous then
                dull; young catkins often recurving; styles less than
                .5 mm long. .... 6. *S. humilis*
              Branchlets pilose when young, becoming glabrous, when
                glabrous usually lustrous; young catkins not recurving;
                styles .5-.7 mm long. .... 16. *S. discolor*
          i. Mature capsules 3-7 mm long.
            k. Mature capsules 6-7 mm long.
              Branchlets finely pubescent to glabrous. .... 14. *S. caprea*
              Branchlets densely and heavily pubescent. .... 27. *S. cinerea*
            k. Mature capsules 3-5 mm long .... 29. *S. sericea*

1. *S. herbácea* L. (herbaceous). Dwarf Willow. Alpine meadows and barrens. June-August. Mt. Washington, N.H. and Mt. Katahdin, ME. Map 783. (Eurasia). Endangered in NH, ME, NY.

S. x. peásei Fern. A hybrid between *S. herbacea* and *S. uva-ursi*. King's Ravine, Mt. Adams, NH

2. *S. úva-úrsi* Pursh. Bearberry Willow. Alpine meadows and barrens. June-July. Rare. Map 784. (Greenland, e. Arctic Amer. and Newfoundland). Endangered in VT.

3. *S. arctóphylla* Cockerell ex Heller (arctic-lover). Alpine meadows and barrens. June-July. (Canada). Endangered in ME; reported for Mt. Katahdin, ME. [*S. groenlandica*].—FACW

4. *S. purpúrea* L. (purple). Basket Willow. Pond and stream margins, shrub swamps. April-May. Map 785. (Europe).

5. *S. pellíta* (Anderss.) Andress. ex Schneid. (clad in skins). Satin Willow. River and stream banks. May-June. Map 786. Endangered in NH.—FACW

6. *S. húmilis* Marsh. (low). Small Pussy-Willow. Abandoned fields, open woods, barrens, roadsides and waste places. April-May. Map 787. [*S. humilis* var. *hyporhysa*; var. *keweenawensis*]. Our plants include var. *humilis* and the following var.:

var. *trístis* (Ait.) Argus. Shrub up to 1 m tall, leaves narrowly oblanceolate (shrub 1-3 m tall, leaves oblanceolate to narrowly obovate in var. *humilis*). [*S. humilis* var. *microphylla*; *S. occidentalis*; *S. tristis*].—FACU

7. S. cándida Flugge ex Willd. (white). Hoary Willow. Calcareous bogs, woodland borders. May. Map 788. Endangered in ME. Our plants include var. *candida* and the following var.:

var. *denudáta* Anderss. Leaves glabrate beneath (flocculent-tomentose in var. *candida*).—OBL

S. x cryptodónta Fern. Similar to *S. candida* but with leaves oblong-lanceolate to ovate, shallowly glandular-crenulate, rugulose beneath, pedicels 1 mm or more long (leaves linear-lanceolate to oblong, entire to undulate, not rugulose beneath, pedicels up to 1 mm long in *S. candida*). From farther north. Reported for MA.

S. x rubélla Bebb. A hybrid between *S. candida* and *S. rigida*.

S. x clàrkei Bebb. A hybrid between *S. candida* and *S. petiolaris*.

8. S. planifólia Pursh (flat-leaved). Tea-leaved Willow. Alpine in NH, ME, and VT. June-July. Map 789. Endangered in NH, ME. [*S. phylicifolia* subsp. *p.*; *S. chlorophylla*]. Our plants are var. *planifolia*.—OBL

S. x grayi Schneid. A hybrid between *S. planifolia* and *S. argyrocarpa*.

783. *Salix herbacea* 784. *Salix uva-ursi* 785. *Salix purpurea*

786. *Salix pellita* 787. *Salix humilis* 788. *Salix candida*

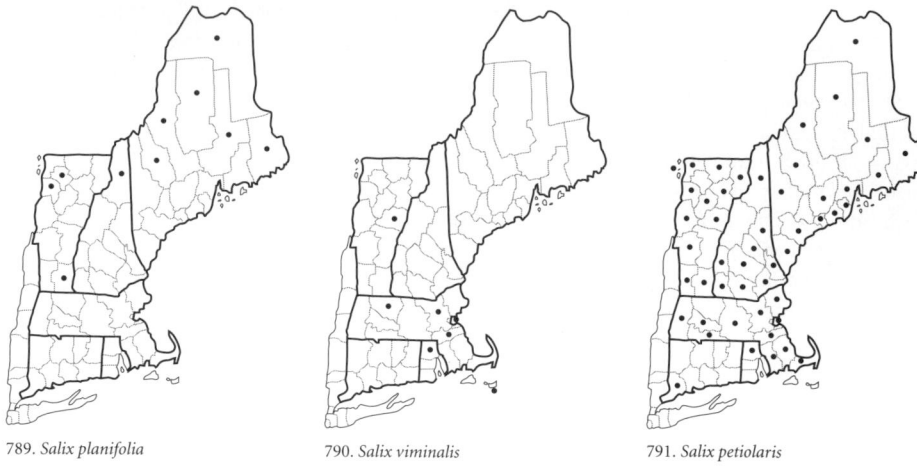

789. *Salix planifolia*   790. *Salix viminalis*   791. *Salix petiolaris*

9. S. viminális L. (bearing withes). Osier Willow. Occasionally escaped from cultivation. May-June. Fig. 358, Map 790. (Introduced from Europe).—FACW-

S. x. smithiána Willd. A hybrid between *S. viminalis* and *S. caprea*.

S. elaeágnos Scop. Differing from *S. viminalis* in having fruiting catkins 2 cm or less long and capsules glabrous and pedicelled (fruiting catkins 3 cm or more long, capsules sessile or subsessile and puberulent in *S. viminalis*). Occasionally escaped from cultivation. Reported for CT, Hancock County ME, Barnstable County MA. [*S. incana*].

10. S. petioláris Smith. Slender Willow. Wet meadows, stream and riverbanks, lake shores. May. Map 791. [*S. gracilis*].—OBL

S. x. subserícea (Anderss.) Schneid. A hybrid between *S. petiolaris* and *S. sericea*.

11. S. bebbiána Sarg. (for M. S. Bebb). Beaked Willow. Stream margins, wet thickets. May-June. Fig. 359, Map 792. [*S. rostrata*].—FACW-

S. x beschèlii Boivin. A hybrid between *S. bebbiana* and *S. discolor*.

12. S. argyrocárpa Anderss. (silvery-carpelled). Silvery Willow. Alpine meadows. June-August. Endangered in ME, NH; reported for Piscataquis County ME, Coos County NH.—FACU

13. S. pedicelláris Pursh (having pedicels). Bog-Willow. Bogs, wet meadows, pond margins and wooded swamps. May-June. Map 793. Endangered in CT.—OBL

14. S. cáprea L. (she-goat). Goat Willow. Spread from cultivation to thickets. March-April. (Introduced from Europe). Reported for Fairfield County CT.

15. S. myricoídes Muhl. (resembling *Myrica*). Blue-leaf Willow. River thickets. May-June. Rare. Fig. 360, Map 794. [*S. glaucophylla; S. glaucophylloides*]. Our plants are var. *myricoides*.—FAC

16. S. díscolor Muhl. (parti-colored; from the leaves). Large Pussy-Willow. Shrub swamps, wooded swamps, moist woodland borders, wet meadows, river and pond margins. March-May. Fig. 361, Map 795. —FACW

S. x conífera Wangenh. Twigs dull, these and lower leaf surfaces sometimes pubescent (twigs lustrous, these and lower leaf surfaces glabrate in *S. discolor*). [*S. discolor* var. *latifolia*].

17. S. babylónica L. (of Babylon). Weeping Willow. Spread from cultivation to river banks and pond margins. April-May. Map 796. (Introduced from Eurasia).—FACW-

18. S. frágilis L. (brittle). Crack Willow. Spread from cultivation to woodland borders, stream margins, roadsides and waste places. April-May. Map 797. (Introduced from Europe).—FAC+

S. x rúbens Schrank. A hybrid between *S. fragilis* and *S. alba*.

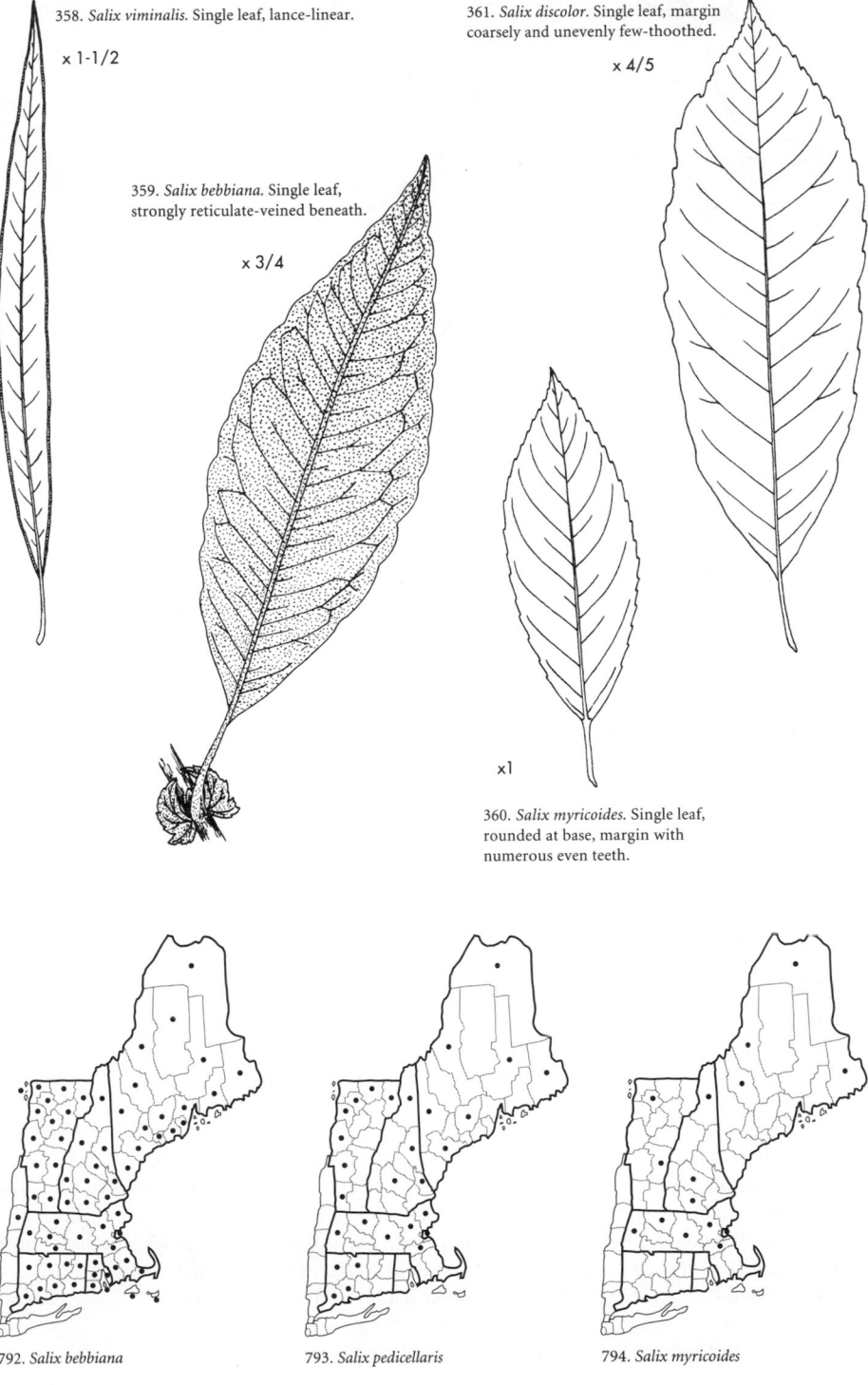

358. *Salix viminalis.* Single leaf, lance-linear.

x 1-1/2

359. *Salix bebbiana.* Single leaf, strongly reticulate-veined beneath.

x 3/4

361. *Salix discolor.* Single leaf, margin coarsely and unevenly few-thoothed.

x 4/5

x1

360. *Salix myricoides.* Single leaf, rounded at base, margin with numerous even teeth.

792. *Salix bebbiana*

793. *Salix pedicellaris*

794. *Salix myricoides*

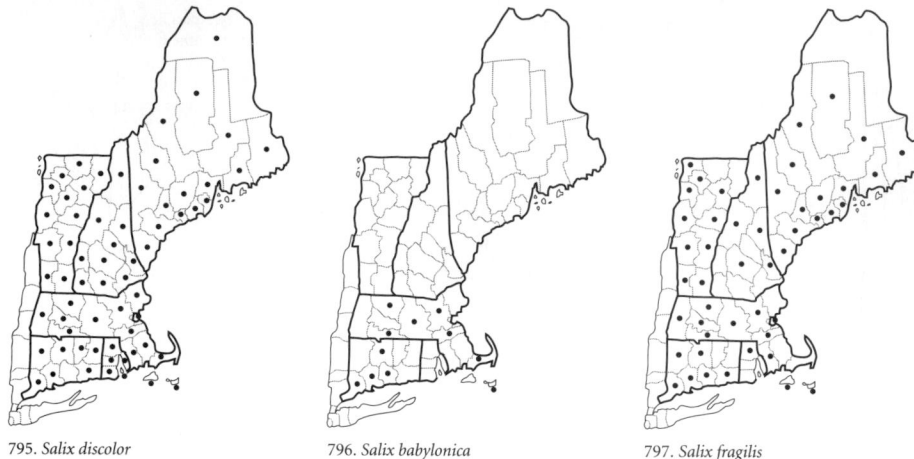

795. *Salix discolor*   796. *Salix babylonica*   797. *Salix fragilis*

19. S. álba L. (white). White Willow. Spread from cultivation to pond and stream margins, wetland edges, mostly in moist soil. April-May. Map 798. (Introduced from Europe). Our plants include var. *alba* and the following vars.:

var. *vitellína* (L.) Stokes. Twigs yellow, these and the leaves glabrate (twigs olivaceous to brown, pubescent, leaves pubescent especially beneath in var. *alba*).

var. *caerúlea* (Sm.) Sm. Twigs erect, brown, these and the leaves glabrate (twigs spreading, these and the leaves pubescent in var. *alba*; twigs spreading and yellow in var. *vitellina*). [*S. alba* var. *calva*].—FACW

20. S. lúcida Muhl. (shining). Shining Willow. Stream and pond margins, shrub swamps. May-June. Fig. 362, Map 799. [*S. lucida* var. *angustifolia;* var. *intonsa*]. Our plants are subsp. *lúcida.*—FACW

S. x jésupii Fern. A hybrid between *S. lucida* and *S. serissima.*

21. S. pentándra L. (with 5 stamens). Bay-leaved Willow. Spread from cultivation to roadsides, meadows, pond and stream margins. May. Map 800. (Introduced from Europe).

22. S. seríssima (Bailey) Fern. (very late). Autumn Willow. Wet meadows, shrub swamps, bogs and river margins. May-June. Map 801.—OBL

23. S. intérior Rowlee (inland). Sandbar Willow. River beaches and sandbars. April-May. Fig. 363, Map 802. Rare. [*S. exigua* subsp. interior var. *angustissima; S. fluviatilis; S. longifolia*].—OBL

S. exígua Nutt. Similar to *S. interior* but with capsules to 5 (rarely 6) mm long, sessile or subsessile, pistillate catkins mostly short and dense, usually up to 5 cm long (capsules 5-9 mm long, distinctly pedicelled, mature pistillate catkins loose and elongating to 8 cm long in *S. interior*). From farther west. Reported for MA, NH.—OBL

24. S. nígra Marsh. (black). Black Willow. River and pond margins, marshes and wooded swamps. May-June. Fig. 364, Map 803. Our plants are var. *nigra.* [*S. marginata*].—FACW+

25. S. cordáta Michx. (heart-shaped). Heart-leaved Willow. Gravelly and sandy stream and lake margins. May-June. Map 804.[*S. adenophylla; S. coactilis; S. syrticola*]. (It has been concluded that 2 vars. formerly recognized under *S. cordata* and *S. rigida* comprise a single species. The distinguishing characteristics of this species are given below under each of the latter species.)—FACW

S. eriocéphala Michx. Twigs petioles and blades glabrate (pubescent in *S. cordata*). [*S. cordata* var. *abrasa*].—FACW

S. x rubélla Bebb. A hybrid between *S. eréocephala* and *S. candida.*

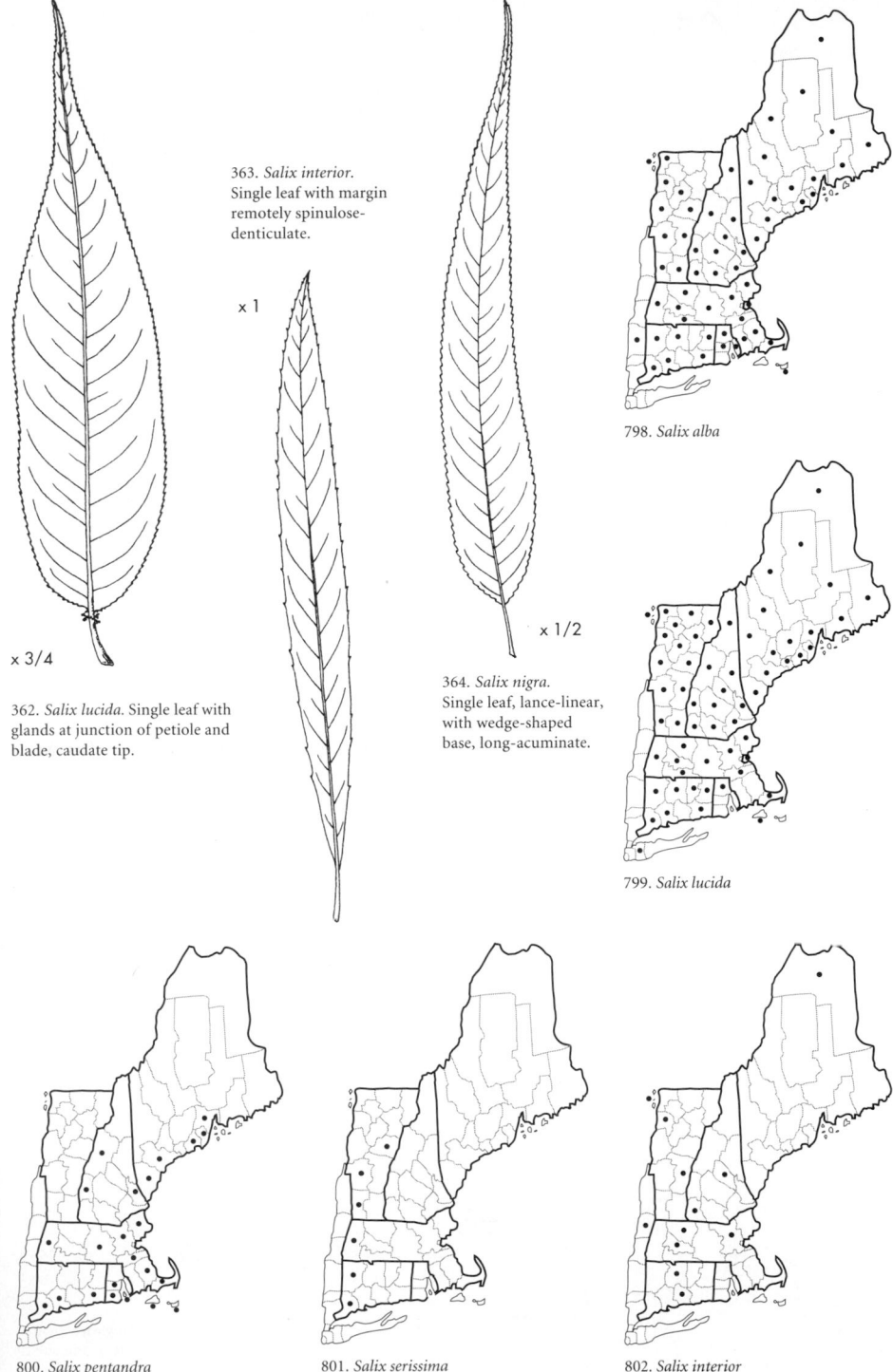

363. *Salix interior.*
Single leaf with margin
remotely spinulose-
denticulate.

x 1

x 3/4

362. *Salix lucida.* Single leaf with
glands at junction of petiole and
blade, caudate tip.

x 1/2

364. *Salix nigra.*
Single leaf, lance-linear,
with wedge-shaped
base, long-acuminate.

798. *Salix alba*

799. *Salix lucida*

800. *Salix pentandra*

801. *Salix serissima*

802. *Salix interior*

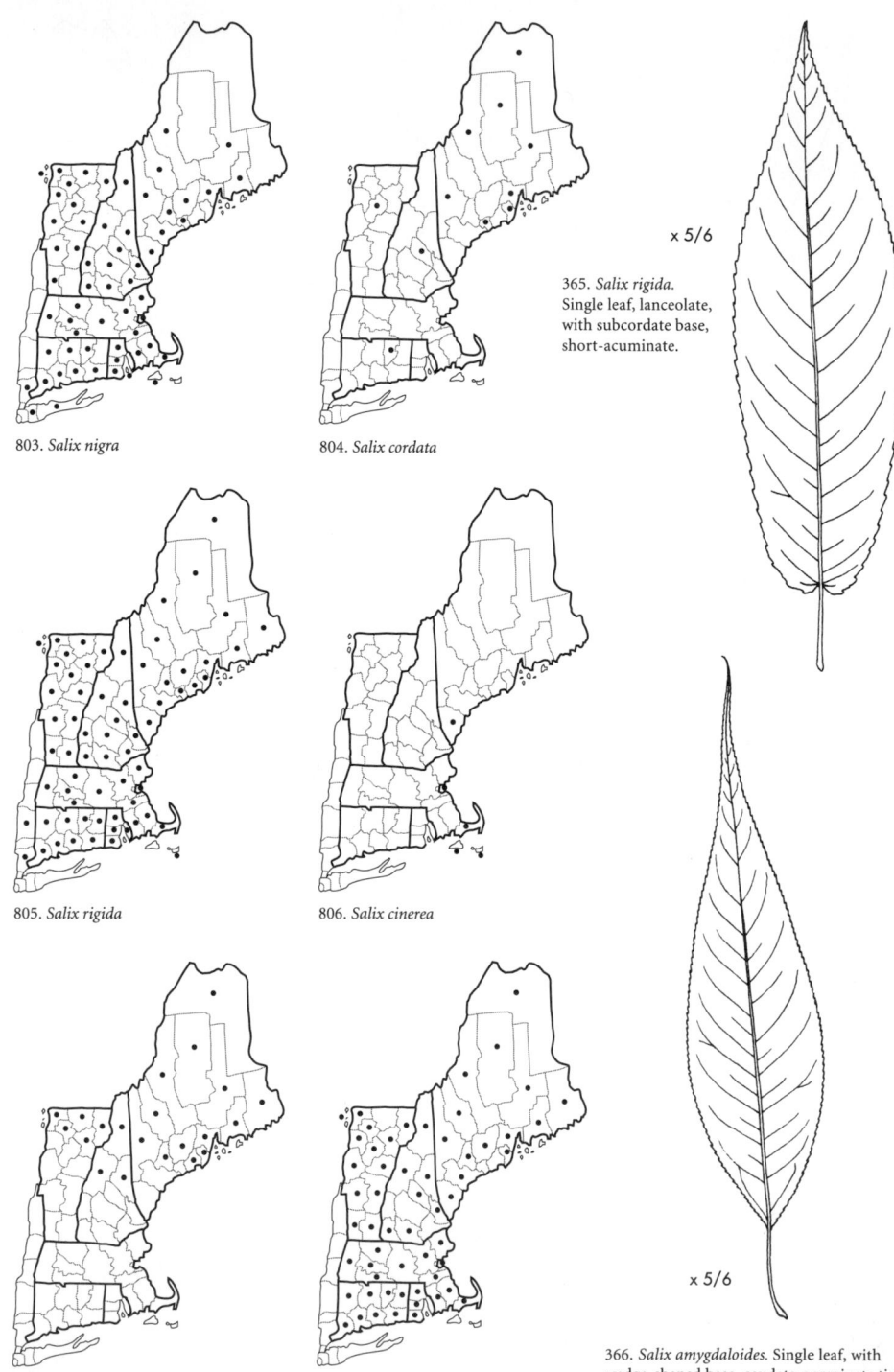

803. *Salix nigra*

804. *Salix cordata*

x 5/6

365. *Salix rigida.*
Single leaf, lanceolate,
with subcordate base,
short-acuminate.

805. *Salix rigida*

806. *Salix cinerea*

807. *Salix pyrifolia*

808. *Salix sericea*

x 5/6

366. *Salix amygdaloides.* Single leaf, with
wedge-shaped base, caudate-acuminate tip.

26. S. rígida Muhl. (stiff). Heart-leaved Willow. Stream and pond margins, wet thickets, ditches. May-June. Fig. 365, Map 805. [*S. cordata*].—OBL

S. eriocéphala Michx. Blades tapering to the base, 4-8 times as long as wide (broadly rounded to subcordate in *S. rigida*; up to 5 times as long as wide). [*S. rigida* var. *angustata*].—FACW

27. S. cinérea L. (ashy). Gray Willow. Rarely spread from cultivation. April-May. Map 806. (Introduced from Europe).

28. S. pyrifólia Anderss. (with leaves of pear). Balsam Willow. Bogs, wet meadows, wet woods, stream and pond margins. May-August. Map 807. [*S. balsamifera*].—FACW

29. S. serícea Marsh. (silky). Silky Willow. Stream and pond margins, wet meadows, marshes, shrub swamps. April-May. Map 808. [*S. coactilis*].—OBL

30. S. amygdaloídes Anderss. (resembling *Amygdalus*, the peach). Peach-leaved Willow. Lake or river shores, wooded swamps. April-May. Fig. 366. Reported for Cheshire County NH, Grand Isle County VT.—FACW

S. x glatfélteri C. K. Schneider. A hybrid between *S. amygdaloides* and *S. nigra*.

2. Pópulus P. Poplar (classical Latin name).

Trees; buds often appressed, frequently lustrous, covered with several-many scales of which the lowermost is immediately above the leaf scar, leaf scars broadly crescent-shaped to triangular, somewhat 3-lobed, bundle traces 3 or in 3 compound groups, stipule scars narrow, pith 5-angled, brown, end bud present; leaves deltoid to widely ovate, toothed, occasionally lobed, on long, sometimes flattened petioles; catkins precocious, usually pendulous, on naked peduncles, their scales deeply dissected, fringed, lobed or densely ciliate, flowers subtended by a cup-shaped disc, staminate flowers with 5 or more stamens; capsule 2-4 valved.—WILDl. 2

a. Mature leaves present.
  b. Petioles strongly flattened.
    c. Blades coarsely dentate, each margin with fewer than 15 teeth. .... 1. *P. grandidentata*
    c. Blades finely dentate or crenulate, each margin with more than 15 teeth.
      d. Blades broadly deltoid or triangular, the teeth raised and terminating in
        an incurved point. (Fig. 367).
        Blades, or many of them, glandular at base, usually longer than wide,
          truncate to subcordate at base .... 2. *P. deltoides*
        Blades not glandular at base, usually wider than long, truncate to
          broadly cuneate at base .... 3. *P. nigra*
      d. Blades ovate to suborbicular, the teeth mostly low and rounded. .... 4. *P. tremuloides*
  b. Petioles terete or nearly so.
    e. Blades lobed and/or coarsely and irregularly toothed, densely tomentose
      beneath (sparsely pubescent to glabrate in *P. X. canescens*). (Fig. 369).
      Blades, at least some of them, lobed, densely tomentose beneath. .... 5. *P. alba*
      Blades merely coarsely toothed, pubescent, becoming glabrate
        beneath. .... 6. *P. x. canescens*
    e. Blades finely and regularly toothed, not lobed, glabrous beneath or
      pubescent only on the main veins.
      Blades rounded or obtuse to merely acute at apex, often with a small,
        pubescent patch above at the intersection of the veins;
        southern NE and NY. .... 7. *P. heterophylla*
      Blades acute to acuminate at apex, glabrous above; boreal.
        Twigs hairy; leaves slightly pubescent beneath, especially on
          main veins. .... 8. *P. x. jackii*
        Twigs glabrous; leaves glabrous beneath .... 9. *P. balsamifera*
a. Mature leaves present or absent; catkins present.
  f. Scales of catkins with 3-several linear or triangular segments long-bearded at
    the apex; stigmas with slender, terete branches; overwintering terminal
    buds 1 cm or less long. (Fig. 368).

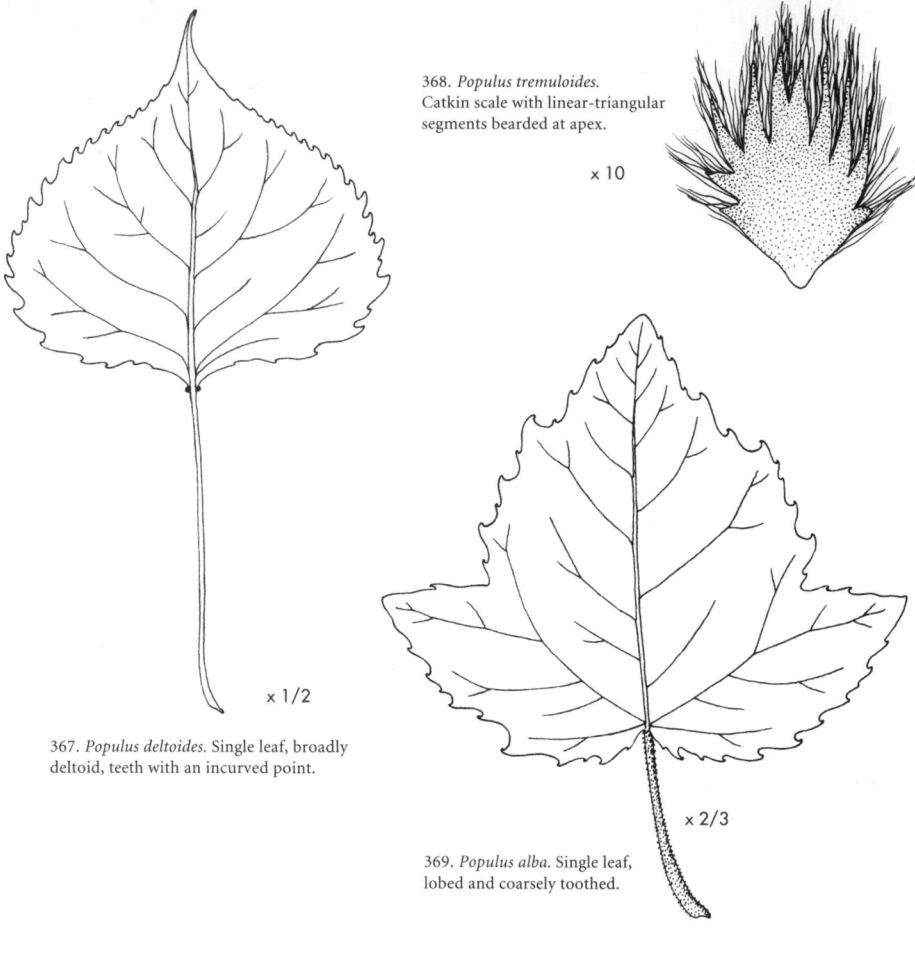

368. *Populus tremuloides.*
Catkin scale with linear-triangular
segments bearded at apex.

x 10

x 1/2

367. *Populus deltoides.* Single leaf, broadly
deltoid, teeth with an incurved point.

x 2/3

369. *Populus alba.* Single leaf,
lobed and coarsely toothed.

g. Overwintering buds glabrous, highly lustrous; expanding leaves glabrate. .... 4. *P. tremuloides*
g. Overwintering buds pubescent or tomentose, dull, or not highly lustrous;
      expanding leaves white-felted beneath.
      Buds and young twigs densely tomentose. .... 5. *P. alba*
      Buds and young twigs finely pubescent to glabrate. .... 1. *P. grandidentata*
f. Scales of catkins fimbriate with numerous filiform, beardless segments;
      stigmas broadly dilated; overwintering terminal buds 1 cm or more long.
    h. Stigmas elevated on long styles; expanding leaves white-felted beneath. .... 7. *P. heterophylla*
    h. Stigmas sessile or nearly so; expanding leaves not white-felted beneath.
      i. Buds very resinous and gummy, fragrant; sprouts and twigs terete;
        stigmas 2.
        Twigs hairy .... 8. *P. x. jackii*
        Twigs glabrous .... 9. *P. balsamifera*
      i. Buds not strongly resinous, nor gummy.
        Twigs and sprouts distinctly angled; stigmas 3. .... 2. *P. deltoides*
        Twigs and sprouts terete; stigmas 2 .... 3. *P. nigra*

1. *P. grandidentáta* Michx. (large-toothed). Large-toothed Aspen. Dry woods, waste places, roadsides, in dry, infertile soil. April-May. Map 809.—FACU-

P. x smìthii B. Boivin. A hybrid between *P. grandidentata* and *P. tremuloides.*

2. *P. deltoides* Bartr. ex Marsh. (deltoid, from the leaf outline). Cottonwood. River and stream bottoms, rich, moist woods, pond margins. April-May. Fig. 367, Map 810. [*P. balsamifera; P. virginiana*]. Our plants are subsp. *deltoides.*—FAC

3. *P. nígra* L. (black). Black Poplar. Escaped from cultivation to roadsides, house lots. Map 811. (Introduced from Europe). [*P. dilatata; P.n.* var. *italica; P. italica*].

4. *P. tremuloídes* Michx. Trembling Aspen. Open woods, old fields, roadsides, cutover areas, waste places, in dry to moist soil. March-May. Fig. 368, Map 812.—FACU

P. trémula L. European Aspen. Similar to trembling aspen but with irregularly sinuate-dentate leaves (leaves finely and regularly toothed in *P. tremuloides*). Sometimes escaped from cultivation. Reported for MA.

5. *P. álba* L. (white). White Poplar. Escaped from cultivation to roadsides and waste places. April-May. Fig. 369, Map 813. (Naturalized from Europe).

6. *P. x canéscens* (Ait.) J. E. Smith (gray). Gray Poplar. Escaped from cultivation to roadsides and waste places. Map 814. (Naturalized from Europe).

7. *P. heterophýlla* L. (with varied leaves). Swamp Cottonwood. Bottomlands, swamps, wet woods. April-May. Map 815. Endangered in CT.—FACW+

8. *P. x jáckii* Sarg. Balm of Gilead. A hybrid between *P. deltoides* and *P. balsamifera.* Escaped from cultivation. Map 816. [*P. x. gileadensis; P. balsamum-gileadense; P. candicans*].

9. *P. balsamífera* L. (balsamic). Balsam Poplar. River and pond margins, mixed moist to dry woods. April-May. Map 817. [*P. tacamahacca; P. trichocarpa*].Our plants include subsp. *balsamifera* and the following subsp.:

subsp. *trichocárpa* (T.&G.) Brayshaw. Ovaries and fruits ovate to globose, pubescent, 3-carpellate, fruit 3-valved, stamens 30 or more (ovaries and fruits lanceolate, glabrous, 2-carpellate, fruit 2-valved, stamens about 20 in subsp. *balsamifera*). [*P. trichocarpa; P. balsamifera* var. *californica*]. —FACW

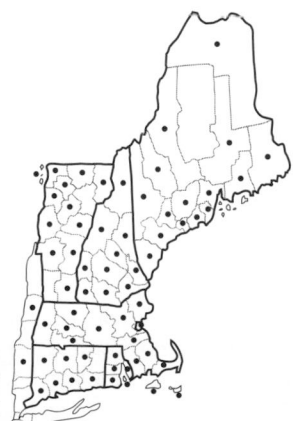
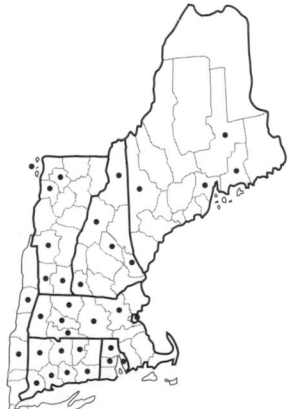

809. *Populus grandidentata*   810. *Populus deltoides*   811. *Populus nigra*

812. *Populus tremuloides*

813. *Populus alba*

814. *Populus x canescens*

815. *Populus heterophylla*

816. *Populus x jackii*

817. *Populus balsamifera*

Family 62. Myricáceae (Sweet Gale Family)

Monoecious or dioecious aromatic shrubs. Buds small, subglobose to ovoid, uniform in size or, in plants with staminate flowers, 6-12 of the buds (often the upper) much larger than the others, leaf scars half elliptic to somewhat 3-sided, bundle traces 3, stipule scars small or absent, pith small, angled, end bud lacking. Leaves deciduous, coriaceous, alternate, simple, entire, toothed, or pinnatifid, mostly short-petioled, stipulate or estipulate, resinous-dotted, aromatic when crushed. Flowers imperfect, the staminate and pistillate in separate, stiff to flexuous, cylindric to globose, axillary catkins, in the same or separate plants, perianth lacking, flower solitary in the axil(s) of 1 or more bracts; staminate flowers of 2-many (usually 4-8) stamens; pistillate flowers consisting of a single pistil, the ovary 1-locular, superior, containing a single ovule, style very short, stigmas 2, linear. Fruit an ovoid to globose nutlet often covered with a waxy coat, often clustered.

Leaves pinnately lobed (Fig. 370) .... 1. *Comptonia peregrina*
Leaves entire or merely toothed .... 2. *Myrica*

1. *Comptónia* L'Her ex Ait. (for H. Compton).

Low, monoecious or dioecious, pubescent shrubs, leaves narrow, deeply pinnatifed, stipulate; staminate catkins flexuous, cylindric, the pistillate ovoid to globose, bur-like, ovary subtended by 8 linear-subulate persistent bractlets overtopping and forming an involucre to the nutlet. [*Myrica*].

1. *C. peregrína* (L.) Coult. (foreign). Sweet-fern. Dry fields, open deciduous woods, roadsides, gravel pits and waste places. April-May. Fig. 370, Map 818. [*Myrica asplenifolia*]. Tea made from the leaves has been used as a cure for diarrhea; crushed leaves were used by Indians as a cure for poison ivy.

2. *Mýrica* L. (Greek name for a fragrant shrub).

Mostly dioecious shrubs; leaves entire or toothed, estipulate; staminate catkins cylindric, the pistillate cylindric to ovoid, ovary subtended by 2-4 bractlets, these not overtopping the nutlet (or bractlets absent); nutlets covered with a waxy coat or resinous atoms. Dried leaves of both species can be used as a substitute for commercially sold bay leaves to flavor stews, roasts etc.—WILDl. 2

Catkins borne at the summits of the twigs; fruit not wax-covered. .... 1. *M. gale*
Catkins borne on the lower portions of the twigs, below the leafy tips; fruit thickly
    wax-covered .... 2. *M. pensylvanica*

1. *M. gále* L. (old generic name). Sweet Gale. Pond margins, bogs, shrub swamps. April-June. Map 819. (Eurasia). [*Gale palustris*]. Our plants include var. *gale* and the following var.:
    var. *subglábra* (Chev.) Fern. Leaves glabrous or subglabrous (somewhat pubescent in var. *gale*). Crushed leaves useful in treating skin eruptions, i.e. poison ivy, boils; dried leaves have been stored with clothing to protect from moths; nutlets have been used as a spice.—OBL

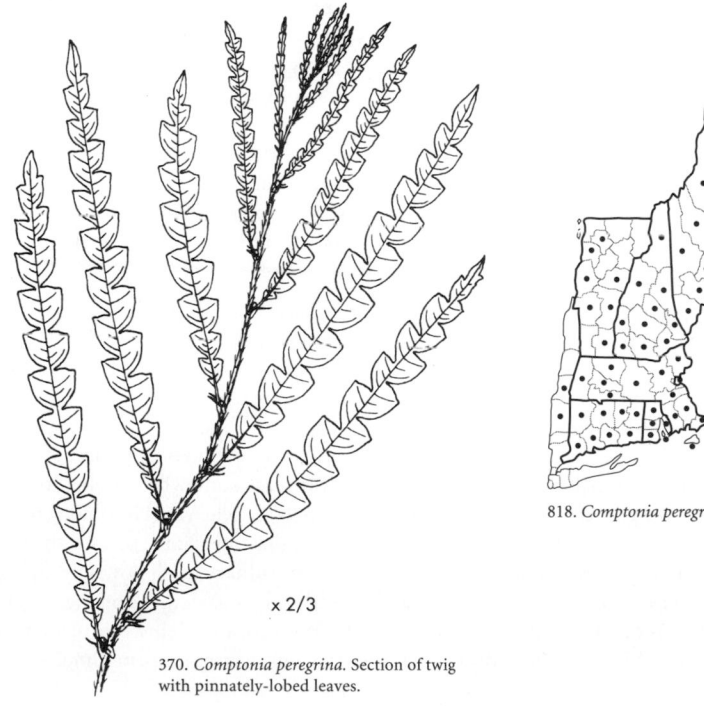

818. *Comptonia peregrina*

× 2/3

370. *Comptonia peregrina*. Section of twig with pinnately-lobed leaves.

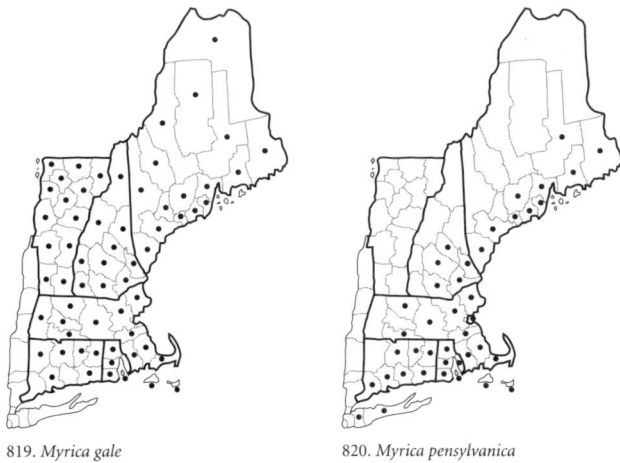

819. *Myrica gale*   820. *Myrica pensylvanica*

2. M. pensylvánica Loisel. (of Pennsylvania). Bayberry. Dry to moist, sandy soil, mostly near the coast. April-May. Map 820. [*M. carolinensis; Cerothamnus c.; Morella p.*]. Waxy fruits are used to make candles. Dried bark of the root is said to have been used by colonists to cure diarrhea, however recent information questions the safety of consuming root preparations of this species.—FAC

Family 63. Juglandáceae (Walnut Family)

Monoecious trees. Leaves deciduous, alternate, estipulate, pinnately compound, the leaflets oppo-site or subopposite, glandular-dotted beneath. Flowers imperfect, the staminate and pistillate in separate inflorescences in the same plant, the staminate in elongate, solitary or fascicled, pendulous catkins at the summit of the previous year's growth, each composed of a primary bract and 2 secondary bracts (sometimes lacking), with a calyx adnate to the bract and 2 bractlets, and few to many stamens on the upper side; pistillate flowers solitary or in small clusters at the tip of the current year's growth, each subtended by a bract (sometimes lacking) and surrounded by a 3-4 lobed, perianth-like involucre adherent to the ovary, this inferior, 2-4 locular, 1 ovulate, styles 2 or absent and 2 sessile stigmas present. Fruit a nut covered by a woody or fibrous, dehiscent or indehiscent husk.

Twigs with a chambered pith; leaflets 9-17, the median lateral the largest. .... 1. *Juglans*
Twigs with a continuous pith; leaflets 5-9, the terminal and upper pair usually
    the largest .... 2. *Carya*

1. Júglans L. Walnut (nut of Jupiter).
Twigs rather stout, with a brown, angular, chambered pith, buds downy, commonly superposed, with several scales, the terminal larger than the laterals, leaf scars somewhat 3-lobed or shield-shaped, bundle traces in 3 groups, stipule scars lacking; leaflets 9-17, nearly sessile, oblong or ovate-lanceolate, acuminate at tip, rounded or cordate and often inequilateral at base, serrate, the median lateral leaflets the longest, pubescent beneath; staminate catkins solitary, each flower composed of a primary bract, 2 secondary bracts and a calyx, all adnate, and with 8-40 stamens on the upper side, pistillate flowers with a 3-lobed involucre and 4 small sepals; fruit with an indehiscent husk enclosing a roughened nut. Nut edible; sap reportedly can be boiled to make syrup in springtime.—Wildl. 2

Leaf scars with a thick, raised mustache across the top; fruit ellipsoid. (Fig. 371) .... 1. *J. cinerea*
Leaf scars without a mustache across the top; fruit ovoid or globose. .... 2. *J. nigra*

1. *J. cinérea* L. (ashy). Butternut. Rich or rocky deciduous woods. April-May. Fig. 371, Map 821. [*Wallia c.*].—FACU+

J. ailanthifólia Carr. Rarely escaped from cultivation in our range; similar to *J. cinerea*, but differs from the latter species in having leaf scars notched at the top and fruits in long racemes (leaf scars not notched and fruits several, not in long racemes in *J. cinerea*). [*J. cordiformis; J. sieboldiana*]. Reported for Knox County ME, Franklin County MA, Providence County RI.

2. *J. nígra* L. (black). Black Walnut. Rich deciduous woods. April-May. Map 822. [*Wallia n.*]. —FACU

2. *Cárya* Nutt. Hickory (ancient Greek name for walnut).

Pith whitish or often brown, angular, continuous, buds commonly superposed, with several scales or 2 valvate scales, the terminal larger than the laterals, leaf scars 3-lobed or shield-shaped, bundle traces either in 3 or 4 distinct groups or scattered, stipule scars lacking; leaflets 5-9, all but the terminal sessile, lanceolate or lance-ovate to elliptic, the terminal oblanceolate or obovate, acute to acuminate at the tip, tapering to rounded and often inequilateral at base, serrate, the terminal and upper pair the largest, glabrous or pubescent; staminate catkins in fascicles of 3, each flower composed of a primary bract and a 2-3 lobed calyx, all adnate, and with 3-8 stamens on the upper side, pistillate flowers with a 4-lobed involucre, sepals absent; fruit with a 4-valved, usually dehiscent husk enclosing a smooth nut. The nuts of all of the species below are edible with the exception of *C. cordiformis*, which is too bitter.—Wildl. 2

a. Buds yellow, their scales in several valvate pairs. .... 1. *C. cordiformis*
a. Buds brown (often somewhat yellowish in *C. ovalis*), their scales imbricated.
  b. Serrations with 1 or more distinct tufts of hairs toward the tips. (Fig. 372) .... 2. *C. ovata*
  b. Serrations glabrous or ciliate but without distinct tufts of hairs.
    c. Terminal buds 12 mm or more long.
      Nut terete to slightly compressed, up to 3 cm long; bark not separating
        into plates .... 3. *C. alba*
      Nut strongly compressed, 3 cm or more long; bark separating into plates. ..... 4. *C. laciniosa*
    c. Terminal buds less than 12 mm long.
      Mature bark rough and furrowed, not separating into plates; husk
        splitting to the middle or remaining closed; nut bitter, not edible. ...... 5. *C. glabra*
      Mature bark separating into long plates; husk promptly splitting to the
        base; nut sweet and edible .... 6. *C. ovalis*

1. *C. cordifórmis* (Wang.) K. Koch (heart-shaped, from the nut). Bitternut. Open deciduous woods, edges of fields. May-June. Map 823. Endangered in ME.—FACU+

C. x láneyi Sarg. A hybrid between *C. cordiformis* and *C. ovata*.

2. *C. ováta* (Mill.) K. Koch (ovate, from the nut). Shagbark. Rich deciduous woods, field fencerows, roadsides. May-June. Fig. 372, Map 824.—FACU-

3. *C. álba* (L.) Nutt. ex Ell. Mockernut. Mixed or deciduous woods, fields, roadsides. May-June. Map 825. [*C. tomentosa*].

4. *C. laciniósa* (Michx. f.) G. Don (slashed, from the plates of bark). Big Shellbark. Floodplains and rich woods. Rare; Concord, MA; from the west or south.—FAC

5. *C. glábra* (P. Mill.) (smooth). Sweet Pignut. Rich, deciduous woods, old fields, roadsides. May-June. Map 826. Our plants include var. *glabra* and the following var.:

var. *hirsúta* (Ashe) Ashe. Petioles, rachises and lower leaf surfaces pubescent (glabrous or glabrate in var. *glabra*). [*C. ovalis* var. *h.*].—FACU-

6. *C. ovális* (Wang.) Sarg. (oval). Sweet Pignut. Rich deciduous woods. May-June. Map 826a. [*C. microcarpa; Hickoria borealis*].

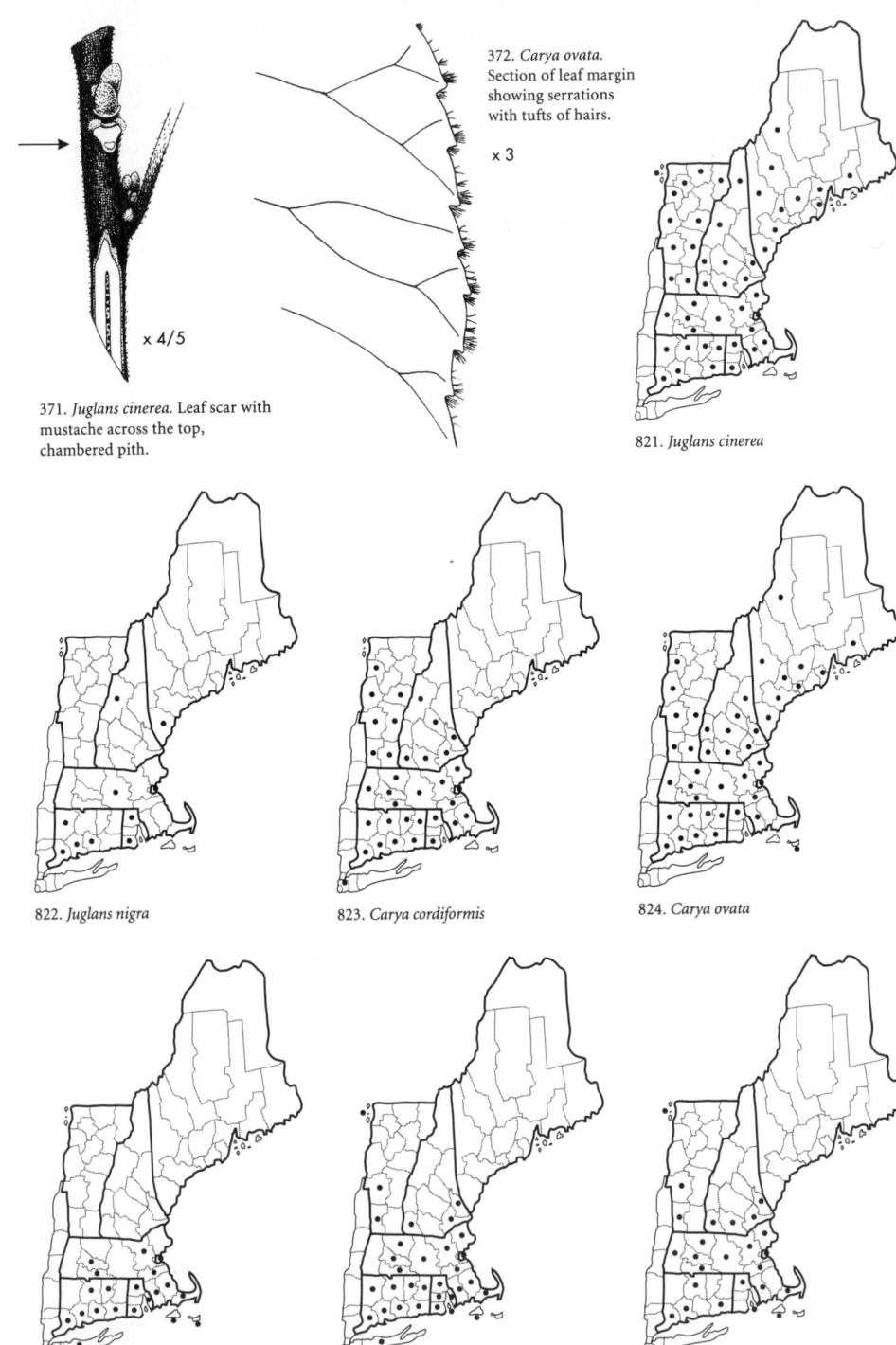

371. *Juglans cinerea*. Leaf scar with mustache across the top, chambered pith.

× 4/5

372. *Carya ovata*. Section of leaf margin showing serrations with tufts of hairs.

× 3

821. *Juglans cinerea*

822. *Juglans nigra*

823. *Carya cordiformis*

824. *Carya ovata*

825. *Carya alba*

826. *Carya glabra*

826a. *Carya ovalis*

Family 64. Betuláceae (Birch Family)

Monoecious trees or shrubs. Leaves deciduous, alternate, stipulate (often deciduous), simple, petiolate, serrate. Flowers imperfect, the staminate and pistillate in separate inflorescences in the same plant, the inflorescence with numerous spirally arranged, separate or imbricated scales, each subtending 1-3 flowers, the perianth lacking or very small; staminate flowers in slender, pendulous catkins, stamens 2-10; pistillate flowers in erect, spreading or drooping clusters, spikes, or catkins, ovary inferior, 2-locular, 4-ovulate, styles 2. Fruit a 1-seeded nut, nutlet or samara.

a. Fruit 1 cm or more long; pistillate flowers clustered in ovoid buds, not in catkins ...... 1. *Corylus*
a. Fruit less than 1 cm long; pistillate flowers in spikes or catkins.
  b. Fruiting catkins pendulous; fruit wingless.
      Fruit enclosed in an inflated, saccate involucre; bark grayish-brown, scaly
        and shredding. (Fig. 374) .... 2. *Ostrya virginiana*
      Fruit subtended by a 2-3 lobed foliaceous bract; bark smooth, the trunk
        vertically fluted. (Fig. 375) .... 3. *Carpinus*
  b. Fruiting catkins erect or if pendulous, fruits winged.
      Pistillate scales unlobed or merely erose, persistent, woody; leaves not paired .... 4. *Alnus*
      Pistillate scales 3-lobed, deciduous with fruits; leaves often paired on short
        shoots .... 5. *Betula*

1. *Córylus* L. Hazel-nut (classical Greek name).

Shrubs or small trees, twigs somewhat slender, zig-zag, pith roundish to somewhat triangular, pale, buds ovoid, with 4-6 scales, end bud lacking, leaf scars half rounded, with 3 distinct or many indistinct bundle scars, stipule scars present, elongate; leaves oblong to ovate, acute to short-acuminate at tip, rounded or subcordate at base, sharply doubly serrate, pubescent beneath; staminate catkins appearing in autumn, solitary or 2-3 together at the ends of the previous year's growth, the scales mucronate, each with a single flower consisting of 8, 1-locular anthers cohering to the inner face of the scale, pistillate flowers in ovoid buds at the ends of the current season's growth, each bud scale subtending a single flower, the flower subtended by a minute bract and 2 bractlets, with 2 exserted, red stigmas, the bract and bractlets enlarging in fruit and forming a leaf-like involucre around the fruit; fruit a nut, the leaf-like involucre distinct or united and forming a beak. Nuts edible.—Wildl. 2

Twigs and leaf petioles stipitate-glandular; involucral bracts united for half or
    less their length, not extended into a beak. .... 1. *C. americana*
Twigs and leaf petioles not stipitate-glandular although often pubescent;
    involucral bracts united to near apex, extended into a beak. (Fig. 373). .... 2. *C. cornuta*

    1. *C. americána* Walt. (American). American H. Deciduous woods and woodland borders, thickets, roadsides and waste places. April-May. Map 827.—FACU-
    2. *C. cornúta* Marsh. (horned). Beaked H. Same habitats as *C. americana*. April-May. Fig. 373, Map 828. [*C. rostrata*.]. Our plants are var. *cornuta*.—FACU-

2. *Ostrya* Scop. Hop Hornbeam (Greek name for a tree with hard wood).

Tree with light grayish-brown scaly bark, twigs and pith as in *Carpinus*, buds ovoid, with 6-8 longitudinally striate scales, end bud lacking, leaf scars crescent-shaped to half-elliptic, with 3 bundle traces, stipule scars present; leaves oblong to ovate, short-acuminate at tip, rounded or subcordate at base, sharply doubly serrate, pubescent beneath; staminate catkins often in 2s or 3s, at the summit of the previous year's growth, the scales mucronate, each subtending a single flower of several stamens, pistillate catkins short, slender, at the tips of the current year's growth, the scales deciduous, each subtending 2 flowers, each enclosed within an ovoid pouch, which becomes enlarged and bladder-like in fruit, these loosely imbricated, drooping, and resembling a strobile like that of hops; fruit an ovoid, compressed nutlet within a bladder-like pouch.—Wildl. 1

1. *O. virginiána* (Mill.) K. Koch (Virginian). Moist, rich to dry deciduous woods. April-May. Fig. 374, Map 829. Our plants are var. *virginiana*.—FACU

3. *Carpínus* L. Ironwood (ancient Latin name).

Tree with vertically fluted trunk having smooth, gray bark, twigs slender, zig-zag, pith small, round or angled, light-colored, buds small, ovoid, 4-angled, with 10-12 scales in 4 ranks, end bud lacking, leaf scars crescent-shaped, with 3 bundle traces, stipule scars present; leaves oblong to ovate, acute or acuminate at tip, rounded or subcordate at base, sharply doubly serrate; staminate catkins linear-cylindric, pendulous, at the summit of the previous year's growth, each scale subtending a single flower of several stamens, pistillate flowers in short, slender catkins at the tips of the current year's growth, the scales deciduous, each subtending 2 flowers, each flower subtended by a bractlet which becomes enlarged, foliaceous, and 3-lobed in fruit, the entire fruiting structure a loose, pendulous cluster; fruit a small, ribbed nutlet, 1 to each 3-lobed bractlet.—Wildl. 1

1. *C. caroliniána* Walt. (of Carolina). Rich, moist, deciduous woods and along streams. April-May. Fig. 375, Map 830. Represented with us as subsp. *virginiana*. (Marsh.) Furlow.—FAC

C. *bétulus* L. European Hornbeam. Differs from the latter species in having larger fruiting bracts (longer than 3 cm) and glabrous or subglabrous buds 6 mm or more long (bracts to 3 cm long and buds pubescent and 5 mm or less long in *C. caroliniana*). Rarely escaped from cultivation. Reported for Suffolk County NY. A preparation made from the leaves has been used as an eye lotion and in a compress to heal small wounds because of its astringent properties.

4. *Álnus* Mill. Alder (ancient Latin name).

Shrubs or small trees, pith triangular, buds stalked, with 2 or 3 valvate scales (sessile, with 3-6 imbricated scales in *A. crispa*), end bud present, leaf scars half rounded, with 3 bundle traces (sometimes compound), stipule scars present; leaves ovate to obovate, cuneate, rounded or subcordate at base, obtuse to short-acuminate at tip, sharply singly or doubly serrate; catkins usually clustered, appearing in autumn, the staminate pendulous, each scale with 3 flowers cohering to the inner face, each flower with a 4-parted calyx and 4 stamens, the pistillate catkins erect, each scale subtending 2 flowers without a calyx, each with 2 styles, the catkins ovoid, cone-like, with woody bracts in fruit; fruit a small, compressed, winged or wingless nutlet.—Wildl. 2

a. Leaves broadly fan-shaped to suborbicular, retuse at apex. (Fig. 376). .... 1. *A. glutinosa*
a. Leaves ovate, elliptic or obovate, acute or obtuse but not retuse at apex.
  b. Racemes of pistillate catkins leafy; leaf buds sessile, with 3 or more unequal,
    imbricate scales. (Fig. 377) .... 2. *A. viridis*
                                                           subsp. *crispa*
  b. Racemes of pistillate catkins leafless; leaf buds stalked, with 2 or 3 valvate scales.
    Leaves widest at or below middle, doubly serrate with unequal teeth, often
      shallowly lobed or wavy-margined .... 3. *A. incana*
                                                           subsp. *rugosa*
    Leaves widest above the middle, simply serrate with nearly equal teeth,
      only rarely wavy-margined .... 4. *A. serrulata*

1. *A. glutinósa* (L.) Gaertn. (gummy). Black Alder. Escaped from cultivation. April-May. Fig. 376, Map 831. (Introduced from Europe). [*A. alnus; A. vulgaris*].—FACW-

2. *A. víridis* (Vill.) Lam. & DC. (Ait.) Turrill. Mountain Alder. River shores, rocky slopes and alpine areas. Fig. 377, Map 832. Our plants are subsp. *críspa*. Turrill. [*A. alnobetula; A. crispa*].—FAC

3. *A. incána* (L.) Moench. Speckled Alder. Pond and stream margins, marshes, shrub swamps. March-May. Map 833. Our plants are subsp. *rugósa* (Du Roi) Clausen. [*A. incana* var. *americana*; *A. rugosa*]. Reported to have been used by Indians as a cure for dropsy.—FACW+

4. *A. serruláta* (Ait.) Willd. (finely saw-toothed). Smooth Alder. Pond and stream margins, marshes, shrub swamps. March-May. Map 834. [*A. rugosa*].—OBL

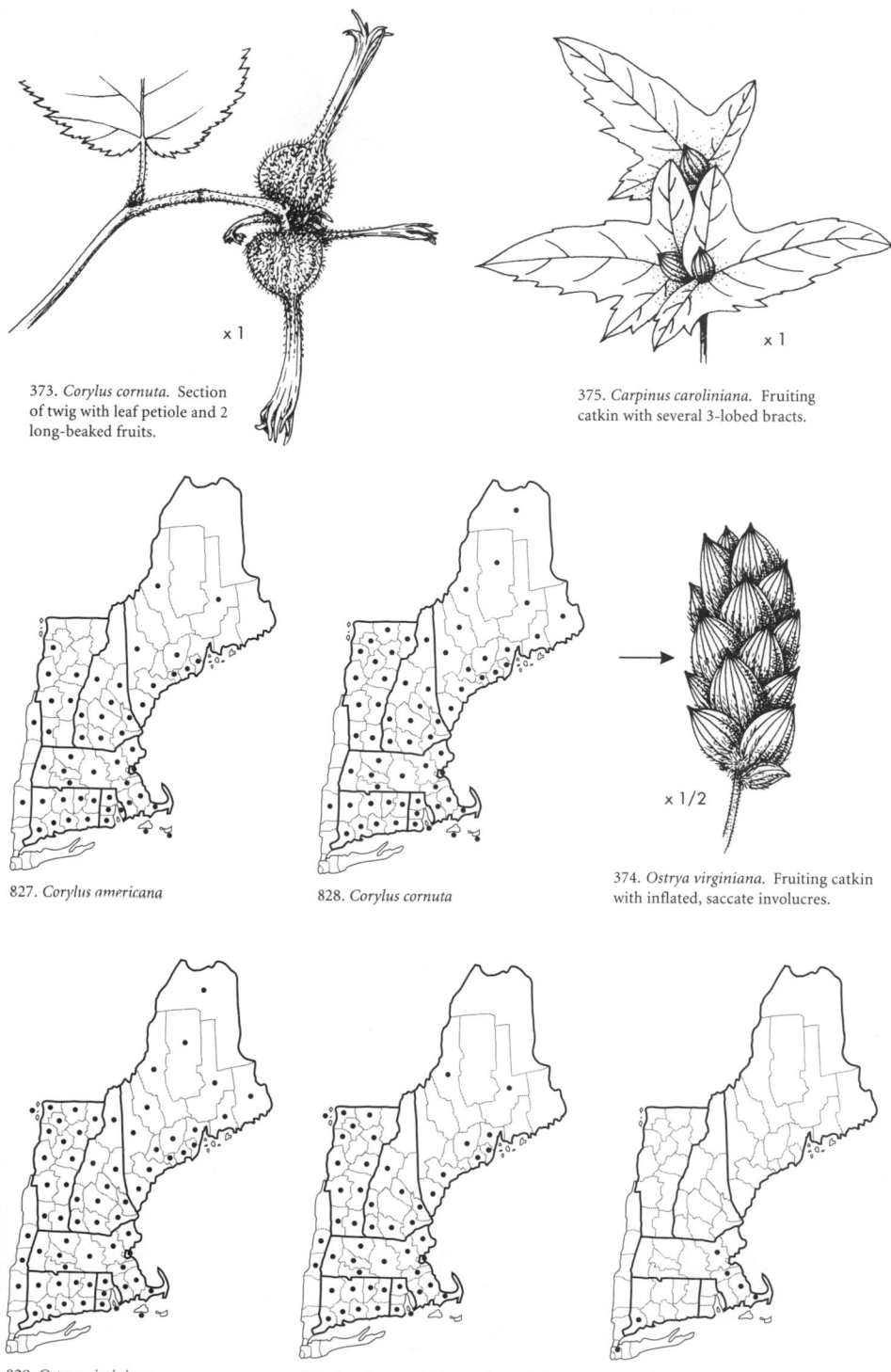

373. *Corylus cornuta.* Section of twig with leaf petiole and 2 long-beaked fruits.

375. *Carpinus caroliniana.* Fruiting catkin with several 3-lobed bracts.

827. *Corylus americana*

828. *Corylus cornuta*

374. *Ostrya virginiana.* Fruiting catkin with inflated, saccate involucres.

829. *Ostrya virginiana*

830. *Carpinus caroliniana* subsp. *virginiana*

831. *Alnus glutinosa*

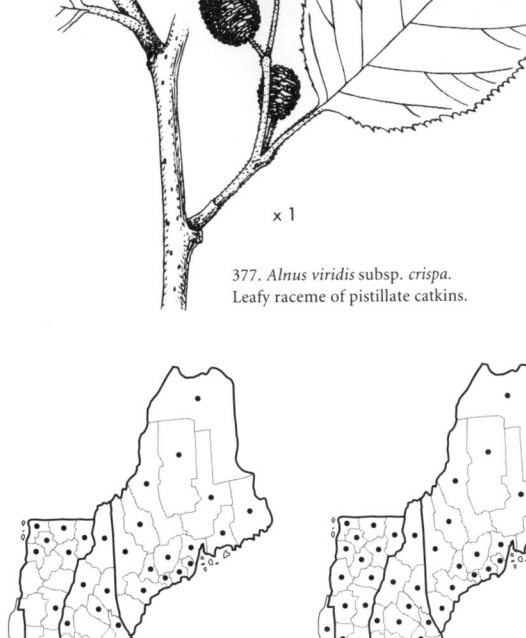

× 1

377. *Alnus viridis* subsp. *crispa*.
Leafy raceme of pistillate catkins.

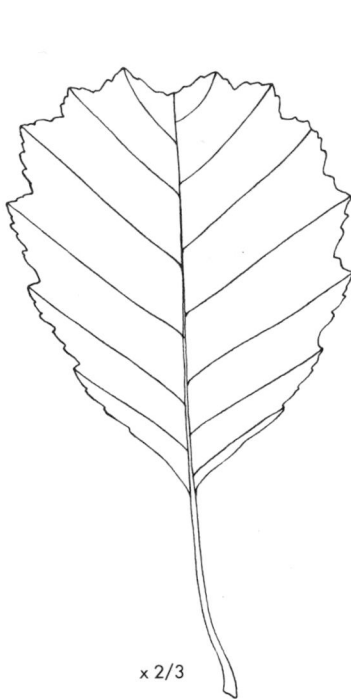

× 2/3

376. *Alnus glutinosa*. Single leaf,
suborbicular with retuse apex.

832. *Alnus viridis* subsp. *crispa*

833. *Alnus incana* subsp. *rugosa*

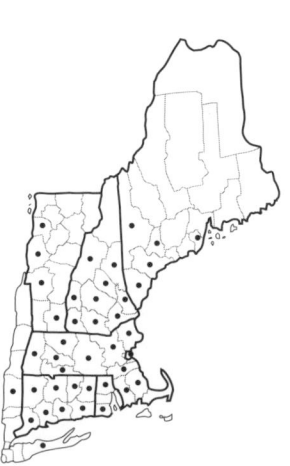

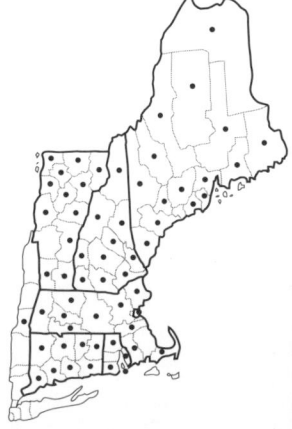

834. *Alnus serrulata*

835. *Betula lenta*

836. *Betula alleghaniensis*

5. Bétula L. Birch (ancient Latin name).

Trees or shrubs with outer bark often peeling in sheets, marked by horizontally elongate lenticels, twigs slender, often developing into short shoots such that the lateral buds appear stalked, pith very small, angled, greenish, buds sessile, ovoid, with 2-3 or more scales, end bud lacking (except on the short shoots), leaf scars crescent-shaped to half-elliptic, bundle traces usually 3, stipule scars present; leaves ovate, oblong or elliptic, singly or doubly serrate, typically occurring in pairs on the short shoots; staminate catkins elongate, sessile, terminal and lateral, pendulous, formed in late summer or early fall, each scale with 3 flowers cohering to the inner face, each flower with a scale-like calyx bearing 4, 1-locular anthers, pistillate catkins usually terminal on the short shoots, erect or spreading, ovoid, the scales usually 3-lobed, each subtending 2-3 flowers without a calyx, each with 2 styles. Fruit a samara composed of a nutlet with 2 lateral wings. The inner bark of the birches is edible raw, cut into strips and boiled or dried and ground into flour.—Wildl. 3

a. Leaves with 9-12 pairs of prominent veins; pistillate catkins sessile or
 subsessile (peduncled in *B. nigra*); wings of samara narrower than body;
 samara not or barely retuse; bark brown, yellowish or grayish.
 b. Leaves rounded to subcordate at base; twigs with odor and taste of wintergreen.
  Bark dark brown, not peeling or flaking; pistillate scales glabrous. .... 1. *B. lenta*
  Bark yellowish to grayish, peeling in thin layers; pistillate scales pubescent .... 2. *B. alleghaniensis*
 b. Leaves cuneate at base; twigs lacking wintergreen odor and taste. (Fig. 378) .... 3. *B. nigra*
a. Leaves usually with fewer than 9 pairs of prominent veins; pistillate catkins peduncled.
 c. Bark of trunk brown or dark; wings of samara narrower than body
  (except *B. x minor*) samara not or barely retuse.
  d. Tree, with exfoliating bark; leaves with 6-10 pairs of prominent veins. .... 3. *B. nigra*
  d. Shrubs, bark not exfoliating; leaves with 3-6 pairs of prominent veins.
   e. Leaves obovate to orbicular, usually rounded at apex.
    Twigs covered with resinous, wart-like glands, glabrous or puberulent. ...... 4. *B. nana*
    Twigs without resinous glands, usually very pubescent with long hairs. .... 5. *B. pumila*
   e. Leaves ovate, acute or obtuse at apex.
    Twigs and leaves glabrous .... 6. *B. minor*
    Twigs and leaves pubescent .... 7. *B. borealis*
 c. Bark of mature trunk white; wings of samara as wide or wider than body;
  samara deeply retuse. (Fig. 379).
  f. Leaves usually pubescent beneath on the veins or in their axils.
   Terminal twigs densely pubescent when mature; leaves mostly 3-5 cm
    long; pistillate catkins 1-3 cm long; occasionally escaped from
    cultivation. ,,.. 8. *B. pubescens*
   Terminal twigs glabrous when mature; leaves mostly 5-10 cm long;
    pistillate catkins 3-5 cm long; native .... 9. *B. papyrifera*
  f. Leaves glabrous beneath.
   g. Bark not exfoliating; small, sapling-like tree; staminate catkins solitary. .... 10. *B. populifolia*
   g. Bark exfoliating; large tree; staminate catkins usually more than 1.
    h. Twigs pendulous; leaves cuneate to truncate at base. .... 11. *B. pendula*
    h. Twigs not pendulous.
     Leaves 4-6 cm long, cuneate to truncate at base. .... 12. *B. platyphylla*
      var. *szechuanica*
     Leaves 6-8 cm long, rounded at base .... 13. *B. x caerulea*
      var. *grandis*

1. B. lénta L. (tough or flexible). Black Birch. Rich woods, streambanks. April-May. Map 835. Inner bark (particularly of the stump and roots) and twigs of this and the next species can be used to make tea; sap is also made into syrup in the same manner as sugar maple.—FACU

2. B. alleghaniénsis Britt. (of the Allegheny Mts.). Yellow Birch. Rich, often moist woods, streambanks. May-June. Map 836. [*B. lutea*]. Our plants include var. *alleghaniensis* and the following var.:

var. *macrólepis* Fern. Bracts of pistillate catkins 8 mm or longer (shorter than 8 mm in var. *alleghaniensis*).—FAC

B. x purpúsii Schneid. A hybrid between *B. alleghaniensis* and *B. pumila*.

3. B. nígra L. (black). River Birch. River and streambanks. April-May. Fig. 378, Map 837.—FACW

4. B. nána L. Dwarf Birch. Alpine areas of the White Mountains and Mt. Katahdin. June-July. Endangered in ME, NY. Reported for VT, Piscataquis County ME, Coos County NH. [*B. glandulosa*].—OBL

5. B. púmila L. (dwarf). Low Birch. Bogs. May-June. Map 838. Endangered in VT, NH. Our plants include var. *pumila* and the following var.:

var. *renifólia* Fern. Leaves of fertile branches orbicular to reniform, rounded at base, nearly or quite as broad as long (leaves obovate, narrowed to base, longer than broad in var. *pumila*).—OBL

6. B. minor (Tuckerm.) Fern. (smaller). Dwarf White Birch. Higher mountains of N. New England. June-July. Endangered in ME, NY.

7. B. boreális Spach. Calcareous soil, often alpine. Canadian. Reported for ME, NH, VT and Franklin County MA.

8. B. pubéscens Ehrh. European White Birch. Escaped from cultivation to roadsides and damp thickets. April-May. Map 839. (Introduced from Europe). [*B. alba*]. Our plants are subsp. *pubéscens*. Sap of this and the next species reportedly has been used to make syrup.—FAC+

9. B. papyrífera Marsh. (paper bearing). Paper Birch. Upland woods. April-May. Fig. 379, Map 840. Our plants include var. *papyrifera* and the following vars.:

var. *commutáta* (Regel) Fern. Bark brownish, peeling only on older trunks (white and peeling on young trunks in var. *papyrifera*).

var. *cordifólia* (Regel) Fern. Leaves truncate to subcordate or cordate at base (leaves cuneate to rounded at base in vars. *papyrifera* and *commutata*). [*B. cordifolia*]. Leaves have been used by Indians to make tea.—FACU

10. B. populifólia Marsh. (poplar-leaved). Gray Birch. Abandoned fields, gravel pits roadsides and waste places, in poor, wet or dry soil. April-May. Map 841.—FAC

11. B. péndula Roth (drooping). European Weeping Birch. Escaped from cultivation to roadsides, thickets and woods. April-May. Map 842.

12. B. platyphýlla Sukat. Asian White Birch. Escaped from cultivation; established along Neponset River, Massachusetts. [*B. mandshurica*]. Represented with us as var. *szechuánica* Schneid.

13. B. x caerúlea Blanch. Dry woods. May-June. Map 843. Our plants are var. *grándis* Blanch. [*B. caerulea-grandis*].

B. x caerúlea var. *caerúlea* is a hybrid between *B. x caerulea* var. *grandis* and *B. populifolia*.

Family 65. Fagáceae (Beech Family)

Monoecious trees or shrubs. Leaves deciduous (ours), alternate, simple, entire, toothed, or lobed, petioled, straight-veined, stipules deciduous. Flowers imperfect, the staminate and pistillate in separate inflorescences in the same plant, the staminate in catkins or heads, subtended by an early-deciduous bract, each with a small 4-8 lobed calyx and 3-20 stamens; pistillate flowers solitary or in small clusters, enclosed within an involucre of bracts, and with a 4-8 (mostly 6) lobed calyx adnate to the ovary, this inferior, 3-6 locular, each locule 1 or 2 ovulate, styles 3-6. Fruit a 1-seeded nut subtended or enclosed within a cup composed of wholly or partly fused, indurated bracts.

a. Leaves serrate; buds not clustered at tips of the twigs; nuts 2-3, enclosed in a spiny
       or bristly, 2-4 lobed involucre.
    Mature buds narrowly cylindric, more than 1 cm long; nut sharply triangular. ...... 1. *Fagus*
    Mature buds ovoid, less than 8 mm long; nut rounded on at least 1 side. .... 2. *Castanea*
a. Leaves usually lobed or crenate, seldom dentate; buds clustered at tips of the twigs;
       nut solitary, the base or rarely all of the nut covered by a scaly cup .... 3. *Quercus*

1. Fágus L. Beech (classical Latin name).

Trees with smooth gray bark, twigs slender, zig-zag, pith small, round, buds divergent, long and narrowly cylindric, with 10 or more scales, end bud present, leaf scars half round, bundle traces 3 or sometimes compound or in irregular clusters, stipule scars nearly meeting around the twig; leaves oblong to ovate, acute to acuminate at tip, cuneate to rounded at base, serrate, pubescent beneath, at least on the veins, some of the dead, brown leaves usually persisting long into winter; flowers appearing with the leaves, the staminate in small pendulous heads from the lower leaf axils, yellowish-green, each subtended by a deciduous bract, the pistillate usually in pairs on a short peduncle, enclosed by an involucre of numerous subulate bracts, ovary 3-locular, styles 3; nut 3-angled, usually in pairs within the involucre, this covered with the recurved bracts and splitting into 4 valves.—Wildl

Leaves acuminate, with more than 9 pairs of veins, distinctly toothed, the teeth
    narrow and sharply acuminate. (Fig. 380). .... 1. *F. grandifolia*
Leaves obtuse to acute, with 9 or fewer pairs of veins, nearly entire to merely
    undulate, or if toothed the teeth wide and obtuse to acute. .... 2. *F. sylvatica*

1. *F. grandifólia* Ehrh. (large-leaved). American Beech. Rich, mixed upland woods. April-May. Fig. 380, Map 844.

Our plants include var. *grandifolia* and the following var.:

var. *caroliniána* (Loudon) Fern. & Rehder. Leaves often merely denticulate, prickles of fruit 3 mm or less long (leaves sharply serrate and prickles of fruit 4 mm or more long in var. *grandifolia*). Nut edible; nut sometimes also roasted, ground and used as a coffee substitute; young leaves can be cooked as a potherb; inner bark can be dried and ground into flour as an emergency food.—FACU

2. *F. sylvática* L. (of woods). European Beech. Escaped from cultivation to roadsides. May. Reported for RI, Hancock County ME, Middlesex County MA.

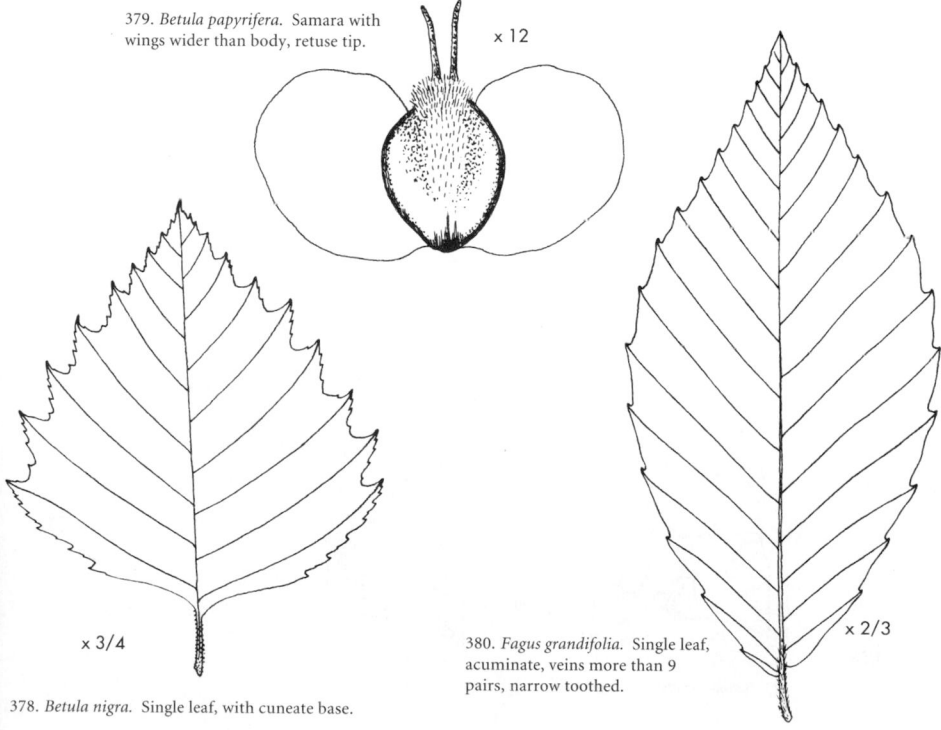

379. *Betula papyrifera.* Samara with wings wider than body, retuse tip.

x 12

x 3/4

378. *Betula nigra.* Single leaf, with cuneate base.

380. *Fagus grandifolia.* Single leaf, acuminate, veins more than 9 pairs, narrow toothed.

x 2/3

837. *Betula nigra*

838. *Betula pumila*

839. *Betula pubescens*

840. *Betula papyrifera*

841. *Betula populifolia*

842. *Betula pendula*

843. *Betula x caerulea* var. *grandis*

844. *Fagus grandifolia*

2. *Castánea* P. Mill. Chestnut (classical Latin name).

Trees or shrubs with smooth (fissured when mature), gray bark, twigs moderate, somewhat fluted, pith moderate, star-shaped, buds ovoid, blunt, with 2 or 3 scales, obliquely positioned over the leaf scar, end bud frequently lacking, leaf scars half round, bundle traces 3, sometimes compound, stipule scars elongate; leaves oblong-lanceolate, acute to acuminate at tip, narrowed to a cuneate or acute base (seldom rounded), sharply serrate, glabrous or pubescent beneath; flowers appearing after the leaves, the staminate in long, narrowly cylindric, interrupted, axillary catkins near the tips of the branches, several flowers in the axil of a minute, deciduous bract, the pistillate usually 2-4 together within an ovoid, prickly involucre, these borne at the bases of staminate catkins or in separate axils, ovary usually 6-locular, styles 6; nuts solitary or 2-3 together within the long-spined, 2-4 valved involucre.

Leaves glabrous or essentially so beneath. .... 1. *C. dentata*
Leaves densely pubescent beneath (sometimes less so in shade leaves). .... 2. *C. pumila*

    1. *C. dentáta* (Marsh.) Borkh. (toothed). American Chestnut. Dry upland deciduous woods. June-July. Fig. 381, Map 845. Occuring mostly as sprouts of trees succumbed to chestnut blight.
    2. *C. púmila* (L.) P. Mill. (dwarf). Chinquapin. Dry upland woods and thickets. June-July. Map 846. Our plants are var. *pumila.*
    C. mollíssima Blume. Resembling *C. pumila* but nuts usually 2-3 together (solitary in *C. pumila*). Rarely escaped from cultivation in our range. Reported for Middlesex County MA, Washington County RI.

3. *Quércus* L. Oak (classical Latin name).

Trees or shrubs, twigs moderate to slender, fluted, pith moderate, star-shaped, buds clustered at the tips of the twigs, usually solitary at the nodes but sometimes collaterally multiple, ovoid or subglobose to conical, distinctly angled or with rounded angles, with numerous scales, leaf scars half round, bundle traces numerous, scattered, stipule scars small; leaves pinnately lobed, crenate,

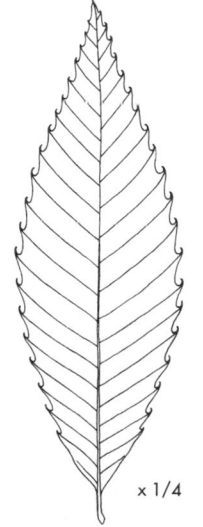

381. *Castanea dentata.* Single leaf, oblong-lanceolate, sharply serrate.

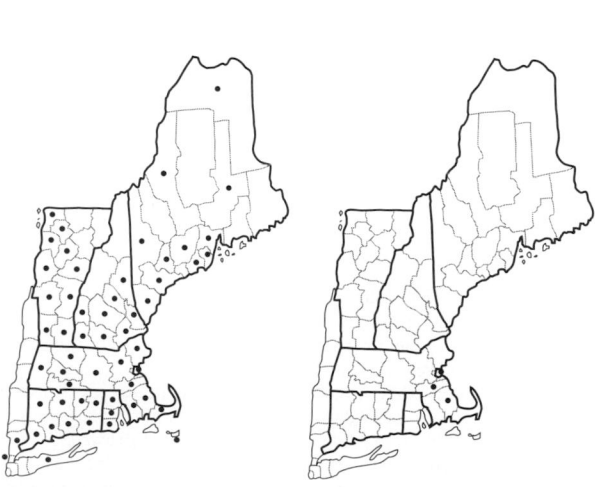

845. *Castanea dentata*

846. *Castanea pumila*

dentate, or rarely entire, some of the dead, brown leaves persisting long into the winter; flowers appearing before the leaves, the staminate in slender, filiform or interrupted pendulous, catkins, these solitary or several from the same lateral bud, subtended by minute, early-deciduous bracts, the pistillate solitary or in short spikes, each flower subtended by a bract and surrounded by an involucre of numerous scales that become indurated and fused forming a cup, ovary 3-locular, stigmas 3; nut solitary within the cup, the cup surrounding the base or nearly covering the nut. Nuts edible, particularly those of the white oak group, after removing hard outer covering, boiling and then roasting or grinding and leaching with water to remove the bitterness caused by tannins; inner bark of the white oaks reported to be useful in treating dysentery after drying and being ground into powder; inner bark of the red oak group has been used as an externally applied astringent. —Wildl. 4

a. Leaves entire or slightly sinuate or shallowly 3-5 lobed at the summit (lobes often
    bristle-tipped).
  b. Leaves obovate, much widened distally and often shallowly 3-5 lobed at the
    summit. (Fig. 382) .... 1. *Q. marilandica*
  b. Leaves lanceolate or linear-oblong, widest near the middle, not lobed.
    Mature leaves pubescent beneath, the petioles mostly longer than .5 cm. .... 2. *Q. imbricaria*
    Mature leaves glabrescent beneath except on midvein or vein axils, nearly
      sessile, the petioles .5 cm long or shorter. .... 3. *Q. phellos*
a. Leaves distinctly toothed or pinnately lobed or dissected.
  c. Lobes of the leaves bristle-tipped.
    d. Mature leaves pubescent beneath over the entire surface.
      Largest buds less than 4 mm long, glabrous or only loosely pubescent;
        scraggly shrub or small tree .... 4. *Q. ilicifolia*
      Largest buds 4 mm or longer, densely pubescent from base to apex;
        large tree. .... 5. *Q. velutina*
    d. Mature leaves glabrous beneath or pubescent only on midvein or vein axils.
      e. Buds tomentose from base to apex; upper scales of acorn cups loosely
        ascending, the free tips forming a loose, marginal fringe. (Fig. 383). .... 5. *Q. velutina*
      e. Buds glabrous, at least at base, or the scales merely ciliate; upper scales of
        acorn cups tightly appressed, not forming a marginal fringe.
        f. Buds densely pubescent on the upper half, acorn cups turbinate, covering
          nearly half of the acorn; leaves deeply lobed. .... 6. *Q. coccinea*
        f. Buds glabrous, or scales merely ciliate; acorn cups saucer-shaped,
          covering a third or less of the acorn.
          Leaves shallowly lobed, the length of the longest dissections mostly
            less than 2 times as long as the width of the uncut central
            portion; lower branches ascending; acorn cups 1.5 cm or more
            wide. (Fig. 384). .... 7. *Q. rubra*
          Leaves deeply lobed, the length of the longest dissections 2 1/2-3 times
            as long as the width of the uncut central portion; lower
            branches horizontal or drooping; acorn cups up to 1.5 cm
            wide. .... 8. *Q. palustris*
  c. Lobes or teeth of the leaves rounded to acute but not bristle-tipped.
    g. Petioles mostly less than 5 mm long.
      Leaf base rounded or cordate, the lobes rounded; tree. .... 9. *Q. robur*
      Leaf base cuneate to attenuate, the lobes ending in a papilla; shrub.
        (Fig. 385) .... 10. *Q. prinoides*
    g. Petioles mostly longer than 5 mm.
      h. Leaves distinctly lobed, the length of the upper side of many of the lobes
        more than 1 cm.
        i. Mature leaves glabrous or only thinly pubescent beneath.
          Leaf lobes 7 or fewer per side; bark not furrowed, light. .... 11. *Q. alba*
          Leaf lobes 8-14 per side; bark deeply furrowed, dark. .... 12. *Q. prinus*
        i. Mature leaves densely pubescent beneath, velvety to the touch
          (except sometimes in *Q. margarettiae*, which has pubescent twigs;
          twigs glabrous in the above 2 species).

j. Lobes not wavy-margined; fruiting peduncles 2 cm or longer; lower
  branches drooping... 13. *Q. bicolor*
j. Lobes, at least some, irregularly wavy-margined; acorns sessile or
  nearly so; lower branches not drooping.
    Leaves with 2-3 main lobes per side, the middle pair larger than
      the others such that leaf resembles a cross; twigs not alate;
      acorn cup scales obtuse to acute .... 14. *Q. margarettiae*
    Leaves with 4-7 main lobes per side; often separated into upper and
      lower parts by a pair of deep sinuses; twigs often alate; acorn
      cup scales caudate-tipped. (Fig. 386) .... 15. *Q. macrocarpa*
  h. Leaves merely toothed or shallowly lobed, the upper sides of the lobes less
    than 1 cm long.
      k. Acorns on peduncles 2 cm or longer, exceeding the petioles; acorn cup
        scales caudate-tipped; lower branches drooping. .... 13. *Q. bicolor*
      k. Acorns sessile or on peduncles not exceeding the petioles; acorn cup
        scales obtuse or acute; lower branches ascending.
          l. Leaf lobes rounded; acorn cup more than 1.8 cm wide. .... 12. *Q. prinus*
          l. Leaf lobes ending in a papilla; acorn cup less than 1.8 cm wide.
            Lobes 8-14 per side; tree, with solitary trunk. .... 16. *Q. muhlenbergii*
            Lobes 7 or fewer per side; shrub, usually with several stems from
              the base. (Fig. 385) .... 10. *Q. prinoides*

1. Q. marilándica Muench. (of Maryland). Black-Jack Oak. Dry, sandy barrens and oak-pine woods. May-June. Fig. 382.
  Q. x búshii Sarg. A hybrid between *Q. marilandica* and *Q. velutina.*
  Q. x rúdkini Britt. (Pro sp.). A hybrid between *Q. marilandica* and *Q. phellos.*
  Q. x brittónii W. T. Davis. A hybrid between *Q. marilandica* and *Q. ilicifolia.*
2. Q. imbricária Michx. (overlapping, from early use for shingles). Shingle-Oak. Dry woods and waste places. Introduced from farther south. April-May. Map 847.—FAC
  Q. x exácta Trel. A hybrid between *Q. imbricaria* and *Q. palustris.*
  Q. x leána Nutt. (Pro. sp.). A hybrid between *Q. imbricaria* and *Q. velutina.*
  Q. x runcináta (A.DC) Engelm. A hybrid between *Q. imbricaria* and *Q. rubra.*
  Q. x tridentáta (A.DC) Engelm. A hybrid between *Q. imbricaria* and *Q. marilandica.*
3. Q. phéllos L. (Greek, for the Cork-Oak). Willow-Oak. Wooded swamps, moist woods, or dry upland fields and woods, along the coast. April-May. CT, NY. Endangered in NY.—FAC+
  Q. x filiális Little. A hybrid between *Q. phellos* and *Q. velutina.*
  Q. x heterophýlla Michx. f. (Pro. sp.). A hybrid between *Q. phellos* and *Q. rubra.*—FAC+
4. Q. ilicifólia Wangenh. (holly-leaved). Scrub-Oak. Dry sandy woods, thickets, barrens and waste places. May. Map 848. Endangered in VT.
  Q. x bríttonii W. T. Davis. (Pro. sp.). A hybrid between *Q. ilicifolia* and *Q. marilandica.*
  Q. x fernáldii Trel. A hybrid between *Q. ilicifolia* and *Q. rubra.*
  Q. x gíffordii Trel. A hybrid between *Q. ilicifolia* and *Q. phellos.*
  Q. x réhderi Trel. A hybrid between *Q. ilicifolia* and *Q. velutina.*
5. Q. velútina Lam. (velvety, from the young foliage). Black Oak. Dry deciduous woods. May. Fig. 383, Map 849.
  Q. x hawkínsiae Sudworth. A hybrid between *Q. velutina* and *Q. rubra.*
6. Q. coccínea Muenchh. (scarlet). Scarlet Oak. Dry deciduous woods. May-June. Map 850. Endangered in ME. Our plants are var. *coccinea*; another var. that has been distinguished is var. *tuberculata* Sarg.
  Q. x bénderi Baenitz. A hybrid between *Q. coccinea* and *Q. rubra.*
  Q. x robbínsii Trel. A hybrid between *Q. coccinea* and *Q. ilicifolia.*
7. Q. rúbra L. (red) Northern Red Oak. Dry to moist, fertile, deciduous or mixed woods. May. Fig. 384, Map 851. [*Q. borealis*]. Our plants include var. *rubra* and the following var.:
  var. *ambígua* (Gray) Fern. A hybrid between *Q. rubra* and *Q. palustris.* [*Q. x richteri*].—FACU

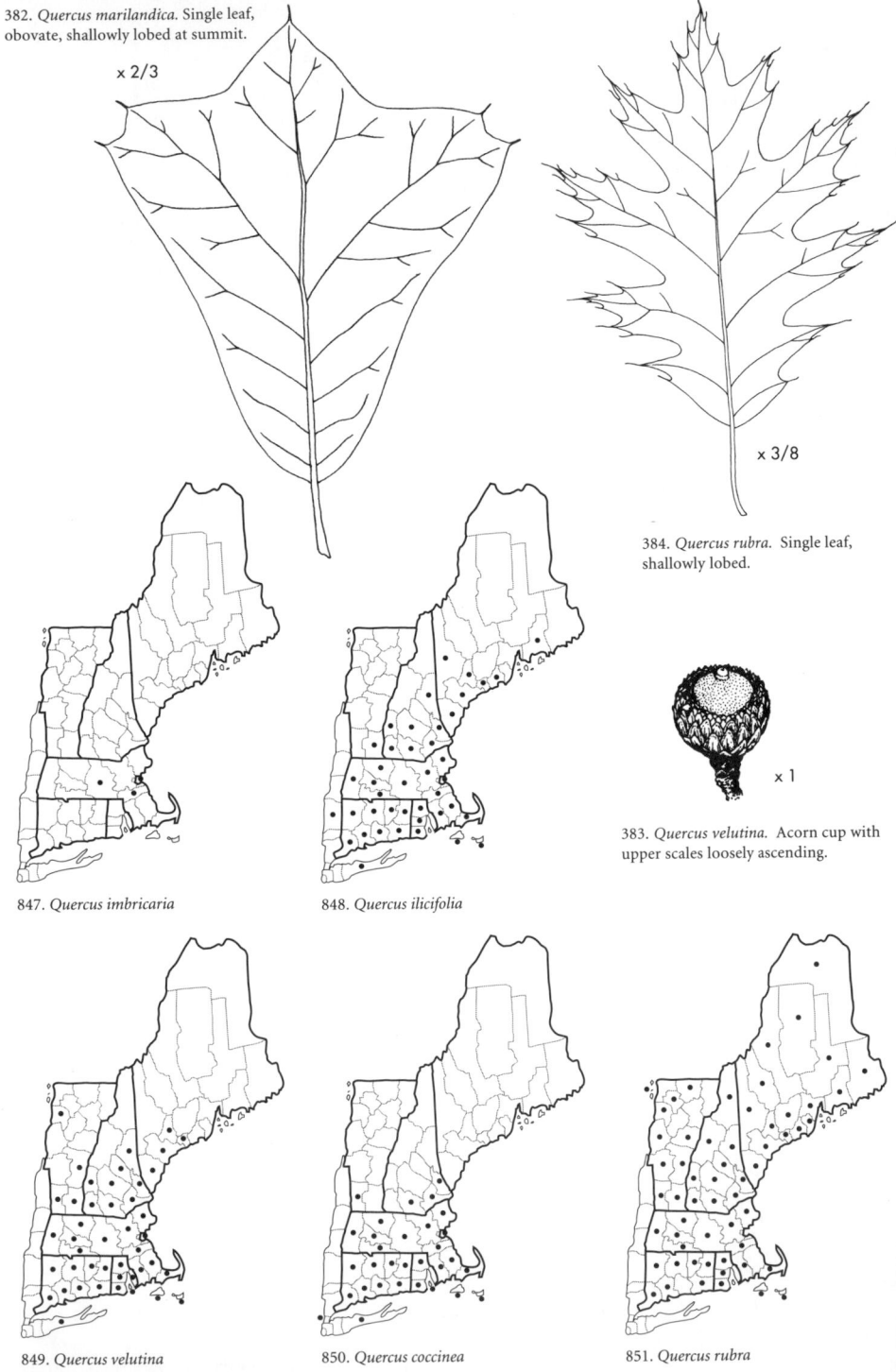

382. *Quercus marilandica.* Single leaf, obovate, shallowly lobed at summit.

x 2/3

x 3/8

384. *Quercus rubra.* Single leaf, shallowly lobed.

x 1

383. *Quercus velutina.* Acorn cup with upper scales loosely ascending.

847. *Quercus imbricaria*

848. *Quercus ilicifolia*

849. *Quercus velutina*

850. *Quercus coccinea*

851. *Quercus rubra*

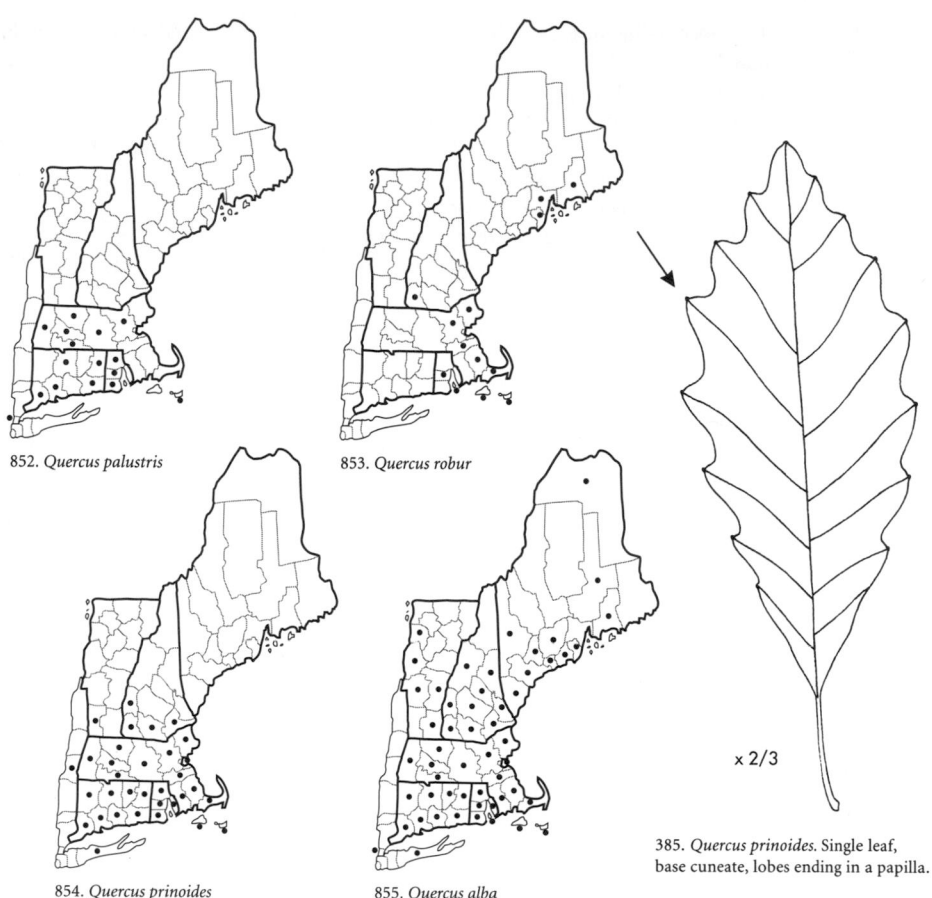

852. *Quercus palustris*

853. *Quercus robur*

854. *Quercus prinoides*

855. *Quercus alba*

x 2/3

385. *Quercus prinoides*. Single leaf, base cuneate, lobes ending in a papilla.

8. Q. palústris Muenchh. (of marshes). Pin Oak. Wooded swamps and wet woods. May-June. Map 852.—FACW

Q. x schochiána Dieck. ex. Palmer. A hybrid between *Q. palustris* and *Q. phellos*.

Q. x vága Palmer & Steyermark. A hybrid between *Q. palustris* and *Q. velutina*.

9. Q. róbur L. (ancient latin name). English Oak. Escaped from cultivation to roadsides and woodland borders. May. Map 853. (Introduced from Europe). Leaves reported as poisonous to livestock.

10. Q. prinoídes Willd. (resembling *Q. prinus*). Dwarf Chestnut Oak. Dry rocky or sandy barrens, fields and thickets. May-June. Fig. 385, Map 854. [*Q. muhlenbergii*].

Q. x stelloídes Palmer. A hybrid between *Q. prinoides* and *Q. stellata*.

11. Q. álba L. (white). White Oak. Dry deciduous or mixed woods and fields. May-June. Map 855.—FACU-

Q. x bebbiána Schneid. A hybrid between *Q. alba* and *Q. macrocarpa*.

Q. x bimundórum Palmer. A hybrid between *Q. alba* and *Q. robur*.

Q. x fernówii Trel. A hybrid between *Q. alba* and *Q. stellata*.

Q. x fáxonii Trel. A hybrid between *Q. alba* and *Q. prinoides*.

Q. x jackiána Schneid. A hybrid between *Q. alba* and *Q. bicolor*.

Q. x saúlii Schneid. A hybrid between *Q. alba* and *Q. prinus*.

12. *Q. prínus* L. (Greek name for European Oak). Chestnut Oak. Dry rocky deciduous woods. May-June. Map 856. Endangered in ME.[*Q. montana*].

Q. x bernardiénsis W. Wolf. (Pro sp.). A hybrid between *Q. prinus* and *Q. stellata*.

Q. x sargéntii Rehd. A hybrid between *Q. prinus* and *Q. robur*.

13. *Q. bícolor* Willd. (two-colored). Swamp White Oak. Bottomlands, stream margins, wooded swamps and wet woods. May-June. Map 857.—FACW+

Q. x schuéttei Trel. A hybrid between *Q. bicolor* and *Q. macrocarpa*.

Q. x substelláta Trel. A hybrid between *Q. bicolor* and *Q. stellata*.

14. *Q. stelláta* Wangenh. Post Oak. Dry upland woods, fields and barrens. May-June. Map 858. [*Q. margarettiae*].

Q. x guadelupénsis Sarg. A hybrid between *Q. stellata* and *Q. macrocarpa*.

15. *Q. macrocárpa* Michx. (large-fruited). Mossy-cup Oak. Bottomlands and moist to dry, rich woods. May-June. Fig. 386, Map 859. Endangered in CT. Our plants are var. *macrocarpa*.—FAC-

Q. x déamii Trel. A hybrid between *Q. macrocarpa* and *Q. muhlenbergii*.

16. *Q. muhlenbérgii* Engelm. (for G.H.E. Muhlenberg). Yellow Oak. Rich bottomlands and calcareous uplands. May-June. Map 860. [*Q. prinoides* var. *acuminata*].

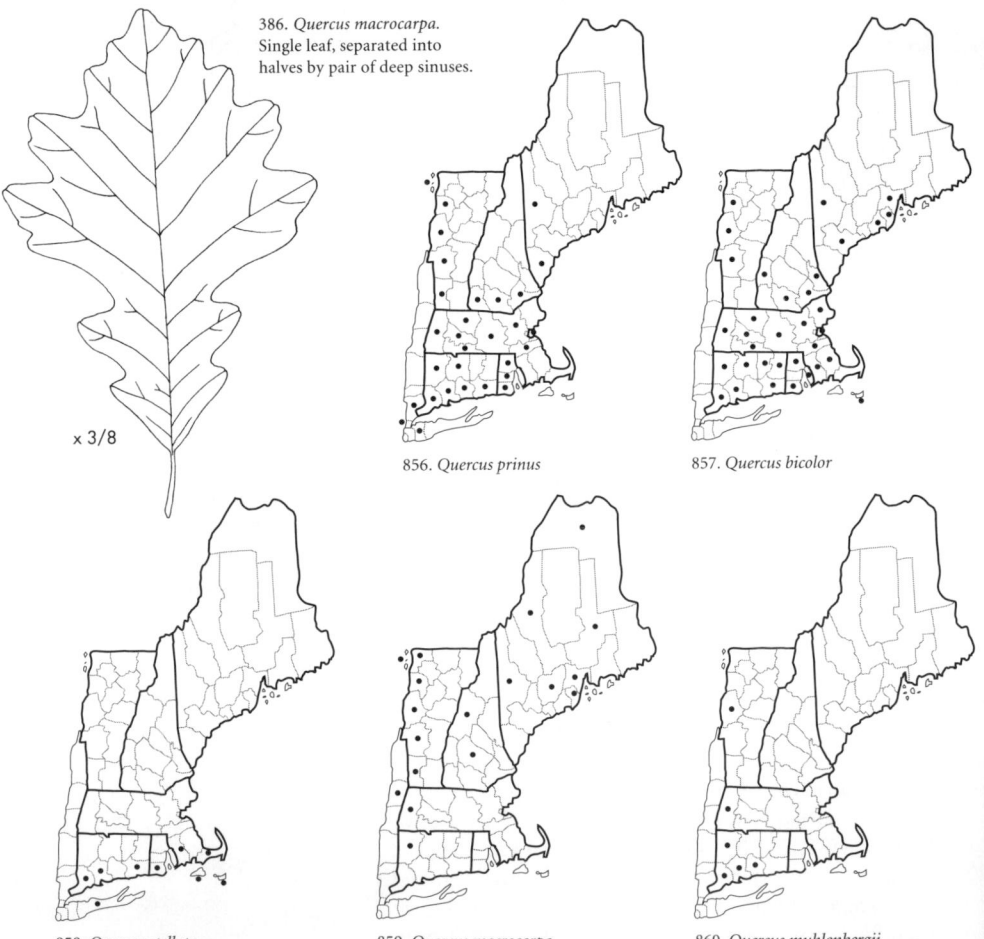

386. *Quercus macrocarpa.*
Single leaf, separated into
halves by pair of deep sinuses.

x 3/8

856. *Quercus prinus*

857. *Quercus bicolor*

858. *Quercus stellata*

859. *Quercus macrocarpa*

860. *Quercus muhlenbergii*

Family 66. Ulmáceae (Elm Family)

Monoecious or polygamous trees. Leaves deciduous, alternate, distichous, simple, serrate (ours), petioled, pinnately veined, mostly obliquely based, stipules deciduous. Flowers perfect or unisexual, small and inconspicuous, in racemes, fascicles or clusters, or the pistillate solitary, petals absent, calyx with 3-9 sepals or lobes, stamens the same number and opposite the sepals or calyx lobes, ovary superior, 2-carpelled, unilocular, with 1 ovule, styles 2. Fruit a samara or drupe.

Leaves with only 1 principal vein; fruit a samara. .... 1. *Ulmus*
Leaves with 3 principal veins from the base; fruit a drupe. (Fig. 389). .... 2. *Celtis occidentalis*

1. *Úlmus* L. Elm (classical Latin name).

Trees with slender, somewhat zig-zag stems, these sometimes corky-winged, pith small, round, buds oblique over the leaf scars, the flower buds much larger than the foliar buds, with about 6, 2-ranked scales, end bud lacking, leaf scars half round, corky, bundle traces 3 or sometimes in 3 compound groups, stipule scars unequal; leaves inequilateral at base, ovate, oblong or obovate, usually doubly serrate, with prominent, straight, pinnate veins, usually pubescent on one or both sides, short-petioled; flowers perfect, in short racemes or fascicles, borne along the twigs of the previous year, appearing before the leaves, calyx campanulate, 4-9 lobed; fruit a flat, oval, 1-seeded, stipitate samara, its wings continuous around the seed except at the tip, which is frequently notched. —Wildl. 2

a. Leaves simply serrate; flowering in autumn. .... 1. *U. parvifolia*
a. Leaves mostly doubly serrate (some of the teeth simple or only slightly toothed in
    U. pumila); flowering in spring.
  b. Principal veins of leaves rarely forking (1 or 2 on an occasional leaf); flowers
      pendulous in racemes or in fascicles on long pedicels of unequal lengths.
      (Fig. 387).
    Second year branches often corky-winged; flowers in racemes; samaras
      pubescent on the sides; scarcely notched at apex .... 2. *U. thomasii*
    Second year branches not corky-winged; flowers in fascicles on long pedicels
      of unequal lengths; samaras glabrous on the sides, notched at apex. .... 3. *U. americana*
  b. Principal veins of leaves often forking (at least 1 or 2 on most leaves); flowers
      not pendulous, not racemose, in fascicles on short pedicels of equal lengths.
      (Fig. 388).
    c. Mature blades less than 4 cm wide, base symmetrical or only slightly
      asymmetrical; calyx glabrous, eciliate; samaras as broad or broader
      than long. .... 4. *U. pumila*
    c. Mature blades mostly 4 cm wide or wider, base strongly asymmetrical; calyx
      pubescent or ciliate; samaras mostly longer than broad.
      d. Blades mostly longer than 10 cm, harshly scabrous above, fragrant in
        drying; calyx pubescent; samaras pubescent on sides; twigs
        mucilaginous. .... 5. *U. rubra*
      d. Blades mostly 10 cm or shorter, smooth or only somewhat scabrous above,
        not fragrant in drying; calyx ciliate; samaras glabrous; twigs not
        mucilaginous.
      Second year branches often corky-winged; seed above the middle of the
        samara. .... 6. *U. minor*
      Second year branches not corky-winged; seed central in samara. .... 7. *U. glabra*

    1. *U. parvifólia* Jacq. (small-leaved). Chinese Elm. Escaped from cultivation to field edges and roadsides. Autumn. Reported for Franklin County MA.
    2. *U. thómasii* Sarg. (for its discoverer). Rock-Elm. Rich, often calcareous woods. April-May. Map 861. [*U. racemosa*].—FACU+
    3. *U. americána* L. (American). American Elm. Wooded swamps, moist woods, stream and pond margins, bottomlands, roadsides and waste places. March-April. Fig. 387, Map 862. Many mature trees killed by Dutch Elm Disease.—FACW-

4. *U. púmila* L. (dwarf). Siberian Elm. Roadsides, woodland borders, abandoned fields, waste places. March-April. Map 863. (Introduced from Asia).

5. *U. rúbra* Muhl. (red). Slippery Elm. Rich, often calcareous or moist deciduous woods, stream borders, woodland borders, roadsides and waste places. March-April. Fig. 388, Map 864. [*U. fulva*]. Inner bark was used as food by Indians; inner bark was also dried and sometimes powdered and used as a remedy for intestinal problems, colds and sore throat.—FAC

6. *U. minor* P. Mill. English Elm. Escaped from cultivation to woodland borders and roadsides. April. Map 865. (Introduced from Europe). [*U procera*].

7. *U. glábra* Huds. (smooth). Wych Elm. Escaped from cultivation to roadsides. April. Map 866. (Introduced from Europe).

2. *Céltis* L. Hackberry (early Greek name for Lotus, with which this genus was confused).

Shrub or tree, the trunks of mature trees often with corky ridges, twigs slender, somewhat zig-zag, pith small, white, closely chambered, buds small, closely appressed, with about 4, 2-ranked scales, end bud lacking, leaf scars oval to crescent-shaped, bundle traces 3 or sometimes the middle one a compound group, stipule scars narrow, twigs often clustered in the crowns as "witches brooms" caused by insect galls; leaves inequilateral at base, ovate to ovate-lanceolate, acuminate at tip, cordate, rounded or cuneate at base, serrate to nearly entire, with 3 principal veins arising from the base, short-petioled, smooth to scabrous above, pubescent on veins below or glabrous; flowers often imperfect, calyx deeply 5-lobed, staminate flowers numerous, in small clusters toward the base of the twigs of the current season, with 5-6 stamens, pistillate flowers solitary or in pairs, on slender pedicels in the axils of the developing leaves, stamens often present; fruit an ovoid to globose drupe with a large stone and thin but sweet flesh.—Wildl. 1

1. *C. occidentális* L. (western). Rich, dry to moist deciduous woods and sand barrens. April-May. Fig. 389, Map 867. Represented with us by the following vars.:

var. *púmila* (Pursh) Gray. Leaves less than twice as long as wide. [*C. georgiana; C. occidentalis* var. *p.*].

var. *canína* (Raf.) Sarg. Leaves more than twice as long as wide. [*C. canina; C. crassifolia*]. The flesh and inner part of the stone are edible.—FACU

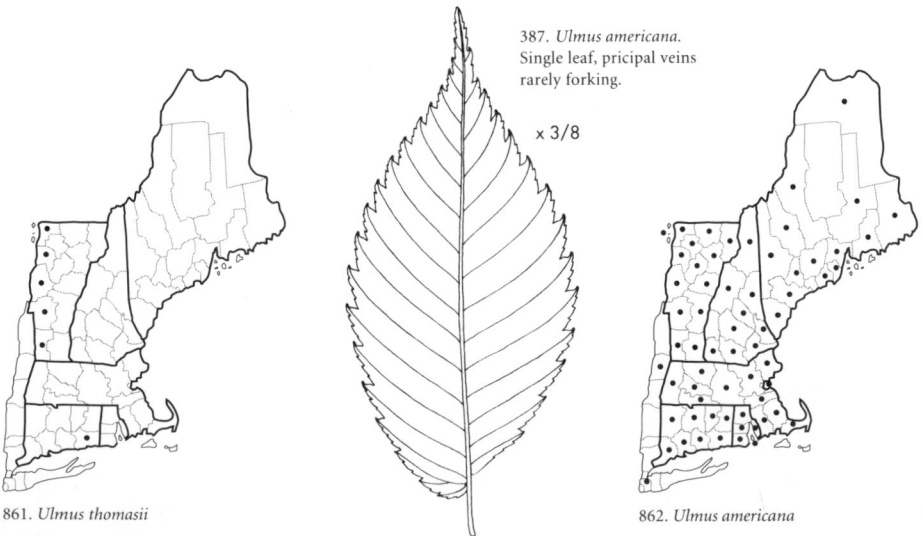

387. *Ulmus americana.*
Single leaf, pricipal veins
rarely forking.

× 3/8

861. *Ulmus thomasii*

862. *Ulmus americana*

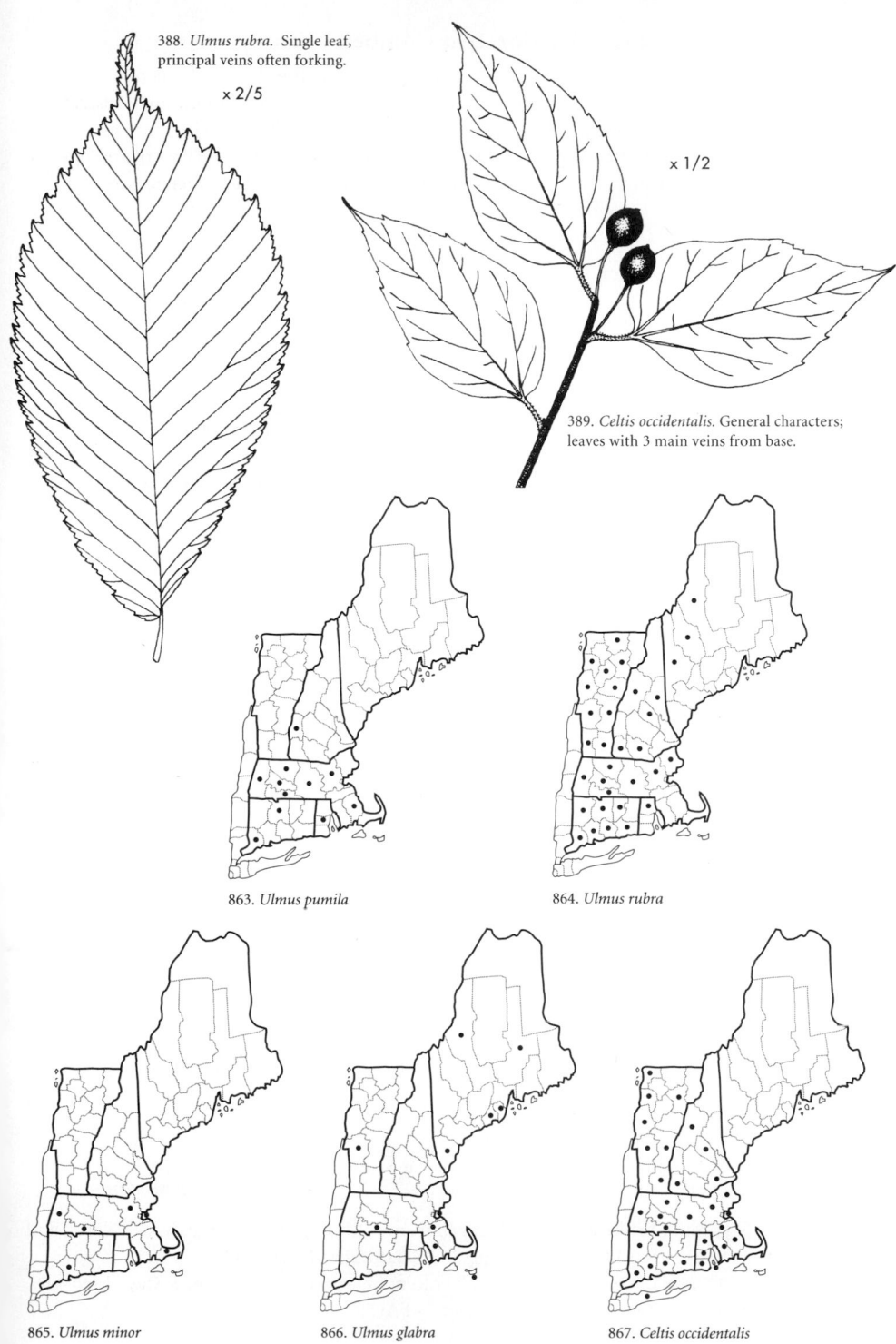

388. *Ulmus rubra.* Single leaf, principal veins often forking.

× 2/5

× 1/2

389. *Celtis occidentalis.* General characters; leaves with 3 main veins from base.

863. *Ulmus pumila*

864. *Ulmus rubra*

865. *Ulmus minor*

866. *Ulmus glabra*

867. *Celtis occidentalis*

Family 67. Moráceae (Mulberry Family)

Monoecious or dioecious trees or shrubs with milky latex. Leaves deciduous, alternate, simple and entire, toothed, or palmately lobed, stipules deciduous. Flowers unisexual, minute, in heads, catkins or dense clusters, calyx 4-5 lobed or parted, petals absent, staminate flowers with stamens as many as the calyx lobes or segments and opposite them, rarely fewer, pistillate flowers with ovary superior to inferior, bicarpellate, usually unilocular, with 1 ovule, styles 1 or 2. Fruit an achene or drupe, often aggregated.

a. Leaves toothed and frequently lobed; twigs unarmed.
    Twigs and petioles hirsute; pistillate catkins globose. (Fig. 390). .... 1. *Broussonetia*
                                          papyrifera
    Twigs and petioles glabrous or cinereous; pistillate catkins cylindric. (Fig. 391) ..... 2. *Morus*
a. Leaves entire; twigs frequently with stout, axillary spines. (Fig. 392). .... 3. *Maclura pomifera*

1. *Broussonétia* L'Her. ex Vent. (for A. Broussonet).

Tree or shrub with milky latex, twigs moderately stout, somewhat zig-zag, pubescent, pith rather large, round, white, buds moderate size, conical-ovoid, with 2 or 3 striate scales, end bud lacking, leaf scars roundish, with about 5 compound bundle scars in an ellipse, stipule scars long and prominent; leaves alternate or opposite, with pubescent petioles, broadly ovate, rounded to cordate at base, acute at apex, serrate, often lobed, scabrous above, velvety-pubescent beneath, stipules large, to 1.5 cm long, deciduous; staminate and pistillate flowers on separate plants, peduncled, axillary, the staminate in cylindric catkins, with a deeply 4-parted, pubescent calyx and 4 stamens, the pistillate in dense globose heads, with a 4-parted, pubescent calyx and 1 long style; fruit a red achene protruding from the fleshy persistent calyx, these aggregated into dense, globose heads.

    Fícus L. *cárica* L. (from Caria). Fig. Leaves palmately 3-5 lobed; flowers borne inside a closed receptacle. Rarely spread from cultivation to clearings and waste places. Reported for Plymouth County MA; Suffolk County NY.

    1. *B. papyrífera* (L.) L'Her ex Vent. Paper Mulberry. Escaped from cultivation to roadsides and abandoned fields. April-May. Fig. 390. Reported for MA, RI and Fairfield County CT. [*Papyrius p.*].

2. *Mórus* L. Mulberry (classical Latin name).

Small trees with milky latex, twigs moderate to slender, pith moderate, round, buds small to moderate, ovoid, pointed, with 5-6, 2-ranked scales, end bud lacking, leaf scars roundish, bundle scars numerous, scattered or in an ellipse, stipule scars narrow; leaves alternate, ovate, cordate, rounded or truncate at base, acute to short-acuminate at apex, serrate, often lobed, glabrous to scabrous above, pubescent beneath, at least on the veins or in their axils; staminate and pistillate flowers on the same or separate plants, in axillary catkins, the staminate consisting of 4 sepals and 4 stamens, the catkins longer and more loosely flowered than the pistillate, the latter with 4 sepals and a deeply 2-parted style, in dense catkins; fruit consisting of an achene covered by the calyx which becomes fleshy and juicy, the catkin becoming a thickened, ellipsoid, multiple fruit resembling a blackberry. Fruit edible.—Wildl. 2

Undersides of leaves glabrous or pubescent only on the main veins or in their axils .... 1. *M. alba*
Undersides of leaves pubescent on all the veins and veinlets. .... 2. *M. rubra*

    1. *M. álba* L. (white). White Mulberry. Escaped from cultivation to roadsides, waste places, and occasionally bottomlands. May. Fig. 391, Map 868. (Naturalized from Asia).
    2. *M. rúbra* L. (red). Red Mulberry. Rich, often limestone woods. April-May. Map 869. Endangered in MA, CT. Our plants are var. *rubra*.—FACU

3. *Maclúra* Nutt. Osage Orange (for W. Maclure).

Tree with milky latex, twigs moderate, with stout, axillary spines, pith moderate, round, buds small, globose, often collateral, with 4-5 scales, end bud lacking, leaf scars elliptic or half round to somewhat triangular, bundle scars several, often arranged in an ellipse, stipule scars small; leaves alternate, ovate to lance-ovate, rounded to cuneate at base, acuminate at tip, entire, glabrous; staminate and pistillate flowers on separate plants, the staminate in loose, spherical to oblong, peduncled, axillary heads, with 4-parted calyx and 4 stamens, the pistillate in dense spherical, peduncled, axillary heads, with 4 lobed calyx and 1 long style; fruit an achene deeply embedded in the enlarged, fleshy calyx, these fused and forming a large, spherical, green multiple fruit.

1. *M. pomífera* (Raf.) Schneid. (pome-bearing). Escaped from cultivation to roadsides, waste places and fields. May-June. Fig. 392, Map 870. [*Toxylon p.*]. Coming in contact with the latex has caused dermatitis in some people.

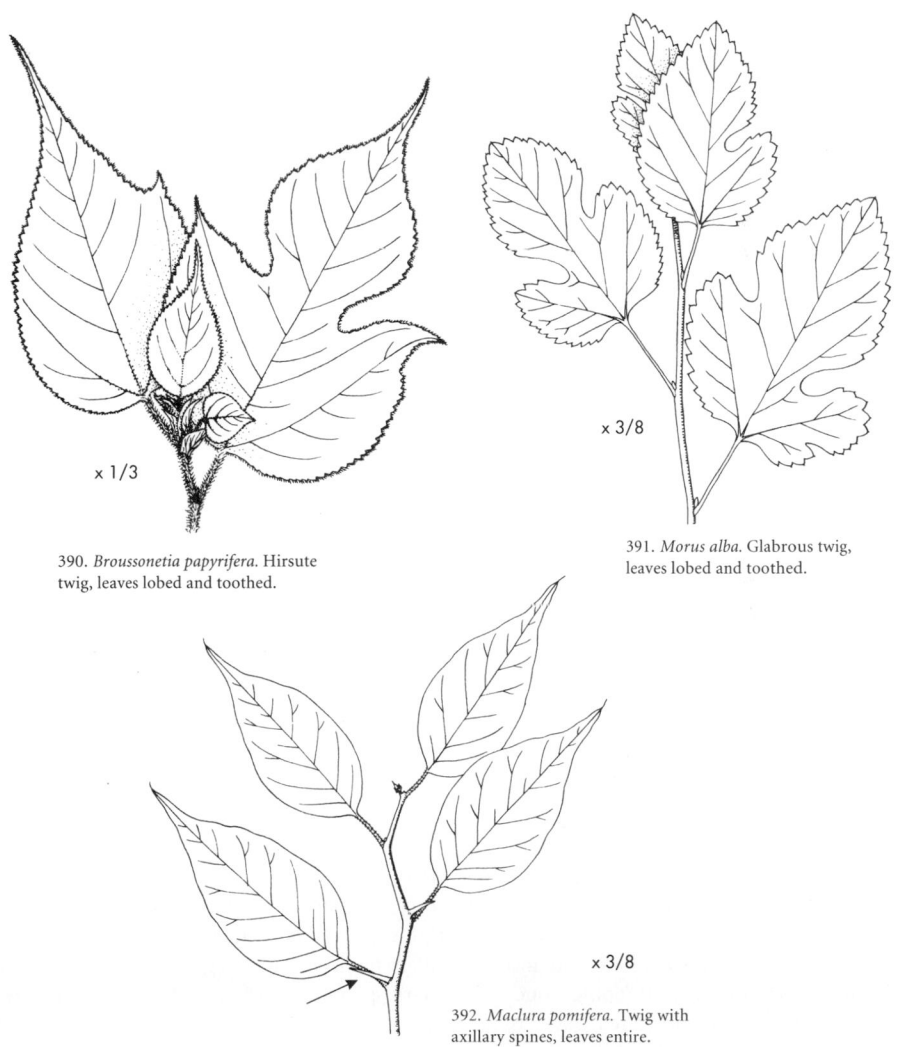

390. *Broussonetia papyrifera.* Hirsute twig, leaves lobed and toothed.

x 1/3

391. *Morus alba.* Glabrous twig, leaves lobed and toothed.

x 3/8

392. *Maclura pomifera.* Twig with axillary spines, leaves entire.

x 3/8

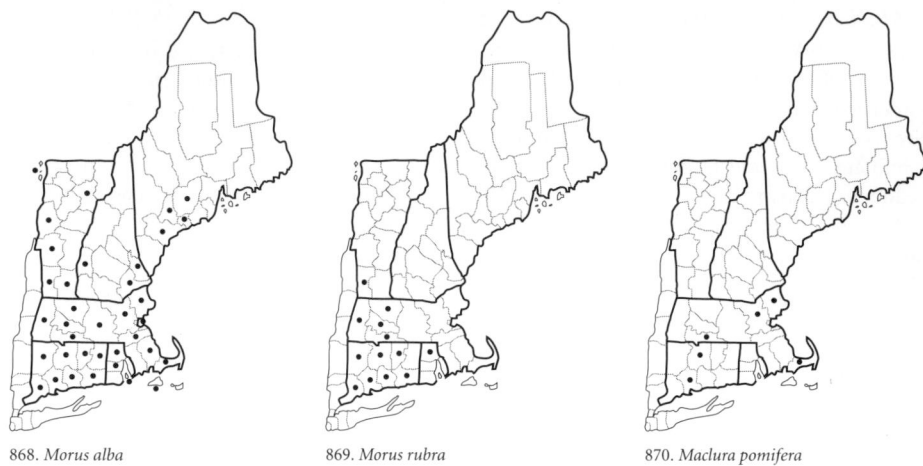

868. *Morus alba*   869. *Morus rubra*   870. *Maclura pomifera*

Family 68. Cannabáceae

Dioecious herbs with watery juice, the stems erect or twining. Leaves opposite or sometimes alternate, palmately lobed or compound, stipules persistent. Flowers unisexual, the staminate in panicled racemes, the pistillate in bracted spikes or clusters, otherwise as in *Moraceae*. Achenes separate, not aggregated. [*Moraceae*].

Plant erect; principal leaves palmately compound. (Fig. 393). .... 1. *Cannabis sativa*
Plant a vine; principal leaves merely palmately lobed. (Fig. 394). .... 2. *Humulus*

1. *Cánnabis* L. Marijuana (ancient Greek name).

Tall, stout, scabrous-stemmed, aromatic, dioecious annual with watery juice and an inner bark of tough fibers, stem unbranched below inflorescence; leaves petiolate, the lower opposite, palmately compound with 5-9 leaflets, the upper alternate, smaller, with fewer leaflets or undivided, stipules persistent, leaflets linear-lanceolate, sharply and coarsely toothed, attenuate to base, acuminate to tip, pubescent; staminate and pistillate flowers in separate plants, the former numerous in small clusters on filiform, bracteolate pedicels from the upper leaf axils forming loose, narrow, leafy, peduncled panicles, with 5 sepals and 5 short stamens, the pistillate densely clustered in short, lateral, leafy branches from the upper leaf axils, each surrounded by an acuminate bract, the calyx unlobed, styles 2; fruit a compressed achene enclosed within the glandular bract.

    1. *C. sativa* L. (Sown). Roadsides and waste places. June-September. Fig. 393, Map 871. (Adventive from Asia). Our plants are subsp. *sativa* var. *sativa*. Long history of use as a narcotic. —FACU

2. *Húmulus* L. Hops (Latin name).

Twining, herbaceous, perennial, dioecious vines without latex; stems, petioles and axis of inflorescence with retrorse prickles; leaves opposite, palmately 3-7 lobed or the upper unlobed, cordate at base, acuminate at tip or lobes acuminate, serrate, stipules persistent; staminate and pistillate flowers in separate plants, the former numerous in loose, axillary panicles, with 5 sepals and 5 short stamens, pistillate flowers in short, drooping, cone-like axillary spikes, in pairs, each pair subtended by a foliaceous bract, these imbricated, calyx unlobed, styles 2; fruit an achene enclosed within the calyx and covered by the bracts.

Leaves 3-lobed (rarely more), occasionally unlobed or with 1 lateral lobe; bracts
of pistillate flowers usually pubescent but not bristly ciliate. (Fig. 394) .... 1. *H. lupulus*
Leaves 5-7 lobed; bracts of pistillate flowers bristly ciliate. .... 2. *H. japonicus*

1. *H. lúpulus* L. (early generic name). Common Hops. Alluvial woods and thickets, roadsides, waste places. July-August. Fig. 394, Map 872. [*H. americanus*]. Our plants include var. *lupulus* and the following var.:

var. *lupuloìdes* E. Small. Midrib of central lobe of most leaves with more than 20 hairs per cm (midrib of central lobe of leaves with fewer than 20 hairs per cm in var. *lupulus*). Hops have long been used in the making of beer. Flowers and seeds used by Indians for food.

2. *H. japónicus* Sieb. & Zucc. (of Japan). Japanese Hops. Escaped from cultivation to roadsides and waste places. July-October. Map 873.—FACU

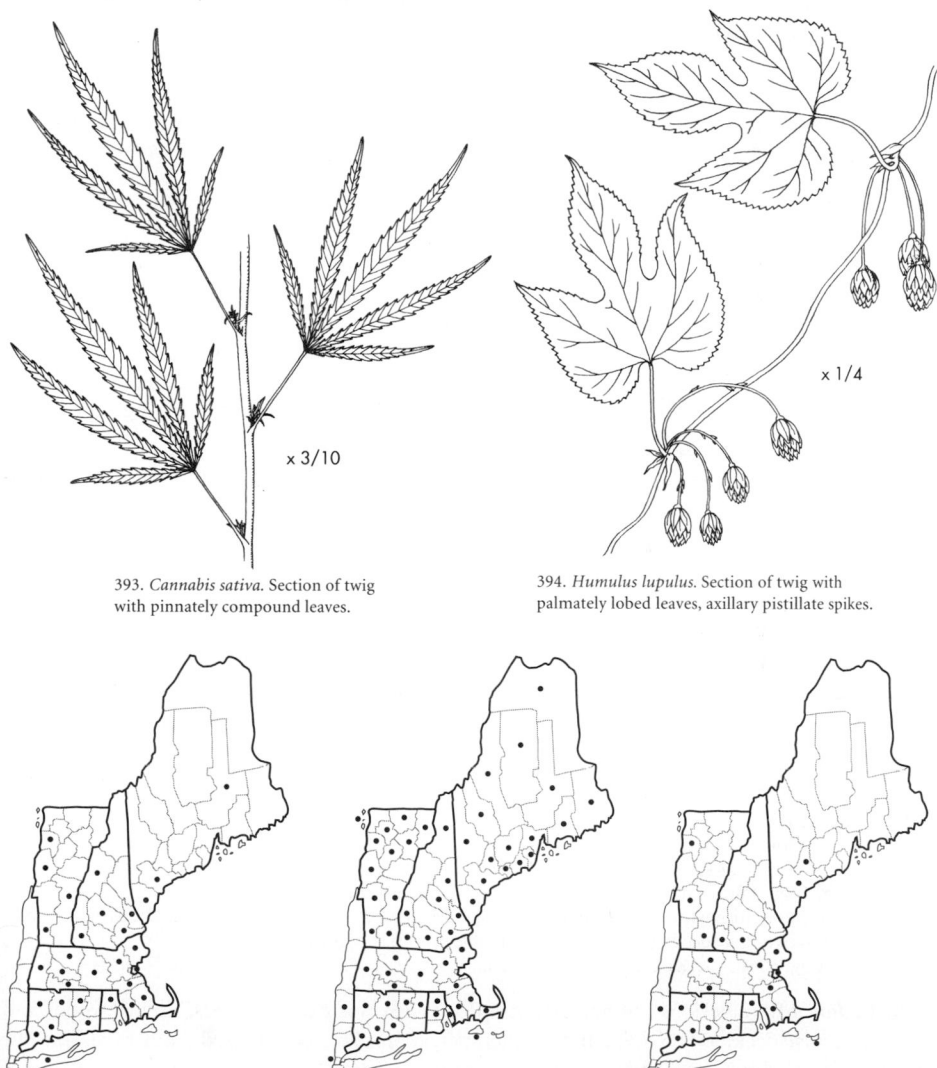

× 3/10

× 1/4

393. *Cannabis sativa.* Section of twig with pinnately compound leaves.

394. *Humulus lupulus.* Section of twig with palmately lobed leaves, axillary pistillate spikes.

871. *Cannabis sativa*

872. *Humulus lupulus*

873. *Humulus japonicus*

Family 69. Urticáceae (Nettle Family)

Monoecious or dioecious, annual or perennial, fibrous herbs (ours), often with stinging hairs. Leaves alternate or opposite, simple, toothed or entire, mostly stipulate. Flowers unisexual, rarely perfect, small, greenish, in axillary, simple or branched clusters, calyx 3-5 lobed or dissected, corolla absent, staminate flowers with stamens as many as the calyx lobes or segments and opposite them, anthers explosive, pistillate flowers with superior ovary, 1-carpelled, unilocular, with 1 ovule, style 1. Fruit an achene, often enclosed in the persistent calyx.

a. Plants with stinging hairs.
    Leaves alternate; staminate inflorescences axillary, pistillate terminal. (Fig. 395) .... 1. *Laportea canadensis*

    Leaves opposite; staminate and pistillate flowers in the same axillary
        inflorescence, or if in separate inflorescences not arranged as above.
        (Fig. 396) .... 2. *Urtica*
a. Plants without stinging hairs.
    b. Leaves alternate, entire. (Fig. 397). .... 3. *Parietaria*
    b. Leaves opposite, toothed.
        Flowers in axillary panicles or glomerules. (Fig. 398). .... 4. *Pilea*
        Flowers in glomerules in interrupted, axillary spikes. .... 5. *Boehmeria cylindrica*

1. *Lapórtea* Gaud. Wood-nettle (for F.L. deLaporte).

Monoecious perennial with stinging hairs; leaves alternate, broadly ovate, rounded to broadly cuneate at base, acuminate at tip, coarsely serrate, pubescent to glabrous, long petioled, with small, deciduous stipules; flowers clustered in loose, axillary, compound cymes, the staminate from the lower axils, with 5 sepals and 5 stamens, the pistillate in spreading, divaricately branched cymes from the upper axils or terminal, with 4 sepals of which 2 are larger, 2 minute, style elongate; fruit a flat, crescent-shaped achene with the 2 larger sepals and style persistent, reflexed on winged pedicels.

    1. *L. canadénsis* (L.) Wedd. (of Canada). Moist woods and stream or river banks. July-September. Fig. 395, Map 874. [*Urticastrum divaricatum*]. Stinging hairs cause itching of short duration.— FACW

2. *Úrtica* L. Nettle (classical Latin name).

Monoecious or dioecious, annual or perennial, with stinging hairs; leaves opposite, lanceolate to ovate, rounded to cordate at base, obtuse to acute at tip, coarsely serrate, pubescent to glabrous, with persistent stipules; flowers in axillary panicles, spikes or glomerulate clusters, staminate and pistillate flowers mixed in the same inflorescence or in separate inflorescences on the same or separate plants, the staminate with 4 subequal sepals and 4 stamens, the pistillate with 4 sepals of which 2 are larger, 2 minute, stigma sessile, tufted; fruit a flat, ovate achene enclosed by the 2 larger sepals. Stinging hairs cause itching of short duration.

a. Inflorescence more than 2 cm long, usually longer than the petioles; stipules 5 mm
    or more long, erect; stiffly erect perennial. .... 1. *U. dioica*
a. Inflorescence less than 1.5 cm long, usually shorter than petioles; stipules less than
    5 mm long, reflexed or spreading; sprawling or weakly ascending annuals.
    Upper leaves reduced; leaf teeth frequently blunt with convex sides. .... 2. *U. chamaedryoides*
    Upper leaves not reduced; leaf teeth frequently sharp, with straight sides.
        (Fig. 396) .... 3. *U. urens*

    1. *U. dioíca* L. (dioecious). Stinging Nettle. Roadsides, waste places, fields, alluvial woods and thickets, moist deciduous woods. June-September. Map 875. (Naturalized from Eurasia). Our plants include subsp. *dioica* and the following subsp.:
    subsp. *grácilis* (Ait.) Seland. Monoecious, sparsely pubescent, with lanceolate to ovate leaves

mostly rounded at the base (dioecious, densely pubescent, with cordate-ovate leaves in subsp. *dioica*). [*U. dioica* var. *procera; U. gracilis; U. procera; U. viridis*]. Young plants and leaves edible after being simmered in water; high in vitamins A and C. An extract made from the root is used as a diuretic.—FACU

2. **U. chamaedryoides** Pursh (resembling Chamaedrys). Weak Nettle. Moist woods and thickets, bottomlands, waste places. April-August. Reported for MA.—FACU

3. **U. úrens** L. (stinging). Dwarf Nettle. Waste places. June-September. Fig. 396, Map 876. (Naturalized from Eurasia). Rare. Young greens edible after cooking.

3. *Parietária* L. Pellitory (ancient Latin name).

Monoecious or polygamous annual without stinging hairs; leaves alternate, lanceolate to ovate, short or long-acuminate at tip, rounded or narrowed to base, entire, roughened with minute dots above and below, estipulate; flowers few in short, axillary, bracteate cymes, the staminate, pistillate and perfect flowers mixed in the same cluster, staminate flowers with a deeply 4-parted calyx and

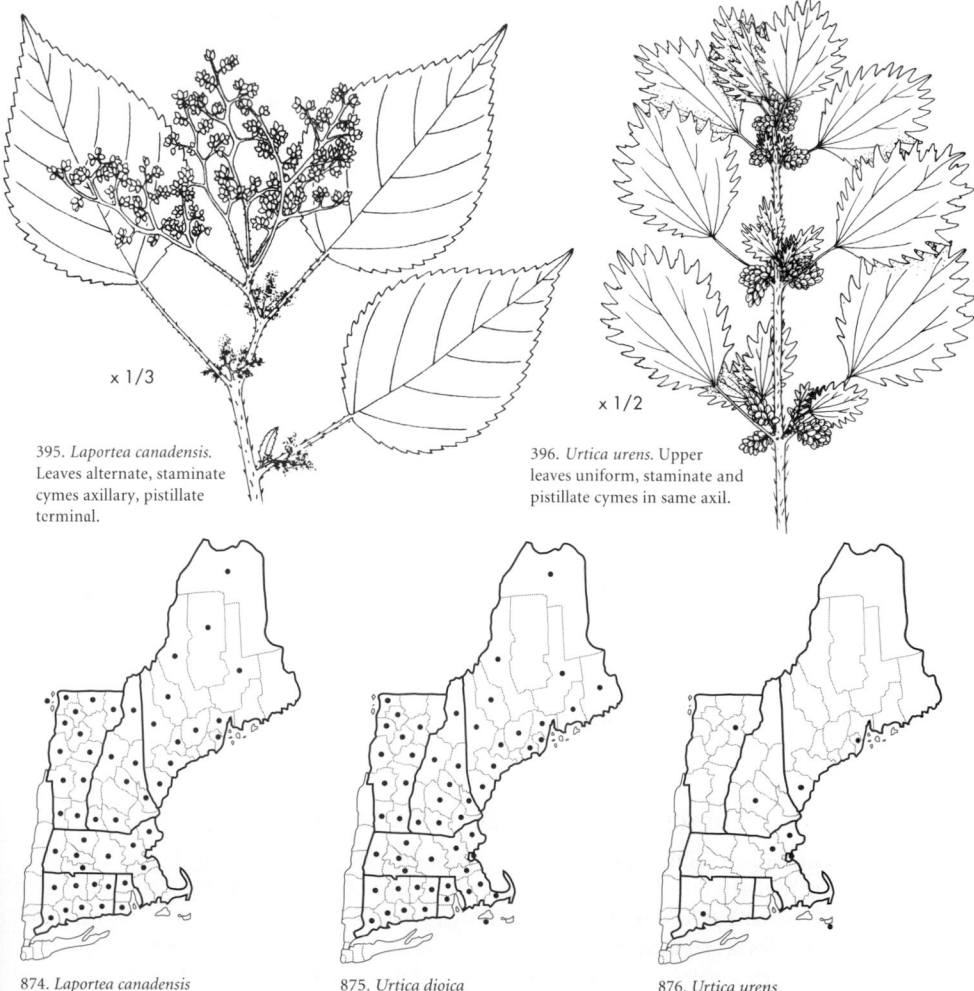

x 1/3

395. *Laportea canadensis.* Leaves alternate, staminate cymes axillary, pistillate terminal.

x 1/2

396. *Urtica urens.* Upper leaves uniform, staminate and pistillate cymes in same axil.

874. *Laportea canadensis*

875. *Urtica dioica*

876. *Urtica urens*

4 stamens, pistillate flowers with tubular, 4-lobed calyx and a sessile, tufted stigma; fruit an ovoid achene loosely enclosed within the persistent calyx.

Bracts 2 or more times as long as the calyces; leaves lanceolate, narrowed to base,
    widest 1/3 of the distance from base, mostly 3 cm or more long. (Fig. 397). .... 1. *P. pensylvanica*
Bracts less than twice as long as the calyces; leaves ovate, rounded and widest at
    or near base, mostly less than 3 cm long. .... 2. *P. floridana*

    1. *P. pensylvánica* Muhl. ex Willd. (of Pennsylvania). Dry woods and slopes, often calcareous. June-September. Fig. 397, Map 877. Our plants are var. *pensylvanica.*—FACU-
    2. *P. floridána* Nutt. (of Florida). Southern, reported for Pawtuckaway Mt., Rockingham County NH.
    P. judáica L. Similar to *P. floridana* but perennial, with leaves subacuminate at apex (*P. floridana* is annual, with leaves obtuse at apex). (Eurasian). From the southwest. Reported for MA.

4. *Pílea* Lindl. Clearweed (from the Latin, based on the shape of the larger sepal of the pistillate flower of one of the species).

Monoecious or dioecious annual without stinging hairs, mostly glabrous, with stout, usually branched, translucent stems; leaves opposite, long petioled, lustrous, translucent, glabrous or sparsely pubescent, ovate, acute to acuminate at tip, cuneate to rounded at base, with coarse, rounded teeth and 3 main veins, stipules inconspicuous, united; staminate and pistillate flowers often mixed in axillary panicles or glomerules from the middle and upper leaf axils, the staminate deeply 3-4 parted, with an equal number of stamens, the pistillate deeply 3-parted, the segments often unequal, each subtending a concave, scale-like staminodium, stigma sessile, tufted; fruit an ovoid, flattened, purple-spotted achene.

Mature achenes stramineous or green, usually with purple markings. .... 1. *P. pumila*
Mature achenes black or dark olive .... 2. *P. fontana*

    1. *P. púmila* (L.) Gray (dwarf). Moist, rich, shaded woods. July-September. Fig. 398, Map 878. [*Adicea p.*]. Our plants are var. *pumila.*—FACW
    2. *P. fontána* (Lunell) Rydb. (of springs). Wet soil. From farther west.
Reported for Franklin County MA; eastern NY. [*P. opaca*].—FACW+

5. *Boehméria* Jacq. False Nettle (for G. Boehmer).

Monoecious or dioecious perennial without stinging hairs, glabrous to pubescent; leaves opposite, long petioled, ovate to ovate-lanceolate, acute or acuminate at tip, cuneate to rounded at base, coarsely serrate, with 3 main veins, stipules distinct; flowers in glomerules in interrupted or continuous axillary spikes frequently terminated by leaves, the staminate and pistillate in the same or separate spikes in the same or separate plants, the staminate with 4 sepals and 4 stamens, the pistillate with calyx entire or 2-4 lobed, style elongate; fruit an ovate achene enclosed within the persistent calyx, the latter flattened and narrowly 2- winged.

    1. *B. cylíndrica* (L.) Sw. (cylindric). Wooded swamps, low woodlands, pond and stream margins. July-September. Map 879. (W.I.)—FACW+

Family 70. Santaláceae (Sandalwood Family)

Hermaphrodite or polygamous, perennial, glabrous herbs (ours) from creeping rhizomes, parasitic on the roots of herbs or shrubs. Leaves alternate, simple, entire, sessile or short petioled, estipulate, the lower often smaller. Flowers perfect or staminate, small, in 2-several-flowered axillary cymules or terminal panicles of cymules, hypanthium partly or entirely enclosing the inferior ovary, bearing 5 erect or spreading sepals on its margin and a 5-lobed disc inside the sepals, stamens 5, inserted

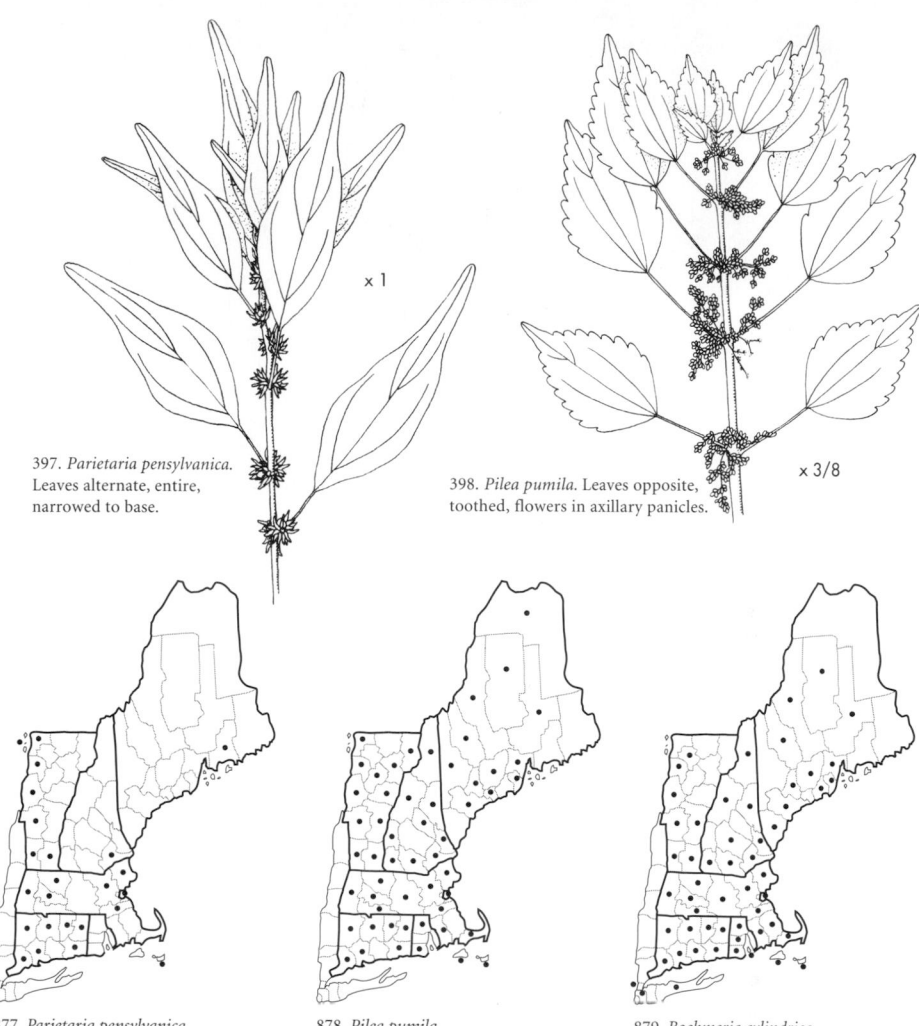

397. *Parietaria pensylvanica.*
Leaves alternate, entire,
narrowed to base.

×1

398. *Pilea pumila.* Leaves opposite,
toothed, flowers in axillary panicles.

×3/8

877. *Parietaria pensylvanica*

878. *Pilea pumila*

879. *Boehmeria cylindrica*

between the lobes of the disc, the anthers often connected to the sepals at the middle by tufts of hairs, 1-carpelled, unilocular, few ovuled, style 1. Fruit a dry or juicy drupe surmounted by the persistent calyx.

Pyrulária Michx. *púbera* Michx. Buffalo-nut. A shrub with flowers in terminal racemes. Southern. Rarely occurring in our range. Reported for Queens County NY.

Flowers in terminal panicles of cymules; sepals ascending to erect. (Fig. 399) .... 1. *Comandra umbellata*
Flowers in axillary, few-flowered cymules; sepals spreading. .... 2. *Geocaulon lividum*

1. *Comándra* Nutt. Bastard-toadflax (from the Greek, based on the hairs of the sepals connected to the anthers).

Hermaphrodite; stem very leafy; leaves oblong to ovate, narrowed to base and tip, sessile or subsessile; flowers perfect, in terminal panicles of cymules, sepals ascending to erect, greenish-white, longer than wide, connected to the anthers by tufts of hairs from their middle; fruit a dry, globose drupe.

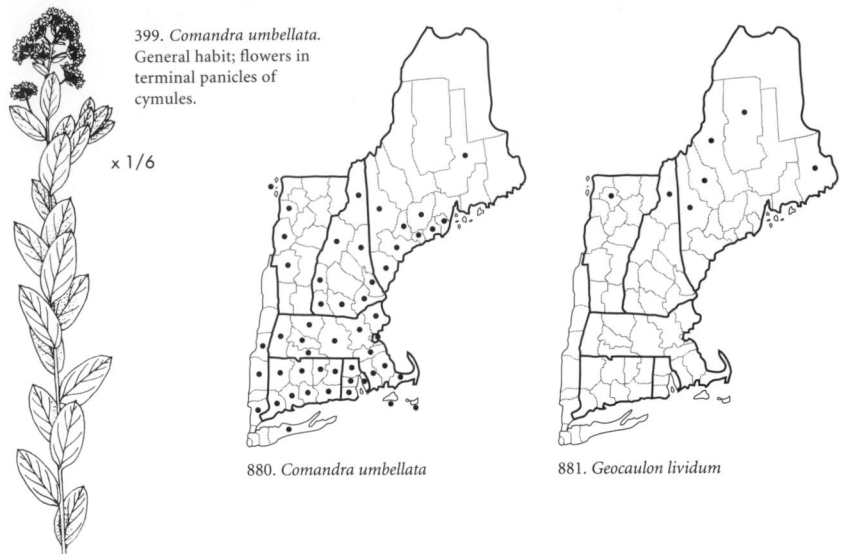

399. *Comandra umbellata.*
General habit; flowers in
terminal panicles of
cymules.

x 1/6

880. *Comandra umbellata*

881. *Geocaulon lividum*

1. C. umbelláta (L.) Nutt. (bearing umbels). Dry fields, thickets, and open deciduous or coniferous woods. May-June. Fig. 399, Map 880. [*C. richardsiana; C. umbellata* var. *decumbens*]. Our plants are subsp. *umbellata.*-FACU-

2. Geocaúlon Fern. Northern Comandra (from the Greek, referring to the creeping rhizomes).
Polygamous; leaves elliptic, obtuse or rounded at tip, narrowed to base, short petioled; central flower in each cymule perfect, the others staminate, the cymules few, axillary, few-flowered, sepals spreading, greenish, about as long as wide, free from the anthers; fruit a juicy drupe.

1. G. lívidum (Richards) Fern. (lead-colored). Bogs and wet, coniferous woods at high altitudes. June-July. Map 881. Endangered in NH. [*Comandra livida*].—FAC

Family 71. Viscáceae (Mistletoe Family)

Dioecious, suffrutescent, minute (ours), inconspicuous plants (up to 2 cm long), glabrous, parasitic on the branches of coniferous trees (mostly *Picea mariana*) but with chlorophyll, attached by root-like suckers. Stem simple or sparingly branched, roundish to somewhat rectangular in cross section. Leaves opposite, reduced to decussate, connate scales, estipulate. Flowers unisexual, on the same or separate trees, solitary or few on short pedicels in the leaf axils, resembling short, lateral branches until expanded, the staminate with a mostly 3-4 parted calyx, the lobes spreading, each lobe bearing a sessile anther, the pistillate with a 2-lobed calyx, the lobes erect, ovary inferior, unilocular, 1 ovuled, stigma sessile. Fruit an ovoid, somewhat flattened berry. [*Loranthaceae*].

1. Arceuthóbium Bieb (from the Greek, based on the plants being parasitic on Juniperous and related conifers).
Same characters as the family.—Wildl. 1

1. A. pusíllum Peck (tiny). Dwarf Mistletoe. Mostly in bogs on black spruce; infrequently on the branches of white spruce, tamarack and other conifers. April-June. Fig. 400, Map 882. Endangered in RI, CT.

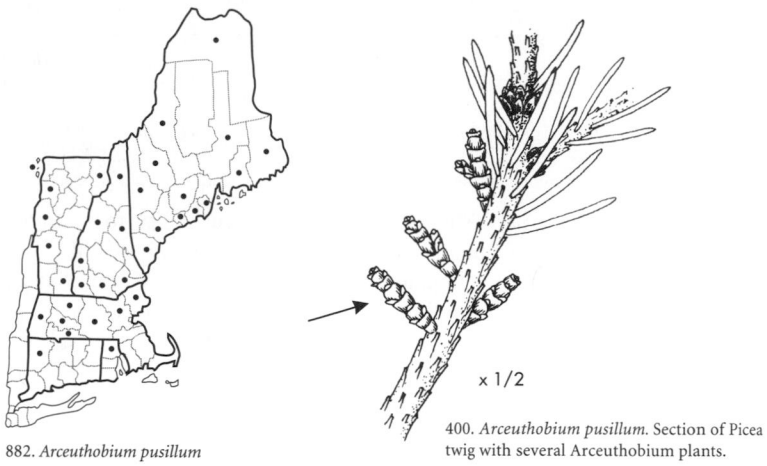

882. *Arceuthobium pusillum*

400. *Arceuthobium pusillum*. Section of Picea twig with several Arceuthobium plants.

x 1/2

Family 72. Aristolochiáceae (Birthwort Family)

Perennial herbs or twining woody vines. Leaves alternate or basal, simple, entire, petioled, mostly broad and cordate, estipulate. Flowers perfect, terminal or axillary, solitary or clustered, regular or irregular, calyx gamosepalous, usually 3-parted, the tube maroon, adnate to the ovary, petals none or minute, stamens 6-12, connivent or adnate with the style, ovary partly or wholly inferior, with usually 6 united carpels, 6-locular, each locule with numerous ovules, styles 6, united in a column, stigma 6-lobed. Fruit a 6-celled septicidal capsule.

Acaulescent herb; calyx regular. (Fig. 401). .... 1. *Asarum canadense*
Caulescent herbs or twining, woody vines; calyx irregular or tube bent. (Fig. 402) .... 2. *Aristolochia*

1. *Ásarum* L. Wild Ginger (ancient Greek name).

Perennial, stemless, pubescent herbs with slender, aromatic rhizomes; leaves basal, 1 or usually 2, reniform to orbicular, cordate at base, abruptly acuminate at tip, long petioled; flower solitary, on a short, stout peduncle arising between the usually paired leaves, calyx regular, 3-parted, the segments acuminate to subulate or mucronate at tip, stamens 12, connivent with the style.

1. *A. canadénse* L. (of Canada). Rich, deciduous woods. April-May. Fig. 401, Map 883. Our plants are var. *canadense*. Rhizomes can be dried and candied; powder made from the dried rhizome has been used as a drink to aid flatulency. Leaves have also been used fresh or dried to flavor foods.

2. *Aristolóchia* L. Birthwort (from the Greek, based on supposed value in aiding childbirth).

Perennial, stemmed, herbs or twining woody vines, glabrous or pubescent; stems swollen at the nodes, pith large, round, buds small, 2 or 3 superposed on a silky patch in the curve of the leaf scar, enclosed in petiole base and not visible until after leaf fall, bud scale single, silky, end bud lacking, leaf scars U-shaped, with 3 bundle traces, stipule scars lacking; leaves alternate, narrowly lanceolate to ovate or orbicular, truncate to hastate or cordate at base, blunt to acute or acuminate at tip; flowers solitary or clustered in the leaf axils, the peduncle sometimes with a perfoliate bract near middle, calyx irregular, 1-lobed or unequally 3-lobed, the tube often bent and/or inflated, much overtopping the stamens and style, stamens 6, the anthers sessile, adnate to the stigma, style column short and stout.

a. Erect or reclining herbs.
    Flowers in axillary clusters to summit of plant; calyx nearly straight, with a
        single terminal lobe .... 1. *A. clematitis*
    Flowers on short scaly peduncles toward the base; calyx curved, with 3 lobes. .... 2. *A. serpentaria*
a. Twining woody vines.
    Twigs, petioles, leaf undersides and perianth tomentose or densely pubescent;
        peduncles bractless .... 3. *A. tomentosa*
    Plant glabrous or nearly so; peduncles with a perfoliate bract near middle. .... 4. *A. macrophylla*

1. *A. clematítis* L. (ancient name, of Clematis). Escaped from cultivation to roadsides and waste places. June-August. (Introduced from Europe). Reported for Suffolk County MA.

2. *A. serpentária* L. (ancient name for plants used to cure snake-bite). Virginia Snakeroot. Rich, often calcareous, moist to dry woods and thickets. May-July. Map 884. Rare.

3. *A. tomentósa* Sims (tomentose). Woolly Pipevine. Escaped to roadsides and cellar holes. May-June. Reported for CT, VT, Franklin and Hampden Counties MA.—FAC

4. *A. macrophýlla* Lam. (large-leaved). Dutchman's Pipe. Rich, often calcareous woods. May-June. Fig. 402. Reported for MA, VT, Fairfield County CT. [*A. durior*].

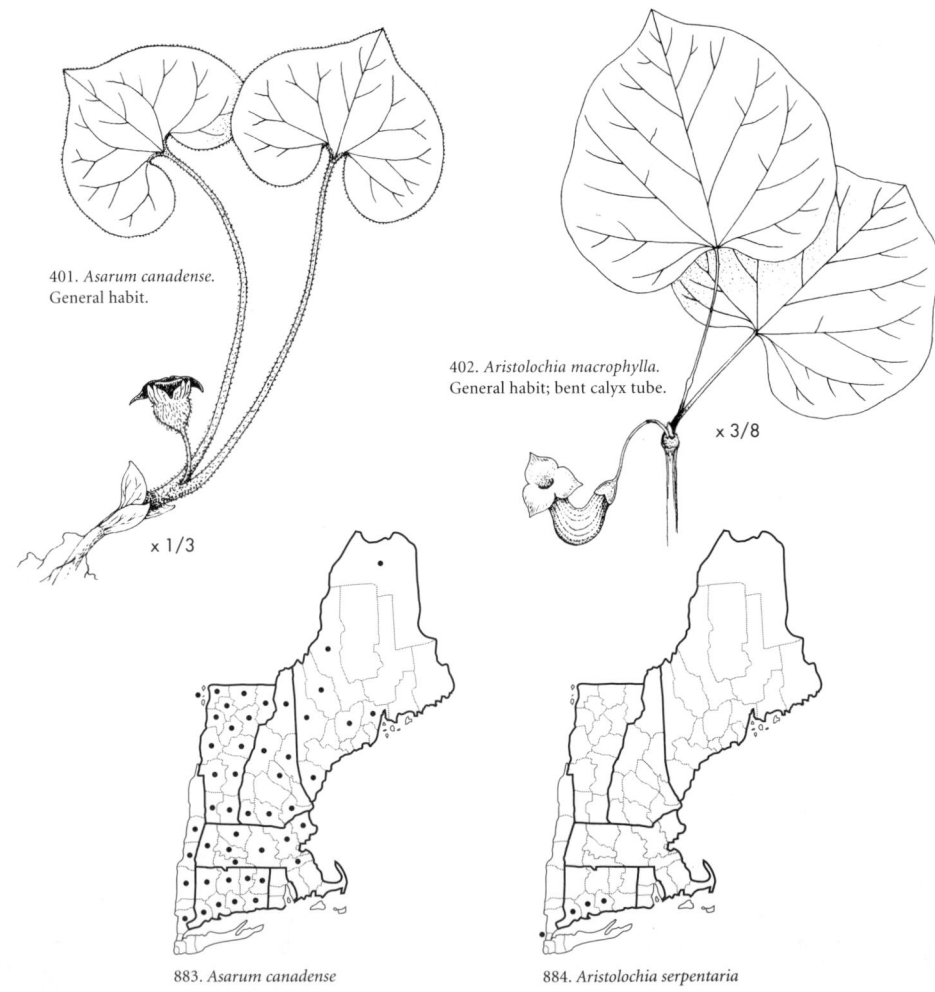

401. *Asarum canadense.*
General habit.

× 1/3

402. *Aristolochia macrophylla.*
General habit; bent calyx tube.

× 3/8

883. *Asarum canadense*

884. *Aristolochia serpentaria*

Family 73. Polygonáceae (Buckwheat Family)

Hermaphrodite, polygamous or dioecious, annual or perennial herbs, sub-shrubs or vines. Stems often swollen at the nodes, usually with sheathing stipules (ocreae) above the nodes at the petiole base. Leaves alternate, rarely opposite, simple, mostly entire. Flowers small, mostly perfect, sometimes unisexual, solitary or in cymes or cymules in the axils of small sheaths (ocreolae) disposed in panicles, racemes, spikes or heads, regular, calyx of 3-6 sepals in 1 or 2 series or 3-6 parted, the segments sometimes winged and/or tubercled in fruit; petals lacking, stamens 4-12, inserted on the base of the calyx, ovary superior, of 2-4 carpels, 1-locular, with 1 ovule, styles 2 or 3. Fruit an achene, flattened or 3 angled, enclosed within the persistent calyx.

Émex Campd. *spinósa* (L.) Camp. Flowers clustered in the branch and leaf axils; fruit enclosed in 3 valves, each tipped by a strong spine. Mediterranean. A waif reported for Suffolk County MA.

a. Leaves reniform to reniform-ovate, less than 1.5 times as long as wide; achenes
    with 2 broad wings. (Fig. 403). .... 1. *Oxyria digyna*
a. Leaves not reniform or reniform-ovate, more than 1.5 times as long as wide;
    achenes wingless or 3-winged.
  b. Achenes 3-winged; leaves mostly basal. .... 1. *Rheum*
                rhaponticum
  b. Achenes wingless (although often 3-angled); leaves mostly cauline (basal leaves
    numerous in some *Polygonum*).
    c. Flowers solitary in the axils of ocreolae; branches appearing internodal.
      (Fig. 404) .... 2. *Polygonella*
                articulata
    c. Flowers mostly clustered in the axils of ocreolae or if solitary then subtended
      by bracteal leaves; branches definitely nodal.
      d. Plant dioecious; leaves hastate or sagittate. .... 3. *Rumex*
      d. Plant not dioecious.
        e. Three inner sepals larger than the outer in fruit; developing wings; leaves
          never hastate or sagittate. (Fig. 407). .... 3. *Rumex*
        e. Three inner sepals smaller than or equal to the outer, not developing
          wings (outer 3 sepals developing wings in some *polygonum*); leaves
          of some species hastate or sagittate.
          Flowers in corymbose racemes; leaves broadly triangular, cordate or
            hastate at base. (Fig. 410) .... 4. *Fagopyrum*
          Flowers in axillary clusters, panicles or spiciform racemes variously
            arranged but not corymbose .... 5. *Polygonum*

1. Oxýria Hill. Mountain-Sorrel (from the Greek, based on the sour tasting leaves). Glabrous, perennial herb from a stout rootstock; stem erect, stout, simple or sparingly branched, 1-2 leaved or leafless, leaves mostly basal, long-petioled, with a reniform to orbicular blade and cylindric ocreae; flowers perfect, small, greenish to red, pedicelled, several pedicels in the axil of each ocreola, in terminal panicles of racemes, sepals persistent, 4 in 2 series, the outer narrower, spreading, the inner broader, erect, stamens 6, stigmas 2, divergent, subsessile, tufted, ovary flattened; achene lenticular, with 2 broad wings, subtended by and exceeding the sepals, stigmas persistent on wings of the achene.

    1. O. dígyna (L.) Hill (with 2 carpels). Alpine, Mt. Washington, NH. June-August. Fig. 403. (N. Eurasia). Rare. High in vitamin C; used in salads where abundant.—FACW
    Rhéum rhapónticum L. Rhubarb. Coarse, stout-stemmed perennial with large basal leaves; flowers numerous in panicled racemes, with 6 unequal sepals and 6 stamens; achene 3-winged. Occasionally escaped from cultivation to roadsides and cellar holes. Map 885. [*R. rhabarbicum*]. Stems well known in cooking; leaves and roots are poisonous.
    In addition, *R. rhabárbarum* has also been reported for MA.

2. *Polygonélla* Michx. (diminutive of *Polygonum*).

Glabrous, annual herb (ours); stem slender, usually freely branched, the branches appearing internodal; leaves linear, articulated to the ocreae; flowers perfect, small, whitish to red, on solitary, jointed pedicels in the axils of ocreolae, densely aggregated in slender, panicled racemes, sepals 5, subequal in width, petaloid, persistent, stamens 8, stigmas 3, capitate, ovary 3-angled; achene 3-angled, loosely invested by the calyx, pedicels recurved.

1. P. articuláta (L.) Meisn. (jointed). Open, sandy soil, often along the coast. July-October.Fig. 404, Map 886. [*Delopyrum a.*].

3. *Rúmex* L. Dock (ancient Latin name).

Hermaphrodite, polygamous or dioecious, annual or perennial herbs; leaves petioled, lanceolate to elliptic, sometimes lobed at base, entire, undulate or crisped, with cylindric ocreae; flowers perfect or unisexual, small, greenish or part red, fascicled and often verticillate in terminal, paniculate racemes, sepals 6, the outer 3 usually small, often reflexed, the inner 3 enlarging and usually developing wings, (these 3 inner sepals called valves in fruit), the valves connivent over the achene, the midrib of 1 or all 3 often bearing a tubercle (called a grain), stamens 6, styles 3, stigmas tufted, ovary 3-angled; achene 3-angled, included within the 3 valves.

In addition to the following species *R. x dissimilis* and *R. x acutus* L. (pro. sp.) have been reported for our range.—Wildl. 2

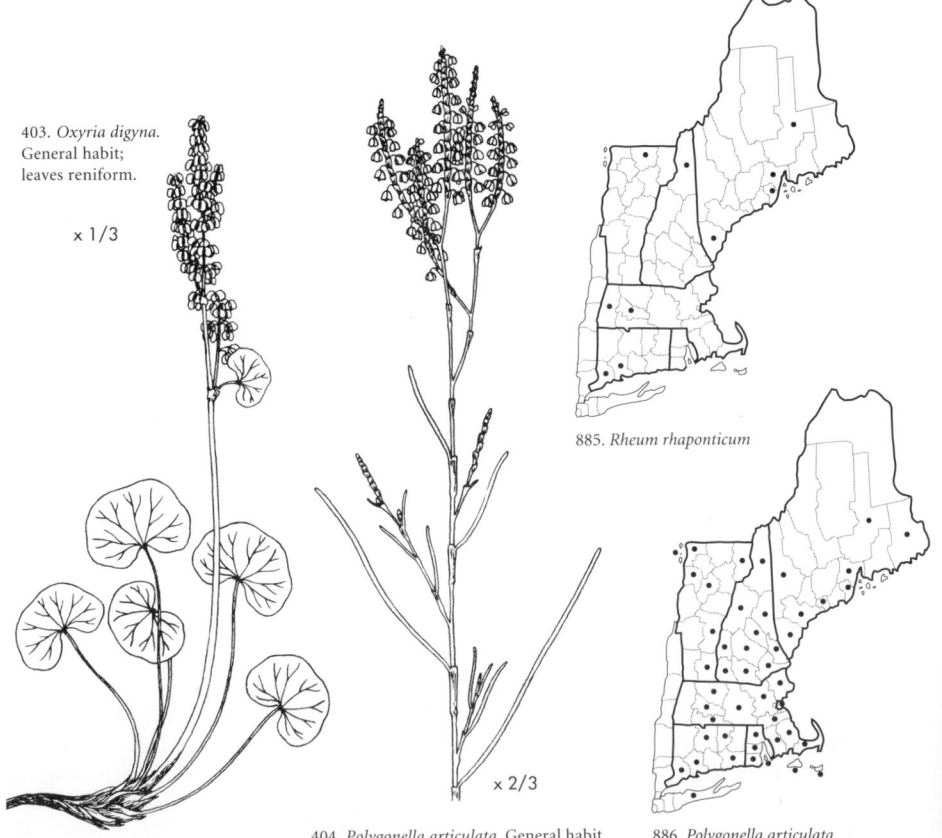

403. *Oxyria digyna*.
General habit;
leaves reniform.

x 1/3

885. *Rheum rhaponticum*

x 2/3

404. *Polygonella articulata*. General habit.   886. *Polygonella articulata*

a. Leaves, at least some, hastate or sagittate; plant dioecious.
  b. Sepals of pistillate flowers only slightly enlarged in fruit, not forming wings;
    plant rhizomatous .... 1. *R. acetosella*
  b. Sepals of pistillate flowers greatly enlarged in fruit, expanded into wings; plant
    not rhizomatous.
    Leaves hastate, the larger ones less than 2 cm wide (excluding lobes), those
      at base of plant numerous; valves without grains. .... 2. *R. hastatulus*
    Leaves sagittate, the larger ones more than 2 cm wide, those at base of plant
      few; valves each with a small grain at base. .... 3. *R. acetosa*
a. Leaves not hastate or sagittate (although sometimes cordate); plant mostly or
    entirely with perfect flowers.
  c. Margins of valves with slender, bristly teeth longer than wide.
    d. Teeth as long or longer than width of valve. .... 4. *R. maritimus*
    d. Teeth shorter than width of valve. (Fig. 405).
      Pedicels shorter than or about equalling valves in fruit; verticels of flowers
      all separate .... 5. *R. pulcher*
      Pedicels much longer than valves in fruit; upper verticels mostly
      contiguous. .... 6. *R. obtusifolius*
  c. Margins of valves entire, undulate, or dentate with teeth wider than long.
    e. Valves without grains.
      f. Largest leaves less than 2 times as long as wide. .... 7. *R. alpinus*
      f. Largest leaves more than 2 times as long as wide.
        g. Pedicel of fruit not visibly jointed. .... 8. *R. aquaticus*
          var. *fenestratus*
        g. Pedicel of fruit with a conspicuous joint near or below the middle.
          Principal leaves rounded to subcordate at base .... 9. *R. patientia*
          Principal leaves narrowed to a cuneate base. .... 10. *R. longifolius*
    e. Valves (at least 1) with a prominent grain.
      h. Valves barely or not wider than face of achene, not expanded into wings.
        (Fig. 406) .... 11. *R. conglomeratus*
      h. Valves definitely wider than face of achene, each expanded into wings
        appressed to the wings of the other valves, the fruit therefore 3-winged.
        i. Pedicel of fruit not visibly jointed; base of grain definitely elevated
          beyond base of valve. (Fig. 407) .... 12. *R. orbiculatus*
            var. *borealis*
        i. Pedicel of fruit with a conspicuous joint near or below the middle; base
          of grain mostly even with or below base of valve.
          j. Pedicels 2 or more times as long as the valves, conspicuously reflexed.
            (Fig. 408) .... 13. *R. verticillatus*
          j. Pedicels mostly less than 2 times as long as the valves, not
            conspicuously reflexed.
            k. Verticels of flowers all separate .... 5. *R. pulcher*
            k. Verticels of flowers mostly contiguous, at least above.
              l. Leaves flat, the margins entire or slightly undulate or denticulate,
              not crisped or ruffled.
               m. Well-developed grain 1 (rarely more in *R. altissimus*).
                  Grain less than half as long as the valve. .... 9. *R. patientia*
                  Grain more than half as long as the valve. .... 14. *R. altissimus*
               m. Well-developed grains 3.
                  Grain considerably shorter and much less than half as wide
                    as the valve. .... 15. *R. salicifolius*
                      var. *mexicanus*
                  Grain nearly as long and about half as wide as the valve. .... 16. *R. pallidus*
             l. Leaves crisped or ruffled on the margins. (Fig. 409). .... 17. *R. crispus*

1. *R. acetosélla* L. (little sorrel). Sheep Sorrel. Fields and waste places. May-August. Map 887.
(Naturalized from Europe). Leaves used in salads; young flowering plant used for soups.

2. *R. hastátulus* Bladw. (slightly hastate). Wild sorrel. Sandy soil along the coast. April-August.
Reported for MA, Suffolk County NY.—FACU-

3. R. acetósa L. (old generic name). Garden sorrel. Fields and roadsides. June-July. Map 888. (Naturalized from Europe). Leaves used for salads and soups.—FACU

4. R. marítimus L. (maritime). Brackish shores and borders of salt marshes. July-October. Map 889. (Adventive from Europe). [*R. fueginus*]. Represented with us by the following 2 vars.:

var. *persicarioídes* (L.) Mitchell. Grain ellipsoid, 0.4 mm or more wide. [*R.persicarioides*].

var. *fúeginus* (Philippi) Dusen. Grain narrowly lanceolate, up to 0.4 mm wide.—FACW

var. *marítimus* is European.—FACW

5. R. púlcher L. (beautiful). Fiddledock. Waste places and roadsides. May-September. (Naturalized from Europe). Reported for Suffolk County MA, Bronx County NY.—FACW-

6. R. obtusifólius L. (blunt-leaved). Bitter dock. Roadsides, waste places, fields and stream borders. June-September. Fig. 405, Map 890. (Naturalized from Europe). Young leaves can be used as a potherb after simmering to remove bitterness.—FACU-

7. R. alpínus L. (alpine). Alpine dock. Fields and roadsides. June-August. Rare. Map 891. (Adventive from Europe).

8. R. aqúaticus L. Borders of lakes, marshes. August-September. Rare. Map 892. [*R. fenestratus; R. occidentalis*]. Represented with us as var. *fenestratus*. (Greene) Dorn.—OBL

9. R. patiéntia L. (old colloquial name). Patience dock. Roadsides and waste places. June-July. Rare. Map 893. (Naturalized from Eurasia). Young leaves can be used as a potherb after simmering to remove bitterness.

10. R. longifólius DC. Fields, roadsides and waste places. July-September. Map 894. (Naturalized from Europe). [*R. domesticus*].—FAC

11. R. conglomerátus Murr. (clustered). Roadsides, waste places and fields. June-July. Fig. 406. (Naturalized from Europe). Reported for Bronx County NY.—FAC

12. R. orbiculátus Gray (disc-shaped; from the valves). Great water dock. Marshes, swamps, ditches, stream and lake margins. July-September. Fig. 407, Map 895. [*R. britannica*]. Represented with us as var. *borealis* Rech. f.—OBL

13. R. verticillátus L. (whorled). Water dock. Pond and lake margins, wooded swamps and wet woods. June-September. Fig. 408, Map 896. [*R. floridanus*]. —OBL

14. R. altíssimus Wood (tallest). Pale dock. Waste places. June-August. Rare. Map 897.—FACW-

15. R. salicifólius Weinm. Willow dock. River margins. Roadsides, waste places. June-September. Map 898. [*R. mexicanus; R. triangulivalvis; R. salicifolius* var. *t.*]. Represented with us as var. *mexicánus* (Meisn.) C. L. Hitchc.—FAC to FACU

16. R. pállidus Bigel. (pale). Seabeach dock. Sandy and rocky coastal beaches. June-September. Map 899. Endangered in NH.—FACW

17. R. críspus L. (curled). Curly dock. Fields, roadsides and waste places. July-September. Fig. 409, Map 900. (Naturalized from Europe). [*R. elongatus*]. Young leaves used as a potherb after simmering in water to remove bitterness; fruits were ground into flour by Indians; a preparation made from the root has been used as a laxative.—FACU

4. Fagopýrum P. Mill. Buckwheat (from the Latin and Greek, based on the resemblance of the achene to the beech nut).

Annual herbs; stem usually freely branched, pubescent in lines above; leaves petioled, broadly triangular, cordate or hastate at base, acute to acuminate at tip, ocreae obliquely truncate; flowers perfect, greenish, white or pink, in fascicles disposed in terminal and axillary, corymbose and solitary racemes, calyx petaloid, deeply 5-parted, the segments unequal in width, persistent, stamens 8, styles 3, stigmas capitate, ovary 3-angled; achene 3-angled, much exceeding the calyx.

Achene without longitudinal grooves, the angles smooth, not undulate or crested .... 1. *F. esculentum*
Achene with a longitudinal groove on each of the 3 faces, the angles undulate or
    irregularly crested, and often with 3 prominent protuberances above the
    middle .... 2. *F. tataricum*

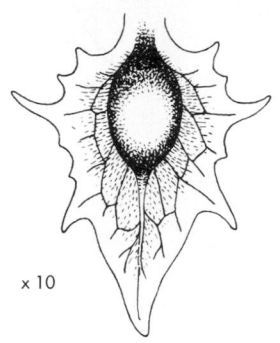

x 10

405. *Rumex obtusifolius.* Single fruit, valves expanded into wings, the margins toothed.

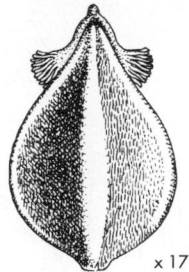

x 17

406. *Rumex conglomeratus.* Single fruit, valves not expanded into wings.

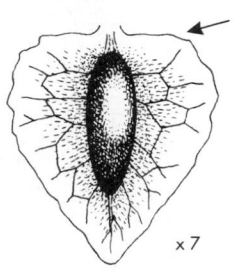

x 7

407. *Rumex orbiculatus.* Single fruit, grain elevated beyond base of valve.

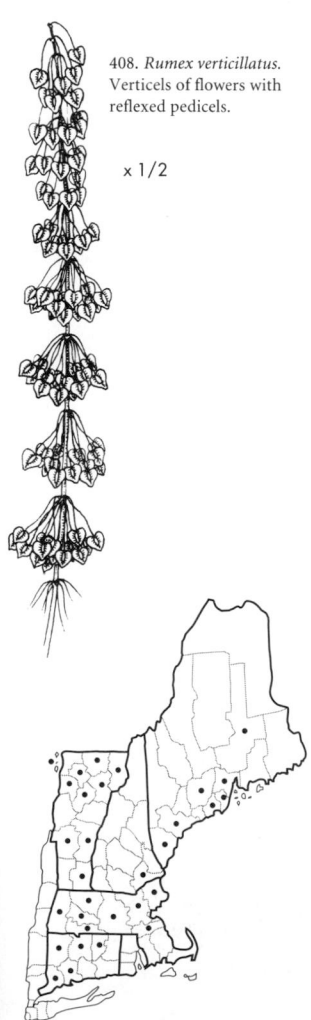

408. *Rumex verticillatus.* Verticels of flowers with reflexed pedicels.

x 1/2

409. *Rumex crispus.* Single leaf with margins crisped.

x 1/4

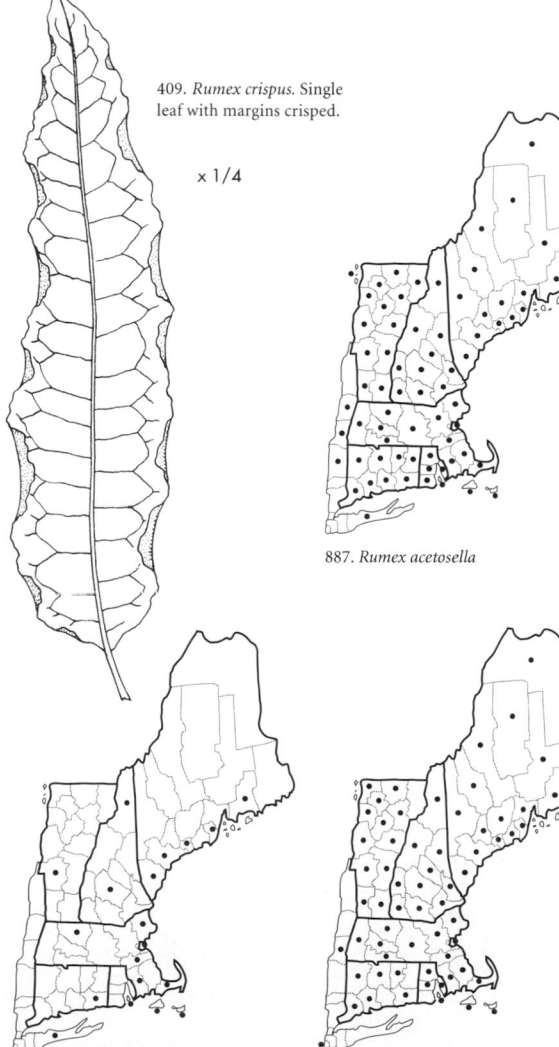

887. *Rumex acetosella*

888. *Rumex acetosa*

889. *Rumex maritimus*

890. *Rumex obtusifolius*

891. *Rumex alpinus*

892. *Rumex aquaticus* var. *fenestratus*

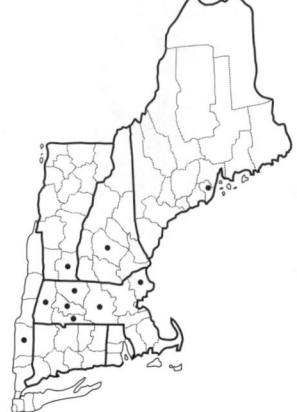

893. *Rumex patientia*

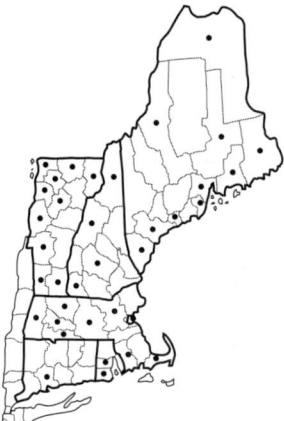

894. *Rumex longifolius*

895. *Rumex orbiculatus* var. *borealis*

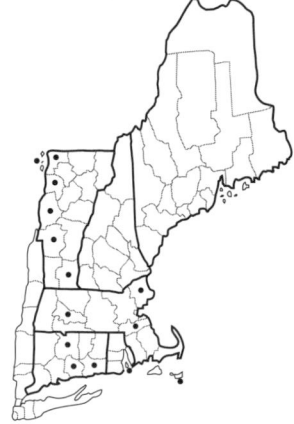

896. *Rumex verticillatus*

897. *Rumex altissimus*

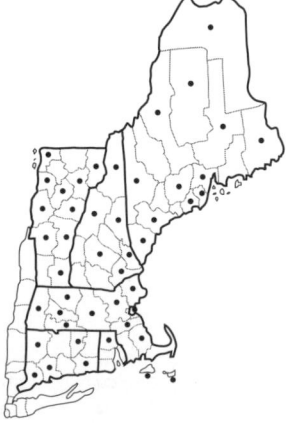

898. *Rumex salicifolius* var. *mexicanus*

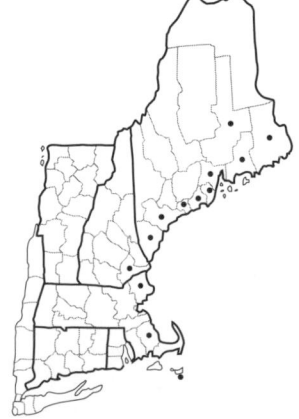

899. *Rumex pallidus*

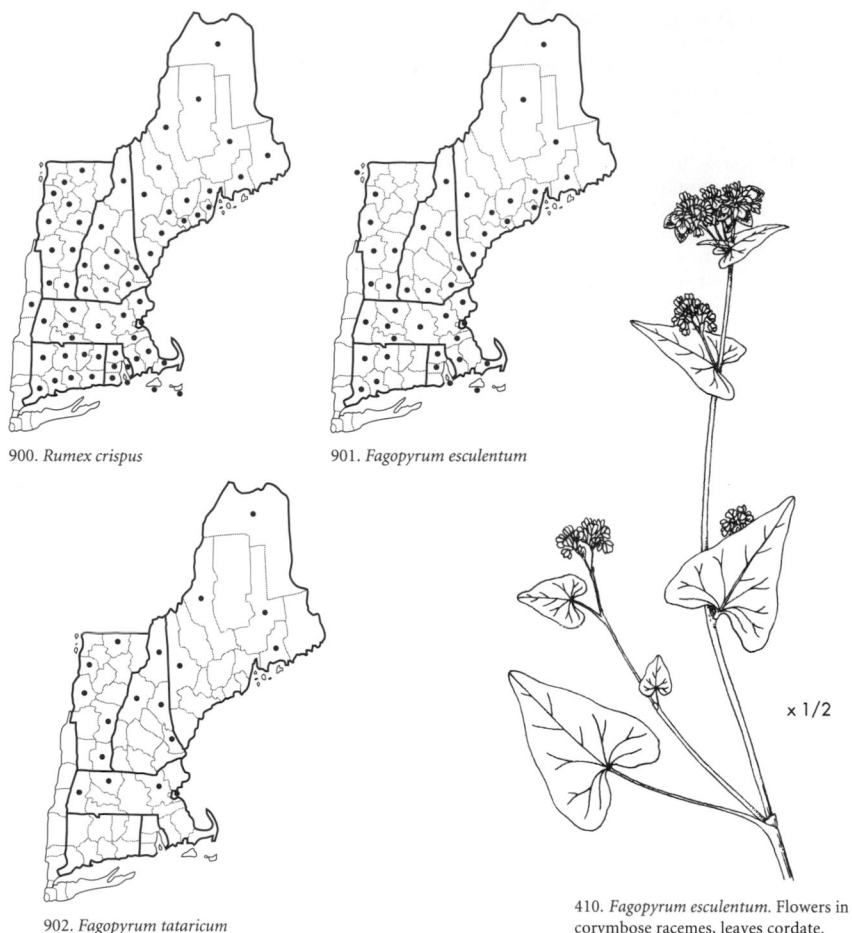

900. *Rumex crispus*

901. *Fagopyrum esculentum*

902. *Fagopyrum tataricum*

× 1/2

410. *Fagopyrum esculentum*. Flowers in corymbose racemes, leaves cordate.

1. F. esculéntum Moench. Buckwheat. Escaped from cultivation to fields, roadsides and waste places. June-September. Fig. 410, Map 901. [*F. sagittatum*]. Long used to make flour for various recipes; certain people may develop a rash from eating buckwheat flour.

2. F. tatáricum (L.) Gaertn. (Tartarian). India-Wheat. Spread from cultivation to fields, roadsides and waste places. July-September. Map 902.

5. Polýgonum L. Smartweed (name based on the thickened nodes of the stem).

Annual or perennial, herbaceous or suffrutescent; stem erect or prostrate; leaves mostly entire, ocreae entire, lobed, lacerate, or fringed with bristles; flowers perfect, in axillary and/or terminal fascicles, spiciform racemes or panicles, calyx 4-6 (usually 5) lobed or parted, greenish, white or pink, stamens 3-8, styles or stigmas 2 or 3, mostly deciduous; achene flattened or trigonous, partly or completely included within the persistent calyx.—Wildl. 4

In addition to the following species *P. chinense* has also been reported for MA.

Chorizánthe R. Br. ex Benth. *púngens* Berth. Similar to Polygonum but differing in having leaves mostly in basal rosettes and opposite, ocreae lacking, upper leaves and calyx lobes spine-tipped. Rarely escaped from cultivation in our range. Reported for Middlesex County MA.

a. Stems glabrous or pubescent, not armed.
    b. Flowers in small clusters or solitary in the axils of bracteal leaves, these
        sometimes much reduced; leaves usually jointed at base. (Fig. 411).
        c. Flowers and fruits (at least some) nodding on recurving pedicels. .... 1. *P. douglasii*
        c. Flowers and fruits on ascending pedicels.
            d. Leaves plicate, with a furrow on each side of the midrib, minutely
                spinulose-serrulate .... 2. *P. tenue*
            d. Leaves flat or revolute-margined, entire or crenulate.
                e. Plant stiffy erect; outer 3 sepals cucullate, exceeding the inner 2 in fruit
                    and mostly concealing them. (Fig. 412).
                    f. Leaves linear to linear-oblong, 4 or more times as long as wide. .... 3. *P. ramosissimum*
                    f. Leaves oval to oblong, 2-3 times as long as wide.
                        Calyx divided to below the middle, below widest part of the achene;
                            pedicels exserted; lower leaves not much longer than upper. .... 4. *P. erectum*
                        Calyx divided to above the middle, above widest part of the achene;
                            pedicels mostly included; lower leaves 2-3 times as long as
                            upper. .... 5. *P. achoreum*
                e. Plant loosely ascending, spreading or trailing, rarely erect; outer 3 sepals
                  usually flat, equalling or shorter than the inner 2.
                    g. Ocreae about 1/3 to 1/2 the length of subtending leaf; sepals spreading
                      in fruit. (Fig. 413) .... 6. *P. glaucum*
                    g. Ocreae less than 1/3 the length of subtending leaf; sepals appressed to
                      fruit.
                      h. Achenes 4-5 mm long .... 3. *P. ramosissimum*
                      h. Achenes 2-4 mm long.
                        i. Achenes exserted 1/4 or more their length. .... 7. *P. fowleri*
                      i. Achenes included or barely exserted.
                        Flowers subtended by reduced bracts, forming a slender,
                          much interrupted raceme .... 8. *P. arenarium*
                        Flowers much overtopped by foliaceous bracts, not forming a
                          raceme. (Fig. 414) .... 9. *P. aviculare*
    b. Flowers in terminal, and often axillary racemes or panicles, these either dense
        or loose (if in small, axillary clusters, leaf bases cordate; bases cuneate or
        rounded in above species); leaves not jointed.
        j. Ocreae with a short, retrorse beard at the base. .... 10. *P. cilinode*
        j. Ocreae without retrorse beard at base.
            k. Stems twining, climbing or trailing.
                Mature calyx broadly winged .... 11. *P. scandens*
                Mature calyx merely keeled .... 12. *P. convolvulus*
            k. Stems not twining, climbing or trailing.
                l. Flowers in axillary and terminal panicles; coarse, bushy-branched,
                  hollow-stemmed plants 1-4 m tall. (Fig. 415).
                    m. Leaves with short, rounded, basal auricles; sepals not winged. .... 13. *P. polystachyum*
                    m. Leaves cordate or truncate at base, not auriculate; mature sepals
                      broadly winged.
                    Leaves truncate to widely cuneate at base, the larger ones usually
                      less than 1.8 dm long .... 14. *P. cuspidatum*
                    Leaves cordate at base, the larger ones usually longer than 1.8 dm. ..... 15. *P. sachalinense*
               l. Flowers in racemes, terminal on the stems and branches. (Fig. 416).
                n. Styles elongate, persistent; flowers deflexed. (Fig. 416). .... 16. *P. virginianum*
                n. Styles short, deciduous; flowers ascending.
                  o. Ocreae not ciliate, entire or merely lacerate.
                    p. Raceme solitary, rarely with a shorter second one present.
                    (Fig. 417).
                    q. Stem simple; leaves basal and cauline; achenes trigonous.
                      Spike 8 mm or less in diameter; lower flowers replaced by
                        bulblets; stem leaves cuneate at base. (Fig. 417) .... 17. *P. viviparum*
                      Spike more than 8 mm in diameter; raceme uniform,
                        without bulblets; stem leaves rounded to cordate at
                        base .... 18. *P. bistorta*
                  q. Stem branched; leaves chiefly cauline; achenes lenticular. .... 19. *P. amphibium*

p. Racemes numerous.
  r. Racemes subtended by a triangular-ovate leaf. .... 20. *P. nepalense*
  r. Racemes not subtended by a triangular ovate leaf.
    Peduncles stipitate-glandular .... 21. *P. pensylvanicum*
    Peduncles glabrous or with sessile glands. .... 22. *P. lapathifolium*
o. Ocreae fringed with cilia or bristles. (Fig. 418).
  s. Stems spreading-hirsute and/or bristly-glandular.
    Stems spreading-hirsute; ocreae with a divergent flange at the
      summit. (Fig. 418) .... 23. *P. orientale*
    Stems bristly-glandular; ocreae without flange. .... 24. *P. careyi*
  s. Stems glabrous or appressed-pubescent.
    t. Calyx glandular-punctate. (Fig. 420).
      u. Glands large, white, occurring only on the inner lobes of
        the calyx. ....25. *P. hydropiperoides*
      u. Glands small, dark or tan, occurring over the entire calyx.
        v. Upper, middle, and often lower ocreae wholly or partly
          enclosing 1-several flowers; achenes dull. (Fig. 419) .... 26. *P. hydropiper*
        v. Flowers confined to the racemes or extending down to
          the upper ocreae; achenes lustrous.
          Racemes loose and much interrupted except at the
            summit. (Fig. 420). .... 27. *P. punctatum*
          Racemes dense, continuous except at base .... 28. *P. robustius*
    t. Calyx not glandular-punctate.
      w. Plant perennial from rhizomes.
        Hairs of ocreae closely appressed, adnate to ocreae at base. . 25. *P. hydropiperoides*
        Hairs of ocreae spreading or not closely appressed, not
          adnate to ocreae at base .... 29. *P. setaceum*
                                      var. *interjectum*
      w. Plant annual.
        Ocreae with cilia less than half as long as sheath, usually
          less than 5 mm long; cilia of ocreolae less than
          2 mm long or absent; leaves often purple blotched .. 30. *P. persicaria*
        Ocreae with cilia more than half as long as sheath, usually
          5 mm or longer; cilia of ocreolae 2 mm or longer,
          equalling or longer than sheath; leaves not
          blotched .... 31. *P. caespitosum*
                                        var. *longisetum*
a. Stems retrorsely barbed. (Fig. 421).
  Leaves hastate; inflorescence of short racemes; achenes lenticular. .... 32. *P. arifolium*
  Leaves sagittate; inflorescence of subcapitate heads; achenes trigonous. (Fig. 421) . 33. *P. sagittatum*

1. *P. douglásii* Greene (for its discoverer). Dry sandy or gravelly soil. August-September. Rare. Map 903. Endangered in VT. Our plants are subsp. *douglasii*.

2. *P. ténue* Michx. (slender). Dry sandy, gravelly or rocky soil. August-September. Fig. 411, Map 904. Endangered in NH. Our plants are var. *tenue*.

3. *P. ramosíssimum* Michx. (much branched). Bushy Knotweed. Borders of salt marshes, roadsides and waste places. July-September. Fig. 412, Map 905. Our plants include var. *ramosissimum* [*P. atlanticum; P. exsertum; P. triangulum*]. and the following var.:

  var. *prolíficum* Small. Flowers included or barely exserted from ocreae (usually exserted in var. *ramosissimum*). [*P. prolificum*].—FAC

4. *P. eréctum* L. (erect). Waste places. August-September. Map 906. Endangered in NH.—FACU

5. *P. achóreum* Blake (without a native land). Roadsides, waste places and gardens. July-September. Rare. Map 907.—FACU

6. *P. glaúcum* Nutt. (blue-green). Seabeach Knotweed. Sandy seabeaches and dunes. July-October. Fig. 413. Map 908. [*P. maritimum*].—FACU

P. bellárdi All. Similar to *P. glaucum* but distinguishable in having a calyx up to 3 mm long and a finely punctate achene 2 mm long (calyx 3 mm or more long and achene smooth and 3 mm or more long in *P. glaucum.*).

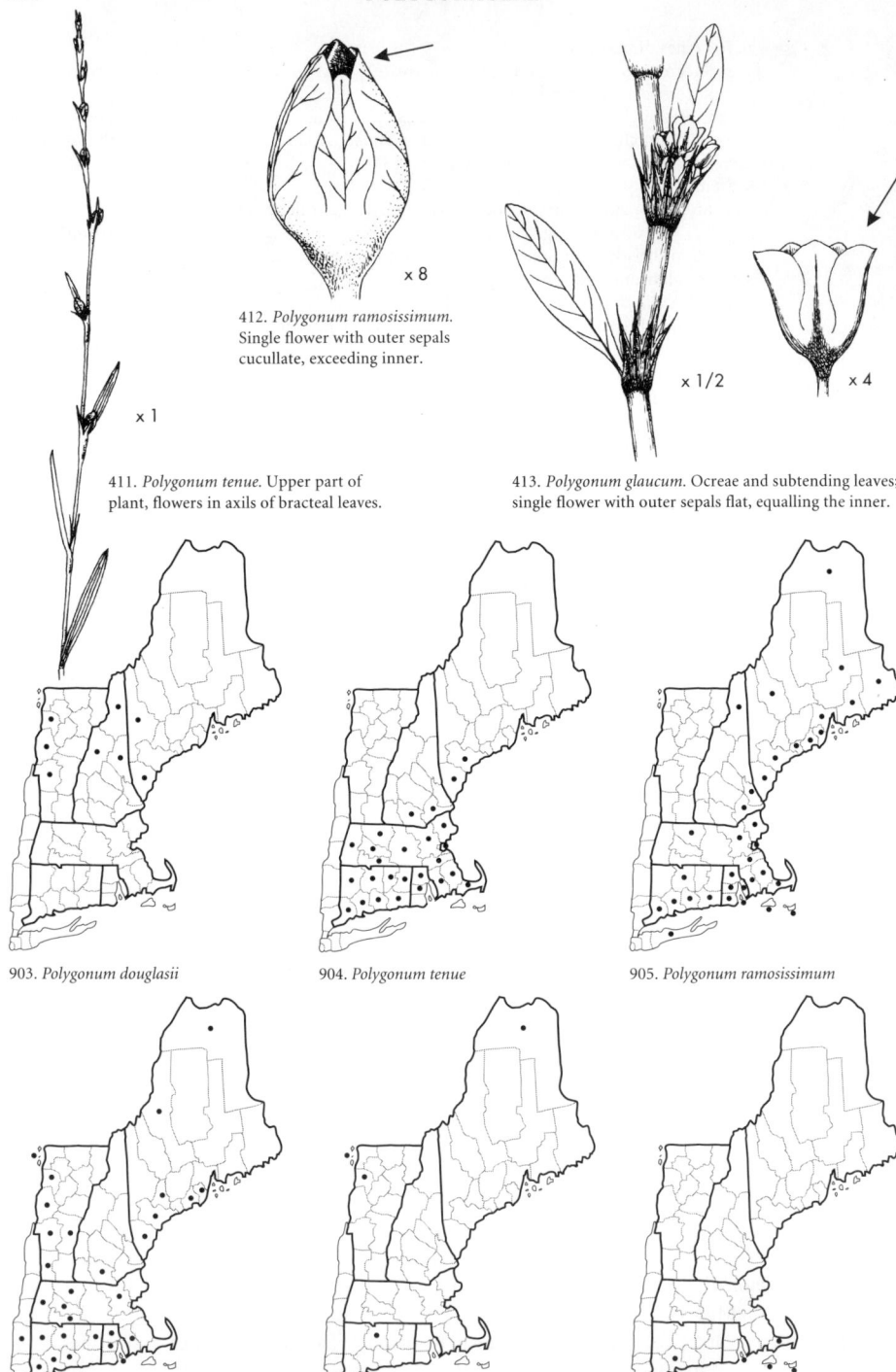

× 8

412. *Polygonum ramosissimum.*
Single flower with outer sepals
cucullate, exceeding inner.

× 1

411. *Polygonum tenue.* Upper part of
plant, flowers in axils of bracteal leaves.

× 1/2

× 4

413. *Polygonum glaucum.* Ocreae and subtending leaves;
single flower with outer sepals flat, equalling the inner.

903. *Polygonum douglasii*

904. *Polygonum tenue*

905. *Polygonum ramosissimum*

906. *Polygonum erectum*

907. *Polygonum achoreum*

908. *Polygonum glaucum*

7. P. fówleri Robins (for its discoverer). Seabeaches and gravelly seacoast. July-September. Map 908a. [*P. allocarpum*].

8. P. arenárium Waldst. & Kit. (of sand). Waste places and roadsides. From Europe and Asia. Reported for RI.

P. argyrocóleon Steud. ex Kuntz. Will key to *P. arenarium* but can be distinguished in having bracts persistent, a calyx 1.5 mm long, and achenes about 1.5 mm long (bracts soon deciduous, leaving a naked raceme, calyx about 2.5 mm long, achenes more than 1.5 mm long in *P. arenarium*). (Asia). From the southwest. Reported for MA, VT.

9. P. aviculáre L. (pertaining to birds). Waste places, roadsides, sidewalk cracks, borders of salt marshes, lawns. July-September. Fig. 414, Map 909. (Naturalized from Europe). [*P. arenastrum; P. exsertum; P. neglectum; P. provinciale*]. Seeds edible, whole or ground into flour; various medicinal uses have also been attributed to this species.—FACU

P. buxifórme Small. Similar to *P. aviculare* but with leaves less than 4 times as long as wide, obtuse (leaves 4 or more times as long as wide and acute in *P. aviculare*). [*P. aviculare* var. *littorale*].

P. arenástrum Jord. Similar to *P. aviculare* and *P. buxiforme* but distinguishable in having leaves of the branches about the same size as those of the stem, fruiting perianth divided to about the middle (leaves of the branches distinctly smaller than those of the stem, fruiting perianth divided past the middle in the latter 2 species). Throughout our range.

10. P. cilinóde Michx. (with ciliate nodes). Fringed Bindweed. Dry, open woods, thickets, roadsides. June-September. Map 910. [*Bilderdykia c.; Tiniaria c.*].

11. P. scándens L. (climbing). False Buckwheat. Moist, low woods and thickets, often along rivers, meadows, fresh marshes, roadsides, waste places. August-September. Map 911. [*Bilderdykia s.; Tiniaria s.*]. Our plants include var. *scandens* and the following vars.:

var. *cristátum* (Engelm. & Gray) Gl. Fruiting calyx 5-7 mm long, with crenate or toothed wings (calyx 7-10 mm long with flat or crisped wings in var. *scandens*). [*P. cristatum*].

var. *dumetórum* (L.) Gl. Fruiting calyx 5-7 mm long with flat, mostly entire wings. [*P. dumetorum*].—FAC

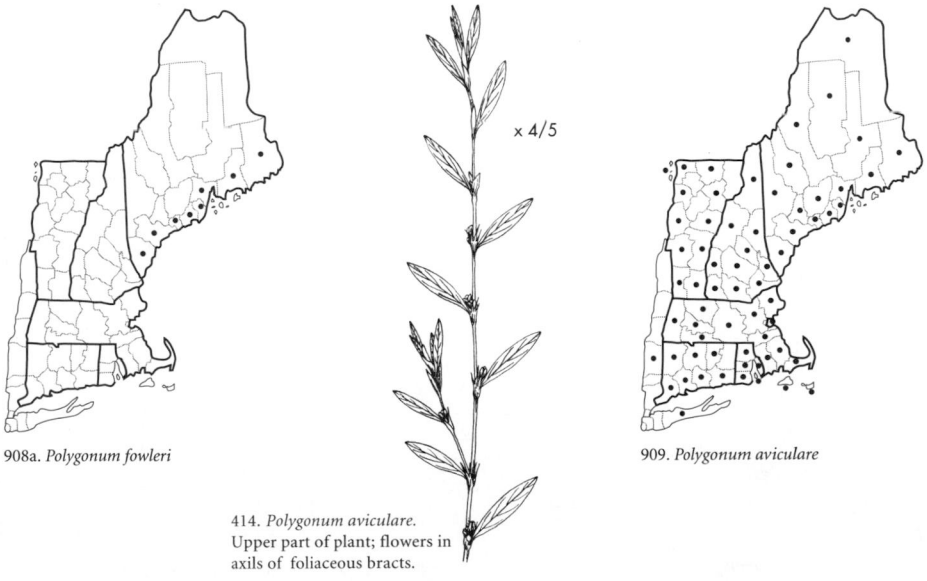

x 4/5

908a. *Polygonum fowleri*

414. *Polygonum aviculare.*
Upper part of plant; flowers in
axils of foliaceous bracts.

909. *Polygonum aviculare*

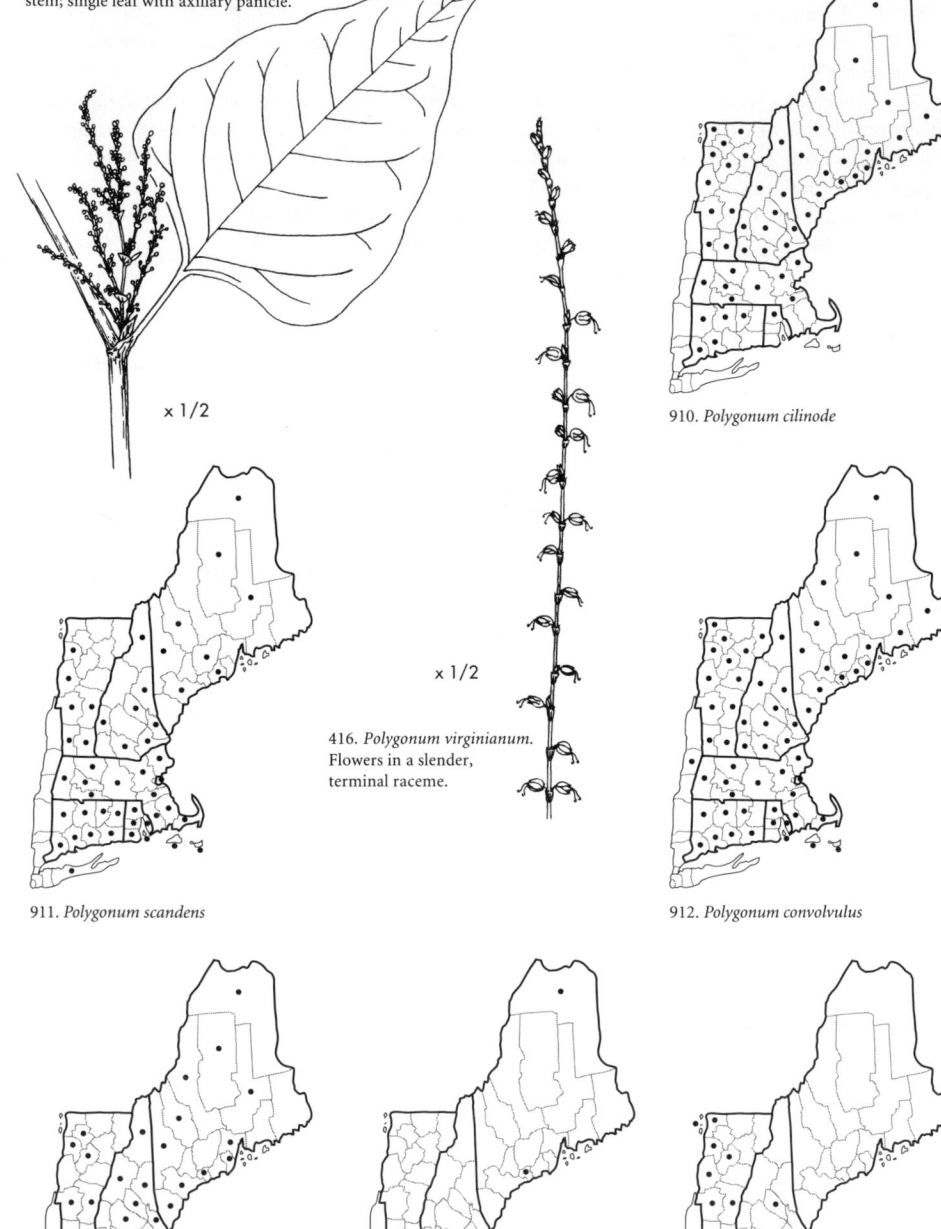

415. *Polygonum cuspidatum*. Section of stem; single leaf with axillary panicle.

x 1/2

x 1/2

416. *Polygonum virginianum*. Flowers in a slender, terminal raceme.

910. *Polygonum cilinode*

911. *Polygonum scandens*

912. *Polygonum convolvulus*

913. *Polygonum cuspidatum*

914. *Polygonum sachalinense*

915. *Polygonum virginianum*

P. aubértii (L.) Henry. Leaves sinuate-margined, acute to obtuse; racemes glandular-pubescent (leaf margins not sinuate, acuminate; racemes not glandular-pubescent in *P. scandens*). Reported for MA.

12. *P. convólvulus* L. (twiner). Black Bindweed. Roadsides and waste places. July-September. Map 912. (Naturalized from Europe). [*Bilderdykia c.; Tiniaria c.*]. Our plants include var. *convolvulus* and the following var.:

var. *subulátum* Lej. & Court. Fruiting calyx 5 mm or more long, with 3 well developed keels (fruiting calyx 4-5 mm long, keels scarcely developed in var. *convolvulus*).—FACU

13. *P. polystáchyum* Wall. (many-spiked). Waste places. August-September. (Introduced from e. Asia). Reported for MA.

14. *P. cuspidátum* Sieb. & Zucc. (abruptly pointed). Japanese Bamboo. Roadsides and waste places. August-September. Fig. 415., Map 913. (Introduced from e. Asia). [*Pleuropteris zuccarinii; Reynoutria japonica*]. Young shoots edible when simmered.—FACU-

15. *P. sachalinénse* F. Schmidt ex Maxim. (of Sachalin Island). Giant Knotweed. Roadsides and waste places. August-September. Rare. Map 914. (Introduced from e. Asia). [*Reynoutria s.*].

16. *P. virginiánum* L. (Virginian). Jumpseed. Rich, moist deciduous woods. July-October. Fig. 416, Map 915. (e. Asia). [*Tovara virginiana*].—FAC

17. *P. vivíparum* L. (with young well developed on the parent plant). Alpine Bistort. Alpine areas in NH, VT (formerly) and ME. July-August. Fig. 417, Map 916. (Eurasia). Endangered in ME. [*Bistorta v.*]. Roots starchy; can be boiled or roasted.—FAC

18. *P. bistórta* L. (double twist, from the often sigmoid rhizome). European Bistort. Rarely escaped from cultivation to thickets, meadows and gardens. May-June. Map 917. (Adventive from Europe). Roots starchy; can be boiled or roasted; young leaves edible as a potherb.—FACW

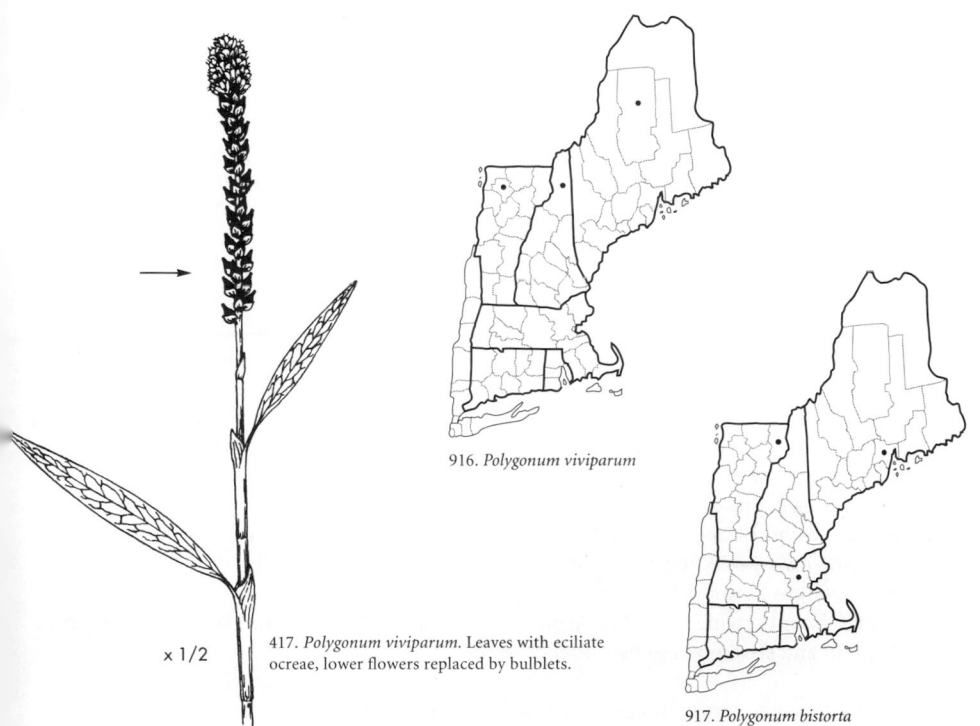

× 1/2

916. *Polygonum viviparum*

417. *Polygonum viviparum*. Leaves with eciliate ocreae, lower flowers replaced by bulblets.

917. *Polygonum bistorta*

19. P. amphíbium L. (amphibious). Water Smartweed. Aquatic form in deep to shallow water, terrestrial form on margins of rivers and ponds. July-September. Map 918. (Adventive from Europe). Represented with us by the following vars.:

var. *emérsum* Michx. On land or emergent; floating leaves not produced; leading spike 4-18 cm long. [*P. coccineum; P. muhlenbergii*].

var. *stipuláceum* Coleman. Aquatic; floating leaves produced; leading spike up to 4 cm long. [*P. natans; P. hartwrightii*].

var. *amphibium* is Eurasian.—OBL

20. P. nepalénse Meisn. (of Nepal). Rarely escaped from cultivation to roadsides and meadows. (Adventive from Asia). Reported for MA, New London County CT.

21. P. pensylvánicum L. (Pennsylvanian). Pinkweed. Meadows, waste places, roadsides and pond margins. July-September. Map 919.—FACW

22. P. lapathifólium L. (dock-leaved). Waste places, fields and pond margins. July-September . Map 920. (Europe). [*P. scabrum; P. tomentosum*]. Our plants include var. *lapathifolum* and the following var.:

var. *salicifólium* Sibth. Leaves white-tomentose beneath (glabrous beneath except often for sessile glands in var. *lapathifolium*). [*P. lapathifolium* var. *incanum*].—FACW+

23. P. orientále L. (eastern). Prince's feather. Escaped from cultivation to roadsides, waste places and cultivated ground. July-September. Fig. 418, Map 921. (Introduced from Eurasia). [*Persicaria o.*].—FACU-

24. P. cáreyi Olney (for its discoverer). Fields, roadsides, waste places, stream and pond margins. July-September. Map 922. [*Persicaria c.*].—FACW

25. P. hydropiperoídes Michx. (resembling *P. hydropiper*). Mild Water-pepper. Pond and stream margins, shallow water, wet meadows, fresh marshes. July-October. Map 923. [*P. opelousanum*]. —OBL

26. P. hydrópiper L. (water-pepper). Common Smartweed. Pond and stream margins, wet meadows and pastures. July-September. Fig. 419, Map 924. [*Persicaria h.*]. Various medicinal uses are cited for this species.—OBL

27. P. punctátum Ell. (dotted). Water-Smartweed. Pond and stream margins, open shrub swamps and wooded swamps, fresh to brackish meadows and marshes. July-October. Fig. 420, Map 925. [*P. acre; Persicaria p.*]. Our plants include var. *punctatum* and the following var.:

var. *confertiflórum* (Meisn.) Fassett. Leaves fleshy, sparsely punctate (not fleshy, strongly punctate in var. *punctatum*). [*P. punctatum* var. *leptostachyum; P.p.* var. *parvum*].—OBL

28. P. robústius (Small) Fern. (more robust). Pond and stream margins, shrub swamps and wooded swamps, wet meadows and fresh marshes, mostly near the coast. August-October. Map 926.—OBL

29. P. setáceum Baldw. (bristly) Stream and pond margins, wooded swamps, and wet woods. August-September. Rare. Reported for Barnstable County MA, Washington County RI. Represented with us as var. *interjéctum* Fern.—OBL

30. P. persicária L. (resembling *Persica*, the peach). Roadsides, waste places, fields and pond margins. June-September. Map 927. [*P. dubium; P. minus; P. maculosum; P. puritanorum; Persicaria persicaria*]. Young plants can be used as a potherb when cooked.—FACW

31. P. cespitósum Blume (tufted). Roadsides and waste places, gardens, meadows, marshes, woodland openings, pond and river margins. July-September. Map 928. [*Persicaria longiseta*]. Represented with us as var. *longisétum* (De Bruyn) Steward.—FACU

32. P. arifólium L. (with the leaf of Arum). Halberd-leaved Tearthumb. Wet meadows, fresh marshes, pond and stream margins, wooded swamps. July-September. Map 929. [*Tracaulon a.*]. —OBL

33. P. sagittátum L. (arrow-shaped). Arrow-leaved Tearthumb. Same habitats as *P. arifolium*. July-September. Fig. 421, Map 930. [*Tracaulon s.*].—OBL

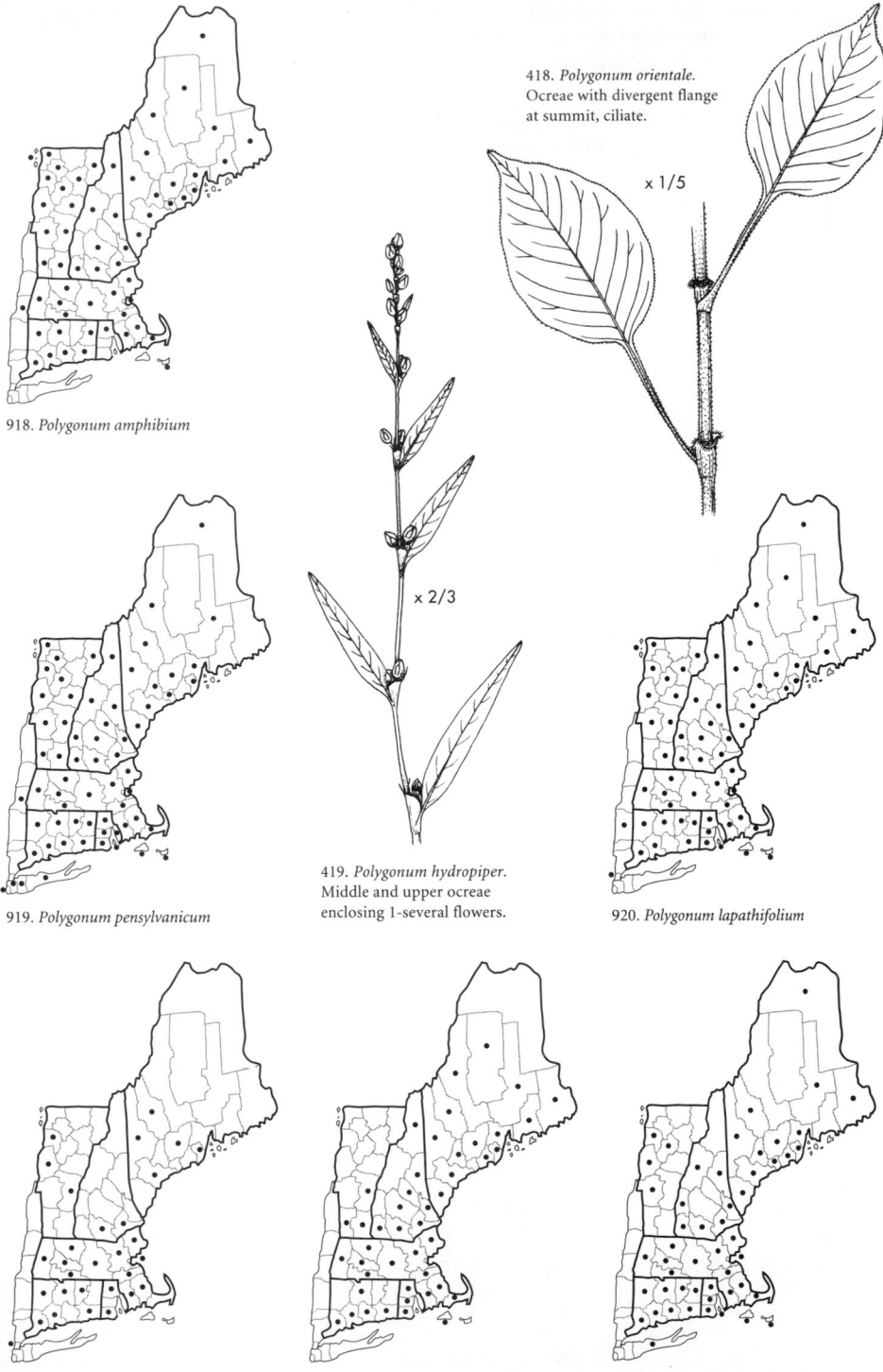

918. *Polygonum amphibium*

418. *Polygonum orientale.* Ocreae with divergent flange at summit, ciliate.

x 1/5

x 2/3

919. *Polygonum pensylvanicum*

419. *Polygonum hydropiper.* Middle and upper ocreae enclosing 1-several flowers.

920. *Polygonum lapathifolium*

921. *Polygonum orientale*

922. *Polygonum careyi*

923. *Polygonum hydropiperoides*

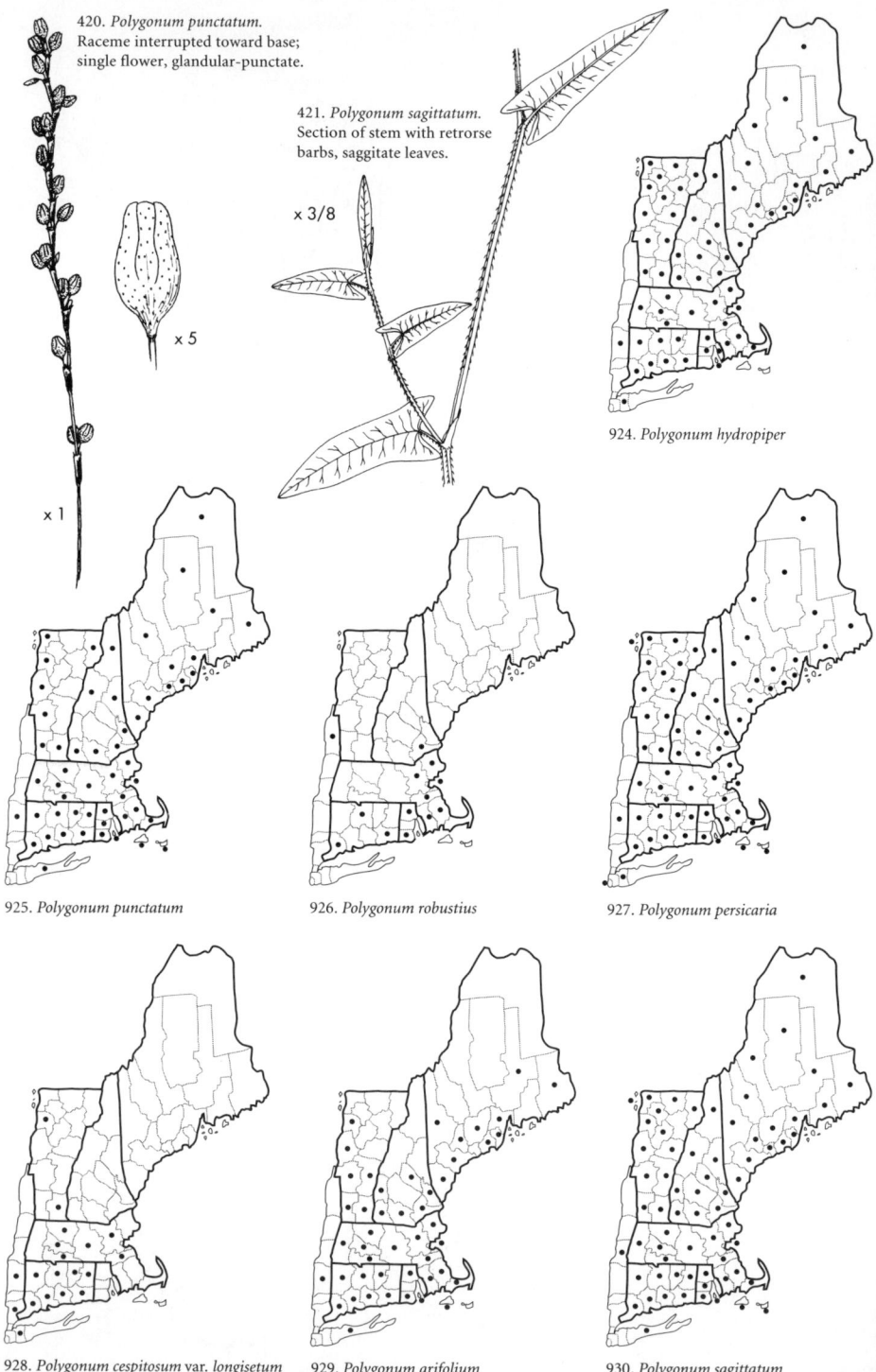

420. *Polygonum punctatum.*
Raceme interrupted toward base;
single flower, glandular-punctate.

421. *Polygonum sagittatum.*
Section of stem with retrorse
barbs, saggitate leaves.

× 3/8

× 5

× 1

924. *Polygonum hydropiper*

925. *Polygonum punctatum*

926. *Polygonum robustius*

927. *Polygonum persicaria*

928. *Polygonum cespitosum* var. *longisetum*

929. *Polygonum arifolium*

930. *Polygonum sagittatum*

Family 74. Chenopodiáceae (Goosefoot Family)

Hermaphrodite, polygamous or monoecious, annual or perennial, somewhat succulent herbs. Leaves mostly alternate, occasionally opposite, sessile or petioled, entire, toothed or lobed, estipulate, sometimes fleshy or reduced to scales. Flowers small, greenish, perfect or unisexual, solitary or clustered in the leaf axils, or aggregated into spikes or glomerules, often bracteate, the bracts herbaceous when present, seldom scarious, mostly regular, calyx 1-5 parted, often fleshy, occasionally lacking, petals lacking, stamens 1-5, inserted on the calyx or hypogynous, ovary superior, of 2-3 carpels, 1- locular, with 1 ovule, styles 1-5. Fruit a utricle, often enclosed by the persistent calyx, seed vertical or horizontal.

a. Leaves all opposite, represented by small scales. (Fig. 422). .... 1. *Salicornia*
a. Leaves alternate, or those at the base of the plant opposite.
  b. Fruit enclosed by 2 valve-like bracts. (Fig. 423). .... 2. *Atriplex*
  b. Fruit not enclosed by 2 valve-like bracts.
    c. Leaves entire, usually less than 5 mm wide.
      d. Leaves and bracts spine-tipped. (Fig. 425). .... 3. *Salsola*
      d. Leaves and bracts not spine-tipped.
        e. Calyx on inner side of the flower only, usually of 1 sepal, the stamens
          and fruit free and exposed .... 4. *Corispermum*
                          hyssopifolium
        e. Calyx completely surrounding stamens and fruit, of 3-5 sepals.
          f. Plants pubescent, especially in the inflorescence.
            g. Pubescence of undersides of leaves stellate; mature sepals
              membranous, erect, not incurved .... 5. *Axyris*
                          amaranthoides
            g. Pubescence simple; mature sepals herbaceous or coriaceous,
              incurved over the flower.
              Fruiting calyx with several or all of the lobes bearing dorsal
                tubercles or hooked spines. (Fig. 427) .... 6. *Bassia*
              Fruiting sepals each bearing a horizontal wing. (Fig. 428). .... 7. *Kochia scoparia*
          f. Plants glabrous, farinose or with resinous dots (glandular-pubescent
            in 1 species of Chenopodium).
            Leaves sessile; flowers mostly in groups of 3. .... 8. *Suaeda*
            Leaves petioled; flowers in groups of irregular numbers. .... 9. *Chenopodium*
    c. Leaves toothed or variously cut or lobed.
      h. Calyx covered with horny, projections, the cluster of flowers appearing
        tuberculate .... 10. *Beta vulgaris*
      h. Calyx not covered with horny projections.
        i. Fruiting calyx encircled by a wheel-like membranous wing. (Fig. 438). .... 11. *Cycloloma*
                          atriplicifolium
        i. Fruiting calyx without a wing.
          Leaves with a pair of teeth near the middle, otherwise entire, 2 or more
            times as long as wide; calyx of 1 bract-like sepal, on one side of
            flower. .... 12. *Monolepis*
                          nuttalliana
         Leaves with more teeth, or less than 2 times as long as wide; calyx
          2-5 parted, surrounding the stamens and fruit .... 9. *Chenopodium*

1. *Salicórnia* L. Glasswort (meaning plants of saline environments with horn-like branches).

Annual or perennial, fleshy, glabrous, freely branched, halophytic herbs, often turning red in autumn, the branches opposite; leaves reduced to minute, opposite scales; flowers perfect, in clusters of 3, each deeply sunk in a pit in the fleshy axis, each cluster above the axil of a scale-like bract, the bracts opposite, in 4 ranks, crowded and forming spikes terminating the branches, calyx obpyramidal, fleshy, unlobed, enclosing the pistil and 1 or 2 stamens, these exserted, styles 2; utricle enclosed in the calyx, seed vertical, pubescent.—Wildl. 1

a. Rhizomatous perennial, often woody; main stems trailing and forming mats; the
    3 flowers in a cluster at or nearly at the same level. .... 1. *S. virginica*
a. Annuals, main stems usually erect; middle flower conspicuously higher than the
    lateral ones. (Fig. 422).
        Bracts mucronate; joints of the spike thicker than long. (Fig. 422). .... 2. *S. bigelovii*
        Bracts obtuse or subacute; joints of the spike mostly longer than thick. .... 3. *S. maritima*

    1. *S. virgínica* L. (Virginian). Perennial Glasswort. Salt and brackish marshes, seabeaches.
August-October. Map 931. Endangered in ME. [*S. ambigua; Sarcocornia perennis*].—OBL
    2. *S. bigelóvii*Torr. (for its discoverer). Dwarf Glasswort. Salt marshes. August-October. Fig. 422,
Map 932.—OBL
    3. *S. marìtima*Wolff. & Jefferies. Slender Glasswort. Salt marshes. August-September. Map 933.
(Africa, Eurasia). [*S. europaea; S. herbacea; S. prostrata*]. Plant used as a potherb, in salads, and
pickled.—OBL
    S. rúbra Nels. (red). Will key to either of the latter 2 species. Bracts are obtuse to subacute and
joints of the spike are as thick or thicker than long. From farther west. Reported for CT.

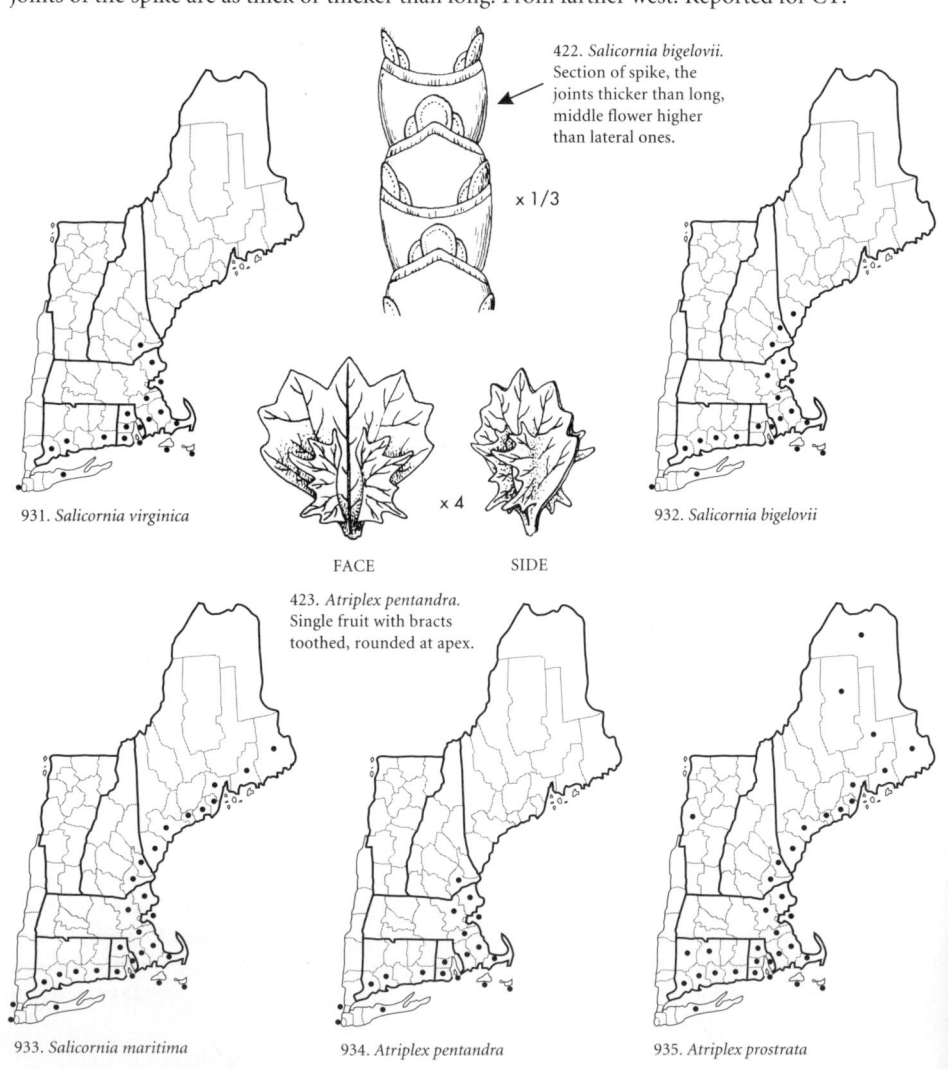

422. *Salicornia bigelovii.*
Section of spike, the
joints thicker than long,
middle flower higher
than lateral ones.

× 1/3

931. *Salicornia virginica*

× 4

FACE   SIDE

932. *Salicornia bigelovii*

423. *Atriplex pentandra.*
Single fruit with bracts
toothed, rounded at apex.

933. *Salicornia maritima*

934. *Atriplex pentandra*

935. *Atriplex prostrata*

2. *Átriplex* L. Orach (ancient Latin name).

Monoecious, annual (ours), usually mealy or scurfy; leaves alternate or the lower opposite, petioled or sessile, variable in shape, linear or lanceolate to elliptic, ovate, rhombic or triangular, entire, lobed or toothed; flowers imperfect, in axillary clusters or the clusters in terminal or panicled spikes, staminate flowers ebracteate, with 3-5 sepals and stamens, the pistillate without sepals (some pistillate flowers ebracteate, with a 3-5 lobed calyx in *A. hortensis*), consisting of a pistil enclosed by a pair of appressed, foliaceous bracts, these enlarged in fruit and sometimes partly united, entire or toothed, their sides flat, with 1 or 2 crests, or tubercled, sometimes with a spongy layer on the inner surface, this strongly or weakly developed, sometimes confined to the base, styles 2; utricle partly or entirely enclosed by the bracts, seed vertical, rarely horizontal, often of 2 kinds, brown and black, the brown larger. Leaves and young shoots edible in salads and as a potherb; starchy seeds were eaten whole or ground into flour by Indians.

a. Margins of fruiting bracts toothed to or nearly to the apex. (Fig. 423).
  b. Lower leaves linear to linear-oblong .... 1. *A. pentandra*
  b. Lower leaves triangular-hastate, lanceolate, oblong or rhombic-ovate.
    c. Lower leaves triangular-hastate with a pair of outward-pointing lobes. .... 2. *A. prostrata*
    c. Lower leaves lanceolate, oblong, oval, or rhombic-ovate without
        outward-pointing lobes.
      d. Leaves entire or remotely toothed; fruiting bracts rounded at apex.(Fig. 423) 1. *A. pentandra*
      d. Leaves coarsely dentate or sinuate-dentate; fruiting bracts acute or
        subacute at apex.
        Staminate flowers in terminal spikes less than 2 cm long. .... 3. *A. rosea*
        Staminate flowers in terminal spikes 3 cm or more long. .... 4. *A. tatarica*
a. Margins of fruiting bracts entire or toothed to or below the middle. (Fig. 424).
  e. Fruiting bracts oval to rotund, rounded at apex, 1-1.5 cm broad. .... 5. *A. hortensis*
  e. Fruiting bracts triangular or rhomboidal, acute or subacute at apex, mostly
    narrower. (Fig. 424).
    f. Fruiting bracts with central part indurated and coriaceous when mature. .... 6. *A. laciniata*
    f. Fruiting bracts entirely herbaceous.
      g. Spikes leafy-bracted to tip .... 7. *A. glabriuscula*
      g. Spikes naked, or flower clusters subtended by minute leaves, or only the
        lower clusters subtended by leafy bracts.
        h. Lower leaves lanceolate or linear-lanceolate.
          Fruiting bracts denticulate, up to 6 mm long, often tubercled on the
            back, leaves variable, often slightly hastate-lobed at the base. ...... 8. *A. patula*
          Fruiting bracts entire-margined, up to 12 mm long, usually smooth
            on the back, leaves lanceolate to oblong, unlobed .... 9. *A. subspicata*
        h. Lower leaves triangular-hastate to lance-hastate; leaf base subcordate,
          truncate or broadly cuneate.
          Bracts 3-5 mm long, with a spongy inner layer present; brown seeds
            1.5-2.5 mm wide .... 2. *A. prostrata*
          Bracts 5-7 mm long, lacking a spongy inner layer; brown seeds 2.5-3.5
            mm wide. .... 10. *A. acadiensis*

  1. *A. pentándra* (Jacq.) Standl. (with 5 stamens). Salt marshes and sheltered bays and sea beaches. August-October. Fig. 423, Map 934. (W.I.). [*A. arenaria*].—FAC-

  2. *A. prostráta* Boucher ex DC. Salt marshes, sea beaches and sand, mud or cobble seashores. August-October. Map 935. (Eurasia). [*A. hastata; A. franktonii; A. patula* var. *hastata; A. triangularis*].—FACW

  3. *A. rósea* L. (roseate). Red Orach. Waste places. August-September. Rare. Map 936. Reported for MA, RI. (adventive from Eurasia).—FACU

  4. *A. tatárica* L. (Tartarian). Around Atlantic seaports. Reported for CT.

  5. *A. horténsis* L. (of the garden). Garden Orach. Spread from cultivation to roadsides and waste places. August-October. Rare. Reported for MA, New Haven County CT. (Introduced from Asia). [*A. nitens*].

  6. *A. laciniáta* L. Seashore; Canadian and European. Reported for Bronx County NY. [*A. sabulosa*].

7. A. glabriúscula Edmonst. (smoothish). Sea beaches, salt marshes and waste places. August-October. Map 937. (Europe). [*A. patula* subsp. *g.*].—FACW

8. A. pátula L. (spreading). Spearscale. Salt and brackish marshes, tidal flats, sea beaches and waste places. August-October. Fig. 424, Map 938. (Eurasia). Our plants are subsp. *patula.*—FACW

A. littorális L. Similar to *A. patula* but with linear leaves rarely over 4 mm broad, fruiting bracts linear to narrowly lanceolate (leaves lanceolate to oblong or ovate, wider than 4 mm, fruiting bracts lanceolate to deltoid in *A. patula*). Throughout our range. [*A. patula* subsp. *l.*].—FACW

9. A. subspicáta (Nutt.) Ryd. Sheltered bays, sea beaches and tidal rivers, and at the upper edges of salt marshes. August-October. Map 939. (Eurasia). [*A. patula* var. *obtusa*].—FACW

10. A. acadiénsis sp. nov. Taschereau and Wright. Salt marshes, sandy and cobble beaches in protected bays and inlets. August-October. Reported for ME.

Spinácia L. (old name) *olerácea* L. (fit for a garden vegetable). Spinach. Occasionally occurring on dumps and in waste places. August-October. Map 940.

3. Sálsola L. Saltwort (from the Latin meaning salty).

Farinose, puberulent, or nearly glabrous, annual herb with freely branched stem; leaves alternate, sessile, entire, fleshy, linear, terete, subulate or filiform, spine-pointed, rigid; flowers perfect, sessile, solitary or several in the leaf axils, often forming terminal spikes, each flower subtended by a pair of spiny bractlets, calyx 5-parted, the lobes incurved over the fruit and forming a short beak, each lobe developing a horizontal wing in maturity, the wings often becoming petaloid, forming a nearly continuous, membranous border, stamens usually 5, ovary dorsiventrally flattened, styles 2; utricle enclosed in the calyx, seed horizontal.

Polýcnemum L. *május* A. Br. Similar to Salsola but distinguishable in having leaves which are merely pointed, not spine-tipped as in Salsola. European. Rarely found in our range. Reported for Westchester County NY.

1. S. austrális R. Br. Russian Thistle. Sea beaches and waste places. August-October. Fig. 425, Map 941. (Eurasia). [*S. iberica; S. kali*]. Young plants can be eaten after boiling until tender.—FACU

S. collína Pallas. Sepals soft with an obscure midvein, inland plants (sepals stiff, ending in a sharp point, maritime in *S. australis*). Map 941a.

4. Corispérmum L. Bugseed (from the Greek, based on fancied resemblence of the seed to a bedbug).

Annual herb, low and branched from the base, glabrous except when young; leaves alternate, sessile, entire, narrowly linear, pointed; flowers perfect, solitary in the axils of leaves (lower flowers) or bracts, forming narrow, terminal spikes, these interrupted or the bracts imbricated and the spike continuous, the spikes sometimes arranged in panicles, bracts ovate to lanceolate, long-acuminate, scarious-margined, concealing the fruits, calyx of usually 1 small, scarious sepal, easily overlooked, stamens 1 or 2, rarely more, ovary laterally flattened, styles 2; fruit oval or elliptic, flat, indurated and indehiscent, plano-convex, with a distinct wing continuous around the margin, seed vertical.

1. C. hyssopifólium L. (hyssop-leaved). Sea beaches, dunes and dry waste places. August-October. Fig. 426. Reported for MA, Dutchess County NY.—FACU

5. Áxyris L. (unshorn).

Monoecious, annual, pubescent herb with numerous short, slender, ascending branches; leaves alternate, entire, petioled, lanceolate to elliptic, becoming reduced above, stellate-pubescent beneath; flowers imperfect, the pistillate each subtended by 3 bracts, in spikes arranged in terminal panicles on naked peduncles, calyx 3-4 parted, pubescent, ovary laterally flattened, minutely 2-winged at summit when mature, styles 2, the staminate in short, slender, naked, terminal spikes, or

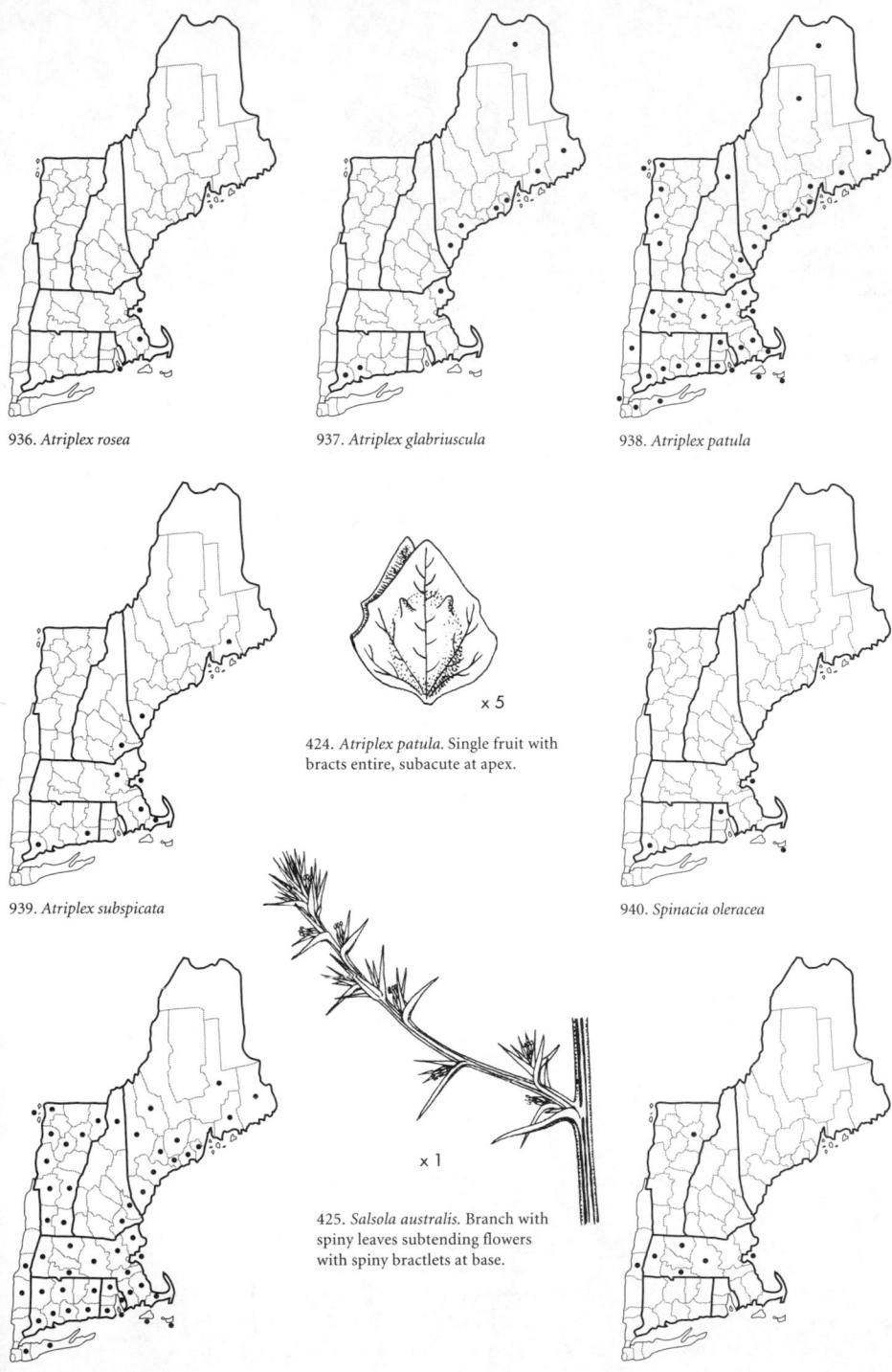

936. *Atriplex rosea*

937. *Atriplex glabriuscula*

938. *Atriplex patula*

424. *Atriplex patula*. Single fruit with bracts entire, subacute at apex. × 5

939. *Atriplex subspicata*

940. *Spinacia oleracea*

425. *Salsola australis*. Branch with spiny leaves subtending flowers with spiny bractlets at base. × 1

941. *Salsola australis*

941a. *Salsola collina*

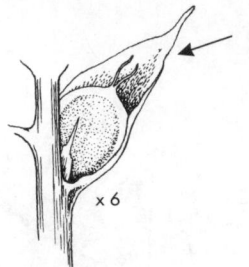

426. *Corispermum hyssopifolium.* Section of spike with ovate-acuminate bract subtending oval fruit.

427. *Bassia hirsuta.* Single fruit, calyx with 2 lobes bearing dorsal tubercles.

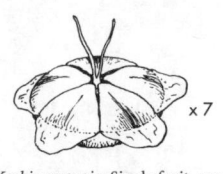

428. *Kochia scoparia.* Single fruit, sepals each bearing a horizontal wing.

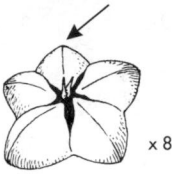

429. *Suaeda linearis.* Single flower, sepals prominently keeled.

942. *Axyris amaranthoides*

943. *Bassia hirsuta*

944. *Bassia hyssopifolia*

945. *Kochia scorparia*

946. *Suaeda linearis*

947. *Suaeda americana*

948. *Suaeda maritima*

few at the tips of the pistillate spikes, calyx 3-5 parted, membranous, stamens 2-5; utricle enclosed in the calyx, 2-winged at the summit, seed vertical.

1. **A. amaranthoídes** L. (like Amaranthus). Russian Pigweed. Waste places, roadsides and cultivated land. June-October. Map 942. (Naturalized from Russia).

6. Bássia All. (for F. Bassi).

Shrubs or annual herbs with much-branched stems; leaves small and numerous, alternate, sessile, pubescent, flat and linear to subterete; flowers perfect, solitary or in short spikes from the upper axils, forming terminal spikes or spike-like panicles, axis of inflorescence and flowers pubescent, calyx 5-parted, the lobes incurved over the flower, keeled, several or all developing dorsal tubercles or spines, stamens 5, ovary dorsiventrally flattened, styles 2-3; utricle enclosed in the calyx, seed horizontal.

Fruiting calyx with 3 or fewer lobes bearing stout dorsal tubercles. (Fig. 427) .... 1. *B. hirsuta*
Fruiting calyx with all 5 lobes bearing slender, hooked dorsal spines. .... 2. *B. hyssopifolia*

1. **B. hirsúta** (L.) Aschers (hirsute). Salt marshes and sea beaches. August-October. Fig. 427, Map 943. (Naturalized from Eurasia). Rare.—OBL
2. **B. hyssopifólia** (Pall.) Volk. (hyssop-leaved). Waste places. August-September. Map 944. (Adventive from Eurasia). Rare.

7. Kóchia Roth (for W. Koch).

Hermaphrodite or polygamous, annual, much branched, usually pubescent (at least above) herb; leaves numerous, alternate, linear to narrowly lanceolate, entire, sessile, often ciliate; flowers perfect or pistillate, sessile, solitary or in small clusters in the axils of bracts forming dense, axillary or terminal spikes, spikes densely villous, calyx 5-lobed, the lobes incurved over the flower, each lobe developing a horizontal wing when mature, stamens 5, ovary dorsiventrally flattened, styles 2-3; utricle enclosed in the calyx, seed horizontal.

1. **K. scopária** (L.) Schrad. (broom-like). Summer-cypress. Waste places and roadsides. September-October. Fig. 428, Map 945. Rare. Tips of the young shoots reported to be edible; seeds may be ground and used as flour.

8. Suaéda Forsk. ex Scop. Sea-blight (Arabic name).

Hermaphrodite or polygamous, annual (ours), fleshy, glabrous, halophytic herbs; leaves very numerous, sessile, entire, alternate, linear, thick and fleshy; flowers perfect or occasionally unisexual, sessile, solitary or clustered in the axils of leaves or leafy bracts, these often forming terminal spikes, calyx deeply 5-parted, fleshy, some or all of the lobes keeled or slightly winged in fruit in some species, sometimes transversely carinate, enclosing the pistil and 5 stamens, ovary dorsiventrally flattened, styles 2-3; utricle enclosed in the calyx, seed horizontal, occasionally vertical. Young plants can be used in salads; seeds may be eaten raw or cooked.

a. Sepals, at least one of them, prominently keeled or winged on the back. (Fig. 429).
    Stems erect, branches spreading or ascending; sepals subequally keeled. .... 1. *S. linearis*
    Stems procumbent, only the flowering tips ascending; 1 or 2 of the sepals very
        strongly keeled, the keel developed as a prominent protuberance. .... 2. *S. americana*
a. Sepals rounded or only obscurely keeled on the back. .... 3. *S. maritima*

1. **S. lineáris** (Ell.) Moq. (linear). Salt marshes and seabeaches. August-October. Fig. 429, Map 946. [*Dondia l.*].—OBL
2. **S. americána** (Pers.) Fern. Salt marshes. August-September. Map 947. Rare. [*Dondia a.*].—OBL
3. **S. marítima** (L.) Dum. (maritime). Salt marshes, sea beaches and muddy or rocky tidal flats. August-September. Map 948. (Eurasia). [*Dondia m.*].
S. ríchii Fern. Leaves rounded in cross section; seeds 1.5 mm or less long (leaves flat on 1 surface and seeds 1.5 mm or longer in *S. maritima*). Endangered in ME.—OBL

9. Chenopódium L. Goosefoot (from the Greek, based on fancied resemblance of the leaf to a goose's foot).

Mostly annual, occasionally perennial, usually white-mealy or glandular-pubescent; leaves alternate, petioled, narrow to broad, entire, toothed or lobed; flowers usually perfect, sessile, bractless, in small clusters which are axillary or aggregated in terminal spikes or panicles, calyx 2-5 parted, the segments usually incurved over and enveloping the fruit, thin or slightly fleshy, stamens mostly 5, styles mostly 2; seed lenticular, horizontal or vertical.—Wildl. 2

a. Calyx shallowly toothed, becoming urceolate to obovoid and reticulate-veined
    when mature. (Fig. 430) .... 1. *C. multifidum*
a. Calyx lobed to the middle or below when mature, not obovoid, urceolate or
    reticulate-veined.
  b. Leaves with yellowish, resinous dots or glandular hairs, at least beneath; calyx
      often glandular; strongly aromatic.
    c. Flowers in dense glomerules in elongate or subglobose spikes. (Fig. 431).
        Calyx not glandular; pericarp glandular-dotted; spikes elongate, often
          panicled .... 2. *C. ambrosioides*
        Calyx with glandular dots; pericarp not glandular-dotted; spikes subglobose,
          not panicled .... 3. *C. carinatum*
    c. Flowers in loose, open panicles, these often numerous, forming large,
      terminal inflorescences. (Fig. 432).
        Plant pubescent with short, glandular hairs; calyx segments not horned. .... 4. *C. botrys*
        Plant glabrous; calyx with yellowish, resinous dots; calyx segments with a
          conical horn toward the tip .... 5. *C. graveolens*
  b. Leaves without yellowish, resinous dots or glandular hairs, although leaves and
      calyx often farinose; calyx not glandular.
    d. Seeds dorsiventrally flattened, wider than high, appearing horizontal.
      (Fig. 435).
      e. Calyx segments, when mature, distinctly keeled, or midvein widened and
        elevated on the back, the calyx thus appearing pentagonal. (Fig. 435).
        f. Leaves linear to narrowly lanceolate, most of them 4 or more times as
          long as wide.
          g. Perianth lobes covering seed at maturity in most flowers; leaves
            1-nerved. .... 6. *C. leptophyllum*
          g. Perianth lobes spreading and exposing seed at maturity in many or
            most flowers; leaves 3-nerved. (Fig. 433).
            Pericarp nonadherent, easily separable from seed; spikes mostly
              compact. .... 7. *C. pratericola*
            Pericarp usually adherent, not easily separable; spikes interrupted. ...... 8. *C. foggii*
        f. Leaves, at least the lower, lanceolate to ovate, oblong or deltoid, less
          than 4 times as long as wide.
        h. Pericarp closely adherent, not readily separable from seed, the latter
          thus appearing to be covered by a translucent film.
          i. Pericarp areolate or honeycombed. (Fig. 434).
            Lower leaves 6 cm or less long; seeds mostly 1.6 mm or
              less wide. .... 9. *C. macrocalycium*
            Lower leaves longer than 6 cm; seeds mostly wider than 1.6 mm. ... 10. *C. bushianum*
          i. Pericarp smooth or minutely roughened.
            Leaves rhombic or rhombic-ovate, less than 3 times as long as
             broad; perianth lobes covering seed at maturity in most
             flowers. (Fig. 435). .... 11. *C. album*
            Leaves oblong-ovate, 3 or more times as long as broad; perianth
             lobes spreading and exposing seed at maturity in many or
             most flowers. .... 12. *C. strictum*
                                 var. *glaucophyllum*
        h. Pericarp loosely covering, easily removed when mature, the seed
          then appearing lustrous.
          Plant low and spreading, densely farinose; leaves hastate-lobed at
            base; calyx mostly covering seed. .... 13. *C. incanum*

Plant erect, green or sparsely farinose; leaves narrowed to base;
   calyx spreading and exposing seed. .... 14. *C. standleyanum*
e. Calyx segments, when mature, rounded on the back, the midvein barely or
   not widened, flat, the calyx not pentagonal. (Fig. 436).
j. Leaves densely farinose beneath .... 15. *C. glaucum*
j. Leaves green or sparsely farinose beneath.
   k. Seed 1.5 mm or more in diameter .... 16. *C. simplex*
   k. Seed less than 1.5 mm in diameter.
      l. Pericarp papery and brittle when mature, readily separable, often
         splitting and exposing shiny seed .... 14. *C. standleyanum*
      l. Pericarp rather closely adherent to seed when mature, not splitting
         and exposing seed (somewhat readily separable in *C.*
         polyspermum, which is totally glabrous; above species is slightly
         mealy on the inflorescence).
         m. Leaves entire .... 17. *C. polyspermum*
         m. Leaves toothed.
            Seed with keeled margins, more than 1 mm wide .... 18. *C. murale*
            Seed with rounded margins, 1 mm or less wide. .... 19. *C. urbicum*
d. Seeds not dorsiventrally flattened, as high or higher than wide, appearing
   vertical. (Fig. 437).
n. Flowers in spherical glomerules, these, in maturity, becoming red and
   berry-like.
   o. Glomerules in upper part of spike not subtended by leaves. .... 20. *C. capitatum*
   o. Glomerules all subtended by leaves.
      Plant upright; glomerules in a terminal spike; seeds channeled around
         the margin .... 21. *C. foliosum*
      Plant branched at base and spreading; glomerules not forming a
         terminal spike; seeds acute around the margin .... 22. *C. humile*
n. Flowers in small clusters in axillary and terminal spikes, not in berry-like
   glomerules.
   p. Leaves densely farinose beneath .... 15. *C. glaucum*
   p. Leaves green or sparsely farinose beneath.
      Styles enlarged, evident in fruit; seed 1.5 mm or more wide; leaves
         triangular-hastate .... 23. *C. bonus-henricus*
      Styles not enlarged or evident in fruit; seed 1 mm or less wide; leaves
         deltoid-ovate to oblong. .... 24. *C. rubrum*

1. C. multifidum L. (much divided). Waste places. July-September. Fig. 430. (Adventive from S. Amer.). [*Roubieva multifida*].

2. C. ambrosioides L. (like Ambrosia). Mexican Tea. Waste places and roadsides. August-October. Fig. 431, Map 949. (Naturalized from Tropical Amer.). Our plants are var. *ambrosioides*. —FACU

3. C. carinátum R. Br. (keeled, from the keeled or hooded sepals). Waste places, roadsides and gardens. July-October. Map 950. (Naturalized from Australia). Rare. [*C. pumilio*].

C. pumilio R. Br. Reportedly distinct from *C. carinatum*, has been documented as occuring in MA.

4. C. bótrys L. (a bunch of grapes, from the inflorescence). Jerusalem-oak. Waste places, roadsides and gardens. July-September. Fig. 432, Map 951. (Introduced from Eurasia). Reported as a possible potherb.

5. C. graveólens Willd. (strong-smelling). Waste places and cultivated soil. August-October. Map 952. (Adventive from Mexico or S. Amer.). Rare. [*C. incisum*].

6. C. leptophýllum (Nutt. ex Moquin) Nutt. ex Wats. (slender-leaved). Dry, sandy soil along the coast, sea beaches and waste places. August-October. Map 953. [*C. pallescens; C. subglabrum*]. Seeds were parched or ground into meal by Indians. —FAC

7. C. pratericola Rydb. (growing in meadows). Waste places and cultivated soil. July-October. Fig. 433. Throughout our range. [*C. desiccatum; C. foggii*].

8. C. fóggii Wahl (for J. Fogg). Dry, sandy waste places. July-October. Reported for ME, NH, VT and MA.

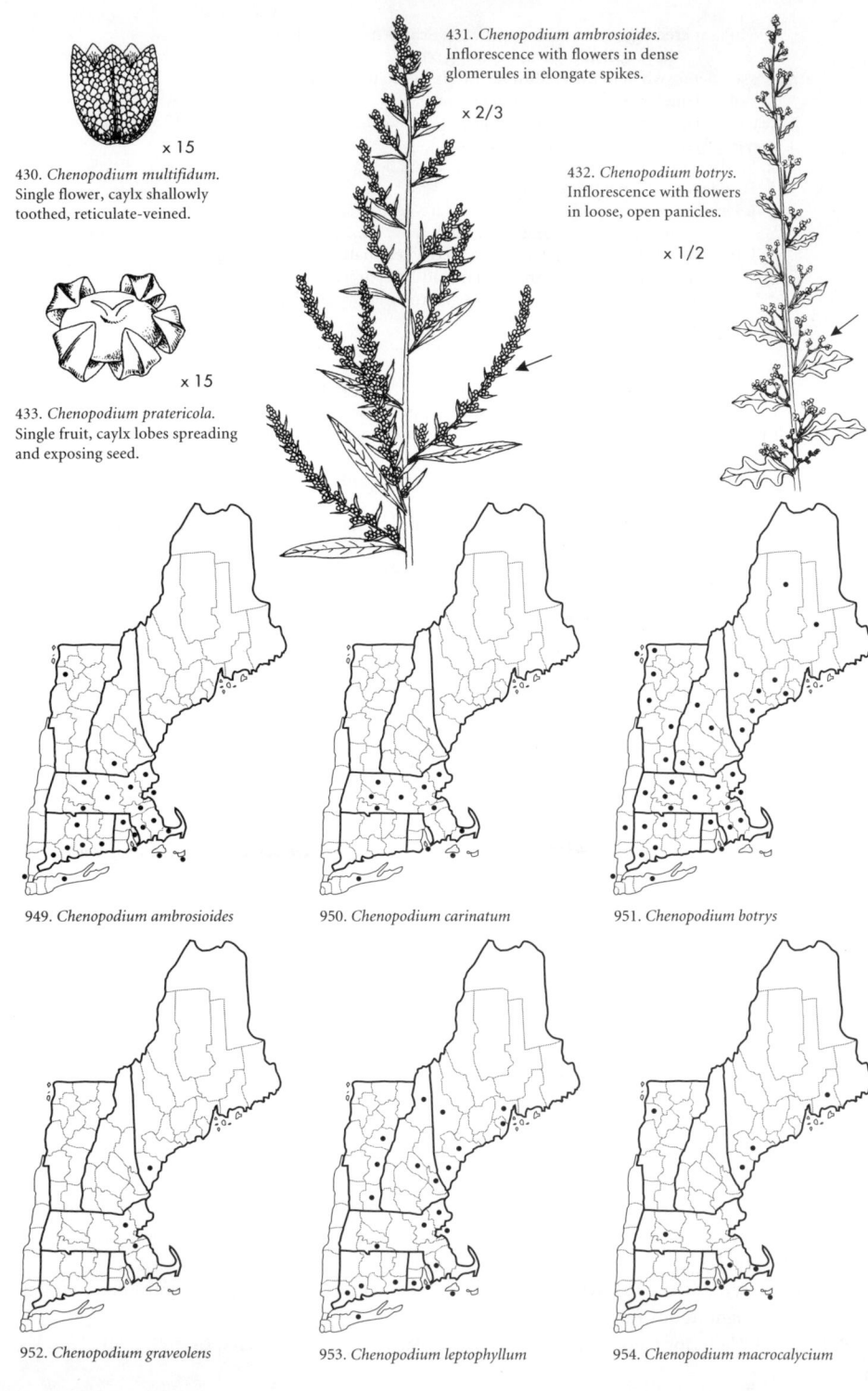

x 15

430. *Chenopodium multifidum.*
Single flower, caylx shallowly
toothed, reticulate-veined.

x 15

433. *Chenopodium pratericola.*
Single fruit, caylx lobes spreading
and exposing seed.

431. *Chenopodium ambrosioides.*
Inflorescence with flowers in dense
glomerules in elongate spikes.

x 2/3

432. *Chenopodium botrys.*
Inflorescence with flowers
in loose, open panicles.

x 1/2

949. *Chenopodium ambrosioides*

950. *Chenopodium carinatum*

951. *Chenopodium botrys*

952. *Chenopodium graveolens*

953. *Chenopodium leptophyllum*

954. *Chenopodium macrocalycium*

9. C. macrocalýcium Aellen (with large calyx). Dry, sandy waste places along coast. September-October. Map 954. [*C. berlandieri* var. *m.*].

C. berlandiéri Moq. Similar to *C. macrocalycium* but with sepals having a keel about half of the width of the sepal, style bases prominent on the seeds (sepals with a keel less than half the width of the sepal and style bases lacking or not prominent in *C. macrocalycium*). From farther south and west. Reported for MA, ME, NH.

Represented with us by the following vars.:

var. *zscháckei* (Murr.) Murr. Pericarp with a light yellowish area at the base of the style.

var. *bosciánum* (Moq.) M. A. Wahl. Pericarp lacking a light yellowish area at base of style; uniformly colored.

C. watsónii A. Nels. Similar to the latter 2 species but with mature pericarp white, seeds about 1 mm wide (pericarp transparent, seeds 1-1.5 mm wide in *C. macrocalycium* and *C. berlandieri*). From farther west. Reported for ME.

10. C. bushiánum Aellen (for B. Bush). Waste places, roadsides, cultivated soil and seashores. August-October. Fig. 434, Map 955. [*C. berlandieri* var. *b.*]. Our plants are var. *bushianum.*

11. C. álbum L. (white). Lamb's-quarters. Waste places, roadsides and cultivated soil. August-September. Fig. 435, Map 956. (Naturalized from Europe). Our plants include var. *album* and the following var.:

var. *missouriénse* (Aellen) Bassett & Crompton. Plant densely branched (sparsely branched in var. *album*). [*C. missouriense*]. Young plants favored as a potherb; seeds may be ground and used as flour.—FACU+

C. opulifólium Schrad. Similar to *C. album* but distinguishable in having leaves about as broad as long, sepals united to or above broadest part of fruit (leaves distinctly longer than broad, sepals not united up to the broadest part of the fruit in *C. album*). Reported for MA, RI.

12. C. strictum Roth (erect) Waste places and roadsides. August-September. Map 957. Represented with us as var. *glaucophýllum* (Aellen) Wahl.

13. C. incánum (Wats.) Heller (hoary). Waste places. July-October. From farther west. Reported for ME. [*C. fremontii* var. *i.*]. Seeds were parched or ground into meal by Indians.

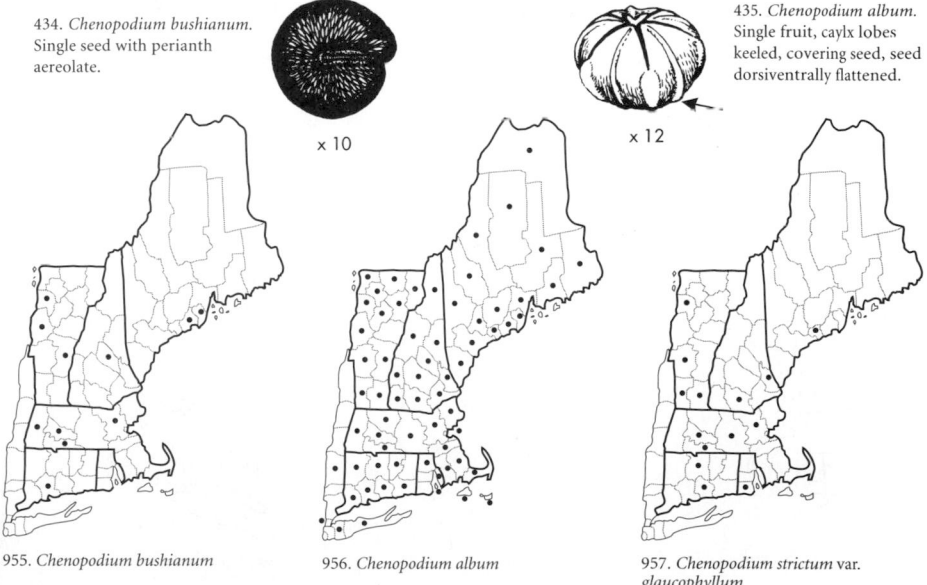

434. *Chenopodium bushianum.* Single seed with perianth aereolate.

× 10

435. *Chenopodium album.* Single fruit, caylx lobes keeled, covering seed, seed dorsiventrally flattened.

× 12

955. *Chenopodium bushianum*

956. *Chenopodium album*

957. *Chenopodium strictum* var. *glaucophyllum*

14. *C. standleyánum* Aellen. (for P. Standley). Dry, often rocky woods, thickets, clearings, waste places and roadsides. August-September. Map 958. Endangered in ME, NH. [*C. boscianum; C. berlanderi* var. *boscianum*].

15. *C. glaúcum* L. (blue-green). Oak-leaved Goosefoot. Waste places, roadsides, cultivated land. July-September. Map 959. (Naturalized from the Old World).—FACW-

C. salínum Standl. Similar to *C. glaucum* but distinguishable in having sharply toothed leaves and continuous spikes (leaves entire, sinuate, or with a few low-teeth and spikes mostly interrupted in *C. glaucum*). From farther west. Reported for NH.

16. *C. símplex* (Torr.) Raf. Maple-leaved Goosefoot. Rocky, open woods, thickets, clearings, waste places and cultivated soil. July-September. Map 960. [*C. gigantospermum; C. gigantospermum* var. *standleyanum; C. hybridum*].

17. *C. polyspérmum* L. (many-seeded). Waste places and cultivated soil. July-September. Map 961. (Adventive from Europe).

18. *C. murále* L. (of walls). Waste places and cultivated soil. August-September. Fig. 436, Map 962. (Naturalized from Europe).

19. *C. úrbicum* L. (of cities). Waste places. August-September. Map 963. (Naturalized from Europe). Young shoots and leaves used as a potherb.

20. *C. capitátum* (L.) Aschers. (with heads). Strawberry-blite. Open woods and clearings, often after a fire, roadsides, waste places. June-August. Map 964. (Eurasia). Rare. [*Blitum c.*]. Reported as a possible potherb.

21. *C. foliósum* (Moench) Aschers. (leafy). Waste places. June-August. Rare. (Adventive from Europe). Reported for ME, Middlesex County MA.

22. *C. húmile* Hook. (low-growing). Along the seacoast. August-September. Rare. Reported for Cumberland County ME, Nantucket County, MA.

23. *C. bónus-henrícus* L. (good Henry). Good King Henry. Waste places and roadsides. June-September. Map 965. (Naturalized from Europe). Young shoots and leaves used as a potherb; leaves used to relieve eruptions of the skin; seeds have laxative effect.

24. *C. rúbrum* L. (red). Coast-blite. Salt marshes. July-September. Fig. 437, Map 966. (Europe). [*C. chenopodioides*].—FACW

10. *Béta* L. Beet.

1. *B. vulgáris* L. (common). Occasional in waste places and around seaports. Map 967.

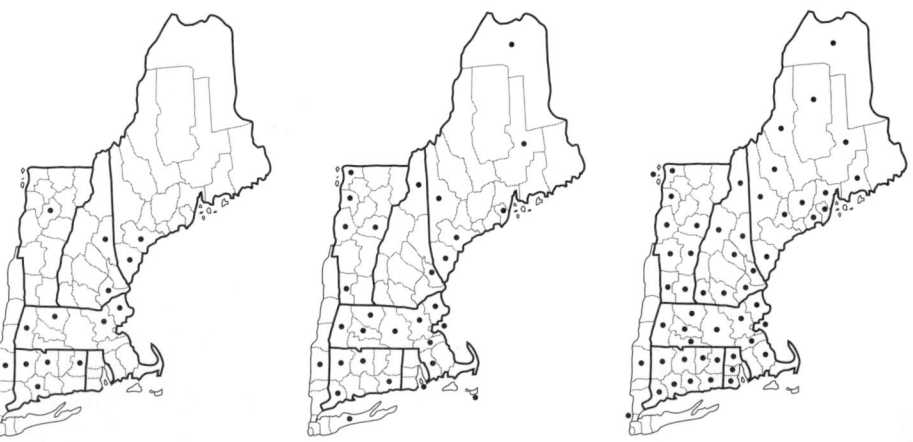

958. *Chenopodium standleyanum*   959. *Chenopodium glaucum*   960. *Chenopodium simplex*

× 15

436. *Chenopodium murale*. Single fruit, caylx lobes not keeled.

961. *Chenopodium polyspermum*

962. *Chenopodium murale*

963. *Chenopodium urbicum*

964. *Chenopodium capitatum*

965. *Chenopodium bonus-henricus*

966. *Chenopodium rubrum*

× 15

437. *Chenopodium rubrum*. Single fruit, seed not dorsiventrally compressed.

967. *Beta vulgaris*

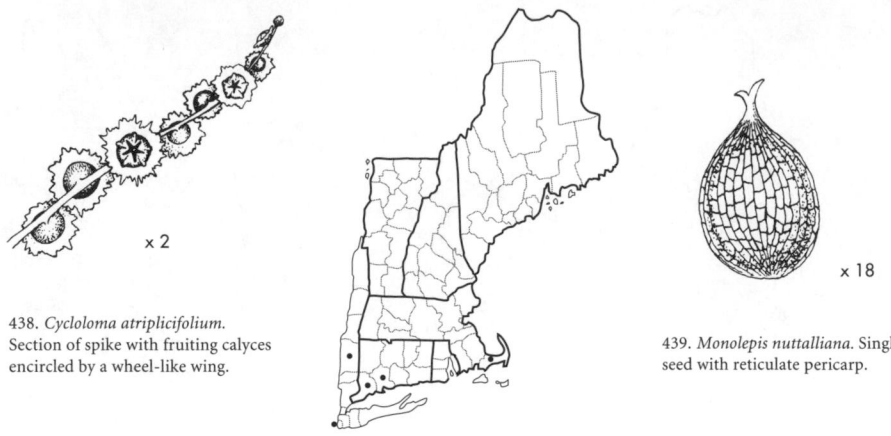

438. *Cycloloma atriplicifolium.*
Section of spike with fruiting calyces
encircled by a wheel-like wing.

439. *Monolepis nuttalliana.* Single
seed with reticulate pericarp.

×2

×18

968. *Cycloloma atriplicifolium*

11. *Cyclolóma* Moq. Winged pigweed (from the Greek, based on the wing encircling the calyx).
Hermaphrodite or polygamous, annual, much-branched herb, glabrous except when young; leaves alternate, petioled, lanceolate, coarsely and irregularly dentate, progressively reduced upward, often deciduous before fruiting; flowers perfect or pistillate, sessile, each subtended by a minute bract, in interrupted spikes arranged in open panicles, calyx 5-lobed, the segments keeled, incurved over the flower, a horizontal, circumferential, broad, membranous, erose wing developing below the lobes, stamens 5, ovary dorsiventrally flattened, styles usually 3; utricle enclosed in the calyx, seed horizontal, bearing scattered, silky, white pubescence.

1. *C. atriplicifólium* (Spreng.) Coult. (with leaves of Atriplex). Dry, sandy waste places. July-September. Fig. 438, Map 968. Seeds can be ground and used as meal.—FACU-

12. *Monólepis* Schrad. (from the Greek, meaning solitary scale).
Glabrous annual herb, low and branched from the base; leaves alternate, short-petioled to sessile, lanceolate to ovate, at least the lower few-toothed or with a pair of teeth near the middle, cuneate to the base; flowers perfect, sessile, in dense clusters in the upper axils forming a leafy terminal spike, calyx of 1 bract-like sepal, stamen 1, ovary laterally flattened, styles 2; seed vertical, pericarp reticulate-honeycombed.

1. *M. nuttalliána* (Schult.) Greene (for T. Nuttall). Dry often alkaline soil in waste places. June-September. Fig. 439. Rare. Reported for York County ME. Can be used as a potherb.

Family 75. Amarantháceae (Amaranth Family)

Hermaphrodite, monoecious, dioecious or polygamous, annual herbs (ours). Leaves alternate or opposite, simple, sessile or petioled, entire or undulate-margined, estipulate. Flowers small, green, purplish, white or colored, perfect or unisexual, variously clustered in axillary or terminal spikes, heads or panicles, each subtended by 3 bracts, these sometimes colored, sometimes concealing the perianth, calyx of 3-5 united or separate sepals (or absent in pistillate flowers of some *Amaranthus* spp.), petals lacking, stamens usually 5, rarely fewer, hypogynous, sometimes partly or completely united into a lobed, petaloid tube, the lobes frequently extending beyond the anthers, ovary superior, of 2-3 carpels, 1-locular, often compressed, with 1-several ovules, stigmas 1-3. Fruit an indehiscent utricle or a pyxis.

a. Leaves opposite. (Fig. 440) .... 1. *Froelichia gracilis*
a. Leaves alternate.
  Ovules 2 or more; inflorescence white, silvery, pink, red or yellow. .... 2. *Celosia cristata*
  Ovule solitary; inflorescence green or dull purplish. .... 3. *Amaranthus*

1. *Froelíchia* Moench Cottonweed (for J. Froelich).

Hermaphrodite, erect, branched, (usually from the base in ours) or simple, woolly herbs; leaves opposite, sessile, or the lower and basal petioled, linear to narrowly lanceolate, entire, pubescent on both sides; flowers perfect, in terminal spikes, calyx tubular, 5-lobed at the summit, densely woolly, becoming indurate and somewhat flattened in fruit, bearing 2 longitudinal rows (ours) of spinose processes and several basal tubercles on the faces, stamens 5, the filaments united into a tube surrounding the ovary and equalling the calyx, the tube 5-cleft at the summit and bearing the 1-celled anthers between the lobes, style slender, stigma capitate, ovule 1; utricle indehiscent, enclosed in the calyx.

Gomphréna L. *globósa* L. Globe Amaranth. Flowers in showy, subglobose, solitary heads. Rarely escaped from cultivation. (Introduced from Tropical Asia). Reported for MA, Suffolk County NY.

  1. *F. grácilis* (Hook.) Moq. (slender). Waste places. July-September. Fig. 440, Map 969.

2. *Celósia* L. Celosia (from the Greek, referring to the silvery appearance of the spikes).

Hermaphrodite, erect, often much branched, glabrous herbs; leaves alternate, entire, lanceolate to linear, short petioled; flowers perfect, clustered into a dense, cristate, fan shaped or flattened, somewhat amorphous terminal structure, white, silvery, pink, red or yellow, sepals 5, distinct, scarious, erect, concealing the utricle, stamens 5, united at the base, style elongate, exserted at maturity, stigma capitate, ovules several; utricle usually circumscissile at the middle, seeds lenticular.

  1. *C. cristáta* L. (crested). Cockscomb. Much cultivated and occasionally escaped to waste places. Fig. 441. (Introduced from the Tropics). Reported for CT, VT. A cultigen derived from *C. argentea*; reports of the latter species for our range have not been substantiated. [*C. argentea* var. *c.*].

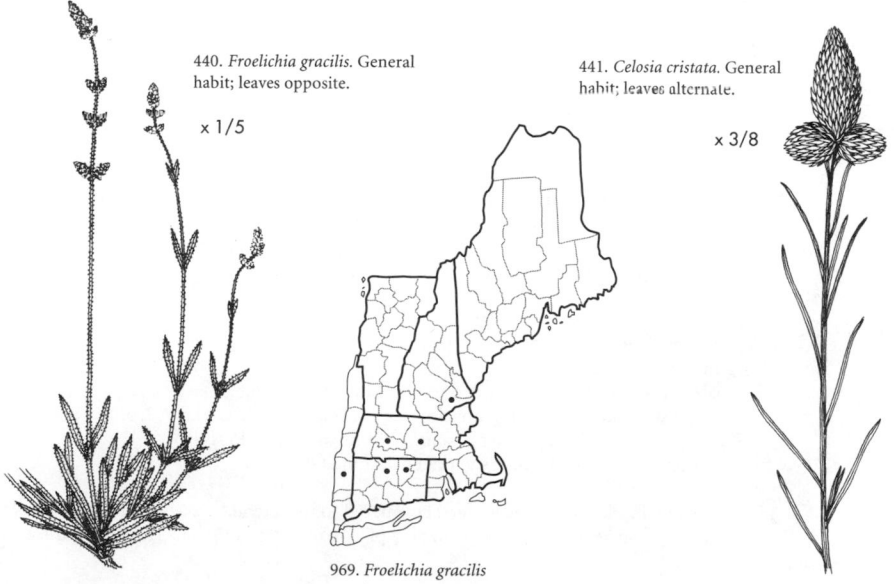

440. *Froelichia gracilis*. General habit; leaves opposite.

x 1/5

441. *Celosia cristata*. General habit; leaves alternate.

x 3/8

969. *Froelichia gracilis*

3. *Amaránthus* L. Amaranth (from the Greek, referring to the persistent bracts and calyx).

Monoecious, dioecious or polygamous, prostrate to erect, usually much branched, glabrous or pubescent herbs; leaves alternate, petioled, entire or undulate-margined; flowers perfect or unisexual, in axillary clusters or in axillary and/or terminal simple or panicled spikes, green or dull purplish, calyx of 1 to 5 separate sepals, often aristate, or absent from pistillate flowers in some species, stamens usually 5, rarely fewer, separate, ovary laterally compressed, stigmas 2-3; utricle ovoid or oblong, 2-3 beaked by the persistent stigmas, indehiscent, or bursting irregularly, or circumscissile across the middle, seed lenticular to round or obovate. (*Acnida*).—Wildl. 2

In addition to the following species *A. dubius* has also been reported for MA.

a. Stem bearing a pair of stipular spines at the base of most leaves .... 1. *A. spinosus*
a. Stem without spines.
  b. Pistillate flowers without sepals (or rarely with 1 or 2 rudimentary sepals less
      than 1 mm long); plants dioecious.
      Seed 1 mm or less long; utricle up to 2 mm long .. . . 2. *A. tuberculatus*
      Seed 2 mm or more long; utricle 2.5-4 mm long. .... 3. *A. cannabinus*
  b. Pistillate flowers with 1-5 well developed sepals 1 mm or more long; plants
      monoecious (*A. palmeri* and *A. rudis* dioecious).
    c. Flowers in axillary clusters and sometimes also in short terminal spikes.
      (Fig. 443).
      d. Utricle circumscissile at the middle, the top falling off as a lid, or
          dehiscence line evident.
          Plant trailing; bracts equalling or slightly exceeding flower; sepals of
             pistillate flowers usually 5. (Fig. 442). .... 4. *A. blitoides*
          Plant erect; bracts 2-3 times as long as the flower; sepals of pistillate
             flowers usually 3 .... 5. *A. albus*
      d. Utricle indehiscent.
          Utricle 4 mm or more long (except in similar species *A. crispus*); sepals
             of pistillate flowers 5 .... 6. *A. pumilus*
          Utricle less than 3 mm long; sepals of pistillate flowers 3. .... 7. *A. blitum*
    c. Flowers in elongate terminal simple or panicled spikes; sometimes also in
      axillary clusters, spikes or panicles. (Fig. 445).
      e. Leaves retuse or emarginate .... 7. *A. blitum*
      e. Leaves acute, obtuse or rounded.
        f. Utricle indehiscent.
          Utricle rugose; sepals of pistillate flowers 3. .... 8. *A. viridis*
          Utricle smooth; sepals of pistillate flowers 2. .... 9. *A. deflexus*
        f. Utricle circumscissile at the middle, the top falling off as a lid, or
          dehiscence line evident.
          g. Bracts less than twice as long as the flower; inflorescence usually red
            or purple.
            Inflorescence pendulous, greatly elongated; inner sepals spatulate,
              obtuse or emarginate .... 10. *A. caudatus*
            Inflorescence spreading to erect, not greatly elongated; inner sepals
              oblong, acute .... 11. *A. cruentus*
          g. Bracts 2-3 times as long as the flower; inflorescence usually green.
            (Fig. 444).
           h. Sepals of pistillate flowers spatulate, recurved; plant dioecious. .... 12. *A. palmeri*
           h. Sepals of pistillate flowers oblong to lanceolate, not recurved; plant
             monoecious.
            i. Sepals of pistillate flowers rounded to truncate, mucronulate,
              conspicuously exceeding utricle. (Fig. 444) .... 13. *A. retroflexus*
            i. Sepals of pistillate flowers sharply acute, as long or slightly longer
              than utricle (conspicuously longer in some flowers in
              A. powellii).
             Terminal spike greatly prolonged compared to the lateral. .... 14. *A. powellii*
             Terminal spike not disproportionately prolonged. (Fig. 445). ..... 15. *A. hybridus*

1. A. spinósus L. (spiny). Thorny Amaranth. Waste places and cultivated ground. July-September. Map 970.—FACU

2. A. tuberculátus (Moq.) Sauer. (with tubercles). Water Hemp. Waste places, cultivated ground and shores of lakes and rivers. July-October. Map 971. [*Acnida altissima; A. subnuda; A. tuberculata*]. —FACW

3. A. cannábinus (L.) Sauer. (like Cannabis). Salt Marsh Hemp. Salt and brackish marshes and tidal rivers. July-September. Map 972. [*Acnida cannabina*].—OBL

4. A. blitoídes Wats. Tumbleweed. Roadsides and waste places. July-October. Fig. 442, Map 973. [*A. graecizans*]. Seeds were used by Indians to make meal.

5. A. álbus L. (white). Tumbleweed. Fields, cultivated ground and waste places. July-September. Fig. 443, Map 974. [*A. graecizans*].—FACU

6. A. púmilus Raf. (dwarf). Seabeach Amaranth. Sea beaches. July-September. Reported for CT, RI, Nantucket and Martha's Vineyard Islands, MA and Suffolk County NY.—FACW

A. críspus (Lesp. & Thev.) A. Br. Similar to *A. pumilus* but distinguishable in having sepals less than 2 mm long and fruits 2 mm or less long (sepals 2 mm or more long and fruits 4 mm or more long in *A. pumilus*). South American; a waif in our range. Reported for Kings County NY.

7. A. blítum L. Waste places, fields, cultivated soil, river shores. August-September. Map 975. (Adventive from the Tropics). [*A. ascendens; A. lividus*].

8. A. víridis L. (green). Waste places. July-September. (Adventive from the Old World). Reported for Suffolk County MA; Bronx County NY. [*A. gracilis*].

9. A. defléxus L. (turned back). Waste places. July-September. Reported for Berkshire County MA.

10. A. caudátus L. (tailed). Escaped from cultivation to waste places. August-September. Map 976. (Introduced from Tropical Amer.).

11. A. cruéntus L. (stained with blood). Roadsides and waste places. August-September. Map 977. (Adventive from Asia). [*A. hybridus* subsp. *c.*]. Seeds can be eaten whole or ground into flour or meal.

A. hypochondríacus L. Prince's feather. Similar to *A cruentus* and *A. caudatus* but with inflorescence stiffly erect, bract equalling the style branches (inflorescence pendulous to spreading or erect, bract shorter than the style branches in the latter 2 species). Occasionally escaped from cultivation. Reported for MA.

A. rúdis Sauer. Will key to *A. cruentus* but is distinguishable from it and *A. hypochondriacus* in being dioecious and having pistillate flowers with 1 well developed sepal and 1 rudimentary one

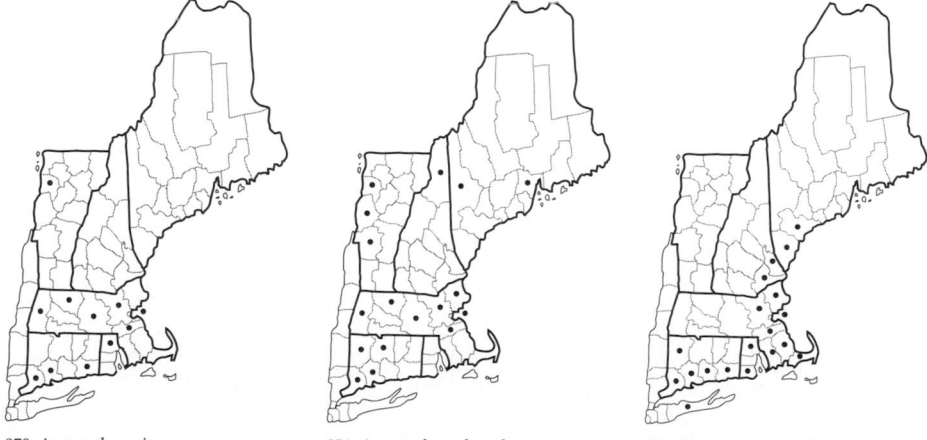

970. *Amaranthus spinosus*   971. *Amaranthus tuberculatus*   972. *Amaranthus cannabinus*

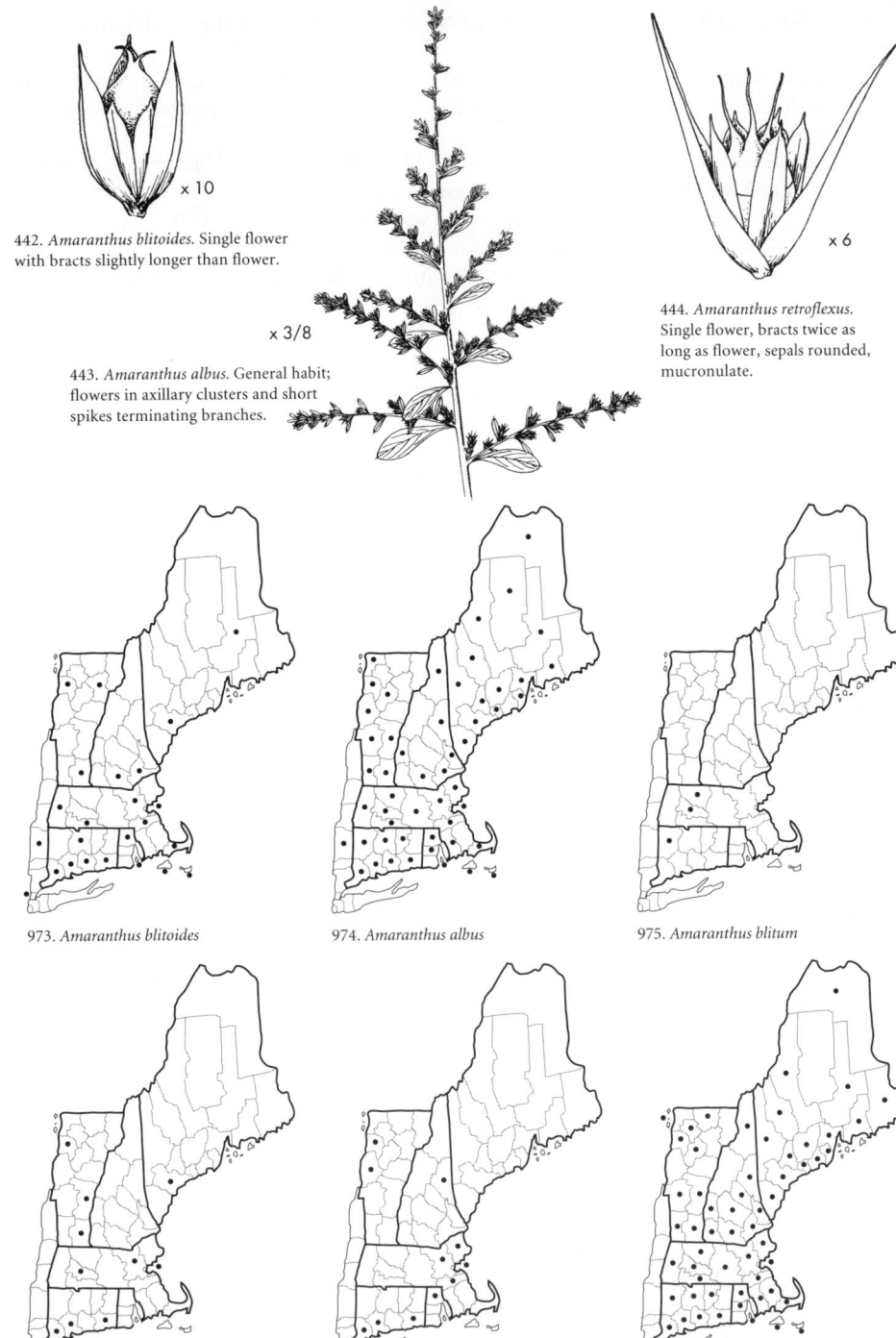

× 10

442. *Amaranthus blitoides*. Single flower with bracts slightly longer than flower.

× 3/8

443. *Amaranthus albus*. General habit; flowers in axillary clusters and short spikes terminating branches.

× 6

444. *Amaranthus retroflexus*. Single flower, bracts twice as long as flower, sepals rounded, mucronulate.

973. *Amaranthus blitoides*

974. *Amaranthus albus*

975. *Amaranthus blitum*

976. *Amaranthus caudatus*

977. *Amaranthus cruentus*

978. *Amaranthus retroflexus*

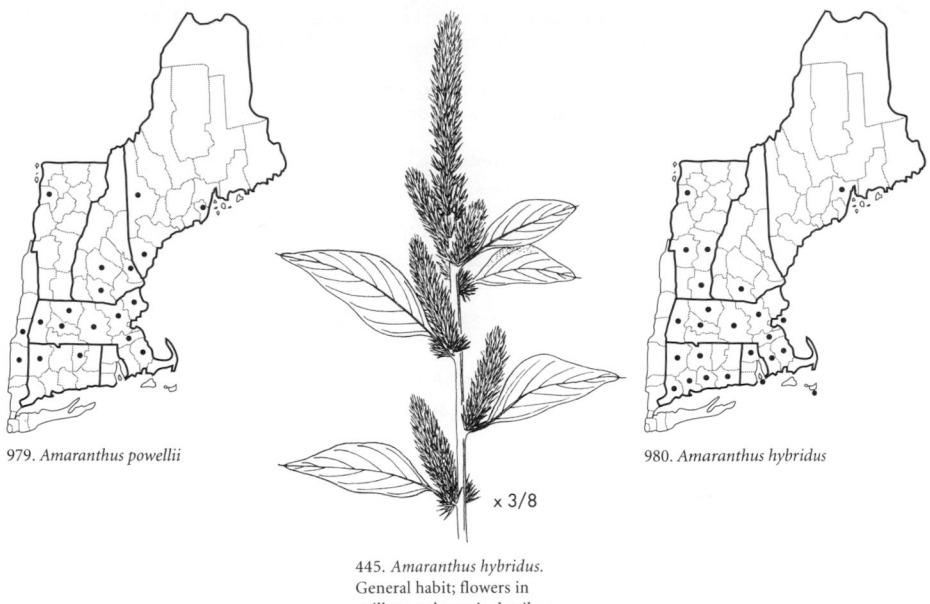

979. *Amaranthus powellii*

980. *Amaranthus hybridus*

x 3/8

445. *Amaranthus hybridus.*
General habit; flowers in
axillary and terminal spikes.

(plant monoecious and pistillate flowers with 2 or more well developed sepals in the latter 2 species). From farther west. Reported for MA, ME, VT. [*Acnida tamariscinus; Amaranthus t.*].—FACW-

12. A. pálmeri Wats. (for its discoverer). Waste places. August-September. From the southwest. Reported for Essex and Middlesex Counties MA. Used as a potherb.—FACU

13. A. retrofléxus L. (bent backward). Pigweed. Roadsides, waste places, fields and cultivated ground. August-October. Fig. 444, Map 978. Young tips and leaves can be cooked as a potherb; seeds can be roasted and ground into flour. Plant also can be eaten raw when young.—FACU

14. A. powéllii Wats. (for its discoverer). Waste places, fields and cultivated ground. From farther west. August-September. Map 979.

15. A. hýbridus L. (hybrid). Pigweed. Roadsides, waste places, fields and cultivated ground. August-October. Fig. 445, Map 980. [*A. cruentus; A. paniculatus*]. Young plants used as a potherb; seeds used to make meal. Plant also has been used in treating intestinal disorders.—Wildl. 1

Family 76. Nyctagináceae (Four-O-Clock Family)

Hermaphrodite, dichotomously branched, perennial herbs with stems swollen at the joints. Leaves opposite, simple, entire, sessile or petioled, estipulate. Flowers perfect, flowers or involucres clustered in the leaf axils or terminal and cymose, often forming dichasial panicles, pink or rose colored to purple, a single flower or several subtended by a green, 5-lobed involucre of partially fused bracts simulating a calyx, calyx campanulate or funnelform, 5-lobed, the tube closely surrounding the ovary and constricted above it, petaloid, corolla absent, stamens 3-5 (ours), hypogynous, distinct, unequal, exserted, ovary superior (although appearing inferior), of 1 carpel, 1-locular, ovule 1, style 1, filiform, exserted, stigma capitate. Fruit an achene enclosed within the calyx tube, obovoid, angled or ribbed.

1. Mirábilis L. (wonderful). Four-O-Clock.
Same characters as the family. [*Oxybaphus*].

a. Calyx-like involucre 1-flowered; calyx tube 2-3 cm long above the ovary. .... 1. *M. jalapa*
a. Calyx-like involucre with 2 or more flowers; calyx tube less than 2 cm long above
    the ovary. (Fig. 446).
  b. Stems pubescent, especially around the nodes and below the inflorescence. .... 2. *M. hirsuta*
  b. Stems glabrous or nearly so, or sometimes pubescent on the peduncles and
      branches of the inflorescence.
      Leaves ovate or deltoid-ovate, distinctly petioled. .... 3. *M. nyctaginea*
      Leaves linear, sessile or nearly so .... 4. *M. linearis*

1. *M. jalápa* L. (old generic name). Occasionally escaped from cultivation to roadsides and waste places. June-October. (Introduced from Tropical Amer.). Reported for RI, VT, Fairfield County CT. Poisonous.

2. *M. hirsúta* (Pursh) MacM. (hirsute). Dry, sandy waste places and roadsides. June-September. Map 981. [*Oxybaphus h.; Allionia h.; A. pilosa*].

M. álbida (Walt.) Heimerl. Similar to *M. hirsuta* but stem with 2 puberulent lines at each internode (stem hirsute with long hairs, especially around the nodes in *M. hirsuta*). [*Oxybaphus a. Allionia a.; A. decumbens*].

3. *M. nyctagínea* (Michx.) MacM. (resembling Nyctago). Waste places and roadsides. June-September. Fig. 446, Map 982. [*Oxybaphus nyctagineus; O. floribunda; Allionia n.*].—FACU-

4. *M. lineáris* (Pursh) Heimerl (linear). Waste places. June-September. From farther west. Reported for New Haven County CT. [*Oxybaphus l.; Allionia l.*].

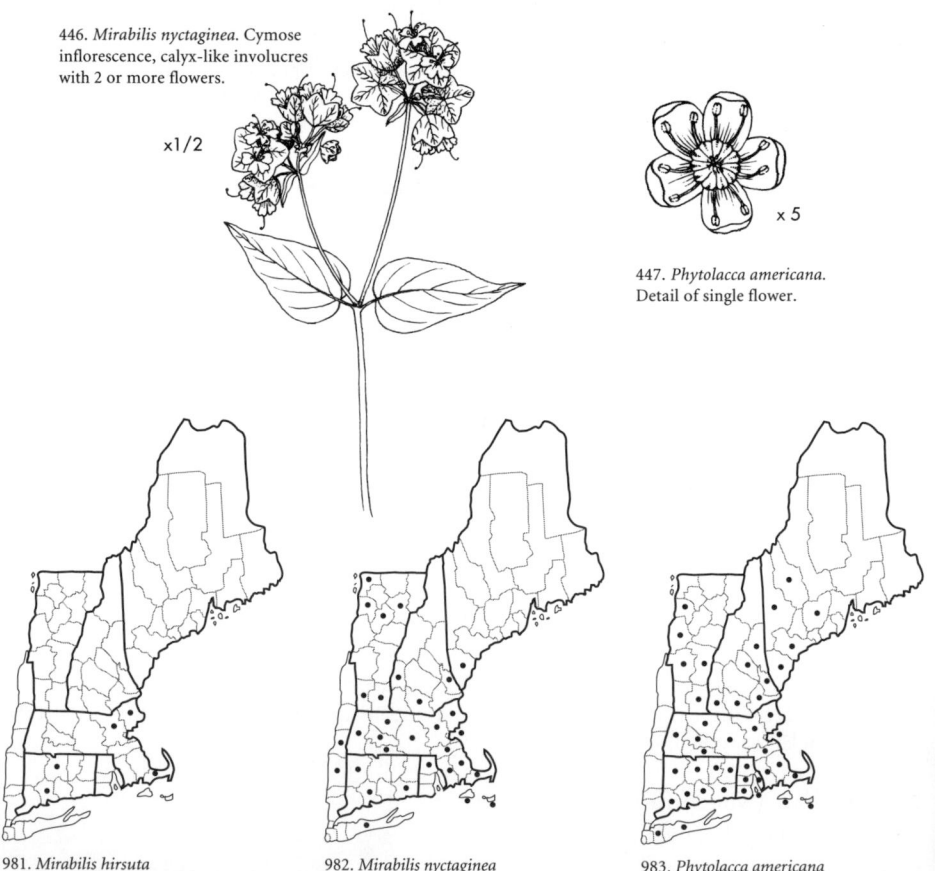

446. *Mirabilis nyctaginea*. Cymose inflorescence, calyx-like involucres with 2 or more flowers.

×1/2

× 5

447. *Phytolacca americana*. Detail of single flower.

981. *Mirabilis hirsuta*

982. *Mirabilis nyctaginea*

983. *Phytolacca americana*

Family 77. Phytolaccáceae (Pokeweed Family)

Hermaphrodite, tall, stout, glabrous, perennial herbs with 1-several stems from a crown (ours), the roots thick and fleshy. Leaves alternate, simple, entire, petioled, estipulate. In ours flowers perfect, small, bracteate, in terminal racemes which become opposite the leaves by further growth of the stem, white or pinkish, with 5 distinct, petoloid sepals, petals lacking, stamens 5-30, hypogynous, distinct or united at the base, as long as the sepals, ovary superior, with a ring of 5-12 separate or partly united carpels, each 1-locular, with 1 ovule and 1 style. Fruit a depressed-globose, juicy, purplish-black, 5-12 locular berry, with a flattened seed in each locule.—WILDl.

1. Phytolácca L. Pokeweed (From the Greek and Latin, based on the red dye yielded by the berries).

Same characters as in the family.

1. P. americána L. (American). Fields, clearings, waste places and roadsides. July-September. Fig. 447, Map 983. [*P. decandra*]. Young sprouts and unfolding leaves can be cooked as a potherb in 2 changes of water; all parts of the mature plant, particularly the roots are very poisonous.—FACU+

Family 78. Aizoáceae (Carpet-weed Family)

Hermophrodite, prostrate, ascending or erect, often succulent, glabrous, mostly annual herbs. Leaves alternate, opposite or subopposite, simple, entire, sessile or petioled, usually estipulate, but petiole bases sometimes dilated. Flowers perfect, solitary or few in the leaf axils, calyx 4-5-lobed, green outside, pink, white or purple inside, separate or united basally, petals absent, stamens 5-10, hypogynous or perigynous, separate or united at the base, (in small groups in *Tetragonia*) ovary mostly superior, of 3-5 carpels (rarely more), 3-8 loculed, styles or stigmas 3-8, ovules one-many in each locule. Fruit a circumscissile capsule or fleshy and indehiscent.

Leaves opposite or subopposite, oblanceolate to obovate or spatulate. (Fig. 448) .... 1. *Sesuvium maritimum*

Leaves alternate, deltoid-ovate .... 2. *Tetragonia tetragonioides*

1. Sesúvium L. Sea-purslane.

Prostrate to ascending, succulent, annual herbs, branched, not rooting at the nodes; leaves opposite to subopposite, oblanceolate to obovate or spatulate, short-petioled or sessile, estipulate, but petioles dilated and clasping at the base; flowers solitary or few, sessile or nearly so in the leaf axils, calyx tubular at the base, 5-lobed, pink to purplish inside, greenish outside, each lobe bearing a short horn near the apex, stamens 5 (ours), inserted on the calyx tube, ovary shorter than to about equalling calyx, of 3 carpels, 3-loculed, stigmas 3, ovules many; fruit a circumscissile capsule.

1. S. marítimum (Walt). B.S.P. (of the sea). Sea beaches. July-September. Suffolk County NY. Fig. 448. (W.I.) Endangered in NY; reported for Suffolk County.—FACW

2. Tetragónia L. (four-angled).

Trailing, succulent, annual, branched herb, scurfy and sometimes with scattered, short pubescence; leaves alternate, deltoid to rhombic-ovate, abruptly narrowed to petioles, estipulate; flowers solitary or few, sessile or short-pedicelled in the leaf axils, calyx cup shaped at base, 4-lobed, green; stamens in small groups, ovary about equalling calyx, with 2-8 carpels, locules and styles, ovule 1 in each carpel; fruit fleshy, indehiscent, tubercled.

1. T. tetragonioídes (Pallas) Kuntze (4-angled). New Zealand Spinach. Escaped from cultivation to waste places. Map 984. (Introduced from e. Asia). [*T. expansa*]. May be used as a potherb.

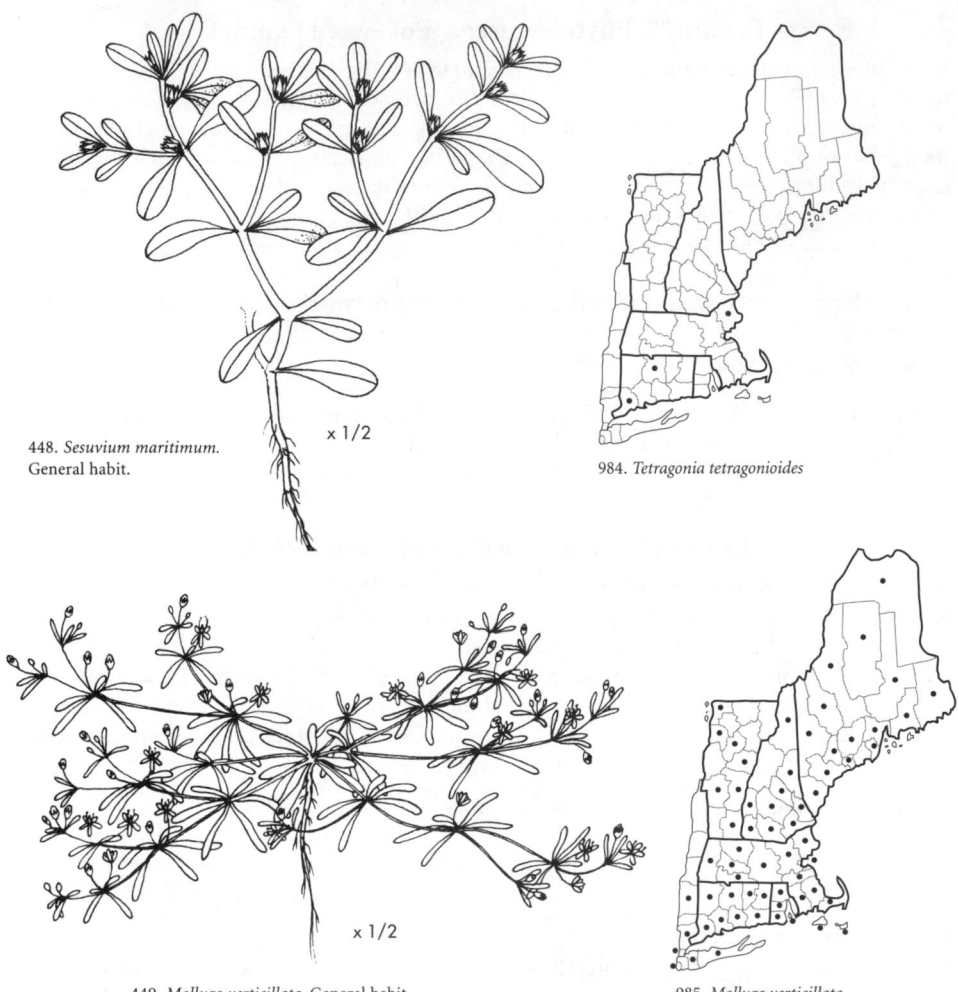

448. *Sesuvium maritimum.*
General habit.

x 1/2

984. *Tetragonia tetragonioides*

x 1/2

449. *Mollugo verticillata.* General habit.

985. *Mollugo verticillata*

Family 79. Mollúginaceae

Mostly decumbent annual, not fleshy, stems radially spreading from a central root, much branched, not rooting at the nodes, forming mats. Leaves whorled; narrowly to broadly oblanceolate or spatulate, attenuate to a short petiole or sessile, stipules none, but petioles sometimes dilated at the base. Flowers in a sessile, bracteate cymule opposite each whorl of leaves, on pedicels 3 mm or more long, sepals 5, separate, green with white margins, stamens usually 3, hypogynous, ovary exceeding the sepals, of 3 carpels, 3-loculed, stigmas 3, ovules many. Fruit a 3-valved loculicidal capsule.

1. Mollúgo L. Carpet-weed.
Same characters as the family.

    1. M. verticilláta L. (whorled). Waste places, roadsides, disturbed areas and cultivated soil. July-September. Fig. 449, Map 985. From Tropical Amer.—FAC

Family 80. Portulacáceae (Purslane Family)

Hermaphrodite, generally succulent, glabrous or pubescent, annual or perennial herbs. Leaves alternate or opposite, simple, entire, sessile or petioled, mostly estipulate. Flowers perfect, solitary or in racemes, cymes, or glomerules, regular or nearly so, sepals 2, petals 5, rarely 3, 4 or 6, sometimes ephemeral, separate or united basally, stamens 5(3)-many, distinct or nearly so, perigynous, ovary superior or half-inferior, of 2-3 carpels, 1-locular, styles 2-several, usually 3, separate or united, ovules few-many. Fruit a capsule with circumscissile or longitudinal dehiscence.

a. Leaves crowded toward the base of the stem, restricted to the lower 1/4.
    (Fig. 450) .... 1. *Talinum*
                                                                 teretifolium
a. Leaves produced well up on the stem.
  b. Flowers sessile, ovaries half-inferior, capsule circumscissile. .... 2. *Portulaca*
  b. Flowers pedicelled, ovary superior, capsule longitudinally dehiscent.
    Stems with a single pair of leaves; flowers in a solitary terminal raceme.
    (Fig. 452) .... 3. *Claytonia*
    Stems with several-many pairs of leaves or leaves alternate; flowers 1 or 2 in
    the axils or in several terminal racemes (Fig. 453). .... 4. *Montia*

1. *Talínum* Adans. Fameflower.

Erect, subscapose, glabrous, perennial herbs from a short taproot; leaves alternate, crowded toward the base, linear-terete, sessile; flowers pedicelled, in a loose, terminal, bracteate cyme on a slender scape much exceeding the leaves, forked several times, bracts prolonged at the base, sepals 2, distinct, deciduous, petals 5, distinct, pink, ephemeral, stamens 10-20, ovary superior, styles united, 3-lobed at the apex, ovules many; capsule ovoid or ellipsoid, longitudinally dehiscent, 3-valved.

    1. *T. teretifólium* Pursh (leaves round in cross section). Dry rocks, particularly serpentine. May-August. Fig. 450. From farther south. Reported for CT.

2. *Portuláca* L. Purslane (ancient Latin name).

Prostrate, ascending or spreading, diffusely branched, glabrous or pubescent, annual herbs; leaves alternate and clustered at the ends of the branches, linear to spatulate, sessile or short-petioled; flowers solitary or in small glomerules at the ends of the stem and branches, sessile, bracteate, sepals 2, united at the base and adnate to part of the ovary, the ovary half-inferior, petals usually 5, distinct, inserted on the calyx, yellow, red, pink or white, stamens 6-many, ovary half-inferior, style deeply 3-9 parted, ovules many; capsule ovoid to subglobose, with circumscissile dehiscence. —Wildl. 1

Leaves linear to subterete, with tufts of long hairs in the axils. .... 1. *P. grandiflora*
Leaves spatulate, without tufts of hairs in the axils. (Fig. 451). .... 2. *P. oleracea*

    1. *P. grandiflóra* Hook. (large-flowered). Portulaca. Occasionally escaped from cultivation to waste places. Map 986. (Introduced from S. Amer.).
    2. *P. olerácea* L. (like a garden vegetable). Pusley. Cultivated ground, roadsides and waste places. July-September. Fig. 451, Map 987. (Naturalized from Europe). Young tips and leaves can be used as salad; entire plant may be used as a potherb, or stems can be pickled or used to thicken soups; seeds can be used in breadstuffs. —FAC

3. *Claytónia* L. Spring-beauty (for J. Clayton).

Ascending or erect, simple-stemmed, glabrous, perennial herbs from a globose corm (1-several stems from a corm), or annual with fibrous roots; leaves basal, petioled, and a pair of opposite (rarely alternate), sessile, connate-perfoliate or petioled stem leaves; flowers pedicelled, in a loose, terminal, bracteate raceme, sepals 2, free from the ovary, petals 5, distinct, spreading, pink or white, stamens

5, ovary superior, styles united, 3-lobed or parted at the apex, ovules 2-6; capsule ovoid to subglobose, longitudinally dehiscent, 3-valved.

a. Stem leaves connate-perfoliate, partly or completely united into a disc. .... 1. *C. perfoliata*
a. Stem leaves not connate-perfoliate.
　　　Leaves lanceolate, elliptic, ovate or oblanceolate, 6 times or less as long as wide
　　　　　　　(including petiole), blade clearly differentiated from petiole. (Fig. 452) ...... 2. *C. caroliniana*
　　　Leaves linear or linear-lanceolate, 7 or more times as long as wide, blade
　　　　　　　scarcely differentiated from petiole. .... 3. *C. virginica*

　　1. *C. perfoliáta* Donn. ex Willd. (perfoliate). Occasionally escaped from cultivation to roadsides and waste places. April-May. From farther west. Reported for Coos County NH. [*Montia perfoliata*]. Young plants used in salads and as a potherb.
　　2. *C. caroliniána* Michx. (of Carolina). Rich open woods. March-May. Fig 452, Map 988. Our plants are var. *caroliniana*. Corm can be cooked like potato and young leaves edible as a potherb. —FACU
　　C. sibírica L. (*Siberian*). Similar to *C. caroliniana* but blade not distinct from petiole is occasionally escaped from cultivation. Reported for Essex County MA. [*Montia sibirica*]. Our plants are var. *sibirica*.
　　3. *C. virgínica* L. (of Virginia). Rich moist and low wet woods and wooded swamps. March-May. Map 989. Corm can be cooked like potato and young leaves edible as a potherb. —FACU

4. *Móntia* L. (for G. Monti).

Densely tufted, weak-stemmed, diffuse or ascending, simple or branched, glabrous, fibrous-rooted, annual herbs; leaves opposite or alternate, linear or oblanceolate to obovate, on petioles dilated and often clasping at the base; flowers small, white, solitary, paired, or racemose, axillary or terminal, pedicelled, nodding, sepals 2, free from the ovary, petals 3, united at the base and split down 1 side, stamens 3, ovary superior, style short, 3-parted, ovules 3; capsule longitudinally dehiscent, 3-valved, seeds flattened.
　　Calandrínia HBK *ciliáta* (R. & P.) DC. Will key to *Montia linearis* but is distinguishable in having usually purplish (rarely white) flowers in leafy-bracted racemes, petals and stamens usually 5 (flowers white, in non-leafy bracted or bractless racemes, petals and stamens usually 3 in Montia linearis). From the west coast. Reported for MA.

Leaves in several opposite pairs, oblanceolate to obovate. .... 1. *M. fontana*
Leaves alternate, linear to linear-spatulate. .... 2. *M. linearis*

　　1. *M. fontána* L. Blinks. Springs and seeps, brooks, wet woods. June-August. Fig. 453, Map 990. (Eurasia). [*M. lamprosperma; M. rivularis*]. Our plants are subsp. *fontana*. —OBL
　　2. *M. lineáris* (Dougl.) Greene. Moist to dry openings and woodlands. June-August. From farther north and west. Reported for MA.

Family 81. Caryophylláceae (Pink Family)

Hermaphrodite, annual or perennial herbs, with stems often swollen at the nodes. Leaves opposite (alternate in *Corrigiola*; whorled in *Spergula*), simple, entire, often united at the base, stipulate or estipulate, usually sessile. Flowers perfect, solitary, or in a bracteate, basically cymose or dichasial inflorescence, 4-5 merous, sepals separate or united, petals of the same number, distinct, often differentiated into a claw and limb, sometimes absent, stamens 1-10, usually of the same number or twice as many as the sepals, distinct or united at the base, hypogynous or perigynous, ovary superior, of 2-5 carpels, mostly 1-locular with free-central placentation, rarely 3-locular in the lower part with axile placentation, styles and stigmas 2-5, as many as the carpels, or styles united up to the stigmas,

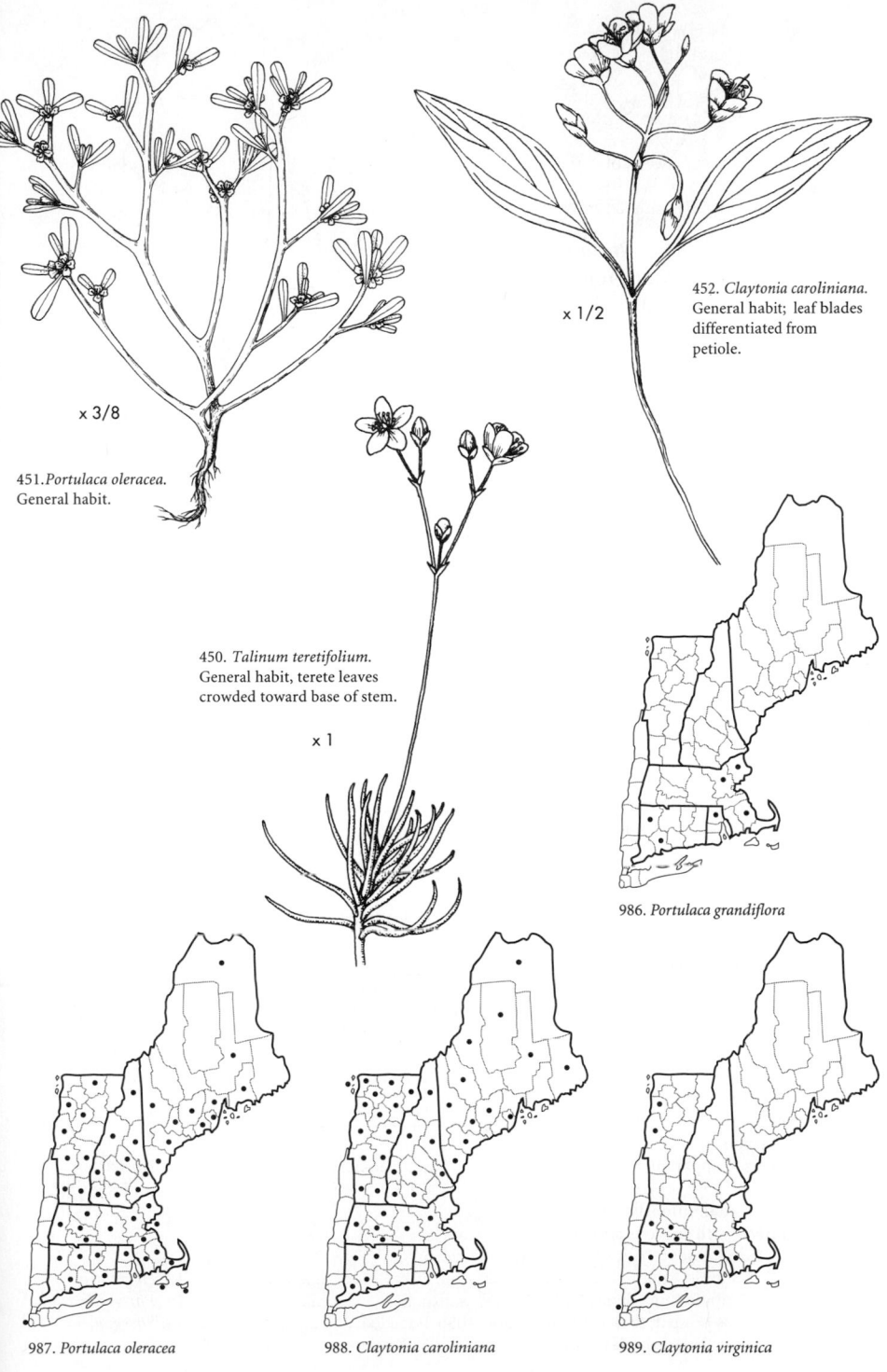

x 3/8

451. *Portulaca oleracea.*
General habit.

452. *Claytonia caroliniana.*
General habit; leaf blades
differentiated from
petiole.

x 1/2

450. *Talinum teretifolium.*
General habit, terete leaves
crowded toward base of stem.

x 1

986. *Portulaca grandiflora*

987. *Portulaca oleracea*

988. *Claytonia caroliniana*

989. *Claytonia virginica*

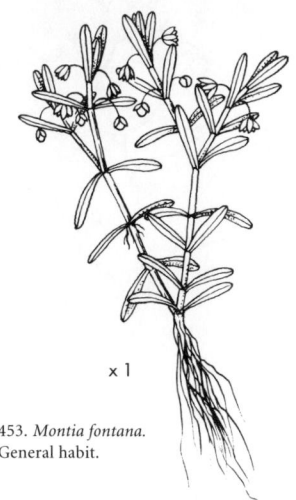

x 1

453. *Montia fontana.*
General habit.

990. *Montia fontana*

ovules solitary to many. Fruit a capsule dehiscing apically by valves or teeth of the same number or twice the number of the styles, the seeds few to many, or a 1-seeded utricle.

a. Sepals united, forming a tube or cup.
    b. Calyx lobes foliaceous, mostly 1.5 cm or more long. .... 1. *Agrostemma githago*
    b. Calyx lobes not foliaceous, mostly less than 1 cm long.
        c. Petals absent; fruit indehiscent, 1-seeded. .... 2. *Scleranthus*
        c. Petals present; fruit dehiscent, more than 1-seeded.
            d. Calyx subtended by 2 or more bracts; seeds flattened. .... 3. *Dianthus*
            d. Calyx ebracteate; seeds not flattened.
                e. Styles 2; capsule dehiscent by 4 valves or teeth.
                    f. Calyx 5 mm or less long .... 4. *Gypsophila*
                    f. Calyx 1 cm or more long.
                        Calyx strongly wing-angled; plant annual from a taproot. .... 5. *Vaccaria hispanica*
                        Calyx terete, not wing-angled; plant perennial with rhizomes. .... 6. *Saponaria officinalis*
                e. Styles 3-5; capsule dehiscent by 5 or more valves or teeth.
                    Capsule dehiscent by 5 teeth .... 7. *Lychnis*
                    Capsule dehiscent by 6 or more teeth.
                      Plant mat-forming, with crowded imbricated leaves not over 2 mm
                          wide; alpine; calyx pubescent more than 1 cm long .... 6. *Saponaria pumilio*
                      Plant not as above or if so calyx glabrous, 1 cm or less long. .... 8. *Silene*
a. Sepals separate, or essentially so.
    g. Leaves alternate .... 9. *Corrigiola litoralis*
    g. Leaves opposite or whorled.
        h. Leaves whorled. (Fig. 464) .... 10. *Spergula arvensis*
        h. Leaves opposite.
            i. Flowers in apparent umbels. (Fig. 465). .... 11. *Holosteum umbellatum*
            i. Flowers not in umbels.
                j. Leaves with scarious stipules.
                    k. Petals absent; fruit indehiscent, 1-seeded.
                      Stipules ciliate .... 12. *Herniaria*
                      Stipules not ciliate .... 13. *Paronychia*
                  k. Petals present; fruit dehiscent, more than 1-seeded. .... 14. *Spergularia*
               j. Leaves without stipules.

l. Petals deeply 2-cleft, rarely wanting.
  m. Capsule cylindric, slightly curved, dehiscent by terminal teeth. .... 15. *Cerastium*
  m. Capsule ovoid or oblong, dehiscent by valves.
      Styles 5; leaves, at least some, cordate-clasping .... 16. *Myosoton*
                                                                                    aquaticum
      Styles 3; leaves not cordate-clasping. .... 17. *Stellaria*
l. Petals entire or merely emarginate, or absent.
  n. Plant fleshy and succulent; petals and stamens inserted on a
      conspicuous, 10-lobed disc. (Fig. 471) .... 18. *Honckenya*
                                                                                    peploides
  n. Plant not fleshy or succulent; disc inconspicuous or absent.
      o. Styles the same number as the sepals (4-5). .... 19. *Sagina*
      o. Styles fewer than the sepals, usually 3.
          p. Leaves linear to setaceous; capsule with 3 valves. (Fig. 473). .... 20. *Minuartia*
          p. Leaves elliptic, ovate or lanceolate; capsule dehiscent by 6
              valves or teeth.
          Leaves 8 mm or less long; seed without a strophiole;
              annual. ....21. *Arenaria*
                                                                                    serpyllifolia
          Leaves mostly longer than 8 mm; seed with a strophiole;
              perennial. ....22. *Moehringia*

1. *Agrostémma* L. Corn-cockle (field crown).

Tall, pubescent, simple or slightly branched, annual herbs; leaves linear to lanceolate, opposite, sessile, acute to acuminate, estipulate; flowers showy, solitary at the ends of long, axillary peduncles, calyx ovoid, with a coarsely 10-ribbed tube and 5 elongate, linear, foliaceous lobes, petals 5, red, shorter than the calyx lobes, slightly retuse, narrowed below into slender, pale claws, stamens 6, perigynous, styles 5, ovary 1-locular; fruit an ovoid capsule dehiscent by 5 teeth, seeds many.

  1. *A. githágo* L. (old generic name). Wheat fields and waste places. June-September. Fig. 454, Map 991. (Naturalized from Europe). Poisonous.

2. *Scleránthus* L. Knawel (from the Greek, referring to the hardened calyx tube).

Low, much-branched, prostrate or spreading, glabrous or puberulent, annual or perennial herbs; leaves linear to subulate, opposite, connate at the base, estipulate; flowers small, greenish, sessile or subsessile in the axils and in congested, terminal cymes, ebracteate, sepals united into a coarsely-ribbed, indurated tube, calyx deeply 5-lobed, petals lacking, stamens usually 5-10 perigynous, styles 2, distinct, ovary 1-locular; fruit an ovoid utricle enclosed within the indurated calyx tube.

Calyx lobes acute to acuminate, narrowly scarious-margined toward tip; plant
    annual. (Fig. 455). .... 1. *S. annuus*
Calyx lobes obtuse, widely scarious-margined toward tip; plant perennial. .... 2. *S. perennis*

  1. *S. ánnuus* L. (annual). Dry fields, roadsides, waste places and lawns. May-September. Fig. 455, Map 992. (Naturalized from Europe). —FACU
  2. *S. pérennis* L. (perennial). Dry roadsides and waste places. May-September. Rare. Reported for CT, MA.

3. *Diánthus* L. (from the Greek meaning Jupiter flower).

Simple to sparingly branched, glabrous to pubescent, perennial or biennial herbs; leaves linear to lanceolate, opposite, sessile, estipulate; flowers solitary or few, or in dense cymes, bracts 2 or more per flower, calyx tube cylindric, coarsely many-nerved, 5-toothed, petals 5, long-clawed, erose, toothed, or laciniate, white to red, stamens 10, perigynous, styles 2, ovary 1-locular; fruit a cylindric or ellipsoid capsule dehiscent by 4 teeth.

Petrorhágia (Ser.) Link *saxifrága* (L.) Link. Similar to Dianthus but calyx has 15 or fewer prominent nerves (20 or more prominent nerves in *Dianthus*). (Europe). Rarely escaped from cultivation. Reported for Worcester County MA. [*Tunica saxifraga*].

P. prolifera (L.) Ball et Heyw. Similar to *P. saxifraga* but with flowers cymose, calyx 1 cm or more long (flowers solitary and calyx up to 6 mm long in *P. saxifraga*). (Europe). Reported for MA.

a. Flowers long-pedicellate, solitary or few. (Fig. 456).
    Calyx 1.8 cm or less long, the tube 4 mm or less in diameter; basal bracts
        1/3-1/2 as long as calyx; petals dentate, the teeth less than 2 mm long. .... 1. *D. deltoides*
    Calyx 1.8 cm or more long, the tube more than 4 mm in diameter; basal bracts
        up to 1/3 as long as calyx; petals laciniate, the lobes more than 2 mm
        long. .... 2. *D. plumarius*
a. Flowers sessile or short-pedicellate, mostly 3 or more in dense, congested cymes.
    Widest leaves less than 8 mm wide; stem pubescent, at least around the nodes. ..... 3. *D. armeria*
    Widest leaves 8 mm or more wide; stem glabrous. .... 4. *D. barbatus*

1. *D. deltoídes* L. (triangular). Maiden-pink. Fields and roadsides. June-August. Fig. 456, Map 993. (Naturalized from Europe).

D. chinénsis L. Similar to *D. deltoides* but bracts 4-6, leaves glabrous, mostly longer than 3 cm, longer than the internodes (bracts usually 2, rarely 4, leaves ciliate on the margins and midrib, mostly shorter than 3 cm, shorter than the internodes in *D. deltoides*). (Asia). Rarely escaped from cultivation. Reported for VT.

2. *D. plumárius* L. (feathery). Garden-pink. Escaped from cultivation to fields and roadsides. June-August. Map 994. (Introduced from Europe).

3. *D. arméria* L. (formerly placed with Armeria). Depford-pink. Fields, roadsides and waste places. June-August. Map 995. (Naturalized from Europe).

4. *D. barbátus* L. (bearded). Sweet William. Escaped from cultivation to roadsides and waste places. June-August. Map 996. (Introduced from Europe).

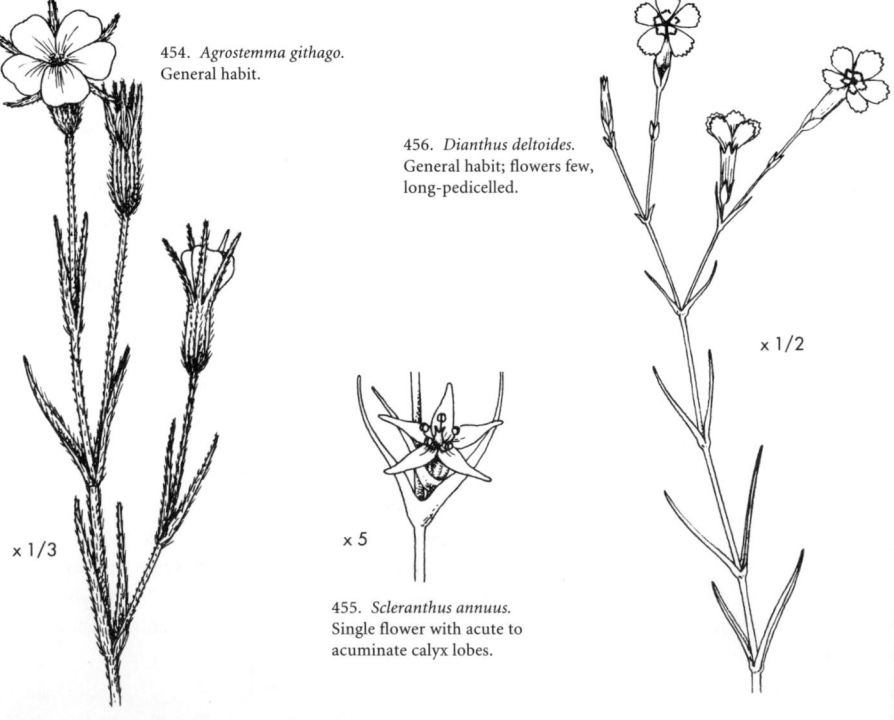

454. *Agrostemma githago.* General habit.

456. *Dianthus deltoides.* General habit; flowers few, long-pedicelled.

x 1/2

x 5

x 1/3

455. *Scleranthus annuus.* Single flower with acute to acuminate calyx lobes.

991. *Agrostemma githago*   992. *Scleranthus annuus*   993. *Dianthus deltoides*

994. *Dianthus plumarius*   995. *Dianthus armeria*   996. *Dianthus barbatus*

D. carthusianórum L. Similar to the latter 2 spp; leaves linear, calyx lobes puberulent, petals consistently dark red (the latter 2 spp. lacking this combination of characters), has been reported as locally escaped in NH.

4. Gypsóphila L. (from the Greek, based on the habitat of some species).

Branched, glabrous or puberulent, often glaucous, annual or perennial herbs; leaves linear to lanceolate or oblanceolate, opposite, sessile, estipulate; flowers small, solitary in the leaf axils or in paniculately branched, bracteate cymes, calyx campanulate to turbinate, 5-toothed, petals 5, white to pink or roseate, stamens 10, perigynous, styles 2, ovary 1-locular; fruit a globose to oblong or ovoid capsule dehiscent by 4 valves.

a. Widest leaves 2 mm or less wide; plant 2 dm or less tall. .... 1. *G. muralis*
a. Widest leaves 3 mm or more wide; plant more than 2 dm tall.
  b. Calyx 3-5 mm long; petals 2-3 times as long as calyx; longest pedicels 12 mm
     or more long .... 2. *G. elegans*
  b. Calyx up to 3 mm long; petals equalling or only slightly exceeding calyx; longest
     pedicels less than 12 mm long.
     Leaves subcordate at base, 3 or more nerved. .... 3. *G. perfoliata*
     Leaves not subcordate at base, 1-nerved. .... 4. *G. paniculata*

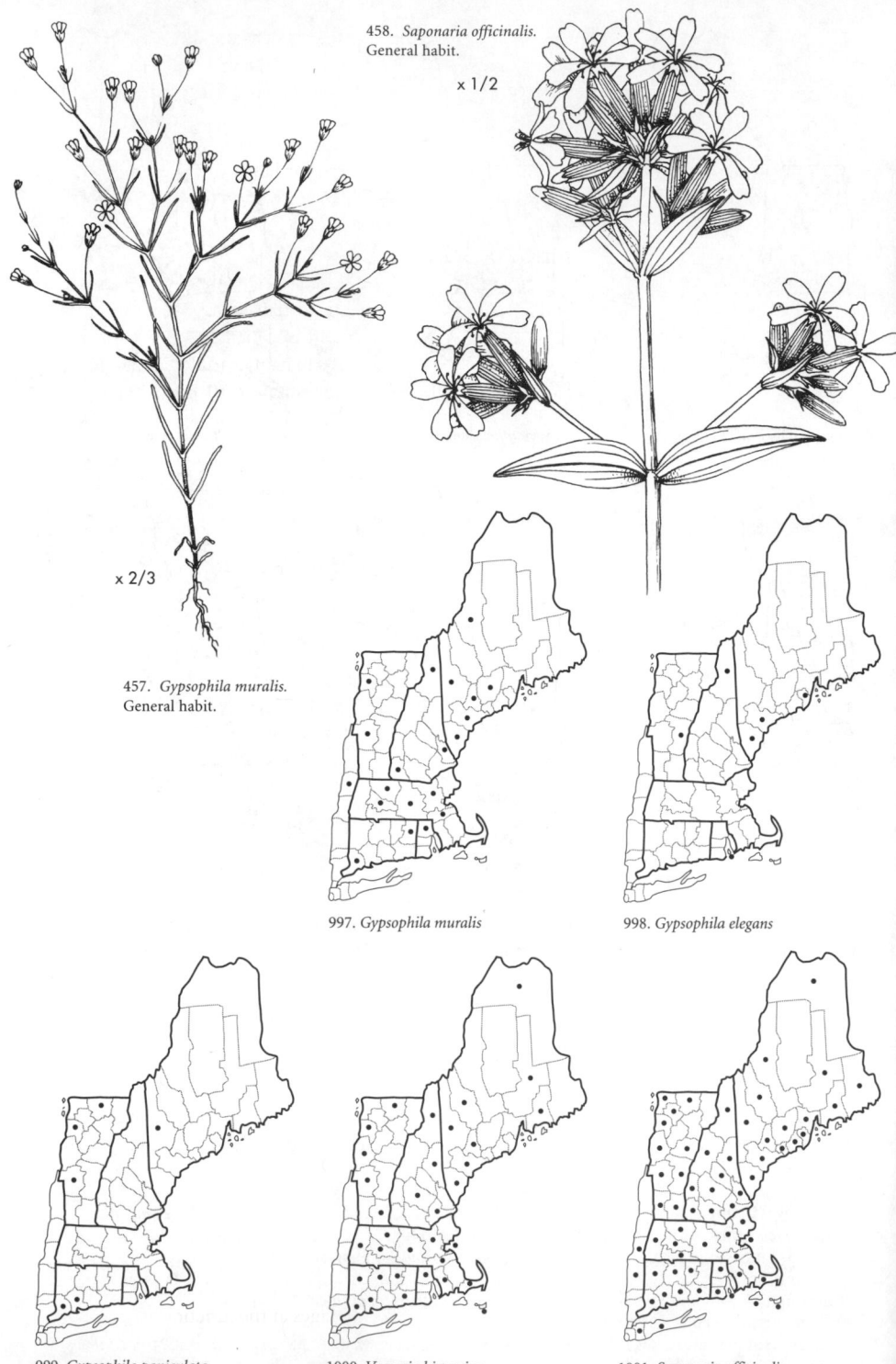

458. *Saponaria officinalis.*
General habit.

x 1/2

x 2/3

457. *Gypsophila muralis.*
General habit.

997. *Gypsophila muralis*

998. *Gypsophila elegans*

999. *Gypsophila paniculata*

1000. *Vaccaria hispanica*

1001. *Saponaria officinalis*

1. G. murális L. (of walls). Roadsides, waste places, fields and cultivated land. July-September. Fig. 457, Map 997. (Naturalized from Europe).

2. G. élegans Bieb. (elegant). Escaped from cultivation to roadsides and waste places. June-July. Map 998. (Introduced from Eurasia).

3. G. perfoliáta L. (perfoliate). Escaped from cultivation to roadsides, waste places and sea beaches. June-September. (Introduced from Eurasia). Reported for Fairfield County CT.

4. G. paniculáta L. (paniculate). Baby's-breath. Escaped from cultivation to roadsides and waste places. June-August. Map 999. (Introduced from Eurasia).

5. Vaccária N. M. Wolf Cow-herb.

Glabrous and glaucous, branched, annual herbs; leaves ovate to lanceolate, sessile, connate or clasping the base, estipulate; flowers numerous, pedicellate, in diffuse, open, bracteate cymes, calyx tube 5-ribbed, becoming inflated and sharply 5-angled or winged in fruit, 5-toothed, petals 5, erose, long-clawed, not appendaged at the junction with the blade, pink, stamens 10, perigynous, styles 2, ovary 1-locular or 2-4 locular at the base; fruit an ovoid to subglobose capsule dehiscent by 4 teeth.

1. V. hispánica (Mill.) Rauschert. Roadsides and waste places. June-September. Map 1000. (Adventive from Europe). [*V. pyramidata; V. segetalis; V. vaccaria; V. vulgaris; Saponaria vaccaria*]. Poisonous.

6. Saponária L. Soapwort (soap, referring to the lather produced from the plant with water).

Stout, rhizomatous, sparingly branched, glabrous, perennial herbs, rarely mat-forming; leaves elliptic, ovate or lanceolate, opposite, strongly 3-nerved, short-petioled to sessile, estipulate, or rarely crowded and imbricated and not over 2 mm wide; flowers in congested, terminal and axillary, leafy and scarious-bracted, peduncled cymes, parts sometimes double, calyx tube cylindric, often deeply split on 1 side, 5-toothed, petals 5, emarginate or entire, long-clawed, appendaged at the junction with the blade, white to pinkish, stamens 10, perigynous, styles 2, rarely 3, ovary 1-locular or 2-4 locular at the base; fruit an ellipsoid to ovoid capsule dehiscent by 4 or rarely by 6 or more teeth.

Plant not mat-forming, stem elongate, leaves not crowded or imbricated, more than
　　2 mm wide; not typically alpine; styles 2; capsule dehiscent by 4 teeth. .... 1. *S. officinalis*
Plant mat-forming, stem very short, with crowded, imbricated leaves not over
　　2 mm wide; alpine; styles 3 or more; capsule dehiscent by 6 or more teeth. .... 2. *S. pumilio*

1. S. officinális L. (of the shops). Roadsides and waste places. July-September. Fig. 458, Map 1001. (Naturalized from Europe). Soapy lather useful in cleaning, can be obtained by boiling the roots or leaves in water; poisonous if eaten.

S. ocymoídes L. Will key to *S. officinalis* but has a slender trailing stem, much-branched, leaves mostly less than 2.5 cm long, petals entire (stem upright, stout, sparingly branched, leaves 5 cm or more long, petals notched in *S. officinalis*). (Europe). Rarely escaped from cultivation and not becoming established. Reported for MA.

2. S. pumílio (L.) Fenzl ex A. Braun (pygmy). Pygmy Pink. Sargents Purchase, NH. Rare. [*Silene p.*].

7. Lýchnis L. Campion (ancient Greek name for a scarlet-flowered species).

Pubescent or glabrous perennial herbs; leaves basal and cauline, the basal oblanceolate to lanceolate, the cauline opposite, ovate to lanceolate or lance-linear, sessile or the lowest petiolate; estipulate; flowers few to many in open or condensed, bracteate cymes, calyx 5-toothed, petals 5, with long, narrow claws, often with a pair of auricles and a pair of appendages at the junction with the blade, white to red, entire to emarginate, bifid, or laciniate, stamens 10, perigynous, styles 5, ovary 1-locular or 3-locular, many ovuled; fruit an ovoid capsule dehiscent by 5 teeth.

a. Plant densely white-tomentose; calyx teeth twisted. .... 1. *L. coronaria*
a. Plant glabrous to pubescent but not white-tomentose; calyx teeth not twisted.
   b. Inflorescence compact, hemispherical; petals scarlet; stem leaves numerous,
      mostly 8 or more pairs, the widest 2 cm or more wide. .... 2. *L. chalcedonica*
   b. Inflorescence open, or if compact, elongate; petals pink; stem leaves mostly 6
      or fewer pairs, the widest 1.5 cm or less wide. (Fig. 459).
      Inflorescence open-paniculate; pedicels, at least some, longer than the calyx;
        petals deeply 2-4 cleft.. 3. *L. flos-cuculi*
      Inflorescence compact and elongate; pedicels all much shorter than the
        calyx; petals entire or emarginate .... 4. *L. viscaria*

    1. *L. coronária* (L.) Desr. (like a crown). Mullein-pink. Escaped from cultivation to roadsides and waste places. June-August. Map 1002. (Naturalized from Europe).

    2. *L. chalcedónica* L. (of Chalcedon). Scarlet Lychnis. Escaped from cultivation to roadsides. June-August. Map 1003. (Introduced from Asia).

    3. *L. flos-cúculi* L. (cuckoo-flower). Ragged Robin. Moist to dry fields and roadsides. June-July. Fig. 459. Map 1004 (Naturalized from Europe). —FACU

    4. *L. viscária* L. (old generic name from the viscid stem). German Catchfly. Escaped from cultivation to roadsides and waste places. June-July. Map 1005. (Introduced from Eurasia). [*Viscaria vulgaris*].

8. *Siléne* L. Catchfly (name from Greek mythology).

Pubescent or glabrous, annual or perennial herbs; leaves basal and cauline, the cauline opposite or whorled, sessile or the lower petiolate, estipulate; flowers perfect or imperfect, solitary or cymose, bracteate, calyx somewhat inflated, 5-toothed, petals 5, with long, narrow claws, often with a pair of auricles and a pair of appendages at the junction with the blade, white, pink or red, entire, erose, emarginate or bifid, stamens 10, perigynous, styles usually 3, rarely 4, ovary 1-locular or 3-locular, many-ovuled; fruit a capsule usually dehiscent by 6 or more teeth.

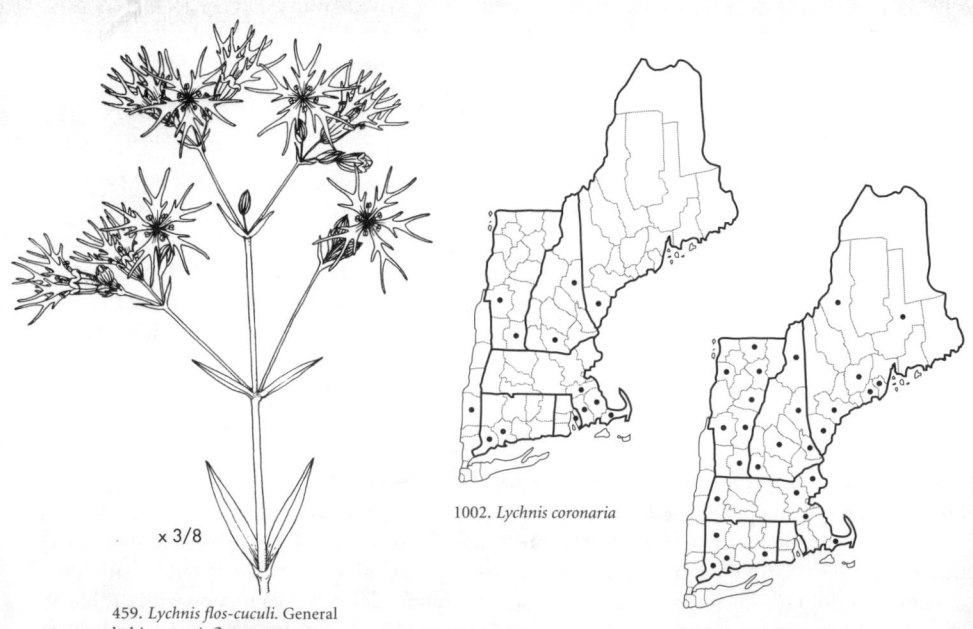

459. *Lychnis flos-cuculi.* General habit; open inflorescence.

× 3/8

1002. *Lychnis coronaria*

1003. *Lychnis chalcedonica*

1004. *Lychnis flos-cuculi*   1005. *Lychnis viscaria*

a. Plant mat-forming, with crowded, imbricated leaves not over 2 mm wide; alpine. ..... 1. *S. acaulis* var. *exscapa*
a. Plant not mat-forming; leaves not crowded or imbricated, more than 2 mm wide; not typically alpine.
  b. Middle stem leaves whorled, mostly in 4s. .... 2. *S. stellata*
  b. Middle (and all) stem leaves opposite.
    c. Stems pubescent.
      d. Calyx with 20-35 nerves .... 3. *S. conica*
      d. Calyx with fewer than 20 nerves (if more styles 5 and flowers imperfect; styles 3 and flowers perfect in *S. conica*).
        e. Flowers in mostly 1-sided simple or dichotomously forking racemes. (Fig. 460).
          f. Styles and stamens conspicuously exserted; flower usually present at fork of dichotomous inflorescence branches; petals cleft to below middle. .... 4. *S. dichotoma*
          f. Styles and stamens not or only slightly exserted; flower usually not present at fork of inflorescence branches; petals cleft to above middle.
            Calyx 1 cm or less long; petals entire or merely emarginate. .... 5. *S. gallica*
            Calyx longer than 1 cm; petals bilobed. .... 6. *S. pendula*
        e. Flowers in open or dense cymose panicles or solitary.
          g. Styles 5; flowers imperfect; capsule opening by 10 teeth.
            Flowers white, opening in the evening; capsule ovoid, with a narrow mouth, teeth erect or ascending .... 7. *S. latifolia* subsp. *alba*
            Flowers mostly red, opening in the morning; capsule globose, with a wide mouth, teeth recurved .... 8. *S. dioica*
          g. Styles 3 (rarely 4); flowers perfect; capsule opening by 6 or fewer teeth.
            h. Calyx lobes 3 mm or less long; plant perennial.
              Petals entire or slightly notched; inflorescence less than 2 times as long as wide; calyx 13 mm or more long .... 9. *S. caroliniana* subsp. *pensylvanica*
              Petals cleft to below middle; inflorescence more than 2 times as long as wide; calyx less than 13 mm long .... 10. *S. nutans*
            h. Calyx lobes 4 mm or more long; annual. .... 11. *S. noctiflora*
    c. Stems glabrous or essentially so (often puberulent below in *S. antirrhina*).
      i. Flowers solitary in the upper leaf axils. (Fig. 461). .... 12. *S. nivea*
      i. Flowers in the axils of small bracts in cymes or cymose panicles.

j. Longest calyx 9 mm or less long; carpophore (stalk of ovary) up to 1 mm
   long; stem usually with glutinous internodal areas. .... 13. *S. antirrhina*
j. Longest calyx longer than 9 mm; carpophore 2 mm or more long; stem
   lacking glutinous internodal areas.
  k. Calyx distinctly inflated, 5 mm or more in diameter (often narrower
    in *S. nutans*); carpophore 2-3 mm long; plant perennial.
    (Fig. 462).
    l. Leaves 1 cm or less wide; calyx glandular-pubescent. .... 10. *S. nutans*
    l. Leaves 1 cm or more wide; calyx glabrous or pubescent but not
      glandular.
      Calyx ovoid, much inflated; seeds 1-1.5 mm. .... 14. *S. vulgaris*
      Calyx cylindric, only slightly inflated; seeds up to 1 mm long. .... 15. *S. cserei*
  k. Calyx not inflated, 4 mm or less in diameter; carpophore 7-8 mm
    long; plant annual .... 16. *S. armeria*

1. S. acaúlis (L.) Jacq. (stemless) Moss-Campion. Alpine summit of Mt. Washington, NH, Piscataquis County ME. June-July. (Eurasia). Rare. [*S. acaulis* subsp. *arctica*]. Represented with us as var. *exscápa* (All.) DC.

2. S. stelláta (L.) Ait. f. (star-like). Starry campion. Dry, open woods. July-September. Map 1006.

3. S. cónica L. (conical). Fields, roadsides and waste places. June-July. (Adventive from Europe). Rare. Reported for Bristol and Nantucket Counties MA.

S. conoídea L. Similar to *S. conica* but with mature calyx 2 cm or more long, much inflated, seeds more than 1 mm wide (mature calyx less than 2 cm long and seeds less than 1 mm wide in *S. conoidea*). Eurasian. Reported for MA.

4. S. dichotóma Ehrh. (forking). Forked Catchfly. Fields, roadsides and waste places. June-September. Fig. 460, Map 1007. (Naturalized from Europe).

5. S. gállica L. (French). Waste places and roadsides. July-September. Map 1008. (Adventive from Europe). [*S. anglica*].

6. S. péndula L. (pendulous). Nodding Catchfly. Spreading from cultivation to roadsides and fields. July-September. (Introduced from Europe). Reported for ME, Franklin County MA.

7. S. latifólia Poir. White campion. Roadsides, fields and waste places. May-September. Map 1009. (Naturalized from Eurasia). [*S. alba; S. pratensis; Lychnis alba*]. Represented with us as subsp. *álba* (Mill.) Greuter & Burdet. —FAC

8. S. dioíca (L.) Clairv. Red campion. Cultivated ground, roadsides and waste places. May-September. Map 1010. (Naturalized from Eurasia). [*Lychnis d.; Melandrium d.*].

9. S. caroliniána Walt. (of Carolina) Dry woods and openings, rocky and gravelly areas. May-June. Map 1011. Represented with us as subsp. *pensylvánica* (Michx.) Clausen.

10. S. nútans L. (nodding). Spread from cultivation to roadsides and waste places. June-September. (Introduced from Eurasia). Reported for Hancock County ME.

11. S. noctiflóra L. (flowering at night). Night-flowering Catchfly. Cultivated ground, fields and waste places. June-August. Map 1012. (Naturalized from Europe).

12. S. nívea (Nutt.) Muhl. ex Otth. (snowy). Snowy Campion. Rich woods and river banks. July-August. From farther south. Reported for Penobscot County ME. Fig. 461. [*S. alba*]. —FAC

13. S. antirrhína L. (with leaves as in Antirrhinum). Sleepy Catchfly. Fields, roadsides, waste places and sandy areas. June-September. Map 1013. (Mexico; S. Amer.).

14. S. vulgáris (Moench) Garcke (common). Bladder-campion. Fields, roadsides, waste places, rocky or gravelly shores. June-September. Fig. 462, Map 1014. (Naturalized from Eurasia). [*S. cucubalis; S. latifolia*].

15. S. csérei Baumg. (for W. von Cserei). Waste places and roadsides. July-August. Map 1015. (Naturalized from Europe).

16. S. arméria L. (like Ameria). Garden Catchfly. Escaped from cultivation to roadsides and waste places. June-October. Map 1016. (Introduced from Eurasia).

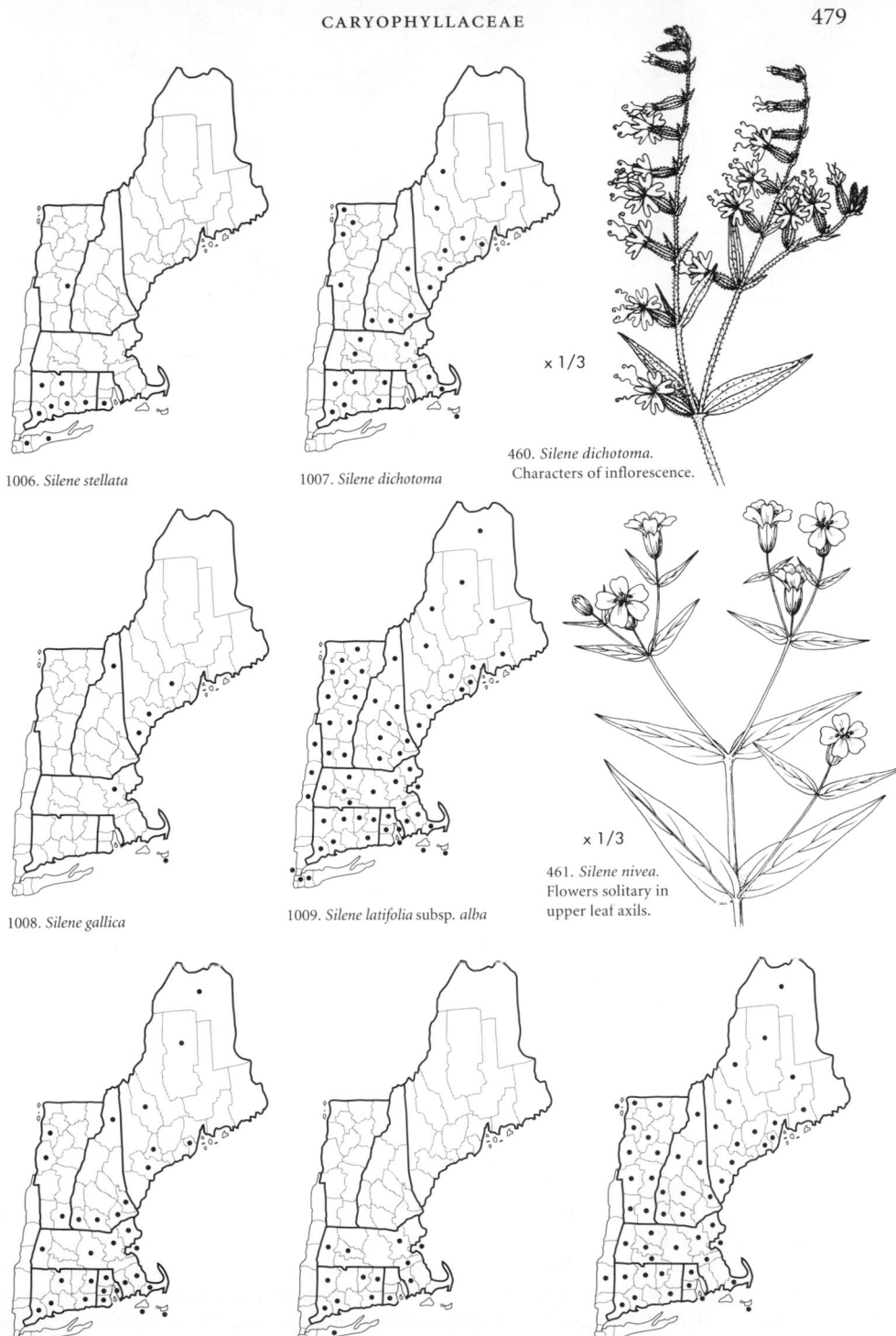

1006. *Silene stellata*

1007. *Silene dichotoma*

x 1/3

460. *Silene dichotoma.*
Characters of inflorescence.

1008. *Silene gallica*

1009. *Silene latifolia* subsp. *alba*

x 1/3

461. *Silene nivea.*
Flowers solitary in
upper leaf axils.

1010. *Silene dioica*

1011. *Silene caroliniana* subsp. *pensylvanica*

1012. *Silene noctiflora*

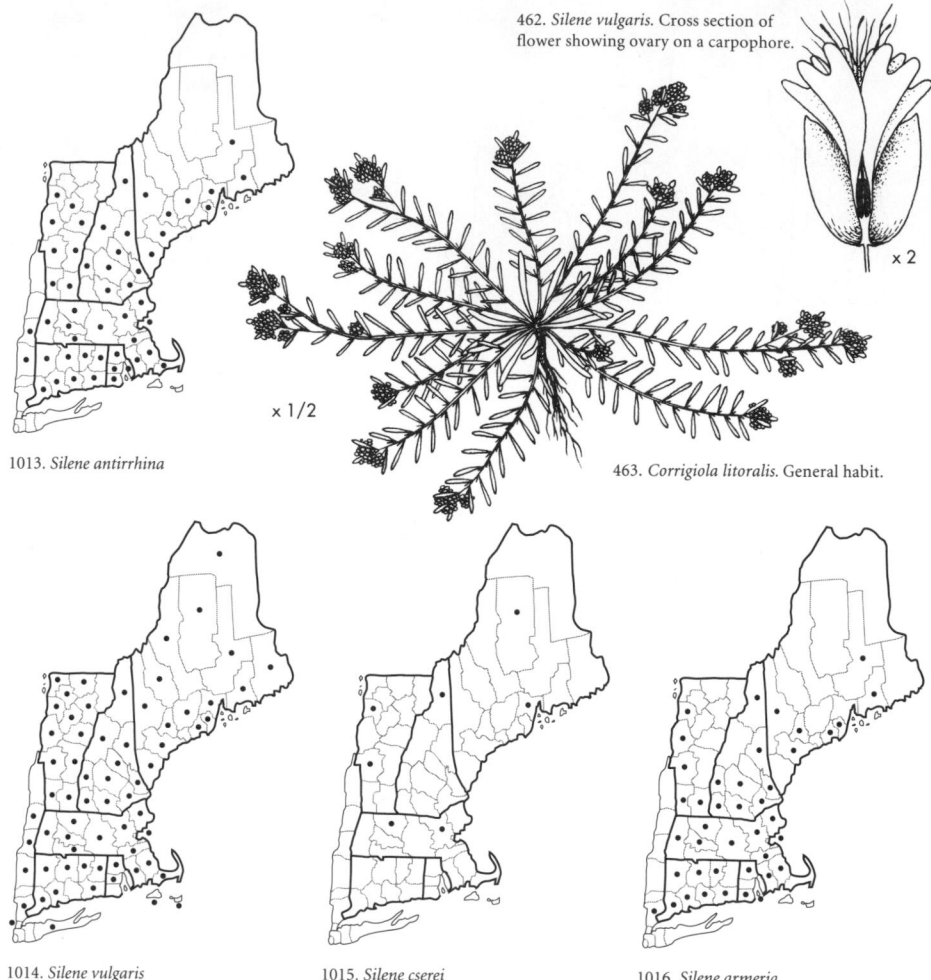

462. *Silene vulgaris.* Cross section of flower showing ovary on a carpophore.

× 2

× 1/2

1013. *Silene antirrhina*

463. *Corrigiola litoralis.* General habit.

1014. *Silene vulgaris*

1015. *Silene cserei*

1016. *Silene armeria*

9. *Corrigíola* L. Strapwort (shoe-string, referring to the slender form).

Low, spreading, slender, glabrous, annual herbs; leaves narrowly oblanceolate, alternate, sessile, with scarious, caudate stipules; flowers in dense, terminal, bracteate cymes, calyx deeply 5-parted, petals 5, whitish, stamens 5, stigmas 3, sessile, ovary 1-locular; fruit a globose, rugose utricle included within the calyx.

1. *C. litorális* L. (of the seashore). Waste places and grassy areas near the coast. June-September. Fig. 463. Reported for MA. (Adventive from Europe).

10. *Spérgula* L. Spurrey (sowing of the seeds).

Low, branched, annual herbs, glabrous or sparingly glandular-puberulent; leaves linear to filiform, sessile, stipulate, apparently whorled; flowers numerous in open, terminal, bracteate, dichotomous cymes, pedicels (at least some of them) reflexed, sepals 5, separate, petals 5, entire, white, stamens 5-10, hypogynous, styles 5, distinct, ovary 1-locular; capsule ovoid, 5-valved, dehiscent to the base, exceeding the calyx, seeds numerous, black, white-papillate and narrowly winged or margined.

1. *S. arvénsis* L. (of cultivated fields). Cultivated ground, fields, roadsides and waste places. May-August. Fig. 464, Map 1017. (Naturalized from Europe). Our plants include var. *arvensis* and the following var.:

var. *satíva* (Boenn.) Reichenb. Glandular-pubescent; seeds not white-papillate (glabrous or sparingly glandular-puberulent, and seeds conspicuously white-papillate in var. *arvensis*). [*S. sativa*].

11. *Holósteum* L. Jagged Chickweed (from the Greek, meaning all bone).

Tufted, simple-stemmed, glandular-pubescent, annual herb; leaves basal and cauline, oblong, lanceolate or oblanceolate, the cauline few, sessile, estipulate; flowers long-pedicelled in a terminal, bracteate umbel borne on a long peduncle, sepals 5, distinct, petals 5, jagged or denticulate, the same length or slightly exceeding sepals, white, stamens 3-5, hypogynous, styles 3, distinct, ovary 1-locular; capsule ovoid-cylindric, many seeded, dehiscent by 6 teeth, seeds rough, yellowish.

1. *H. umbellátum* L. (with umbels). Fields, cultivated ground, and roadsides. April-May. Fig. 465, Map 1018. (Naturalized from Europe).

12. *Herniária* L. Herniary (name based on its reputed medicinal value).

Low, spreading, diffusely branched, glabrous or puberulent, annual or perennial herbs; leaves opposite, sessile, oblong, elliptic or obovate, small and crowded, with minute, connate, scarious, ciliate stipules; flowers small, green, in dense, axillary, bracteate cymes, calyx deeply 5-parted, petals lacking, stamens 2-5, perigynous, style 2-cleft at the apex, ovary 1-locular; fruit an indehiscent, 1-seeded capsule partly enclosed within the calyx.

1. *H. glábra* L. (smooth). Native of Europe sparingly occurring in waste places. Reported for Penobscot County ME.

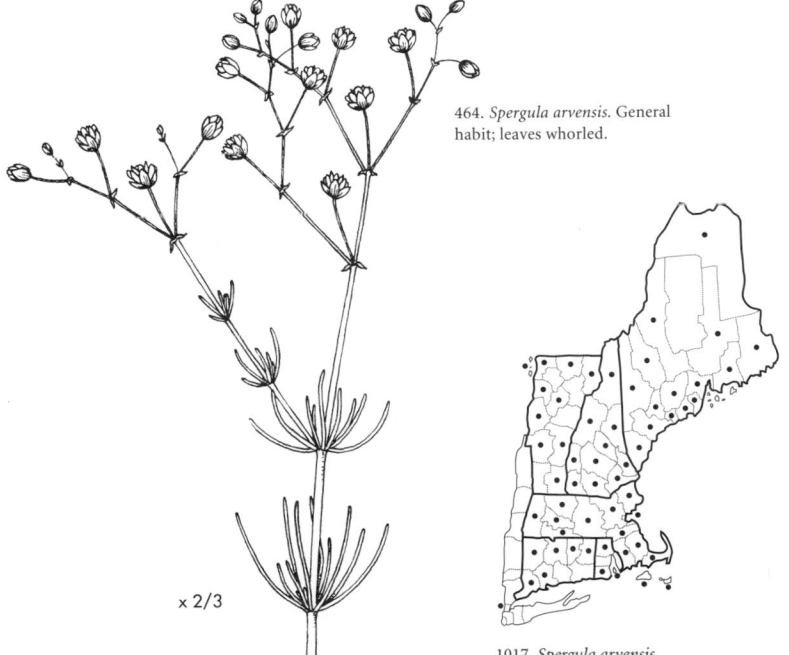

464. *Spergula arvensis*. General habit; leaves whorled.

× 2/3

1017. *Spergula arvensis*

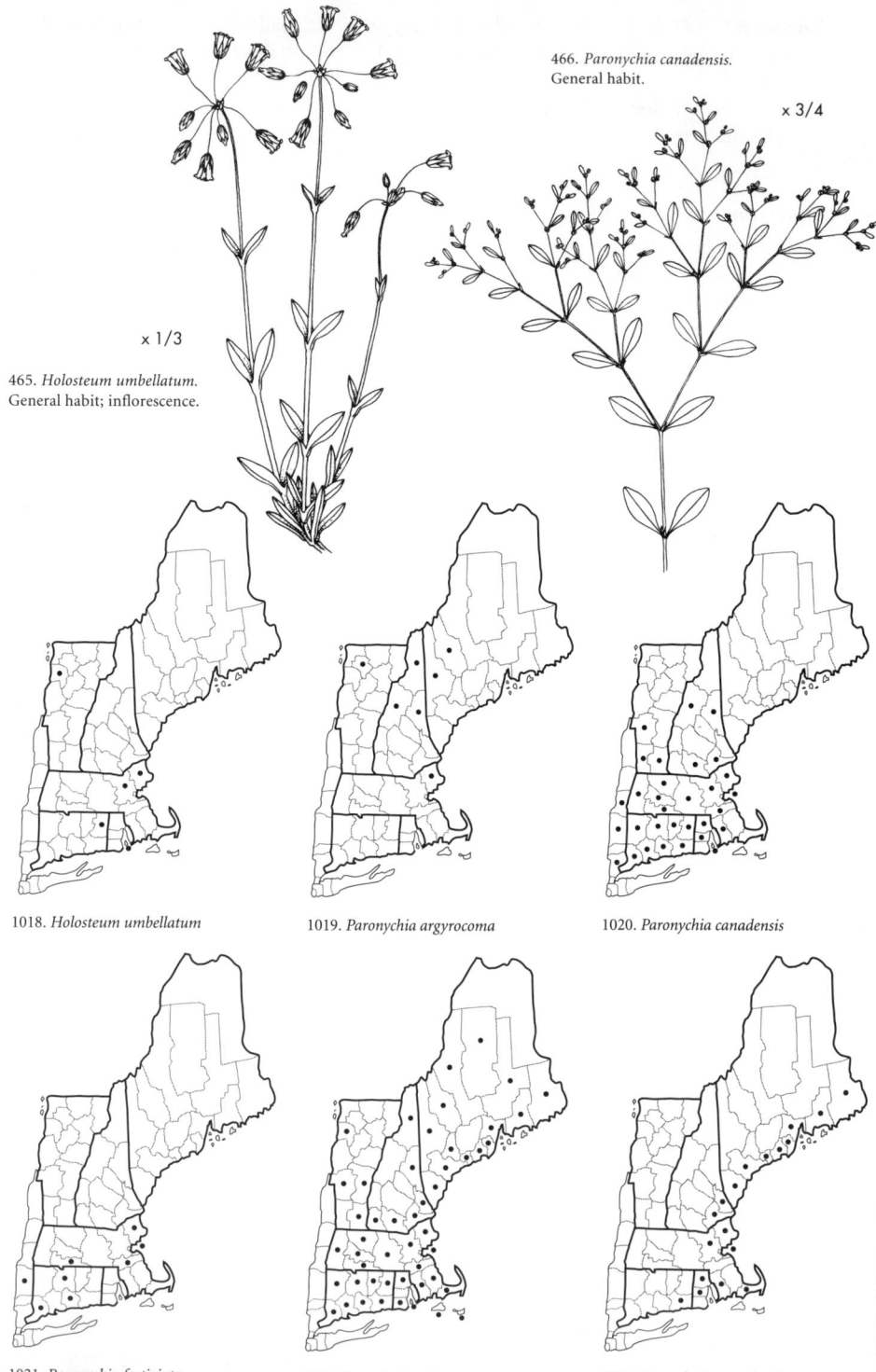

466. *Paronychia canadensis.*
General habit.

× 3/4

× 1/3

465. *Holosteum umbellatum.*
General habit; inflorescence.

1018. *Holosteum umbellatum*

1019. *Paronychia argyrocoma*

1020. *Paronychia canadensis*

1021. *Paronychia fastigiata*

1022. *Spergularia rubra*

1023. *Spergularia canadensis*

H. cinérea DC. Similar to the latter species but grayish-hispid rather than glabrous or puberulent. (Adventive from Europe). Reported for Bronx County NY.

H. hirsùta L. A slender annual closely resembling *H. cinerea* has been reported for MA.

13. Paronýchia Mill. Whitlow-wort (from the Greek, named for a plant with whitish scales able to cure disease of the nails).

Tufted, glabrous or pubescent, annual or perennial herbs; leaves linear to lanceolate or elliptic, opposite, sessile, with conspicuous, hyaline stipules; flowers small, numerous, sessile or subsessile, in loose or congested, forked, scarious or leafy-bracted cymes, sepals 5, distinct or united at the base, cucullate to awned at the apex, petals lacking, stamens usually 5, inserted at the base of the calyx, style 2-cleft at the apex, ovary 1-locular; fruit an ovoid, obovoid or globose, membranous, 1-seeded, utricle included within or slightly exceeding the calyx. Reported to be useful applied as a poultice, to relieve discomfort caused by hangnails or other inflammation of the nails.

a. Perennial; leaves linear to lance-linear. .... 1. *P. argyrocoma*
a. Annual; leaves oval, elliptic or spatulate.
    Stems glabrous; sepals flat, blunt or indistinctly mucronulate. .... 2. *P. canadensis*
    Stems pubescent; sepals usually longitudinally ribbed, distinctly mucronulate. ...... 3. *P. fastigiata*

1. *P. argyrócoma* (Michx.) Nutt. (with silvery locks). Silverling. Rocky slopes in mountains of N.H. and Maine, and ledges near mouth of Merrimack River, MA. June-September. Map 1019. Endangered in MA.

P. virgínica Spreng. Will key to *P. argyrocoma* but is distinguishable in having flowers in open, repeatedly forked cymes, not concealed by the bracts, the plant not appearing silvery (flowers in dense cymes, concealed by large, scarious bracts such that the plant appears silvery in *P. argyrocoma*). From farther south. Reported for RI. Our plants are var. *virginica* [*P. dichotoma*].

2. *P. canadénsis* (L.) Wood (Canadian). Dry rocky, sandy, or rich deciduous woods and openings. June-September. Fig. 466, Map 1020. [*Anychia c.*].

3. *P. fastigiáta* (Raf.) Fern. (with crowded, erect branches). Dry woods and openings. July-September. Map 1021. Our plants are var. *fastigiata*

14. Spergulária (Pers.) J. & K. Presl. Sand-Spurrey (name derived from *Spergula*).

Low, glabrous or glandular-pubescent, annual or perennial herbs; leaves linear or filiform, sessile, stipulate, often subtending clusters of smaller leaves; flowers in terminal, bracteate or leafy cymes, sepals 5, separate, petals 5, entire, pink or white, stamens 2-10, hypogynous, styles usually 3, distinct, ovary 1-locular; capsule ovoid to globose, 3-valved, dehiscent to the base, many-seeded, seeds surrounded by a membranous wing or wingless, smooth or sculptured.

a. Leaves strongly mucronate, the mucro 0.2 mm or more long; sepals about as long
    as the capsule; stamens 6 or more; inland species of dry soil. .... 1. *S. rubra*
a. Leaves obtuse or with a mucro 0.1 mm or less long; sepals as long as to shorter
    than capsule; stamens 5 or fewer (6 or more in *S. media*); species of salt
    marshes or sea beaches.
        Leaves obtuse, not mucronate; stipules truncate, mostly broader than long. .... 2. *S. canadensis*
        Leaves short-mucronate; stipules triangular, as long or slightly longer than
        broad. (Fig. 467). .... 3. *S. salina*

1. *S. rúbra* (L.) J. & K. Presl (red). Gravelly soil of roadsides and waste places. May-September. Map 1022. (Naturalized from Europe). [*Tissa r.*]. —FACU

2. *S. canadénsis* (Pers.) G. Don (Canadian). Muddy or sandy tidal areas, salt marshes. July-September. Map 1023. [*Tissa c.*]. Our plants are var. *canadensis.* —OBL

3. *S. sálina* J. & K. Presl Fig. 467. Brackish and saline marshes and shores. July-September. Map 1024. (southwestern US, Eurasia, S. Amer.). [*S. leiosperma; S. marina; Tissa m.*]. Our plants are var. *salina.* —OBL

467. *Spergularia salina*. Two pairs of opposite leaves, short mucronate, triangular stipules.

×1

1024. *Spergularia salina*

1025. *Cerastium tomentosum*

1026. *Cerastium arvense* subsp. *strictum*

1027. *Cerastium nutans*

1028. *Cerastium semidecandrum*

S. média (L.) C. Presl.　Similar to *S. salina* but distinguishable in having fascicled leaves and flowers with 9 or 10 stamens (leaves not fascicled and stamens 5 or fewer in *S. salina*). (Naturalized from Europe). Coastal environments, e. NY. [*S. maritima*]. —FACW

S. diándra (Guss.) Held. & Sart. European species with black seeds (the above species have brown seeds). (Adventive from Europe). Reported for MA.

15. Cerástium L. Mouse-ear Chickweed (from the Greek, based on the curved capsules).

Low, usually pubescent, annual or perennial herbs; leaves sessile, or the lowest short-petioled, estipulate; flowers usually in terminal, dichotomous, bracteate cymes, sepals 5, distinct, petals 5, usually 2-lobed or retuse, rarely entire, sometimes absent in some flowers, the same length as or longer than the sepals, white, stamens 10, rarely fewer, hypogynous, styles 5, rarely 3 or 4, distinct, ovary 1-locular; capsule cylindric, often curved, usually longer than the sepals, dehiscent by twice as many teeth as the styles, many-seeded, seeds rough, reddish-brown.

a. Leaves densely white-woolly or tomentose; petals much longer than sepals,
often 2-3 times as long .... 1. *C. tomentosum*
a. Leaves green, sometimes densely hairy but not white-woolly or tomentose.
  b. Petals much longer than sepals, often 2-3 times as long; median stem leaves 5
    or more times as long as wide.
      Mat-forming perennial; leaves (in ours) 4 mm or less wide. .... 2. *C. arvense*
      Tufted or solitary-stemmed annual; largest leaves 5 mm or more wide. .... 3. *C. nutans*
  b. Petals as long, slightly exceeding, or shorter than sepals or lacking; median stem
    leaves 4 times or less as long as wide (except in *C. nutans*). (Fig. 468).
    c. Bracts of inflorescence scarious at the tip or on the margins.
      Plant annual; capsule straight, up to 7 mm long.
        Bracts with upper half scarious; petals shallowly notched. .... 4. *C. semidecandrum*
        Bracts with narrow scarious margins and tips; petals deeply bifid. .... 5. *C. pumilum*
      Plant perennial; capsule curved, longer than 7 mm. .... 6. *C. glomeratum*
    c. Bracts of inflorescence herbaceous.
      Pedicels usually not longer than sepals, not over 7 mm long; median stem
        leaves 4 times or less as long as wide. .... 7. *C. fontanum*
      Pedicels longer than sepals, 1 cm or more long; median stem leaves 5 or
        more times as long as wide .... 3. *C. nutans*

1. *C. tomentósum* L. (tomentose). Snow in Summer. Occasionally escaped from cultivation. Map 1025. (Introduced from Eurasia).

C. bieberstéinii DC. Similar to *C. tomentosum* but with lanceolate leaves more than 2 cm long and 3-6 mm wide (leaves linear lanceolate, up to 2 cm long and 3 mm wide in *C. tomentosum*). (Asia). Rarely escaped from cultivation. Reported for ME.

2. *C. arvénse* L. (of cultivated ground). Field Chickweed. Dry fields, woodlands, waste places and seashore. May-June. Map 1026. (Eurasia). [*C. campestre; C. oreophilum; C. strictum; C. velutinum*]. Represented with us as subsp. *strictum*. Ugborogh.

3. *C. nútans* Raf. (nodding). Nodding Chickweed. Fields and wooded hillsides, often calcareous. May-June. Map 1027. Endangered in MA. —FAC

C. diffúsum Pers. Similar to *C. nutans* but flowers 4-merous and capsule straight or nearly so (flowers 5-merous and capsules curved in *C. nutans*). From farther south and west. (Adventive from Europe). Reported for Middlesex county MA. [*C. tetrandrum*].

4. *C. semidecándrum* L. (with half of 10 stamens). Sandy fields and waste places. Map 1028. (Naturalized from Europe).

5. *C. púmilum* Curt. (dwarf). Sandy fields and waste places. (Adventive from Europe). Reported for CT, Hampden County MA. Our plants are var. *pumilum*.

6. *C. glomerátum* Auct. non L. Common Chickweed. Fields, cultivated ground, roadsides and waste places. May-September. Fig. 468, Map 1029. (Naturalized from Eurasia). [*C. viscosum*].—FACU-

7. *C. fontánum* Baumg. Fields, roadsides and waste places. May-July. Map 1030. (Naturalized from Europe). [*C. vulgatum*].

16. *Myosóton* Moench. Giant Chickweed (mouse ear).

Branched, decumbent or spreading and ascending, perennial herb; stems angled, glandular-pubescent above, nearly glabrous below; leaves ovate to ovate-lanceolate, mostly sessile and somewhat cordate-clasping, the lowest short-petioled; flowers solitary and in open, leafy, terminal cymes, pedicelled, the pedicels glandular, reflexed in fruit, sepals 5, glandular-pubescent, distinct, petals 5, deeply 2-cleft, white, much exceeding the sepals, stamens 10, hypogynous, styles 5, distinct, ovary many ovuled, 1-locular; capsule ovoid, dehiscent by 5 valves, each valve 2-cleft. [*Alsine; Stellaria*].

1. *M. aquáticum* (L.) Moench (aquatic). Riverbanks, stream and pond margins, moist meadows and waste places. June-October. Map 1031. (Naturalized from Europe). [*Alsine aquatica; Stellaria aquatica*]. —FACW

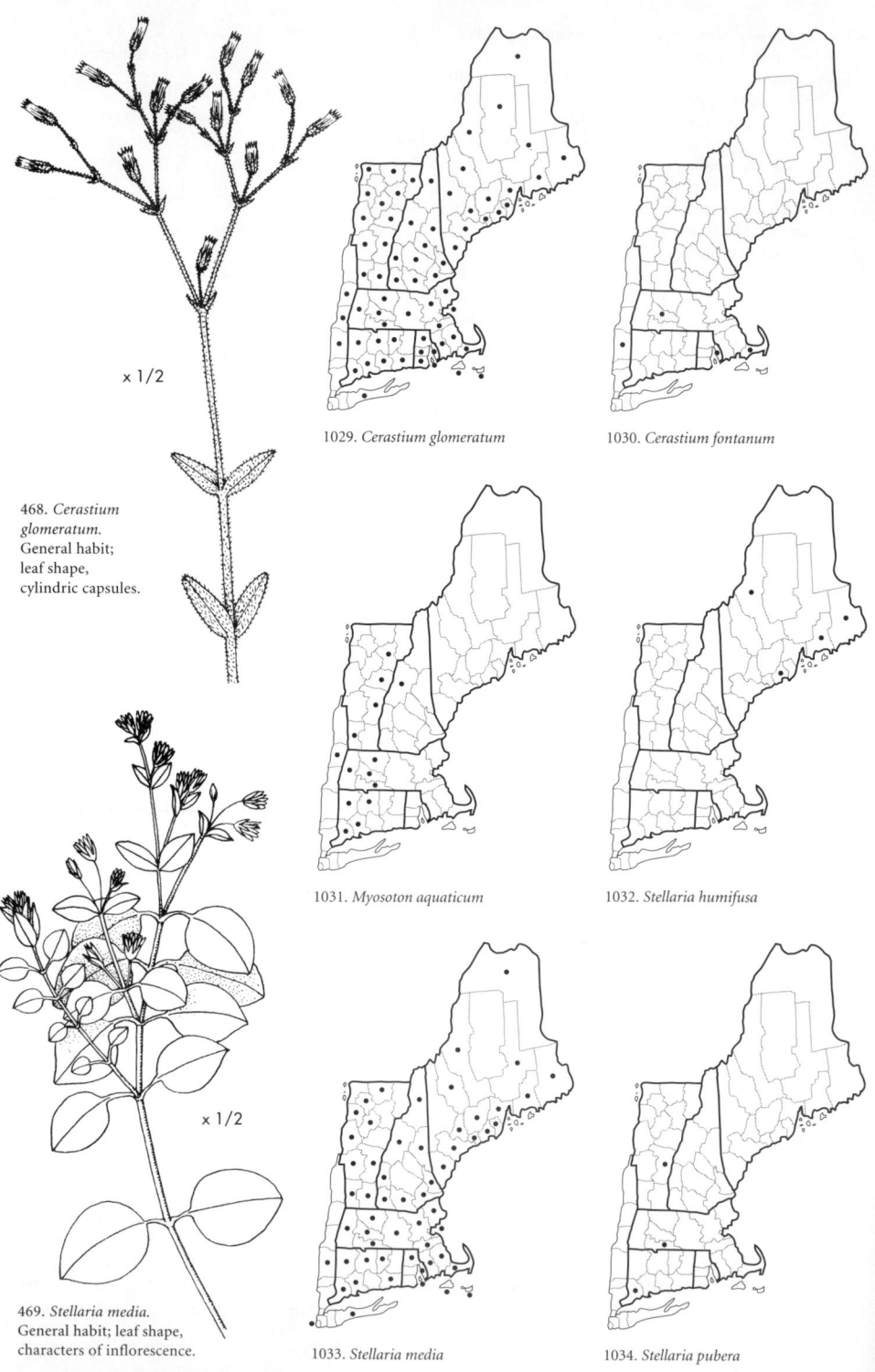

× 1/2

468. *Cerastium glomeratum.* General habit; leaf shape, cylindric capsules.

1029. *Cerastium glomeratum*

1030. *Cerastium fontanum*

1031. *Myosoton aquaticum*

1032. *Stellaria humifusa*

× 1/2

469. *Stellaria media.* General habit; leaf shape, characters of inflorescence.

1033. *Stellaria media*

1034. *Stellaria pubera*

17. Stellária L. Chickweed (star, from the star-shaped flowers).

Low, often matted, generally diffuse and branched, annual or perennial, sometimes rhizomatous herbs; stems decumbent, ascending or erect, round or usually 4-angled, glabrous or pubescent, sometimes in lines; leaves sessile or petioled, estipulate; flowers solitary or in terminal and/or axillary, bracteate cymes, sepals 5, distinct, petals 5, usually deeply 2-cleft, white, sometimes lacking, stamens 10 or fewer, hypogynous, styles 3, distinct, ovary few to many ovuled, 1-locular; capsule ovoid to globose, opening by twice as many valves as styles. [*Alsine*].

a. Leaves ovate to elliptic, 3 times or less as long as wide; flowers solitary in the leaf
    axils or in leafy-bracted cymes. (Fig. 469).
    b. Stems and sepals glabrous; leaf blades up to 1 cm long and 4 mm wide. .... 1. *S. humifusa*
    b. Stems pubescent, often in lines; sepals often pubescent; leaf blades longer than
        1 cm and wider than 4 mm (except sometimes in *S. media*).
        Lower and middle leaves petioled; stems round; sepals usually pubescent;
            seeds less than 1.5 mm long or broad. (Fig. 469). .... 2. *S. media*
        Only the lowermost leaves petioled; stems angled; sepals glabrous or only
            ciliate; seeds more than 1.5 mm long or broad. .... 3. *S. pubera*
a. Leaves linear to linear-lanceolate or lance-elliptic, mostly 4 or more times as long
    as wide, or if broader then the cymes scarious-bracted, or sepals 3 mm or less
    long (longer than 3 mm in the above species). (Fig. 470).
    c. Cymes with foliaceous bracts (or the uppermost bracts just below the flowers
        occasionally scarious in *S. calycantha*).
        Petals conspicuously exceeding the sepals; sepals 6 mm or longer. .... 4. *S. holostea*
        Petals shorter than sepals or lacking; sepals 3 mm or less long. .... 5. *S. calycantha*
    c. Cymes entirely scarious-bracted.
        d. Petals shorter than sepals or lacking; cymes all or nearly all axillary. .... 6. *S. alsine*
        d. Petals as long or longer than sepals; cymes terminal or pseudolateral.
            Cymes few-flowered; sepals usually 3.5 mm or less long, weakly 3-nerved. ...... 7. *S. longifolia*
            Cymes many-flowered; sepals longer than 3.5 mm, strongly 3-nerved.
            (Fig. 470). .... 8. *S. graminea*

    1. S. humifúsa Rottb. (spreading on the ground). Salt-marsh Stitchwort. Salt marshes and brackish or saline soil. July-August. Map 1032. (Eurasia). [*Alsine h.*].

    2. S. média (L.) Villars (intermediate). Common Chickweed. Fields, cultivated land, roadsides and waste places. May-September. Fig. 469, Map 1033. (Naturalized from Eurasia). [*Alsine m.*]. Can be eaten in salad or lightly cooked. —Wildl. 1

    S. córei Shinners. Will key to *S. media* or *S. pubera* but has sepals 7 mm or more long and acuminate (sepals 6 mm or less long and acute or obtuse in the latter 2 species). Reported for CT, MA, ME, VT. [*S. pubera* var. *silvatica; S. silvatica*].

    3. S. púbera Michx. (puberulent). Rich woods. April-May. Map 1034. [*Alsine p.*]. Our plants are var. *pubera*.

    4. S. holóstea L. (like Holosteum). Spread from cultivation to roadsides and dry, rocky woods. April-June. Map 1035. (Introduced from Europe). [*Alsine h.*].

    5. S. calycántha (Ledeb.) Bong. (calyx-flowered). Alpine Stitchwort. Alpine areas, wooded swamps, wet woods and springy places. June-August. Map 1036. (Eurasia).

    S. boreális Bigelow. Similar to *S. calycantha* but with larger leaves 2.5-7 cm long (leaves up to 2.5 cm long in *S. calycantha*). Reported for all the New England states. [*Alsine b.; S. calycantha* var. *floribunda*]. Our plants are subsp. *borealis*.

    6. S. alsíne Grimm (like Alsine). Streams, springy places and marshes. May-August. Map 1037. (Europe). [*Alsine uliginosa*].

    7. S. longifólia Muhl. ex Willd. (long-leaved). Moist meadows and woods, pond and river margins. May-July. Map 1038. (Eurasia). [*Alsine l.*].

    S. lóngipes Goldie. Similar to *S. longifolia* and the following species but distinguishable in having ascending pedicels (pedicels spreading or reflexed in *S. longifolia* and *S. graminea*). From farther south and west. Reported for ME. [*Alsine l.*]. Our plants are subsp. *longipes*.

S. palústris Retz. Similar to *S. longipes* but sepals 5 mm or more long, acuminate, seeds wider than 1 mm (sepals less than 5 mm long, acute or obtuse, and seeds up to 1 mm wide in *S. longipes*). [*S. glauca*]. (Naturalized from Europe). From farther north and west. Reported for ME.

8. *S. gramínea* L. (grass-like). Common Stitchwort. Fields and roadsides. May-July. Fig. 470, Map 1039. (Naturalized from Europe). [*Alsine g.*]. Represented with us as var. *graminea* and the following var.:

var. *latifolia* Peterm. Leaves lanceolate (linear to linear-lanceolate in var. *graminea*).

18. *Honckénya* Ehrh. Seabeach Sandwort.

Simple to much branched, erect, procumbent or ascending, thick-stemmed, glabrous, perennial herbs, fleshy throughout; leaves sessile, clasping, ovate, elliptic or lance-ovate, acute or mucronate, estipulate; flowers solitary in the upper leaf axils and in the forks of the stem and branches, or terminal, sepals 5, separate, ovate or lanceolate, petals 5, spatulate-obovate, about equalling the sepals, stamens 10 or in some flowers reduced in number or abortive, the petals and stamens inserted on a 10-lobed disc surrounding the base of the ovary, styles 3-5, distinct, ovary 3-5 locular, with few ovules; capsule globose or subglobose, longer than the calyx, 1-locular, dehiscing by 3-5 valves, few-seeded. [*Arenaria*].

1. *H. peploídes* (L.) Ehrh. (resembling Peplis portula). Sea beaches and sand dunes. June-July. Fig. 471, Map 1040. (Eurasia). Endangered in NH. [*Arenaria p.*]. Represented with us as subsp. *robusta* (Fern.) Hulten. —FACU

19. *Sagína* L. Pearlwort (fattening; name based on use of a related plant for forage).

Low, tufted or matted, delicate, glabrous or pubescent, annual or perennial herbs; leaves connate, linear or subulate, estipulate; flowers terminating the stem or branches, sepals 4 or 5, distinct, petals 4 or 5 or none, entire or emarginate, shorter or longer than the sepals, white, stamens 4 or 5, less often fewer or more, hypogynous, styles 4 or 5, separate, ovary 1-locular; capsule ovoid or oblong, many-seeded, 4-5 valved, dehiscent to the base at maturity.

a. Leaves of upper stem and branches usually bearing axillary bulb-like tufts, giving a
    moniliform appearance; petals nearly twice the length of the sepals (Fig. 472). .. 1. *S. nodosa*
a. Leaves not bearing axillary bulb-like tufts, or if subtending axillary shoots or leaf
    clusters, not appearing moniliform; petals shorter than to barely exceeding sepals.
      Plant annual without persistent basal rosettes or axillary fascicles of reduced
        leaves; sepals usually 5 .... 2. *S. decumbens*
      Plant perennial usually with persistent basal rosettes and fascicles of reduced
        leaves in the axils of the stem leaves; sepals usually 4. .... 3. *S. procumbens*

1. *S. nodósa* (L.) Fenzl. Rocks and cliffs, and gravelly or sandy soil along the coast. July-September. Fig. 472, Map 1041. (Europe). Our plants include subsp. *nodosa* and the following subsp.:
subsp. *boreális* Crow. Stems glabrous (glandular-pubescent in subsp. *nodosa*). —FAC

2. *S. decúmbens* (Ell.) T. & G. (depressed but with ascending tips). Moist or dry sandy fields, open woods, lawns, paths and roadsides. May-Aug. Map 1042. Our plants are subsp. *decumbens*. —FAC

S. japónica (Sw.) Ohwi. Similar to *S. decumbens* but distinguishable by its glandular-pubescent pedicels, capsules as broad as long and seeds with a dorsal groove (pedicels glabrous, capsules longer than broad and seeds lacking dorsal groove in *S. decumbens*). From the west. Reported for CT, MA and NY.

S. máxima Gray. Annual or sometimes perennial, pedicels glandular-pubescent as in *S. japonica* but capsules longer than broad, seeds lustrous, lacking a dorsal groove, not marked with slender ridges as in *S. decumbens*. From the west coast. Reported for MA. Our plants are subsp. *maxima*.

3. *S. procúmbens* L. (lying on the ground). Moist gravelly soil along pond and river margins, springy areas, wet rocks, roadsides, lawns and paths. May-September. Map 1043. (Eurasia). —FACW-

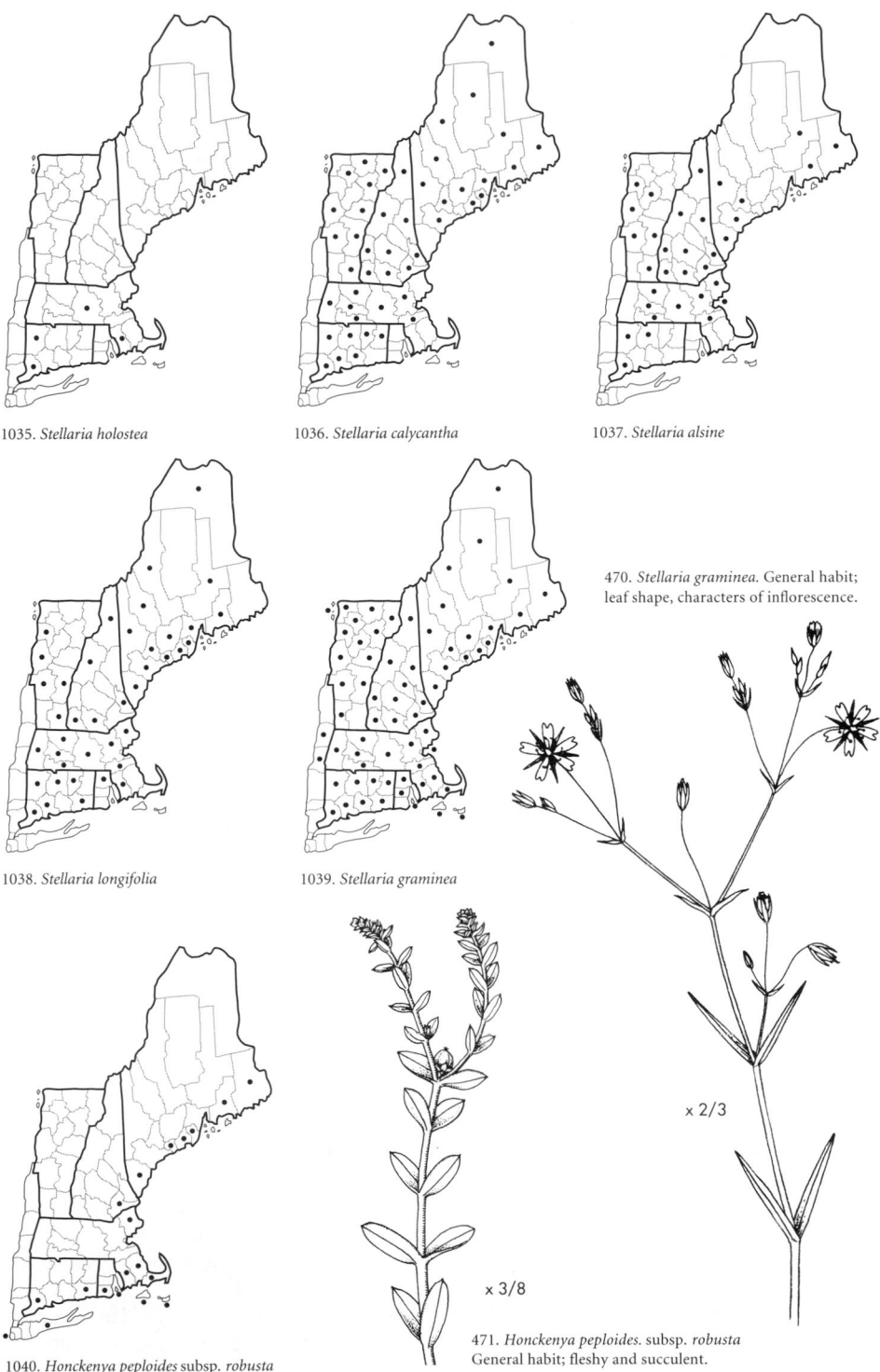

1035. *Stellaria holostea*

1036. *Stellaria calycantha*

1037. *Stellaria alsine*

1038. *Stellaria longifolia*

1039. *Stellaria graminea*

470. *Stellaria graminea.* General habit; leaf shape, characters of inflorescence.

× 2/3

× 3/8

1040. *Honckenya peploides* subsp. *robusta*

471. *Honckenya peploides.* subsp. *robusta* General habit; fleshy and succulent.

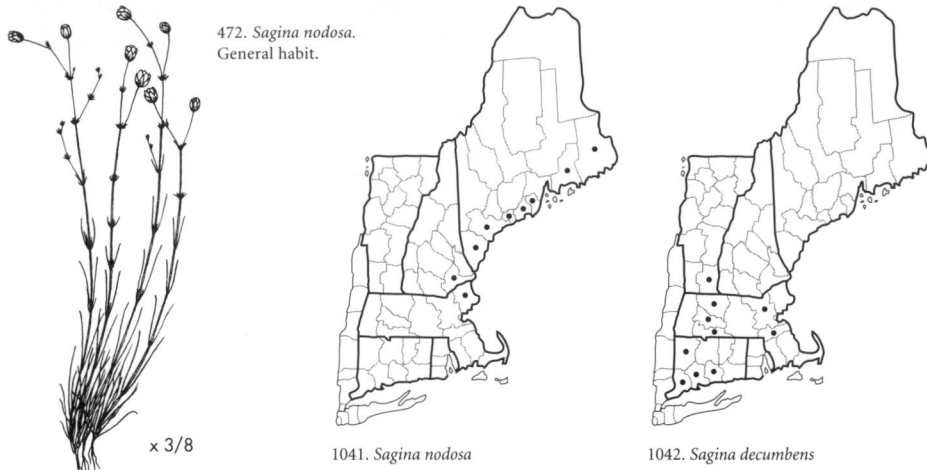

472. *Sagina nodosa.*
General habit.

× 3/8

1041. *Sagina nodosa*

1042. *Sagina decumbens*

20. *Minuártia* L. Sandwort.

Loosely to densely tufted and mat-forming, decumbent or erect, simple to freely branched, glabrous or pubescent, annual or perennial herbs, sometimes bearing short, leafy, sterile shoots; leaves linear or subulate, sessile, sometimes crowded on the lower part of the stem and becoming separated above, or subtending dense fascicles, estipulate; flowers few to many in open bracteate cymes, sepals 5, separate, petals 5, shorter or longer than the sepals, stamens 10, hypogynous, styles 3, distinct, ovary 1-locular, with many ovules; capsule cylindric to ovoid, equalling or exceeding the calyx, with 3-5 valves, many-seeded [*Arenaria; Sabulina*].

a. Sepals acute to acuminate, strongly 3-nerved.
    Primary stem leaves subtending fascicles of shorter leaves; petals much longer
        than sepals; stems usually glabrous .... 1. *M. michauxii*
    Primary stem leaves only present; petals equalling or shorter than sepals; stems
        usually pubescent .... 2. *M. rubella*
a. Sepals obtuse to subacute, nerveless or weakly nerved (distinctly 3-nerved in
    M. marcescens).
  b. Leaves rigid, linear-subulate .... 3. *M. caroliniana*
  b. Leaves not rigid, linear, obtuse.
    c. Sepals faintly 1-nerved; petals often emarginate.
        Forming mats, with many leafy shoots; sepals 4 mm or more long. .... 4. *M. groenlandica*
        Seldom forming mats, with few or no leafy shoots; sepals 4 mm or less long. . 5. *M. glabra*
    c. Sepals distinctly 3-nerved; petals entire. .... 6. *M. marcescens*

    1. *M. micháuxii* (Fenzl) Farw. (for A. Michaux). Rock Sandwort. Dry, usually calcareous gravel and ledges. May-July. Map 1044. Endangered in RI, NH. [*M. stricta; Arenaria stricta* var. *s.; Sabulina s.*]. Our plants are var. *michauxii*.

    2. *M. rubélla* (Wahlenb.) Hiern (reddish). Calcareous rocks and gravel at high elevations. June-August. (Eurasia). Endangered in ME. Reported for Aroostook County ME; Lamoille County VT. [*Arenaria r.; A. verna; Sabulina propinqua*].

    M. pátula (Michx.) Mattf. Similar to *M. rubella* but distinguishable in having leaves with midrib stronger than the lateral nerves, not alpine (leaves with 3 strong nerves, alpine in *M. rubella*). From farther south. Reported for ME. Represented with us as var. *robusta* (Steyerm.) McNeill. [*Arenaria patula* var. *r.*].

    3. *M. caroliniána* (Walt.) Mattf. (of Carolina). Pine-Barren Sandwort. Sandy soil in oak or pine woods and in the open. June-July. Reported for Suffolk County NY; Washington County RI. [*Arenaria c.; A. squarrosa; Sabulina c.*].

4. *M. groenlándica* (Retz.) Ostenf. (of Greenland). Mountain Sandwort. Rocks, gravel and ledges in alpine areas. June-August. Fig. 473, Map 1045. Endangered in RI. [*Arenaria g.; Sabulina g.*].

5. *M. glábra* (Michx.) Mattf. (smooth). Rocky, gravelly and ledgy woods of foothills and lower mountains. May-August. Map 1046. [*Arenaria groenlandica* var. *glabra; Sabulina g.*].

6. *M. marcéscens* (Fenzl) House (retaining old dry leaves). Serpentine Sandwort. Reported for NH and Haystack Mountain, Vermont. Only known localities in the U.S.

21. *Arenária* L. Sandwort (sand; referring to the habitat in which the species often occurs).

Delicate, diffuse and widely branched, puberulent, annual herbs; leaves sessile, ovate, cuneate at the base, estipulate; flowers small, white, pedicelled, in a panicle of dichotomous, bracteate, cymes, sepals 5, separate, acuminate, petals 5, entire, shorter than the sepals, stamens 10, hypogynous, styles 3, distinct, ovary 1-loculed, with many ovules; capsule ovoid to conic, longer than the sepals, dehiscent by 6 teeth, many-seeded, seeds strongly rugose.

1043. *Sagina procumbens*

1044. *Minuartia michauxii*

1045. *Minuartia groenlandica*

× 1

473. *Minuartia groenlandica.*
General habit; linear leaves.

1046. *Minuartia glabra*

1. A. serpyllifólia L. (with leaves of Serpyllum, Thyme). Thyme-leaved Sandwort. Dry fields, lawns, roadsides and waste places. May-August. Fig. 474, Map 1047. (Naturalized from Europe). Our plants include subsp. *serpyllifolia* and the following subsp.:

subsp. *leptoclados* (Reichenb.) Nyman. Fruiting calyx 2-3 mm long; seeds 0.5 mm or less long (fruiting calyx 3-4 mm long and seeds 0.6 mm long in subsp. *serpyllifolia*). [*A. serpyllifolia* var. *tenuior; A. leptoclados*]. —FAC

22. Moehríngia L. Sandwort.

Simple to sparingly branched, puberulent, rhizomatous, perennial herbs; leaves sessile or short petioled, estipulate, ovate, oblong, or lanceolate; flowers solitary in the axils or in terminal, few-flowered, bracteate cymes, sepals 5, separate, obtuse to acuminate, petals 5, entire, shorter or longer than the sepals, stamens 10, hypogynous, styles 3, distinct, ovary 1-loculed, with few ovules; capsule ovoid to ellipsoid, shorter or longer than the calyx, dehiscent by 6 valves to the middle or nearly to the base, few-seeded, seeds usually with a pale, spongy appendage (strophiole) at the hilum. [*Arenaria*].

Petals longer than sepals, leaves oval to elliptic, obtuse to subacute. .... 1. *M. lateriflora*
Petals shorter than or equalling sepals; leaves lanceolate, acute to acuminate .... 2. *M. macrophylla*

1. M. lateriflóra (L.) Fenzl (flowering on the side). Dry to damp woods and thickets, woods edges, shores and meadows. May-July. Fig. 475, Map 1048. (Eurasia). [*Arenaria l.*]. —FAC

2. M. macrophýlla (Hook.) Fenzl (large-leaved). Dry woods, rocky slopes and ledges. May-July. Map 1049. (Asia). Endangered in CT. [*Arenaria m.*].

Family 82. Ceratophylláceae (Hornwort Family)

Monoecious, rootless, submerged, aquatic herbs with prolonged, branching stems. Leaves whorled, sessile, estipulate, once to several times dichotomously divided. Flowers unisexual, minute, solitary

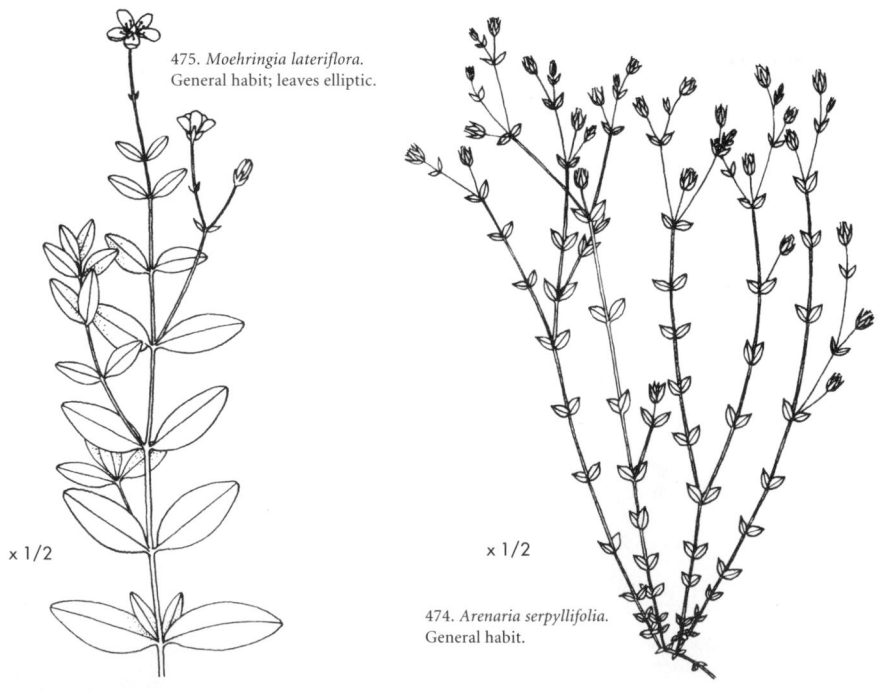

475. *Moehringia lateriflora.*
General habit; leaves elliptic.

× 1/2

× 1/2

474. *Arenaria serpyllifolia.*
General habit.

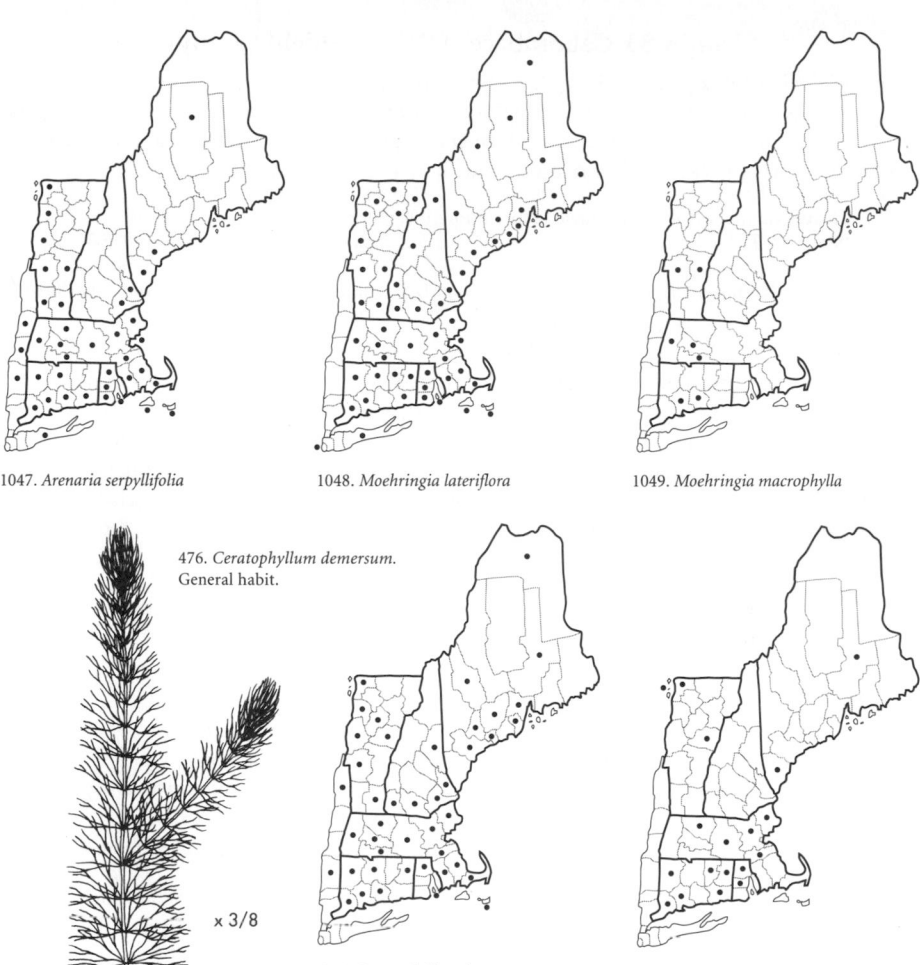

1047. *Arenaria serpyllifolia*

1048. *Moehringia lateriflora*

1049. *Moehringia macrophylla*

476. *Ceratophyllum demersum.*
General habit.

× 3/8

1050. *Ceratophyllum demersum*

1051. *Ceratophyllum echinatum*

and sessile in the leaf axils, each subtended by 8-20 involucral bracts, perianth none, staminate flowers of 10-20 stamens with sessile or subsessile anthers, pistillate flowers with a superior, 1-locular, 1-ovulate ovary and a solitary style. Fruit an achene with a persistent style and 2 or more spines.

1. Ceratophýllum L. Coontail (from the Greek, meaning horn leaf).
Same characters as the family. —Wildl. 1

Leaf segments distinctly spinulose-serrate, at least on 1 side; achenes with 2 spines
near the base .... 1. *C. demersum*
Leaf segments entire or remotely serrate; achenes with basal as well as several lateral
spines .... 2. *C. echinatum*

   1. C. demérsum L. (submerged). Quiet water of lakes and streams. July-September. Fig. 476, Map 1050. —OBL
   2. C. echinátum Gray. Quiet water of lakes and streams. August-September. Map 1051. [*C. muricatum*]. —OBL

Family 83. Cabombáceae (Water-shield Family)

Perennial caulescent, aquatic herbs with creeping rhizimes. Leaves floating and peltate, alternate (opposite submersed leaves also present in Cabomba). Flowers solitary, axillary, sepals and petals each 3 or 4, stamens 3-many, carpels 3-8, distinct and unilocular with 1 stigma and several ovules per locule, ovary superior. Fruit coriaceous, indehiscent. [*Nymphaeaceae*].

Principal leaves submersed, opposite, divided into numerous filiform or linear
 segments. (Fig. 477) 1.*Cabomba*
 caroliniana
Principal leaves floating, alternate, centrally peltate. (Fig. 478). .... 2. *Brasenia schreberi*

1. *Cabómba* Aubl. (an aboriginal name).

Caulescent herbs from a creeping rhizome giving rise to slender, branching stems; leaves dimorphic, the submersed ones mostly opposite, petioled, rotund, palmately and dichotomously divided into numerous linear or filiform segments, the floating ones mostly alternate, few, linear-elliptic, petioled, peltate, often slightly constricted at the middle and/or notched at one end; flowers from the upper leaf axils, small, white, or yellow at the base within, sepals and petals each 3, the petals slightly longer, auriculate near the base, stamens 3-6, carpels usually 3 (2-4), separate, each containing 2-3 ovules, stigmas capitate; fruit ovoid, indehiscent, 2-3 seeded.

 1. *C. caroliniána* Gray (of Carolina). Fanwort. Aggressive weed of ponds and quiet streams. June-September. Fig. 477, Map 1052. Our plants are var. *caroliniana*. —OBL

2. *Brasénia* Schreb. Water shield (for C. Brasen).

Caulescent herbs from a creeping rhizome giving rise to slender, branching stems, the submersed parts of the plant heavily coated with mucilage; leaves alternate, crowded toward the summit of the stem, long petioled, floating, oval, centrally peltate; flowers small, dull purple, sepals and petals each 3 or 4, the petals slightly longer and narrower; stamens 12-18, carpels 4-8, separate, each containing 2-3 ovules, stigmas linear; fruit ellipsoid, ovoid or obovoid, indehiscent, 1 or 2 seeded. —Wildl. 1

 1. *B. schréberi* Gmel. (for J.C.D. Schreber). Ponds and quiet streams. June-September. Fig. 478, Map 1053. (Africa, Asia, Australia, Tropical Amer.). Starchy rhizome can be peeled, cooked and eaten or dried and ground into flour. —OBL

Family 84. Nelumbonáceae (Sacred Bean Family)

Large, acaulescent herbs from a thick, horizontal, tuberiferous rhizome. Leaves arising directly from the rhizome on long petioles, sometimes floating but usually raised high out of the water, large and orbicular with a depressed center, peltate. Flowers raised out of the water on long peduncles, pale yellow, showy, perianth segments numerous, sepals grading into petals, the outermost segments green and sepaloid, stamens numerous, the anthers with a terminal, somewhat hooked appendage, carpels numerous, contained in separate pits on top of a wide, convex receptacle, styles short and stout. Fruits indehiscent, nut-like, ellipsoid or subglobose, 1-seeded. [*Nymphaeaceae*].

1. *Nelúmbo* Adans. Sacred Bean.
Same characters as the family.

 1. *N. lútea* (Willd.) Pers. (Yellow). Lotus lily. Ponds and quiet water of rivers. July-August. Map 1054. (W.I.). Fruits edible after cracking shell and then boiling; rhizome was dried and cooked by Indians. —OBL

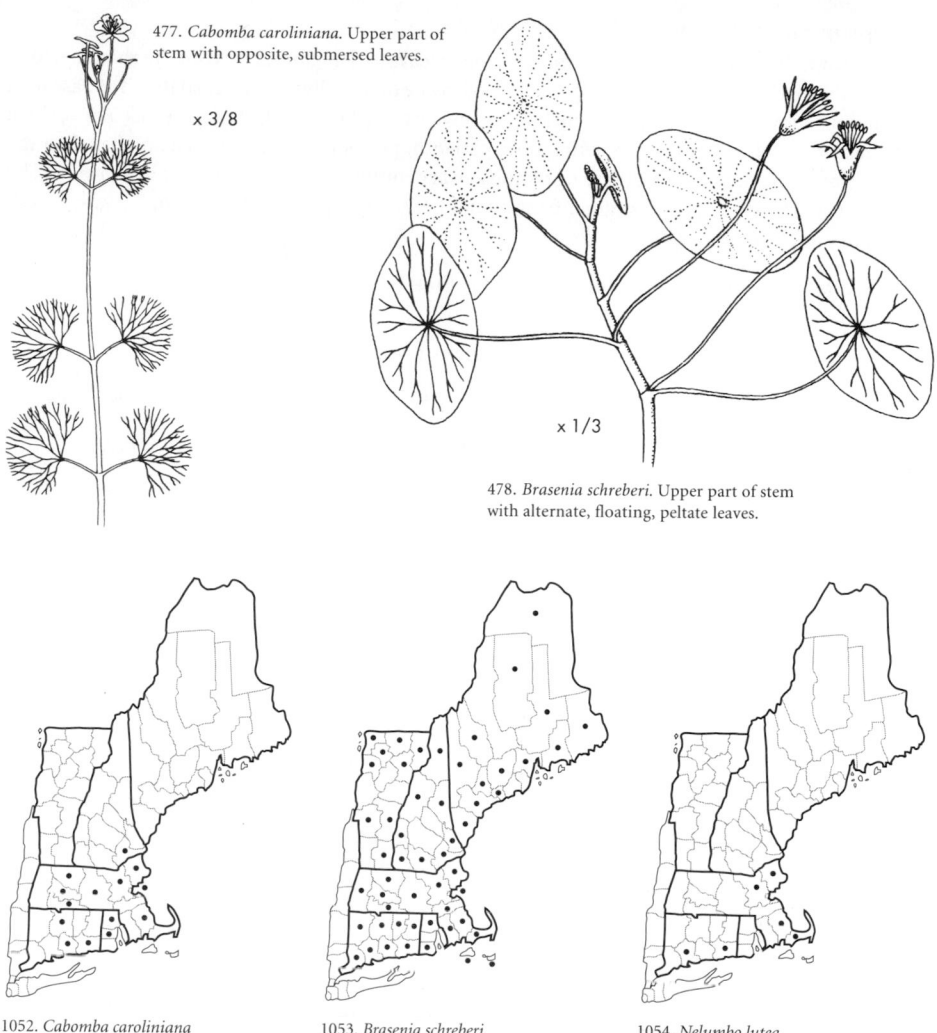

477. *Cabomba caroliniana*. Upper part of stem with opposite, submersed leaves.

x 3/8

x 1/3

478. *Brasenia schreberi*. Upper part of stem with alternate, floating, peltate leaves.

1052. *Cabomba caroliniana*

1053. *Brasenia schreberi*

1054. *Nelumbo lutea*

Family 85. Nymphaeáceae (Water-lily Family)

Hermaphrodite, perennial, acaulescent, aquatic herbs with mostly horizontal rhizomes. Leaves floating, emersed, or submersed, cordate, alternate. Flowers perfect, solitary, axillary, long peduncled, sepals 4-6, distinct, usually green but sometimes colored and resembling the petals, petals many, distinct, often grading into the stamens, stamens many, hypogynous, carpels many, united into a compound ovary, the ovary superior with many locules, the stigmas united into a disc with radiating stigmatic lines, each locule with many ovules. Fruit a leathery, many-seeded berry.

Flowers yellow to red or purple, subglobose; sepals petaloid; leaves pinnately veined.
(Fig. 479). .... 1. *Nuphar lutea*
Flowers white or pink, expanded; sepals green; leaves with veins mostly radiating
from base of sinus. (Fig. 480). .... 2. *Nymphaea*

1. *Núphar* Sm. Yellow water lily.

Acaulescent herbs from a thick, horizontal rhizome; leaves arising directly from the rhizome, long petioled, the blade submersed, floating or emersed, ovate to broadly elliptic, cordate at the base with a basal sinus; flowers floating on the surface, yellow or tinged with red, showy, sepals 5 or 6, thick and concave, petaloid, forming a subglobose perianth, petals numerous, much smaller than the sepals, resembling the stamens, these numerous, ovary compound, with many locules, crowned by a disc-like, 6-25 rayed, sessile stigma; fruit ovoid, berry-like, naked, ripening underwater, seeds numerous, not arillate. —Wildl. 1

1. *N. lutéa* (L.) Sibthorp & Sm. Represented with us by the following subsp.:

Anthers shorter than the filaments; stigmatic disc red. .... subsp. *pumila*
Anthers longer than the filaments and stigmatic disc green or yellowish.
   Petioles terete or oval in cross section. .... subsp. *advena*
   Petioles flattened on the upper side and narrowly winged. .... subsp. *variagata*

subsp. *púmila* (Timm.) E. O. Beal. Ponds. June-September. Map 1055. [*N. microphylla; N. pumila; N. x rubrodisca*].

subsp. *ádvena* (Ait.) Kartesz & Gandhi (immigrant). Pond margins and fresh tidal rivers. June-September. Map 1056. (W.I.). [*N. advena; N. luteum* subsp. *macrophyllum; N. fluviatilis; N. macrophylla; N. puteorum*].

subsp. *variegáta* (Dur.) E. O. Beal (variegated). Ponds. June-September. Fig. 479, Map 1057. [*N. variegata; N. fraterna*]. Seeds edible; can be prepared like popcorn after drying; starchy rhizome was boiled or roasted by Indians, then peeled and used like a vegetable or ground into flour. —OBL

2. *Nymphaéa* L. Water lily (ancient name).

Acaulescent herbs from a thick, horizontal (rarely erect) rhizome, this simple or branched, or producing numerous knotty tubers; leaves arising directly from the rhizome, long petioled, the blade floating, suborbicular to ovate or elliptic, with a basal sinus; flowers floating on the surface, pink or white, showy, sepals 4, green, petals numerous, imbricately inserted on the ovary in many

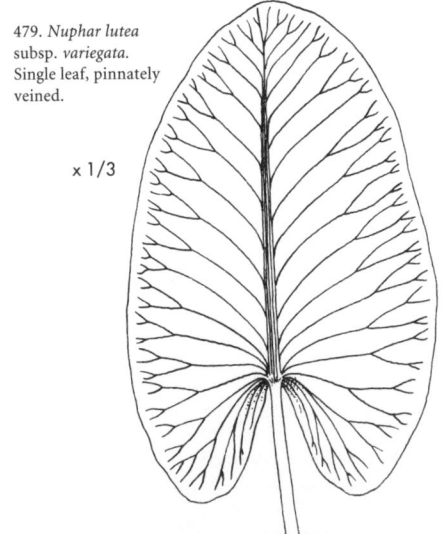

479. *Nuphar lutea*
subsp. *variegata*.
Single leaf, pinnately
veined.

x 1/3

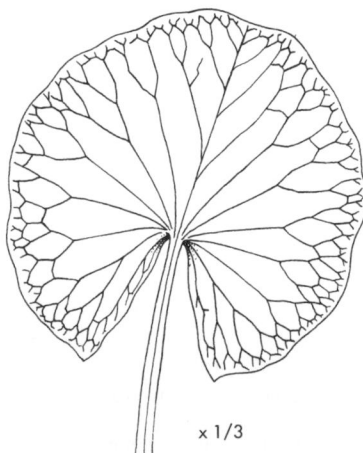

x 1/3

480. *Nymphaea odorata*. Single leaf with veins
mostly radiating from base of sinus.

series, the inner gradually passing into stamens, these numerous, ovary compound, with many locules, crowned by numerous, radiating, linear, incurved stigmas; fruit depressed-globose, berry-like, covered with the bases of the petals, ripening under water, seeds numerous, enveloped by a sac-like aril. [*Castalia*]. —OBL; Wildl. 1

a. Leaves elliptic, longer than wide; petals 8-17; stigmas 6-9. .... 1. *N. tetragona*
a. Leaves orbicular, as wide as long; petals 17-32; stigmas 10-25.
    Petals oblanceolate, rounded above; leaves usually green beneath; petiole usually
       striped with brown above .... 2. *N. tuberosa*
    Petals elliptic to lanceolate, subacute; leaves usually purple or red beneath;
       petiole not striped .... 3. *N. odorata*

1. *N. tetragóna* Georgi (four angled). Ponds and quiet streams. June-September. Map 1058. [*Castalia leibergia*].

2. *N. tuberósa* Paine (bearing tubers). Ponds and quiet streams. June-September. Map 1059. [*N. odorata*].

3. *N. odoráta* Soland in Ait. (fragrant). Ponds and quiet streams. June-September. Fig. 480, Map 1060. Our plants are var. *odorata*.

1055. *Nuphar lutea* subsp. *pumila*   1056. *Nuphar lutea* subsp. *advenu*   1057. *Nuphar lutea* subsp. *variegata*

1058. *Nymphaea tetragona*   1059. *Nymphaea tuberosa*   1060. *Nymphaea odorata*

Family 86. Cercidiphylláceae (Katsura Tree Family)

1. *Cercidiphýllum* Sieb. & Zucc. Katsura Tree.
Dioecious, deciduous, small tree with short shoots; leaves opposite on the shoots, solitary on the spurs, simple, petioled, broadly ovate, subcordate, serrulate; flowers unisexual in small clusters of several from opposite buds on the shoots or solitary buds terminating the short shoots, each subtended by a bract, perianth lacking, stamens 8-12, ovary superior, 1-locular, with numerous ovules, style 1; fruit a follicle.

1. *C. japónicum* Sieb. & Zucc. Asian. A waif in our range; rarely escaped from cultivation. Reported for Berkshire County MA.

Family 87. Ranunculáceae (Crowfoot Family)

Hermophrodite, rarely dioecious, annual or perennial herbs, occasionally shrubs or vines, with clear, acrid sap. Leaves alternate, sometimes opposite or whorled, cauline and/or basal, compound or simple, mostly estipulate, but petiole base often clasping or sheathing. Flowers perfect or rarely unisexual, solitary or in cymose, racemose, umbellate or paniculate inflorescences, regular or irregular, perianth segments mostly all distinct, sepals 3-15, imbricated, in some genera small and early deciduous, in others petal like, petals about as many as the sepals or absent, stamens usually numerous, hypogynous, distinct, often some modified into nectariferous staminodia, these frequently petaloid, carpels usually many, separate, rarely 1, superior, 1-locular, ovules 1-many, style or stigma 1, terminal or lateral. Fruit an achene, utricle, follicle or berry.

Myosúrus L. *mínimus* L. Mouse Tail. Small annual with basal linear leaves and 1-flowered scapes; sepals 5, spurred at the base, petals 5 or lacking, stamens 5-20, carpels numerous, on a long slender receptacle. Southern. Reported for Bristol County MA. —FACW+

a. Stem leaves absent (flower subtended by a calyx-like involucre of 3 bracts in
 Hepatica but true stem leaves lacking).
  Leaves divided into 3 leaflets; rhizomes trailing, bright yellow. (Fig. 481). .... 1. *Coptis trifolia*
   subsp.
   groenlandica

  Leaves 3 or more lobed, but not divided into 3 leaflets; trailing, yellow rhizomes
   absent. (Fig. 482) .... 2. *Hepatica nobilis*
a. Stem leaves present (stems repent and rooting at the nodes, sometimes bearing
 scapes in *Ranunculus lapponicus*).
 b. Stem leaves opposite or whorled, dissected or compound.
  c. Plant a soft-wooded, trailing or climbing vine more than 1.5 m long.
   (Fig. 483) .... 3. *Clematis*
  c. Plant an erect herb less than 1.5 m tall.
   Stem leaves ternately compound, sessile, the leaflets long petioled, broadly
    ovate, typically rounded and 3-toothed apically. (Fig. 484). .... 4. *Thalictrum*
   Stem leaves deeply divided, or if compound, the leaflets subsessile, typically
    obtuse or acute apically with more than 3 teeth. (Fig. 485). .... 5. *Anemone*
 b. Stem leaves alternate.
  d. Flowers strongly irregular.
   Upper sepal long-spurred; petal with a spur extending into the spur of the
    calyx .... 6. *Consolida*
   Upper sepal hooded or helmet-like; petals not spurred. (Fig. 487). .... 7. *Aconitum*
  d. Flowers regular (petals long-spurred in *Aquilegia* but flower not irregular).
   e. Rhizomes or roots and stems yellow when cut.
    Shrub with pinnate leaves; flowers in racemes or panicles. (Fig. 488). .... 8. *Xanthorhiza*
     simplicissima
    Herb with palmate leaves; flower solitary, terminal. (Fig. 489). .... 9. *Hydrastis*
     canadensis

e. Rhizomes, roots and stems not yellow.
    f. Stem leaves 2-3 times compound.
        g. Leaflets mostly with obtuse to rounded lobes.
            Petals long-spurred; fruit a cluster of follicles. (Fig. 490). .... 10. *Aquilegia*
            Petals absent; fruit a cluster of achenes. .... 4. *Thalictrum*
        g. Leaflets sharply toothed.
            Raceme solitary, in flower less than 7 cm long; fruit a red or white
               berry. . (Fig. 491) .... 11. *Actaea*
            Racemes usually more than 1, in flower more than 8 cm long; fruit
               a follicle. (Fig. 492) .... 12. *Cimicifuga*
                                                                      racemosa
    f. Stem leaves palmately parted or unlobed.
        h. Sepals and petals present; fruit a head of achenes. .... 13. *Ranunculus*
        h. Sepals petaloid, petals absent (staminodes present in *Trollius*); fruit
            an aggregate of follicles.
            Leaves palmately parted; staminodes present. (Fig. 499). .... 14. *Trollius laxus*
            Leaves ovate to reniform, cordate, not lobed or dissected, merely
               crenate or dentate; staminodes none. (Fig. 500). .... 15. *Caltha palustris*

1. *Cóptis* Salisb. Goldthread (name derived from the Latin).

Low, perennial, stemless herbs from slender, trailing, bright-yellow rhizomes; leaves basal, ever-green, slender-petioled, ternately compound, the leaflets cuneate-obovate, slightly lobed or crenate, with mucronate teeth; flowers solitary-few on the slender, minutely bracteate scapes, perfect, white, sepals 5-7, petaloid, petals none, stamens numerous, staminodes 5-7, smaller than the sepals, carpels 3-9, stipitate, with several ovules, style short and slender; fruit a spreading cluster of follicles, each with a persistent beak, several seeded.

    1. *C. trifólia* (L.) Salisb. (three-leaved). Wooded swamps and wet woods. May-July. Fig. 481, Map 1061. [*C. groenlandica*]. Represented with us as subsp. *groenlándica* (Oeder) Hulten. The rhizome, finely chopped and lightly boiled, can be used as a mouthwash to relieve mouth sores. —FACW

2. *Hepática* Mill. Liverleaf (from the Latin based on shape of the leaves).

Scapose, perennial herbs from a short rhizome; leaves basal, simple, 3-lobed (occasionally more), cordate, on long, pubescent petioles, evergreen; flowers white, pink or purple, perfect, solitary on several pubescent, 1-flowered scapes, subtended by a calyx-like involucre of 3 bracts, sepals 5-12, petaloid, petals none, stamens numerous, carpels numerous, 1 ovuled, style short; fruit an aggregate of short-beaked, pubescent achenes.

    1. *H. nobílis* Schreb. Rich dry woods and openings. April-May. Represented with us by the following vars.:

    var. *acúta* (Pursh) Steyerm. Leaf lobes and bracts acute. Map 1062. [*H. acutiloba*].

    var. *obtúsa* (Pursh) Steyerm. Leaf lobes and bracts rounded or obtuse. Fig. 482, Map 1063. [*H. americana; H. hepatica; H. triloba*].

3. *Clématis* L. (Greek name for a slender, climbing plant).

Soft-wooded vines (except *C. ochroleuca* and *C. recta*) climbing by prehensile leaf rachises, dioecious or hermaphrodite, stem angled, pith angled, buds rather small, ovoid, sessile and solitary, with 1-3 pairs of somewhat hairy scales, leaf petioles persistent such that scars and bundle traces are not visible, stipule scars none; leaves opposite, slender-petioled, ternately or pinnately compound, (except *C. ochroleuca*) leaflets ovate, entire to crenate or toothed; flowers axillary, solitary on long peduncles or cymose-paniculate, white or purple, perfect or imperfect, sepals usually 4, petaloid, petals none, stamens numerous, staminodes sometimes present, carpels numerous, 1-ovuled, style long, plumose, persistent; fruit a plumose head of achenes. Poisonous.

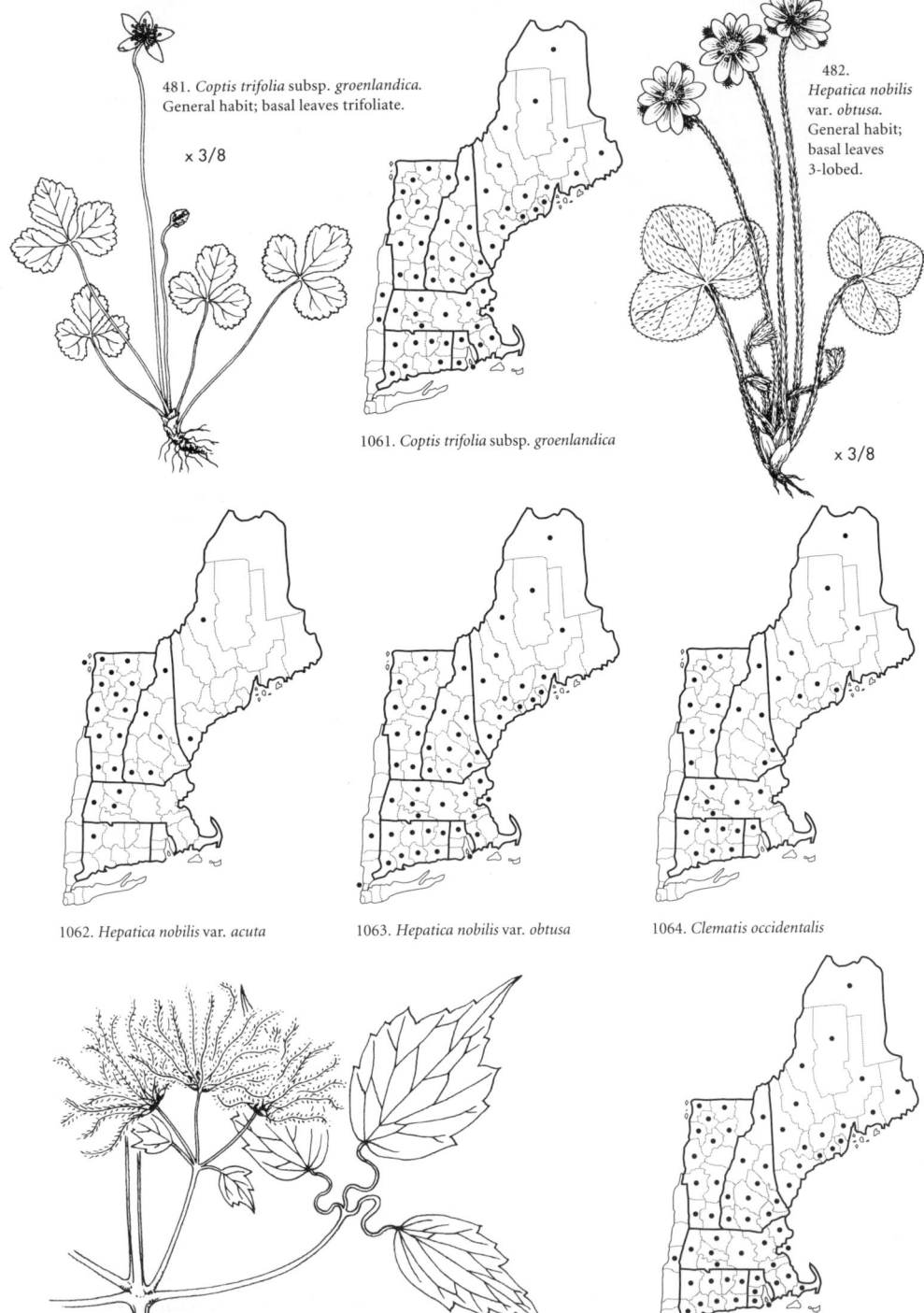

481. *Coptis trifolia* subsp. *groenlandica*.
General habit; basal leaves trifoliate.

× 3/8

482.
Hepatica nobilis
var. *obtusa*.
General habit;
basal leaves
3-lobed.

1061. *Coptis trifolia* subsp. *groenlandica*

× 3/8

1062. *Hepatica nobilis* var. *acuta*

1063. *Hepatica nobilis* var. *obtusa*

1064. *Clematis occidentalis*

× 1/2
483. *Clematis virginiana*. Section of stem with
opposite, trifoliate leaves; axillary panicle.

1065. *Clematis virginiana*

a. Flowers solitary or 2-3 together, purple or yellowish; sepals large, more than 2 cm
long .... 1. *C. occidentalis*
a. Flowers numerous, cymose-paniculate, white; sepals small, less than 2 cm long.
    Leaflets usually coarsely toothed; leaves mostly 3-foliate. (Fig. 483). .... 2. *C. virginiana*
    Leaflets entire or merely undulate; leaves mostly 5-foliate. .... 3. *C. terniflora*

1. *C. occidentális* (Hornem.) DC. (western). Open rocky woods and slopes, calcareous ledges, thickets, river borders. May-June. Map 1064. Endangered in RI. [*C. verticillaris; Atragene americana*]. Our plants are var. *occidentalis*.

    C. flórida Thunb. Leaves usually twice ternate; flowers white (leaves once ternate and flowers purple in *C. occidentalis*). Chinese. Rarely escaped from cultivation. Reported for New Haven County CT.

    C. vitálba L. Leaves pinnate; sepals thick and leathery (leaves ternate and sepals thin and petaloid in *C. occidentalis* and *C. florida*). Rich, moist woods and thickets. From farther south and west. Reported for Hancock County ME.

    C. ochroleúca Ait. Erect herb; leaves simple, ovate. From farther south. Reported for Kings County NY.

2. *C. virginiána* L. (Virginian). Virgin's bower. Thickets and woodland borders. July-August. Fig. 483, Map 1065. —FAC

3. *C. terniflóra* DC. Escaped from cultivation to roadsides and thickets. August-September. Map 1066. (Introduced from e. Asia). [*C. dioscoreifolia; C. maximowicziana; C. paniculata*]. —FACU-

    C. récta L. Differing *C. virginiana* and *C. terniflora* in being an erect herb, not woody and climbing. Rarely escaped from cultivation in our range. Reported for Grafton County NH.

4. *Thalíctrum* L. Meadow Rue (from the Greek).

Erect perennial, dioecious or rarely hermaphrodite, herbs; leaves basal and cauline, the latter alternate, 2-3 times ternately compound, rarely opposite or whorled and trifoliate, sessile or petioled, the divisions and leaflets stalked, the leaflets variously lobed, the petioles dilated at the base; flowers in terminal panicles, or rarely umbellate, perfect or unisexual, small and usually numerous, pedicellate, greenish, white or purplish, the color due to the stamens, sepals 4-5(10), green or petaloid, mostly early deciduous, petals absent, stamens numerous, the filaments elongate, filiform or clavate, carpels numerous, 1-ovulate, style short or absent, stigma elongate; fruit an achene, usually coarsely ribbed, stigma persistent.

a. Stem leaves opposite or whorled, forming an involucre subtending an umbel or
    solitary flower, usually with 3 leaflets; sepals persistent, 6 mm or more long.
    (Fig. 484) .... 1. *T. thalictroides*
a. Stem leaves alternate, with more than 3 leaflets; inflorescence paniculate; sepals
    early deciduous, up to 5 mm long.
  b. Leaflets all or mostly all with 4 or more lobes or teeth.
    Stem leaves subtending panicle branches (at least the lowest) long petioled;
        flowering in April-May .... 2. *T. dioicum*
    Stem leaves subtending panicle branches sessile; flowering in June-July. .... 3. *T. venulosum*
  b. Leaflets all or mostly all entire or with 2 or 3 lobes or teeth, a few leaves
    sometimes with more.
    c. Leaflets bearing minute sessile or short-stalked rounded glands beneath, the
      surface appearing mealy .... 4. *T. revolutum*
    c. Leaflets glabrous or puberulent beneath, not bearing rounded glands or
      appearing mealy.
      Filaments dilated above; anthers blunt; achene narrowed to a stipitate base. ... 5. *T. pubescens*
      Filaments filiform, not dilated above; anthers apiculate; achene obtuse at
        the sessile or subsessile base .... 6. *T. dasycarpum*

1. *T. thalictroídes* (L.) Eames & Boivin (like *Thalictrum*). Rue Anemone. Open mesic woods. April-May. Fig. 484, Map 1067. [*Anemonella t.*].

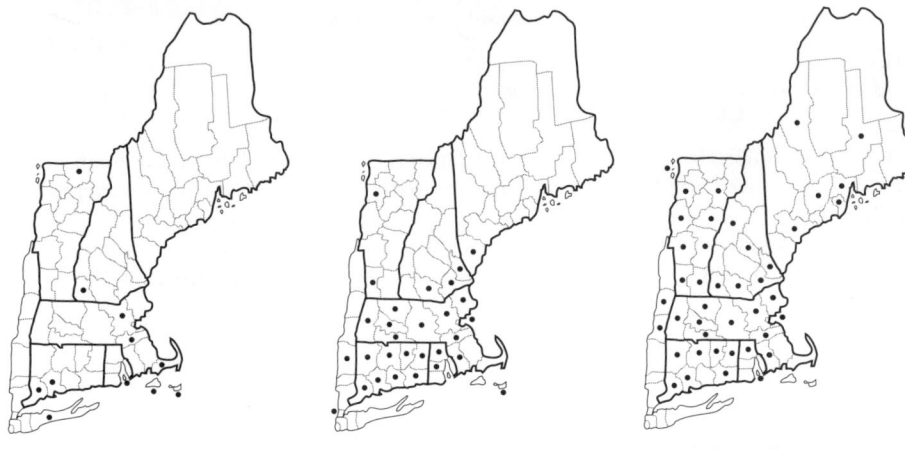

1066. *Clematis terniflora*   1067. *Thalictrum thalictroides*   1068. *Thalictrum dioicum*

2. T. dioícum L. (dioecious). Early Meadow Rue. Rich, moist, often rocky deciduous woods. April-May. Map 1068. —FAC

3. T. venulósum Trel. Gravelly or rocky river or lake shores. June-July. Map 1069. Endangered in NY. [*T. confine; T. lunellii*]. —FACW

4. T. revolútum DC. (with edge rolled back). Wax-leaved Meadow Rue. Dry, open deciduous woods and thickets. June-July. Map 1070.

5. T. pubéscens Pursh (pubescent). Tall Meadow Rue. Wet meadows and thickets, wet woods, stream and riverbanks. June-July. Map 1071. [*T. polygamum*]. —FACW+

6. T. dasycárpum Fisch. & Ave-Lall. (hairy-carpelled). Purple Meadow Rue. Wet meadows and streambanks. June-July. Reported for CT, MA, RI, VT. —FACW

5. Anemóne L. Windflower (name derived from the ancient Greek and Latin).

Erect, perennial herbs from a rhizome or thickened base; leaves basal and cauline, the former deeply palmately divided, the latter opposite or in whorles of 3 or more, forming an involucre subtending one or more elongate peduncles; flowers solitary on one or more elongate peduncles, perfect, sepals 4-many, petal-like, white, greenish or red, petals none, stamens numerous, carpels numerous, 1-ovuled, pubescent, in a cylindric to subglobose head, style short or long; fruit a beaked achene.

   Clématis récta and *C. ochroleúca* will key to *Anemone* but *C. recta* has pinnately compound leaves and *C. ochroleuca* has simple leaves (leaves neither pinnate nor simple in Anemone).

a. Leaves deeply divided into numerous linear or narrowly lanceolate lobes. (Fig. 485) . 1. *A. multifida*
a. Leaves variously divided into broadly lanceolate to obovate lobes. (Fig. 486).
   b. Involucral leaves sessile or nearly so. .... 2. *A. canadensis*
   b. Involucral leaves distinctly petioled.
      c. Basal leaves absent or not at the base of the flowering stem; sepals glabrous
        or essentially so; achenes thinly pubescent. .... 3. *A. quinquefolia*
      c. Basal leaves present; sepals densely pubescent outside; achenes densely
        long-woolly.
        Involucral leaves generally more than 3; peduncles above the involucre
          naked. .... 4. *A. cylindrica*
        Involucral leaves 3; peduncles often with an additional pair of involucral
        leaves .... 5. *A. virginiana*

   1. A. multífida Poir. (much cleft). Cut-leaved Anemone. River shores in calcareous gravel and limestone ledges. May-June. Fig. 485, Map 1072. (S. Amer.).

   2. A. canadénsis L. (Canadian). River and lake margins, wet meadows. May-July. Map 1073. Endangered in CT. —FACW

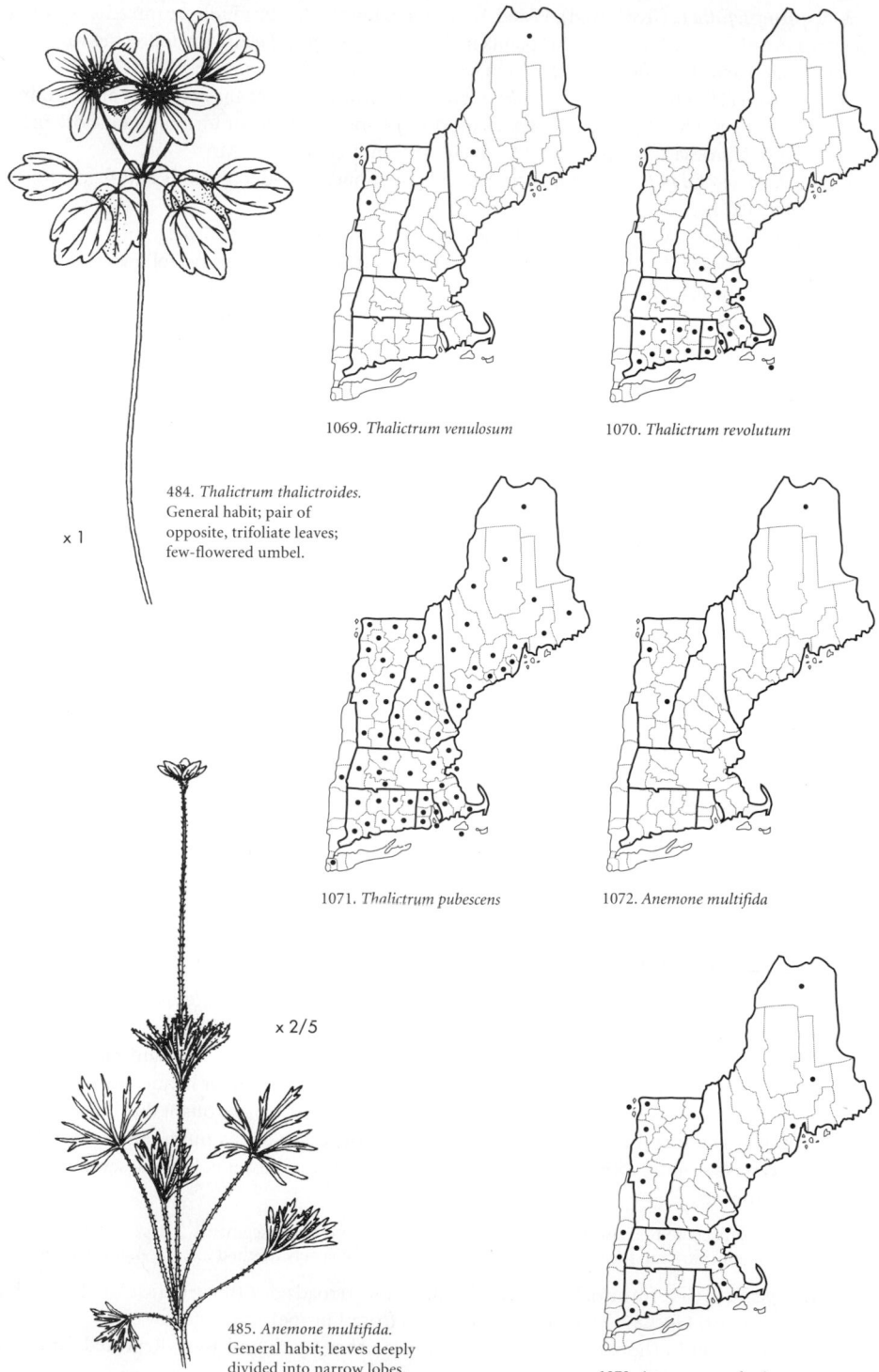

484. *Thalictrum thalictroides.*
General habit; pair of
opposite, trifoliate leaves;
few-flowered umbel.

× 1

1069. *Thalictrum venulosum*

1070. *Thalictrum revolutum*

1071. *Thalictrum pubescens*

1072. *Anemone multifida*

× 2/5

485. *Anemone multifida.*
General habit; leaves deeply
divided into narrow lobes.

1073. *Anemone canadensis*

3. A. quinquefólia L. (five leaved). Wood Anemone. Moist to dry deciduous or mixed woods and openings. April-June. Map 1074. Our plants include var. *quinquefolia* and the following var.:

var. *bifólia* Farw. Involucral leaves 2 (3 in var. *quinquefolia*). [var. *interior*]. —FACU

A. nemorósa L. Similar to *A. quinquefolia* but having sepals with veins anastomosing and forming a network below the free tips (veins of sepals mostly not anastomosing or forming a network in *A. quinquefolia*). (Eurasia). Rarely escaped from cultivation. Reported for MA.

4. A. cylíndrica Gray (cylindric). Long-headed Anemone. Dry, open woods and fields. June-August. Map 1075.

5. A. virginiána L. (Virginian). Thimbleweed. Dry open woods, river borders. July-August. Fig. 486, Map 1076. [*A. riparia*]. Our plants include var. *virginiana* and the following var.:

var. *ripária* (Fern.). Boivin. Divisions of leaves mostly cuneate below; fruiting heads cylindric, around 1 cm thick (divisions of leaves convex below, fruiting heads ellipsoid, well over 1 cm thick in var. *virginiana*). [*A.v.* var. *alba; A. riparia*].

6. Consolída S. F. Gray Larkspur.

Branched, erect annual herbs from a taproot; leaves alternate, palmately finely dissected into numerous narrowly linear to filiform segments, the lower petioled, the upper sessile or nearly so; flowers showy, blue, purple, pink or white, perfect, in short corymbiform or long, narrow, terminal, bracteate racemes, irregular, calyx of 5 petaloid sepals, the upper one prolonged into a spur, petals 2, united into 1, with 1 spur, this extending into the spur of the calyx, stamens numerous, the filaments dilated basally, carpel 1, pubescent, or glabrous, many ovuled, with a short style; fruit a beaked, hairy, many-seeded follicle. [*Delphinium*].

Delphínum L. Larkspur. Similar to *Consolida* but with 4 distinct petals, 3 or more carpels, and perennial. Two species are occasionally found in our range: *D. exaltátum* Ait. with stem below the inflorescence glabrous, leaf segments lanceolate, 1 cm or more wide, flowers many in an elongate raceme. From farther south. Reported for ME. *D. grandiflórum* L. Stem pubescent, leaf segments linear, less than 1 cm wide, flowers few in a short raceme. (*Siberia; Asia*). Escaped from cultivation. Reported for VT.

1. C. ajácis (L.) Schur. Escaped from cultivation to fields, roadsides and waste places. July-September. Map 1077. (Adventive from Europe). [*C. abiguum; Delphinium a.; D. ajacis*].

C. regális S. F. Gray. Similar to *C. ajacis* but with a short-corymbiform raceme and glabrous carpel (raceme elongate and carpel pubescent in *C. ajacis*). Escaped from cultivation. Reported for CT, RI. [*Delphinium consolida*].

7. Aconítum L. Monkshood (ancient Greek and Latin name).

Tall, erect, perennial herbs from a short tuber; leaves numerous, alternate, petioled, palmately divided, the divisions deeply cleft into numerous linear segments; flowers showy, perfect, often numerous, blue or purple, and crowded in a long, narrow, terminal, bracteate raceme, calyx irregular, of 5 sepals, the upper (helmet) the largest, shaped like a hood or helmet, its tip broadly rounded to a beak, 2 petals concealed under the helmet, clawed, nectariferous at the tip, prolonged backward into a spur, other petals wanting or much reduced, stamens numerous, with dilated filaments, carpels several, with several ovules, style slender; fruit a cluster of beaked, several-seeded follicles. Poisonous.

Leaves divided entirely to the base, the divisions cleft into numerous linear segments ... 1. *A. napellus*
Leaves divided only partly to the base, the divisions (3-5) merely coarsely toothed .... 2. *A. uncinatum*

1. A. napéllus L. (like turnip). Escaped from cultivation to roadsides, thickets, fields and old cellar holes. July-August. Fig. 487. Map 1078. (Introduced from Europe).

2. A. uncinátum L. (hooked). Woodlands. From farther south and west. Reported for Coos County NH.

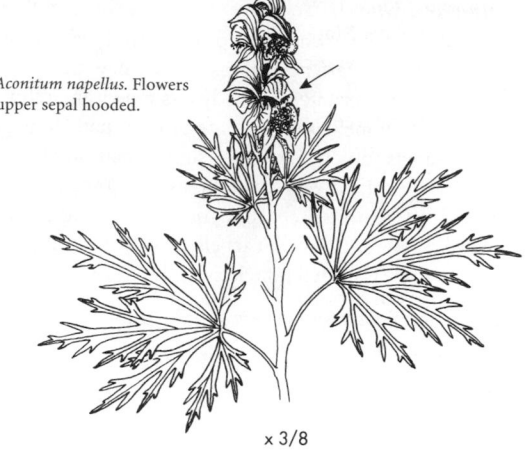

487. *Aconitum napellus.* Flowers
with upper sepal hooded.

x 3/8

x 1/4

486. *Anemone virginiana.*
General habit; leaves divided
into broad lobes.

1074. *Anemone quinquefolia*

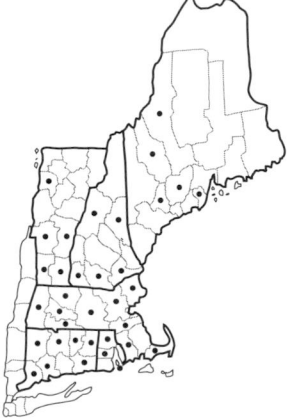

1075. *Anemone cylindrica*

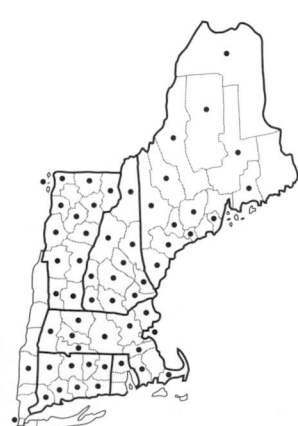

1076. *Anemone virginiana*

1077. *Consolida ajacis*

1078. *Aconitum napellus*

8. *Xanthorhíza* Marsh. Yellowroot (from the Greek, meaning Yellow-root).

Low shrub, wood yellow when cut, pith relatively large, round, buds unequal, the lateral solitary, sessile, ovoid-oblong, flattened against the stem, with 2-3 scales, the terminal larger, fusiform, with 4-5 scales, leaf scars alternate, shallowly U-shaped, encircling the twig by half or more, bundle traces 9-11, stipule scars none; leaves pinnate or bipinnate, long petioled, crowded toward the tip of the short stem, leaflets mostly 5, ovate, acute to acuminate, cuneate at the base, serrate to cleft, the terminal often 3-cleft; flowers small, in several drooping, open racemes or panicles borne at the tip of the stem, polygamous, sepals 5, maroon, spreading, deciduous, petals none, stamens 5-10, staminodia 5, clawed, 2-lobed, carpels mostly 5-10, 2-ovulate, style short; fruit a cluster of 4-8, inflated, yellowish, 1-seeded follicles.

 1. *X. simplicíssima* Marsh. (very simple, unbranched). Moist woods, bottomlands, and borders of streams and creeks. April-May. Fig. 488, Map 1079. [*Zanthorhiza apiifolia*]. —FACW

9. *Hydrástis* Ellis.

Erect, pubescent, perennial herbs from a thick, knotty, yellow rhizome; leaves basal and cauline, the former long petioled, arising apart from the flowering stem, cauline leaves 2, alternate, borne at the top of the stem, the lower long petioled, the upper sessile and subtending a single flower, blades palmately 5-9 lobed, cordate at the base, doubly serrate, up to 2.5 dm wide at maturity; flower solitary at the top of the stem, perfect, sepals 3, greenish-white, petaloid, falling when the flower opens, petals none, stamens and carpels numerous, carpels 2-ovulate, style very short; fruit a head of 1-2 seeded, red berries, somewhat resembling a raspberry.

 1. *H. canadénsis* L. (Canadian). Golden Seal. Rich woods. April-May. Fig. 489, Map 1080. Endangered in MA, CT. Tonic made from the rhizome reported to have various medicinal uses, including relief from gastric disorders and mouth sores; was used by Indians to treat skin diseases.

10. *Aquilégia* L. Columbine.

Erect, branching, perennial herbs from a short, stout rhizome or caudex; leaves basal and cauline, 2-3 times ternately compound, petioled, the cauline alternate, reduced upward, leaflets broadly obovate, lobed; flowers large and showy, few, terminating the branches of the bracteate inflorescence, nodding, perfect, red, yellow, blue or white, sepals 5, short clawed, colored like the petals, petals 5, prolonged backward below the flower into long, hollow spurs, (lacking in 1 rare form) stamens numerous, often connivent, the inner ones staminodial, these scarious and dilated, carpels 5, many-ovuled, with a slender style; fruit a cluster of follicles.

 Nigélla L. Leaves finely dissected; sepals petaloid, petals none; follicles connate. Two species occasionally escaped from cultivation: *N. damascéna* L. Love in a mist. Reported for MA, ME, Fairfield County CT, Chittenden County VT; *N. satíva* L. Reported for Fairfield County CT.

Flowers red and yellow, spurs nearly straight; styles on mature fruit more than 1 cm
  long .... 1. *A. canadensis*
Flowers blue or purple to pink or white; styles on mature fruit 1 cm or less long .... 2. *A. vulgaris*

 1. *A. canadénsis* L. (Canadian). Rocky wooded, springy slopes, dry woods and open areas in rich soil. April-June. Fig. 490, Map 1081. [*A. coccinea; A. latiuscula*]. —FAC
 2. *A. vulgáris* L. (common). Escaped from cultivation to roadsides, fields and woodland edges. May-July. Map 1082. (Introduced from Europe).

11. *Actaéa* L. Baneberry (ancient name for the Elder, later transferred to this genus).

Erect, perennial herbs; leaves large, alternate, 2-3 times compound, leaflets ovate, sharply cleft and toothed; flowers small, white, perfect, in a dense, short, long-peduncled terminal raceme,

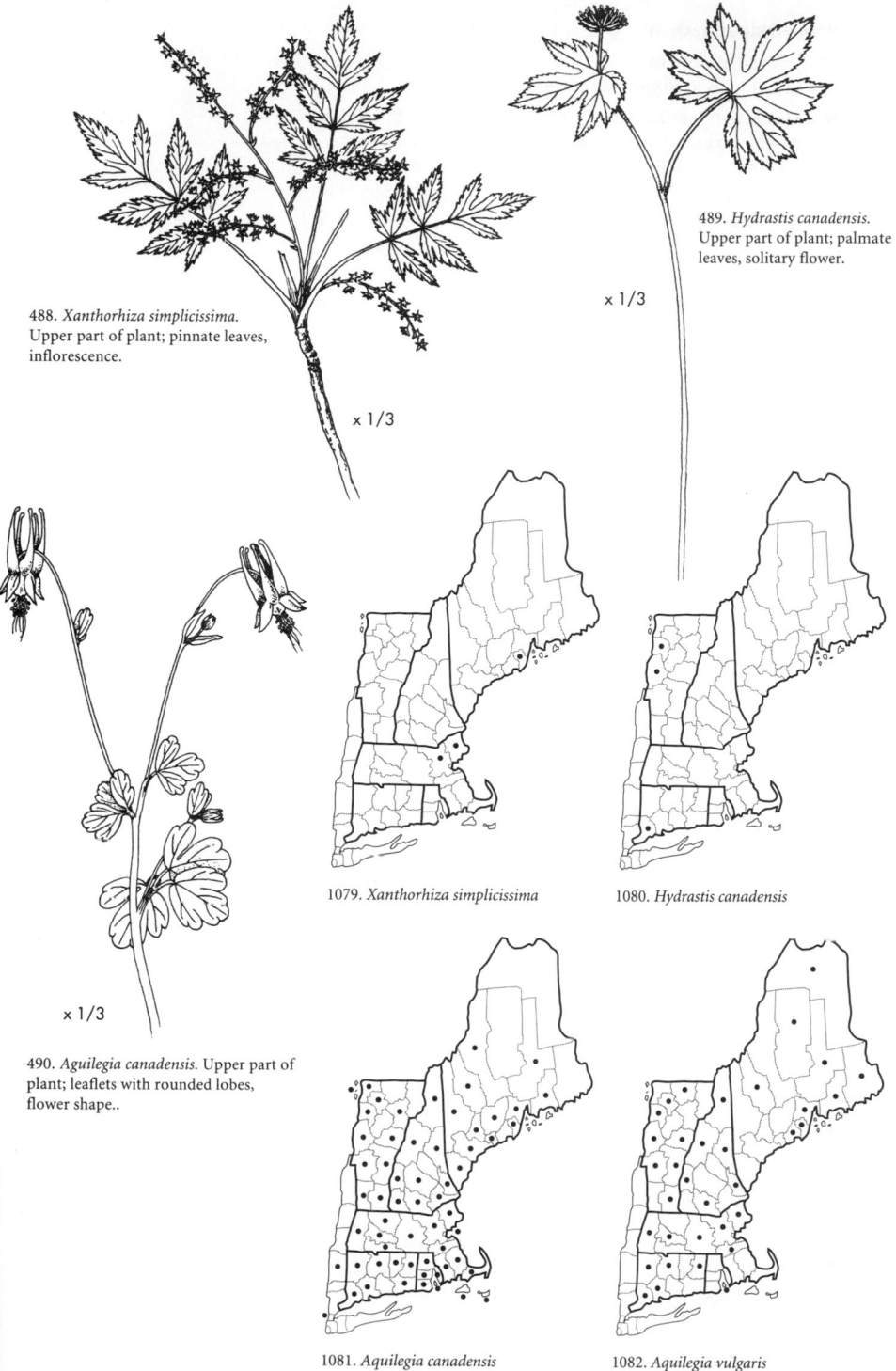

489. *Hydrastis canadensis.*
Upper part of plant; palmate
leaves, solitary flower.

x 1/3

488. *Xanthorhiza simplicissima.*
Upper part of plant; pinnate leaves,
inflorescence.

x 1/3

x 1/3

490. *Aguilegia canadensis.* Upper part of
plant; leaflets with rounded lobes,
flower shape..

1079. *Xanthorhiza simplicissima*

1080. *Hydrastis canadensis*

1081. *Aquilegia canadensis*

1082. *Aquilegia vulgaris*

sepals 4-5, petaloid, caducous, petals 4-10, clawed, early-deciduous, stamens numerous, with long slender, white filaments, these slightly clavate upward, carpel 1, with many ovules, stigma broad and sessile, bilobed; fruit a subglobose, many-seeded berry. Poisonous.

Fruit white, rarely red; fruiting pedicels stout, 1-2 mm thick; flowering pedicels 8 mm
    or less long. (Fig. 491). .... 1. *A. pachypoda*
Fruit red, rarely white; fruiting pedicels slender, up to 0.8 mm thick; flowering
    pedicels 10 mm or more long. .... 2. *A. rubra*

    1. *A. pachypóda* Ell. (with thick pedicels). White Baneberry. Dolls' Eyes. Rich woods and thickets. May-June. Fig. 491, Map 1083. (Hybridizes with *A. rubra*). [*A. alba*].

    2. *A. rúbra* (Ait.) Willd. (red). Red Baneberry. Rich woods and thickets. May-June. Map 1084. [*A. alba; A. eburnea; A. erythrocarpa; A. spicata* var. *rubra*]. Our plants are subsp. *rubra*.

12. *Cimicífuga* L. Bugbane (meaning to drive away bugs).

Tall, perennial herbs from knotty rhizomes; leaves alternate, petioled, ternate, with the divisions once or twice pinnately compound, leaflets ovate or oblong, cleft or serrate, obtuse to acute or acuminate, cuneate to cordate at the base; flowers numerous in an elongate, terminal, panicle or raceme, perfect, white, sepals 4-5, petaloid, caducous, petals none, stamens numerous, with long filaments, staminodia short, 4-8, 2-lobed, petaloid, carpel 1, sessile, with several ovules, style short and thick; fruit an ellipsoid, several-seeded follicle.

    1. *C. racemósa* (L.) Nutt. (with racemes). Black Cohosh. Rich woods. June-August. Fig. 492, Map 1085. Endangered in MA. Various medicinal uses are cited but can also cause poisoning if used in improper doses.

13. *Ranúnculus* L. Buttercup (Latin name for frog).

Annual or perennial herbs; leaves alternate, simple, lobed or palmately dissected; flowers solitary or in cymes, yellow, rarely white, perfect, sepals and petals mostly 5, rarely fewer or more, petals often with a nectariferous pit or scale at the base of the blade inside, stamens mostly numerous, rarely few, carpels numerous, in a globose, oblong, or cylindric head, ovule 1; fruit an achene, mostly beaked. Poisonous, except for the seeds which were parched and ground into flour by Indians. Contact with leaves of *R. acris* and *R. sceleratus* is reported to cause dermatitis in some people. Dried Ranunculus, however, can be fed to cattle in forage without harm, since drying drives off the poison. —Wildl. 1

    Adónis L. Pheasant's eye. Resembling *Ranunculus* but petals lacking the nectariferous pit or scale at the base of the blade. Represented in our range by *A. vernális* L. Rarely escaped from cultivation. Reported for Westchester County NY. Poisonous.

a. Plants aquatic, with most of the leaves submersed, often finely dissected. (Fig. 493).
  b. Petals white.
    Leaves flaccid, collapsing when withdrawn from water, with a petiole about
      as long as the stipular part. (Fig. 493). .... 1. *R. trichophyllus*
    Leaves firmer, holding their form when withdrawn from water, petiole much
      shorter than the stipular part or blade sessile at summit of stipule. .... 2. *R. longirostris*
  b. Petals yellow.
    Leaf segments less than 2 mm wide; margin of mature achenes prominently
      corky-thickened below middle; achene beak .7-1.5 mm long. .... 3. *R. flabellaris*
    Leaf segments 2 mm or more wide; margin of mature achenes not
      corky-thickened; achene beak .4-.7 mm long .... 4. *R. gmelini*
                                                  var. *purshii*
a. Plants terrestrial or subaquatic, with most leaves emersed, lobed or divided but
    not finely dissected.
  c. Leaves not lobed or divided, entire or merely toothed or crenate.
    d. Leaves all reniform to ovate. (Fig. 494).
      Leaves mostly 2 cm or more wide; roots tuberous-thickened, sepals 3-4. .... 5. *R. ficaria*
                                                       var. *bulbifera*

Leaves mostly less than 2 cm wide; roots slender; sepals 5. .... 6. *R. cymbalaria*
d. Leaves linear to lanceolate, the basal sometimes ovate.
   e. Perennial, stems often rooting at the lower, and sometimes the middle
      nodes; petals 5 or more; achenes 1.3 mm or more long.
      Stem leaves up to 1 cm wide; sepals 2-4 mm long; achene beak less than
         0.6 mm long .... 7. *R. flammula*
      Stem leaves mostly 1-3 cm wide; sepals 5-7 mm long; achene beak 0.6
         mm or more long .... 8. *R. ambigens*
   e. Annual, stems erect or ascending; petals 5 or fewer; achenes less than 3 mm
      long .... 9. *R. pusillus*
c. Leaves lobed or divided.
   f. Plant repent, rooting at some of the nodes.
      g. Stem filiform, bearing slender-petioled, 3-lobed leaves and erect scapes
         (sometimes with 1 leaf); sepals usually 3. .... 10. *R. lapponicus*
      g. Stem not filiform, thicker, leafy, not bearing scapes; sepals 5.
        h. Achenes strongly flattened, with a distinct, narrowly winged margin.
           (Fig. 495).
           Beak of achene less than 1.5 mm long. .... 11. *R. repens*
           Beak of achene 1.5 mm or more long .... 12. *R. hispidus*
        h. Achenes not strongly flattened, lacking a narrowly winged margin.
           Petals mostly less than 8 mm long; margins of mature achenes not
             corky-thickened; achene beak .4-.7 mm long. .... 4. *R. gmelini*
                                                  var. *purshii*
           Petals mostly 8 mm or more long; margins of mature achenes
             corky-thickened; achene beak .7-1.5 mm long .... 3. *R. flabellaris*
   f. Plant erect or ascending.
      i. Basal and cauline leaves unlike, some or all of the basal undivided, merely
         crenate, the cauline deeply divided. (Fig. 496).
        j. Achenes mostly longer than 1.5 mm; achene beak longer than 0.5 mm. .... 13. *R. allegheniensis*
        j. Achenes up to 1.5 mm long; achene beak less than 0.5 mm long.
           Stems glabrous or nearly so, or puberulent above; basal leaves
             (at least some) cordate at base. (Fig. 496) .... 14. *R. abortivus*
           Stems pubescent, at least below; basal leaves mostly cuneate to
             rounded or truncate, occasionally subcordate .... 15. *R. micranthus*
      i. Basal and cauline leaves alike in general form, all divided.
        k. Terminal segment or all segments of the principal leaves stalked.
           (Fig. 497).
           l. Base of plant bulbous .... 16. *R. bulbosus*
           l. Base of plant not bulbous.
              m. Petals 5 mm or less long .... 17. *R. pensylvanicus*
              m. Petals longer than 5 mm.
                 n. Beak of achene 0.5 mm or less long. .... 18. *R. sardous*
                 n. Beak of achene more than 0.5 mm long.
                    o. Beak of achene up to 1.4 mm long, stigmatose along the
                       upper side. .... 11. *R. repens*
                    o. Beak of achene mostly more than 1.4 mm long, stigmatose
                       only at the tip.
                      Principal leaves mostly longer than wide; petals less than half
                       as wide as long. (Fig. 497) .... 19. *R. fascicularis*
                      Principal leaves mostly as wide or wider than long; petals
                       often more than half as wide as long .... 12. *R. hispidus*
        k. Terminal and lateral segments of the principal leaves sessile. (Fig. 498).
          p. Petals more than 6 mm long.
            Achene beak less than 1 mm long; stigmatose along the upper side. ... 20. *R. acris*
           Achene beak more than 1 mm long; stigmatose only at the tip. .... 12. *R. hispidus*
          p. Petals 6 mm or less long.
            q. Achenes spiny on the faces .... 21. *R. parviflorus*
           q. Achenes smooth or minutely pitted or pebbled on the faces.
              Achene less than 1.5 mm long, nearly beakless. .... 22. *R. sceleratus*
              Achene more than 1.5 mm long, with a beak 0.5-1.2 mm long and
                distinctly hooked .... 23. *R. recurvatus*

1. *R. trichophýllus* Chaix (with hair-like leaves). White Water Crowfoot. Ponds and streams. June-September. Fig. 493, Map 1086. (Eurasia). [*R. aquatilis* var. *capillaceus*]. Our plants are var. *trichophyllus*. —OBL

2. *R. longiróstris* Godr. (long-beaked). White Water Crowfoot. Ponds and sluggish streams. June-September. Map 1087. [*R. circinatus* var. *subrigidus; R. subrigidus*]. —OBL

3. *R. flabelláris* Raf. (fan-like). Yellow Water Crowfoot. Ponds, sluggish streams and muddy shores. May-June. Map 1088. [*R. delphinifolius*]. —OBL

4. *R. gmélini* DC (for its discoverer). Small Yellow Water Crowfoot. Shallow pools, ditches and muddy shores. June-August. (Asia). Rare. Reported for Aroostook and Penobscot Counties ME. Represented with us as var. *púrshii* (Richards.) Hara. [*R. gmelini* var. *hookeri*]. —FACW

5. *R. ficária* L. (like figworts). Lesser Celandine. Spread from cultivation to waste places, etc. May-June. Map 1089. (Introduced from Europe). Represented with us as var. *bulbifera* Marsden-Jones.

6. *R. cymbalária* Pursh (like *Cymbalaria*). Seaside Crowfoot. Saline and brackish shores, flats, and marshes, in mud or sand. May-September. Fig. 494, Map 1090. (Eurasia; S. Amer.). Endangered in CT, NY. Our plants are var. *cymbalaria*. —OBL

7. *R. flámmula* L. (old generic name). Spearwort. Pond and river shores. June-August. Map 1091. Represented with us by the following vars.:

var. *ovális* (Bigel.) Benson. Leaves lanceolate to oval 1.5-7 mm wide. [*R. reptans* var. *ovalis*].

var. *filifórmis* DC. Leaves filiform to linear, up to 1.5 mm wide. [*R. flammula* var. *reptans; R. reptans* var. *reptans*]. —FACW

8. *R. ámbigens* Wats. (uncertain). Water Plantain Spearwort. Ditches, swamps, pond and stream margins. June-August. Map 1092. Endangered in NH, CT. [*R. obtusiusculus*]. —OBL

9. *R. pusíllus* Poir. (very small). Spearwort. Ditches, mud flats along pond and river margins, wet fields and wet deciduous woods, shallow water. May-June. Reported for se NY. —OBL

R. laxicaúlis (T. & G.) Darby. Similar to *R. pusillus* but petals mostly 5, 3 mm or more long, much exceeding the sepals (petals mostly fewer than 5, less than 3 mm long, about equalling the sepals in *R. pusillus*). From farther south and west. Reported for VT. [*R. oblongifolius; R. subcordatus; R. texensis*]. Our plants are var. *laxicaulis*. —OBL

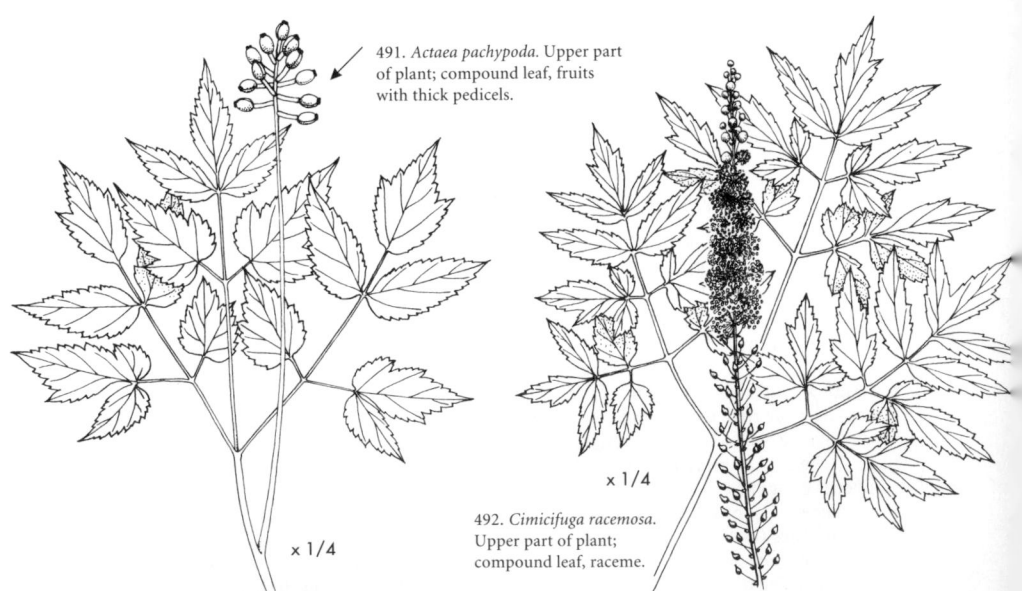

491. *Actaea pachypoda.* Upper part of plant; compound leaf, fruits with thick pedicels.

× 1/4

× 1/4

492. *Cimicifuga racemosa.* Upper part of plant; compound leaf, raceme.

× 1/4

1083. *Actaea pachypoda*

1084. *Actaea rubra*

1085. *Cimicifuga racemosa*

1086. *Ranunculus trichophyllus*

1087. *Ranunculus longirostris*

1088. *Ranunculus flabellaris*

1089. *Ranunculus ficaria*

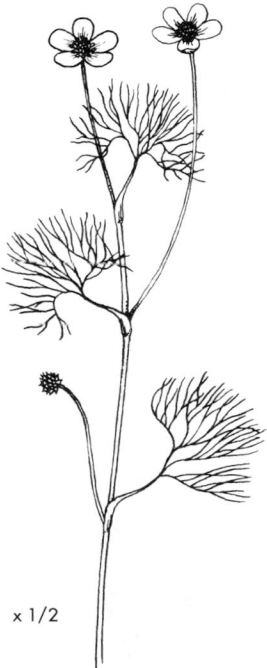

× 1/2

493. *Ranunculus trichophyllus.*
Upper part of stem with finely
dissected submersed leaves.

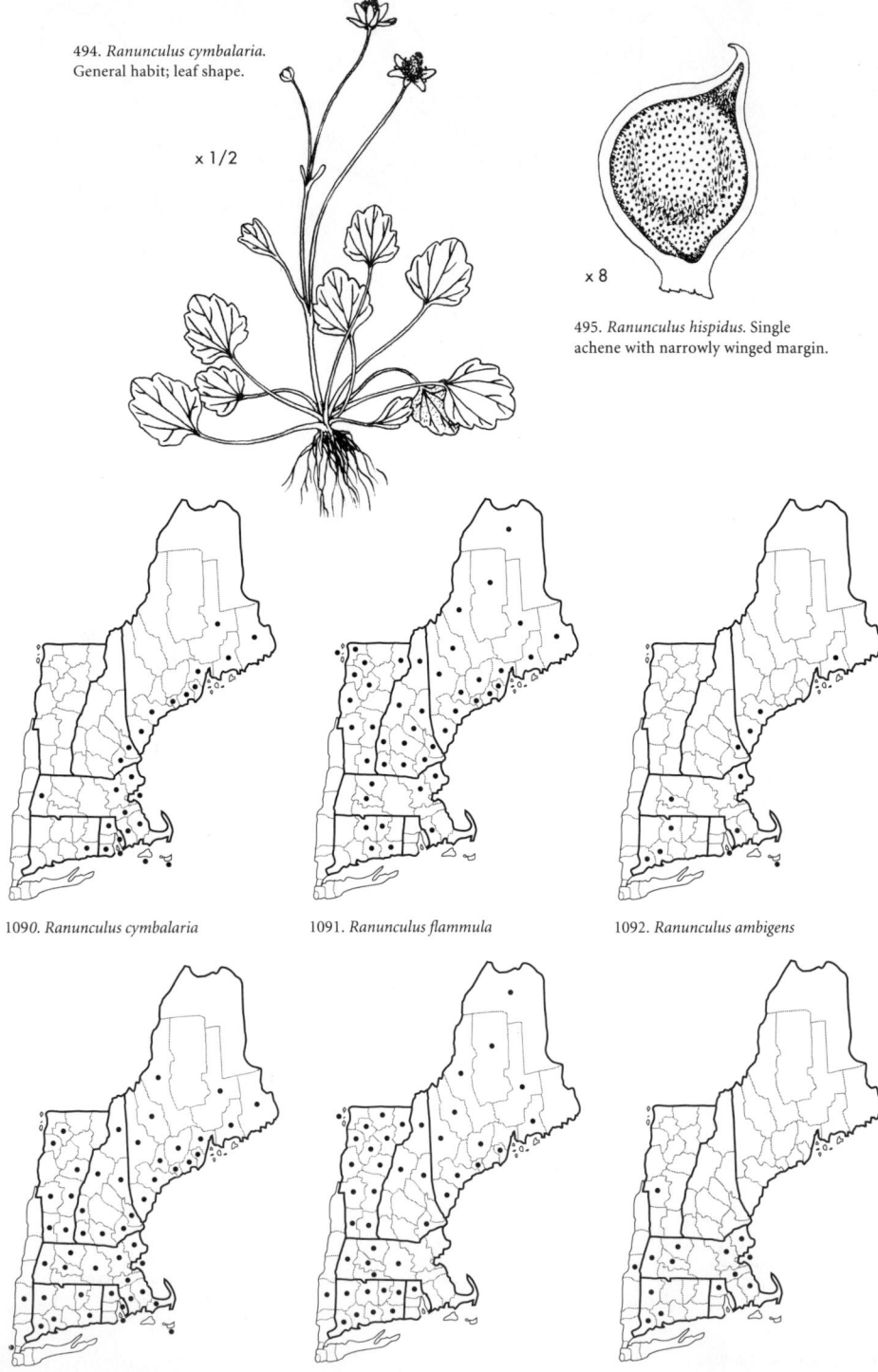

494. *Ranunculus cymbalaria.*
General habit; leaf shape.

x 1/2

x 8

495. *Ranunculus hispidus.* Single
achene with narrowly winged margin.

1090. *Ranunculus cymbalaria*

1091. *Ranunculus flammula*

1092. *Ranunculus ambigens*

1093. *Ranunculus repens*

1094. *Ranunculus hispidus*

1095. *Ranunculus allegheniensis*

10. R. lappónicus L. (of Lapland). Lapland Buttercup. Moss and wet woods. June-July. (Eurasia). Reported for Aroostook County ME. —OBL

11. R. répens L. (creeping). Creeping Buttercup. Wet or dry fields, river bottoms, wet woods, ditches, roadsides and waste places. May-August. Map 1093. (Naturalized from Europe). Our plants include var. *repens* and the following vars.:

var. *glabrátus* DC. Stems and petioles glabrous or subglabrous (pubescent in var. *repens*). [*R. repens* var. *erectus*].

var. *degenerátus* Schur. Flowers with numerous petals (petals 5-9 in vars. *glabratus* and *repens*). [*R. repens* var. *pleniflorus*]. —FAC

12. R. híspidus Michx. (stiffly hairy). Dry, open woods. April-May. Fig. 495, Map 1094. Our plants include var. *hispidus* [*R. marilandicus*]. and the following vars.: —FAC

var. *nítidus* (Chapman) T. Duncan. Stipules conspicuous, rounded at the summit; plants of wet soil (stipules inconspicuous, tapering to the petiole, plants of dry soil in var. *hispidus*). [*R. carolinianus; R. nitidus; R. septentrionalis*]. —OBL

var. *caricetórum* (Greene) T. Duncan. Similar to var. *nitidus* but with sepals spreading (reflexed in var. *nitidus*). [*R. caricetorum; R. septentrionalis* var. *c.*]. —OBL

13. R. allegheniénsis Britt. (of the alleghenies). Mountain Crowfoot. Rich, often calcareous, moist or dry deciduous woods. May-June. Map 1095. —FAC

R. rhombóideus Goldie. Will key to *R. allegheniénsis* but is distinguishable in having petals 4 mm or more long and fruiting heads 6 mm or more thick (petals less than 4 mm long and fruiting heads less than 6 mm thick in *R. allegheniensis*). From farther west. Reported for MA, RI. [*R. ovalis*].

14. R. abortívus L. (abortive). Kidneyleaf Crowfoot. Rich, moist to dry deciduous woods, alluvial woods. May-June. Fig. 496, Map 1096. Our plants include var. *abortivus* and the following var.:

var. *eucýclus* Fern. Basal leaves suborbicular, with a narrow sinus (reniform, with a broad sinus in var. *abortivus*). —FACW-

15. R. micránthus Nutt. (tiny flowered). Rich, rocky woods. April-May. Map 1097. —FACU

16. R. bulbósus L. (bulbous). Bulbous Buttercup. Fields, roadsides and waste places. April-July. Map 1098. (Naturalized from Europe).

17. R. pensylvánicus L.F. (of Pennsylvania). Bristly Crowfoot. Pond margins, wet meadows, ditches. July-September. Map 1099. —OBL

18. R. sardoús Crantz (ancient name). Roadsides, waste places, etc. May-July. (Naturalized from Europe). Reported for Bronx County NY.

19. R. fasciculáris Muhl. ex Bigelow (clustered). Early Buttercup. Dry, wooded hillsides and ledges (often calcareous). April-May. Fig. 497, Map 1100. Endangered in NH. —FACU

20. R. ácris L. (acrid). Tall Buttercup. Fields and roadsides. May-August. Fig. 498, Map 1101. (Naturalized from Europe). [*R. boreanus*]. Our plants are var. *acris*. —FAC+

21. R. parviflórus L. (small flowered). Small Flowered Crowfoot. Roadsides and waste places. May-July. (Naturalized from Europe). Reported for e. NY. —FAC

22. R. scelerátus L. (cursed). Cursed Crowfoot. Marshes, wet meadows, ditches and waste places in moist soil. May-July. Map 1102. (Eurasia). Our plants are var. *sceleratus*. —OBL

23. R. recurvátus Poir. (bent backward). Moist, rich, deciduous woods, wooded swamps, borders of woodland streams. May-July. Map 1103. —FAC+

14. Tróllius L. Globe-flower (name of Latin derivation, meaning globe).

Erect or ascending, perennial herbs; leaves palmately 5-7 parted, the divisions obovate, cuneate, lobed and toothed, basal leaves long-petioled, stem leaves 1-3, alternate, the lower petioled, the upper sessile or subsessile and often approximate; flower solitary, terminal, perfect, large, greenish-yellow, sepals 5-15, petaloid, petals none, stamens numerous, with slender filaments, staminodes numerous, shorter than the stamens, carpels few to many, with numerous ovules, style subulate; fruit a head of follicles, each tipped by a straight, subulate beak, many-seeded.

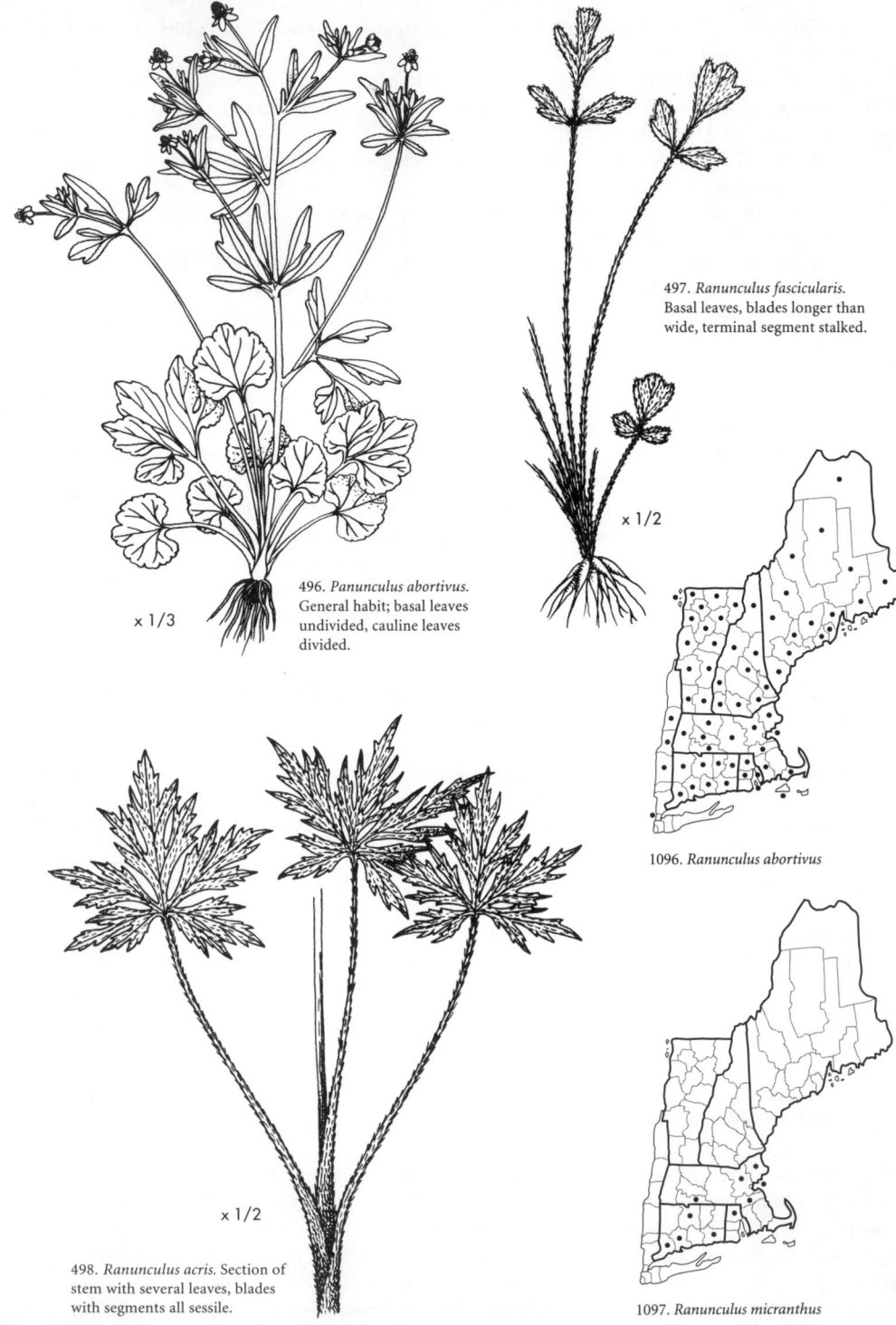

497. *Ranunculus fascicularis.*
Basal leaves, blades longer than
wide, terminal segment stalked.

× 1/2

496. *Panunculus abortivus.*
General habit; basal leaves
undivided, cauline leaves
divided.

× 1/3

1096. *Ranunculus abortivus*

× 1/2

498. *Ranunculus acris.* Section of
stem with several leaves, blades
with segments all sessile.

1097. *Ranunculus micranthus*

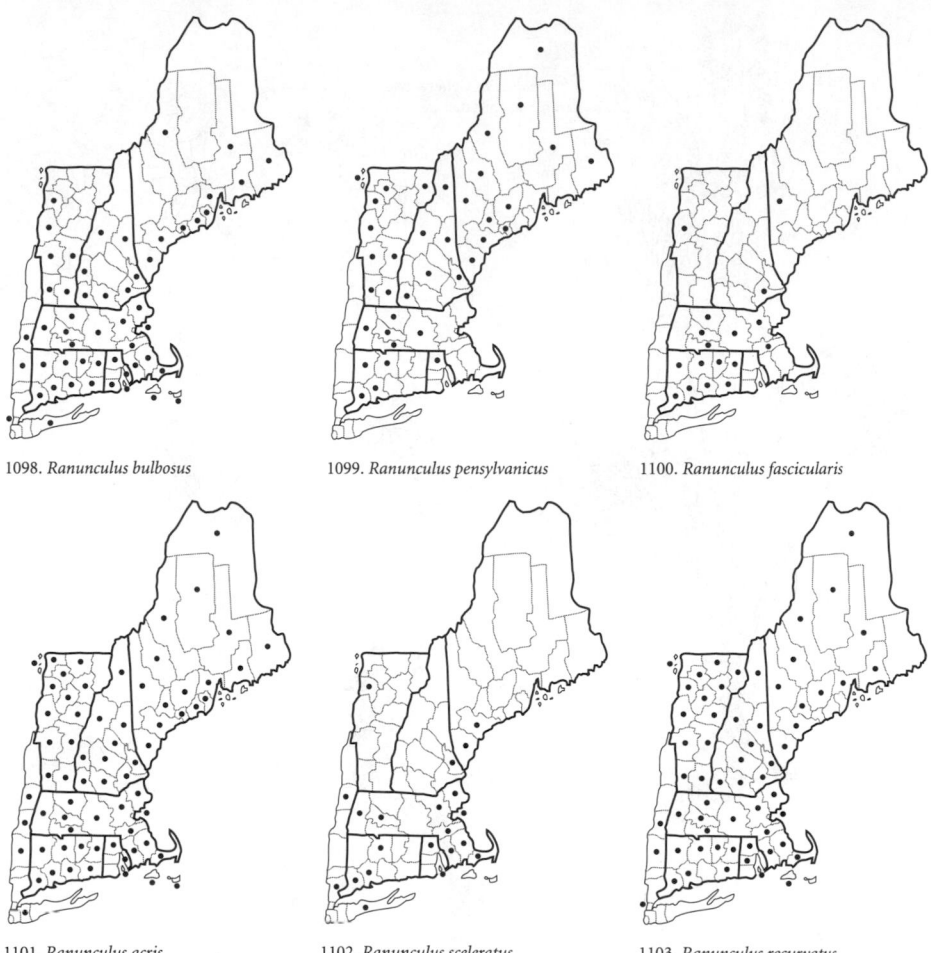

1098. *Ranunculus bulbosus* 1099. *Ranunculus pensylvanicus* 1100. *Ranunculus fascicularis*

1101. *Ranunculus acris* 1102. *Ranunculus sceleratus* 1103. *Ranunculus recurvatus*

1. **T. láxus** Salisb. (loose). Wooded swamps and wet meadows. April-May. Fig. 499. Reported for ME, CT. Endangered in Litchfield County, CT. Our plants are subsp. *laxus.* —OBL

15. *Cáltha* L. Marsh-Marigold (from the Latin, meaning cup).

Succulent, glabrous, branched, perennial herbs with stout, erect or decumbent stems (ours); leaves basal and cauline, ovate to reniform, cordate, crenate or dentate, the basal long petioled, the cauline short petioled to sessile, alternate, sometimes nearly truncate at the base; flowers few, showy, bright yellow, perfect, on terminal and axillary peduncles, sepals 5-9, petaloid, petals none, stamens numerous, carpels 5-10, with numerous ovules, style very short; fruit a cluster of spreading or ascending, many-seeded follicles.

1. **C. palústris** L. (of swamps). Wooded swamps, shrub swamps, wet woods and wet meadows. April-June, and occasionally September-October. Fig. 500, Map 1104. (Eurasia). Our plants are var. *palustris.* Leaves can be used as a potherb and unopened flower buds can be pickled and used as a substitute for capers, but both must first be blanched in 2 waters to remove the poisonous substance; the parts can then be simmered until tender. —OBL

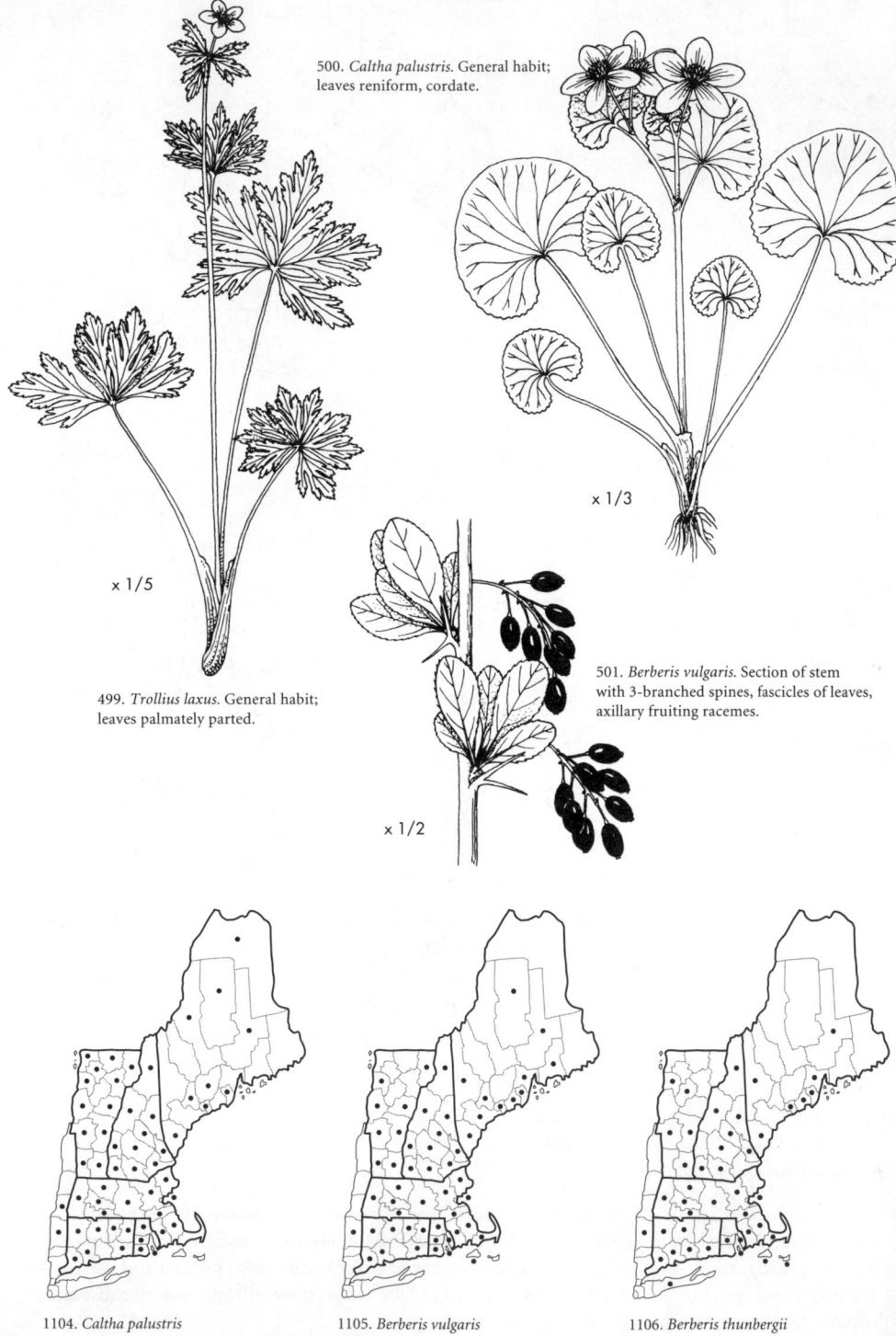

500. *Caltha palustris.* General habit; leaves reniform, cordate.

× 1/3

× 1/5

499. *Trollius laxus.* General habit; leaves palmately parted.

501. *Berberis vulgaris.* Section of stem with 3-branched spines, fascicles of leaves, axillary fruiting racemes.

× 1/2

1104. *Caltha palustris*

1105. *Berberis vulgaris*

1106. *Berberis thunbergii*

Family 88. Berberidáceae (Barberry Family)

Hermaphrodite, rhizomatous, perennial herbs or shrubs. Leaves alternate, opposite or basal, simple or compound, estipulate, but often dilated at the base. Flowers perfect, solitary, umbellate, racemose or paniculate, regular, perianth segments all distinct, sepals 6, sometimes petaloid, often early deciduous, petals 6-9, or reduced to nectaries, stamens as many or twice as many as the petals, hypogynous, distinct, ovary 1, superior, carpel 1, 1-loculed, with 1-many ovules, style 1, short or absent. Fruit a berry, or mature seed not enclosed in an ovary in *Caulophyllum*.

Spiny shrubs with numerous simple, unlobed leaves . (Fig. 501). .... 1. *Berberis*
Smooth herbs with 2 compound or lobed leaves.
    Leaves alternate, 2 or more times ternately compound; flowers paniculate.
        (Fig. 502) .... 2. *Caulophyllum*
    Leaves opposite, merely palmately lobed; flowers solitary. (Fig.503). .... 3. *Podophyllum*
                                                   peltatum

1. *Bérberis* L. Barberry (name based on Arabic name for the fruit).

Deciduous shrubs with yellow wood, inner bark and pith, and a simple or 3-branched spine at each node, these alternate, pith relatively large, round, buds small to moderate, ovoid, sessile and solitary, in the axils of the spines, with 5 or 6 scales, giving rise to a spur shoot containing the persistent bases of several leaves, leaf scars small, terminating the dilated leaf bases, bundle traces 3, minute, sometimes indistinct, stipule scars lacking; leaves short petioled, in fascicles on spur shoots in the axils of the spines, small, simple, obovate, entire or serrulate; flowers small, yellow, solitary, umbellate or racemose, sepals 6, petaloid, subtended by 2-3 bractlets, petals 6, smaller than the sepals, each with 2 glands inside near the base, stamens 6; fruit a red, 1-few-seeded berry. —FACU; WILDL. 1

Leaves serrulate; flowers in racemes 3 cm or more long; spines, or many of them,
    3-branched .... 1. *B. vulgaris*
Leaves entire or at most, slightly crenulate; flowers solitary or in umbellate clusters
    less than 3 cm long; spines all simple. .... 2. *B. thunbergii*

    1. *B. vulgáris* L. (common). Common Barberry. Thickets, pastures, woodland borders and open woods. May-June. Fig. 501, Map 1105. (Naturalized from Europe). Fruits edible, used commonly to make jams and jellies.

    2. *B. thunbérgii* DC. (for C.P. Thunberg). Japanese Barberry. Thickets, pastures, woodland borders, open woods and roadsides. May-June. Map 1106. (Introduced from Asia).

    B. x ottawénsis Schneid. A hybrid between *B. thunbergii* and *B. vulgaris.*

2. *Caulophýllum* Michx. Blue Cohosh (from the Greek, based on the compound leaves).

Perennial, glabrous, herbs (bluish-glaucous, at least when young) from thick, knotted rhizomes; leaves 2, alternate, the first large, sessile, above the middle of the stem, triternate and simulating 3 long-petioled biternate leaves, the second smaller, biternate, subtending the inflorescence, leaflets oblong to obovate, 2-3 or more lobed; flowers in 1-several terminal panicles of cymes, yellowish green to greenish purple, sepals 6, pataloid, subtended by 3 or 4 bractlets, petals 6, reduced to reniform, gland like bodies much smaller than the sepals, one at the base of each sepal, stamens 6; seeds 2 together, on short, thick stalks, becoming large and globose, enclosed in a membranous covering which turns blue, the seeds then resembling berries.

    1. *C. thalictroídes* (L.) Michx. (resembling *Thalictrum*). Rich woods. April-May. Fig. 502, Map 1107. (e. Asia). Reported to have been used by Indians to stimulate uterine contractions to hasten childbirth, and to induce menstruation; plant also listed as poisonous and must be used with extreme caution.

C. gigànteum (Farw.) Loconte & Blackwell. Similar to *C. thalictroides* but with uniformly purple sepals 6 mm or more long (sepals green, yellow or purple, up to 5 mm long in *C. thalictroides*). Reported for MA, NH, VT. [*C. thalictroides* var. *g.*].

3. *Podophýllum* L. May Apple (from the Greek).

Perennial, glabrous herbs from a creeping rhizome; leaves basal and cauline, suborbicular, the former arising apart from the stems, long petioled, large, centrally peltate, deeply, palmately 5-9 lobed, the cauline usually 2 (rarely 3 or none), opposite, long petioled, smaller, but deeply palmately lobed like the basal; flower solitary, terminal and nodding on a short peduncle between the 2 leaves, white, subtended by 3 bractlets which fall early when in bud, sepals 6, petaloid, early deciduous, petals 6-9, longer than the sepals, stamens 12-18; fruit a large, yellow, (sometimes red) ovoid, many-seeded berry, the seeds enclosed in fleshy arils.

1. *P. peltátum* L. (shield-shaped). Rich, open woods and pastures. May. Fig. 503, Map 1108. Various medicinal uses, including use as a cathartic, have been ascribed to the rhizome, which is poisonous and cannot be taken in large doses. Ripe fruits are edible. —FACU

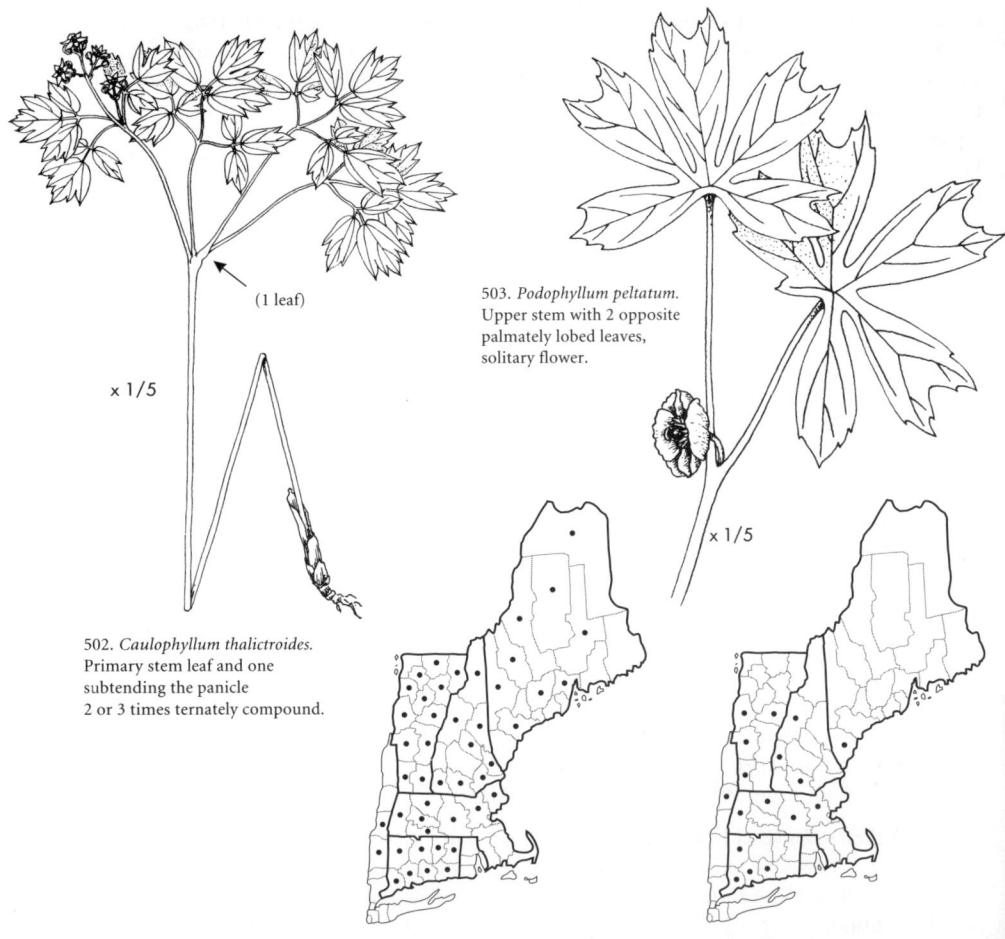

(1 leaf)

x 1/5

503. *Podophyllum peltatum.* Upper stem with 2 opposite palmately lobed leaves, solitary flower.

x 1/5

502. *Caulophyllum thalictroides.* Primary stem leaf and one subtending the panicle 2 or 3 times ternately compound.

1107. *Caulophyllum thalictroides*

1108. *Podophyllum peltatum*

Family 89. Lardizabaláceae (Lardizabala Family)

Monoecious, woody, climbing and twining deciduous vines (ours), stems slender, pith small, buds small, sessile, ovoid, with numerous scales, sometimes multiple, leaf scars alternate, half round, conspicuously raised, bundle traces 5-6, stipule scars lacking. Leaves alternate, palmately compound, with 5 leaflets, petioled and petiolulate, estipulate, leaflets elliptic, entire, retuse. Flowers imperfect, regular, in axillary racemes, the lower flowers in the raceme pistillate, the upper staminate and smaller, sepals 3, purple and petaloid, petals none, staminate flowers with 6 hypogenous stamens, pistillate flowers with 3 or more superior, 1-locular carpels, each containing many ovules, stigmas sessile. Fruit an ovoid, fleshy, purple follicle.

1. Akébia Dcne. (Japenese name).
Same characters as the family.

   1. A. quináta (Houtt.) Dcne. Sometimes escaped from cultivation around old homesites and fields, roadsides, open woodlands, etc. Fig. 504, Map 1109. (Introduced from Asia).

Family 90. Menispermáceae (Moonseed Family)

Dioecious, woody, twining and climbing, deciduous vines, stems fluted, pith relatively large, buds small, pubescent, superposed, one visible above the leaf scar, or at some nodes developing into an inflorescence, the other 1 or 2 covered by the leaf scar, scales 2 or 3, leaf scars alternate, elliptical, raised and concave, bundle traces 3 or more, stipule scars lacking. Leaves alternate, petioled, broadly ovate, 3-7 lobed or angled, or nearly entire, palmately veined, cordate and peltate at the base, estipulate. Flowers imperfect, small and greenish to whitish, regular, in axillary panicles, sepals 4-8, petals 4-8, shorter than the sepals, staminate flowers with 12-24 hypogenous stamens, carpels 2-4, superior, 1-locular, 1 ovuled, stigmas sessile. Fruit a blue, 1-seeded drupe.

1. Menispérmum L. Moonseed (from the Greek, meaning moon seed).
Same as characters as the family.

   1. M. canadénse L. (Canadian). Rich limey woods and thickets, particularly along streams and rivers. June. Fig. 505, Map 1110. Root has been used to make a diuretic; fruits are poisonous.

Family 91. Magnoliáceae (Magnolia Family)

Hermaphrodite, trees or tall shrubs, deciduous (ours), bark aromatic and bitter. Leaves alternate, simple, entire or lobed, petioled, pinnately veined, stipulate. Flowers perfect, regular, large, solitary and terminal, white or greenish-yellow, hypogynous, sepals and petals alike or scarcely differentiated, arranged in 3 or more cycles of 3s, deciduous, stamens numerous, distinct, spirally arranged on the basal portion of an elongate receptacle, carpels numerous, superior, distinct or coherent, spirally arranged on the receptacle, 1-locular, ovules 1-2, style and stigma 1. Fruit a cone of follicles or samaras.

Leaves 4 or more lobed, truncate or broadly retuse at the apex. (Fig. 506). .... 1. *Liriodendron*
                                                                                                     tulipifera
Leaves entire, acute, acuminate or obtuse at the apex. (Fig. 507). .... 2. *Magnolia*

1. Liriodéndron L. Tulip Tree (from the Greek, meaning tulip tree).
Large tree; twigs moderate, pith moderately large, with diaphrams, buds solitary or superposed, the lateral small, rounded and sessile, the terminal larger oblong, compressed and 2-edged, short-stalked, with 2 valvate scales, leaf scars alternate, elliptic to round, bundle traces numerous, scattered, stipule scars encircling the twig; leaves large, with 4 main lobes and sometimes several

smaller lobes, 2 of the main lobes at the base and 2 at the apex, appearing truncate or broadly retuse; sepals 3, green, soon reflexed, petals 6, forming a cup, greenish-yellow with an orange spot at the base inside; fruit a cone of samaras, long-persistent. —Wildl. 1

1. *L. tulipífera* L. (tulip-bearing). Rich, deciduous woods and woodland borders. June. Fig. 506, Map 1111. —FACU

2. *Magnólia* L. Magnolia (for P. Magnol).

Trees or tall shrubs; twigs moderate to stout, pith moderately large, buds solitary, ovoid, sessile, the terminal often larger than the lateral, glabrous or pubescent, with a single keeled scale, leaf scars alternate, rounded or U-shaped, bundle traces numerous, scattered, stipule scars encircling the twig; leaves large, entire, oblong to elliptic or oblanceolate, acute or rounded to truncate at the base, obtuse, acute or acuminate at the tip; flowers white to greenish-yellow, sepals 3, petaloid, petals 6-12, in 2-3 whorles of 3, scarcely differentiated from the sepals; fruit a cone of red or brown follicles, each follicle containing 2 arillate, berry-like seeds suspended on slender, filamentous threads. —Wildl. 1

Leaves glaucous-whitened beneath; petals 5 cm or less long. .... 1. *M. virginiana*
Leaves green beneath; petals more than 5 cm long.
    Mature leaves more than 2.5 dm long; buds glabrous and glaucous; flowers white ..... 2. *M. tripetala*
    Mature leaves less than 2.5 dm long; buds pubescent; flowers greenish-yellow. .... 3. *M. acuminata*

1. *M. virginiána* L. (Virginian). Sweet Bay. Wooded swamps and wet woods. June-July. Fig. 507. From farther south. Endangered in MA. Reported for Essex County. Leaves are used to flavor roasts and gravies. —FACW+

2. *M. tripétala* (L.) L. (with three petals). Umbrella tree. Rich woods. May. From farther south. Reported for Hartford County CT, Hampshire County MA. —FACU

3. *M. acumináta* (L.) L. (acuminate). Cucumber tree. Rich woods. May-June. Map 1112. [*Tulipastrum acuminatum*].

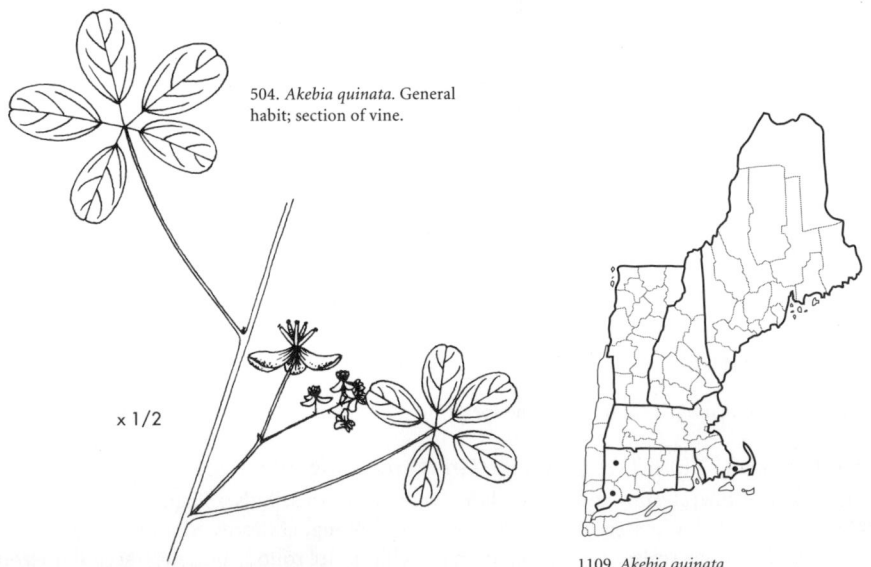

504. *Akebia quinata.* General habit; section of vine.

x 1/2

1109. *Akebia quinata*

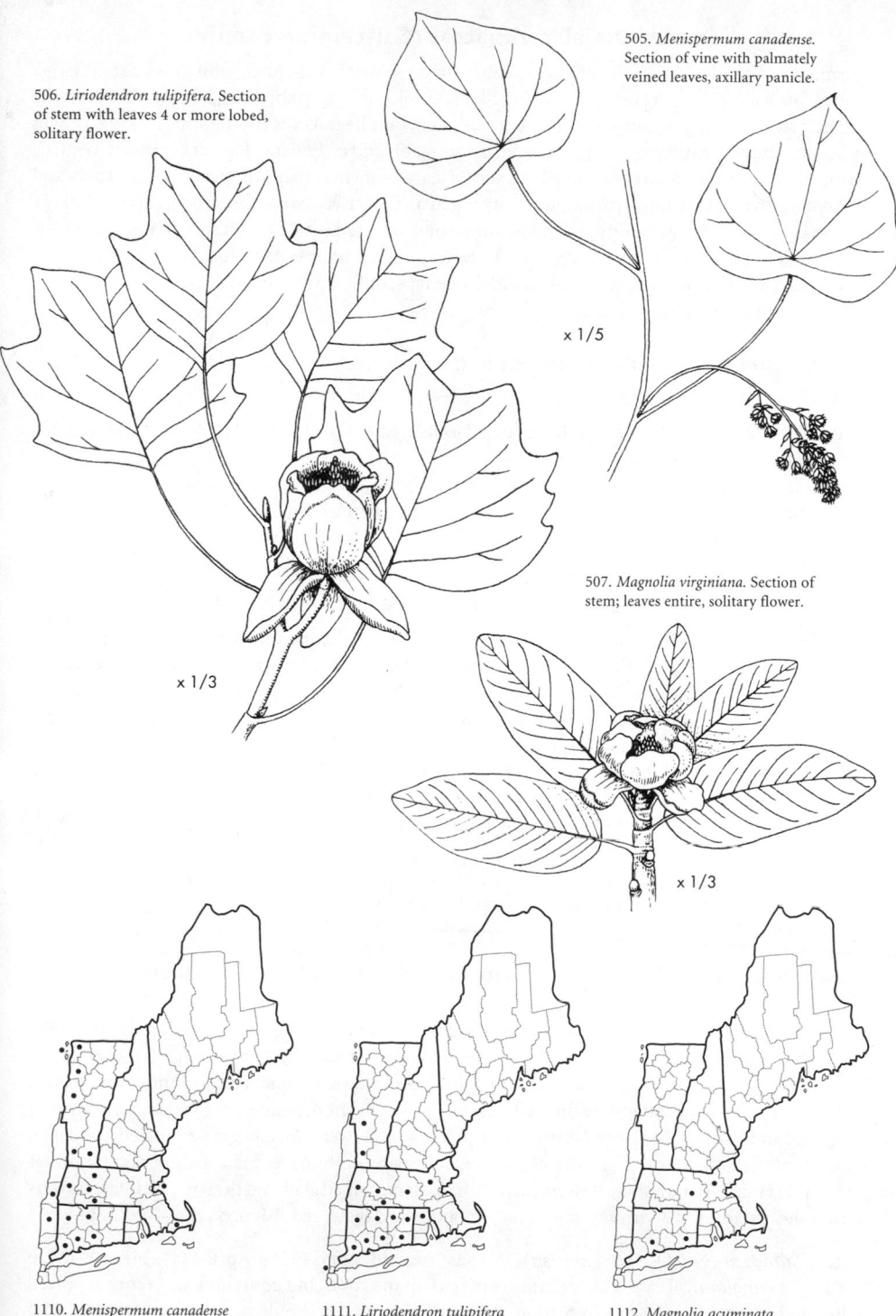

505. *Menispermum canadense.* Section of vine with palmately veined leaves, axillary panicle.

506. *Liriodendron tulipifera.* Section of stem with leaves 4 or more lobed, solitary flower.

x 1/5

x 1/3

507. *Magnolia virginiana.* Section of stem; leaves entire, solitary flower.

x 1/3

1110. *Menispermum canadense*

1111. *Liriodendron tulipifera*

1112. *Magnolia acuminata*

Family 92. Calycantháceae (Calycanthus Family)

Hermaphrodite, deciduous, aromatic shrubs, twigs somewhat 4-sided, pith moderately large, angled, buds closely superposed, appearing like 1, sessile, oblong, pubescent, lacking visible scales, end bud lacking, leaf scars opposite, U-shaped, raised, bundle traces 3, stipule scars lacking. Leaves opposite, simple, entire, ovate to oblong, short-petioled, estipulate. Flowers perfect, regular, terminal and solitary, short pedicelled on short, leafy branches, maroon, perigynous, sepals and petals undifferentiated, numerous, spirally arranged on the outer rim of a thickened, cuplike, hollow receptacle with a narrow mouth, stamens numerous, inserted inside the perianth, the innermost staminodial, carpels numerous, at or near the bottom of the receptacle inside, 1-locular, with 1 or 2 ovules, styles filiform, elongate. Fruit an indehiscent pseudocarp consisting of the fleshy receptacle within which are enclosed numerous achenes.

1. Calycánthus L. Carolina allspice (from the Greek, meaning cup flower).
Same characters as the family.

    1. C. flóridus L. From farther south. Reported for CT, MA. May-June. Fig. 508. Our plants include var. *floridus* and the following var.:
    var. *gláucus* (Willd.) Torr. & Gray. Leaves glabrous beneath or sparsely pilose when young (leaves downy beneath in var. *floridus*). [*C.f.* var. *laevigatus; C. fertilis*]. Seeds reported to be poisonous. —FACU

Family 93. Lauráceae (Laurel Family)

Dioecious or polygamodioecious, deciduous (ours), aromatic, trees or shrubs. Leaves alternate, simple, entire or lobed, petioled, punctate, estipulate. Flowers imperfect, regular, in sessile or subsessile, lateral, umbellate clusters, or clustered in peduncled, umbelled racemes at the branch tips of the previous year, involucrate, with scaly bracts, (the bud scales) small, yellowish, appearing before or with the leaves, sepals and petals undifferentiated, in 2 cycles of 3, persistent or deciduous, staminate flowers with 9 stamens, (ours) arranged in 3 cycles of 3s on the base of the calyx, pistillate flowers with staminodia, carpel 1, superior, 1-locular, with a single ovule, style 1. Fruit a 1-seeded, berry-like drupe, usually surrounded at the base by the persistent, cuplike, perianth tube.

Leaves, at least some, 1-3 lobed; inflorescence terminal on previous year's twigs,
    peduncled, 2.5 cm or more broad; fruit blue. (Fig. 509). .... 1. *Sassafras albidum*
Leaves all unlobed; inflorescence lateral, sessile, less than 2 cm broad; fruit red.
    (Fig. 510) .... 2. *Lindera benzoin*

1. Sássafras Nees & Eberm. Sassafras (name applied by early French settlers in Florida).

Dioecious trees; twigs green, mucilaginous, moderate, often crooked or irregular, pith moderate, somewhat angled, buds usually solitary, sessile, ovoid to subglobose, the terminal larger than the laterals, ovoid and pointed, bud scales about 4, leaf scars alternate, small, half-round, bundle trace a single, transverse line sometimes divided into 3, stipule scars none; leaves mucilagenous, some oval or elliptic and entire, others with 1-several irregular lobes; flowers clustered in peduncled, umbelled racemes at the branch tips of the previous year, appearing with the leaves, sepals persistent, inner series of 3 stamens in staminate flowers each with a pair of stalked glands at the base, pistillate flowers with 6 short staminodia; drupe ovoid, blue, on a thick, clavate, reddish pedicel. —Wildl. 1

    1. S. álbidum (Nutt.) Nees (whitish). Woods, roadsides and fields. April-May. Fig. 509, Map 1113. [*S. variifolium*]. Tea is widely made from bark of the roots, but contains a substance reported to be carcinogenic; dried leaves have been used to thicken soups; should be used sparingly and with caution. —FACU-

2. *Líndera* Thunb. Spicebush (for J. Linder).

Polygamodioecious shrubs; twigs green, olive or brownish, slender, with pale lenticels, pith relatively large, buds superposed, the upper of 2 kinds on flowering branches, the flower buds larger and globose, stalked, arranged in pairs at the nodes, one on each side of a leaf bud, the latter smaller and pointed, with about 3 scales, end bud lacking, leaf scars small, alternate, crescent-shaped to half-round, bundle traces 3, sometimes indistinct, stipule scars none; leaves entire, oblong to obovate, tapered to the base, acute to acuminate tipped; flowers in sessile or subsessile, lateral, umbellate clusters, appearing before the leaves, sepals deciduous, inner series of 3 stamens in staminate flowers lobed and glandular at the base, pistillate flowers with few to many staminodia of 2 forms; drupe ellipsoid, red.—Wildl. 1

1. *L. benzóin* (L.) Blume (old generic name). Wooded swamps, wet woods and along streams. April-May. Fig. 510, Map 1114. [*Benzoin aestivale*]. Our plants are var. *benzoin*. Twigs and leaves are used to make a tea and dried fruits are used as a substitute for allspice. —FACW-

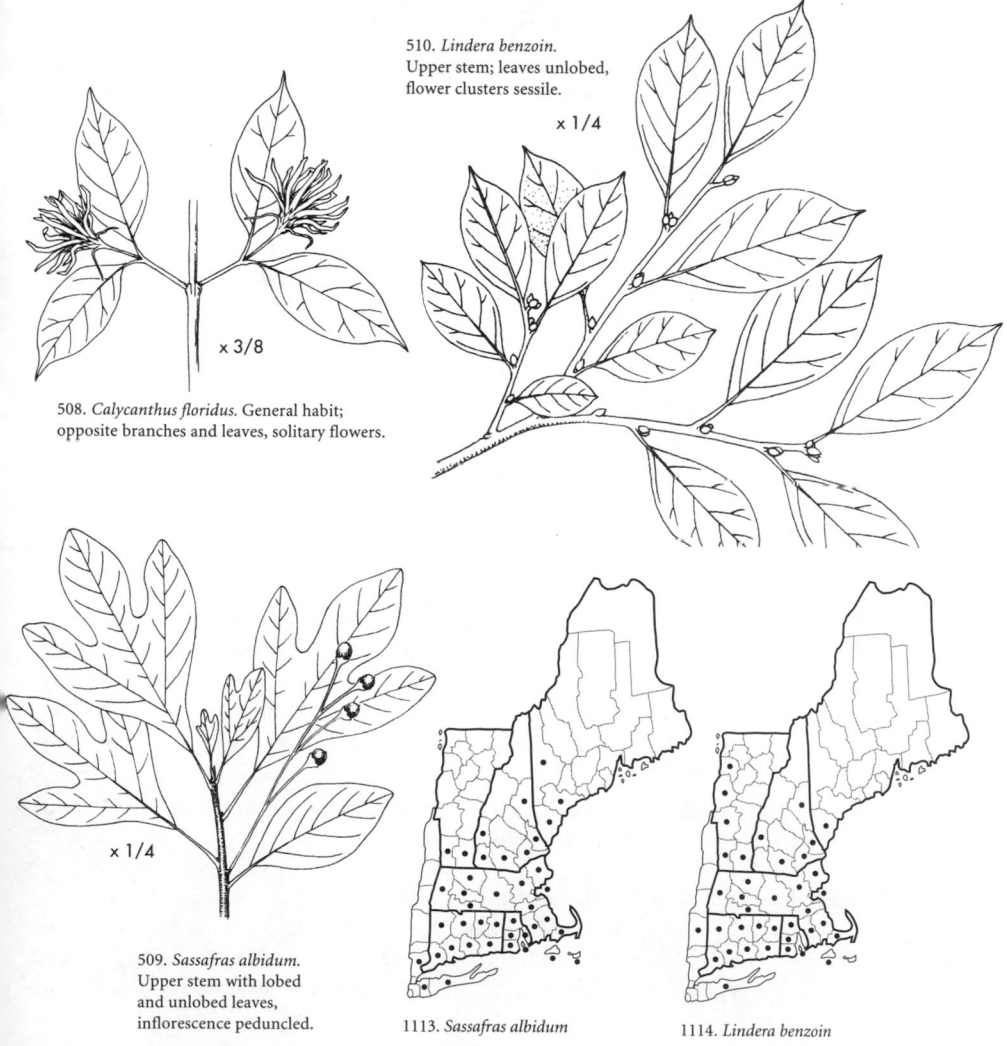

510. *Lindera benzoin.*
Upper stem; leaves unlobed,
flower clusters sessile.

x 1/4

x 3/8

508. *Calycanthus floridus.* General habit;
opposite branches and leaves, solitary flowers.

x 1/4

509. *Sassafras albidum.*
Upper stem with lobed
and unlobed leaves,
inflorescence peduncled.

1113. *Sassafras albidum*

1114. *Lindera benzoin*

Family 94. Papaveráceae (Poppy Family)

Hermaphrodite, annual or perennial herbs with milky or colored juice. Leaves basal or cauline or both, simple or pinnately or palmately lobed or dissected, alternate, sessile or petioled, estipulate. Flowers perfect, regular, solitary or in cymose or umbellate clusters, (paniculate in *Macleaya*) large and showy, sepals 2 or 3, caducous, petals 4-12 (absent in *Macleaya*), stamens numerous, hypogynous, distinct, ovary superior, 1 or 2-locular, of 2-many carpels, ovules numerous, style 1, short, with a simple or lobed stigma. Fruit a capsule dehiscent by valves or a pore.

a. Plant prickly. (Fig. 511) .... 1. *Argemone*
a. Plant not prickly.
   b. Stem leaves absent, plant acaulescent. (Fig. 512). .... 2. *Sanguinaria*
                                                 canadensis
   b. Stem leaves present, plant caulescent.
      c. Leaves cordate and petioled; flowers paniculate; petals absent; capsule 6 or
         fewer seeded. (Fig. 513) .... 3. *Macleaya cordata*
      c. Leaves not cordate, or if so then sessile and clasping; flowers solitary or
         umbellate; petals present; capsule more than 6-seeded.
         d. Flowers yellow; capsule long and linear, 5 or more times as long as thick,
            dehiscent to the base by 2 valves.
            Flowers solitary; capsule more than 10 cm long. (Fig. 514). .... 4. *Glaucium flavum*
            Flowers in lateral umbels; capsule up to 5 cm long. (Fig. 515). .... 5. *Chelidonium*
                                      majus
         d. Flowers white, red or purple; capsule globose to clavate, less than 5 times
            as long as thick, dehiscent by many pores. (Fig. 516). .... 6. *Papaver*

1. *Argemóne* L. Prickly Poppy (ancient Greek name).

Annual, prickly herbs with yellow juice; leaves sessile and auriculate-clasping, pinnately lobed, spiny-toothed, sometimes mottled with paler green; flowers solitary and terminal on the branches or in open cymes, sessile or peduncled, closely subtended by the upper leaves, sepals 2-3, prickly, petals 4-6, carpels 4-6, style very short or none, stigma 4-6 lobed; capsule spiny, ellipsoid, dehiscent by 4-6 apical valves. Poisonous.

Flowers white to pink, 6-10 cm wide .... 1. *A. albiflora*
Flowers yellow to cream-colored, 3-6 cm wide. .... 2. *A. mexicana*

   1. *A. albiflóra* Hornem. (white flowered). From farther south. June-August. Rare. Reported for MA, Fairfield and New Haven Counties CT. [*A. alba; A. intermedia*]. Our plants are subsp. *albiflora*.
   2. *A. mexicána* L. (Mexican). Escaped from cultivation to waste places. June-September. Fig. 511, Map 1115.

2. *Sanguinária* L. Bloodroot (name based on the red color of the juice).

Perennial, acaulescent herbs from a thick rhizome with red juice; leaf 1, at the base of the flower stalk, reniform, long petioled, palmately 3-9 lobed, the lobes crenate to coarsely toothed; flower solitary, rarely 2, scapose, large and white to pink, sepals 2, petals 8-12, early deciduous, 4 usually longer than the others, carpels 2, style short, stigma 2 lobed; capsule fusiform, 2-valved, 1-locular, overtopped by the mature leaves, seeds numerous.

   1. *S. canadénsis* L. (Canadian). Rich woods and thickets. April-May. Fig. 512, Map 1116. Various medicinal uses are reported but is also poisonous. —FACW+

3. *Macleáya* R. Br. Plume (for A. Macleay).

Tall, perennial herbs; leaves large, roundish, cordate, deeply lobed, the lobes toothed or crenate, petioled, whitened beneath; flowers in panicles in the upper leaf axils and terminating the stem, sepals 2, cream-colored, petals none, carpels 2, style absent, stigma 2-lobed; capsule oblanceolate, 2-valved, 2-locular, 6 or fewer seeded.

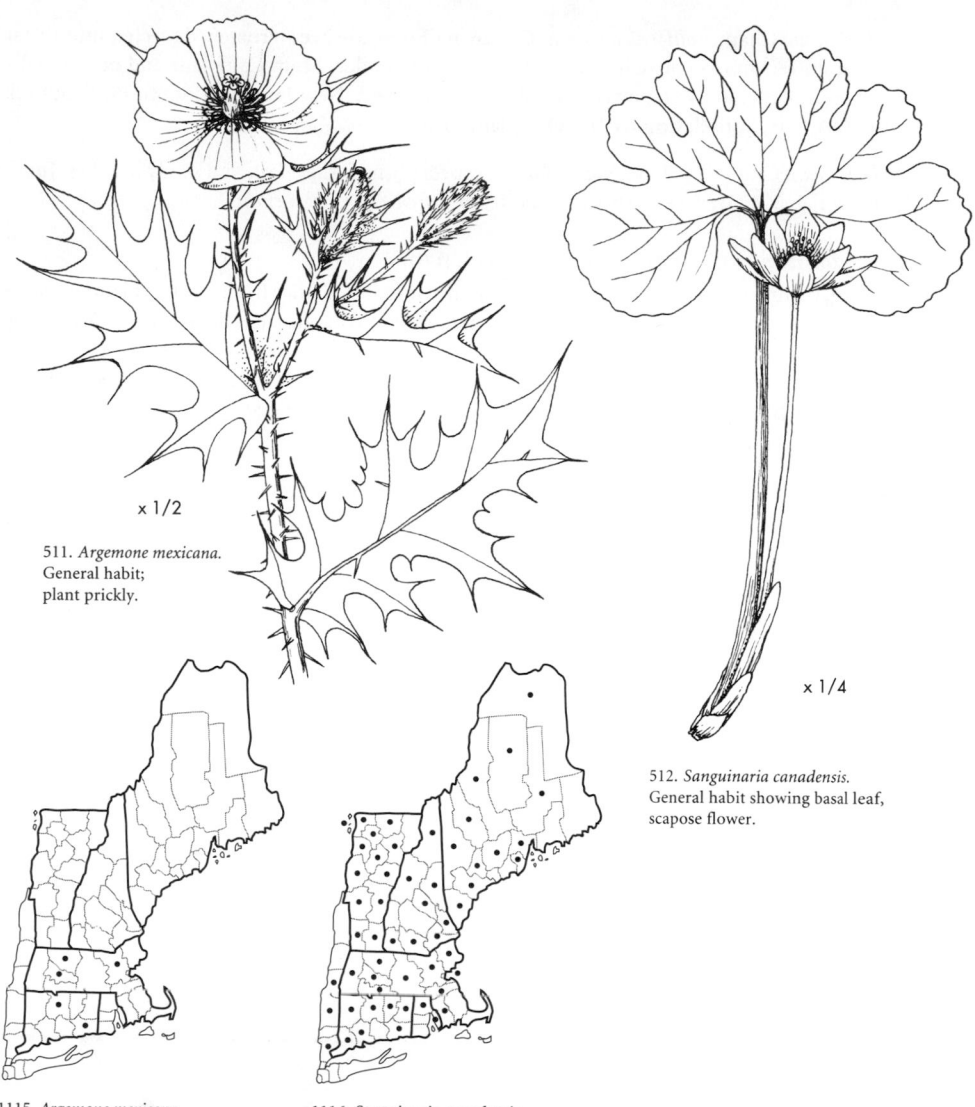

511. *Argemone mexicana.*
General habit;
plant prickly.

x 1/2

x 1/4

512. *Sanguinaria canadensis.*
General habit showing basal leaf,
scapose flower.

1115. *Argemone mexicana*

1116. *Sanguinaria canadensis*

1. M. cordáta (Willd.) R. Br. (heart-shaped). Waste places. July-August. Rare. Fig. 513, Map 1117. (Introduced from e. Asia).

4. Glaúcium Mill. Sea Poppy (from the Greek, based on the glaucous foliage).

Stout, branching, biennial or perennial herbs with saffron-colored juice; leaves basal and cauline, pubescent, the basal and lower stem leaves petioled, the others sessile and cordate clasping, oblong to ovate, pinnatifid, with toothed divisions, the uppermost leaves merely sinuate lobed and toothed; flowers large and yellow, solitary, terminal and in the upper leaf axils, sepals 2, petals 4, carpels 2, style absent, stigma 2-lobed; capsule very long and linear, curved, 2-valved and 2-locular, seeds numerous.

Eschschóltzia Cham. *califórnica* Cham. California Poppy. Leaves ternately dissected into linear segments; flowers orange or yellow, capsules long and slender. From California and occasionally escaped from cultivation. Reported for Fairfield, Litchfield, New London Counties CT, Suffolk County MA, NH, Suffolk County NY. Our plants are subsp. *californica.*

1. *G. flávum* Crantz. (yellow). Waste places, especially near the coast, and sandy beaches. June-July. Rare. Fig. 514, Map 1118. (Naturalized from Europe). [*G. glaucium*].

5. *Chelidónium* L. Celandine (ancient Greek name).

Branching, biennial herbs with brittle stems and saffron-colored juice from a stout rhizome; leaves basal and cauline, short or long petioled, 1 or 2 times pinnatifid or pinnately dissected into 5-7 widely elliptic to obovate segments, these coarsely and irregularly lobed, crenate or toothed, glaucous beneath; flowers yellow, in few-flowered, lateral, pedunculate umbels, sepals 2, petals 4 (sometimes doubled) carpels 2, style short, stigma 2-lobed; capsule linear, subcylindric, 2-valved, dehiscent from the base upward, seeds numerous.

1. *C. május* L. (larger). Waste places and roadsides, occasionally woodlands, often in moist soil. May-August. Fig. 515, Map 1119. (Naturalized from Europe). Our plants include var. *majus* and the following vars:

var. *plénum* Wehrhaln. Petals more than 4 (4 in var. *majus*).

Another var. that has been distinguished is var. *laciniatum.* Various medicinal uses have been reported but plant is also poisonous.

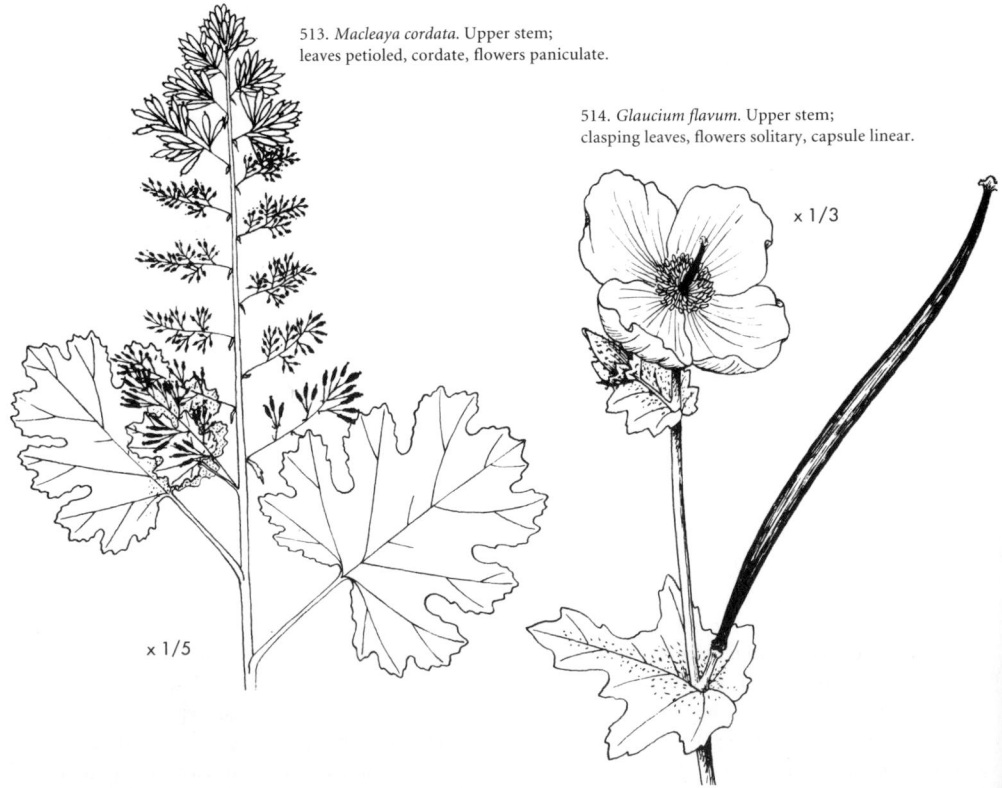

513. *Macleaya cordata.* Upper stem; leaves petioled, cordate, flowers paniculate.

514. *Glaucium flavum.* Upper stem; clasping leaves, flowers solitary, capsule linear.

x 1/3

x 1/5

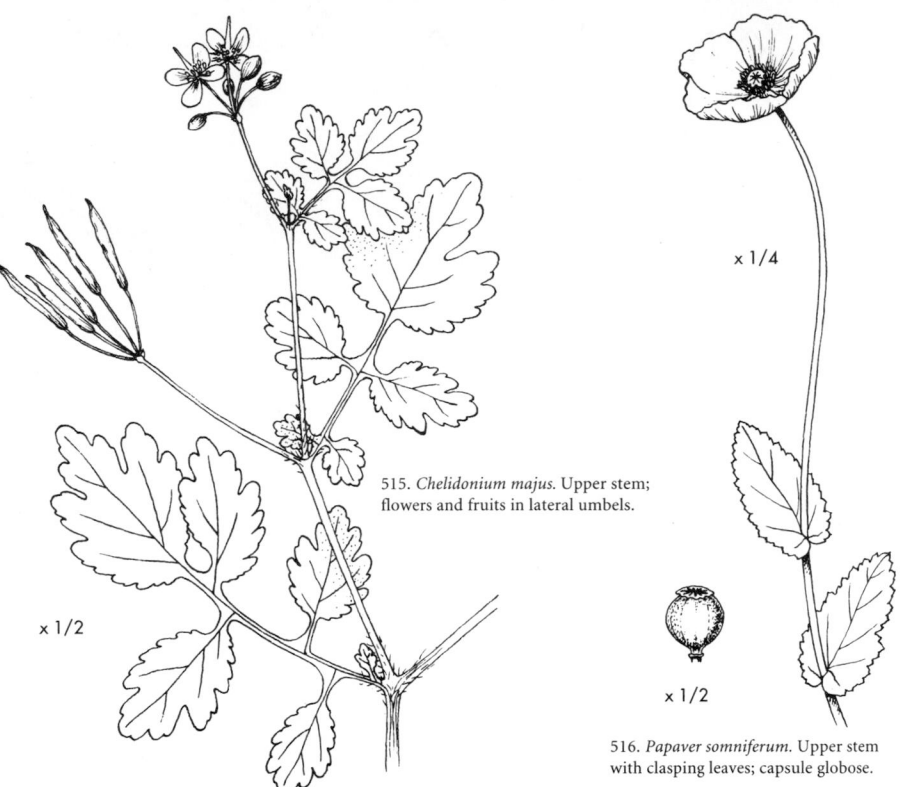

515. *Chelidonium majus*. Upper stem; flowers and fruits in lateral umbels.

x 1/4

x 1/2

x 1/2

516. *Papaver somniferum*. Upper stem with clasping leaves; capsule globose.

6. *Papáver* L. Poppy (ancient name).

Annual or biennial, glabrous or hispid herbs with white, milky juice; leaves basal and cauline, sessile or petioled, lobed or toothed, pinnatifid or pinnately dissected; flowers large and showy, long-peduncled, solitary, terminating the stem and branches, white, red or purple, sepals 2, petals usually 4, carpels 4-many, stigmas as many as the carpels, sessile and radiating on a flat disc on the summit of the ovary and capsule; capsule globose to clavate, opening by pores under the edge of the stigmatic disc, seeds numerous.

Stem glabrous and glaucous; stem leaves clasping, merely lobed or toothed. .... 1. *P. somniferum*
Stem spreading-pubescent; stem leaves not clasping, pinnatifid or pinnately dissected.
    Capsule subglobose to broadly obovoid, less than twice as long as broad; stigmatic
        rays 9(8)-14 .... 2. *P. rhoeas*
    Capsule narrowly obovoid to clavate, twice or more as long as broad; stigmatic
        rays 5-8(9) .... 3. *P. dubium*

    1. *P. somníferum* L. (sleep-bringing). Opium Poppy. Escaped from cultivation to waste places. June-September. Fig. 516, Map 1120. (Introduced from Europe). Juice from this and the next species has well known sedative properties.

    2. *P. rhoéas* L. (old Greek name). Corn Poppy. Escaped from cultivation to waste places. July-September. Map 1121. (Adventive from Europe).

    3. *P. dúbium* L. (doubtful). Escaped from cultivation to fields and waste places. June-July. Map 1122. (Naturalized from Europe).

    P. argemóne L. Petals red with black markings at the base; fruits bristly (glabrous in the above species). Occasionally escaped from cultivation to waste places. Reported for Bronx County NY.

1117. *Macleaya cordata*

1118. *Glaucium flavum*

1119. *Chelidonium majus*

1120. *Papaver somniferum*

1121. *Papaver rhoeas*

1122. *Papaver dubium*

Family 95 Fumariáceae (Fumitory Family)

Hermaphrodite, annual, biennial or perennial, erect or climbing, glabrous herbs with watery juice. Leaves basal or cauline or both, alternate, bi- or tri-ternately or pinnately compound, sessile or petioled, estipulate. Flowers perfect, irregular or bilaterally symmetrical, in terminal or axillary racemes or panicles, sepals 2, scale-like, often caducous, petals 4 in 2 pairs, the 2 outer connivent below, free and spreading above, 1 or both spurred or saccate at the base, the inner 2 narrower, crested or winged and united over the stigma, stamens 6, hypogynous, in 2 sets of 3, their filaments connate, ovary superior, 2-carpelled, 1-locular, ovules 1-several, style 1, stigma 2-lobed. Fruit a 1-seeded, indehiscent nut or a 2-valved, several-many-seeded capsule.

a. Corolla bilaterally symmetrical, 2 of the petals spurred at the base or saccate, with
    the corolla bigibbous.
    Plant acaulescent, leaves basal; corolla 2-spurred or distinctly cordate at base.
        (Fig. 517) .... 1. *Dicentra*
    Plant a vine, leaves cauline, alternate; corolla subcordate at base. (Fig. 518) .... 2. *Adlumia fungosa*

a. Corolla irregular, only 1 petal spurred or saccate at the base. (Fig. 519).
    Flowers purple; ovary and fruit globose or subglobose; fruit indehiscent. .... 3. *Fumaria officinalis*
    Flowers yellow or pink and yellow; ovary and fruit elongate; fruit dehiscent by
        2 valves .... 4. *Corydalis*

1. *Dicéntra* Bernh. (from the Greek, meaning 2-spurred).

Perennial, acaulescent herbs from rhizomes or tuber-bearing rootstocks; leaves basal, long-petioled, ternately-pinnately decompound, the ultimate segments linear to elliptic or obovate, entire or coarsely toothed, glaucous beneath; flowers nodding, on 2-bracted pedicels, in a scapose raceme or panicle, white to pink, corolla bilaterally symmetrical, the outer 2 petals spurred or saccate at the base, the inner 2 narrower, spatulate, dorsally crested or winged, united above; capsule oblong to linear, 2-valved, many seeded. Poisonous. —Wildl. 1

Inflorescence paniculate, the flowers in clusters in the panicle. .... 1. *D. eximia*
Inflorescence a simple raceme. (Fig. 517).
    Petal spurs rounded, not over 5 mm long from pedicel to tip. .... 2. *D. canadensis*
    Petal spurs subacute, 6-10 mm long from pedicel to tip. .... 3. *D. cucullaria*

    1. *D. éximia* (Ker-Gawl.) Torr. (choice). Wild Bleeding Heart. Rocky woods; from farther south. May-July. Endangered in NY. Reported for MA, Orange and Windham Counties VT.
    D. formósa (Andr.) Walp. Western Bleeding Heart. Similar to *D. eximia* but corolla with a short neck, petals united to above the middle (corolla tapering into a narrow neck, petals united to well below the middle in *D. eximia*). From the west coast. Reported for MA.
    2. *D. canadénsis* (Goldie) Walp. (Canadian). Squirrel-corn. Rich woods. April-May. Map 1123.
    D. spectábilis Lem. Bleeding Heart. Similar to *D. canadensis* but rootstocks not bearing tubers and flowers rose colored (rootstocks bearing tubers and flowers greenish-white in *D. canadensis*). (Japan). Rarely spread from cultivation. Reported for Ct, ME.
    3. *D. cucullária* (L.) Bernh. (hood-like). Dutchman's-breeches. Rich woods. April-May. Fig. 517, Map 1124.

2. *Adlúmia* Raf. ex DC. Climbing Fumitory (for J. Adlum).

Slender, glabrous, biennial vine, climbing by the leaf rachises (acaulescent the first year, the basal leaves non-prehensile); leaves petioled, ternately-pinnately decompound, the ultimate segments elliptic to obovate, lobed, toothed or entire, pale beneath, the uppermost leaflets reduced, the rachises elongate and prehensile; flowers white to purplish, nodding, in axillary panicles, corolla of 4 united petals, bilaterally symmetrical, narrowly ovoid, flattened, subcordate at the base, 4-lobed at the apex, 2 of the lobes united above over the stigma, stamens adherent to the petals, monodelphous below, diadelphous above, corolla persistent, becoming spongy; capsule cylindric, 2-valved, few-seeded, enclosed within the persistent corolla.

    1. *A. fungósa* (Ait.) Greene ex B.S.P. (spongy). Wet or rocky woods, moist, usually calcareous ledges. June-August. Fig. 518, Map 1125. Endangered in ME, RI.

3. *Fumária* L. Fumitory (Smoke).

Trailing or erect, diffusely branched, glabrous, annual herbs; leaves pinnately decompound, petioled, the ultimate segments linear, oblong or obovate, entire or lobed; flowers small and numerous, in peduncled axillary and terminal racemes, bracteate, purplish, sepals 2, dentate, corolla irregular, of 4 connivent petals, the upper petal spurred at the base, style deciduous; fruit a 1-seeded, indehiscent, globose or subglobose nut.

    1. *F. officinális* L. (of the shops). Waste places and cultivated ground. May-August. Fig. 519, Map 1126. (Adventive from Europe). Reported to have various medicinal values.

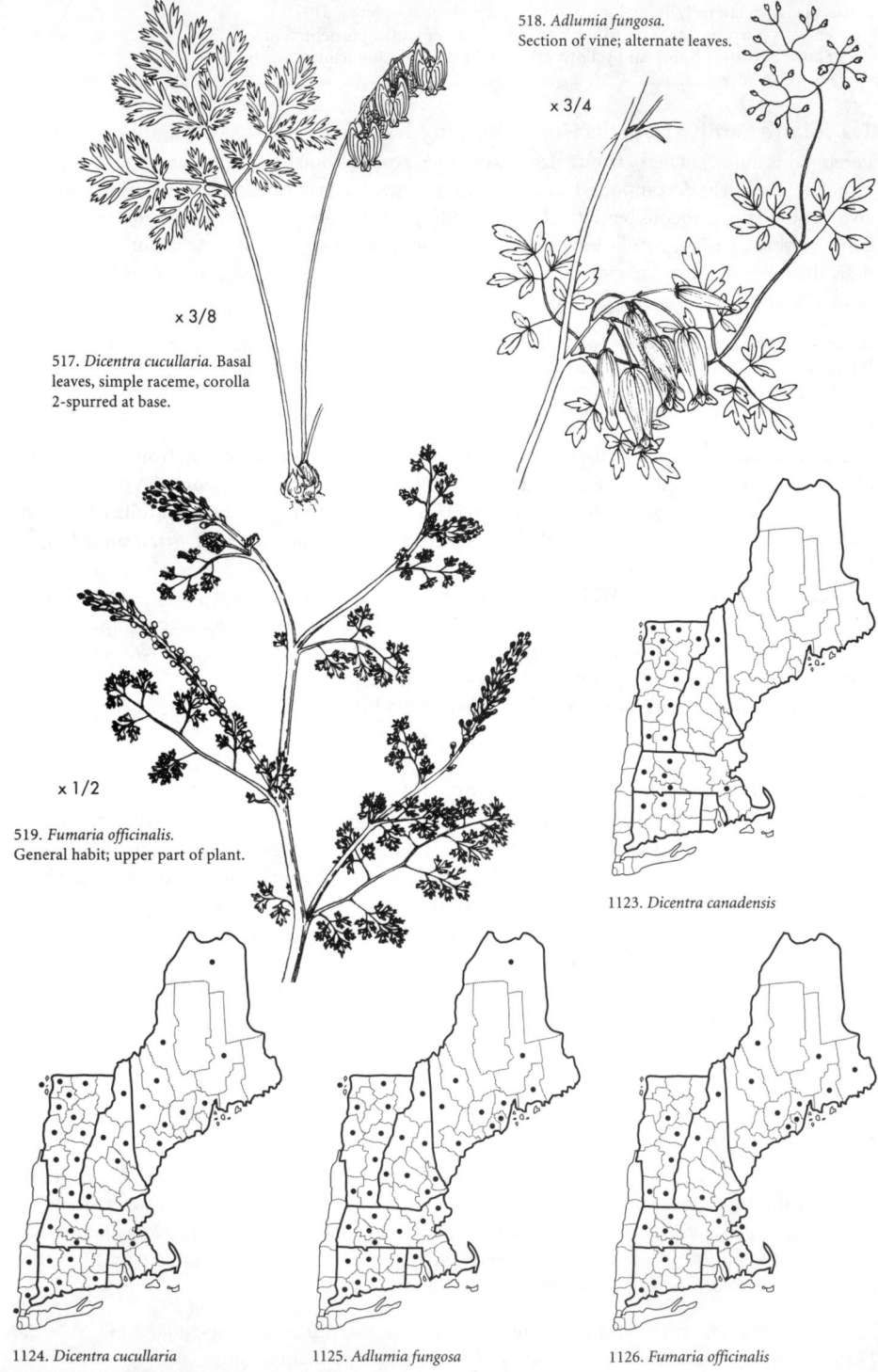

× 3/8

517. *Dicentra cucullaria.* Basal
leaves, simple raceme, corolla
2-spurred at base.

518. *Adlumia fungosa.*
Section of vine; alternate leaves.

× 3/4

× 1/2

519. *Fumaria officinalis.*
General habit; upper part of plant.

1123. *Dicentra canadensis*

1124. *Dicentra cucullaria*

1125. *Adlumia fungosa*

1126. *Fumaria officinalis*

4. Corýdalis Vent. Corydalis (ancient Greek name for the crested lark).

Trailing or erect, diffusely branched, glabrous, pale or glaucous, annual or biennial herbs; leaves pinnately decompound, the lower petioled, the upper subsessile, the ultimate segments linear, oblong or obovate, entire, lobed or toothed; flowers in terminal panicles or lateral racemes, bracteate, pink, tipped with yellow, or all yellow, corolla irregular, of 4 connivent petals, all somewhat dilated above and dorsally crested or winged, the upper petal saccate at the base, style persistent; capsule cylindric, 2-valved, many-seeded, sometimes torulose, seeds arillate. Poisonous.

Flowers pink with yellow tips; capsules mostly longer than 2.5 cm (excluding style);
      apex of lowest fruit overtopping apex of the rachis. .... 1. *C. sempervirens*
Flowers yellow; capsules mostly 2.5 cm or less long (excluding style), or if occasionally
      longer, apex of lowest fruit below apex of the rachis.
   Corolla (including spur) 9 mm or less long; longest fruiting pedicels mostly more
      than 9 mm long; seed distinctly pebbled along the margin. .... 2. *C. flavula*
   Corolla (including spur) more than 1 cm long; longest fruiting pedicels mostly less
      than 9 mm long; seed smooth or minutely pitted. .... 3. *C. aurea*

1. C. sempervirens (L.) Pers. (evergreen). Pale Corydalis. Dry, rocky woods and clearings, gravelly, rocky areas and ledges. June-August. Fig. 520, Map 1127.

C. solída (L) Swartz. Similar to *C. sempervirens* but plant arises from a tuberous base and stem is 2-3 leaved (plant not tuberous and stem with more than 2 leaves in *C. sempervirens*). Rarely escaped from cultivation. Reported for Suffolk County MA, Chittenden County VT.

2. C. flávula (Raf.) DC. (yellowish). Yellow Fumewort. Rocky woods, slopes and openings, floodplains. April-May. Reported for New Haven County CT, Dutchess County NY. —FACU

3. C. áurea Willd. (golden). Golden Corydalis. Rocky woods and calcareous slopes, sandy or gravelly river or lake shores. May-June. Map 1128. Our plants are subsp. *aurea*.

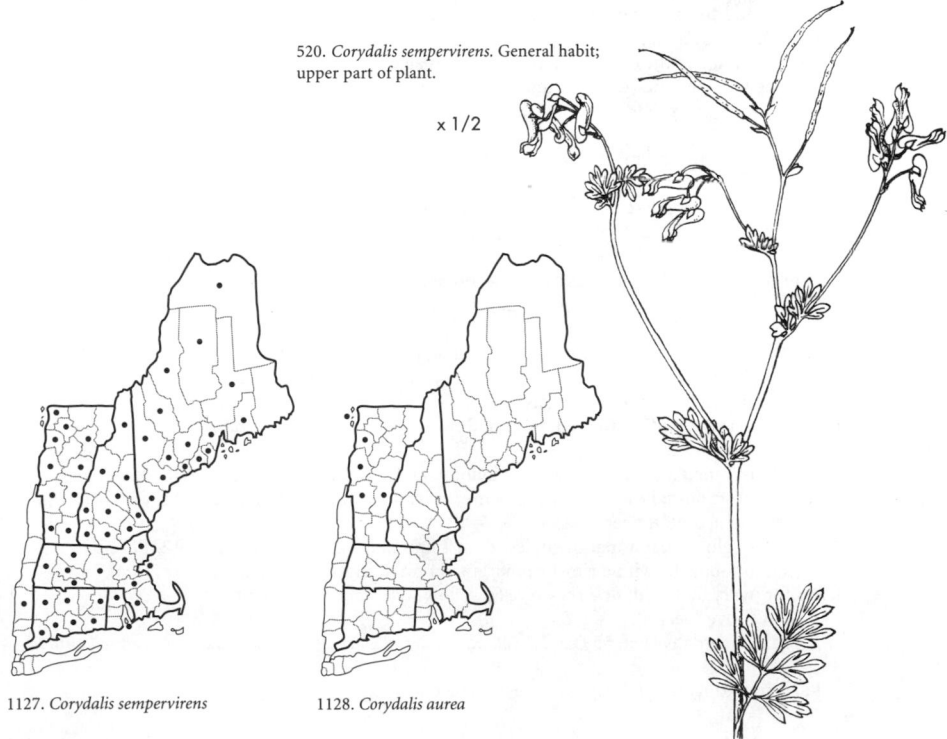

520. *Corydalis sempervirens.* General habit; upper part of plant.

x 1/2

1127. *Corydalis sempervirens*

1128. *Corydalis aurea*

Family 96. Brassicáceae (Mustard Family)

Hermaphrodite, annual or perennial herbs with acrid, watery sap. Leaves basal or cauline, simple to compound, alternate, rarely opposite or subverticillate, sessile or petioled, estipulate. Flowers perfect, usually regular, racemose or corymbose, mostly ebracteate, sepals 4, petals 4 or rarely absent, usually clawed, stamens usually 6, 4 long and 2 short, rarely fewer, hypogynous, distinct, usually subtended by minute glands, ovary superior, usually 2-locular, the locules separated by a thin septum, 2-carpelled, with few to many ovules, rarely indehiscent with a single ovule, style usually 1 or sometimes none, stigma usually 2-lobed. Fruit usually a 2-valved capsule, the valves separating from the septum, the latter persistent on the pedicel, either much longer than broad (a silique) or not much longer than broad (a silicle), sometimes transversely septate and lomentaceous, occasionally an indehiscent, 1-celled nut. [*Cruciferae*].

A. Plant scapose, with only rosette leaves, or with a basal rosette and 1 stem leaf.
　　(Fig. 521).
　　B. Petals yellow; fruit more than 2 cm long; seeds in 2 rows in each locule. .... 1. *Diplotaxis*
　　B. Petals white or absent; fruit 2 cm or less long, or if longer, seeds in 1 row in
　　　　each locule.
　　　　C. Basal leaves entire or toothed.
　　　　　　D. Leaves subulate. (Fig. 522) .... 2. *Subularia aquatica*
　　　　　　　　　　　　　　　　　　　　　　　　　　　　　　　　　　　　　　var. *americana*
　　　　　　D. Leaves not subulate, oblanceolate to obovate or oval.
　　　　　　　　E. Fruit terete or angled, less than 1 mm wide; stems mostly branched. .... 3. *Arabidopsis*
　　　　　　　　　　　　　　　　　　　　　　　　　　　　　　　　　　　　　　　thaliana
　　　　　　　　E. Fruit flattened, more than 1 mm wide, or if less, then leaves ovate
　　　　　　　　　　(oblanceolate to oblong in *Arabidopsis*); stems mostly simple.
　　　　　　　　　　Leaves long petioled, ovate .... 4. *Cardamine*
　　　　　　　　　　Leaves sessile, oblanceolate to obovate. .... 5. *Draba*
　　　　C. Basal leaves pinnately lobed or dissected.
　　　　　　F. Fruit a silique, longer than 1 cm .... 6. *Arabis*
　　　　　　F. Fruit a silicle, less than 5 mm long.
　　　　　　　　Raceme sessile in the center of a rosette; petals all equal. .... 7. *Coronopus*
　　　　　　　　Raceme long peduncled; petals unequal, the outer pair larger than the
　　　　　　　　　　inner. (Fig. 531) .... 8. *Teesdalia*
　　　　　　　　　　　　　　　　　　　　　　　　　　　　　　　　　　　　　　　nudicaulis
A. Plant leafy-stemmed, with several-many stem leaves, with or without a basal
　　rosette.
　　G. Leaves all entire, serrate or crenate, not lobed or dissected.
　　　　H. Stem leaves auriculate-clasping, the lobes extending beyond other side of
　　　　　　stem. (Fig. 532).
　　　　　　I. Fruit or ovary more than 4 times as long as broad.
　　　　　　　　Fruit 4-sided; flowers yellow; plant glaucous. .... 9. *Conringia*
　　　　　　　　　　　　　　　　　　　　　　　　　　　　　　　　　　　　　　　orientalis
　　　　　　　　Fruit terete or flattened; flowers white or pink; plant usually not
　　　　　　　　　　glaucous. .... 6. *Arabis*
　　　　　　I. Fruit or ovary up to 4 times as long as broad.
　　　　　　　　J. Fruit or ovary scarcely flattened, plump; flowers yellow (white in *Cardaria*).
　　　　　　　　　　K. Fruit indehiscent.
　　　　　　　　　　　　Fruit reticulated; flowers yellow, in loose racemes. .... 10. *Neslia paniculata*
　　　　　　　　　　　　Fruit smooth; flowers white, in dense, corymbose racemes. .... 11. *Cardaria draba*
　　　　　　　　　　K. Fruit dehiscent, flowers yellow.
　　　　　　　　　　　　Fruit globose, not margined, less than 4 mm long. .... 12. *Rorippa*
　　　　　　　　　　　　Fruit obovate, with a rim-like margin, 5 mm or more long. .... 13. *Camelina*
　　　　　　　　J. Fruit or ovary flattened; flowers white (if yellow style wanting; present
　　　　　　　　　　in above species).
　　　　　　　　　　L. Fruit obcordate. (Fig. 539) .... 14. *Capsella bursa-*
　　　　　　　　　　　　　　　　　　　　　　　　　　　　　　　　　　　　　　　pastoris
　　　　　　　　　　L. Fruit oblong, subglobose, cordate or orbicular.

M. Fruit oblong, pendulous; flowers yellow. .... 15. *Isatis tinctoria*
M. Fruit subglobose, cordate or orbicular, ascending; flowers white.
   N. Fruit subglobose or cordate, indehiscent, not keeled or winged. .... 11. *Cardaria draba*
   N. Fruit orbicular, dehiscent, keeled or winged.
      Fruit 6 mm or less long; seeds 1 or 2 in each fruit. .... 16. *Lepidium*
      Fruit 7 mm or more long; seeds several in each fruit. .... 17. *Thlaspi*
H. Stem leaves not auriculate clasping or only slightly so.
  O. Plant in flower.
    P. Flowers yellow.
      Q. Leaves entire or essentially so. (Fig. 544).
        Ovary or fruit ovate to orbicular .... 18. *Alyssum*
                                                                alyssoides
        Ovary or fruit long and linear .... 19. *Erysimum*
      Q. Leaves toothed.
        R. Ovary or fruit transversely segmented into 2 unlike members.
          (Fig. 546). .... 20. *Rapistrum*
                                                                rugosum
        R. Ovary or fruit not transversely segmented.
          Plant glabrous or with pubescence of simple hairs; fruit not over
            1 cm long. .... 12. *Rorippa*
          Plant pubescent with forked hairs; fruit longer than 1 cm. .... 19. *Erysimum*
    P. Flowers white, pink or purple.
      S. Plant thick and fleshy; sandy beaches; ovary 2-jointed, the upper
        member longer than the lower .... 21. *Cakile*
      S. Plant not thick and fleshy; various habitats; ovary not 2-jointed.
        T. Leaves, at least the lower, more than 2 cm wide.
          U. Leaves deltoid, cordate-based.
            Ovary or fruit broadly elliptic; flowers purple. (Fig. 548). .... 22. *Lunaria annua*
            Ovary or fruit long and linear; flowers white. .... 23. *Alliaria petiolata*
          U. Leaves lanceolate or oblong.
            V. Ovary or fruit ellipsoid, obovoid or subglobose. .... 24. *Armoracia*
            V. Ovary or fruit elongate.
              Petals longer than 1 cm.. 25. *Hesperis*
                                                           matronalis
             Petals shorter than 1 cm .... 6. *Arabis*
        T. Leaves all less than 2 cm wide.
          W. Ovary or fruit orbicular to elliptic or oblong, 3 times or less as
            long as wide.
          X. Petals deeply 2-cleft. .... 26. *Berteroa*
          X. Petals rounded or merely emarginate, not deeply cleft.
            Y. Plant with a rosette at the base of the flowering stem or
              with rosettes on basal offshoots .... 5. *Draba*
            Y. Plant without basal rosettes.
              Z. Plant pubescent with stellate or appressed, forked hairs.
                Pubescence of stellate hairs .... 18. *Alyssum*
                                                                              alyssoides
                Pubescence of appressed, forked hairs. .... 27. *Lobularia*
                                                                                maritima
             Z. Plant glabrous, or with pubescence of very short, simple
              hairs.
               Petals unequal, the outer pair larger than the inner. .... 28. *Iberis*
               Petals all equal .... 16. *Lepidium*
         W. Ovary or fruit elongate, 4-many times as long as wide.
          a. Plant without a rosette at the base of the flowering stem;
            leaves, at least the lower, orbicular or nearly so .... 4. *Cardamine*
         a. Plant with a rosette at the base of the flowering stem or with
            rosettes on basal offshoots (sometimes absent in *Arabis*);
            leaves oblong to elliptic or lanceolate.
           b. Fruit flattened.

Fruit linear-oblong to lanceolate, mostly 2 cm or less
long; seeds in 2 rows in each locule .... 5. *Draba*
Fruit linear, 2.5 cm or more long; seeds in 1 row in each
locule. .... 6. *Arabis*
b. Fruit terete or subterete.
Plant annual, from a slender taproot; leaves oblong to
oblanceolate; fruit not torulose .... 3. *Arabidopsis*
thaliana

Plant perennial, from a branched caudex; leaves
linear-oblanceolate; fruit often torulose.
(Fig. 553) .... 29. *Braya humilis*
O. Plant in fruit.
c. Fruit transversely segmented into 2 unlike members.
Upper member subglobose, abruptly narrowed to a slender beak. .... 20. *Rapistrum*
rugosum

Upper member lanceolate to ovoid, gradually narrowed to a stout
beak. .... 21. *Cakile*
c. Fruit not transversely segmented into unlike members, though
sometimes constricted between the seeds and/or beaked.
d. Fruit 3 times or less as long as wide.
e. Fruit flattened at right angles to the septum, this indicated by a
vertical line on the center of both faces; often notched.
Fruit broadly winged in the upper half. .... 28. *Iberis*
Fruit wingless or uniformly narrowly winged. .... 16. *Lepidium*
e. Fruit scarcely flattened or flattened parallel to the septum, not
notched.
f. Fruit inflated, obovoid, ellipsoid or subglobose (sometimes not
fully developing in *Rorippa*).
Fruit tipped by a broad, conspicuous stigma; basal leaves
mostly 2 dm or more long .... 24. *Armoracia*
Fruit not tipped by a conspicuous stigma; basal leaves less
than 2 dm long. .... 12. *Rorippa*
f. Fruit distinctly flattened.
g. Fruit elliptic to oblong or lanceolate. (Fig. 552).
Plant low, tufted, the stems arising from a basal rosette or
with rosettes on basal offshoots .... 5. *Draba*
Plant tall, not tufted; basal rosettes lacking. .... 26. *Berteroa*
g. Fruit orbicular or nearly so, or broadly elliptic and more than
1 cm long and 6 mm wide (shorter and narrower in
above species). (Fig. 548).
h. Fruit more than 1 cm long .... 22. *Lunaria annua*
h. Fruit less than 1 cm long.
Pubescence of stellate hairs; fruit with a broad, rim-like
margin. .... 18. *Alyssum*
alyssoides

Pubescence of appressed, forked hairs; fruit with a
narrow, wire-like margin. .... 27. *Lobularia*
maritima
d. Fruit 4-many times as long as wide.
i. Fruit 4 cm or more long and largest leaves more than 2 cm wide.
Cauline leaves deltoid, cordate-based, with odor of onions.
(Fig. 549). .... 23. *Alliaria petiolata*
Cauline leaves lanceolate to ovate, without odor of onions. .... 25. *Hesperis*
matronalis
i. Fruit less than 4 cm long or largest leaves 2 cm or less wide
(sometimes wider in *Arabis* but fruits flat; fruits terete or
angled in above species).
j. Basal leaves more or less orbicular; plants glabrous. .... 4. *Cardamine*
j. Basal leaves not orbicular, or if somewhat so, plants pubescent.

k. Fruit flattened.
    Fruit less than 2 cm long .... 5. *Draba*
    Fruit more than 2 cm long .... 6. *Arabis*
k. Fruit terete or angled.
    l. Fruit less than 1 cm long... 12. *Rorippa*
    l. Fruit 1 cm or more long.
        m. Principal stem leaves 1-5, mostly entire. .... 3. *Arabidopsis*
                                                  thaliana
        m. Principal stem leaves more than 5, or fewer and
           distinctly toothed.
           Plant perennial, with many stems from base. .... 29. *Braya humilis*
           Plant annual or perennial, with usually only 1 stem
               from base. .... 19. *Erysimum*
G. Leaves, or some of them, lobed or dissected.
  n. Ovary or fruit transversely segmented into 2 unlike members.
    Upper member subglobose, abruptly narrowed to a slender beak; flowers
      yellow. .... 20. *Rapistrum*
                                                            rugosum
    Upper member lanceolate to ovoid, gradually narrowed to a stout beak;
      flowers white, pink or purple .... 21. *Cakile*
  n. Ovary or fruit not transversely segmented into unlike members, though
    sometimes constricted between the seeds and/or beaked.
    o. Plant in flower.
      p. Petals white, pink, green or absent.
        q. Plants aquatic.
          r. Leaves, at least the lower, dissected into numerous filiform
             segments. (Fig. 550) .... 24. *Armoracia*
          r. Leaf segments not filiform, broader.
             Stems rooted at lower nodes; plants forming mats. .... 12. *Rorippa*
             Stems not rooted at lower nodes, or plants not forming mats. .... 4. *Cardamine*
        q. Plants terrestrial.
          s. Leaves palmately divided into 3 or more segments. .... 4. *Cardamine*
          s. Leaves pinnately lobed or divided.
             t. Petals, including claw, 9-20 mm long.
                u. Lower leaves pinnatifid or lyrate; stem usually pubescent,
                   at least below. (Fig. 554).
                   Root thickened; pedicels 6 mm or more long. .... 30. *Raphanus*
                   Root not thickened; pedicels 5 mm or less long. .... 31. *Eruca vesicaria*
                                                           subsp. *sativa*
                u. Lower leaves pinnately divided, the leaflets orbicular or nearly
                   so, usually petiolulate; stem glabrous .... 4. *Cardamine*
             t. Petals, including claw, 8 mm or less long.
                v. Petals unequal, the outer pair larger than the inner. .... 8. *Teesdalia*
                                                      nudicaulis
                v. Petals equal, or essentially so.
                  w. Basal leaves mostly 2 dm or more long; petals 5-8 mm long. .. 24. *Armoracia*
                  w. Basal leaves less than 2 dm long or absent; petals less than
                    5 mm long (if longer ovary long and slender; ovary
                    ellipsoid, obovoid or suborbicular in the above species).
                  x. Leaves all pinnate or deeply divided.
                    y. Ovary or fruit long and slender .... 4. *Cardamine*
                    y. Ovary or fruit suborbicular or obovate.
                      Depressed and mat-forming; flowers in short,
                        lateral racemes. .... 7. *Coronopus*
                    Erect, not mat-forming; flowers in long, terminal
                        racemes. .... 16. *Lepidium*
                  x. Leaves, at least the upper, not pinnate or deeply divided.
                    z. Ovary or fruit long and slender .... 6. *Arabis*
                    z. Ovary or fruit suborbicular, obovate or obdeltoid.

Ovary or fruit obdeltoid; seeds several in each locule.
(Fig. 539). .... 14. *Capsella bursa-pastoris*

Ovary or fruit orbicular to obovate; seed 1 in each
locule. .... 16. *Lepidium*

p. Petals yellow.
  a.a. Plants pubescent, some or all of the hairs forked or branched;
        leaves bipinnate or bipinnatifid, with linear segments no more
        than 2 mm wide. (Fig. 556) .... 32. *Descurainia*
  a.a. Plants glabrous or with pubescence of all simple hairs; leaves once
        divided into coarser segments more than 2 mm wide (more
        divided with narrower segments in some species of *Sisymbrium*
        and *Rorippa*). (Fig. 557).
    b.b. Racemes with pinnatifid bracts subtending all, or all but the
        uppermost pedicels .... 33. *Erucastrum gallicum*

    b.b. Racemes bractless or bracts subtending only the lowest pedicels.
      c.c. Stem leaves auriculate-clasping.
        d.d. Ovary or fruit elliptic, oblong or suborbicular, 4 times or
          less as long as wide.
          Upper cauline leaves subrotund, entire. .... 16. *Lepidium*
          Upper cauline leaves oblong to lanceolate, lobed or toothed. 12. *Rorippa*
        d.d. Ovary or fruit elongate, many times longer than wide.
          Ovary or fruit prominently beaked, this longer than 5 mm
            when mature; mature pedicels 1 cm or more long ... 34. *Brassica*
          Ovary or fruit not prominently beaked, this shorter than 5
            mm when mature; mature pedicels 8 mm or less
            long .... 35. *Barbarea*
      c.c. Stem leaves not auriculate-clasping.
        e.e. Petals, including claw, 1-2 cm long.
          f.f. Ovary with spongy cross partitions separating the ovules;
            fruit indehiscent .... 30. *Raphanus*
          f.f. Ovary lacking cross partitions; fruit dehiscent.
            Petals 14 mm or less long, without violet veins. .... 34. *Brassica*
            Petals 15-20 mm long, with violet veins. .... 31. *Eruca vesicaria*
                                    subsp. *sativa*
        e.e. Petals, including claw, less than 1 cm long.
          g.g. Ovary or fruit elliptic, oblong or obliquely ovoid, 4 times
            or less as long as wide.
            Stem and inflorescence glandular; ovary and fruit
              obliquely ovoid, glandular, indehiscent.
              (Fig. 560) .... 36. *Bunias orientalis*
            Stem and inflorescence not glandular; ovary and fruit
               elliptic or oblong, not glandular, dehiscent .... 12. *Rorippa*
          g.g. Ovary or fruit elongate, many times longer than wide.
            h.h. Ovules or seeds in 2 rows in each locule (fruit sometimes
              not fully developing in *Rorippa*).
              Flowers 5 mm or less wide .... 12. *Rorippa*
              Flowers 8 mm or more wide .... 1. *Diplotaxis*
            h.h. Ovules or seeds in 1 row in each locule.
             i.i. Ovary and fruit not prominently beaked. .... 37. *Sisymbrium*
            i.i. Ovary and fruit prominently beaked.
              Beak flat; ovary and fruit bristly or sometimes
               glabrous. .... 38. *Sinapis*
              Beak terete; ovary and fruit glabrous. .... 34. *Brassica*

o. Plant in fruit.
  j.j. Fruit 3 times or less as long as wide.
    k.k. Fruit strongly flattened.
      l.l. Fruit flattened at right angles to the septum, this indicated by a
        vertical line on the center of both faces.

m.m. Fruit obdeltoid. (Fig. 539) .... 14. *Capsella bursa-pastoris*

m.m. Fruit orbicular, obovate, or wider than long.
   n.n. Fruits in lateral racemes, rugose or tuberculate, broader
      than long. .... 7. *Coronopus*
   n.n. Fruits in terminal racemes, smooth, as long as broad or
      longer.
      Seeds 2 in each locule; leaves small, few, occurring mostly
         below middle of stem. (Fig. 531) .... 8. *Teesdalia nudicaulis*
      Seeds 1 in each locule; leaves moderate, few to many,
         occurring above and below middle of stem .... 16. *Lepidium*
l.l. Fruit flattened parallel to the septum. .... 32. *Descurainia*
k.k. Fruit turgid, subglobose ovoid or obovoid.
  o.o. Fruit indehiscent.
     Fruit obliquely ovoid, rugose, less than 1 cm long (including
      beak); beak less than half as long as the body. (Fig. 560). 36. *Bunias orientalis*
     Fruit globose to cylindric, smooth, longer than 1 cm
      (including beak); beak more than half as long as the
      body. .... 30. *Raphanus*
  o.o. Fruit longitudinally dehiscent, the valves separating and exposing
     the septum and seeds.
     Plant aquatic, with submersed leaves divided into capillary
      segments, or terrestrial and basal leaves mostly 2 dm
      or more long. (Fig. 550). .... 24. *Armoracia*
     Plant terrestrial, with basal leaves less than 2 dm long, or if
      aquatic, submersed leaves not divided into capillary
      segments. .... 12. *Rorippa*
j.j. Fruit 4-many times as long as wide.
  p.p. Fruit indehiscent .... 30. *Raphanus*
  p.p. Fruit dehiscent.
    q.q. Plants pubescent, some or all of the hairs forked or branched;
      leaves bipinnate or bipinnatifid, with linear segments no
      more than 2 mm wide. (Fig. 556) .... 32. *Descurainia*
    q.q. Plants glabrous or with pubescence of all simple hairs (some
      hairs branched in *Arabis*); leaves once divided into coarser
      segments more than 2 mm wide (more divided with narrower
      segments in some species of *Sisymbrium* and *Rorippa*).
      r.r. Seeds in 2 rows in each locule of the fruit (fruit sometimes not
        fully developing in *Rorippa*).
        s.s. Plants aquatic, succulent, forming mats; stems rooted at
          lower nodes. .... 12. *Rorippa*
        s.s. Plant terrestrial or bordering, not succulent or mat-forming;
          stems not rooting at lower nodes.
          t.t. Fruit with a flat, lanceolate-triangular beak 5 mm or more
            long. .... 31. *Eruca vesicaria* subsp. *sativa*
          t.t. Fruit with a terete, somewhat slender beak 4 mm or less
            long.
            Fruits mostly 2 cm or more long, with a distinct
             midnerve on each valve. .... 1. *Diplotaxis*
            Fruits mostly less than 2 cm long, the valves nerveless or
             indistinctly nerved .... 12. *Rorippa*
      r.r. Seeds in 1 row in each locule of the fruit.
        u.u. Fruits flattened.
          Plant glabrous or with simple hairs; seeds wingless. .... 4. *Cardamine*
          Plant with pubescence of simple and branched hairs; seeds
            narrowly winged. .... 6. *Arabis*
        u.u. Fruits terete or angled.
          v.v. Fruit with a beak 5 mm or more long.

Beak flat; fruit bristly or glabrous. .... 38. *Sinapis*
Beak terete; fruit glabrous .... 34. *Brassica*
v.v. Fruit with a beak 4 mm or less long.
  w.w. Stem leaves auriculate-clasping. (Fig. 559). .... 35. *Barbarea*
  w.w. Stem leaves not auriculate-clasping.
    Fruits with 1 nerve on each valve, at least the lower
      ones subtended by leafy bracts.......................... 33. *Erucastrum*
                                          gallicum
    Fruits with 1 main nerve and 2 less prominent ones
      on each valve, none subtended by leafy bracts . 37. *Sisymbrium*

1. *Diplotáxis* DC. (from the Greek, referring to the 2 rows of seeds).

Erect or decumbent, branching, annual or perennial herbs, glabrous or with pubescence of simple hairs; leaves oblanceolate to narrowly oblong, the basal sometimes forming rosettes, pinnatifid to coarsely toothed, petioled; flowers yellow (rarely white or purple; sometimes purple on drying), in terminal racemes; capsule a flattened silique, the valves 1-nerved, short-beaked, seeds in 2 irregular rows in each cell.

Leaves in basal rosettes, and sometimes 1 or 2 on the lower part of the stem; fruit
  not stipitate. (Fig. 521) .... 1. *D. muralis*
Leaves extending up the stem nearly to the inflorescence; fruit on a stipe up to
  2 mm long .... 2. *D. tenuifolia*

  1. *D. murális* (L.) DC. (growing on walls). Sand-rocket. Waste places. Fruit: July-September. Fig. 521, Map 1129. (Naturalized from Europe).

  2. *D. tenuifólia* (L.) DC. (slender leaved). Wall-rocket. Waste places. Fruit: July-September. Map 1130. (Naturalized from Europe).

  D. erucoídes (L.) DC. Differing from the above 2 species in being hirsute on the pedicels and backs of the sepals and in having white or purple petals with purple veins (pedicels and backs of sepals glabrous and petals yellow in the above 2 species). European. Occurring as a waif. Reported for Suffolk County NY.

2. *Subulária* L. Awlwort (an awl; based on the awl-shaped leaves).

Small, scapose, glabrous, aquatic, submerged or emergent, annual herbs; leaves all in a basal rosette, linear and awl-shaped, cauline leaves none; flowers minute, white, few and sparse, in a raceme on a naked scape; fruit an ovoid to ellipsoid or globose, inflated silicle, long pedicelled, somewhat flattened perpendicular to the septum, seeds several in each locule.

  1. *S. aquàtica* L. (aquatic). Submerged in shallow water along the margins of freshwater ponds and lakes, rarely emergent. Fruit: July-October. Fig. 522, Map 1131. (Eurasia, Greenland). Represented with us as var. *americána* (Mulligan & Calder) Boivin. —OBL

3. *Arabidópsis* Heynh. Mouse-ear-Cress (name based on resemblance to Arabis).

Low, annual herbs with slender, simple or branched stems and pubescence of simple or forked hairs; leaves basal and cauline, the former oblong to oblanceolate, entire or toothed, petiolate, forming rosettes, stem leaves smaller, linear to narrowly oblong, often entire, sessile; flowers white, racemose; fruit a slender, subterete or somewhat 4-sided silique, glabrous, seeds in 1 or 2 rows in each locule, the siliques widely spaced in the mature, open raceme.

  Choríspora ténella, a species with beaked fruit possibly keying here, is described under *Braya* (genus 29).

  1. *A. thaliána* (L.) Heynh. (for J. Thal). Fields, roadsides and waste places. Fruit: May-June. Map 1132. (Naturalized from Europe). [*Sisymbrium t.*].

4. *Cardámine* L. Bitter cress (ancient Greek name for a cress).

Essentially glabrous (rarely hirsute), annual or perennial herbs; leaves pinnately or palmately compound or lobed, or simple and crenate or entire, sessile or petioled, alternate, subopposite or subwhorled, some species forming basal rosettes, with or without stem leaves, or arising apart from the stem, other species only with stem leaves; flowers white, pink or purple, in racemes or corymbs; petals rarely absent, stamens fewer than 6 in some species; fruit a linear silique, usually flattened, with a persistent style, valves coiling from the base at maturity, seeds in 1 row in each locule.

Choríspora tenélla, a species with beaked fruit possibly keying here, is described under Braya (genus 29).

a. Leaves ternately or palmately compound. (Fig. 523).
  b. Rhizome long and continuous, of constant diameter or with constrictions;
      rachis of inflorescence glabrous or essentially so; leaflets mostly ovate,
      coarsely crenate-dentate.
      Rhizome of constant diameter; stem leaves usually 2; hairs on the margins
        of the leaflets appressed .... 1. *C. diphylla*
      Rhizome with enlarged and constricted regions; stem leaves often 3; hairs on
        the margins of the leaflets spreading. .... 2. *C. maxima*
  b. Rhizome not continuous, of readily separable segments; rachis of inflorescence
      pubescent; leaflets mostly linear or lanceolate, sharply laciniate-toothed .... 3. *C. concatenata*
a. Leaves simple, or pinnately compound or lobed.
  c. Leaves simple, entire or coarsely toothed, not compound or deeply divided.
      (Fig. 524).
    d. Tuberous based; upper leaves sessile; pedicels (at least the lower) usually
      1 cm or more long; petals longer than 5 mm.
      Sepals purple; petals pink to purple; stem somewhat pubescent. .... 4. *C. douglassii*
      Sepals green to yellow; petals white; stem glabrous. .... 5. *C. rhomboidea*
    d. Fibrous-rooted; leaves all petioled; pedicels usually less than 1 cm long
      (sometimes longer in *C. pensylvanica*); petals shorter than 5 mm
      or absent.
      e. Dwarf, alpine, 1 dm or less tall; axis of raceme scarcely elongating after
        anthesis, the silicles approximate and erect. (Fig. 524). .... 6. *C. bellidifolia*
      e. Mostly 1 dm or more tall; axis of raceme elongating after anthesis; the
        silicles ascending.
      Flowers more than 5 mm long, apetalous, siliques mostly less than
        1.5 cm long. .... 7. *C. longii*
      Flowers less than 5 mm long, petaliferous; siliques mostly more than
        1.5 cm long .... 8. *C. pensylvanica*
  c. Leaves, or most of them, pinnately compound or deeply divided. (Fig. 525).
    f. Cauline leaves with prolonged, sagittate bases. .... 9. *C. impatiens*
    f. Cauline leaves without sagittate bases.
      g. Petals more than 5 mm long; flower 6 mm or more wide. .... 10. *C. pratensis*
      g. Petals less than 5 mm long; flower less than 6 mm wide.
      Terminal leaflet of cauline leaves usually significantly wider than the
        lateral; leaves mostly 4-8 cm long; leaflets often decurrent along
        the rachis. (Fig. 525) .... 8. *C. pensylvanica*
      Terminal leaflet of cauline leaves not usually significantly wider than
        the lateral; leaves mostly 4 cm or less long; leaflets distinct,
        not decurrent.
      Basal leaves few or absent; petioles of stem leaves glabrous. .... 11. *C. parviflora*
      Basal leaves numerous; petioles of stem leaves hirsute at the base. .... 12. *C. hirsuta*

1. *C. diphýlla* (Michx.) Wood (two-leaved). Two-leaved Toothwort. Rich, moist woods. April-May. Fig. 523, Map 1133. [(*Dentaria d.*]. The roots of this and the next 2 species can be eaten plain or made into a condiment similar to horseradish. —FACU

    C. x anómala (Eames) K. Schum. (pro sp.). A hybrid between *C. diphylla* and *C. concatenata*.

    2. *C. máxima* (Nutt.) Wood (greatest). Large Toothwort. Rich, moist woods. April-May. Map 1134. [*Dentaria m.*].

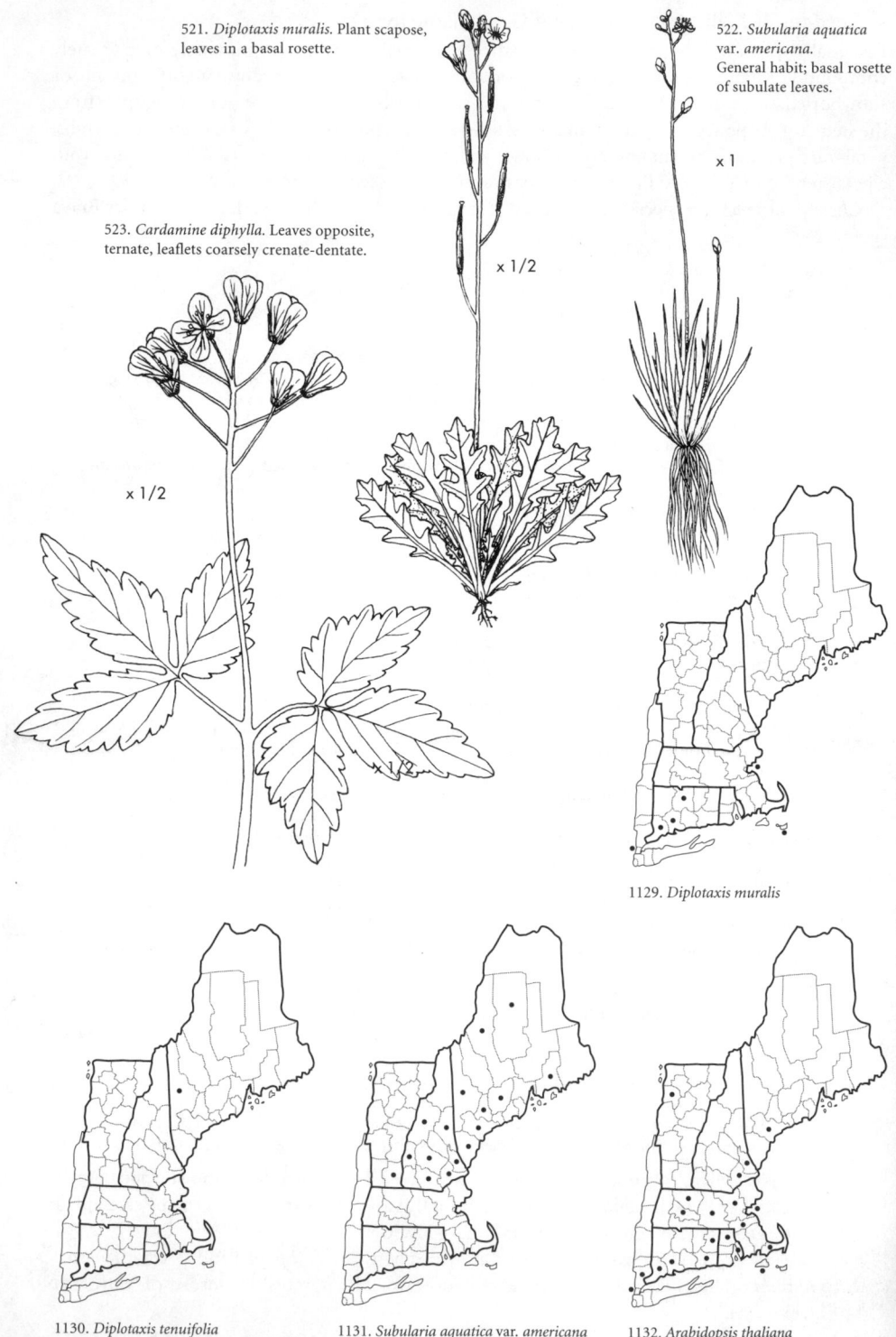

521. *Diplotaxis muralis.* Plant scapose, leaves in a basal rosette.

522. *Subularia aquatica* var. *americana.* General habit; basal rosette of subulate leaves.

× 1

523. *Cardamine diphylla.* Leaves opposite, ternate, leaflets coarsely crenate-dentate.

× 1/2

× 1/2

× 1/2

1129. *Diplotaxis muralis*

1130. *Diplotaxis tenuifolia*

1131. *Subularia aquatica* var. *americana*

1132. *Arabidopsis thaliana*

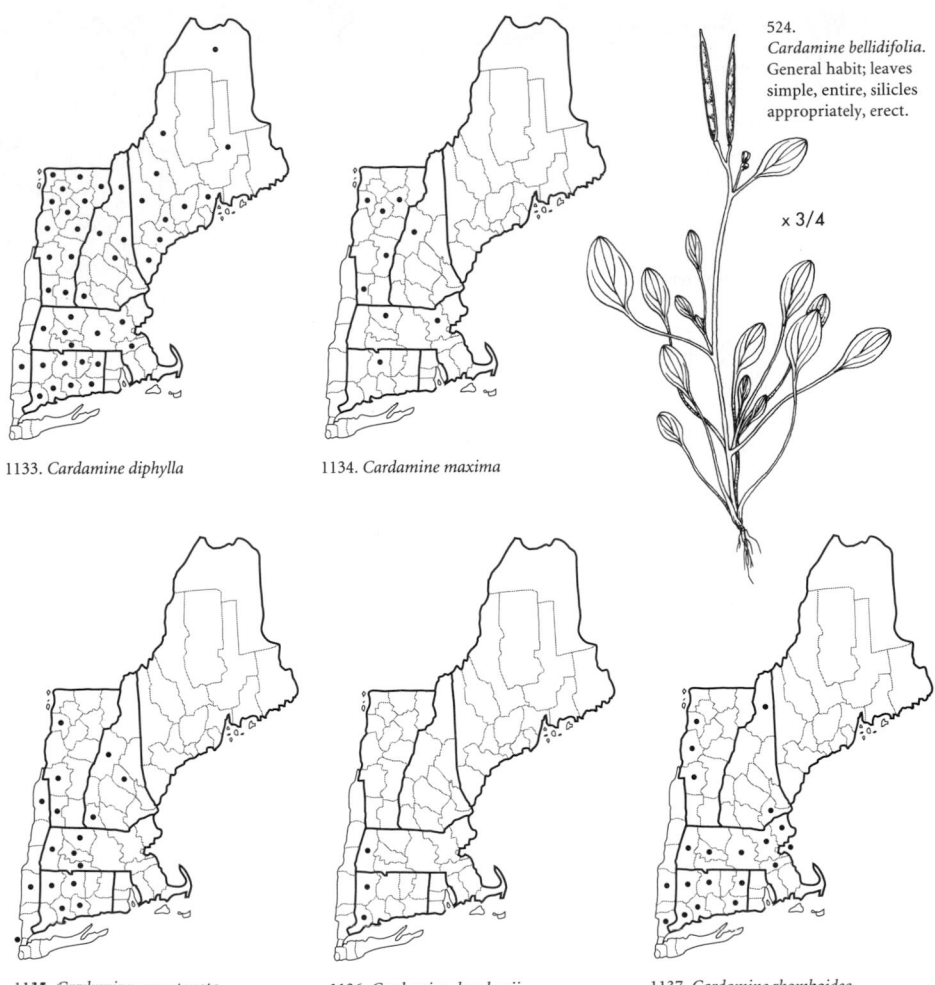

524.
Cardamine bellidifolia.
General habit; leaves
simple, entire, silicles
appropriately, erect.

x 3/4

1133. *Cardamine diphylla*

1134. *Cardamine maxima*

1135. *Cardamine concatenata*

1136. *Cardamine douglassii*

1137. *Cardamine rhomboidea*

3. C. concaténata (Michx.) Sw. Cut-leaved Toothwort. Rich, moist woods, April-May. Map 1135. [*Dentaria laciniata*]. —FACU

C. x. incísa K. Schum. (pro sp.). A hybrid between *C. concatenata* and *C. maxima*.

4. C. douglássii Britt. (for its discoverer). Rich, moist woods. March-May. Map 1136. Endangered in MA. —FACW+

5. C. rhomboídea (Pers.) DC. Spring-Cress. Wet woods. April-June. Map 1137. Rare. Endangered in NH. [*C. bulbosa*]. —OBL

6. C. bellidifólia L. (with leaves like Bellis). Alpine Cress. Alpine summits in the White Mountains, N.H., and on Mt. Katahdin, ME. Fruit: June-August. Fig. 524, Map 1138. (n. Eurasia). Endangered in NH, ME. Our plants are var. *bellidifolia*. —FACW

7. C. lóngii Fern. (for one of its discoverers). Borders of tidal estuaries, Bowdoinham, ME, and Charles River, MA. Fruit: June-September. Map 1139. Endangered in MA, RI. —OBL

8. C. pensylvánica Muhl. ex Willd. (of Pennsylvania). Common Bitter Cress. Swamps, wet woods, wet meadows, stream and pond margins and shallow water. Fruit: June-September. Fig. 525, Map 1140. Can be used in salads as a substitute for watercress. —OBL

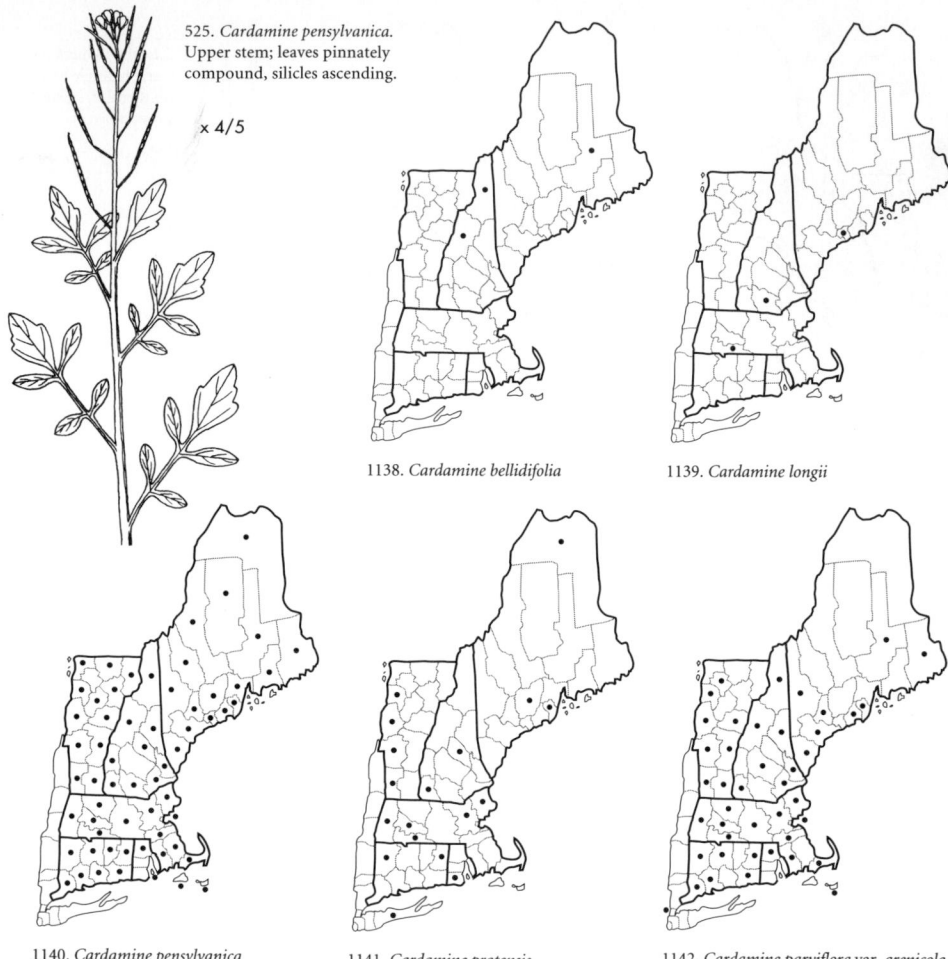

525. *Cardamine pensylvanica.*
Upper stem; leaves pinnately
compound, silicles ascending.

× 4/5

1138. *Cardamine bellidifolia*

1139. *Cardamine longii*

1140. *Cardamine pensylvanica*

1141. *Cardamine pratensis*

1142. *Cardamine parviflora* var. *arenicola*

9. C. impátiens L. (impatient). Shaded meadows and lawns. Fruit: July-August. (Adventive from Europe). Reported for CT, Hillsboro County NH.

10. C. praténsis L. (of meadows). Cuckoo-flower. Meadows, lawns and roadsides in moist soil. May-June. Map 1141. (Naturalized from Europe). Can be used in salads as a substitute for watercress. —OBL

11. C. parviflóra L. (small-flowered). Dry rocky or sandy woods. Fruit: May-September. (Eurasia). Our plants include var. *pariflora* (reported for ME, RI) and the following var.:

var. *arenicola* (Britt.) O. E. Schulz. Leaflets of basal leaves usually obovate to suborbicular and with 1 or more pairs of teeth; petals 2.5 mm or more long (leaflets of basal leaves oblong, usually entire, and petals 2.5 mm or less long in var. *parviflora*). Map 1142. —FACU

12. C. hirsúta L. (with stiff hairs). Old fields, lawns, roadsides. March-April. (Naturalized from Europe). From farther south and west. Reported for CT, MA, Suffolk and Westchester Counties NY. —FACU

C. flexuósa With. Similar to *C. hirsuta* but with stems hirsute, stem leaves similar to the basal (stems glabrous and stem leaves unlike the basal in *C. hirsuta*). From farther north. Reported for NH. —OBL

5. _Dràba_ L. (ancient Greek name for a cress).

Low, tufted, scapose or leafy-stemmed, annual or perennial herbs with basal rosettes and simple, branched or stellate pubescence; leaves alternate or the lower subopposite in some species, simple, toothed or entire; flowers in terminal racemes, the petals white (ours), rounded, emarginate, bifid, or rarely none; fruit a silicle or silique, elliptic, oblong or linear, flattened parallel to the septum, seeds in 2 rows in each locule.

a. Siliques densely stellate-pubescent. .... 1. _D. cana_
a. Siliques glabrous or essentially so.
  b. Leaves with simple, forked or stellate pubescence.
    c. Stems leafless, or with leaves restricted to the lower third; plants annual.
      (Fig. 526).
      Stem leaves absent; longest fruiting pedicels more than 6 mm long; petals
        deeply cleft .... 2. _D. verna_
      Stem with several leaves occurring on the lower third; longest fruiting
        pedicels 6 mm or less long; petals rounded or absent. .... 3. _D. reptans_
    c. Stems with leaves occurring above the lower third, often to the base of the
      raceme; plants perennial, often forming mats.
      Siliques twisted; cauline leaves narrowed to an acute base. .... 4. _D. arabisans_
      Siliques flat; cauline leaves mostly rounded at the base. .... 5. _D. glabella_
  b. Leaves glabrous although often ciliate; stems leafless or with 1 leaf occurring
    near the base .... 6. _D. lactea_

1. _D. càna_ Rydb. Cliffs and rocks in the mountains of ME, NH, and VT. Fruit: June-August. Map 1143. (Asia). Endangered in ME. [_D. lanceolata; D. stylaris_].

    D. incàna L. Will key either to _D. cana_ or _D. glabella_ depending upon whether the fruits are glabrous or stellate; distinguishable from the latter 2 species in having numerous stem leaves similar to and merging with the rosette leaves (stem leaves few and different from the rosette leaves in the latter 2 species). (Canada, Eurasia). Reported for Orleans County VT.

    2. _D. vérna_ L. (of spring). Whitlow-grass. Fields, cultivated ground, roadsides and waste places. Fruit: April-May. Map 1144. (Naturalized from Europe). [_Erophila v._].

    3. _D. réptans_ (Lam.) Fern. (creeping). Dry sandy or rocky fields. Fruits: April-June. Fig. 526, Map 1145. [_D. caroliniana; D. micrantha_]. Our plants are var. _reptans_.

    4. _D. aràbisans_ Michx. (passing to _Arabis_) Ledges, cliffs and gravelly soil. Fruit: July. Map 1146.

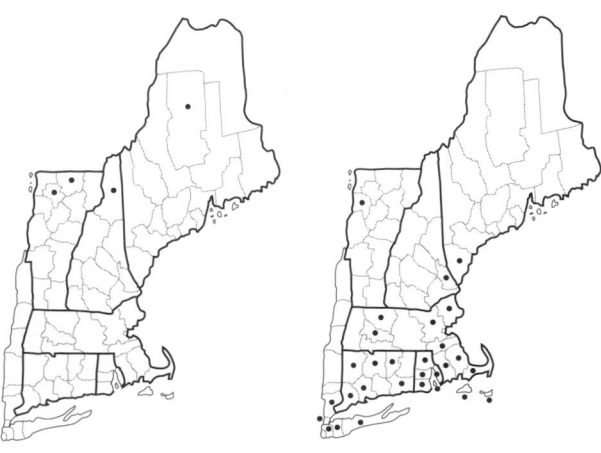

1143. _Draba cana_   1144. _Draba verna_

5. *D. glabélla* Pursh (becoming smooth). Calcareous rock. (Eurasia). Reported for VT, NY. Endangered in NY. Our plants include var. *glabella* and the following var.:

var. *orthocárpa* (Fern. & Knowlt.) Fern. Stem leaves 5 or more (5 or fewer in var. *glabella*).

6. *D. láctea* M. F. Adams. Mt. Katahdin, ME. Rare. [*D. allenii*].

6. *Árabis* L. Rock-cress (from Arabia).

Simple stemmed to much branched, annual or perennial herbs, glabrous or with pubescence of simple, forked or stellate hairs; leaves basal and cauline, the former petioled, entire, toothed or pinnatifid, forming rosettes in some species, cauline leaves entire or toothed, usually sessile, sagittate-based in some species; flowers white, yellowish or purplish, in terminal racemes; fruit a linear silique, flattened or subterate, seeds in 1 or 2 rows, often winged.

Iodánthus T. & G. *pinnatífidus* (Michx.) Steud. Often keying to *Arabis* but is distinguishable in having leaves pinnatifid only at the base with a much larger terminal lobe (when deeply divided leaves are present), fruits widely divergent (*Arabis* is more evenly pinnatifid, with lobes about the same size and shape and fruits are closely appressed). From farther south and west. Reported for CT. —FACW

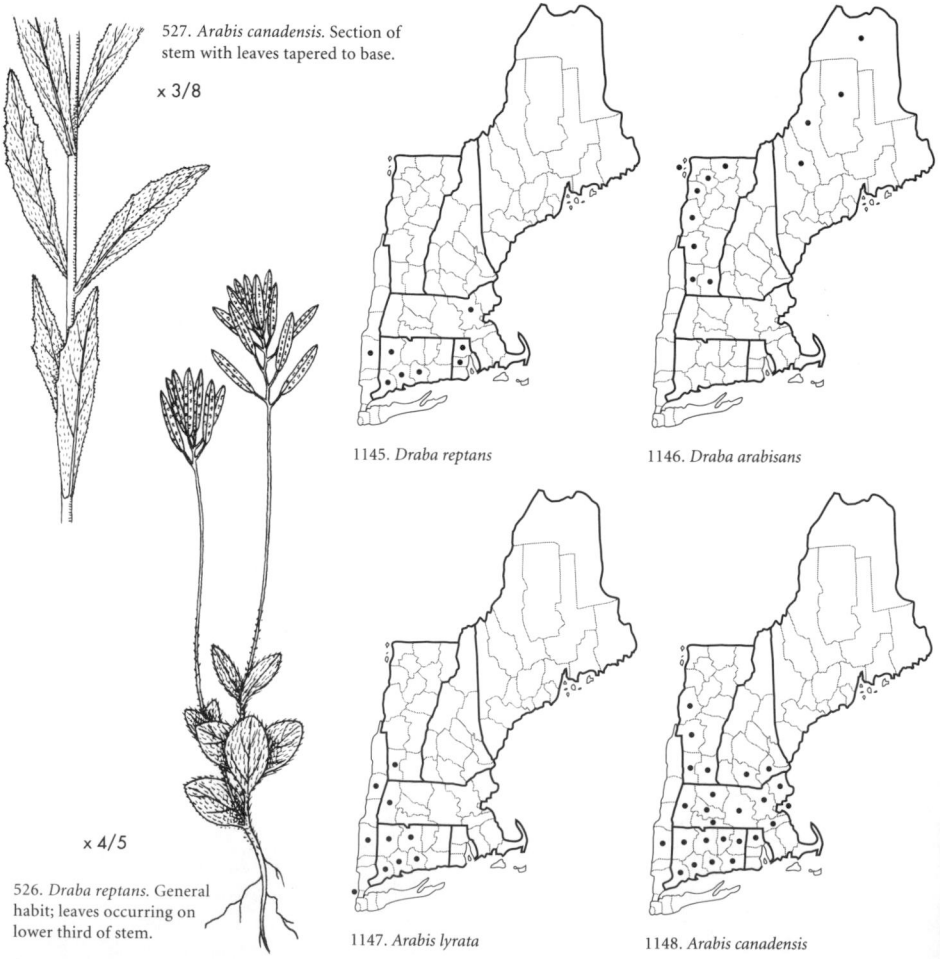

527. *Arabis canadensis*. Section of stem with leaves tapered to base.

x 3/8

x 4/5

526. *Draba reptans*. General habit; leaves occurring on lower third of stem.

1145. *Draba reptans*

1146. *Draba arabisans*

1147. *Arabis lyrata*

1148. *Arabis canadensis*

a. Cauline leaves not auricled or sagittate at the base. (Fig. 527).
  b. Siliques less than 5 cm long; largest leaves 4 cm or less long; plant usually
     several-branched from the base. .... 1. *A. lyrata*
  b. Siliques 5 cm or more long; largest leaves more than 4 cm long; plant
     simple-stemmed or with 1 or 2 basal branches.
     Cauline leaves pubescent; lowest part of stem sparsely pubescent. .... 2. *A. canadensis*
     Cauline leaves glabrous; lowest part of stem glabrous. .... 3. *A. laevigata*
a. Cauline leaves, at least the median, mostly auricled or sagittate at the base.
  (Fig. 528).
  c. Lowest part of stem pubescent.
    d. Fruiting pedicels ascending to spreading.
     Stems matted, several-branched at the base, densely spreading-pubescent
     below. .... 4. *A. alpina*
     Stems erect or strongly ascending, simple or with 1 or 2 basal branches,
     sparsely appressed-pubescent below .... 5. *A. divaricarpa*
    d. Fruiting pedicels appressed or subappressed. (Fig. 528).
     Lower cauline leaves glabrous; siliques terete or nearly so; seeds merely
     margined .... 6. *A. glabra*
     Lower cauline leaves pubescent; siliques flat; seeds distinctly winged. .... 7. *A. hirsuta*
        var. *pycnocarpa*
  c. Lowest part of stem glabrous.
    e. Fruiting pedicels appressed or subappressed. (Fig. 528).
     Siliques terete or nearly so; seeds merely margined; rosette leaves often
     pubescent .... 6. *A. glabra*
     Siliques flat; seeds distinctly winged; rosette leaves glabrous. .... 8. *A. drummondii*
    e. Fruiting pedicels ascending to spreading.
     f. Stem leaves 10 or fewer, if more then some of them 7 cm or more long and
      serrate toward apex; petals 3-5 mm long. .... 3. *A. laevigata*
     f. Stem leaves more than 10; less than 7 cm long or if longer entire; petals
      5-8 mm long.
      Rosette leaves glabrous, these and the lower cauline leaves pinnately
      dissected or laciniate. (Fig. 529) .... 9. *A. missouriensis*
      Rosette leaves stellate-pubescent, these and the lower cauline leaves
      dentate to entire .... 5. *A. divaricarpa*

1. *A. lyráta* L. (lyre-shaped). Ledges, rocky or sandy woods, clearings and fields. Fruit: May-July. Map 1147. Our plants are var. *lyrata*. —FACU

A. procúrrens Waldst. & Kit. Resembling *A. lyrata* but basal leaves entire or with 1 tooth on each side and stem leaves broad at the base (basal leaves usually pinnatifid or dentate and stem leaves narrowed to base in *A. lyrata*). Rarely escaped from cultivation. Reported for Middlesex County MA.

2. *A. canadénsis* L. (Canadian). Sickle-pod. Rich or rocky woods and thickets. Fruit: June-September. Fig. 527, Map 1148.

3. *A. laevigáta* (Muhl. ex Willd.) Poir. (smoothed). Dry, rocky woods and slopes, ledges. Fruit: June-August. Map 1149. Endangered in ME. Our plants are var. *laevigata*.

4. *A. alpína* L. (alpine). Rocky, gravelly or springy slopes and meadows. Fruit: July-September. (Europe). Rare. Reported for Knox County ME. —FAC+

A. caucásica Willd. Similar to *A. alpina* but with leaves whitish-tomentose beneath with 3 or fewer teeth on each margin, petals to 1.5 cm long (leaves thinly to moderately pubescent, with up to 6 teeth on each margin, petals less than 1 cm long in *A. alpina*). Escaped from cultivation. Reported for ME.

5. *A. x divaricárpa* A. Nels. (with spreading fruit). Ledges, gravelly, sandy or rocky areas. Fruit: June-August. Map 1150. [*A. brachycarpa; A. confinis*]. —FACU

6. *A. glábra* (L.) Bernh. (smooth). Tower Mustard. Open woods, fields, ledges and waste places. Fruit: June-September. Fig. 528, Map 1151. (Eurasia). [*Turritis g.*]. Our plants are var. *glabra*.

7. *A. hirsúta* (L.) Scop. (hirsute). Limestone ledges and rocks, rich woods, waste places. Fruit: June-August. Map 1152. Endangered in NH. Represented with us as var. *pycnocarpa* (Hopkins) Rollins. —FACU

8. A. drummóndii Gray (for its discoverer). Ledges, rocky slopes, woodlands and thickets. Fruit: May-August. Map 1153. Endangered in VT. —FACU

9. A. missouriénsis Greene (of Missouri). Ledges and rocky woods. Fruit: June-September. Fig. 529, Map 1154. [*A. viridis*].

7. Corónopus Zinn Wart-cress (from the Greek, based on the pinnatifid leaves).

Procumbent or diffuse, foetid, annual or biennial herbs with freely branched, radiating stems, glabrous or with pubescence of simple hairs; leaves oblong, pinnatifid, petioled to sessile; flowers minute, white, in axillary or lateral racemes, stamens often only 2; fruit a silicle, suborbicular in outline, notched at the apex or not, rugose or tuberculate, flattened perpendicular to the septum, indehiscent, seed 1 in each locule.

Silicles didymous, notched at the apex, rugose but not tuberculate, less than 3 mm
    wide. (Fig. 530) .... 1. *C. didymus*
Silicle valves not distinctly separate, silicle not notched at apex, tuberculate, mostly
    3 mm or more wide. .... 2. *C. squamatus*

1. C. dídymus (L.) Sm. (twin). Waste places, roadsides and fields. Fruit: June-September. Fig. 530, Map 1155. (Naturalized from Europe). [*Carara d.*].

2. C. squamátus (Forsk.) Aschers. Waste places. Fruit: June-September. Map 1156. (Adventive from Europe). [*C. procumbens*].

8. Teesdália Ait. f. Shepherd-cress (for R. Teesdale).

Small, erect, simple or slightly branched, glabrous, annual herbs; leaves in a basal rosette, oblanceolate, pinnatifid, petioled, stem leaves absent or few, small, occurring mostly below the middle, sessile or petioled; flowers small, white, in terminal racemes, 2 of the petals much longer than the other 2; fruit an orbicular to obovate silicle, winged in the upper half, retuse at the apex, flattened perpendicular to the septum, seeds 2 in each locule.

1. T. nudicaúlis Ait. f. (naked-stemmed). Sandy fields, roadsides and waste places. Fruit: May-July. Fig. 531. (Naturalized from Europe). Reported for CT, Barnstable and Nantucket Counties MA.

9. Conríngia Heister ex Fabr. Hare's-ear mustard (for H. Conring).

Erect, glabrous, simple to slightly branched, annual herbs; leaves oval to elliptic, entire, the middle and upper auriculate-clasping, the lower tapered to the base; flowers yellow to creamy-white, racemose; siliques long and slender, terete, becoming 4-angled, gradually tapering to a short beak, seeds in 1 row in each locule.

1. C. orientális (L.) Andrz. (eastern). Roadsides, waste places, cultivated ground. Fruit: June-August. Fig. 532, Map 1157. (Naturalized from Europe). Feeding on grain containing large quantities of seeds may cause poisoning in livestock.

10. Néslia Desv. Ball Mustard (for J. de Nesle).

Erect annual herbs, simple up to the inflorescence, pubescent with forked hairs; leaves oblong to lanceolate, sagittate-clasping, entire or denticulate; flowers small, yellow, in terminal racemes; fruit a small, subglobose, indehiscent silicle with a reticulated surface and a persistent style, long-pedicelled, or obscurely 2-locular, 1 (rarely 2) seeded.

1. N. paniculáta (L.) Desv. (with panicles). Waste places. Fruit: June-September. Fig. 533, Map 1158. (Naturalized from Europe).

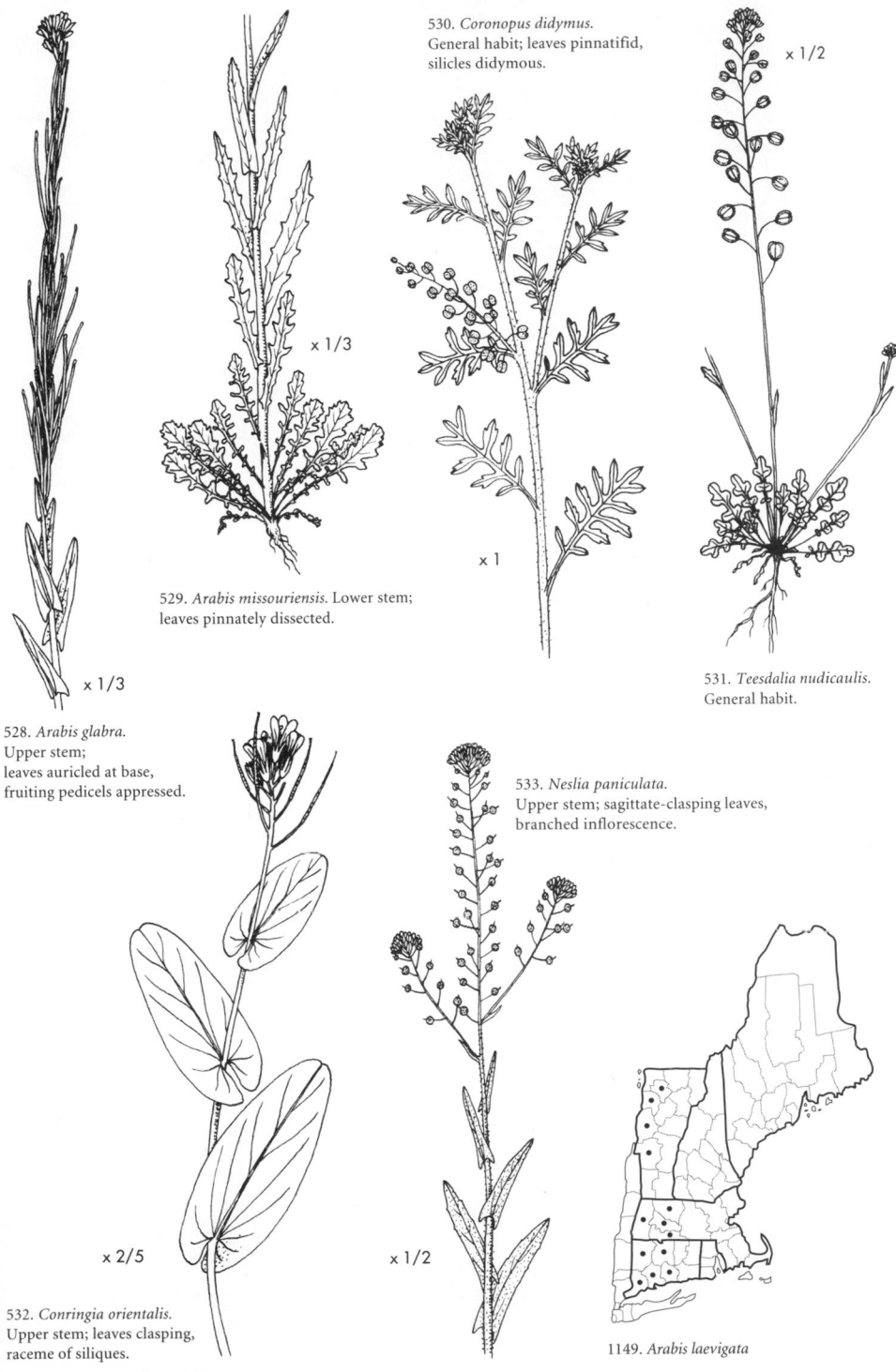

530. *Coronopus didymus.*
General habit; leaves pinnatifid,
silicles didymous.

× 1/2

× 1/3

529. *Arabis missouriensis.* Lower stem;
leaves pinnately dissected.

× 1

531. *Teesdalia nudicaulis.*
General habit.

× 1/3

528. *Arabis glabra.*
Upper stem;
leaves auricled at base,
fruiting pedicels appressed.

533. *Neslia paniculata.*
Upper stem; sagittate-clasping leaves,
branched inflorescence.

× 2/5

× 1/2

532. *Conringia orientalis.*
Upper stem; leaves clasping,
raceme of siliques.

1149. *Arabis laevigata*

1150. *Arabis x divaricarpa*

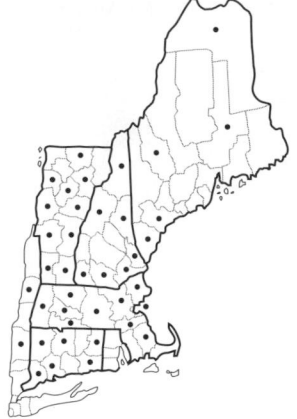

1151. *Arabis glabra*

1152. *Arabis hirsuta* var. *pycnocarpa*

1153. *Arabis drummondii*

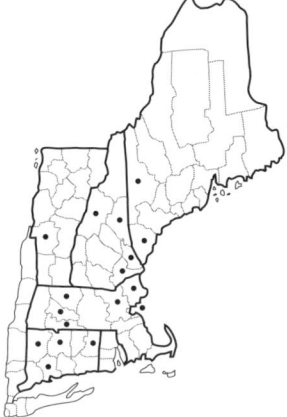

1154. *Arabis missouriensis*

1155. *Coronopus didymus*

1156. *Coronopus squamatus*

1157. *Conringia orientalis*

1158. *Neslia paniculata*

11. Cardária Desv. (name based on the cordiform fruit of another species).

Erect, short-pubescent, perennial herbs from rhizomes; leaves oblong to ovate, dentate to entire, the basal petioled, the cauline sessile and auriculate-clasping; flowers small, white, numerous in short, dense, terminal, corymbose racemes; fruit a subglobose or ovate, somewhat inflated silicle, rounded to subcordate at the base, sometimes obcordate, tipped by the persistent style, flattened perpendicular to the septum, indehiscent, seed 1 in each locule.

1. C. drába (L.) Desv. (formerly included with *Draba*). Hoary Cress. Roadsides, waste places and fields. Fruit: June-August. Fig. 534, Map 1159. (Naturalized from Europe) [*Lepidium d.*]. Our plants are subsp. *draba*.

12. Roríppa Scop. Yellow Cress (ancient Saxon name).

Branched or simple, aquatic to terrestrial, annual or perennial herbs; stems erect or sprawling, glabrous or remotely pubescent with short, thick hairs; leaves pinnately compound, pinnatifid or dentate; glabrous or pubescent, sagittate-based in some species; flowers yellow or white, racemose or corymbose-paniculate; fruit a silicle or silique, subterete or cylindric, varying from slender to subglobose, seeds in 2 rows in each locule in most species.

In addition to the following species *R. cantoniensis* has also been reported for MA; *Tropidócarpum* Hook. *grácile* Hook. may sometimes key to *Rorippa*. See note under *Descurainia* (genus 32).

a. Plants aquatic, succulent, forming mats; stems rooted at lower nodes; flowers
　　white. (Fig. 535).
　　Silique 1.5 mm or more broad, beakless or with a thick style. .... 1. *R. nasturtium-*
　　　　　　　　　　　　　　　　　　　　　　　　　　　　　　　　　　　　aquaticum
　　Silique up to 1.5 mm broad, tapering to a slender style. .... 2. *R. microphylla*
a. Plants terrestrial or bordering, not succulent or mat-forming; stems not rooting
　　at lower nodes; flowers yellow.
　　b. Mature pedicels not more than 1.5 times as long as the fruit; cauline leaves all
　　　　deeply pinnately divided, or if not, plant annual or biennial. (Fig. 536).
　　　　Petals shorter than the sepals; silique less than 9 mm long; plant annual or
　　　　　　biennial .... 3. *R. palustris*
　　　　Petals longer than sepals; silique 9 mm or more long, or often aborted; plant
　　　　　　perennial .... 4. *R. sylvestris*
　　b. Mature pedicels 2 or more times as long as the fruit; cauline leaves dentate to
　　　　irregularly pinnatifid, but usually not deeply pinnately divided; plant
　　　　perennial. (Fig. 537).
　　　　c. Fruit globose, 1-3 mm long; style 1-3 mm long; cauline leaves auricled. .... 5. *R. austriaca*
　　　　c. Fruit ellipsoid or oblong, 3-5 mm long.
　　　　　　Style 1-2 mm long; cauline leaves usually not auricled. .... 6. *R. amphibia*
　　　　　　Style up to 1 mm long; cauline leaves usually auricled. .... 7. *R. prostrata*

1. R. nastúrtium-aquáticum (L.) Hayek. Watercress. Brooks and streams. Fruit: June-September. Fig. 535, Map 1160. (Introduced from Europe). [*Nasturtium officinale* var. *siifolium; Radicula n.; Sisymbrium n.*]. Well known as a salad herb; the next species may be similarly used. —OBL

　　R. x stérilis Airy-Shaw. A hybrid between *R. nasturtium-aquaticum* and *R. microphylla.*

2. R. microphýlla (Boen. ex Reichenb.) Hyl. ex A. & D. Love. Brooks and streams. Fruit: June-September. [*Nasturtium officinale* var. *microphyllum; N. microphyllum*]. —OBL

3. R. palústris (L.) Bess. (of marshes). Pond and stream margins, wet meadows, waste places, and wet spots in exposed soil. Fruit: July-September. Fig. 536, Map 1161. (Eurasia, Greenland). [*R. indica; R. islandica*]. Our plants include subsp. *palustris* and the following subsp.:

　　subsp. *híspida* (Desv.) Jonsell. Upper leaves merely dentate; (leaves all pinnate or pinnatifid in subsp. *palustris*).

　　subsp. *fernáldiana* (Butters & Abbe) Jonsell. Similar to subsp. *hispida* but with leaves glabrous on lower surface and stems glabrous to sparsely hispid below (leaves hirsute on lower surface and stem hispid below in subsp. *hispida*). [*R. p.* subsp. *glabra*]. —OBL

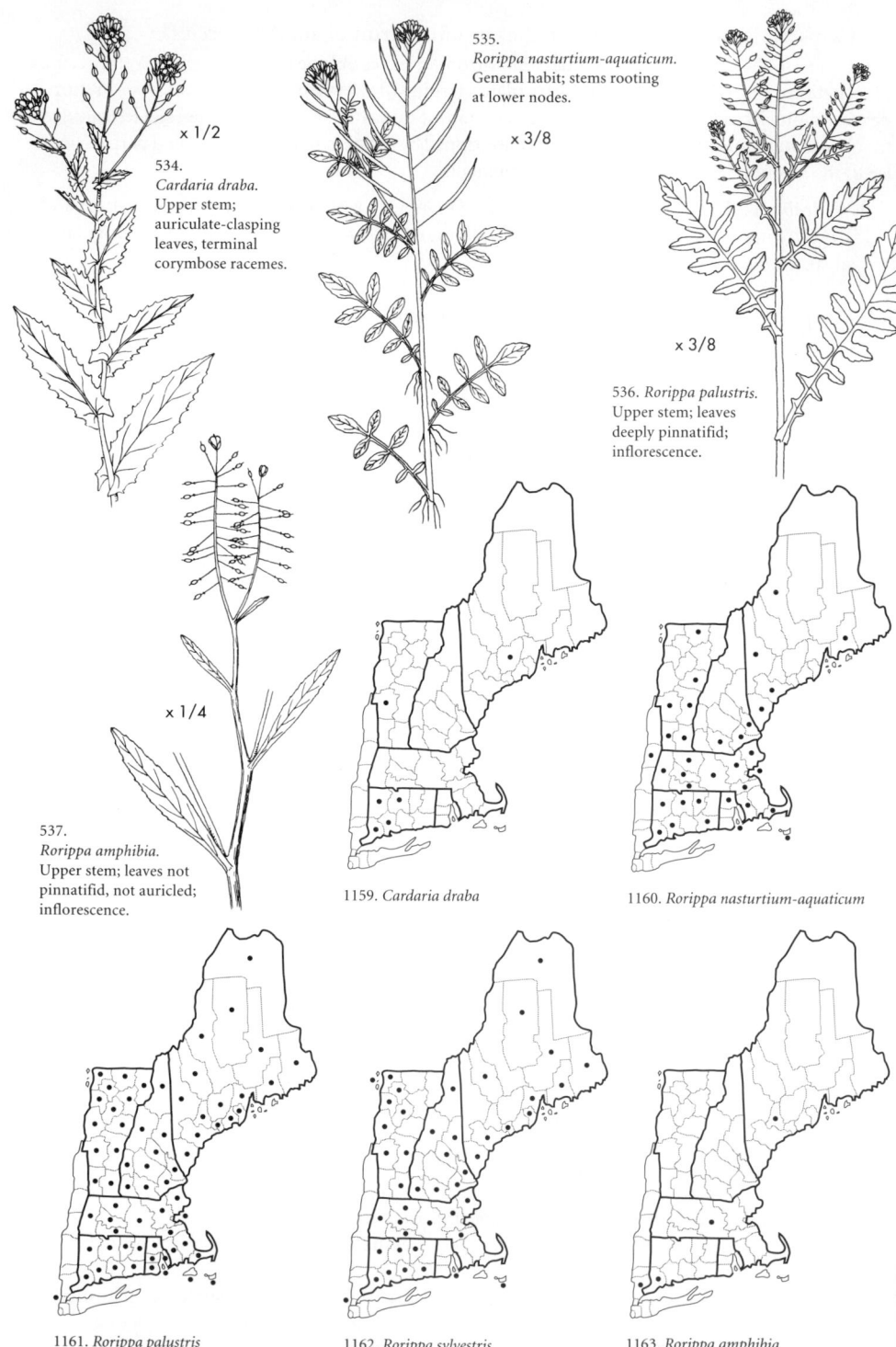

× 1/2

534.
Cardaria draba.
Upper stem;
auriculate-clasping
leaves, terminal
corymbose racemes.

535.
Rorippa nasturtium-aquaticum.
General habit; stems rooting
at lower nodes.

× 3/8

× 3/8

536. *Rorippa palustris.*
Upper stem; leaves
deeply pinnatifid;
inflorescence.

× 1/4

537.
Rorippa amphibia.
Upper stem; leaves not
pinnatifid, not auricled;
inflorescence.

1159. *Cardaria draba*

1160. *Rorippa nasturtium-aquaticum*

1161. *Rorippa palustris*

1162. *Rorippa sylvestris*

1163. *Rorippa amphibia*

R. sessiflóra (Nutt.) Hitchc. Will key to *R. palustris* but is distinguishable in having pedicels usually not over 3 mm long and fruits more than twice as long as the pedicels (pedicels longer than 3 mm and fruits up to twice as long as the pedicel in *R. palustris*). From farther south and west. Reported for MA. [*Radicula s.*]. —OBL

Euclídium R. Br. *syríacum* (L.) R. Br. Will key to *Rorippa palustris* vars. but has oblanceolate leaves and small, ovoid, long-beaked, 2-seeded silicles. (Adventive from Eurasia.) Reported for MA.

4. R. sylvéstris (L.) Bess. (of woods). Pond and stream margins, wet meadows, cultivated ground and waste places. Fruit: June-September. Map 1162. (Naturalized from Europe). [*Radicula s.*]. —FACW

5. R. austríaca (Crantz) Bess. (Austrian). Fields. Fruit: June-July. (Adventive from Europe). Reported for Hampshire County MA, Rockingham County NH. —FAC-

6. R. amphíbia (L.) Bess. (on land or in the water). Margins and shallow water of ponds and quiet streams, waste places. Fruit: July-September. Fig. 537, Map 1163. (Naturalized from Europe). —FACW

7. R. prostráta (Bergeret) Schinz & Thellung (prostrate). Wet meadows and waste places. (Adventive from Europe). Reported for Fairfield County CT. —FAC

13. *Camélina* Crantz False Flax (from the Greek meaning dwarf flax).

Erect, simple or branched annual herbs, glabrous, or with simple, branched or stellate pubescence; leaves basal and cauline, the former spatulate to oblanceolate, petioled, entire or sinuate-margined, stem leaves lanceolate, mostly entire, with a sagittate-auriculate base; flowers small, yellow, racemose; fruit a turgid, obovoid silicle with a rim-like margin, seeds in 2 rows in each locule.

Base of stem rough-hairy, with long spreading hairs as well as short, stellate ones;
    silicles 6 mm or less long .... 1. *C. microcarpa*
Base of stem glabrous or with scattered stellate and short, simple hairs; silicles
    longer than 6 mm .... 2. *C. sativa*

1. C. microcárpa Andrz. ex DC. (small-fruited). Roadsides, fields, waste places and cultivated soil. Fruit: June-September. Fig. 538, Map 1164. (Naturalized from Europe). Forage containing seeds of this species may be toxic to livestock if eaten in large quantities.

2. C. satíva (L.) Crantz. (sown). Roadsides, waste places and cultivated soil. Fruit: May-August. Map 1165. (Adventive from Europe). Our plants are subsp. *sativa.*

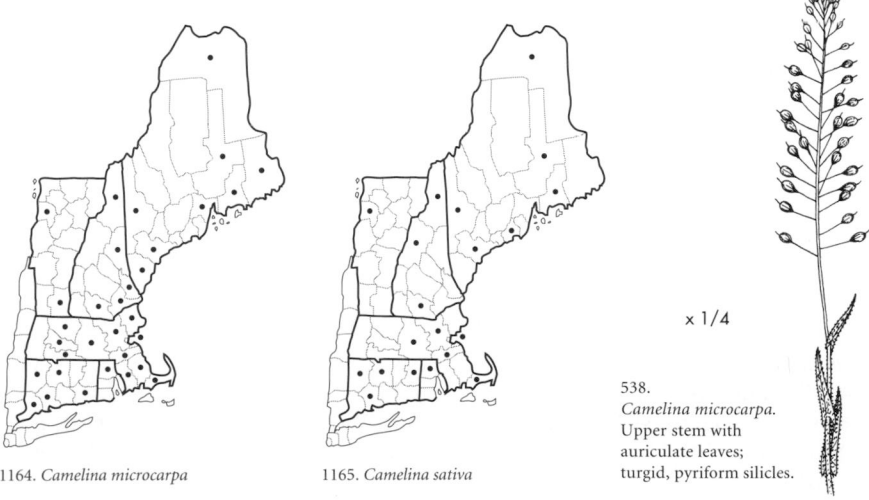

x 1/4

538.
Camelina microcarpa.
Upper stem with
auriculate leaves;
turgid, pyriform silicles.

1164. *Camelina microcarpa*

1165. *Camelina sativa*

14. _Capsélla_ Medik. Shepherd's-purse (diminutive of capsa, a box).

Erect, slightly branched, annual herbs, stellate-pubescent below, glabrous above; basal leaves in rosettes, oblong to oblanceolate, dentate to pinnatifid, petioled, cauline leaves reduced, lanceolate to linear, denticulate to entire, auriculate-sagittate; flowers small, white, in racemes that become much elongated in fruit; fruit an obcordate-triangular silicle, truncate to retuse at the apex, flattened perpendicular to the septum, seeds numerous in each locule.

 1. _C. búrsa-pastóris_ (L.) Medik. (shepherd's pouch). Roadsides, fields, waste places. Fruit: May-October. Fig. 539, Map 1166. (Naturalized from Europe). [_C. gracilis; C. rubella_]. Used in salads when young and as a potherb when older; also has been used as a styptic among other medicinal uses. —FACU

15. _Ísatis_ L. Woad (greek name for a dye-producing plant).

Erect, coarse, branched, glabrous annual or perennial herbs; basal leaves obovate to oblong, petioled, coarsely toothed, cauline leaves lanceolate, auriculate-clasping, entire or subentire; flowers small, yellow, in a large, terminal corymb of numerous racemes; fruit an oblong, ovate or obovate silicle, flat, indehiscent, lacking a septum, these drooping on slender pedicels, 1-seeded.

 1. _I. tinctória_ L. (used for dying). Roadsides and waste places. Fruit: June-October. Rare. Fig. 540. (Introduced from Europe).

16. _Lepídium_ L. (Greek name, referring to the shape of the fruit).

Erect, simple to branched, annual to perennial herbs from basal rosettes, these often absent at flowering or fruiting, glabrous or with pubescence of simple hairs; leaves pinnatifid to entire, petioled to sessile; flowers small, racemose, petals white to yellowish, short, or sometimes none, stamens often fewer than 6; fruit a silicle, orbicular to obovate in outline, often notched at the summit, flattened perpendicular to the septum, often winged, seed 1 in each locule. —Wildl. 1

 In addition to the following species _L. hirtum_ has also been reported for ME.

a. Median and upper stem leaves auriculate-clasping or perfoliate. (Fig. 541).
  Basal and lower leaves 2 or more times pinnatifid; flowers yellow. .... 1. _L. perfoliatum_
  Basal and lower leaves lyrate-pinnatifid to merely crenate, toothed or entire;
   flowers white. .... 2. _L. campestre_
a. Stem leaves not auriculate-clasping or perfoliate.
 b. Larger stem leaves 1 cm or more wide, finely toothed or entire; silicles not
   notched at the apex .... 3. _L. latifolium_
 b. Larger stem leaves less than 1 cm wide, or if wider than dissected or coarsely
   toothed; silicles distinctly notched at apex. (Fig. 542).
  c. Silicles more than 4 mm long, on closely ascending pedicels; basal and lower
    stem leaves commonly bipinnatifid .... 4. _L. sativum_
  c. Silicles 4 mm or less long, on spreading or loosely ascending pedicels.
   d. Petals equalling or exceeding the sepals; silicles mostly 3 mm or more long. .. 5. _L. virginicum_
   d. Petals none or rumentary and shorter than the sepals; silicles mostly less
    than 3 mm long.
    Racemes loose, with 10 or fewer fruiting pedicels per cm of rachis;
     basal leaves commonly bipinnatifid .... 6. _L. ruderale_
    Racemes dense, with more than 10 fruiting pedicels per cm of rachis;
     basal leaves pinnatifid to coarsely toothed. .... 7. _L. densiflorum_

 1. _L. perfoliàtum_ L. (through the leaf). Waste places, roadsides and fields. Fruit: June-August. Map 1167. (Naturalized from Europe).
 2. _L. campéstre_ (L.) Ait. f. (of fields). Field-Pepper-grass. Waste places, roadsides and fields. Fruit: June-September. Fig. 541, Map 1168. Seeds of this species are reported to be harmful to livestock if eaten in large quantities in forage. (Naturalized from Europe).

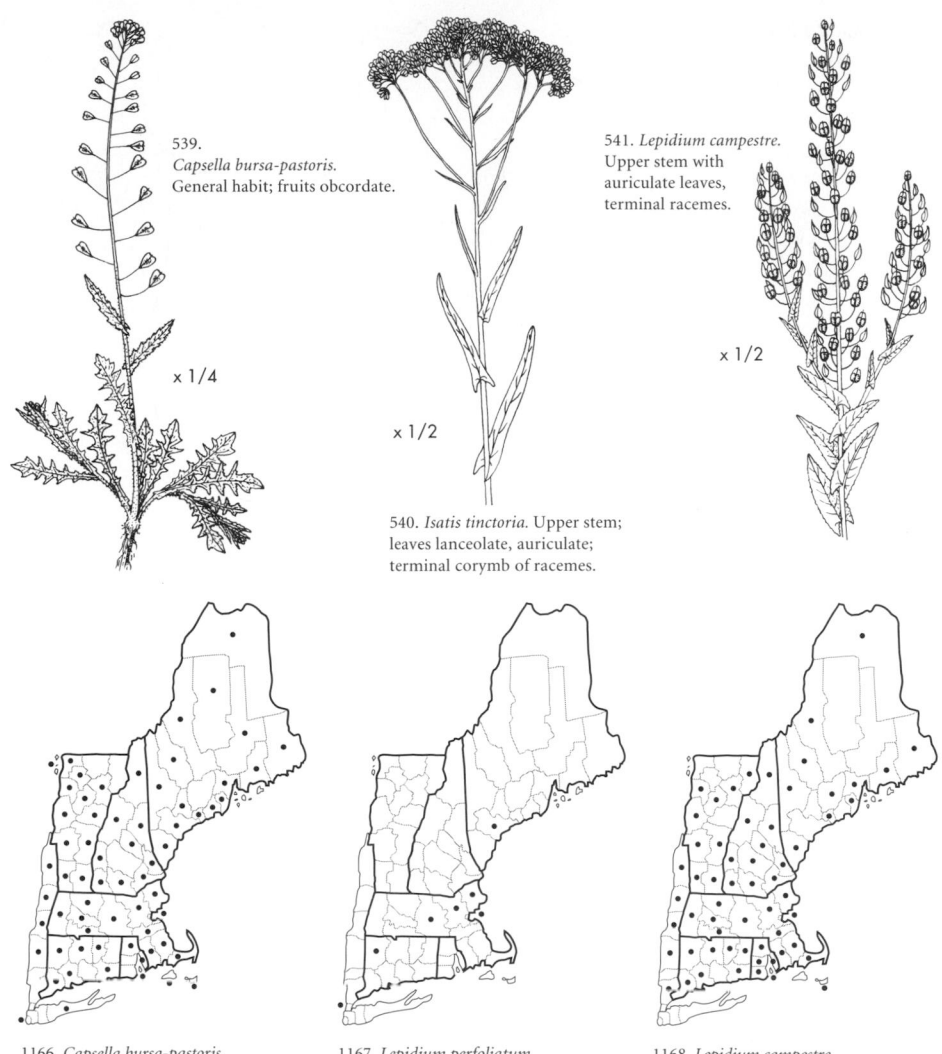

539.
Capsella bursa-pastoris.
General habit; fruits obcordate.

x 1/4

541. *Lepidium campestre.*
Upper stem with
auriculate leaves,
terminal racemes.

x 1/2

x 1/2

540. *Isatis tinctoria.* Upper stem;
leaves lanceolate, auriculate;
terminal corymb of racemes.

1166. *Capsella bursa-pastoris*

1167. *Lepidium perfoliatum*

1168. *Lepidium campestre*

L. heterophýllum Benth. Similar to *L. campestre* but perennial with numerous stems, anthers purple, silicles not or only slightly papillose (*L. campestre* is annual or biennial with yellow anthers, silicles usually papillose). (European). From the northwest. Reported for MA.

3. *L. latifòlium* L. (broad-leaved). Waste places and along the coast. Fruit: August-October. Map 1169. (Naturalized from Europe). —FACU

4. *L. satìvum* L. (sown). Garden-Pepper-grass. Roadsides and waste places, cultivated ground. Fruit: July-September. Fig. 542. Map 1170. (Introduced from Europe).

5. *L. virgínicum* L. (Virginian). Pepper-grass. Roadsides, fields and waste places. Fruit: June-September. Map 1171. (Adventive in Europe). Our plants are var. *virginicum.* Young plants are used as a garnish and in salads; seeds mixed with vinegar are used as a condiment. —FACU

6. *L. ruderàle* L. (of rubbish). Narrow-leaved Pepper-grass. Roadsides and waste places. Fruit: May-August. Map 1172. (Naturalized from Europe).

x 1

542. *Lepidium sativum.* Section of
raceme with silicles notched at apex.

1169. *Lepidium latifolium*

1170. *Lepidium sativum*

7. L. densiflòrum Schrad. (densely flowered). Pepper-grass. Roadsides, waste places and fields. Fruit: June-September. Map 1173. [*L. apetalum; L. neglectum*]. Our plants are var. *densiflorum.* —FAC

17. **Thláspi** L. Penny-cress (from the Greek based on the flattened fruit).

Erect, simple or branched, glabrous, annual herbs; basal leaves oblanceolate, petioled, in rosettes, usually withered or absent during flowering, stem leaves ovate to oblong or lanceolate, entire or dentate, auriculate-clasping or the lower merely sessile; flowers small, white to purplish, in terminal racemes; fruit an orbicular to obovate or obcordate silicle, winged, retuse at the apex, flattened perpendicular to the septum, seeds several in each locule.

Silicles more than 7 mm long .... 1. *T. arvense*
Silicles less than 7 mm long .... 2. *T. perfoliatum*

1. T. arvénse L. (of cultivated land). Waste places, roadsides, fields and cultivated ground. Fruit: May-August. Fig. 543, Map 1174. (Naturalized from Europe). Young plants are used in salads; forage containing the seeds is said to be harmful to livestock if eaten in large quantities.

2. T. perfoliátum L. (perfoliate). Waste places, roadsides and fields. Fruit: April-June. (Naturalized from Europe).

18. **Alýssum** L. (Greek name of a plant reputed to cure hydrophobia).

Low, erect, simple or branched, annual herbs, hoary with stellate pubescence; leaves linear, oblong or obovate, tapered to the base, obtuse at the apex, entire, short-petioled to sessile; flowers whitish to pale yellow, in terminal racemes; fruit a small, ovate to orbicular silicle, the valves convex toward the center, flattened and sharp around the margin, flattened parallel to the septum, sepals often persisting at the base, seeds 1-several in each locule.

Aurínia Desv. *saxátilis* (L.) Desv. Similar to *Alyssum alyssoides* but is a matted perennial with bright yellow flowers and glabrous fruits (plant annual with erect stems, flowers white to pale yellow, and fruits pubescent in *Alyssum alyssoides*). (Introduced from Europe). Sometimes escaped from cultivation. Reported for MA, NH.

1. A. alyssoídes (L.) L. (like *Alyssum*). Waste places, roadsides, fields. Fruit: June-July. Fig. 544, Map 1175. (Naturalized from Europe). [*Clypeola a.*].

19. Erýsimum L. (from the Greek, based on the medicinal value of some species).
Erect, simple or branched, annual or perennial herbs, with dense, appressed pubescence of 2-4
parted hairs; leaves linear to narrowly lanceolate or oblanceolate, simple and entire or dentate,
sessile, or the lower short-petiolate; flowers yellow, racemose; fruit a silique, this elongate, linear,
terate to slightly 4-angled, seeds in 1 row in each locule. [*Cheirinia*].

Iodanthus pinnatifidus, sometimes keying here, is described under *Arabis* (genus 6).

a. Pedicels filiform, less than 0.5 mm thick; petals less than 6 mm long. (Fig. 545) .... 1. *E. cheiranthoides*
a. Pedicels stout, mostly 0.5 mm or more thick; petals 6 mm or more long.
    Siliques widely spreading, 5 cm or more long; pedicel scarcely differentiated
        from silique .... 2. *E. repandum*
    Siliques erect or nearly so, less than 5 cm long; pedicels, or many of them,
        clavate at the junction with the silique. .... 3. *E. inconspicuum*

    1. E. cheiranthoídes L. (resembling *Cheiranthus*). Wormseed-mustard. Fields, roadsides, waste
places and cultivated soil. Fruit: June-September. Fig. 545, Map 1176. (Naturalized from the Old
World). [*Cheirinia c.*]. Forage containing seeds of this species is reported to be harmful to livestock
if seeds are eaten in large quantities. —FAC
    2. E. repándum L. (wavy). Waste places. June-July. Reported for Middlesex and Norfolk Counties
MA. [*Cheirinia r.*].
    3. E. inconspícuum (S. Wats.) Macm. (inconspicuous). Waste places. Fruit: June-August. Map
1177. [*Cheirinia inconspicua; C. syrticola; E. parviflorum*]. Our plants are var. *inconspicuum*.

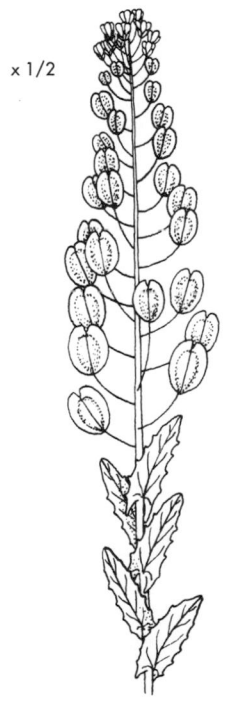

x 1/2

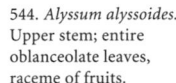

544. *Alyssum alyssoides.*
Upper stem; entire
oblanceolate leaves,
raceme of fruits.

x 1

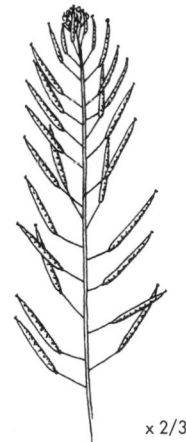

x 2/3

545. *Erysimum cheiranthoides.*
Fruiting raceme with spreading-
ascending, filiform pedicels.

543. *Thlaspi arvense.* General
characters; upper stem and raceme.

1171. *Lepidium virginicum*

1172. *Lepidium ruderale*

1173. *Lepidium densiflorum*

1174. *Thlaspi arvense*

1175. *Alyssum alyssoides*

1176. *Erysimum cheiranthoides*

1177. *Erysimum inconspicuum*

1178. *Cakile edentula*

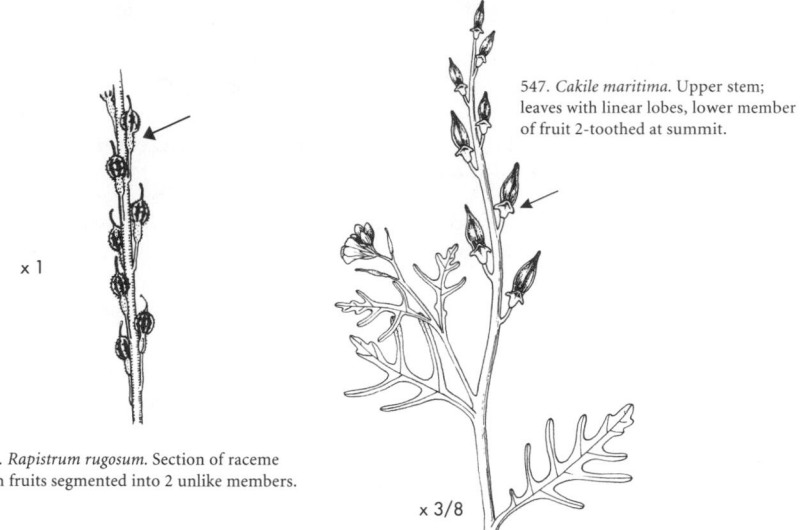

547. *Cakile maritima.* Upper stem; leaves with linear lobes, lower member of fruit 2-toothed at summit.

x 1

546. *Rapistrum rugosum.* Section of raceme with fruits segmented into 2 unlike members.

x 3/8

20. *Rapistrum* Crantz (Latin name for wild rape).

Erect, branching, annual herbs, subglabrous or with pubescence of simple hairs; leaves oblanceolate to obovate, pinnatifid to coarsely dentate, petioled, or the upper sessile; flowers yellow, racemose, short-pedicelled; fruits appressed, on short, thick pedicels, short, terete, densely pubescent to glabrous, transversely 2-jointed, the lower joint cylindric, dehiscent by 2 valves, 1-several seeded, the upper joint larger, subglobose, indehiscent, 5-ribbed, 1-seeded, abruptly tipped by a long, slender beak.

1. *R. rugósum* (L.) All. (wrinkled). Waste places. Fruit: July-September. Rare. Fig. 546. (Adventive from Europe). Reported for Essex and Suffolk Counties MA. Our plants include var. *rugosum* and the following var.:

var. *venósum* (Pers.) DC. Fruits eventually glabrous (pubescent in var. *rugosum*).

21. *Cakíle* P. Mill. Sea-rocket (old Arabic name).

Succulent, glabrous, annual herbs, simple or freely branched, with spreading to ascending stems; leaves obovate to oblanceolate, thick and fleshy, deeply pinnatifid to pinnately lobed, dentate, crenate or subentire, short petioled to sessile; flowers purplish, pink or white, racemose, on short, thick pedicels; fruit short, terete, transversely 2-jointed, the upper member larger than the lower, deciduous at maturity, both members indehiscent, 1-locular, angled or ribbed, 1-seeded or the lower seedless, short-beaked.

Leaves deeply pinnatifid, with linear segments; lower member of silique usually
    2-toothed at summit. (Fig. 547). .... 1. *C. maritima*
Leaves toothed or lobed but not deeply pinnatifid, the segments not linear; lower
    member of silique not toothed at summit, or teeth barely developed. .... 2. *C. edentula*

1. *C. marítima* Scop. (maritime). Waste places along the coast. Fruit: August-September. Fig. 547. Reported for ME. (Adventive from Europe).

2. *C. edéntula* (Bigelow) Hook. (without teeth). Seabeaches. Fruit: August-September. Map 1178. (Azores, Iceland). Our plants are subsp. *edentula* var. *edentula*. Leaves used in salads or as a potherb; root has been dried, ground and mixed with flour to make bread. —FACU

22. *Lunária* L. (moon).

Erect, branching, annual herbs with simple pubescence; leaves deltoid, cordate based, acuminate at the apex, coarsely dentate, the lower subopposite, becoming alternate upwards, petioled, the uppermost truncate to rounded at the base and sessile; flowers large, purple, in terminal racemes; fruit a silicle, broadly elliptic and rounded at both ends, with a persistent style, long-pedicelled, flattened parallel to the septum, seeds several in each locule.

    1. *L. ánnua* L. (annual). Honesty. Occasionally escaped from cultivation to roadsides and waste places. Fruit: July-August. Fig. 548, Map 1179. (Introduced from Europe).

23. *Alliária* Heister ex Fabr. Garlic Mustard (name from Allium, based on the garlic-like odor).

Tall, erect, simple or branching, biennial herbs with the odor of garlic, glabrous or with pubescence of simple hairs toward the base of the stem; leaves simple, the basal reniform, the cauline cordate to deltoid, coarsely dentate or crenate, petioled, the upper smaller, sessile or subsessile; flowers white, racemose; fruit a long, linear, 4-angled silique, these widely divergent on short, thick pedicels, seeds in 1 row in each locule.

    1. *A. petioláta* (Bieb.) Cavara & Grande (petioled). Roadsides, open woods, waste places, cultivated soil. Fruit: May-June. Fig. 549, Map 1180. (Naturalized from Europe). [*A. alliaria; A. officinalis*]. Young leaves can be used in salads to impart a garlic flavor. —FACU

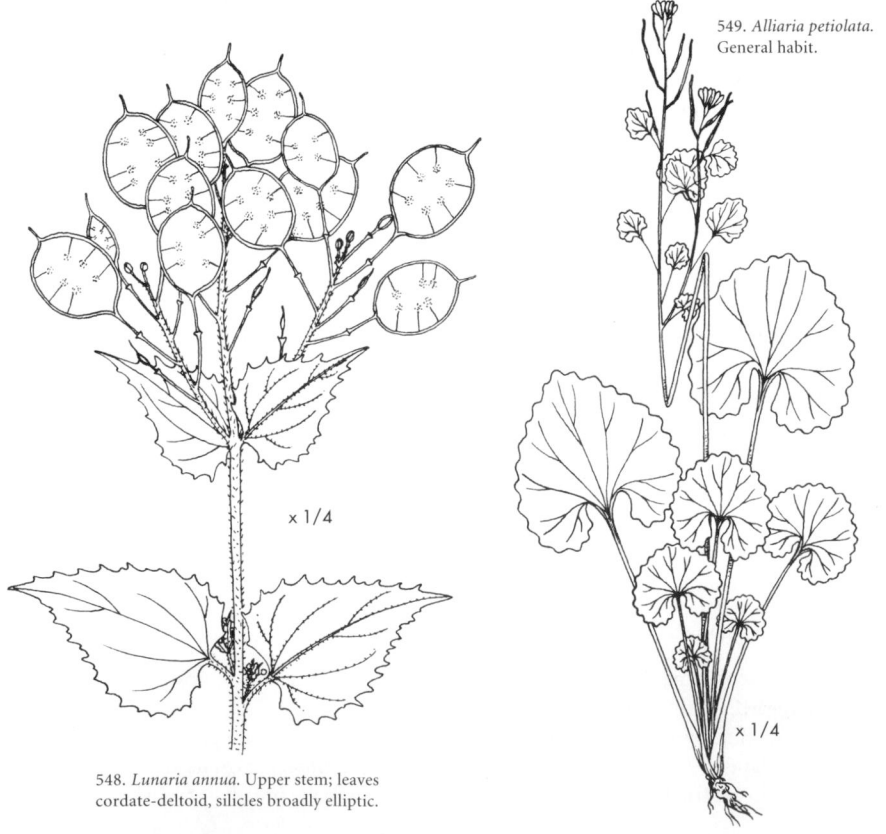

549. *Alliaria petiolata.* General habit.

x 1/4

x 1/4

548. *Lunaria annua.* Upper stem; leaves cordate-deltoid, silicles broadly elliptic.

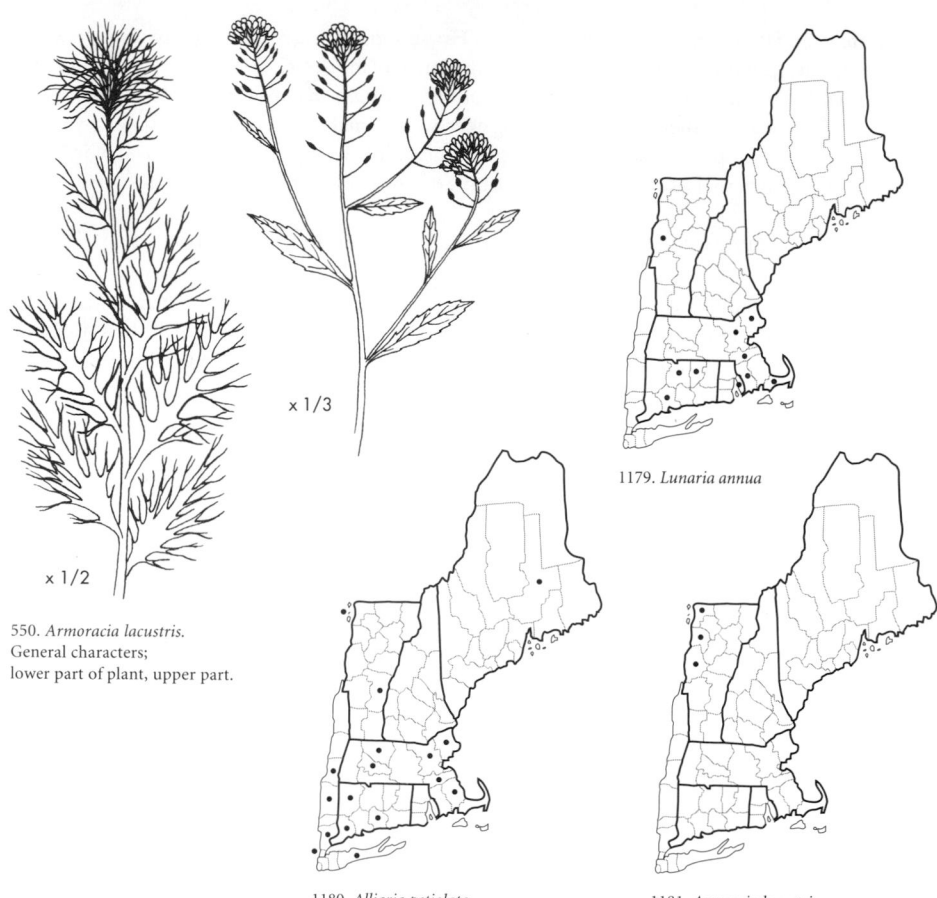

x 1/3

x 1/2

550. *Armoracia lacustris.*
General characters;
lower part of plant, upper part.

1179. *Lunaria annua*

1180. *Alliaria petiolata*

1181. *Amoracia lacustris*

24. Armorácia P. G. Gaertn., B. Mey. & Scherb. (ancient name for horseradish).

Glabrous, perennial herbs, terrestrial, tall and erect, from a thick, vertical root, or aquatic, with submersed or prostrate, simple or branched stems from a horizontal rhizome; leaves highly polymorphic, terrestrial species with lower leaves large, oblong, merely crenate to deeply pinnatifid or bipinnatifid, petioled, the upper leaves progressively reduced, lanceolate, pinnately lobed to crenate or dentate, sessile or short petioled, aquatic species with submersed leaves divided into numerous filiform segments, emersed leaves, when present, oblong or lanceolate, pinnatifid, dentate or entire, (or dissected like the lower leaves in 1 form); flowers white, in terminal and axillary racemes; fruit a silicle, obovoid, ellipsoid or subglobose, inflated, the valves convex, with a persistent style, and a broad, persistent stigma, flattened parallel to the septum, 1 or 2 locular, several seeded (fruit seldom developed in our area).

Plant aquatic, with lax stems and submersed leaves divided into capillary segments.
   (Fig. 550) .... 1. *A. lacustris*
Plant terrestrial, with upright stems; lower leaves merely toothed or pinnatifid .... 2. *A. rusticana*

1. A. lacústris (Gray) Al-Shehbaz & Bates. Lake-cress. Lakes, quiet streams and muddy shores. Fruit: July-August. Fig. 550, Map 1181. [*A. aquatica; Radicula a.; Neobeckia a.*]. —OBL

2. *A. rusticána* P. G. Gaertn., B. Mey. & Scherb. Horse-radish. Escaped from cultivation to waste places, roadsides, pond and stream margins and other areas of moist soil. Fruit: June-July. Map 1182. (Naturalized from Europe). [*A. armoracia; A. lapathifolia; Radicula armoracia*]. Young leaves are useable in salads or as a potherb; roots have long been used to make the familiar condiment; various medicinal uses have also been ascribed to this plant including use as a diuretic, removal of internal parasites, and for external uses similar to a mustard or onion plaster.

25. *Hésperis* L. Dame's rocket (from the Greek, based on the evening fragrance of the flowers).

Tall, erect, simple-stemmed, biennial or perennial herbs with pubescence of simple or forked hairs; leaves simple, lanceolate to ovate, acuminate, denticulate, sessile to short-petiolate; flowers large and showy, purple or white, racemose; fruit a silique, this elongate, slender, subcylindric, widely divergent on thick pedicels, seeds in 1 row in each locule.

Choríspora tenélla, a species with beaked fruit sometimes keying here, is described under *Braya* (genus 29.).

Iodanthus pinnatifidus sometimes keys here and is described under *Arabis* (genus 6).

1. *H. matronális* L. (matronly). Roadsides, waste places and open woods. Fruit: June-August. Fig. 551, Map 1183. (Naturalized from Europe).

26. *Berteróa* DC. (for C. Bertero).

Tall, stellate-pubescent, annual or perennial herbs, usually branched above; leaves lanceolate or oblanceolate, narrowed to the base, acute or obtuse at the apex, entire or slightly undulate-margined, sessile or short petioled; flowers white, in terminal racemes, the petals deeply 2-cleft; fruit an oblong to elliptic silicle, somewhat inflated, with a persistent style, densely pubescent to glabrous, flattened parallel to the septum, seeds several in each locule.

Silicles densely pubescent, plump, the valves convex. .... 1. *B. incana*
Silicles glabrous or subglabrous, flattened. .... 2. *B. mutabilis*

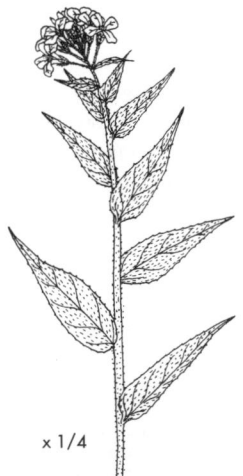

x 1/4

551. *Hesperis matronalis.* General habit; upper part of plant.

1182. *Armoracia rusticana*

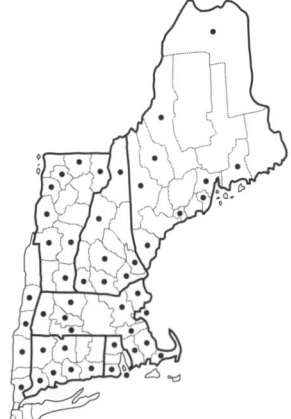

1183. *Hesperis matronalis*

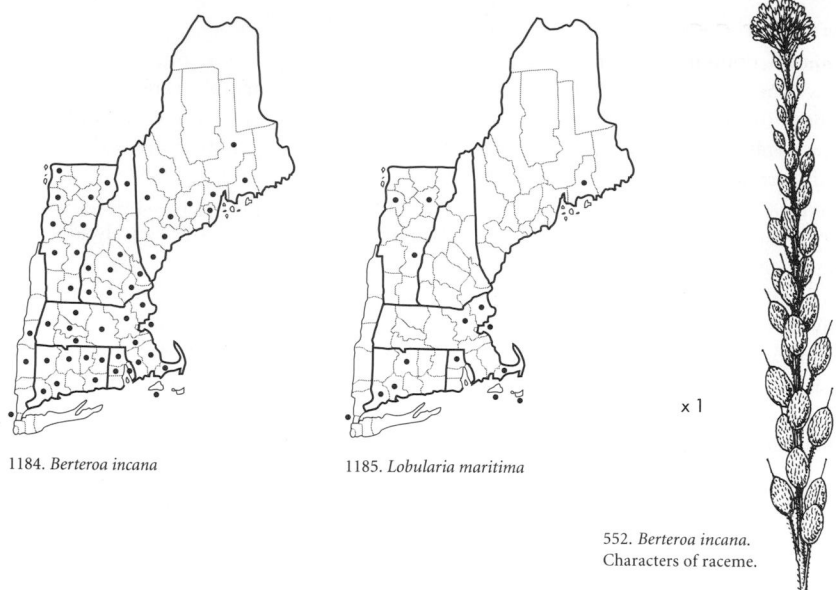

1184. *Berteroa incana*

1185. *Lobularia maritima*

x 1

552. *Berteroa incana.*
Characters of raceme.

1. B. incána (L) DC. (hoary). Hoary Alyssum. Waste places, roadsides and fields. Fruit: July-October. Fig. 552, Map 1184. (Naturalized from Europe).

2. B. mutábilis (Vent.) DC. (changeable). Waste places, roadsides and cultivated ground. Fruit: July-October. (Adventive from Europe). Reported for Norfolk County MA.

27. Lobulária Desv. (from the Latin, based on the forked hairs).

Low, procumbent to ascending, branching, annual or perennial herbs with forked, appressed pubescence; leaves linear-lanceolate or oblanceolate, tapered to the base, acute at the apex, entire, sessile or short petioled; flowers small, white, fragrant, in terminal racemes; fruit as in Alyssum, long pedicelled, calyx not persistent, style persistent, seeds 1 in each locule.

1. L. marítima (L.) Desv. (of the sea). Sweet alyssum. Escaped from cultivation to roadsides and waste places. Fruit: June-October. Map 1185. (Introduced from Europe). [*Koniga m.*].

28. Ibéris L. Candytuft (ancient Greek name).

Similar to *Teesdalia* (genus 8) except 1 species perennial, cauline leaves numerous and well developed, entire or toothed but not pinnatifid, flowers larger, (5 mm or more wide compared to 2 mm or less wide in *Teesdalia*), white, pink or purple, fruits longer (5 mm or longer compared to 4 mm or less in *Teesdalia*).

Plant perennial, suffrutescent; leaves evergreen. .... 1. *I. sempervirens*
Plant annual, herbaceous; leaves withering.
    Inflorescence elongating after anthesis and becoming a raceme. .... 2. *I. amara*
    Inflorescence not elongating, remaining corymbose .... 3. *I. umbellata*

1. I. sempervírens L. Occasionally escaped from gardens. Reported for Belknap County NH.

2. I. amára L. (bitter). Occasionally escaped from gardens. Map 1186. (Introduced from Europe).

3. I. umbelláta L. (umbellate). Occasionally escaped from gardens. Reported for Knox County ME, Coos County NH.

29. Bráya Sternb. & Hoppe (for F. de Bray).

Low, perennial herbs with clustered, simple or branched stems arising from a stout caudex, sparsely pubescent with mostly branched hairs; leaves basal and cauline, linear-oblanceolate, toothed to entire, the basal forming overwintering rosettes; flowers white to purplish, racemose; fruit a linear, terete, often torulose silique, ours glabrous, the septum of characteristic structure with elongate cells, seeds in 1 row in each locule.

Choríspora DC. *tenélla* (Pallis) DC. Will key nearest to Braya, but petals are clawed, fruits are transversely septate and beaked, and plant is sparsely stipitate-glandular. Western, rarely adventive in our range. Reported for Middlesex County MA.

Malcólmia Ait. f. *marítima* (L.) Ait. f. Similar to *Chorispora tenella* but eglandular and fruits not transversely septate. European. Reported for Coos County NH.

Mathíola R. Br. *incána* (L.) R. Br. Similar to *Chorispora* and *Malcolmia* but is a perennial with entire leaves and winged seeds (the latter 2 taxa are annual, with few-toothed leaves and wingless seeds). Occasionally escaped from cultivation. Reported for VT.

Iodánthus pinnatífidus sometimes keying here, is described under *Arabis* (genus 6).

1. B. húmilis (C. A. Mey.) B. L. Robins. New England Rock-cress. Limestone cliffs and talus, Willoughby, Vermont. Fruit: June-July. Rare. Fig. 553. (Asia). From farther north. Reported for Orleans County VT. [*B. novae-angliae*].

30. Ráphanus L. (from the Greek, based on the rapid germination).

Coarse, erect, branching, annual herbs from a stout taproot, with pubescence of simple hairs; leaves ovate to obovate or oblong, petioled or the upper sessile, the lower lyrate-pinnatifid, the upper lobed, coarsely dentate or crenate, sometimes entire, progressively reduced; flowers yellow, white, pink or lavender, racemose, long pedicelled; fruit a torulose or cylindric silique, indehiscent, 2-8 seeded, with the seeds in a single row, separated by constrictions or spongy cross partitions, with a long, slender conical beak.

Iodanthus pinnatífidus, sometimes keying here, is described under *Arabis* (genus 6).

Flowers yellow or white; siliques less than 6 mm thick, constricted between each seed... 1. *R. raphanistrum*
Flowers pink, white or lavender; siliques mostly 6 mm or more thick, not constricted
between the seeds .... 2. *R. sativus*

1. R. raphanístrum L. (old generic name). Wild Radish. Fields, roadsides, waste places, cultivated ground. Fruit: July-September. Fig. 554, Map 1187. (Naturalized from Europe). [*R. innocuum*]. Seeds of this species if eaten in large quantities in forage are reported to be harmful to cattle.

2. R. satívus L. (planted). Garden Radish. Escaped from cultivation to fields and roadsides. Fruit: July-September. Map 1188. (Introduced from Europe).

31. Erúca P. Mill. Garden-rocket (Classical Latin name).

Coarse, erect, branching, annual (ours) herbs, glabrous or with pubescence of simple hairs; leaves ovate to obovate, the lower pinnatifid or pinnately lobed and lyrate, petioled, the upper lobed to coarsely dentate, progressively reduced, sessile; flowers white or yellowish-white to purplish, with purple veins, large, racemose, on short, thick pedicels; capsule a slightly flattened to somewhat angled silique, the valves 1-nerved, with a flat, narrowly triangular, elongate beak, seeds in 2 rows in each cell.

Diplotaxis erucoídes (genus 1) Will key to *Eruca* but is distinguished in having petals 1 cm or less long (petals 1.5 cm or more long in *Eruca*).

1. E. vesicária (L.) Cav. Waste places and cultivated ground. Fruit: June-October. Fig. 555. (Naturalized from Europe). Reported for CT, MA, Lamoille and Rutland Counties VT. [*E. sativa*]. Represented with us as subsp. *satíva* P. Mill.

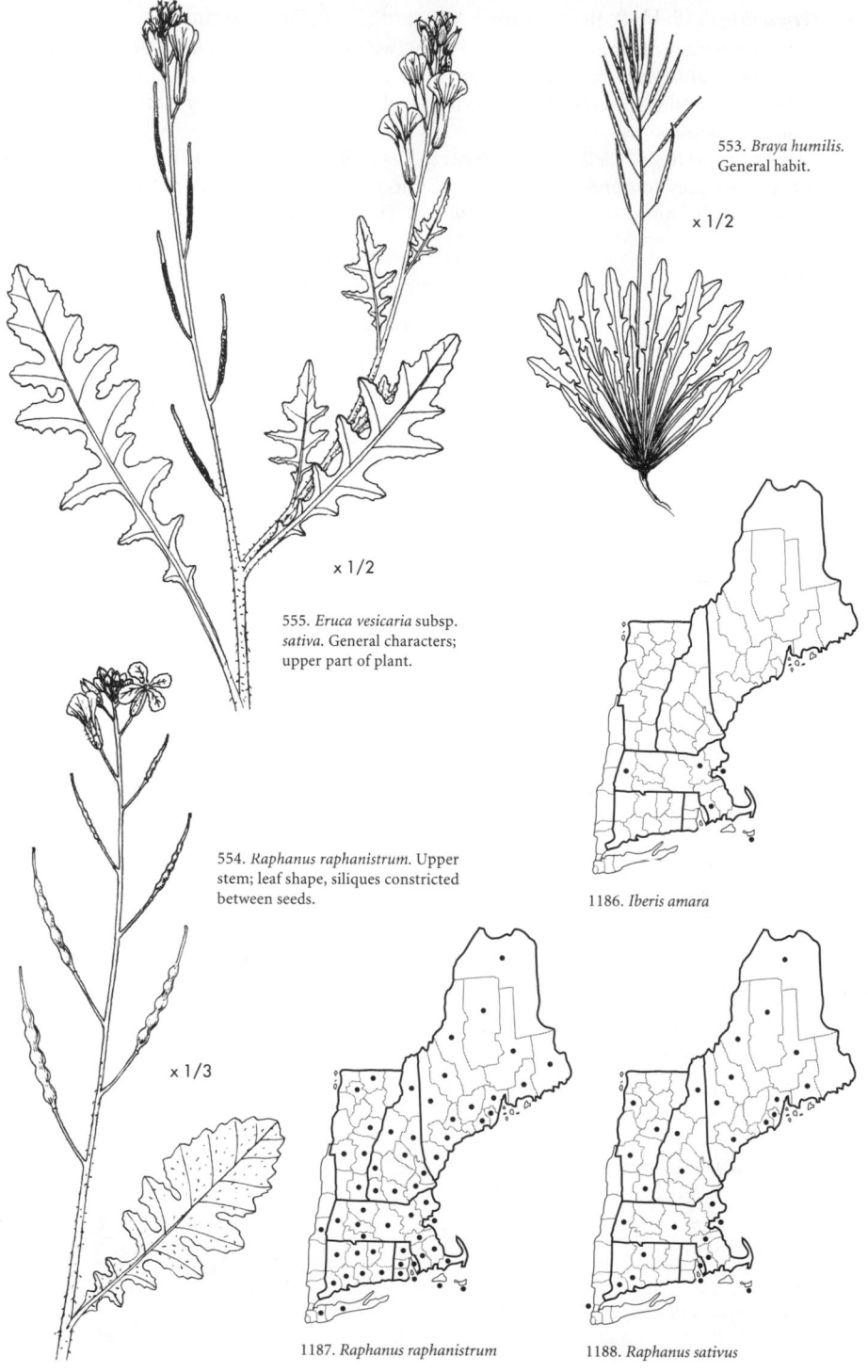

553. *Braya humilis.*
General habit.

x 1/2

x 1/2

555. *Eruca vesicaria* subsp.
sativa. General characters;
upper part of plant.

554. *Raphanus raphanistrum.* Upper
stem; leaf shape, siliques constricted
between seeds.

1186. *Iberis amara*

x 1/3

1187. *Raphanus raphanistrum*

1188. *Raphanus sativus*

32. *Descuraínia* Webb & Berth. Tansy-Mustard (for F. Descourain).

Erect, slender, branched, annual or biennial herbs, with pubescence of simple or branched hairs; leaves 1-3 times pinnately dissected, with numerous small divisions; flowers small, yellow, racemose; fruit a silique, these linear to clavate, cylindric to slightly angled, on slender pedicels, seeds in 1 or 2 rows in each locule.

Tropidocárpum Hook. *grácile* Hook. will key to *Descurainia* but is distinguishable in having leafy racemes and siliques compressed at right angles to the septum (racemes not leafy and siliques compressed parallel to the septum in *Descurainia*). From the southwest. Reported for MA.

a. Seeds in 2 rows in each locule; inflorescence usually glandular; siliques somewhat
    clavate .... 1. *D. pinnata*
                                                                  subsp. *brachycarpa*

a. Seeds in 1 row in each locule; inflorescence not glandular; siliques linear to
    lanceolate.
    Mature siliques 15 mm or more long; leaves 2-3 times pinnate; fruiting pedicels
        spreading-ascending. (Fig. 556). .... 2. *D. sophia*
    Mature siliques less than 15 mm long; leaves mostly once pinnate; fruiting
        pedicels strongly ascending .... 3. *D. incana*

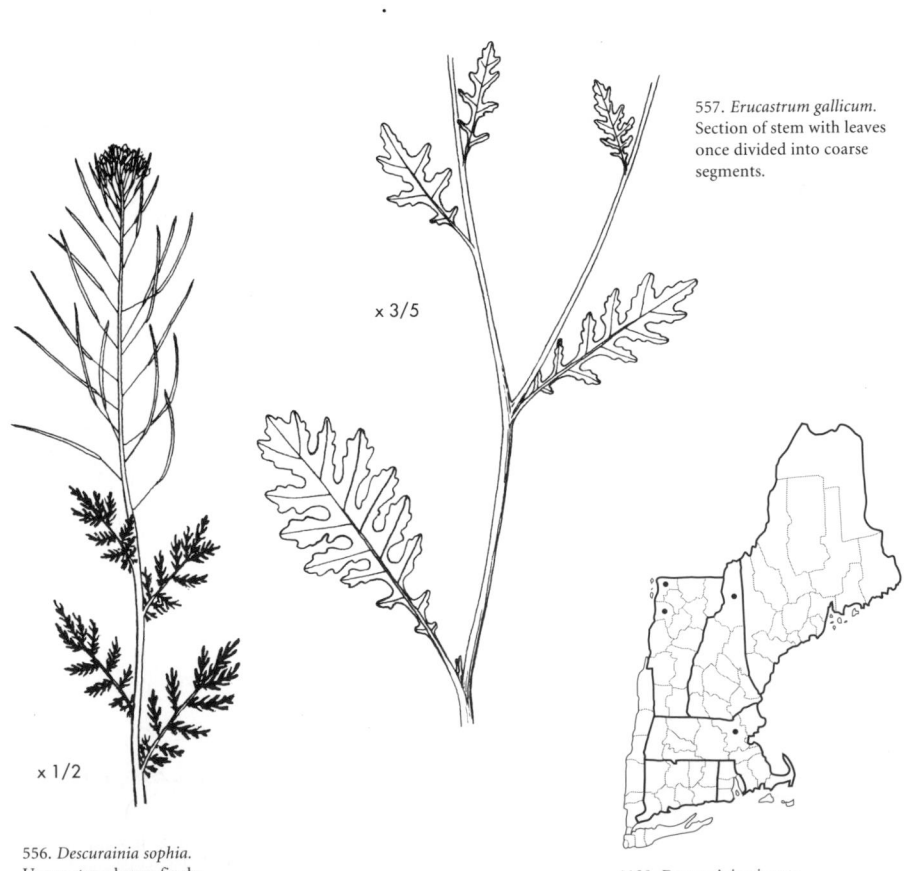

557. *Erucastrum gallicum.*
Section of stem with leaves once divided into coarse segments.

× 3/5

× 1/2

556. *Descurainia sophia.*
Upper stem; leaves finely dissected, raceme of long siliques.

1189. *Descurainia pinnata*
subsp. *brachycarpa*

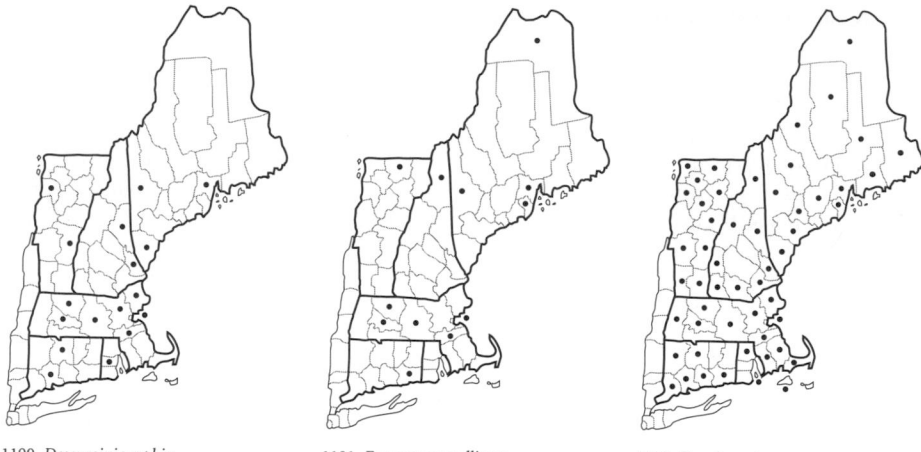

1190. *Descurainia sophia*   1191. *Erucastrum gallicum*   1192. *Brassica rapa*

1. D. pinnáta (Walt.) Britt. (pinnate). Dry fields, roadsides, lake shores and waste places. Fruit: June-August. Map 1189. [*Sophia p.; S. incisa; S. intermedia; S. millefolia*]. Represented with us as subsp. *brachycarpa* (Richards.) Delting. Poisonous.

2. D. sóphia (L.) Webb. ex Prantl (old generic name). Fields, roadsides and waste places. Fruit: June-September. Fig. 556, Map 1190. (Naturalized from Europe). [*Sophia multifida; S. sophia; Sisymbrium sophia*].

3. D. incána (Bernh. ex Fisch & C. A. Mey.) Dorn. Roadsides and waste places. Fruit: July-September. Reported for New Haven County CT, Somerset County ME. [*D. richardsonii; Sophia richardsoniana; S. hartwegiana; Sisymbrium incisum*]. Our plants are subsp. *incana*.

33. Erucástrum K. Presl. (name based on resemblance to Eruca).

Erect, branching, annual or biennial herbs, glabrous or with pubescence of simple hairs; basal and lower leaves oblong to oblanceolate, deeply pinnatifid to bipinnatifid, lyrate, petioled, stem leaves progressively reduced, pinnatifid to coarsely toothed, sessile or short petioled; flowers in terminal racemes, the lower flowers subtended by small, leafy bracts, yellow; capsule a slender, 4-angled silique with keeled valves, tapering to a distinct, conic beak, torulose, seeds in 1 row in each cell.

Iodánthus pinnatífidus, sometimes keying here, is described under *Arabis* (genus 6).

1. E. gállicum (Willd.) O. E. Schulz. Waste places. Fruit: July-September. Fig. 557, Map 1191. (Naturalized from Europe).

34. Brássica L. Mustard (Latin name for cabbage).

Similar to *Sinapis* (genus 38) except some species biennial instead of annual, and beak terete, not 2-edged, seedless, valves of silique and the beak with fewer than 3 distinct nerves. —Wildl. 1

Median and upper leaves auriculate-clasping.
  Glaucous; often sparsely hispid .... 1. *B. rapa*
  Green, glabrous .... 2. *B. napus*
Median and upper leaves not clasping.
  Mature siliques appressed, less than 2 cm long excluding beak; beak 4 mm or less
    long. (Fig. 558) .... 3. *B. nigra*
  Mature siliques ascending, more than 2 cm long excluding beak; beak longer than
    4 mm .... 4. *B. juncea*

1. *B. rápa* L. Bird's Rape. Waste places, fields, cultivated ground and roadsides. Fruit: June-September. Map 1192. (Naturalized from Eurasia). [*B. campestris*]. Our plants are var. *rápa*.

2. *B. nápus* L. Turnip. Waste places, abandoned farmland. Throughout our range. (Introduced from Eurasia).

B. olerácea L. Cabbage. Seldom persistent after cultivation.

3. *B. nígra* (L.) W. D. J. Koch. Black mustard. Waste places, fields, cultivated ground and roadsides. Fruit: June-September. Fig. 558, Map 1193. (Naturalized from Eurasia). Young leaves can be used as a potherb; clusters of flower buds may also be lightly cooked and eaten; seeds can be ground to make the familiar condiment.

4. *B. júncea* (L.) Czern. (rush-like). Indian mustard. Waste places, roadsides, cultivated ground and roadsides. Fruit: June-September. Map 1194. (Naturalized from Eurasia).

35. *Barbaréa* Ait. f. Winter-cress (herb of St. Barbara).

Erect, simple or branched, mostly glabrous, biennial or perennial herbs with angled stems; leaves pinnately divided, pinnatifid, toothed or entire, the basal petioled, forming overwintering basal rosettes, the cauline with clasping bases; flowers yellow, racemose; fruit a linear, terete or somewhat 4-angled silique, tipped by the persistent style, seeds in 1 row in each locule. —Wildl. 1

Iodánthus pinnatífidus, sometimes keying here, is described under *Arabis* (genus 6).

Basal leaves with 5 or more pairs of lateral segments; silique more than 4 cm long .... 1. *B. verna*
Basal leaves with 4 or fewer pairs of lateral segments; silique less than 4 cm long.
   (Fig. 559).
   Beak of silique 1.5 mm or more long .... 2. *B. vulgaris*
   Beak of silique less than 1.5 mm long. .... 3. *B. orthoceras*

1. *B. vérna* (P. Mill.) Aschers. (of spring). Early Winter-cress. Fields, roadsides and waste places. Fruit: May-July. Map 1195. (Naturalized from Europe). [*Campe v.*]. Young leaves and flower buds of this and the next species may be used as a potherb.

2. *B. vulgáris* Ait. f. (common). Common Winter-cress. Fields, roadsides and waste places, often in moist soil. Fruit: June-September. Fig. 559, Map 1196. (Naturalized from Europe). [*B. barbarea*; *B. stricta; Campe barbarea; C. stricta*]. —FACU

3. *B. orthóceras* Ledeb. (with straight horns). Stream borders, wooded swamps, wet woods and other wet soil in the open or shaded. Fruit: June-August. (Asia). Reported for Aroostook County ME, Coos County NH. [*B. americana*]. —OBL

36. *Búnias* L. (ancient Greek name).

Tall, coarse, branching, biennial herbs, glandular, glabrous or with simple pubescence; basal and lower stem leaves lyrate-pinnatifid to coarsely toothed, oblong to lanceolate, acuminate, petioled, somewhat resembling those of dandelion, stem leaves ovate to lanceolate, acuminate, progressively reduced upward, petioled to sessile; flowers yellow, in terminal racemes with sessile glands; fruit obliquely ovoid, coarsely rugose, beaked, long-pedicelled, indehiscent, several-seeded.

1. *B. orientális* L. (oriental). Waste places. Fruit: June-August. Fig. 560. (Adventive from Asia). Reported for CT, Hampshire County MA.

37. *Sisýmbrium* L. (Latinized from an ancient Greek name).

Tall, erect, branching, annual or biennial herbs, glabrous or with pubescence of simple hairs; leaves, at least the lower, pinnatifid, petioled, the upper sometimes merely dentate to nearly entire and sessile; flowers small, yellow, racemose; fruit a silique, this elongate, linear or subulate, terete or slightly angled, seeds in one row in each locule.

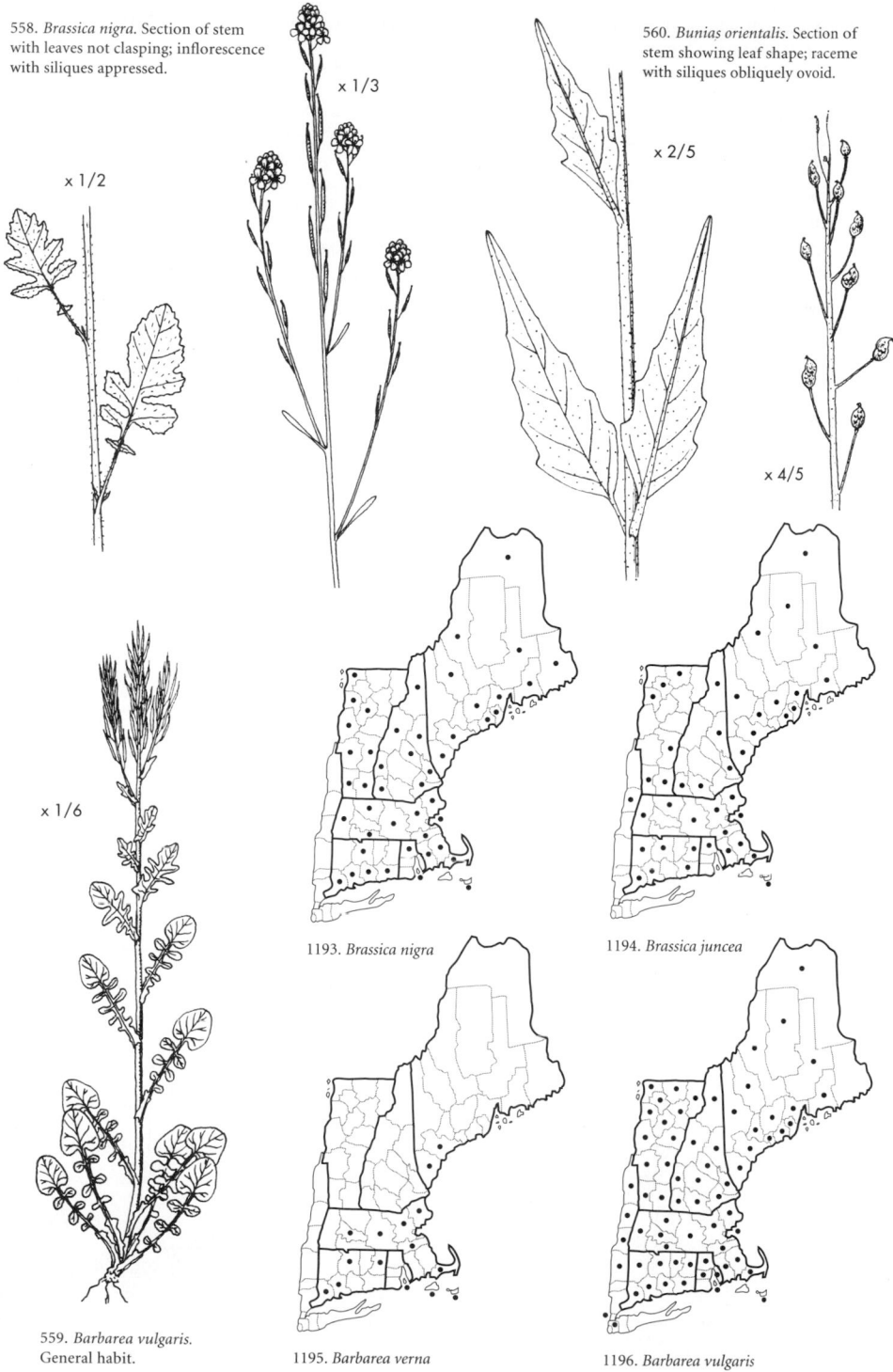

558. *Brassica nigra.* Section of stem with leaves not clasping; inflorescence with siliques appressed.

× 1/3

× 1/2

560. *Bunias orientalis.* Section of stem showing leaf shape; raceme with siliques obliquely ovoid.

× 2/5

× 4/5

× 1/6

1193. *Brassica nigra*

1194. *Brassica juncea*

559. *Barbarea vulgaris.* General habit.

1195. *Barbarea verna*

1196. *Barbarea vulgaris*

a. Siliques closely appressed to rachis, subulate; pedicels less than 5 mm long .... 1. *S. officinale*
a. Siliques spreading to loosely ascending, linear; pedicels 5 mm or more long.
   b. Siliques 5 cm or more long; fruiting pedicels about as thick as the siliques; leaf
      segments linear to lanceolate. (Fig. 561). .... 2. *S. altissimum*
   b. Siliques less than 5 cm long; fruiting pedicels much more slender than the
      siliques; leaf segments triangular to ovate.
      Petals much exceeding sepals, nearly twice their length; pistil scarcely
        projecting above the flower .... 3. *S. loeselii*
      Petals only slightly exceeding sepals; pistil clearly projecting above the flower .... 4. *S. irio*

1. *S. officinále* (L.) Scop. (of the shops). Hedge-mustard. Roadsides and waste places. Fruit: June-September. Map 1197. (Naturalized from Europe). Preparations made from fresh plants are reported to be useful as a decongestant for irritations of the larynx.

2. *S. altíssimum* L. (tallest). Tumble-mustard. Fields, roadsides and waste places. Fruit: June-September. Fig. 561, Map 1198. (Naturalized from Europe). [*Norta a.*]. Reported to be harmful to livestock if seeds are eaten in large quantities in forage. —FACU-

S. orientále L. Similar to *S. altissimum* but short-pilose, leaf segments ovate, siliques sparsely puberulent (sparsely hirsute at base, leaf segments linear to lanceolate, and siliques glabrous in *S. altissimum*). (Adventive from Eurasia). Reported for MA.

3. *S. loesélii* L. (for J. Loeselius). Roadsides and waste places. Fruit: July-September. Map 1199. (Adventive from Europe).

4. *S. írio* L. (Latin name). Roadsides and waste places. Fruit: July-September. (Adventive from Europe). Reported for Bronx County NY. [*Norta i.*].

561. *Sisymbrium altissimum.* Upper stem; leaves with linear segments, siliques spreading.

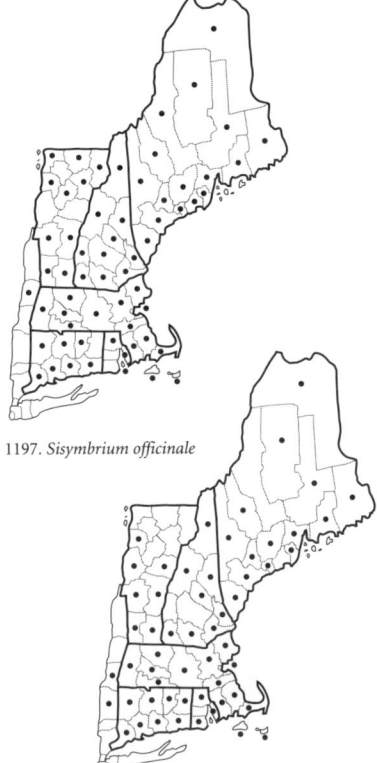

1197. *Sisymbrium officinale*

1198. *Sisymbrium altissimum*

× 1/4

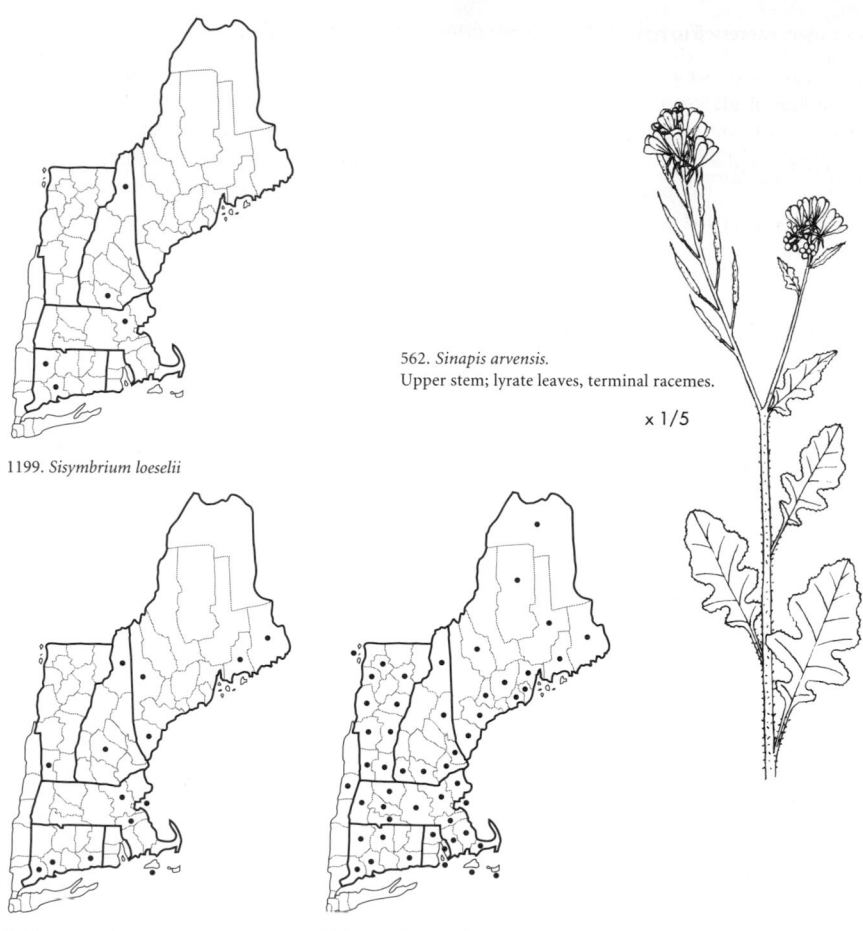

562. *Sinapis arvensis.*
Upper stem; lyrate leaves, terminal racemes.

x 1/5

1199. *Sisymbrium loeselii*

1200. *Sinapis alba*

1201. *Sinapis arvensis*

38. *Sinápis* L. Mustard.

Erect, branching, pubescent to subglabrous, annual herbs; leaves obovate, the lower deeply pinnatifid and lyrate or lobed, petioled, the upper less lobed or merely toothed, progressively smaller, sessile or short petioled; flowers in terminal racemes, large and yellow; capsule a silique, this linear, subterete, seeds in 1 row in each cell, somewhat constricted between the seeds, glabrous or hispid, each valve 3-nerved, with a flat or angled, 2-edged, indehiscent, beak, this 3-nerved on each side, often with a basal seed.

Siliques hispid; with a beak 1-2 times as long as the body. .... 1. *S. alba*
Siliques glabrous, rarely hispid, with a beak shorter than the body. (Fig. 562) .... 2. *S. arvensis*

    1. *S. álba* L. (white). White Mustard. Fields, waste places and roadsides. Fruit: June-August. Map 1200. (Introduced from Eurasia). [*Brassica a.; B. hirta*]. Young leaves and flower buds may be cooked as a potherb; seeds can be ground and used to make the familiar condiment.
    2. *S. arvénsis* L. (of cultivated ground). Charlock. Roadsides, waste places, fields and cultivated ground. Fruit: June-September. Fig. 562, Map 1201. (Naturalized from Eurasia). [*Brassica a.; B. kaber*].

Family 97. Capparáceae (Caper Family)

Hermaphrodite, viscid or glandular-pubescent, annual herbs. Leaves palmately compound, alternate, petioled, estipulate or stipules short and spinose, with entire or serrulate leaflets. Flowers perfect, regular (ours), in terminal leafy or bracteate racemes, sepals 4, distinct or slightly united at the base, petals 4, equal or nearly so, clawed, stamens 6-many, equal or somewhat unequal but not tetradynamous, distinct, hypogynous, ovary superior, 1-locular, 2-carpelled, with numerous ovules, bearing a gland at the base, style 1. Fruit an elongate capsule, dehiscent by 2 valves, lacking a septum. [*Capparidaceae*].

Leaflets 3; stipular spines absent; petals retuse; fruit sessile or short-stipitate above the
     pedicel. (Fig. 563). .... 1. *Polanisia*
                                                                                                                                 dodecandra

Leaflets 5 or more; stipular spines often present; petals entire; fruit long-stipitate
     above the pedicel. (Fig. 564). .... 2. *Cleome*

1. *Polanísia* Raf. Clammy-weed. (from the Greek, based on the many unequal stamens).

Branched, glandular-pubescent herbs; leaves trifoliate, estipulate, with oblong, ovate or elliptic, entire leaflets; flowers white to pinkish, in leafy racemes, the petals retuse, stamens 8-many; fruit linear to lance-linear, turgid, veiny, sessile to short-stipitate above the pedicel.

   1. *P. dodecándra* (L.) DC. Gravelly and sandy soil of waste places, shores of streams and lakes. July- September. Fig. 563, Map 1202. Our plants include subsp. *dodecandra* [*P. graveolens*] and the following subsp.

   subsp. *trachyspérma* (Torr. & Gray) Iltis. Petals 8-12 mm long; stamens 12 mm or more long (petals 4-8 mm long and stamens 10 mm or less long in subsp. *dodecandra*). [*Polanisia t.*]. —FACU

2. *Cleóme* L.

Branched, viscid, glandular-pubescent or glabrous herbs; leaves commonly with a pair of short stipular spines at the base of the petiole, leaflets 3-5 or more, lanceolate to oblanceolate, entire or

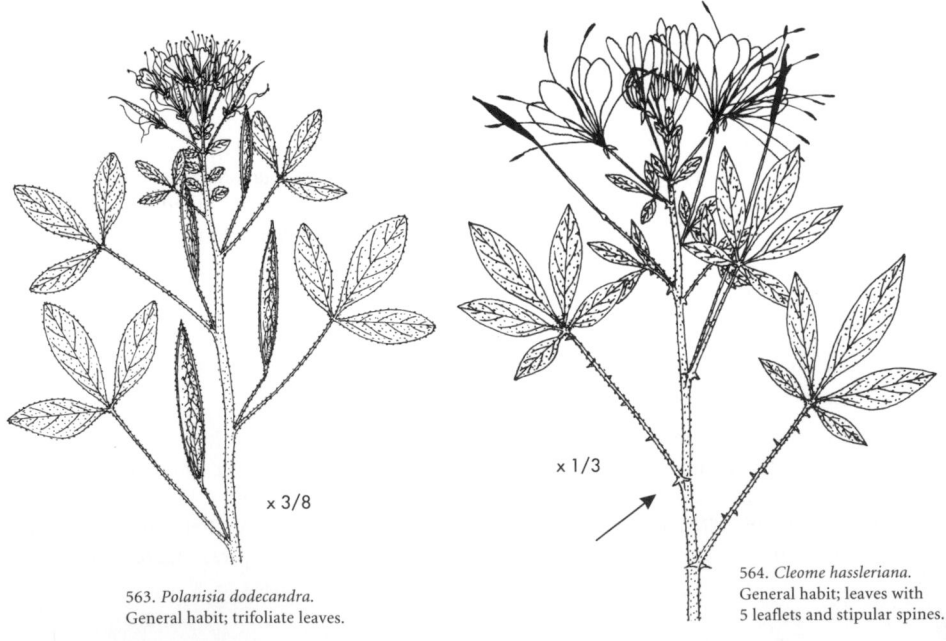

× 3/8

× 1/3

563. *Polanisia dodecandra.*
General habit; trifoliate leaves.

564. *Cleome hassleriana.*
General habit; leaves with
5 leaflets and stipular spines.

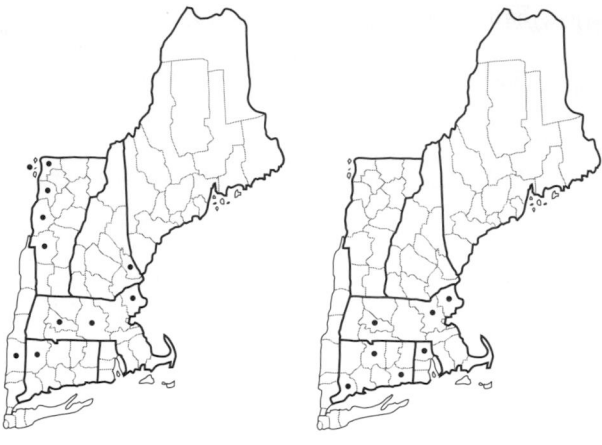

1202. *Polanisia dodecandra*   1203. *Cleome hassleriana*

serrulate; flowers white to pink, in bracteate racemes, the petals entire, stamens 6, with long, slender filaments; fruit linear to lance-linear, long-stipitate above the pedicel.

Stem viscid, glandular-pubescent; leaflets 5 or more. .... 1. *C. hassleriana*
Stem glabrous, or sparsely pubescent when young; leaflets 3. .... 2. *C. serrulata*

1. *C. hassleriána* Chodat. Spider-flower. Waste places. July- October. Rare. Fig. 564, Map 1203. (Naturalized from the Tropics). [*C. spinosa*]. —FACU-

2. *C. serruláta* Pursh. Stinking clover. Western; rarely adventive in our range. Reported for CT, ME, Essex County MA.

Family 98. Resedáceae (Mignonette Family)

Hermaphrodite, mostly glabrous, annual or perennial herbs. Leaves simple, lobed or pinnately divided, alternate, petioled or sessile, with minute, gland-like stipules. Flowers small, perfect, irregular, whitish, greenish or yellow, in dense terminal bracteate spikes or racemes, sepals 4-8, nearly equal, petals 4-8, unequal, entire to variously cleft or lobed, stamens numerous, borne on a large, fleshy, 1-sided disc above the petals, distinct, ovary superior, 1-locular, of 3-6 carpels, with numerous ovules, styles or stigmas 3-6. Fruit a capsule, this 3-6 lobed and with 3-6 horns, opening at the top.

1. *Reséda* L. Mignonette (name based on reputed sedative value).
Same characters as the family.

a. Sepals reflexed in flower; capsules pendant or horizontally spreading. (Fig. 565) .... 1. *R. odorata*
a. Sepals mostly ascending in flower; capsules ascending.
    b. Stem leaves not dissected .... 2. *R. luteola*
    b. Stem leaves dissected.
        Bracts subtending pedicels deciduous at anthesis or shortly after; leaves
            irregularly pinnatifid, with few segments. .... 3. *R. lutea*
        Bracts subtending pedicels persistent until maturity of fruit; leaves regularly
            pinnatifid, with more numerous segments. .... 4. *R. alba*

1. *R. odoráta* L. (fragrant). Escaped from cultivation to waste places. Fig. 565, Map 1204.

2. *R. luteóla* L. (yellowish). Dyer's Rocket. Waste places. (Introduced from Europe). Reported for MA, RI, New Haven County CT, Bronx County NY.

3. *R. lútea* L. (yellow). Fields, roadsides and waste places. June-September. Map 1205. (Adventive from Europe).

4. *R. álba* L. (white). Roadsides and waste places. June-October. Map 1206. (Adventive from Europe).

Family 99. Sarraceniáceae (Pitcher-plant Family)

Hermaphrodite, scapose, insectivorous, evergreen perennial herbs. Leaves rosulate, hollow and pitcher-shaped, with a broad wing along the adaxial side, and a broad, arching hood at the apex, the hood and tube with reflexed bristles inside, usually partially filled with water and decayed insects. Flowers perfect, regular, large, solitary (ours), nodding, scapose, purple, calyx subtended by 3 bracts, sepals 5, broad and spreading, persistent, petals 5, oblong or obovate, incurved, deciduous, stamens numerous, hypogynous, ovary superior, large, subglobose, 5-locular, of 5 carpels, with numerous ovules, style short, expanded into a thin broad, peltate, 5-angled and 5-rayed umbrella-shaped body, the rays each terminating in a small, hooked stigma beneath. Fruit a 5-valved, loculicidal capsule.

1. *Sarracénia* L. Pitcher-plant (for M. Sarrasin de l'Etang).

Same characters as the family

    1. *S. purpúrea* L. (purple). Sphagnum bogs. June-July. Fig. 566, Map 1207. Our plants are subsp. *purpurea.* —OBL

Family 100. Droseráceae (Sundew Family)

Hermaphrodite, glandular-pubescent, scapose, or occasionally leafy-stemmed, insectivorous, annual or perennial herbs. Leaves rosulate (cauline and alternate in submersed plants), filiform or linear to orbicular, unrolling from base to tip when young, petioled, covered with stalked, reddish

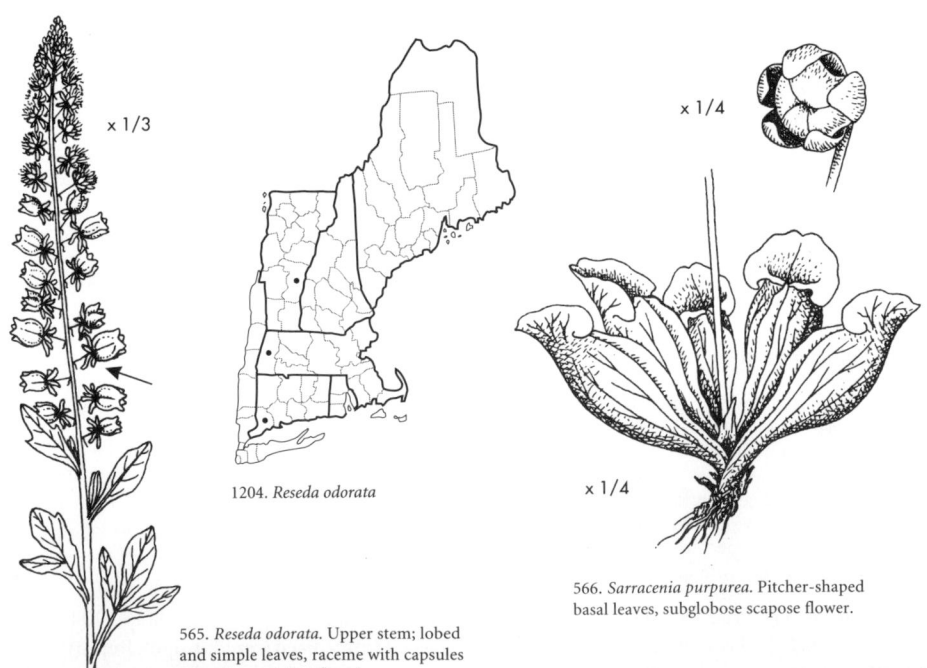

× 1/3

1204. *Reseda odorata*

× 1/4

× 1/4

565. *Reseda odorata.* Upper stem; lobed
and simple leaves, raceme with capsules
spreading, sepals reflexed.

566. *Sarracenia purpurea.* Pitcher-shaped
basal leaves, subglobose scapose flower.

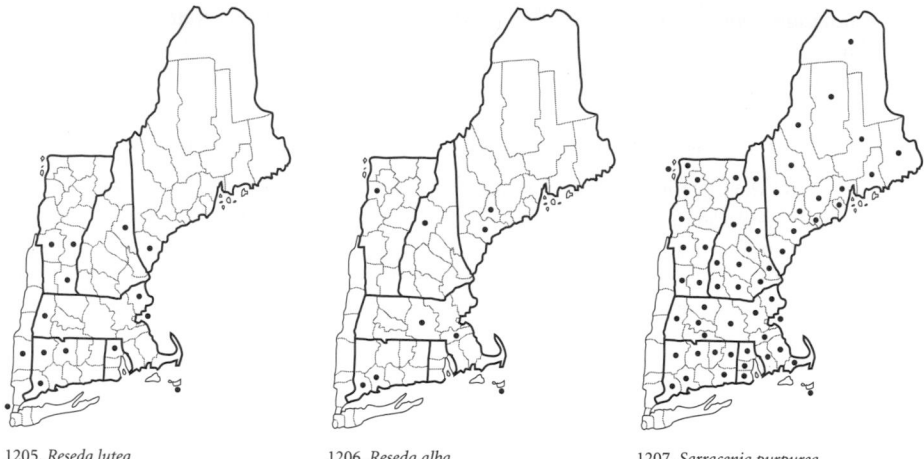

1205. *Reseda lutea*   1206. *Reseda alba*   1207. *Sarracenia purpurea*

glands which secrete a viscid fluid that entraps insects, stipulate, the stipules variously fringed or divided. Flowers perfect, regular, in a terminal, 1-sided, usually simple racemose inflorescence, white to pink or purple, sepals, petals and stamens each 5, withering-persistent, hypogynous, ovary superior, 1-locular, of usually 3 carpels, with numerous ovules, styles usually 3, deeply divided so as to appear 6. Fruit a usually 3-valved, loculicidal capsule.

1. *Drosera* L. Sundew (from the Greek, meaning dewy).

Same characters as the family. —OBL

a. Leaf blades filiform, not distinct from the petiole, the glandular portion more than
    5 cm long; petals rose-purple. .... 1. *D. filiformis*
a. Leaf blades linear, spatulate or suborbicular, distinct from petiole, 5 cm or less
    long; petals white, rarely pink.
    b. Leaf blades suborbicular, as wide or wider than long; petioles pubescent. .... 2. *D. rotundifolia*
    b. Leaf blades linear to spatulate, longer than wide; petioles glabrous.
        Stipules adnate to the petiole. (Fig. 567).
            Leaf blades linear; seeds rhomboid .... 3. *D. linearis*
            Leaf blades elongate-spatulate; seeds fusiform. .... 4. *D. anglica*
        Stipules free (sometimes inconspicuous in forma *natans* which has alternate
            stem leaves; leaves all basal in *D. linearis* and *D. anglica*). .... 5. *D. intermedia*

    1. *D. filifórmis* Raf. (thread-like). Dew-thread. Sandy pond margins and damp sand along the coast. July-August. Map 1208. Endangered in RI, CT. Our plants are var. *filiformis*.
    2. *D. rotundifólia* L. (round-leaved). Round-leaved Sundew. Bogs, pond margins, wet depressions. June-August. Map 1209. (Eurasia). Our plants include var. *rotundifolia* and the following var.:
    var. *comósa* Fern. Inflorescence capitate; carpels modified into leaves, petals greenish to red (inflorescence loose, carpels not modified, petals white in var. *rotundifolia*). Reported to be of value in treating whooping cough.
    3. *D. lineáris* Goldie (linear). Bogs and wet, calcareous lake shores. July-August. Fig. 567. Endangered in ME; reported for Aroostook County.
    4. *D. ánglica* Huds. (English). Bogs and peaty areas. June-August. (Eurasia; Hawaii). From farther north and west. Reported for ME. [*D. longifolia*].
    5. *D. intermédia* Hayne (intermediate). Bogs, pond margins, wet depressions. July-August. Map 1210. (Eurasia; W.I.). Endangered in ME. [*D. longifolia*].

forma *nátans* Heuser. Stem prolonged; leaves scattered, alternate; shallow water (stem not greatly prolonged, leaves basal and plant usually growing in wet soil but not shallow water in forma *intermedia*).

Family 101. Podostemáceae (Riverweed Family)

Hermaphrodite, densely tufted, submerged, aquatic, perennial herbs, attached to stones in running water by fleshy discs, stem usually branched. Leaves alternate, 2-ranked, with adnate stipules, the base dilated and sheathing, usually forked above into numerous linear or filiform segments, sometimes long, narrowly linear and simple. Flowers perfect, much reduced, solitary in the leaf axils, subtended by a membranous, spathe-like involucre, perianth none, stamens 2, hypogynous, attached to one side of the ovary near the base, united for more than half their length, staminodia 2, minute, filiform, ovary superior, 2-locular, of 2 carpels, with numerous ovules, styles 2, short. Fruit a ribbed, 2-valved capsule on an elongate pedicel, one valve deciduous, the other persistent.

1. Podostémum Michx. Riverweed (from the Greek, based on the position of the stamens). Same characters as the family.

1. P. ceratophýllum Michx. Attached to stones in rapidly flowing water. July-September. Fig. 568, Map 1211. —OBL

Family 102. Crassuláceae (Orpine Family)

Hermaphrodite or dioecious, mostly succulent, annual or perennial herbs. Leaves simple, alternate, opposite or whorled, entire or toothed, mostly sessile, estipulate. Flowers perfect or rarely unisexual, regular, mostly cymose, occasionally solitary in the leaf axils, bracteate, sepals and petals usually 3-5, or occasionally more, distinct or united at the base, petals, occasionally none, stamens as many or twice as many as the sepals, distinct, usually hypogynous, ovary superior, 1-locular, with numerous ovules, style 1, carpels of the same number as the sepals, each usually with a scale at the base, carpels distinct or sometimes united below. Fruit a follicle or these united below and forming a lobed capsule.

a. Plants minute; flowers solitary in the axils of opposite leaves; stamens 3 or 4.
   (Fig. 569) .... 1. *Crassula aquatica*
a. Plants not minute; flowers in terminal cymes, corymbs or panicles; stamens 8 to
   many.
   b. Plants not succulent; petals usually absent; fruit an angular, 5-lobed and beaked
      capsule. (Fig. 570) .... 2. *Penthorum*
                                                                                             sedoides
   b. Plants succulent; petals present; fruit a cluster of distinct or barely united
      (at base) follicles.
      Basal leaves in dense, subglobose rosettes, abruptly pointed; sepals and petals
      6-many. (Fig. 571) .... 3. *Sempervivum*
                                                                                              tectorum
      Basal leaves, if present, neither in dense, subglobose rosettes nor abruptly
      pointed; sepals and petals 4-5 .... 4. *Sedum*

1. Cróssula L. Pygmy-weed.
Minute, tufted or matted, glabrous, annual herbs with slender, branched stems, aquatic or growing in mud; leaves opposite, linear, succulent, connate-based, entire; flowers minute, whitish or greenish, solitary and sessile or short pedicelled in the leaf axils, sepals and petals each 3-4, distinct or united at the base, stamens and carpels each 3-4; follicles divergent, several-seeded. [*Tillaea*].
   In addition to the following species *C. saginoides* has also been reported for MA.

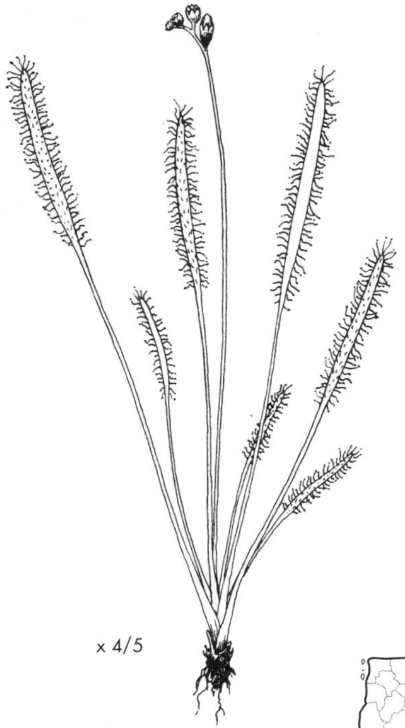

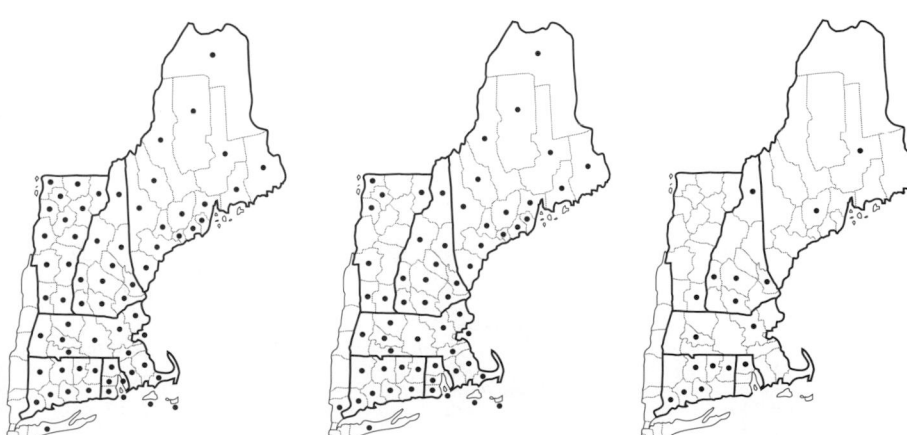

568. *Podostemum ceratophyllum.*
General habit; leaves forked
into linear segments.

567. *Drosera linearis.* General
habit; leaf blades linear.

x 4/5

x 1

1208. *Drosera filiformis*

1209. *Drosera rotundifolia*

1210. *Drosera intermedia*

1211. *Podostemum ceratophyllum*

1. *C. aquática* (L.) Schoenl. (aquatic). Tidal mud flats usually within the limits of the tide, and margins of freshwater pools and rivers. July-September. Fig. 569. Map 1212. (Europe, n. Africa). [*Tillaea aquatica*]. —OBL

2. *Pénthorum* L. Ditch stonecrop (from the Greek, based on the flower parts in 5s).

Rhizomatous, non-succulent, perennial herbs with glabrous, simple or branched stems; leaves alternate, lanceolate to narrowly elliptic, sessile or short petioled, acuminate to base and tip, sharply serrate; flowers on the upper side of spreading, leafless branches of a terminal, 2-4 branched, stipitate-glandular cyme, yellowish-green, sepals 5, petals usually lacking, stamens 10, carpels 5, united to or above the middle; fruit an angular, 5-lobed and beaked, 5-locular capsule formed from the 5 united carpels, each lobe circumscissile above the middle, many-seeded.

1. *P. sedoídes* L. (like sedum). Marshes, pond and stream margins, and wet depressions. July-October. Fig. 570, Map 1213. —OBL

3. *Sempervívum* L. Houseleek (name based on the hardiness of the plant).

Fleshy, pubescent, perennial herbs; leaves basal and cauline, entire, the former ovate or obovate, abruptly pointed, in dense, subglobose rosettes at the base of the flowering stem and on short, lateral offshoots, the cauline alternate, imbricated, oblong to obovate, sessile; flowers rose-purple, sessile along the branches of a usually dense, compound cyme, this compact with short branches or open, with spreading or recurved branches, sepals and petals 6-many, the latter 2-3 times as long as the sepals, stamens twice as many as the petals, carpels 6-many, distinct; fruit follicular, seeds many.

1. *S. tectórum* L. (of roofs). Hens-and-chickens. Escaped from cultivation. July-August. Fig. 571, Map 1214. (Introduced from Europe). The steeped leaves are reported to be of value in soothing burns and bruises and in removing corns and warts. There may be a variety of other medicinal uses for this plant.

4. *Sédum* L. Stonecrop (name based on the ability of some species to attach to ledges and rocks).

Fleshy, glabrous, perennial herbs or sub-shrubs, erect or more often decumbent and mat-forming; leaves alternate, opposite or whorled, often dense and imbricated, with linear, terete or expanded blades, sessile, entire or toothed; flowers perfect or imperfect (plant dioecious), white, yellow, pink

1212. *Crassula aquatica*   1213. *Penthorum sedoides*   1214. *Sempervivum tectorum*

x 1

569. *Crassula aquatica.*
General habit.

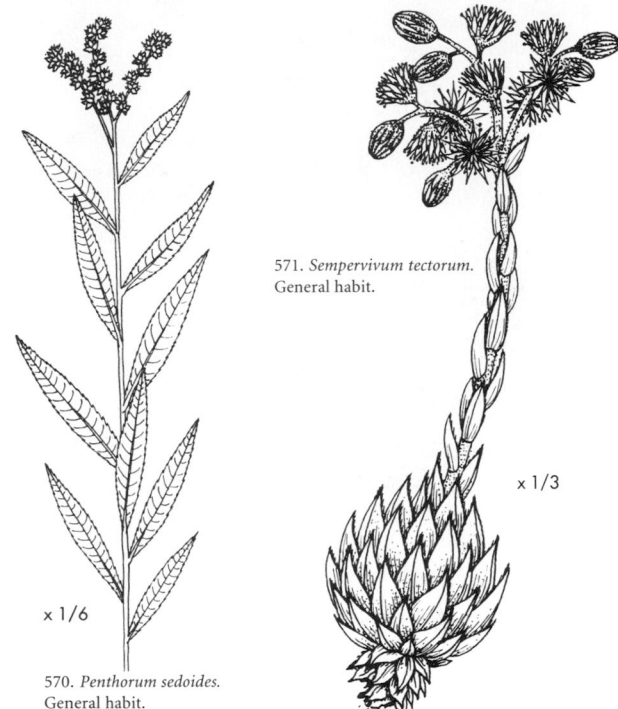

571. *Sempervium tectorum.*
General habit.

x 1/6

570. *Penthorum sedoides.*
General habit.

x 1/3

or purple, in a terminal, sometimes 1-sided cyme, or a corymb or panicle, calyx 4-5 lobed, petals 4-5, distinct, stamens 8-10, perigynous, carpels 4-5, distinct or united at the base; fruit follicular, seeds many.

a. Leaves mostly in whorles of 3 on non-flowering branches.
    Leaves obovate, less than 2.5 times as long as wide; flowers white. .... 1. *S. ternatum*
    Leaves oblong-lanceolate or lanceolate; more than 3 times as long as wide;
        flowers yellow .... 2. *S. sarmentosum*
a. Leaves mostly alternate or opposite.
  b. Leaves less than 4 mm wide.
    c. Leaves 5 mm or less long, imbricated. (Fig. 572).
      Leaves ovoid, more than 1.5 mm wide .... 3. *S. acre*
      Leaves oblong, less than 1.5 mm wide. .... 4. *S. sexangulare*
    c. Leaves 6 mm or more long, at least those of the flowering stems not imbricated.
      d. Leaves flat; inflorescence branches with stalked glands .... 5. *S. hispanicum*
      d. Leaves terete or subterete; inflorescence branches glabrous.
        Sepals 2-3 mm long; petals 6 mm or less long .. . . 6. *S. reflexum*
        Sepals 4-6 mm long; petals longer than 6 mm. .... 7. *S. ochroleucum*
  b. Leaves more than 5 mm wide.
    e. Leaves mostly opposite.
      Stems creeping and rooting at the lower nodes, plant mat-forming;
        inflorescence forking at the base into several secund cymes.
        (Fig. 573). .... 8. *S. spurium*
      Stems erect, plant not mat forming; inflorescence repeatedly branched,
        not secund .... 9. *S. alboroseum*
    e. Leaves alternate.
      Flowers all or mostly unisexual; leaves less than 1.5 cm wide. .... 10. *S. rosea*
      Flowers perfect (although often not produced); leaves, at least the larger,
        more than 1.5 cm wide .... 11. *S. telephium*

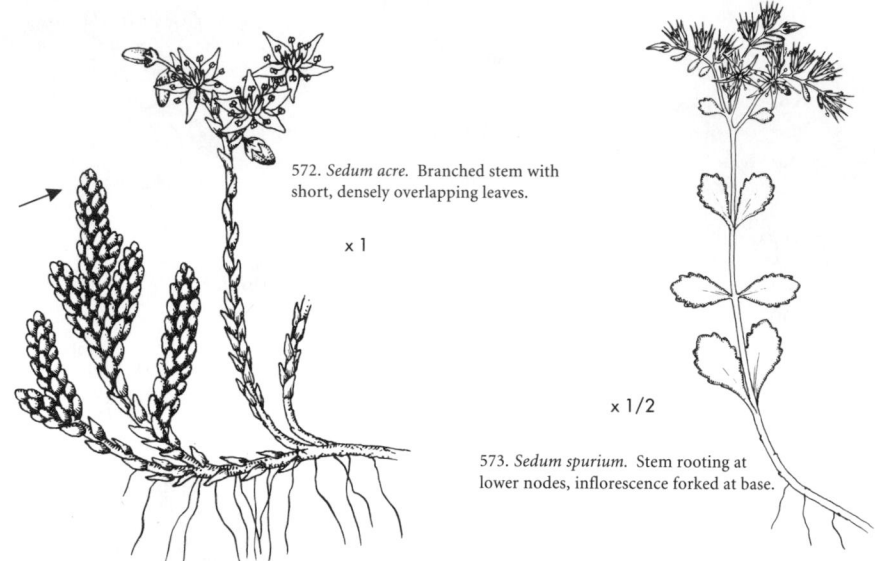

572. *Sedum acre.* Branched stem with short, densely overlapping leaves.

x 1

x 1/2

573. *Sedum spurium.* Stem rooting at lower nodes, inflorescence forked at base.

1. S. ternátum Michx. (in threes). Spread from cultivation to damp roadsides, near buildings, rocks and streambanks. May-June. Map 1215.

2. S. sarmentósum Bunge (producing lithe runners). Escaped from cultivation to roadsides and waste places. June. Map 1216. (Introduced from e. Asia).

3. S. ácre L. (pungent-tasting). Mossy Stonecrop. Escaped from cultivation to streambanks, ledges, rocks and roadsides. June-July. Fig. 572, Map 1217. (Naturalized from Europe). Reported to be of value in removing corns and in bringing boils to a head.

4. S. sexanguláre L. (six-angled). Escaped from cultivation to roadsides and waste places. June-July. Map 1218.

5. S. hispánicum L. Escaped from cultivation to rocks, roadsides and waste places. Reported for MA, Addison County VT.

6. S. refléxum L. Escaped from cultivation to roadsides and waste places. June-July. Map 1219. (Introduced from Europe). [*S. rupestre*].

S. rupéstre L. Similar to *S. reflexum* but with leaves subterete, flat on the upper surface (leaves terete in *S. reflexum*). Rarely spread from cultivation. Reported for MA.

7. S. ochroléucum Chaix. Escaped from cultivation to roadsides, fields and waste places. July - August. (Naturalized from Europe). Reported for MA, Lincoln County ME. [*S. anopetalum*].

S. álbum L. A similar species with white flowers (flowers are yellow or cream colored in *S. ochroleucum*). Escaped from cultivation. (Introduced from Eurasia). Reported for Lincoln County ME.

8. S. spúrium Bieb. (false). Escaped from cultivation to roadsides, fields and waste places. July-August. (Naturalized from Eurasia). Fig. 573, Map 1220.

9. S. alboróseum Baker (whitish pink). Escaped from cultivation to roadsides and waste places. July-August. Map 1221. (Introduced from Asia). [*S. x erythrostrictum*].

S. spectábile Boreau. Resembling *S. alboroseum* but with stamens much exceeding the petals (stamens equalling or only slightly exceeding petals in *S. alboroseum*); may also key to *S. ternatum* or *S. sarmentosum* but has pink petals and upright stems (petals white in *S. ternatum* and *S. sarmentosum* and stems creeping). Rarely escaped from cultivation. Reported for New London County CT, Suffolk County NY.

10. S. rósea (L.) Scop. (old generic name). Ledges and rocks, along the coast and inland. June-August. Map 1222. (Eurasia). Endangered in NY. [*Rhodiola r.*]. Young leaves and roots are reported as good for salads.

11. S. teléphium L. Live-forever. Escaped from cultivation to roadsides, waste places and thickets. August-September. Map 1223. (Naturalized from Eurasia). [*S. fabaria; S. purpureum*].

S. kamtscháticum Fisch. & C. A. Mey. Rarely escaped from cultivation; distinguishable from *S. telephium* in having yellow flowers (red-purple in *S. telephium*). (Introduced from Asia). Reported for Strafford County NH, Dutchess and Suffolk Counties NY. [*S. ellacombianum*]. Represented with us as subsp. *ellacombiánum* (Praeg.) R. T. Clausen.

S. aízoon L. Differing from *S. kamtschaticum* in having leaves broadest at or below the middle and toothed from below the middle (leaves broadest above the middle and toothed above the middle in *S. kamtschaticum*). (Asia). Rarely spread from cultivation. Reported for MA.

S. telephioídes Michx. Similar to *S. telephium* but with pale pink flowers and glaucous leaves (flowers red-purple and leaves not glaucous in *S. telephium*). Southern. Reported for CT, Dutchess County NY. [*Anacampseros t.*].

1215. *Sedum ternatum*

1216. *Sedum sarmentosum*

1217. *Sedum acre*

1218. *Sedum sexangulare*

1219. *Sedum reflexum*

1220. *Sedum spurium*

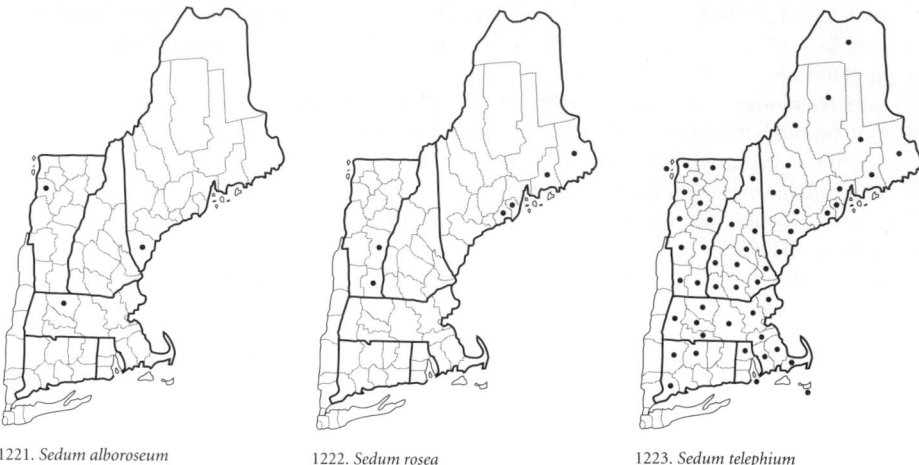

1221. *Sedum alboroseum*   1222. *Sedum rosea*   1223. *Sedum telephium*

Family 103. Hydraneáceae (Hydrangea Family)

Shrubs, rarely a vine. Leaves opposite, occasionally whorled, simple, entire or toothed to lobed, estipulate. Flowers solitary or in cymes, racemes or panicles, perfect, or the marginal ones sterile, or all sterile, calyx 4-5-lobed, petals 4-5, stamens twice as many as the petals or numerous, epigynous, ovary inferior, of 2-5 united carpels, 2-5 locular, ovules numerous, styles 2-5. Fruit a capsule. [*Hydrangeaceae; Saxifragaceae*].

a. Sepals and petals mostly 4; calyx lobes more than 3 mm long; stamens 20 or more .... 1. *Philadelphus*
a. Sepals and petals mostly 5 or more; calyx lobes (of fertile flowers) 3 mm or less
     long; stamens 10 or fewer or plant a vine (plant not a vine in *Philadelphus*).
        Styles 2; capsule 2-locular, poricidally dehiscent; marginal (sometimes all)
           flowers frequently enlarged and sterile; stellate hairs lacking. (Fig. 575). ...... 2. *Hydrangea*
        Styles 3-5; capsule 3-5-locular, dehiscent by 3-5 valves; flowers all fertile;
           stellate hairs present on twigs, leaves and inflorescence. .... 3. *Deutzia scabra*

1. *Philadélphus* L. Mock Orange (named for an early King of Egypt).

Shrubs, with outer bark often exfoliating, twigs with fine vertical lines or ridges, pith roundish, pale, buds small, ovoid, solitary and sessile, with 2 valvate, pubescent scales, imbedded under the leaf scars and bursting through in winter, end bud lacking, leaf scars opposite, half-rounded, becoming crescent shaped when bud bursts through, transversely connected, bundle scars 3, stipule scars lacking; leaves opposite, short petioled, mostly ovate, acuminate, serrate or entire; flowers conspicuous, solitary, cymose or racemose, terminal or axillary, calyx with a turbinate or campanulate tube adnate to the ovary, usually 4-lobed, usually pubescent within, petals 4, large and white, stamens 20 or more, carpels 4, united into a 4-locular, inferior ovary, styles 4, united to or beyond the middle; fruit a 4 celled, loculicidal, 4-valved capsule with many seeds.

a. Flowers solitary or in cymules of 3, or if more the lowest in leaf axils. .... 1. *P. inodorus*
a. Flowers 5 or more in terminal, leafless racemes. (Fig. 574).
     Leaves hairy beneath over their entire surface; bark of second year branches
          persistent, not exfoliating .... 2. *P. pubescens*
     Leaves hairy beneath only on the main veins, otherwise glabrous; bark of
          second year branches exfoliating .... 3. *P. coronarius*

1. P. inodórus L. (odorless). Escaped from cultivation to roadsides. May-June. Map 1224. [*P. grandiflorus*].

2. P. pubéscens Loisel. (hairy). Limestone river bluffs. May-June. Map 1225.

3. P. coronárius L. (suitable for wreath). Escaped from cultivation to roadsides. June-July. Fig. 574, Map 1226. (Introduced from Europe).

2. Hydrangéa L. Hydrangea (from the Greek, based on the shape of the capsule).

Shrubs, with outer bark sometimes exfoliating, pith moderate to large, roundish, pale, buds solitary and sessile to subsessile, subglobose to oblong-conical, with 2-3 pairs of scales, leaf scars opposite, sometimes whorled, crescent shaped or 3-5 angled, often transversely connected, bundle scars usually 3, sometimes 5-7, stipule scars lacking; leaves opposite, sometimes whorled, petioled, ovate or oblong to elliptic, acute to acuminate, subcordate to rounded at the base, serrate or 5-7 lobed; flowers numerous, in an ovoid or flat-topped compound terminal cyme, all perfect, or the marginal frequently sterile, or all sterile, the fertile flowers small, white, calyx with a hemispherical tube adnate to the ovary, 4-5 lobed, petals 4-5, stamens 8-10, carpels usually 2, united into a 2-locular, inferior ovary, styles usually 2, short and stout, sterile flowers consisting only of 3-4 large, spreading, white or variously colored sepals; fruit a strongly ribbed, 2-locular, 2-beaked, poricidally dehiscent, many-seeded capsule. The leaves and buds of various species are reported as poisonous.

a. Leaves sharply 5-7 lobed, resembling oak leaves. .... 1. *H. quercifolia*
a. Leaves merely toothed.
    Inflorescence ovoid to oblong .... 2. *H. paniculata*
    Inflorescence flat to round-topped. (Fig. 575). .... 3. *H. arborescens*

1. H. quercifólia Bartr.(oak-leaved). Escaped from cultivation. Reported for Fairfield County CT.

2. H. paniculáta Siebold (panicled). Escaped from cultivation to roadsides and wooded swamps. August-September. Map 1227. (Introduced from Asia). —FAC

3. H. arboréscens L. (tree-like). Roadsides, thickets, woods and woodland borders. June-July. Fig. 575, Map 1228. Reported for CT, MA. [*H. radiata*]. Preparations made from roots have been used as a diuretic and in treating kidney stones. —FACU

H. cinérea Small. Similar to *H. arborescens* but with leaves grayish beneath with dense minute pubescence (leaves glabrous beneath in *H. arborescens*). From farther south and west. Reported for MA. [*H. arborescens* var. *discolor*; var. *deamii*].

H. radiáta Walt. Similar to *H. cinerea* but leaves thick and leathery, tomentum white (leaves membranous, tomentum gray in *H. cinerea*). From farther south. Reported for CT.

3. Deútzia Thunb. (for J. van der Deutz).

Shrubs with exfoliating outer bark, the twigs, leaves and inflorescence with stellate and branched pubescence, pith brown, excavated and twigs hollow between the nodes, buds mostly solitary, sessile, ovoid to oblong, with 2-6 pairs of scales, leaf scars opposite, occasionally whorled, narrowly triangular, transversely connected, bundle scars 3, stipule scars lacking; leaves opposite, occasionally whorled, short petioled, lance-ovate, acute, subcordate to rounded at the base, serrulate to subentire; flowers white, in peduncled, axillary cymes and in cymose-paniculate inflorescences terminating the stem and branches, sometimes double, calyx with a hemispherical tube adnate to the ovary, 5-lobed, petals 5, stamens 10, carpels 3-5, united into a 3-5-locular inferior ovary, styles 3-5; fruit a hemispherical, 3-5 celled, many-seeded capsule tardily dehiscent by 3-5 valves.

Decumária L. *barbáta* L. Similar to *Deutzia* but is a woody vine climbing by aerial rootlets. Southern Reported for Suffolk County NY.

1. D. scábra Thunb. (harsh). Escaped from cultivation to roadsides, thickets and open woodlands. June-July. Rare. Fig. 576, Map 1229. (Introduced from e. Asia).

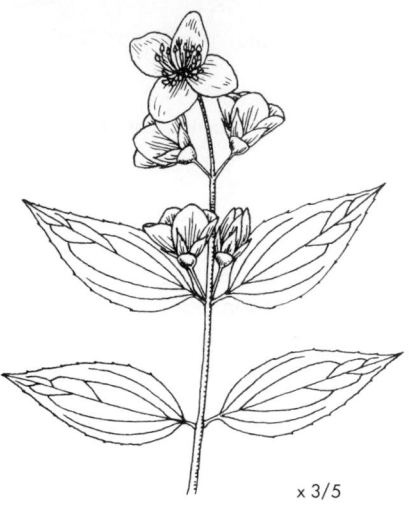

574. *Philadelphus coronarius.* Upper stem
with 5 flowers in leafless raceme.

575. *Hydrangea arborescens.* Upper stem;
inflorescence round-topped with marginal
flowers enlarged and sterile.

x 1/4

576. *Deutzia scabra.* General habit.

1224. *Philadelphus inodorus*

1225. *Philadelphus pubescens*

1226. *Philadelphus coronarius*

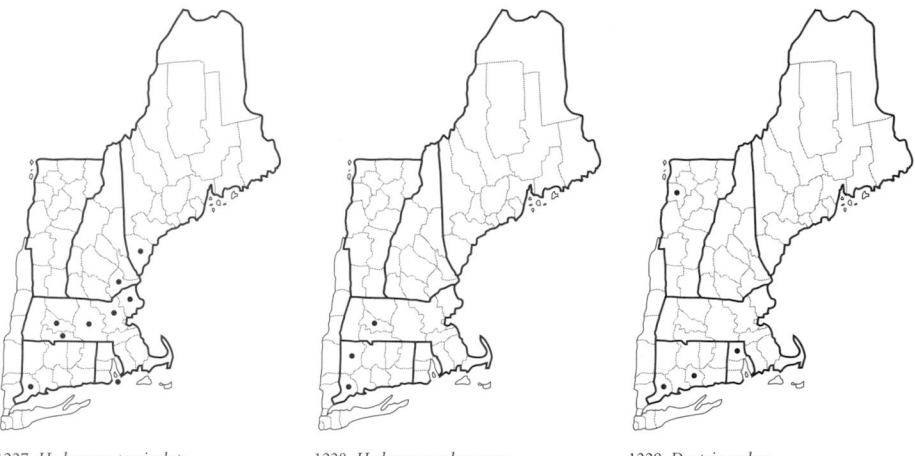

1227. *Hydrangea paniculata*   1228. *Hydrangea arborescens*   1229. *Deutzia scabra*

Family 104. Grossulariáceae (Gooseberry Family)

Low, erect or decumbent, loosely branching shrubs with exfoliating outer bark, internodal bristles and nodal spines sometimes present, the twigs with decurrent ridges from the nodes, sometimes malodorous when broken, pith moderately large, round, pale, buds small, ovoid, solitary, sessile to short-stalked, with 2-3 pairs of scales, leaf scars alternate, U-shaped to crescent-shaped, bundle scars 3, stipule scars lacking. Leaves alternate or fascicled on short spur branches, petioled, palmately veined and lobed or cleft, the base cordate to rounded. Flowers small, white to greenish-yellow or purplish, solitary or in several to many-flowered racemes, occurring with the leaf fascicles on the spur branches or arising from separate lateral buds, calyx with tube adnate to the ovary and sometimes prolonged beyond, 5-lobed, petals 5, smaller than the calyx lobes, stamens 5, included or exserted, carpels 2, united into a 1-locular inferior ovary, styles 2, distinct or united. Fruit a berry with the calyx persisting at the summit, the berry smooth or sometimes bristly or prickly, seeds numerous.

1. ***Ribes*** (Danish name for the red current).

Same characters as the family. The fruits of all species below are edible raw or cooked; Ribes is also host to the white pine blister rust and has been eradicated where white pine is grown as a forest product. —Wildl. 1

a. Flowers or fruit mostly fewer than 4 in a raceme.
  b. Stamens much longer than the calyx lobes.
      Nodal spines (at least the larger ones) 7 mm or more long; stamens mostly
            longer than 8 mm; pedicels shorter than peduncles. (Fig. 577). .... 1. *R. missouriense*
      Nodal spines less than 7 mm long; stamens 8 mm or less long; pedicels
            mostly equalling to longer than peduncles .... 2. *R. rotundifolium*
  b. Stamens shorter than, equalling or barely exceeding (by 1-1.5 mm) the calyx
    lobes.
    c. Calyx lobes shorter than the tube (above the ovary); peduncles mostly longer
        than 6 mm. (Fig. 578) .... 3. *R. cynosbati*
    c. Calyx lobes as long or longer than the tube; peduncles mostly 6 mm or less
      long.

Calyx, ovary and fruit usually glabrous, sometimes hirtellous. .... 4. *R. hirtellum*
Calyx pubescent; ovary and fruit pubescent to glandular. .... 5. *R. uva-crispa*
var. *sativum*
a. Flowers or fruit mostly more than 4 in a raceme.
  d. Ovary and fruit bristly with stalked glands.
    Stems bristly on the internodes and with longer nodal spines. .... 6. *R. lacustre*
    Stems unarmed .... 7. *R. glandulosum*
  d. Ovary and fruit smooth or with sessile glands.
    e. Leaves resinous-glandular beneath.
      Bracts as long or longer than the subtended pedicel; calyx glabrous to
        sparsely villous; ovary eglandular. (Fig. 579). .... 8. *R. americanum*
      Bracts shorter than the subtended pedicel; calyx densely short-pubescent;
        ovary often with sessile glands .... 9. *R. nigrum*
    e. Leaves not resinous-glandular beneath.
      f. Calyx with a long, slender tube, yellow; fruit black. .... 10. *R. aureum*
      var. *villosum*

      f. Calyx tube saucer shaped or campanulate, greenish; fruit red. (Fig. 580).
        Pedicels mostly with stalked glands; anther sacs parallel or nearly so;
          plant decumbent; flowers purplish .... 11. *R. triste*
        Pedicels mostly eglandular; anther sacs widely divergent; plant erect;
          flowers yellowish or greenish .... 12. *R. rubrum*

1. R. missouriénse Nutt. (of Missouri). Open woods, thickets, roadsides. April-May. Fig. 577. Reported for Fairfield County CT.

2. R. rotundifólium Michx. (round-leaved). Rocky open woods. April-May. Map 1230.

3. R. cynósbati L. (dogberry). Moist or rocky woods and thickets. May-June. Fig. 578, Map 1231.

4. R. hirtéllum Michx. (bristly). Woods, wooded swamps and thickets. May-June. Map 1232. [*R. huronense*]. —FAC

R. oxyacanthoídes L. Similar to *R. hirtellum* but differing in having bristly middle and upper internodes of fruiting canes, and glandular leaf blades and inflorescence bracts. Northern and western. Reported for Dutchess County NY. Our plants are var. *oxyacanthoides*.

5. R. úva-críspa L. Garden Gooseberry. Spread from cultivation to woods, thickets and roadsides. May. Map 1233. (Introduced from Europe). [*R. grossularia; Grossularia reclinata*]. Represented with us as var. *sativum* DC. Preparations made from the leaves are reported to be useful in treating dysentery and for skin wounds.

6. R. lacústre (Pers.) Poir. (of lakes). Swamp Current. Moist or rocky mixed or deciduous woods, wooded swamps, pond and stream borders. May-June. Map 1234. [*Limnobotrya lacustris*]. —FACW

7. R. glandulósum Grauer (glandular). Skunk Current. Wooded swamps and wet woods. May-June. Map 1235. [*R. prostratum*]. —FACW

8. R. américánum Mill. (American). Wild Black Current. Moist woods, wooded swamps and thickets. May-June. Fig. 579. Map 1236. [*R. floridanum*]. —FACW

9. R. nígrum L. (black). Black Current. Escaped from cultivation to roadsides and thickets. May. Map 1237. (Introduced from Europe). Seeds of this species may be of value in treating PMS; preparations made from the leaves are used to relieve rheumatism.

10. R. aúreum Pursh. Golden Current. Escaped from cultivation to roadsides and thickets. May-June. Map 1238. [*R. odoratum*]. Represented with us as var. *villosum* DC.

11. R. tríste Pall. (sad). Red Current. Moist woods and wooded swamps. May-June. Map 1239. (Asia). —OBL

12. R. rúbrum L. Garden Current. Woods, wooded swamps, thickets, river borders, roadsides. May. Fig. 580, Map 1240. (Naturalized from Europe). [*R. sativum*]. Preparations made from the leaves are used to relieve rheumatism and to treat sprains.

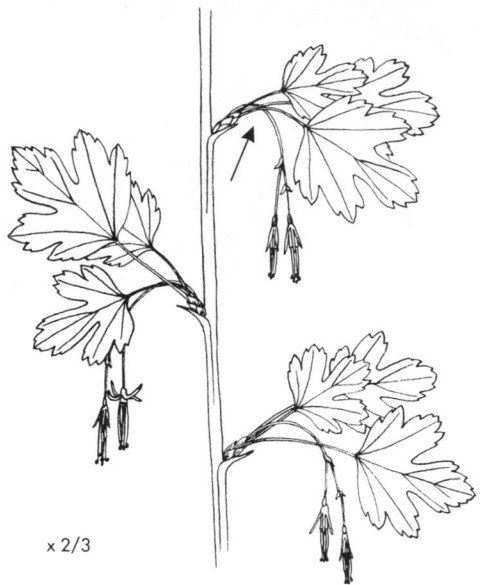

x 2/3

577. *Ribes missouriense*. Section of stem with axillary inforescences, peduncle longer than pedicels.

x 1

578. *Ribes cynosbati*. Several flowers, calyx lobes shorter than tube.

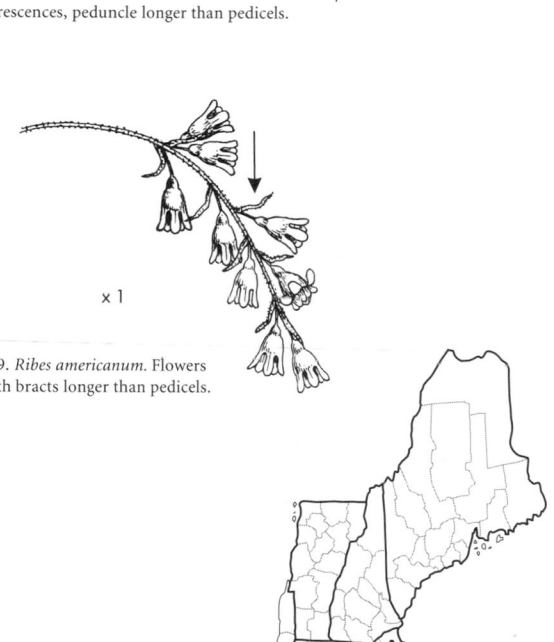

x 1

579. *Ribes americanum*. Flowers with bracts longer than pedicels.

x 3

580. *Ribes rubrum*. Single flower, saucer-shaped calyx tube.

1230. *Ribes rotundifolium*

1231. *Ribes cynosbati*

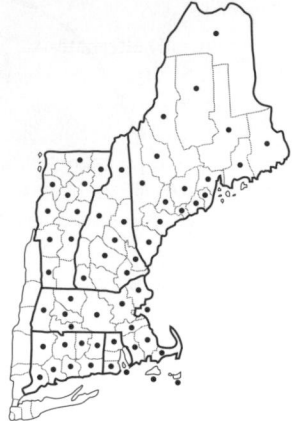

1232. *Ribes hirtellum*

1233. *Ribes uva-crispa* var. *sativum*

1234. *Ribes lacustre*

1235. *Ribes glandulosum*

1236. *Ribes americanum*

1237. *Ribes nigrum*

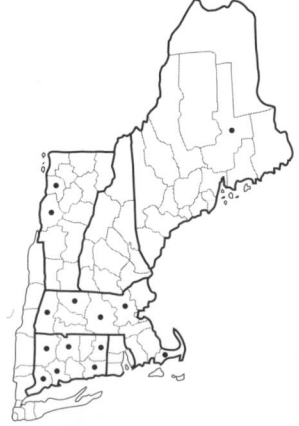

1238. *Ribes aureum* var. *villosum*

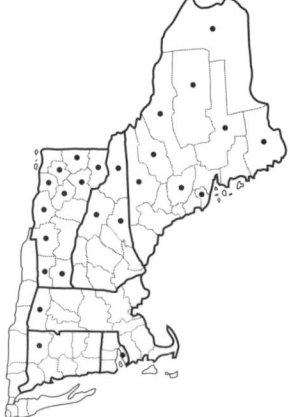

1239. *Ribes triste*

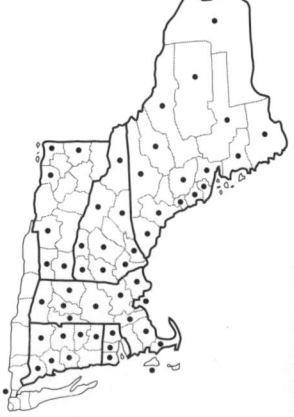

1240. *Ribes rubrum*

Family 105. Saxifragáceae (Saxifrage Family)

Mostly hermaphrodite, rarely polygamodioecious, perennial herbs. Leaves mostly alternate, occasionally opposite or all basal, mostly simple, entire or toothed to lobed or deeply cleft, rarely compound, mostly estipulate. Flowers perfect or rarely unisexual, mostly regular, solitary or in racemes, panicles or cymes, bracteate, sepals 4-5, free or united, petals 4-5, separate, sometimes reduced or absent, sepals and petals rarely more than 5, stamens as many or twice as many as the petals (or calyx lobes in apetalous genera), distinct, perigynous or epigynous, ovary superior, inferior or half-inferior, of 2-4 distinct or united carpels, 1-2-locular, with usually numerous ovules, styles 1-2 (4 stigmas in *Parnassia*). Fruit a capsule or 2-3 follicles.

a. Leaves ternately decompound. (Fig. 581). .... 1. *Astilbe japonica*
a. Leaves simple, lobed or unlobed.
  b. Stems with several to many pairs of opposite leaves.
    Flower solitary on the stem; petals purple; capsule more than 3 mm long. .... 2. *Saxifraga*
    Flowers several on each stem, terminal or appearing axillary; petals absent,
      flower greenish-yellow; capsule 3 mm or less long . (Fig. 584). .... 3. *Chrysosplenium*
                                            americanum
  b. Stems with alternate or 1 pair of opposite leaves or scapose.
    c. Flowers and fruit in racemes (rarely paniculate below in *Tiarella* with 2
      unequal carpels; plants in second half of couplet have equal carpels).
      (Fig. 585).
      Petals pinnately divided to fimbriate; capsule with 2 equal valves. .... 4. *Mitella*
      Petals entire; capsule with 2 unequal valves. .... 5. *Tiarella cordifolia*
    c. Flowers and fruit in panicles, cymes or solitary.
      d. Flower solitary; leaves entire. (Fig. 587). .... 6. *Parnassia glauca*
      d. Flowers in panicles or cymes, or if solitary leaves lobed. (Fig. 588).
        Stamens 5; ovary 1-locular; petioles of basal leaves longer than the
        blades ; rich upland woods .... 7. *Heuchera*
                                                  americana
        Stamens 10; ovary 2-locular; petioles of basal leaves (if present) shorter
        than the blades (or if longer, plant alpine.). .... 2. *Saxifraga*

1. *Astilbe* Hamilton. False Goatsbeard (from the Greek, based on the lustreless foliage of one of the species).

Tall, perennial, polygamodioecious herbs, glandular-pubescent above; leaves alternate, 2-3 times ternately compound, the leaflets serrate and often lobed; flowers perfect or unisexual, small, white or yellowish, in a large, terminal panicle of spikes or racemes, calyx 4-5 parted, petals 5, minute or absent in the pistillate flowers, stamens 10, these and the petals inserted at the base of the calyx, ovary superior, carpels 2, connate in anthesis, styles 2, short; fruit of 2 separate follicles, seeds numerous.

    1. *A. japónica* (Morren & Decne.) Gray (Japanese). Escaped from cultivation to roadsides and waste places. Fig. 581. (Introduced from Japan). Reported for Fairfield County CT, Providence County RI.

2. *Saxífraga* L. Saxifrage (from the reputed value of certain European species in dissolving kidney stones).

Perennial herbs arising from a rootstalk; leaves basal and cauline, simple and lobed, toothed, or entire, the former in basal rosettes or on short, lateral offshoots, the cauline lacking or few and alternate (rarely opposite); flowers regular to slightly irregular, in terminal cymes or panicles, or solitary, calyx 5 cleft or parted, petals 5, often clawed, sometimes deciduous, stamens 10, ovary superior to half inferior, carpels 2, connate, at least at the base, styles 2; fruit a bilobed, 2-locular capsule or 2 nearly distinct follicles, many seeded.

a. Basal, and often the stem leaves (at least the lower) 3-5 lobed. (Fig. 582).
    Bulblets usually present in the axils of the upper leaves; petals 6-10 mm long .... 1. *S. cernua*
    Bulblets not present in the leaf axils; petals 5 mm or less long. .... 2. *S. hyperborea*
a. Basal and stem leaves (if present) entire or toothed, not lobed.
  b. Cauline leaves present below the inflorescence.
    c. Leaves mostly opposite, bristly-ciliate; flowers purple. .... 3. *S. oppositifolia*
    c. Leaves alternate; flowers white or yellow.
      Leaves linear-oblong, entire, without lime encrusted pores; flowers yellow. ... 4. *S. aizoides*
      Leaves oblong to obovate, serrulate, many of the teeth with a lime
        encrusted pore at the base; flowers white .... 5. *S. paniculata*
  b. Cauline leaves absent, the branches of the inflorescence often subtended by
    leaves or bracts.
    d. Basal leaves (at least the larger) 8 cm or more long; petals greenish-white,
      yellowish or purple .... 6. *S. pensylvanica*
    d. Basal leaves less than 8 cm long; petals usually white or flowers replaced by
      leafy tufts.
      Flowers mostly all replaced by tufts of small leaves, a single normal
        terminal flower sometimes present. (Fig. 583) .... 7. *S. foliolosa*
      Flowers normal, not replaced by leafy tufts .. . . 8. *S. virginiensis*

1. S. cérnua L. (nodding). Wet ledge, Mt. Washington, NH. July. Rare. Fig. 582. (Eurasia). Endangered in NH.

2. S. hyperbórea R. Br. Alpine-brook Saxifrage. Wet moss, Mt. Washington, NH. July. (Eurasia). Endangered in NH. Rare. [*S. rivularis*]. —OBL

3. S. oppositifólia L. (opposite-leaved). Purple Mountain Saxifrage. Cliffs. May-July. (Eurasia). Rare. Reported for Lamoille and Orleans Counties VT. [*Antiphylla o.*]. Our plants are subsp. *oppositifolia*. —FAC

4. S. aizoídes L. (resembling *Aizoon*). Yellow Mountain Saxifrage. Cliffs. July-September. (Eurasia). Rare. Reported for Lamoille and Orleans Counties VT. [*Leptasea a.*]. —FACW

5. S. paniculáta P. Mill. Cliffs. June-July. Map 1241. Endangered in NH. [*S. aizoon; Chondrosea a.*].

6. S. pensylvánica L. (of Pennsylvania). Swamp Saxifrage. Wooded swamps, bogs and wet meadows. May-June. Map 1242. [*Micranthes p.; S. forbesii*]. —OBL

7. S. foliolósa R. Br. Mt. Katahdin, ME. July-August. (Eurasia). Rare. Fig. 583. Endangered in ME. [*Hydatica f.; S. stellaris* var. *comosa*].

8. S. virginiénsis Michx. (of Virginia). Early Saxifrage. Ledges, rocky woods, mixed woods. April-May. Map 1243. [*Micranthes v.*]. Our plants are var. *virginiensis*. —FAC-

3. Chrysosplénium L. Golden Saxifrage (from the Greek, based on its reputed medicinal value).

Low, glabrous, semi-aquatic, often mat-forming, perennial herbs; stems slender, decumbent and branched; leaves short-petioled, primarily opposite, or the uppermost sometimes alternate, widely ovate to suborbicular, the base rounded to somewhat cordate, entire to obscurely lobed or crenate; flowers small, greenish tinged with yellow or purple, mostly solitary or in small, leafy-bracted cymes, terminal or appearing axillary by branching of the stem, sessile or subsessile, calyx with a short, turbinate tube and 4 lobes, petals none, stamens 4-8, short, inserted in the notches of a conspicuous 8-lobed disc, carpels 2, united into a 1-locular, inferior ovary, styles 2, protruding through the center of the disc; fruit a short, somewhat flattened, obcordate or 2-lobed capsule, 2-valved at the top, seeds many.

1. C. americánum Schwein. ex Hook. (American). Wooded swamps and wet woods, streams and springy areas, in shade. May-June. Fig. 584, Map 1244. —OBL

4. Mitélla L. Miterwort (name based on shape of the immature fruit).

Rhizomatous, glandular-pubescent, perennial herbs, with or without stolons; stem erect, leafless or few-leaved; leaves closely alternate toward the tip of the rhizome at the base of the flowering stem,

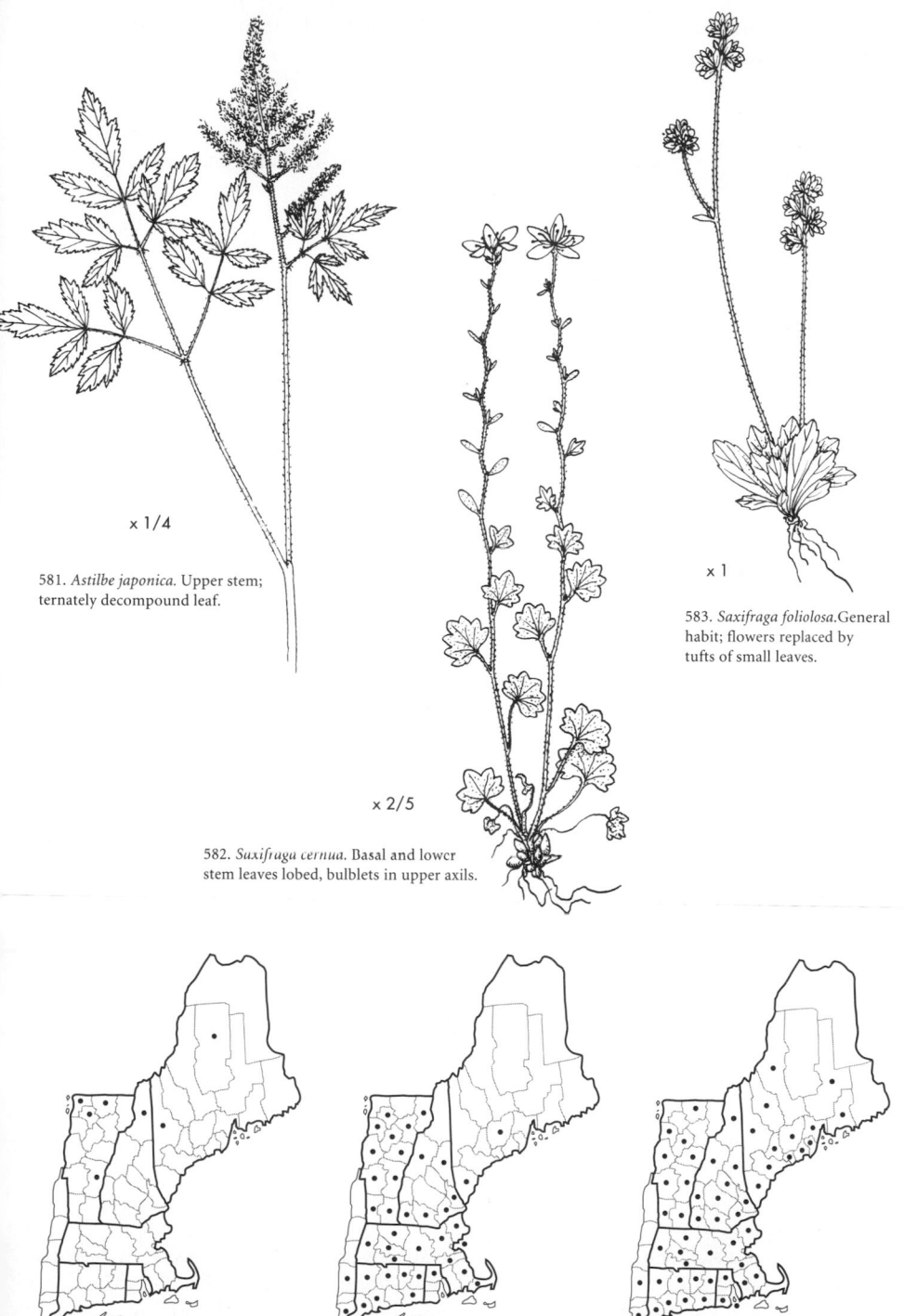

× 1/4

581. *Astilbe japonica*. Upper stem; ternately decompound leaf.

× 2/5

582. *Saxifraga cernua*. Basal and lower stem leaves lobed, bulblets in upper axils.

× 1

583. *Saxifraga foliolosa*.General habit; flowers replaced by tufts of small leaves.

1241. *Saxifraga paniculata*

1242. *Saxifraga pensylvanica*

1243. *Saxifraga virginiensis*

and sometimes also more loosely alternate on stolons, long-petioled, cordate-ovate or suborbicular to reniform, obscurely or shallowly lobed, crenate, the cauline leaves when present, similar but smaller, usually sessile or subsessile, opposite or sometimes alternate; flowers small, white or greenish, in a terminal, spiciform raceme, the rachis and pedicels glandular-pubescent, calyx with a short, campanulate tube adherent to the base of the ovary, 5-lobed, petals 5, pinnately divided to fimbriate, stamens 5-10, included, carpels 2, united below into a 1-locular, inferior ovary, styles 2, short; fruit a 1-celled, 2-valved, many-seeded capsule.

Stem leaves 2, opposite (rarely a 3rd leaf above the pair); flowers white. (Fig. 585) .... 1. *M. diphylla*
Stem leaves none or 1 (if more then alternate); flowers greenish. .... 2. *M. nuda*

 1. *M. diphýlla* L. (two-leaved). Rich, often moist woods. May-June. Fig. 585, Map 1245. —FACU
 M. prostráta Michx., considered an aberrant form of *M. diphylla*, has 4 alternate stem leaves. Reported from sw. CT and Lake Champlain, VT.
 2. *M. núda* L. (naked). Wet mossy woods, borders of woodland streams, wooded swamps and bog forests. May-July. Map 1246. (Asia).
 forma *countrymániae* Seymour has purple flowers. —FACW-

5. *Tiarélla* L. Foamflower (name based on shape of the pistil).

Rhizomatous, pubescent, perennial herbs, usually with long stolons; stem erect, usually leafless (rarely with 1 or 2 leafy bracts); leaves at the base of the flowering stem terminating the rhizome, and/or alternate on the stolons, long petioled, with small, adnate stipules, broadly cordate-ovate, palmately 3-5 lobed, crenate or serrate; flowers white, in a raceme (rarely a panicle) terminating the flowering stem, the rachis and pedicels glandular-pubescent, calyx with a short, campanulate tube, this nearly or quite free from the base of the ovary, 5-lobed, petals 5, clawed, stamens 10, long and slender, carpels 2, unequal, united below into a 1-locular, superior ovary, styles 2; fruit a 1-celled capsule with 2 unequal valves, seeds numerous.

 1. *T. cordifólia* L. (heart-leaved). Rich, moist woods. May-June. Fig. 586, Map 1247. Our plants include var. *cordifolia* and the following var.:
 var. *collína* Wherry. Non-stoloniferous (var. *cordifolia* usually has long stolons). [*T. wherryi*]. —FAC-

6. *Parnássia* L. Grass of Parnassus (name from Mt. Parnassus).

Glabrous, often scapose, perennial herbs from a short, stout rhizome; leaves long petioled, basal, ovate, entire, with a rounded to subcordate base, the scape usually with a single sessile or short petioled leaf at or below the middle; flower solitary, terminal, white, sepals and petals each 5, free from the ovary, the petals with conspicuous greenish veins, stamens 5, staminodia 5, each consisting of 3 or more sterile stamens united below and separate above, shorter than to equalling the stamens, carpels 4, united into a 1-locular, superior ovary, stigmas 4, nearly sessile; fruit a 1-celled, loculicidal, 4-valved, many-seeded capsule.

 1. *P. glaúca* Raf. (blue-green). Wet meadows, bogs and river borders in calcareous soil. August-September. Fig. 587, Map 1248. [*P. americana; P. caroliniana*]. —OBL

7. *Heúchera* L. Alumroot (for J. Heucher).

Glabrous to minutely glandular-pubescent, perennial herbs from a stout caudex; stems naked or with scattered bracts; leaves basal, long-petioled, ovate to suborbicular, cordate-based, with 5-9 crenate to coarsely-toothed lobes; flowers regular, purplish, loosely clustered in a terminal panicle, the panicle branches, pedicels and hypanthium glandular-puberulent, calyx with a short campanu-

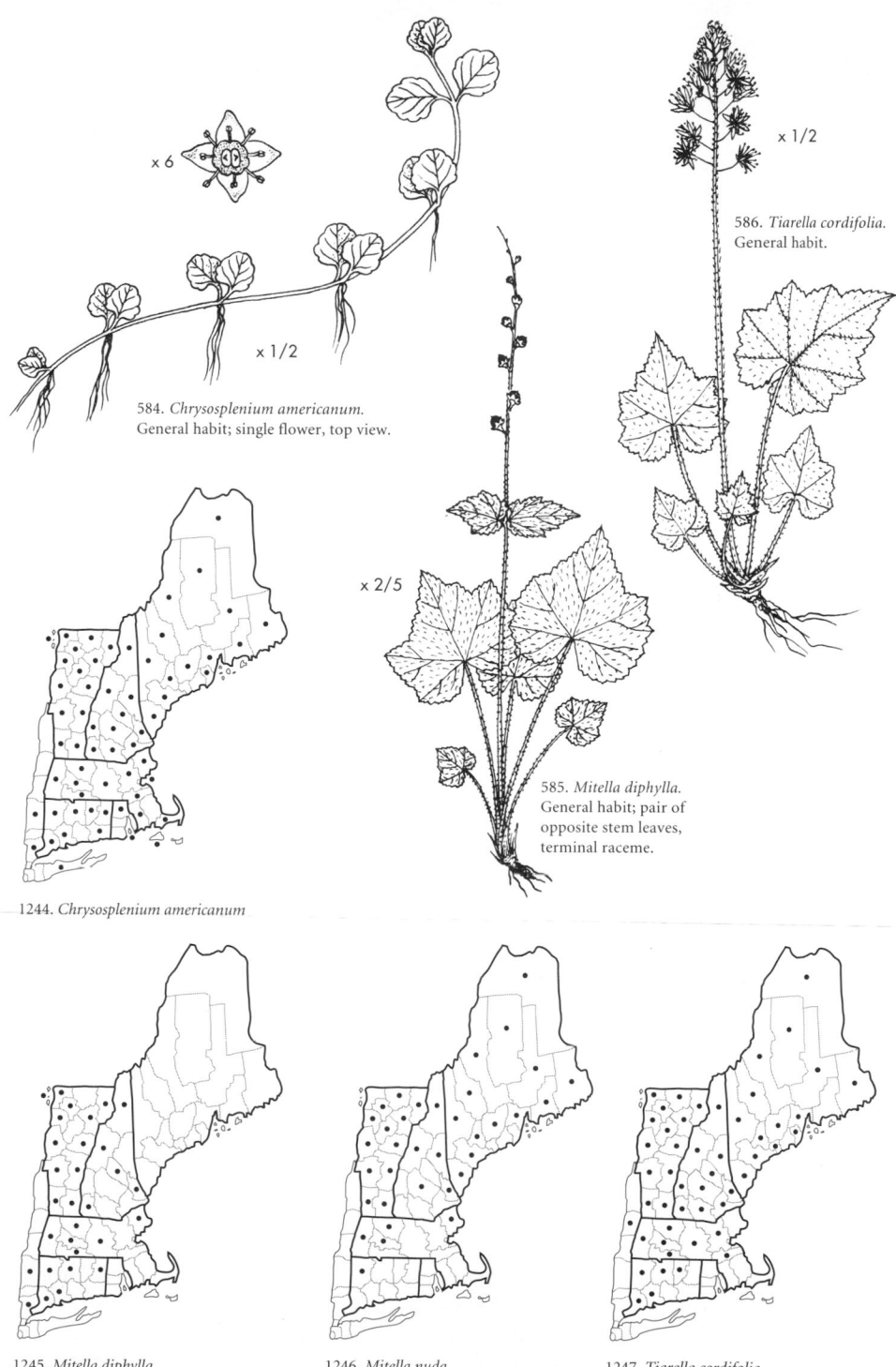

× 6

× 1/2

584. *Chrysosplenium americanum.*
General habit; single flower, top view.

× 1/2

586. *Tiarella cordifolia.*
General habit.

× 2/5

585. *Mitella diphylla.*
General habit; pair of
opposite stem leaves,
terminal raceme.

1244. *Chrysosplenium americanum*

1245. *Mitella diphylla*

1246. *Mitella nuda*

1247. *Tiarella cordifolia*

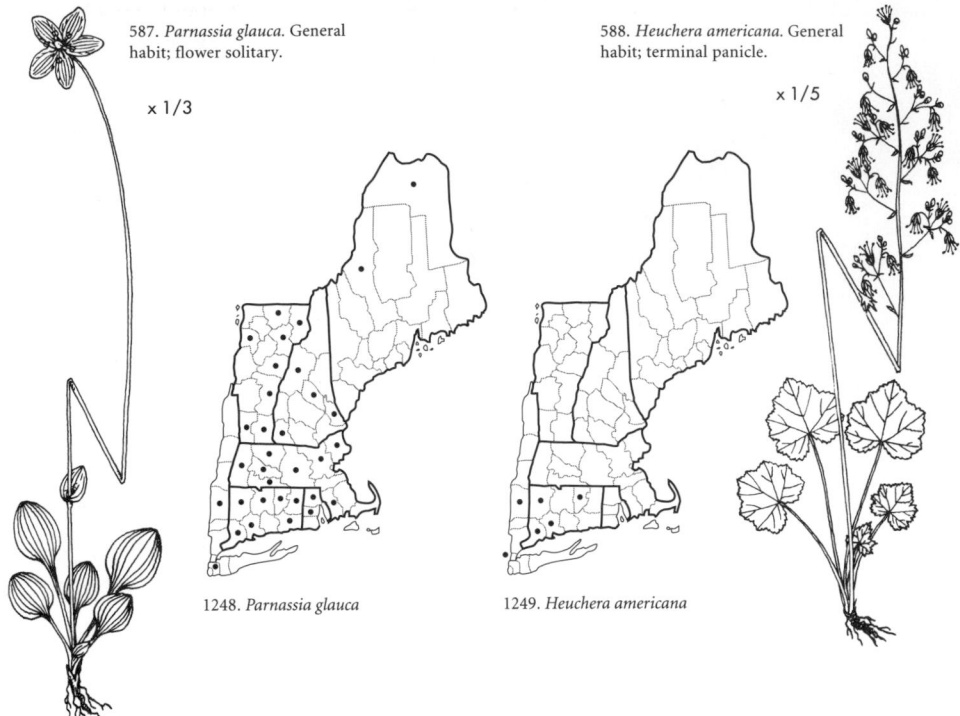

587. *Parnassia glauca*. General habit; flower solitary.

× 1/3

588. *Heuchera americana*. General habit; terminal panicle.

× 1/5

1248. *Parnassia glauca*

1249. *Heuchera americana*

late tube adnate to the base of the ovary, 5-lobed, petals small, usually not exceeding the calyx lobes, entire, narrowly spatulate, stamens 5, much exserted, carpels 2, united below into a 1-locular, inferior ovary, styles 2, long-exserted; fruit a 1-celled, 2-valved, 2-beaked capsule with many seeds.

1. *H. americána* L. (American). Rich, upland woods. May-June. Rare. Fig. 588, Map 1249. Our plants are var. *americana*. Roots, eaten raw, are useful in treating diarrhea. —FACU-

Family 106. Hamamelidáceae (Witch Hazel Family)

Hermaphrodite, monoecious or polygamous trees or shrubs. Leaves alternate, simple toothed or lobed, with deciduous stipules. Flowers perfect or unisexual, regular, in heads or axillary clusters, sessile or subsessile, bracteate, calyx tube adnate to the base of the ovary, calyx lobes 4 or absent, petals 4 or absent, stamens 4-many, some often sterile, distinct, perigynous, ovary half inferior, compound, of 2 united carpels, 2-locular, with 1-many ovules per cell, styles 2. Fruit a 2-locular, 2-beaked woody capsule dehiscent across the top.

Leaves palmately lobed; flowers in dense, globose heads. (Fig. 589). .... 1. *Liquidambar styraciflua*

Leaves, coarsely toothed; flowers in small, axillary clusters. (Fig. 590). .... 2. *Hamamelis virginiana*

1. *Liquidámbar* L. Sweet Gum (name referring to the fragrant resinous sap produced). Monoecious tree with furrowed bark and resinous sap, the smaller branches frequently corky-winged, twigs moderate, sometimes developing as short shoots, pith angled, brownish, buds solitary, sessile or subsessile, ovoid, pointed, the lateral sometimes reduced, normal buds with about 6 scales, leaf scars crescent-shaped to half-elliptic or heart-shaped, bundle traces 3, stipule scars lacking; leaves long-petioled, cordate to truncate at the base, palmately 5-7 lobed, the lobes triangular, divergent, finely serrate, the leaf distinctly star-shaped; flowers imperfect, in heads, perianth lacking, but flowers subtended by small scales, the pistillate heads solitary, globose, on long, axillary peduncles, the flowers cohering, consisting of a 2-locular ovary with 2 long styles, rudimentary stamens present, staminate heads ovoid, in terminal racemes, the flowers consisting of numerous stamens; capsules cohering and hardening, forming a spinose head, each locule 1-2 seeded. —Wildl. 1

1. *L. styraciflua* L. (old generic name, flowering gum). Wooded swamps and wet woods. April-May. Fig. 589, Map 1250. (Central Amer.). Gum used as an expectorant and as a weak antiseptic; also used as chewing gum. —FAC

2. *Hamamélis* L. Witch Hazel (ancient Greek name for a similar plant).

Hermaphrodite, or polygamous shrubs or small trees, twigs somewhat zig-zag, slender, stellate tomentose when young, becoming glabrate, pith small, buds oblong, flattened, stalked, naked, and pubescent, leaf scars half-round to 3-lobed, bundle traces 3, stipule scars unequal; leaves short petioled, ovate, elliptic or obovate, oblique and rounded or subcordate at the base, sometimes stellate pubescent beneath, coarsely toothed; flowers perfect or imperfect, yellow, sessile in small, capitate clusters on short peduncles in the leaf axils, calyx with several bracts at the base, pubescent, lobes 4, ovate, petals 4, long and narrow, stamens 4, short, alternating with 4 scale-like staminodes, styles short; capsule oblong, densely pubescent, each locule 1-seeded. —Wildl. 1

1. *H. virginiána* L. (Virginian). Rich, moist woods. October-November; fruit ripe a year later. Fig. 590, Map 1251. Preparations made from twigs, leaves and bark have long been used to sooth cuts, bruises and insect bites, as well as a variety of other ailments, including varicose veins; first introduced to the settlers by the Indians. —FAC-

Family 107. Platanáceae (Plane-tree Family)

Monoecious tree, with outer bark freely exfoliating, exposing the greenish-gray to white inner layers. Leaves alternate, simple, palmately 3-5 or more lobed, sharply serrate, cordate to truncate at the base, densely pubescent when young, becoming glabrate, petioled, the petiole dilated basally and enclosing the bud, stipules foliaceous, toothed, encircling the twig. Flowers unisexual, very small, in 1 or 2 separate, dense, globose heads, on a pendulous peduncle, minutely bracteate, calyx and corolla tiny and insignificant, staminate flowers consisting of numerous stamens, the pistillate consisting of several, 1-locular, 1-ovulate, superior ovaries, each with a long, recurved style. Fruit a head of clavate achenes, each subtended by tawny bristles.

1. *Plátanus* L. Sycamore (ancient Greek name, based on the broad leaves).

Large tree with spreading branches when mature, twigs zig-zag, pith moderate, pale to brownish, buds solitary, sessile, conical, with a single scale, end bud lacking, leaf scars narrow, encircling the bud, bundle traces 5-7, stipule scars narrow, encircling the twig. —Wildl. 1

1. *P. occidentális* L. (western). Along streams and river floodplains, often planted as a roadside shade tree. May-June. Fig. 591, Map 1252. —FACW-

P. hýbrida Brot. London Plane Tree. Closely resembling the above species but distinguishable in having fruiting heads mostly borne in 2s on the stalk (heads mostly borne solitary in *P. occidentalis*). Possibly a hybrid between *P. occidentalis* and *P. orientalis*, the latter having fruiting heads mostly borne in 3s. Often planted as a shade tree. Reported for MA. [*P. acerifolia*].

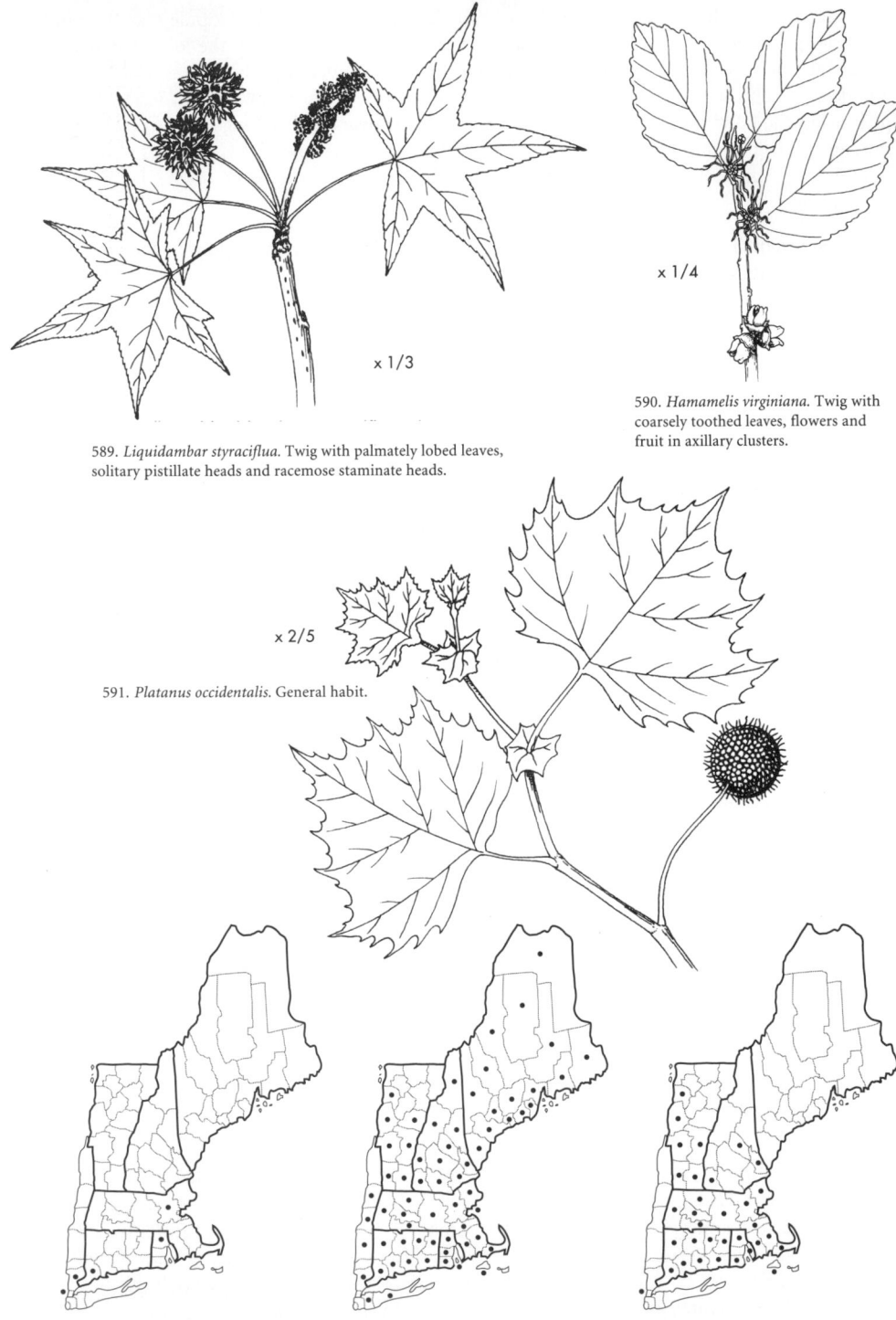

589. *Liquidambar styraciflua*. Twig with palmately lobed leaves, solitary pistillate heads and racemose staminate heads.

590. *Hamamelis virginiana*. Twig with coarsely toothed leaves, flowers and fruit in axillary clusters.

x 1/3

x 1/4

x 2/5

591. *Platanus occidentalis*. General habit.

1250. *Liquidambar styraciflua*

1251. *Hamamelis virginiana*

1252. *Platanus occidentalis*

Family 108. Rosáceae (Rose Family)

Hermaphrodite, rarely dioecious, trees, shrubs or herbs, sometimes armed. Leaves alternate, rarely opposite, simple or pinnately, palmately or ternately compound, stipules present, sometimes caducous, rarely wanting. Flowers perfect, rarely unisexual, solitary, cymose, corymbose, racemose or paniculate, regular, calyx of usually 5 sepals, united at the base, often alternating with bracts and appearing double, hypanthium saucer-shaped to cup-shaped, petals usually 5, rarely absent or numerous, distinct, stamens 5 to many, distinct, sometimes of different lengths, inserted with the petals on the rim of the hypanthium, rarely hypogynous, carpels 1-many, superior, inserted within the hypanthium, usually distinct, or sometimes united into a compound, inferior ovary adnate to the hypanthium, 1-locular and 1-ovulate to several-locular and many-ovulate, style 1 (several when ovary compound). Fruit an achene, drupe, follicle, or pome, the hypanthium often enlarged and modified.

a. Leaves opposite. (Fig. 592) .... 1. *Rhodotypos scandens*

a. Leaves alternate.
  b. Plant a tree or shrub, or woody and trailing.
    c. Leaves compound.
      d. Leaflets 9 or more, pinnate; plant unarmed; carpels 5 or fewer. (Fig. 593).
        Flowers and fruit in elongate panicles. .... 2. *Sorbaria sorbifolia*
        Flowers and fruit in round-topped or flattened compound cymes. .... 3. *Sorbus*
      d. Leaflets 7 or fewer, if pinnate and more than 7, plant prickly or bristly
        and or/ carpels numerous.
        e. Leaflets entire .... 4. *Pentaphylloides floribunda*
        e. Leaflets uniformly toothed, or at least partly so.
          Hypanthium urceolate to globose, contracted at the mouth, enclosing
            the carpels; fruit a cluster of achenes .... 5. *Rosa*
          Hypanthium hemispheric to flattish, not enclosing the carpels, these
            inserted on a receptacle and exposed; fruit a cluster of
            drupelets resembling a berry. .... 6. *Rubus*
    c. Leaves simple.
      f. Leaves palmately lobed; ovaries numerous; fruit a cluster of drupelets
        resembling a berry .... 6. *Rubus*
      f. Leaves not palmately lobed (except in *Physocarpus* and some *Crataegus*);
        ovaries mostly 5 or fewer; fruit not as above.
        g. Leaves with a row of glands along the midvein on the upper side.
          (Fig. 605). .... 7. *Aronia*
        g. Leaves lacking a row of glands along the midvein on the upper side.
          h. Ovary superior, of 1 or more simple carpels; fruit a drupe, aggregate
            of follicles, or winged capsule.
            i. Ovary solitary; fruit a fleshy drupe with a single stone. .... 8. *Prunus*
            i. Ovaries mostly 2-5; fruit an aggregate of follicles (rarely achenes)
              or a winged capsule.
              j. Leaves lobed. (Fig. 611) .... 9. *Physocarpus opulifolius*
              j. Leaves entire or serrate.
                Leaves serrate; flowers small, less than 1 cm wide; fruit an
                  aggregate of follicles .... 10. *Spiraea*
                Leaves mostly entire; flowers moderately large, more than
                  1 cm wide; fruit a 5-winged capsule or an aggregate of
                  achenes. .... 11. *Exochorda racemosa*
         h. Ovary inferior, of (1) 2-5 carpels united into a compound ovary;
           fruit a pome.
           k. Plant usually armed with sharp spines; mature carpels bony. .... 12. *Crataegus*
          k. Plant unarmed (spine like lateral spurs common in *Malus* and
            Pyrus which have the flowers in umbel-like cymes on the

spurs; flowers are mostly in terminal, compound corymbs
[rarely 1-several] in *Crataegus*); mature carpels papery or
cartilaginous.
  l. Flowers and fruit mostly in racemes (1-several on leafy twigs
     in 1 species); locules twice as many as the styles; fruit
     easily crushed, without a distinct central core .... 13. *Amelanchier*
  l. Flowers and fruit in umbel-like cymes or rarely solitary;
     locules the same number as the styles; fruit usually not
     easily crushed, with a distinct central core.
       Leaves coarsely serrate; flowers usually pinkish; styles united
          at the base; fruit without grit cells .... 14. *Malus*
       Leaves entire to serrulate; flowers white; styles separate to the
          base; fruit containing grit cells .... 15. *Pyrus communis*
b. Plant herbaceous or merely woody at the base.
  m. Leaves bi or triternately compound. (Fig. 620). .... 16. *Aruncus dioicus*
  m. Leaves not as above, simple, trifoliate, palmate or pinnate.
    n. Leaves pinnately compound with 5 or more leaflets. (Fig. 621).
      o. Flowers and fruit in racemes, spikes or heads.
          Petals none; sepals 4, white, green or purple; hypanthium unarmed. ...... 17. *Sanguisorba*
          Petals 5, yellow; hypanthium armed with hooked bristles. .... 18. *Agrimonia*
      o. Flowers and fruit not in racemes, spikes or heads.
        p. Carpels 5-15; flowers numerous, mostly more than 30, paniculate,
           white or pink.
             Terminal leaflet deeply lobed or laciniate; panicle flat-topped, the
                lateral branches equalling or exceeding the central.
                (Fig. 623). .... 19. *Filipendula*
             Terminal leaflet regularly toothed; panicle pyramidal, the lateral
                branches shorter than the central. (Fig. 593) .... 2. *Sorbaria sorbifolia*
        p. Carpels numerous; flowers mostly fewer than 20, solitary, cymose or
           corymbose, yellow, white or purplish.
             Styles elongate, jointed or plumose, persistent. .... 20. *Geum*
             Styles short, inconspicuous, deciduous.
                Aquatic or subaquatic; stems decumbent, woody and rooting
                   below; flowers purple; aggregate fleshy in fruit .... 21. *Comarum*
                                                                                             palustre
                Terrestrial; stems erect, or if decumbent and rooting, not woody;
                   flowers yellow to white; aggregate not fleshy in fruit.
                   Flowers solitary-axillary, or terminal and not in cymes; plant
                      trailing and rooting at intervals. (Fig. 627) .... 22. *Argentina*
                   Flowers in terminal cymes, these often leafy; plant erect to
                      spreading-ascending .... 23. *Potentilla*
    n. Leaves simple, ternate, palmate, or pinnate and with fewer than 5 leaflets.
      q. Leaves simple.
        r. Sepals 4; stamens and pistils 4 or fewer .... 24. *Alchemilla*
        r. Sepals 5 or more; stamens and pistils 5 or more.
             Flowers solitary, scapose, pistils 5-10; fruit dry. (Fig. 633). .... 25. *Dalibarda repens*
             Flowers more than 1 or not scapose; pistils many; fruit fleshy. .... 6. *Rubus*
      q. Leaves ternate, palmate, or pinnate and with fewer than 5 leaflets.
        s. Styles elongate, jointed or plumose .... 20. *Geum*
        s. Styles short, inconspicuous.
          t. Bracts present in the calyx, alternating with the 5 sepals; carpels
             more than 10 (except in *Sibbaldia*).
          u. Bracts widest at the apex, 3-5 toothed. .... 26. *Duchesnea indica*
          u. Bracts narrowed to the apex, entire.
            v. Petals white; leaflets obtuse or acute, toothed on the sides;
               receptacle fleshy .... 27. *Fragaria*
            v. Petals yellow, or white and leaflets widest and 3-5 toothed at
               the apex; receptacle not fleshy.
               Petals less than 3 mm long, yellow; carpels 10 or fewer. .... 28. *Sibbaldia*
                                                                                          procumbens
               Petals 5 mm or more long, white or yellow; carpels more than 10.

Leaflets evergreen, mostly 3-toothed, otherwise entire; flowers white. .... 29. *Sibbaldiopsis tridentata*

Leaflets not evergreen, with regularly toothed margins or with more than 3 teeth; flowers yellow .... 23. *Potentilla*

t. Bracts not present in the calyx (rarely present in *Waldsteinia*, having leaflets with toothed sides; leaflets are 3-5 toothed at the apex in *Sibbaldia*); carpels fewer than 10 (except in *Rubus*).

w. Acaulescent; petals yellow; fruit an achene .. . . 30. *Waldsteinia fragarioides*

w. Leafy stemmed; petals white to pinkish; fruit a follicle or cluster of drupelets resembling a berry.

Carpels 10 or fewer; fruit a follicle .... 31. *Porteranthus trifoliatus*

Carpels numerous; fruit a cluster of drupelets resembling a berry. .... 6. *Rubus*

1. *Rhodótypos* Sieb & Zucc. (having the characters of a rose).

Shrubs, pith moderate, white, buds opposite, solitary to collateral, sessile to slightly stalked, ovoid, with 6-8 scales, leaf scars crescent-shaped, ciliate across the top, connected by a line, bundle traces 3, stipule scars small; leaves simple, opposite, short petioled, elliptic, abruptly acuminate, rounded at the base, sharply, doubly serrate; flowers solitary and terminal on the branches, with 4 large sepals and 4 large white petals, stamens numerous, unequal, carpels 4; fruits 4, black, shining, drupe-like.

1. *R. scándens* (Thunb.) Makino (climbing). Spread from cultivation to waste places, thickets and woods. May-June. Fig. 592, Map 1253. (Introduced from e. Asia).

2. *Sorbária* (Seringe) A. Br. False Spiraea (name from Sorbus, because of similar foliage).

Shrubby to somewhat suffrutescent, twigs moderate, pith moderately large, brown, buds solitary to collateral, sessile to stalked, ovoid, with 4-5 scales, leaf scars half-round to elliptic, end bud lacking, bundle traces 3, stipule scars lacking; leaves pinnately compound, with 12-20 leaflets, stipules large, foliose, leaflets lanceolate, acuminate, sharply doubly serrate; flowers small, white, numerous, in a large, terminal panicle, hypanthium cup-shaped, sepals 5, reflexed, petals 5, stamens numerous, carpels 5, connate below, with a long style, each with several ovules; fruits follicular, dehiscent along both sutures.

1. *S. sorbifólia* (L.) A. Br. (with leaves of *Sorbus*). Spread from cultivation to thickets, roadsides and waste places. June-July. Fig. 593, Map 1254. (Naturalized from Asia). [*Schizonotus s.*].

3. *Sórbus* L. Mountain-ash.

Shrubs or small trees, glabrous or pubescent, twigs moderate, with conspicuous, scattered, large, pale lenticels, pith moderate, brown, buds solitary, sessile, dark red or purplish, woolly or somewhat gummy, with 2 or 3 scales, the terminal bud rather large, conical, the lateral often much reduced, leaf scars crescent-shaped, bundle traces usually 3-5, stipule scars lacking; leaves pinnately compound, with 11-17 leaflets, these oblong to lanceolate, acute or acuminate, serrate; flowers white, numerous, in terminal, round-topped or flattened, compound cymes, hypanthium obconic, sepals 5, petals 5, stamens 15-20, ovary compound, half-inferior, of 2-4 carpels adnate below to the hypanthium and free above, styles 2-4, separate, ovules 1 or 2 in each carpel; fruit a small, berry-like, orange-red pome, with 2-4 papery locules imbedded in the flesh. [*Pyrus*].

In addition to the following species *S. x thuringiaca* has been reported for our range. The fruits of the species below, particularly European and American Mountain Ash can be eaten raw or made into jams or jellies. —Wildl. 2

a. Winter buds and hyphanthium densely pubescent. .... 1. *S. aucuparia*
a. Winter buds glabrous or essentially so (at least the outer scales; inner scales often
      pubescent); hypanthium glabrous or essentially so.
  b. Leaflets 2-3 times as long as wide; petals about equaling the stamens; fruit
      8-10 mm thick.
      Leaflets short-acuminate, whitish beneath . ... 2. *S. decora*
      Leaflets long-acuminate, merely pale green beneath. .... 3. *S. groenlandica*
  b. Leaflets over 3 times as long as wide; petals conspicuously longer than the
      stamens; fruits 4-7 mm thick. (Fig. 594). .... 4. *S. americana*

1. *S. aucupária* L. (attractive to birds). European Mountain ash. Escaped from cultivation to woodland borders, woods, roadsides and waste places. May-June. Map 1255. (Introduced from Europe). [*Pyrus a.*].

S. hýbrida Schneid. Similar to *S. aucuparia* but with terminal leaflet conspicuously larger than the others (terminal leaflet not conspicuously larger than the others in *S. aucuparia*). Reported for ME, NH, VT. [x *Aronia h.*].

x *Sorbarónia* Schneid. *fállax* Schneid. A hybrid between *S. aucuparia* and *Aronia arbutifolia* or *A. melanocarpa.* [x *Pyrus f.*].

2. *S. decóra* (Sarg.) C. K. Schneid. (handsome). Northern Mountain ash. Woods and rocky slopes. May-July. Map 1256. Endangered in MA. [*Pyrus d.; Sorbus subvestita*]. —FAC

3. *S. groenlándica* (C. K. Schneid.) A. & D. Loeve (of Greenland). High mountain slopes. May-July. Northern New England.

4. *S. americána* Marsh. (American). American Mountain ash. Moist woods. May-June. Fig. 594, Map 1257. [*Pyrus a.*]. —FACU

x *Sorbarónia* Schneid. *hýbrida* (Moench) Schneid. A hybrid between *S. americana* and *Aronia arbutifolia.* [*Aronia h.; Sorbus h.*].

x *Sorbaronia sorbifólia* (Poir.) Schneid. A hybrid between *S. americana* and *Aronia melanocarpa.* [*Sorbus s.; Pyrus s.; x P. mixta*].

4. *Pentaphylloídes* Duham.

Similar to *Potentilla* (genus 23), but with leaflets entire. [*Potentilla*]. —Wildl. 1

1. *P. floribúnda* (Pursh) A. Love. Shrubby Cinquefoil. Pastures, wet meadows, bogs, wooded swamps, pond and stream margins, often in calcareous soil. June-September. Map 1258. (Eurasia). [*Potentilla fruticosa; Dasiphora f.*]. —FACW

5. *Rósa* L. Rose (ancient Latin name).

Shrubs, with upright, arching or trailing, usually prickly stems, pubescent or glabrous, pith moderately large, brownish, buds solitary, sessile, ovoid, with 3-4 scales, leaf scars narrow, U-shaped to somewhat linear, bundle traces 3, stipule scars lacking; leaves pinnately compound, with 3-11 serrate leaflets, stipules conspicuous, adnate to the petioles; flowers white, yellow, pink or red, solitary or corymbose at the tips of the stems and branches, hyphantheum urceolate to globose, contracted at the mouth, sepals 5, long-attenuate or with a foliaceous tip, deciduous or persistent, petals 5 (or more in double flowered forms), inserted with the numerous stamens near the mouth of the hypanthium, carpels numerous, inserted on the bottom and/or sides of the hypanthium, commonly pubescent, styles separate or united into a column; fruit a bony achene, these numerous, enclosed in the berry-like hypanthium which is commonly fleshy and colored in fruit. The rose hips of all species are high in vitamin C and are edible raw or cooked; the petals are also used for jams and tea. —Wildl. 1

a. Twigs and bases of prickles conspicuously tomentose; petals 3-5 cm long. .... 1. *R. rugosa*
a. Twigs and bases of prickles glabrous or inconspicuously hairy; petals mostly
    2-3 cm long.

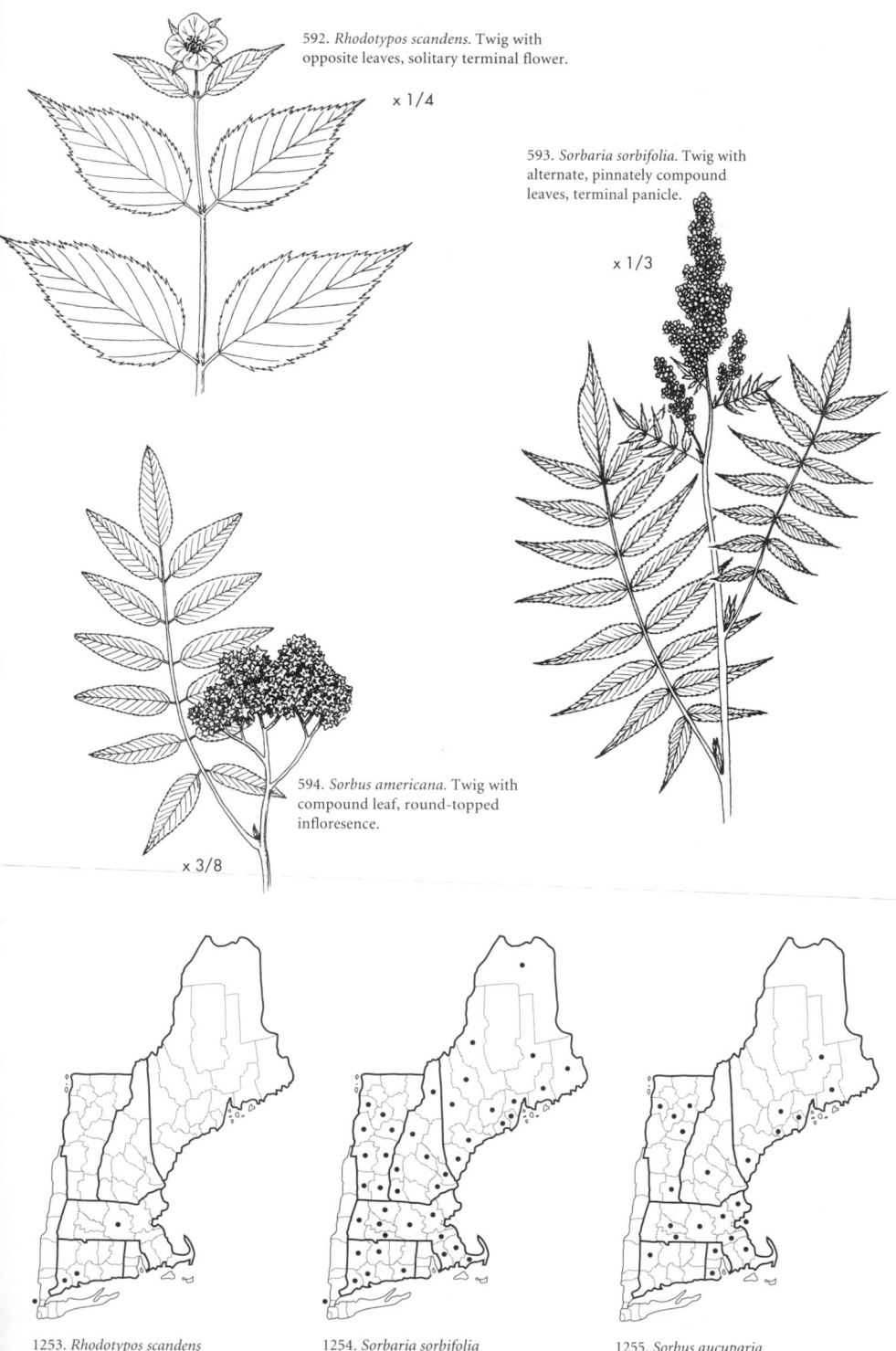

592. *Rhodotypos scandens.* Twig with opposite leaves, solitary terminal flower.

× 1/4

593. *Sorbaria sorbifolia.* Twig with alternate, pinnately compound leaves, terminal panicle.

× 1/3

594. *Sorbus americana.* Twig with compound leaf, round-topped infloresence.

× 3/8

1253. *Rhodotypos scandens*

1254. *Sorbaria sorbifolia*

1255. *Sorbus aucuparia*

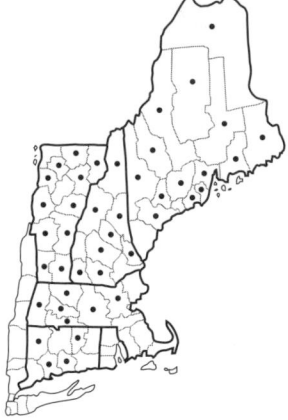
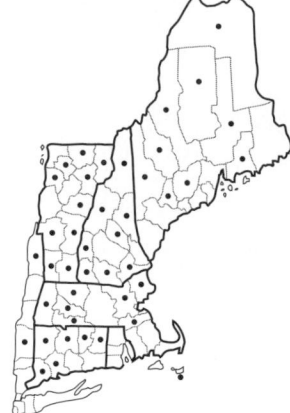

1256. *Sorbus decora*   1257. *Sorbus americana*   1258. *Pentaphylloides floribunda*

b. Leaflets glandular-dotted beneath.
    Styles pubescent .... 2. *R. eglanteria*
    Styles glabrous or essentially so .... 3. *R. micrantha*
b. Leaflets not glandular-dotted beneath (except sometimes along the mid-rib or
    margin).
    c. Stipules fimbriate-pectinate; styles united into a protruding column.
        (Fig. 595) .... 4. *R. multiflora*
    c. Stipules entire or merely dentate; styles distinct (except in *R. setigera*).
        d. Styles united into a protruding column; leaflets mostly 3 (7-9 in *R.*
            wichuriana). (Fig. 596) .... 5. *R. setigera*
        d. Styles distinct; leaflets mostly more than 3.
            e. Hypanthium and pedicel glabrous; sepals erect or ascending, persistent
                in fruit (except in *R. carolina* and *R. johannensis*).
                f. Leaves, at least some of them, with 5 or more pairs of lateral leaflets;
                    flowers usually solitary, the pedicel not subtended by a bract. .... 6. *R. spinosissima*
                f. Leaves with 4 or fewer pairs of lateral leaflets; flowers often
                    corymbose, when solitary, with pedical subtended by a bract.
                    g. Infrastipular prickles present, stout and differentiated from the
                        internodal ones (when present). (Fig. 597).
                        Flowers double (petals 6-many); leaflets simply serrate. .... 7. *R. cinnamomea*
                        Flowers single (petals 5); leaflets often doubly serrate. .... 8. *R. canina*
                    g. Infrastipular prickles none or scarcely differentiated from the
                        internodal ones. (Fig. 598).
                      h. Infrastipular prickles usually paired; sepals usually spreading
                        widely or reflexed in fruit .... 9. *R. carolina*
                      h. Infrastipular prickles absent or not paired.
                        Stems unarmed or with prickles only toward the base. .... 10. *R. blanda*
                        Stems with prickles extending nearly to the inflorescence. .... 11. *R. acicularis*
                                                  subsp. *sayi*
            e. Hypanthium and pedicel stipitate-glandular; sepals spreading to
                reflexed, deciduous in fruit (except *R. blanda*).
                i. Leaflet margins usually glandular-ciliate; flowers usually
                  solitary, the pedicel not subtended by a bract. (Fig. 599). .... 12. *R. gallica*
                i. Leaflet margins not glandular-ciliate (teeth sometimes gland tipped);
                  flowers often corymbose, when solitary, with pedicel subtended
                  by a bract.
                  j. Leaflets finely toothed, the teeth near and above the middle
                      averaging 0.5-0.75 mm high measured along the distal margin.
                  Infrastipular prickles present at many nodes, these stout,

wide-based and recurved; internodal prickles few or none .. 13. *R. palustris*
Infrastipular prickles straight and slender, scarcely differentiated
from the numerous internodal ones .... 14. *R. nitida*
j. Leaflets coarsely toothed, the teeth near and above the middle
averaging 1 mm or more high measured along the distal
margin.
k. Infrastipular prickles absent or not in pairs; sepals erect or
ascending in fruit .... 10. *R. blanda*
k. Infrastipular prickles in pairs; sepals widely spreading to reflexed
in fruit.
Infrastipular prickles stout, wide-based; internodal prickles
commonly absent. .... 15. *R. virginiana*
Infrastipular prickles slender, scarcely differentiated from the
numerous internodal ones .... 9. *R. carolina*

1. R. rugósa Thunb. (rugose). Dunes and sea beaches, sandy roadsides and waste places. June-September. Map 1259. (Naturalized from e. Asia). —FACU-

2. R. eglantéria L. (latinization of an old French and English name). Sweetbriar. Frequently escaped from cultivation to roadsides, thickets and pastures. June-July. Map 1260. (Naturalized from Europe). [*R. rubiginosa*].

3. R. micrántha Borrer ex Smith (small-flowered). Sweetbriar. Occasionally escaped from cultivation to roadsides and thickets. June-July. Map 1261. (Naturalized from Europe). —FACU

4. R. multiflóra Thunb. ex Murr. (many-flowered). Multiflora Rose. Thickets, fields, pastures, woodland borders, roadsides and waste places. May-June. Fig. 595, Map 1262. (Naturalized from e. Asia). —FACU

5. R. setígera Michx. (bearing bristles, a misnomer). Prairie Rose. Thickets and roadsides (from farther west and south and escaped from cultivation). June-July. Fig. 596, Map 1263. Our plants include var. *setegera* and the following var.:

var. *tomentósa* Torr. & Gray. Leaflets pubescent beneath (glabrous beneath or pubescent only on nerves in var. *setigera*). [*R. rubrifolia*]. —FACU

R. wichuraiána Crepin. Differing from *R. setigera* in having 7-9 leaflets. Spread from cultivation. (Introduced from Asia). Reported for CT, Franklin County MA.

6. R. spinosíssima L. (mostly spiny). Scotch Rose. Occasionally escaped from cultivation to roadsides and thickets. June-July. Map 1264. (Naturalized from Europe). [*R. pimpinellifolia*].

7. R. cinnamómea L. (like Cinnamon). Cinnamon-rose. Occasionally escaped from cultivation to roadsides and old cellar holes. June-July. Map 1265. (Naturalized from Eurasia). [*R. majalis*].

8. R. canína L. (of a dog). Dog-rose. Escaped from cultivation to roadsides and thickets. June-July. Fig. 597, Map 1266. (Naturalized from Europe). Dried leaves can be used as a coffee substitute.

9. R. carolína L. (Carolinian). Thickets, fields and dunes. June-July. Map 1267. [*R. humilis; R. lyoni; R. obovata; R. housei*].

Our plants include var. *carolina*, with leaflets glabrous or nearly so beneath, and the following 2 vars., having leaflets pubescent beneath:

var. *setígera* Crepin. Calyx with glandular hairs.

var. *villósa* (Best) Rehd. Calyx lacking glandular hairs.

10. R. blánda Ait. (mild, from its lack of prickles). River shores, rocky slopes, thickets, fields and roadsides. June-July. Map 1268. [*R. subblanda*]. Our plants include var. *blanda* and the following vars.:

var. *glábra* Crepin. Sepals widely spreading to reflexed in fruit; leaf rachis and undersides of leaflets glabrous (sepals erect or ascending in fruit; leaf petiole and rachis tomentose and/or glandular; undersides of leaflets often tomentose in var. *blanda*). [*R. johannensis*].

var. *carpohíspida* Schuette. Pedicels and hypanthium with stalked glands (without stalked glands in the above vars.). —FACU

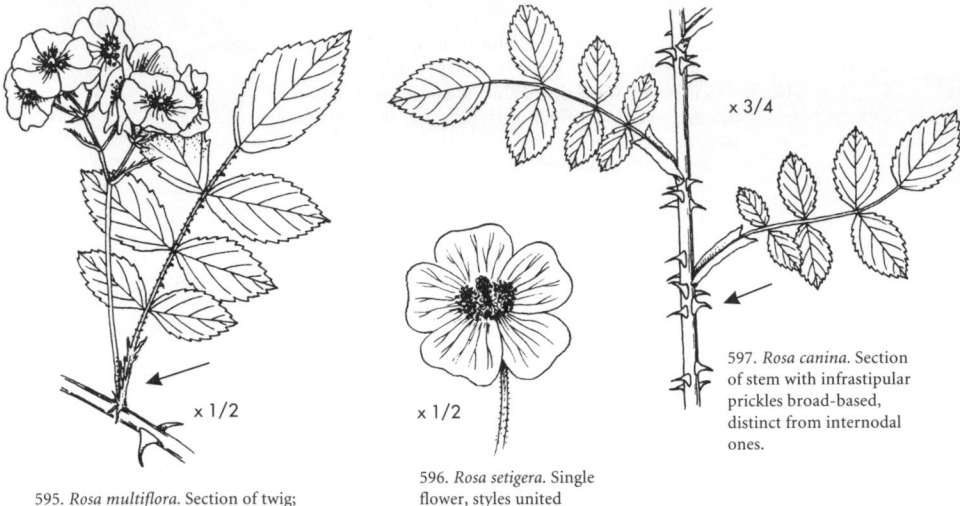

595. *Rosa multiflora*. Section of twig;
leaf with fimbriate-pectinate stipules.

596. *Rosa setigera*. Single
flower, styles united
into a column.

597. *Rosa canina*. Section
of stem with infrastipular
prickles broad-based,
distinct from internodal
ones.

x 3/4

x 1/2

x 1/2

R. rubrifólia Ait. Similar to *R. blanda* var. *glabra* but with leaflets finely toothed and red-tinged (leaflets coarsely toothed and green in *R. blanda* var. *glabra*). European. Reported for MA, ME.

R. x palustrifórmis Rydb. A hybrid between *R. blanda* and *R. palustris.*

11. *R. aciculáris* Lindl. (needle-like). River and lake shores, waste places. June-July. Rare. Fig. 598, Map 1269. (e. Asia). Endangered in VT, MA, NH. [*R. bourgeauiana; R. majalis*]. Represented with us as subsp. *sáyi* (Schweinitz) W. H. Lewis. [*R. sayi*]. —FACU

R. arkansána Porter. Resembling *R. acicularis* but distinguishable in having glandless, merely pilose foliage (foliage glandular in *R. acicularis*). From farther west. Reported for MA. [*R. conjuncta; R. pratincola; R. suffulta*]. Represented with us as var. *suffúlta* (Greene) Cockerell.

12. *R. gállica* L. (French). French Rose. Escaped from cultivation to roadsides, pastures and old cellar holes. June-July. Fig. 599, Map 1270. (Naturalized from Europe). Used for rose oil for perfume.

13. *R. palústris* Marsh. (of marshes). Swamp-rose. Pond and stream margins, shrub swamps, wooded swamps and marshes. July-August. Map 1271. —OBL

R. rubrifólia, with red-tinged leaves may sometimes key here; see note under *R. blanda* (10).

14. *R. nítida* Willd. (shining). Wooded swamps, bogs, pond margins. June-July. Map 1272. —FACW+

15. *R. virginiána* Mill. (Virginian). Wooded swamps, thickets, pond and river margins, waste places. June-August. Map 1273. [*R. lucida*]. Our plants are var. *virginiana.*

Another var. that has been distinguished is var. *lamprophylla.* —FAC

6. *Rúbus* L. Bramble (Roman name).

Hermaphrodite or rarely dioecious, shrubs or infrequently perennial herbs, with erect, arching, or trailing, usually bristly or prickly stems; the new shoots, termed primocanes, are usually unbranched and do not bear flowers, in their second year they are termed floricanes, developing branches that bear flowers and then usually dying; pith moderately large, brownish, round or sharply angled, buds solitary or often superposed, with the lower bud covered by the persistent petiole base, sessile, ovoid to oblong, with 5-6 scales, leaf scars torn on the petiole base, bundle traces 3, evident only when the petiole is cut at the base, stipule scars lacking; leaves usually ternately, palmately or pinnately

1259. *Rosa rugosa*

1260. *Rosa eglanteria*

1261. *Rosa micrantha*

1262. *Rosa multiflora*

1263. *Rosa setigera*

1264. *Rosa spinosissima*

1265. *Rosa cinnamomea*

1266. *Rosa canina*

1267. *Rosa carolina*

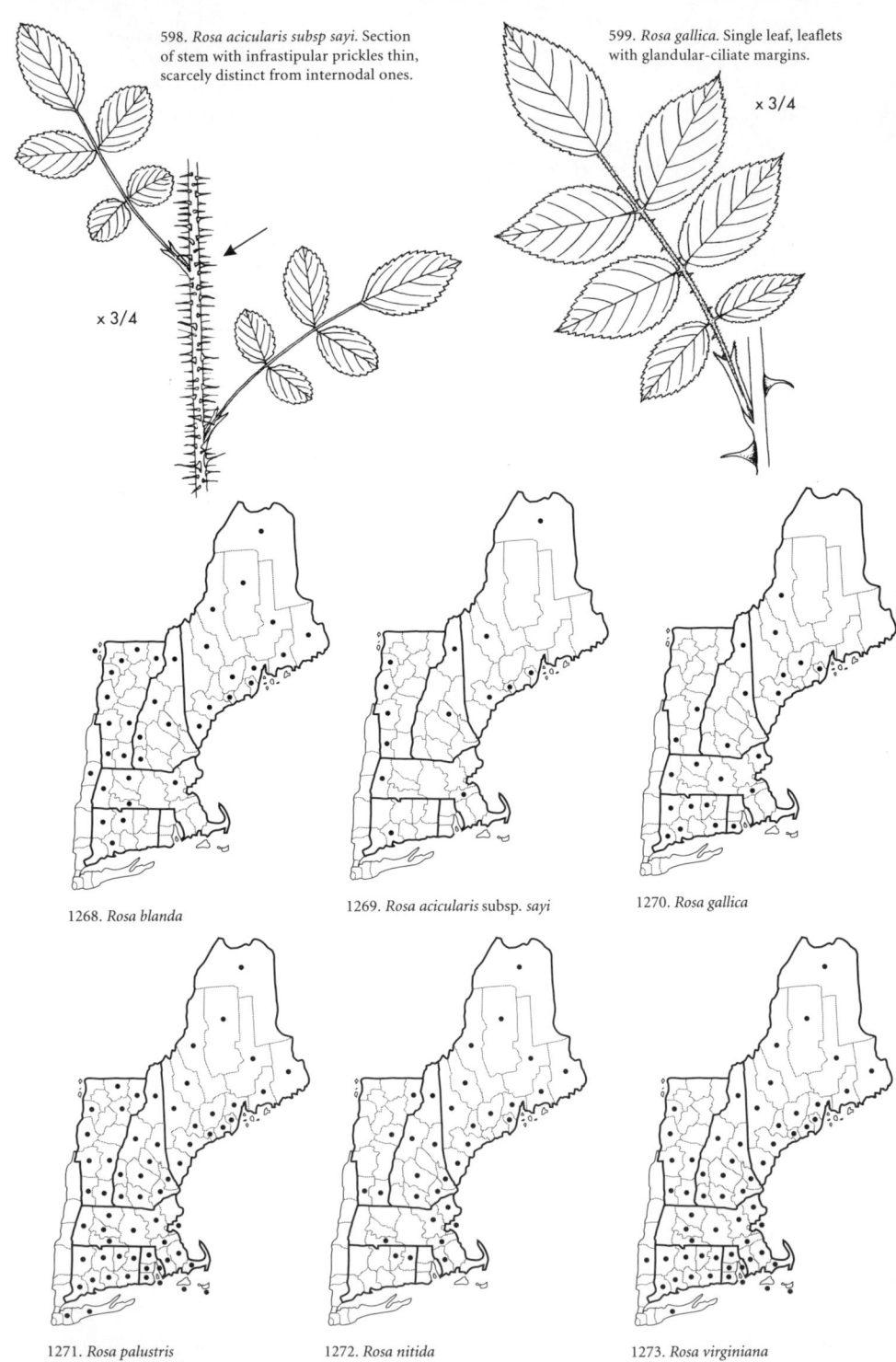

598. *Rosa acicularis subsp sayi.* Section of stem with infrastipular prickles thin, scarcely distinct from internodal ones.

x 3/4

599. *Rosa gallica.* Single leaf, leaflets with glandular-ciliate margins.

x 3/4

1268. *Rosa blanda*

1269. *Rosa acicularis* subsp. *sayi*

1270. *Rosa gallica*

1271. *Rosa palustris*

1272. *Rosa nitida*

1273. *Rosa virginiana*

compound, less often simple or merely lobed, serrate, stipules persistent, usually adnate to the petiole; flowers perfect, rarely unisexual, white or occasionally pink, terminal on the branches, solitary or in cymes, corymbs, racemes or panicles, hypanthium small, hemispheric to flattish, sepals 5, often ending in a caudate tip, petals 5, stamens numerous, carpels numerous, inserted on a convex or conic receptacle; fruit a cluster of drupelets resembling a berry, falling separately or together, the receptacle falling with the aggregate or remaining attached to the pedicel. (The taxonomy of this genus is very complex and not well understood. Other floras covering the greater New England region have described several hundred species. The following treatment, based largely on the work of Harry Ahles, is highly condensed and subject to substantial modification as future studies shed light on this difficult group). —Wildl. 4

In addition to the species in the following treatment *R. thyrsoides* has been reported for MA, NH, VT. The fruits of all species are edible as are the young shoots; fruits and medicine made from root bark are reportedly useful in treating diarrhea.

a. Leaves lobed or dissected but not compound. (Fig. 600).
  b. Stems herbaceous; leaves 1-3; flowers solitary, terminal, dioecious. .... 1. *R. chamaemorus*
  b. Stems woody; leaves numerous; flowers several to many, hermaphrodite.
    Leaves white-tomentose beneath, the lobes not triangular; flowers white. .... 2. *R. idaeus*
    Leaves merely pubescent on the veins beneath, the lobes broadly triangular;
      flowers rose purple. (rarely white) .... 3. *R. odoratus*
a. Leaves pinnate, palmate or ternate.
  c. Leaflets white or gray tomentose beneath, the tomentum obscuring the surface.
    d. Petals equalling or shorter than sepals; fruit separating from receptacle, which
      is persistent on the pedicel; prickles, if present, not expanded at base or
      if so, stems terete.
      e. Stems, petioles and inflorescence densely shaggy with long, reddish,
        glandular hairs .... 4. *R. phoenicolasius*
      e. Stems, petioles and inflorescence only sparsely if at all glandular pubescent,
        not densely long-shaggy as above.
        Stems bristly or hispid to smooth, with or without prickles having
          expanded bases; primocane leaves pinnate, with 5 or more
          leaflets; fruit red. .... 2. *R. idaeus*
        Stems with prickles having expanded bases, without bristles; primocane
          leaves ternate, or with 5 leaflets and palmate; fruit black. .... 5. *R. occidentalis*
    d. Petals longer than sepals; fruit separating from pedicel with the receptacle
      included; prickles expanded at the base; stems angled.
      Terminal leaflet obovate; inflorescence cymose; flowers usually white. .... 6. *R. cuneifolius*
      Terminal leaflet ovate to elliptic; inflorescence paniculate; flowers usually
        pink .... 7. *R. bifrons*
  c. Leaflets glabrous or pubescent beneath but not white or gray tomentose, the
    green of the surface evident.
    f. Leaves pinnate, with 5-9 leaflets; fruit separating from the receptacle, which is
      persistent on the pedicel. (Fig. 601). .... 8. *R. illecebrosus*
    f. Leaves ternate, or if with 5 or more leaflets, palmate; fruit separating from
      pedicel with the receptacle included.
      g. Stems herbaceous or woody only near base, unarmed, or rarely with a few
        bristles .... 9. *R. pubescens*
      g. Stems woody throughout, with broad-based prickles and/or bristles or
        narrow-based prickles (*R. canadensis* usually unarmed).
        h. Leaflets pinnately dissected and deeply lobed ... . 10. *R. laciniatus*
        h. Leaflets merely toothed to shallowly lobed.
          i. Stems trailing, usually rooting at the tip; flowers solitary or if more
            then the lateral flowers on pedicels 3 cm or more long.
            Armature of bristles or slender-based prickles; broad-based prickles
              sometimes also present .... 11. *R. hispidus*
            Armature of stout, broad-based, often hooked prickles; bristles and
              slender-based prickles lacking.

Inflorescence leafy, the flowers all or all except the terminal 1 or
    2 subtended by a simple or ternate leaf .... 12. *R. flagellaris*
Inflorescence leafless, the flowers, except often for the lowest,
    subtended by stipules only .... 13. *R. arenicola*
i. Stems erect or arching, or if trailing, flowers more numerous, the
  lateral on shorter pedicels.
  j. Pedicels with numerous stipitate glands. (Fig. 602).
    k. Stems erect or nearly so, either bearing broad-based prickles or
      prickleless; inflorescence an elongate raceme. .... 14. *R. allegheniensis*
    k. Stems arching, the tips usually coming back to the ground,
      bearing bristles or slender-based prickles; inflorescence a
      short raceme or corymb.
      Armature of soft bristles, the primocane densely covered with
        30 or more per cm. (Fig. 603) .... 15. *R. setosus*
      Armature of slender-based prickles resistent to touch, the
        primocane with fewer than 30 per cm .... 16. *R. vermontanus*
  j. Pedicels eglandular, or glands few.
    l. Armature of bristles or slender-based prickles; broad-based
      prickles sometimes also present. (Fig. 603).
      m. Stems trailing, usually rooting at the tip .... 11. *R. hispidus*
      m. Stems arching, not rooting at the tip.
        Armature of soft bristles, the primocane densely covered
          with 30 or more per cm .... 15. *R. setosus*
        Armature of slender-based prickles resistent to touch, the
          primocane with fewer than 30 per cm .... 16. *R. vermontanus*
    l. Armature of stout, broad-based, often hooked prickles; bristles
      and slender-based prickles lacking, or stems sometimes
      unarmed. (Fig. 604).
      Stem trailing, usually rooting at the tip. .... 12. *R. flagellaris*
      Stem erect or arching, not rooting at tip.
      n. Leaves glabrous beneath or pubescent only on veins. .... 17. *R. canadensis*
      n. Leaves pubescent over the entire lower surface.
        Terminal leaflet of the primocane leaves less than twice as
          long as wide. .... 18. *R. argutus*
        Terminal leaflet of the primocane leaves 2-3 times as long as
          wide. .... 19. *R. pensilvanicus*

1. *R. chamaemórus* L. (old generic name for ground-mulberry). Baked-apple Berry. Wet alpine slopes, coastal areas. June-July. Map 1274. (Eurasia). Endangered in NH. —FACW

2. *R. idaéus* L. (of Mt. Ida). Red Raspberry. Clearings, fields, thickets, roadsides and waste places. May-June. Map 1275. (Naturalized from Europe). Our plants include subsp. *idaeus* and the following subsp.:

subsp. *strigósus* (Michx.) Focke. Inflorescence bearing glands and bristles (inflorescence without glands or bristles in subsp. *idaeus*). [*R. strigosus*]. —FAC-

3. *R. odorátus* L. (fragrant). Flowering raspberry. Open woods, woodland borders, thickets, roadsides and waste places. June-August. Fig. 600, Map 1276. [*R. parviflorus; Rubacer o.*].

4. *R. phoenicolásius* Maxim. (with purple-red hairs). Wineberry. Woodland borders, open woods, thickets, roadsides and waste places. June-July. Map 1277. (Introduced from e. Asia).

5. *R. occidentális* L. (western). Black raspberry. Open woods and clearings, woodland borders, thickets, roadsides and waste places. May-June. Map 1278.

R. triphýllus Thunb. Similar to *R. occidentalis* but with young stems pilose and flowers purple (young stems not pilose and flowers white in *R. occidentalis*). (Adventive from Japan). Reported for Boston, MA.

6. *R. cuneifólius* Pursh. Sand blackberry. Dry fields, open woods and open areas, mostly on the coastal plain. May-July. Map 1279. Endangered in NH. [*R. longii*]. —FAC

7. *R. bífrons* Vest. ex Tratt. (having 2 kinds of leaves). Escaped from cultivation to roadsides and waste places. May-July. Map 1280. (Introduced from Europe). [*R. discolor*].

8. R. illecebrósus Focke (enticing). Strawberry-Raspberry. Escaped from cultivation to roadsides and thickets. July-September. Fig. 601. (Introduced from Japan). Reported for Fairfield County CT, Cumberland County ME.

9. R. pubéscens Raf. (hairy). Dwarf blackberry. Moist woods, wooded swamps, bogs. May-July. Map 1281. [*R. arcticus; R. triflorus*]. Our plants include var. *pubescens* and the following var.:

var. *pilosifólius* A. F. Hill. Leaves pilose beneath (glabrous or nearly so in var. *pubescens*). —FACW

10. R. laciniátus Willd. (slashed). Cut-leaved Blackberry. Escaped from cultivation to roadsides and waste places. June-August. Map 1282.

11. R. híspidus L. (bristly). Stream and pond margins, wet or dry fields, open, often moist woods, roadsides, power lines, waste places. June-August. Map 1283. [*R. aculiferus; R. adjacens; R. alter; R. arcuans; R. bicknellii; R. blanchardianus; R. cubitans; R. harmonicus; R. jacens; R. laevior; R. multiformis; R. novanglicus; R. paludivagus; R. parlinii; R. permixtus; R. pervarius; R. provincialis; R. severus; R. spiculosus; R. tardatus; R. trifrons*]. —FACW

12. R. flagelláris Willd. (like a whip-lash). Dewberry. Roadsides, waste places, fields and woodland borders. May-June. Map 1284. [*R. baileyanus; R. curtipes; R. enslenii; R. felix; R. invisus; R. jactus; R. jaysmithii; R. maniseesensis; R. multifer; R. plicatifolius; R. roribaccus*]. —FACU

13. R. arenícola Blanch. (for Arundel, York Co., Me.). Clearings, thickets and woodland borders. June-July. Map 1285. [*R. arundelanus; R. biformispinus; R. eflagellaris; R. fraternalis; R. multispinus; R. obsessus; R. particeps; R. positivus; R. prosper; R. recurvicaulis; R. tholiformis*].

14. R. allegheniénsis Porter (of the Alleghenies). Common blackberry. Waste places, roadsides, thickets, clearings, power lines, woodland borders. May-July. Fig. 602, Map 1286. [*R. abbrevians; R. alumnus; R. aptatus; R. auroralis; R. flavinanus; R. frondisentus; R. glandicaulis; R. gnarus; R. latens; R. longissimus; R. orarius; R. ortivus; R. paulus; R. perinvisus; R. pugnax; R. ravus; R. rosa; R. saltuensis; R. sceleratus*]. Our plants include var. *allegheniensis* and the following var.:

var. *grávesii* Fern. Stems lacking prickles (with prickles in var. *alleghaniensis*). —FACU-

15. R. setósus Bigel. (bristly). Woodland borders, thickets, fields, roadsides and waste places. June-August. Fig. 603, Map 1287. [*R. ascendens; R. bigelovianus; R. gulosus; R. hispidioides; R. lawrencei; R. notatus; R. regionalis; R. semisetosus; R. univocus*]. —FACW+

16. R. vermontánus Blanch. (of Vermont). Woodland borders, thickets, fields, roadsides and waste places. June-August. Map 1288. [*R. junceus; R. multilicius*].

17. R. canadénsis L. (Canadian). Smooth Blackberry. Roadsides, waste places, thickets, woodland borders, rocky woods. June-July. Map 1289. (*R. amnicola; R. elegantulus; R. miscix; R. multilicius; R. pauper; R. perpauper; R. tantalus*].

18. R. argútus Link (sharply serrate). Woodland borders, thickets, waste places. May-June. Fig. 604, Map 1290. [*R. blakei; R. jugosus*]. —FACU

19. R. pensilvánicus Poir. (Pennsylvanian). Woodlands, clearings and woodland borders. June-July. Map 1291. [*R. acer; R. amnicola; R. andrewsianus; R. barbarus; R. bellobatus; R. brainerdii; R. burnhamii; R. conanictuensis; R. facetus; R. floricomus; R. frondosus; R. insons; R. insulanus; R. ostryifolius; R. pergratus; R. philadelphicus; R. recurvans; R. rossbergianus*].

7. Arónia Medic. Chokeberry.

Shrubs, often colonial, twigs moderate, pubescent to glabrous, pith moderate, the latter pale, buds solitary, sessile, oblong, pointed, red, the lateral flattened and appressed to the twig, pubescent to glabrous with 5-6 scales, leaf scars U-shaped, bundle traces 3, stipule scars lacking; leaves simple, petioled, elliptic, or oblong to obovate, acute to short acuminate, cuneate at the base, finely glandular-serrate, with a row of glands along the midvein on the upper side, pubescent to glabrous beneath; flowers white to pink-tinged, in terminal, round-topped or flattened, compound cymes, hypanthium obconic to urceolate, tomentose to glabrous, sepals 5, bearing stipitate glands or glandless, petals 5, spreading, stamens 15-20, ovary compound, half-inferior, pubescent at the

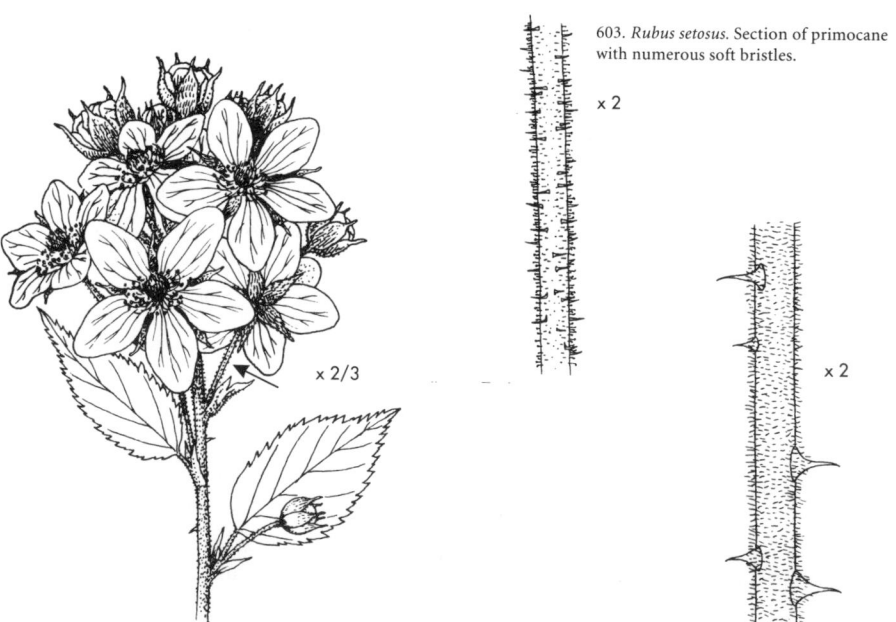

× 1/2

600. *Rubus odoratus.* Upper stem with
several simple, lobed leaves.

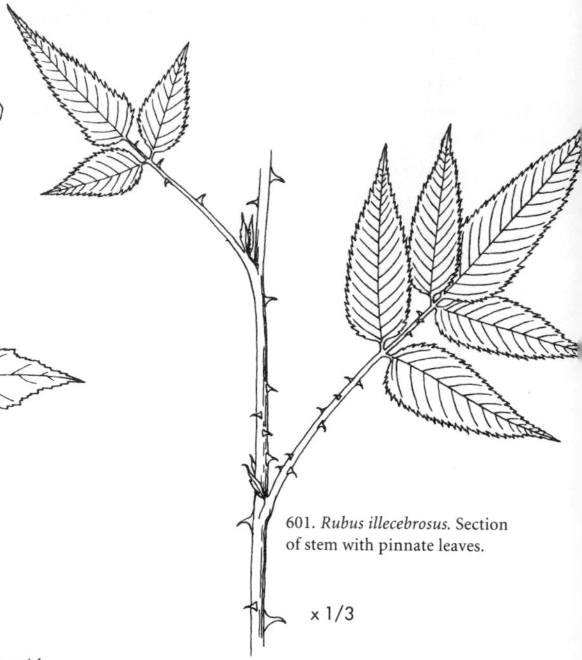

601. *Rubus illecebrosus.* Section
of stem with pinnate leaves.

× 1/3

603. *Rubus setosus.* Section of primocane
with numerous soft bristles.

× 2

× 2/3

602. *Rubus allegheniensis.* Raceme,
pedicels with numerous stipitate glands.

× 2

604. *Rubus argutus.* Section of primocane
with stout, broad-based prickles.

1274. *Rubus chamaemorus*

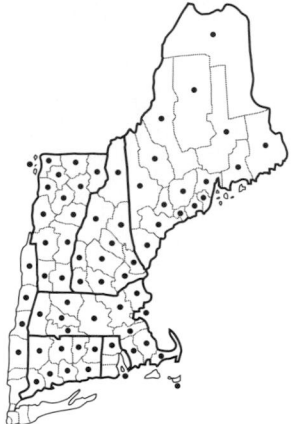

1275. *Rubus idaeus*

1276. *Rubus odoratus*

1277. *Rubus phoenicolasius*

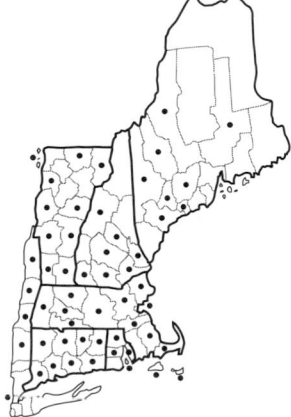

1278. *Rubus occidentalis*

1279. *Rubus cuneifolius*

1280. *Rubus bifrons*

1281. *Rubus pubescens*

1282. *Rubus laciniatus*

1283. *Rubus hispidus*

1284. *Rubus flagellaris*

1285. *Rubus arenicola*

1286. *Rubus allegheniensis*

1287. *Rubus setosus*

1288. *Rubus vermontanus*

1289. *Rubus canadensis*

1290. *Rubus argutus*

1291. *Rubus pensilvanicus*

summit, of 5 carpels adnate to the hypanthium, styles 5, connate at the base, ovules 2 in each carpel; fruit a small, red to black pome, with 5 locules imbedded in the flesh. [*Pyrus*]. Fruits edible. —Wildl. 1

a. Twigs, rachis, pedicels and lower leaf surfaces glabrous or nearly so; buds glabrous; fruit black .... 1. *A. melanocarpa*
a. Twigs, rachis, pedicels and usually the lower leaf surfaces pubescent (leaves sometimes subglabrate in *A. prunifolia*).
    Fruit red; sepals very glandular; buds somewhat pubescent. .... 2. *A. arbutifolia*
    Fruit black; sepals glandless or with few glands; buds quickly glabrous. .... 3. *A. x prunifolia*

    1. A. melanocárpa (Michx.) Ell. (black-fruited). Black Chokeberry. Bogs, moist woods and borders of wooded swamps, thickets and dunes. April-June. Map 1292. [*Pyrus m.*]. —FAC
    2. A. arbutifólia (L.) Pers. (with leaves of *Arbutus*). Red Chokeberry. Wet woods, borders of wooded swamps, bogs, thickets. April-June. Fig. 605, Map 1293. [*Pyrus a.*]. —FACW
    3. A. x prunifólia (Marsh.) Rehder. (plum-leaved). Purple Chokeberry. Wet woods, borders of wooded swamps, bogs, thickets. April-June. Map 1294. A hybrid between *A. melanocarpa* and *A. arbutifolia*. [*A. atropurpurea; Pyrus floribunda*]. —FACW

8. Prúnus L. Plum, Peach, Cherry (ancient Latin name for plum).

Shrubs or small trees, sometimes rhizomatous or root sprouting, bark frequently peeling or breaking into plates or scales, twigs and bark often with the odor of bitter almond when broken, twigs moderate, often producing short lateral spur shoots or spines, the branches and trunks often with conspicuous, scattered lenticels, pith moderate, pale or brown, buds ovoid or conical, solitary or collaterally multiple, sessile, brownish, with 4-6 scales, leaf scars half-elliptic, raised on a cushion, bundle traces 3, stipule scars present but sometimes indistinct, end bud present or absent; leaves simple, lanceolate, ovoid, oblong, or obovate, obtuse, acute or acuminate, serrate, the teeth and petiole often glandular; flowers white or pink, solitary or in lateral fascicles, corymbs, or umbels, or in terminal racemes, hypanthium campanulate, obconic, or urceolate, sepals 5, spreading or reflexed, usually small, deciduous, petals 5, stamens 10-many, carpel 1, with 2 ovules, style 1; fruit a fleshy drupe with a single stone. The fruits of the majority of the species below are reported as edible (information regarding the edibility of *P. mahaleb*, *P. cerasifera* and *P. spinosa* was not provided in the reference sources reviewed); the pits are poisonous, although they were crushed by Indians and leached with water to remove the poison and then eaten. The leaves are reported as poisonous to livestock. Medicinal values are cited for *P. avium* and *P. domestica*. —Wildl. 4

a. Inflorescence an elongate raceme of 20 or more flowers, or a short raceme of 10 or fewer flowers, the lower pedicels subtended by foliceous bracts. (Fig. 606).
    b. Pedicels, at least some, more than 1 cm long; racemes with 10 or fewer flowers ..... 1. *P. mahaleb*
    b. Pedicels all less than 1 cm long; racemes with 20 or more flowers.
        Leaves crenate, with blunt, incurved teeth, mostly elliptic, often pubescent along the midvein beneath, lustrous above .. . . 2. *P. serotina*
        Leaves sharply serrate, mostly obovate, glabrous beneath or pubescent in the axils of the main veins, dull above .... 3. *P. virginiana*
a. Inflorescence a sessile umbel, flowers 10 or fewer or solitary (short racemes also sometimes present in *P. pensylvanica*, the lower pedicels not subtended by bracts).
    c. Flowers and fruit sessile or subsessile; fruit velvety-tomentose; twigs green, at least on one side .... 4. *P. persica*
    c. Flowers and fruit on pedicels 5 mm or more long; fruit glabrous or essentially so; twigs not green.
        d. Key based primarily on vegetative characteristics.
            e. Leaves, even when very young (except *P. alleghaniensis*) glabrous beneath.
                f. Leaves long-acuminate, the teeth glandular, glands near the sinuses. .... 5. *P. pensylvanica*
                f. Leaves acute to short-acuminate, the teeth glandless or with glands at the apices.

Leaves toothed to base, the teeth glandless; plant 6 or more feet tall. .... 6. *P. alleghaniensis*
Leaves entire toward base, the teeth with glands at the apices; plant
    usually less than 5 feet tall. (Fig. 607) .... 7. *P. pumila*
e. Leaves pubescent beneath, at least on the midrib.
  g. Leaves acuminate, often doubly serrate or crenate.
    h. Teeth sharp, glandless .... 8. *P. americana*
    h. Teeth blunt, gland-tipped (glands sometimes represented only by
      scars or callous remnants in mature leaves).
      i. Base of pedicels with an involucre of large bracts; seed globose.
        (Fig. 608).
        Leaves pubescent beneath primarily along the midrib and in the
          axils of the veins; glands of the teeth nearer the sinuses;
          bracts erect at anthesis. .... 9. *P. cerasus*
        Leaves pubescent on the lateral veins and elsewhere as well as on
          the midrib and axils; glands of the teeth nearer the apices;
          bracts reflexed at anthesis .... 10. *P. avium*
      i. Base of pedicels lacking bracts; seed compressed. .... 11. *P. nigra*
  g. Leaves acute or obtuse, mostly simply serrate or crenate.
    j. Leaves pubescent beneath only along the midrib and in the axils of the
      veins.
      Leaves with glandular teeth; flowers 1 or 2 in each umbel; sepals
        with marginal glands.. 12. *P. cerasifera*
      Leaves with glandless teeth; flowers 3 or more in each umbel; sepals
        without marginal glands .... 6. *P. alleghaniensis*
    j. Leaves pubescent beneath along the lateral veins and elsewhere as well
      as on the midrib and axils.
      k. Short lateral branches ending in spines. (Fig. 610).
        Flowers mostly paired in each umbel; pedicels pubescent. .... 13. *P. domestica*
        Flowers mostly solitary at each node, pedicels glabrous. .... 14. *P. spinosa*
      k. Short lateral branches, when present, ending in buds.
        Pubescence of petioles short and felt-like; leaf teeth glandless. .... 15. *P. maritima*
        Pubescence of petioles longer, not felt-like, the individual hairs
          distinct; leaf teeth gland-tipped .... 16. *P. hortulana*
d. Key based on flowers or fruit as well as vegetative characteristics.
  l. Base of pedicels with an involucre of large bracts. (Fig. 608).
    Leaves pubescent beneath primarily along the midrib and in the axils of
      the veins; glands of the teeth nearer the sinuses; bracts erect at
      anthesis. .... 9. *P. cerasus*
    Leaves pubescent on the lateral veins and elsewhere as well as on the
      midrib and axils; glands of the teeth nearer the apices; bracts
      reflexed at anthesis. .... 10. *P. avium*
  l. Base of pedicels lacking bracts.
    m. Sepals glandless or nearly so; leaf teeth glandless (except *P. pensylvanica*).
      n. Leaf teeth glandular; sepals glabrous; seed globose. .... 5. *P. pensylvanica*
      n. Leaf teeth glandless; sepals pubescent; seed compressed.
        o. Leaves acuminate, often doubly serrate or crenate . ... 8. *P. americana*
        o. Leaves acute or obtuse, mostly simply serrate or crenate.
          Pedicels and lower surfaces of mature leaves pubescent. .... 15. *P. maritima*
          Pedicels and lower surfaces of mature leaves glabrous. .... 6. *P. alleghaniensis*
    m. Sepals with marginal glands; leaf teeth glandular (glands sometimes
      represented only by scars or callous remnants in mature leaves).
      p. Leaves entire toward the base; mature plant usually less than 5 feet
        tall; seed globose. (Fig. 607) .... 7. *P. pumila*
      p. Leaves toothed to the base; mature plant usually 6 or more feet tall;
        seed compressed.
        q. Flowers mostly solitary or paired.
          r. Short lateral branches ending in spines; leaves pubescent beneath
            along the lateral veins and elsewhere as well as on the midrib
            and axils.
            Flowers mostly paired in each umbel; pedicels pubescent. .... 13. *P. domestica*
            Flowers mostly solitary at each node; pedicels glabrous. .... 14. *P. spinosa*

r. Short lateral branches, when present, ending in buds; leaves
pubescent beneath only along the midrib and in the axils
of the veins. .... 12. *P. cerasifera*

q. Flowers mostly 3 or more in each umbel. (Fig. 609).
Leaves 2 or more times as long as wide; petals less than 1 cm
long. .... 11. *P. nigra*
Leaves less than twice as long as wide; petals 1 cm or more
long. .... 16. *P. hortulana*

1. *P. máhaleb* L. (Arabic name). Mahaleb-cherry. Occasionally escaped from cultivation to roadsides, waste places and woodland borders. April-May. Map 1295. (Naturalized from Eurasia).

2. *P. serótina* Ehrh. (late-ripening). Black-cherry. Woodland borders and dry woods, thickets, abandoned fields, roadsides, waste places, dunes. May-June. Fig. 606, Map 1296. Our plants are var. *serotina*. —FACU

3. *P. virginiána* L. (Virginian). Choke-cherry. Woodland borders, thickets, roadsides and waste places. May-June. Map 1297. Our plants are var. *virginiana*. —FACU

4. *P. pérsica* (L.) Batsch (old generic name). Peach. Occasionally escaped from cultivation to roadsides, thickets and waste places. April-May. Map 1298. (Introduced from Asia).

5. *P. pensylvánica* L. f. (Pennsylvanian). Pin-cherry. Dry to moist woods, woodland openings, recent burns, roadsides and waste places. April-May. Map 1299. —FACU-

P. serruláta Lindl. Japanese Flowering Cherry. Similar to *P. pensylvanica* but distinguishable by sepals erect or slightly spreading. (reflexed in *P. pensylvanica*). Escaped from cultivation; reported for West Hatfield MA.

6. *P. alleghaniénsis* Porter (of the Alleghanies). Alleghany-Plum. Dry woods, woodland borders and thickets. May. Map 1300. Our plants are var. *allegheniensis*.

7. *P. púmila* L. (dwarfish). Sand-cherry. Sandy, gravelly, or rocky pond and river margins, beaches, dunes, barrens and clearings, ledges. May-June. Fig. 607. Represented with us by the following vars.:

var. *susquehánae* Hort. ex Willd. Plants erect, often diffusely branched but not prostrate and mat-forming. Map 1301. [*P. pumila* var. *cuneata*; *P. susquehanae*].

var. *depréssa* (Pursh) Gl. Plants prostrate, mat-forming. Map 1302. [*P. depressa*].

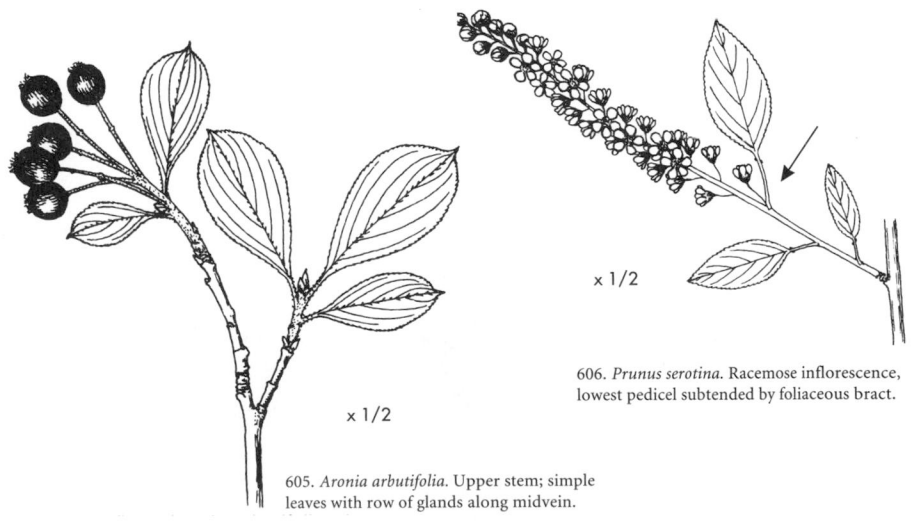

x 1/2

x 1/2

606. *Prunus serotina*. Racemose inflorescence, lowest pedicel subtended by foliaceous bract.

605. *Aronia arbutifolia*. Upper stem; simple leaves with row of glands along midvein.

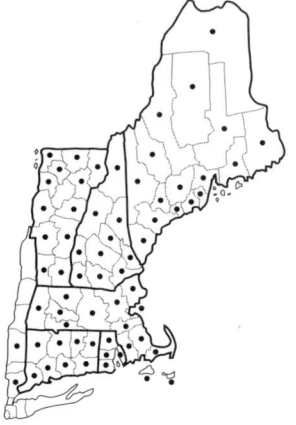

1292. *Aronia melanocarpa*

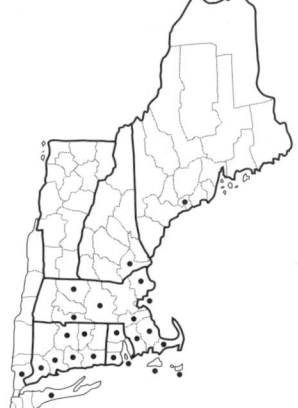

1293. *Aronia arbutifolia*

1294. *Aronia x prunifolia*

1295. *Prunus mahaleb*

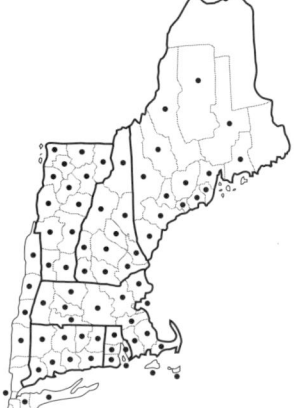

1296. *Prunus serotina*

1297. *Prunus virginiana*

1298. *Prunus persica*

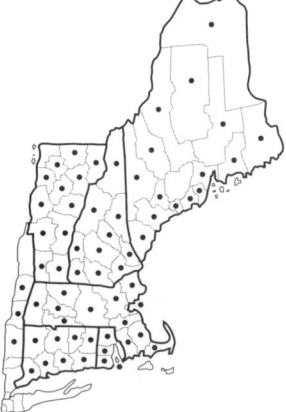

1299. *Prunus pensylvanica*

1300. *Prunus alleghaniensis*

8. P. americána Marsh. (American). Wild Plum. Moist woods, woodland borders, stream borders, thickets and roadsides. May. Map 1303. —FACU-

9. P. cérasus L. (cherry, brought to Europe from Cerasus). Sour cherry. Occasionally escaped from cultivation to woodland borders, thickets, roadsides and waste places. May. Fig. 608, Map 1304. (Naturalized from Asia).

10. P. ávium (L.) L. (of birds). Sweet cherry. Escaped from cultivation to woodland borders, thickets, roadsides and waste places. April-May. Map 1305. (Naturalized from Eurasia).

11. P. nígra Ait. (black). Canada-plum. Pond and stream margins, woodland borders, thickets and roadsides. April-May. Fig. 609, Map 1306.

12. P. cerasífera Ehrh. (bearing cherries). Cherry-Plum. Occasionally escaped from cultivation to old cellar holes and roadsides. May. Map 1307. (Introduced from Europe).

13. P. doméstica L. (domesticated). Garden-Plum. Occasionally escaped from cultivation to woodland borders, thickets, roadsides, and old cellar holes. May. Fig. 610, Map 1308. (Naturalized from Europe). Our plants include var. *domestica* and the following var.:

var. *institia* (L.) Fiori & Paoletti. Leaves 4-7 cm long, sparsely pubescent beneath, fruit 1.5-3 cm long. (leaves 6-10 cm long, densely pubescent beneath, fruit 3-7 cm long in var. *domesticus*). Map 1309. [*P. institia*].

14. P. spinósa L. (spiny). Blackthorn. Occasionally escaped from cultivation to roadsides and waste places. Reported for MA, New London County CT, Lincoln County ME.

15. P. marítima Marsh. (maritime). Beach-plum. Dunes, sandy roadsides and thickets mostly along the coast, occasionally inland. May. Map 1310. Our plants include var. *maritima* and the following var.:

var. *grávesii* (Small) G. J. Anderson. Leaves about as long as wide, suborbicular, 4 cm or less long (leaves longer than wide, elliptic to ovate, longer than 4 cm in var. *maritima*). Endangered in CT. [*P. gravesii*].

16. P. hortulána Bailey (of the garden). Moist thickets and woodland borders, floodplain forest. April-May. Reported for Plymouth County MA.

9. Physocárpus Maxim. Ninebark (from the Greek, referring to the inflated carpels).

Shrubs, with bark separating in numerous thin layers, twigs terete but lined from the nodes, moderate, pith relatively large, brownish, buds ovoid to conical, solitary, sessile, with 4-5 scales, leaf scars half-elliptic, raised on a cushion, bundle traces 5, stipule scars present, small; leaves simple, petioled, ovate, usually with 3 lobes and 3 principal veins, occasionally with a few smaller, upper lobes, cordate, truncate, or cuneate at the base, irregularly crenate to serrate; flowers small, white, numerous in terminal, round-topped corymbs, hypanthium campanulate; sepals 4-5, petals 5, stamens numerous, carpels mostly 3-5, inflated, ovules few, style elongate; fruit an inflated follicle, dehiscent on both sutures.

1. P. opulifólius (L.) Maxim. (with leaves of *Viburnum opulus*). Borders of streams and rivers, thickets, and waste places. June. Fig. 611, Map 1311. [*Opulaster o.; O. australis*]. Our plants are var. *opulifolius*. —FACW-

10. Spiraéa L. (from the Greek, meaning wreath).

Shrubs, twigs terete but lined from the nodes, slender to moderate, pith moderate, brownish, buds small, globose to ovoid, solitary or occasionally collaterally multiple, sessile, with 5-6 scales, leaf scars half-round to crescent-shaped, often raised, bundle trace 1, stipule scars lacking; leaves simple, petioled, oblong, lanceolate or oblanceolate, serrate; flowers small, white or pink, in simple or compound, terminal or axillary corymbs, umbels, or panicles, hypanthium campanulate, sepals and petals each 5, stamens 15-many, carpels usually 5, not inflated, ovules 2-several, style rather short; fruit a follicle, dehiscent on the ventral suture.

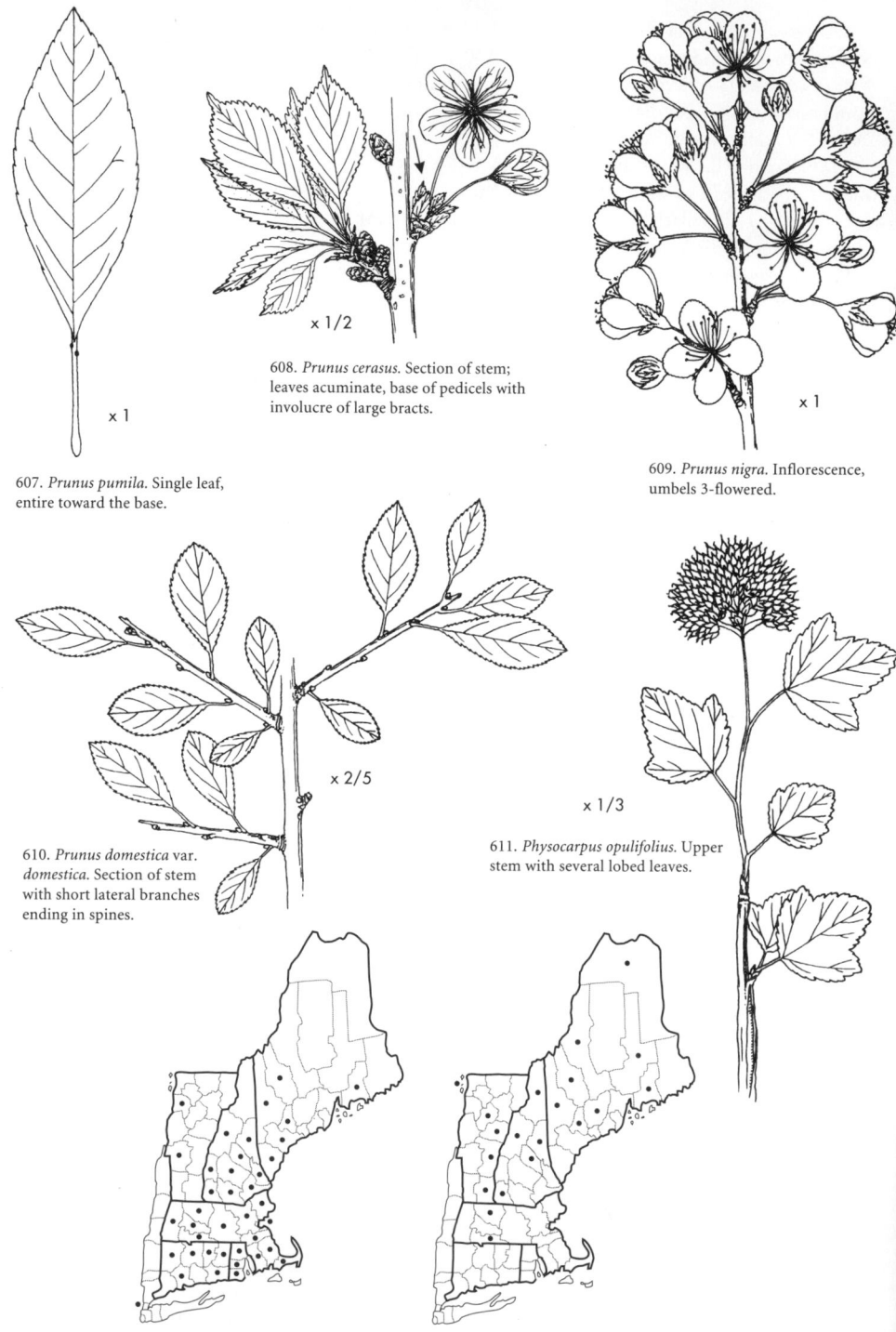

x 1/2

608. *Prunus cerasus.* Section of stem; leaves acuminate, base of pedicels with involucre of large bracts.

x 1

607. *Prunus pumila.* Single leaf, entire toward the base.

609. *Prunus nigra.* Inflorescence, umbels 3-flowered.

x 1

x 2/5

610. *Prunus domestica* var. *domestica.* Section of stem with short lateral branches ending in spines.

x 1/3

611. *Physocarpus opulifolius.* Upper stem with several lobed leaves.

1301. *Prunus pumila* var. *susquehanae*

1302. *Prunus pumila* var. *depressa*

1303. *Prunus americana*

1304. *Prunus cerasus*

1305. *Prunus avium*

1306. *Prunus nigra*

1307. *Prunus cerasifera*

1308. *Prunus domestica* var. *domestica*

1309. *Prunus domestica* var. *institia*

1310. *Prunus maritima*

1311. *Physocarpus opulifolius*

a. Inflorescence paniculate, usually longer than broad. (Fig. 612).
    Leaves densely tomentose beneath; panicle spire-like; follicles tomentose. .... 1. *S. tomentosa*
    Leaves glabrous beneath or nearly so, or if pubescent, not tomentose; panicle
        open-pyramidal (ovoid to cylindric in similar sp.); follicles glabrous.
        (Fig. 612) .... 2. *S. alba*
a. Inflorescence of compound corymbs or simple corymbs or umbels, usually
    broader than long.
  b. Inflorescence of compound corymbs.
    Leaves long-acuminate; calyx densely pubescent; flowers pink. .... 3. *S. japonica*
    Leaves obtuse to acute; calyx glabrous; flowers white. .... 4. *S. betulifolia*
                                       var. *corymbosa*
  b. Inflorescence of simple umbels or corymbs.
    c. Inflorescence of sessile or subsessile umbels. (Fig. 613).
      Leaves ovate to oblong; pedicels pubescent; flowers often double. .... 5. *S. prunifolia*
      Leaves lance-linear; pedicels glabrous; flowers with single perianth. .... 6. *S. thunbergii*
    c. Inflorescence corymbose, the corymbs terminating leafy branches.
      Stamens equalling or shorter than the petals; leaves few toothed near the tip. 7. *S. x vanhouttei*
      Stamens longer than the petals; leaves usually toothed at least to the middle.. 8. *S. chamaedryfolia*

1. *S. tomentósa* L. (tomentose). Steeple-bush. Dry to wet meadows, fields and pastures. July-August. Map 1312. Our plants include var. *tomentosa* and the following var.:
    var. *rósea* (Raf.) Fern. Flowers loosely clustered on the panicle branches (densely crowded in var. *tomentosa*). —FACW

2. *S. álba* Du Roi (white). Meadow-sweet. Dry to wet meadows, fields, waste places. July-August. Fig. 612, Map 1313. Our plants include var. *alba* (—FACW+) and the following var.:
    var. *latifólia* (Ait.) H. E. Ahles. Branchlets of panicle glabrous (branchlets puberulent in var. *alba*). Map 1314. [*S. latifolia*]. —FAC+

S. septentrionális Fern. Similar to *S. alba* but distinguishable in having panicles ovoid to cylindric, without elongated lower branches; northern or alpine (panicles open-pyramidal, with elongated lower branches, habitats various in *S. alba*). Reported for NH, ME. Endangered in ME. [*S. latifolia* var. *septentrionalis*]. —FAC+

S. salicifólia L. Similar to *S. alba* and *S. septentrionalis* but with leaves broadest below the middle and pink flowers (leaves oblong to obovate, broadest at or above the middle and flowers white in the latter 2 species). Eurasian. Occasionally escaped from cultivation. Reported for VT. —FACW+

3. *S. japónica* L. f. (Japanese). Escaped from cultivation to roadsides, thickets and waste places. July. Map 1315. (Naturalized from Asia). —FACU

4. *S. betulifólia* Pall. Mt. woods and streambanks. June-July. Throughout our range. Represented with us as var. *corymbósa*. (Raf.) Wats.

5. *S. prunifólia* Sieb. & Zucc. (plum-leaved). Occasionally escaped from cultivation to roadsides and old cellar holes. May-June. Fig. 613, Map 1316.

S. hypericifólia L. Similar to *S. prunifolia* but differs in having leaves entire or toothed only around the tip (leaves serrate all along the margin in *S. prunifolia*). Rarely escaped from cultivation. Reported for Fairfield County CT.

6. *S. thunbérgii* Sieb. ex Blume. Occasionally escaped from cultivation to roadsides and old cellar holes. May-June. Reported for MA, Fairfield County CT.

7. *S. x vanhoúttei* (Briot) Zabel. Bridal Wreath. Occasionally escaped from cultivation to roadsides and old cellar holes. May-June. Map 1317. [*S. vanhouttei*].

8. *S. chamaedryfólia* L. (with leaves of *Chamaedrys*). Occasionally escaped from cultivation to roadsides and old cellar holes. May-June. Reported for CT. Our plants include var. *chamaedryfolia* and the following var.:
    var. *ulmifólia* (Scop.) Maxim. Leaves rounded at the base, doubly toothed (cuneate at the base and singly toothed in var. *chamaedryfolia*).

11. *Exochórda* Lindl. Pearlbush.

Shrubs, with exfoliating bark, twigs slender, glabrous, with conspicuous lenticels, pith small, pale, buds solitary, sessile, ovoid, with numerous fringed scales, leaf scars shallowly U-shaped to linear, bundle traces 3, stipule scars lacking; leaves simple, petioled, elliptic to obovate, cuneate at the base and rounded at the tip, mucronate, entire to undulate-margined, sometimes dentate around the tip; flowers moderately large, white, in terminal racemes, sepals and petals each 5, stamens numerous, carpels 5, weakly united; fruit a 5-winged capsule, the carpels eventually separating.

Kérria DC. *japónica* (L.) DC. Occasionally escaped from cultivation; will key to *Exochorda* or *Spiraea* but differs in having green branches, yellow flowers, and fruit consisting of 5 or more drupe-like achenes. Reported for RI, Fairfield County CT, Strafford County NH.

Drýas L. *integrifólia* Vahl. Matted, trailing boreal or arctic shrub, keying to *Exochorda*; leaves coriaceous, whitened beneath, flowers scapose, solitary, 8-10 merous, fruit a head of achenes. Reported for NH.

1. *E. racemósa* (Lindl.) Rehd. (with racemes). Occasionally escaped from cultivation to roadsides and around buildings. May. Map 1318. [*E. grandiflora*].

12. *Crataégus* L. Hawthorn (from the Greek, meaning strength).

Shrubs or small trees, usually with stiff and sharply pointed spines on their stems and branches, twigs moderate to slender, often lustrous, pith rather small, white to brownish, buds solitary or collaterally multiple, sessile, round or ovoid, with about 6 scales, leaf scars narrowly crescent-shaped, bundle traces 3, stipule scars small; leaves simple, petioled, toothed and often lobed, those on the vegetative branches often differently shaped, larger and more deeply cut than those on the flowering branches; flowers white, rarely pink, in terminal simple or compound cymes or rarely solitary, hypanthium campanulate, sepals and petals each 5, stamens 5-25, ovary inferior,

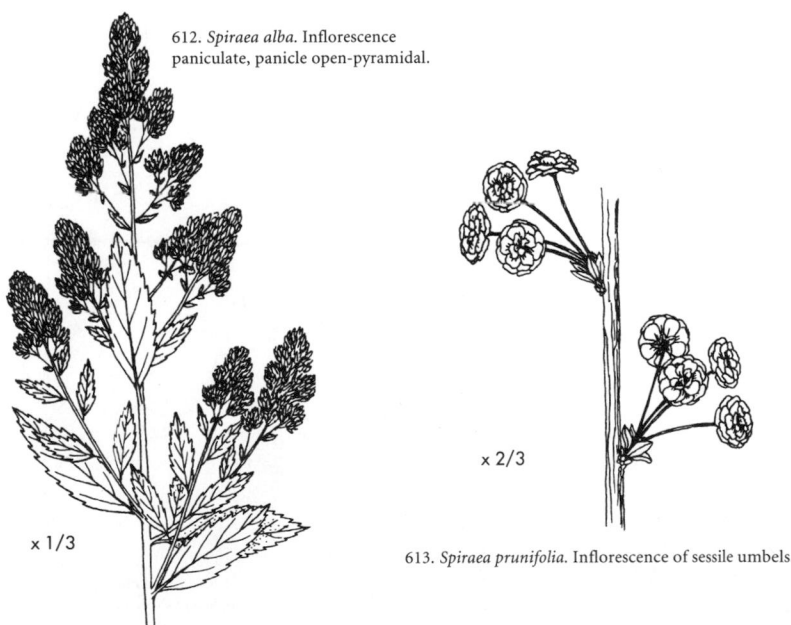

612. *Spiraea alba.* Inflorescence paniculate, panicle open-pyramidal.

x 2/3

x 1/3

613. *Spiraea prunifolia.* Inflorescence of sessile umbels.

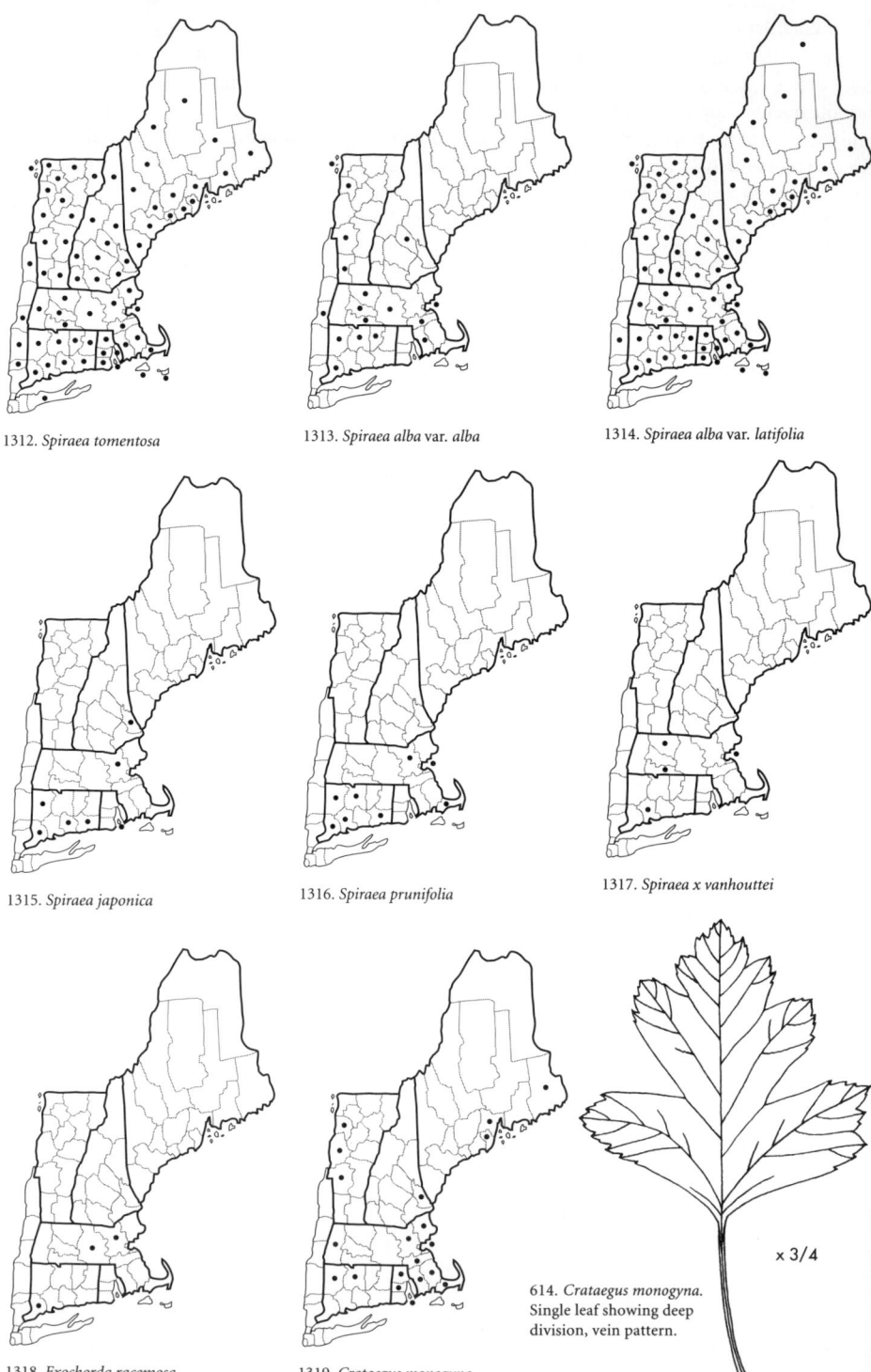

1312. *Spiraea tomentosa*

1313. *Spiraea alba* var. *alba*

1314. *Spiraea alba* var. *latifolia*

1315. *Spiraea japonica*

1316. *Spiraea prunifolia*

1317. *Spiraea x vanhouttei*

1318. *Exochorda racemosa*

1319. *Crataegus monogyna*

x 3/4

614. *Crataegus monogyna*.
Single leaf showing deep
division, vein pattern.

compound, of 1-5 carpels, with as many separate styles, ovule usually 1 in each carpel; fruit a small, apple-like pome containing 1-5 bony, 1-seeded nutlets. (The taxonomy of this genus is very complex and not well understood. Other floras covering the greater New England region have described several hundred species. The following treatment, based largely on the work of Harry Ahles, is highly condensed and subject to substantial modification as future studies shed light on these difficult groups). The fruits of all species are edible raw or as jams or jellies; the bark, leaves, flowers and fruits are reported to be of value in treating heart ailments and circulatory disorders. —Wildl. 2

Choenómeles Lindl. Flowering Quince. Similar to *Crataegus* but differs in having large stipules, styles joined at the base and fruits more than 1 inch in diameter (stipules none or small, styles separate and fruit less than 1 inch in diameter in *Crataegus*); 2 species rarely escaped from cultivation in our range: *C. speciósa* (Sweet) Naki. Twigs glabrous, leaves sharply serrate, reported for CT, Barnstable County MA [*C. lagenaria*], and *C. japónica* (Thunb.) Lindl. ex Spach. Twigs scabrous, leaves coarsely crenate-serrate, reported for MA, Fairfield and Litchfield Counties CT, Chittenden County VT.

a. Veins of the leaves usually running to the sinuses as well as to the points of the
    lobes; leaves usually deeply cleft. (Fig. 614).
  b. Spines mostly less than 2 cm long; leaves cuneate at the base; styles 1-2(3).
    Leaf divisions cut more than halfway to midrib, the lobes toothed only toward
      the tips; style 1. (Fig. 614) .... 1. *C. monogyna*
    Leaf divisions cut up to halfway to midrib, the lobes serrate; styles 2(3). .... 2. *C. curvisepala*
  b. Spines mostly longer than 2 cm; leaves deltoid, mostly rounded to cordate at the
    base; styles 3-5 .... 3. *C. phaenopyrum*
a. Veins of the leaves running only to the points of the lobes or larger teeth; leaves
    lobed or toothed but not deeply cleft.
  c. Leaves of reproductive branches mostly cuneate, acute or attenuate at base.
    d. Flowers solitary or rarely 2-3 together; petioles stout, not over 5 mm long. .... 4. *C. uniflora*
    d. Flowers cymose; petioles, at least some or most, over 5 mm long.
      e. Leaves mostly simply serrate, not, or rarely obscurely lobed. .... 5. *C. crus-galli*
      e. Leaves doubly serrate or lobed.
        f. Petioles strongly glandular; inflorescence conspicuously glandular-
          bracteolate, the glands stalked. (Fig. 615). .... 6. *C. intricata*
        f. Petioles eglandular or nearly so; inflorescence bracteoles lacking or few,
          when present, glands sessile (if stalked-glandular styles and nutlets
          2-3; 3-5 in *C. intricata*).
          g. Leaves with veins impressed above, attenuate at the base. .... 7. *C. punctata*
          g. Leaves with veins not impressed above, or if so, not attenuate at the
            base.
            h. Leaves pubescent beneath, at least on the veins; styles and nutlets
              2-3; nutlets deeply pitted on the inner side, the ends rounded .... 8. *C. succulenta*
            h. Leaves essentially glabrous beneath; styles and nutlets (2)3-5;
              nutlets not pitted, or if slightly so, the ends acute.
              Leaves usually obtuse or acute at the apex and points of the lobes;
                nutlets not pitted. (Fig. 616) .... 9. *C. chrysocarpa*
              Leaves usually acuminate at the apex and points of the lobes;
                 nutlets shallowly pitted on the inner side, the ends acute. ... 10. *C. brainerdii*
  c. Leaves of reproductive branches mostly rounded, truncate or cordate at base.
    (Fig. 617).
    Leaves distinctly pubescent beneath, at least along the veins; inflorescence
      tomentose .... 11. *C. mollis*
    Leaves glabrous or lightly pubescent beneath; inflorescence glabrous or
      pubescent but not tomentose.. 12. *C. pedicellata*

1. *C. monógyna* Jacq. (having 1 ovary). English Hawthorn. Escaped from cultivation to roadsides and woodland borders. May-June. Fig. 614, Map 1319. (Introduced from Eurasia and the Mediterranean). [*C. oxyacantha*].

C. laevigàta (Poir.) DC. Similar to *C. monogyna* but leaves are distinctly cuneate (leaves broadly based in *C. monogyna*). European. Reported for MA.

2. C. curvisépala Lindm. Occasionally escaped from cultivation to roadsides. May-June. Map 1320.

3. C. phaenópyrum (L. f.) Medik. (with the appearance of pear). Washington Thorn. Roadsides, thickets, and around buildings; escaped from cultivation and from further south. June. Map 1321. —FAC

4. C. uniflóra Muenchh. (one flowered). Dry woodlands and barrens. May. Reported for Suffolk County, NY.

5. C. crús-gálli L. (spur of a cock). Cockspur-thorn. Thickets, fields and open woods. May-June. Map 1322. [*C. schizophylla*]. —FACU

6. C. intricáta Lange (entangled). Roadsides, thickets and open woods. May. Fig. 615, Map 1323. [*C. biltmoreana; C. foetida; C. stonei*].

7. C. punctáta Jacq. (dotted). Pastures, thickets and roadsides. May-June. Map 1324. [*C. suborbiculata*].

8. C. succulénta Schrad. ex Link (succulent). Thickets, woodland borders. May-June. Map 1325. [*C. laxiflora; C. calpodendron; C. macrantha; C. spatiosa*].

9. C. chrysocárpa Ashe (golden fruited). Thickets and stream borders. May-June. Fig. 616, Map 1326. [*C. bicknellii; C. brunetiana; C. dodgei; C. faxoni; C. irrasa; C. jonesae; C. oakesiana; C. rotundifolia*].

10. C. brainérdii Sarg. (for E. Brainerd). Old pastures, thickets, roadsides and open woods. May. Map 1327. [*C. scabrida*].

11. C. móllis Scheele (soft). Open woods, often in floodplains. May-June. Map 1328. [*C. arnoldiana; C. submollis*]. —FACU

12. C. pedicelláta Sarg. (pedicelled). Open woods, thickets, borders of streams. May-June. Fig. 617, Map 1329. [*C. basilica; C. beckwithae; C. brumalis; C. coccinea; C. compta; C. dilatata; C. dissona; C. flabellata; C. haemocarpa; C. holmesiana; C. iracunda; C. jesupi; C. lemingtonensis; C. levis; C. lucorum; C. macrosperma; C. porteri; C. pringlei; C. pruinosa; C. schuetii*].

Some *Crataegus* hybrids that have been named:

C. anomala Sarg.	- *C. coccinea x mollis*
C. chadsfordiana Sarg.	- *C. pruinosa x succulenta*
C. ideae Sarg.	- *C. brainerdi x rotundifolia*
C. kennedyi Sarg.	- *C. brainerdi x pruinosa*
C. littoralis Sarg.	- *C. intricata x pruinosa*
C. membranacea Sarg.	- *C. pruinosa x succulenta*
C. pilosa Sarg.	- *C. intricata x pruinosa*
C. randiana Sarg.	- *C. brainerdi x flabellata*
C. rotundata Sarg.	- *C. pruinosa x rotundifolia*
C. shirleyensis Sarg.	- *C. brainerdi x punctata*
C. spatiosa Sarg.	- *C. pruinosa x succulenta*
C. websteri Sarg.	- *C. brainerdi x calpodendron*

13. Amelánchier Medik. Shadbush (name of a European species).

Small trees or shrubs, the shrubs sometimes stoloniferous, twigs slender, pith small, pale, buds solitary, sessile, elongate and narrowly conical, often slightly twisted, with about 6 reddish to greenish scales, leaf scars narrowly crescent-shaped, bundle traces 3, stipule scars lacking; leaves simple, petioled, serrate; flowers white or pink, in short, often leafy-bracted, terminal racemes (or in fascicles of 1-3 in 1 species), appearing with or before the leaves, hypanthium campanulate, sepals and petals both 5, the latter oblong and strap-shaped, stamens mostly 20, ovary inferior, compound,

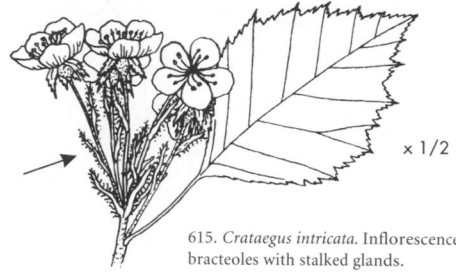

615. *Crataegus intricata*. Inflorescence, bracteoles with stalked glands.

× 2/3

616. *Crataegus chrysocarpa*. Leaf subtending inflorescence, acute apex and lobes.

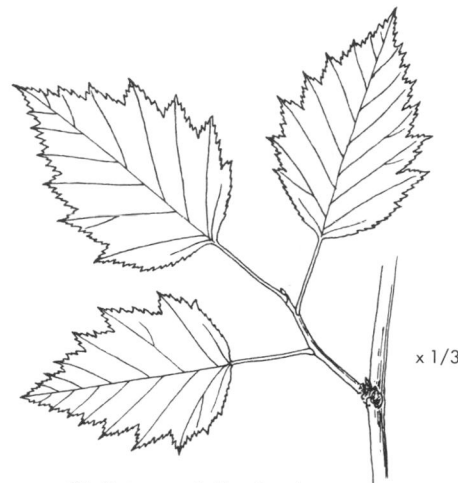

× 1/3

617. *Crataegus pedicellata*. Branch with several leaves rounded at base.

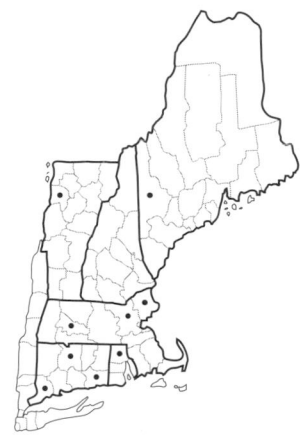

1320. *Crataegus curvisepala*

1321. *Crataegus phaenopyrum*

1322. *Crataegus crus-galli*

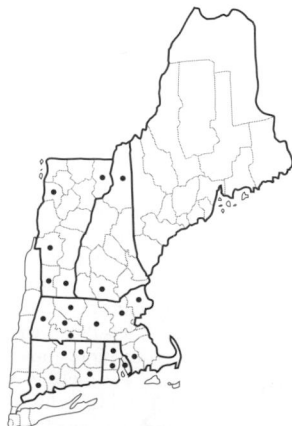

1323. *Crataegus intricata*

1324. *Crataegus punctata*   1325. *Crataegus succulenta*   1326. *Crataegus chrysocarpa*

1327. *Crataegus brainerdii*   1328. *Crataegus mollis*   1329. *Crataegus pedicellata*

of 5 carpels, 5-locular, with 2 ovules in each carpel, each pair of ovules separated by a false partition, the ovary thereby appearing 10-locular and 10-seeded, styles 5, united toward the base; fruit a small, berry-like, 10-locular and 10-seeded pome, the partitions cartilaginous. The fruits of all species are edible. —Wildl. 3

a. Leaves coarsely toothed, teeth mostly 5 or fewer per cm; flowers in racemes; ovary
    tomentose and rounded at the summit. .... 1. *A. sanguinea*
a. Leaves finely toothed, teeth mostly 6 or more per cm.
    b. Flowers 1-3; ovary summit tomentose, tapering to the styles; mature leaves
        mostly cuneate at the base, glabrous; rachis of fruiting inflorescence, when
        present, less than 1 cm long. (Fig. 618). .... 2. *A. bartramiana*
    b. Flowers mostly more numerous, racemose; ovary summit rounded to flat;
        mature leaves mostly rounded to subcordate at the base, pubescent beneath,
        or if glabrous, rachis of fruiting inflorescence more than 1 cm long.
        c. Ovary tomentose and rounded at the summit .... 3. *A. stolonifera*
        c. Ovary glabrous at the summit or only sparsely and temporarily pubescent.

d. Stoloniferous, colonial shrubs; primary veins of leaves mostly up to 9 pairs;
    petals up to 7 mm long.
  Young leaves densely pubescent; petioles and pedicels permanently pilose;
    sepals up to 2 mm long .... 4. *A. obovalis*
  Young leaves sparsely pubescent; petioles and pedicels glabrate; sepals
    2 mm or more long .... 5. *A. nantucketensis*
d. Clumped shrubs or small trees, primary veins more than 9 pairs; petals
    7 mm or more long.
  Petals mostly 11 mm or less long; sepals spreading to irregularly reflexed
    in fruit; racemes ascending .... 6. *A. canadensis*
  Petals mostly 11-18 mm long; sepals reflexed in fruit; racemes often
    divergent or pendant .... 7. *A. arborea*

1. A. sanguínea (Pursh.) DC. (blood-red). Riverbanks, open woods, rocky slopes. May-June. Map 1330. Endangered in CT, ME. [*A. humilis; A. huronensis; A. wiegandii*]. Our plants include var. *sanguinea* and the following var.:

var. *gaspénsis* Wieg. Veins of leaf forking at tip, mostly not extending to the teeth, blades glabrous from the first; petals 1 cm or less long (veins of leaf mostly not forking, extending to the teeth, blades pubescent at first; petals 1-1.5 cm long in var. *sanguinea*). [*A. fernaldii; A. gaspensis*].

A. húmilis Wieg. Similar to *A. sanguinea* var. *sanguinea* but teeth of leaves with narrow sinuses, racemes densely pubescent, petals 1 cm or less long (teeth with broad, open sinuses, racemes soon glabrate, petals 1-1.5 cm long in *A. sanguinea* var, *sanguinea*). Reported for ME, VT.

2. A. bartramiána (Tausch.) Roemer. Moist thickets and woods, frequently at high altitudes. May-June. Fig. 618, Map 1331. —FAC

A. x neglécta Egglest. A hybrid between *A. bartramiana* and *A. laevis*.

3. A. stolonífera Wieg. Dry open woods and fields. May-June. Map 1332. [*A. mucronata; A. spicata*]. —FACU

4. A. obovális (Michx.) Ashe (obovate). Pine barrens, open woods along the coastal plain. April. From farther south. Reported for Barnstable County MA. —FACU

5. A. nantucketénsis Bickn. (of Nantucket). Pine barrens and pond margins. May-June. Nantucket and Martha's Vineyard Islands, MA. [*A. canadensis*].

6. A. canadénsis (L.) Medic. Wooded swamps and damp to dry woods and thickets. April-May. Map 1333. [*A. lucida*]. —FAC

A. x intermédia Spach Similar to *A. canadensis* but with leaves well developed at anthesis, sparsely pubescent, often purple-tinged, mature leaves with 7 or fewer teeth per/cm, mature sepals glabrate (leaves barely developed at anthesis, tomentose, without purple tinge, mature leaves, at least the larger ones, with 7 or more teeth/cm, mature sepals tomentose above in *A. canadensis*). Reported for CT, ME, VT. [*A. canadensis*].

7. A. arbórea (Michx. f.) Fern. Dry to moist woods and thickets. April-June. Map 1334. [*A. arborea* var. *cordifolia*]. Our plants are var. *arborea*. —FAC-

14. *Málus* Mill. Apple.

Trees or large shrubs, twigs moderately stout, often woolly toward the ends, spine-like lateral spurs common along the branches, pith moderate, pale, buds solitary, ovoid, blunt, with 3-4 scales, woolly, leaf scars linear, bundle traces 3, stipule scars lacking; leaves simple, petioled, coarsely crenate or serrate, pubescent to glabrous beneath; flowers white to pinkish, in umbel like cymes on the lateral spurs, hypanthium campanulate or urceolate, open at the mouth, sepals and petals both 5, stamens numerous, ovary inferior, compound, of 5 carpels, 5-locular, with 2 ovules in each carpel, styles 5, united at the base; fruit a fleshy, 5-locular, 10-seeded, depressed-globose pome lacking grit cells, the partitions cartilaginous. Fruit edible raw or cooked; crushed pulp will heal inflammation or small flesh wounds. —Wildl. 3

In addition to the following species *M. x arnoldiana* has been reported for MA.

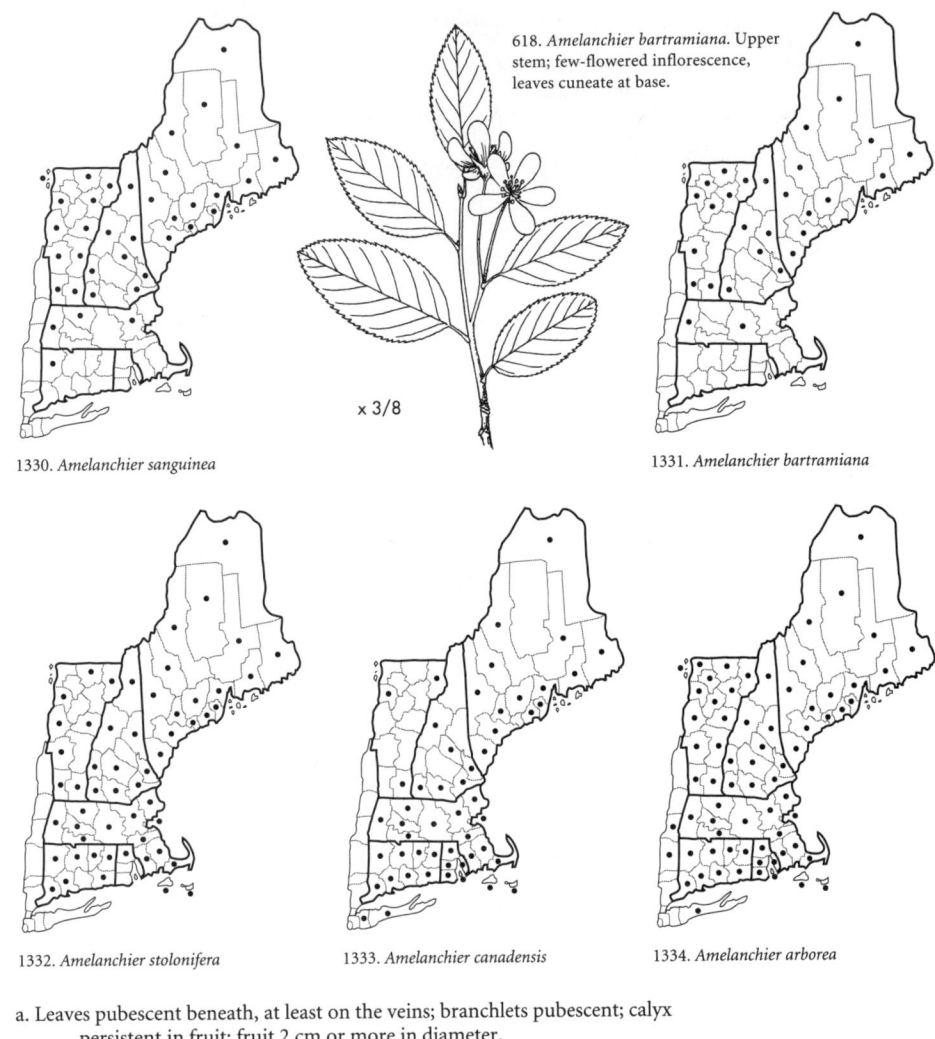

618. *Amelanchier bartramiana*. Upper stem; few-flowered inflorescence, leaves cuneate at base.

x 3/8

1330. *Amelanchier sanguinea*

1331. *Amelanchier bartramiana*

1332. *Amelanchier stolonifera*

1333. *Amelanchier canadensis*

1334. *Amelanchier arborea*

a. Leaves pubescent beneath, at least on the veins; branchlets pubescent; calyx
    persistent in fruit; fruit 2 cm or more in diameter.
    Leaves pubescent only on the veins beneath, sharply serrate; hypanthium
        glabrous .... 1. *M. prunifolia*
    Leaves pubescent on the surface as well as the veins beneath, crenate-serrate;
        hypanthium tomentose .... 2. *M. pumila*
a. Leaves and branchlets glabrous; calyx deciduous in fruit; fruit 1 cm or less in
    diameter .... 3. *M. baccata*

1. *M. prunifólia* (Willd.) Borkh. (plum-leaved). Crab-Apple. Occasionally spread from cultivation to roadsides and waste places. May. Map 1335. (Introduced from e. Asia). [*Pyrus p.*].

2. *M. púmila* Mill. (dwarf). Apple. Open woods, thickets, pastures and roadsides. May-June. Fig. 619, Map 1336. (Naturalized from Eurasia). [*M. malus; Pyrus malus*].

In addition, *M. sylvestris*, reportedly a distinct species, has been documented for RI and VT.

3. *M. baccáta* (L.) Borkh. (berry-like). Siberian Crab. Occasionally escaped from cultivation to roadsides and waste places. May. Map 1337. (Introduced from Asia). [*Pyrus b.*].

M. siebóldii (Regel) Rehder, the Toringo Crabapple which differs in having 3-5-lobed shoot leaves has also been reported as an escape. [*Pyrus s.*].

15. Pýrus L. Pear (classical name of the Pear).

Similar to *Malus*; leaves finely toothed; hypanthium nearly closed at the mouth around the base of the styles, styles separate to the base; pome pear-shaped, the flesh containing grit cells.

Cydónia P. Mill. *oblónga* P. Mill. Quince. Similar to *Pyrus* but differs in having entire leaf margins (leaf margins finely toothed or crenate in *Pyrus*). (*C. vulgaris* Pers.) Rarely escaped from cultivation. Reported for VT, Fairfield County CT, Middlesex County MA, Dutchess County NY. Fruit edible.

1. P. commúnis L. (common). Common Pear. Occasionally escaped from cultivation to roadsides, thickets and waste places. May. Map 1338. (Introduced from Eurasia). Fruit edible.

16. Arúncus Adans. Goat's-beard (ancient Greek name).

Dioecious, tall, perennial, rhizomatous herbs; leaves large, long-petioled, bi or triternately compound, leaflets lanceolate to elliptic, rounded to cordate at the base, acuminate, doubly serrate, stipules lacking; flowers imperfect, small, white, numerous, sessile or subsessile, in a large terminal panicle of spiciform racemes, hypanthium saucer-shaped, sepals and petals each 5, staminate flowers with 15-20 unequal stamens and several vestigial carpels, pistillate flowers with usually 3 carpels and several vestigial stamens; fruit a follicle.

1. A. dioícus (Walt.) Fern. (dioecious). Rich woods. May-June. Fig. 620, Map 1339. —FACU

17. Sanguisórba L. Burnet (name based on reputed value in stanching blood).

Hermaphrodite, monoecious or polygamous, erect, perennial herbs from a thick rhizome; leaves unequally pinnately compound, petioled, the leaflets serrate to pinnatifid, the stipules foliaceous, adnate to the petiole; flowers small, white, green or purple, perfect or unisexual, in dense, terminal spikes or heads, hypanthium urceolate, constricted at the throat, angled or winged (roughened between the wings in *S. minor*), sepals 4, petal-like, deciduous, petals none, stamens 4-many, carpels 1 or 2, tipped by a brush-like stigma, ovule usually 1; fruit an achene enclosed within the hypanthium. Young leaves taste like cucumber and can be used in salads.

a. Leaflets dissected nearly to the midvein; plant annual. .... 1. *S. annua*
a. Leaflets merely toothed; plant perennial.
  b. Longest spikes more than 4 cm long; sepals white. .... 2. *S. canadensis*
  b. Longest heads 3 cm or less long; sepals green or purple.
    Principal leaflets of basal leaves usually not over 2 cm long; stamens
      numerous .... 3. *S. minor*
                                                           subsp. *muricata*
    Principal leaflets of basal leaves usually more than 2 cm long; stamens 4. .... 4. *S. officinalis*

1. S. ánnua Nuttall ex T. & G. A waif in our region. Reported for MA.

2. S. canadénsis L. (Canadian). Canadian Burnet. Wet meadows, wooded swamps, river shores and floodplains. July-September. Fig. 621, Map 1340. Endangered in RI, ME. —FACW+

3. S. mínor Scop. (smaller). Garden Burnet. Fields, roadsides and waste places. June-July. Map 1341. (Adventive from Eurasia). [*Poterium sanguisorba*]. Represented with us as subsp. *muricáta* (Spach) Nordb. —FAC

4. S. officinális L. (of the shops). Great Burnet. Rarely escaped from cultivation to fields, thickets and roadsides. July-September. (Adventive from Eurasia). Reported for Waldo and York Counties ME. —FACW

18. Agrimónia L. Agrimony (ancient Greek name).

Erect, pubescent to glabrous, perennial, often glandular herbs from short, stout, knotty rhizomes; leaves pinnately compound, petioled, with much smaller leaflets interspersed between the larger ones, the leaflets crenate-serrate, the stipules prominent, foliaceous, usually toothed or laciniate; flowers small, yellow, in a long, terminal, interrupted, spicate raceme, or panicle of racemes, the peduncle subtended by a laciniate bract, the short pedicel and the flower each by a 3-lobed bract, hypanthium turbinate or hemispheric, with several rows of hooked bristles, becoming indurate in fruit, sepals 5, spreading in flower, becoming erect and connivent in fruit and forming a beak, petals 5, stamens 5-15, carpels 2, enclosed within the hypanthium, styles terminal, ovule 1 in each carpel; fruit a pair of achenes enclosed within the grooved, bristly hypanthium.

a. Hypanthium densely long-hirsute, concealing most or all of the surface. .... 1. *A. eupatoria*
a. Hypanthium remotely pubescent to glabrous or glandular, the surface clearly visible.
  b. Principal stem leaves with 11 or more primary leaflets. .... 2. *A. parviflora*
  b. Principal stem leaves mostly with 9 or fewer primary leaflets.
    c. Rachis of the inflorescence glandular, pubescent or glabrous.
      Stem spreading-pubescent; rachis of inflorescence densely glandular-
        puberulent and with scattered long hairs intermixed; mature
        hypanthium (including beak) 5 mm or more long .... 3. *A. gryposepala*
      Stem glabrous or sparsely appressed-pubescent; rachis of inflorescence
        merely glandular, rarely sparsely hirsute; mature hypanthium less
        than 5 mm long. .... 4. *A. rostellata*
    c. Rachis of the inflorescence eglandular, densely short-pubescent.
      Leaves sparsely pubescent and covered with minute resinous glands
        beneath; fruit (including beak) 5 mm or more long; roots not
        fusiform-thickened. .... 5. *A. striata*
      Leaves densely pubescent and eglandular or sparsely resinous-glandular
        beneath; fruits less than 5 mm long; roots fusiform-thickened. .... 6. *A. pubescens*

Dates are for mature fruit.

1. *A. eupatória* L. (from the name Eupatorium). Old fields and waste places. July-August. (Adventive from Europe). Reported for MA.

2. *A. parviflóra* Ait. (small-flowered). Wet to dry meadows, thickets and woodlands. August-September. Map 1342. Endangered in MA. —FAC

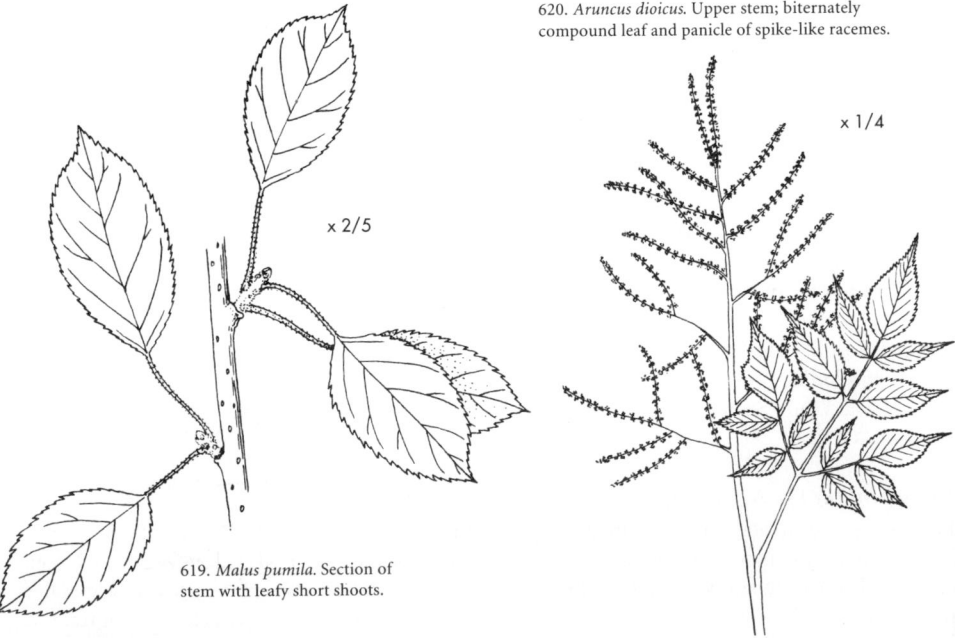

620. *Aruncus dioicus.* Upper stem; biternately compound leaf and panicle of spike-like racemes.

x 1/4

x 2/5

619. *Malus pumila.* Section of stem with leafy short shoots.

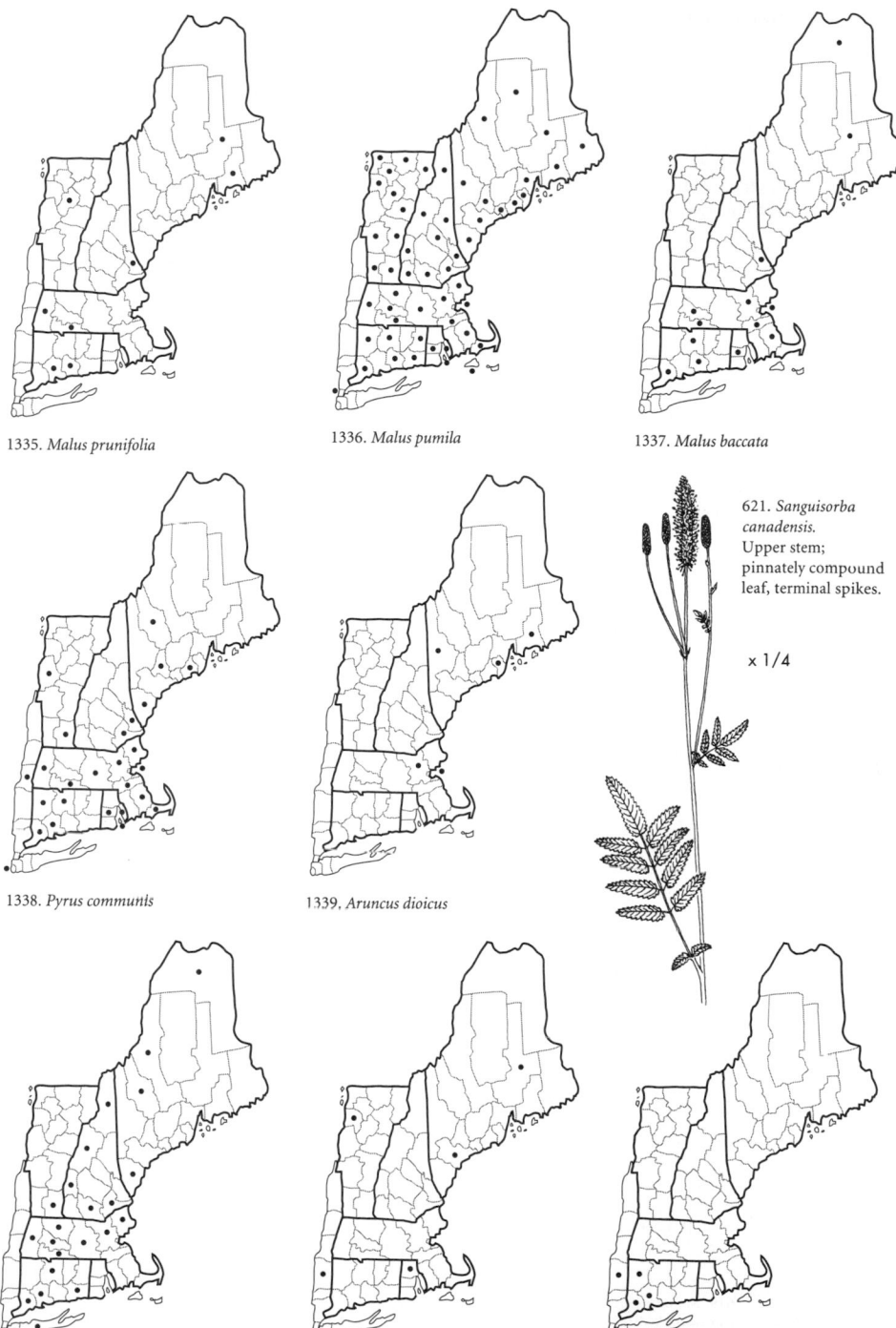

1335. *Malus prunifolia*

1336. *Malus pumila*

1337. *Malus baccata*

1338. *Pyrus communis*

1339. *Aruncus dioicus*

621. *Sanguisorba canadensis.* Upper stem; pinnately compound leaf, terminal spikes.

x 1/4

1340. *Sanguisorba canadensis*

1341. *Sanguisorba minor*

1342. *Agrimonia parviflora*

3. *A. gryposépala* Wallr. (having hooked sepals). Woods, thickets and roadsides. July-September. Fig. 622, Map 1343. Reported to be of value for kidney stones and for relieving sore throat. —FACU

4. *A. rostelláta* Wallr. (with a small beak). Moist to dry woodlands. August-September. Map 1344. —FACU

5. *A. striáta* Michx. (grooved). Moist to dry thickets and woods. July-September. Map 1345. —FACU-

6. *A. pubéscens* Wallr. (hairy). Rich open woods and thickets. July-September. Map 1346.

A. bicknéllii, reportedly a distinct species, has been documented for MA.

19. *Filipéndula* Mill. (name based on the thin roots of one of the species).

Tall, perennial, rhizomatous herbs; leaves pinnately compound, petioled, the leaflets deeply divided, lobed, or merely serrate, often with much smaller leaflets between the larger ones, stipules foliaceous; flowers small, pink or white, in a large, terminal, somewhat flat-topped panicle with ascending branches, hypanthium cup-shaped, sepals and petals each usually 5, stamens numerous, hypogynous, carpels 5-15, distinct, ovules 2; fruit indehiscent, 1-seeded, resembling a follicle, sometimes twisted.

a. Leaves with 2-5 pairs of lateral leaflets.
  Leaves white or grayish-tomentose beneath (except in subsp.); lateral leaflets
    coarsely single or double-toothed; flowers white .... 1. *F. ulmaria*
  Leaves green to slightly pale beneath, not tomentose; lateral leaflets distinctly
    3-5 lobed; flowers pink. (Fig. 623). .... 2. *F. rubra*
a. Leaves with 8 or more pairs of lateral leaflets. .... 3. *F. vulgaris*

1. *F. ulmária* (L.) Maxim. (old generic name). Queen of the meadow. Occasionally escaped from cultivation to roadsides, around buildings and in wet to dry meadows and thickets. July-August. Map 1347. Our plants include subsp. *ulmaria* and the following subsp.:

subsp. *denudáta* (J.&K. Presl.) Hayek. Leaves green and glabrous beneath (tomentose in subsp. *ulmaria*).

2. *F. rúbra* (Hill) Robins. (red). Queen of the prairie. Occasionally escaped from cultivation to roadsides and wet meadows. July-August. Fig. 623, Map 1348. —FACW

3. *F. vulgáris* Moench. (common). Dropwort. Occasionally escaped from cultivation to roadsides and waste places. Map 1349. [*F. hexapetala*].

20. *Géum* L. Avens (ancient Greek name).

Perennial, rhizomatous herbs; lower leaves pinnately compound or lyrate, those at the base of the plant commonly in rosettes, the lateral leaflets often smaller than the terminal, or rarely absent, often with much smaller leaflets interspersed or on the lower part of the petiole, middle leaves smaller, often trifoliate, the upper often simple, stipules foliaceous; flowers yellow, white or purple, solitary or in terminal corymbs, hypanthium hemispheric or campanulate, sepals 5, usually alternating with as many smaller, sepal-like bractlets, petals 5, stamens many, hypogynous, carpels numerous, on a cylindric to conical, non-fleshy receptacle, styles long, persistent, usually hooked; fruit an achene tipped by the long, persistent style.

a. Plant in flower.
  b. Sepals (and often the petals) purplish to reddish, spreading to ascending at
      anthesis; petals erect .... 1. *G. rivale*
  b. Sepals greenish, reflexed at anthesis (except *G. peckii*); petals spreading, white
      to yellow.
    c. Petals white or cream colored.
      d. Pedicels densely pubescent with long spreading hairs 1-2 mm long. .... 2. *G. laciniatum*
      d. Pedicels minutely velvety puberulent; long hairs, if present, sparse and
          scattered.

Petals white, slightly shorter than longer than the sepals; stems glabrous to
  sparsely hirsute below, often minutely pubescent above. .... 3. *G. canadense*
Petals cream-colored, much shorter than the sepals; stems densely
  hirsute below and usually throughout .... 4. *G. virginianum*
 c. Petals deep yellow.
  e. Stem leaves below the flower(s) (not counting the one immediately
   subtending) 1 or 2, simple; styles not jointed ... . 5. *G. peckii*
  e. Stem leaves below the flower(s) 3 or more, at least some compound; styles
   jointed.
   f. Calyx without bractlets; petals 1-2 mm long. .... 6. *G. vernum*
   f. Calyx usually with bractlets; petals longer.
    g. Petals much shorter than the sepals .... 4. *G. virginianum*
    g. Petals equaling to longer than the sepals.
     h. Stipules mostly as wide or wider than long. (Fig. 625). .... 7. *G. urbanum*
     h. Stipules longer than wide.
      Central lobe of most stem leaves obtuse to broadly rounded;
       pedicels minutely velvety puberulent, without or with
       few long, spreading hairs. (Fig. 626). .... 8. *G. macrophyllum*
      Central lobe of most stem leaves acute; pedicels with long
       spreading hairs 1-2 mm long, may also be puberulent .... 9. *G. aleppicum*
a. Plant in fruit
 i. Head of achenes raised above the sepals on a stipe. (Fig. 624).
  Sepals 7 mm or more long; bractlets present; head, including styles, more
   than 1.5 cm wide .... 1. *G. rivale*
  Sepals 3 mm or less long; bractlets none; head, including styles, less than
   1.5 cm wide .... 6. *G. vernum*
 i. Head of achenes sessile.
  j. Stem leaves below the flower(s) (not counting the one immediately subtending)
   1 or 2, simple; styles not jointed nor hooked at the tip. .... 5. *G. peckii*
  j. Stem leaves below the flower(s) 3 or more, at least some compound; style
   jointed, the upper part deciduous, the lower hooked at the tip.
   k. Stipules reniform to hemispheric, mostly as wide or wider than long; styles
    mostly purplish. (Fig. 625) ....7. *G. urbanum*
   k. Stipules ovate to lanceolate, mostly longer than wide; styles mostly greenish
    (except sometimes in *G. macrophyllum*).
    l. Central lobe of most stem leaves obtuse to broadly rounded; pedicels
     minutely velvety-puberulent, without or with few long spreading
     hairs; receptacle glabrous or short-hispid. (Fig. 626). .... 8. *G. macrophyllum*
    l. Central lobe of most stem leaves acute; if pedicels velvety-puberulent,
     without long spreading hairs, receptacle densely hirsute.
     m. Pedicels minutely velvety-puberulent, without or with few long
      spreading hairs; receptacle densely hirsute.
      Stems glabrous to sparsely hirsute below, often minutely pubescent
       above. .... 3. *G. canadense*
      Stems densely hirsute below and usually throughout. .... 4. *G. virginianum*
     m. Pedicels with long spreading hairs 1-2 mm long, may also be
      puberulent.
      Pedicels densely pubescent, the median area with more than 40 hairs
       per cm; head globose .... 2. *G. laciniatum*
      Pedicels less pubescent, the median area with less than 30 hairs per
       cm; head more or less obovoid .... 9. *G. aleppicum*

1. G. riválé L. (of brooksides). Purple Avens. Wooded swamps, wet woods, wet meadows. May-July. Fig. 624, Map 1350. (Eurasia). Root is used to make a chocolate colored drink used as a cocoa substitute, which is also of value in treating dysentery. —OBL

G. x púlchrum Fern. A hybrid between *G. rivale* and *G. macrophyllum*.

2. G. laciniátum Murr. (slashed). Wet to dry meadows and woodlands, stream and river edges, roadsides. June-July. Map 1351. Our plants include var. *laciniatum* and the following var.:
var. *trichocárpum* Fern. Achenes bristly at summit (glabrous in var. *laciniatum*). —FAC+

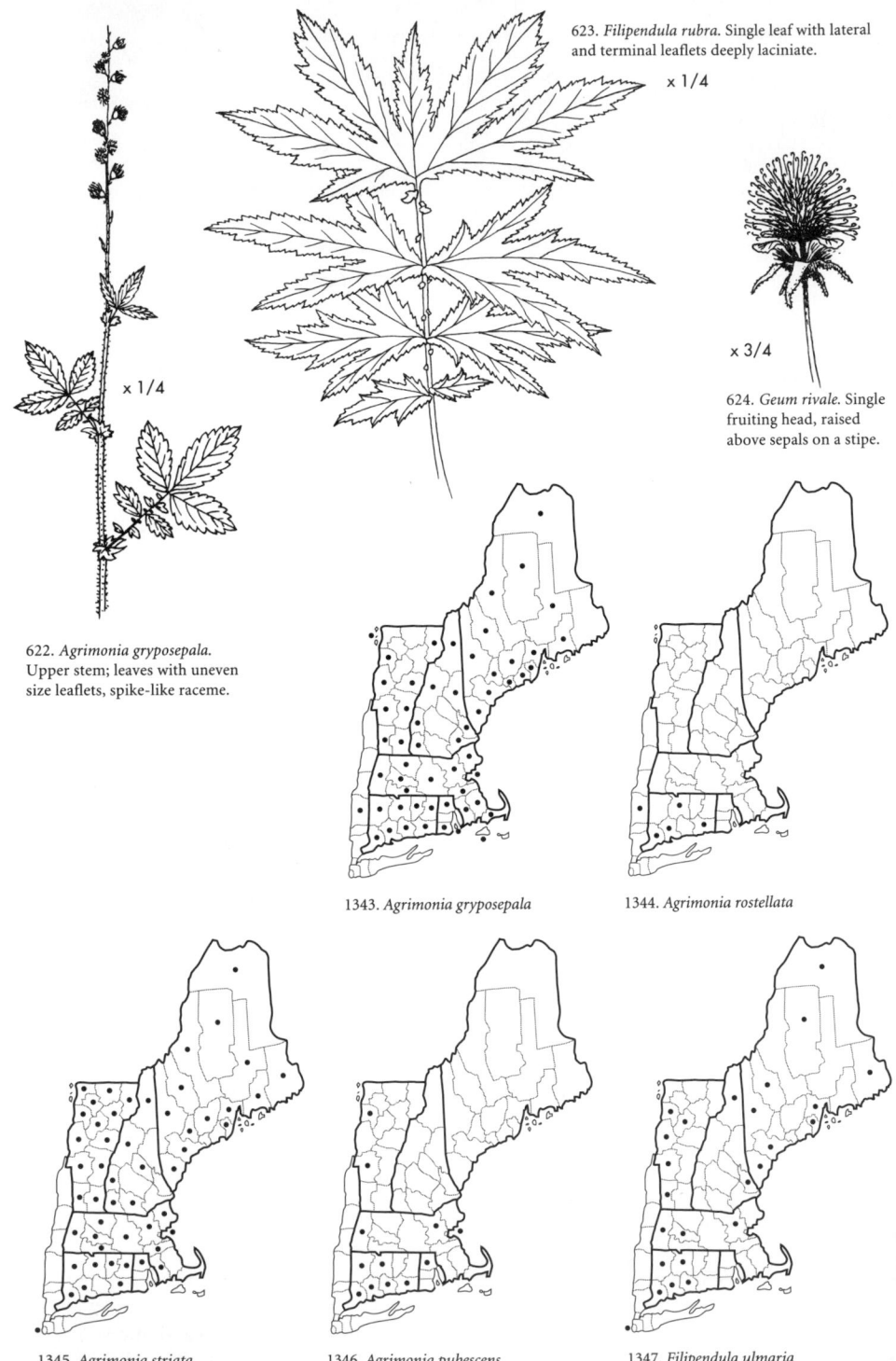

623. *Filipendula rubra*. Single leaf with lateral and terminal leaflets deeply laciniate.

x 1/4

x 3/4

624. *Geum rivale*. Single fruiting head, raised above sepals on a stipe.

x 1/4

622. *Agrimonia gryposepala*. Upper stem; leaves with uneven size leaflets, spike-like raceme.

1343. *Agrimonia gryposepala*

1344. *Agrimonia rostellata*

1345. *Agrimonia striata*

1346. *Agrimonia pubescens*

1347. *Filipendula ulmaria*

1348. *Filipendula rubra*

1349. *Filipendula vulgaris*

1350. *Geum rivale*

1351. *Geum laciniatum*

1352. *Geum canadense*

1353. *Geum virginianum*

3. G. canadénse Jacq. (Canadian). Wet to rich, moist meadows and woodlands, roadsides. June-August. Map 1352. Our plants include var. *canadense* and the following var.:

var. *campórum* (Rydb.) Fern. & Weath. Carpels 60 or more, 3 mm or more long when mature (carpels up to 60, up to 3 mm long when mature in var. *canadense*). [*G. camporum*]. —FACU

4. G. virginiánum L. (Virginian). Rich woodlands. June-August. Map 1353. [*G. flavum*].

5. G. péckii Pursh (for its discoverer). Mountain Avens. Known only from alpine slopes and meadows, VT, White Mountains, NH, and Brier Island, NS. Map 1354. June-August. [*Sieversia p.*]. —OBL

6. G. vérnum (Raf.) Torr. & Gray (vernal). Rich woods. April-June. Reported for VT, Bronx and Dutchess Counties NY. —FACU

7. G. urbánum L. (of towns). Roadsides and around buildings. Fig. 625, Map 1355. (Adventive from Europe).

8. G. macrophýllum Willd. (large-leaved). Rich, moist woods. June-July. Fig. 626, Map 1356. (e. Asia; Europe). Our plants are var. *macrophyllum*. —FACW

9. G. aléppicum Jacq. (of Aleppo). Dry to moist meadows, thickets, woodland openings and borders, and roadsides. June-August. Map 1357. —FAC

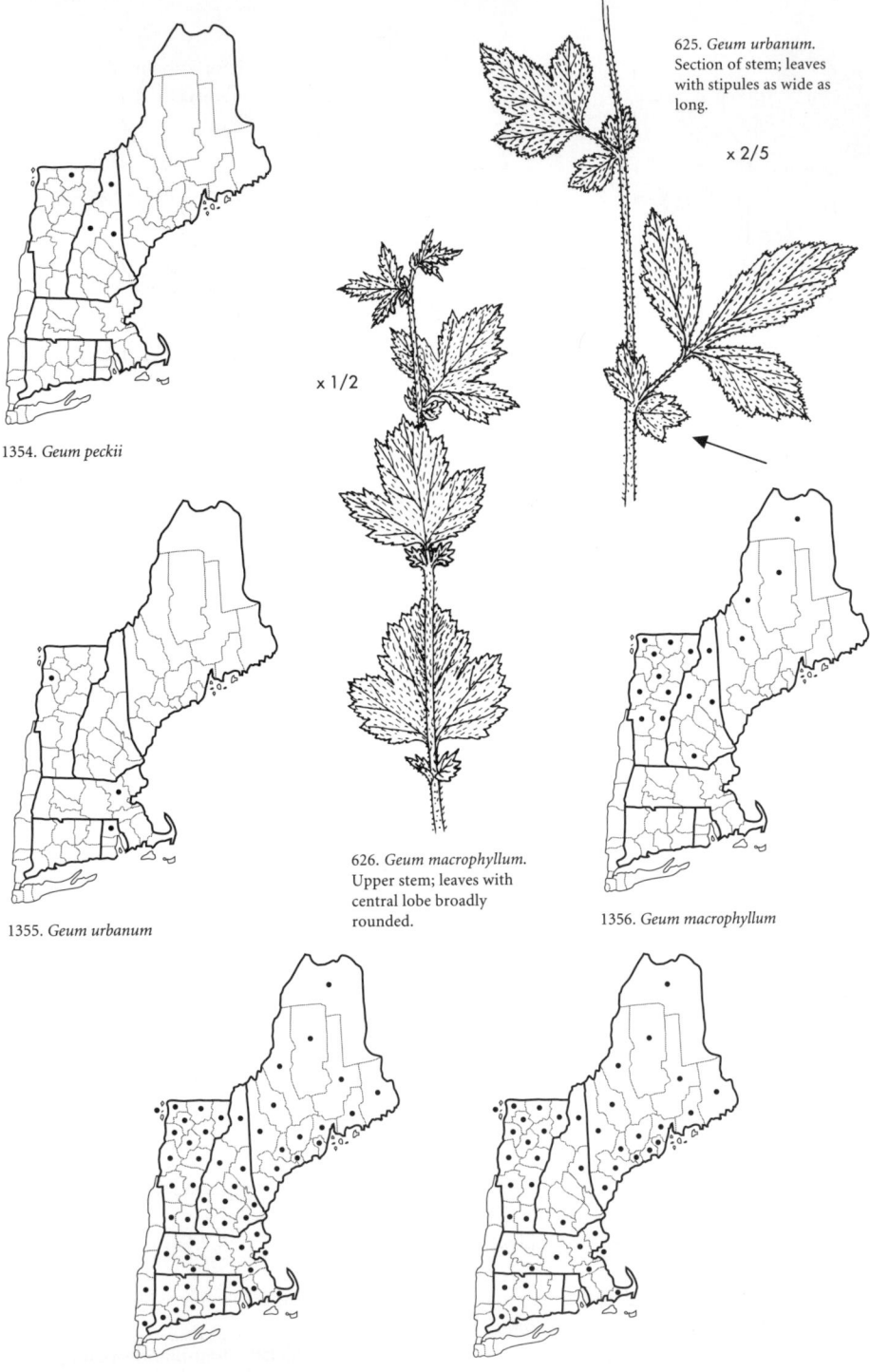

1354. *Geum peckii*

× 1/2

625. *Geum urbanum.*
Section of stem; leaves
with stipules as wide as
long.

× 2/5

1355. *Geum urbanum*

626. *Geum macrophyllum.*
Upper stem; leaves with
central lobe broadly
rounded.

1356. *Geum macrophyllum*

1357. *Geum aleppicum*

1358. *Comarum palustre*

21. Comárum L.

Similar to *Potentilla* (genus 23), but distinguishable in being aquatic or subaquatic, with stems decumbent, woody and rooting below; flowers purple; aggregate fleshy in fruit. [*Potentilla*]. —Wildl. 1

1. C. palústre L. Marsh Five-finger. Bogs, inundated meadows and swamps, pond and stream margins in shallow water or in muck. June-July. Map 1358. (Eurasia). [*Potentilla palustris*]. —OBL

22. Argentína Hill.

Similar to *Potentilla* (genus 23), but trailing and rooting at intervals; flowers solitary-axillary, or terminal and not in cymes. —Wildl. 1

1. A. anserína (L.) Rydb. Silverweed. Lake and river shores. June-July. Fig. 627, Map 1359. (Eurasia). [*Potentilla a.*]. Roots edible steamed, boiled or roasted with a taste like parsnip; tea can be made from the young leaves; preparations of the dried plant are reported to have various medicinal uses such as treatment of skin disorders, diarrhea, menstrual pain and intestinal disorders. —OBL

A. egédii (Wormskj.) Rydb. Similar to *A. anserina* but with leaf margins distinctly revolute; pubescence of undersides of leaflets tightly appressed, not extending over margin; pedicels and petioles glabrous or only slightly pubescent (leaf margins indistinctly or not revolute; pubescence of undersides of leaflets loose, extending over the margins; pedicels and petioles pubescent in *A. anserina*). Salt marshes and sandy beaches. Reported throughout our range. [*Potentilla e.* var. *groenlandica*; *P. anserina* subsp. *egedii*; *P. pacifica*; *Anserina p.*]. Represented with us as subsp. *groenlandica* (Tratt.) A. Löve.

23. Potentílla (name based on reputed medicinal value of one of the species).

Annual or perennial herbs, sometimes suffruticose, erect to spreading-ascending; leaves ternately, palmately or pinnately compound, leaflets serrate or toothed, stipules prominent, adnate; flowers yellow, in terminal cymes, these often leafy, hypanthium saucer-shaped to hemispheric, sepals 5, alternating with 5 similar bracts and adnate to them, petals 5, (flowers rarely 4-merous) stamens numerous, carpels numerous, borne on a dry, usually pubescent receptacle, style lateral or terminal, deciduous, ovule 1 in each carpel; fruit a head of achenes, often enclosed by the persistent calyx. —Wildl. 1

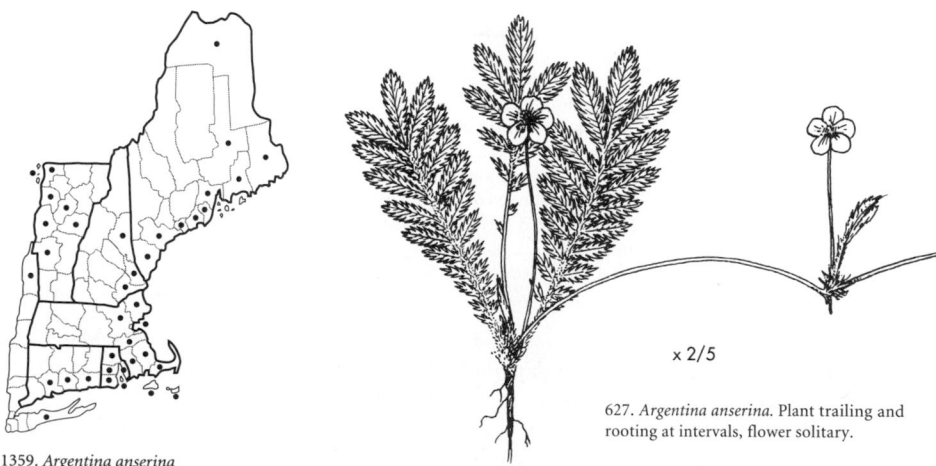

x 2/5

627. *Argentina anserina*. Plant trailing and rooting at intervals, flower solitary.

1359. *Argentina anserina*

a. Leaves pinnate.

    Leaflets dissected into narrow, linear teeth; rachis (not including naked portion)
        usually shorter than terminal leaflet (leaf sometimes appearing subdigitate).
        (Fig. 628) .... 1. *P. pensylvanica*
                                                            var. *pectinata*

    Leaflets merely toothed, the teeth not linear; rachis usually longer than terminal
        leaflet .... 2. *P. arguta*

a. Leaves ternate or palmate.

  b. Leaves with mostly 3 leaflets, occasionally 4 or 5 on some basal leaves (in *P. erecta*
      the stipules may resemble leaflets; in the species in second part of couplet,
      stipules are unlike the leaflets). (Fig. 629).

    c. Plants dwarf, less than 5 cm tall, tufted; flowers solitary, terminal. .... 3. *P. robbinsiana*

    c. Plants taller; flowers solitary-axillary or in terminal cymes.

      d. Stem leaves sessile or on petioles less than 5 mm long. .... 4. *P. erecta*

      d. Stem leaves petiolate, with petioles mostly over 5 mm long.

        Achenes smooth, less than 0.8 mm long .... 5. *P. rivalis*
                                                  var. *millegrana*

        Achenes rugose, 0.8 mm or more long .... 6. *P. norvegica*

  b. Leaves with 5 or more leaflets. (Fig. 630).

    e. Flowers axillary or terminal, solitary or few and scarcely cymose; plant often
      trailing.

      f. Flowers from the axils of reduced leaves, the leaves becoming progressively
        smaller upward .... 7. *P. tabernaemontani*

      f. Flowers from normal leaf axils, except perhaps the lowest flower.

        g. Flowers all or nearly all 4-merous .... 8. *P. anglica*

        g. Flowers 5-merous.

          h. Stems radiating from a vertical, thick, tap-like root system; flowers
            more than 1.5 cm wide .... 9. *P. reptans*

          h. Stems radiating from a short, horizontal rhizome; flowers 1.5 cm or
            less wide.

            First flower usually borne from the axil of the first well developed
              leaf; leaflets toothed from the apex to approximately the
              middle. (Fig. 630). .... 10. *P. canadensis*

            First flower usually borne from the axil of the second well developed
              leaf; leaflets toothed from apex to well below the middle . . .. 11. *P. simplex*

    e. Flowers in terminal cymes, these often leafy; plant erect to spreading-ascending.

      i. Some leaves, particularly the basal, with more than 5 leaflets. (Fig. 631).

        Surface of underside of leaflets tomentose .... 12. *P. gracilis*

        Surface of underside of leaflets strigose-pubescent but not
          tomentose. .... 13. *P. recta*

      i. Leaves with 5 leaflets.

        j. Surface of underside of leaflets tomentose.

          k. Leaflet margins revolute.

            Leaflets densely tomentose, the surface usually concealed, without
              longer hairs, the tomentum white or silvery .... 14. *P. argentea*

            Leaflets thinly tomentose with longer hairs intermixed, the
              tomentum grayish. .... 15. *P. intermedia*

          k. Leaflet margins flat, at least on the basal leaves. .... 16. *P. inclinata*

        j. Surface of underside of leaflets glabrous or hirsute but not tomentose.

          Flowering stem with more than 3 leaves below first flower or branch
           of inflorescence .... 16. *P. inclinata*

          Flowering stem with 0-1 leaf below first flower or branch of
           inflorescence. .... 7. *P. tabernaemontani*

1. *P. pensylvánica* L. Dry fields, rocks and ledges along the coast. June-July. Fig. 628, Map 1360. Endangered in VT. [*P. pensylvanica* var. *bipinnatifida*; *P.p.* var. *glabrata*; *P. glabrella*; *P. litoralis*; *P. pectinata*; *P. strigosa*]. Represented with us as var. *pectináta* (Raf.) Boivin.

2. *P. argúta* Pursh (acute). Tall Cinquefoil. Dry woods, roadsides. June-August. Map 1361. [*Drymocallis agrimonioides*]. Our plants are subsp. *arguta*.

3. P. robbinsiána Oakes ex Rydb. (for its discoverer). Alpine; VT, Mt. Washington, NH. June-July. Federally Endangered.

4. P. erécta (L.) Raeusch. (erect). Moist open woods. June-August. (Azores; Eurasia). Reported for MA. [*P. tormentilla*]. Preparations made from the plant are reported to be of value in treating toothache and gum disease and in external application to reduce skin wrinkles.

5. P. rivális Nutt. Waste places. June-August. Reported for Cumberland County ME, Suffolk County MA. [*P. millegrana; P. pentandra*]. Represented with us as var. *millegrána*. (Engelm. ex Lehm.) S. Wats.

6. P. norvégica L. (Norwegian). Fields, roadsides and waste places. June-August. Fig. 629, Map 1362. (Europe). —FACU

7. P. tabernaemontáni Aschers. Roadsides. May-June. (Adventive from Europe). Reported for Fairfield County CT. [*P. verna*].

8. P. ánglica Laichard. (English). Fields, roadsides and waste places. July-September. (Azores; Europe). Reported for Knox County ME. [*P. procumbens*].

9. P. réptans L. (creeping). Fields, roadsides, waste places and lawns. June-July. (Adventive from Europe). Reported for Middlesex County MA. Young leaves are edible in salads; a preparation made from the roots is said to relieve toothache, and is used also in external applications to reduce skin wrinkles.

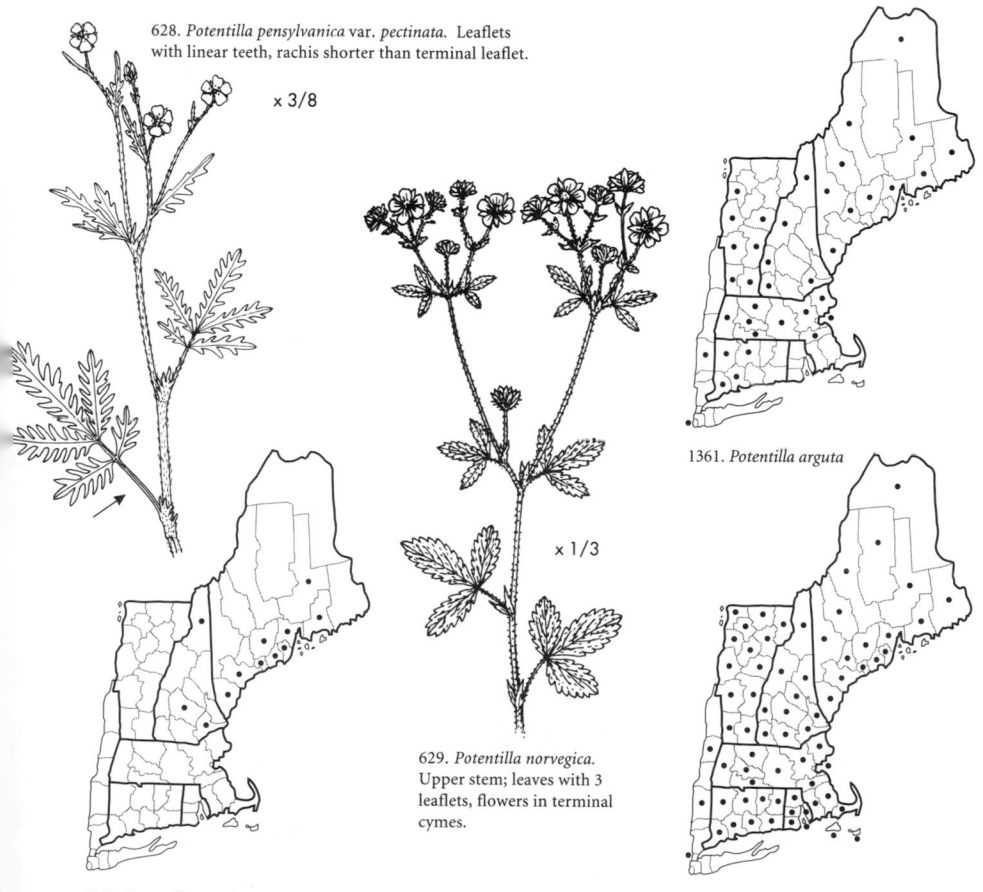

628. *Potentilla pensylvanica* var. *pectinata*. Leaflets with linear teeth, rachis shorter than terminal leaflet.

x 3/8

x 1/3

1361. *Potentilla arguta*

629. *Potentilla norvegica*. Upper stem; leaves with 3 leaflets, flowers in terminal cymes.

1360. *Potentilla pensylvanica* var. *pectinata*

1362. *Potentilla norvegica*

10. P. canadénsis L. (of Canada). Early Cinquefoil. Dry fields, open woods, and waste places. April-June. Fig. 630, Map 1363. [*P. pumila*]. Our plants are var. *canadensis*.

11. P. símplex Michx. (unbranched). Old-field-Cinquefoil. Fields, open woods, roadsides and waste places. May-June. Map 1364. —FACU-

12. P. grácilis Dougl. ex Hook. (slender). Fields and waste places. June-July. Reported for Coos County NH. [*P. flabelliformis*]. Our plants are var. *gracilis*.

P. pulchérrima Lehm. Similar to *P. gracilis* but with leaflets densely white tomentose beneath, appressed-pilose above, margin crenate-serrate (leaflets gray tomentose beneath, sparsely pilose above, margin sharply toothed in *P. gracilis*). Reported for CT, NH. [*P. gracilis* var. *pulcherrima*].

13. P. récta (upright). Fields, roadsides and waste places. June-August. Fig. 631, Map 1365. (Naturalized from Europe). [*P. sulphurea*]. Suspected of being poisonous but there is no direct evidence to support this.

14. P. argéntea L. (silvery). Silvery Cinquefoil. Fields, roadsides, waste places and lawns. June-August. Map 1366. (Naturalized from Europe). Our plants are var. *argentea*.

15. P. intermédia L. (intermediate). Fields, roadsides and waste places. June-August. Map 1367. (Naturalized from Europe).

16. P. inclináta Vill. Fields, roadsides and waste places. June-August. Map 1368. (Naturalized from Europe). [*P. canescens*].

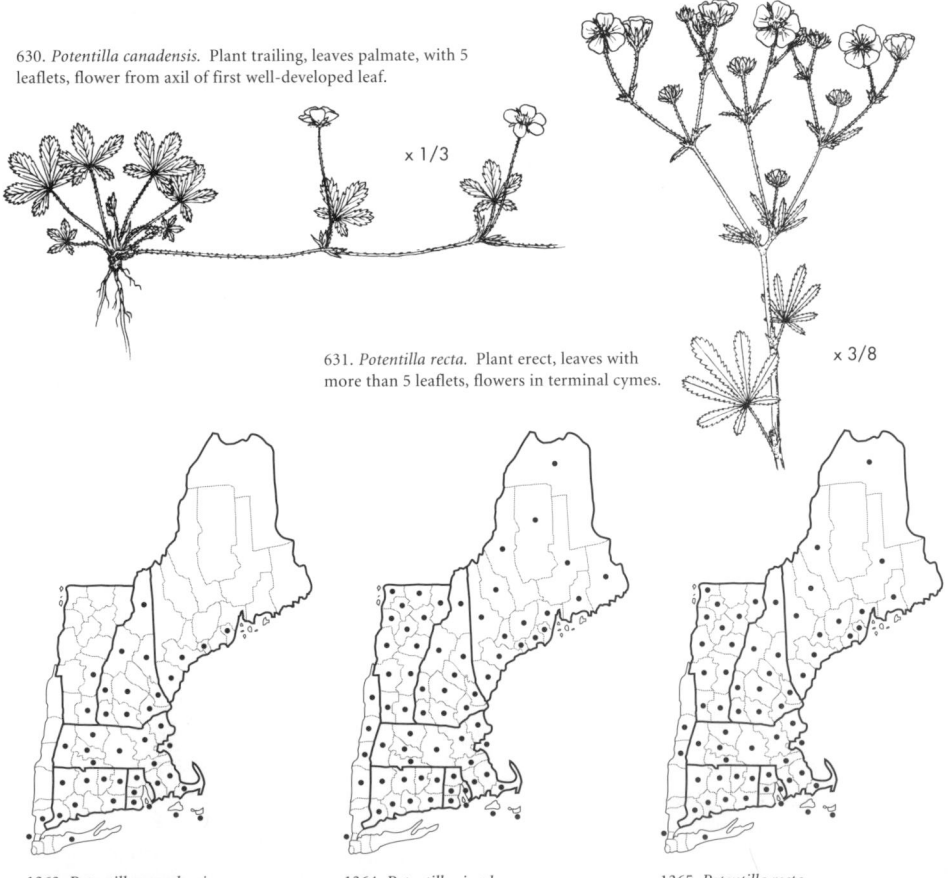

630. *Potentilla canadensis.* Plant trailing, leaves palmate, with 5 leaflets, flower from axil of first well-developed leaf.

× 1/3

631. *Potentilla recta.* Plant erect, leaves with more than 5 leaflets, flowers in terminal cymes.

× 3/8

1363. *Potentilla canadensis*   1364. *Potentilla simplex*   1365. *Potentilla recta*

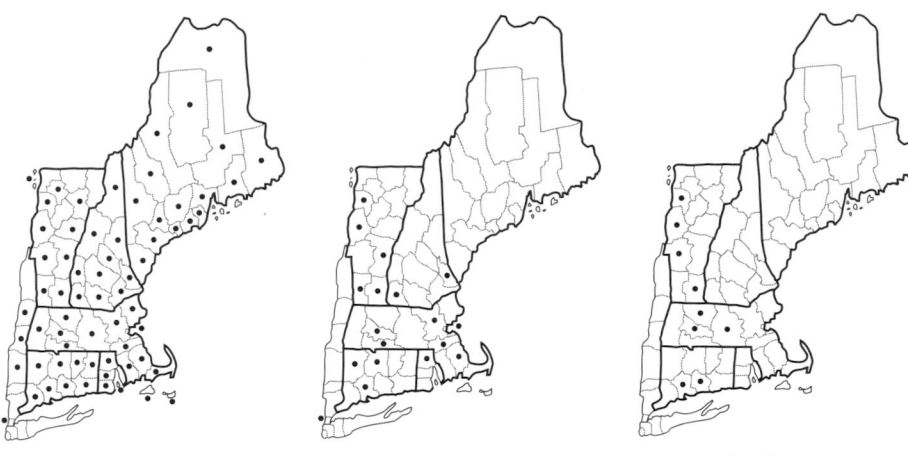

1366. *Potentilla argentea*   1367. *Potentilla intermedia*   1368. *Potentilla inclinata*

24. *Alchemílla* L. Lady's Mantle (Arabic name).

Pubescent to glabrate, diffusely branched, annual or perennial herbs from a thick rhizome; stem leaves petioled or sessile, the basal, when present, long petioled, blade palmately lobed or divided, the lobes or divisions lobed or toothed, stipules foliaceous, lobed or toothed, adnate and clasping; flowers small, greenish, in small axillary clusters surrounded and partly enclosed by the stipules or in terminal and axillary peduncled, leafy-bracteate corymbs, hypanthium ellipsoid to campanulate, sepals 4, alternating with as many smaller, sepal-like bractlets, or the bractlets sometimes absent, petals none, stamens 1 or 4, carpel usually solitary, sometimes 2-3, style slender, arising from near the base; fruit an achene enclosed in the hypanthium. The various species are said to be of medicinal value as an astringent and a styptic.

Leaves deeply 3-parted, the lowest on petioles 1 cm or less long; flowers in sessile,
    axillary clusters surrounded and partly enclosed by the stipules. .... 1. *A. microcarpa*
Leaves 5 or more lobed, the lowest on petioles more than 3 cm long; flowers in
    peduncled terminal and axillary corymbs. (Fig. 632).
  Branches of inflorescence and hypanthium hirsute; leaves pilose above.
    Mature hypanthium up to 1.5 mm high, obscurely ribbed; pedicels glabrous. .... 2. *A. monticola*
    Mature hypanthium 1.5 mm or more high, strongly ribbed; pedicels often
      hirsute .... 3. *A. filicaulis*
                                         subsp. *vestita*
  Branches of inflorescence and hypanthium glabrous or nearly so; leaves glabrous
    above .... 4. *A. xanthochlora*

    1. *A. microcárpa* Wallr. (tiny-fruited). Fields, lawns, roadsides and waste places in dry, sandy soil. May-June. (Naturalized from Europe). Reported for Suffolk County NY. [*Aphanes m.*].

    2. *A. montícola* Opiz (of mountains). Fields, lawns, and roadsides. May-August. Fig. 632, Map 1369. (Adventive from Europe). [*A. pratensis; A. vulgaris*].

    3. *A. filicaúlis* Buser (stems thread-like). Wet calcareous slopes and stream margins. June-September. (from Europe). Reported for MA. Represented with us as subsp. *vestita* (Buser) M. E. Bradsh. [*A. minor; A. vulgaris* var. *vestita*].

    4. *A. xanthochlóra* Rothmmal. Thickets, fields, roadsides. June-September. (Naturalized from Europe). Reported for CT, MA. [*A. pratensis*].

25. *Dalibárda* L. False Violet (for T. Dalibard).

Perennial, downy-pubescent herbs with slender, creeping, tufted stems; leaves arising directly from the stems, orbicular to reniform, cordate, crenate, pubescent on both sides, long petioled, stipules setaceous; flowers solitary on axillary peduncles, of 2 kinds, petaliferous and apetalous, sepals 5 or 6, often unequal, 3 larger and usually toothed at the apex (or sometimes all sepals toothed) bracts none; petaliferous flowers few, on peduncles as long or longer than the petioles, petals white, flowers usually sterile, stamens numerous, pistils few, abortive, apetalous flowers numerous, on short recurved peduncles, fertile, stamens numerous, pistils 5-10, style terminal; fruit a dry, achene-like, 1-seeded drupe.

   1. *D. répens* L. (creeping). Rich, moist, deciduous or mixed woods, wet woods, wooded swamps. June-August. Fig. 633, Map 1370. Endangered in RI, CT. —FAC

26. *Duchésnea* Smith. Indian Strawberry (for A. Duchesne).

Hirsute, perennial herbs from a short rhizome which bears several long petioled basal leaves and slender, leafy stolons which are erect at first, soon prostrate; leaves all long-petioled, trifoliate, the leaflets ovate to elliptic, crenate to doubly crenate, stipules small; flowers solitary, axillary, on long peduncles arising from the nodes, hypanthium saucer-shaped, sepals 5, alternating with 5 bracts, these foliaceous, much larger than the sepals, widened upward, with 3, rarely 5 teeth at the apex, petals 5, yellow, stamens numerous, in several lengths, pistils numerous, inserted on a receptacle, style lateral; fruit an aggregate of achenes, the receptacle becoming fleshy and red at maturity but not juicy or edible.

   1. *D. índica* (Andr.) Focke (of India). Waste places. April-June. Rare. Fig. 634, Map 1371. (Naturalized from Asia). —FACU-

27. *Fragária* L. Strawberry (from the Latin based on fragrance of the fruit).

Similar vegetatively to *Duchesnea* except leaves tufted at the nodes, stipules membranous and sheathing and leaflets often serrate instead of crenate; flowers white, few to several in a raceme or corymb terminating an often leafy-bracteate scape, hypanthium saucer-shaped, sepals 5, alternating with 5 similar, but slightly shorter and narrower bracts, petals 5, stamens usually 20, pistils numerous, on a conical receptacle, style lateral; fruit an aggregate of achenes, the receptacle becoming fleshy, red, juicy and edible at maturity. Fruit edible as is the entire green plant; plant possibly toxic when wilted, but when thoroughly dried the crushed leaves are used as a tea substitute useful in treating diarrhea. —Wildl. 2

Petals mostly 7 mm or more long, 1.5 or more times as long as the sepals; achenes
    imbedded in the receptacle; longest flowering peduncle usually shorter than
    the longest petiole; terminal tooth of the leaflets usually surpassed by
    the adjacent lateral ones .... 1. *F. virginiana*
Petals mostly less than 7 mm long, less than 1.5 times as long as the sepals; achenes
    not imbedded in the receptacle; longest flowering peduncle usually as long or
    longer than the longest petiole; terminal tooth of the leaflets usually surpassing
    the adjacent lateral ones. .... 2. *F. vesca*

   1. *F. virginiána* Duchesne (Virginian). Fields, open hillsides, roadsides. May-June. Map 1372. [*F. australis; F. canadensis*]. Our plants include subsp. *virginiana* and the following subsp.:
   subsp. *grayána* (Vilm. ex J. Gay) Staudt. Terminal leaflet with 8 or more teeth on each margin (8 or fewer in subsp. *virginiana*). [var. *illinoensis; F. grayana; F. terrae-novae*].
   subsp. *glaúca* (S. Wats.) Staudt. Scapes and petioles with appressed pubescence or glabrous

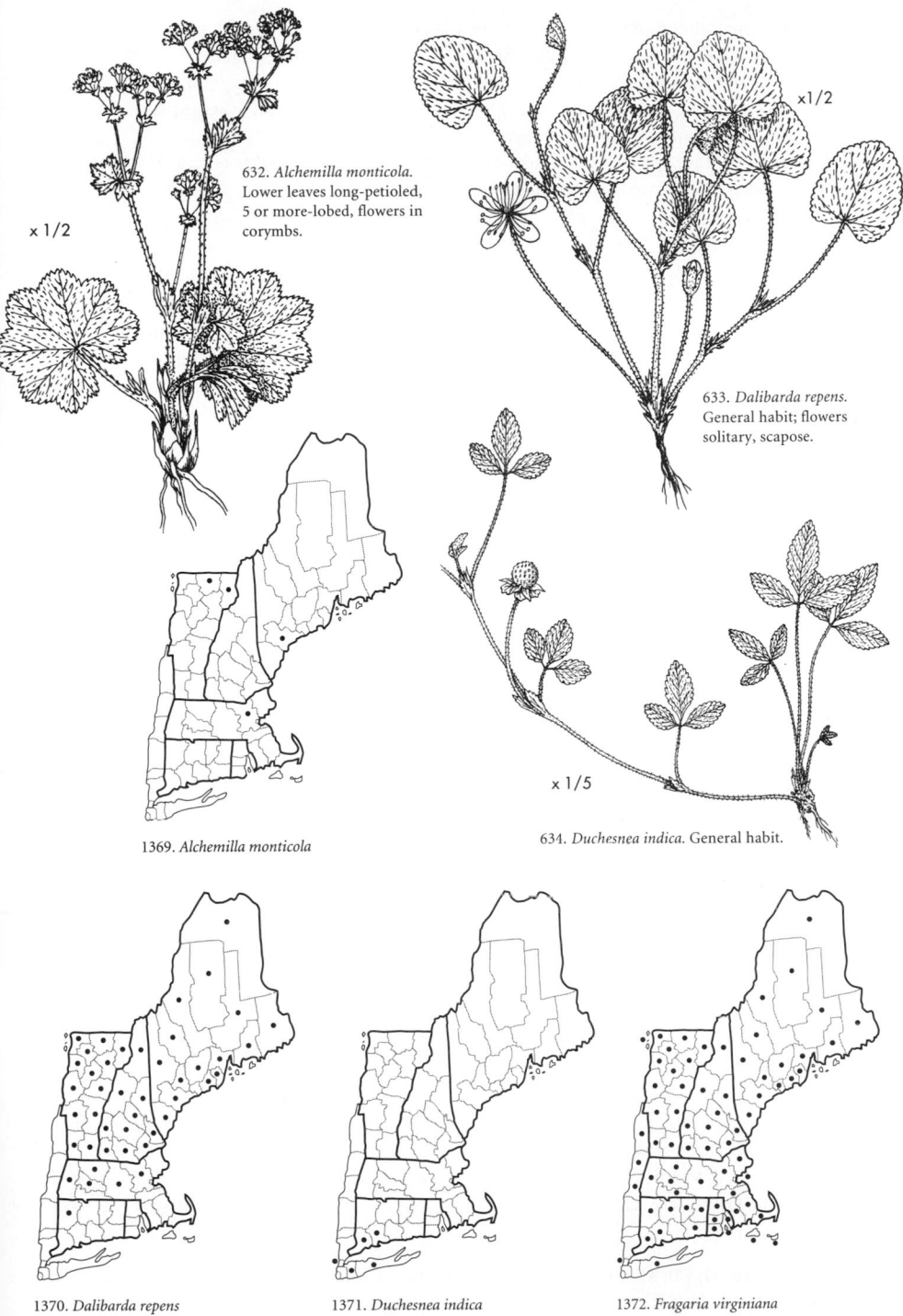

x 1/2

632. *Alchemilla monticola.*
Lower leaves long-petioled,
5 or more-lobed, flowers in
corymbs.

x1/2

633. *Dalibarda repens.*
General habit; flowers
solitary, scapose.

x 1/5

1369. *Alchemilla monticola*

634. *Duchesnea indica.* General habit.

1370. *Dalibarda repens*

1371. *Duchesnea indica*

1372. *Fragaria virginiana*

(pubescence spreading in the above subspecies). [var. *terrae-novae; Fragaria t.*].

Another subsp. that has been distinguished is subsp. *platypetala.* —FACU

F. x ananássa Duchesne, the cultivated strawberry, a hybrid between *F. virginiana* and *F. chiloensis* Duchesne, occasionally escapes along roadsides, near cultivated land, and in waste places. Map 1373. [*F. ananassa*]. Our plants are var. *ananassa.*

2. F. vésca L. (weak). Open woodlands, openings, roadsides and waste places. May-June. Map 1374. (Introduced from Europe). Our plants are subsp. *vesca.*

28. Sibbáldia L. (for R. Sibbald).

Low, depressed, densely tufted, perennial herbs from a multicipital caudex, stem woody; leaves trifoliate, primarily basal, these long petioled, flowering stems leafless or few-leaved, leaflets obovate or oblanceolate, mostly 3 toothed at the apex, stipules membranous, adnate; flowers small, yellow, cymose, on leafless or few-leaved peduncles, hypanthium saucer-shaped, sepals 5, alternating with 5 sepal-like bracts, petals 5, much smaller than the sepals, stamens 5, carpels 5-10, style lateral; fruit an achene.

1. S. procúmbens L. (lying on the ground). Alpine, White Mts., NH. July-August. Fig. 635. (Eurasia). Endangered in NH.

29. Sibbaldiópsis Rydb.

Similar to *Potentilla* (genus 23), but leaflets evergreen, mostly 3-toothed, otherwise entire; flowers white. [*Potentilla*].

1. S. tridentáta (Ait.) Rydb. (three-toothed). Dry, rocky or gravelly, open soil, often at high altitudes, and along shores. June-August. Map 1375. Endangered in CT. [*Potentilla t.*].

30. Waldsteínia Willd. Barren Strawberry (for F. Adam, Count of Waldstein Wartenburg).

Perennial herbs from long, creeping rhizomes, resembling *Fragaria*; leaves arising directly from the rhizome, long petioled, the petioles hirsute, trifoliate, leaflets broadly cuneate, obovate, lobed and crenate or dentate, stipules membranous; flowers small, yellow, few to several in a bracteate cyme terminating an often bracteate scape, this often forked and the cymes paired, hypanthium obconic, contracted at the mouth by a disc, sepals 5, usually without alternating bracts, petals 5, stamens numerous, carpels 2-6, inserted on a pubescent receptacle enclosed in the hypanthium, styles protruding from the mouth of the hypanthium, terminal, deciduous; fruit an achene, receptacle not fleshy.

1. W. fragarioídes (Michx.) Tratt. (like *Fragaria*). Moist to dry woods, clearings and edges. May-June. Map 1376. Endangered in CT. Our plants are subsp. *fragarioides.*

31. Porteránthus Britton ex Small. Indian-physic.

Perennial, rhizomatous, branched, herbs; leaves trifoliate, subsessile, leaflets lanceolate to oblong or oblanceolate, tapered to base and tip, simply to doubly serrate, stipules linear or subulate; flowers white to pinkish, long-pedicelled, in a leafy, loosely paniculate-corymbose inflorescence, hypanthium cylindric to turbinate, somewhat narrowed at the throat, sepals 5, petals 5, somewhat unequal, linear-lanceolate, stamens 10-20, carpels 5, enclosed in the hypanthium, with few ovules; fruit a follicle. [*Gillenia*].

1. P. trifoliátus (L.) Britton (3-leaved). Dry to moist, rich woods. May-June. Fig. 636. Reported for RI, Essex and Hampshire Counties MA. [*Gillenia trifoliata*].

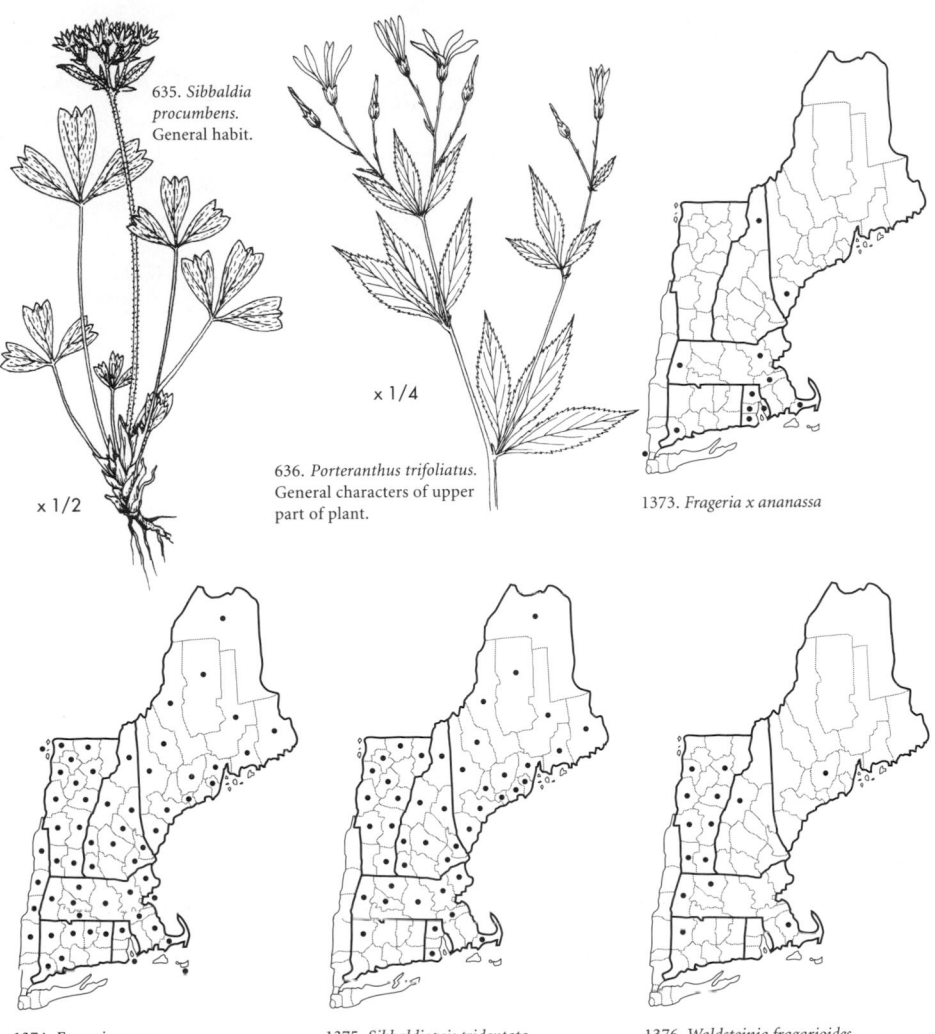

635. *Sibbaldia procumbens.* General habit.

x 1/2

636. *Porteranthus trifoliatus.* General characters of upper part of plant.

x 1/4

1373. *Frageria x ananassa*

1374. *Fragaria vesca*

1375. *Sibbaldiopsis tridentata*

1376. *Waldsteinia fragarioides*

Family 109. Fabáceae (Bean Family)

Hermaphrodite, rarely polygamous trees, shrubs, vines or herbs. Leaves alternate, simple or compound, usually stipulate. Flowers perfect, rarely unisexual, in racemes, panicles, spikes or heads, mostly irregular, calyx usually 5-parted, gamosepalous and tubular, hypanthium small or well developed, corolla of 5 petals, nearly regular, or more typically irregular (papilionaceous), the upper petal (the standard) larger than the others, the 2 side petals (wings) outside the 2 lower, which are usually somewhat united (the keel), and enclose the stamens and pistil, stamens mostly 10, distinct, monadelphous or diadelphous, pistil 1, superior, ovary 1-locular or rarely several-many locular, ovules 1-many, style 1. Fruit usually a pod (legume) dehiscent along both sutures, or rarely indehiscent, or transversely divided into 1-seeded joints (loments).

In addition to the following species *Kummerowia striata* has been reported for CT.

A. Plant a tree, shrub or woody vine.
  B. Leaves simple.
    C. Leaves about as long as wide, long petioled, flowers pink. .... 1. *Cercis canadensis*
    C. Leaves more than twice as long as wide, short petioled or sessile; flowers
        yellow.
        Leaves and branches sharply spine-tipped. (Fig. 637). .... 2. *Ulex europaeus*
        Leaves and branches not spine-tipped .... 3. *Genista tinctoria*
  B. Leaves compound.
    D. Leaves pinnate or bipinnate; leaflets 5 or more.
      E. Leaflets mostly crenulate, rarely entire; leaves, at least some of them,
          bipinnate; corolla regular or nearly so. .... 4. *Gleditsia*
                  triacanthos
      E. Leaflets entire (except for an occasional leaflet); leaves pinnate; corolla of 1
        petal or papilionaceous.
        F. Woody, twining vines .... 5. *Wisteria*
        F. Shrubs or trees.
          G. Calyces, fruit and often the leaflets glandular-punctate; corolla of 1
            petal; fruit 1 cm or less long .... 6. *Amorpha fruticosa*
          G. Calyces, fruit and leaflets eglandular; corolla papilionaceous, of 5
            petals; fruit more than 2 cm long.
            H. Corolla yellow; fruit inflated and bladder-like. (Fig. 641). .... 7. *Colutea*
                      arborescens
            H. Corolla not yellow; fruit flattened, not bladder-like.
                Leaflets mostly 5-8, alternately arranged; stamens distinct. .... 8. *Cladrastis*
                      kentukea
                Leaflets mostly 9 or more, oppositely or suboppositely arranged;
                  stamens diadelphous .... 9. *Robinia*
    D. Leaves ternate; leaflets 3 or 1. (Fig. 643). .... 10. *Cytisus scoparius*
A. Plant an herb.
  I. Leaves palmate, or pinnate with 2, 4 or more leaflets.
    J. Leaves palmate. (Fig. 644) .... 11. *Lupinus*
    J. Leaves pinnate.
      K. Leaves even-pinnate, the terminal leaflet absent, the rachis usually
          terminated with a bristle (sometimes lacking) or tendril. (Fig. 645).
        L. Leaf rachis usually terminated by a bristle or not by a tendril.
          Corolla regular or nearly so; fruit less than 10 cm long or longer and
            pubescent; leaf petiole or rachis with 1 or more glands.
            Leaflets mostly 2 cm or more long; pairs of leaflets mostly 8 mm or
               more apart .... 12. *Senna*
            Leaflets mostly 1.8 cm or less long; pairs of leaflets mostly 6 mm or
               less apart .... 13. *Chamaecrista*
          Corolla papilionaceous; fruit more than 10 cm long, glabrous; leaf
            petiole and rachis eglandular .... 14. *Sesbania exaltata*
        L. Leaf rachis terminated with tendrils.
          M. Leaflets 2 .... 15. *Lathyrus*
          M. Leaflets more than 2.
            N. Peduncles absent or less than 5 mm long. .... 16. *Vicia*
            N. Peduncles more than 5 mm long.
              O. Flowers 8 mm or less long, or longer and more than 10 in
                raceme; style bearded all around tip; fruit 3 cm or less long .... 16. *Vicia*
              O. Flowers more than 8 mm long, mostly fewer than 10 in a raceme;
                style bearded down one side, fruit longer than 3 cm.
                Calyx lobes shorter than the tube .... 15. *Lathyrus*
                Calyx lobes longer than the tube .... 17. *Pisum sativum*
      K. Leaves odd-pinnate, the terminal leaflet present. (Fig. 652).
        P. Leaflets serrulate from above the middle. .... 18. *Cicer arietinum*
        P. Leaflets entire.
          Q. Flowers and fruit in heads or umbels.
            R. Heads subtended by several 3 or more-cleft bracts. .... 19. *Anthyllis*
                      vulneraria

R. Heads or umbels not subtended by cleft bracts (heads often closely
  subtended by a pinnate leaf or 3-foliate bract).
    S. Leaflets 5, the lowest pair simulating stipules. (Fig. 651). .... 20. *Lotus*
    S. Leaflets more than 5, the lowest pair not simulating stipules.
      Flowers less than 1 cm long, in heads of 6 or fewer; legume
        flattened. ....21. *Ornithopus*
                                                                                                    sativus
      Flowers 1 cm or more long, in umbels of 10 or more; legume
        angled. ....22. *Coronilla varia*
  Q. Flowers and fruit in racemes or spikes (may be dense and congested in
    some species). (Fig. 653).
    T. Stipules with sagittate appendages, persistent. .... 23. *Galega officinalis*
    T. Stipules without sagittate appendages, often early deciduous.
      U. Plant a twining vine; leaflets mostly 5-7. .... 24. *Apios americana*
      U. Plant erect to ascending; leaflets 9 or more.
        V. Inflorescence terminal or apparently so.
          Plant acaulescent or nearly so; inflorescence terminating a
            long peduncle. (Fig. 654) .... 25. *Oxytropis*
                                                                                                    campestris
          Plant leafy stemmed, inflorescence terminating the stem.
            (Fig. 655). ....26. *Tephrosia*
                                                                                                    virginiana
        V. Inflorescence axillary. (Fig. 656).
          W. Herbage glandular-viscid or gland-dotted; fruit spiny. .... 27. *Glycyrrhiza*
                                                                                                    lepidota
          W. Herbage not glandular-viscid or gland-dotted; fruit not
            spiny.
            Legume flattened, with 2-5 disarticulating segments
              (rarely with a single 1-seeded joint, this indehiscent,
              spiny); lowest stipules 1-2 cm long, lanceolate,
              widest at the base. ....28. *Hedysarum*
                                                                                                    alpinum
                                                                                                    var. *americanum*
            Legume usually turgid, without disarticulating segments;
              lowest stipules less than 1 cm long or ovate, widest
              above the base, usually dehiscent, not spiny. .... 29. *Astragalus*
I. Leaves trifoliate or unifoliate.
  X. Leaves unifoliate.
    Y. Leaves and branches sharply spine-tipped. (Fig. 637). .... 2. *Ulex europaeus*
    Y. Leaves and branches not spine-tipped.
      Plant annual, pubescent; calyx equalling or exceeding corolla; legume
        inflated. (Fig. 659) ....30. *Crotalaria*
                                                                                                    sagittalis
      Plant woody, at least at the base, glabrous; calyx shorter than corolla;
        legume not inflated ....3 *Genista tinctoria*
  X. Leaves trifoliate.
    Z. Leaflets serrulate (sometimes only at the apex).
      a. Flowers in heads or non-leafy racemes.
        b. Flowers in slender, elongate racemes. (Fig. 660). .... 31. *Melilotus*
        b. Flowers in heads or head-like racemes.
          Corolla withering and persistent in fruit; legume straight, often
            hidden in the corolla ....32. *Trifolium*
          Corolla deciduous, not persistent in fruit; legume visible, usually
            curved, spirally twisted, or falcate, rarely straight. .... 33. *Medicago*
      a. Flowers solitary or paired in the axils, forming terminal leafy racemes. .... 34. *Ononis*
    Z. Leaflets entire, sometimes lobed.
      c. Terminal leaflet sessile or the petiolule approximately the same length as
        those of the lateral leaflets, or if longer (rarely in Lotus) stipules
        minute and gland-like.

d. Flowers cream-colored to pink; fruit 1-seeded; plant very pubescent. ..... 35. *Lespedeza*
d. Flowers yellow or blue (rarely pink in Lotus); fruit 2 or more seeded,
or 1 seeded and plant essentially glabrous.
  e. Flowers and fruits in elongate racemes, the rachis more than 1 cm
    long; stamens completely free. (Fig. 668).
    Largest stipules more than 1 cm wide; rachis of inflorescence and
      pedicels densely pubescent; legume flat, linear. .... 36. *Thermopsis*
    Largest stipules less than 1 cm wide; rachis of inflorescence and
      pedicels glabrous or essentially so; legume inflated, ovoid. .. 37. *Baptisia*
  e. Flowers and fruits in capitate umbels or solitary, or in short clusters,
    the rachis less than 1 cm long; stamens monadelphous or
    diadelphous.
    Lowest pair of leaflets as large as the others, simulating stipules;
      fruit several seeded. (Fig. 651) .... 20. *Lotus*
    Lowest pair of leaflets not simulating stipules; stipules adnate to
      the petiole and sheathing the stem; fruit 1-seeded.
      (Fig. 669). .... 38. *Stylosanthes biflora*

c. Terminal leaflet with petiolule distinctly longer than those of the lateral
leaflets, at least on the lower leaves; stipules not minute and
gland-like.
  f. Stipules adnate to the petiole and sheathing the stem; flowers yellow;
    fruit 1-seeded, solitary. (Fig. 669) .... 38. *Stylosanthes biflora*

  f. Stipules not adnate to the petiole and sheathing the stem; flowers white,
    pink, blue or cream-colored; fruit, if 1-seeded, in racemes or
    heads.
    g. Flower 4 cm or more long, the standard 2 cm or more wide; seeds
      very viscid. .... 39. *Clitoria mariana*
    g. Flowers 3 cm or less long, the standard less than 1.5 cm wide; seeds
      not viscid.
      h. Fruit indehiscent and 1-seeded or 2-several-seeded and
        transversely septate into 1-seeded indehiscent segments;
        inflorescences usually terminal as well as axillary; plant
        prostrate to erect but not a vine.
        Fruit 2-several-seeded, the segments covered with minute
          hooked hairs making them adhesive; leaflets usually
          stipellate. ....40. *Desmodium*
        Fruit 1-seeded, glabrous or pubescent but non-adhesive; leaflets
          not stipellate ....35. *Lespedeza*
      h. Fruit dehiscent, 2-several-seeded, not transversely septate;
        inflorescences usually only axillary; plant often a vine.
        i. Flowers and fruits in long peduncled heads; style bearded. .... 41. *Strophostyles*
        i. Flowers and fruits in racemes or sessile fascicles; style glabrous
          (except in *Phaseolus*).
          j. Stipules sagittate-auriculate, the auricle several mm long;
            flowers 2 cm or more long; half woody vine .... 42. *Pueraria montana* var. *lobata*

          j. Stipules not sagittate-auriculate; flowers less than 2 cm long;
            herbaceous.
            k. Flowers of 2 kinds, petaliferous and apetalous; calyx of
              petaliferous flowers ebracteolate; stipules ovate to
              obovate. .... 43. *Amphicarpaea bracteata*

            k. Flowers all petaliferous; calyx with a pair of subtending
              bracteoles; stipules linear to lanceolate.
              l. Flowers and fruit in fascicles or racemes usually much
                shorter than subtending petioles; ovary and legume
                densely long-pubescent. .... 44. *Glycine max*

l. Flowers and fruit in racemes usually longer than
    subtending petioles; ovary and legume glabrous
    to densely short-pubescent. (Fig. 675).
    Terminal leaflet ovate, acuminate; keel petals coiled. .... 45. *Phaseolus*
    Terminal leaflet elliptic, obtuse or retuse; keel petals
        merely slightly curved .... 46. *Galactia*

1. *Cércis* L. Redbud (ancient name of the Judas tree).

Small trees or shrubs, twigs slender, light to dark brown, lustrous, pith pale to pink, buds small, ovoid, blunt, somewhat appressed, often superposed or collateral, with 2, or in the flower buds several scales, leaf scars inversely triangular, fringed along the upper margin, decurrently ridged from the corners, bundle traces 3, stipule scars and end bud lacking; leaves simple, long-petioled, widely cordate, abruptly acuminate, entire, petioles swollen just beneath the blade; flowers pink to purplish, pedicellate in sessile, umbel-like clusters borne along the branches of the preceding years, appearing before the leaves, hypanthium short, campanulate, calyx somewhat oblique, 5-toothed, corolla somewhat papilionaceous, the standard smaller than the wings, the keel petals the largest and not united, stamens 10, distinct; legume narrowly oblong, flat, tapering to both ends, margined along the upper suture, many-seeded.

    1. *C. canadénsis* L. (Canadian). Rich woods. April-May. Map 1377. Our plants are var. *canadensis*. Unopened flower buds are used in salads and are also reported to be useful in treating diarrhea. —FACU-

2. *Úlex* L. Gorse (ancient Greek name).

Much branched shrubs, twigs green, modified into short, slender spines, pith small, buds small, positioned between the persistent leaf spine and spiny twig immediately above, with several scales, stipules lacking; leaves without blades (except sometimes the lowest), consisting only of triangular spiny petioles, these numerous and crowded; flowers yellow, solitary or paired in the axils of the spiny leaves along the twigs, the latter appearing like racemes, these forming terminal panicles, each flower subtended by a bract, calyx bracteolate at the base, deeply bilabiate, upper lip 2-toothed, lower 3-toothed, corolla papilionaceous, stamens 10, monadelphous, alternately longer and shorter; legume short, oblong, few-seeded.

    1. *U. europaéus* L. (European). Sandy areas and waste places near the coast. May-June. Fig. 637, Map 1378. (Naturalized from Europe).

3. *Genísta* L. (Celtic name for bush).

Small, branching shrubs with striate stems and branches, twigs slender, greenish, pith small, buds small, sessile, ovoid, with several scales, leaf scars small, raised, bundle trace 1, stipules usually present at the edges of the petiole base; leaves simple, sessile, elliptic to lanceolate, usually stipulate; flowers yellow, nearly sessile in bracteate racemes or panicles, calyx bracteolate at the base, bilabiate, the upper lip 2-toothed, the lower 3-toothed, corolla papilionaceous, the petals clawed, stamens 10, monadelphous, anthers alternately large and small; legume linear, flat, several-seeded.

    Coronilla scorpióides, an herb with yellow flowers in umbels, sometimes keying here, is described under *Coronilla* (genus 22).

    1. *G. tinctória* L. (used in dyeing). Dyer's greenweed. Dry fields, roadsides, woodland borders. June-July. Fig. 638, Map 1379. (Naturalized from Europe).

4. *Gledítsia* L. Honey Locust (for J. Gleditsch).

Monoecious or polygamous trees, usually armed with simple or branched, supra-axillary thorns, twigs moderate, swollen at the joints, lustrous, pith pale, buds indistinct, sunken with only the tips exposed, often superposed, leaf scars U-shaped, bundle traces 3, stipule scars and end bud lacking; leaves pinnate or bipinnate, with oblong-lanceolate, somewhat crenate leaflets; flowers usually imperfect, small, greenish, in solitary or clustered, axillary, spicate racemes, the staminate densely flowered, the pistillate looser, with fewer flowers, hypanthium campanulate, sepals and petals each 3-5, all nearly equal, distinct, or the 2 lower petals sometimes united, stamens 3-10, distinct, those of the pistillate flowers smaller, abortive, pistil rudimentary or wanting in the staminate; legume oblong, flattened, twisted, 1-many seeded, indehiscent.

Gymnócladus Lam. *dióicus* (L.) K. Koch. Kentucky Coffee-tree. Similar to *Gleditsia* but differs in being unarmed, with leaflets entire, 2 cm or more wide and flowers in panicles. From farther west and south; rarely found in our range. Reported for ME, Fairfield and Hartford Counties CT, Hampden County MA, Columbia County NY. Seeds can be roasted, ground, and used as a coffee substitute; Indians roasted and ate the seeds.

1. *G. triacánthos* L. (three-thorned). Roadsides, riverbanks. June. Map 1380. Pods contain a pulp between and around the seeds which is edible. —FAC-

5. *Wistéria* Nutt. Wisteria (for C. Wistar).

High climbing, woody, twining vines, stems moderate, somewhat angled, pith moderate, pale to brownish, buds solitary, sessile, oblong, pointed, with 2 imbricate scales, leaf scars raised, transversely elliptic, with a horn-like or wart-like protuberance at each side, bundle trace 1, stipule scars lacking; leaves odd-pinnate, petioled, with numerous, lanceolate to ovate, acuminate, entire leaflets which are pubescent when young, glabrate at maturity, stipules caducous; flowers showy, blue to purple, in large, cylindric, drooping, terminal, bracteate racemes, calyx tube campanulate, somewhat bilabiate, the upper lip of 2 short teeth, the lower of 3 longer teeth, corolla papilionaceous, the standard with 2 callosities at the base of the blade, stamens diadelphous; legume long and linear, flattened, many-seeded, deshiscent into 2 valves. Seeds are very poisonous.

Leaflets gradually acuminate, 13 or more; flowers opening gradually from base of
    raceme to apex; racemes 2-5 dm long. .... 1. *W. floribunda*
Leaflets abruptly acuminate, 13 or fewer; flowers opening almost simultaneously;
    racemes 2 dm or less long. (Fig. 639). .... 2. *W. sinensis*

1. *W. floribúnda* (Willd.) DC. (full of flowers). Occasionally escaped from cultivation to open woods, roadsides, old cellar holes. April-June. (Naturalized from Asia). Reported for MA, Knox County ME, Strafford County NH.

2. *W. sinénsis* (Sims) DC. (Chinese). Occasionally escaped from cultivation to open woods, roadsides, old cellar holes. April-May. Fig. 639, Map 1381. (Naturalized from Asia).

W. frutéscens (L.) Poir. Differing from the above 2 species in having glabrous ovary and fruit. From farther south, rarely adventive in our range. Reported for RI, New Haven County CT., Hampshire County MA, Suffolk County NY. [*W. macrostachya*]. —FACW

6. *Amórpha* L. (Greek name based on absence of 4 of the petals).

Tall, branching, pubescent to glabrate shrubs, twigs slender, angled or ridged, pith moderate, pale, buds small, ovoid, superposed, with 2-4 scales, leaf scars somewhat triangular, bundle traces 3, stipule scars small, end bud lacking; leaves odd-pinnate, with numerous leaflets, petioled, leaflets elliptic, entire, mucronate, glandular-punctate and sparsely pubescent beneath, stipules linear, caducous or withered-persistent; flowers purple, bracteate, in dense, spiciform, terminal and

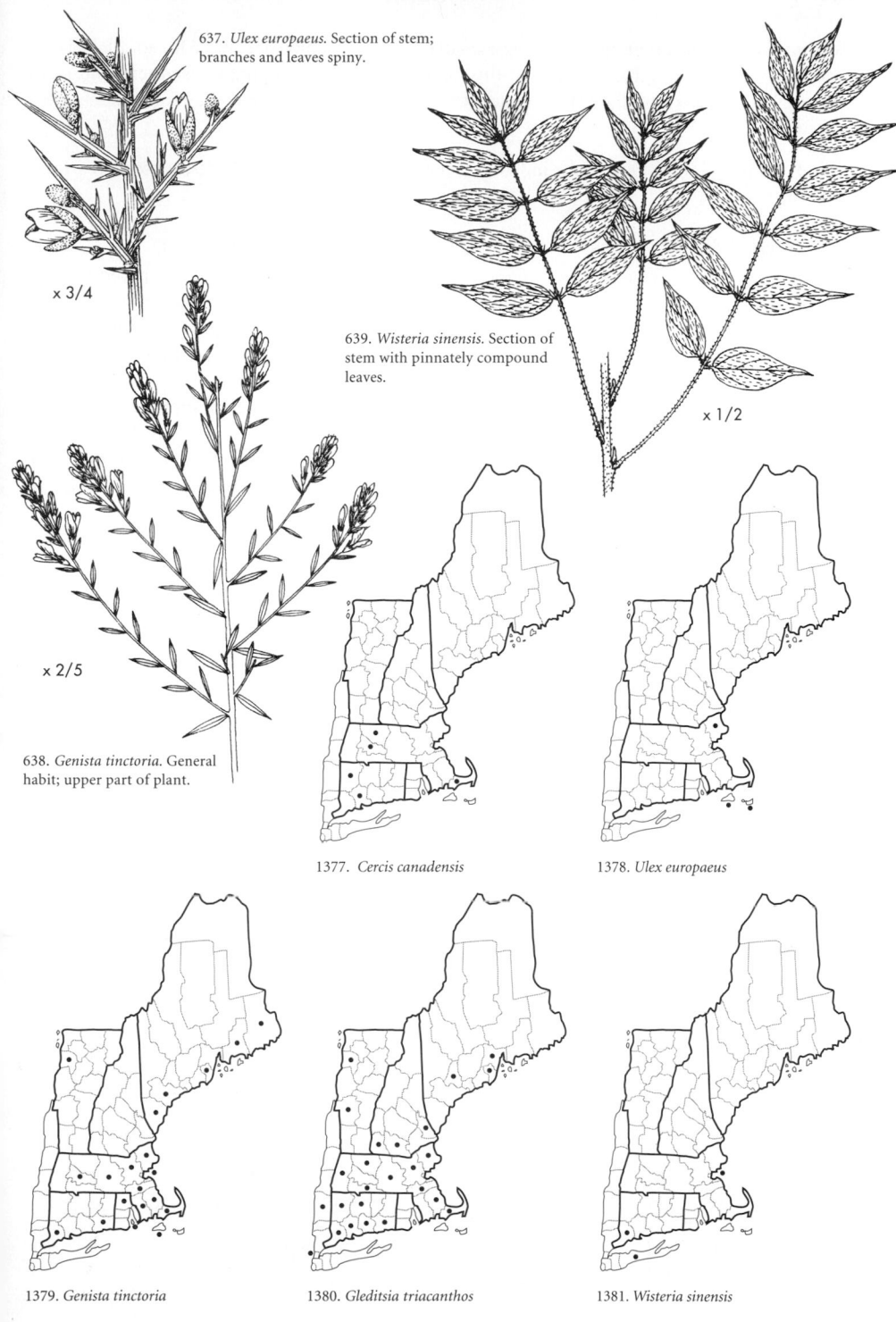

637. *Ulex europaeus.* Section of stem; branches and leaves spiny.

x 3/4

639. *Wisteria sinensis.* Section of stem with pinnately compound leaves.

x 1/2

x 2/5

638. *Genista tinctoria.* General habit; upper part of plant.

1377. *Cercis canadensis*

1378. *Ulex europaeus*

1379. *Genista tinctoria*

1380. *Gleditsia triacanthos*

1381. *Wisteria sinensis*

axillary racemes, these solitary or forming a small panicle, calyx tube obconic, 5 lobed, 1 lobe larger than the others, petal 1 (the standard), this clawed, basally enveloping the stamens and pistil, stamens 10, united below, distinct above; legume oblong, curved, punctate-glandular, indehiscent, 2-seeded.

1. *A. fruticósa* L. (shrubby). False indigo. River and pond margins, roadsides, waste places. June-July. Fig. 640, Map 1382. —FACW

7. *Colútea* L. Bladder-senna (classical name for a plant with inflated fruit).

Shrubs, twigs moderate, appressed-pubescent, with short, decurrent lines from the nodes, pith white, buds small, often superposed, with 1 or 2 pairs of scales, leaf scars elevated, broadly crescent-shaped, bundle traces 3, sometimes 1, stipules persistent; leaves odd-pinnate, petioled, leaflets oval to obovate, entire; flowers yellow, in short, axillary, bracteate racemes, calyx tube hemispheric, oblique, with 5, acuminate, nearly equal lobes, corolla papilionaceous, stamens diadelphous, style hooked, pubescent toward the tip; legume inflated and bladder-like, membranous, ovoid, many-seeded, indehiscent.

Caragána Fabr. *arboréscens* Lam. Pea Tree. May key to *Colutea* in flower but differs in having even-pinnate leaves (leaves odd-pinnate in *Colutea*). Rarely escaped from cultivation in our range. Reported for MA, Hancock County ME and Bronx County NY.

1. *C. arboréscens* L. (becoming tree-like). Rarely escaped from cultivation to roadsides and waste places. June-September. Fig. 641, Map 1383. (Introduced from Europe).

8. *Cladrástis* Raf. Yellow-wood (from the Greek).

Trees with smooth, gray bark, the freshly cut wood bright yellow, twigs moderate, pith white, buds naked, woolly, several superposed so as to appear as a single bud, surrounded by the leaf scar, which contains 3-7 bundle traces, stipule scars and end bud lacking; leaves odd-pinnate, the leaflets alternate, ovate to elliptic, entire, petiole base swollen and hollow, covering the buds; flowers showy, white, in large drooping, terminal panicles, calyx campanulate, 5-lobed, corolla papilionaceous, the petals clawed, those of the keel distinct, stamens 10, distinct; legume linear, flat, tapered to both ends, 4-6 seeded, tardily dehiscent.

1. *C. kentúkea* (Dum.-Cours.) Rudd. Rarely escaped from cultivation. May-June. Reported for CT, MA, ME. [*C. lutea; Sophora k.*].

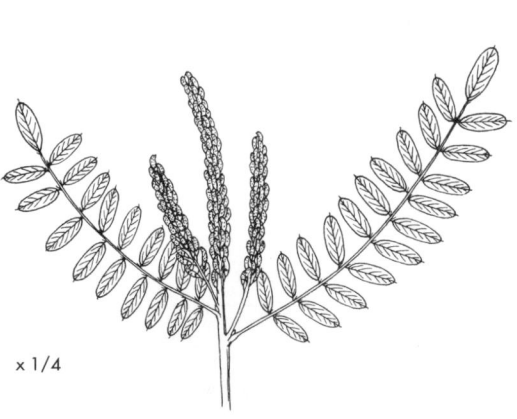

x 1/4

640. *Amorpha fruticosa.* General habit; upper part of plant.

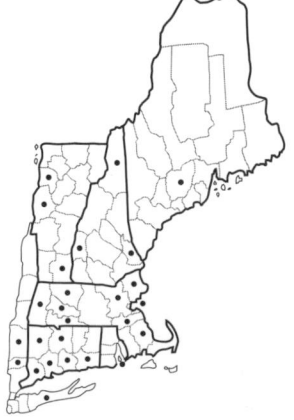

1382. *Amorpha fruticosa*

641. *Colutea arborescens.* General habit; fruit inflated and bladder-like.

x 1/4

1383. *Colutea arborescens*

9. *Robínia* L. Locust (for J. Robin).

Trees with coarse, deeply furrowed bark or shrubs, often spreading from underground stems, twigs zig-zag, somewhat angled, smooth to viscid or bristly, pith brown, buds small, superposed beneath a membrane remaining after leaf fall, leaf scars inversely triangular or 3-lobed, bundle traces 3, stipules commonly modified into spines or bristles, end bud lacking; leaves odd-pinnate, petioled, the petiole bases covering next year's buds, leaflets oval to oblong or elliptic, entire; flowers showy, white, pink or purple, few to numerous in short or long, ascendent to pendulous, axillary, bracteate racemes, calyx tube campanulate, bilabiate, corolla papilionaceous, the petals clawed, stamens diadelphous, one stamen united with the others to the middle, legume long and linear, flat, many-seeded, dehiscent into 2 valves. Flower clusters and seeds reported as edible by some sources; all parts of the plant reported as poisonous by others; perhaps best avoided.

Caragána Fabr. *arboréscens* Lam. Pea Tree. May key to *Robinia* but differs in having even-pinnate leaves and yellow flowers (leaves odd-pinnate and flowers white, pink or purple in Robinia). Rarely escaped from cultivation in our range. Reported for Hancock County ME and Bronx County NY.

a. Twigs and peduncles hispid; flowers deep pink to purple. (Fig. 642). .... 1. *R. hispida*
a. Twigs and peduncles not hispid; flowers pale pink to white.
    Twigs, peduncles and often the petioles glandular-viscid; stipular spines lacking
        or setaceous; flowers pale pink. .... 2. *R. viscosa*
    Twigs, peduncles and petioles glabrous or essentially so (twigs with pale lenticels
        not to be mistaken for glands, these dark in *R. viscosa*), stout stipular
        spines often present; flowers white. .... 3. *R. pseudoacacia*

    1. *R. híspida* L. (with bristles). Bristly locust. Roadsides, waste places, thickets and old cellar holes. May-June. Fig. 642, Map 1384.

    Our plants include var. *hispida* and the following var.:

    var. *fértilis* (Ashe) Clausen. Leaflets elliptic, acute, flowers to 2.5 cm long (leaflets oblong, mucronate, flowers 2.5 cm or more long in var. *hispida*). [*R. fertilis*].

    2. *R. viscósa* Vent. (sticky). Clammy locust. Roadsides and thickets. May-August. Map 1385. Our plants are var. *viscosa*.

    3. *R. pseudoacácia* L. (false *Acacia*). Black locust. Upland woods, thickets, fields, roadsides and waste places. May-June. Map 1386. —FACU-

10. Cýtisus L. Broom (ancient Greek name of a plant).

Much branched shrubs with dark green stems and branches, the latter slender, stiff, ribbed and angled, pith small, buds small, sessile, ovoid, with several scales, leaf scars small, raised, bundle trace 1, stipules present at the edges of the petiole base or lacking; leaves digitately 3-foliate below, often 1-foliate above, short-petioled, leaflets obovate, entire, stipules minute or more typically lacking; flowers showy, yellow, solitary or in pairs in the leaf axils, forming long, terminal, leafy racemes, papilionaceous, similar to *Genista*, style long and spirally coiled; legume flat, broadly linear, several seeded.

    1. *C. scopárius* (L.) Link (broom-like). Scotch Broom. Sandy roadsides, fields, beaches and dunes. May-June. Fig. 643, Map 1387. (Naturalized from Europe). Our plants are var. *scoparius*. A preparation made from the young shoots is reported to be useful as a diuretic; roasted seeds have been used as a coffee substitute.

11. Lupínus L. Lupine (ancient name of the lupine).

Glabrous or pubescent perennial (rarely annual) herbs; leaves palmately compound, with several (rarely single)-many entire, oblanceolate leaflets, petioled, stipules adnate to the base of the petiole; flowers showy, white, pink or purple, in terminal, bracteate racemes or spikes, calyx deeply bilabiate, upper lip 2-toothed, the lower 3-toothed or entire, corolla papilionaceous, standard with reflexed margins, wings united toward the apex, keel sometimes beaked, stamens 10, monadelphous, the filaments alternately longer with small, oblong anthers and shorter with linear anthers; legume oblong, flattened, several-seeded, often constricted between the seeds. Poisonous, particularly the seeds and fruits.

a. Stems glabrous to appressed-pubescent or sparsely villous; leaves glabrous to
      short-strigose beneath; lower lip of calyx less than 8 mm long.
    Lower leaves with mostly fewer than 11 leaflets, these mostly 5 cm or less long ...... 1. *L. perennis*
    Lower leaves with mostly 11 or more leaflets, these mostly 6 cm or more long. ...... 2. *L. polyphyllus*
a. Stems densely long-villous; leaves densely long-villous beneath; lower lip of calyx
      8 mm or more long .... 3. *L. nootkatensis*

    1. *L. perénnis* L. (perennial). Roadsides, waste places, fields and openings in sandy soil. May-July. Fig. 644, Map 1388. Our plants include subsp. *perennis* var. *perennis* and the following var.:
    var. *occidentális* S. Wats. Upper half of stem sparsely villous (glabrous to appressed-pubescent in var. *perennis*).
    2. *L. polyphýllus* Lindl. (many-leaved). Fields and roadsides. June-July. Map 1389. From the northwest.
    3. *L. nootkaténsis* Donn. ex Sims (of Nootka Sound, Vancouver Island). Fields and roadsides. June-July. From the northwest. Reported for n. New England.
    L. angustifólius L. Differs from the above species in having narrowly linear leaflets (leaflets oblanceolate in the above species). Mediterranean. Reported for ME.

12. Sénna P. Mill.

Similar to *Chamaecrista* (Genus 13), but with larger leaflets, the pairs more widely spaced (see key to genera); stamens all perfect. [*Cassia*].

    1. *S. hebecárpa* (Fern.) Irwin & Barneby (hairy fruited). Wild senna. Fields, open woods, roadsides. July-August. Fig. 645, Map 1390. Endangered in MA, NH. [*Cassia hebecarpa; C. marilandica; Ditremexa m.*].
    Three species resembling *S. hebecarpa* are rarely adventive in our range from farther South:
    S. obtusifólia (L.) Irwin & Barneby differs from the latter and the following species in having obovate leaflets, broadly rounded above. Reported for Franklin County MA. [*Cassia o.*].

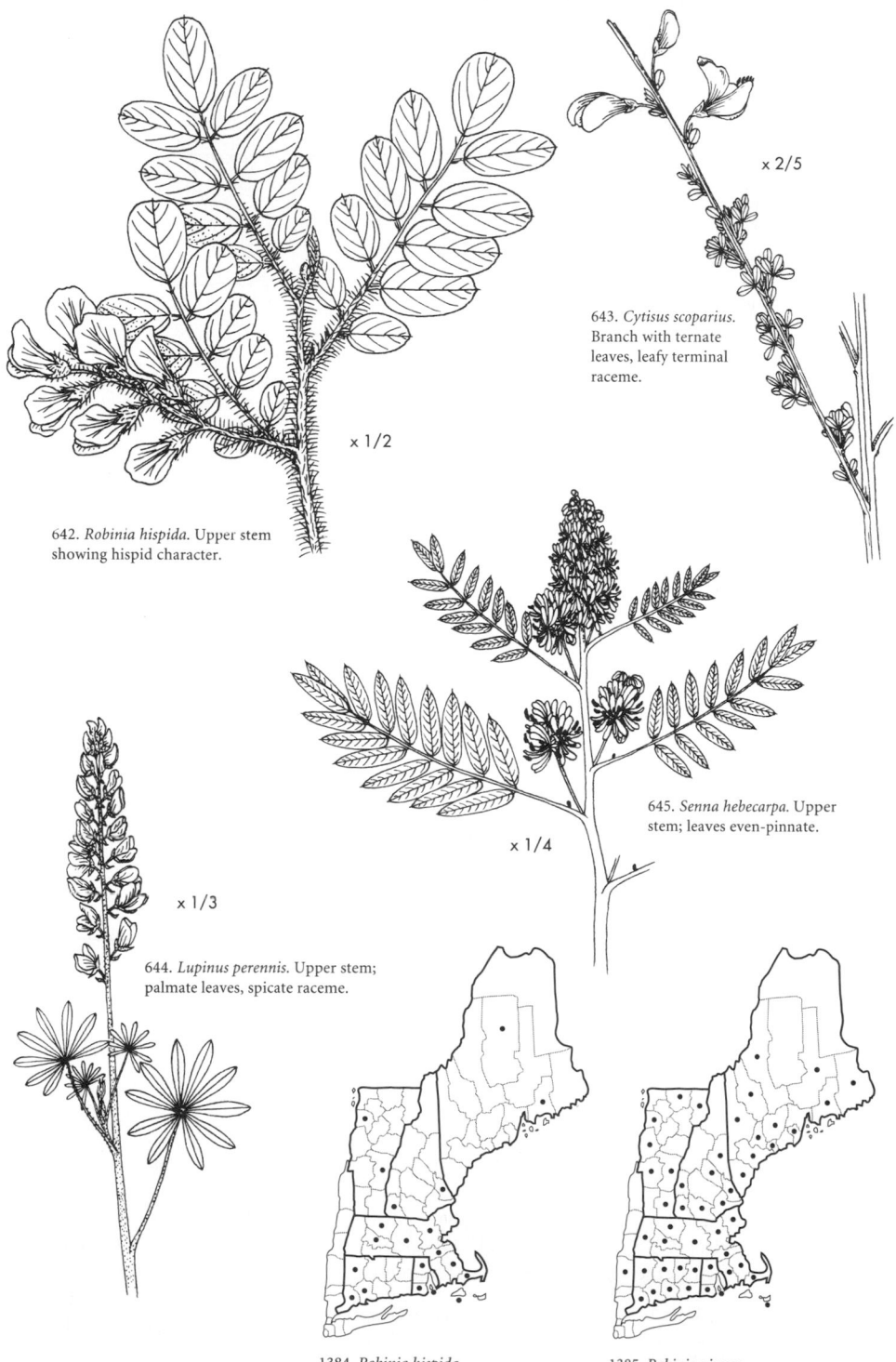

642. *Robinia hispida.* Upper stem showing hispid character.

×1/2

643. *Cytisus scoparius.* Branch with ternate leaves, leafy terminal raceme.

×2/5

644. *Lupinus perennis.* Upper stem; palmate leaves, spicate raceme.

×1/3

645. *Senna hebecarpa.* Upper stem; leaves even-pinnate.

×1/4

1384. *Robinia hispida*

1385. *Robinia viscosa*

1386. *Robinia pseudoacacia*   1387. *Cytisus scoparius*   1388. *Lupinus perennis*

1389. *Lupinus polyphyllus*   1390. *Senna hebecarpa*   1391. *Chamaecrista nictitans*

S. marilándica (L.) Link differs from *S. hebecarpa* in having the gland at base of petiole short-cylindric to dome-shaped (gland is clavate in *S. hebecarpa*). Reported for Dutchess County NY. [*Cassia m.; C. medsgeri; Ditremexa medsgeri*]. Useful as a laxative if used in proper, measured amounts; in the wrong amounts can cause nausea and diarrhea; also used by Indians for other medicinal purposes.

13. *Chamaecrísta* (L.) Moench.

Annual or perennial, pubescent to glabrous herbs (ours); leaves pinnate, often sensitive to the touch, usually with 1 or more conspicuous glands on the petiole or rachis, stipules persistent or deciduous; flowers yellow, solitary or in few flowered axillary clusters or racemes, or in terminal racemes, hypanthium short and inconspicuous, sepals and petals each 5, slightly unequal, stamens 5-10, unequal, some often sterile; legume linear, flat, few-many seeded, often septate. [*Cassia*].

Petiolar gland distinctly short-stalked; pedicels 4 mm or less long; petals less than 1
     cm long .... 1. *C. nictitans*
Petiolar gland sessile; pedicels 1 cm or more long; petals 1 cm or more long. .... 2. *C. fasciculata*

1. C. níctitans (L.) Moench (winking). Wild sensitive plant. Pond and river margins, woods, roadsides and waste places, in sandy soil. July-August. Map 1391. Endangered in NH. [*C. procumbens; Cassia n.*]. Our plants are subsp. *nictitans* var. *nictitans.* —FACU

2. C. fasciculáta (Michx.) Greene (in bunches). Partridge-pea. Fields, thickets and waste places in sandy soil. July-September. Map 1392. [*C. chamaecrista; Cassia f.; Cassia chamaecrista*]. —FACU

14. Sesbánia Scop. (name Latinized from an earlier Arabic name).

Tall, branched, glabrous, annual herbs; leaves long, even pinnate, petioled, with numerous small, narrowly oblong, entire, mucronate leaflets, stipules caducous; flowers yellow, often streaked or spotted with purple, in short, bracteate, few-flowered, axillary racemes, calyx tube campanulate, equally 5-toothed, corolla papilionaceous, stamens diadelphous; legume flattened, long and linear, slender, septate, many seeded.

Árachis L. *hypogáea* L. Common Peanut. Similar to *Sesbania* but differs in having a bilabiate calyx and large stipules adnate to the petiole. Occasionally escaped from cultivation. Reported for New Haven County CT, Bristol, Middlesex and Suffolk Counties MA.

1. S. exaltáta (Raf.) Rydb. ex A. W. Hill (tall). Fields and waste places. July-September. Fig. 646. From further south. Reported for Essex County MA. [*S. macrocarpa*]. —FAC

15. Láthyrus L. Wild pea (Greek name, based on the reputed aphrodisiac properties of one of the species).

Trailing or climbing, glabrous, perennial herbs; leaves pinnate, petioled, terminated by a tendril, lateral leaflets entire, stipules conspicuous, often foliaceous, with 1 or 2 basal lobes; flowers purple, yellow or white, in bracteate, axillary peduncled racemes, calyx tube campanulate, usually gibbous at the base, 5-toothed, regular to irregular, corolla papilionaceous, wing not adherent to the keel, stamens diadelphous, style laterally compressed and bearded along the upper side; legume 2-many-seeded, laterally compressed to terete, dehiscent into 2 valves.

a. Leaflets 2.
  b. Stems wingless although usually angled; leaflets 4 cm or less long.
    Leaflets oblong to obovate, obtuse; flowers red-purple. .... 1. *L. tuberosus*
    Leaflets lance-linear to lanceolate, acute; flowers yellow. .... 2. *L. pratensis*
  b. Stems distinctly winged; leaflets mostly longer than 4 cm.
    Leaflets lanceolate to oval, the larger ones wider than 1.5 cm; standard more
      than 1.7 cm wide; legumes mostly more than 6 cm long. ...., 3. *L. latifolius*
    Leaflets narrowly lanceolate, the larger ones mostly less than 1.5 cm wide;
      standard 1.7 cm or less wide; legumes mostly 6 cm or less long. .... 4. *L. sylvestris*
a. Leaflets 4 or more.
  c. Stipules with 2 basal lobes, somewhat hastate, essentially symmetrical. (Fig. 647) .. 5. *L. japonicus*
  c. Stipules with one basal lobe, semicordate or semisagittate, asymmetrical.
    (Fig. 648).
    d. Stipules semicordate, the basal lobe rounded; flowers yellowish-white. .... 6. *L. ochroleucus*
    d. Stipules semisagittate, the basal lobe sharp pointed; flowers purple.
      Stems usually winged; leaflets 8 or fewer; racemes usually 8 or fewer
        flowered. (Fig. 648) .... 7. *L. palustris*
      Stems wingless; leaflets mostly more than 8; racemes usually with more
        than 8 flowers .... 8. *L. venosus*

1. L. tuberósus L. (with tubers). Fields and roadsides. July-August. Map 1393. (Naturalized from Europe).

2. L. praténsis L. (of meadows). Fields, roadsides and waste places. June-August. Map 1394. —FACU

3. L. latifólius L. (broad-leaved). Everlasting pea. Occasionally escaped from cultivation to roadsides and waste places. June-August. Map 1395. (Introduced from Europe).

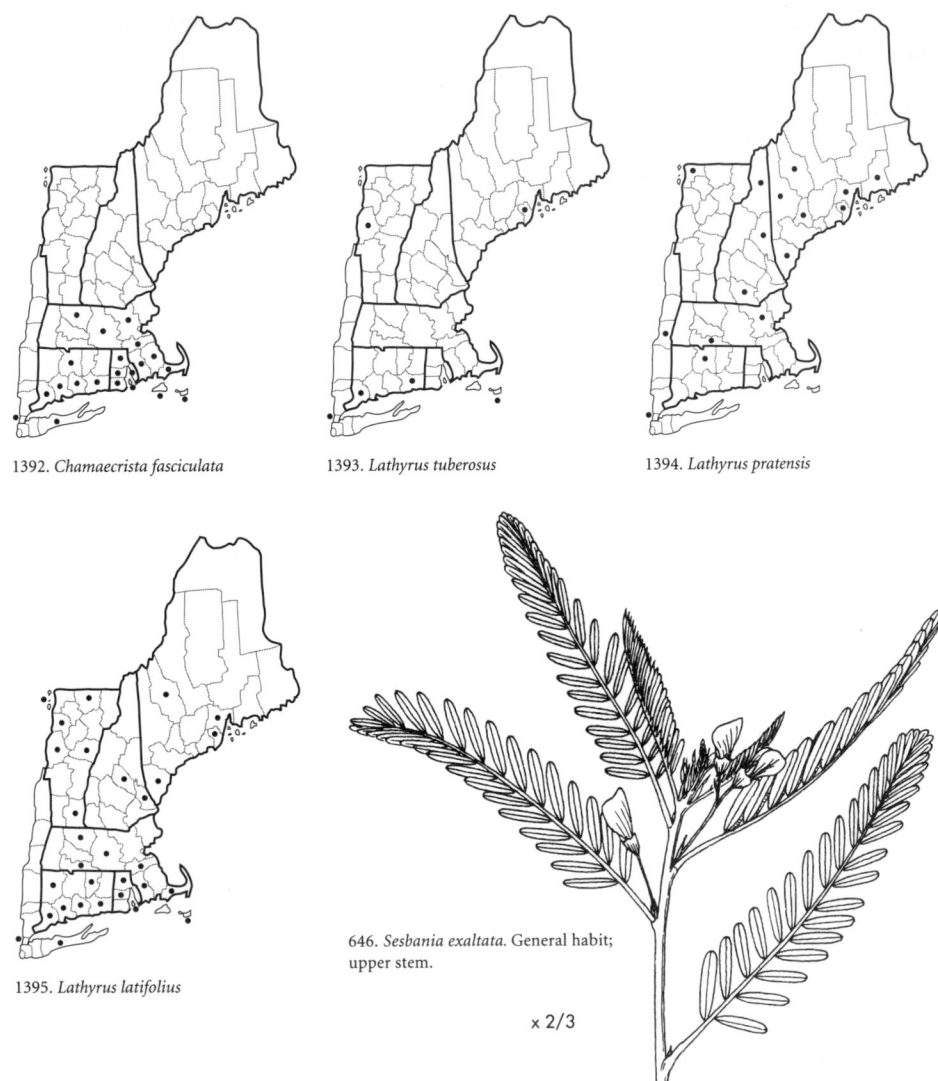

1392. *Chamaecrista fasciculata*

1393. *Lathyrus tuberosus*

1394. *Lathyrus pratensis*

1395. *Lathyrus latifolius*

646. *Sesbania exaltata.* General habit; upper stem.

× 2/3

L. odorátus L. Sweet Pea. Peduncles 3 or fewer flowered (4 or more flowers in racemes in *L. latifolius*). Occasionally escaped from cultivation. (Introduced from Europe). Reported for ME, Fairfield County CT.

L. satívus L. Differing from the latter 2 species in having calyx lobes equal or nearly so. (calyx lobes are very unequal in *L. latifolius* and *L. odoratus*). Rarely adventive from Europe. Reported for Middlesex County MA. Mature plants poisonous if eaten in large quantities; young plants are non-toxic.

4. L. sylvéstris L. (of woods). Occasionally escaped from cultivation to fields, roadsides and waste places. June-July. Map 1396. (Introduced from Europe).

5. L. japónicus Willd. (Japanese). Beach Pea. Sea beaches and dunes. June-August. Fig. 647, Map 1397. (Chile, Canada, Greenland, Japan). [*L. maritimus*]. Represented with us by the following vars.:

var. *marítimus* (Ser.) Fern. Plant glabrous or sparsely hairy and glabrate. [*L. maritimus* var. *glaber; L. japonicus* var. *g.*].

var. *pellítus* Fern. Plant pubescent on the upper stem, lower leaf surfaces and inflorescence. [*L. maritimus* var. *p.*]. Fruit edible raw or cooked; ripe peas reported as poisonous if eaten in large quantities. —FACU-

6. L. ochroleúcus Hook. (yellowish-white). Dry upland woods and banks. May-July. Reported for Chittenden and Grand Isle Counties VT.

7. L. palústris L. (of marshes). River and lake shores, wet meadows. June-July. Fig. 648, Map 1398. (Eurasia). —FACW+

8. L. venósus Muhl. ex Willd. (veiny). Moist woods and thickets. May-June. Represented with us as var. *intónsus* Butters & St. John. —FACW

L. apháca L. Differing from all of the above species in that the leaves are represented by unbranched tendrils with foliaceous, triangular stipules connate at the base. European. Rarely adventive in our range. Reported for Berkshire County MA.

16. Vícia L. Vetch (classical Latin name).

Trailing or climbing, less commonly erect, annual or perennial herbs; leaves pinnate, petioled to subsessile, with the terminal leaflet usually modified into a simple or branched tendril, lateral leaflets entire or apically toothed, stipules small, usually half-sagittate; flowers purplish or yellow, in few flowered, axillary clusters or short to elongate, axillary racemes, calyx tube campanulate, 5-toothed, regular to irregular, corolla papilionaceous, wings adherent to the keel, stamens diadelphous, style with a ring or tuft of hairs beneath the stigma; legume 2-many-seeded, laterally compressed to terete, dehiscent into 2 valves. —Wildl. 1

Léns Mill. *culinàris* Medik. Lentil. Resembling Vicea but calyx parted nearly to the base, occasionally escapes from cultivation. (Introduced from the Old World). Reported for Fairfield and New Haven Counties CT. [*L. esculenta*].

a. Peduncles distinctive, longer than the subtending petiole, usually 1 cm or more long. (Fig. 649).
  b. Flowers 8 mm or less long, solitary or in racemes of 2-8; legume 1.5 cm or less long.
    Calyx lobes nearly equal; legume pubescent, usually 2-seeded. .... 1. *V. hirsuta*
    Calyx lobes very unequal; legume glabrous, usually 4(3)-seeded. .... 2. *V. tetrasperma*
  b. Flowers 9 mm or more long, usually in racemes of more than 8; legume more than 1.5 cm long.
    c. Stems and racemes spreading-pubescent. .... 3. *V. villosa*
    c. Stems and racemes appressed-pubescent to glabrous.
      Calyx tube very gibbous at the base, the pedicel appearing laterally
        attached. .... 3. *V. villosa*
                                            subsp. *varia*
      Calyx tube rounded to slightly gibbous at the base, the pedicel appearing
        basally attached .... 4. *V. cracca*
a. Peduncles shorter than the subtending petiole or absent, less than 5 mm long. (Fig. 650).
  d. Leaflets 6 or fewer.
    Tendrils lacking; flowers 2-6, 2-3 cm long; legume 10 cm or more long. .... 5. *V. faba*
    Tendrils present, simple; flowers usually solitary or 2, less than 1 cm long;
      legume 3 cm or less long .... 6. *V. lathyroides*
  d. Leaflets mostly 8 or more.
    e. Calyx lobes very unequal, broadly triangular at the base, abruptly narrowed
      to a slender tip; peduncle short but distinct. .... 7. *V. sepium*
    e. Calyx lobes nearly equal, linear lanceolate, gradually narrowed; peduncle
      absent or if present flowers yellow (purple in *V. sepium*).
      Flowers reddish-purple, rarely white. .... 8. *V. sativa*
      Flowers yellow or yellow and purple .... 9. *V. grandiflora*

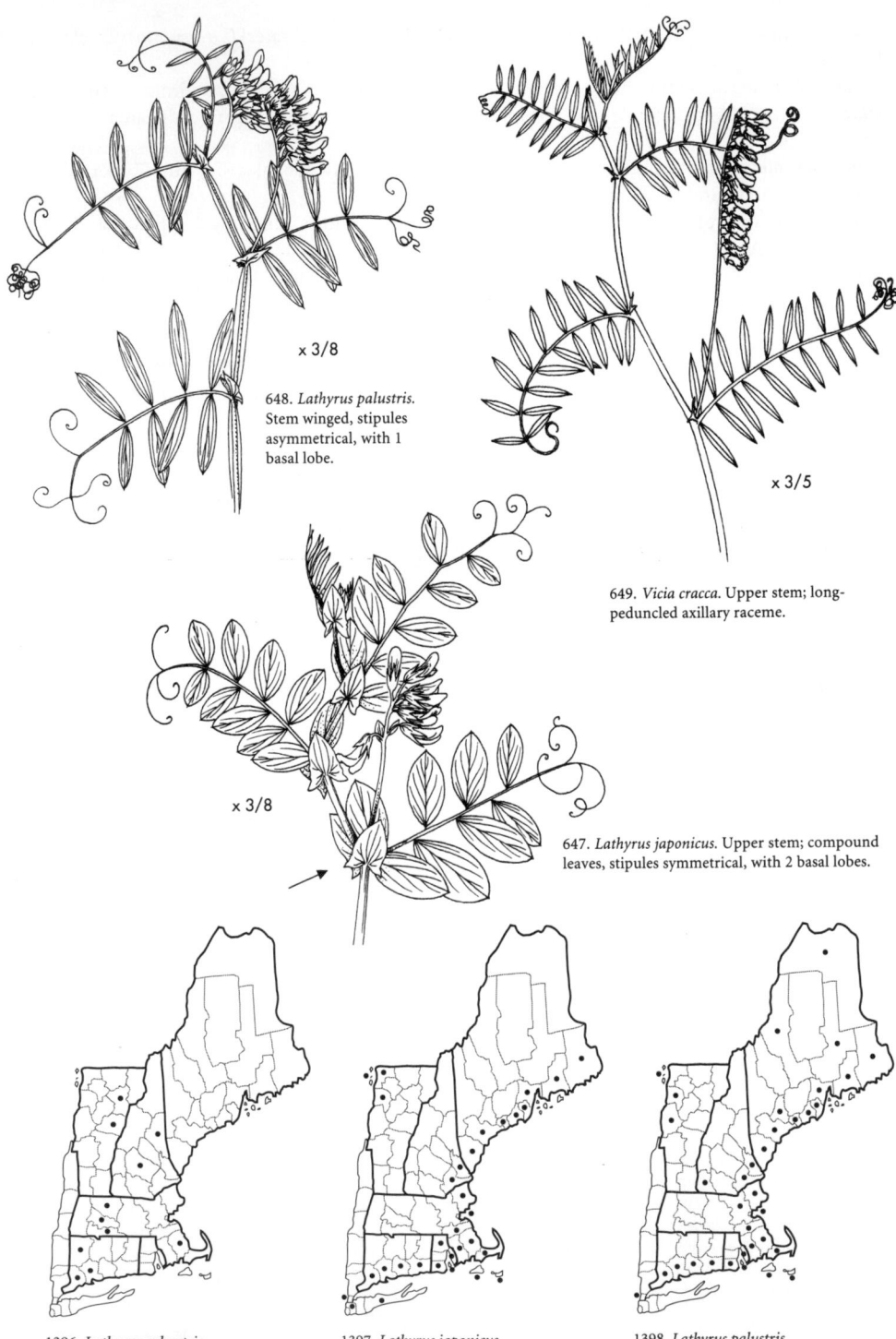

x 3/8

648. *Lathyrus palustris.*
Stem winged, stipules
asymmetrical, with 1
basal lobe.

x 3/5

649. *Vicia cracca.* Upper stem; long-
peduncled axillary raceme.

x 3/8

647. *Lathyrus japonicus.* Upper stem; compound
leaves, stipules symmetrical, with 2 basal lobes.

1396. *Lathyrus sylvestris*

1397. *Lathyrus japonicus*

1398. *Lathyrus palustris*

1. V. hirsúta (L.) S. F. Gray (hirsute). Roadsides and waste places. June-August. Map 1399. (Naturalized from Europe).

2. V. tetraspérma (L.) Schreb. (four-seeded). Fields, roadsides and waste places. June-August. Map 1400. (Naturalized from Europe). Our plants include var. *tetrasperma* and the following var.:

var. *tenuíssima* Druce. Leaflets of upper leaves linear, tapering to slender tips (leaflets oblong, round at the tip in var. *tetrasperma*).

3. V. villósa Roth (long-hairy). Fields, roadsides and waste places. June-August. Map 1401. (Naturalized from Europe). Our plants include subsp. *villosa* and the following subsp.

subsp. *vária* (Host) Corb. Stems and racemes appressed-pubescent to glabrous (spreading-pubescent in subsp. *villosa*). [*V. dasycarpa; V. villosa* subsp. *eriocarpa; V.v.* var. *glabrescens*].

4. V. crácca L. (ancient Latin name). Fields, roadsides and waste places. June-August. Fig. 649, Map 1402. (Naturalized from Europe).

5. V. fába L. (old generic name). Broad bean. Rarely escaped from cultivation. Map 1403. (Introduced from Europe). Fruit edible but can be toxic if eaten raw in large amounts.

6. V. lathyroídes L. (similar to *Lathyrus*). Disturbed areas. May-June. (Adventive from Europe). Barnstable and Nantucket Counties MA.

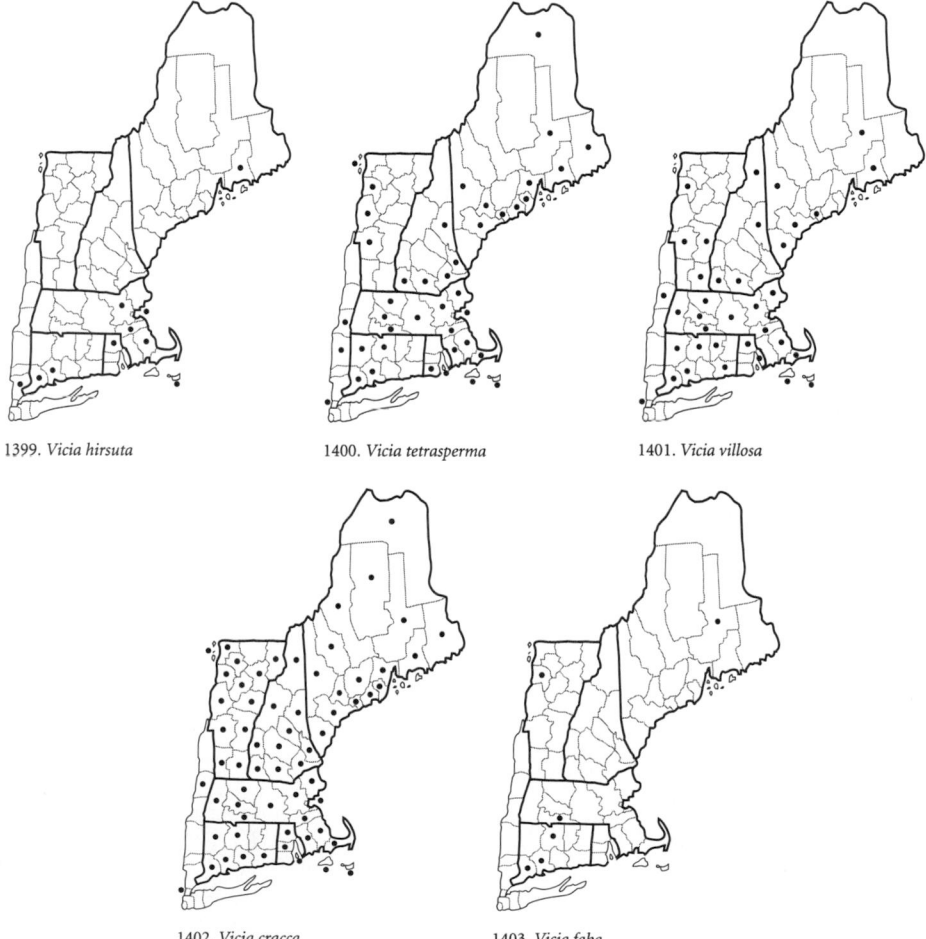

1399. *Vicia hirsuta*

1400. *Vicia tetrasperma*

1401. *Vicia villosa*

1402. *Vicia cracca*

1403. *Vicia faba*

V. narbonénsis L. Differing from *V. lathroides* in having very unequal calyx teeth (teeth equal or nearly so in *V. lathroides*). Cultivated; rarely escaped in our region. (Introduced from Europe). Reported for Kings County NY.

7. *V. sépium* L. (of hedges). Fields, roadsides and waste places. June-August. Fig. 650, Map 1404. (Naturalized from Europe). Our plants include var. *sepium* and the following var.:

var. *montána* W. D. J. Koch. Leaflets tapering to an acute tip (leaflets rounded or emarginate at the tip in var. *sepium*).

8. *V. sativa* L. (sown). Fields, roadsides and waste places. June-September. Map 1405. (Introduced from Europe). Our plants include subsp. *sativa* and the following subsp.:

subsp. *nígra* Ehrh. Flowers up to 1.8 cm long; legume terete (flowers longer than 1.8 cm and legume compressed in subsp. *sativa*). [*V. angustifolia*]. —FACU-

9. *V. grandiflóra* Scop. (large-flowered). Fields, roadsides and waste places. May-June. (Naturalized from Europe). Reported for MA, Bronx and Westchester Counties NY.

V. pannónica Crantz. Hungarian Vetch. Will key to *V. grandiflora* but leaflets are 7-9 pairs and flowers are yellowish white, less than 2 cm long (leaflets up to 6 pairs and flowers yellow, sometimes marked with purple, well over 2 cm long in *V. grandiflora*). (Europe). Reported for CT.

17. *Písum* L. Garden Pea (ancient name).

Sprawling or climbing, glabrous, annual, vine; leaves pinnate, petioled, terminated by tendrils, leaflets ovate to oblong, entire, glaucous, stipules large and foliaceous; flowers white, in short,

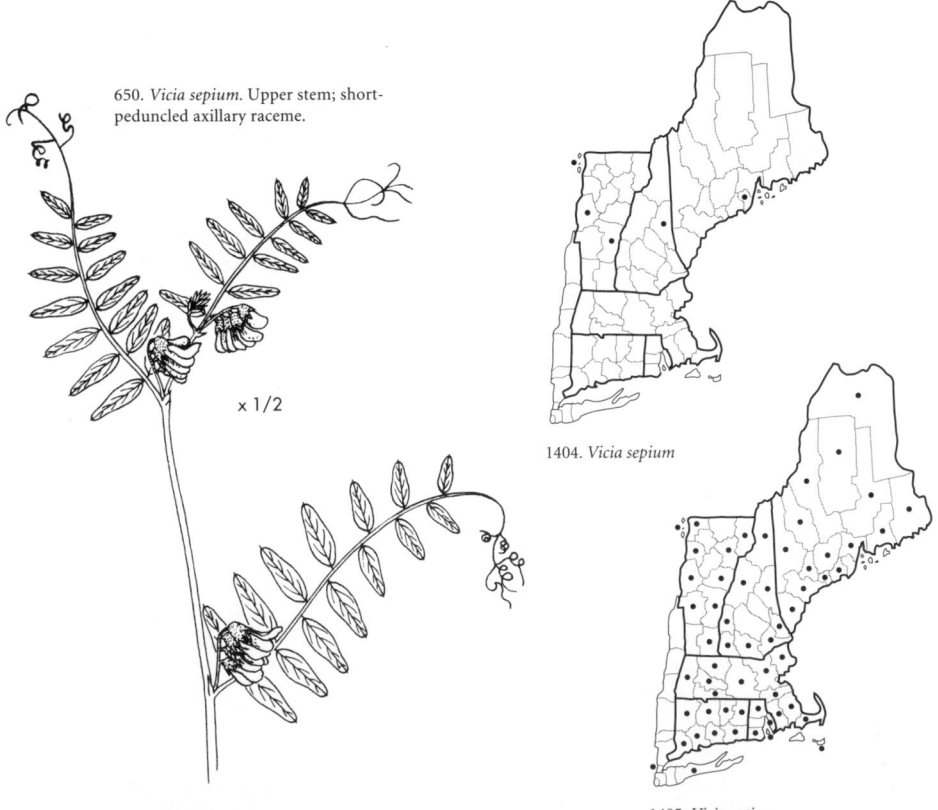

650. *Vicia sepium.* Upper stem; short-peduncled axillary raceme.

x 1/2

1404. *Vicia sepium*

1405. *Vicia sativa*

axillary racemes, calyx tube campanulate, oblique, with 5 subequal lobes twice as long as the tube, corolla papilionaceous, stamens diadelphous, style flattened, bearded along 1 side; legume flattened to terete, many-seeded, dehiscent into 2 valves.

1. P. sativum L. (sown). Occasionally escaped from cultivation to roadsides and around dwellings. July-September. Map 1406. (Introduced from Eurasia). Edible, and the fresh peas are also useful in treating various skin complaints such as acne and wrinkles.

18. Cicer L. (classical name).

Erect, densely pubescent, annual herbs; leaves odd-pinnate, petioled, stipulate, with small, ovate to obovate leaflets, these cuneate-based, toothed from above the middle; flowers pink to white, solitary in the leaf axils, on long, geniculate pedicels, calyx tube short, lobes elongate, about equal in length, corolla papilionaceous, stamens diadelphous; legume oblong-ovate, turgid, 1 or 2-seeded, indehiscent.

1. C. arietinum L. (like a ram's head). Chick-pea. Occasionally escaped from cultivation to waste places. May-August. Map 1407. (Introduced from sw. Asia). Widely cultivated for food.

19. Anthýllis L. Lady's-fingers (ancient Greek name).

Perennial herbs, pubescent and branched from the base; leaves pinnate, subsessile, of 5-13 leaflets, the terminal leaflet often the largest, the basal leaves often with fewer or a solitary leaflet, stipules small or none; flowers yellow or red, numerous in large, terminal, peduncled heads subtended by several 3 or more-cleft bracts, calyx pubescent, inflated, 5-toothed, bilabiate with an oblique orifice, corolla papilionaceous, the petals clawed, free from the staminal tube, wing and keel petals coherent, stamens 10, monadelphous; legume ovoid, several-seeded, indehiscent, enclosed in the calyx.

1. A. vulneraria L. (old generic name). Fields and waste places. June-July. (Adventive from Europe). Reported for VT, Middlesex County CT, Hillsboro County NH.

20. Lótus L. (ancient Greek name).

Perennial herbs with numerous prostrate to ascending, glabrous to sparsely appressed-pubescent stems; leaves pinnately 3-5-foliate, subsessile, leaflets elliptic to oblanceolate, entire, the lowest pair simulating stipules, stipules none or minute and gland-like; flowers yellow to red, rarely pink, in long-peduncled, capitate umbels from the upper axils, the umbel often closely subtended by a 3-foliate bract, calyx tube campanulate, with 5 long subequal lobes, corolla papilionaceous, the petals clawed, free from the staminal tube, wing and keel petals coherent below, the keel beaked, stamens 10, unequal, diadelphous; legume linear, terete, straight, several-seeded, dehiscent.

Coronilla scorpioides, a trifoliate herb with yellow flowers in small umbels, sometimes keying here, is described under *Coronilla* (genus 22).

Leaflets 5; stipules lacking; flowers yellow, in umbels. .... 1. *L. corniculatus*
Leaflets 1-3; stipules minute and gland-like; flowers pink, solitary in the upper axils ..... 2. *L. unifoliolatus*

1. L. corniculátus L. (horned). Birds-foot trefoil. Fields, roadsides and waste places. June-September. Fig. 651, Map 1408. (Adventive from Europe). Reported to be useful in treating skin inflammation if applied externally in compresses. —FACU-

L. ténuis Waldst. & Kit. Similar to *L. corniculatus* but with flowers 1 cm or less long, in umbels of 4 or fewer; (flowers usually longer than 1 cm, in umbels of 5 or more in *L. corniculatus*). From farther west. Reported for RI. [*L. corniculatus* var. *tenuifolius*].

2. L. unifoliolátus (Hook.) Benth. Prairie-Trefoil. Dry fields. June-September. From farther west. Occasionally adventive in our range. Reported for Fairfield County CT, Norfolk County MA. [*L. americanus; L. purshianus; Hosackia a.; Acmispon a.*]. Our plants are var. *unifoliatus*.

21. *Ornithopus* L.

Pubescent, annual herbs; leaves sessile or petioled, odd-pinnate, with numerous leaflets, leaflets small, oblong, entire, often mucronate, stipules connate to the petiole; flowers pink, bracteate, in few flowered, peduncled heads from the upper axils, the heads often closely subtended by a leaf, calyx tube campanulate, with 5 nearly equal teeth, corolla papilionaceous, stamens 10, diadelphous; legume linear, flattened, with 2-5 disarticulating, 1-seeded segments.

1. *O. sativus* Brot. (of the garden). Waste places. June-August. Reported for Suffolk County NY.

22. *Coronilla* L. Crown-vetch (diminutive of corona, referring to the inflorescence).

Glabrous, branching, perennial herbs with ascending stems; leaves odd-pinnate, with numerous leaflets, sessile, leaflets obovate to oblong, entire, mucronate, stipules persistent; flowers pink, or pink and white, rarely yellow (*C. scorpioides*), bracteate, in dense, axillary, peduncled umbels, calyx tube campanulate, bilabiate, the 2 upper lobes more or less united, the 3 lower separate, corolla papilionaceous, petals clawed, keel beaked, stamens 10, diadelphous; legume linear, 4-angled, with 3-7, disarticulating, 1-seeded segments.

1. *C. vária* L. (variable). Roadsides, waste places, old cellar holes. June-August. Fig. 652, Map 1409. (Naturalized from Europe). Plant, especially the seed, is poisonous.

C. scorpioides (L.) Koch. Leaflets 1-3, flowers yellow, in umbels of 2-5. (From s. Europe). Reported for MA.

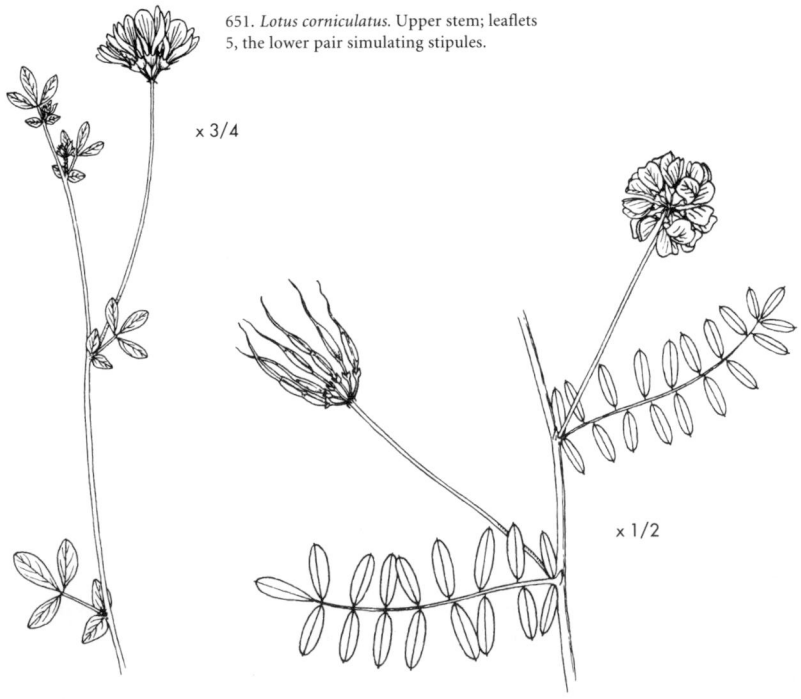

651. *Lotus corniculatus.* Upper stem; leaflets 5, the lower pair simulating stipules.

x 3/4

x 1/2

652. *Coronilla varia.* Section of stem; leaves odd-pinnate, flowers in peduncled, axillary umbels.

1406. *Pisum sativum*

1407. *Cicer arietinum*

1408. *Lotus corniculatus*

1409. *Coronilla varia*

1410. *Galega officinalis*

23. *Galéga* L. Goat's Rue.

Tall, branching, mostly glabrous, perennial herbs; leaves pinnate, petioled, leaflets numerous, lance-oblong to narrowly elliptic, entire, mucronate, stipules sagittate; flowers purple, pink, or white, in long, axillary, bracteate, racemes, calyx tube campanulate, with 5 equal, linear-setaceous lobes, corolla papilionaceous, stamens monadelphous; legume linear-cylindric, somewhat torulose, several-seeded, 1-celled, dehiscent.

1. G. officinális L. (of the shops). Occasionally escaped from cultivation to borders of fields and roadsides. June-August. Map 1410. Preparations made from the entire plant are reported to increase milk yield.

24. *Ápios* Fabr. Groundnut (Greek name for pear, based on shape of the tuberous thickenings of the rhizome).

Twining, often climbing, pubescent to glabrate, perennial, herbaceous vines from slender rhizomes bearing fleshy, tuberous thickenings; leaves pinnate, petioled, leaflets mostly 5-7, ovate-lanceolate, entire, stipules subulate, deciduous; flowers brownish-purple, bracteate, in dense, peduncled, axillary racemes, these often branched at the base, the nodes swollen, calyx tube broadly campanulate, somewhat bilabiate, the 4 upper lobes very short or obsolete, the lower one long, corolla papilionaceous, the keel strongly curved, stamens diadelphous, style curved, glabrous; legume linear, straight or slightly curved, flattened, several-many seeded, dehiscing by 2 spirally twisted valves.

1. *A. americána* Medik. (American). Riverbanks, thickets, fields and roadsides. July-September. Fig. 653, Map 1411. [*A. tuberosa; Glycine apios*]. Tubers edible raw or cooked. —FACW

25. *Oxýtropis* DC (from the Greek, meaning sharp keel).

Low, nearly acaulescent, perennial herbs, the leaves and peduncles crowded on the crown of a multicipital taproot; leaves odd-pinnate, petioled, leaflets numerous, lance-linear to oblong, entire, stipules adnate to the petiole; flowers purple, in a dense, bracteate spike terminating a long peduncle, keel abruptly short-beaked, otherwise as in *Astragalus*; legumes nearly erect, thick-cylindric, incompletely 2-locular, dehiscent. Certain western species that are not part of our flora are reported as poisonous.

1. *O. campéstris* (L.) DC. (of fields). Shores of St. John River, Maine. June-July. Fig. 654. Represented with us as var. *johannensis*. Fern. [*O. johannensis*].

26. *Tephrósia* Pers. (from the Greek meaning hoary).

Erect, pubescent, perennial herbs from long, fibrous roots; leaves odd-pinnate, short-petioled, leaflets linear-oblong to elliptic, entire, mucronate, pubescent beneath, stipules small; flowers showy, bicolored, purple and yellow, in dense, terminal, subsessile, bracteate, often leafy racemes, calyx teeth 5, about equal, corolla papilionaceous, the standard yellow, wings and keel rose or purple, coherent, stamens monadelphous, style bearded along the inner side; legume linear, flat, pubescent, several-seeded, dehiscent into 2 valves.

Dálea L. Similar to *Tephrosia* but differs in usually being glandular-punctate, flowers white, legume indehiscent, 1-seeded. Western; 2 species occurring as waifs in our range: *D. leporína* (Ait.) Bullock. Plant annual, keel to 3 mm long, stamens 9 or 10. [*D. alopecuroides; Parosela a.*]. Reported for Suffolk County MA; *D. candída* Michx. ex Willd. Plant perennial, keel longer than 3 mm, stamens 5. From farther west. Reported for NH. Our plants are var. *candida*. [*Petalostemum c.*].

1. *T. virginiána* (L.) Pers. Goat's-rue. Open deciduous or pine woods and clearings, barrens, dunes and roadsides in sandy soil. June-July. Fig. 655, Map 1412. Endangered in NH. [*Cracca v.*].

27. *Glycyrrhíza* L.

Tall, branching, perennial herbs from a thick root, the upper stem and branches glandular; leaves odd-pinnate, petioled, leaflets numerous, oblong-lanceolate, entire, mucronate, dotted beneath with minute glands, stipulate; flowers yellowish-white, in dense, bracteate, axillary racemes, calyx tube campanulate, slightly bilabiate, the 2 upper teeth partly united, corolla papilionaceous, stamens diadelphous, anthers alternately larger and smaller; legumes oblong, densely covered with hooked prickles, several-seeded, 1-celled, indehiscent.

1. *G. lepidóta* Pursh (scaly). Wild Licorice. Fields and waste places. June-July. Rare. Fig. 656, Map 1413. Our plants are var. *lepidota*. Root edible, with a taste like licorice.

28. *Hedýsarum* L. (ancient Greek name for another plant).

Perennial herbs with few-many, erect or ascending stems; leaves odd-pinnate, with numerous leaflets, short-petioled, leaflets oblong, entire, often mucronate, stipules opposite the petioles, connate at the base; flowers pink to purple, bracteate, in loose, elongate, axillary, peduncled, 1-sided

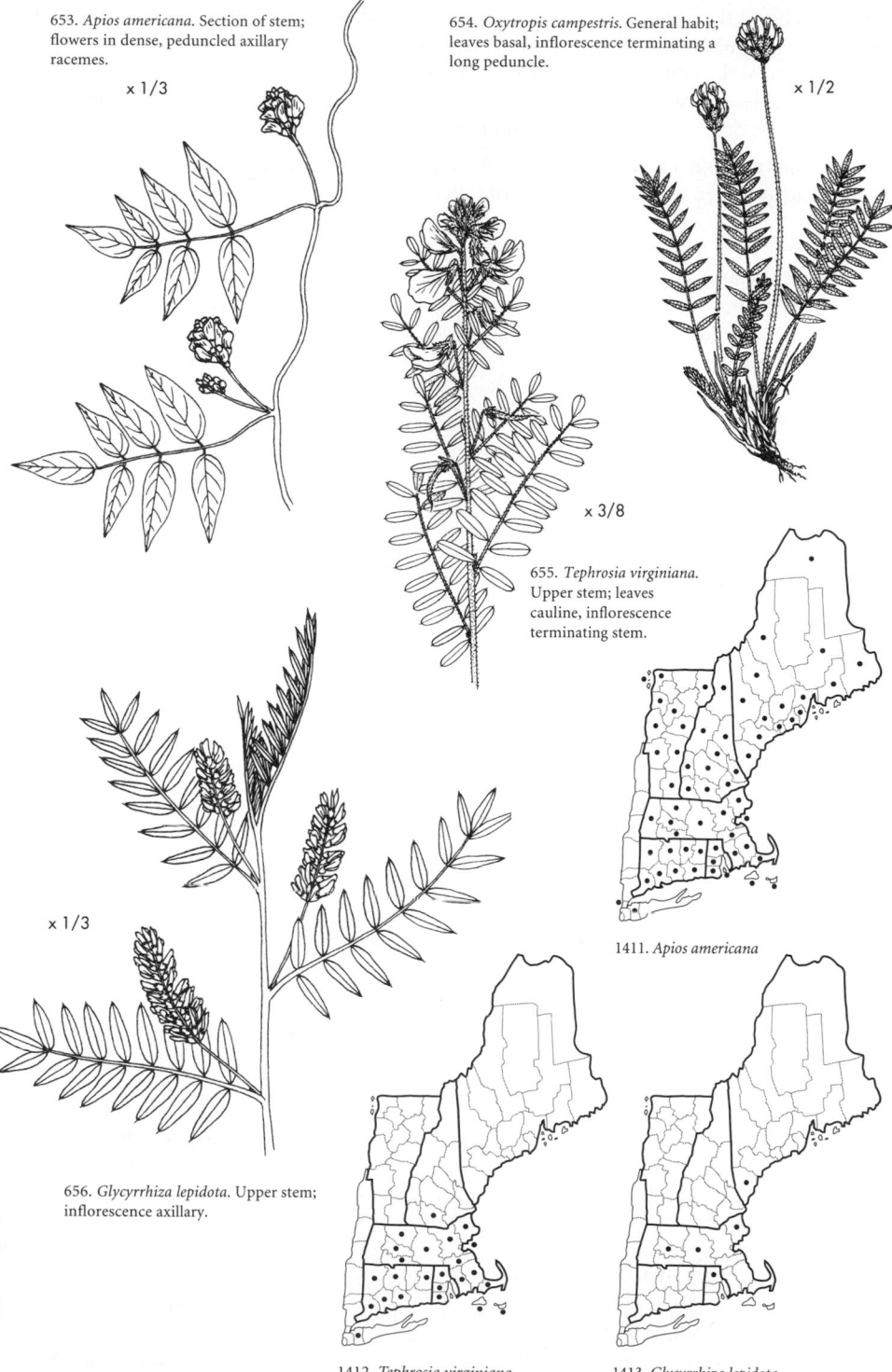

653. *Apios americana*. Section of stem; flowers in dense, peduncled axillary racemes.

× 1/3

654. *Oxytropis campestris*. General habit; leaves basal, inflorescence terminating a long peduncle.

× 1/2

× 3/8

655. *Tephrosia virginiana*. Upper stem; leaves cauline, inflorescence terminating stem.

× 1/3

656. *Glycyrrhiza lepidota*. Upper stem; inflorescence axillary.

1411. *Apios americana*

1412. *Tephrosia virginiana*

1413. *Glycyrrhiza lepidota*

racemes, calyx tube campanulate, with 5 nearly equal teeth, corolla papilionaceous, stamens 10, diadelphous; legume linear, flattened, with 2-5, disarticulating, 1-seeded segments.

Onóbrychis Mill. *viciifólia* Scop. Will key to *Hedysarum* but is distinguishable in having flowers in dense racemes, these not 1-sided, fruit a single 1-seeded, spiny joint (joints 2 or more and not spiny in *Hedysarum*). Sporadically adventive from Europe. Reported for MA, VT.

1. *H. alpínum* L. Rocky slopes and river shores, limestone. June-July. Fig. 657, Map 1414. [*H. boreale*]. Represented with us as var. *americánum* Michx. Root edible with a taste like licorice. —FAC-

29. *Astrágalus* L. Milk-vetch (ancient Greek name for a leguminous plant).

Decumbent or erect, often rhizomatous, glabrous to sparingly pubescent perennial herbs; leaves odd-pinnate, petioled, leaflets usually numerous, oblong to oval, entire, stipules present; flowers white to yellowish or purple, in axillary, bracteate racemes, calyx tube campanulate to cylindric, with 5, subequal, short-triangular to subulate lobes, corolla papilionaceous, usually long and narrow, petals clawed, stamens diadelphous; legume variable, usually turgid, several-many seeded, 1 or 2 celled, usually dehiscent. Certain western species that are not part of our flora are reported as poisonous.

a. Stipules, at least the lower, 1-2 cm long, ovate, widest above the base. .... 1. *A. contortuplicatus*
a. Stipules less than 1 cm long, setaceous to lanceolate or triangular, widest at the base.
  b. Corolla yellowish; fruits erect, imbricate, completely 2-locular. (Fig. 658) .... 2. *A. canadensis*
  b. Corolla pink, purple or white; fruits spreading to pendulous, not imbricate,
    1-locular or incompletely 2-locular (only a partial partition present).
    c. Most leaves with more than 15 leaflets; stems decumbent or creeping at the
      base; keel about equalling the standard. .... 3. *A. alpinus*
                                                var. *brunetianus*
    c. Most leaves with 15 or fewer leaflets; stems erect or ascending; keel much
      shorter than standard.
      Flowers 9 mm or more long; legume 14 mm or more long on a stipe 2 mm
        or more long .... 4. *A. robbinsii*
      Flowers 8 mm or less long; legume 13 mm or less long, essentially sessile. ...... 5. *A. eucosmus*

1. *A. contortuplicátus* L. Fields, roadsides and waste places. May-July. (Adventive from Europe). Reported for Suffolk County MA. [*A. glycyphyllos*].

2. *A. canadénsis* L. (Canadian). River and lake shores. July-August. Fig. 658, Map 1415. [*A. carolinianus*]. Our plants are var. *canadensis*. —FAC

3. *A. alpínus* L. (alpine). Calcareous, gravelly, river shores. June-July. Map 1416. Represented with us as var. *brunetiánus* Fern. [*A. labradoricus*]. —FACU

4. *A. robbinsii* (Oakes) Gray (for its discoverer). Calcareous ledge, Winooski River, VT. May-June. Map 1417. Our plants include var. *robbinsii* (reported for VT, now thought to be extinct) and the following vars. which are distinguishable from the typical phase in having larger flowers (1 cm or more long); flowers are less than 1 cm long in var. *robbinsii*.

    var. *jésupi* Egglest. & Sheld. Leaflets glabrous beneath; fruit beaked. Banks of Connecticut River in NH and Vt. Federally endangered.

    var. *mínor* (Hook.) Barneby. Leaflets strigose beneath; fruit beakless. Calcareous cliffs and ledges [var. *blakei*].

5. *A. eucósmus* B. L. Robins. (elegant). Calcareous, gravelly, river shores. June-July. Reported for Aroostook County ME. [*Atelophragma elegans*]. —FACU

30. *Crotalária* L. Rattlebox (based on the Greek name for rattle).

Low, pubescent, usually branched annual (ours) herbs; leaves simple, the lower elliptic, the upper lanceolate to linear, entire, sessile or subsessile, stipules conspicuous, united and decurrent on the stem, inversely sagittate, or absent from the lower leaves; flowers yellow, in 2-4-flowered, bracteate racemes terminating the stem and branches, calyx bracteolate at the base, deeply 5-lobed, corolla papilionaceous, stamens 10, monadelphous, the sheath cleft above the middle, filaments alternately longer with small, roundish anthers and shorter with larger, linear anthers; legume oblong-cylindric, inflated, many-seeded, the seeds loose and rattling in the pods when plant shaken.

Scorpiúrus L. *muricátus* L. Will key to *Crotalaria* but has oblanceolate leaves, flowers in long peduncled, axillary clusters of 3 and spiny legumes (leaves lanceolate, flowers in racemes terminating the stem and branches and legume inflated, not spiny in *Crotalaria*). Reported as a waif in MA. [*S. sulcatus*].

1. *C. sagittális* L. (like an arrow-head). Gravel pits, sandy fields, roadsides and waste places. July-August. Fig. 659, Map 1418. (W.I.). Endangered in NH. Poisonous.

31. *Melilótus* Mill. Sweet clover (Greek name for a leguminous plant).

Annual or biennial herbs, fragrant in drying; leaves pinnately 3-foliate, petioled, the leaflets serrulate or denticulate, stipules lanceolate to subulate, partly adnate to the petiole; flowers small, white or yellow, pedicillate and bracteate, numerous in spike-like, peduncled racemes from the upper axils, calyx eventually deciduous, 5-lobed, the lobes subulate to lanceolate, subequal, corolla papilionaceous, deciduous after anthesis, free from the staminal tube, the wing and keel petals coherent below, stamens 10, diadelphous; legume ovoid to subglobose, exceeding the calyx, 1-2-seeded, usually indehiscent.

a. Corolla white .... 1. *M. albus*
a. Corolla yellow.
    Flowers 3 mm or less long; fruit less than 2.5 mm long. .... 2. *M. indicus*
    Flowers 4 mm or more long; fruit 2.5 mm or more long. .... 3. *M. officinalis*

1. *M. álbus* Medik. (white). White sweet clover. Fields, roadsides, waste places. June-September. Fig. 660, Map 1419. (Naturalized from Europe). —FACU

2. *M. índicus* (L.) All. (of India). Fields, roadsides, waste places. June-September. Map 1420. (Adventive from Eurasia). —FACU

3. *M. officinális* (L.) Lam. (of the shops). Yellow sweet clover. Fields, roadsides, waste places. May-October. Map 1421. (Naturalized from Europe). A preparation made from the inflorescence is reported to be effective as an eye lotion. —FACU-

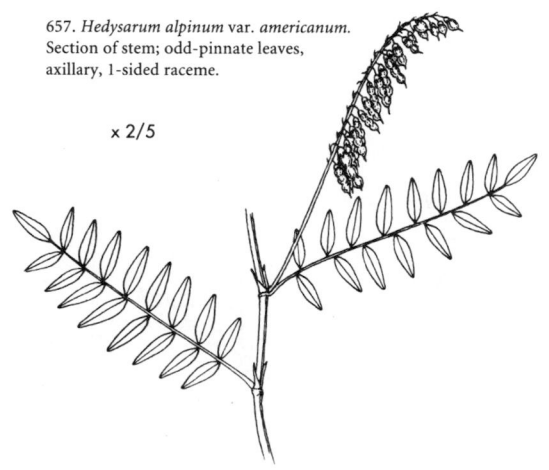

657. *Hedysarum alpinum* var. *americanum*.
Section of stem; odd-pinnate leaves,
axillary, 1-sided raceme.

x 2/5

1414. *Hedysarum alpinum*

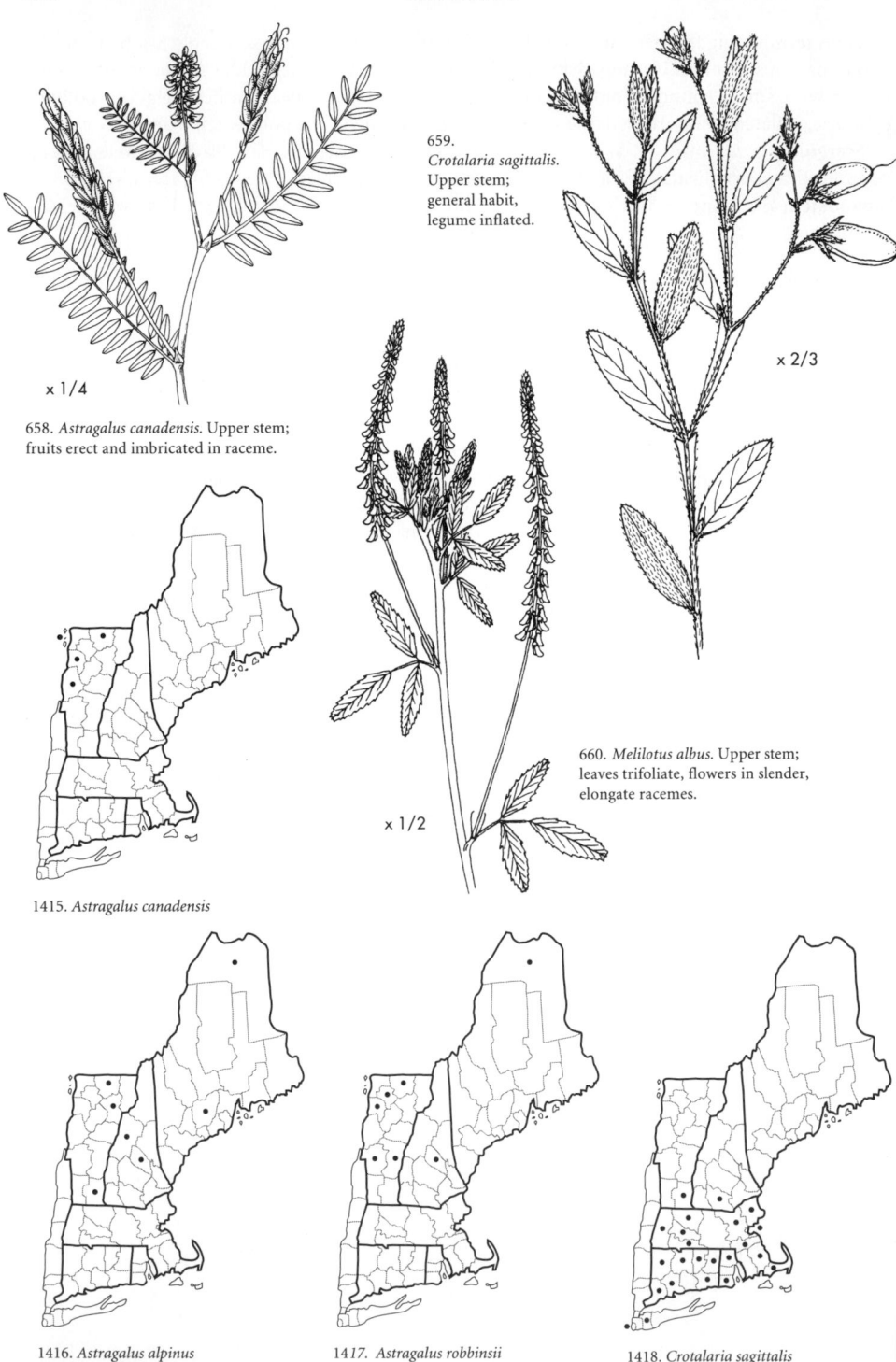

659.
Crotalaria sagittalis.
Upper stem;
general habit,
legume inflated.

x 2/3

x 1/4

658. *Astragalus canadensis.* Upper stem;
fruits erect and imbricated in raceme.

660. *Melilotus albus.* Upper stem;
leaves trifoliate, flowers in slender,
elongate racemes.

x 1/2

1415. *Astragalus canadensis*

1416. *Astragalus alpinus*
var. *brunetianus*

1417. *Astragalus robbinsii*

1418. *Crotalaria sagittalis*

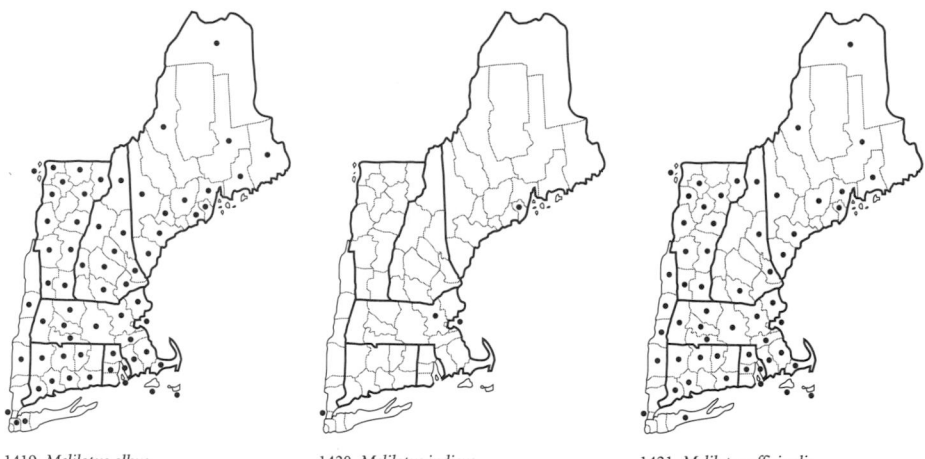

1419. *Melilotus albus* 1420. *Melilotus indicus* 1421. *Melilotus officinalis*

32. *Trifólium* L. Clover (3-leaved).

Annual, biennial or perennial, erect or prostrate herbs; leaves mostly palmately (rarely pinnately) trifoliate (rarely 4 or more-foliate), with serrulate leaflets, stipules adnate to the petiole; flowers purple, pink, red, white or yellow, small, sessile or pedicellate, in dense, terminal or axillary heads, calyx 5-lobed, the lobes usually setaceous, nearly equal or calyx strongly bilabiate, corolla papiliona-ceous, the petals all separate (in the yellow-flowered species) or united below with the staminal tube, withering and persistent after anthesis, stamens 10, diadelphous, 1 separate from the others for part of its length; legume short, oblong, often enclosed by the persistent calyx, indehiscent or tardily dehiscent, several-seeded. Various species of clover, particularly *T. pratense* have been eaten raw or cooked (the entire plant) by the Indians and colonists. —Wildl. 2

Several species of *Trigonélla* L. native to Europe and Asia and rarely escaped from cultivation in our range, may be distinguished from *Trifolium* in having the fruit exserted from the calyx (enclosed within the persistent calyx in *Trifolium*). Reported for Suffolk and Middlesex Counties MA.

a. Calyx tube densely pubescent on 1 side, glabrous or nearly so on the other, in fruit
    becoming inflated and bladdery; corolla blue to purple. .... 1. *T. resupinatum*
a. Calyx tube glabrous or uniformly pubescent, in fruit not becoming inflated or
    bladdery; corolla white, pink, red or yellow (can be purple in *T. medium* and
    T. pratense).
    b. Terminal leaflet with petiolule conspicuously longer than petiolules of lateral
        leaflets; corolla yellow. (Fig. 661).
        Heads more than 8 mm broad, usually 20 or more flowered; standard striate-
            sulcate .... 2. *T. campestre*
        Heads 8 mm or less broad, usually less than 20 flowered; standard not striate-
            sulcate .... 3. *T. dubium*
    b. Terminal leaflet sessile or on a very short petiolule not conspicuously longer
        than the laterals.
        c. Calyx glabrous or essentially so.
            d. Stems creeping and rooting at the nodes, the petioles and peduncles arising
                from the prostrate stems .... 4. *T. repens*
            d. Stems erect or ascending, not rooting at the nodes, the petioles and
                peduncles arising from upright stems.
                Corolla yellow; petioles less than twice as long as the stipules. .... 5. *T. aureum*

Corolla pink to whitish; petioles (at least the lower) more than twice as
long as the stipules .... 6. *T. hybridum*
c. Calyx pubescent (only in the throat and on the lobes in *T. medium*).
e. Heads on long, naked peduncles, not involucrate.
f. Corolla shorter than the calyx lobes; heads mostly less than 1.5 cm broad. ... 7. *T. arvense*
f. Corolla longer than the calyx lobes; heads mostly more than 1.5 cm broad.
Stipules obtuse to acute, usually darkened apically; heads ovoid or
cylindric. .... 8. *T. incarnatum*
Stipules acuminate to caudate, not darkened apically, heads
subglobose. .... 9. *T. medium*
e. Heads sessile or short peduncled, involucrate from a pair of opposite leaves
or their stipules. (Fig. 662).
g. Heads less than 1.5 cm broad; flowers less than 1 cm long, whitish to
pink. .... 10. *T. striatum*
g. Heads more than 1.5 cm broad; flowers more than 1 cm long, purplish
or red, rarely white to pink.
Stipules abruptly narrowed to a short point, the free part shorter than
the adnate part; calyx tube pubescent, throat glabrous. .... 11. *T. pratense*
Stipules acuminate to caudate, the free part longer than the adnate
part; calyx tube glabrous, throat pubescent .... 9. *T. medium*

1. *T. resupinátum* L. (upside down). Occasional in lawns, fields and roadsides. May-September. (Adventive from Europe). Reported for Suffolk County MA, Chittenden County VT.

2. *T. campéstre* Schreb. (of fields). Hop-clover. Fields, roadsides and waste places. May-September. Fig. 661, Map 1422. (Naturalized from Europe). [*T. procumbens*].

3. *T. dúbium* Sibth. (doubtful). Hop-clover. Fields, roadsides and waste places. May-September. Map 1423. (Naturalized from Europe).

4. *T. répens* L. (creeping). White clover. Fields, roadsides and waste places. May-September. Map 1424. (Naturalized from Europe). —FACU-

5. *T. áureum* Poll. Yellow clover. Fields, roadsides and waste places. June-September. Map 1425. (Naturalized from Europe). [*T. agrarium*].

T. subterráneum L. Will key to *T. aureum* or possibly to species 2 or 3 but distinguishable in having calyx lobes nearly equal (calyx strongly bilabiate in the other 3 species). (Naturalized from Europe); a waif in our range. Reported for Worcester County, MA.

6. *T. hýbridum* L. (hybrid, a misnomer). Alsike clover. Fields, roadsides and waste places. June-September. Map 1426. (Introduced from Europe). —FACU-

7. *T. arvénse* L. (of cultivated fields). Rabbit-foot clover. Fields, roadsides and waste places. June-September. Map 1427. (Naturalized from Europe). Reported to be useful in treating gum disease if used as a mouthwash, and in treating skin eruptions if applied externally.

8. *T. incarnátum* L. (blood-red). Crimson clover. Fields, roadsides and waste places. May-August. Map 1428. (Introduced from Europe).

9. *T. médium* L. (intermediate). Zig-zag clover. Occasionally escaped from cultivation to fields and roadsides. June-August. Map 1429. (Naturalized from Europe).

T. dichótomum Hook & Arn. Similar to *T. medium* but annual, with corolla not over 1 cm long (*T. medium* biennial or perennial with corolla over 1 cm long). From the west coast. Reported for MA [*T. macraei*].

T. caroliniánum Michx. Will key to *T. medium* but is distinguishable from it and *T. dichotomum* in having the flowers distinctly pedicelled in the heads (sessile in the heads in the latter 2 species). From farther south. Reported for VT.

10. *T. striátum* L. (striped). Knotted clover. Fields and roadsides on Cape Cod, MA. June-August. (Adventive from Europe).

11. *T. praténse* L. (of meadows). Red clover. Fields, roadsides and waste places. May-September. Fig. 662, Map 1430. (Naturalized from Europe). —FACU

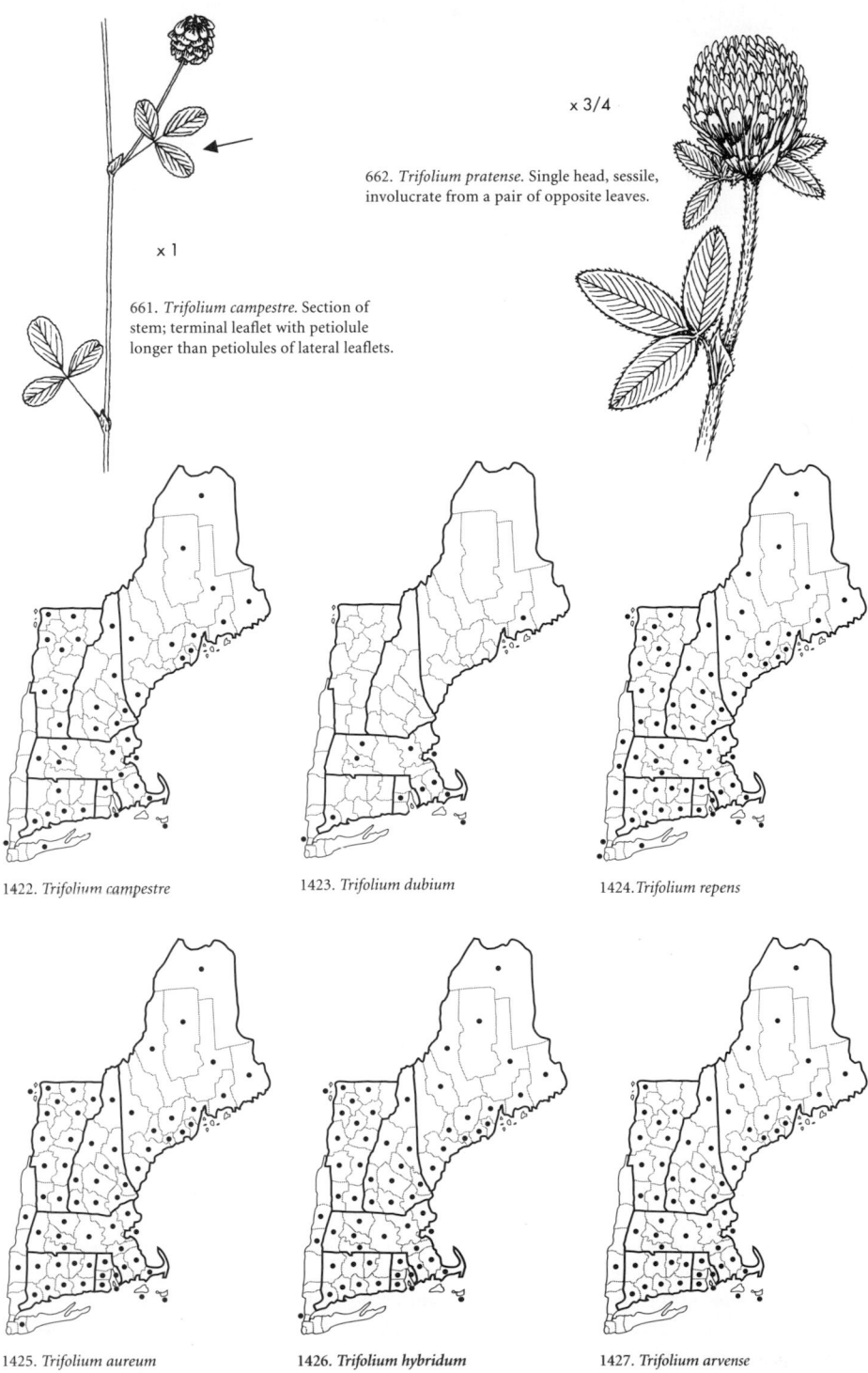

× 3/4

662. *Trifolium pratense.* Single head, sessile, involucrate from a pair of opposite leaves.

× 1

661. *Trifolium campestre.* Section of stem; terminal leaflet with petiolule longer than petiolules of lateral leaflets.

1422. *Trifolium campestre*

1423. *Trifolium dubium*

1424. *Trifolium repens*

1425. *Trifolium aureum*

1426. **Trifolium hybridum**

1427. *Trifolium arvense*

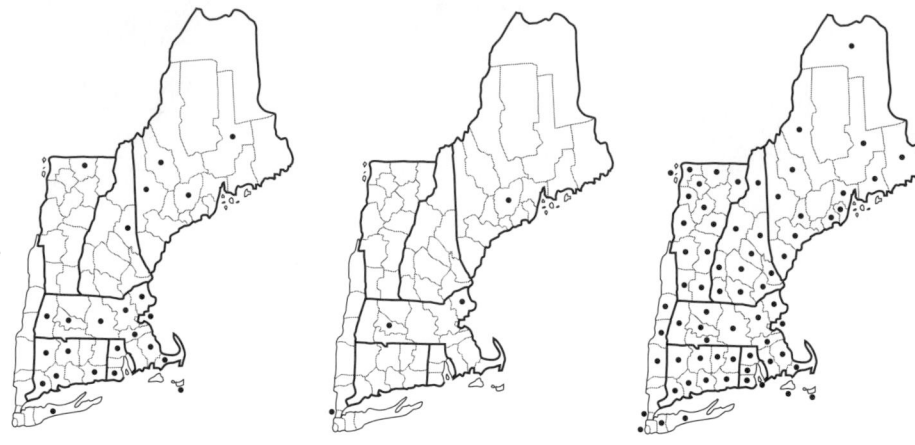

1428. *Trifolium incarnatum*   1429. *Trifolium medium*   1430. *Trifolium pratense*

33. *Medicágo* L. (based on the Greek name for Alfalfa).

Annual or perennial, prostrate or ascending herbs; leaves pinnately 3-foliate, petioled, the leaflets serrulate or denticulate to pectinate or lacerate, stipules ovate to lanceolate, entire, toothed or lacerate, partly adnate to the petiole; flowers small, yellow, white or blue, pedicillate and bracteate, in axillary heads or capitate racemes, calyx tube campanulate, lobes 5, subequal, corolla papilionaceous, similar to *Melilotus,* stamens 10, diadelphous; legume exceeding the calyx, straight, reniform or coiled, 1-several-seeded, usually indehiscent, smooth to spiny. —Wildl. 1

In addition to the following species *M. monspeliaca* has been reported for MA.

a. Flowers 6 mm or more long; legume coiled into a loose spiral open at the center,
　　or falcate to straight, unarmed. .... 1. *M. sativa*
a. Flowers less than 6 mm long; legume coiled into a tight spiral closed at the center
　　and armed with spines, or reniform and unarmed.
　　b. Flowers and fruit mostly more than 8; legume reniform, unarmed. (Fig. 663). ...... 2. *M. lupulina*
　　b. Flowers and fruit 8 or fewer; legume coiled into a tight spiral, armed. (Fig. 664).
　　　　c. Stipules entire or short-toothed; stems and upper surfaces of leaflets densely
　　　　　　pilose .... 3. *M. minima*
　　　　c. Stipules pectinate or deeply lacerate; stems and upper surfaces of leaflets
　　　　　　glabrous or sparsely pilose.
　　　　　　d. Leaflets mostly pectinate or laciniate. .... 4. *M. laciniata*
　　　　　　d. Leaflets merely shallowly toothed or denticulate.
　　　　　　　　Leaflets as wide as or wider than long, usually with a reddish-black mark
　　　　　　　　　　on the upper surface; the 2 rows of spines along the coils of the
　　　　　　　　　　legume separated by a furrow .... 5. *M. arabica*
　　　　　　　　Leaflets longer than wide, without a mark; the 2 rows of spines along the
　　　　　　　　　　coils of the legume separated by a keeled ridge. .... 6. *M. polymorpha*

1. M. satíva L. (sown). Alfalfa. Fields, roadsides and waste places. June-September. Map 1431. (Naturalized from the Old World). Our plants include subsp. *sativa* and the following subsp.:

subsp. *falcáta* (L.) Arcang. (sickle-shaped). Corolla yellow; legume falcate to nearly straight (corolla blue, violet or white; legume loosely coiled, of 1-3 complete turns in subsp. *sativa*). [*M. falcata*]. Young leaves can be used in a salad.

2. M. lupulína L. (hop-like). Black medick. Fields, roadsides and waste places. May-September. Fig. 663, Map 1432. (Naturalized from Europe). Seeds were eaten by Indians; eating large quantities reported to cause blood abnormalities.

3. M. mínima (L.) L. (tiny). Bur-clover. Fields, roadsides and waste places. May-September. Fig. 664, Map 1433. (Adventive from Europe).

4. M. laciniáta (L.) Mill. (slashed). Occasional in waste places. May-September. Map 1434. (Adventive from Europe).

5. M. arábica (L.) Huds. (Arabian). Spotted medick. Occasional in waste places. April-September. Map 1435. (Adventive from the Old World).

6. M. polymórpha L. (of many forms). Occasional in waste places. June-September. Map 1436. (Adventive from Europe). [*M. hispida*].

M. praécox DC. Similar to *M. polymorpha* but with leaflets up to 4 mm long, flowers 2 mm long (leaflets 6 mm or more long, flowers 4 mm or more long in *M. polymorpha*). From the southwest. Reported for MA.

34. Onónis L. (classical name).

Perennials, herbaceous or suffruticose, glandular-pubescent, prostrate or creeping, branches often ending in spines; leaves trifoliate, or reduced to 1 leaflet when subtending flowers, leaflets oblong to elliptic, the blades serrate, stipules adnate to the petiole; flowers red to purplish, solitary or paired in the axils, forming terminal leafy racemes, calyx deeply 5-lobed, corolla papilionaceous, keel beaked, stamens monadelphous, with alternately long and short filaments; legume small, oblong to ovate, few-seeded.

Branches, some or most, ending in spines. (Fig. 665). .... 1. *O. campestris*
Branches not ending in spines .... 2. *O. repens*

    1. O. campéstris G. Koch. Occasional in waste places around coastal cities. May-September. Fig. 665. (Adventive from Europe). [*O. spinosa*].

    2. O. répens L. (creeping). Occasional in waste places around coastal cities. May-September. (Adventive from Europe). Reported for Kings County NY.

35. Lespedéza Michx. Bush-clover (for V. de Cespedes, later misspelled as de Lespedez).

Procumbent, erect or ascending perennial herbs or sub-shrubs; leaves pinnately 3-foliate, petioled, leaflets entire, stipules small, setaceous, withering or deciduous; flowers small, purple or whitish, bracteate, solitary, in small clusters, spicate, racemose or capitate, in sessile or peduncled, loose to compact, axillary or terminal inflorescences, both apetalous (cleistogamous) and petaliferous flowers present in most species, calyx tube campanulate, the lobes nearly equal or the 2 upper partly united, corolla of petaliferous flowers papilionaceous, the wing and keel petals connivent, stamens 10, diadelphous; legume 1-seeded, indehiscent, oval to elliptic, similar or different in the apetalous and petaliferous flowers, often not developing in the latter.

a. Plants procumbent.
    Stems spreading-pubescent .... 1. *L. procumbens*
    Stems appressed-pubescent to glabrate .... 2. *L. repens*
a. Plants erect to ascending.
    b. Petioles mostly less than half as long as lateral leaflets; flowers in dense heads,
        yellowish-white (in racemes and purple in *L. x nuttalii* and *L. x brittonii*,
        solitary or few in the upper axils in *L. cuneata*); apetalous flowers. few or
        none.
        c. Leaflets linear to narrowly oblong, mostly 4 times or more as long as wide;
            petiolules of terminal leaflets mostly less than 3.5 mm long. .... 3. *L. angustifolia*
        c. Leaflets oblong to oval or elliptic, mostly less than 4 times as long as wide;
            petiolules of terminal leaflets 3.5 mm or more long.
        Leaflets oblong to narrowly elliptic, mostly 2 times or more as long as wide;
            peduncles usually much shorter than subtending leaves. .... 4. *L. capitata*

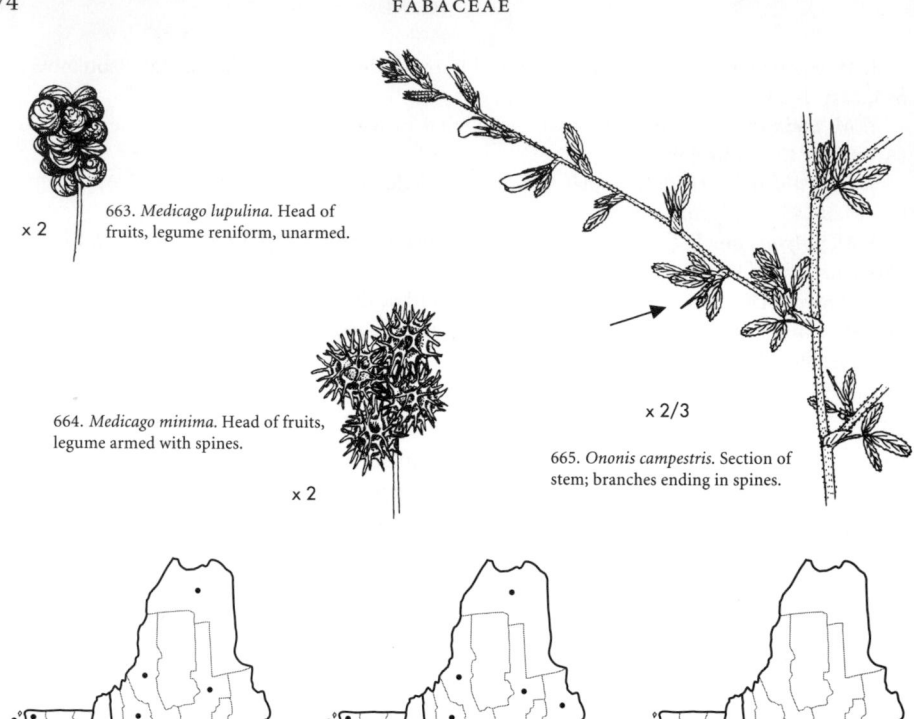

663. *Medicago lupulina.* Head of
fruits, legume reniform, unarmed.

× 2

664. *Medicago minima.* Head of fruits,
legume armed with spines.

× 2

× 2/3

665. *Ononis campestris.* Section of
stem; branches ending in spines.

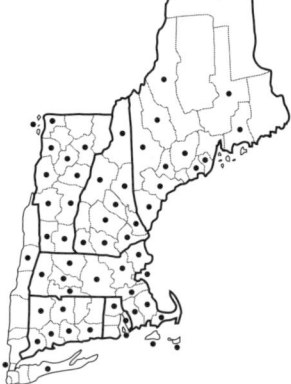

1431. *Medicago sativa*

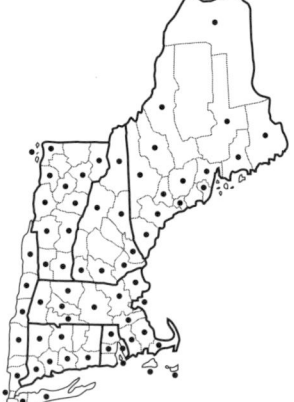

1432. *Medicago lupulina*

1433. *Medicago minima*

1434. *Medicago laciniata*

1435. *Medicago arabica*

1436. *Medicago polymorpha*

Leaflets oval or suborbicular to widely obovate, less than 2 times as long as
wide; peduncles mostly longer than subtending leaves. (Fig. 666). ...... 5. *L. hirta*
b. Petioles mostly more than half as long as lateral leaflets; flowers in loose to
compact racemes but not in dense heads, purplish or bluish; apetalous
flowers often numerous, in sessile axillary clusters. (Fig. 667).
d. Leaflets densely spreading-pubescent beneath; stems spreading-pubescent. .... 6. *L. stuevei*
d. Leaflets appressed-pubescent beneath or glabrous except on midrib; stems
usually appressed-pubescent to glabrate, rarely spreading-pubescent.
e. Leaflets linear to narrowly oblong, 3.5 or more times as long as wide. .... 7. *L. virginica*
e. Leaflets elliptic to oblong, less than 3.5 times as long as wide.
Peduncles of petaliferous racemes longer than subtending leaves. .... 8. *L. violacea*
Peduncles of petaliferous racemes mostly shorter than subtending leaves. . 9. *L. intermedia*

1. *L. procúmbens* Michx. (trailing). Dry open woods, woodland borders, thickets. August-September. Map 1437. Endangered in NH.

2. *L. répens* (L). W. Bart. (creeping). Dry open woods, woodland borders, fields. June-September. Map 1438.

3. *L. angustifólia* (Pursh) Ell. (narrow-leaved). Dry, open, sandy soil along the coast. August-September. Map 1439. —FAC

L. cuneáta (Dum.-Cours.) G. Don. Resembling *L. angustifolia* but differing in having flowers solitary or few in the upper axils (flowers are in spikes in *L. angustifolia*). Spread from cultivation farther south; rarely found in our range. (Naturalized from e. Asia). Reported for CT, Barnstable County MA, Suffolk County NY.

4. *L. capitáta* Michx. (in heads). Fields, thickets, open woods, roadsides. August-September. Map 1440. —FACU-

L. x simuláta Mackenzie & Bush (pro sp.). A hybrid between *L. capitata* and *L. virginica* or *L. intermedia.*

5. *L. hírta* (L.) Hornem. (stiffly-hairy). Dry open woods, woodland borders, fields, roadsides. July-September. Fig. 666, Map 1441. Our plants are subsp. *hirta.*

L. x longifólia DC. (pro sp.). A hybrid between *L. hirta* and *L. capitata.*

L. x nuttállii Darl. (pro sp.). A hybrid between *L. hirta* and *L. intermedia.*

L. x brittónii Bickn. (pro sp.). A hybrid between *L. procumbens* and *L. virginica.*

6. *L. stuévei* Nutt. (for its discoverer). Dry open woods, fields and barrens. August-September. Fig. 667. Map 1442.

7. *L. virgínica* (L.) Britt. (Virginian). Dry open woods and barrens. August-September. Map 1443.

8. *L. violácea* (L.) Pers. (violet). Dry open woods and openings. August-September. Map 1444. [*L. prairea*].

L. thunbérgii (DC.) Nakai. Petaliferous flowers more than 1 cm long; legumes 7 mm or more long (petaliferous flowers 1 cm or less long and legumes mostly less than 7 mm long in *L. violacea*). Spread from cultivation. (Introduced from e. Asia). Reported for MA, Fairfield County CT, Suffolk County NY.

L. bícolor Turcz. A shrub 1-3 m tall similar to *L. thunbergii* but distinguishable in having calyx teeth shorter than the tube (longer than the tube in *L. thunbergii*). Southern. Reported for CT, MA, Columbia County NY.

9. *L. intermédia* (S. Wats.) Britt. (intermediate). Dry open woods, fields and roadsides. July-September. Map 1445. [*L. frutescens*].

L. crytobótrya Miq. Similar to *L. intermedia* but distinguishable in having a corolla 8 mm or more long (corolla 7 mm or less long in *L. intermedia*). Reported for CT, MA.

L. stipulácea Maxim. Will key to *L. intermedia* or possibly *L. repens* but is distinguishable from those species and *L. cyrtobotrya* in having lance-ovate, persistent stipules (stipules are subulate and deciduous or withering in the latter 2 species). Southern. (Naturalized from e. Asia). Reported for the Eastern NY Counties.

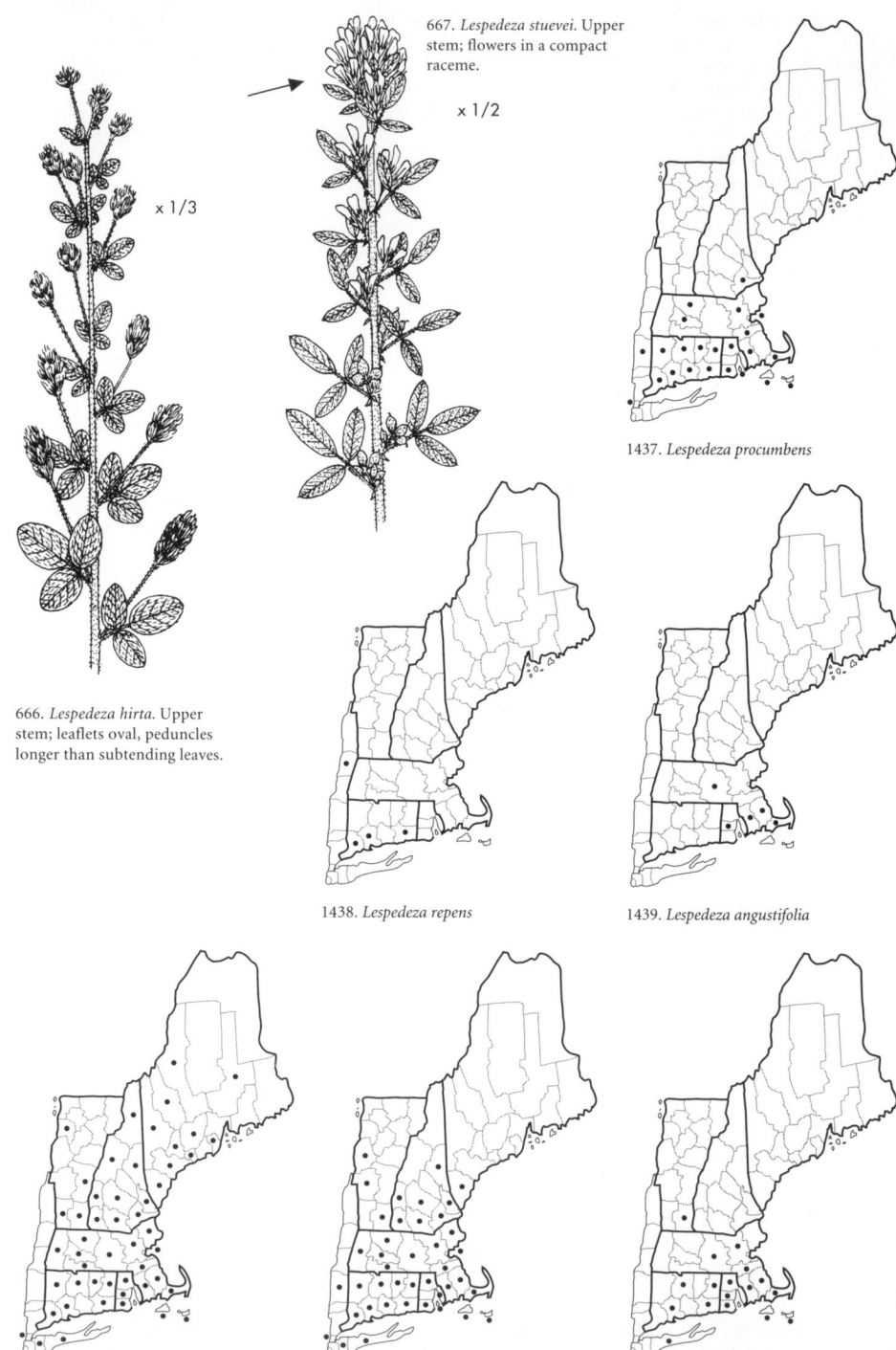

667. *Lespedeza stuevei.* Upper stem; flowers in a compact raceme.

x 1/2

x 1/3

666. *Lespedeza hirta.* Upper stem; leaflets oval, peduncles longer than subtending leaves.

1437. *Lespedeza procumbens*

1438. *Lespedeza repens*

1439. *Lespedeza angustifolia*

1440. *Lespedeza capitata*

1441. *Lespedeza hirta*

1442. *Lespedeza stuevei*

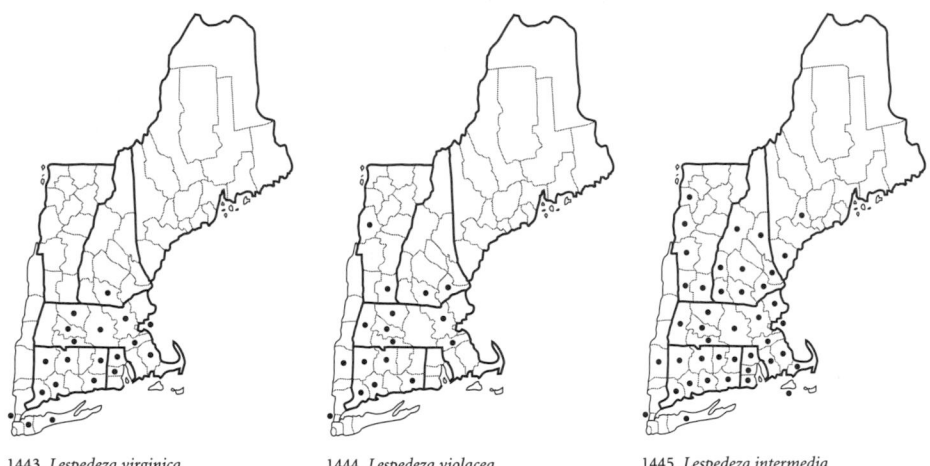

1443. *Lespedeza virginica*   1444. *Lespedeza violacea*   1445. *Lespedeza intermedia*

36. Thermópsis R. Br. ex Ait. f (from the Greek, based on fancied resemblance to Lupine).

Perennial herbs, stems finely appressed-pubescent; leaves digitately 3-foliate, petioled, leaflets rhombic-elliptic, entire, stipules foliaceous; flowers yellow, in terminal, bracteate racemes, papilionaceous, similar to *Baptisia*; legume linear, flat, straight or curved, several-seeded.

1. T. móllis (Michx.) M. A. Curtis ex Gray (soft). Bush pea. Occasional on roadbanks and in waste places. May-June. Map 1446. Our plants are var. *mollis*.

T. villósa (Walt.) Fern. & Schub. Differing from *T. mollis* in having clasping stipules and ovate bracts (stipules not clasping the stem and bracts linear to lanceolate in *T. mollis*). Southern, reported from Walpole, NH, Windham County VT, Middlesex and Hampshire Counties MA, and Dutchess and Columbia Counties NY. [*T. caroliniana*].

T. rhombifólia Nutt. Differing from the latter 2 species in having the ovary long-stipitate within the calyx, the stipe 4 mm or more long, legume strongly recurved, sometimes forming nearly a circle (ovary sessile or short-stipitate, the stipe 3 mm or less long, legume straight or slightly curved in *T. mollis* and *T. villosa*). From the west. Reported for ME.

37. Baptísia Vent. Wild indigo (from the Greek, based on use of some species in dyeing).

Much branched perennial herbs from thick rhizomes, often blackening on drying; leaves digitately 3-foliate or rarely simple, petioled to almost sessile, leaflets obovate to oblanceolate, cuneate, entire, stipules minute and deciduous or larger and persistent; flowers yellow or blue, in terminal racemes, calyx campanulate, bilabiate, the upper lip entire or 2-lobed, lower lip 3-lobed, corolla papilionaceous, stamens 10, distinct; legume inflated, subglobose to ovoid or cylindric, many-seeded.

Corolla blue; legume more than 2 cm long. .... 1. *B. australis*
Corolla yellow; legume less than 2 cm long. .... 2. *B. tinctoria*

1. B. austrális (L.) R. Br. (southern). Blue false indigo. Rarely found around buildings and in open, rocky or gravelly soil. May-June. Map 1447. Our plants are var. *australis*.

2. B. tinctória (L.) R. Br. (used in dyeing). Dry open woods, clearings and fields. June-July. Fig. 668, Map 1448. Endangered in ME. Has been used to treat ulcers; young shoots are used as an asparagus substitute; plant poisonous if ingested in large quantities.

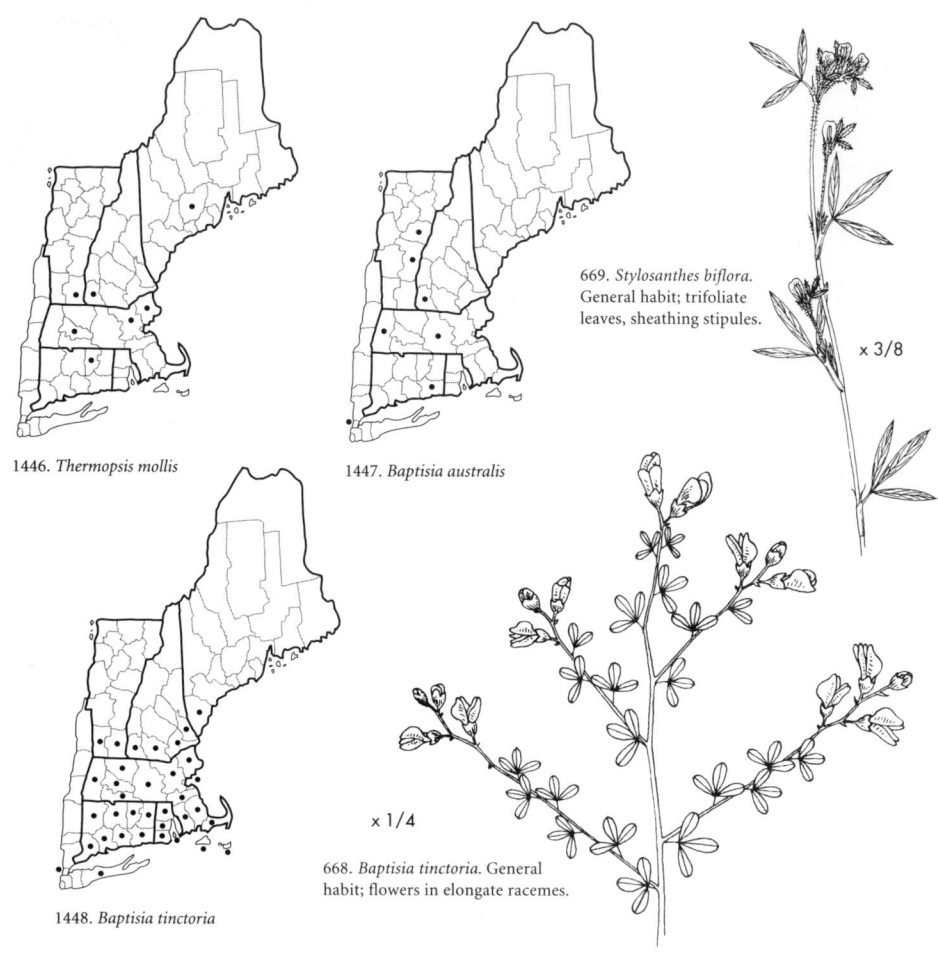

1446. *Thermopsis mollis*

1447. *Baptisia australis*

669. *Stylosanthes biflora.* General habit; trifoliate leaves, sheathing stipules.

× 3/8

× 1/4

668. *Baptisia tinctoria.* General habit; flowers in elongate racemes.

1448. *Baptisia tinctoria*

B. bracteàta Muhl. ex Ell. Plant somewhat pubescent, with persistent bracts 1 cm or more long (plant glabrous, with bracts deciduous and less than 1 cm long in *B. tinctoria*). Western; rarely escaped from cultivation in our range. Reported for Barnstable County MA. Represented with us as var. *leucopháea* (Nutt.) Kartesz & Gandhi. [*B.b.* var *glabrescens; B. leucophaea*].

38. *Stylosánthes* Sw. Pencil-flower (from the Greek, based on the pedicel-like hypanthium).

Erect or ascending to prostrate perennial herbs, with wiry, puberulent to glabrate stems branched from the base; leaves pinnately 3-foliate, short petioled, leaflets narrowly elliptic to lanceolate or oblanceolate, acute and subulate-tipped, entire, stipules adnate to the petiole and sheathing the stem, subulate-tipped; flowers small, yellow, in short, few-flowered, terminal or axillary clusters subtended by an involucre of crowded, usually 1-foliate leaves, these with bristly-ciliate blades and stipules, hypanthium elongate, pedicel-like, calyx tube short, campanulate above the hypanthium, its lobes unequal, one larger than the other 4, the upper 2 partly united, corolla papilionaceous, stamens 10, monadelphous, anthers alternately larger-oblong and smaller-subglobose; legume obliquely ovate, 2-jointed, only the uppermost developing, with a hooked, persistent style, the lowest pedicel-like.

1. S. biflóra (L.) B.S.P. (two-flowered). Dry woods, openings and barrens. June-August. Fig. 669. Reported for Suffolk County NY. [*S. riparia*].

39. Clitória L. Butterfly-pea (based on size of the keel, suggesting the mammalian clitoris).
Trailing or twining to ascending, glabrous, perennial herbs; leaves pinnately 3-foliate, petioled, the leaflets ovate to lanceolate, ovate-oblong or somewhat elliptic, entire, mucronate, stipulate; flowers large and showy, pale blue, solitary or in 2-3-flowered axillary racemes, bracteate, calyx tube cylindric, somewhat bilabiate, the 2 upper teeth partly united, corolla papilionaceous, wings and keel partly united, stamens monadelphous; legume oblong-linear, flattened, several-seeded, 1-celled, dehiscent, the valves longitudinally twisting upon dehiscence.

1. C. mariána L. (of Maryland). Dry, open woods and barrens. June-July (from farther south). Reported for Suffolk County NY. [*Martiusia m.*].

40. Desmódium Desv. Tick-trefoil (from the Greek, based on the connected articles of the loment).
Prostrate, erect, or ascending perennial herbs; leaves pinnately 3 (rarely 1 or 5) foliate, petioled or subsessile, leaflets entire, stipules caducous to persistent, foliaceous to setaceous; flowers small, white or purple, bracteate, in axillary or terminal racemes or panicles, calyx slightly to conspicuously bilabiate, the upper lip variously bifid, the lower usually deeply 3-toothed, corolla papilionaceous, stamens 10, monadelphous or more commonly diadelphous; fruit a loment, transversely segmented, flattened, mostly uncinate-pubescent, separating into 2-many, 1-seeded, indehiscent articles. [*Meibomia*]. —Wildl. 1

a. Leaves approximate at summit of stem (except in occasional forms) the flowers in
    a naked, long-peduncled panicle from the top or on a scape from the base,
    this usually naked or with 1-3 distant leaves; stamens monadelphous, their
    persistent remains exceeded by the loment stipe. (Fig. 670).
    Inflorescence terminating the leafy stem. .... 1. *D. glutinosum*
    Inflorescence borne on a usually leafless stem arising from the base. (Fig. 670) ...... 2. *D. nudiflorum*
a. Leaves uniformly scattered on stem from near base to apex; stamens diadelphous
    (9 and 1), their persistent remains exceeding the loment stipe (except
    sometimes in *D. laevigatum*).
  b. Plant trailing or prostrate.
    Terminal leaflets rhombic-ovate to suborbicular, as wide as long or wider. .... 3. *D. rotundifolium*
    Terminal leaflets ovate to rhombic-ovate, about 2 or more times as long
        as wide .... 4. *D. humifusum*
  b. Plant erect or ascending.
    c. Stipules ovate-attenuate, persistent, usually 4 mm or more wide. (Fig. 671). ...... 5. *D. canescens*
    c. Stipules setaceous to lanceolate, often promptly deciduous, less than 4 mm wide.
      d. Terminal leaflet 1.5 cm or less wide, 4 or more times as long as wide.
        Leaves subsessile, the longest petioles 4 mm or less long; flowers mostly
          less than 6 mm long; loment articles 3 or fewer. .... 6. *D. sessilifolium*
        Leaves with petioles more than 1 cm long; flowers 6 mm or more long;
          loment articles 4 or more. .... 7. *D. paniculatum*
      d. Terminal leaflet wider than 1.5 cm or less than 4 times as long as wide.
        e. Stem glabrous or essentially so (inconspicuously puberulent and sparsely
          pilose in *D. glabellum*); loment articles 3 or more, the lower suture
          abruptly angular, flowers mostly 6 mm or more long (except
          D. marilandicum). (Fig. 672).
          f. Terminal leaflets (mature) mostly 3 cm or less long; loment articles
            1-3, the lower suture gradually curved; flowers 4-6 mm long. .... 8. *D. marilandicum*
          f. Terminal leaflets longer than 3 cm; loment articles 3 or more, the lower
            suture abruptly angular; flowers 6-12 mm long.
            g. Leaflets lanceolate-ovate, usually 3 or more times as long as wide. ...... 7. *D. paniculatum*
            g. Leaflets ovate, oblong or elliptic, usually less than 3 times as long
              as wide.

Leaflets moderately to densely short-pubescent at least beneath. .... 9. *D. glabellum*
Leaflets glabrous to sparsely pubescent along the veins.
  Bracts of inflorescence at anthesis more than 5 mm long;
    mature loment articles more than 7 mm long; pedicels
    7 mm or less long. .... 10. *D. cuspidatum*
  Bracts of inflorescence at anthesis less than 5 mm long; mature
    loment articles 7 mm or less long; pedicels 8 mm or
    more long. .... 11. *D. laevigatum*
e. Stem distinctly pubescent; loment articles 1-3, flowers 6 mm or less long
    (except *D. canadense, D. perplexum* and *D. viridiflorum*); lower
    suture of articles gradually curved (except *D. perplexum* and
    sometimes *D. viridiflorum*).
  h. Terminal leaflets (mature) mostly 3 cm or less long, and/or less than
      2 times as long as wide .... 12. *D. ciliare*
  h. Terminal leaflets mostly longer than 3 cm and/or more than 2 times
      as long as wide.
    i. Racemes densely flowered, the flowers overlapping; bracts at anthesis
        lance-ovate; loment articles 3 or more, the lower suture
        gradually curved. (Fig. 673) .... 13. *D. canadense*
    i. Racemes loosely flowered, the flowers (except sometimes the
        terminal) well-spaced; bracts at anthesis absent or setaceous;
        loment articles 3 or fewer or the lower suture abruptly angled.
      Petioles (at least the lower and middle) mostly 2.5 cm or more
          long; loment segments 3 or more or the lower suture
          abruptly angled. .... 14. *D. perplexum*
      Petioles mostly less than 2.5 cm long; loment segments 3 or
          fewer, the lower suture gradually curved .... 15. *D. obtusum*

1. *D. glutinósum* (Muhl. ex Willd.) Wood (glutinous). Rich woods. July-September. Map 1449. [*D. acuminatum; D. grandiflorum*].

2. *D. nudiflórum* (L.) DC. (with naked flowering scape). Rich, dry woods. August-September. Fig. 670, Map 1450.

3. *D. rotundifólium* DC. (round-leaved). Rich or dry, often rocky woods. August-September. Map 1451. [*Meibomia michauxii*].

4. *D. humifúsum* (Muhl. ex Bigelow) Beck (spread on the ground). Dry woods. July-August. Map 1452. Endangered in MA, CT. [*D. glabellum*].

5. *D. canéscens* (L.) DC. (gray or hoary). Fields, waste places, dry woods. August-September. Fig. 671, Map 1453.

6. *D. sessilifólium* (Torr.) Torr. & Gray (with sessile leaves). Roadsides, in sandy soil. August-September. Map 1454. Endangered in RI.

D. strictum (Pursh) DC. Similar to *D. sessilifolium* but leaves with petioles 4 mm or more long (leaves subsessile, the petioles 4 mm or less long in *D. sessilifolium*). From farther south along the coastal plain. Reported for MA.

7. *D. paniculátum* (L.) DC. (paniculate). Dry woods, woodland borders and fields. August-September. Map 1455. Our plants are var. *paniculatum*.

8. *D. marilándicum* (L.) DC. (of Maryland). Dry woods, thickets, woodland borders, fields. August-September. Map 1456. Endangered in NH.

9. *D. glabéllum* (Michx.) DC. Dry fields and open woods. July-August. From farther south. Reported for CT, MA.

10. *D. cuspidátum* (Muhl. ex Willd.) DC. (ex Loud.) (made pointed). Dry woods, woodland borders, roadsides. August-September. Fig. 672, Map 1457. Endangered in VT. [*D. bracteosum; D. grandiflorum*]. Our plants are var. *cuspidatum*.

11. *D. laevigátum* (Nutt.) DC. (smooth). Dry woods, woodland borders, fields, roadsides. July-August. Reported for Suffolk County NY.

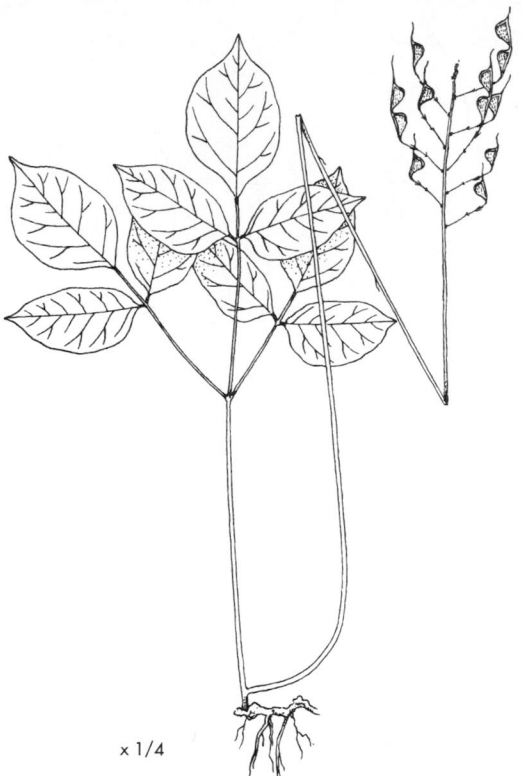

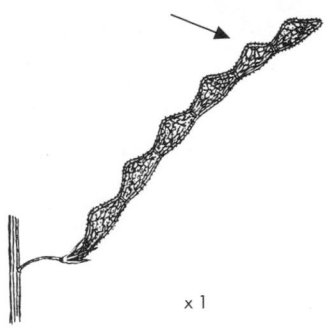

672. *Desmodium cuspidatum.* Single loment, lower suture of articles abruptly angular.

× 1/4

670. *Desmodium nudiflorum.* General habit; leaves approximate at suumit of stem, inflorescence on a scape from the base.

1449. *Desmodium glutinosum*

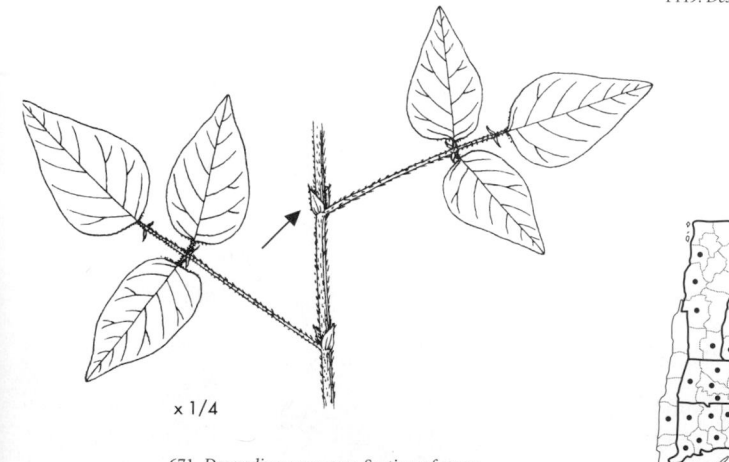

× 1/4

671. *Desmodium canescens.* Section of stem; leaves with ovate-attenuate stipules.

1450. *Desmodium nudiflorum*

FABACEAE

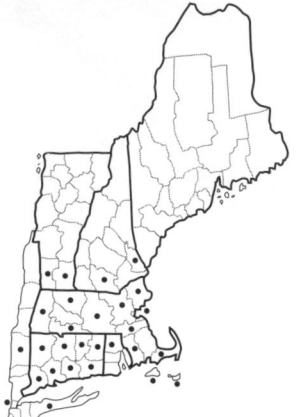

1451. *Desmodium rotundifolium*

1452. *Desmodium humifusum*

1453. *Desmodium canescens*

1454. *Desmodium sessilifolium*

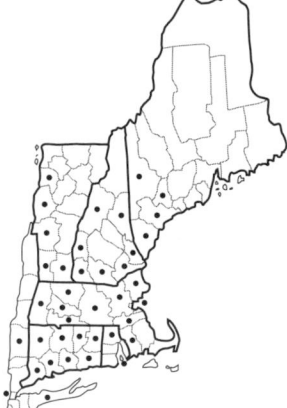

1455. *Desmodium paniculatum*

1456. *Desmodium marilandicum*

1457. *Desmodium cuspidatum*

1458. *Desmodium ciliare*

12. D. ciliáre (Muhl. ex Willd.) DC. (ciliate). Dry woods, woodland borders, fields, roadsides. August-September. Map 1458. (W.I.). [*D. obtusum*]. Our plants are var. *ciliare.*

13. D. canadénse (L.) DC. (of Canada). Dry woods, riverbanks, thickets, roadsides. July-September. Fig. 673, Map 1459. —FAC

14. D. perpléxum Schub. Dry woods, fields and roadsides. August-September. Map 1460. [*D. dillenii; D. glabellum*].

D. viridiflórum (L.). DC. Similar to *D. perplexum* but is distinguishable in having terminal leaflets velvety-tomentose beneath (terminal leaflets glabrous to pubescent beneath but not velvety tomentose in *D. perplexum*). From farther south and west. Reported for Kings and Bronx Counties NY. [*D. nuttallii*].

15. D. obtúsum (Muhl. ex Willd.) DC. Dry woods and thickets. August-September. Map 1461. Endangered in NH. [*D. rigidum*].

41. Strophostýles Ell. Wild Bean (from the Greek, referring to the curved style).

Trailing, twining or weakly climbing, branching, pubescent or glabrous, annual or perennial herbaceous vines; leaves pinnately 3-foliate, petioled, the leaflets ovate or oblong to elliptic, often basally lobed on one or both sides, entire, stipules small, persistent; flowers pink-purple to white, few to several, bracteate, in capitate clusters on long, axillary peduncles, calyx tube campanulate, more or less bilabiate, appearing 4-lobed through fusion of the 2 upper lobes, the lowermost lobe the longest, corolla papilionaceous, the keel beaked and strongly curved, stamens diadelphous, style curved, bearded along the inner side; legume linear, nearly terete, straight, with several woolly seeds, 1-celled, the valves twisted after dehiscence.

Calyx tube and bractlets glabrous or nearly so; flowers 8 mm or more long.
    Bractlets lanceolate, acute, equalling or exceeding the sinuses of the calyx tube;
        peduncle usually 4 times or less as long as the subtending petiole; leaflets
        often lobed .... 1. *S. helvula*
    Bractlets ovate or oblong, obtuse, reaching up to 2/3 the distance to the sinuses
        of the calyx tube; peduncle usually 4.5 or more times as long as the
        subtending petiole; leaflets unlobed .... 2. *S. umbellata*
Calyx tube and bractlets densely pubescent; flowers 8 mm or less long. .... 3. *S. leiosperma*

1. S. hélvula (L.) Ell. (yellowish). Dry thickets and waste places near the coast. July-September. Map 1462. [*S. helveola; S. missouriensis*]. —FACU-

2. S. umbelláta (Muhl. ex Willd.) Britt. (umbelled). Dry woods and fields near the coast. July-September. Reported for Washington County RI. —FACU

3. S. leiospérma (T. & G.) Piper (smooth-seeded). Dry woods, dunes and shores. July-September. Reported for CT. [*S. pauciflora*].

42. Puerária DC (for W. Puerari).

Climbing, twining, half woody vines, the young stems pubescent; leaves pinnately trifoliate, petioled, leaflets large, ovate to rotund, entire or 2-3 lobed, abruptly acuminate, stipules sagittate-auriculate; flowers reddish-purple, in dense, axillary, bracteate, densely pubescent, racemes or panicles, calyx tube campanulate, 4 lobed through fusion of the 2 upper lobes, the lowest lobe the longest, corolla papilionaceous, the wings cohering to the keel, stamens monadelphous, one stamen free at the base; legume linear-oblong, compressed, several-seeded, pubescent, dehiscent.

1. P. montána (Lour.) Merr. Kudzu-vine. Fields, woodland borders, roadsides and waste places. Spreading to the northeast from the southeast. August-September. Reported for Fairfield County CT, Plymouth County MA. [*P. lobata; P. thunbergii*]. Represented with us as var. lobáta (Willd.) Maesen & S. Almedia.

43. Amphicárpaea Ell. ex Nutt. Hog-peanut (from the Greek, based on the two kinds of fruit produced).

Twining, climbing, perennial, herbaceous vine, the slender stems sparsely to densely pubescent; leaves pinnately trifoliate, petioled, the leaflets ovate to rhombic-ovate, entire, stipules persistent; plants producing both petaliferous, and apetalous-cleistogamous flowers, the petaliferous flowers purplish to white, in bracteate racemes from the upper axils, calyx tube narrowly campanulate, appearing 4-lobed through fusion of the 2 upper lobes, corolla papilionaceous, stamens diadelphous; apetalous flowers inconspicuous, in racemes from the lower axils and solitary at the ends of long, filiform branches, stamens few, free; legume of petaliferous flowers oblong-linear, flattened, several-seeded, the valves twisted after dehiscence, legume of cleistogamous flowers fleshy, indehiscent, those solitary on the long, filiform branches, often subterranean. (*Amphicarpa*). —Wildl. 1

1. **A. bracteáta** (L.) Fern. (bracted). Rich woods and thickets. July-September. Fig. 674, Map 1463. [*A. monoica; A. pitcheri*]. Fruits produced by the cleistogamous flowers are edible, resembling a pea. —FAC

44. Glycíne L. (sweet).

Erect, bushy-branched, densely pubescent annual herbs; leaves pinnately trifoliate, petioled, stipulate, leaflets ovate, entire; flowers small, purple, pink or white, bracteate, in axillary fascicles or racemes, calyx densely pubescent, the upper 2 lobes united, corolla papilionaceous, wings adherent to the keel, stamens monadelphous or becoming diadelphous; legumes pendulous, oblong, compressed, densely pubescent, few-seeded, septate, dehiscent.

1. **G. máx** (L.) Merr. (old name). Soy-bean. Occasionally escaped from cultivation to fields, roadsides and waste places. August-September. Map 1464. (Introduced from e. Asia). Widely cultivated for food.

45. Phaséolus L. (ancient name for the Kidney-Bean).

Twining or trailing to ascending or erect, finely pubescent, annual or perennial herbs; leaves pinnately 3-foliate, petioled, the leaflets ovate to rhombic-ovate, abruptly acuminate, entire, stipulate; flowers blue, in elongate, loose, axillary racemes, these simple or often branched at the base, bracteate, calyx tube campanulate, with 5 subequal lobes, the 2 upper sometimes partly united and shorter than the others, corolla papilionaceous, wings cohering to the spirally coiled keel petals, stamens diadelphous, style coiled and bearded along the upper surface; legume terete to compressed, straight or curved, few to several-seeded, 1-celled, dehiscent.

Dólichos L. *láblab* L. Hyacinth Bean. Similar to *Phaseolus* but is distinguishable in having 4 calyx lobes and incurved keel petals (calyx lobes 5 and keel petals coiled in *Phaseolus*). Rarely escaped from cultivation. Reported for Westchester County NY.

Stem twining or trailing; plant perennial. .... 1. *P. polystachios*
Stem ascending or erect, bushy-branched; plant annual. .... 2. *P. vulgaris*

1. **P. polystáchios** (L.) B.S.P. (many-spiked). Wild Bean. Deciduous or coniferous woods and thickets. July-August. Fig. 675, Map 1465. Our plants are var. *polystachios*. The seeds can be prepared as in the domestic variety.

2. **P. vulgáris** L. (common) var. *húmilis* Alef. (low). Bush Bean. Rarely spread from cultivation to waste places and around buildings. Map 1466. Preparations made from the seeds are reported to be of value in treating skin disorders such as eczema and ulcerations when externally applied.

P. coccíneus L. Scarlet Runner. Rarely spread from cultivation and apparently not persisting in our range. Reported for Middlesex County MA.

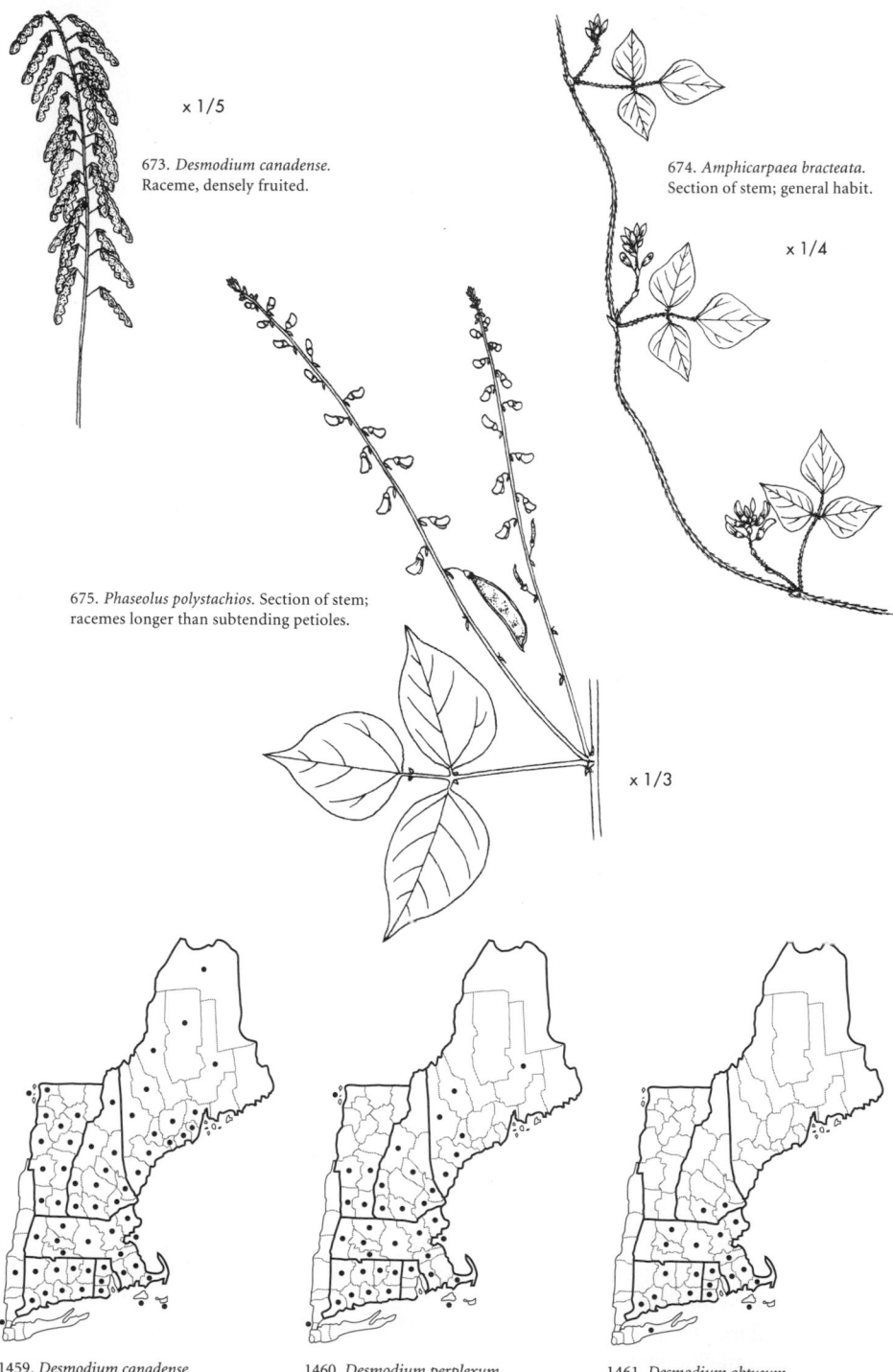

x 1/5

673. *Desmodium canadense.*
Raceme, densely fruited.

674. *Amphicarpaea bracteata.*
Section of stem; general habit.

x 1/4

675. *Phaseolus polystachios.* Section of stem;
racemes longer than subtending petioles.

x 1/3

1459. *Desmodium canadense*

1460. *Desmodium perplexum*

1461. *Desmodium obtusum*

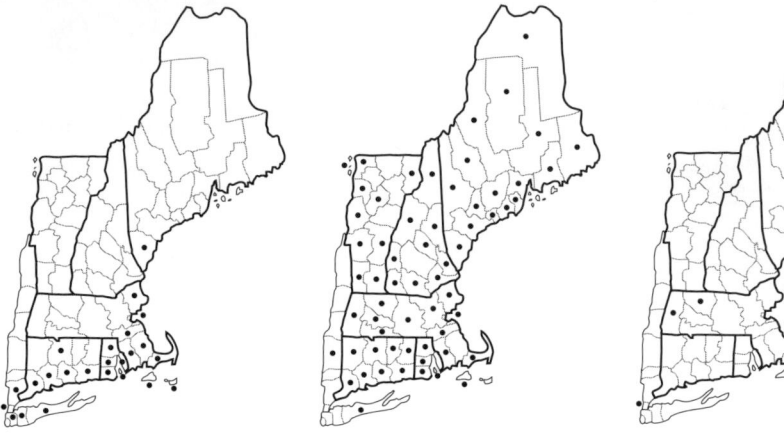

1462. *Strophostyles helvula*   1463. *Amphicarpaea bracteata*   1464. *Glycine max*

1465. *Phaseolus polystachios*   1466. *Phaseolus vulgaris*

46. *Galáctia* P. Br. Milk-pea (milky).

Trailing or twining, pubescent to glabrous, perennial herbs; leaves pinnately trifoliate, petioled, leaflets elliptic to ovate-oblong or narrowly oblong, entire, stipules small and deciduous; flowers purplish, in loose or dense, bracteate, axillary racemes, borne solitary or 2-3 at a node, calyx nearly regular, 4-lobed through fusion of the 2 upper lobes, corolla papilionaceous, stamens diadelphous; legume oblong-linear, flattened, several-seeded, the valves twisted after dehiscence.

Stems twining; flowers up to 12 mm long. .... 1. *G. volubilis*
Stems trailing, sometimes twining at the tip; flowers 12 mm or more long. .... 2. *G. regularis*

    1. *G. volúbilis* (L.) Britt. (twining). Dry open woods, woodland borders and thickets. July-August. Reported for Bronx and Suffolk Counties NY.
    2. *G. reguláris* (L.) B.S.P. (according to rule). Dry open woods and barrens. July-August. Reported for Suffolk County NY. [*G. glabella*].

Family 110. Lináceae (Flax Family)

Hermaphrodite, annual or perennial, fibrous herbs. Leaves alternate or opposite, simple, sessile, narrow, entire, estipulate, often with glands in place of stipules. Flowers perfect, regular, usually numerous, in a leafy panicle of racemes or cymes, regular, calyx of 4-5 separate sepals imbricated in an outer and an inner series, corolla of 4-5 petals, sometimes early deciduous, fertile stamens 4-5, monadelphous at the base, sometimes alternating with as many toothlike staminodes, pistil 1, superior, 4-5-carpellate, each carpel completely or partly divided at maturity, the pistil then appearing 8-10-carpellate, each locule with 2 ovules, styles 4-5. Fruit an 8-10-locular, septicidal capsule surrounded by the persistent calyx.

Flowers 5-merous; sepals entire or ciliate; plants 1 dm or more tall. .... 1. *Linum*
Flowers 4-merous; sepals 3-lobed; plants less than 1 dm tall. .... 2. *Radiola linoides*

1. *Línum* L. Flax. (classical name of flax). Parts of flower all in 5s. [*Cathartolinum*].

a. Petals blue; capsule 5 mm or more long.
   Sepals acuminate, the inner ciliate; leaves distinctly 3-nerved; plant annual,
      stems solitary .... 1. *L. usitatissimum*
   Sepals obtuse, mucronate, eciliate; leaves obscurely nerved at the base; plant
      perennial, stems clustered .... 2. *L. lewisii*
a. Petals yellow or white; capsule less than 4 mm long.
  b. Outer as well as inner sepals glandular-ciliate. (Fig. 676).
    Leaves all or mostly alternate; petals yellow; lower pedicels 1 cm or more long .. 3. *L. sulcatum*
    Leaves all or mostly opposite; petals white; lower pedicels less than 1 cm long ... 4. *L. catharticum*
  b. Outer sepals (and the inner in some species) not glandular-ciliate. (Fig. 677).
    c. Inner sepals entire, or ciliate with eglandular hairs; glandular hairs, if present,
      very few and promptly deciduous.
    Inflorescence corymbosely branched; all but the lowest leaves alternate; stem
      usually with one wing decurrent from each leaf base. .... 5. *L. virginianum*
    Inflorescence paniculately branched; all but the upper leaves opposite; stem
      usually with 3 wings decurrent from each leaf base. .... 6. *L. striatum*
    c. Inner sepals distinctly glandular-ciliate.
      Capsule beaked, the individual carpels sharp pointed. .... 7. *L. intercursum*
      Capsule beakless, the individual carpels blunt. .... 8. *L. medium*
                var. *texanum*

1. *L. usitatíssimum* L. (most useful). Common flax. Fields, roadsides, railroads, waste places. June-September. Map 1467. (Introduced from Europe). [*L. humile*]. Source of commercial flax from which linen is made and linseed oil from the seeds. Various medicinal uses are also cited. Waste materials are used as fattening foods for livestock, but immature or wilted plants are said to cause poisoning.

2. *L. lewísii* Pursh. Grasslands. June-July. From farther west. Reported for ME. [*L. perenne* var. *l.*]. Our plants are var. *lewisii*. Seeds were cooked and eaten by Indians.

3. *L. sulcátum* Riddell (furrowed). Dry roadsides, fields and upland woods. July-September. Fig. 676, Map 1468. Endangered in RI. [*Cathartolinum s.*]. Our plants are var. *sulcatum*.

4. *L. cathárticum* L. (cathartic). Fields and roadsides. July-August. Rare; from Europe. Map 1469. [*L. pratense; Cathartolinum c.*].

5. *L. virginiánum* L. (Virginian). Dry roadsides, fields and upland woods. July-August. Map 1470. [*Cathartolinum v.*]. —FACU

6. *L. striátum* Walt. (furrowed). Wet meadows, pond margins, bogs, damp open woods. June-August. Map 1471. [*Cathartolinum s.*]. —FACW

7. *L. intercúrsum* Bickn. (running between). Dry beaches and barrens. June-August. Map 1472. Endangered in RI. [*Cathartolinum i.*].

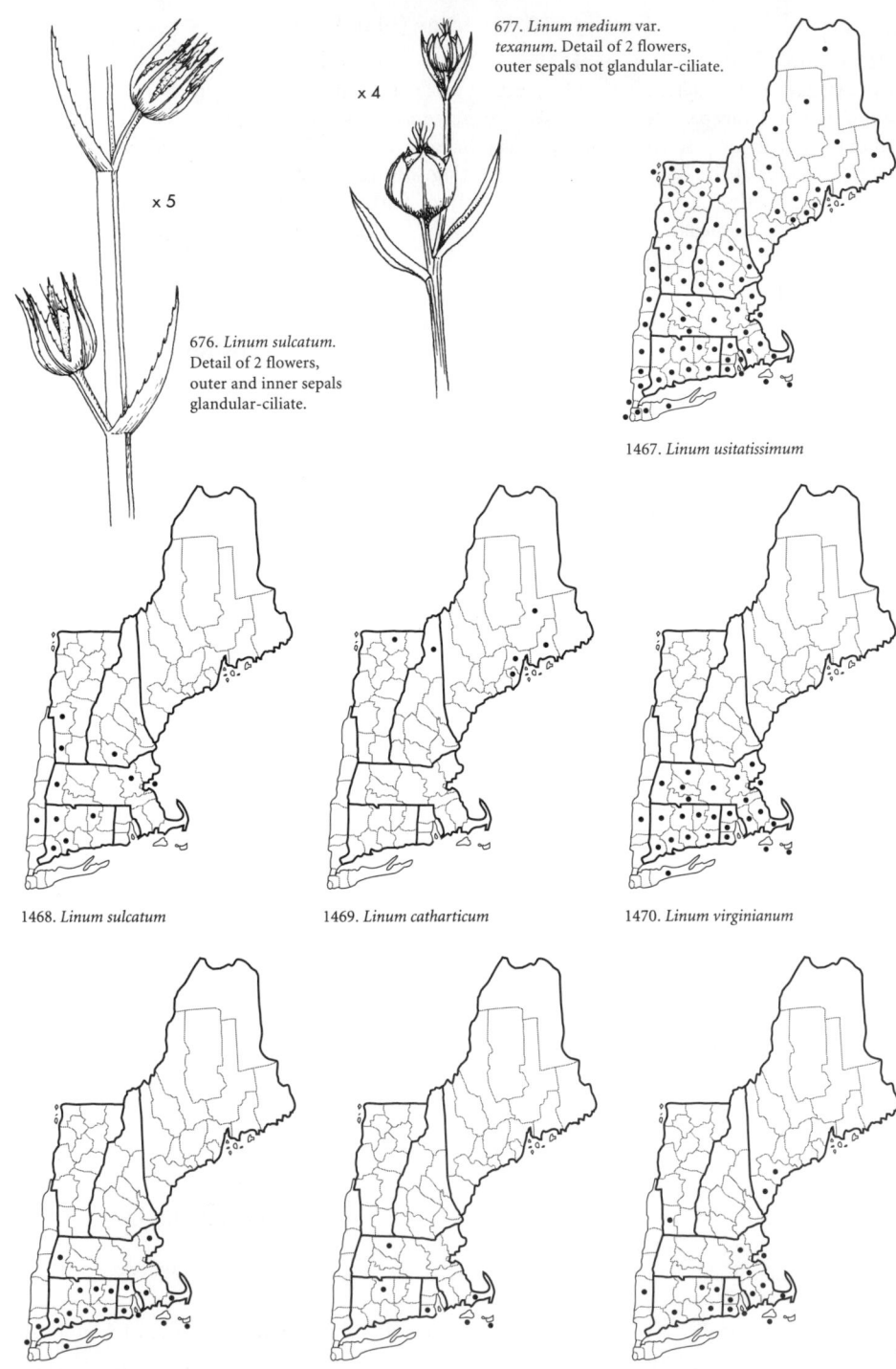

676. *Linum sulcatum.*
Detail of 2 flowers,
outer and inner sepals
glandular-ciliate.

× 5

× 4

677. *Linum medium* var.
texanum. Detail of 2 flowers,
outer sepals not glandular-ciliate.

1467. *Linum usitatissimum*

1468. *Linum sulcatum*

1469. *Linum catharticum*

1470. *Linum virginianum*

1471. *Linum striatum*

1472. *Linum intercursum*

1473. *Linum medium* var. *texanum*

8. L. médium (Planch.) Britt. (intermediate). Dry fields, roadsides and open woods. June-August. Fig. 677; Map 1473. Represented with us as var. *texánum* (Planch.) Fern. [*Cathartolinum m.*]. —FACU

L. floridánum (Planch.) Trel. Similar to *L. medium* but with an ovoid capsule (capsule subglabose in *L. medium*). From farther south. Reported for CT. [*Cathartolinum f.*]. Our plants are var. *floridanum.* —FAC

2. Radióla Hill Druce. Tiny annual; parts of flower all in 4s.

1. R. linoídes Roth. Fields and ditches near the coast, from Europe. July-August. Rare. Reported for Knox County Me. [*Millegrana radiola*].

Family 111. Oxalidáceae (Wood-sorrel Family)

Hermaphrodite, caulescent or acaulescent, trailing or erect, annual or perennial herbs, often with rhizomes, stolons or bulbs, the sap sour. Leaves alternate or basal, petioled, ternately compound with obcordate leaflets, these often folded back, estipulate. Flowers perfect, regular, pedunculate, in bracteate umbels, cymes or solitary, calyx of 5, persistent, imbricated sepals, corolla of 5 petals, separate or basally connate, stamens 10, of 2 lengths, usually united at the base, hypogynous, ovary superior, 5-carpelled, 5-locular, each locule with 2 or more ovules, styles 5. Fruit a loculicidal capsule.

1. Óxalis L. Wood-sorrel. (Greek name for sorrel).

Same characters as the family. The various species are used sparingly in salads, but are poisonous in large doses due to the presence of oxalic acid. —Wildl. 1

a. Plants acaulescent, the leaves and scapes basal; flowers white, pink or purple.
    Peduncles 1-flowered; sepals not callous-tipped; from a slender rhizome. .... 1. *O. montana*
    Peduncles 2-several flowered; sepals with callous-tips; from a scaly bulb. .... 2. *O. violacea*
a. Plants caulescent; flowers yellow or greenish.
  b. Stems creeping, rooting at the nodes. .... 3. *O. corniculata*
  b. Stems erect or decumbent but not creeping and rooting at the nodes.
    Inflorescence cymose, the lateral branches often only bracteate by abortion
    of the lateral flowers; hairs of the stem and petioles often septate.
    (Fig. 678). .... 4. *O. stricta*
    Inflorescence umbellate, rarely with an occasional cymose branch; hairs of the
    stem and petioles nonseptate .... 5. *O. dillenii*

   1. O. montána Raf. (of the mountains). Rich, moist woods. June-August. Map 1474. [*O. acetocella*]. —FAC-
   2. O. violácea L. (violet). Rich, moist to dry woods. May-June. Map 1475. [*Ionoxalis v.*]. Reported to be of value in treating cancerous growths on the lips, boils and abscesses; also said to have an astringent effect on wounds.
   3. O. corniculáta L. (horned). Roadsides, waste places, and around gardens and greenhouses. July-August. Map 1476. [*O. repens; Xanthoxalis c.*]. —FACU
   4. O. stricta L. (erect). Fields, roadsides, waste places, cultivated soil. June-August. Fig. 678, Map 1477. [*O. corniculata; O. europaea; Xanthoxalis s.; X. bushii; X cymosa; X. rufa*].
   5. O. dillénii Jacq. Fields, roadsides, waste places, cultivated soil. June-July. Map 1478. [*O. florida; O. stricta; Xanthoxalis brittoniae; X. colorea*]. Our plants include subsp. *dillenii* and the following subsp.:
    subsp. *fílipes* (Small.) Eiten. Lourteig. Pubescence of lower stems appressed or none, styles about 2 mm long (pubescence of lower stems spreading, styles 3-4 mm long in subsp. *dillenii*). [*O. dillenii* subsp. *prostrata; O. filipes*].

678. *Oxalis stricta*. Cymose
inflorescence.

x 3/8

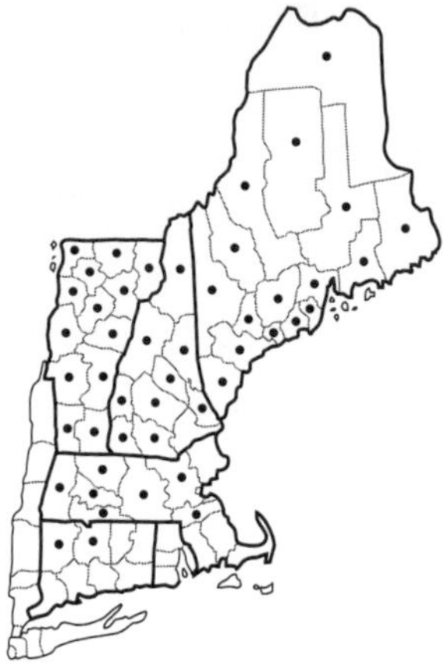

1474. *Oxalis montana*

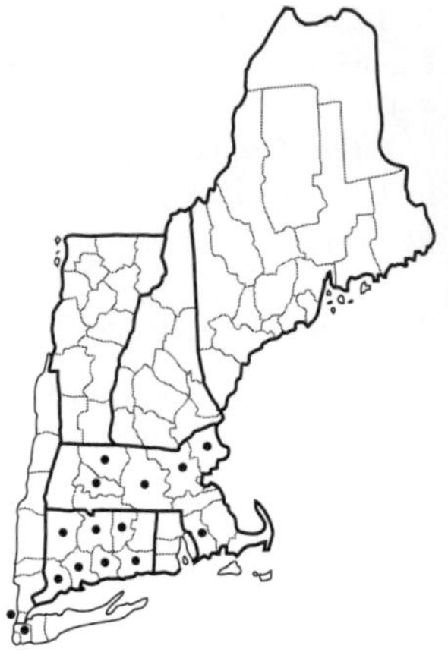

1475. *Oxalis violacea*

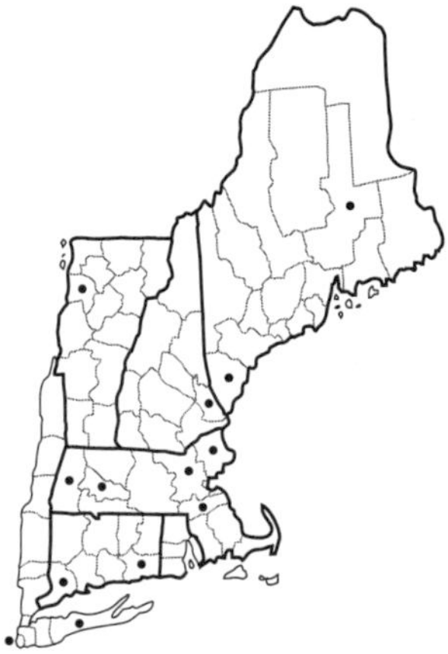

1476. *Oxalis corniculata*

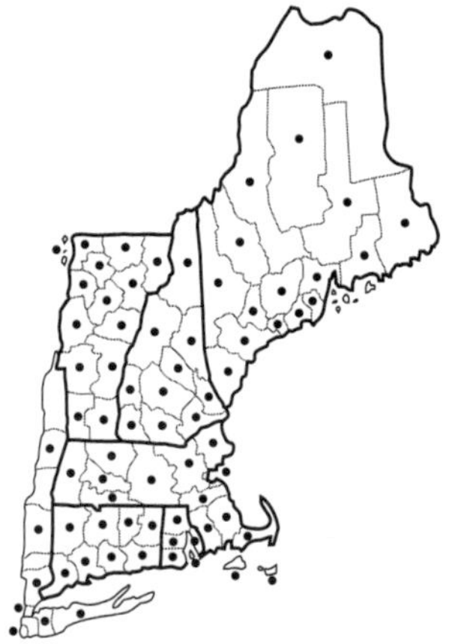

1477. *Oxalis stricta*

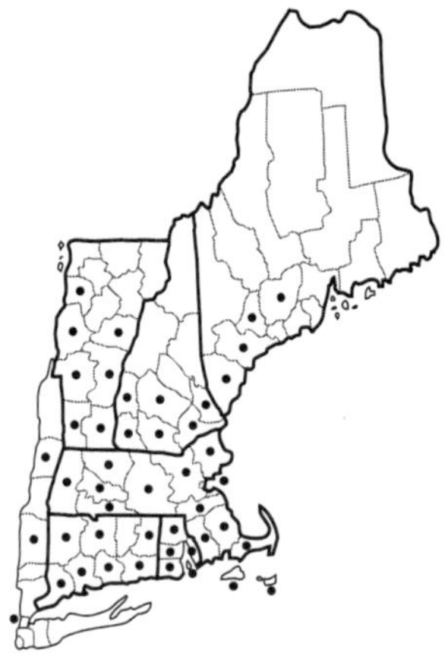

1478. *Oxalis dillenii*

Family 112. Geraniáceae (Geranium Family)

Hermaphrodite, annual or perennial herbs with erect, spreading or procumbent stems. Leaves basal, alternate or opposite, petioled, palmately or pinnately dissected or compound, stipulate. Flowers perfect, regular or nearly so, often paired at the summit of axillary peduncles or umbellate, bracteate, sepals and petals each 5, distinct, the petals alternating with 5 glands at the base, stamens 10, often connate at the base, the inner whorl often sterile, pistil 5-lobed, ovary superior, the axis prolonged into a long beak, carpels 5, each 1-locular, ovules 2 in each locule, styles 5. Fruit a capsule, septicidally dehiscing into 5 mericarps, the long styles adhering to the ovarian beak toward the tip, the basal portions coiling outwardly or spirally, each mericarp 1-seeded, remaining attached to the style or not.

Leaves pinnately dissected or compound. (Fig. 679). .... 1. *Erodium*
Leaves palmately dissected or compound. (Fig. 680). .... 2. *Geranium*

1. Eródium L'Her ex Ait. Stork's bill (from the Greek, based on the long beak of the fruit).

Small, annual or biennial; leaves basal or alternate, opposite when subtending peduncles, pinnately dissected or compound; flowers pink or purple, in axillary umbels, petals slightly unequal, 2 smaller than the others, stamens 10, 5 fertile and 5 sterile; styles of mericarps separating from the ovarian beak from the tip downward, eventually completely free, spirally twisted below when free.

a. Leaves not divided to the rachis or if so then rachis winged.
  b. Leaves cleft about halfway to the rachis into wide lobes.
    Lobes of leaves acute .... 1. *E. botrys*
    Lobes of leaves rounded or leaves undivided, merely crenate. .... 2. *E. malacoides*
  b. Leaves cleft nearly or quite to the rachis into narrow lobes, the rachis winged or
    with projecting lobes of tissue.
    Rachis with projecting lobes of tissue between the lobes. .... 3. *E. ciconium*
    Rachis with narrowly cuneate wings connecting the lobes. .... 4. *E. stephenianum*
a. Leaves divided to the rachis into distinct, separate leaflets, the rachis not winged.
    Leaf pinnae sessile, deeply cleft to beyond the middle; awns of sepals terminated
      with 1 or 2 bristles equal to it in length. (Fig. 679). .... 5. *E. cicutarium*
    Leaf pinnae short stalked, less deeply cleft to merely toothed or lobed; awns of
      sepals terminated with a very short bristle or bristle absent. .... 6. *E. moschatum*
                           var. *praecox*

    1. E. bótrys (Cav.) Bertol. Rarely escaped from cultivation. Reported for ME, Middlesex and Norfolk Counties MA, Chittenden County VT.

    E. laciniánum (Cav.) Willd. Similar to *E. botrys* but with stems retrorsely pubescent with short hairs (stems with spreading pubescence in *E. botrys*). Reported for MA.

    2. E. malacoídes (L.) L'Her. European. Rarely found as a waif in our range. Reported for Essex County MA.

    3. E. cicónium (L.) L'Her. Mediterranean. Rarely found as a waif in our range. Reported for MA.

    4. E. stepheniánum Willd. European. Rarely found as a waif in our range. Reported for MA.

    E. cygnórum Nees. Will key to *E. stephenianum*; leaves somewhat cordate at base, 3-5-parted into cuneate-lobed divisions, stipules ovate, petals blue, 7-8 mm long. From the southwest. Reported for MA.

    5. E. cicutárium (L.) L'Her ex Ait. (like *Cicuta*). Sandy waste places, roadsides. May-October. Fig. 679, Map 1479. (Naturalized from Europe). Young leaves can be used in salad.

    6. E. moschátum (L.) L'Her ex Ait. (with smell of musk). Waste places. May-October. From Europe. Map 1480. (Adventive from Europe). Represented with us as var. *práecox* Lange.

    E. grúinum (L.) L'Her. Differing from the above species in having the lower leaves undivided and the upper divided into 3 toothed and/or lobed leaflets (leaves pinnatifid or pinnately compound in the above species). Mediterranean. Reported for Westchester County NY.

2. Geránium L. Wild Geranium (from the Greek, based on fancied resemblance of the fruiting beak to a crane's bill).

Annual or perennial; leaves basal or opposite, palmately lobed, dissected or compound; flowers pink or purple, paired, on axillary peduncles, stamens 10, all fertile; styles of mericarp separating from the base upward, coiling backward and remaining attached at the tip to the ovarian beak.

a. Leaves divided to the petiole into 3-5 distinct leaflets, at least the terminal one with
    a distinct petiolule. (Fig. 680). .... 1. *G. robertianum*
a. Leaves divided but not to the petiole into distinct leaflets.
  b. Petals 1.3 cm or more long; perennial from rhizomes or with separate stems
    from a single crown.
    Peduncles, pedicels, calyx and style column stipitate-glandular. .... 2. *G. pratense*
    Peduncles, pedicels, calyx and style column eglandular or essentially so. .... 3. *G. maculatum*

    b. Petals less than 1.3 cm long; annual or biennial from a taproot and a single stem
       from the crown (*G. ibericum* and *G. pyrenaicum* perennial).
      c. Sepals with subulate tips 0.7 mm or more long.
        d. Pedicels mostly more than 2 cm long; appressed-pubescent. .... 4. *G. columbianum*
        d. Pedicels less than 2 cm long, or longer and spreading-pubescent.
          e. Peduncles terminated mostly with 1 flower; sepals uniformly pubescent. ... 5. *G. sibiricum*
          e. Peduncles terminated mostly with 2 flowers; sepals with longer
            pubescence on the veins.
            f. Beak of mature style column (including stigmas) 4 mm or more long;
              mature pedicels often more than twice as long as the calyx. .... 6. *G. bicknellii*
            f. Beak of mature style column 3 mm or less long; mature pedicels up to
              twice as long as the calyx (often longer in *G. ibericum*).
              g. Plant perennial from a stout rhizome; mature pedicels often more
                than twice as long as the calyx .... 7. *G. ibericum*
              g. Plant annual or biennial; mature pedicels up to twice as long as the
                calyx.
                Petals pale pink; carpel body with hairs 0.8 mm or more long. .... 8. *G. carolinianum*
                Petals dark pink; carpel body with hairs 0.6 mm or less long. .... 9. *G. dissectum*
      c. Sepals obtuse to acute or with a short, blunt mucro less than 0.5 mm long.
        h. Beak of mature style column (excluding stigmas) less than 1 mm long or
          lacking; carpels not cross-wrinkled.
          Sepals up to 4 mm long; petals about as long; fruit, including calyx,
            12 mm or less long; annual or biennial .... 10. *G. pusillum*
          Sepals longer than 4 mm; petals twice as long; fruit 13 mm or more long;
            perennial .... 11. *G. pyrenaicum*
        h. Beak of mature style column 1 mm or more long; carpels usually
          conspicuously cross-wrinkled. (Fig. 681) .... 12. *G. molle*

    1. *G. robertiánum* L. (for St. Robert). Herb-Robert. Rocky woods, stream borders. May-October.
Fig. 680, Map 1481. (Eurasia; n. Africa). [*Robertiella r.*]. Lotion made from the plant is reported to
be of value in treating eye complaints and to relieve rheumatism.
    2. *G. praténse* L. (of meadows). Fields and roadsides. June-July. Map 1482. (Naturalized from
Europe).
    3. *G. maculátum* L. (spotted). Woodlands, thickets, fields and roadsides. May-June. Map 1483.
Powder made from the dried rhizome is useful in treating mouth sores and sore throat; can cause
severe constipation however. —FACU
    G. sanguíneum L. Petals retuse; fruit with stylar beak less than 5 mm long (petals entire and stylar
beak 5 mm or more long in *G. maculatum*). Rarely escaped from cultivation in our range.
(Introduced from Europe). Reported for ME, MA, Merrimack County NH, Newport County RI.
    4. *G. columbiánum* L. (of a dove). Fields, roadsides, waste places. June-September. (Naturalized
from Europe). Reported for MA, Dutchess County NY.
    5. *G. sibíricum* L. (Siberian). Fields, roadsides, waste places. July-September. Map 1484. (Natu-
ralized from Eurasia).
    6. *G. bicknéllii* Britt. (for E. Bicknell). Open woods, ledges, roadsides, waste places. June-August.
Map 1485. Our plants are var. *bicknellii*.
    G. rotundifólium L. Leaves divided to about the middle, the segments shallowly lobed (leaves cleft
nearly to the base, the segments deeply lobed in *G. bicknellii*). Rarely found in our range. (Eurasia).
Reported for Suffolk County NY.
    7. *G. ibéricum* Cav. Cultivated ground, waste places. Map 1486. (Adventive from e. Asia). [*G.
nepalense* var. *thunbergii*].
    8. *G. carolinianum*, L. Cultivated soil, dry waste places, fields, roadsides. June-September. Map
1487. Endangered in NH. Our plants include var. *carolinanum* and the following vars.:
    var. *confertiflórum* Fern. Inflorescence of compact, many-flowered, terminal corymbs (inflores-
cence loose and open in var. *carólinianum*).

var. *sphaerospérmum* (Fern.) Breitung. Sepals relatively wide and seeds relatively plump (this combination lacking in the above vars.). [*G. sphaerospermum*].

9. *G. disséctum* L. (dissected). Roadsides and waste places. May-August. Map 1488. (Adventive from Europe).

10. *G. pusíllum* L. (very small). Roadsides, fields, waste places. June-September. Map 1489. (Naturalized from Europe).

11. *G. pyrenaícum* Burm. f. (of the Pyrenees). Roadsides and waste places. June-September. (Adventive from Europe). Reported for Windsor County VT.

12. *G. mólle* L. (soft). Lawns, waste places. June-September. Fig. 681, Map 1490. (Adventive from Europe).

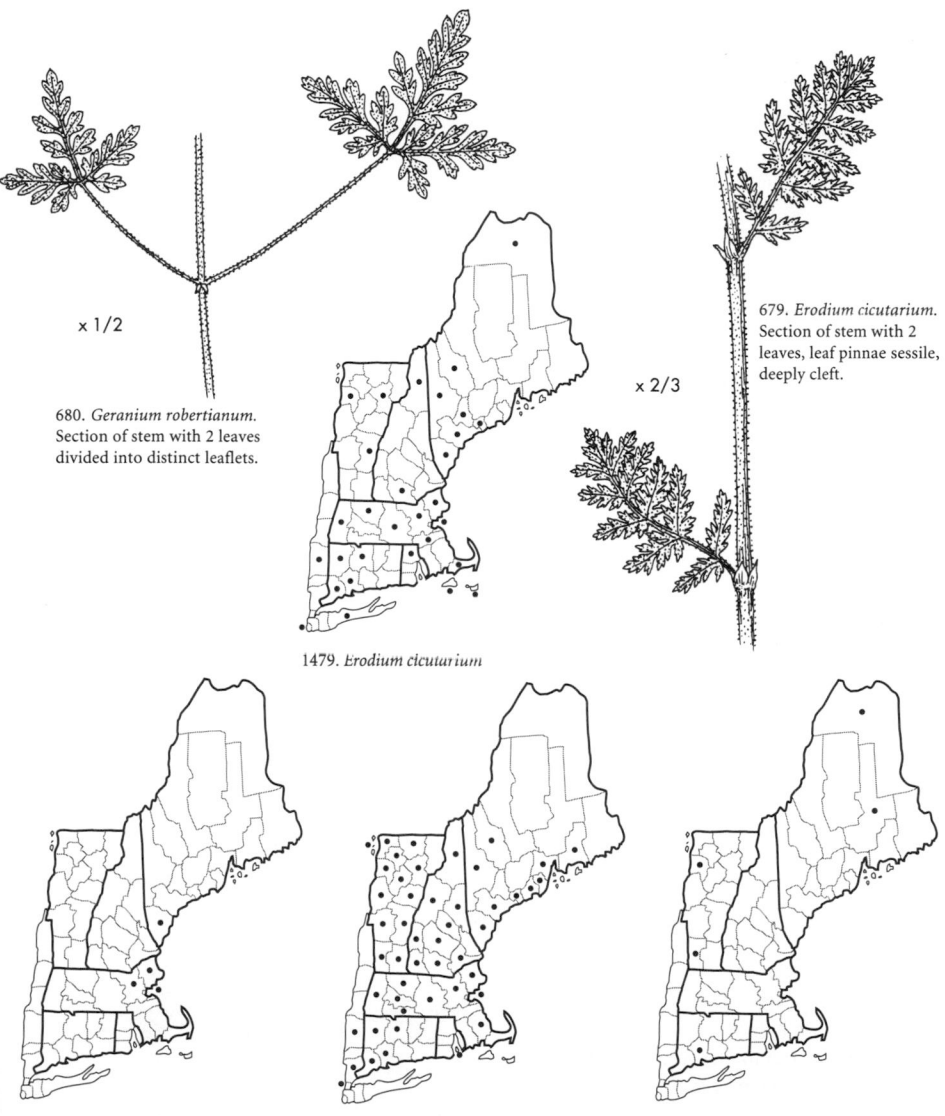

x 1/2

680. *Geranium robertianum.* Section of stem with 2 leaves divided into distinct leaflets.

679. *Erodium cicutarium.* Section of stem with 2 leaves, leaf pinnae sessile, deeply cleft.

x 2/3

1479. *Erodium cicutarium*

1480. *Erodium moschatum var. praecox*

1481. *Geranium robertianum*

1482. *Geranium pratense*

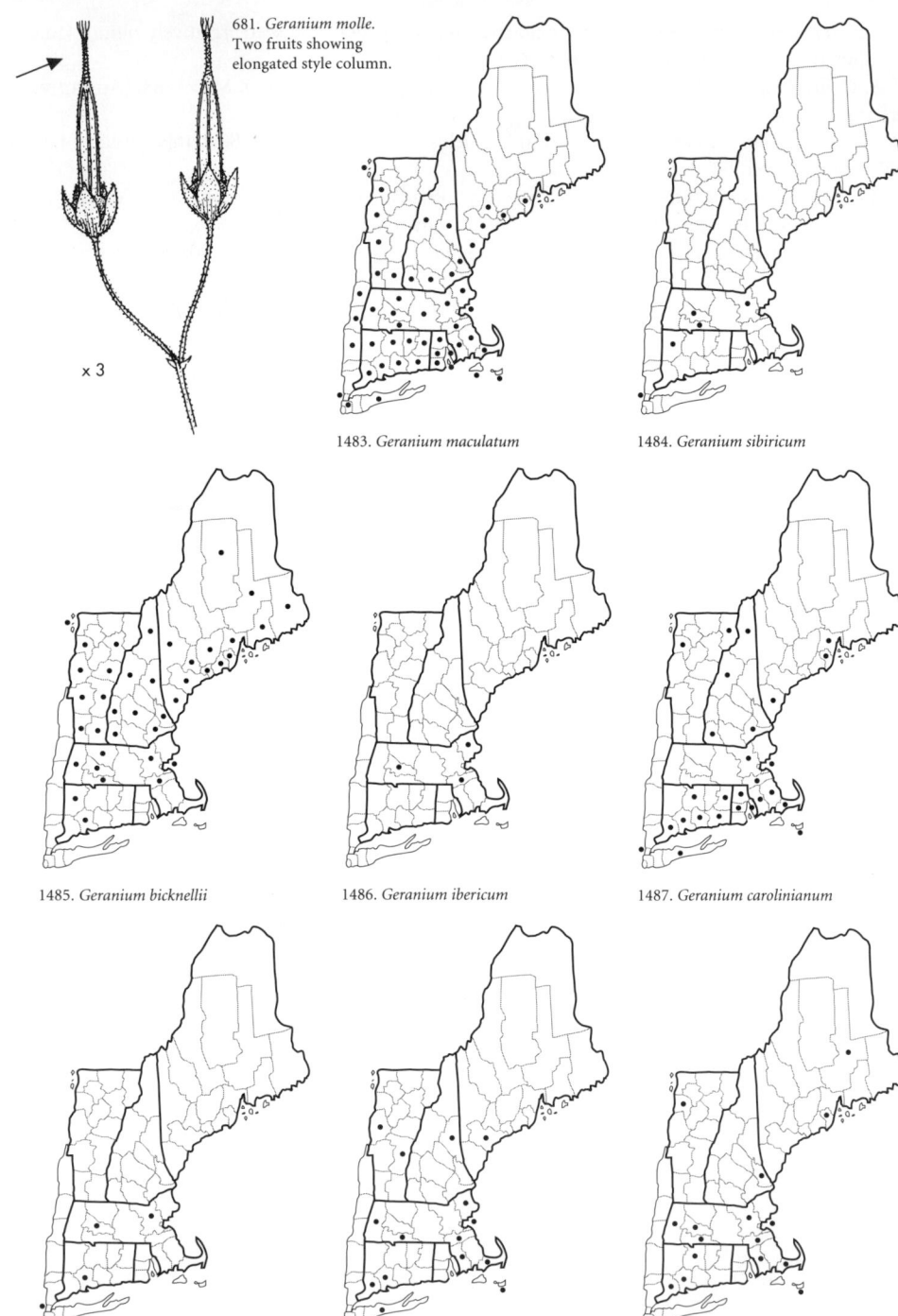

681. *Geranium molle.*
Two fruits showing
elongated style column.

x 3

1483. *Geranium maculatum*

1484. *Geranium sibiricum*

1485. *Geranium bicknellii*

1486. *Geranium ibericum*

1487. *Geranium carolinianum*

1488. *Geranium dissectum*

1489. *Geranium pusillum*

1490. *Geranium molle*

Family 113. Zygophylláceae (Caltrop Family)

Hermaphrodite, pubescent annual herbs (ours), the stems branched from the base, prostrate and radiating from a central crown, forming mats, when branched above, branching alternate, from the same leaf axils as the flowers. Leaves opposite, petioled, evenly pinnate, one leaf of each pair distinctly smaller than the other, leaflets opposite, stipules small. Flowers perfect, regular, small and yellow, solitary, on pedicels from the axils of the small leaves, sepals and petals each 5, distinct, stamens 10, hypogynous, ovary superior, carpels 5, locules 5, each 3-5 ovulate, style 1. Fruit a schizocarp of 5 mericarps, each with 2 stout lateral spines toward the middle and an irregular row of tubercles forming a crest down the back.

1. *Tríbulus* L. (Latin name for the Caltrop). Same characters as the family.

    1. *T. terréstris* L. (terrestrial). Puncture-weed. Dry, sandy roadsides and waste places. June-September. Rare. Fig. 682. (Naturalized from the Old World). Reported for Hunters Point NY. Poisonous.

Family 114. Rutáceae (Rue Family)

Hermaphrodite, dioecious or polygamous, trees, shrubs or sub-shrubs, often glandular-punctate and strong-smelling. Leaves alternate or occasionally opposite, petioled, pinnately compound, trifoliate or occasionally simple, with translucent dots, estipulate. Flowers perfect or unisexual, regular, small, whitish or greenish, in axillary or terminal cymes, fascicles or panicles, sepals 3-7 or none, distinct, petals the same number, distinct, stamens as many or twice as many as the petals, hypogynous, pistils 1-5, separate or united, ovary superior, carpels and locules 1-5, ovules 1-several in each locule, styles 2-5, distinct or connate into 1. Fruit a follicle, drupe, capsule or samara.

a. Leaves trifoliate. (Fig. 683) .... 1. *Ptelea trifoliata*
a. Leaves pinnately dissected or compound.
  b. Plant a perennial, suffrutescent herb, 10 dm or less tall. .... 2. *Ruta graveolens*
  b. Plant a shrub 12 dm or more tall or tree.
    Leaves alternate; branches and petioles prickly; plant a shrub. (Fig. 684). .... 3. *Zanthoxylum americanum*
    Leaves opposite; branches and petioles unarmed; plant a tree. .... 4. *Phellodendron*

1. *Ptélea* L. Hop-tree (Greek name for Elm, earlier applied to *Ptelea* because of the similar fruit).

Polygamous, shrubs or small trees, glabrous or essentially so, bark ill-scented and bitter, twigs moderate, warty-dotted, pith large, white, buds small to moderate, blunt, silvery-pubescent, without evident scales, often in pairs, beneath the leaf scars at first, leaf scars U-shaped after buds break through, nearly surrounding them, bundle traces 3, stipule scars and end bud lacking; leaves alternate, trifoliate, leaflets sessile, ovate, pointed at both ends, crenate to entire, glabrous to pubescent beneath; flowers perfect and unisexual on the same plant, in terminal, compound cymes, sepals, petals and stamens each 3-5, the latter lacking or imperfect in pistillate flowers, pistil 1, 2-locular, with 2 ovules in each locule, styles 2, short; fruit a 2-seeded samara, with a thin wing all around, circular.

    1. *P. trifoliáta* L. (three-leaved). Woods, roadsides and waste places. May-June. Fig. 683, Map 1491. Our plants are subsp. *trifoliata* var. *trifoliata*. Samaras have been used as a substitute for hops. —FAC

2. *Rúta* L. Rue (ancient name).

Hermaphrodite, suffrutescent, glandular-punctate, strong-smelling plants; leaves alternate, the principal ones 2-3 times pinnatifid, the upper ones often simple, the ultimate divisions or lobes oblanceolate, crenate to entire; flowers perfect, in dichasial panicles in the upper axils, sepals and petals 4-5, petals yellow, stamens 8-10, the anthers in 2 sizes, ovary 4-5 locular, each locule with several ovules, style 1; fruit a 4-5 lobed, loculicidal capsule, dehiscent in the upper half.

Dictámnus L. *álbus* L. Dittany. Will key to *Ruta* but is distinguishable in having leaves once pinnately compound with ovate leaflets and showy white, pink or purple flowers (Ruta has leaves 2-3 times pinnatifid with oblanceolate segments, flowers yellow, not showy). (Europe, China). Rarely escaped from cultivation. Reported for VT.

1. *R. gravéolens* L. (strong-smelling). Occasionally escaped from cultivation to fields, roadsides and waste places. June-July. Map 1492. (Introduced from Europe). Contact with the leaves can cause dermatitis; also poisonous if taken internally.

3. *Zanthóxylum* L. Prickly ash (Greek name, meaning yellow wood).

Dioecious, shrubs or small trees, the stems and branches usually armed with broad-based prickles, these paired or solitary at the nodes, twigs moderate, pith moderate, white, buds moderate, closely superposed, blunt, pubescent, without distinct scales, leaf scars triangular, bundle traces 3, stipule scars lacking; leaves alternate, odd-pinnately compound, the petioles and rachis often prickly, leaflets sessile or on short petiolules, ovate or oblong, crenate to entire, pubescent beneath, at least when young; flowers imperfect, in small, sessile, umbellate, axillary clusters on the previous year's twigs, appearing before the leaves, sepals none, petals 4-5, stamens 4-5 in staminate flowers, pistils 3-5 in pistillate flowers, each 1-locular with 2 ovules, their styles connivent above; fruit a cluster of fleshy, 1-2 seeded follicles, the seeds often remaining attached by a long, slender thread (funiculus).

1. *Z. americánum* Mill. (American). Woods, thickets and roadsides. April-May. Fig. 684, Map 1493. Endangered in NH.

4. *Phellodéndron* Rupr. Cork-tree (Greek name).

Dioecious, small trees with soft, corky bark, twigs moderate, pith moderate, brown, buds pubescent, without distinct scales, leaf scars horseshoe-shaped, almost surrounding the buds, bundle traces 3, sometimes split and multiple, stipule scars, and usually the end bud lacking; leaves opposite, odd-pinnately compound, leaflets ovate or obliquely ovate, acuminate, sessile or on short petiolules, crenate to entire; flowers imperfect, in axillary or terminal panicles, sepals and petals 5-8, staminate flowers with 5-6 stamens and a rudimentary ovary, pistillate flowers with a 5-locular ovary and 5-6 staminodia, stigma 5-lobed; fruit a 5-stoned drupe.

1. *P. amurénse* Rupr. Occasionally escaped from cultivation to roadsides and woods. May-July. Reported for Fairfield County CT, Hampshire County MA.

P. japónicum Maxim. Occasionally spread from cultivation. (Introduced from e. Asia). Reported for Essex County MA.

Family 115. Simaroubáceae (Quassia Family)

1. *Ailánthus* Desf. Tree of Heaven.

Polygamous, malodorous trees often spreading by root sprouts, bark smooth, with prominent lenticels; twigs stout, pith large, light brown, buds small, pubescent, with several scales, leaf scars large, shield-shaped, bundle traces several, in a curved line, stipule scars and end bud lacking; leaves alternate, petioled, odd-pinnately compound, leaflets lanceolate, acuminate, entire except for a few coarse, glandular teeth toward the base, estipulate; flowers perfect and unisexual on the same plant, small, greenish, in large terminal panicles, regular, calyx 5-parted, petals 5, stamens hypogynous, 10 in staminate flowers, 2-3 in perfect flowers, absent in pistillate flowers, carpels 2-5, unilocular, basally connate, each with a single ovule, ovary superior, styles 2-5; fruit a schizocarp with 2-5 samaroid mericarps, each with a single seed near the center.

1. A. altissima (Mill.) Swingle (tallest). Roadsides, waste places, especially in cities. June-July. Map 1494. (Naturalized from Asia). [*A. glandulosa*]. Cases of dermatitis have been reported from contact with the leaves.

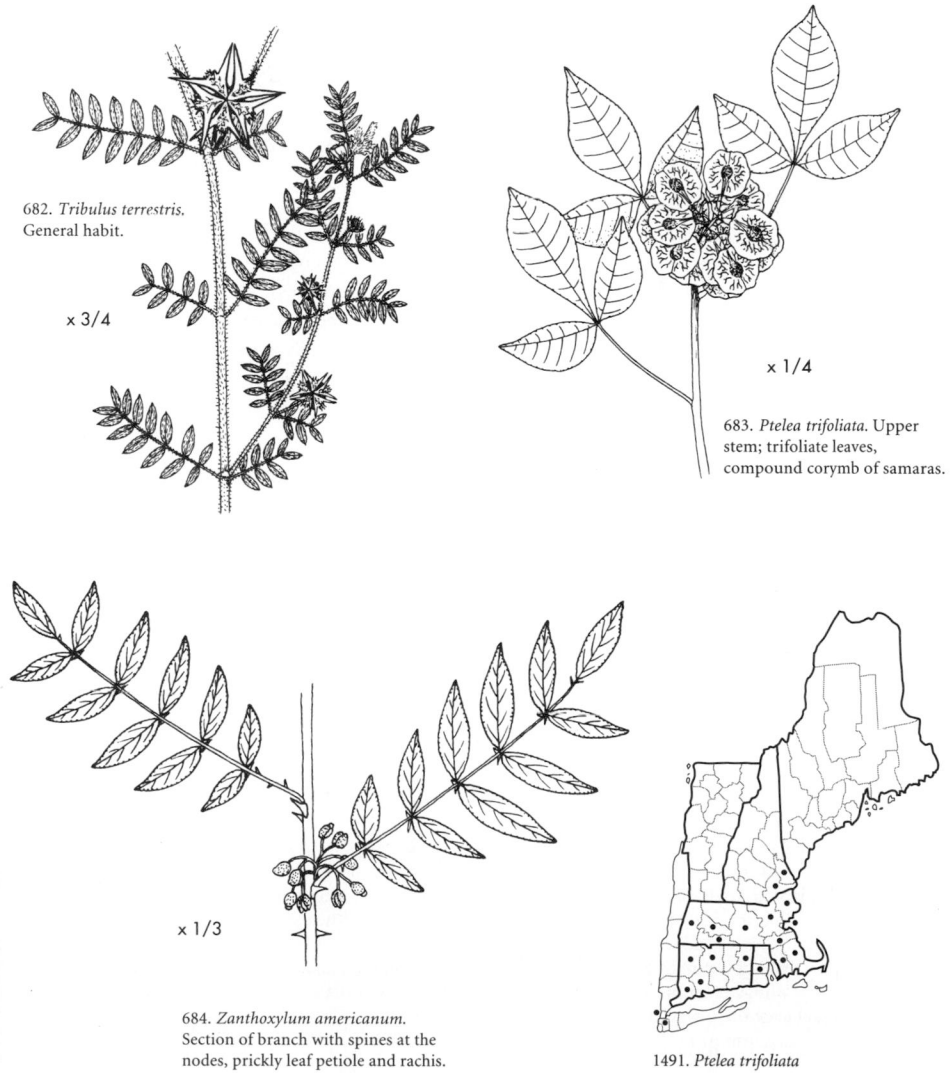

682. *Tribulus terrestris.* General habit.

× 3/4

× 1/4

683. *Ptelea trifoliata.* Upper stem; trifoliate leaves, compound corymb of samaras.

× 1/3

684. *Zanthoxylum americanum.* Section of branch with spines at the nodes, prickly leaf petiole and rachis.

1491. *Ptelea trifoliata*

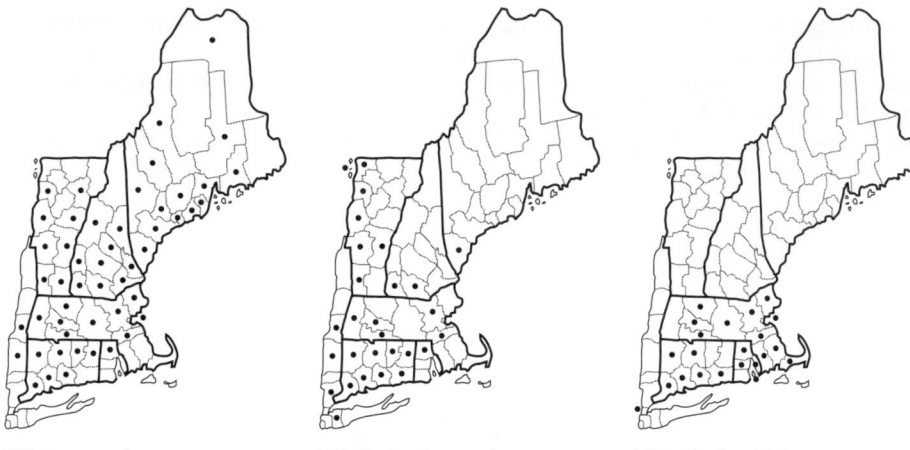

1492. *Ruta graveolens*   1493. *Zanthoxylum americanum*   1494. *Ailanthus altissima*

Family 116. Polygaláceae (Milkwort Family)

1. Polýgala L. Milkwort (ancient Greek name).

Hermaphrodite, annual or perennial herbs; leaves alternate, rarely whorled, petioled, simple, entire estipulate; flowers perfect, irregular, bracteate, in terminal racemes or spikes, (cleistogamous flowers produced from the base of the plant or subterranean in 2 species) calyx of 3 small and 2 larger sepals colored like the petals (the wings), corolla of 3 petals, united with each other and the stamen tube, the 2 lateral petals similar, the central one keel-shaped and usually with a lacerate crest, stamens 6-8, hypogynous, in 2 sets, their filaments united below into a split sheath, which is united with the corolla, pistil 1, ovary superior, 2-locular, with a single ovule in each locule, style 1; fruit a small, 2-seeded loculicidal capsule.

a. Flowers 1.3 cm or more long, 1-4; well developed leaves few and crowded toward
  top of stem .... 1. *P. paucifolia*
a. Flowers 1 cm or less long, numerous; leaves in whorles or scattered along the stem.
 b. Flowers orange, yellow on drying; sepals decurrent on the pedicels, forming
   narrow wings .... 2. *P. lutea*
 b. Flowers pink, lavender, white or green; sepals not decurrent on the pedicels as
   wings.
  c. Leaves alternate.
   d. Corolla 2 or more times as long as the wings, 6.5 mm or more long. .... 3. *P. incarnata*
   d. Corolla less than 2 times as long as the wings, less than 6.5 mm long.
    e. Flowers in loose racemes; cleistogamous flowers produced at the base of
     the plant and subterranean; perennial. (Fig. 685). .... 4. *P. polygama*
                                     var. *obtusata*
    e. Flowers in dense racemes; cleistogamous flowers not produced; annual
     or perennial.
     f. Plant perennial; stems usually several from the base or if solitary, from
      a thick root; leaves, or many of them, 5 mm or more wide. .... 5. *P. senega*
     f. Plant annual; stems solitary from a small, slender root, frequently
      branched above but not from the base; leaves mostly less than
      5 mm wide.
     Wings 3 mm or more long, exceeding the corolla. .... 6. *P. sanguinea*
     Wings 2.7 mm or less long, about equalling the corolla. .... 7. *P. nuttallii*
  c. Leaves, at least the lower (and sometimes all) whorled.
   Racemes 8 mm or more broad; bracts persistent. .... 8. *P. cruciata*
                                     var. *aquilonia*
   Racemes 5 mm or less broad; bracts deciduous. .... 9. *P. verticillata*

1. P. paucifólia Willd. (few-leaved). Gay-wings. Moist, rich woods. May-June. Map 1495. [*Triclisperma p.*]. —FACU

2. P. lútea L. (yellow). Wet sandy soil, sandy swamps and bogs along the coastal plain. May-August. Endangered in NY. [*Pilostaxis l.*]. —FACW+

3. P. incarnáta L. (flesh-colored). Dry woods, fields, barrens and roadsides. June-August. Reported for Suffolk County NY. [*Galypola i.*].

4. P. polýgama Walt. (polygamous). Dry sandy fields and open soil. June-August. Fig. 685. Map 1496. Represented with us as var. *obtusáta* Chod.

5. P. sénega L. (for the Seneca Indians). Seneca snakeroot. Fields and woods, particularly on limestone soils. May-June. Map 1497. Endangered in CT. Our plants are var. *senega*. Preparations of the root used for controlling coughs and related throat irritations; was also used by the Seneca Indians for snakebite; can cause stomach upset if taken in large doses. —FACU

6. P. sanguínea L. (blood-red). Fields, roadsides, pond margins. July-September. Map 1498. [*P. viridescens*]. —FACU

P. mariána Mill. Resembling *P. sanguinea* but flowers with wings only slightly exceeding the corolla (wings about twice as long as the corolla in *P. sanguinea*). Southern. Rarely occurring in our range. Reported for Suffolk County NY. [*P. harperi*]. —FACW

7. P. nuttállii T. & G. (for its discoverer). Dry, sandy fields and barrens. July-September. Map 1499. Endangered in CT. —FAC

8. P. cruciáta L. (cross-shaped) Wet meadows, pond margins, wet sand and boggy areas. Map 1500. [*P. ramosior*]. Represented with us as var. *aquilónia* Fern. & Schub. —FACW+

9. P. verticilláta L. (whorled). Fields, open woods. July-September. Map 1501. Our plants include var. *verticillata* and the following vars.:

var. *isócycla* Fern. Pedicels 0.3 mm or less long (longer in var. *verticillata*).

var. *ambígua* (Nutt.) Wood. Leaves, except for the lowest 1-3 nodes, alternate (all or mostly all whorled in the above vars.). [*P. ambigua*].

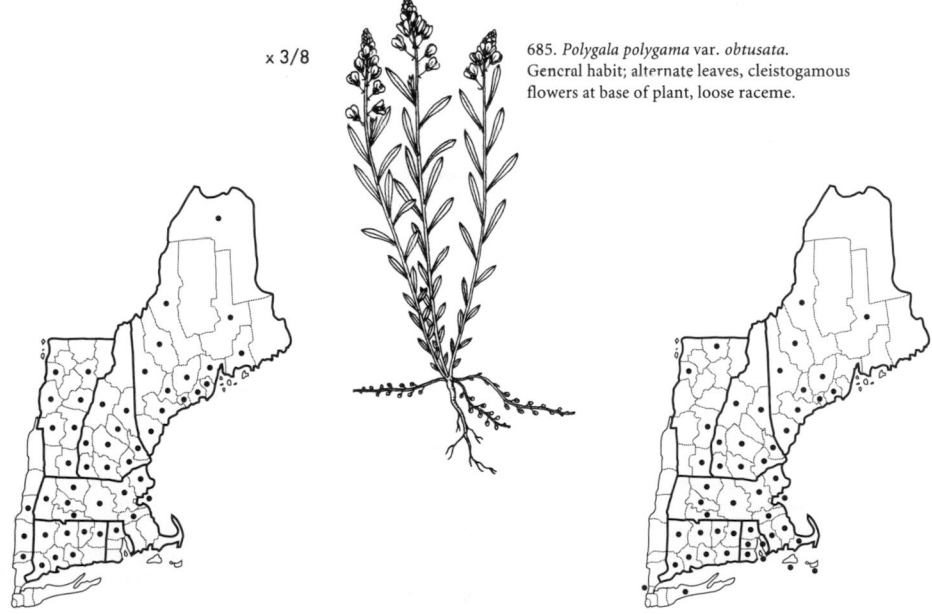

× 3/8

685. *Polygala polygama* var. *obtusata*. General habit; alternate leaves, cleistogamous flowers at base of plant, loose raceme.

1495. *Polygala paucifolia*

1496. *Polygala polygama* var. *obtusata*

1497. *Polygala senega*   1498. *Polygala sanguinea*   1499. *Polygala nuttallii*

1500. *Polygala cruciata* var. *aquilonia*   1501. *Polygala verticillata*   1502. *Ricinus communis*

Family 117. Euphorbiáceae (Spurge Family)

Monoecious or occasionally dioecious herbs (ours), often with milky juice. Leaves alternate or opposite, petioled, simple, entire, serrate or lobed, stipules usually present, often in the form of glands. Flowers imperfect, regular, usually small, often subtended by a calyx-like involucre (*cyathium*), in terminal or axillary racemes, spikes, cymes or clusters, sepals and petals present or absent, when present usually 5-merous, stamens 1-many, hypogynous, the filaments sometimes branched, pistil 1, ovary superior, 3 (occasionally 1- locular), with 1 or 2 ovules in each locule, styles 3, often bifid or branched. Fruit a 3-locular capsule or 1-seeded utricle.

a. Leaves palmately lobed, peltate .... 1. *Ricinus communis*
a. Leaves unlobed.
    b. Plants with stellate pubescence and/or scales.
        Pubescence stellate; fruit with 2-3 cells and seeds, dehiscent. .... 2. *Croton*
        Pubescence stellate and also of small, round scales; fruit 1-celled and
          1-seeded, indehiscent .... 3. *Crotonopsis*
                                            elliptica
    b. Plants with pubescence of simple hairs or glabrous.

c. Plants dioecious; staminate flowers in interrupted spikes, pistillate in axillary
    fascicles not surrounded by bracts. .... 4. *Mercurialis annua*
c. Plants monoecious; staminate and pistillate flowers usually in the same
    inflorescence.
    d. Staminate and pistillate flowers in the same head (cyathium) appearing as
        a solitary flower; plant with latex.
        Leaves symmetrical; most species erect; glands of the involucre with 5
           petaloid appendages or these lacking (Fig. 687). .... 5. *Euphorbia*
        Leaves oblique at base; most species prostrate to ascending; glands of the
           involucre with 4 petaloid appendages (Fig. 688). .... 6. *Chamaesyce*
    d. Staminate and pistillate flowers separate, the staminate terminal in heads
        or spikes, the pistillate basal, surrounded by a leaf-like bract; plant
        without latex .... 7. *Acalypha*

1. Rícinus L. Castor-bean (named for the Mediterranean sheep tick Ricinus, because of the resemblance of the seed to a tick).

Monoecious, tall, annual, glabrous herbs; leaves large, long petioled, alternate, peltate, palmately 5-11 lobed, the lobes with gland-tipped teeth; flowers in a terminal thyrse, appearing lateral, the staminate flowers in the lower part, the pistillate above, sepals 5, petals absent, stamens numerous, with repeatedly branched filaments, styles 3, each bifid and plumose; capsule large, 3-lobed, covered with soft spines, each locule 1-seeded.

    1. R. commúnis L. Occasionally escaped from cultivation to waste places. Map 1502. (Introduced from the Tropics). Very poisonous. However oil from the seeds is the source of the well known castor oil, which is used for constipation and as a hair tonic.

2. Cróton L. (Greek name for tick, based on resemblance of the seeds of another *Euphorb* to a tick).

Dioecious or monoecious annual herbs with repeatedly forking branching, stellate-pubescent throughout, pistillate plants usually stouter than staminate, leaves alternate or subopposite, lance-oblong to linear, toothed or entire; flowers in axillary and terminal racemes, sepals 5, petals as many as the sepals or none, staminate plants with numerous flowers, stamens 8-12, pistillate plants with fewer flowers, styles 3, each 2 or 3 times bifid; capsule 3-locular, 3-seeded. Various species are reported to be poisonous.

Leaves toothed and with 1 or 2 glands at the base. .... 1. *C. glandulosus*
                                                                 var. *septentrionalis*
Leaves entire or undulate, eglandular.
    Plants monoecious; staminate flowers with petals. .... 2. *C. capitatus*
    Plants dioecious; staminate flowers apetalous. .... 3. *C. texensis*

    1. C. glandulósus L. (glandular). Dry woods, fields and waste places. June-October. From farther south and west. Reported for CT. Represented with us as var. *septentrionalis* Muell. Arg.

    2. C. capitátus Michx. (in heads). Hogwort. Dry fields, barrens and waste places. June-October. Rarely adventive from farther west. Reported for Suffolk County MA. Our plants are var. *capitatus*.

    3. C. texénsis (Klotzsch) Muell. Arg. (Texan). Skunkweed. Dry fields and barrens, waste places. June-October. From farther west. (Mexico). Reported for Suffolk County MA.

3. Crotonópsis Michx. (from similarity in appearance to *Croton*).

Monoecious, annual herbs with repeatedly forked branching, the entire plant, except the upper leaf surfaces, densely stellate-pubescent and also covered with small round scales; leaves alternate or the upper often opposite, elliptic to linear-lanceolate, entire, the upper surfaces stellate-pubescent;

flowers minute, in short axillary and terminal spikes, the upper flowers staminate, the lower pistillate, staminate flowers with 5 sepals, 5 petals and 5 stamens, pistillate flowers with a 3-5 parted calyx, petals none, ovary 1-locular, with 1 ovule, style 1, 2-3 parted; fruit a utricle.

1. *C. elliptica* Willd. (elliptical). Dry sandy fields, open woods and waste places. July-September. Fig. 686. Reported for New Haven County CT.

4. *Mercuriális* L. Mercury (named for the god mercury).

Dioecious, annual herbs; leaves opposite, lanceolate to lance-ovate, crenate-serrate; in staminate plants flowers in peduncled, axillary, interrupted spikes, in pistillate plants in sessile and peduncled axillary clusters, sepals 3, petals none, stamens 8-20, ovary 2-locular, with 2 ovules, styles 2; capsule 2-locular, 2-seeded, hispid.

1. *M. ánnua* L. (annual). Herb-mercury. Waste places. Map 1503. (Adventive from Europe). Poisonous.

5. *Euphórbia* L. Spurge (for *Euphorbus*).

Monoecious, mostly erect, annual or perennial herbs (ours) with milky, acrid juice; leaves alternate or opposite, entire, symmetrical, crenate or serrate; flowers borne in cyathia (cupulate involucres subtending flowers), each cyathium 5 lobed, usually bearing glands in the sinuses, these often with white or colored marginal petaloid, appendages containing several staminate flowers surrounding a single pistillate flower, the staminate flower consisting of a single stamen, the pistillate pedicelled, the pedicel becoming exserted, consisting of a 3-locular ovary with 3 ovules and 3 styles, the cyathia in cymose inflorescences with umbelliform branching; fruit a 3-lobed capsule. The majority of species are poisonous if taken internally, and can also cause dermatitis in some individuals. —Wildl. 1

a. Leaves, at least those among the inflorescences, with white margins. .... 1. *E. marginata*
a. Leaves without white margins.
　　b. Glands of the involucre with 5 conspicuous petaloid appendages, or appendages
　　　　　　inconspicuous and cyathia on peduncles more than 1 cm long.
　　　　　　Petaloid appendages conspicuous, usually white, 1.5 mm or more long. .... 2. *E. corollata*
　　　　　　Petaloid appendages inconspicuous, consisting of a very narrow greenish or
　　　　　　　　yellowish border on the gland less than 1 mm long. .... 3. *E. ipecacuanhae*
　　b. Glands of the involucre lacking petaloid appendages, cyathia on peduncles less
　　　　　　than 1 cm long.
　　　　c. Stems pubescent; gland of involucre usually 1, bilabiate. .... 4. *E. dentata*
　　　　c. Stems glabrous; glands of involucre usually 4, not bilabiate.
　　　　　　d. Leaves pubescent beneath, particularly near the margin; glands of involucre
　　　　　　　　transversely oval to elliptic .... 5. *E. platyphyllos*
　　　　　　d. Leaves glabrous beneath.
　　　　　　　　e. Leaves toothed; glands of involucre transversely oval to elliptic. .... 6. *E. helioscopia*
　　　　　　　　e. Leaves entire; glands of involucre horseshoe to crescent-shaped.
　　　　　　　　　　f. Stem leaves opposite and decussate .... 7. *E. lathyris*
　　　　　　　　　　f. Stem leaves alternate.
　　　　　　　　　　　　g. Rays of the umbel usually 5 or fewer; seeds pitted; plants annual,
　　　　　　　　　　　　　　stem solitary from a tap root .... 8. *E. peplus*
　　　　　　　　　　　　g. Rays of the umbel usually more than 5; seeds smooth; plants perennial,
　　　　　　　　　　　　　　stems several from a crown.
　　　　　　　　　　　　　　Bracteal leaves mucronate; larger stem leaves more than 3 mm
　　　　　　　　　　　　　　　　wide and 2 cm long .... 9. *E. esula*
　　　　　　　　　　　　　　Bracteal leaves not mucronate; larger stem leaves less than 3 mm
　　　　　　　　　　　　　　　　wide and 2 cm long .... 10. *E. cyparissias*

1. *E. margináta* Pursh (margined). Snow-on-the-mountain. Fields and waste places; from farther west. July-September. Map 1504. [*Dichrophyllum m.; Lepadena m.*].

2. E. corolláta L. (with corollas). Flowering spurge. Fields, roadsides, railroads; from farther west. July-September. Fig. 687, Map 1505. [*Tithymalopsis c.*]. Our plants are var. *corollata*.

E. pubentíssima Michx. Similar to *E. corollata* but distinguishable in having 15 or fewer leaves or leaf scars on the main stem below the inflorescence (leaves or scars 25 or more below the inflorescence in *E. corollata*). From farther south. Reported for NH. [*E. apocynifolia*].

3. E. ipecacuánhae L. (having the emetic properties of Brazilian Ipecacuanha). Wild Ipecac. Pinelands, barrens, sandy soil, of the coastal plain. April-July. Reported for CT, Suffolk County NY. [*Tithymalopsis i.*].

4. E. dentáta Michx. (toothed). Railroads, roadsides and waste places. July-September. Map 1506. [*Poinsettia d.*].

5. E. platyphýllos L. (broad-leaved). Lake shores, waste places; from Europe. June-August. Map 1507. (Naturalized from Europe). [*E. platyphylla; Tithymalus p.; Galarhoeus p.*].

6. E. helioscópia L. (turning toward the sun). Wartweed. Lake shores, roadsides, waste places; from Europe. July-September. Map 1508. (Naturalized from Europe). [*Tithymalus h.; Galarhoeus h.*].

7. E. láthyris L. (a kind of wolf's milk). Escaped from cultivation to roadsides and waste places. June-September. (Naturalized from Europe). Reported for MA, Fairfield County CT. [*Tithymalus l.; Galarhoeus l.*].

8. E. péplus L. (ancient name). Cultivated soil and waste places; from Europe. July-October. Map 1509. (Naturalized from Europe). [*Tithymalus p.; Galarhoeus p.*].

9. E. ésula L. (sharp). Wolf's milk. Fields, roadsides, waste places; from Europe. May-October. Map 1510. (Naturalized from Europe). [*E. intercedens; E. podperae; E. virgata; Tithymalus e.; Galarhoeus e.*]. Our plants are var. *esula*.

E. agrária Bieb. Similar to *E. esula* but with the main leaves 1 cm or more wide and distinctly pinnately veined (main leaves up to 1 cm wide and with only the midvein distinct, the lateral veins obscure in *E. esula*). European. Rarely occurring as a waif in our range. Reported for MA. [*E. lucida; Tithymalus l.; Galarhoeus l.*].

10. E. cyparíssias L. (ancient name). Fields, roadsides, waste places; May-September. Map 1511. (Naturalized from Europe). [*Tithymalus c.; Galarhoeus c.*].

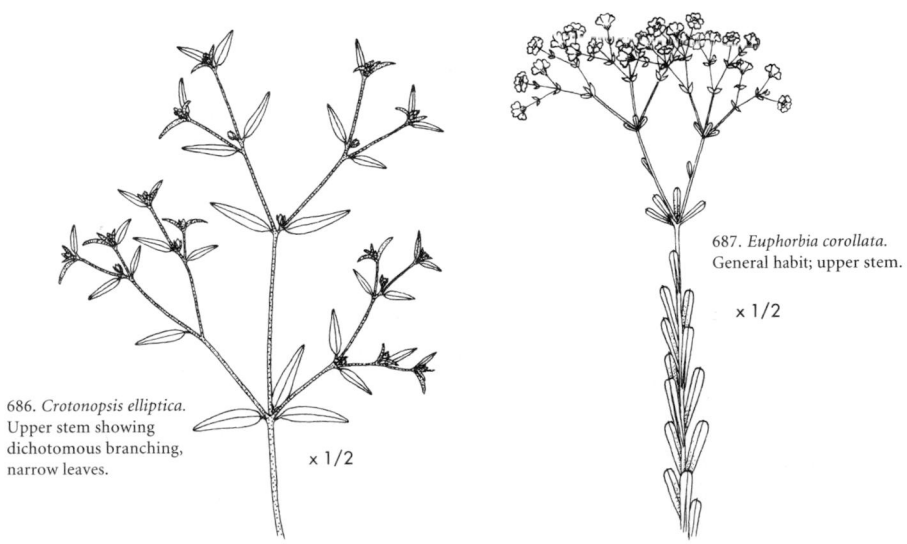

686. *Crotonopsis elliptica.*
Upper stem showing
dichotomous branching,
narrow leaves.

x 1/2

687. *Euphorbia corollata.*
General habit; upper stem.

x 1/2

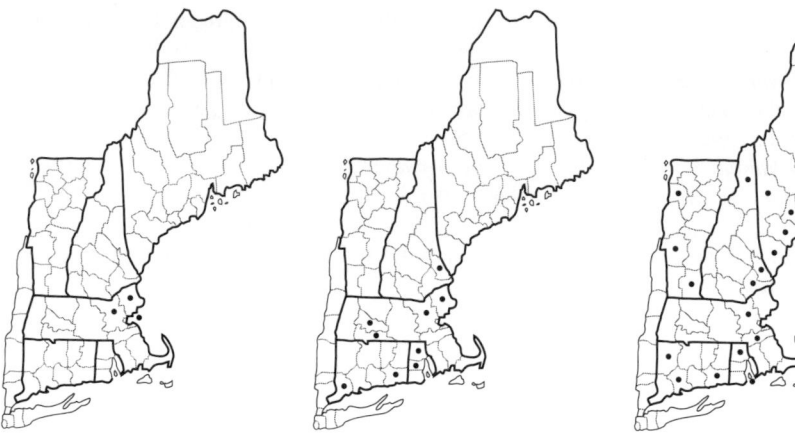

1503. *Mercurialis annua*   1504. *Euphorbia marginata*   1505. *Euphorbia corollata*

6. *Chamaesýce* S. F. Gray.

Similar to *Euphorbia*; most species prostrate to ascending, leaves oblique at the base, glands of the involucre with 4 petaloid appendages. [*Euphorbia*]. Poisonous; may also cause dermatitis. —Wildl. 1

a. Capsule and ovary pubescent.
    Involucre cleft on 1 side for half its length. .... 1. *C. humistrata*
    Involucre cleft on 1 side for up to a third its length. .... 2. *C. maculata*
a. Capsule and ovary glabrous.
  b. Stems glabrous or essentially so (often pubescent in lines or on all sides when
      young or on the younger parts).
    c. Leaves entire.
      Leaves 2 times as long as wide or shorter; stipules united into a triangular
        scale, this often lacerate; other habitats. .... 3. *C. serpens*
      Leaves more than 2 times as long as wide; stipules separate; sand dunes and
        sea beaches .... 4. *C. polygonifolia*
    c. Leaves serrulate, at least around the tip.
      Larger leaves usually more than 1.5 cm long; plant erect, at least in the
        upper half; leaves serrulate all along the margins. .... 5. *C. nutans*
      Larger leaves less than 1.5 cm long; plant prostrate or barely ascending;
        leaves serrulate only around the tip. .... 6. *C. glyptosperma*
  b. Mature stems evenly and uniformly spreading or curly-pubescent. .... 7. *C. vermiculata*

1. *C. humistráta* Engelm. (carpeting). River banks and floodplains. August-September. From farther west. Reported for NH, VT. [*Euphorbia h.*]. —FACU

2. *C. maculáta* (L.) Small (spotted). Roadsides, waste places, railroads. July-October. Map 1512.[*Euphorbia m.; E. supina*]. —FACU-

C. prostráta (Ait.) Small. Similar to *C. maculata* but differing in having seeds with several distinct transverse ridges (in *C. maculata* seeds are inconspicuously ridged). From farther south. (Naturalized from Tropical Amer.). Reported for Middlesex County MA. [*Euphorbia p.; E. chamaesyce*].

3. *C. sérpens* (Kunth) Small (crawling). Fields and waste places. July-October. (S. Amer.) [*Euphorbia s.*].

4. *C. polygonifólia* (L.) Small (with leaves of Polygonum). Seaside spurge. Sand dunes and seabeaches. July-October. Fig. 688, Map 1513. [*Euphorbia p.*]. —FACU

5. *C. nútans* Lag. Cultivated soil, roadsides, waste places. June-October. Reported for MA, RI. [*Euphorbia n.; E. maculata; C. preslii; Euphorbia p.; C. rafinesquii*]. —FACU

6. *C. glyptospérma* (Engelm.) Small (with engraved seeds). Railroads, waste places. July-October. Map 1514. [*Euphorbia g.*].

C. serpyllifólia Pers. Similar to *C. glyptosperma* but having seeds smooth or minutely pitted (seeds with 4-6 distinct transverse ridges in *C. glyptosperma*). [*Euphorbia s.*]. From farther west. Reported for NH. Our plants are var. *serpyllifolia.*

7. *C. vermiculáta* (Raf.) House (like tracks of worms). Roadsides, waste places railroads. July-September. Map 1515. [*C. rafinesquii; Euphorbia v.; E. hirsuta*].

7. *Acalýpha* L. Three-seeded mercury (Greek name for nettle).

Monoecious, pubescent annual herbs; leaves alternate, crenate or crenate-serrate; flowers minute, the staminate clustered in axillary peduncled heads or short spikes, the pistillate solitary or few at the base of the staminate spike or sometimes in separate clusters, the pistillate or pistillate-staminate clusters surrounded by a large, toothed-lobed, leaf-like bract at the base, 1-several bracted clusters occurring per leaf axil, petals absent, staminate flowers with 4 sepals and 8 or more stamens, pistillate flowers with 3-5 sepals, styles 3; capsule 3-locular, 3-seeded.

1506. *Euphorbia dentata*

1507. *Euphorbia platyphyllos*

1508. *Euphorbia helioscopia*

1509. *Euphorbia peplus*

1510. *Euphorbia esula*

1511. *Euphorbia cyparissias*

Teeth of the bracts lanceolate; petioles a third or more the length of the blades,
   usually exceeding the bracts. .... 1. *A. virginica*
Teeth of the bracts triangular; petioles less than a third the length of the blades,
   usually shorter than the bracts. .... 2. *A. gracilens*

1. *A. virginica* L. (Virginian). Fields, open woods, roadsides and waste places. August-September. Map 1516. Our plants include var. *virginica* and the following var.:

var. *rhomboídea* (Raf.) Cooperider. Teeth of the bracts usually 7 or fewer, usually glandular; stems glabrous or puberulent with incurved hairs, rarely with spreading hairs (teeth of the bracts 9 or more, eglandular; stems with some straight spreading hairs in var. *virginica*). Fig. 689, Map 1517. [*A. rhomboidea*]. —FACU-

A. austrális L. Similar to *A. virginica* var. *rhomboidea* but distinguishable in having fruiting bracts which are cordate at the base (bracts not cordate-based in var. *rhomboidea*). Asiatic; recently reported from the boroughs of NY City, Bronx, Manhatten, Kings and Queens Counties.

2. *A. grácilens* Gray (slender). Fields and open woods. August-October. Map 1518. Our plants are var. *gracilens*.

Family 118. Callitricháceae (Water Starwort Family)

Monoecious, slender, glabrous, aquatic or rarely terrestrial, annual or perennial herbs. Leaves opposite, the upper often rosulate in aquatic species, sessile, entire, linear to obovate, estipulate. Flowers imperfect, minute, solitary or 2-3 in the leaf axils, flowers of both sexes usually not in the same axil, perianth lacking, the flower sometimes subtended by a pair of bracts, the staminate flower consisting of a single stamen with a filament and a 4-locular anther, the pistillate of a 2-carpellate, 4-locular superior ovary with 2 styles. Fruit a schizocarp splitting into 4 achene-like mericarps.

1. *Callítriche* L. Water starwort. (from the Greek, based on the slender stems). Same characters as the family.

In addition to the following species *C. intermedia* has been reported for MA.

a. Plants terrestrial; stems 5 cm or less long. .... 1. *C. terrestris*
a. Plants aquatic or on muddy shores; stems usually more than 5 cm long (except
      sometimes in *C. heterophylla*).
   b. Flowers ebracteate; halves of fruit divided by a deep groove extending from the
         margin nearly to the axis, easily separated; leaves all linear. .... 2. *C. hermaphroditica*
   b. Flowers 2-bracted at base; halves of fruit divided by a shallow groove, not easily
         separated; upper leaves often spatulate or oblanceolate.
      c. Fruit 1.3 mm or more wide; mature carpels distinctly wing-margined. .... 3. *C. stagnalis*
      c. Fruit less than 1.3 mm wide; mature carpels acute or rounded at the margin.
         Fruit longer than wide; carpels acute at the margin. .... 4. *C. palustris*
         Fruit as wide as long; carpels rounded at the margin. .... 5. *C. heterophylla*

1. *C. terréstris* Raf. Moist woodlands, along paths and trails. Fruit: May-September. Map 1519. [*C. deflexa* var. *austini*]. —FACW+

2. *C. hermaphrodítica* L. (hermaphrodite). Lakes and quiet streams. Fruit: July-October. Map 1520. (Eurasia). [*C. autumnalis*]. —OBL

3. *C. stagnális* Scop. (of pools). Ponds and quiet streams. Fruit: July-October. Map 1521. (Naturalized from Europe). —OBL

4. *C. palústris* L. Ponds, quiet streams, wet shores. Fruit: July-October. Fig. 690, Map 1522. (Eurasia). [*C. verna*]. —OBL

5. *C. heterophýlla* Pursh (diverse-leaved). Ponds, quiet streams, wet shores. Fruit: June-October. Map 1523. [*C. anceps*]. Our plants are subsp. *heterophylla*. —OBL

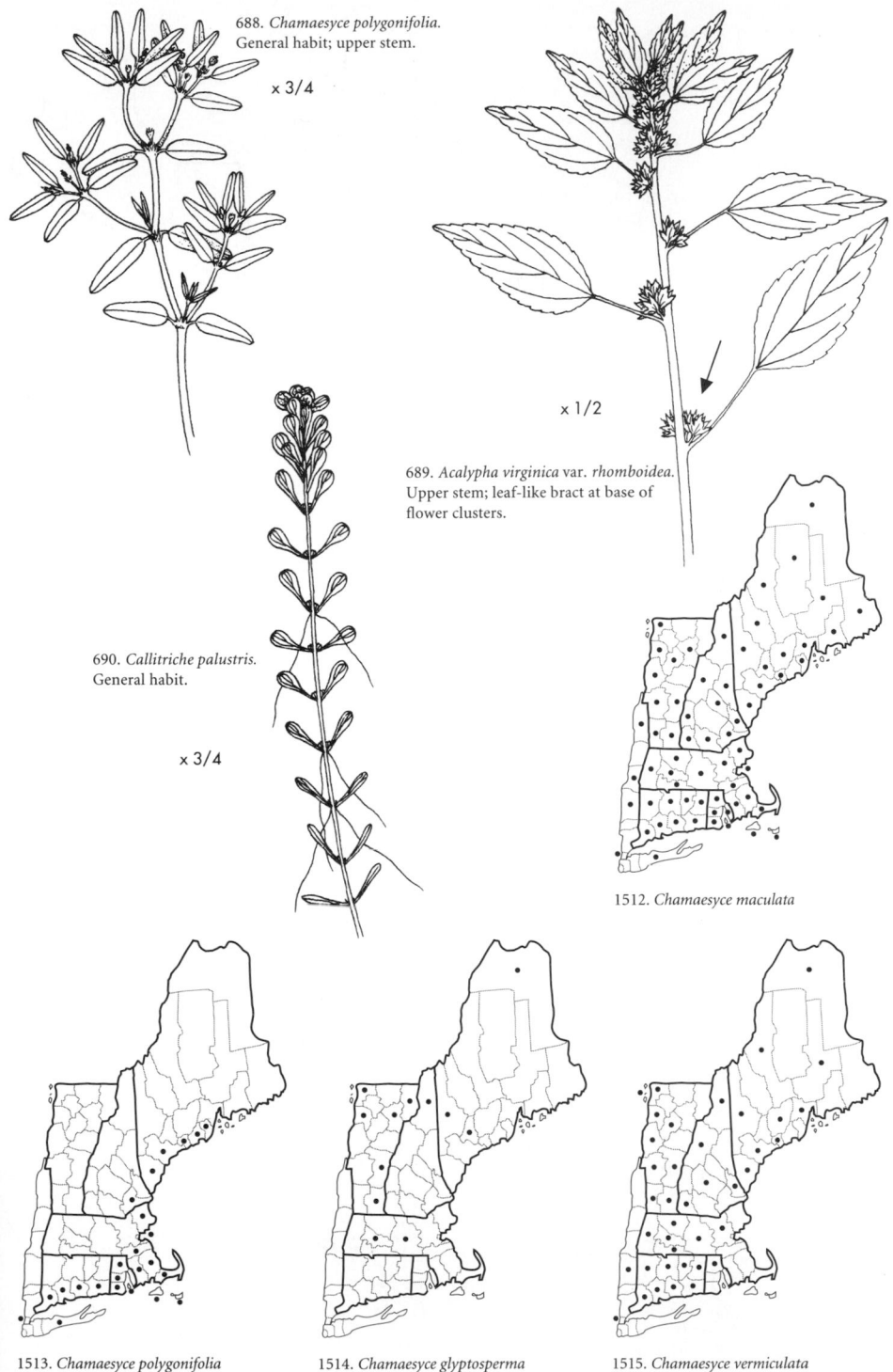

688. *Chamaesyce polygonifolia.*
General habit; upper stem.

x 3/4

689. *Acalypha virginica* var. *rhomboidea.*
Upper stem; leaf-like bract at base of
flower clusters.

x 1/2

690. *Callitriche palustris.*
General habit.

x 3/4

1512. *Chamaesyce maculata*

1513. *Chamaesyce polygonifolia*

1514. *Chamaesyce glyptosperma*

1515. *Chamaesyce vermiculata*

1516. *Acalypha virginica* var. *virginica*

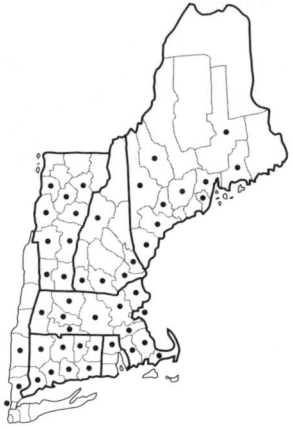

1517. *Acalypha virginica* var. *rhomboidea*

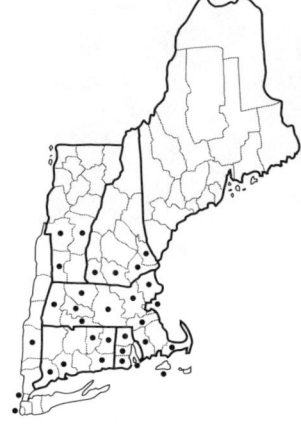

1518. *Acalypha gracilens*

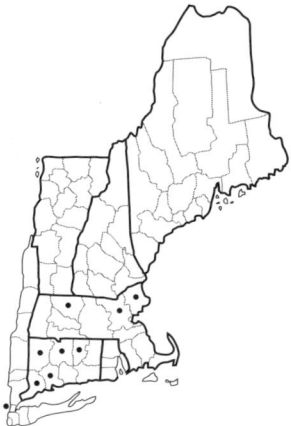

1519. *Callitriche terrestris*

1520. *Callitriche hermaphroditica*

1521. *Callitriche stagnalis*

1522. *Callitriche palustris*

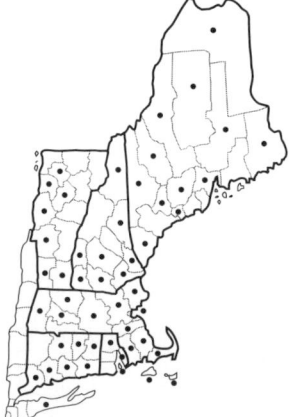

1523. *Callitriche heterophylla*

Family 119. Buxáceae (Box Family)

1. *Pachysándra* Michx. (Greek name, based on the stout stamen filaments).
Monoecious, suffrutescent, glabrous, perennial herbs with long rhizomes. Leaves evergreen, alternate, mostly approximate in the middle and upper parts of the stem, ovate to obovate, coarsely toothed, petioled, estipulate. Flowers imperfect, regular, small and whitish, in terminal bracteate spikes (ours), the staminate flowers above, the pistillate few, basal, sepals 4-5, petals none, stamens 4, hypogynous, with stout, flattened filaments, ovary superior, of 3 carpels and 3 locules, with 3 stout styles. Fruit a 3-beaked capsule with 2 seeds in each locule.

    1. *P. terminális* Sieb. & Zucc. (terminal). Occasionally escaped from cultivation to railroads, waste places. Fig. 691. Reported for Fairfield County CT, Hampshire County MA.

    Búxus L. *sempervírens* L. Common Boxwood. A shrub or small tree with opposite evergreen, entire leaves and flowers in axillary or terminal clusters. Rarely escaped from cultivation. Reported for Suffolk County NY. Poisonous; various medicinal uses are also cited.

Family 120. Empetráceae (Crowberry Family)

Monoecious, dioecious or polygamous, sometimes hermaphrodite, low, heathlike, evergreen shrubs. Leaves alternate, narrow, revolute, subsessile, jointed to pulvini visible as short stubs when leaves are removed, estipulate, numerous and crowded. Flowers imperfect or sometimes perfect, small, regular, axillary or in terminal clusters, bracteate, calyx of 3-4 sepals, corolla of 3 petals or none, stamens 3-4, hypogynous, with long filaments, ovary superior, of 2-9 carpels and locules, with 1 ovule in each locule, style 1, stigmas as many as the carpels. Fruit a dry or juicy, berry-like drupe with 2-9 nutlets.

Flowers and fruits in terminal clusters; leaves narrowly linear, the midrib on the
    underside indistinct, deeply sunken. (Fig. 692). .... 1. *Corema conradii*
Flowers and fruits axillary; leaves linear -oblong, the midrib on the underside usually
    distinct, slightly sunken, lighter colored than rest of leaf. .... 2. *Empetrum*

1. *Coréma* D. Don. Broom-crowberry (from the Greek, based on the diffusely branched habit).
Dioecious, low, diffusely branched shrubs, twigs slender, ridged below the leaf scars, pith small, buds solitary, sessile, small, leaf scars minute; leaves subverticillate, narrowly linear; flowers in terminal clusters, purplish (at least the staminate) calyx of 3-4 sepals, corolla none, ovary usually 3-locular, stigmas usually 3; drupe small, dry, usually with 3 nutlets.

    1. *C. conrádii* (Torr.) Torr. ex Loud. (for its discoverer). Sandy pine barrens and dunes, mostly near the coast. April-May. Fig. 692, Map 1524. Endangered in NY. Fruit edible.

2. *Émpetrum* L. Crowberry (ancient Greek name).
Monoecious, dioecious or polygamous, sometimes hermaphrodite, low, spreading, diffusely branched shrubs, twigs, buds, leaf scars as in *Corema*; leaves subverticillate, linear-oblong; flowers solitary or few in the leaf axils, greenish or purplish, sepals, petals and stamens each 3, ovary 6-9-locular, stigmas 6-9; drupe juicy, with 6-9 nutlets. Fruit edible, especially after cooking. —Wildl. 1

Young twigs white-tomentose, not glandular. .... 1. *E. eamesii* subsp.
                                                          atropurpureum
Young twigs minutely stipitate glandular, not tomentose. .... 2. *E. nigrum*

1. E. eámesii Fern. & Wieg. Purple Crowberry. Gravel and rocks in mountainous areas. Fruit: July-September. Map 1525. [*E. atropurpureum; E. rubrum* subsp. *eamesii* var. *atropurpureum*]. Represented with us as subsp. *atropurpúreum* D. Love. —FAC

2. E. nígrum L. (black). Black Crowberry. Gravel and rocks in mountainous areas and along the coast. Fruit: July-September. Map 1526. (Eurasia).

Our plants include subsp. *nigrum* and the following subsp.:

subsp. *hermaphrodítum* (Lange) Boecher. Flowers mostly perfect, sometimes partly unisexual (flowers unisexual, the plants dioecious in subsp. *nigrum*). —FACW

Family 121. Limnantháceae (False Mermaid Family)

1. Floérkea Willd. False Mermaid (for H. Floerke).

Hermaphrodite, decumbent, branching, glabrous annual herbs; leaves alternate, pinnately divided into 3-5 lanceolate to oblong leaflets, these entire or cleft, petioled, estipulate; flowers perfect, regular, minute, white, solitary on axillary peduncles, sepals and petals each 3, the latter much shorter than the sepals, glands alternating with the petals, stamens 6, hypogynous, ovary superior, of 3 carpels and locules, with 1 ovule in each locule, style 1, arising from the center of the deeply divided ovary, stigmas 3; fruit deeply divided, separating when ripe into 3 fleshy nutlets.

1. F. proserpinacoídes Willd. (like *Prosperinaca*). Rich, moist, often alluvial woods. April-May. Rare. Fig. 693, Map 1527. Endangered in CT. —FAC

Family 122. Anacardiáceae (Cashew Family)

Hermaphrodite or polygamous shrubs, small trees or vines with resinous or milky sap. Leaves alternate, pinnately or ternately compound or simple, petioled, estipulate. Flowers perfect or imperfect, regular, small,yellowish or greenish to white, in terminal or axillary panicles, calyx 5-parted, petals 5, stamens 5, hypogynous, ovary superior, of 3 carpels, 1-locular, 1-ovuled, styles 3. Fruit a dry, 1-seeded, pubescent or glabrous drupe.

Leaves simple .... 1. *Cotinus coggyria*
Leaves compound.
   Inflorescence axillary, loose and spreading or drooping; fruits whitish. (Fig. 694) ...... 2. *Toxicodendron*
   Inflorescence terminal, crowded, erect; red. (Fig. 695). .... 3. *Rhus*

1. Cótinus Mill. Smoke-tree (ancient Greek name for the wild olive).

Shrubs or small trees, twigs moderate, with prominent lenticels, pith moderate, brownish, buds small, solitary, ovoid, with several scales, leaf scars raised, crescent shaped or somewhat 3-lobed, bundle traces 3, stipule scars lacking; leaves simple, ovate to obovate, entire; flowers perfect (ours) yellowish, slender-pedicelled, in large, terminal panicles that appear plumose due to the plumose pedicels of numerous aborted flowers, styles in fertile flowers lateral, persistent and clearly visible on the fruits.

1. C. coggýgria Scop. (modification of the name Coccygea). Occasionally escaped from cultivation to waste places. Map 1528. (Introduced from Eurasia).

2. Toxicodéndron Mill. (Poison tree).

Shrubs, small trees or vines, poisonous to touch, twigs slender to stout, with dark lenticels, pith rather large, brownish, buds small to moderate, solitary, ovoid, with several scales or scales obscured by dense pubescence, leaf scars broadly crescent or shield shaped, bundle traces 5-7 or numerous in several indistinct groups, end bud present, stipule scars lacking; leaves pinnately or ternately

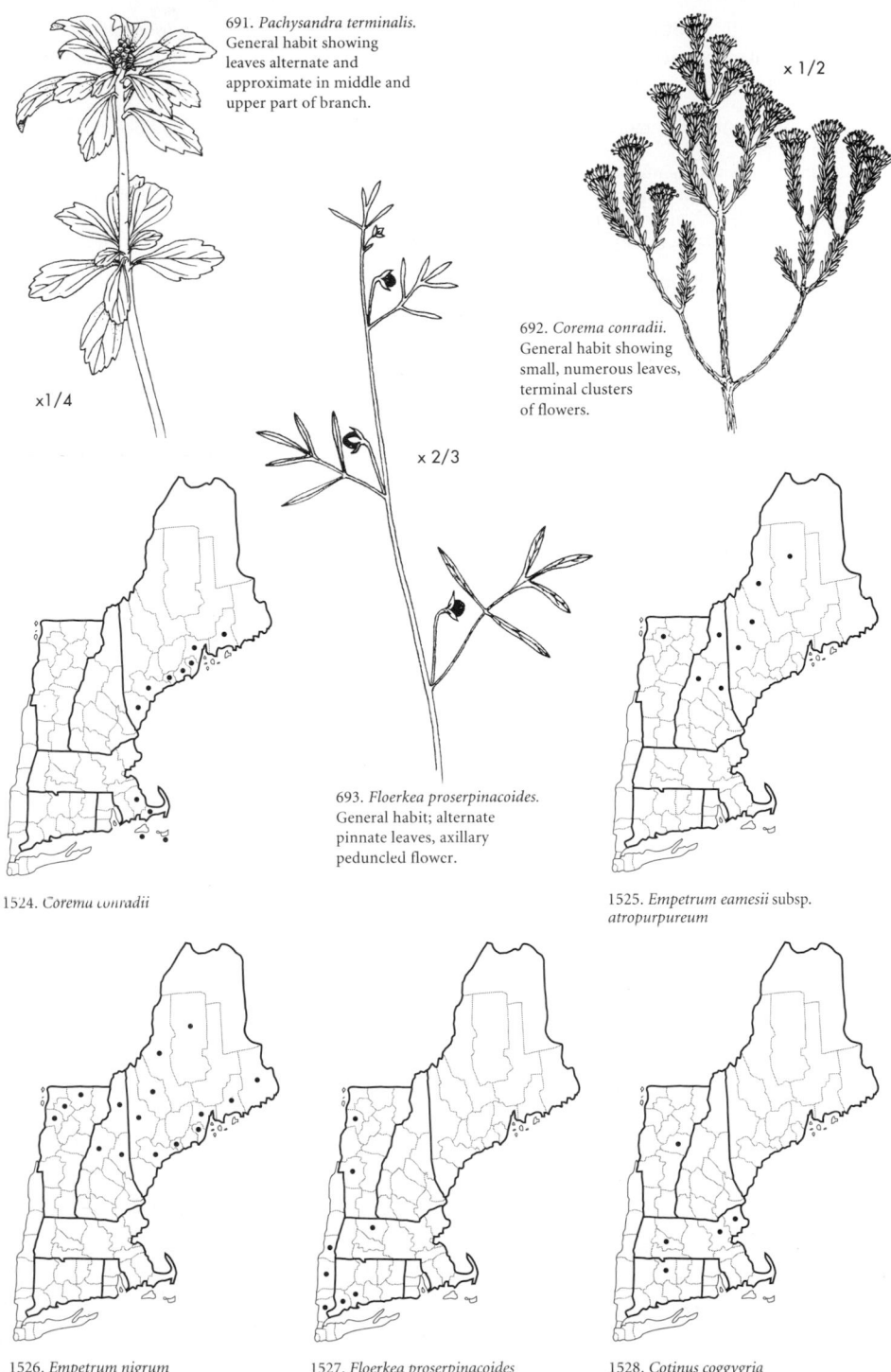

691. *Pachysandra terminalis.* General habit showing leaves alternate and approximate in middle and upper part of branch.

x1/4

x 1/2

692. *Corema conradii.* General habit showing small, numerous leaves, terminal clusters of flowers.

x 2/3

693. *Floerkea proserpinacoides.* General habit; alternate pinnate leaves, axillary peduncled flower.

1524. *Corema conradii*

1525. *Empetrum eamesii* subsp. *atropurpureum*

1526. *Empetrum nigrum*

1527. *Floerkea proserpinacoides*

1528. *Cotinus coggygria*

compound, leaflets entire, lobed or toothed; flowers perfect or imperfect, in loose, spreading or drooping, axillary panicles, styles terminal; drupes whitish or grayish. [*Rhus*]. Foliage poisonous to touch; smoke from burning foliage also poisonous and can cause injury if inhaled. —Wildl. 2

a. Leaves pinnate, with 7 or more leaflets. (Fig. 694). .... 1. *T. vernix*
a. Leaves ternate.
    Stems woody throughout, much branched, straggling or climbing and producing
        aerial roots; terminal leaflet gradually acuminate. .... 2. *T. radicans*
    Stems woody only above the rhizomatous base, simple to sparingly branched,
        not climbing or producing aerial roots; terminal leaflet abruptly acute. ...... 3. *T. rydbergii*

1. T. vérnix (L.) Kuntze. (varnish). Poison Sumac. Wooded swamps, pond and stream margins. Fruit: July-November. Fig. 694, Map 1529. [*Rhus vernix*]. —OBL

2. T. rádicans (L.) Kuntze. (rooting). Poison Ivy. Open woods, roadsides, stone walls, sand dunes. Fruit: July-November. Map 1530. [*Rhus radicans; R. toxicodendron*]. Our plants are subsp. *radicans*. —FAC

3. T. rydbérgii (Small ex. Rydb.) Greene. (for P. A. Rydberg). Poison Ivy. Same habitats as *T. radicans*. Fruit: July-November. Map 1531. [*Rhus radicans* var. *rydbergii*]. —FAC-

T. pubéscens Miller Poison Oak. Similar to *T. rydbergii* but with pubescent petiole and leaflets with blunt lobes or teeth (petiole glabrous and leaflets with pointed lobes or teeth in *T. rydbergii*. Reported for Suffolk County, NY. [*T. toxicaria; Rhus quercifolia; R. toxicodendron*].

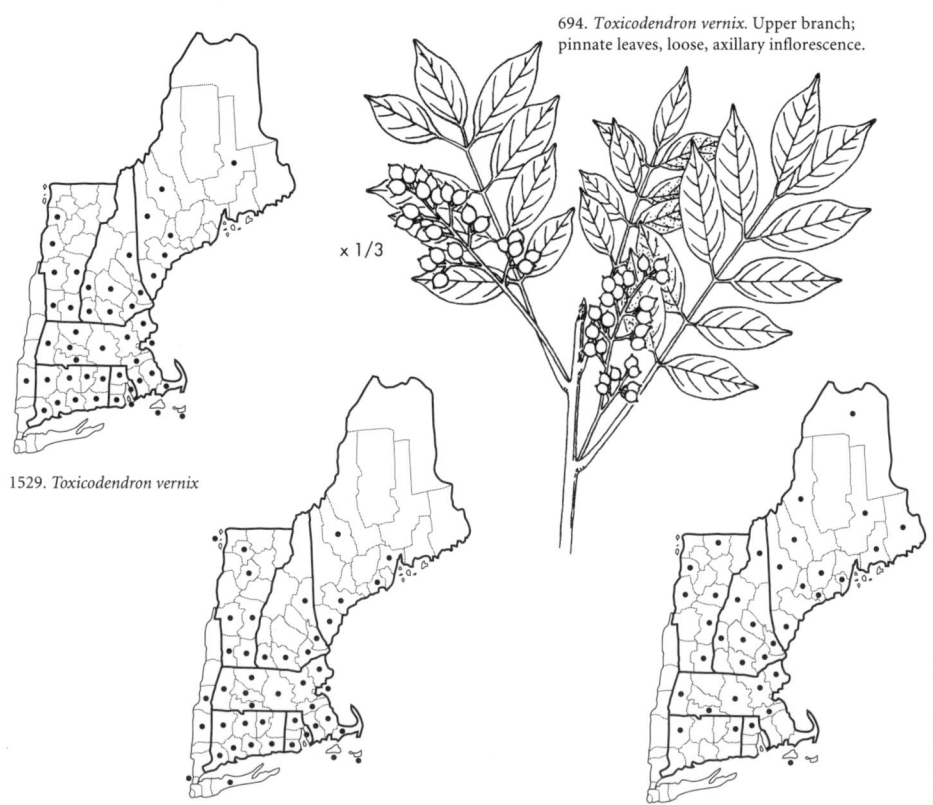

694. *Toxicodendron vernix*. Upper branch; pinnate leaves, loose, axillary inflorescence.

x 1/3

1529. *Toxicodendron vernix*

1530. *Toxicodendron radicans*

1531. *Toxicodendron rydbergii*

3. *Rhús* L. Sumac (classical Greek and Latin name).

Shrubs or small trees, similar to *Toxicodendron* except not poisonous to touch, end bud lacking, flowers in crowded, erect, terminal panicles, drupes red. The fruiting clusters may be steeped in hot water and used to make a drink that can serve as a substitute for lemonade. —Wildl. 3

a. Leaves ternate .... 1. *R. aromatica*
a. Leaves pinnate, with 7 or more leaflets.
  b. Leaf rachis winged. (Fig. 695) .... 2. *R. copallinum*
  b. Leaf rachis wingless.
    Twigs and petioles glabrous or merely puberulent. .... 3. *R. glabra*
    Twigs and petioles densely velvety-pubescent. .... 4. *R. hirta*

1. *R. aromática* Ait. (aromatic). Fragrant sumac. Dry, open woodlands, rocks and ledges. Fruit: June-August. Map 1532. [*Schmaltzia aromatica; S. crenata; Rhus canadensis*]. Our plants are var. *aromatica*.

2. *R. copallínum* L. (from the copal-like resinous atoms). Shining sumac. Thickets, fields, openings. Fruit: August-October. Fig. 695, Map 1533. Our plants include var. *copallinum* and the following var.:

var. *latifólia* Engler. Leaflets rounded to the base on the upper side of the oblique base (leaflets attenuate to the base in var. *copallinum*). A preparation made from the roots was used by Indians to treat hemorrhoids.

3. *R. glábra* L. (glabrous). Smooth sumac. Thickets, fields, openings. Fruit: August-October. Map 1534. Leaves have been smoked to treat asthma; other medicinal uses are also cited.

R. x pulvináta Greene. A supposed hybrid between *R. glabra* and *R. hirta* [*R. x borealis*].

4. *R. hírta* (L.) Sudworth. Staghorn sumac. Fields, roadsides, thickets, woodland borders. Fruit: July-September. Map 1535. [*R. typhina*].

Family 123. Aquifoliáceae (Holly Family)

Polygamodioecious shrubs or trees. Leaves alternate, simple, petioled, entire, serrate or crenate, evergreen or deciduous, stipules minute or lacking. Flowers perfect or imperfect, regular, small, whitish or greenish, solitary or clustered in the axils, calyx lobes, petals and stamens each 4-7 or calyx absent, stamens hypogynous, ovary superior, 4-7 locular, each with 1 ovule, stigmas 4-7. Fruit a berry-like drupe with 4-7 nutlets.

Calyx persistent in fruit; minute stipules or stipule scars usually present; petals elliptic,
  united at base; stamens attached to base of corolla; fruit on pedicels mostly
  less than 1 cm long .... 1. *Ilex*
Calyx promptly deciduous; stipules and stipule scars lacking; petals linear, separate;
  stamens free; fruit on pedicels 1 cm or more long. .... 2. *Nemopanthus*
                                                   mucronatus

1. *Ílex* L. Holly (ancient Latin name for the Holly-Oak).

Twigs slender, often producing spurs with densely crowded leaf scars, pith small, buds small, with several scales, solitary or superposed, leaf scars crescent-shaped, raised, bundle trace 1, end bud present, minute stipule scars or tiny pointed stipules present; leaves usually minutely stipulate; calyx persistent, petals united at the base, stamens attached to base of the corolla. Fruits poisonous; both leaves and fruits have been used as an emetic. —Wildl. 2

a. Leaves coriaceous and evergreen; fruit black or leaves spiny-margined or tipped.
  Leaves spine-tipped and usually with several spine-tipped teeth on each margin;
    fruit red or yellow. (Fig. 696). .... 1. *I. opaca*
  Leaves crenate above the middle; fruit black. .... 2. *I. glabra*

a. Leaves membranous, deciduous; fruit red to yellowish; leaves crenate to serrate.
  b. Calyx lobes eciliate; fruit usually orange-red. .... 3. *I. laevigata*
  b. Calyx lobes ciliate, even on mature fruit; fruit usually scarlet.
    Petals entire or minutely erose; nutlets smooth and even. .... 4. *I. verticillata*
    Petals ciliate; nutlets grooved on the back. .... 5. *I. montana*

1. *I. opáca* Ait. (opaque). American holly. Moist woods, mostly near the coast. May-June. Fig. 696, Map 1536. Our plants are var. *opaca*. —FACU+

2. *I. glábra* (L.) Gray (smooth). Inkberry. Wooded swamps, bogs, wet woods, pond margins. June-July. Map 1537. (N.S.). Endangered in ME, NH. —FACW-

3. *I. laevigáta* (Pursh) Gray. (smooth). Smooth winterberry. Wooded swamps, wet woods, bogs, pond margins. June. Map 1538. —OBL

4. *I. verticilláta* (L.) Gray. (whorled). Winterberry. Wooded swamps, wet woods, pond margins. May-June. Map 1539. —FACW+

5. *I. montána* (T. & G.) Gray. Mountain winterberry. Woodlands. June. Rare. Reported for Berkshire County MA. [*I. ambigua; I. monticola*].

2. Nemopánthus Raf. Mountain holly (Greek name).

Shrubs, similar to *Ilex* except buds solitary, ovoid, stipules and stipule scars lacking, calyx promptly deciduous, petals and stamens free.

1. *N. mucronátus* (L.) Loes. (abruptly short-pointed). Wooded swamps, shrub swamps, wet woods, bogs, pond margins. May-June. Map 1540. —OBL

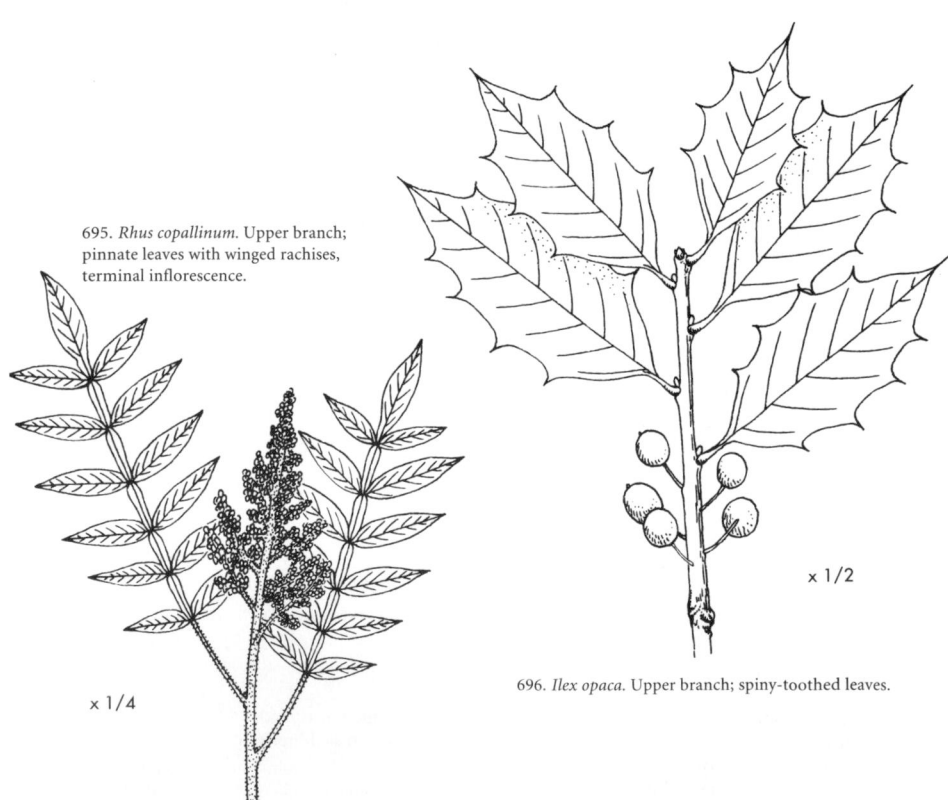

695. *Rhus copallinum*. Upper branch; pinnate leaves with winged rachises, terminal inflorescence.

× 1/2

× 1/4

696. *Ilex opaca*. Upper branch; spiny-toothed leaves.

1532. *Rhus aromatica*

1533. *Rhus copallinum*

1534. *Rhus glabra*

1535. *Rhus hirta*

1536. *Ilex opaca*

1537. *Ilex glabra*

1538. *Ilex laevigata*

1539. *Ilex verticillata*

1540. *Nemopanthus mucronatus*

Family 124. Celastráceae (Staff-tree Family)

Hermaphrodite or polygamodioecious vines, shrubs or small trees. Leaves alternate or opposite, simple, petioled, stipules none or small and caducous. Flowers perfect or imperfect, regular, small, greenish, whitish or purplish, in axillary cymes or terminal panicles, sepals and petals each 4-5, stamens 4-5, all inserted at the margin of a flattened, fleshy disc, ovary superior, inserted on or surrounded by the disc (then appearing inferior), 2-4-locular, each with 2 ovules, style short, stigma 2-4 lobed. Fruit a leathery, loculicidal capsule with several seeds, each enclosed in a colorful, fleshy aril.

Leaves alternate; twining vines .... 1. *Celastrus*
Leaves opposite; shrubs or small trees; if a vine, climbing by aerial rootlets, not
    twining .... 2. *Evonymus*

1. Celástrus L. Bittersweet (ancient Greek name for an evergreen tree).

Polygamodioecious, climbing and twining woody vines, stems somewhat slender, pith large, white, buds small, solitary, projecting at right angles from the stem, scales 4-6, leaf scars half-elliptic, bundle trace 1, stipule scars minute; leaves alternate, petioled, serrulate; flowers 5-merous, ovary inserted on the disc, 3-locular, stigma 3-lobed; capsule orange, 3-valved, splitting and exposing 1 or 2 scarlet, arillate seeds. Poisonous. —Wildl. 1

Flowers and fruits in terminal panicles. (Fig. 697). .... 1. *C. scandens*
Flowers and fruits in axillary cymes .... 2. *C. orbiculata*

    1. C. scándens L. (climbing). American bittersweet. Roadsides, thickets, often along rivers and woodland edges. May-June. Fig. 697, Map 1541. —FACU-
    2. C. orbiculáta Thunb. (round). Asian bittersweet. Roadsides, thickets. Map 1542. (Naturalized from e. Asia).

2. Evónymus L. (ancient Greek name).

Hermaphrodite, shrubs or small trees, sometimes a vine, twigs moderate, green, 4-lined or winged, pith greenish, buds small to moderate, solitary, scales 5-8, leaf scars half elliptic, bundle trace 1, stipule scars minute; leaves opposite, petioled, serrulate; flowers perfect, greenish or purplish, in axillary cymes, 4 (5)-merous, ovary surrounded by and concealed within the disc, 2-4-locular, stigma 2-4-lobed; capsule 2-4-lobed (sometimes only 1-lobed by abortion), pink to purple. [*Euonymus*]. Poisonous.

Twigs corky-winged; petiole less than 5 mm long. .... 1. *E. alata*
Twigs lined and angled but not winged, or if so (*E. phellomana*) petiole 5 mm or
      more long.
    Leaves pubescent beneath; flowers purple; aril red. .... 2. *E. atropurpurea*
    Leaves glabrous beneath; flowers greenish; aril orange (red in *E. americana*). .... 3. *E. europaea*

    1. E. aláta (Thunb.) Sieb. (winged). Winged Spindle-tree. Occasionally escaped from cultivation to roadsides. Map 1543. (Introduced from e. Asia).
    2. E. atropurpúrea Jacq. (dark purple). Burning bush. Roadsides, old foundations. June-July. Map 1544. From farther west or south. Our plants are var. *atropurpurea*. —FACU
    3. E. europaéa L. (European). Occasionally escaped from cultivation to roadsides, waste places and woodlands. May-June. Map 1545. (Naturalized from Europe).
    E. phellomána Loes. Branches 4-sided or with corky wings; petioles 5 mm or more long; seeds brown (branches not angled or winged, seeds white in *E. europaea*). From China. Reported for MA, CT.

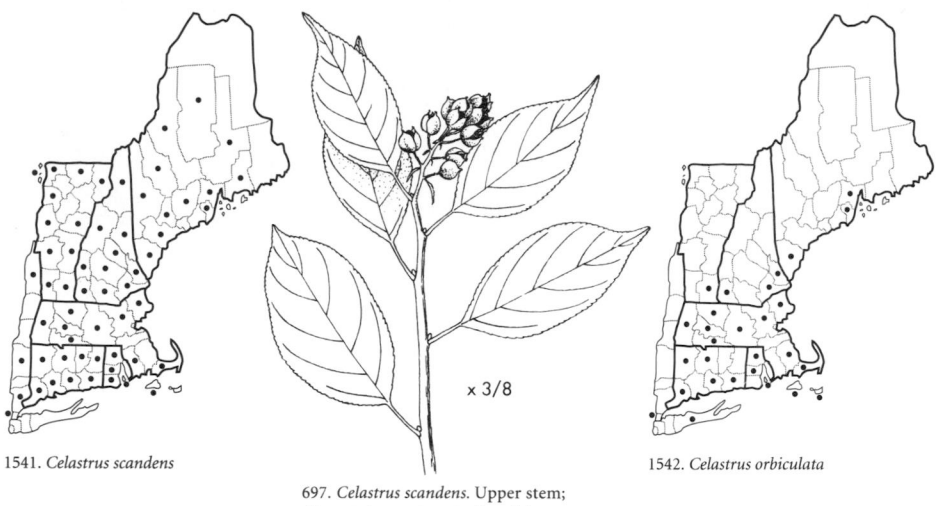

1541. *Celastrus scandens*

697. *Celastrus scandens*. Upper stem; alternate leaves, terminal panicle.

× 3/8

1542. *Celastrus orbiculata*

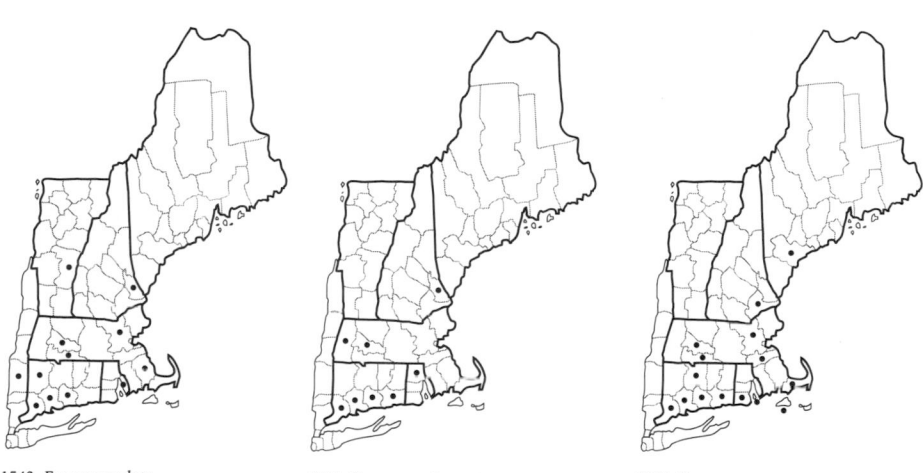

1543. *Evonymus alata*

1544. *Evonymus atropurpurea*

1545. *Evonymus europaea*

E. fortúnei (Turcz.) Hand-Maz. Evergreen, climbing by aerial rootlets, leaves simple, elliptic (*E. europaea* and *E. phellomana* are deciduous shrubs). (Introduced from Asia). Occasionally spread from cultivation. Reported for Hampshire County MA. Our plants include var. *fortunei* and the following var.:

var. *rádicans* Rehd. Leaves obtuse, sharply serrate (leaves acute to acuminate and crenate-serrate in var. *fortunei*). [*E. radicans*].

E. americána L. Strawberry-bush. Flowers 5-merous and fruits strongly tubercled (flowers 4-merous and fruits smooth in the latter 3 species). Rarely adventive from farther west and south. Reported for Bronx County NY. —FAC

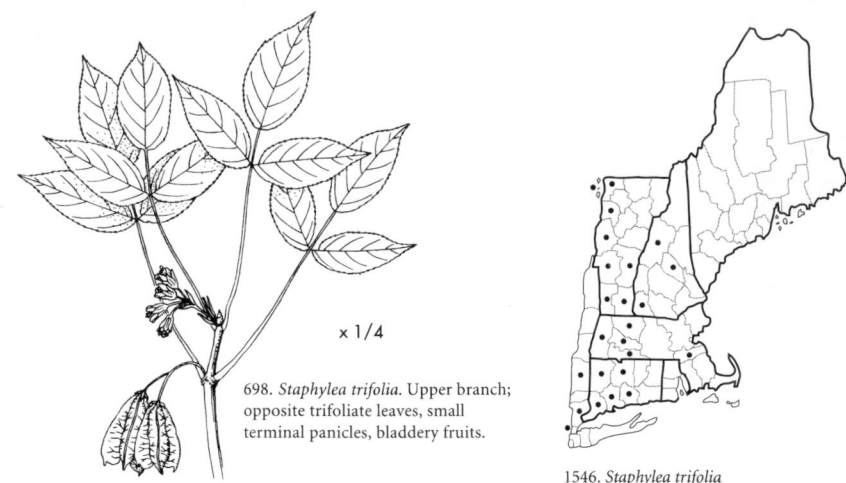

x 1/4

698. *Staphylea trifolia*. Upper branch;
opposite trifoliate leaves, small
terminal panicles, bladdery fruits.

1546. *Staphylea trifolia*

Family 125. Staphyleáceae (Bladdernut Family)

Represented with us by the following genus:

1. Staphyléa L. Bladdernut (Greek name meaning cluster of grapes).

Hermaphrodite, shrubs or small trees, bark greenish-striped, twigs moderate, pith relatively large, white, buds moderate, solitary, scales 1-several, leaf scars half-round, bundle traces 3-6, stipule scars present, end bud lacking; leaves opposite, trifoliate, long-petioled, stipulate, leaflets elliptic to ovate, serrate, sometimes oblique at the base; flowers perfect, regular, greenish-white, campanulate, in small, drooping panicles terminating the branches, sepals and petals each 5, stamens 5, all inserted at the margin of a large disc, ovary superior, inserted on the disc, pubescent, 3-locular, each with several ovules, styles 3, united; fruit an inflated, bladdery, 3-lobed capsule dehiscing apically.

1. **S. trifólia** L. (three-leaved). Woodlands, thickets, borders. Fruit: June-September. Fig. 698, Map 1546. —FAC

Family 126. Aceráceae (Maple Family)

Represented with us by the following genus:

1. Ácer L. Maple (Latin name for the maple).

Polygamodioecious, trees or shrubs, often with sugary or milky sap, twigs moderate, pith pale, buds moderate, solitary or collaterally multiple, highly variable in shape, stalked or sessile, scales 2-numerous, leaf scars V or U-shaped, bundle traces 3 or in 3 groups, stipule scars lacking, end bud present (ours); leaves opposite, simple and palmately lobed or rarely pinnately compound, petioled, estipulate; flowers perfect, or more commonly imperfect, regular, small, in various kinds of terminal and axillary inflorescences, calyx usually 5 (4-12) parted, petals the same number or absent, stamens 4-10, all inserted inside or at the margin of a disc (disc wanting in a few species), stamens long-exsert in the staminate flowers, ovary superior, 2-locular, flattened and 2-lobed, ovules 2 in each locule, stigmas 2, elongate; fruit a schizocarp of 2, 1-seeded samaras. —Wildl. 3

In addition to the following species *A. x freemánii* has been reported for ME. Syrup and sugar are mostly made from *A. saccharum*, but can also be made from the other large species including species 1, 5, 7, 8 and 10.

a. Leaves compound .... 1. *A. negundo*
a. Leaves simple.
  b. Leaf lobes blunt or rounded with entire margins or leaves rarely unlobed, merely
      serrate; petioles usually with milky sap. (Fig. 699). .... 2. *A. campestre*
  b. Leaf lobes acute or acuminate, with margins usually toothed or serrate.
    c. Twigs distinctly puberulent, particularly toward the tip; bud scales 2, valvate ..... 3. *A. spicatum*
    c. Twigs glabrous or essentially so; bud scales more than 2, imbricate
      (2 and valvate in *A. pensylvanicum*).
      d. Buds stalked, scales 2, valvate; flowers and fruits in a raceme; bark of young
          trunk and branches green, with longitudinal stripes. .... 4. *A. pensylvanicum*
      d. Buds sessile, scales more than 2, imbricate; flowers and fruits in clusters,
          corymbs or panicles; bark brownish, not striped.
        e. Sinuses between the principal leaf lobes usually rounded; lobes bearing a
           few large teeth; petioles with milky sap or buds conical and acute,
           tan, with numerous scales. (Fig. 700).
           Petioles with milky sap; buds ovoid and blunt, greenish or reddish;
              samara wings widely spreading, nearly horizontal. .... 5. *A. platanoides*
           Petioles lacking milky sap; buds conical and acute, tan; samara wings
              forming a U, the sides essentially parallel .... 6. *A. saccharum*
        e. Sinuses between the principal leaf lobes sharp (except sometimes in *A.*
          saccharinum); lobes regularly coarsely or finely toothed; petioles
          lacking milky sap; buds without above combination of characters.
          f. Twigs usually reddish; collateral buds common on older growth; flowers
            and fruits in sessile or subsessile lateral clusters; flowering before
            the leaves.
            Terminal leaf lobe less to slightly more than the length of the blade,
              broadest at base; sinuses between lobes always sharp; twigs
              not malodorous when broken .... 7. *A. rubrum*
            Terminal leaf lobe well over half the length of the blade, narrowed
              at base; sinuses between lobes sometimes rounded; twigs
              malodorous when broken. .... 8. *A. saccharinum*
          f. Twigs brown; buds solitary; flowers and fruits in terminal panicles;
            flowering with the leaves.
            Leaf blades longer than wide, 3-lobed. (Fig. 701). .... 9. *A. ginnala*
            Leaf blades as long as wide or wider, 5-lobed. .... 10. *A. pseudoplatanus*

1. *A. negúndo* L. (aboriginal name). Boxelder. Roadsides, waste places, riverbanks. April-May. Map 1547. [*Negundo n.; N. nuttallii*]. Our plants include var. *negundo* and the following var.: var. *violáceum* (Kirsch.) Jaeg. Twigs glaucous (green in var. *negundo*). —FAC+

2. *A. campéstre* L. (of fields). Hedge-maple. Occasionally escaped from cultivation to waste places and around dwellings. Fig. 699. (Introduced from Europe). Reported for Barnstable County MA.

A. tatáricum L. Similar to *A. campestre* but differs in having leaves unlobed, cordate-based and doubly serrate (leaves blunt-lobed with entire margins in *A. campestre*). Rarely escaped from cultivation. Reported for Middlesex County MA, Newport County RI.

3. *A. spicátum* Lam. (spiked). Mountain-maple. Rich, moist woods. May-June. Map 1548. —FACU-

4. *A. pensylvánicum* L. (of Pennsylvania). Striped-maple. Rich, moist woods. May-June. Map 1549. —FACU-

5. *A. platanoídes* L. (like Plane-tree). Norway-maple. Roadsides, waste places, around dwellings. April-May. Map 1550. (Introduced from Europe).

6. *A. sáccharum* Marsh. (sugar). Sugar-maple. Rich woods. April-May. Fig. 700, Map 1551. [*A. saccharophorum; Saccharodendron s.*]. Our plants are var. *saccharum*. —FACU-

A. nígrum Michx. f. Similar to *A. saccharum* but having leaves with drooping sides (leaves with flat sides in *A. saccharum*). Reported for CT, MA, NH, VT. [*A. saccharum* var. *nigrum; A.s.* var. *viride; Saccharodendron n.*].

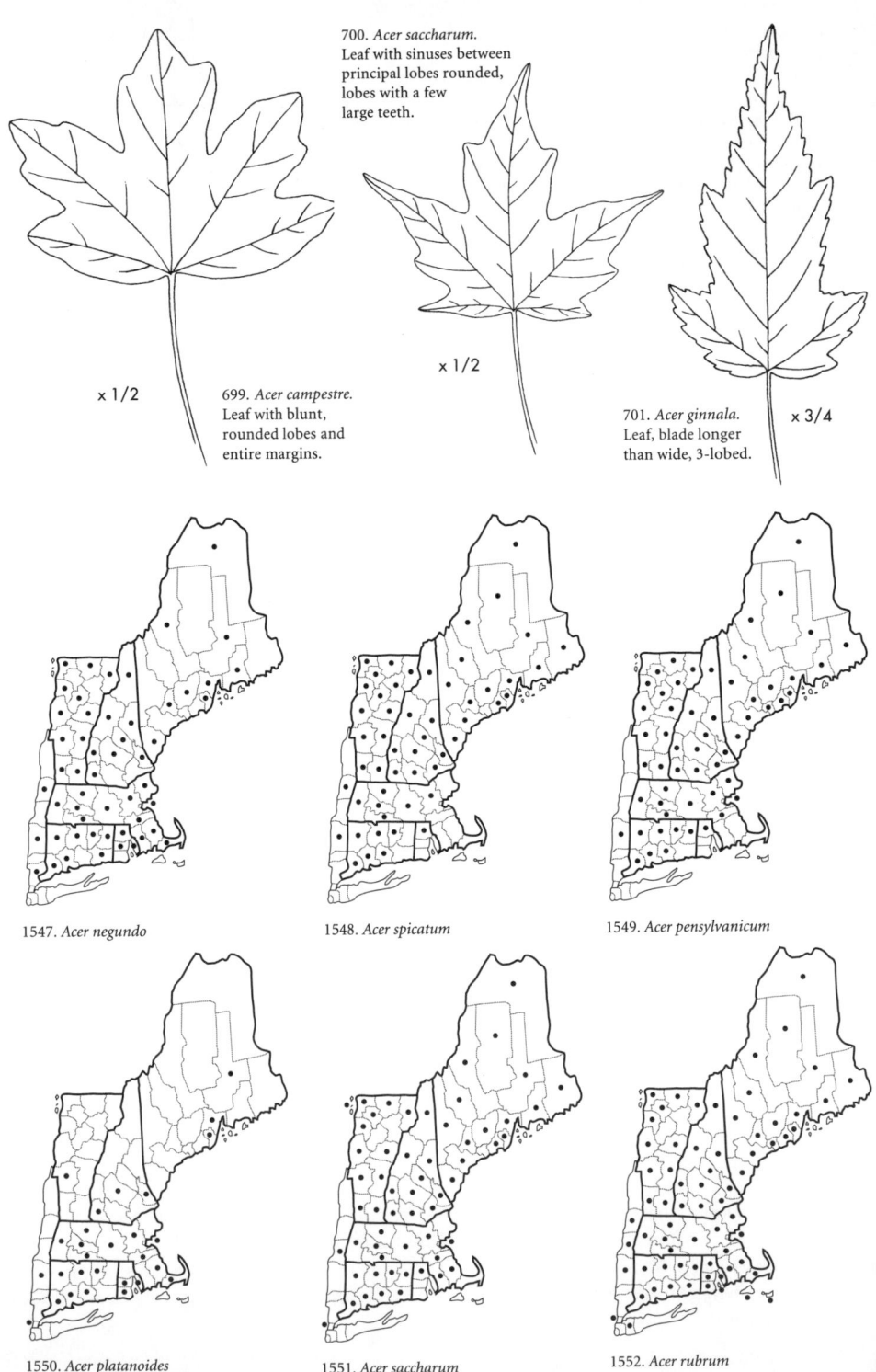

700. *Acer saccharum.*
Leaf with sinuses between
principal lobes rounded,
lobes with a few
large teeth.

x 1/2

699. *Acer campestre.*
Leaf with blunt,
rounded lobes and
entire margins.

x 1/2

701. *Acer ginnala.*
Leaf, blade longer
than wide, 3-lobed.

x 3/4

1547. *Acer negundo*

1548. *Acer spicatum*

1549. *Acer pensylvanicum*

1550. *Acer platanoides*

1551. *Acer saccharum*

1552. *Acer rubrum*

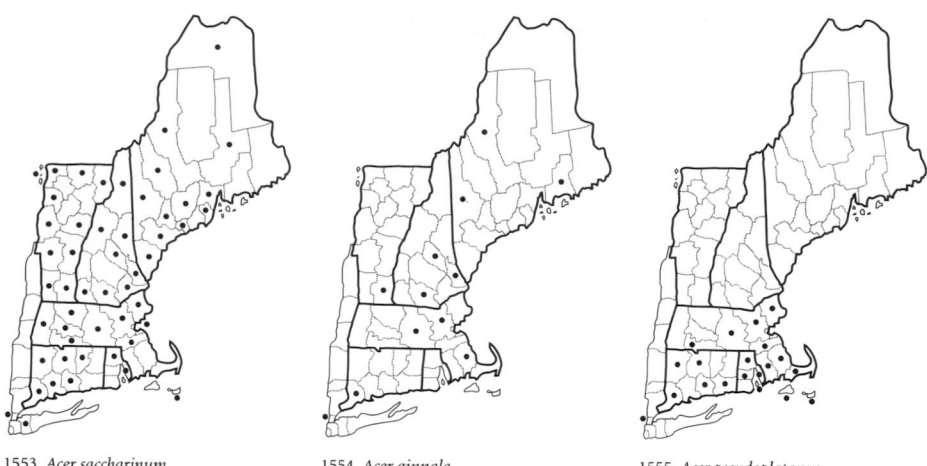

1553. *Acer saccharinum*   1554. *Acer ginnala*   1555. *Acer pseudoplatanus*

7. A. rúbrum L. (red). Red maple. Wooded swamps, pond and river margins, uplands. April-May. Map 1552. [*A. carolinianum; A. stenocarpum; Rufacer r.; R. drummondii*]. Our plants include var. *rubrum* and the following var.:

var. *trílobum* Torr. & Gray ex K. Koch. Blades with 3 minor lobes (distinctly 3-5-lobed in var. *rubrum*). —FAC

8. A. saccharínum L. (sugary). Silver maple. Typically river bottomlands. March-April. Map 1553. [*Argentacer s.*]. —FACW

9. A. gínnala Maxim. (native name). Occasionally escaped from cultivation to roadsides, borders of woods and fields. May. Fig. 701, Map 1554. (Introduced from Asia).

10. A. pseudoplátanus L. (false plane-tree). Escaped from cultivation to roadsides, waste places and woodlands. May. Map 1555. (Introduced from Europe).

Family 127. Hippocastánaceae (Horse-Chestnut Family)

Represented with us by the following genus:

1. Aésculus L. (ancient name for some mast-bearing tree).

Polygamomonoecious trees, twigs stout, pith large, pale, buds large, solitary, ovoid and pointed, often resinous, with several scales, leaf scars large, shield-shaped or inversely triangular, bundle traces in 3 distinct groups or 7-9 in a curved line, stipule scars lacking; leaves opposite, palmately compound, with 5-7 serrate leaflets, long-petioled, estipulate; flowers perfect and staminate, in a terminal panicle, irregular, showy, white with red or yellowish, calyx unequally 5-lobed, petals 4-5, clawed, unequal, stamens 5-8, conspicuously exserted, hypogynous, ovary superior, 3-locular, with 2 ovules in each locule, style and stigma 1; fruit a spiny (ours) 3-valved, usually 1-locular capsule with a single large, brown, shiny seed with a large pale scar. Poisonous.

Leaflets usually 7, abruptly acuminate; pubescence of the leaf undersides and
    inflorescence, at least in the axils, tawny, long and matted; petals usually 5 .... 1. *A. hippocastanum*
Leaflets usually 5, gradually acuminate; pubescence of the leaf undersides and
    inflorescence whitish, short, not matted; petals usually 4. .... 2. *A. glabra*

1. A. hippocástanum L. (Horse-chestnut). Horse-chestnut. Occasionally escaped from cultivation to roadsides and waste places. May. Map 1556. (Introduced from Europe).

2. A. glábra Willd. (smooth). Ohio Buckeye. River bottomlands. Rare. From farther south or west. Reported for ME, Strafford County NH. Our plants are var. *glabra*. —FACU+

Family 128. Sapindáceae (Soapberry Family)

Represented with us by the following genera:

1. Koelreutéria Laxm. Golden rain tree (for J. Koelreuter).
Polygamodioecious trees, rarely herbaceous vines, twigs rather large, pith moderate, whitish, buds moderate, solitary, conical, projecting at right angles from the stem, scales usually 2, leaf scars moderately large, shield-shaped, raised, bundle traces in an irregular line, stipule scars and end bud lacking; leaves alternate, pinnate or bipinnate, leaflets lobed and coarsely toothed, estipulate; flowers imperfect or functionally so, regular, yellow, in showy, terminal panicles, calyx lobes and petals 5, stamens 8-10, extrastaminal disc present, ovary superior, 3-locular, each cell with 1 ovule, style 1; fruit an inflated, membranous, 3-lobed capsule.

    Cardiospérmum L. *halicácabum* L. Balloon-vine. Annual herb climbing by tendrils, leaves biternate, flowers white, in small clusters, 4-merous. (Introduced from tropical Amer.). Escaped from cultivation in the southeastern U.S., rarely found in our range. Reported for CT, Middlesex County MA. —FACU

    1. K. paniculáta Laxm. (panicled). Occasionally escaped from cultivation. Reported for MA. (Introduced from e. Asia).

Family 129. Balsamináceae (Touch-me-not Family)

Represented with us by the following genus:

1. Impátiens L. Jewelweed (impatient; referring to the sudden bursting of the capsules when touched).
Hermaphrodite, often succulent, annual or perennial herbs with hollow stems and watery juice; leaves alternate or whorled, simple, coarsely dentate, petioled, estipulate; flowers perfect, irregular, showy, pedicellate and bracteate, 1-3 or racemose in the leaf axils, often resupinate, sepals 3, colored, 2 lateral ones small, middle one larger, saccate and prolonged into a spur, petals 3, the 2 lateral ones cleft into 2 dissimilar lobes, stamens 5, hypogynous, the filaments short, flattened, united above, covering the ovary like a hood, ovary superior, 5-locular, ovules several in each locule, stigma minutely toothed; fruit an oblong, elastically dehiscent capsule, the 5 valves spirally coiling after expelling the seeds. Young shoots edible as a potherb; juice from the crushed stems useful in treating poison ivy and other types of skin rash. —Wildl. 1

a. Leaves opposite or whorled .... 1. *I. glandulifera*
a. Leaves alternate.
  b. Flowers and fruit on axillary pedicels, not racemose; sepals and fruit pubescent ..... 2. *I. balsamina*
  b. Flowers and fruit in peduncled clusters forming axillary racemes; sepals and
    fruit glabrous. (Fig. 702).
    Spur 5 mm or less long, at a right angle to the yellow or cream-colored corolla . 3. *I. pallida*
    Spur 6 mm or more long, curved parallel to the usually orange to reddish
    corolla .... 4. *I. capensis*

    1. I. glandulífera Royle (bearing glands). Occasionally escaped from cultivation to roadsides and waste places. August-September. Map 1557. (Introduced from Asia). [*I. roylei*].

    2. I. balsámina L. (old generic name). Balsam. Occasionally escaped from cultivation. (Introduced from Asia). Reported for Washington County RI.

    3. I. pállida Nutt. (pale). Moist woods, often calcareous. July-September. Map 1558. —FACW

    4. I. capénsis Meerb. (of the Cape). Wooded swamps, moist woods, stream borders. July-September. Fig. 702, Map 1559. [*I. biflora; I. nortonii*]. —FACW

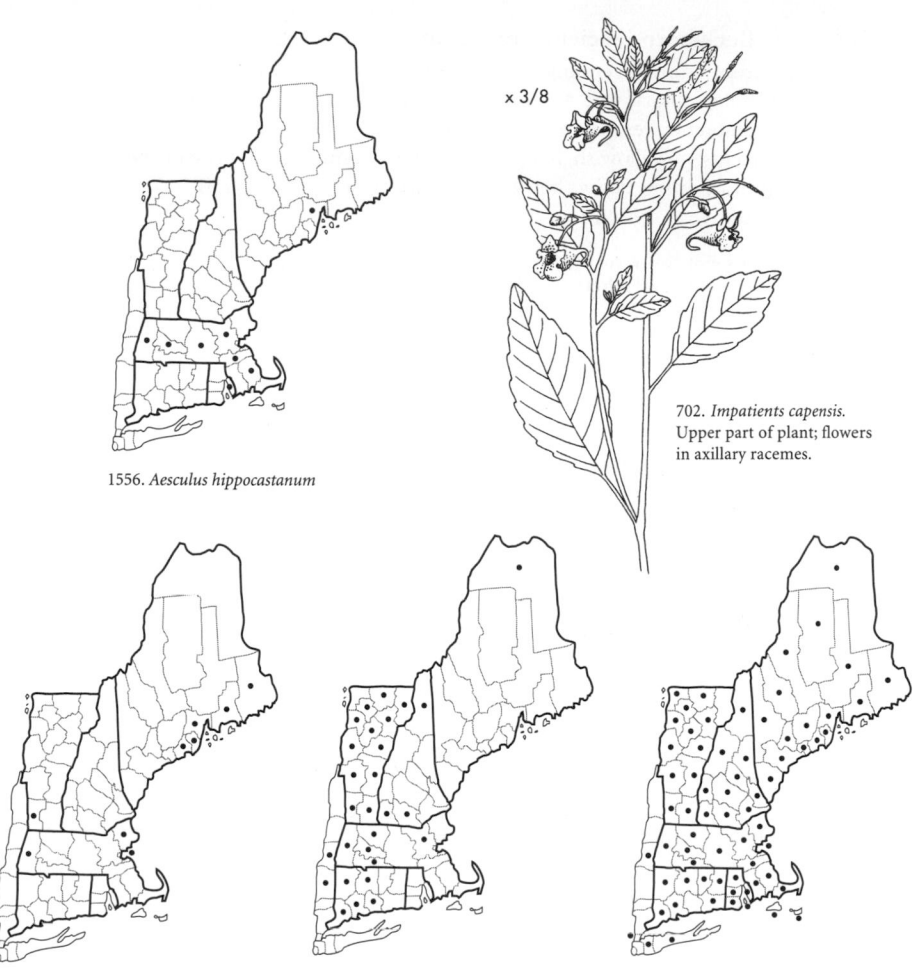

1556. *Aesculus hippocastanum*

× 3/8

702. *Impatients capensis.*
Upper part of plant; flowers
in axillary racemes.

1557. *Impatiens glandulifera*

1558. *Impatiens pallida*

1559. *Impatiens capensis*

Family 130. Rhamnáceae (Buckthorn Family)

Hermaphrodite or polygamous, shrubs or small trees. Leaves alternate or opposite, simple, petioled, stipules small, deciduous. Flowers perfect or imperfect, regular, small and greenish, yellowish or whitish, solitary or in umbellate cymes or panicles of cymes, axillary or terminal, calyx lobes and petals 4-5 or petals absent, stamens 4-5 and borne opposite the petals on a disc that rims the hypanthium, ovary superior, inserted on or surrounded by the disc (then appearing inferior), 2-4-locular, with 1 ovule per locule, stigmas 2-4. Fruit a dry or fleshy, capsule-like or berry-like drupe.

a. Leaves pinnately-nerved; longer peduncles less than 1 cm long, axillary; flowers
    greenish to yellowish; drupe berry-like.
      Leaves distinctly serrate to crenate; winter buds scaly. .... 1. *Rhamnus*
      Leaves entire or obscurely crenulate; winter buds naked. .... 2. *Frangula*
a. Leaves 3-nerved from the base; longer peduncles more than 2 cm long or
    inflorescences terminal; flowers white; drupe capsule-like. (Fig. 703). .... 3. *Ceanothus*

1. *Rhámnus* L. Buckthorn (ancient Greek name).

Shrubs or small trees, branches ending in spines, or spineless, twigs and pith moderate, the latter white, buds moderate, solitary, with 4-6 imbricated scales, leaf scars crescent-shaped, bundle traces 3, stipule scars minute; leaves alternate, opposite or subopposite, serrate or crenate, pinnately veined; flowers greenish to yellowish, in umbellate, axillary cymes, petals present, ovary inserted on the disc, free from it; drupe fleshy, berry-like. Fruits of the species below have been used as a purgative and a laxative. —Wildl. 1

a. Leaves opposite or subopposite; many of the branches ending in short spines.
    Larger leaves 2 times or less as long as wide, widely elliptic to nearly orbicular .... 1. *R. cathartica*
    Larger leaves more than 2 times as long as wide, narrowly elliptic to oblong. .... 2. *R. davurica*
                                                      subsp. *nipponica*
a. Leaves alternate; branches spineless .... 3. *R. alnifolia*

    1. *R. cathártica* L. (cathartic). Common Buckthorn. Open woods and woodland borders, roadsides, waste places. May-June. Map 1560. (Naturalized from Europe).

    2. *R. davúrica* Pall. Rarely found in waste places and along roadsides. (Introduced from Japan and Korea). Reported for RI, Hartford County CT. [*Rhamnus citrifolia; Frangula c.*]. Represented with us as subsp. *nipponica* (Makino) Kartesz & Gandhi.

    3. *R. alnifólia* L'Her (alder-leaved). Alder-leaved Buckthorn. Bogs and wooded swamps. May-June. Map 1561. [*Frangula a.*]. —OBL

2. *Frángula* P. Mill.

Similar to *Rhamnus*, but with winter buds naked and leaves entire or obscurely crenulate. [*Rhamnus*].

    1. *F. álnus* P. Mill. Glossy Buckthorn. Damp woodlands, wetland borders, roadsides. May-June. Map 1562. (Naturalized from Europe). [*Rhamnus frangula*]. Dried bark has been used as a purgative and laxative; charcoal was used for making gunpowder. —FAC

3. *Ceanóthus* L. Redroot (ancient Greek name).

Shrubs, from a reddish root, twigs moderate, puberulent, pith rather large, white, buds solitary, ovoid, with several scales, leaf scars half elliptic, slightly raised, bundle traces 1-3, stipule scars minute; leaves alternate, serrate, strongly 3-nerved from the base; flowers white, in terminal or

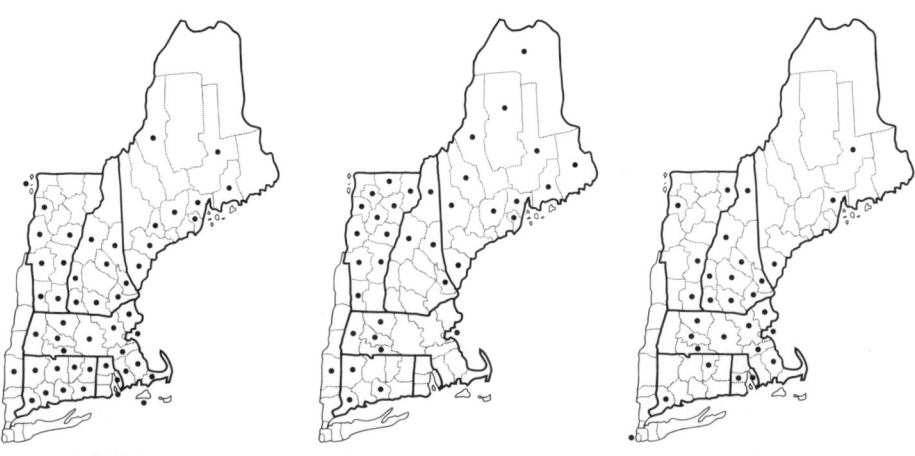

1560. *Rhamnus cathartica*   1561. *Rhamnus alnifolia*   1562. *Frangula alnus*

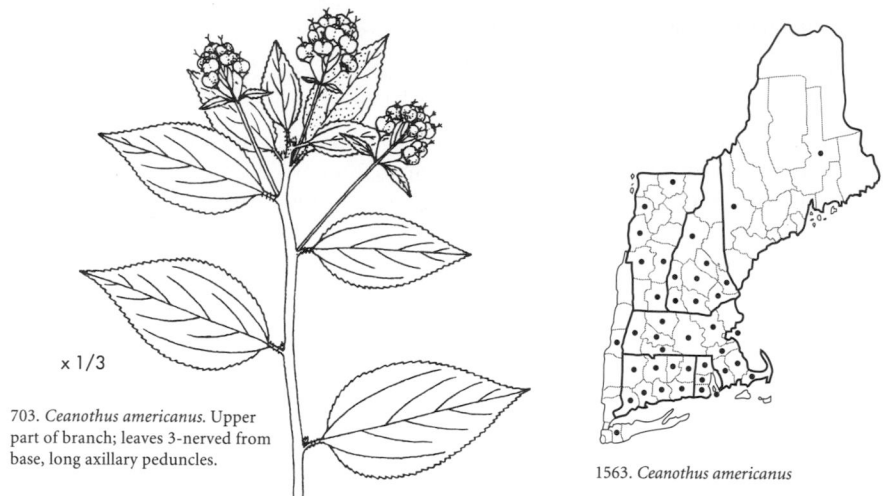

703. *Ceanothus americanus.* Upper part of branch; leaves 3-nerved from base, long axillary peduncles.

1563. *Ceanothus americanus*

axillary panicles of umbellate cymes, calyx 5-lobed, petals 5, ovary surrounded by the disc, adnate to the hypanthium at the base; drupe dry, capsule-like, 3-lobed, subtended by the persistent hypanthium, loculicidally dehiscent into 3 carpels when ripe.

Inflorescences terminating long, axillary peduncles, these naked or with 1-several
   reduced leaves subtending the panicle; leaves mostly ovate. (Fig. 703) .... 1. *C. americanus*
Inflorescences short-peduncled, these terminating regular leafy branches; leaves
   mostly elliptic to elliptic-lanceolate. .... 2. *C. herbaceus*

   1. *C. americánus* L. (American). New Jersey Tea. Dry, open woods and thickets. June-July. Fig. 703, Map 1563. Dried leaves can be prepared as a substitute for tea.
   2. *C. herbáceus* Raf. (herbaceous). Dry sandy or rocky woods and open areas. May-June. Reported for Essex County MA, Chittenden County VT. Endangered in VT. [*C. ovatus; C. pubescens*].

Family 131. Vitáceae (Grape Family)

Hermaphrodite or polygamous, woody vines, usually climbing by tendrils opposite the leaves. Leaves alternate, simple or compound, petioled, with deciduous stipules. Flowers perfect or imperfect, regular, small, greenish, in bracteate cymes or panicles on peduncles opposite the leaves or terminal, usually with a disc or cup, calyx entire or 4-5-lobed, petals 5, separate or coherant, stamens 5, ovary superior, 2-locular, 2-4 ovulate, style and stigma solitary. Fruit a berry.

a. Leaves with 5-7 leaflets, or simple and tendrils tipped by adhesive discs. .... 1. *Parthenocissus*
a. Leaves simple; tendrils, when present, not tipped by adhesive discs.
   Inflorescence a dichotomously forked cyme; petals separate; pith white. .... 2. *Ampelopsis*
   Inflorescence paniculate; petals cohering at summit, falling off like a cap; pith
   brown .... 3. *Vitis*

1. *Parthenocíssus* Planch. Virginia Creeper (from the Greek, meaning virgin ivy).
Tendrils often tipped by adhesive discs which serve as holdfasts, twigs moderate, pith rather large, whitish or greenish, buds solitary or often 2 at a node, 1 large and 1 small, ovoid to roundish, with several scales, leaf scars circular or nearly so, raised, bundle traces numerous, in a circle or ellipse, stipule scars present, end bud lacking; leaves palmately compound, with 3-7 serrate leaflets, or palmately lobed with a cordate base; flowers in compound cymes or panicles of cymes, disc small, adnate to the ovary, calyx obscurely lobed, petals thick, spreading; berry with thin flesh. —Wildl. 2

a. Leaves of mature vine palmately lobed, not compound. .... 1. *P. tricuspidata*
a. Leaves of mature vine compound, with 5-7 leaflets.
    Tendrils tipped by adhesive discs; inflorescence with a distinct central axis. .... 2. *P. quinquefolia*
    Tendrils without adhesive discs; inflorescence dichotomously forked. (Fig. 704) ... 3. *P. vitacea*

1. P. tricuspidáta (Sieb. & Zucc.) Planch. (with three cusps). Boston Ivy. Occasionally escaped from cultivation to waste places. Map 1564. (Introduced from Asia).

2. P. quinquefólia (L.) Planch. (5-leaved). Woodlands, roadsides, thickets, waste places. June-July. Map 1565. [*P. hirsuta; Psedera q.*]. —FACU

3. P. vitácea (Knerr) Hitchc. (grape-like). Woodlands, thickets, commonly along rivers, roadsides, waste places. June-August. Fig. 704, Map 1566. [*P. inserta; Psedera v.*]. —FACU

2. Ampelópsis Michx. (from the Greek, meaning appearance like a vine).

Glabrous or pubescent, tendrils few to none, when present not tipped by adhesive discs, twigs moderate, pith moderate, white, buds solitary, roundish, with several scales, leaf scars circular, raised, bundle traces numerous in a circle or ellipse, stipule scars present, end bud lacking; leaves simple, lobed or unlobed, truncate or cordate at the base, serrate; flowers in a dichotomously forked cyme, disc saucer-shaped, free from the ovary except at the base, calyx lobes usually obsolete, petals separate; berry with thin flesh.

Leaves distinctly 3 (occasionally 5)-lobed. .... l. *A. brevipedunculata*
Leaves unlobed or very obscurely lobed, mostly merely coarsely serrate. .... 2*A. cordata*

1. A. brevipedunculáta (Maxim.) Trautv. (short-peduncled). Pond margins, thickets, waste places. Map 1567. (Introduced from Asia).

2. A. cordáta Michx. (heart-shaped). Alluvial woods. May-June. From farther south. (*Cissus ampelopsis*]. —FAC+

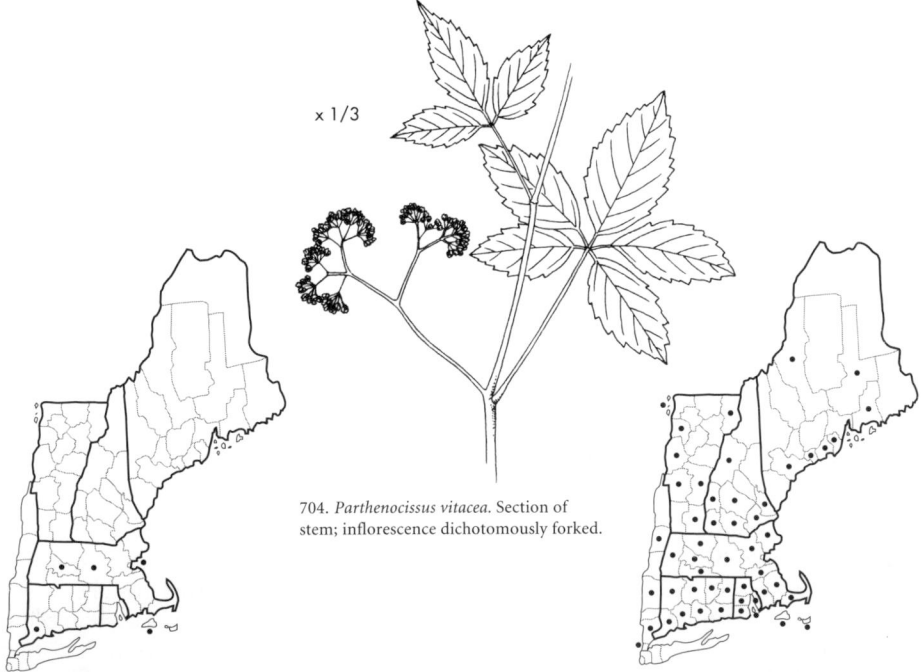

x 1/3

704. *Parthenocissus vitacea.* Section of stem; inflorescence dichotomously forked.

1564. *Parthenocissus tricuspidata*

1565. *Parthenocissus quinquefolia*

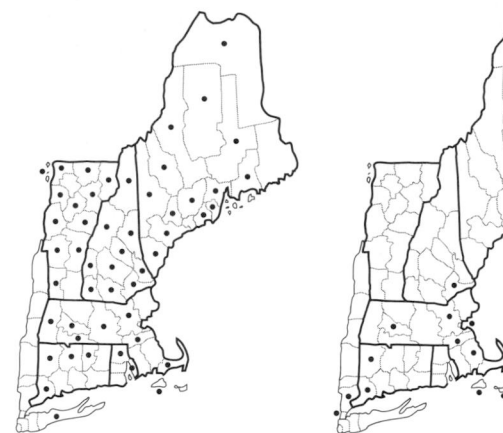

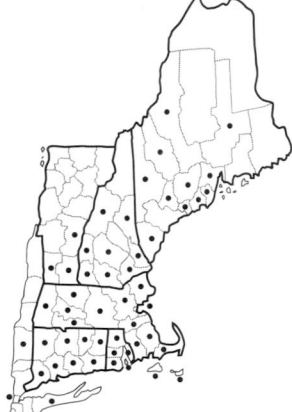

1566. *Parthenocissus vitacea*   1567. *Ampelopsis brevipedunculata*   1568. *Vitis labrusca*

3. Vítis L. Grape (classical Latin name).

Bark or older growth often flaking, tendrils not tipped by adhesive discs, stems striate, glabrous or pubescent, moderate, pith moderate, brown, discontinuous through the nodes (ours) buds solitary or collateral, subglobose, with 2-3 scales, leaf scars half-round or crescent-shaped, bundle traces numerous, scattered, stipule scars present, end bud lacking; leaves simple, lobed or unlobed, serrate, cordate at the base; flowers paniculate, disc of 5 connate or separate glands, calyx lobes obsolete, petals cohering at the summit, separating at the base, falling off like a cap; berry pulpy and juicy, dark purple. Fruit and leaves edible. —Wildl. 4

a. Leaves permanently tomentose or floccose beneath, or if pubescent only on the
    veins, the exposed surface whitened or glaucous.
    Leaves permanently tomentose beneath, the surface completely concealed;
        tendrils or inflorescences produced at 3 or more successive nodes. .... 1. *V. labrusca*
    Leaves floccose beneath, portions of the surface clearly visible, whitened or
    glaucous; tendrils or inflorescences not produced at more than 2
    successive nodes .... 2. *V. aestivalis*
a. Leaves glabrous beneath when mature, or pubescent only on the principal veins,
    or rarely with some scattered bunched hairs (*V. vinifera*), the exposed surface
    green, the expanding leaves sometimes pubescent over the surface but soon
    glabrate.
    b. Teeth of leaves long-acuminate, longer than wide. (Fig. 705). .... 3. *V. riparia*
    b. Teeth of leaves obtuse or acute, mostly wider than long.
      c. Tendrils or inflorescences usually produced at 3 or more consecutive nodes;
        fruits 1.2 cm or more in diameter .... 4. *V. novae-angliae*
      c. Tendrils or inflorescences not produced at more than 2 successive nodes; fruits
        1 cm or less in diameter.
        Leaves unlobed to slightly lobed, glabrous beneath or pubescent only on
          the veins .... 5. *V. vulpina*
        Leaves usually deeply lobed, usually with some scattered, bunched hairs
        beneath .... 6. *V. vinifera*

    1. V. labrúsca L. (early Latin name). Fox-grape. Open woods, roadsides, thickets. Fruit: September-October. Map 1568. —FACU

    V. x labruscána Bailey. A hybrid between *V. labrusca* and 1 or more of a variety of popular cultivated strains.

2. *V. aestivális* Michx. (of summer). Summer-grape. Open woods, roadsides, thickets. Fruit: September-October. Map 1569. Our plants include var. *aestivalis* and the following var.:

var. *argentifólia* (Munson) Fern. Leaves glaucous beneath, flocculent or pubescent mostly only on the principal and smaller veins (not glaucous beneath and flocculent over the surface in var. *aestivalis*). [*V. bicolor*]. —FACU

3. *V. ripária* Michx. (of river-banks). River-bank grape. Riverbanks, thickets and roadsides. Fruit: August-September. Fig. 705, Map 1570. [*V. vulpina*].—FACW

4. *V. nóvae-ángliae* Fern. Very doubtfully a species and most probably a hybrid between *V. labrusca* and *V. riparia*. Fruit: September-October. Map 1571.

5. *V. vulpína* L. Riverbanks, floodplains, thickets. Fruit: September-October. From farther south. Reported for MA. [*V. cordifolia*]. —FAC

6. *V. vinífera* L. Oriental. A waif in our area in refuse. Reported for MA.

Family 132. Tiliáceae (Linden Family)

Represented with us by the following genus:

1. *Tília* L. Basswood (classical Latin name).

Hermaphrodite trees, twigs moderate, pith moderate, pale, buds obliquely divergent over the leaf scars, inequilaterally ovoid, with 2-3 red or greenish scales, leaf scars elevated, half-elliptic, bundle traces several, scattered, stipule scars present, end bud lacking; leaves alternate, simple, petioled, widely ovate to suborbicular, acuminate-tipped, obliquely cordate to truncate at the base, serrate, glabrous or with simple or stellate pubescence; stipules deciduous; flowers perfect, regular, white to yellowish, in long-peduncled, axillary cymes, the peduncle adnate to about the middle of a long, narrow, foliaceous bract, sepals 5, petals 5, often with tiny, scale-like bodies at the base (staminodia), stamens numerous, in clusters, ovary superior, tomentose, 5-locular, with 2 ovules per locule, style 1, stigma shallowly several-lobed; fruit tomentose, hard, indehiscent, nut-like. Tea is made from the flowers, which has a sedative effect but is reported to cause heart damage in people with cardiac problems if used too often; inner bark was used by Indians to make cord and rope. —Wildl. 1

a. Leaves glabrous beneath except for tiny tufts often present in the vein axils, or with
    sparse, scattered pubescence.
  b. Twigs and petioles pubescent .... 1. *T. platyphyllos*
  b. Twigs and petioles glabrous.
    Petals with tiny, scale-like bodies (staminodia) at the base; largest leaves
      longer than 1 dm .... 2. *T. americana*
                                      var. *americana*
    Petals lacking staminodia; largest leaves 1 dm or less long. .... 3. *T. europaea*
a. Leaves densely and finely tomentose beneath. .... 2. *T. americana*
                                          var. *heterophylla*

1. *T. platyphýllos* Scop. (broad-leaved). Rarely escaped from cultivation to roadsides and waste places. (Introduced from Europe). Reported for York County ME.

T x vulgáris Hayne (pro sp.) A hybrid between *T. platyphyllos* and *T. cordata*.

2. *T. americána* L. (American). Basswood. Rich, moist woods. July. Fig. 706, Map 1572. [*T. neglecta; T. palmeri*]. Our plants include var. *americana* and the following var.:

var. *heterophýlla* (Vent.) Loud. Leaves densely and finely tomentose beneath (leaves glabrous beneath except for tiny tufts often present in the vein axils or with sparse, scattered pubescence in var. *americana*). [*T. heterophylla; T. monticola; T. michauxii; T. pubescens*]. —FACU

T. petioláris DC. Will key to *T. americana* var. *heterophylla* but is distinguishable in having pendulous branchlets and suborbicular leaves (branchlets not pendulous and leaves ovate to oblong in *T. americana* var. *heterophylla*). Eurasian. Sometimes spread from cultivation to waste places. Reported for MA.

3. *T. europaéa* L. (European). Rarely escaped from cultivation to roadsides and waste places. (Introduced from Europe). Reported for Middlesex and Barnstable Counties MA; Hartford County CT.

T. cordáta Mill. Resembling *T. europaea* but leaves are nearly orbicular and glaucous beneath (ovate and green beneath in *T. europaea*). (Introduced from Europe). Occasionally escaped from cultivation in our range. Reported for Fairfield County CT, Kennebec County ME, Middlesex, Plymouth and Worcester Counties, MA.

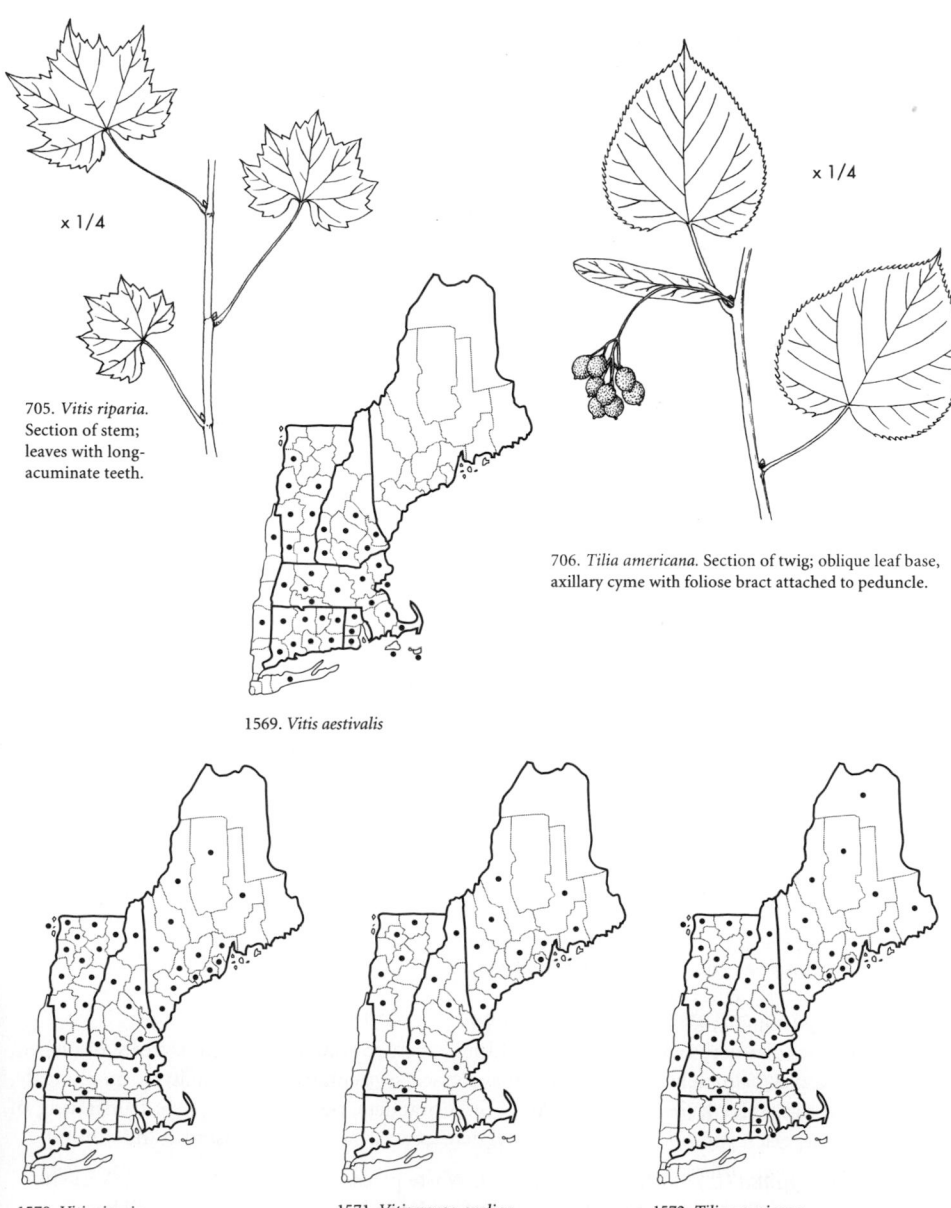

705. *Vitis riparia.* Section of stem; leaves with long-acuminate teeth.

706. *Tilia americana.* Section of twig; oblique leaf base, axillary cyme with foliose bract attached to peduncle.

1569. *Vitis aestivalis*

1570. *Vitis riparia*

1571. *Vitis novae-angliae*

1572. *Tilia americana*

Family 133. Malváceae (Mallow Family)

Hermaphrodite, rarely dioecious herbs; rarely shrubs (ours), commonly stellate-pubescent. Leaves alternate, simple, lobed or unlobed, petioled, usually palmately veined, stipulate. Flowers perfect, regular, solitary or fascicled in the leaf axils, or in terminal panicles, sepals 5, united, at least at the base, often subtended by an involucre of bractlets, petals 5, distinct, stamens numerous, monadelphous, forming a column around the ovary and style, filaments separate near the apex, ovary superior, of 5-many carpels, either forming a ring around the base of the style or united into a 5-locular ovary, ovules 1-several in each locule, style branched at the apex into as many branches as carpels, usually projecting above the stamen column. Fruit a ring of easily separated dehiscent or indehiscent carpels or a loculicidal capsule.

Napaéa L. *dioíca* L. Glade-Mallow. A dioecious perennial herb with palmately lobed leaves, and white flowers lacking an involucel of bractlets and occurring in large terminal panicles is rarely spread from cultivation in our range; from farther south and west. Reported for Windsor County VT. —FACW

Sphaerálcea St. Hil. Gray False Mallow. With 0-3 bractlets subtending calyx, petals emarginate, stigmas terminal, capitate, and carpels beakless, differentiated into a lower indehiscent part and stellete pubescent. *S. féndleri* Gray. Leaves triangular-ovate, much longer than wide. From the southwest. Reported for Middlesex County MA; *S. munroána* (Dougl.) Spach. Leaves round-ovate to orbicular, about or nearly as long as wide. From the northwest. Reported for MA. Represented with us as subsp. *munroana*.

Lavátera L. *triméstris* L. Tree-Mallow. Annual, flowers solitary in the leaf axils, 1 dm across; Mediterranean; rarely escaped from cultivation in our range. Reported for Fairfield County CT, Addison County VT.

a. Calyx subtended by an involucel of bractlets.
  b. Bractlets 3.
    Petals red-purplish; carpels 2-horned at summit. .... 1. *Modiola caroliniana*
    Petals white or pink to purple; carpels rounded, not horned. .... 2. *Malva*
  b. Bractlets 5 or more.
    c. Leaves glabrous or essentially so above; carpels several-seeded; fruit a
      5-locular capsule .... 3. *Hibiscus*
    c. Leaves definitely with forked or stellate pubescence above; carpels 1-seeded.
      Stigmas and carpels 10 or more; fruit a ring of carpels, separating at maturity.
        Calyx lobes 5 mm or less wide across the base; petals less than 4 cm long;
          plant less than 1.5 m tall .... 4. *Althaea officinalis*
        Calyx lobes 6 mm or more wide across the base; petals 4 cm or more
          long; plant 1.5 m or more tall .... 5. *Alcea rosea*
      Stigmas and carpels 5; fruit a 5-locular capsule. .... 6. *Kosteletskya virginica*
a. Calyx not subtended by bractlets.
  Petioles of principal stem leaves more than 4 cm long; blades broadly ovate,
    crenate to entire .... 7. *Abutilon theophrasti*
  Petioles of principal stem leaves less than 4 cm long; blades lance-ovate to
    oblong or blades deeply palmately lobed. .... 8. *Sida*

1. *Modíola* Moench (name based on shape of the fruit).

Annual or biennial herbs, prostrate to ascending, often rooting at the nodes, freely branched, pubescent; leaves palmately 3-5 cleft, the lobes incised or dentate; flowers solitary, on elongate, axillary pedicels, calyx pubescent, subtended by 3 bractlets, petals red-purplish; fruit a ring of numerous carpels, separating at maturity, each dehiscent, 2-horned and hispid at the summit.

    1. *M. caroliniána* (L.) G. Don. (of Carolina). Waste places and around buildings. April-June. (Tropical Amer.). From farther south. Reported for Hampshire County MA. —FACU

2. *Málva* L. Mallow (ancient Latin and Greek name).

Annual or perennial, prostrate to erect, pubescent to glabrous herbs; leaves orbicular or reniform, toothed or crenate to lobed or dissected; flowers solitary or fascicled in the leaf axils, calyx subtended by 3 bractlets, petals white or pink to purple, style branches stigmatose along the inner side; fruit a ring of numerous carpels, separating at maturity, each indehiscent, beakless.

Malvástrum Gray *coromandeliánum* (L.) Garcke. Will key to *Malva* but is distinguishable in having style branches terminating in capitate stigmas, carpels dehiscent. From farther west. Reported for MA. [*M. americanum*].

Gossýpium L. *hirsútum* L. Cotton. Similar to Malva but differs from it and Malvastrum in having an involucel of 3 large, foliaceous, cordate and laciniate bractlets and white-woolly seeds. Spread from cultivation in the south, rarely found in waste places in our range. Reported for Middlesex and Suffolk Counties MA. [*G. herbaceum*].

a. Upper leaves divided beyond the middle; flowers in crowded, leafy-bracted, terminal
    clusters and solitary in the upper leaf axils, surpassing petioles of subtending
    stem leaves. (Fig. 707).
    Pubescence of stems stellate; bractlets ovate. .... 1. *M. alcea*
    Pubescence of stems simple; bractlets linear to narrowly lanceolate. .... 2. *M. moschata*
a. Upper leaves merely lobed, seldom as far as the middle; flowers in fascicles in the
    leaf axils, surpassed by petioles of subtending stem leaves. (Fig. 708).
    b. Bractlets oblong to ovate-lanceolate; petals 2 cm or more long; stem erect. .... 3. *M. sylvestris*
    b. Bractlets linear to linear-lanceolate; petals less than 2 cm long; stem prostrate to
        ascending (erect in *M. verticillata*).
        c. Stems stiffly erect; individual flowers mostly sessile or subsessile. .... 4. *M. verticillata*
        c. Stems prostrate to ascending; individual flowers mostly pedicelled (often
            mostly short-pedicelled in *M. parviflora*).
            Mature carpels smooth to very obscurely reticulate on the back, the lateral
                faces not radially veined .... 5. *M. neglecta*
            Mature carpels distinctly rugose-reticulate on the back, the lateral faces
                radially veined .... 6. *M. parviflora*

1. *M. álcea* L. (from the genus *Alcea*). Vervain-mallow. Fields, roadsides and around dwellings. June-August. Map 1573. (Naturalized from Europe).

2. *M. moscháta* L. (musky). Musk-mallow. Fields, roadsides and waste places. June-September. Fig. 707, Map 1574. (Naturalized from Europe).

3. *M. sylvéstris* L. (of woodlands). High mallow. Occasionally escaped from cultivation to roadsides and waste places. May-August. Map 1575. (Introduced from Europe). Used as a potherb; various medicinal uses are also cited.

4. *M. verticilláta* L. (whorled). Whorled mallow. Occasionally escaped from cultivation to waste places and around buildings and gardens. July-September. Fig. 708, Map 1576. (Adventive from Europe). Used as a potherb.

M. críspa L. Similar to *M. verticillata* but with leaves crisped or curled (flat in *M. verticillata*). Throughout our range. (Adventive from Europe). [*M. verticillata* var. *c.*].

5. *M. neglécta* Wallr. (overlooked). Cheeses. Waste places, gardens, around buildings. June-September. Map 1577. (Naturalized from Europe). Used as a potherb.

6. *M. parvifióra* L. (small-flowered). Waste places, around buildings. June-September. (Naturalized from Europe). Reported for Middlesex County MA. Used as a potherb.

M. pusílla Sm. Similar to *M. parviflora* but with claws of petals bearded, calyx slightly reticulate (claws of petals glabrous, calyx distinctly reticulate in *M. parviflora*). From farther west. Map 1577a. [*M. rotundifolia*]. Used as a potherb; various medicinal uses are also cited.

3. *Hibíscus* L. (ancient Latin and Greek name for a mallow).

Annual or perennial herbs, or shrubs with twigs fluted toward the tip, pith small, white, buds hidden above the leaf scars by branch or pedicel scars or bases, leaf scars half-round, raised, with short,

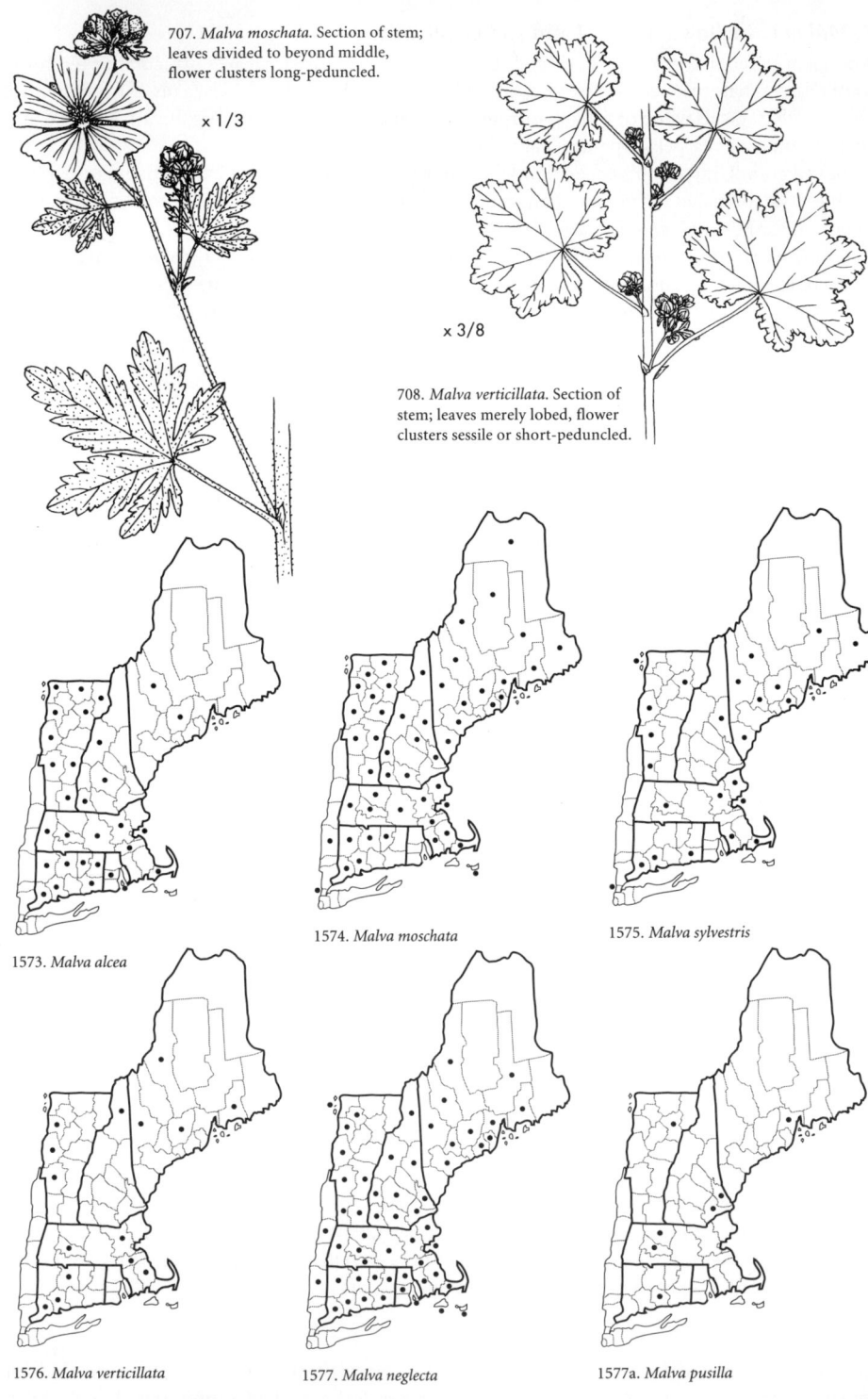

707. *Malva moschata*. Section of stem; leaves divided to beyond middle, flower clusters long-peduncled.

x 1/3

x 3/8

708. *Malva verticillata*. Section of stem; leaves merely lobed, flower clusters sessile or short-peduncled.

1573. *Malva alcea*

1574. *Malva moschata*

1575. *Malva sylvestris*

1576. *Malva verticillata*

1577. *Malva neglecta*

1577a. *Malva pusilla*

decurrent ridges, bundle traces scattered or forming an ellipse, stipule scars small; leaves usually long-petioled, ovate, unlobed to lobed, coarsely dentate; flowers large and showy, solitary or few in the upper leaf axils, calyx subtended by numerous linear bractlets, petals pink to purple or yellow with a purple base, carpels united into a 5-locular ovary, style branches 5; fruit a 5-locular, loculicidal capsule subtended or enclosed by the persistent calyx.

Abelmóschus Medik. *esculéntus* (L.) Moench. Okra. Leaves up to 3 dm in diameter, 3-9-lobed, flowers yellow, calyx spathe-like, fruit a pod 1 dm or more long. Rarely escaped from cultivation. Reported for Fairfield County CT. (*Hibiscus esculentus*). Widely planted as a vegetable.

a. Plant woody .... 1. *H. syriacus*
a. Plant herbaceous.
    Leaves deeply 3-parted, nearly to the base; fruiting calyx inflated, papery; petals
        yellow with purple base; annual. (Fig. 709). .... 2. *H. trionum*
    Leaves unlobed or shallowly 3-lobed sometimes to the middle or only slightly
        beyond; fruiting calyx not inflated or papery; petals pink to white;
        perennial .... 3. *H. moscheutos*

1. *H. syríacus* L. (Syrian). Rose of Sharon. Occasionally escaped from cultivation to roadsides and thickets. July-September. Reported for Fairfield County CT.

2. *H. triónum* L. (old generic name). Flower of an hour. Fields, roadsides, waste places, cultivated soil. July-September. Fig. 709, Map 1578.

3. *H. moscheútos* L. (Musk-rose). Rose-mallow. Salt or brackish to fresh marshes. July-September. Map 1579. (Naturalized from Europe). [*H. moscheutos* subsp. *palustris; H. oculiroseus*]. Our plants are subsp. *moscheutos*. —OBL

4. *Althaéa* L. (ancient Greek and Latin name).

Robust, pubescent, perennial herbs; leaves ovate, coarsely toothed and often shallowly lobed, with forked or stellate pubescence; flowers large and showy, in peduncled clusters from the upper axils and in axillary and terminal racemes, calyx subtended by a 6-9-lobed involucel, petals pink to purple; fruit a ring of numerous carpels, separating at maturity, each indehiscent, beakless.

1. *A. officinális* L. (of the shops). Marshmallow. Borders of salt marshes. August-September. Map 1580. (Introduced from Europe). A mucilagenous extract of the roots is reported to have various medicinal uses as well as do the dried leaves and flowers. Roots are also edible. —FACW+

5. *Alcéa* L.

Similar to *Althaea* but with larger proportions; distinguishing measurements given in key to genera. [*Althaea*].

1. *A. rósea* L. (rose-colored). Hollyhock. Occasionally escaped from cultivation to roadsides and waste places. July-August. Map 1581. (Introduced from Eurasia). [*Althaea r.*]. Reported to have medicinal uses similar to those of the latter species.

6. *Kostelétzkya* K. Presl. Seashore-mallow (for V. Kosteletzky).

Stellate-pubescent, perennial herbs; leaves triangular-ovate to triangular-lanceolate, hastate, cordate or truncate at the base, coarsely toothed; flowers axillary or in terminal, often leafy-bracted racemes or panicles, calyx subtended by 6-10 linear bractlets, petals pink to rose, carpels united into a 5-locular ovary, stigmas 5; fruit a 5-locular, loculicidal capsule subtended by the persistent calyx.

1. *K. virgínica* (L.) K. Presl. ex Gray (Virginian). Salt or brackish marshes. August-September. Reported for Nassau County NY. Represented with us as var. *aquilónia* Fern. —OBL

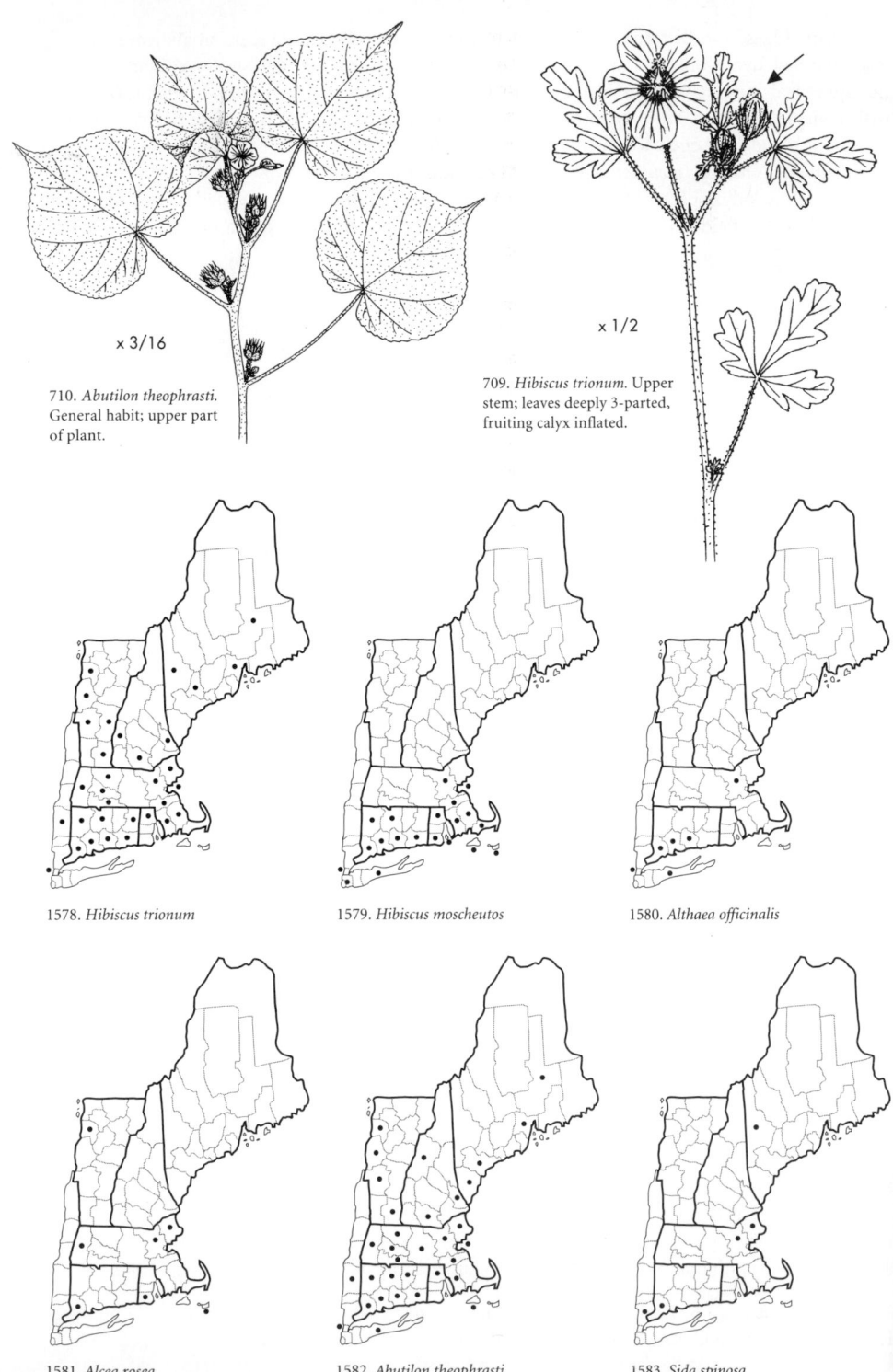

710. *Abutilon theophrasti.* General habit; upper part of plant.

×3/16

709. *Hibiscus trionum.* Upper stem; leaves deeply 3-parted, fruiting calyx inflated.

×1/2

1578. *Hibiscus trionum*

1579. *Hibiscus moscheutos*

1580. *Althaea officinalis*

1581. *Alcea rosea*

1582. *Abutilon theophrasti*

1583. *Sida spinosa*

7. Abútilon P. Mill. (modified from the original name *Aubuitilun*).

Tall, velvety-pubescent, annual herbs; leaves long-petioled, ovate, cordate, acuminate, crenate to entire; flowers axillary or in leafy-bracted racemes, involucral bractlets none, petals yellow, styles 5-many; fruit a ring of numerous united carpels, separating at maturity, each carpel dehiscent into 2 valves, each valve beaked by a slender awn.

  1. **A. theophrásti** Medik. (for Theophrastus). Butter-print. Roadsides, waste places, cultivated ground. August-September. Fig. 710, Map 1582. (Naturalized from India). [*A. abutilon*].

8. Sída L. (ancient Greek name for a related plant).

Annual or perennial herbs; leaves lobed or unlobed, crenate or toothed, stipules sometimes persistent as tiny tubercles at the base of the petiole; flowers solitary or in axillary and terminal clusters or corymbose panicles, involucral bractlets none, petals white or yellow, styles 5-10; fruit a ring of 5-10 united carpels, separating at maturity, enclosed by the persistent calyx, carpels indehiscent with a single beak or dehiscent into 2 valves, each valve beaked.

  Anóda Cav. *cristáta* (L) Schlechtendahl. Similar to Sida but flowers blue and carpels divergent in a depressed capsule which eventually breaks up, the partitions evanescent. Reported for CT, Middlesex County MA.

Leaves deeply palmately lobed; petals white. .... 1. *S. hermaphrodita*
Leaves not lobed; petals yellow .... 2. *S. spinosa*

  1. **S. hermaphrodíta** (L.) Rusby (hermaphrodite). Moist soil, often along rivers. July-September. Rare. Reported for Middlesex and Suffolk Counties MA. —FAC
  2. **S. spinósa** L. (spiny). Roadsides and waste places. July-September. Map 1583. (Naturalized from the tropics).

Family 134. Actinidiáceae (Actinidia Family)

Represented with us by the following genus:

1. Actinídia Lindl.

Dioecious or polygamous climbing shrub; leaves alternate, simple, long petioled, broadly ovate, truncate to subcordate at the base, finely serrate, abruptly acuminate; flowers unisexual in axillary cymes or solitary, sepals 5, persistent, petals 5, deciduous, stamens numerous, ovary superior, with several-many locules and many ovules, styles several-many; fruit a berry.

  1. **A. argúta** Miq. Bower Actinidia. (Introduced from Asia). A waif in our range, rarely escaped from cultivation. Reported for Berkshire County MA.

Family 135. Clusiáceae (St. John's-wort Family)

Hermaphrodite herbs, rarely shrubs. Leaves opposite, simple, entire, sessile or subsessile, usually pellucid-punctate and often also black-dotted, estipulate. Flowers perfect, regular, usually yellow, solitary or cymose, terminal or axillary, bracteate, sepals 4-5, persistent, petals 4-5, deciduous, stamens few, or more typically numerous, hypogynous, separate or basally connate in 3 or more clusters, ovary superior, of 2-5 carpels, 1-locular or partly or completely 2-5-locular, ovules numerous, styles as many as the carpels, sometimes fused below. Fruit a septicidal capsule. [*Hypericaceae*].

Petals pink or flesh-color to purplish; stamens in 3 clusters, the clusters alternating
    with 3 large glands .... 1. *Triadenum*
Petals yellow; glands none .... 2. *Hypericum*

1. *Triadénum* Raf. Marsh St. John's-wort.

Perennial herbs; leaves oblong, ovate or elliptic, cordate or clasping at the base, glaucous beneath; sepals and petals 5, petals pink or flesh-color to purplish; stamens 9, in 3 clusters of 3, the clusters alternating with 3 large glands, ovary 3-locular, styles 3. [*Hypericum*].

Mature sepals 5-8 mm long; styles 2-3 mm long. .... 1. *T. virginicum*
Mature sepals 3-5 mm long; styles less than 2 mm long. .... 2. *T. fraseri*

1. *T. virginicum* (L.) Raf. (Virginian). Marshes, bogs, pond and stream borders. July-August. Map 1584. [*Hypericum v.*]. —OBL

2. *T. fráseri* (Spach) Gleason (for its discoverer). Same habitats as *T. virginicum.* July-August. [*Hypericum f.; H. virginicum* var. *fraseri*]. —OBL

2. *Hypericum* L. St. John's-wort (ancient Greek name).

Herbs, or shrubs with exfoliating bark, twigs slender, wing-angled, at least below the nodes, pith small, brown or pale, buds minute, with 2-several scales, often developed as spurs or branches covered with scars, leaf scars minute, sometimes raised, triangular, bundle trace 1; leaves linear, lanceolate, or elliptic to ovate, rarely reduced and subulate; sepals 2, 4 or 5, often subequal, petals 4-5, yellow, stamens few or more typically many, separate or basally connate into 3 or more clusters, ovary 1-locular or partly or completely 3-5-locular, styles 2-5, sometimes fused below; capsule 1-5 locular, styles persistent, sometimes as a beak.

a. Sepals 4, of 2 sizes, or 2; petals 4.
    Larger leaves 7 mm or less wide; bracteoles on pedicels reaching base of calyx
        or beyond; styles 2 .... 1. *H. hypericoides*
                                                                              subsp. *multicaule*
    Larger leaves 8 mm or more wide; bracteoles on pedicels not reaching base of
        calyx; styles 3-4 .... 2. *H. crux-andreae*
a. Sepals and petals 5.
  b. Plant distinctly shrubby, the woody portion comprising more than two-thirds
    of the plant.
    c. Leaves 0.8 cm or less wide; sepals equal, 5 mm or less long, not foliaceous;
      capsule body 7 mm or less long .... 3. *H. densiflorum*
    c. Leaves, at least the larger ones, wider than 0.8 cm; sepals often unequal, some
      of them longer than 5 mm, foliaceous; capsule body longer than 7 mm.
      Capsule completely 3-locular .... 4. *H. prolificum*
      Capsule incompletely 3-locular, the placentae not reaching the central axis. .. 5. *H. frondosum*
  b. Plant herbaceous or suffrutescent, the woody portion, if any, comprising less
    than half the plant.
    d. Styles 5; capsule 5-locular, 1.5 cm or more long. .... 6. *H. ascyron*
    d. Styles 3 or united into 1; capsule 1 or 3-locular, 1 cm or less long.
      e. Leaves linear-subulate and scale-like, less than 4mm long. .... 7. *H. gentianoides*
      e. Leaves not linear-subulate and scale-like, 5 mm or more long.
        f. Styles united or closely connivent below, persistent as a beak on the capsule,
          becoming distinct due to its dehiscence; stigmas minute, not capitate.
          Largest leaves mostly 3 cm or less long; sepals oblanceolate to
            narrowly obovate .... 8. *H. ellipticum*
          Largest leaves more than 3 cm long; sepals lanceolate to ovate. .... 9. *H. adpressum*
        f. Styles 3, distinct, often divergent, not forming a beak on the capsule;
          stigmas capitate.
          g. Capsule 3-locular; stamens numerous, more than 20, in several
            distinct clusters.
            Branches ridged below each leaf; leaves with pellucid dots; petals
              black-dotted along the margin .... 10. *H. perforatum*
            Branches not ridged; leaves with both pellucid and dark dots; petals
              with both streaks and dots .... 11. *H. punctatum*
          g. Capsule 1-locular; stamens 20 or fewer, not in distinct clusters.
            h. Ultimate bracts of the inflorescence dilated and resembling the
              foliage leaves but smaller. (Fig. 711) .... 12. *H. boreale*

h. Ultimate bracts of the inflorescence setaceous to linear-subulate.
    i. Leaves linear, linear-oblong or linear-oblanceolate, with 1-3
        principal nerves. (Fig. 712) .... 13. *H. canadense*
    i. Leaves lanceolate, elliptic, ovate or deltoid, with more than 3
        principal nerves (at least the larger leaves).
        j. Leaves lanceolate or deltoid-lanceolate, tapered from base to
            apex, acute; sepals lanceolate; capsule conical, narrowed
            above. (Fig. 713).
            Leaves deltoid-lanceolate, 3 times or less as long as wide. .... 14. *H. gymnanthum*
            Leaves lanceolate, more than 3 times as long as wide. .... 15. *H. majus*
        j. Leaves elliptic to oblong, mostly obtuse; sepals linear-oblong;
            capsule ellipsoid, rounded above .... 16. *H. mutilum*

    1. *H. hypericóides* (L.) Crantz (like *Hypericum*). St. Andrew's cross. Dry, rocky or sandy, open soil. July-August. Endangered in MA, NY. Reported for Nantucket County MA. Represented with us as subsp. *multicaule* (Michx. ex Willd.) Robson. [*Ascyrum hypericoides* var. *multicaule; H. stragulum*]. —FACU

    2. *H. crúx-andreae* Crantz. St. Peter's-wort. Sandy fields and barrens. July-August. Reported for Suffolk County, NY. [*Ascyrum stans*]. —FACU

    3. *H. densiflórum* Pursh (densely flowered). Wet soil. July-September. From farther south. Endangered in NY. Reported for Middlesex County MA. —FAC+

    4. *H. prolíficum* L. (prolific). Woodlands and fields. July-September. Map 1585. From farther west or south. [*H. spathulatum*]. —FACU

    5. *H. frondósum* Michx. (full of leaves). Rarely escaped from cultivation. June-August. Map 1586. [*H. aureum*].

    6. *H. ascýron* L. Pond and river thickets. July-August. Map 1587. [*H. pyramidatum*]. —FAC

    7. *H. gentianoídes* (L.) B.S.P. (gentian-like). Waste places, roadsides, fields. July-August. Map 1588. [*Sarothra g.*].

    8. *H. ellípticum* Hook. (elliptical). Pond and stream margins, wet ditches, wet meadows. July-August. Map 1589. —OBL

    9. *H. adpréssum* Bart. (appressed). Pond margins and wet meadows. July-August. Map 1590. Endangered in NY. —OBL

    10. *H. perforátum* L. (perforated). Fields, roadsides, waste places. June-September. Map 1591. (Naturalized from Europe). Has been recommended as a remedy in herbals since the middle ages; tea made from the plant is reported to be of value as a nerve tonic in treating anxiety, depression and insomnia, as a diuretic and in treating stomach disorders; can cause dermatitis if used in excessive quantities.

    11. *H. punctátum* Lam. (dotted). Fields, roadsides, waste places, open woods, in dry to moist soil. June-September. Map 1592. [*H. subpetiolatum*]. —FAC-

    12. *H. boreále* (Britt). Bickn. (northern). Pond margins, wet meadows, bogs, wet sand. July-September. Fig. 711, Map 1593.

    forma *callitrichoídes* Fassett. Submersed plants with simple sterile stems and roundish leaves. —OBL

    13. *H. canadénse* L. Pond margins, wet meadows, ditches, wet sand. July-September. Fig. 712, Map 1594. (Includes *H. dissimulatum*, an apparent hybrid between *H. canadénse* and *H. boreale* or *H. mutilum*). —FACW

    14. *H. gymnánthum* Engelm. & Gray (with naked flowers). Moist to wet, usually sandy soil. July-September. From farther south or west. —OBL

    15. *H. május* (Gray) Britt. (larger). Pond margins, roadsides, waste places, meadows in moist to wet soil. July-September. Fig. 713, Map 1595. —FACW

    16. *H. mútilum* L. (cut off). Pond and stream margins, wet meadows, roadsides and waste places in moist to wet soil. July-September. Map 1596. [*H. parviflorum*]. —FACW

Family 136. Elatináceae (Waterwort Family)

Represented with us by the following genus:

1. *Elátine* L. Waterwort (classical name for a low-creeping plant).

Hermaphrodite, small, creeping or erect, often submerged, succulent-stemmed, annual herbs of wet soil or shallow water; leaves opposite or whorled, simple, sessile or subsessile, obovate or oblong to linear-lanceolate, entire, stipulate; flowers perfect, regular, minute, sessile and mostly solitary in the leaf axils, sepals, petals, stamens and stigmas each 2-3; ovary superior; fruit a 2-3-locular capsule with several seeds per locule, seeds areolate. —OBL

a. Seeds basal, all terminating at about the same level, mostly straight; flowers
    mostly 2-merous .... 1. *E. minima*
a. Seeds axile, terminating at different levels, mostly curved; flowers mostly
    3-merous.
    Leaves linear, lanceolate or oblong to narrowly spatulate. .... 2. *E. triandra*
    Leaves obovate to broadly spatulate .... 3. *E. americana*

    1. *E. mínima* (Nutt.) Fisch. & Mey. (smallest). Pond and river margins, often submerged. Fruit: July-October. Fig. 714, Map 1597.

    2. *E. triándra* Schkuhr (with three stamens). Pond margins. Fruit: July-October. (Eurasia). Reported for MA, Somerset County ME.

    3. *E. americána* (Pursh) Arn. (American). Muddy pond and stream margins, often tidal. Fruit: July-October. Map 1598. Endangered in MA. [*E. triandra* var. *a.*].

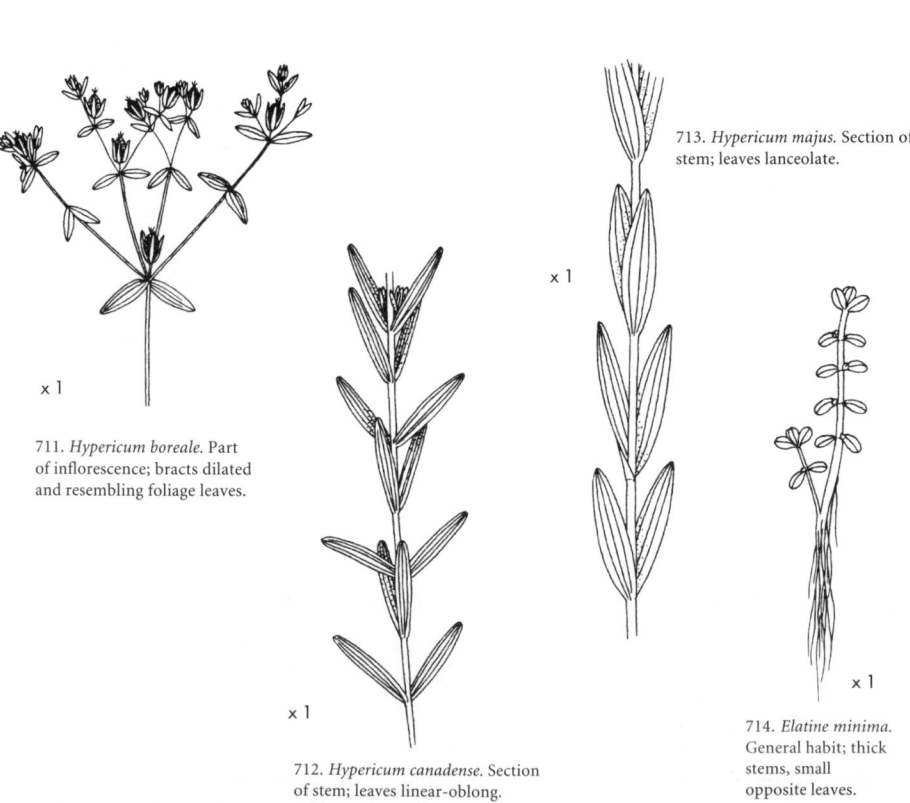

713. *Hypericum majus.* Section of stem; leaves lanceolate.

× 1

711. *Hypericum boreale.* Part of inflorescence; bracts dilated and resembling foliage leaves.

× 1

712. *Hypericum canadense.* Section of stem; leaves linear-oblong.

× 1

714. *Elatine minima.* General habit; thick stems, small opposite leaves.

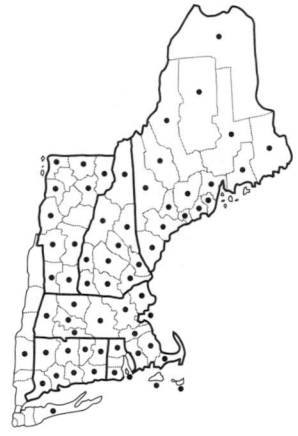

1584. *Triadenum virginicum*

1585. *Hypericum prolificum*

1586. *Hypericum frondosum*

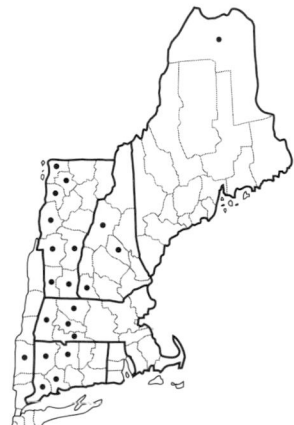

1587 *Hypericum ascyron*

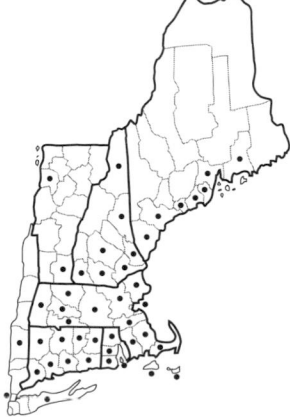

1588. *Hypericum gentianoides*

1589. *Hypericum ellipticum*

1590. *Hypericum adpressum*

1591. *Hypericum perforatum*

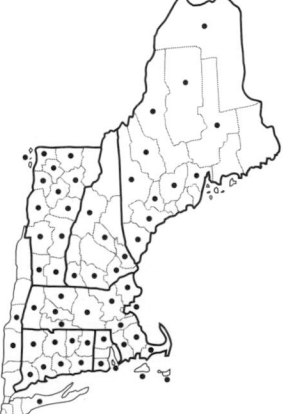

1592. *Hypericum punctatum*

1593. *Hypericum boreale*

1594. *Hypericum canadense*

1595. *Hypricum majus*

1596. *Hypericum mutilum*

1597. *Elatine minima*

1598. *Elatine americana*

Family 137. Tamaricáceae (Tamarisk Family)

Represented with us by the following genus:

1. *Támarix* L. Tamarisk (classical name).

Hermaphrodite, shrubs or small trees, twigs slender, pith small, white, slightly off center, buds small, ovoid, solitary or multiple, with several scales, subtended by a persistent leaf base, leaf scars, bundle traces and stipule scars lacking; leaves minute and scale-like, alternate and often imbricated on very slender, deciduous foliar shoots, these superficially resembling foliage of *Chamaecyparis*, stipules lacking; flowers perfect, regular, small and pink or white, ebracteate, crowded in slender, spike-like racemes borne singly on the old wood or aggregated into terminal panicles, sepals, petals and stamens 4-5, distinct, persistent, all arising from the margin of a hypogynous disc, ovary superior, 1-locular, with 3-5 short styles; fruit a 3-5-valved conical capsule, seeds numerous, comose.

Flowers 5-merous .... 1. *T. gallica*
Flowers 4-merous .... 2. *T. parviflora*

1. T. gállica L. (French). Occasionally escaped from cultivation to roadsides and waste places. May-September. Fig.715, Map 1599. (Naturalized from Europe). [*T. chinensis; T. pentandra; T. ramosissima*]. Reported to be used in parts of Europe in compresses applied to wounds to stop bleeding.

2. T. parviflóra DC. (small-flowered). Occasionally escaped from cultivation to roadsides and waste places. April-June. (Naturalized from Europe). Reported for Fairfield County CT.

Family 138. Cistáceae (Rockrose Family)

Hermaphrodite herbs or low, evergreen shrubs. Leaves alternate, opposite or whorled, simple, entire, sessile or short-petioled, stipulate or estipulate. Flowers perfect, regular except for the calyx, solitary, cymose or paniculate, sepals 5, the 2 outer smaller than the 3 inner, petals 3 or 5, often fugacious, or none in cleistogamous flowers, stamens numerous, hypogenous, ovary superior, 1-locular, style 1 or none, stigmas 1-3. Fruit a 3-valved, loculicidal capsule enclosed in the persistent calyx, seeds few-many.

a. Low, spreading shrub with imbricated, evergreen, scale-like or linear-subulate
   leaves. (Fig. 716) .... 1. *Hudsonia*
a. Upright herbs with leaves not imbricated or evergreen, dilated (although often
   narrow).
   Petals (in petaliferous flowers) 5, yellow, conspicuous; both petaliferous and
      apetalous (cleistogamous) flowers usually produced; bases of plants
      without overwintering basal shoots .... 2. *Helianthemum*
   Petals 3, red, minute; only petaliferous flowers produced; bases of plants usually
      with procumbent overwintering basal shoots. .... 3. *Lechea*

1. Hudsónia L. False Heather (for W. Hudson).

Low, diffusely branched, spreading and often mat-forming shrubs, twigs slender, pith minute, buds and leaf scars not evident; leaves evergreen, pubescent, alternate, crowded, scale-like or linear-subulate, estipulate; flowers numerous, yellow, at the tips of short branches, calyx 5-lobed, 2 of them subulate, the other 3 oblong, petals 5, distinct, much longer than calyx, fugacious, style long and slender, stigma minute; capsule few-seeded.

Leaves lance-ovate, mostly 2 mm or less long, obscured by a hoary tomentum;
   flowers sessile or subsessile (except in Var.). .... 1. *H. tomentosa*
Leaves linear-subulate, mostly more than 2 mm long, villous, the surface not
   obscured; flowers pedicellate .... 2. *H. ericoides*

1. H. tomentósa Nutt. (tomentose). Beaches, dunes and open sandy soil. Fig. 716, Map 1600. Endangered in VT. Our plants include var. *tomentosa* and the following var.:
   var. *intermédia* Peck. Flowers pedicellate (sessile or subsessile in var. *tomentosa*). [*H. intermedia*].
2. H. ericoídes L. (heath-like). Beaches, dunes and open sandy soil. May-July. Map 1601. Endangered in CT.

2. Heliánthemum Mill. Frostweed (from the Greek, meaning sun flower).

Herbaceous or suffrutescent, rhizomatous perennials, stellate-pubescent; leaves alternate, linear, oblong, or oblanceolate to elliptic; flowers solitary or clustered, calyx 5-lobed, 2 lobes much narrower than the others, the first flowers of the season showy, yellow, with 5 large, fugacious petals, those produced later in the season much smaller, apetalous, cleistogamous, style short, stigma capitate; capsules of first flowers many-seeded, those of the later flowers usually much smaller, several-seeded.

H. salicifólium (L.) Mill., a small, hairy, annual, Mediterranean species, has been reported for Westchester County NY.

a. Petaliferous flowers in corymbs of 2-several; cleistogamous flowers numerous,
    crowded, their mature capsules uniform in size, less than 3 mm wide.
    Stems clustered; petaliferous flowers rarely surpassed by the branches, their
        outer sepals two-thirds or more as long as the inner; leaves gray above. ...... 1. *H. bicknellii*
    Stems solitary; petaliferous flowers often surpassed by the branches, their outer
        sepals mostly less than two-thirds as long as the inner; leaves green above . 2. *H. propinquum*
a. Petaliferous flowers solitary or rarely 2; cleistogamous flowers 1-several, when
    several, their capsules unequal in size, the larger (or only one) 3 mm or more
    wide. (Fig. 717).
    Cleistogamous flowers solitary or 2; seeds pebbled. .... 3. *H. dumosum*
    Cleistogamous flowers several; seeds papillose. .... 4. *H. canadense*

   1. *H. bicknéllii* Fern. (for E. P. Bicknell). Fields, roadsides, waste places, open woods, in dry, sandy
soil. Petaliferous flowers: June-July. Map 1602. [*H. majus; Crocanthemum m.; C. bicknellii*].
   2. *H. propínquum* Bickn. (near). Waste places, dunes, open woods, in dry, sandy soil. Petaliferous
flowers: May-June. Map 1603. Endangered in CT.
   3. *H. dumósum* (Bickn.) Fern. (bushy). Dunes, barrens, open woods, in dry, sandy soil.
Petaliferous flowers: May-June. Map 1604. Endangered in RI.
   4. *H. canadénse* (L.) Michx. (Canadian). Roadsides, waste places, dunes, barrens, open woods,
in dry, sandy soil. Petaliferous flowers: May-June. Fig. 717, Map 1605. [*Crocanthemum c.; H. majus*].
Used by Indians as a diuretic and astringent; reported to be of value for other medicinal uses but there
are also cautionary notes.

3. *Léchea* L. Pinweed (for J. Leche).

Perennial herbs, often woody at the base, erect, branched above, producing procumbent, leafy,
overwintering basal shoots late in the season; leaves small, alternate, opposite or subverticillate,
sessile or short petioled; flowers minute, very numerous in large, leafy panicles, reddish, sepals 5, the
outer 2 linear, the inner 3 elliptic to ovate, petals 3, usually shorter than the sepals, marcescent,
stigmas 3, red, plumose; capsule few-seeded.

a. Stems spreading-pubescent .... 1. *L. mucronata*
a. Stems with appressed or strongly ascending pubescence.
    b. Narrow outer sepals equalling, or usually longer than the wider inner ones.
        Leaves lanceolate to elliptic, more than 1 mm wide. .... 2. *L. minor*
        Leaves linear, usually less than 1 mm wide. .... 3. *L. tenuifolia*
    b. Narrow outer sepals shorter than the wider inner ones.
        c. Fruiting calyx and fruit pyriform to narrowly obovoid, approximately twice
            as long as thick (measured from base before dehiscence). (Fig. 718). .... 4. *L. racemulosa*
        c. Fruiting calyx and fruit globose to ovoid or ellipsoid, less than twice as long
            as thick.
            d. Plant canescent with copious appressed hairs; leaves pilose over the surface
                beneath (sometimes thinly so) .... 5. *L. maritima*
            d. Plant green, thinly appressed-pilose; leaves pilose beneath only on the
                midrib and margin.
                Fruiting calyx obovoid; seeds flattened. .... 6. *L. pulchella*
                Fruiting calyx subglobose; seeds prominently 3-sided. .... 7. *L. intermedia*

   1. *L. mucronáta* Raf. Dry fields, clearings, roadsides and waste places. Fruit: July-October. Map
1606. Endangered in VT. [*L. villosa*].
   2. *L. mínor* L. (smaller). Dry fields, sandy pond margins. Fruit: August-October. Map 1607.
   3. *L. tenuifólia* Michx. (slender-leaved). Dry fields, barrens, and open woods. Fruit: July-
October. Map 1608. Endangered in NH.
   4. *L. racemulósa* Michx. (with small racemes). Dry fields, roadsides, open woods. Fruit: August-
October. Fig. 718.
   5. *L. marítima* Leggett ex B.S.P. (maritime). Dunes, sandy pond margins, barrens, open woods.
Fruit: August-October. Map 1609.

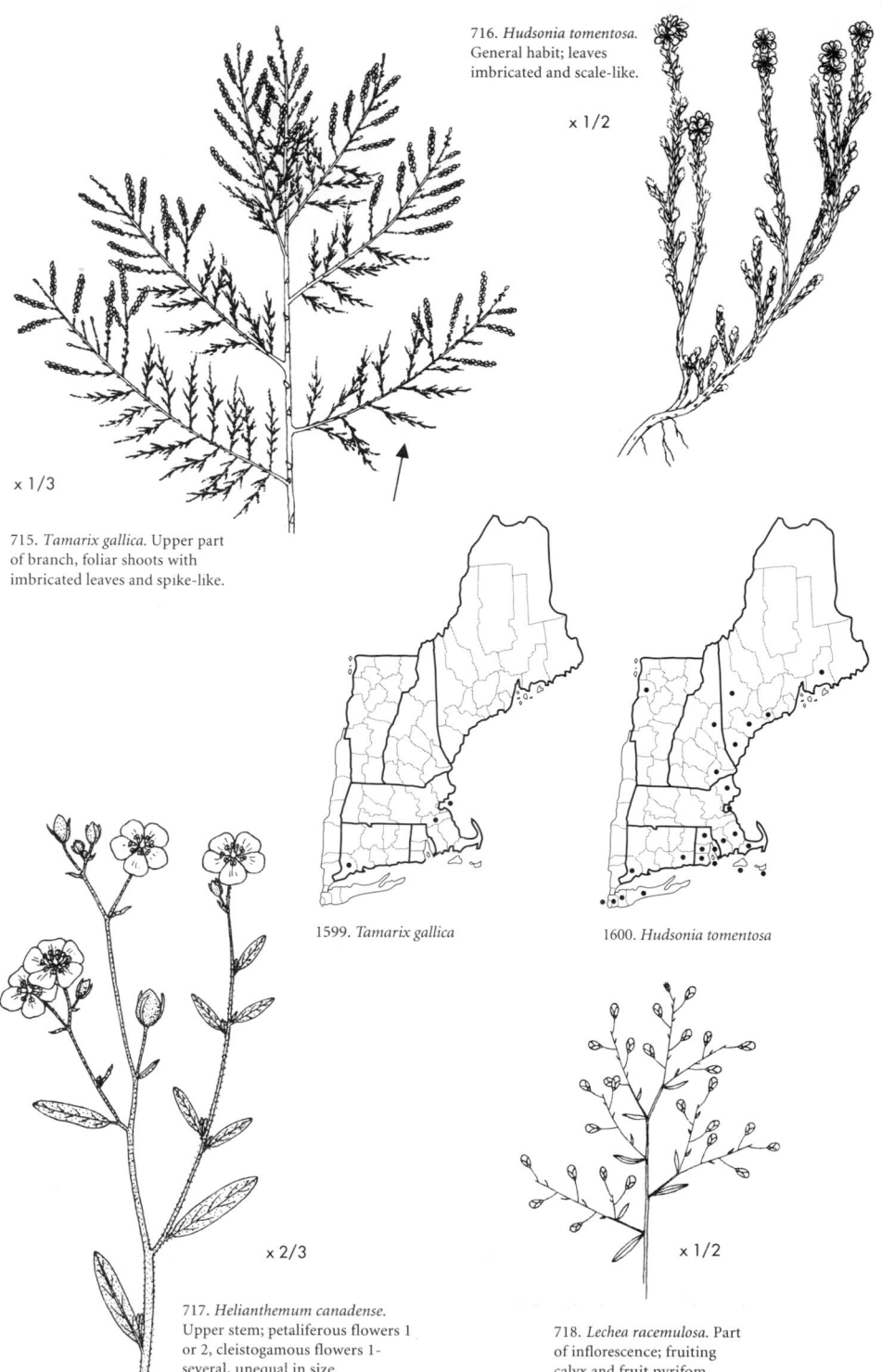

716. *Hudsonia tomentosa.*
General habit; leaves
imbricated and scale-like.

x 1/2

x 1/3

715. *Tamarix gallica.* Upper part
of branch, foliar shoots with
imbricated leaves and spike-like.

1599. *Tamarix gallica*

1600. *Hudsonia tomentosa*

x 2/3

717. *Helianthemum canadense.*
Upper stem; petaliferous flowers 1
or 2, cleistogamous flowers 1-
several, unequal in size.

x 1/2

718. *Lechea racemulosa.* Part
of inflorescence; fruiting
calyx and fruit pyrifom.

1601. *Hudsonia ericoides*

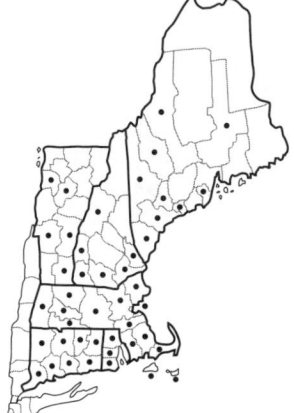

1602. *Helianthemum bicknellii*

1603. *Helianthemum propinquum*

1604. *Helianthemum dumosum*

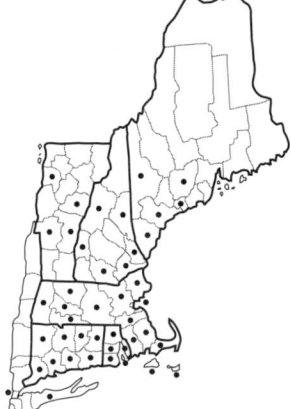

1605. *Helianthemum canadense*

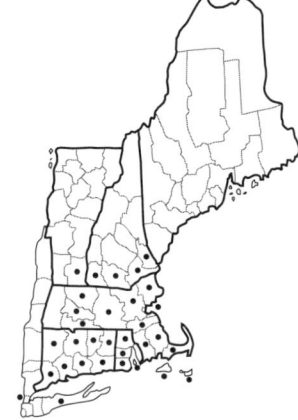

1606. *Lechea mucronata*

1607. *Lechea minor*

1608. *Lechea tenuifolia*

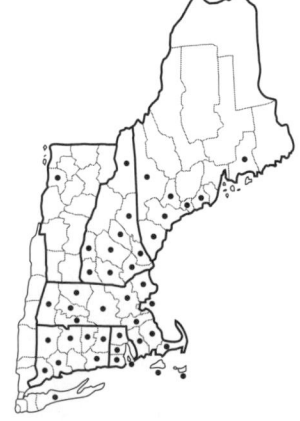

1609. *Lechea maritima*

6. L. pulchélla Raf. Dry fields, open woods and pond margins. Fruit: August-October. Map 1610. Endangered in MA. [*L. leggettii*]. Our plants are var. *pulchélla*.

7. L. intermédia Leggett ex Britt. (intermediate). Dry fields, roadsides, open woods, pond margins. Fruit: July-October. Map 1611. (*L. juniperina*].

Family 139. Violáceae (Violet Family)

Hermaphrodite, annual or perennial, caulescent or acaulescent herbs. Leaves basal or alternate, petioled, simple, crenate, serrate or rarely entire, lobed or unlobed, stipulate. Flowers perfect, irregular, basal or axillary, solitary, sepals 5, distinct, petals 5, the lower usually larger or spurred, stamens 5, hypogynous, connate or connivent around the ovary, ovary superior, 1-locular, style and stigma 1, both petaliferous and cleistogamous flowers usually produced. Fruit a 3-valved, loculicidal capsule, seeds few-many.

Sepals without basal auricles; stamens united into a sheath; petals green; capsule
    1.5 cm or more long .... 1. *Hybanthus*
                                           concolor
Sepals with basal auricles; stamens not united, merely connivent; petals not green;
    capsules usually less than 1.5 cm long. .... 2. *Viola*

1. Hybánthus Jacq. Green violet (from the Greek based on shape of the flowers).
Leafy stemmed perennials; leaves alternate, elliptic to oblong-lanceolate, attenuate at the base, acuminate at the tip, entire or sparingly toothed; flowers small, greenish-white, 1-3 together on short, recurved, axillary pedicels, sepals linear, subequal, about equalling the corolla, petals subequal, the lower wider than the others and saccate at the base, stamens connate into a sheath around the ovary, with white appendages, style hooked at the tip, seeds large. [*Cubelium*].

    1. H. cóncolor (T. F. Forst.) Spreng. (of one color). Rich woods, often in calcarous soils. April-June. From farther south. Reported for New Haven County CT. [*Cubelium c.*]. —FACU-

2. Vióla L. Violet (classical name).
Leafy stemmed or stemless, annuals or rhizomatous or stoloniferous perennials; leaves crenate or crenate-serrate, dissected, lobed or unlobed; flowers on axillary (caulescent) or basal (acaulescent) 1-flowered peduncles with 2 small bracts near the middle, sepals usually with posterior appendages (auricles), petals somewhat unequal, the 2 lateral often bearded, the lower one usually spurred or saccate at the base, sometimes bearded, stamens closely connivent around the ovary, with orange appendages, the lower 2 spurred, the spurs projecting into the spur of the corolla; most species produce petaliferous flowers in spring and cleistogamous flowers in summer, the latter produced on peduncles or stolons, sometimes concealed underground; hybrids very numerous. The leaves and flowers of violets may be used in salads and as a potherb; plant is high in vitamin C; also reported to be of medicinal value when applied externally to treat skin sores, or taken internally to treat a variety of symptoms. —Wildl.1

a. Plants leafy-stemmed, the flowers borne from the leaf axils.
  b. Stipules leaflike and lyrate, widened to the apex; winter annuals. (Fig. 719).
      Lateral petals equalling or shorter than the sepals. .... 1. *V. arvensis*
      Lateral petals much longer than the sepals. .... 2. *V. tricolor*
  b. Stipules neither leaflike (usually) nor lyrate, narrowed to the apex; perennials.
    c. Stipules pectinate, toothed or fringed; petals blue or violet. (Fig. 720).
      d. Peduncles and stems puberulent .... 3. *V. adunca*
      d. Peduncles and stems glabrous.
        e. Spur 8 mm or more long; lateral petals beardless; middle and upper
          leaves acute to acuminate .... 4. *V. rostrata*

e. Spur less than 8 mm long; lateral petals bearded; middle and upper leaves
obtuse to rounded.
Stipules ovate-lanceolate, the longer teeth more than 1 mm (up to
2 mm) long. .... 5. *V. conspersa*
Stipules linear-lanceolate, the longer teeth mostly 1 mm or less long. ..... 3. *V. adunca*
c. Stipules entire or merely serrulate; petals yellow or white suffused with
purple outside.
Petals white, often suffused with purple outside; upper stipules narrowly
lanceolate, less than 3 mm wide, hyaline and pale. .... 6. *V. canadensis*
Petals yellow; upper stipules usually 3 mm or more wide, green. .... 7. *V. pubescens*
a. Plants stemless, the leaves and peduncles borne from the base.
f. Leaves, or some of them, palmately or pedately divided or lobed, or at least
lobed or coarsely toothed toward the base. (Fig. 721).
g. None of the petals bearded; cleistogamous flowers none. .... 8. *V. pedata*
g. One or more of the petals bearded; cleistogamous flowers developed.
h. Petioles and lower leaf surfaces pubescent.
Blades cordate-ovate, at least some palmately or pedately lobed or
divided. (Fig. 721) ....9. *V. palmata*
Blades lanceolate to oblong or oblong-ovate, lobed or coarsely toothed
only toward the base .... 10. *V. sagittata*
h. Petioles and lower leaf surfaces glabrous or essentially so.
i. Blades lanceolate to lance-oblong, sagittate to hastate at the base.
(Fig. 722) .... 10. *V. sagittata*
i. Blades deltoid-ovate to broadly ovate, subcordate to truncate at the base.
(Fig. 723).
Blades coarsely toothed at the base .... 11. *V. x emarginata*
Blades sharply or pectinately toothed to more often deeply dissected
or lobed. .... 12. *V. brittoniana*
f. Leaves all merely crenate-serrate around the margin.
j. Petals yellow; cleistogamous flowers on trailing, leafless stolons. .... 13. *V. rotundifolia*
j. Petals white, blue or violet; cleistogamous flowers not on trailing stolons or
the stolons leafy.
k. Petals white with purple veins; rhizome slender (mostly 4 mm or less thick)
and elongate; plants stoloniferous (except in *V. renifolia*).
l. Leaves truncate to rounded or cuneate at the base, lanceolate to oblong
or ovate. (Fig. 724).
Leaves narrowly to widely lanceolate or oblanceolate, more than 3
times as long as wide, attenuate at the base .... 14. *V. lanceolata*
Leaves oblong to ovate, less than 3 times as long as wide, truncate,
rounded or slightly cuneate at the base. (Fig. 724). .... 15. *V. x primulifolia*
l. Leaves cordate at the base, ovate to orbicular. (Fig. 725).
m. Style hooked at the tip; stolons leafy throughout. .... 16. *V. odorata*
m. Style capitate, with a beak on one side, but not hooked; stolons
leafless or sparsely leafy toward the tip.
n. Leaves reniform; plants non-stoloniferous; petals all beardless.
(Fig. 725) .... 17. *V. renifolia*
n. Leaves ovate, or if reniform lateral petals bearded; plants
stoloniferous.
o. Lateral petals distinctly bearded .... 18. *V. incognita*
o. Lateral petals beardless or essentially so.
Peduncle pink to reddish near summit; lateral petals somewhat
reflexed and twisted; leaves sometimes with scattered
hairs above. .... 19. *V. blanda*
Peduncle green; lateral petals not recurved or twisted; leaves
glabrous. .... 20. *V. macloskeyi*
subsp. *pallens.*
k. Petals blue to violet (except in white-flowered forms of some species, these
having stout rhizomes and being non-stoloniferous).
p. Rhizome slender (mostly 4 mm or less thick) and elongate; plants
stoloniferous (except in *V. selkirkii*).

q. Style hooked at the tip; lateral petals usually bearded; stolons leafy
throughout .... 16. *V. odorata*
q. Style capitate, with a beak on one side but not hooked; lateral petals
beardless or essentially so; stolons absent or leafy toward the tip.
Leaves strigose above, sinus narrow with converging or overlapping
lobes; spur 3 mm or more long; non-stoloniferous .... 21. *V. selkirkii*
Leaves glabrous, sinus open, the lobes not converging or overlapping;
spur 2.5 mm or less long; stoloniferous .... 22. *V. palustris*
p. Rhizome stout (mostly 4 mm or more thick), and often short;
non-stoloniferous.
r. Blades lanceolate, lance-oblong or narrowly triangular, mostly 1.5 or
more times as long as wide.
s. Plants distinctly pubescent on the petioles and often on the blades
and peduncles. .... 23. *V. novae-angliae*
s. Plants glabrous or at most sparsely pubescent.
t. Blades cordate at base, teeth uniform. .... 24. *V. affinis*
t. Blades truncate or subcordate to hastate at base, teeth longer
toward base. (Fig. 723).
Blades narrowly triangular, mostly less than 2 times as long as
wide, truncate to subcordate at base .... 11. *V. x emarginata*
Blades lanceolate to lance-oblong, mostly 2 or more times as
long as wide, hastate at base. (Fig. 722) .... 10. *V. sagittata*
r. Blades reniform, ovate or broadly triangular, mostly less than 1.5
times as long as wide to wider than long (occasionally narrowly
ovate in *V. cucullata*, which is separated from the above species by
the petal characteristics).
u. Plants distinctly pubescent on the petioles or blades and often on
the peduncles.
v. Blades pubescent only on the upper surface; petioles glabrous;
sepals eciliate or nearly so .... 25. *V. hirsutula*
v. Blades pubescent on the lower and often the upper surface;
petioles pubescent, at least near the top; sepals ciliate.
Spurred petal bearded; sepals ciliate to tip. .... 26. *V. septentrionalis*
Spurred petal glabrous or nearly so; sepals ciliate only on the
lower half. .... 27. *V. sororia*
u. Plants glabrous or at most sparsely pubescent or minutely
granular-puberulent.
w. Beard of lateral petals knobbed at apex; petals usually with
a darker bluish spot at the base .... 28. *V. cucullata*
w. Beard of lateral petals slender to thickened but not knobbed;
petals not darkened at the base.
Blades broadly ovate to reniform, obtuse to rounded;
sepals obtuse to rounded. .... 29. *V. nephrophylla*
Blades narrowly ovate, acute; sepals acute. .... 24. *V. affinis*

1. V. arvénsis Murr. (of fields). Wild Pansy. Cultivated or abandoned fields, waste places. May-August. Fig. 719, Map 1612. (Naturalized from Europe).

2. V. trícolor L. (three-colored). Pansy. Cultivated ground and around dwellings. April-September. Map 1613. (Introduced from Europe).

V. rafinésquii Greene. Wild Pansy. Similar to *V. tricolor* but is distinguishable in having middle lobe of stipules linear and entire (middle lobe is spatulate and toothed or crenate in *V. tricolor*). (Naturalized from Eurasia). Reported for MA, Dutchess County NY. [*V. kitaibeliana* var. *rafinesquii*].

3. V. adúnca Sm. (hooked). Dry, open woods, thickets, waste places. May-June. Map 1614. Endangered in MA. Our plants are var. *adunca*. [*V. arenaria*; *V. subvestita*]. —FAC

V. labradórica Schrank. Similar to *V. adunca* but glabrous, or essentially so (*V. adunca* is puberulent). (Greenland). [*V. adunca* var. *labradorica*; var. *minor*]. —FAC

4. V. rostráta Pursh (beaked). Long-spurred violet. Rich, often calcareous woods. April-June. Map 1615. —FACU

5. V. conspérsa Reichenb. (sprinkled). American dog-violet. Moist to dry, rich woods, meadows, roadsides. April-June. Fig. 720, Map 1616. —FACW

V. striáta Ait. Similar to *V. conspersa* but differs in having ciliate sepals and white flowers (sepals eciliate and flowers violet in *V. conspersa*). From farther west and south. Reported for NH, Fairfield and Tolland Counties CT, Middlesex County MA, Addison County VT, and Dutchess County NY. —FACW

6. V. canadénsis L. (Canadian). Rich, often calcareous woods. May-July. Map 1617. Our plants are var. *canadensis*.

7. V. pubéscens Ait. (pubescent). Downy yellow violet. Rich, dry woods. May-June. Map 1618. [*V. eriocarpa; V. pensylvanica*]. Our plants include var. *pubescens* and the following vars.:

var. *leiocárpon* (Fern. & Weig.) B. Boiv. Capsules glabrous (white-tomentose in var. *pubescens*). [*V. pensylvanica* var. *leiocarpa*].

var. *péckii* House. Capsules glabrous as in var. *leiocarpon* but leaves deeper green. —FACU-

8. V. pedáta L. (foot-like). Bird-foot violet. Dry, sandy fields, open woods and barrens. April-June. Map 1619.

9. V. palmáta L. (palmate). Rich, dry woods. April-June. Map 1620. Endangered in NH. Represented with us by the following vars.:

var. *trilóba* (Schwein.) Gingins ex DC. Blades both lobed and unlobed, the lobed ones usually with 3-5 primary lobes, these lobulate. Fig. 721. [*V. triloba*].

var. *dilatáta* Ell. Lobed blades divided nearly to the base into 5 or more narrow-lobes. [*V. triloba* var. *d.*].

10. V. sagittáta Ait. (arrow-shaped). Wet to dry meadows. May-June. Fig. 722, Map 1621. [*V. fimbriatula*]. —FACW

V. x multifórdiae Pollard. A hybrid between *V. sagittata* and *V. brittoniana*.

11. V. x emargináta (Nutt.) Le Conte (emarginate). Woods and clearings. April-May. Fig. 723, Map 1622.

12. V. brittoniána Pollard (for N. L. Britton). Wet to dry sandy open soil near the coast. May-June. Map 1623. Endangered in CT.[*V. pectinata*]. —FAC

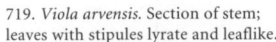

719. *Viola arvensis.* Section of stem;
leaves with stipules lyrate and leaflike.

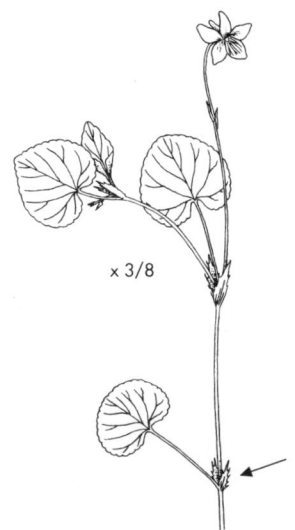

720. *Viola conspersa.* Upper stem;
leaves with fringed-toothed stipules.

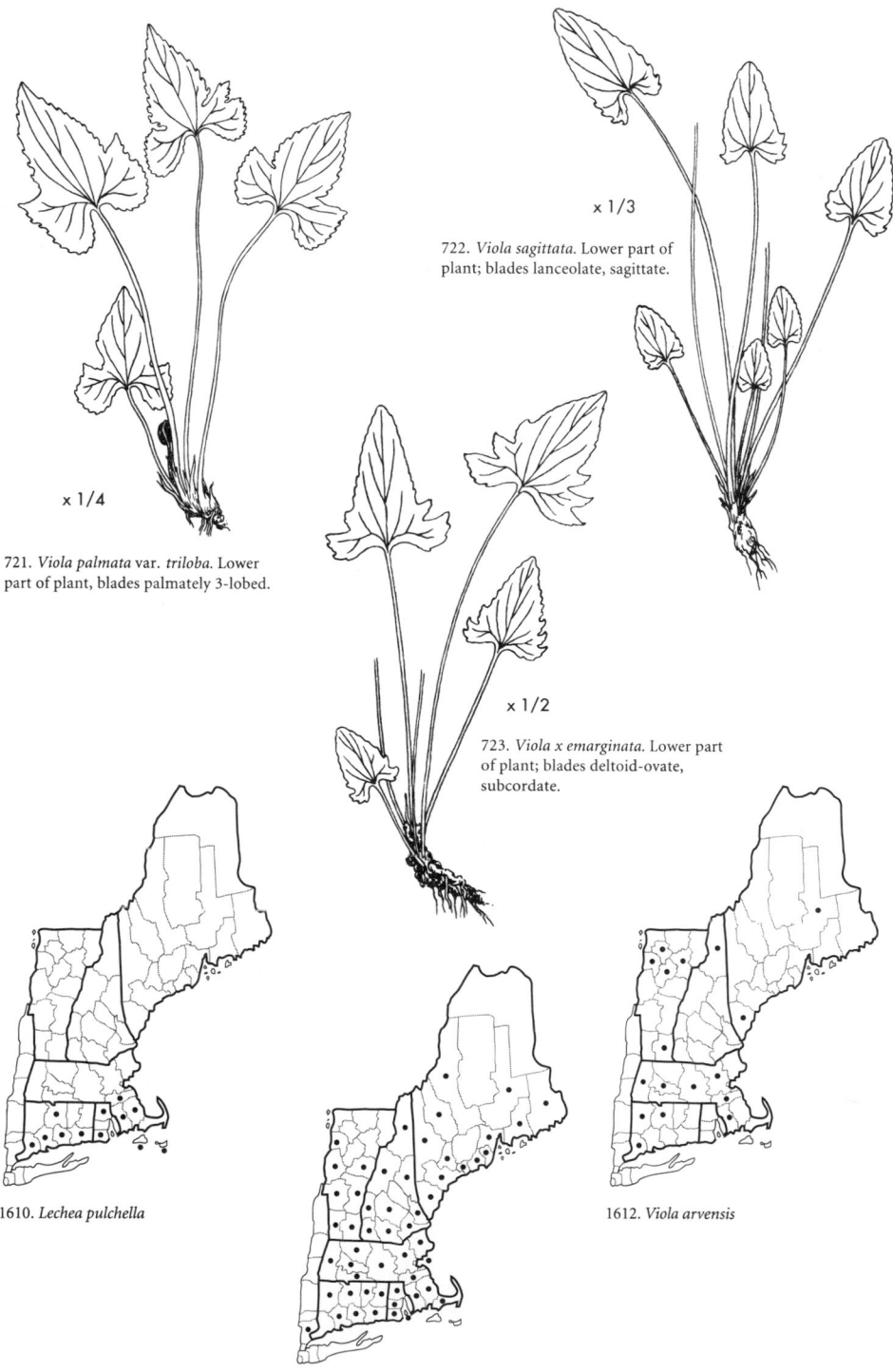

x 1/3

722. *Viola sagittata.* Lower part of plant; blades lanceolate, sagittate.

x 1/4

721. *Viola palmata* var. *triloba.* Lower part of plant, blades palmately 3-lobed.

x 1/2

723. *Viola x emarginata.* Lower part of plant; blades deltoid-ovate, subcordate.

1610. *Lechea pulchella*

1611. *Lechea intermedia*

1612. *Viola arvensis*

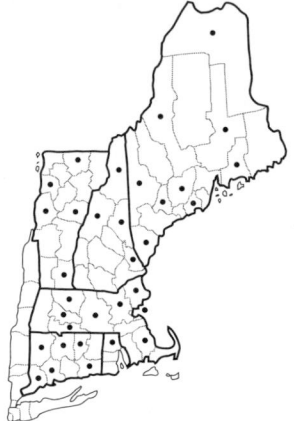

1613. *Viola tricolor*

1614. *Viola adunca*

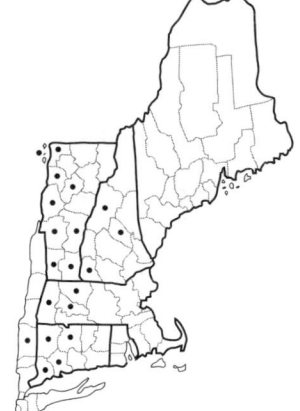

1615. *Viola rostrata*

1616. *Viola conspersa*

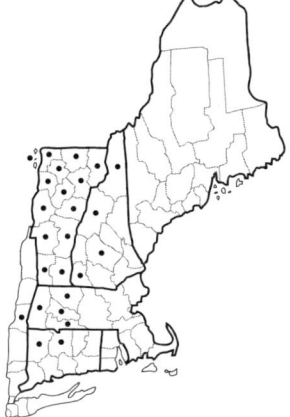

1617. *Viola canadensis*

1618. *Viola pubescens*

1619. *Viola pedata*

1620. *Viola palmata*

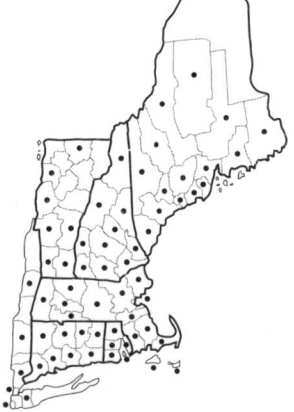

1621. *Viola sagittata*

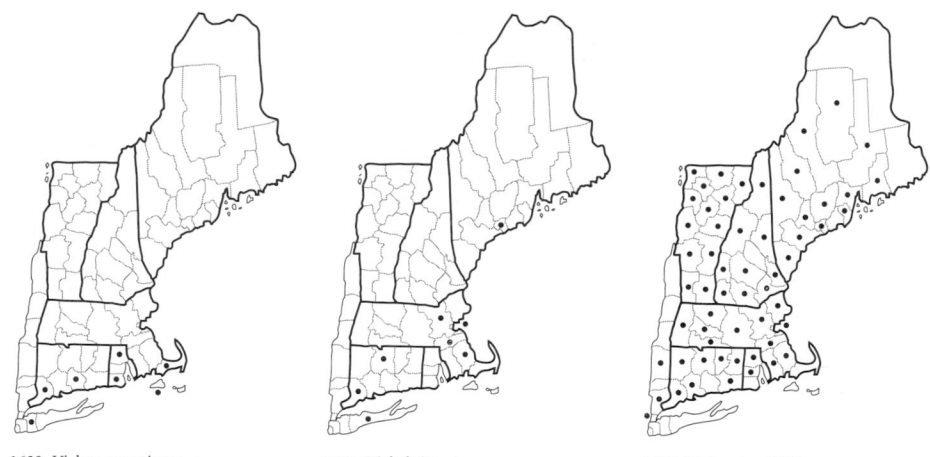

1622. *Viola x emarginata*   1623. *Viola brittoniana*   1624. *Viola rotundifolia*

V. stoneána House. Similar to *V. brittoniana* but distinguishable from it and the next species in having a glabrous spurred petal (spurred petal is bearded at the base in *V. brittoniana* and *V. septemloba*). Endangered in NY.

V. septemlóba Le Conte. Similar to *V. brittoniana* and *V. stoneana* but with lateral leaf lobes 2-4 parted, the middle lobe uncleft (in *V. brittoniana* and *V. stoneana* the blades are divided into 5 or more narrow lobes). From farther south on the coastal plain. Reported for CT, RI. —FACW

13. V. rotundifólia Michx. (round-leaved). Round-leaved yellow violet. Rich woods. April-May. Map 1624. —FAC+

14. V. lanceoláta L. (lanceolate). Pond margins, wet meadows, moist open soil. April-June. Map 1625. Our plants are var. *lanceolata*. —OBL

15. V. x primulifólia L. (primrose-leaved). Moist meadows, pond margins, open soil. May-June. Fig. 724, Map 1626. —FAC+

16. V. odoráta L. (fragrant). Sweet violet. Cultivated ground, roadsides and around dwellings. April-May. Map 1627. (Naturalized from Europe).

17. V. renifólia Gray (kidney-leaved). Rich, often wet woods, fields, bogs. May-July. Fig. 725, Map 1628. Our plants include var. *renifolia* and the following var.:

var. *brainérdii* (Greene) Fern. Leaves glabrous above (pubescent in var. *renifolia*). —FACW

18. V. incógnita Brainerd (unknown). Rich moist woods. May-June. Map 1629. —FACW

19. V. blánda Willd. (mild). Sweet white violet. Rich moist woods. April-June. Map 1630. Our plants include var. *blanda* and the following var.:

var. *palustrifórmis* Gray. Upper leaf surface with scattered hairs (upper leaf surface glabrous in var. *blanda*). [*V. incognita* var. *forbesii*]. —FACW

20. V. maclóskeyi Lloyd. Moist woods and thickets, stream borders. April-June. Map 1631. Represented with us as subsp. *pállens* (Banks ex DC.) M.S. Baker [*V. pallens*]. —OBL

21. V. selkírkii Pursh ex Goldie (for the Earl of Selkirk). Rich woods. May-July. Map 1632. (n. Eurasia).

22. V. palústris L. (of marshes). Alpine marsh violet. Damp soil in alpine areas. June-August. Map 1633. (Eurasia). Endangered in ME. Our plants are var. *palustris*. —FACW+

23. V. nóvae-ángliae House (of New England). Gravelly river shores. May-June. Endangered in NY. Reported for NH, VT, Aroostook and Penobscot Counties ME. —OBL

24. V. affínis Le Conte (related). Moist meadows, woods and stream banks. May-June. Map 1634. Endangered in NH. [*V. latiuscula*]. —FACW

25. V. hirsutúla Brainerd (slightly hirsute). Moist to dry woods and openings. April-May.

26. V. septentrionális Greene (northern). Moist to dry woods, clearings, river shores and meadows. May-June. Map 1635. Our plants are var. *septentrionalis.* —FACU

V. x párca House. A hybrid between *V. septentrionalis* and *V. sagittata.*

27. V. sorória Willd. (sisterly). Woolly blue violet. Rich, often moist woods and fields. April-June. Map 1636. [*V. latiuscula; V. missouriensis; V. papilionacea; V. pratincola*]. —FAC-

V. x montívaga House. A hybrid between *V. sororia* and *V. septentrionalis.*

28. V. cullláta Ait. (hooded). Blue marsh violet. Wet woods, stream and river borders, meadows, roadsides. April-June. Map 1637. [*V. obliqua*]. —FACW+

V. x porteriána Pollard. A hybrid between *V. cucullata* and *V. sagittata.*

V. x ryóniae House. A hybrid between *V. cucullata* and *V. palmata.*

29. V. nephrophýlla Greene (with kidney-shaped leaves). Moist woods, fields, river borders, bogs. May-June. Map 1638.

V. x subaffínis House. A hybrid between *V. nephrophylla* and *V. affinis.* —FACW

Family 140. Loasáceae (Loasa Family)

Represented with us by the following genus:

1. Mentzélia L.

A perennial herb armed with stiff, barbed pubescence, no stipules, simple, alternate, coarsely toothed and lobed leaves, large, regular, 5-merous terminal yellow flowers with numerous stamens, and a 1-locular inferior ovary with 3 stigmas, fruit capsular.

    1. M. oligospérma Nutt. ex Sims. Western; rarely found in our range. Reported for Worcester County MA.

Family 141. Cactáceae (Cactus Family)

1. Opúntia Mill. Prickly pear (ancient Greek name for another plant).

Hermaphrodite, fleshy, succulent plants, prostrate or spreading, with branched stems composed of flattened, suborbicular to ovoid segments separated by constrictions; leaves scale-like, spirally arranged, promptly deciduous, the axils with cushions of hairs (areoles), usually also with tufts of barbed bristles (glochids) at the areoles, spineless or sometimes with 1 or 2 spines also present; flowers perfect, regular, mostly solitary, sessile, borne at the axils, showy, yellow, perianth poorly differentiated, the segments numerous, imbricated, the sepals gradually grading into the petals, stamens numerous, inserted on the hypanthium, ovary inferior, of several carpels, 1-locular, style 1, stigma several-rayed; fruit a fleshy berry beset with glochids, many-seeded.

    1. O humifúsa (Raf.) Raf. (spreading on the ground). Sandy fields, dunes and rocks. June-July. Fig. 726, Map 1639. [*O. calcicola; O. compressa; O. opuntia; O. pollardii; O. rafinesquii; O. vulgaris*]. Our plants are var. *humifusa.* Pulp of fruit edible, as are the young stem segments after removing spines and cooking; juice from the stems can be used as emergency water.

Family 142. Thymelaeáceae (Mezereum Family)

Hermaphrodite shrubs with very tough, fibrous bark. Leaves alternate, simple, short-petioled, entire, estipulate. Flowers perfect, regular, in sessile or subsessile, lateral clusters of 2-4, from buds on twigs of the preceding season, appearing before the leaves, calyx corolla-like, tubular or funnelform, 4-lobed to merely undulate, petals none, stamens 8, perigynous, ovary superior, 1-locular, 1-ovuled, style 1. Fruit a berry-like drupe.

Leaves 2.5 cm or more wide; twigs swollen and with a spur at the nodes; perianth
    yellowish, obscurely lobed; stamens and style exserted. (Fig. 727). .... 1. *Dirca palustris*
Leaves 2 cm or less wide; twigs not swollen or spurred at the nodes; perianth pink to
    purple, distinctly lobed; stamens and style included. .... 2. *Daphne mezereum*

1. *Dírca* L. Leatherwood (name based on ancient Greek mythology).

Twigs jointed and swollen at the nodes, each node having a short, upward-pointing spur, pith small, white, buds small, solitary, ovoid, silky, leaf scars almost encircling the buds, bundle traces 5, stipule scars and end bud lacking; leaves widely elliptic to obovate, the petiole bases concealing next season's buds; flowers pale yellow, calyx obscurely toothed, stamens and style exserted.

    1. *D. palústris* L. (of swamps). Wicopy. Rich, moist woods. April-May. Fig. 727, Map 1640. Bark can cause skin irritations in susceptable individuals. —FAC

2. *Dáphne* L. Mezereum (name based on ancient Greek mythology).

Twigs somewhat angled or fluted, pith small, white, buds small, ovoid, solitary or sometimes superposed or collateral, with several bud scales, leaf scars crescent-shaped, bundle trace 1, stipule scars lacking; leaves lanceolate to oblanceolate; flowers pink to purple, calyx with 4 spreading lobes, stamens and style included.

    1. *D. mezéreum* L. (from the Arabic name). Roadsides, thickets, fields. April-May. Map 1641. (Naturalized from Europe). Poisonous.

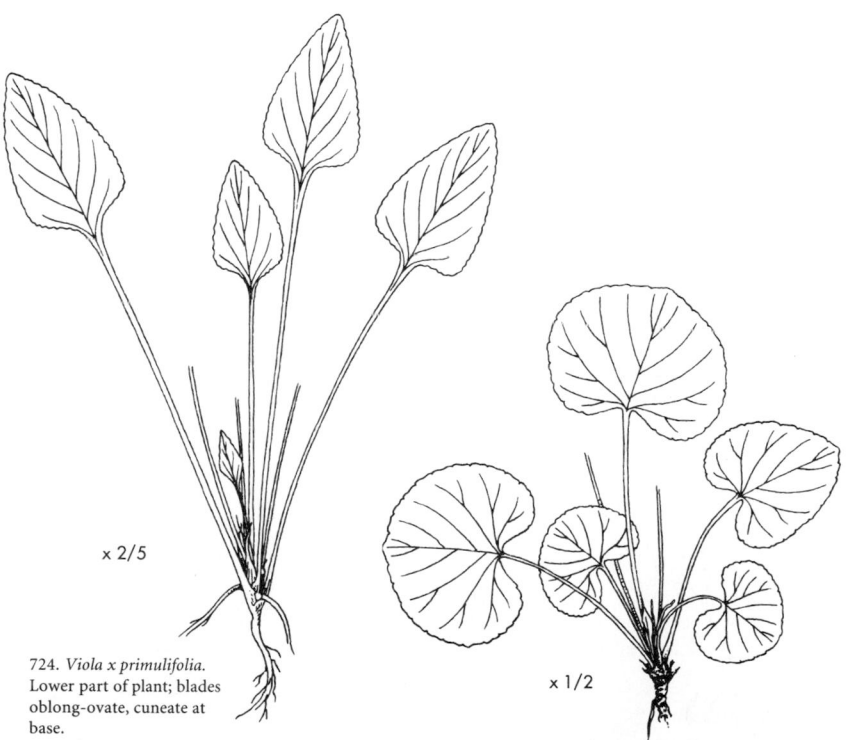

x 2/5

724. *Viola x primulifolia.*
Lower part of plant; blades
oblong-ovate, cuneate at
base.

x 1/2

725. *Viola renifolia.* Lower part of
plant; leaves reniform, cordate.

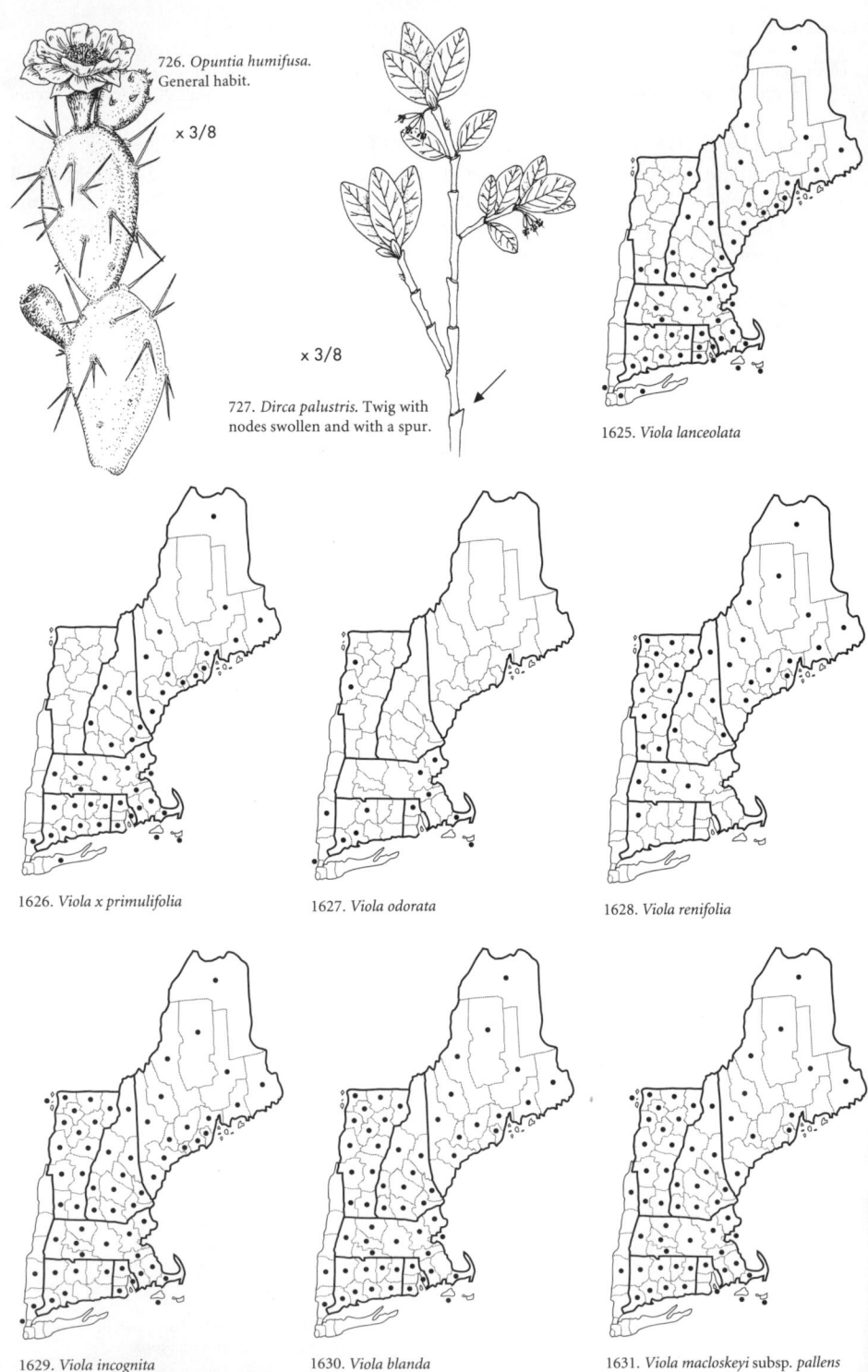

726. *Opuntia humifusa.*
General habit.

× 3/8

× 3/8

727. *Dirca palustris.* Twig with
nodes swollen and with a spur.

1625. *Viola lanceolata*

1626. *Viola x primulifolia*

1627. *Viola odorata*

1628. *Viola renifolia*

1629. *Viola incognita*

1630. *Viola blanda*

1631. *Viola macloskeyi* subsp. *pallens*

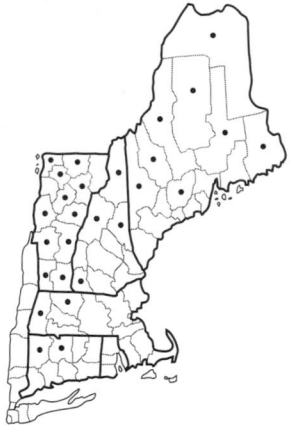

1632. *Viola selkirkii*

1633. *Viola palustris*

1634. *Viola affinis*

1635. *Viola septentrionalis*

1636. *Viola sororia*

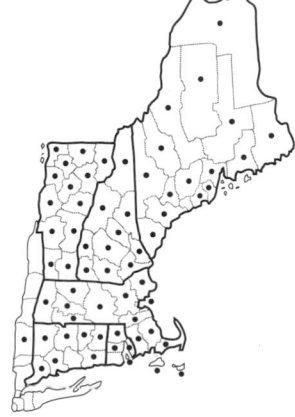

1637. *Viola cucullata*

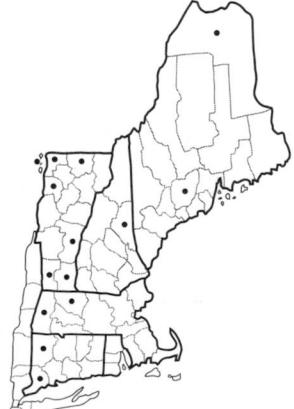

1638. *Viola nephrophylla*

1639. *Optuntia humifusa*

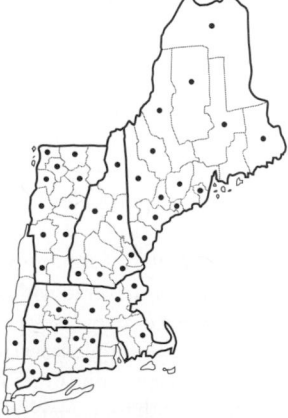

1640. *Dirca palustris*

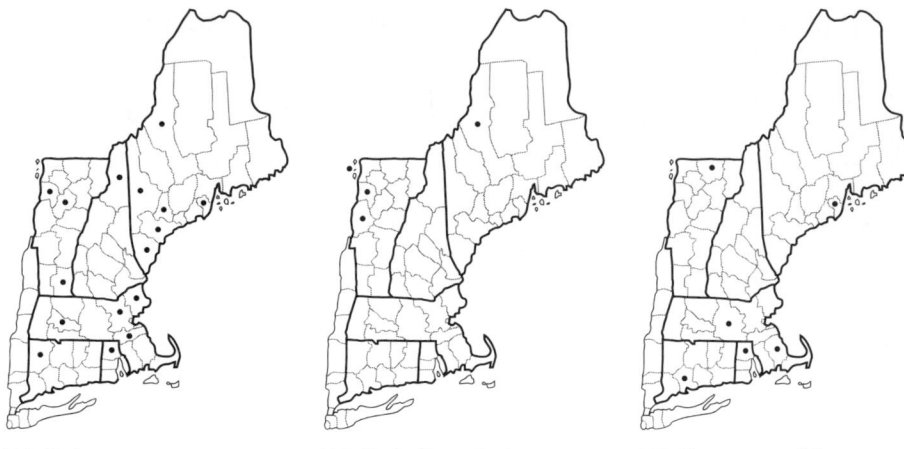

1641. *Daphne mezereum*   1642. *Shepherdia canadensis*   1643. *Elaeagnus angustifolia*

Family 143. Elaeagnáceae (Oleaster Family)

Hermaphrodite, dioecious or polygamodioecious, silvery or brown-scaly or stellate-pubescent shrubs. Leaves alternate or opposite, simple, petioled, entire, estipulate. Flowers perfect or imperfect, regular, solitary or in small clusters in the leaf axils or at the nodes of the twigs, calyx corolla-like, cupulate to campanulate or urceolate, with 4 spreading lobes, petals none, stamens 4 or 8, borne at the rim or in the throat of the calyx tube, ovary superior, enclosed in the calyx tube and appearing inferior but free from the tube, 1-locular, 1-ovuled, style 1. Fruit drupe-like, enclosed in the fleshy, persistent calyx tube.

Leaves opposite; plant dioecious; stamens 8. .... 1. *Shepherdia*
Leaves alternate; plants hermaphrodite or polygamodioecious; stamens 4. .... 2. *Elaeagnus*

1. Shephérdia Nutt. (for J. Shepherd).

Plants densely covered with reddish-brown scales, pith small, brown, buds oblong, stalked, solitary or multiple, with 2 valvate scales, leaf scars raised, half-round, small, bundle trace 1, stipule scars lacking; leaves opposite, ovate to elliptic, green and nearly glabrous above, densely brownish-scaly and stellate-pubescent beneath; plants dioecious, calyx of staminate flowers cupulate, stamens 8, alternating with 8 lobes on a disc at the summit of the perianth tube, calyx of pistillate flowers urceolate, nearly closed at the mouth by the disc.

    1. S. canadénsis (L.) Nutt. (Canadian). Buffalo-berry. Calcareous banks and ledges, particularly along rivers. April-May. Map 1642. Endangered in ME.

    S. argéntea Nutt. (silvery). Differing from *S. canadensis* in having leaves that are silvery-lepidote on both sides (green and nearly glabrous above in *S. canadensis*). From farther west; rarely found in our range. Reported for Rensselaer County NY. Ripe fruit edible.

2. Elaeágnus L. (ancient Greek name for a tree).

Plants densely covered with silvery and/or brown scales or silvery pubescence, pith small, brown, buds oblong or ovoid, sessile, solitary or multiple, with several scales, leaf scars half-round, small, bundle trace 1, stipule scars lacking; leaves alternate, ovate to lanceolate, silvery on one or both sides; plants hermaphrodite or polygamodioecious, calyx campanulate, stamens 4, inserted in the throat of the perianth tube. —Wildl. 1

E. púngens Thunberg. Has evergreen leaves puberulent or glabrous above (the 3 species below have deciduous leaves), the lower surface covered with both silvery and reddish-brown scales, flowers 1-3 in the leaf axils, is rarely escaped from cultivation. Reported for MA.

a. Leaves densely silvery-scaly on both sides; twigs silvery, without any brown scales
   (except in *E. commutata*). .... 1. *E. angustifolia*
a. Leaves soon glabrous or only sparsely silvery-scaly above; twigs reddish-brown,
   sometimes also with silvery scales.
   Calyx tube about as long or only slightly longer than the lobes; fruiting pedicels
       more than 1 cm long; twigs with only reddish-brown scales. .... 2. *E. multiflora*
   Calyx tube much longer (about twice as long) than the lobes; fruiting pedicels
       1 cm or less long; twigs usually with both reddish-brown and silvery scales. 3. *E. umbellata*

1. *E. angustifólia* L. (narrow-leaved). Russian Olive. Escaped from cultivation to thickets, roadsides, along streams. June-July. Map 1643. (Introduced from Eurasia). —FACU

E. commutáta Bernh. Similar to *E. angustifolia* but twigs are covered with brown scales (twigs silvery, brown scales lacking in *E. angustifolia*). From farther north and west. Reported for RI. [*E. argentea*]. Fruit edible.

2. *E. multiflóra* Thunb. (many-flowered). Occasionally escaped from cultivation. (Introduced from e. Asia). Reported for RI, Rockingham and Strafford Counties NH.

3. *E. umbelláta* Thunb. (with umbels). Autumn Olive. Escaped from cultivation to roadsides and thickets. Map 1644. (Introduced from e. Asia). Represented with us as var. *parviflora* (Royale) Schneid.

Family 144. Lythráceae (Loosestrife Family)

Hermaphrodite, annual or perennial herbs, stems 4-sided, at least above. Leaves opposite or whorled, occasionally alternate, simple, sessile or petioled, entire, estipulate. Flowers perfect, regular or irregular, solitary or clustered in the leaf axils, calyx tube present, cylindric to subglobose, usually conspicuously nerved, 4-7-toothed, intersepalary appendages present or absent, petals 4-7 or none, borne at the rim of the calyx tube, stamens 4-14, borne in the throat of the calyx tube, of unequal lengths, ovary superior, often subtended by a hypogynous disc, enclosed by but free from the calyx tube, 2-6-locular, many-ovulate, style 1, varying in length. Fruit a capsule, regularly or irregularly dehiscent.

a. Flowers regular, calyx not gibbous at the base nor oblique at the mouth, petals
   equal.
   b. Calyx tube cylindrical, much longer than broad. .... 1. *Lythrum*
   b. Calyx tube campanulate to globose, about as broad as long.
       Flowers densely clustered in the upper axils; appendages much longer than
           calyx lobes; petals conspicuous; stems arching. (Fig. 729). .... 2. *Decodon*
                                                                                              verticillatus
       Flowers mostly solitary in the axils; appendages about equalling calyx lobes;
           petals minute or absent; stems not arching. (Fig. 730). .... 3. *Rotala ramosior*
a. Fowers irregular; calyx gibbous on one side at the base, oblique at the mouth,
   petals unequal .... 4. *Cuphea*

1. *Lýthrum* L. Loosestrife (based on an ancient Greek name used for *L. salicaria*).
Erect perennial, seldom annual, glabrous or pubescent herbs; leaves alternate, opposite or whorled, sessile, reduced in the inflorescence; flowers regular, pink or purple, axillary, solitary, paired or in clusters or cymules aggregated into terminal, spike-like panicles, calyx tube cylindrical, 4-6-toothed, alternating with as many appendages in the sinuses, petals 4-6, stamens as many or twice as many as the petals, these and the style often variable in length; capsules subcylindrical, 2-locular, septicidal, enclosed by the calyx tube.

a. Flowers mostly in clusters of 3 or more in the axils of reduced leaves forming
    terminal, spike-like panicles; larger leaves 6 cm or more long. (Fig. 728).
    Leaves rounded to cordate at the base; plant usually pubescent. .... 1. *L. salicaria*
    Leaves narrowed to the base; plant glabrous. .... 2. *L. virgatum*
a. Flowers solitary or paired in the leaf axils; larger leaves 5 cm or less long.
    b. Leaves mostly opposite or subopposite. .... 3. *L. lineare*
    b. Leaves mostly alternate, the lower ones sometimes opposite.
        Leaves obtuse; petals 3 mm or less long; plant annual. .... 4. *L. hyssopifolia*
        Leaves acute; petals 4 mm or more long; plant perennial. .... 5. *L. alatum*

1. L. salicária L. (willow-like). Purple loosestrife. Marshes, pond and river margins. July-September. Fig. 728, Map 1645. (Naturalized from Europe). Preparations made from the leaves are reported to be of value in treating gastric disorders and skin wounds; twigs are chewed to treat bleeding gums. —FACW+

2. L. virgátum L. (wand-like). Occasionally escaped from cultivation. Reported for MA. (Introduced from Europe).

3. L. lineáre L. (linear). In and around the borders of brackish and saline marshes. July-September. Reported for Fairfield County CT, Long Island, NY. Endangered in NY. —OBL

4. L. hyssopifólia L. (hyssop-leaved). Edges of salt marshes and wet depressions near the coast. June-September. Map 1646. (Europe). —OBL

5. L. alátum Pursh (winged). Wet meadows and ditches. July-September. Map 1647. Our plants are var. *alátum*. [*L. dacotanum*]. —FACW+

2. Décodon J.F. Gmel. Water-willow (ten-toothed, referring to the summit of the calyx).

Perennial, stems somewhat woody below, arching and rooting at the tips and starting new plants, plants pubescent or glabrous; leaves opposite or whorled, lanceolate, cuneate at the base, acuminate-tipped, short-petioled; flowers regular, pink or purple, densely clustered in the upper axils, calyx tube campanulate to globose, 5-7-toothed, alternating with as many longer, linear appendanges in the sinuses, petals 5, stamens 10, 5 included or nearly so and 5 exserted, style variable in length; capsules depressed-globose, 3-5-locular, loculicidally dehiscent.

1. D. verticillátus (L.) Ell. (whorled). Pond and river margins, in shallow water. July-August. Fig. 729, Map 1648. Our plants are var. *verticillatus*.—OBL

3. Rotála L. (name based on the whorled leaves of another species).

Low, glabrous, annual herbs, often diffusely branched from the base; leaves opposite, sessile or subsessile, linear to lanceolate or oblanceolate, obtuse, tapered to the base; flowers regular, small, pink to white, mostly solitary in the leaf axils, calyx tube globose to campanulate, 4-toothed, alternating with as many appendages in the sinuses, petals 4, minute, caducous, stamens 4, short, style short; capsules subglobose, 2-4-locular, septicidal, enclosed by the calyx tube.

1. R. ramósior (L.) Koehne (very branching). Tooth-cup. Pond margins, damp depressions. July-September. Fig. 730, Map 1649. Endangered in MA, RI, CT. —OBL

4. Cúphea R. Br. (from the Greek, based on the shape of the calyx).

Viscid-pubescent, annual herbs; leaves opposite, long-petioled, lanceolate to ovate-lanceolate; flowers irregular, purple, solitary or paired in the upper leaf axils, calyx tube tubular, obliquely gibbous on 1 side at the base, oblique at the mouth, 6-toothed, alternating with as many appendages in the sinuses, petals 6, unequal, stamens 11 or 12, unequal, ovary with a minute curved gland at the base; capsule ovoid to oblong, 2-locular, splitting on 1 side, enclosed by the calyx tube.

1. C. viscosíssima (Jacq.). Blue waxweed. Fields, roadsides, waste places. August-September. Map 1650. [*C. petiolata*]. —FAC-

C. procúmbens Cav. Similar to *C. viscosissima* but flowers 2.5 cm wide with woolly anthers (flowers much smaller and anthers not woolly in *C. viscosissima*). From Mexico. Reported for MA.

Family 145. Melastomatáceae (Melastoma Family)

Represented with us by the following genus:

1. Rhéxia L. Meadow-beauty (ancient Greek name for another plant).

Hermaphrodite, perennial herbs; stems terete to 4-angled, glandular-pubescent to nearly glabrous, arising from tuberous-thickened roots or horizontally spreading stoloniform roots; leaves opposite, simple, sessile to short-petioled, lanceolate to lance-ovate or oblong, ciliate-serrulate, estipulate; flowers perfect, regular in terminal cymes, showy, purplish to white, calyx tube cylindrical in flower, urceolate in fruit, narrowed in the throat, 4-lobed, petals 4, these and the 8 stamens borne on the summit of the calyx tube, anthers yellow, ovary superior, closely surrounded by but free from the calyx tube, 4-locular, many-ovulate, style 1; fruit a globose or subglobose loculicidal capsule, enclosed by the calyx tube.

Stem narrowly 4-winged, the faces essentially equal, glabrous to sparsely hirsute; neck
    of fruiting calyx tube shorter than the body; roots tuberous-thickened .... 1. *R. virginica*
Stem merely 4-ridged, 2 of the faces narrower than the other 2, densely hirsute, neck
    of fruiting calyx tube as long or longer than body; roots stoloniform .... 2. *R. mariana*

1. R. virgínica L. (Virginian). Moist meadows and pond margins. July-September. Fig. 731, Map 1651. Leaves edible in salads. —OBL

2. R. mariána L. (of Maryland). Pond margins. July-September. Endangered in MA; reported for Barnstable County. —OBL

Family 146. Onagráceae (Evening-primrose Family)

Hermaphrodite, annual or perennial herbs. Leaves opposite or alternate, simple, sessile to petioled, entire or toothed, estipulate or with glands in their places. Flowers perfect, regular or nearly so, solitary in the leaf axils or in terminal or axillary racemes or spikes, hypanthium present, adnate to the ovary, frequently prolonged beyond it as a calyx tube, calyx lobes and petals 2-4, persistent or deciduous, or petals sometimes none, stamens as many or twice as many as the calyx lobes or petals, inserted with the petals on the summit of the calyx tube or on a perigynous disc, ovary inferior, 1-4-locular, few-many-ovulate, style 1. Fruit a capsule or indehiscent and nut-like.

a. Sepals and petals 2; fruit 1-seeded, bristly. .... 1. *Circaea*
a. Sepals and petals 4; fruit more than 1-seeded or 1-seeded and not bristly.
  b. Hypanthium much prolonged beyond the summit of the ovary as a narrow
      tube; fruit dehiscent by 4 valves or indehiscent and 1-seeded; seed not
      comose.
    c. Petals pink to whitish; fruit indehiscent, 1-seeded. .... 2. *Gaura*
    c. Petals yellow; fruit dehiscent, many-seeded.
        Hypanthium tubular; stigma deeply 4-lobed or (rarely) unlobed. .... 3. *Oenothera*
        Hypanthium funnelform; stigma shallowly 4-lobed. .... 4. *Calylophus*
                                 serrulatus
  b. Hypanthium not or only scarcely prolonged beyond the summit of the ovary;
      fruit dehiscent by a terminal pore or by 4-valves and seeds comose.
    Petals pink to whitish or purplish; fruit dehiscent by 4 valves; seeds comose. ...... 5. *Epilobium*
    Petals yellowish or absent; fruit dehiscent by a terminal pore; seeds not
      comose .... 6. *Ludwigia*

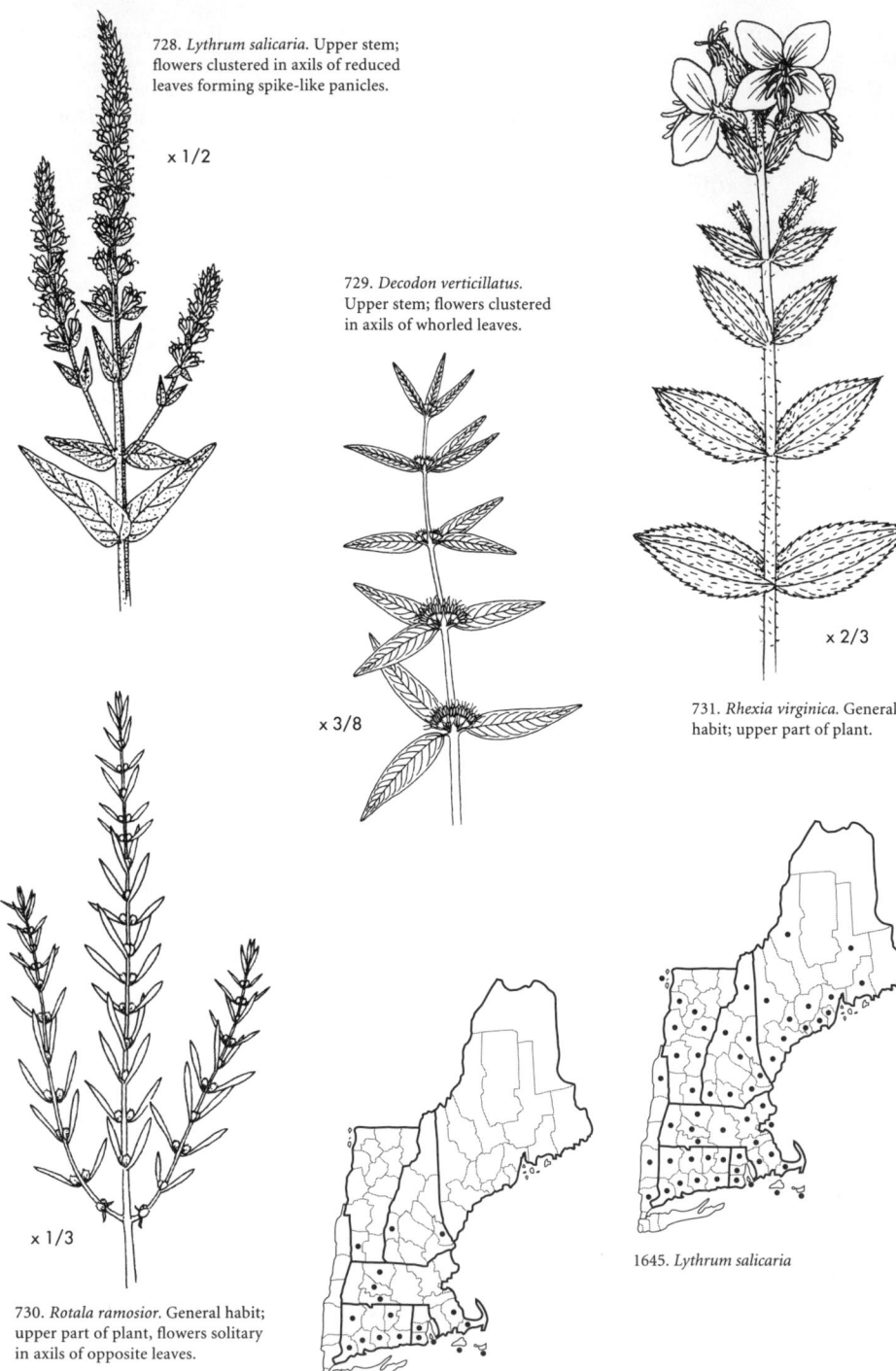

728. *Lythrum salicaria.* Upper stem; flowers clustered in axils of reduced leaves forming spike-like panicles.

x 1/2

729. *Decodon verticillatus.* Upper stem; flowers clustered in axils of whorled leaves.

x 3/8

x 2/3

731. *Rhexia virginica.* General habit; upper part of plant.

x 1/3

730. *Rotala ramosior.* General habit; upper part of plant, flowers solitary in axils of opposite leaves.

1645. *Lythrum salicaria*

1644. *Elaeagnus umbellata var. parviflora*

1646. *Lythrum hyssopifolia*
1647. *Lythrum alatum*
1648. *Decodon verticillatus*

1649. *Rotala ramosior*
1650. *Cuphea viscosissima*
1651. *Rhexia virginica*

1. Circáea L. Enchanter's nightshade (name based on Greek mythodology).

Low, slender perennial herbs; leaves opposite, petioled, ovate, dentate or denticulate; flowers small, white to pink, in 1-several terminal and/or axillary racemes, hypanthium slightly prolonged beyond the ovary, calyx lobes, petals and stamens each 2, ovary 1-2-locular, ovules 1 in each locule, stigma 2-lobed; fruit obovoid, nut-like, indehiscent, covered with hooked bristles.

Pedicels pubescent; fruit, including bristles, more than 3 mm broad, furrowed. .... 1. *C. lutetiana*
Pedicels glabrous; fruit, including bristles, 3 mm or less broad, not furrowed .... 2. *C. alpina*

1. C. lutetiána L. Moist woods. June-August. Fig. 732; Map 1652. [*C. lutetiana* subsp. *quadrisulcata*; *C. quadrisulcata*; *C. latifolia*]. Represented with us as subsp. *canadénsis* (L.) Aschers. & Magnus —FACU

2. C. alpína L. (alpine). Moist to wet woods and bogs. June-August. Map 1653. (Eurasia). Our plants are subsp. *alpína*. —FACW

C. x intermédia Ehrh. (pro sp.) A hybrid between the latter 2 species; will key to *C. alpina* but differs in having a slender rhizome and 2-locular fruit (*C. alpina* has a tuberous-thickened rhizome and 1-locular fruit). From farther north. Map 1654. (Europe). [*C. canadensis*].

2. *Gaúra* L. (from the Greek meaning superb).

Coarse, branched, pubescent, annual or biennial herbs; leaves basal and cauline, the former oblanceolate, the latter alternate, sessile to short-petioled, sometimes with axillary fascicles, lanceolate to elliptic, tapered at both ends, remotely or obscurely denticulate; flowers small, pink to whitish, numerous in terminal, solitary or paniculate spikes, hypanthium much prolonged beyond the ovary as a narrow tube, deciduous, calyx lobes 4, reflexed, petals 4, clawed, slightly unequal, deciduous, stamens 8, ovary 1-locular, 1-4 ovulate, stigma 4-lobed; fruit hard, indehiscent, 4-angled, 1-seeded.

a. Sepals longer than 3 mm; fruit canescent or spreading-pubescent; spikes usually
    paniculate. (Fig. 733).
    Leaves 1 cm or more wide; fruit obtusely angled. .... 1. *G. biennis*
    Leaves up to 1 cm wide; fruit acutely angled. .... 2. *G. longiflora*
a. Sepals 3 mm or less long; fruit glabrous or nearly so; spikes usually solitary .... 3. *G. parviflora*

   1. *G. biénnis* L. (biennial). Roadsides and waste places. July-September. Fig. 733, Map 1655. From farther west and south. —FACU
   2. *G. longiflóra* Spach. Roadsides and waste places. June-September. From farther south. Reported for CT, MA. [*G. angustifolia*; *G. biennis* var. *pitcheri*].
   3. *G. parviflóra* Dougl. ex Lehm. (small-flowered). Roadsides and waste places. July-September. From farther west. Reported for Middlesex County MA.

3. *Oenothéra* L. Evening-primrose (early Greek name for a species of *Epilobium*).

Annual, biennial or perennial, usually pubescent herbs; basal rosettes often formed, stem leaves alternate, sessile or short-petioled, entire, toothed or sinuate; flowers yellow or rarely white or pink, solitary in the leaf axils or forming a terminal raceme, hypanthium much prolonged beyond the ovary as a narrow tube, deciduous, calyx lobes 4, at first ascending and connate, separating at anthesis and reflexed, petals 4, often showy, deciduous, stamens 8, ovary 4-locular, ovules many, stigma deeply 4-lobed; capsule oblong to obovoid, somtimes angled, 4-valved, many-seeded.

Camissónia Link. Similar to *Oenothera* but differing in having a capitate unlobed stigma. From the west coast. Three species occurring with us as waifs: *C. bistórta* (Nutt. ex Torr. & Gray) Raven ex Hook. Petals 8 mm or more long, capsules 4-angled. Reported for Middlesex County MA; *C. contórta* (Dougl. ex Lehm.) Kearn. Petals less than 4 mm long, capsules terete. Reported for ME, NH, VT, RI; *C. campéstris* Raven. Petals 5-8 mm long, capsules terete. Reported for MA. Our plants are subsp. *campestris*.

a. Ovary and capsule clavate to ellipsoid, broadest toward the middle or tip, usually
    4-angled or winged. (Fig. 734).
    b. Calyx tube 1.5 cm or more long .... 1. *O. pilosella*
    b. Calyx tube less than 1.5 cm long.
        c. Hypanthium and ovary glabrous or if pubescent with some gland-tipped hairs.
            Petals 1 cm or more long; capsule wing-angled. (Fig. 734). .... 2. *O. fruticosa*
            Petals less than 1 cm long; capsule not decidedly wing-angled. .... 3. *O. perennis*
        c. Hypanthium and ovary pubescent, the hairs not gland-tipped. .... 2. *O. fruticosa*
a. Ovary and capsule cylindric or subcylindric, broadest toward the base, not winged
    or angled or only obscurely so. (Fig. 735).
    d. Flowers white or pink; flower buds nodding. .... 4. *O. speciosa*
    d. Flowers yellow, flower buds erect.
        e. Leaves (at least some of them) deeply coarsely toothed to pinnatifid; seeds
            pitted. (Fig. 735) .... 5. *O. laciniata*
        e. Leaves shallowly toothed to entire; seeds not pitted.
            f. Reflexed calyx lobes with a prominent corniculate appendage below the
                tip; tips of calyx lobes in unexpanded bud distinct, not connivent.
                (Fig. 736). .... 6. *O. parviflora*

f. Reflexed calyx lobes lacking an appendage; tips of calyx lobes in unexpanded
  bud partly connivent.
  g. Petals 3 cm or more long .... 7. *O. grandiflora*
  g. Petals less than 3 cm long.
    Calyx lobes, ovaries and capsules canescent. .... 8. *O. villosa*
    Calyx lobes; ovaries and capsules glabrous or with scattered
      pubescence. .... 9. *O. biennis*

1. *O. pilosélla* Raf. (finely pilose). Fields, woods, waste places. May-July. Map 1656. [*O. fruticosa* var. *hirsuta; O. pratensis; Kneiffia pratensis*]. Our plants are subsp. *pilosella*. —FAC

2. *O. fruticósa* L. (shrubby). Fields, open woods, wet meadows. May-June. Fig. 734, Map 1657. Our plants include subsp. *fruticosa* [*O. linearis; O. longipedicellata; Kneiffia alleni; K. fruticosa*] and the following subsp.:

subsp. *glaúca* (Michx.) Straley. Pubescence of hypanthium and ovary with some minute gland-tipped hairs (hairs all eglandular in subsp. *fruticosa*). [*O. tetragona; O. glauca; Kneiffia g.; K. hybrida; K. latifolia; K. tetragona*]. —FAC

3. *O. perénnis* L. (perennial). Moist to dry meadows, fields and open woods. May-June. Map 1658. [*O. pumila; Kneiffia pumila; K. perennis*]. —FAC

4. *O. speciósa* Nutt. (showy). From farther west; rarely found in our range. Reported for Fairfield County CT. [*Hartmannia s.*].

5. *O. laciniáta* Hill (slashed). Waste places, roadsides, in dry sandy soil. May-June. Fig. 735, Map 1659. [*Raimannia l.*]. —FACU-

O. grándis Rydb. Similar to *O. laciniata* but distinguishable in having the hypanthium tube 3 cm or more long, sepals longer than 1.5 cm and petals 2 cm or more long (hypanthium tube less than 3 cm long, sepals shorter than 1.5 cm and petals less than 2 cm long in *O. laciniata*). From farther west. Reported for CT. [*O. laciniata* var. *grandiflora*].

6. *O. parviflóra* L. (small-flowered). Roadsides and waste places. May-June. Fig. 736, Map 1660. [*O. angustissima; O. cruciata*]. —FACU-

O. oakesiána (Gray) J.W. Robbins ex S. Wats. & Coult. (for its discoverer).Similar to *O. parviflora* but densely puberulent, rarely with a few scattered strigose hairs (upper part of stem, undersides of leaves, calyx and capsules glabrous or with scattered strigose hairs in *O. parviflora*). Throughout our range. [*O. parviflora* var. *o.*].

7. *O. grandiflóra* L'Her. ex Ait. (large-flowered). Escaped from cultivation to fields, roadsides and waste places. July-August. Map 1661. (Naturalized from Europe). [*O. lamarckiana*].

O. glazioviána Micheli. Similar to *O. grandiflora* but with sessile leaves, pubescent sepals and ovary, and capsules 4 mm or more thick (leaves petioled, sepals and ovary glabrous or nearly so and capsule about 3 mm thick in *O. grandiflora*). Throughout our range. [*O. erythrosepala; O. lamarckiana*].

O. eláta H.B.K. Similar to the latter 2 species; leaves petioled, sepals, ovary and capsules as in *O. glazioviana*, petals up to 4 cm long (petals generally longer than 4 cm in the latter 2 species). From farther west. Reported for VT. Represented with us as subsp. *hirsutíssima* (Gray ex S. Wats.) Dietrich.

8. *O. villósa* Thunb. Roadsides and waste places. June-July. Map 1662. From farther west. [*O. biennis* var. *canescens; O. biennis* var. *hirsutissima; O. depressa; O. strigosa; O. rydbergii*]. —FAC

9. *O. biénnis* L. (biennial). Fields, roadsides, waste places. May-July. Map 1663. Young roots edible when cooked, as are the young shoots and leaves; syrup made from the flowers is said to be beneficial for treating whooping cough. —FACU-

4. *Calylóphus* Spach. Evening-Primrose.

Similar to *Oenothera* except hypanthium funnelform and stigma shallowly 4-lobed. [*Oenothera*].

1. *C. serrulátus* (Nutt.) Raven (finely serrate). Dry fields. May-June. From farther west. Reported for Chittendon County VT. [*Oenothera serrulata; Meriolix serrulata; M. intermedia*].

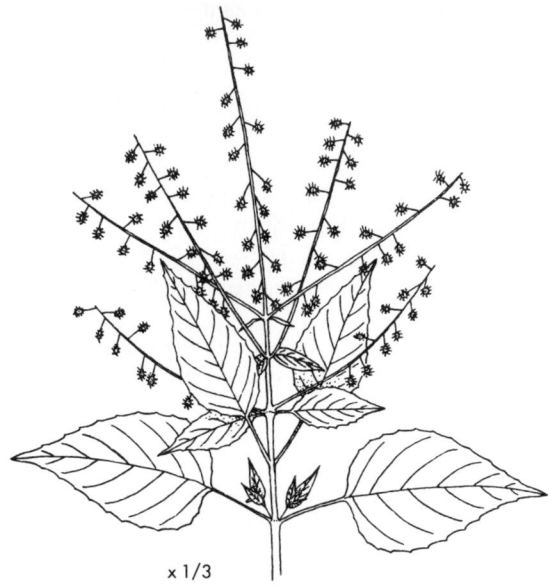

×1/3

732. *Circaea lutetiana.* General
habit; upper part of plant.

× 1

734. *Oenothera fruticosa.* Fruiting
inflorescence; capusule clavate
and wing-angled.

×2/3

733. *Gaura biennis.* Upper
stem; spikes paniculate.

736. *Oenothera parviflora.* Flowers, calyx
lobes reflexed, with an appendage, bud
with tips of calyx lobes distinct.

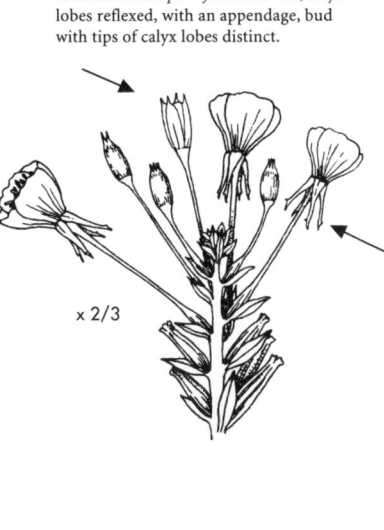

× 2/3

×3/5

735. *Oenothera laciniata.* Upper stem;
leaves coarsely toothed to pinnatifid,
capsules cylindric, not winged.

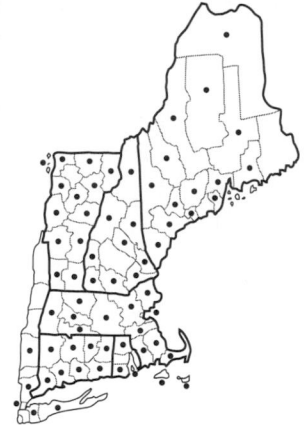

1652. *Circaea lutetiana* subsp. *canadensis*

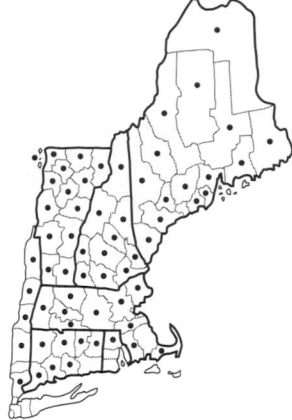

1653. *Circaea alpina*

1654. *Circaea x intermedia*

1655. *Gaura biennis*

1656. *Oenothera pilosella*

1657. *Oenothera fruticosa*

1658. *Oenothera perennis*

1659. *Oenothera laciniata*

1660. *Oenothera parviflora*

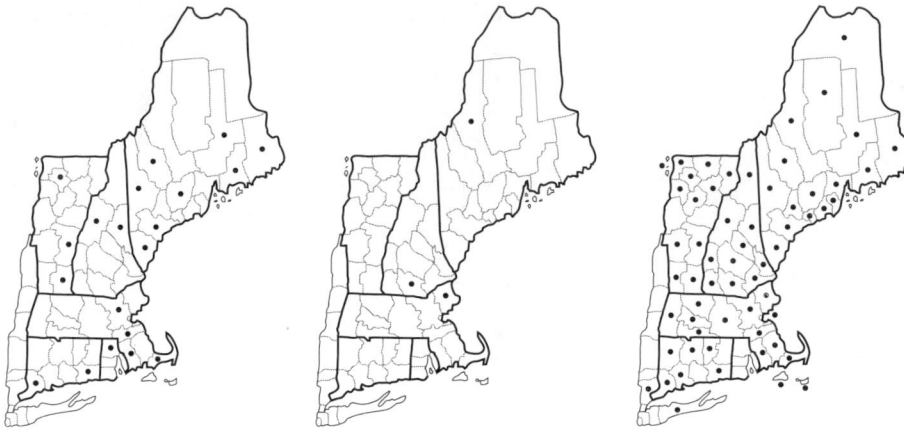

1661. *Oenothera grandiflora*   1662. *Oenothera villosa*   1663. *Oenothera biennis*

5. *Epilóbium* L. Willow-herb (from the Greek, referring to the perianth surmounting the capsule).

Perennial (ours) herbs; leaves alternate or opposite, sessile or subsessile, entire or toothed; flowers pink to whitish or purplish, few to many in short or elongate terminal racemes, or solitary, calyx tube long and narrow, scarcely or not produced beyond the ovary, calyx lobes 4, deciduous, petals 4, stamens 8, ovary 4-locular, stigma entire or 4-lobed; fruit a long, linear, 4-valved capsule, seeds small, numerous, with a tuft of hairs (coma) at the tip.

Clárkia Pursh. Similar to *Epilobium* but differs in that the seeds are not comose. Several species occasionally escape from cultivation in our range. Reported for Fairfield and Hartford Counties CT; Franklin, Hampshire and Middlesex Counties MA; Rutland and Windsor Counties VT.

a. Plants with pubescence of dense, horizontally divergent hairs.
　　Leaves entire or essentially so, mostly less than 1 cm wide; stigma entire. .... 1. *E. strictum*
　　Leaves serrulate, the larger ones 1 cm or more wide; stigma 4-lobed. .... 2. *E. hirsutum*
a. Plants with pubescence of appressed or incurved hairs or glabrous, or if
　　　　spreading-pubescent (rarely) lacking other characteristics of the above
　　　　species.
　　b. Stigma 4-lobed; stems glabrous; robust plants, generally well over 1 m tall when
　　　　mature .... 3. *E. angustifolium*
　　b. Stigma entire; stems puberulent, at least above; mature plants generally 1 m or
　　　　less tall.
　　　　c. Leaves entire or essentially so, margins usually revolute, linear to lance-linear,
　　　　　　mostly 8 mm or less wide; stem lacking ribs, puberulence not in
　　　　　　decurrent lines.
　　　　　　Leaves minutely puberulent above .... 4. *E. leptophyllum*
　　　　　　Leaves glabrous above or essentially so. .... 5. *E. palustre*
　　　　c. Leaves usually toothed, the larger wider than 8 mm (sometimes entire or
　　　　　　narrower in *E. anagallidifolium*), margins flat, lanceolate to ovate; stem
　　　　　　with ribs and/or puberulent lines decurrent from the leaf bases, at
　　　　　　least above.
　　　　　　d. Stems commonly tufted or matted, mostly simple to slightly forked; leaves
　　　　　　　　mostly ovate to oblong; rhizomes well developed, not ending in
　　　　　　　　globose bulbs; chiefly alpine. (Fig. 737) .... 6. *E. anagallidifolium*
　　　　　　d. Stems solitary or few, mostly freely branched; leaves mostly narrow to
　　　　　　　　broadly lanceolate (sometimes ovate to elliptic in *E. ciliatum*);
　　　　　　　　rhizomes short, or well developed and ending in globose bulbs;
　　　　　　　　not chiefly alpine. (Fig. 738).

Coma whitish; rhizomes sometimes well developed and ending in
  globose bulbs. .... 7. *E. ciliatum*
Coma brownish; rhizomes short, not ending in globose bulbs. .... 8. *E. coloratum*

1. E. stríctum Muhl. ex Spreng. (pressed together). Bogs, wooded swamps. Fruit: July-September. Map 1664. [*E. densum; E. molle*]. —OBL

2. E. hirsútum L. (hirsute). Meadows, marshes, pond margins, waste places. Fruit: July-September. Map 1665. (Naturalized from Europe). —FACW

3. E. angustifólium L. (narrow-leaved). Clearings, burned-over land, roadsides. Fruit: July-September. Map 1666. (Eurasia). [*Chamaenerion a.; C. spicatum*]. Our plants are subsp. *angustifolium*. Young shoots and flower buds edible; tea can be made from the dried leaves and pith of the stems can be used in soups; hairs on the seeds can be used as tinder; various medicinal uses are also cited. —FAC

4. E. leptophýllum Raf. (narrow-leaved). Bogs, cedar swamps, wet meadows, marshes, pond margins. Fruit: July-September. Map 1667. [*E. densum; E. lineare; E. nesophyllum*]. —OBL

5. E. palústre L. (of marshes). Bogs, wooded swamps, wet meadows, marshes. Fruit: July-September. Map 1668. (Eurasia). [*E. oliganthum*]. —OBL

6. E. anagallidifólium Lam. (pimpernel-leaved). Wet soil in alpine areas of Mt. Katahdin, ME, and White Mts., NH. Fruit: July-August. Fig. 737, Map 1669. (Eurasia). Endangered in ME, NY. [*E. alpinum* var. *alpinum*]. —FACW

E. lactiflórum Haussk. Similar to *E. anagallidifólium* but with white or pink-tipped petals (petals entirely pink in *E. anagallidifolium*). Alpine areas in ME, NH. [*E. alpinum* var. *l.*]. (Eurasia). —FACW

E. hornemánni Reichenb. Similar to the latter 2 species but seeds papillate and petals 5-8 mm long (seeds smooth and petals 3-6 mm long in the latter 2 species). (Eurasia). Alpine areas in ME, NH. [*E. alpinum* var. *nutans*]. Our plants are subsp. *hornemanni*. —FACW

7. E. ciliátum Raf. (with marginal hairs). Wet meadows, marshes, wooded swamps. Fruit: July-September. Map 1670. Reported for Aroostook County ME, Strafford County NH. Our plants include subsp. *ciliátum* [*E. adenocaulon; E. americanum; E. perplexans*] and the following subsp.:

subsp. *glandulósum* (Lehm.) P.C. Hoch. Rhizomes well developed and ending in globose bulbs; leaves sessile or subsessile (rhizomes very short and leaves definitely petioled in subsp. *ciliatum*). [*E. glandulosum; E. boreale; E. saximontanum; E. steckerianum*]. —FAC-

E. halleánum Hausskn. Similar to *E. ciliatum* subsp. *glandulosum* but with slender terete stems, flowers up to 5 mm long (stems 4 angled and flowers mostly longer than 5 mm in *E. ciliatum* subsp. *glandulosum*). From farther north and west. Reported for NH. [*E. glandulosum* var. *macouneii; E. leptocarpum* var. *m.*].

8. E. colorátum Biehler (colored). Wet meadows, marshes, wooded swamps, stream margins. Fruit: July-September. Fig. 738, Map 1671. —OBL

6. Ludwígia L. (for C. Ludwig).

Perennial herbs with stems slightly 4-angled; leaves opposite or alternate, sessile or short petioled, entire or essentially so, narrowly to broadly lanceolate to ovate; flowers solitary, sessile or short-pedicelled in the upper axils, calyx tube cylindric to obpyramidal, often 4-sided, not produced beyond the ovary, calyx lobes 4, persistent, petals 4, deciduous, yellow to greenish, stamens 4, ovary 4-locular, stigma entire or 4-lobed; fruit a cubical to short-cylindric or subglobose capsule, dehiscing by a terminal pore (ours), many-seeded.

a. Leaves, or most of them, opposite; flowering stems creeping and/or submerged
    or floating. (Fig. 739) .... 1. *L. palustris*
a. Leaves alternate; flowering stems erect, not submerged or floating.
  b. Flowers and fruits distinctly pedicelled; petals yellow, conspicuous. .... 2. *L. alternifolia*

b. Flowers and fruits sessile or subsessile; petals greenish and minute or none.
   Capsule glabrous; bractlets reaching well beyond the middle of the
      hypanthium. .... 3. *L. polycarpa*
   Capsule puberulent; bractlets wanting or barely reaching middle of the
      hypanthium .... 4. *L. sphaerocarpa*

1. L. palústris (L.) Ell. (of marshes). Pond and stream margins, creeping on mud or submerged in shallow water. July-September. Fig. 739, Map 1672. (Bermuda). —OBL

L. x lacústris Eames (pro sp.). A sterile hybrid between *L. palustris* and *L. brevipes*.

2. L. alternifólia L. (alternate-leaved). Seedbox. Pond and river margins, wet meadows. June-August. Map 1673. Reported as having medicinal value. —FACW+

3. L. polycárpa Short & Peter (many-fruited). Pond and river margins, wet meadows. July-September. Map 1674. Endangered in VT. —OBL

4. L. sphaerocárpa Ell. (spherical-fruited). Pond and river margins. July-September. Map 1675. Endangered in RI, CT. —OBL

Family 147. Trapáceae (Water-chestnut Family)

Hermaphrodite, annual, aquatic herbs with submersed stems up to several feet long. Submersed leaves verticillate, pinnately divided into capillary segments; scattered, caducous, linear submersed leaves also formed; floating leaves in a rosette, petioles inflated, the upper progressively shorter, blades rhombic-ovate, broadly cuneate and entire below, dentate above. Flowers perfect, regular, white, axillary, solitary, on short, thick peduncles, hypanthium adnate to the lower half of the ovary, calyx lobes and petals 4, stamens 4, perigynous, ovary half-inferior, 2-locular, 2-ovulate, style 1. Fruit indehiscent, nut-like, with 2-4 stout spines, 1-locular, 1-seeded. [*Hydrocaryaceae*].

1. Trápa L. Water-chestnut. (name based on the spreading spines on the fruit).
Same characters as the family. Fruit edible.

1. T. nátans L. (floating). Rivers and ponds. Fruit: August-September. Fig. 740, Map 1676. (Naturalized from Eurasia). —OBL

Family 148. Haloragáceae (Water-milfoil Family)

Hermaphrodite, monoecious or polygamous, perennial, aquatic or marsh herbs. Leaves alternate, opposite or whorled, once pinnately dissected to merely serrate, estipulate. Flowers small, perfect or unisexual, regular, sessile and solitary or in small clusters in the axils of leaves or bracts, usually above water, often forming interrupted, emersed, terminal spikes, sepals 3 or 4, petals 4 or none, stamens 3-8, ovary inferior, 3-4-locular, stigmas 3-4. Fruit indehiscent or eventually splitting into 4 mericarps.

Flowers 3-merous; fruit triangular, indehiscent; emersed leaves foliaceous. .... 1. *Proserpinaca*
Flowers 4-merous; fruit quadrangular, eventually splitting into 4 mericarps;
   emersed leaves reduced, often bract-like. (Fig. 743). .... 2. *Myriophyllum*

1. Proserpináca L. Mermaid-weed (ancient Greek name used for another plant).
Marsh or amphibious herbs with stems creeping or decumbent at the base; leaves alternate, the submersed ones pinnatifid, with very narrow divisions, the emersed ones either serrate or pinnatifid; flowers perfect, solitary or in small clusters in the axils of the emersed leaves, sepals 3, petals none, stamens 3, ovary 3-locular, stigmas 3; fruit indehiscent, triangular. —OBL

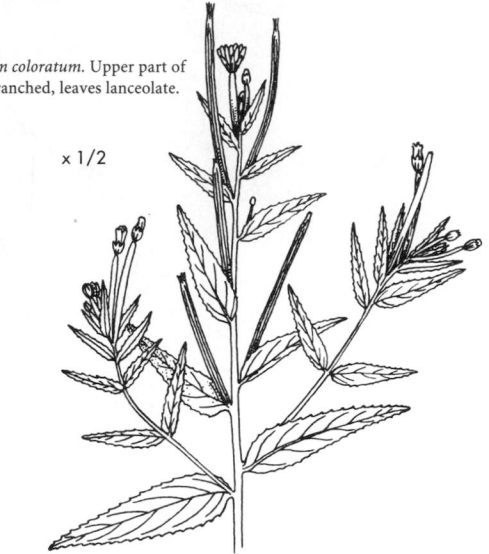

738. *Epilobium coloratum.* Upper part of plant; stem branched, leaves lanceolate.

x 1/2

x 1

737. *Epilobium anagallidifolium.* General habit; stem simple, leaves oblong or ovate.

x 1/2

x 2/5

739. *Ludwigia palustris.* General habit; flowering stem creeping, leaves opposite.

740. *Trapa natans.* General habit; submerged and floating leaves, single fruit.

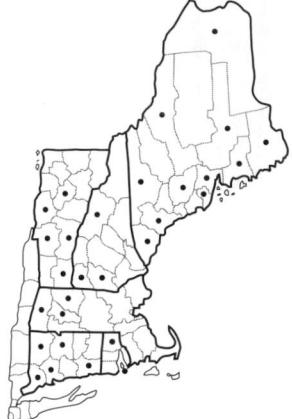

1664. *Epilobium strictum*

1665. *Epilobium hirsutum*

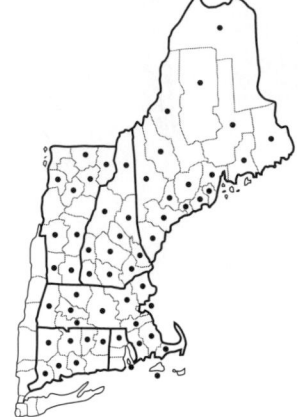

1666. *Epilobium angustifolium*

1667. *Epilobium leptophyllum*

1668. *Epilobium palustre*

1669. *Epilobium anagallidifolium*

1670. *Epilobium ciliatum*

1671. *Epilobium coloratum*

1672. *Ludwigia palustris*

1673. *Ludwigia alternifolia*   1674. *Ludwigia polycarpa*   1675. *Ludwigia sphaerocarpa*

1676. *Trapa natans*   1677. *Proserpinaca palustris*   1678. *Proserpinaca pectinata*

Bracteal leaves merely serrate, the teeth shorter than the width of the central lamina.
    (Fig. 741) .... 1. *P. palustris*
Bracteal leaves pinnatifid or deeply pinnatisect, the teeth (or divisions) as long or
    longer than the width of the central lamina. .... 2. *P. pectinata*

1. P. palústris L. (of marshes). Shallow water and muddy shores of ponds and streams. June-September. Fig. 741, Map 1677. (W.I.). Our plants include var. *palustris* [*P. platycarpa*] and the following var.:

var. *crébra* Fern & Grisc. Sides of fruit flat or convex, angles wingless (concave with winged angles in var. *palustris*).

2. P. pectináta Lam. (comb-like). Wet or muddy depressions and pond margins on the coastal plain. June-September. Map 1678. Endangered in NH.

P. intermédia Mackenz. Similar to *P. pectinata* but with emersed leaves shallowly pinnatifid, the uncleft median portion more than 1 mm wide (emersed leaves deeply pinnatifid or pinnatisect, the uncleft median portion up to 1 mm wide in *P. pectinata*). Reported for MA, RI. Possibly a hybrid between *P. palustris* and *P. pectinata*.

2. *Myriophýllum* L. Water-milfoil (from the Greek, referring to the finely divided leaves).

Aquatic or amphibious herbs; leaves alternate, opposite or whorled, the submersed ones usually pinnatifid into capillary segments, the emersed ones reduced, often bract-like, pinnatifid to dentate or entire; flowers perfect or unisexual, solitary in the upper leaf axils, often forming an emersed, interrupted, terminal spike, calyx 4-lobed or toothed, petals 0 or 4, stamens 4-8, ovary 4-locular, stigmas 4; fruit quadrangular, eventually splitting into 4 mericarps. —OBL; Wildl. 1

a. Stems leafless or with scattered, minute, entire, scale-like leaves. .... 1. *M. tenellum*
a. Stems leafy, at least the submersed leaves pinnatifid (sometimes entire in the
    emergent form of *M. humile* but not minute or scale-like).
  b. Foliage leaves alternate and often also subopposite or whorled on the same plant.
    c. Plant with all leaves submersed and pinnatifid into capillary segments; flowers
      and fruits scattered in the leaf axils.
      Leaves usually with minute black spicules in the axils of the capillary
        segments; mature mericarps tuberculate on the back. .... 2. *M. farwellii*
      Leaves lacking spicules in the axils of the capillary segments; mature
        mericarps smooth or minutely roughened on the back. .... 3. *M. humile*
    c. Plant with some or all leaves emersed; flowers and fruits in sequential
      order forming interrupted terminal spikes. (Fig. 742).
      Mature mericarps tuberculate on the back. .... 4. *M. pinnatum*
      Mature mericarps smooth or minutely roughened on the back. .... 3. *M. humile*
  b. Foliage leaves all distinctly whorled.
    d. Leaves 1.2 cm or less long; flowers, except the lower ones, alternate. .... 5. *M. alterniflorum*
    d. Leaves, at least some or most of them, longer than 1.2 cm; flowers whorled.
      e. Bracts all pinnatisect. (Fig. 743) .... 6. *M. verticillatum*
      e. Bracts mostly entire to serrate, sometimes only the lowermost pinnatisect.
        Bracts shorter than to equalling flowers or fruit. .... 7. *M. sibericum*
        Bracts 2 or more times longer than flowers or fruit. .... 8. *M. heterophyllum*

1. *M. tenéllum* Bigelow (delicate). Shallow, quiet water and pond margins. July-September. Map 1679.

2. *M. farwéllii* Morong (for its discoverer). Quiet water of rivers and ponds. July-September. Map 1680.

3. *M. húmile* (Raf.) Morong (lowly). Pond margins, totally emergent or in shallow water. July-October. Map 1681.

4. *M. pinnátum* (Walt.) B.S.P. (pinnate). Shallow water, pond and stream margins, ditches. July-October. Fig. 742, Map 1682. (W.I.). [*M. scabratum*].

5. *M. alterniflórum* DC. (alternate-flowered). Quiet water of ponds and streams. July-September. Map 1683. (Europe; Greenland).

M. aquáticum (Vell.) Verdc. Parrot-feather. Differing from the following 3 species in having the flowers borne in the axils of the submersed foliage leaves (flowers borne in the axils of bracts in an emersed spike in the following 3 species.) (South Amer.). Escaped from aquaria. Reported for Nassau and Suffolk Counties NY. [*M. brasiliense*; *M. proserpinacoides*].

6. *M. verticillátum* L. (whorled). Quiet water of ponds and streams. July-September. Fig. 743, Map 1684. (Eurasia). [*M. hippuroides*].

7. *M. sibericum* Komarov. Quiet water of ponds and streams, sometimes brackish. July-September. Map 1685. [*M. exalbescens*; *M. spicatum* var. *exalbescens*].

M. spicátum L. Similar to *M. sibericum* but distinguishable in having leaves around middle portion of plant with 12 or more divisions on each side and stem below the inflorescence distinctly thicker than the lower stem (middle leaves with fewer than 12 divisions on each side and stem of uniform thickness in *M. sibericum*). Reported for CT, MA, NH, VT.

8. *M. heterophýllum* Michx. (diverse-leaved). Quiet water of ponds and streams. July-September. Map 1686.

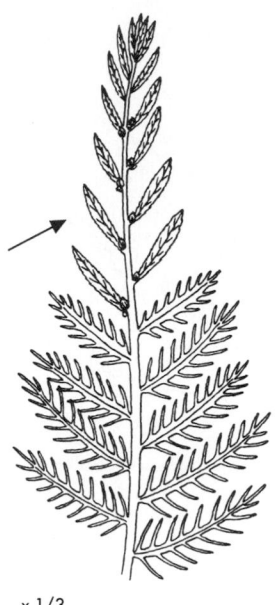

× 1/3

741. *Proserpinaca palustris.* Upper
stem; bracteal leaves merely serrate.

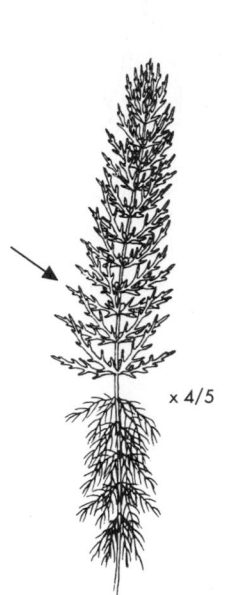

× 4/5

742. *Myriophyllum pinnatum.*
Branch with flowers and fruits in
axils of emersed leaves forming an
interrupted spike.

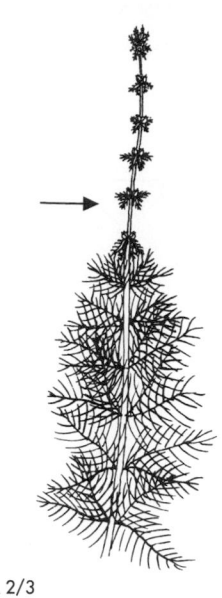

× 2/3

743. *Myriophyllum verticillatum.*
Branch with terminal spike
having pinnatisect bracts.

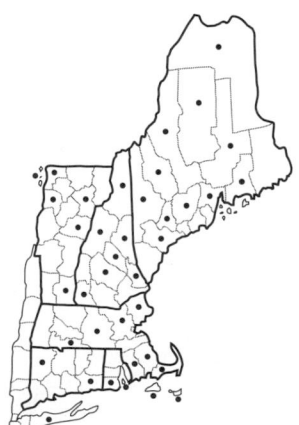

1679. *Myriophyllum tenellum*

1680. *Myriophyllum farwellii*

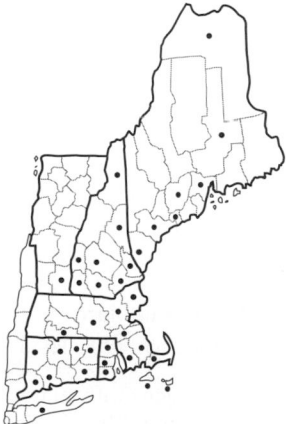

1681. *Myriophyllum humile*

1682. *Myriophyllum pinnatum*   1683. *Myriophyllum alterniflorum*   1684. *Myriophyllum verticillatum*

1685. *Myriophyllum sibericum*   1686. *Myriophyllum heterophyllum*   1687. *Hippuris vulgaris*

Family 149. Hippuridáceae (Mare's-tail Family)

Hermaphrodite or polygamous, rhizomatous, perennial, aquatic or amphibious herbs. Leaves whorled, numerous, simple, sessile, linear, the submersed ones longer and more flaccid than the upper, the lowest scale-like. Flowers perfect or pistillate, minute, sessile and solitary in the upper leaf axils, perianth lacking, stamen 1, ovary inferior, 1-locular, style 1. Fruit hard and nut-like, ellipsoid, beaked with the persistent style, 1-seeded.

1. Hippúris L. Mare's tail. (from the Greek meaning horse tail).
Same characters as the family.

   1. H. vulgáris L. (common). Shallow water and borders of ponds and streams. July-September. Fig. 744, Map 1687. (Eurasia). Endangered in VT. —OBL

Family 150. Araliáceae (Ginseng Family)

Hermaphrodite or polygamous, perennial herbs, shrubs or trees. Leaves alternate or whorled, petioled, pinnate, ternate or palmately compound (rarely simple), with stipules adnate to the petiole. Flowers perfect or polygamous, regular, small, bracteate, in umbels, these sometimes corymbose, racemose or paniculate, calyx tube adnate to the ovary, lobes 5 or none, petals and stamens 5, inserted on the calyx tube, ovary inferior, 2-5-locular, styles 2-5, ovules 2-5. Fruit a 2-5-seeded berry.

Hédera L. *hélix* L., with stems creeping or climbing by aerial roots and with simple leaves is occasionally escaped from cultivation in our range. Reported for Barnstable and Dukes Counties MA. Poisonous if taken internally and, in some individuals, can cause dermatitis if touched; however, administered in the proper amounts extractions of the plant are reported to be used in external applications to treat rheumatism and various skin disorders, and taken internally for whooping cough.

Leaves whorled, once palmately compound; umbel solitary. (Fig. 745). .... 1. *Panax*
Leaves alternate or solitary and basal, the ultimate divisions pinnate (rarely palmate);
        umbels 2 or more, in corymbs or panicles. (Fig. 746). .... 2. *Aralia*

1. *Pánax* L. Ginseng (Greek name, based on the reputed medicinal value).

Perennial herbs, with simple stems arising from a thickened fusiform or globose root; leaves usually 3 in a single whorl at the summit of the stem, palmate, leaflets 3-5, sessile or petiolulate, lanceolate to oblong or obovate, serrate; flowers in a simple, long-peduncled, terminal umbel, white or greenish, locules, styles and ovules 2-3; berry red or yellow.

Leaflets long-stalked, acuminate; root fusiform. (Fig. 745). .... 1. *P. quinquefolius*
Leaflets sessile or subsessile, obtuse or acute; root globose. .... 2. *P. trifolius*

    1. *P. quinquefólius* L. (five-leaved). Ginseng. Rich woods. June-July. Fig. 745, Map 1688. Long regarded in the Orient as valuable in preventing illness, curing a variety of illnesses and in prolonging life; there is no proven scientific evidence of any actual medicinal value.
    2. *P. trifólius* L. (three-leaved). Dwarf Ginseng. Rich woods. April-June. Map 1689.

2. *Arália* L. (early French-Canadian name).

Perennial herbs, shrubs or small trees, armed or unarmed, when woody twigs stout, these and the stem or trunk armed with stout prickles, pith large, whitish, buds ovoid, solitary and sessile, with several scales, leaf scars narrow, half or more encircling the stem, remnants of the petiole base often forming a thin raised border, bundle traces numerous in a curved line, stipule scars lacking; leaves alternate (1 species with a solitary, basal ternate leaf), pinnately or ternately compound or decompound, petioles sheathing at the base; flowers whitish or greenish, umbels several in a corymb or many in a large panicle, locules, styles and ovules 5; berry purple or black. —Wildl. 1

a. Plant a shrub or small tree, the stem and branches armed with stout prickles;
    umbels numerous in a large compound panicle. .... 1. *A. spinosa*
a. Plant an herb, or woody only at the base, unarmed or merely bristly-hispid.
  b. Plant acaulescent or nearly so, the single ternate leaf and peduncle arising from
      the rhizome .... 2. *A. nudicaulis*
  b. Plant leafy-stemmed.
    Stem bristly at the base; leaflets cuneate at base; umbels several, corymbose.
      (Fig. 746) .... 3. *A. hispida*
    Stem unarmed; leaflets cordate at base; umbels numerous,
      racemose-paniculate. .... 4. *A. racemosa*

1. A. spinósa L. (spiny). Hercules club. Moist woods and woodland borders. July-September. Map 1690. From farther west or south. Dermatitis is caused in susceptible individuals by handling the bark and roots. —FAC

A. eláta *(Miq.)* Seem. Japanese Angelica Tree. Resembling *A. spinosa* but differing in having subsessile, lanceolate leaflets (leaflets distinctly stalked and ovate in *A. spinosa*). Rarely escaped from cultivation in our range. Reported for NH, Fairfield County CT.

Acanthopánax (Dcne & Planch.) Miq. Prickly shrubs or trees resembling *Aralia spinosa* but distinguishable by the palmately dissected or lobed leaves (leaves pinnately dissected in *Aralia spinosa*). Two species occasionally escape from cultivation in our range: *A. sieboldiánus* Makino has palmately dissected leaves. Reported for: Hartford County CT, Franklin and Hampshire Counties MA.; *A. ricinifólius* Seem., has palmately lobed leaves. Reported for New Haven County CT. [*Kalopanax pictus*].

2. A. nudicaúlis L. (naked-stemmed). Wild Sarsaparilla. Moist to dry woods. May-June. Map 1691. Extractions of the root have been used as a substitute for sarsaparilla and to treat coughs. —FACU

3. A. híspida Vent. (with straight hairs). Bristly Sarsaparilla. Dry woods and clearings. June-August. Fig. 746, Map 1692.

4. A. racemósa L. (racemose). Spikenard. Rich woods. July-August. Map 1693. Endangered in RI. Our plants are subsp. *racemosa*. Extracts of the root have been used to treat rheumatism and as a cough remedy; fruits have been used as an ingredient in root beer.

Family 151. Apiáceae (Parsley Family)

Hermaphrodite, or polygamomonoecious, often aromatic, usually hollow-stemmed herbs. Leaves alternate or basal, simple or ternately, palmately or pinnately dissected or compound, petiole usually expanded and sheathing at the base, stipules none or minute. Flowers usually perfect, sometimes imperfect, regular, small, in simple or compound umbels (rarely heads), the umbels and umbellets often subtended by an involucre of bracts or an involucel of bractlets, calyx entire or minutely 5-toothed, petals and stamens 5, inserted on the calyx tube, ovary inferior, 2-locular, styles 2, usually swollen and disc-like at the base (the stylopodium), ovules 2. Fruit a schizocarp of 2 mericarps, attached by the inner face (the commissure), separating when ripe from the base upward and remaining attached to the summit of a wiry prolongation of the axis (the carpophore), each mericarp with 5 primary ribs and sometimes 4 intermediate ones, the spaces between the ribs and/or commissural surfaces usually containing oil tubes (vittae). [*Umbelliferae*].

a. Leaves all simple or represented by phyllodes.
　b. Leaves palmately lobed or divided; ovary and fruit bristly. .... 1. *Sanicula*
　b. Leaves not palmately lobed or divided; ovary and fruit not bristly.
　　c. Leaves perfoliate, ovate to elliptic. (Fig. 748). .... 2. *Bupleurum*
　　c. Leaves not perfoliate, shapes various.
　　　d. Leaves (phyllodes) linear, 3.5 mm or less wide, septate. (Fig. 749). .... 3. *Lilaeopsis chinensis*
　　　d. Leaves (normally developed) not linear or wider than 3.5 mm, not septate.
　　　　e. Leaves linear.
　　　　　Leaves more than 10 cm long; flowers in heads, each flower subtended
　　　　　　by a bractlet .... 4. *Eryngium*
　　　　　Leaves less than 10 cm long; flowers in umbels, each flower not
　　　　　　subtended by a bractlet .... 2. *Bupleurum*
　　　　e. Leaves not linear.
　　　　　Leaves orbicular to reniform; umbels simple or flowers in whorles. .... 5. *Hydrocotyle*
　　　　　Leaves ovate to lanceolate; umbels compound. .... 6. *Sium suave*
a. Leaves (at least some) compound.
　f. Leaves once ternately, palmately or pinnately compound.
　　g. Ovary and fruit bristly.
　　　Leaves palmately divided; stems glabrous. .... 1. *Sanicula*

Leaves pinnate-ternate; stems pubescent. (Fig. 751). .... 7. *Torilis*
g. Ovary and fruit glabrous (pubescent in *Heracleum* with principal leaflets
    1 dm or more wide; leaflets less than 8 cm wide in above genera).
  h. Leaves once ternately compound.
    i. Stems pubescent; outer flowers of umbellets irregular, the outer petals
      much larger than the inner .... 8. *Heracleum*
    i. Stems glabrous or essentially so; flowers regular.
      j. Leaflets linear-lanceolate; involucre of several to many filiform bracts.
        (Fig. 752) .... 9. *Falcaria vulgaris*
      j. Leaflets lanceolate-ovate; involucre none or inconspicuous.
        k. Leaflets mostly doubly serrate; umbels very irregular; flowers white;
          fruit linear-oblong.. 10. *Cryptotaenia*
                                                     canadensis
        k. Leaflets mostly singly serrate; umbels regular; flowers yellow or
          purple; fruit ovoid or oblong to elliptic.
          Central flower or fruit of each umbellet sessile; flowers yellow;
            fruit not winged .... 11. *Zizia*
          Central (and all) flowers and fruits of each umbellet pedicelled;
            flowers purple; fruit winged .... 12. *Thaspium*
                                                            trifoliatum
  h. Leaves once pinnately compound.
    l. Leaflets lanceolate to linear, the principal ones 3 cm or more long.
      Flowers in heads .... 4. *Eryngium*
      Flowers in umbels.
        Involucre of several to many linear-lanceolate bracts; leaflets with
          numerous teeth; fruit wingless .... 6. *Sium suave*
        Involucre none or of few linear bracts; leaflets with only up to 4 or
          5 teeth per side; fruit winged .... 13. *Oxypolis rigidior*
    l. Leaflets oblong to ovate or obovate, or if sometimes lanceolate to linear
      (*Pimpinella*) less than 3 cm long.
      m. Principal leaflets less than 2.5 cm wide; leaves mostly near base of
        plant, few on the stem; fruit wingless. (Fig. 753). .... 14. *Pimpinella*
      m. Principal leaflets more than 2.5 cm wide; leaves distributed all along
        the stem; fruit winged.
        Flowers white; upper leaf sheaths dilated, 1 cm or more wide when
          flattened. .... 8. *Heracleum*
        Flowers yellow; upper leaf sheaths not dilated, less than 1 cm wide
          when flattened .... 15. *Pastinaca sativa*
f. Leaves two or more times ternately or pinnately compound.
  n. Leaves decompound into distinct leaflets or numerous divisions less than
    1 cm wide (in which case the leaflets are indistinct).
    o. Ovary and fruit bristly to minutely puberulent (*Pimpinella*); stems usually
      pubescent (sometimes sparsely so).
      p. Involucre of long, pinnately dissected bracts. .... 16. *Daucus carota*
      p. Involucre none or of short, linear bracts.
        q. Involucels of lanceolate, often lobed bractlets; fruit with a long,
          bristly beak .... 17. *Scandix*
                                                  pecten-veneris
        q. Involucels none or of linear bractlets; fruit not beaked.
        Ovary and fruit bristly .... 7. *Torilis*
        Ovary and fruit minutely puberulent... 14. *Pimpinella*
    o. Ovary and fruit glabrous; stems glabrous or essentially so (except
      sometimes in *Anthriscus*).
    r. Ultimate leaf divisions filiform. (Fig. 754).
      s. Flowers yellow; involucre none or of 1 or 2 bracts.
        Plant with odor of anise; perennial; fruit winged, the styles not
          evident. .... 18. *Foeniculum*
                                            vulgare
        Plant with odor of dill; annual; fruit wingless, the styles evident. .... 19. *Anethum*
                                                   graveolens

    s. Flowers white; involucre of several-many filiform bracts (rarely none or
       1 or 2 minute bracts). .... 20. *Ptilimnium*
                                                         capillaceum

r. Ultimate leaf divisions linear or broader (in genera for which
    distinction is questionable flowers are white and involucre is
    absent or of 1-few bracts; in above genera flowers are yellow or
    involucre is present and of several-many bracts).
  t. Leaves with distinct, linear-lanceolate leaflets, the principal ones
    mostly 2.5 cm or more long. (Fig. 752).
    Axils (of at least the upper leaves) often bearing bulbs; involucre
       none or of few linear-lanceolate bracts; leaf rachis wingless. ..... 21. *Cicuta*
    Axils not bearing bulbs; involucre of several to many filiform
       bracts; leaf rachis winged .... 9. *Falcaria vulgaris*
  t. Leaves decompound into numerous divisions less than 2 cm long,
    the leaflets indistinct. (Fig. 756).
    u. Bractlets of involucels ovate to broadly lanceolate.
    Leaf sheaths pubescent; fruit 2.5 or more times as long as broad;
       stem not purple-spotted .... 22. *Anthriscus*
    Leaf sheaths glabrous; fruit 2 times or less as long as broad; stem
       purple-spotted .... 23. *Conium*
                                                             maculatum
    u. Bractlets of involucels none or linear to narrowly lanceolate.
    v. Fruit winged, dorsally flattened .... 24. *Conioselinum*
                                                              chinense
    v. Fruit often prominently ribbed but not winged; laterally flattened
      to globose.
    w. Fruit more than 2.5 times as long as broad. .... 22. *Anthriscus*
    w. Fruit 2 times or less as long as broad.
      x. Fruit subglobose, not readily separating into mericarps;
        flowers irregular. .... 25. *Coriandrum*
                                                             sativum
      x. Fruit flattened, readily separating into mericarps.
      y. Ribs of mature fruit wider than the intervals between;
        flowers irregular. .... 26. *Aethusa*
                                                             cynapium
      y. Ribs of mature fruit much narrower than the intervals
        between; flowers regular.
        Flowers yellow; leaves mostly ternately compound,
          the petiole forking into 3 primary divisions .... 27. *Petroselinum*
                                                            crispum
        Flowers white or pink; leaves pinnately compound, the
          petiole not ternately forked .... 28. *Carum carvi*
n. Leaves decompound into distinct leaflets mostly 1 cm or more wide.
  z. Ovary and fruit bristly or pubescent.
    Rays of the umbel 10 or fewer; fruit attenuate to base. (Fig. 757). .... 29. *Osmorhiza*
    Rays of the umbel more than 10; fruit not attenuate to base. .... 30. *Angelica*
  z. Ovary and fruit glabrous or essentially so.
    a.a. Leaflets usually entire; flowers yellow. .... 31. *Taenidia*
                                                                integerrima
    a.a. Leaflets serrate or lobed.
      b.b. Involucre of several to many bracts.
      Bracts filiform; leaflets linear-lanceolate; leaf rachis broadly winged;
        flowers white. (Fig. 752) .... 9. *Falcaria vulgaris*
      Bracts lance-linear; leaflets ovate to oblong; leaf rachis not winged;
        flowers yellow .... 32. *Levisticum*
                                                             officinale
      b.b. Involucre none or of 1-few bracts.
        c.c. Plant in flower.
          d.d. Flowers yellow or purple.

e.e. Leaves pinnately compound; stems coarse and angular or
corrugated. .... 15. *Pastinaca sativa*
e.e. Leaves mostly ternately compound, the petiole forking into
3 primary divisions; stems not coarse and angular or
corrugated.
f.f. Leaflets divided into numerous segments or lobes. .... 27. *Petroselinum*
crispum
f.f. Leaflets merely toothed.
Central flower of each umbellet sessile; flowers yellow. .... 11. *Zizia*
Central (and all) flowers of each umbellet pedicelled;
flowers purple. .... 12. *Thaspium*
trifoliatum
d.d. Flowers white.
g.g. Upper leaf sheaths dilated, 1 cm or more wide when
flattened. .... 30. *Angelica*
g.g. Upper leaf sheaths not dilated, less than 1 cm wide when
flattened.
h.h. Leaflets mostly 9 or fewer; lateral veins from midvein
traceable directly to a tooth.
Involucels none; calyx teeth none .... 33. *Aegopodium*
podagraria
Involucels of linear bractlets; calyx teeth present. .... 34. *Ligusticum*
scothicum
h.h. Leaflets mostly more than 9; lateral veins from midvein
traceable to a sinus between teeth, then branching to
each tooth. (Fig. 755). .... 21. *Cicuta*
c.c. Plant in fruit.
i.i. Fruit winged, dorsally flattened.
j.j. Dorsal and lateral ribs winged .... 12. *Thaspium*
trifoliatum
j.j. Dorsal ribs wingless, only the lateral ribs winged.
Involucels usually none; upper leaf sheaths not dilated; less
than 1 cm wide when flattened .... 15. *Pastinaca sativa*
Involucels of several to many small, linear bractlets usually
present; upper leaf sheaths dilated, 1 cm or more
wide when flattened. .... 30. *Angelica*
i.i. Fruit often prominently ribbed but not winged, laterally
flattened.
k.k. Fruit 6 mm or more long .... 34. *Ligusticum*
scothicum
k.k. Fruit 5 mm or less long.
l.l. Leaflets divided into numerous segments or lobes. .... 27. *Petroselinum*
crispum
l.l. Leaflets merely toothed.
m.m. Lateral veins from midvein traceable to a sinus
between the teeth, then branching to each tooth.
(Fig. 755) .... 21. *Cicuta*
m.m. Lateral veins from midvein traceable directly to a tooth.
Rays of fruiting umbel very unequal, the outer much
longer than the inner; stylopodium lacking .... 11. *Zizia*
Rays of fruiting umbel equal or approximately so;
stylopodium conspicuous on the fruit .... 33. *Aegopodium*
podagraria

1. *Sanicula* L. Black snakeroot (name based on reputed medicinal value).

Tall, glabrous, perennial or biennial herbs; leaves palmately lobed or divided, serrate, long-petioled
toward the base, becoming progressively shorter petioled above; umbels compound, few-rayed, the
rays unequal, umbellets capitate, flowers perfect or staminate in the same or separate umbellets,

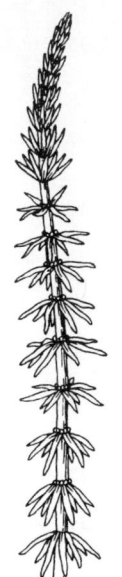

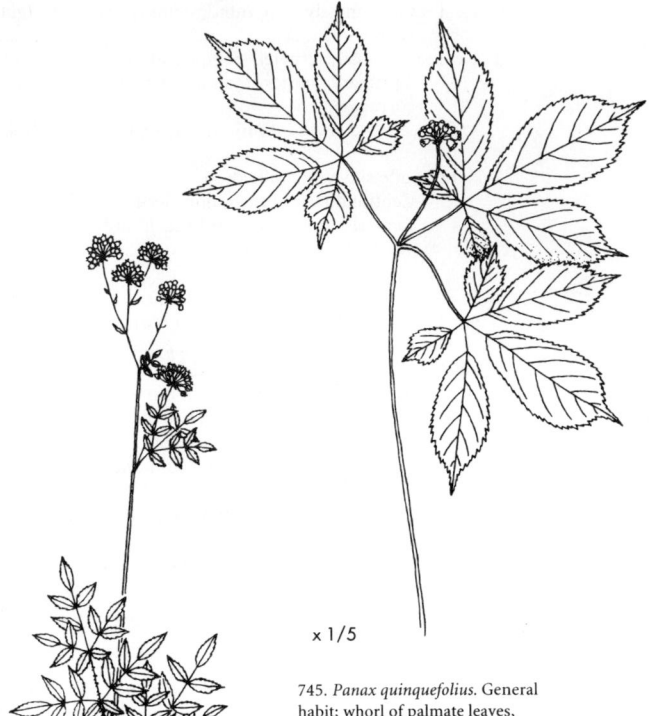

x 1/2

744. *Hippuris vulgaris*. General
habit of part of stem; crowded,
whorled leaves of varying lengths.

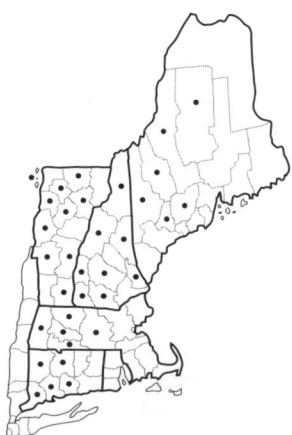

x 1/5

746. *Aralia hispida*. General habit;
leaves alternate, with pinnate
divisions, umbels corymbose.

x 1/5

745. *Panax quinquefolius*. General
habit; whorl of palmate leaves,
leaflets long-stalked, acuminate.

1688. *Panax quinquefolius*

1689. *Panax trifolius*

1690. *Aralia spinosa*

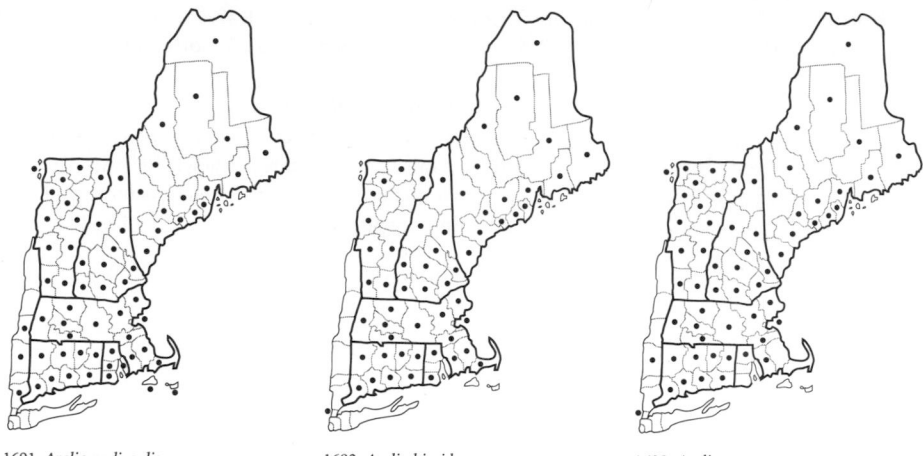

1691. *Aralia nudicaulis*   1692. *Aralia hispida*   1693. *Aralia racemosa*

white to yellowish, the staminate pedicelled, the perfect sessile or subsessile, involucre and involucels foliaceous, calyx 5 toothed; fruit globose to ellipsoid, ribs lacking, covered with hooked bristles.

a. Styles longer than the bristles of the fruit. (Fig. 747).
    Calyx teeth ovate to deltoid; less than 1 mm long; fruit (including bristles)
        mostly 4 mm or less long, short-stipitate. .... 1. *S. odorata*
    Calyx teeth lance-subulate, 1 mm or more long; fruit mostly more than 4 mm
        long, sessile .... 2. *S. marilandica*
a. Styles shorter than the bristles of the fruit.
    Calyx teeth connivent into a conspicuous beak, equalling or exceeding the
        bristles; staminate flowers on long pedicels, conspicuously exceeding the
        fertile .... 3. *S. trifoliata*
    Calyx teeth with beak inconspicuous, hidden among the bristles; staminate
        flowers on short pedicels, hidden among the fertile. .... 4. *S. canadensis*

    1. S. odoráta (Raf.) K.M. Pryer & L.R. Phillippe. Rich woods. Fruit: July-August. Map 1694. [*S. gregaria*]. —FACU
    2. S. marilándica L. (of Maryland). Woods and meadows. Fruit: July-September. Fig. 747, Map 1695.
    3. S. trifoliáta Bickn. (with 3 leaflets). Rich woods. Fruit: July-September. Map 1696.
    4. S. canadénsis. L. (Canadian). Rich woods, borders of streams. Fruit: July-September. Map 1697. Our plants include var. *canadensis* and the following var.:
    var. *grándis* Fern. Fruit cluster 1 cm or more in diameter, larger leaflets of petioled leaves up to more than 10 cm long (fruit cluster less than 1 cm in diameter and larger leaflets of petioled leaves up to 8 cm long in var. *canadensis*).

2. Bupleúrum L. (from the Greek meaning ox-rib).

Branched, glabrous and glaucous, annual herbs; leaves simple, entire, mucronate, the lower ovate or obovate, sessile to short petioled, the middle and upper ovate to elliptic, perfoliate, or leaves all linear and not perfoliate; umbels compound, terminal and lateral, few-rayed, flowers greenish-yellow, involucre present or absent, involucels of 5, foliaceous, ovate to elliptic, mucronate bractlets much surpassing the flowers, calyx teeth none; fruit oblong to ellipsoid, glabrous, obscurely ribbed.

    1. B. rotundifólium L. (round-leaved). Thoroughwax. Fields, roadsides, waste places. May-June. Fig. 748, Map 1698. (Adventive from Europe).

B. fontánesii Caruel. Leaves linear, not perfoliate, involucre present (leaves not linear, the middle and upper perfoliate, involucre none in *B. rotundifolium*). (Europe, Asia). Reported as a waif for MA.

3. Lilaeópsis Greene (name based on resemblance to *Lilaea*).

Small, glabrous, perennial herbs with stems prostrate and rooting at the nodes; leaves 1-several at each node, represented by hollow, linear-spatulate, transversely septate petioles (phyllodes); umbels simple, axillary, peduncled, flowers few, white, involucre of several small bracts, calyx teeth none; fruit broadly ovoid to subglobose, glabrous to minutely puberulent, prominently ribbed.

    1. **L. chinénsis** (L.) Kuntze. (of China, a misnomer). Tidal mud, salt and brackish marshes. Fig. 749, Map 1699. June-September. [*L. lineata*]. —OBL

4. Erýngium L. Eryngo (classical name for a prickly plant).

Glabrous, perennial herbs, the stems simple or slightly branched at the inflorescence; leaves simple (rarely pinnatifid), coriaceous, elongate-linear (rarely oblong to ovate), clasping at the base, parallel-veined, remotely bristly-margined; flowers in dense, ovoid to subglobose heads, stout-peduncled in a cymosely branched inflorescence, flowers white to greenish, involucre of ovate-lanceolate, cuspidate bracts, each flower subtended by a similar but smaller bractlet, bracts and bractlets sometimes dissected, calyx with 5, pungent teeth; fruit ovoid to obovoid, covered with small, hyaline scales.

    1. **E. yuccifólium** Michx. (with leaves of Yucca). Rattlesnake-master. Fields and waste places. July-August. From farther west or south. Reported for Fairfield County CT. [*E. aquaticum*]. Our plants are var. *yuccifolium*. A drink made from the plant was used as an emetic by Indians. —FAC
    E. plánum L. Basal leaves oblong or ovate and involucres exceeding the heads (basal leaves elongate-linear and involucres shorter than the heads in *E. yuccifolium*). (Introduced from Eurasia). Rarely spread from cultivation. Reported for Fairfield County CT, Nantucket County MA.
    E. amethystínum L. Leaves pinnatifid (simple in the above 2 species). Rarely escaped from cultivation. Reported for Essex County MA.

5. Hydrocótyle L. Water-pennywort (from the Greek, based on the somewhat cup-shaped leaves of same species).

Small, glabrous, perennial herbs, with slender, creeping or ascending stems; leaves solitary at the nodes, simple, long-petioled, orbicular to reniform, sometimes peltate, crenate to shallowly lobed, petioles not sheathing, the base with a pair of scale-like stipules; flowers white or greenish, in simple umbels or in whorles forming an interrupted spike, the involucre reduced or none, the peduncle axillary, elongate or very short, calyx nearly entire; fruit laterally flattened, ellipsoid to ovate, the ribs obscure or evident, oil tubes none, mericarps not separating.

Leaf blades attached by the margin; umbels sessile or subsessile. (Fig. 750). .... 1. *H. americana*
Leaf blades peltate; umbels on peduncles more than 1 cm long.
    Inflorescence usually a simple umbel, rarely proliferating into a second one. .... 2. *H. umbellata*
    Inflorescence a simple or forked spike bearing 2 or more verticels of flowers. .... 3. *H. verticillata*

    1. **H. americána** L. (American). Wet woods and thickets, wooded swamps, wet meadows, stream margins. July-September. Fig. 750, Map 1700. —OBL
    2. **H. umbelláta** L. (with umbels). Pond margins, ditches. July-September. Map 1701. (Tropical Amer.). —OBL
    3. **H. verticilláta** Thunb. (whorled). Pond and stream margins, wet woods and meadows. July-August. Reported for Barnstable and Dukes Counties MA. Endangered in NY. Our plants include var. *verticillata* and the following var.:

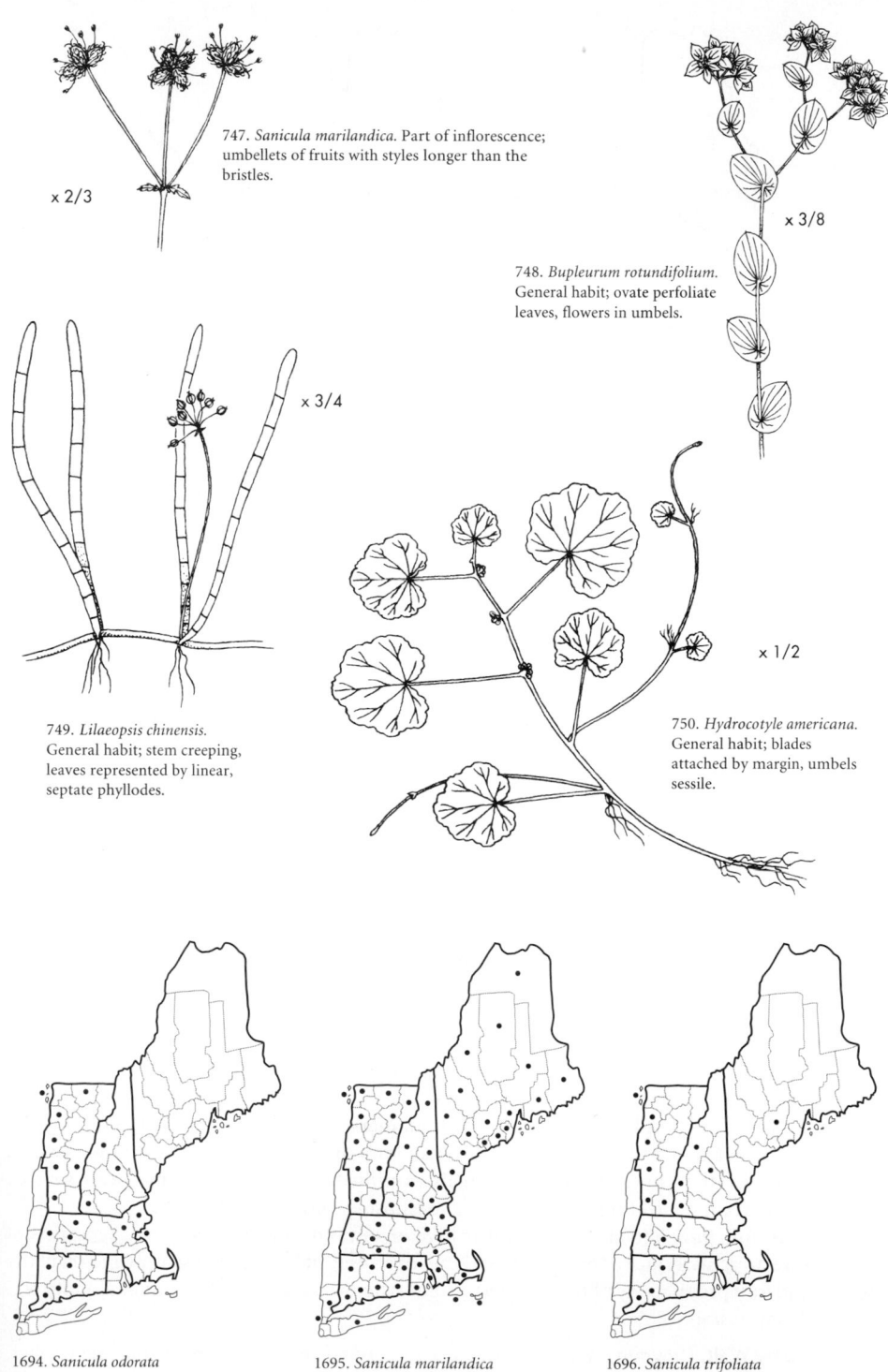

747. *Sanicula marilandica.* Part of inflorescence; umbellets of fruits with styles longer than the bristles.

x 2/3

748. *Bupleurum rotundifolium.* General habit; ovate perfoliate leaves, flowers in umbels.

x 3/8

x 3/4

749. *Lilaeopsis chinensis.* General habit; stem creeping, leaves represented by linear, septate phyllodes.

750. *Hydrocotyle americana.* General habit; blades attached by margin, umbels sessile.

x 1/2

1694. *Sanicula odorata*

1695. *Sanicula marilandica*

1696. *Sanicula trifoliata*

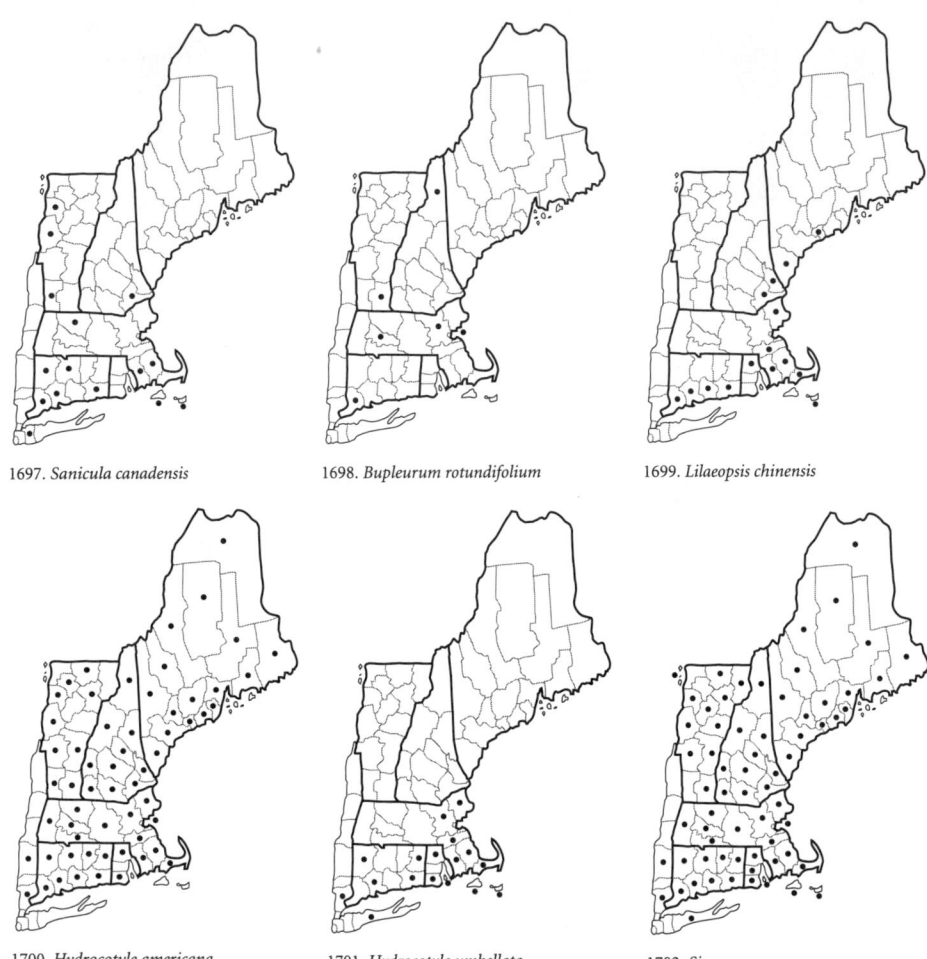

1697. *Sanicula canadensis*

1698. *Bupleurum rotundifolium*

1699. *Lilaeopsis chinensis*

1700. *Hydrocotyle americana*

1701. *Hydrocotyle umbellata*

1702. *Sium suave*

var. *triradiáta* (A. Rich.). Fern. Flowers distinctly pedicelled; spikes often forked (flowers sessile or subsessile and spikes always simple in var. *verticillata*). [*H. australis; H. canbyi*]. —OBL

6. *Síum* L. Water-parsnip (Greek name for a marsh plant).

Tall, branched, glabrous, perennial, marsh or aquatic herbs with corrugated stems; leaves once pinnately compound, the leaflets linear to lance-oblong, sharply serrate, lower leaves long-petioled, becoming shorter-petioled and reduced upward, submersed leaves, when present, pinnately decompound, with linear to filiform segments; umbels compound, terminal and lateral, flowers white, involucre of linear to linear-lanceolate, sometimes pinnately lobed bracts, involucels similar, smaller, calyx teeth none or minute; fruit ovoid to ellipsoid, prominently ribbed.

Bérula Hoffm. *pusílla* (Nutt.) Fern. Similar to *Sium* but is distinguishable in having leaflets of upper leaves irregularly incised or laciniate and fruit obscurely ribbed (leaflets sharply and regularly serrate and fruit prominently ribbed in *Sium*). From farther west. Reported for Suffolk County NY. [*B. erecta* var. *incisa*].

    1. *S. suáve* Walt. (fragrant). Wet meadows, marshes, pond and river margins. July-September. Map 1702. (e. Asia). Poisonous. —OBL

S. carsónii Durand. Weak-stemmed, aquatic or subaquatic species with 3-7 oblong to ovate leaflets, or leaves occasionally simple (stems stout and erect, leaflets more than 7, linear to lanceolate in *S. suave*). —OBL

7. Torílis Adans. Hedge-parsley.

Branching, hispidulous, annual herbs; leaves pinnately or ternately once or twice compound, the ultimate segments narrowly lanceolate, pinnatifid or serrate; flowers white, densely clustered in compound, terminal and lateral umbels, involucres and involucels of linear bracts, calyx teeth triangular; fruit ovoid, densely covered by hooked bristles.

Cùminum L. cýminum L. Cumin. Similar to *Torilis* but is glabrous except for its bristly fruits, the bristles not hooked. Rarely spread from cultivation. Reported for Suffolk County MA.

1. *T. japónica* (Houtt.) DC. (Japanese). Fields and waste places. Fruit: July-August. Fig. 751. (Naturalized from Eurasia). Reported for Berkshire County MA, Dutchess and Columbia Counties NY. [*T. arvensis; T. anthriscus*].

T. leptophýlla (L.) Reichenb. Distinguishable from *T. jáponica* in having peduncles up to 3 cm long (peduncles longer than 3 cm in *T. japonica*). Reported for MA.

8. Heracléum L. Cow-parsnip (ancient Greek name, based on reputed medicinal value of one of the species).

Tall, stout, pubescent, perennial herbs with grooved stems; leaves once-ternate or pinnate, petioled, the ultimate segments palmately lobed and toothed; umbels large, compound, terminal and lateral, flowers perfect and staminate in the same umbellets, white, the outer flowers of at least the marginal umbellets irregular, the outer petals commonly larger and 2-cleft; involucre none or of few, deciduous, lance-linear bracts, involucels of numerous, linear bractlets, calyx teeth none or minute; fruit oval or obovate, dorsally flattened, glabrate or puberulent, ribbed and winged. Roots reported to be edible when boiled as are young leaves and shoots.

Principal leaves ternate, with 3 leaflets. .... 1. *H. maximum*
Principal leaves pinnate, with 5 or more leaflets. .... 2. *H. sphondylium*

1. *H. máximum* Bartr. Roadsides, waste places, woodland borders, meadows. June-August. Map 1703. [*H. lanatum; H. sphondylium* subsp. *montanum*]. —FACU-

H. mantegazziánum Sommier & Levier. Resembling *H. maximum* but distinguishable by the fruits, which are rounded at the base and with ribs extending beyond the middle (narrowed to the base and with ribs extending to or below the middle in *H. maximum*). (Europe). Reported for York County ME.

2. *H. sphondýlium* L. (old generic name). Fields, roadsides and waste places. June-August. Map 1704. (Naturalized from Eurasia). Represented with us as subsp. *sibíricum* (L.) Simonkai [*H. sphondylium* var. *angustifolium*].

9. Falcária Fabr. Sickleweed (sickle, referring to the arching lobes of the perianth).

Branched, glabrous and glaucous, perennial herbs from a deep taproot; leaves ternately compound, the lower petioled, the upper sessile, each of the 3 principal divisions simple or again ternate, pinnate or palmately divided or lobed, the ultimate segments long, linear-lanceolate, often falcate, sharply serrate; umbels compound, terminal and lateral, flowers perfect and staminate in the same or different umbellets, white, involucre and involucels of filiform bracts and bractlets, calyx tube cylindric in the perfect flowers, absent in the staminate, calyx teeth 5; fruit oblong, laterally flattened, ribbed.

1. *F. vulgáris* Bernh. (common). Waste places. July-September. Fig. 752. (Adventive from Europe). Reported for MA. [*F. sioides*].

10. Cryptotaénia DC. Honewort (Greek name, referring to the concealed oil tubes of the fruit).

Branching, glabrous, perennial herbs; leaves ternately compound, the lower long-petioled, becoming progressively shorter-petioled above, leaflets ovate, irregularly or doubly serrate or lobed; flowers in compound, unequal-rayed, open umbels, these terminal and in the upper leaf axils, umbellets few-flowered, on unequal pedicels, involucre and involucels none or inconspicuous, calyx teeth none, petals white; fruit linear-oblong, often curved, strongly ribbed, beaked.

  1. *C. canadénsis* (L.) DC. (Canadian). Rich woods. Fruit: July-September. Map 1705. [*Deringa c.*]. Tops, young leaves and roots edible. —FAC

11. Zízia W.D.J. Koch Golden Alexanders (for J. Ziz).

Glabrous, simple or branched, perennial herbs; leaves simple to 1-3 times ternately compound, the ultimate segments ovate to lanceolate, serrate, sometimes lobed, lower petioles long, the upper short; umbels compound, flowers yellow, numerous in the umbellets, the central flower of each umbellet often sessile, involucre none, involucels none or of few, linear-lanceolate bractlets, calyx 5-toothed; fruit oblong to ellipsoid, laterally flattened, glabrous.

Lowest leaves cordate, undivided, or at most once-ternate. .... 1. *Z. aptera*
Lowest leaves 2 or more times ternately compound. .... 2. *Z. aurea*

  1. *Z. áptera* (Gray) Fern. (without wings). Open woods and fields. May-June. Map 1706. Endangered in CT. From farther west and south. [*Z. cordata*].
  2. *Z. aúrea* (L.) W.D.J. Koch. (golden). Wet to dry fields and woodlands, pond and stream margins, roadsides. May-June. Map 1707.

12. Tháspium Nutt. Meadow-parsnip (name based on that of a related genus).

Branched perennial herbs, glabrous or essentially so; basal leaves simple, ovate to orbicular, cordate, or sometimes ternate, stem leaves ternate or rarely biternate, the leaflets ovate-lanceolate, serrate or crenate, sometimes lobed; umbels compound, terminal and lateral, flowers purple (ours), involucre none, involucels of several inconspicuous, triangular bractlets, calyx 5-toothed; fruit ovoid to ellipsoid, winged.

  1. *T. trifoliátum* (L.) Gray (three-leaved). Woodlands. April-June. From farther south. Reported for RI. [*T. atropurpureum*]. Our plants are var. *trifoliatum*.

13. Oxýpolis Raf. Hog-fennel (from the Greek, referring to the subulate involucels and white flowers).

Glabrous, perennial herbs from a cluster of tuberous roots; leaves once pinnately compound, sessile or subsessile, leaflets linear to lanceolate, entire or remotely serrate; umbels compound, terminal and sometimes also axillary, flowers white, involucre and involucels none or of few linear bracts and bractlets, calyx 5-toothed; fruit ovoid to ellipsoid, dorsally flattened, winged and strongly ribbed.

  1. *O. rigídior* (L.) Raf. (stiff). Wet meadows, pond margins, wooded swamps. June-September. From farther south and west. Reported for Suffolk County NY. [*O. turgida*]. —OBL

14. Pimpinélla L. (ancient name).

Glabrous to puberulent, branched, perennial herbs; leaves pinnately compound or decompound, mostly near base of plant, rosulate, leaflets varying from ovate to narrowly oblong, serrate to deeply pinnately dissected, stem leaves becoming much reduced, the upper often consisting of only the sheath; umbels compound, terminal and lateral, flowers white (rarely yellow), the outer ones in the umbellet often irregular, involucre and involucels none or occasionally of 1-few narrow bracts or bractlets, calyx teeth none; fruit ovate to oblong, laterally flattened, prominently ribbed, glabrous (rarely puberulent).

Ápium L. *gravéolens* L. Celery. Will usually key to *Pimpinella* but has leaflets sharply toothed (leaflets blunt-toothed in *Pimpinella*). Occasionally escaped from gardens. Reported for Fairfield County CT, Essex County MA, Rensselaer County NY. [*Celeri g.*].

1. P. saxífraga L. (like Saxifrage). Burnet-saxifrage. Fields, roadsides, waste places. June-August. From Europe. Fig. 753, Map 1708. (Naturalized from Europe). Our plants are subsp. *saxifraga*.

P. anísum L. Anise, with yellowish flowers and puberulent fruit, reported for Suffolk County MA, and *P. májor* (L.) Huds. with hollow stem (pithy in *P. saxifraga*), reported for Westchester County NY, rarely escape from cultivation.

15. *Pastináca* Parsnip (Latin name).
Tall, coarse, branched, glabrous to puberulent biennial herbs, with grooved stems arising from a fleshy taproot; leaves pinnately or bipinnately compound, the ultimate segments lanceolate to ovate, serrate, often lobed or divided, the lower leaves long-petioled, the upper becoming shorter-petioled and smaller; umbels large, compound, terminal and lateral, many-rayed, flowers yellow, involucre and involucels usually none, calyx teeth none; fruit ellipsoid, strongly flattened dorsally, prominently ribbed and winged.

1. P. satíva L. (sown). Wild parsnip. Fields, roadsides, waste places. May-July. Map 1709. (Naturalized from Europe). Reported to be poisonous.

16. *Daúcus* L. Carrot (ancient Greek name).
Pubescent, annual or biennial herbs from a thick, fleshy taproot; leaves pinnately decompound, petioled or the upper subsessile, the ultimate segments linear to lanceolate, pinnatifid, lobed or serrate; umbels compound, long-peduncled, terminal and lateral, flowers white to yellowish or pinkish, numerous in the umbellets, the outer ones often larger and irregular, involucre of foliaceous bracts pinnately dissected into linear or filiform segments, involucels of linear, entire or toothed bractlets, or these sometimes pinnate, calyx teeth none; fruit ovoid or oblong, flattened, bristly. —Wildl. 1

1. D. caróta L. (old generic name). Queen Anne's Lace. Fields and waste places. June-October. Map 1710. (Naturalized from Europe). Plant breeding over time has produced the garden carrot from this species; the wild carrot can be collected and eaten in spring when the new growth begins after boiling to tenderize; the root, leaves and seed are also of value for various medicinal uses; ground seed can be used as a spice.

17. *Scándix* L. Venus' comb.
Small, branched, pubescent to subglabrous, annual herbs; leaves pinnately decompound into numerous, linear segments, the lower leaves long-petioled, the upper subsessile; umbels compound, terminal and lateral, flowers white, petals mostly unequal, involucre none or sometimes of 1 narrow bract, involucels of several lanceolate, often lobed bractlets, calyx teeth minute or none; fruit linear, prolonged into a beak much longer than the body.

1. S. pécten-venéris L. (comb of Venus). Waste places. May-July. Map 1711. Mediterranean region.

18. *Foeniculum* Mill. Fennel (from the Latin, based on the finely dissected leaves).
Tall, stout, branched, glabrous and often glaucous, anise-scented, perennial herbs; leaves pinnately decompound into numerous filiform segments, petioled to subsessile, the petiole sheaths expanded

and clasping; umbels large, compound, many-rayed, terminal and lateral, flowers yellow, involucre and involucels none, calyx teeth none; fruit oblong-ellipsoid, glabrous, prominently ribbed.

1. F. vulgáre Mill. (common). Fields, roadsides, waste places. June-September. Map 1712. (Naturalized from Europe). Preparations made from the fruits are of value as an aid to digestion and in treating colic and coughs.

19. Anéthum L. Dill (ancient Greek name for dill).

Slender, branched, glabrous and glaucous, pungent-scented, annual herbs; leaves pinnately decompound into numerous filiform segments, the lower long- petioled, the upper smaller and shorter-petioled; umbels large, compound, terminal and lateral, many-rayed, flowers yellow, involucre and involucels usually none, calyx teeth none; fruit oblong to ovoid, flattened, prominently ribbed and winged.

1. A. gravéolens L. (strong-smelling). Occasionally escaped from cultivation to waste places. July-August. Map 1713. (Naturalized from Asia).

20. Ptilímnium Raf. Mock bishop's-weed (Greek name, based on the finely dissected leaves and the habitat).

Branched, slender, glabrous, annual herbs; leaves pinnately decompound into numerous, filiform segments, the lower leaves petioled, the upper sessile; umbels compound, terminal and lateral, flowers white, involucre of filiform, often pinnately divided bracts, involucels of filiform bractlets, calyx teeth 5, minute; fruit ovoid, prominently ribbed, the adjacent, lateral nerves of the 2 mericarps contiguous and forming a broad corky band.

Bíflora Hoffm. *rádians* Bieb. Similar to *Ptilimnium* but involucre lacking or of 1 or 2 minute bracts, fruit of 2 subglobose, ribless mericarps (involucre of filiform, often pinnately divided bracts, mericarps prominently ribbed, the adjacent lateral nerves contiguous and forming a broad-corky band in *Ptilimnium*). (Europe). A waif reported in our range from RI.

1. P. capilláceum (Michx.) Raf. (hair-like). Fresh to brackish marshes along the coast. July-October. Fig. 754, Map 1714.—OBL

21. Cicúta L. Water-hemlock (ancient Latin name for the poison hemlock).

Tall, branched, glabrous perennial herbs from a cluster of usually thickened roots; leaves pinnate to pinnately decompound or ternate-pinnate, the ultimate segments linear to lanceolate, often irregular in shape, coarsely serrate or pinnatifid to entire, lower leaves long-petioled, becoming reduced and shorter-petioled upward; umbels compound, many-rayed, terminal and lateral, flowers white, involucre none or of few linear-lanceolate bracts, involucels of linear-lanceolate bractlets, calyx 5-toothed; fruit ovoid to subglobose, laterally flattened, prominently ribbed. Very poisonous.

Leaflets linear, 5 mm or less wide (not including teeth or lobes); axils of upper leaves
        usually bearing clustered bulblets. ....1. *C. bulbifera*
Leaflets linear-lanceolate, wider than 5 mm (not including teeth or lobes); axils of
        leaves without bulblets. (Fig. 755). ....2. *C. maculata*

1. C. bulbífera L. (bulb-bearing). Marshes, pond and river margins. July-August. (fruit seldom maturing). Map 1715. —OBL
2. C. maculáta L. (spotted). Marshes, pond and river margins. July-August. Fig. 755, Map 1716. [*C. mexicana*]. —OBL

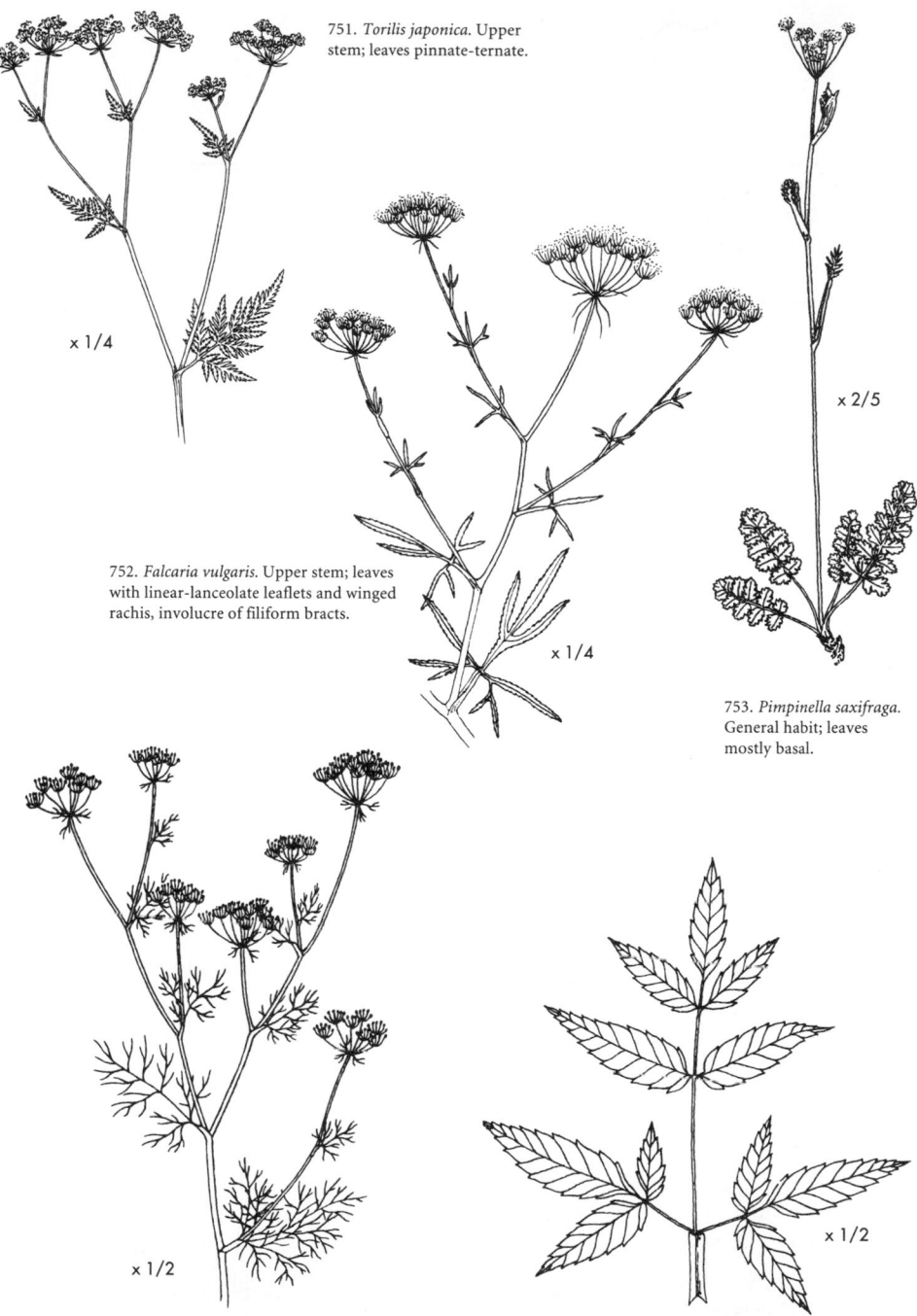

751. *Torilis japonica*. Upper stem; leaves pinnate-ternate.

x 1/4

752. *Falcaria vulgaris*. Upper stem; leaves with linear-lanceolate leaflets and winged rachis, involucre of filiform bracts.

x 1/4

x 2/5

753. *Pimpinella saxifraga*. General habit; leaves mostly basal.

x 1/2

754. *Ptilimnium capillaceum*. Upper stem; leaves several times pinnate, the ultimate divisions filiform.

x 1/2

755. *Cicuta maculata*. Single leaf, leaflets lanceolate, lateral veins to sinus between teeth.

1703. *Heracleum maximum*

1704. *Heracleum sphondylium*
    subsp. *sibiricum*

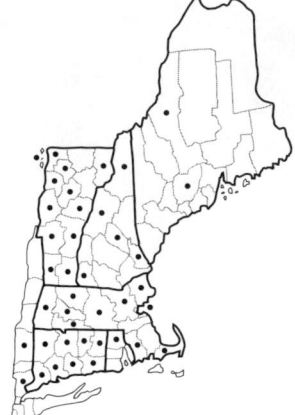

1705. *Cryptotaenia canadensis*

1706. *Zizia aptera*

1707. *Zizia aurea*

1708. *Pimpinella saxifraga*

1709. *Pastinaca sativa*

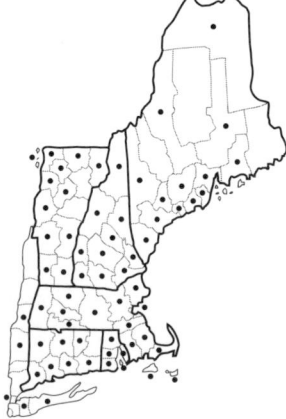

1710. *Daucus carota*

1711. *Scandix pecten-veneris*

1712. *Foeniculum vulgare*

1713. *Anethum graveolens*

1714. *Ptilimnium capillaceum*

1715. *Cicuta bulbifera*

1716. *Cicuta maculata*

22. *Anthriscus* Pers. Chervil (ancient Roman name).

Annual or biennial, freely branched herbs, glabrous to sparsely puberulent; leaves pinnately-ternately decompound, the ultimate segments lanceolate, pinnatifid, lobed or serrate, lower leaves petioled, the upper sessile; umbels compound, short-peduncled or sessile, few-rayed, terminal and axillary, umbellets few-flowered, flowers white, petals unequal, involucre usually none or occasionally of 1-few bracts, involucels of several ovate to lanceolate, ciliate bractlets, calyx teeth none; fruit linear to ovoid, beaked, glabrous and without ribs (beak ribbed), laterally flattened.

Chaerophýllum L. *tainturiéri* Hook. Similar to *Anthriscus* but distinguishable in having fruits with prominent ribs, beakless or short-beaked (fruits without ribs and with a distinct, ribbed beak in *Anthriscus*). From farther south. Reported for RI. [*C. floridanum*]. —FACW

Primary rays up to 6, usually pubescent; bractlets lance-linear; beak of fruit distinct,
    about a third as long as the body. .... 1. *A. cerefolium*
Primary rays 6 or more, usually glabrous; bractlets lance-ovate; beak of fruit
    indistinct, only slightly narrower than the body, much less than a third
    as long .... 2. *A. sylvestris*

1. *A. cerefolium* (L.) Hoffm. (old generic name). Rarely escaped from cultivation to roadsides and waste places; from Europe. May-August. Reported for Litchfield County CT. [*Cerefolium c.*].

2. *A. sylvéstris* (L.) Hoffm. (of woodlands). Fields, waste places, roadsides; from Europe. May-August. Map 1717. (Naturalized from Europe).

23. *Conium* L. (ancient Greek name for the poison hemlock).

Tall, freely branched, glabrous, biennial herbs with purple-spotted stems from a thick taproot; leaves pinnately decompound, the ultimate segments ovate-lanceolate, pinnatifid or toothed, lower leaves petioled, the upper sessile or subsessile; umbels compound, many-rayed, lateral and terminal, often several together at the top of the stem and/or branches, flowers white, petals unequal, involucre and involucels of several ovate to lanceolate-acuminate bracts and bractlets, calyx teeth none; fruit ovoid-ellipsoid, glabrous, with strong, wavy ribs, laterally flattened.

Peucedánum L. *palústre* (L.) Moench. Similar to *Conium* but distinguishable in having stems not purple-spotted (although sometimes uniformly purplish), ultimate leaf segments oblong-linear, entire, and fruit with straight ribs (stems purple-spotted, ultimate leaf segments ovate-lanceolate, pinnatifid or toothed, and fruit with wavy ribs in *Conium*). European; a waif with us. Reported for Essex and Middlesex Counties MA.

1. *C. maculátum* L. (spotted). Poison hemlock. Roadsides and waste places.June-July. Fig. 756, Map 1718. (Naturalized from Europe). Very poisonous. —FACW

24. *Conioselínum* Hoffm. Hemlock-parsley (name compounded from Conium and Selinum, from its resemblance to these genera).

Branched, glabrous, perennial herbs from a cluster of thickened roots; leaves ternately-pinnately decompound, the leaflets lanceolate, pinnatifid, the lower leaves long-petioled, the upper sessile; umbels compound, terminal and axillary, many-rayed, flowers white, involucre none or of a few short linear bracts, involucels of linear bractlets, calyx teeth none; fruit oblong-ovoid, dorsally flattened, winged and prominently ribbed.

1. *C. chinénse* (L.) B.S.P. (of China). Wooded swamps, wet woods, river margins. July-September. Map 1719. —FACW

25. *Coriándrum* L. Coriander (classical name).

Slender, glabrous, annual herbs; leaves petioled to subsessile, the lower cleft into obovate, incised, toothed lobes, the middle and upper ternately-pinnately divided into numerous linear segments; umbels compound, few-rayed, terminal and lateral, umbellets few flowered, flowers white to pink, the outer ones larger and irregular, involucre none or of a single bract, involucels of several linear bractlets, calyx unequally 5-toothed; fruit globose, glabrous, the mericarps not readily separating.

1. *C. satívum* L. (sown). Waste places. June-July. Map 1720. (Introduced from Eurasia).

26. *Aethúsa* L. Fool's parsley (from the Greek, based on the lustrous foliage).

Branched, glabrous, annual herbs; leaves ternately or pinnately decompound into narrow, coarsely toothed or lobed segments, lower leaves petioled, the upper subsessile; umbels compound, terminal and lateral, flowers white, the outer ones irregular, involucre none or of a single linear bract, involucels of long, linear bractlets, all on one side of the umbellet, calyx teeth none; fruit globose-ovoid, prominently ribbed, the ribs wider than the intervals between.

1. *A. cynápium* L. (old generic name). Roadsides and waste places. June-August. Map 1721. (Naturalized from Europe). Poisonous.

27. *Petroselínum* J. Hill Parsley (from the Greek, meaning rock parsley).

Branched, glabrous, biennial herbs from a taproot; leaves ternate-pinnately or pinnately decompound, the ultimate segment linear to lanceolate or ovate, entire, toothed or variously lobed, lower leaves petioled, the upper sessile; umbels compound, terminal and axillary, flowers yellowish, involucre none or of several linear-lanceolate bracts, involucels similar but smaller, calyx lobes none; fruit ovoid, laterally flattened, prominently ribbed.

1. *P. crispum* (Mill.) Nyman ex A.W. Hill. Occasionally escaped from cultivation to waste places. Map 1722. (Introduced from the Mediterranean region). [*P. hortense; Apium petroselinum*]. In addition to its popular use as a garnish parsley is also used to aid digestion, as a diuretic and to aid menstrual flow; seeds can be toxic to pregnant woman.

28. *Cárum* L. (based on the old Latin name).

Glabrous, biennial herbs from a thick taproot; leaflets pinnately decompound into numerous linear to filiform segments, the lower leaves long-petioled, the upper nearly sessile; umbels compound, terminal and lateral, flowers white to pink, involucre and involucels none or of few linear bracts or bractlets, calyx teeth none; fruit ovate or oblong, laterally flattened, prominently ribbed, glabrous.

Peucedánum L. *palústre* (L.) Moench. May key to *Carum* but is distinguishable in having involucels conspicuous, of lanceolate bractlets (involucels none or of few linear bractlets in *Carum*). European; a waif with us. Essex and Middelsex Counties MA.

1. *C. cárvi* L. (old name). Caraway. Fields, roadsides, waste places. May-July. Map 1723. (Naturalized from Europe).

29. *Osmorhíza* Raf. Sweet cicely (from the Greek, meaning scented root).

Pubescent to glabrous or subglabrous perennial herbs from thick, aromatic roots; leaves twice ternately compound, petioled toward the base, becoming subsessile above, the ultimate segments ovate to lanceolate, pinnately lobed or serrate; umbels compound, few-rayed, terminal and lateral, umbellets few-flowered, flowers white, perfect and staminate in the same umbellet, involucres and involucels of few narrow bracts or none, calyx teeth none; fruit linear to narrowly ellipsoid, attenuate to a thin, bristly base, the ribs also bristly. [*Washingtonia*].

a. Involucels present (some or most of the bractlets often deciduous at maturity of
    the fruit); styles (including stylopodium) mostly 1 mm or more long.
    Styles more than 1.5 mm long; roots anise-scented. .... 1. *O. longistylis*
    Styles 1.5 mm or less long; roots not anise-scented. .... 2. *O. claytonii*
a. Involucels mostly absent (or an occasional bractlet sometimes present); styles
    (including stylopodium) mostly 1 mm or less long.
    Stylopodium conical, higher than broad; fruit narrowed to a stout, beak-like tip.
      (Fig. 757) .... 3. *O. chilensis*
    Stylopodium depressed, broader than high; fruit gradually narrowed but not to
      a distinct, beak-like tip .... 4. *O. depauperata*

1. *O. longistýlis* (Torr.) DC. (long-styled). Anise-root. Rich, often alluvial woods. Fruit: July-August. Map 1724. [*Washingtonia l.*]. The root has the taste of anise and is often chewed; reported also to be of value in treating upset stomach. —FACU

2. *O. claytónii* (Michx.) C.B. Clarke (for J. Clayton). Rich woods. Fruit: July-August. Map 1725. [*Washingtonia c.*]. —FACU-

3. *O. chilénsis* Hook. & Arn. (of Chile). Rich woods. Fruit: July-August. Fig. 757, Map 1726. (Temperate w., S. Amer.). Endangered in NH. [*O. divaricata; Washingtonia d.*].

4. *O. depauperáta* Phil. (impoverished). Rich woods. Fruit: July-September. Map 1727. [*O. obtusa*].

30. *Angélica* L. Angelica (name based on the medicinal value of some species).

Tall, stout, branched perennial herbs; leaves pinnately or ternately decompound, the ultimate segments lanceolate to oblong or ovate, serrate, lower leaves long-petioled, the upper becoming reduced, the uppermost often consisting of only the sheath; umbels large, compound, terminal and lateral, many-rayed, flowers greenish-white, involucre none or of few, linear bracts, involucels of numerous small, linear bractlets, calyx teeth none or minute; fruit oblong to ellipsoid, dorsally flattened, glabrous or puberulent, prominently ribbed or winged.

a. Fruit and upper part of stem below inflorescence pubescent; sheaths of upper
     leaves slenderly cylindric, 1 cm or less in diameter. .... 1. *A. venenosa*
a. Fruit glabrous or essentially so; upper part of stem below inflorescence glabrous
     or pubescent; sheaths of upper leaves inflated, usually more than 1 cm in
     diameter.
     Ribs of fruit all thick and corky, nearly equal, none winged; upper part of stem
          pubescent or glabrous; upper sheaths usually blade-bearing; plants
          maritime. (Fig. 758) .... 2. *A. lucida*
     Ribs of fruit not equal, the lateral with thin, broad wings; upper part of stem
          glabrous or essentially so; upper sheaths usually not blade-bearing;
          plants not maritime .... 3. *A. atropurpurea*

    1. *A. venenósa* (Greenway) Fern. Dry woods, thickets and fields. Fruit: August-October. Map 1728. [*A. villosa*].

    2. *A. lúcida* L. (shining). Seabeaches, rocky and gravelly seashores, fields and thickets near the coast. Fruit: July-September. Fig. 758, Map 1729. (Greenland). Endangered in NY. [*Coelopleurum actaeifolium; C. lucidum*]. —FAC

    3. *A. atropurpúrea* L. (dark purple). Wet to dry woods, thickets and meadows, bottomlands. Fruit: July-October. Map 1730. The young stems are eaten in salads and as a potherb; root also used to flavor drinks such as gin and vermouth; various medicinal uses have also been ascribed to this plant including use as a diuretic, antiflatulent and to promote menstrual flow; large quantities taken internally are known to cause poisoning.

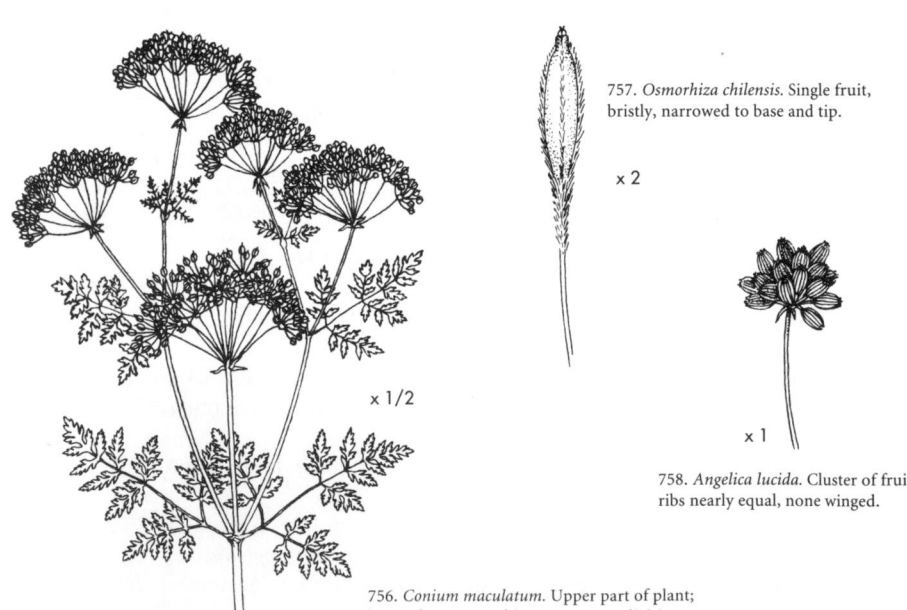

757. *Osmorhiza chilensis.* Single fruit, bristly, narrowed to base and tip.

× 2

× 1/2

× 1

758. *Angelica lucida.* Cluster of fruits, ribs nearly equal, none winged.

756. *Conium maculatum.* Upper part of plant; leaves decompound into numerous divisions.

1717. *Anthriscus sylvestris*

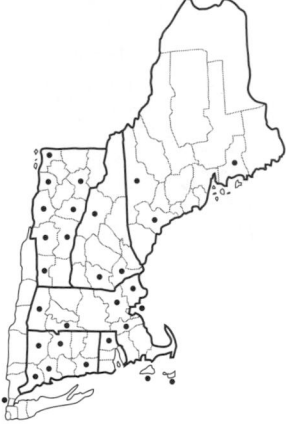

1718. *Conium maculatum*

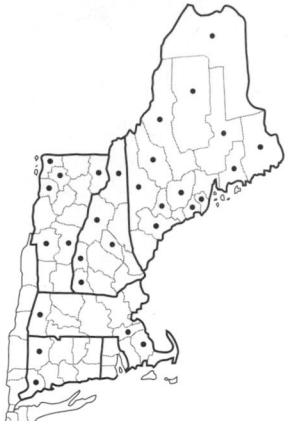

1719. *Conioselinum chinense*

1720. *Coriandrum sativum*

1721. *Aethusa cynapium*

1722. *Petroselinum crispum*

1723. *Carum carvi*

1724. *Osmorhiza longistylis*

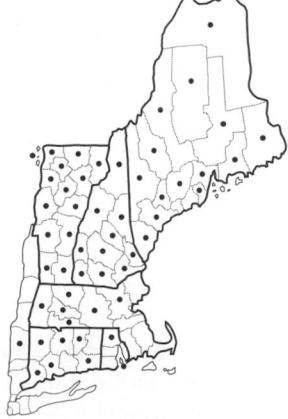

1725. *Osmorhiza claytonii*

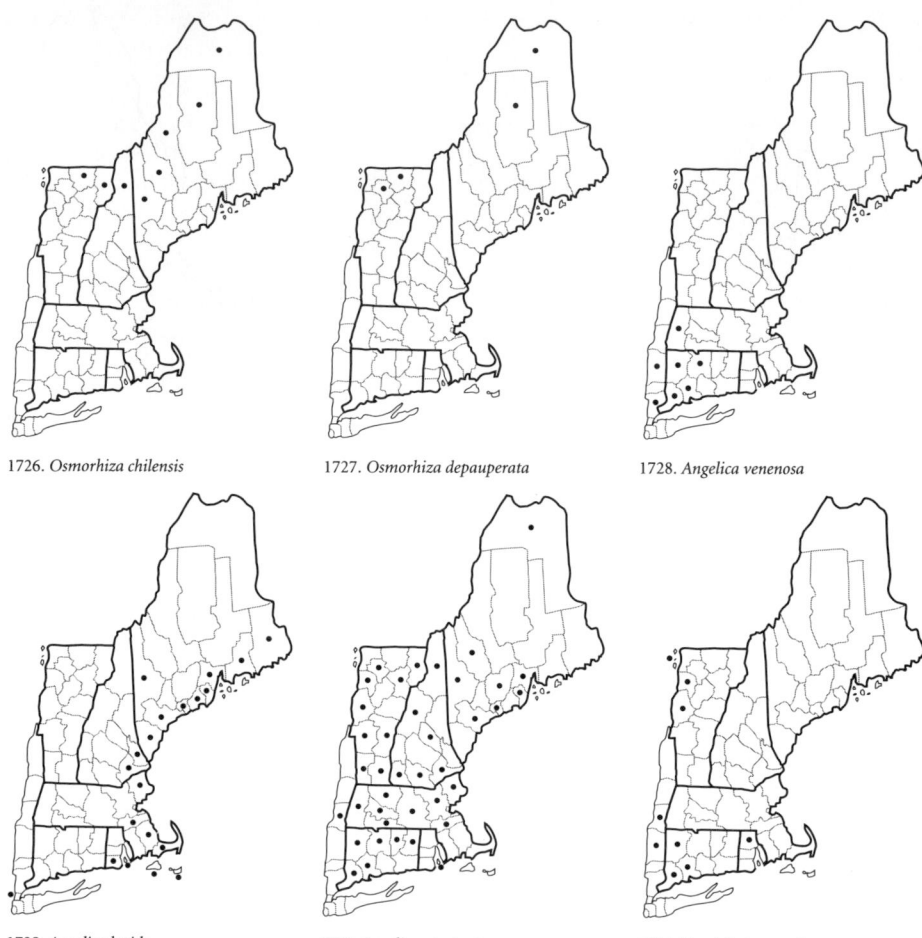

1726. *Osmorhiza chilensis*   1727. *Osmorhiza depauperata*   1728. *Angelica venenosa*

1729. *Angelica lucida*   1730. *Angelica atropurpurea*   1731. *Taenidia integerrima*

31. Taenídia (Torr. & Gray) Drude. Yellow Pimpernel (from the Greek, referring to the scarcely prominent ribs of the fruit).

Slender, branched, glabrous and often glaucous, perennial herbs from a deep taproot; leaves ternately or pinnately 2-3 times compound, the ultimate segments ovate to elliptic or lanceolate, entire or sometimes lobed, often mucronulate, lower petioles long, the upper short; umbels compound, rays numerous, variable in length, terminal and lateral, flowers yellow, perfect and staminate in the same umbellet, involucre and involucels none, calyx teeth none; fruit oblong to elliptic, laterally flattened, glabrous, ribs not prominent.

    1. T. integérrima (L.) Drude (quite entire). Rocky or gravelly woods and thickets. May-June. Fig. 759, Map 1731.

32. Levísticum J. Hill. Lovage (a corruption of the name *Ligusticum*).

Tall, stout, branched, essentially glabrous, perennial herbs from a stout rhizome; leaves pinnately decompound, the ultimate segments ovate to oblong, broadly cuneate and entire toward the base, serrate and often lobed or divided above, the upper leaves becoming reduced, less divided, and shorter-petioled, the uppermost sometimes simple; umbels compound, many-rayed, flowers greenish-yellow, involucre and involucels of numerous lance-linear bracts and bractlets, calyx teeth none; fruit oblong to elliptic, prominently ribbed.

1. *L. officinále* W.D.J. Koch (of the shops). Occasionally escaped from cultivation to roadsides, waste places, and around buildings. May-July. Map 1732. (Introduced from Europe). [*Hipposelinum levisticum*]. Leaves and chopped roots are used to flavor soups and stews; root has medicinal value as a diuretic and digestive in addition to other purported values; is also used as a flavoring ingredient in liqueurs, herb bitters and sauces.

33. *Aegopódium* L. Goutweed (from the Greek, based on shape of the leaflets).
Coarse, branched, glabrous perennial herbs from a creeping rhizome; lower leaves long-petioled and biternately or ternately-pinnately compound, the upper short-petioled and once ternate, leaflets oblong to ovate, rounded or cordate at the base, often irregular in shape, sharply toothed, often lobed or dissected, umbels compound, terminal and lateral, flowers white, involucre and involucels none, calyx teeth none; fruit oblong-ovate, laterally flattened, ribs inconspicuous.

1. *A. podagrária* L. (old generic name). Waste places, roadsides, woodlands, cultivated ground. July-August. (Forms cultivated for ornament have white-variegated leaves). Map 1733. (Naturalized from Europe). Young leaves are reported to be of use as a fresh green in springtime. —FACU

34. *Ligústicum* L. Lovage (name in reference to the country where the garden lovage is abundant).
Glabrous, perennial herbs from thick, aromatic roots; leaves biternately compound, the lower petioled, the upper subsessile, the ultimate segments rhombic to ovate or obovate, mostly cuneate and entire toward the base, coarsely toothed above the middle, often lobed or dissected, thick and fleshy; umbels compound, terminal and lateral, flowers white, involucre none or of few linear, deciduous bracts, involucels of linear bractlets, calyx 5-toothed; fruit oblong, prominently ribbed.

1. *L. scóthicum* L. (scotch). Scotch lovage. Salt marshes, sandy or rocky seashores and tidal portions of rivers. July-September. Map 1734. (Europe). Endangered in NY, CT. Our plants are subsp. *scothicum.* —FAC

Family 152. Cornáceae (Dogwood Family)

Hermaphrodite trees, shrubs or rarely herbs. Leaves opposite or alternate, simple, entire, petioled, estipulate. Flowers perfect, regular, small, in axillary or terminal cymes or heads, calyx tube adherent to the ovary, calyx minutely 4 toothed, petals 4, small, stamens 4, inserted with the petals on the margin of an epigynous disc, ovary inferior, 1-2 locular, style 1, ovules 2. Fruit a drupe.

1. *Córnus* L. Dogwood (Latin name, referring to the hardness of the wood).
Twigs slender to moderate, pith moderate, white or tan, continuous, buds oblong to ovoid (flower buds sometimes subglobose) stalked, with 2-4 scales, leaf scars crescent-shaped, raised on persistent petiole bases on the first year's twigs, bundle traces 3, stipule scars none; leaves opposite (alternate in 1 species), entire, mostly lanceolate to ovate or elliptic; flowers perfect, 4-merous, in open cymes or in heads subtended by a corolla-like involucre of 4 bracts; drupes red, blue or white. -Wldl. 3

C. sanguínea L. Bloodtwig Dogwood. Opposite-leaved, and distinguishable from species 4-6 in having black or green fruits (species 4-6 have blue or white fruits). Rarely escaped from cultivation. Reported for Middlesex and Plymouth Counties MA. Leaves are astringent and are used externally for inflammations of the skin; seeds are used in Europe for soap making.

a. Leaves alternate, often crowded at apex of twigs. .... 1. *C. alternifolia*
a. Leaves opposite or appearing verticillate.
  b. Plant a low herb; principal leaves approximate, appearing verticillate; flowers in
    compact clusters subtended by 4 usually white petaliferous bracts; fruit red.
    (Fig. 760) .... 2. *C. canadensis*
  b. Plant a tree or shrub; leaf pairs well spaced.
    c. Flowers in compact clusters subtended by 4 usually white petaliferous bracts;
      leaf scars of first year's twigs covering the buds; fruit red, tree. .... 3. *C. florida*
    c. Flowers in open cymes, not subtended by petaliferous bracts; leaf scars not
      covering the buds; fruit blue or white; shrub.
      d. Pith of second year or older wood brown; first year's twigs densely
        pubescent, reddish; fruit blue .... 4. *C. amomum*
      d. Pith of second year or older wood whitish; first year's twigs glabrous or
        pubescent; fruit white or if blue twigs greenish with purple blotches.
        e. Leaves with 4 or fewer lateral veins on each side; inflorescence usually
          paniculiform, somewhat conical; fruit white. (Fig. 761). .... 5. *C. racemosa*
        e. Leaves with 5 or more lateral veins on each side; inflorescence usually
          cymose, flat or somewhat convex.
          Twigs greenish with purple blotches, not rooting at the tip; leaves
            broadly ovate to rotund; fruit bluish .... 6. *C. rugosa*
          Twigs red, often rooting at the tips; leaves lanceolate to ovate; fruit
            white. .... 7. *C. sericea*

1. C. alternifólia L. f. (alternate-leaved). Rich woods and thickets. Fruit: July-September. Map 1735. [*Svida a.*].

2. C. canadénsis L. (Canadian). Bunchberry. Moist, often coniferous woods. Fruit: July-October. Fig. 760, Map 1736. (ne. Asia). [*Chamaepericlymenum c.*]. Fruit edible but tasteless. —FAC-

3. C. flórida L. (flowering). Flowering dogwood. Rich woods. Fruit: August-October. Map 1737. Endangered in ME. [*Cynoxylon f.*]. Due to its astringent properties the bark has been chewed to relieve mouth sores and harden gums, as well as for external application to treat skin inflammations. —FACU-

4. C. amómum P. Mill. (old generic name). Silky dogwood. Wooded swamps, shrub-swamps, borders of streams, wet woods. Fruit: August-October. Map 1738. [*Svida a.*]. Our plants include subsp. *amomum* and the following subsp.:

  subsp. *oblíqua* (Raf.) J. S. Wilson. Leaves cuneate at base, pubescence of the lower surfaces not reddish (leaves rounded at base and pubescence of the lower surfaces often reddish in subsp. *amomum*). [*C. amomum* var. *schuetzeana; C. obliqua; C. purpusii*]. —FACW

  C. x arnoldiána Rehd. A hybrid between *C. amomum* subsp. *obliqua* and *C. racemosa*.

5. C. racemósa Lam. Gray dogwood. Abandoned fields, thickets, roadsides. Fruit: July-October. Fig. 761, Map 1739. [*C. foemina* subsp. *racemosa; C. paniculata; Svida femina*]. —FAC

6. C. rugósa Lam. (wrinkled). Round-leaved dogwood. Dry woods and thickets. Fruit: August-October. Map 1740. [*C. circinata; Svida r.*].

  C. x slavínii Rehd. A hybrid between *C. rugosa* and *C. sericea*.

7. C. serícea L. Red osier. Shrub swamps, stream borders. Fruit: July-October. Map 1741. [*C. stolonifera*]. Our plants are subsp. *sericea*. It is reported that the inner bark of the stems was dried and smoked by the Indians and pioneers to produce a narcotic effect. —FACW+

Family 153. Nyssáceae (Tupelo Family)

Dioecious or polygamo dioecious trees, twigs moderate, short spur shoots often developed, pith moderate, white, with transverse woody partitions when cut lengthwise (diaphragmed), buds ovoid, with 4-5 scales, the terminal somewhat larger than the laterals, leaf scars broadly crescent-shaped, corky, bundle traces 3, stipule scars none. Leaves alternate, elliptic to obovate, cuneate at the base, abruptly acuminate, entire or occasionally coarsely toothed. Flowers mostly imperfect, greenish, borne at the summit of axillary peduncles, calyx minutely 5 toothed, petals 5, small or none, stamens 5-10, pistillate flowers solitary or 2-8 in capitate clusters, bracteate, stamens sometimes present, staminate flowers in umbels or umbellate racemes. Drupe blue to black. [*Cornaceae*].

1. Nýssa L. Tupelo. (name based on Greek mythology).
Same characteristics as the family. —Wildl. 2

    1. N. sylvática Marsh. (of the woods). Black gum. Moist to wet woods, wooded swamps, bottomlands. May-June. Map 1742. Our plants are var. *sylvatica*. —FACW+

Family 154. Clethráceae (White Alder Family)

Represented with us by the following genus:

1. Cléthra L. Sweet pepper-bush (ancient Greek name for alder).
Hermaphrodite shrubs, the new growth minutely stellate-pubescent, the second year's growth with bark peeling, short spur shoots often developed, pith moderate, white, buds minutely pubescent, the terminal ovoid, with 3 caducous scales, the lateral small and inconspicuous, leaf scar triangular, bundle trace 1, prominent, stipule scars none; leaves alternate, simple, obovate, cuneate at the base, obtuse or acute, sharply serrate above the middle, petioled, estipulate; flowers perfect, regular, white, fragrant, in dense, terminal, solitary or clustered racemes, with deciduous bracts, calyx lobes 5, petals 5, stamens 10, hypogynous, ovary superior, 3-locular, style 1, stigma 3-lobed, ovules numerous; fruit a globose, 3-valved, loculicidal capsule, enclosed by the persistent calyx.

    1. C. alnifólia L. (alder-leaved). Wooded swamps, shrub swamps and their borders, pond and stream borders. July-September. Fig. 762, Map 1743. —FAC+

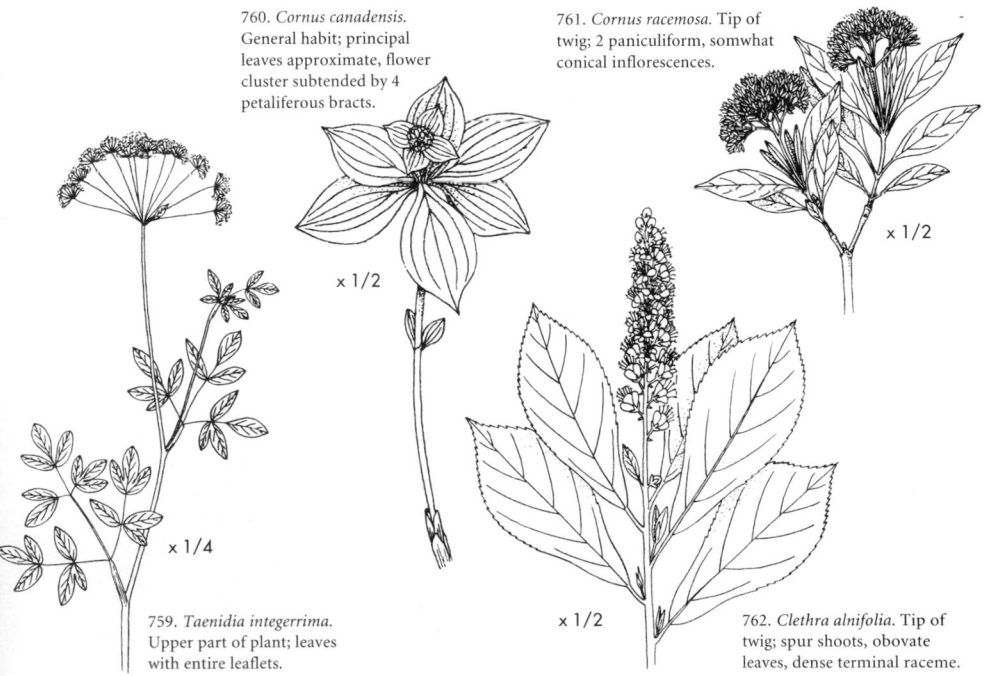

760. *Cornus canadensis.* General habit; principal leaves approximate, flower cluster subtended by 4 petaliferous bracts.

761. *Cornus racemosa.* Tip of twig; 2 paniculiform, somwhat conical inflorescences.

× 1/2

× 1/2

× 1/4

759. *Taenidia integerrima.* Upper part of plant; leaves with entire leaflets.

× 1/2

762. *Clethra alnifolia.* Tip of twig; spur shoots, obovate leaves, dense terminal raceme.

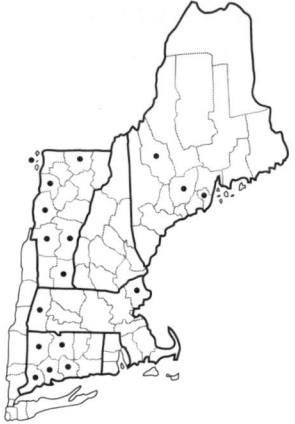

1732. *Levisticum officinale*

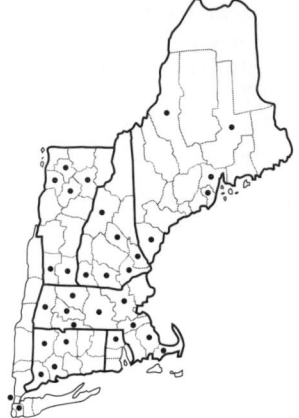

1733. *Aegopodium podagraria*

1734. *Ligusticum scothicum*

1735. *Cornus alternifolia*

1736. *Cornus canadensis*

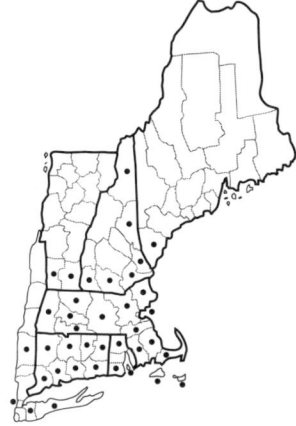

1737. *Cornus florida*

1738. *Cornus amomum*

1739. *Cornus racemosa*

1740. *Cornus rugosa*

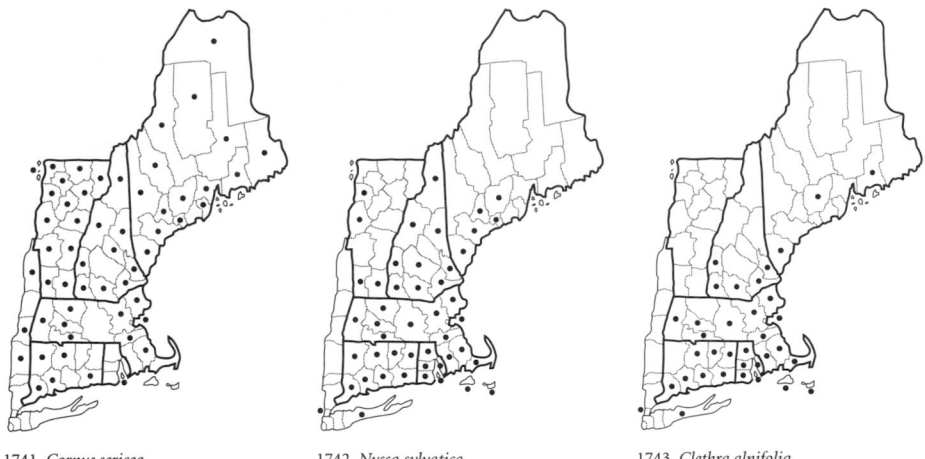

1741. *Cornus sericea*   1742. *Nyssa sylvatica*   1743. *Clethra alnifolia*

Family 155. Monotropáceae (Indian Pipe Family)

Fleshy saprophytes or root parasites, lacking green color, arising from a ball or dense mass of matted mycorrhizae. Leaves reduced to scales, scattered, deciduous. Flowers perfect, regular, solitary or racemose, bracteate, sepals 0-5 or calyx deeply 5-parted, petals or corolla lobes 3-5, flowers and fruit otherwise as in *Pyrolaceae*. [*Pyrolaceae*].

Corolla gamopetalous, urceolate; fruits nodding; plants glandular-pubescent. (Fig. 763) .. 1. *Pterospora andromedea*

Corolla of separate petals, not urceolate; fruits erect; plants glabrous or pubescent
 but not glandular .... 2. *Monotropa*

1. Pteróspora J. Hill. Pine-drops (from the Greek, based on the winged seeds).

Fleshy root parasites from a dense ball of mycorrhizae, without green color, glandular-pubescent, purplish or brown; leaves reduced and scale-like, scattered; flowers numerous in a long raceme, nodding, white to reddish, calyx and corolla deeply 5-parted, corolla urceolate, stamens 10, stigma capitate, obscurely 5-lobed; capsule depressed-globose, deeply umbilicate.

   1. P. andromedéa Nutt. (like Andromeda). Dry, pine woods. June-August. Rare. Fig. 763, Map 1744. Endangered in NY.

2. Monótropa L. Indian pipe (from the Greek, based on the summit of the flowering stem being turned to 1 side).

Fleshy saprophytes or root parasites from a ball or dense mass of matted mycorrhizae, without green color, glabrous to somewhat pubescent, white, yellowish, pink or red, often blackened on drying; leaves reduced and scale-like, scattered; flower terminal, solitary, nodding, or several to many in a nodding raceme which becomes erect at anthesis, sepals 0-5, petals 4-5, gibbous at the base, stamens 8-10; stigma concave, obscurely 5-lobed; capsule ovoid to subglobose, erect.

Flower solitary; stems glabrous .... 1. *M. uniflora*
Flowers several to many in a raceme; stems pubescent. .... 2. *M. hypopithys*

   1. M. uniflóra L. (one-flowered). Rich woods. June-August. Map 1745. (Asia, Mexico). Reported to be edible raw or cooked. —FACU-
   2. M. hypópithys L. Pinesap. Deciduous, coniferous or mixed woods. June-September. Map 1746. (Eurasia, Mexico). [*Hypopitys americana; H. monotropa*].

Family 156. Pyroláceae (Wintergreen Family)

Hermaphrodite, rhizomatous, evergreen, perennial herbs, sometimes suffrutescent. Leaves evergreen and basal, opposite, scattered or whorled, simple, toothed or entire, petioled, estipulate. Flowers perfect, regular, racemose, corymbose or solitary, bracteate, calyx 5-parted, petals 5, stamens twice as many as the petals, hypogynous, ovary superior, 5-locular, style 1, stigmas 5, ovules numerous. Fruit a 5-valved loculicidal capsule.

a. Flowers in umbels or corymbs, rarely solitary; style very short or absent. (Fig. 764) ... 1. *Chimaphila*
a. Flowers in racemes or solitary; style elongate, mostly longer than the ovary.
  b.Flower and fruit solitary .... 2. *Moneses uniflora*
  b.Flowers and fruits several in a raceme.
    Raceme secund; style straight, exserted at anthesis, 4 mm or more long.
    (Fig. 765) .... 3. *Orthilla secunda*
    Raceme not secund; style declined or if straight not exserted at anthesis and
    3 mm or less long .... 4. *Pyrola*

1. *Chimáphila* Pursh (from the Greek).

Low, rhizomatous, suffrutescent, perennial herbs; leaves alternate, opposite or subverticillate, lanceolate to oblanceolate, thick and shining, toothed; flowers white or pink, few, in terminal umbels or corymbs on a long peduncle, rarely solitary, calyx 5-parted, petals 5, stamens 10, the filaments dilated and pubescent or ciliate in the middle, style very short or absent, stigma shallowly 5-lobed; capsule subglobose.

Leaves oblanceolate, uniformly green .... 1. *C. umbellata*
                                                             subsp. *cisatlantica*
Leaves lanceolate, whitish above along the midrib and principal side veins. .... 2. *C. maculata*

    1. *C. umbelláta* (L.) Bart. (umbellate). Pipsissewa. Dry woods. July-August. Map 1747. Represented with us as subsp. *cisatlántica* Blake [*C. corymbosa*]. Indians used a lotion prepared from the plant to treat blisters, and the dried leaves as an astringent or for rheumatism.
    2. *C. maculáta* (L.) Pursh. Spotted wintergreen. Dry woods. July-August. Fig. 764, Map 1748. Our plants are var. *maculata*.

2. *Monéses* Salisb. ex S. F. Gray (from the Greek, referring to the solitary flower).

Similar to *Pyrola* except flower solitary and terminal. [*Pyrola*].

    1. *M. uniflóra* (L.) Gray (one-flowered). Moist to dry coniferous or mixed woods, wooded swamps. June-August. Map 1749. (Eurasia). Endangered in CT. [*Pyrola u.*].

3. *Orthílla* Raf.

As in *Pyrola* except raceme secund and style straight, exserted at anthesis. [*Pyrola*].

    1. *O. secúnda* (L.) House (one-sided). Moist to dry woods, wooded swamps. June-July. Fig. 765, Map 1750. (Eurasia). [*Pyrola s.; Ramschia s.*]. —FAC

4. *Pýrola* L. Shinleaf (diminutive of *Pyrus*, from resemblance of the foliage).

Low, rhizomatous, perennial herbs; leaves basal, opposite or whorled, toothed to entire; flowers whitish or pink, in a simple raceme on a long peduncle, calyx 5-parted, petals 5, stamens 10, filaments glabrous, style elongate, stigma shallowly to deeply 5-lobed; capsule subglobose.

a. Style 3 mm or less long, straight, not exserted at anthesis. .... 1. *P. minor*
a. Style 4 mm or more long, declined, exserted at anthesis.
  b. Calyx lobes triangular, as wide or wider than long.

Leaves mostly 3.5 cm or more long, conspicuously longer than wide, blade
usually longer than petiole; calyx lobes short-acuminate; bracts of
raceme linear-subulate .... 2. *P. elliptica*
Leaves mostly less than 3.5 cm long, about as wide as long or only slightly
longer, blade usually as long or shorter than petiole; calyx lobes acute
or obtuse; bracts of raceme linear-lanceolate. .... 3. *P. chlorantha*
  b. Calyx lobes oblong-lanceolate, conspicuously longer than wide. (Fig. 766).
Calyx lobes slightly overlapping at the base; petals pink or purplish. .... 4. *P. asarifolia*
Calyx lobes not overlapping at base; petals white, rarely pinkish. .... 5. *P. americana*

1. P. *minor* L. (smaller). Cool, moist woods. June-August. Map 1751. (Eurasia). Endangered in
VT. [*Braxilia m.; Erxlebenia m.*]. —FAC

2. P. *elliptica* Nutt. (elliptic). Moist to dry woods. June-August. Map 1752. (Japan).

3. P. *chlorantha* Swartz. Dry woods. June-July. Map 1753. (Eurasia). [*P. oxypetala; P. virens*].

4. P. *asarifólia* Michx. (with leaves of *Asarum*). Rich, dry to moist woods, bogs. June-August.
Map 1754. Endangered in NH, MA. [*P. uliginosa*]. Our plants are subsp. *asarifolia*. —FACW

5. P. *americána* Sweet (American). Dry to moist woods. June-August. Fig. 766, Map 1755. [*P.
rotundifolia* var. *americana*]. Reported to be of value as an astringent and diuretic. —FAC

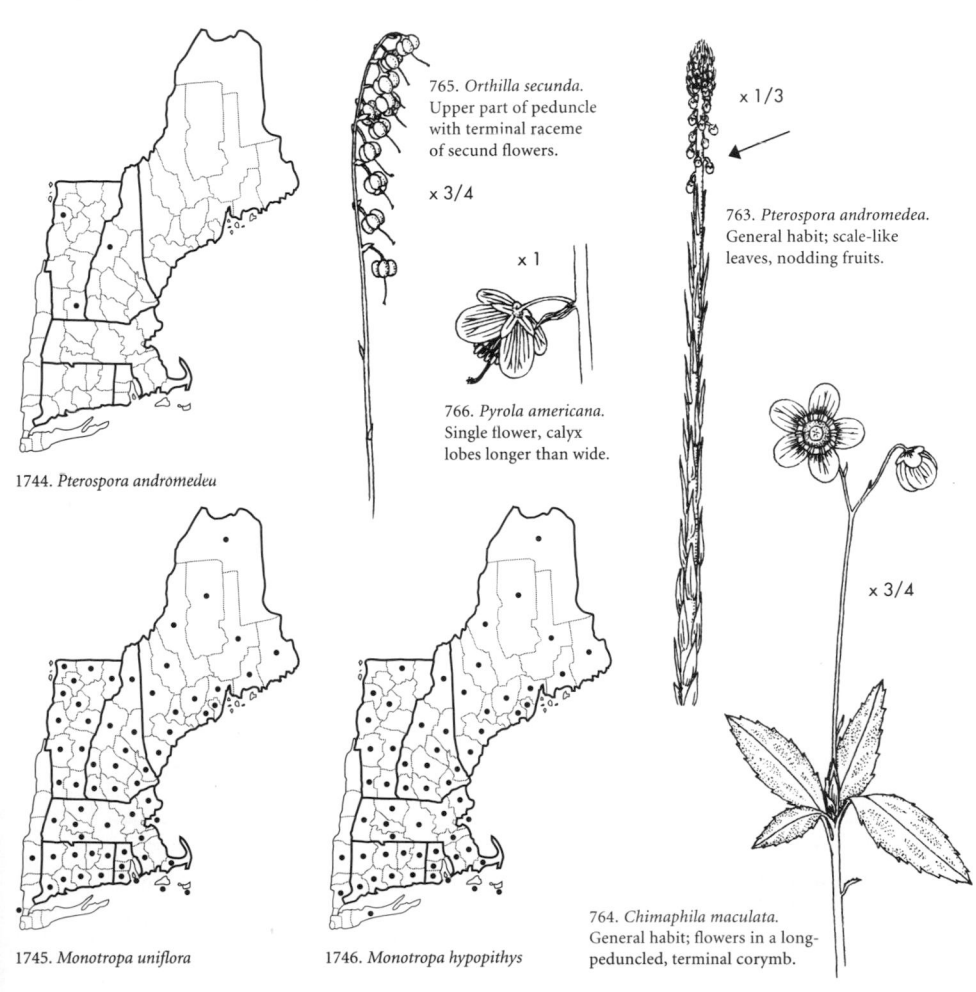

765. *Orthilla secunda.*
Upper part of peduncle
with terminal raceme
of secund flowers.

x 3/4

x 1

766. *Pyrola americana.*
Single flower, calyx
lobes longer than wide.

x 1/3

763. *Pterospora andromedea.*
General habit; scale-like
leaves, nodding fruits.

x 3/4

1744. *Pterospora andromedeu*

1745. *Monotropa uniflora*

1746. *Monotropa hypopithys*

764. *Chimaphila maculata.*
General habit; flowers in a long-
peduncled, terminal corymb.

1747. *Chimaphila umbellata*
subsp. *cisatlantica*

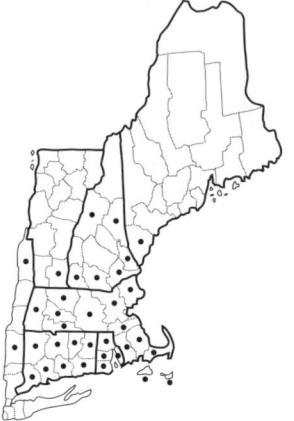

1748. *Chimaphila maculata*

1749. *Moneses uniflora*

1750. *Orthilla secunda*

1751. *Pyrola minor*

1752. *Pyrola elliptica*

1753. *Pyrola chlorantha*

1754. *Pyrola asarifolia*

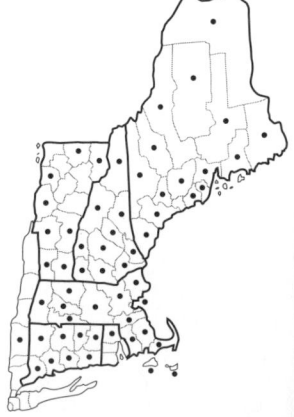

1755. *Pyrola americana*

Family 157. Ericáceae (Heath Family)

Hermaphrodite, shrubs or suffrutescent herbs, rarely trailing, often evergreen. Leaves simple, alternate, or occasionally opposite or whorled, sessile or petioled, toothed or entire, estipulate. Flowers perfect, regular, rarely irregular, solitary in the leaf axils or in axillary or terminal racemes, panicles or clusters, calyx and corolla, 4-5 parted, or of 4-5 separate sepals or petals, often campanulate or urceolate, stamens as many or twice as many as the corolla lobes or petals, hypogynous or epigynous, usually opening by a terminal pore, ovary superior or inferior, 2-10-locular, style 1, ovules few to many. Fruit a capsule, berry or drupe.

a. Leaves scale-like, bristle-like, or linear to narrowly oblong (ovate in *Gaultheria* and *Vaccinium*), 1 cm or less long and 3 mm or less wide, evergreen. (Figs. 767, 768).
   b. Leaves (most of them) 2-auricled at the base, opposite. .... 1. *Calluna vulgaris*
   b. Leaves not auricled at the base.
      c. Plants moss-like; leaves bristle-like, 4 mm or less long, alternate. (Fig. 768) .... 2. *Harrimanella hypnoides*
      c. Plants not moss-like; leaves not bristle-like, or if so (*Erica*) then whorled, mostly longer than 4mm.
         d. Leaves opposite or whorled.
            Leaves opposite; flowers 5-merous. (Fig. 769). .... 3. *Loiseleuria procumbens*
            Leaves whorled; flowers 4-merous .... 4. *Erica*
         d. Leaves alternate.
            e. Stems prostrate and trailing; flowers 4-merous; fruit a berry; not alpine. (Fig. 770).
               Leaves sparsely setose beneath; ovary partly inferior; berry white, with wintergreen taste .... 5. *Gaultheria*
               Leaves glabrous; ovary completely inferior; berry red, with cranberry taste. .... 6. *Vaccinium*
            e. Stems diffusely branched; flowers 5-merous; fruit a capsule; plant of alpine summits .... 7. *Phyllodoce caerulea*
a. Leaves not scale-like or bristle-like, longer than 1 cm and/or wider than 3 mm.
   f. Plant prostrate or trailing; fruit a berry.
      g. Flowers 4-5-merous; ovary inferior.
         Leaves sparsely setose beneath; ovary partly inferior; berry white with wintergreen taste .... 5. *Gaultheria*
         Leaves glabrous; ovary completely inferior; berry red or blue, without wintergreen taste .... 6. *Vaccinium*
      g. Flowers 5-merous; ovary superior.
         Corolla salverform; calyx subtended by 2 ovate bracts; leaves elliptic to ovate .... 8. *Epigaea repens*
         Corolla urceolate; calyx without bracts; leaves obovate to oblanceolate. .... 9. *Arctostaphylos*
   f. Plant erect or ascending.
      h. Petals separate; leaves densely brown to whitish-woolly beneath. .... 10. *Ledum groenlandicum*
      h. Petals united, at least at the base; leaves glabrous, pubescent or densely puberulent beneath but not woolly.
         i. Ovary inferior; fruit a berry.
             Leaves resinous-dotted on one or both sides. .... 11. *Gaylussacia*
             Leaves not resinous-dotted .... 6. *Vaccinium*
         i. Ovary superior.
            j. Corolla campanulate to funnelform or rotate.
               Corolla campanulate to funnelform, the anthers not in pouches in the corolla; capsule oblong to cylindric, 2 or more times as long as thick. .... 12. *Rhododendron*
               Corolla rotate, the anthers in pouches in the corolla; capsule subglobose, less than twice as long as thick .... 13. *Kalmia*
            j. Corolla urceolate, not or only slightly wider than the tube at the apex.

k. Leaves deciduous (evergreen in 1 species of *Leucothoe*); flowers mostly in lateral inflorescences, rarely terminal.
Pedicels bracteolate at the base; inflorescence racemose, rarely paniculate. (Fig. 779) .... 14. *Leucothoe*
Pedicels not bracteolate at base; inflorescence mostly in clusters or panicles. (Fig. 780) .... 15. *Lyonia*
k. Leaves evergreen; flowers solitary in the leaf axils or in terminal inflorescences.
l. Flowers solitary in the leaf axils.
Upper leaves becoming progressively smaller; leaves lepidote-scaly; fruit a capsule. (Fig. 781) .... 16. *Chamaedaphne calyculata*
Upper leaves not reduced; leaves glabrous; fruit a red berry. .... 5. *Gaultheria*
l. Flowers in terminal inflorescences.
Leaves revolute, whitened beneath with close, minute puberulence. .... 17. *Andromeda polifolia* var. *glaucoplylla*
Leaves not revolute, not whitened beneath, glabrous. .... 9. *Arctostaphylos*

1. ***Callúna*** Salisb. Heather (from the Greek, meaning to sweep, brooms being made from the twigs).

Much branched, evergreen shrubs, twigs slender, pith very small, pale, buds and leaf scars small; leaves small, evergreen, opposite, crowded and imbricated, sessile, mostly 2-auricled at the base; flowers small, white to pink or rose-purple, in dense, one-sided, bracteate, spike-like, terminal racemes, each closely subtended by 2-3 pairs of decussate bracts, sepals 4, petaloid, much exceeding the 4-lobed corolla, stamens 8, ovary superior, 4-locular; fruit a 4-valved capsule enclosed by the persistent perianth.

1. *C. vulgáris* (L.) Hull (common). Roadsides, fields, pond margins, woods, in sandy soil. July-September. Fig. 767, Map 1756. (Naturalized from Europe). Inflorescences have been used as a substitute for hops in making beer; a liniment made from macerating the plant is used in parts of Europe for arthritis and rheumatism. —FAC

2. ***Harrimanélla*** Coville.

Small, tufted, procumbent, matted, moss-like, evergreen shrubs, twigs slender, pith very small, buds and leaf scars small, the latter raised; leaves small and needle-like, evergreen, alternate, crowded and imbricated, sessile, flowers white to pink, solitary, terminal, nodding on slender peduncles, sepals 5, corolla 5-lobed, campanulate, stamens 10, anthers 2-awned, ovary superior, 5-locular; fruit a subglobose, 4-valved, loculicidal, many-seeded capsule. [*Cassiope*].

1. *H. hypnoídes* (L.) Coville (like *Hypnum*, a moss). Alpine summits. June-August. Fig. 768. (Eurasia). Endangered in ME. Reported for Piscataquis County ME, Coos County NH. [*Cassiope hypnoides*].

3. ***Loiseleúria*** Desv. Alpine azalea (for J. Loiseleur-Delongchamps).

Low, depressed or decumbent, diffusely branched and tufted, glabrous, evergreen shrubs, twigs slender, pith minute, buds ovoid, appressed, with 2-3 scales, leaf scars small, crescent-shaped, elevated, bundle trace 1, stipule scars lacking; leaves opposite, crowded, coriaceous and evergreen, revolute-margined, narrowly elliptic, puberulent beneath, midrib wide, short-petioled; flowers small, pink or white, 1-several from a single terminal or small cluster of terminal buds, calyx and corolla 5-parted, the latter campanulate, stamens 5, epigynous, ovary superior, 2-3-locular; fruit a 2-3 valved, many-seeded capsule, each of the valves 2-cleft.

1. **L. procúmbens** (L.) Desv. Barren, rocky or gravelly alpine regions. June-August. Fig. 769. (Eurasia) Endangered in ME, NY. Reported for NY, Piscataquis County ME, Coos County NH. [*Chamaecistus p.*].

4. Eríca L. Heath (ancient Greek and Latin name).

Much branched, evergreen shrubs, twigs as in *Calluna*; leaves small, evergreen, mostly whorled, narrow and revolute, subsessile; flowers small, white to pink or purple, in terminal or axillary clusters, otherwise as in *Calluna* except sepals are shorter than the corolla; fruit a 4-valved capsule enclosed by the persistent corolla.

Calyx and leaves ciliate with long-stipitate glands. .... 1. *E. tetralix*
Calyx and leaves glabrous to canescent but not glandular-ciliate.
    Stems pubescent; corolla tubular; anthers included. .... 2. *E. cinerea*
    Stems glabrous; corolla campanulate; anthers exserted .... 3. *E. vagans*

1. **E. tétralix** L. (with 4 spirals). Dry open woods, clearings, barrens, pond margins. July-September. Map 1757. (Naturalized from Europe). —FACU
2. **E. cinérea** L. (ashy). Barrens, dry open woods. July-August. (Introduced from Europe). Reported for Nantucket County MA.
3. **E. vágans** L. (wandering). Open pine woods. July-September. (Introduced from Europe). Reported for Nantucket County MA.

5. Gaulthéria L. (for J. Gaultier).

Colonial, branching, evergreen shrubs with stems creeping or erect from a horizontal rhizome, pubescent or glabrous, stems slender, pith minute to moderate, buds small, ovoid, with several scales, leaf scars small, crescent-shaped to half-round, bundle trace 1; leaves coriaceous and evergeen, alternate, petioled, elliptic, obovate or suborbicular, slightly revolute, entire or crenulate; flowers white, solitary in the leaf axils, the pedicels with 2-bracteoles subtending the calyx, calyx deeply 4-5 lobed, corolla urceolate to campanulate, 4-5 lobed or toothed, stamens 8 or 10, ovary superior to partly inferior, 4-5-locular; fruit a many-seeded berry enclosed by the enlarged, fleshy hypanthium forming a mealy, red or white berry.

Leafy stems erect; leaves clustered toward the tips of the stems, 1.5 cm or more
    long, glabrous beneath .... 1. *G. procumbens*
Leafy stems prostrate; leaves 2-ranked along the stems, 1 cm or less long, pubescent
    beneath. (Fig. 770) .... 2. *G. hispidula*

1. **G. procúmbens** L. (lying flat). Wintergreen. Moist to dry upland woods. July-August. Map 1758. Fruits and young leaves edible; tea can be made from older leaves. —FACU; Wildl. 1
2. **G. hispídula** (L.) Muhl. ex Bigelow (finely rough-hairy). Creeping snowberry. Moist, mostly coniferous woods, wooded swamps and bogs. May-June. Fig. 770, Map 1759. [*Chiogenes h.*]. Fruits edible; tea can be made from stems and leaves. —FACW

6. Vaccínium L. (ancient name).

Upright shrubs, rarely trailing, twigs slender, pith small, vegetative buds small, the 2 outer scales often with hair-like points and the flower buds often larger and subglobose in the upright shrubby species, leaf scars small, crescent-shaped, bundle trace 1, end bud and stipule scars lacking; leaves alternate, deciduous or evergreen; flowers solitary in the leaf axils or in axillary or terminal racemes or clusters, calyx and corolla 4-5-parted, corolla urceolate, campanulate or cylindric, stamens 8 or 10, epigynous, ovary inferior, 4-10-locular; fruit a many-seeded blue, black, yellow or red berry. Fruits of all of the species treated below are edible raw or cooked —Wildl. 3 (blueberries), 1 (cranberries).

a. Stems trailing or creeping; leaves coriaceous and evergreen (not coriaceous and
    deciduous in *V. cespitosum*). (Fig. 771).
  b. Corolla 4-parted to below the middle, with reflexed lobes; pedicels 1 cm or
      more long.
      Pedicels bearing a pair of green foliaceous bracts above the middle. .... 1. *V. macrocarpon*
      Pedicels bearing a pair of red scale-like bracts below the middle. .... 2. *V. oxycoccos*
  b. Corolla 4-5 parted to above the middle, with erect or spreading lobes; pedicels
      less than 1 cm long.
    c. Flowers and fruits in terminal clusters; anthers not 2-awned; leaves with
        scattered dark glands beneath. (Fig. 772). .... 3. *V. vitis-idaea*
                                                                                                          subsp. *minus*
    c. Flowers and fruits solitary in the leaf axils or 1-4 from scaly axillary buds;
        anthers 2-awned; leaves usually lacking dark glands beneath. (Fig. 773).
        Flowers and fruits solitary in the leaf axils; leaves not coriaceous,
            deciduous, serrulate; flowers 5-merous. .... 4. *V. cespitosum*
        Flowers and fruits 1-4 from scaly axillary buds; leaves coriaceous,
            evergreen, entire; flowers 4-merous .... 5. *V. uliginosum*
a. Stems erect or ascending; leaves not coriaceous, deciduous (coriaceous and
    evergreen in *V. uliginosum*).
  d. Flowers and fruits in leafy bracted racemes, solitary in the leaf axils, or 1-4 from
      scaly axillary buds; anthers 2-awned.
    e. Flowers and fruits in leafy bracted racemes; corolla campanulate; berry
        usually yellowish (ours). (Fig. 774) .... 6. *V. stamineum*
    e. Flowers and fruits solitary in the leaf axils or 1-4 from scaly axillary buds;
        corolla ovoid or urceolate; berry blue to blackish.
        Flowers and fruits solitary in the leaf axils; leaves not coriaceous,
            deciduous, serrulate; flowers 5-merous. .... 4. *V. cespitosum*
        Flowers and fruits 1-4 from scaly axillary buds; leaves coriaceous,
            evergreen, entire; flowers 4-merous .... 5. *V. uliginosum*
  d. Flowers and fruits in dense, non-leafy-bracted terminal or lateral racemes or
      clusters; anthers not 2-awned.
    f. Plants mostly 6 dm or less tall; leaves mostly 3 cm or less long.
      g. Leaves entire or essentially so.
          Leaves bright green, the lower surfaces (at least on the veins) and twigs
              with dense, spreading pubescence .... 7. *V. myrtilloides*
          Leaves pale green beneath and glabrous, glaucous or sparsely pubescent;
              twigs glabrous or sparsely pubescent .... 8. *V. pallidum*
      g. Leaves serrulate.
          Leaves 8 mm or less wide, bright green on both sides. .... 9. *V. angustifolium*
          Leaves (the larger ones) more than 8 mm wide. .... 8. *V. pallidum*
    f. Plants mostly 9 dm or more tall; larger leaves mostly longer than 3 cm.
        Leaves 5 cm or more long, 2-4 cm wide; corolla 6 mm or more long. .... 10. *V. corymbosum*
        Leaves 5 cm or less long, 2 cm or less wide; corolla 6 mm or less long. .... 11. *V. caesariense*

1. *V. macrocárpon* Ait. (large-fruited). Large Cranberry. Bogs. June-August. Fig. 771, Map 1760.
[*Oxycoccus m.*]. Cranberry juice is reported to be of value in treating urinary tract and kidney
infections. —OBL

2. *V. oxycóccos* L. (old generic name). Small Cranberry. Bogs. May-July. Map 1761. (Eurasia).
[*Oxycoccus o.; O. palustris; O. quadripetalus*]. —OBL

3. *V. vítis-idaéa* L. (Grape of Mt. Ida). Mountain-cranberry. Alpine open rocky or gravelly areas.
June-July. Fig. 772, Map 1762. (e. Asia; Greenland). Endangered in MA. [*Vitis-idaea v.; Vitis-idaea
punctata*]. Represented with us as subsp. *mínus* Lodd. —FAC

4. *V. cespitósum* Michx. (in tufts). Dwarf bilberry. Alpine open rocky or gravelly areas,
riverbanks. June-July. Map 1763. Endangered in NY. Our plants are var. *cespitosum*. —FACW

5. *V. uliginósum* L. (of swamps). Alpine bilberry. Alpine open rocky or gravelly areas. June-July.
Fig. 773, Map 1764. —FACU

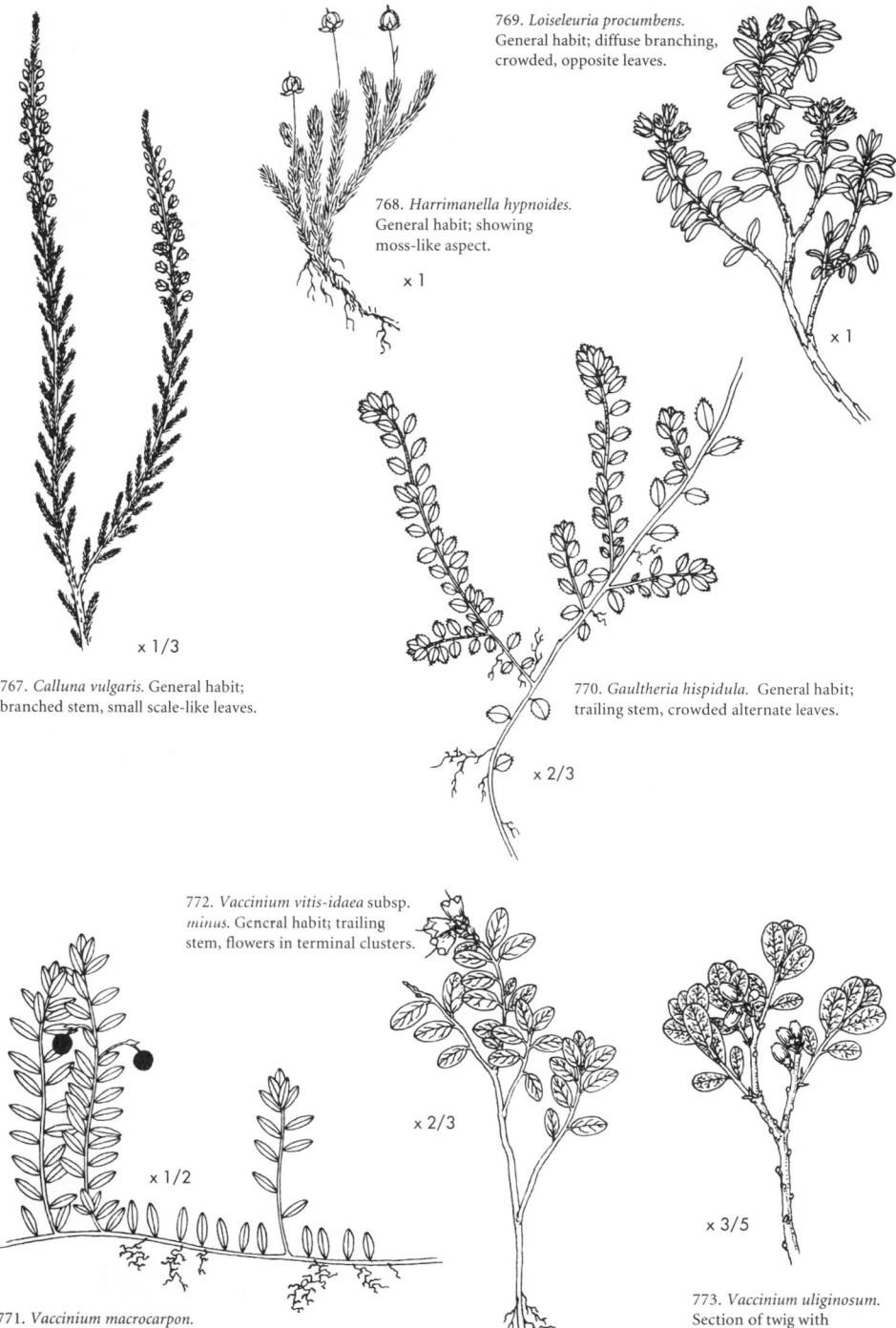

769. *Loiseleuria procumbens.* General habit; diffuse branching, crowded, opposite leaves.

768. *Harrimanella hypnoides.* General habit; showing moss-like aspect.

× 1

× 1

× 1/3

767. *Calluna vulgaris.* General habit; branched stem, small scale-like leaves.

770. *Gaultheria hispidula.* General habit; trailing stem, crowded alternate leaves.

× 2/3

772. *Vaccinium vitis-idaea* subsp. *minus.* General habit; trailing stem, flowers in terminal clusters.

× 2/3

× 1/2

771. *Vaccinium macrocarpon.* General habit; trailing stem.

× 3/5

773. *Vaccinium uliginosum.* Section of twig with flowers in leaf axils.

ERICACEAE

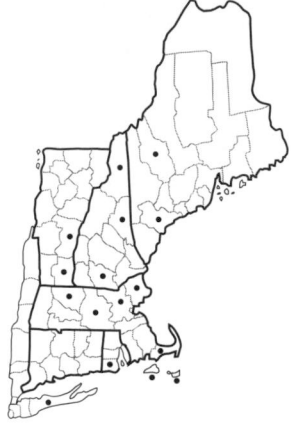

1756. *Calluna vulgaris*

1757. *Erica tetralix*

1758. *Gaultheria procumbens*

1759. *Gaultheria hispidula*

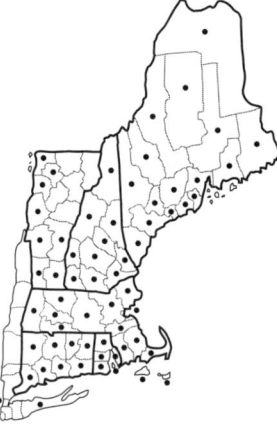

1760. *Vaccinium macrocarpon*

1761. *Vaccinium oxycoccos*

1762. *Vaccinium vitis-idaea* subsp. *minus*

1763. *Vaccinium cespitosum*

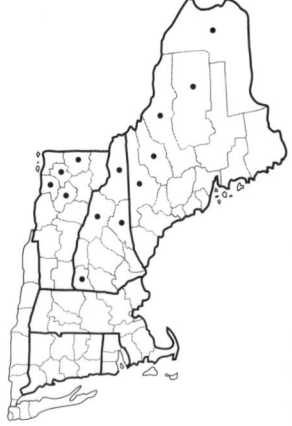

1764. *Vaccinium uliginosum*

6. V. stamíneum L. (with prominent stamens). Squaw-huckleberry. Dry woods, roadsides. May-June. Fig. 774, Map 1765. [*V. caesium; V. melanocarpum; V. neglectum; Polycodium s.; P. candicans*]. —FACU-

7. V. myrtilloídes Michx. (like *V. myrtillus*). Velvet-leaf blueberry. Moist to dry woods, bogs. May-June. Map 1766. [*V. canadense; Cyanococcus c.*]. —FAC

8. V. pállidum Ait. Lowbush blueberry. Dry woods, clearings and fields. May-June. Map 1767. [*V. altomontanum; V. vacillans; Cyanococcus liparis; C. subcordatus; C. vacillans*].

9. V. angustifólium Ait. (narrow-leaved). Lowbush blueberry. Dry woods, clearings and barrens. May-June. Map 1768. [*V. boreale; V. brittonii; V. lamarckii; V. nigrum; V. pensylvanicum; Cyanococcus a.*]. —FACU-

V. boreále I.V. Hall & Aald. Similar to *V. angustifolium* but dwarf, 1 dm or less toll, corolla up to 4 mm long, fruit up to 5 mm thick (plant taller than 1 dm, corolla 4 mm or more long, fruit 5 mm or more thick in *V. angustifolium*. Alpine areas. Reported for ME, NH, VT.

10. V. corymbósum L. Highbush blueberry. Wooded swamps, shrub swamps, wet to dry woods and fields. May-June. Map 1769. [*V. atrococcum; V. australe; V. constablei; V. marianum; V. simulatum; Cyanococcus c.; C. atrococcus*]. —FACW-

V. fuscátum Ait. Similar to *V. corymbosum* but distinguishable in having subcoriaceous leaves and a red, cylindric corolla about twice as long as wide (leaves deciduous and corolla white to pink, urceolate to ovoid, less than twice as long as wide in *V. corymbosum*). From farther south on the Coastal Plain. Throughout our range.

11. V. caesariénse Mackenz. (of New Jersey). Wooded swamps, shrub swamps, bogs near the coast. May-June. Map 1770. —OBL

7. *Phyllódoce* Salisb. (name based on Greek mythodology).

Low, branched, matted, evergreen shrubs, twigs slender, pith minute, buds and lear scars very small; leaves evergreen, yew-like, alternate, crowded, linear, minutely serrulate, short-petioled; flowers pink to purple, on glandular pedicels from the axils of the upper leaves, solitary or forming a small umbelliform cluster, sepals 5, corolla urceolate to campanulate, 5-lobed, stamens 10, ovary superior, 5-locular; fruit a subglobose, 5-valved, septicidal, many-seeded capsule.

1. P. caerúlea (L.) Bab. (sky-blue). Alpine summits. June-July. Map 1771. (Eurasia). Endangered in ME.

8. *Epigaéa* L. Trailing arbutus (Greek name, based on the trailing habit).

Prostrate, creeping, branched, pubescent, evergreen shrub, twigs slender, pith moderate, brown, vegetative buds solitary, flower buds clustered, with 2-several scales, leaf scars usually not visible; leaves alternate, coriaceous and evergreen, elliptic to ovate, rounded or cordate at the base, entire, pubescent or glabrous, petioled; flowers pink or white, fragrant, in short, congested, terminal and axillary clusters, each subtended by 2 ovate bracts, sepals 5, corolla salverform, 5-lobed, stamens 10, epigynous, ovary superior, 5-locular; fruit a many-seeded, subglobose capsule, fleshy and berry-like; hirsute.

1. E. répens L. (running on the ground). Woods and clearings. April-May. Map 1772.

9. *Arctostáphylos* Adans. (Greek name).

Trailing or spreading, branched, mat-forming shrubs, the older branches and stems with papery, shredding bark, twigs slender, tomentulose or glabrous, pith small, buds small, ovoid, with several scales, leaf scars crescent-shaped, elevated, bundle trace 1; leaves alternate, coriaceous and evergreen or marcescent, petioled, obovate to oblanceolate, entire or crenulate; flowers white to pink, in few-flowered terminal, bracteate racemes or clusters, sepals 5, corolla urceolate, 5-toothed, stamens 10,

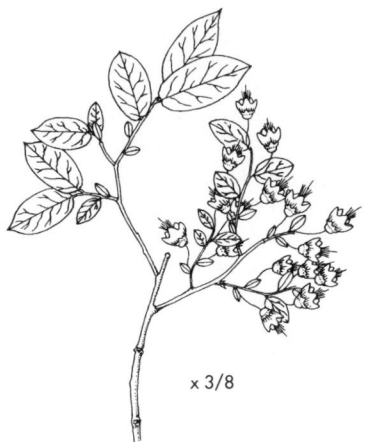

774. *Vaccinium stamineum*. Section of twig with flowers in leafy bracted racemes.

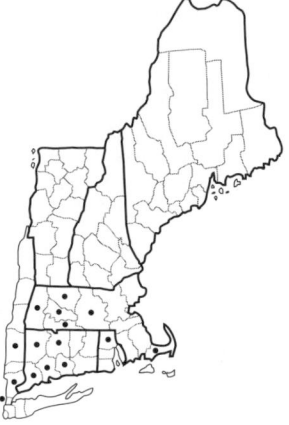

1765. *Vaccinium stamineum*

1766. *Vaccinium myrtilloides*

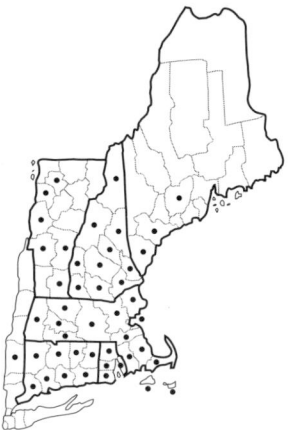

1767. *Vaccinium pallidum*

1768. *Vaccinium angustifolium*

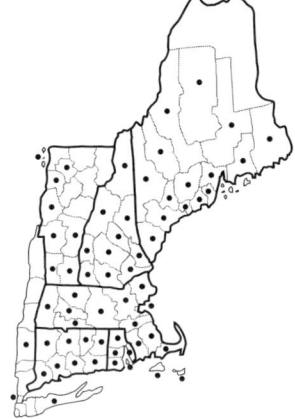

1769. *Vaccinium corymbosum*

1770. *Vaccinium caesariense*

1771. *Phyllodoce caerulea*

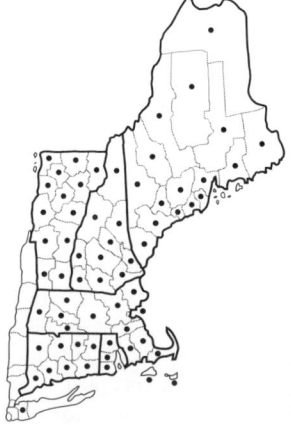

1772. *Epigaea repens*

ovary superior, 5-locular; fruit a dry, mealy, red or a juicy purplish drupe with 5 seeds, these separate or fused into a single stone.

Píeris D. Don *floribúnda* (Pursh) Benth. & Hook. f. Similar to *Arctostaphylos* but is an upright shrub with flowers in panicles and fruit a capsule. Southern. Rarely escaped from cultivation in our range. Reported for Windham County VT. [*Andromeda f.*].

Leaves crenulate, reticulate-rugose; twigs glabrous; fruit purplish. .... 1. *A. alpina*
Leaves entire, not reticulate-rugose; twigs tomentulose; fruit red. .... 2. *A. uva-ursi*

1. *A. alpína* (L.) Spreng. (alpine). Alpine bearberry. Alpine barrens. June-July. Endangered in ME. Reported for Piscataquis County ME, Coos County NH. [*Arctous a.; Mairania a.*]. —FAC
2. *A. úva-úrsi* (L.) Spreng. (bear's grape). Bearberry. Dry, rocky or sandy open areas and sandy, open pine or oakwoods. May-June. Map 1773. (Eurasia). [*Uva-ursi u.*]. Preparations made from the leaves are useful in treating urinary infections; leaves should be macerated and soaked overnight in cold water.

10. *Lédum* L. (based on an ancient Greek name for another aromatic plant).
Erect, branched, evergreen shrubs, twigs densely tomentose, pith small, brownish, vegetative buds small, with 2 or 3 scales, the terminal flower buds larger, with more scales, leaf scars somewhat heart-shaped to half-elliptic, bundle trace 1, stipule scars lacking; leaves coriaceous and evergreen, alternate, densely brown to whitish-tomentose beneath, oblong to lanceolate, sessile to subsessile, revolute-margined, aromatic when crushed; flowers white, in terminal, umbellate or corymbose clusters, calyx small, 5-toothed, petals 5, spreading, stamens 5-10, ovary superior, 5-locular; fruit a canescent, ovoid, 5-valved, septicidal, many-seeded capsule splitting from the base upward.

1. *L. groenlándicum* Oeder (of Greenland). Labrador-tea. Bogs. May-July. Map 1774. Leaves can be used to make tea; one source states that if used more than a few cups at a time it may have a cathartic effect. —OBL

11. *Gaylussácia* HBK Huckleberry (for L. Gay-Lussac).
Freely branched shrubs, often colonial, twigs slender, pith small, buds small, ovoid, with several scales, the flower buds often larger than the vegetative buds, leaf scars crescent-shaped, bundle trace 1, stipule scars and end bud lacking; leaves alternate, petioled, elliptic to oblong or obovate, resinous-dotted on one or both sides, entire, sessile or subsessile; flowers white to pink, in lateral, bracted racemes, calyx 5-lobed, corolla urceolate to campanulate, 5-lobed, stamens 10, ovary inferior, 10-locular; fruit a usually dark blue to black, berry-like drupe with 10 bony seeds. Fruits edible. —Wildl. 1

a. Bracts of racemes foliaceous, persistent, as long or longer than the usually
   2-bracteolate pedicels; sepals, pedicels, bracts and often the leaves
   stipitate-glandular. (Fig. 775) .... 1. *G. dumosa*
a. Bracts of racemes nearly scarious, deciduous, mostly shorter than the 2-bracteolate
   pedicels; sepals, pedicels, bracts and leaves with sessile glands.
   Leaves glandular on both surfaces; rachis of racemes 1.5 cm or less long; young
      twigs usually pubescent .... 2. *G. baccata*
   Leaves glandular only beneath; rachis of racemes 1.8 cm or more long; young
      twigs glabrous or essentially so .... 3. *G. frondosa*

1. *G. dumósa* (Andr.) Torr. & Gray (bushy). Bogs or barrens, mostly near the coastal plain. May-July. Fig. 775, Map 1775. [*Lasiococcus d.*]. Our plants include var. *dumosa* and the following var.:
   var. *bigeloviána* Fern. Leaves and bracts conspicuously and persistently glandular above as well as beneath (glandless or sparsely glandular above in var. *dumosa*). —FAC
2. *G. baccáta* (Wang.) K. Koch (berry-bearing). Black Huckleberry. Dry woods, thickets, clearings, bogs. May-July. Map 1776. [*Decachaena b.*]. —FACU

3. G. frondósa (L.) Torr. & Gray ex Torr. (leafy). Dry woods, thickets, clearings, bogs. May-June. Map 1777. [*Decachaena f.*]. Our plants are var. *frondosa.* —FAC

12. Rhododéndron L. (Greek name, meaning rose-tree).

Branching, deciduous or evergreen shrubs (ours), twigs slender to stout, those of the season's growth often clustered so as to appear whorled, pith small to moderate, buds solitary on the older growth, clustered toward the tips of the twigs, these buds larger than the lower, solitary buds, one greatly enlarged flower bud present in the cluster, the larger terminal buds with 6 or more scales, the lower buds with fewer scales, leaf scars shield shaped, bundle trace 1, stipule scars lacking; leaves alternate, deciduous or coriaceous and evergreen, toothed or entire, petioled; flowers usually large and showy, in terminal umbellate or corymbose clusters, calyx small, 5-lobed, corolla campanulate to funnelform, regularly or irregularly 5-lobed, stamens 5 or 10, epigynous, ovary superior, 5-locular; fruit a 5-valved, septicidal, many-seeded capsule. The species of Rhododendron are for the most part poisonous. —Wildl. 1

a. Leaves coriaceous, evergreen.
    Dwarf shrub 3 dm or less tall; leaves 2 cm or less long. (Fig. 776). .... 1. *R. lapponicum*
    Large shrub 4 dm or more tall; leaves 6 cm or more long. .... 2. *R. maximum*
a. Leaves membranaceous, deciduous.
  b. Corolla bilabiate, divided nearly to the base; capsules glaucous and puberulent;
      leaves puberulent beneath, rounded at tip. .... 3. *R. canadense*
  b. Corolla not bilabiate, with a funnelform tube; capsules not glaucous; leaves if
      puberulent beneath, acute.
    c. Corolla red, orange or yellow; leaves usually canescent beneath, at least on
        the midrib .... 4. *R. japonicum*
    c. Corolla pink to purple, rarely white; leaves glabrous or setose beneath on the
        midrib (canescent in *R. roseum*).
      d. Plant in flower.
        e. Leaves fully developed at anthesis; anthesis mid-June or later. .... 5. *R. viscosum*
        e. Leaves not fully developed at anthesis; anthesis before mid-June.
          f. Corolla tube glabrous, one-third or less as long as the limb. .... 6. *R. vaseyi*
          f. Corolla tube pubescent, more than one-third as long as the limb.
            Ovary hirsute and glandular; leaves canescent beneath, at least
            along the midrib, with or without setae on midrib. .... 7. *R. prinophyllum*
            Ovary hirsute, not glandular; leaves mostly glabrous beneath,
            setose on the midrib .... 8. *R. periclymenoides*
      d. Plant in fruit.
        g. Leaves canescent beneath, at least along the midrib, with or without
          setae on midrib; capsule canescent and often also sparsely
          glandular. .... 7. *R. prinophyllum*
        g. Leaves mostly glabrous beneath or setose on the midrib; capsule
          glabrous to sparsely glandular or setose.
          h. Capsule glabrous or sparsely glandular. .... 6. *R. vaseyi*
          h. Capsule setose. (Fig. 777).
            Pedicels usually abundantly stipitate-glandular; largest mature
            leaves mostly less than 6 cm long .... 5. *R. viscosum*
            Pedicels usually not or sparsely stipitate-glandular; largest mature
            leaves mostly 6 cm or more long .... 8. *R. periclymenoides*

1. R. lappónicum (L.) Wahl. (of Lapland). Alpine barrens. June. Fig. 776. (Eurasia). Endangered in ME. Reported for Piscataquis County ME, Coos County NH. Our plants are var. *lapponicum*.

2. R. máximum L. (greatest). Rhododendron. Moist woods. June-July. Map 1778. —FAC

R. catawbiénse Michx. Red Laurel. Similar to *R. maximum* except pedicels, ovary and capsule puberulent (stipitate-glandular in *R. maximum*). Southern; rarely escaped from cultivation in our range. Reported for Hampshire County MA.

R. caroliniánum Rehder. Lower surface of leaves and petioles glandular-punctate (lower leaf

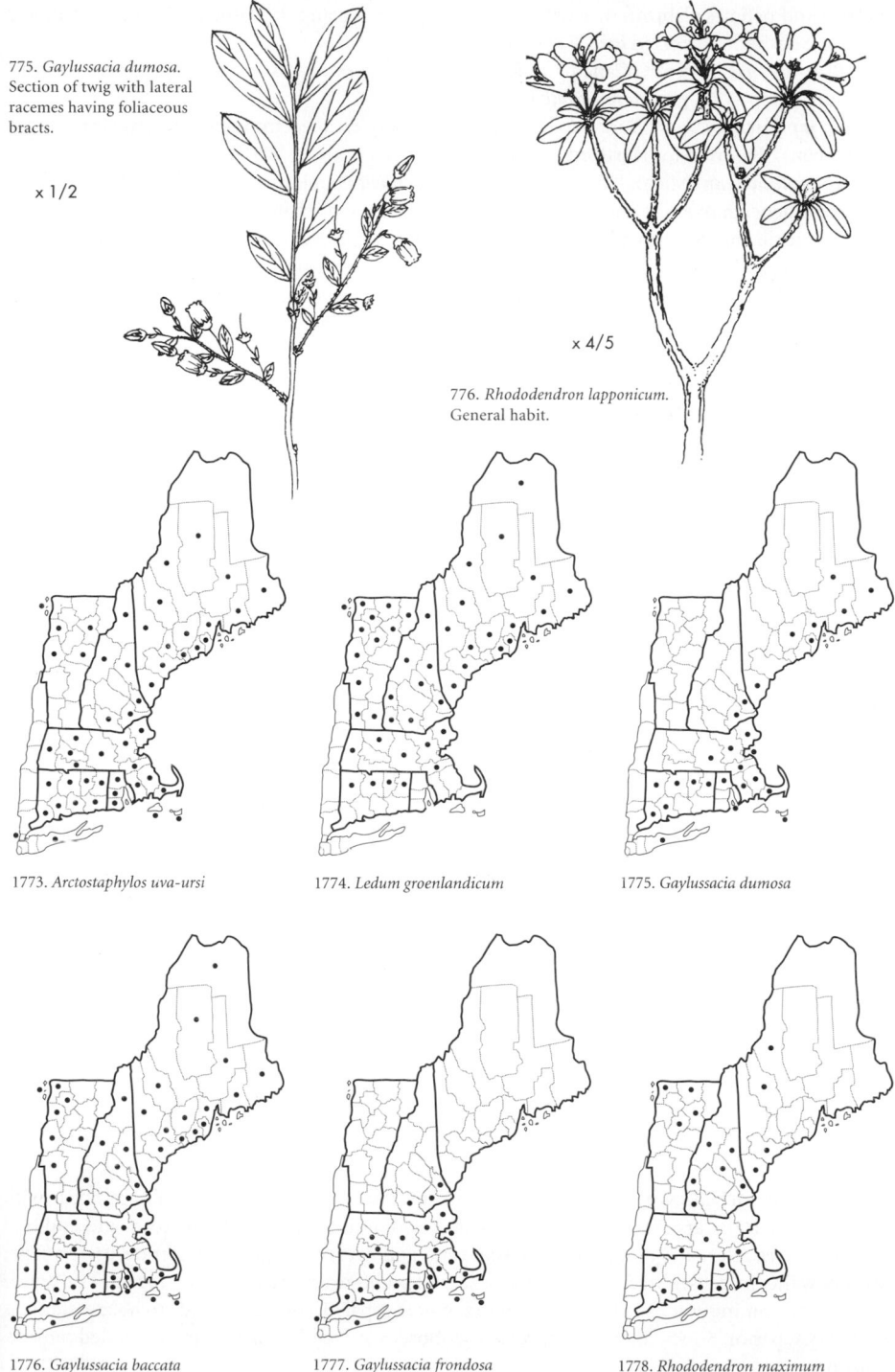

775. *Gaylussacia dumosa.*
Section of twig with lateral
racemes having foliaceous
bracts.

x 1/2

x 4/5

776. *Rhododendron lapponicum.*
General habit.

1773. *Arctostaphylos uva-ursi*

1774. *Ledum groenlandicum*

1775. *Gaylussacia dumosa*

1776. *Gaylussacia baccata*

1777. *Gaylussacia frondosa*

1778. *Rhododendron maximum*

surfaces and petioles glabrous or scurfy-tomentose but not glandular punctate in the preceding 2 species). Southern. Reported for CT. [*R. minus*].

3. *R. canadénse* (L.) Torr. (Canadian). Rhodora. Bogs, wooded swamps, shrub swamps, marshes. May-June. Map 1779. [*Rhodora canadensis*]. —FACW

4. *R. japónicum* (Gray) Sur. (Japanese). Occasionally escaped from cultivation. (Introduced from Japan). Reported for Hartford County CT.

R. calenduláceum (Michx.) Torr. Similar to *R. japonicum* but is distinguishable in having leaves pubescent beneath over the surface and flowers with exserted stamens (leaves canescent beneath only on midrib and flowers with stamens included in *R. japonicum*). Southern; rarely found in our range. Reported for Westchester County NY. [*Azalea c.*].

5. *R. viscósum* (L.) Torr. (sticky). Swamp-azalea. Wooded swamps, shrub swamps, wet woods, pond margins. June-July. Fig. 777, Map 1780. Endangered in ME. [*Azalea viscosa*]. —OBL

6. *R. váseyi* Gray (for G. R. Vasey). Pinkshell-azalea. Occasionally escaped from cultivation. From farther south. Reported for CT, Plymouth County MA.

7. *R. prinóphyllum* (Small) Millais (saw-tooth leaved). Mountain-azalea. Moist to dry woods and thickets, borders of ponds and rivers. May-June. Map 1781. [*R. roseum; R. canescens; Azalea c.; A. prinophylla; A. rosea*]. —FAC

8. *R. periclymenoídes* (Michx.) Shinners. (like Honeysuckle). Pinkster flower. Moist to dry woods, bogs. April-May. Map 1782. Endangered in NH. [*R. nudiflorum; Azalea n.*]. —FAC

13. *Kálmia* L. Laurel (for P. Kalm).

Branched, evergreen shrubs, twigs slender to moderate, pith small, tan, buds small, naked or with 2 scales, leaf scars half round or shield shaped, sometimes sunken and partly obscured, bundle trace 1, often a transverse line, end bud and stipule scars lacking; leaves coriaceous and evergreen, alternate, opposite or whorled in 3s, entire, petioled; flowers showy, white to pink or purple, in terminal or lateral corymbs, calyx deeply 5-lobed, corolla shallowly 5-lobed, stamens 10, the anthers fitting into small pockets in the corolla, ovary superior, 5-locular; fruit a subglobose, 5-valved, septicidal, many-seeded capsule. Poisonous.

a. Corymbs lateral; leaves mostly whorled in 3s. (Fig. 778). .... 1. *K. angustifolia*
a. Corymbs terminal; leaves opposite or alternate.
    Leaves opposite, whitened beneath; twigs 2-edged. .... 2. *K. polifolia*
    Leaves mostly alternate (crowded and sometimes opposite or whorled toward
        the tips of the twigs), not whitened beneath; twigs terete. .... 3. *K. latifolia*

1. *K. angustifólia* L. (narrow-leaved). Sheep-laurel. Bogs, wooded swamps, pond margins, upland woods, old pastures. June-July. Fig. 778, Map 1783. —FAC

2. *K. polifólia* Wang. (with leaves of *Polium*). Bog-laurel. Bogs, pond margins, alpine barrens. May-June. Map 1784. —OBL

3. *K. latifólia* L. (broad-leaved). Mountain-laurel. Woods, old pastures. May-July. Map 1785. —FACU; Wildl. 1

14. *Leucóthoe* D. Don Fetterbush (named for the daughter of an ancient King of Babylon).

Usually tall, branched, evergreen or deciduous shrubs, pith white to tan, buds small, roundish, with several scales, leaf scars crescent-shaped or half-round, bundle trace 1, stipule scars and end bud lacking; leaves alternate, deciduous or coriaceous and evergreen, petioled, serrate or serrulate; flowers white, in dense, bracteate, axillary or lateral and terminal racemes, the racemes of flower buds for the coming year usually conspicuous in winter, sepals 5, corolla 5-lobed, urceolate, stamens 10, ovary superior, 5-locular; fruit a depressed-globose, 5-valved, loculicidal, many-seeded capsule. Poisonous.

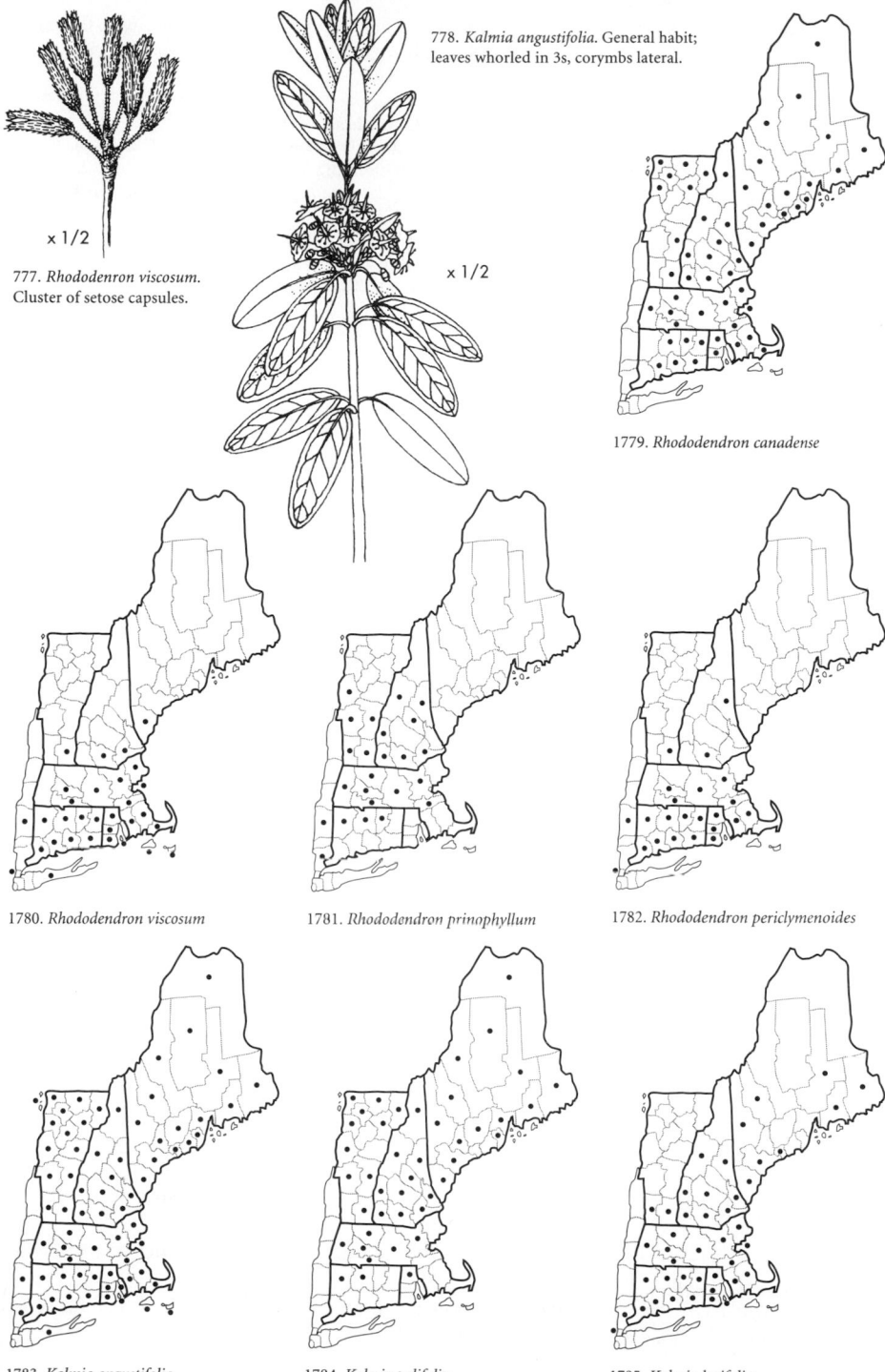

× 1/2

777. *Rhododenron viscosum.* Cluster of setose capsules.

778. *Kalmia angustifolia.* General habit; leaves whorled in 3s, corymbs lateral.

× 1/2

1779. *Rhododendron canadense*

1780. *Rhododendron viscosum*

1781. *Rhododendron prinophyllum*

1782. *Rhododendron periclymenoides*

1783. *Kalmia angustifolia*

1784. *Kalmia polifolia*

1785. *Kalmia latifolia*

Oxydéndrum DC. *arbóreum* (L.) DC. Sourwood. Similar to *Leucothoe* but is a tree with flowers in terminal panicles, the capsules ovoid. Southern. Rarely found in our range. Reported for Providence County RI.

Leaves deciduous; racemes one-sided; pedicels with or without a bract at the base
    (bracts deciduous) and with 2 bractlets just beneath the calyx. (Fig. 779) .... 1. *L. racemosa*
Leaves evergreen; racemes not one-sided; pedicels with a persistent bract and
    2 bractlets at the base, none beneath the calyx. .... 2. *L. axillaris*

    1. *L. racemósa* (L.) Gray (with racemes). Wooded swamps, shrub swamps, wet woods, pond and stream margins, mostly toward the coast. May-June. Fig. 779, Map 1786. [*Eubotrys r.*]. —FACW
    2. *L. axilláris* (Lam.) D. Don (axillary). Rare, from farther south. Reported for Nantucket County MA. [*L. fontanesiana*]. —FACW+

15. *Lyónia* Nutt. (for J. Lyon).

Tall, much-branched shrubs with the aspect of highbush blueberry, twigs slender, yellowish, pith small, buds reddish, oblong and pointed, somewhat flattened against the twig, with 2 scales, or ovoid, not flattened, with 4 scales, leaf scars half-round or crescent-shaped, bundle trace 1, stipule scars and end bud lacking, leaves alternate, short-petioled, entire or serrulate; flowers white to pink, on long, bracteolate pedicels, in lateral and terminal clusters or panicles, calyx and corolla 5-lobed, the latter globose or urceolate, stamens 10, ovary superior, 5-locular; fruit an ovoid to globose, 5-valved, loculicidal, many-seeded capsule, thickened along the sutures. Poisonous.

Corolla and capsule 5 mm or less long; buds flattened against twig, with 2-scales;
    leaves often serrulate .... 1. *L. ligustrina*
Corolla and capsule more than 5 mm long; buds pointing outward from twig, with
    3 or more scales; leaves entire .... 2. *L. mariana*

    1. *L. ligustrína* (L.) DC. (resembling *Ligustrum*). Male-berry. Wooded swamps, shrub swamps, pond and stream margins, wet to dry woods and thickets. June-July. Fig. 780, Map 1787. [*Arsenococcus l.; Xolisma l.*]. Our plants are var. *ligustrina*. —FACW
    2. *L. mariána* (L.) D. Don (of Maryland). Stagger-bush. Open deciduous or pine woods in sandy soil. May-June. Map 1788. [*Neopieris m.*]. —FAC-

16. *Chamaedáphne* Moench. Leather-leaf (from the Greek, meaning ground-laurel).

Branched, evergreen shrub, young twigs puberulent and scurfy, older growth with shredding bark, finally becoming smooth, buds small, roundish, leaf scars small, crescent-shaped, bundle trace 1; leaves alternate, coriaceous and evergreen, short-petioled, oblong to elliptic, densely covered on one or both sides with brown lepidote scales, crenulate and often somewhat revolute-margined, the upper leaves becoming progressively smaller, the uppermost reduced to floral bracts; flowers white, in the axils of the reduced upper leaves, forming terminal and lateral, 1-sided, leafy racemes, sepals 5, closely subtended by a pair of bracteoles, corolla urceolate, 5-toothed, stamens 10, ovary superior, 5-locular; fruit a drepessed-globose, 5-valved, loculidical, many-seeded capsule. [*Cassandra*].

    1. *C. calyculáta* (L.) Moench (with an outer calyx). Bogs and pond margins. April-June. Fig. 781, Map 1789. (e. Asia). Represented with us by the following 2 vars.:
    var. *latifólia* (Ait.) Fern. Depressed to ascending, up to 6 dm tall; leaves about twice as long as wide; sepals obtuse, up to half as long as the corolla.
    var. *angustifólia* (Ait.) Rehd. Up to 1 m or more tall; leaves 2.5 to 4 times as long as wide, sepals acute, up to a third as long as the corolla. —OBL

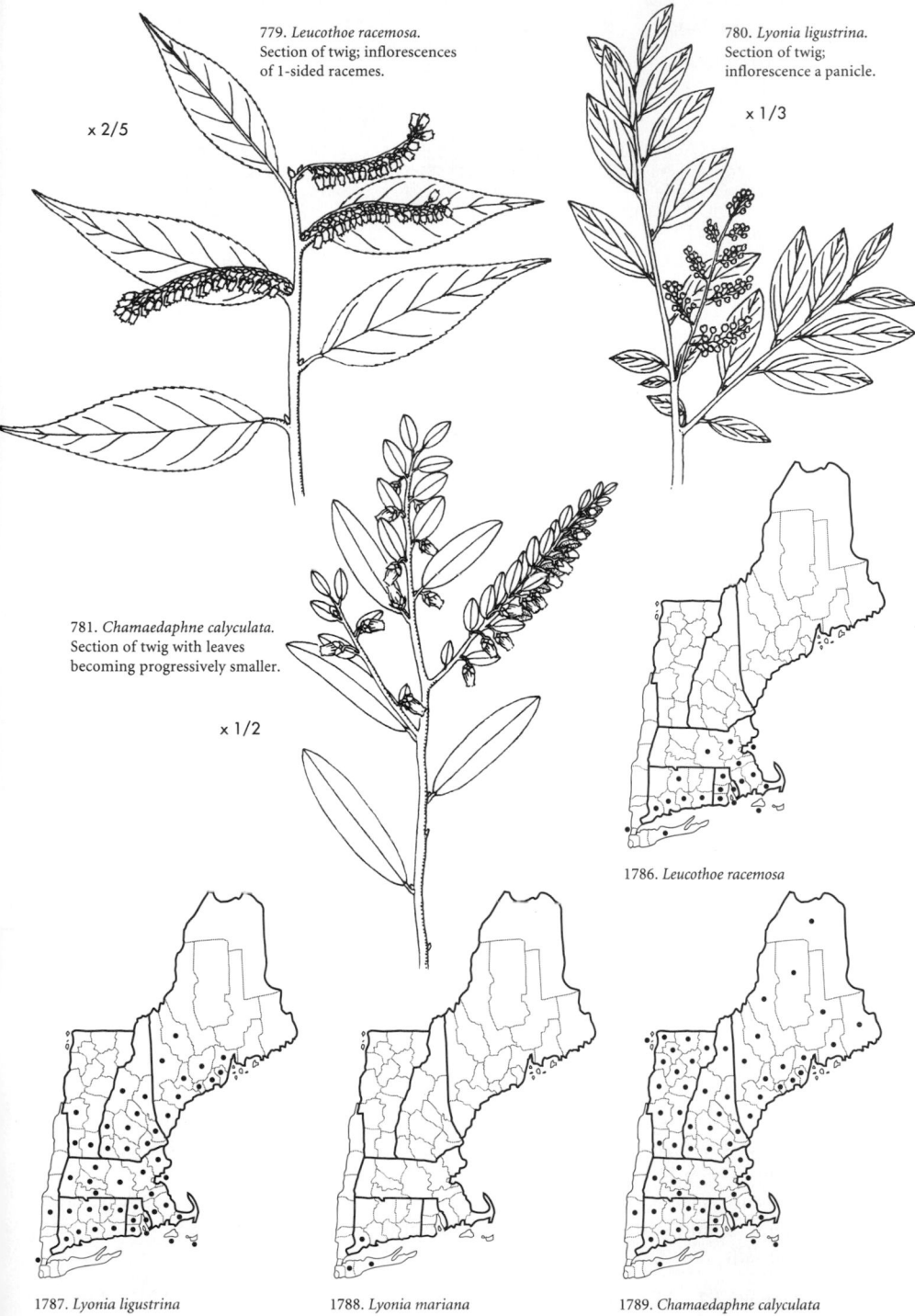

779. *Leucothoe racemosa.*
Section of twig; inflorescences
of 1-sided racemes.

× 2/5

780. *Lyonia ligustrina.*
Section of twig;
inflorescence a panicle.

× 1/3

781. *Chamaedaphne calyculata.*
Section of twig with leaves
becoming progressively smaller.

× 1/2

1786. *Leucothoe racemosa*

1787. *Lyonia ligustrina*

1788. *Lyonia mariana*

1789. *Chamaedaphne calyculata*

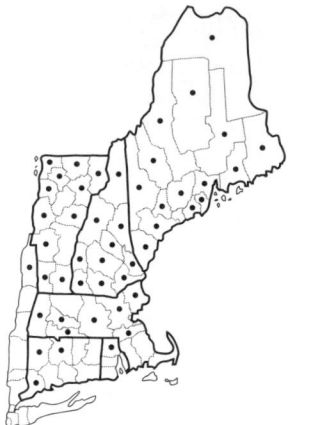

x 1

1790. *Andromeda polifolia*
var. *glaucophylla*

782. *Diapensia lapponica*. General
habit; densely imbricated leaves,
flowers solitary on long peduncles.

1791. *Diapensia lapponica*

17. *Andrómeda* L. Bog-rosemary (name based on Greek mythology).

Low, evergreen shrubs with an elongate, creeping base, twigs slender, pith small, buds small, roundish, leaf scars small, crescent-shaped, bundle trace 1; leaves alternate, coriaceous and evergreen, short-petioled, linear to narrowly oblong, revolute, whitened beneath with close, minute puberulence; flowers white to pink, in terminal and lateral, bracteate umbels, sepals 5, corolla 5-toothed, urceolate, stamens 10, ovary superior, 5-locular; fruit a subglobose, 5-valved, loculicidal, many-seeded capsule.

   1. *A. polifólia* L. Bogs. May-June. Map 1790. Endangered in CT, RI. Represented with us as var. *glaucophlla* (Link) DC.[*A. glaucophylla*]. Poisonous —OBL

Family 158. Diapensiaceae (Diapensia Family)

1. *Diapénsia* L. (ancient name for another plant).

Hermaphrodite, evergreen shrubs, branched and matted, forming dense, convex, cushion-like tussocks; leaves simple, coriaceous and evergreen, sessile and entire, narrowly spatulate, densely crowded and imbricated, the lower, older sections of stems densely covered by the persistent leaf remnants; flowers perfect, regular, white, solitary on a terminal peduncle, closely subtended by 3 bracts, calyx deeply 5-lobed, corolla campanulate, 5-lobed, deciduous, stamens 5, adnate to the corolla up to the sinuses, ovary superior, 3-locular, style 1, ovules many; fruit a 3-valved, loculicidal capsule.

   Pyxidánthera Michx. *barbátula* Michx. Flowering Moss. Flowers numerous, sessile on short leafy branches (flowers few, on peduncles in *Diapensia*). Southern. Endangered in NY; Reported for Suffolk County. —FACU-

   Gálax Sims *urceoláta* (Poir.) Brummitt. An evergreen herb with long petioled basal leaves and a scapose raceme. Southern. Rarely escaped from cultivation in our range. Reported for Essex County MA. [*G. aphylla*].

   1. *D. lappónica* L. (of Lapland). Alpine barrens. June-July. Fig. 782, Map 1791. (Eurasia). Endangered in VT. Our plants are var. *lapponica*.

Family 159. Primuláceae (Primrose Family)

Hermaphrodite, annual or perennial herbs. Leaves simple or rarely pinnately dissected (*Hottonia*), alternate, opposite, whorled or basal, entire or toothed, often glandular or farinose beneath, sessile or petioled, estipulate. Flowers perfect, regular, solitary, racemose, umbellate or corymbose, bracteate, calyx usually 5-parted, corolla usually 5-lobed (absent in *Glaux*), stamens usually 5, hypogynous or perigynous, ovary superior (half inferior in *Samolus*), 1-locular, style 1, ovules many. Fruit a many-seeded, 5-valved or circumscissile capsule.

a. Plants aquatic; leaves deeply pinnatifid into narrow, linear segments.(Fig. 783) .... 1. *Hottonia inflata*
a. Plants terrestrial or amphibious; leaves entire or toothed.
  b. Leaves all basal, toothed, rarely entire; inflorescence a bracteate umbel terminating
    a naked scape. (Fig. 784) .... 2. *Primula*
  b. Leaves cauline, basal leaves sometimes also present, entire or nearly so;
    inflorescence not as above.
    c. Leaves clustered in a single whorl at the top of the stem. (Fig. 785). .... 3. *Trientalis borealis*
    c. Leaves distributed throughout the stem.
      d. Leaves alternate.
        e. Flowers solitary in the leaf axils .... 4. *Anagallis*
        e. Flowers in terminal, often paniculate racemes.
          Pedicels with bracts at base; ovary superior. .... 5. *Lysimachia*
          Pedicels with bracts near middle; ovary half-inferior ... . 6. *Samolus valerandi*
                                                       subsp. *parviflorus*
      d. Leaves opposite or whorled.
        f. Flowers red, white or blue; stems 4-angled; capsule circumscissile. .... 4. *Anagallis*
        f. Flowers white, pink, or yellow (sometimes red in *Glaux*); stems round;
          capsule not circumscissile.
          Leaves fleshy; petals none; calyx white to red; saline or brackish. .... 7. *Glaux maritima*
          Leaves not fleshy; petals present, yellow, calyx green; fresh or terrestrial. 5. *Lysimachia*

1. *Hottónia* L. Featherfoil (for P. Hotton).

Aquatic herbs, stems submersed, spongy-thickened, rooting at the base; leaves deeply pinnatifid into narrow, linear segments, central lamina wide, numerous, crowded at the base of the peduncles; flowers small, white, whorled at the constricted nodes of an inflated, hollow, peduncled raceme, sessile or pedicelled, each flower subtended by an entire, foliaceous bract, the peduncles several in a cluster terminating the stem and branches, partly emersed, corolla salverform, stamens perigynous; capsule globose.

  1. *H. infláta* Ell. (inflated). Ponds, pools and ditches. May-June. Fig. 783, Map 1792. Rare. —OBL

2. *Prímula* L. Primrose (diminutive of *primus*, from the flowering of true primrose in spring).

Perennial, scapose herbs; leaves basal, oblanceolate to obovate, sessile or short-petioled, toothed, often white or yellowish-mealy beneath; flowers pink to purple and/or yellow, in an involucrate umbel terminating a naked scape, calyx and corolla tubular to campanulate, corolla lobes notched or 2-lobed, stamens perigynous; capsule ellipsoid to oblong.

  Andrósace L. *occidentális* Pursh. Differs from *Primula* in having the corolla tube equalling or exceeded by the calyx (corolla tube longer than calyx in *Primula*). Western. Rarely occurring in our range. Reported for Essex County MA.

  A. máxima L. A European waif, has been reported for Westchester County NY. Distinguishable from *A. occidentalis* by the toothed leaves (leaves entire to sparsely denticulate in *A. occidentalis*).

a. Calyx, umbel rays and scape densely pubescent. .... 1. *P. veris*
a. Calyx, umbel rays and scape glabrous or essentially so.
  Calyx and involucral bracts 5 mm or less long; leaves not or only slightly
    farinose beneath .... 2. *P. mistassinica*
  Calyx and involucral bracts more than 5 mm long; leaves farinose beneath. .... 3. *P. laurentiana*

1. P. véris L. (of spring). European Cowslip. Occasionally escaped from cultivation. Map 1793. Compresses made from the crushed plant are said to be useful in treating inflammation of the skin when applied externally; other medicinal uses are also cited.

2. P. mistássinica Michx. (of Lake Mistassini). Wet cliffs and ledges, gravelly river shores. May-June. Fig. 784, Map 1794. [*P. intercedens*]. —FACW

3. P. laurentiána Fern. (of the Gulf and St. Lawrence River). Ledges, cliffs, lake and sea-shores. June-July. Map 1795. —FAC

P. anisódora Balf. f. & Forrest. Differing from the above 3 species in having odor of anise and scape bearing several superimposed umbels. Asian. Rarely escaped from cultivation. Reported for Berkshire County MA.

3. Trientális L. Starflower (Latin name, referring to the height of the plant).

Low, perennial herbs from a slender rhizome, stems simple, erect; leaves clustered in a single whorl at the top of the stem, sessile or short-petioled, somewhat unequal, lanceolate, acuminate, undulate and crenulate-margined, 1-several minute, scattered, scale-like leaves usually also present on the stem below; flowers white, solitary or few on long slender pedicels from the axils of the whorled leaves, usually 7-merous, lobes of the calyx and corolla nearly separate, corolla rotate, the filaments of the 7 stamens united in a ring at the base of the corolla; capsule globose.

1. T. boreális Raf. (northern). Dry to moist, coniferous or deciduous woods. May-June. Fig. 785, Map 1796. [*T. americana*]. Our plants are subsp. *borealis*. —FAC

4. Anagállis L. Pimpernel (ancient Greek name, referring to its habit of closing its flowers in cloudy weather).

Diffuse, usually much-branched annual herbs from a slender tap root, the stem terete or 4-angled; leaves opposite or alternate, sessile or subsessile, elliptic to ovate or obovate, entire; flowers scarlet to white, pink or blue, solitary on long pedicels or sessile in the leaf axils, corolla rotate or campanulate, its lobes crenulate and minutely glandular to entire, stamens perigynous; capsule globose or subglobose, circumscissile, often covered by the marcescent corolla.

Leaves opposite .... 1. *A. arvensis*
Leaves alternate .... 2. *A. minima*

1. A. arvénsis L. (of cultivated fields). Scarlet Pimpernel. Dry fields, waste places and roadsides. June-August. Map 1797. (Naturalized from Europe). Poisonous.

A. foémina Mill. Blue pimpernel. Flowers blue, pedicels usually shorter than the leaves (flowers scarlet or rarely white and pedicels usually longer than the leaves in *A. arvensis*). (Europe). Reported for ME, VT. [*A. arvensis* var. *caerulea; A. caerulea*].

2. A. mímina (L.) Krause (smallest). Damp sand and mud. Sporadic, from outside the northeast. [*Centunculus minimus*]. —FACW

5. Lysimáchia L. Loosestrife (name based on Greek mythology).

Erect or trailing perennial herbs; leaves opposite or whorled, rarely alternate, entire, often glandular-punctate; flowers yellow or rarely white, often marked with dots or lines, solitary in the leaf axils or in axillary or terminal racemes or panicles, corolla campanulate to rotate, stamens perigynous, distinct or united at the base, staminodes 5 or absent; capsule ovoid to globose. [*Naumbergia; Steironema*].

L. clethroídes Duby. Differing from all other species in our range in having alternate leaves and white flowers. Native to China and Japan. Rarely escaped from cultivation in our range. Reported for Hartford County CT, Androscoggin County ME, Suffolk County NY.

a. Flowers in short, peduncled racemes from the lower and middle leaf axils.
(Fig. 786) .... 1. *L. thyrsiflora*
a. Flowers not in racemes or racemes terminating leafy branches.
  b. Flowers in terminal racemes or panicles; subtending bracts much smaller than
      the stem leaves (lower flowers in axils of stem leaves in *L. x producta*).
      (Fig. 787).
    c. Inflorescence paniculate; corolla not dotted or streaked.
        Calyx lobes 6 mm or more long; corolla lobes glandular-ciliolate. .... 2. *L. punctata*
        Calyx lobes 5 mm or less long; corolla lobes entire. .... 3. *L. vulgaris*
    c. Inflorescence racemose or mostly so; corolla dark-dotted or streaked.
        Flowers (except sometimes for the very lowest) all in the axils of reduced
          bracts .... 4. *L. terrestris*
        Lower flowers in the axils of the upper stem leaves. .... 5. *L. x producta*
  b. Flowers axillary or terminal, not racemose or paniculate; subtending leaves not
      bract-like but resembling those of the stem. (Fig. 788).
    d. Plant trailing, rooting at the nodes; leaves broadly ovate to orbicular. .... 6. *L. nummularia*
    d. Plant erect, not rooting at the nodes; leaves longer than wide.
      e. Principal leaves whorled or stems densely pubescent.
          Stems densely pubescent; corolla not dotted or streaked. .... 2. *L. punctata*
          Stems glabrous or sparsely hairy; corolla dark-dotted or streaked. .... 7. *L. quadrifolia*
      e. Principal leaves opposite; stems glabrous or essentially so.
        f. Leaves ovate to broadly lanceolate, rounded to subcordate at base. .... 8. *L. ciliata*
        f. Leaves linear to lanceolate or narrowly oblong, gradually narrowed
            to base.
            Plants from long, slender rhizomes; leaves ciliate at base. .... 9. *L. lanceolata*
            Plants from short, stout rhizomes; leaves not ciliate at base. .... 10. *L. hybrida*

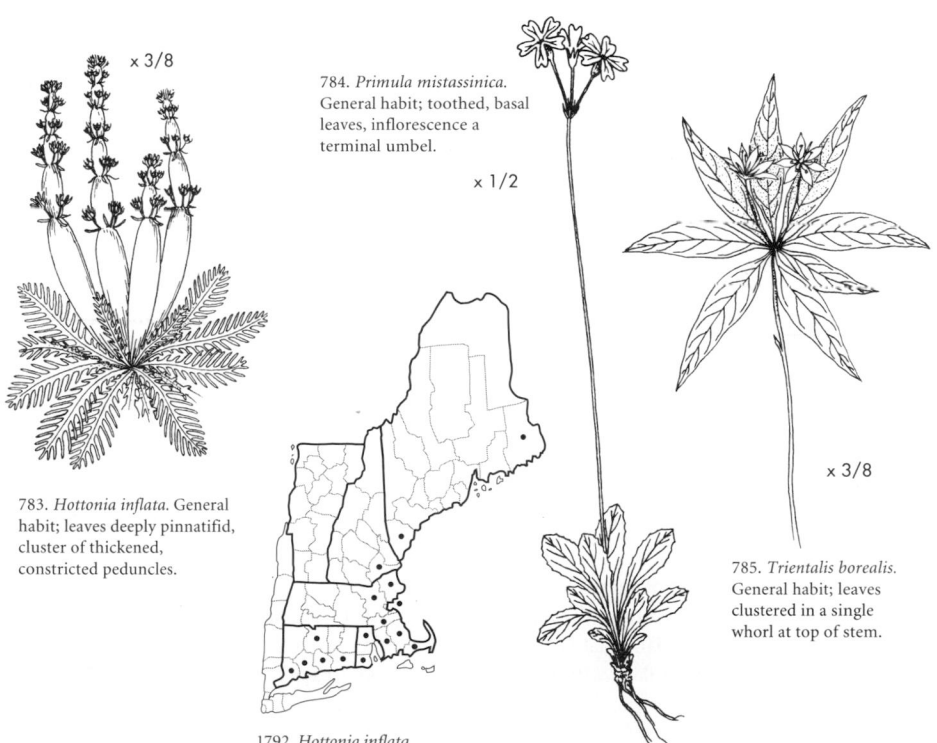

x 3/8

784. *Primula mistassinica.*
General habit; toothed, basal
leaves, inflorescence a
terminal umbel.

x 1/2

783. *Hottonia inflata.* General
habit; leaves deeply pinnatifid,
cluster of thickened,
constricted peduncles.

x 3/8

785. *Trientalis borealis.*
General habit; leaves
clustered in a single
whorl at top of stem.

1792. *Hottonia inflata*

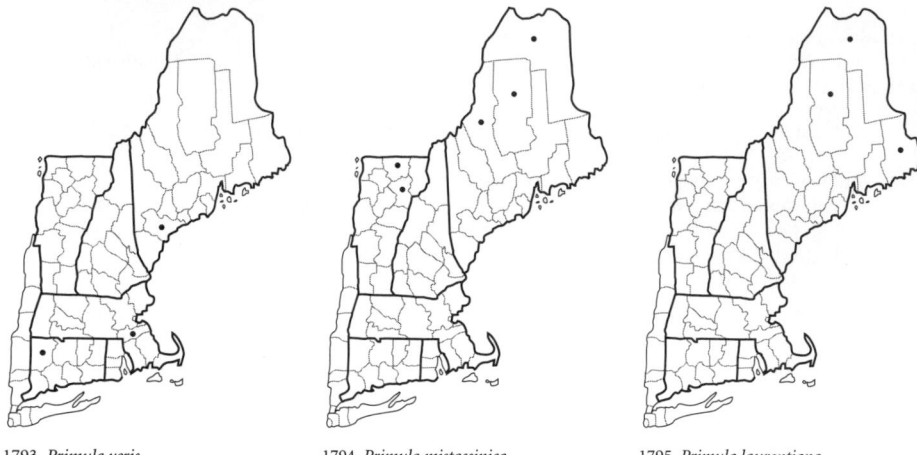

1793. *Primula veris*　　　1794. *Primula mistassinica*　　　1795. *Primula laurentiana*

1. L. thyrsiflóra L. (flowers in a thyrse). Bogs and wooded swamps. May-July. Fig. 786, Map 1798. (Eurasia). [*Naumbergia t.*]. —OBL

2. L. punctáta L. (dotted). Waste places, roadsides, old cellar holes. June-July. Map 1799. (Naturalized from Europe). —OBL

3. L. vulgáris L. (common). Roadsides, waste places, riverbanks. July-August. Fig. 787, Map 1800. (Naturalized from Europe). —FAC

4. L. terréstris (L.) B.S.P. (terrestrial). Swamp-candles. Marshes, wet meadows, pond margins. June-August. Map 1801. —OBL

L. x commíxta Fern. A hybrid between *L. thyrsiflora* and *L. terrestris*.

5. L. x prodúcta (Gray) Fern. (elongated). Woodlands, roadsides, waste places, wet or dry meadows. June-August. Map 1802. A hybrid between *L. terrestris* and *L. quadrifolia*.

6. L. nummulária L. (coin-like). Moneywort. Wet meadows, stream margins, damp roadsides. June-July. Map 1803. (Naturalized from Europe). —OBL

7. L. quadrifólia L. (four-leaved). Whorled loosestrife. Woodlands, clearings, roadsides and waste places. June-July. Map 1804. [*Steironema q.*]. —FACU-

8. L. ciliáta L. (with marginal hairs). Wet woods, thickets and meadows, stream margins. July-August. Fig. 788, Map 1805. [*Steironema c.*]. —FACW

9. L. lanceoláta Walt. (lance-shaped). Open woods, thickets, pond margins. June-July. Reported for Fairfield County CT; Waldo County ME. [*Steironema l.; S. heterophyllum*]. —FAC

10. L. hýbrida Michx. (hybrid, a misnomer). Wet woods, stream margins. July-August. Map 1806. [*Steironema h.*]. —OBL

6. Samólus L. Water-pimpernel (ancient name referring to value in treating diseases of livestock).

Slender, branched, perennial herbs; leaves alternate and often in a basal rosette, entire, obovate to spatulate, attenuate or cuneate at the base, petioled or sessile, the basal often larger; flowers small, white, in terminal, often paniculate racemes, on long, slender pedicels, each bracteolate midway, corolla somewhat campanulate, with 5 scale-like staminodia, each in a sinus of the corolla, stamens perigynous, ovary half inferior; capsule globose.

1. S. valerándi L. Fresh to brackish pond and stream margins, ditches. May-September. Map 1807. (Tropical Amer.). [*S. floribundus; S. parviflorus*]. Represented with us as subsp. *parviflórus* (Raf.) Hulten. —OBL

7. Glaúx L. Sea-milkwort (ancient Greek name meaning sea-green).

Small, fleshy, diffusely branched and often prostrate, or erect and simple, perennial, rhizomatous herbs; leaves fleshy, opposite, linear to oblong, sessile, entire; flowers white to red, solitary and subsessile in the leaf axils, calyx campanulate, petaloid, corolla none, stamens hypogynous; capsule globose to ovoid.

1. G. marítima L. (of the sea). Salt marshes, saline or brackish shores, sea beaches. June-July. Fig. 789, Map 1808. (Eurasia). Our plants include subsp. *maritima* and the following subsp.:

subsp. *obtusifólia* Fern. Leaves less than 3 times as long as wide; capsule 2.5 mm or more broad (leaves more than 3 times as long as wide and capsule 2.5 mm or less broad in subsp. *maritima*). —OBL

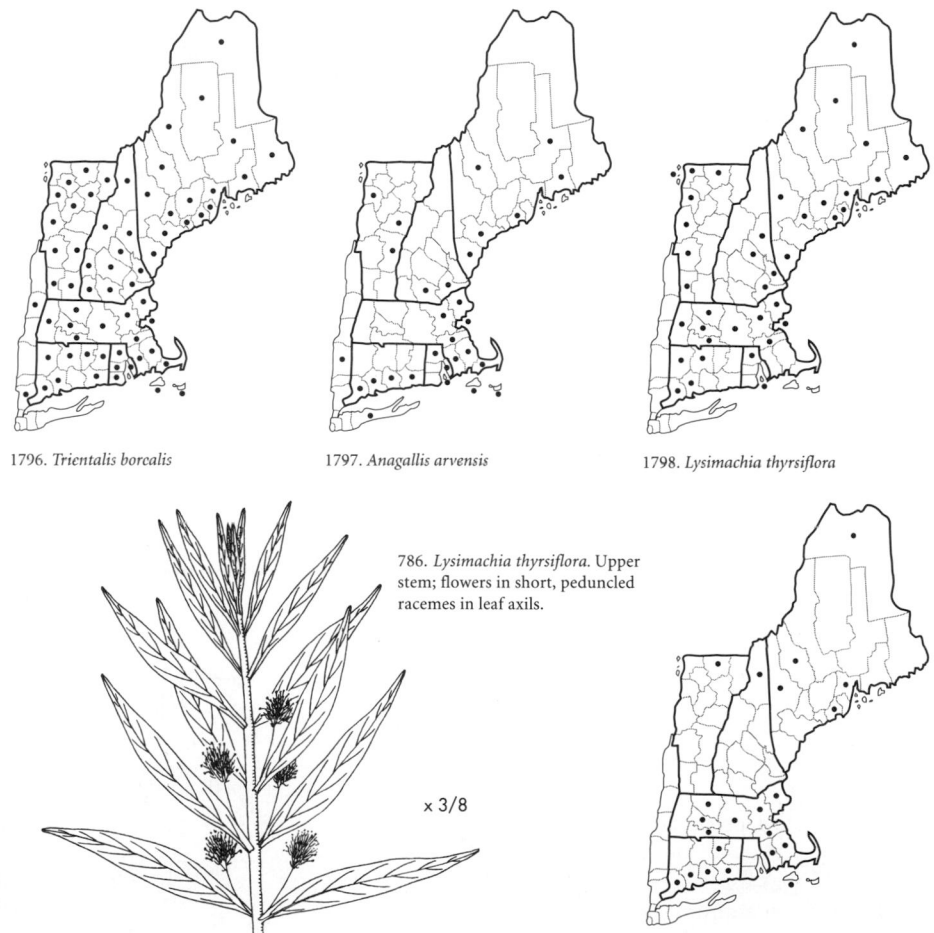

1796. *Trientalis borealis*

1797. *Anagallis arvensis*

1798. *Lysimachia thyrsiflora*

786. *Lysimachia thyrsiflora.* Upper stem; flowers in short, peduncled racemes in leaf axils.

× 3/8

1799. *Lysimachia punctata*

787. *Lysimachia vulgaris*. Upper stem;
flowers in a terminal panicle.

x 1/4

x 1/4

788. *Lysimachia ciliata*. Upper stem; flowers solitary in
leaf axils and terminating axillary branches.

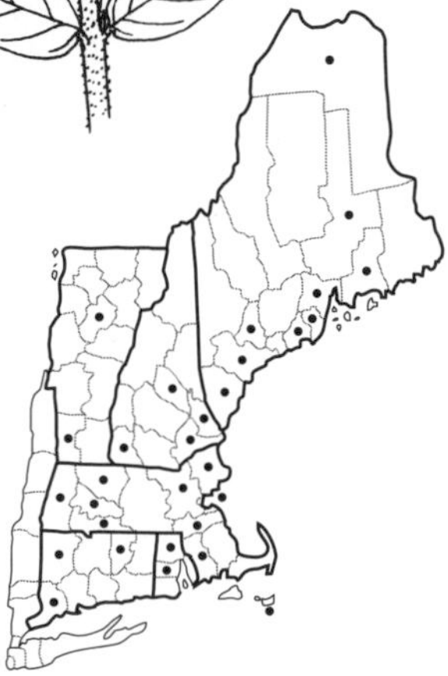

1800. *Lysimachia vulgaris*

1801. *Lysimachia terrestris*

1802. *Lysimachia x producta*

1803. *Lysimachia nummularia*

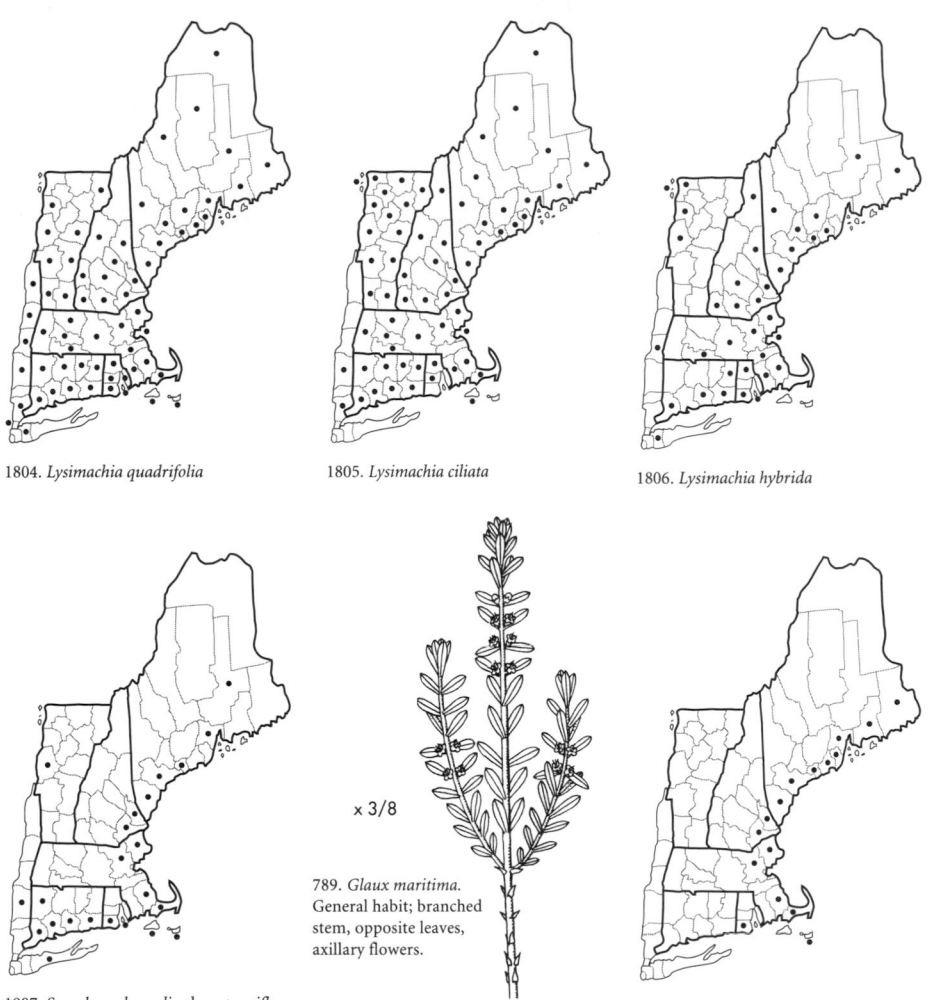

1804. *Lysimachia quadrifolia*

1805. *Lysimachia ciliata*

1806. *Lysimachia hybrida*

x 3/8

789. *Glaux maritima.*
General habit; branched
stem, opposite leaves,
axillary flowers.

1807. *Samolus valerandi* subsp. *parviflorus*

1808. *Glaux maritima*

Family 160. Plumbagináceae (Leadwort Family)

1. Limónium P. Mill. Sea-lavender (ancient Greek name).

Hermaphrodite, scapose, perennial herbs from a thick woody root. Leaves simple, basal, fleshy, oblong to obovate or oblanceolate, entire to undulate or crenulate, mucronate, the base attenuate to a petiole. Flower perfect, regular, minute, 1-3 at a node, surrounded at the base by 2-3 bracteoles forming loose, 1-sided spikes in a large, diffusely branched, bracteate panicle, calyx white, tubular, 5-toothed, often with a minute tooth in each sinus, petals 5, purple, clawed, stamens 5, attached to the petals at the bases, ovary superior, 1-locular, styles 5, ovule 1. Fruit a 1-seeded utricle enclosed by the calyx.

    1. *L. caroliniánum* (Walt.) Britt. (of Carolina). Salt marshes. July-September. Fig. 790, Map 1809. [*L. nashii*]. —OBL

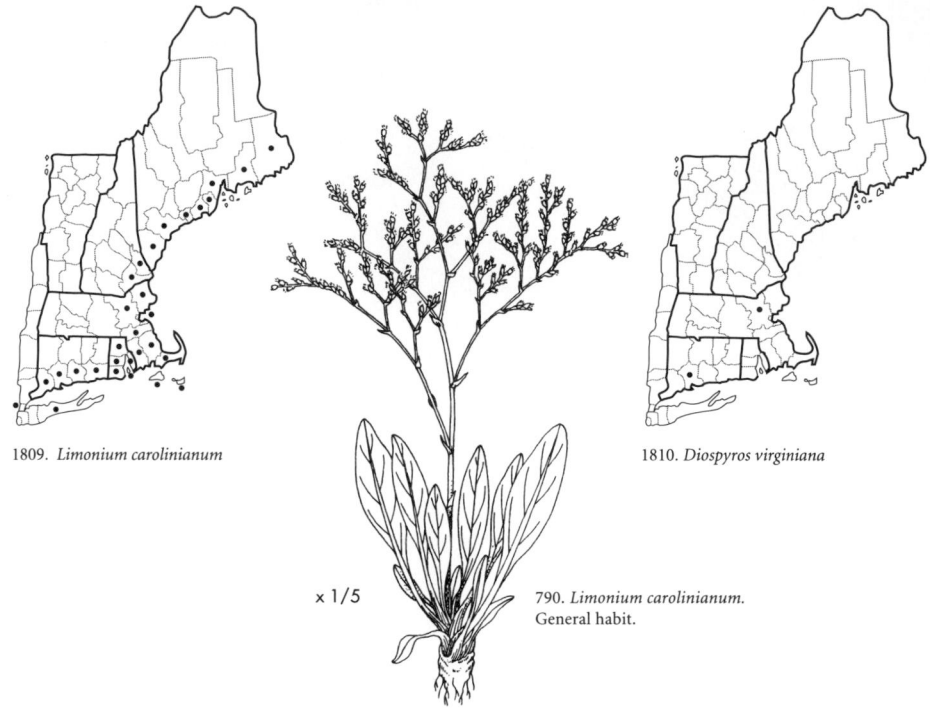

1809. *Limonium carolinianum*

× 1/5

790. *Limonium carolinianum.*
General habit.

1810. *Diospyros virginiana*

Family 161. Ebenáceae (Ebony Family)

1. Diospýros L. Persimmon (Greek name).

Dioecious trees, twigs moderate, with conspicuous lenticels, pith moderate, greenish to white, often chambered, buds small, ovoid, with 2-3 scales, leaf scars broadly crescent-shaped, bundle scar 1, stipule scars and end bud lacking. Leaves simple, alternate, ovate to oblong, entire, petioled, estipulate. Flowers imperfect, regular, yellowish, axillary, the pistillate usually solitary, the staminate 1-several, smaller than the pistillate, calyx and corolla usually 4-lobed, stamens 16 in the staminate flowers, perigynous, the pistillate with 8 staminodes, ovary superior, usually 8-locular, styles 4. Fruit a pulpy, yellowish, 3-8 seeded berry, surrounded at the base by the persistent calyx. —Wildl. 1

1. D. virginiána L. (Virginian). Woodlands and abandoned fields. May-June. Map 1810. From farther south. Fruit edible; bark and unripe fruit have astringent qualities useful for various medicinal purposes such as treating unfirm skin, diarrhea and sore throat. —FAC-

Family 162. Styracáceae (Storax Family)

1. Halésia Ellis ex L. Silverbell-tree (for S. Hales).

Hermaphrodite, shrubs or small trees. Leaves alternate, deciduous, simple, serrulate. Flowers perfect, regular, in lateral clusters, white, calyx 4-toothed, corolla campanulate, 4-lobed, stamens 8-16, ovary inferior, 4-locular, with 4 ovules per locule, style 1. Fruit a dry, 4-winged drupe.

1. H. carolína L. Southern. A waif in our range. Reported from Kent County RI. [*H. tetraptera*]. —FACU

Family 163. Oleáceae (Olive Family)

Dioecious, monoecious, polygamous or hermaphrodite trees or shrubs. Leaves simple or ternately or pinnately compound, opposite, toothed or entire, estipulate. Flowers perfect or imperfect, regular, in lateral or terminal fascicles, racemes or panicles, calyx entire or 4-toothed or lobed, corolla 4-lobed, 4-petalous or none, stamens usually 2, ovary superior, 2-locular, usually 4-ovulate, style 1. Fruit a samara, capsule or drupe.

a. Leaves pinnately compound; flowers imperfect, corolla none; fruit a samara.
(Fig. 791) .... 1. *Fraxinus*
a. Leaves simple (3-lobed or with 3 leaflets in *Forsythia*); flowers perfect, corolla present; fruit a capsule or drupe.
  b. Flowers in lateral fascicles, or rarely panicles, appearing before the leaves; leaves simple to 3-lobed or with 3 leaflets .... 2. *Forsythia*
  b. Flowers in terminal panicles, appearing with or after the leaves; leaves simple.
    Leaves rounded to truncate or cordate at base; petioles mostly 1 cm or more long; twigs glabrous; fruit a capsule .... 3. *Syringa*
    Leaves rounded to cuneate at base; petioles mostly 6 mm or less long; twigs usually puberulent; fruit a drupe .... 4. *Ligustrum*

1. *Fráxinus* L. Ash (classical Latin name).

Dioecious, monoecious, or polygamous trees, twigs stout, pith moderate, white, buds broad and stout, the terminal usually conspicuously larger than the lateral, with 4-6 scales, leaf scars broadly U-shaped to crescent-shaped or vertically elliptical, bundle traces numerous, in an elliptical or U-shaped aggregate, stipule scars lacking; leaves pinnately compound, petioled, leaflets entire to undulate or serrate; flowers perfect or imperfect, in axillary fascicles, racemes or panicles, calyx small, 4-toothed or absent, corolla none; fruit a 1-seeded samara. Inner bark has been long used as a cathartic and diuretic; chewed bark is also used as a dressing for sores. —Wildl. 2

a. Upper margin of leaf scars deeply concave or notched; wing of samara decurrent a third or less the body length. .... 1. *F. americana*
a. Upper margin of leaf scars convex or truncate (concave in *F. profunda* with twigs and petioles pubescent; these glabrous in *F. americana*); wing of samara decurrent half or more the body length.
  b. Leaflets sessile; samara winged to base; buds blue-black.
    Leaf rachis tomentose at base of leaflets; largest leaflets mostly 10 cm or more long and/or 3 cm or more wide .... 2. *F. nigra*
    Leaf rachis glabrous to puberulent; largest leaflets mostly less than 10 cm long and 3 cm wide .... 3. *F. excelsior*
  b. Leaflets petioluled; samara not winged to base; buds brown. (Fig. 791).
    Leaflets, at least the lower, wing-petioluled; samara wing usually less than 7 mm wide .... 4. *F. pennsylvanica*
    Leaflets not wing-petioluled; samara wing usually 7 mm or more wide. .... 5. *F. profunda*

1. *F. americána* L. (American). White Ash. Rich, often moist woods, pond and stream margins, bottomlands. Fruit: June-September. Map 1811. —FACU

2. *F. nígra* Marsh. (black). Black Ash. Wooded swamps, wet woods, pond and stream margins, bottomlands. Fruit: July-September. Map 1812. —FACW

3. *F. excélsior* L. (taller). European Ash. Rarely escaped from cultivation to roadsides. Map 1813. (Eurasia).

4. *F. pennsylvánica* Marsh. (of Pennsylvania). Moist to wet woods, wooded swamps, pond and stream margins, bottomlands. Fruit: July-September. Fig. 791, Map 1814. [*F. campestris*]. Typical *F. pennsylvanica*, with densely pubescent twigs, lower leaf surfaces and inflorescence is called Red Ash, and glabrous plants, distinguished as var. *subintegerrima* (Vahl) Fern. are called Green Ash. [*F. lanceolata*]. The distinction is doubtful. —FACW

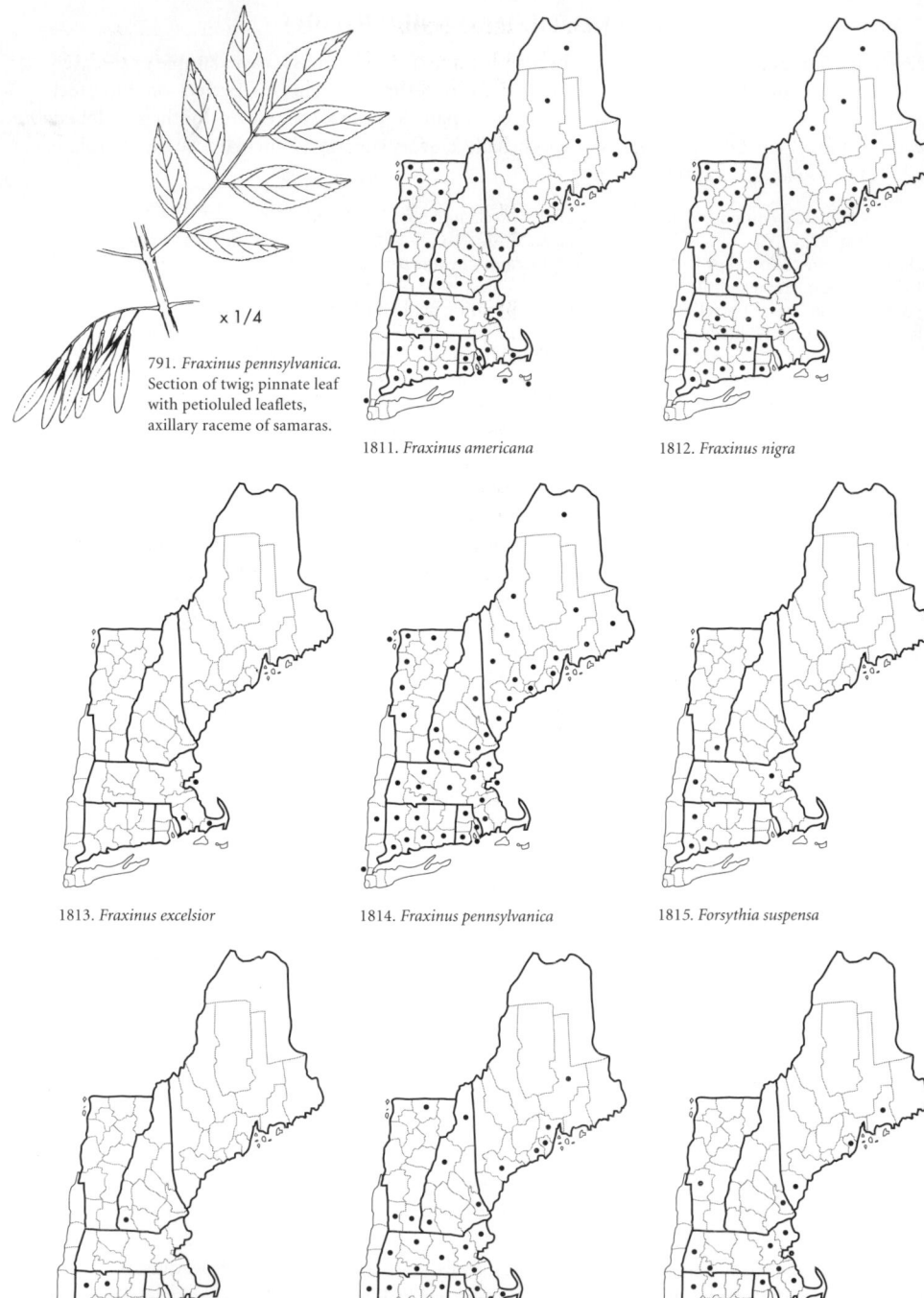

× 1/4

791. *Fraxinus pennsylvanica.*
Section of twig; pinnate leaf
with petioluled leaflets,
axillary raceme of samaras.

1811. *Fraxinus americana*

1812. *Fraxinus nigra*

1813. *Fraxinus excelsior*

1814. *Fraxinus pennsylvanica*

1815. *Forsythia suspensa*

1816. *Forsythia virridissima*

1817. *Syringa vulgaris*

1818. *Ligustrum vulgare*

5. *F. profúnda* (Bush) Bush. Pumpkin Ash. Wooded swamps and wet woods, bottomlands. Fruit: June-September. From farther west and south. Reported for Bronx County NY. [*F. michauxiii; F. tomentosa*]. —OBL

2. *Forsýthia* Vahl. Golden bell (for W. Forsyth).

Hermaphrodite, loosely branched shrubs, twigs somewhat 4-sided, with conspicuous lenticels, pith moderate, chambered, or twigs hollow between the nodes, buds cylindrical, pointed, often collateral or multiple, with numerous scales, the flower buds larger than the vegetative, leaf scars shield-shaped, raised, bundle trace 1, stipule scars lacking; leaves simple and entire or toothed, 3-lobed, or divided into 3 leaflets, petioled; flowers perfect, showy, yellow, appearing before the leaves, in lateral fascicles, calyx and corolla deeply 4-lobed; fruit a many-seeded capsule.

Chionánthus L. *virgínicus* L. Fringe-tree. Similar to *Forsythia* but differs in having numerous white flowers in large drooping panicles. From farther south. Spread from cultivation. Reported for Middlesex County MA. Bark of the roots and trunk is used as an astringent, diuretic, and in treating various skin irritations. —FAC+

Several species of Forsythia occasionally escape from cultivation to roadsides and persist around abandoned dwellings; in our area the species that occur include *F. suspénsa* (Thunb.) Vahl with branches hollow except at the nodes, Map 1815, *F. virridíssima* Lindl. Map 1816, with chambered pith and narrowly oblong to lanceolate leaves (this and the latter species both introduced from China), and *F. ováta* Nakai, similar to *F. virridissima* but with ovate leaves (from Korea). Reported for MA, ME, RI. Fuller treatment should be sought in works on cultivated plants.

3. *Syrínga* L. Lilac (Greek name meaning pipe, originally applied to *Philadelphus*, from use of its branches for pipes).

Hermaphrodite, much branched shrubs, twigs usually lined or finely ridged, pith moderate, white, buds usually solitary, ovoid, with several pairs of scales, leaf scars crescent-shaped, raised, bundle trace a transverse line, stipule scars and usually the end bud lacking; leaves ovate, acuminate, rounded to truncate or cordate at base, entire, petioled; flowers perfect, purple or lavender to white, in terminal panicles, calyx 4-toothed, corolla salverform, 4-lobed; fruit a 4-seeded capsule.

1. *S. vulgáris* L. (common). Occasionally escaped from cultivation to roadsides and around abandoned dwellings and fields. May-June. Map 1817. (Introduced from Asia).

S. x pérsica L. A hybrid between *S. afighanica* and *S. lacinata* differing from *S. vulgaris* in having lanceolate leaves attenuate to the base (leaves are ovate and truncate to subcordate at base in *S. vulgaris*). Rarely escaped from cultivation. Reported for MA.

4. *Ligústrum* L. Privet (classical name of *L. vulgare*).

Hermaphrodite, much branched shrubs, twigs usually lined or finely ridged, pith moderate, white, buds small, usually solitary, ovoid, with several pairs of scales, leaf scars crescent-shaped to half round, raised, bundle trace 1, transverse, stipule scars lacking; leaves lance-ovate to elliptic, entire, short-petioled, tardily deciduous; flowers perfect, white, in small panicles terminating the main stem and branches, calyx truncate or obscurely 4-lobed, corolla salverform, 4-lobed; fruit a small, black drupe.

Twigs minutely puberulent to glabrescent. .... 1. *L. vulgare*
Twigs densely pilose .... 2. *L. obtusifolium*

1. *L. vulgáre* L. (common). Escaped from cultivation to roadsides, around old buildings, thickets, open woods. June-July. Map 1818. (Naturalized from Europe). Poisonous if taken internally; reported to be of value in treating skin conditions when preparations are applied externally. —FACU

L. ovalifólium Hassk. California Privet. Differs from *L. vulgare* in having a corolla tube 4 mm or more long (tube less than 4 mm long in *L. vulgare*). (Naturalized from Japan). Rarely spread from cultivation in our range. Reported for Fairfield County CT, Franklin County MA.

2. *L. obtusifólium* Sieb. & Zucc. (blunt-leaved). Escaped from cultivation to roadsides, open woods. June-July. Map 1819. (Naturalized from Japan).

L. sinénse Lour. Differs from *L. obtusifolium* in having a corolla tube less than 4 mm long (tube 4 mm or more long in *L. obtusifolium*). Occasionally escaped from cultivation in our range. (From Asia). Reported for Middlesex County CT; Hampshire, Middlesex, and Plymouth Counties MA; Newport County RI. —FACU

L. amurénse Carr. Corolla tube 4 mm or more long and calyx mostly glabrous (pubescent over the entire surface in *L. obtusifolium*). (From Asia). Rarely escaped from cultivation. Reported for Knox County ME.

Family 164. Buddlejáceae (Buddleia Family) [*Loganiaceae*]

Represented with us by the 2 genera described below.

1. *Polyprémum* L. (from the Greek, meaning many-stemmed).

Hermaphrodite, diffusely branched, annual herbs. Leaves simple, opposite, narrowly linear, minutely serrulate, connected at base by a stipular membrane. Flowers perfect, regular, small, white, sessile, in terminal, dichotomous, leafy cymes, calyx of 4 subulate sepals, scarious-margined below, corolla 4-lobed, rotate, bearded in the throat, stamens 4, perigynous, ovary superior, 2-locular, style 1. Fruit an ovoid, 2-valved, loculicidal, many-seeded capsule.

1. *P. procúmbens* L. (prostrate). Dry, sandy fields, roadsides, waste places. June-September. Fig. 792. (Tropical Amer.). From farther south and west. Reported for Suffolk County NY.

Buddléia L. *dávidi* Franch. A shrub with lanceolate, serrate leaves tomentose beneath, and lilac orange-throated flowers in slender panicles. (China); occasionally escaped from cultivation in our range. Reported for Fairfield and New Haven Counties CT, Nantucket County MA, Westchester and Suffolk Counties NY.

Family 165. Menyantháceae

Similar to *Gentianaceae* (Family 166) except plant aquatic with floating, cordate leaves and flowers umbellate, often apparently borne on the petiole beneath the blade, or not aquatic and with trifoliate leaves.

Plant aquatic; leaves floating, cordate; flowers umbellate, often apparently borne on
the petiole below the blade. (Fig. 793). .... 1. *Nymphoides*
Plant not aquatic; leaves trifoliate, not floating or cordate; flowers not borne as
above. (Fig. 794) .... 2. *Menyanthes trifoliata*

1. *Nymphoídes* Hill. Floating heart (being similar in appearance to *Nymphaea*).

Aquatic, perennial herbs from slender rhizomes, stems filiform to moderately slender, bearing at the summit one or more short to long-petioled floating leaves; leaf blades ovate to orbicular, cordate; flowers white to yellow, umbellate at the summit of the stems at the base of the petioles (often apparently borne on the petiole below the blade); often accompanied by a cluster of long, thick or slender tubers, calyx and corolla deeply 5-parted nearly to the base, stamens 5; capsule ellipsoid. —OBL

a. Fertile stem with a pair of opposite leaves at the summit, subtending the umbel,
    often extending beyond it and producing one or more additional umbels;
    calyx more than 8 mm long; flowers yellow. .... 1. *N. peltata*
a. Fertile stem with a single leaf at the summit at the base of the umbel, not
    extending beyond it; calyx 8 mm or less long; flowers white to cream colored.
    (Fig. 793).
   Calyx lobes streaked or spotted with purple, more than 3.5 mm long at anthesis;
        leaves entirely green above; capsule 6 mm or more long. .... 2. *N. aquatica*
   Calyx lobes entirely green, 3.5 mm or less long at anthesis; leaves usually mottled
        green and purple above; capsule 5 mm or less long. .... 3. *N. cordata*

   1. *N. peltáta* (Gmel.) Kuntze (shield-shaped). Quiet waters. June-September. Map 1820. (Introduced from Europe).
   2. *N. aquática* (Gmel.) Kuntze (aquatic). Quiet waters. July-September. From farther south and
west. Reported for southern NY. [*N. lacunosa*].
   3. *N. cordáta* (Ell.) Fern. (heart-shaped). Quiet waters. July-September. Fig. 793, Map 1821. [*N. lacunosa*].

2. *Menyánthes* L. Buckbean (ancient Greek name, based on progressive expansion of
the flowers in the raceme).
Perennial herbs with a thick, creeping rhizome, the older portion covered with the scars or petiole
bases of former leaves; leaves alternate, often crowded toward the end of the rhizome, with long
petioles sheathing the rhizome, trifoliate, leaflets sessile, oblong to ovate or obovate, entire; flowers
white to pinkish, in a bracteate raceme terminating a naked scape arising from the rhizome near or
among the leaves, calyx 5-lobed, corolla 5-lobed, white-bearded inside, stamens 5, capsule ovoid,
rupturing irregularly.

   1. *M. trifoliáta* L. (three-leaved). Bogs, pond margins. May-June. Fig. 794, Map 1822. Has been
used commercially as a substitute for hops in beer making and as a flavoring for various alcoholic
drinks; preparations made from the dried leaves were used as herbal tonics in the past. —OBL

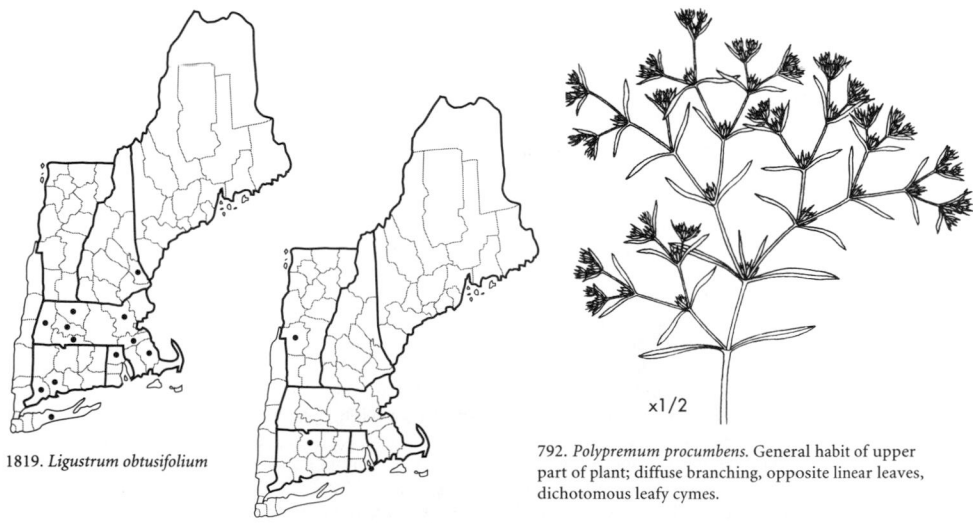

1819. *Ligustrum obtusifolium*

1820. *Nymphoides peltata*

x1/2

792. *Polypremum procumbens*. General habit of upper
part of plant; diffuse branching, opposite linear leaves,
dichotomous leafy cymes.

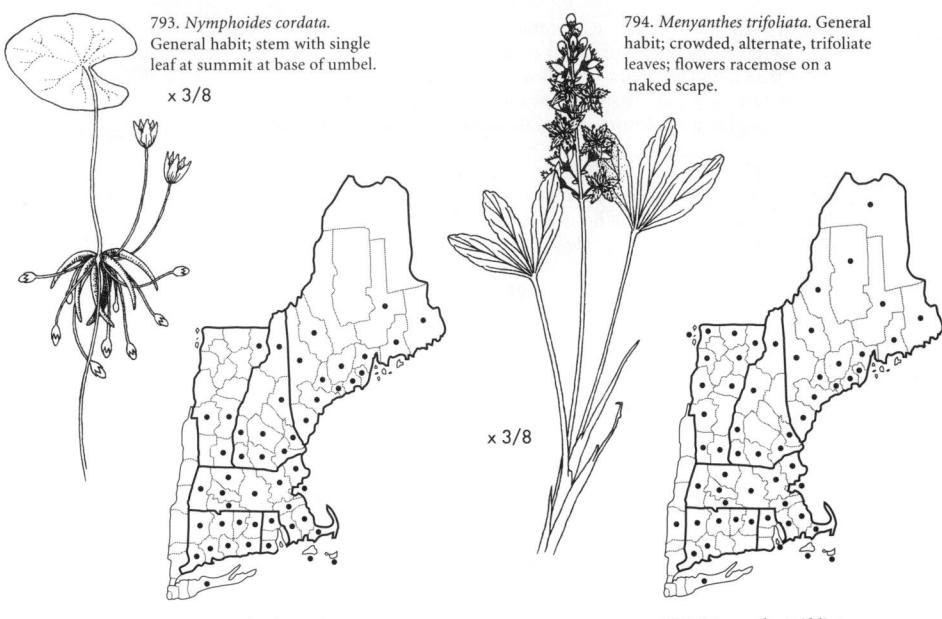

793. *Nymphoides cordata.* General habit; stem with single leaf at summit at base of umbel.

x 3/8

794. *Menyanthes trifoliata.* General habit; crowded, alternate, trifoliate leaves; flowers racemose on a naked scape.

x 3/8

1821. *Nymphoides cordata*

1822. *Menyanthes trifoliata*

Family 166. Gentianáceae (Gentian Family)

Hermaphrodite, glabrous, annual or perennial herbs. Leaves simple and entire, alternate, opposite or whorled, sessile or petioled, estipulate. Flowers perfect, regular, in bracteate, terminal or axillary cymes, panicles, or racemes, or solitary in the leaf axils or at the ends of the stem or branches, calyx and corolla 4-12 (usually 4-5) lobed, corolla rotate, salverform or campanulate, mostly marcescent, stamens as many as the corolla lobes, perigynous, ovary superior, 1-locular, 2-carpellate, ovules numerous, style 1 or absent. Fruit a mostly 2-valved, septicidal capsule.

a. Leaves all scale-like, 5 mm or less long. (Fig. 795). .... 1. *Bartonia*
a. Leaves, at least the upper, larger, foliaceous.
  b. Corolla lobes spurred at base. (Fig. 796). .... 2. *Halenia deflexa*
  b. Corolla lobes not spurred.
    c. Corolla rotate, the lobes much longer than the tube.
      Style none; corolla lobes each bearing a pair of scale-like appendages at
        base, blue, rarely white; fruit flattened. .... 3. *Lomatogonium rotatum*
      Style present; corolla lobes without scale-like appendages, pink or rose,
        rarely white; fruit turgid .... 4. *Sabatia*
    c. Corolla campanulate, funnelform or tubular, the lobes as long or shorter
      than the tube.
      d. Corolla salverform, the tube 2 mm or less wide, pink or rose, rarely white;
        calyx lobes carinate; fruit turgid .... 5. *Centaurium*
      d. Corolla not salverform, the tube 3 mm or more wide, blue or purple,
        rarely white; calyx lobes not carinate; fruit flattened.
        e. Corolla with plaits, secondary lobes or teeth in the sinuses; leaves
          broadest above the base, mostly more than 5 cm long; plant
          perennial. .... 6. *Gentiana*
        e. Corolla lacking plaits, secondary lobes or teeth in the sinuses; leaves
          broadest at base, mostly 5 cm or less long; plant annual.
          Calyx and corolla 4-lobed; corolla lobes fringed across the summit. .... 7. *Gentianopsis crinita*
          Calyx and corolla 5-lobed; corolla lobes entire or nearly so. .... 8. *Gentianella*

1. *Bartónia* Muhl. ex Willd. (for B. Barton).

Small, annual herbs with very slender, wiry, sometimes twining stems; leaves minute and scale-like, subulate, opposite, subopposite or alternate, appressed to ascending; flowers small, white to yellowish or purple, in terminal racemes or panicles, the branches and pedicels often opposite, calyx and corolla deeply 4-parted, almost to the base, stamens 4, inserted at bases of petals; capsule ovoid to oblong, flattened, abruptly beaked.

Leaves mostly opposite; petals oblong, obtuse to acute, often mucronulate, entire to
    erose. (Fig. 795) .... 1. *B. virginica*
Leaves, except sometimes the lowest, mostly alternate; petals lanceolate, acute to
    acuminate (except in subsp. *iodandra*), entire. .... 2. *B. paniculata*

    1. *B. virgínica* (L.) B.S.P. (Virginian). Wet to dry woodlands, thickets and fields, bogs. August-September. Fig. 795, Map 1823. —FACW
    2. *B. paniculáta* (Michx.) Muhl. (panicled). Wooded swamps, wet meadows, wet sand. August-September. Map 1824. Endangered in ME. [*B. lanceolata*]. Our plants include subsp. *paniculata* and the following subsp.:
        subsp. *iodándra* (B. L. Robins.) J.M. Gillett. Calyx cleft up to three-fourths the way to base, petals obtuse to acute (calyx cleft to base or nearly so and petals acute to acuminate in subsp. *paniculata*). —OBL

2. *Halénia* Borkh. Spurred Gentian (for J. Halenius).

Simple or branched, annual herbs; lowest leaves oblong-spatulate, narrowed to petioles, other leaves opposite, sessile or subsessile, oblong-lanceolate to ovate, acuminate; flowers purplish-green, in cymes terminating the stem and branches, calyx 4-lobed, corolla 4-lobed, each lobe prolonged underneath into a spur, or spurs sometimes lacking, stamens 4; capsule oblong.

    1. *H. defléxa* (Sm.) Griseb. (bent downward). Moist woods, river and stream margins. July-August. Fig. 796, Map 1825. Endangered in MA, NH. Our plants are subsp. *deflexa*. —FAC

3. *Lomatogónium* A.Braun (Greek name, based on shape of the stigmas).

Slender, simple or branched, annual herbs; leaves opposite, sessile, linear to lanceolate; flowers showy, blue or white, terminating the stem and branches and on slender, axillary pedicels, calyx deeply 4-5 parted, lobes narrow, corolla deeply 4-5 parted, rotate, each lobe bearing a pair of small, scale-like appendages at base, stamens 4-5, style none; capsule narrowly oblong.

    1. *L. rotátum* (L.) Fries ex Fern. (wheel-shaped). Seashores, edges of salt marshes. July-August. Fig. 797. Reported for NH, Hancock County ME. [*Pleurogyne r.*]. —OBL

4. *Sabátia* Adans. (for L. Sabbati).

Branched annual or perennial herbs; leaves opposite, linear to ovate, sessile; flowers showy, white to pink or rose, terminal, solitary or loosely cymose, calyx 5-12 parted, lobes narrow, united at base, corolla rotate, deeply 5-12 parted, stamens 5-12; capsule ovoid to ellipsoid, enclosed in the marcescent corolla.

a. Flowers usually 5-merous.
  b. Branches of inflorescence all opposite, the cyme appearing trichotomous.
    (Fig. 798) .... 1. *S. angularis*
  b. Branches of inflorescence mostly alternate, the cyme appearing dichotomous.
    (Fig. 799).
    c. Calyx tube 5-winged or strongly 5-ribbed. .... 2. *S. campestris*
    c. Calyx tube not winged, weakly ribbed or ribless.

Plant annual; lateral peduncles usually bractless, calyx lobes usually
  distinctly shorter than corolla .... 3. *S. stellaris*
Plant perennial; lateral peduncles usually bracteate; calyx lobes usually
  nearly equalling to exceeding corolla. (Fig. 799). .... 4. *S. campanulata*
a. Flowers 7-12-merous.
  Calyx tube strongly nerved .... 5. *S. dodecandra*
  Calyx tube nerveless or faintly nerved. .... 6. *S. kennedyana*

1. *S. anguláris* (L.) Pursh (with angles). Open woods, clearings and fields. July-August. Fig. 798. Reported for CT, MA, NY. From farther west and south. Endangered in NY. —FAC

2. *S. campéstris* Nutt. (of the plains). Fields and upland woods. July-August. From farther west. Reported for Fairfield County CT, Franklin County ME. —FACU

3. *S. stelláris* Pursh (star-like). Brackish or salt marshes. July-September. From farther south. Map 1826. Endangered in MA. —FACW

4. *S. campanuláta* (L.) Torr. (bell-shaped). Pond margins, along the coast, salt or brackish marshes. July-September. Fig. 799. From farther south. Reported for NY, Barnstable and Nantucket Counties MA. Endangered in MA, NY. [*S. gracilis*]. —FACW

5. *S. dodecándra* (L.) B.S.P. (having 12 stamens). Salt or brackish marshes. July-September. Map 1827. From farther south. —OBL

6. *S. kennedyána* Fern. (for G.G. Kennedy). Borders of fresh ponds near the coast. July-September. Map 1828. Endangered in RI. —OBL

5. *Centaúrium* Hill. Centaury (ancient name, based on medicinal value).

Annual herbs; leaves opposite, sessile, lanceolate to oblong or elliptic, the basal sometimes forming a rosette; flowers small, white to pink or roseate, numerous in spikes or corymbiform cymes terminating the stem and branches, calyx cleft into 4-5 narrow, keeled lobes, corolla salverform, 4-5 lobed, stamens 4-5, the anthers often spiralled, capsule oblong to ovoid.

a. Flowers in spikes .... 1. *C. spicatum*
a. Flowers in corymbiform or paniculate cymes.
  Flowers in flat-topped, corymbiform cymes, sessile or subsessile (bracteoles
    present at or very near base of calyx). (Fig. 800). .... 2. *C. erythraea*
  Flowers in paniculate cymes, on pedicels more than 2 mm long. .... 3. *C. pulchellum*

1. *C. spicátum* (L.) Fritsch. Salt marshes. July-August. (Naturalized from Europe). Reported for Nantucket County MA. —FACW+

2. *C. erýthraea* Rafn. Waste places and roadsides. August-September. Fig. 800, Map 1829. (Naturalized from Europe). [*C. centaurium; C. umbellatum*]. Plant has bitter qualities which, taken before a meal, can aid digestion. —FAC

3. *C. pulchéllum* (Swartz) Druce. Waste places and roadsides. July-August. (Naturalized from Europe). Reported for CT, MA, Bennington and Windham Counties VT. —FAC

6. *Gentiána* L. Gentian (named for an ancient king who discovered the medicinal value of the plant).

Annual or perennial herbs; leaves opposite, rarely whorled, sessile or short-petioled; flowers showy, blue or purple to white, solitary or in dense cymes, terminal or axillary, pedicelled or sessile, calyx mostly 5 lobed, tubular, corolla mostly 5 lobed, campanulate, funnelform or tubular, the lobes alternating with plaits or folds in the sinuses, these often of a different color and terminating in secondary lobes or teeth, open or closed, stamens as many as the corolla lobes, the anthers coherent in a ring around the style; capsule ellipsoid. [*Dasystephana*]. Various species of this and the following 2 closely related genera are used in various drinks, largely alcoholic preparations that include bitters, as an appetite stimulant and digestive aid; other medicinal uses, such as expellation of intestinal worms, fever reduction and stimulating menstrual flow are also cited.

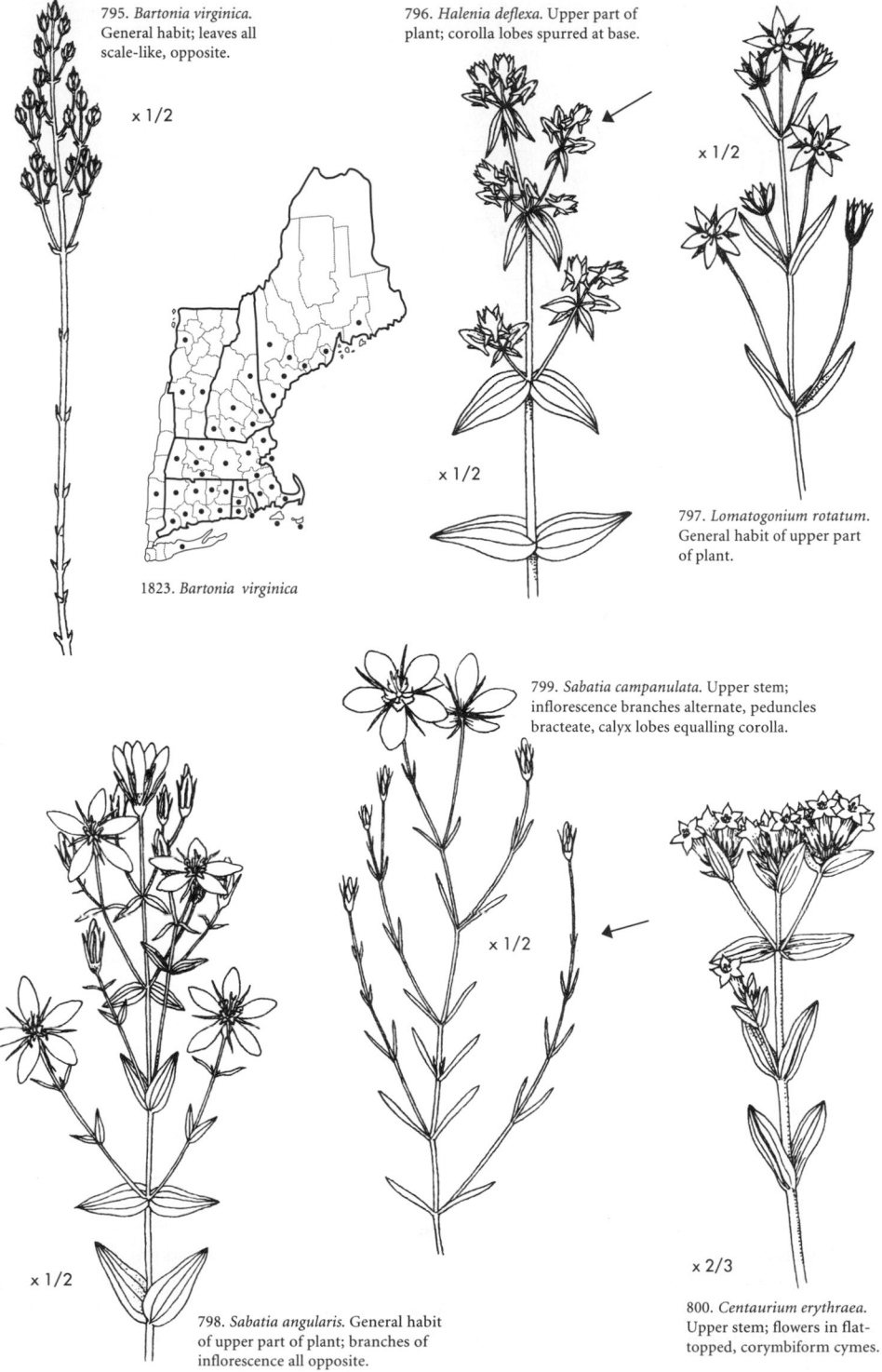

795. *Bartonia virginica.* General habit; leaves all scale-like, opposite.

x 1/2

1823. *Bartonia virginica*

796. *Halenia deflexa.* Upper part of plant; corolla lobes spurred at base.

x 1/2

x 1/2

797. *Lomatogonium rotatum.* General habit of upper part of plant.

x 1/2

799. *Sabatia campanulata.* Upper stem; inflorescence branches alternate, peduncles bracteate, calyx lobes equalling corolla.

x 1/2

798. *Sabatia angularis.* General habit of upper part of plant; branches of inflorescence all opposite.

x 2/3

800. *Centaurium erythraea.* Upper stem; flowers in flat-topped, corymbiform cymes.

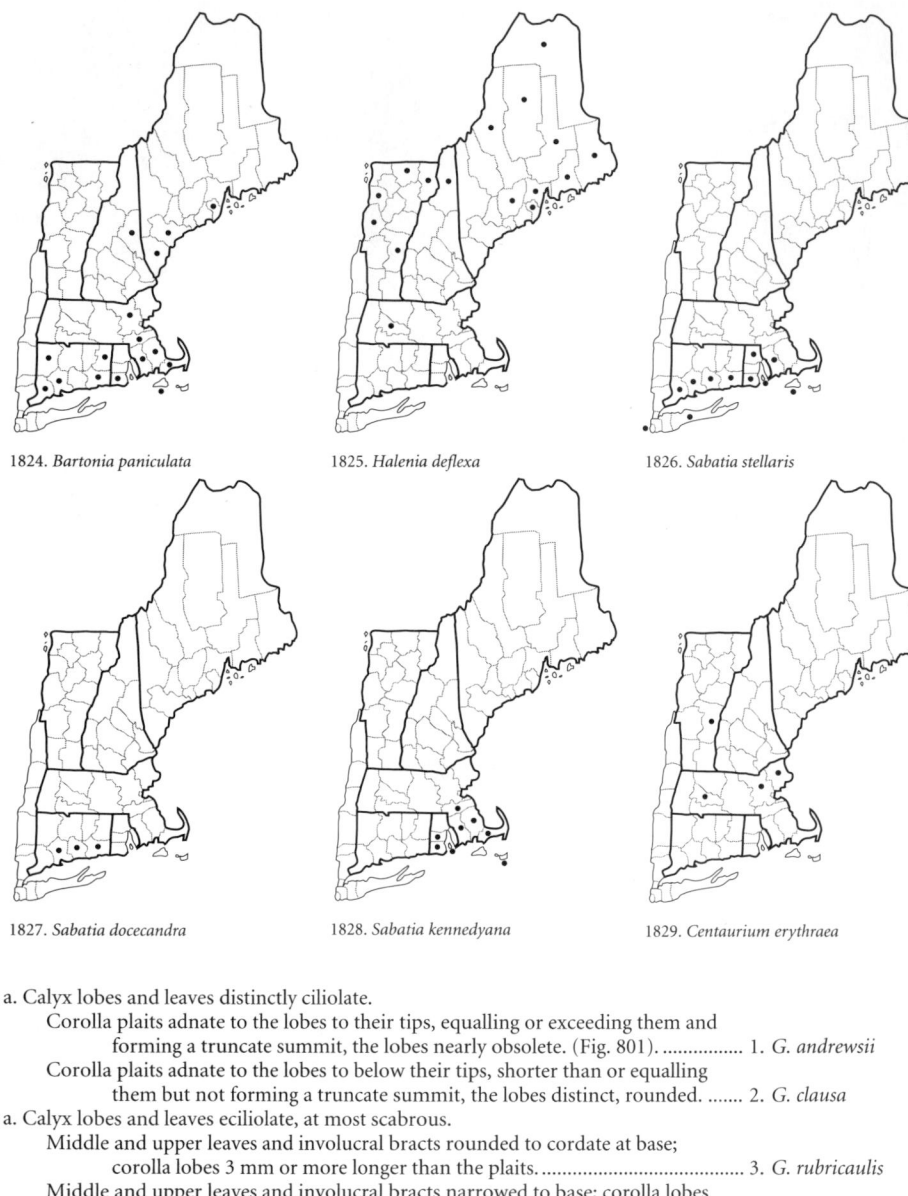

1824. *Bartonia paniculata*   1825. *Halenia deflexa*   1826. *Sabatia stellaris*

1827. *Sabatia docecandra*   1828. *Sabatia kennedyana*   1829. *Centaurium erythraea*

a. Calyx lobes and leaves distinctly ciliolate.
    Corolla plaits adnate to the lobes to their tips, equalling or exceeding them and
        forming a truncate summit, the lobes nearly obsolete. (Fig. 801). .... 1. *G. andrewsii*
    Corolla plaits adnate to the lobes to below their tips, shorter than or equalling
        them but not forming a truncate summit, the lobes distinct, rounded. .... 2. *G. clausa*
a. Calyx lobes and leaves eciliolate, at most scabrous.
    Middle and upper leaves and involucral bracts rounded to cordate at base;
        corolla lobes 3 mm or more longer than the plaits. .... 3. *G. rubricaulis*
    Middle and upper leaves and involucral bracts narrowed to base; corolla lobes
        less than 3 mm longer than the plaits .... 4. *G. linearis*

    1. G. andréwsii Griseb. (for H.C. Andrews). Closed gentian. Meadows, wet woods, stream margins. August-October. Fig. 801, Map 1830. [*Dasystephana a.*]. Our plants are var. *andrewsii*. —FACW
    2. G. claúsa Raf. (closed). Closed gentian. Pond and stream margins, meadows, moist woods. August-October. Map 1831. —FACW
    3. G. rubricaúlis Schwein. (red-stemmed). Wet meadows, moist woods. August-September. Reported for Aroostook and Somerset Counties ME. [*G. linearis* var. *latifolia; Dasystephana grayi*]. —OBL

4. G. lineáris Froel. (linear). Wet meadows, moist woods, pond and stream margins. August-September. Map 1832. [*Dasystephana l.*]. —OBL

7. Gentianópsis Ma.

Similar to *Gentiana* except plant annual, leaves broadest at instead of above the base, corolla lacking plaits, with secondary lobes or teeth in the sinuses.

1. G. criníta (Froel.) Ma. (fringed). Fringed gentian. Wet meadows and woods, stream borders. August-October. Map 1833. [*Gentiana c.; Anthopogon c.*].

8. Gentianélla Moench.

Similar to *Gentianopsis* except calyx and corolla 5 instead of 4-lobed, corolla lobes entire or nearly so instead of fringed across the summit. [*Gentiana*].

Corolla bearing a fringe of hairs in the throat at the base of the lobes. .... 1. *G. amarella*
                                                                                                                                                                subsp. *acuta*
Corolla without a fringe of hairs in the throat. .... 2. *G. quinquefolia*

1. G. amarélla (L.) Boerner (old generic name). Moist gravelly soil, streambanks. July-September. Reported for Aroostook County ME, Lamoille County VT. Endangered in ME. [*Gentiana a.; G. acuta; Amarella acuta*]. Represented with us as subsp. *acúta* (Michx.) J. M. Gillett. —FAC
2. G. quinquefólia (L.) Small (five-leaved). Meadows, moist or rich woods, streambanks. August-October. Map 1834. Endangered in CT. [*Gentiana q.*]. Our plants are subsp. *quinquefolia.* —FAC

Family 167. Apocynáceae (Dogbane Family)

Hermaphrodite, perennial herbs, stems erect, or trailing and slightly woody, sap usually milky. Leaves simple, opposite or alternate, entire, herbaceous or evergreen, estipulate. Flowers perfect, regular, solitary-axillary or in terminal, bracteate cymes, calyx and corolla deeply 5-lobed, the corolla salverform, campanulate to urceolate, stamens 5, inserted on the corolla tube, ovaries 2, superior, each 1-locular, ovules numerous, styles or stigmas united into 1. Fruit of 2 long, slender follicles.

Leaves alternate, sometimes a few subopposite. .... 1. *Amsonia*
Leaves opposite.
    Flowers solitary in the axils; corolla salverform; seeds naked. .... 2. *Vinca*
    Flowers in terminal cymes; corolla campanulate to urceolate; seeds comose.
      (Fig. 802) .... 3. *Apocynum*

1. Amsónia Walt. (for Dr. Amson).

Perennial herbs, simple or branched, the upper branches sometimes overtopping the inflorescence, stems usually clustered; leaves alternate, petioled, lanceolate to ovate; flowers pale blue, numerous, in terminal cymes, calyx small, corolla salverform, pubescent outside and within; seeds naked.

1. A. tabernaemontána Walt. (for J.T. Tabernaemontanus). Rarely escaped from cultivation; from farther west or south. Reported for Hampden County MA. [*A. amsonia*]. Our plants are var. *tabernaemontana.* —FACW
A. illústris Woodson. Differing from *A. tabernaemontana* in having leaves lustrous above, calyx hirsute and fruit torulose (leaves not lustrous, calyx glabrous and fruit continuous in *A. tabernaemontana*). Rarely escaped from cultivation. From farther west. Reported for Nassau County NY.

2. Vínca L. Periwinkle (abbreviated from the ancient name).

Trailing or creeping perennial herbs or slightly woody; leaves opposite, petioled, lanceolate to oblong or elliptic, herbaceous or coriaceous and evergreen; flowers blue, rarely white, solitary in 1 axil of each pair of leaves, pedicelled, corolla salverform; seeds naked.

Leaf margins smooth .... 1. *V. minor*
Leaf margins scabrous-ciliate .... 2. *V. herbacea*

1. V. *minor* L. (smaller). Spread from cultivation to roadsides, waste places, open woods. April-June. Map 1835. (Introduced from Europe). Crushed leaves, applied to skin wounds, are reported to have healing value.

2. V. *herbácea* Waldst. & Kit. (herbaceous). Occasionally escaped from cultivation. May-June. (Introduced from Europe). Reported for Franklin County MA.

V. *májor* L. Will key to the latter species but leaves are deltoid-ovate (lanceolate to narrowly elliptic in *V. herbacea*). (Introduced from Europe). Excaped from cultivation farther south. Reported for MA.

3. *Apócynum* L. Dogbane (ancient Greek name for the dogbane).

Branched, perennial herbs with tough, fibrous bark; leaves opposite, petioled to sessile, ovate or elliptic to lanceolate, mucronate; flowers white, pink or greenish, cymose, the cymes terminal and often in the upper axils, corolla campanulate to urceolate, the tube bearing 5 small scales inside, anthers connivent around and adherent to the stigma; paired follicles pendant, seeds comose. Roots are reported to be of value as an emetic, cathartic and diuretic; also poisonous if taken in overdoses.

a. Corolla 4.5 mm or less long, the lobes erect or ascending, white to greenish;
      branches usually opposite .... 1. *A. cannabinum*
a. Corolla more than 4.5 mm long, the lobes spreading to recurved, pinkish to white;
      branches mostly alternate.
    Corolla approximately twice the length of the calyx, its lobes spreading but not
      recurving .... 2. *A. x floribundum*
    Corolla approximately three times the length of the calyx, its lobes recurving .... 3. *A. androsaemifolium*

1. A. *cannábinum* L. (hemp-like). Indian Hemp. Fields, waste places, stream margins. June-August. Map 1836. [*A. sibiricum; A. hypericifolium*]. —FACU

2. A. *x floribúndum* Greene. A hybrid between *A. cannabinum* and *A. androsaemifolium*. Map 1837. [*A. medium*].

3. A. *androsaemifólium* L. (with leaves of *Androsaemum*). Fields, roadsides, waste places, thickets. June-August. Fig. 802, Map 1838. Represented with us as subsp. *androsaemifolium* var. *incánum* A.DC.

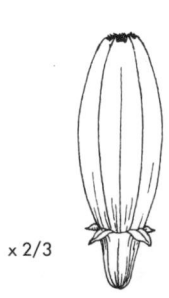

x 2/3

801. *Gentiana andrewsii*. Single flower; corolla plaits adnate to the lobes to their tips, the lobes nearly obsolete.

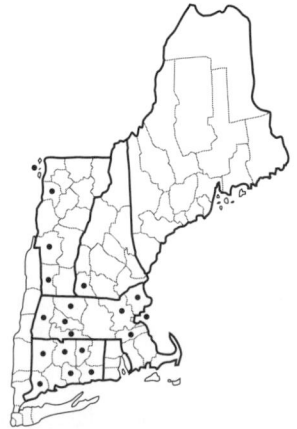

1830. *Gentiana andrewsii*

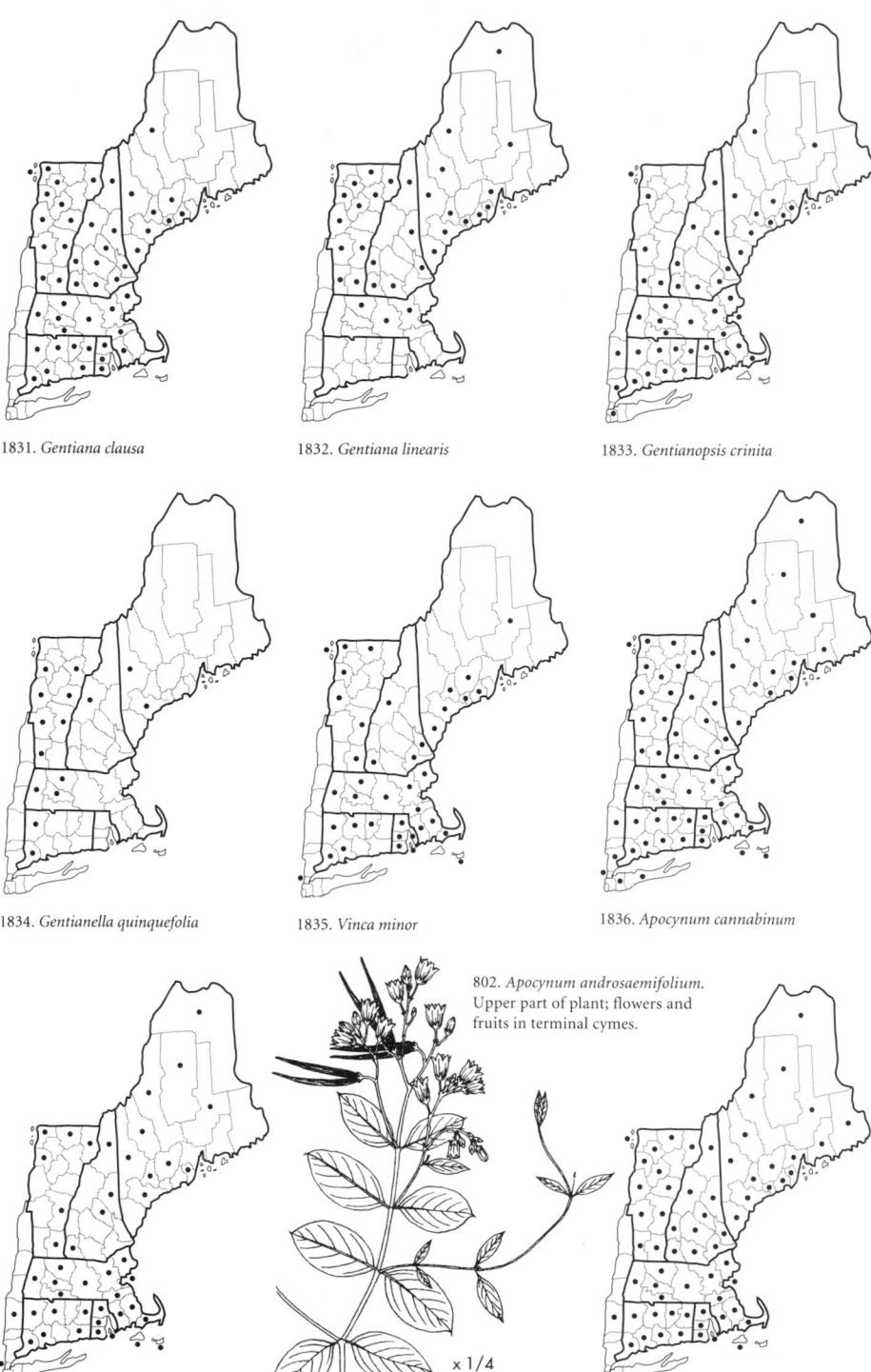

1831. *Gentiana clausa*

1832. *Gentiana linearis*

1833. *Gentianopsis crinita*

1834. *Gentianella quinquefolia*

1835. *Vinca minor*

1836. *Apocynum cannabinum*

802. *Apocynum androsaemifolium.*
Upper part of plant; flowers and
fruits in terminal cymes.

x 1/4

1837. *Apocynum x floribundum*

1838. *Apocynum androsaemifolium*

Family 168. Asclepiadáceae (Milkweed Family)

Hermaphrodite, erect, decumbent or twining perennial herbs or twining woody vines, sap usually milky. Leaves simple, usually opposite, sometimes alternate or whorled, entire, estipulate. Flowers perfect, regular, umbellate or cymose, 5-merous, corolla deeply lobed, the segments often reflexed, often with a corona (a 5-lobed or 5-parted crown between the corolla and stamens and adnate to one or the other), stamens 5, perigynous, anthers adnate to the stigma, forming a gynostegium, the anther sacs sometimes with a membranous appendage, the pollen of each anther sac united into a single mass (a pollinium) or rarely (in *Periploca*) 2 masses, the pollinia from adjacent anthers united and forming a pair, ovaries 2, superior, each 1-locular, ovules numerous, styles 2, stigma 1, often much enlarged. Fruit of usually 2, linear to ovoid follicles, seeds usually comose.

a. Stems erect or decumbent, not twining; flowers umbellate.
a. Stems twining; flowers cymose or paniculate. .... 1. *Asclepias*
    Corolla lobes less than 5 mm long; corona with shallow lobes, equalling to
      slightly exceeding gynostegium; stems herbaceous. .... 2. *Cynanchum*
                                         louiscae

    Corolla lobes 6 mm or more long; corona with long, slender appendages,
      greatly exceeding gynostegium; stems woody .... 3. *Periploca graeca*

1. *Asclépias* L. Milkweed (Ancient Greek name).

Perennial herbs from a stout root or rhizome, stems erect or decumbent, usually simple; leaves opposite or whorled, rarely alternate, sessile, clasping or petioled; flowers in simple, usually peduncled, terminal or axillary umbels, corolla segments reflexed, rarely spreading, corona of 5 hood-like structures, attached at the base of the gynostegium, each usually bearing an incurved horn at the base, filaments connate into a tube which encloses the pistil, anthers tipped with a membranous appendage, stigma large, 5-angled; follicles 1 or 2, ovoid or lanceolate, acuminate, seeds comose (ours). Most species are poisonous; several species are edible as noted below but should never be eaten without cooking thoroughly to remove the bitter, poisonous sap.

a. Leaves narrowly linear, 5 mm or less wide, very numerous and mostly in whorles
    of 3-6, some alternate .... 1. *A. verticillata*
a. Leaves broader, the principal ones wider than 5 mm, not both very numerous and
    mostly whorled.
    b. Leaves mostly alternate; flowers orange to yellow. .... 2. *A. tuberosa*
    b. Leaves mostly opposite or whorled (some alternate in *A. viridiflora*); flower
      color various.
      c. Umbels sessile or subsessile, the peduncles less than 1 cm long; hoods lacking
        a horn .... 3. *A. viridiflora*
      c. Umbels (at least the axillary) on peduncles 1 cm or more long; hoods each
        bearing a horn.
        d. Stems branched above .... 4. *A. incarnata*
        d. Stems simple, unbranched.
          e. Leaves usually in 3(4) cycles, the upper and lower opposite, the middle
            with 1 or 2 whorles of usually 4 larger leaves. .... 5. *A. quadrifolia*
          e. Leaves usually in 4 or more cycles, all opposite and similar in size.
            f. Leaves sessile or petioles less than 5 mm long.
              Leaves rounded to obtuse at tips, undulate-margined; flowers
                greenish-purple .... 6. *A. amplexicaulis*
              Leaves acuminate at tip, not undulate-margined; flowers purplish-red ... 7. *A. rubra*
            f. Leaves with petioles mostly 5 mm or more long (sometimes shorter in
              A. incarnata).
              g. Hoods about equalling or shorter than the gynostegium, the horns
                longer than the hoods.
              Lateral margins of hood divergent from near middle, entire;
                flowers pink to rose-purple .... 4. *A. incarnata*
              Lateral margins of hood not divergent, the hood thick-tubular, each
                margin terminating in a tooth; flowers white to greenish. .... 8. *A. exaltata*

g. Hoods conspicuously longer than the gynostegium, the horns about
equalling the hoods.
   h. Leaves glabrous beneath or with scattered hairs along the midvein.
      Leaves lanceolate to ovate-lanceolate, acuminate; lateral margins
         of hood each with a prominent tooth near the middle. .... 5. *A. quadrifolia*
      Leaves ovate to elliptic, obtuse and short-pointed or cuspidate;
         lateral margins of hood entire to obscurely toothed. .... 9. *A. variegata*
   h. Leaves distinctly pubescent to tomentulose over the surface beneath.
      Lateral margins of hood each with a prominent lobe near the
         middle; follicles muricate .... 10. *A. syriaca*
      Lateral margins without prominent lobes, merely widened or
         obscurely lobed; follicles not muricate .... 11. *A. purpurascens*

1. *A. verticilláta* L. (whorled). Dry woods and fields. July-August. Map 1839.

2. *A. tuberósa* L. (tuberous). Butterfly-weed. Dry fields, roadsides and waste places. July-August. Map 1840. Endangered in NH, ME. Our plants include subsp. *tuberosa* and the following subsp.:

subsp. *intérior* Woods. Leaves widest below middle, tapering gradually to tip (widest above middle and abruptly tapered in subsp. *tuberosa*). Edible as in *A. syriáca*; roots were also cooked and eaten by Indians.

3. *A. viridiflóra* Raf. (green-flowered). Dry fields, barrens and woodlands.July-August. Map 1841. [*Acerates v.*].

4. *A. incarnáta* L. (flesh-colored). Swamp-milkweed. Wooded swamps, pond and river shores. July-August. Map 1842. Our plants are subsp. *incarnata*. Edible as in *A. syriaca*. —OBL

5. *A. quadrifólia* Jacq. (four-leaved). Dry woods. May-July. Map 1843.

6. *A. amplexicaúlis* Smith (clasping the stem). Dry fields and open woods. June-July. Map 1844.

7. *A. rúbra* L. (red). Wooded swamps, bogs, wet pine woods. June-July. Rare, from farther south. Reported for Suffolk County NY. —OBL

8. *A. exaltáta* L. (very tall). Woods and woodland borders. June-July. Map 1845. [*A. phytolaccoides*]. —FACU

9. *A. variegáta* L. (variegated). Woods and thickets. June-July. Map 1846. Endangered in CT. From farther south and west. [*Biventraria v.*]. —FACU

10. *A. syriáca* L. (Syrian). Fields and roadsides. June-August. Map 1847. [*A. kansana*]. Young shoots (up to 6 inches), young leaves, unopened flower buds and young pods can be eaten after first boiling in several waters to remove the milky sap.

11. *A. purpuráscens* L. (purplish). Woods, woodland borders, fields. June-July. Map 1848. —FACU

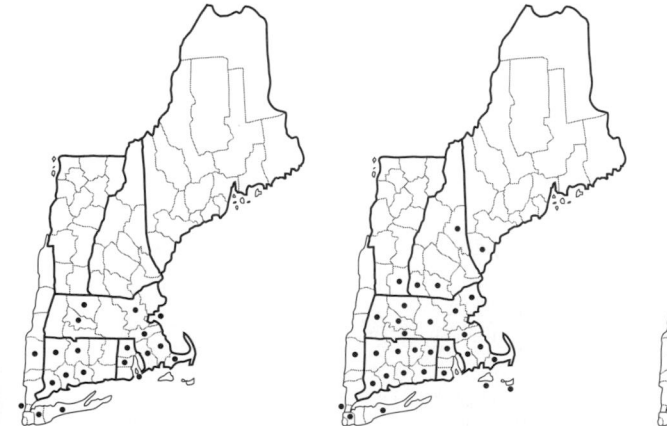

1839. *Asclepias verticillata*   1840. *Asclepias tuberosa*   1841. *Asclepias viridiflora*

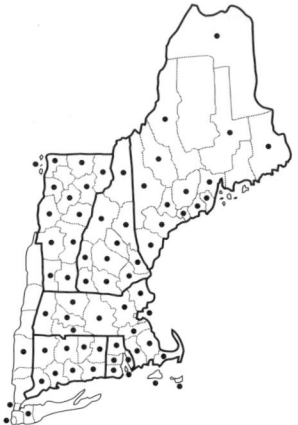

1842. *Asclepias incarnata*

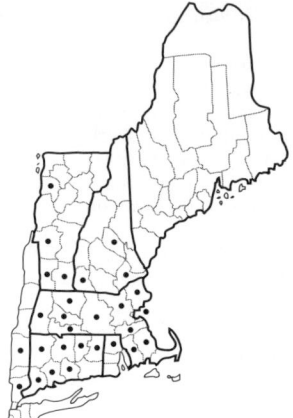

1843. *Asclepias quadrifolia*

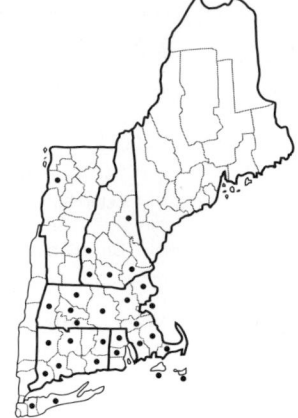

1844. *Asclepias amplexicaulis*

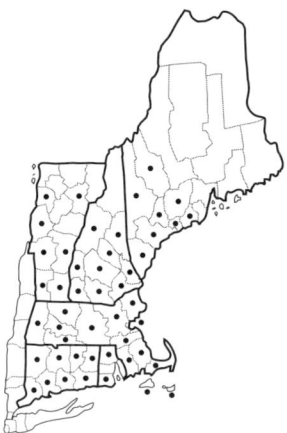

1845. *Asclepias exaltata*

1846. *Asclepias variegata*

1847. *Asclepias syriaca*

1848. *Asclepias purpurascens*

1849. *Cynanchum louiscae*

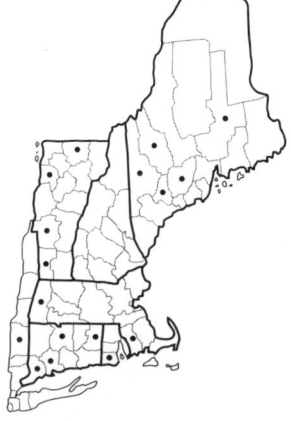

1850. *Cuscuta epithymum*

2. Cynánchum L. (ancient name for a plant reputed to be poisonous to dogs).
Slender, twining, perennial, herbaceous or slightly woody vines; leaves opposite, rarely alternate or whorled, petioled, ovate to lance-ovate, acuminate at tip, rounded to subcordate at base; flowers small, purple in axillary, peduncled cymes, corolla lobes spreading, corona cup-like, shallowly 5-lobed, the lobes equalling or slightly surpassing the gynostegium, much shorter than the corolla, filaments connate into a tube and anthers tipped with a membranous appendage as in *Asclepias*; follicles slender, seeds comose. [*Vincetoxicum*].

   1. C. louíscae Kartesz & Gandhi. Black swallow-wort. Waste places, roadsides and river thickets, open woods. June-August. Map 1849. (Naturalized from Europe). [*C. nigrum; Vincetoxicum n.*].

3. Períploca L. Silk-vine (from the Greek, referring to the twining habit).
Twining, woody vines, pith white, excavated, buds small, concealed by the persistent petiole bases, leaf scars raised, half-round to elliptic, bundle trace 1, stipule scars lacking; leaves opposite, petioled, lance-ovate; flowers brownish-purple, in axillary and terminal panicles, corolla lobes elongate, pubescent above, corona with 5, long, slender appendages, greatly exceeding the gynostegium, anthers bearded; follicles slender.

   1. P. graéca L. (Greek). Rarely escaped from cultivation to roadsides and around buildings. May-August. (Introduced from Europe). Reported for Fairfield County CT and Newport County RI.

Family 169. Cuscutáceae (Dodder Family)

White, yellow or orange, twining vines with filiform stems, parasitic on herbs and shrubs by means of numerous minute suckers, the root and lower part of stem soon withering. Leaves reduced to minute, alternate scales. Flowers perfect, regular, small, white to yellowish, in cymose clusters, 4-5 merous, calyx lobes united at the base or sepals distinct, corolla urceolate to cylindric or campanulate, lobed, stamens 4-5, inserted on the corolla, with a fringed or toothed scale at the base, ovary superior, 2-locular, styles 2. Capsule ovoid to globose, sometimes indehiscent. [*Convolvulaceae*].

1. Cuscúta L. Dodder (Arabic name).
Same characters as the family.

a. Stigmas linear-filiform, elongate; capsule circumscissile toward the base.
    Style and stigmas longer than the ovary, soon exsert from the corolla. .... 1. *C. epithymum*
    Style and stigmas about as long as the ovary, included .... 2. *C. epilinum*
a. Stigmas capitate; capsule indehiscent or rupturing irregularly but not
    circumscissile.
  b. Flowers all or mostly 5-merous.
    c. Calyx of distinct sepals subtended by 1-several bracts. .... 3. *C. compacta*
    c. Calyx of sepals united at base, not subtended by bracts.
      Corolla lobes acute; calyx about equalling corolla tube .... 4. *C. pentagona*
      Corolla lobes obtuse; calyx about half as long as corolla tube. .... 5. *C. gronovii*
  b. Flowers all or mostly 4-merous.
    d. Corolla lobes obtuse to rounded; styles about as long as capsule. .... 6. *C. cephalanthi*
    d. Corolla lobes acute; styles shorter than capsule.
      Tips of corolla lobes incurved; flowers, at least some, distinctly pedicelled ..... 7. *C. coryli*
      Tips of corolla lobes erect or ascending; flowers sessile or subsessile . ... 8. *C. polygonorum*

   1. C. epíthymum L. (on thyme). On herbs, often legumes. June-September. Map 1850. (Naturalized from Europe).
   2. C. epílinum Weihe (on flax). On herbs, often on flax. June-August. Map 1851. (Adventive from Europe).

C. europaéa L. Similar to *C. epilinum* but differs in having obtuse calyx lobes and 4 corolla lobes (calyx lobes acute and corolla lobes 5 in *C. epilinum*). (Adventive from Europe). Reported for Oxford County ME.

3. *C. compácta* Juss. ex Choisy (compact). Shrubs and coarse herbs, often those occurring on edges of ponds and wetlands. July-October. Map 1852. [*C. paradoxa*]. Our plants are var. *compacta*.

4. *C. pentagóna* Engelm. (5-angled). On a wide variety of herbs. July-October. Map 1853. Endangered in NH. [*C. arvensis; C. campestris*]. Our plants are var. *pentagona*.

5. *C. gronóvii* Willd. ex J.A. Schultes (for J.F. Gronovius). Shrubs and coarse herbs. July-October. Map 1854. Our plants are var. *gronovii*.

Another var. that has been distinguished is var. *latifólia*.

6. *C. cephalánthi* Engelm. (of *Cephalanthus*). Shrubs and coarse herbs. August-September. Map 1855. From farther south and west.

7. *C. córyli* Engelm. (of *corylus*). On a variety of herbs. July-September. Map 1856.

8. *C. polygonórum.* Engelm. (of *Polygonums*). On coarse herbs. July-September. Map 1857.

Family 170. Convolvuláceae (Morning-glory Family)

Hermaphrodite, annual or perennial herbs (ours), often twining vines, sap often milky. Leaves usually simple, alternate, petioled, entire or lobed, estipulate. Flowers perfect, regular, solitary or cymose in the leaf axils, usually 5-merous, sepals usually distinct, often subtended by 2 bracts, corolla deeply lobed, or unlobed and funnelform or campanulate, stamens 5, inserted on the corolla, ovary superior, 2-4-locular, styles 1 or 2. Fruit a 2-6 seeded capsule.

a. Calyx closely subtended by 2 large, foliaceous bracts .... 1. *Calystegia*
a. Calyx not subtended by 2 large bracts, the bracts when present scale-like and
      inserted well below the calyx.
    Calyx lobes rounded at apex, 7 mm or less long; stigmas 2, filiform .... 2. *Convolvulus
                                                                arvensis*

    Calyx lobes acute to acuminate or caudate, or rounded and more than 1 cm
        long; stigma capitate, entire or shallowly lobed. .... 3. *Ipomoea*

1. *Calystégia* R. Br. Bindweed.

Erect, trailing or twining perennial herbs; leaves oblong to ovate or lanceolate, truncate to cordate or sagittate; flowers large and showy, white to pink, solitary or few on axillary peduncles, 5-merous, calyx closely subtended by 2 large, foliaceous bracts, corolla funnelform to campanulate, entire or lobed, style 1, stigmas 2; capsule globose or subglobose, 2-4-celled. [*Convolvulus*]. Eating the seeds can cause nausea and hallucinations; taken in large quantities they are poisonous.

a. Corolla double, 3 cm or less long .... 1. *C. pellita*
a. Corolla single, 3.5 cm or more long
    Leaves subtending flowers with petioles more than half as long as the midvein;
        flowers from many axils; stems twining or trailing; freely branched .... 2. *C. sepium*
    Leaves subtending flowers with petioles less than half as long as midvein;
        flowers 1-4, from lower and median leaf axils; stems erect, sometimes
        twining near the tip; simple to sparingly branched .... 3. *C. spithamaea*

1. *C. péllita* (Ledeb.) G. Don. Japanese bindweed. Occasionally escaped from cultivation to roadsides, waste places and old fields. Map 1858. (Naturalized from China). [*C. japonicus; C. hederacea; Convolvulus j.; C. pellitus; C. pubescens*].

2. *C. sépium* (L.) R. Br. (of hedges) Hedge-bindweed. Fields, roadsides, thickets, pond and river margins. May-September. Map 1859. (Eurasia; N.Z.). [*Convolvulus s.*]. Our plants include subsp. *sepium* and the following subsp.:

1851. *Cuscuta epilinum*

1852. *Cuscuta compacta*

1853. *Cuscuta pentagona*

1854. *Cuscuta gronovii*

1855. *Cuscuta cephalanthi*

1856. *Cuscuta coryli*

1857. *Cuscuta polygonorum*

1858. *Calystegia pellita*

1859. *Calystegia sepium*

subsp. *americána* (Sims) Brummit. Basal lobes of leaves obtuse (basal lobes truncate to angulate or slightly 2-lobed in subsp. *sepium*).

subsp. *anguláta* and subsp. *appalachiána* have also been reported for our range. —FAC-

C. silvática (Kit.) Griseb. Similar to *C. sepium* but leaves with quadrangular sinuses, the sides nearly parallel (leaf sinuses v or u-shaped with divergent sides in *C. sepium*). From farther west. Reported for CT, VT. Represented with us as subsp. *fraterniflóra* (Mack. & Bush) Brummitt. [*C. sepium* var. *fraterniflorus*].

3. C. spithamaéa (L.) Pursh (a span high). Fields and waste places. June-July. Map 1860. Endangered in MA. [*Convolvulus spithameus; C. purshianus; C. catesbianus*]. Our plants are subsp. *spithamaea*.

2. Convólvulus L. Bindweed (to entwine).

Similar to *Calystegia* except bracts small and often scale-like, inserted well below the calyx. Eating the seeds can cause nausea and hallucinations; eaten in large quantities they can cause poisoning.

1. C. arvénsis L. (of fields). Field-bindweed. Fields, roadsides and waste places. June-August. Map 1861. (Naturalized from Eurasia). [*Strophocaulos a.*]. Of medicinal value as a purgative.

C. tricolor L. Dwarf Morning Glory. Distinguishable from *C. arvensis* in having 3-flowered peduncles and an ebracteate calyx (peduncles 1-2-flowered and bracts present but inserted well below calyx in *C. arvensis*). (Europe). Rarely escaped from cultivation in our range. Reported for Middlesex County MA.

3. Ipomoéa L. Morning-glory (Greek name, referring to the twining habit).

Twining or trailing, annual or perennial herbs; leaves ovate to orbicular, entire, deeply lobed or coarsely toothed, acute to acuminate at apex, cordate at base; flowers showy, solitary or several on axillary peduncles, 5-merous, sepals often unequal, corolla salverform to companulate, entire or shallowly lobed, style 1, stigma entire or lobed; capsule globose or subglobose, 2-4 celled. Eating the seeds can cause nausea and hallucinations; eaten in large quantities can cause poisoning.

a. Corolla salverform, scarlet; sepals less than 1 cm long. .... 1. *I. coccinea*
a. Corolla funnelform to campanulate, not scarlet; sepals 1 cm or more long
    (shorter in *I. tricolor*).
  b. Sepals glabrous, obtuse, often unequal, the outer considerably shorter; stigmas
      2-lobed or entire; ovary 2-locular; corolla 4 cm or more long. .... 2. *I. pandurata*
  b. Sepals hirsute and/or ciliate, acute, acuminate or caudate, mostly equal; stigmas
      3-lobed and ovary 3-locular (except in *I. lacunosa*).
    c. Sepals narrowed into prolonged caudate tips; leaves often 3-lobed. .... 3. *I. hederacea*
    c. Sepals acute to short-acuminate; leaves not 3-lobed.
      Peduncles papillose, essentially glabrous; corolla 2.5 cm or less long;
        stigmas 2-lobed or entire; overy 2-locular. .... 4. *I. lacunosa*
      Peduncles not papillose; usually pubescent with reflexed hairs; corolla 3
        cm or more long; stigmas 3-lobed and ovary 3-locular. .... 5. *I. purpurea*

1. I. coccínea L. (scarlet). Red morning-glory. Occasionally escaped from cultivation to roadsides and waste places. August-October. Map 1862. (Naturalized from Tropical Amer.). [*Quamoclit c.*]. —FACU

I. hederifólia L. Similar to *I. coccinea* but with leaves 3-5-lobed or parted (leaves entire, toothed or angulate in *I. coccinea*). Tropical. Reported in our range from MA, VT. [*I. coccinea* var. *h.*].

I. quámoclit L. Similar to *I. coccinea* but distinguishable from it and *I. hederifolia* in having leaves pinnately divided into numerous narrow lobes (leaves cordate and entire to toothed or angulate in *I. coccinea*, and leaves 3-5 lobed or parted in *I. hederifolia*). (Adventive from Tropical Amer.). Rarely spread from cultivation. Reported for Windsor County VT. [*Quamoclit vulgaris; Quamoclit q.*].

2. I. panduráta (L.) G.F.W. Mey. (fiddle-shaped). Wild Potato-vine. Fields, roadsides, open woods. June-September. Reported for Litchfield County CT, Norfolk County MA. Large, fleshy root resembles sweet potato and was cooked and eaten by Indians. —FACU

I. trícolor Cav. Similar to *I. pandurata* but with blue to purplish-red flowers (flowers white in *I. pandurata*). Occasionally escaped from cultivation. Reported for MA.

3. I. hederácea Jacq. (resembling *Hedera*). Roadsides, waste places, cultivated fields. July - September. Map 1863. (Naturalized from Tropical Amer.). [*Pharbitis h.*]. —FACU

I. nil (L.) Roth. Similar to *I. hederacea* but with sepals erect and flowers 3.8 cm or more long (tips of sepals spreading to recurved and flowers up to 3.8 cm long in *I. hederacea*). Occasionally spread from cultivation. Reported for MA.

4. I. lacunósa L. (with air spaces). Fields, waste places, roadsides and thickets, especially in bottomlands. August-October. Map 1864. From farther south and west. —FACW

5. I. purpúrea (L.) Roth (purple). Common morning-glory. Occasionally escaped from cultivation to fields, roadsides, waste places. July-September. Map 1865. (Naturalized from Tropical Amer.). [*Pharbitis p.*].

1860. *Calystegia spithamaea*   1861. *Convolvulus arvensis*   1862. *Ipomoea coccinea*

1863. *Ipomoea hederacea*   1864. *Ipomoea lacunosa*   1865. *Ipomoea purpurea*

Family 171. Polemoniáceae (Phlox Family)

Hermaphrodite, annual or perennial herbs. Leaves simple, pinnately compound or pinnatifid, alternate or opposite, estipulate. Flowers perfect, regular, thyrsoid, cymose or corymbose, calyx 5-lobed, tubular to campanulate, corolla 5-lobed, salverform to campanulate or funnelform, stamens 5, inserted on the corolla, ovary superior, 3-locular, style 1, stigmas 3. Fruit a 3-valved, loculicidal capsule.

a. Leaves pinnately compound or divided.
    Leaves pinnately compound, with lanceolate to ovate leaflets 3 mm or more
        wide (at least the larger); corolla campanulate, mostly blue, rarely white. ... 1. *Polemonium*
    Leaves pinnately divided, with linear-filiform segments 2 mm or less wide;
        corolla salverform, scarlet and yellow. .... 2. *Ipomopsis rubra*
a. Leaves simple, entire.
    Leaves mostly alternate; corolla limb 8 mm or less wide .... 3. *Collomia linearis*
    Leaves mostly opposite (alternate in one cultivated escape); corolla limb 1 cm
        or more wide. .... 4. *Phlox*

1. Polemónium L. Jacob's ladder (ancient Greek name).

Perennial herbs; leaves alternate, pinnately compound; flowers blue, rarely white, in bractless corymbs, thyrses or cymes terminating the stem and branches, corolla short-funnelform to broadly campanulate; capsule ovoid.In addition to the following species *P. cuspidatum* has been reported for ME.

a. Inflorescence loose and open, with long, remote branches terminated by
    few-flowered corymbs; pedicels often longer than calyx; stamens equalling
    or shorter than corolla. (Fig. 803) .... 1. *P. reptans*
a. Inflorescence a compact thyrsoid or cymose panicle; pedicels shorter than calyx.
    Stamens long-exserted; pedicels densely pubescent but not glandular; calyx
        with scattered long hairs .... 2. *P. van-bruntiae*
    Stamens not or barely exserted; pedicels densely pubescent and with stalked
        glands; calyx short-pubescent, lacking scattered long hairs.
    Stamens included in the corolla, distinctly surpassed by the style. .... 3. *P. occidentale*
    Stamens slightly exserted from the corolla, the style not greatly surpassing
        the stamens .... 4. *P. acutiflorum*

1. P. réptans L. (creeping). Rich, moist woods. May-June. Fig. 803, Map 1866. From farther south and west. Our plants are var. *reptans*. —FACU

2. P. van-brúntiae Britt. (for Mrs. C. Van Brunt). Bogs, wet meadows, stream banks. June-July. Endangered in ME. Also reported for CT, Addison County VT. —FACW

3. P. occidentále Greene. Arbor vitae bogs. June-July. Western. Reported for MA, VT. Our plants are subsp. *occidentale*. [*P. caeruleum* subsp. *o.*].

4. P. acutiflórum Willd. Wet meadows, wooded swamps. June-July. Northwestern. Reported for ME, NH. [*P. caeruleum* subsp. *villosum*].

P. micránthum Benth. Differing from the above species in being annual, with a white corolla equalling or shorter than the calyx (the above species are perennial, with a blue corolla much exceeding the calyx). Western. Reported for MA.

2. Ipomópsis Michx.

Tall, pubescent, usually simple-stemmed, biennial herbs; leaves alternate, crowded, subsessile, pinnately divided into linear-filiform segments; flowers typically scarlet outside, yellow inside, in a slender, elongate panicle, corolla salverform to narrowly funnelform; capsule oblong. [*Gilia*].

1. I. rúbra (L.) Wherry. (red). Rarely escaped from cultivation to roadsides and fields. June-August. From farther south. [*Gilia r.*].

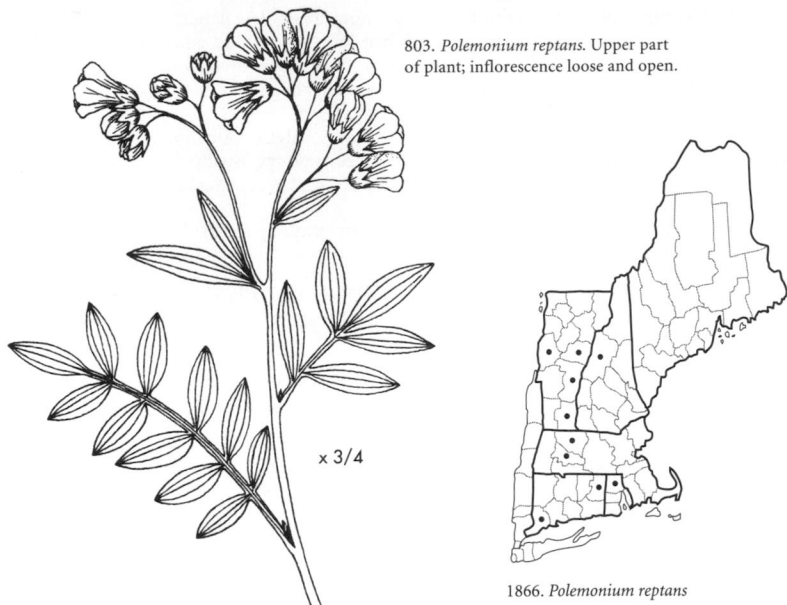

803. *Polemonium reptans.* Upper part of plant; inflorescence loose and open.

x 3/4

1866. *Polemonium reptans*

Several annual species of *Gilia* Ruiz & Pavon having differently colored flowers (not scarlet outside) occasionally adventive from the west, have been reported for VT, ME and Franklin and Middlesex Counties MA but these apparently do not persist.

Navarrétia Ruiz and Pavon *leucocéphala* Benth. with calyx lobes divided, spinulose-tipped and unequal, and flowers in dense, cymose heads is also sometimes adventive from the west and apparently not persistent. Reported for Middlesex County MA.

3. *Collómia* Nutt. (Greek name, referring to the mucilaginous seeds).

Pubescent, annual herbs; leaves simple, alternate, entire, sessile or subsessile, linear to lanceolate; flowers purplish to whitish, sessile in leafy-bracted clusters terminating the stem and branches, corolla salverform to tubular-funnelform; capsule ovoid to obovoid.

1. *C. lineáris* Nutt. (linear). Dry, open, sandy and gravelly soil. June-August. Fig. 804, Map 1867. From farther west. [*Gilia l.*].

4. *Phlóx* L. (ancient name for *Lychnis*, transferred to this genus).

Perennial herbs (rarely annual); leaves opposite or the upper ones subopposite (rarely alternate), sessile or subsessile, entire; flowers bracteate, in terminal or axillary cymes, calyx 5-ribbed or angled, corolla salverform; capsule ovoid.

a. Leaves linear, 2 cm or less long and 3 mm or less wide, often with axillary fascicles;
    stem suffruticose, prostrate; petals notched. (Fig. 805). .... 1. *P. subulata*
a. Leaves broader, at least the larger ones 3 cm or more long and/or wider than
    3 mm, usually without axillary fascicles; stem herbaceous, erect or decumbent
    at base; petals not notched (except sometimes in *P. divaricata*).
  b. Calyx lobes longer than tube; style short, scarcely or not longer than the stigmas
     or ovary.
    Corolla tube usually pubescent; plant without sterile basal offshoots .... 2. *P. pilosa*
    Corolla tube glabrous; plant with sterile basal offshoots. .... 3. *P. divaricata*
  b. Calyx lobes shorter than or equalling tube (sometimes longer in *P. stolonifera*);
     style elongate, greatly exceeding the stigmas or ovary.

c. Leaves with conspicuous lateral veins beneath forming an areolate pattern;
    leaf margins ciliolate; calyx glabrous or puberulent. (Fig. 806). .... 4. *P. paniculata*
c. Leaves with inconspicuous lateral veins beneath, not forming an areolate
    pattern; leaf margins not ciliolate (often pilose beneath and on the
    margins in *P. stolonifera*, with a long-hairy calyx).
        Plant with sterile basal offshoots with spatulate leaves; calyx long-hairy. .... 5. *P. stolonifera*
        Plant without sterile basal offshoots or spatulate leaves; calyx usually
            glabrous or sparsely pubescent. .... 6. *P. maculata*

1. *P. subuláta* L. (awl-shaped). Moss-pink. Sandy or gravelly roadsides, cemetaries. April-June. Fig. 805, Map 1868. From farther south and west. Our plants are subsp. *subulata*. [*P. ciliata*].

2. *P. pilósa* L. (soft-pubescent). Open woods and fields, May-June. From farther west and south. Reported for New Haven County CT. Our plants are subsp. *pilosa*. —FACU

P. drummóndii Hook. Will key to *P. pilosa* but is distinguishable in being an annual with upper leaves alternate (plant perennial and upper leaves opposite or subopposite in *P. pilosa*). (Introduced from Texas). Occasionally escaped from cultivation to waste places. Reported for VT. Our plants are subsp. *drummondii*.

3. *P. divaricáta* L. (strongly divergent). Rich woods. April-June. Map 1869. Our plants are subsp. *divaricata*. —FACU

4. *P. paniculáta* L. (panicled). Open woods,streambanks, roadsides, near former dwellings. July-September. Fig. 806, Map 1870. From farther south and west. —FACU

5. *P. stolonífera* Sims (bearing stolons). Moist woods, streambanks. April-May. Map 1871. From farther south and west.

6. *P. maculáta* L. (spotted). Wild Sweet William. Meadows, near former dwellings. June-July. Map 1872. [*P. pyramidalis*]. Our plants are subsp. *maculata*. —FACW

P. latifólia Michx. Will key to *P. maculata* but lower cymes are on long peduncles, the upper on shorter ones forming a flattened to rounded inflorescence (cymes are short-peduncled, forming a subcylindric inflorescence in *P. maculata*). From farther south and west. Reported for MA. [*P. ovata*].

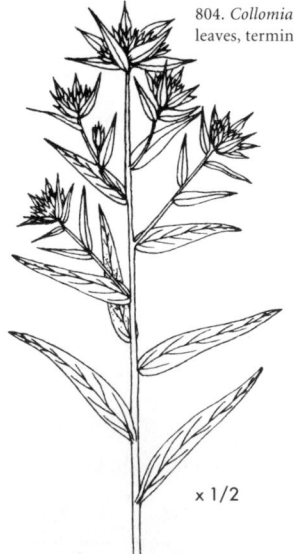

804. *Collomia linearis*. Upper part of plant; alternate leaves, terminal, leafy-bracted clusters of flowers.

x 1/2

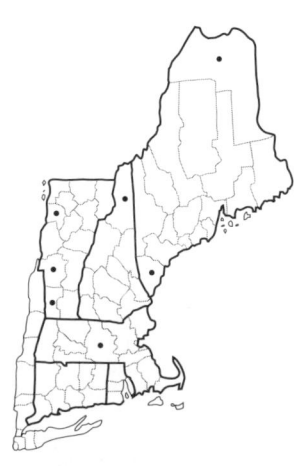

1867. *Collomia linearis*

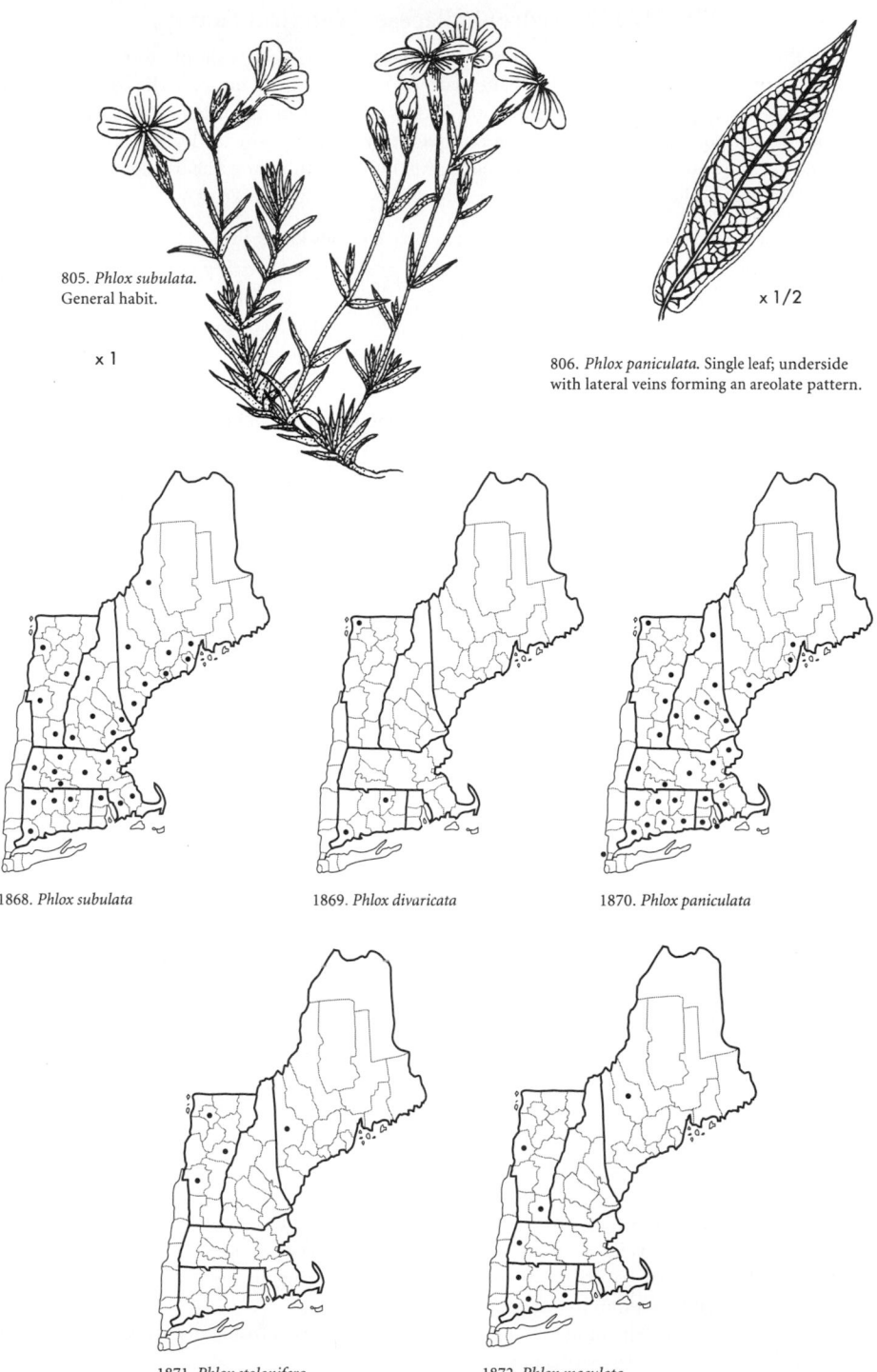

805. *Phlox subulata.* General habit.

× 1

× 1/2

806. *Phlox paniculata.* Single leaf; underside with lateral veins forming an areolate pattern.

1868. *Phlox subulata*

1869. *Phlox divaricata*

1870. *Phlox paniculata*

1871. *Phlox stolonifera*

1872. *Phlox maculata*

Family 172. Hydrophylláceae (Waterleaf Family)

Hermaphrodite, annual or perennial usually pubescent herbs. Leaves simple to pinnately compound, pinnatifid or palmately lobed, alternate or rarely opposite, at least the lower petioled, estipulate. Flowers perfect, regular, blue, purple or white, in terminal or lateral, ebracteate, often helicoid or scorpioid cymes or racemes, or rarely solitary in or opposite the leaf axils, calyx 5-lobed or of almost separate sepals, corolla 5-lobed, campanulate to tubular or nearly rotate, stamens 5, inserted on the corolla, ovary superior, 1 or 2-locular, style 1, 2-cleft. Fruit a 2-valved capsule.

Flowers solitary in or opposite the leaf axils; corolla as long or slightly longer than
    calyx .... 1. *Ellisia nyctelea*
Flowers in cymes or racemes; corolla substantially longer than the calyx.
    Axis of the inflorescence a simple monochasium, unbranched. .... 2. *Phacelia*
    Axis of the inflorescence a compound dichasium, repeatedly forked. (Fig. 807). .... 3. *Hydrophyllum*

1. *Ellísia* L. (for J. Ellis).

Branched, annual herbs; leaves pinnatifid, with oblong to lanceolate, entire or few-toothed segments, the lower leaves opposite, upper alternate; flowers white to bluish, solitary in or opposite the leaf axils, corolla campanulate, equalling or slightly longer than the calyx; capsule globose.

    1. *E. nyctélea* (L.) L. (nocturnal). Rich, moist woods and margins of streams. May-June. From farther south and west. Reported for Middlesex County MA. [*Nyctelea n.*]. —FACU

2. *Phacélia* Juss. (Greek name, based on type of inflorescence).

Annual (rarely perennial) herbs, simple or branched from the base; leaves simple to pinnately compound or pinnatifid, with oblong to lanceolate, entire or toothed segments or divisions; flowers bluish to white, in simple, monochasial cymes, corolla campanulate, rotate or tubular; capsule globose to ovoid.

a. Corolla with fringed lobes .... 1. *P. purshii*
a. Corolla lobes not fringed.
    b. Plant perennial from a short, underground caudex. .... 2. *P. heterophylla*
    b. Plant annual often from a taproot.
        c. Leaves simple, entire to deeply toothed or pinnately lobed.
            Stamens slightly exserted, with hairy appendages at base; seeds reticulated. ... 3. *P. minor*
            Stamens included, lacking hairy appendages; seeds not reticulated. .... 4. *P. linearis*
        c. Leaves pinnately compound.
            d. Calyx lobes 6 mm or more long; stamens exserted 1.5 or more times the
                length of the corolla; capsule up to 4 mm long, seeds usually 2. .... 5. *P. tanacetifolia*
            d. Calyx lobes 5 mm or less long; stamens included or barely exserted.
                Corolla blue; capsule globose, to 3 mm long; seeds 2-4. .... 6. *P. distans*
                Corolla white to pink with a yellow tube; capsule oblong, 4 mm or more
                long; seeds more than 4, numerous .... 7. *P. brachyloba*

    1. *P. púrshii* Buckl. (for its discoverer). Miami mist. Rich, moist woods and fields. April-June. From farther south and west. Reported for CT, Providence County RI.

    2. *P. heterophýlla* Pursh. Western; rarely adventive in our range. Reported for Middlesex County MA.

    P. egéna (Greene ex Brand) Const. Similar to *P. heterophylla* but with inflorescence short, open and widely branched; corolla white, 6 mm or more long (inflorescence elongate, of many short cymes; corolla yellowish to greenish-white, 5 mm or less long in *P. heterophylla*). From the southwest. Occurring as a waif in our range. Reported for MA.

    3. *P. mínor* (Harvey) Thellung ex Zimmerman. Rarely escaped from cultivation. Reported for MA. Touching can cause dermatitis in some individuals.

P. campanulária Gray. Resembling *P. minor* but corolla blue, corolla tube about twice as long as the lobes and appendages glabrous (corolla purple, tube about 3 times as long as the lobes and appendages puberulent in *P. minor*). From California; rarely escaped from cultivation in our range. Reported for Washington County NY.

4. *P. lineáris* (Pursh) Holz. Western; rarely adventive in our range. Reported for Hartford County CT, Hancock County ME.

P. víscida (Benth.) Torr. Will key to *P. linearis* but is hirsute and glandular, leaves doubly serrate, corolla lacking scales (*P. linearis* is hirsute but not glandular, leaves entire to pinnately lobed, corolla with scales at the base). From the southwest. Reported for CT.

5. *P. tanacetifólia* Benth. Rarely escaped from cultivation. Reported for MA, Hancock County ME.

6. *P. dístans* Benth. From the southwest. Occurring in our range as a waif. Reported for MA.

7. *P. brachylóba* (Benth.) Gray. From the southwest. Occurring as a waif in our range. Reported for MA. Touching can cause dermatitis in some individuals.

3. *Hydrophýllum* L. Water-leaf (from the Greek).

Perennial herbs from scaly rhizomes, glabrous or nearly so, simple to sparingly branched; leaves petioled, pinnately compound, deeply pinnately divided or palmately lobed, the divisions or lobes toothed; flowers white to blue or purple, in compound, dichasial cymes, corolla campanulate to tubular, the tube bearing 5 narrow appendages within, opposite the lobes; capsule globose.

Stem leaves pinnate; calyx lobes with cilia longer than the width of the lobe. (Fig. 807) . 1. *H. virginianum*
Stem leaves palmately 5-lobed; calyx lobes eciliate, or cilia shorter than the width
    of the lobe .... 2. *H. canadense*

1. *H. virginiánum* L. (Virginian). Rich, deciduous, often wet woods. May-July. Fig. 807, Map 1873. Young plants were used in salad and as a potherb by the Indians and early settlers. —FAC

2. *H. canadénse* L. (Canadian). Damp, rich woods. June-July. Endangered in ME. Reported for Berkshire County MA, Bennington County VT. —FACU

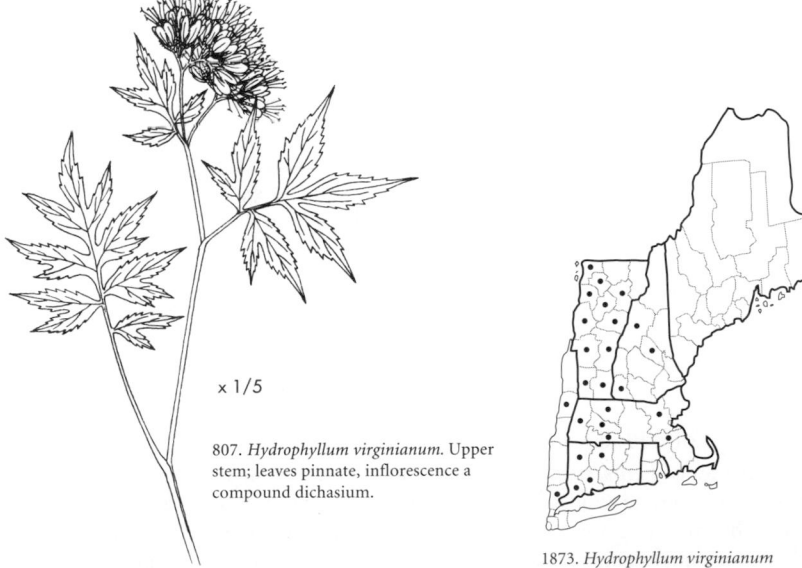

x 1/5

807. *Hydrophyllum virginianum.* Upper stem; leaves pinnate, inflorescence a compound dichasium.

1873. *Hydrophyllum virginianum*

Family 173. Boragináceae (Borage Family)

Hermaphrodite, annual or perennial, often bristly herbs. Leaves simple, alternate or rarely opposite, entire, or sometimes shallowly toothed, estipulate. Flowers perfect, usually regular, mostly blue, in one-sided scorpioid cymes, racemes or rarely axillary, bracteate or not, calyx 5-lobed or of 5 distinct sepals, corolla 5-lobed, often with 5 appendages in the throat, alternating with the stamens, stamens 5, inserted on the corolla, ovary superior, usually shallowly 4-lobed and 4-locular, style 1. Fruit mostly of 4, 1-seeded nutlets, sometimes fewer than 4 maturing.

a. Stem and leaves glabrous, glaucous .... 1. *Mertensia*
a. Stem and/or leaves pubescent.
    b. Leaves with at least 2 lateral veins paralleling midrib; nutlets smooth and
        shining, globose or ovoid. (Fig. 809).
        Corolla lobes obtuse; style included or short-exsert. .... 2. *Lithospermum*
        Corolla lobes acute to acuminate; style long-exsert. .... 3. *Onosmodium*
    b. Leaves with pinnate venation, the lateral veins not particularly parallel; nutlets
        not smooth and shining or if so then flattened.
      c. Flowers 1-3 in the leaf axils, blue; stems retrorsely prickly-hispid. (Fig. 810) ...... 4. *Asperugo*
                                                  procumbens
      c. Flowers in racemes or cymes or if axillary then not blue.
        d. Nutlets armed with barbed prickles, these evident before full maturity;
           stems with soft, appressed or spreading pubescence.
          e. Flowers all bracted .... 5. *Lappula*
          e. Flowers bractless, or only the basal ones bracted, or bracts alternating
            with or opposite the flowers.
            Leaves, at least the upper, auriculate-clasping or closely sessile by a
                rounded base; nutlets attached to the receptacle near the apex,
                their bases divergent. (Fig. 811) .... 6. *Cynoglossum*
            Leaves petioled or sessile, tapered to the base; nutlets attached to the
                receptacle near the middle, their bases not divergent . (Fig. 812). 7. *Hackelia*
        d. Nutlets smooth or roughened but lacking prickles.
          f. Stems with soft, appressed or spreading pubescence.
           g. Flowers and fruits sessile; upper leaves petioled. .... 8. *Heliotropium*
           g. Flowers and fruits pedicelled or upper leaves sessile.
             Flowers bractless except sometimes the lowest 1-4. .... 9. *Myosotis*
             Flowers all leafy-bracted .... 2. *Lithospermum*
         f. Stems with bristly-hispid, spreading pubescence.
           h. Pedicels mostly 1 cm or more long; corolla rotate; anthers with an
               appendage .... 10. *Borago officinalis*
           h. Pedicels mostly less than 1 cm long; corolla with a tube; anthers
             without an appendage.
            i. Corolla irregular, oblique, with unequal lobes, the tube often bent
               or curved.
              Stamens exserted; throat of corolla tube without appendages. .... 11. *Echium*
              Stamens included; throat of corolla tube with appendages ... . 12. *Anchusa*
            i. Corolla regular.
             j. Flowers all or mostly all bracted .... 12. *Anchusa*
             j. Flowers bractless except sometimes the lowest 1-3.
                Corolla tubular-campanulate, the upper part of the tube 3 mm
                  or more in diameter; plant perennial .... 13. *Symphytum*
                Corolla salverform or funnelform, the upper part of the tube
                  less than 3 mm in diameter; plant annual .... 14. *Amsinckia*

1. *Merténsia* Roth. Bluebell (for F. Mertens).

Glabrous, perennial herbs, stems erect or ascending to spreading or decumbent; leaves alternate, oblong to ovate, obovate or oblanceolate, petioled or the uppermost sometimes sessile; flowers blue or pink, in bractless or leafy-bracted cymes terminating the stem and branches, corolla tubular, funnelform or campanulate, appendages lacking or small and inconspicuous.

Flowers 1.3 cm or more long, not leafy-bracted; plant erect or ascending; woodlands.... 1. *M. virginica*
Flowers less than 1 cm long, usually leafy-bracted; plant spreading or decumbent;
    beaches. (Fig. 808) .... 2. *M. maritima*

1. M. virgínica (L.) Pers. ex Link (Virginian). Rich, moist woods. April-May. From farther south and west. Reported for Sagadahoc County ME, Norfolk County MA. —FACW

2. M. marítima (L.) S. F. Gray (of seashores). Gravel, sandy and rocky seacoast. June-July. Fig. 808, Map 1874. (Arctic; Eurasia). Endangered in MA. [*Pneumaria m.*]. Our plants are var. *maritima*. —FACW

2. Lithospérmum L. Gromwell (from the Greek, referring to the hard nutlets).

Branched, soft-pubescent or puberulent, annual or perennial herbs; leaves alternate, sessile or subsessile, linear to lanceolate or oblanceolate, with a single midvein or with at least 2 lateral veins paralleling midrib; flowers white to yellowish-white, sessile and solitary in the axils of the upper leaves, forming leafy spikes or racemes, corolla funnelform, appendages lacking or small and inconspicuous. [*Buglossoides*].

Leaves with 2 or more lateral veins on each side of the midvein; nutlets white,
    smooth and shining; flowers yellowish; perennial (Fig. 809). .... 1. *L. officinale*
Leaves with only a midvein, lateral veins absent; nutlets brown, wrinkled and pitted,
    dull; flowers white; annual .... 2. *L. arvense*

1. L. officinále L. (of the shops). European Gromwell. Fields, roadsides, waste places. May-July. Fig. 809, Map 1875. (Naturalized from Europe).

L. latifólium Michx. Similar to *L. officinale* but with leaves 2 cm or more wide, scattered, the internodes mostly longer than 2 cm (leaves less than 2 cm wide, somewhat overlapping, the internodes mostly shorter than 2 cm in *L. officinale*). From farther west. Reported for MA.

2. L. arvénse L. (of cultivated fields). Corn Gromwell. Fields, roadsides, waste places. May-June. Map 1876. (Naturalized from Europe). [*Buglossoides a.*].

3. Onosmódium Michx. False Gromwell (name based on resemblance to the genus *Onosma*).

Branched, appressed-pubescent perennial herbs; leaves alternate, oblong to oblong-lanceolate, sessile or the lower narrowed to petioles, with at least 2 strong lateral veins paralleling midrib; flowers yellowish (or rarely whitish or greenish), in terminal, leafy-bracted, scorpioid cymes, calyx lobes often unequal, corolla cylindric, with erect lobes, appendages lacking, style long-exserted; nutlets white to tan, smooth and shining.

1. O. virginiánum (L.) A. DC. (Virginian). Dry sandy barrens and woodlands. May-July. Map 1877. Endangered in CT.

O. mólle Michx. Corolla whitish or greenish, the lobes acute (corolla yellowish, the lobes acuminate in *O. virginianum*). Southern. Reported for New Haven County CT. Represented with us as subsp. *occidentále* (Mack.) Johnst.

4. Asperúgo L. Madwort (name referring to the harsh leaves).

Annual herbs with recurved, prickly-hispid pubescence and slender, procumbent, freely branched stems; leaves opposite, or some alternate or whorled, oblanceolate or the upper elliptic, narrowed to margined petioles; flowers on short, recurved pedicels, 1-3 together in the leaf axils and forks of the branches, calyx longer than the corolla, each lobe with a pair of smaller lobes or teeth at the base, becoming enlarged, reticulate-veiny, and compressed in fruit, corolla small, campanulate, with well developed appendages.

1. A. procúmbens L. (ascending from a prostrate base). Waste places. May-July. Fig. 810, Map 1878. (Adventive from Europe).

5. Láppula Moench. Stickseed (diminutive of *lappa*, a bur, referring to the armed nutlets).

Branched, rough-pubescent, annual herbs; leaves alternate, sessile or the lower petioled, linear to narrowly lanceolate or oblong; flowers blue or white, all bracted, in scorpioid cymes terminating the branches, corolla salverform or funnelform, the throat with appendages; fruiting pedicels erect, nutlets tuberculate, armed with 1 or more rows of prickles.

Prickles on each nutlet in 2 rows .... 1. *L. squarrosa*
Prickles on each nutlet in a single row. ....2. *L. occidentalis*

1. L. squarrósa (Retz.) Dumort. Waste places and roadsides. May-September. Map 1879. (Naturalized from Europe). [*L. echinata; L. lappula*].

L. cenchrusoides reportedly a distinct species, has been documented for CT and MA.

2. L. occidentális (Wats.) Greene. Waste places and roadsides. May-September. Map 1880. (*Patagonia*). [*L. redowskii*]. Our plants are var. *occidentalis*.

6. Cynoglóssum L. (from the Greek meaning dog tongue, from the leaf shape and texture).

Mostly tall, soft-pubescent, annual or perennial herbs; leaves alternate, the basal petioled, the upper sessile by a rounded base or clasping; flowers purplish, blue or white, in bractless, panicled, somewhat scorpioid racemes, corolla salverform to funnelform, with a short tube and 5 appendages in and partially closing the throat; nutlets covered with barbed prickles. In addition to the following species *C. microglochin* and *C. wallichii* have been reported as waifs in MA.

Racemes occurring in the leaf axils or terminating axillary branches. (Fig. 811) .... 1. *C. officinale*
Racemes with a naked common peduncle. ....2. *C. virginianum*

1. C. officinále L. (of the shops). Hound's tongue. Pastures, fields, waste places. May-June. Fig. 811, Map 1881. (Naturalized from Europe). Contact with skin can cause dermatitis; preparations are used to treat hemorrhoids and insomnia; large doses can produce narcotic effects.

C. amábile Staph. & Drummond. Chinese Forget-Me-Not. Similar to *C. officinale* but with calyx up to 3 mm long, flowers blue, occasionally white to pink (calyx 3 mm or more long, flowers reddish-purple in *C. officinale*). Occasionally escaped from cultivation. Reported for MA, NH.

2. C. virginiánum L. (Virginian). Wild Comfrey. Open woods. May-June. Map 1882. Endangered in NH, ME. From farther west and south. Our plants include var. *virginianum* and the following var.:

var. *boreále* (Fern.) Cooperrider. Calyx at anthesis 2.5 mm or less long; nutlets 5 mm or less long (calyx at anthesis 3 mm or more long and nutlets more than 5 mm long in var. *virginianum*). [*C. boreale*].

7. Hackélia Opiz. Beggar's-lice (for P. Hackel).

Similar to *Lappula* except median stem leaves mostly petioled, flowers bractless or only the basal ones bracted, or bracts alternating with or opposite the flowers, and fruiting pedicels deflexed.

Nutlets prickly over the entire surface. .... 1. *H. virginiana*
Nutlets prickly only on the margins, the dorsal area unarmed or with a few short
   bristles .... 2. *H. deflexa*
                                                                                                                 var. *americana*

1. H. virginiána (L.) Johnst. Rich woods and thickets. July-September. Fig. 812, Map 1883. [*Lappula v.*]. —FACU

x 3/5

808. *Mertensia maritima.* General habit; plant decumbent, flowers in leafy-bracted, terminal cymes.

x 2/3

809. *Lithospermum officinale.* Upper stem; leaves with lateral veins paralleling midrib.

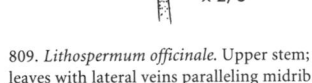

x 1/4

810. *Asperugo procumbens.* Section of stem; stem retrorsely hispid, flowers 1-several in the leaf axils.

x 1/2

811. *Cynoglossum officinale.* Upper part of plant; leaves sessile by a rounded base, flowers axillary and terminating axillary branches.

x 1/3

812. *Hackelia virginiana.* Upper part of plant; median leaves petioled, upper sessile.

1874. *Mertensia maritima*

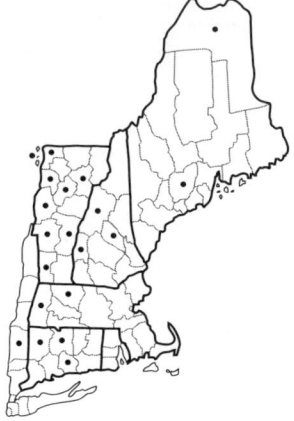

1875. *Lithospermum officinale*

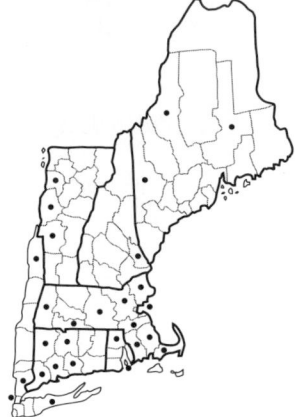

1876. *Lithospermum arvense*

1877. *Onosmodium virginianum*

1878. *Asperugo procumbens*

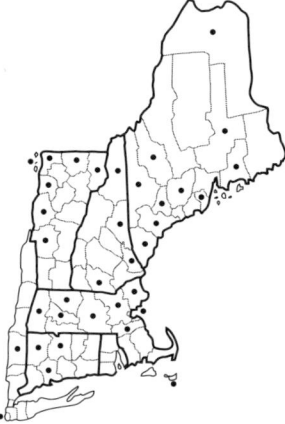

1879. *Lappula squarrosa*

1880. *Lappula occidentalis*

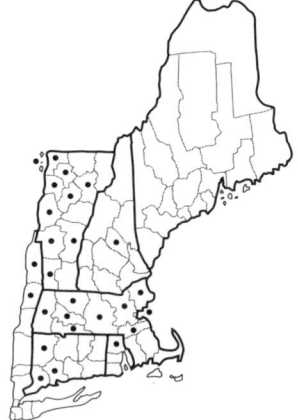

1881. *Cynoglossum officinale*

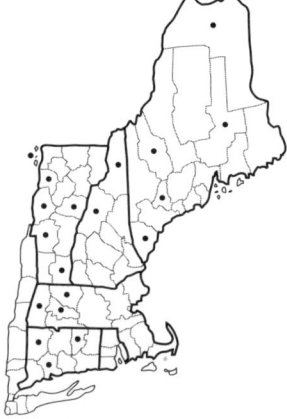

1882. *Cynoglossum virginianum*

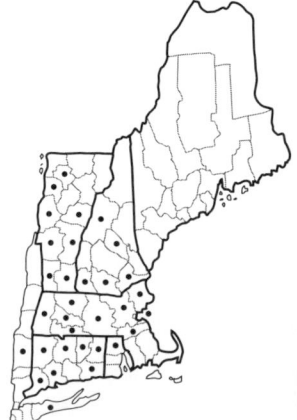

1883. *Hackelia virginiana*

2. *H. defléxa* (Wahlenb.) Opiz. Rocky woods. July-August. Map 1884. Endangered in NH, ME. From farther north and west. [*H. americana; Lappula a.; L. deflexa*]. Represented with us as var. *americána* (Gray) Fern. & I.M. Johnst.

8. Heliotrópium L. Heliotrope (ancient name based on the belief that the plant turns toward the sun in flowering).

Branched, soft-pubescent, annual herbs; leaves alternate, long-petioled, elliptic to ovate; flowers blue to white, sessile, in bractless scorpioid cymes, the lateral often solitary, the terminal in peduncled clusters of 2 or more, corolla funnelform, appendages lacking; nutlets puberulent and tuberculate.

1. *H. europaéum* L. (European). Roadsides and waste places. June-August. (Naturalized from Europe). Reported for Middlesex County MA, Bronx County NY. Three other species, two native to South America and one native to India (*H. indicum*) and introduced in the southern U.S. have been recorded in our range:

H. índicum L. Fruits separating into 2 halves, each with 2 nutlets, axis of inflorescence and calyx sparsely hirsute, annual, leaves ovate, reported for Middlesex County MA. [*Tiaridium i.*] —FAC; *H. amplexicáule* Vahl. Similar to *H. indicum* but perennial with lanceolate leaves, reported for Middlesex and Norfolk Counties MA [*Cochranea anchusaefolia*]; *H. curassávicum* L. Fruit 4-lobed, separating into 4 nutlets, axis of inflorescence and calyx glabrous, leaves linear to oblanceolate, reported for York County ME —OBL. (In *H. europaeum* fruits are similar to *H. curassavicum* but axis of inflorescence and calyx are densely pubescent and leaves are ovate).

9. Myosótis L. Forget-me-not (Greek name based on the short soft leaves of some species).

Low, erect or decumbent, usually soft-pubescent, annual or perennial herbs; leaves alternate, sessile or the lower petioled; flowers blue to white, in terminal, bractless, scorpioid cymes or occasionally the lower ones in the leaf axils, calyx lobes sometimes unequal, corolla salverform to funnelform, the throat with appendages; nutlets compressed, smooth and shining, with a conspicuous rim.

a.Hairs of calyx straight, closely appressed, none spreading or hooked.
    Corolla more than 5 mm wide; style as long or longer than the nutlets. .... 1. *M. scorpioides*
    Corolla 5 mm or less wide (first flowers may be somewhat larger); style
        distinctly shorter than the nutlets .... 2. *M. laxa*
a.Hairs of calyx, at least some, spreading or hooked.
  b. Lowest flowers of inflorescence in leaf axils. (Fig. 813).
    Calyx somewhat bilabiate, the lobes unequal; corolla white. .... 3. *M. verna*
    Calyx not bilabiate, the lobes equal or nearly so; corolla blue. .... 4. *M. stricta*
  b. Lowest flowers of inflorescence not in leaf axils, the cymes naked.
    c. Pedicels 3 mm or less long .... 5. *M. discolor*
    c. Pedicels, at least the longer ones, 4 mm or more long.
      Corolla 4 mm or less wide .... 6. *M. arvensis*
      Corolla 4.5 mm or more wide .... 7. *M. sylvatica*

1. *M. scorpioídes* L. (like a scorpion). Shallow-water, pond and stream margins, wet meadows, marshes, open wet soil. May-September. Map 1885. (Naturalized from Europe). [*M. palustris*]. —OBL

2. *M. láxa* Lehm. (loose). Same habitats as *M. scorpioides*. May-September. Map 1886. (Chile; Eurasia). —OBL

3. *M. vérna* Nutt. (spring). Dry woods and fields. April-June. Fig. 813, Map 1887. (s. S. Amer.). [*M. virginica*]. —FAC-

4. *M. stricta* Link ex Roemer & J.A. Schultes. Fields, roadsides and waste places. May-July. Map 1888. (Naturalized from Europe). [*M. micrantha*].

5. *M. díscolor*Pers. (parti-colored). Fields and roadsides. May-July. Reported for MA. (Adventive from Europe). [*M. versicolor*].

6. *M. arvénsis* (L.) Hill (of cultivated soil). Fields, roadsides, waste places. June-August. Map 1889. (Naturalized from Europe).

7. *M. sylvática*(Ehrh.) Hoffm. (of the woods). Occasionally escaped from cultivation to roadsides and around buildings. May-July. Map 1890. (Introduced from Europe).

10. *Borágo* L. Borage (old name).

Coarse, branched, hispid, annual herbs from a taproot; leaves alternate, oblong to obovate, narrowed into margined petioles, the upper sessile and often clasping, entire to crenulate; flowers blue, in loose, terminal cymes, these leafy-bracted, at least below, corolla rotate, with appendages, anthers appendaged, connivent around the style, forming a cone.

1. *B. officinális* L. (of the shops). Waste places. July-September. Map 1891. (Introduced from Europe). Leaves and flowers can be added to salads or to cold drinks; also reported to be useful as a diuretic, in treating throat irritations and in imparting an exhilarating effect.

11. *Échium* L. Viper's Bugloss (Greek name, based on fancied resemblance of the nutlets to a viper's head).

Branched, rough-hispid, biennial herbs from a taproot; leaves alternate, oblong to linear-lanceolate, sessile or the lower petioled; flowers blue, in short, bracted, scorpioid cymes forming an elongate, leafy thyrse, corolla funnelform, irregularly lobed, appendages lacking, stamens and style exserted; nutlets roughened.

In addition to the following species *E. creticum* has been reported for MA and ME.

1. *E. vulgáre* L. (common). Fields, roadsides and waste places. June-September. Fig. 814, Map 1892. (Naturalized from Europe). Contact with skin causes dermatitis, however young leaves can be eaten in salads; preparations made from the plant have been used in treating skin eruptions and irritations.

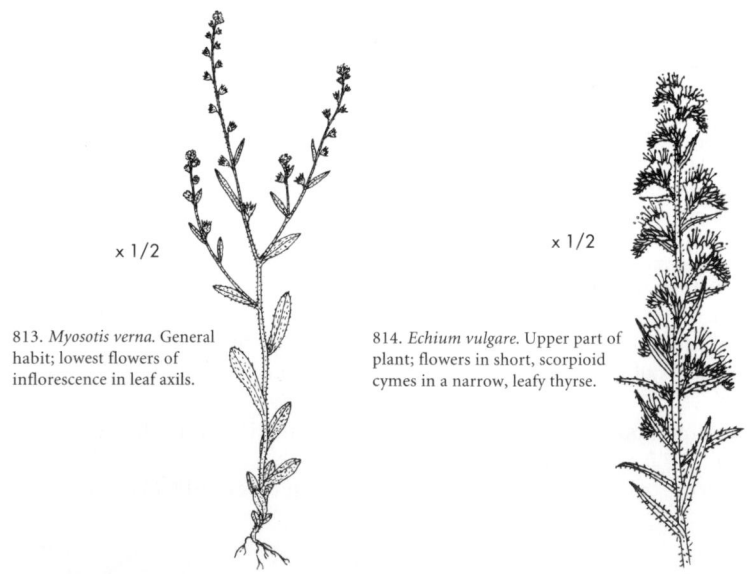

x 1/2

x 1/2

813. *Myosotis verna.* General habit; lowest flowers of inflorescence in leaf axils.

814. *Echium vulgare.* Upper part of plant; flowers in short, scorpioid cymes in a narrow, leafy thyrse.

1884. *Hackelia deflexa* var. *americana*

1885. *Myosotis scorpioides*

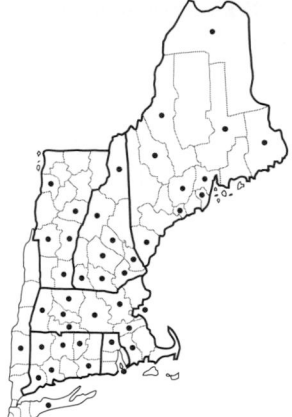

1886. *Myosotis laxa*

1887. *Myosotis verna*

1888. *Myosotis stricta*

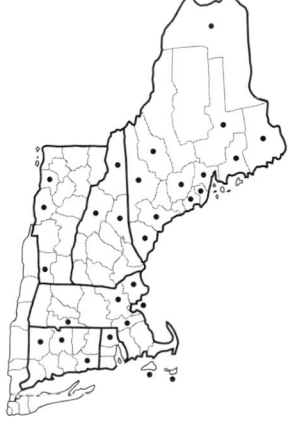

1889. *Myosotis arvensis*

1890. *Myosotis sylvatica*

1891. *Borago officinalis*

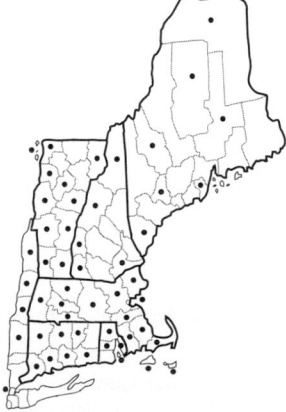

1892. *Echium vulgare*

E. pustulátum Sibthorp & Sm. Similar to *E. vulgare* but distinguishable in having pubescence with pustular bases and a broad, pyramid-shaped thyrse (pubescence not pustulate at base and inflorescence a long narrow thyrse in *E. vulgare*). (Adventive from Europe). Reported for MA. [*E. vulgare* var. *p.*].

12. Anchúsa L. Alkanet (Greek name).

Branched, hispid, annual, biennial or perennial herbs; leaves alternate, the lower petioled, oblanceolate, the others sessile and lanceolate; flowers blue, bracted, in single or paired scorpioid cymes in a leafy panicle or cyme, corolla regular to slightly irregular, funnelform, appendaged in the throat; nutlets reticulate or tuberculate.

Nónea Medic. rósea (Bieb.) Link. Will key to *Anchusa* but is distinguishable from it in having a long-tubular rose-colored corolla unappendaged in the throat (corolla funnelform, blue, appendaged in the throat in *Anchusa*). (Adventive from Europe.) Reported for ME.

Pentaglóttis Tausch *sempervírens* (L.) Tausch ex Bailey. Resembling *Anchusa* but distinguishable from it and *Nonea rosea* by the ovate, acuminate, conspicuously netted-veined leaves (leaves oblong to lanceolate and not conspicuously veined in the latter 2 species). European; rarely found in our range. Reported for Hancock County ME. [*Anchusa s.; Caryolopha s.*].

Plagiobóthrys Fisch. & Mey. *trachycárpus* (Gray) Jtn. Will key to *Anchusa* but is distinguishable from it, *Nonea* and *Pentaglottis* in having lower leaves opposite, linear, corolla white, short-salverform to rotate. From the southwest. Reported for MA.

a. Plant annual; corolla slightly irregular, the tube bent or curved. .... 1. *A. arvensis*
a. Plant perennial; corolla regular.
  b. Corolla 6 mm or less wide, the tube equalling or only slightly longer than the calyx .. 2. *A. barrelieri*
  b. Corolla more than 6 mm wide, the tube (in fully developed flowers) distinctly
      longer than the calyx.
    Nutlets oblique, longer than high, creating a broadly rounded base to the
      calyx; corolla less than 12 mm wide .... 3. *A. officinalis*
    Nutlets erect, higher than long, the calyx base tapered; corolla 12 mm or
      more wide .... 4. *A. azurea*

1. *A. arvénsis* (L.) Bieb. (of cultivated fields). Waste places. June-August. Map 1893. (Naturalized from Europe). [*Lycopsis*].

2. *A. barreliéri* (All.) Vitm. (for J. Barrellier). Waste places. (Adventive from Europe). Reported for Fairfield County CT.

3. *A. officinális* L. (of the shops). Roadsides and waste places. May-September. Map 1894. (Adventive from Europe).

4. *A. azúrea* Mill. (sky-blue). Roadsides and waste places. May-September. Map 1895. (Adventive from Europe). Preparations made from the plant have been used in external applications to treat skin inflammation.

13. Sýmphytum L. Comfrey (Greek name, based on its reputed medicinal value).

Coarse, branched, sparsely to densely hispid, perennial herbs from a thick, mucilaginous taproot; leaves alternate, lanceolate to ovate-lanceolate, narrowed into margined petioles, the bases sometimes decurrent by wings along the stem, the uppermost leaves sessile and sometimes opposite; flowers yellowish to blue or pink, in single or paired, terminal, scorpioid cymes, bractless, tubular-campanulate, the throat with appendages.

In addition to the following species *S. x uplandicum* has been reported for CT.

a. Leaf bases decurrent, nearly or quite to the next leaf. (Fig. 815). .... 1. *S. officinale*
a. Leaf bases not decurrent or only slightly so.
    Pubescence of broad-based, flattened, often recurved spinules; root thickened
      and fleshy but not a tuber .... 2. *S. asperum*
    Pubescence of slender hairs, these not broad-based or flattened; root a rounded
      tuber .... 3. *S. tuberosum*

1. S. officinále L. (of the shops). Fields, roadsides, waste places. May-September. Fig. 815, Map 1896. (Introduced from Europe). Preparations of the plant are used in externally applied poultices for healing wounds; despite claims as to beneficial uses of the roots and leaves taken as medicine or as food or drink, recent research has shown that this plant is poisonous and can produce harmful effects if taken internally.

2. S. ásperum Lepechin (harsh). Fields, roadsides, waste places. June-August. Map 1897. (Introduced from the Caucasus). [*S. asperrimum*].

3. S. tuberósum. L. (tuberous). Fields, roadsides. June-July. (Adventive from Europe). Reported for CT, Middlesex County MA.

14. *Amsínckia* Lehm. (for W. Amsinck).

Decumbent to ascending, branched, spreading-hispid, annual herbs; leaves alternate, sessile or the lowest petioled, lanceolate to ovate-lanceolate, denticulate or entire; flowers yellow, in terminal scorpioid cymes, bractless or the lower flowers bracted, corolla salverform or funnelform, append-ages present or absent; nutlets roughened.

Cryptántha Lehm. ex G. Don. Similar to *Amsinckia* but distinguishable in being copiously pustulate-hispid and in having white flowers (plant hispid but hairs not pustulate and flowers yellow in *Amsinckia*). Northwestern; 2 species occur as waifs in our range: *C. ambígua* (Gray) Greene. Limb of corolla up to 2.5 mm broad. Reported for Middlesex County MA; *C. intermédia* (Gray) Green. Limb of corolla 4 mm or more broad. Reported for MA.

Plagiobóthrys Fisch. & Mey. *scoúleri* (H. & A.) Johnston. Will key to *Amsinckia* but is distinguish-able from it and *Cryptantha* in having the lower leaves opposite (lower leaves alternate in the latter 2 genera). West coast. Reported for MA, ME. Represented with us as var. *scouleri*.

1. A. lycopsoídes Lehm. Sporadically occurring in fields and waste places. April-June. Map 1898. (Adventive from B.C.). From farther west. [*A. barbata*].

Several other species adventive from the west have been reported as waifs for our range: these include *A. spectábilis, A. douglasiana, A. menziesii;* and *A. intermedia* all of which are very similar; they differ in minor features of the leaf margins, pubescence of the calyx, length of the corolla tube and the nutlets but the distinctions are unclear and inconsistent. The latter species is reported to be poisonous.

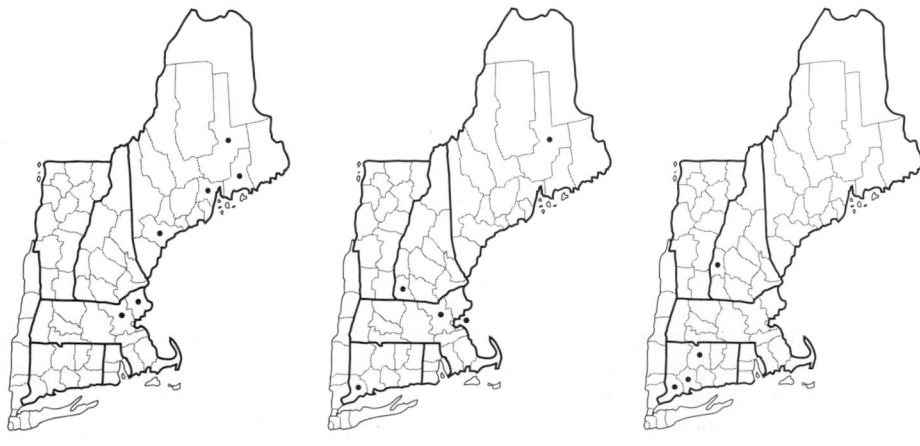

1893. *Anchusa arvensis*   1894. *Anchusa officinalis*   1895. *Anchusa azurea*

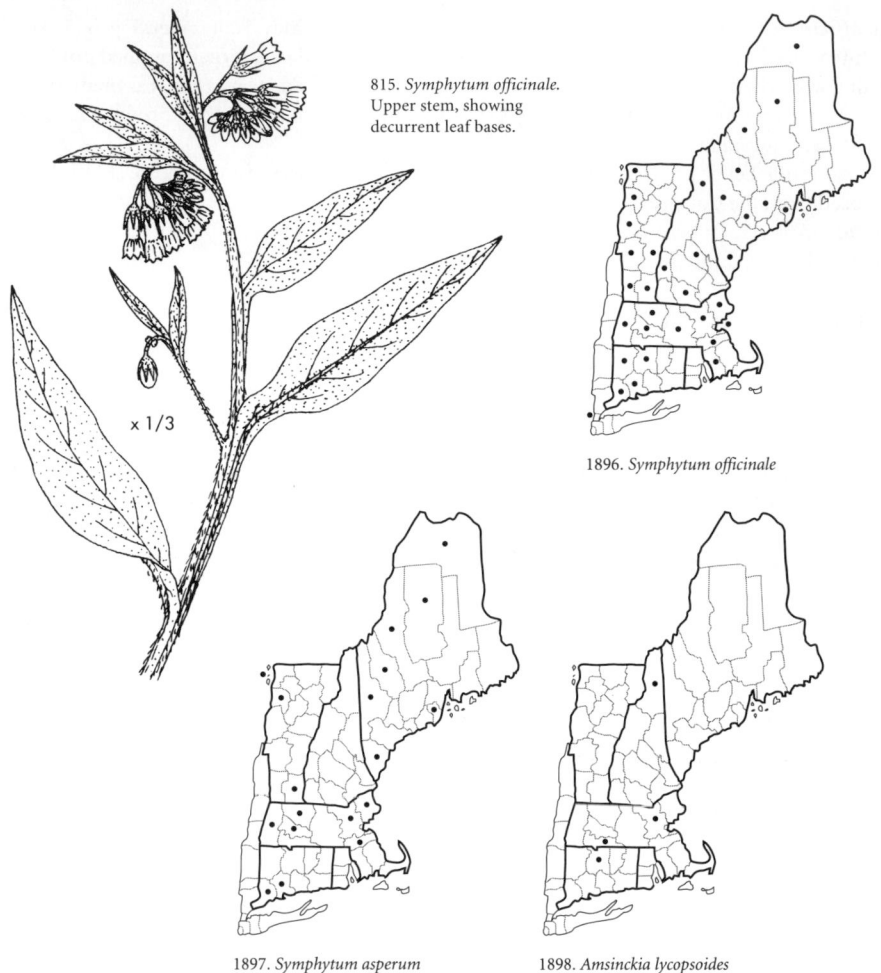

815. *Symphytum officinale.*
Upper stem, showing
decurrent leaf bases.

× 1/3

1896. *Symphytum officinale*

1897. *Symphytum asperum*

1898. *Amsinckia lycopsoides*

Family 174. Verbenáceae (Vervain Family)

Represented with us by the 3 genera described below.

Ovary 4-locular; fruit of 4, 1-seeded nutlets. .... 1. *Verbena*
Ovary 1-locular; fruit a single achene. .... 2. *Phryma*
                                                                                                    leptostachya

1. Verbéna L. Vervain (Latin name).

Hermaphrodite, annual or perennial herbs with quadrangular stems; leaves simple, opposite, toothed, lobed or dissected, estipulate; flowers perfect, irregular to nearly regular, blue, purple, pink or white, bracted, sessile, in terminal solitary, cymose or paniculate spikes, calyx tubular, unequally 5-toothed, corolla salverform, somewhat unequally 5-lobed, slightly 2-lipped, the tube often curved, stamens 4, didynamous, inserted on the corolla, ovary superior, 4-locular, style 1, 2-lobed; fruit of 4, 1-seeded nutlets enclosed within the persistent calyx. —Wildl. 1

Glandulária J. F. Gmel. *canadénsis* (L.) Small. Similar to *Verbena* but with showy flowers, the corolla 1 cm or more broad, sterile lobe of the style protruding well beyond the stigmatic lobe, fruiting calyx usually more than twice as long as the fruit, its tips constricted or contorted beyond it (in *Verbena* corollas are less than 1 cm broad, sterile lobe of the style not protruding beyond the stigmatic lobe, fruiting calyx rarely more than twice as long as the fruit and not contorted beyond it). From farther south and west. Reported for CT. [*G. lambertii; G. drummondii; Verbena c.; V. drummondii*].

V. hýbrida Voss. Similar to the latter species but with flowers up to 2.5 cm broad and densely pubescent leaves (flowers up to 1.5 cm broad and leaves glabrous or appressed-pubescent in *Glandularia canadensis*). Occasionally escaped from cultivation. Reported for MA.

a. Leaves deeply dissected or lobed. (Fig. 816).
  b. Subtending bracts leafy, 2 or more times as long as the calyx; plant usually
    decumbent. .... 1. *V. bracteata*
  b. Subtending bracts not leafy, as long or shorter than the calyx; plant erect.
    Spikes very slender and elongate, with mostly remote fruiting calyces. .... 2. *V. officinalis*
    Spikes pencil-like, with mostly imbracted fruiting calyces. .... 3. *V. hastata*
a. Leaves not dissected or lobed, often coarsely or doubly toothed.
  c. Leaves with subcordate, auriculate-clasping base. .... 4. *V. bonariensis*
  c. Leaves petioled or tapered to the base.
    d. Spikes panicled at the tips of the stems and branches; mature calyces mostly
      3 mm or less long. (Fig. 817).
      Spikes very slender and elongate, with mostly remote fruiting calyces. .... 5. *V. urticifolia*
      Spikes pencil-like, with mostly imbricated fruiting calyces. .... 3. *V. hastata*
    d. Spikes 1-3 at the tips of the stems and branches; mature calyces mostly longer
      than 3 mm.
      Stems densely pubescent; leaves ovate to elliptic, the larger more than 1.5
        cm wide .... 6. *V. stricta*
      Stems glabrous to sparsely pubescent; leaves narrowly lanceolate or
        oblanceolate, the larger 1.5 cm or less wide. .... 7. *V. simplex*

1. *V. bracteáta* Lag. & Rodr. (with bracts). Roadsides, waste places and fields. Fruit: July-September. Fig. 816, Map 1899. From farther south and west. [*V. bracteosa*].

V. lasiostáchys Link. Resembling *V. bracteata* but distinguishable in having bracts not surpassing the calyx (bracts much longer than the calyx in *V. bracteata*). Western. Reported for Kings County NY.

2. *V. officinális* L. (of the shops). Roadsides, waste places and fields. Fruit: July-October. Map 1900. (Naturalized from Europe). Has been used as a bitter in making liquors and as a substitute for tea. —FACU-

3. *V. hastáta* L. (halberd-shaped). Wet meadows, marshes, pond and stream margins. Fruit: July-October. Fig. 817, Map 1901. Our plants are var. *hastata*. —FACW+

V. x blanchárdii Moldenke. A hybrid between *V. hastata* and *V. simplex.*

4. *V. bonariénsis* L. Cultivated soil, waste places. From farther south. Reported for Hampshire County MA. Represented with us as var. *conglomeráta* Briq.

5. *V. urticifólia* L. (nettled-leaved). Fields, thickets, roadsides, waste places. Fruit: July-September. Map 1902. Our plants include var. *urticifolia* and the following var.:
  var. *leiocárpa* Perry & Fern. Leaves velutinous beneath; calyx puberulent; nutlets smooth (leaves strigose or glabrous beneath, calyx strigose and nutlets corrugated in var. *urticifolia*). —FACU

V. x engelmánnii Moldenke. A hybrid between *V. urticifolia* and *V. hastata.*

6. *V. stricta*. Vent. (strict). Roadsides, fields, barrens. Fruit: July-September. Map 1903. From farther west.

7. *V. símplex* Lehm. (simple). Dry fields and woods. Fruit: July-September. Map 1904. Endangered in MA. [*V. angustifolia*].

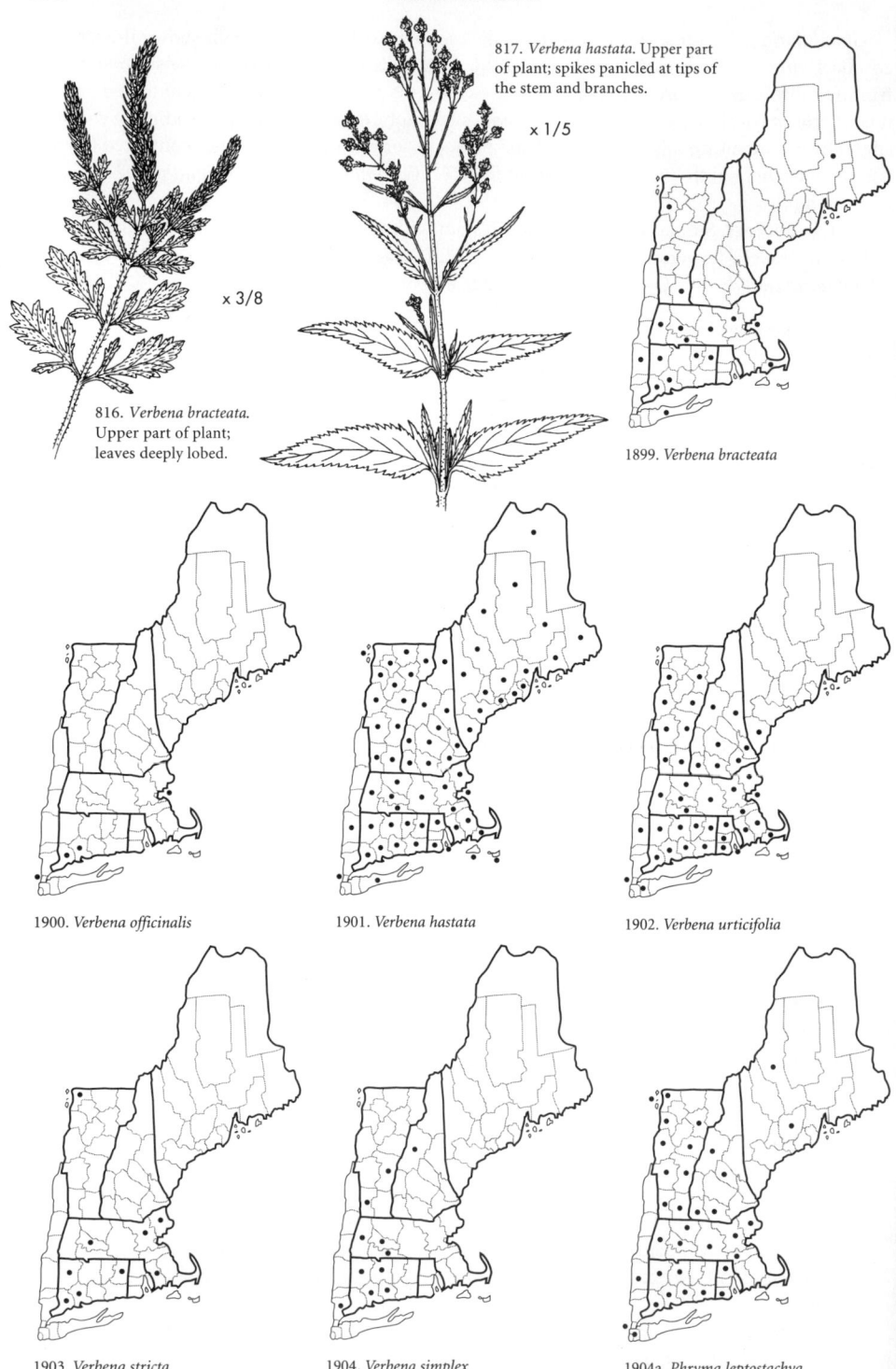

817. *Verbena hastata*. Upper part of plant; spikes panicled at tips of the stem and branches.

x 1/5

x 3/8

816. *Verbena bracteata*. Upper part of plant; leaves deeply lobed.

1899. *Verbena bracteata*

1900. *Verbena officinalis*

1901. *Verbena hastata*

1902. *Verbena urticifolia*

1903. *Verbena stricta*

1904. *Verbena simplex*

1904a. *Phryma leptostachya*

2. Phrýma L. Lopseed.

Hermaphrodite, perennial herbs with stems somewhat 4-sided; leaves simple, opposite, petioled or the upper sessile, ovate, acute to acuminate, coarsely and often doubly dentate, estipulate; flowers perfect, irregular, small, white to purplish, opposite, horizontal, distant, in slender, elongate, spiciform racemes terminating the stem and branches and often in the upper axils, each flower subtended by a bract and 2 bractlets, becoming reflexed in fruit, calyx bilabiate, 5-lobed, 3 lobes much longer than the other 2, subulate, corolla tubular, bilabiate, the upper lip emarginate, the lower much larger, 3-lobed, stamens 4, inserted on the corolla tube, ovary superior, 1-locular, style 1; fruit an achene, enclosed by the persistent calyx, the latter with the 3 elongate lobes hooked at the tip. [*Phrymaceae*].

    1. P. leptostáchya L. (slender-spiked). Rich woods. June-August. Map 1904a (Asia).

Family 175. Lamiáceae (Mint Family)

Hermaphrodite, annual or perennial, mostly aromatic herbs (ours), usually with square stems. Leaves simple, opposite, entire or toothed to deeply lobed, estipulate. Flowers perfect, usually irregular, in axillary cymose clusters, these often aggregated into leafy-bracted racemes, spikes, heads or panicles, or flowers solitary in the leaf axils, bracteolate or not, calyx usually 5-lobed (rarely 4-lobed), regular or bilabiate, corolla tubular, 4-5 lobed, usually irregular and bilabiate, rarely nearly regular, stamens 2, or 4 and didynamous, inserted on the corolla tube, ovary superior, 4-lobed or parted, 2-4-locular, style 1, 2-lobed. Fruit of 4, 1-seeded nutlets, sometimes fewer than 4 maturing. [*Labiatae*].

A. Calyx tube with a distinct protuberance or cap.
    Calyx 2-lipped, the lips entire, the tube with a protuberance. (Fig. 820). .... 1. *Scutellaria*
    Calyx 5-lobed, the upper lobe broad and rounded, its margins decurrent along
        the tube and forming a cap. (Fig. 822). .... 2. *Ocimum basilicum*
A. Calyx tube without a protuberance or cap.
  B. Flowers solitary in the axil of each bract, scattered or opposite, the verticels up
    to 2-flowered; inflorescence terminal, or terminal and axillary. (Fig. 824).
    C. Inflorescence a terminal panicle.
      D. Flowers in dense clusters forming trichotomous panicles; calyx regular;
        bracts colored. (Fig. 823) .... 3. *Origanum vulgare*
      D. Flowers in a loose, irregularly branched, leafy panicle or a panicle of
        racemes; calyx 2-lipped; bracts not colored.
        Flowers in a loose, irregularly branched, leafy panicle, blue; leaves
          oblong, entire or nearly so .... 4. *Trichostema*
        Flowers in a panicle of racemes, yellow; leaves ovate to elliptic, coarsely
          serrate .... 5. *Collinsonia*
                                                   serotina
    C. Inflorescence of terminal and axillary racemes. (Fig. 825).
      E. Leaves lanceolate, sessile .... 6. *Physostegia*
                                                   virginiana
      E. Leaves ovate to oblong, petioled.
        Leaves truncate to cordate at base, crenate; corolla 1-lipped, the lip
          pinnately 5-lobed. (Fig. 826) .... 7. *Teucrium*
        Leaves narrowed to base, coarsely serrate to laciniate; corolla 2-lipped,
          1 lobe slightly larger than the other 4 .... 8. *Perilla frutescens*
  B. Flowers 2 or more in the axil of each bract, the verticels 4 or more flowered.
    F. Calyx teeth 10, spreading, hooked and spiny. .... 9. *Marrubium*
                                                   vulgare
    F. Calyx teeth 5 or fewer.
      G. Upper lip of the corolla very short, or corolla 1-lipped and the lip
        pinnately 5-lobed.

Upper lip very short; lower lip 3 or 4-lobed. (Fig. 827). .... 10. *Ajuga*
Upper lip lacking; lower lip pinnately 5-lobed. (Fig. 826). .... 7. *Teucrium*
G. Upper lip of the corolla well developed or corolla regular, its lobes equal
    or nearly so.
  H. Calyx regular, its lobes equal or nearly so. (Fig. 829).
    I. Stamens 2.
      J. Corolla regular, its lobes equal or nearly so. (Fig. 829). .... 11. *Lycopus*
      J. Corolla 2-lipped.
        Flowers distinctly pedicelled in loose, cymose clusters.
        (Fig. 831) .... 12. *Cunila marina*
        Flowers sessile or nearly so, in compact verticels. .... 13. *Monarda*
    I. Stamens 4.
      K. Inflorescence axillary, the clusters subtended by foliage leaves and
        separated by normal internodes, the uppermost leaves
        sometimes smaller and the internodes shorter (plants with
        axillary spikes or racemes not included here).
       L. Corolla regular, its lobes equal or one slightly larger than the
         others, sometimes notched.
         Flowers 2 or 3 in each axil, mostly distinctly pedicelled; leaves
          entire. .... 4. *Trichostema*
         Flowers numerous in each axil, subsessile; leaves serrate. .... 14. *Mentha*
       L. Corolla irregular, distinctly 2-lipped.
        M. Flowers pedicelled or the cymes open and loosely branched;
          leaves round or ovate, toothed or crenate. (Fig. 836).
          Stems prostrate, rooting at the nodes; leaves reniform to
            round-cordate. .... 15. *Glecoma*
                    hederacea
          Stems erect; leaves ovate .... 16. *Ballota nigra*
        M. Flowers sessile, the cymes dense and compact (often open
          and loosely branched in *Satureja* but leaves lance-linear,
          entire).
         N. Upper flower clusters subtended by bracts much smaller
          than the foliage leaves; herbage not glandular-punctate.
          (Fig. 837). .... 17. *Stachys*
         N. Upper flower clusters subtended by leafy bracts similar to
          the foliage leaves (except in *Satureja* which has
          glandular-punctate herbage and loose, open cymes).
          O. Calyx lobes prolonged into stiff spines. (Fig. 838).
            Leaves palmately 3-5 lobed .... 18. *Leonurus*
                    cardiaca
            Leaves merely toothed or entire .... 19. *Galeopsis*
          O. Calyx lobes acuminate but not spiny.
            Leaves mostly ovate, cordate, and dentate, crenate or
             pinnatifid. .... 20. *Lamium*
            Leaves lance-linear, entire .... 21. *Satureja hortensis*
      K. Inflorescence terminal, the clusters subtended by bracteal leaves
        conspicuously different from the foliage leaves, the internodes
        shorter (plants with axillary spikes or racemes included
        here).
       P. Stamens ascending under the upper lip of the corolla, equalling
        or shorter than the lip. (Fig. 841).
        Lower verticels distinctly (although often shortly) peduncled. .... 22. *Nepeta cataria*
        Lower verticels sessile .... 17. *Stachys*
       P. Stamens, at least some of them, protruding from the corolla,
        not ascending under the upper lip. (Fig. 842).
        Q. Corolla regular or only obscurely bilabiate, its lobes equal or
         one slightly larger than the others, sometimes notched.
         Corolla tube included in calyx tube .... 14. *Mentha*
         Corolla tube exserted from calyx tube. (Fig. 842). .... 23. *Elsholtzia ciliata*

Q. Corolla irregular, distinctly 2-lipped.
  R. Inflorescence of dense, head-like cymes terminating the
        stem and branches and often in the upper leaf axils .... 24. *Pycnanthemum*
  R. Inflorescence of continuous or interrupted spikes.
    Leaves coarsely serrate .... 25. *Agastache*
    Leaves entire .... 26. *Hyssopus*
                                   officinalis
H. Calyx bilabiate, 2 of the lobes definitely different in size, shape, and/or
    spacing than the other (1)3.
  S. Inflorescence axillary, the clusters subtended by foliage leaves and
    separated by normal internodes, the uppermost leaves
    sometimes smaller and the internodes shorter (plants with
    axillary spikes or racemes not included here).
  T. Stamens 2; calyx bearded in the throat. .... 27. *Hedeoma*
  T. Stamens 4; calyx not bearded in the throat.
    U. Corolla regular, its lobes equal or one slightly larger than the
      others, sometimes notched .... 14. *Mentha*
    U. Corolla irregular, distinctly 2-lipped.
      V. One calyx lobe distinctly wider and/or longer than the others
        and/or bracts spinose-serrate. (Fig. 847) .... 28. *Dracocephalum*
      V. One calyx lobe not distinctly wider or longer than the others;
        bracts not spinose-serrate.
        W. Largest leaves 1.5 cm or less long .... 29. *Acinos arvensis*
        W. Largest leaves 2 cm or more long.
          Calyx more than 6 mm long, its lobes subulate; stamens
            ascending under the upper lip of the corolla,
            equalling or shorter than it . ... 30. *Melissa officinalis*
          Calyx 6 mm or less long, its lobes acute; stamens, at least
            some of them, protruding from the corolla .... 24. *Pycnanthemum*
  S. Inflorescence terminal, the clusters subtended by bracteal leaves
    conspicuously different from the foliage leaves, the internodes
    shorter (plants with axillary spikes or racemes included here).
  X. One calyx lobe distinctly wider and/or longer than the others
    and/or bracts spinose-serrate. (Fig. 847) .... 28. *Dracocephalum*
  X. One calyx lobe not distinctly wider and/or longer than the others;
    bracts not spinose-serrate (although long-ciliate in *Satureja*).
    Y. Stamens 2.
      Verticels often more than 5, loosely flowered, the pedicels
        conspicuous although often short, bases of the calyces
        usually visible. .... 31. *Salvia*
      Verticels 5 or fewer, dense and head-like, the pedicels not
        conspicuous, bases of the calyces hidden .... 32. *Blephilia*
    Y. Stamens 4.
      Z. Corolla regular, its lobes equal or one slightly larger than the
        others, sometimes notched .... 14. *Mentha*
      Z. Corolla irregular, distinctly 2-lipped.
        a. Bracts ovate-orbicular, cuspidate .... 33. *Prunella*
        a. Bracts setaceous, linear or minute.
          b. Bracts linear-subulate, long-ciliate; stamens ascending
            under the upper lip of the corolla, equalling or
            shorter than it. .... 34. *Clinopodium*
                                vulgare
          b. Bracts linear or minute; stamens, at least some of them,
            protruding from the corolla.
             Inflorescence of hemispherical or head-like cymes;
              calyx not bearded in the throat; bracts linear;
              plant erect .... 24. *Pycnanthemum*
            Inflorescence spike-like; calyx bearded in the throat;
              bracts minute; plant creeping .... 35. *Thymus*

1. *Scutellária* L. Skullcap (name based on the crested upper calyx lip).

Perennial, mostly rhizomatous, non-aromatic herbs; leaves petioled or sessile, crenate, serrate or entire; flowers mostly blue to violet, occasionally white or pink, solitary to several in the leaf axils or in axillary or terminal, bracted, racemes or spikes, calyx 2-lipped, the lips entire, the upper one crested, the crest very small in flower and enlarging in fruit, upper lip often deciduous in fruit, corolla tube elongate and curved, 2-lipped, the upper lip galeate, 3-lobed, lower lip unlobed, or sometimes notched, stamens 4, ovary deeply 4-parted.

S. *altíssima* L. Leaves long-petioled, deltoid-ovate, flowers in elongate terminal racemes, upper lip of the corolla dark blue, lower lip pale blue. Reported as naturalized in Suffolk County MA.

a. Median stem leaves widest at rounded, subcordate or truncate base and sessile, or
    petioles 4 mm or less long; flowers mostly solitary in the axils of the stem
    leaves. (Fig. 818).
  b. Principal leaves entire or remotely crenate; rhizomes moniliform-thickened. .... 1. S. *parvula*
  b. Principal leaves uniformly crenate; rhizomes slender.
    Corolla 1.5 cm or more long; leaves mostly more than 2.5 times as long as
      wide; pubescence of recurved hairs .... 2. S. *galericulata*
    Corolla less than 1.5 cm long; leaves mostly 2.5 times or less as long as wide;
      pubescence of incurved-ascending hairs. .... 3. S. *x churchilliana*
a. Median stem leaves widest above and narrowed to cuneate or acute base, or
    petioles longer than 4 mm; flowers in the axils of reduced bracts, in terminal
    or axillary racemes.
  c. Flowers mostly in axillary racemes, or also in a few terminal racemes. (Fig. 819).
    Corolla 9 mm or less long .... 4. S. *lateriflora*
    Corolla longer than 9 mm .... 3. S. *x churchilliana*
  c. Flowers mostly in terminal racemes, or also in a few lateral racemes from the
    upper axils. (Fig. 821).
    d. Median and upper stem leaves entire, undulate or remotely crenate,
      lanceolate, less than 1.5 cm wide .... 5. S. *integrifolia*
    d. Median and upper stem leaves uniformly toothed, or crenate, ovate to
      elliptic, the larger more than 1.5 cm wide.
      Stem pubescent; calyx with spreading, glandular hairs; leaves crenate. (Fig. 821) ...... 6. S. *elliptica*
      Stem glabrous or essentially so; calyx with appressed, eglandular hairs;
      leaves serrate .... 7. S. *serrata*

1. S. *párvula* Michx. (very small). Fields, open woods. May-July. Map 1905.
Our plants include var. *parvula* and the following vars.:
var. *austrális* Fassett. Leaves with a submarginal vein (vein undeveloped in var. *parvula*).
var. *leonárdii* (Epling) Fern. Stem and calyx eglandular; leaves mostly with 2 pairs of lateral veins (stem and calyx glandular; leaves mostly with 3 or more pairs of lateral veins in the above vars.). Endangered in CT. [S. *ambigua*; S. *leonardii*].

2. S. *galericuláta* L. Wet meadows, shrub swamps, wooded swamps, pond and stream margins. June-August. Fig. 818, Map 1906. [S. *epilobiifolia*]. Potentially toxic to the liver if taken internally (see discussion for S. *lateriflora*). —OBL

3. S. *x churchilliána* Fern. (pro sp.) A hybrid between S. *galericulata* and S. *lateriflora*. Map 1907. —FACW

S. *nervósa* Pursh. Resembling S. *x churchilliana* but distinguishable in having petioles of median leaves mostly less than 3 mm long (3 mm or longer in S. *churchilliana*). From farther south and west. Reported for Dutchess County NY. —FAC

4. S. *lateriflóra* L. (lateral-flowered). Pond and stream margins, wooded swamps, wet woods. July-August. Figs. 819, 820, Map 1908. Our plants are var. *lateriflora*. Was recommended in the past as a sedative, but recent findings have shown that preparations of this plant can be toxic to the liver if taken internally. —FACW+

5. S. *integrifólia* L. (entire-leaved). Fields, open woods, woodland borders. May-July. Map 1909. —FACW

6. S. ellíptica Muhl. ex Spreng. (elliptic). Fields and open woods. May-July. Fig. 821. From farther south and west. Reported for Suffolk County NY. [*S. ovalifolia; S. pilosa*]. Our plants are var. *elliptica*.

7. S. serráta Andr. (saw-toothed). Rich woods. May-June. From farther south. Reported for Manhattan NY.

2. Ócimum L.

Annual herbs; leaves sessile or subsessile, ovate to lance-ovate, entire; flowers small, white, in bracteate verticels forming long, terminal spikes, calyx 5-lobed, the upper lobe broad and rounded, its margins decurrent along the tube and forming a cap, corolla bilabiate, the upper lip 4-lobed, the lower entire, stamens 4, turned downward along the lower lip.

1. O. basílicum L. Basil. Occasionally escaped from cultivation. Fig. 822, Map 1910. This well known garden herb is also reported to act as a mosquito repellent if used on the skin.

3. Oríganum L. Wild marjoram (ancient Greek name).

Pubescent, rhizomatous, perennial herbs; leaves petioled, ovate, entire or crenate; flowers pink to purple, subtended by colored bracts, in dense clusters forming rounded, once or repeatedly trichotomous, terminal panicles, calyx regular, 5-toothed, pubescent in the throat, corolla bilabiate, the upper lip 2-lobed, the lower longer with 3 nearly equal lobes, stamens 4, at least 2 exserted, ovary deeply 4-lobed.

1. O. vulgáre L. (common). Fields, roadsides, waste places. June-October. Fig. 823, Map 1911. (Naturalized from Europe). Widely used culinary herb; also reported to be antiseptic.

4. Trichostéma L. Blue curls (from the Greek, based on the thread-like filaments).

Branched annual herbs, minutely glandular-pubescent; leaves sessile or short petioled, linear to oblong or ovate, entire; flowers small, blue, in a leafy panicle of bracteate cymes, calyx regular, nearly equally 5-toothed or 2-lipped and the upper lip with 3 teeth, the lower 2-toothed, shorter than the upper, corolla exserted, the lowest lobe lip-like, larger than the other 4, stamens 4, exserted, ovary shallowly 4-lobed.

a. Calyx regular, nearly equally 5-toothed .... 1. *T. brachiatum*
a. Calyx irregular, distinctly 2-lipped, the upper lip with 3 teeth, the lower with 2.
    Leaves oblong to lanceolate, the larger 5 mm or more wide; stems with long,
        spreading hairs and stipitate glands .... 2. *T. dichotomum*
    Leaves linear, less than 5 mm wide; stems uniformly retrorsely puberulent. .... 3. *T. setaceum*

1. T. brachiátum L. Dry fields, roadsides, waste places. July-September. Map 1912. Endangered in MA. [*Isanthus brachiatus*].

2. T. dichótomum L. (regularly forking in pairs). Dry fields, roadsides, waste places. July-September. Fig. 824, Map 1913.

3. T. setáceum Houtt. (bristle-like). Dry fields, roadsides, waste places. July-September. Reported for CT. [*T. dichotomum* var. *lineare; T. lineare*].

5. Collinsónia L. Horse-balm (for P. Collinson).

Tall, stout, branched, perennial herbs from a thick, woody rhizome; leaves large, petioled, ovate to elliptic, acute to acuminate, coarsely serrate; flowers small, yellow, bracteate, mostly opposite, in a terminal panicle of racemes, calyx 2-lipped, the upper lip with 3 short teeth, the lower with 2 long teeth, corolla much longer than calyx, expanded in the throat, somewhat 2-lipped, the 4 upper lobes nearly equal, the lower lobe much larger, deeply fringed, stamens 2, long-exserted, ovary deeply 4-parted.

1. C. serótina Walt. Rich woods. July-September. Map 1914. [*C. canadensis*]. Preparations made from various parts of this plant are reported to be of value as a sedative. —FAC+

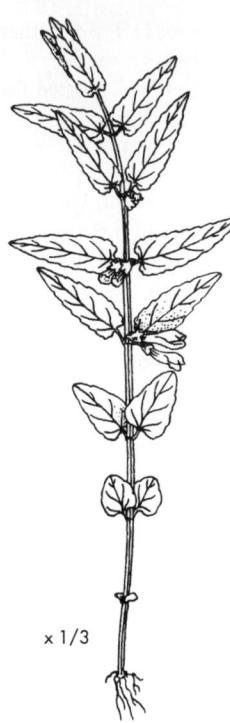

820. *Scutellaria lateriflora*. Single flower; calyx tube with a protuberance.

819. *Scutellaria lateriflora*. Upper stem; leaves widest above, narrowed to base, flowers in axillary racemes.

818. *Scutellaria galericulata*. General habit; leaves widest at base, short-petioled, flowers solitary in the axils.

822. *Ocimum basilicum*. Single flower; calyx tube with a cap.

821. *Scutellaria elliptica*. Upper stem; leaves crenate, flowers in a terminal raceme and in lateral racemes.

823. *Origanum vulgare*. Upper stem; flowers in dense clusters forming trichotomous panicles.

824. *Trichostema dichotomum*. Panicle branch; flowers solitary in the axil of each bract.

1905. *Scutellaria parvula*

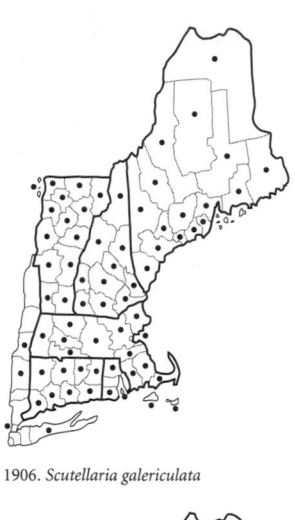

1906. *Scutellaria galericulata*

1907. *Scutellaria x churchilliana*

1908. *Scutellaria lateriflora*

1909. *Scutellaria integrifolia*

1910. *Ocimum basilicum*

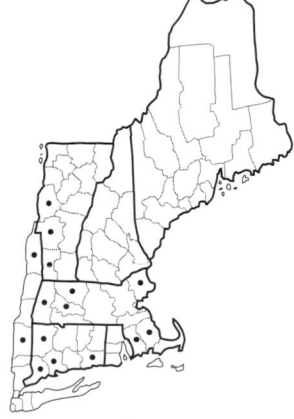

1911. *Origanum vulgare*

1912. *Trichostema brachiatum*

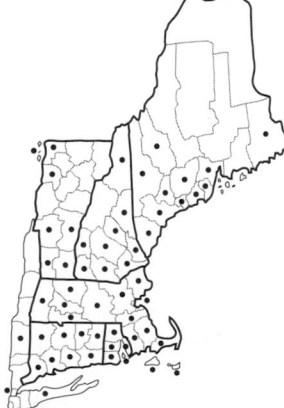

1913. *Trichostema dichotomum*

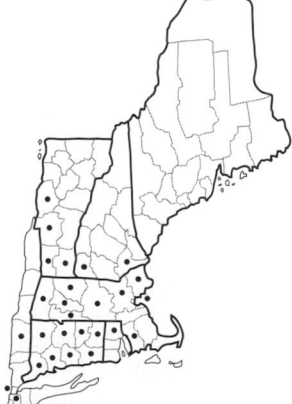

1914. *Collinsonia serotina*

6. *Physostégia* Benth. False Dragonhead (from the Greek, referring to the calyx becoming somewhat inflated in maturity).

Stout, glabrous, perennial herbs; leaves sessile, lanceolate, sharply serrate; flowers pink or purple, showy, bracteate and numerous in elongate, terminal and axillary racemes, calyx regular, 5-toothed, corolla funnelform, bilabiate, the upper lip entire or nearly so, the lower 3-lobed, the middle lobe the larger, stamens 4, ovary deeply 4-parted.

1. *P. virginiána* (L.) Benth. (Virginian). River edges, woodlands, roadsides, fields. July-September. Fig. 825, Map 1915. [*P. denticulata; P. formosior; Dracocephalum virginianum*]. Our plants are subsp. *virginiana.* —FAC+

7. *Teúcrium* L. Wood-sage (ancient Greek name for a related plant).

Annual, or perennial rhizomatous, pubescent herbs; leaves petioled, toothed, crenate or divided; flowers pink, purple or yellowish, in verticels in the upper leaf axils and/or in terminal and axillary, bracteate, spiciform, cylindric or 1-sided racemes, calyx bilabiate or nearly equally 5-lobed, often saccate at base, corolla 1-lipped, the lip pinnately 5-lobed, lateral lobes much smaller than the middle (terminal), stamens 4, exserted, ovary shallowly 4-lobed.

a. Leaves deeply divided into linear to oblong segments. .... 1. *T. botrys*
a. Leaves merely crenate or toothed.
   Flowers 1 or 2 at each node, forming a 1-sided raceme; leaves cordate to
      truncate at base .... 2. *T. scorodonia*
   Flowers numerous, in verticels at each node, forming a cylindric raceme; leaves
      tapered to rounded at base .... 3. *T. canadense*

1. *T. bótrys* L. (bunch of grapes). Calcareous pastures, waste places. July-September. (Naturalized from Europe). Reported for CT, Berkshire and Franklin Counties MA.

2. *T. scorodónia* L. (old generic name). Waste places. (Adventive from Europe). Reported for Norfolk County MA.

3. *T. canadénse* L. (Canadian). Roadsides, waste places, fields, thickets, borders of salt marshes and sea beaches, bottomlands. July-September. Fig. 826, Map 1916. Our plants include var. *canadense* [*T. littorale*] and the following vars.:

   var. *occidentále* (Gray) McClintock & Epling. Inflorescence with gland-tipped hairs (hairs eglandular in var. *canadense*). [*T. boreale; T. occidentale*].

   var. *virgínicum* (L.) Eat. Leaves up to 5 mm wide, sparsely pubescent beneath (2 cm or less wide and densely pubescent beneath in var. *canadense*). Endangered in NH. —FACW+

8. *Perílla* L. (east Indian name).

Stout, branched, often purplish annual herbs; leaves long-petioled, ovate, acuminate, coarsely serrate to laciniate; flowers small, white or purple, bracteate, bracts folded, deciduous in fruit, numerous, in terminal and axillary racemes, calyx 2-lipped, enlarging and becoming more bilabiate in fruit, long-pubescent, the upper lip with 3 short teeth, the lower with 2 long teeth, corolla tube shorter than calyx, corolla somewhat 2-lipped, 1 lobe slightly larger than the other 4, stamens 4, exserted beyond the corolla throat, ovary deeply 4-parted.

1. *P. frutéscens* (L.) Britt. (shrubby). Occasionally escaped from cultivation to roadsides and waste places. August-September. Map 1917. (Introduced from e. Asia). Our plants include var. *frutescens* and the following var.:

   var. *críspa* (Benth.) Deane. Leaves laciniate-dentate (leaves blunt-toothed in var. *frutescens*). —FACU+

9. Marrúbium L. Horehound (ancient Hebrew name, meaning bitter juice).

Strongly aromatic, white-woolly, perennial herbs from a taproot, branched at the base; leaves petioled, round-ovate, crenate-toothed; flowers small, white, in dense, axillary clusters, calyx nearly regular, with 10 spreading, hooked, spiny teeth, corolla 2-lipped, the upper lip 2-lobed, the lower 3-lobed, the middle lobe the largest, stamens 4, included, ovary deeply 4-lobed.

   1. **M. vulgáre** L. (common). Roadsides, waste places, around buildings. June-September. Map 1918. (Naturalized from Europe). Preparations of the young stems and leaves have long been used to make cough syrup, lozenges and candy that are of value as an expectorant and for treating coughs; in large doses can have a laxative effect.

10. Ájuga L. Bugle-weed (from the Greek and Latin, based on shape of the lower corolla lip).

Perennial, often stoloniferous herbs; leaves oblong, ovate, obovate or oblanceolate, the lower ones and those of the stolons (when present) petioled, the upper sessile, toothed, undulate, or entire; flowers blue, in several, somewhat approximate whorles subtended by foliaceous bracts, forming an interrupted, terminal, leafy spike, and/or in the upper axils, calyx regular, 5-toothed, corolla bilabiate, the upper lip short, 2-lobed, the lower 3-lobed, the middle lobe the larger, emarginate or 2-lobed, stamens 4, exserted beyond the corolla throat, ovary shallowly 4-lobed.

Plant with leafy stolons .... 1. *A. reptans*
Plant without stolons .... 2. *A. genevensis*

   1. **A. réptans** L. (creeping). Fields and roadsides. May-June. Fig. 827, Map 1919. (Naturalized from Europe). Preparations of this plant are reported to be useful in treating mouth sores and throat irritation; young shoots can be used in salads.
   2. **A. genevénsis** L. (of Geneva). Fields, roadsides, around dwellings. May-June. Map 1920. (Naturalized from Europe).

11. Lýcopus L. Water-horehound (Greek name based on fancied resemblance of the leaves to a wolf's foot).

Perennial, usually stoloniferous herbs; leaves petioled or sessile, serrate to pinnatifid; flowers small, white, in dense, compact, axillary clusters, calyx regular, 4-5 toothed, corolla nearly regular, nearly equally 4-lobed, or one of the lobes larger than the other 3, entire or emarginate, stamens 2, exserted, ovary deeply 4-lobed, nutlets triangular-obovoid, flattened, with thickened margins. —OBL

a. Calyx teeth shorter than mature nutlets, obtuse to acute, 1 mm or less long.
 Inner angle of nutlet shorter than the two lateral angles, the summit of the
  cluster of 4 nutlets appearing concave; stamens mostly exserted beyond
   throat of corolla. (Fig. 828) .... 1. *L. uniflorus*
 Inner angle of nutlet as long as the two lateral angles, the summit of the cluster
  of 4 nutlets nearly flat; stamens mostly included. .... 2. *L. virginicus*
a. Calyx teeth longer than mature nutlets, acuminate, longer than 1 mm.
 b. Lower and median stem leaves pinnatifid, at least at base, the teeth more than
  3 mm long (measured from upper margin); inner angle of nutlet shorter
  than the 2 lateral angles, the summit of the cluster of nutlets concave.
  (Fig. 830).
  Upper surface of leaf strigose (the hairs sometimes sparse); corolla about
   equalling the calyx teeth .... 3. *L. europaeus*
  Upper surface of leaf glabrous or scabrous; corolla exceeding the calyx teeth. .... 4. *L. americanus*
 b. Lower and median stem leaves merely serrate, the teeth 3 mm or less long;
  inner angle of nutlet as long as the 2 lateral angles, the summit of the
  cluster of nutlets nearly flat (concave in *L. asper*).
  Leaves sessile, rounded to widely cuneate at the base. .... 5. *L. amplectens*
  Leaves petioled or gradually narrowed to a petiolar base. .... 6. *L. rubellus*

1. L. uniflórus Michx. (one-flowered). Damp to wet, open or shaded ground. July-September. Fig. 828, Map 1921. (e. Asia). [*L. virginicus* var. *pauciflorus*].

2. L. virgínicus L. (Virginian). Damp to wet, open or shaded ground, particularly around pond and river margins. July-September. Fig. 829, Map 1922. [*L. membranaceus*]. Reported to have medicinal value as an astringent and sedative.

3. L. europaéus L. (European). Roadsides and waste places, wet soil, especially near the coast. August-September. (Adventive from Europe). Reported for Norfolk and Plymouth Counties MA.

4. L. americánus Mulh. ex W. Bact. (American). Damp to wet, open or shaded ground. July-September. Fig. 830, Map 1923.

5. L. ampléctens Raf. (clasping). Damp open soil, pond margins, on the coastal plain. August-September. Map 1924. [*L. sessilifolius*].

L. ásper Greene. Similar to *L. amplectens* except inner angle of nutlet shorter than the 2 lateral angles, the summit of the cluster of nutlets concave, larger leaves with more than 6 teeth on each side (summit of cluster of nutlets nearly flat and larger leaves with up to 6 teeth on each side in *L. amplectens*). Western. Reported for Essex County MA. [*L. lucidus* var. *americanus*].

6. L. rubéllus Moench (reddish). Pond and river margins, wooded swamps. July-September. Map 1925.

12. Cuníla D. Royen ex L. Dittany (ancient Latin name for a fragrant plant).
Branched, perennial herbs; leaves sessile or subsessile, ovate to lance-ovate, acute at the tip, rounded, truncate or subcordate at base, serrate, punctate; flowers white or purplish, in peduncled, bracteate, trichotomous cymes terminating the stem and in the upper leaf axils, calyx 5-toothed, nearly regular, pubescent in the throat, corolla 2-lipped, the upper lip emarginate, the lower 3-lobed, stamens 2, exserted, ovary deeply 4-lobed.

x 1-1/2

826. *Teucrium canadense.* Single flower; corolla 1-lipped, the lip pinnately 5-lobed.

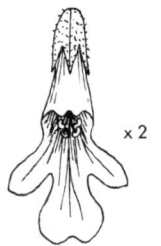

x 2

827. *Ajuga reptans.* Single flower; upper lip of corolla very short, lower lip 3-4 lobed.

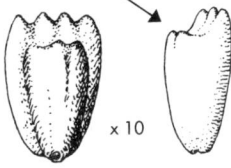

x 10

828. *Lycopus uniflorus.* Single nutlet, 2 views; inner angle shorter than the 2 lateral angles.

x 1/2

825. *Physostegia virginiana.* Upper part of plant; inflorescence of terminal and axillary racemes.

x 4

829. *Lycopus virginicus.* Single flower; calyx and corolla regular.

x 3/8

830. *Lycopus americanus.* Section of stem; median stem leaves pinnatifid.

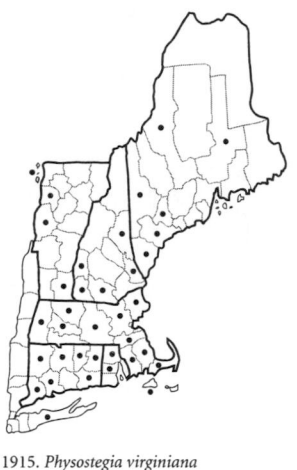

1915. *Physostegia virginiana*

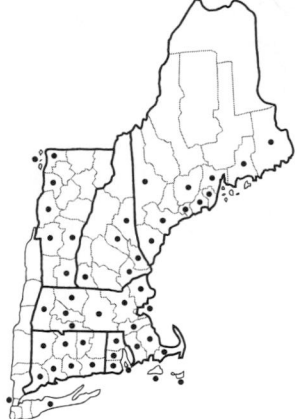

1916. *Teucrium canadense*

1917. *Perilla frutescens*

1918. *Marrubium vulgare*

1919. *Ajuga reptans*

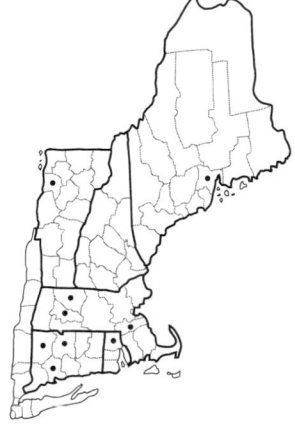

1920. *Ajuga genevensis*

1921. *Lycopus uniflorus*

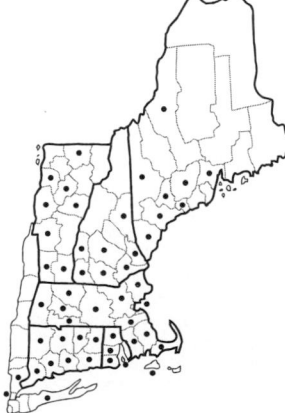

1922. *Lycopus virginicus*

1923. *Lycopus americanus*

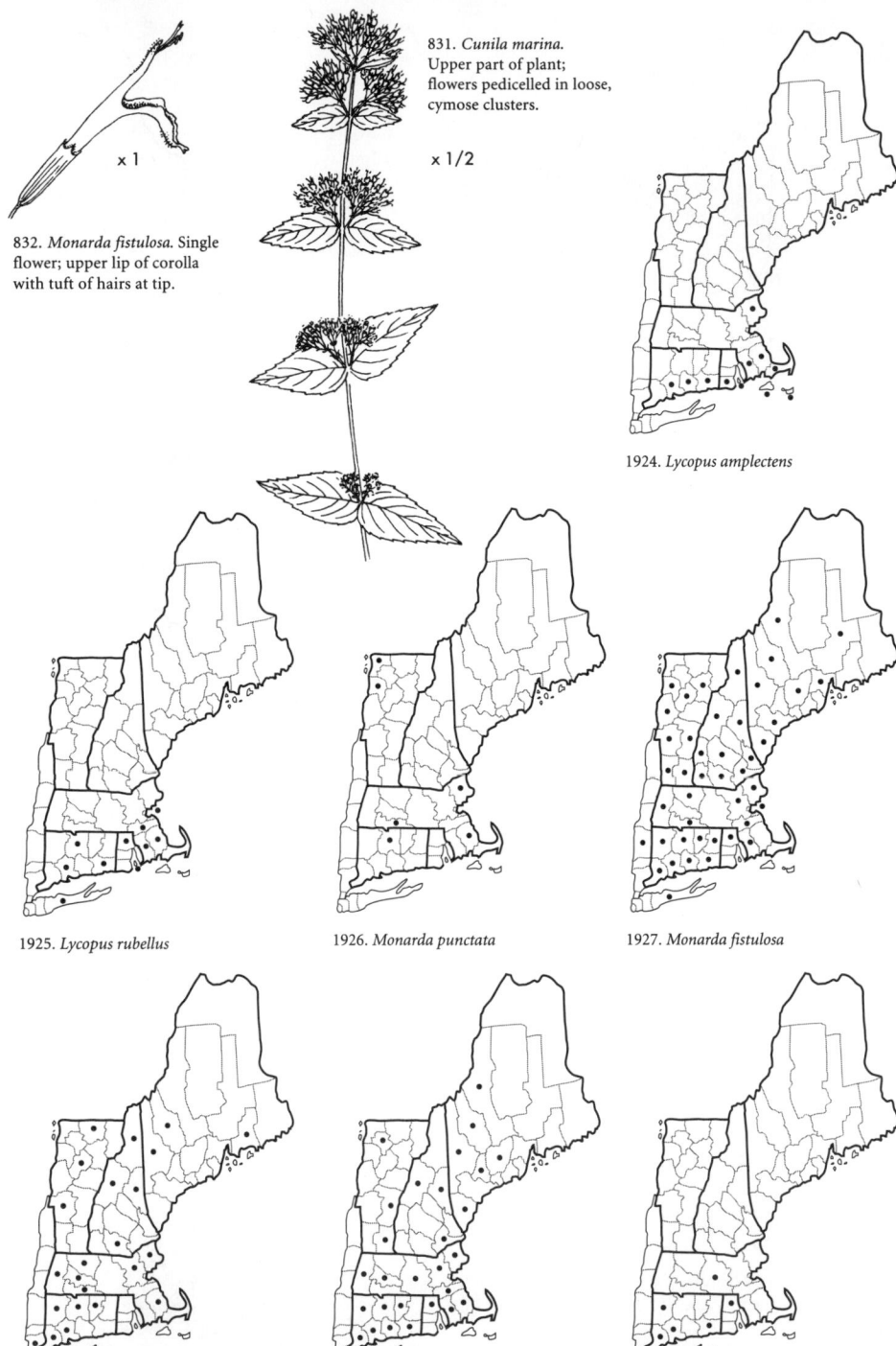

× 1

832. *Monarda fistulosa.* Single
flower; upper lip of corolla
with tuft of hairs at tip.

831. *Cunila marina.*
Upper part of plant;
flowers pedicelled in loose,
cymose clusters.

× 1/2

1924. *Lycopus amplectens*

1925. *Lycopus rubellus*

1926. *Monarda punctata*

1927. *Monarda fistulosa*

1928. *Monarda didyma*

1929. *Monarda media*

1930. *Monarda clinopodia*

1. C. márina L. Dry, rocky woods and thickets. July-October. Fig. 831. From farther west and south. Reported for Suffolk and Westchester Counties and Manhatten NY. [*C. origanoides*]. Reported to have been used to make a mild stimulating drink because of its aromatic properties.

13. Monárda L. Horse-mint (for N. Monardes).

Aromatic, annual or perennial herbs; leaves petioled, toothed, lanceolate to ovate; flowers purple, red, white, yellowish or spotted, showy, bracteolate, in terminal head-like clusters or in several whorles, subtended by foliaceous bracts, these sometimes colored, calyx regular, 5-toothed, corolla bilabiate, the upper lip entire, the lower 3-lobed, the middle lobe wider or longer than the laterals, stamens 2, exserted beyond the corolla throat, ovary deeply 4-lobed.

a. Flowers in 2 or more whorles at apex of stem; stamens not exserted beyond the
　　upper corolla lip; leaves narrowed to base. .... 1. *M. punctata*
a. Flowers in a terminal head, rarely topped by a second one; stamens exserted
　　beyond the upper corolla lip; leaves widest near base.
　　b. Upper lip of corolla with a conspicuous tuft of hairs at the tip. (Fig. 832) .... 2. *M. fistulosa*
　　b. Upper lip of corolla without a tuft of hairs at the tip.
　　　　c. Corolla 3 cm or more long, scarlet .... 3. *M. didyma*
　　　　c. Corolla 3 cm or less long, reddish-purple to white, yellowish or pink.
　　　　　　Corolla and bracts reddish-purple .... 4. *M. media*
　　　　　　Corolla white, yellowish or pink; bracts green to whitish .. .. 5. *M. clinopodia*

1. M. punctáta L. (dotted). Dry, sandy fields, roadsides. July-September. Map 1926. Our plants include subsp. *punctata* var. *punctata* and the following var.:

var. *villicaúlis* (Pennell) Palmer & Steyermark. Stem with long, spreading pubescence; leaves densely pubescent beneath (stem with pubescence of short, recurved hairs and leaves glabrous to minutely puberulent beneath in var. *punctata*).

M. citriodóra Cerv. Similar to *M. punctata* but distinguishable in being annual with calyx lobes 2 mm or more long, corolla white or pink (*M. punctata* is perennial, with calyx teeth less than 2 mm long, corolla yellow). From farther west. Reported for MA.

2. M. fistulósa L. (tubular). Fields, roadsides, waste places, thickets, woodlands. July-September. Fig. 832, Map 1927. Our plants include subsp. *fistulosa* var. *fistulosa* and the following var.:

var. *móllis* (L.) Benth. Leaves puberulent to glabrous beneath (with long hairs on veins beneath in var. fistulosa). Leaves of this species and the next have been used to make tea.

var. *rubra* has also been reported for MA and ME.

3. M. dídyma L. (twin). Oswego-tea. Around former dwellings, roadsides, thickets. July-September. Map 1928. —FAC+

4. M. média Willd. (intermediate). Roadsides, thickets. July-August. Map 1929.

5. M. clinopódia L. (resembling *Clinopodium*). Roadsides, thickets. July-August. Map 1930. From farther west or south.

14. Méntha L. Mint (ancient name based on Greek mythodology).

Perennial herbs from rhizomes or stolons; leaves sessile or petioled, serrate or crenate, mostly punctate; flowers purple to whitish, in verticels forming terminal, bracteate heads or continuous or interrupted spikes, or verticels axillary, calyx 5-toothed, regular or nearly so, corolla slightly irregular, 4-lobed, the upper lobe slightly larger, entire or notched or corolla sometimes equally 5-lobed, stamens 4, exserted, ovary deeply 4-lobed.

a. Flowers all in verticels in the leaf axils. (Fig. 833).
　　Leaves subtending the flower clusters conspicuously smaller than the lower
　　　　leaves. (Fig. 833) .... 1. *M. x gracilis*
　　Leaves subtending the flower clusters the same size as the lower leaves. .... 2. *M. arvensis*
a. Flowers in terminal spikes or heads, sometimes also with several peduncled heads
　　in the upper leaf axils.

b. Flowers in a globose to ovoid head, sometimes also with several peduncled
   heads in the upper leaf axils. (Fig. 834).
   Stem glabrous; calyx glabrous below the teeth. .... 3. *M. x piperita*
   Stem pubescent; calyx pubescent below the teeth. .... 4. *M. aquatica*
b. Flowers in a dense spike(s), sometimes interrupted at the base. (Fig. 835).
   c. Leaves glabrous or with scattered hairs beneath; calyx tube glabrous.
      Spike, including corollas, 1 cm or more thick; petioles of principal leaves
         3.5 mm or more long; calyx 2.5 mm or more long. .... 3. *M. x piperita*
      Spike, including corollas, less than 1 cm thick; petioles of principal leaves
         3 mm or less long; calyx 2 mm or less long. .... 5. *M. spicata*
   c. Leaves pubescent above, densely so below; calyx tube pubescent.
      d. Leaves 2 or more times as long as wide, acute to acuminate at tip, cuneate
         to rounded at the base .... 6. *M. longifolia*
      d. Leaves less than twice as long as wide, obtuse to acute at tip, broadly
         rounded to subcordate at base .... 7. *M. suaveolens*
         Spikes 1 cm or less thick, often interrupted. .... 8. *M. x rotundifolia*
         Spikes more than 1 cm thick, continuous. .... 9. *M. x villosa*

1. M. x grácilis Sole (pro sp.). A hybrid between *M. arvensis* and *M. spicata*. Fig. 833, Map 1931. (Introduced from Europe). [*M. cardiaca; M. x gentilis*]. —FACW

2. M. arvénsis L. (of cultivated ground). Wet meadows, pond and stream margins. July-September. Map 1932. (Naturalized from Europe). Leaves are used to flavor drinks and foods. —FACW

M. canadénsis L. Similar to *M. arvensis* but with leaves lanceolate to lance-ovate (ovate to elliptic in *M. arvensis*). Throughout our range. [*M. arvensis* var. *canadensis; M. a.* var. *glabrata; M. a.* var. *villosa*].

3. M. x piperíta L. (peppery). Peppermint. Pond and stream margins, wet meadows. July-September. Map 1933. (Introduced from Europe). A hybrid between *M. aquatica* and *M. spicata*. Widely used in flavoring drinks and foods and in salads; various medicinal uses are also cited including treating indigestion and stimulating appetite. —FACW+

4. M. aquática L. (aquatic). Wet soil on roadsides and ditches. August-September. Fig. 834, Map 1934. (Introduced from Europe). [*M. citrata*]. Our plants include var. *aquatica* and the following var.:
var. **críspa** (L.) Benth. Leaves strongly crisped and lacerate-toothed (merely toothed in var. *aquatica*). [*M. crispa*]. Leaves are used to flavor drinks and foods. —OBL

M. x verticilláta L. A hybrid between *M. aquatica* and *M. arvensis*.

5. M. spicáta L. (spiked). Spearmint. Pond and stream margins, wet meadows, wet soil of roadsides, ditches and waste places. July-September. Fig. 835, Map 1935. (Introduced from Europe). Leaves are used to add flavoring to drinks and foods. —FACW+

6. M. longifólia L. (long-leaved). Escaped from cultivation to roadsides, waste places and fields. July-September. Map 1936. (Introduced from Europe). Leaves are used to flavor drinks and foods. —FACU

7. M. suaveólens Ehrh. Excaped to roadsides and waste places. July-September. (Introduced from Europe). Reported for CT, MA.

8. M. x rotundifólia (L.) Huds. (pro sp.) A hybrid between *M. longifolia* and *M. suaveolens*. Map 1937. (Introduced from Europe). —FACW

9. M. x villósa Huds. (pro sp.). A hybrid between *M. spicata* and *M. suaveolens*. Map 1938. (Introduced from Europe). [*M. x alopecuroides*].

15. Glechóma L. Ground-Ivy (old Greek name for pennyroyal).

Repent, perennial herbs rooting at the nodes, with erect flowering branches; leaves long-petioled, reniform to round-cordate, coarsely crenate or toothed; flowers blue, short-pedicelled, few in bracteate, axillary clusters, bracts linear-setaceous, calyx unequally 5-toothed, the teeth aristate, corolla bilabiate, speckled with purple, the upper lip small, shallowly 2-lobed, the lower larger, with middle lobe larger than the laterals, stamens 4, ascending under the upper lip, slightly exserted from the corolla throat, ovary deeply 4-lobed.

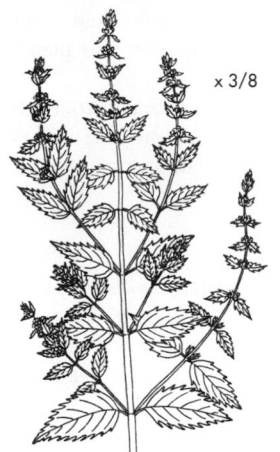

833. *Mentha x gracilis.* Upper part of plant; leaves subtending flower clusters smaller than lower leaves.

834. *Mentha aquatica.* Upper part of plant; flowers in globose heads.

835. *Mentha spicata.* Upper part of plant; flowers in dense spikes.

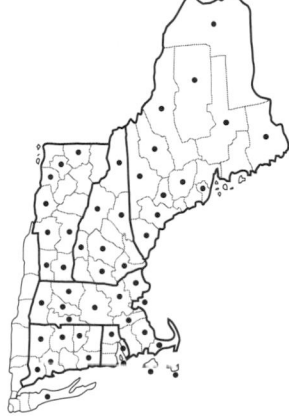

1931. *Mentha x gracilis*

1932. *Mentha arvensis*

1933. *Mentha x piperita*

1934. *Mentha aquatica*

1935. *Mentha spicata*

1936. *Mentha longifolia*

1. G. hederácea L. (ivy-like). Gill-over-the-ground. Roadsides, waste places, woodlands, and around dwellings. April-June. Map 1939. (Naturalized from Europe). [*Nepeta h.*]. Our plants include var. *hederacea* and the following var.:

var. *micrántha* Moricand. Corolla 1.5 cm or less long (longer than 1.5 cm in var. *hederacea*). High in vitamin C; leaves are used for tea, as a bitter in liquors and to improve appetite; was once used as a flavoring for beer; various medicinal uses are also cited, particularly as treatment for coughs. —FACU

16. *Ballóta* L. Black horehound (Greek name).

Pubescent perennial herbs; leaves petioled, ovate, coarsely dentate or crenate; flowers purplish, numerous, in sessile or short peduncled, bracteate cymes from the upper leaf axils, calyx regular, 5-toothed, corolla 2-lipped, the upper lip pubescent, entire or emarginate, the lower 3-lobed, the middle lobe emarginate, stamens 4, exserted and ascending under the upper lip, ovary deeply 4-lobed.

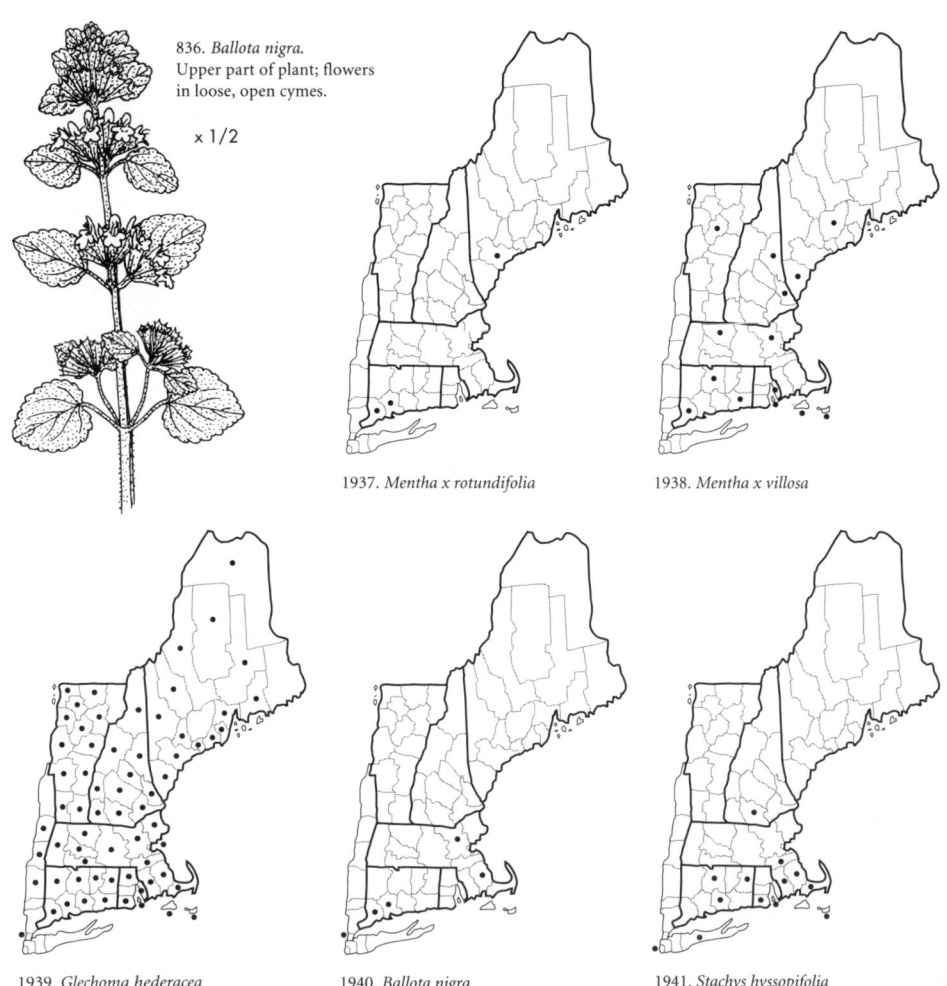

836. *Ballota nigra.*
Upper part of plant; flowers in loose, open cymes.

× 1/2

1937. *Mentha x rotundifolia*

1938. *Mentha x villosa*

1939. *Glechoma hederacea*

1940. *Ballota nigra*

1941. *Stachys hyssopifolia*

1. **B. nígra** L. (black). Waste places. June-September. Fig. 836, Map 1940. (Adventive from Europe). Our plants include var. *nigra* and the following var.:

var. *foétida* Vis. Calyx teeth abruptly narrowed to short points (gradually acuminate to long points in var. *nigra*).

17. Stáchys L. Hedge-nettle (from the Greek, referring to the spicate inflorescence).

Annual or perennial herbs; leaves sessile or petioled, serrate, crenate or entire; flowers purplish, white or yellow, in clusters in the axils of reduced leaves, or also in the axils of the upper foliage leaves, forming a terminal, continuous or interrupted spike, calyx 5-toothed, regular or nearly so, corolla 2-lipped, the upper lip galeate, entire or emarginate, lower lip 3-lobed, the middle lobe the largest, sometimes emarginate, stamens 4, exserted and ascending under the upper lip, ovary deeply 4-lobed.

Lavándula L. *angustifólia* Miller. Will key to *Stachys* but is woody, at least at the base, leaves narrowly linear, entire, flowers blue (*Stachys* not woody, lacking the remaining combination of characters). European. Reported for VT. Widely used for its aromatic qualities.

a. Plant densely white-woolly .... 1. *S. germanica*
a. Plant glabrous or pubescent but not white-woolly.
  b. Flowers yellow; plant annual; stem glabrous or appressed-pubescent. .... 2. *S. annua*
  b. Flowers purplish; plant perennial or if annual (*S. arvensis*) stem
    spreading-pubescent.
    c. Stem glabrous or pubescent only on the angles, the sides rarely with a few
      remote hairs.
      d. Bracts and calyx lobes eciliate; stem glabrous or with scattered hairs on the
        angles; leaves entire or few-toothed. .... 3. *S. hyssopifolia*
      d. Bracts and calyx lobes ciliate; stem copiously pubescent on the angles;
        leaves serrate or crenate .... 4. *S. tenuifolia*
    c. Stem pubescent on the sides as well as on the angles.
      e. Leaves sessile or subsessile, the petioles less than 5 mm long. .... 5. *S. palustris*
      e. Leaves, at least the lower and middle on petioles longer than 5 mm.
        Leaves acute to acuminate; plant perennial, stoloniferous . ... 6. *S. sylvatica*
        Leaves obtuse to rounded; plant annual, not stoloniferous. .... 7. *S. arvensis*

1. **S. germánica** L. (German). Fields, roadsides, waste places. June-August. Rare. (Naturalized from Europe). Reported for RI.

2. **S. ánnua** (L.) L. (annual). Fields and waste places. June-September. (Adventive from Europe). Reported for ME, Worcester County MA, Providence County RI.

3. **S. hyssopifólia** Michx. (hyssop-leaved). Sandy pond margins near the coast. July-September. Map 1941. Endangered in CT, RI. [*S. atlantica*]. Our plants are var. *hyssopifolia.* —FACW+

4. **S. tenuifólia** Willd. River and pond margins, thickets. June-September. Map 1942. [*S. hispida; S. tenuifolia* var. *hispida; S. tenuifolia* var. *platyphylla; S. aspera*]. Our plants are var. *tenuifólia.* —FACW+

5. **S. palústris** L. (of marshes). Fields, river margins. June-September. Fig. 837, Map 1943. (Naturalized from Europe). [*S. ampla; S. arenicola; S. arguta; S. borealis; S. brevidens; S. homotricha; S. pustulosa; S. schweinitzii*]. Our plants include subsp. *palustris* and the following subsp.:

subsp. *pilósa* (Nutt.) Epl. Calyx with both glandular hairs and longer, glandless hairs (calyx uniformly short glandular-pubescent in subsp. *palustris*).

subsp. *arenícola* (Britt.) Gill. Calyx with pubescence characteristics of subsp. *pilosa* but leaves narrowly oblong to lanceolate (broadly oblong to ovate in subsp. *pilosa*). [*S. palustris* var. *homotricha*]. —OBL

6. **S. sylvática** L. (of the woods). Waste places. June-September. (Adventive from Europe). Reported for NY.

S. officinális (L.) Trev. Resembling *S. sylvatica* but distinguishable in having obtuse lower leaves and purple flowers (lower leaves acute to acuminate and flowers purple variegated with white in *S. sylvatica*). (Introduced from Europe). Rarely spread from cultivation. Reported for ME, Rensselaer County NY. Reported to be of value in treating diarrhea, irritations of the throat and mouth, and headache; overdoses can cause excessive stomach irritation.

7. *S. arvénsis* (L). L. (of fields). Fields and waste places. July-October. Map 1944. (Adventive from Europe).

18. *Leonúrus* L. Motherwort (from the Greek, meaning lion's tail).

Tall, branched, perennial herbs, stems puberulent on the angles; leaves long-petioled, palmately 3-5-lobed, the lobes acuminate, entire to coarsely toothed, the upper gradually reduced and less cleft; flowers white to pink, in dense verticels in the upper leaf axils and subtended by linear bracts, calyx regular, 5-lobed, the lobes prolonged into spines, 2 of them usually reflexed, corolla bilabiate, the upper lip entire, flat or galeate, bearded, the lower 3-lobed, the middle lobe the larger, stamens 4, ovary deeply 4-parted.

1. *L. cardíaca* L. (for the heart). Waste places, roadsides around dwellings. July-August. Fig. 838, Map 1945. (Naturalized from Europe). Our plants are subsp. *cardiaca*. Contact with skin can cause dermatitis in some individuals; reported to have been used in Europe for treating heart conditions and asthma.

19. *Galeópsis* L. Hemp-nettle (from the Greek, based on fancied resemblance of the corolla to the head of a weasel).

Branched, pubescent, annual herbs; sometimes swollen just below the nodes in fresh specimens; leaves petioled, linear to lanceolate to ovate, toothed or entire; flowers red, purple, white or variegated, in dense verticels in the upper leaf axils, calyx nearly regular, with 5 spincscent teeth, corolla bilabiate, the upper lip galeate, entire, the lower 3-lobed, with a pair of projections on the upper side near the base, stamens 4, exserted and ascending under the upper lip, ovary deeply 4-lobed.

Stem spreading-pubescent, with coarse, bristly hairs; petioles mostly 1 cm or more long.
 Leaves rounded at the base; fruiting calyx with teeth mostly longer than 8 mm;
  corollas mostly 1.5 to over 2 cm long, middle lobe of the lower lip not
   emarginate .... 1. *G. tetrahit*
 Leaves narrowed to base; fruiting calyx with teeth up to 8 mm long; corollas
  seldom much over 1.5 cm long, middle lobe of the lower lip emarginate. ... 2. *G. bifida*
Stem appressed-pubescent, with fine hairs; petioles mostly less than 1 cm long .... 3. *G. ladanum*

1. *G. tetráhit* L. Fields, roadsides, waste places. June-September. Map 1946. (Naturalized from Eurasia). Our plants are var. *tetrahit*.

2. *G. bífida* Boenn. Fields, roadsides, waste places. Throughout our range. (Naturalized from Europe). [*G. tetrahit* var. *b.*].

3. *G. ládanum* L. (old generic name). Waste places, often near the coast. June-September. Map 1947. (Adventive from Europe). Our plants include var. *ladanum* [*G. l.* var. *angustifolia; G. angustifolia*] and the following var.:

 var. *latifólia* (Hoffm.) Wallr. Leaves 1 cm or more wide (less than 1 cm wide in var. *ladanum*). [*G. l.* var. *ladanum*].

20. *Lámium* L. Dead nettle (old Latin name for a nettle-like plant).

Annual or perennial herbs, often branched and decumbent or creeping at the base; leaves petioled, mostly ovate, cordate, dentate or crenate to pinnatifid; flowers purplish or white, in verticels in the upper leaf axils, calyx nearly regular, 5-toothed, corolla 2-lipped, the upper lip entire or emarginate,

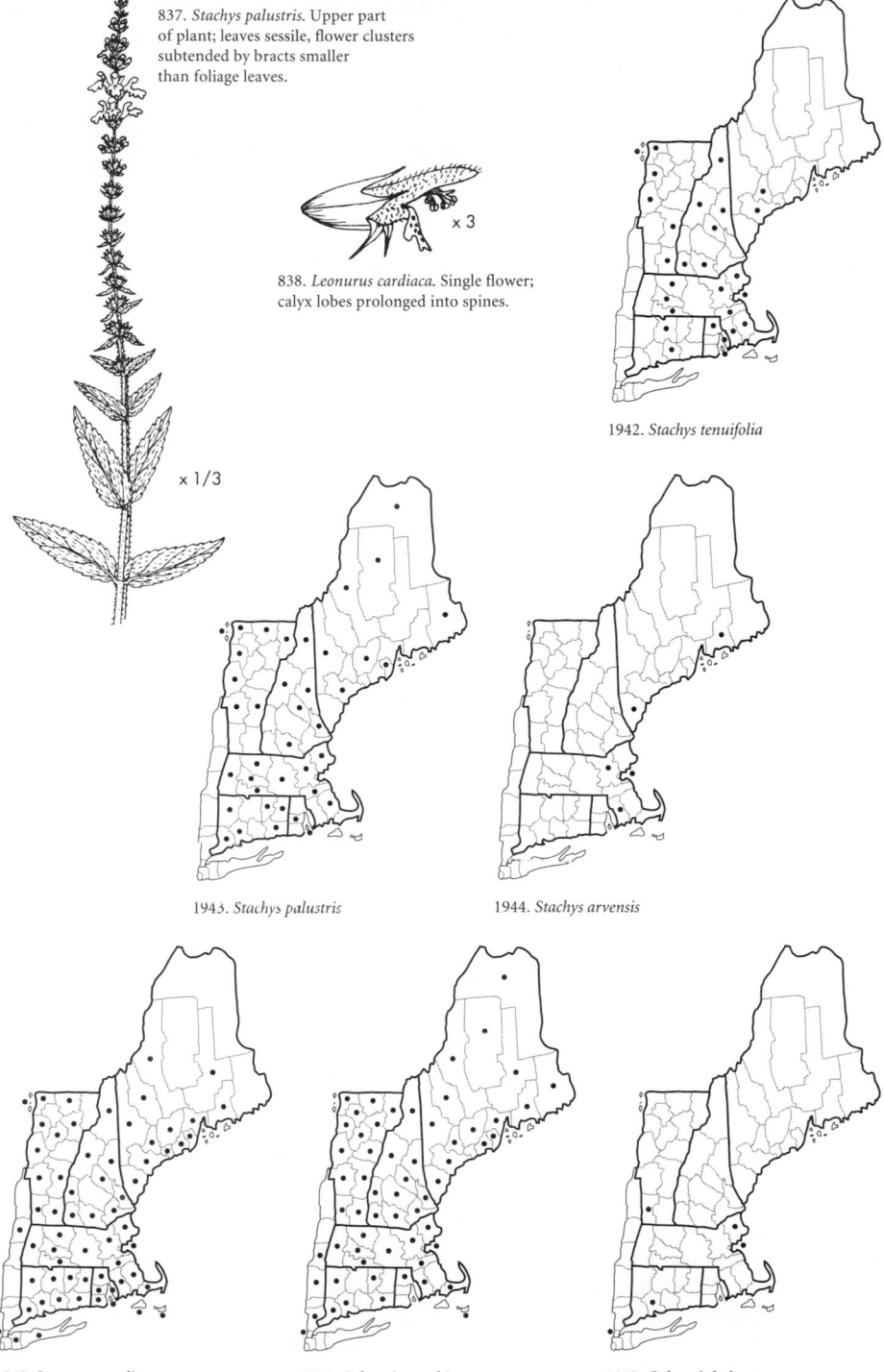

837. *Stachys palustris.* Upper part of plant; leaves sessile, flower clusters subtended by bracts smaller than foliage leaves.

× 3

838. *Leonurus cardiaca.* Single flower; calyx lobes prolonged into spines.

× 1/3

1942. *Stachys tenuifolia*

1943. *Stachys palustris*

1944. *Stachys arvensis*

1945. *Leonurus cardiaca*

1946. *Galeopsis tetrahit*

1947. *Galeopsis ladanum*

galeate, the lower 3-lobed, middle lobe constricted at the base, emarginate, the lateral lobes small, borne at the margin of the throat, each terminating in a tooth, stamens 4, exserted and ascending under the upper lip, ovary deeply 4-lobed.

a. Leaves subtending the verticels of flowers sessile and clasping or the lowest
    sometimes petioled .... 1. *L. amplexicaule*
a. Leaves, at least those subtending the lower and middle verticels, petioled. (Fig. 840).
  b. Upper lip of corolla 6 mm or more long; plant perennial.
    Corolla purple, the tube with a transverse ring of hairs inside near the base;
        leaves obtuse to acute, often with a white band along the midvein. .... 2. *L. maculatum*
    Corolla white, the tube with an oblique ring of hairs inside near the base;
        leaves, at least the middle and upper, acuminate, lacking a white band.
        (Fig. 839) .... 3. *L. album*
  b. Upper lip of corolla 5 mm or less long; plant annual. .... 4. *L. purpureum*

1. *L. amplexicaúle* L. (clasping stem). Fields, cultivated ground, waste places, roadsides. May-September. Map 1948. (Naturalized from Europe). May be boiled and used as a potherb.

2. *L. maculátum* L. (spotted). Roadsides, waste places, around buildings. May-September. Map 1949. (Introduced from Europe).

Lamiástrum Heister ex Fabr. *galeóbdolon* (L) Ehrend & Polatschek. Will key to *Lamium maculatum* or *L. album* but is distinguishable in having yellow flowers streaked with green or brown (flowers purple or white in the latter 2 species). European; a waif in our range. Reported for Middlesex County MA. [*Lamium g.*].

3. *L. álbum* L. (white). Roadsides, waste places, cultivated ground. May-September. Fig. 839, Map 1950. (Introduced from Europe). The young tips can be cooked and used as a potherb; distillation of the leaves and flowers can be used as an effective eye lotion.

4. *L. purpúreum* L. (purple). Fields, cultivated ground, waste places, roadsides. May-September. Fig. 840, Map 1951. (Naturalized from Europe). Our plants include var. *purpureum* and the following var.:

var. *incísum* (Willd.) Pers. Leaves crenate-serrate, the teeth mostly longer than wide; leaves all green; corolla tube naked inside (leaves crenate, the teeth mostly as wide or wider than long; upper leaves purplish; corolla tube with a ring of hairs inside near the base in var. *purpureum*). Map 1951a [*L. hybridum*].

21. *Satureja* L. (ancient Latin name for savory).

Puberulent, annual herbs; leaves petioled, entire, sometimes with smaller ones fascicled in the axils; flowers pink-purplish, to white, in terminal and axillary, bracteate clusters, calyx regular, 5-toothed, mostly naked in the throat, corolla bilabiate, the upper lip entire or emarginate, the lower 3-lobed, stamens 4, exserted and ascending under the upper lip, ovary deeply 4-lobed.

1. *S. horténsis* L. (of the gardens). Savory. Occasionally escaped from cultivation to roadsides and waste places. July-September. Map 1952. (Introduced from Europe). Reputed to be of value as a digestive aid.

22. *Népeta* L. (Latin name).

Branched, puberulent, perennial herbs; leaves long-petioled, deltoid to deltoid-oblong, acute at the tip, truncate or cordate at the base, coarsely toothed; flowers whitish to pale purple dotted with dark purple, in verticels subtended by reduced foliaceous leaves or also in the axils of the upper foliage leaves forming continuous or interrupted spikes terminating the stem and branches, calyx slightly irregular, 5-toothed, corolla bilabiate, the upper lip notched or 2-lobed, the lower 3-lobed, the middle lobe the largest and crenulate, stamens 4, exserted and ascending under the upper lip, ovary deeply 4-lobed.

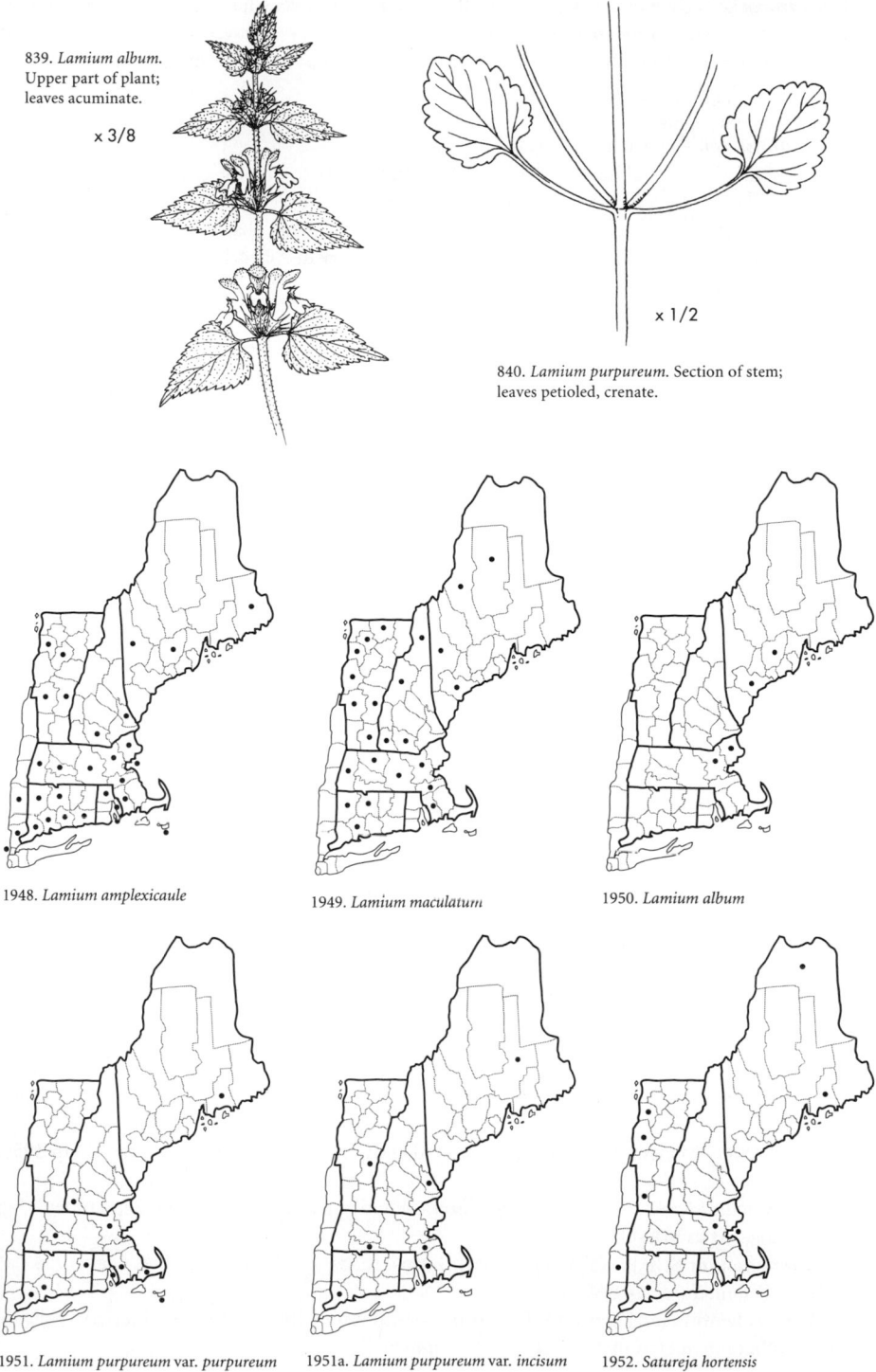

839. *Lamium album.* Upper part of plant; leaves acuminate.

x 3/8

x 1/2

840. *Lamium purpureum.* Section of stem; leaves petioled, crenate.

1948. *Lamium amplexicaule*

1949. *Lamium maculatum*

1950. *Lamium album*

1951. *Lamium purpureum* var. *purpureum*

1951a. *Lamium purpureum* var. *incisum*

1952. *Satureja hortensis*

1. N. catária L. (old generic name). Catnip. Roadsides, waste places, near former dwellings, fields. July-September. Fig. 841, Map 1953. (Naturalized from Europe). Leaves are used to make tea; various medicinal uses have also been ascribed to this plant such as use as a tranquilizer, as a digestive aid, and to restore menstrual flow. —FACU

23. Elshóltzia Willd. (for J. Elsholtz).

Branched, glabrous, annual herbs; leaves petioled, lance-ovate to oblong, crenate-serrate; flowers small, blue to purplish, several in the axils of ovate, mucronate bracts, these overlapping, forming dense, terminal and axillary spikes, calyx regular, 5-toothed, corolla obscurely bilabiate, the upper lobe emarginate, the lower 3-lobed, stamens 4, exserted ovary deeply 4-lobed.

1. E. ciliáta (Thunb.) Hyl. (ciliate). Roadsides, waste places. July-September. Fig. 842, Map 1954. (Naturalized from Asia).

24. Pycnánthemum Michx. Mountain-mint (Greek name, referring to the compact inflorescence).

Branched, rhizomatous, perennial herbs with a mint-like odor and flavor; leaves short-petioled or sessile, serrate to entire, linear to ovate; flowers small, white to purple or purple-dotted, in dense, bracteate, head-like cymes terminating the stem and branches or in clusters in the upper leaf axils, bracts often foliaceous, calyx 5-toothed, nearly regular to bilabiate, the upper lip entire or emarginate, the lower 3-lobed, stamens 4, mostly exserted beyond the corolla throat, ovary deeply 4-lobed.

a. Principal stem leaves, at least the larger ones, mostly more than 1.5 cm
   wide.
  b. Leaves subtending flower clusters and foliaceous bracts distinctly whitened with
       hairs; leaves ovate or lance-ovate, a third or more as wide as long.
      Heads open, the branches visible; calyx teeth usually with long bristles at or
          near the tips. (Fig. 843) .... 1. *P. incanum*
      Heads dense and compact, the branches not visible; calyx teeth without long
          bristles at or near the tips .... 2. *P. muticum*
  b. Leaves subtending the flower clusters and foliaceous bracts not or very slightly
       whitened; leaves lanceolate, less than a third as wide as long. .... 3. *P. clinopodioides*
a. Principal stem leaves 1.5 cm or less wide.
  c. Stem glabrous; leaves 4 mm or less wide. .... 4. *P. tenuifolium*
  c. Stem pubescent, at least on the angles; leaves, at least the larger ones, mostly
       wider than 4 mm.
      d. Calyx teeth 1 mm or more long.
          Calyx bilabiate; leaves pubescent beneath, especially on the veins. .... 3. *P. clinopodioides*
          Calyx nearly regular; leaves glabrous beneath or puberulent on the
              midvein. .... 5. *P. torrei*
      d. Calyx teeth less than 1 mm long.
          Outermost foliaceous bracts glabrous above or essentially so. .... 6. *P. virginianum*
          Outermost foliaceous bracts densely fine-pubescent above. .... 7. *P. verticillatum*

1. P. incánum (L.) Michx. (gray). Dry, rocky woods. Fig. 843, Map 1955. July-September. Endangered in VT, NH.

2. P. múticum (Michx.) Pers. (awnless). Woodlands and fields. July-September. Map 1956. —FACW

3. P. clinopodioídes T. & G. (like *Clinopodium*). Woodlands and thickets. July-September. Map 1957. Endangered in MA, CT.

4. P. tenuifólium Schrad. (slender-leaved). Fields, roadsides. July-September. Map 1958. [*P. flexuosum; P. linifolium*]. —FACW

5. P. tórrei Benth. (for J. Torrey). Dry woods and thickets. July-September. Map 1959. From farther south. Endangered in NH, NY, CT. [*P. leptodon*].

6. P. virginiánum (L.) T. Dur. & B.D. Jackson ex B.L. (Virginian). Fields, thickets, pond and river margins. July-September. Map 1960. Endangered in NH. —FAC

7. P. verticillátum (Michx.) Pers. (whorled). Woods, fields and thickets. July-September. Map 1961. [*P. leptodon*]. Our plants include var. *verticillatum* and the following var.:

var. *pilósum* (Nutt.) Cooperrider. Lower leaf surfaces and sides of the stem (as well as the angles) pubescent (lower leaf surfaces glabrous or puberulent only on the veins; stem pubescent only on the angles, glabrous or puberulent on the sides in var. *verticillatum*). [*P. pilosum*]. —FAC

25. Agástache Clayton ex Gronov. Giant hyssop (from the Greek, referring to the numerous spikes in the inflorescence).

Tall, stout, perennial herbs; leaves petioled, ovate, acute, coarsely serrate; flowers small, yellowish, purple or blue, in dense bracteate whorles forming terminal, interrupted or continuous spikes, calyx nearly regular, 5-toothed, corolla 2-lipped, the upper lip 2-lobed, the lower 3-lobed, the middle lobe the largest, erose, stamens 4, exserted, ovary deeply 4-lobed.

a. Leaves whitened beneath with a uniform, dense, close puberulence; calyx
       puberulent, its lobes blue; corolla blue. .... 1. *A. foeniculum*
a. Leaves green beneath, glabrous, or if pubescent, not as above; calyx glabrous, its
       lobes green, whitish or pink; corolla yellowish or purplish.
   Calyx teeth ovate to oblong, obtuse to subacute, less than 2 mm long; corolla
           yellowish; stem usually glabrous, occasionally puberulent . ... 2. *A. nepetoides*
   Calyx teeth lanceolate, acute to acuminate, 2 mm or more long; corolla
           purplish; stem usually pubescent, occasionally glabrous. (Fig. 844) .... 3. *A. scrophulariifolia*

1. A. foenículum (Pursh) Kuntze. (odor resembling that of fennel). Fields and woods. June-August. From farther west. Reported for NH, Hartford County CT. [*A. anethiodora*]. Used as a flavoring by Indians and for making a beverage.

2. A. nepetoídes (L.) Kuntze. (resembling *Nepeta*). Open woods. August-September. Map 1962. —FACU

3. A. scrophulariifólia (Willd.) Kuntze. (with leaves of *Scrophularia*). Open woodlands. July-August. Fig. 844, Map 1963.

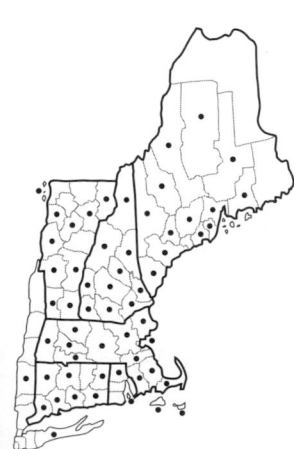

1953. *Nepeta cataria*

1954. *Elsholtzia ciliata*

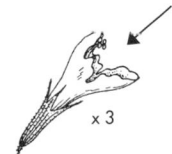

841. *Nepeta cataria*. Single flower; stamens ascending under upper lip of corolla, equalling the lip.

842. *Elsholtzia ciliata*. Single flower; stamens protruding from corolla, not ascending under the upper lip.

843. *Pycnanthemum incanum.*
Upper part of plant; heads open,
the branches visible.

x 1/2

x 3

844. *Agastache scrophulariifolia.*
Single flower; calyx teeth lanceolate,
acute to acuminate.

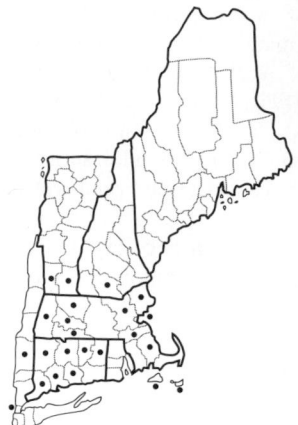

1955. *Pycnanthemum incanum*

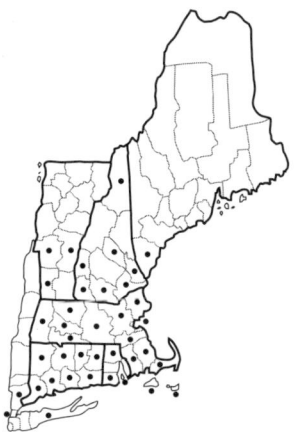

1956. *Pycnanthemum muticum*

1957. *Pycnanthemum clinopodioides*

1958. *Pycnanthemum tenuifolium*

1959. *Pycnanthemum torrei*

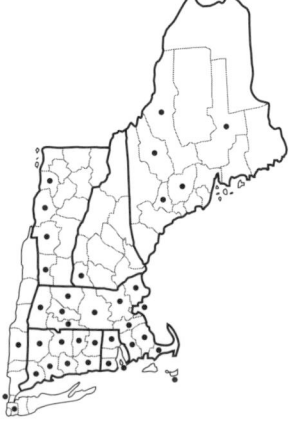

1960. *Pycnanthemum virginianum*

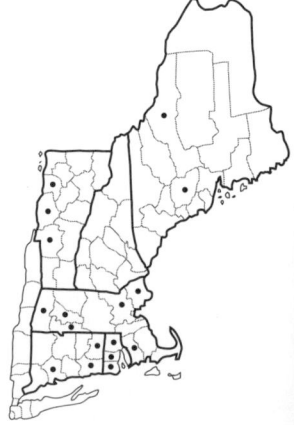

1961. *Pycnanthemum verticillatum*

1962. *Agastache nepetoides*   1963. *Agastache scrophulariifolia*

26. Hyssópus L. Hyssop (ancient Greek name).

Perennial herbs, somewhat woody at the base, from a rhizome, stems puberulent; leaves sessile or subsessile, linear to lanceolate or oblong, entire, often with smaller ones or short leafy branches in their axils; flowers blue, bracteate, in dense clusters, the lower clusters in the axils of foliage leaves, the upper subtended by reduced bracteal leaves, becoming closer together and forming interrupted spikes, calyx regular, 5-toothed, puberulent and usually glandular-dotted, corolla bilabiate, the upper lip obscurely 2-lobed, the lower much larger, 3-lobed, the middle lobe the larger and 2-lobed, stamens 4, exserted, ovary deeply 4-lobed.

1. *H. officinális* L. (of the shops). Roadsides, waste places, around old dwellings. July-October. Fig. 845, Map 1964. (Introduced from Europe). Has been used as a flavoring agent for liquors, and medicinally as an aromatic stimulant, for treatment of coughs and bronchial irritations and as a healing agent for skin wounds.

27. Hedeóma Pers. Mock Pennyroyal (from the Greek, meaning sweet scent).

Low, pubescent, strongly aromatic, annual herbs; leaves sessile or petioled, toothed or entire, pellucid-dotted; flowers small, blue, few in bracteate, axillary clusters, calyx 2-lipped, 5-toothed, gibbous on the lower side at the base, bearded in the throat, corolla weakly 2-lipped, the upper lip emarginate, the lower 3-lobed, stamens 2, exserted and ascending under the upper lip, ovary deeply 4-lobed.

Siderítis L. *montána* L. Will key to *Hedeoma hispida* but calyx teeth are expanded at the base, subulate only in the upper half or third, calyx not gibbous at the base (calyx teeth entirely subulate, calyx gibbous at the base in *Hedeoma hispida*). Europe. Reported for CT.

Leaves lanceolate to ovate, mostly wider than 3 mm, often serrate; 3 upper calyx
    teeth triangular; bracts subtending flower clusters leaf-like. .... 1. *H. pulegioides*
Leaves linear, 3 mm or less wide, entire; 3 upper calyx teeth subulate; bracts
    subtending flower clusters setaceous .... 2. *H. hispida*

1. *H. pulegioídes* (L.) Pers. (like *Mentha pulegium*). American pennyroyal. Dry fields, woods and waste places. July-September. Map 1965. Tea made from this plant is used as a stimulant and an expectorant; can be toxic if taken in large quantities (more than a few cups at a time).

2. *H. híspida* Pursh (with stiff hairs). Dry fields, barrens, roadsides, waste places. June-August. Map 1966. [*H. hispidum*].

28. *Dracocéphalum* L. Dragonhead (Greek name, referring to the shape of the corolla in one of the species).

Branched, annual or perennial herbs; leaves petioled, toothed or incised; flowers blue, in verticels in the leaf axils or in bracteate terminal heads or interrupted racemes, calyx 2-lipped, 5-toothed, 1 tooth wider than the other 4, corolla weakly 2-lipped, the upper lip 2-lobed, lower lip 3-lobed, the middle lobe largest and notched, stamens 4, exserted and ascending under the upper lip, ovary deeply 4-lobed.

a. Bracts entire or subentire, not spinose-serrate. .... 1. *D. thymiflorum*
a. Bracts spinose-serrate. (Fig. 846).
    Calyx tube puberulent; flowers in verticels in the leaf axils forming elongate,
        interrupted racemes. (Fig. 846). .... 2. *D. moldavica*
    Calyx tube with long, spreading hairs; flowers in dense, terminal heads and
        often also in the upper axils .... 3. *D. parviflorum*

    1. *D. thymiflórum* L. (thyme-flavored). Waste places, fields. June-July. (Adventive from Europe). Reported for Middlesex County MA.

    2. *D. moldávica* L. (old generic name). Waste places, cultivated soil. June-September. Fig. 846. (Adventive from Europe). Reported for VT, Hartford County CT.

    3. *D. parviflórum* Nutt. (small-flowered). Waste places, cultivated soil. June-July. Fig. 847, Map 1967. From farther west. Seeds have been used by some Indians to make flour. —FACU-

29. *Ácinos* P. Mill.

Pubescent annual herbs; leaves petioled, entire or crenate-toothed; flowers purplish, in axillary bracteate clusters, calyx 2-lipped, 5-toothed, gibbous on the lower side at the base, corolla bilabiate, the upper lip entire or emarginate, the lower 3-lobed, stamens 4, exserted and ascending under the upper lip, ovary deeply 4-lobed [*Satureja*].

    Calamíntha Lam. *népeta* (L.) Savi. Similar to *Acinos arvensis* but stoloniferous, with axillary clusters peduncled, each cluster 5 or more-flowered (*Acinos arvensis* is non-stoloniferous, with axillary clusters sessile, each cluster with 3 or fewer flowers). From farther south. Reported for RI. [*Satureja calamintha; Clinopodium nepeta*]. Represented with us as subsp. *glandulosa* (Riquien) P. W. Ball.

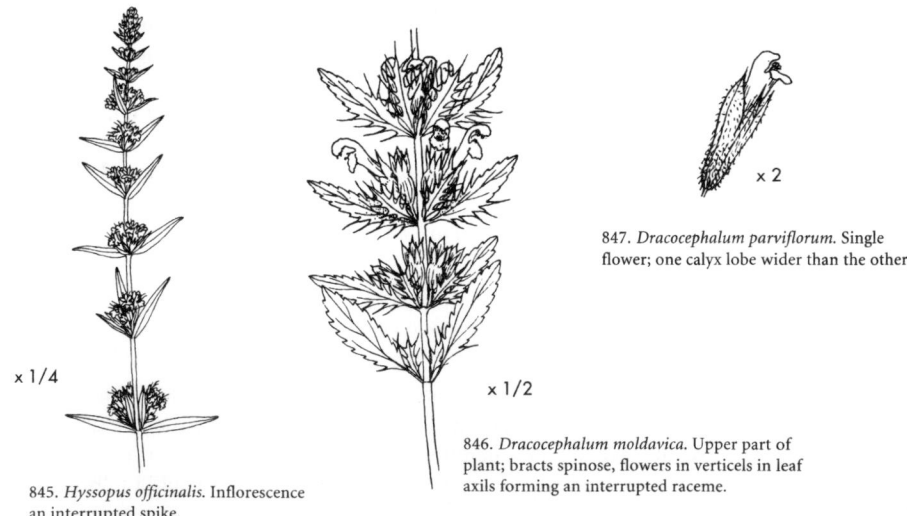

847. *Dracocephalum parviflorum.* Single flower; one calyx lobe wider than the others.

845. *Hyssopus officinalis.* Inflorescence an interrupted spike.

846. *Dracocephalum moldavica.* Upper part of plant; bracts spinose, flowers in verticels in leaf axils forming an interrupted raceme.

1964. *Hyssopus officinalis*

1965. *Hedeoma pulegioides*

1966. *Hedeoma hispida*

1967. *Dracocephalum parviflorum*

1968. *Acinos arvensis*

1969. *Melissa officinalis*

1. *A arvénsis* (Lam.) Dandy. Roadsides and waste places. June-September. Map 1968. (Naturalized from Europe). [*Satureja acinos; Clinopodium acinos*].

30. *Melíssa* L. Balm (from the Greek, meaning bee, the flowers yielding abundant honey).

Branched, lemon-scented, perennial herbs; leaves petioled, ovate, crenate-toothed; flowers white, few in bracteate, axillary clusters, calyx 2-lipped, 5-toothed, corolla bilabiate, with a curved-ascending tube, the upper lip 2-lobed, the lower 3-lobed, the middle lobe the largest, stamens 4, exserted and ascending under the upper lip, ovary deeply 4-lobed.

1. *M. officinális* L. (of the shops). Roadsides and waste places. June-August. Map 1969. (Introduced from Europe). Used in seasonings to make beverages, as a flavoring for liquors, and in the perfume industry; also reported to have sedative qualities.

31. Sálvia L. Sage (old Latin name for Sage).

Annual or perennial herbs; leaves basal and/or cauline, petioled or stem leaves sometimes sessile, lobed or toothed; flowers blue, purple, or red, rarely white, mostly showy, in verticels subtended by reduced bracteal leaves, forming terminal, continuous or interrupted, spikes or racemes, calyx bilabiate, the upper lip entire to 3-lobed, the lower 2-toothed or lobed, corolla bilabiate, the upper lip entire or notched, the lower 3-lobed, the middle lobe the larger, stamens 2, ascending under the upper lip, exserted from the corolla throat, often only 1-locular, ovary deeply 4-lobed.

a. Upper lip of calyx entire or with a single pointed lobe.
    Calyx obscurely bilabiate, the upper lip entire; leaves linear to lanceolate,
        obtuse or acute .... 1. *S. azurea*
                                                                var. *grandiflora.*
    Calyx distinctly bilabiate, the upper lip with a single pointed lobe; leaves ovate,
        abruptly acuminate .... 2. *S. splendens*
a. Upper lip of calyx 3-lobed or toothed, the teeth sometimes small.
    b. Pedicels as long or nearly as long as fruiting calyx; flowers 12 or more per node .... 3. *S. verticillata*
    b. Pedicels much shorter than fruiting calyx; flowers mostly fewer than 12 per
        node.
        c. Lobes of upper calyx lip short and close together, sometimes inconspicuous.
            (Fig. 848).
            Leaves mostly in a basal rosette, stem leaves only 1-3 pair. .... 4. *S. pratensis*
            Leaves mostly cauline, mostly more than 3 pair. .... 5. *S. nemorosa*
        c. Lobes of upper calyx lip conspicuous, distinctly separated by flat or rounded
            sinuses. (Fig. 849).
            Leaves mostly basal, often lyrate, stem leaves only 1-3 pair; anthers with
                both locules present although separated. .... 6. *S. lyrata*
            Leaves mostly cauline, not lyrate, mostly more than 3 pair; anthers with
                only 1 locule present .... 7. *S. officinalis*

    1. S. azúrea Michx. ex Lam. (sky-blue). Occasionally escaped from cultivation. July-September. From farther west and south. Reported for Fairfield County CT, Bronx County NY. Represented with us as var. *grandiflóra* Benth. [*S. pitcheri*].

    S. farinácea Benth. Resembling *S. azurea* var. *grandiflora* but distinguishable by a densely tomentose calyx (calyx finely pubescent in *S. azurea* var. *grandiflora*). Southwestern. Reported for Fairfield County CT.

    2. S. spléndens Sellow ex Roemer & J.A. Schultes (shining). Rarely escaped from cultivation. From South America. Reported for Fairfield County CT, Essex County MA.

    S. tiliifólia Vahl. Similar to *S. splendens* but distinguishable in having deltoid leaves acute or obtuse at the tip and truncate or widely cuneate at the base (leaves ovate, abruptly acuminate in *S. splendens*). European. A waif in our range. Reported for Middlesex County, MA.

    3. S. verticilláta L. (whorled). Roadsides, waste places, fields. June-August. Map 1970. (Adventive from Europe).

    4. S. praténsis L. (of meadows). Waste places, fields. June-August. Fig. 848, Map 1971. (Naturalized from Europe).

    5. S. nemorósa L. Waste places, fields. June-July. (Naturalized from Europe). Reported for MA. [*S. sylvestris*].

    6. S. lyráta L. (lyre-shaped). Open woods, fields, waste places. May-June. Rare; from farther west and south. Reported for New Haven County CT, Westchester County NY.

    7. S. officinális L. (of the shops). Garden Sage. Occasionally escaped from cultivation. Fig. 849, Map 1972. Well known for culinary uses and for teas; long reported to have various medicinal benefits but these claims have been discounted by modern researchers.

    S. scláorea L. Clary. Similar to *S. officinalis* but stem leaves and bracteal leaves are ovate (stem leaves and bracteal leaves lance-ovate in *S. officinalis*). Mediterranean, occasionally escaped from cultivation. Reported for Fairfield County CT, Middlesex County MA.

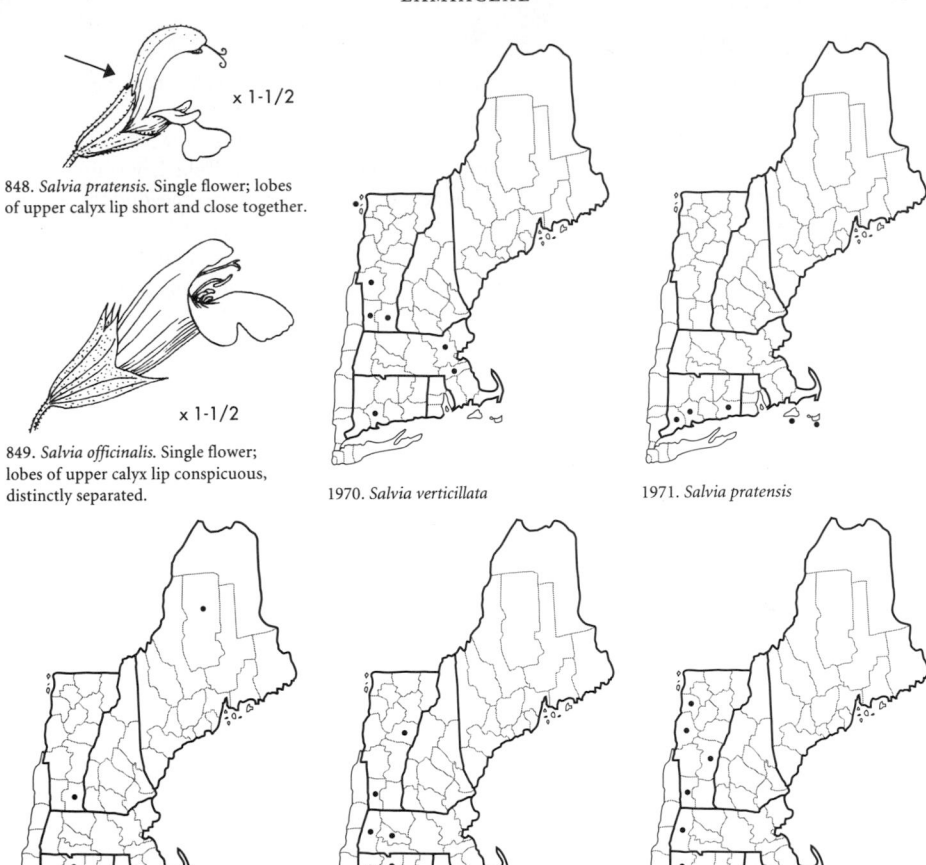

848. *Salvia pratensis.* Single flower; lobes
of upper calyx lip short and close together.

849. *Salvia officinalis.* Single flower;
lobes of upper calyx lip conspicuous,
distinctly separated.

1970. *Salvia verticillata*

1971. *Salvia pratensis*

1972. *Salvia officinalis*

1973. *Blephilia ciliata*

1974. *Blephilia hirsuta*

32. Blephília Raf. (from the Greek, referring to the pubescence of the bracts and calyx).
Pubescent, perennial herbs; leaves sessile or petioled, lanceolate to ovate, entire to serrate; flowers
purple or bluish, in dense verticels in the upper leaf axils and/or forming a continuous or interrupted
bracteate, terminal spike, calyx bilabiate, covered with long, spreading hairs, the upper lip 3-
toothed, the lower 2-toothed, teeth setaceous, corolla 2-lipped, pubescent, the upper lip entire, the
lower 3-lobed, the lateral lobes broader than the middle one, stamens 2, exserted, ovary deeply 4-
lobed.

Lobes of lower calyx lip extending beyond sinuses of upper lip. .... 1. *B. ciliata*
Lobes of lower calyx lip not reaching sinuses of upper lip. .... 2. *B. hirsuta*

    1. B. ciliáta (L.) Benth. (with marginal hairs). Fields, roadsides. June-July. Map 1973. Endangered
in MA.
    2. B. hirsúta (Pursh) Benth. (with straight hairs). Moist woodlands. July-August. Map 1974.
Endangered in MA. Our plants include var. *hirsuta* and the following var.:
    var. *glabráta* Fern. Stem and leaves becoming glabrous (permanently pubescent in var. *hirsuta*).
—FACU-

33. *Prunélla* L. Seal-heal.

Low, perennial herbs, often with leafy basal offshoots; leaves petioled, ovate, lanceolate or oblong, entire, crenate or serrate (rarely pinnatifid); flowers blue, purple or white, in dense, continuous, bracteate, terminal and axillary spikes or heads, calyx 2-lipped, the upper lip 3-toothed, the lower deeply 2-parted, corolla bilabiate, the upper lip unlobed, galeate, the lower 3-lobed, the middle lobe the largest, erose to laciniate, stamens 4, curved under the upper lip, exserted beyond the corolla throat, ovary deeply 4-lobed.

Oríganum L. *marjorána* L. Sweet Marjoram. Similar to *Prunella* but is distinguishable in having a paniculate inflorescence and calyx split on one side (inflorescence spicate and calyx not split in Prunella). Rarely escaped from cultivation. Reported for Suffolk County MA [*Marjorana hortensis*]. Commonly used as garden herb.

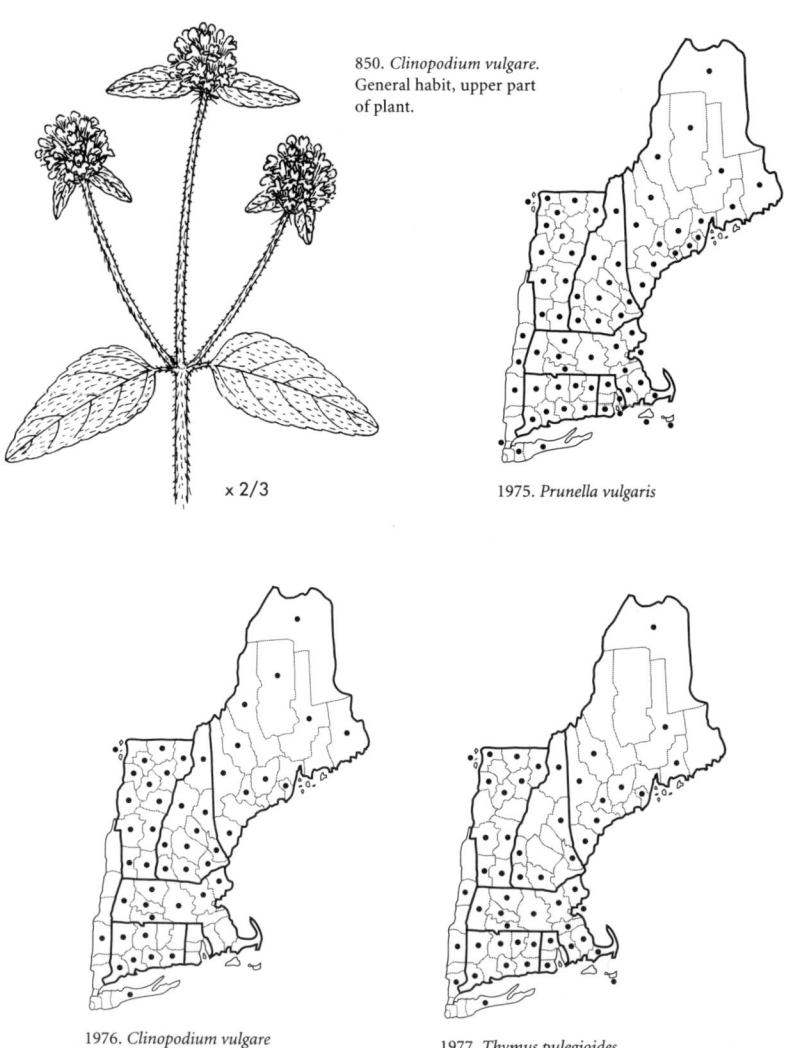

850. *Clinopodium vulgare.* General habit, upper part of plant.

× 2/3

1975. *Prunella vulgaris*

1976. *Clinopodium vulgare*

1977. *Thymus pulegioides*

1. P. vulgáris L. (common). Fields, roadsides, waste places. June-September. Map 1975. (Naturalized from Eurasia). Our plants include subsp. *vulgaris* and the following subsp.:

subsp. *lanceoláta* (Bart.) Hulten. Principal leaves lanceolate, a third as wide as long, cuneate at the base (ovate, half as long as wide, rounded at the base in subsp. vulgaris). Used as a mouthwash and gargle and to aid healing of skin wounds. —FACU+

P. laciniáta (L.) L. Upper leaves pinnatifid (entire or obscurely toothed in *P. vulgaris*). Eurasian; reported for Dukes County, MA.

34. Clinopódium L.

Pubescent, perennial herbs from short stolons; leaves petioled, entire or crenate-toothed; flowers purplish, pink or white in dense, subglobose clusters, terminal and in the upper axils, subtended by numerous, long-ciliate bracts, calyx 2-lipped, 5-toothed, somewhat gibbous on the lower side at the base, corolla bilabiate, the upper lip entire or emerginate, the lower 3-lobed, stamens 4, exserted and ascending under the upper lip, ovary deeply 4-lobed. [*Satureja*].

1. C. vulgáre L. (common) Wild basil. Fields, thickets, woods, roadsides, waste places. June-August. Fig. 850, Map 1976. (Naturalized from Europe). [*Satureja vulgaris*].

35. Thýmus L. (ancient Greek name for Thyme).

Suffrutescent, creeping, diffusely branched, mat-forming, strongly aromatic perennial with puberulent stems; leaves sessile to short-petioled, ovate to elliptic, entire; flowers small, purplish to whitish, in bracteate verticels forming dense, terminal spikes and often also in the upper axils, calyx bilabiate, 5-toothed, pubescent in the throat, corolla bilabiate, the upper lip emarginate, the lower 3-lobed, stamens 4, usually exserted, ovary deeply 4-lobed.

1. T. pulegióides L. (old generic name). Wild thyme. Fields, pastures, roadsides. June-September. Map 1977. (Naturalized from Europe). [*T. serpyllum*]. Can be used as a food flavoring in the same manner as garden thyme; also reputed to have numerous medicinal uses.

T. práecox Opiz. Similar to *T. pulegioides* but with flowering stems densely pubescent on 2 of the 4-sides with both short and longer hairs, the other 2 sides sparsely pubescent to glabrous (flowering stems equally short-pubescent on all 4 sides in *T. pulegioides*). [*T. arcticus*]. (Europe). Reported for MA, NH, RI. Represented with us as subsp. *árcticus* (Dur.) Jalas.

T. vulgáris Garden Thyme. Differs from the latter 2 species in having sessile leaves with revolute margins (leaves short-petioled and flat in the above species). A garden escapee. Reported for MA.

Family 176. Solanáceae (Nightshade Family)

Hermaphrodite, annual or perennial herbs, shrubs or vines. Leaves simple, alternate or rarely opposite, entire, toothed or divided, estipulate. Flowers perfect, regular or nearly so, in ebracteate, cymose inflorescences, calyx and corolla usually 5-lobed, sometimes obscurely lobed or entire, usually plaited, stamens 5, inserted on the corolla tube, ovary superior, 3-5 (usually 2)- locular, style 1. Fruit a capsule or berry.

a. Plant a shrub or vine; flowers bluish to purplish, rarely white; fruit a red berry.
　Flowers and fruit solitary or in sessile fascicles. .... 1. *Lycium*
　Flowers and fruit in peduncled cymes. .... 2. *Solanum*
a. Plant herbaceous, not shrubby or viney.
　b. Plant in flower.
　　c. Corolla rotate, widely spreading, the lobes often longer than the short tube; plants sometimes spiny. (Fig. 852).
　　　d. Corolla distinctly lobed, the lobes usually longer than the tube or plant spiny. (Fig. 852).

Anthers opening by terminal pores; leaves entire, toothed, or deeply
pinnatifid but not compound; plant sometimes spiny. .... 2. *Solanum*
Anthers opening longitudinally; leaves pinnately or bi-pinnately
compound; plant not spiny .... 3. *Lycopersicon esculentum*
d. Corolla obscurely lobed or merely 5-angled; plant not spiny. .... 4. *Leucophysalis grandiflora*
c. Corolla funnelform to salverform or campanulate, the lobes shorter than the
tube; plant not spiny. (Fig. 854).
e. Flowers sessile or subsessile; leaves (except sometimes the lowest) sessile
or clasping. (Fig. 854) .... 5. *Hyoscyamus niger*
e. Flowers pedicelled; leaves petioled (often sessile or clasping in *Nicotiana*).
f. Flowers in terminal panicles or racemes. .... 6. *Nicotiana*
f. Flowers solitary, lateral or axillary.
g. Corolla 3 cm or more long.
Calyx tube 2 cm or more long .... 7. *Datura*
Calyx tube less than 2 cm long.
Corolla salverform, white, the tube longer than 3 cm. .... 8. *Petunia axillaris*
Corolla funnelform, purple, the tube 3 cm or less long. .... 9. *Calibrachoa parviflora*
g. Corolla less than 3 cm long.
Calyx lobes auriculate at the base; corolla blue. .... 10. *Nicandra physalodes*
Calyx lobes not auriculate; corolla white to yellowish .. . . 11. *Physalis*
b. Plant in fruit.
h. Fruit a berry.
i. Calyx longer than and completely enclosing or surrounding fruit, not spiny.
j. Calyx parted nearly to the base, the lobes auriculate at base. (Fig. 857). .... 10. *Nicandra physalodes*
j. Calyx parted only to or just below summit of fruit, the lobes not
auriculate at base.
Calyx closely surrounding berry, its lobes 5 mm or more long;
pedicels mostly 2 or more at each node .... 4. *Leucophysalis grandiflora*
Calyx inflated and loosely surrounding berry, its lobes less than 5 mm
long; pedicels solitary at each node .... 11. *Physalis*
i. Calyx shorter than fruit or longer and spiny.
Fruit pulpy, not juicy, 2.5 cm or less thick; calyx often spiny. .... 2. *Solanum*

Fruit juicy, 3 cm or more thick, calyx not spiny. .... 3. *Lycopersicon esculentum*
h. Fruit a capsule.
k. Calyx lobes absent, the calyx circumscissile after flowering, the base
persisting as a collar; fruit usually spiny. .... 7. *Datura*
k. Calyx lobes present in fruit; fruit not spiny.
l. Capsules sessile or subsessile, circumscissile. .... 5. *Hyoscyamus niger*
l. Capsules distinctly pedicelled, longitudinally dehiscent.
Capsules solitary .... 8. *Petunia axillaris*
Capsules in terminal panicles or racemes. .... 6. *Nicotiana*

1. *Lýcium* L. Matrimony-vine (ancient Greek name for a prickly shrub).

Shrub with long, slender, spreading or climbing branches, 5-ridged, often weakly and sparsely thorny, pith moderate, tan, spongy, buds small, multiple, subglobose, leaf scars small, crescent-shaped, bundle trace 1, stipule scars lacking; leaves short-petioled, entire or wavy-margined, elliptic to lanceolate or oblanceolate, often fascicled; flowers greenish-purple, 1-several in the leaf axils, pedicelled, corolla funnelform, lobes spreading, stamens and style exserted; fruit a red berry.

Cápsicum L. *ánnuum* L. Red Pepper. Will key to *Lycium* but is distinguishable in being unarmed and having a rotate corolla and pod-like fruit. Rarely escaped from cultivation. Reported for

Fairfield and Hartford Counties CT. [*C. frutescens*]. Widely used as a spice; also has value as a digestive aid and in relieving pain following surgery when externally applied; a variety of other medicinal uses are also reported.

Solándra Sw. *grandiflóra* Sw. Chalice Vine. Distinguishable from *Lycium* and *Capsicum* in having leathery leaves, and a yellowish corolla 1 dm or more long; plant unarmed, fruit a pulpy berry with large seeds. (Mexico). Rarely escaped from cultivation. Reported for CT.

Corolla lobes shorter than the tube .... 1. *L. barbatum*
Corolla lobes equalling or longer than the tube. .... 2. *L. chinense*

1. *L. barbátum* L. Occasionally escaped from cultivation to roadsides and waste places. June-September. Fig. 851, Map 1978. (Introduced from Europe). [*L. halimifolium; L. chinense*]. Leaves and young shoots poisonous.

2. *L. chinénse* Mill. (Chinese). Occasionally escaped from cultivation to roadsides and waste places. June-September. Map 1979. (Introduced from Asia).

2. *Solánum* L. Nightshade (classical Latin name).

Annual or perennial herbs or woody vines, sometimes prickly, when woody stems slender, terate or irregularly 3-sided, pith moderate, tan, spongy, or twigs hollow in older growth, buds small, globose, scales pubescent, leaf scars semi-circular, bundle scars 1-3, stipule scars lacking; leaves petioled, entire, toothed, lobed or pinnatifid; flowers bluish, purple, yellow or white, in cymes, umbels or racemes, the inflorescences generally lateral and extra-axillary, corolla rotate, the lobes spreading or reflexed, filaments short, anthers connivent around the style, opening by two terminal pores; fruit a berry. All of the species below have properties that have been reported as causing poisoning under certain conditions. —Wildl.1

a. Plant, at least the stem, armed with prickles or spines; lower leaf surfaces, and
    often other parts of the plant, stellate-pubescent.
  b. Calyx merely pubescent, or with 1-several short spines on the tube; leaves
      wavy-margined to coarsely toothed or shallowly lobed. .... 1. *S. carolinense*
  b. Calyx tube and usually the lobes abundantly spiny; leaves deeply pinnately or
      bipinnately lobed. (Fig. 853).
    c. Inflorescence with pubescence containing gland-tipped hairs; corolla blue,
       purple or white.
      Anthers unequal, one longer and distinctly curved .. . . 2. *S. citrullifolium*
      Anthers equal or nearly so, straight or only slightly curved. (Fig. 853). .... 3. *S. sisymbriifolium*
    c. Inflorescence with pubescence not containing gland-tipped hairs; corolla
      yellow .... 4. *S. rostratum*
a. Plant unarmed; pubescence of simple hairs.
  d. Woody climbing or twining vine or an upright shrub; leaves often with a pair
    of smaller basal lobes or leaflets .... 5. *S. dulcamara*
  d. Herbs, erect or diffuse, not climbing or twining; leaves entire, shallowly or
    obscurely lobed, pinnate or irregularly pinnatifid.
    e. Leaves pinnate or irregularly pinnatifid. .... 6. *S. tuberosum*
    e. Leaves entire, shallowly or obscurely lobed.
      f. Stem glabrous or sparsely appressed-pubescent; fruit black. .... 7. *S. americanum*
      f. Stem densely spreading-pubescent; fruit greenish or yellow.
        Calyx cupping the lower half of the fruit; fruit greenish or yellowish. .... 8. *S. physalifolium*
        Calyx not cupping the fruit; fruit yellow to orange or red. .... 9. *S. villosum*

1. *S. carolinénse* L. (of Carolina). Horse-nettle. Dry fields and waste places. June-September. Fig. 852, Map 1980. Our plants are var. *carolinense*. Various medicinal uses are reported for the ripe fruit and the root; should be used with caution because of poisonous properties.

2. *S. citrullifólium* A.Br. (with leaves of *citrullus*). Roadsides and waste places. From the southwest. Reported for Middlesex County MA. [*Androcera c.*]. Our plants are var. *citrullifolium*.

3. S. sisymbriifólium Lam. (with leaves of *Sisymbrium*). Roadsides and waste places. Fig. 853, Map 1981. (Adventive from S. Amer.).

4. S. rostrátum Dunal (beaked). Buffalo-bur. Waste places, cultivated ground. July-September. Map 1982. From farther west. [*S. cornutum*].

5. S. dulcamára L. (bittersweet). Climbing Nightshade. Thickets, clearings and open woods. May-September. Map 1983. (Naturalized from Europe). Our plants include var. *dulcamara* and the following var.:

var. *villosíssimum* Desv. Branches and leaves abundantly pubescent (branches and leaves glabrous or nearly so in var. *dulcamara*). Poisonous; however external application of the chopped leaves is reported to be successful in treating cellulite. —FAC-

S. pseúdo-cápsicum L. Jerusalem-cherry. Upright shrub with oblong or spatulate leaves and white flowers (leaves ovate-acuminate and flowers blue or purple in *S. dulcamara*). Occasionally escaped from cultivation. (Introduced from Europe). Reported for Fairfield County, CT, Middlesex and Suffolk Counties, MA.

6. S. tuberósum L. (tuberous). Potato. Occasionally escaped from cultivation to waste places and dumps. July-September. Map 1984. (Introduced from S. Amer.). Various medicinal uses are reported in addition to its wide use as a food; can cause poisoning if eaten green.

S. triflórum Nutt. Similar to *S. tuberosum* but differs in having deeply pinnatifid but simple leaves (leaves pinnately compound in *S. tuberosum*). Adventive from the west. Reported for Dukes County MA.

7. S. americánum Mill. (American). Waste places, roadsides. June-October. Map 1985. (Naturalized from Europe). [*S. nigrum* var. *virginicum; S. ptychanthum*]. Leaves and unripe fruits are poisonous; ripe fruits can be cooked and used for preserves; juice of the fruits is reported to have analgesic properties useful when applied to the skin or to relieve toothache. —FACU

8. S. physalifólium Rusby. Waste places, cultivated ground. Map 1986. (Adventive from S. Amer.). [*S. sarrachoides*].

x 2/5

x 1/2

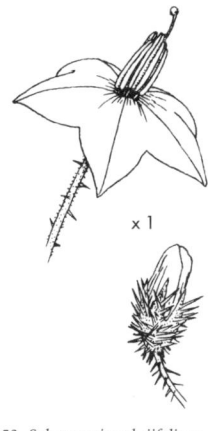

x 1

853. *Solanum sisymbriifolium.* Single flower, 2 views; calyx spiny, anthers slightly curving.

851. *Lycium barbatum.* General habit, upper part of plant.

852. *Solanum carolinense.* Several flowers; corolla rotate, distinctly lobed.

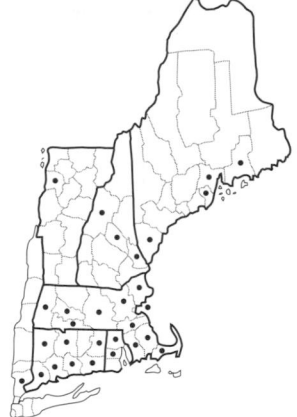

1978. *Lycium barbatum*

1979. *Lycium chinense*

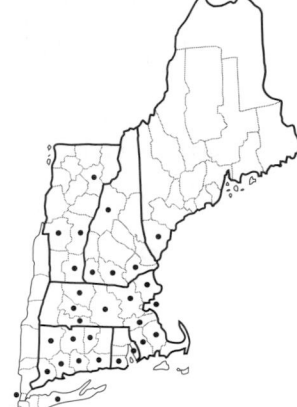

1980. *Solanum carolinense*

1981. *Solanum sisymbriifolium*

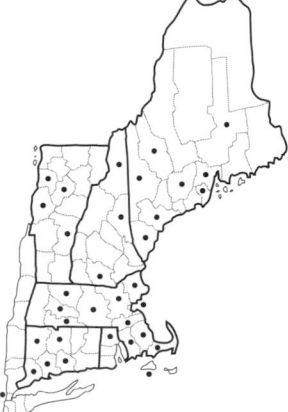

1982. *Solanum rostratum*

1983. *Solanum dulcamara*

1984. *Solanum tuberosum*

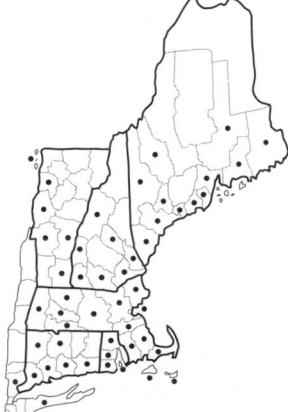

1985. *Solanum americanum*

1986. *Solonum physalifolium*

9. S. villósum Miller. Waste places, cultivated ground. Map 1987. (Adventive from Eurasia).

S. melongéna L. Eggplant. Occasionally found in garden refuse but not persistent. Reported for Essex County MA. Reported to be of value in regulating cholesterol and in relief of hemorrhoidal discomfort when applied externally.

3. Lycopérsicon Mill. Tomato (wolf peach).

Similar to *Solanum* except anthers connate into a cone prolonged into a long, sterile tip and opening by longitudinal slits instead of by terminal pores.

1. L. esculéntum Mill. (edible). Occasionally escaped from cultivation to waste places, sea beaches. July-September. Map 1988. Various medicinal uses are reported in addition to its wide use as a food.

4. Leucophýsalis Rydb.

Villous and viscid annual herbs with angled or ridged stems; leaves large, petioled, ovate to lance-ovate, entire; flowers large, white, with a yellowish center, pedicelled, in clusters of 2-4 from the upper leaf axils, corolla rotate; fruit a dry berry, closely enclosed, or nearly so, within the persistent calyx. [*Chamaesaracha; Physalis*].

1. L. grandiflóra (Hook.) Rydb. (large-flowered). White-flowered Ground-cherry. Sandy lake shores, rocky open woods. June-August. Reported for Grand Isle, VT. [*Chamaesaracha g.; Physalis g.*].

5. Hyoscýamus L. Henbane (from the Greek, meaning hog-bean).

Coarse, viscid-pubescent, rank-smelling, narcotic annual or biennial herbs; leaves large, sessile to clasping, irregularly lobed or pinnatifid; flowers yellowish with purple veins, sessile or subsessile in the axils of the leaves and branches, and forming 1-sided, terminal racemes or spikes, calyx campanulate to urceolate, corolla funnelform, slightly irregular; fruit a 2-locular, circumscissile capsule enclosed in the persistent calyx.

1. H. níger L. (black). Roadsides and waste places. June-September. Fig. 854, Map 1989. (Naturalized from Europe). All parts poisonous; in external applications it is used to relieve arthritis and rheumatism; helpful in relieving toothache; properly used it has long been valued as a sedative; was used in medieval Europe to cause visual hallucinations.

6. Nicotiána L. Tobacco (for J. Nicot).

Coarse, viscid-pubescent, rank-smelling, narcotic annual herbs; leaves large, sessile and clasping to subsessile or petioled, entire or slightly undulate, lanceolate to ovate; flowers greenish, yellow, white, or pink to red, in terminal panicles or racemes, corolla cylindric or salverform to funnelform; fruit a 2-locular capsule. Leaves are poisonous if eaten.

Browállia L. *americána* L. Sometimes keying to *Nicotiana* but distinguishable in having 4 stamens in 2 pairs and capsule with lobed valves (stamens 5 and valves of capsule not lobed in *Nicotiana*). Tropical. Rarely escaped from cultivation. Reported for Norfolk County MA.

Schizánthus Ruiz & Pavon *pinnátus* Ruiz & Pavon. Butterfly Flower. Similar to *Nicotiana* but distinguishable from it and *Browallia* by its pinnately divided leaves. Rarely escaped from gardens. Reported for Penobscot County ME.

Corolla short-cylindric, 2 cm or less long. .... 1. *N. rustica*
Corolla salverform to funnelform, 3 cm or more long. (Fig. 855). .... 2. *N. tabacum*

1. N. rústica L. (of the country). Wild Tobacco. Fields and waste places. September-October. Map 1990. Formerly cultivated by Indians.

2. N. tabácum L. (aboriginal name). Tobacco. Occasionally escaped from cultivation to waste places. August-September. Fig. 855. (Introduced from Tropical Amer.).

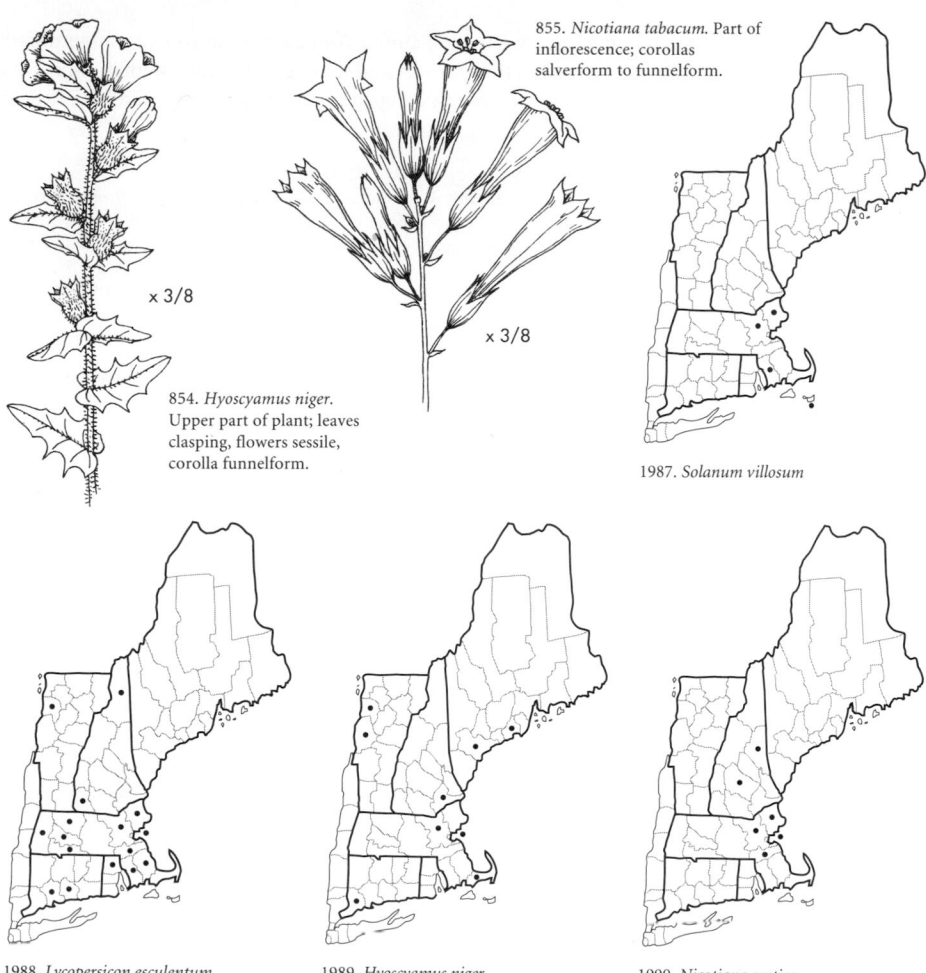

855. *Nicotiana tabacum*. Part of inflorescence; corollas salverform to funnelform.

x 3/8

x 3/8

854. *Hyoscyamus niger*. Upper part of plant; leaves clasping, flowers sessile, corolla funnelform.

1987. *Solanum villosum*

1988. *Lycopersicon esculentum*

1989. *Hyoscyamus niger*

1990. *Nicotiana rustica*

N. longiflóra Cav. Resembling the above species but differing in that the corolla tube much exceeds the calyx (only up to 2/3 longer in the above species). Occasionally escaped from cultivation to waste places. Reported for New Haven and Tolland Counties CT; Dukes, Essex and Suffolk Counties MA; Strafford County VT.

Other species of *Nicotiana* rarely or occasionally escape from cultivation and are not treated here; accounts for these species should be sought in works on cultivated plants.

7. *Datúra* L. (name altered from Hindustani).

Tall, branched, coarse, rank smelling, narcotic-poisonous, annual herbs; leaves petioled, ovate, entire to undulate-margined or irregularly lobed; flowers large and showy, solitary, on short pendundles in the forks of the branches, white or purplish, calyx prismatic or cylindric, circumscissile near the base, leaving a persistent, reflexed, flaring collar at the base of the fruit, corolla funnelform, shallowly lobed and with subulate teeth; fruit an ovoid to subglobose, usually spiny, 4-locular capsule subtended by the persistent base of the calyx. Poisonous, but also has various medicinal values when administered in the proper amounts by medical professionals; has also been used as a hallucinogen by Indians in the southwest.

Salpiglóssis Ruiz & Pavon *sinuáta* Ruiz & Pavon. Painted Tongue. Similar to *Datura* but differs in having flowers subtended by bracts rather than solitary and ebracteate in the forks of the branches as in *Datura,* and in having a smooth capsule. Rarely escaped from gardens. Reported for Fairfield County CT.

Flowers less than 12 cm long and 6 cm wide; calyx tube strongly prismatic and
    narrowly 5-winged, the remnant in fruit less than 1 cm long. .... 1. *D. stramonium*
Flowers 12 cm or more long and 6 cm or more wide; calyx tube terete or slightly
    angled, wingless, the remnant in fruit mostly 1 cm or more long. .... 2. *D. innoxia*

    1. *D. stramónium* L. (old generic name). Jimson-weed. Waste places, cultivated ground, around old cellar holes. June-August. Fig. 856, Map 1991. (Naturalized from Asia).
    Forms lacking prickles occasionally occur.
    2. *D. innóxia* Mill. (harmless). Waste places. July-September. Map 1992. (Adventive to the southwest from Tropical Amer.). [*D. meteloides*].

8. *Petúnia* Juss. Petunia (an aboriginal name for Tobacco).

Branched, viscid-pubescent, annual herbs; leaves alternate, or the upper ones opposite, sessile or petioled, entire, ovate to obovate; flowers white, solitary, on terminal and axillary or lateral peduncles, calyx deeply 5-cleft to below the middle, corolla salverform, shallowly lobed, one stamen conspicuously smaller than the other 4; fruit a 2-valved capsule.

Browállia L. *americána* L. May key to *Petunia* in fruit but is distinguishable in having a capsule with lobed valves (valves not lobed in *Petunia*). Tropical. Rarely escaped from cultivation. Reported for Norfolk County MA.

Salpiglóssis Ruiz & Pavon *sinuáta* Ruiz & Pavon. Painted Tongue. May key to *Petunia* in fruit but is distinguishable from it and *Browallia* in having fruit with 2-cleft valves. Rarely escaped from gardens. Reported for Fairfield County CT.

    1. *P. axilláris* (Lam.) B.S.P. (axillary). Occasionally escaped from cultivation to waste places. July-September. Map 1993. (Introduced from S. Amer.).

9. *Calibráchoa* Llave & Lex.

Similar to *Petunia,* distinguished in having a purple, funnelform corolla. [*Petunia*].

    1. *C. parviflóra* (Juss.) D'Arcy. Occasionally escaped from cultivation to waste places. July-October. Map 1994. (Introduced from S. Amer.). [*Petunia integrifolia*; *P. violacea*]. Has been used by S. American Indians as a hallucinogen.

10. *Nicándra* Adans. Apple of Peru (for Nicander).

Branched, glabrous, annual herbs with angled stems; leaves petioled, ovate to oblong, coarsely and unevenly toothed or lobed; flowers light blue, solitary, nodding on peduncles in or adjacent to the leaf axils, calyx 5-angled, the segments auriculate at the base, the auricles acute, calyx inflated in fruit, corolla broadly campanulate, shallowly lobed, ovary 3-5 locular; fruit a dry berry enclosed within the inflated calyx.

    1. *N. physalódes* (L.) Gaertn. (resembling *Physalis*). Roadsides and waste places. July-September. Fig. 857, Map 1995. (Introduced from Peru). [*Physalodes p.*].

11. *Phýsalis* L. Ground-cherry (Greek name for bladder, referring to the inflated calyx).

Branched, annual or perennial herbs; leaves petioled, ovate to ovate-lanceolate, entire or toothed; flowers white to yellowish, often with a darker center, solitary from the leaf axils, calyx inflated in

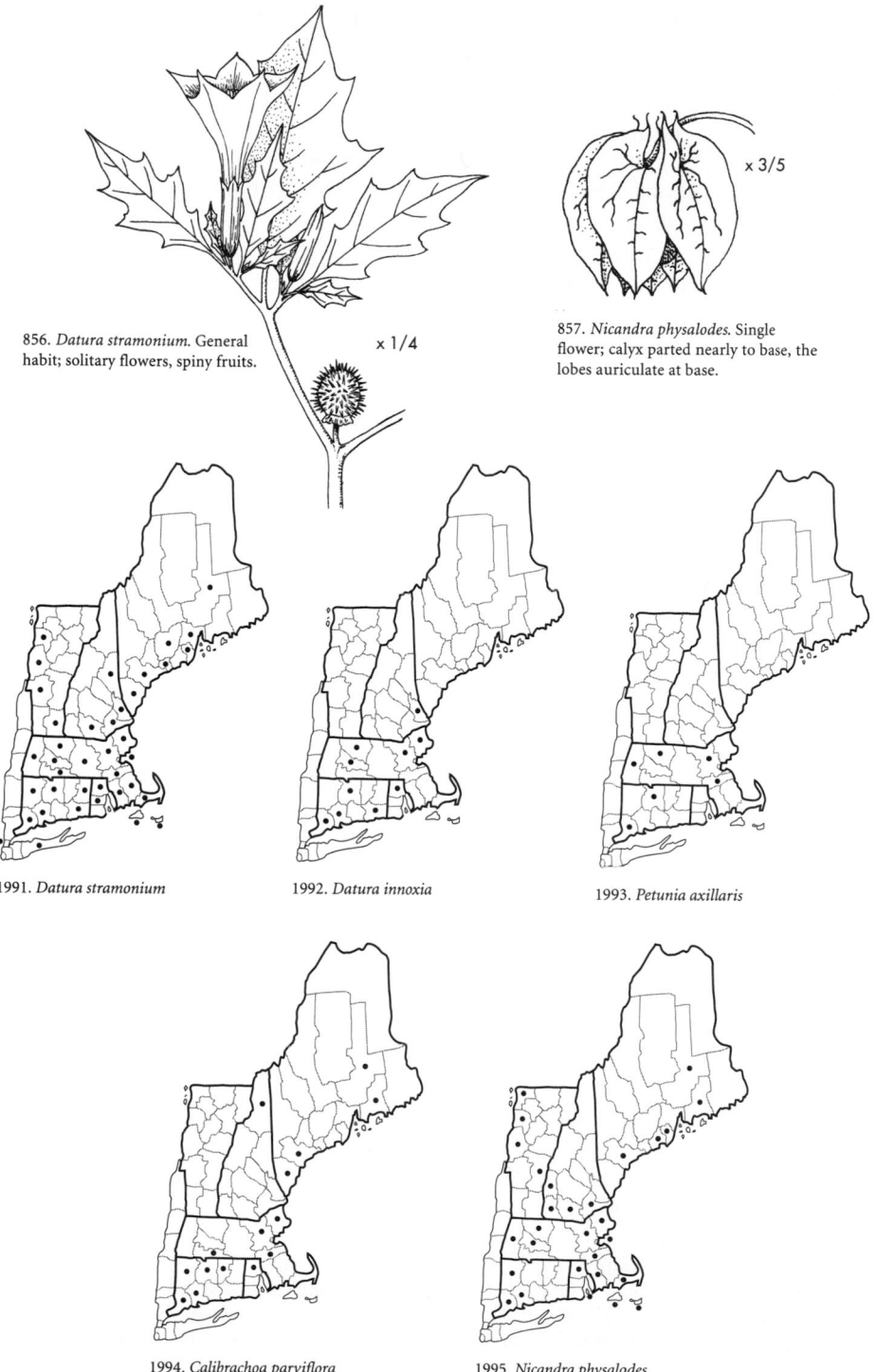

856. *Datura stramonium*. General habit; solitary flowers, spiny fruits.

× 1/4

× 3/5

857. *Nicandra physalodes*. Single flower; calyx parted nearly to base, the lobes auriculate at base.

1991. *Datura stramonium*

1992. *Datura innoxia*

1993. *Petunia axillaris*

1994. *Calibrachoa parviflora*

1995. *Nicandra physalodes*

fruit, often ribbed or angled, corolla campanulate or funnelform, shallowly or obscurely lobed, fruit a berry enclosed within the inflated calyx. Foliage poisonous; the ripe fruits of all species are edible, although species vary in size and quantity of fruit produced; the unripe fruits of some species are poisonous; those species that are considered to produce the best fruits for use raw or in preserves as well as those with reported cases of poisoning from unripe fruits are noted below. —Wildl. 1

Browállia L. *americána* L. May key to *Physalis* but is distinguishable in having 4 stamens in 2 pairs (stamens 5 in *Physalis*) and a capsular fruit. Tropical. Rarely escaped from cultivation. Reported for Norfolk County MA.

a. Corolla white; fruiting calyx orange or red. .... 1. *P. alkekengi*
a. Corolla yellowish, often with a darker center; fruiting calyx green to brown.
  b. Stem with dense, spreading pubescence.
    c. Corolla more than 1 cm long; plant perennial; stem usually not branched
      below the first 3 internodes. (Fig. 858). .... 2. *P. heterophylla*
    c. Corolla 1 cm or less long; plant annual; stem usually branched from near
      the base.
      Corolla uniformly yellow; calyx lobes triangular; leaves tapered to
        rounded at base .... 3. *P. missouriensis*
      Corolla yellow with a darker center; calyx lobes acuminate; leaves rounded
        to cordate at base .... 4. *P. pruinosa*
  b. Stem glabrous or with curved or appressed pubescence.
    d. Plant annual, from fibrous roots; corolla usually 1 cm or less long (sometimes
      longer in *P. ixocarpa*).
      Flowering pedicels 5 mm or less long; fruiting pedicels less than 1 cm
        long; corolla yellow with a darker center .... 5. *P. philadelphica*
                                                        var. *immaculata.*
      Flowering pedicels longer than 5 mm; fruiting pedicels 1 cm or more
        long; corolla uniformly yellow .... 6. *P. angulata*
    d. Plant perennial, from a horizontal rhizome; corolla usually more than 1 cm
      long.
      Leaves pubescent beneath over the entire surface, and often above; calyx
        tube pubescent over the entire surface .... 7. *P. virginiana*
      Leaves glabrous beneath and above, or sparsely pubescent along the main
        veins beneath; calyx tube glabrous or sparsely pubescent along the
        main veins. .... 8. *P. longifolia*
                                                       var. *subglabrata*

1. *P. alkekéngi* L. (Arabic name). Chinese lantern plant. Occasionally escaped from cultivation to waste places. Map 1996. (Introduced from Asia). Ripe fruit edible.

2. *P. heterophýlla* Nees (variabled-leaved). Fields, roadsides, waste places. June-September. Fig. 858, Map 1997. Our plants are var. *heterophylla*. Can cause poisoning if unripe fruits are eaten in large quantities.

P. peruviána L. Similar to *P. heterophylla* but leaves are long-acuminate and pedicels are shorter than 1 cm (leaves acute and pedicels 1 cm or more long in *P. heterophylla*). (Introduced from S. Amer.). Occasionally escaped from cultivation. Reported for Norfolk County MA.

P. hederifólia Gray. Leaves obtuse, pedicels less than 1 cm long. From farther west. Reported for VT, RI. Our plants are var. *hederifolia*.

3. *P. missouriénsis* Mackenz. & Bush (of Missouri). Waste places, barrens, cultivated ground, open woods. June-September. From the southwest.

4. *P. pruinósa* L. Abandoned fields, waste places. July-September. Map 1998. (Tropical Amer.). [*P. pubescens* var. *grisea*]. Ripe fruit edible.

P. pubéscens L. Similar to *P. pruinosa* but with thin, translucent leaves, entire or with 3-4 teeth on each side (leaves thicker, not translucent, toothed to the base in *P. pruinosa*). From farther south and west. Reported for MA, VT. Represented with us as var. *integrifolia* (Dunal) Waterfall. Fruit edible when ripe. —FACU-

5. P. philadélphica Lam. Tomatillo. Occasionally escaped from cultivation to waste places. Map 1999. (Introduced from southwestern US and Mexico). [*P. ixocarpa*]. Represented with us as var. *immaculáta* Waterfall. Ripe fruit edible.

6. P. anguláta L. (angled). Waste places, thickets. July-September. (Asia, S. Amer., W.I.). From the south. Reported for Hartford County CT, Essex County MA. Our plants are var. *angulata*. —FAC

7. P. virginiána Mill. (Virginian). Fields, roadsides, waste places, woods. June-September. Map 2000. From farther west and south. [*P. monticola*]. Our plants are var. *virginiana*.

P. lanceoláta Michx. Similar to *P. virginiana* but differing primarily in having oblanceolate, spatulate or oblong leaves (leaves lanceolate to ovate in *P. virginiana*). From farther west. Reported for NH. [*P. virginiana* var. *hispida; P. hispida*].

8. P. longifólia Nutt. (long-leaved). Fields, roadsides, waste places. June-September. Map 2001. From farther west and south. Represented with us as var. *subglabráta* (Mackenz. & Bush) Cronq. [*P. macrophysa; P. subglabrata*]. Can cause poisoning if unripe fruits are eaten in large quantities.

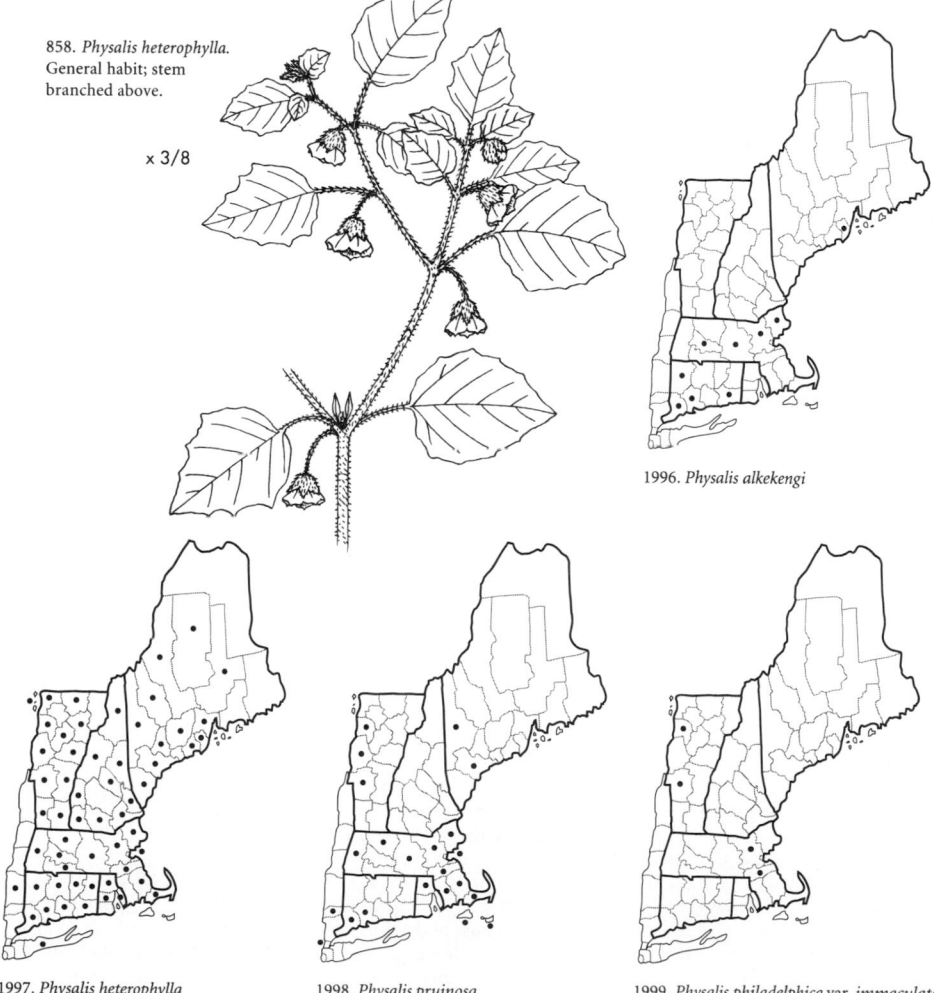

858. *Physalis heterophylla.*
General habit; stem
branched above.

x 3/8

1996. *Physalis alkekengi*

1997. *Physalis heterophylla*

1998. *Physalis pruinosa*

1999. *Physalis philadelphica* var. *immaculata*

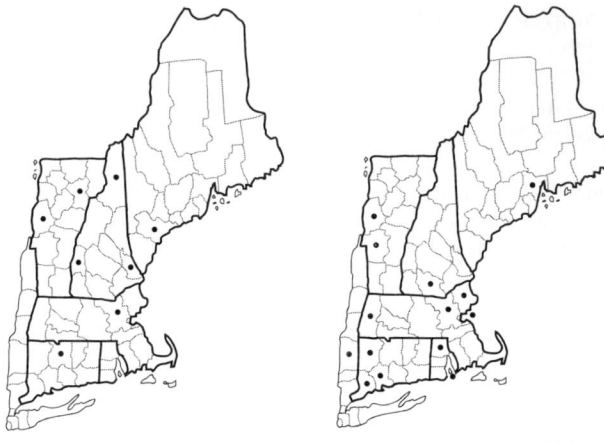

2000. *Physalis virginiana*   2001. *Physalis longifolia* var. *subglabrata*

Family 177. Scrophulariáceae (Figwort Family)

Hermaphrodite, annual or perennial herbs or rarely trees (*Paulownia*). Leaves simple, alternate, opposite or rarely whorled (*Veronicastrum*), entire, toothed, pinnatifid or lobed, estipulate. Flowers perfect, irregular to regular or nearly so, bracteate, in various kinds of inflorescences, calyx 4-5 toothed or divided, corolla 4-5 parted, usually tubular, the tube long or short, usually 2-lipped, sometimes spurred or saccate, stamens usually 2 or 4, occasionally 5, inserted on the corolla tube near the base, ovary superior, 2-locular, style 1, ovules numerous. Fruit a capsule.

a. Stem leaves in whorles of 3-7, at least the larger ones 1 cm or more wide. .... 1. *Veronicastrum*
                                                                            virginicum

a. Stem leaves mostly opposite or alternate, or if whorled (sometimes in *Collinsia*
    and *Linaria*) less than 1 cm wide.
  b. Plant a tree .... 2. *Paulownia*
                                                                tomentosa
  b. Plant herbaceous.
    c. Leaves all basal, plant scapose .... 3. *Limosella australis*
    c. Leaves alternate or opposite, plant not scapose.
      d. Foliage leaves (not including bracteal leaves subtending flowers) alternate.
        e. Corolla spurred at the base. (Fig. 860).
          f. Leaves ovate to orbicular or hastate, less than twice as long as wide;
            plants procumbent.
            Leaves round-ovate to triangular-ovate or hastate. (Fig. 859). .... 4. *Kickxia*
            Leaves reniform-orbicular, shallowly 3-7-lobed. .... 5. *Cymbalaria*
                                                                    muralis
        f. Leaves linear to lance-linear or lance-ovate, more than twice as long
          as wide; plants erect.
          Flowers solitary in the leaf axils; spur less than 3 mm long. .... 6. *Chaenorrhinum*
                                                                    minus
          Flowers in terminal, bracted racemes; spur 3 mm or more long.
            Flowers yellow or orange, or if whitish or blue then corolla with
               purple stripes or an orange palate, spur usually more
               than 1 mm wide at base and/or pedicels, or some of
               them, 5 mm or more long. .... 7. *Linaria*
            Flowers blue, not marked with purple or orange, spur of corolla
               less than 1 mm wide at base and 6 mm or less long;
               pedicels all less than 5 mm long. .... 8. *Nuttalanthus*
                                                                canadensis

e. Corolla not spurred.
  g. Corolla rotate, nearly regular.
    Corolla 4-lobed; stamens 2; capsule flattened, obcordate . ... 9. *Veronica*
    Corolla 5-lobed; stamens 5; capsule turgid, globose to oblong. .... 10. *Verbascum*
  g. Corolla tubular to campanulate, bilabiate (weakly bilabiate in
    Digitalis).
    h. Leaves entire or divided into long, linear lobes.
      i. Calyx lobes 2 or 4 .... 11. *Castilleja*
      i. Calyx lobes 5.
        Corolla 1.5 times or more as long as calyx; calyx closely
          subtended by a pair of bractlets .... 12. *Schwalbea*
                                                            americana
        Corolla barely exceeding calyx, less than 1.5 times as long;
          calyx not subtended by bractlets .... 13. *Digitalis*
    h. Leaves serrate, crenate or pinnatifid.
      Leaves deeply toothed to pinnatifid .... 14. *Pedicularis*
      Leaves crenate to merely serrate, not deeply toothed. .... 13. *Digitalis*
d. Foliage leaves (not including bracteal leaves subtending flowers) opposite.
  j. Calyx lobes or sepals 4 or fewer.
    k. Corolla nearly regular; stamens 2; capsule obcordate. .... 9. *Veronica*
    k. Corolla bilabiate; stamens 4 (except in *Hemianthus*); capsule oblong,
      ovate or suborbicular.
      l. Foliage leaves (not including bracteal leaves) entire. .... 15. *Melampyrum*
                                                         lineare
      l. Foliage leaves serrate or toothed to pinnatifid.
        m. Leaves pinnately lobed, the lobes crenate. .... 14. *Pedicularis*
        m. Leaves simple (although sometimes coarsely) serrate.
          n. Leaves ovate to orbicular, usually 2 times or less as long as
            wide. .... 16. *Euphrasia*
          n. Leaves lanceolate to oblong-lanceolate, more than 3 times as
            long as wide.
            Calyx ovoid, in fruit much inflated and papery. .... 17. *Rhinanthus*
            Calyx campanulate, in fruit not inflated or papery. .... 18. *Odontites vernus*
  j. Calyx lobes or sepals 5.
    o. Inflorescence a panicle of cymes. (Fig. 869).
      Stem leaves sessile or sometimes clasping. .... 19. *Penstemon*
      Stem leaves petioled .... 20. *Scrophularia*
    o. Inflorescence of terminal and/or lateral spikes or racemes, or flowers
      solitary in the leaf axils.
      p. Flowers usually in whorles; corolla gibbous on one side near the
        base, the middle lobe folded and enclosing the stamens.
        (Fig. 870). .... 21. *Collinsia*
                                                         parviflora
      p. Flowers not in whorles; corolla not gibbous (although sometimes
        spurred), the middle lobe not folded and enclosing the
        stamens.
      q. Corolla spurred at the base.
        r. Leaves round-ovate, less than twice as long as wide, plants
          procumbent. (Fig. 859) .... 4. *Kickxia*
        r. Leaves linear to lance-linear or lance-ovate, more than twice
          as long as wide; plants erect.
          Flowers solitary in the leaf axils; spur less than 3 mm long. ..... 6. *Chaenorrhinum*
                                                           minus
          Flowers in terminal, bracted racemes; spur 3 mm or more
            long.
            Flowers yellow or orange, or if whitish or blue then
               corolla with purple stripes or an orange palate,
               spur usually more than 1 mm wide at base
               and/or pedicels, or some of them, 5 mm or more
               long. ....7. *Linaria*

Flowers blue, not marked with purple or orange, spur of
corolla less than 1 mm wide at base and 6 mm or
less long; pedicels all less than 5 mm long. .... 8. *Nuttalanthus*
canadensis
q. Corolla not spurred.
s. Flowers in dense, terminal spikes or loose, terminal racemes
with bracts unlike the foliage leaves, these either sepaloid
or minute and scale-like.
Flowers in dense, terminal spikes with large, ovate bracts.
(Fig. 871). .... 22. *Chelone*
Flowers in loose, terminal racemes with minute bracts. .... 23. *Mazus*
s. Flowers solitary in the leaf axils, the leaves subtending flowers
sometimes reduced but resembling the foliage leaves.
t. Leaves linear; flowers not or indistinctly bilabiate
(Fig. 872). .... 24. *Agalinus*
t. Leaves lanceolate to oblong or ovate; flowers distinctly
bilabiate (leaves sometimes linear in *Gratiola* but
flowers are bracteolate; flowers indistinctly bilabiate in
Aureolaria but yellow; flowers pink or purple and not
bracteolate in *Agalinus*).
u. Calyx closely subtended by a pair of sepaloid
bractlets. .... 25. *Gratiola*
u. Calyx not subtended by bractlets.
v. Calyx tube as long or longer than the lobes; corolla
1.4 cm or more long.
Corolla indistinctly bilabiate; leaves mostly
pinnatifid or bipinnatifid; capsule longer
than calyx tube .... 26. *Aureolaria*
Corolla distinctly bilabiate; leaves entire to merely
toothed; capsule included in calyx tube .... 27. *Mimulus*
v. Calyx tube much shorter than the lobes; corolla 1 cm
or less long. .... 28 *Lindernia dubia*

1. *Veronicástrum* Heist. ex Fabr. Culver's root (false Veronica).

Tall, stout, perennial herbs; leaves whorled, petioled, lanceolate to elliptic-lanceolate, acuminate,
sharply serrate; flowers white or bluish, in terminal, solitary or panicled spikes, calyx deeply 4-5
lobed, corolla tubular, 4 lobed, nearly regular, stamens 2, strongly exserted; capsule ovoid.

1. *V. virgínicum* (L.) Farw. Rich woods, thickets and fields. June-August. Map 2002. [*Veronica
v.; Leptandra v.*]. Has been used for various medicinal purposes including treatment of scurvy and
as a cathartic and emetic; overdose of root extracts may be toxic. —FACU

2. *Paulównia* Sieb. & Zucc. Princess-tree (for A. Paulowna).

Trees, twigs stout, with prominent lenticels, pith large, white, usually chambered or hollowed, lateral
buds small, often superposed, with several scales, leaf scars oval, somewhat notched at the top,
bundle traces numerous in a circle or ellipse, stipule scars and terminal bud lacking, large, terminal
panicles of tan, velvety flower buds naked, those of the following season conspicuous throughout
winter; leaves large, opposite, long-petioled, broadly ovate, acuminate, cordate, entire or slightly
lobed, pubescent on one or both sides; flowers white or bluish, showy, in large, terminal panicles,
calyx deeply 5-parted, regular, corolla tubular, irregular, with 5, somewhat unequal lobes, stamens
4; capsules large, ovoid, woody, in panicles from the previous season persisting over winter. [Placed
in *Bignoniaceae* by some authors].

1. *P. tomentósa* (Thunb.) Sieb. & Zucc. ex Steud. Rarely escaped from cultivation. April-May.
Map 2003. (Naturalized from Asia).

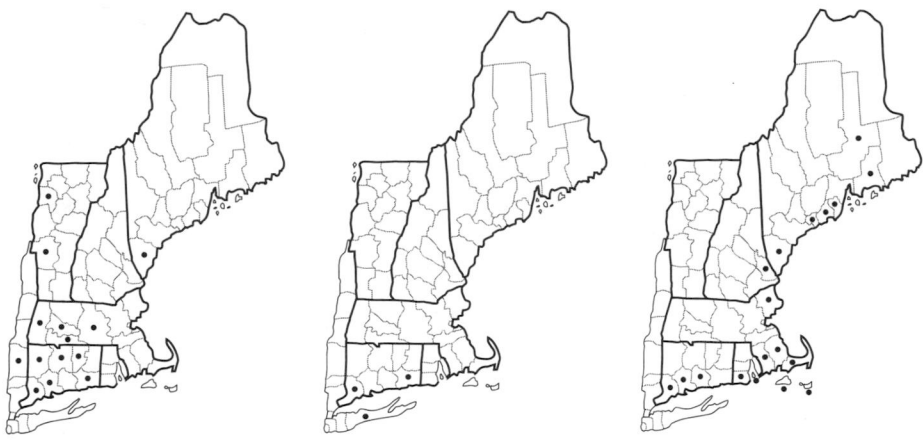

2002. *Veronicastrum virginicum*   2003. *Paulownia tomentosa*   2004. *Limosella australis*

3. Limosélla L. Mudwort (diminutive of mud, referring to typical habitat).

Small, scapose, annual herbs, the stems prostrate and rooting at the nodes; leaves basal, arising in a cluster at each node, linear to filiform, grass-like; flowers small, white, solitary on filiform peduncles, several peduncles arising at each node, shorter than the leaves, calyx and corolla 5-lobed, campanulate, regular or nearly so, stamens 4; capsule globose.

    1. L. austrális R. Br. Tidal sand and mud. July-September. Map 2004. Endangered in NH. [*L. aquatica* var. *tenuiflora; L. subulata*]. —OBL

4. Kíckxia Dum. Cancerwort (for J. Kickx).

Procumbent, usually branched, pubescent, annual herbs; leaves opposite below, subopposite to alternate above, short petioled, entire, toothed or lobed, ovate to suborbicular or triangular-ovate; flowers yellowish and purple variegated, solitary in the leaf axils, long-pedicelled, calyx deeply 5-parted, regular, corolla irregular, bilabiate, with a spur at the base, the throat closed by the palate, stamens 4; capsule subglobose.

Pedicels glabrous or only sparsely pubescent, mostly near the base and summit; leaves
    triangular-ovate to hastate. (Fig. 859). .... 1. *K. elatine*
Pedicels densely villous their entire length; leaves round-ovate. .... 2. *K. spuria*

    1. K. elatíne (L.) Dum. (early name). Roadsides and waste places in sandy soil. June-September. Fig. 859, Map 2005. (Naturalized from Europe). [*Linaria e.*]. —FAC
    2. K. spúria (L.) Dum. (illegitimate). Roadsides, waste places, fields in sandy soil. June-September. (Naturalized from Europe). Reported for RI. [*Linaria s.*].

5. Cymbalária Hill. Kenilworth ivy (a cymbal, referring to the leaf shape).

Glabrous, annual herbs, the stems trailing, branched, often rooting at the nodes; leaves alternate, long-petioled, reniform-orbicular, shallowly 3-7 lobed; flowers purple with a yellow palate, solitary in the leaf axils on long peduncles, calyx deeply 5-parted, regular, corolla irregular, bilabiate, with a spur at the base, the throat closed by the palate, stamens 4; capsule globose, with 2 terminal pores; these eventually splitting to the base.

    1. C. murális Gaertn. Mey. and Scherb. (of walls). Waste places, roadsides. June-August. Map 2006. (Introduced from Europe). [*C. cymbalaria; Linaria c.*].

859. *Kickxia elatine*. General habit; procumbent stems, leaf shape.

2005. *Kickxia elatine*

2006. *Cymbalaria muralis*

2007. *Chaenorrhinum minus*

2008. *Linaria vulgaris*

2009. *Linaria genistifolia*

6. *Chaenorrhínum* (DC. ex Duby) Reichenb. Dwarf Snapdragon (Greek name, based on flower shape).

Branched, glandular-pubescent, annual herbs; leaves mostly alternate, but the lowest opposite, linear to linear-lanceolate or linear-obovate, narrowed to a sessile or subsessile base, entire; flowers purple with a yellow palate, solitary in the leaf axils, long-pedicelled, calyx deeply 5-parted, regular, corolla irregular, bilabiate, with a short spur at the base, stamens 4; capsule subglobose, with 2 terminal pores.

    1. *C. mínus* (L.) Lange (smaller). Roadsides, waste places, fields. June-September. Map 2007. (Naturalized from Europe). [*Linaria m.*].

7. *Lináría* P. Mill. Toadflax (name based on similarity of foliage to that of flax).

Annual or perennial, generally glabrous herbs; leaves alternate, or the lower and those of basal offshoots opposite or whorled, sessile or short petioled, entire, linear to lanceolate or lance-ovate; flowers yellow, white, blue or multi-colored, in terminal bracted racemes, calyx deeply 5-parted, corolla irregular, bilabiate, spurred at the base, upper lip 2-lobed, the lower 3-lobed, throat open or closed by a palate, stamens 4; capsule ovoid to globose.

In addition to the following species *L. angustissima* has been reported for MA and *L. incarnata* has been reported for CT.

a. Flowers yellow, or yellow and orange.
  b. Lower leaves whorled; axis of inflorescence and sepals with glandular hairs .... 1. *L. supina*
  b. Lower leaves alternate; axis of inflorescence and sepals not glandular.
    Leaves linear, short-petioled, less than 5 mm wide. .... 2. *L. vulgaris*
    Leaves linear-lanceolate to ovate, sessile, the larger ones often wider than
      5 mm .... 3. *L. genistifolia*
a. Flowers blue to whitish, sometimes marked with orange or yellow.
  Spur of corolla short and conic, usually more than 1 mm in diameter at base,
    5 mm or less long; corolla with purple stripes. (Fig. 860). .... 4. *L. repens*
  Spur of corolla filiform, less than 1 mm in diameter at base or if wider, then
    7 mm or more long; corolla without purple stripes.
    Spur nearly straight .... 5. *L. maroccana*
    Spur strongly curved .... 6. *L. bipartita*

1. *L. supina* (L.) Chaz. Waste places and ballast, mostly near the coast. (From Europe). Reported for Hunters Point and N. Terminus of 8th Ave. NY.

2. *L. vulgáris* P. Mill. (common). Butter-and-eggs. Fields, roadsides, waste places. May-September. Map 2008. (Naturalized from Europe). [*L. linaria*]. In some areas the young shoots are boiled and used as a potherb; also used in external applications for healing minor flesh wounds, as an eye lotion and for hemorrhoids.

L. spártea (L.) Chaz. Similar to *L. vulgaris* but is distinguishable in having flowers in a loose, open raceme, lacking an orange palate (flowers in a compact raceme with an orange palate in *L. vulgaris*). Mediterranean; a waif in our range. Reported for Fairfield County CT.

3. *L. genistifólia* (L.) Mill. (with leaves of *Genista*). Broomleaf Toadflax. Waste places. Map 2009. (From Europe).

L. dalmática (L.) Mill. Similar to *L. genistifolia* but with lance-ovate to ovate, clasping leaves and flowers well over 2 cm long including spur (leaves lanceolate, not clasping and flowers 2 cm or less long including spur in *L. genistifolia*). Throughout our range. [*L. genistifolia* subsp. *d.*]. Our plants include subsp. *dalmatica* and the following subsp.:

subsp. *macedónica* (Griseb.) D.A. Sutton. Calyx lobes less than 3 mm long, ovate (calyx lobes 3 mm or longer and lanceolate in subsp. *dalmatica*). [*L. macedonica*].

4. *L. répens* (L.) Mill. (creeping). Fields, roadsides. June-September. Fig. 860, Map 2010. (Naturalized from Europe).

860. *Linaria repens.*
Part of inflorescence;
flowers with corolla
spurred at base.

× 2/3

2010. *Linaria repens*

5. L. maroccána J.D. Hook. (of Morocco). Roadsides, waste places. June-September. Map 2011. (Introduced from n. Africa).

L. aerugínea (Gouan) Cav. Similar to *L. maroccana* but distinguishable in having very densely crowded, overlapping leaves, pedicels all less than 5 mm long, and lower lip lacking an orange palate (leaves remote, some pedicels longer than 5 mm, and lower lip with an orange palate in *L. maroccana*). Mediterranean; a waif in our range. Reported for Fairfield County CT.

6. L. bipártita (Vent.) Willd. Waste places. Reported for CT.

8. Nuttalánthus D. A. Sutton.

Similar to *Linaria*, except flowers blue, not marked with purple or orange. [*Linaria*].

1. N. canadénsis (L.) D.A. Sutton. Roadsides, fields, waste places, mostly in sandy soil. May-September. Map 2012. [*Linaria canadensis*].

9. Verónica L. Speedwell (for St. Veronica).

Annual or perennial herbs; leaves opposite or alternate, sessile or petioled, toothed or entire; flowers small, blue or white, solitary in the leaf axils or in terminal or axillary spikes or racemes, calyx deeply 4-lobed, corolla rotate, unequally 4-lobed, stamens 2; capsule somewhat flattened, usually obcordate or emarginate. Used for various medicinal purposes such as treating scurvy, and as a cathartic and emetic; preparations made from the root may be toxic if used in excessive quantities.

a. Flowers in axillary racemes; leaves all opposite. (Fig. 861).
  b. Leaves linear to narrowly lanceolate, 6 or more times as long as wide, mostly
          10 mm or less wide; capsule flattened, conspicuously obcordate. (Fig. 861) ... 1. *V. scutellata*
  b. Leaves lanceolate to ovate or elliptic, mostly less than 6 times as long as wide
      and 10 mm or less wide, or capsule turgid, scarcely notched.
    c. Plants decidedly pubescent.
      d. Leaves ovate to lanceolate, rounded to truncate at base; pedicels as long or
          longer than the calyx lobes or calyx lobes very unequal; inflorescence
          merely pubescent, or with few glandular hairs.
          Calyx lobes very unequal; style more than 5 mm long. .... 2. *V. austriaca*
          Calyx lobes about equal; style 5 mm or less long. .... 3. *V. chamaedrys*
      d. Leaves elliptic to elliptic-obovate, narrowed to base; pedicels shorter than
          the nearly equal calyx lobes; inflorescence densely
          glandular-pubescent. .... 4. *V. officinalis*
    c. Plants glabrous or essentially so.
      e. Leaves of flowering stems (at least the middle and upper) sessile. .... 5. *V. anagallis-*
                                       aquatica
      e. Leaves all short petioled.
        Leaves mostly broadest at or above the middle; style less than
          2.5 mm long. .... 6. *V. beccabunga*
        Leaves mostly broadest near the base; style 2.5 mm or more long. .... 7. *V. americana*
a. Flowers in terminal racemes, the bracteal leaves mostly alternate, or flowers
    solitary in the axils of mostly alternate leaves.
  f. Flowers in terminal racemes, the bracteal leaves abruptly smaller than the
      foliage leaves. (Fig. 862).
    g. Leaves sharply serrate, the larger ones more than 3.5 cm long. .... 8. *V. longifolia*
    g. Leaves entire to obscurely toothed or crenate, 3.5 cm or less long.
      Stem spreading-pubescent, erect or ascending; capsules longer than wide. ..... 9. *V. wormskjoldii*
      Stem glabrous or closely puberulent, often creeping at the base; capsules
        wider than long .... 10. *V. serpyllifolia*
  f. Flowers solitary in the axils of mostly alternate leaves, these only gradually
      reduced. (Fig. 863).
    h. Pedicels up to 2 mm long.
      Foliage leaves 3 or more times as long as wide; stem glabrous or glandular. ... 11. *V. peregrina*
      Foliage leaves less than 3 times as long as wide; stem spreading-pubescent,
        the hairs not glandular .... 12. *V. arvensis*

h. Pedicels longer than 2 mm.
 i. Leaves, or many of them, 3-5 lobed, mostly wider than long. (Fig. 863). .... 13. *V. hederifolia*
 i. Leaves merely coarsely crenate-dentate, mostly longer than wide.
  j. Perennials, from slender rhizomes; stems creeping and often rooting
   from most of the nodes .... 14. *V. filiformis*
  j. Annuals; stems ascending or prostrate, sometimes rooting from the
   lower nodes.
   Mature pedicels less than 15 mm long; corolla up to 8 mm wide;
    capsule up to 5 mm wide .... 15. *V. agrestis*
   Mature pedicels 15 mm or more long; corolla more than 8 mm wide;
    capsule more than 5 mm wide .... 16. *V. persica*

1. *V. scutelláta* L. (platter-like). Marsh-speedwell. Pond and stream margins, ditches, wooded swamps, marshes and wet meadows. May-September. Fig. 861, Map 2013. (Eurasia). —OBL

2. *V. austriáca* L. Roadsides and waste places. June-July. Map 2014. (Introduced from Europe). [*V. latifolia; V. teucrium*]. Represented with us as subsp. *teucrium*. D. A. Webb.

3. *V. chamaédrys* L. (ground-oak). Roadsides, waste places, lawns, fields. May-June. Map 2015. (Naturalized from Europe).

4. *V. officinális* L. (of the shops). Woodlands, fields and roadsides. May-July. Map 2016. (Eurasia). Our plants include var. *officinalis* and the following var.:
 var. *tournefórtii* (Vill.) Reichenb. Peduncles filiform (peduncles stout in var. *officinalis*). —FACU

5. *V. anagállis-aquática* L. (aquatic-*Anagallis*). Pond and stream margins, ditches, often in shallow water. May-September. Map 2017. (Indigenous and also Naturalized from Europe). Endangered in MA. From farther south and west. [*V. aquatica; V. catenata; V. comosa; V. connata; V. glandifera; V. salina*]. —OBL

6. *V. beccabúnga* L. (old generic name). Brooklime. Pond and stream margins, ditches. June-August. (Naturalized from Europe). Reported for Hampshire County MA, Dutchess County NY. —OBL

7. *V. americána* Schwein. ex Benth. (American). Stream margins, wet meadows, marshes, springs and seeps. May-July. Map 2018. Used in salads. —OBL

8. *V. longifólia* L. (long-leaved). Roadsides, waste places, fields. June-August. Map 2019. (Naturalized from Europe). [*V. maritima; V. spicata*].

V. spúria L. Will key to *V. longifolia* or *V. wormskjoldii* but is distinguishable in having racemes in panicles and pedicels as long or longer than the calyx (racemes not panicled and pedicels shorter than calyx in the latter 2 species). Rarely escaped from cultivation. Reported for Rockingham County NH, Windsor County VT.

9. *V. wormskjóldii* Roem. & Schult. Alpine Speedwell. Alpine areas; White Mts. of N.H., Mt. Katahdin, Maine. July-August. Endangered in ME, NH. Reported for Piscataquis County, ME, Coos County, NH. [*V. alpina* var. *unalaschensis*]. —FAC

10. *V. serpyllifólia* L. (thyme-leaved). Fields, lawns, roadsides, open woods. May-July. Fig. 862, Map 2020. (Naturalized from Europe). Our plants include subsp. *serpyllifolia* and the following subsp.:
 subsp. *humifúsa* (Dickson) Syme. Rachis and pedicels with glandular pubescence (finely puberulent in subsp. *serpyllifolia*). [*V. humifusa; V. tenella*]. —FAC+

11. *V. peregrína* L. (wandering). Fields, roadsides, waste places. May-July. Map 2021. (Europe). Our plants include var. *peregrina* and the following var.:
 var. *xalapénsis* (H.B.K.) Pennell. Stem and capsule glandular-pubescent (glabrous in var. *peregrina*). —FACU-

12. *V. arvénsis* L. (of cultivated ground). Corn-speedwell. Cultivated ground, fields, waste places, roadsides. May-August. Map 2022. (Naturalized from Europe).

13. *V. hederifólia* L. (with leaves of *Hedera*). Fields and waste places. April-May. Fig. 863. (Naturalized from Europe). Reported for CT, N. Terminus of 8th Ave., NY.

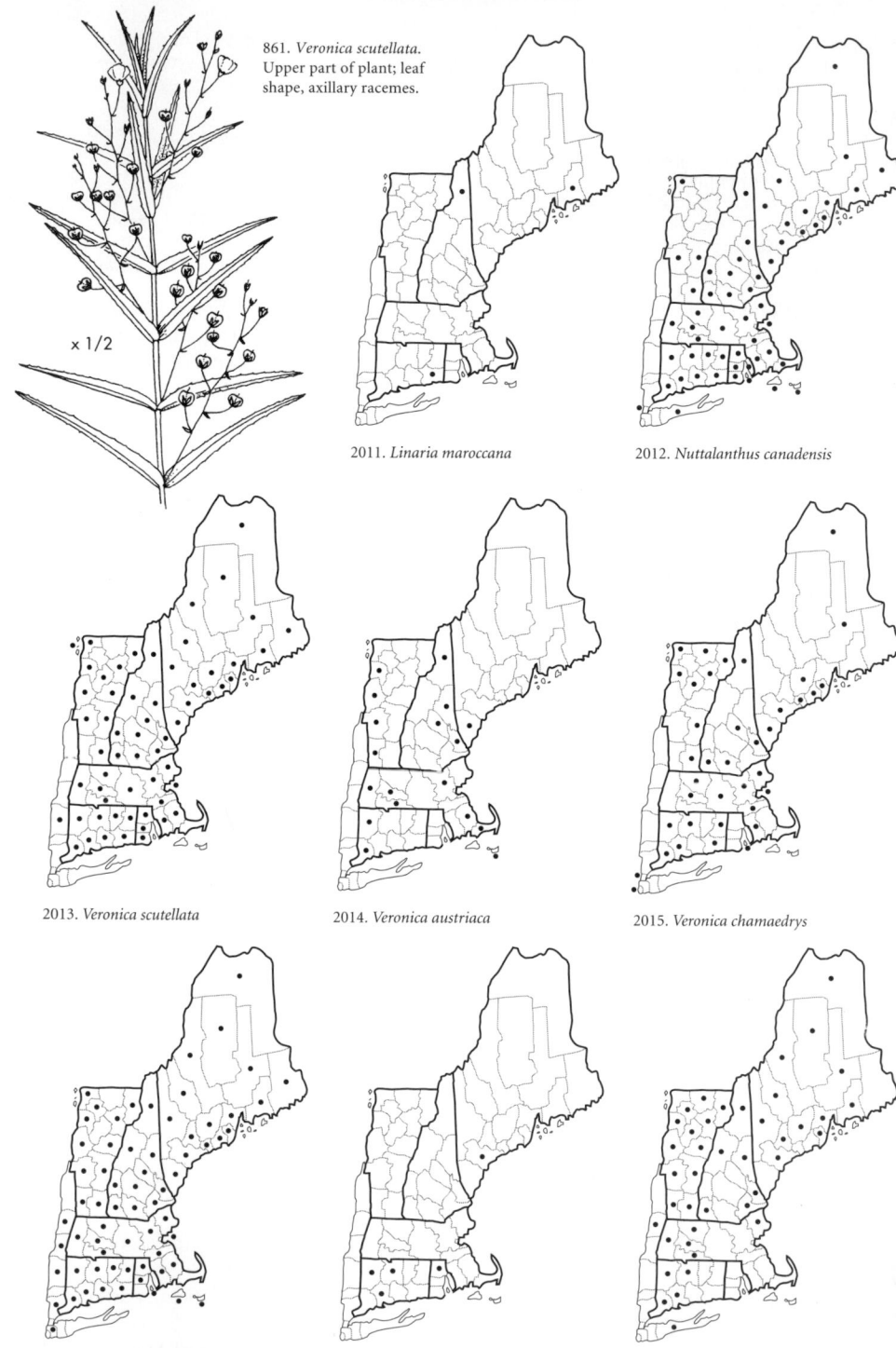

861. *Veronica scutellata.*
Upper part of plant; leaf
shape, axillary racemes.

× 1/2

2011. *Linaria maroccana*

2012. *Nuttalanthus canadensis*

2013. *Veronica scutellata*

2014. *Veronica austriaca*

2015. *Veronica chamaedrys*

2016. *Veronica officinalis*

2017. *Veronica anagallis-aquatica*

2018. *Veronica americana*

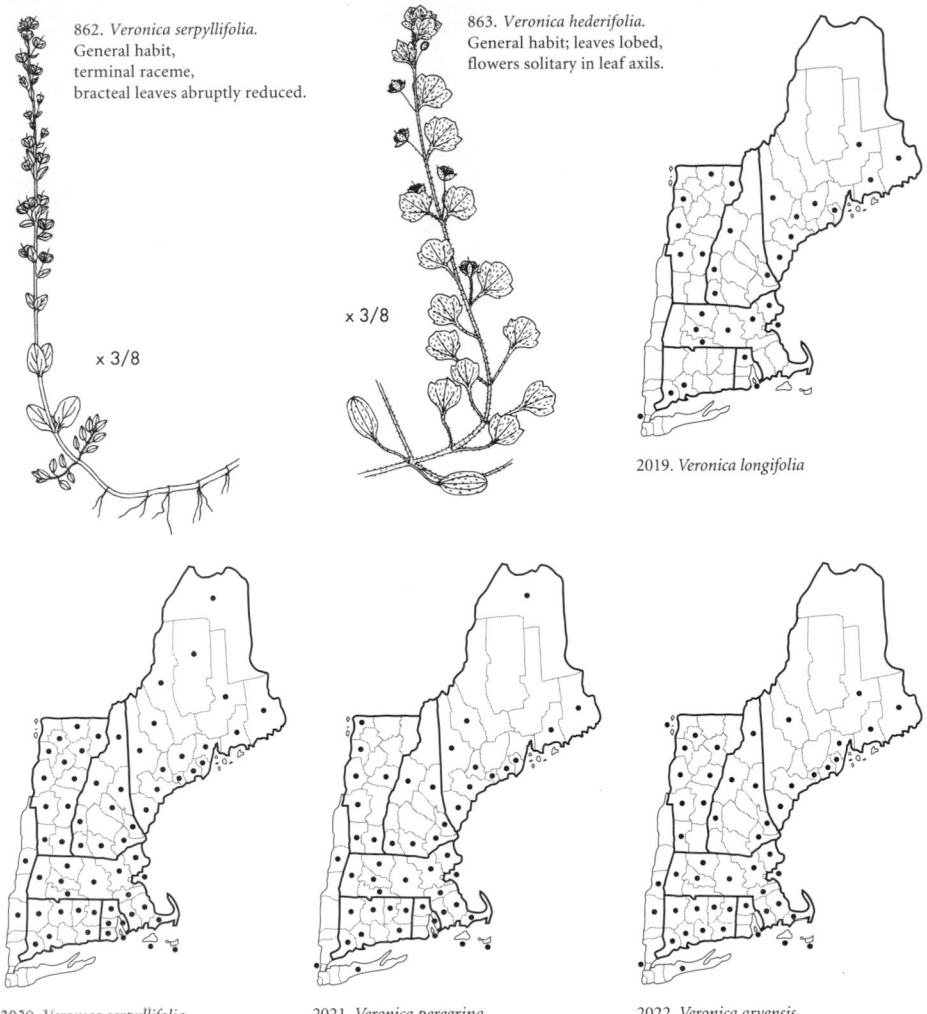

862. *Veronica serpyllifolia*. General habit, terminal raceme, bracteal leaves abruptly reduced.

x 3/8

863. *Veronica hederifolia*. General habit; leaves lobed, flowers solitary in leaf axils.

x 3/8

2019. *Veronica longifolia*

2020. *Veronica serpyllifolia*

2021. *Veronica peregrina*

2022. *Veronica arvensis*

14. V. filifórmis Sm. (hair-like). Lawns and gardens. Map 2023. (Introduced from Eurasia).

15. V. agréstis L. (of fields). Fields, roadsides, waste places. May-August. Map 2024. (Naturalized from Europe). [*V. didyma; V. opaca; V. polita*).

16. V. pérsica Poir. (Persian). Lawns, cultivated ground, waste places, roadsides. May-August. Map 2025. (Naturalized from Eurasia). [*V. tournefortii*].

10. **Verbáscum** L. Mullein (ancient Latin name).

Tall, stout, usually pubescent biennial herbs; leaves in a basal rosette produced the first year, the flowering stem produced the following year, stem leaves alternate, sessile or petioled, often decurrent, toothed or entire; flowers yellow, white or purple, in large terminal spikes, racemes or panicles, calyx deeply 5-lobed, corolla rotate, nearly regular, deeply 5-lobed, stamens 5; capsule globose to oblong, 2-valved.

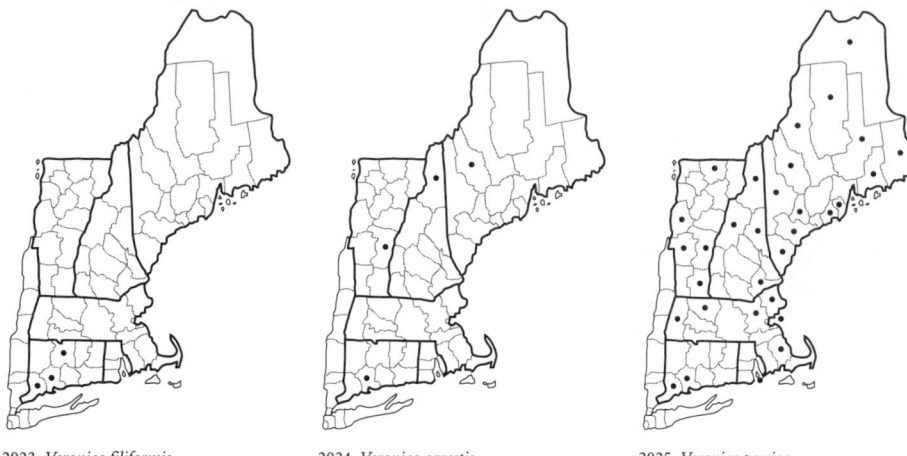

2023. *Veronica filiformis*   2024. *Veronica agrestis*   2025. *Veronica persica*

a. Pubescence of branched or stellate, non-glandular hairs; stems and/or leaves
    (at least the undersides) tomentose.
  b. Leaves tomentose on both sides, decurrent down the stem or cordate/clasping;
      inflorescence simple.
      Leaves long-decurrent, usually as far as the next leaf; spike dense, not
        interrupted .... 1. *V. thapsus*
      Leaves short-decurrent or cordate/clasping; spike interrupted. (Fig. 864). .... 2. *V. phlomoides*
  b. Leaves tomentose or densely pubescent only beneath, glabrous or nearly so
      above, not decurrent, not or rarely cordate; inflorescence often branched,
      forming a panicle .... 3. *V. lychnitis*
a. Pubescence all, or predominantly simple, glandular; stems and/or leaves glabrous
    or pubescent but not tomentose.
  c. Pedicels mostly shorter than calyx, 5 mm or less long. .... 4. *V. virgatum*
  c. Pedicels mostly longer than calyx, 7 mm or more long.
      Corolla yellow or white .... 5. *V. blattaria*
      Corolla purple .... 6. *V. phoeniceum*

    1. V. thápsus L. (from ancient *Thapsus*). Dry fields, roadsides, banks. June-August. Map 2026. (Naturalized from Europe). Preparations made from the leaves and flowers are used to treat coughs and various bronchial conditions.
    V. densiflórum Vis. Similar to *V. thapsus* but with corolla 2.5 cm or more wide (corolla less than 2.5 cm wide in *V. thapsus*). From Europe. Occurring as a waif in our range. Reported for MA. [*V. thapsiforme*].
    2. V. phlomoídes L. (resembling *Phlomis*). Dry fields, roadsides, waste places. July-August. Fig. 864, Map 2027. (Naturalized from Europe).
    3. V. lychnítis L. (ancient name). White mullein. Fields, roadsides, waste places. June-September. Map 2028. (Adventive from Europe).
    V. nígrum L. Similar to *V. lychnitis* but distinguishable in having purple hairs on the stamen filaments (hairs on the stamen filaments light-colored in *V. lychnitis*). Eurasian. Reported for Essex and Norfolk Counties MA, Coos County NH.
    4. V. virgátum Stokes (wand-like). Roadsides, waste places. (Adventive from Europe).
    5. V. blattária L. (pertaining to a moth). Moth-mullein. Dry fields, roadsides, waste places. June-September. Map 2029. (Naturalized from Europe).
    6. V. phoenícium L. Purple mullein. Waste places. May-August. (From Europe). Reported for Suffolk County NY.

11. *Castilléja* Mutis (for D. Castillejo).

Annual or perennial, root-parasitic herbs; rosette-leaves, when present, mostly entire, stem leaves alternate, sessile, entire to pinnatifid; flowers large, yellowish-green, in dense, terminal, leafy-bracted spikes, the bracts large, colored, entire or 3-5 cleft, calyx tubular, deeply cleft into 2 halves, each half entire or 2-lobed, corolla bilabiate, the tube included in the calyx, the upper lip laterally flattened, enclosing the stamens, the lower lip much shorter, 3-lobed, stamens 4, capsule oblong to ovoid. Flowers edible.

Orthocárpus Nutt. *purpuráscens* Benth. Similar to *Castilleja* but corolla 2 or more times as long as calyx (less than twice as long as calyx in *Castilleja*). Western; rarely adventive in our range. Reported for Middlesex County, MA.

Stem leaves and bracts entire or bracts with a few teeth; stems glabrous. .... 1. *C. septentrionalis*
Stem leaves and bracts deeply cleft or lobed; stems pubescent. (Fig. 865). .... 2. *C. coccinea*

1. *C. septentrionális* Lindl. (northern). Alpine areas in Maine, New Hampshire and Vermont. June-August. Map 2030. [*C. acuminata; C. pallida* var. *s.*].

2. *C. coccínea* (L.) Spreng. (scarlet). Painted cup. Wet meadows. May-August. Fig. 865, Map 2031. Endangered in CT. Rare, formerly common. —FAC

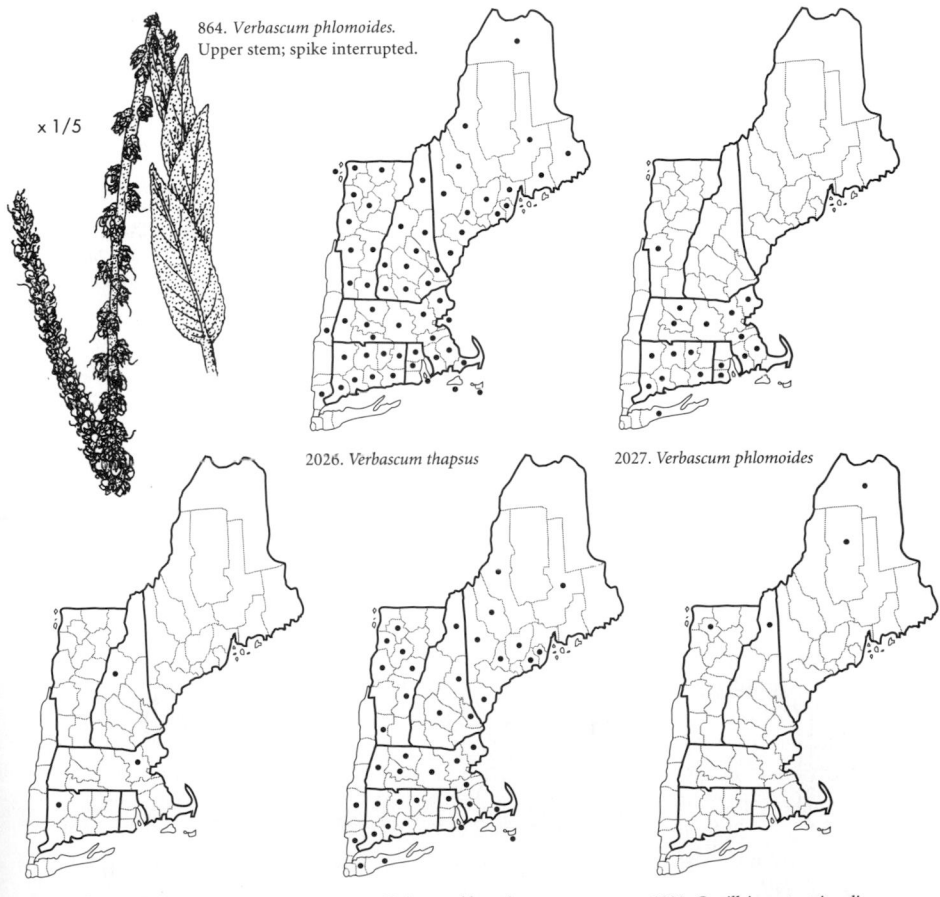

864. *Verbascum phlomoides.*
Upper stem; spike interrupted.

x 1/5

2026. *Verbascum thapsus*

2027. *Verbascum phlomoides*

2028. *Verbascum lychnitis*

2029. *Verbascum blattaria*

2030. *Castilleja septentrionalis*

12. *Schwálbea* L. Chaffseed (for C. Schwalbe).

Simple or sparingly branched, puberulent, perennial herbs; leaves alternate, sessile, lanceolate, entire; flowers large, purplish-yellow, solitary in the axils of the reduced upper leaves forming a loose, bracted, terminal spike, calyx tubular, 5-toothed, irregular, bilabiate, closely subtended by 2 bractlets, corolla tubular, irregular, bilabiate, stamens 4; capsule narrowly ovoid.

    1. *S. americána* L. (American). Woodlands and openings, fields. May-July. Map 2032. From south and southwest. [*S. australis*]. —FACU

13. *Digitális* L. Foxglove (name based on fancied resemblance of the corolla to a small glove).

Tall, biennial or perennial herbs; leaves alternate, sessile or petioled, lanceolate to ovate or oblong, crenate, serrate or entire; flowers showy, purple to white or cream colored, with purple dots or lines, in long, terminal usually 1-sided racemes, calyx deeply 5-parted, corolla tubular to campanulate, somewhat irregular, 5-lobed, slightly 2-lipped, stamens 4; capsule ovoid to globose.

    Antirrhínum L. Snapdragon. Differing from *Digitalis* in having the throat of the corolla closed by a prominent palate. One species and a closely related genus rarely escape from cultivation in our range; *A. május* L. having a corolla 2 cm or more long, reported for Fairfield County CT and Essex County MA; used in external applications for treating hemorrhoids and skin irritations and as a gargle for mouth sores.

    Misópates Raf. *oróntium* (L.) Raf. with the corolla 1.5 cm or less long, reported for Fairfield County CT. [*Antirrhinum o.*].

a. Stem leaves narrowed to base, the lower and middle petioled. .... 1. *D. purpurea*
a. Stem leaves rounded at base, sessile and usually clasping.
  b. Plant entirely glabrous except for ciliate sepals. .... 2. *D. lutea*
  b. Plant pubescent, at least in the inflorescence.
    Stem glabrous below, pubescent only in the inflorescence. .... 3. *D. lanata*
    Stem pubescent below as well as in the inflorescence. .... 4. *D. grandiflora*

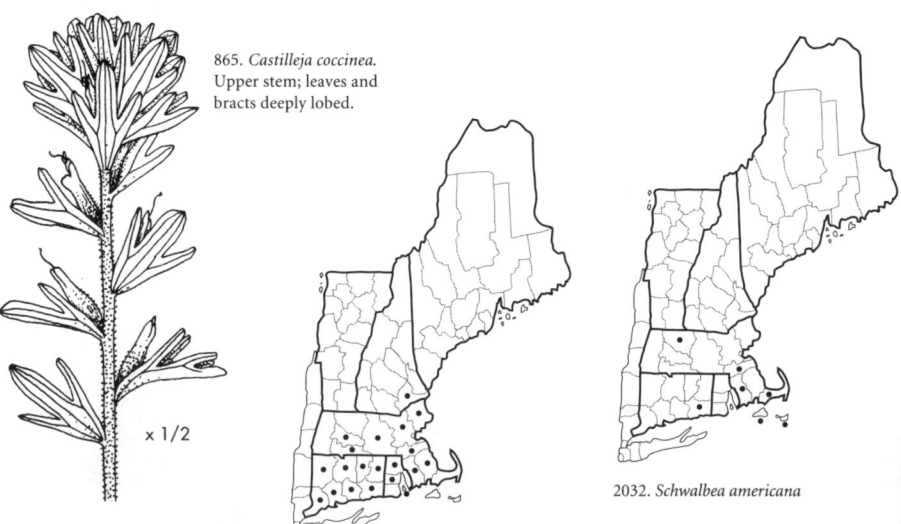

865. *Castilleja coccinea.*
Upper stem; leaves and
bracts deeply lobed.

x 1/2

2032. *Schwalbea americana*

2031. *Castilleja coccinea*

1. *D. purpúrea* L. (purple). Occasionally escaped from cultivation to fields, roadsides and waste places. Map 2033. (Naturalized from Europe). Our plants are var. *purpurea*. Has long been used in treating heart failure; poisonous if taken in overdoses.

2. *D. lutéa* L. (yellow). Rarely escaped from cultivation. (Europe). Reported for CT, MA, Cheshire and Grafton Counties NH, Addison County VT.

3. *D. lanáta* Ehrh. (woolly). Rarely escaped from cultivation. (Introduced from Europe). Reported for MA, NH, VT.

4. *D. grandiflóra* P. Mill. Rarely escaped from cultivation. Map 2034. (Europe). [*D. ambigua*].

14. *Pediculáris* L. Lousewort (louse, from an early European belief that cattle became infested with lice when grazing near one of the species).

Perennial herbs, stems simple or sparingly branched; leaves alternate or opposite, sessile or petioled, lanceolate, toothed to pinnatifid or bipinnatifid; flowers yellow to purple, in terminal and axillary, leafy-bracteate spikes, calyx tubular, obliquely 2-5-lobed, corolla bilabiate, tube cylindric, the upper lip laterally flattened, arched or galeate, often minutely toothed or beaked, the lower lip 3-lobed, 2-crested below the sinuses, stamens 4, included within the upper lip; capsule oblong to ovoid, compressed, usually curved or oblique, beaked.

a. Stem leaves mostly opposite, sessile or subsessile, stem glabrous or nearly so .... 1. *P. lanceolata*
a. Stem leaves scattered or alternate, petioled (at least the lower and middle); stem
  pubescent, at least above.
    Stem leaves with connective blade tissue along the midrib between all the
      segments; calyx 2-lobed .... 2. *P. canadensis*
    Stem leaves (the lower and middle), without connective blade tissue along the
      midrib between the lower segments; calyx 5-lobed. (Fig. 866). .... 3. *P. furbishiae*

1. *P. lanceoláta* Michx. (lanceolate). Pond and stream margins, wet meadows, wooded swamps, wet woods. August-September. Map 2035. Endangered in MA. —FACW

2. *P. canadénsis* L. (Canadian). Fields, thickets, woodlands. May-June. Map 2036. Reported to have been used by Indians to cure rattlesnake bites. —FACU

3. *P. furbíshiae* S. Wats (for its discoverer). Wooded banks of rivers, Maine. July-August. Fig. 866. Endangered in ME; reported for Aroostook County. —FACW+

15. *Melampýrum* L. Cow-wheat (from the Greek, based on the seed color of some species).

Slender, branched, puberulent annual herbs; leaves opposite, short-petioled, linear to ovate-lanceolate, the lower entire, the upper floral ones sometimes sharply toothed near the base; flowers white, white and yellow or purplish, solitary in the upper axils, calyx campanulate, 4-toothed, 2 teeth somewhat longer than the other 2, corolla bilabiate, the tube gradually widened above, the upper lip hooded, pubescent within, the lower 3-lobed, ascending, stamens 4, ascending under the upper lip; capsule flattened, ovate, asymmetrical.

Hemiánthus Nutt. *micranthemoídes* Nutt. Similar to *Melampyrum* but distinguishable in creeping on muddy shores and having 2 stamens (plant upright and stamens 4 in *Melampyrum*). Reported for Dutchess County NY along the Hudson River. [*Micranthemum m.*]. —OBL

1. *M. lineáre* Desr. (linear). Woodlands and woodland edges, heaths. July-August. Map 2037. Our plants include var. *lineare* and the following vars.:

var. *latifólium* Bart. Leaves lanceolate to ovate, the larger 1 cm or more wide (narrower in var. *lineare* and the following two varieties).

var. *pectinátum* (Pennell) Fern. Bracteal leaves sharply toothed near the base; (bracteal leaves entire or nearly so in vars. *lineare* and *latifolium*).

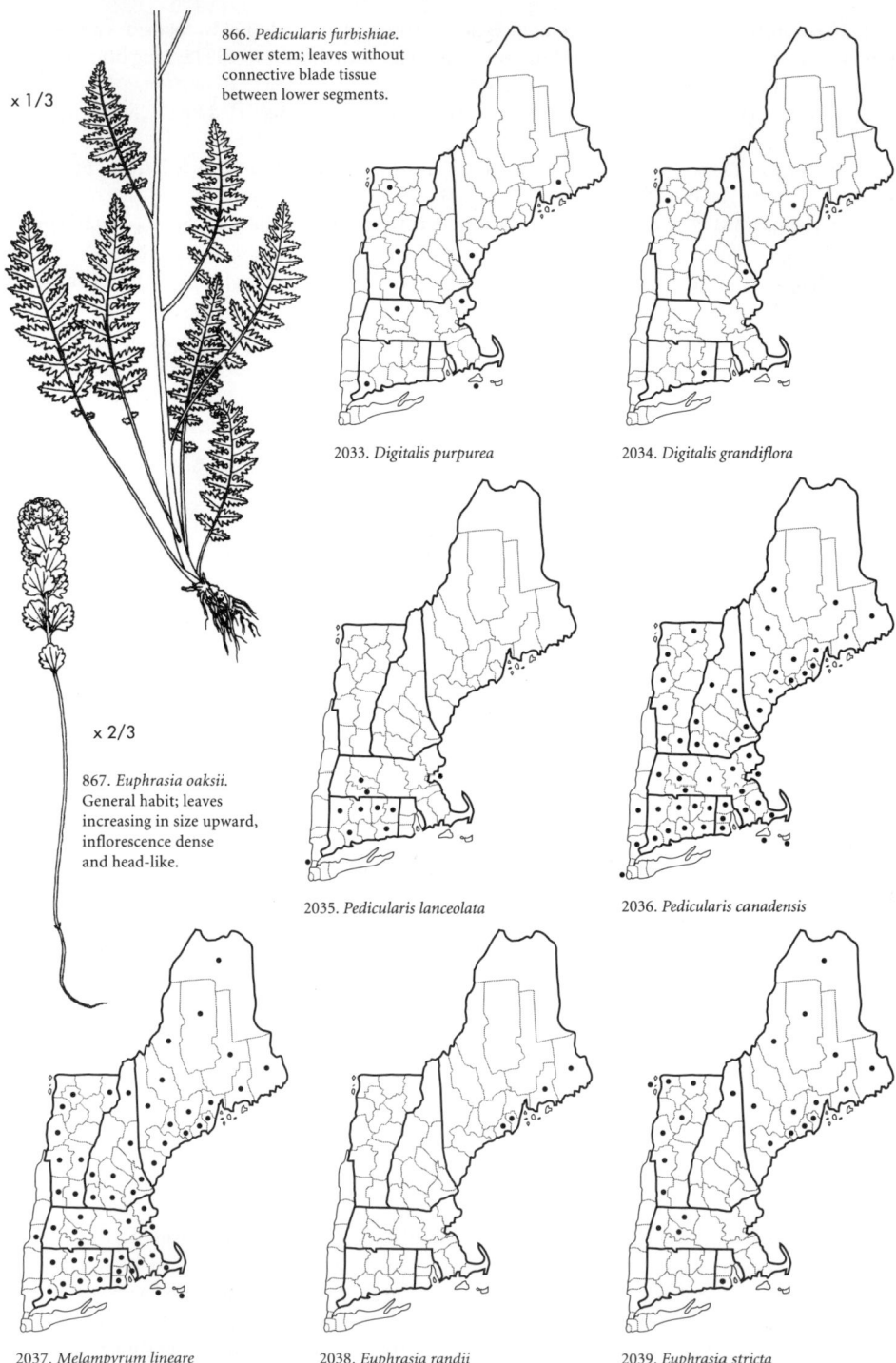

× 1/3

866. *Pedicularis furbishiae.*
Lower stem; leaves without
connective blade tissue
between lower segments.

× 2/3

867. *Euphrasia oaksii.*
General habit; leaves
increasing in size upward,
inflorescence dense
and head-like.

2033. *Digitalis purpurea*

2034. *Digitalis grandiflora*

2035. *Pedicularis lanceolata*

2036. *Pedicularis canadensis*

2037. *Melampyrum lineare*

2038. *Euphrasia randii*

2039. *Euphrasia stricta*

var. *americánum* (Michx.). Beauverd. Similar to var. *pectinatum* but plants few-branched or simple, teeth of the middle and upper bracts shorter than width of the undivided portion (plants much branched and teeth of middle and upper bracts usually as long as width of the undivided portion in var. *pectinatum*).—FACU

16. Euphrásia L. Eyebright (from the Greek, based on reputed value in improving eyesight).

Low, annual herbs; leaves opposite, sessile, coarsely toothed, ovate to orbicular; flowers small, white or purplish, sometimes bicolor, sessile or subsessile, in terminal, leafy-bracted spikes, calyx 4-lobed, corolla bilabiate, the upper lip 2-lobed, the lower 3-lobed, stamens 4; capsule oblong, flattened.

a. Teeth of bracteal leaves mostly rounded to obtuse; corollas mostly 4 mm or less
    long, the upper lip merely emarginate.
    Leaves increasing in size upwards; flowers and bracts closely crowded, forming
        a dense, head-like inflorescence. (Fig. 867). .... 1. *E. oaksii*
    Leaves decreasing in size upwards; flowers and bracts not crowded, the
        inflorescence loose, racemose .... 2. *E. randii*
a. Teeth of bracteal leaves mostly acute to aristate; corollas mostly longer than 4 mm,
    the upper lip prominently bilobed.
    b. Teeth of bracteal leaves aristate; calyx glabrous or essentially so, occasionally
        ciliate.
        In maturity spikes produced in the upper two-thirds of the stem, sometimes
            nearly to the base .... 3. *E. stricta*
        In maturity spikes produced only in the upper third to half of the stem and
            branches .... 4. *E. nemorosa*
    b. Teeth of bracteal leaves merely acute, calyx decidedly pubescent. .... 5. *E. disjuncta*

   1. E. óaksii Wettst. (for its discoverer). Alpine areas; White Mts., Coos County NH; Mt. Katahdin, Piscataquis County ME. July-August. Fig. 867. Endangered in ME, NH. [*E. williamsii*].
   2. E. rándii B. Rob. Rocks, gravel, fields along the coast. July-August. Map 2038. [*E. bottnica*]. —FACW
   3. E. strícta D. Wolff ex J.F. Lehm. Fields, roadsides, disturbed areas. July-September. Map 2039. [*E. borealis; E. canadensis; E. condensata; E. curta; E. micrantha; E. officinalis; E. rigidula; E. tatarica; E. tetraquetra*]. A lotion made from the plant has long been used in Europe as a remedy for various eye diseases, although its unsupervised use in home remedies is not recommended by the medical profession.
   4. E. nemorósa (Pers.) Ettst. Fields, roadsides, waste places. July-September. Throughout our range. [*E. americana*].
   5. E. disjúncta Fern. & Wieg. (separated). Damp open soil. July-September. Reported for ME. [*E. arctica* var. *disjuncta*].
   E. micrántha Reichenb. Similar to *E. disjuncta* but corolla not yellow in the throat, leaves up to 6 mm long (corolla yellow in the throat, leaves up to over 1 cm long, in *E. disjuncta*). From Europe. Reported for MA.

17. Rhinánthus L. Yellow rattle (Greek name based on shape of the flower of plants transferred to another genus).

Annual herbs; leaves opposite, sessile, serrate, lanceolate to oblong-lanceolate; flowers yellow, in a terminal, 1-sided, leafy-bracted, spiciform raceme, calyx flattened, 4-toothed, reticulate-veined, much inflated in fruit, corolla bilabiate, the upper lip strongly arched, flattened, minutely 2-toothed below the apex, lower lip 3-lobed, stamens 4, ascending under the upper lip; capsule suborbicular, flattened.

1. R. mínor L. Fields, roadsides. Fruit: June-July. Map 2040. (Eurasia). [*R. crista-galli; R. kyrollae; R. stenophyllus*]. Our plants include subsp. *minor* and the following subsp.:

subsp. *groenlándicus* (Ostenf.) L. Nenin. Leaves oblong, crenate-dentate, bracts with obtuse teeth, corolla not brown-mottled (leaves lance-attenuate, serrate-dentate, bracts with acute teeth, lower lip of corolla brown-mottled in subsp. *minor*). [*R. borealis; R. oblongifolius; R. groenlandicus*]. —FAC

R. alectorólophus (Scop.) Pollich. Similar to the above species but differing in having a corolla about 2 cm long, the teeth of the upper lip more than 1 mm long (corolla 1.7 cm or less and teeth of the upper lip less than 1 mm long in *R. minor*). Reported for Plymouth County MA. [*R. major*].

18. Odontítes Ludwig (ancient Greek name for a plant used for toothache).

Pubescent, usually branched, annual herbs; leaves opposite, sessile, coarsely toothed, lanceolate; flowers small, pink or red, subsessile, in long, loose, leafy-bracted, somewhat 1-sided, terminal, spiciform racemes, calyx 4-lobed, corolla bilabiate, the upper lip entire, the lower 3-lobed, stamens 4, ascending under the upper lip; capsule oblong-elliptic.

1. O. vérnus (Bellardi) Dumort. Fields and roadsides. June-August. Map 2041. (Naturalized from Europe). [*O. odontites; O. serotina*]. Represented with us as subsp. *serótinus* (Dumort.) Corb.

19. Penstémon Schmidel Beard-tongue (Greek name based on presence of 4-fertile stamens and a fifth sterile stamen).

Perennial herbs, from a basal rosette; leaves of the basal rosette petioled, stem leaves opposite, sessile or sometimes clasping, toothed or entire, mostly lanceolate; flowers showy, white, purple or bicolor (rarely red), in a terminal panicle or thyrse, calyx deeply 5-parted, corolla long-tubular, the throat dilated, bilabiate, the upper lip 2-lobed, the lower 3-lobed, fertile stamens 4, the fifth sterile, usually bearded, at least toward the tip, all included; capsule ovoid.

a. Throat of corolla minutely glandular-puberulent inside. .... 1. *P. tubiflorus*
a. Throat of corolla eglandular, although usually pubescent inside.
   b. Corolla with a distinct basal tube and strongly dilated throat, the latter only
       slightly ridged inside. (Fig. 868).
      Corolla white or slightly purple-tinged outside; anthers usually with a few
         stiff hairs .... 2. *P. digitalis*
      Corolla purple outside; anthers glabrous or essentially so. .... 3. *P. calycosus*
   b. Corolla not differentiated, only gradually dilated upward, the throat strongly
       ridged inside.
      Base of lower lip of corolla arched against the upper one closing the throat. .... 4. *P. hirsutus*
      Base of lower lip of corolla not arched against the upper one, the throat open. .. 5. *P. pallidus*

1. P. tubiflórus Nutt. (with tubular flowers). Fields, open woods. May-July. Map 2042. From farther west. [*P. tubaeflorus*]. Our plants include var. *tubiflorus* and the following var.:

var. *achóreus* Fern. Lowest peduncles of inflorescence 1.5 cm or more long (lowest peduncles up to 1.5 cm long in var. *tubiflorus*, rarely longer).

2. P. digitális Nutt. ex Sims (like *Digitalis*). Fields, roadsides, streambanks. June-July. Fig. 868, Map 2043. —FAC

3. P. calycósus Small (with prominent calyx). Fields, open woods. June-July. Map 2044. From farther west and south.

P. laevigátus Soland. Similar to *P. calycosus* but with mature calyx about 5 mm long, corolla up to 2.2 cm long (mature calyx 5.5 mm or more long, corollas mostly longer than 2.2 cm in *P. calycosus*). From farther south. Reported for CT, MA. [*P. calycosus*]. —FACU

4. P. hirsútus (L.) Willd. (hirsute). Fields, open woods, roadsides. May-July. Map 2045. Endangered in MA.

5. P. pállidus Small (pale). Fields, open woods, roadsides. May-July. Map 2046. From farther west and south. [*P. arkansanus*]. —FACU

2040. *Rhinanthus minor*

2041. *Odontites vernus* subsp. *serotinus*

2042. *Penstemon tubiflorus*

x 2/3

868. *Penstemon digitalis*. Part of inflorescence; corolla with basal tube and dilated throat.

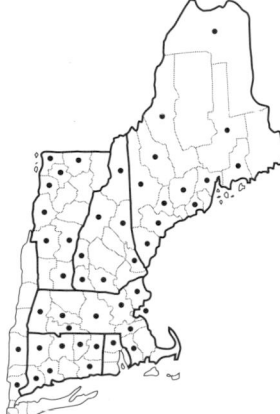

2043. *Penstemon digitalis*

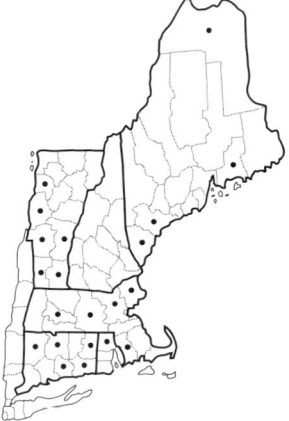

2044. *Penstemon calycosus*

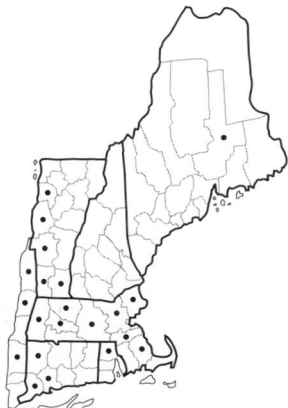

2045. *Penstemon hirsutus*

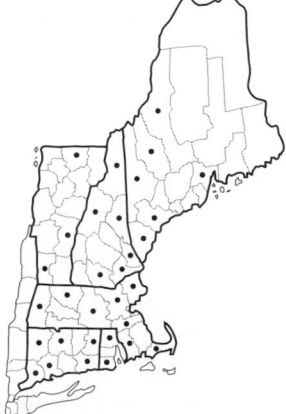

2046. *Penstemon pallidus*

P. grandiflórus Nutt. Differing from the above species in having a corolla longer than 3.5 cm and with inflorescence usually being glabrous and glaucous throughout (corolla 3.5 cm or less long and inflorescence usually glandular-pubescent in the above species). Western; rarely occurring in our range. Reported for CT, Hampden County MA. [*P. bradburyi*].

P. barbátus (Cav.) Roth. Differing from all the above species in having red flowers (flowers white, purple or bicolor but not red in the above species). Western; rarely found in our range. Reported for Suffolk County MA.

20. Scrophulária L. Figwort (name based on value in treating skin disorders according to the doctrine of signatures).

Tall, coarse, perennial herbs with 4-angled stems; leaves opposite, petioled, toothed, rarely pinnate, ovate to lanceolate; flowers small, greenish to purplish, numerous, in a large, terminal, panicle of cymes, calyx deeply 5-lobed, the lobes ovate, corolla bilabiate, the tube short and wide, the upper lip 2-lobed, the lower 3-lobed, fertile stamens 4, the fifth sterile, reduced, all included or slightly exserted; capsule ovoid.

a. Leaves mostly cuneate to truncate at base; petioles narrowly margined to base, a
  third or less as long as the blade; sterile stamen greenish-yellow. (Fig. 869) .... 1. *S. lanceolata*
a. Leaves mostly rounded to cordate at base; sterile stamen purple or brown.
  Petioles narrowly margined to base, a third or less as long as the blade. .... 2. *S. nodosa*
  Petioles not margined, mostly a third to half as long as the blade. .... 3. *S. marilandica*

 1. *S. lanceoláta* Pursh (lanceolate). Fields, thickets, roadsides. May-July. Fig. 869, Map 2047. [*S. leporella; S. occidentalis*]. —FACU+

 2. *S. nodósa* L. (knotty). River shores, thickets, waste places. June-July. Map 2048. (Europe).

 3. *S. mariländica* L. (of Maryland). Open woods, thickets, roadsides. July-August. Map 2049. [*S. neglecta*]. Various medicinal uses are reported such as diuretic and use in treating hemorrhoids. —FACU-

 S. cánina L. Differing from the above species in having lobed or pinnate leaves (in the above species leaves are merely toothed). Mediterranean; a waif in our range. Reported for 107th St., NY.

21. Collínsia Nutt. (for Z. Collins).

Slender, branched, puberulent annual herbs; leaves opposite, or sometimes whorled at some nodes, sessile or short petioled, linear to oblong-lanceolate, entire or nearly so; flowers blue, white, or variegated, in whorles of 2-several from the upper leaf axils, calyx deeply 5-parted, somewhat irregular and bilabiate, corolla bilabiate, gibbous on one side near the base, the upper lip 2-lobed, the lower 3-lobed, the middle lobe folded and enclosing the stamens, stamens 4; capsule globose.

 1. *C. parviflóra* Lindl. (small-flowered). Dry woods and openings. May-July. Fig. 870. From farther west and north. Reported for Rutland County VT. Our plants are var. *parviflora*.

22. Chelóne L. Turtlehead (from the Greek, based on fancied resemblance of the corolla to a turtle's head).

Glabrous, perennial herbs, simple or sparingly branched; leaves opposite, subsessile to petioled, serrate, linear to lanceolate or ovate; flowers white, pink, purple or bicolor, in dense spikes terminating the stem and branches, each flower closely subtended by 2-several ovate bracts, calyx deeply 5-lobed, corolla bilabiate, the upper lip arched, emarginate, the lower 3-lobed, throat bearded, almost closed, fertile stamens 4, 1 smaller sterile stamen also present; capsule broadly ovoid.

Petioles 1 cm or less long; leaves linear to lance-ovate, mostly narrowed at the base;
  corolla white, often tinged with green or pink. (purple in *C. obliqua*) .... 1. *C. glabra*
Petioles 1.5 cm or more long; leaves ovate, mostly rounded or truncate at the base;
  corolla rose pink .... 2. *C. lyonii*

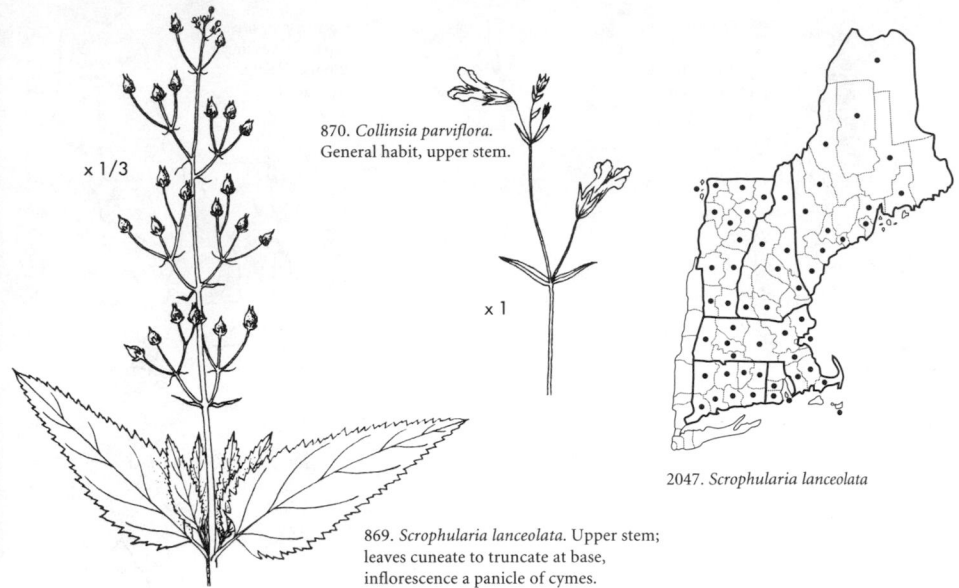

x 1/3

870. *Collinsia parviflora.*
General habit, upper stem.

x 1

2047. *Scrophularia lanceolata*

869. *Scrophularia lanceolata.* Upper stem;
leaves cuneate to truncate at base,
inflorescence a panicle of cymes.

1. *C. glábra* L. (smooth). Pond and stream margins, wooded swamps, wet meadows, ditches. July-September. Fig. 871, Map 2050. Leaves are reported to be of value in treating intestinal worms and reducing inflammation. —OBL

C. oblíqua L. Leaves distinctly petioled; corolla purple (leaves subsessile or obscurely petioled and corolla white in *C. glabra*). Reported for MA. —OBL

2. C. lýonii Pursh (for its discoverer). Occasionally escaped from cultivation to wet soil. July-September. Map 2051. —FACW+

23. *Mázus* Lour. (Greek name, based on the swellings in the throat of the corolla).

Low, erect or creeping, annual or perennial herbs, often branched from near the base; leaves often mostly basal, petioled, spatulate or obovate, irregularly toothed, stem leaves similar, opposite, petioled or subsessile; flowers blue, variegated with yellow or white and red, solitary in the axils of minute, alternate bracts, forming a loose, terminal raceme longer than the stem at maturity, calyx deeply 5-lobed, corolla bilabiate, the upper lip emarginate, the lower much longer, 3-lobed, stamens 4; capsule globose to ovate or orbicular.

Plant not stoloniferous, annual; corolla 1 cm or less long. .... 1. *M. pumilus*
Plant stoloniferous, perennial; corolla 1.5 cm or more long. .... 2. *M. miquelii*

1. M. púmilus (Burm. f.) Steenis. Lawns, fields, roadsides. July-September. (Naturalized from e. Asia). Reported for Hampshire County MA. [*M. japonicus*]. —FACU-

2. M. miquélii Makino. Lawns, fields, roadsides. July-September. (From e. Asia). [*M. reptans*].

24. *Agalínus* Raf.

Branched, annual herbs; leaves opposite, or on the branches alternate, sessile, entire, linear; flowers showy, pink to purple, often with yellow markings in the throat, solitary in the leaf axils, terminal, or in terminal and/or lateral leafy-bracted racemes, calyx campanulate, 5-lobed, corolla slightly irregular, campanulate, 5-lobed, slightly 2-lipped, stamens 4; capsule globose or subglobose. [*Gerardia*].

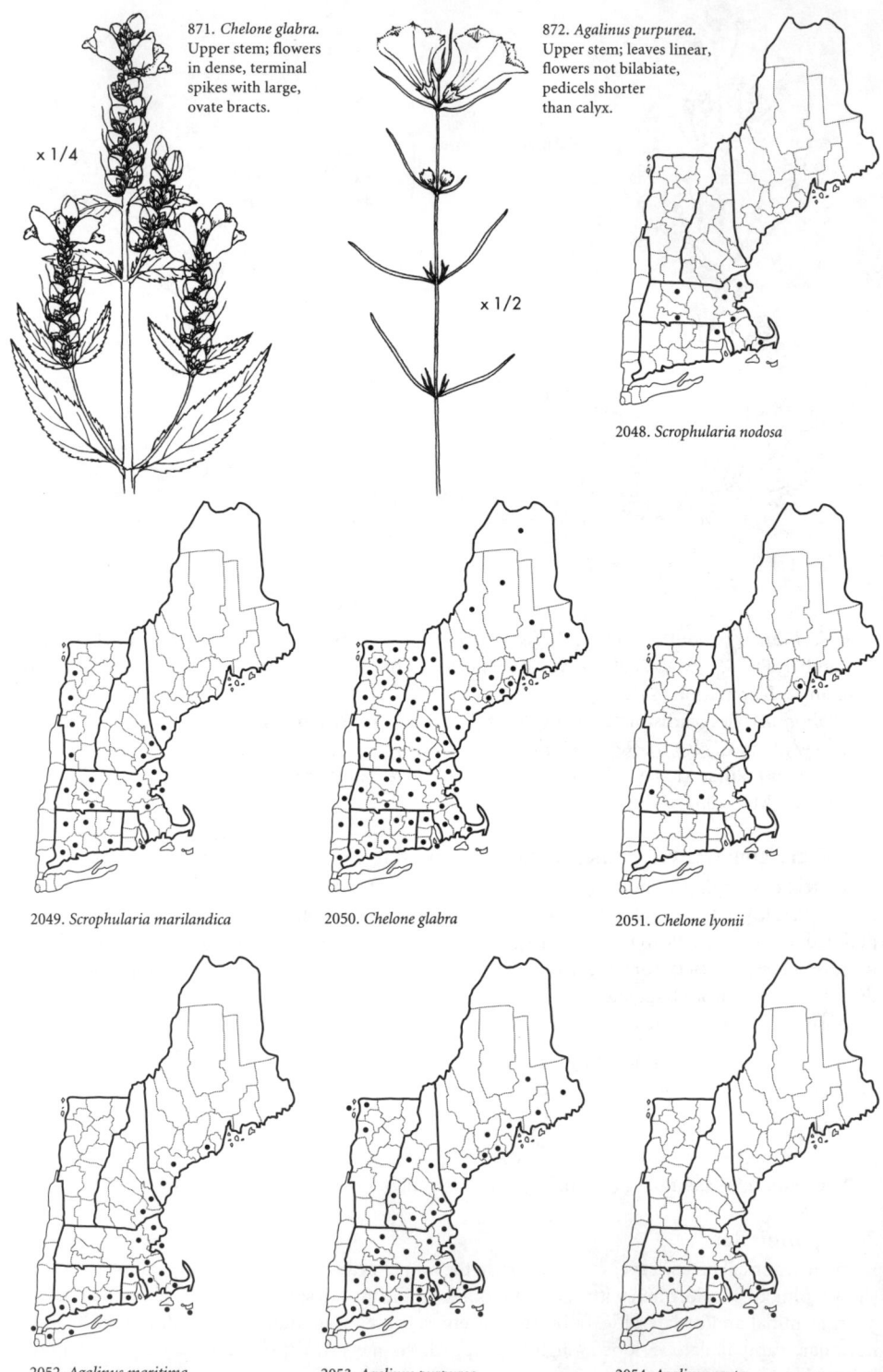

871. *Chelone glabra.* Upper stem; flowers in dense, terminal spikes with large, ovate bracts.

× 1/4

872. *Agalinus purpurea.* Upper stem; leaves linear, flowers not bilabiate, pedicels shorter than calyx.

× 1/2

2048. *Scrophularia nodosa*

2049. *Scrophularia marilandica*

2050. *Chelone glabra*

2051. *Chelone lyonii*

2052. *Agalinus maritima*

2053. *Agalinus purpurea*

2054. *Agalinus acuta*

a. Calyx lobes rounded to obtuse; plant fleshy, occurring in brackish areas. .... 1. *A. maritima*
a. Calyx lobes acute to acuminate; plant not fleshy, usually not in brackish areas.
  b. Pedicels shorter than or equalling the calyx. (Fig. 872). .... 2. *A. purpurea*
  b. Pedicels longer than the calyx.
    c. Calyx tube distinctly reticulate-veined; pedicels, at least the upper ones, 2 or
      more times as long as the subtending leaves; plants not blackened in
      drying .... 3. *A. acuta*
    c. Calyx tube not or only obscurely reticulate-veined; pedicels mostly shorter to
      slightly longer than subtending leaves (sometimes longer in *A. setacea*
      with corolla 1.5 cm or more long; corolla less than 1.5 cm long in *A.*
      acuta); plants blackened in drying.
      Leaves narrowly linear to filiform, less than 1 mm wide; upper lip of corolla
        erect to reflexed; corolla throat pubescent. .... 4. *A. setacea*
      Leaves linear, mostly 1 mm or more wide; upper lip of corolla arched over
        the stamens; corolla throat glabrous .... 5. *A. tenuifolia*

1. *A. marítima* (Raf.) Raf. (of the sea). Salt or brackish marshes. July-August. Map 2052. [*Gerardia m.*]. Our plants are var. *maritima*. —FACW+

2. *A. purpúrea* (L.) Pennell (purple). Wet or dry fields, pond and sea shores, roadsides, barrens. July-September. Fig. 872, Map 2053. (W.I.). [*Gerardia p.*]. Our plants are var. *purpurea*. —FACW-

A. paupércula (Gray) Britt. Similar to *A. purpurea* but with calyx lobes mostly half or more as long as the tube and corollas mostly 1.5-2 cm long (calyx lobes mostly up to half as long as the tube and corolla longer than 2 cm in *A. purpurea*). Throughout our range. [*A. purpurea* var. *parviflora; Gerardia paupercula*]. Our plants include var. *paupercula* and the following var.:

  var. *boreális* Pennell. Corolla up to 1.7 cm long, style to 8 mm long (corolla up to 2 cm and style 8 mm or longer in var. *paupercula*). —FACW+

A. neoscótica (Greene) Fern. Calyx lobes from nearly as long to up to twice as long as the tube and corollas up to 1.5 cm long (calyx lobes up to nearly as long as the tube and corollas mostly 1.5 cm or more long in the latter 2 species). Reported for ME. Endangered in ME. [*A. purpurea* var. *n.*; *Gerardia n.*].

A. virgáta Raf. Strongly virgate (not strongly virgate in the latter 3 species). Reported for Suffolk County NY. [*Gerardia purpurea* var. *racemulosa; Gerardia r.*]. —FAC

3. *A. acúta* Pennell (acute). Dry fields, woodland openings. August-September. Map 2054. Federally endangered. [*Gerardia a.*].

4. *A. setácea* (J.F. Gmel.) Raf. (bristleform). Dry fields, woodland openings. August-September. Reported for Suffolk County NY. [*Gerardia s.*].

5. *A. tenuifólia* (Vahl) Raf. (slender-leaved). Wet or dry fields, woodland openings. August-September. Map 2055. Our plants include var. *tenuifolia* and the following vars.:

  var. *macrophýlla* (Benth.) S. F. Blake. Capsule 5 mm or more thick (less than 5 mm thick in var. *tenuifolia*). [*A. besseyana; Gerardia tenuifolia* var. *m.*].

  var. *parviflóra* (Nutt.) Pennell. Capsule 5 mm or more thick; anthers sparsely pilose (densely pilose in vars. *macrophylla* and *tenuifolia*). [*Gerardia tenuifolia* var. *p.*]. —FAC

25. *Gratíola* L. Hedge-hyssop (name based on reputed medicinal value).

Glabrous or glandular-puberulent, annual or perennial herbs, erect or creeping at the base; leaves opposite, sessile, entire or remotely serrulate, linear to lanceolate, oblong or ovate; flowers small, yellow or white, on solitary pedicels in the leaf axils, usually with a pair of bractlets subtending the calyx, sepals 5, subequal, corolla bilabiate, the upper lip entire to 2-lobed, the lower 3-lobed, fertile stamens 2, sterile stamens 2, rudimentary or absent; capsule globose to ovoid.

Leaves broad at base, these, the bracts and sepals glandular-punctate; stems glabrous
    or nearly so; corolla usually bright yellow. .... 1. *G. aurea*
Leaves narrowed to base, these, the bracts and sepals not glandular-punctate; stems
    usually glandular-puberulent above; corolla white to cream color. .... 2. *G. neglecta*

1. G. aúrea Pursh (golden). Pond and lake shores. June-September. Map 2056. [*G. lutea*].
forma *pusílla* Fassett. A submersed, dwarf, sterile form with sharply acuminate, linear-lanceolate leaves less than 1 cm long. —OBL
2. G. neglécta Torr. (overlooked). Pond and river shores, ditches, wet meadows. June-August. Map 2057. [*G. virginiana*]. —OBL

26. *Aureolária* Raf. False foxglove.

Similar to *Agalinus* (genus 24) except leaves lanceolate to lance-ovate, mostly sinuate-margined, pinnatifid or bipinnatifid; flowers yellow. [*Gerardia; Dasystoma*].

a. Stems glabrous .... 1. *A. flava*
a. Stems densely puberulent.
    Calyx lobes usually crenate or serrate; pedicels and calyx stipitate-glandular;
        leaves pinnatifid, with serrate lobes. .... 2. *A. pedicularia*
    Calyx lobes entire; pedicels and calyx eglandular, the pubescence simple; leaves
        entire, sinuate-margined, or pinnatifid with lobes entire or nearly so. .... 3. *A. virginica*

1. A. fláva (L.) Farw. (yellow). Dry woodlands. July-September. Map 2058. [*Gerardia f.; G. virginica*]. Our plants are var. *flava*.
2. A. pediculária (L.) Raf. (resembling pedicularis). Dry woodlands. August-September. Map 2059. [*Gerardia p.; Dasystoma p.*]. Our plants are var. *pedicularia*.
3. A. virgínica (L.) Pennell (Virginian). Dry woodlands. July-September. Map 2060. [*Gerardia flava; G. virginica*].

27. *Mímulus* L. Monkey-flower (name based on fancied resemblance of corolla to a grinning buffoon).

Erect or decumbent, rhizomatous or stoloniferous, perennial herbs; leaves opposite, sessile or petioled, toothed or entire, lanceolate, oblong, ovate or oblanceolate; flowers showy, blue, yellow or rarely white, on solitary pedicels in the leaf axils, calyx 5-angled, 5-toothed, 1 tooth sometimes longer than the others, corolla bilabiate, the upper lip 2-lobed, the lower 3-lobed, throat partly or entirely closed, stamens 4; capsule oblong. —OBL

a. Leaves subtending flowers sessile or auriculate-clasping.
    Leaves subtending flowers ovate to obovate; corolla yellow; calyx lobes in fruit
        triangular to ovate, the upper one the longest. (Fig. 873). .... 1. *M. guttatus*
    Leaves subtending flowers lanceolate or oblong to oblanceolate; corolla blue,
        rarely white; calyx lobes in fruit linear to lanceolate, all about equal. .... 2. *M. ringens*
a. Leaves subtending flowers distinctly petioled (the uppermost occasionally sessile).
    Stems glabrous or essentially so; corolla blue or purple, rarely white. .... 3. *M. alatus*
    Stems viscid-pubescent or tomentose; corolla yellow. .... 4. *M. moschatus*

1. M. guttátus DC. (spotted). Brooksides, springy meadows. June-July. Fig. 873. From farther west. Reported for Litchfield County, CT. [*M. langsdorfii*].
2. M. ríngens L. (gaping). Pond and stream borders, wet meadows, marshes. July-August. Map 2061. Our plants include var. *ringens* and the following var.:
    var. *colpóphilus* Fern. Internodes less than 3 cm long, pedicels less than 2 cm long (internodes and pedicels longer in var. *ringens*).
M. brévipes Benth. Similar to *M. ringens* but distinguishable by the yellow corolla (corolla blue or white in *M. ringens*). Southwestern. Reported for Middlesex County MA.
3. M. alátus Ait. (winged). Wet woods, wet meadows, shores of ponds and streams. July-August. Endangered in MA. From farther south and west. Map 2062.
4. M. moschátus Dougl. ex Lindl. (musky). Borders of streams and rivers, roadside ditches. June-August. Map 2063. Endangered in NH. From farther north and west.

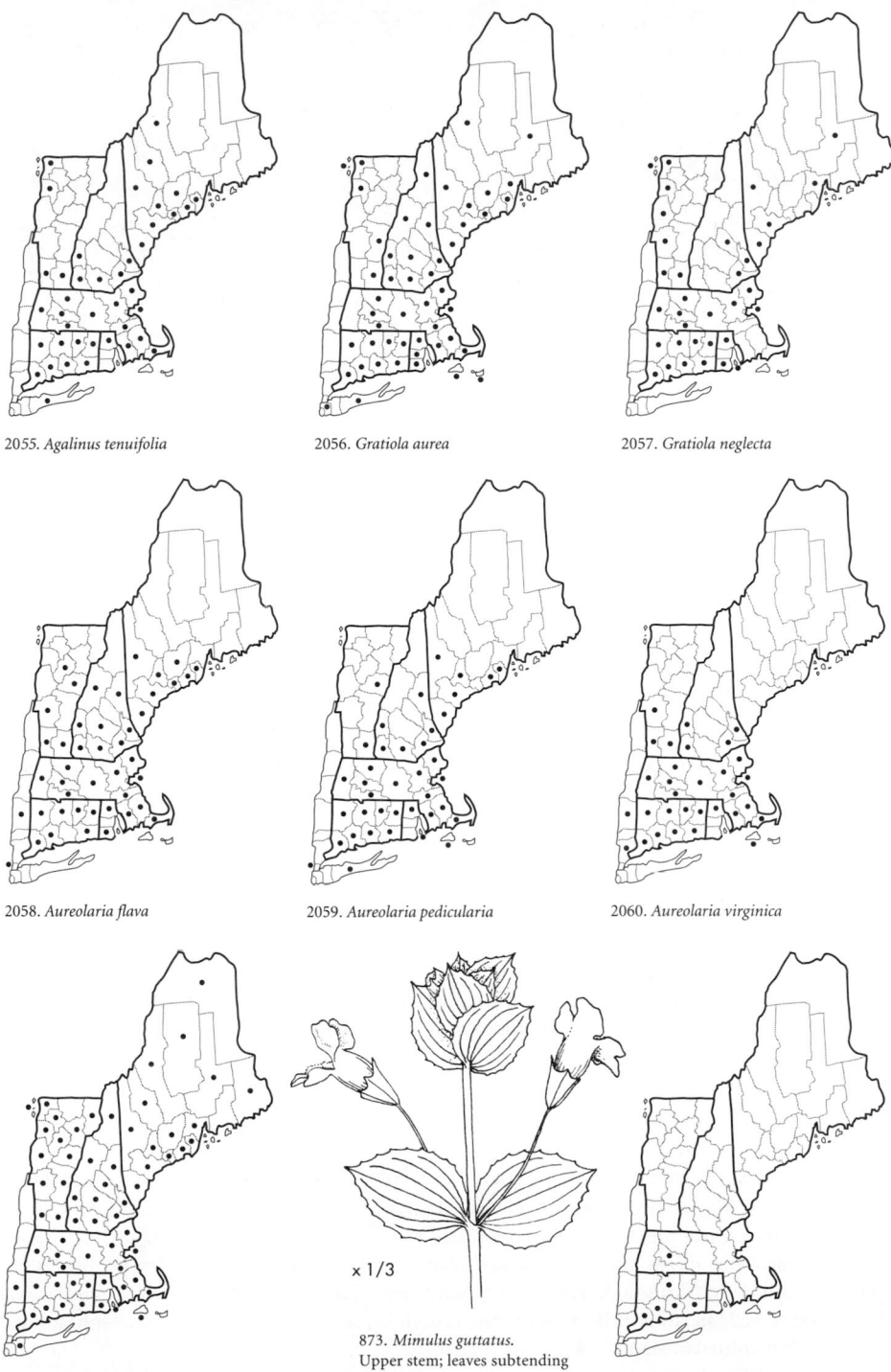

2055. *Agalinus tenuifolia*

2056. *Gratiola aurea*

2057. *Gratiola neglecta*

2058. *Aureolaria flava*

2059. *Aureolaria pedicularia*

2060. *Aureolaria virginica*

2061. *Mimulus ringens*

× 1/3

873. *Mimulus guttatus.*
Upper stem; leaves subtending
flowers sessile, ovate.

2062. *Mimulus alatus*

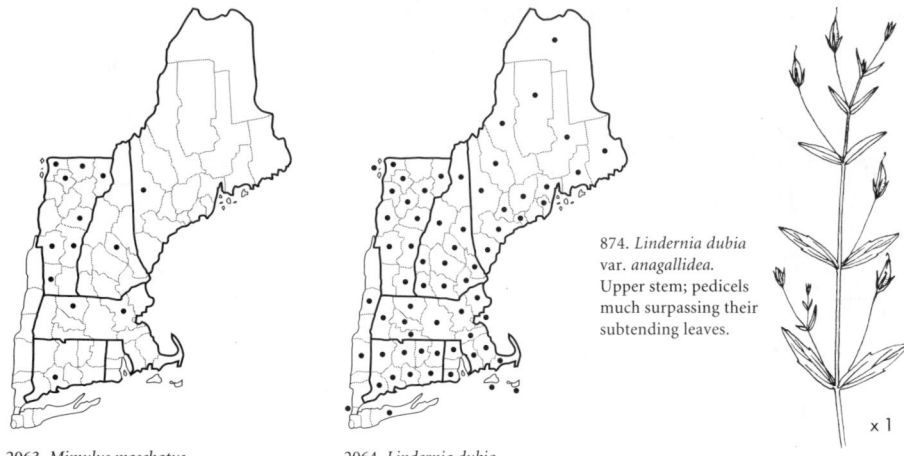

874. *Lindernia dubia*
var. *anagallidea.*
Upper stem; pedicels
much surpassing their
subtending leaves.

x 1

2063. *Mimulus moschatus*   2064. *Lindernia dubia*

28. *Lindérnia* All. False pimpernel (for F. Balthasar von Lindern).

Small, branched, glabrous, annual herbs; leaves opposite, sessile, entire or serrulate, oblong to ovate or obovate; flowers small, purplish, on solitary bractless pedicels in the leaf axils, calyx deeply 5-lobed, corolla bilabiate, the upper lip 2-lobed, the lower 3-lobed, stamens 4, 2 fertile, 2 sterile; capsule ovoid to ellipsoid.

    1. *L. dúbia* (L.) Pennell (doubtful). River and pond shores, inland or tidal. July-September. Map 2064. Our plants include var. *dubia* [*Ilysanthes d.; I. attenuata*] and the following vars.:

    var. *inundáta* Pennell. Flowers cleistogamous; leaves rounded at tip (flowers expanding and leaves tapering to tip in var. *dubia*).

    var. *anagallídea* (Michx.) Cooperrider. Pedicels conspicuously surpassing their subtending leaves (pedicels shorter than to rarely surpassing their subtending leaves in the above vars.). Fig. 874. Endangered in NH. [*L. anagallidea; Ilysanthes a.; I. inaequalis.*]. —OBL

Family 178. Bignoniáceae (Trumpet Creeper Family)

Hermaphrodite, trees or woody vines. Leaves simple or pinnately compound, opposite or rarely whorled, estipulate. Flowers perfect, somewhat irregular, showy, bracteate, in terminal panicles or corymbs, calyx 2-5-lobed, corolla tubular to campanulate, 5-lobed, somewhat 2-lipped, stamens 2 or 4, inserted on the corolla tube, ovary superior, 2-locular, style 1. Fruit an elongate capsule; seeds numerous, flat and winged.

Plant a vine with pinnately compound leaves. .... 1. *Campsis radicans*
Plant a tree with simple leaves .... 2. *Catalpa*

1. *Cámpsis* Lour. Trumpet-creeper (from the Greek, referring to the curved stamens).

Woody vines trailing or climbing by aerial rootlets along the stem; pith moderate, tan, continuous or hollow, buds small, solitary, with several scales, leaf scars elliptical or shield-shaped, connected by hairy transverse ridges, bundle trace 1, C-shaped, stipule scars lacking; leaves petioled, odd-pinnately compound, leaflets short-stalked, lanceolate to ovate, acuminate, coarsely serrate; flowers large, orange-red, on stout pedicels in terminal corymbs, calyx 5-lobed, corolla tubular to funnel-form, slightly irregular, stamens 4.

1. C. radícans (L.) Seem. ex Bureau (rooting). Occasionally escaped from cultivation around buildings, waste places, roadsides. July-September. Map 2065. [*Bignonia r.; Tecoma r.*]. —FAC

2. Catálpa Scop. Catalpa (aboriginal name).

Trees; twigs slender to stout, pith large, white, buds small and inconspicuous, solitary, leaf scars oval, bundle traces numerous, in an oval, end bud and stipule scars lacking; leaves simple, petioled, opposite or whorled, broadly ovate or cordate-ovate, entire or shallowly lobed, short to long-acuminate; flowers white or yellow, often mottled with purple or yellow, in terminal panicles, calyx 2-lobed, corolla campanulate, somewhat 2-lipped, stamens 2 or 4; capsule long and slender, cylindric.

a. Leaves glabrous beneath, often lobed; corolla yellow . ... 1. *C. ovata*
a. Leaves pubescent beneath, seldom lobed; corolla white mottled with yellow or purple.
    Corolla 4 cm or less broad, densely spotted with purple; capsules mostly 1 cm
      or less thick .... 2. *C. bignonioides*
    Corolla more than 4 cm broad, sparsely spotted with purple; capsules mostly
      more than 1 cm thick .... 3. *C. speciosa*

1. C. ováta G. Don (egg-shaped). Occasionally escaped from cultivation to roadsides and waste places. June-August. Map 2066. (Introduced from e. Asia).

2. C. bignonioídes Walt. (like *Bignonia*). Occasionally escaped from cultivation to roadsides and waste places. June-August. Map 2067. From farther south. Various medicinal uses are reported; preparations made from the fruit have been used to treat respiratory conditions and also as an eye lotion.

3. C. speciósa (Warder ex Barney) Warder ex Engelm. (showy). Occasionally escaped from cultivation to roadsides and waste places. May-June. Map 2068. From farther west. —FAC

Family 179. Pedaliáceae (Pedalium Family)

Represented with us by the 2 genera described below. [*Martyniaceae*].

Flowers in terminal racemes; ovary 1-locular; capsule terminated by a hooked horn,
    this splitting into 2 at maturity. .... 1. *Proboscidea*
                                                  louisianica
Flowers solitary in the leaf axils; ovary 4-locular; capsule somewhat 4-sided, velvety,
    opening at the summit .... 2. *Sesamum orientale*

1. Proboscídea Schmidel. Unicorn-plant (from the Greek, referring to the resemblance of the beak of some fruit to a proboscis).

Hermaphrodite, coarse, branched, glandular-pubescent, annual herbs; leaves simple, opposite, or the upper alternate, long-petioled, ovate to orbicular, cordate at base, entire or undulate, estipulate; flowers perfect, irregular, large, whitish or yellowish mottled with purple, in terminal racemes, calyx 1 or 2 bracteolate at base, unequally 5-lobed and cleft, corolla campanulate, subequally 5-lobed, stamens 4, inserted on the corolla tube, ovary superior, 1-locular, style 1; fruit a capsule terminated by a hooked horn, this splitting into 2 at maturity.

1. P. louisiánica (P. Mill.) Thellung (of Louisiana). Cultivated ground, waste places. July-September. From farther south and west. Reported for ME, Chittenden County VT, Strafford & Rockingham Counties NH, Suffolk County MA, Bristol County RI, New Haven County CT. [*P. jussieui; P. louisiana; Martynia louisiana*]. Our plants are subsp. *louisianica*. Young fruit can be boiled or pickled and eaten. —FACU

2065. *Campsis radicans*

2066. *Catalpa ovata*

2067. *Catalpa bignonioides*

2068. *Catalpa speciosa*

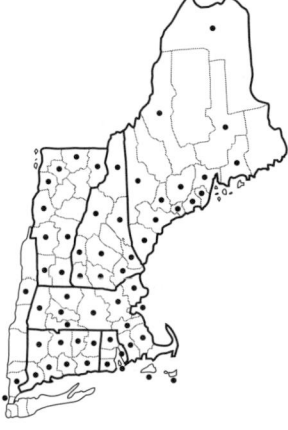

2069. *Orobanche uniflora*

x 1/2

875. *Epifagus virginiana.*
Inflorescence; flowers
scattered in spiciform racemes.

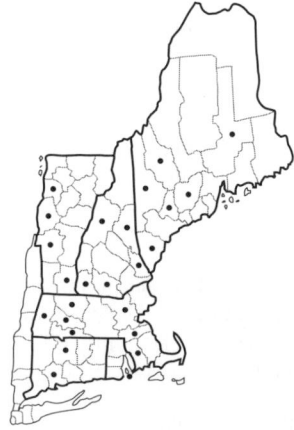

2070. *Conopholis americana*

2071. *Epifagus virginiana*

2. Sésamum L. Sesame (ancient name).

Hermaphrodite, annual herbs; leaves simple, petioled, opposite, or the upper alternate, lanceolate to ovate, entire, divided, or coarsely toothed, estipulate; flowers perfect, irregular, white to pink, solitary in the leaf axils, calyx 5-cleft, corolla 5-parted, campanulate, bilabiate, stamens 4, epipetalous, ovary superior, 4-locular, style 1; fruit an oblong, somewhat 4-sided, velvety capsule opening at the summit.

    1. S. orientále L. Occasionally escaped from cultivation to waste places. (Adventive from the old world). Reported for Essex County MA. [*S. indicum*].

Family 180. Orobancháceae (Broom-rape Family)

Hermaphrodite, root-parasitic herbs without chlorophyll and lacking green color, brownish or yellowish. Leaves reduced to scales, alternate. Flowers mostly perfect, irregular, (rarely cleistogamous) withering-persistent, solitary and ebracteate on long pedicels (ours) or sessile in a terminal bracteate spike or raceme, these sometimes paniculate, calyx 4-5-toothed, sometimes split on 1 side, corolla bilabiate, 4-5-lobed, stamens 4, inserted on the corolla tube, ovary superior, 1-locular, style 1. Fruit a capsule.

a. Flowers solitary on long, naked, scapose pedicels. .... 1. *Orobanche uniflora*

a. Flowers racemose-spiciform or paniculate.
    Bracts covering lower half of flower or fruit; flowers crowded in a dense spike, axis of spike 5 mm or more in diameter, spike simple. .... 2. *Conopholis americana*

    Bracts not covering lower half of flower or fruit; flowers scattered in spiciform racemes, the axis less than 5 mm in diameter, racemes usually paniculate. (Fig. 875) .... 3. *Epifagus virginiana*

1. Orobánche L. (Greek name for vetch applied to this genus).

Stem short, with several scale-like leaves, subterranean or slightly prolonged above the ground; pedicels 1-3, finely glandular-puberulent, without bractlets, each bearing a solitary white to purple flower, calyx 5-lobed, corolla usually curved, the upper lip 2-lobed, lower lip 3-lobed; capsule ovoid.

    1. O. uniflóra L. (one-flowered). Cancer-root. Moist woods, thickets, streambanks, roadsides. May-July. Map 2069. [*Anoplanthus u.; Thalesia u.*]. —FACU

2. Conópholis Wallr. Squaw-root (from the Greek, based on fancied resemblance of the plant to a pine cone).

Stems simple, stout and fleshy, usually clumped; leaf scales numerous, overlapping, the plant somewhat resembling a dead pine cone; flowers yellowish, subsessile, numerous and imbricated in a dense, bracted spike, calyx subtended by 1 or 2 minute bractlets, irregularly 4-5-toothed, split on 1 side, corolla curved, the upper lip concave, emarginate, lower lip 3-lobed; capsule ovoid.

    1. C. americána (L.) Wallr. (American). Rich woods. May-June. Map 2070.

3. Epifágus Nutt. Beech-drops (from the Greek, meaning upon beech).

Slender, branched, parasitic on roots of beech; leaf scars few, small and scattered; flowers subsessile, bracteate, scattered in spiciform racemes on the branches, usually forming a panicle, dimorphic, the lower cleistogamous, the upper sterile, calyx 5-toothed, corolla of upper flowers curved, 4-lobed, white, often purple-striped; capsule subglobose.

    1. E. virginiána (L.) W. Bart. (Virginian). Under beech trees. August-October. Fig. 875, Map 2071. [*Epiphegus v.; Leptamnium v.*].

Family 181. Lentibulariáceae (Bladderwort Family)

Hermaphrodite, aquatic or wetland, mostly insectivorous herbs. Leaves simple or capillary-dissected, basal, alternate, whorled, root-like or absent. Flowers perfect, irregular, scapose, solitary or in short bracteate racemes, calyx often bilabiate, 2-5-lobed, corolla bilabiate, the upper lip entire or 2-lobed, the lower 3-lobed, prolonged into a basal spur or sac, stamens 2, inserted at the base of the corolla tube, ovary superior, 1-locular, style 1, short or absent. Fruit a capsule.

Leaves entire, more than 5 mm wide in a basal rosette; bladders absent; flowers
    solitary, on bractless peduncles. (Fig. 876). .... 1. *Pinguicula vulgaris*
Leaves capillary-dissected or less than 2 mm wide, not in rosettes; leaves or
    specialized branches bearing bladders in most species; flowers solitary or
    racemose, bracteate. (Fig. 878) .... 2. *Utricularia*

1. *Pinguícula* L. Butterwort (from the Latin, referring to the fleshy leaves).

Scapose, perennial herbs; leaves in a basal rosette, entire, ovate or elliptic, fleshy, the upper surface viscid, catching small insects; flowers purple, solitary, on 1 or more bractless penduncles, calyx somewhat bilabiate, 5-lobed, upper lip of corolla 2-lobed, the lower 3-lobed, lacking a palate, prolonged into a basal spur.

    1. *P. vulgáris* L. (common). Wet rocks and open areas at high altitudes. June-July. Fig. 876, Map 2072. (Eurasia). Endangered in NH. A rennet for curdling milk to make cheese can be obtained from the leaves; crushed leaves applied externally are reported to have a healing effect; preparations of the plant are also reported to be useful in treating whooping cough. —OBL

2. *Utriculária* L. Bladderwort (name meaning little bladder).

Aquatic plants with stems submersed or subterranean; leaves capillary-dissected, the divisions mostly dichotomously forking, alternate or whorled, bearing small bladders which float the plant and capture small aquatic animals, or when stems subterranean, leaves simple, linear, the bladders borne on the leaves or underground branchlets; flowers yellow or purple, solitary or in short racemes, bracteate, calyx 2-lobed, upper lip of corolla entire or 2-lobed, the lower entire or 3-lobed, usually with a palate at the base, prolonged into a basal spur or sac. Species of *Utricularia*, particularly *U. inflata*, are reported to be useful as a diuretic. —OBL

a. Leaves linear or filiform, minute, attached to subterranean stems in wet soil, often
    overlooked and the plant apparently leafless; bladders minute or none; plants
    terrestrial or only partly submersed. (Fig. 877).
  b. Flowers each subtended only by a bract, bractlets lacking; pedicels, at least the
    longer ones, 3 mm or more long.
    Flowers solitary, purple; bract at base of pedicel tubular. .... 1. *U. resupinata*
    Flowers usually more than 1, yellow, the bract(s) peltate. .... 2. *U. subulata*
  b. Flowers each subtended by a bract and 2 smaller bractlets; pedicels 2.5 mm or
    less long.
    Bractlets linear, subulate; corolla, from tip of spur to tip of upper lip, less than
      1.5 cm long; spur 7.5 mm or less long. .... 3. *U. juncea*
    Bractlets oblong, acute; corolla 1.5 cm or more long; spur more than 7.5 mm
      long .... 4. *U. cornuta*
a. Leaves dichotomously forking, usually conspicuous; bladders usually well
    developed; plants aquatic, usually submersed. (Fig. 878).
  c. Leaves, at least the upper ones, whorled.
    Leaves of the uppermost whorl subtending the scape each with the rachis
      inflated, forming floats; flowers yellow. .... 5. *U. radiata*
    Leaves all capillary-dissected; flowers purple. .... 6. *U. purpurea*
  c. Leaves all or mostly alternate.

d. Leaf segments flat; lower lip of corolla nearly twice as long as the upper.
Bladders borne on separate leafless branches. .... 7. *U. intermedia*
Bladders borne on the leaves .... 8. *U. minor*
d .Leaf segments terete or filiform; lower lip of corolla as long or only slightly
longer than the upper.
e. Leaves mostly forking 4-many times; leafy stems free-floating.
Peduncles, below the lowest bract, with 1-several scattered scales; corolla,
from tip of spur to tip of upper lip more than 1 cm long. .... 9. *U. macrorhiza*
Peduncles, below the lowest bract, without scales; corolla less than 1 cm
long. .... 10. *U. geminiscapa*
e. Leaves mostly forking 1-3 times; leafy stems creeping on the bottom in
shallow water.
Leaves dimorphic, some forking twice and with bladders, others forking
3 times and without bladders .... 11. *U. fibrosa*
Leaves uniform, with scattered bladders .... 12. *U. gibba*

1. *U. resupináta* B.D. Greene ex Bigelow (turned upside down). Pond margins, in wet soil or very shallow water. July-September. Fig. 877, Map 2073. [*Leticula r.*].

2. *U. subuláta* L. (awl-shaped). Pond margins, in wet soil or very shallow water. June-September. Map 2074. (W.I.). [*Setiscapella s.*].

3. *U. júncea* Vahl (rush-like). Pond margins in wet soil, bogs near the coast. July-September. (S. Amer., W.I.). From farther south. Reported for Suffolk County, NY. [*U. virgulata; Stomoisia j.; S. virgulata*].

4. *U. cornúta* Michx. (horned). Pond margins in wet soil, bogs. July-September. Map 2075. [*Stomoisia c.*].

5. *U. radiáta* Small. Ponds. June-October. Map 2076. Rare. (S. Amer.). [*U. inflata* var. *minor*].

U. infláta Walt. Similar to *U. radiata* but with peduncles 6 or more-flowered, 7 cm or more long, floats mostly 4 cm or more long (peduncles with up to 5 flowers, up to 5 cm long, floats mostly up to 4 cm long in *U. radiata*). From farther south along the coastal plain. Reported for MA.

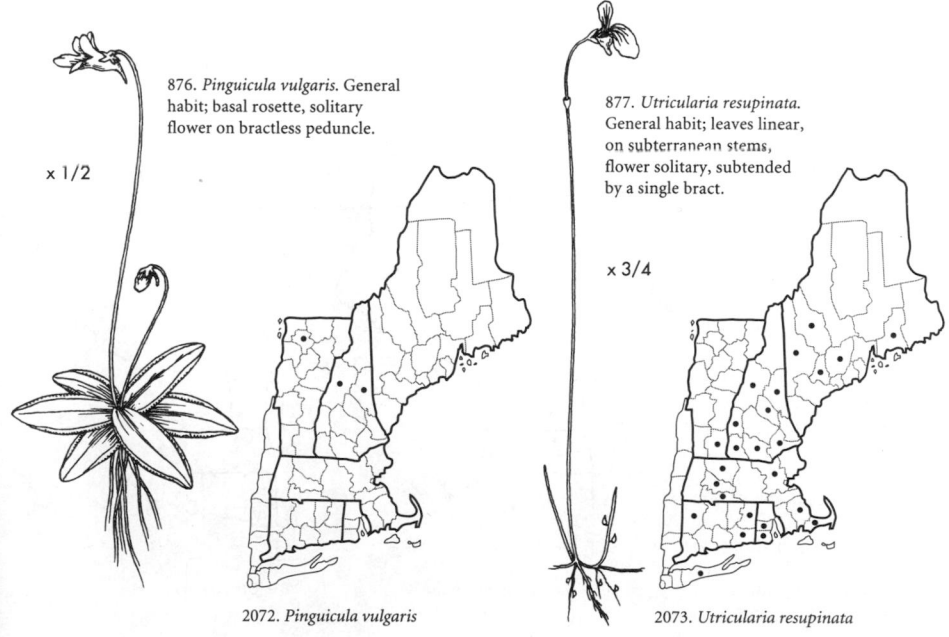

× 1/2

876. *Pinguicula vulgaris*. General habit; basal rosette, solitary flower on bractless peduncle.

877. *Utricularia resupinata*. General habit; leaves linear, on subterranean stems, flower solitary, subtended by a single bract.

× 3/4

2072. *Pinguicula vulgaris*

2073. *Utricularia resupinata*

6. ***U. purpúrea*** Walt. (purple). Ponds and lakes. July-September. Map 2077. (Central Amer.; W.I.). [*Vesiculina p.*].

7. ***U. intermédia*** Hayne (intermediate). Creeping on bottom of shallow ponds, pools, bog ponds. June-August. Map 2078. (Eurasia).

8. ***U. mínor*** L. (smaller) Shallow ponds, bog ponds, pools. May-July. Map 2079. (Eurasia).

9. ***U. macrorhíza*** Le Conte. Ponds and lakes. June-September. Fig. 878, Map 2080. (Eurasia). [*U. vulgaris*]. Of value in treating minor skin wounds because of its mildly astringent effect.

10. ***U. geminiscápa*** Benj. (with twin scapes). Ponds and pools. July-September. Map 2081. [*U. clandestina*].

11. ***U. fibrósa*** Walt. (fibrous). Shallow ponds and pools near the coast. July-September. Map 2082. From farther south and west. [*U. pumila*].

12. ***U. gíbba*** L. (humped). Shallow ponds and pools. July-September. Map 2083. (Central Amer.; W.I.). [*U. biflora*].

2074. *Utricularia subulata*

2075. *Utricularia cornuta*

2076. *Utricularia radiata*

2077. *Utricularia purpurea*

2078. *Utricularia intermedia*

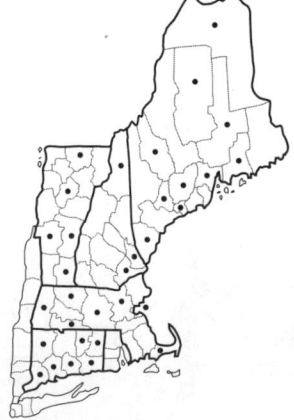

2079. *Utricularia minor*

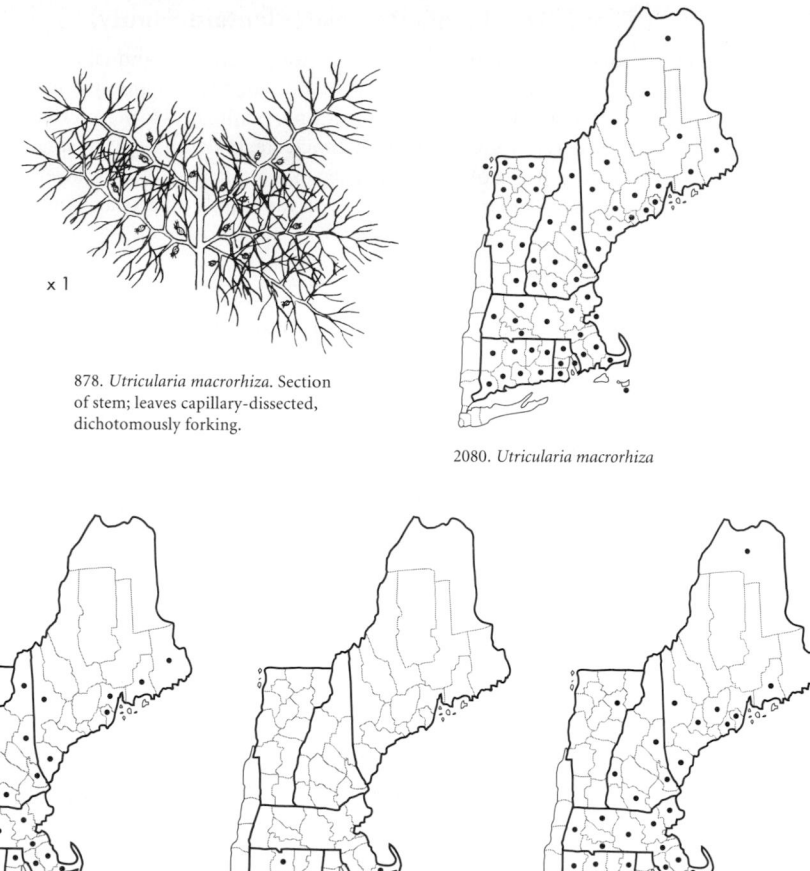

878. *Utricularia macrorhiza*. Section of stem; leaves capillary-dissected, dichotomously forking.

2080. *Utricularia macrorhiza*

2081. *Utricularia geminiscapa*

2082. *Utricularia fibrosa*

2083. *Utricularia gibba*

Family 182. Acantháceae (Acanthus Family)

1. Justícia L. Water-willow (for J. Justice).

Hermaphrodite, rhizomatous, glabrous, perennial herbs. Leaves simple, opposite, sessile or subsessile, linear to lanceolate, entire, estipulate. Flowers perfect, irregular, small, white to purple, in short, dense, long-peduncled, axillary spikes, calyx minutely 3-bracteolate at base, calyx deeply 5-parted, corolla tubular, bilabiate, the upper lip entire or emarginate, the lower 3-lobed, stamens 2, inserted on the corolla tube, ovary superior, 2-locular, style 1. Fruit a laterally compressed, clavate capsule.

   1. J. americána (L.) Vahl. (American). Margins and shallow water of lakes and rivers. June-August. Reported for Addison County VT. [*J. mortuifluminis; Dianthera a.*]. —OBL

Family 183. Plantagináceae (Plantain Family)

Hermaphrodite or monoecious, acaulescent or rarely leafy-stemmed, annual or perennial herbs. Leaves simple, toothed or entire, rarely pinnately dissected, basal or rarely opposite, sessile or petioled, linear to broadly ovate, the bases often sheathing, estipulate. Flowers perfect or imperfect, mostly regular, small, greenish, white, or purplish, bracteate, in dense heads or spikes terminating long scapes, or rarely solitary, calyx of 3-4 lobes or sepals, corolla urceolate or salverform, 4-lobed, scarious, mostly marcescent, stamens 2 or 4, inserted on the corolla tube, ovary superior, 2-locular, style 1. Fruit a circumscissile capsule or an achene.

Flowers solitary; fruit indehiscent; plant aquatic. .... 1. *Littorella americana*

Flowers in dense heads or spikes; fruit a circumscissile capsule; plant terrestrial .... 2. *Plantago*

1. *Littorélla* Berg. (name based on occurrence along shores).

Monoecious, low, acaulescent, fibrous-rooted, stoloniferous, perennial herbs, usually growing in mats; leaves basal, sessile, entire, linear; flowers imperfect, the staminate solitary or 2 together at the summits of short scapes, these naked or bearing a small bract near the middle, the scapes usually much overtopped by the leaves, the pistillate sessile at the bases of the leaves, calyx 3-4-parted, persistent, corolla urceolate, 4-lobed or toothed, stamens 4, long-exsert; fruit an achene, enclosed by the persistent calyx.

1. *L. americána* Fern. (American). Pond and lake shores, often in shallow water. July-September. Map 2084. [*L. uniflora* var. *americana*]. —OBL

2. *Plantágo* L. Plantain (from the Latin, meaning footprint).

Hermaphrodite, acaulescent or rarely leafy-stemmed, annual or perennial herbs; leaves basal or opposite when cauline, sessile or petioled, toothed or entire, rarely pinnately dissected, linear to lanceolate or ovate, often ribbed; flowers perfect, in bracteate spikes or heads terminating naked scapes arising from the leaf axils, sepals typically 4, 2 often larger than the other 2, corolla salverform, 4-lobed, papery, persistent, stamens 2 or 4, short or long-exsert; fruit a circumscissile capsule, the summit invested by the persistent corolla. The various species of *Plantago* have long been used in Europe and by American Indians to heal wounds, bruises and skin irritations, crushing the whole plant and soaking and applying to the affected area; an eye lotion is also made from the leaves; young leaves are high in vitamins A and C and can be used in salads, particularly the narrow-leaved species; older leaves can be used as a potherb; tea can also be made from the leaves; seeds of *P. media* and *P. psyllium* act as a laxative. —Wildl. 2

a. Leaves all cauline, opposite; heads on axillary peduncles. .... 1. *P. psyllium*
a. Leaves mostly or entirely basal; heads or spikes on scapes arising from the basal
     leaves.
  b. Bracts conspicuously exserted from the spikes. (Fig. 879). .... 2. *P. aristata*
  b. Bracts inconspicuous, mostly hidden in the spikes.
    c. Bracts and sepals distinctly pubescent.
        Leaves linear, mostly 7 mm or less wide; corolla lobes spreading to
             reflexed. .... 3. *P. patagonica*
        Leaves obovate to oblanceolate, mostly wider than 7 mm; corolla lobes
             ascending to erect .... 4. *P. virginica*
    c. Bracts and sepals glabrous or merely scabrous (sepals ciliate toward tip in
        P. lanceolata but otherwise glabrous).
      d. Leaves linear, less than 8 mm wide. (Fig. 880).
          Corolla tube pubescent outside; calyx 2 mm or more long; leaves thick
             and fleshy; plant of salt or brackish areas. .... 5. *P. maritima* var. *juncoides*

Corolla tube glabrous; calyx less than 2mm long; leaves thin, not fleshy;
  plant usually of disturbed areas .... 6. *P. pusilla*
d. Leaves lanceolate to ovate, mostly 8 mm or more wide (at least the larger
  leaves).
  e. Inflorescence a dense head or short spike less than a quarter as long as
    remainder of scape. (Fig. 881).
    Leaves ovate, broadly elliptic or obovate, less than 5 times as long as
      wide; sepals 4, separate .... 7. *P. media*
    Leaves lanceolate to lance-elliptic, 5 or more times as long as wide;
      sepals 3, 2 of them united .... 8. *P. lanceolata*
  e. Inflorescence a long slender spike, dense or loose, more than a quarter as
    long as remainder of scape.
    f. Bracts and sepals distinctly keeled; capsules less than 2.5 mm broad.
      Capsule circumscissile below the middle, the upper portion about
        twice as long as the lower; bracts narrowly lanceolate. .... 9. *P. rugelii*
      Capsule circumscissile near the middle; bracts broadly ovate. .... 10. *P. major*
    f. Bracts and sepals not or indistinctly keeled; capsules mostly 2.5 mm or
      more broad .... 11. *P. cordata*

1. P. psýllium L. (old generic name). Waste places, especially along railroad tracks. July-September. Map 2085. (Naturalized from Europe). [*P. arenaria; P. indica*].

2. P. aristáta Michx. (bearing bristles). Roadsides and waste places. June-September. Fig. 879, Map 2086.

3. P. patagónica Jacq. Waste places, especially railroad tracks. May-August. Map 2087. (From farther west). [*P. purshii*].

4. P. virgínica L. (Virginian). Fields, roadsides, waste places. May-June. Map 2088.

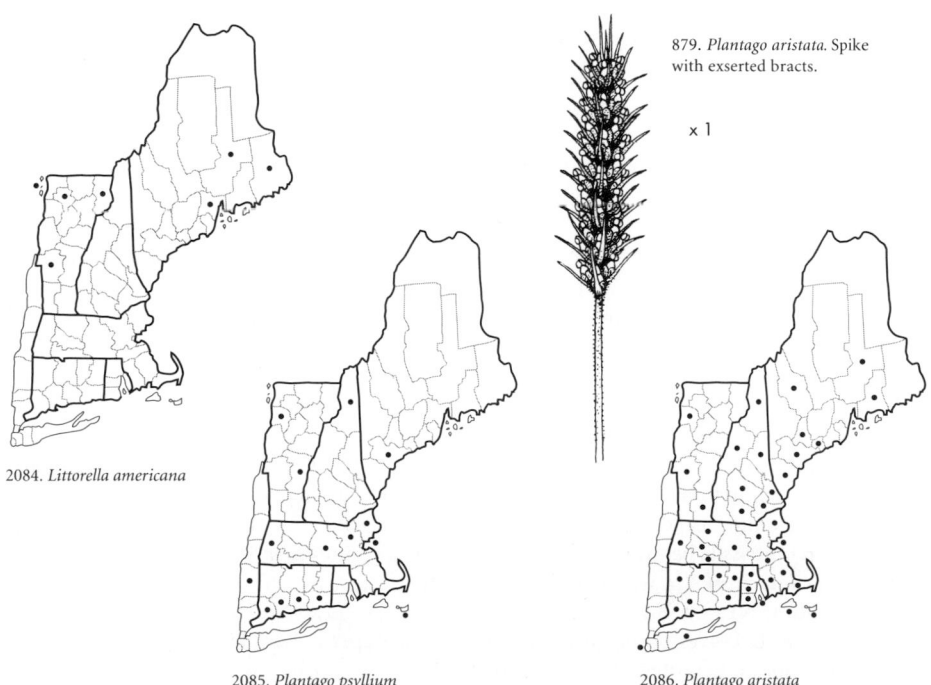

2084. *Littorella americana*

879. *Plantago aristata.* Spike with exserted bracts.

x 1

2085. *Plantago psyllium*

2086. *Plantago aristata*

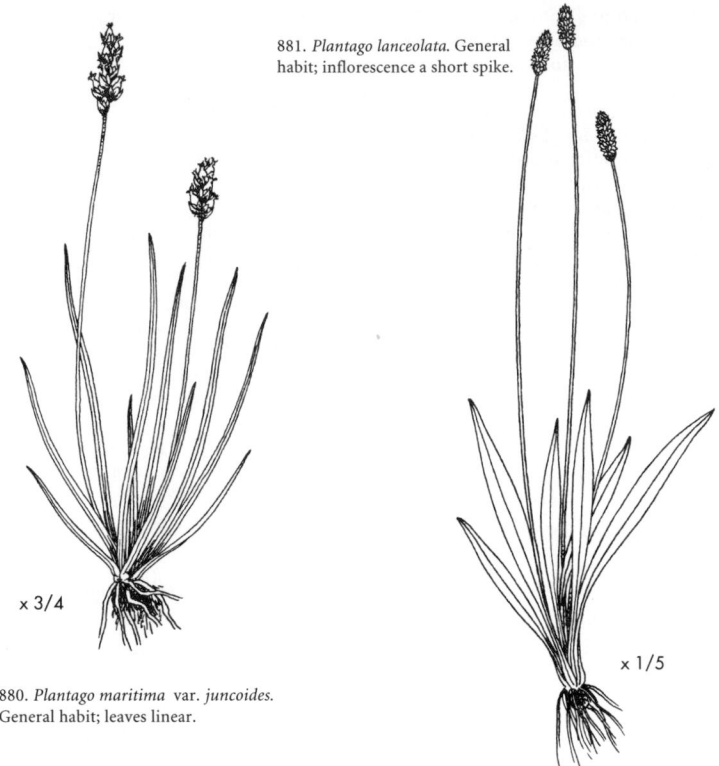

881. *Plantago lanceolata.* General
habit; inflorescence a short spike.

× 3/4

880. *Plantago maritima* var. *juncoides.*
General habit; leaves linear.

× 1/5

5. *P. marítima* L. (of the sea). Seaside plantain. Brackish and salt marshes, sea beaches, rocks along the coast. June-September. Fig. 880, Map 2089. Represented with us as var. *juncoídes* (Lam.) Gray. [*P. juncoides; P. oliganthos*]. —FACW

6. *P. pusílla* Nutt. (very small). Fields and roadsides. May-June. Map 2090. From farther west.

7. *P. média* L. (intermediate). Fields, cultivated ground, waste places. June-August. Map 2091. (Adventive from Europe).

8. *P. lanceoláta* L. (lance-shaped). English plantain. Fields, roadsides, waste places, cultivated ground. May-October. Fig. 881, Map 2092. (Naturalized from Europe). [*P. altissima*].

9. *P. rugélii* Dcne. (for its discoverer). Roadsides, waste places, cultivated ground. July-October. Map 2093. —FACU

10. *P. májor* L. (larger). Roadsides, waste places, cultivated ground. July-October. Map 2094. (Naturalized from Europe). Very variable. [*P. asiatica*]. Our plants include var. *major* and the following confluent vars.:

var. *intermédia* (DC.) Pilger. Scapes decumbent at base, capsule broadly rounded at tip (scapes erect, capsule conical to the tip in vars. *major* and *pilgeri*). [*var. scopulorum*].

var. *pílgeri* Domin. Scapes and capsule conical as in var. *major* but capsule circumscissile at tips of sepals (circumscissile below tips of sepals in vars. *major* and *intermedia*). —FACU

11. *P. cordáta* Lam. (heart-shaped). Margins of streams, marshes. May-July. Reported for Dutchess County NY. —OBL

P. corónopus L. Leaves pinnately dissected (the above species have leaves which are entire to toothed). European. Reported for Suffolk County, MA.

2087. *Plantago patagonica*

2088. *Plantago virginica*

2089. *Plantago maritima* var. *juncoides*

2090. *Plantago pusilla*

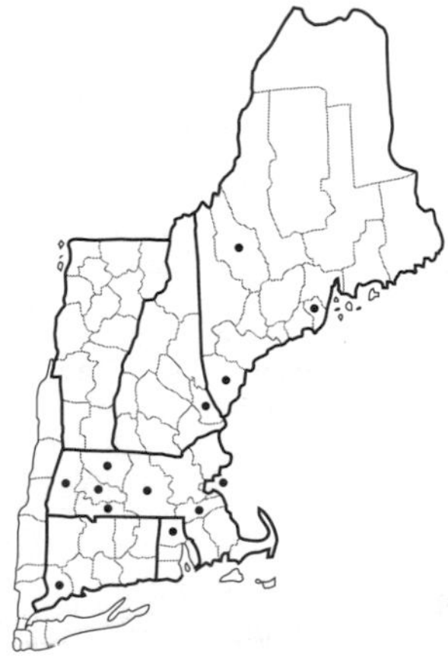

2091. *Plantago media*

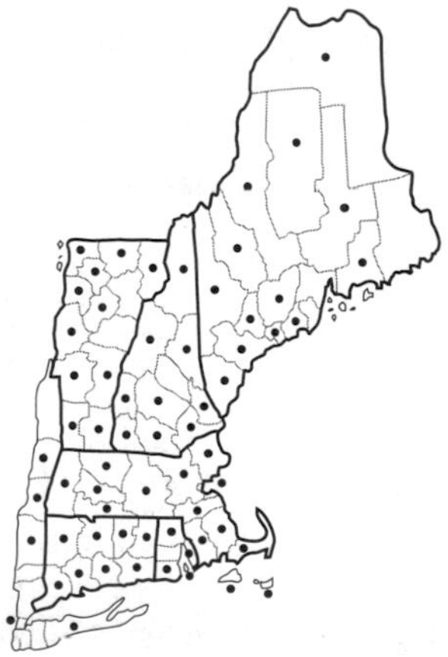

2092. *Plantago lanceolata*

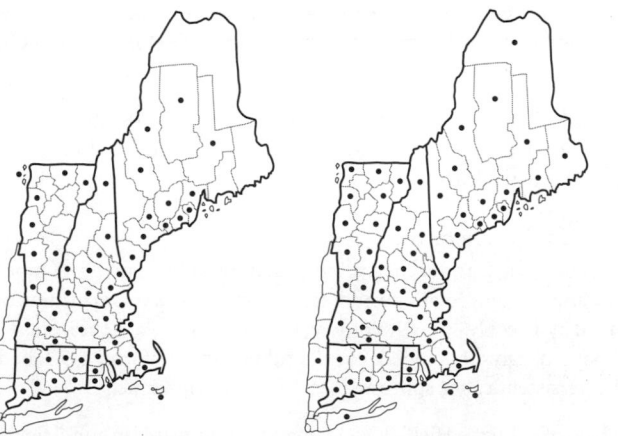

2093. *Plantago rugelii*

2094. *Plantago major*

Family 184. Rubiáceae (Madder Family)

Hermaphrodite, annual or perennial herbs, shrubs or small trees. Leaves simple, entire, opposite or whorled, stipulate (stipules sometimes resembling leaves), sessile or petioled. Flowers perfect, regular, solitary or in various types of inflorescences, calyx lobes mostly 4 or (in *Galium*) none, corolla rotate, funnelform or salverform, 3-5-lobed, stamens 4-5, inserted on the corolla tube, ovary inferior, 2-4-locular, styles 1 or 2. Fruit a berry, capsule, drupe or nutlet.

In addition to the species treated under the genera below *Canthium odoratum* has been reported for MA.

a. Plant a shrub or small tree; flowers in spherical heads. .... 1. *Cephalanthus occidentalis*
a. Plant an herb; flowers not in spherical heads.
  b. Principal leaves in whorles.
    c. Flowers in involucrate heads; calyx with lanceolate lobes. .... 2. *Sherardia arvensis*
    c. Flowers not involucrate (although sometimes in heads in *Asperula*); calyx lobes absent.
      Flowers in simple or branched, terminal or axillary cymes. .... 3. *Galium*
      Flowers sessile, in an involucrate head. .... 4. *Asperula arvensis*
  b. Principal leaves opposite.
    d. Flowers paired, their hypanthia fused; fruit a red berry; leaves about as wide as long, evergreen .... 5. *Mitchella repens*
    d. Flowers not paired or if so hypanthia not fused; fruit a capsule; leaves longer than wide, deciduous.
      e. Flowers solitary on peduncles or pedicelled in terminal cymes. .... 6. *Houstonia*
      e. Flowers sessile or subsessile, solitary in the leaf axils or in compact terminal and axillary clusters.
        Stipular sheath bearing 3 or more linear divisions or bristles of approximately the same length; ovules solitary in each locule. .... 7. *Diodia*
        Stipular sheath irregularly fimbriate or lacerate; ovules more than 1 in each locule .... 8. *Hedyotis*

1. Cephalánthus L. Buttonbush (Greek name, referring to the dense head of flowers).
Shrubs or small trees, twigs floriferous at the tips or dying back, pith moderate, tan, buds small, in depressions above the leaf scars, leaf scars roundish, bundle trace 1, stipule scars or persistent stipules present, end bud lacking; leaves opposite or in whorles of 3 or 4, petioled, ovate to oblong, stipules triangular; flowers small, white, bracteolate, densely aggregated in globose, penduncled heads terminating some of the twigs and in the upper leaf axils, hypanthium inversely pyramidal, calyx 4-toothed, corolla tubular-funnelform, with 4 short lobes, style elongate; fruit obpyramidal, splitting into 2-4 nutlets.

    1. C. occidentális L. (western). Pond and stream margins, shrub swamps, usually in shallow water. June-August. Map 2095. (W.I.). Reported to have various medicinal uses; also reported as poisonous, particularly the leaves. —OBL

2. Sherárdia L. (for W. Sherard).
Slender, diffusely branched, annual herbs, stems square, pubescent, procumbent at the base; leaves whorled, sessile, linear to lanceolate, cuspidate, pubescent; flowers small, pink or blue, in penducled heads surrounded by a deeply-lobed involucre, the lobes lanceolate, the heads terminal and axillary, hypanthium obovoid, calyx 4-5-lobed, corolla tubular-funnelform, 4-5-lobed, stamens 4-5; fruit crowned by the persistent calyx, splitting into 2 indehiscent carpels.

    1. S. arvénsis L. (of cultivated fields). Field-madder. Cultivated ground, fields, waste places. May-July. Map 2096. (Adventive from Europe).

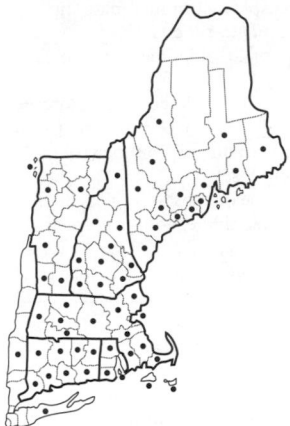

2095. *Cephalanthus occidentalis*   2096. *Sherardia arvensis*

3. *Gálium* L. Bedstraw (from the Greek, referring to the curdling of milk caused by some of the species).

Slender, annual or perennial herbs, stems 4-sided, often scabrous or prickly; leaves whorled, sessile; flowers small, in simple or branched, terminal or axillary cymes, calyx lobes obsolete, corolla rotate (funnelform, with a definite tube in *G. glaucum*), with 3-4 lobes, stamens 4, styles 2; fruit 1 or 2 indehiscent, globose or subglobose, smooth or bristly carpels.

Rúbia L. *tinctória* L. Madder. Resembling *Galium* but distinguishable by the 5-merous flowers and fleshy fruits (flowers 3-4 merous and fruits dry in *Galium*). Rarely escaped from cultivation. Reported for Hampshire County MA; Washington County NY.

a. Flowers sessile, in an involucrate head. .... 1. *G. glaucum*
a. Flowers in simple or branched, terminal or axillary cymes.
  b. Leaves sharply cuspidate or mucronate, the principal ones in whorles of 5-8.
    c. Ovary and/or fruit pubescent or bristly. (Fig. 882).
      Leaves retrorsely ciliate on the margins; plants annual, from a taproot. .... 2. *G. aparine*
      Leaves antrorsely ciliate on the margins; plants perennial from rhizomes. ...... 3. *G. triflorum*
    c. Ovary and fruit smooth to granular or muricate but not pubescent or bristly.
      d. Stems retrorsely prickly (sometimes obscurely so in *G. parisiense* but plant
        annual from a taproot; plants in second part of couplet perennial
        from rhizomes); stems weak, reclining, ascending or matted.
      e. Margins of leaves antrorsely ciliate; plant annual from a taproot. .... 4. *G. parisiense*
      e. Margins of leaves retrorsely ciliate; plant perennial, from rhizomes.
        Ovary and fruit granular or muricate; inflorescence of axillary,
          few-flowered penduncles shorter than to slightly exceeding
          the leaves. (Fig. 883). .... 5. *G. tricornutum*
        Ovary and fruit smooth; inflorescence a leafy-bracteate panicle of
          cymes, the cymes longer than the bracteal leaves. .... 6. *G. asprellum*
      d. Stems smooth to pubescent but not prickley; stems erect.
        f. Leaves linear-acicular; branches of inflorescence usually densely
          puberulent; flowers yellow.
          Panicle dense, its lower branches much exceeding the internodes. .... 7. *G. verum*
          Panicle looser and more interrupted, its lower branches shorter than
            the internodes .... 8. *G. wirtgenii*
        f. Leaves narrowly lanceolate to linear-oblong or oblanceolate; branches of
          inflorescence glabrous or essentially so; flowers white.
          Leaves (the larger ones) 2.5 cm or more long, lanceolate. .... 9. *G. sylvaticum*
          Leaves usually 2 cm or less long (rarely to 2.5 cm), linear-oblong to
            oblanceolate .... 10. *G. mollugo*

b. Leaves obtuse to acute or acuminate, not sharply cuspidate or mucronate (tip
    rounded with a very short, blunt mucro in *G. pilosum* and *G.*
    kamtschaticum), the principal ones in whorles of 4 (sometimes more in *G.*
    trifidum, G. tinctorium and *G. palustre*).
  g. Ovary and/or fruit pubescent or bristly; leaves, at least the larger ones, more
      than 6 mm wide, (except usually in *G. boreale*), with 3 (5) prominent
      parallel veins (sometimes narrower and/or with only a prominent
      midvein in *G. pilosum* but stems spreading-pilose).
    h. Lateral flowers and fruits, or some of them, sessile or subsessile. (Fig. 884).
        Leaves oval, elliptic or oblong, widest near the middle, obtuse; corollas
          usually pubescent outside .... 11. *G. circaezans*
        Leaves lanceolate, widest below the middle, acute to acuminate; corollas
          glabrous .... 12. *G. lanceolatum*
    h. Lateral flowers and fruits all pedicelled.
      i. Leaves linear-lanceolate .... 13. *G. boreale*
      i. Leaves elliptic, ovate or obovate. (Fig. 885).
        Stems spreading-pilose; leaves in numerous whorles. .... 14. *G. pilosum*
        Stems glabrous or essentially so; leaves in 6 or fewer whorles. .... 15. *G. kamtschaticum*
  g. Ovary and fruit smooth; leaves usually 6 mm or less wide, with only a
      prominent midvein (3 prominent parallel veins in *G. boreale*); stems
      glabrous, appressed-pubescent or scabrous.
    j. Leaves with 3 prominent parallel veins; stems erect. .... 13. *G. boreale*
    j. Leaves with only a prominent midvein; stems mostly weak, reclining,
      ascending or matted.
      k. Flowers numerous in repeatedly branched cymes. (Fig. 886). .... 16. *G. palustre*
      k. Flowers solitary-several in simple to twice-branched cymes.
        l. Corolla 3-lobed .... 17. *G. trifidum*
        l. Corolla 4-lobed.
          Leaves loosely spreading to ascending; mature fruits 1.75 mm or
            more wide. .... 18. *G. obtusum*
          Leaves reflexed; mature fruits 1.5 mm or less wide. .... 19. *G. labradoricum*

1. G. glaúcum L. Fields, waste places. (Introduced from Europe). Reported for CT. [*Asperula glauca; A. galioides*].

2. G. aparíne L. (old generic name). Woodlands, thickets, fields, roadsides, waste places. Fruit: June-August. Fig. 882, Map 2097. (Eurasia). Young plants can be steamed and eaten as a potherb; leaves can be used for tea; fruits can be roasted and used as a coffee substitute; also has medicinal value as a diuretic; preparations made from the leaves can be used to treat skin eruptions and other skin complexion problems. —FACU

3. G. triflórum Michx. (three-flowered). Woodlands, thickets, fields, roadsides, waste places. Fruit: June-September. Map 2098. (Greenland, Eurasia). —FACU

G. odorátum (L.) Scop. Similar to *G. triflorum* but with stems pubescent at the nodes, corolla funnelform, 4 mm or more wide (stems often scabrous on the angles but not pubescent at the nodes, corolla rotate, up to 3 mm wide in *G. triflorum*). (Introduced from Europe). Reported for MA, RI. [*Asperula o.*].

4. G. parisiénse L. (Parisian). Fields and roadsides. Fruit: June-August. (Naturalized from Europe). Reported for VT. [*G. divaricatum*]. —FACU

5. G. tricornútum Dandy (three-pronged). Waste places and cultivated ground. Fruit: June-July. Fig. 883, (Adventive from Europe). Reported for Providence County, RI. [*G. tricorne*].

6. G. aspréllum Michx. (slightly rough). Margins of streams and ponds, wet meadows, marshes, wooded swamps. Fruit: July-September. Map 2099. —OBL

7. G. vérum L. (true). Fields, roadsides, waste places. Fruit: June-September. Map 2100. (Naturalized from Europe). The same uses may be made for this plant as for *G. aparine*.

G. x pomeránicum Retz. A hybrid between *G. verum* and *G. mollugo*.

8. G. wirtgénii F. Schultz (for P. Wirtgen). Fields. Fruit: June-September. Map 2101. (Naturalized from Europe).

9. ***G. sylváticum*** L. (of the woods). Scotch-mist. Fields, thickets, roadsides. Fruit: July-September. Map 2102. (Introduced from Europe).

10. ***G. mollúgo*** L. (old generic name). Fields, roadsides, waste places. Fruit: June-September. Map 2103. (Naturalized from Europe). [*G. erectum*].

G. álbum Miller. Very similar to *G. mollugo* but corolla 3 mm or more wide and leaves for the most part linear-lanceolate with a long, tapering base (corolla up to 3 mm wide and leaves more typically oblanceolate and abruptly tapered to base in *G. mollugo*). European. Reported for CT. [*G. mollugo* var. *erectum*].

11. ***G. circaézans*** Michx. (resembling *Circaea*). Wild Licorice. Woodlands and thickets. Fruit: July-September. Map 2104. Our plants include var. *circaezans* and the following var.:

var. *hypomálacum* Fern. Angles of stems and undersides of leaves densely pubescent (sparsely pubescent to glabrous in var. *circaezans*).

12. ***G. lanceolátum*** Torr. (lance-shaped). Wild Licorice. Woodlands and thickets. Fruit: June-September. Fig. 884, Map 2105.

13. ***G. boreále*** L. (northern). Fields and woodland borders. Fruit: July-August. Map 2106. (Eurasia). Endangered in MA. —FACU

14. ***G. pilósum*** Ait. (soft-hairy). Woods, thickets, fields. Fruit: August-September. Fig. 885, Map 2107. Endangered in NH. Our plants include var. *pilosum* and the following var.:

var. *punticulósum* (Michx.) T. & G. Stem and leaves with pubescence of dense, short, upwardly incurved hairs (stem and leaves with pubescence of sparse to dense straight hairs in var. *pilósum*).

15. ***G. kamtscháticum*** Steller ex J. A. & J. H. Schultes (of Kamtchatka). Woodlands at high altitudes. Fruit: June-August. Map 2108. (Aleutian Islands, Asia).

16. ***G. palústre*** L. (of marshes). Marshes, wet meadows, stream and river edges. Fruit: July-September. Fig. 886, Map 2109. (Eurasia). —OBL

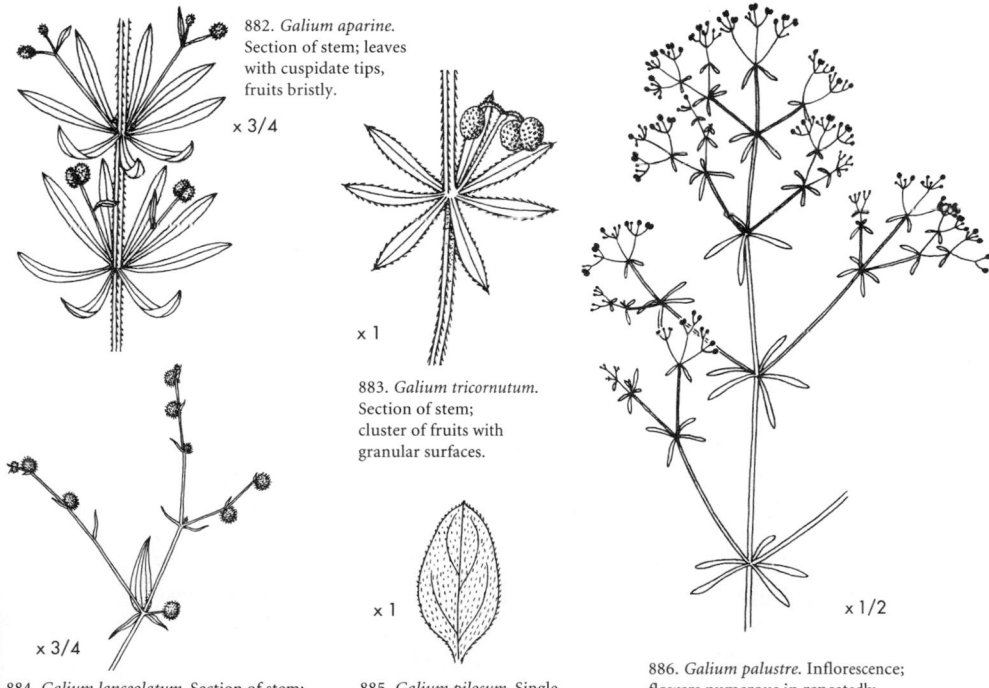

882. *Galium aparine.* Section of stem; leaves with cuspidate tips, fruits bristly.

x 3/4

x 1

883. *Galium tricornutum.* Section of stem; cluster of fruits with granular surfaces.

x 3/4

884. *Galium lanceolatum.* Section of stem; lateral fruits, some sessile, some pedicelled.

x 1

885. *Galium pilosum.* Single leaf showing elliptic shape.

x 1/2

886. *Galium palustre.* Inflorescence; flowers numerous in repeatedly branched cymes.

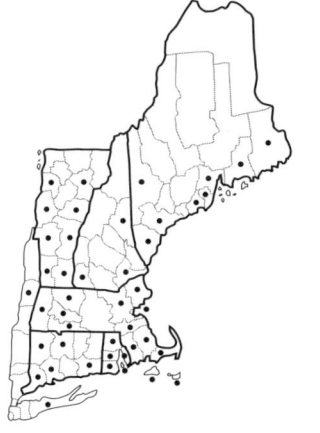

2097. *Galium aparine*

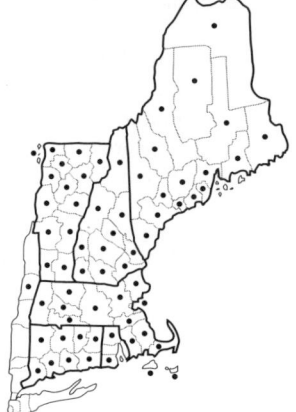

2098. *Galium triflorum*

2099. *Galium asprellum*

2100. *Galium verum*

2101. *Galium wirtgenii*

2102. *Galium sylvaticum*

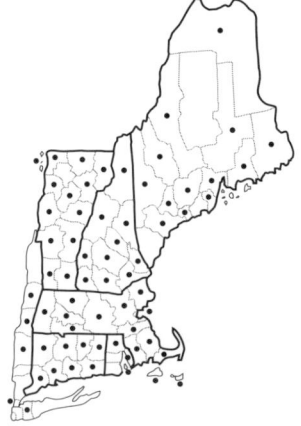

2103. *Galium mollugo*

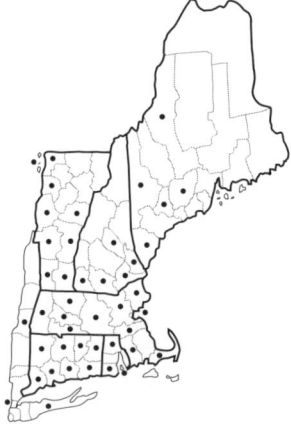

2104. *Galium circaezans*

2105. *Galium lanceolatum*

2106. *Galium boreale* 2107. *Galium pilosum* 2108. *Galium kamtschaticum*

2109. *Galium palustre* 2110. *Galium trifidum* 2111. *Galium obtusum*

17. G. trífidum L. (three-cleft). Pond and stream margins, marshes, wooded swamps. Fruit: July-September. Map 2110. (Eurasia). Our plants include subsp. *trifidum* and the following subsp.:

subsp. *halophílum* (Fern. & Wieg.) Puff. Fleshy seaside plant, totally glabrous (not fleshy, scabrous on the stem angles, leaf margins and pedicels in subsp. *trifidum* and subsp. *subbiflorum*).

subsp. *subbiflórum* (Wieg.) Puff. Principal leaves 5-6 in a whorl (4 in a whorl in the above subsp). [*G. subbiflorum; G. trifidum* var. *pacificum; G. tinctorium* var. *s.*]. —FACW+

G. tinctórium (L.) Scop. Similar to *G. trifidum*, leaves 5-6 in a whorl, pedicels 3 terminating a peduncle, to 6 mm long (pedicels 1 or 2 terminating each peduncle, to 20 mm long, or if pedicels 3 leaves 4 in a whorl in *G. trifidum*). Throughout our range. [*G. trifidum* var. *tinctorium; G. claytoni*]. —OBL

G. brévipes Fern. & Wieg. Similar to the latter 2 species; leaves 4 in a whorl, pedicels 5 mm or less long, 1-flowered, as long or shorter than the subtending leaves (latter 2 species lacking this combination of characters). Reported for ME, NH, VT. [*G. brandegei; G. trifidum*]. —OBL

18. G. obtúsum Bigel (obtuse). Wooded swamps and wet woods. Fruit: July-September. Map 2111. Endangered in NH. [*G. tinctorium*]. Our plants are subsp. *obtusum.* —FACW+

19. G. labradóricum (Wieg.) Wieg. (of Labrador). Northern cedar swamps and bogs. Fruit: July-August. Map 2112. Endangered in NH. —OBL

4. Aspérula L. (slightly harsh).

Similar to *Galium* except flowers are sessile, in involucrate heads.

1. A. arvénsis L. (of cultivated fields). Waste places. Map 2113. (Introduced from Europe).

5. Mitchélla L. Partridge-berry (for J. Mitchell).

Creeping, often mat-forming, evergreen, perennial herbs; leaves opposite, petioled, entire or undulate, round-ovate; flowers white, in pairs on a usually terminal peduncle, their hypanthia and bases of the 2 calyces fused, their common limb 6-8 toothed, corolla funnelform, usually 4-lobed, lobes pubescent on the inner surface, style 1; fruit a twin, usually red berry crowned with the calyx teeth of the 2 flowers. —Wildl.1

1. M. répens L. (creeping). Woodlands. June-July. Map 2114. Fruit edible; dried plant was used by Indians to ease childbirth. —FACU

6. Houstónia L. (for W. Houstoun).

Small, usually tufted, perennial herbs; leaves opposite, petioled or sessile; flowers blue, purple or white, solitary on terminal and axillary peduncles or pedicelled in terminal cymes, calyx and corolla 4-lobed, the latter salverform or funnelform, the lobes often pubescent on the inner surface, style 1; fruit a capsule, its upper half protruding beyond the hypanthium, thus half-inferior, the apex loculicidal. [*Hedyotis*].

a. Flowers on peduncles 1.5 cm or more long, usually not more than 1-3 per stem .... 1. *H. caerulea*
a. Flowers on pedicels less than 1.5 cm long, numerous in corymbed cymes. (Fig. 887).
    Calyx lobes less than 2.5 mm long; leaves linear to narrowly oblong, 5 mm or
        less wide, narrowed to the base .... 2. *H. longifolia*
    Calyx lobes 2.5 mm or more long; leaves lance-ovate to oblong, more than
        5 mm wide (at least the larger ones), rounded at the base. .... 3. *H. purpurea*
                var. *calycosa*

1. H. caerúlea L. (blue). Bluets. Fields, roadsides, open woods. April-July. Map 2115. [*H. faxonorum; Hedyotis c.*]. —FACU
2. H. longifólia Gaertn. (long-leaved). Fields, open woods. June-July. Fig. 887, Map 2116. Endangered in RI, CT. [*Hedyotis l.*]. Our plants are var. *longifolia*.
3. H. purpúrea L. (purple) Fields, open woods. June-July. Map 2117. From farther south and west. [*H. lanceolata; Hedyotis p.*]. Represented with us as var. *calycósa* Gray.

7. Diódia L. Buttonweed (from the Greek, based on the plants' occurrence along travelled ways).

Decumbent to spreading or ascending, annual or perennial herbs, branched from near the base; leaves opposite, sessile, linear to oblong-lanceolate or narrowly elliptic, stipular sheath bearing conspicuous setaceous to linear divisions; flowers small, white to pink or purple, 1 or 2 in each axil, sessile, calyx lobes 2-4, sometimes unequal, corolla salverform to funnelform, 4-lobed, style 1; fruit splitting into 2 nutlets.

Stipular sheath bearing 3-4 linear divisions between each pair of leaves; calyx lobes
    2; corolla salverform .... 1. *D. virginiana*
Stipular sheath bearing 5 or more setaceous bristles between each pair of leaves;
    calyx lobes 4; corolla funnelform. .... 2. *D. teres*

1. D. virginiána L. (Virginian). Pond and stream margins, ditches, marshes, wet meadows. June-August. From farther south and west. Reported for New Haven County, CT. Our plants are var. *virginiana.* —FACW

2. D. téres. Walt. (circular in cross-section). Dry sandy soil in waste places, beaches. June-August. Map 2118. From farther south and west. [*Diodella t.*]. Our plants are var. *teres.*

8. Hedýotis L.

Erect or diffuse, simple or branched annual or perennial herbs; leaves opposite, sessile or subsessile, linear, lanceolate or ovate, stipules irregularly fimbriate or lacerate; flowers small, white to purple, sessile or subsessile, solitary in the leaf axils or in compact terminal and axillary clusters, calyx and corolla 4-lobed, the latter rotate or salverform, style 1; fruit a small capsule, three quarters to fully inferior. [*Oldenlandia*].

Plant annual; leaves lanceolate to oval; inflorescence few-flowered; corolla
        nearly rotate .... 1. *H. uniflora*
Plant perennial; leaves linear; inflorescence many-flowered; corolla salverform .... 2. *H. nigricans*

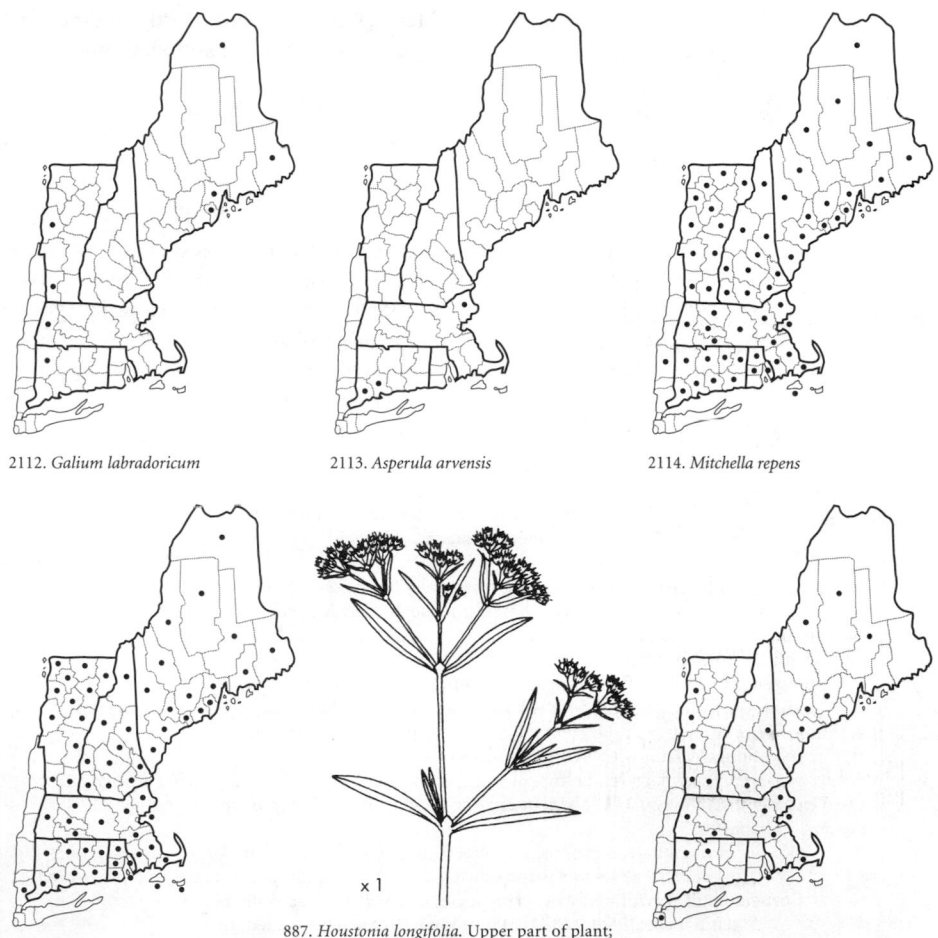

2112. *Galium labradoricum*

2113. *Asperula arvensis*

2114. *Mitchella repens*

2115. *Houstonia caerulea*

887. *Houstonia longifolia.* Upper part of plant; flowers numerous in corymbed cymes.

× 1

2116. *Houstonia longifolia*

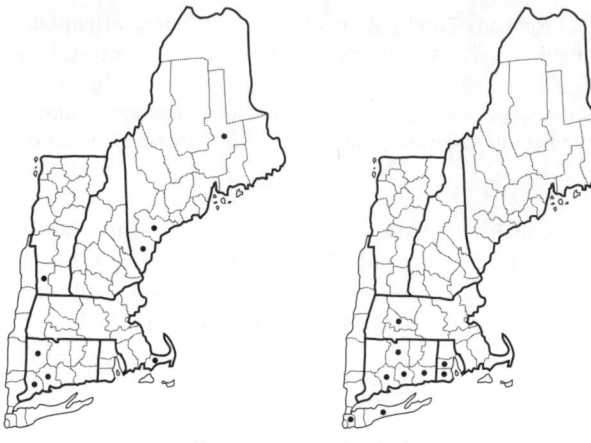

2117. *Houstonia purpurea* var. *calycosa*   2118. *Diodia teres*

1. H. uniflóra L. (one-flowered). Pond margins, ditches, wet depressions, mostly on the coastal plain. July-September. (W.I.) From farther south. Reported for Kings and Suffolk Counties, NY. [*Oldenlandia u.*].

2. H. nígricans (Lam.) Fosb. (blackening). Dry open areas. June-October. From farther south and west. Reported for NH. [*Houstonia n.; H. lanceolata; H. angustifolia*]. Our plants are var. *nigricans*.

Family 185. Caprifoliáceae (Honeysuckle Family)

Hermaphrodite, shrubs, vines or perennial herbs, rarely suffrutescent. Leaves simple or pinnately compound, opposite, sessile or petioled, toothed, lobed or entire, mostly estipulate. Flowers perfect (sterile flowers also produced in some *Virburnum*), regular or irregular, in basically cymose inflorescences, occasionally solitary or paired, terminal and/or axillary, calyx regular, 3-5 toothed or lobed, corolla 3-5-lobed, rotate to tubular, the tube sometimes gibbous at the base, regular or bilabiate, stamens 3-5, inserted on the corolla tube, ovary inferior, 1-5-locular, style 1. Fruit a capsule, berry or drupe (rarely an achene).

a. Leaves pinnately compound .... 1. *Sambucus*
a. Leaves simple.
   b. Stems creeping and trailing, bearing short, erect branches 1.5 cm or less tall;
       leaves short-petioled, 2 cm or less long, evergreen . (Fig. 889). .... 2. *Linnaea borealis*
                                                                    subsp. *longiflora*
   b. Stems erect, 2 cm or more tall, or if trailing (occasionally in *Lonicera*) leaves
       (uppermost) connate and/or longer than 2 cm, usually deciduous.
      c. Plant herbaceous .... 3. *Triosteum*
      c. Plant woody, a shrub or vine.
         d. Inflorescence a terminal, flat-topped, compound cyme or panicle; style
            none, the stigmas sessile; fruit with 1 flattened seed .. (Fig. 892). .... 4. *Viburnum*
         d. Inflorescence of axillary and terminal clusters, simple cymes or spikes;
            style elongate; fruit with 2 or more seeds or an achene.
           e. Leaves evenly serrulate; fruit a capsule. .... 5. *Diervilla lonicera*
           e. Leaves entire to irregularly lobed, crenate or dentate; fruit a berry, drupe
              or achene.
              Corolla campanulate, 8 mm or less long; fruit 2-seeded, more than 3
                 in each axil or terminal and white .... 6. *Symphoricarpos*
              Corolla tubular or funnelform (campanulate in *Kolkwitzia*, a similar
                 genus), usually more than 8 mm long; fruit several-seeded, or
                 an achene, paired or 3 in each axil and/or terminal, not white. ... 7. *Lonicera*

1. Sambúcus L. Elder (from the Greek, based on use of parts of the plant for musical instruments).

Shrubs, usually colonial, the younger growth often suffrutescent, twigs stout, lenticels usually prominent, the bark warty, pith large, white or brown, buds solitary or multiple, ovoid, with several scales, leaf scars broadly crescent-shaped, sometimes lobed, connected by transverse lines, bundle traces 3 or more, end bud and stipule scars lacking; leaves once or occasionally twice pinnately compound, petioled, leaflets serrate, rarely laciniate, lanceolate to ovate, acuminate; flowers small, white, numerous, in flat or ovoid paniculate, terminal, compound cymes, calyx minutely 5-lobed, corolla 5-lobed, regular, rotate, stamens 5; fruit a red to black berry. —Wildl. 3

a. Inflorescence a flat-topped cyme, lacking a main axis, the rays all arising from the
   base; pith of second year wood white; berries usually black or purple.
   (Fig. 888).
   Plant colonial, spreading from rhizomes; berries purplish-black; leaflets mostly
      more than 5 .... 1. *S. canadensis*
   Plant neither colonial nor spreading from rhizomes; berries black; leaflets
      mostly 5 .... 2. *S. nigra*
a. Inflorescence ovoid-paniculate, with a main axis; pith of second year wood brown;
   berries usually red .... 3. *S. racemosa*

1. S. canadénsis L. (Canadian). Shrub swamps, wooded swamps, wet woods. June-July. Fig. 888, Map 2119. Flower clusters can be dipped in batter and fried; pickled flower buds can be used as a substitute for capers; fruits popular for jams, pies and wine; bark and leaves are poisonous, but a poultice made from the leaves is said to be effective in treating bruises and sprains; dried flowers were used as a tea by Indians for colic, cough syrup can be made from the fruits. —FACW-

2. S. nígra L. (black). Rarely escaped from cultivation to waste places. Reported for Fairfield County, CT. Much the same uses described for the preceding species apply to this species.

3. S. racemósa L. (racemed). Woods and thickets. May-June. Map 2120. [*S. pubens*]. Represented with us as subsp. *púbens* (Michx.) House var. *leucocárpa* (T&G) Cronq. Fruits distasteful, even toxic. —FACU

2. Linnaéa L. (for *Linnaeus*).

Suffrutescent, evergreen sub-shrub, stems slender, creeping and trailing, bearing short, erect branches; leaves short-petioled, oval to obovate, obscurely crenate; flowers pink to white, pedicelled and nodding, usually in pairs at the ends of long, slender, terminal peduncles, calyx and corolla 5-lobed, regular, the latter funnelform, stamens 4; fruit dry, subglobose, enclosed in the persistent calyx.

1. L. boreális L. (northern). Twinflower. Coniferous or deciduous woods, wooded swamps, bogs. June-August. Fig. 889, Map 2121. [*L. americana; L. borealis* var. *americana*]. Represented with us as subsp. *longiflóra* Torr. —FAC

3. Triósteum L. Horse Gentian (name based on reference to the 3 bony nutlets).

Coarse, pubescent, perennial herbs; leaves sessile or connate-perfoliate, entire, oblanceolate to obovate or ovate; flowers greenish to yellowish or red, solitary or clustered in the axils, sessile, calyx with 5 elongate, foliaceous lobes, corolla tubular, gibbous at the base, unequally 5-lobed, stamens 5; fruit a red, orange or yellow drupe.

Calyx lobes hispid-ciliate, glabrous on the back or with pubescence of hairs
   conspicuously shorter than the marginal cilia; leaves usually 5 cm or less
   wide .... 1. *T. angustifolium*
Calyx lobes uniformly pubescent on the back and margin, the hairs all approximately
   the same length; leaves, at least the largest, usually wider than 5 cm .... 2. *T. perfoliatum*

1. *T. angustifólium* L. (narrow-leaved). Woods and thickets. May-June. Map 2122. From farther south. Our plants include var. *angustifolium* and the following var.:

var. *eámesii* Wieg. Leaves soft-pubescent over the surface beneath (glabrous beneath or pubescent only on the veins in var. *angustifolium*).

2. *T. perfoliátum* L. (with leaves fused around the stem). Dry woods, thickets and openings. May-June. Fig. 890, Map 2123. Endangered in MA. Dried, roasted berries have been used as a coffee substitute; a preparation made from the plant was used by Indians for fevers, colds and other medicinal purposes.

T. aurantiacum Bickn. Leaves tapering to the base, usually not connate; hairs of the stem mostly longer than .5 mm (leaves, or the middle ones, connate-perfoliate and hairs of stem .5 mm or shorter in *T. perfoliatum*). Endangered in NH. [*T. perfoliatum* var. *aurantiacum*]. Our plants are var. *aurantiacum*.

4. *Vibúrnum* L. (classical Latin name).

Shrubs or small trees, twigs slender to moderate, pith moderate, white or brownish, buds usually solitary, ovoid to oblong or linear, naked, or with a pair of valvate scales, or with 3 or more separate scales, leaf scars crescent-shaped, with 3 bundle traces, stipule scars lacking; leaves petioled, toothed, lobed or rarely entire, stipules present or absent; flowers small, usually white, in compound cymes terminating the stem and branches, rarely paniculate, the marginal flowers sometimes enlarged and sterile, calyx 5-toothed, corolla rotate to short-campanulate, regular (marginal sterile flowers, when present, irregular), 5-lobed, stamens 5, style absent, stigmas 3; fruit a fleshy, blue, black or red drupe containing a single compressed stone. —Wildl. 2

a. Leaves, or many of them, mostly 3-lobed; palmately 3-5-veined. (Fig. 891).
  b. Petioles with 1-several prominent glands below the junction with the blade;
    sterile marginal flowers present, much larger than the fertile and irregular..... 1. *V. opulus*
  b. Petioles glandless, glands sometimes present on blade just above the junction
    with the petiole; flowers all fertile, uniform.
    Petioles and/or undersides of leaves densely stellate-pubescent; fruit purplish
      or black .... 2. *V. acerifolium*
    Petioles and undersides of leaves glabrous or with pubescence of sparse,
      simple hairs; fruit red .... 3. *V. edule*
a. Leaves not lobed, pinnately veined.
  c. Inflorescence paniculate, with a main axis. (Fig. 892)................................. 4. *V. sieboldii*
  c. Inflorescence cymose, lacking a main axis, the rays all arising from the base.
    d. Leaves with lateral veins simple or 1-2 times forked, each vein extending to a
      tooth, coarsely toothed; winter buds with 3 or more separate scales. (Fig. 893).
      Stipules present in one or more pairs of leaves on each branch;
        stylopodium glabrous.. 5. *V. rafinesquianum*
      Stipules mostly absent; stylopodium pubescent. .... 6. *V. dentatum*
    d. Leaves with lateral veins branching and anastomosing before reaching the
      margin, subentire to finely serrate or serrulate; winter buds naked or with
      a pair of valvate scales.
      e. Leaves stellate-pubescent beneath; winter buds naked.
        Cymes sessile; marginal flowers sterile, larger than the fertile flowers in
          the inner part of the cyme.. 7. *V. lantanoides*
        Cymes peduncled; flowers all perfect, uniform. .... 8. *V. lantana*
      e. Leaves glabrous beneath or pubescence not stellate; winter buds with a pair
        of valvate scales.
        f. Leaves without reddish-brown dots beneath, rounded to obtuse or acute;
          cymes sessile .... 9. *V. prunifolium*
        f. Leaves with minute reddish-brown dots beneath (visible with 10x hand
          lens); cymes peduncled or if sessile (*V. lentago*) leaves (at least
          some) sharply acuminate.

Cymes sessile; leaves (some) long-acuminate; winter buds smooth,
    grayish-purple. (Fig. 894) .... 10. *V. lentago*
Cymes peduncled; leaves obtuse, acute or abruptly blunt-acuminate;
    winter buds loosely scurfy, tan .... 11. *V. nudum*

1. *V. ópulus* L. (old generic name). Guelder Rose. Occasionally escaped from cultivation to fields and roadsides. June-July. Fig. 891, Map 2124. Our plants include var. *opulus* and the following var.:

var. *americánum* Ait. High-bush Cranberry. Petiolar glands round-topped; stipules usually filiform-clavate (petiolar glands concave-topped and stipules usually filiform-attenuate in var. *opulus*). Map 2125. [*V. trilobum*]. Fruit edible; can be used as a substitute for cranberries in jams and juice; a tea made from the bark was used by Indians to ease menstrual cramps. —FACW

2. *V. acerifólium* L. (maple-leaved). Maple-leaved Viburnum. Moist or dry woods. May-June. Map 2126. Our plants include var. *acerifolium* and the following var.:

var. *ovátum* (Rehd.) Mcatee. Leaves unlobed, 2-lobed or short-lobed (leaves with 3 well developed lobes in var. *acerifolium*).

3. *V. edúle* (Michx.) Raf. (edible). Squashberry. Alpine areas in ME, NH and VT. June-July. Map 2127. (ne Asia). [*V. eradiatum; V. pauciflorum*]. Fruit edible. —FACW

4. *V. siebóldii* Miq. (for P.F. von Siebold). Occasionally escaped from cultivation. Fig. 892. (Introduced from Japan). Reported for Fairfield County, CT; Hampshire County, MA.

5. *V. rafinesquiánum* J. A. Schultes (for its discoverer). Downy Arrow-wood. Rocky woods and slopes. May-June. Fig. 893, Map 2128. Endangered in NH. [*V. pubescens*]. Our plants are var. *rafinesquianum*.

V. plicátum. Thunb. Japanese Snowball. Will key to *V. rafinesquianum* or *V. dentatum* but inflorescence is a globose head with all the flowers sterile (inflorescence cymose and some or all flowers fertile in the latter two species). Reported for Norfolk County, MA. [*V. tomentosum*].

6. *V. dentátum* L. (toothed). Arrow-wood. Wooded swamps, shrub swamps. May-July. Map 2129. Our plants include var. *dentatum* [*V. semitomentosum*] and the following vars.:

var. *lúcidum* Ait. Petioles glabrous (stellate in the other vars.). [*V. recognitum*].

var. *venósum* (Brit.) Gl. Petioles stellate; stipules and glandular hairs none; differs from var. *dentatum* in having round leaves, often broader than long, thickly pubescent beneath (leaves ovate, thinly pubescent to glabrate beneath in var. *dentatum*). [*V. venosum*].

var. *deámii* (Rchd.) Fern. Petioles stellate; stipules and glandular hairs often present. —FAC to FACW-

7. *V. lantanoídes* Michx. (like *V. lantana*). Witch-hobble. Coniferous or deciduous woods. May-June. Map 2130. [*V. alnifolium*]. Fruit edible. —FAC

8. *V. lantána* L. (flexible). Wayfaring-tree. Occasionally escaped from cultivation to roadsides and waste places. May-June. Map 2131. (Introduced from Europe).

9. *V. prunifólium* L. (plum-leaved). Black Haw. Woods, thickets and roadsides. April-May. Map 2132. From farther south and west. [*V. bushii*]. Fruit edible; tea made from the bark was used by Indians to ease menstrual cramps. —FACU

10. *V. lentágo* L. (flexible). Nannyberry. Woods, thickets, fields, pond and stream borders, roadsides, waste places. May-June. Fig. 894, Map 2133. Fruit and bark used as in the preceding species. —FAC

11. *V. núdum* L. (naked). Possum Haw. Wooded swamps. May-July. Our plants include var. *nudum* (from farther south; reported for Fairfield and New Haven Counties, CT, Wading River, NY; fruit and bark used as in *V. prunifolium*) and the following var.:

var. *cassinoídes* (L.) Torr. & Gray (like *Ilex cassine*). Wild-raisin. Leaves not pilose beneath, the margins mostly not revolute; leaves subtending inflorescence widely cuneate (leaves often sparsely pilose beneath, especially near the margins, the margins mostly revolute; leaves subtending

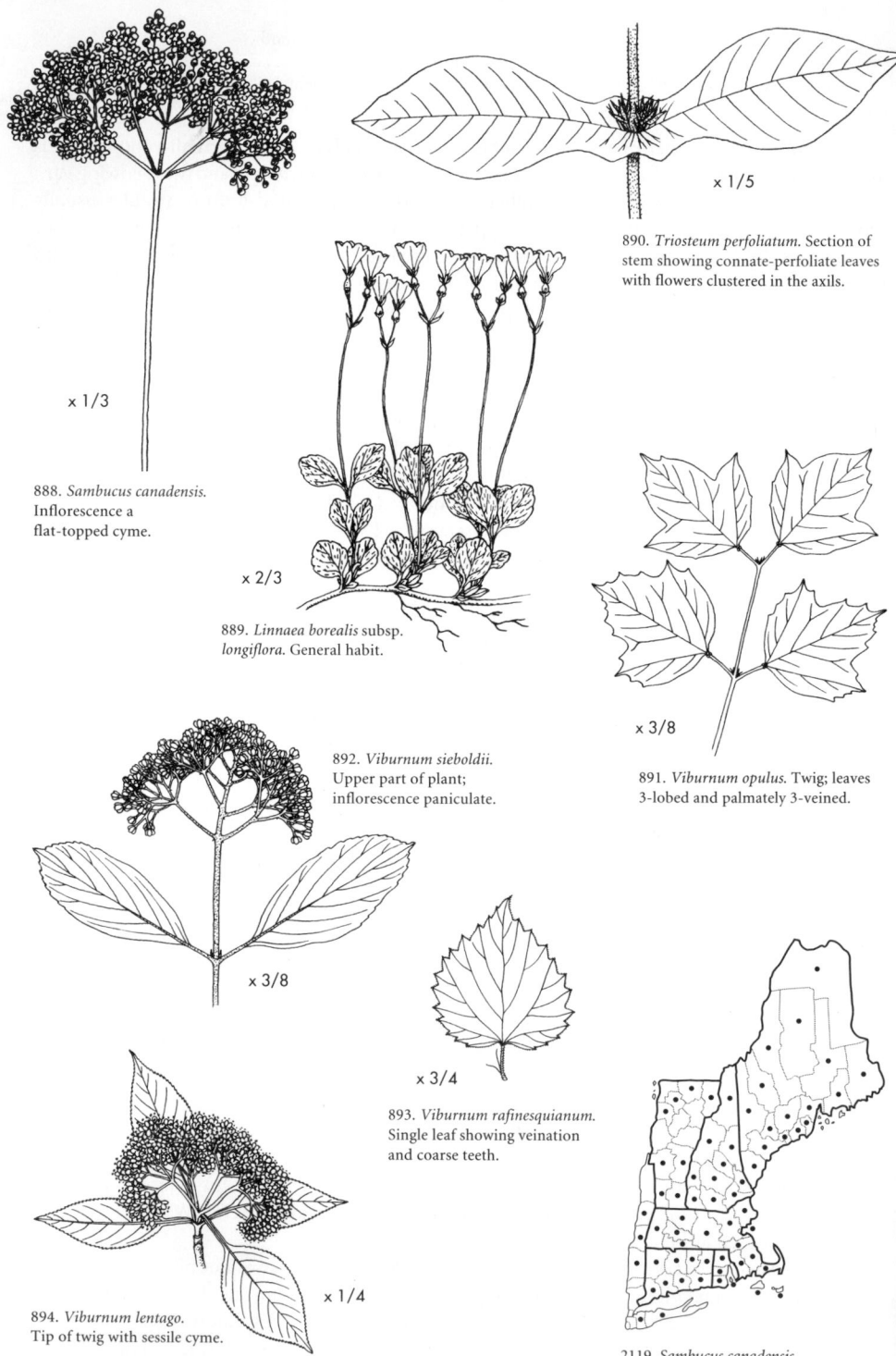

× 1/3

888. *Sambucus canadensis.*
Inflorescence a
flat-topped cyme.

× 1/5

890. *Triosteum perfoliatum.* Section of
stem showing connate-perfoliate leaves
with flowers clustered in the axils.

× 2/3

889. *Linnaea borealis* subsp.
longiflora. General habit.

892. *Viburnum sieboldii.*
Upper part of plant;
inflorescence paniculate.

× 3/8

891. *Viburnum opulus.* Twig; leaves
3-lobed and palmately 3-veined.

× 3/8

× 3/4

893. *Viburnum rafinesquianum.*
Single leaf showing veination
and coarse teeth.

× 1/4

894. *Viburnum lentago.*
Tip of twig with sessile cyme.

2119. *Sambucus canadensis*

2120. *Sambucus racemosa* subsp. *pubens* var. *leucocarpa*

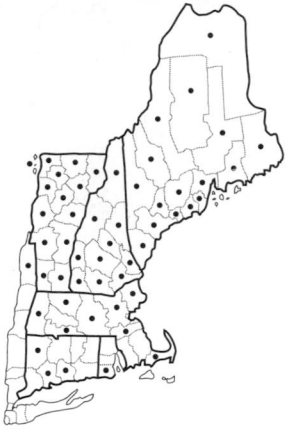

2121. *Linnaea borealis* subsp. *longiflora*

2122. *Triosteum angustifolium*

2123. *Triosteum perfoliatum*

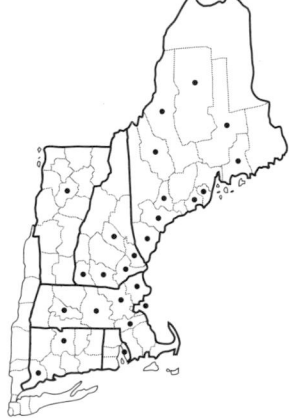

2124. *Viburnum opulus* var. *opulus*

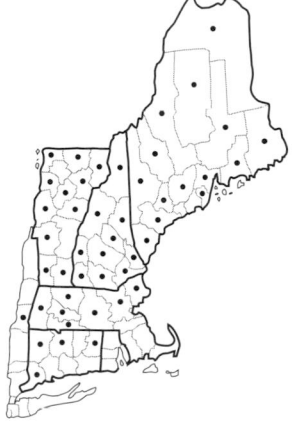

2125. *Viburnum opulus* var. *americanum*

2126. *Viburnum acerifolium*

2127. *Viburnum edule*

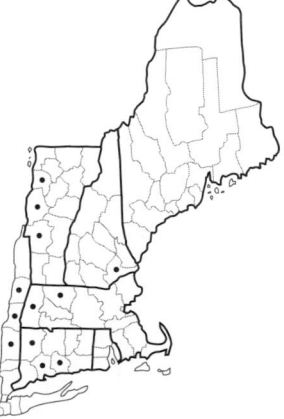

2128. *Viburnum rafinesquianum*

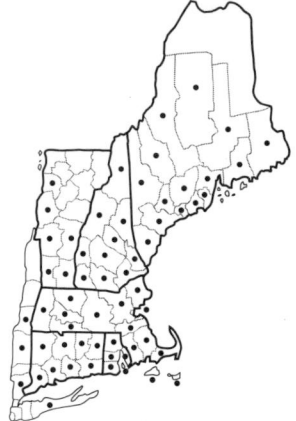

2129. *Viburnum dentatum*

2130. *Viburnum lantanoides*

2131. *Viburnum lantana*

2132. *Viburnum prunifolium*

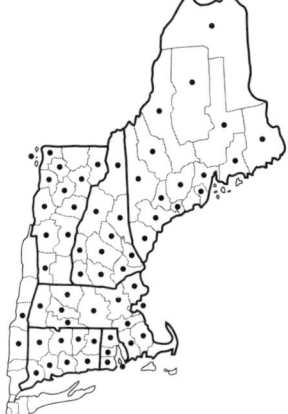

2133. *Viburnum lentago*

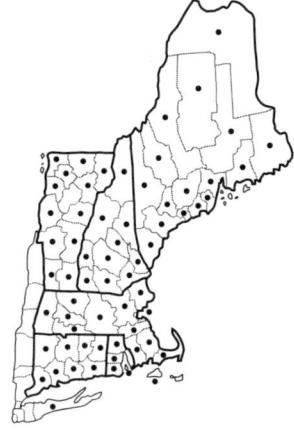

2134. *Viburnum nudum* var. *cassinoides*

2135. *Diervilla lonicera*

2136. *Symphoricarpos orbiculatus*

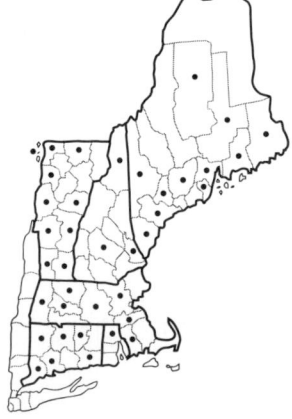

2137. *Symphoricarpos albus*

inflorescence narrowly cuneate in var. *nudum*). Wooded swamps, shrub swamps, wet woods, pond and stream margins. May-July. Map 2134. [*V. cassinoides*]. Fruit edible; leaves can be used to make tea. —FACW to OBL

5. Diervílla Mill. Bush Honeysuckle (for N. Diereville).

Shrubs, twigs glabrous, with 2 or sometimes 4 ridges decurrent from the nodes, moderate, pith moderate, white, buds solitary or superposed, oblong, appressed, with several pairs of scales, leaf scars crescent-shaped, connected by transverse lines, bundle traces 3, stipule scars lacking; leaves petioled, serrulate, lanceolate to ovate, acuminate, rounded at the base; flowers yellow, turning reddish, solitary or in few-flowered cymes terminating the stem and in the upper axils, calyx with 5 linear lobes, corolla tubular-funnelform, 5-lobed, slightly irregular, stamens 5, exsert, style exsert; fruit a narrowly oblong, long-beaked capsule with calyx lobes persistent at the tip.

Weígela Thunb. *floribúnda* (Sieb. & Zucc.) C. A. Mey. Resembling Diervilla but distinguishable in having flowers deep rose colored or white. Rarely escaped from cultivation. Reported for Fairfield County, CT; Essex County, MA. [*W. florida*].

1. D. lonícera Mill. (resembling Honeysuckle). Open woods, clearings, thickets. June-August. Map 2135. [*D. diervilla*].

6. Symphoricárpos Duham (from the Greek, referring to the clustered berries).

Small shrubs, often rhizomatous and colonial, bark on older growth often shreddy, twigs puberulent or glabrous, slender, hollow, or with a light tan pith, buds small, solitary or collaterally multiple, with several pairs of keeled scales, leaf scars raised, crescent-shaped, torn, somewhat connected by transverse ridges, bundle trace 1, stipule scars lacking; leaves short-petioled, ovate, entire to crenate, dentate or shallowly lobed; flowers small, white to pink, bracteate, in terminal and axillary clusters or dense or interrupted spikes, calyx 4-5-toothed, corolla campanulate, 4-5-lobed, regular or nearly so, stamens 4-5; fruit a rather large, white or red, globose or ovoid, berry-like drupe.

a. Corolla 3-4 mm long; fruit red; pith continuous. .... 1. *S. orbiculatus*
a. Corolla 5 mm or more long; fruit white; pith excavated.
    Style 3 mm or less long, glabrous; stamens and style included; twigs usually
        glabrous .... 2. *S. albus*
    Style 4 mm or more long, usually pilose near the middle; stamens and style
        slightly exserted; twigs usually puberulent. .... 3. *S. occidentalis*

1. S. orbiculátus Moench. (round). Coralberry. Thickets, open woods, roadsides, waste places. July-August. Map 2136. [*S. symphoricarpos*].

2. S. álbus (L.) Blake (white). Snowberry. Roadsides, waste places, cliffs and slopes. May-July. Map 2137. Endangered in MA. Our plants include var. *albus* and the following var.:

var. *laevigátus* (Fern.) Blake. Inconsistently separable from var. *albus* in having leaves glabrous beneath, fruits 1.2 cm or more in diameter (leaves usually pubescent beneath and fruits usually less than 1.2 cm in diameter in var. *albus*). [*S. racemosus*]. —FACU-

3. S. occidentális Hook. (western). Wolfberry. Roadsides, waste places. June-August. From farther west. Reported for Suffolk County, MA.

7. Lonícera L. Honeysuckle (for A. Lonitzer).

Shrubs or woody vines, twigs slender to moderate, pith moderate, white or brown, sometimes excavated, buds solitary or superposed, with several-many ranked scales, leaf scars small and raised, crescent-shaped, somewhat connected by transverse lines, bundle traces 3, stipule scars lacking; leaves petioled or sessile, sometimes connate, mostly entire; flowers paired in the leaf axils, their ovaries sometimes united, or in one-several 6-flowered whorles in the upper axils or terminal, forming interrupted spikes or dense heads, calyx minutely 5-toothed, corolla tubular or funnelform, often gibbous at the base, 5-lobed, 2-lipped to essentially regular, stamens 5; fruit a several-seeded red, blue, black or rarely yellowish berry. —Wildl. 1

Kolkwitzia Graebn. *amábilis* Graebn. Will key to *Lonicera* but differs in having a campanulate corolla, 4 stamens and fruit an achene. Rarely spread from cultivation. Reported for MA.

a. Plant a climbing, twining or trailing vine; uppermost leaves below the flowers
　　connate (except in *L. japonica* and *L. periclymenum*); flowers sessile in
　　6-flowered whorles in the upper axils or terminal, forming interrupted
　　spikes or dense heads (paired on axillary peduncles in *L. japonica*).
　　b. None of the leaves connate.
　　　　Flowers in pairs terminating axillary peduncles. .... 1. *L. japonica*
　　　　Flowers sessile, in several 6-flowered whorles forming a dense, terminal spike
　　　　　　or head .... 2. *L. periclymenum*
　　b. Uppermost leaves below the flowers connate. (Fig. 895).
　　　　c. Twigs glandular-pubescent; upper leaf surface strigose-pubescent; leaves green
　　　　　　both sides .... 3. *L. hirsuta*
　　　　c. Twigs and upper leaf surfaces glabrous or nearly so; leaves glaucous on one
　　　　　　or both sides.
　　　　　　d. Disc of uppermost connate leaves orbicular or suborbicular, glaucous
　　　　　　　　above. .... 4. *L. reticulata*
　　　　　　d. Disc of uppermost connate leaves elliptic or oval, green above.
　　　　　　　　Leaves of flowering twigs sessile or subsessile; corolla distinctly bilabiate;
　　　　　　　　　　fruiting spike dense, with crowded whorles. .... 5. *L. dioica*
　　　　　　　　Leaves of flowering twigs mostly petioled; corolla nearly regular; fruiting
　　　　　　　　　　spike usually interrupted .... 6. *L. sempervirens*
a. Plant an erect or spreading shrub; no leaves connate; flowers paired on solitary
　　axillary peduncles. (Fig. 896).
　　e. Pith of twigs brownish, usually excavated between the nodes.
　　　　f. Twigs, buds, petioles, undersides of leaves and peduncles glabrous or
　　　　　　essentially so .... 7. *L. tatarica*
　　　　f. Twigs and/or 1 or more of the above structures pubescent.
　　　　　　g. Leaves abruptly acuminate .... 8. *L. maackii*
　　　　　　g. Leaves acute.
　　　　　　　　Sepals glandular-ciliate and/or ovary glandular; corolla strongly bilabiate;
　　　　　　　　　　buds fusiform .... 9. *L. xylosteum*
　　　　　　　　Sepals and ovary not glandular; corolla nearly regular, almost evenly
　　　　　　　　　　deeply lobed; buds short-conical to ovoid .... 10. *L. morrowii*
　　e. Pith of twigs white, continuous between the nodes.
　　　　h. Ovaries or fruits separate or united only at base, divergent; bracts more than
　　　　　　1 mm long; corolla nearly regular. .... 11. *L. canadensis*
　　　　h. Ovaries or fruits united half or more their length, or bracts less than 1 mm
　　　　　　long or obsolete and corolla strongly bilabiate.
　　　　　　i. Ovaries or fruits united to apex; corolla nearly regular; peduncles shorter
　　　　　　　　than flowers; fruit red .... 12. *L. villosa*
　　　　　　i. Ovaries or fruits, at least toward apex, usually free; corolla strongly
　　　　　　　　bilabiate; peduncles longer than flowers or if equalling or shorter
　　　　　　　　leaves acuminate (obtuse in *L. villosa*); fruit blue.
　　　　　　　　Leaves acuminate; peduncles equalling or shorter than flowers. .... 13. *L. standishii*
　　　　　　　　Leaves obtuse or acute; peduncles longer than flowers. .... 14. *L. oblongifolia*

1. *L. japónica* Thunb. (Japanese). Japanese Honeysuckle. Woods and woodland borders, thickets, waste places. May-August. Map 2138. (Naturalized from Asia). [*Nintooa j.*]. —FAC-

2. *L. periclýmenum* L. (old generic name). Woodbine. Occasionally escaped from cultivation to thickets and roadsides. July-August. Map 2139. (Introduced from Europe).

3. *L. hirsúta* Eat. (stiffly hairy). Hairy Honeysuckle. Ledges, bluffs, woodlands and thickets in calcareous soil. May-July. Map 2140. —FAC

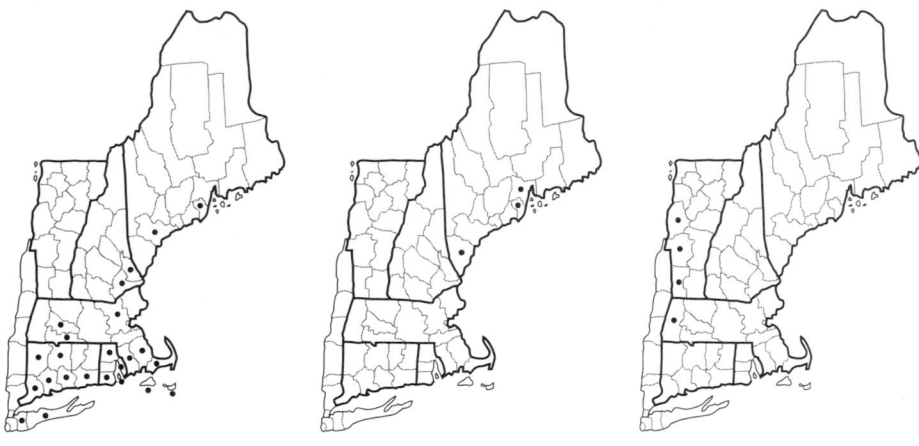

2138. *Lonicera japonica*   2139. *Lonicera periclymenum*   2140. *Lonicera hirsuta*

4. L. reticuláta Raf. Wild Honeysuckle. Occasionally escaped from cultivation to woods and thickets. May-June. Fig. 895. Reported for Hampshire County, MA. [*L. prolifera*].

5. L. dioíca L. (dioecious). Open woods and thickets. May-June. Map 2141. Endangered in ME. Our plants are var. *dioica*. —FACU

6. L. sempérvirens L. (evergreen). Trumpet Honeysuckle. Woods and thickets. May-September. Map 2142. Endangered in ME. Our plants are var. *sempervirens*. —FACU

7. L. tatárica L. (Tartarian). Tartarian Honeysuckle. Woodlands, thickets, river shores, waste places. May-June. Map 2143. (Introduced from Eurasia). [*Xylosteum tatarícum*]. —FACU

8. L. máackii (Rupr.) Maxim. Woodlands, waste places. From Asia. Reported for Bristol and Hampshire Counties, MA.

9. L. xylósteum L. (bonewood). European Fly Honeysuckle. Occasionally escaped from cultivation to woods and thickets. May-June. Map 2144. (Introduced from Eurasia).

10. L. mórrowii Gray (for its discoverer). Occasionally escaped from cultivation to woods, thickets, fields, roadsides, and waste places. May-June. Map 2145. (Introduced from Eurasia).

L. x bélla Zabel. A hybrid between *L. morrowii* and *L. tatarica*. Map 2146. (Introduced from Asia). —FACU-

11. L. canadénsis Bartr. (Canadian). Fly Honeysuckle. Woodlands. April-June. Fig. 896. Map 2147. [*Xylosteum canadense; X. ciliatum*]. —FACU

12. L. villósa (Michx.) R. & S. (soft-hairy). Mountain Fly Honeysuckle. Wooded swamps, wet woods, wet meadows, bogs, sometimes subalpine. May-July. Map 2148. Our plants include var. *villosa* [*L. caerulea* var. *v.*] and several intergrading vars.:

var. *villósa* has densely villous to subtomentose twigs and leaves, ciliate calyx and pubescent corolla; the following vars. have an eciliate calyx and glabrous corolla, and variable twig and leaf pubescence characters.

var. *calvéscens* (Fern. & Wieg.) Fern. Twigs puberulent.

var. *solónis* (Eat.) Fern. Twigs both puberulent and hirsute.

var. *tónsa* Fern. Twigs glabrous to sparsely hirsute.

var. *fúlleri* Fern. Twigs glabrous; corolla tube not gibbous at base (strongly gibbous on 1 side in the other vars.). —FACW+

13. L. standíshii Jacques (for J.S. Standish). Occasionally escaped from cultivation to thickets. April. Reported for Suffolk County NY. (Introduced from Asia).

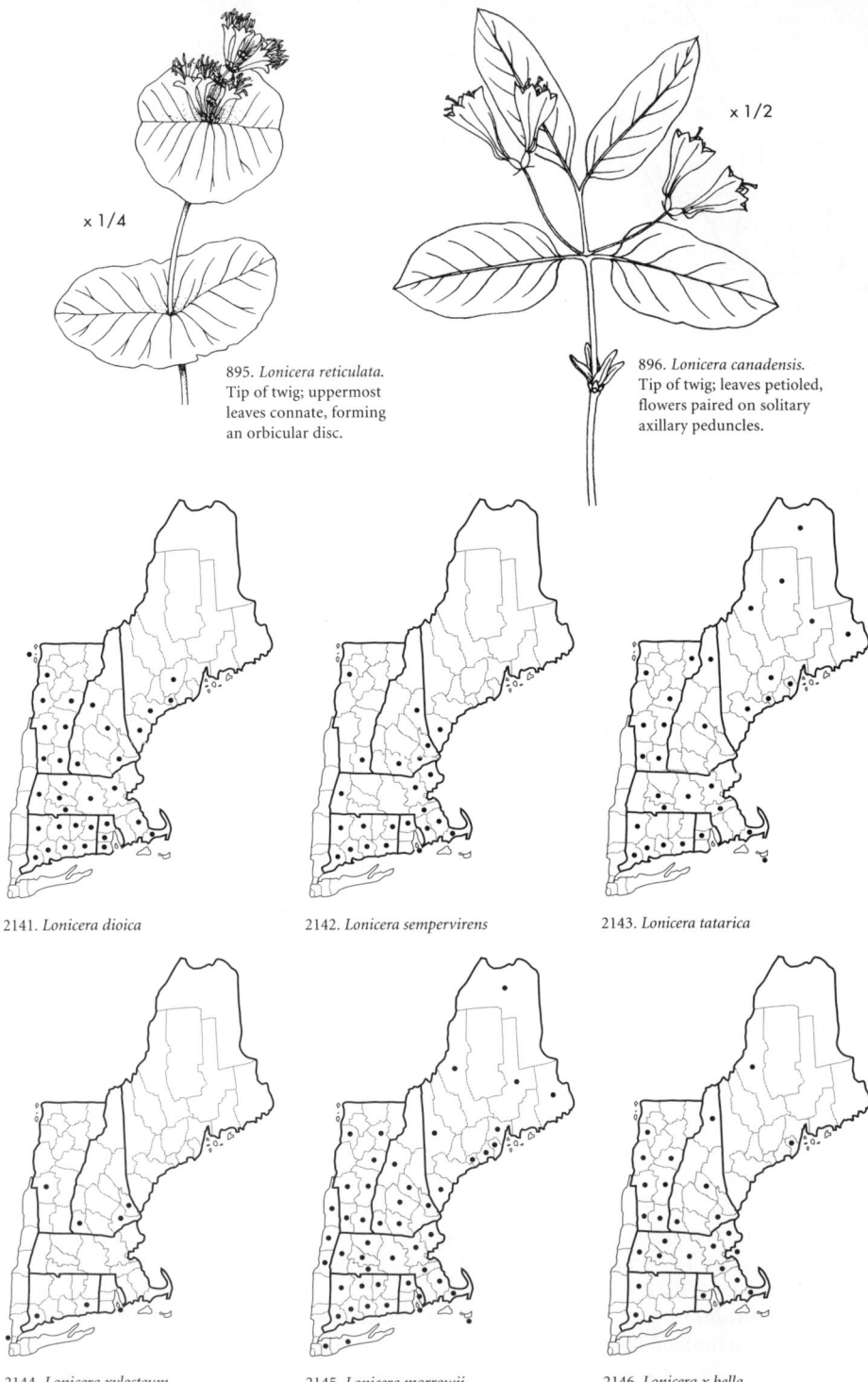

x 1/4

895. *Lonicera reticulata.*
Tip of twig; uppermost
leaves connate, forming
an orbicular disc.

x 1/2

896. *Lonicera canadensis.*
Tip of twig; leaves petioled,
flowers paired on solitary
axillary peduncles.

2141. *Lonicera dioica*

2142. *Lonicera sempervirens*

2143. *Lonicera tatarica*

2144. *Lonicera xylosteum*

2145. *Lonicera morrowii*

2146. *Lonicera x bella*

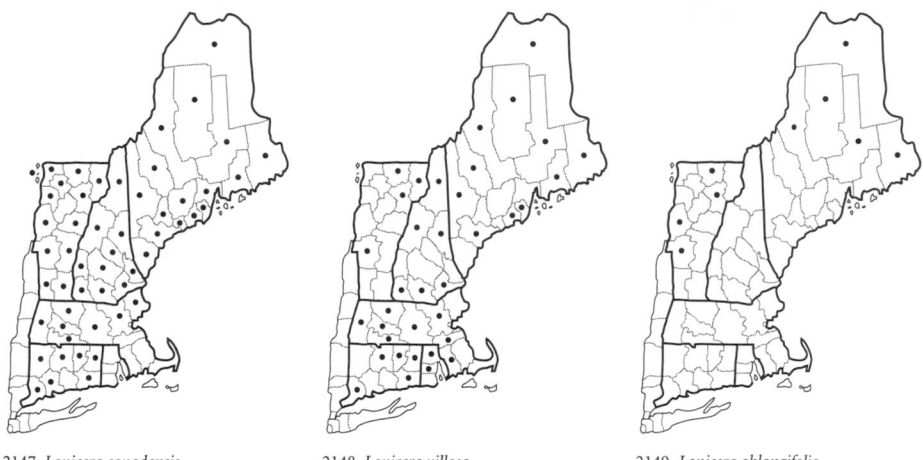

2147. *Lonicera canadensis*   2148. *Lonicera villosa*   2149. *Lonicera oblongifolia*

14. L. oblongifólia (Goldie). Hook. (oblong-leaved). Swamp Fly Honeysuckle. Wooded swamps and bogs. May-June. Map 2149. [*Xylosteon oblongifolium*]. Our plants include var. *oblongifolia* and the following var.:

var. *altíssima* (Jennings) Rehd. Branchlets and undersides of leaves glabrous or essentially so (Minutely pubescent in var. *oblongifolia*). —OBL

Family 186. Valerianáceae (Valerian Family)

Hermaphrodite or polygamo-dioecious, annual or perennial herbs. Leaves basal and opposite, sessile or petioled, entire, dentate or pinnately divided, estipulate. Flowers perfect or imperfect, small, pink or white, regular or slightly irregular, bracteate, in terminal panicled or variously clustered cymes, calyx lobes minute or obsolete or spreading in fruit and modified into few-many pappus-like, plumose segments, corolla tubular or funnelform, sometimes gibbous at the base, 5-lobed, lobes equal or subequal, stamens 3, inserted on the corolla tube, ovary inferior, 1-3-locular, style 1. Fruit indehiscent, 1-seeded.

Stem leaves pinnately divided .... 1. *Valeriana*
Stem leaves entire or toothed at the base. .... 2. *Valerianella*

1. Valeriána L. Valerian (Medieval name, said to be in honor of a Roman emperor). Tall, coarse, perennial herbs; leaves petioled, the basal entire to pinnately divided, the cauline pinnately divided, the segments entire or dentate; flowers perfect or imperfect, in paniculate or corymbose cymes, calyx lobes inconspicuous in flower, but spreading in fruit and modified into few-many pappus-like, plumose segments, corolla sometimes gibbous at the base, the lobes equal or subequal; fruit 1-locular.

Basal leaves evenly pinnately divided like the cauline. .... 1. *V. officinalis*
Basal leaves simple, entire to coarsely toothed or irregularly and shallowly lobed,
    only the cauline pinnately divided. (Fig. 897). .... 2. *V. uliginosa*

1. V. officinális L. (of the shops). Garden heliotrope. Occasionally escaped from cultivation to roadsides, thickets and around dwellings. June-July. Map 2150. (Naturalized from Europe). A preparation made from the root is used as a sedative to treat nervousness, insomnia and hysteria.

2. V. uliginósa (Torr. & Gray) Rydb. (growing in marshes). Calcareous bogs and swamps often with *Thuja*. June-July. Fig. 897, Map 2151. Endangered in VT, NH. From farther north and west. [*V. sitchensis* subsp. *uliginosa; V. septentrionalis* var. *u.*]. —OBL

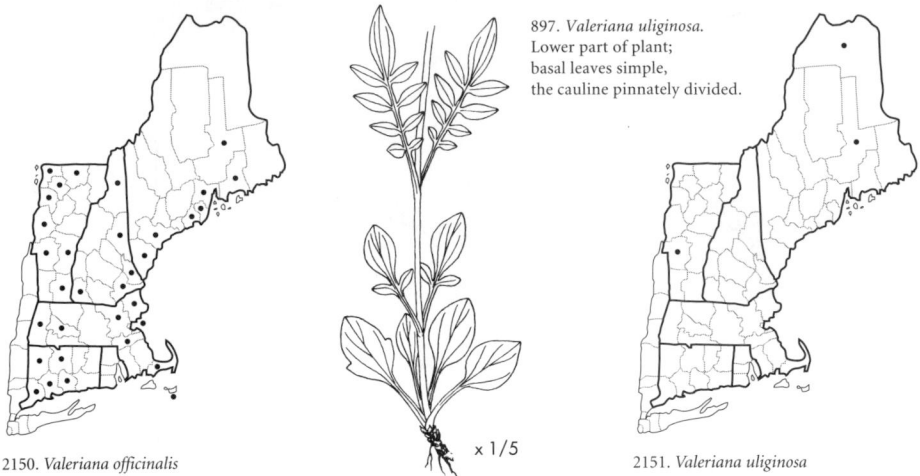

897. *Valeriana uliginosa.*
Lower part of plant;
basal leaves simple,
the cauline pinnately divided.

x 1/5

2150. *Valeriana officinalis*

2151. *Valeriana uliginosa*

2. Valerianélla P. Mill. Corn-salad (diminutive of *Valeriana*).

Dichotomously branched, annual herbs; leaves simple, the basal petioled, the cauline sessile, sometimes connate, entire or toothed at the base, spatulate to oblong or lanceolate; flowers perfect, in small, compact terminal cymes often aggregated into a loosely corymbose or paniculate inflorescence, calyx lobes minute or obsolete, corolla lobes subequal; fruit 3-locular, only 1 locule seed-bearing.

1. **V. radiáta** (L.) Dufr. Fields, roadsides, waste places. May-June. From farther south and west. Reported for CT. —FAC

V. umbilácata (Sulliv.) Wood. Differing from *V. radiata* in having the fertile locule much narrower than the 2 sterile ones (fertile locule and the 2 sterile ones subequal in *V. radiata*). From farther south. Reported for CT, Hampden County MA, Rensselaer County, NY. [*V. patellaria; V. radiata* var. *intermedia; V. intermedia*]. —FAC

V. locústa (L.) Betcke. Differing from *V. radiata* and *V. umbilacata* in having the fertile locule of the fruit with a thickened corky back (fertile locule without a thickened corky back in the latter 2 species. (Introduced from Europe). Reported for Fairfield County, CT; Penoboscot County, ME; Manhattan, NY. [*V. olitoria*].

Family 187. Dipsacáceae (Teasel Family)

Hermaphrodite, annual, biennial or perennial, sometimes prickly herbs. Leaves opposite or whorled, entire to toothed or pinnatifid, sessile or petioled, estipulate. Flowers perfect, irregular, white, pink or blue, borne on a subglobose or cylindric receptacle subtended by involucral bracts forming dense, terminal heads, the receptacle often with chaffy bracts, each flower enveloped by a toothed or subentire epicalyx of bracteoles, true calyx cup-shaped and unlobed, or with 4-many teeth or bristles, corolla 4-5-lobed, often bilabiate, stamens usually 4, inserted on the corolla tube, ovary inferior, 1-locular, style 1. Fruit an achene enclosed within the epicalyx and often crowned by the persistent calyx.

a. Stems, and usually the leaves and involucre, prickly .... 1. *Dipsacus*
a. Stems, leaves and involucre not prickly.
    b. Upper part of peduncles with long, widely-spreading hairs; receptacle without
        bracts but densely pubescent .... 2. *Knautia arvensis*

b. Upper part of peduncle with short-appressed, loosely ascending or reflexed
hairs; receptacle with chaffy bracts.
  c. Leaves all simple.
      Epicalyx densely pubescent, 4-angled; true calyx 4-5-awned. .... 3. *Succisa pratensis*
      Epicalyx glabrous or essentially so, 8-ribbed; true calyx with 4-5 short
          lobes, not awned .... 4. *Succisella inflexa*
  c. Some leaves pinnately divided .... 5. *Scabiosa*

1. Dípsacus L. Teasel (Greek name for teasel).

Tall, biennial or perennial herbs with prickly stems; leaves large, opposite, sessile or connate,
sometimes prickly, entire, lobed, toothed or pinnatifid; heads ovoid to ellipsoid, involucral bracts
numerous, linear, spreading or ascending, chaffy bracts of the receptacle with awns surpassing the
flowers, epicalyx ribbed, truncate or 4-toothed, true calyx short, cup-shaped, densely pubescent,
shallowly 4-lobed, corolla 4-lobed, stamens 4.

Leaves, at least the lower, pinnatifid or bipinnatifid; longest involucral bracts usually
    shorter than to equalling head. .... 1. *D. laciniatus*
Leaves entire to merely toothed or shallowly lobed; longest involucral bracts usually
    conspicuously longer than head. .... 2. *D. fullonum*

  1. *D. laciniátus* L. (slashed). Waste places. July-September. (Introduced from Europe). Reported
for Hampshire and Middlesex Counties, Ma.
  2. *D. fullónum* L. Roadsides and waste places. July-September. Map 2152. (Naturalized from
Europe). [*D. sylvestris*]. A preparation made from the plant is used in treating skin diseases; mature
heads of this and the preceding species were used to card wool.

2. Knaútia L. (for C. Knaut).

Pubescent, perennial herbs; leaves opposite, the lowest usually lobed or coarsely toothed, sometimes
pinnatifid, petioled, the upper pinnatifid and sessile; heads depressed-hemispheric, involucral
bracts lanceolate, shorter than to equalling head, receptacle without bracts but densely pubescent,
epicalyx strongly compressed, long-hairy, ribbed, minutely 2-toothed at summit, true calyx
pubescent, with 8 or more awns, corolla 4-lobed, the marginal ones larger, stamens 4. [*Scabiosa*].

  1. *K. arvénsis* (L.) Coult. (of cultivated ground). Bluebuttons. Cultivated ground, fields, roadsides, waste places. June-September. Map 2153. (Naturalized from Europe). [*Scabiosa a.*].

3. Succísa Haller (name based on the rootstock appearing as if bitten off).

Slender, annual or biennial herbs; leaves basal and opposite, petioled or the upper sessile, entire,
undulate or toothed, oblanceolate to narrowly lanceolate; heads hemispheric, involucral bracts
narrowly lanceolate, shorter than to equalling head, chaffy bracts of the receptacle equalling or
shorter than the flowers, epicalyx 4-angled, densely pubescent, 4-lobed at summit, true calyx 4-5-
awned, corolla blue, 4-5-lobed, stamens 4. [*Scabiosa*].

  1. *S. praténsis* Moench. Fields and waste places. August-September. (Adventive from Europe).
Reported for MA, RI. [*Scabiosa succisa*]. A compress of the fresh chopped leaves has been used in
treating eczema and other skin complaints.

4. Succisélla G. Beck (diminutive of Succisa).

Similar to *Succisa* but with epicalyx glabrous or essentially so, 8-ribbed, true calyx with 4-5 short
lobes, not awned. [*Scabiosa*].

  1. *S. infléxa* (Kluk) G. Beck. Fields, often wet, and waste places. July-September. Map 2154.
(Naturalized from Europe). [*Scabiosa australis; Succisa a.; S. inflexa*].

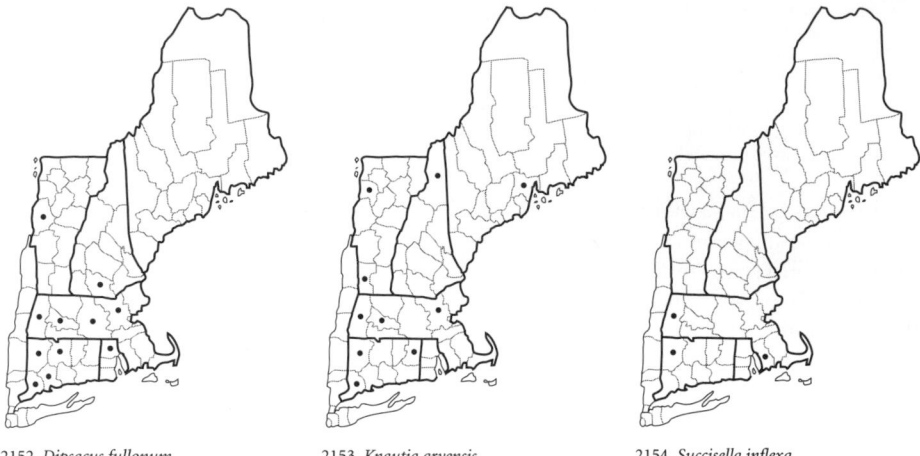

2152. *Dipsacus fullonum*   2153. *Knautia arvensis*   2154. *Succisella inflexa*

5. *Scabiósa* L.

Similar to *Succisa* but differing in having some of the leaves pinnately divided; flowers rose white or purple.

    1. *S. atropurpúrea* L. (Europe). Rarely adventive in our range. Reported for ME, Suffolk County, MA.

    S. ochroléuca L. Resembling *S. atropurpurea* but distinguishable in being perennial and by pubescent stems and limb of epicalyx erect and cup-like (plant annual, stems glabrous or nearly so and limb of epicalyx crenate and inflexed in *S. atropurpurea*). (Europe). Rarely adventive in our range. Reported for Berkshire County, MA.

    S. columbária L. Limb of epicalyx erect and cup like as in *S. ochroleuca* but flowers purplish (flowers yellowish-white in *S. ochroleuca*). (Europe). Rarely escaped from cultivation. Reported for MA.

Family 188. Cucurbitáceae (Gourd Family)

Monoecious or dioecious, herbaceous, annual or perennial vines, trailing or climbing by tendrils, these spirally coiled, simple or branched. Leaves simple, alternate, usually palmately lobed (occasionally unlobed or pinnately lobed or dissected), petioled, estipulate. Flowers imperfect, regular, white, greenish or yellow, axillary, solitary or in clusters, racemes or panicles, the pistillate and staminate in the same or different axils (in monoecious plants), calyx and corolla 5-6-lobed, the latter rotate or campanulate, stamens 3 or 5, distinct or often united, ovary inferior, 1-3-locular, style 1. Fruit fleshy with a soft or firm rind, usually indehiscent (pepo) or membranous and dehiscent, or dry and indehiscent, 1-many-seeded.

a. Leaves unlobed except for cordate base, not angled; stamens free. .... 1. *Thladiantha dubia*
a. Leaves lobed (often shallowly) or angled; stamens united, at least in part.
    b. Ovary and fruit prickly; staminate flowers in racemes or panicles several cm
        long (including peduncles). (Fig. 898).
        Fruit less than 2 cm long, indehiscent, 1-seeded, corolla 5-lobed. .... 2. *Sicyos angulatus*
        Fruit 3 cm or more long, dehiscent, 2 or more-seeded; corolla 6-lobed. .... 3. *Echinocystis lobata*
    b. Ovary and fruit smooth or pubescent, not prickly (except in the cultivated
        cucumbers); staminate flowers solitary in the leaf axils, fascicled, or in
        racemes 1 cm or less long.

c. Leaves deeply pinnately lobed or dissected. .... 4. *Citrullus lanatus*
c. Leaves shallowly to deeply palmately lobed or angled.
   Tendrils simple; corolla less than 4 cm long. .... 5. *Cucumis*
   Tendrils forked; corolla more than 4 cm long. .... 6. *Cucurbita*

1. Thladiántha Bunge (name based on an earlier impression that the flowers are sterile).
Dioecious, climbing, perennial vines; leaves ovate, cordate at base, otherwise unlobed, acuminate, finely toothed, scabrous-pubescent, tendrils simple or sometimes forked; flowers yellow, peduncled, solitary or in small clusters, calyx and corolla deeply 5-lobed, lobes reflexed, corolla campanulate, stamens free, style short, stigmas 3; fruit ellipsoid, strongly ribbed and cross-ribbed, pubescent.

   1. T. dúbia Bunge (doubtful). Occasionally escaped from cultivation to roadsides and waste places. June-July. (Introduced from Asia). Reported for NH, Worcester County, MA.

2. Sícyos L. Bur-cucumber (Greek name for cucumber).
Monoecious, climbing, annual vines; leaves suborbicular, 3-5-angled or lobed, the lobes acute, base deeply cordate, margins denticulate, tendrils branched; flowers whitish, the staminate and pistillate mostly in the same axils, the former racemose or paniculate, the latter in compact cymes, shorter peduncled than the staminate inflorescence, calyx 5-toothed, corolla rotate, 5-lobed, stamens united, ovary 1-locular, stigmas 3; fruits in clusters, indehiscent, not fleshy, covered by prickly bristles, 1-seeded.

   1. S. angulátus L. (angular). Along rivers, thickets, waste places. July-September. Fig. 898, Map 2155. —FACU

3. Echinocýstis Torr. & Gray. Wild Cucumber (from the Greek, based on the inflated, prickly fruit).
Monoecious, climbing, annual vines; leaves orbicular, 3-7 (usually 5) angled or lobed, the lobes acute, aristate, base deeply cordate, margins denticulate to serrulate, tendrils branched; flowers whitish, the staminate and pistillate mostly in the same axils, the former in long, narrow racemes or panicles, the latter solitary or in small clusters, much shorter peduncled than the staminate inflorescence, calyx 6-lobed, corolla rotate, deeply 6-lobed, stamens united, ovary 2-locular, stigma broad and lobed; fruit ovoid, fleshy, becoming dry, bladdery-inflated and fibrous-netted within, covered with soft prickles, dehiscent by 2 pores at apex, 4-seeded.

   1. E. lobáta (Michx.) Torr. & Gray (lobed). Riverbanks, thickets, fields, woodland edges, waste places. July-September. Map 2156. [*Micrampelis l.*].

4. Citrúllus Schrad. Ex. Ecklon & Zeyh. *lanátus* (Thunb.) Matsumura & Nakai var. *lanátus* (watermelon) Map 2157.
   C. colocynthis has also been reported for MA.

5. Cúcumis L. *satívus* L. (cucumber). Reported for MA; *C. mélo* L. (muskmelon) Map 2158.
   C. angúria (bur gherkin). Similar to cucumber but with deeply lobed leaves (leaves shallowly lobed or toothed in cucumber). Reported for MA.
   Momórdica L. *charántia* L. (balsam pear). Peduncles conspicuously bracted; fruit oblong, yellow or orange, seed scarlet. Reported for CT.

6. Cucúrbita L. *máxima* Duchesne (squash) Map 2159; *C. pépo* L. (pumpkin) Map 2160.
   Lagenária Seringe *sicerária* (*Molina*) Standl. (gourd). Reported for MA. The above cultivated plants frequently occur in dumps, waste places and along sea beaches.

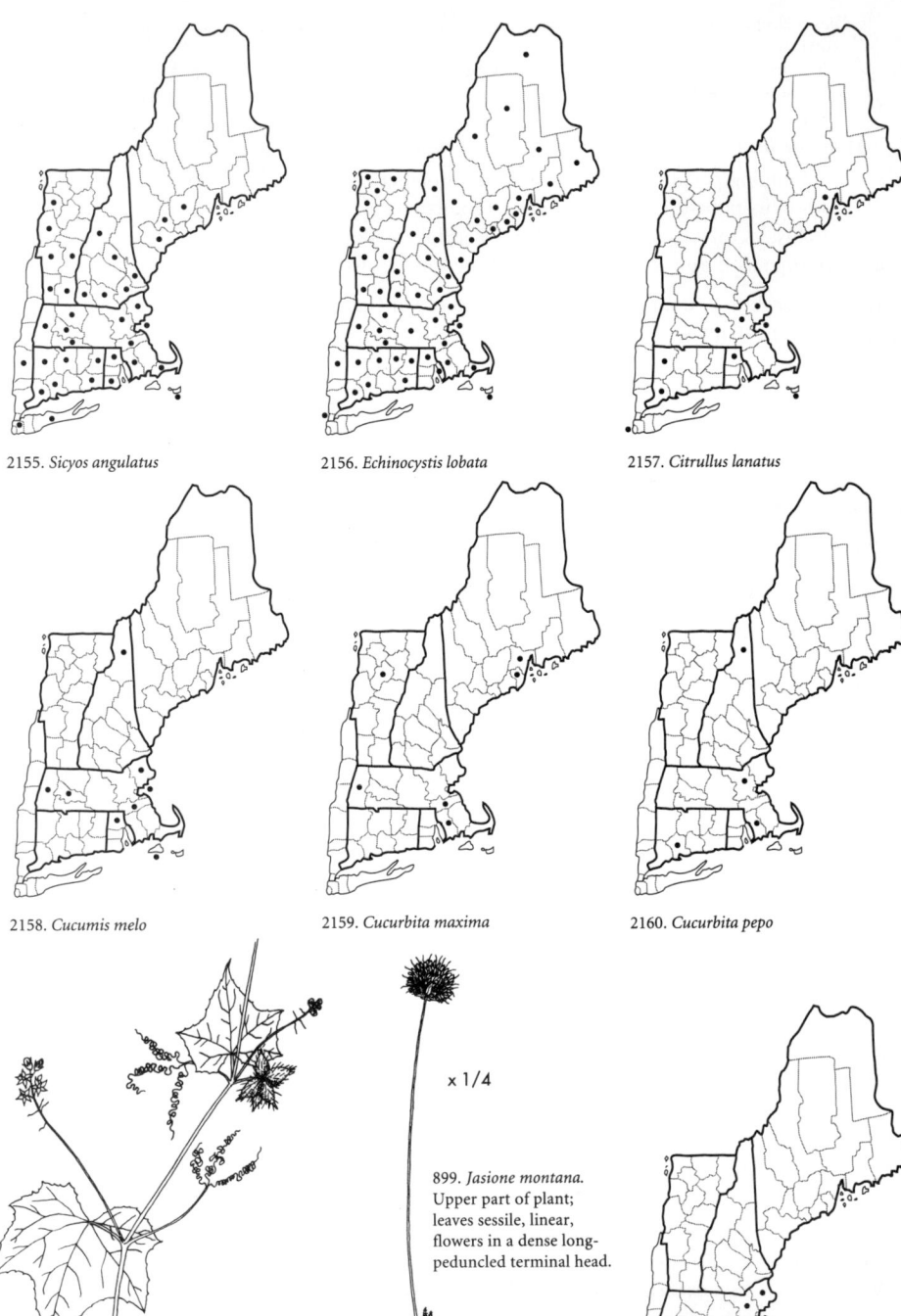

2155. *Sicyos angulatus*

2156. *Echinocystis lobata*

2157. *Citrullus lanatus*

2158. *Cucumis melo*

2159. *Cucurbita maxima*

2160. *Cucurbita pepo*

× 3/8

898. *Sicyos angulatus*. Section of stem; lobed leaves, staminate racemes, cluster of prickly fruits.

× 1/4

899. *Jasione montana*. Upper part of plant; leaves sessile, linear, flowers in a dense long-peduncled terminal head.

2161. *Jasione montana*

Family 189. Campanuláceae (Bluebell Family)

Hermaphrodite, annual or perennial herbs, often with milky sap. Leaves simple, basal or alternate, sessile or petioled, estipulate. Flowers perfect, solitary in the leaf axils, or in axillary and/or terminal involucrate heads, bracteate cymes, racemes or panicles, calyx of 5 equal or unequal sepals, corolla 5-lobed, regular and campanulate, rotate or tubular, or bilabiate and split down 1 side, stamens 5, free from the corolla, distinct or united, sometimes in a tube around the style, ovary inferior or half-inferior, 2-5-locular, style 1. Fruit a capsule opening by pores or terminal valves.

a. Flowers and fruits in dense, long-peduncled, terminal heads; leaves sessile, linear,
    less than 5 mm wide; calyx lobes less than 4 mm long. (Fig. 899). .... 1. *Jasione montana*
a. Flowers and fruits in racemes, panicles, small clusters or solitary, or if in heads
    (some *Campanula*) leaves, at least the lower, petioled, lanceolate or
    lance-ovate, more than 5 mm wide; calyx lobes more than 4 mm long.
    b. Ovary 3 or more times as long as broad or flowers in the axils of ovate,
        cordate-clasping leaves; corolla rotate.
        Flowers sessile in the axils of cordate-clasping, ovate leaves; ovary oblong to
            obovoid. (Fig. 900) .... 2. *Triodanis*
                                                                    perfoliata
        Flowers in 2s or 3s terminating the stem and branches; leaves narrowly
            ovate to lanceolate, not cordate-clasping; ovary linear-cylindric. .... 3. *Legousia*
                                                          speculum-veneris
    b. Ovary 2 or less times as long as broad; flowers not in the axils of ovate,
        cordate-clasping leaves; corolla funnelform, campanulate, or bilabiate.
        Corolla regular; capsule 3-locular, opening by lateral pores. .... 4. *Campanula*
        Corolla bilabiate; capsule 2-locular, opening by apical pores. .... 5. *Lobelia*

1. Jasióne L. Sheep's bit (ancient Greek name, based on reputed medicinal value). Annual herbs, stems few to many from a central crown and tap root, simple or branched; leaves numerous, basal and alternate, sessile, linear to lanceolate, entire, pubescent; flowers blue, in dense, long-peduncled, terminal heads subtended by a leafy-bracted involucre, the bracts coarsely few-toothed, corolla at first tubular, soon splitting into linear lobes, regular, anthers united at base into a ring around the style, filaments free, ovary 2-locular.

    1. J. montána L. (of mountains). Fields, roadsides, waste places. June-September. Fig. 899, Map 2161. (Naturalized from Europe).

2. Triodánis Raf. ex Greene.
Annual herbs, simple to sparingly branched near base; leaves numerous, cordate-clasping, ovate, crenate to serrate; flowers sessile or subsessile, usually with 2 subtending bracts, solitary or several in axils of the upper, middle and often lower leaves, also terminal, the lowest flowers cleistogamous, with 3-4 calyx lobes, the corolla reduced or absent, the upper flowers blue to purple, calyx 5-lobed, corolla regular, rotate, 5-lobed, stamens free, ovary 3-locular; capsule oblong, opening by lateral pores. [*Specularia*].

    1. T. perfoliáta (L.) Nieuwl. (with leaf surrounding stem). Woodlands, thickets, waste places. May-August. Fig. 900, Map 2162. (Tropical Amer.). [*Specularia p.*]. Our plants are var. *perfoliata*. —FAC

3. Legoúsia Durande.
Annual herbs, branched to summit; leaves clasping or merely sessile, narrowly ovate to lanceolate, entire to crenate; flowers all normal, none cleistogamous, in 2s or 3s terminating the stem and branches, short-pedicelled, ovary linear-cylindric, otherwise as in *Triodanis*. [*Specularia*].

    1. L. spéculum-véneris (L.) Fisch. ex A. DC. (mirror of Venus). Rarely found in waste places. (Adventive from Europe). [*Specularia s.*].

4. *Campánula* L. Bellflower (from the Latin, based on shape of the corolla).

Annual or perennial herbs; leaves basal and/or alternate; flowers blue or purple to white, solitary, in small clusters, racemose, paniculate or glomerulate, terminal and/or axillary, sepals 5, corolla regular, funnelform or campanulate, 5-lobed, stamens free, ovary 3-locular; capsule opening by lateral pores.

a. Flowers sessile, in terminal glomerules subtended by a leafy-bracted involucre,
   often also in small clusters in the upper axils. (Fig. 901). .... 1. *C. glomerata*
a. Flowers pedicelled, solitary, clustered, racemose or paniculate but not in glomerules.
   b. Corolla rotate; flowers in elongate spiciform racemes. .... 2. *C. americana*
   b. Corolla campanulate or funnelform; flowers not in long spiciform racemes.
      c. Hypanthium and calyx lobes bristly with pale hairs. .... 3. *C. trachelium*
      c. Hypanthium and calyx lobes glabrous or pubescent but not bristly.
         d. Stem weak and reclining on other plants, somewhat 3-angled,
            retrorsely-scabrous on the angles; leaves retrorsely-scabrous on the
            margins and midrib. .... 4. *C. aparinoides*
         d. Stem erect or ascending, terete or obscurely angled, not retrorsely scabrous;
            leaves not retrorsely-scabrous.
            e. Leaves serrate, mostly lanceolate to ovate-lanceolate.
               Inflorescence a secund raceme .... 5. *C. rapunculoides*
               Inflorescence a panicle .... 6. *C. divaricata*
            e. Leaves entire or essentially so, mostly linear to linear-lanceolate. (Fig. 902).
               Inflorescence a raceme; corollas mostly longer than 2.5 cm. .... 7. *C. persicifolia*
               Inflorescence a panicle or flowers solitary; corollas mostly 2.5 cm or
               less long. (Fig. 902) .... 8. *C. rotundifolia*

1. *C. glomeráta* L. (clustered). Clustered bellflower. Rarely escaped from cultivation to roadsides and waste places. June-July. Fig. 901, Map 2163. (Introduced from Europe).

2. *C. americána* L. Tall bellflower. Woodlands. Rarely occurring in our range. Reported for Rensselaer County, NY. [*Campanulastrum a.*]. —FAC

3. *C. trachélium* L. (old generic name). Throatwart. Roadsides, waste places. August-September. Map 2164. (Introduced from Europe).

***C. latifólia* L.** Similar to *C. trachelium* but differing in having 1-flowered peduncles and corollas 4 cm or more long (peduncles 2 or more flowered and corollas less than 4 cm long in *C. trachelium*). (Europe). Rarely escaped from cultivation to waste places. Reported for ME, Fairfield County, CT; Windsor County, VT.

4. *C. aparinoídes* Pursh (like *Galium aparine*). Marsh-bellflower. Wet meadows and marshes. June-August. Map 2165. [*C. uliginosa*]. —OBL

5. *C. rapunculoídes* L. (like *C. rapunculus*). Roadsides, waste places, around buildings. July-September. Map 2166. (Naturalized from Europe). Root reported to be edible after boiling.

Two European species resemble *C. rapunculoides* but differ in having corollas 4 cm or more long (corollas 3 cm or less long in *C. rapunculoides*): *C. punctáta* Lam. Flowers drooping, corollas 5 cm or more long, reported for Coos County, NH; *C. médium* L. Flowers ascending, corollas 4-5 cm long, reported for Fairfield and Litchfield Counties, CT; a third European species *C. bononiénsis* L., differs from *C. rapunculoides* in having finely pubescent stem and leaves, clasping upper leaves and corollas 2 cm or less long (stem glabrous or finely pubescent above, leaves not clasping, corollas 2-3 cm long in *C. rapunculoides*). Reported for ME. The latter three species occur sporadically in waste places and abandoned dwellings but do not persist.

6. *C. divaricáta* Michx. (widely divergent). Dry woods. July-September. From farther south. Reported for CT, Coos County, NH. [*C. flexuosa*].

Gadéllia Schulkina *lactiflóra* (Bieb.) Schulkina. Resembling *Campanula divaricata* but with ascending flowers 1.5 cm or more long (flowers drooping and 1 cm or less long in *C. divaricata*). Rarely escaped from cultivation. Reported for Coos County, NH.

900. *Triodanis perfoliata.* Upper part of plant; flowers in the axils of ovate, cordate-clasping leaves.

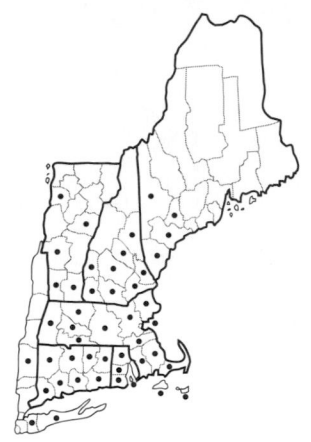

2162. *Triodanus perfoliata*

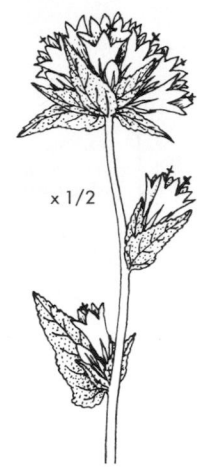

901. *Campanula glomerata.* Upper stem; flowers in terminal glomerules and in clusters in the upper axils.

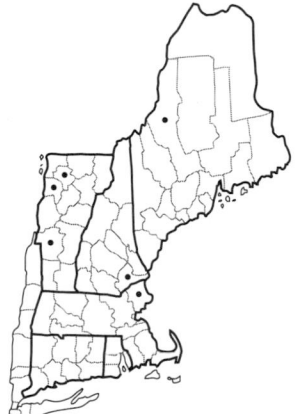

2163. *Campanula glomerata*

2164. *Campanula trachelium*

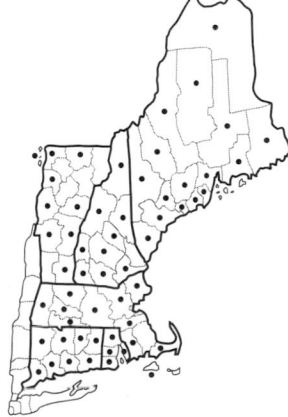

2165. *Campanula aparinoides*

C. carpática Jacq. Will key to *C. divaricata*, but is distinguishable from it and from *Gadellia* in having long-petioled, ovate stem leaves and large, solitary flowers (leaves lanceolate and short petioled, flowers in a panicle in *C. divaricata* and *Gadellia*). From Europe. Rarely spread from cultivation. Reported for CT.

7. *C. persicifólia* L. (peach-leaved). Rarely escaped from cultivation to roadsides and waste places. Map 2167. (Eurasia).

8. *C. rotundifólia* L. (round-leaved). Harebell. Ledges, rock outcrops, river shores, meadows, alpine areas, often calcareous. June-September. Fig. 902, Map 2168. (Eurasia). —FACU

C. pátula L. Similar to *C. rotundifolia* but differing in fruit opening near top (opening near base in *C. rotundifolia*). (Europe). Rarely escaped from cultivation. Reported for NH, Windham County, CT.

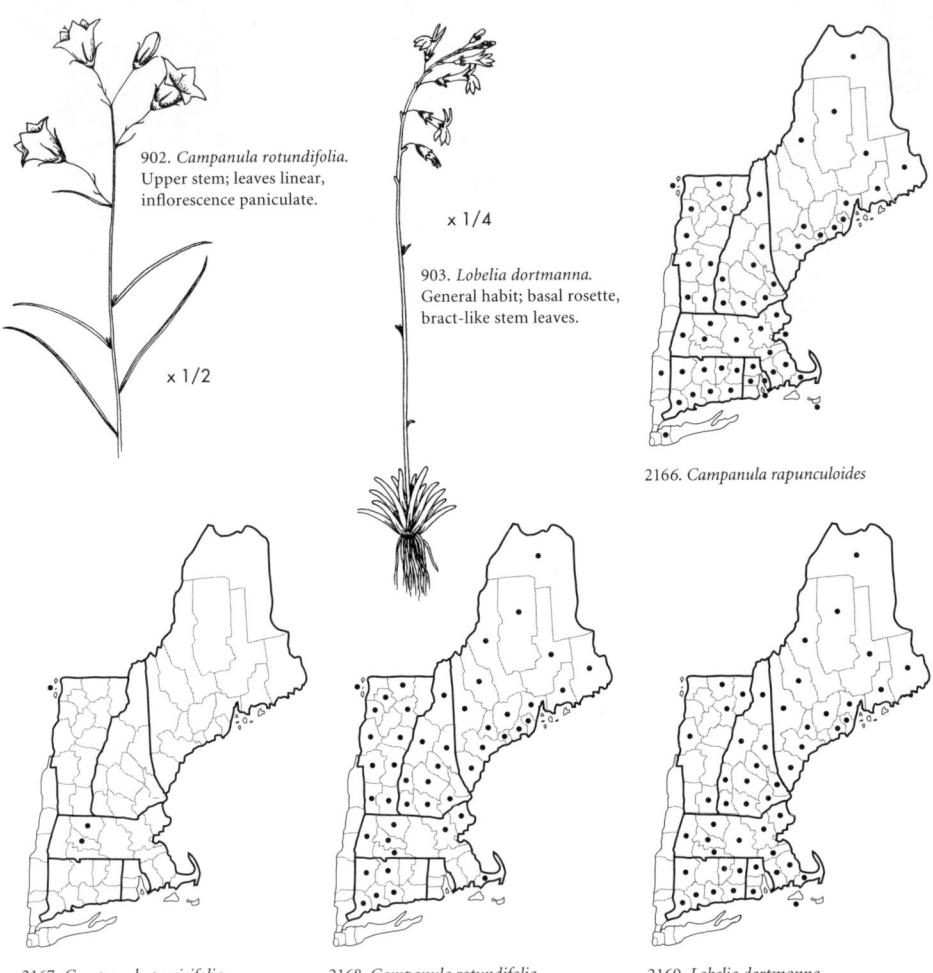

902. *Campanula rotundifolia.*
Upper stem; leaves linear,
inflorescence paniculate.

× 1/2

× 1/4

903. *Lobelia dortmanna.*
General habit; basal rosette,
bract-like stem leaves.

2166. *Campanula rapunculoides*

2167. *Campanula persicifolia*

2168. *Campanula rotundifolia*

2169. *Lobelia dortmanna*

5. *Lobélia* L. Lobelia (for M. de l'obel).

Annual or perennial herbs; leaves basal and/or alternate; flowers red, blue or white, in terminal, bracteate racemes or in the upper axils, calyx 5-lobed, corolla split to the base on 1 side, bilabiate, the upper lip 2-lobed, the lower 3-lobed, stamens united in a tube around the style, ovary 2-locular; capsule dehiscent by apical pores.

a. Plant aquatic; primary leaves in a basal rosette, in cross section like two hollow
    tubes, those of the stem, when present, minute and bract-like, 5 mm or less
    long (1 or 2 just above the rosette sometimes longer). (Fig. 903). .... 1. *L. dortmanna*
a. Plant terrestrial, primary leaves basal and cauline, those of the stem longer than
    5 mm.
  b. Calyx lobes with basal auricles; hypanthium and/or calyx lobes usually hirsute;
    calyx lobes 6 mm or more long. (Fig. 904). .... 2. *L. siphilitica*
  b. Calyx lobes not auriculate or if so (small auricles present in *L. spicata*)
    hypanthium and/or calyx lobes glabrous (except 1 var. of *L. spicata*) and
    calyx lobes 5 mm or less long.

c. Calyx lobes 6 mm or more long; corolla red. .... 3. *L. cardinalis*
c. Calyx lobes 5 mm or less long; corolla blue, rarely white.
    d. Stem leaves 5 mm or less wide.
        Pedicels bracteolate at or above the middle. .... 4. *L. kalmii*
        Pedicels bracteolate at or near the base. .... 5. *L. nuttallii*
    d. Stem leaves (at least the lower and/or median ones) more than 5 mm wide.
        Lower bracts of central raceme foliaceous, scarcely different from the
            upper leaves; stem long-pubescent; hypanthium much inflated
            in fruit. .... 6. *L. inflata*
        Lower bracts of central raceme bract-like, distinctly different from the
            upper leaves; stem glabrous or hirtellous; hypanthium not or
            barely inflated in fruit ....7. *L. spicata*

1. *L. dortmánna* L. (for Dortmann). Sandy pond margins in shallow water. July-September. Fig. 903, Map 2169. (Europe). Poisonous. —OBL

2. *L. siphilítica* L. (formerly supposed to have curative properties). Wooded swamps and wet woods. August-September. Fig. 904, Map 2170. Our plants are var. *siphilitica*. Poisonous. —FACW+

3. *L. cardinális* L. (of the Cardinal). Cardinal-flower. Pond and stream margins, wooded swamps, wet woods. July-September. Map 2171. Our plants are subsp. *cardinalis* var. *cardinalis*. —FACW+

4. *L. kálmii* L. (for its discoverer). Calcareous pond and stream margins, wet meadows, bogs, wooded swamps and wet ledges. July-September. Map 2172. [*L. strictiflora*].

5. *L. núttallii* J.A. Schultes (for its discoverer). Sandy wet to dry meadows and deciduous or pine woods on the coastal plain. July-September. From farther south. Reported for Suffolk County, NY. —FACW

6. *L. infláta* L. (inflated). Indian tobacco. Fields, roadsides, waste places, open woods. July-September. Map 2173. Poisonous; preparations made from the leaves and flowers have been used to treat respiratory ailments and to break the smoking habit but only under medical supervision. —FACU

7. *L. spicáta* Lam. (spicate). Fields, roadsides, thickets. June-August. Map 2174. Our plants include var. *spicata* and the following vars.:

    var. *hirtélla* Gray. Plant hirtellous throughout (densely pubescent only at base in var. *spicata*).

    var. *campanuláta* McVaugh. Corolla dark blue, anthers white (corolla light blue to white, anthers blue in the other 2 vars.) [var. *spicata*]. —FAC-

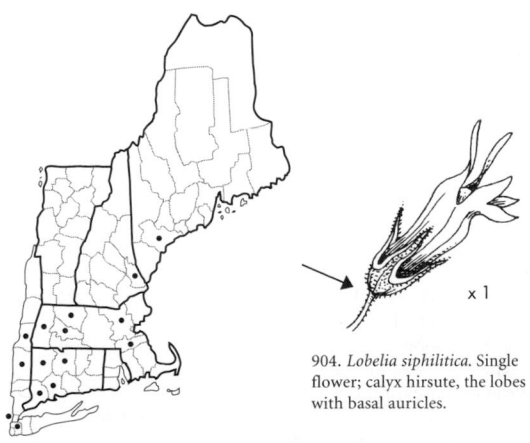

904. *Lobelia siphilitica.* Single flower; calyx hirsute, the lobes with basal auricles.

2170. *Lobelia siphilitica*

2171. *Lobelia cardinalis*

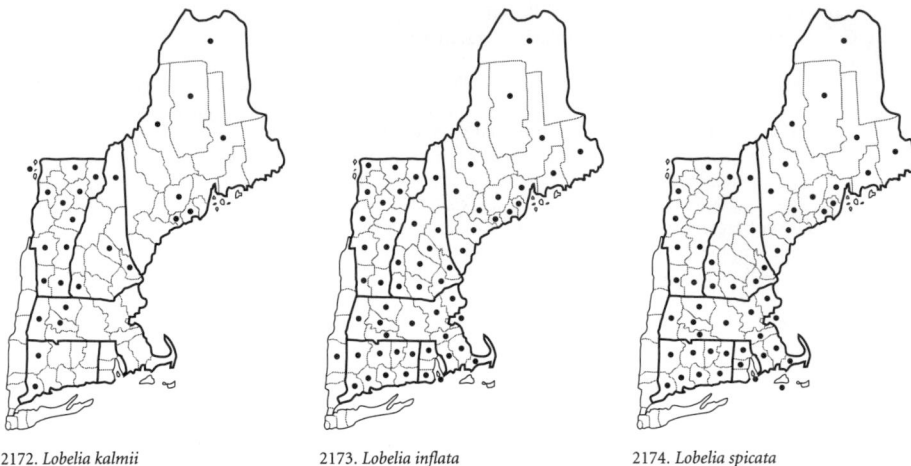

2172. *Lobelia kalmii*   2173. *Lobelia inflata*   2174. *Lobelia spicata*

Family 190. Asteráceae (Composite Family)

Hermaphrodite, monoecious, dioecious or polygamous herbs, rarely shrubs, sap sometimes milky. Leaves simple, entire, toothed or pinnatifid to pinnately compound, alternate, opposite and/or basal, rarely whorled, estipulate. Flowers sessile on a receptacle subtended by an involucre of bracts forming a dense head, the heads solitary or in corymbs or panicles, each flower sometimes also subtended by a bract (these bracts called chaff) or bracts lacking, the receptacle flat or convex, smooth or pitted, naked, chaffy or bristly; calyx represented by a pappus of bristles, scales or teeth, or pappus lacking, corolla of 2 types, 1 type tubular and regular, 5-lobed (disc flower) or strap-shaped (ligulate) usually with several apical teeth (ray flower); a single head may be composed exclusively of disc flowers (the head then discoid), the flowers usually all perfect, or sometimes imperfect and the plants monoecious or dioecious, or a head may be composed entirely of ray flowers (the head then ligulate), the flowers usually all perfect; a single head may also be composed of both ray and disc flowers (the head then radiate), the disc flowers then usually occupying the center of the head and perfect or sometimes staminate, the ray flowers restricted to the periphery of the head and either pistillate or neutral; stamens 5, inserted on the corolla, the anthers united in a tube around the style, ovary inferior, unilocular, style 1, 2-cleft (in perfect flowers). Fruit an achene, usually crowned with the pappus, sometimes naked. [*Compositae*].

In addition to the species treated under the genera below *Dendranthema morifolium* has been reported for MA, *Chamaemelum nobile* and *Leucanthemilla serotina* for CT, *Machaeranthera gracilis* for ME.

A. Leaves opposite (at least the lower) or whorled.
  B. Rays absent or less than 4 mm long.
    C. Leaves in whorles or 4 or more, 1.5 mm or less wide. (Fig. 905). .... 1. *Sclerolepis uniflora*
    C. Leaves opposite, or if whorled, more than 1.5 mm wide.
      D. Leaves (at least the lower) dissected or deeply lobed.
        E. Staminate and pistillate flowers in separate heads, the staminate in racemes or spikes, the pistillate at the bases of the staminate inflorescences .... 2. *Ambrosia*
        E. Staminate and pistillate flowers in the same head or flowers perfect, not in spikes or racemes.

  F. Involucral bracts united nearly to the apex. .... 3. *Tagetes*
  F. Involucral bracts separate.
    Pappus of capillary bristles.
      Leaves opposite or whorled, involucral bracts imbricated in 2 or
        3 series. (Fig. 909) .... 4. *Eupatorium*
      Leaves opposite, involucral bracts equal or nearly so. .... 5. *Ageratina*
    Pappus absent or a crown of 2-4 awns.
      Involucral bracts in 2 series; achenes 2-4-awned.
        Plant terrestrial or emergent; leaves if dissected, with broader
          segments; achenes flat or linear-tetragonal .... 6. *Bidens*
        Plant aquatic; submersed leaves dissected, with filiform
          segments; achenes terete .... 7. *Megalodonta beckii*
      Involucral bracts in 1 series; achenes not awned. .... 8. *Polymnia*
                                  canadensis
 D. Leaves not dissected or lobed, toothed or entire.
  G. Staminate and pistillate flowers in separate heads, the staminate in
    racemes or spikes, the pistillate at the bases of the staminate
    inflorescences .... 2. *Ambrosia*
  G. Staminate and pistillate flowers in the same head or flowers perfect, not
    in spikes or racemes (except in *Iva*).
    H. Pappus of capillary bristles.
      Twining and climbing vines; involucral bracts 4. .... 9. *Mikania scandens*
      Erect herbs; involucral bracts more than 4.
        Leaves opposite or whorled, involucral bracts inbricated in 2 or
          3 series. .... 4. *Eupatorium*
        Leaves opposite, involucral bracts equal or nearly so. .... 5. *Ageratina*
    H. Pappus absent or of scales or a crown of awns, not of capillary bristles.
     I. Pappus a crown of awns or achenes enclosed within a prickly,
       star-shaped bur.
       Pappus a crown of 2-4 awns; achenes not enclosed within a
         prickly bur; stems erect.
        Plant terrestrial or emergent; leaves if dissected, with broader
          segments; achenes flat or linear-tetragonal .... 6. *Bidens*
        Plant aquatic; submersed leaves dissected, with filiform
          segments; achenes terete .... 7. *Megalodonta beckii*
       Pappus none; achenes enclosed within a prickly bur, stems
         trailing. (Fig. 918) .... 10. *Acanthospermum*
                               australe
     I. Pappus absent or of scales, not a crown of awns; achenes not
       enclosed within a bur.
      J. Rays present, white; heads not in spikes or racemes.
        Leaves attenuate to sessile or subsessile bases; rays more than
         5; pappus absent or a crown. .... 11. *Eclipta prostrata.*
        Leaves obtuse or rounded to petioled bases; rays 5 or fewer;
         pappus of scales. .... 12. *Galinsoga*
      J. Rays absent; heads in spikes or racemes. .... 13. *Iva*
B. Rays present, 4 mm or more long.
 K. Involucre of 2 dimorphic series of bracts, the inner wider than the outer, or
    the outer foliaceous and often larger and the inner membranous.
   L. Pappus of 2 smooth or antrorsely barbed teeth or short awns or none;
      achenes frequently wing-margined .... 14. *Coreopsis*
   L. Pappus of 2-4, usually retrorsely barbed teeth or awns; achenes not
      wing-margined.
      Achenes beaked .... 15. *Cosmos*
      Achenes beakless.
        Plant terrestrial or emergent; leaves if dissected, with broader
          segments; achenes flat or linear-tetragonal .... 6. *Bidens*
        Plant aquatic; submersed leaves dissected, with filiform segments;
          achenes terete .... 7. *Megalodonta beckii*
 K. Involucre not of 2 distinct series, the bracts not dimorphic.

M. Involucral bracts in 1 series, united nearly to apex. .... 3. *Tagetes*
M. Involucral bracts in 1 or more series, not united, or united only at base.
  N. Rays white, rarely yellow or orange; leaves, at least the lower, pinnatifid.... 8. *Polymnia*
      canadensis
  N. Rays yellow; leaves entire or toothed, none pinnatifid.
    O. Leaves connate-perfoliate or clasping.
      Leaves connate-perfoliate; disc flowers sterile, the styles undivided. ... 16. *Silphium*
      perfoliatum
      Leaves merely clasping, not connate-pinnatifid; disc flowers fertile,
        the styles divided .... 17. *Guizotia*
      abyssinica
    O. Leaves petioled or sessile but not connate-perfoliate or clasping.
      P. Pappus of capillary bristles; receptacle naked; plant of alpine areas. .... 18. *Arnica*
      P. Pappus of scales or awns or none; receptacle chaffy; plants of other
        habitats.
        Q. Rays marcescent on the achenes; receptacle conic. .... 19. *Heliopsis*
        helianthoides
        Q. Rays deciduous; receptacle flat to convex.
          R. Achenes strongly flattened, broadly winged; pappus of 2
            persistent awns, not enlarged and chaffy at base .... 20. *Verbesina*
          R. Achenes not strongly flattened or winged; pappus of 2
            deciduous awns, enlarged and chaffy at base .... 21. *Helianthus*
A. Leaves alternate or all basal.
  S. Leaves basal, stem leaves absent or reduced to bracts.
    T. Heads discoid or radiate; plants lacking latex.
      U. Heads discoid.
        Leaves entire, narrowed or rounded at base. .... 22. *Antennaria*
        Leaves angulate, toothed or lobed, cordate to reniform at base. .... 23. *Petasites*
      U. Heads radiate.
        V. Rays yellow; leaves cordate, angled or toothed; heads solitary.
          (Fig. 931). .... 24. *Tussilago farfara*
        V. Rays white to pink; leaves not as above or if so, heads racemose or
          corymbose.
          Leaves dentate or denticulate, narrowed or rounded at base, not
            white-tomentose beneath; heads solitary .... 25. *Bellis perennis*
          Leaves angulate, lobed or toothed, cordate to reniform at base,
            usually white-tomentose beneath; heads racemose or
            corymbose. .... 23. *Petasites*
    T. Heads ligulate; plants with latex.
      W. Pappus none; involucral bracts with a pale, thickened midrib in fruit. .... 26. *Arnoseris minima*
      W. Pappus present, of scales or bristles; involucral bracts lacking a pale,
        thickened midrib.
        X. Pappus in 2 series, the outer of short, chaffy scales, the inner of simple,
          capillary bristles .... 27. *Krigia*
        X. Pappus in 1 series, capillary, simple or plumose, or if an outer series of
          scales present, inner series plumose.
          Y. Pappus of simple, capillary bristles.
            Achenes muricate, at least at summit, tipped by a slender beak. .... 28. *Taraxacum*
            Achenes not muricate, beakless .... 29. *Hieraceum*
          Y. Pappus of plumose bristles, at least in part.
            Receptacle naked .... 30. *Leontodon*
            Receptacle chaffy .... 31. *Hypochaeris*
  S. Leaves alternate, basal leaves sometimes also present.
    Z. Heads discoid (species with inconspicuous rays also included here).
      AA. Staminate and pistillate flowers in separate heads, often on separate
        plants.
        BB. Plant a shrub .... 32. *Baccharis*
        halimifolia
        BB. Plant an herb.
          CC. Leaves spiny .... 33. *Cirsium*
          CC. Leaves not spiny.

DD. Plant monoecious; involucre of pistillate flowers bearing spines
    or tubercles; leaves not woolly or tomentose beneath.
       Staminate heads in long, slender spikes or racemes; pistillate
          involucre with 1 series of spines or tubercles at apex. ...... 2. *Ambrosia*
       Staminate heads in short, spicate clusters; pistillate involucre
          covered with hooked prickles. (Fig. 941) .... 34. *Xanthium*
DD. Plant dioecious or polygamodioecious; involucre of pistillate
    flowers not bearing spines or tubercles; leaves usually woolly
    or tomentose beneath.
      EE. Basal leaves palmately divided, cordate or reniform, large,
         more than 5 cm wide .... 23. *Petasites*
      EE. Basal leaves absent or narrowed to base, less than 5 cm wide.
         Basal leaves persistent in rosettes, mostly obovate, stem leaves
            few. .... 22. *Antennaria*
         Basal leaves early deciduous, not persistent in rosettes,
            linear-lanceolate, stem leaves numerous .... 35. *Anaphalis*
                                             margaritacea
AA. Staminate and pistillate flowers in the same head or flowers perfect.
  FF. Leaves spiny and/or involucral bracts fringed, spiny-margined, or
    tipped by a hooked or straight spine; corollas cleft into long,
    ray-like lobes.
    GG. Leaves not spiny.
      Involucral bracts terminated by hooked spines. .... 36. *Arctium*
      Involucral bracts erose, lacerate, pectinate, or terminated by 1 or
        more straight spines .... 37. *Centaurea*
    GG. Leaves spiny.
      HH. Involucres 1-flowered, numerous, in a globose head with a
        reflexed, hidden outer involucre .... 38. *Echinops*
                                         sphaerocephalus
      HH. Involucres many-flowered, heads not globose.
        II. Receptacle honeycombed, not or scarcely bristly on the
          partitions. .... 39. *Onopordum*
                                           acanthium
        II. Receptacle densely bristly or chaffy.
          JJ. Leaves white-mottled; filaments united below. .... 40. *Silybum*
                                            marianum
          JJ. Leaves not white-mottled; filaments separate.
            KK. Pappus biseriate, an outer series of long awns and an
              inner of short ones .... 41. *Cnicus benedictus*
            KK. Pappus of a single series of capillary bristles or rarely
              absent or scale-like.
               Pappus bristles plumose .... 33. *Cirsium*
               Pappus bristles not plumose .... 42. *Carduus*
  FF. Leaves not spiny; involucral bracts not fringed, spiny-margined or
    tipped; corollas merely toothed or shallowly lobed (except in
    Vernonia).
  LL. Leaves dissected or lobed.
    MM. Heads extremely strong-scented when bruised, discoid; pappus
      none or a short crown.
    NN. Heads in spikes, racemes or panicles. .... 43. *Artemisia*
    NN. Heads in corymbs or solitary.
      OO. Suffruticose; receptacle chaffy. .... 44. *Santolina*
                                        chamaecyparissus
      OO. Herbaceous; receptacle naked.
        PP. Achenes, particularly the marginal ones, stipitate. .... 45. *Cotula*
                                     coronopifolia
        PP. Achenes sessile.
          Plant with pineapple odor when crushed; receptacle
            conical. .... 46. *Matricaria*
          Plant without pineapple odor, merely strong-scented;
            receptacle flat to convex .... 47. *Tanacetum*

MM. Heads not extremely strong-scented when bruised, discoid or
 radiate, pappus of capillary bristles or of awned or awnless scales
 (heads somewhat strong-scented and pappus none in *Achillea*
 which has radiate heads).
 QQ. Leaves with broad central lamina, merely lobed; heads discoid
  and pappus of capillary bristles or radiate (*Parthenium*) and
  pappus of 2 scales.
  RR. Basal leaves palmately lobed .... 23. *Petasites*
  RR. Basal leaves pinnately lobed.
   SS. Flowers yellow, all perfect; pappus of capillary bristles. .... 48. *Senecio*
   SS. Flowers white, some imperfect.
    Involucres cylindric; pappus of capillary bristles. .... 49. *Erechtites*
      hieracifolia
    Involucres hemispheric; pappus of 2 scales. .... 50. *Parthenium*
 QQ. Leaves dissected to or nearly to midrib; heads radiate and
  pappus none or of awned or awnless scales (pappus capillary
  in *Senecio*).
  TT. Involucral bracts in 1 series, united nearly to apex. .... 3. *Tagetes*
  TT. Involucral bracts imbricated, or if in 1 series not united
   except at base.
   UU. Flowers yellow; pappus of capillary bristles. .... 48. *Senecio*
   UU. Flowers white, pink or yellowish; pappus none or of scales.
    Involucral bracts scarious-margined; pappus none. .... 51. *Achillea*
    Involucral bracts not scarious-margined (although often
     scarious at base); pappus of 2 or more scales .... 50. *Parthenium*
LL. Leaves not dissected or lobed, toothed, crenate or entire.
 VV. Disc flowers purple or pink.
  WW. Flowers all perfect.
   Heads in spikes or racemes; pappus in 1 series. .... 52. *Liatris*
   Heads in corymbose cymes; pappus double. .... 53. *Vernonia*
  WW. Outer flowers, or in some heads all flowers, pistillate.
   XX. Leaves densely white-tomentose beneath. .... 23. *Petasites*
   XX. Leaves not densely white-tomentose beneath.
    Leaves lanceolate to elliptic .... 54. *Pluchea*
    Leaves linear to narrowly oblanceolate. .... 55. *Conyza*
      canadensis
 VV. Disc flowers yellow, greenish or white.
  YY. Leaves densely white-tomentose, at least beneath.
   ZZ. Pappus none .... 43. *Artemisia*
   ZZ. Pappus of capillary bristles.
    Plant perennial, rhizomatous; involucral bracts
     pearly-white. .... 35. *Anaphalis*
      margaritacea
    Plant annual or perennial, not rhizomatous; involucral
     bracts greenish, tan, purplish or yellowish-white.
     Heads in corymbose or paniculate inflorescences, or in
      terminal glomerules overtopped by their
      subtending leafy bracts and plant a diffusely
      branched non-alpine annual with numerous stem
      leaves and glabrous achenes, pappus bristles
      distinct .... 56. *Gnaphalium*
     Heads in spiciform-thyrsoid inflorescences, or if in
      terminal glomerules pappus bristles united in a
      ring at the base or distinct and plant a simple or
      sparingly branched alpine perennial with few stem
      leaves and sparsely strigose achenes.
      Basal and lower leaves rounded to obtuse (although
      usually mucronate); achenes glabrous,
      papillate; annual. (Fig. 953). .... 57. *Gamochaeta*
      purpurea

Basal and lower leaves acute; achenes sparsely
  strigose; perennial. .... 58. *Omalotheca*
YY. Leaves not white-tomentose (although often pubescent)
  beneath.
  a. Involucral bracts in 1 series, sometimes also with a short outer
    series.
    b. Lower and middle stem leaves triangular to
      lanceolate-hastate; flowers all perfect. (Fig. 955) .... 59. *Synosma*
        suaveolens
    b. Leaves not hastate.
      c. Flowers all perfect .... 48. *Senecio*
      c. Outer flowers, or in some heads all flowers, pistillate.
        Involucres more than 1 cm long; rays absent; flowers all
          with pappus. .... 49. *Erechtites*
            hieracifolia
        Involucres 1 cm or less long; rays present; outer flowers
          lacking pappus. .... 60. *Trimorpha acris*
  a. Involucral bracts in 2 or more series.
    d. Pappus none or a short crown or of 2 scales.
      e. Pappus of 2 scales; receptacle chaffy. .... 50. *Parthenium*
      e. Pappus none or a short crown; receptacle naked.
        f. Heads in spikes, racemes or panicles. .... 43. *Artemisia*
        f. Heads in corymbs or solitary.
          Heads corymbose; achenes sessile .... 61. *Balsamita major*
          Heads solitary; achenes, particularly the marginal
            ones, stipitate. .... 45. *Cotula*
              coronopifolia
    d. Pappus of capillary bristles.
      Heads scattered or corymbose; pappus bristles smooth. ...... 62. *Aster*
      Heads in spikes or racemes; pappus bristles barbellate. .... 52. *Liatris*
Z. Heads ligulate or radiate.
  g. Heads ligulate; stems with latex.
    h. Pappus absent or of scales, or both bristles and scales.
      i. Flowers blue to pink or white; pappus of small, chaffy scales. .... 63. *Cichorium*
      i. Flowers yellow or orange; pappus none or of bristles and scales.
        j. Pappus of an outer series of short, chaffy scales and an inner series
          of capillary bristles .... 27. *Krigia*
        j. Pappus none.
          Peduncles conspicuously upwardly thickened; stem leaves much
            reduced. .... 26. *Arnoseris minima*
          Peduncles not inflated; stem leaves not reduced. .... 64. *Lapsana*
            communis
    h. Pappus present, of simple capillary or plumose bristles.
      k. Pappus of plumose bristles, at least in part.
        Involucral bracts in 1 series; plume branches of pappus
          interwebbed. .... 65. *Tragopogon*
        Involucral bracts in 2 or more series; plume branches of pappus not
          interwebbed. (Fig. 976) .... 66. *Picris*
      k. Pappus of simple capillary bristles.
        l. Achenes strongly flattened.
          Achenes with a long or short, stout beak; flowers mostly 50 or
            fewer per head.
          Involucres urceolate, mostly more than 1 cm long and/or more
            than 2 mm wide; flowers 6 or more per head; leaves
            prickly along midrib beneath or not. .... 67. *Lactuca*
          Involucres narrowly cylindric, mostly 1 cm or less long and
            2 mm or less wide; flowers 5 per head; leaves not prickly
            along midrib beneath. (Fig. 977) .... 68. *Mycelis muralis*
          Achenes not beaked; flowers 60 or more per head. .... 69. *Sonchus*
        l. Achenes prismatic or terete, not flattened.

      m. Flowers pink to white or cream color; heads usually nodding. .... 70. *Prenanthes*
      m. Flowers bright yellow to red or orange; heads usually erect.
          Plant annual, biennial or perennial, from a taproot or several
              main roots, rhizomes lacking; achenes tapered to apex. ... 71. *Crepis*
          Plant perennial, from a rhizome (sometimes short), taproot
              lacking; achenes usually truncate at apex. .... 29. *Hieraceum*
g. Heads radiate.
  n. Rays white, pink, red, purple or blue.
    o. Rays actually enlarged disc flowers; involucral bracts erose, lacerate,
        pectinate or terminated by a spine .... 37. *Centaurea*
    o. Rays normal; involucral bracts entire.
      p. Receptacle chaffy.
        q. Heads solitary; rays more than 5 mm long.
          Leaves 1-3 times pinnately dissected; chaff not
             spinescent-tipped. .... 72. *Anthemis*
          Leaves toothed or entire; chaff spinescent-tipped. .... 73. *Echinacea*
        q. Heads corymbose; rays 5 mm or less long.
          Involucral bracts scarious-margined; pappus none. .... 51. *Achillea*
          Involucral bracts not scarious-margined; pappus of 2 scales. .... 50. *Parthenium*
      p. Receptacle naked.
        r. Pappus none, or a short crown, or of bristles.
          Leaves entire .... 74. *Boltonia*
                                         asteroides
          Leaves toothed to pinnately dissected.
            Leaves toothed to pinnatifid, with broad lobes.
              Heads corymbose; disc less than 1 cm wide; rays 8 mm or
                less long; leaves bipinnatifid .... 47. *Tanacetum*
              Heads solitary; disc 1 cm or more wide; rays longer than
                8 mm; leaves serrate or pinnatifid .... 75. *Leucanthemum*
                                                vulgare
            Leaves pinnately dissected, with linear to filiform lobes. .... 46. *Matricaria*
        r. Pappus of capillary bristles.
          s. Stem leaves reduced to bracts .... 23. *Petasites*
          s. Stem leaves normally developed.
            t. Rays numerous, white or purplish, narrow and
              inconspicuous, involucral bracts imbricated,
              inflorescence open .... 55. *Conyza*
                                                canadensis
           t. Plants without above combination of characters.
            u. Involucral bracts foliaceous or with chartaceous base and
              herbaceous tip, usually imbricated.
              Inflorescence a narrow, elongate, interrupted, thyrsoid
                panicle. .... 76. *Solidago*
              Inflorescence not as above .... 62. *Aster*
            u. Involucral bracts neither foliaceous nor with chartaceous
             base and herbaceous tip, usually in 1 series .... 77. *Erigeron*
  n. Rays yellow (sometimes also partly red, purple or brownish).
    v. Leaves dissected.
      w. Involucral bracts in 1 series, united nearly to apex. .... 3. *Tagetes*
      w. Involucral bracts in 1 or more series, not united or united only at
        base.
        x. Pappus of capillary bristles .... 48. *Senecio*
        x. Pappus none, or a short crown, or of 2 awns or teeth, or of scales.
          y. Receptacle naked.
             Rays 5 mm or less long .... 47. *Tanacetum*
             Rays more than 5 mm long .... 78. *Chrysanthemum*
          y. Receptacle chaffy or rarely bristly.
           z. Involucral bracts scarious-margined .... 72. *Anthemis*

z. Involucral bracts not scarious-margined.
    aa. Receptacle flat or nearly so .... 14. *Coreopsis*
    aa. Receptacle columnar or conical. (Fig. 992).
        Achenes flattened, sharp-margined or winged; rays
            subtended and partly embraced by the chaff .... 79. *Ratibida*
        Achenes angled; rays not subtended or partly embraced
            by the chaff. .... 80. *Rudbeckia*
v. Leaves entire or merely toothed.
  bb. Stem leaves reduced to bracts .... 24. *Tussilago farfara*
  bb. Stem leaves normally developed.
    cc. Pappus of capillary bristles.
      dd. Involucral bracts in 1 series, sometimes also with a short
          outer series. ....48. *Senecio*
      dd. Involucral bracts imbricated, in 2 or more series.
        ee. Leaves densely tomentose beneath; involucres more than
            1.5 cm broad. .... 81. *Inula*
        ee. Leaves glabrous or pubescent beneath but not tomentose;
           involucres 1.5 cm or less broad.
           Pappus double, of short outer bristles and long inner ones.
              Stem leaves lanceolate to elliptic, mostly more than
                5 mm wide, pinnately veined.
                Ray flowers epappus, only the disc flowers with
                    pappus of capillary bristles. .... 82. *Heterotheca*
                                  subaxillaris
                Ray and disc flowers all with pappus of capillary
                    bristles. .... 83. *Chrysopsis*
                                    mariana
              Stem leaves linear, mostly 5 mm or less wide,
                parallel-veined. .... 84. *Pityopsis falcata*
            Pappus simple, bristles in 1 series.
               Inflorescence, leaves, and involucre variable; if with
                the combination below, disc flowers 4
                or fewer .... 76. *Solidago*
              Inflorescence a flat-topped, compound corymb;
                leaves linear to linear-lanceolate, the larger
                ones usually less than 1 cm wide; involucre
                  5 mm or less high; disc flowers 5 or more.
                (Fig. 994). .... 85. *Euthamia*
    cc. Pappus none, a short crown, or of scales or awns.
      ff. Stems narrowly winged by the decurrent leaf bases. (Fig. 995).
        Receptacle naked; achenes angled .... 86. *Helenium*
        Receptacle chaffy; achenes flattened, winged. .... 20. *Verbesina*
      ff. Stems not winged.
        gg. Receptacle naked.
          Pappus none or a short crown .... 78. *Chrysanthemum*
          Pappus of 2-8 awns .... 87. *Grindelia*
        gg. Receptacle chaffy or rarely bristly.
          hh. Involucral bracts in 1 series; stems viscid-glandular;
             receptacle chaffy only near margin .... 88. *Madia*
          hh. Plants without the above combination of characters.
            ii. Receptacle conical or columnar .... 80. *Rudbeckia*
            ii. Receptacle flat or nearly so.
              Involucral bracts in 2 distinct series; achenes winged,
                not embraced by the chaff .... 14. *Coreopsis*
             Involucral bracts imbricated in several series, achenes
               thick, wingless, embraced by the chaff .... 21. *Helianthus*

1. Sclerólepis Cass. (from the Greek, based on the pappus of scales).

Slender, rhizomatous, glabrous, perennial, aquatic herbs, stems decumbent at base, creeping; leaves in whorles of 4-6, sessile, linear, entire; heads terminal, usually solitary, discoid, involucral bracts in 1 or 2 series, receptacle conic, naked, flowers perfect, purplish, 5-lobed, pappus of 5 ovate, chaffy scales; achenes 5-angled.

    1. S. uniflóra (Walt.) B. S. P. (one-flowered). Shallow water and shores near the coast. July-October. Fig. 905, Map 2175. Endangered in MA, NH, RI. —OBL

2. Ambrósia L. Ragweed (Greek and Latin name used for other plants; also meaning food of the gods).

Monoecious, coarse, branched, pubescent, annual or perennial herbs; leaves opposite or the upper alternate, toothed, lobed or dissected, sessile or petioled; heads small, greenish, the staminate and pistillate flowers in separate heads, the staminate heads in bractless racemes or spikes, the involucre of united bracts, receptacle chaffy, corolla 5-lobed, the pistillate heads solitary or several in the axils of the upper leaves at the bases of the staminate inflorescences, involucre hard and closed, bearing a series of tubercles or spines at the apex, 1-flowered, corolla none, pappus none; achenes ellipsoid or ovoid. The pollen produced by various species of ragweed is the cause of most cases of hay fever in late summer and fall. —Wildl. 4

a. leaves sessile, usually with 1 or 2 pairs of sharp teeth near the base, entire above; staminate heads sessile, the involucres extended into a retrorsely projected lobe. (Fig. 906) .... 1. *A. bidentata*
a. Leaves usually petioled (*A. coronopifolia* subsessile), uniformly toothed, palmately lobed or pinnatifid; staminate heads penduncled, the involucre not extended into a lobe.
    b. Leaves unlobed or palmately 3-5-lobed. .... 2. *A. trifida*
    b. Leaves once to 2 or more times pinnatifid.
        Plant annual, from a taproot; leaves usually bi- or tri-pinnatifid. .... 3. *A. artemisiifolia*
        Plant perennial from a spreading root system; leaves usually once-pinnatifid. .... 4. *A. coronopifolia*

    1. A. bidentáta Michx. (two-toothed). Roadsides and waste places. July-October. Fig. 906. From farther west. Reported for Fairfield County, CT.

    2. A. trífida L. (three-cleft). Roadsides and waste places. July-September. Map 2176. Our plants include var. *trifida* [*A. striata*] and the following var.:

    var. *texána* Scheele. Petioles wingless, ribs of fruit etuberculate or with short obtuse tubercles (petioles slightly winged, ribs of fruit with acute tubercles in var. *trifida*). [*A. aptera*]. —FAC

    3. A. artemisiifólia L. (with leaves of *Artemisia*). Roadsides, waste places, cultivated ground. July-October. Map 2177. [*A. elatior; A. media*].

    Our plants include var. *artemisiifolia* and the following vars., which are distinguishable from the typical form in having leaves bi or tripinnatifid (leaves simple to once pinnatifid, rarely bipinnatifid in the typical form).

    var. *elátior* (L.) Descourtils. Staminate involucres 2.5 mm or more broad.

    var. *paniculáta* (Michx.) Blankinship. Staminate involucres 2.5 mm or less broad. —FACU

    4. A. coronopifólia T. & G. Roadsides, waste places, fields. July-September. Map 2178. From farther west. [*A. cumanensis; A. psilostachya*]. —FACU-

3. Tagétes L. Marigold (name based on early mythodology).

Strong-scented, glabrous, annual herbs; lower leaves opposite, the upper alternate, pinnately compound, with 11-17, sharply serrate, linear to lanceolate leaflets, glandular-punctate, petioled; heads solitary, corymbed, or in a panicle of corymbs, narrow, radiate, involucre cylindric, the bracts

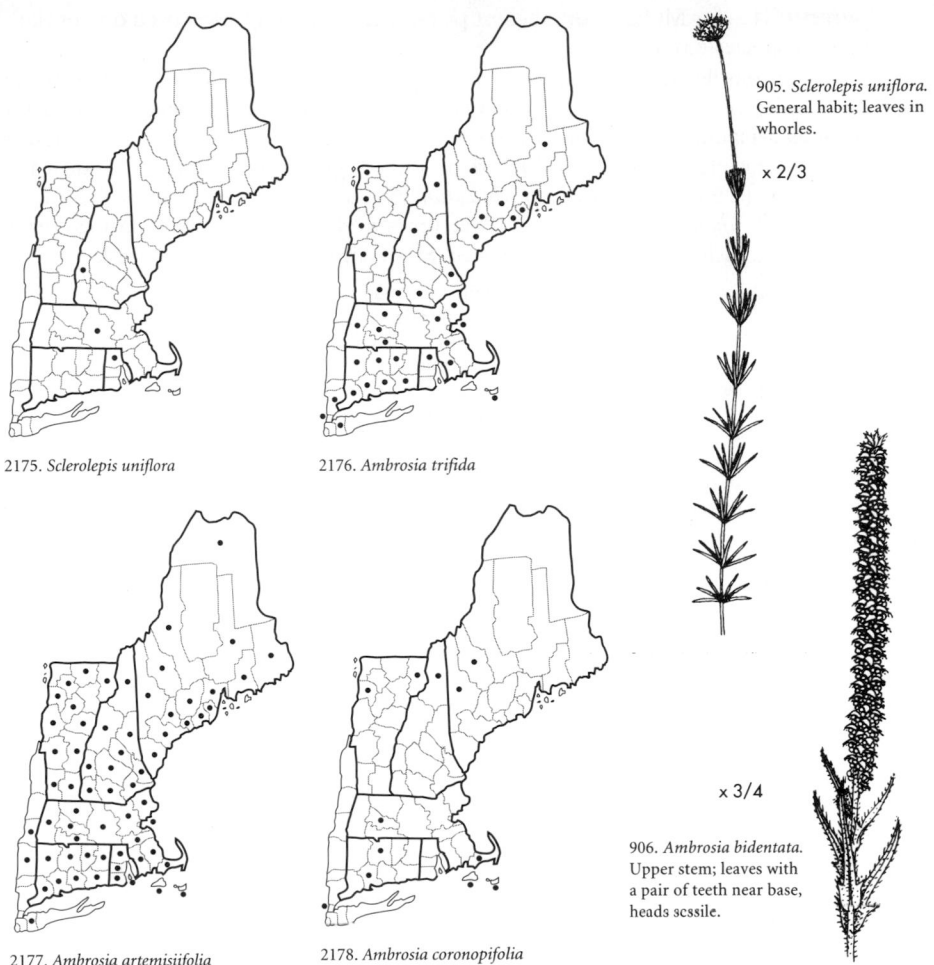

905. *Sclerolepis uniflora.*
General habit; leaves in whorles.

x 2/3

2175. *Sclerolepis uniflora*

2176. *Ambrosia trifida*

2177. *Ambrosia artemisiifolia*

2178. *Ambrosia coronopifolia*

x 3/4

906. *Ambrosia bidentata.*
Upper stem; leaves with
a pair of teeth near base,
heads sessile.

in 1 series, united nearly to the apex, glandular-punctate, rays yellow, orange or reddish, pistillate, receptacle flat, naked, disc flowers perfect, pappus of about 5, unequal, often united scales, 1 or more of them awned; achenes linear. Some species of marigold are reported to provide insect-repellant values in gardens.

a. Involucres 4 mm or less broad; rays 3 mm or less long.. .... 1. *T. minuta*
a. Involucres 5 mm or more broad; rays 5 mm or more long.
    Rays more than 1.5 cm long; plant often 5 cm or more tall. .... 2. *T. erecta*
    Rays 1.5 cm or less long; plant usually less than 5 cm tall. .... 3. *T. patula*

    1. *T. minúta* L. (minute). Roadsides and waste places. August-October. (Introduced from S. Amer.). Reported for CT, Middlesex and Norfolk Counties, MA.

    2. *T. erécta* L. (erect). Occasionally escaped from cultivation to roadsides and waste places. (Introduced from Mexico). Reported for MA, New Haven County, CT.

    3. *T. pátula* L. Occasionally escaped from cultivation to roadsides and waste places. (Introduced from Mexico). [*T. signata; T. tenuifolia*].

4. Eupatórium L. (for M. Eupator, ancient physician, reputed to have used one of the Eupatorium species in medicine).

Perennial herbs, mostly branching; leaves mostly opposite or whorled, entire or toothed (rarely palmately lobed), sessile or petioled, often glandular-punctate; heads relatively small, in corymbs or panicles, discoid, involucral bracts imbricated in several series (in ours), receptacle naked, flowers perfect, white, pink, bluish or purplish, 5-lobed, pappus of capillary bristles; achenes 5-angled.

In addition to the following species *E. x truncatum* has been reported for RI and VT.

Brickéllia Ell. *grandiflóra* (Hook.) Nutt. Sometimes keying to *Eupatorium;* distinguishable primarily in having achenes 10-ribbed, not angled. From farther west. Reported for RI.

a. Leaves whorled; flowers usually purple to pink (white in *E. hyssopifolium*).
  b. Leaves 2 cm or more wide; flowers usually pink or purple.
    c. Leaves with 3 main nerves, one of the lower pairs of lateral veins longer and
      more prominent than the others, rather abruptly contracted to the
      petiole. (Fig. 907) .... 1. *E. dubium*
    c. Leaves pinnately veined and/or gradually narrowed to petiole.
      d. Stems hollow .... 2. *E. fistulosum*
      d. Stems usually solid (sometimes hollowed by borders, then evident by pink
        fragments).
        Stems green, often purplish at the nodes; heads with 7 or fewer flowers. .... 3. *E. purpureum*
        Stems purplish or heavily spotted with purple throughout; heads with 8
          or more flowers .... 4. *E. maculatum*
  b. Leaves 1 cm or less wide; flowers white. .... 5. *E. hyssopifolium*
a. Leaves opposite.
  e. Leaves connate-perfoliate. (Fig. 908). .... 6. *E. perfoliatum*
  e. Leaves not connate-perfoliate.
    f. Leaves, at least the larger ones, on petioles 5 mm or more long. .... 7. *E. serotinum*
    f. Leaves sessile or subsessile.
      g. Involucral bracts acuminate. (Fig. 910).
        Leaves, at least the larger ones, 1.5 mm or more wide; involucral bracts
          glabrous or sparsely pubescent .... 8. *E. album*
        Leaves less than 1.5 cm wide; involucral bracts densely pubescent. .... 9. *E. leucolepis*
      g. Involucral bracts obtuse to acute.
        h.Leaves attenuate to base. (Fig. 911). .... 10. *E. altissimum*
        h. Leaves truncate, rounded, or widely cuneate at base.
          Leaves acuminate; stems glabrous below inflorescence. .... 11. *E. sessilifolium*
          Leaves rounded to obtuse or acute; stems pubescent. .... 12. *E. rotundifolium*

1. E. dúbium Willd. ex Poir. (doubtful). Joe-Pye-Weed. Wet meadows, pond and stream margins. July-September. Fig. 907, Map 2179. Endangered in ME. [*Eupatoriadelphus dubius*]. —FACW

2. E. fistulósum Barratt (tubular). Joe-Pye-Weed. Wet meadows, thickets, woods. July-September. Map 2180. Endangered in NH, ME. [*Eupatoriadelphus fistulosus*]. —FACW

3. E. purpúreum L. (purple). Joe-Pye-Weed. Moist to dry thickets, open woods, and woodland borders. July-September. Map 2181. [*E. trifoliatum; Eupatoriadelphus purpureus*].

Our plants include var. *purpureum* and the following var.:

var. *amoénum* (Pursh) Gray. Leaves lanceolate, subglabrous beneath (leaves ovate, pilose beneath in var. *purpureum*). Reported to be of value as a diuretic. —FAC

4. E. maculátum L. (mottled). Joe-Pye-Weed. Wet meadows, marshes, pond and stream margins. July-September. Map 2182. [*Eupatoriadelphus maculatus*]. Our plants include var. *maculatum* and the following var.:

var. *foliósum* (Fern.) Wieg. Upper leaves below the corymb mostly longer than the height of the corymb (upper leaves shorter than the height of the corymb in var. *maculatum*). —FACW

5. E. hyssopifólium L. (hyssop-leaved). Fields, roadsides, mostly near the coast. August-September. Map 2183. Our plants include var. *hyssopifolium* and the following var.:

var. *calcarátum* Fern. & Schub. Leaves linear, up to 5 mm wide (leaves lanceolate, wider than 5 mm in var. *hyssopifolium*).

6. E. perfoliátum L. (through the leaf). Boneset. Wet meadows, marshes, pond and stream margins. July-September. Fig. 908, Map 2184. Our plants include var. *perfoliatum* and the following var.:

var. *colpóphilum* Fern. & Griscom. Glabrate to sparsely pubescent (densely pubescent or villous in var. *perfoliatum*). Tea made from the dried leaves and inflorescences has been used to induce sweating, break up colds and flu and provide relief for associated aches and pains. —FACW+

7. E. serótinum Michx. (late-flowering). Fields, thickets, open woods. August-October. Fig. 909, Map 2185. From farther south and west. —FAC-

8. E. álbum L. (white). Dry, open woods. July-September. Endangered in CT; also reported for Suffolk County, NY. [*E. petaloideum; E. a.* var. *glandulosum*].

9. E. leucólepis (DC.) Torr. & Gray (white-scaled). Wet meadows, pond margins near the coast. August-September. Fig. 910. From farther south. Reported for eastern NY, Washington County, RI; Barnstable and Plymouth Counties MA. Endangered in RI, NY. Our plants include var. *leucolepis* and the following var.:

var. *nóvae-ángliae* Fern. Leaves sharply toothed (blunt-toothed to entire in var. *leucolepis*). Endangered in MA. —FACW+

10. E. altíssimum L. (tallest). Woods and clearings. August-September. Fig. 911, Map 2186.

11. E. sessilifólium L. (sessile-leaved). Woods and clearings. August-September. Map 2187. Endangered in VT, NH. Our plants include var. *sessilifolium* and the following var.:

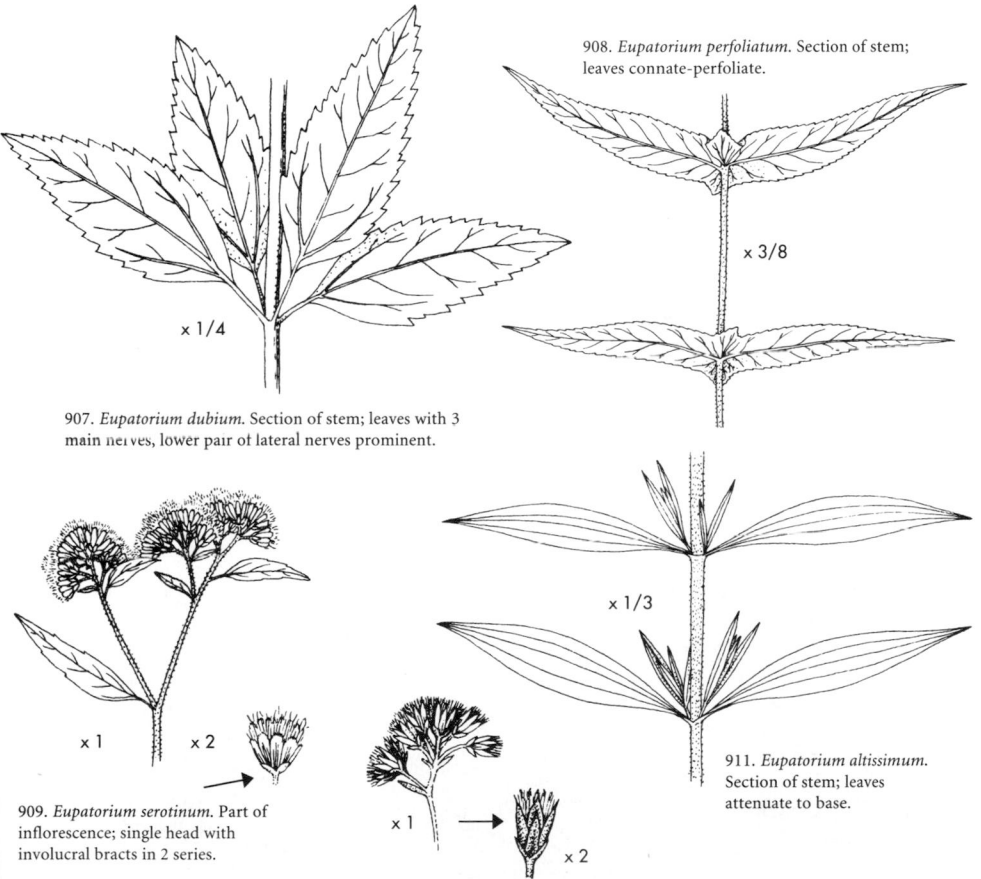

908. *Eupatorium perfoliatum*. Section of stem; leaves connate-perfoliate.

× 3/8

× 1/4

907. *Eupatorium dubium*. Section of stem; leaves with 3 main nerves, lower pair of lateral nerves prominent.

× 1/3

911. *Eupatorium altissimum*. Section of stem; leaves attenuate to base.

× 1   × 2

909. *Eupatorium serotinum*. Part of inflorescence; single head with involucral bracts in 2 series.

× 1   × 2

910. *Eupatorium leucolepis*. Part of inflorescence and single head with acuminate involucral bracts.

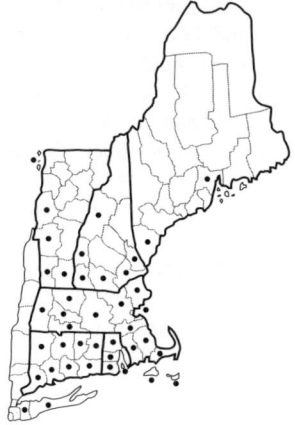

2179. *Eupatorium dubium*

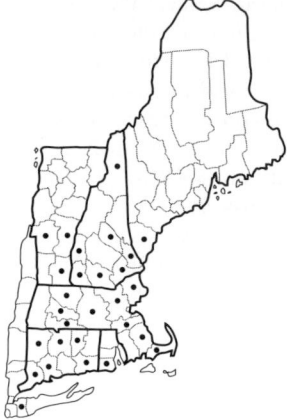

2180. *Eupatorium fistulosum*

2181. *Eupatorium purpureum*

2182. *Eupatorium maculatum*

2183. *Eupatorium hyssopifolium*

2184. *Eupatorium perfoliatum*

2185. *Eupatorium serotinum*

2186. *Eupatorium altissimum*

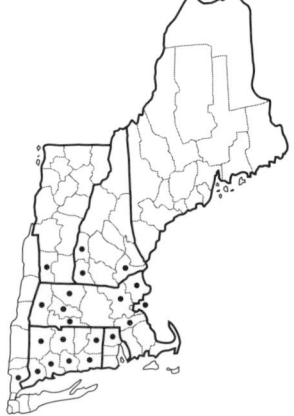

2187. *Eupatorium sessilifolium*

var. *brittoniánum* Porter. Leaves ovate-lanceolate to ovate, averaging 3 times as long as wide (leaves lanceolate, averaging 5 times as long as wide in var. *sessilifolium*).

12. E. rotundifólium L. (round-leaved). Woods, clearings, thickets, fields. August-September. Map 2188. Our plants include var. *rotundifolium* and the following var.:

var. *ovátum* (Bigel.) Torr. Leaves rounded to cordate at base, rounded to obtuse at tip (subtruncate to cuneate at base, acute at tip in var. *rotundifolium*). Endangered in NH. [*E. pubescens*]. —FAC-

E. pilósum Walt. Leaves lance-ovate to elliptic; inflorescence branches alternate (leaves ovate and inflorescence branches opposite in *E. rotundifolium* vars. *rotundifolium* and *ovatum*). Reported for MA, RI, CT. [*E. rotundifolium* var. *saundersii; E. verbenaefolium*]. —FACW

E. cannabínum L. Differing from other opposite leaved *Eupatoriums* (species 6-12) in having palmately 3-5 lobed leaves, the lobes serrate (leaves entire to merely toothed in the above species). European; a waif in our range. Reported for the *N. Terminus* of 8th Ave. NY. Preparations of this species have been used as a laxative.

5. Agerátina Spach.

Similar to *Eupatorium*; leaves opposite, petioled or sessile; involucral bracts equal or nearly so; heads with 8 or more flowers. [*Eupatorium*].

Petioles 1.5 cm or less long; blades crenate-serrate. .... 1. *A. aromatica*
Petioles, at least the longer ones, more than 1.5 cm long; blades sharply serrate .... 2. *A. altissima*

1. A. aromática (L.) Spach (aromatic). Dry, open woods. August-September. Map 2189. Endangered in MA, CT. [*Eupatorium aromaticum*]. Our plants are var. *aromatica*.

2. A. altíssima (L.) R. M. King & H. Rob. (tallest). White snakeroot. Woods and thickets. August-September. Map 2190. [*Eupatorium rugosum; E. urticaefolium*]. Our plants are var. *altissima*. Poisonous; poison can also be transmitted to humans in the milk and meat of contaminated livestock; milk sickness was a frequent cause of death among early settlers when livestock fed upon this plant. —FACU-

6. Bídens L. Beggar-ticks (from the Latin, meaning two-toothed).

Annual or perennial herbs; leaves simple, pinnately or ternately divided, opposite, sessile or petioled; heads solitary to many, terminal or axillary, radiate or discoid, involucral bracts in 2 series, the outer green, often foliaceous, the inner membranous, rays, if present, yellow to white or pink, neutral,

2188. *Eupatorium rotundifolium*   2189. *Ageratina aromatica*   2190. *Ageratina altissima*

receptacle flat or nearly so, chaffy, disc flowers perfect, yellow, pappus of usually 2-4 awns or teeth, these usually retrorsely or antrorsely barbed; achenes flattened or angled, usually crowned with the persistent pappus awns or teeth, beakless. —Wildl. 1

In addition to the following species *B. alba* var. *radiata* has been reported for CT, and *B. x multiceps* for MA.

a. Leaves simple, sometimes deeply lobed or laciniate.
  b. Leaves (except sometimes the lowest) sessile, sometimes narrowed to the base
    but not petioled.
    c. Heads campanulate; outer involucral bracts erect or ascending; chiefly
      estuarine .... 1. *B. hyperborea*
    c. Heads hemispheric; outer involucral bracts reflexed or spreading; mostly
      other habitats. (Fig. 912).
      Chaff reddish-tipped; rays 1.5 cm or more long. .... 2. *B. laevis*
      Chaff greenish or yellowish-tipped; rays absent or mostly 1.5 cm or less
        long. .... 3. *B. cernua*
  b. Leaves with distinct (although sometimes winged) petioles mostly 1 cm or
    more long. (Fig. 915).
    d. Achenes linear-tetragonal, glabrous. (Fig. 913). .... 4. *B. pilosa*
    d. Achenes flattened, or if angled then narrowly cuneate.
      e. Heads narrow, longer than broad; chiefly estuarine. (Fig. 914).
      Achenes densely pubescent .... 5. *B. bidentoides*
      Achenes sparsely pubescent .... 6. *B. eatonii*
      e. Heads as long as broad; estuaries and other habitats.
        f. Achenes convex and cartilaginous at summit; heads usually nodding in
          fruit. .... 3. *B. cernua*
        f. Achenes truncate or concave at summit, not cartilaginous; heads erect
          in fruit.
          Inner achenes 2 mm or less wide, flat. .... 6. *B. eatonii*
          Inner achenes more than 2 mm wide, or compressed-angled. .... 7. *B. tripartita*
a. Leaves one or more times pinnatifid, or pinnately compound or trifoliate.
  g. Rays 1 cm or more long.
    Achenes obovate to elliptic-obovate; peduncles pubescent. .... 8. *B. aristosa*
    Achenes oblanceolate, or narrowly oblong; peduncles glabrous. .... 9. *B. coronata*
  g. Rays absent or 5 mm or less long.
    h. Leaves bipinnately divided .... 10. *B. bipinnata*
    h. Leaves pinnately or ternately divided.
      i. Achenes linear-tetragonal. (Fig. 913). .... 4. *B. pilosa*
      i. Achenes flattened, or if angled then narrowly cuneate.
        j. Outer involucral bracts 5 or fewer, eciliate; awns of achenes not barbed
          or antrorsely barbed .... 11. *B. discoidea*
        j. Outer involucral bracts 5 or more, ciliate, at least toward the base; awns
          of achenes often retrorsely barbed.
          Tissue of lowest segments of divided leaves mostly decurrent on the
          petioles. (Fig. 915) .... 7. *B. tripartita*
          Tissue of lowest segments of divided leaves tapered to the base but
          not decurrent on the petioles .... 12. *B. frondosa*

1. *B. hyperbórea* Greene (northern). Estuaries. August-September. Map 2191. Endangered in MA. Our plants include var. *hyperborea* and the following var.:
var. *svensónii* Fassett. Outer achenes 5 mm or more long, inner more than 7 mm long (outer achenes up to 5 mm long, the inner up to 7 mm long in var. *hyperborea*). —OBL

2. *B. laévis* (L.) B.S.P. (smooth). Marshes and borders of ponds and streams, fresh to brackish. August-October. Map 2192. (Hawaii, S. Amer.). —OBL

3. *B. cérnua* L. (nodding). Pond and stream margins. August-September. Fig. 912, Map 2193. (Eurasia). [*B. elliptica; B. filamentosa; B. glaucescens; B. gracilenta; B. leptopoda; B. prinophylla*]. —OBL

4. B. pilósa L. (hairy). Waste places. Fig. 913. (Adventive from Tropical Amer.). Reported for Hartford County CT; Middlesex County MA.

5. B. bidentoídes (Nutt.) Britt. (resembling *Bidens*). Estuaries. August-September. Fig. 914. From farther south. [*B. mariana*]. —FACW

6. B. eátonii Fern. (for its discoverer). Estuaries. August-September. Map 2194. —OBL

B. heterodóxa (Fern.) Fern. & St. John. Similar to *B. eatonii* but with outer achenes up to 5 mm long (over 5 mm long in *B. eatonii*). Reported for CT. Represented with us by the following 2 vars.:

var. *monardifólia* Fern. Awns of achenes retrorsely barbed.

var. *agnóstica* Fern. Awns smooth to scabrous, but not barbed. —FACW+

7. B. tripartíta L. (three-parted). Borders of ponds and streams, marshes and wet meadows, wet ditches and depressions. August-October. Fig 915, Map 2195. (Adventive from Europe). [*B. acuta; B. comosa*]. —OBL

B. connáta. Muhl. Similar to *B. tripartita* but with achenes compressed-angular (achenes flat in *B. tripartita*). Throughout our range. —FACW+

8. B. aristósa (Michx.) Britt. (bearing bristles). Wet waste places. August-October. Map 2196. From farther south and west. —FACW-

9. B. coronáta (L.) Britt. (crowned). Wet meadows, borders of ponds and streams, wet ditches. August-September. Map 2197. [*B. trichosperma*]. —OBL

10. B. bipinnáta L. (twice-pinnate). Wet waste places. August-October. Map 2198. (Tropical Amer.). From farther south and west. [*Cosmos bipinnatus*]. Leaves are reported to be useable as a potherb. —FACU-

B. tenuisécta Gray. Similar to *B. bipinnata* but ultimate leaf segments are linear and achenes are 2-awned (ultimate leaf segments lanceolate to ovate and achenes 2-4 awned in *B. bipinnata*). Western. Reported for MA.

11. B. discoídea (Torr. & Gray) Britt. Borders of ponds and streams, marshes and wet meadows. August-September. Map 2199. Endangered in NH. —FACW

12. B. frondósa L. (leafy) Borders of ponds and streams, marshes and wet meadows, wet waste places and cultivated ground. August-October. Map 2200. —FACW

B. vulgáta Greene. Similar to *B. frondosa* but with 10 or more outer involucral bracts (outer involucral bracts fewer than 10 in *B. frondosa*). Throughout our range. [*B. puberula*].

7. Megalodónta Greene (from the Greek, meaning large tooth).

Similar to *Bidens* except aquatic, having submersed leaves dissected, with filiform segments and terete achenes. [*Bidens*].

1. M. béckii (Torr. ex Spreng.) Greene (for its discoverer). Ponds and slow rivers and streams. August-September. Map 2201. [*Bidens b.*]. —OBL

8. Polýmnia L. Leaf-cup (name based on ancient Greek mythology).

Perennial herbs, glandular-pubescent, at least above; leaves opposite, or the upper alternate, large, the lower pinnatifid, the upper shallowly lobed, toothed or entire, with stipule-like appendages at base, petioled; heads small, in corymbs or a panicle of corymbs, radiate, or discoid, involucral bracts in 1 series, rays whitish and pistillate or obsolete, receptacle flat, chaffy, disc flowers hermaphrodite but sterile, yellow, pappus none; achenes thick, slightly compressed.

Dyssódia Cav. *pappósa* (Vent.) A. S. Hitchc. Resembling *Polymnia* but rays yellow or orange. Adventive from farther west. Reported for York County, ME; Norfolk County, MA; Chittenden County, VT. [*Boebera p.*].

1. P. canadénsis L. (Canadian). Rich woods. June-September. Fig. 916, Map 2202. Endangered in CT.

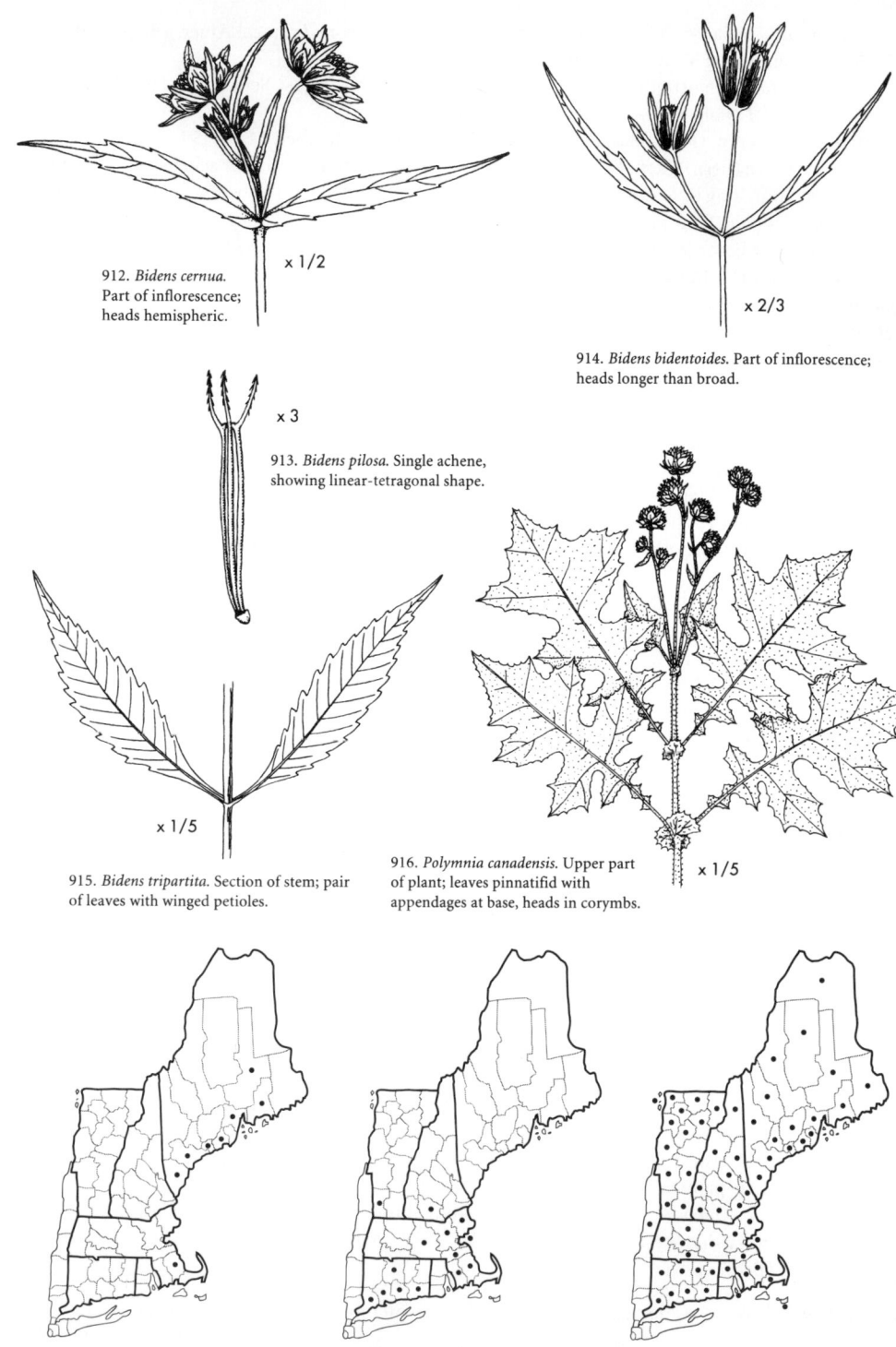

912. *Bidens cernua.*
Part of inflorescence;
heads hemispheric.

× 1/2

× 2/3

914. *Bidens bidentoides.* Part of inflorescence;
heads longer than broad.

× 3

913. *Bidens pilosa.* Single achene,
showing linear-tetragonal shape.

× 1/5

915. *Bidens tripartita.* Section of stem; pair
of leaves with winged petioles.

916. *Polymnia canadensis.* Upper part
of plant; leaves pinnatifid with
appendages at base, heads in corymbs.

× 1/5

2191. *Bidens hyperborea*

2192. *Bidens laevis*

2193. *Bidens cernua*

2194. *Bidens eatonii*

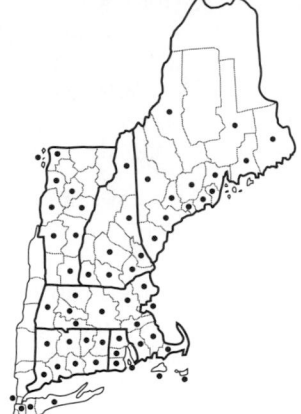

2195. *Bidens tripartita*

2196. *Bidens aristosa*

2197. *Bidens coronata*

2198. *Bidens bipinnata*

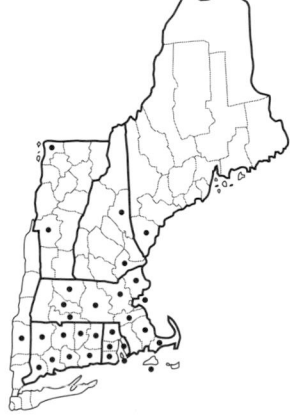

2199. *Bidens discoidea*

2200. *Bidens frondosa*

2201. *Megalodonta beckii*

2202. *Polymnia canadensis*

9. Mikánia Willd. Climbing hempweed (for J. Mikan).

Twining and climbing, perennial vines, stems pubescent to glabrous, somewhat angled; leaves opposite, petioled, triangular-ovate, cordate at base, acuminate, entire to sinuate-margined, palmately-veined; heads in corymbs on axillary peduncles, discoid, 4-flowered, involucre of 4, mostly equal bracts and sometimes 1-few smaller ones, receptacle small, naked, flowers perfect, white to pink, pappus of capillary bristles; achenes 4-5-angled.

1. **M. scándens** (L.) Willd. (climbing). Wooded swamps and streambanks, climbing on shrubs. August-October. Fig. 917, Map 2203. —FACW+

10. Acanthospérmum Schrank (from the Greek, based on the prickly fruit cluster).

Pubescent, annual herbs with stems trailing, usually rooting at the nodes; leaves opposite, toothed above the middle, petioled, rhombic-ovate, glandular-punctate; heads solitary in the forks of the branched stem and in the leaf axils, small, radiate, involucral bracts in 2 series, the outer herbaceous, the inner larger, prickly, rays small, yellow, pistillate, receptacle conical, chaffy, disc flowers yellow, perfect, sterile, pappus none; achenes oblong, slightly flattened, enclosed within the inner involucral bracts, the cluster of usually 5 remaining attached and forming a star-shaped bur.

1. **A. austrále** (Loefl.) Kuntze. Roadsides and waste places. July-October. Fig. 918. (Adventive from Tropical Amer.). From farther south. Reported for Suffolk County, MA.

11. Eclípta L. (from the Greek, referring to the absence of pappus).

Erect or spreading, rough-pubescent, annual herbs, the stem branched and often rooting at the nodes; leaves simple, opposite, sessile or subsessile, narrowly to broadly lanceolate, narrowed at both ends, entire to remotely serrate; heads small, numerous, solitary or in small clusters, terminal and axillary, radiate, involucral bracts in 1 or 2 series, rays very short, pistillate, white, receptacle flat to slightly convex, with awn-like or bristly chaff, disc flowers perfect, white, pappus none; achenes of the rays angled, those of the disc laterally flattened.

1. **E. prostráta** (L.) L. Waste places. August-October. Fig. 919, Map 2204. From farther west or south. [*E. alba; E. erecta; Verbesina alba*]. —FAC

Sigesbéckia L. *orientális* L. Similar to *Eclipta* but with involucral bracts stipitate-glandular, dimorphic, the outer linear-oblanceolate, spreading, the inner shorter and broader (involucral bracts not stipitate-glandular, not distinctly dimorphic in *Eclipta*). (Asia). Occurring as a waif in MA.

12. Galinsóga Ruiz & Pavon (for M. de Galinsoga).

Branched, annual herbs; leaves simple, opposite, petioled, toothed or entire, lanceolate, to lance-ovate; heads small, numerous, in leafy cymes, radiate, involucral bracts few, rays white to pink, pistillate, receptacle conical, chaffy, the chaff linear, disc flowers perfect, yellow, pappus of several to many fimbriate or aristate scales, sometimes lacking; achenes angled to flattened.

Rays lacking pappus; pappus of disc flowers conspicuously fimbriate but divisions
    not aristate, merely acute, as long or longer than the corolla. .... 1. *G. parviflora*
Rays with pappus; pappus of disc flowers fimbriate, the divisions aristate or if not
    then only about half as long as the corolla. (Fig. 920). .... 2. *G. quadriradiata*

1. **G. parviflóra** Cav. (small-flowered). Roadsides, waste places, cultivated ground. June-October. Map 2205. (Naturalized from Tropical Amer.). Tops of plant edible as a potherb.

2. **G. quadriradiáta** Ruiz & Pavon. Roadsides, waste places, cultivated ground. June-October. Fig. 920, Map 2206. (Naturalized from Tropical Amer.). [*G. ciliata; G. caracasana; G. bicolorata*].

13. Íva L. Marsh-elder (old name for a medicinal plant).

Monoecious, puberulent to scabrous, annual or suffrutescent perennial herbs; leaves opposite or the upper alternate, short to long petioled, dentate; heads small, greenish-white, nodding, solitary in the leaf axils or in axillary and terminal racemes, spikes or panicles, discoid, flowers imperfect, the staminate and pistillate in the same head, the pistillate corollas marginal, barely lobed at apex, or none, the staminate distinctly 5-lobed, involucral bracts few, imbricated, receptacle chaffy, pappus none; achenes compressed.

Agératum L. houstoniánum P. Mill. Similar to *Iva* but distinguishable in having leaves cordate at base and heads clustered (leaves not cordate and heads in spikes or racemes in *Iva*). From Mexico. Rarely escaped from cultivation in our range. Reported for Fairfield County, CT; Essex County, MA.

Heads in panicled spikes, not subtended by leafy bracts. .... 1. *I. xanthifolia*
Heads in the axils of leaves or leafy bracts, forming spikes or racemes. (Fig. 921).
    Perennial herb or somewhat shrubby; leaves sessile or short-petioled; coastal
        plants .... 2. *I. frutescens*
                                                                subsp. *oraria*
    Annual; leaves long-petioled; inland plants. .... 3. *I. annua*

1. I. xanthifólia Nutt. (with leaves of *Xanthium*). Roadsides and waste places. July-September. Map 2207. [*Cyclachaena x.*]. Contact with leaves causes dermatitis in some people; pollen is a cause of hay fever in autumn. —FAC

2. I. frutéscens L. (shrubby). Salt marshes, at the limit of normal high tide. August-October. Fig. 921, Map 2208. Represented with us as subsp. *orária* (Bartlett) R. C. Jackson. —FACW+

3. I. ánnua L. (annual). Waste places, moist soil, river bottoms. July-October. Reported for MA, ME. Adventive from farther west. [*I. caudata; I. ciliata*]. Our plants are var. *annua*. —FAC

14. Coreópsis L. Tickseed (Greek name, referring to fancied resemblance of the achene to an insect).

Annual or perennial herbs; leaves entire or serrate to pinnatifid or ternate, opposite or rarely alternate, sessile or petioled; heads solitary or in corymbs or panicles, radiate, involucral bracts in 2 series, the outer green, foliaceous, usually spreading, narrower and usually shorter than the inner, the inner more membraneous, appressed, rays yellow or rarely pink or white, sometimes bicolored, neutral, receptacle flat or nearly so, chaffy, disc flowers perfect, yellow or red, pappus of 2 smooth or antrorsely barbed teeth or short awns or none; achenes flattened, winged or sometimes wingless.

a. Rays pink, white, or yellow with reddish base; achenes wingless.
  b. Rays pink or white; leaves mostly entire, occasionally irregularly lobed;
    rhizomatous perennial .... 1. *C. rosea*
  b. Rays yellow with reddish base; leaves pinnately divided; annual.
    Leaf segments linear to narrowly lanceolate; outer involucral bracts much
      shorter than the inner .... 2. *C. tinctoria*
    Leaf segments lanceolate to oblong or elliptic; outer involucral bracts about
      as long as the inner .... 3. *C. basalis*
a. Rays entirely yellow; achenes winged.
  c. Rays entire or minutely toothed; chaff linear, rounded to acute at tip; leaves
    mostly trifoliate, the lateral leaflets or divisions at least half as long as the
    terminal one. (Fig. 922).
    Leaves sessile, ternately parted to the base and thus appearing whorled.
      Leaf segments entire, not again divided, the ultimate segments lanceolate
      to oval .... 4. *C. major*
      Leaf segments, or at least the central one, pinnate or again ternate, the
      ultimate segments linear to filiform .... 5. *C. verticillata*
    Leaves petioled, ternately parted but not to the base, not appearing whorled. .... 6. *C. tripteris*
  c. Rays coarsely toothed or lobed; chaff narrowly lanceolate, attenuate to long,
    filiform tips; leaves mostly entire or pinnatifid, or if with 1 pair of basal
    segments these mostly less than half as long as the terminal one. (Fig. 924).

d. Stem leafy in the lower half. (Fig. 923). .... 7. *C. lanceolata*
d. Stem leafy beyond the middle.
    Leaves pinnatifid, with linear to lance-linear segments. .... 8. *C. grandiflora*
    Leaves entire or with 1 or 2 pairs of oblong to elliptic basal segments. .... 9. *C. pubescens*

1. *C. rósea* Nutt. (rose-colored). Pond margins. July-September. Map 2209. —FACW

2. *C. tinctória* Nutt. (used in dyeing). Roadsides and waste places. July-September. Map 2210. From farther west. Our plants are var. *tinctoria.* —FAC-

3. *C. basális* (Dietr.) Blake (with basal branching). Occasionally escaped from cultivation to roadsides and waste places. Reported for Fairfield and New London Counties, CT. [*C. drummondii*].

4. *C. májor* Walt. (larger). Open woods and clearings. June-July. From farther south. Reported for Essex County, MA.

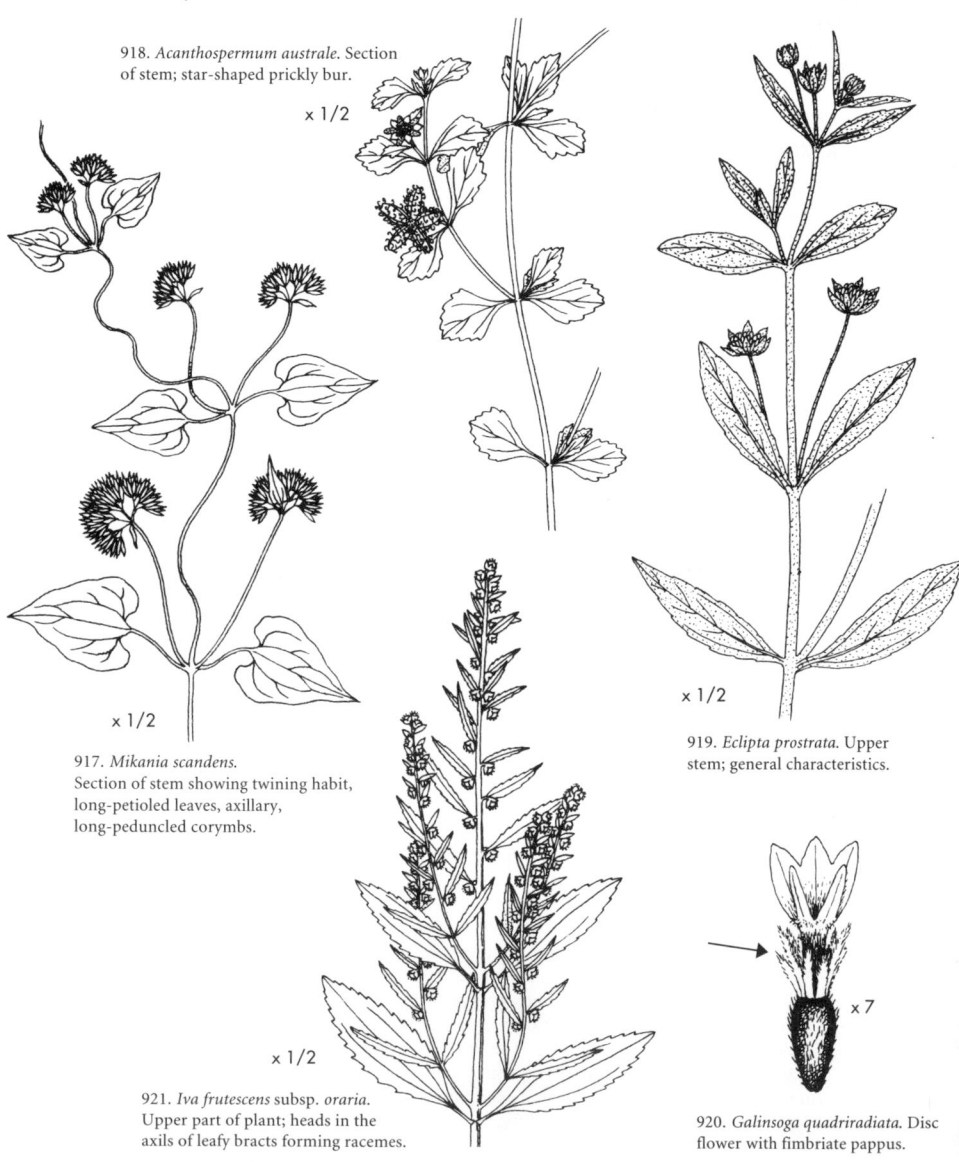

918. *Acanthospermum australe.* Section of stem; star-shaped prickly bur.

x 1/2

x 1/2

917. *Mikania scandens.* Section of stem showing twining habit, long-petioled leaves, axillary, long-peduncled corymbs.

919. *Eclipta prostrata.* Upper stem; general characteristics.

x 1/2

x 1/2

921. *Iva frutescens* subsp. *oraria.* Upper part of plant; heads in the axils of leafy bracts forming racemes.

x 7

920. *Galinsoga quadriradiata.* Disc flower with fimbriate pappus.

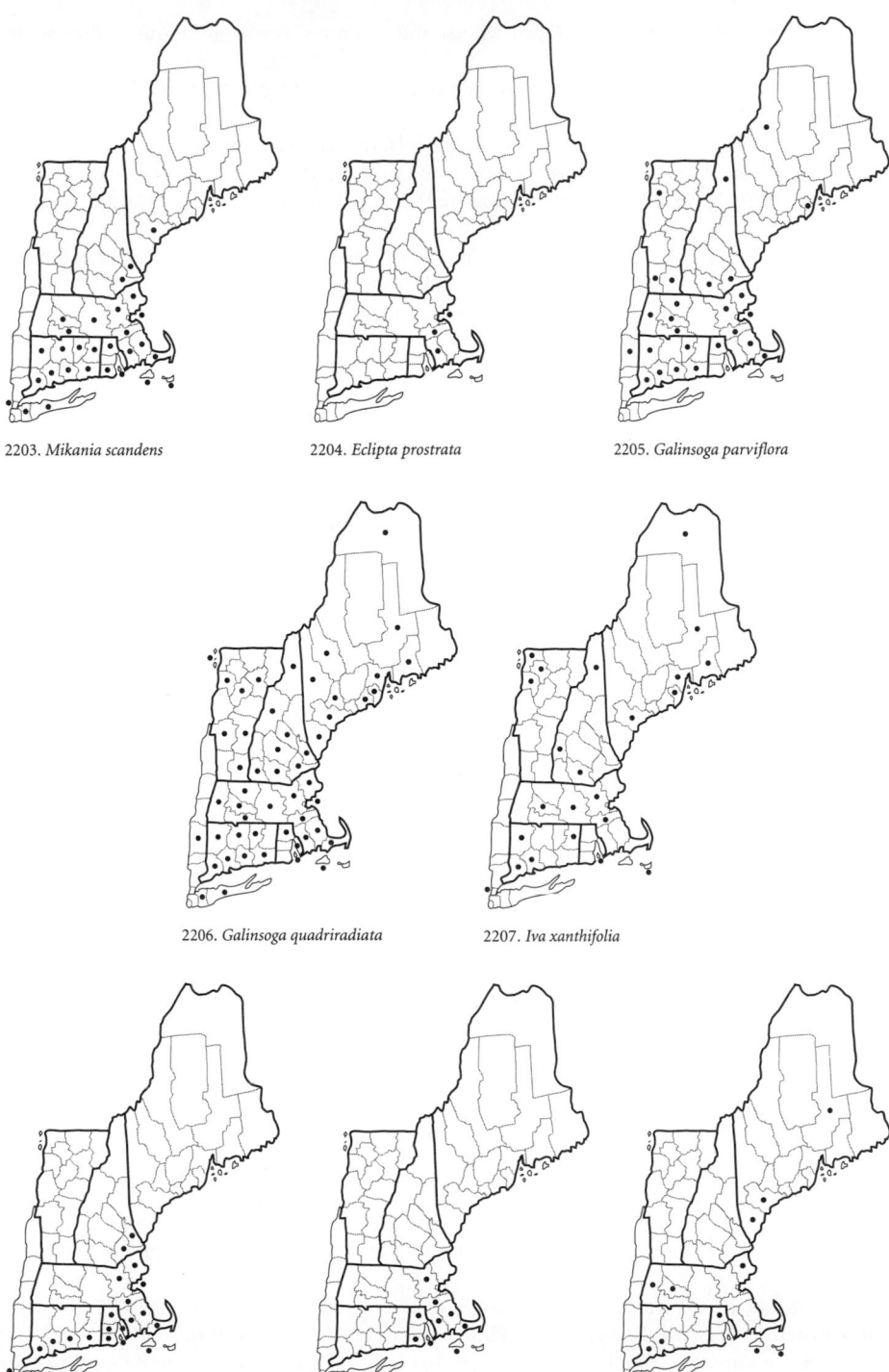

2203. *Mikania scandens*

2204. *Eclipta prostrata*

2205. *Galinsoga parviflora*

2206. *Galinsoga quadriradiata*

2207. *Iva xanthifolia*

2208. *Iva frutescens* subsp. *oraria*

2209. *Coreopsis rosea*

2210. *Coreopsis tinctoria*

5. *C. verticilláta* L. (whorled). Open woods and clearings. June-July. From farther south. Reported for CT, MA.

6. *C. trípteris* L. (three-winged). Open woods, thickets, fields. August-September. Fig. 922, Map 2211. From farther south and west. —FAC

7. *C. lanceoláta* L. (lance-shaped). Dry sandy fields, roadsides and waste places. June-August. Figs. 923 and 924, Map 2212. From farther south and west. [*C. crassifolia; C. heterogyna*]. —FACU

8. *C. grandiflóra* Hogg ex Sweet (large-flowered). Dry fields, roadsides, waste places. May-July. From farther south.

9. *C. pubéscens* Ell. (hairy). Open woods. June-September. Map 2213. From farther south and west. Our plants include var. *pubescens* and the following var.:

var. *robústa* Gray. Herbage glabrous or nearly so (pubescent in var. *pubescens*).

15. *Cósmos* Cav. (from the Greek, meaning decoration).

Annual herbs; leaves pinnately or bipinnately compound, opposite, sessile to short-petioled; heads solitary, on terminal and axillary peduncles, radiate, the same as in *Bidens* (genus 6) except achenes are beaked, awns deciduous.

Rays white, pink or red; achenes with beaks less than half the length of the body;
    leaf segments linear to linear-filiform. .... 1. *C. bipinnatus*
Rays orange or yellow; achenes with beaks half or more the length of the body; leaf
    segments mostly linear-lanceolate to elliptic. .... 2. *C. sulphureus*

1. *C. bipinnátus* Cav. (twice pinnately divided). Roadsides and waste places. August-October. Map 2214. (Introduced from Mexico). —FACU-

2. *C. sulphúreus* Cav. (sulphur-colored). Roadsides and waste places. August-October. Fig. 925. (Introduced from Mexico). Reported for Fairfield County, CT.

C. parviflórus (Jackq.) H.B.K. Similar to the latter species but with rays 1 cm or less long (rays 1.3 cm or more long in *C. sulphureus*). From farther west. Reported for MA, ME, RI.

16. *Sílphium* L. Rosin-weed (based on an ancient Greek name for a resinous plant).

Tall, coarse, square-stemmed, glabrous, perennial herbs with resinous juice; leaves opposite, connate-perfoliate by their blades or by winged petioles, ovate to deltoid-ovate, coarsely toothed, scabrous on both sides; heads corymbose or paniculate, radiate, involucral bracts subequal or in 2 or more indistinct series, elliptic or ovate, rays yellow, pistillate, imbricated in 2 or 3 rows, receptacle flat, with linear chaff, disc flowers yellow, perfect, sterile, pappus none or of 2 teeth or awns; achenes broad and flat, winged, usually notched at the apex.

1. *S. perfoliátum* L. (leaf-base surrounding stem). Thickets, roadsides, waste places. July-September. Map 2215. Rare; from farther west or south. Our plants are var. *perfoliatum*. —FACU

17. *Guizótia* Cass. (for F. Guizot).

Branched, annual herbs; leaves simple, opposite (or the upper alternate), sessile and clasping, serrate or entire, lance-oblong; heads in cymes terminating the stem and branches, radiate, involucral bracts few, in 1 series, rays yellow, pistillate, several-toothed at the apex, receptacle convex or conical, chaffy, disc flowers perfect, yellow, the tube short and densely woolly, pappus none; achenes flattened.

Flavéria Juss. *trinérvia* (Spreng.) C. Mohr. Similar to *Guizotia* but differs in having receptacle naked or setose. Western. Reported for Middlesex County, MA. [*F. bidentis*].

Zínnia L. *violácea* Cav. Similar to *Guizotia* but has large orange or red heads and rays persistent on the achenes. Occasionally escaped from cultivation. Reported for Fairfield County, CT. [*Z. elegans*].

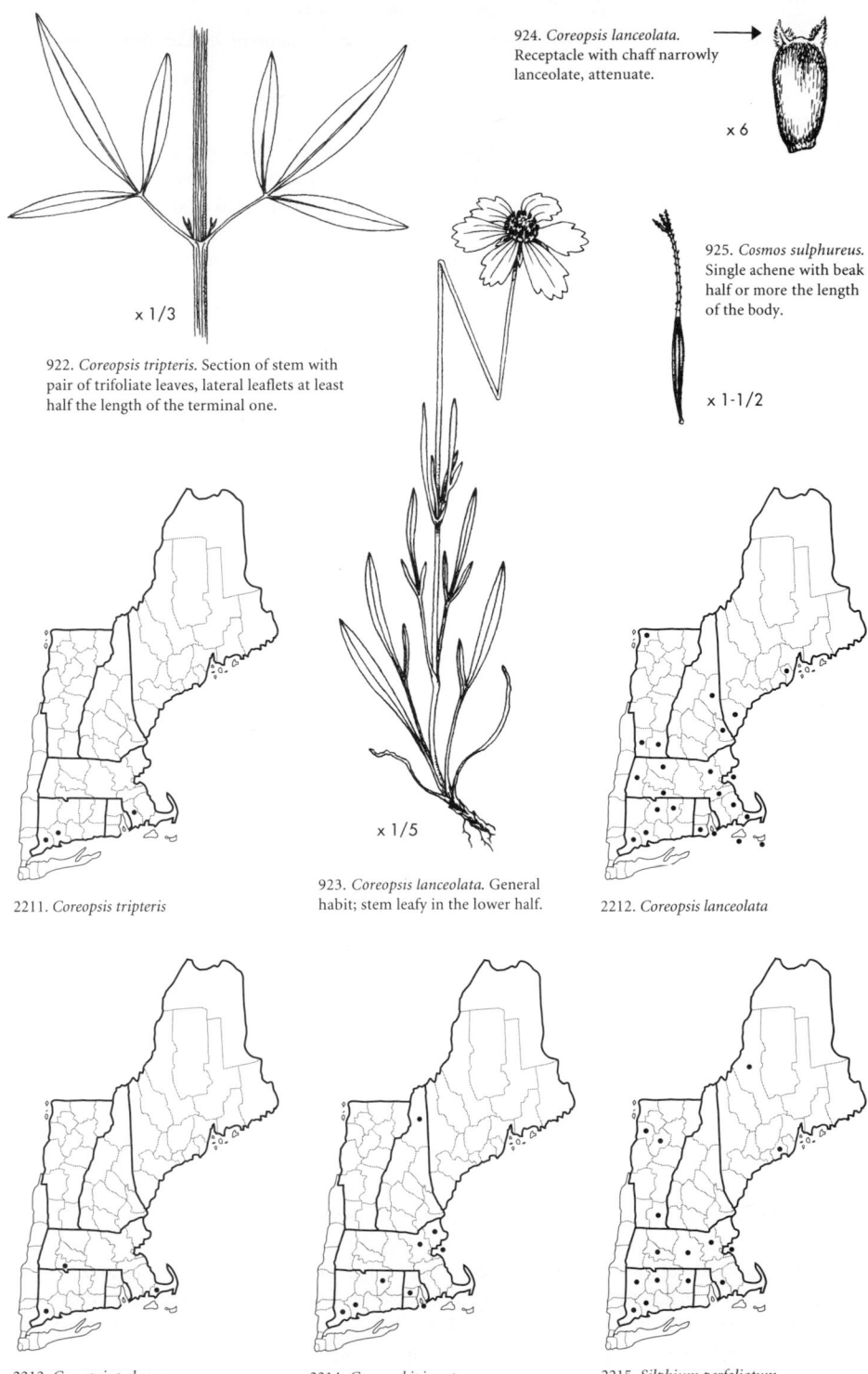

924. *Coreopsis lanceolata*. Receptacle with chaff narrowly lanceolate, attenuate.

x 6

925. *Cosmos sulphureus*. Single achene with beak half or more the length of the body.

x 1-1/2

x 1/3

922. *Coreopsis tripteris*. Section of stem with pair of trifoliate leaves, lateral leaflets at least half the length of the terminal one.

x 1/5

923. *Coreopsis lanceolata*. General habit; stem leafy in the lower half.

2211. *Coreopsis tripteris*

2212. *Coreopsis lanceolata*

2213. *Coreopsis pubescens*

2214. *Cosmos bipinnatus*

2215. *Silphium perfoliatum*

1. G. abyssínica (L.f.) Cass. (of *Abyssinia*). Waste places. September-October. Map 2216. (Adventive from Tropical Africa).

18. Árnica L.

Simple-stemmed, annual herbs, the stems spreading-pubescent, often glandular above; leaves opposite, dentate or denticulate, all but the lowest sessile, lanceolate to lance-ovate or oblanceolate; heads large, yellow, solitary or corymbose, radiate, involucral bracts equal or subequal, somewhat biseriate, spreading-pubescent and glandular, rays pistillate, receptacle flat, naked, disc flowers perfect, pappus of tawny, sub-plumose, bristles; achenes cylindric, pubescent.

1. A. móllis Hook. (soft). Alpine areas, wet ledges, river shores. July-August. Map 2217. Endangered in NY. —FAC

A. lanceoláta Nutt. Similar to *A. mollis* except with all but the upper leaves narrowed to petioles, heads up to 4 cm wide, involucral bracts less than 1 cm long, occuring at lower altitudes(leaves rounded to a sessile base, heads 4 cm or more wide, bracts 1 cm or more long in *A.mollis*). Reported for ME, NH. [*A. mollis* var. *petiolaris*]. —FAC

19. Helíópsis Pers. Ox-eye (from the Greek, based on similarity of appearance to the sunflower).

Perennial herbs with glabrous stems; leaves simple, opposite, petioled, lanceolate to ovate-lanceolate, 3-ribbed, serrate; heads showy, on long peduncles terminating the stem and branches, radiate, involucral bracts in 1 or 2 series, rays yellow, pistillate, persistent, receptacle conical, with linear chaff, disc flowers perfect, yellow, pappus none or a minute, obscurely-toothed crown; achenes thick, slightly angled.

Sanvitália Lam. *procúmbens* Lam. Similar to *Heliopsis* but annual, with margins of leaves entire (*Heliopsis* is perennial with coarsely toothed leaves). (Mexico). Rarely spread from cultivation in our range. Reported for VT.

1. H. helianthoídes (L.) Sweet. Open woods, thickets, fields, waste places. July-September. Map 2218. From farther west and south. Our plants include var. *helianthoides* and the following var.: var. *scábra* (Dunal) Fern. Leaves harshly scabrous above (smooth to slightly scabrous in var. *helianthoides*). [*H. scabra*].

20. Verbesína L. Crownbeard (based on the name Verbena).

Annual or perennial herbs; leaves simple, alternate or opposite, petioled, the petioles often decurrent on the stem, toothed to subentire; heads in corymbs or panicles, radiate, involucral bracts subequal, scarcely imbricated, rays yellow, pistillate or neutral, receptacle convex, chaffy, disc flowers perfect, yellow, pappus of usually 2 awns; achenes strongly flattened, usually winged.

Involucral bracts reflexed in flower and fruit; leaves alternate; petioles usually
    decurrent on stem; perennial .... 1. *V. alternifolia*
Involucral bracts erect or spreading in flower and fruit; leaves, at least the lower,
    opposite; petioles not decurrent; annual. .... 2. *V. encelioides*

1. V. alternifólia (L.) Britt. ex Kearney (alternate-leaved). Rich woodlands. June-September. Rare; from farther west. Reported for RI. [*Actinomeris a.; Ridan a.*]. —FAC

2. V. encelioídes (Cav.) Benth. & Hook. f. ex Gray (resembling *Encelia*). (without auricles). Roadsides and waste places. June-September. From farther west. Reported for Essex and Norfolk Counties, MA. [*Ximenesia e.*]. Our plants include subsp. *encelioides* and the following subsp.: subsp. *exauriculáta* (Robins. & Greenm.) J. R. Petioles not auriculate at the base (petioles auriculate at the base in subsp. *encelioides*). [*X. exauriculata*]—FACU

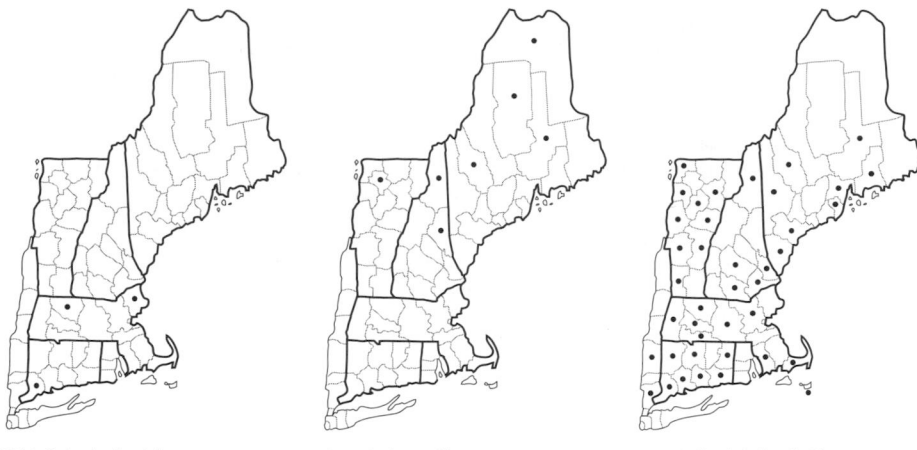

2216. *Guizotia abyssinica*   2217. *Arnica mollis*   2218. *Heliopsis helianthoides*

21. *Heliánthus* L. Sunflower (Greek name for sunflower).

Stout, annual or perennial herbs; leaves simple, opposite or alternate, petioled or sessile, toothed or entire; heads solitary or corymbose, radiate, involucral bracts in several series, rays large and yellow, neutral, receptacle flat or convex, chaffy, disc flowers perfect, brown, purplish or yellow, pappus of 2 awned scales, promptly deciduous; achenes thick, compressed or angled, embraced by the persistent chaff. —Wildl. 1

In addition to the species in the following treatment *H. x divariserratus* has been reported for CT and *H. x intermedius* has been reported for ME.

Flavéria Juss. *trinérvia* (Spreng.) C. Mohr. May sometimes key to *Helianthus* but differs in having receptacle naked or setose and no pappus. Western. Reported for Middlesex County, MA.

Lasthénia Cass. Similar to *Helianthus* but distinguishable in being slender annuals having flowers with pappus of 5 or more acuminate scales or pappus sometimes absent (*Helianthus* is a robust annual or perennial having flowers with pappus of 2 awned scales). Southwestern; two species occur as waifs in our range: *L. califórnica* DC. ex Lindl, has entire leaves. Reported for Middlesex County, MA. [*L. chrysostoma*]; *L. mínor* (DC.) Ornduff, has leaves pinnately lobed or cleft. Reported for MA.

Hemizónia DC. *fasciculáta* (DC.) Torr. & Gray. Will key to *Helianthus* but is distinguishable from it as well as the above 2 similar genera in having a chaffy receptacle (usually), involucral bracts each clasping the outer half of a ray achene, and rays small and inconspicuous. Southwestern; a waif in our range. Reported for Middlesex County, MA.

a. Plants annual; leaves mostly alternate; petioles mostly longer than 2 cm, not
    winged with blade tissue; receptacle flat or nearly so. (Fig. 926).
  b. Involucral bracts long-ciliate .... 1. *H. annuus*
  b. Involucral bracts eciliate or with marginal hairs about the same length as those
    on the back.
    Central bracts of receptacle long-bearded at summit; stems not mottled. .... 2. *H. petiolaris*
    Central bracts of receptacle not bearded; stem usually dark-mottled. .... 3. *H. debilis*
a. Plants perennial; leaves mostly opposite (except usually the uppermost) or if
    mostly alternate the petioles shorter or distinctly winged with blade tissue;
    receptacle usually convex.
  c. Leaves, except sometimes the lowest, rounded, truncate or subcordate, sessile,
    or petioles 5 mm or less long. (Fig. 927).
    Stems glabrous or essentially so .... 4. *H. divaricatus*
    Stems densely pubescent .... 5. *H. mollis*
  c. Leaves tapered to bases or if rounded with petioles longer than 5 mm. (Fig. 928).

d. Stems smooth, glabrous or essentially so.
  e. Leaves narrowly lanceolate, mostly 4 or more times as long as wide and
    3.5 cm or less wide .... 6. *H. grosseserratus*
  e. Leaves broadly lanceolate to ovate-lanceolate, mostly 3 times or less as long
    as wide and more than 3.5 cm wide (at least the larger ones).
    Leaves coarsely serrate, thin-textured. .... 7. *H. decapetalus*
    Leaves obscurely serrate or crenate, thick-textured. .... 8. *H. strumosus*
d. Stems rough, scabrous, or pubescent, or if subglabrous, involucral bracts
  appressed (bracts loose, not evidently appressed or imbricated in the
  species in first part of couplet).
  f. Leaves linear or lance-linear, mostly 1 cm or less wide, sessile or subsessile ..... 9. *H. angustifolius*
  f. Leaves lanceolate to ovate, more than 1 cm wide, petioled.
    g. Leaves mostly alternate.
      h. Leaves lanceolate, mostly 4 or more times as long as wide and 3.5 cm
        or less wide.
        Involucral bracts long-ciliate .... 10. *H. giganteus*
        Involucral bracts eciliate or with marginal hairs about the same length
          as those on the back .... 11. *H. maximilianii*
      h. Leaves lanceolate to ovate, mostly 3 times or less as long as wide and
        4 cm or more wide .... 12. *H. tuberosus*
    g. Leaves mostly opposite (except usually the uppermost).
      Involucral bracts appressed; leaves mostly less than 5 cm wide. .... 13. *H. x laetiflorus*
      Involucral bracts spreading or loosely ascending; leaves, at least the
        larger ones, 6 cm or more wide .... 12. *H. tuberosus*

1. H. ánnuus L. (annual). Common sunflower. Roadsides and waste places. July-September. Fig. 926, Map 2219. [*H. aridus; H. lenticularis*]. Hulled seeds can be roasted and eaten, ground into flour or used as a coffee substitute; oil produced from the seeds is used in cooking. —FAC-

2. H. petioláris Nutt. (petioled). Roadsides and waste places. July-September. Map 2220. From farther west. Our plants are subsp. *petiolaris*.

3. H. débilis Nutt. (weak). Roadsides and waste places. July-October. Map 2221. Represented with us as subsp. *cucumerifólius* (Torr. & Gray) Heiser. [*H. cucumerifolius*].

4. H. divaricátus L. (spread asunder). Dry woods and thickets. July-September. Fig. 927, Map 2222.

5. H. móllis Lam. (soft). Dry woods and fields. July-September. Map 2223. From farther west and south.

6. H. grosseserrátus Martens (coarsely serrate). Fields, roadsides, waste places. July-October. Map 2224. From farther west. —FACW

H. x luxúrians E. E. Watson. A hybrid between *H. grosseserratus* and *H. giganteus.*

H. x kellermánii Britton. A hybrid between *H. grosseserratus* and *H. salicifolius.*

H. salicifólius A. Dietr. Similar to *H. grosseserratus* but differing in having linear leaves mostly 5 mm or less wide (leaves lanceolate and 1 cm or more wide in *H. grosseserratus*). From farther west. Reported for Bronx and Columbia Counties, NY. [*H. orgyalis*].

7. H. decapétalus L. (with ten petals). Open woods, stream borders, thickets. August-October. Map 2225. [*H. trachelifolius*]. —FACU

8. H. strumósus L. (scrofulous). Open woods and thickets. July-September. Map 2226. [*H. chartaceus; H. trachelifolius*].

9. H. angustifólius L. (narrow-leaved). Moist woods and thickets near the coast. August-October. From farther south. Reported for Suffolk County NY. —FACW

10. H. gigantéus L. (gigantic). Fields and moist thickets. August-September. Fig. 928, Map 2227. From farther west. [*H. subtuberosus*]. —FACW

11. H. maximiliánii Schrad. (for its discoverer). Fields and waste places. July-September. Map 2228. From farther west.

12. H. tuberósus L. (tuberous). Jerusalem Artichoke. Waste places, thickets. August-October. Map 2229. Tuber edible; was cultivated by Indians. —FAC

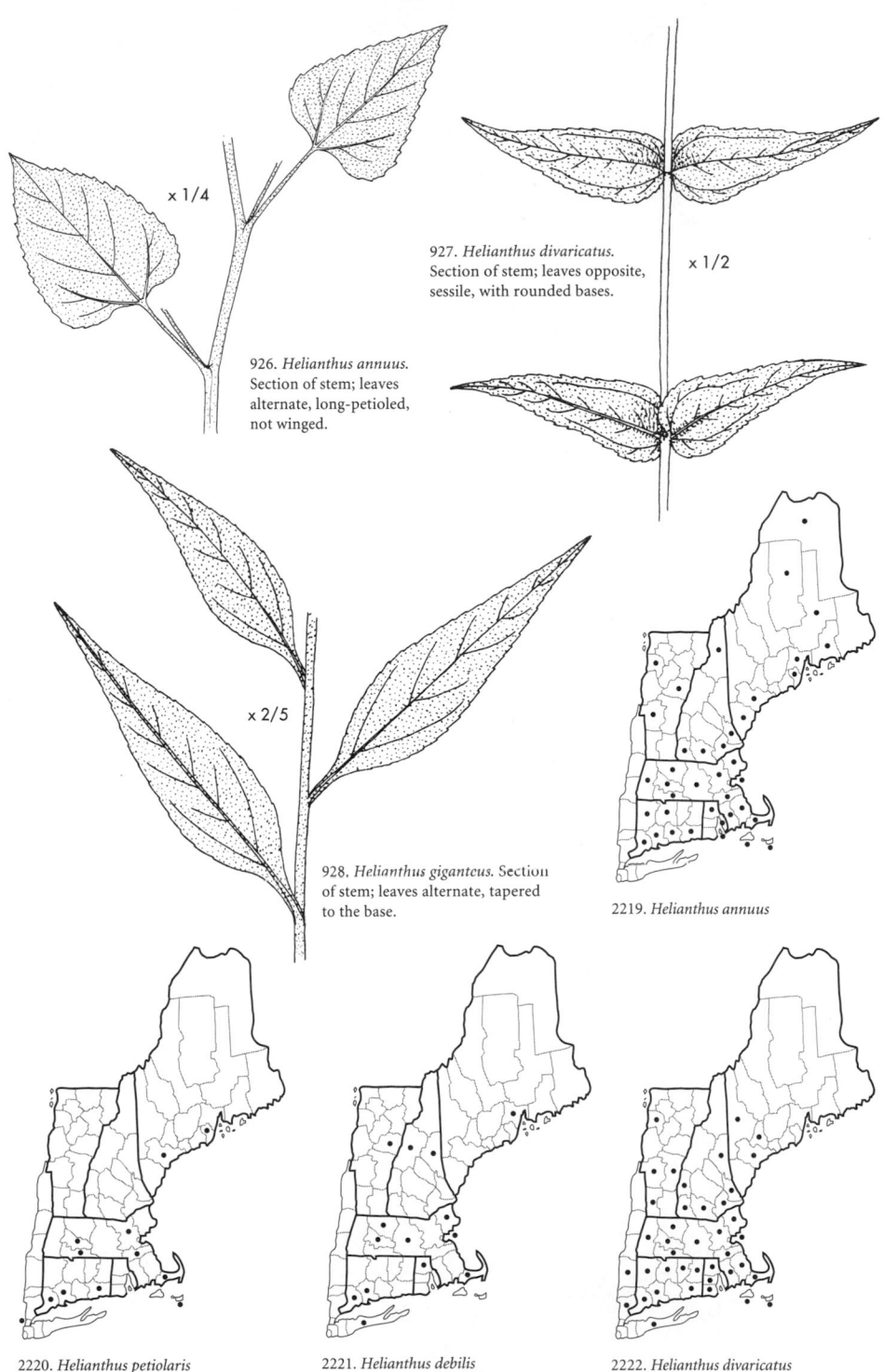

× 1/4

927. *Helianthus divaricatus.*
Section of stem; leaves opposite,
sessile, with rounded bases.

× 1/2

926. *Helianthus annuus.*
Section of stem; leaves
alternate, long-petioled,
not winged.

× 2/5

928. *Helianthus giganteus.* Section
of stem; leaves alternate, tapered
to the base.

2219. *Helianthus annuus*

2220. *Helianthus petiolaris*

2221. *Helianthus debilis*
subsp. *cucumerifolius*

2222. *Helianthus divaricatus*

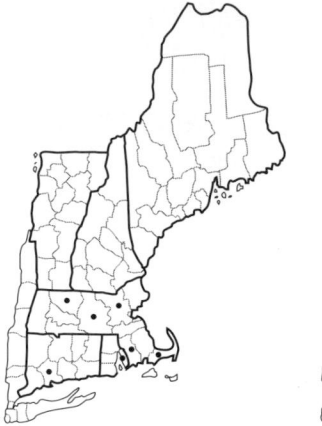

2223. *Helianthus mollis*

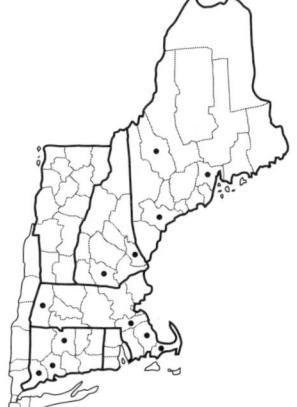

2224. *Helianthus grosseserratus*

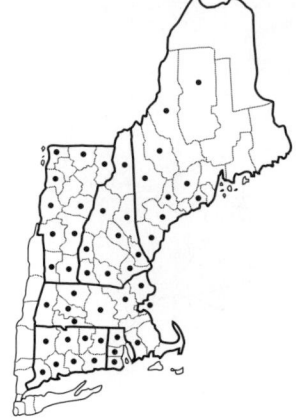

2225. *Helianthus decapetalus*

2226. *Helianthus strumosus*

2227. *Helianthus giganteus*

2228. *Helianthus maximilianii*

2229. *Helianthus tuberosus*

2230. *Helianthus x laetiflorus*

13. H. x laetiflórus Pers. (pro. sp.) (beautifully flowered). A hybrid between *H. paucifloris* and *H. tuberosus*. Fields, roadsides, waste places. August-September. Map 2230. From farther west. [*H. scaberrimus*]. Tuber edible.

H. pauciflórus Nutt. Will key to *H. x laetiflorus* but is distinguishable primarily in having a reddish-purple disc (disc yellow in *H. x laetiflorus*). From farther west. Our plants include subsp. *pauciflorus* (reported throughout our range) [*H. rigidus*] and the following subsp.:

subsp. *subrhomboídeus* (Rydb.) O. Spring & E. Schilling. Leaves 10 or fewer pairs below the inflorescence, obtuse to acute, up to 12 cm long (leaves mostly more than 10 pairs, acuminate, mostly longer than 12 cm in subsp. *pauciflorus*). Reported for CT, MA, ME, NH [*H. subrhomboideus*].

22. Antennária Gaertn. Pussy-toes (name based on fancied resemblance of the pappus of the staminate flowers to the antennae of certain insects).

Dioecious, stoloniferous, woolly, perennial herbs, the stolons leafy-bracteate, producing new rosettes at their apices; leaves in basal rosettes and alternate, entire, woolly beneath; heads corymbose, discoid, staminate and pistillate flowers on separate plants, involucral bracts imbricated in several series, scarious, often colored, receptacle flat or convex, naked, pistillate flowers 5-lobed, staminate flowers unlobed, pappus of capillary bristles, copious in pistillate flowers, scanty in the staminate; achenes small, smooth. (Staminate plants are unknown in most species, the seeds being produced without fertilization. Numerous species have been described based on characteristics of the stolons, size, shape and pubescence of the leaves, and characteristics of the involucre, but these overlap, making the distinctions unclear. The following treatment represents the view currently held for the species in our range.) Mucilage from the stems of various species has been reportedly used to make chewing gum. —Wildl. 1

a. Basal leaves distinctly 3-5-veined, the lateral veins reaching nearly to the apex.
  b. Basal leaves glabrous above from the first or nearly so. Map 2231. [*A. plantaginifolia* var. *arnoglossa*, var. *parlinii*; *A. brainerdii*] .... 1. *A. parlínii* Fern. subsp. *parlínii*
  b. Basal leaves pubescent above, at least when young.
    Pistillate involucres 7 mm or more high. Map 2232. [*A. plantaginifolia* var. *ambigens*; *A. fallax*; *A. farwellii*; *A. munda*; *A. obovata*; *A. occidentalis*]. ... 1. *A. parlínii* Fern. subsp. *fállax* (Greene) Bayer & Stebbins
    Pistillate involucres up to 7 mm high. Throughout our range.
    [*A. plantaginifolia* var. *p.*] ....2. *A. plantaginifólia* (L.) Richards
a. Basal leaves 1-veined or obscurely 3-veined, the lateral veins extending only about half the length of the blade.
  c. Basal leaves abruptly contracted to a petiole-like base; stolons short, decumbent. (Fig. 929).
    Pistillate involucres 5-7 mm high, Map 2233. From farther south. [*A. neglecta* var. *argillicola*] .... 3. *A. virgínica* Stebbins
    Pistillate involucres 7 mm or more high. Fig. 929, Map 2234. [*A. neglecta* var. *attenuata*, var. *neodioica*; *A. brainerdii*; *A. neodioica*; *A. rupicola*]. .... 4. *A. hówellii* Greene subsp. *neodióica* (Greene) Bayer
  c. Basal leaves gradually attenuate to the base; stolons long, procumbent, or basal leaves glabrous above or promptly glabrate, or less than 5 mm wide (basal leaves canescent above, tardily glabrate, and wider than 5 mm in species in the first part of couplet).
    d. Basal leaves 5 mm or less wide. From farther north. Reported for ME.
    [*A. neglecta* var. *gaspensis*; *A. gaspensis*]. .... 5. *A. rósea* Greene subsp. *pulvináta* (Greene) Bayer

d. Basal leaves, at least the larger ones, more than 5 mm wide.
    e. Basal leaves glabrous or promptly glabrate above. Map 2235. [*A. neglecta*
        var. *canadensis*, var. *randii*; *A. canadensis*]. .... 4. *A. hówellii* Greene
                                                        subsp. *canadénsis*
                                                        (Greene) Bayer

    e. Basal leaves canescent above, tardily glabrate.
        Middle and upper stem leaves of pistillate plant terminated by a long
            colored subulate tip. Throughout our range. [*A. petaloidea*;
            A. neglecta var. *p.*]. .... 4. *A. hówellii* Greene
                                                          subsp. *petaloidea*
                                                         (Fern) Bayer

        Middle and upper stem leaves of pistillate plant terminated by a
            lance-attenuate flat or involute tip. Throughout our range.
            [*A. campestris*; *A. longifolia*] .... 6. *A. neglécta* Greene

929. *Antennaria howellii*
subsp. *neodioica.*
General habit;
basal leaves abruptly
contracted to petiole-like base.

× 1/3

2231. *Antennaria parlinii* subsp. *parlinii*

2232. *Antennaria parlinii* subsp. *fallax*

2233. *Antennaria virginica*

2234. *Antennaria howellii* subsp. *neodioica*

2235. *Antennaria howellii* subsp. *canadensis*

23. Petasítes P. Mill. Sweet coltsfoot (Greek name for coltsfoot).

Dioecious or polygamodioecious, perennial herbs; leaves large, basal, long-petioled, angled and toothed to lobed and toothed, usually white-tomentose beneath, stem leaves reduced to alternate bracts; heads racemose or corymbose, the female heads all or nearly all pistillate, whitish and radiate or purple and discoid, the male heads all or nearly all perfect but sterile, with undivided style, whitish or purplish and discoid, involucral bracts in 1 series, or with a few bracteoles at the base, receptacle flat, naked, pappus of numerous white, capillary bristles; achenes ribbed.

Leaves palmately divided; usually some of the bracts on flowering stems deeply
    toothed; flowers whitish, the pistillate radiate. (Fig. 930). .... 1. *P. frigidus*
                                     var. *palmatus*
Leaves merely angulate to dentate; bracts on flowering stems entire to shallowly
    toothed; flowers purplish, all discoid. .... 2. *P. hybridus*

1. P. frígidus (L.) Fries. Wooded swamps and wet woods. April-June. Fig. 930, Map 2236. Endangered in NH. Represented with us as var. *palmátus* (Ait.) Cronq. [*P. palmatus; P. speciosa*]. Leaves can be cooked and used as a potherb; dried leaves can be burned and the ashes used as salt. —FACW

2. P. hýbridus (L.) P. G. Gaertn., B. Mey. & Scherb. (hybrid). Waste places. April-May. Map 2237. (Introduced from Europe).

24. Tussilágo L. Coltsfoot (name based on reputed value in alleviating cough).

Rhizomatous, perennial herbs; leaves large, basal, long-petioled, rounded-cordate, angled or toothed, persistently white-tomentose beneath, stem leaves reduced to alternate bracts; heads solitary, terminal, blooming before the basal leaves develop, radiate, involucral bracts in 1 series, or with a few bracteoles at the base, rays yellow, pistillate, receptacle flat, naked, disc flowers perfect, sterile, with undivided style, pappus of numerous white, capillary bristles; achenes ribbed.

1. T. fárfara L. (Latin name for coltsfoot). Pond and stream margins, wet ditches and roadsides. April-June. Fig. 931, Map 2238. (Introduced from Europe). Preparations made from the leaves have long been regarded as valuable medicine for treating coughs and bronchial congestion; however recent studies have demonstrated that the plant contains a liver toxin and its use in herbal medicine is no longer recommended. —FACU

25. Béllis L. English daisy (Latin name for daisy).

Pubescent, perennial herbs, scapose or nearly so; leaves basal, obovate to elliptic, dentate or denticulate, narrowed to margined petioles; heads solitary on naked scapes, radiate, involucral bracts in 1 series, foliaceous, rays pistillate, white to pink, receptacle conical, naked, disc flowers perfect, yellow, pappus none; achenes flattened, ribbed near the margins.

1. B. perénnis L. (perennial). Lawns and waste places. April-July. Map 2239. (Introduced from Europe). Young leaves can be used in salads; an oil made from the plant was used at one time in external applications for eczema; tea made from the leaves is reported to help insomnia.

26. Arnóseris Gaertn. Dwarf Nipplewort (Greek name meaning lamb-chicory).

Branched, lactiferous, annual herbs; leaves basal, oblanceolate to obovate, toothed; heads small, solitary, at the ends of conspicuously upwardly thickened peduncles, ligulate, involucral bracts in 1 series, with a pale, thickened midrib in fruit, flowers perfect, 5-toothed, yellow, pappus none; achenes ovoid, flattened, strongly ribbed.

1. A. mínima (L.) Schweigg. & Koerte. (smallest). Fields, roadsides, waste places. June-September. (Adventive from Europe). Reported for NH, Hancock County ME.

27. *Krígia* Schreb. Dwarf dandelion (for D. Krieg).

Annual or perennial herbs with milky latex; leaves all basal or basal and cauline, the latter alternate or subopposite, leaves entire to pinnatifid, the basal petioled, the cauline sessile; heads solitary or few, terminal, ligulate, involucral bracts in 1 series, flowers perfect, 5-toothed, yellow or orange, pappus in 2 series, the outer of short, chaffy scales, the inner of capillary bristles; achenes ribbed or angled.

Scolýmus L. *hispánicus* L. Golden Thistle. Similar to *Krigia* but differs in being thistle-like with spiny leaves having bases decurrent in spinose wings and spinose involural bracts. European. Rarely occurring in our range. Reported for Queens County NY.

Stems leafy only near base; leaves ciliate at base; pappus bristles 10 or fewer; plant
    annual. (Fig. 932) .... 1. *K. virginica*
Stems leafy half way up or more; leaves eciliate; pappus bristles more numerous;
    plant perennial .... 2. *K. biflora*

    1. *K. virgínica* (L.) Willd. (Virginian). Dry fields, roadsides, waste places. May-August. Fig. 932, Map 2240.

    2. *K. biflóra* (Walt.) Blake (two-flowered). Fields and roadsides. May-August. Map 2241. Rare; from farther south and west. [*K. amplexicaulis*]. —FACU

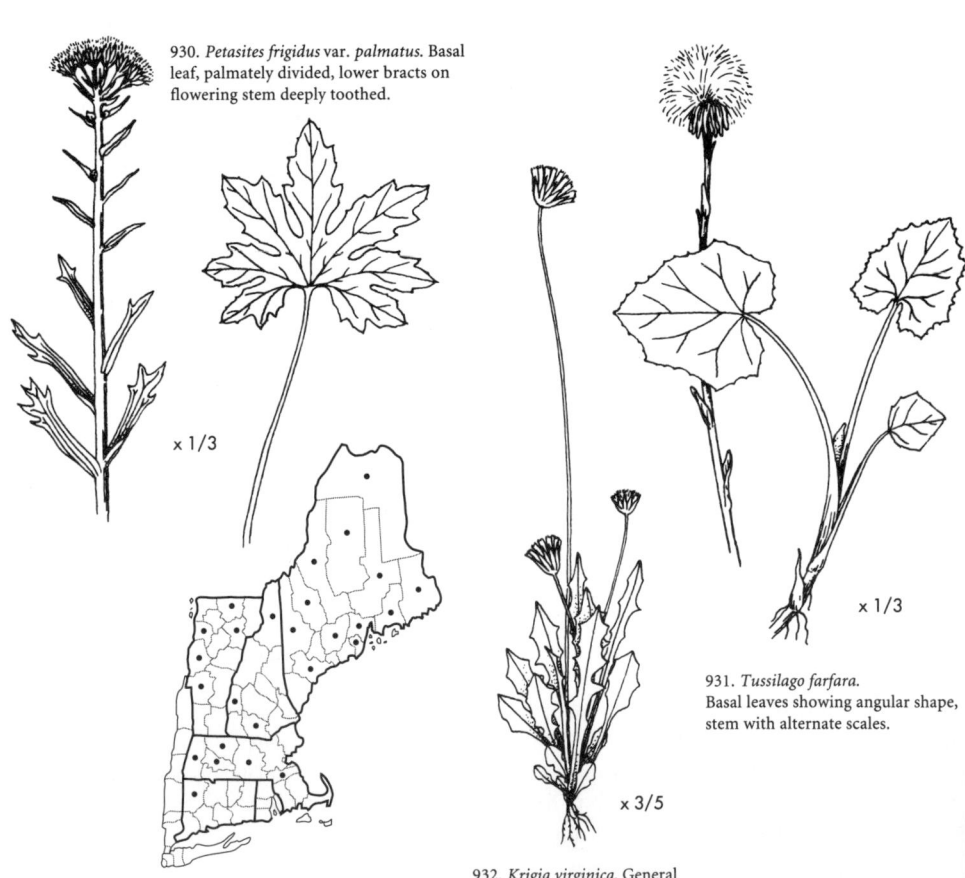

930. *Petasites frigidus* var. *palmatus*. Basal leaf, palmately divided, lower bracts on flowering stem deeply toothed.

x 1/3

x 1/3

931. *Tussilago farfara*. Basal leaves showing angular shape, stem with alternate scales.

x 3/5

2236. *Petasites frigidus* var. *palmatus*

932. *Krigia virginica*. General habit; stem leafy toward base.

2237. *Petasites hybridus*

2238. *Tussilago farfara*

2239. *Bellis perennis*

2240. *Krigia virginica*

2241. *Krigia biflora*

2242. *Taraxacum laevigatum*

28. *Taráxacum* G. H. Weber ex Wiggers. Dandelion (based on Arabic name).

Acaulescent, lactiferous, perennial herbs from a taproot; leaves in a basal rosette, oblanceolate, entire to runcinate or pinnatifid; heads solitary, terminating a hollow scape, ligulate, involucral bracts in 2 series, flowers perfect, 5-toothed, yellow, numerous, pappus of white, capillary bristles; achenes ribbed, muricate, at least at summit, tapering to a slender beak which bears the pappus. Roots can be cooked as a vegetable or roasted, ground, and used as a coffee substitute; crowns and young leaves can be used in salads or as a potherb; older leaves can also be used as a potherb, as can the young heads; mature heads can be used to make wine; entire plant is a rich source of vitamins and minerals; medicinally the root is reported to be of value as a diuretic, laxative, and as an aid to digestion and appetite stimulator. —Wildl. 2

Achenes red or reddish-purple; leaves mostly dissected nearly or quite to midrib .... 1. *T. laevigatum*
Achenes greenish, yellowish or brownish; leaves usually not as deeply dissected .... 2. *T. officinale*

    1. *T. laevigátum* (Willd.) DC. Fields, roadsides, waste places. May-July. Map 2242. (Naturalized from Europe). [*T. erythrospermum; Leontodon e.*].

2. T. officinále G. H. Weber ex Wiggers (of the shops). Fields, lawns, waste places; widespread, common. April-September. Map 2243. (Naturalized from Europe). [*Leontodon taraxacum*]. Our plants include subsp. *officinale* and the following subsp.:

subsp.*ceratóphorum* (Ledeb.) Schinz ex Thellung (horn-bearing). Outer involucral bracts appressed to ascending (reflexed in subsp. *officinale*). Meadows, rocky areas, mostly high altitudes. July-August. Map 2244. (Asia). [*T. ceratophorum; T. lapponicum; T. latilobum*].Another subsp. that has been distinguished is subsp. *vulgare.* —FACU-

29. Hieráceum L. Hawkweed (name based on belief by the early Greeks that plant was used by eagles to strengthen eyesight).

Pubescent and often glandular to glabrous, perennial herbs with milky latex; leaves alternate and sessile or basal and petioled, toothed or entire; heads solitary, corymbose or paniculate, ligulate, involucral bracts in 1-several series, flowers perfect, 5-toothed, yellow to red or orange, pappus of capillary bristles, whitish to sordid or tan; achenes ribbed. —Wildl. 1

In addition to the species treated below *H. x fuscatrum* has been reported for CT.

Microséris D. Don *douglásii* (DC). Sch. Bip. Similar to *Hieraceum* but differs in having pappus, at least in part, of slender, attenuate scales. Western. Reported for Middlesex County MA.

Chondrílla L. *júncea* L. Also similar to *Hieraceum* but distinguishable from it and *Microseris* in having achenes spinulose above and beaked. Eurasian. Reported for Suffolk County NY.

a. Stems leafy, with 9 or more leaves below the inflorescence, without a distinct cluster
    of basal leaves. (Fig. 933).
  b. Leaves usually coarsely and sharply toothed and/or principal involucral bracts
      imbricated in 2-3 series.
    c. Lower part of stem and lower leaf surfaces with bulbous-based hairs. .... 1. *H. sabaudum*
    c. Lower part of stem and lower leaf surfaces glabrous or with slender hairs not
       bulbous-based.
      d. Leaf margins with short, subconic hairs. (Fig. 934). .... 2. *H. umbellatum*
      d. Leaf margins naked or with slender cilia.
        e. Involucral bracts obtuse at apex .... 3. *H. canadense*
        e. Involucral bracts, at least the longer ones, attenuate to apex. (Fig. 935).
          Hairs of the peduncles mostly gland-tipped. .... 4. *H. lachenalii*
          Hairs of the peduncles all or mostly glandless. .... 5. *H. robinsonii*
  b. Leaves entire, denticulate or remotely serrate; principal involucral bracts mostly
      in 1 series, with a few much smaller bracts at the base.
    f. Inflorescence long and cylindric; achenes distinctly tapering toward the apex.
      (Fig. 936) .... 6. *H. gronovii*
    f. Inflorescence usually open-paniculate or corymbiform (sometimes
      long-cylindric in *H. scabrum*); achenes not or scarcely narrowed toward
      apex.
      Involucres 5 mm or more in diameter; inflorescence corymbiform; heads
        40 or more flowered .... 7. *H. scabrum*
      Involucres less than 5 mm in diameter; inflorescence open-paniculate;
        heads 30 or fewer flowered .... 8. *H. paniculatum*
a. Stems not leafy, or if so with fewer than 9 leaves, with a distinct cluster of basal
    leaves, these often rosulate. (Fig. 937).
  g. Leaves (or some of them) coarsely and sharply toothed, at least toward the base.
    h. Stems with only 1 or 2 leaves; leaves cordate, rounded or truncate at base. .... 9. *H. murorum*
    h. Stems with more than 2 leaves; leaves tapered to base.
      Hairs of the peduncles mostly gland-tipped. .... 4. *H. lachenalii*
      Hairs of the peduncles all or mostly glandless. .... 5. *H. robinsonii*
  g. Leaves entire or denticulate.
    i. Inflorescence long and cylindric. (Fig. 936). .... 6. *H. gronovii*
    i. Inflorescence corymbose or heads solitary.
      j. Heads solitary or fewer than 5 and long-peduncled. .... 10. *H. pilosella*
      j. Heads mostly 5 or more, short-peduncled in corymbs (long peduncled in
        H. venosum). (Fig. 937).

k. Rachis of inflorescence and upper stem essentially glabrous to
stipitate-glandular; veins of basal leaves usually purple. .... 11. *H. venosum*
k. Rachis of inflorescence and upper stem densely short-pubescent,
sometimes also stipitate-glandular; veins of basal leaves not purple.
l. Flowers red-orange .... 12. *H. aurantiacum*
l. Flowers yellow.
m. Leaves setose on upper surface, not glaucous. .... 13. *H. caespitosum*
m. Leaves glabrous on upper surface or with scattered hairs near the
margin; usually glaucous.
Plants stoloniferous; rhizome elongate. .... 14. *H. floribundum*
Plants not stoloniferous; rhizome short. .... 15. *H. piloselloides*

1. *H. sabaúdum* L. (of Savoy). Fields, roadsides, waste places. August-October. Fig. 933, Map 2245. (Naturalized from Europe).

2. *H. umbellátum* L. (umbelled) Thickets, beaches, shores. July-September. Fig. 934. (Eurasia). Endangered in NH; reported for Cheshire County. [*H. scabriusculum*].

3. *H. canadénse* Michx. (Canadian). Fields, thickets, roadsides, waste places. July-September. Map 2246. Our plants include var. *canadense* and the following var.:

var. *fasciculátum* (Pursh) Fern. Leaves 25 or more, involucre dark brown to black (leaves mostly fewer than 25 and involucre light green in var. *canadense*).

H. x fernáldii Lepage. A hybrid between *H. canadense* and *H. scabrum.*

H. kálmii L. Similar to *H. canadense* but distinguishable in having the upper leaves rounded to cuneate at the base, styles brown (upper leaves truncate to subcordate at base and styles yellow in *H. canadense*). From farther north. Reported for ME. [*H. canadense* var. *k.*]. Our plants include var. *kalmii* and the following var.:

var. *fasciculátum* (Pursh) Lepage. Leaves with teeth irregular in size (leaves uniformly toothed in var. *kalmii*). [*H. canadense* var. *f.*].

4. *H. lachenálii* K. C. Gmel. Fields, roadsides, waste places. June-August. Fig. 935, Map 2247. (Naturalized from Europe). [*H. vulgatum*].

5. *H. robinsónii* (Zahn) Fern. Ledges and rocky borders of streams. June-September. Map 2248. Endangered in NH.

6. *H. gronóvii* L. (for J.F. Gronovius). Open woods, clearings, fields. July-September. Fig. 936, Map 2249.

H. x mariánum Willd. A hybrid between *H. gronovii* and *H. venosum* or of the latter and *H. scabrum.*

7. *H. scábrum* Michx. (harsh). Open woods, clearings, fields. July-September. Map 2250. Our plants include var. *scabrum* and the following var.:

var. *tónsum* Fern. & St. John. Lower stem hispidulous with hairs less than 1 mm long or becoming glabrous; leaves glabrous beneath (lower stem and midribs of leaves beneath with hairs 2 mm or more long in var. *scabrum*).

8. *H. paniculátum* L. (panicled). Dry, open woods. July-September. Map 2251.

9. *H. murórum* L. (of walls). Roadsides and waste places. June-July. Map 2252. (Adventive from Europe).

10. *H. pilosélla* L. (slightly hairy). Fields, lawns, roadsides. June-August. Map 2253. (Naturalized from Europe). Our plants include var. *pilosella* and the following var.:

var. *níveum* Muell. Arg. Leaves permanently covered beneath with a close, white pubescence (stellate tomentose when young, less pubescent later in var. *pilosella*). A preparation of the fresh plant is used as a diuretic.

H. x flagelláre Willd. A hybrid between *H. pilosella* and *H. caespitosum.*

11. *H. venósum* L. (veiny). Dry woods and clearings. July-September. Map 2254. Endangered in ME. Our plants include var. *venosum* and the following var.:

var. *nudicaúle* (Michx.) Farw. Basal leaves glabrous above (basal leaves, or some of them with sparse long coarse hairs above in var. *venosum*).

× 1/4

× 1

936. *Hieraceum gronovii.*
Inflorescence,
showing long,
cylindric shape.

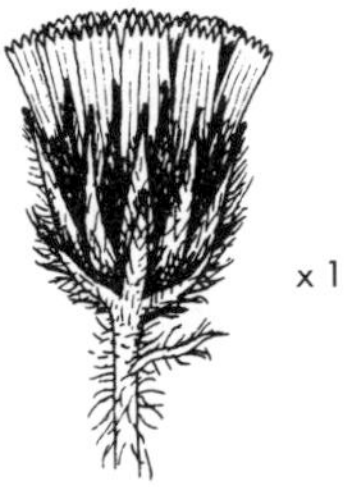

× 1/2

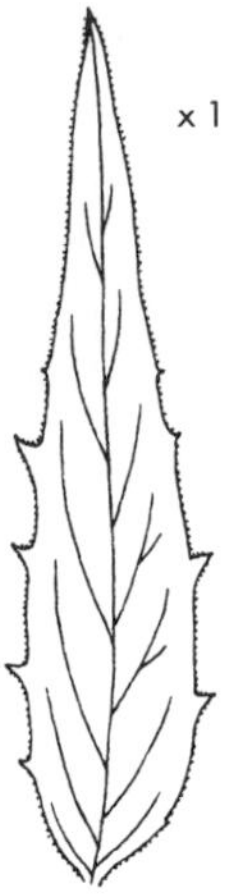

934. *Hieraceum umbellatum.*
Single leaf; general characteristics.

× 1

933. *Hieraceum sabaudum.* General
habit; stem leafy, without a distinct
cluster of basal leaves.

935. *Hieraceum lachenalii.* Single head;
involucral bracts in several distinct
series, attenuate to apex.

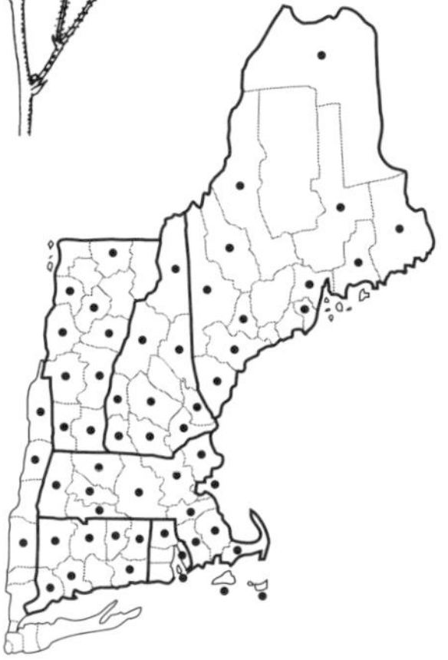

2243. *Taraxacum officinale* subsp. *officinale*

2244. *Taraxacum officinale* subsp.
ceratophorum

2245. *Hieraceum sabaudum*

2246. *Hieraceum canadense*

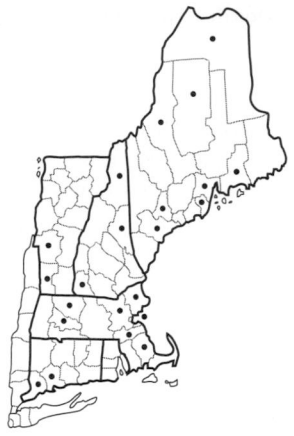

2247. *Hieracium lachenalii*

2248. *Hieracium robinsonii*

2249. *Hieracium gronovii*

2250. *Hieracium scabrum*

2251. *Hieracium paniculatum*

2252. *Hieracium murorum*

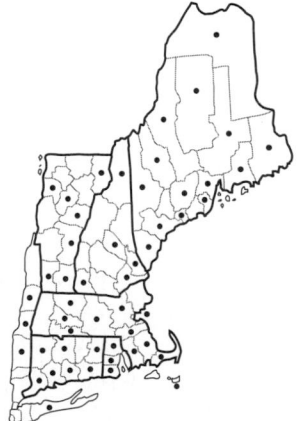

2253. *Hieracium pilosella*

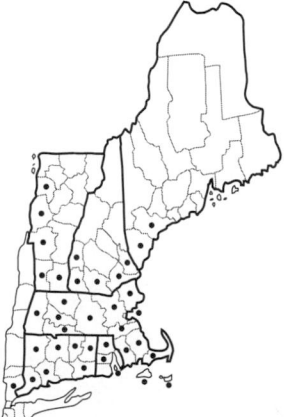

2254. *Hieracium venosum*

12. *H. aurantíacum* L. (orange-colored). King-devil. Fields, roadsides, waste places. June-August. Map 2255. (Naturalized from Europe).

13. *H. caespitósum* Dumort. Fields, roadsides, waste places. June-August. Fig. 937, Map 2256. (Naturalized from Europe). [*H. pratense*].

H. praeáltum Vill. ex Gochnat. Resembling *H. caespitosum* but differing in having short thick rhizomes and leaves stellate-pubescent beneath (rhizomes long and slender and leaves setose beneath in *H. caespitosum*). Map 2257. (Naturalized from Europe). Represented with us as var. *decípiens* W.D.J. Koch.

14. *H. floribúndum* Wimm. & Grab. (abounding with flowers). Fields, roadsides. June-July. Map 2258. (Naturalized from Europe).

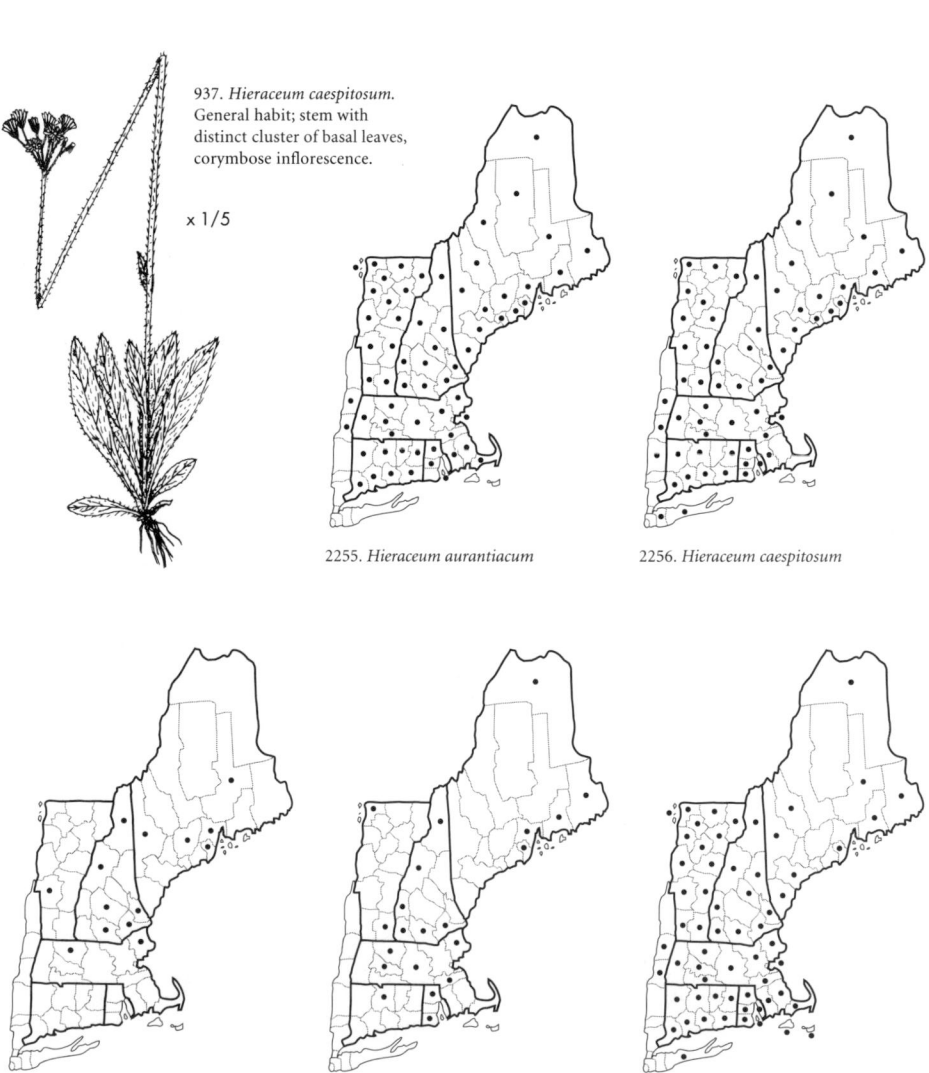

937. *Hieraceum caespitosum.*
General habit; stem with
distinct cluster of basal leaves,
corymbose inflorescence.

x 1/5

2255. *Hieraceum aurantiacum*

2256. *Hieraceum caespitosum*

2257. *Heiraceum praealtum*

2258. *Hieraceum floribundum*

2259. *Hieraceum piloselloides*

15. *H. piloselloídes* Vill. Fields, roadsides, waste places. June-August. Map 2259. (Naturalized from Europe). [*H. florentinum; H. praealtum*].

30. *Leóntodon* L. Hawkbit (from the Greek, referring to the toothed leaves).

Scapose, lactiferous, perennial herbs, the scapes naked or scaly-bracted; leaves basal, oblanceolate, mostly toothed to pinnately lobed; heads solitary, terminal on the scape or its branches, ligulate, principal involucral bracts in 1 or 2 series, 1 or more short outer series often also present, flowers perfect, 5-toothed, yellow, pappus of plumose bristles, the outer sometimes shorter and non-plumose or scale-like; achenes fusiform, striate, distinctly beaked or merely narrowed upward. [*Apargia*].

a. Scape branched, with 2 or more heads, scaly-bracted above; pappus of plumose
    bristles only. (Fig. 938) .... 1. *L. autumnalis*
a. Scape simple, with a solitary head, naked; pappus of plumose bristles and short
    outer scales or bristles.
    Involucres 1 cm or less long; pappus of some of the outer flowers consisting
        only of short scales, the inner of both short scales and plumose bristles. ...... 2. *L. taraxacoides*
    Involucres more than 1 cm long; pappus of all flowers similar, of both short
        scales or bristles and long, plumose bristles. .... 3. *L. hispidus*

1. *L. autumnális* L. (autumnal). Fields, lawns, roadsides, waste places. June-September. Fig. 938, Map 2260. (Naturalized from Europe). [*Apargia a.*]. Our plants include subsp. *autumnalis* and the following subsp.:
    subsp. *praténsis* (Less.) Koch. Involucre densely pubescent (glabrous to slightly pubescent in var. *autumnalis*).

2. *L. taraxacoídes* (Vill.) Merat. Fields, lawns, waste places. June-September. Map 2261. (Adventive from Europe). [*L. leysseri; L. nudicaulis*]. —FACU

3. *L. hispidus* L. (stiffly hairy). Fields and waste places. June-September. Map 2262. (Adventive from Europe). [*L. hastilis; Apargia hispidus*]. Our plants are subsp. *hispidus*.
    Another subsp. that has been distinguished is subsp. *danubiális*.

31. *Hypochaéris* L. Cat's ear (ancient Greek name).

Similar to *Leontodon* except receptacle chaffy.

1. *H. radicáta* L. (having roots). Fields, roadsides, waste places. May-September. Map 2263. (Naturalized from Europe).

H. glábra L. Similar to *H. radicata* but outer achenes are beakless (all achenes are beaked in *H. radicata*). (Europe). Reported for Penobscot County ME; Middlesex County MA.

32. *Báccharis* L. Groundsel tree (ancient name for a shrub).

Dioecious shrubs, twigs slender, ridged or angled, glabrous but somewhat glutinous or scurfy, pith small, buds small, resinous, leaf scars narrowly crescent-shaped, with decurrent ridges from the angles, bundle traces 3, stipule scars and end bud lacking, inflorescence or remnants usually persistent; leaves alternate, short-petioled, elliptic to obovate, coarsely angular-dentate or the upper entire, resinous, fleshy; heads in numerous small, pedunculate clusters of 1-several, forming a terminal, leafy panicle, staminate and pistillate flowers on separate plants, heads discoid, yellowish, involucral bracts imbricated in several series, receptacle flat, naked, pistillate flowers unlobed, with copious pappus much exceeding corollas, staminate flowers 5-lobed, with scanty pappus barely or not exceeding the corollas; achenes ribbed.

1. *B. halimifólia* L. (with leaves of *Halimus*). Salt and brackish marshes and edges, beaches, thickets near the coast. August-October. Map 2264. (Tropical Amer.). —FACW

33. Círsium Mill. Plumed Thistle (from the Greek, based on reputed value in treating varicose veins).

Similar to *Carduus* (genus 42) except stems not always winged and pappus bristles plumose. Various species of plumed thistle have food value; the roots may be roasted and the young stem can be peeled and eaten raw or cooked; the pappus makes good tinder for starting fires.

a. Stem spiny-winged by the decurrent leaf bases. (Fig. 939).
   b. Plant perennial from rhizomes, forming colonies; heads dioecious. .... 1. *C. arvense*
   b. Plant biennial, from a taproot; heads with perfect flowers.
      Heads clustered; involucres 2 cm or less long, the inner bracts attenuate but
         not spine-tipped .... 2. *C. palustre*
      Heads scattered; involucres mostly more than 2 cm long, the bracts all
         spine-tipped .... 3. *C. vulgare*
a. Stem not or scarcely winged.
   c. Involucres subtended by a whorl of strongly spiny, leaf-like bracts. (Fig. 940) .... 4. *C. horridulum*
   c. Involucres lacking a whorl of leaf-like bracts, although sometimes subtended by
      1 or 2 such bracts.
      d. Involucres 2 cm or less long; heads dioecious. .... 1. *C. arvense*
      d. Involucres mostly more than 2 cm long; heads with perfect flowers.
         e. Involucral bracts acute to mucronate but not spine-tipped. .... 5. *C. muticum*
         e. Involucral bracts, at least the outer ones, spine-tipped.
            f. Leaves glabrous to thinly arachnoid and green beneath, not
               white-tomentose, margins not revolute .... 6. *C. pumilum*
            f. Leaves densely white-tomentose beneath, margins slightly revolute.
               g. Stems and upper leaf surfaces white-tomentose. .... 7. *C. flodmanii*
               g. Stems and upper leaf surfaces glabrous to hirsute but not
                 white-tomentose.
                 Leaves toothed to shallowly lobed .... 8. *C. altissimum*
                 Leaves deeply pinnatifid .... 9. *C. discolor*

1. C. arvénse (L.) Scop. (of fields). Canada thistle. Fields, roadsides, waste places. July-August. Map 2265. (Naturalized from Europe). [*C. arvense* var. *mite; C. setosum*]. —FACU

2. C. palústre (L.) Scop. (of marshes). Damp woods, clearings, thickets. June-August. Reported for Suffolk County MA.

3. C. vulgáre (Savi) Tenore (common). Bull thistle. Fields, roadsides, waste places. July-October. Fig. 939, Map 2266. (Naturalized from Europe). [*C. lanceolatum*]. —FACU-

C. cánum (L.). All. Heads solitary or scattered as in *C. vulgare* but involucres and bracts are as in *C. palustre*. (Europe). Reported for MA.

4. C. horrídulum Michx. (somewhat bristly). Fields, roadsides, in sandy soil along the coastal plain, borders of salt marshes. May-August. Fig. 940, Map 2267. Endangered in NH. [*C. spinosissimum*]. —FACU-

5. C. múticum Michx. (without points). Swamp thistle. Wooded swamps, wet thickets and meadows, borders of streams. July-September. Map 2268. —OBL

6. C. púmilum (Nutt.) Spreng. (dwarf). Open woods, fields, roadsides, waste places. July-September. Map 2269. [*C. odoratum*].

7. C. flodmánii (Rydb.) Arthur (for its discoverer). Wet meadows, stream and lake margins. July-September. From farther west. Reported for Essex County VT. [*C. canescens*].

8. C. altíssimum (L.) Hill. (very tall). Open woods, fields, river-bottoms, waste places. July-September. From farther south and west. Reported for CT and MA. [*C. iowense*].

9. C. díscolor (Muhl. ex Willd.) Spreng. (parti-colored). Fields, thickets, river-bottoms, waste places. July-October. Map 2270.

34. Xánthium L. Cocklebur (Greek name for a plant used to dye hair).

Monoecious, coarse, branched, pubescent, annual herbs; leaves alternate, petioled, entire, toothed or lobed; staminate and pistillate flowers in separate heads, the staminate heads globose or

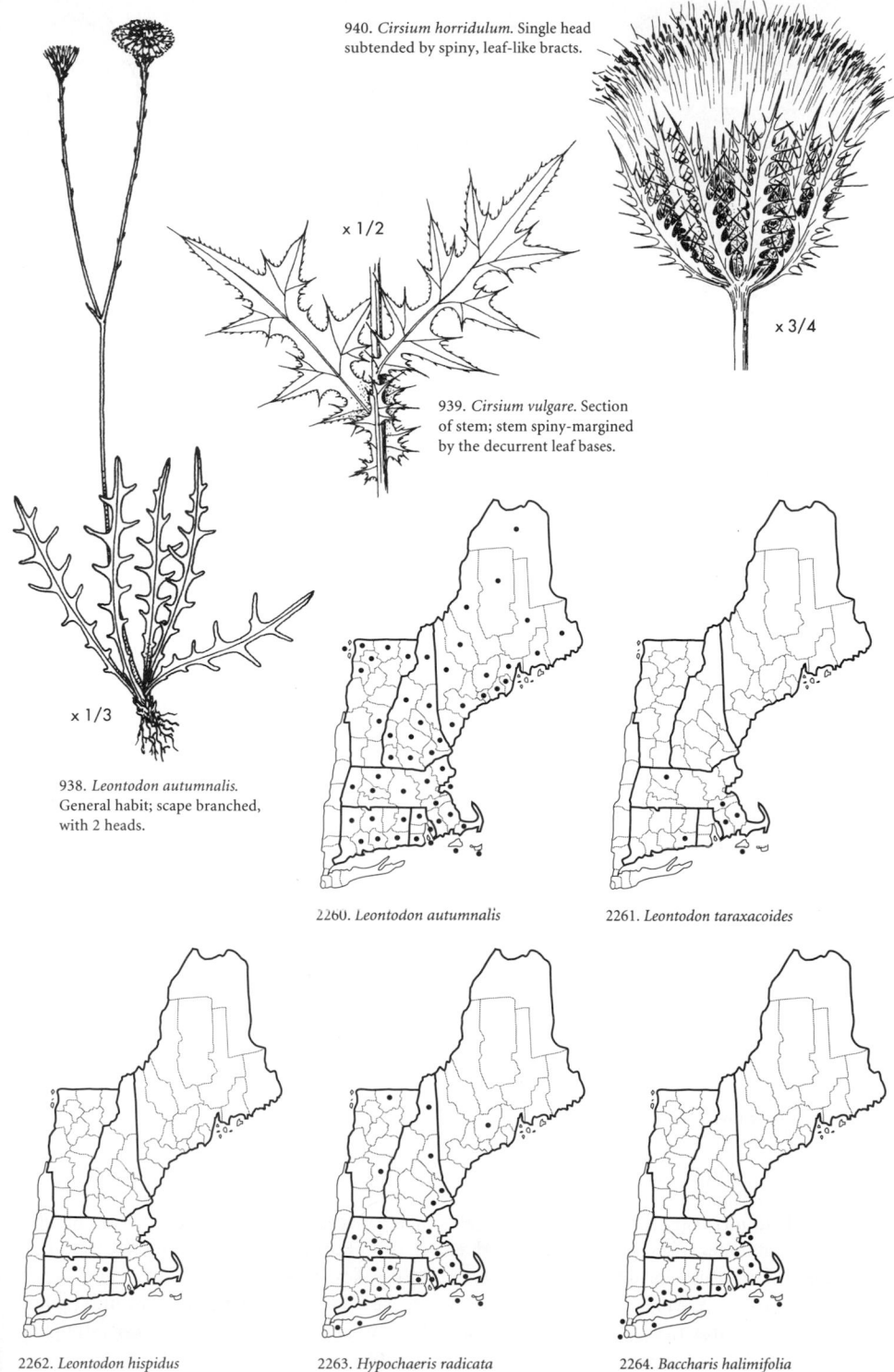

940. *Cirsium horridulum.* Single head subtended by spiny, leaf-like bracts.

× 1/2

939. *Cirsium vulgare.* Section of stem; stem spiny-margined by the decurrent leaf bases.

× 3/4

× 1/3

938. *Leontodon autumnalis.* General habit; scape branched, with 2 heads.

2260. *Leontodon autumnalis*

2261. *Leontodon taraxacoides*

2262. *Leontodon hispidus*

2263. *Hypochaeris radicata*

2264. *Baccharis halimifolia*

2265. *Cirsium arvense*   2266. *Cirsium vulgare*   2267. *Cirsium horridulum*

2268. *Cirsium muticum*   2269. *Cirsium pumilum*   2270. *Cirsium discolor*

hemispheric, in short spikes terminating the branches, the involucre of separate bracts, receptacle chaffy, corolla 5-lobed, the pistillate heads solitary or in short clusters in the leaf axils, each head an oblong or ovoid involucre covered with hooked prickles and 2 terminal spines forming a bur, the bur 2-locular, with a pistillate flower in each locule, corolla none, pappus lacking; achenes oblong, flat, 1 in each locule of the bur. Poisonous.

Stem lacking spines; leaves ovate to suborbicular, usually cordate or rounded
    at base, not white-canescent beneath. (Fig. 941). .... 1. *X. strumarium*
Stem with 3-forked spines at the nodes; leaves lanceolate, tapered to the base, white
    or grayish-canescent beneath. .... 2. *X. spinosum*

1. *X. strumárium* L. (cure for tumors). Fields, waste places, river and lake shores, sea beaches. August-September. Fig. 941, Map 2271. (Adventive from Europe). [*X. curvescens; X. oviforme; X. wootonii*]. Our plants include var. *strumarium* and the following vars.:

var. *canadénse* (P. Mill.) Torrey & Gray. Lower part of prickles spreading-pubescent and stipitate-glandular; beaks incurved (bur and its prickles glabrous to merely puberulent and beaks straight in var. *strumarium*). [*X. echinatum; X. italicum; X. pensylvanicum; X. speciosum*].

var. *glabrátum* (DC.) Cronq. Burs puberulent and nonstipitate-glandular to subglabrous; beaks incurved. [*X. americanum; X. cylindricum; X. echinellum; X. globosum; X. inflexum; X. chinense; X. orientale*]. —FAC

2. X. spinósum L. (spiny). Waste places. August-October. Map 2272. (Naturalized from Europe). [*Acanthoxanthium s.*]. —FACU

35. Anáphalis DC. Pearly everlasting (based on the name *Gnaphalium*).

Dioecious or polygamo-dioecious, rhizomatous, woolly, perennial herbs; leaves alternate, sessile, entire, linear-lanceolate, often revolute, woolly beneath; heads corymbose, discoid, staminate and pistillate flowers on separate plants or some flowers with both stamens and pistils, involucral bracts imbricated, scarious and pearly white, receptacle flat, naked, pistillate flowers 5-lobed, staminate flowers unlobed, pappus of capillary bristles; achenes small, smooth.

1. A. margaritácea (L.) Benth. & Hook. f. (pearly). Fields, roadsides, waste places. July-September. Map 2273. (e. Asia).

36. Árctium L. Burdock (Greek name, based on the spinous involucre).

Coarse, branched, biennial herbs; leaves large, alternate, petioled, toothed or entire, ovate to round, mostly cordate, often tomentose beneath; heads in corymbose, racemose or paniculate inflorescences, discoid, involucre hemispheric, bracts imbricated, spine-tipped, with hooked apex, receptacle bristly, flowers perfect, purple, with long, slender lobes, pappus of short, barbed bristles; achenes oblong, flattened, roughened.

a. Heads in a corymbose, more or less flat-topped inflorescence, mostly on
    peduncles longer than 1.5 cm. (Fig. 942).
    Involucral bracts distinctly arachnoid-tomentose. .... 1. *A. tomentosum*
    Involucral bracts glabrous or essentially so to the naked eye. .... 2. *A. lappa*
a. Heads in a racemose or paniculate, more or less pyramidal inflorescence, mostly
    sessile or on shorter peduncles. .... 3. *A. minus*

1. A. tomentósum Mill. (tomentose). Waste places. July-September. Map 2274. (Naturalized from Europe).

2. A. láppa L. (a bur). Fields, roadsides, waste places. July-September. Fig. 942, Map 2275. (Naturalized from Europe). Roots from the first year plants can be eaten after peeling and boiling; young leaves can be cooked like a potherb; young leaf petioles can be peeled and eaten raw or as a potherb; the stem just below the heads can also be cooked as a potherb after peeling if harvested before the flowers mature.

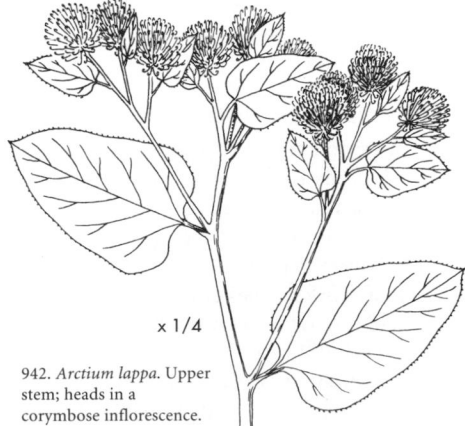

x 1/4

x 1/4

941. *Xanthium strumarium*. Upper stem; leaves ovate, cordate, pistillate involucres prickly.

942. *Arctium lappa*. Upper stem; heads in a corymbose inflorescence.

2271. *Xanthium strumarium*   2272. *Xanthium spinosum*   2273. *Anaphalis margaritacea*

2274. *Arctium tomentosum*   2275. *Arctium lappa*   2276. *Arctium minus*

3. *A. mínus* Bernh. (smaller). Fields, roadsides, waste places. July-October. Map 2276. (Naturalized from Europe). The same uses can be made for this species as described for *A. lappa*.

A. vulgáre A. H. Evans. Similar to *A. minus* but with middle and inner involucral bracts equalling or exceeding corolla, heads 2.5 cm or more wide (middle and inner involucral bracts shorter than corollas and heads up to 2.5 cm wide in *A. minus*). Throughout our range. [*A. nemorosum*].

37. *Centaúrea* L. Star-thistle (based on an ancient Greek name).

Annual or perennial herbs; leaves alternate, entire, toothed or pinnatifid, sessile or the lower petioled; heads solitary and terminal or paniculate, discoid or falsely radiate (marginal, sterile flowers larger and simulating rays), involucre ovoid to globose, bracts imbricated in several-many series, outer bracts sometimes spine-tipped or more often erose, lacerate or pectinate, receptacle bristly, flowers, at least the central ones, perfect, purple, blue or yellowish, with long, slender lobes, pappus of bristles, scales or none; achenes obovate or oblong, compressed or angled.

In addition to the following species *C. debeauxii* subsp. *thuillieri* has also been attributed to our range. —Wildl. 1

Carthámus L. *tinctórius* L. Safflower. Outer involucral bracts foliaceous; flowers orange. Rarely escaped from cultivation. Reported for Barnstable County MA.

a. Involucral bracts, at least the outer ones, terminated by a distinct, rigid spine.
  Stems winged by the decurrent leaf bases; spines divergent, the larger ones 1 cm
  or more long .... 1. *C. solstitialis*
  Stems not winged, merely angled; spines ascending, 5 mm or less long. .... 2. *C. diffusa*
a. Involucral bracts not terminated by a spine, merely erose, lacerate or pectinate.
  b. Median, and often the upper stem leaves pinnatifid.
    Involucres 1.5 cm or more long .... 3. *C. scabiosa*
    Involucres 1.4 cm or less long .... 4. *C. biebeesteinii*
  b. Median and upper stem leaves entire, toothed, or shallowly lobed.
    c. Involucre 2 cm or more high; pappus well developed, more than 5 mm
      long. .... 5. *C. americana*
    c. Involucre less than 2 cm high; pappus not well developed, less than 5 mm
      long or absent.
      d. Median and upper involucral bracts gradually tapered to apex. .... 6. *C. cyanus*
      d. Median and upper involucral bracts abruptly widened at apex.
        e. Tips of the median and upper involucral bracts irregularly dentate to
          lacerate, not regularly pectinate, brownish. .... 7. *C. jacea*
        e. Tips of the median and upper (but not the inner) involucral bracts
          regularly pectinate, blackish.
          f. Pectinate tips of involucral bracts, or at least the larger ones, 4 mm or
            more long; involucres mostly higher than broad. .... 8. *C. transalpina*
          f. Pectinate tips of involucral bracts less than 4 mm long; involucres
            broader than high.
            Green or pale lower portion of median involucral bracts hidden
              behind the blackish tips .... 9. *C. nigra*
            Green or pale lower portion of median involucral bracts conspicuous
              among the blackish tips .... 10. *c. nigrescens*

1. ***C. solstitiális*** L. (of the summer solstice). Fields, roadsides, waste places. July-October. (Naturalized from the Mediterranean region). Reported for CT, RI, Worcester County MA; Sullivan County NH.

C. meliténsis L. Resembling *C. solstitialis* but differing in having spines of the involucral bracts less than 1 cm long (spines are more than 1 cm long in *C. solstitialis*). (Europe). Rarely found in our range. Reported for Norfolk and Suffolk Counties, MA.

2. ***C. diffúsa*** Lam. (spreading). Fields, roadsides, waste places. July-September. Fig. 943, Map 2277. (Naturalized from Europe).

C. áspera L. Similar to *C. diffusa* but is distinguishable in having involucral bracts with 3-5 distinct spines (bracts with a single distinct spine in *C. diffusa*). (Europe). Reported for northern terminus of Hunters Point NY.

3. ***C. scabiósa*** L. (scurfy). Fields, roadsides, waste places. July-September. Map 2278. (Naturalized from Europe).

4. ***C. biebeestéinii*** DC. Fields, roadsides, waste places. July-September. Map 2279. (Naturalized from Europe). [*C. maculosa*].

5. ***C. americána*** Nutt. (American). From the southwest. Rarely adventive in our range. Reported for RI.

6. ***C. cyánus*** L. (ancient name). Bachelor's button. Fields, roadsides, waste places. June-September. Map 2280. (Introduced from Europe). A preparation made from the plant is used as an eye lotion; seeds are used as a laxative.

C. phýrgia L. Similar to *C. cyanus* but median and upper involucral bracts long-pinnate fringed, the fringe several mm long (bracts merely deeply lacerate, the teeth under 1 mm long in *C. cyanus*). European. Reported for VT.

7. ***C. jácea*** L. (old generic name). Fields, roadsides, waste places. June-September. Fig. 944, Map 2281. (Naturalized from Europe). A preparation made from this plant is used to aid digestion and treat indigestion; is also reported to reduce fever; a preparation made from the leaves is used as an eye lotion.

8. C. transalpína Schleich. ex DC. Fields, roadsides, waste places. June-September. Reported for MA, VT. [*C. dubia* subsp. *vochinensis; C. vochinensis*].

9. C. nígra L. (black). Fields, roadsides, waste places. June-October. Fig. 945, Map 2282. (Naturalized from Europe).

C. montána L. Similar to *C. nigra* but differing in having decurrent leaves (leaves petioled to sessile in *C. nigra*). Rarely escaped from cultivation. Reported for Waldo County ME.

10. C. nigréscens Willd. (blackish). Fields, roadsides, waste places. July-October. Map 2283. (Naturalized from Europe). [*C. dubia*].

C. uniflóra Turra. Similar to *C. nigra* and *C. nigrescens* but distinguishable in having the bracts with elongate, thread-like, recurving appendages. (Europe). Reported for Washington County NY. Represented with us as subsp. *nervósa* (Willd.) Bonnier & Layens.

38. Echínops L. Globe-thistle (from the Greek, meaning having the appearance of a hedgehog, referring to the spinescent leaves and bracts).

Coarse, branched, spiny, tomentose, perennial herbs; leaves alternate, sessile, the upper clasping, pinnatifid, spiny; heads 1-flowered, aggregated into dense, globose, secondary heads terminating the branches, the secondary heads often with an involucre of several small, reflexed bracts, primary heads with a cylindrical involucre of bracts imbricated in several series, the bracts often spinescent, primary involucre subtended by a ring of capillary bristles, flowers bluish, perfect, with long, slender lobes, pappus coroniform, of numerous very short, narrow scales; achenes pubescent.

1. E. sphaerocéphalus L. (spherical-headed). Fields, roadsides, waste places. July-September. Map 2284. (Introduced from Europe).

39. Onopórdum L. Scotch thistle (early Greek and Latin name, based on belief that the plant caused flatulence in donkeys).

Coarse, branched, spiny, tomentose, biennial herbs, stems winged by decurrent leaf bases; leaves alternate, sessile, or the lower petioled, coarsely dentate to shallowly lobed, spiny; heads large, solitary at the ends of the branches, discoid, involucre subglobose, bracts imbricated, spine-tipped, receptacle honey-combed, flowers perfect, purple, with long, slender lobes, pappus bristles capillary; achenes obovate, slightly corrugated.

1. O. acánthium L. (prickly). Roadsides and waste places. July-September. Map 2285. (Naturalized from Europe).

943. *Centaurea diffusa.* Single head; general characteristics.

944. *Centaurea jacea.* Single head; general characteristics.

945. *Centaurea nigra.* Single head; general characteristics.

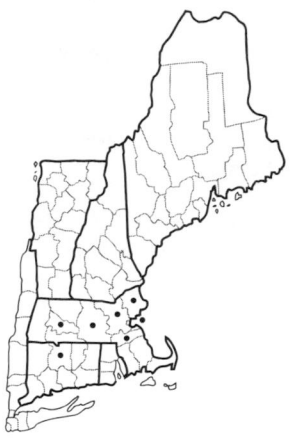

2277. *Centaurea diffusa*

2278. *Centaurea scabiosa*

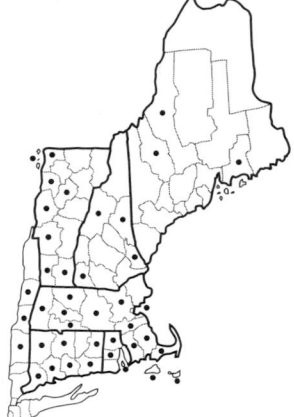

2279. *Centaurea biebeesteinii*

2280. *Centaurea cyanus*

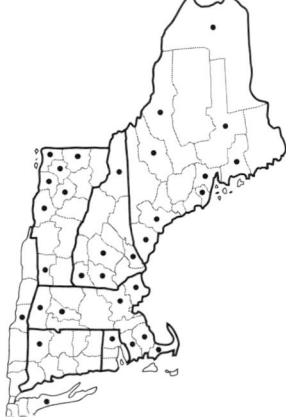

2281. *Centaurea jacea*

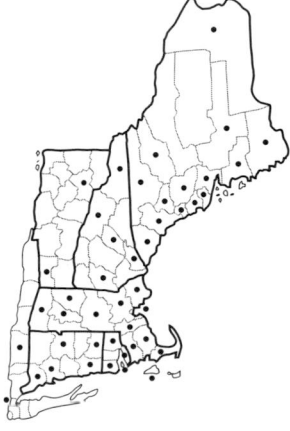

2282. *Centaurea nigra*

2283. *Centaurea nigrescens*

2284. *Echinops sphaerocephalus*

2285. *Onopordum acanthium*

40. *Sílybum* Adans. Milk-thistle.

Glabrous to slightly pubescent, annual or biennial herbs; leaves alternate, the lower petioled, the upper sessile and auriculate-clasping, pinnately-lobed, spiny, white-mottled; heads large, solitary at the ends of the branches, discoid, involucre subglobose, involucral bracts imbricated, spiny-margined, some of the bracts also tipped with very long spines, receptacle bristly, flowers perfect, purple, with long, slender lobes, pappus bristles capillary; achenes obovate.

1. *S. mariánum* (L.) Gaertn. (of the Virgin Mary). Waste places. June-August. (Introduced from Europe). Reported for MA, Litchfield County CT; Rockingham County NH. [*Mariana m.*]. Preparations made from the achenes with the pappus removed have been used to treat various liver ailments such as hepatitis and cirrhosis.

41. *Cnícus* L. Blessed Thistle (Latin name for safflower).

Pubescent annual herbs similar to *Centaurea;* leaves alternate, spinulose-toothed or lobed, sessile, or the lower petioled; heads terminal, closely subtended by leaves, heads discoid (not falsely radiate); outer bracts of involucre spine-tipped, the inner bracts pinnately-spinescent, receptacle bristly, flowers all perfect, yellow, pappus capillary, biseriate; achenes strongly ribbed, with a crown of 10 teeth.

1. *C. benedíctus* L. (blessed). Roadsides and waste places. May-September. Map 2286. (Adventive from Europe). [*Centaurea b.*]. Preparations of this plant have been used as a bitter in flavoring liquors; has been used to treat hepatitis and jaundice.

42. *Cárduus* L. Plumeless Thistle (ancient Latin name).

Spiny, biennial herbs, stems winged by decurrent leaf bases; leaves alternate, serrate to pinnately lobed or pinnatifid, spiny, sessile; heads large, solitary or clustered at the ends of the branches, discoid, involucral bracts imbricated, usually spine-tipped, receptacle bristly, flowers perfect, purple to white or yellowish, with long, slender lobes, pappus of capillary bristles; achenes obovate. Various species have food value; pith of the stems can be boiled and eaten and the dried flowers can be used to curdle milk.

Carthámus L. *lanátus* L. Safflower. Similar to *Carduus* but distinguishable in having a chaffy receptacle; pappus none or scale-like. Rarely escaped from cultivation. Reported for Hampshire County MA.

a. Involucres 2 cm or more long; involucral bracts mostly 2 mm or more wide; heads
        nodding .... 1. *C. nutans*
a. Involucres less than 2 cm long; involucral bracts mostly less than 2mm wide
        (except in *C. pycnocephalus*); heads erect or ascending.
    Leaves floccose beneath, more so between the veins than on them. .... 2. *C. crispus*
    Leaves glabrous beneath, or if floccose more so on the veins than between them ... 3. *C. acanthoides*

1. *C. nútans* L. (nodding). Fields, roadsides, waste places. June-October. Map 2287. (Adventive from Europe). [*C. thoermeri*].

2. *C. críspus* L. (crisped). Fields, roadsides, waste places. July-September. Map 2288. (Adventive from Europe).

C. pycnocéphalus L. Similar to *C. crispus* but distinguishable in that the middle involucral bracts are 2-3 mm wide (mostly less than 2 mm wide in *C. crispus*). Mediterranean. A waif in our range. Reported for Hunters Point, NY.

3. *C. acanthoídes* L. (resembling *Acanthus*). Fields, roadsides, waste places. June-September. Map 2289. (Adventive from Europe).

43. *Artemísia* L. Wormwood (ancient name for mugwort, species 12 and 14).
Aromatic, annual or perennial herbs, occasionally suffrutescent; leaves alternate, entire, toothed, dissected, or 1-3 times pinnatifid; heads small, often nodding, in spikes, racemes, or panicles, discoid, involucral bracts scarious, at least on the margins, often pubescent, imbricated in several series, receptacle flat to convex, naked or with long hairs, flowers yellowish to greenish, the marginal ones pistillate, the others perfect or sterile, pappus none; achenes obovoid to oblong.

a. Leaves glabrous or essentially so.
  b. Leaves mostly entire, or the lowest 3-5-cleft at apex . . .. 1. *A. dracunculus*
                                                                  subsp. *glauca*
  b. Leaves mostly pinnatifid or dissected.
    c. Plant woody in the lower half; leaves mostly 3-parted into filiform segments ..... 2. *A. filifolia*
    c. Plant not woody; leaves 1 or more times pinnatifid.
      d. Ultimate leaf segments entire .... 3. *A. campestris*
      d. Ultimate leaf segments toothed. (Fig. 946).
          Inflorescence dense, spiciform; heads essentially sessile. .... 4. *A. biennis*
          Inflorescence open, paniculate; heads distinctly pendunculate. .... 5. *A. annua*
a. Leaves tomentose on one or both sides.
  e. Leaves mostly with only 3 apical teeth. .... 6. *A. tridentata*
  e. Leaves with more teeth or dissected (lowest leaves sometimes 3-cleft at apex in
    A. dracunculus but involucres are glabrous; involucres tomentose in
    A. tridentata).
    f. Involucres glabrous, or if occasionally pubescent disc flowers sterile, with
      undivided style.
      Leaves mostly entire, or the lowest 3-5-cleft at apex. .... 1. *A. dracunculus*
                                                           subsp. *glauca*
      Leaves pinnatifid or dissected .... 3. *A. campestris*
    f. Involucres tomentose or arachnoid; disc flowers fertile, with style 2-cleft.
      g. Leaves or ultimate leaf segments mostly 1.5 mm or less wide.
        h. Leaves 2-3-times pinnatifid.
          Leaves green and glabrous above, the longest ultimate segments 5 mm
            or more long .... 7. *A. abrotanum*
         Leaves usually tomentose on both sides, the longest ultimate segments
            less than 5 mm long .... 8. *A. pontica*
        h. Leaves once pinnatifid or 3-parted.
         i. Heads less than 2 mm long.. 2. *A. filifolia*
         i. Heads 2 mm or more long.
          Leaves green and not, or less tomentose above than below. .... 9. *A. curruthii*
          Leaves white to grayish and about equally tomentose above and
            below. .... 10. *A. frigida*
      g. Leaves or ultimate leaf segments wider than 1.5 mm.
        j. Involucres mostly longer than 5 mm; leaf segments mostly rounded;
          plant of sea beaches. (Fig. 947) .... 11. *A. stelleriana*
        j. Involucres 5 mm or less long; leaf segments acute or obtuse; plants of
         other habitats.
         k. Leaves entire, or toothed, or if lobed or dissected, the segments entire;
          bases of leaves lacking stipule-like lobes. .... 12. *A. ludoviciana*
         k. Leaves dissected, the segments again dissected or toothed; or if entire
          (var. of *A. vulgaris*) bases of leaves with stipule-like lobes.
          Upper surfaces of leaves usually densely pubescent; receptacle beset
           with long hairs .... 13. *A. absinthium*
          Upper surfaces of leaves glabrous or essentially so; receptacle smooth. 14. *A. vulgaris*

    1. *A. dracúnculus* L. Fields and waste places. July-September. (Siberia). From farther west. Reported for CT, Essex County MA. (*A. cernua; A. dracunculoides; A. glauca*]. Represented with us as subsp. *gláuca* (Pallas) H.M. Hall & Clem.
    2. *A. filifólia* Torr. Fields and waste places. July-September. Rare; from farther west. Reported for New Haven County CT.

2286. *Cnicus benedictus*

2287. *Carduus nutans*

2288. *Carduus crispus*

2289. *Carduus acanthoides*

2290. *Artemisia campestris*

2291. *Artemisia biennis*

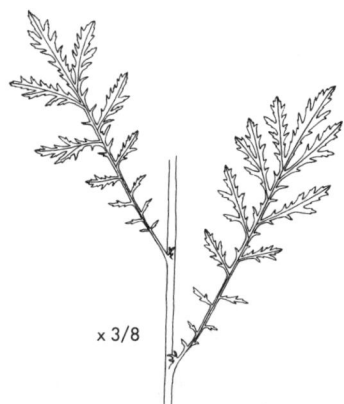

x 3/8

946. *Artemisia biennis.* Section of stem;
leaves with ultimate segments toothed.

2292. *Artemisia annua*

2293. *Artemisia abrotanum*

3. A. campéstris L. Dry, sandy, open soil. July-September. Map 2290. Represented with us by the following subsp:

subsp. *caudáta* (Michx.) Hall & Clem. Involucres 3 mm or less long [*A. caudata*].

subsp. *boreális* (Pall.) Hall & Clem. var. *borealis*. Involucres 3 mm or more long. Endangered in MA. [*A. canadensis; A. campestris* var. *c.*].

4. A. biénnis Willd. (biennial). Roadsides and waste places. August-October. Fig. 946, Map 2291.—FACU-

5. A. ánnua L. (annual). Roadsides, waste places, cultivated ground. August-October. Map 2292. (Naturalized from Eurasia). —FACU

6. A. tridentáta Nutt. (three-toothed). Sagebrush. Fields and waste places. From farther west. Reported for Middlesex County MA. Seeds were dried and ground into meal by Indians or eaten raw; tea made from the leaves was used to treat colds.

7. A. abrótanum L. (aromatic plant). Roadsides and waste places. August-September. Map 2293. (Introduced from Europe). Leaves are used in salads and in the preparation of aromatic vinegars; used also to restore menstrual flow and for children as a disinfectant against parasites; also used to stanch blood from small wounds.

8. A. póntica L. (from the Black Sea). Roadsides and waste places. August-September. Map 2294. (Introduced from Europe).

9. A. carrúthii Wood ex Carruth. (for its discoverer). Roadsides and waste places. August-October. From farther west. Reported for Providence County RI.

10. A. frígida Willd. (of cold regions). Roadsides and waste places. July-September. Map 2295. (Asia). From farther west.

11. A. stelleriána Besser (for its discoverer). Dusty Miller. Sea beaches and dunes. May-September. Fig. 947, Map 2296. (Naturalized from ne. Asia). —FACU

12. A. ludoviciána Nutt. (of St. Louis). Western Mugwort. Roadsides and waste places. July-September. Map 2297. (Europe). Our plants include subsp. *ludoviciana* and the following subsp.:

subsp. *mexicána* (Willd.) Keck. Leaves generally with several long narrow lobes (leaves entire, irregularly toothed or with short broad lobes in subsp. *ludoviciana*). [*A. mexicana*].

A. serráta Nutt. Similar to *A. ludoviciana* but is distinguishable in having leaves regularly serrate (leaves entire to irregularly toothed or lobed in *A. ludoviciana*). Rarely found in our range; from farther west. Reported for Rensselaer County NY.

13. A. absínthium L. (wormwood). Absinthe. Fields, roadsides, waste places. July-September. Map 2298. (Introduced from Europe). Leaves formerly used to flavor the drink Absinth; tea made from the leaves improves appetite and serves as a diuretic; can be toxic taken in large doses or over a long time.

14. A. vulgáris L. (common). Common Mugwort. Fields, roadsides, waste places. July-September. Map 2299. (Naturalized from Europe). Our plants include var. *vulgaris* and the following vars.:

var. *glábra* Ledeb. Divisions of the primary leaves entire (toothed or lacerate in var. *vulgaris*).

var. *latilóba* Ledeb. Divisions of the primary leaves obtuse or acute (acuminate in var. *vulgaris*). Used as a bitter in preparing some liquors.

44. Santolína L.

Branched, aromatic, tomentose subshrub; leaves small and narrow, alternate, pectinate or pinnatifid, sessile or short-petioled; heads solitary, terminating long peducles or in terminal corymbs, discoid, globose or hemispheric, flowers all tubular and perfect, yellow, involucral bracts scarious, at least on the margins, in several series, receptacle convex, chaffy, pappus none; achenes angled.

1. S. chamaecyparíssus L. (dwarf Cypress). Lavender-cotton. Rarely escaped from cultivation to roadsides and waste places. May-August. Reported for MA. (Introduced from Europe). Useful when finely ground in soothing pain and irritation from insect bites; when applied to skin wounds hastens healing.

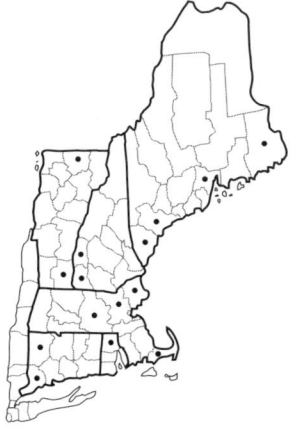

2294. *Artemisia pontica*

2295. *Artemisia frigida*

x 1/2

947. *Artemisia stelleriana*. Section of stem; leaves with rounded segments.

2296. *Artemisia stelleriana*

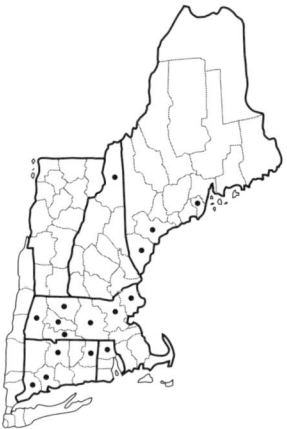

2297. *Artemisia ludoviciana*

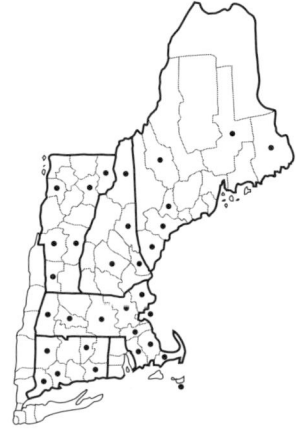

2298. *Artemisia absinthium*

2299. *Artemisia vulgaris*

2300. *Matricaria discoidea*

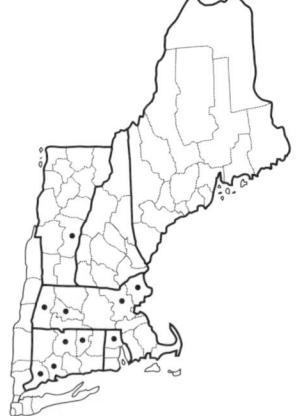

2301. *Matricaria recutita*

45. Cótula L. (from the Greek and Latin, referring to the hollow formed by the sheathing leaf bases).

Glabrous, strongly aromatic, often decumbent, perennial herbs, branched from the base; leaves alternate, entire to irregularly toothed or pinnately lobed, linear to oblong, sessile and sheathing at the base; heads solitary and terminal, yellow, discoid, involucral bracts in 2 series, receptacle flat to conical, naked, marginal flowers pistillate, the others perfect, pappus none; achenes, particularly the marginal ones, stipitate.

    1. C. coronopifólia L. (with leaves of *Coronopus*). Tidal flats and meadows. July-September. From farther north. Reported for Suffolk County MA.

46. Matricária L. Wild Chamomile (name based on reputed medicinal value).

Glabrous, branched, often aromatic, annual herbs; leaves alternate, 1-3 times pinnatifid, the ultimate segments linear to filiform, sessile; heads solitary and terminal or corymbose, radiate or discoid, involucral bracts scarious-margined, in several series, rays white, pistillate, receptacle hemispheric to elongate, naked, disc flowers perfect, yellow, pappus none or a short crown; achenes ribbed.

a. Heads discoid, the rays absent .... 1. *M. discoidea*
a. Heads radiate, the rays present.
    Involucres less than 1 cm broad; achenes faintly ribbed, otherwise smooth;
        plant aromatic .... 2. *M. recutita*
    Involucres mostly 1 cm or more broad; achenes with strong, almost wing-like
        ribs, papillose between the ribs; plant not aromatic. .... 3. *M. maritima*

    1. M. discoídea DC. Pineapple-weed. Fields, roadsides, waste places. June-September. Map 2300. [*M. matricarioides; M. suaveolens; Chamomilla s.*]. —FACU
    2. M. recútita L. Fields, roadsides, waste places. June-September. Map 2301. (Naturalized from Europe). [*M. chamomilla*]. The heads are dried and used to make tea, which is reported to have many healthful and medicinal values.
    3. M. marítima L. (of the sea shore). Fields, roadsides, waste places. June-September. Map 2302. (Adventive from Europe). [*M. inodora; M. perforata; Chamomilla inodora; C. maritima*]. Our plants are subsp. *maritima*.
    M. perforáta Merat. Similar to *M. maritima* but with leaves having narrow segments 5-20 mm long and heads 3 cm or more broad (leaf segments up to 5 mm long and heads up to 3 cm broad in *M. maritima*). Reported for CT, MA, ME, NH. [*M. maritima* var. *agrestis; M. inodora; Chamomilla i.*].

47. Tanacétum L. Tansy.

Strongly aromatic, perennial herbs; leaves 1-3 times pinnately dissected, alternate, sessile or short-petioled; heads numerous, small, corymbose, discoid or nearly so, involucral bracts scarious-margined, in several series, rays usually absent or if present very small, yellow, pistillate, receptacle flat or convex, naked, disc flowers perfect, yellow, the marginal ones usually pistillate; pappus none or a short crown; achenes ribbed or angled.

a. Rays absent or if present yellow, and 4 mm or less long.
    Heads 1 cm or less broad, usually numerous, more than 8 per stem; leaves,
        peduncles and involucres glabrous or essentially so. .... 1. *T. vulgare*
    Heads more than 1 cm broad, usually 8 or fewer per stem; leaves, peduncles and
        involucres villous-pubescent .... 2. *T. bipinnatum*
                                     subsp. *huronense*
a. Rays present, white, 4 mm or more long. .... 3. *T. parthenium*

    1. T. vulgáre L. (common). Fields, roadsides, waste places. August-September. Map 2303. (Introduced from Europe). Leaves have been used in salads and for restoring menstrual flow; was used on meat to discourage insects in the days before refrigeration; the plant is also reported as poisonous if eaten or taken in tea in large quantity.

2. *T. bipinnátum* (L.) Schultz-Bip. St. John River and tributaries. July-August. Reported for Aroostook County ME. Represented with us as subsp. *huronénse* (Nutt.) Breitung. [*T. huronense* var. *johannense*].

3. *T. parthénium* (L.) Schultz-Bip. Feverfew. Roadsides and waste places. June-September. Map 2303a. (Introduced from Europe). [*Chrysanthemum p.; Matricaria p.*]. Used as a bitter to flavor foods and liquors.

48. Senécio L. Squaw-weed (Latin name, meaning old, based on the hoary appearance of some species).

Annual or perennial herbs; leaves basal and alternate, entire to variously divided; heads solitary or corymbose, radiate or discoid, yellow, involucral bracts equal, in 1 series or also with a very short outer series, rays pistillate, receptacle flat, naked, disc flowers perfect, pappus of white bristles; achenes terete.

Arnoglóssum Raf. *atriplicifólium* (L.) H. Rob. Will key to those species of Senecio with rays lacking or inconspicuous but can be distinguished in having heads with 5 involucral bracts and 5 white to greenish or light pinkish flowers (*Senecio* has more numerous bracts and flowers, the latter yellow or orange). Fom the midwest. Reported for MA. [*Cacalia atriplicifolia*].

Láyia Hook. & Arn. *platyglóssa* (Fisch. & C.A. Mey.) Gray. Will key to *Senecio* or possibly *Heterotheca* (genus 82) but differs; may be distinguished from these genera and *Arnoglossum* in having solitary heads and 3-toothed rays. Southwestern. Rarely escaped from cultivation in our range. Reported for Middlesex County MA.

a. Rays absent or less than 5 mm long; plant annual.
  b. Involucre with a short, distinct, outer series of black-tipped phyllaries; rays
     none .... 1. *S. vulgaris*
  b. Involucre without an outer series of phyllaries or if present inconspicuous or
     few, and not black-tipped; rays present, minute.
     Plant densely glandular-pubescent throughout. .... 2. *S. viscosus*
     Plant sparsely pubescent to subglabrate, scarcely glandular. .... 3. *S. sylvaticus*
a. Rays present, 5 mm or more long; plant perennial or biennial.
  c. Disc 2 cm or more wide; involucres 1 cm or more long; plant of the seashore .... 4. *S. pseudoarnica*
  c. Disc less than 2 cm wide; involucres less than 1 cm long; plants of other habitats.
    d. Principal leaves mostly 2-3 times pinnatifid. .... 5. *S. jacobaea*
    d. Principal leaves entire, toothed or once pinnatifid.
      e. Plants, at least the stems, undersides of leaves and involucres persistently
        tomentose .... 6. *S. plattensis*
      e. Plants not persistently tomentose, or if so, only at the base and in the leaf axils.
        f. Basal leaves, or some of them, subtruncate to deeply cordate at base.
          Basal leaves subtruncate to shallowly cordate, more than 1.5 times as
           long as wide. (Fig. 948) .... 7. *S. schweinitzianus*
          Basal leaves, or some of them, deeply cordate, 1.5 times or less as long
           as wide .... 8. *S. aureus*
        f. Basal leaves tapering or abruptly contracted to the base.
          Plant stoloniferous, the stolons 4 cm or more long. .... 9. *S. obovatus*
          Plant not stoloniferous or if so, stolons very short. .... 10. *S. pauperculus*

1. *S. vulgáris* L. (common). Fields, roadsides, cultivated ground. June-October. Map 2304. (Naturalized from Europe). Preparations of this plant have been used in external applications in the treatment of hemorrhoids. —FACU

2. *S. viscósus* L. (sticky). Waste places. July-September. Map 2305. (Naturalized from Europe).

3. *S. sylváticus* L. (of the woods). Beaches and rocks along the coast, waste places. July-September. Map 2306. (Naturalized from Europe).

2302. *Matricaria maritima*

2303. *Tanacetum vulgare*

2303a. *Tanacetum parthenium*

2304. *Senecio vulgaris*

2305. *Senecio viscosus*

2306. *Senecio sylvaticus*

4. S. pseudoárnica Less. (false *Arnica*). Sea beaches. July-September. (ne. Asia). From farther north. Reported for ME.

5. S. jacobaéu L. (of St. James). Fields, waste places. July-October. (Naturalized from Europe). Reported for Cumberland County ME; Essex County MA. Poisonous.

S. eremóphilus Richards. Similar to *S. jacobaea* but with more laciniate leaves (leaves 2-3 times pinnatifid in *S. jacobaea*). From farther north and west. Reported for MA. Represented with us as var. *macdoúgalii* (A. Heller) Cronq. —OBL

6. S. platténsis Nutt. (of the Platte River). Dry fields, waste places. May-July. From farther west. Reported for VT.

7. S. schweinitziánus Nutt. Wet meadows, wet woods. June-August. Fig. 948, Map 2307. [*S. robbinsii*]. —FACW

8. S. aúreus L. (golden). Wooded swamps, wet woods. May-August. Map 2308. [*S. gracilis*]. Although used in early herbal medicine, preparations of this plant have recently been shown to be poisonous to the liver and its use is not recommended. —FACW

9. S. obovátus Muhl. ex Willd. (obovate). Rich woods. April-June. Map 2309. [*S. rotundus*]. —FACU-

10. S. paupérculus Michx. (poor). River shores, cliffs, rocks, fields. May-July. Map 2310. [*S. balsamitae*]. —FAC

49. *Erechtítes* Raf. (ancient Greek name used for another plant).

Robust, annual herbs; leaves alternate, elliptic to lanceolate, irregularly serrate or lobed, the lower tapered to a short petiole, the upper often auriculate; heads corymbose-paniculate, discoid, whitish, involucre swollen at the base, its bracts in 1 series, or with a few bracteoles at the base, receptacle flat, naked, marginal flowers pistillate, the inner perfect, pappus of numerous white, capillary bristles; achenes ribbed, pubescent.

1. E. hieracifólia (L.) Raf. ex DC. (with leaves of Hawkweed). Roadsides, waste places, clearings. July-September. Map 2311. Our plants include var. *hieracifolia* and the following var.:

var. *megalocárpa* (Fern.) Cronq. Receptacle 1 cm or more wide; achenes 4 mm or more long; plant of the seashore (receptacle less than 1 cm wide; achenes less than 4 mm long; plant mostly of other habitats in var. *hieracifolia*). [*E. megalocarpa*]. —FACU

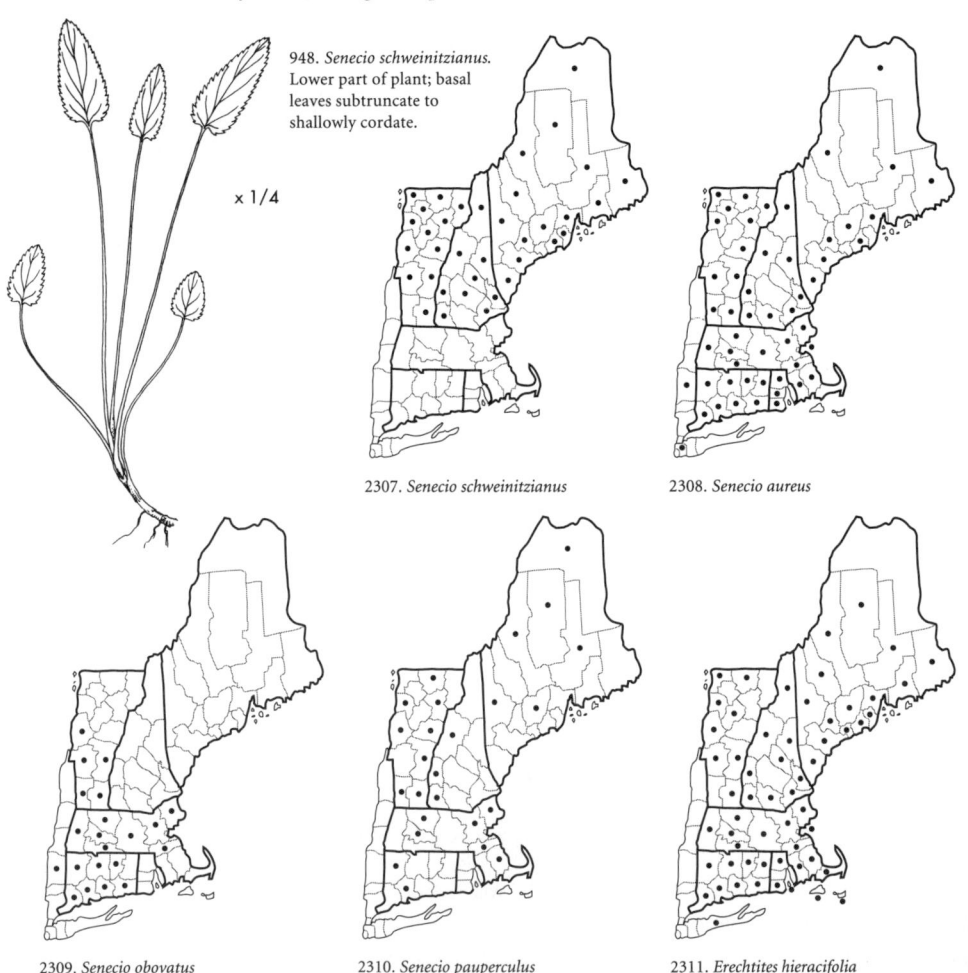

948. *Senecio schweinitzianus.* Lower part of plant; basal leaves subtruncate to shallowly cordate.

× 1/4

2307. *Senecio schweinitzianus*

2308. *Senecio aureus*

2309. *Senecio obovatus*

2310. *Senecio pauperculus*

2311. *Erechtites hieracifolia*

50. Parthénium L. (ancient Greek name for another plant).

Branched, pubescent, annual or perennial herbs; leaves alternate, pinntifid to bipinnatifid or merely toothed, sessile or petioled; heads small, in corymbs, radiate, involucral bracts in 2 or more series, rays few, white, minute, pistillate, receptacle conical, chaffy, disc flowers perfect, sterile, white, pappus a pair of scales; achenes flattened, joined to their subtending chaff and crowned by the persistent rays at the apex.

Crupína (Pers.) DC. *vulgáris* Cass. Similar to *Parthenium* but distinguishable in having purple disc flowers with long, narrow lobes and pappus consisting of an outer series of scales and an inner series of bristles (in *Parthenium* disc flowers are white, the corolla 5-toothed, and pappus is a single pair of scales). Mediterranean; a waif in our range. Reported for Suffolk County MA.

Chaenáctis DC. *glabriúscula* DC. Will key to *Parthenium*; heads discoid, yellow, pappus of 4 scales. From the southwest. Reported for MA.

Leaves pinnatifid or bipinnatifid .... 1. *P. hysterophorus*
Leaves merely crenate or serrate or shallowly lobed at the base. .... 2. *P. integrifolium*

1. P. hysteróphorus L. (old generic name). Waste places. July-October. (Adventive from Tropical Amer.). Reported for Fairfield County CT; Middlesex County MA.

2. P. integrifólium L. (entire-leaved). Wild Quinine. Waste places, cultivated ground. June-September. Map 2312. From farther west or south. Our plants are var. *integrifolium*.

51. Achilléa L. Yarrow (name based on reputed medicinal value, said to have been discovered by Achilles).

Perennial herbs; leaves subentire to serrate or 2-3 times pinnately dissected, stem leaves alternate, sessile (except sometimes the lowermost), basal leaves, when present, petioled; heads in terminal corymbs, radiate, involucral bracts scarious-margined, pubescent, in several series, rays white to pink, pistillate, receptacle convex, chaffy, disc flowers perfect, white, very small, pappus none; achenes compressed. —Wildl. 1

Leaves subentire to finely serrate .... 1. *A. ptarmica*
Leaves 2-3 times pinnately dissected .... 2. *A. millefolium*

1. A. ptármica L. (causing to sneeze). Fields, roadsides, waste places. July-September. Map 2313. (Naturalized from Europe).

2. A. millefólium L. (thousand-leaved). Fields, roadsides, waste places. June-September. Map 2314. (Naturalized from Europe). [*A. ligustica*]. Our plants include var. *millefolium* and the following vars.:

var. *occidentális* DC. Median stem leaves mostly less than 2 cm wide, the segments in several planes (median stem leaves mostly more than 2 cm wide, the segments mostly on 1 plane in var. *millefolium*). [*A. millefolium* subsp. *lanulosa; A. lanulosa*].

var. *boreális* (Bong.) Farw. Margins of involucral bracts dark brown or black (not edged in brown or black in the above vars.) [*A. borealis; A. millefolium* var. *nigrescens*]. Dried heads and leaves are used to make tea, which is reported to have many healthful and medicinal values. —FACU

A. filipendulína Lam. Similar to *A. millefolium* but distinguishable in having a subglobose inflorescence and the stem leafless for 5 cm or more below the inflorescence (inflorescence rounded to flat-topped and stem leafy to inflorescence in *A. millefolium*). Rarely escaped from cultivation. Reported for Rutland County VT.

52. Liátris Gaertn. ex Schreb. Blazing star.

Simple-stemmed, perennial herbs from a roundish corm; leaves alternate, crowded, entire, linear, punctate, decreasing in size upward and becoming sessile, the lowest petioled; heads in spikes or racemes, discoid, involucral bracts imbricated in several series, receptacle naked, flowers perfect, rose-purple, rarely white, pappus of barbellate bristles; achenes ribbed, pubescent.

a. Heads hemispheric; involucres mostly 1.3 cm or more thick. (Fig. 949). .... 1. *L. scariosa*
a. Heads cylindric to campanulate; involucres 1.2 cm or less thick.
    Involucral bracts erect, appressed, rounded or obtuse. .... 2. *L. spicata*
    Involucral bracts squarrose-tipped, acute to acuminate. .... 3. *L. pycnostachya*

1. *L. scariósa* (L.) Willd. Dry open woods, clearings, barrens, in sandy soil. August-September. Fig. 949, Map 2315. Endangered in RI, NH. Represented with us by the following vars.:
    var. *nóvae-ángliae* Lunell. Lower leaves seldom over 2 cm wide. [*L. novae-angliae; L. borealis*].
    var. *nieuwlándii* Lunell. Lower leaves 2-5 cm wide [*Liatris n.*].
    L. ligulistýlis (A. Nels.) K. Schum. Similar to *L. scariosa* but with middle involucral bracts having broad conspicuous, lacerate scarious margins (middle involucral bracts with narrow, ciliate but not lacerate scarious margins in *L. scariosa*). Western. Reported for CT.
    2. *L. spicáta* (L.) Willd. (spicate). Wet meadows, ditches. July-September. From farther south and west. Reported for Middlesex County MA; Fairfield County CT. Reported to be of value as a diuretic and to promote menstrual flow. —FAC+
    3. *L. pycnostáchya* Michx. (with crowded spike). Fields, barrens. July-September. Map 2316. From farther south and west. —FACU

53. *Vernónia* Schreb. Ironweed (for W. Vernon).

Perennial herbs; leaves alternate, serrate or entire, sessile or short-petioled, linear to lanceolate, acute to acuminate; heads in corymbose cymes, discoid, involucral bracts imbricated, receptacle flat, naked, flowers purple, perfect, pappus double, the inner of capillary bristles, the outer of short, scale-like bristles; achenes ribbed.
    Palafóxia Lag. *texána* DC. Similar to *Vernonia* but differs in having pappus of short rounded scales or no pappus. Western. Reported for Middlesex County MA.

a. Involucral bracts narrowed to long, filiform tips. .... 1. *V. noveboracensis*
a. Involucral bracts obtuse to acute.
    Leaves glabrous beneath or essentially so; heads with 30 or fewer flowers. .... 2. *V. fasciculata*
    Leaves tomentose beneath, at least on the veins; heads with more than 30 flowers . 3. *V. missurica*

    1. *V. noveboracénsis* (L.) Michx. (of New York). Pond and stream margins, wet meadows, wet thickets. August-September. Map 2317. —FACW+
    2. *V. fasciculáta* Michx. (bunched). Pond and stream margins, wet meadows. July-September. From farther west. Reported for Middlesex County MA. Our plants are var. *fasciculata*. —FAC+
    3. *V. missúrica* Raf. (of Missouri). Fields and barrens. July-September. Rare; from farther west. Reported for Middlesex County MA. FACU+

54. *Plúchea* Cass. Marsh-fleabane (for Abbe Nat. Ant. Pluche).

Annual herbs, usually glandular-puberulent; leaves alternate, sessile or short petioled, toothed to nearly entire, lanceolate to elliptic, cuneate to attenuate at the base; heads in a leafy, flat-topped to rounded corymb of cymes, discoid, involucral bracts imbricated in several series, often pink or purple, receptacle flat, naked, flowers small, pink to purple, the outer pistillate, the inner perfect, pappus of whitish, capillary bristles; achenes ribbed.

    1. *P. odoráta* (L.) Cass. Salt-marsh-fleabane. Salt to brackish marshes. August-September. Fig. 950, Map 2318. Represented with us as var. *succulénta* (Fern.) Cronq. [*P. purpurascens* var. *s*]. —OBL
    P. camphoráta (L.) DC. Similar to *P. odorata* but with involucral bracts glabrous or with a granular surface (bracts pubescent in *P. odorata*). From farther south and west. Reported for RI. [*P. petiolata*]. —FACW

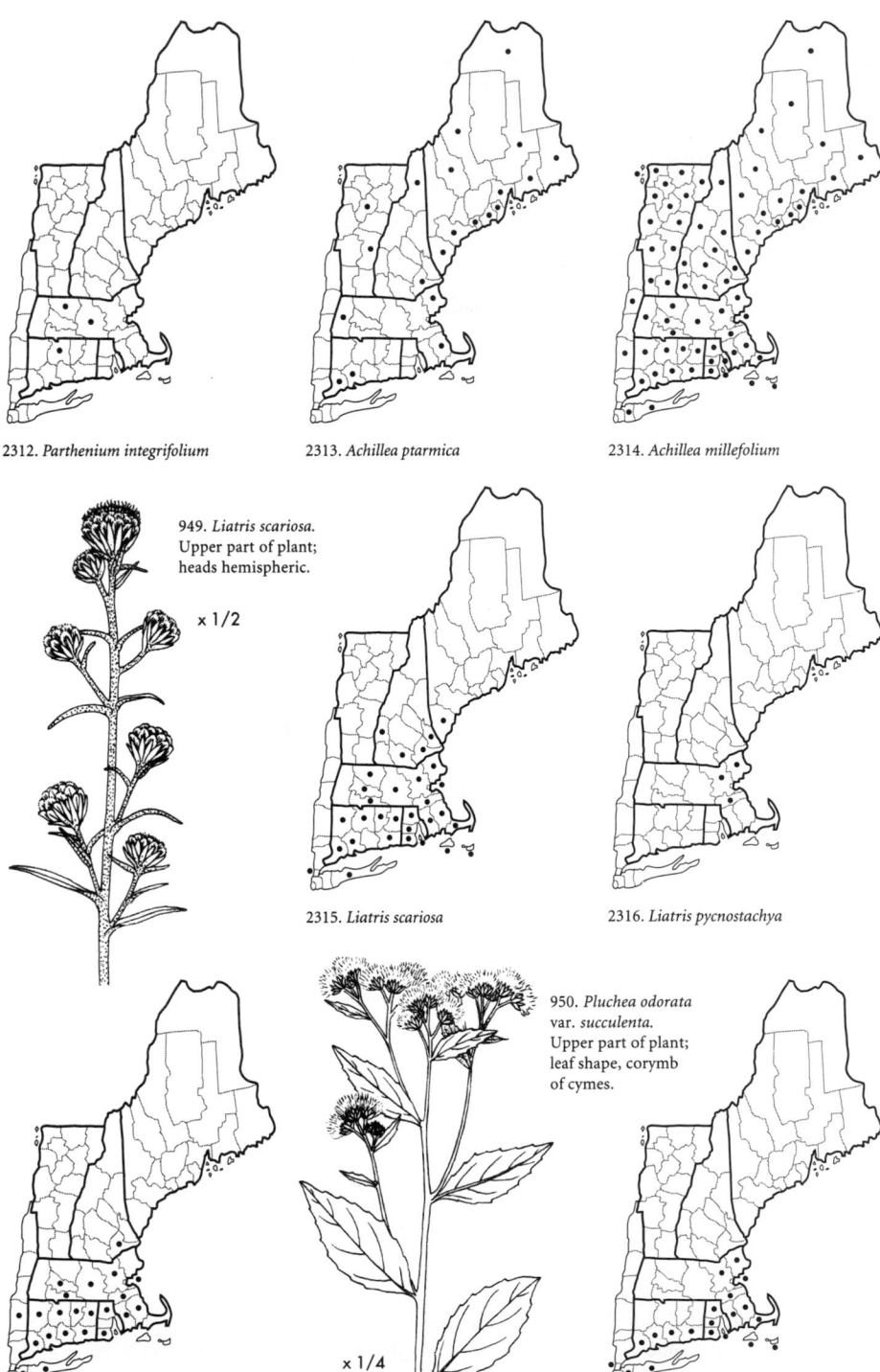

2312. *Parthenium integrifolium*

2313. *Achillea ptarmica*

2314. *Achillea millefolium*

949. *Liatris scariosa*.
Upper part of plant;
heads hemispheric.

× 1/2

2315. *Liatris scariosa*

2316. *Liatris pycnostachya*

2317. *Vernonia noveboracensis*

950. *Pluchea odorata*
var. *succulenta*.
Upper part of plant;
leaf shape, corymb
of cymes.

× 1/4

2318. *Pluchea odorata* var. *succulenta*

55. Conýza Less.

Similar to *Erigeron* (genus 77) but involucral bracts imbricated, rays white or purplish, barely or not exceeding the pappus, heads small and numerous, the involucres 4 mm or less broad (more than 4 mm broad in *Erigeron*). [*Erigeron; Leptilon*].

1. **C. canadénsis** (L.) Cronq. Horseweed. Fields, roadsides, waste places. July-September. Map 2319. [*Erigeron c.; Leptilon c.*]. Our plants include var. *canadense* and the following vars.:

var. *pusílla* (Nutt.) Cronq. Stems glabrous; involucral bracts tipped with purple (stems spreading-pubescent and bracts uniformly green in var. *canadensis*). [*Erigeron pusillus; Leptilon pusillum*].

var. *glabráta* (Gray) Cronq. Bracts uniformly green as in var. *canadensis* but stem glabrous or sparsely appressed-pubescent. Preparation made from the plant has been used as a tonic, diuretic, and to treat bleeding piles.

56. Ghaphálium L. Cudweed (ancient Greek name, meaning lack of wool, applied to some woolly plant).

Woolly, annual or biennial herbs; leaves alternate, sessile or decurrent, usually entire, usually woolly beneath; heads in glomerules, corymbs or panicles, discoid, involucral bracts imbricated in several series, receptacle flat, naked, flowers small, whitish or yellowish, the outer pistillate, the inner perfect, pappus of distinct, capillary bristles; achenes small, smooth or papillate.

Filágo L. *mínima* Fries. Will key to *Gnaphalium*; distinguishable in having heads in a glomerule terminating the stem, this usually subtended by several leafy branches also bearing terminal glomerules, these often again giving rise to leafy branches bearing terminal glomerules; receptacle chaffy. (Europe). Reported for MA, Suffolk County, NY.

a. Heads in terminal glomerules overtopped by their subtending leafy bracts; pappus
    bristles distinct. (Fig. 951) .... 1. *G. uliginosum*
a. Heads in corymbose or paniculate inflorescences. (Fig. 952).
    b. Leaf bases decurrent down the stem .... 2. *G. viscosum*
    b. Leaf bases not decurrent.
        Stems with spreading stipitate-glandular pubescence. .... 3. *G. helleri*
                                                                                                    var. *microdenium*
        Stems with appressed woolly pubescence. .... 4. *G. obtusifolium*

1. **G. uliginósum** L. (growing in marshes). Roadsides, waste places, pond and stream borders. July-September. Fig. 951, Map 2320. (Eurasia). [*Filaginella uliginosa*]. —FAC

2. **G. viscósum** Kunth (sticky). Fields, clearings, roadsides, waste places. July-September. Fig. 952, Map 2321. [*G. macounii*].

3. **G. hélleri** Britt. (for its discoverer). Dry woodlands. August-October. Map 2322. Represented with us as var. *microdénium* (Weatherby) Mahler. [*G. obtusifolium* var. *m.*].

4. **G. obtusifólium** L. (obtuse-leaved). Fields, roadsides, waste places. August-October. Map 2323. Our plants are var. *obtusifolium*. Was used by Indians and Europeans for a variety of medicinal purposes.

57. Gamocháeta Wedd.

Similar to *Gnaphalium* except inflorescence spiciform-thyrsoid and pappus bristles united in a ring at the base. [*Gnaphalium*].

1. **G. purpúrea** (L.) Cabrera (purple). Fields, roadsides, waste places. July-September. Fig. 953, Map 2324. (Tropical Amer.). Endangered in MA. [*Gnaphalium purpureum; G. pensylvanicum; G. peregrinum; G. spathulatum*].

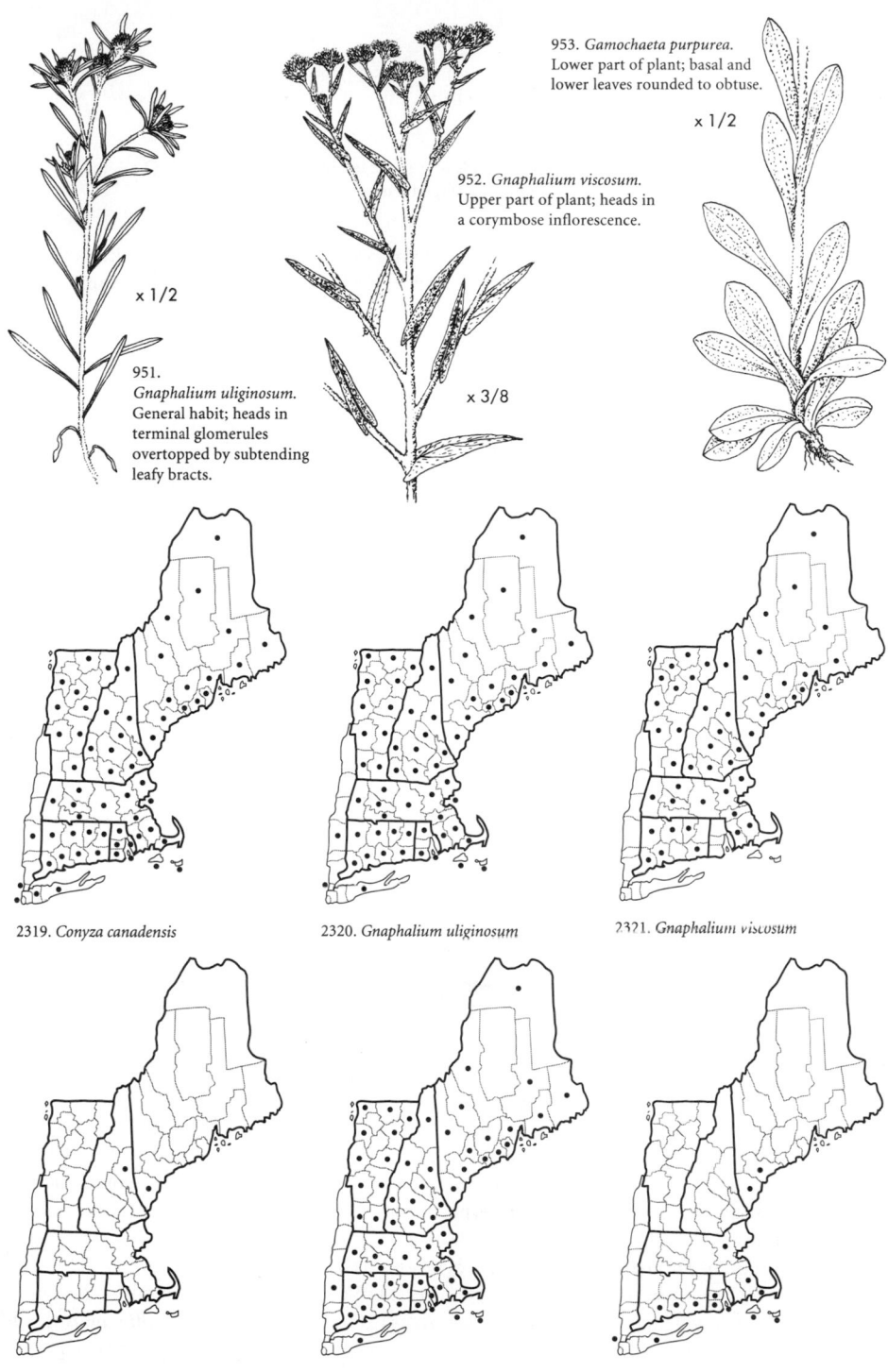

951.
Gnaphalium uliginosum.
General habit; heads in
terminal glomerules
overtopped by subtending
leafy bracts.

x 1/2

x 3/8

952. *Gnaphalium viscosum.*
Upper part of plant; heads in
a corymbose inflorescence.

953. *Gamochaeta purpurea.*
Lower part of plant; basal and
lower leaves rounded to obtuse.

x 1/2

2319. *Conyza canadensis*

2320. *Gnaphalium uliginosum*

2321. *Gnaphalium viscosum*

2322. *Gnaphalium helleri* var. *microdenium*

2323. *Gnaphalium obtusifolium*

2324. *Gamochaeta purpurea*

58. *Omalothéca* Cass.

Similar to *Gnaphalium*; perennial, heads in spiciform-thyrsoid inflorescences or in terminal glomerules, pappus bristles distinct or united in a ring at the base, achenes sparsely strigose. [*Gnaphalium*].

Plants 1 cm or less tall; pappus bristles distinct; heads 8 or fewer; alpine areas .... 1. *O. supina*
Plants 1 cm or more tall; pappus bristles united in a ring at base; heads mostly more
    than 8; mostly other habitats. .... 2 *O. sylvatica*

    1. *O. supína* (L.) DC. (lying on its back). Alpine areas of Mt. Katahdin, Maine and Mt. Washington, New Hampshire. July-September. Endangered in ME, NH. Piscataquis County ME; Coos County NH. [*Gnaphalium supinum*].
    2. *O. sylvática* (L.) Schultz-Bip. & F. W. Schultz (of woodland). Woodlands, openings, fields. August-September. Fig. 954, Map 2325. (Europe). Endangered in VT. [*Gnaphalium sylvaticum*].

59. *Synósma* (L.) Raf. ex Britt. and A. Br. Indian plantain (ancient name).

Glabrous, perennial herbs, stem striate; leaves alternate, triangular-hastate to lanceolate-hastate, sharply toothed, petioled, the blade decurrent on the petiole; heads in flat corymbs, discoid, whitish, involucral bracts in 1 series or also with a short outer series, receptacle flat, naked, flowers all perfect, pappus of numerous white, capillary bristles; achenes cylindric, ribbed. [*Cacalia; Hasteola*].

    1. *S. suavéolens* L. (sweet-smelling). Riverbanks. August-September. Fig. 955, Map 2326. From farther south and west. [*Cacalia s.; Hasteola s.*].

60. *Trimórpha* Andrz. ex Bess.

Similar to *Erigeron* (genus 77) except rays inconspicuous, not or barely exceeding the pappus. [*Erigeron*].

    1. *T. ácris* (L.) Nesonn. Clearings, thickets. July-August. (e. Asia). From farther north and west. Reported for Aroostook and Franklin Counties, ME. [*Erigeron a.* var. *kamtschaticus; Erigeron asteroides; E. angulosus* var. *kamtschaticus; E. droebachensis*]. Represented with us as var. *kamtschatica* (DC.) Nesonn. —FACU

61. *Balsamíta* P. Mill.

Similar to *Chrysanthemum* (genus 78) except rays usually absent or minute. [*Chrysanthemum*].

    1. *B. májor* Desf. (old generic name). Costmary. Roadsides and waste places. August-October. Fig. 956, Map 2327. (Introduced from Europe). [*Chrysanthemum balsamita; Tanacetum b.*].

62. *Áster* L. Aster (from the Greek, meaning star, based on the radiate heads of flowers).

Perennial, rarely annual herbs, stems mostly branched; leaves alternate, sessile or petioled, entire or variously toothed; heads mostly corymbose or paniculate, rarely solitary, radiate, involucral bracts usually imbricated, sometimes equal, rays blue, purple, pink or white, pistillate, receptacle naked, flat, disc flowers perfect, yellow, red or purple, pappus of capillary bristles, sometimes accompanied by a short outer series; achenes small, mostly flattened. —Wildl. 1
    In addition to the species treated below *A. x gravesii* has been reported for CT.
    Callistéphus Cass. *chinénsis* (L). Nees. China Aster. Similar to Aster but distinguishable from it and the following 2 genera in having much larger heads (5 cm or more across in *Callistephus*, much narrower across in Aster and the following 2 genera). Rarely escaped from flower gardens. Reported for CT, Hancock County ME.

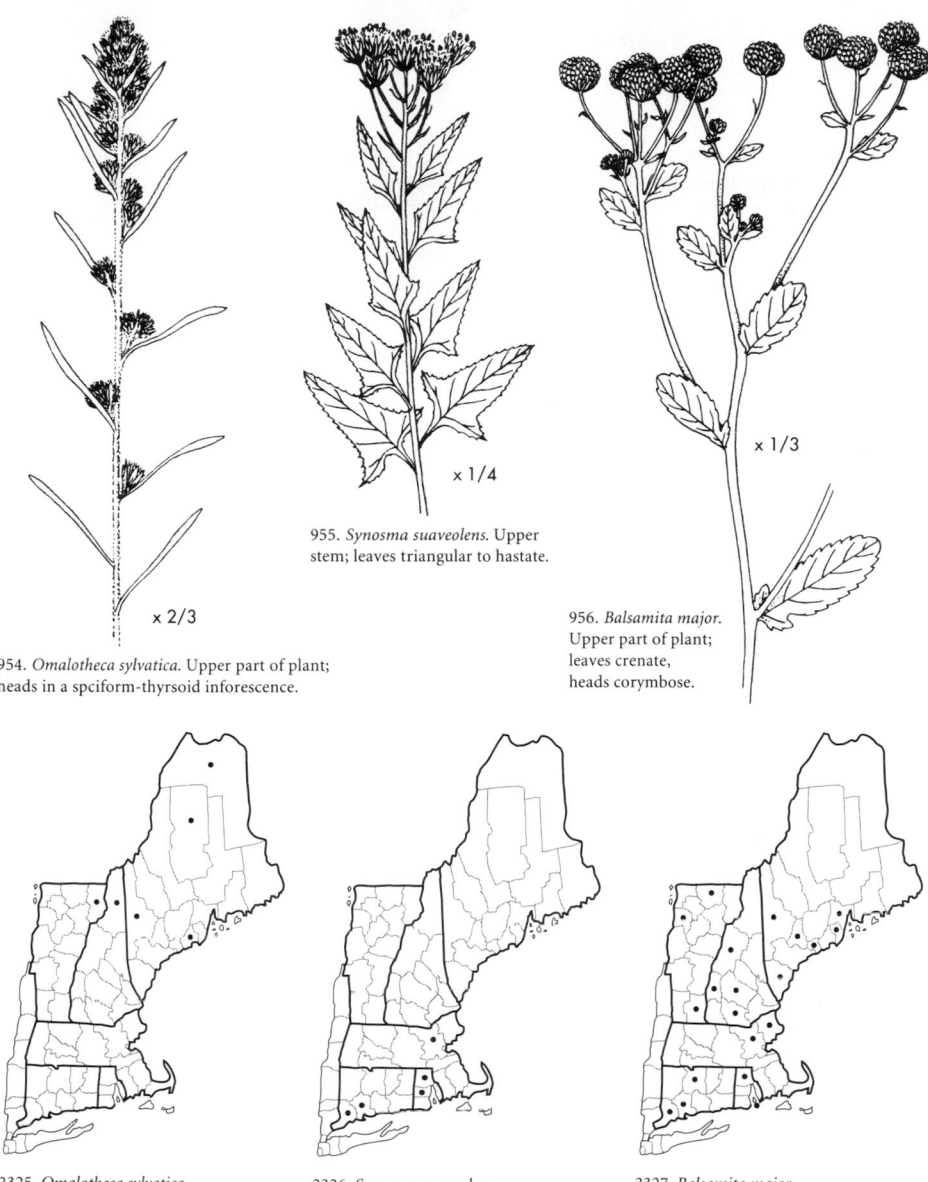

× 2/3

954. *Omalotheca sylvatica.* Upper part of plant;
heads in a spciform-thyrsoid inforescence.

955. *Synosma suaveolens.* Upper
stem; leaves triangular to hastate.

× 1/4

× 1/3

956. *Balsamita major.*
Upper part of plant;
leaves crenate,
heads corymbose.

2325. *Omalotheca sylvatica*

2326. *Synosma suaveolens*

2327. *Balsamita major*

Brickéllia Ell. *grandiflóra* (Hook.) Nutt. Sometimes keying to *Aster*; heads discoid, corymbose in an open panicle, flowers all perfect (rays sometimes inconspicuous but heads not truly discoid in *Aster*, the outer flowers pistillate). From farther west. Reported for RI.

Helichrýsum Gaertn. *bracteátum* Andr. Strawflower. Similar to Aster but distinguishable from it and the above 2 genera in having solitary discoid heads (rays sometimes inconspicuous but heads not truly discoid in Aster; heads discoid in *Brickellia* but corymbose in an open panicle; rays well developed in *Callistephus*). Rarely escaped from cultivation. Reported for Fairfield County CT; Essex County MA.

A. Leaves, at least the basal or lower ones, cordate and petioled. (Fig. 957).
  B. Inflorescence a flat or round-topped corymb; outer involucral bracts broad,
     mostly less than 3 times as long as wide. (Fig. 957).
    C. Peduncles glandular; rays purplish .... 1. *A. macrophyllus*
    C. Peduncles eglandular; rays white.
      Plants with well developed tufts of basal leaves on separate shoots. .... 2. *A. schreberi*
      Plants usually without well developed tufts of basal leaves. .... 3. *A. divaricatus*
  B. Inflorescence paniculate, often elongate; outer involucral bracts narrow, mostly
     3 or more times as long as wide. (Fig. 958).
    D. Median and upper stem leaves (at least some) sessile and cordate-clasping or
      petioles auriculate-clasping. (Fig. 958). .... 4. *A. undulatus*
    D. Median and upper stem leaves or petioles not clasping or auriculate but
      often petioled and cordate.
      Inflorescence branches and peduncles mostly sparsely bracteate. (Fig. 959). .. 5. *A. ciliolatus*
      Inflorescence branches and peduncles mostly abundantly bracteate. .... 6. *A. cordifolius*
A. Leaves not both cordate and petioled.
  E. Stem leaves sessile and cordate or auriculate-clasping.
    F. Involucral bracts glandular or puberulent or both.
      Leaves cordate-clasping, ovate to oblong. .... 7. *A. patens*
      Leaves auriculate, but not cordate-clasping, lanceolate. (Fig. 960). .... 8. *A. novae-angliae*
    F. Involucral bracts glabrous or essentially so or ciliate, not glandular or puberulent.
      G. Involucral bracts, at least the inner ones, linear-attenuate. (Fig. 961). .... 9. *A. puniceus*
      G. Involucral bracts mostly obtuse to acute.
        H. Outer involucral bracts, at least some of them, green and foliaceous,
          conspicuously exceeding the inner .... 10. *A. novi-belgii*
                                              var. *tardiflorus*
        H. Outer involucral bracts not foliaceous, usually with scarious margins or
          base, equalling or shorter than the inner.
          I. Stem and leaves glaucous, the latter leathery; involucral bracts with
            green band strongly widened and diamond-shaped at apex. .... 11. *A. laevis*
          I. Stem and leaves not glaucous, leaves not leathery; involucral bracts
            with green band not or only gradually widened at apex.
            J. Leaves, at least the lower ones, abruptly contracted below the
              middle into a winged base .... 12. *A. prenanthoides*
            J. Leaves gradually tapered to the base.
              Involucral bracts, at least some of them, with spreading or
                recurved tips; leaves mostly wider than 5 mm. (Fig. 962). ... 10. *A. novi-belgii*
              Involucral bracts appressed; leaves mostly 5 mm or less wide. .... 13. *A. borealis*
  E. Stem leaves sessile or petioled, tapered or rounded, not cordate or
    auriculate-clasping.
    K. Leaves silvery-pubescent on both sides, entire. .... 14. *A. concolor*
    K. Leaves pubescent or glabrous but not silvery, entire or toothed.
      L. Involucral bracts glandular.
        Lowest leaves abruptly contracted to the petiole. .... 15. *A. x herveyi*
        Lowest leaves narrowed to the petiole .... 16. *A. spectabilis*
      L. Involucral bracts eglandular.
        M. Annuals with rays absent or short and not or barely exceeding the
          pappus. (Fig. 965) .... 17. *A. subulatus*
        M. Perennials with rays conspicuous and distinctly exceeding the pappus.
          N. Pappus double, the inner series of long bristles, the outer of short
            ones. (Fig. 966).
            O. Leaves linear, less than 5 mm wide; inner pappus bristles
              slender-tipped, not clavate .... 18. *A. linariifolius*
            O. Leaves lanceolate to elliptic, more than 5 mm wide; inner pappus
             bristles clavate.
             Achenes sparsely to densely pubescent; involucres 5 mm or less
              long; inflorescences mostly compact, heads numerous. .... 19. *A. umbellatus*
             Achenes glabrous; involucres 5 mm or more long; inflorescences
              mostly open, heads sparse and scattered .... 20. *A. infirmus*
         N. Pappus single, consisting only of a series of long bristles.

P. Involucral bracts cartilaginous, whitish with green tips; rays 8 or
    fewer; achenes densely sericeous.
    Leaves, or some of them, toothed, the larger ones 1 cm or more
        wide, elliptic. ....21. *A. paternus*
    Leaves entire, mostly less than 1 cm wide, linear to linear-oblong. ... 22. *A. solidagineus*
P. Involucral bracts herbaceous, not cartilaginous; rays 8 or more;
    achenes glabrous to pubescent but not densely sericeous.
    Q. Leaves fleshy, narrowly linear; salt marshes. (Fig. 967). .... 23. *A. tenuifolius*
    Q. Leaves not fleshy, linear or broader; widespread in mostly
        other habitats.
        R. Inflorescence mostly corymbose or heads solitary; achenes
            glandular or some of the pappus bristles clavate.
            (Fig. 968).
            S. Leaves below the inflorescence mostly fewer than 25,
                coarsely toothed, the largest mostly wider than 2.5 cm,
                often appearing nearly whorled below inflorescence.
                (Fig. 968) ....24. *A. acuminatus*
            S. Leaves below the inflorescence mostly 25 or more, entire to
                shallowly toothed, the largest 2.5 cm or less wide, not
                appearing whorled below the inflorescence.
                Leaves below the inflorescence mostly fewer than 40, the
                    largest mostly wider than 8 mm .... 25. *A. x blakei*
                Leaves below the inflorescence mostly more than 40, the
                    largest 8 mm or less wide .... 26. *A. nemoralis*
        R. Inflorescence mostly paniculate or racemose; if corymbose
            or heads solitary achenes not glandular; pappus bristles
            not clavate.
            T. Involucres mostly longer than 7 mm, the larger bracts
                mostly 1 mm or more wide; rays usually purple or blue.
                U. Lower leaves the largest, more than 2.5 cm wide................. 27. *A. tataricus*
                U. Lower leaves reduced and deciduous; largest leaves
                  2.5 cm or less wide.
                Involucral bracts pale-coriaceous except for the tip;
                    inflorescence mostly corymbose or heads
                    solitary .... 28. *A. radula*
                Involucral bracts green throughout or with scarious
                    margins; inflorescence mostly paniculate .... 10. *A. novi-belgii*
            T. Involucres 7 mm or less long, the bracts mostly less than
                1 mm wide (except sometimes in *A. falcatus*, a species
                similar to *A. ericoides*); rays usually white (except *A.*
                novi-belgii).
                V. Involucral bracts with subulate or mucronate tips.
                  Involucral bracts subulate-tipped, ascending. .... 29. *A. pilosus*
                  Involucral bracts spinulose-mucronate, at least some
                    of them with spreading or recurved tips .... 30. *A. ericoides*
                V. Involucral bracts obtuse to acute but not subulate or
                  mucronate-tipped.
                  W. Involucral bracts, at least some of them, with spreading
                    or recurved tips. (Fig. 962) .... 10. *A. novi-belgii*
                  W. Involucral bracts appressed or ascending.
                    X. Lobes of disc corollas half to three-quarters the length
                    of the tube; leaves often pubescent beneath
                    along midrib ....31. *A. lateriflorus*
                  X. Lobes of disc corollas less than half the length of the
                  tube; leaves glabrous beneath.
                  Y. Involucres less than 4 mm long; rays 6 mm or less
                    long; heads numerous, often secund along
                    the inflorescence branches. (Fig. 970). .... 31. *A. lateriflorus*
                  Y. Involucres and rays longer or heads few, seldom
                    secund.

Z. Veinlets of leaves forming a conspicuous
reticulum of isodiametric areolae. (Fig. 971) . 32. *A. praealtus*
Z. Veinlets of leaves not forming a conspicuous
reticulum, or if so, the areolae definitely
longer than broad (sometimes somewhat
isodiametric in *A. lateriflorus* var.
hirsuticaulis but involucres are 5 mm or less
long; 5 mm or more long in *A. praealtus*).
a. Peduncles long, copiously small-bracteolate;
involucral bracts with midrib
conspicuously upwardly dilated to a
broad green tip. (Fig. 972). .... 33. *A. dumosus*
a. Peduncles short or bracteoles sparse, or
foliaceous; involucral bracts with
midrib not or only gradually upwardly
dilated.
b. Inflorescence short and broad, loose and
open, the heads mostly few and
scattered; involucres 5 mm or more
long; bogs. (Fig. 964). .... 13. *A. borealis*
b. Inflorescence elongate, compact, the heads
numerous; involucres mostly 5 mm or
less long; other habitats.
Plants 6 dm or less tall; stems less than
3 mm in diameter near base. .... 31. *A. lateriflorus*
Plants taller than 6 dm; stems usually 3
mm or more in diameter near
base. .... 34. *A. lanceolatus*

1. A. macrophýllus L. (large-leaved). Woodlands and openings. July-September. Fig. 957, Map 2328. Highly variable; the following weakly defined vars. are recognized in our area.:

var. *iánthinus* (Burgess) Fern. Glands on the pedicels minute, rarely stipitate (glands stipitate in the following vars.). [*A. ianthinus; A. multiformis; A. nobilis; A. violaris*].

var. *apricénsis* Burgess. Stem branching well below middle (stem branching well above middle in the following vars.):

var. *velútinus* Burgess. Stem and petioles pubescent with long soft hairs (glabrous in vars. *excelsior, macrophýllus* and *pinguifolius*).

var. *sejúnctus* Burgess. Similar to var. *velutinus* but stem leaves rounded or cordate at base (stem leaves truncate or tapered to base in var. *velutinus*).

var. *macrophýllus* Basal and usually the stem leaves harshly scabrous, pedicels with numerous glands (basal and usually stem leaves smooth or slightly scabrous, pedicels with few glands in the following vars.). [*A. roscidus*].

var. *pinguifólius* Burgess. Stem not glaucous, leaves smooth, principal stem leaves widely ovate, long-petioled.

var. *excélsior* Burgess. Similar to the latter var. but fresh stems glaucous, leaves slightly scabrous, principal stem leaves narrowly ovate to lanceolate, sessile to short-petioled.

2. A. schréberi Nees (for J. von Schreber). Woodlands. July-September. Map 2329. [*A. chasei; A. curvescens; A. glomeratus*].

3. A. divaricátus L. (widely branched). Woodlands. August-October. Map 2330. [*A. carmesinus; A. castaneus; A. excavatus; A. stelletiformis; A. tenebrosus*].

4. A. undulátus L. (undulate). Fields, open woods, roadsides. August-October. Fig. 958, Map 2331. [*A. claviger; A. corrigiatus; A. gracilescens; A. sylvestris; A. triangularis; A. truellius*]. Our plants include var. *undulatus* and the following var.:

var. *lorifórmis* Burgess. Principal stem leaves narrowly lanceolate (ovate to oblong in var. *undulatus*). [*A. loriformis*].

5. A. ciliolátus Lindl. (slightly ciliate). Woods, clearings, fields, roadsides. August-September. Fig. 959, Map 2332. [*A. lindleyanus; A. saundersii; A. wilsoni*]. Our plants include var. *ciliolatus* and the following var.:

var. *comátus* Fern. Upper stem, petioles and undersides of leaves pubescent (glabrous in var. *ciliolatus*).

6. A. cordifólius L. (heart-leaved). Woods, thickets, roadsides. August-October. Map 2333. Our plants include var. *cordifolius* and the following vars.:

var. *polycéphalus* Porter. Similar to var. *cordifolius* but upper stem leaves truncate or tapered at the base (cordate at the base in var. *cordifolius*).

var. *racemiflórus* Fern. Involucre 5 mm or more high, inflorescence with primary branches simple to slightly branched (involucre up to 5 mm high and inflorescence much branched in the latter 2 vars.).

var. *furbíshiae* Fern. Similar to the latter var. but with stem and petioles densely pubescent (glabrous or sparsely pubescent in var. *racemiflorus*).

var. *laevigátus* Porter. Petioles conspicuously winged; leaves smooth above, glabrous below (petioles scarcely winged; leaves somewhat scabrous above, sparsely to densely pubescent below in the above vars.) [*A. lowrieanus*].

var. *lanceolátus* Porter. Similar to var. *laevigatus* but with lower leaves narrowly ovate to lanceolate, gradually rounded at the base (lower leaves ovate, cordate at the base in var. *laevigatus*). [*A. lowrieanus* var. *l.*].

var. *sagittifólius* (Wedemeyer ex Willd.) A. G. Jones. Inflorescence a narrow panicle; involucral bracts with green band narrow, not strongly widened or diamond-shaped at apex (inflorescence an open panicle; involucral bracts with green band strongly widened and diamond-shaped at apex in the above vars.) [*A. sagittifolius*].

7. A. pátens Ait. (spreading). Woods, fields. August-October. Map 2334. Our plants include var. *patens* and the following var.:

var. *phlogifólius* (Muhl. ex Willd.) Nees. Leaves often constricted above the base (rarely constricted above base in var. *patens*). [*A. phlogifolius*].

8. A. nóvae-ángliae L. (of New England). New England Aster. Fields, roadsides, waste places. August-October. Fig. 960, Map 2335. —FACW-

A. x amethystínus Nutt. A hybrid between *A. novae-angliae* and *A. ericoides*.

9. A. puníceus L. (red or purple). Wet woods, thickets, meadows, marshes. August -October. Fig. 961, Map 2336. Our plants include var. *puniceus* and the following vars.:

var. *fírmus* (Nees) Torr. & Gray. Stem glabrous or nearly so below inflorescence (pubescent in var. *puniceus*). [*A. firmus; A. lucidulus*].

var. *perlóngus* Fern. Differing from the latter 2 vars. in having the inner bracts mostly concealed by the foliaceous outer ones, outer bracts 1 mm or more wide (inner bracts not concealed in the latter 2 vars., the outer bracts less than 1 mm wide). —OBL

10. A. nóvi-bélgii L. (of New Belgium). Salt marshes, moist thickets and fields, river borders near the coast. July-October. Fig. 962, Map 2337. [*A. longifolius*]. Highly variable; in addition to var. *novi-belgii* the following vars. appear to be the best defined:

var. *tardiflórus* (L.) A. G. Jones. Outer involucral bracts, at least some of them, green and foliaceous, conspicuously exceeding the inner (outer involucral bracts not foliaceous, usually with scarious margins or base, equalling or shorter than the inner in the other vars.). Endangered in NH. [*A. crenifolius; A. tardiflorus*]. —FACW+

A. foliáceus L. Similar to *A. novi-belgii* var. *tardiflorus* but with leaves entire or remotely serrate, midrib beneath glabrous or sparsely pubescent (leaves distinctly crenate, midrib beneath densely pubescent in the latter var.). Reported for ME, NH, VT. Our plants are var. *foliaceus*. —FAC

var. *johannénsis* (Fern.) A. G. Jones. Bracts strongly ascending to appressed, disc corollas and pappus 6 mm or more long (bracts, or at least the outer ones, recurving, disc corollas and pappus

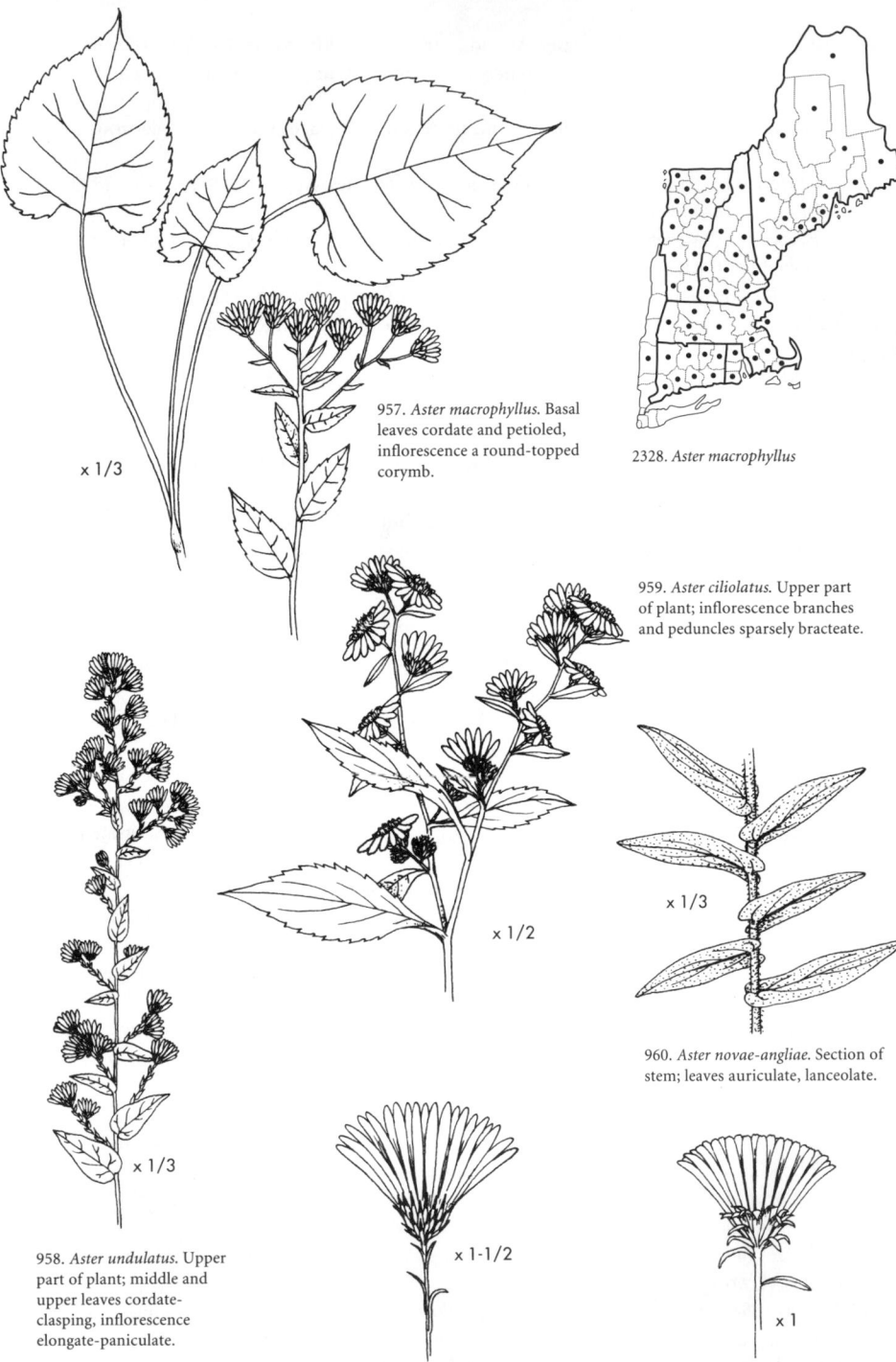

x 1/3

957. *Aster macrophyllus*. Basal leaves cordate and petioled, inflorescence a round-topped corymb.

2328. *Aster macrophyllus*

959. *Aster ciliolatus*. Upper part of plant; inflorescence branches and peduncles sparsely bracteate.

x 1/2

x 1/3

960. *Aster novae-angliae*. Section of stem; leaves auriculate, lanceolate.

x 1/3

958. *Aster undulatus*. Upper part of plant; middle and upper leaves cordate-clasping, inflorescence elongate-paniculate.

x 1-1/2

961. *Aster puniceus*. Single head; inner involucral bracts linear-attenuate.

x 1

962. *Aster novi-belgii*. Single head; involucral bracts spreading.

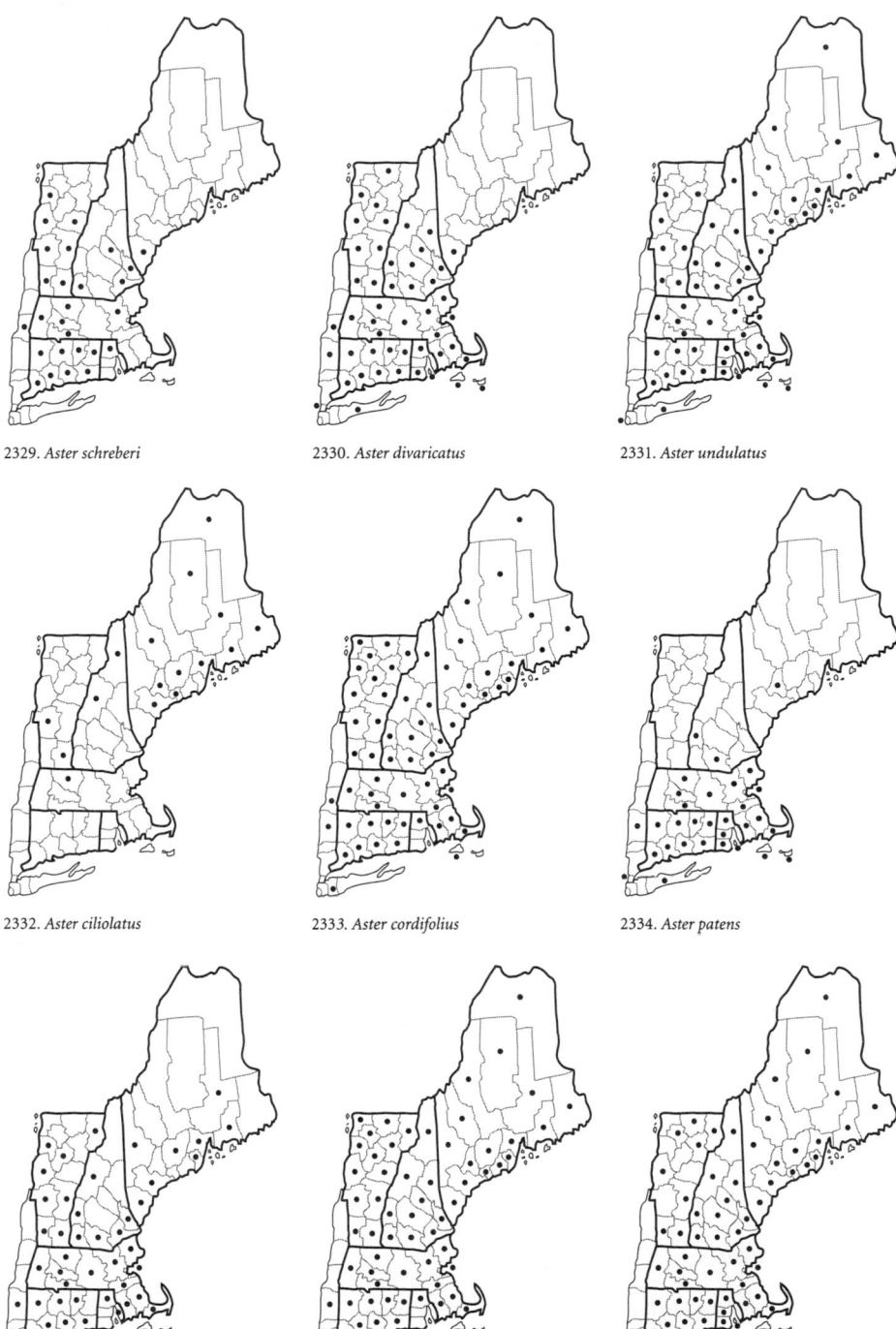

2329. *Aster schreberi*

2330. *Aster divaricatus*

2331. *Aster undulatus*

2332. *Aster ciliolatus*

2333. *Aster cordifolius*

2334. *Aster patens*

2335. *Aster novae-angliae*

2336. *Aster puniceus*

2337. *Aster novi-belgii*

up to 6 mm long in vars. *novi-belgii,* elodes and litoreus). [*A. johannensis; A. anticostensis; A. gaspensis*].

A. longifólius, reportedly a distinct species, has been documented for CT.

var. *villicáulis* (Gray). Boivin. Similar to var. *johannensis* but stems densely pubescent (glabrous in var. *johannensis*). [*A. johannensis* var. *v.*].

var. *elódes* (T. & G.) Gray. Leaves narrowly linear-lanceolate, 10 or more times as long as wide, scarcely clasping at base (leaves oblong or broadly lanceolate, less than 10 times as long as wide, clasping at base in vars. *novi-belgii* and *litoreus*). [*A. elodes*].

var. *litóreus* Gray. Similar to var. *novi-belgii* but compact, with crowded branching, blades wide at base (branching open, blades usually narrow at base in var. *novi-belgii*).

11. A. láevis L. (smooth). Fields, roadsides. August-October. Fig. 963, Map 2338. [*A. falcidens; A. steeleorum*]. Our plants are var. *laevis.*

12. A. prenanthoídes Muhl. ex Willd. (like *Prenanthes*). Moist woods, thickets, meadows, streambanks. August-September. Map 2339. From farther south and west. [*A. oticus*]. —FAC

13. A. boreális (Torr. & Gray) Prov. Bogs, wet meadows, river borders. July-September. Fig. 964, Map 2340. [*A. junceus; A. junciformis*]. —OBL

14. A. cóncolor L. (of uniform color). Open woods, barrens, roadsides. August-October. Map 2341. Endangered in MA, NY.

15. A. x hérveyi Gray (for its discoverer). Open woods and clearings. August-October. Map 2342. A hybrid between *A. macrophyllus* and *A. spectabilis.*

16. A. spectábilis Ait. (showy). Open woods, clearings, roadsides and waste places. August-October. Map 2343. Our plants are var. *spectabilis.*

17. A. subulátus Michx. (awl-shaped). Salt and brackish marshes. July-October. Fig. 965, Map 2344. Endangered in ME. Our plants include var. *subulatus* and the following var.:

var. *euroaúster* Fern. & Grisc. Basal and principal stem leaves narrowly linear, heads mostly scattered, on long peduncles (basal and principal stem leaves mostly lanceolate, heads crowded, on short peduncles or subsessile in var. *subulatus*). —OBL

Brachyáctis Ledeb. *ciliáta* (Ledeb.) Ledeb. Resembling *A. subulatus* but differing in having foliaceous involucral bracts and ligules absent or less than 1 mm long (bracts not foliaceous and ligules longer than 1 mm in *A. subulatus*). Canadian. Reported for York County ME. [*Aster laurentianus*]. Represented with us as subsp. *laurentiána* (Fern.) Ledeb.

B. frondósa (Nutt.) Gray. Resembling *A. subulatus* but with involucral bracts obtuse and ligules pinkish (involucral bracts attenuate and ligules blue or purple in *A. subulatus*). From the southwest. Reported for ME. [*Aster frondosus*].

18. A. linariifólius L. (with leaves of *Linaria*). Woodland borders, roadsides. July-October. Map 2345. [*Ionactis l.*]. Our plants are var. *linariifolius.*

19. A. umbellátus Mill. (umbellate). Moist woods, thickets, meadows. August-September. Fig. 966, Map 2346. [*Doellingeria u.*]. Our plants are var. *umbellatus.* —FACW

20. A. infirmus Michx. (weak). Woodlands. July-September. Map 2347. Endangered in ME. From farther south. [*Doellingeria i.*].

21. A. patérnus Cronq. Dry woodlands. July-August. Map 2348. [*Sericocarpus asteroides*].

22. A. solidagíneus Michx. Dry woodlands and fields. July-August. Map 2349. [*Sericocarpus linifolius*].

23. A. tenuifólius L. (slender-leaved). Salt and brackish marshes and shores. August-October. Fig. 967, Map 2350. Endangered in NH. —OBL

24. A. acuminátus Michx. (acuminate). Woodlands. July-September. Fig. 968, Map 2351. Our plants are var. *acuminatus.*

25. A. x blákei (Porter) House (for its discoverer). Moist woods and thickets, pond and stream borders, bogs, roadsides. August-September. Map 2352. Endangered in CT. A hybrid between *A. acuminatus* and *A. nemoralis.* —FACW+

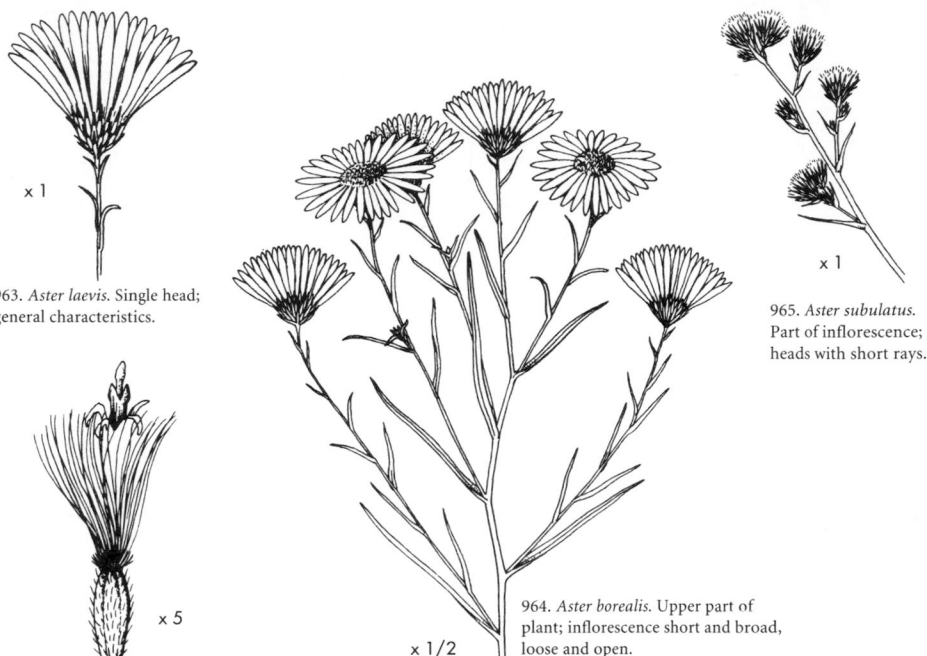

x 1

963. *Aster laevis*. Single head; general characteristics.

x 5

966. *Aster umbellatus*. Single achene; pappus double, the inner series of long bristles, the outer of short ones.

x 1

965. *Aster subulatus*. Part of inflorescence; heads with short rays.

964. *Aster borealis*. Upper part of plant; inflorescence short and broad, loose and open.

x 1/2

968. *Aster acuminatus*. Upper part of plant; leaves appearing nearly whorled below corymbose inflorescence.

x 1/2

967. *Aster tenuifolius*. Upper part of plant; leaves narrowly linear, general character of inflorescence.

x 1/2

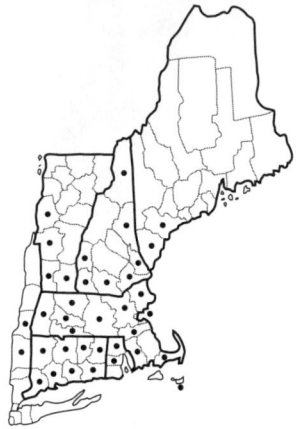

2338. *Aster laevis*

2339. *Aster prenanthoides*

2340. *Aster borealis*

2341. *Aster concolor*

2342. *Aster x herveyi*

2343. *Aster spectabilis*

2344. *Aster subulatus*

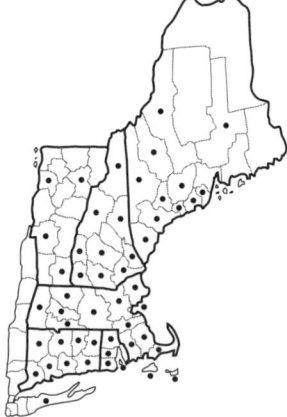

2345. *Aster linariifolius*

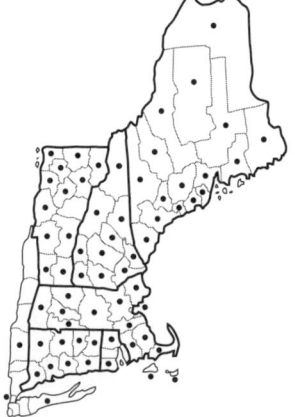

2346. *Aster umbellatus*

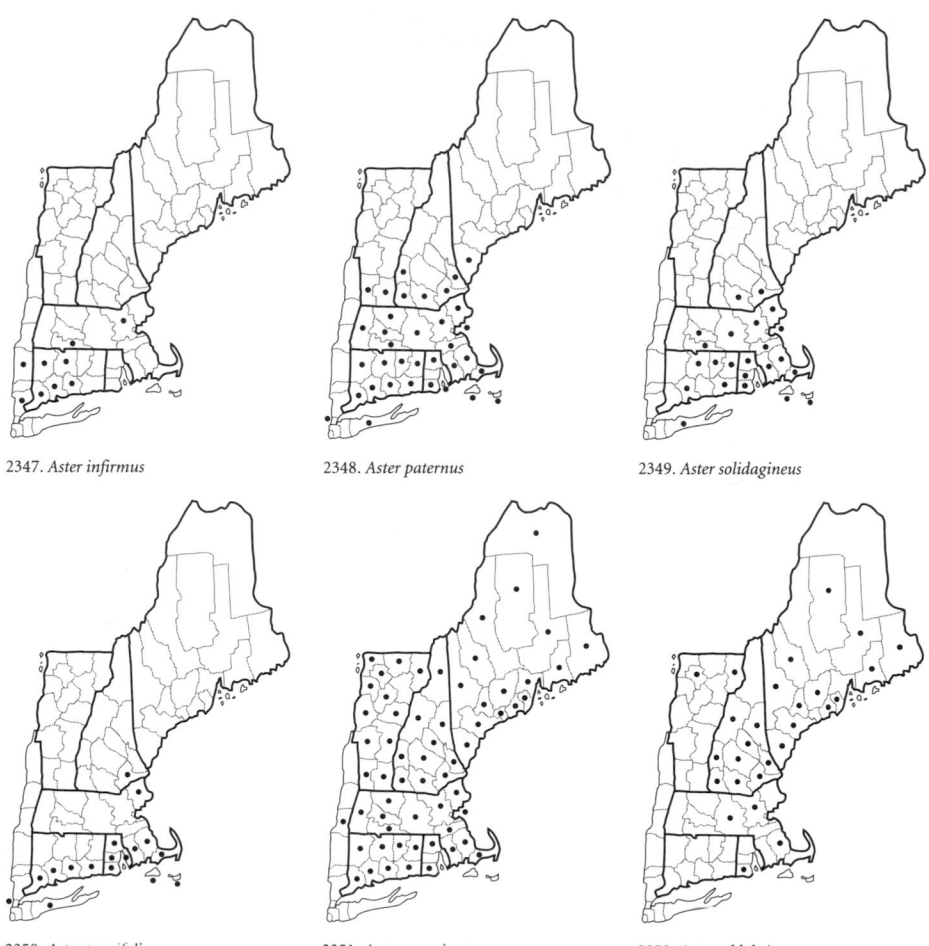

2347. *Aster infirmus*

2348. *Aster paternus*

2349. *Aster solidagineus*

2350. *Aster tenuifolius*

2351. *Aster acuminatus*

2352. *Aster x blakei*

26. A. nemorális Ait. (of woodland). Bog Aster. Bogs. August-September. Map 2353. —FACW+

27. A. tatáricus L. f. (Tartarian). Escaped from cultivation to roadsides and waste places. October. Map 2354. (Introduced from ne. Asia).

28. A. rádula Ait. (a scraper). Wooded swamps, open springy and boggy areas. August-October. Map 2355. Endangered in CT. Our plants include var. *radula* and the following var.:

var. *stríctus* (Pursh) Gray. Involucral bracts not in 3 or more lengths, subequal (bracts in 3 or more lengths in var. *radula*). —OBL

29. A. pilósus Willd. (pilose). Fields, roadsides, waste places. August-October. Fig. 969, Map 2356. Our plants include var. *pilosus* and the following vars.:

var. *demótus* Blake. Stem and leaves glabrous (pubescent in var. *pilosus*). [*A. glabellus; A. ramosissimus*].

var. *prínglei* (Gray) Blake. Stem and leaves glabrous; inflorescence corymbose-paniculate (racemose-paniculate in var. *demotus*). [*A. faxoni; A. polyphyllus; A. pringlei*].

30. A. ericoídes L. (like *Erica*). Fields, thickets, waste places. August-October. Map 2357. [*A. multiflorus*]. Our plants include var. *ericoides* and the following var.:

var. *prostrátus* (Kuntze) Blake. Pubescence on the stem spreading (appressed or stiffly ascending in var. *ericoides*). —FACU

ASTERACEAE

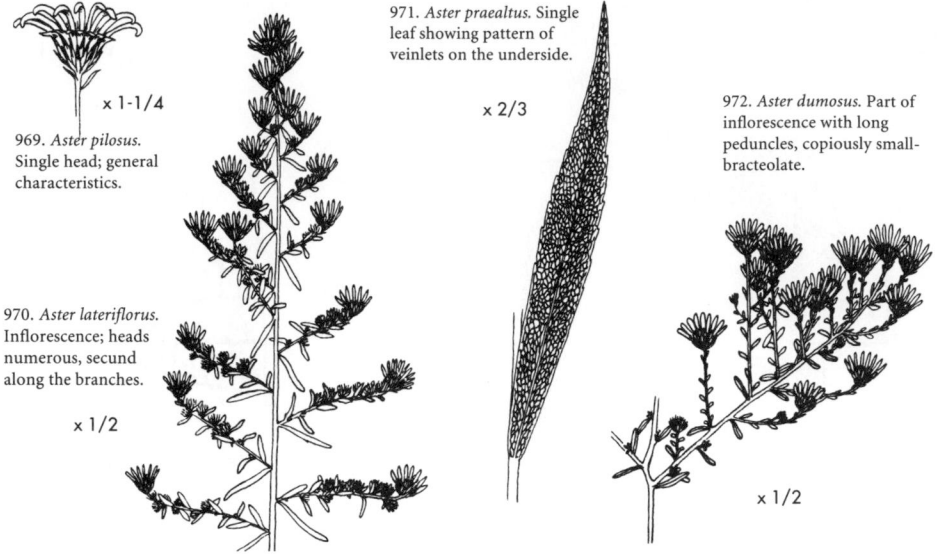

x 1-1/4

969. *Aster pilosus.*
Single head; general
characteristics.

971. *Aster praealtus.* Single
leaf showing pattern of
veinlets on the underside.

x 2/3

972. *Aster dumosus.* Part of
inflorescence with long
peduncles, copiously small-
bracteolate.

970. *Aster lateriflorus.*
Inflorescence; heads
numerous, secund
along the branches.

x 1/2

x 1/2

A. falcátus Lindl. Similar to *A. ericoides* but with heads solitary or in small clusters, not secund, involucres mostly 5-7 mm high, bracts not in distinct series, the outer and inner nearly the same length, rays 20 or more (heads numerous, often secund, involucres up to 5 mm high, bracts in 3 or 4 distinct series, rays up to 20 in *A. ericoides*). Western. Reported for MA. Represented with us as var. *commutátus* (Torr. & Gray) A. G. Jones. [*A. commutatus*].

31. A. lateriflórus (L.) Britt. (with 1-sided flower clusters). Open woods, fields, roadsides, waste places. August-October. Fig. 970, Map 2358. [*A. agrostifolius; A. vimineus*]. Our plants include var. *lateriflorus* and the following vars. that freely intergrade into the typical phase:

var. *angustifólius* Wieg. Similar to var. *lateriflorus* but with leaves more than 6 times as long as wide (up to 6 times as long as wide in var. *lateriflorus*).

var. *hirsuticaúlis* (Lindl. ex DC.) Porter. Inflorescence open-paniculate, the ultimate branchlets and pedicels 1-4 times as long as the involucre (inflorescence racemose-paniculate, the ultimate branchlets and pedicels shorter than the involucre in the latter 2 vars.). [*A. hirsuticaulis; A. acadiensis; A. lateriflorus* var. *tenuipes; A. saxatilis; A. tradescanti*].

var. *horizontális* (Desf.) Farw. Distinguished from the above vars. in having long, divaricate branches with leaves of the branches very small, mostly entire. —FACW to FACW-

32. A. praeáltus Poir. (very tall). Fields, barrens, roadsides. August-October. Fig. 971, Map 2359. [*A. salicifolius*]. Our plants include var. *praealtus* and the following var.:

var. *angústior* Wieg. Leaves, more than 10 times as long as wide (up to 10 times as long as wide in var. *praealtus*). —FACW

33. A. dumósus L. (bushy). Open woods, fields. August-October. Fig. 972, Map 2360. Endangered in ME. [*A. coridifolius*]. Our plants include var. *dumosus* and the following var.:

var. *stríctior* T. & G. Inflorescence branches stiffly ascending, simple or slightly forked (inflorescence branches spreading, usually forking). —FAC

34. A. lanceolátus Willd. Fields, pond and stream borders, roadsides, waste places. August-September. Map 2361. [*A. acutidens; A. lamarckianus; A. paniculatus; A. simplex*]. Our plants are subsp. *lanceolatus* var. *l.*.

Another var. that has been distinguished is var. *hirsuticaúlis.*

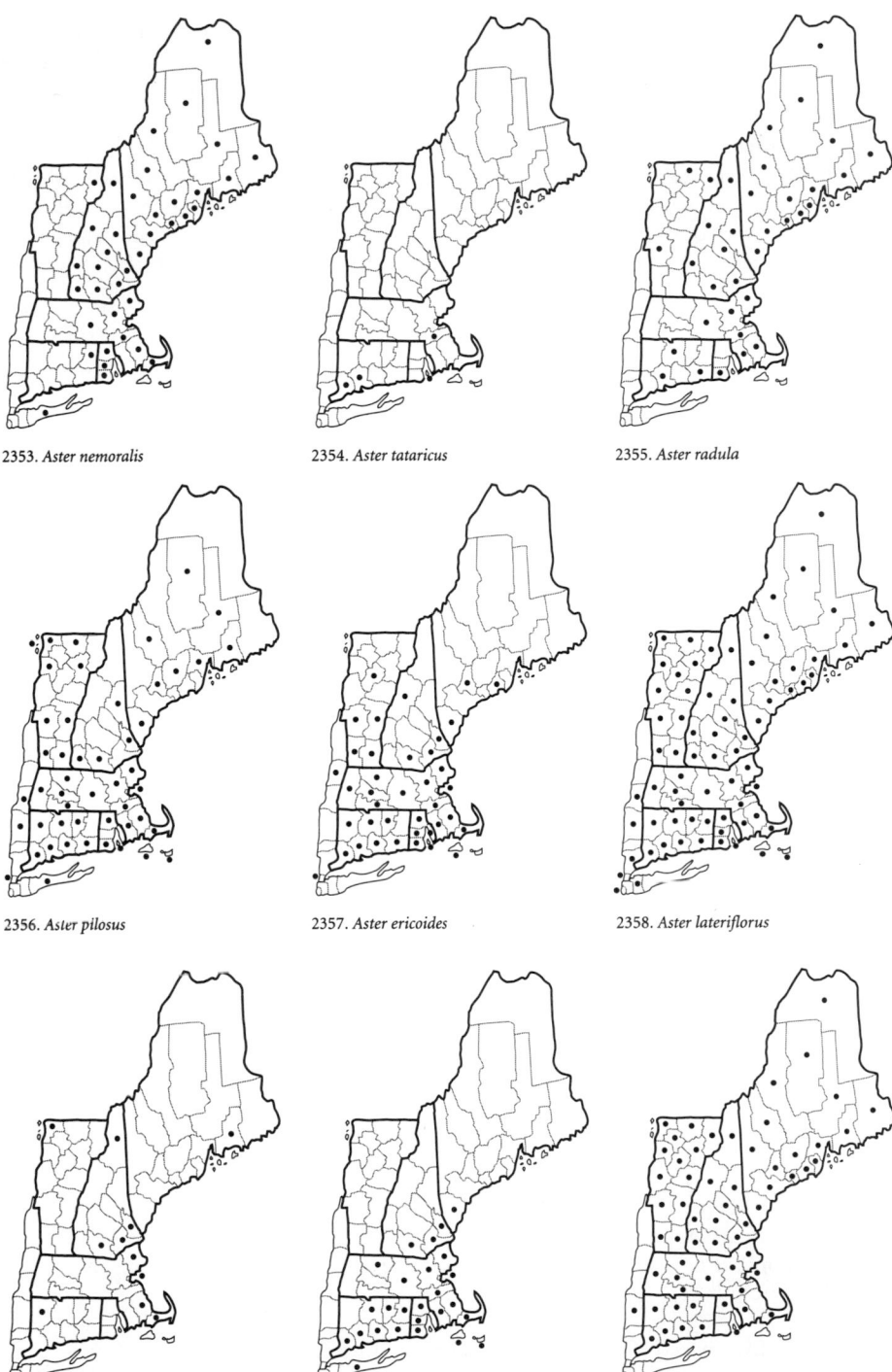

2353. *Aster nemoralis*

2354. *Aster tataricus*

2355. *Aster radula*

2356. *Aster pilosus*

2357. *Aster ericoides*

2358. *Aster lateriflorus*

2359. *Aster praealtus*

2360. *Aster dumosus*

2361. *Aster lanceolatus*

A. racemósus Elliott. Similar to *A. lanceolatus* but with leaves of the branches becoming much reduced, mostly less than 1.5 cm long (leaves of the branches, or many of them, 1.5 cm or more long in *A. lanceolatus*). Reported for CT, RI, VT. [*A. fragilis* var. *subdumosus; A. brachypholis*].

63. Cichórium L. Chicory (based on the Arabian name).

Branched, lactiferous, perennial herbs from a taproot; leaves basal and alternate, the basal and lower stem leaves petioled, toothed to runcinate or pinnatifid, becoming sessile or auriculate, smaller and less divided upward on the stem; heads 1-3, sessile or short peduncled, terminal and in the axils of reduced leaves along the branches, ligulate, involucral bracts in 2 series, flowers perfect, 5-toothed, blue to pink or white, pappus a crown of small chaffy scales; achenes angled or ribbed.

1. C. íntybus L. (old generic name). Fields, roadsides, waste places. July-September. Fig. 973, Map 2362. Young leaves can be eaten in salads and used as a potherb; roots can be roasted and used as a coffee substitute; a preparation of the roots also is used as a tonic, laxative and diuretic.

C. endívia L. Endive. Differing from *C. intybus* in having foliaceous involucral bracts exceeding the heads (bracts not foliaceous nor exceeding heads in *C. intybus*). Occasionally escaped from cultivation. Reported for Fairfield and New Haven Counties, CT; Knox County ME.

64. Lápsana L. Nipplewort (ancient Greek name for some plant).

Branched, lactiferous, annual herbs; leaves alternate, petioled, the lower ovate, dentate, and often with 1 or more pairs of lobes on the petiole, becoming shorter petioled to sessile, narrower, toothed to entire upward on the stem; heads small, corymbose to paniculate, ligulate, principal involucral bracts in 1 series, a short outer series also present, flowers perfect, 5-toothed, yellow, pappus none; achenes oblanceolate, somewhat flattened, curved, strongly nerved.

1. L. commúnis L. (common). Fields, roadsides, waste places. June-September. Fig. 974, Map 2363. (Naturalized from Europe).

65. Tragopógon L. Goat's-beard (from the Greek, meaning goat beard).

Stout, usually branched, glabrate, lactiferous, biennial herbs from a taproot; leaves alternate, linear, grass-like, entire, clasping; heads large, solitary at the tips of the branches, ligulate, involucral bracts in 1 series, flowers perfect, 5-toothed, yellow or purple, pappus of plumose bristles, the plume branches interwebbed; achenes fusiform, ribbed, mostly beaked, the ribs muricate. Roots of the species below can be cooked like carrots when young; leaves can be used as a potherb; preparations made from the flowers are reported to be of value as a skin lotion and cough syrup.

Peduncle not or scarcely enlarged just below head; rays yellow. .... 1. *T. pratensis*
Peduncle enlarged just below head; rays yellow or purple. (Fig. 975).
    Rays yellow .... 2. *T. dubius*
    Rays purple .... 3. *T. porrifolius*

1. T. praténsis L. (of meadows). Fields, roadsides, waste places. May-August. Map 2364. (Naturalized from Europe). Our plants are subsp. *pratensis.*

2. T. dúbius Scop. (doubtful). Fields, roadsides, waste places. May-July. Fig. 975, Map 2365. (Naturalized from Europe). [*T. major*].

3. T. porrifólius L. (with leaves of leek). Salsify. Fields, roadsides, waste places. Map 2366. (Introduced from Europe).

66. Pícris L. Bitterweed (Greek name for a related bitter plant).

Branched, hispid, lactiferous, annual or biennial herbs; leaves alternate, the lower petioled, the upper sessile to clasping, oblanceolate to lanceolate, dentate, sinuate-dentate or entire; heads corymbose to paniculate, ligulate, involucral bracts in 2 or more series, flowers perfect, 5-toothed, yellow, pappus of plumose bristles; achenes angled or ribbed, beaked or beakless.

Crépis (genus 71) *foétida* L. Will key to *Picris* but can be distinguished in having a combination of pinnately lobed leaves, involucral bracts not spinose-margined, merely pubescent, and achenes beaked. Southern; rarely found in our range. Reported for Middlesex County MA. [*Hypochaeris elata*].

Involucral bracts biseriate, the outer ovate, spinose-margined, the inner narrow.
(Fig. 976) .... 1. *P. echioides*
Involucral bracts in more than 2 series, all uniformly narrow, none spinose-margined.. 2. *P. hieracioides*

1. P. echioídes L. (like *Echium*). Ox-tongue. Fields, roadsides, waste places. July-September. Fig. 976, Map 2367. (Adventive from Europe).

2. P. hieracioídes L. (like *Hieracium*). Fields, roadsides, waste places. July-September. Map 2368. (Adventive from Europe). Our plants are subsp. *hieracioides*.

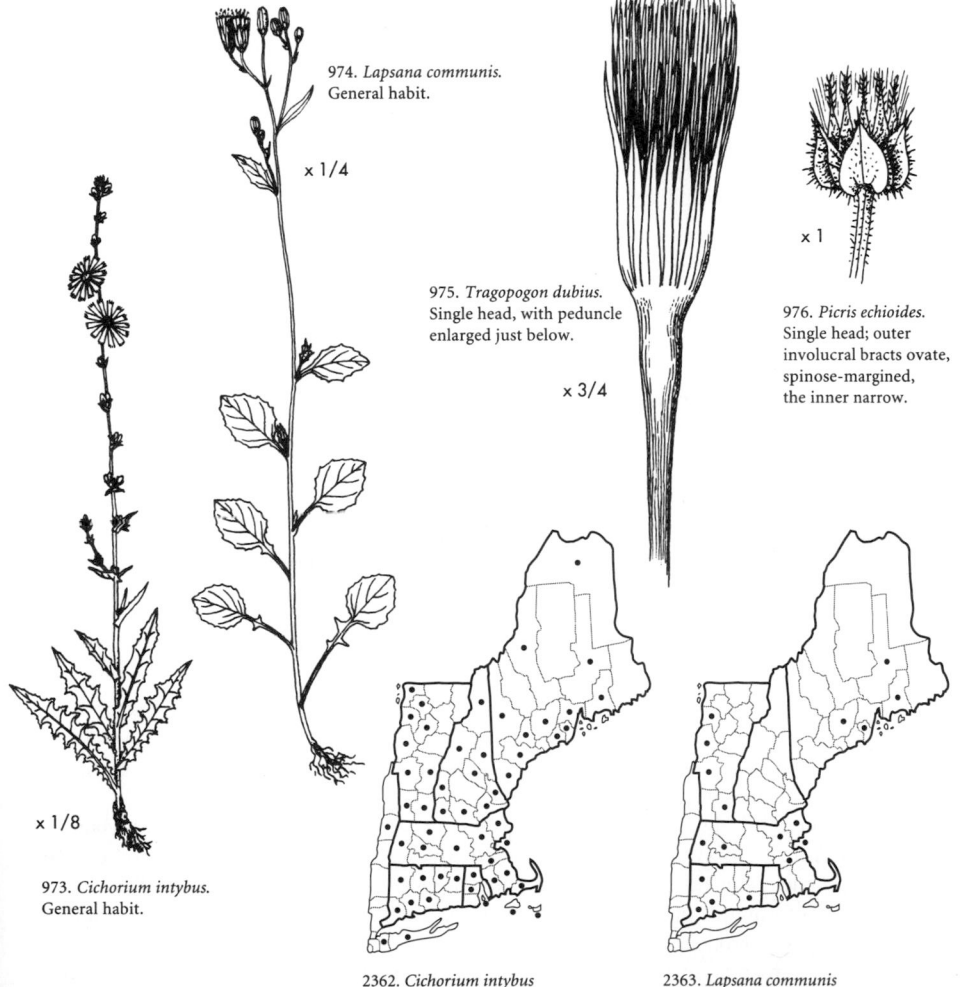

974. *Lapsana communis.*
General habit.

x 1/4

975. *Tragopogon dubius.*
Single head, with peduncle
enlarged just below.

x 3/4

x 1

976. *Picris echioides.*
Single head; outer
involucral bracts ovate,
spinose-margined,
the inner narrow.

x 1/8

973. *Cichorium intybus.*
General habit.

2362. *Cichorium intybus*

2363. *Lapsana communis*

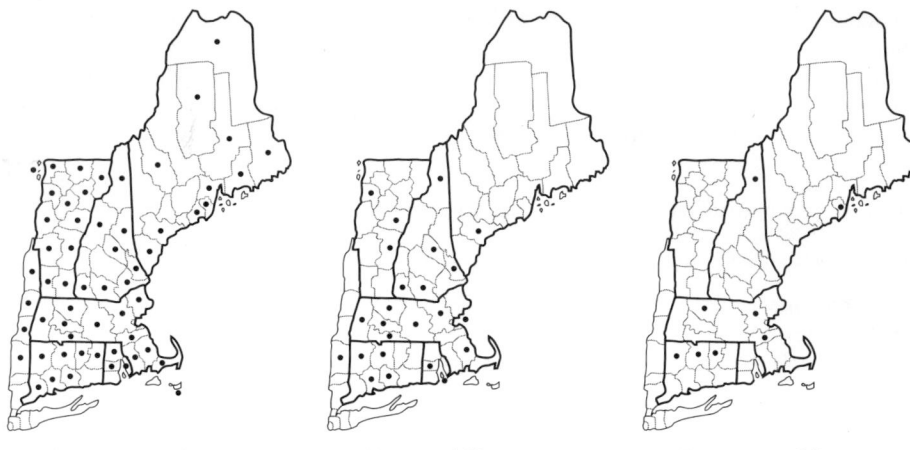

2364. *Tragopogon pratensis*   2365. *Tragopogon dubius*   2366. *Tragopogon porrifolius*

67. Lactúca L. Lettuce (ancient name for lettuce).

Tall, annual, biennial or perennial herbs with milky latex; leaves alternate, sessile to auriculate, or the lower petioled, entire, toothed or pinnatifid, sometimes spiny on the margins and/or veins beneath; heads usually numerous, paniculate, ligulate, involucre usually becoming widened at base in maturity, the bracts usually imbricated, flowers perfect, 5-toothed, yellow, blue or white, pappus of white, gray or brown, capillary bristles; achenes flat, ribbed, with or without a beak. —Wildl. 1

a. Involucres, at least the larger ones, longer than 15 mm.
    Plant perennial; rays blue to purple; achenes with several distinct nerves on each face .... 1. *L. tatarica*
                         var. *pulchella*
    Plant annual or biennial; rays yellow; achenes with only a distinct median nerve
        on each face, other nerves lacking or obscure. .... 2. *L. hirsuta*
                         var. *sanguinea*
a. Involucres 15 mm or less long.
    b. Leaves prickly along the midrib beneath. .... 3. *L. serriola*
    b. Leaves not prickly along the midrib beneath, although sometimes hairy.
        Achenes abruptly contracted to a filiform beak, with only a distinct median
            nerve on each face, other nerves obscure; pappus white. .... 4. *L. canadensis*
        Achenes beakless or with a short stout beak, with several distinct nerves on
            each face; pappus tan or grayish .... 5. *L. biennis*

1. L. tatárica (L.) C. A. Mey. Meadows, thickets. July-September. From farther west. Reported for Cumberland County ME. [*L. pulchella; L. oblongifolia*]. Represented with us as var. *pulchélla* (Pursh) DC. —FAC

2. L. hirsúta Muhl. ex Nutt. (hirsute). Open woods and clearings. July-September. Map 2369. Represented with us as var. *sanguínea* (Bigelow). Fern.

L. graminifólia Michx. Similar to *L. hirsuta* but with leaves crowded at the base, linear and entire or with several linear-lanceolate to oblanceolate falcate-recurving lobes (leaves not crowded at the base, pinnatifid [except the upper ones], the lobes oblong-obovate, not falcate-recurving in *L. hirsuta*). From farther south. Reported for ME.

3. L. serrióla L. Prickly lettuce. Fields, roadsides and waste places. July-September. Map 2370. (Introduced from Eurasia). [*L. scariola*]. Stems and leaves can be eaten as salad or as a potherb when very young (up to about 4 dm tall); when the stems appear they become very bitter; the leaves and gum that forms from the milky latex is reported to be mildly sedative; latex can cause burning if it gets into the eyes. —FAC-

L. satíva L. Garden Lettuce. Frequently occurring in dumps but not naturalized. Reported for MA, ME. —FAC-

4. L. canadénsis L. (Canadian). Clearings, thickets, fields, roadsides, waste places. July–September. Map 2371. [*L. sagittifolia; L. steelei*]. Our plants include var. *canadensis* and the following vars.:

var. *obováta* Wieg. Main stem leaves oblanceolate to obovate, usually toothed (main stem leaves lanceolate to lance-ovate, usually entire, rarely toothed in var. *canadensis*).

var. *longifólia* (Michx.) Farw. Leaves, except sometimes the uppermost, lobed or pinnatifid (leaves entire or toothed, the lowermost sometimes lobed in the above vars.).

var. *latifólia* Kuntze. Similar to var. *longifolia* but with lobes broadly falcate to obovate (lobes linear-falcate in var. *longifolia*). This plant can be used in the same manner as *L. serriola.* —FACU-

5. L. biénnis (Moench) Fern. (biennial). Clearings, thickets, fields, roadsides, waste places. July–September. Map 2372. [*L. spicata*]. —FACU

L. x mórssii Robins. A hybrid between *L. biennis* and *L. canadensis*.

68. Mycélis Cass.

Similar to *Lactuca* but with narrowly cylindric involucres, flowers 5 or fewer per head. [*Lactuca*].

1. M. murális (L.) Dumort. (growing on walls). Roadsides and waste places. July–September. Fig. 977. (Adventive from Europe). Reported for MA, VT, Hancock County ME; Sullivan County NH. [*Lactuca m.*].

2367. *Picris echioides*

2368. *Picris hieracioides*

2369. *Lactuca hirsuta* var. *sanguinea*

2370. *Lactuca serriola*

2371. *Lactuca canadensis*

2372. *Lactuca biennis*

69. Sónchus L. Sow-thistle (ancient Greek name).
Annual or perennial herbs with milky latex; leaves alternate and basal, mostly auriculate, entire, toothed or pinnatifid, often spiny-margined; heads solitary, corymbose or umbellate, ligulate, involucre often becoming widened at base in maturity, the bracts imbricated in several series, flowers perfect, 5-toothed, yellow, numerous, pappus of white, capillary bristles; achenes flattened, ribbed, not beaked.

Callistéphus Cass. *chinénsis* (L.) Nees. China Aster. Similar to *Sonchus* in cultivated varieties having only ray flowers but distinguishable in that the ray flowers are never yellow. Rarely escaped from flower gardens. Reported for CT, Hancock County ME.

a. Plant annual, from a vertical taproot; flowering heads (from tip to tip of rays) less
    than 3 cm wide; fruiting involucres mostly less than 14 mm long.
      Basal auricles of leaves acute; achenes transversely tuberculate-rugulose. .... 1. *S. oleraceus*
      Basal auricles of leaves rounded; achenes not transversely rugulose. .... 2. *S. asper*
a. Plant perennial, from a creeping rootstalk; flowering heads 3 cm or more wide;
    fruiting involucres mostly 14 mm or more long. .... 3. *S. arvensis*

1. S. oleráceus L. (fit to be a vegetable). Fields, roadsides, waste places. July-October. Map 2373. (Naturalized from Europe). Can be used in salads when very young; later as a potherb after simmering to remove the bitterness.

2. S. ásper (L.) Hill (rough). Fields, roadsides, waste places. July-October. Map 2374. (Naturalized from Europe). Our plants are subsp. *asper.* —FAC

3. S. arvénsis L. (of cultivated ground). Fields, roadsides, waste places. July-October. Fig. 978, Map 2375. (Naturalized from Europe). Our plants include subsp. *arvensis* and the following subsp.:

subsp. *uliginósus* (Bieb) Nyman. Involucres and peduncles glabrous or pubescent but not glandular (glandular-pubescent in subsp. *arvensis*). [*S. uliginosus; S. arvensis* var. *glabrescens*].

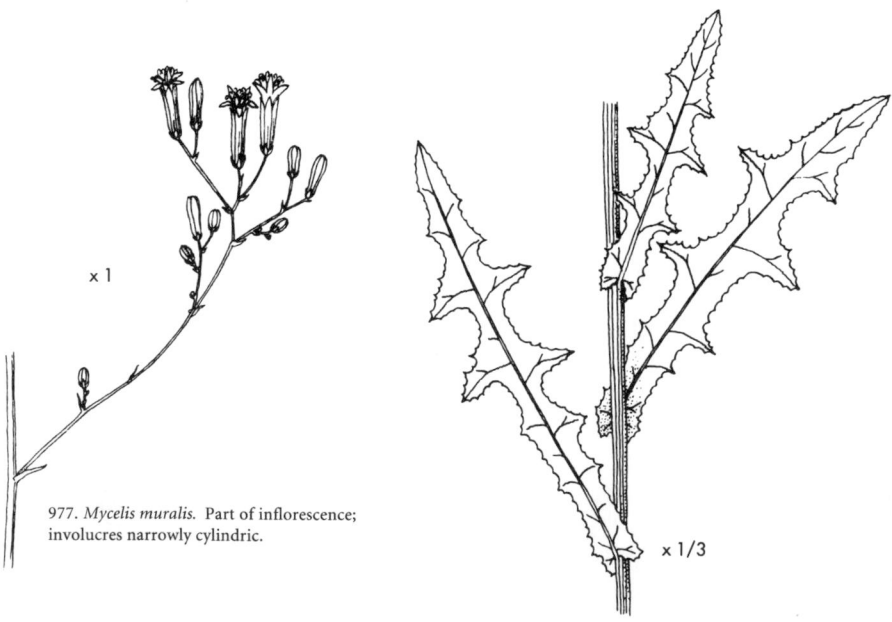

977. *Mycelis muralis.* Part of inflorescence; involucres narrowly cylindric.

x 1

x 1/3

978. *Sonchus arvensis.* Section of stem with auriculate, pinnatifid, spiny-margined leaves.

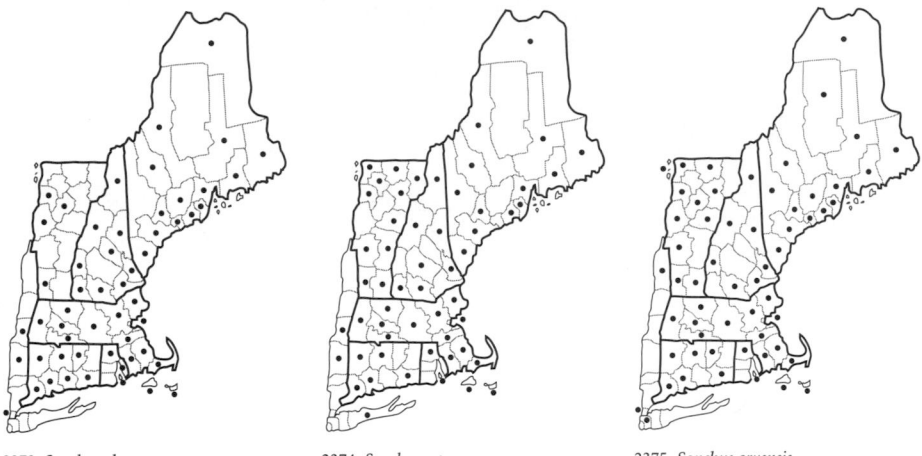

2373. *Sonchus oleraceus*   2374. *Sonchus asper*   2375. *Sonchus arvensis*

70. Prenánthes L. Rattlesnake-root (from the Greek, meaning nodding flower).

Perennial herbs with milky latex from tuberous roots; leaves alternate, petioled or sessile, toothed or hastate to pinnately or palmately lobed or dissected; heads thyrsoid to racemose-paniculate, usually nodding, ligulate, principal involucral bracts in 1 series with several short ones at the base, flowers perfect, 5-lobed, pink to white or cream color, pappus of capillary bristles; achenes cylindric, striate.

a. Involucral bracts sparsely to densely hirsute.
　　Median stem leaves sessile; flowers pink; inflorescence cylindric. .... 1. *P. racemosa*
　　Median stem leaves petioled; flowers whitish or yellowish; inflorescence
　　　paniculate .... 2. *P. serpentaria*
a. Involucral bracts glabrous or essentially so.
　b. Flowers and principal bracts 6 or fewer. .... 3. *P. altissima*
　b. Flowers and principal bracts 7 or more.
　　c. Involucres blackish; plants alpine, mostly 4 dm or less tall.
　　　Peduncles densely pubescent; leaves entire or merely toothed. .... 4. *P. boottii*
　　　Peduncles glabrous or sparsely pubescent; lower leaves often lobed. .... 5. *P. nana*
　　c. Involucres greenish or purplish; plants not alpine, mostly taller than 4 dm.
　　　d. Pappus dark reddish-brown .... 6. *P. alba*
　　　d. Pappus white, cream-colored or light brown.
　　　　Short, outer involucral bracts lanceolate; principal bracts usually with at
　　　　　least a few hairs. (Fig. 979) .... 2. *P. serpentaria*
　　　　Short, outer involucral bracts deltoid; principal bracts glabrous. .... 7. *P. trifoliolata*

　1. P. racemósa Michx. (racemose). River shores and banks. August-September. Reported for VT, Aroostook County ME. —FACW-
　P. x mainénsis Gray. A hybrid between *P. racemosa* and *P. trifoliolata*.
　2. P. serpentária Pursh (of serpents). Dry open woods and thickets. August-October. Fig. 979, Map 2376. Endangered in MA. From farther south.
　3. P. altíssima L. (very tall). Rich, moist woods. August-October. Map 2377. —FACU-
　4. P. boóttii (DC.) Gray. Alpine areas. July-August. Map 2378. Endangered in VT, NY.
　5. P. nána (Bigelow) Torr. Alpine Areas. July-September. Reported for ME, NH, VT. Endangered in ME. [*P. trifoliolata* var. *n.*].
　6. P. álba L. (white). Woodlands. August-September. Map 2379. A preparation made from this species is reported to have been used in treating rattlesnake bite and dysentery. —FACU
　7. P. trifoliólata (Cass.) Fern. Woodlands and clearings. August-September. Map 2380.

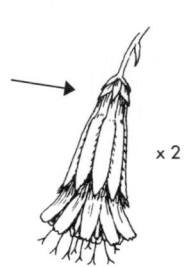

x 2

979. *Prenanthes serpentaria.* Single
head with short, outer series of
involucral bracts lanceolate.

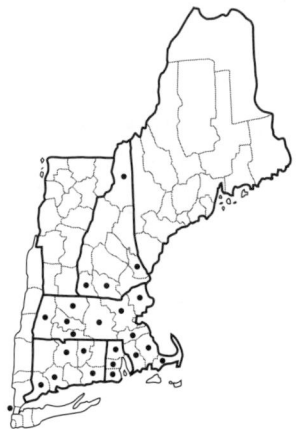

2376. *Prenanthes serpentaria*

2377. *Prenanthes altissima*

2378. *Prenanthes boottii*

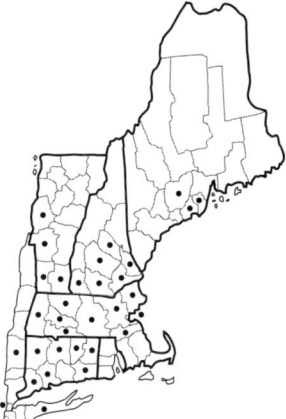

2379. *Prenanthes alba*

2380. *Prenanthes trifoliolata*

71. Crépis L. Hawk's-beard (Greek name for boot, applied to some plant).
Similar to *Hieracium* (genus 29) but plant annual or biennial (*C. runcìnata* perennial), from a taproot or several main roots, rhizomes lacking, basal leaves often pinnatifid, achenes tapered to apex.

In addition to the following species *C. pannonica* has been reported for CT.

1. C capilláris (L.) Wallr. (hair-like). Fields, roadsides, waste places. June-September. Map 2381. (Adventive from Europe).

One western species, one southern species and several European species are rarely adventive in our range and not persistent:

C. runcináta (James) Torr. & Gray. May be distinguished from *C. capillaris* and the following species in being perennial with 1 or more well developed roots and basal rosettes (plants annual or biennial and basal rosettes lacking in *C. capillaris* and the following species). Western; rarely occurring in our range. Reported for Nassau County NY. Our plants are subsp. *runcinata.* [*C. glaucella*].

C. vesicária L. Achenes beaked (beakless in *C. capillaris* and all other species below except *C. setosa*). Reported for Hartford County CT. Represented with us as subsp. *haenseleri* (Boiss. ex DC.) P. D. Sell.

C. setósa Hall. Similar to the latter species but distinguished by the stem and involucres strongly setose with stiff yellow bristles, achenes up to 5 mm long (stem and involucres pubescent or setose with short black setae, achenes 5 mm or more long in *C. vesicaria*). Reported for CT, VT, Suffolk County NY.

C. tectórum L. Distinguished from the other species below (except *C. biennis*) and *C. capillaris* in having the inner involucral bracts pubescent within and mature achenes dark-colored (glabrous within and achenes light-colored in the other species). Reported for CT, RI, Middlesex County MA; Hunters Point, NY.

C. biénnis L. Similar to *C. tectorum* but with involucres 1 cm or more long (less than 1 cm long in *C. tectorum*). Reported for VT.

C. nicaeénsis Balb. Similar to *C. capillaris* but involucre 8 mm or more long and achenes 2.5 mm or more long (involucre up to 8 mm long and achenes up to 2.5 mm long in *C. capillaris*). Reported for MA, VT.

C. fóetida L. May be distinguished from the above species in having plumose pappus (pappus capillary, not plumose in the above species). Southern; rarely occurring in our range. Reported for Middlesex County MA. [*Hypochaeris elata*].

72. *Ánthemis* L. Chamomile (ancient name for chamomile).

Branched, aromatic, annual or perennial herbs; leaves 1-3 times pinnately dissected, with filiform, linear or lanceolate segments, alternate, sessile; heads solitary, peduncled, terminal, radiate, rarely discoid, involucral bracts scarious-margined, pubescent, in several indistinct series, rays white or yellow, pistillate or neutral, receptacle convex or conical, with slender chaff, at least toward the middle, disc flowers perfect, yellow, pappus none; achenes terete or angled.

a. Rays yellow .... 1. *A. tinctoria*
a. Rays white.
    Rays pistillate and fertile; receptacle chaffy throughout. .... 2. *A. arvensis*
    Rays sterile and neutral, rarely with abortive pistils, receptacle chaffy only toward
      the middle .... 3. *A. cotula*

1. *A. tinctória* L. (used in dyeing). Fields, roadsides, waste places, cultivated ground. June-August. Map 2382. (Naturalized from Europe).[*Cota t.*].

2. *A. arvénsis* L. (of cultivated fields). Fields, roadsides, waste places. May-August. Map 2383. (Naturalized from Europe). Our plants include var. *arvensis* and the following var.:

    var. *agréstis* (Wallr.) DC. Chaff shorter than disc flowers (longer than disc flowers in var. *arvensis*).

3. *A. cótula* L. (like *Cotula*). Fields, roadsides, waste places. June-September. Fig. 980, Map 2384. (Naturalized from Europe). [*Maruta c.*]. —FACU

73. *Echinácea* Moench. Purple Coneflower (from the Greek, referring to the spiny chaff).

Perennials from thick roots, stems simple or little branched; leaves simple, alternate, petioled, toothed or entire; heads large and showy, solitary and terminal, radiate, involucral bracts imbricated in 2 obscure series, spreading or reflexed, rays purple to white, neutral or pistillate, drooping, receptacle conical, with spinescent-tipped chaff exceeding the disc flowers, these perfect, purplish, pappus a minute crown; achenes angled. Preparations from the roots of the two species of *Echinacea* in our range have been reported to be of value in preventing and treating colds and sore throat and in external applications to heal skin wounds and for treating respiratory and urinary infections.

Gaillárdia Foug. *pulchélla* Foug. Will key to *Echinacea* or possibly the last genus (*Anthemis*), but differs from these genera in having receptacle bristly rather than chaffy and pappus of awned scales. From farther west. Reported for ME, NH, Fairfield, Litchfield and New Haven Counties, CT; Windham County VT. Represented with us as var. *picta* (D. Don) Gray. [*G. picta; G. drummondii*].

Leaves ovate-lanceolate to ovate, mostly up to 5 times as long as wide. .... 1. *E. purpurea*
Leaves linear to lance-linear, mostly more than 5 times as long as wide. .... 2. *E. pallida*

   1. *E. purpúrea* (L.) Moench (purple). Open woods and fields. June-October. From farther south and west. Reported for New Haven County CT.
   2. *E. pállida* (Nutt.) Nutt. (pale). Fields and waste places. May-August. Map 2385. From farther south and west.

74. *Boltónia* L'Her. (for J. Bolton).
Branched, glabrous, perennial herbs, stems striate or corrugated; leaves alternate, sessile, entire, linear to lanceolate; heads few to numerous, corymbose, radiate, involucral bracts imbricated in 2 or more series, scarious-margined, rays white to pink or blue, pistillate, receptacle hemispheric to conic, naked, disc flowers perfect, yellow, pappus of several minute bristles and 2-4 longer bristles; achenes flat, obovate, wing-margined.

   1. *B. asteroídes* (L.) L'Her. (resembling *Aster*). Roadsides and waste places. August-October. Map 2386. From farther west and south. Our plants include var. *asteroides* and the following vars.:
   var. *latisquáma* (Gray) Cronq. Heads usually more than 25 (25 or fewer in var. *asteroides*); involucral bracts, at least the outer, spatulate and rounded or obtuse. [*B. latisquama*].
   var. *recógnita* (Fern. & Griscom) Cronq. Similar to var. *latisquama*; involucral bracts linear and acute. —FACW

75. *Leucánthemum* P. Mill.
Similar to *Chrysanthemum* (genus 78) except rays white and ray achenes merely strongly ribbed. [*Chrysanthemum*].
Chrysánthemum carinátum may key to *Leucanthemum* but is distinguished in having a purple disc, rays white, red or purple, yellow or purple at the base (see genus 78).

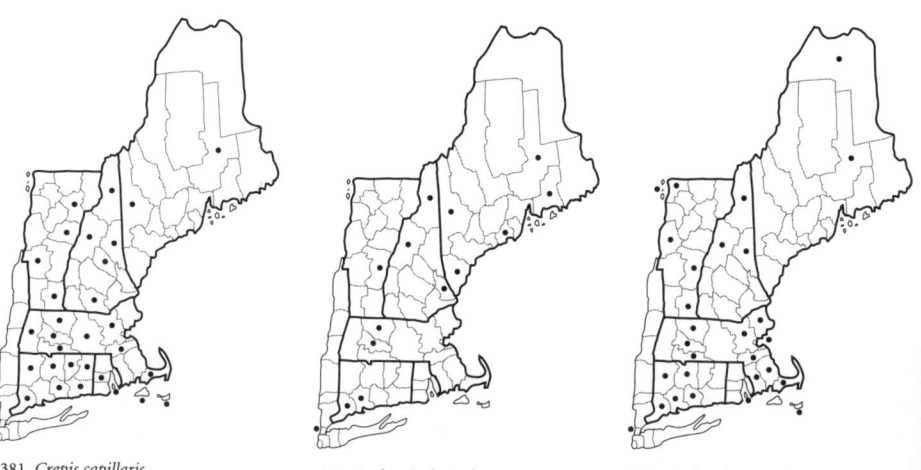

2381. *Crepis capillaris*   2382. *Anthemis tinctoria*   2383. *Anthemis arvensis*

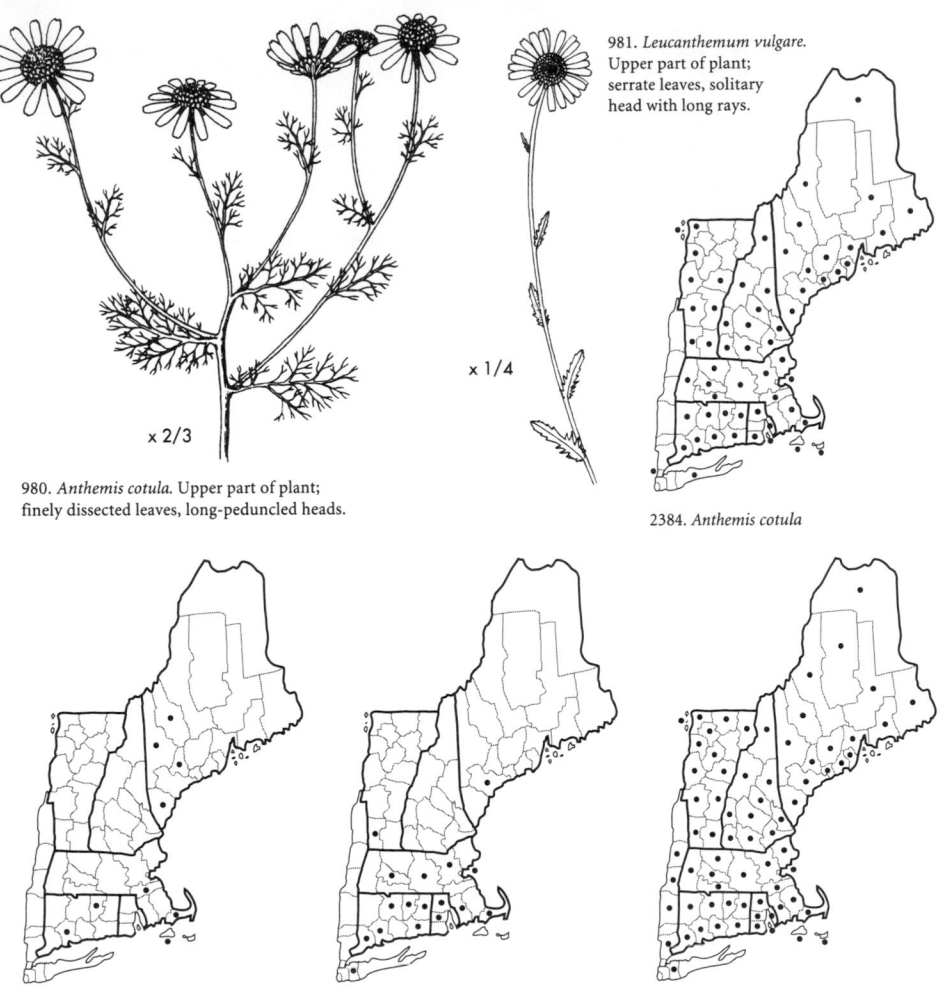

981. *Leucanthemum vulgare.*
Upper part of plant;
serrate leaves, solitary
head with long rays.

980. *Anthemis cotula.* Upper part of plant;
finely dissected leaves, long-peduncled heads.

× 2/3

× 1/4

2384. *Anthemis cotula*

2385. *Echinacea pallida*

2386. *Boltonia asteroides*

2387. *Leucanthemum vulgare*

1. *L. vulgáre* Lam. Fields, roadsides, waste places. June-September. Fig. 981, Map 2387. (Naturalized from Europe). [*Chrysanthemum leucanthemum; Leucanthemum 1.*]. Young shoots can be used in salad; a preparation made from the plant is reported to be useful as an eye lotion.

76. *Solidágo* L. Goldenrod (Latin name based on reputed value in healing wounds).

Perennial herbs, stems mostly simple or sparingly branched; leaves alternate, sessile or petioled, entire or variously toothed; heads small, in terminal or axillary corymbs, panicles, or thyrses, radiate, involucral bracts imbricated in several series, rays yellow (rarely white), pistillate, receptacle small, naked, disc flowers perfect, yellow, pappus of capillary bristles, usually white; achenes ribbed. —Wildl. 1

Dorónicum L. *pardaliánches* L. Leopards-Bane. Will key to *Solidago* or possibly *Heterotheca* (genus 82) but is distinguishable by the large heads (3.5 cm or more across) solitary or several at the tips of the stems, and cordate basal leaves. Rarely escaped from cultivation. Reported for Suffolk County MA.

a. Rays and disc flowers white; inflorescence open, corymbiform. .... 1. *S. ptarmicoides*
a. Rays and disc flowers yellow, or if rays white, inflorescence a narrow, interrupted,
    thyrsoid panicle.
  b. Inflorescence a flat-topped, compound corymb.
      Leaves ovate to oblong, the larger ones usually 1 cm or more wide; involucre
          more than 5 mm long, its bracts striate. .... 2. *S. rigida*
      Leaves linear to linear-lanceolate, the larger ones usually less than 1 cm wide;
          involucre 4.5 mm or less long, its bracts not striate. .... 3. *S. ulmifolia*
  b. Inflorescence axillary, thyrsoid, racemose or paniculate, but not as above.
    c. Inflorescence of reduced axillary clusters or a terminal thyrse or panicle with
        heads spirally arranged on the branches (not secund). (Figs. 982, 986).
      d. Involucral bracts with strongly recurved tips. .... 4. *S. squarrosa*
      d. Involucral bracts with tips appressed to slightly spreading.
        e. Involucres 8 mm or more long, bracts acuminate. .... 5. *S. macrophylla*
        e. Involucres less than 8 mm long or if longer bracts obtuse to acute.
          f. Basal and lower stem leaves mostly smaller than the median and upper
            ones, deciduous, all usually uniform in shape. (Fig. 984).
            g. Involucral bracts acute to acuminate; leaves weakly to strongly
              triple-nerved (ie. midvein paralleled by a pair of prominent
              lateral veins); stems pubescent (sometimes glabrous in
              S. calcicola). (Fig. 983).
              Plant rhizomatous ....6. *S. canadensis*
              Plant not rhizomatous ....7. *S. calcicola*
            g. Involucral bracts rounded or obtuse; leaves not triple-nerved; stems
              glabrous.
              Stems distinctly angled; leaves ovate to widely elliptic, abruptly
                acuminate to base and tip, coarsely and sharply serrate. ...... 8. *S. flexicaulis*
              Stems terete; leaves lanceolate to narrowly elliptic, gradually
                acuminate to base and tip, low-serrate .... 9. *S. caesia*
          f. Basal and lower stem leaves mostly larger than the median and upper
            ones, usually persistent, generally of a different shape. (Fig. 985).
            h. Stems, and often also the leaves distinctly pubescent or puberulent.
              i. Heads more than 30-flowered; alpine species. .... 10. *S. multiradiata*
              i. Heads with 30 or fewer flowers; mostly lowland species.
                j. Achenes pubescent .... 11. *S. simplex*
                j. Achenes glabrous or essentially so.
                  k. Involucral bracts acuminate .... 12. *S. puberula*
                  k. Involucral bracts obtuse to rounded.
                    l. Leaves pubescent on one or both sides.
                      Rays white .... 13. *S. bicolor*
                      Rays yellow .... 14. *S. hispida*
                    l. Leaves glabrous .... 15. *S. speciosa*
             h. Stems and leaves below the inflorescence glabrous or essentially so.
              m. Heads more than 30-flowered; alpine .... 10. *S. multiradiata*
               m. Heads with 30 or fewer flowers; mostly lowland.
                n. Achenes pubescent .... 11. *S. simplex*
                n. Achenes glabrous or essentially so.
                  Lower stem leaves with sheathing bases; bog or marsh species.
                    (Fig. 987). .... 16. *S. uliginosa*
                  Lower stem leaves without sheathing bases; upland species. .... 15. *S. speciosa*
    c. Inflorescence a terminal panicle or thyrse, the heads borne on the upper sides
        of the branches (secund). (Fig. 989).
      o. Stem leaves entire.
        p. Stems pubescent, at least above the middle; leaves triple-nerved.(Fig. 983) 6. *S. canadensis*
        p. Stems glabrous or pubescent in lines; leaves not triple-nerved.
          q. Lower stem leaves with bases sheathing half or more of the stem.
            (Fig. 987).
            Leaves fleshy; maritime species .... 17. *S. sempervirens*
            Leaves not fleshy; bog or marsh species. .... 16. *S. uliginosa*
         q. Lower stem leaves not sheathing, petioled or merely sessile.

Leaves sessile, glandular-punctate, usually anise-scented. .... 18. *S. odora*
Leaves, at least the lower, neither glandular-punctate nor
    anise-scented. .... 19. *S. juncea*
o. Stem leaves, at least some of them, toothed.
  r. Stems pubescent, at least above the middle.
    s. Leaves triple-nerved. (Fig. 983) .... 6. *S. canadensis*
    s. Leaves not triple-nerved.
      Leaves coarsely serrate; stems spreading-hirsute; plant rhizomatous. ... 20. *S. rugosa*
      Leaves crenate; stems puberulent; plant not rhizomatous. .... 21. *S. nemoralis*
  r. Stems glabrous.
    t. Leaves triple-nerved .... 22. *S. gigantea*
    t. Leaves not triple-nerved.
      u. Basal and lower stem leaves mostly smaller than the median and
        upper ones, deciduous, all usually uniform in shape.
        v. Leaves pubescent beneath, at least on the main veins . ... 3. *S. ulmifolia*
        v. Leaves glabrous beneath.
          Involucral bracts 4 mm or less long, linear. .... 20. *S. rugosa*
                                                    var. *sphagnophila*
          Involucral bracts 4 mm or more long, oblong. .... 23. *S. latissimifolia*
      u. Basal and lower stem leaves mostly larger than the median and
        upper ones, usually persistent, generally of a different shape.
        w. Stems strongly angled, at least below; leaves strongly scabrous above. ...... 24. *S. patula*
        w. Stems terete or striate, not strongly angled.
          x. Lower stem leaves with sheathing bases; bog or marsh species.
            (Fig. 987). .... 16. *S. uliginosa*
          x. Lower stem leaves without sheathing bases; upland species.
            Upper leaves usually subtending axillary fascicles of leaves
               more than 1 cm long; panicle branches glabrous to
               sparsely pubescent. (Fig. 988). .... 19. *S. juncea*
            Upper leaves rarely subtending axillary fascicles of leaves, if
               so the leaves less than 1 cm long; panicle branches
               densely pubescent . ... 25. *S. arguta*

1. S. ptarmicoides (Nees) Boivin. Open woods, ledges, fields, mostly calcareous, roadsides. July-September. Map 2388. Endangered in NH, CT. [*Aster p.; Unamia alba*].

2. S. rígida L. (stiff). Dry open woods and fields. August-October. Map 2389. Endangered in CT. [*Oligoneuron r.*]. Our plants are subsp. *rigida*.

S. ohioénsis Riddell. Similar to *S. rigida* but distinguishable in having glabrous stems and leaves 6 or more times as long as wide (stems pubescent and leaves up to 6 times as long as wide in *S. rigida*). From farther west. Reported for Rensselaer County NY. —OBL

3. S. ulmifólia Muhl. ex Willd. (elm-leaved) var. *ulmifólia*. Dry open woods and thickets. August-October. Map 2390. Endangered in VT. [*S. helleri; Euthamia minor*].

S. gymnospermóides (Greene) Fern. Will key to the latter 2 species but is distinguishable in having involucres mostly 5 mm or more long (5 mm or less long in the latter 2 species). Western. Reported for Nassau and Suffolk Counties NY. [*Euthamia g.*].

4. S. squarrósa Nutt. (recurved). Dry, rocky woods. August-September. Fig. 982, Map 2391.

5. S. macrophýlla Pursh (large leaved). Moist woods, often subalpine. July-September. Map 2392.

6. S. canadénsis L. (Canadian). Fields, roadsides, waste places. July-September. Fig. 983, Map 2393. Our plants include var. *canadensis* and the following vars.:

var. *hárgeri* Fern. Leaves beneath and stems above pilose with loosely spreading hairs (pubescence of minute hairs in var. *canadensis*).

var. *salebrósa* (Piper) Jones. Involucres 3 mm or more long; rays 1.5 mm or more long (involucres less than 3 mm long and rays less than 1.5 mm long in vars. *canadensis and hargeri*). [*S. elongata*].

var. *subserráta* (DC.) Cronq. Inflorescence paniculiform (thyrsoid in var. *salebrosa*); involucres and rays as in var. *salebrosa*. [*S. lepida*].

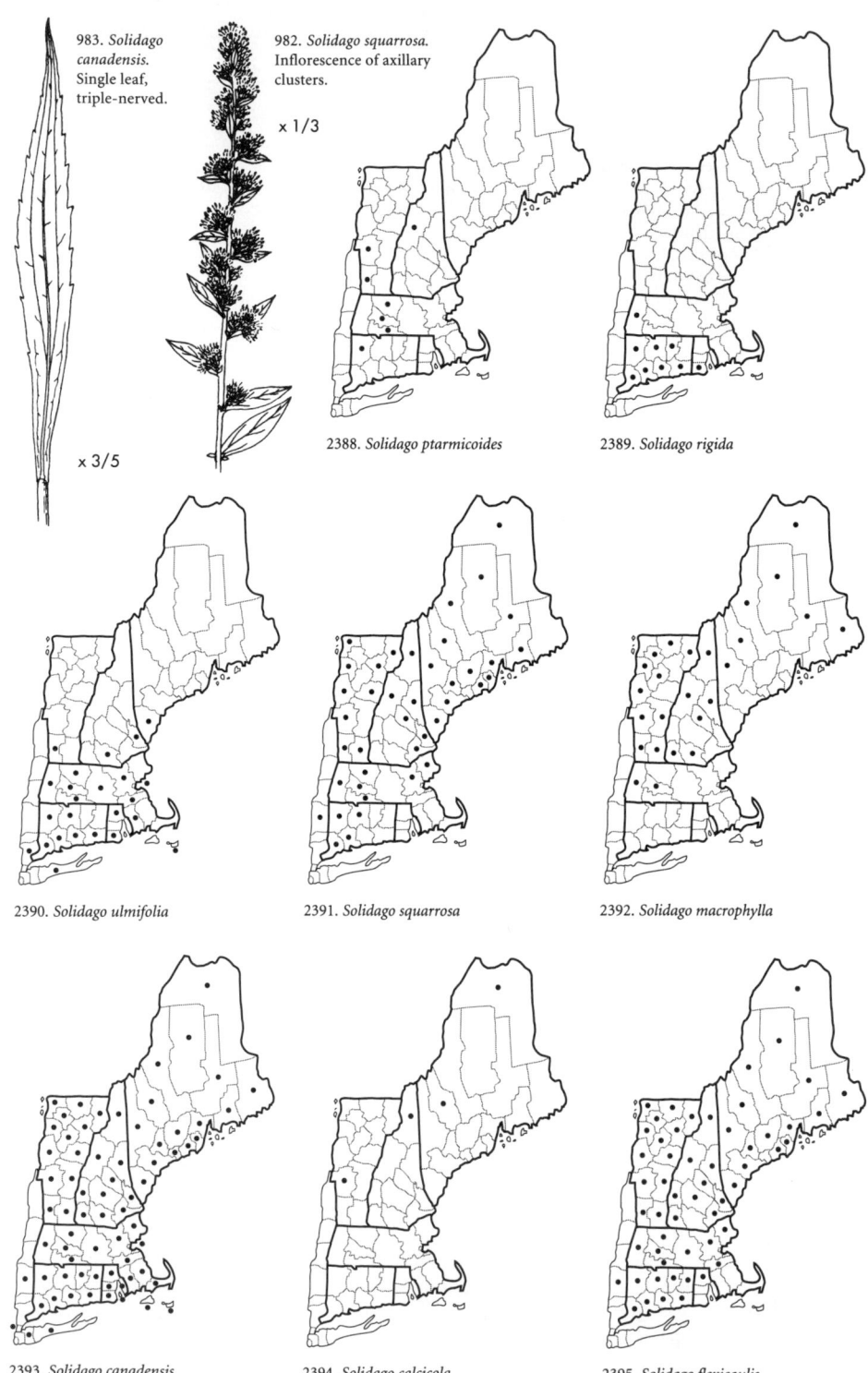

983. *Solidago canadensis.* Single leaf, triple-nerved.

× 3/5

982. *Solidago squarrosa.* Inflorescence of axillary clusters.

× 1/3

2388. *Solidago ptarmicoides*

2389. *Solidago rigida*

2390. *Solidago ulmifolia*

2391. *Solidago squarrosa*

2392. *Solidago macrophylla*

2393. *Solidago canadensis*

2394. *Solidago calcicola*

2395. *Solidago flexicaulis*

var. *scábra* Torr. & Gray. Leaves beneath and stems densely pubescent (sparsely pubescent in the above vars.). [*S. altissima*]. —FACU to FACU-

7. S. calcícola Fern. (living on lime). Rich, damp woods. August-September. Map 2394.

8. S. flexicaúlis L. (zigzag stem). Rich woods. August-October. Fig. 984, Map 2395. [*S. latifolia*]. —FACU

9. S. caésia L. (bluish-gray). Rich woods. August-October. Map 2396. —FACU

10. S. multiradiáta Ait. Alpine areas. July-September. Map 2397. [*S. cutleri*]. Our plants are var. *multiradiata*.

11. S. símplex Kunth. Rocks, gravel, cliffs, often alpine. July-September. Map 2398. Endangered in MA. [*S. glutinosa* subsp. *randii; S. humilis; S. randii; S. spathulata* subsp. *randii*]. Represented with us as subsp. *rándii* (Porter) Kartesz & Gandhi var. *rándii* and the following var.:

var. *racemósa* (Greene) Kartesz & Gandhi. Inflorescence loosely subracimiform (racimiform to densely thyrsoid in var. *randii*). [*S. racemosa; S. spathulata* var. *racemosa*].

12. S. pubérula Nutt. (short-pubescent). Dry fields, roadsides, waste places. August-October. Fig. 985, Map 2399. —FACU-

13. S. bícolor L. (two-colored). Silverrod. Open woods, fields. August-September. Map 2400.

14. S. híspida Muhl. ex Willd. (stiffly hairy). Open woods, ledges, river borders. July-October. Map 2401. Our plants include var. *hispida* and the following var.:

var. *lanáta* (Hook.) Fern. Stems densely woolly or villous (stems pilose in var. *hispida*).

15. S. speciósa Nutt. (showy). Fields, roadsides. August-October. Fig. 986, Map 2402. Our plants include var. *speciosa* and the following var.:

var. *erécta* (Pursh) MacM. Inflorescence virgate, spiciform-thyrsoid, often interrupted, or an open panicle of virgate branches (inflorescence usually a dense panicle with crowded, densely flowered branches in var. *speciosa*). [*S. erecta*].

16. S. uliginósa Nutt. (of marshes). Bogs. August-October. Fig. 987, Map 2403. [*S. neglecta; S. uniligulata*]. Our plants include var. *uliginosa* and the following vars.:

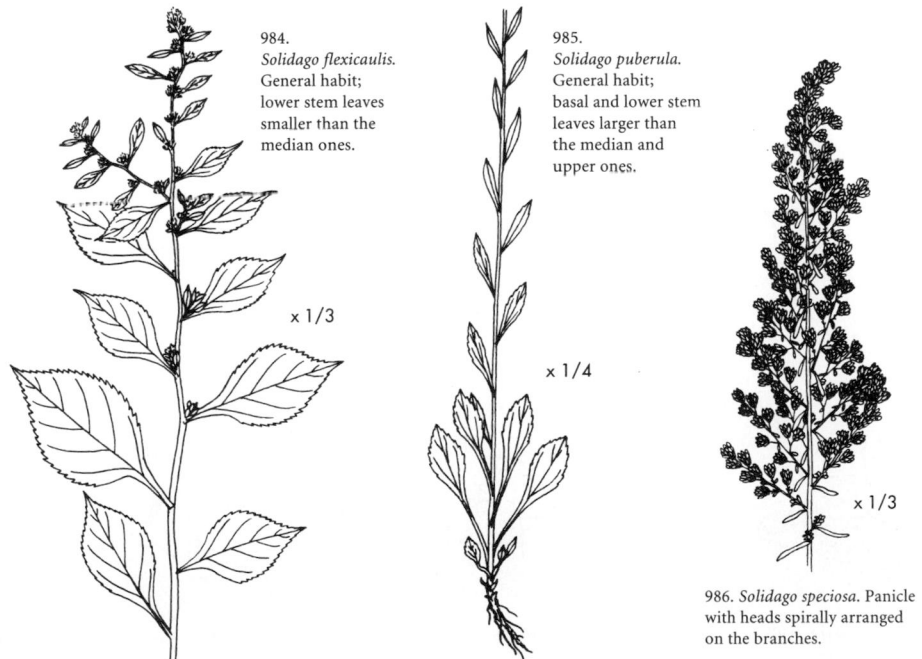

984.
Solidago flexicaulis.
General habit;
lower stem leaves
smaller than the
median ones.

x 1/3

985.
Solidago puberula.
General habit;
basal and lower stem
leaves larger than
the median and
upper ones.

x 1/4

986. *Solidago speciosa.* Panicle
with heads spirally arranged
on the branches.

x 1/3

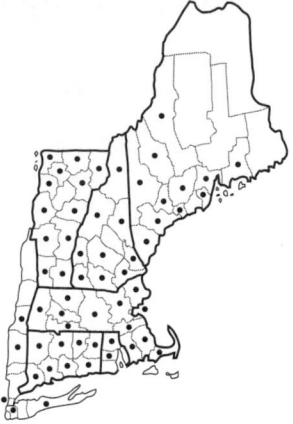

2396. *Solidago caesia*

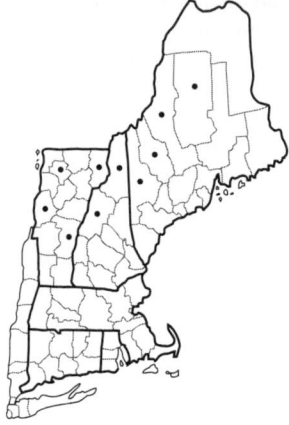

2397. *Solidago multiradiata*

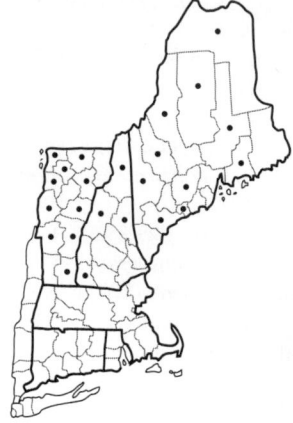

2398. *Solidago simplex* subsp. *randii*
var. *randii*

2399. *Solidago puberula*

2400. *Solidago bicolor*

2401. *Solidago hispida*

2402. *Solidago speciosa*

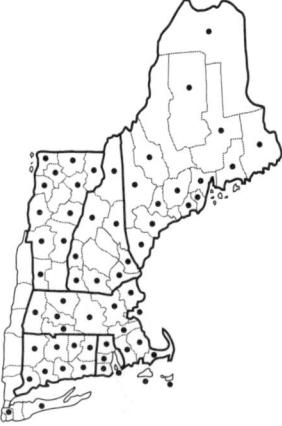

2403. *Solidago uliginosa*

2404. *Solidago sempervirens*

var. *linoídes* (T. & G.) Fern. Stem leaves mostly 20 or fewer, the lower up to 3 cm wide (stem leaves more than 20, the lower 3 cm or more wide in var. *uliginosa*). [*S. linoides*].

var. *peracúta* (Fern.) Friesner. Branches of inflorescence not secund; leaves entire or nearly so (branches of inflorescence secund and leaves serrate in vars. *uliginosa and linoides*). [*S. humilis; S. purshii*]. —OBL

17. S. sempervírens L. (evergreen). Seaside Goldenrod. Salt and brackish marshes, seashores, dunes, tidal rivers. July-October. Map 2404. Our plants include var. *sempervirens* and the following var.:

var. *mexicána* (L.) Fern. Involucres mostly 4 mm or less long; rays 11 or fewer (involucres 4 mm or more long and rays 12 or more in var. *sempervirens*). —FACW

S. x aspérula Desf. Representing a series of hybrids between *S. sempervirens* and *S. rugosa*. —OBL

18. S. odóra Ait. (fragrant). Anise-Scented Goldenrod. Dry, open woods and clearings, thickets. July-September. Map 2405. The dried leaves can be used to make a tea.

19. S. júncea Ait. (stiff). Open woods, fields, roadsides, waste places. July-September. Fig. 988, Map 2406. Our plants are var. *juncea*.

20. S. rugósa P. Mill. (wrinkled). Fields, thickets, roadsides, waste places. August-October. Map 2407. [*S. altissima*].

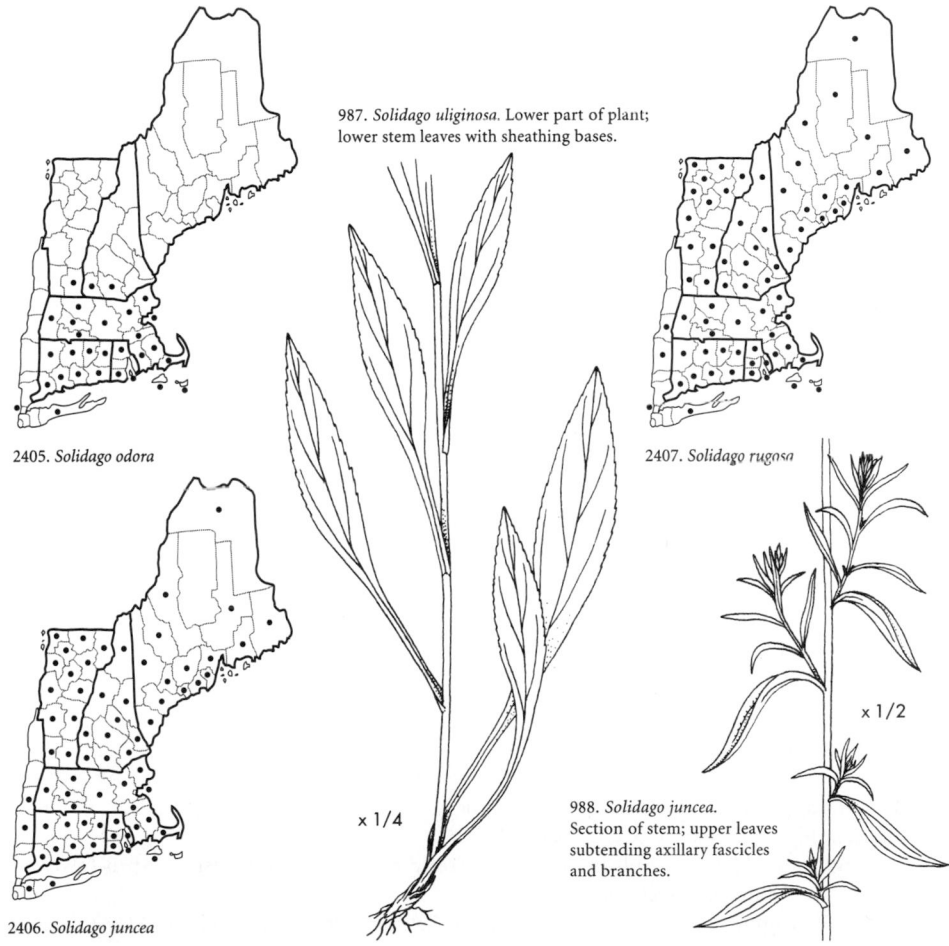

987. *Solidago uliginosa.* Lower part of plant; lower stem leaves with sheathing bases.

2405. *Solidago odora*

2407. *Solidago rugosa*

x 1/4

x 1/2

988. *Solidago juncea.* Section of stem; upper leaves subtending axillary fascicles and branches.

2406. *Solidago juncea*

S. x beáudryi Boivin. A hybrid between *S. rugosa* and *S. uliginosa.*
Our plants include subsp. *rugosa* var. *rugosa,* the following vars., and subsp. *aspera.*

var. *villósa* (Pursh.) Fern. Panicle narrow, often cylindric, the lower branches not or barely exceeding the subtending leaves (broadly pyramidal; the lower branches much exceeding the subtending leaves in var. *rugosa*).

var. *sphagnóphila* Graves. Stem and leaves glabrous (stem pubescent at least above, leaves pubescent, at least on the veins beneath in the other vars.). [*S. aestivalis*].

subsp. *áspera* (Ait.) Cronq. Leaves strongly rugose, blunt-toothed; stems puberulent or hispidulous (leaves not strongly rugose, sharply toothed and stems villous in subsp. *rugosa*). [*S. aspera; S. celtidifolia*]. —FACU- to FAC

21. S. nemorális Ait. (of woodland). Dry fields, roadsides, waste places. July-September. Map 2408. Our plants include the typical phase and the following var.:

var. *longipetioláta* (Mackenz. & Bush) Palmer & Steyerm. Basal and stem leaves narrowly lanceolate to linear or linear-oblanceolate; involucres mostly 4.5 mm or more high (basal and stem leaves broadly oblanceolate to obovate, involucres mostly less than 4 mm high in the typical phase). [*S. nemoralis* var. *decemflora; S. pulcherrima*].

22. S. gigantéa Ait. (very large). Fields, woodland borders, edges of streams and rivers, roadsides. July-September. Fig. 989, Map 2409. [*S. serotina*]. —FACW

23. S. latissimifólia P. Mill. Wet thickets, marshes, wet meadows, near the coast. August-October. Map 2410. [*S. elliottii*]. —OBL

24. S. pátula Muhl. ex Willd. (spreading). Wooded swamps, wet meadows. August-September. Map 2411. —OBL

25. S. argúta Ait. (sharp). Dry open woods, clearings, fields, roadsides. July-September. Map 2412. Our plants are var. *arguta.*

77. Erígeron L. Fleabane (ancient name for a downy, early-flowering plant).
Annual or perennial herbs; leaves alternate, often also basal, sessile or petioled, toothed or entire; heads solitary, corymbose or paniculate, usually radiate, involucral bracts narrow, usually in 1 series, rays narrow, white, pink, purple or blue, pistillate, receptacle flat, naked, disc flowers perfect, yellow, pappus of capillary bristles, a short outer series of minute bristles or scales sometimes also present; achenes flattened, ribbed, usually pubescent.

a. Leaves 4 mm or less wide, 3 cm or less long, numerous, all nearly uniform(Fig. 990) . 1. *E. hyssopifolius*
a. Leaves, at least the larger, wider than 4 mm and/or longer than 3 cm, relatively few,
    the lower usually of a distinctly different size and shape.
  b. Stem leaves subamplexicaul or rounded at the base; pappus of ray flowers of
      capillary bristles several mm long.
    Stolons present; heads of disc flowers mostly 1 cm or more wide; disc corollas
      4 mm or more long .... 2. *E. pulchellus*
    Stolons absent; heads of disc flowers mostly less than 1 cm wide; disc corollas
      less than 4 mm long .... 3. *E. philadelphicus*
  b. Stem leaves narrowed to the base; pappus of ray flowers absent or
    inconspicuous, 1 mm or less long. (Fig. 991).
    Stems spreading-pubescent; stem leaves broadly lanceolate to ovate, mostly
      toothed. (Fig. 991) .... 4. *E. annuus*
    Stems often appressed-pubescent; stem leaves linear to lanceolate, mostly
      entire .... 5. *E. strigosus*

1. E. hyssopifólius Michx. (hyssop-leaved). Rocky ledges, shores, banks, often calcareous. June-September. Fig. 990, Map 2413. Our plants are var. *hyssopifolius.* —FACW

2. E. pulchéllus Michx. (handsome). Woods, stream borders, fields, roadsides. April-July. Map 2414. Our plants are var. *pulchellus.* —FACU

3. E. philadélphicus L. (Philadelphian). Woods, fields, roadsides, waste places. May-July. Map 2415. [*E. purpureus; E. provancheri*]. —FACU

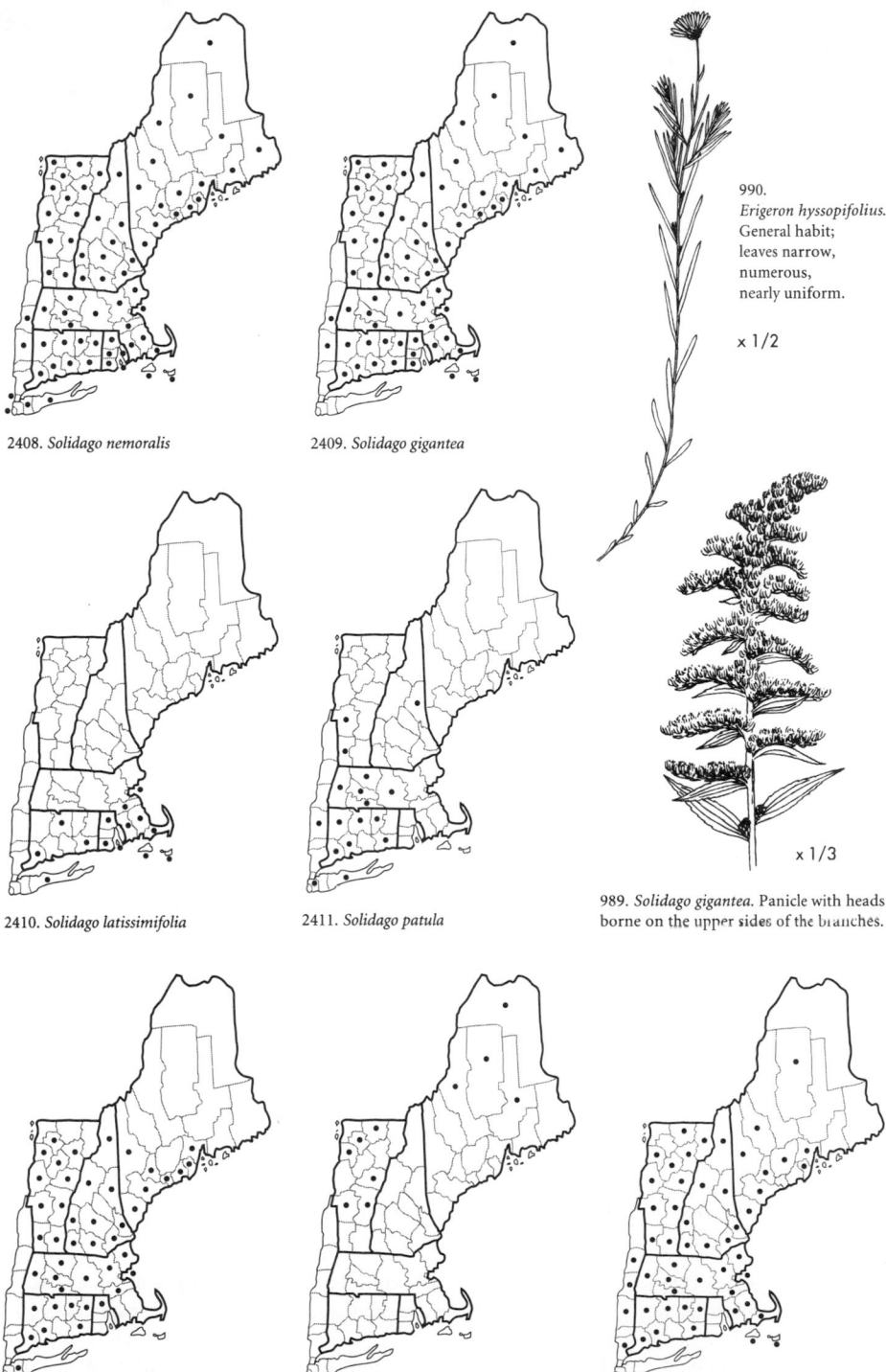

2408. *Solidago nemoralis*

2409. *Solidago gigantea*

990.
Erigeron hyssopifolius.
General habit;
leaves narrow,
numerous,
nearly uniform.

x 1/2

2410. *Solidago latissimifolia*

2411. *Solidago patula*

989. *Solidago gigantea.* Panicle with heads borne on the upper sides of the branches.

x 1/3

2412. *Solidago arguta*

2413. *Erigeron hyssopifolius*

2414. *Erigeron pulchellus*

4. E. ánnuus (L.) Pers. (annual). Daisy-fleabane. Fields, roadsides, waste places. June-August. Fig. 991, Map 2416. —FACU

5. E. strigósus Muhl. ex Willd. (with straight, appressed hairs). Fields, roadsides, waste places. June-August. Map 2417. [*E. ramosus*]. Our plants include var. *strigósus* [includes var. *discoideus*] and the following vars.:

var. *beyríchii* (Fisch. & Mey.) Gray. Inflorescence diffuse, leafless or nearly so (inflorescence not diffuse or if so, with leaves).

var. *septentrionális* (Fern. & Wieg.) Fern. Stems glabrous or sparsely spreading-pubescent (appressed-pubescent in vars. *strigosus* and *beyrichii*).—FACU+

78. Chrysánthemum L. Chrysanthemum (ancient Greek name meaning golden flower).

Annual or perennial herbs; leaves entire, dentate or pinnatifid, alternate, sessile or petioled; heads terminal, solitary, radiate, involucral bracts scarious-margined, in several series, rays usually yellow, pistillate, receptacle flat or convex, naked, disc flowers perfect, usually yellow, pappus none or a short crown; achenes terete or wing-angled.

Caléndula L. *officinális* L. Pot-marigold. Similar to *Chrysanthemum* but is distinguishable in having leaves entire or remotely denticulate and involucral bracts in 1 or 2 series (leaves are serrate or pinnatifid and bracts are in 3 or more series in *Chrysanthemum*). Occasionally escaped from gardens. Reported for MA, Fairfield County CT; Aroostook, Piscataquis, Washington Counties, ME; Coos County NH.

Hymenóxys Cass. *odoráta* DC. Similar to *Chrysanthemum* but distinguishable from it and the latter genus in having heads numerous in a corymbose inflorescence and a pappus of 5 or more acuminate scales (heads solitary and pappus none or a short crown in *Chrysanthemum* and *Calendula*). From the southwest. Reported for ME.

Leaves mostly serrate or pinnatifid; achenes with 2 wings. .... 1. *C. segetum*
Leaves bipinnatifid; achenes with 3 wings. .... 2. *C. coronarium*

1. C. ségetum L. (weed among crops). Corn-marigold. Fields, roadsides, waste places. July-September. Map 2418. (Adventive from Europe).

2. C. coronárium L. (used in garlands). Occasionally escaped from cultivation. July-September. Map 2419. (Introduced from Europe).

C. carinátum L. Tricolor Chrysanthemum. Differing from the latter 2 species in having a purple disc, the rays white, red or purple, yellow or purple at the base, the head appearing tricolored. From the southwest. A waif in our range reported for MA.

79. Ratíbida Raf. Prairie Coneflower.

Perennial herbs; leaves alternate, pinnatifid, the leaf segments linear to lanceolate, toothed or entire; heads showy, terminal, long-peduncled, radiate, involucral bracts in 1 series, spreading, rays yellow or partly brownish-purple, neutral, spreading or reflexed, receptacle columnar, chaffy, the chaff bearded at the tip, disc flowers perfect, pappus none or of 2 teeth, 1 longer than the other, achenes flattened, sharp-margined or winged.

Receptacle columnar, 2 or more times as long as wide, usually longer than the rays.
  (Fig. 992)   .... 1. *R. columnifera*
Receptacle oblong to elliptic, less than 2 times as long as wide, usually shorter than
  the rays   .... 2. *R. pinnata*

1. R. columnífera (Nutt.) Woot. & Standl. (bearing columns). Fields, waste places. June-August. Fig. 992. From farther west. Reported for MA, Hartford County, CT. [*R. pulcherrima; Lepachys columnaris*].

2. R. pinnáta (Vent.) Barnh. (pinnate). Fields, waste places. June-August. Map 2420. From farther west and south. [*Lepachys p.*].

991. *Erigeron annuus.*
Upper part of plant; leaves
lanceolate, toothed, narrowed
to base.

992. *Ratibida columnifera.*
Single head showing
columnar receptacle.

2415. *Erigeron philadelphicus*

2416. *Erigeron annuus*

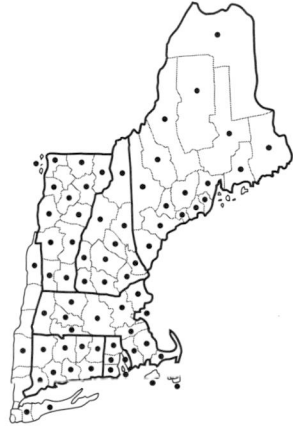

2417. *Erigeron strigosus*

2418. *Chrysanthemum segetum*

2419. *Chrysanthemum coronarium*

2420. *Ratibida pinnata*

80. *Rudbeckia* L. Coneflower (for Professor Rudbeck).

Perennial (rarely annual)herbs; leaves simple, basal and alternate, serrate, lobed or pinnatifid, sessile or petioled; heads showy, long peduncled, terminal, radiate, rarely ligulate, involucral bracts in 1 or 2 series, spreading or reflexed, rays yellow, neutral, receptacle conical or columnar, chaffy, disc flowers perfect, yellow to brown or purple, pappus none or a minute crown; achenes angled.

Gaillárdia Foug. *aristáta* Pursh. Similar to *Rudbeckia* but differs in having a bristly receptacle and a pappus of awned scales. From farther west. Reported for CT, Berkshire County MA; Coos County NH; Suffolk County NY.

a. Leaves, at least some of them, pinnatifid or deeply trilobed. (Fig. 993).
  b. Stems glabrous and smooth; disc green to yellow or disc flowers absent and
      head entirely of ray flowers .... 1. *R. laciniata*
  b. Stems pubescent, somewhat scabrous; disc purplish-black.
    Stems and leaves densely pubescent; chaff merely acute. .... 2. *R. subtomentosa*
    Stems and leaves with scattered pubescence; chaff extended into sharp
    awns. .... 3. *R. triloba*
a. Leaves entire or merely toothed.
  c. Receptacular chaff densely pubescent at apex. .... 4. *R. hirta*
  c. Receptacular chaff glabrous or essentially so at apex.
    Chaff extended into sharp awns .... 3. *R. triloba*
    Chaff merely acute .... 5. *R. fulgida*
                            var. *speciosa*

1. *R. laciniáta* L. (slashed). Borders of ponds and streams, marshes, wet open woods and thickets. July-September. Fig. 993, Map 2421. Our plants are var. *laciniata*.
    Another var. which has been distinguished is var. *bipinnáta*. —FACW
    2. *R. subtomentósa* Pursh (somewhat tomentose). Wet fields, bottomlands. July-September. From farther west. Reported for Hartford County CT; Berkshire County MA. —FAC
    3. *R. tríloba* L. (three-lobed). Fields, thickets, open woods, waste places. July-September. Map 2422. From farther west. Our plants are var. *triloba*.—FACU
    4. *R. hírta* L. (rough). Black-eyed Susan. Fields, thickets. June-October. Map 2423. Our plants include var. *hirta* and the following var.:
    var. *pulchérrima* Farw. Leaves entire or finely toothed (coarsely toothed in var. *hirta*). [*R. serotina*]. —FACU-
    R. bícolor Nutt. Similar to *R. hirta* but distinguishable in being annual without a basal cluster of leaves, stem leaves nearly uniform, obtuse (*R. hirta* is perennial, with a basal cluster of leaves, stem leaves decreasing in size upward, acute to acuminate). From farther south. Reported for MA.
    5. *R. fulgida* Ait. Woods and bottomlands. July-September. From farther west. Reported for Fairfield County CT; Franklin County MA. [*R. deamii; R. fulgida* var. *sullivantii; R. speciosa*]. Represented with us as var. *speciosa* (Wenderoth) Perd. —FAC

81. *Ínula* L. (ancient Latin name).

Stout, pubescent, perennial herbs; leaves basal and alternate, large, scabrous above, tomentose beneath, irregularly dentate, the basal long-petioled, elliptic, the cauline sessile and partly clasping, lance-ovate; heads large, few, in corymbs, radiate, involucral bracts imbricated, the outer foliaceous, rays numerous, yellow, pistillate, receptacle flat or convex, naked, disc flowers perfect, yellow, pappus of tan, capillary bristles; achenes ribbed and striate, naked.

    1. *I. helénium* L. (old generic name). Elecampane. Fields, roadsides, clearings. June-September. Map 2424. (Naturalized from Europe). Root has been candied and eaten as a confection; syrup made from the root is reported to be of value in treating bronchial infection and asthma.
    I. salícina L. Disc. less than 3 cm wide (3 cm or more wide in *I. helenium*). A waif in our range, reported for MA but not known to have persisted.

I. británnica L. Differing from the latter 2 species in having entire or serrulate leaves and linear outer bracts (leaves coarsely and doubly serrate and outer bracts ovate in *I. helenium* and *I. salicina*) Eurasian. Rarely occurring in our range. Reported for Nassau County NY.

82. Heterothéca Cass. (from the Greek, referring to the differences in the achenes). Branched, perennial herbs, woolly or villous, at least when young; leaves alternate, sessile or the lower petioled, entire or denticulate, linear or broader; heads corymbose, radiate, involucral bracts imbricated in several series, rays yellow, pistillate, receptacle flat, naked, disc flowers yellow, perfect, pappus in disc flowers double, the outer of short, coarse bristles, the inner of long, tawny, capillary bristles, ray flowers without pappus; achenes flattened, pubescent.

1. *H. subaxilláris* (Lam.) Britt. & Rusby. Camphor-weed. Dunes, sandy fields. July-September. (Tropical Amer.). From farther south and west. Reported for CT.

83. Chrysópsis (Nutt.) Ell. (from the Greek, referring to the golden inflorescence). Similar to *Heterotheca* except ray flowers with pappus. [*Heterotheca*].

1. *C. mariána* (L.) Ell. (of Maryland). Sandy woods, fields, roadsides. August-October. From farther south and west. Reported for RI. [*Heterotheca m.*].

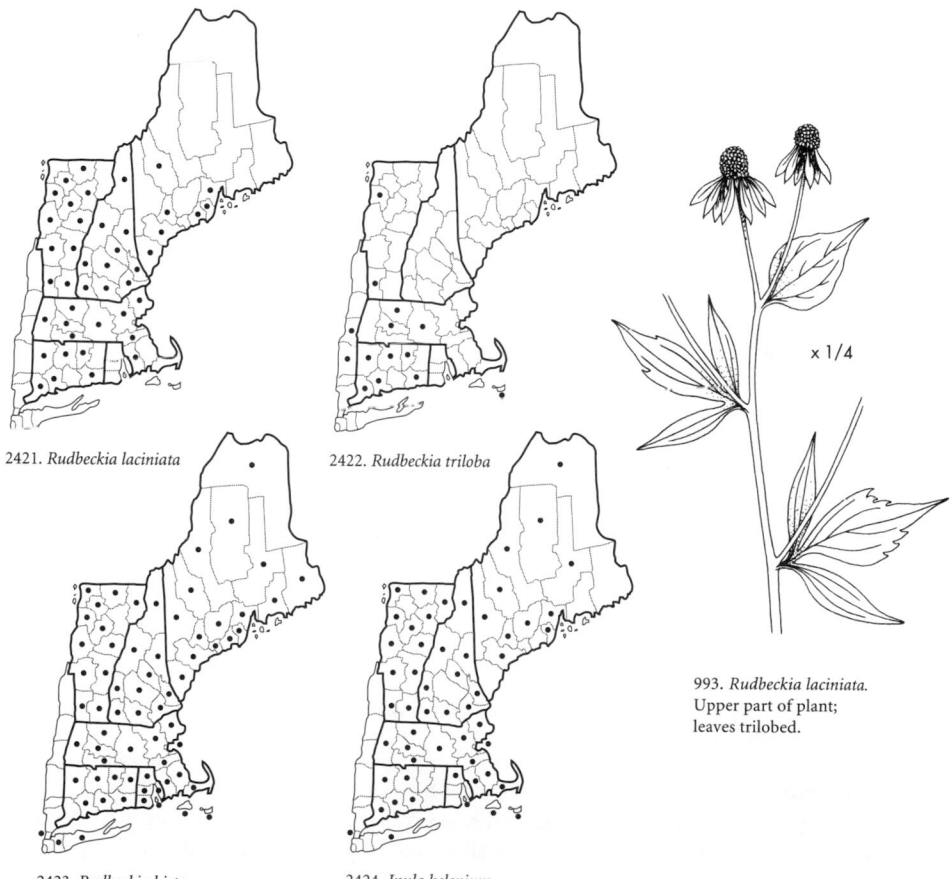

2421. *Rudbeckia laciniata*

2422. *Rudbeckia triloba*

x 1/4

2423. *Rudbeckia hirta*

2424. *Inula helenium*

993. *Rudbeckia laciniata.*
Upper part of plant;
leaves trilobed.

84. Pityópsis Nutt.

Similar to *Heterotheca* except stem leaves linear, parallel veined. [*Heterotheca; Chrysopsis*].

1. P. falcáta (Pursh) Nutt. (sickle-shaped). Sandy fields, thickets, roadsides, mostly near the coast. July-September. Map 2425. Endangered in CT. [*Heterotheca f.; Chrysopsis f.*].

85. Euthámia Nutt.

Similar to *Solidago* (genus 76), except inflorescence a flat-topped, compound corymb, leaves linear to linear-lanceolate, involucre 5 mm or less high, disc flowers 5 or more. [*Solidago*].

Leaves with 3-5 principal veins; heads mostly 20 or more-flowered. .... 1. *E. graminifolia*
Leaves with 1 principal vein and sometimes 2 faint lateral veins; heads mostly 20 or
    fewer-flowered .... 2. *E. tenuifolia*

1. E. graminifólia (L.) Nutt. Fields, thickets, roadsides, waste places. August-October. Fig. 994, Map 2426. [*E. floribunda; Solidago g.*]. Our plants include var. *graminifólia* and the following var.: var. *nuttállii* (Greene) W. Stone. Branches, leaves, and sometimes stems densely pubescent with fine hairs (glabrous or nearly so in var. *graminifolia*). [*E. nuttallii; Solidago graminifolia* var. *n.*].

2. E. tenuifólia (Pursh) Nutt. (slender-leaved). Sandy shores of rivers and lakes, sandy fields, roadsides, waste places. August-October. Map 2427. [*E. galetorum; Solidago t.*]. Our plants include var. *tenuifólia* and the following var.: var. *pycnocéphala* (Fern.) C.&J. Taylor. Primary stem leaves strongly ascending, not acuminate, without or with scarcely developed fascicles of leaves in the axils (primary stem leaves acuminate, with well developed fascicles of leaves in the axils in var. *tenuifolia*). [*Solidago tenuifolia* var. *p.*].

86. Helénium L. Sneezeweed (ancient Greek name for some plant).

Annual or perennial herbs, often branched, stem usually narrowly winged by the decurrent leaf bases; leaves simple, alternate, sessile and usually decurrent on the stem, toothed or entire, glandular-punctate; heads terminal, solitary or corymbed, few to numerous, mostly radiate, involucral bracts in 1 or 2 series, reflexed, rays mostly yellow, pistillate or neutral, several-toothed at the apex, drooping, receptacle convex to oblong or subglobose, naked, disc flowers perfect, yellow or purplish, the lobes glandular-pubescent, pappus of several aristate or acuminate scales; achenes angled and ribbed, pubescent. Poisonous.

a. Leaves filiform to linear, mostly 2 mm or less wide, very numerous, not decurrent
    on the stem or branches; plant annual. .... 1. *H. amarum*
a. Leaves lance-linear to ovate or elliptic, mostly 3 mm or more wide, not very
    numerous, decurrent on the stem and branches; plant perennial. (Fig. 995).
    Disc flowers yellow; rays usually pistillate. .... 2. *H. autumnale*
    Disc flowers purple or brownish; rays neutral. .... 3. *H. flexuosum*

1. H. ámarum (Raf.) H. Rock (bitter). Roadsides and waste places. June-October. Map 2428. (W.I.). From farther south and west. [*H. tenuifolium*]. —FACU-

2. H. autumnále L. (autumnal). River shores, fields. August-October. Map 2429. From farther south and west. [*H. altissimum; H. latifolium*].

Our plants include var. *autumnale* and the following var.: var. *parviflórum* (Nutt.) Fern. Rays less than 1.5 cm long, mature disc up to 1.5 cm wide (rays longer than 1.5 cm, mature disc wider than 1.5 cm in var. *autumnale*). [*H. parviflorum*]. —FACW+

3. H. flexuósum Raf. (zigzag). Fields, roadsides, waste places. July-October. Fig. 995, Map 2430. [*H. nudiflorum; H. polyphyllum*].

87. Grindélia Willd. Tarweed (for D. Grindel).

Branched, glabrous, biennial or perennial herbs; leaves alternate, sessile or clasping, serrate, oblong to obovate-oblong, resinous-punctate; heads large, solitary and terminal on the branches, radiate,

2425. *Pityopsis falcata*

2426. *Euthamia graminifolia*

994. *Euthamia graminifolia.*
Upper stem; inflorescence a
flat-topped compound corymb.

x 1/2

2427. *Euthamia tenuifolia*

2428. *Helenium amarum*

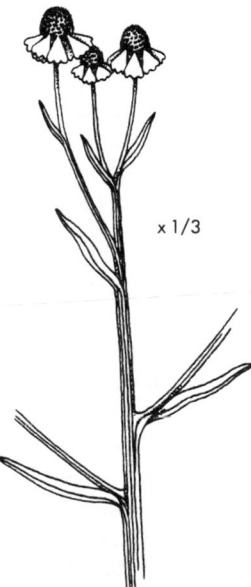

x 1/3

995. *Helenium flexuosum.*
Upper part of plant;
leaves decurrent on the
stem and branches.

2429. *Helenium autumnale*

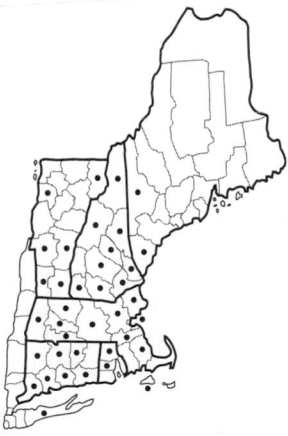

2430. *Helenium flexuosum*

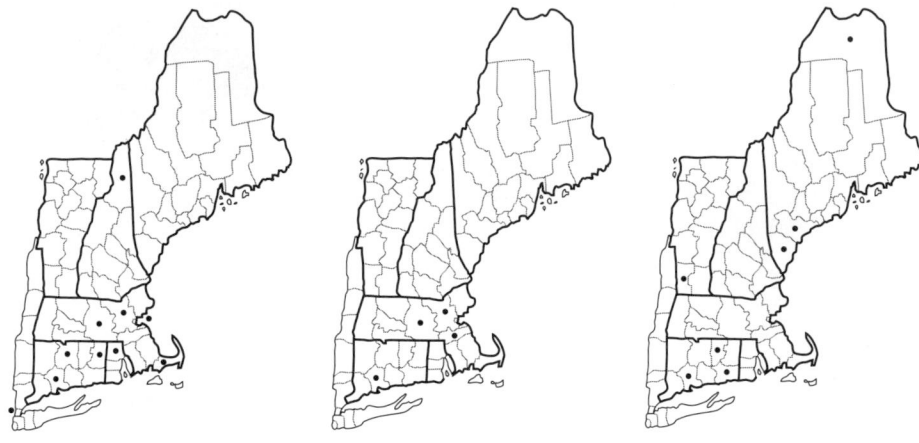

2431. *Grindelia squarrosa*   2432. *Madia capitata*   2433. *Madia glomerata*

involucral bracts imbricated in several series, slightly to strongly resinous, rays yellow, pistillate, receptacle flat or convex, naked, disc flowers perfect or sometimes only staminate, yellow, pappus of 2-8, deciduous, mostly serrulate awns; achenes short and thick.

1. *G. squarrósa* (Pursh) Dunal (with recurved tips). Fields, roadsides, waste places. July-September. Map 2431. From farther west. Our plants include var. *squarrosa* and the following var.:
var. *serruláta* (Rydb.) Stey. Principal stem leaves linear-oblong to oblanceolate, rays 1 cm or more long (principal stem leaves mostly ovate to oblong, rays up to 1 cm long in var. *squarrosa*). —FACU

G. robústa Nutt. Similar to *G. squarrosa* but distinguishable from it in having sharply toothed to entire leaves and heads 3-5 cm wide (leaves with teeth blunt or rounded and heads up to 3 cm wide in *G. squarrosa*). From the southwest. Reported for MA. Preparations of this species have been reported as useful in treating asthma and in external applications for inflamed or irritated skin.

G. lanceoláta Nutt. Similar to *G. squarrosa* but distinguishable from it and *G. robusta* in having involucral bracts spreading to ascending but not reflexed (strongly reflexed in *G. squarrosa* and *G. robusta*). From farther west. Reported for CT.

88. *Mádia* Molina Tarweed (based on a Chilean name).
Glandular, strongly-scented, annual herbs; leaves alternate, toothed or entire, sessile, linear to lanceolate; heads axillary or terminal, solitary or in clusters, radiate, involucral bracts in 1 series, rays yellow, pistillate, or rarely absent, receptacle convex, chaffy only near the margin, disc flowers perfect or sterile, yellow, pappus none; achenes compressed.

Heads subglobose, about as long as wide. .... 1. *M. capitata*
Heads narrowly elliptic, about twice as long as wide. .... 2. *M. glomerata*

1. *M. capitáta* Nutt. Cultivated ground and waste places. June-September. Map 2432. From the west coast. [*M. sativa* var. *congesta*].

M. satíva Molina. Similar to *M. capitata* but inflorescence more open, with scattered heads, these up to 8 mm high (heads crowded in glomerules, 9 mm or more high in *M. capitata*). From the west coast. Reported for VT. A meal is sometimes made by grinding the fruits.

M. grácilis (Sm.) Keck. & J. Clausen ex Applegate. Similar to the above species but plant is stipitate-glandular usually only above the middle (stipitate-glandular from the base in *M. capitata* and *M. sativa*). Rarely adventive in our range from the west coast. Reported for Cumberland County ME; Plymouth County MA. [*M. dissitiflora*; *M. racemosa*].

2. *M. glomeráta* Hook. (clustered). Cultivated ground and waste places. June-September. Map 2433. From the west coast.

PARTIAL BIBLIOGRAPHY
FOR USEFUL PLANTS

Angier, B. 1974. *Field Guide to Edible Wild Plants.* Harrisburg, PA: Stackpole Books.

Chiej, R. 1984. *The Macdonald Encyclopedia of Medicinal Plants.* London: Macdonald & Co.

Coon, N. 1974. *The Dictionary of Useful Plants.* Emmaus, PA: Rodale Press.

Gibbons, E. 1962. *Stalking the Wild Asparagus.* New York: David McKay Co.

Gibbons, E. 1966. *Stalking the Healthful Herbs.* New York: David McKay Co.

James, W.R. 1973. *Know Your Poisonous Plants.* Healdsburg, CA: Naturegraph Pub.

Medsger, O. P. 1973. *Edible Wild Plants.* New York: Macmillan.

Muenscher, W. C. 1975. *Poisonous Plants of the United States.* New York: Collier Books, Macmillan.

Schultes, R. E. 1976. *Hallucinogenic Plants.* New York: Golden Press.

Tyler, V. E. 1992. *The Honest Herbal.* Binghamton, NY: Pharmaceutical Products Press.

MATRIX OF DIAGNOSTIC CHARACTERISTICS FOR DICOTS

In preparing the keys for dicot families and genera a matrix of the 40-odd characteristics listed below was constructed as an aid. This matrix has been included because of its potential usefulness as a teaching tool and for identifying plant specimens on which only certain structures are present.

Because of space limitations in the matrix, variability within a genus could only be touched on in a rudimentary fashion. Also, for a few features, as for example Characteristic 19 "Leaves Sheathing" information was included in the matrix only to the extent to which it was relevant in constructing the keys, i.e. information was not included for all genera. For the vast majority of features, however, the information is inclusive of all the genera treated in the manual. A few genera treated in the manual were not included in the matrix such as genera recently reported as waifs in our area and genera newly recognized as a result of splitting, as for example in the case of Potentilla; the three other genera now recognized as distinct from Potentilla, i.e. Pentaphylloides, Comarum and Argentina, were not included in the matrix because it was not necessary to do so in order to prepare the keys.

Based on the above considerations, the matrix should be used to assist in narrowing the range of possibilities in identifying a plant, and in finding examples of plants having certain features for teaching. For a more complete understanding of a genus the user should refer to the full description of the family and genus in the Descriptive Flora as well as keys to the genus and any species treated within the genus.

Below, the 40-odd features that have been abbreviated in the matrix are fully listed, and inflorescence types, fruit types and flower color are also listed along with the corresponding abbreviations used in the matrix; other abbreviations and clarifications for the matrix have also been included below.

Diagnostic Characteristics:
1. Plant Aquatic
2. Epiphyte/Parasite
3. Flowers Replaced by Bulblets or Leafy Tufts
4. Vine (climbing/trailing)
5. Rhizomes Present; includes woody plants that spread underground and form colonies.

6. Latex Present
7. Plant Armed
8. Woody/Suffrutescent/Herbaceous
9. Evergreen
10. Plant Pubescent/Glabrous; refers to the condition of any part of the plant, i.e. stem, leaves, etc.
11. Leaves Alternate/Opposite/Subopposite/Whorled
12. Leaves Simple/Compound
13. Leaves Compound (pinnate/palmate); the palmately compound category includes trifoliate leaves.
14. Leaves Lobed/Toothed/Sinuate/Entire; in a compound leaf the designation refers to the condition of the leaflets. In most cases toothed and sinuate conditions were not distinguished and a toothed designation may include margins having a sinuate condition; a toothed designation also includes leaves with a distinct cusp or mucro.
15. Leaves Sessile/Petioled
16. Leaves Stipulate
17. Leaves Basal/Cauline
18. Leaves Reduced/Modified
19. Leaves Sheathing; includes the auriculate or clasping condition.
20. Plant Hermaphrodite/Monoecious, Dioecious, Polygamous/Polygamomonoecious/Polygamodioecious
21. Inflorescence Type
22. Flowers Bracteate/Ebracteate
23. Flowers/Inflorescence/Axillary/Terminal
24. Calyx/Corolla; Cl=calyx; Co=corolla; CC=calyx & corolla; T=tepals; CC/Cl indicates that conditions in which calyx and corolla are present or only calyx present may both apply; in some genera only the calyx tube is present and lobes or teeth are lacking; such a condition is indicated by a 0 under number of calyx lobes.
25. Flowers Regular/Irregular
26. Ovary Superior/Inferior/Half-Inferior; S/I refers to the condition of a superior ovary that appears inferior.
27. Ovary Lobed
28. Perianth Parts Equal/Unequal
29. Flower Color
30. Perianth United/Separate; U/B=perianth united at base only.
31. Number Sepals/Petals/or Lobes; single numbers refer to sepals only; ♀ or ♂ = character applies only to that gender; 2/5=upper # sepals, lower # petals; in Asteraceae number of corolla lobes refers to the disc flowers only.
32. Number Styles/Stigmas/Stigma Lobes
33. Number Carpels; S=several; 00=many
34. Number Locules; 2-4/B=2-4 locular at base, 1 locular at top, or 1/2-4=1 locular above 2-4 locular below
35. Carpels United/Separate
36. Number Stamens/Anthers
37. Stamens Hypogenous/Perigynous
38. Stamens United/Separate; U/B=united at base only
39. Fruit Type; in capsular fruits C/2=capsule 2-valved
40. Dehiscence - Septicidal/Loculicidal/Circumscissile/Poricidal/Indehiscent

Inflorescence Types:

Cat. Catkin
Cl. Cluster
Co. Corymb
Cy. Cyme
D Dichasium
F Fascicle
H Head
P Panicle
R Raceme
S Spike
So. Solitary
T Thyrse
U Umbel
V Variable
Ve. Verticels

Fruit Types:

A Achene
B Berry
C Capsule
D Drupe
Dl. Drupelet
F Follicle
L Legume
M Mericarp
N Nut
Nl. Nutlet
P Pome
Pe. Pepo
Py. Pyxis
Sa. Samara
Sc. Schizocarp

Se. Seed
Sl. Silicle
Sq. Silique
U Utricle

Flower Color:

B Blue
C Cream
G Green
M Maroon
O Orange
Pi. Pink
Pu. Purple
R Red
Ro. Rose
S Scarlet
V Variable
W White
Y Yellow

Other Abbreviations/Clarifications:

✓ = character applicable to some or all members of a genus; ✓/- = character may either be present or not present.

1 sp. = this designation indicates that the character applies to only 1 member of a genus.

W/H = a designation of 2 characters, as in Diagnostic Characteristic 8. woody/herbaceous, indicates that the genus contains members exhibiting both conditions.

H,D,P = A combination of 3 conditions, as in Diagnostic Characteristic 20. hermaphrodite, dioecious, polygamous, indicates that the genus exhibits all 3 conditions.

The **V** designation indicates condition variable where 3 or more conditions apply.

Other Distinguishing Characteristics: **Cleist.** = cleistogamous; **Subt.** = subtending; **Inv.** = involucre; **Adn.** = adnate to.

Diagnostic Characteristics	Salix	Populus	Myrica	Comptonia	Juglans	Carya	Carpinus	Ostrya	Corylus	Alnus	Betula	Fagus	Castania	Quercus	Ulmus	Celtis	Broussonetia	Morus	Maclura	Cannabus	Humulus	Laportea	Urtica
1. Plant Aquatic																							
2. Epiphyte/Parasite																				✓			
3. Fl. Repl. by Bulbl./Leafy Tufts	1 sp.																						
4. Vine (climbing/trailing)																					✓		
5. Rhizomes Present																							
6. Latex Present																	✓	✓	✓				
7. Plant Armed																			✓			✓	✓
8. Woody/Suffr./Herb.	W/H	W	W	W	W	W	W	W	W	W	W	W	W	W	W	W	W	W	W	H	H	H	H
9. Evergreen																							
10. Plant Pubscent/Glabrous	P/G	G	G	P	P/G	G	G	G	G	P/G	P/G	P/G	G	P/G	P/G	P	P/G	G	P	G	P/G	P/G	
11. Lvs Alt./Opp./Sub./Wh.	A/O	A	A	A	A	A	A	A	A	A/O	A	A	A	A	A	A	A	A	A/O	O	O	O	
12. Lvs Simple/Compound	S	S	S	C	C	C	S	S	S	S	S	S	S	S	S	S	S	S	S	S	S	S	S
13. Lvs Cmpnd. (pinn./palm.)					Pi	Pi													Pa				
14. Lvs Lobed/Toothed/Sin./Ent.	T/E	L/T	L	T	T	T	T	T	T	T	T	T	L/T	T	T	L/T	L/T	E	T	L/T	T	T	T
15. Lvs Sessile/Petioled	P	P	P	P	P	P	P	P	P	P	P	P	P	P	P	P	P	P	P	P	P	P	
16. Lvs Stipulate	✓	✓	✓	✓	✓	✓	✓	✓	✓	✓	✓	✓	✓	✓	✓	✓	✓	✓	✓	✓	✓	✓	✓
17. Lvs Basal/Cauline	C	C	C	C	C	C	C	C	C	C	C	C	C	C	C	C	C	C	C	C	C	C	
18. Lvs Red./Modified																							
19. Lvs Sheathing																							
20. Plant Her./M/D/P/Prm/Pd	D	D	M/D	M	M	M	M	M	M	M	M	M	M	M/P	M/P	D	M/D	D	D	D	M	M/D	M/D
21. Inflorescence Type	Cat.	Cat.	Cat.	Cat.	Cat.	Cat.	Cat.	Cat.	Cat.	Cat.	Cat.	Cat.	Cat.	F	F	Cat./H	Cat.	H	P/S	P/S	Cy	P/S	
22. Flwrs. Bracteate/Ebrac.	B	B	B	B	B	B	B	B	B	B	B	B	B	B	E	E	E	E	B	B	E	E	E
23. Flwrs./Infl. Axil./Term.	A	A	A	A/T	A/T	A/T	A/T	A/T	T	A/T	A	A	A	A	A	A	A	A	A	A/T	A/T	A	A

24. Calyx/Corolla		Cl	Cl								Cl					Cl	Cl	Cl	Cl	Cl	Cl	Cl	Cl	Cl
25. Flwrs. Regular/Irreg.		S	S	S	I	I	I	I	I	I	I	I	S	S	S	S	S	I	I
26. Ovary Sup./Inf./Hlf Inf.		S	S	S	I	I	I	I	I	I	S	S	S	S	S	S	S	I	I
27. Ovary Lobed																			
28. Per. Parts Equal/Uneq.										U	U							U	U
29. Flwr. Color																			
30. Per. United/Sep.		U	U			U	U	U	U	U	U							
31. No. sepals/Petals/or Lobes		4	2-3	2	2	4	4·d	4-8	4-8	4-8	5	4	4	2	1	1	5	5	4
32. No. Styles/Stigmas/St. Lobes		2	2	1	1	2	2	3-6	3-6	3-6	2	2	2	1	2	2	2	1	1
33. No. Carpels		1	1	1	1	1	1	1	1	1	2	1	2	1	2	2	1	1	1
34. No. Locules		1	2-4	2	2	2	2	3	6	3	6	3	2	1	1	1	1	1	1
35. Carpels United/Separate																			
36. No. Stamens/Anthers		2-8	5-00	8-40	3-8	2-10	2-10	4	4	8-16	$\frac{12}{20}$	3-12	3-9	3-9	4	4	5	5	4
37. Stamens Hypog./Perig.																			
38. Stamens United/Sep.		S	S	S	S	S	S	S	S	S	S	S	S	S	S	S	S	S	A
39. Fruit Type		C/2-4	NI	N	N	N	NI	NI	N	N	N	N	N	Sa	D	A	A	A	A
40. Dehiscence S/L/C/P/I		$\frac{C/}{2-4}$	NI	N	N	N	NI												
41. Other Disting. Char.																			

Column distinguishing characteristics (diagonal labels, left to right):
1 herb. sp.; 1 sp. w. opp. lvs • 1 sp. w. lobed lvs • lvs are oblique at base • lvs oblique at base; forms witches brm. • multiple fruit • multiple fruit • multiple fruit • stinging hairs • stinging hairs • stinging hairs

Diagnostic Characteristics	Parietaria	Pilea	Boehmeria	Comandra	Geocaulon	Arceuthobium	Asarum	Aristolochia	Oxyria	Polygonella	Rumex	Fagopyrum	Polygonum	Salicornia	Atriplex	Salsola	Corispermum	Axyris	Bassia	Kochia	Suaeda	Chenopodium	Cycloloma
1. Plant Aquatic												✓–	✓–										
2. Epiphyte/Parasite				✓	✓	✓																	
3. Fl. Repl. by Bulbl./Leafy Tufts						✓						1 sp											
4. Vine (climbing/trailing)						✓	✓	✓				✓–	✓–										
5. Rhizomes Present				✓	✓	✓	✓	✓		✓													
6. Latex Present																							
7. Plant Armed												✓			✓								
8. Woody/Suffr./Herb.	H	H	H	H	S	H	H	H	H	H	H	H	H	H	H	H	H	H	H	H	H	H	
9. Evergreen																							
10. Plant Pubscent/Glabrous	G	P/G	G	G	G	P	P/G	G	G	P/G	P	P/G	G	G	G	G	P	P	P	G	P/G	P/G	
11. Lvs Alt./Opp./Sub./Wh.	A	O	O	A	O	P	A	A	A	A	A	A	A	O	A	A	A	A	A	A	A	A	
12. Lvs Simple/Compound	S	S	S	S	S	S	S	S	S	S	S	S	S	S	S	S	S	S	S	S	S	S	
13. Lvs Cmpnd. (pinn./palm.)																							
14. Lvs Lobed/Toothed/Sin./Ent.	E	T	E	E	E	E	E	E	E	L,S/E	L/E	E	E	L,T/E	E	E	E	E	E	E	L,T/E	T	
15. Lvs Sessile/Petioled	P	P	P	P	P	P	P	P	P	P	P	P	P	S/P	S	S	P	S	S	S	P	P	
16. Lvs Stipulate		✓	✓							✓	✓	✓	✓										
17. Lvs Basal/Cauline	C	C	C	C	C	B	C	B	C	C	C	B/C	C	C	C	C	C	C	C	C	C	C	
18. Lvs Red./Modified						✓								✓									
19. Lvs Sheathing																							
20. Plant Her./M/D/P/Pm/Pd	M/P	M/D	H	P	D	H	H	H	H	H,D/P	H	H	H	M	H	H	M	H	H/P	H/P	H	H/P	
21. Inflorescence Type	Cy	P	P	C	So.	So.	Cl	P	P	P/R	Co/R	PR/Cl.	S	PS/Cl.	S	S/P	P/S	P/S	S/Cl.	So./S	PS/S	PS/Cl.	
22. Flwrs. Bracteate/Ebrac.	B	E	E	E	E	E	E	E	E	B	B	B/E	B/E	B/E	B	E	E	E	B	B	E	B	
23. Flwrs./Infl. Axil./Term.	A	A	T	A	A	A	A	T	T	A/T	A/T	A/T	A/T	A/T	A/T	A/T	T	A/T	A/T	A/T	T	T	

Taxon (41. Other Disting. Char.)	24. Calyx/Corolla	25. Flwrs. Reg./Irreg.	26. Ovary Sup./Inf./Hlf Inf.	27. Ovary Lobed	28. Per. Parts Equal/Uneq.	29. Flwr. Color	30. Per. United/Sep.	31. No. sepals/Petals/or Lobes	32. No. Styles/Stigmas/St. Lobes	33. No. Carpels	34. No. Locules	35. Carpels United/Separate	36. No. Stamens/Anthers	37. Stamens Hypog./Perig.	38. Stamens United/Sep.	39. Fruit Type	40. Dehiscence S/L/C/P/I
Continuous wing below calyx lobes	Cl	R	S		E		U	5	5	3	2-3		5	H	S	U	U
Sepals Keeled or winged in some spp.	Cl	R	S		E		U	2-5	2	2-3	2-3		5	H/P	S	U	U
Calyx lobes devel., horizontal wing	Cl	R	S		E	G/W	U	3-5	3-5	2-3	2-3		3-5	H	S	U	U
Calyx tubercles or spines	Cl	R	S		E	G/Pi	U	2	2	2	2-3		1-2	H/P	S	U	U
Fruit winged	Cl	R	S		E	G/Pi	U	2	6	2-4	2-4		5	H	S	U	U
Bracts and lvs. spinose	Cl	R	S		E	G/Pi	U	3	6	3	2-4		5	H/P	S	U	U
Pl. mealy/scurfy; lower lvs. opp.	Cl	R	S		U	W/R	U	5	5	6	6	U	8	P	S	A	A
Flwrs. imbedded in pits	Cl	R	S		U	G/R	S	4	5	8	8	U	8	P	S	A	A
3 inner sepals modified into valves	Cl	R	S		U	M	S	4	6	8	6	U	6	P	S	A	A
Buds covered by petiole bases	Cl	R	I	I	E	M	U	2-4	12	6	6	U	12	U	U	B	C
Parasitic on branches of conifers	Cl	R	I	I	E		U	2-4	1	1	1	U	5	U	S	B	B
Root parasite	Cl	S	S			G/W		1	1	1	1		4	S	S	A	D
Root parasitic; anthers att. to cal. by hairs	Cl	S	S			G/W		3-4	1	1	1		4	S	S	A	A

Diagnostic Characteristics	Monolepis	Amaranthus	Froelichia	Celosia	Mirabilis	Phytolacca	Mollugo	Sesuvium	Tetragonia	Talinum	Portulaca	Claytonia	Montia	Agrostemma	Scleranthus	Dianthus	Gypsophila	Vaccaria	Saponaria	Lychnis	Silene	Corrigiola	Spergula
1. Plant Aquatic													✓										
2. Epiphyte/Parasite																							
3. Fl. Repl. by Bulbl./Leafy Tufts																							
4. Vine (climbing/trailing)																							
5. Rhizomes Present																							
6. Latex Present																							
7. Plant Armed	✓																						
8. Woody/Suffr./Herb.	H	H	H	H	S	H	H	H	H	H	H	H	H	H	H	H	H	H	H	H	H	H	H
9. Evergreen																							
10. Plant Pubscent/Glabrous	G	P	G	P/G	G	G	G	P	G	P/G	G	G	P	P/G	G	P/G	G	G	G	P/G	G	P/G	P/G
11. Lvs Alt./Opp./Sub./Wh.	A	A	A	A	O	A	W	O	A	A/O	O	O	O	O	O	O	O	O	O	O/W	A	A	W
12. Lvs Simple/Compound	S	S	S	S	S	S	S	S	S	S	S	S	S	S	S	S	S	S	S	S	S	S	S
13. Lvs Cmpnd. (pinn./palm.)																							
14. Lvs Lobed/Toothed/Sin./Ent.	T/E	E	E	E	E	E	E	E	E	E	E	E	E	E	E	E	E	E	E	E	E	E	E
15. Lvs Sessile/Petioled	S/P	S/P	P	S/P	P	S/P	S/P	P	S	S/P	S/P	P	S	S	S	S	S	S/P	S/P	S/P	S	S	S
16. Lvs Stipulate																						✓	✓
17. Lvs Basal/Cauline	C	C	C	C	C	C	C	C	C	C	B/C	C	C	C	C	B/C	B/C	B/C	B/C	B/C	C	C	C
18. Lvs Red./Modified																							
19. Lvs Sheathing																							
20. Plant Her./M/D/P/Pm/Pd	H (M,D,P)	H	H	H	H	H	H	H	H	H	H	H	H	H	H	H	H	H	H	H	H	H	H
21. Inflorescence Type	S/Cl	S	S	P/Cy	R	Cy	So/Cl	So/Cl	Cy	So/Cl	R	So/Cl	So	So/Cy	So/Cy	So/Cy	Cy	Cy	Cy	So/Cy	Cy	Cy	Cy
22. Flwrs. Bracteate/Ebrac.	B	B	B	B	B	B	E	E	B	B	B	B	E	E	B	B	B	B	B	B	B	B	B
23. Flwrs./Infl. Axil./Term.	A/T	A/T	T	A/T	T	A/T	A	A	T	T	T	A	A	A/T	T	A/T	T	A/T	A/T	A/T	T	T	T

24. Calyx/Corolla	CC	CC	CC	CC	CC	CC	CC	CC	CC	CC	CC	CC	CC	CC	Cl	Cl	Cl	Cl	Cl	Cl	Cl	Cl
25. Flwrs. Regular/Irreg.	R	R	R	R	R	R	R	R	R	R	R	R	R	R	R	R	R	R	R	R	R	R
26. Ovary Sup./Inf./Hlf Inf.	S	S	S	S	S	S	S	C	C	S	S	HI	C	C	S	S	S	S	S	S	S	S
27. Ovary Lobed																						
28. Per. Parts Equal/Uneq.	E	E	E	E	E	E	E	E	U	E	E	E	E	E	E	E	E	E	E	E	E	U
29. Flwr. Color	W	W	W/Pi	W/R	Pl	W/Pi/W	W/R	R	W	V	P	P/W	G	Pi	W/Pi/G/W	G	V	Pl	V	Pi	V	G/Pi
30. Per. United/Sep.	S	S	CoS	CoS	U/S	U/S	U/S	U	S	U	S	S	U/B	S	U/B	S	U	S	U	S	U	S
31. No. sepals/Petals/or Lobes	5/5	5/5	5/5	5/5	5/5	5/5	5/5	2/3	2/5	2/3	2/5	2/5	4	5	5	5	5	5	5	5	5	0-5
32. No. Styles/Stigmas/St. Lobes	5	3	3	3	2	2	2	3	3	3	3	3	2-8	3	5-12	3	1	1	1	5	3	3
33. No. Carpels	5	3	3	3	2	2	2	2-3	2-3	2-3	2-3	2-3	2-8	3	5-12	3	2-3	1	2-3	5	2-3	2-3
34. No. Locules	1	1	1-3	1-3	1/2-4	1	1	1	1	1	1	1	2-8	3	5-12	3	1	1	1	1	1	1
35. Carpels United/Separate	U	U	U	U	U/S	U	U	U	U	U	U	U	S	S	U/S	S	U	U	U	S	U	U
36. No. Stamens/Anthers	U	5	10	10	10	5-10	10	3	5	10	5	10-20	6-00	3	5-30	3	5	5	1	3-5	5	5
37. Stamens Hypog./Perig.	H	P	P	P	P	P	P	P	P	P	P	P		H	H	H	H	H	H	H	H	H
38. Stamens United/Sep.	S	S	S	S	S	S	S	S	S	S	S	S	U	S	U/B	S	U/B	U	S	S	U/B	S
39. Fruit Type	C	U	C	C	C	C	C	C	C	C	C	L	U	C	B	C	A	U	U	C	U	C
40. Dehiscence S/L/C/P/I	C								L	L	L	I			L							
41. Other Disting. Char.																						

Diagonal labels (Other Distinguishing Characteristics):
- Single sepal
- Calyx woolly, bearing spines
- Flowers subtended by 5-lobed involucre
- Carpels in a ring
- Calyx lobes with horn near apex
- Fruit indehiscent and tubercled
- Lvs subterete, clustered near base
- Sepals united into an indurated tube
- Calyx winged in fruit; per. long-clawed
- Petals long - clawed
- Capsule dehiscent by 5 teeth
- Capsule dehiscent by 6-10 teeth

Diagnostic Characteristics

Diagnostic Characteristics	Holosteum	Herniaria	Paronychia	Spergularia	Cerastium	Myosoton	Stellaria	Honckenya	Sagina	Minuartia	Arenaria	Moehringia	Ceratophyllum	Cabomba	Brasenia	Nelumbo	Nuphar	Nymphaea	Coptis	Hepatica	Clematis	Thalictrum	Anemone
1. Plant Aquatic													√	√	√	√	√	√					
2. Epiphyte/Parasite																				√			
3. Fl. Repl. by Bulbl./Leafy Tufts																							
4. Vine (climbing/trailing)																					√		
5. Rhizomes Present							√							√	√	√	√	√	√			√	
6. Latex Present																			√				
7. Plant Armed																							
8. Woody/Suffr./Herb.	H	H	H	H	H	H	H	H	H	H	H	H	H	H	H	H	H	H	H	H	W	H	H
9. Evergreen																		√	√	√			
10. Plant Pubscent/Glabrous	P	P/G	P/G	P	P	P	G	P/G	P/G	P	P	G	G	G	G	G	P/G	P/G	P	P/G	P/G	G	G
11. Lvs Alt./Opp./Sub./Wh.	O	O	O	O	O	O	O	O	O	O	O	W	A/O	A	A	A	A	A		O	A,O,W	A,O/O,W	
12. Lvs Simple/Compound	S	S	S	S	S	S	S	S	S	S	S	C	C	S	S	S	S	C	S	C	C	C	
13. Lvs Cmpnd. (pinn./palm.)													Pa					Pa		Pv/Pa	Pv/Pa	Pa	
14. Lvs Lobed/Toothed/Sin./Ent.	E	E	E	E	E	E	E	E	E	E	E	E		E	E	E	L/E	L/E	L	L	L	L/T	L/T
15. Lvs Sessile/Petioled	S	S	S	S/P	S/P	S/P	S	S	S	S	S/P	S	P	P	P	P	P	P	P	P	S/P	S/P	
16. Lvs Stipulate	√	√	√																				
17. Lvs Basal/Cauline	B/C	C	C	C	C	C	C	C	C	C	C	C	C	B	B	B	B	B	B	C	B/C	B/C	
18. Lvs Red./Modified																							
19. Lvs Sheathing																							
20. Plant Her./M/D/P/Pm/Pd	U	H	H	H	H	H	H	H	H	H	H	M	H	H	H	H	H	H	H	H	H/D	H	H
21. Inflorescence Type	Cy	Cy	Cy	Cy	Cy	Cy	So.	So./Cy	So./Cy	P/Cy	So./Cy	So.	So.	So.	So.	So.	So.	So.	So.	So./Cy	P	So.	
22. Flwrs. Bracteate/Ebrac.	B	B	B	B	B	B	E	E	B	B	B	B	E	E	E	E	E	B	B	B	B	B	
23. Flwrs./Infl. Axil./Term.	T	A	T	T	T	A/T	A/T	A/T	T	T	A/T	A	A	A	A	A	A	A	T	T	A	T	T

24.	Calyx/Corolla	CC	Cl	CC	CC	CC	CC	CC	CC	CC	CC	CC	CC/C	CC	CC	CC	CC	CC	CC	CC	CC	CC	CC	Cl	Cl	Cl	Cl	Cl
25.	Flwrs. Regular/Irreg.	R	R	R	R	R	R	R	R	R	R	R	R	R	R	R	R	R	R	R	R	R	R	R	R	R	R	R
26.	Ovary Sup./Inf./Hlf Inf.	S	S	S	S	S	S	S	S	S	S	S	S	S	S	S	S	S	S	S	S	S	S	S	S	S	S	S
27.	Ovary Lobed															R												
28.	Per. Parts Equal/Uneq.	E	E	E	E	E	E	E	E	E	E	E	E	E	E	E	E	E	E	E	E	E	E	E	E	E	E	E
29.	Flwr. Color	W	G	W/Pi	W	W	W	W	W	W	W	W	Pu	W/Y		Pu	Y	Y	W/Pi	W	Pu	Pi/Pu	W	Pi/Pu	W	W/Pu	Pu	W/GR
30.	Per. United/Sep.	S	S	S	S	S	S	S	S	S	S	S	S	S	S	S	S	S	S	S	S	S	S	S	S	S	S	S
31.	No. sepals/Petals/or Lobes	5/5	5/0	5/5	5/5	5/5	5/3	4-5/4-5	5/5	5/5	5/5	5/5	3/3	3-4/3-4		3/3	00	5-6/00	4-00	4-00	5-7/0	5-12/0	4/0	4/0	4-5/0	4-00/0		
32.	No. Styles/Stigmas/St. Lobes	3	2	3	5	5	3-5	4-5	3	3	3	3	2-4	2-4	1	2-4		00			1	1	1	1	1	1		
33.	No. Carpels	3	2	3	5	5	3-5	4-5	3	3	3	3	2-4	2-4	1	2-4	00	00	00	00	3-9	00	00	00	00	00		
34.	No. Locules	1	1	1	1	1	3-5	1	1	1	1	1	2-4	2-4	1	2-4	00	00	00	00	1	1	1	1	1	1		
35.	Carpels United/Separate	U	U	U	U	U	U	U	U	U	U	U	S	S	S	S	S	S	S	S	S	S	S	S	S	S		
36.	No. Stamens/Anthers	3-5	5	2-10	10	10	10	4-5	10	10	10	10	3-6	12-18	10-30	3-6	00	00	00	00	00	00	00	00	00	00		
37.	Stamens Hypog./Perig.	H	P	P	H	H	H	H	H	H	H	H	S	S	H	S	H	H	H	H	H	H	H	H	H	H		
38.	Stamens United/Sep.	S	S	S	S	S	S	S	S	S	S	S	S	S	S	S	S	S	S	S	S	S	S	S	S	S		
39.	Fruit Type	C	C	C	C	C	C	C	C	C	C	C	U	U	A	C	B	B	B	B	F	A	A	A	A	A		
40.	Dehiscence S/L/C/P/I	C	C	U	C	C	C	C	C	C	C	C	I	I	A													
41.	Other Disting. Char.																											

Row 41 — Other Distinguishing Characteristics (by column, from left to right):
- Petals jagged on margin
- Petals 2-cleft
- Petals 2-cleft
- Petals 2-cleft
- Fleshy; per. & stamens on a 10 lobed dis.
- Leaves linear
- Lvs 1 - several times dichot. divided
- Seed with a strophiole
- Leaves peltate
- Leaves peltate, emersed
- Ovary crowned with stigmatic disc
- Ovary crowned with incurved stigmas

Diagnostic Characteristics	Consolida	Aconitum	Xanthorhiza	Hydrastis	Aquilegia	Actaea	Cimicifuga	Ranunculus	Trollius	Caltha	Berberis	Caulophyllum	Podophyllum	Akebia	Menispermum	Liriodendron	Magnolia	Calycanthus	Sassafras	Lindera	Argemone	Sanguinaria	Macleaya
1. Plant Aquatic																							
2. Epiphyte/Parasite																							
3. Fl. Repl. by Bulbl./Leafy Tufts																							
4. Vine (climbing/trailing)													✓	✓	✓								
5. Rhizomes Present			✓				✓					✓	✓						✓		✓		
6. Latex Present											✓									✓	✓	✓	
7. Plant Armed										✓										✓	✓	✓	
8. Woody/Suffr./Herb.	H	W	H	H	H	H	H	H	H	W	H	H	W	W	W	W	W	W	W	W	H	H	H
9. Evergreen																							
10. Plant Pubscent/Glabrous	A	G	P	A	P/G	G	P/G	G	A	G	G	G	A	A	A	A	A	O	A	A	G	G	
11. Lvs Alt./Opp./Sub./Wh.	A	A	A	A	A	A	A	A	A	A	A	A	O	A	A	A	A	O	A	A	A	A	
12. Lvs Simple/Compound	C	C	S	S	C	C	S/C	C	S	S	C	C	C	C	S	S	S	S	S	S	S	S	
13. Lvs Cmpnd. (pinn./palm.)	Pa	Pi		Pa	Pa	Pa	Pa	Pa			Pa	Pa	Pa										
14. Lvs Lobed/Toothed/Sin./Ent.		L/T	L/T	L	L/T	L/T	L,T/E	L,T	E	T/E	L	L	E	L	L	L	E	L	E	L/T	L/T	L/T	
15. Lvs Sessile/Petioled	S/P	P	S/P	P	P	P	S/P	S/P	S/P	P	P	P	P	P	P	P	P	P	P	P	P	P	
16. Lvs Stipulate	C	C	B/C	B/C	C	C	C	B/C	B/C	C		B/C	C	C	C	✓	C	C	C	C	C	C	
17. Lvs Basal/Cauline	C	C	B/C	B/C	C	C	B/C	B/C	C	C	C	B/C	C	C	C	C	C	C	C	C	B	C	
18. Lvs Red./Modified																							
19. Lvs Sheathing																							
20. Plant Her./M/D/P/Prm/Pd	H	H	H	H	H	H	H	H	H	H	H	H	M	D	H	H	H	D	P/D	H	H	H	
21. Inflorescence Type	R	R/P	So.	S	R	P/R	So./Cy	S	R,U So.	So.	P	So.	R	P	So.	So.	So.	R	Cl.	So./Cy.	So.	P	
22. Flwrs. Bracteate/Ebrac.	B	B	B	B	E	E	B/E	E	B	B	B	B	B	B	B	P	P	B	B	B	B		
23. Flwrs./Infl. Axil./Term.	T	T	T	T	T	T	T	T	A/T	A	T	T	A	A	A/T	T	T	A/T	A	T	T	A/T	

This is a dense, rotated diagnostic chart. The characteristics (rows 24–41) are listed at the left; the 20 taxon columns are identified by the slanted descriptions at the right (legend below). Best-effort reading of the data grid:

#	Characteristic	Data (20 taxon columns, left → right)
24	Calyx/Corolla	CC, CC, Cl, CC, CC, CC, CC, CC, CC, Cl, CC, CC, CC, Cl, CC, T, T, T, Cc, CC
25	Flwrs. Regular/Irreg.	I, I, R, R, R, R, R, R, R, R, R, R, R, R, R, R, R, R, R, R
26	Ovary Sup./Inf./Hlf Inf.	S, S, S, S, S, S, S, S, S, S, S, S, S, S, S, S, S, S, S, S
27	Ovary Lobed	U, , , , , , , , , , , , , , , , , , , E
28	Per. Parts Equal/Uneq.	U, U, U, U, E, E, E, E, E, E, E, E, E, E, E, E, E, E, U, E
29	Flwr. Color	W/PU, B/PU, M, WG, V, W, W/Y, G/Y, Y, G/Y, W, Pu, G/W, G/Y, G/Y, M, Y, Y, W/Pi, c
30	Per. United/Sep.	Cl S, S, S, S, S, S, S, S, S, S, S, S, S, S, S, S, S, S, S, S
31	No. sepals/Petals/or Lobes	5/2, 5/2, 5/0, 3/0, 5/5, 4-10/4-10, 4-5/0, 5/5, 4-15/0, 5-9/0, 6/6, 6/6, 6/9, 3, 4-8/4-8, 3/6, 3/6-9, 3/3, 2-3/4-6, 2/8-12
32	No. Styles/Stigmas/St. Lobes	1, 1, 1, 2, 1, 2, 1, 1, 1, 1, 1, 1, 1, 1, 1, 1, 1, 1, 1, 1
33	No. Carpels	1, 5, 5-10, 1, 1, 1, 00, 00, 1, 5-10, 1, 3, 1, 1, 2-4, 00, 00, 1, 4-6, 2
34	No. Locules	1, 1, 1, 1, 1, 1, 1, 1, 1, 5-10, 1, 1, 1, 1, 1, 1, 1, 1, 1-2, 2
35	Carpels United/Separate	S, S, S, S, S, S, S, S, S, S, S, S, S, S, S, S, S, S, S, S
36	No. Stamens/Anthers	00, 00, 5-10, 00, 00, 00, 00, 00, 6, 6, 6, 12-18, 12-24, 00, 8, 00, 9, 9, 00, 00
37	Stamens Hypog./Perig.	H, H, H, H, H, H, H, H, H, H, H, H, H, H, H, H, P, P, H, H
38	Stamens United/Sep.	S, S, S, S, S, S, S, S, S, S, S, S, S, S, S, S, S, S, S, S
39	Fruit Type	F, F, B, B, F, F, F, Se, B, F, F, F, D, Sa, D, F, D, D, C,
40	Dehiscence S/L/C/P/I	, , , , , , , , , , , I, , , , , , , ,
41	Other Disting. Char.	

Taxon column descriptions (slanted headers, as printed):

- Tall coarse plant
- Plant with red juice; fl. scapose
- Prickly with yellow juice
- Aromatic; fl. in umbellate clusters
- Aromatic; fl. in umbelled racemes
- Flowers perigynous; fr. a pseudocarp
- Vine with lobed leaves
- Vine with compound leaves
- Lg. peltate lvs; yellow berry
- Lvs triternately cmpnd; seeds naked
- Armed w/1-3 spines subt. short roots
- Flowers have many staminodes
- Flowers have many staminodes
- Sepals and petals falling early
- Petals prolonged into spur
- 2 petals united into 1

Diagnostic Characteristics	Glaucium	Chelidonium	Papaver	Dicentra	Adlumia	Fumaria	Corydalis	Sinapis	Brassica	Erucastrum	Diplotaxis	Eruca	Raphanus	Rapistrum	Cakile	Conringia	Lepidium	Coronopus	Cardaria	Isatis	Thlaspi	Teesdalia	Iberis
1. Plant Aquatic																							
2. Epiphyte/Parasite																							
3. Fl. Repl. by Bulbl./Leafy Tufts																							
4. Vine (climbing/trailing)					√																		
5. Rhizomes Present	√	√	√	√	√	√	√											√					
6. Latex Present	√	√	√	√	√	√																	
7. Plant Armed																							
8. Woody/Suffr./Herb.	H	H	H	H	H	H	H	H	H	H	H	H	H	H	H	H	H	H	H	H	H	H	H
9. Evergreen																							
10. Plant Pubscent/Glabrous	P	P/G	G	G	G	G	P/G	P/G	P/G	P/G	P/G	P	P/G	G	G	G	P/G	P	G	G	G	G	G
11. Lvs Alt./Opp./Sub./Wh.	A	A	A	A	A	A	A	A	A	A	A	A	A	A	A	A	A	A	A	A	A	A	A
12. Lvs Simple/Compound	S	S	Pi/Pa	Pi/Pa	Pi	Pi	S	S	S	S	S	S	S	S	S	S	S	S	S	S	S	S	S
13. Lvs Cmpnd. (pinn./palm.)																							
14. Lvs Lobed/Toothed/Sin./Ent.	L/T	L/T	L/T	L/T	L/T	L/T	L/T	L/T	L/T	L/T	L/T	L/T	L/T	L/T	E	E	L/T	T/E	E	T/E	L/T	T/E	T/E
15. Lvs Sessile/Petioled	P/S	P/S	P	P	P	S/P	S/P	S/P	S/P	P	S/P	S/P	S/P	S/P	S	S	S/P	S/P	S	S	S	S/P	S/P
16. Lvs Stipulate																							
17. Lvs Basal/Cauline	B/C	B/C	B	C	C	C	C	C	C	B/C	C	C	C	C	C	C	B/C	C	B/C	B/C	B/C	B/C	B/C
18. Lvs Red./Modified																							
19. Lvs Sheathing																							
20. Plant Her./M/D/P/Pm/Pd	H	H	H	H	H	H	H	H	H	H	H	H	H	H	H	H	H	H	H	H	H	H	H
21. Inflorescence Type	So.	U	P/R	R	R	P/R	R	R	R	R	R	R	R	R	R	R	R	Co./R	Co./R	R	R	R	R
22. Flwrs. Bracteate/Ebrac.			B	B	B	B	E	E	B/E	E	E	E	E	E	E	E	E	E	E	E	E	E	E
23. Flwrs./Infl. Axil./Term.	A/T	T	T	A	A/T	A/T	T	T	T	T	T	T	T	T	T	T	A	T	T	T	T	T	T

Column key (left → right):

1. Plant with yellow juice
2. Yellow juice; lvs. pinnatid
3. White juice; lvs pinnatifid
4. Corolla 2-spurred; st. didynamous
5. Corolla bigibbous; st. didynamous
6. Corolla 1-spurred; st. didynamous
7. Corolla 1-saccate; st. didynamous
8. Silique torulose, beaked
9. Silique torulose, beaked
10. Silique 4-angled, torulose, beaked
11. Silique flattened
12. Silique with long, flat beak
13. Fruit 2-jointed, upper joint ind.
14. Fruit 2-jointed, both joints ind.
15. Fruit inflated
16. Lvs. auriculate
17. Lvs. auriculate; fruit winged

Characteristic	1	2	3	4	5	6	7	8	9	10	11	12	13	14	15	16	17
24. Calyx/Corolla	cc	cc	cc	cc	cc	cv/cc	cc	cc	cc	cc	cc	cc	cc	cc	cc	cc	cc
25. Flwrs. Regular/Irreg.	R	R	R	R	R	R	R	I	R	R	R	R	R	R	R	R	R
26. Ovary Sup./Inf./Hlf Inf.	S	S	S	S	S	S	S	S	S	S	S	S	S	S	S	S	S
27. Ovary Lobed				U	U	U	U										U
28. Per. Parts Equal/Uneq.	E	E	E	U	U	U	U	E	E	E	E	E	E	E	E	E	U
29. Flwr. Color	Y	W,R/Pu	W,Pu/Pi	Y	Pu	V	Pi/Y	Y	Y	Y/W	Y/W	W	W	W/Y	W	Y	V
30. Per.United/Sep.	S	S	S	U	U	U	U	S	S	S	S	S	S	S	S	S	S
31. No. sepals/Petals/or Lobes	2/4	2/4	2/4	2/4	2/4	2/4	2/4	4/4	4/4	4/4	4/4	4/4	4/4	4/4	4/4	4/4	4/4
32. No. Styles/Stigmas/St. Lobes		1	1	1	1	1	1	1	1	1	1	1	1	1	1	1	1
33. No. Carpels	2	4-00	2	2	2	2	2	2	2	2	2	2	2	2	2	2	2
34. No. Locules	2		2	1	1	1	1	2	2	2	2	1	2	2	2	2	2
35. Carpels United/Separate	S	S	S	U	U	U	U	S	S	S	S	S	S	S	S	S	S
36. No. Stamens/Anthers	00	00	6	6	6	6	6	6	6	6	6	6	6	6	2-6	6	6
37. Stamens Hypog./Perig.	H	H	H	H	H	H	H	H	H	H	H	H	H	H	H	H	H
38. Stamens United/Sep.	S	S	U	U	U	U	U	S	S	S	S	S	S	S	S	S	S
39. Fruit Type	C	C	C	C	C	N	C	Sq	Sq	Sq	Sq	Sq	Sq	Sq	Sl	Sl	Sl
40. Dehiscence S/L/C/P/I		P		I				I	I	I	I	I	I			I	I
41. Other Disting. Char.																	

Diagnostic Characteristics	Capsella	Subularia	Neslia	Bunias	Lunaria	Alyssum	Lobularia	Berteroa	Armoracea	Cardamine	Draba	Arabis	Rorippa	Barbarea	Hesperis	Erysimum	Alliaria	Sisymbrium	Braya	Arabidopsis	Camelina	Descurania	Polanisia
1. Plant Aquatic	✓							✓	✓	✓		✓											
2. Epiphyte/Parasite																							
3. Fl. Repl. by Bulbl./Leafy Tufts																							
4. Vine (climbing/trailing)																							
5. Rhizomes Present									✓	✓		✓											
6. Latex Present										✓													
7. Plant Armed																							
8. Woody/Suffr./Herb.	H	H	H	H	H	H	H	H	H	H	H	H	H	H	H	H	H	H	H	H	H	H	
9. Evergreen																							
10. Plant Pubscent/Glabrous	P/G	P	P/G	P/G	P	P	P	G	P/G	P/G	P/G	P/G	G	P	P	G	P/G	P	P	P/G	P	P	
11. Lvs Alt./Opp./Sub./Wh.	A	A	A	A/O	A	A	A	A	A,O/W	A/O	A	A	A	A	A	A	A	A	A	A	A	A	
12. Lvs Simple/Compound	S	S	S	S	S	S	S	S	S	S	S	S	S	S	S	S	S	S	S	S	C	S	
13. Lvs Cmpnd. (pinn./palm.)								Pi	Pi/Pa			Pi/Pi	Pi/Pi									Pi	
14. Lvs Lobed/Toothed/Sin./Ent.	L/T B	T/E	L/T	T	E	E	E	L/T B	L/T B	T/E	L/T B	L/T B	L/T B	T	T/E	T	L/T B	T/E	T/E	T/E		E	
15. Lvs Sessile/Petioled	S/P	S	S/P	S/P	S/P	S/P	S/P	S/P	S/P	S/P	S/P	S/P	S/P	S/P	S/P	S/P	S/P	S/P	S/P	S/P	S/P	S/P	
16. Lvs Stipulate																							
17. Lvs Basal/Cauline	B/C	C	B/C	C	C	C	C	C	B/C	B/C	B/C	B/C	B/C	C	C	B/C	B/C	B/C	B/C	B/C	B/C	C	
18. Lvs Red./Modified	B																						
19. Lvs Sheathing																							
20. Plant Her./M/D/P/Prn/Pd	H	H	H	H	H	H	H	H	H	H	H	H	H	H	H	H	H	H	H	H	H	H	
21. Inflorescence Type	R	R	R	R	R	R	R	R	R Co.	R	R	RP Co.	R	R	R	R	R	R	R	R	R	R	
22. Flwrs. Bracteate/Ebrac.	E	E	E	E	E	E	E	E	E	E	E	E	E	E	E	E	E	E	E	E	E	B	
23. Flwrs./Infl. Axil./Term.	T	T	T	T	T	T	T	A/T	T	T	T	T	T	T	T	T	T	T	T	T	T	T	

	1	2	3	4	5	6	7	8	9	10	11	12	13	14	15	16	17	18	19	20	21
24. Calyx/Corolla	CC	CC	CC	CC	CC	CC	CC	CC	CC	CC	CC/D	CC	CC	CC	CC	CC	CC	CC	CC	CC	CC
25. Flwrs. Regular/Irreg.	R	R	R	R	R	R	R	R	R	R	R	R	R	R	R	R	R	R	R	R	R
26. Ovary Sup./Inf./Hlf Inf.	S	S	S	S	S	S	S	S	S	S	S	S	S	S	S	S	S	S	S	S	S
27. Ovary Lobed																					
28. Per. Parts Equal/Uneq.	E	E	E	E	E	E	E	E	E	E	E	E	E	E	E	E	E	E	E	E	E
29. Flwr. Color	W	Y	Pu.	W/Y	Y	W/Y	W	W	W	W	W	V	W/Y	Y	Pi/Pa	Y	W	W/Pi	W	Y	W/Pi
30. Per. United/Sep.	S	S	S	S	S	S	S	S	S	S	S	S	S	S	S	S	S	S	S	S	S
31. No. sepals/Petals/or Lobes	4/4	4/4	4/4	4/4	4/4	4/4	4/4	4/4	4/4	4/4	4/0-4	4/0-4	4/4	4/4	4/4	4/4	4/4	4/4	4/4	4/4	4/4
32. No. Styles/Stigmas/St. Lobes	1	1	1	1	1	1	1	1	1	1	1	1	1	1	1	1	1	1	1	1	1
33. No. Carpels	2	2	2	2	2	2	2	2	2	2	2	2	2	2	2	2	2	2	2	2	2
34. No. Locules	2	2	2	2	2	2	2	2	1/2	2	2	2	2	2	2	2	2	2	2	2	1
35. Carpels United/Separate	S	U	S	S	S	S	S	S	U/S	S	S	S	S	S	S	S	S	S	S	S	U
36. No. Stamens/Anthers	6	6	6	6	6	6	6	6	6	6 or √	6	6	6	6	6	6	6	6	6	6	8-00
37. Stamens Hypog./Perig.	H	H	H	H	H	H	H	H	H	H	H	H	H	H	H	H	H	H	H	H	H
38. Stamens United/Sep.	S	S	S	S	S	S	S	S	S	S	S	S	S	S	S	S	S	S	S	S	S
39. Fruit Type	Sl	Sl	Sl	Sl	N	Sl	Sl	Sl	Sl	Sq	Sl	Sl	Sl/Sq	Sq	Sq	Sq	Sq	Sq	Sq	Sq	Sq
40. Dehiscence S/L/C/P/I	I	I																			
41. Other Disting. Char.	Fruit an obcordate silicle	Silicle inflated, septum purple	Silicle globose; lvs clasping	Fruit obliquely ovoid	Silicle large flat; lvs cordate	Pubescence stellate; lvs oblanceolate	Pubescence of forked hairs	Pubescence stellate; petals bifid	lvs. capillary dissected in 1 sp.	Basal rosettes produced in some spp.	Rosettes formed in all spp.	Rosettes in some spp.; lvs auriculate	Rosettes formed			Basal lvs. uniform; garlic odor	Rosettes formed	Rosettes formed; raceme open	Silicle pyriform	Lvs. 2-3 x pinnately compound	Glandular-pubescent; trifoliate

Diagnostic Characteristics	Cleome	Reseda	Saracenia	Drosera	Podostemum	Crassula	Penthorum	Sempervivum	Sedum	Astilbe	Saxifraga	Tiarella	Mitella	Heuchera	Parnassia	Chrysosplenium	Philadelphus	Hydrangea	Deutzia	Ribes	Liquidambar	Hamamelis	Platanus
1. Plant Aquatic			✓	✓	✓											✓							
2. Epiphyte/Parasite																							
3. Fl. Repl. by Bulbl./Leafy Tufts																							
4. Vine (climbing/trailing)																							
5. Rhizomes Present										✓	✓	✓	✓	✓	✓	✓							
6. Latex Present																							
7. Plant Armed	✓																			✓			
8. Woody/Suffr./Herb.	H	H	H	H	H	H	H	H	H	H	H	H	H	H	H	H	W	W	W	W	W	W	
9. Evergreen		✓						✓			✓												
10. Plant Pubscent/Glabrous	P/G	P	P	G	G	G	G	G	P	P	P	P	P	G	G	P/G	P/G	P	P/G	P/G	G	G	
11. Lvs Alt./Opp./Sub./Wh.	A	S	A	A	O	A	A	A,O/W	A,O	A/O	A/O	A/O			A/O	O	O/W	O/W	A	A	A	A	
12. Lvs Simple/Compound	S	S	S	S	S	S	S	S	S		S	S	S	S	S	S	S	S	S	S	S	S	
13. Lvs Cmpnd. (pinn./palm.)	Pi								Pa														
14. Lvs Lobed/Toothed/Sin./Ent.	T/E	E	E	E	E	E	T/E	T/E	T	L/T_R	L/T_R	L/T	L/T	E	L/T_R	T/E	L/T	T/E	L/T	L/T	L/T	L/T	
15. Lvs Sessile/Petioled	P	S	P	P	S	S/P	S/P	S	P	P	P	P	P	S/P	P	P	P	P	P	P	P	P	
16. Lvs Stipulate	✓	✓										✓							✓	✓	✓	✓	
17. Lvs Basal/Cauline	C	C	B/C	C	C	C	B/C	C	C	B/C	B	B	B	B/C	C	C	C	C	C	C	C	C	
18. Lvs Red./Modified			✓	✓	✓																		
19. Lvs Sheathing					✓																		
20. Plant Her./M/D/P/Pm/Pd	H	H	H	H	H	H	H	H/D	Pd	H	H	H	H	H	H	H	H	H	H	M	H/P	M	
21. Inflorescence Type	R	R/S	R	So.	So.	Cy	Cy	Co.P/Cy	Co.P/Cy	So.Cy	R	R	R	So.	So.Cy.	So.R.Cy.	Cy	Cy.P	So.R	R	Cl	H	
22. Flwrs. Bracteate/Ebrac.	B	B	B	E	E	B	B	B	B	B	B	B	B	B	B	B	B	B	B	B	B	B	
23. Flwrs./Infl. Axil./Term.	T	T	T	A	A	T	T	T	T	T	T	T	T	T	A/T	A/T	T	A/T	A	A/T	A	A	

Columns (taxa, left → right):
1. Gland.-pub.; stipular spines
2. Stamens borne on fleshy, 1-sided disc
3. Pitcher-shaped lvs.; stigmatic disc
4. Lvs. with stalked glands; 1-sided rac.
5. Plant attached by fleshy discs
6. Minute succulent; matted or tufted
7. Carpels united into 5-lobed capsule
8. Basal lvs. forming dense rosettes
9. Often succulent; most spp. escaped
10. Carpels separating in fruit
11. 2-connate carpels; bilobed ovary
12. Carpels unequal; ovary bilobed
13. Petals pinnatifid to fimbriate
14. Pet. smaller than sepals; stamens exsert.
15. Flowers with 5 staminodes
16. Flowers with 8-lobed disc
17. Infl. with outer fl. sterile
18. Fl. in axillary cymes & term. cymes
19. Petals smaller than calyx lobes
20. ♀ heads solitary, ♂ heads racemose
21. 4 staminodes; unequal leaf base

Characteristic	1	2	3	4	5	6	7	8	9	10	11	12	13	14	15	16	17	18	19	20	21
24. Calyx/Corolla	CC	CC	CC	CC	CC	CC	CC	Cl	CC	CC	CC/CC	CC	CC	CC	CC	CC	Cl	CC	CC	CC	CC
25. Flwrs. Regular/Irreg.	R	I	I	I	R	R	R	R	R	R	R	R	R	R	R	R	R	R	R	R	R
26. Ovary Sup./Inf./Hlf Inf.	S	S	S	S	S	S	S	S	S	S	S	I/R	S	S/HI	I	S	I	I	S	S	S
27. Ovary Lobed			✓	✓							✓		✓	✓	✓		✓				
28. Per. Parts Equal/Uneq.	E	U	U	U	E	E	E	E	E	E	E	E/U	E	E	E	E	E	E	E	E	E
29. Flwr. Color	W/Pi	V	V	V	V		W/G/Y	W/G/Y	Ro/Pu	V	W/Y	V	W	W/G	Pu	W	G/Y	W	W	V	Y
30. Per.United/Sep.	S	S	S	S	S	S	S	S	S	S	U	U	U	U	U	S	CoS	U	U	U	U
31. No. sepals/Petals/or Lobes	4/4	4-8/4-8	4/4	4-8/4-8	5/5	5/5	3-4/3-4	5	6-00/6-00	4-5/4-5	4-5/5	5/5	5/5	5/5	5/5	5/5	4/4	4-5/4-5	5/5	5/5	4/4
32. No. Styles/Stigmas/St. Lobes	1	1	3-6	1	3-5	2	1	1	1	2	2	2	2	2	2	4	4	2	3-5	2	2
33. No. Carpels	2	5	3-6	5	3-5	1	3-4	5	1	2	2	2	2	2	2	4	2	2	3-5	1	2
34. No. Locules	2	1	1	5	1	1	1	1	1	1	2	2	1	1	1	1	4	2	1	1	2
35. Carpels United/Separate	U	U	U	U	U	S	S	S	S	S	S	S	U	U	U	U	U	U	U	U	U
36. No. Stamens/Anthers	4-8	∞	∞	∞	5	2	3-4	10	∞	8-10	10	10	10	5-10	5	5	4-8	8-10	10	5	4
37. Stamens Hypog./Perig.	H	H	H	H	H	H	H	H	H	P	P	P	P	P	P	P	P	P	P	P	P
38. Stamens United/Sep.	S	S	S	S	S	S	S	S	S	S	S	S	S	S	S	S	S	S	S	S	S
39. Fruit Type	C	C	C	C	C	C	F	C	F	F	F	C/F	C	C	C	C	C	C	C	B	C
40. Dehiscence S/L/C/P/I	L	L	L	L	L	S	C	C	C				C	C			L	P			
41. Other Disting. Char.																					

Diagnostic Characteristics	Rhodotypos	Sorbaria	Sorbus	Aronia	Potentilla	Rosa	Rubus	Prunus	Physocarpus	Spiraea	Crataegus	Amelanchier	Malus & Pyrus	Agrimonia	Sanguisorba	Filipendula	Geum	Alchemilla	Duchesnea	Fragaria	Sibbaldia	Dalibarda	Waldsteinia
1. Plant Aquatic																✓							
2. Epiphyte/Parasite																							
3. Fl. Repl. by Bulbl./Leafy Tufts																							
4. Vine (climbing/trailing)					✓	✓	✓															✓	✓
5. Rhizomes Present		✓		✓	✓	✓	✓				✓			✓		✓	✓	✓	✓	✓	✓	✓	✓
6. Latex Present																							
7. Plant Armed					✓	✓	✓	✓			✓								✓				
8. Woody/Suffr./Herb.	W	W	W	W	H/W	H/W	W	W	W	W	W	W	W	H	H	H	H	H	H	H	H	H	H
9. Evergreen				✓																			
10. Plant Pubscent/Glabrous	G	G	P/G	P/G	P/G	P/G	P/G	P	P/G	P/G	P/G	P/G	P/G	G	P/G	P/G	P	P	P	P/G	P	P	P
11. Lvs Alt./Opp./Sub./Wh.	O	A	A	A	A	A	A	A	A	A	A	A	A	A	A	A	A	A	A	A	A	A	A
12. Lvs Simple/Compound	S	C	C	S	C	C	C	S	S	S	S	S	S	C	C	C	S/C	S/C	C	C	C	C	C
13. Lvs Cmpnd. (pinn./palm.)	Pi	Pi	Pi	Pi/Pa	Pi/Pa	Pi	Pi						Pi	Pi	Pi	Pi/Pa	Pa	Pa	Pa	Pa	Pa		Pa
14. Lvs Lobed/Toothed/Sin./Ent.	T	T	T	T/E	T	L/T	L/T	L/T	L/T	L/T	T	T	T	T	L/T	L/T	L/T	T	T	T	T	L/T	L/T
15. Lvs Sessile/Petioled	P	P	P	S/P	P	P	P	P	P	P	P	P	P	P	P	P/S	P/S	P	P	P	P	P	P
16. Lvs Stipulate	✓	✓	✓	✓	✓	✓	✓	✓	✓	✓	✓	✓	✓	✓	✓	✓	✓	✓	✓	✓	✓	✓	✓
17. Lvs Basal/Cauline	C	C	C	B/C	C	C	C	C	C	C	C	C	C	B/C	B/C	B/C	B/C	B/C	B/C	B/C	B	B	B
18. Lvs Red./Modified																							
19. Lvs Sheathing																							
20. Plant Her./M/D/P/Pm/Pd	H	H	H	H	H	H/D	H	H	H	H	H	H	H	H	H	H	H	H	H	H	H	H	H
21. Inflorescence Type	So.	Cy	Cy	Cy	So./Co.	v	v	Co.	Co./Pa	Cy./Co.	So./Co./Cl.P	Cy	R	S/H	P	So./Co.	Co./Cl	So.	Co./R	Cy.	So.	So.	So./Cy.
22. Flwrs. Bracteate/Ebrac.	B	B	B	B	B/E	B	B	B	B	B/E	B	B	B	B	B	B	B	B/E	B/E	B/E	B	B	B
23. Flwrs./Infl. Axil./Term.	T	T	T	A/T	T	T	A/T	T	A/T	T	T	T	T	T	T	T	A/T	A	A	A	A	T	T

	1	2	3	4	5	6	7	8	9	10	11	12	13	14	15	16	17	18	19	20	21
24. Calyx/Corolla	CC	CC	CC	CC	CC	CC	CC	CC	CC	CC	CC	CC	CC	CC	CC	C	C	C	C	CC	CC/C
25. Flwrs. Regular/Irreg.	R	R	HI	R	R	R	R	R	R	R	R	R	R	R	R	R	R	R	R	I	R
26. Ovary Sup./Inf./Hlf Inf.	S	S	HI	S	S	S	S	S	S	S	S	S	S	S	S	S	S	I	I	S	S
27. Ovary Lobed																					
28. Per. Parts Equal/Uneq.	E	E	E	E	E	E	E	E	E	E	E	E	E	E	E	E	E	E	E	U	E
29. Flwr. Color	W	W	W	V	W	W/Pk	W	W/Pk	W/Pk	W	Y	W/Pk	Y	V	W/Pk	V	G	Y	W	W	Y
30. Per.United/Sep.	S	S	S	S	S	S	S	S	S	S	S	S	S	S	S	S	S	S	S	S	S
31. No. sepals/Petals/or Lobes	4/4	5/5	4-5/4-5	4-5/5	5/5	5/5	5/5	5/5	5/5	5/5	5/5	5/5	5/5	5/5	5/5	4	5/5	5/5	5/5	5-6/5	5/5
32. No. Styles/Stigmas/St. Lobes	5	5	1	∞	∞	∞	1	1-5	1-5	5	10	5	2	1-2	5	4	1-3	∞	∞	5-10	2-6
33. No. Carpels	2-4	2-4	∞	∞	∞	∞	1	1-5	1-5	5	20	5	2	1-2	5-15	1	1-3	∞	∞	5-10	2-6
34. No. Locules	2-4	2-4	∞	∞	∞	∞	1	1-5	1-5	5	10	5	2	1-2	5-15	1	1	∞	∞	5-10	2-6
35. Carpels United/Separate	S	S	S	S	S	S	S	S	S	S	S	S	S	S	S	S	S	S	S	S	S
36. No. Stamens/Anthers	∞	15-20	15-20	∞	∞	10-80	10-80	15-80	5-25	20	∞	15-80	4-80	4-80	∞	1-4	20-25	20-25	5	∞	∞
37. Stamens Hypog./Perig.	P	P	P	P	P	P	P	P	P	P	P	P	P	H	H	H	P	P	P	P	P
38. Stamens United/Sep.	S	S	S	S	S	S	S	S	S	S	S	S	S	S	S	S	S	S	S	S	S
39. Fruit Type	D	F	P	A	DL	D	F	P	F	P	P	P	A	A	A	H	A	A	A	D	A
40. Dehiscence S/L/C/P/I														I							
41. Other Disting. Char.	Plant suffrutescent	Stipules deciduous	Stip. dec.; lvs. with glandular midvein	Sometimes suffrutescent	Hypanthium colored & fleshy in fruit	Some species trailing	Some spp. with spiny spur shoots	Bark peeling; twigs lined; fr. inflated	Fruit resembles a small apple	Ovary 5-loc., each with a partition	short shoots; umbel-like cymes	Uneven leaflets; hypanthium bristly	Hypanthium angled or winged	Fruit res. a follicle but indehiscent	Styles usually jointed and hooked	Basal lvs. palm.-lobed; stip. sheathing	Plant with leafy stolons; fr. dry	Fruit fleshy, juicy	Plant with woody base	Fertile fl. apetalous, sterile petalous	Fruit not fleshy

Diagnostic Characteristics	Exochorda	Porteranthus	Aruncus	Cercis	Gleditsia	Senna	Cladrastis	Baptisia	Thermopsis	Genista	Cytisus	Ulex	Lupinus	Crotalaria	Ononis	Trifolium	Melilotus	Medicago	Lotus	Anthyllis	Amorpha	Coronilla	Hedysarum
1. Plant Aquatic																							
2. Epiphyte/Parasite																							
3. Fl. Repl. by Bulbl./Leafy Tufts																							
4. Vine (climbing/trailing)																							
5. Rhizomes Present	✓	✓					✓						✓										
6. Latex Present																							
7. Plant Armed				✓	✓							✓		✓									
8. Woody/Suffr./Herb.	W	H	H	W	W	W	W	H	H	W	W	W	H	H	H	H	H	H	H	W	H	H	
9. Evergreen										✓	✓	✓											
10. Plant Pubscent/Glabrous	G	P/G	P/G	G	G	G	G	P	G	G	P	P/G	P	P	P	P/G	P/G	P/G	P	P/G	P/G	P/G	
11. Lvs Alt./Opp./Sub./Wh.	A	A	A	A	A	A	A	A	A	A	A	A	A	A	A	A	A	A	A	A	A	A	
12. Lvs Simple/Compound	s	C	C	s	C	C	C	C	C	s	s	s	C	s	S/C	S/C	C	C	C	C	C	C	
13. Lvs Cmpnd. (pinn./palm.)	Pa	Pi	Pi		Pi	Pi	Pi	Pa	Pa	Pa	Pa	Pa	Pa	Pa	Pa	Pa	Pa	Pi	Pi	Pi	Pi	Pi	
14. Lvs Lobed/Toothed/Sin./Ent.	T/E	T	T	T	E	E	E	E	E	E	E	E	E	E	T	T	T	T	E	E	E	E	
15. Lvs Sessile/Petioled	P	P	P	P	P	P	P/S	P	s	s	P/S	P	P/S	P	P	P	P	s	s	s	P	P	
16. Lvs Stipulate	✓	✓	✓	✓	✓	✓	✓	✓	✓	✓	✓	✓	✓	✓	✓	✓	✓	✓	✓	✓/−	✓	✓	
17. Lvs Basal/Cauline	C	C	C	C	C	C	C	C	C	C	C	C	C	C	B/C	C	C	C	C	C	C	C	
18. Lvs Red./Modified											✓	✓											
19. Lvs Sheathing																							
20. Plant Her./M/D/P/Pm/Pd	H	D	H	MP	H	H	H	H	H	H	H	H	H	H	H	H	H	H	H	H	H	H	
21. Inflorescence Type	R	P/R	Cl	R	Cl/R	P	R	R	R/P	R	P	S/R	R	R	H	S/R	H/R	U	H	R	U	R	
22. Flwrs. Bracteate/Ebrac.	B/E	B/E	E	E	E	E	B	B	B	B	B	B	B	B	B/E	B/E	B/E	B/E	B	B	B	B	
23. Flwrs./Infl. Axil./Term.	T	T	A	A	A/T	T	T	T	T	T	T	T	T	A	A/T	A	A	A	T	A/T	A/T	A	

Column key (row 41, Other Disting. Char.):

1. Sep. & pet both white; fr. 5-winged
2. Stamens included in hypanthium
3. Tall; lvs 2-3 times compound
4. Glandular petiole; lvs sensitive to touch
5. Petiole covers buds
6. Plant blackens on drying
7. Stems striate; stamens monadelphous
8. Stems green, striate; style spiral
9. Twigs & lvs modified into spines
10. Lvs digitately compound
11. Stipules inversely sagittate
12. Flowers in leafy racemes
13. Stamens diadelphous
14. Lvs pinnately trifoliate
15. Fruit often coiled & spiny
16. Lowest leaflets resemble stipules
17. Head subt. by 3 or >3-5 lobed bracts
18. Leaves & fruit punctate
19. Raceme 1-sided

Character	1	2	3	4	5	6	7	8	9	10	11	12	13	14	15	16	17	18	19
24. Calyx/Corolla	CC	CC	CC	CC	CC	CC	CC	CC	CC	CC	CC	CC	CC	CC	CC	CC	CC	CC	CC
25. Flwrs. Regular/Irreg.	R	I	R	R	R	I	I	I	I	I	I	I	I	I	I	I	I	I	I
26. Ovary Sup./Inf./Hlf Inf.	S	S	S	S	S	S	S	S	S	S	S	S	S	S	S	S	S	S	S
27. Ovary Lobed	✓																		
28. Per. Parts Equal/Uneq.	E	U	U	E/U	U	U	U	U	U	U	U	U	U	U	U	U	U	U	U
29. Flwr. Color	W/P	W/Pi	G	W	Pi/Y	Pi/Y	Y	Y	Y	Y	Y	Y	R/Pu	V	W/Y	Y,R	Y,R	Pu	Pi
30. Per. United/Sep.	S	S	S	CoS	CoS	CoS	CoS	CoS	CoS	CoS	CoS	CoS	CoS	CoS	U	U	U	U	U
31. No. sepals/Petals/or Lobes	5/5	5/5	5/5	4-5/5	4-5/5	5/5	5/5	5/5	5/5	5/5	5/5	5/5	5/5	5/5	5/5	5/5	5/1	5/5	5/5
32. No. Styles/Stigmas/St. Lobes	5	5	5	1	1	1	1	1	1	1	1	1	1	1	1	1	1	1	1
33. No. Carpels	5	5	5	1	1	1	1	1	1	1	1	1	1	1	1	1	1	1	1
34. No. Locules	5	5	5	1	1	1	1	1	1	1	1	1	1	1	1	1	1	1	1
35. Carpels United/Separate	S	S	S	S	S	S	S	S	S	S	S	S	S	S	S	S	S	S	S
36. No. Stamens/Anthers	10-20	15-20	∞	10	5-10	3-10	10	10	10	10	10	10	10	10	10	10	10	10	10
37. Stamens Hypog./Perig.	P	P	P	P	P	P	P	P	P	P	P	P	P	P	P	P	P	P	P
38. Stamens United/Sep.	S	S	S	S	S	S	S	U	U	U	U	U	U	U	U	U	U	U	U
39. Fruit Type	C	F	L	L	L	L	L	L	L	P	P	P	P	U	U	L	L	L	L
40. Dehiscence S/L/C/P/I	F	F	L	L	L	L	L	L	L	L	L	L	L	L	L	L	L	L	L
41. Other Disting. Char.	(1)	(2)	(3)	(4)	(5)	(6)	(7)	(8)	(9)	(10)	(11)	(12)	(13)	(14)	(15)	(16)	(17)	(18)	(19)

Diagnostic Characteristics	Ornithopus	Desmodium	Lespedeza	Stylosanthes	Vicia	Lathyrus	Tephrosia	Wisteria	Sesbania	Robinia	Colutea	Pisum	Astragalus	Oxytropis	Galega	Glycyrrhiza	Clitorea	Phaseolus	Strophostyles	Apios	Amphicarpaea	Galactia	Pueraria
1. Plant Aquatic																							
2. Epiphyte/Parasite																							
3. Fl. Repl. by Bulbl./Leafy Tufts																							
4. Vine (climbing/trailing)				✓	✓	✓		✓				✓					✓	✓	✓	✓	✓	✓	✓
5. Rhizomes Present									✓										✓	✓			
6. Latex Present																							
7. Plant Armed										✓													
8. Woody/Suffr./Herb.	H	H	H	H	H	H	W	H	W	W	H	H	H	H	H	H	H	H	H	H	H	H	S
9. Evergreen																							
10. Plant Pubscent/Glabrous	P	P/G	P/G	P/G	G	P	P/G	G	P/G	P	G	G	P/G	G	G	G	P	P/G	P/G	P/G	P/G	P	P
11. Lvs Alt./Opp./Sub./Wh.	A	A	A	A	A	A	A	A	A	A	A	A	A	A	A	A	A	A	A	A	A	A	A
12. Lvs Simple/Compound	C	C	C	C	C	C	C	C	C	C	C	C	C	C	C	C	C	C	C	C	C	C	C
13. Lvs Cmpnd. (pinn./palm.)	Pi	Pi	Pi	Pi	Pi	Pi	Pi	Pi	Pi	Pi	Pi	Pi	Pi	Pi	Pi	Pi	Pi	Pi	Pi	Pi	Pi	Pi	Pi
14. Lvs Lobed/Toothed/Sin./Ent.	E	E	E	T	E	E	E	E	E	E	E	E	E	E	E	E	E	L	E	E	E	L	L
15. Lvs Sessile/Petioled	S/P	P	P	P	P	P	P	P	P	P	P	P	P	P	P	P	P	P	P	P	P	P	P
16. Lvs Stipulate	✓	✓	✓	✓	✓	✓	✓	✓	✓	✓	✓	✓	✓	✓	✓	✓	✓	✓	✓	✓	✓	✓	✓
17. Lvs Basal/Cauline	C	C	C	C	C	C	C	C	C	C	C	C	B	C	C	C	C	C	C	C	C	C	C
18. Lvs Red./Modified																							
19. Lvs Sheathing																							
20. Plant Her./M/D/P/Pm/Pd	H	H	H	H	H	H	H	H	H	H	H	H	H	H	H	H	H	H	H	H	H	H	H
21. Inflorescence Type	R/P	Cl/H	Cl/R	Cl/R	Cl/R	R	R	R	R	R	R	R	R	R	R	So./R	R	R/H	R	R	R	R	R/P
22. Flwrs. Bracteate/Ebrac.	B	B	B	B/E	B	B	B	B	B	B	B	B/E	B	B	B	B	B	B	B	B	B	B	B
23. Flwrs./Infl. Axil./Term.	A	A/T	A/T	A	A	A/T	A/T	A/T	A	A	A	A	T	A	T	A	A	A	A	A/T	A	A	A

Column key (left to right across the table):

1. Small leaflets; heads subt. by lvs.
2. Fruit a loment w 2-00 articles
3. Many spp. with cleist. & petal. flwrs.
4. Stipules sheathing; flwrs subt. by inv.
5. Lvs. with tendrils; wings adn. to keel
6. Lvs. with tendrils
7. Flowers showy; leaflets linear
8. Twining vine
9. Long lvs. with many small leaflets
10. Stipular spines sometimes present
11. Style hooked; legume bladdery
12. Stipules foliaceous
13. Racemes dense, axillary
14. Keel petals abruptly pointed
15. Stipules sagittate
16. Plant glandular-viscid
17. Trailing or twining; flwrs large
18. Trailing or erect; long racemes
19. Trailing or climbing; long peduncle
20. Tuberous thickening along rhizome
21. Cleist. flwrs.; subterranean fruits
22. Twining or trailing
23. Stipules sagittate-auriculate

Character	1	2	3	4	5	6	7	8	9	10	11	12	13	14	15	16	17	18	19	20	21	22	23
24. Calyx/Corolla	CC	CC	CC	CC	CC	CC	CC	CC	CC	CC	CC	CC	CC	CC	CC	CC	CC	CC	CC	CC	CC	CC	CC
25. Flwrs. Regular/Irreg.	I	I	I	I	I	I	I	I	I	I	I	I	I	I	I	I	I	I	I	I	I	I	I
26. Ovary Sup./Inf./Hlf Inf.	S	S	S	S	S	S	S	S	S	S	S	S	S	S	S	S	S	S	S	S	S	S	S
27. Ovary Lobed																							
28. Per. Parts Equal/Uneq.	U	U	U	U	U	U	U	U	U	U	U	U	U	U	U	U	U	U	U	U	U	U	U
29. Flwr. Color	Pi	W/Pu	Pi/Y	Y	Pu	Y	V	V	Y	W	V	YW	B	B	Pu/W	V	YW	B	Pu/W	Pu/W	Pi/W	Pu	Pu
30. Per. United/Sep.	U	U	U	U	U	U	U	U	U	U	U	U	U	U	U	U	U	U	U	U	U	U	U
31. No. sepals/Petals/or Lobes	5/5	5/5	5/5	5/5	5/5	5/5	5/5	5/5	5/5	5/5	5/5	5/5	5/5	5/5	5/5	5/5	5/5	5/5	5/5	5/5	5/5	5/5	5/5
32. No. Styles/Stigmas/St. Lobes	1	1	1	1	1	1	1	1	1	1	1	1	1	1	1	1	1	1	1	1	1	1	1
33. No. Carpels	1	1	1	1	1	1	1	1	1	1	1	1	1	1	1	1	1	1	1	1	1	1	1
34. No. Locules	1	1	1	1	1	1	1	1	1	1	1	1	1	1/2	1	1	1	1	1	1	1	1	1
35. Carpels United/Separate	S	S	S	S	S	S	S	S	S	S	S	S	S	U/S	S	S	S	S	S	S	S	S	S
36. No. Stamens/Anthers	10	10	10	10	10	10	10	10	10	10	10	10	10	10	10	10	10	10	10	10	10	10	10
37. Stamens Hypog./Perig.	P	P	P	P	P	P	P	P	P	P	P	P	P	P	P	P	P	P	P	P	P	P	P
38. Stamens United/Sep.	U	U	U	U	U	U	U	U	U	U	U	U	U	U	U	U	U	U	U	U	U	U	U
39. Fruit Type	L	L	L	L	L	L	L	L	L	L	L	L	L	L	L	L	L	L	L	L	L	L	L
40. Dehiscence S/L/C/P/I																							
41. Other Disting. Char.																							

Diagnostic Characteristics	Glycine	Cicer	Linum	Radiola	Oxalis	Erodium	Geranium	Tribulus	Ptelea	Zanthoxylum	Phellodendron	Ruta	Ailanthus	Polygala	Ricinus	Crotonopsis	Croton	Mercurialis	Acalypha	Euphorbia	Callitriche	Pachysandra	Corema
1. Plant Aquatic																					✓		
2. Epiphyte/Parasite																							
3. Fl. Repl. by Bulbl./Leafy Tufts																							
4. Vine (climbing/trailing)				✓																		✓	
5. Rhizomes Present							✓												✓				
6. Latex Present																			✓	✓			
7. Plant Armed										✓													
8. Woody/Suffr./Herb.	H	H	H	H	H	H	H	W	W	W	S	W	H	H	H	H	H	H	H	H	S	W	W
9. Evergreen																					✓	✓	
10. Plant Pubscent/Glabrous	P	P	G	G	P/G	P/G	P	P/G	P/G	G	G	G	P/G	G	P	P	G	P	P/G	G	G	G	G
11. Lvs Alt./Opp./Sub./Wh.	A	A/O	A	A	A/O	O	O	O	A	O	A	A	A/W	A	A/O	A	O	A	A/O/W	O	A	A	A
12. Lvs Simple/Compound	C	S	S	C	S/C	S/C	S/C	C	C	C	S/C	C	S	S	S	S	S	S	S	S	S	S	S
13. Lvs Cmpnd. (pinn./palm.)	Pi	Pi		Pa	Pa	Pi	Pa	Pi	Pi	Pi	Pi	Pi											
14. Lvs Lobed/Toothed/Sin./Ent.	E	E	E	E	L/T	L/T	E	E/S	E/S	E/S	E/L	E	E	L/T	E	E/T	T	T	E/T	E	E	T	T
15. Lvs Sessile/Petioled	P	P	S	P	P	P	P	P	P	P	P	P	P	P	P	P	P	P	S/P	S	P	P	P
16. Lvs Stipulate	✓	✓			✓	✓	✓							✓	✓	✓	✓	✓	✓				
17. Lvs Basal/Cauline	C	C	C	B/C	B/C	B/C	B/C	C	C	C	C	C	C	C	C	C	C	C	C	C	C	C	C
18. Lvs Red./Modified																							
19. Lvs Sheathing																							
20. Plant Her./M/D/P/Pm/Pd	H	H	H	H	H	H	H	P	D	D	D	P	H	H	M	M/D	D	M	M	M	M	D	D
21. Inflorescence Type	Cl/R	P/S	Cy/Co	v	U	So./Cl.	So./Cl.	Cy.	Cl.	P	P	P	R	T	S	S/R	S/Cl	CL	CL	So.	S	CL	CL
22. Flwrs. Bracteate/Ebrac.	B	B	B	B	B	B	B	B	E	E	E	B	B	B	B	B	B	B	B	B/E	B	B	B
23. Flwrs./Infl. Axil./Term.	A	A	T	T	A	A	A	T	A	A/T	A/T	T	T	T	A/T	A/T	A	A	A/T	A	T	T	T

	Very pubescent	Leaflets toothed; legume inflated	Filaments in ring; staminodes present	Plant tiny	3 obcordate leaflets; st. U at base	5 fertile and 5 sterile st.	Mericarps attached at tip	Mericarps spiny	Malodorous; winged samara	Plant prickly	Staminodia in ♀ flwrs.	Plant glandular - punctate	Mericarps samaroid	Cal. 2 larger wing-like sep.	St. w branched filaments	Plant w dichotomous branching	Plant w dichotomous branching	Foliaceous bract subt. flwr. cl.	Flwrs. in cyathia	Perianth o; 1 terrest. sp.	Lvs. approximate	Lvs. crowded, subverticillate
24. Calyx/Corolla	CC	CC	CC	CC	CC	CC	CC	CC	CC	Cc	Cc	Cc	Cc	Cc	Ca	Ca	Ca	Ca	Ca	Ca	Ca	Ca
25. Flwrs. Regular/Irreg.	I	R	R	R	R	R	R	R	I	R	R	R	R	I	R	R	R	R	R	R	R	R
26. Ovary Sup./Inf./Hlf Inf.	S	S	S	S	S	S	S	S	S	S	S	S	S	S	S	S	S	S	S	S	S	S
27. Ovary Lobed			✓	✓	✓	✓	✓	✓		✓	✓	✓		✓				✓				
28. Per. Parts Equal/Uneq.	U	E	E	E	E	E	U	E	E	E	E	E	E	U	E	E	E	E	E	E	E	E
29. Flwr. Color	V	W	V	V	Y	Pi/Pi/Pu	Y	G	Y	G	G	G	Y	G/Y	G/Y	G/Y	Co.U	G	G	W	W	Pu
30. Per. United/Sep.	U	U	S	S	S	S	S	S	S	S	S	S	S	S	S	S	S	S	U	S	S	S
31. No. sepals/Petals/or Lobes	5/5	5/5	5/5	5/5	4/4	5/5	5/5	1	1	1	3-5/3-3	4-5/4-5	5/5	2-3/10	5/5	3/0	3-5/0	5/0	0/0	3-5/0	3/0	4-5/0
32. No. Styles/Stigmas/St. Lobes	1	5	5	4	4	5	5	1	1	1	5	5	1	10	1	2	1	3	3	2	3	3
33. No. Carpels	1	5	5	4	8	5	5	5	5	5	5	5	5	10	5	2	2	3	3	2	3	3
34. No. Locules	1	10	5	8	5	5	5	5	5	5	5	5	5	2-5	5	2	2	6-8	3	2	3	3
35. Carpels United/Separate	S	S	S	S	S	S	S	S	S	S	S	S	S	S	S	S	S	S	S	S	S	S
36. No. Stamens/Anthers	10	10	5	4	4	10	10	10	10	5	8-10	8-10	10	2-3/10	6-8	5	5	8-12	8-20	8-16	4	3-4
37. Stamens Hypog./Perig.	P	P	H	H	H	H	H	H	H	U	S	H	H	H	U	H	H	H	H	H	H	H
38. Stamens United/Sep.	U	U	S	U	U	U	S	U	S	S	U	S	S	S	U	S	S	S	S	S	S	S
39. Fruit Type	L	L	C	C	C	C	C	Sc.	Sc.	C	Sc.	C	C	Sc.	C	U	C	C	C	C	C	C
40. Dehiscence S/L/C/P/I		S	S	L			L			L		L		L	L							D
41. Other Disting. Char.																						

Diagnostic Characteristics — Genera

Diagnostic Characteristics	Empetrum	Floerkea	Cotinus	Toxicodendron	Rhus	Ilex	Nemopanthus	Celastrus	Evonymus	Staphylea	Acer	Aesculus	Koelreutera	Impatiens	Rhamnus	Ceanothus	Parthenocissus	Ampelopsis	Vitis	Tilia	Modiola	Malva	Hibiscus
1. Plant Aquatic																							
2. Epiphyte/Parasite																							
3. Fl. Repl. by Bulbl./Leafy Tufts																							
4. Vine (climbing/trailing)				✓				✓									✓	✓	✓				
5. Rhizomes Present										✓													
6. Latex Present			✓	✓	✓																		
7. Plant Armed															✓								
8. Woody/Suffr./Herb.	W	H	W	W	W	W	W	W	W	W	W	W	W	H	W	W	W	W	W	H	H	H	H
9. Evergreen	✓				1 sp.																		
10. Plant Pubscent/Glabrous	P/G	G	G	P/G	P/G	G	G	G	G	G	G	G	P/G	G	G	G	P/G	P/G	P/G	P	P/G	P/G	
11. Lvs Alt./Opp./Sub./Wh.	A	A	A	A	A	A	A	A	O	O	O	O	A/O/W	A/O/S	A	A	A	A	A	A	A	A	A
12. Lvs Simple/Compound	S	C	S	C	C	S	S	S	S	C	S/C	C	C	S	S	S	C	S	S	S	S	S	S
13. Lvs Cmpnd. (pinn./palm.)		Pi		Pi/Pa	Pi					Pi	Pi	Pa	Pi				Pa						
14. Lvs Lobed/Toothed/Sin./Ent.	T	L/E	T/E	T/E	T	T/E	T	T	T	T	L/T	T	L/T	T	T	T	L/T	L/T	T	L/T	L/T	L/T	L/T
15. Lvs Sessile/Petioled	P	P	P	S/P	P	P	P	P	P	P	P	P	P	P	P	P	P	P	P	P	P	P	P
16. Lvs Stipulate								✓	✓	✓					✓	✓	✓	✓	✓	✓	✓	✓	✓
17. Lvs Basal/Cauline	C	C	C	C	C	C	C	C	C	C	C	C	C	C	C	C	C	C	C	C	C	C	C
18. Lvs Red./Modified																							
19. Lvs Sheathing																							
20. Plant Her./M/D/P/Prn/Pd	MD/P	H	P	P	Pd	Pd	Pd	H	H	H	Pd	Pd	H	H	H/P	H/P	H/P	H/P	H	H	H	H	H
21. Inflorescence Type	So./Cl.	So.	P	P	So.	So.	P	Cy.	P	P	V	P	P	R/Cl.	So./Cy.	Cy./P	C	C	C	Cy./So.	So./F.	So.	So.
22. Flwrs. Bracteate/Ebrac.	B	B	B	B	B	E	E	E	B	B	E	E	E	B	B	B	B	B	B	B	B	B	B
23. Flwrs./Infl. Axil./Term.	A	A	A/T	A	A	A	A/T	A	A	A/T	T	T	A	A	A/T	A/T	A/T	A/T	A	A	A	A	A

24. Calyx/Corolla	CC	CC	CC	CC	CC	CC	CC	CC	CC	CC	CC/ Ca.	CC	CC	CC	CC/ Ca.	CC	CC	CC/ Co.	CC/ Co.	CC	CC	CC	CC
25. Flwrs. Regular/Irreg.	R	R	R	R	R	R	R	R	R	R	R	I	R	I	R	R	R	R	R	R	R	R	R
26. Ovary Sup./Inf./Hlf Inf.	S	S	S	S	S	S	S	S/I	S/I	S	S	S	S	S	S/I	S/I	S	S	S	S	S	S	S
27. Ovary Lobed		√							√	√	√					√					√	√	√
28. Per. Parts Equal/Uneq.	E	E	E	E	E	E	E	E	E	E	E	U	E	U	E	E	E	E	E	E	E	E	E
29. Flwr. Color	G Pu	W	Y	G	G	W/G	W/G	W/G	G Pu	G/W	G	W/Y	Y	V	G/Y	W	G	G	G	W/Y	R Pu	V	V
30. Per. United/Sep.	S	S	S	S	S	U/B	S	S	S	S	S	S	S	U	S	S	S	S	U	S	S	S	S
31. No. sepals/Petals/or Lobes	3/3	3/3	5/5	5/5	5/5	0-7 4-7	0-7 4-7	5/5	4/4	5/5	4-12 0-12	5 4-5	5/5	3/3	4-5 0-5	5/5	5/5	0/5	0/5	5/5	5/5	5/5	5/5
32. No. Styles/Stigmas/St. Lobes	6-9	1	3	3	3	4-7	4-7	3	2-4	3	2	1	1	4-5	2-4	3	1	1	1	1	1	1	1
33. No. Carpels	6-9	3	3	3	3	4-7	4-7	3	2-4	3	2	3	3	5	2-4	3	2	2	2	5	00	00	5
34. No. Locules	6-9	3	1	1	1	4-7	4-7	3	2-4	3	2	3	3	5	2-4	3	2	2	2	5	00	00	5
35. Carpels United/Separate	S	S	U	U	U	S	S	S	S	S	S	U	U	S	S	S	S	S	S	U	S	S	U
36. No. Stamens/Anthers	3	6	5	5	5	4-7	4-7	5	4	5	4-10	5-8	8-10	5	4-5	5	5	5	5	00	00	00	00
37. Stamens Hypog./Perig.	H	H	H	H	H	P	H	H	H	H	H	H	H	H	P	P	P	P	P	H	H	H	H
38. Stamens United/Sep.	S	S	S	S	S	S	S	S	S	S	S	S	S	U	S	S	S	S	U	U	U	U	U
39. Fruit Type	D	N	D	D	D	D	D	C	C	C	Sc.	C	C	C	D	D	B	B	B	N			C
40. Dehiscence S/L/C/P/I								L	L			L		L									L
41. Other Disting. Char.	Leaves crowded, subverticillate	Leaflets sometimes lobed	Plumose panicle due to pedicels	Plant poisonous to touch		Minute persistent stipules		Pet. sep. stamens on a disc	Ovary appears inf.; is sup.	Capsule bladdery				Stam. united apically		Hypanthium persistent	Tendrils often with adhes. discs			Peduncle with a foliose bract	Fruit a ring of carpels	Cal. subt. by 3 bractlets	Fruit a loculicidal capsule

Diagnostic Characteristics	*Althaea*	*Kosteletskya*	*Abutilon*	*Sida*	*Hypericum*	*Elatine*	*Tamarix*	*Hudsonia*	*Helianthemum*	*Lechea*	*Hybanthus*	*Viola*	*Opuntia*	*Dirca*	*Daphne*	*Shepherdia*	*Elaeagnus*	*Decodon*	*Lythrum*	*Rotala*	*Cuphea*	*Rhexia*	*Circaea*
1. Plant Aquatic					√/_																		
2. Epiphyte/Parasite																							
3. Fl. Repl. by Bulbl./Leafy Tufts																							
4. Vine (climbing/trailing)					√/_				√														
5. Rhizomes Present				√/_				√	√/_									√					
6. Latex Present	√										√												
7. Plant Armed													√										
8. Woody/Suffr./Herb.	H	H	H	H	W/H	W	W	H	H	H	H	H	W	W	W	W	S	H	H	H	H	H	
9. Evergreen							√																
10. Plant Pubscent/Glabrous	P	P	P	G	G	G	P	P	P	P	P/G	G	G	G	G	G	P/G	P/G	G	P	P	G	
11. Lvs Alt./Opp./Sub./Wh.	A	A	A	A	O/W	A	A	A	A/O/W	A	A	A	A	A	A	O	A O/W	A O/W	O	O	O	O	
12. Lvs Simple/Compound	S	S	S	S	S	S	S	S	S	S	S	S	S	S	S	S	S	S	S	S	S	S	
13. Lvs Cmpnd. (pinn./palm.)																							
14. Lvs Lobed/Toothed/Sin./Ent.	L/T	L/T R	L/T B	L/T	E	E	E	E	E	T/E	L/T	L/T	E	E	E	E	E	E	E	E	L	L	
15. Lvs Sessile/Petioled	P	P	P	S/P	S/P	S	S	S	S/P	P	S	S	S	P	P	P	P	S/P	S	S/P	S/P	P	
16. Lvs Stipulate	√	√	√	√	√					√	√	√											
17. Lvs Basal/Cauline	C	C	C	C	C	C	C	C	B/C	C	B/C	C	C	C	C	C	C	C	C	C	C	C	
18. Lvs Red./Modified												√											
19. Lvs Sheathing																							
20. Plant Her./M/D/P/Pm/Pd	H	H	H	H	H	H	H	H	H	H	H	H	H	H	D	H/Pd	H	H	H	H	H	H	
21. Inflorescence Type	So.	So./R	So./Cy.	So./Cy.	So./Cy.	R	So.	So./Co.	P	So./Cl.	So.	So.	Cl.	Cl.	Cl.	Cl.	Cl.	Cl.	So.	So.	Cy.	R	
22. Flwrs. Bracteate/Ebrac.	B	B	B	B	E	E	E	E	B	E	B	E	E	E	E	E	E	B	B	B	E	E	
23. Flwrs./Infl. Axil./Term.	A/T	A	A/T	A/T	A/T	A/T	T	A/T	A/T	A	A/T	A	A	A	A	A	A	A	A	A	T	A/T	

Characteristic	Cal. subt. by united bracteoles	Plant stellate-pubescent	Carpels deh. into 2 valves	Fruit a ring of carpels	Tiny aquatic	Lvs minute, scale-like	Lvs minute, scale-like	Both petal. and cleist. flwrs	Overwintering rosettes produced	Stamens in sheath	St. connivent, w. white append.	Areoles and glochids in lf. axils	Funneliform calyx	Funneliform calyx; tough bark	Covered with red scales	Silvery and/or red scales	Cal. lobes with append. in sinuses	Cal. lobes with append. in sinuses	Plant viscid-pubescent	Cal. closely surrounding ovary	Fruit covered with hooked bristles
24. Calyx/Corolla	CC	CC	CC	CC	CC	CC	CC	CC	CC/Cl	Cl	CC	CC	CC	Cl	Cl	Cl	Cl	Cl	CC	CC	CC
25. Flwrs. Regular/Irreg.	R	R	R	R	R	R	R	R	R	R	R	R	R	R	R	R	R	R	R	I	R
26. Ovary Sup./Inf./Hlf Inf.	s	s	s	s	s	s	s	s	s	s	s	s	I	I	s	s	s	s	s	s	I
27. Ovary Lobed	✓	✓	✓	✓												✓				✓	✓
28. Per. Parts Equal/Uneq.	E	E	E	E	E	E	E	E	U	E	E	E	E	E	E	E	E	E	E	U	E
29. Flwr. Color	Pi/Pa	Pi/Pa	Y	W/Y	Y/Pi	W/Pi	R	G/W	Wy		Y	Y	Y	U	Pi/Pa	Pi/Pa	Y	W	W/Pi	Pu	W/Pi
30. Per. United/Sep.	s	s	s	s	s	s	s	s	s	s	s	s	s	U	Cl/U	Cl/U	Cl/U	Cl/U	Cl/U	Cl/U	Cl/U
31. No. sepals/Petals/or Lobes	5/5	5/5	5/5	4-5/4-5	2-3/2-3	2-5	5/5	5/5	5/5	5/5	5/5	1	0/0	4/0	4/0	4/0	4/0	1	4-6/4-6	4/4	2/2
32. No. Styles/Stigmas/St. Lobes	1	1	00	00	3-5	2-3	1	1	1	1	1	1	3-7	1	1	1	1	3-5	2	2	2
33. No. Carpels	00	5	00	5	3-5	2-3	3	3	1	1	1	1	1	1	1	1	1	3-5	2	2	2
34. No. Locules	00	5	00	5	1	2-3	1	1	1	1	1	1	1	1	1	1	1	10	2-4	2	2
35. Carpels United/Separate	s	U	s	S	U/S	s	U	U	U	U	U	U	U	U	U	U	U	s	s	s	s
36. No. Stamens/Anthers	00	00	00	00	00	2-3	4-5	00	00	5	5	00	00	8	8	8	4	10	4	11/12	8
37. Stamens Hypog./Perig.	H	H	H	H	H	H	H	H	H	H	H	H	P	P	P	P	P	P	P	P	P
38. Stamens United/Sep.	U	U	U	U	s	s	s	s	s	U	U	s	s	s	s	s	s	s	s	s	s
39. Fruit Type					C	C	C	C	L	L	L	L	B	D	D	D	D	L	C	C	L
40. Dehiscence S/L/C/P/I					s	s		L	L	L	L	L							s	s	
41. Other Disting. Char.																					

Diagnostic Characteristics	Gaura	Oenothera	Epilobium	Ludwigia	Trapa	Proserpinaca	Myriophyllum	Hippuris	Panax	Aralia	Hydrocotyle	Sanicula	Cryptotaenia	Torilis	Osmorhiza	Daucus	Coriandrum	Anthriscus	Conium	Foeniculum	Taenidia	Zizia	Pimpinella
1. Plant Aquatic				✓/-	✓	✓	✓	✓															
2. Epiphyte/Parasite																							
3. Fl. Repl. by Bulbl./Leafy Tufts																							
4. Vine (climbing/trailing)									✓	✓													
5. Rhizomes Present	✓/-	✓							✓	✓	✓												
6. Latex Present									✓/-														
7. Plant Armed																							
8. Woody/Suff./Herb.	H	H	H	H	H	H	H	H	W/H	H	H	H	H	H	H	H	H	H	H	H	H	H	
9. Evergreen																							
10. Plant Pubscent/Glabrous	P	P	P/G	P	P	P	P	P	P/G	P	P	P	G	G	P/G	G	P/G	P	P	P	P	P	
11. Lvs Alt./Opp./Sub./Wh.	A	A/O	A/O	A/W	A	A/O/W	W	W	A	A	A	A	A	A	A	A	A	A	A	A	A	A	
12. Lvs Simple/Compound	S	S	S	S/C	S/C	S/C	S	S	C	C	S/C	C	C	C	C	C	C	C	C	C	S/C	C	
13. Lvs Cmpnd. (pinn./palm.)				Pi	Pi	Pi			Pa	Pa	Pa	Pa	Pi/Pa	Pa	Pi	Pi	Pi	Pi	Pi	Pi	Pa	Pi	
14. Lvs Lobed/Toothed/Sin./Ent.	L/T (E)	T/E	E	T/E	L/T	L/T (B)	E	E	T	L/T	L/T	L/T	L/T	L/T	L/T	L/T	L/T	L/T	L/T	L/E	L/T	L/T	
15. Lvs Sessile/Petioled	S/P	S/P	S/P	P	S/P	S/P	S	P	P	P	P	S/P	P	S/P	P	S/P	S/P	S/P	S/P	P	P	S/P	
16. Lvs Stipulate									✓	✓	✓												
17. Lvs Basal/Cauline	B/C	B/C	B/C	C	C	C	C	C	B/C	C	C	C	C	C	C	C	C	C	C	C	B/C	B/C	
18. Lvs Red./Modified																			✓			✓/-	
19. Lvs Sheathing									✓		✓	✓	✓	✓	✓	✓	✓	✓	✓	✓	✓	✓	
20. Plant Her./M/D/P/Pm/Pd	H	H	H	H	H	H/P	H/P	H/P	H/P	H	H/Pm	H	H/Pm	H/Pm	H	H	H	H	H	H/Pm	H	H	
21. Inflorescence Type	So./R	So./R	So.	So.	So./Cl	So.	So.	U	U	U	U	U	U	U	U	U	U	U	U	U	U	U	
22. Flwrs. Bracteate/Ebrac.	B	B	E	E	B	B	E	B	B	B/E	B	B/E	B	B	B	B	B	B	B	E	B/E	B/E	
23. Flwrs./Infl. Axil./Term.	A/T	A/T	A	A	A	A/T	A/T	A	T	A	T	A/T	A/T	A/T	A/T	A/T	A/T	A/T	A/T	A/T	A/T	A/T	

24. Calyx/Corolla	CC	CC	CC	CC	CC	Cl	CC Cl		CC Co	CC Co	Co	CC	Co	CC	Co	Co	CC	Co	Co	Co	Co	CC	Co
25. Flwrs. Regular/Irreg.	I	R	R	R	R	R	R	R	R	R	R	R	R	R	R	R/I	R/I	I	I	R	R	R	R/I
26. Ovary Sup./Inf./Hlf Inf.	S	S	S	I	HI	I	I	I	I	I	I	I	I	I	I	I	I	I	I	I	I	I	I
27. Ovary Lobed		✓				✓	✓				✓												
28. Per. Parts Equal/Uneq.	U	E	E	E	E	E	E	E	E	E	E	E	E	E	E	E/U	E/U	U	U	E	E	E	E/U
29. Flwr. Color	W Pi	Y	W Pi	G/Y	W				W/G	W/G	W/G	W/Y	W	W	W	V	W Pi	W	W	Y	Y	Y	W
30. Per.United/Sep.	Cl U	Cl U	Cl U	Cl /U	Cl /U	S	S		Cl /U	Cl /U	Cl /U	Cl /U	Cl /U	Cl /U	Cl /U	Cl /U	Cl /U	Cl /U	Cl /U	Cl /U	Cl /U	Cl /U	Cl /U
31. No. sepals/Petals/or Lobes	4/4	4/4	4/4	4/4	4/4	3	4 0-4	0/0	0-5 /5	0-5 /5	0/5	5/5	0/5	5/5	0/5	0/5	5/5	0/5	0/5	0/5	0/5	5/5	0/5
32. No. Styles/Stigmas/St. Lobes	1	1	1	1	1	3	4	1	2-3	5	2	2	2	2	2	2	2	2	2	2	2	2	2
33. No. Carpels	2-4	4	4	4	2	3	4	1	2-3	5	2	2	2	2	2	2	2	2	2	2	2	2	2
34. No. Locules	1	4	4	4	2	3	4	1	2-3	5	2	2	2	2	2	2	2	2	2	2	2	2	2
35. Carpels United/Separate	U	S	S	S	U	S	S	S	S	S	S	S	S	S	S	S	S	S	S	S	S	S	S
36. No. Stamens/Anthers	8	8	8	4	4	3	4-00	1	5	5	5	5	5	5	5	5	5	5	5	5	5	5	5
37. Stamens Hypog./Perig.	P	P	P	P	P	P	P	P	P	P	P	P	P	P	P	P	P	P	P	P	P	P	P
38. Stamens United/Sep.	S	S	S	S	S	S	S	S	S	S	S	S	S	S	S	S	S	S	S	S	S	S	S
39. Fruit Type		C	C	C			M		B	B	Sc	Sc	Sc	Sc	Sc	Sc	Sc	Sc	Sc	Sc	Sc	Sc	Sc
40. Dehiscence S/L/C/P/I																							
41. Other Disting. Char.	Fr. indehiscent	Hypanth. prolonged above ovary	Seeds comose	Stems slightly 4-angled	Fl. lvs. w infl. pet.; fr 4 horned	Emersed lvs. foliaceous	Em. lvs. reduced; per. none	Fruit nut-like; beaked	Root fusiform or bulbous			Fruit w. hooked bristles	Umbel w. irregular rays	Fruit w. hooked bristles			Outer fl. lgr. and irregular	Petals irregular	Petals irregular	Leaf segments filiform			Lower lvs. rosulate; upper reduced

Genera

Diagnostic Characteristics	Carum	Liaeopsis	Eryngium	Anethum	Pastinaca	Levisticum	Angelica	Heracleum	Falcaria	Sium	Ptilimnium	Ligusticum	Aegopodium	Cicuta	Aethusa	Conoselinum	Thaspium	Oxypolis	Scandix	Petroselinum	Bupleurum	Cornus	Nyssa
1. Plant Aquatic										✓													
2. Epiphyte/Parasite																							
3. Fl. Repl. by Bulbl./Leafy Tufts																							
4. Vine (climbing/trailing)																							
5. Rhizomes Present					✓							✓											
6. Latex Present																							
7. Plant Armed																							
8. Woody/Suffr./Herb.	H	H	H	H	H	H	H	H	H	H	H	H	H	H	H	H	H	H	H	H	W	W	
9. Evergreen		✓																					
10. Plant Pubscent/Glabrous	P	P	G	P/G	G	P/G	P	P	G	G	G	G	G	G	G	G	G	P/G	G	G	G	G	
11. Lvs Alt./Opp./Sub./Wh.	A	A	A	A	A	A	A	A	A	A	A	A	A	A	A	A	A	A	A	A	A	O	A
12. Lvs Simple/Compound	C	S	C	C	C	C	C	C	C	C	C	C	C	C	C	C	C	C	C	C	S	S	S
13. Lvs Cmpnd. (pinn./palm.)	Pi		Pi	Pi	Pi	Pi/Pa	Pi/Pa	Pi/Pa	Pi	Pi	Pa	Pa	Pi	Pi	Pa	Pa	Pi	Pi	Pa	Pa			
14. Lvs Lobed/Toothed/Sin./Ent.	E	T		L/T	L/T	T	L/T	L/T	T		T	T	L/T	L/T	L/T	L/T	T/E		L/T	E	E	T/E	
15. Lvs Sessile/Petioled	S	S	P	P	S/P	S/P	P	S/P	P	S/P	P	P	P	S/P	S/P	P	S	S/P	S/P	S/P	P	P	
16. Lvs Stipulate																							
17. Lvs Basal/Cauline	C	B/C	C	C	C	C	C	C	C	C	C	B/C	B/C	C	C	B/C	C	B/C	C	C	C	C	
18. Lvs Red./Modified		✓				✓																	
19. Lvs Sheathing	✓	✓	✓	✓	✓	✓	✓	✓	✓	✓	✓	✓	✓	✓	✓	✓	✓	✓	✓	✓			
20. Plant Her./M/D/P/Pm/Pd	U	U	H	H	H	H	Pm	Pm	H	U	U	U	U	U	U	U	U	U	H	H	H	D	Pd
21. Inflorescence Type	U	H	H	U	U	U	U	U	U	U	U		U	U	U	U	U	U	U	U	U	Cy	H
22. Flwrs. Bracteate/Ebrac.	B/E	B	B	E	B	B	B	B	B	B	B	B	B	B	B	B	B	B	B/E	B	E	B	B
23. Flwrs./Infl. Axil./Term.	A/T	A/T	A/T	A/T	A/T	A/T	A/T	A/T	A/T	A/T	A/T	A/T	A/T	A/T	A/T	A/T	A/T	A/T	A/T	A/T	A/T	A/T	A

	1	2	3	4	5	6	7	8	9	10	11	12	13	14	15	16	17
24. Calyx/Corolla	Co	Co	CC	CC	CC	CC	CC	CC	CC	CC	CC	CC	CC	CC	CC	CC	CC/C
25. Flwrs. Regular/Irreg.	R	R	R	R	R	R	R	R/I	R	R	R	R	R	R	R	R	R
26. Ovary Sup./Inf./Hlf Inf.	I	I	I	I	I	I	I	I	I	I	I	I	I	I	I	I	I
27. Ovary Lobed																	
28. Per. Parts Equal/Uneq.	E	E	E	E	E	E	E	E/U	E	E	E	E	E	E	E	U	E
29. Flwr. Color	W/Pi	W	Y	Y	Y	G/W	W	W	W	W	W	W	W	P/U	W	Y	G
30. Per.United/Sep.	U/U	U/U	Cl/Ru	Cl/Ru	Cl/Ru	Cl/Ru	Cl/Ru	Cl/Ru	Cl/Ru	Cl/Ru	Cl/Ru	Cl/Ru	Cl/Ru	Cl/Ru	Cl/Ru	Cl/Ru	Cl/Ru
31. No. sepals/Petals/or Lobes	0/5	5/5	0/5	0/5	5/5	5/5	0/5	5/5	0/5	5/5	5/5	5/5	0/5	0-3/5	5/5	0/5	0-5
32. No. Styles/Stigmas/St. Lobes	2	2	2	2	2	2	2	2	2	2	2	2	2	2	2	2	2
33. No. Carpels	2	2	2	2	2	2	2	2	2	2	2	2	2	2	1-2	1	1
34. No. Locules	2	2	2	2	2	2	2	2	2	2	2	2	2	2	1-2	1-2	1-2
35. Carpels United/Separate	S	S	S	S	S	S	S	S	S	S	S	S	S	S	S	S	S
36. No. Stamens/Anthers	5	5	5	5	5	5	5	5	5	5	5	5	5	5	5	4	5-10
37. Stamens Hypog./Perig.	P	P	P	P	P	P	P	P	P	P	P	P	P	P	P	P	P
38. Stamens United/Sep.	S	S	S	S	S	S	S	S	S	S	S	S	S	S	S	S	S
39. Fruit Type	Sc	Sc	Sc	Sc	Sc	Sc	Sc	Sc	Sc	Sc	Sc	Sc	Sc	Sc	Sc	Sc	D
40. Dehiscence S/L/C/P/l																D	D
41. Other Disting. Char.	Leaf segments filiform	Lvs. parallel veined	Lvs. red. to phyllodes	Leaf segments filiform	Upper lvs. red. to sheaths	Lflets. palmately divided	Lflts w linear, falcate segs.	Submersed lvs. sometimes pr.	Leaf segments filiform	Leaves biternate	Leaves biternate	Bublets pr. in lf. axis in 1 sp.	Involucel on 1 side of umbellet	Basal lvs. simple; stem l. ternate	Lf. segs. filiform; fr. long beaked	Leaves perfoliate	Flwrs. w. an epigynous disc

Diagnostic Characteristics — Genera

Diagnostic Characteristics	Cletra	Monotropa	Pterospora	Chimaphila	Pyrola	Vaccinium	Loiseleuria	Rhododendron	Epigaea	Kalmia	Calluna	Erica	Harrimanella	Phyllodoce	Ledum	Gaylussacia	Lyonia	Leucothoe	Andromeda	Chamaedaphne	Arctostaphylos	Gaultheria	Diapensia
1. Plant Aquatic																							
2. Epiphyte/Parasite		✓	✓																				
3. Fl. Repl. by Bulbl./Leafy Tufts																							
4. Vine (climbing/trailing)																					✓/–		
5. Rhizomes Present		✓	✓	✓	✓																		
6. Latex Present																							
7. Plant Armed																							
8. Woody/Suffr./Herb.	W	H	S	H	H	W	W	W	W	W	W	W	W	W	W	W	W	W	W	W	W	W	
9. Evergreen				✓	✓/–	✓/–	✓/–	✓	✓	✓	✓	✓	✓	✓	✓		✓/–	✓	✓	✓	✓	✓	
10. Plant Pubscent/Glabrous	P/G	P	G	G	P/G	G	P/G	P	P/G	P/G	P/G	G	G	P	P/G	P/G	P/G	G	P	P/G	P/G	G	
11. Lvs Alt./Opp./Sub./Wh.	A	A	A/O/W	A/O/W	A	A	O	A	A/O/W	O/W	O/W	A	A	A	A	A	A	A	A	A	A	A	
12. Lvs Simple/Compound	S	S	S	S	S	S	S	S	S	S	S	S	S	S	S	S	S	S	S	S	S	S	
13. Lvs Cmpnd. (pinn./palm.)																							
14. Lvs Lobed/Toothed/Sin./Ent.	T/E	E	T	T/E	T/E	E	T/E	E	E	E	E	E	T	E	E	T/E	T	E	T	T/E	T/E	E	
15. Lvs Sessile/Petioled	P	S	P	P	S/P	P	P	P	P	S	P	S	P	S/P	P	P	P	P	P	P	P	S	
16. Lvs Stipulate																							
17. Lvs Basal/Cauline	C	C	B/C	B/C	C	C	C	C	C	C	C	C	C	C	C	C	C	C	C	C	C	C	
18. Lvs Red./Modified		✓	✓							✓	✓	✓											
19. Lvs Sheathing																							
20. Plant Her./M/D/P/Pm/Pd	H	H	H	H	H	H	H	H	H	H	H	H	H	H	H	H	H	H	H	H	H	H	
21. Inflorescence Type	So./R	R	Co.	So./U	V	So./Cl.	Co./Cl.	Co./Cl.	R	R	Cl	So.	So./U	U/Co.	R	R	R	U	R	R/Cl	So.	So.	
22. Flwrs. Bracteate/Ebrac.	B	B	B	B	B/E	E	E	E	E	B	B	B	E	B	B	B	B	B	B	B	B	B	
23. Flwrs./Infl. Axil./Term.	T	T	T	A/T	A/T	T	T	A/T	A/T	T	A/T	T	A	T	A	T/A	T/A	T/A	T/A	T/A	A	T	

	Pl. arising from mycorrhizae	Pl. arising from mycorrhizae	Leaves revolute margined	Plant creeping	Anthers in pouches in corolla	Fl in 1-sided spike-like rac.	Small overlapping scale-like lvs.	Moss-like aspect	Leaves yew-like	Rusty tomentum under lvs.	Rac. of fl. buds over winter	Lvs. revolute, whitened below	Lvs. progressively smaller	Wintergreen taste	Forms cushion-like tussocks
24. Calyx/Corolla	CC	CC	CC	CC	CC	CC	CC	CC	CC	CC	CC	CC	CC	CC	CC
25. Flwrs. Regular/Irreg.	R	R	R	R	R/I	R	R	R	R	R	R	R	R	R	R
26. Ovary Sup./Inf./Hlf Inf.	S	S	S	S	S	S	S	S	S	S	I	S	S	HI	S
27. Ovary Lobed	✓	✓	✓		✓										
28. Per. Parts Equal/Uneq.	E	E	E	E	E/U	E	E	E	E	E	E	E	E	E	E
29. Flwr. Color	W	V	WR	W/Pl	W/Pi	V	W/Pl	W	W/Pl	W/Pi	W	W/Pl	W/Pl	W	W
30. Per. United/Sep.	Cl/U	U	U	Cl/U	U	U	U	Co/U	Co/U	Co/U	Cl/U	U	Co/U	Co/U	U
31. No. sepals/Petals/or Lobes	5/5	0-5/4-5	5/5	5/5	5/5	5/5	5/5	4/4	4/4	5/5	5/5	5/5	5/5	4-5/4-5	5/5
32. No. Styles/Stigmas/St. Lobes	1	1	1	1	1	1	1	1	1	1	1	1	1	1	1
33. No. Carpels	3	5	5	5	5	5	5	4	4	5	10	5	5	4-5	5
34. No. Locules	3	5	5	5	5	5	5	4	4	5	10	5	5	4-5	5
35. Carpels United/Separate	S	S	S	S	S	S	S	S	S	S	S	S	S	S	S
36. No. Stamens/Anthers	10	8-10	10	10	5-10	5	10	8	8	10	10	5-10	10	8-10	5
37. Stamens Hypog./Perig.	H	H	H	H	P	P	P	H	H	H	H	H	H	P	P
38. Stamens United/Sep.	S	S	S	S	S	S	S	S	S	S	S	S	S	S	S
39. Fruit Type	C	C	C	C	C	C	C	C	C	C	D	C	C	D	C
40. Dehiscence S/L/C/P/I	L	L	L	L	S	S	S	C	C	C	B	C	C	B	C
41. Other Disting. Char.	L	L	L	L	S	S		L		L		L	L	L	L

Diagnostic Characteristics	Amsonia	Halenia	Menyanthes	Lomatogonium	Sabatia	Gentiana	Nymphoides	Centaurium	Bartonia	Polypremum	Ligustrum	Syringa	Forsythia	Fraxinus	Diospyros	Limonium	Lysimachia	Samolus	Glaux	Anagallis	Trientalis	Primula	Hottonia
1. Plant Aquatic							√																√
2. Epiphyte/Parasite																							
3. Fl. Repl. by Bulbl./Leafy Tufts																		√/−				√/−	
4. Vine (climbing/trailing)																							
5. Rhizomes Present						√/−	√											√/−				√	
6. Latex Present	√																						
7. Plant Armed																							
8. Woody/Suffr./Herb.	H	H	H	H	H	H	H	H	H	H	W	W	W	W	W	H	H	H	H	H	H	H	H
9. Evergreen																							
10. Plant Pubscent/Glabrous	G	P/G	G	G	G	G	G	G	G	G	G	G	G	G	P/G	G	G	P/G	G	G	G	G	P/G
11. Lvs Alt./Opp./Sub./Wh.	A	O	O	O	O	O	O/W	A/O	A/O	A/O	O	O	O	O	A	A	O	A/O/W	O	O	A/O	W	U
12. Lvs Simple/Compound	S	S	C	S	S	S	S	S	S	S	S	S	S	C	S	S	S	S	S	S	S	S	S
13. Lvs Cmpnd. (pinn./palm.)			Pa.											Pi									Pi
14. Lvs Lobed/Toothed/Sin./Ent.	E	E	E	E	E	E	E	E	E	E	E	E	E	LT/E	T/E	E	T/E	E	E	E	E	T	T
15. Lvs Sessile/Petioled	S/P	P	S/P	S	S	S	S/P	P	S	S	P	P	P	P	P	P	P	S/P	S/P	S	S	S/P	S/P
16. Lvs Stipulate																							
17. Lvs Basal/Cauline	C	C	B	C	C	C	C	C	C	C	C	C	C	C	C	B	C	B/C	C	C	C	B	C
18. Lvs Red./Modified										√												√/−	
19. Lvs Sheathing				√																			
20. Plant Her./M/D/P/Pm/Pd	H	H	H	H	H	H	H	H	H	H	H	H	H	H	MD/P	D	H	H	H	H	H	H	H
21. Inflorescence Type	Cy	A	Cy	A	So	So/Cy	Cy	U	S/U	P/R	Cy	P	P	F	V	So/Cy	S/P	V	R/P	So	So	So	U
22. Flwrs. Bracteate/Ebrac.	B	E	B	B	E	B/E	B	E	B	B	B	E	E	E	E	E	B	B	B	E	E	E	B
23. Flwrs./Infl. Axil./Term.	T	A/T	A/T	T	A/T	T	A/T	A	T	T	T	T	T	A	A	A	A	A/T	T	A	A	A	A

24. Calyx/Corolla	CC	CC	CC	CC	Cl	CC	CC	CC	CC	Cl	CC	CC	CC	CC	CC	CC	CC	CC	CC	CC	CC	CC	CC
25. Flwrs. Regular/Irreg.	R	R	R	R	R	R	R	R	R	R	R	R	R	R	R	R	R	R	R	R	R	R	R
26. Ovary Sup./Inf./Hlf Inf.	S	S	S	S	S	HI	S	S	S	S	S	S	S	S	S	S	S	S	S	S	S	S	S
27. Ovary Lobed																							
28. Per. Parts Equal/Uneq.	E	E	E	E	E	E	E	E	E	E	E	E	E	E	E	E	E	E	E	E	E	E	E
29. Flwr. Color	W	V	W	V	W/R	W	Y/W	Pu	Y	G/Y	Y	W Pi	W	W	V	W Pu	W/Y	V	V	W/B	W Pi	G Pu	B
30. Per.United/Sep.	U	U	U	U	U	U	U	Cl U	U	U	U	U	U	Co U	U	U	U	U	U	U	U	U	U
31. No. sepals/Petals/or Lobes	5/5	5/5	7/7	4-5 4-5	5/0	5/5	5/5	5/5	4/4	0-4 0	4/4	4/4	4/4	4/4	4/4	4-5 4-5	5/5	4-5 4-5	5-12 5-12	4-5 4-5	5/5	4/4	5/5
32. No. Styles/Stigmas/St. Lobes	1	1	1	1	1	1	1	5	4	1	1	1	1	1	1	1	1	1	1	0	1	1	1
33. No. Carpels	5	5	5	5	5	5	5	5	4	2	2	2	2	2	2	2	2	2	2	2	2	2	2
34. No. Locules	1	1	1	1	1	1	1	1	8	2	2	2	2	2	1	1	1	1	1	1	1	1	2
35. Carpels United/Separate	U	U	U	U	U	U	U	U	S	S	S	S	S	S	U	U	U	U	U	U	U	U	S
36. No. Stamens/Anthers	5	5	7	5	5	5	5	5	16	2	2	2	2	4	4	4-5	5	4-5	5-12	4-5	5	4	5
37. Stamens Hypog./Perig.	P	P	P	P	H	P	P	P	P	H	P	P	P	P	P	P	P	P	P	P	P	P	P
38. Stamens United/Sep.	S	S	U/B	S	S	S	S	S	S	S	S	S	S	S	S	S	S	U	S	S	S	S	S
39. Fruit Type	C	C	C	C	C	C	C	U	B	Sa	C	C	D	C	C	C	C	C	C	C	C	C	F
40. Dehiscence S/L/C/P/I				C										L	S	S	S	S	S	S		S	
41. Other Disting. Char.	Peduncles and rac. inflated	Leaves basal; petals notched	Stamens in ring at base of cor.		Plant fleshy			Panicle diffuse						Leaves connected by stipules	Leaves scale-like		Cl. of tubers below umbel	Plaits often in cor. sinuses		Cor. lobes w scales at base	Cor. bearded inside	Cor. lobes usually spurred	Follicles paired

Diagnostic Characteristics

Diagnostic Characteristics	Vinca	Apocynum	Asclepias	Cynanchum	Periploca	Convolvulus	Ipomoea	Cuscuta	Polemonium	Collomia	Ipomopsis	Phlox	Ellisia	Phacelia	Hydrophyllum	Asperugo	Mertensia	Lithospermum	Onosmodium	Cynoglossum	Heliotropium	Myosotis	Lappula
1. Plant Aquatic	√/-																						√/-
2. Epiphyte/Parasite			√		√	√	√	√															
3. Fl. Repl. by Bulbl./Leafy Tufts								√															
4. Vine (climbing/trailing)	√/-			√	√	√	√	√															
5. Rhizomes Present		√/-			√				√/-		√/-												
6. Latex Present	√	√	√	√	√																		
7. Plant Armed															√								
8. Woody/Suffr./Herb.	H/S	H	H	W	W	H	H	H	H	H	H	H	H	H	H	H	H	H	H	H	H	H	
9. Evergreen	√/-										√/-												
10. Plant Pubscent/Glabrous	G	P/G	P	G	G	P/G	G	P/G	P	P	P/G	P	P	G	P	G	G	P	P	P	P	P	
11. Lvs Alt./Opp./Sub./Wh.	O	A/O/W	A/O/W	O	O	A	A	A	A	A	O	A/O	A	A	A/O/W	A	A	A	A	A	A	A	
12. Lvs Simple/Compound	S	S	S	S	S	S	S	C	S	S	S	S	S/C	S/C	S	S	S	S	S	S	S	S	
13. Lvs Cmpnd. (pinn./palm.)								Pi	Pi				Pi	Pi/Pa									
14. Lvs Lobed/Toothed/Sin./Ent.	E	T/E	E	E	L/E	L/T/E	E	E	E	L	E	L/T	L/T	E	E	E	E	E	E	E	E	E	
15. Lvs Sessile/Petioled	P	S/P	P	P	P	P	S	P	S	S	S	P	S/P	P	S/P	P	S/P	S/P	S/P	P	S/P	S/P	
16. Lvs Stipulate																							
17. Lvs Basal/Cauline	C	C	C	C	C	C	C	B/C	C	C	C	C	C	C	C	B/C	C	C	B/C	C	C	B/C	
18. Lvs Red./Modified								√															
19. Lvs Sheathing																							
20. Plant Her./M/D/P/Pm/Pd	So	H	H	H	H	H	H	H	H	H	H	H	H	H	H	H	H	H	H	H	H	H	
21. Inflorescence Type	Cy	U	Cy	P	So/Cl	So/Cl	Cy	Cy/T	Cy	P	Cy	So	Cy	Cy	So/Cl	Cy	So	Cy	R	Cy	Cy	Cy	
22. Flwrs. Bracteate/Ebrac.	B	B	B	B	B	B	B	B	B	B	B	B	E	E	E	B/E	B	B	E	E	E	B	
23. Flwrs./Infl. Axil./Term.	A/T	A/T	A	A/T	A	A	A	A/T	T	T	A/T	A	T	T	A	T	A	T	A/T	A/T	A/T	T	

Characteristic	Plant creeping; fl. slight. irreg.	Anthers adherent to stigma	Flowers in 5 hood-like struct.	Twining vine	Corona with long lobes	Mostly twining vines	Mostly twining vines	Non-green parasites	Flowers in dense, leafy bracted cl.	Leaves pinnately divided	Scorpioid cyme; petals fringed	Ovary deeply 4-lobed	Flowers in axils of upper leaves	Flowers in bracted scorpioid cy.	Flowers in bracted scorpioid cy.	Flowers in bracted scorpioid cy.	Flowers in bracted scorpioid cy.	Scorpioid cyme; fruit prickly
24. Calyx/Corolla	CC	CC	CC	CC	CC	CC	CC	CC	CC	CC	CC	CC	CC	CC	CC	CC	CC	CC
25. Flwrs. Regular/Irreg.	R/I	R	R	R	R	R	R	R	R	R	R	Cl	Cl	Cl	R	R	I	R
26. Ovary Sup./Inf./Hlf Inf.	S	S	S	S	S	S	S	S	S	S	S	S	S	S	S	S	S	S
27. Ovary Lobed				✓	✓							✓	✓	✓	✓	✓	✓	✓
28. Per. Parts Equal/Uneq.	E/U	E	E	E	E	E	E	E	E	E	U	U	Cl	E	E	E	E	E
29. Flwr. Color	B/W	Pu/W	V	W/Pi	W/Y	W/Y	B/Pi	V	B	W/B	W/B	V	S/Y	V	B	W/B	V	W/B
30. Per. United/Sep.	U	U	U	U	U	U	U	U	U	U	U	U	U	U	U	U	U	U
31. No. sepals/Petals/or Lobes	5/5	5/5	5/5	5/5	5/5	5/5	5/5	5/5	5/5	5/5	5/5	5/5	5/5	5/5	5/5	5/5	5/5	5/5
32. No. Styles/Stigmas/St. Lobes	1	2	2	1	2	2	2	1	1	1	1	1	1	1	1	1	2	1
33. No. Carpels	2	2	2	2	2	2	2	3	3	3	2	2	3	3	3	2	2	2
34. No. Locules	2	2	2	2-4	2-4	2	2	1	3	3	1-2	1	4	4	4	4	4	4
35. Carpels United/Separate	S	U/S	S	U/S	S	S	S	S	S	S	U/S	U	S	S	S	S	S	S
36. No. Stamens/Anthers	5	5	5	5	5	5	5	5	5	5	5	5	5	5	5	5	5	5
37. Stamens Hypog./Perig.	P	P	P	P	P	P	P	P	P	P	P	P	P	P	P	P	P	P
38. Stamens United/Sep.	S	U	U	S	S	S	S	S	S	S	S	S	S	S	S	S	S	S
39. Fruit Type	F	F	F	F	F	F	F	C	C	C	C	U	N	NI	NI	NI	NI	NI
40. Dehiscence S/L/C/P/I						F	C	C	L	L	L	L	L	L				
41. Other Disting. Char.																		

Diagnostic Characteristics	Hackelia	Amsinckia	Symphytum	Borago	Echium	Anchusa	Verbena	Phryma	Scutellaria	Leonurus	Physostegia	Collinsonia	Perilla	Trichostema	Marrubium	Agastache	Prunella	Origanum	Blephilia	Glechoma	Salvia	Hyssopus	Teucrium
1. Plant Aquatic																							
2. Epiphyte/Parasite																							
3. Fl. Repl. by Bulbl./Leafy Tufts																							
4. Vine (climbing/trailing)																							
5. Rhizomes Present											✓										✓	✓/_	
6. Latex Present																							
7. Plant Armed																							
8. Woody/Suffr./Herb.	H	H	H	H	H	H	H	H	H	H	H	H	H	H	H	H	H	H	H	H	H	H	
9. Evergreen																							
10. Plant Pubscent/Glabrous	P	P	P	P	P	P/G	P/G	P/G	P	G	P/G	P/G	P/G	P/G	P/G	P/G	P	P	P/G	P/G	P	P	
11. Lvs Alt./Opp./Sub./Wh.	A	A	A	A	A	O	O	O	O	O	O	O	O	O	O	O	O	O	O	O	O	O	
12. Lvs Simple/Compound	S	S	S	S	S	S	S	S	S	S	S	S	S	S	S	S	S	S	S	S	S	S	
13. Lvs Cmpnd. (pinn./palm.)																							
14. Lvs Lobed/Toothed/Sin./Ent.	E	E	T/E	E	E	L/T	T	T/E	L/T, E	T	T	T	E	E	T	T/E	T/E	T/E	T	L/T	E	L/T	
15. Lvs Sessile/Petioled	S/P	S/P	S/P	S/P	S/P	S/P	P	S/P	P	S	P	P	S/P	P	P	P	P	S/P	P	S/P	S/P	P	
16. Lvs Stipulate																							
17. Lvs Basal/Cauline	B/C	C	C	B/C	B/C	C	C	C	C	C	C	C	C	C	C	C	C	C	C	B/C	C	C	
18. Lvs Red./Modified																							
19. Lvs Sheathing																							
20. Plant Her./M/D/P/Pm/Pd	H	H	H	H	H	H	H	H	H	H	H	H	H	H	H	H	H	H	H	H	H	H	
21. Inflorescence Type	Cy	Cy	Cy	Cy	Cy	S	R	V	Cl	R	P/R	R	Cy/P	Cl	S	S/H	Cy/P	Cl	Cl	Cl	Cl/S	Cl/S	
22. Flwrs. Bracteate/Ebrac.	B/E	B	B	B	B	B	B	B	B	B	B	B	B	B	B	B	B	B	B	B	B	B	
23. Flwrs./Infl. Axil./Term.	T	T	T	T	T	T	A/T	A/T	A	T	T	A/T	A/T	A	T	A/T	T	A/T	A	T	A/T	A/T	

	Scorpioid cyme; Fruit prickly	Scorpioid cyme	Stems rough-hispid	Scorpioid cyme	Scorpioid cyme in a thyrse	Scorpioid cyme in a cy. or pan.	Sp. sol. or in cy. or pan.	Fl. long-ped. in spiciform R.	Cal. w crest; fl. in verticils	Cal. with spiny teeth	Lower cor. lip largest, fringed	Plant purplish	Cl. R or T; pan. of cymes	Pl. white woolly; cl teeth hooked	Fl. in dense bracteate whorles	Bracts each subt. 3 flowers	Flowers subt by colored bracts	Verticils subt. by leaves	Trailing and rooting at nodes	Flowers in verticils in S or R	Flowers in verticils in S	Flowers in verticils in S
24. Calyx/Corolla	CC	CC	CC	CC	CC	CC	CC	CC	CC	CC	CC	CC	CC	CC	CC	CC	CC	CC	CC	CC	CC	CC
25. Flwrs. Regular/Irreg.	R	R	R	R/I	R/I	R/I	R/I	R/I	I	I	I	I	I	I	I	I	I	I	I	I	Cl R	R/I
26. Ovary Sup./Inf./Hlf Inf.	s	s	s	s	s	s	s	s	s	s	s	s	s	s	s	s	s	s	s	s	s	s
27. Ovary Lobed	✓	✓	✓	✓	✓	✓	✓	✓	✓	✓	✓	✓	✓	✓	✓	✓	✓	✓	✓	✓	✓	✓
28. Per. Parts Equal/Uneq.	E	E	E/U	E/U	E	U	U	U	U	U	U	U	U	U	U	U	U	U	U	U	U	E/U
29. Flwr. Color	W/B	Y	B	B	B	W/Pu	W/B	W/Pi	W/Pi/R	B	Y	W/B	W	V	V	Pi/Pu	Pi/B	V	Pi/B	B	B	V
30. Per.United/Sep.	U	U	U	U	U	U	U	U	U	U	U	U	U	U	U	U	U	U	U	U	U	U
31. No. sepals/Petals/or Lobes	5/5	5/5	5/5	5/5	5/5	5/5	5/4	5/5	5/5	5/5	5/4	5/5	5/5	5/5	10/5	5/5	5/4	5/5	5/4	5/5	2/5 2/5	5/5
32. No. Styles/Stigmas/St. Lobes	1	1	1	1	1	1	1	1	1	1	1	1	1	1	1	1	1	1	1	1	1	1
33. No. Carpels	2	2	2	2	2	2	2	2	2	2	2	2	2	2	2	2	2	2	2	2	2	2
34. No. Locules	4	4	4	4	4	4	1	4	4	4	4	4	4	4	4	4	4	4	4	4	4	4
35. Carpels United/Separate	s	s	s	s	s	s	s	s	s	s	s	s	s	s	s	s	s	s	s	s	s	s
36. No. Stamens/Anthers	5	5	5	5	4	4	4	4	2	4	4	4	4	4	4	4	4	4	4	4	2	4
37. Stamens Hypog./Perig.	P	P	P	P	P	P	P	P	P	P	P	P	P	P	P	P	P	P	P	P	P	P
38. Stamens United/Sep.	s	s	U	s	s	s	s	s	s	s	s	s	s	s	s	s	s	s	s	s	s	s
39. Fruit Type	NI	NI	NI	NI	NI	NI	NI	NI	A	NI	NI	NI	NI	NI	NI	NI	NI	NI	NI	NI	NI	NI
40. Dehiscence S/L/C/P/I																						
41. Other Disting. Char.																						

#	Diagnostic Characteristics	Monarda	Ajuga	Lycopus	Pycnanthemum	Cunila	Mentha	Stachys	Ballota	Lamium	Galeopsis	Nepeta	Dracocephalum	Hedeoma	Melissa	Satureja	Thymus	Ocimum	Elsholtzia	Lycium	Solanum	Datura	Petunia	Hyoscyamus
1.	Plant Aquatic																							
2.	Epiphyte/Parasite																							
3.	Fl. Repl. by Bulbl./Leafy Tufts																							
4.	Vine (climbing/trailing)																		√/−	√/−				
5.	Rhizomes Present			√																√				
6.	Latex Present																		√/−	√/−				
7.	Plant Armed																							
8.	Woody/Suffr./Herb.	H	H	H	H	H	H	H	H	H	H	H	H	H	H	S	H	H	W	W/H	H	H	H	H
9.	Evergreen																							
10.	Plant Pubscent/Glabrous	P/G	P/G	P/G	P/G	P/G	P/G	P	P/G	P/G	P	P/G	P	P/G	P	P	P	P	G	G	P/G	P	P	
11.	Lvs Alt./Opp./Sub./Wh.	O	O	O	O	O	O	O	O	O	O	O	O	O	O	O	O	O	O	A	A	A/O	A	A
12.	Lvs Simple/Compound	S	S	S	S	S	S	S	S	S	S	S	S	S	S	S	S	S	S	S	S	S	S	S
13.	Lvs Cmpnd. (pinn./palm.)																							
14.	Lvs Lobed/Toothed/Sin./Ent.	T	L/T	T/E	T	T	T	T	T	L/T	T	T	T/E	T	T/E	E	E	T	T	T/E	T/E	T/E	E	L/T
15.	Lvs Sessile/Petioled	S/P	S/P	S/P	S/P	S/P	S/P	P	S/P	S/P	P	P	S/P	P	P	S/P	S	P	P	P	P	S/P	S	
16.	Lvs Stipulate																							
17.	Lvs Basal/Cauline	C	B/C	C	C	C	C	C	C	C	C	C	C	C	C	C	C	C	C	C	C	C	C	
18.	Lvs Red./Modified																							
19.	Lvs Sheathing																							
20.	Plant Her./M/D/P/Pm/Pd	H	H	H	H	H	H	H	H	H	H	H	H	H	H	H	H	H	H	H	H	H	H	H
21.	Inflorescence Type	Cl/S	Cl	Cy	Cy	HS	Cl/S	Cy	Ve	Ve	S	Ve/H	Cl	Cl	Cl	S	S	S	So/Cl	V	So	So	So/R	
22.	Flwrs. Bracteate/Ebrac.	B	B	B	B	B	B	B	B	B	B	B	B	B	B	B	B	B	B	E	E	E	B	E
23.	Flwrs./Infl. Axil./Term.	A/T	A	A/T	A/T	A/T	T	A	A	A	T	T/A	A	A	T/A	T/A	T	A/T		A	A	A/T	A/T	A/T

	Other Distinguishing Characters (row 41, read diagonally per column)
24. Calyx/Corolla	CC throughout
25. Flwrs. Regular/Irreg.	Cl/R, Cl/R, R/I, Cl/R, Cl/R, Cl/R, Cl/R, Cl/R, Cl/R, Cl/R, Cl/R, I, I, I, I, I, I, I, Cl/R, Cl/R, Cl/R, R, R, R, R, R, Cl/R
26. Ovary Sup./Inf./Hlf Inf.	S throughout
27. Ovary Lobed	✓ (present in most columns; blank in several)
28. Per. Parts Equal/Uneq.	E/U, U, Cl/E, Cl/E, U, U, Cl/E, Cl/E, Cl/E, Cl/E, U, U, U, U, U, U, U, Cl/E, Cl/E, Cl/E, Cl/E, E, E, E, E, E, Cl/E
29. Flwr. Color	W, B, W, W/Pu, W/Pu, W/Pu, V, Pu, V, W/Pu, B, B, W, Pu, W, W, W/Pi, B, W/Pu, V, Gr/Pi, V, W/Pu, V, Pu, W/Pu, Cl/R
30. Per.United/Sep.	U throughout
31. No. sepals/Petals/or Lobes	5/5, 5/5, 4-5/4, 5/5, 5/5, 4-5/5, 4-5/5, 4-5/5, 4-5/5, 4-5/5, 5/4, 5/4, 4-5/5, 5/4, 5/4, 5/4, 5/4, 5/4, 5/4, 5/5, 3-5/5, 5/5, 5/5, 5/5, 5-5/5, 5/5, 5/5
32. No. Styles/Stigmas/St. Lobes	1 throughout
33. No. Carpels	2 throughout
34. No. Locules	4 (most columns); 2 in several
35. Carpels United/Separate	S throughout
36. No. Stamens/Anthers	4 / 2 (left columns); 5 (right columns)
37. Stamens Hypog./Perig.	P throughout
38. Stamens United/Sep.	S throughout
39. Fruit Type	N (most columns); B, C (right columns)
40. Dehiscence S/L/C/P/I	(blank in most columns); B, B, C, C, C, C, C (right columns)
41. Other Disting. Char.	See diagonal labels below

Diagonal column labels (row 41, "Other Disting. Char."), read left to right:

- Flowers in head-like cl.
- Flowers in clusters in spike
- Plant stoloniferous
- Fl. in H like Cy; mint odor
- Fl. ped. in trichotomous Cy.
- Fl. in verticils in head or spike
- Plant stoloniferous
- Fl. pedicelled in peduncled Cy
- Fl. sessile in verticils
- Calyx teeth spiny
- Cor. strongly bilab.; dotted
- Prostrate and mat forming
- Calyx tube with a cap
- Spike with overlapping bracts
- Spr. or climbing; wkly thorny
- Capsules usually spiny

Diagnostic Characteristics	Agalinus	Melampyrum	Scrophularia	Penstemon	Euphrasia	Digitalis	Pedicularis	Castilleja	Linaria	Verbascum	Veronica	Collinsia	Schwalbea	Chaenorrhinum	Paulownia	Cymbalaria	Kickxia	Limosella	Veronicastrum	Physalis	Leucophysalis	Nicandra	Nicotiana
1. Plant Aquatic																							
2. Epiphyte/Parasite																							
3. Fl. Repl. by Bulbl./Leafy Tufts																							
4. Vine (climbing/trailing)																							
5. Rhizomes Present																							
6. Latex Present																							
7. Plant Armed																							
8. Woody/Suffr./Herb.		H	H	H	H	H	H	H	H	H	H	H	H	H	H	W	H	H	H	H	H	H	H
9. Evergreen																							
10. Plant Pubscent/Glabrous		P/G	P	P/G	P/G	P/G	P/G	P/G	P/G	G	P	P/G	P	P	P	P	G	P	G	P/G	P	G	P
11. Lvs Alt./Opp./Sub./Wh.		A/O	O	O	O	O	A	A/O	A	A/O/W	A	A/O	O/W	A	A/O	O	A/O	A/O	W	A	A	A	A
12. Lvs Simple/Compound		S	S	S	S	S	S	S	S	S	S	S	S	S	S	S	S	S	S	S	S	S	S
13. Lvs Cmpnd. (pinn./palm.)																							
14. Lvs Lobed/Toothed/Sin./Ent.		E	T/E	T	T	T/E	L/T/E	L/E	L/E	E	T/E	L/T/E	E	E	E	L/E	L	L/T	E	T	T/E	E	T/E
15. Lvs Sessile/Petioled		S	P	P	S	S	S/P	S/P	S	S/P	S/P	S/P	S/P	S	S	P	P	P	S	P	P	P	S/P
16. Lvs Stipulate																							
17. Lvs Basal/Cauline		C	C	C	B/C	C	C	B/C	B/C	C	B/C	C	C	C	C	C	C	C	B	C	C	C	C
18. Lvs Red./Modified																					B		
19. Lvs Sheathing																							
20. Plant Her./M/D/P/Pm/Pd		H	H	H	H	H	H	H	H	H	H	H	H	H	H	H	H	H	H	H	H	H	H
21. Inflorescence Type		So/R	So	P/Cy	P/T	S	R	S	S	R	R/P	So/R	Ve	S	So	P	So	So	So	S/P	So	So	R/P
22. Flwrs. Bracteate/Ebrac.		B	B	B	B	B	B	B	B	B	B	B	B	B	B	E	E	E	E	E	E	E	B
23. Flwrs./Infl. Axil./Term.		A/T	A	T	T	T	T	A/T	T	T	T	A/T	A	A	A	T	A	A	A	A	A	A	T

Diagonal column headers (selected columns), read bottom to top:

- Sepals with auriculate bases
- Corolla nearly regular
- Lvs. linear; scapes < lvs.
- Each cell of capsule circum.
- Capsules flat, obcordate
- Corolla spurred
- Leaves and bracts entire or lobed
- 4 fertile and 1 sterile stamen
- 4 fertile and 1 sterile stamen

24. Calyx/Corolla	CC	CC	CC	CC	CC	CC	CC	CC	CC	CC	CC	CC	CC	CC	CC	CC	CC	CC	CC	CC	CC	CC	CC	CC	CC	CC	CC
25. Flwrs. Regular/Irreg.	R	R	R	R	R	R	R	R	I	I	I	I	R	R	I	I	I	I	I	I	I	I	I	I	I	I	I
26. Ovary Sup./Inf./Hlf Inf.	S	S	S	S	S	S	S	S	S	S	S	S	S	S	S	S	S	S	S	S	S	S	S	S	S	S	S
27. Ovary Lobed												√															
28. Per. Parts Equal/Uneq.	E	E	E	E	E	E	U	U	U	U	E	Co U	E	U	U	U	U	U	U	U	U	U	U	U	U	U	U
29. Flwr. Color	V	B	W	W/Y	W/B	W	Y/Pi	Y/Pi	U	Pu	V	W/B	V	W/B	V	G/Y	Y/Pi	Y/Pi	W/Pi	G/Pu	W/Pi	Pu	Pu	G/Pu	W/Y	Pu	Pu
30. Per.United/Sep.	U	U	U	U	U	U	U	U	U	U	U	U	U	U	U	U	U	U	U	U	U	U	U	U	U	U	U
31. No. sepals/Petals/or Lobes	5/5	5/5	5/5	4-5/4	5/5	5/5	5/5	5/5	5/5	5/5	5/5	4/4	5/5	5/5	5/5	2-4/4	2-5/4	5/5	4/5	5/5	5/5	4/4	5/5	5/5	4/4	5/5	5/5
32. No. Styles/Stigmas/St. Lobes	1	1	1	1	1	1	1	1	1	1	1	1	1	1	1	1	1	1	1	1	1	1	1	1	1	1	1
33. No. Carpels	2	3-5	2	2	2	2	2	2	2	2	2	2	2	2	2	2	2	2	2	2	2	2	2	2	2	2	2
34. No. Locules	2	3-5	2	2	2	2	2	2	2	2	2	2	2	2	2	2	2	2	2	2	2	2	2	2	2	2	2
35. Carpels United/Separate	U	U	U	S	S	S	S	S	S	S	S	S	S	S	S	S	S	S	S	S	S	S	S	S	S	S	S
36. No. Stamens/Anthers	5	5	5	2	4	2	4	4	4	4	5	5	4	2	4	4	4	4	4	4	4	4	4	4	4	4	4
37. Stamens Hypog./Perig.	P	P	P	P	P	P	P	P	P	P	P	P	P	P	P	P	P	P	P	P	P	P	P	P	P	P	P
38. Stamens United/Sep.	S	S	S	S	S	S	S	S	S	S	S	S	S	S	S	S	S	S	S	S	S	S	S	S	S	S	S
39. Fruit Type	C	B	B	C	C	C	C	C	C	C	C	C	C	C	C	C	C	C	C	C	C	C	C	C	C	C	L
40. Dehiscence S/L/C/P/I				P	S	C	P	S	L	S	L	L/S	S	S	P	L	L	S	L	S	S	L	S	S	S	L	L
41. Other Disting. Char.																											

Genera

Diagnostic Characteristics	Aureolaria	Chelone	Rhinanthus	Odontites	Lindernia	Gratiola	Mimulus	Mazus	Campsis	Catalpa	Orobanche	Conopholis	Epifagus	Pinguicula	Utricularia	Proboscidea	Justicia	Littorella	Plantago	Cephalanthus	Sherardia	Galium	Mitchella
1. Plant Aquatic															√			√					
2. Epiphyte/Parasite											√	√	√										
3. Fl. Repl. by Bulbl./Leafy Tufts																							
4. Vine (climbing/trailing)									√														
5. Rhizomes Present							√	√								√	√	√					
6. Latex Present																	√						
7. Plant Armed																					√/−	√	
8. Woody/Suffr./Herb.	H	H	H	H	H	H	H	W	W	W	H	H	H	H	H	H	H	H	W	H	H	H	H
9. Evergreen												√											
10. Plant Pubscent/Glabrous	P/G	P/G	P	G	G	P/G	P	G	G	P	G	G	P	G	P	G	G	P/G	G	P	P/G	P/G	P/G
11. Lvs Alt./Opp./Sub./Wh.	A/O	O	O	O	O	O	O	O	O/W	A	A	A		A/W	A/W	O	O	A/O	A/O	W	W	W	O
12. Lvs Simple/Compound	S	S	S	S	S	S	S	C	C	S	S	S	S	S/C	S/C	S	S	S	S	S	S	S	S
13. Lvs Cmpnd. (pinn./palm.)								Pi	Pi														
14. Lvs Lobed/Toothed/Sin./Ent.	L/T	T	T	T/E	T/E	T/E	T	T	L/E	E	E	E	E	E	T/E	E	E	E	E	E	E	E	
15. Lvs Sessile/Petioled	S	P	S	S	S	S/P	S/P	P	P	S	S	S	S	S	S	S	S	S/P	P	S	S	S	P
16. Lvs Stipulate	C	C	C	C	C	C	B/C	C	C	C	C	C	B	C	C	C	B	B/C	C	C	C	C	C
17. Lvs Basal/Cauline																		√					
18. Lvs Red./Modified										√	√	√				√							
19. Lvs Sheathing																	√	√					
20. Plant Her./M/D/P/Pm/Pd	H	H	H	H	H	H	H	H	H	H	H	H	H	H	H	H	M	H	H	H	H	H	H
21. Inflorescence Type	So/R	R	R	So	So	So	R	R	P	P	S	S	So	SoR	R	S	So	S/H	H	H	Cy	Cy	H
22. Flwrs. Bracteate/Ebrac.	B	B	B	B	B	E	B	B	B	E	B	B	E	E	E	E	B/E	B	B	B	E	E	E
23. Flwrs./Infl. Axil./Term.	A/T	T	T	A	A	A	T	T	C	T	T	T	T	T	T	A	A/T	T	A/T	A/T	A/T	A/T	A/T

	4 fertile and 1 sterile stamen	Raceme 1-sided, spiciform	Raceme 1-sided, spiciform	2 fertile and 2 sterile stamens	2 fertile and 2 sterile stamens	Climbing by aerial rootlets	Capsules long and linear	Yellow or brown root parasite	Yellow or brown root parasite	Lower flowers cleist.; upper sterile	Leaves dichot. forked; bladders	Calyx bracteolate	Spikes long peduncled	Male fl. sol.on scapes; female basal	Leaves basal in most spp.	6-8 lobed involucre present	Ovaries usually paired	Fl. paired, united at base
24. Calyx/Corolla	CC	CC	CC	CC	CC	CC	CC	CC	CC	CC	CC	CC	CC	CC	CC	CC	Co	CC
25. Flwrs. Regular/Irreg.	I	I	I	I	I	I	I	I	I	I	I	I	I	I	R	R	R	R
26. Ovary Sup./Inf./Hlf Inf.	S	S	S	S	S	S	S	S	S	S	S	S	S	S	S	I	I	I
27. Ovary Lobed																		
28. Per. Parts Equal/Uneq.	U	U	U	U	U	U	U	U	U	U	U	U	U	U	E	E	E	E
29. Flwr. Color	V	Y	Pu	Y/W	V	Pu	R/O	W/Y	W/Pu	Y	W	Y/Pu	V	V/Pu	V	V	Pi/B	V
30. Per.United/Sep.	U	U	U	U	U	U	U	U	U	U	U	U	U	U	U	U	U	U
31. No. sepals/Petals/or Lobes	5/5	5/4	4/4	5/5	5/5	1	5/5	2/5	5/5	4-5/4	5/4	2/4-5	5/5	5/5	3-4/4	3-4/4	4-5/4-5	0/3-4
32. No. Styles/Stigmas/St. Lobes	1	1	1	1	1	1	1	1	1	1	1	1	1	2	1	1	1	2
33. No. Carpels	2	2	2	2	2	2	2	2	2	2	2	2	2	2	2	2	2	2
34. No. Locules	2	2	2	2	2	2	2	2	1	1	1	1	1	2	2	2-4	2-4	2
35. Carpels United/Separate	S	S	S	S	S	S	S	S	S	U	S	S	U	S	S	S	S	S
36. No. Stamens/Anthers	4	4	4	2	4	4	4	2-4	4	4	4	2	4	2	4	2-4	4-5	4
37. Stamens Hypog./Perig.	P	P	P	P	P	P	P	P	P	P	P	P	P	P	P	P	P	P
38. Stamens United/Sep.	S	S	S	S	S	S	S	S	S	P	S	P	P	P	A	S	S	S
39. Fruit Type	C	C	C	C	C	C	C	C	C	C	C	C	C	C	C	NI		B
40. Dehiscence S/L/C/P/I	L	L	L	L/S	L	L	L	L	C	C	C	C	C	L	A	C	I	I
41. Other Disting. Char.																		

Diagnostic Characteristics (rows) × **Genera** (columns)

Diagnostic Characteristics	Houstonia	Diodia	Hedyotis	Asperula	Sambucus	Linnaea	Triosteum	Viburnum	Symphoricarpos	Lonicera	Diervilla	Valeriana	Dipsacus	Knautia	Scabiosa	Thaladiantha	Sicyos	Echinocystis	Jasione	Campanula	Triodanus	Legousia	Lobelia
1. Plant Aquatic																							√/_
2. Epiphyte/Parasite																							
3. Fl. Repl. by Bulbl./Leafy Tufts																							
4. Vine (climbing/trailing)									√/_								√	√					
5. Rhizomes Present				√				√							√	√							
6. Latex Present												√											
7. Plant Armed																							
8. Woody/Suffr./Herb.	H	H	H	W	W	S	H	W	W	W	W	H	H	H	H	H	H	H	H	H	H	H	
9. Evergreen					√																		
10. Plant Pubscent/Glabrous	P/G	P	G	P/G	P	P	P/G	P/G	P/G	G	P/G	G	P	P/G	P	P	P	P/G	P	P	P	P/G	
11. Lvs Alt./Opp./Sub./Wh.	O	O	W	O	O	O	O	O	O	O	O	O	O	O	O	A	A	A	A	A	A	A	
12. Lvs Simple/Compound	S	S	S	S	S	S	S	S	S	S	S	S	S	S	S	S	S	S	S	S	S	S	
13. Lvs Cmpnd. (pinn./palm.)				Pt																			
14. Lvs Lobed/Toothed/Sin./Ent.	E	E	E	T	T/E	E	L-T/B	L-T/B	T/E	T	L-T/B	L-T/B	L/T	T/E	L/T	L/T	L/T	E	T/E	T	T	T/E	T/E
15. Lvs Sessile/Petioled	S/P	S/P	S	P	P	S	P	P	S/P	P	P	S	S/P	S/P	P	P	P	P	S	S	S	S/P	S/P
16. Lvs Stipulate	√	√	√				√/_															√/_	
17. Lvs Basal/Cauline	B/C	C	C	C	C	C	C	C	C	C	B/C	C	B/C	B/C	C	C	C	C	B/C	C	C	B/C	
18. Lvs Red./Modified																						√/_	
19. Lvs Sheathing																							
20. Plant Her./M/D/P/Pm/Pd	H	H	H	H	H	H	H	H	H	H	H/Pd	H	H	H	D	D	M	H	H	H	H	H	H
21. Inflorescence Type	So/Cy	So/Cl	Cy/H	Cy/P	Cl	So/Cl	Cy/P	So/Cy/Cl	Cl/Cy	So/Cy	Co/P	H	H	H	So/R	Cy/R	Cy/R	H	V	Cl	So/Cl	So/Cl/R	So/R
22. Flwrs. Bracteate/Ebrac.	B	E	B	E	B	E	E	B	B/E	E	B	B	B	B	E	E	E	E	B	B	B	B	B
23. Flwrs./Infl. Axil./Term.	A	A/T	A	A/T	T	A	A/T	A/T	A/T	A/T	T	T	T	T	A	A	A	T	A/T	A/T	A/T	A/T	A/T

24. Calyx/Corolla	CC	CC	CC	CC	CC	CC	CC	CC	CC	CC	CC	CC	CC	CC	CC	CC	CC	CC	CC	CC	CC	CC	CC
25. Flwrs. Regular/Irreg.	R	R	R	R	R	R	I	R/I	R	R/I	R	R	I	I	I	R	R	R	R	R	R	R	I
26. Ovary Sup./Inf./Hlf Inf.	I	I	I	I	I	I	I	I	I	I	I	I	I	I	I	I	I	I	I	I	I	I	I
27. Ovary Lobed																							
28. Per. Parts Equal/Uneq.	Ca U	Ca U	E	E	E	E	U	E/U	E	E/U	E	E	U	U	U	E	E	E	E	E	E	E	U
29. Flwr. Color	V	V	W	W	W	W Pi	V	W	W Pi	V	W Pi	W Pi	V	Pu	W Pu	Y	W	W	B	V	B Pu	B Pu	V
30. Per.United/Sep.	U	U	U	U	U	U	U	U	U	U	U	U	U	U	U	U	U	U	U	U	U	U	U
31. No. sepals/Petals/or Lobes	4/4	2-4 4	4/4	0/4	5/5	5/5	5/5	5/5	4-5 4-5	5/5	5/5	3-00 5	4/4	8-12 4	4-5 4-5	5/5	5/5	6/6	5/5	5/5	5/5	5/5	5/5
32. No. Styles/Stigmas/St. Lobes	1	1	1	2	1	1	1	3	1	1	1	1	1	1	1	3	1	1	1	1	1	1	1
33. No. Carpels	2	2	2	2	3-5	3	3	3	4	2-3	2	1	1	1	1	3	1	2	2	3	3	3	2
34. No. Locules	2	2	2	2	3-5	3	3	3	4	2-3	2	1	1	1	1	3	1	2	2	3	3	3	2
35. Carpels United/Separate	S	S	S	S	S	S	S	S	S	S	S	S	S	S	S	S	S	S	S	S	S	S	S
36. No. Stamens/Anthers	4	4	4	4	5	4	5	5	4-5	5	5	3	4	4	4	3	3	3	5	5	5	5	5
37. Stamens Hypog./Perig.	P	P	P	P	P	P	P	P	P	P	P	P	P	P	P	P	P	P	H	H	H	H	H
38. Stamens United/Sep.	S	S	S	S	S	S	S	S	S	S	S	S	S	S	S	S	U	U	U	S	S	S	U
39. Fruit Type	C	Nl	C		B		D	D	D	B	C		A	A	A	Pe			C	C	C	C	C
40. Dehiscence S/L/C/P/I	L		L	I							S	I					I	P		P	P	P	P
41. Other Disting. Char.	Stipules setaceous or linear		Flowers in involucrate head		Flowers paired; fruit dry		Plant malodorous		Flowers paired in some species		Cal. lobes plumose in fruit	Ea. flower subt. by epicalyx	Calyx with 8 or > awns		Vine climbing by tendrils	Tendrils; fruit prickley	Fr. bladdery; fibrous within	Long ped. head subt. by involucre	Capsule opening by lat. pores	Fl. in lower lf. axils cleist.		Cor. split down 1 side	

Diagnostic Characteristics	Anthemis	Xanthium	Ambrosia	Iva	Parthenium	Silphium	Acanthospermum	Polymnia	Tagetes	Madia	Coreopsis	Cosmos	Bidens	Guizotia	Galinsoga	Helenium	Ratibida	Echinacea	Rudbeckia	Heliopsis	Eclipta	Verbesina	Helianthus
1. Plant Aquatic													√/-										
2. Epiphyte/Parasite																							
3. Fl. Repl. by Bulbl./Leafy Tufts																							
4. Vine (climbing/trailing)																							
5. Rhizomes Present				√								√							√				√
6. Latex Present																							
7. Plant Armed			√/-																				
8. Woody/Suffr./Herb.		H	H	H	S/H	H	H	H	H	H	H	H	H	H	H	H	H	H	H	H	H	H	H
9. Evergreen																							
10. Plant Pubscent/Glabrous		P/G	P	P	P	P	G	P	P	G	P	P/G	P/G	P/G	P/G	P/G	P	P	P	P/G	G	P	P/G
11. Lvs Alt./Opp./Sub./Wh.		A	A	A/O	A	O	O	O	A/O	A/O	A	O	O	O	O	A	A	A	A	A	O	O	A/O
12. Lvs Simple/Compound		C	S	S/C	S	S	S	S	C	S	S	S/C	C	S/C	S	S	S	S	S	S	S	S	S
13. Lvs Cmpnd. (pinn./palm.)		Pi	Pi	Pi	Pi				Pi	Pi		Pi/Pa	Pi/Pa	Pi/Pa									
14. Lvs Lobed/Toothed/Sin./Ent.		L/T	L/T	L/T	L/T	L/T	T	T	L/T	T	T/E	L,T	T	L/T	T/E	T/E	L/T	L/T	T/E	T/E	T	T/E	T/E
15. Lvs Sessile/Petioled		S	P	S/P	P	S/P	S/P	P	P	P	S	S/P	S/P	S/P	S	P	S	S/P	P	S/P	P	S	S/P
16. Lvs Stipulate																							
17. Lvs Basal/Cauline		C	C	C	C	C	C	C	C	C	C	B/C	C	C	C	C	B/C	C	C	C	C	C	C
18. Lvs Red./Modified																							
19. Lvs Sheathing																							
20. Plant Her./M/D/P/Pm/Pd		H	M	M	M	H	H	H	H	H	H	H	H	H	H	H	H	H	H	H	H	H	H
21. Inflorescence Type		So	Cl/S	S/R	V	Co	Co/P	So	So/P	V	So/Co	So/Co	So	So/Cy	Cy	Cy	So/Co	So	So	So	So	So/Cl	So/Co
22. Flwrs. Bracteate/Ebrac.		B	B	B	B	B	B	B	B	E	B	B	B	B	B	B	E	B	B	B	B	B	B
23. Flwrs./Infl. Axil./Term.		T	A/T	A/T	A/T	A/T	T	A	A/T	A/T	A/T	A/T	A/T	A/T	T	T	T	T	T	T	T	A/T	T

#	24. Calyx/Corolla	25. Flwrs. Reg./Irreg.	26. Ovary Sup./Inf./Hlf Inf.	27. Ovary Lobed	28. Per. Parts Equal/Uneq.	29. Flwr. Color	30. Per. United/Sep.	31. No. sepals/Petals/or Lobes	32. No. Styles/Stigmas/St. Lobes	33. No. Carpels	34. No. Locules	35. Carpels United/Separate	36. No. Stamens/Anthers	37. Stamens Hypog./Perig.	38. Stamens United/Sep.	39. Fruit Type	40. Dehiscence S/L/C/P/I	41. Other Disting. Char.
1	Co	R	I		E	Y	U	5	1	2	1	U	5	P	U	A		Rays neutral, disc. perfect
2	Co	R	I		E	W	U	4	1	2	1	U	5	P	U	A		Achenes usually winged
3	Co	R	I		E	Y	U	5	1	2	1	U	5	P	U	A		Rays very short, pappus 0
4	Co	R	I		E	Y/Pu	U	5	1	2	1	U	5	P	U	A		Rays persist.; papery; pappus 0
5	Co	R	I		E	W/Pu	U	5	1	2	1	U	5	P	U	A		Pappus 0
6	Co	R	I		E	Y/Pu	U	5	1	2	1	U	5	P.	U	A		Chaff spinescent; pappus 0
7	Co	R	I		E	Wy/Pl	U	5	1	2	1	U	5	P	U	A		Recept. columnar; pappus 0 or 2T.
8	Co	R	I		E	Y	U	5	1	2	1	U	5	P	U	A		Stems usually winged
9	Co	R	I		E	Y	U	5	1	2	1	U	5	P	U	A		Pappus 0
10	Co	R	I		E	V	U	5	1	2	1	U	5	P	U	A		Achenes awned (pappus)
11	Co	R	I		E	Y	U	5	1	2	1	U	5	P	U	A		Achenes beaked with decid. awns
12	Co	R	I		E	V	U	5	1	2	1	U	5	P	U	A		Chaff covers only perim. of disc
13	Co	R	I		E	Y	U	5	1	2	1	U	5	P	U	A		Receptacle naked
14	Co	R	I		E	V	U	5	1	2	1	U	5	P	U	A		Pappus 0
15	Co	R	I		E	W/Y	U	5	1	2	1	U	5	P	U	A		Fr. clusters forming bur.; pappus 0
16	Co	R	I		E	Y	U	5	1	2	1	U	5	P	U	A		Leaves connate-perfoliate
17	Co	R	I		E	W/G	U	0-5	1	2	1	U	5	P	U	A		Leaves in some spp. bipinnate
18	Co	R	I		E	G	U	0-5	1	2	1	U	5	P	U	A		1 sp. suffr.; pappus 0
19	Co	R	I		E	G	U	0-5	1	2	1	U	5	P	U	A		Head w hooked prickles; pappus 0
20	Co	R	I		E	W/Y	U	5	2	2	1	U	5	P	U	A		Leaves finely 1-3 divided; pappus 0

Diagnostic Characteristics	Achillea	Santolina	Chrysanthemum	Tanacetum	Matricaria	Cotula	Artemisia	Arnica	Senecio	Erechtites	Synosma	Tussilago	Petasites	Heterotheca	Grindelia	Solidago	Aster	Boltonia	Erigeron	Baccharis	Bellis	Pluchea	Gnaphalium
1. Plant Aquatic																							
2. Epiphyte/Parasite																							
3. Fl. Repl. by Bulbl./Leafy Tufts		✓																					
4. Vine (climbing/trailing)																							
5. Rhizomes Present	✓							✓				✓				✓	✓	✓		✓			
6. Latex Present																							
7. Plant Armed																							
8. Woody/Suffr./Herb.	S	H	H	H	H	S/H	H	H	H	H	H	H	H	H	H	H	H	H	W	H	H	H	
9. Evergreen																							
10. Plant Pubscent/Glabrous	P/G	P/G	G	G	G	P/G	P	P/G	P/G	G	G	P/G	P/G	G	G	P/G	G	P/G	G	P	P/G	P	
11. Lvs Alt./Opp./Sub./Wh.	A	A	A	A	A	A	A	O	A	A	A	A	A	A	A	A	A	A	A	A	A	A	
12. Lvs Simple/Compound	S/C	S	C	C	S/C	S/C	S	S/C	S	S	S	S	S	S	S	S	S	S	S	S	S	S	
13. Lvs Cmpnd. (pinn./palm.)	Pi	Pi	Pi	Pi	Pi	Pi	Pi	Pi															
14. Lvs Lobed/Toothed/Sin./Ent.	T/E	LT/E			LT/E	LT/E	L/T	LT/E	LT/E	T	L/T	L/T	L/T	T	T/E	T/E	E	T/E	T	T	T/E	E	
15. Lvs Sessile/Petioled	S	P/S	S	S	S	S/P	S/P	S/P	S/P	S	S/P	S/P	S/P	S	S/P	S/P	S	S/P	P	P	S/P	S	
16. Lvs Stipulate																							
17. Lvs Basal/Cauline	B/C	C	B/C	C	C	C	B/C	B/C	C	C	B/C	B/C	B/C	B/C	C	B/C	C	C	C	B	C	B/C	
18. Lvs Red./Modified												✓	✓										
19. Lvs Sheathing					✓										✓/-								
20. Plant Her./M/D/P/Pm/Pd	H	H	H	H	H	H	H	H	H	H	H	D/Pd	H	H	H	H	H	H	D	H	H	H	
21. Inflorescence Type	So/Co	So/Co	Co	So/Co	So	V	So/Co	So/P	Co/P	Co/P	So	So/R	Co	Co	T/P	Co/P	Co	V	Cl/P	So/S	Co/Cy	Co/V	
22. Flwrs. Bracteate/Ebrac.	B	B	E	E	E	B/E	E	E	E	E	E	E	E	E	E	E	E	E	E	E	E	E	
23. Flwrs./Infl. Axil./Term.	T	T	T	T	T	T	T	T	T	T	T	T	T	T	A/T	T	T	T	T	T	T	A/T	

Column legend (left → right):

1. Pappus 0
2. Pappus 0
3. Receptacle naked; pappus 0
4. Aromatic; chaff(c)0; pappus(p) 0
5. Some spp. aromatic; c:0; p.0
6. chaff 0, pappus 0
7. Some spp. aromatic; p.0
8. Chaff 0
9. Chaff 0
10. Involucres swollen base; c.0
11. Chaff 0
12. Stem leaves reduced; chaff 0
13. Stem leaves reduced; chaff 0
14. Leaves parallel veined in 1 sp.; c. 0
15. Leaves and bracts resinous; c.0
16. Chaff 0
17. Chaff 0
18. Chaff 0; pappus of bristles
19. Involucre in 1 series; c. 0
20. Chaff 0
21. Chaff 0; pappus 0
22. Chaff 0
23. Chaff 0

Character	1	2	3	4	5	6	7	8	9	10	11	12	13	14	15	16	17	18	19	20	21	22	23
24. Calyx/Corolla	Co	Co	Co	Co	Co	Co	Co	Co	Co	Co	Co	Co	Co	Co	Co	Co	Co	Co	Co	Co	Co	Co	Co
25. Flwrs. Regular/Irreg.	R	R	R	R	R	R	R	R	R	R	R	R	R	R	R	R	R	R	R	R	R	R	R
26. Ovary Sup./Inf./Hlf Inf.	I	I	I	I	I	I	I	I	I	I	I	I	I	I	I	I	I	I	I	I	I	I	I
27. Ovary Lobed																							
28. Per. Parts Equal/Uneq.	E	E	E	E	E	E	E	E	E	E	E	E			E	E	E	E	E	E	E	E	E
29. Flwr. Color	W	Y	W/Y	Y	Y	W	Y	G/Y	Y	W	W	W/Pu	Y	W	V	V	V	W	W/Y	Y	Pi/Pu	W/Y	R
30. Per. United/Sep.	U	U	U	U	U	U	U	U	U	U	U	U	U	U	U	U	U	U	U	U	U	U	U
31. No. sepals/Petals/or Lobes	5	0-5	0-5	0-5	1	1	1	1	1	1	1	1	1	1	1	1	1	1	1	1	1	1	1
32. No. Styles/Stigmas/St. Lobes	1	1	1	1	2	2	2	2	2	2	2	2	2	2	2	2	2	2	2	2	2	2	2
33. No. Carpels	2	2	2	2	2	2	2	2	2	2	2	2	2	2	2	2	2	2	2	2	2	2	2
34. No. Locules	1	1	1	1	1	1	1	1	1	1	1	1	1	1	1	1	1	1	1	1	1	1	1
35. Carpels United/Separate	U	U	U	U	U	U	U	U	U	U	U	U	U	U	U	U	U	U	U	U	U	U	U
36. No. Stamens/Anthers	5	5	5	5	5	5	5	5	5	5	5	5	5	5	5	5	5	5	5	5	5	5	5
37. Stamens Hypog./Perig.	P	P	P	P	P	P	P	P	P	P	P	P	P	P	P	P	P	P	P	P	P	P	P
38. Stamens United/Sep.	U	U	U	U	U	U	U	U	U	U	U	U	U	U	U	U	U	U	U	U	U	U	U
39. Fruit Type	A	A	A	A	A	A	A	A	A	A	A	A	A	A	A	A	A	A	A	A	A	A	A
40. Dehiscence S/L/C/P/I																							
41. Other Disting. Char.																							

Diagnostic Characteristics

Diagnostic Characteristics	Anaphalis	Antennaria	Inula	Sclerolepis	Eupatorium	Mikania	Liatris	Vernonia	Arctium	Cirsium	Onopordum	Echinops	Centaurea	Cnicus	Prenanthes	Hieraceum	Taraxacum	Sonchus	Lactuca	Cichorium	Krigia	Lapsana	Arnoseris
1. Plant Aquatic																							
2. Epiphyte/Parasite																							
3. Fl. Repl. by Bulbl./Leafy Tufts																							
4. Vine (climbing/trailing)						✓																	
5. Rhizomes Present	✓	✓	✓	✓													✓	✓					
6. Latex Present															✓	✓	✓/-	✓/-	✓	✓	✓	✓	
7. Plant Armed									✓	✓	✓												
8. Woody/Suffr./Herb.	H	H	H	H	H	H	H	H	H	H	H	H	H	H	H	H	H	H	H	H	H	H	
9. Evergreen																							
10. Plant Pubscent/Glabrous	P	P	G	P/G	P/G	P/G	P/G	P	P	P	P	P/G	P	P/G	P/G	P/G	P/G	P/G	P	P/G	G	P/G	
11. Lvs Alt./Opp./Sub./Wh.	A	A	W	O/W	O	O	A	A	A	A	A	A	A	A	A	A	A	A	A	A	A	A	
12. Lvs Simple/Compound	S	S	S	S	S	S	S	S	S	S	S	S	S	S	S	S	S	S	S	S	S	S	
13. Lvs Cmpnd. (pinn./palm.)																							
14. Lvs Lobed/Toothed/Sin./Ent.	E	T	E	T/E	T/E	E	L/T(E)	T/E	L/T	L/T	L/T	L/T	L/T	L/T	L/T(E)	L/T(E)	L/T(E)	L/T(E)	L/T(E)	L/T(E)	L/T(E)	T	
15. Lvs Sessile/Petioled	S/P	S/P	S	S/P	P	S/P	S/P	P	S	S/P	S/P	S/P	S/P	S/P	S/P	P	S	S	S/P	S/P	S/P	P	
16. Lvs Stipulate																							
17. Lvs Basal/Cauline	C	B/C	C	C	C	C	C	B/C	B/C	B/C	B/C	B/C	B/C	C	B/C	B	B/C	B/C	B/C	B/C	C	B	
18. Lvs Red./Modified		✓/-	✓														✓	✓/-					
19. Lvs Sheathing			✓																				
20. Plant Her./M/D/P/Pm/Pd	D/Pd	H	H	H	H	H	H	H	H	H	H	H	H	H	H	H	H	H	H	H	H	H	
21. Inflorescence Type	Co	Co	So	Co/P	Co	R	Co	Co	So/Cl	So	H	So/P	So	TP	V	So	V	P	Cl	So/Co/P	Co/P	So	
22. Flwrs. Bracteate/Ebrac.	E	E	E	E	E	E	E	B	B	B	B	B	B	B	E	E	E	E	E	E	E	E	
23. Flwrs./Infl. Axil./Term.	T	T	T	T	A	T	T	T	T	T	T	T	T	T	T	T	T	T	A/T	T	T	T	

Character	1	2	3	4	5	6	7	8	9	10	11	12	13	14	15	16	17	18	19	20	21	22	23
24. Calyx/Corolla	Co	Co	Co	Co	Co	Co	Co	Co	Co	Co	Co	Co	Co	Co	Co	Co	Co	Co	Co	Co	Co	Co	Co
25. Flwrs. Regular/Irreg.	R	R	R	R	R	R	R	R	R	R	R	R	R	R	R	R	R	R	R	R	R	R	R
26. Ovary Sup./Inf./Hlf Inf.	I	I	I	I	I	I	I	I	I	I	I	I	I	I	I	I	I	I	I	I	I	I	I
27. Ovary Lobed																							
28. Per. Parts Equal/Uneq.	E	E	E	E	E	E	E	E	E	E	E	E	E	E	E	E	E	E	E	E	E	E	E
29. Flwr. Color	W	W	Y	W/Pi	V	Y	Pu	Pu	Pu	B	Pu	Pu	Y	Y	Y/O	Y	V	V	V	Y/O	Y	Y	Y
30. Per.United/Sep.	U	U	U	U	U	U	U	U	U	U	U	U	U	U	U	U	U	U	U	U	U	U	U
31. No. sepals/Petals/or Lobes	5	5	5	5	5	5	5	5	5	5	5	5	5	5	5	5	5	5	5	5	5	5	5
32. No. Styles/Stigmas/St. Lobes	1	1	1	1	1	1	1	1	1	1	1	1	1	1	1	1	1	1	1	1	1	1	1
33. No. Carpels	2	2	2	2	2	2	2	2	2	2	2	2	2	2	2	2	2	2	2	2	2	2	2
34. No. Locules	1	1	1	1	1	1	1	1	1	1	1	1	1	1	1	1	1	1	1	1	1	1	1
35. Carpels United/Separate	U	U	U	U	U	U	U	U	U	U	U	U	U	U	U	U	U	U	U	U	U	U	U
36. No. Stamens/Anthers	5	5	5	5	5	5	5	5	5	5	5	5	5	5	5	5	5	5	5	5	5	5	5
37. Stamens Hypog./Perig.	P	P	P	P	P	P	P	P	P	P	P	P	P	P	P	P	P	P	P	P	P	P	P
38. Stamens United/Sep.	U	U	U	U	U	U	U	U	U	U	U	U	U	U	U	U	U	U	U	U	U	U	U
39. Fruit Type	A	A	A	A	A	A	A	A	A	A	A	A	A	A	A	A	A	A	A	A	A	A	A
40. Dehiscence S/L/C/P/I																							
41. Other Disting. Char.	Chaff 0	Stems leafy or with scales; c. 0	Leaves partly clasping; c. 0	Chaff 0	Chaff 0	Twining climbing vine; c. 0	Chaff 0	Inv. bracts hooked, rec. bristly	Receptacle bristly	Woolly; receptacle naked	Hds 1 fl, aggr. in secondary hds.	Inv. bracts pectinate	Inv. subt. by lvs	Receptacle naked	Receptacle naked	Achenes muricate	Leaves spiny margined	Leaves spiny margined	Receptacle naked	Receptacle naked	Receptacle naked	Pappus 0; receptacle naked	Peduncles thickened upwards

Diagnostic Characteristics	Picris	Leontodon	Tragopogon
1. Plant Aquatic			
2. Epiphyte/Parasite			
3. Fl. Repl. by Bulbl./Leafy Tufts			
4. Vine (climbing/trailing)			
5. Rhizomes Present			
6. Latex Present	✓	✓	✓
7. Plant Armed			
8. Woody/Suffr./Herb.	H	H	H
9. Evergreen			
10. Plant Pubscent/Glabrous	P	P/G	G
11. Lvs Alt./Opp./Sub./Wh.	A	A	A
12. Lvs Simple/Compound	S	S	S
13. Lvs Cmpnd. (pinn./palm.)			
14. Lvs Lobed/Toothed/Sin./Ent.	T/E	T/E L/T	E
15. Lvs Sessile/Petioled	S/P	S/P	S
16. Lvs Stipulate			
17. Lvs Basal/Cauline	B/C	B	C
18. Lvs Red./Modified			
19. Lvs Sheathing			
20. Plant Her./M/D/P/Pm/Pd	H	H	H
21. Inflorescence Type	Co P	So Co	So
22. Flwrs. Bracteate/Ebrac.	E	E	E
23. Flwrs./Infl. Axil./Term.	T	T	T

24. Calyx/Corolla	Co	Co	Co	Co
25. Flwrs. Regular/Irreg.	R	R	R	R
26. Ovary Sup./Inf./Hlf Inf.	I	I	I	I
27. Ovary Lobed				
28. Per. Parts Equal/Uneq.	E	E	E	E
29. Flwr. Color	Y	Y	Y/Pu	Y/Pu
30. Per.United/Sep.	U	U	U	U
31. No. sepals/Petals/or Lobes	5	5	5	5
32. No. Styles/Stigmas/St. Lobes	1	1	1	1
33. No. Carpels	2	2	2	2
34. No. Locules	1	1	1	1
35. Carpels United/Separate	U	U	U	U
36. No. Stamens/Anthers	5	5	5	5
37. Stamens Hypog./Perig.	P	P	P	P
38. Stamens United/Sep.	U	U	U	U
39. Fruit Type	A	A	A	A
40. Dehiscence S/L/C/P/I				
41. Other Disting. Char.				

Receptacle naked
Receptacle naked or chaffy
Receptacle naked

MATRIX OF
DIAGNOSTIC CHARACTERISTICS
FOR WOODY PLANTS IN WINTER CONDITION

In preparing the general key to genera of woody plants in winter condition a matrix of the 36-odd characteristics listed below was constructed as an aid. This matrix has been included because of its potential usefulness as a teaching tool and for identifying plant specimens on which only certain structures are present.

Because of space limitations in the matrix variability within a genus could only be touched on in rudimentary fashion. For some characteristics information was included in the matrix only to the extent to which it was useful in constructing the keys. For the majority of characteristics, however, the information is complete for the woody genera in winter condition treated in the manual. Genera with persistent evergreen leaves were not included in the matrix.

Based on these considerations, the matrix should be used only as a guide to find genera having certain characteristics for teaching and to narrow the range of possibilities in identifying a plant. Once a genus is identified as having a certain feature(s) the user should then refer to the description of the genus and perhaps also the family and any winter keys that have been completed in the Descriptive Flora for more information on winter characteristics.

Below, the 36-odd characteristics that have been abbreviated in the matrix are fully listed, and leaf scar shape, bud shape and twig, pith and bud color are also listed along with the corresponding abbreviations used in the matrix. Other abbreviations and clarifications for the matrix have also been included below.

Diagnostic Characteristics:
 1. Thorns/Spines present
 2. Twigs St = Stout / M = Moderate / Sl = Slender
 3. Twigs Ridged or Lined (including twigs which are angled).
 4. Twigs R = Rough (scurfy or scaly); P = Pubescent
 5. Bark Exfoliating
 6. Twig Color
 7. Latex Present
 8. Twigs with Odor or Taste Wintergreen/Spicy (including malodorous twigs)
 9. Pith Small / Medium / Large
10. Pith D = Diaphragmed / Ch.= Chambered / E = Excavated / C = Continuous
11. Pith Color
12. Pith Shape R = Round / A = Angled / Star = Star Shaped
13. Leaf Scars A=Alternate / O=Opposite / S=Subopposite / W=Whorled
14. Leaf Scar Shape

15. Leaf Scar Length S=Short / M=Medium / L=Long
16. Leaf Scars in Ranks (no. of ranks)
17. Leaf Scars Raised
18. Stipule Scars Present
19. Stipule Scar Length S=Short / M=Medium / L=Long
20. Bud Color
21. Bud Length S=Short / M=Medium / L=Long
22. Bud Shape
23. Buds Pubescent / Glabrous
24. Buds Naked
25. Bud Scales 1=Single / V=Valvate / I=Imbricated; No.=number of Scales / S=Several; unless otherwise specified bud scales are imbricated.
26. Terminal Buds Clustered
27. Terminal Bud Stalked
28. Terminal Bud P=Present / Pt=Pseudoterminal
29. Buds S=Solitary / Su=Superposed / C=Collateral
30. Buds Resinous
31. Lateral Buds A=Absent / H=Hidden / M=Minute
32. Lateral Buds A=Ascending / Ap=Appressed / D=Divergent
33. Bud Scales (no. ranks)
34. Bundle Traces 1/3/5/or more / S=Scattered / G=Groups (including compound bundle traces)
35. Bundle Traces D=Distinct / I=Indistinct / L=Line / E=Ellipse / S=Scattered
36. Fruit Type

Leaf Scar Shape:

A   3 or more angled
BC   Broadly crescent-shaped
C   Crescent-shaped
Cs   C-shaped
D   Deltoid
E   Elliptical
H   Horseshoe
He   Half-elliptical
Hr   Half-round
Ht   Half-triangular
L   Lobed
Li   Linear
NC   Narrowly crescent-shaped
O   Obdeltoid
Ov   Oval
R   Round
S   Shield-shaped
U   U-shaped
V   V-shaped
Va   Variable
3s   3-sided

Bud Shape:

A   Angled
C   Cylindrical
Co   Conical
D   Deltoid
Dg   Depressed-globose
F   Fusiform
G   Globose
H   Hemispherical
He   Half-elliptical
L   Lanceolate
Li   Linear
Nc   Narrowly conical
O   Oblong
Ob   Obtuse
Oq   Oblique
Ov   Ovoid
P   Pointed
R   Round
S   Subglobose
T   Terete
V   Variable
2e   Two-edged

Twig Color:

B   Brown
Gr   Green
Gy   Gray
L   Lustrous
P   Purple
V   Variable
W   White
Y   Yellow

Pith Color:

B   Brown
G   Green
P   Pale
Pi   Pink
W   White
Y   Yellow

Bud Color:

B   Brown
G   Green
L   Lustrous
P   Purple
R   Red

Other Abbreviations/Clarifications:

✓ = Character applicable to some or all members of a genus; ✓/- = character may either be present or not present.

Other Distinguishing Characteristics: **Appr.** = appressed; **Aro.** = aromatic; **Br.** = Branches; **Cmpnd.** = Compound; **Consp.** = Conspicuous; **Enc.** = Encircling; **Fr.** = Fruits; **Infl.** = Inflorescence; **Mal.** = Malodorous; **Mod.** = Modified; **Mucro.** = Mucronate; **Pers.** = Persistent; **Resin.** = Resinous; **Somet.** = Sometimes; **Stip.** = Stipules.

Genera

Diagnostic Characteristics	Salix	Populus	Myrica	Juglans	Carya	Carpinus	Ostrya	Corylus	Alnus	Betula	Fagus	Castanea	Quercus	Ulmus	Celtis	Broussonetia	Morus	Maclura	Xanthorhiza	Berberis	Liriodendron	Magnolia	Calycanthus
1. Thorns/Spines Present																	✓	✓		✓			
2. Twigs St./M/Sl.	M	Sl	St	M	M	Sl	Sl	Sl/M	M	Sl	M	Sl/M	M	Sl	Sl	Sl/M	M	M	M	M	M/Sl	Sl/M	
3. Twigs Ridged or Lined	✓		✓					✓	✓			✓							✓		✓		
4. Twigs R/P			✓				✓		✓	✓													
5. Bark Exfoliating									✓	✓				✓/-			✓						
6. Twig Color	Gr/Gy																✓	✓					
7. Latex Present																✓	✓	✓					
8. Twigs with Odor or Taste W/S		S							W/-														
9. Pith Small /Med./ Lg.	S	S	M	M	M	S	S	S	S	S	S	M	S	S	M/L	M	M	L	L	M	L	S	S
10. Pith D/Ch/E/C	C	C	Ch	Ch	C	C	C	C	C	C	C	C	C	Ch	C	C	C	C	C	D	C	C	
11. Pith Color	W	B	G	W/B	P	P	P	P	G	G			W	W	W	P	P		G/Y	P	W	W	
12. Pith Shape R/A/Star	R	A	A	R/A	R/A	A	A	A	A	A	A	A	A	A	A	A	A	A	R	R	R	A	
13. Leaf Scars A/O/S/W	A/O	A	A	A	R/AR	A	A	A	A	A	A	A	A	A	A	A	A	A	A	A	A	A	
14. Leaf Scar Shape	U	CD	S/L	S/L	C	C	HeC/HeD	Hr	HeC	Hr	Hr	Hr	Hr	HeC	R	R/O	R/O	UHe	Hr	R	R/U/H	O	
15. Leaf Scar Length S/M/L					S	S	S	S	S	S	S	S/M	M	S	M/L	M	M/L	S		M/L	S/M	S/M	
16. Leaf Scars in Ranks		3s			2	2	2		2/-	2/-			2		2						2/-		
17. Leaf Scars Raised	✓/-	✓/-			✓	✓/-	✓/-	✓/-	✓	✓		✓/-	✓	✓	✓	✓/-	✓						
18. Stipule Scars Present	✓/-	✓/-	✓		✓	✓	✓	✓	✓	✓	✓	✓	✓	✓	✓	✓	✓/-			✓	✓	✓	
19. Stipule Scar Length S/M/L	S	S	S			L	L	L	M	L	L	S	M	M	L	L	S/M			L	M	S/M	
20. Bud Color	L																			L			

Characteristic																						
21. Bud Length S/M/L	S	S/M	S	M	M	S	M	M	L	M	M	M	S	M	S/M	S	S/L	S	S	S/L	S/L	S/M
22. Bud Shape	Ōv/s	Ōv/O	Ōv/s	Ōv/O	Ōv/A	Ov	R/Ōv	Ōv/F	Ov	Ov	Ov	Ōv/D	Co	Ōv/Og	Dg	T	Ov	Ōv/R	Ōv/R	Ov	O/R	P
23. Buds Pubescent/Glabrous	P/G											P									P/G	P
24. Buds Naked			✓																			✓
25. Bud Scale(s) 1/V/I (No.)/S	1 / S-00	2-4	10/-12	6-8	V S 3-6	3>	10>	2-3	00	6	4	1-3	5-6	4-5	3-5	3	6	V	1		00	3
26. Term. Buds Clustered			✓			✓				✓												
27. Term. Bud Stalked			✓			✓											✓					
28. Term. Bud P./Pt.	Pt	P	P	Pt	Pt	Pt	Pt	Pt	P	P/Pt	P	Pt	Pt	Pt	Pt	P	P	P	P			Pt
29. Buds S/Su/C	S/C	S	S/Su/Su	S	S	S	S	S	S/C/S/C	S/C/S/C	S	S	S/C/S/C	S/C/S/C	S	S	S/Su	S	S/Su		S	Su
30. Buds Resinous	✓		✓		✓																	
31. Lat. Buds A/H/M																	M					
32. Lat Buds A/AP/D	Ap Ap							D			Ap		Ap				Ap Ap					
33. Bud Scales (No. Ranks)		4					5	2	2	2		2										
34. Bundle Tr. 1/3/5 or >/S/G	3	3/3g	3g	3	3/3g	3	3/3g	3	12	3/3g	3/3g	5	00	S	9-11	3	12>	00	3			
35. Bundle Tr. D/I/L/E/S	Ni	N	N	Ni	Ni	D/	D/	E	E/S	E/S	E	E/S	E/S/S	E/S	S	E/S	E/S	E/S				
36. Fruit Type	C	C	N	N	Ni	Ni	N	N	N	N	N	E	D	Sa	A	A	A	F	B	Sa	S	F
37. Other Disting. Characteristics	Single bud scale	1st bud scale over leaf scar	Spicy odor	Trunk Fluted	Bark Scaly	Female flowers with red stigmas	Horizontal lenticels	Short shoots, hor. lent.; 2 spp. aro.	Lf scar nearly encircling twig	Buds oblique over leaf scar	Buds oblique over leaf scar	Stipules persistent	Yellow wood; long term. bud	Bundle traces indistinct						Lf scar encir. twig; buds 2 edged	Lf scar encircl. twig; buds 2 edged	

Diagnostic Characteristics	Sassafras	Lindera	Philadelphus	Hydrangea	Deutzia	Ribes	Liquidambar	Hamamelis	Platanus	Rhodotypos	Sorbaria	Sorbus	Aronia	Potentilla	Rosa	Rubus	Prunus	Physocarpus	Spiraea	Crataegus	Amelanchier	Pyrus/Malus	Exochorda
1. Thorns/Spines Present						√/_								√	√	√/_				√		Sl	
2. Twigs St./M/Sl.	M	Sl	M/St	Sl	M	M	Sl/M	M	M/L	M	M	M	Sl	M	M	Sl/M	M	Sl/M	Sl/M	Sl	M	Sl	
3. Twigs Ridged or Lined	√	√			√	√/_												√/_	√/_		√/_	√	√/_
4. Twigs R/P			P/_	P/_	√	√/_	P/_														P/_	√	
5. Bark Exfoliating		√	√	√	√			√									√	√					
6. Twig Color	Gr	Gr										B							L/_				
7. Latex Present						√										√							
8. Twigs with Odor or Taste W/S	S	S																					
9. Pith Small /Med./ Lg.	M	L	M/L	M	M/L	M	S/M	M	M	M/L	M	M	S	M/L	M/L	M	M/L	M/L	S	S	S	S	
10. Pith D/Ch/E/C	C	C	C	E	E	C	C	C	C	C	C	C	E	C	C	C	C	C	C	C	C	C	
11. Pith Color	W	W	P	B	P	B	P/B	P/B	W	B	B	P	B	B	B	P/B	B	B	W/B	P	P	P	R
12. Pith Shape R/A/Star	A/S	R	R	R	R	A/S	R	R	R	R	R	R	R	A	R/A	R/A	A	R	R	A/S	A/S	R	
13. Leaf Scars A/O/S/W	A	A	O/W	A	A	A	A	A	O	A	A	A	A	A	A	A	A	A	A	A	A/S	A	
14. Leaf Scar Shape	Hr/C	Hr/C	C/A	D/N/C	BC/U/H	CB/C/H	Hr/L	L	C/3./B	Hr/B	C/Li	U	U/R/Li	U/Li	C/U	Hr/C/U	Hr/L	Hr/C	NC	NC	L	U/Li	
15. Leaf Scar Length S/M/L	S	S							M	M/L	S		S	S	S	S		S	S				
16. Leaf Scars in Ranks							2	2												2/_			
17. Leaf Scars Raised	√						√	√	√/_	√				√	√	√	√	√	√	√/_	√/_	√/_	√/_
18. Stipule Scars Present							√	√	√								√	√	√				
19. Stipule Scar Length S/M/L							M	L									S	S	S				
20. Bud Color										R	R/P					B			R	R/G			

No.	Characteristic	Values (across taxa, left → right)
21.	Bud Length S/M/L	M · S · S · M · M · S/M · M · M · L · M · M · M/L · M · M/LS/M · M · M · S/M · S · M · M · M
22.	Bud Shape	Ov/s · Gp · Ov · OS · Ov/O · Ov/F · O · Ov · Co · Ov · Ov · O/Co · Ov · Ov · Ov · Ov/C · Ov/C · Ov/G · Ov/R · Ov/Ob · Ov
23.	Buds Pubescent/Glabrous	G · G · P · G · G · G · P · G · G · G · P/G/P/G · P · G · O · O · G · C · · · P ·
24.	Buds Naked	· · · · √ · · √ · · · · · · · · · · · · · ·
25.	Bud Scale(s) 1/V/I (No.)/S	4 · 3 · 2 V · 4-6 · 4-12 · 6 · 6 · 1 · 10-12 · 4 · 5 · 4 / 3-4 · 6 · 4-5 · 6 · 6 · 6 · 6 · 3-4 · 3-4 · 10
26.	Term. Buds Clustered	· · √ · √/√ · √/√ · √ · √ · · √/√ · · · · · · · · · · · ·
27.	Term. Bud Stalked	
28.	Term. Bud P./Pt.	P · Pt · P · P · P · Pt · P · P · P · P · P · P · P · P · P · P/Pt · P · P · P · P/Pt · P
29.	Buds S/Su/C	S · SuC · S · S · S/C · S/C · S · S/C · S · S/C · S · S · S · S · SC/SU · S · S/C · S/C · S/C · S · S
30.	Buds Resinous	
31.	Lat. Buds A/H/M	· H/ · · M/ · · Ap/ · M/ · · · · · M/ · · · · · · · · ·
32.	Lat Buds A/AP/D	· · · · Ap/ · · Ap · · · · · · · · · · · · · ·
33.	Bud Scales (No. Ranks)	
34.	Bundle Tr. 1/3/5 or >/S/G	3 · 3 · 3 · 3-7 · 3 · 3 · 3/G · 5-9 · 3 · 1 · 3 · 3-7 · 3 · 5 · 1 · 3 · 3 · 6 · 3 · 3 · 3
35.	Bundle Tr. D/I/L/E/S	D/L/D/L · D · D · D · D · D · D · D · D · D · D · D · D · D · D · D · D · D · D · D · D
36.	Fruit Type	D · C · C · C · B · C · A · D · F · D · P · P · A · D · F · Di · F · F · P · P · A
37.	Other Disting. Characteristics	(see distinguishing notes below)

Row 37 — Other Distinguishing Characteristics (one per taxon column):

- Bud scales fleshy, keeled
- Fl. buds Gl, foliar buds Pub.
- Yng. buds covered by membrane
- Capsule 2 - beaked
- Somet. dying back at tip
- Some spp. malodorous
- Twigs somet. corky winged
- Auxiliary buds somet. pr.
- Lf. scars and stipule scars enc.
- Stipule scars ciliate at top
- Lenticels consp; buds off. resin
- Stipules persistent
- Rose hips pers. over winter
- Lf scars torn; stip. off. pers.
- Lf scars on cushion; 3 spp. malod.
- Follicles clustered
- Inflorescence persistent
- Spines often cumpd. on stems
- Buds slightly twisted
- Short shoots present
- Consp. lenticels; bud scales fringed

Diagnostic Characteristics	Cercis	Gleditsia	Cladrastis	Genista	Cytisus	Ulex	Amorpha	Robinia	Colutea	Ptelea	Zanthoxylum	Phellodendron	Ailanthus	Cotinus	Toxicodendron	Rhus	Ilex	Nemopanthus	Evonymus	Staphylea	Acer	Aesculus	Koelreuteria
1. Thorns/Spines Present	✓					✓		✓/_			✓												
2. Twigs St./M/Sl.	M	M	Sl	Sl	Sl	Sl	M	M	M	M	M	St	M	St	St	Sl	Sl	M	M	M	M	St	M/St
3. Twigs Ridged or Lined			✓	✓	✓	✓	✓/_	✓/_										✓					
4. Twigs R/P								P							P/_								
5. Bark Exfoliating																				✓			
6. Twig Color			Gr	Gr	Gr								BP										
7. Latex Present												✓		✓	✓	✓				✓/_			
8. Twigs with Odor or Taste W/S									✓	S	S	✓	✓	✓	✓								
9. Pith Small/Med./Lg.	S	M	S	S	S	S	M	M	L	M	M	L	L	M/L	M/L	S	S	M	M	M	L	M/L	
10. Pith D/Ch/E/C	C	C	C	C	C	C	C	C	C	C	C	C	C	C	C	C	C	C	C	C	C	C	
11. Pith Color	P Pi	P W				P	B	W	W	W	B	B	B	B/Pi	B/Pi	B/Pi		G	G	W	P	W	
12. Pith Shape R/A/Star	R	R	R	R	R	R	R	R	R	R	R	R	R	R	R	R/A	R	R/A	R	R	R	A/S	
13. Leaf Scars A/O/S/W	A	A	A	A	A	A	A	A	A	A	O/S	A	A	A	A	A	A	O	O	O	O	O	
14. Leaf Scar Shape	O	U				D	D	L D B C	C/H	L D H	H	S	L/C	BC/Cs	U/Cs	C	D/C	D/C	H/C	V/U/D/S	V/U/D/S	S	
15. Leaf Scar Length S/M/L	L	L	S	S				L	L	L		L	L		L	L	S	S	S	S	L	L	M/L
16. Leaf Scars in Ranks	2	2																					
17. Leaf Scars Raised	✓/_		✓	✓	✓	✓			✓	✓	✓			✓/_	✓/_	✓/_		✓/_	✓/_	✓			✓
18. Stipule Scars Present			✓	✓														✓	✓	✓			
19. Stipule Scar Length S/M/L							S											S	M/L	S			M/L
20. Bud Color																							

21. Bud Length S/M/L	S			S	S		S	S	S	S/M	M	M	S	S	S/M	S/M	S	S	S/L	M	M	L	M
22. Bud Shape	Ov Ob			Ov	Ov		Ov			Co	G	L	H	Ov R	Ov R	Ov R	Ov R	Ov		Ov	Ov C	Ov P	He
23. Buds Pubescent/Glabrous			P							P	P	P	P			P/G							
24. Buds Naked			N																				
25. Bud Scale(s) 1/V/I (No.)/S	2 S	S		S-6	S	S	2-4		2-4			2 S	S	2-4	3-4		2-6	2	6-10	1-4	2-00	10+	2/V
26. Term. Buds Clustered									√/–								√/–	√/–					
27. Term. Bud Stalked	√																				√/–		
28. Term. Bud P./Pt.	Pt	Pt	Pt	Pt	P		Pt	Pt	P	Pt	P	Pt	Pt	P	P	Pt	P	P	P	Pt	P	P	Pt
29. Buds S/Su/C	SSu	SSu	Su	S	S	SSu	Su	Su	Su/–	Su	Su	S	S	S	S	S	Su/–	S	S	S	S/C	S	S
30. Buds Resinous																						√/–	
31. Lat. Buds A/H/M								H		H													
32. Lat Buds A/AP/D	Ap																	D					D
33. Bud Scales (No. Ranks)																							
34. Bundle Tr. 1/3/5 or >/S/G	3	3	3-7	1	1		3	3	1-3	3	3	3/G	S	3	3/G	3-9	1	1	1	3G 5-7	3-9 C	3/g	3/g
35. Bundle Tr. D/I/L/E/S	D	D	D	I	I		D	D	D	D	D	D	L	D	D	D	D	D	L	D/E	D	D	D/S
36. Fruit Type	L	L	L	L	L	L	L	L	L	Sa	F	D	Sc	D	D	D	D	D	C	C	Sc	C	C
37. Other Disting. Characteristics	Decurr. ridges from lf. scars	Buds sunken; partly covered	Wood yellow; lf. scars enc. buds	Twigs striate; stipules pers.	Twigs ribbed; stipules pers.	Twigs and lvs. mod. into spines	Stem angled or ridged	Buds hidden; stip. pers., mod.	Lined from nodes; stip. pers.	Lf scars nearly enc. buds; mal.	Often prickly at nodes	Bark corky; lf. scars enc. buds	Lenticels prominent; malodorous	Lent. prom.; sap gummy	Sap poisonous on contact	Lf. scars nearly enc. twig	Stipules pers.; bark mottled		Twigs 4 - lined or angled	Capsule bladdery	Fr. a schizocarp of 2 mericarps	Capsule usually spiny	

Diagnostic Characteristics	Rhamnus	Ceanothus	Tilia	Hypericum	Tamarix	Dirca	Daphne	Shepherdia	Elaeagnus	Aralia	Cornus	Nyssa	Clethra	Vaccinium	Rhododendron	Gaylussacia	Lyonia	Leucothoe	Diospyros	Fraxinus	Forsythia	Syringa	Ligustrum
1. Thorns/Spines Present	√/-								√/-														
2. Twigs St./M/Sl.	Sl/M/Sl	M	Sl	Sl	Sl/M	Sl/M	Sl	Sl	Sl	St	M	M	S/M/M	Sl/M	Sl	Sl	Sl	Sl	St	M	M	M	Sl
3. Twigs Ridged or Lined		√	√		√/-	√/-				√/-	√/-	√/-	√/-	√/-		√/-			√/-	√/-	√	√	
4. Twigs R/P	P/-			R				R		P/-		P/-	P/-										
5. Bark Exfoliating			√					R															
6. Twig Color	GrB															Y	Y						
7. Latex Present																							
8. Twigs with Odor or Taste W/S																							
9. Pith Small /Med./ Lg.	M	M/L	S	S	S	S	S	S	L	L	M	M/L	S	S/M	S	S	S	S	M	M	M	M	M
10. Pith D/Ch/E/C	C	C	C	C	E	C	C	C	C	C/E	D	D	C	C	C	C	C	C		Ch/√	C	C	
11. Pith Color	W	P/Y	G/B	W	W	W	B	B	P	W/B	W	W/B	W/B					W/BG/W	W		W	W	
12. Pith Shape R/A/Star	R	R/A		R	R	R	R	R	R		R	R	R	R	R/A			R/A	R/A	R	R		
13. Leaf Scars A/O/S/W	A/O S	A	A	O	A	A	O	A	A	A/O	A	A	A	A	A	A	A	A	O	O	O	O/S	
14. Leaf Scar Shape	He Hr C	Hr He	D/E			C	Hr	Hr	U	C U C	C U C D	C D	Hr C	S	C 3s	Hr C	Hr C	He Bc	U/C		C/S	C Hr	
15. Leaf Scar Length S/M/L	S	S	S	S	L	S	S	S	M		S	S	S	S	S	S	S	S		S	S	S	
16. Leaf Scars in Ranks		2			2	2-4												2-5					
17. Leaf Scars Raised	√/-	√/-			√	√				√			√/-	√/-				√/-	√/-	√	√	√	
18. Stipule Scars Present	√	√																					
19. Stipule Scar Length S/M/L	S	S	M																				
20. Bud Color																R							

21. Bud Length S/M/L	M		M/L	S	S	S	S	S	S	M	M	M	M	S		S	S/M	S	S	M	M	M	S
22. Bud Shape		Ov	Ov Oq		R	Co	Ov	O	Co O	Co Ov	O	Ov	Ov		Ov	Ov	O	Ov G	Ov D	Ov D	C	Ov	Ov
23. Buds Pubescent/Glabrous						P							P										
24. Buds Naked	√/–																						
25. Bud Scale(s) 1/V/I (No.)/S	6	S	2/I	2-3	3	4	4-6	2/V	4	S	2/V -4	4	3	2-6	6	2-5	2-4	3-4	2-3	4-6	00	5	5
26. Term. Buds Clustered															√								
27. Term. Bud Stalked								√			√												
28. Term. Bud P./Pt.	P	P	Pt	P	P	P	Pt	P	P	P	P	P	P	Pt	P	Pt	Pt	Pt	Pt	P	P	Pt	P
29. Buds S/Su/C	S	S	S/C	S	S	S	S	S Su	S	S/C	S	S	S	S	S	S	S	S	S	Su	S/C	S	S Su
30. Buds Resinous																							
31. Lat. Buds A/H/M													M										
32. Lat Buds A/AP/D					Ap												Ap						
33. Bud Scales (No. Ranks)																							
34. Bundle Tr. 1/3/5 or >/S/G	3/G	1	3	1		5	1	1	1	15	3	3	1	1	1	1	1	1	1	00	1	1/G	1
35. Bundle Tr. D/I/L/E/S	D	D	D/S	I		I	D	D	D		D	D	D	D	D	D	D	D	D	E			
36. Fruit Type	D	D	N	C	C	D	D	D	D	B	D	D	C	B	C	D	C	C	B	Sa	C	C	D
37. Other Disting. Characteristics	Spiny shoots somet. present	Base of fruit persistent	Buds oblique over lf. scars		Lf. bases pers.; lf. scars 0	Twigs jointed, w. short spurs at nodes		Twigs w. reddish peltate scales	Twigs w. silvery peltate scales	Lf. scars w. remnants of pet. bases	Petiole bases persistent	Short shoots; corky lf. scars	Raceme pers.; bud scales caducous	Outer scales of foliar buds mucro.	Twigs clustered at end of yrly.growth		Young twigs yellow; buds appr.	Racemes of next yr. flwr. buds consp.	Bundle trace C-shaped	Twigs very stout	Pith somet. hollow between nodes	Bundle traces transverse & cmpnd.	

Diagnostic Characteristics

Diagnostic Characteristics	Lycium	Paulownia	Catalpa	Cephalanthus	Sambucus	Viburnum	Symphoricarpos	Lonicera	Diervilla	Baccharis
1. Thorns/Spines Present	√/-									
2. Twigs St./M/Sl.	Sl	St	M/St	Sl/M	St	Sl/M	Sl/M	M	Sl/M	Sl/M
3. Twigs Ridged or Lined	√		√/-	√/-					√	√
4. Twigs R/P						P/-			R	
5. Bark Exfoliating										
6. Twig Color									Gr	
7. Latex Present									√	
8. Twigs with Odor or Taste W/S										
9. Pith Small /Med./ Lg.	M	L	L	L	L	S	M	M	S	S
10. Pith D/Ch/E/C	Ch	C	C	C	C	C	C/E	C	C	C
11. Pith Color	W	W	B	W/Bw/B	W/Bw/B	B	W/B	P	P	
12. Pith Shape R/A/Star	R	R	A			R		A	A	A
13. Leaf Scars A/O/S/W	A	O/W	O/W	O/W	O	O	O	O/W	O/W	A
14. Leaf Scar Shape	C	Ov	R	BC	C	C	C	C	NC	
15. Leaf Scar Length S/M/L	S	M	L	L	L	S	S	M	S	
16. Leaf Scars in Ranks										
17. Leaf Scars Raised	√/-	√	√/-		√/-	√	√			
18. Stipule Scars Present			√/-							
19. Stipule Scar Length S/M/L										
20. Bud Color										

	Spreading or climbing w. long br.	Pers. infl. of flwr. buds consp.	Long capsules pers. over winter	Twigs dying back; fr. heads pers.	Lenticels prominent, bark warty	Plant malodorous	Twigs somet. hollow; fr. consp.	Ridges decurrent from nodes	Infl. remnants pers.; buds resin.
21. Bud Length S/M/L	S	S	S	S	M	S	M	M	S
22. Bud Shape	S	H	G	Co	Ov	O/Li	O	V	O/S
23. Buds Pubescent/Glabrous									
24. Buds Naked									
25. Bud Scale(s) 1/V/I (No.)/S		S	S	I	S	V/I	S	S-00	4
26. Term. Buds Clustered									
27. Term. Bud Stalked				✓	✓/	✓			
28. Term. Bud P./Pt.	P	Pt	Pt	Pt	Pt	P	P	P	Pt
29. Buds S/Su/C	S	Su	S	S	S	S/Co	S/Su	S/Su	S
30. Buds Resinous									✓
31. Lat. Buds A/H/M									
32. Lat Buds A/AP/D								Ap	
33. Bud Scales (No. Ranks)						1	4	3	
34. Bundle Tr. 1/3/5 or >/S/G	1	00	1	3>	3	1	3	3	
35. Bundle Tr. D/I/L/E/S	D	E	D	D	D	I	D	D	
36. Fruit Type	B	C	Nl	B	D	D	B	C	
37. Other Disting. Characteristics									

GLOSSARY OF TERMS

Abaxial   The side away from the axis.

Abortive   Not developing, or development starting normally and then stopping prior to normal maturity.

Acaulescent   Without a stem.

Achene   A small, dry, hard, 1-locular, 1-seeded, indehiscent fruit as in Carex and Ranunculus.

Actinomorphic   Radially symmetrical, as in a regular flower.

Acuminate   Gradually long-tapering to a sharp point.

Acute   Sharp pointed (but not long-tapering).

Adaxial   The side toward the axis.

Adnate   Fusion of unlike structures, as in stamens with the corolla.

Adventitious   Developing in an irregular or unusual position as in buds or roots that originate from a stem.

Adventive   Introduced but not naturalized.

Aggregate   Crowded into a cluster but not cohering.

Alate   Winged.

Alternate   Borne singly at each node, as in leaves on a stem, or borne singly between parts of a different kind, as in stamens alternating with petals.

Alveolate   Honeycombed; having angular cavities separated by thin partitions.

Ament   See catkin.

Amplexicaul   Clasping the stem, as in the base of some leaves.

Anastomosing   Branching and rejoining to form a network.

Androgynous   A spike composed of both staminate and pistillate flowers, the staminate positioned above the pistillate, as in some Carex.

Angiosperm   Plants having the ovules enclosed in an ovary.

Annual   Plants completing their life cycle in one year or growing season.

Annular   In the form of a ring.

Anther   The part of the stamen that contains 1 or 2 pollen-bearing sacs.

Anthesis   The period of flowering.

Antrorse   Directed upward or forward.

Apetalous   Lacking petals.

Apiculate   Terminating abruptly in a short, distinct point.

Appressed   Lying close and flat against.

Arborescent   Tree-like, approaching the size and form of a tree, or becoming a tree.

Arcuate   Curved or bowed.

Areolate   Marked into small spaces, i.e., reticulated.

Aril   A fleshy thickening of the seed coat.

Aristate   Tipped with an awn or bristle.

Articulate   Jointed.

Ascending   Rising obliquely upward.

Attenuate   Gradually tapering, usually applied to the base.

Auricle   An ear-shaped appendage or lobe.

Auriculate   With 1 or more auricles.

Awn   A bristle, usually terminal or dorsal, as in the grasses.

Axil   The angle formed between 2 structures.

Axillary   Located in an axil.

Axis   The central part of a plant along which parts arise.

Banner   The upper, usually larger petal of a papilionaceous flower (see standard).

Barbed   Bearing short, reflexed bristles or barbs.

Beak   A firm terminal appendage, as on a fruit or seed.

Bearded   Bearing a tuft or ring of long or bristle-like hairs.

Berry   A fleshy fruit developed from a single pistil containing several to many seeds; more generally, any pulpy or fleshy fruit i.e., raspberry, strawberry.

Bi   A Latin prefix meaning 2.

Biennial   Living for two years and flowering the second year.

Bifid   Cleft from the tip into two segments.

Bifurcate   Forked, as in some styles or trichomes.

Bilabiate   Two lipped.

Bipinnate   With the primary pinnae again pinnate.

Bisexual   With both stamens and pistils.

Bivalvate   Opening by two valves.

Blade   The expanded portion of a flat structure such as a leaf or petal.

Bloom   A whitish powdery or waxy covering of the surface that makes it glaucous.

Boreal   Northern.

Bract   A reduced leaf subtending a flower or associated with an inflorescence.

Bracteal   Having the form or position of a bract.

Bracteate   Having bracts.

Bracteole, Bractlet   A small bract.

Bristle   A strong, stiff, slender hair.

Bud   An undeveloped leafy shoot or flower, often enclosed by scales.

Bulb   A short underground stem with fleshy leaves or scales.

Bulbil, Bulblet   A small bulb arising from a parent bulb, or in an inflorescence in place of flowers, or in the axils of leaves.

Bulbous   Swollen at the base, or having true bulbs.

Caducous   Falling off very early.

Callus   A hard thickening; in grasses the hard, swollen point of insertion of the lemma or palea.

Calyculate   Having small bracts around the base of the calyx or (in Asteraceae) the involucre simulating an outer calyx.

Calyx   All of the sepals of a flower.

Cambium   A one-cell thick layer of meristem which produces xylem to the inside and phloem to the outside.

Campanulate   A bell-shaped calyx or corolla.

Canescent   Hoary, with grayish or whitish pubescence.

Capillary   Very slender and hair-like.

Capitate   Head-like, or clustered into a head.

Capsule   A dry, dehiscent fruit developed from 2 or more carpels.

Carina   A keel.

Carinate   Keeled.

Carpel   The fertile leaf of an angiosperm, which bears the ovules; a simple pistil or one member of a compound pistil.

Carpophore   The part of the receptacle that in some flowers is prolonged as a central axis between the carpels, as in the Apiaceae; in Silene the stalk of the ovary.

Cartilaginous   Firm and tough but flexible.

Caryopsis   The fruit in Poaceae, which is dry, indehiscent, with the thin pericarp usually fused to the single seed.

Castaneous   Dark reddish-brown; chestnut-colored.

Catkin   A dense, usually flexuous, scaly-bracted spike or raceme bearing many small, naked or apetalous flowers, as in the Betulaceae.

Caudate   Having a slender, tail-like appendage.

Caudex   The thickened, persistent base, usually of an herbaceous perennial.

Caulescent   Having an evident leafy, above ground stem with visible internodes.

Cauline   On or pertaining to an evident stem.

Cernuous   Nodding.

Cespitose   Growing in dense, low tufts.

Chaff   Small, thin, dry scales or bracts, as in many of the Asteraceae.

Channeled   Deeply grooved longitudinally.

Chartaceous   Having a papery texture.

Ciliate   Having a fringe of marginal hairs.

Ciliolate   Minutely ciliate.

Cinereous   Having a covering of short, ash-colored hairs.

Circinate   Coiled from the tip downward, as in the fiddlehead in some ferns.

Circumscissile   Dehiscing by an encircling transverse line such that the top part separates as a cap, as in Plantago.

Clasping   The base partly or entirely surrounding another structure, as in some leaves clasping stems.

Clavate   Shaped like a club, being gradually thickened toward the tip.

Clavellate   Diminutive of clavate.

Claw   The narrow base or stalk of some sepals and petals.

Cleft   Cut, lobed, or parted, i.e., as some leaves are cut half the distance from the margin to midrib.

Cleistogamous   A self-pollinated flower that remains closed, setting seed without ever opening as in the Violaceae.

Clone   A group of plants originating by vegetative reproduction from a single plant, as in some Cornus.

Coalescent   A union of parts of the same kind, forming a single unit.

Coherent   Sticking together of parts of the same kind, although not united.

Collateral   Side by side.

Colonial   Forming colonies, with all plants connected by common roots, rhizomes, or stolons.

Column   The united filaments, as in Malvaceae; the united style and filaments.

Coma   A tuft of usually long, soft hairs, as on the seeds of Epilobium.

Commissure   The surface by which two carpels cohere, as in the Apiaceae.

Comose   Having a coma.

Complete Flower   Having sepals, petals, pistil, and stamens.

Compound Leaf   A leaf divided into separate leaflets.

Compound Ovary   An ovary composed of more than one carpel.

Compressed   Flattened, especially laterally.

Conduplicate   Folded together lengthwise.

Cone   A globose or cylindrical aggregation of sporophylls or ovuliferous scales on an axis.

Connate   Similar structures united into one unit, as in some leaves, or the anthers in some Solanaceae.

Connective   The tissue of an anther that connects the two locules.

Connivent   Converging, or coming into contact but not actually united.

Contorted   Twisted or bent.

Convolute   Rolled up longitudinally.

Coralloid   Coral-like.

Cordate   Having a sinus and rounded lobes at the base; heart-shaped with the point facing upward.

Coriaceous   Having a leathery texture.

Corm   The enlarged, fleshy but solid, bulb-like base of a stem, lacking the fleshy leaves of a true bulb.

Corniculate   Covered with minute horns or crests.

Corolla   All of the petals of a flower.

Corona   A crown of petal-like structures between the corolla and stamens derived by modification of the corolla, as in Narcissus, or the anthers, as in Asclepias.

Corrugated   Wrinkled or in folds.

Corymb   A short, round or flat-topped, contracted raceme having the outer pedicels progressively longer than the inner.

Corymbiform   Shaped like but not necessarily with the structure of a corymb.

Corymbose   In corymbs.

Creeping   Running at or just below the ground surface and rooting at intervals.

Crenate   Shallowly round-toothed along the margin.

Crenulate   Finely crenate.

Crested   Having an elevated ridge, appendage, or projection on the surface or tip.

Crisped   Irregularly curled or twisted so as to be 3-dimensional instead of flat, as in the leaves of Rumex crispus.

Crown   An inner appendage to a petal or to the throat of a corolla.

Cruciform   Cross-shaped.

Cucullate   Hooded or hood-shaped.

Culm   The aboveground stem of a grass or sedge.

Cultigen   A plant derived through cultivation.

Cuneate   Wedge-shaped or triangular, with the narrow end at the point of attachment, as in the bases of certain leaves.

Cuspidate   Bearing a cusp or sharp firm point.

Cyathium   The specialized inflorescence of Euphorbia, consisting of a cup-like involucre (often with petaloid appendages) bearing the flowers from the base.

Cycle   A series of similar parts of a flower.

Cyme   A broad, flattish, determinate inflorescence having the central or terminal flowers blooming first.

Cymose   Like a cyme, or bearing cymes.

Cymule   A small cyme or a portion of a larger one.

Deciduous   Not persistent or evergreen; falling after completing its function, as in a deciduous tree that loses its leaves before winter.

Declined   Bent or curved downward or forward.

Decompound   Repeatedly compound or divided, as in a leaf divided into numerous leaflets.

Decumbent   Prostrate or reclining at the base but with the tip ascending or erect.

Decurrent   With an adnate wing extending downward from the point of insertion, as in the leaf base of Verbascum thapsus.

Decussate   Alternating in pairs at successive levels, each pair at right angles to the pair above and the one below.

Deflexed   Bent downward.

Dehiscent   Opening at maturity and releasing or exposing the contents, as in a fruit or an anther.

Deltoid   Shaped like a triangle with equal sides.

Dentate   Toothed, usually with the teeth spreading outward.

Denticulate   Minutely dentate.

Depauperate   Smaller than usual or poorly developed; stunted.

Depressed   Flattened from above.

Determinate Inflorescence   An inflorescence in which the terminal flower in the inflorescence or in each branch of the inflorescence blooms first, stopping the elongation of the axis; a cymose inflorescence.

Diadelphous   Arranged in 2 fascicles, as in the stamens of some flowers.

Diandrous   With 2 stamens.

Diaphragm   A dividing partition, as in the pith of some woody plants.

Dichasium   A cyme with 2 lateral axes.

Dichotomous   Forking into 2 branches of similar size.

Didymous   Occurring in pairs.

Didynamous   Having stamens in 2 pairs of unequal length.

Diffuse   Widely or loosely spreading or branching.

Digitate   Compound, with the segments diverging from a common point, as in the fingers of a hand.

Dilated   Enlarged or widened.

Dimorphic   Having 2 forms.

Dioecious   Having stamens and pistils in separate flowers on different plants.

Disarticulating   Separating at a predetermined point.

Discoid   Resembling a disc; in the Asteraceae with the flowers in a head all tubular, ray flowers lacking.

Disk or disc   An outgrowth from the receptacle of a flower that surrounds the base of the ovary; in the Asteraceae the central portion of the head that bears the tubular flowers.

Dissected - Divided or cut into narrow segments.

Distal - Toward or at the tip or far end.

Distichous   In 2 vertical ranks on opposite sides of the stem in the same plane.

Distinct   Separate and evident, not united.

Diurnal   Occurring during the day.

Divaricate   Widely spreading or divergent.

Divergent   Spreading away from each other.

Divided   Cut or separated to the rachis or base into distinct parts.

Dorsal   The back or outer surface.

Dorsiventral or dorsoventral   Flattened from front to back as opposed to from 1 side to another.

Downy   Pubescent with fine, soft hairs.

Drupe   A fleshy fruit with the usually solitary seed enclosed in a stony endocarp.

Drupelet   A small drupe, as in a blackberry or raspberry.

E- or ex   A Latin prefix meaning without or lacking, or away from.

Echinate   Bearing prickles.

Ellipsoid   Having an elliptical outline but 3-dimensional.

Elliptic   Widest at or about the middle and narrowed to rounded ends.

Emarginate   Having a shallow notch at the tip.

Endemic   Restricted to a limited geographic area.

Endocarp   The inner layer of the pericarp.

Ensiform   Sword-shaped, as in the leaf of Iris.

Entire   A margin without teeth, lobes, or divisions.

Ephemeral   A flower that lasts for 1 day or less; an annual that completes its growth cycle by spring or early summer.

Epi   Greek prefix meaning upon, often used to mean outermost.

Epicalyx   A series of bracts immediately subtending the calyx, simulating a second outer calyx.

Epigynous   Having the perianth and stamens attached at the summit of the ovary (ovary inferior) instead of beneath it or near the middle.

Epipetalous   Attached to the petals or corolla.

Epiphyte   A plant growing upon another plant but not deriving food or water from it nor attached to the ground.

Equitant   Distichous, with the bases overlapping, as in the leaves of iris.

Erose   Having an irregular margin, as if gnawed.

Eu   Greek prefix, meaning true or typical.

Even-pinnate   Pinnately compound but lacking a terminal leaflet such that there are an even number of leaflets.

Evergreen   Remaining green all winter.

Ex   Latin prefix meaning without or lacking or away from.

Excentric   Off-center or 1-sided.

Excurrent   With a continuing axis, as in the midvein of a leaf projecting beyond the margin.

Exfoliating   Peeling off in layers.

Exocarp   The outer layer of the pericarp.

Exserted   Projecting out of, as the stamens from a corolla.

Extra   Latin prefix meaning outside of.

Extrorse   Facing outward.

Falcate   Curved and flat, gradually tapering, as in a sickle.

Farinose   Covered with a meal-like powder.

Fascicle   A close bundle or cluster.

Fascicled   In fascicles.

Fastigiate   Close together and nearly erect.

Fertile   Capable of reproduction.

Fibrillose   Composed of or breaking down into fibers.

Fibrous   Same as Fibrillose.

-Fid   Suffix meaning deeply cut.

Filament   The stalk of the stamen, which supports the anther; a thread like body.

Filamentous   Composed of threads.

Filiform   Long, very slender, and thread-like.

Fimbriate   Fringed with narrow or filiform projections along the margin.

Fimbrillate   Having a minute fringe.

Flabellate or Flabelliform   Fan-shaped or broadly wedge-shaped.

Flaccid   Lax and weak, not rigid.

Flange   A rim or collar.

Fleshy   Succulent or pulpy; thick and juicy.

Flexuous   Curved alternately in opposite directions.

Floccose   Covered with long, soft, fine, loosely spreading, tangled hairs.

Flocculent   Diminutive of floccose.

Floret   A small flower, usually one of a cluster, as in the head of a composite or the spikelet of a grass.

Floricane   The second year flowering stem in Rubus.

Floriferous   Flower-bearing.

Foliaceous   Leaf-like in appearance or texture.

Foliar   Relating to a leaf or leaves.

-Foliate   Suffix meaning the number of leaves in a cluster, i.e., trifoliate, having 3 leaves.

-Foliolate   Suffix meaning the number of leaflets in a compound leaf.

Foliose   Having numerous or crowded leaves.

Follicle   A dry fruit developing from a single carpel, dehiscent along 1 suture.

Foveolate   Covered with small pits.

Free   Not attached to other structures.

Frond   The leaf of a fern; in plants such as Lemnaceae the thallus-like stem.

Fruit   The part of a plant that bears seed.

Frutescent, Fruticose   Shrubby or becoming so.

Fugacious   Falling or disappearing early.

Fulvous   Tawny or dull yellow.

Furcate   Forked.

Fuscous   Grayish-brown.

Fusiform   Spindle-shaped; thickened in the middle and tapered to both ends.

Galeate   Hooded or helmet-shaped, as in the upper sepal of an irregular calyx and the upper lip of a bilabiate corolla.

Gametophyte   A generation in which gametes are produced as reproductive bodies; in angiosperms consisting of the embryo-sac in the female gametophyte and the pollen-grain in the male.

Gamo   Greek prefix meaning a union of similar parts such as leaves, sepals, or petals.

Geniculate   Abruptly bent.

Gibbous   Abruptly swollen on one side, often near the base.

Glabrate, Glabrescent   Becoming glabrous with age.

Glabrous   Smooth, lacking pubescence or glands.

Gladiate   Sword-shaped, straight or slightly curved.

Gland   A protuberance or depression that secretes a sticky, viscous substance.

Glandular, Glanduliferous   Bearing glands or functioning as a gland.

Glandular-pubescent   Pubescent, with glands on the ends of the hairs.

Glaucescent   Becoming glaucous with age.

Glaucous   Covered with a fine waxy or powdery whitish or bluish bloom that can be rubbed off.

Globose   Spherical.

Glochidia   Apically barbed hairs or bristles.

Glomerate   Densely compacted in clusters or heads.

Glomerule   A small compact cluster or head.

Glume   One of usually 2 empty bracts at the base of a grass spikelet.

Glutinous   Covered with a sticky exudation.

-Gonous   Greek suffix meaning angled; as in trigonous (3-angled)

Gymnosperm   Plants having ovules that are naked, not enclosed in an ovary.

Gynandrous   Having the stamens adnate to the pistil, as in the Orchidaceae.

Gynecandrous   A spike composed of both staminate and pistillate flowers, the pistillate positioned above the staminate, as in some Carex.

Gynobase   An enlargement or prolongation of the receptacle bearing the ovary, as in the Lamiaceae.

Habit   The general appearance or manner of growth of a plant.

Habitat   The kind of place in which a plant grows.

Halberd-shaped   The same as hastate.

Halophyte   A plant adapted to growing in saline soil.

Hastate   Shaped like an arrowhead but with the basal lobes pointing outward at a wide angle.

Head   A dense cluster of sessile or nearly sessile flowers or fruits at the top of a peduncle or on a receptable.

Helicoid Cyme   Having the main axis coiled or spiralled like a snail shell, the successive lateral branches that make up the axis all arising on the same side.

Hemi   Greek prefix meaning half.

Herb   A vascular plant lacking a woody stem.

Hermaphrodite   Having the pistils and stamens in the same flower.

Hetero   Greek prefix meaning unlike, or having differing sorts.

Heterosporous   Producing two different kinds of spores usually of unequal size, one giving rise to male gametophytes, the other to female.

Hexa   Greek prefix meaning six.

Hilum   The scar on a seed indicating its point of attachment.

Hirsute   Pubescent with somewhat coarse or stiff hairs (but less stiff than hispid).

Hirsutulous   Slightly hirsute.

Hirtellous   Minutely hirsute.

Hispid   Pubescent with coarse, rigid hairs or bristles.

Hispidulous   Minutely hispid.

Hoary   Grayish-white with a fine, close pubescence.

Homo   Greek prefix meaning alike, or all of the same sort.

Homosporous   Producing only one kind of spore.

Hyaline   Transparent or translucent.

Hydrophyte   A plant adapted to growing in the water.

Hypanthium   A ring or cup surrounding the ovary, formed either by the enlargement of the receptacle, or by the union of the lower parts of the sepals, petals, and stamens.

Hypo   Greek prefix meaning beneath.

Hypogynous   Having the perianth and stamens attached to the receptacle beneath the ovary and free from it (ovary superior).

-Iferous   Latin suffix meaning having or carrying.

Imbricate   Overlapping or shingled, either vertically or spirally.

Immersed   Growing wholly under water.

Imperfect Flower   A flower having stamens or pistil(s) but not both; sepals and/or petals present or absent.

Incised   Cut irregularly and often deeply and sharply.

Included   Contained within, not projecting beyond; the opposite of exserted.

Incomplete Flower   A flower lacking 1 or more of the structures found in a complete flower, i.e., sepals, petals, pistil(s), stamens.

Indehiscent   Not opening by valves, pores, etc.; remaining closed at maturity.

Indeterminate Inflorescence   An inflorescence in which the flowers bloom from the base upward such that the inflorescence could elongate indefinitely.

Indigenous   Native to an area.

Indument   A hairy or glandular covering.

Indurated   Hardened.

Indusium   In ferns the specialized, flap-like structure that covers the sorus.

Inferior Ovary   An ovary having the perianth and stamens attached at the summit instead of beneath it or at the middle.

Inflated   Swollen or bladdery.

Inflexed   Bent inward; incurved.

Inflorescence   The flowering part of a plant; the mode of arrangement of the flowers.

Infra   Latin prefix meaning below.

Innovation   An offshoot from the base of the stem.

Inserted   Attached to or growing out of.

Inter   Latin prefix meaning between or among.

Internode   The portion of a stem between 2 successive nodes.

Intra   Latin prefix meaning within.

Introduced   Brought in from another region intentionally.

Introrse   Turned inward; opposite of extrose.

Involucel   An involucre of the second order.

Involucre   A collection of bracts beneath a flower cluster or single flower.

Involute   With the margin rolled inward toward the upper side, such that the lower side of an organ is exposed and the upper concealed.

Irregular Flower   A flower in which the sepals or petals are unequal in size, form, or union of similar parts.

Keel   A central dorsal ridge; the 2 united lower petals of a papilionaceous flower.

Labiate   Lipped, as in bilabiate (2-lipped, referring to a calyx or corolla with united upper and lower sets of lobes).

Lacerate   Torn or irregularly cleft or cut.

Laciniate   Divided into long, narrow segments.

Lactiferous   Producing a milky latex.

Lacuna   A space, as in the area between the anastomosing veins of a leaf.

Lacustrine   Pertaining to or growing around lakes.

Lamina   The blade of a leaf, sepal, or petal.

Lanate   Covered with long, curled hairs; woolly.

Lanceolate   Lance-shaped, much longer than wide, widest below the middle, tapering to the tip and tapered or rounded to the base.

Lateral   On or at the side.

Latex   The milky or colored juice produced by some plants.

Leaflet   A single division of a compound leaf.

Legume   The fruit in Fabaceae, composed of a single carpel, dry and usually dehiscing along 2 sutures.

Lemma   The lower of typically 2 bracts enclosing the flower in Poaceae.

Lenticel   A slightly raised corky area in the bark.

Lenticular   Shaped like a biconvex lens.

Lepidote   Covered with small, scurfy scales.

Liana   A climbing, woody vine.

Ligulate   Having a ligule; in the Asteraceae a head composed solely of ligulate flowers.

Ligule   An appendage at the junction of the leaf sheath and blade in some Poaceae and Cyperaceae; the flattened part of the ray corolla in some Asteraceae.

Limb   The expanded part of a sympetalous corolla above the throat; the expanded portion of a petal or leaf.

Linear   Long and narrow with parallel margins.

Lip   The upper or lower segment of a 2-lipped calyx or corolla; in Orchidaceae the odd petal.

Litoral, Littoral   Growing along or pertaining to shores.

Livid   Pale lead-colored.

Lobe   A usually rounded segment of an organ.

Lobed   Divided usually less than half way from margin to midrib or base into lobes.

Lobulate   Divided into small lobes.

Locule   The compartment of an ovary, fruit, or anther.

Loculicidal   Dehiscent along the midrib or median dorsal line of a locule into the cavity.

Lodicule   One of the small scales at the base of the flower in grasses that represent a vestigial perianth.

Loment   A legume composed of 1-seeded articles or joints.

Lunate   In the shape of a half-moon or crescent.

Lyrate   Pinnatifid, with a large, usually rounded terminal lobe and smaller lateral lobes.

Macro   Latin prefix meaning large.

Maculate   Spotted.

Marbled   With irregular colored streaks.

Marcescent   Withering but persistent.

Marginate   Having a distinct margin.

Maritime   Pertaining to or under the influence of the sea.

Median   Central, middle.

Mega   Greek prefix meaning large.

Megaspore   The larger spore giving rise to the female gametophyte compared to the smaller spore that gives rise to the male gametophyte.

Membranaceous, Membranous   Thin, somewhat translucent, and flexible.

Mericarp   The individual carpel of a schizocarp.

-Merous   Greek suffix referring to the number of parts.

Mesic   Medium conditions with respect to moisture and light.

Mesophyte   A plant adapted to growing under medium conditions of moisture and light.

Micro   Greek prefix meaning small.

Microspore   The smaller spore that gives rise to the male gametophyte.

Midrib   The central or main rib of a leaf or other structure.

Monadelphous Stamens   Stamens having the filaments or anthers united into a tube.

Moniliform   Cylindrical, with constrictions at regular intervals, resembling a string of beads.

Mono   Greek prefix, meaning 1.

Monochasium   A 2-flowered cyme having a terminal and a lateral flower.

Monoecious   Having stamens and pistils in separate flowers on the same plants.

Montane   Of or pertaining to the mountains.

Mucilaginous   Slimy.

Mucro   A small, sharp, abrupt tip.

Mucronate   Tipped with a mucro.

Mucronulate   Diminutive of mucronate.

Multi   Latin prefix meaning many.

Multicipital   Many-headed, referring to having several caudices or to a rootcrown from which several to many stems arise.

Multiple Fruit   A fruit derived from several to many flowers, as in mulberry.

Muricate   A surface beset with small, sharp points.

Muriculate   Very finely muricate.

Mycorrhiza   A symbiotic association between a fungus and the root of a vascular plant.

Naturalized   Thoroughly established but originally coming from another area.

Navicular   Boat-shaped.

Nectariferous   Producing nectar.

Nectary   A structure or area where nectar is secreted.

Nerve   A simple unbranched vein or slender rib.

Net-veined   With the veins forming a pattern or network.

Neutral Flower   A flower having neither stamens nor pistil.

Nigrescent   Blackish.

Node   A place on a stem where 1 or more leaves are or have been attached; a constriction or knob-like enlargement on a stem.

Nodose   Beset with knobs or knots.

Nodulose   Beset with small knobs or knots.

Nut   A hard, dry, indehiscent, usually 1-seeded fruit.

Nutlet   A small nut or a hard mericarp.

Ob   Latin prefix meaning inverted, as in obovate.

Obcordate   Cordate, with the tip basal and the notch apical.

Oblanceolate   Lanceolate, with the broadest part above the middle and tapering to the base.

Oblate   Shorter from base to tip than across the middle.

Oblique   Unequal-sided.

Oblong   Shaped like a rectangle; 2-3 times longer than broad.

Obovate-obovoid   Like ovate but thicker toward the distal end.

Obsolete   Reduced so as to be scarcely evident; rudimentary; entirely suppressed.

Obtuse   Blunt, rounded at the end.

Ochrea, Ocrea   A sheath around the stem just above the base of the leaf; sheathing stipules, as in the Polygonaceae.

Ochroleucous   Yellowish-white.

Ocreolae   The smaller, secondary sheaths surrounding fascicles of flowers in the inflorescence in the Polygonaceae.

Odd-pinnate   A pinnately compound leaf with a terminal leaflet such that there is an odd number of leaflets.

Olivaceous   Olive-green.

Opaque   Dull; not shiny or translucent.

Orbicular   A flat structure circular in outline.

Oriface   Any opening.

Oval   Broadly elliptic.

Ovary   The basal part of the pistil that encloses the ovules.

Ovate   A flat structure with an outline like that of an egg, with the broader end toward the base.

Ovoid   A 3-dimensional structure shaped like an egg.

Ovule   The immature structure in the ovary which after fertilization becomes the seed.

Palate   A projection of the lower lip of a corolla closing the throat.

Pale   A chaffy scale such as often subtends the fruit in Asteraceae.

Palea   The upper of typically 2 bracts enclosing the flower in Poaceae.

Paleaceous   Chaffy.

Palmate   With 3 or more structures (leaflets, nerves, etc.) radiating from a common point in a hand-like manner; digitate.

Paludal, Paludose   Of or growing in marshes.

Pandurate   Fiddle-shaped.

Panicle   An indeterminate, branching inflorescence with pedicelled flowers, often broadest toward the base.

Panicled, Paniculate   Arranged in a panicle.

Paniculiform   Resembling a panicle but not necessarily having the same structure.

Pannose   With a layer having a felt-like appearance or texture.

Papilionaceous Flower   Having a corolla consisting of a standard (banner) petal, 2 wing petals and 2 partly united keel petals as in the Fabaceae.

Papillate, Papillose   Covered with minute, rounded, blunt projections.

Pappus   The modified calyx at the summit of the ovary or achene in Asteraceae, consisting of scales, bristles, or a combination.

Parallel-veined   Having several to many veins paralleling the midvein.

Parasitic   Growing on and deriving its food, water, or both from another plant to which it is attached.

Parted   Cut usually more than half the distance from the margin to midvein or base.

Pectinate   Having a single row of narrow, closely set segments, like the teeth of a comb.

Pedate   Palmately divided, with the lateral segments 2-cleft.

Pedicel   The stalk of a single flower in an inflorescence.

Pedicellate   Borne on a pedicel.

Peduncle   The stalk of an inflorescence, or a solitary flower when it is the only flower comprising the inflorescence.

Pedunculate   Borne on a peduncle.

Pellucid   Clear, transparent, or translucent.

Peltate   Attached to the stalk by the lower surface inside the margin.

Pendulous   Drooping or hanging downward.

Penta   Greek prefix meaning 5.

Pepo   A fleshy fruit covered by a rind, lacking a pit or core, as in some Cucurbitaceae.

Perennial   A plant that lasts for more than 2 years.

Perfect Flower   Having both a functional pistil and stamens; sepals and petals present or absent.

Perfoliate Leaf   A sessile leaf with the basal margins united around the stem, the stem apparently passing through the leaf.

Peri   Greek prefix meaning around or enclosing.

Perianth   The sepals and petals collectively.

Pericarp   The wall of a matured ovary.

Perigynium   The sheath or sac enclosing the ovary or achene in Carex.

Perigynous   Having the perianth and stamens united with or borne on a cup (the hypanthium) around the ovary near the middle (ovary half-inferior).

Persistent   Remaining attached after maturity, not falling off.

Petal   One unit of the corolla.

Petaloid   Resembling a petal in color and/or texture.

Petiolate   Having a petiole.

Petiole   The stalk of a leaf.

Petiolule   The stalk of a leaflet.

-Phile   Greek suffix meaning loving.

Phyllary   An involucral bract in the Asteraceae.

Phylloclade   A stem having the appearance and function of a leaf.

Phyllode   An expanded, bladeless petiole having the appearance and function of a leaf.

Pilose   Covered with long, soft hairs.

Pinna   One of the primary divisions of a pinnately compound leaf.

Pinnate   Having the leaflets of a compound leaf or the veins of a leaf in rows on each side of a common axis, as in the parts of a feather.

Pinnatifid   Pinnately divided to or nearly to the midvein.

Pinnule   An ultimate pinna (leaflet) of a compound leaf that is 2 or more times divided.

Pistil   The seed-bearing part of a flower, consisting of 1 or more carpels differentiated into an ovary, style (sometimes lacking), and stigma.

Pistillate Flower   A flower with 1 or more pistils but without fertile stamens.

Pith   The spongy center of a stem consisting of homogeneous, unspecialized cells.

Pitted   Covered with pits.

Plaited, Plicate   Folded, usually lengthwise, like a fan.

Plumose   Having a feathery appearance due to long, dense pubescence, as in the pappus of some Asteraceae.

Pod   A dry, dehiscent fruit, such as a legume or a capsule.

Pollen   The male gametophytes of a seed plant (pollen grains) contained in the anther.

Pollinium   A mass of coherent pollen grains, as in many Orchidaceae and Asclepiadaceae.

Poly   Greek prefix meaning many.

Polygamo-dioecious   Mainly dioecious but having some perfect flowers.

Polygamo-monoecious   Mainly monoecious but having some perfect flowers.

Polygamous   Bearing hermaphrodite and unisexual flowers on the same plant or on different plants of the same species.

Polymorphic   Having several different forms.

Polypetalous   Having the petals separate from each other.

Polysepalous   Having the sepals separate from each other.

Pome   A fleshy fruit developed from an inferior ovary having a bony or cartilagenous core with several locules.

Poricidal   Opening by pores.

Prickle   A small, slender, sharp outgrowth from the bark.

Primary   The part that developed first; a main division.

Primocane   The first year stem in Rubus, usually not producing flowers.

Prismatic   Angulate with flat sides.

Procumbent   Prostrate on the ground or trailing but not rooting at the nodes.

Prophyll   One of a pair of bracteoles at the base of a flower, as in some Juncus.

Prostrate   Lying flat on the ground.

Proximal   Toward or at the base or near end.

Pruinose   Having a whitish powdery or waxy bloom on the surface.

Puberulent   Minutely pubescent with short, soft hairs, barely visible to the naked eye.

Pubescent   A general term for a covering of hairs.

Punctate   Dotted with colored or translucent pits or glands.

Puncticulate   Minutely punctate.

Pungent   With a rigid, sharp point; acrid.

Pustular, Pustulate   Having blisters or pustules.

Pyriform   Pear-shaped.

Pyxis   A capsule with circumscissle dehiscence, the top coming off as a lid, as in Plantago.

Raceme   An elongate, indeterminate inflorescence with pedicelled flowers arising along an un-branched axis.

Racemiform   With the form but not necessarily the structure of a raceme.

Racemose   In racemes or resembling a raceme.

Rachilla   A secondary axis; the axis of a spikelet in Poaceae and Cyperaceae.

Rachis   A primary axis, such as that of a compound leaf or an inflorescence.

Radiate   Spreading from a common point; in the Asteraceae a head bearing ray flowers on the margin and tubular flowers toward the center.

Radical   Of or pertaining to the root.

Rameal   Pertaining to or located on a branch.

Ray   A single branch of an umbel or similar inflorescence; the strap-shaped ligulate flower on the margin of the head in the Asteraceae.

Receptacle   The expanded apex of an axis which bears the floral parts of a single flower or, in the Asteraceae, the flowers of the head.

Recurved   Curved or bent downward or backward.

Reflexed   Abruptly bent downward or backward.

Regular Flower   A flower in which the sepals or petals are similar in size, form or union of similar parts.

Remote   Spaced widely apart.

Reniform   Kidney-shaped.

Repand   Having a slightly wavy margin.

Repent   Prostrate and rooting at the nodes.

Resupinate   Inverted or turned upside-down.

Reticulate   Forming a network, as in the veins of some leaves.

Retrorse   Bent or directed backward or downward.

Retuse   Having a shallow notch in an otherwise rounded apex.

Revolute   With the margin rolled outward toward the lower side, such that the upper side of an organ is exposed and the lower concealed.

Rhizomatous   Producing or bearing rhizomes.

Rhizome   An underground stem usually rooting at the nodes.

Rhombic   Having the outline of an oblique angle.

Rib   A primary or prominent vein of a leaf or other organ.

Ringent   Gaping; wide open, as in the mouth of a bilabiate corolla.

Riparian   Growing along streams or rivers.

Root   The part of the plant that grows in the opposite direction from the stem, usually underground, lacking nodes.

Rootstock   The same as rhizome.

Rosette   A cluster of leaves or other organs arranged in circular form, usually at or near the base of the plant.

Rostellate   Diminutive of rostrate; somewhat beaked.

Rostrate   Beaked, with a short, stout, terminal structure.

Rosulate   Arranged in a rosette.

Rotate   Flat and circular in outline, as in a sympetalous corolla, with spreading lobes and lacking a definite tubular part.

Rotund   Round or rounded in outline.

Ruderal   Growing in waste or disturbed places or among rubbish.

Rudimentary   Poorly or imperfectly developed and non-functional, reflecting an early evolutionary stage.

Rufous   Reddish-brown.

Rugose   Wrinkled.

Rugulose   Finely or minutely wrinkled.

Runcinate   Sharply incised or pinnatifid, with the segments pointing backward toward the base.

Runner   A long, very slender prostrate stem rooting at the nodes and tip; a very slender stolon.

Rupturing   Bursting irregularly.

Saccate   Sac-shaped or pouch-like.

Sagittate   Shaped like an arrowhead, with the basal lobes directed downward.

Salverform   With a slender tube abruptly expanded into a flat, spreading limb, as in primrose or phlox.

Samara   An indehiscent, winged fruit, as in Ulmus.

Saprophyte   A plant that lives on dead organic matter.

Scaberulous, Scabridulous   Minutely or slightly scabrous.

Scabrous   Rough to the touch due to the texture of the surface or to the presence of short, stiff pubescence.

Scale   Any small, usually dry, thin flattish structure.

Scandent   Climbing.

Scape   A leafless (or merely bracteate) peduncle arising from the ground in plants lacking a stem.

Scapose   With the flowers borne on a scape.

Scarious   Thin, dry, and membranaceous, not green, often translucent.

Schizocarp   A fruit that splits into separate, 1-seeded fruits at maturity called mericarps, as in the Apiaceae.

Scorpioid Cyme   A cyme with an elongated zigzag rachis, the successive lateral branches that make up the rachis borne on different sides; sometimes incorrectly applied to helicoid cyme.

Scurfy   Covered with small, bran-like scales.

Secund   Directed to 1 side of the axis and appearing as if borne from 1 side, often by twisting of the branches or pedicels.

Seed   A ripened ovule.

Semi   Latin prefix meaning half.

Sepal   One unit of the calyx.

Sepaloid   Having the texture, color, or otherwise resembling a sepal.

Septate   Divided by 1 or more partitions.

Septicidal   Dehiscent through the partitions and between the locules, such that the carpels are separated.

Septum   A partition; in an ovary formed by the united walls of adjacent carpels.

Sericeous   Silky, covered with long, slender, soft hairs.

Serrate   Having sharp, forward-pointing teeth along the margin.

Serrulate   Minutely serrate.

Sessile   Lacking a stalk, attached directly.

Seta, Setae   A bristle, or bristles.

Setaceous   Resembling a bristle.

Setose   Bearing bristles.

Setulose   Bearing minute bristles.

Sheath   A tubular structure partly or entirely surrounding an organ, as in the sheath of a grass leaf surrounding the stem.

Shrub   A woody perennial, smaller than a tree, usually branching from the base with several main stems.

Siliceous   Containing or composed of silica.

Silicle   In Brassicaceae a short fruit like a silique, usually not, or little longer than wide.

Silique   In Brassicaceae a long capsule in which the 2 valves are deciduous from a persistent partition to which the seeds are attached.

Silky   Covered with a close pubescence of soft, straight hairs.

Simple   A leaf that is not divided into leaflets, an unbranched inflorescence, a pistil composed of a single carpel.

Sinuate   Having a strongly wavy margin.

Sinus   The space or recess between 2 lobes or segments of a leaf or other expanded organ.

Smooth   Lacking roughness, but not necessarily pubescence.

Sordid   Having a dirty or dingy hue, as in pappus that is not pure white.

Sorus   The cluster of sporangia in ferns.

Spadix   A spike with small, crowded flowers imbedded in a thickened, fleshy axis, as in the Araceae.

Spathe   In the monocots a large, usually solitary bract subtending and often enclosing or surrounding an inflorescence.

Spatulate   Oblong but attenuated to the base, like a spatula.

Spicate   Arranged in or resembling a spike.

Spiciform   Having the form but not necessarily the structure of a spike.

Spike   A more or less elongated, simple inflorescence with sessile or subsessile flowers.

Spikelet   A small or secondary spike; in grasses and many sedges consisting of 1-many flowers with their subtending scales.

Spine   A strong, slender, sharp-pointed structure representing a leaf or stipule; a sharp-pointed structure on a leaf or fruit.

Spinose, Spinous   Spine-like or bearing spines.

Spinulose   With small spines over the surface or along the margin.

Sporangium   A spore case.

Spore   An asexual, 1-celled reproductive body.

Sporocarp   A case within which sporangia are contained.

Sporophyll   A leaf bearing sporangia.

Spray   A small, foliage-bearing branchlet of a tree or shrub.

Spur   A hollow tubular or sac-like extension from a petal or sepal; a short branch having a compact cluster of leaves.

Squarrose   Abruptly spreading or recurved above the base, as in the tips of involucral bracts.

Stamen   The pollen-bearing organ in the flower of a seed plant, consisting of an anther and usually a filament.

Staminate Flower   A flower with 1 or more stamens but no functional pistil.

Staminode   A sterile stamen, or a modified stamen that does not produce pollen.

Standard   The uppermost, expanded petal of a papilionaceous flower; the banner.

Stellate   Star-shaped with radiating branches, as in certain pubescence.

Sterile   Infertile, as in a flower lacking a pistil or not producing seeds, or a stamen without an anther or not producing pollen.

Stigma   The part of the pistil that is receptive to pollen.

Stigmatic   Pertaining to the stigma.

Stipe   A general term for the stalk of a structure.

Stipitate   Borne on a stipe.

Stipulate   Having stipules.

Stipule   One of a pair of appendages at the base of a leaf, sometimes fused.

Stolon   An elongate stem or shoot on the ground surface rooting at the tip.

Stoloniferous   Producing stolons.

Stramineous   Straw-colored.

Striate   With fine, longitudinal lines.

Strict   Very straight and upright.

Strigose   With straight, stiff, sharp appressed hairs.

Strigulose   Minutely strigose.

Strobile   An inflorescence having a cluster of imbricated bracts or scales on an axis, as in a pine cone.

Strophiole   An appendage at the hilum of certain seeds.

Style   The slender portion of the pistil between the ovary and the stigma.

Stylopodium   An enlargement at the base of the style as in many Apiaceae.

Sub   Latin prefix meaning below, or almost or somewhat.

Subtend   Arranged beneath and close to.

Subulate   Awl-shaped; tapering to the tip.

Succulent   Fleshy and juicy; a plant that accumulates or stores water.

Suffrutescent, Suffruticose   Somewhat shrubby or woody or becoming so, or having a persistent woody base.

Sulcate   Having longitudinal grooves or furrows.

Super, Supra   Latin prefix meaning above, upon, or more than.

Superior Ovary   An ovary having the perianth and stamens attached beneath it instead of at the summit or at the middle.

Surculose   Producing suckers.

Suture   A usually longitudinal seam or line of dehiscence.

Sym, Syn   Greek prefix meaning united.

Sympetalous   With the petals united, at least toward the base; equals gamopetalous.

Syncarp   A multiple fruit, as in mulberry.

Synonymy   A series of names for a taxon that are no longer in use.

Synsepalous   Having united sepals; equals gamosepalous.

Taproot   The primary descending root from which branch roots originate.

Taxon   Any level of classification, as genus, species, etc.

Taxonomy   A classification of organisms that best reflects their differences and similarities.

Tendril   A slender twining organ representing a modified stem or leaf which enables a climbing plant to attach to its support.

Tepal   A member of a perianth in which sepals and petals cannot be differentiated.

Terete   Circular in cross section.

Ternate   In 3's.

Tetra   Greek prefix meaning 4.

Tetradynamous Stamens   Having 4 long and 2 shorter stamens, as in many Brassicaceae.

Tetramerous   Having 4 parts.

Thalloid   Consisting of or resembling a thallus.

Thallus   A plant body not differentiated into roots, stem or leaves.

Thorn   A stiff, sharp, woody outgrowth from the stem.

Throat   The oriface of a united calyx or corolla; the expanded area between the tube and the limb.

Thyrse   A narrow, elongate, panicle consisting of cymules in a racemose arrangement, as in the Vitaceae.

Thyrsoid   Resembling a thyrse.

Tomentose   Densely pubescent with matted, woolly hairs.

Tomentulose   Minutely tomentose.

Tomentum   A pubescence of matted, woolly hairs.

Torose   Cylindrical with constrictions and swellings at intervals.

Torulose   Minutely torose.

Torus   The receptacle of a flower, or a head (as in Asteraceae).

Trailing   Prostrate but not rooting.

Tree   A woody perennial having a main stem.

Tri, Triplo   Latin or Greek prefix meaning 3.

Trichome   Any simple or branched hair-like structure.

Trichotomous   Forking in 3's.

Trifoliate, Trifoliolate   Having 3 leaves or 3 leaflets.

Trigonous   Having 3 angles.

Triquetrous   Having 3 sharp or projecting angles.

Truncate   With base or apex straight across as if transversely cut, not tapered.

Tuber   A fleshy, thickened part of a rhizome, usually at the end, as in Solanaceae.

Tubercle   A small swelling or protuberance on the surface.

Tuberculate   Bearing tubercles.

Tuberous   Thickened and tuber-like in appearance.

Tuft   A cluster of hairs, leaves, etc.

Tumid   Swollen.

Tunicate   Covered with concentric, sheathing leaf bases, as in an onion.

Turbinate   Top-shaped; inversely conical.

Turgid   Swollen; expanded by pressure from within.

Umbel   An inflorescence having peduncles or pedicels arising from a common point.

Umbellate   In an umbel, umbel-like.

Umbellet   A secondary umbel of a compound umbel.

Umbelliform   Having the shape but not necessarily the form of an umbel.

Umbo   A stout, blunt elevated area or protuberance, as on the scales of some pine cones.

Umbonate   Bearing an umbo.

Undulate   Having a wavy surface or margin.

Uni   Latin prefix meaning 1.

Unisexual Flower   A flower having stamens or pistils but not both.

Urceolate   Hollow and cylindrical, contracted at or below the mouth like an urn, as in some Ericaceae.

Utricle   A small, bladder-like, 1-seeded, usually indehiscent fruit.

Vaginate   Sheathed.

Valvate   Opening by valves, as a capsule; having the margins of petals, sepals, bud scales, etc. meeting along the edges without overlapping.

Valve   One of the sections into which a capsule splits at maturity; the lid of an anther which coveres the pore.

Vascular   Having conducting vessels, i.e., xylem and phloem and associated tissues.

Vein   A bundle or strand of vascular tissue in a leaf or other flat organ.

Velum   The membranous covering over the sporangium in Isoetes.

Velutinous   Velvety.

Ventral   The front or inner surface.

Ventricose   Swelling unequally on 1 side only, as in the corolla of some Scrophulariaceae.

Vernal   Appearing in spring.

Verrucose   Having a warty or nodular surface.

Versatile Anther   Attached to the filament near the middle and capable of swinging freely.

Verticil   A whorl.

Verticillate   Arranged in whorles.

Vestigial   Poorly or imperfectly developed and nonfunctional, reflecting evolutionary reduction.

Vestiture   A covering on a surface.

Villous   Bearing long and soft but not matted or interwoven hairs.

Vine   A plant that climbs, or that creeps or trails on the ground.

Virgate   Wand-like, slender, straight and erect.

Viscid   Sticky or glutinous.

Viviparous   Sprouting or germinating on the parent plant.

Weed   An aggressive plant that colonizes places where it is not wanted.

Whorl   An arrangement of 3 or more similar structures in a ring.

Wing   A thin, flat projection from the margin or tip of an organ; 1 of the 2 lateral petals of a papilionaceous flower.

Winter Annual   An annual plant that persists in a vegetative state throughout winter, flowering in late winter or early spring.

Woolly   Covered with long, soft, matted hairs.

Xerophyte   A plant adapted to dry habitats.

Zygomorphic   Bilaterally symmetrical, as in an irregular flower.

INDEX

Dennis W. Magee is a vice president at Normandeau Associates Environmental Consultants, Bedford, New Hampshire. He is author of *Freshwater Wetlands: A Guide to Common Indicator Plants of the Northeast* (University of Massachusetts Press, 1981), among other books.

The late **Harry E. Ahles** was curator of the Herbarium at the University of Massachusetts Amherst and of the Herbarium at the University of North Carolina, Chapel Hill. He was coauthor of the *Manual of the Vascular Flora of the Carolinas* (1965).